2004

Our Sunday Visitor's

CATHOLIC ALMANAC

Matthew Bunson, D.Min.
General Editor

OUR SUNDAY VISITOR'S CATHOLIC ALMANAC

2004 Edition

STAFF

Greg Erlandson
Editor-in-Chief

Matthew E. Bunson
General Editor

Cathy A. Dee
Production Editor

Contributors to the 2004 Edition
Dr. John Borelli
Barbara Fraze
Dr. Eugene Fisher
Brother Jeffrey Gros, F.S.C.
Rev. C. Eugene Morris
Rev. Ronald Roberson, C.S.P.
Russell Shaw

Jane Cavolina, Editorial Consultant

Carrie Bannister, Assistant

ACKNOWLEDGMENTS: Catholic News Service, for coverage of news and documentary texts; *The Documents of Vatican II*, ed. W. M. Abbott (Herder and Herder, America Press: New York 1966), for quotations of Council documents; *Annuario Pontificio* (2003); *Statistical Yearbook of the Church* (2003); *L'Osservatore Romano* (English editions); *The Official Catholic Directory* — Excerpts of statistical data and other material, reprinted with permission of *The Official Catholic Directory*, © 2003 by Reed Reference Publishing, a division of Reed Publishing (USA) Inc. Trademark used under license from Reed Publishing (Nederland) B.V.; *The Papal Encyclicals*, 5 vols., ed. C. Carlen (Pierian Press, Ann Arbor, Mich.); Newsletter of the U.S. Bishops' Committee on the Liturgy; The United States Catholic Mission Assoc. (3029 Fourth St. N.E., Washington, D.C. 20017), for U.S. overseas-mission compilations and statistics; *Catholic Press Directory* (2003); *Annuaire Directiore*, Canadian Conference of Catholic Bishops, for latest available Canadian Catholic statistics; Rev. Thomas J. Reese, S.J., for names of dioceses for which U.S. bishops were ordained; other sources as credited in particular entries.

Special thanks are owed to His Excellency Most Reverend John P. Foley, President of the Pontifical Council for Social Communications; Bruce Egnew, Associate General Secretary, USCCB; Secretariat for Pro-Life Activities, USCCB; Rev. Mr. William Kokesch, Dir.-Communications Service, Canadian Conference of Catholic Bishops; Msgr. Michael Servinsky; Rev. John Byrnes; Suzanne Lea; and Rev. Jorge Francisco Vázquez Moreno, adjunct secretary of the *Conferencia delEpiscopado Mexicano*.

2004 Catholic Almanac

Copyright © 2003 Our Sunday Visitor Publishing Division, Our Sunday Visitor, Inc.
Published annually by Our Sunday Visitor Publishing Division, Our Sunday Visitor, Inc., 200 Noll Plaza, Huntington, IN 46750
ISBN 10931709-93-9
T50
Library of Congress Catalog Card No. 73-641001
International Standard Serial Number (ISSN) 0069-1208

Editorial Note: The Catholic Almanac is pleased to announce that the 2004 edition marks the inclusion of several new information resources. These include: a Chronology of American Catholic History and expanded statistics on Women Religious. Comments, corrections, and suggestions should be addressed to the editorial offices of the *Catholic Almanac*: 2017 Scenic Sunrise Dr., Las Vegas, NV 89117; (702) 254-2678; E-mail: almanac@osv.com.

Visit us online at www.CatholicAlmanac.com,
and at the Our Sunday Visitor web site at www.OSV.com.

TABLE OF CONTENTS

DEDICATION

The 2004 edition is dedicated to the staff of *Our Sunday Visitor's Catholic Almanac*, in particular Cathy Dee, Production Editor; Carrie Bannister, Editorial Assistant; and Jane Cavolina, Editorial Consultant. Without their patience and tireless efforts, publication of the *Catholic Almanac* would not be possible.

Matthew Bunson, General Editor

THE 100TH ANNIVERSARY OF THE CATHOLIC ALMANAC

The 2004 edition of *Our Sunday Visitor's Catholic Almanac* marks the 100th anniversary of the publication's foundation. The origins of the *Catholic Almanac* are traced to a publication known as the *St. Antony's Almanac*, a 64-page annual with a calendar, feature articles, and an emphasis on devotion and prayer, but its chief purpose was to foster knowledge and devotion to St. Antony of Padua. *St. Antony's Almanac* was published by the Franciscans of Holy Name province from 1904 to 1929 under that name, save for 1911 when the title *Franciscan Almanac* was adopted.

No edition was published in 1930, but recognizing a genuine need in Catholic social communications, the editors of *The Franciscan Magazine* received permission to start up the *Almanac* once more with a revised organization and mission. The result was what was described by the editors of the time as a work "to serve as a factual handbook of basic and current information on matters pertaining to the Catholic Church and its members"; the new Almanac also, but secondarily, included general information in the style of an "almanac." The new version was published under the title *The Franciscan Almanac* and was 320 pages with a general sense of organization that would be vaguely recognizable to readers today. The early

years of the Great Depression prevented continuous publication, however, so there were no editions in 1934 and 1935.

In 1936, however, the St. Anthony's Guild renewed the life of the *Almanac*, establishing a relationship with the volume that lasted until 1971. From the 320 page count, the *Almanac* grew in size and scope steadily over the next years, reaching a massive length of 808 pages by the 1940's. Content was by now well-established with a stress upon the Liturgical Calendar and events pertaining to each year. The *Almanac* also eventually included over 100 pages of useful secular information, including the United States government, the Constitution, census information, postal regulations, the United Nations, and a chart on governments and rulers around the globe.

The title *The National Catholic Almanac* was used for the editions from 1940 to 1968; in 1969, the present title, *Catholic Almanac*, was adopted. In a statement of the influence of the Church in the United States, an agreement was made in 1959 to have the *Almanac* distributed each year by the New York publisher, Doubleday. The arrangement was in effect until 1971, with several editions sometime being printed throughout the year when events warranted.

For most of its first decades, the *Almanac* was pro-

duced every year by a large staff. The 50th anniversary edition in 1954, for example, declared: "The work of preparing material for each edition of the *Almanac* is divided between two staffs. Franciscan students for the priesthood at Holy Name College, Washington. D.C. compile most of the statistical information, conduct surveys, check standard articles for revision, write portions of the new copy, and do the preliminary work necessary to keep material up-to-date . . . From beginning to end, editorial work is under the over-all supervision of a professional staff at St. Anthony's Guild, which shares the tasks of the editors at Holy Name College and completes the work of preparing all materials for publication."

In 1951, meanwhile, a general editor was named to oversee the complex process of research and production, Fr. Felician Foy, OFM. In an interview shortly before his passing in February 2002, Father Felician remembered that he had been serving as a teacher in a high school and had just returned from an ice-skating outing when informed of a new appointment as editor of the *Almanac*. Father Foy confessed that he would have though it impossible to imagine at the time of his appointment, but his tenure as general editor of the *Almanac* endured from 1952 to 1998, meaning that he served as editor for over 45 years. Throughout most of that service, he was assisted by Miss Rose Avato (1927-97).

In 1971, Our Sunday Visitor acquired the publishing rights to the *Almanac*. The guiding force in the acquisition was Father Albert J. Nevins, M.M., then editor-in-chief of Our Sunday Visitor. Father Nevins considered the *Almanac* a prestigious work and the key element of his plans to improve and expand OSV's presence as a publisher. The first edition was launched in 1972, and OSV has remained the publisher of the *Almanac*.

The change in publisher from the St. Anthony Guild and Doubleday to Our Sunday Visitor meant as well a challenge for Fr. Foy and Rose Avato. Each summer, they drove from New Jersey to Huntington, Indiana, just outside of Fort Wayne, and spent several months readying the vast amounts of information for publication. Their work entailed not only finishing the news and other vital updates but laboring with the typesetters and printing staff on the pages and then proof-reading what was by then a 700 page annual. Their annual trek ended only with the entry of the *Almanac* into the digital age in 1991.

While the *Almanac* demanded much of Father

Foy's time, he remained always first and foremost a Franciscan. His ministry included prison visits, direction of Third Order Franciscans, outreach programs for the growing Latino population in New Jersey, and chaplain work in a local hospital. In order to serve the Spanish-speaking people of the diocese of Patterson, Foy taught himself Spanish. He was also an accomplished guitar player.

In 1996, he and Rose received a commendation by the Catholic Press Association for their decades of service. Two years later, Father Foy was awarded the *Pro Ecclesia et Pontifice* Medal for his contributions to the life of the Church. Rose died in her sleep on October 20, 1997 after she had just completed the final corrections for the 1998 edition of the *Almanac*. She had been suffering from amyotrophic lateral sclerosis, also known as Lou Gehrig's disease, since 1995, yet did not let the disease interfere with her work. Foy stepped down officially as general editor starting with the 2000 edition, although he remained actively involved with the *Almanac* until his death on February 21, 2002, from complications of heart surgery.

Matthew Bunson began working with Father Foy with the 1999 edition, taking over the editorship for the 2000 edition. The Jubilee edition of the *Catholic Almanac* began an extensive revision and updating of long-standing material and introduced sections with revised material in order to reflect current developments in the life of the Church. The current 640-page edition is a one-of-a-kind factual volume of basic and contemporary information on an encyclopedic range of subjects pertaining to the Catholic Church and its activity in the world. The centennial of the *Almanac* serves as a reminder of the vitality and stability of the Catholic Church in the United States whose activities, statistics, and commitment to the Gospel the *Almanac* has documented and celebrated for 100 years.

The 2004 edition of the *Catholic Almanac* honors to the hundreds of priests, women and men religious, and laity who have contributed to the success of the *Almanac* over the last ten decades. It is hoped that their commitment and zeal will continue to inspire the work of the *Almanac* in this new century.

ONE HUNDRED YEARS OF THE CATHOLIC ALMANAC

Our Sunday Visitor has been publishing the *Catholic Almanac* for 32 of its 100 years, having acquired the publishing rights in 1972. In many ways it was a perfect match.

Our Sunday Visitor is known for its commitment to the Church, its solid resources, its trustworthy approach to matters of the Faith, and its dedication to make these materials accessible to the average Catholic, as well as to those who are professionals on the educational and pastoral levels.

The *Catholic Almanac* is dedicated to that same audience. For all of its 100 years, it has sought to educate, inform, support and reinforce the faith of all Catholics who opened its covers.

In its early years in the last century, it served as a forum for promoting the devotional cause of St. Anthony of Padua, not much resembling the information-packed resource it has now become. As the Church it served became more of a presence in the life of our country, as its people grew in confidence, as its school systems and parish structures blossomed, the *Catholic Almanac* blossomed as well. By the 1930s, the *Catholic Almanac* was devoted to chronicling the facts about this robust Church, and documenting the facts and history of America as well.

This Golden Age of the Catholic laity and lay organizations saw the *Catholic Almanac* become a resource that would serve them at home, in the parish, at school or on the job.

With the tremendous changes that accompanied the Second Vatican Council, the *Catholic Almanac* found itself taking on a new task: providing trustworthy reports on the Council documents and their aftermath, and chronicling the changes and developments that grew out of this epic pastoral council.

For the last 25 years, it has also found itself devoting dozens of pages to the magnificent pontificate of

John Paul II. You might call him a pope made for an almanac. How else to assemble the record of his many travels, his numerous documents, and the groundbreaking historical actions he has taken year after year since 1978?

The *Catholic Almanac* exists today because of the hard work invested in it by many, many dedicated authors and editors over the years. For the last half-century, the team of Father Felician Foy, O.F.M., and Rose Avato carried this Herculean burden as they reported on all the changes that occurred from Pius XII to John Paul II. Since 2000, an equally impressive team headed by Matthew Bunson and Cathy Dee has done the same.

Matthew and Cathy have overhauled almost every section of the *Catholic Almanac*, bringing in new contributors and new resources, and incorporating changes that reflect the demands of our digital world, including the creation of Our Sunday Visitor's www.CatholicAlmanac.com website.

In their hands is entrusted the beginning of the *Catholic Almanac's* second century. Each year they strive to do better than the last, providing journalists, professors, pastors, students, moms and dads with a phenomenal amount of information at their fingertips. It is an entire resource shelf in one volume, a compendium that should be on every Catholic shelf.

Through all the changes that have occurred at Our Sunday Visitor and that have occurred in the Church it serves, the mission of the *Catholic Almanac* remains unchanged: To provide accurate, trustworthy and accessible information that serves the truth and encourages the faith of every generation of Catholics it is honored to serve.

All for the greater glory of God. All for his Church.
Gregory R. Erlandson, President and Publisher
Our Sunday Visitor Publishing Division

Year in Review: September 2002 to August 2003

SEPTEMBER 2002

Vatican

Christian Life: Pope John Paul II described Christian life as the act of facing "ordinary things extraordinarily." The Holy Father addressed pilgrims on Sept. 1 at Castel Gandolfo adding "Sanctity is required by following Jesus, not by avoiding reality and its trials, but facing them in the light and strength of His Spirit."

Mutual Understanding: Pope John Paul II sent a message to the leaders of the world gathered in Palermo, Sicily. On Sept. 2 he made an appeal for dialogue and mutual understanding to further the strides made at the Assisi meeting in 1986 and to new "lamps of light" in the Holy Land and Mediterranean region.

"Olympic Truce": Pope John Paul II renewed his appeal to the world to establish an "Olympic Truce" on Sept. 2, while meeting with the new ambassador from Greece. The Holy Father stated that the return of the Olympic games could foster such a worldwide observance of peace.

Care in Ordinations: Pope John Paul II instructed Brazilian bishops to be cautious in screening for the priesthood, it was reported on Sept. 5. The Holy Father said he had a duty to renew concerns about vocations and the moral state of seminary entrants. He warned that any bishop who does not perform diligence in this regard would have to render an accounting to God. The bishops of Rio de Janeiro, Brazil, were making their *ad limina* visit to the Vatican required every five years.

Vatican Coins: It was announced on Sept. 5 that Vatican E'uro coins bearing the image of Pope John Paul II are popular around the world. A second set of E'uro coins planned by the Vatican is expected to arouse more interest among collectors. The Holy Father's image and depictions of his coat of arms distinguish the coins.

Letter to Putin: It was announced on Sept. 5 that Pope John Paul II sent a letter to Russian president Vladimir Putin asking for an explanation of the recent banishment of a Catholic bishop and priest from Russia. News sources in Italy said that Putin had responded in writing and had stated that the banishments were "normal measures" and not part of a plot. A Vatican official reported that "forbidding" a bishop from his flock has always been regarded throughout history as a very serious matter.

Iranian Message: It was announced on Sept. 6 that Iranian President Mohammed Khatami sent Pope John Paul II a message calling for reinforcement of dialogue among religions. The Iranian state television reported the action. Iran and the Vatican have stable relations, easing the situation for the 250,000 Christians in that region.

Russian Orchestra: On Sept. 8, the Russian State Symphonic Orchestra performed for Pope John Paul II in the courtyard of Castel Gandolfo, the summer residence south of Rome. The Holy Father then addressed the musicians in Russian and thanked the representatives of the Russian government present.

European Union: On Sept. 13, Pope John Paul II stated that the European Union must view its purpose as an obligation to promote human rights. The Holy Father announced: "The ever stronger unity of Europe understands itself not as a movement of delimitation in regard to other continents, but involves a decided openness to the world." Pope John Paul II made these remarks while receiving the newest ambassador from Germany, Gerhard Westdickenberg.

Repentant Archbishop: It was reported on Sept. 13 that Archbishop Emmanuel Milingo, formerly of Zambia, admitted to pride, naiveté and isolation as the causes for his marriage in the Moon cult. His book, *Fished Out of the Mud*, which examines the episode, has now been published.

Symbol of Love: Pope John Paul II announced on Sept. 13 at Castel Gandolfo that it is crucial to see the cross as a source of blessing and salvation in a secularized world. He added: "In a word, the cross is the supreme symbol of love." The Holy Father noted that the cross has become the sign of the Church, saying: "Christian young people carry it with pride through the streets of the world."

Plea to Bishops: On Sept. 14, Pope John Paul II urged bishops to take seriously and to implement Vatican and papal documents. Addressing a group of Brazilian bishops, the Holy Father stressed that the unity among bishops and the Vatican is an important element in maintaining the missions of the Church. He asked them to become models of communion.

Land Mines: Archbishop Diarmuid Martin and other Vatican officials urged the international community to implement a worldwide ban on land mines and to care for the victims of these weapons. Speaking at Geneva on Sept. 17, the archbishop linked antipersonnel mines with the search for a just peace among nations and people.

Choral Groups: On Sept. 20, the Vatican issued an invitation to choral groups from around the world to take part in a 24-hour telecast and webcast to mark the 25th Christmas celebrated by Pope John Paul II. Praxes Ltd. of Bozeman, MT, was designated as the coordinator of the webcast. The invitation requested tapes be submitted to the Vatican.

Bishops' Priorities: On Sept. 23, Pope John Paul II announced two priorities for the bishops around the world. Meeting with 120 bishops from 33 countries, the Holy Father said that fostering an authentic desire for holiness is a primary role for bishops. The second priority is the spiritual care of the priests of each diocese. The pope also called attention to the fact that Christian truth can "imprint strong direction to human existence," part of the evangelical mission of the Church especially in this era of "restricted and relative horizons," devoid of true values.

Clericalized Laity: On Sept. 23, Pope John Paul II warned against efforts to "clericalize" the laity. The Holy Father said that Second Vatican Council's liturgical reform was designed to include all the faithful, not to confuse the people about the functions reserved to the priestly ministry. The pope cited abuses, such as homilies delivered by lay people.

Swiss Guard: The commander of the Swiss Guard of the Vatican, Colonel Pius Segmüller, visited Pope John Paul II to say farewell. He was asked by the Holy Father to reform the Swiss Guard four years ago. New disciplinary efforts and promotions were instituted during his tenure.

Mother Teresa: It was reported on Sept. 24 that the Cause of Mother Teresa had advanced with the recognition by the Congregation for Sainthood Causes of her lifelong "heroic" virtues. Approval for her beatification was later granted. (See October News.)

Mass for Russians: Pope John Paul offered Mass on Sept. 26 for the Catholic community in Russia deprived of their bishops and priests. Bishop Jerzy Mazur of the Siberian Diocese of St. Joseph in Irkutsk and priests have been denied residence in Russia.

Mozambican Gifts: It was announced on Sept. 29 that a group of Mozambican artists had prepared a chair and hoe for Pope John Paul II. The gifts were crafted from weapons collected in Mozambique at the end of the ten-year civil war. The weapons were gathered by the Christian Council of Mozambique, in the JAE initiative, a sword-into-plowshares campaign to promote peace in that devastated land

General Audience Topics
• Meditation on Canticle in Isaiah 2 (Sept. 4)
• Anniversary of 9/11 Attacks (Sept. 11)
• Meditation on Psalm 95(96) (Sept. 18)
• Meditation on Psalm 84 (85) (Sept. 25)

International

World's End: The Neo-Pháre sect of France believed that the world would end on Oct. 24 and accordingly prepared for "the last trip to Venus" in a Nantes villa, it was announced on Sept.1. The sect considered the Sept. 11 attacks a sure sign of the end of the world.

Last Supper: Natalia Tsarkova's "Last Supper" was on display in the Shrine of Santa Maria delle Grozie in Milan, it was reported on Sept. 2. Leonardo da Vinci's "The Last Supper" is part of the decorations of the shrine. The modern version was blessed by Pope John Paul II and was open to public viewing from Sept. 4-11. The painting is owned by the Vatican Museums.

Opus Dei: Opus Dei, a personal prelature, ordained 37 new priests, it was announced on Sept. 2. Bishop Javier Echevarria presided over the ceremony held in Torreciudad, Spain. The new priests come from the U.S. and 13 other counties.

"Brother's Day": A celebration of the legacy of Mother Teresa was held in Rome in observance of the fifth anniversary of her death, it was announced on Sept. 2. The planned gathering was intended to promote prayer and works of mercy. Father Miguel Elias Aderete Garrido initiated the celebration, which will be held annually.

Ecological Conversion: Archbishop Renato R. Martino, Vatican representative at the U.N., called for an "ecological conversion" on Sept. 3, recommending that human beings must be at the center of environment concerns. Archbishop Martino addressed a U.N. summit in Johannesburg, South Africa, repeating Pope John Paul II's plea for "globalization of solidarity." The Church has warned against modern programs that dehumanize people instead of nurturing a culture of life.

Family Focus: The presidents of the bishops' conferences of the Americas met in Santo Domingo, Dominican Republic, on Sept. 3 to discuss current legislation in their countries concerning life and families. Cardinal Giovanni Battista Re, prefect of the Congregation for Bishops presided.

TV Toxicity: Archbishop Hector Aguer, of La Plata, Argentina, said on Sept. 4.that environmental efforts should counteract current programming on television that debases the human spirit and contaminates the minds and hearts of children. The archbishop cited so-called "investigative reports," talk shows and "reality shows." Obscenity, lewdness and other evils are apparent on such broadcasts, he commented, and he appealed for discernment by parents and other viewers.

Cuban Catholics: The vicar general of the archdiocese of Havana, Monsignor Carlos Manuel de Cespedes, announced on Sept. 4 that the visit of Pope John Paul II to Cuba in 1998 provided the Catholics of the island nation with revival. The Church is no longer "on the defensive," he stated, but involved in missionary programs and growth. Polls taken in 1994 and 1998 demonstrated 86 percent of the population consider themselves believers. Since the Holy Father's visit, many feel compelled to demonstrate their Catholicism.

Clash of Catholicism: In Palermo, Sicily, delegates on Sept. 4 to the Sant' Egidio sponsored meetings on "Peoples and Religions" listened to speakers who predicted that a "clash of civilizations" would destroy all world civilizations. Present civilizations were defined as the legacies of cultures that formed human development, and a clash between the West and Islam was described as having the potential to destroy all civilizations.

Liberalism's Assaults: Cardinal Cormac Murphy O'Connor, the archbishop of Westminster, England, assailed the assaults of liberalism against the Catholic Church, it was reported on Sept. 4. The Church confronts secular society, and liberals attack the faith in order to reduce the effectiveness of the ongoing mission of Catholics. The cardinal also urged Catholics not to be discouraged by weakness or demoralized. Catholicism, he stated, is the force that demonstrates the feeble claims and goals of liberalism today.

Vietnam Hospital: *Thien Phuoc,* the "Grace of God" clinic, was established in Ho Chi Minh City, Vietnam, it was announced by Vatican Radio on Sept. 6. Staffed by 24 doctors and 26 nurses, mostly women religious, the hospital is dedicated to serving the needy and is authorized by the Vietnamese officials.

Mexican Dialogue: It was announced on Sept. 10 that the bishops of Mexico called for a national dialogue on the status and role of Indians in the various regions. The Church is following the words of Pope John Paul II during his July 30-August 1 visit to Mexico, strengthening its commitment to the indigenous peoples. Other groups called for reform of the Law of Indian Rights and Culture. The Mexican Supreme Court of Justice rejected 300 cases asking for such reforms.

Russian Blacklist: Russia has a blacklist of Roman Catholic priests that it intends to expel in "a new wave of persecution." Bishop Joseph Werth of Novosibirsk, Siberia, made the charge on Sept. 15, and Orthodox attempts to rally the Russian people have not been successful to date. Bishop Werth addressed the group Aid to The Church and cited a bishop and four priests already expelled by the Russian authorities.

Missionaries Released: Comboni Missionaries Father Ponziano Velluto and Father Alex Pizzi were released by Ugandan rebels, it was reported on Sept. 15. The two Comboni of Heart of Jesus were kidnapped in Opiti, Uganda, and held for 12 hours. This was the second time that Father Velluto was taken prison by the Lord's Resistance Army and then freed.

Ugandan Martyrs: It was announced on Sept. 15 that the two martyrs of slated for beatification on Oct. 20 will bring to twenty-four the number of Ugandan martyrs who have been raised to the altars of the Church as saints or blesseds. Daudi Okelo and Jildo Irwa were 16 and 14 and among group of catechumens baptized in the faith.

Anglican Rifts: Retiring Archbishop George Carey of Canterbury, the ranking Anglican prelate, announced on Sept. 16 in Hong Kong that his church is facing a split. The adoption of what he termed "local options" has been going on for years but it is reaching a crisis stage. The archbishop fears that decisions made by dioceses and bishops will lead to rifts that will result in two or more Anglican churches.

Turin Shroud: Cardinal Severino Poletto of Turin announced on Sept. 21 that the 40-day cleaning and restoration of the Shroud of Turin was to protect the cloth and the sacred image it bears. The work removed patches and a backing attached to the relic in 1534 after a fire. Removing this backing, called the Holland Cloth, also permitted photographic studies of the shroud. Trapped dirt and bits of scorched fabric had stained the shroud, dimming the sacred image.

Archaeological Find: It was announced on Sept. 25 that Father Ken Boland, a Blessed Sacrament priest of Melbourne, Australia, found the bones of a *Thylacoleo carnifex,* the predatory marsupial lion. The find was made on the Nullabor Plain in Western Australia. Father Bollard and friends have made annual trips to the region for the last 20 years. The *Thylacoleo* was the largest marsupial in the world.

Illegal Occupations: Cardinal Jean-Marie Lustiger of Paris and eight French bishops issued a statement reported on Sept. 27 calling on illegal immigrants to stop occupying churches. The Church leaders in France originally approved illegal immigrants to obtain residency papers. Such occupations now, however, are of little value for immigrant concerns. The Church's open-door policy provided the immigrants with national attention.

Colombian Slayings: Father Sanchez Ramirez was reported slain on Sept. 29 along with three companions. The murders were carried out in Restrepo, Cauca Valley, in Colombia, probably by guerrillas. Another priest, Father José Luis Arroyave, was slain in Medellin. Father Ramirez began a home program for the poor, designed to construct 50 homes in Restrepo.

Congo Death: It was reported on Sept. 29 that Father Jean Guth, a Spiritan missionary, died in the hands of his captors. He was kidnapped on Easter by guerrillas who follow former Prime Minister Bernard Kotelas. Reportedly Father Guth, a Frenchman, was wounded and had a tendon of his foot cut. The guerrillas are called "Ninjas."

Karachi Massacre: On Sept. 29 the Christians of Karachi, Pakistan, buried three of their members in the offices of an aid organization. One victim, Aslam Martin, was coordinator of the Institute for Peace and Justice, serving as a member of the charitable group serving Karachi for three decades. Pakistan President Pervez Musharraf condemned what he termed "terrorist fanaticism."

Return to Rome: Pope John Paul II on Sept. 30 thanked the mayor of Castel Gandolfo, Italy, and other civic authorities for their hospitality during his residence there. Looking refreshed, the Holy Father relaxed in his 136-acre villa in Castel Gandolfo.

National

Black Catholics: On Sept. 1, the four day National Black Congress ended in Chicago, with the adoption of St. Josephine Bakhita as patron of the organization. Black Catholics also celebrated the chapel dedicated to Mary Mother of Africa in the Basilica of the National Shrine of the Immaculate Conception in Washington, DC. There are 11 active black prelates in the U.S., and an estimated 2.3 million African-American faithful. Conferees focused on spirituality and the problems America and Africa.

L.A. Cathedral: Cardinal Roger Mahoney dedicated the new cathedral for the archdiocese of Los Angeles on Sept. 2, calling the structure an "anchor for the ages." The cathedral is 12 stories high and over 300 feet in length. The original cathedral, dating to the early eras in California, was St. Vibiana's. The cardinal announced that the $189 million cathedral had been fully funded "by cash."

Campus Ministry: An estimated 15.6 million college and university students are being served by campus ministers nationwide, it was announced on Sept. 3. New methods of reaching those students are being used alongside the traditional programs. Viewing college and university experiences as periods of change and growth, the campus ministers have faced a more challenging era in their labors.

Donations Decline: After Sept. 2001, charitable organizations saw a decline in donations, it was announced on Sept. 3. The vast donations to relief causes brought about decreases in other program supports. New York and Washington received the relief money.

Priest Acquitted: Fr. Felician Komlan Dem, an African priest working in the archdiocese of Detroit, was acquitted of sexual misconduct, it was reported on Sept. 3. A woman in a Harper Woods parish made the original accusations, charges that were dropped because of lack of evidence. The matter is being reviewed by the archdiocese.

Memorial Planned: It was announced on Sept. 4 that the Somerset County Commission planned a memorial for Flight 93 victims on Sept. 11, at Shanksville, PA. About 6,000 people have visited the site of the downed plane each month since the event.

Vandalism Acts: Two acts of vandalism in Brooklyn, NY, were reported in early Sept. A statue of St. Gregory the Great in Bellerose was toppled. The 7-foot statue had stood in front of the parochial school since 1964. Also, Our Lady of the Blessed Sacrament in Bayside was the scene of anti-Catholic graffiti. The Bayside graffiti attacked Cardinal Bernard Law and Father Patrick Shanley, both involved in the sexual abuse case scandal in Boston.

Redemptorist Exit: The Redemptorists, pioneers in the Alaskan missions, have ended their work in the region. The Redemptorist priests have served Alaska's Kenai Peninsula since 1961. When they arrived only one church served the entire peninsula. The Redemptorists opened six other parishes. The last Redemptorist in the area, Father Richard Strauss, departed on Aug. 29, assigned to Thailand.

Ground Zero: St. Peter's, the closest Catholic church to Ground Zero, held a special service on Sept. 8, in honor of Sept. 11. The service was commissioned by Communion and Liberty, a lay movement founded in Italy. A choir formed by lay group provided hymns

Fulton Sheen's Cause: On Sept. 9, the diocese of Peoria, IL, delivered papers to the Vatican as part of a campaign for the canonization of Archbishop Fulton J. Sheen. If canonized, he would be the first American male to receive such honors. He died in 1979 and was buried in St. Patrick's Cathedral, NY. The Vatican will study Archbishop Sheen's writings and examine any miracles attributed to his intercession. (*See* **Vatican News** for **October**.)

9/11: Cardinal Edward M. Egan of New York, while celebrating a memorial Mass at St. Patrick's Cathedral on Sept. 11, said that the anniversary was one "that stings and scars the soul." He also said that the event caused " 'the best of us' to march into the harm's way for others."

Shanksville Memorial: The 40 passengers and crew on board United Airlines Flight 93 were honored on Sept. 11 in the rural Pennsylvania field where their plane crashed.

Priest's Concerns: Seventy-seven priests of the diocese of Worcester, MA, sent a letter to the Vatican asking for a study of the sexual abuse policy adopted by the U.S. bishops, it was reported on Sept. 15. The priests called for more equitable processes that will protect those falsely accused and will value the "perfect" of the Church, despite the hysteria promoted by coverage of scandals. The group asked for Vatican intervention to remedy the "injustices" toward priests in the adapted policy.

Seminarians: On Sept. 15, the Department of Communications of the U.S. Conference of Catholic Bishops reported that 3,400 men are enrolled in college or post-college seminaries. Diverse in age and background, these seminarians are also younger generally. This survey does not include religious programs for the priesthood within orders or congregations.

Franciscan University: The Franciscan University of Steubenville, OH, announced on Sept. 15 that a new semester abroad is being based in Rome. Students will study at the Angelicum and live in a guest house overlooking the Roman Forum. Ten graduate students of the university will inaugurate the program in Rome at the end of the month.

Indiana Statue: On Sept. 15, USCCB general council, Mark Chopko, praised the 7th U.S. Circuit Court of Appeals for upholding an Indiana statute requiring women contemplating abortion to have an informal session with a healthcare professional. An injunction had blocked enforcement of the statute, passed in 1995, but was reversed.

Names Revealed: Oklahoma Gov. Frank Keating announced on Sept. 16 that the names of bishops who were not responding to the U.S. bishops child protection charter would be released to the public. Gov. Keating heads the U.S. Bishops National Review Board that is charged with reviewing compliance among the American bishops.

Catholic Dominance: A report released on Sept. 19 recorded a 16 percent increase in membership in the Catholic Church in the U.S. in the 1990s. The Catholic population in the nation numbered 62 million in 2000. Glenmary Research Center in Nashville, TN., published the report.

L.A Layoffs: The archdiocese of Los Angeles announced in Sept. it would close offices and layoff workers to cover $4.3 million dollar deficit. Some offices were subsequently kept open through various donations.

U.S. Policy: Cardinal Theodore McCarrick of Washington, DC, addressed the Council for Christians Associated for Defense and Disarmament on Sept. 18, speaking on the moral dimensions of U.S. foreign policy, particularly in regard to the war on terrorism.

Hispanic Ministry: On Sept. 23, it was reported that the Buen Pastor Award in Hispanic ministry would be given to Msgr. John Coffield of the diocese of Orange, CA, and Father Pedro Perez, a Cuban exile working in Miami, FL. The award is bestowed annually by the National Association of Hispanic Priests.

New Campaign: Serrin Foster, president of Feminists For Life, stated on Sept. 23 that it is time to redirect the abortion debate. A new campaign, "Women Deserve Better," is being introduced.

Hispanic Role: Cardinal Theodore McCarrick of Washington, DC, celebrated Mass on Sept. 24 and stated that Hispanics are the key to the future of U.S. Catholicism. He advised Church leaders to be well grounded in Spanish and in Hispanic culture. The Mass commemorated Hispanic Heritage Month.

New Priests: The ordination class of 2002 was reported on Sept. 25, as reflecting an increase in priests born outside the United States, particularly Mexico and Vietnam. An estimated 15 percent are Hispanic and nine percent are Asians or Pacific Islanders.

Project Rachel: It was announced on Sept. 25 that Project Rachel held a conference in San Antonio to focus on the clinical, pastoral and sacramental implications of the group's ministry to women suffering from post-abortion experiences.

OCTOBER 2002

Vatican

Mother Teresa: The Congregation for the Causes of Saints accepted on Oct. 3 a miracle attributed to the intercession of Mother Teresa of Calcutta. This miracle opens the way to the beatification of the beloved foundress of the Missionaries of Charity.

St. Bridget: Pope John Paul II celebrated the Seventh Centenary of the birth of St. Bridget of Sweden on Oct. 4. In a message to the abbess of St. Bridget's Order of the Most Holy Savior, the pope addressed St. Bridget of Sweden as a role model for today's women. Princess Victoria of Sweden and ecumenical leaders were invited to attend the celebration on Oct. 8.

Eucharistic Vigils: On October 4, it was announced that Pope John Paul II encouraged all-night Eucharistic vigils. The Holy Father made this recommendation in a message to the Spanish All-Night Adoration in Madrid. The group was celebrating the 125th anniversary of the organization, founded in 1848.

Sheen Cause: The Vatican Congregation for the Causes of the Saints approved a petition from the diocese of Peoria, IL, to open the canonization cause of Archbishop Fulton J. Sheen, it was reported on Oct. 4. Archbishop Sheen was prominent in the 1950s as the host of *Life Is Worth Living* and evangelized Americans through books, appearances and television productions. He died in 1979 in New York.

Rome Canonization: On Oct. 6, Pope John Paul II canonized Josemaria Escrivá de Balaguer, the founder of Opus Dei. The Mass held in St. Peter's Square drew 300,000 people, who heard the Holy Father praise the new saint who stood up to "a materialistic culture that threatens to dissolve the most genuine identity of the disciples of Christ." The Holy Father also called the saint's teaching as "timely and urgent." The people attending the canonization represented 84 countries and several non-Catholic beliefs.

Romanian Patriarch: On Oct. 7, Pope John Paul II welcomed Romanian Orthodox Patriarch Teoctist to St. Peter's Square along with 200,000 pilgrims attending the canonization of Josemaria Escrivá de Balaguer. This was the first visit of the patriarch to Rome. He signed a joint declaration with the Holy Father, a step toward unifying the two Churches, separated since 1054.

Catechism Praised: Cardinal Joseph Ratzinger hailed the *Catechism of the Catholic Church* as a true manual for happiness on Oct. 8 at the gathering of top theologians in Rome. As Prefect of the Congregation for the Doctrine of the Faith, Cardinal Ratzinger opened the conference. He said: "Appealing to Sacred Scriptures and to the global richness of Tradition in its multiple forms, and inspired by the Second Vatican Council, [*Catechism*] offers an organic view of the totality of the Catholic faith, which is beautiful precisely because of its vitality, a beauty, rich in the splendors of truth."

Rosary Recommendation: On Oct. 9, at the general audience in St. Peter's Square, Pope John Paul II recommended praying the rosary. The Holy Father declared: "October, the month of the holy rosary, encourages us to value ever this prayer so loved by the Christian tradition."

European Honor: It was reported on Oct. 9 that Pope John Paul II is among candidates for "European of the Year." *European Voice*, an English language newspaper published in Brussels, made the selection. Fifty candidates were selected for 10 categories.

Theologians Criticized: Cardinal Dario Castrillon Hoyos was reported on Oct. 9 as criticizing the "ruinous positions" assumed by some Catholic theologians in interreligious dialogue. Cardinal Hoyos stated that such theologians mistakenly present non-Christian religions as "equally valid" to Christians. He cited in particular Belgian Jesuit Father Jacques Dupuis and his book on religious pluralism as an example of such mistaken stances.

Gabon Ambassador: Pope John Paul II received on Oct. 10 the new ambassador of Gabon to the Vatican, Désiré Koumba. In an interview, the Holy Father urged African peoples to work hand-in hand to make their land hospitable to humans and their aspirations. The Holy Father stressed the need for "integral development, characterized by solidarity."

Vatican Radio: It was announced on Oct.10 that Vatican Radio has begun a daily broadcast in Hausa, a Chadic language of western Africa. The 15-fifteen-minute program was requested by bishops of that region. Vatican Radio broadcasts in 40 languages.

Vatican Council II: On Oct. 13, Pope John Paul II defined the Second Vatican Council as the start of the new evangelization and as a compass for Christians in the new century. Romanian Orthodox Patriarch Teoctist was present when the Holy Father made these remarks. He stated that the Council document serve to guide the Church in the path of the new century.

Bali Attacks: On Oct. 4 it was announced that Pope John Paul II sent a message of condolence to Indonesia to condemn the "cruel and misguided violence." About the Bali disco, a bombing that claimed 187 lives, the Holy Father said the assault "must be condemned by all who aspire a world peace built on respect for the inviolable dignity of every human life."

Case Opened: The pope's vicar for Rome, Cardinal Camillo Ruini, announced on Oct. 14 that the cause for beatification of Giovanni Palatucchi had been opened. Giovanni Palatucchi was a policeman who saved thousands of Jews during the Holocaust. He paid for his life in Dachau concentration camp in February 1945, at the age of 35. The Roman Jewish community attended the ceremony for the opening of the cause. Giovanni Palatucchi was proclaimed "Righteous Among the Nations" in 1990, and a street in Tel Aviv, Israel, bears his name.

Apostolic Letter: Pope John Paul II issued an apostolic letter on the Rosary on Oct. 16, proclaiming as well the Year of the Rosary. The Holy Father signed the document during his weekly audience in St. Peter's Square. He also proclaimed five new mysteries to the Rosary, the "mysteries of light." These include moments in the public life of Jesus. The Holy Father used the occasion to announce again his determination to remain pope and entrusted the life of the Church and that of sorely tried humanity into the hands of the Blessed Virgin Mary. (*See* **Special Reports** for other details.)

Vatican Meeting: On Oct. 17, Pope John Paul II held a series of discussions with U.S. Church leaders to study the bishops' norms on clerical sex abuse. These sessions, which included the president and vice president of the U.S. Conference of the Catholic Bishops, centered on the Vatican's official response to the proposed norms, which called for study and revisions to bring the norms into line with the universal law of the Church.

Eucharistic Adoration: On Oct. 18, the Vatican issued a new instruction for parish priests that prescribed an intensive prayer life and Eucharistic adoration as cures for priestly "disaffection, disillusionment, or even failure." The 38-page instruction was issued by the Congregation for the Clergy and was entitled: "The Priest; Pastor and Leader of the Parish Community."

Life-Giving Waters: In a message in honor of World Food Day, on Oct. 16 Pope John Paul II announced that all Christians must safeguard water. The Holy Father said any baptized Christian should recognize the importance of water as a true life-giving substance as well as a symbolic entity. The pope supports the U.N.'s Food and Agricultural Organization in its efforts to focus the world's attention on the use and depletion of water supplies.

Women Deacons: The International Theological Commission announced on Oct. 17 that recent studies and documents exclude the possibility of ordaining women to the diaconate. Two important indications were evident in the Commission's studies. To begin with, early deaconesses in the Church cannot be seen in a light similar to the male modern diaconate, as the rite of institution and their functions were different from ordained deacons. Secondly, the unity of the sacrament of holy orders prevents the ordination of women. The Commission devoted five years to this study at the request of the Congregation for the Doctrine of the Faith.

Beatifications: On Oct. 20, Pope John Paul II beatified six individuals in St. Peter's Square. Two catechists in northern Uganda, Daudi Okelo and Jildo Irwa, aged 16 and 12 , were honored as martyrs, having been slain for the faith on Oct. 18, 1918. The Holy Father recommended them as models for catechists around the world. Also beatified was Mary of the Passion, born Marie de la Passion Hélène Marie de Chappotin de Neuville (1839-1904), the foundress of the Missionaries of Mary in India. Another beatus was Liduina Maneguzzi (190-1941), a Sister of St. Francis de Sales who served as a missionary in Ethiopia. Also beatified were Andrea Giacinto Longhin (1863-1936), the Capuchin bishop of Treviso, and Marcantonio Durando (1801-1880) a priest of the Mission Congregation and the founder of the Nazarene Sisters. Pope John Paul II has beatified 1,303 individuals during his pontificate.

Cultural Manipulation: It was reported on Oct. 20 that Cardinal Alfonso López Trujillo, president of the Pontifical Council for the Family, warned members at that group's plenary assembly that the modern family is under grave assault. The cardinal stated that the media depicts the family as an obstacle for a woman's fulfillment, depicts marriage as personal, without social or moral consequences and recognizes homosexual couples as equal to those participating in sacramental or civil marriages. Efforts are being made by the Council to identify cultural efforts and to educate family members to the dangers in their own world.

Carmelite Mission: On Oct. 20, Pope John Paul II sent a message to the Carmelites of the world, exhorting them to become beacons of light in a troubled era. "Carmel reminds people, preoccupied with so many cares, that the absolute priority must be to search for the 'Kingdom of God and his justice,'" the Holy Father declared.

Church Art: On Oct. 29, it was revealed that Pope John Paul II had stated that sacred art works are not historical artifacts but assets that can effect the entire community. The Holy Father encouraged pastors and administrators to take such sacred articles out of the storerooms and restore them to their rightful places in worship ceremonies and gatherings. The pope was addressing members of the Pontifical Commission for the Cultural Goods of the Church.

Papal Knighthood: On Oct. 24, it was announced that Pope John Paul II conferred a papal knighthood on Yosef Neville Lamdan, the Israeli ambassador to the Vatican. Other ambassadors were also named. Lamdan also received the Grand Cross of the Pian Order.

Papal Visits: On Oct. 29, it was revealed that Pope John Paul II, who has made 301 visits to Roman parishes during his pontificate, introduced a new method of conducting such pastoral ministries. As he is no longer able to visit the parishes, the people are coming to visit him. The Holy Father will receive parishioners in the Paul VI Audience Hall on Sunday mornings.

Honorary Citizen: On Oct. 31, Pope John Paul II became the first pope to receive the distinction of honorary citizen of Rome since the creation of the Italian republic. The mayor of Rome, Walter Veltroni, conferred the honor, accompanied by other Roman dignitaries.

General Audience Topics:
• Comment on Canticle in Isaiah 26 (Oct. 2).
• Address on Psalm 66 (67) (Oct. 9).
• Address at Presentation of Apostolic Letter on Rosary (Oct. 16).
• Meditation on Psalm 85 (86) (Oct. 23).
• Address on Canticle in Isaiah 33 (Oct. 30).

International

Church Attacks: Archbishop Baltazar Porras, the president of the Venezuelan episcopal conference announced on Oct. 1 that recent aggressions against Catholics were worsening in his country. Father Ivan Fernández and an acolyte were wounded by gunshots recently, adding to tensions.

Wanton Terrorism: It was reported on Oct. 1 that Pakistani President Pervez Musharraf had condemned the massacre of six Catholics and one Protestant in a recent attack. Islamic militants killed the Christians, part of the staff of the Committee for Justice and Peace in Karachi. The Karachi Archdiocese was united with Protestants in this ministry for ecumenical justice and peace. President Musharraf termed the attacks an "act of wanton terrorism and fanaticism," and declared it a poor way of promoting Islam.

Papal Exhibit: It was announced on Oct. 3 that the Palazzo Ruspolli was exhibiting the Borgia family objects in nine separate sections. Artifacts of Pope Alexander VI, a Borgia; his son, Cesare; and daughter, Lucrezia, were prominently displayed. The exhibit recreated the historical elements of the 15th century and the beginnings of the Renaissance. Some 234 Borgia weapons, jewelry, sculptures, paintings and documents were in the exhibition.

Swiss Crisis: It was reported on Oct. 3 that not one single young man entered the Catholic seminary in 2002. Local authorities believe that media coverage of pedophilia scandals involving priests had stifled vocations. The decline is being countered through the *Eucharistein* community, founded by a former hermit. These young men are responding to the call of the priesthood.

Palestinian Students: Latin Patriarch Michael Sabbah urged students in the area to use dedication and enthusiasm to overcome the circumstances of their lives, it was reported on Oct. 3. He addressed the students in Manger Square in Bethlehem. Patriarch Sabbah asked the students to overcome fear and fatigue during their new scholastic year, despite ongoing Israeli-imposed occupation of the region.

Belarusian Laws: It was announced on Oct. 3 that the Belarus' upper house of Parliament passed a restrictive law on religion, an act that will threaten Catholics in Belarus. Predictions were made that the nation's Catholics, some 700,000 of a total population of 10 million, will meet with problems as a result. The act is part of the Russian Orthodox Church's efforts to block "Catholic expansion."

Jerusalem Protests: On Oct. 8, religious leaders in Jerusalem sent a message to U. S. President George W. Bush protesting a law that recognizes Jerusalem as the capital of Israel. The leaders of Christian communities and churches stated such recognition ignored the ongoing peace agreements between the Israelis and Palestinians.

St. Maximilian Kolbe: In honor of the 20th anniversary of the canonization of Maximilian Kolbe, the Conventual Friars Minor of Poland opened the archives at Niepokalanow, it was announced on Oct. 10. The saint's last letter, addressed to his mother, assured her of his health and well-being at Auschwitz concentration camp. The saint was slain at the camp on Aug. 4, 1941.

Nepal Attacks: On Oct. 13, Father Anthony Sharma, prefect of Nepal's Apostolic Prefecture, announced from Katmandu that recent Maoist rebel assaults on Catholic schools have not dimmed the Church's mission there. The Maoists have conducted campaigns in Nepal but do not have public support and are not dimming the esteemed reputation of the Church there.

Archbishop Cleared: Archbishop George Pell, Sydney, Australia, was cleared of the accusation of pedophilia, it was reported on Oct. 14. The Australian Churches National Committee for Professional Standards set up the investigation entrusted to Judge Southwell, a respected figure in Australian jurisprudence.

West African Dialogue: It was reported on Oct. 15 that the Association of Episcopal Conference of Anglophone, West Africa, issued a statement calling for interreligious dialogue to eradicate violence and to promote religious rights. The leaders of other religious groups in the region took part in a meeting studying the growing violence. The Association represents bishops' conferences from Gambia, Ghana, Liberia, Nigeria and Sierra Leone.

Environmental Degree: The Pontifical Athenaeum Regina Apostolorum announced on Oct. 16 that a master's degree in environmental sciences is being offered in Rome. A one-year program, from October to June, with six parts, the academic sessions are directed at qualified personnel concerned about the environment and the Church's social doctrine on related issues.

Deportation Anniversary: It was reported on Oct. 20 that the people of Rome remembered the deportation of 1,022 Jews to Auschwitz concentration camp in 1944. A special Day of Remembrance was organized on the 16th to recall the Nazi's deportation. A congress was convened and a silent march was conducted.

Legal Sterilization: It was announced on Oct. 20 that the Catholic bishops of Panama had voiced their opposition to legislation concerning the sterilization of women in that country. The bishops stated that the government prefers to eliminate human mouths rather than provide food. They also warned the government, "not everything possible is ethically valid."

Shrine Bombing: On Oct. 20, a bomb exploded inside a Catholic shrine in Zamboanga, Philippines, the second in three days. One person died in that blast at Fort Pilar, an open-air shrine, and 13 were injured. The bomb was in a bicycle parked near the gate.

Ossuary Findings: Biblical scholars in Jerusalem reported on Oct. 25 that the ossuary linked to the "brother of Jesus" was found interesting, but also a possible fake. The limestone ossuary, a container for human skeletal remains, surfaced with no documentation. The ossuary was subsequently declared a fake by antiquities experts.

Japan Bible: It was reported on Oct. 25 that the last installment in the Japanese Bible had been completed with the publishing of the "Book of Jeremiah." The Franciscan Biblical Study of Tokyo started the translations in 1956. Within the next five years the Study plans to publish the Bible in one volume.

Slain Diplomat: Authorities in Amman, Jordan, prepared to send the body of U.S. diplomat Lawrence Foley, slain on Oct. 28, to Washington. Foley, a Catholic, was killed by a lone gunman at close range. Foley served as an executive administrator for international development.

National

Respect Life: In a statement issued by Cardinal Anthony J. Bevilacqua of Philadelphia on Oct. 1, the reality of contempt for life in the modern world was deplored. Cardinal Bevilacqua said that: "Contempt for human life can take many forms." He added, "such views of life are not restricted to certain troubled areas on the globe."

Marian Film: Ignatius Press has released *Mary of God*, a video on the life on the Blessed Mother, it was reported on Oct. 1. This film is the second in a 10-part series being released. The first was on the life of St. Peter.

Benedictine Settlements: Abbot John Klassen of St. John's Abbey announced on Oct. 1 that all sexual abuse suits against the abbey had been settled. The settlements were reached in an intensive session with professional mediators. The abbey hoped to "heal the wounds" and put methods in place to prevent further difficulties.

Knight's Urgings: Supreme Knight Carl A. Anderson was reported on Oct. 3 as urging members to nurture a culture of service and volunteerism. The

Knights of Columbus established its $1 million Heroes Fund after the Sept. 11 attacks and promotes service, sacrifice, heroism and compassion.

Priests For Life: On Oct. 3, Father Frank Pavone, director of Priests For Life, announced that the organization prepared election-related materials for the nation's parishes. The organization does not endorse candidates or political parties but has programs to advance the culture of life in the election process.

Pope Days: Plans were reported on Oct. 4 for the celebration of "Pope Days" in New York, Philadelphia, Washington, DC, Minneapolis/St. Paul and in other cities and counties. Votive Masses for the Holy Father, distribution of papal writings and evangelical events are part of the "Pope Days" celebrations. Events are scheduled in Canada, Trinidad, Belarus and Slovakia.

Family Life: It was announced on Oct. 7 that the National Association of Family Life Ministers, who just ended their 22nd annual conference, have counseled that America needs Catholic ministers to families more now than in any era of the past. Workshops were conducted to develop pastoral responses to the many crises facing American Catholic families. Some 200 lay ministers attended the conference.

Visions Judged: It was reported on Oct. 7 that Baltimore archdiocesan theological investigators studying visions and messages of the Blessed Virgin Mary alleged to have been received by Gianna Talone-Sullivan at her home near Emmitsburg, MD, had concluded their inquiries. The commission deemed that the alleged apparitions and messages were not supernatural. Cardinal William H. Keeler decreed that no Catholic Church property may provide a platform for activities associated with the alleged apparitions.

Free Choice: The general secretary of the U.S. Conference of Catholic Bishops, it was announced on Oct. 7, asked the Democratic National Committee to remove Catholics for a Free Choice from its listings on its web site. A syndicated column by Mark Shields accused the Democrats of "a deliberate act of political bigotry" in listing that organization as a Catholic site.

Target Donation: It was reported on Oct. 7 that Target Corporation gave $2.5 million to the Center for Nonprofit Management at the University of St. Thomas in Minneapolis, MN. The center provides educational programs and seminars and served 1,900 participants last year.

Religious Threats: On Oct. 9, the U.S. State Department issued its annual International Religious Freedom Report, a study that notes that in some parts of the world practicing a religion is dangerous. Afghanistan was cited as a country in which there was some significant improvement in religious freedom. Much of the world's population, however, lives in places where religious freedom is restricted or forbidden entirely.

Abortion Figures: It was reported on Oct. 13 that there were 21 abortions per 1,000 women in 2000. This is a decline in numbers but also a marked increase in the rate of abortions for lower income women. Various economic and emotional factors are cited for the increase among low-income women.

Seminary Screening: On Oct. 16, it was reported that seminary screening processes had been changed. The U.S. Bishops' Committee on Priestly Formation issued a memorandum concerning new implementations in the process. The seminaries now seek men who are able "to live chaste celibacy." The alterations and new areas of emphasis will strengthen seminaries and future priests.

Support For Vatican: The U.S. Bishops' National Review Board on clergy sexual abuse announced on Oct. 18 that it was comforted by the Vatican response to the sexual norms adopted in the United States. A joint commission of four U.S. bishops and four Vatican officials studied and revised the "essential norms" to reconcile them with the universal law of the Church.

Catholic Media: Archbishop John P. Foley, president of the Pontifical Council for Social Communications, stated that Catholics in the media are called to higher standards of quality on moral issues, it was reported on Oct. 18. Addressing the Catholic Academy for Communication Arts Professionals, Abp. Foley warned that the media has a critical role in modern affairs. The media in America advocate moral permissiveness and increasing regulations, he stated, something that Catholics cannot condone or abet.

Mass Regulation: The U.S. Bishops Committee on Liturgy announced on Oct. 21 that standing during the eucharistic prayer at Mass in the United States is permitted "only on exceptional and extraordinary occasions." The custom may not be used on a regular basis. Listed in the committee's newsletter, the announcement also made clear that the regulation that the only licit posture during the prayer is kneeling. The general norms of the Vatican-approved U.S. Roman Missal adaptations took effect on April 25. (*See* **Special Reports**.)

NOVEMBER 2002

Vatican

Quake Victims: On Nov. 1, Pope John Paul II sent condolences and the promise of prayer for the victims, 26 schoolchildren, of the earthquake in the region of Malise, near Naples. The San Giuliano di Puglia school collapsed during the quake, which caused the death of three adults also.

World "Prisoners": On Nov. 3, Pope John Paul II announced that without faith, modern culture is vulnerable to fear and humans find themselves "prisoners" in the world.

Name Day: On Nov. 4, Pope John Paul II celebrated his name day, the feast of St. Charles Borromeo. Born Karol Wojtyla, the Holy Father honored the day by calling Carlo Azeglo Ciampi to exchange name-day greetings. He also had a luncheon with elderly cardinals who reside in Rome. Some 500 Polish pilgrims celebrated the day with the pope.

Memorial Mass: On Nov. 4, Pope John Paul II presided at a Mass for deceased cardinals and bishops, honoring their memories. The Holy Father praised the deceased as pastors, noting their "hands blessed, their words comfort, their presence — even silent — witnessed eloquently that God's mercy has no end."

Holy Land: It was reported on Nov. 6 that Pope John Paul II was donating $400,000 in humanitarian aid to encourage Christians to remain in the region. Archbishop Paul Josef Cordes, the head of the Vatican's *Cor Unum* aid office will deliver the funds.

New Diplomat: Pope John Paul II named Archbishop Antonio Mennini as the new papal diplomat to Russia, it was announced on Nov. 6. The archbishop previously served as papal nuncio to Bulgaria. His appointment comes at a crucial moment in Vatican-Russian relations.

Catholic Hospitals: The 17th international conference promoted by the Pontifical Council for Health Care workers is exploring the identity of Catholic hospitals, it was reported on Nov. 6. The Church administers 6,038 hospitals, 17,189 ambulatories, 799 leprosaria, and 13,238 centers for elders, chronically ill and the handicapped, as well as other charitable institutions. Social, cultural, religious and political changes demand awareness among health care-givers, who face new challenges and imperatives.

Food Program: The Vatican announced on Nov. 6 that it would make a donation to the World Food Program of the United Nations to demonstrate the Catholic Church's commitment to the eradication of poverty and programs to insure the right of humans to access to food and adequate nutrition.

Christian Zeal: On Nov. 8, Pope John Paul II met with representatives of the John Paul II Cultural Center in Washington, DC, thanking these Americans for their contribution to the work of evangelization. The Holy Father identified the center's mission as one centered in Christ, the core of human history and the key that unlocks the mystery of man.

"Empty Culture": Pope John Paul II addressed the Daughters of Mary Help of Christians, the Salesian Sisters, on Nov. 8, urging them to give hope to the world. The Holy Father described the modern culture as "empty and senseless" and he asked Catholics and the Salesians to "bear witness to hope on so many frontiers of the modern world."

Charismatic Witness: In a letter reported on Nov. 9, Pope John Paul II addressed members of the Catholic Fraternity of Charismatic Covenant Communities and Fellowships, meeting in Rome. The Holy Father commended the charismatics, urging them to bring the Good News of Christ to others and said that the 35 years of charismatic renewal in the Catholic Church has helped people recognize the "beauty of the grace given them at baptism" and the power of the Holy Spirit. The Holy Father called the charismatic renewal "a powerful witness to the anchor of truth which the world so needs."

Media Imperatives: On Nov. 9, Pope John Paul II urged media professionals to protect audiences from programs that feature violence and immorality. The Holy Father announced that the primary duty of the mass media is "service to the individual and society." He warned the absence of vigilance and control over the media "is no guarantee of freedom, as so many would have it believed."

Swiss Guard: It was announced on Nov. 9 that Pope John Paul II has named Elmar Theodor Mäder as the new commander of the Vatican's Swiss Guard. Mäder served as second in command prior to his elevation to the rank of captain. He implemented the extensive reform of the Swiss Guard during the tenure of Col. Pius Segmüller, who resigned in October. The Swiss Guard has heightened its screening process for recruits, revived training and promotion regulations and strengthened its ties with the Swiss military.

Pope At Parliament: On Nov. 14, Pope John Paul II addressed the Italian Parliament, the first time that a pope has ever been received by both chambers of the Parliament in the presence of all state authorities. In the past there were severe tensions between the Italian state and the Vatican, but the Holy Father was warmly received, and his speech was applauded by those present. Over 800 foreign and Italian journalists covered this historic event.

Canonization Causes: It was reported on Nov. 14 that the Coordinating Commission of Religious Historians met to study the Causes, Sanctity, Hagiography and Research on the Sacred. Postulators of the Causes of the Saints were present to clarify aspects of the process by which the saints are recognized and given honors in the Church. Such processes are generally prolonged and involved in uncovering the facts of each individual life. The Cause of St. Pio of Pietrelcina, Padre Pio, was studied in detail.

Additional Studies: The Vatican decreed on Nov. 14 that one extra year of studies will be required for candidates in Vatican-authorized programs in canon law. The Congregation for Catholic Education changed the required years of study for a licentiate degree from two to three years. This insures that candidates receive the degree of knowledge necessary to perform preparation in canon law.

Vatican Archives: It was reported on Nov. 15 that documents from the Vatican Secret Archive document the Church's opposition to the Nazis and the persecution it endured under Hitler's regime. These documents, reporting on activities pertinent to World War II and the rise of the Nazis in 1933, will be made available to scholars.

Qatar Relations: On Nov. 18, the Vatican announced that full diplomatic relations had been opened with Qatar, the Muslim nation in the Persian Gulf. The current diplomatic delegate to Qatar is Archbishop Giuseppe De Andrea, from the diocese of Greensburg, PA. He serves as well as apostolic nuncio to Kuwait, Bahrain and Yemen. The population of Qatar has a population of almost 800,000, 95 percent of which is Muslim.

Eastern Rites: On Nov. 21, Pope John Paul II met with representatives in the plenary assembly of the Vatican Congregation for Eastern Churches, urging them not to be imprisoned by the past. Acknowledging the difficulties faced by the Alexandrian, Antiochan, Armenian, Chaldean and Constantinopolitan churches, "numerical scarcity, lack of means, isolation, minority conditions," the Holy Father promoted a "wise harmony between the new and the old" in carrying out their missions.

Yachting Missions: On Nov. 22, the Pontifical Council for Migrants and Travelers announced the development of a program to link parish priests and chaplains to the world of yachting and coastal leisure-craft navigation. This group of travelers is rapidly expanding and in need of pastoral services.

Parish Role: On Nov. 25, Pope John Paul II called the parish the heart of the community's sacramental life and the key to resisting secular culture. Addressing the Pontifical Council for the Laity, the Holy Father praised the parish as the heart of liturgical life, and "the privileged place of catechesis and education in the faith." He urged parish communities to reach out to bring a profound personal relationship with Christ in the Eucharist to others.

Vocations: On Nov. 23, Pope John Paul II urged young people to consider the priesthood and religious life to serve humanity. The message was released as part of next year's World Vocation Day.

Catholic Websites: It was announced on Nov. 25 that the Catholic World Wide Web Corporation has been established to fund Catholic Internet projects around the world. The Vatican website will receive an estimated $5.5 million to modernize and hire new staff.

Catholic Perceptions: On Nov. 26, Pope John Paul II stated that while Catholic faith does not embrace any particular political or economic system, the faith does hold principles and values that possess clear political or economic implications. Addressing the bishops of Brazil, the Holy Father that only the Catholic faith, with its strong ethical commitment and constant involvement in the service of humanity, can resolve human problems in this age.

General Audience Topics:
· Address on Psalm 97 (98) (Nov. 6).
· Address on Psalm 86 (87) (Nov. 13).
· Meditation on Canticle in Isaiah 40 (Nov. 20).
· Address on Psalm 98 (99) (Nov. 27).

International

Cloning Opposition: It was reported on Nov. 5 that at least 29 countries had united to request a U.N. statement banning all forms of cloning. Spain introduced the initiative, which is supported by the U.S., Italy, Argentina and other nations. The European Convention on Human Rights and Biomedicine, the Oviedo Convention, prohibits the creation of human embryos for experimentation.

Gerardi Murder: On Nov. 5, the episcopal conference of Guatemala called for justice in the 1998 murder of Bishop José Gerardi Conedara. Various judicial acts have allowed three members of the Guatemalan military and a priest to go unpunished. Bishop Gerardi was beaten to death in April 1998 after exposing the military in their criminal activities.

Cloning Ban: On Nov. 6, it was reported that the U.S. has stalled a Franco-German proposal on human cloning at the U.N. This proposal bans only the cloning of humans but does not halt experimental cloning of human embryos, which are then killed for medical research. The delay is hailed by pro-lifers as a crucial victory on behalf of the cloned human embryos.

Galilee Site: On Nov. 7, archaeologists at the Kursi excavation in Galilee stated that the site was one of the earliest Christian stopping places for pilgrims to the Holy Land. Some of these pilgrims were slaughtered by a Persian army invasion in 614. A bathhouse and other ruins indicate that pilgrims did reside in Kursi briefly. The site may have been one of the largest pilgrim rest stops in the region.

Ukraine Cathedral: It was reported on Nov. 8 that the foundation stone for a new Eastern Catholic cathedral was laid in Kiev, Ukraine. Cardinal Lubomyr Husar presided and plans to move his headquarters to Kiev from Lviv. He described the ceremony saying: "The present undertaking is only a step on the way to something much greater and more beautiful."

Sudan Recognition: A Comboni nun, Sister Callista Cozzi, 81, received an award from the Islamic government of Sudan, it was reported on Nov. 8. Sister Callista, who was honored by the Sudanese President Omar Al-Beshir in Khartoum, received an honorary doctorate. She has served the Sudanese people in Omdurman, a village near Khartoum, where she found a 200-bed hospital. She also received the Order of Merit, Sudan's most important honor. She started working in the Sudan in 1964.

Plane Disaster: Bishop José P. Salazar of Batanese and the Babuyanes Islands of the Philippines was in a plane crash that killed 18 passengers on Nov. 11. At least four children were among the dead. Bishop Salazar was hospitalized in serious condition in Manila.

Colombian Kidnapping: Bishop Jorge Jiménez Carvajal, president of the Latin American Bishops Council, was kidnapped by the Armed Revolutionary Forces, it was reported on Nov. 12. Father Desidario Orjuela, pastor of San Antonio de Aquilera, the parish being visited by Bishop Carvajal, is a Eudist religious.

Bethlehem Siege: It was announced on Nov. 13 that correspondents for the RAI, the Italian State Television, have written a book detailing the siege of the Basilica of the Nativity from April 2 to May 10. Palestinians invaded the basilica, and the Israeli army surrounded the complex. Father Ibrahim Faltas, custodian of the basilica, allowed the authors to use information recorded in his diary. *The Siege of the Nativity*, published by Ponte alle Grazie and presented in Rome, cites the urgency for international juridical protection of the area, already defined by the U.N. as a holy place.

Albanian Cathedral: The consecration of the new cathedral of Rrëshen, Albania, reported on Nov. 13, is a symbol of the rejuvenation of the Catholic Church in Albania, after decades of Communist repression. Cardinal Crescenzio Sepe, prefect for the Evangelization of Peoples, praised the new cathedral as a place in which the Catholic community in Rrëshen can celebrate the sacred mysteries after the dark years of prosecution. He attended the ceremonies.

Albanian Beati: It was announced on Nov. 13 that the diocesan phase of beatification of 40 Albanian martyrs has been opened. Cardinal Crescenzio Sepe, prefect of the Congregation of Evangelization of Peoples, initiated the process during his visit to Tirana, Albania. The 40 Catholic martyrs, including bishops, priests, nuns, and lay people, died between 1913 and 1990 and serve now as models for modern Albanians.

Bishop Rescued: It was reported on Nov. 15, that Bishop Jorge Jiménez Carvajal and Father Desidario Orjuela were rescued by a Colombian army unit after a firefight with the men's guerrilla captors. Bishop Jimenez is the president of the Latin American Bishops Council, CELAM. The army unit hunted for the bishop and his companion for four days before freeing them.

Russian Opposition: It was announced on Nov. 15 that the Russian government did not approve of the creation of four Catholic dioceses that country. Yuri Fedotov, Vice-Minister for Foreign Affairs, stated that the plan is "unacceptable." He also announced that some Catholic priests "are not welcome in Russia."

Bali Aid: It was reported on Nov. 19 that Indonesian Catholic officials had been aiding the victims of the terrorist attack on Bali. Indonesia is the most populous Muslim country. Catholic leaders and agencies have joined many groups helping the victims of the assault.

Seminary Enrollments: The new figures on seminary enrollments, reported on Nov. 19, indicated an increase in Eastern Europe and a decline in Western Europe. Experts caution that such figures are subject to change in the future because of events and situations.

Salesian Slain: It was announced on Nov. 19 that Father Declan Collins was slain in Ennerdale, Johannesburg Diocese, South Africa. Father Collins was noted for his hard work among the homeless and unemployed. He was struck on his head and stabbed in the throat while in his own home. This marked the second attack on a priest in the diocese.

Cloning Ban: The European Parliament approved a resolution on Nov. 21 that favors a universal ban on all types of human cloning at all stages of development. The Parliament also called for a ban at the level of the U.N. on the cloning of human beings at all stages of formation and development. The members reaffirmed that the life and dignity of all human beings must be respected.

Little Flower: The relics of St. Thérèse of the Child Jesus were welcomed in Baghdad, Iraq, on Nov. 21, with a Mass and celebration among Iraqi Catholics. The relics are considered a sign of peace. A Day of Prayer for Peace was arranged as part of the Little Flower's visit to Iraq.

Family Support: On Nov. 21, Industrialist François Michelin, co-director of Michelin Group, addressed the International Congress on Catholics and Public Life in Madrid, Spain. Michelin announced that the family must come before profits and that all business ethics must be grounded in respect for the nature of the human person. The Michelin Group produces 844,000 tires daily, along with related items.

Miss World Riot: A Nigerian priest and two Catholic churches and a center were attacked on Nov. 22-22, in Keduna, Nigeria. The priest was seriously wounded, and the buildings were destroyed during riots sparked by a newspaper article about the Miss World pageant. At least 105 people died in the riots.

Bethlehem Siege: On Nov. 22, Israeli tanks returned to Bethlehem, on the West Bank, placing the area under curfew and halting school programs. Two tanks took up position in Manger Square, part of the Church of the Nativity complex. Christmas plans were complicated by the renewed Israeli occupation.

Demographic Crisis: On Nov. 22, Cardinal Camillo Ruini, president of the Catholic Bishop Conference of Italy, announced that the demographic crisis of that nation has assumed importance. The average women in Italy has 1.25 babies, marking a decline. The cardinal urged the Italians to restore the nation's fundamental confidence in life.

Cardinal's Accuser: It was reported on Nov. 25 that an Italian attorney, Alfredo Ormanni, who has accused Cardinal Ricardo Maria Carles Gordó, the archbishop of Barcelona, of collusion with the Mafia, is now facing fraud charges. The cardinal endured a period of living under suspicion until charges were dropped. The lawyer is now accused of a fund's implication.

New Church: It was announced on Nov. 25 that Cardinal Jósef Glemp, archbishop of Warsaw, Poland, broke ground for the Temple of Holy God's Providence in Warsaw. The church was originally planned in 1791. An earlier attempt to erect the shrine took place in 1918. The cornerstone was blessed by Pope John Paul II in 1999. This gilded metal tube holds fragments of the 1791 cornerstone and of the Warsaw Cathedral, destroyed during WWII.

Web Site: A web site about the cause of Mother Teresa of Calcutta was launched in Rome on Nov. 25. The web site, www.motherteresacause.info, details Mother Teresa's spiritual life. A healing was approved by Vatican officials. The miracle opened the door for Mother Teresa's beatification in 2003.

National

Proposed Norms: On Nov. 1, Bishop Wilton D. Gregory, president of the U.S. Conference of Catholic Bishops, noted that the U.S. bishops' proposed norms for dealing with sex abuse matters was not rejected or softened by the Vatican. Rome substantially confirmed the norms, and if adopted by the U.S. bishops they will become "particular law" for the American Church.

L.A. Losses: Five administrators of the archdiocese of Los Angeles, it was reported on Nov. 1, submitted their resignations to Cardinal Roger M. Mahony. Leaving were the chancellor and the administrators for community services and education. Msgr. Terence Fleming, the cardinal's chief of staff, also resigned. A new moderator of the curia was appointed by Cardinal Mahony, and the administrators were resigning so he could appoint his own leadership team.

Catholic Schools: It was reported on Nov. 4 that Catholic schools, no longer run by nuns or religious brothers, face an erosion of Catholic culture. The Chief Administrators of Catholic Education, meeting in Denver, CO, stated that maintaining a Catholic identity is one of their most important challenges. The lay men and women replacing religious in the schools threaten the "charism" that once distinguished Catholic schools in the nation.

Internet Courses: It was announced on Nov. 4 that the University of Notre Dame is instituting STEP, the Satellite Theological Education on the Internet. Members of the university's theological department have formulated 10 online courses in the sacraments, Scriptures, Christian ethics and Christian doctrine. No credits will be available for these courses, but individuals who complete the courses will receive certificates.

Haitian Detainees: On Nov. 5, it was reported that Archbishop John C. Favalora of Miami, FL, visited with some of 214 Haitians being detained after their attempt to seek asylum in the U.S. The archbishop declared that these detainees are not being treated justly or fairly. He is asking for the detainees to receive the same due processes accorded other refugees.

Motorcycle Ministers: The Knights of St. Michael the Archangel, a Catholic motorcycle group, was reported as accepting new members on Nov. 5. The group was started by Keven Jandreau in Michigan and supports outreach programs in the motorcycle community. Jandreau, a social worker, has been riding for over 37 years.

Slave Priest: It was reported on Nov. 6 that Bishop Wilton D. Gregory, president of the U.S. Conference of Catholic Bishops, dedicated a statue of Father Augustine Totten. Father Totten, the first U.S.-born-African-American priest, was born into slavery. The six-foot, 1,200-pound statue stands in a park across the street from St. Patrick's Cathedral in East St. Louis, IL. Bishop Gregory is from the diocese of Belleville.

McChesney Appointed: Kathleen L. McChesney, the executive assistant director for law enforcement services, was named on Nov. 7 as the head of the U.S. Bishops' new Office for Child and Youth Protection. McChesney said, "I believe the Catholic Church has suffered because of the acts of a few."

Call Of Christ: Cardinal Avery Dulles, speaking at Columbia University's chapel, St. Paul's, on Nov. 7, became a Catholic "because I heard the call of Christ resonating in the Catholic Church." He was raised a Presbyterian and converted to the Church while a student at Harvard in 1940. He subsequently became one of the America's foremost theologians.

Nuncio Leaves U.N.: Archbishop Renato R. Martino, the Vatican observer of the U.N., spoke on Nov. 8 to a General Assembly Committee, his last speech before that international body. The archbishop was named president of the Pontifical Council for Justice and Peace in Rome. Archbishop Martino announced: "Religion expresses the deepest dreams, hopes and desires of the human person."

Newman Award: On Nov. 9, Thomas Monaghan, the founder and former CEO of Domino's Pizza, received the annual John Henry Newman award, presented by the Cardinal Newman Society. Monaghan's service to Catholic higher education was honored, and he was praised as a successful Catholic whose gifts have contributed significantly to the life of the Church.

Pro-Life Gains: It was announced Nov. 12 that the U.S. bishops see positive signs that efforts by the pro-life movement in America are aiding in the crusade against abortion. The bishops cited the fact that fewer abortions are being performed and fewer doctors are willing to be involved in abortions. More Americans, especially among the young, identify themselves as pro-life. State legislatures are also moving to restrict or regulate abortions.

Norms Approved: On Nov. 13, the U.S. bishops overwhelmingly approved the revived norms dealing with the removal from ministry of any priest or deacon who has sexually abused a minor. By a vote of 246-7, the document, on which the Vatican was consulted, was accepted. A "Charter for the Protection of Children and Young People" was accepted in a revised form. (*See* **News in Depth**)

Hispanic Ministry: It was reported on Nov. 13 that the U.S. bishops approved a new program for Hispanic Catholics in the U.S. There are 25 million Hispanic Catholics in the U.S., making up about 40 percent of the entire Catholic population. These Latinos are new challenges as the largest minority group in the country. (*See* **Minorities**.)

New Building: The Catholic Relief Service announced on Nov. 13 that it would erect a new eight-story headquarters in Baltimore's Inner Harbor. The structure will adjoin a 1,000-bed motel. Kenneth Hackett, CRS executive director, said: "We are extremely excited about this potential partnership with the city after a lengthy and extensive search for an appropriate location for our agency's new headquarters."

Navajo School: Catholic Extension, the largest supporter of Catholic missions in the U.S., asked for assistance on Nov. 15 in raising $250,000 to save St. Michael Catholic School on a Navajo reservation in Arizona. The school was founded in 1902 by St. Katherine Drexel. The Arizona fire marshal has ordered the school to upgrade its fire system or face closing.

Defrocked Priest: Anthony J. Cipolla, a long-suspended priest in Pittsburgh, was dismissed from the clerical state by the Vatican, it was announced on Nov. 19. Bishop Donald W. Wuerl barred Cipolla from all public ministry in 1988 because of a sexual abuse lawsuit. Cipolla was reinstated and then suspended again by the Apostolic Signatura in Rome.

Medjugorje Priest It was reported on Nov. 21 that Father Jozo Zovko, the priest closely associated with Medjugorje, the site of reported Marian apparitions, has been denied the privilege of celebrating Mass at the Basilica of the National Shrine of the Immaculate Conception in Washington, DC. Authorities denied him permission when it was learned that Father Zovko's faculties had been revoked by the diocese of Mostar-Duvno in Bosnia-Herzegovina.

Aids Prevention: On Nov. 27, the U.S. Conference of Catholic Bishops released a letter asking parishes across the United States to become involved in AIDS programs, especially among African-Americans and Hispanics. Bishop Howard J. Hubbard of Albany, NY, is episcopal moderator of the National Catholic AIDS Network, and he sent the letter to the parishes.

DECEMBER 2002

Vatican

Migrants Day: On Dec. 2, Pope John Paul II appealed to the world to halt racism, xenophobia, and ultra-nationalism. Communicating for the World Day of Migrants and Refugees, the Holy Father said that the Church must lead the way in the name of Christ, accepting all who profess faith in Jesus and in baptism in the name of the Holy Trinity.

Priest Requirements: The Vatican announced on Dec. 2 that men who are homosexuals or who have homosexual tendencies should not be ordained to the priesthood. Cardinal Jorge Medina Estevez, prefect for the Congregation for Divine Worship and the Sacraments, called such candidates "very risky" and said that their ordination would be imprudent.

Filipino Community: It was reported on Dec. 2 that Pope John Paul II celebrated the start of Advent with the Filipino community of Rome, inviting the parishioners of Santa Pudenziana to the Vatican. Some 4,000 Filipino parishioners attended the papal Mass and heard the words of the Holy Father.

Clash Of Civilizations: Pope John Paul II, it was reported on Dec. 2, called modern terrorism an international evil capable of provoking a "clash of civilizations." The Holy Father believes the global dimensions of terrorism demand special and careful deterrence. He said international terrorism has assumed a "fearful dimension."

Images: The news photographers at the Vatican met with Pope John Paul II on Dec. 3 to present him with the new book, *Immagini, Images*, a collection of papal portraits. Archbishop John P. Foley, the president of Pontifical Council for Social Communication, had invited the photographers to donate their favorite photos of the pope. *Images* was a gift for the pope's 25th Christmas at the Vatican. It will not be made available commercially.

Human Globalization: On Dec. 5, Pope John Paul II announced that Catholic universities have not only the resources but the obligation to encourage the protection of human dignity in all aspects of modern globalization. Meeting with 300 Catholic university leaders, the Holy Father stressed that these institutions are uniquely situated to insinuate true human values into decisions concerning the economic, juridical, political and scientific spheres of modern life.

Electronic Inventory: It was announced on Dec. 5 that the Italian government has agreed to finance an electronic inventory of the Congregation of the Doctrine of the Faith's historical archives. This will be a four-year project that will categorize materials from the 16th century through 1903, and additional historic records.

Catholic Journalists: On Dec. 6, Pope John Paul II met with Catholic journalists of the International Catholic Union of the Press. At the audience, the Holy Father defined their role as "striving for the highest ideals of professional excellence, being a man or woman of prayer who seeks to give the best that they have to offer." The pope encouraged the journalists to seek and report the truth and remain sensitive to aspects of human life. Pope John Paul II stated the journalists have obligation to be saints.

New Lexicon: The "Lexicon of the Family," to be released in 2003, is a project of the Pontifical Council for the Family, it was announced on Dec. 6. The lexicon, some 1,000 pages long, defines new terms used in some secular circles to hide ideological objectives and clarifies words used to dim moral connotations. No date has been announced for an English edition.

World Peace: On Dec. 8, Pope John Paul II celebrated a homage to the Immaculate Conception by entrusting world peace to Mary. In the Piazza di Spagna of Rome, the Holy Father stood before a 100-foot statue of the Immaculate Conception, praying for the Middle East. He also visited the Basilica St. Mary Major to venerate an ancient icon of the Blessed Virgin, known as the "Salvation of the Roman People," as patroness of the Eternal City.

Peruvian Visitor: On Dec. 8, Pope John Paul II met with Peruvian President Alejandro Toledo Manrique in his private study. The audience provided an opportunity for Church-state relations in Peru and other international issues to be discussed.

Media Coverage: Cardinal Joseph Ratzinger, the prefect of the Vatican's Congregation for the Doctrine of the Faith, stated a definite media bias in the U.S. media coverage of the clerical sex-abuse cases in the American Church. The cardinal contrasted the less than one percentage of U.S. priests involved in these cases and the overlapping coverage in the media. He stated that the "constant presence of these news items does not correspond to the objectivity of the information or to the statistical objectivity of the facts."

St. Francis De Sales: On Dec. 9, Pope John Paul II defined St. Francis de Sales as a "man of goodness and gentleness, who knew how to manifest God's mercy to those he encountered." The Holy Father presented St. Francis de Sales to journalists, writers and workers in the media as the traditional patron of such activities since 1923.

Beda College: On Dec. 9, Pope John Paul II publicly expressed the gratitude of Catholics to the Beda College of Rome for 150 years of service to English missions. Members of the college were received by the Holy Father and heard him recite the memorable history of the institution and the service still being offered to the Church.

Homosexuals And Ordination: On Dec. 9, it was reported that the Congregation for Divine Worship has written a position on homosexuals and ordination. The congregation stated that a homosexual or one with homosexual tendencies is "not fit" to receive priestly ordination. The written statement was published in the November-December issue of *Notitiae*, the dicastery's bulletin, in response to a query from a bishop.

Religious Orders: On Dec. 10, Pope John Paul II stated there is a great need for religious-order priests, brothers and nuns even in mature dioceses. The orders bring a realization of a varied presence and the multifaceted dynamism of the incarnate Word of God and the community of those who believe in him.

Israeli Visitor: Israeli President Moshe Katsav was received by Pope John Paul II on Dec. 12. Katsav is the first Israeli president to visit the Vatican. The Holy Father asked him to ensure that Christians can celebrate Christmas in Bethlehem, a city occupied by Israeli forces, and Katzav stated that the Israeli Defense Forces would re-deploy outside of Bethlehem and would assist in pilgrimage events.

Singapore President: On Dec. 12, Singapore President Sellapan Ramanathan Nathan visited Pope John Paul II in the Vatican, where the two leaders spoke of a need for interreligious dialogue. Some 13 percent of Singapore's 4.4 million inhabitants are Christian. The island's Catholics are served by 30 parishes.

U.S. Abuse Norms: On Dec. 16, the Vatican released the *recognitio*, or decree of recognition, signed by Cardinal Siovanni Battista Re, prefect of the Congregation for Bishops, making the U.S. bishops' revised norms for dealing with clerical sex abuse binding on all bishops and dioceses. Cardinal Re urged the American bishops to "devote every available resource to restoring the public image of the Catholic priesthood as a worthy and noble vocation of generous and often sacrificial service to the people of God."

Pope's Christmas: On Dec. 17, the Vatican released the Christmas schedule of Pope John Paul II. He spent Christmas in the Vatican, celebrated midnight Mass and performed the other traditional rituals. The Christmas blessing was delivered from St. Peter's Square. This was the 25th Christmas season for the 82-year-old pontiff in the Vatican.

Pipe Organ: It was announced on Dec. 17 that a 787-pipe organ had been installed in the Sistine Chapel in the Vatican. The organ, worth $443,000, was donated by the Peter Kaiser Memorial Foundation and built by the Swiss organ manufacturer, Mathis Orgelbau.

World Day Of Peace: On Dec. 17, Pope John Paul II proposed four "pillars" of peace in his message for the World Day of Peace. The pillars, four essentials for conditions in human affairs, are truth, justice, love and freedom. Such conditions, the Holy Father stated, depend upon individuals and families, as well as the heads of state.

Catholic Action: On Dec. 20, Pope John Paul II met with children of Catholic Action in the Clementine Hall of the Apostolic Palace. The Holy Father used this year's motto: "Hands for All: All Holding Hands," as the basis for his address to the children. He urged them to remember that human hands were created to embrace material goods but open to embrace the love of God.

Mother Teresa: It was announced on Dec. 20 that Mother Teresa of Calcutta would be beatified on Oct. 19, 2003. The Church officially recognized a miracle connected to her intercession. Six others were listed as receiving promulgated decrees as well. Seven decrees of recognition of a second miracle were also promulgated, opening the way for canonization.

Italian Prince Prince Victor Emmanuel of Savoy, the son of the last king of Italy, had an audience with Pope John Paul II on Dec. 23. The prince was in Italy after a 50-year exile from his country. His wife, Marina Doria and his son, Emmanuel Philbert, were also received by the Holy Father. The male members of the Savoy family were exiled by the Italians for having collaborated with Benito Mussolini's Fascist regime.

Urbi Et Orbi: The *Urbi et Orbi* message, the greeting to the city of Rome and the world made by Pope John Paul II on Christmas, urged the world to seek peace. The Holy Father read the Christmas message in 62 languages before a crowd of some 20,000 in St. Peter's Square. The evening before he celebrated Mass in St. Peter's Basilica.

Papal Poetry: It was announced on Dec. 30 that Pope John Paul II, a prolific poet, had written a new religious meditation work that would be published in the coming year. The book will consider death and eternal life, coming as a spiritual last testament.

New Year: Pope John Paul II presided over an evening prayer service in St. Peter's Basilica on Dec. 31, including a *Te Deum* in thanksgiving for the gifts of God. The Holy Father spent the last hours of 2002 in prayer and adoration.

General Audience Topics:
• Address on Psalm 50 (51) (Dec. 4).
• Address on canticle of Jeremiah 14:17-21 (Dec. 11).
• Address dedicated to the last days of Advent (Dec. 18).

International

Christ The Savior: On Dec. 2, Cardinal Joseph Ratzinger addressed the congress on "Christ: Way, Truth, and Life" in Murcia, Spain, proclaiming the rights of Christians to proclaim Christ as the only Savior of humanity. The cardinal commented on modern relativism and the need to announce truth, which the Christian mission makes intelligible.

Forced Sterilization: It was announced on Dec. 2 that the U.N., the Clinton administration and Peruvian and Japanese organizations bear the responsibility for thousands of forced sterilization's in Peru. The sterilization procedures were financed by the U.N., the U.S. Agency for International Development, and other family planning agencies. The program of forced sterilization was aimed at the rural poor.

Philippine Corruption: On Dec. 2, Archbishop Oscar Cruz of Lingayen-Dagupan asked his fellow countrymen to pursue honesty and to defeat the swelling miasma of corruption in the land. The Philippines has a poor ranking in a recent international report on corruption. Archbishop Cruz especially focused on Jueteng, an illegal gambling game called the "lottery of the poor."

Ecumenical Franciscans: Members of Anglican, Lutheran and Presbyterian faiths gathered at the Franciscan headquarters in Rome for an exploratory meeting, Dec. 2-8. These members of non-Catholic churches are vowed Franciscans in their own denominations and are welcomed in the headquarters of St. Francis Order. There are 20 non-Catholic congregations of Franciscans, including cloisters, and many non-Catholic lay Franciscans.

Bethlehem Occupation: It was reported on Dec. 2 that plans for celebrating Christmas on the site of the Nativity were hampered by an Israeli occupation of that city. Curfews, unrest and the presence of weapons of war shelved plans for the holy season.

Korean Protest: On Dec. 2, a group of South Korean Catholic priests launched a weeklong hunger strike to protest the acquittal of two U.S. soldiers whose armored vehicles crushed two Korean girls in June. Some 100 nuns and many lay people joined the prayers for the victims.

Romanian Appeal: A Romanian Catholic coalition was reported on Dec. 5 as making an urgent appeal for the return of churches seized by Communist authorities in the past in Romania. The present government there is also accused of religious discrimination.

Religious Liberty: It was announced on Dec. 6 that the defense minister of Colombia, Marta Lucía Ramírez de Rincón, had charged that a 300 percent rise in attacks against religious leaders in Colombia is a direct assault on the Church. She added that the Catholic Church is "one of our most respected and effective civil institutions," and urged Colombians to defend the Church "as symbol of faith and hope of all."

Russian Report: The Russian government released a report claiming that the Roman Catholic Church poses the greatest threat to national security of all the 69 religious groups operating there. The report on Dec. 6 that Russia views the Church as more dangerous than Satanists. Archbishop Tadeuz Kondrusiewicz of Moscow, the leading Roman Catholic bishop, responded to the report with shock.

Christians of Europe: On Dec. 8, a convention of Christians for Europe ended in Barcelona, Spain, with a declaration calling for the recognition of the historic role of Christians on the continent over the centuries. The convention also insisted that respect for fundamental rights to life and religious liberty be respected by the European Union.

Father Jerzy Popieluszko: On Dec. 9, it was announced that Wladyslaw Ciaston, a former Polish secret police general, was acquitted a second time of murdering Father Popielusko, the outspoken enemy of the Communist regime in Poland. The trial in Warsaw ended in acquittal for Ciaston. Father Jerzy's body was recovered in Oct. 1984.

Bishop To Marry: It was announced on Dec. 9 that Canadian retired Bishop Raymond Dumais, 52, will ask for a dispensation from the Vatican to marry the woman he has been living with in Québec. Bishop Dumais retired from Gaspe in July 2001, stating that he had always been troubled by the vow of celibacy.

Irish Raffle: Archbishop Dermot Clifford of Cashel, Ireland, was reported on Dec. 9 to be as the winner of the first prize in a local sport's club raffle. He won a trip to the Canary Islands. He is an enthusiastic fan of Gaelic football and hurling. Abp. Clifford is a national patron of the Gaelic Athletic Association, the administrator of both sports.

Catholic Press: It was announced on Dec. 10 that the International Catholic Union of the Press plans a new press and teaching technology education center in Rome. The ICUP celebrated its 75th anniversary with a papal audience and dinner. Abp John Foley, president of the Pontifical Council for Social Communications, addressed the group in the Gregorian University to honor the occasion.

St. Juan Diego: On Dec. 10, it was reported that the first celebration of the feast of St. Juan Diego was held yesterday at the Basilica of Guadalupe in Mexico City. Some 30,000 pilgrims attended the Mass presided over by Cardinal Norberto Rivera Carrera. The cardinal led a procession from the basilica to the site of St. Juan Diego's shrine.

Priest Killed: It was reported on Dec. 15 that Father Jean Claude Kilamong was murdered in Bossangoa, Central African Republic, by local rebels. Five Capuchin Franciscans missionaries who stayed in the area to aid victims were taken hostage. Three other Franciscans were taken prisoner, beaten and threatened with death before they escaped from the rebels.

Moonies: It was reported on Dec. 17 that the Bishop's Conference of Zambia has warned Catholics there not to join a new sect led by seven priests and founded by the Family Federation for World Peace and Unification, founded by the Reverend Sun Myung Moon. Joining the sect will lead to automatic excommunication.

Ávila University: The Order of Discalced Carmelites announced on Dec. 17 that a new university is planned in Ávila, Spain. This will be the first university dedicated to the study of mysticism. A center with a capacity for 160 students will be built with a library, residential area, auditorium, administrative offices, and seminar room. The first core buildings will cost $8.1 million.

BBC Documentary: On Dec. 18, Bishop Crispian Hollis of Portsmouth, England, stated that a projected documentary on the Virgin Mary by the BBC was offensive to all Christian believers. The documentary reportedly presents the theory that Jesus was the offspring of a Roman soldier who raped her, or possibly the offspring of an illicit affair. The bishop addressed his concerns to the BBC and plans to write on behalf of Christians.

Russian Church: It was reported on Dec. 20 that a new Catholic parish has been erected in Magadan, Russia, a city on that nation's east coast. The area was a hub for Stalin slave labor camps. The Nativity of Jesus parish is composed of former prisoners who were sent to labor camps because they were Catholics.

Priest Cleared: On Dec. 20, Father Macario Apuya was exonerated by a regional Quezon City, Philippines, court of rape and child abuse. The Divine Word priest had already served four years for the alleged crime. He told reporters that he forgave his accusers.

Germany's Woes: Cardinal Joachim Meisner on Dec. 23 expressed concerns over Germany's loss of family values. The archbishop of Cologne stated, "only someone who knows God knows man." He described the crisis in the family as a "disaster" and stated his regrets that no efforts are being made to halt the disintegration of marriage and families. In Germany maternity and paternity are disparaged.

Mexican Orphanage: In Miacatlan, Mexico, Father Phil Cleary, director of Our Little Brothers, cares for almost 1,000 orphans. He recently accepted 140 such children who tried to survive by scavenging in a nearby garbage dump. "Most would never go to school if they didn't come to us," he said. The orphanage operates in a 19th-century hacienda.

Bethlehem Christmas: A somber Christmas was celebrated in the Church of the Nativity, Bethlehem, because of Israeli's occupation forces. The city was not decorated in its usual holiday lights, and Manger Square was empty.

National

Pietá Reproductions: The American Bronze Five Art Foundry of Sanford, FL, announced on Dec. 2, that it has been granted an exclusive license from the Vatican to reproduce Michelangelo's Pietá sculpture. The foundry has been contracted to produce 3,000 bronze busts of the statue. Another 1,000 reproductions will be made in silver.

Sheen Foundation: It was reported on Dec. 2 that the Archbishop Fulton J. Sheen Foundation is being started in Peoria, IL. The foundation is assisting the

Cause of the archbishop by gathering testimonials from individuals who knew him or have obtained favors from God through his intercession. The cause of Archbishop Sheen, a process that could lead to his canonization, was approved by the Vatican Congregation for the Causes of Saints in September.

Airport Chaplains: On Dec. 4, the National Conference of Catholic Airport Chaplains made the first deposit of archival materials at its repository, the Center for Migration Studies. The aviation ministry documents deposited record activities in the 1980s and 1900s at 99 U.S. and world airports.

Boston Bankruptcy: On Dec. 4, the Boston archdiocese finance council voted to allow Cardinal Bernard F. Law to pursue reorganizing the archdiocese under Chapter 11 of the Federal Bankruptcy Code. The archdiocese must have Vatican approval to pursue this course. The archdiocese of Boston faces 450 alleged sexual abuse cases.

Benedictine Honored: On Dec. 4, Benedictine Father Cyprian Davies received the Catholic University of America 15th annual Johannes Quasten Medal for Excellence in Scholarship and Leadership in Religious Studies. Father Davies is a professor of church history at the St. Meinrad School of Theology in Indiana and a history professor at the Institute for Black Catholic Studies at Xavier University of Louisiana, in New Orleans. He has written books and articles about the Black Catholics of the nation.

Priest Slain: On Dec. 7, Father William Gulas, the pastor of St. Stanislaus Church in Ohio, was killed by a gunshot and a blow to the head. The police arrested Brother Daniel Montgomery. He is accused of killing Father Gulas and then setting fire to the rectory.

Las Posadas: On Dec. 10, a Las Posada ceremony was held on Capital Hill in Washington, DC, as part of a Maryknoll and Oblate campaign for migrants. Las Posadas is a traditional ceremony that re-enacts of the Blessed Virgin and St. Joseph the efforts to find shelter for the Nativity. The Conference of Major Superior of Men and the Leadership Conference for Women Religious and other denominational representatives also sponsored the demonstration.

Ongoing Dialogue: It was announced on Dec. 10 that the ongoing dialogue between U.S. Lutherans and U.S. Catholics had provided common concern about the structure of communion. A recent meeting between the U.S. Conference of Catholic Bishops and the Evangelical Lutheran Church representatives focused on review of a draft document concerning dioceses, synods and the ministries that serve the parishes involved.

Pope Days: "Pope Days" events dedicated to prayers, Masses and expositions of papal accomplishments has been launched by the Marians of the Immaculate Conception, it was reported on Dec. 12. The "Pope Days" will be celebrated on the third Saturday of each month until Oct. 18, 2003. The events honor the 25th anniversary of Pope John Paul II.

Charitable Grants: On Dec. 13, President George W. Bush signed executive orders to aid religious social service organization with government grants and contracts. The faith-based initiative failed to gain Senate support. President Bush stated that the "government must recognize the power, and unique contribution of faith-based groups in every part of our country."

Pastoral Initiative: Two laymen, Joe Lilly and Rick Redman, have started an Internet website, it was reported on Dec. 17, called "Thank You Father" (www.thankyoufather.com). It is dedicated to expressing appreciation for the priests who have faithfully served Catholics over the years. The website counsels Catholics to thank priests in person during the crisis. Both men are former television news workers who recognized the devastating effects of the abuse scandals and wanted to provide a way for Catholics counter the negative aspects that are unfair to faithful priests.

Catholic Heritage: Cardinal Anthony J. Bevilacqua of Philadelphia announced on Dec. 17 that the archdiocesan Catholic Heritage Center would be delayed because of the slow U.S. economy. Originally slated to open this year, the center will serve as a multipurpose center the preservation of Catholic art, history and culture.

Haitian Defense: The Florida Catholic Conference reported on Dec. 24 that it was joining the appeal of the Catholic Charities Legal services. Asking for due process for Haitians who arrive in Florida, the Catholic groups appealed to the U.S. Senate and to President George W. Bush. The arrival of 220 Haitian refugees at Key Biscayne prompted the appeal because of the manner in which their deportations are being handled.

Dominican Merger: The Dominican Sisters of Edmonds, Washington, voted to merge with the Dominican Sisters of Adrian, Michigan, it was reported on Dec. 24. The Sisters have served in the archdiocese of Seattle for more than a century. The Vatican was petitioned for confirmation of the voting. Some 56 Dominican Sisters of the Congregation of the Holy Cross became members of the Adrian Dominicans of the Most Holy Rosary. The merge allowed a continuation of the apostolate and increased membership.

Navajo School: St. Michael's Indian School celebrated its 100th anniversary, it was reported on Dec. 25, attended by Indian tribes and Catholics from the diocese of Gallup, NM. St. Katherine Drexel founded the institution, and the Sisters of the Blessed Sacrament continue to teach there.

Ecumenical Donation: The closure of the Los Angeles Archdiocesan Ecumenical and Interreligious Affairs office was halted by a donation of $4.3 million by an anonymous supporter, it was announced on Dec. 28. Father Alexei Smith, director, stated that a non-Catholic made the donation, which covers the cost of the office ministry until June 2005, the remainder of Father Smith's term.

JANUARY 2003

Vatican

Historical Archives: It was announced on Jan. 1, that researchers would be allowed to consult the Vatican Secret Archives on relations between the Holy See and Germany during Pope Pius XI's pontificate, documents dating back to 1922. Other archives, containing documents from 1931 to 1934, were destroyed or missing as a result of the 1945 bombing in Berlin and the fire at the apostolic nunciature there.

Vatican Meetings: Pope John Paul II was reported on Jan. 1 as having met with more than 2.8 million people during 2002. If his international trips and interaction with individual countries are included, the figure would reach about 8 million. The data were released by the prefecture of the Papal Household and listed 2,823,500 people attending general audiences, liturgical ceremonies, special audiences, and celebration of the Angelus.

Slain Missionaries: *Fides*, the Vatican news agency of the Conference for the Evangelization of Peoples, announced on Jan. 2 that at least 25 priests, religious and lay missionaries were killed in the missions in 2002. Most were slain in Latin America, where 13 died. Africa lost 10, and a Chaldean nun was killed in Baghdad, Iraq. The annual "martyrology" is made public each year.

New Bishops: Pope John Paul II ordained new bishops on Jan. 6, urging them to "become a light to guide the way of nations, weighed by darkness and confusion. "Four of the new bishops are from Italy, and the others are from Benin, Iraq, Ireland, South Korea, Slovakia, Spain, and Ukraine. Following Mass, a parade of the Three Magi and 1,000 participants in national costume entered St. Peter's Square to honor the new prelates.

Beatitudes Community: It was announced on Jan. 6 that the Vatican's Pontifical Council for the Laity had recognized the Community of the Beatitudes as a "private association of faithful of pontifical rights with juridical personality." The Community of the Beatitudes was founded in France by a convert, Ephraim Croissant, his wife, and another couple. The Community is active in 32 countries and is supported by the "Family of the Beatitudes."

Eastern Christmas: Pope John Paul II sent Christmas greetings to the Eastern Christian Churches, who celebrate the feast on Jan. 7. The Holy Father prayed: "May the Lord, born for us from the Virgin Mother, bring serenity and peace to all these ecclesial communities." The Holy Father also received a Christmas message from Patriarch Alexei II of the Russian Orthodox Church.

Mother Teresa: It was announced on Jan. 7 that more than a dozen physicians in Rome and India were consulted about the cure of an Indian women related to the cause of canonization for Mother Teresa. The decree recognizing the miracle opened the way for the Oct. 19 beatification of the Mother Teresa at the Vatican. A website is available for those interested in the Cause: www.motherteresacause.info.

Confessional Rules: The Vatican announced on Jan. 9 that electronic means such as e-mail and faxes may not be used to consult about matters covered by the secrecy of the sacrament of reconciliation. Use of such of electronic means might degenerate into the viola-tion of the constitutive and inherent elements of the sacrament of penance. All priests must exclude technological mechanisms and "use only epistolary means in communication with the Apostolic Penitentiary on all matters covered by the sacramental secrecy of conscience and other prudential reasons."

America's Cup: The Holy See sent a priest and a layman to the America's Cup. Father Gerard Tronche of the Missionaries of Africa and Ludovico Massimo Lancellotti flew from Auckland, New Zealand, to offer their services to participate in the prestigious yachting competitions. The Church operates a ministry to sea-going individuals through the Stella Maris Centers for the Apostleship of the Sea.

Orthodox Petition: It was reported on Jan. 9 that the Holy See had not accepted a petition from the Russian Orthodox patriarchate to remove Archbishop Tadeusz Kondrusiewicz, the Catholic prelate of the archdiocese of the Mother of God in Moscow. The petition had not been recognized because bishops of the Catholic Church are appointed by the pope, not by leaders of other churches.

Cuban Visitor: Pope John Paul II met with Cuban human rights activist Oswaldo Paya Sardinas at a general audience in the Vatican, it was reported on Jan. 9. Paya Sardinas started the Christian Freedom Movement in 1987 and has promoted the Varela Project, seeking non-violent democratic reforms in Cuba.

Holy Childhood: On Jan. 10, Pope John Paul II sent a message concerning the Holy Childhood Association, the charitable organization designed to aid children around the world financially and spiritually. The Holy Father declared: "In poor and needy children, you can see the face of Christ." The Holy Childhood Association has been serving the needs of poor children for 160 years.

Prayerful Solidarity: Pope John Paul II met with 380 U.S. bishops, priests, and seminarians on Jan. 10, telling them that he was in "prayerful solidarity" with U.S. Catholics facing sexual abuse case scandals. Some 200 alumni of the North American College, the U.S. seminary in Rome, and staff and administrators took part in the Vatican gathering.

Papal Baptism: Pope John Paul II baptized 22 infants, including triplets, on Jan.12, at the feast of the Baptism of the Lord. A Mass was celebrated in the Sistine Chapel for the feast, at which the Holy Father defined baptism as the reception of "a new life, which is the very life of God." During his pontificate, Pope John Paul II has baptized 1,370 infants in the Vatican in Italy and abroad.

Sex Changes: A confidential report from the Vatican's Congregation for the Doctrine of the Faith was reported on Jan. 14, stating that a conclusion has been reached that "sex-change" procedures do not alter a person's gender in the eyes of the Church. Parish baptism records are not changed, and the medical procedures do not make an individual eligible to marry, be ordained to the priesthood or enter religious life. The transsexual surgical procedures are deemed so superficial that they do not change the personality.

Papal Cell Phones: It was announced on Jan. 14 that Pope John Paul's teachings would soon be heard on Italian cell phones as daily messages. The Vatican and the Italian mobile phone company, TIM, agreed to a new service called "Through the Holy Father." The text will be selected by the Vatican.

Catholic Politicians: A new Vatican document was reported on Jan 16, concerning Catholic politicians and their responses to issues and moral values. The "Doctrinal Note on Some Questions Regarding the Participation of Catholics in Political Life," written by the Congregation for Doctrine of the Faith and approved by Pope John Paul II, rejects the modern "cultural relativism" and "ethical pluralism" that deny absolute truth. The political figures who do not uphold political stands compatible with the faith and natural moral lawdamage the unity and interior coherence of the faithful. The document also treats organizations founded on Catholic principles that support political movements or forces that are contrary to the moral and social teachings of the Church. (*See* **News in Depth**.)

Families Vital: Pope John Paul II expressed his concern about families during a meeting with administrators of the city of Rome and the region of Lazio, it was announced on Jan. 17. The Holy Father cited the scarcity of births and the aging of the population as a modern crisis. He also called for a "renewed awareness of the importance and sacredness of the family."

"Catholic School Day": On Jan. 19, Pope John Paul II appealed for the rights of parents to send their children to Catholic schools. In his observance of "Catholic School Day" in Rome, the Holy Father greeted Catholic teachers and students at the Angelus in St. Peter's Square. He expressed his hope "that every family will have the concrete possibility to choose this new type of school for its children."

Papal Blessing: On Jan. 21, it was announced that Pope John Paul II blessed two live lambs whose wool will be used for the *palliua* that he will present to new archbishops. The *pallium* has two small white woolen bands with sewn black crosses. Following the blessing, performed in honor of St. Agnes, the lambs were taken the Roman convert of St. Cecilia, where they were shorn. The nuns in the convent make the *palliums*.

Papal Mountains: It was reported on Jan. 22 that a snowy peak at the South Pole, previously nameless, is now "Mount John Paul II." The nearly 3,700-foot mountain was named by the expedition organized by Msgr. Liberio Andreatta, head of the Vatican's pilgrimage tour agency.

Diocesan Affairs: On Jan. 24, Pope John Paul II urged bishops to maintain diocesan governance to avoid the modern trend to ignore the juridical weight of formal doctrinal teachings. The Holy Father asked bishops to conduct "pastoral service" necessary to prevent "true injustices.

Ratisbonne Institute: On Jan. 24, it was announced that the Vatican would not reopen the Ratisbonne Institute for Jewish studies in Jerusalem in the fall. Judaic studies will be strengthened instead at Rome's Gregorian University. The reasons for the discontinuance cited included increased violence, financial problems, declining enrollment, and academic concerns.

Double Speak Book: The Vatican announced on Jan. 28 that it had completed a book to counter the manipulation of terminology regarding family and life issues. The *Dictionary of Family* reveals the ambiguity of terms used, such as "reproductive health," as a code for abortion. Also treated is the modern "antilanguage," the changing of language to cloak truths. The word "abortion" is now replaced by "voluntary interruption of the pregnancy." Translation of the work will be made available later in the year.

General Audience Topics:
• Meditation on Psalm 99(100) (Jan. 8)

International

Hindu Denunciation: It was reported on Jan. 3 that a prominent Hindu organization in New Delhi, India, opposed the participation of President Avul Pakir Jainulabdeen Abdul Kalam in a Jesuit meeting in Calcutta. The organization stated that the Jesuits have taken an oath that "prescribes violent and barbaric means to decimate all those who don't follow the Roman Catholic religion." The volunteer corps, the opposing organization, wants India to become a theocratic Hindu nation that serves as an umbrella for allied Hindu groups.

Sudan Peril: It was announced on Jan. 6 that Bishop Cesare Mazzolari, M.C.C.I., of Rumbek in southern Sudan had warned that the nation's ongoing draught will result in thousands of victims. Bishop Mazzolari has four million Sudanese in his diocese and warns that the population, which has suffered two decades of disaster, is no longer able endure any more conflict.

Peace Climb: On Jan. 7, it was reported that a group representing seven religions has made plans to climb Mount Everest, the world's highest mountain. Lance Trumbull, a resident of Katmandu, Nepal, is the organizer of the climb. He is an American citizen who hopes to promote interreligious dialogue and raise $1 million for charities.

Irish Terror: It was reported on Jan. 7 that a bomb was left at the entrance to a Catholic girls' school in Belfast, Northern Ireland, delaying a Mass there. A homemade pipe bomb was defused by a British Army bomb squad. The school, Holy Cross Girls' Primary, has been a focal point of Protestant protests for nearly two years, and police and soldiers have had to escort students to and from the buildings and grounds.

Korean Award: The first foreigner to win the $4,200 Cheju Culture Prize was announced on Jan. 7, in Seoul, South Korea. An Irish missionary, Columban Father Patrick J. McGlinchey, 75, received the award. He arrived in Korea in 1954 and began his work with farmers. Father McGlinchey started 26 farm-operated credit unions, benefiting 120,000 people. Local farmers have also increased their livestock because off the Columban priest's efforts.

AIDS Crisis: On Jan. 7, the AIDS Office of the Southern African Catholic Bishops Conference urged the South African government to provide cheaper medicinal products to HIV patients. Patent laws prevent the sale of generic anti-retroviral drugs in South Africa, and present costs make the drugs prohibitive to HIV victims. An association of HIV/AIDS patients is working to make pharmaceutical companies provide such drugs for free.

Lithuanian Catholics: The Catholic Church in Lithuania, persecuted during the Communist regime era, is making a comeback, it was reported on Jan. 18. There are 200 students in Lithuania's four seminaries, young men eager to take the place of priests imprisoned by the Communists or forced to leave the country. Lay ministers and ecclesial groups are also laboring as Catholics in Lithuania propose evangelical programs to aid the nation.

Internet Safeguards: The Catholic Agency for Social Concern in London was reported on Jan. 12 as releasing a statement concerning Internet use by children. The statement, entitled "Children and the Net: A Short Guide for Parents," lists inappropriate contacts, exposure to inappropriate materials and other dangers on the Internet. Guidelines and simple elements of parental control are available. The statement is posted on the website of the Catholic Communications Service of the bishops in England and Wales.

Opus Dei: A Mass was celebrated in Rome on the anniversary of the birth of St. Josemaria Escriva, it was announced on Jan. 12. Bishop Javier Echevarriá, prelate of the Opus Dei, celebrated the Mass and spoke of the ongoing programs being conducted. He calls the founder of Opus Dei "a saint within reach of everyone."

Franciscan Harassment: It was reported on Jan 12, that an ethics panel of Russian journalists condemned the two news outlets that libeled a community of Catholic Conventual Franciscans by implicating the friars in a prostitution ring. The media used false information to authenticate their charges, which have been denied by the Franciscan superiors. The Vatican Press assailed the smear tactics.

Hong Kong Poll: A poll in Hong Kong released on Jan. 12 ranked Hong Kong Bishop Joseph Zen Zekiun as the most significant person of the year 2002. *The Apple Daily,* the most popular Chinese-language newspaper in the territory, conducted the poll. Other surveys in Hong Kong's leading daily paper and on an English-language radio station selected Bishop Zen as the person of the year for being an outspoken prelate "who has led the church into the life of society."

Gang Mediation: It was reported on Jan. 14 that Auxiliary Bishop Romulo Emiliani of San Pedro-Sula, Honduras, announced his determination to halt gang wars in the area. The corpses of too many young people are being found in the region, the result of an ongoing war between two local gangs. There are over 200 such gangs in Honduras, affecting the lives of members aged eight to 35.

Holy Lands Needs: On Jan. 15, Father Marun Lahham, rector of the seminary of the Latin Patriarchate of Jerusalem, stated he believed that the Holy Land needs material assistance, especially for schools, and pilgrim visitors. The schools are in an emergency state due to the economic and social conditions there. The region also needs the presence of Christian pilgrims, which will give spiritual and material support.

Homosexual Rights: On Jan. 17, the European Parliament narrowly approved a report asking the 15 member states to provide live-in couples, including homosexuals, the legal rights that married couples enjoy. The amended report was approved 277-269, with 14 abstentions. The vote is not binding on member states.

Cardinal Acquitted: Cardinal Michele Giordano of Naples was acquitted in an appeal on Jan. 17 of charges that he misappropriated funds. He was also charged with being in a loan-shark ring. Both charges were deemed false, but the Italian prosecutors appealed. The appeal court in Potenza upheld the lower court's acquittal.

Israeli Interference: It was reported on Jan.19 that Latin-rite Patriarch Michael Sabbah of Jerusalem was not allowed to leave Tel Aviv airport because of a security search by Israeli officials. The patriarch's Vatican diplomatic passport should have spared him from such interference. The Israelis made him open his suitcase and tried to search his personal documents, a violation of the 1993 agreement between the Vatican and the State of Israel. As a result, the patriarch was unable to attend a symposium in Rome that he was scheduled to address concerning interreligious dialogue.

Bogota Slain: Four gunmen invaded a Catholic Church during Mass and killed two people, it was reported on Jan. 20. Four attending the Mass were wounded in the Bogota, Colombia, parish. The shooting was apparently caused by a grudge. Ten suspects were arrested.

Britain Is Pagan: On Jan. 20, Cardinal Cormac Murphy O'Connor reportedly called Britain "a pagan nation." He stated that the past 50 years created a vacuum that robbed people of their faith. He also commented: "Christianity as a culture has been gravely diminished in the land."

"Subiaco Charter": Abbot Mauro Meacci of Subiaco presented the "Subiaco Charter" to the European Convention, it was announced on Jan. 24. The convention has been given the task of writing a future Constitution for the continent. The "Subiaco Charter," also sponsored by the Italian ambassador to the Vatican and by the president of the Forum of Family Associations, promotes the fundamental rights of the human person. St. Benedict of Nursia played an important role in his lifetime and founded monasteries in Subiaco. He was recognized as the patron of Europe by Pope Paul VI. The "Subiaco Charter" reflects on St. Benedict's labor and visions of human life.

National

Retiring Bishops: It was reported on Jan. 2 that as many as 33 active U.S. bishops could retire this year. They have reached or passed the normal age for retirement. That is the largest number of retirees in one year in the nation's history. Of the 17 active bishops who turned 75 in 2002, Pope John Paul II allowed only five to retire from service. The bishops are required to submit their resignation at age 75, but the Holy Father may refuse or delay in accepting such resignations.

Guantanamo Detainees: Father Raymond A. Tetreault, pastor of St. John the Evangelist Church in Slaterville, RI, stated that the detainees in U.S. custody at Guantanamo Bay, Cuba, are being treated very well, as detention conditions there meet all provisions of international treaties for treatment of prisoners of war. Father Tetreault spent seven months as a chaplain on duty at Guantanamo. He is a lieutenant colonel in the 43rd Police Brigade of the Rhode Island Army National Guard and was called to active duty.

Abortion Funding: It was announced on Jan. 3 that the Texas Supreme Court ruled that the state does not have to fund abortions for women with health complications who receive Medicaid. The case of Low Income Women vs. Raiford was rejected by the court.

Canonical Process: It was reported on Jan. 6 that Bishop Alvaro Corrada of Tyler, TX, had initiated a canonical process against Father Anthony Alphonse to prohibit from serving as a priest anywhere in the world. Father Alphonse was censured in February 2002 after reportedly leaving the diocese without permission and raising funds inappropriately.

Papal Portrait: A portrait of Pope John Paul II was reported on Jan. 6 as being part of a traveling exhibit of Vatican art in Philadelphia. The work of Nelson Shanks, the portrait will also be exhibited at the Cathedral Basilica of SS. Peter and Paul in Philadelphia. The Holy Father did not pose for the portrait.

Catholic Charities: It was announced on Jan. 6 that Catholic Charities U.S.A. has made plans to increase its legislative activities, especially concerning reforms involving farm workers, many of whom are illegal immigrants. The organization is asking for federal benefits to illegal immigrants, the improvement of programs and more funding for farm worker educational, health and housing programs.

Vatican-U.S. Relations: On Jan. 7, a report was issued about the address by Jim Nicholson, the U.S. ambassador to the Vatican. Ambassador Nicholson, speaking to the John Carroll Society, a lay organization in Washington, DC, stated that the U.S. and the Vatican could collaborate concerning freedom and the dignity of human beings. He added that the U.S. and the Vatican fundamentally agree on the urgent need to give people "a world of freedom, justice, well being and peace."

Catholic Press: It was reported on Jan. 7 that Archbishop John P. Foley, president of the Pontifical Council for Social Communications, and Bishop Joseph A. Galante, Coadjutor of Dallas and chairman of the U.S. Bishops' Communication Committee, sent messages for the observance of the Catholic Press Month, held in February each year. Archbishop Foley said that the Catholic Press continues to report the "full story of the Catholic Church in the United States," alleviating damage caused by the news of scandals. Bishop Galante praised the Catholic Press, which has "also supported and pointed the good work of many."

Confessional Threat: The Kentucky House of Representatives filed a bill that challenged the sacramental seal of confession in the Catholic Church, it was reported on Jan. 9. The bill seeks to amend the clergy-penitent privilege, prohibiting the seal from extending to any communication relating to neglect or abuse of a minor child. The Catholic Conference of Kentucky opposed the bill.

Little Flower: The National Shrine of St. Thérèse of the Little Flower in Darien, IL, announced on Jan. 13 that it had received new memorabilia of the saint. The shrine houses the second-largest collection of St. Thérèse memorabilia in the world. New additions include an earthen water-jar, a lap-desk, and a piece of the bed-spread used by the saint. Other memorabilia in the shrine includes a first-class relic of the saint, as well as personal articles.

Rural Life: The National Catholic Rural Life Conference joined other advocacy organizations in urging changes in federal farm policies, it was reported on Jan. 14. The changes requested were not included in last year's farm bill. The agency is asking for a fair market and a share in the funds inserted into the food and agricultural economy.

Lourdes Center: On Jan. 14, it was reported that Archbishop Charles J. Chaput of Denver, CO, blessed a new Marian center that will be allowed to distribute water from Lourdes, where the Blessed Virgin appeared to St. Bernadette in 1858. The Denver Lourdes Marian Center is only the second facility to distribute holy water from Lourdes. The bishop of Lourdes, France, attended the ceremonies.

Historical Awards: It was announced on Jan. 14 that David Burr, professor emeritus at Virginia Polytechnic and State University, Blacksburg, VA, won two prizes from the American Catholic Historical Society for his book, *The Spiritual Franciscan: From Protest to Persecution in the Century After St. Francis.* Burr won the John Gilmary Shea Award and the Howard R. Marraro Prize, named in memory of a professor at Columbia University.

Pro-Abortion Politicians: On Jan. 22, Bishop William K. Weigand of Sacramento, CA, stated that Catholics who support abortion should abstain from receiving Holy Communion until they have a change of heart. In a homily at the Cathedral of the Blessed Sacrament, Bishop Weigand singled out Governor Gray Davis and upheld a recent decision of a pastor to bar the governor from distributing at St. Patrick's Home.

Church Vandalism: It was reported on Jan. 24 that a wave of vandalism in New Jersey centered on Catholic churches in Newark. A hospital was vandalized. Statues were targeted in parishes and at a hospital. Jamil Gadsen, 20, was arrested in connection with the attack on a statue of Mary with the Child Jesus at St. Thomas Aquinas Church.

Seminary Closing: It was announced on Jan. 29 that St. John's Seminary in Camarillo, CA, would close its Seminary College at the end of the academic year. The Archdiocese of Los Angeles owns the school. The decision to close was described as purely fiscal.

Los Angeles: On Jan. 30, it was reported that the Archdiocese of Los Angeles had an operating deficit of $11.2 million in its last fiscal year. Some $1.5 million was used by the archdiocese to settle legal cases created by the sexual abuse of minors by several members of the clergy.

FEBRUARY 2003

Vatican

Lebanon Visitor: Pope John Paul II received Rafiq Hariri, the Muslim president of Lebanese Council of Ministers, it was announced on Feb. 1. The leader of the ministers stated that he was in the Vatican to pay his respects to the Holy Father, adding that the Lebanese Council "must maintain close relations with the Vatican." Pope John Paul was warmly received when he visited Lebanon in May 1977. The Prime Minister also explained that the Islam and the extremism now being displayed are not synonymous.

Pope Mourns: On Feb. 2, Pope John Paul II prayed for the victims of the U.S. space shuttle *Columbia* disaster, expressing condolences and his unity with the surviving relatives of the lost astronauts. The Holy Father expressed his distress to a group of pilgrims in St. Peter's Square, calling the news of the explosion of the shuttle as it reentered the atmosphere "tragic." He also stated that he was spiritually close to the relatives.

Asian New Year: On Feb. 2, Pope John Paul II congratulated the peoples of Asia, who celebrated the Lunar New Year the day before with fireworks, prayers and traditional dances. The Holy Father declared: "May the New Year be a period of peace, founded on four precise needs of human spirit: truth, justice, love and liberty."

Consecrated Life: Honoring the World Day of Consecrated Life, Pope John Paul II declared that the consecrated are signs of God's love. He described poverty, chastity, and obedience as distinct characteristics of the redeemed, those freed from the "slavery of egoism." He addressed religious in a homily in St. Peter's Square marking the occasion. The Statistical Yearbook of the Church states that at the start of 2002, there were 138,619 religious priests, 578 religious deacons, 54,970 men religious (not ordained priests), 792,317 and professed religious women. There were 625 men and 29,221 women in secular institutes.

Christian Charity: Pope John Paul II, it was announced on Feb. 6, said that charity is essential to Christian life. "Christians must not think that they can seek the good of their brothers and sisters without embodying the charity of Christ," the Holy Father declared in his message for Lent 2003. He prayed that each Catholic would practice charity during Lent.

No "Bureaucratization": On Feb. 7, it was reported that Pope John Paul II was against "bureaucratization" in the Church. Meeting with bishops of the Brazilian Episcopal Conference, the Holy Father stressed the fact that organizations and episcopal conferences must serve the bishops and not take their place. He also commented on the "excess" of organizations and meetings that bishops frequently encounter outside of their dioceses.

Kazakstan President: On Feb. 7, it was reported that Pope John Paul II received in audience President Nursultan Nazerbayev of Kazakstan, accompanied by his wife and entourage. Nazarbayev was re-elected after a mandate and is currently dismantling the nuclear arsenal inherited from the Cold War. He offered his county's mediation in the Iraq crisis. The Holy Father visited Kazakstan in Sept. 2001.

New Age: Cardinal Paul Poupard, president of the Pontifical Council for Culture announced on Feb. 7 that a 93-page report, "Jesus Christ, Bearer of the Water of Life: A Christian Reflection on the New Age," was ready for distribution. The Pontifical Council for Interreligious Dialogue also participated in the report's preparation. Cardinal Poupard stated: "The New Age seems to offer its spiritual view of the world, insisting on the profound unhappiness of the contemporary happiness, because of the promises cosmic harmony…. However," he added, "the authentic community receives Christ in salvific encounters." (*See* **Special Report** in **News in Depth**.)

Rebirth in Belarus: On Feb. 10, Pope John Paul II encouraged a rebirth of the Catholic Church in Belarus. Receiving Catholic bishops of that country, the Holy Father announced that the Church there has endured "the winter of violent persecution that lasted several decades." In Oct. 2002, Belarus President Aleksandr Lukashenko approved one of the most repressive pieces of legislation in Europe concerning religious freedom. The law prohibits the registration of religious communities not established in the republic at the time of Soviet Union. The Holy Father asked the Catholics of Belarus to support the family and seek always for dialogue with the Orthodox Church.

Priest Decline: It was reported on Feb. 10 that the latest statistics from the *Annuario*, the Vatican yearbook, show a continuing decline in the number of priests worldwide. Seminarians, however, have increased 1.5 percent. The worldwide Catholic population reached 1.06 billion at the end of 2001, an increase of 1 percent. The number of priests declined 111 during 2001, a decrease of 778 in religious order priests and an increase of 667 in diocesan priests.

St. Francis: Pope John Paul II on Feb. 11 invited Franciscans to be more faithful witnesses of St. Francis in a world needs the faith, hope and charity of the *Poverello*. The Holy Father addressed a group of Friar Minors on the occasion of their 550th anniversary of their ministry in Poland and Russia. The pope said God has created and needs peace and goodness to reign in families, society, and among nations.

Universal Ethic: On Feb. 11, Archbishop Javier Lozano Barragán, president of the Pontifical Council for Health Care Workers, was reported as warning of a plan to supplant Christian values with a "universal ethic." The plan involves a new context of globalization, a "New Paradigm," that is rooted in the end called "quality of life." Objective truth is denied by this plan, which stresses individual self-determination and the introduction of a new spirituality centered on the concept of the earth, Gaia, as divine and inviolable. This plan is viewed as new spirituality that will supplant all religions and will secularize a religion without God.

Highway Ministry: On Feb. 12, the Pontifical Council for Migrants and Travelers conducted the European Meeting of National Directors for Highway Patrol Care in Rome. A call was made for appropriate and creative ministries, including education concerning highway conduct. An effort was devised to sensitize the media to ongoing tragedies and problems of modern traffic.

Papal Praise: It was reported on Feb. 12 that Mikhail Gorbachev, the former Soviet president, stated: "Pope John Paul is one of the most distinguished representatives of the intellectual and political elite of contemporary society." He also wrote the prologue for a new book on the Holy Father's views on social issues. The book, *John Paul II's Ethical and Political Thought,* was written by José Ramón Garitagoitia Equía and published by the Center of Political and Constitutional Studies of Spain. The author details the two main themes of the pope: a continual concern for man and the unity that must be achieved between faith and daily experience.

Roman Rabbi: Pope John Paul II received Riccardo Di Segni, the chief Rabbi of Rome, in audience on Feb. 13. Other rabbis and Jewish leaders were also present as the Holy Father expressed hope that the reciprocal trust completed to date will aid relations between the two communities, and will aid in serving as agents for peace.

Edith Stein: St. Edith Stein (St. Teresa Benedicta of the Cross) was reported on Feb. 19 as having sent Pope Blessed Pius IX a letter, asking his intercession at the start of the persecution of Catholics and Jews in Germany. The document, dated April 12, 1933, possibly prompted *Mit Brennender Sorge,* an encyclical taken secretly to Germany and distributed clandestinely to all parishes and young people. The letter surfaced when the Vatican archives were recently opened.

Call To Contemplation: Pope John Paul II called the Church to be more contemplative during his World Mission Sunday message, reported on Feb. 21. The Holy Father also asked Catholics to be more mission-oriented, grounding their labors in fervent prayers.

Tony Blair: British Prime Minister Tony Blair and his family attended a Mass celebrated by Pope John Paul II, it was announced on Feb. 24. The Blairs were staying at the Pontifical Irish College and were invited to attend Mass by the Holy Father.

Papal Plans: An advance team from the Vatican arrived in Ulan Bator, Mongolia, it was reported on Feb. 28, to assess a tentative program for a visit by Pope John Paul II. A Catholic cathedral is being inaugurated in late August, and the Mongolians have already extended an invitation to the Holy Father.

General Audience Topics:

• Meditation on Psalm 116(117) (Feb. 2)
• Meditation on passages from Psalm 117(118) (Feb. 12)
• Meditation on canticle of the three young ben, in the Book of Daniel (Feb. 19)
• Meditation on Psalm 150 (Feb. 26)

International

Cannibalism Condemned: Bishop Melchisedech Sikuli Paluku of Butembo-Beni, Congo, strongly condemned reports of cannibalism by militant Congolese rebels, it was reported on Feb. 2. The bishop said that everyone in Congo condemns cannibalism, and he pointed out that cannibalism was not a matter of tribal rituals. The militant rebels forced family members to eat their own relatives.

Polish Anniversary: It was reported Feb. 3 that the Catholic Church in Poland celebrated the 200th anniversary of Krakow's Rakowice Cemetery. The parents of Pope John Paul II and a brother are buried there. Auxiliary Bishop Jan Szkodon of Krakow stated: "The pope comes here whenever he can as a sign of his love and faithfulness. Like other Poles, he knows the graves of parents is a place where your whole life stands before your eyes."

Ugandan Plea: On Feb. 5, the major interreligious association in northern Uganda made an urgent plea to all sides to end the regional violence. The Acholi Religious Leaders' Peace Initiatives, presided by Catholic Archbishop John Baptist Odama of Gulu, described the situation as desperate. Both rebel groups, the Lord's Resistance Army and the government's military forces, are massacring civilians and committing crimes against the people. Displaced persons in Uganda now number over 800,000.

Korean Bible: A long-awaited Korean translation of the Catholic Bible has been completed, it was reported on Feb. 5. The version is now being examined by the Korean Bishops' Conference and is to be issued by 2005. This is the first Catholic edition of the Bible in the Korean language. Translators labored to produce a work that is faithful to the original texts and easily readable.

Angelicum Chair: It was reported on Feb. 6 that the University of St. Thomas Aquinas in Rome, the Angelicum, has plans to inaugurate a chair in ecumenical studies. The Tillard Chair, named after a Dominican of Canada, was designed to promote research and to emphasize contact with non-Catholic academies in the cause of ecumenism. Father Jean-Marie Tillard, O.P., instituted ecumenical associations and programs and was a noted author. Tillard died in 2000.

Priests Slain: Two priests of the Archdiocese of Medellín, Colombia, were slain by unknown assailants, it was reported on Feb. 6. Father Carlos Mario González González, a pastor, and Father Luis Ángel Hurtado Henao, a parish vicar, were beaten to death. The priests' automobile was set on fire by two men who accosted them on a motorcycle. The priests had received a warning by telephone.

Virtual Pilgrims: On Feb. 11, would-be pilgrims who feared travel to the Holy Land were invited to take part in a new campaign to support the Christians of the Holy Land. The campaign, called the "virtual pilgrims of solidarity," asks the faithful to contribute the planned expenses of a pilgrimage, estimated at about $700, to aid the Holy Land Christians. The campaign originated in the Pesaro, Italy, diocesan Office of Pilgrims, in collaboration with Caritas-Pesaro, Caritas-Italy and Caritas-Jerusalem.

Ecumenical Obligations: It was reported on Feb. 11 that Cardinal Jean-Marie Lustiger of Paris urged Christians and Jews to work together to confront the enemies that both faiths face today. The cardinal, speaking at a dinner for French priests and scholars in New York, stated that new mutual respect is finally allowing real dialogue. Cardinal Lustiger was born to a non-observant Jewish family and lost his mother in Auschwitz. He converted as a teenager, having received shelter in a Christian family.

Chiapas Visitor: Archbishop Giuseppe Bertello, the ambassador of Pope John Paul II to Mexico was reported on Feb. 11 as visiting the ancient Mayan temples of Palenque in Chiapas. He was there to preside over a Catholic religious ceremony and to serve as a bridge between the Holy See and the local Mexicans. He also looked at the high rate of deacons in San Cristobal de Las Casas, which has a population of 1.5 million people.

"Sexual Health": On Feb. 12, it was reported that a judge in Buenos Aires, Argentina, told a Minister for Health and Social Action to halt the National Program of "Sexual Health" and Responsible Procreation, particularly the controversial provisions for chemical abortions. Charges have been made that the World Bank and the International Monetary Fund have imposed "sexual health" as a fundamental element of assistance.

Euro Rights: On Feb. 12, it was announced that the European Parliament recognized homosexual couples as it does heterosexual married couples. By a vote of 269-225, the Parliament recognized the term "family" as having no determination of sex, using the definition of "lasting relationship, without the existence of marriage," although national relations must be respected. The initiative was supported by the European Socialist Party, the Greens, the Communists and part of the European Liberal Democratic Reform Party. The initiative faces a second reading after member nations study it and propose modifications.

Chinese Arrests: Father Dong Yingmu was reported on Feb. 12, as having been arrested by the Chinese government. He is now a prisoner in Quyang County. Two bishops and eight other priests all belonging to the underground Diocese of Baoding are missing or are in prison labor camp.

Spanish Decline: Thirty of Spain's 68 seminaries were reported on Feb. 12 as having no seminary admissions in 2002. Some 28 dioceses have not recruited candidates for the 2002-03 year. There are 230 men studying for the priesthood in Madrid, nearly 180 in Toledo, about 70 in Seville, Barcelona and Valencia, but there are only 1,800 seminarians nationwide, compared to 7,000 in 1953.

Bulgarian Policies: It was reported on Feb. 14 that the Bulgarian Office of Cults had denied visas to the Missionary Sisters of Charity and the Salesians. A new Bulgarian law requires all religious communities to register with the tribunals, with the traditional Orthodox being exempted. No visas are being issued under the new law, which also affects Protestant and Muslims.

UK Faith: A new census, reported on Feb. 16, indicates that only 71.1% of the people in England and Wales still consider themselves Christians. Only 11% of these individuals attend religious services once a month. Islam has emerged in the census as the second largest religion in the United Kingdom, with 1.54 million member. There are also 552,000 Hindus, 329 Sikhs and 7.7 million who say they have no religion.

Forensic Find: It was reported on Feb. 21 that Honduran forensic specialists believe that a skeleton recently recovered may belong to Father James Carney of St. Louis. Father Carney, known in Honduras as "Padre Guadalupe," disappeared in Sept. 1983. He had left the Jesuits to become a chaplain to leftist guerrillas.

Congo Clinic: The Mater Misericordiae Center, founded in the Kivu region of the Congo, itwas announced on Feb. 23, was serving children and adults in this war-torn nation. Child soldiers and raped women are also patients at the clinic. Dr. Colette Kitoga founded Mater Misericordiae in 1999.

Priest Expelled: It was announced on Feb. 23 that another Polish priest was expelled from Russia. Father Bronislaw Czaplicki, who had worked for 10 years in Pushkin, had his visa canceled and was ordered to depart from the country.

Korean "Angels": Father Shen Don Wen and a group of Korean Sisters at a leper center near Shaanxi province, China, are being called "Angels to the Lepers" by grateful patients and their families. The Korean Church supports this Chinese apostolate.

National

Phone Sting: Life Dynamics, a Pro-Life group, uncovered evidence against Planned Parenthood's Alaska clinics, it was reported on Feb. 3. A woman called Planned Parenthood clinics in the area, stating that she was 13 and that her 22-year-old boyfriend had made her pregnant. An adult having sex with a 13-year old is considered statutory rape in Alaska. None of three Planned Parenthood clinics called reported the matter to authorities, and one encouraged the caller to lie about the boyfriend's age to keep out of trouble. The taped conversations are evidence relating to a court case over a state law requiring consent of a judge before a girl 16 or younger before has an abortion.

Asian-American: It was announced that Ignatius Wang, a 12th generation Catholic born in Beijing, China, is the nation's first Asian-American bishop. He was consecrated in St. Mary's Cathedral in San Francisco and serves as an auxiliary to Archbishop William J. Levada. Auxiliary Bishop John Fong Hon of Hong Kong was present for the ceremony.

Ban On Clones: On Feb. 5, Supreme Knight Carl Anderson of the Knights of Columbus, joined with prominent religious and academic political-policy leaders at Capitol Hill in calling for a total ban on human cloning, including so-called "therapeutic" cloning. Each of the leaders signed "The Sanctity of Human Life in a Brave World: A Manifesto on Biotechnology and Human Dignity,"

Evangelical Barrier: On Feb. 5, it was reported that Archbishop John P. Foley described the greatest barrier to evangelization in the country as the bad example offered by some Catholics. The archbishop made the observation while addressing a group 200 Catholic media representations at the New Evangelization of the Americas Conference. The archbishop urged the Catholic media to focus on good news and not to be depressed by the bad news frequently found in the media. He declared, "Ironically, the good news about the Church is more likely to be believed when it is made known through the secular media, first, because they are viewed as not having a vested interest in telling such good news and, second, because they are better known for having published so much bad news."

Emory U. Fellowships: It was announced on Feb. 5, that Emory University's Candela School of Theology in Atlanta was accepting applications for a postgraduate fellowship in practical theology and religious practices. The fellowships are intended to assist those with recently competed doctorates who wish to teach in a seminary setting.

Rose Hawthorne: On Feb. 6, it was reported that Cardinal Edward M. Egan of New York opened the canonization process for Rose Hawthorne, known in religious life as Mother Alphonsa. The daughter of Nathaniel Hawthorne, Rose Hawthorne was a wife, mother, widow and a convert to Catholicism. She founded the Dominican Sisters, Servants of Relief for Incurable Cancers, also known as the Hawthorne Dominicans, in 1900.

Vatican Treasures: A four city U.S. tour of Vatican art treasures was announced on Feb. 6. The tour began in Houston, TX, and included Fort Lauderdale, FL, Cincinnati, OH, and San Francisco, CA. Described as the largest collection of objects from the Vatican ever to tour the United States, the exhibit is entitled, "St. Peter and the Vatican: The Legacy of the Popes." It included a full-size representation of the tomb of St. Peter, found beneath St. Peter's Basilica, as well as a Bernini sculpture, papal portraits, busts, and liturgical vestments and sacred furnishings.

Abortion Ad: It was reported that Bishop Michael A. Saltarelli of Wilmington, DE, announced his support of Ursuline Academy in firing Michele Curay-Cramer. Curay-Cramer, a religious teacher at the academy, signed a newspaper ad that supports legal abortion. The ad appeared Jan. 22 in the *Wilmington News Journal*. Curay-Cramer had worked at the Catholic school for 18 months.

Prayer Breakfast: On Feb. 6, President George W. Bush addressed the 51st National Prayer Breakfast in Washington, announcing that "this is a testing time" for our country. Attended by government, military and spiritual leaders, the breakfast is an annual tradition in the nation's capital. President Bush also stated that the United States is "a nation of prayer." He asked for divine assistance in the face of terrorism and the likelihood of impending war.

Southern Bishops: It was reported on Feb.7 that the Bishops' Advisory Committee of the Catholic Committee of the South has outlined 10 issues that need re-examination in the criminal justice process. The bishops urged southerners to study the justice system in order to transform its unjust aspects so that it respects "the essential human dignity of each and every victims and each and every offender." This is the first in a series of pastoral statements on the subject.

Permanent Deacons: The International Diaconate Center in Rottenburg, Germany, reported on Feb. 10 that the number of permanent deacons rose 17% during the period of 1998-2001, with half the world's deacons serving in the United States. The rate of the U.S. increase was 10%.

Water Woes: It was announced on Feb. 10 that the National Catholic Rural Life Conference conducted a forum entitled "Water: A Sacramental Commons." The quality and availability of water will become an issue in America in a short time. A shortage of available water and increased contamination demand Christian responses.

"Source Book": It was reported on Feb. 11 that the U.S. Conference of Catholic Bishops had distributed its 2003 "Source Book" that provides an explanation of the USCCB structure and information on Church personnel and programs. Also included is a list of USCCB staff members who can provide expertise to media covering Church affairs. The book also includes relevant statistics on the Catholic Church in the United States.

Spiritual "Care Packages": The United States Archdiocese for the Military Services was reported on Feb. 12 as having a spiritual "care packages" available for Catholics serving in the U.S. military. The packages contain copies of the New Testament, rosaries, religious medals, crucifixes, Catholic prayer books and holy cards. Anonymous donors funded the programs, which is providing the packages at no cost.

Cloning Ban: Legislation to ban human cloning for any purpose, including medical research, was approved 19-12 by the U.S. House Judiciary Committee, it was announced on Feb. 13. The ban, the Human Cloning Prohibition Act, was introduced Jan. 8 by Reps. Dave Weldon, R-Fla., and Bart Stupak, D-Mich., and has received broad support, but debate has continued on "therapeutic cloning" for medical research.

Christopher Head: It was reported on Feb. 13 that Dennis W. Heaney, executive publisher of *The Tidings* and *Vida Nueva*, the newspaper of the Los Angeles archdiocese, has been named president of the Christophers. The first layperson to head the Catholic multimedia organization, Heaney will also serve with a priest-director. The Christophers were founded in 1945 Maryknoll Father James Keller.

Sacrament of Penance: The U.S. Conference of Catholic Bishops announced on Feb. 16 that a new booklet, "Celebrating the Sacrament of Penance: Questions and Answers," is now available. The work was designed for parishes, especially in Lent.

Cathedral Attacked: On Feb. 22, an unidentified attacker threw a Molotov cocktail into Holy Name Cathedral in Chicago. This incendiary device was tossed into the State Street vestibule just after noon. The devise was quickly extinguished.

RICO Charges Dismissed: It was reported on Feb. 26 that the U.S. Supreme Court ruled that federal extortion and racketeering laws may not be used against pro-life groups. Joseph Scheidler and Operation Rescue, who have been brought into the court by the National Organization for Women, were vindicated by the decision. (*See* **Special Reports** in **News in Depth**)

MARCH 2003

Vatican

Latino Priests: The Holy See announced on March 2 that the priority of the Catholic Church in Latin America is priests. Cardinal Giovanni Battista Re, president of the Pontifical Commission for Latin America, stressed that vocations are vital. His announcement came in a letter sent on the Day of Spanish-Speaking America. The shortage is grave, to the point that many Latin American villages see a priest only once a month.

Papal Trials: It was reported on Mar. 3 that Pope John Paul II recounted the perils of the days in which he was studying for the priesthood in Poland when meeting with seminarians of Rome. The studies that the Holy Father undertook had to be clandestine because of the Nazi occupation of Poland. The Holy Father confided that he learned trust in the clandestine seminary. His meeting with seminarians and their families marked the feast of Our Lady of Trust.

Papal Envoy: Cardinal Pio Laghi, the personal envoy of Pope John Paul II, met on March 5 in Washington with President George W. Bush. The cardinal presented the American president with a personal message concerning the hopes of the Holy Father for a peaceful solution to the Iraq crisis.

Scottish Evangelization: On Mar. 4, it was reported that Pope John Paul II made an urgent appeal to Scottish bishops to substitute a "new evangelization" for modern culture. The bishops of the Scottish Episcopal conference were visiting Rome and met with the Holy Father, who said that reports indicate that in Scotland "there no longer exists the reality of a Christian society." He added that "the new evangelization must be marked by hope." The theme of hope was consistent with the Holy Father's appeal and vision for Europe in the subsequently published post-synodal apostolic exhortation, *Ecclesia in Europa*.

Ash Wednesday: Pope John Paul II received the imposition on Ash Wednesday, Mar. 5, at the Basilica of St. Sabina in Rome. At the service he called for an end to injustice, saying: "There will beno peace on earth while the oppression of peoples, injustices and economic imbalances, which still exist, endure." He urged: "In the name of Christ we implore you: Be reconciled with God.... I ask from all of you this prayer and this fast. May these be the concrete gestures of involvement on the part of those who believe in the mission of reminding the world that it is never too late for peace."

Pius XII Letter: It was reported on Mar. 5 that the magazine *Inside the Vatican* obtained a letter written by Pope Pius XII from the Vatican archives that demonstrates his opposition to Hitler. Dated Nov. 14, 1923, and written by then Archbishop Paccelli, serving as the Holy See's ambassador in Bavaria, in southern Germany, to Cardinal Pietro Gasparri, Vatican secretary of state under Pope Pius XI. The letter clearly denounces the National Socialist movement, citing the condemnation by the cardinal of Munich of the persecution of Bavaria's Jewish population.

Papal Pondering: Pope John Paul II's new book of poetry was presented on Mar. 6. *Roman Triptych Meditation* contains the thoughts of the Holy Father in three parts. Part one is "The Stream;" the second part is "On the Book of Genesis at the Threshold of the Sistine Chapel"; and the third is "A Hill in the Land of Moorish." The volume was published in Polish. The Vatican Press is signing agreements for the rights of translation.

Little Compromises: On Mar. 6, Pope John Paul II met with pastors from the Diocese of Rome and admonished them and all priests to strive daily for holiness. The Holy Father said: "If we do not try, humbled and trustingly, to progress on the path of our sanctification, we will end by accepting little compromises that gradually become more serious and can lead to betrayal...."

Condolence Message: It was reported on Mar. 7 that Pope John Paul II sent a message of condolence to the religious and civil authorities and to all the families of victims of the plane crash in Tamanrasset, Algeria. The Holy Father stated that he "entrusts to the mercy of the All Powerful to those who have lost their lives in this drama, that they rest in peace." The death toll of the Air Algeria disaster stood at 102.

Swiss Visit: It was announced on Feb. 10 that the Catholic bishops of Switzerland have invited Pope John Paul II to visit their country to meet young Swiss Catholics in spring of 2004. The invitation was reported at the close of an ordinary assembly of the Swiss episcopal conference, held at Lucerne. The youth meeting being planned is in preparation for the next World Youth Day in Cologne, Germany.

Vatican Denial: On Mar. 11, Vatican spokesman Joaquín Navarro-Valls denied that the Holy See was promoting an initiative with Arab leaders to provide exile for Saddam Hussein. Various news sources had reported such efforts. Navarro-Valls stated: "This information is totally unfounded."

Papal Iraqi View: On Mar. 11, Andrea Riccardi, the founder of the Community of Sant'Egidio, explained the global diplomatic efforts of Pope John Paul II as an attempt to avoid any kind of cultural confrontations. The Holy Father has been consistent in his analysis that Catholics are not struggling against Islam, which cannot be reduced to any concept of extremism. Any conflict between the West and Islam is unthinkable because "religions neither desire nor justify war."

Stolen Hand: The hand holding the key on the statute of St. Peter Enthroned was stolen on Mar.11 from the 13th century masterpiece in St. Peter's Basilica in the Vatican. St. Peter stands at the exit of the grotto under St. Peter's Basilica. The hand actually is a replacement copy of the original which was damaged and restored in the late 1700s and was connected to the wrist by a tightly fitting metal rod.

Barbarous Act: Pope John Paul II condemned the assassination of Prime Minister Zoran Djindjic of Serbia and Montenegro on Mar. 12 as a barbarous act of violence. Djindjic was shot and killed in Belgrade. The Vatican sent telegrams of condolence in the Holy Father's name.

Vatican Treasures: It was announced on Mar. 13 that a small trove of funerary monuments was unearthed by workers excavating a new underground parking lot. The finds include a sarcophagus from the reign of Emperor Nero, with marble decorations and Latin inscriptions. Early Christian tombs were part of the treasures discovered in the excavations.

"Deep Pain": On Mar. 20, just after U.S. air strikes began in Iraq, the Vatican announced that "the Holy See noted with deep pain the evolution of latest events in Iraq. Vatican spokesman Joaquín Navarro-Valls said the Holy See lamented Iraq's failure to comply with the U.N. disarmament resolution and other countries' abandonment of international diplomacy to resolve the crisis.

Current Tensions: It was reported on Mar. 28 that the top ecumenical officers of the Roman Catholic and Russian Orthodox churches desired to overcome current tensions. Cardinal Walter Kasper, president of the Pontifical Council for Promoting Christian Unity, met with Metropolitan Kirill of Smolensk and Kaliningrad, president of the Moscow Patriarchate's Department for External Church Relations, and agreed to further consultation to relieve the problems that exist between the two churches.

Peace Rosary: *L'Osservatore Romano,* the Vatican newspaper, invited believers to pray the Rosary, it was reported on Mar. 21. The paper said that the beginning of military operations in Iraq was the time to intensify prayers to the Queen of Peace. Iraqi Catholics and Christians planned to consecrate their country to the Blessed Virgin, the Queen of Peace, in St. Joseph's Cathedral in Baghdad.

Beatifications: On Mar. 23, Pope John Paul II conducted a ceremony of beatification in Rome, proclaiming five new Blesseds. The new beatified were raised to the altars in the presence of church officials and Otto von Hapsburg, 90, the son of the last Austro-Hungarian emperor. Hungarian President Ferenc Madl was also present. The beatified were Hungarian László Batthyány-Strattmann, the "doctor of the poor," María Dolores Rodríguez Sopeña and María Condesa Lluch, two Spanish women religious who aided women, Swiss religious María Caridad Brader, an apostle to Latin American Indians, and a French priest, Father Pierre Bonhomme, a founder of a religious congregation for women.

Lutheran Dialogue: Lutheran Bishop Mark S. Hansen of the Evangelical Lutheran Church in the U.S. and 17 other Lutherans met Pope John Paul II on Mar. 24. Bishop Hansen expressed his desire to find ways in which to celebrate baptismal unity, to lead to full communion even before organic unity can be achieved.

Trip Announced: On Mar. 25, the Vatican formally announced that Pope John Paul had made plans to visit Spain during the first weekend in May to canonize Blessed Pedro Poveda Castroverde, a founder and martyr, Blessed José María Rubio y Peralta, a Jesuit priest, Blessed Genoveva Torres Morales, a foundress, Blessed Angela de la Cruz, another foundress,and Blessed María Maravillas de Jesus, a Discalced Carmelite who died in 1974.

Rome Video Conferencing: It was reported on Mar. 26 that the "Primacy of Peter" is the theme of the video conference organized in Rome this week by the Vatican Conference for Clergy. This conference is in response to Pope John Paul II's encyclical *Ut Unum Sint* on ecumenical dialogue. Theologians from around the world gathered for the conference, introduced by Cardinal Darío Castrillón Hoyos.

Hang-Glider A 26-year-old hang-gliding Austrian landed in St. Peter's Square on Mar. 28 and was promptly questioned by the Roman police. Joined by other Austrians, the hang-glider was protesting the Iraq war. The peace demonstrators may face charges for "unauthorized manifestation and violation of the airspace" of the Vatican City State.

General Audience Topics:
• Lessons of St. Joseph, Patron of Workers (March 19)
• Reflection on Psalm 89 (90) (March 26)

International

Bethlehem Wall: "A wall isolates Bethlehem," declared the Latin-rite patriarch Michel Sabbah of Jerusalem in his message to the presidents of bishops' conference around the world. The Israeli military forces are building a wall that will enclose the entrance to the city of Bethlehem. The patriarch begged Christians everywhere to contact Israeli authorities to convince them to halt construction.

Cuban Church: On Mar. 3, it was announced that the archbishop of Havana, Cuba, Cardinal Jaime Ortega, published a letter defending the Church's authority in Cuba. He also asked the Cuban people to abandon mediocrity in order to insure the island's future. The letter was issued on the 150th anniversary of the death of the Servant of God Father Felix Varela. The pastoral was entitled: "There Is No Homeland Without Virtue." The cardinal stated as well that Cuba has severely suffered from the process of de-Christianization, and that the Church has been ousted from public life.

Korean Mass: It was reported on Mar. 4 that North Koreans who were visiting Seoul, South Korea, attended Mass at Myongong Cathedral. This was the first time that these Catholics could attend a Mass since the Korean peninsula was divided more than 50 years ago. The groups confirmed, "that even without priests, North Koreans have strong faith."

"Me Too": The archdiocese of Santo Domingo, in the Dominican Republic, announced on Mar. 4 that a home for the city street children is reclaiming these victims of the modern society. Called *Yo Tambien,* "Me Too," the home provides shelter, education, health care and incentives to help the city's abandoned small boys.

Caritas Founding: It was announced on Mar. 5 that the Catholic Bishops' Conference of England and Wales had organized a new agency, Caritas-Social Action. The launching took place at the House of Commons with Cardinal Cormac Murphy O'Connor explaining the goals of the new agency, which is a union of the Catholic Agency for Social Concerns, the Catholic Child Welfare Council and the Social Welfare Committee of the Bishop's Conference. Caritas will administer volunteer sectors and social care on behalf of the Church.

Bangladesh Easter: The Christians in Bangladesh, it was reported on Mar. 5, made a formal request to the government to declare Easter Sunday a national holiday. Demonstrations are planned to convey the Christians' urgency in this matter. They also requested more media coverage and appropriate decorations for the holy observances. The Christians in Bangladesh celebrate Christmas as a recognized holiday. The nation is 88.1% Muslim.

Illegal Mosque: An Israeli court issued a demolition order on a mosque being constructed across from the Basilica of the Annunciation in Nazareth, it was announced on Mar. 7. Over strong Vatican objections, Israeli authorities had approved the construction, but the mosque was deemed illegal and violated previous injunctions. The mosque raises serious questions about free access to holy places in the area.

Iraqi Dominicans: It was announced on Mar. 10 that the Dominican Fathers of Iraq had made plans to open a novitiate in Mosul within the next two years. The Dominicans direct a theological center in Baghdad and conduct pastoral ministers, including the publication of a periodical called *Christian Thought*. They are already in Mosul, working with the poor and operating an audiovisual center and catechetical programs.

"Living Stones": Catholic World Mission reported on Mar. 10 that it is serving the victims of three earthquakes in El Salvador by building a development called "Living Stones." This will be the first community of its type in El Salvador and will include 232 homes, a training facility, sports complexes, and recreation area. Clean drinking water and storage facilities will safeguard the new settlement.

Cuban Convent: President Fidel Castro attended the inauguration of a new Brigittine convent in Havana, it was reported on Mar. 11. Cardinal Crescenzio Sepe, Prefect of the Congregation for the Evangelization for the Peoples, traveled to Cuba to bless the convent. President Castro reportedly asked for the Brigittine Sisters to come to Havana, so that the words of Pope John Paul II can come to fruition in opening Cuba to the world and the world to Cuba.

Political Goals: Archbishop John Olorunfemi Onaiyekan of Abuja, Nigeria, urged Catholics entering politics to be guided by the Church's social teaching. He stated the need for the Church's guidance at a plenary assembly of the country's Catholic bishops. Archbishop Felix Alaba Job of Ibadan said that the sad condition of Nigeria and the world compels the children of the light. Archbishop Job gave the homily during the opening Mass of the assembly.

Thai Women: Bishop Lawrence Thienchai Samanchit of Chanthaburi, Thailand, stated in a pastoral letter that Catholics in his country had to work to eliminate violence and discrimination against women. The letter was reported on Mar. 16, and it recalls that the condition of women in Asia is still a serious problem. In 2000, the Thai Bishops' Conference set up a Commission for Women's Issues.

Comboni Year: A Eucharistic celebration was scheduled for Mar. 16, in Nairobi, Kenya, to honor the coming canonization of Blessed Daniel Comboni, the founder of missionary congregations. In Khartoum, Sudan, Archbishop Gabriel Zubeir Wako of Khartoum launched a campaign for a Comboni University of the Sudan. Blessed Daniel Comboni, the first bishop of Central Africa, died in Khartoum in 1881. He is called one of the "Fathers of the Faith in Africa."

Hans Küng: It was reported on Mar. 21 that Swiss theologian Father Hans Küng hopes that his teaching rights at Catholic universities will be restored. Now 75, he said he wanted to be considered a "loyal Catholic theologian," despite his disagreements on certain matters. Father Küng is seeking "toleration of his views" by the Vatican. Under an injunction issued in 1979, he is not allowed to teach as a Catholic theologian because of his views on papal infallibility and other doctrinal issues.

Holy Land: A Catholic committee reported on Mar. 26 g that Israel is hampering the Church's Holy Land ministry by denying entry visas to priests and religious. Visas have been denied to Church personnel for nearly two years, negatively impacting on Catholic institutions. Latin-Maronite and Melkite rite Catholics have been affected. Some 86 applications for entry have been denied.

Hong Kong Guidelines: It was announced on Mar. 26 that the diocese of Hong Kong had issued special guidelines for Church activities to prevent the spread of acute respiratory syndrome, SARS. The guidelines concerned sterilization procedures, contact during Mass, confessions, and Sunday school. The disease had killed 10 people in the area. The use of holy water fonts had been discontinued during the emergency.

National

Christian Unity: A proposal called Christian Churches Together in the U.S.A was reported on Mar. 3 as having been sent to 46 Christian church bodies. Cardinal William H. Keeler of Baltimore, a supporter of the plan to foster a greater unity in Christian witness in the nation, was quoted as saying: "Please God we are moving toward creating an instrument that will help make more visible the bonds among Christians in the United States." The proposed plan will result in the most inclusive Christian organizations ever in the United States.

New Evangelization: The U.S. Conference of Catholic Bishops, the Canadian Conference of Canadian Bishops, and the Latin American Bishops Conference released statistics on the challenges facing the Church and noting where the Church has lost ground in recent years. Fewer 20- to 40-year-olds participate in the faith in Canada, evangelical sects and New Age doctrines are luring Catholics away from the faith in Latin America, and in the United States 50 percent have no religious affiliation. The statistics were studied at a continental congress on "The New Evangelization and Catechesis."

Catholic Schools: It was reported on Mar. 6 that Catholic school advocates went to Capital Hill to urge school choice initiatives and the inclusion of students and teachers at private and religious institutions in planned education legislation. The Department of Education of the U.S. Conference of Catholic Bishops provided two days of information on key issues before the advocates went to lobby Congress.

Best-sellers: The Catholic Book Publishers Association reported on Mar. 7 that Professor Scott Hahn was the leading author for Catholic hardcover books in America. Johann Christoph Arnold was the top selling paperback author last year. Doubleday printed seven of the top hardcover books and three of the top 20 paperbacks. *Watch for the Light* was the top selling hardcover book in 2002, and the *Catechism of the Catholic Church* was the leading paperback.

Operation Rice Bowl: The Catholic Relief Services distributed materials in March to approximately 12 million Catholic parishioners, students, and teachers, who were expected to participate in Operation Rice Bowl, the Lenten program of giving. Operation Rice Bowl had been called an opportunity for Catholics in the United States to pray, fast, learn and donate.

Partial Birth Abortion: Cardinal Anthony J. Bevilacqua, chairman of the U.S. Catholic Bishops' Association on Pro-Life activities, urged the Senate to approve the Partial Birth Operation Ban Act of 2003, it was reported on Mar. 11. The cardinal also asked the U.S. senators not to allow amendments to the bill that would weaken the ban. President Clinton vetoed two earlier bills banning this form of abortion. (*See* **Special Reports**.)

Penance Booklet: The U. S. Conference of Catholic Bishops published a new booklet, it was announced on Mar. 11, to coincide with Lent 2003. The booklet focused on the sacrament of penance and was designed for parishes. Entitled, "Celebrating the Sacrament of Penance: Questions and Answers," the booklet contained a section on confession and was aimed at individuals who have not been to confession for some time.

Navajo School: A school in Arizona, founded in 1902 by St. Katherine Drexel, received funds from all across the nation and avoided closure. St. Michael School on a Navajo reservation needed $250,000 to upgrade its fire safety system or face closure. The school also sought aid from Catholic Extension.

Uninsured Aided: On Mar. 14, it was reported that National Catholic organizations joined leaders of other faiths to draw attention to the 41 million uninsured Americans, calling the problem a spiritual and moral issue. Cardinal Theodore McCarrick of Washington, DC, was one of the Catholic leaders who signed the letter to Congress about the problem.

Catholic-Muslim Institute: Twelve Catholic bishops attended the three-day institute for bishops on Islam and Catholic-Muslim relations, it was reported on Mar. 11. Cardinal William Keeler of Baltimore was one the prelates who attended the program at St. Mary's Seminary and University in Baltimore.

Indian Scholarships: The Bureau of Catholic Indian Missions was reported on Mar. 21 as having awarded two million dollars in undergraduate scholarships for Catholic Native Americans. The Catholic University of America and Xavier University in New Orleans received the awards. The grants are from the Bureau of Catholic Indian Missions — Carl A. Westerkamp American Indian Scholarship fund.

Guide Issued: It was announced on Mar. 24 that the Canon Law Society of America had issued a 47-page guide concerning the implementation by the U.S. bishops of the clerical sexual abuse norms. The booklet provides guidelines on the rights of accused and the practices to be followed when an allegation is made against a priest or deacon.

Press Circulation: On Mar. 24, it was announced that the combined circulation of Catholic periodicals in the U.S. and Canada has risen over the past years, nearing the 26.9 million mark. The rise was listed in the 2003 edition of the *Catholic Press Directory*.

Magazine circulation dropped but the Catholic newspapers, newsletters and foreign language editions showed an increase. (*See* **Communications**.)

Civility Offered: It was reported on Mar. 25 that Archbishop Timothy M. Dolan of Milwaukee received standing ovations when he addressed the Wisconsin legislature recently. Archbishop Dolan stated that civility is a key factor in American life and something that "we all agree that our society desperately needs." He said, "Sometimes we can't do much about all those other issues, but we can always do something about courtesy and civility."

Maronite Gathering: It was reported on Mar. 25 that Maronite Catholics from St. Louis and other national areas held the first convocation of the Eparchy of Lady of Lebanon at St. Raymond Co-Cathedral in St. Louis. Archbishop Justin F. Rigali, head of the Latin rite, participated. More than 500 Maronites and 25 Maronite priests were also there. The Eparchy covers 34 states.

Catholic Symposium: It was announced on Mar. 26 that a symposium at the Catholic University of America explored the dramatic changes that have taken place in Ireland, the United States, and Quebec since 1950. Titled "Decline and Fall," the symposium detailed the social and economic factors that impacted on Catholics, resulting in authority issues and lay disagreements with some policies. Canadian theologian Fr. Gregory Baum also praised what he called "the extraordinary creativity the post World War II Catholicism."

Roe v. Wade: The original plaintiff in the infamous legal cases Roe v. Wade and Doe v. Bolton joined 700 women in asking the Supreme Court of the United States to seek a "definition of what women injured by abortions have under the law." Reported on Mar. 26, the newly filed case, Donna Santa Marie et al vs. Whitman et al., was the first case of its kind heard by the court.

New Directory: It was reported on Mar. 26 that the U.S. Bishops' Secretariat for Family, Laity, Women and Youth had published the 2002-03 Directory of Lay Movements, Organizations and Professional Associations. Listings for 100 organizations and details are included.

Nun Slain: Sister Philomena Fogarty, 68, a member of the Franciscan Missionaries of Mary, was murdered in Virginia Beach, VA. Her body was found in a parking lot there, and her head, hands and feet had been cut off. A companion religious, Sister Lucie Kristofic, 72, escaped from a motel room in Norfolk, having been kidnapped with Sister Philomena and left alone. The sisters served at Christ the King Mission in Hamilton, GA. The suspected killer was arrested according to Mar. 27 reports.

APRIL 2003

Vatican

"Penitential March": In a letter published on Apr. 1, Pope John Paul II stated that peace at any level is linked to a true conversion and a change of lifestyle. This message was sent on the occasion of the first "Penitential March," a gathering of young people sponsored by the Order of Minims. The march was scheduled to take place in the city of Paola, Italy.

Bolivian Victims: Pope John Paul II sent a telegram on Apr. 1, to Chima, a mining town in northern Bolivia, where 15 died when a hillside collapsed. The Holy Father assured the relatives and survivors that they and the deceased are in his prayers. He also called for effective assistance to those involved in the catastrophe, "with the charity and spirit of fraternal solidarity."

Way Of The Cross: It was announced on Apr. 3 that Pope John Paul II had written the meditations for this year's Stations of the Cross on Good Friday at the Roman Coliseum. The meditations have Marian significance, relating to the Virgin Mary, Queen of Peace. They also reflect an earlier retreat given by the Holy Father before ascending the Throne of Peter.

Catholic Responsibility: Capuchin Father Raniero Cantalamessa, the preacher of the papal household, on Apr. 4 stated that all Catholics share the responsibility for the Church's failure to live up to Christ's call to holiness and perfection. Pope John Paul II and Vatican officials heard the Lenten reflection of Father Cantalemessa. He focused on the New Testament image of the Church as the beloved Bride of Christ.

Sexual Tourism: Archbishop Piero Monni, the permanent observer of the Vatican to the World Tourism Organization, addressed a European Conference for the Protection of Children from Sexual Exploitation, and expressed dismay over the legal vacuum that is exploited in regard to sexual tourism. The conference ended on April 4, in Rome. The archbishop cited the lack of effective measures to protect children from being offered in private premises and centers as prostitutes. He repeated Pope John II's description of child prostitution as "world scourge."

Pedophilia Meeting: A scientific meeting on the problem of pedophilia was held from Apr. 2-5 in the Vatican, sponsored by the Pontifical Academy for Life. Qualified experts on the subject from Canada, Germany and the U.S. took part in the symposium. Reports presented at the gathering will be published. Specialists in recovery therapy for the problem of pedophilia also participated, as did officials from the Vatican Secretariat of State and the congregations for doctrine, clergy, Catholic education, religious and bishops.

End Of War: Pope John Paul II appealed on Apr. 6 for a quick ending to the war in Iraq and expressed his hope that the conflict's cessation would open the way for a new era of forgiveness, love and peace. The Holy Father made his appeal before a crowd of thousands gathered in St. Peter's Square before the midday Angelus. He spoke as well as of the encyclical *Pacem in Terris* by Pope Bl. John XXIII.

Argentine Visitor: Pope John Paul II met with Argentine President Eduardo Alberto Duhalde, it was announced on Apr. 7. Duhalde, who leaves office in May, came to make a farewell visit to the pope. At the meeting, the Holy Father presented the Church's social doctrine as an invaluable instrument to ease Argentina's crisis.

Ecumenical Pilgrimage: On Apr. 7, Pope John Paul II welcomed Archbishop William J. Levada of San Francisco and other leading religious figures from that city who were making an ecumenical pilgrimage throughout Europe. Episcopal Bishop William E. Swing of California and Greek Orthodox Bishop Anthony of San Francisco were in the company of Archbishop Levada. The Holy Father told the pilgrims: "At a time of conflict and grave unrest in our world, I pray that your witness to the Gospel message of reconciliation, solidarity and love will be a sign of hope and a promise of the unity of a humanity reborn and renewed in the grace of Christ."

No Ambiguities: It was reported on Apr. 7 that Pope John Paul II announced that the challenge facing Christians now is to proclaim Christ "clearly and without ambiguities." The Holy Father addressed his words to bishops of the Episcopal Conference of Scandinavia, representing Denmark, Finland, Iceland, Norway and Sweden. The Holy Father welcomed the bishops and also urged them to persevere in their moral teachings and in ecumenical programs.

Eucharistic Essence: On Apr. 8, Cardinal Joseph Ratzinger discussed his new book, *Il Dio Vicino, A God Who Is Near*, concerning the real meaning of the sacrament of the Eucharist. He stated that: "The Eucharist is sacrifice," adding, "the first thing it tells us is that God gives himself to us so that we, in turn, can give ourselves. The initiative in the sacrifice of Jesus Christ comes from God. In the beginning, it was he himself who lowered himself." The book is published by St. Paul Editions.

Pope Pius XII: It was reported on Apr. 8 that documents reveal that at least 800 Jews in three Italian cities were saved from Nazi persecution in 1943 and 1944 thanks in part to an appeal from Pope Pius XII. Various Church groups were asked by Pope Pius XII to assist in the work of saving Jews, and evidence in Livorno, Lucca and Pisa, for example, demonstrates the effectiveness of such efforts.

Mary's Youth: Pope John Paul II entrusted the young men and women of the world to the Blessed Virgin Mary on April 10, asking her to bring them closer to Christ and to help them to be true peacemakers. Thousands of young people gathered in St. Peter's Square on that day to pray with the Holy Father as part of Palm Sunday local celebrations of World Youth Day.

Human Rights: It was announced on Apr. 13 that the Vatican has just published a book entitled *Human Rights in the Teachings of the Church, from John XXIII to John Paul II*. The book contains papal texts on the rights and duties of the human person. Published originally in Italian, the work will soon be available in other languages.

Long Pontificate: On Apr. 24, Pope John Paul II's pontificate became the fourth longest in Church history. The Holy Father is also looking forward to the 25th anniversary of his election in October 1978. The pontiff was elected to the papacy on Oct. 16, 1978, although the formal calculation of his pontificate is from the solemn inauguration of his papacy on Oct. 22, 1978.

New Blesseds: On Apr. 27, during a Mass at St. Peter's Square, Pope John Paul II beatified six Italian nuns and priests. Capuchin Father Marco d'Aviano was beatified for holiness and labors to encourage Viennese to resist a Turkish invasion; Father Giacomo Alberione, the founder of the St. Paul Ministry in the mass media; Sister María Christina Borando, who devoted her life to eucharistic spirituality; Sister Eugenia Ravasco, who founded schools; María Domenica Mantovani, who cared for the sick and the poor; and Sister Guilia Salzano, who ministered to the religiously indifferent, were also beatified.

Biblical Commission: Pope John Paul II met with members of the Pontifical Biblical Commission on Apr. 29, and encouraged the group's new study on "the Bible and morality." The Holy Father declared: "The person of today, disappointed by so many unsatisfactory responses to the fundamental questions of living, seems more open to the voice that comes from transcendence and expresses itself in the biblical message."

General Audience Topics:
• Reflection on Isaiah 42:10-17 (April 2)
• Reflection on Psalm 134 (135):1-12 (April 9)
• Three days to relive the Passion, Death and Resurrection of Christ (April 16)
• Focuses on Christ's Easter message "Peace Be With You!" (April 23)
• Meditation on Psalm 100 (101) (April 30)

International

"Dream" Work: It was reported on Apr. 1 that the Italian project called "Dream" will begin treating AIDS victims in Mozambique, providing care over the next years for some 30,000 patients. The Community of Sant'Egidio has been assisting the program and the Italian government will finance the care. The project is being called a "Second War" in Mozambique.

Mobile Gospel: On Apr. 1, it was announced that the bishops of the Netherlands have initiated the SMS, the "short message service," which will provide an excerpt of the Gospel for mobile phones. The service costs 70 euro cents (76 U.S. cents), which will be allocated to organizations aiding the Third World.

Caritas- Iraq: Caritas-Iraq made an appeal on Apr. 1 for financial help from other Caritas groups around the world. Some 260,000 Iraqis were affected by the war and in need of aid. Caritas-Iraq distributes basic foods and relief services to ease the need. Children, pregnant women and nursing mothers receive priority aid.

Papal Visits: It was reported on Apr. 1 that the `Croatian Bishops' Conference is preparing for a visit from Pope John Paul II from June 5-9. The Holy Father has made plans to beatify a religious, Mary of the Jesus Crucified (1982-1966), during his stay in Zagreb.

Massacre Deplored: Christians in India were reported on Apr. 1 as protesting a recent massacre in which 24 individuals, including women and children, were slain in the Kashmir Valley. The massacre was a terrorist attack, described as an effort to intimidate the local population and to damage the ongoing peace process in the region.

Dominican College: It was announced on Apr. 2 that Spanish Dominican Father Jesus Espeja is currently providing an informal university education for 900 students despite the fact that Catholic schools are illegal in Cuba. His center in Havana gives certificates to students who successfully complete the courses. The Cuban government does not recognize the certificates but has sent government workers to the center for courses in English and computers.

Hong Kong SARS: The Catholic Church in Hong Kong curtailed Holy Week services because of the deadly pneumonia virus, called acute respiratory syndrome. Other affiliated dioceses, including the Singapore Archdiocese, were studying the traditional rites of the season and taking steps to protect worshippers from the highly contagious disease.

Phillipine Bombing: Sister Dulce de Guzman of the Franciscan Sisters of the Immaculate Conception was killed on Apr. 2, one of the victims of a terrorist bomb attack in Davao City, in the southern Philippines. Sister de Guzman was inside an automobile at Sasa Wharf on Apr. 2, when the blast occurred. Three other nuns and a lay associate in the automobile escaped unhurt.

Peace Talks: Archbishop Orlando Quevedo, president of the Philippines Bishops' Conference, stated on Apr. 4 that he has hopes of peace because of a government and rebel initiative to have a truce and to a return to peace talks in Mindanao. Both sides agreed to end hostilities and return to refugees. The rebels are members of the Moorish Front of Islamic Liberation.

Nigerian University: The Nigerian Bishop's Conference announced on Apr. 4 that a campaign to raise funds for a Catholic university has been approved. The Church in Nigeria already has ecclesial institutions at the university level, as seminarians are affiliated with Nigerian and Catholic universities. The campaign is the first of several planned institutions of higher learning for the nation.

Contested Law: On Apr. 6, Archbishop Stanislaus Fernandes of Gandhinagar, India, condemned a document on religious freedom approved in the Gujarat State without any discussion in the Assembly. Under the law, anyone wanting to convert to another religion must receive permission from the civil authorities. Christians in the region were warned by the Gujarat government to anticipate discrimination, possibly by a program designed to limit Christian influence.

Pidgin Catechism: The Catholics of New Guinea will soon have catechisms written in English and pidgin English for easier understanding by various age groups. The South Pacific island nation was reported on Apr. 6 as planning a shorter, inculturated version of the *Catechism of the Catholic Church* in English as well. At this time catechism classes use only a book of questions and answers.

Internet Patron: A poll reported on Apr. 6 from Gerona, Spain, indicates that people favor the angel Gabriel as the patron of the modern Internet. More than 2,100 users participated in the Internet poll. Gabriel announced to Mary that she would become the Mother of the Christ. Results were forwarded to the Vatican's Congregation for the Causes of Saints, which has responsibility for naming patrons for other innovations and careers.

EU Constitution: It was reported on Apr. 6 that the new drafts of the European Constitution include recognition of the legal status of churches, a condition that the Vatican has long recommended. Some Christian groups note that Article 37 of the European Constitution represents a significant step but does not express completely the religious dimension of the Continental union. The Vatican also asks for explicit recognition of the institutional autonomy of churches.

Haitian Slayings: The Haitian Bishops' Justice and Peace Commission was reported on Apr. 7 as charging that murders in Port-au-Prince, the capital of the island, involved the police. At least one murder a day has been documented by the commissioner as having police involvement or complicity. Haiti is described in the report as having a "climate of insecurity and impunity that has taken hold."

Allied Cemetery: It was announced on Apr. 7 that French and British Church leaders were shocked by a desecration of a memorial to the Allied dead in a World War I military cemetery in France. Estaples Military Cemetery near Calais experienced the vandalism, which includes a message that read: "Take away your rubbish which is polluting our soil."

Peaceful Election: It was reported on Apr. 15 that the legislative election in Nigeria proved peaceful despite fears of violence. Nevertheless, the country's bishops called upon the government to respond to claims of rampant election fraud. Archbishop John Olorunfemi Onaiyekan of Abuja, president of the Nigerian Bishops' Conference, said: "We prayed hard that it would be a peaceful election, and our prayers were heard." Still, the archbishop requested that the government respond quickly to the allegations of fraud.

Renewed Easter: On Apr. 21, it was reported that Catholics in remote parishes in northern Vietnam celebrated Easter for the first time in 40 years. Thousands of Catholics, including the Hmong, attended Masses and other services allowed by the Vietnamese government. The priest of the area was arrested and imprisoned in 1963.

Consider Families: It was announced on Apr. 24 that the Scottish bishops urged consideration of Scotland's family rights, access to religious education and support for the poor and immigrants. The plea was given in regard to the May 1 parliamentary elections, considered a milestone for the Scottish Parliament, re-established in 1999.

Nuns Mourned: It was reported on Apr. 24 that the Sisters of Charity of St. Louis in Calgary, Canada, are mourning the death of four nuns killed on Easter Sunday. A tractor-trailer crashed into the nun's vehicle, killing four and seriously wounding a fifth member of the Sisters of Charity. The driver of the truck survived the accident in which the tractor-trailer rear-ended the nuns' car.

Chinese Persecution: The Chinese underground Catholics were harassed during Easter Week, it was revealed on Apr. 23. Seminarians were sentenced to a month's imprisonment in Fujian Province. Father Zheng Ruipin of Fuzhou Diocese also expects imprisonment. The priest and seminarians were arrested for praying in a park.

Mongolian Masks: The Catholic Church in Mongolia on Apr. 26 implemented a government order that requires people to wear masks in public places to prevent the spread of SARS. Two SARS cases were confirmed, with at least five probable cases as well. The Vatican representatives were in Ulan Bator, the capital, investigating the possibility of a papal visit in August.

Blasphemy Charge: Ranha Masih was reported on Apr. 30 as having been sentenced for life for violating Pakistan's blasphemy law. A Catholic, Masih was charged with throwing stones at Quranic verses on a wall. The name of Muhammad was in those verses, and anyone insulting Muhammad can be executed or given life in prison. He was arrested at a memorial procession for Bishop John Joseph of Faisalabad, who committed suicide to protest the Pakistani blasphemy laws.

National

Moynihan Funeral: It was reported on Apr. 1 that U.S. Senator Daniel Patrick Moynihan was honored at a funeral Mass in St. Patrick's Church in Washington, DC, on Mar. 31. The Democratic Senator served four terms in the United States Senate before retiring in 2001. He was buried in Arlington National Cemetery. Senator Moynihan also served as U.S. Ambassador to India and to the United Nations.

Florida Catholic: Kathi Williams, the bureau manager for *The Florida Catholic* newspaper, was reported on Apr. 1 as having been arrested on charges of grand theft. An audit revealed missing funds. The editor and general manager, Steve Paradis, was not implicated in any way in the charges, but resigned so that the newspaper could move forward.

Church Fatality: It was announced on Apr. 1 that Gjek Isufaj was killed in a shooting in St. Paul Albanian Catholic Church in the Detroit suburb of Rochester Hills. Isufaj was slain because of a long standing-feud with Gjon Pepaj, a former friend from Albania. A rape had fostered the feud and the retaliation conducted by two feuding families. Isufaj was the third victim of the feud.

Joint Study: Catholic and Mennonite scholars were reported on Apr. 2 as having planned a combined study of the 16th-century Anabaptist Martyrs. Part of ongoing Bridgefolk conferences, an annual series of informal Catholic-Mennonite dialogues at St. John's Abbey in Collegeville, the conference was scheduled to bring into focus the deaths of thousands of Anabaptists at the hands of the rulers of the Netherlands, Tirol, Bavaria and Switzerland. The Mennonites are one branch of the Anabaptists.

Diocese vs. Archdiocese: It was announced on Apr. 2 that the diocese of San Bernardino, facing a lawsuit over a Boston priest, had sued the Boston Archdiocese to recover any damages incurred. In 1990, the Boston Archdiocese attested to the good standing of Father Paul Shanley when he moved to San Bernardino. Father Shanley faces charges of sexually abusing minors from the 1960s through the 1980s.

Alleged Visions: On April 2, Cardinal William H. Keeler reported in a letter the Feb. 15 ruling of Cardinal Joseph Ratzinger, prefect of the Congregation for the Doctrine of the Faith, concerning Cardinal Keeler's decision in Sept. 2000 to prohibit prayer services at a Maryland church in which a woman claimed to receive messages from the Blessed Virgin Mary. Gianna Talone-Sullivan had claimed to receive messages from the Blessed Virgin Mary during Thursday evening prayer services at St. Joseph Church in Emmitsburg from 1993 until the archdiocesan ban was installed. Cardinal Ratzinger stipulated in the Congregation's ruling that the Baltimore archbishop was correct to issue a decree that the alleged apparitions are clearly not miraculous (*constat de non supernaturalitate*).

Priests Convicted: Several priests in the United States were convicted or sentenced for child sexual abuse in March, it was reported on Apr. 2. Father Louis E. Miller, the most noted offender, was named in more than 80 civil lawsuits against the Archdiocese of Louisville and pleaded guilty to charges involving 21 children.

Abbey Anniversary: It was announced on Apr. 3 that Subiaco Abbey in Arkansas celebrated its 125th anniversary as a Benedictine monastery in America. Father Isidor Hobi was sent to Arkansas in 1877 to find a suitable site for a foundation. St. Meinrad Abbey, IN, was the founding house. Subiaco Abbey has undertaken a $10 million capital campaign to modernize facilities and to provide scholarships.

Keep God Visible: Bishop Donald Wuerl of Pittsburgh was reported on April 3 as urging U.S. Catholics to fight efforts "to bleach out God from our public life." Bishop Wuerl was addressing a symposium on law and conscience at the Columbus School of Law at the Catholic University of America. He stressed the ongoing exclusion of values and faith from public life in the nation, a trend that he termed a serious threat to the well-being of the common good.

Prince Honored: It was announced on April 4 that Notre Dame University had selected Prince El Hassan bin Talal of Jordan as the winner of the Notre Dame Award for international humanitarian service. Father Edward A. Malloy, the Holy Cross president of the university, described the prince as "a devout son of Islam," and added, "he also exemplifies the socially engaged Muslim intellectuals."

Ephesus Shrine: A new oratory to Our Lady of Ephesus was dedicated at the Basilica of the National Shrine of the Immaculate Conception on April 4. Archbishop Giuseppe Bernardini of Izmir was in Washington to join Cardinal Theodore E. McCarrick for the dedication. The archbishop also serves as custos, or spiritual caretaker, of an ancient stone house in Ephesus that is reputed to have been the house where the Blessed Virgin Mary lived her last years. Over one million pilgrims visit the house each year.

Mikulski Vote: Cardinal William H. Keeler of Baltimore criticized a vote against a federal ban on partial-ban abortion by Sen. Barbara A. Mikulski in the U.S. Senate. Sen. Mikulski is a Catholic Democrat, and Cardinal Keeler sent her a letter, it was reported on April 7, stating, "I am deeply troubled by your continuing insistence that such a heinous procedure should be available in the United States of America." The Senate passed the ban by a vote of 64-33.

Appeal Theme: It was reported on April 7 that the theme for the 2003 American Bishops' Overseas Appeal is "Jesus in Disguise." Established 60 years ago as the Bishops' Welfare Emergency Relief Fund, the appeal benefits Catholic Relief Services and other vital emergency care agencies working worldwide to alleviate human suffering.

Catholic Healthcare: Dr. Edmund Pellegrino, professor emeritus of medicine and medical ethics at the Center for Clinical Bioethics at Georgetown University, in Washington, DC, was quoted on April 7 as saying that there is an attempt to remove the religious dimension from the work of Catholic health care providers. Dr. Pellegrino, addressing a three-day symposium at the Catholic University of America, warned that modern secularism has reached the level of a "substitute religion."

Media Distortion: On April 8, it was reported that Archbishop Harry Flynn of St. Paul-Minneapolis said that media coverage of the clergy sexual-abuse scandal created "a largely distorted impression" of the bishops' work to deal with the problem. Speaking at a symposium at Siena College, the archbishop cited the efforts of the United States bishops that date back to 1992. Archbishop Flynn headed the Bishops' Ad Hoc Committee on Sexual Abuse for the past year.

San Antonio Cathedral: San Fernando Cathedral in San Antonio, TX, founded 272 years ago, was reported on April 9 as having been restored and rededicated in San Antonio, TX. Archbishop Gabriel Montalvo, apostolic nuncio to the United States, joined other prelates at the Mass celebrated by Archbishop Patrick F. Flores and brought greetings from Pope John Paul II.

Catholic Home Missions: Grants totaling $11.1 million have been designated by Catholic Home Missions, it was announced on April 22. The grants will be awarded to 87 U.S. dioceses and to 27 U.S. organizations and religious orders.

Regeneration Needed: Cardinal Avery Dulles was reported on April 24 as saying that the Catholic Church in America "stands in urgent need of far-reaching intellectual, spiritual, and moral regeneration." Speaking at Fordham University, Cardinal Dulles added that "the majority of Catholics have little appreciation of their mission to spread the faith as a precious gift intended for all."

Steubenville Scholarship: It was announced on April 28 that the Franciscan University of Steubenville would be offering a scholarship for African-American men who discern a priestly vocation. Given in the name St. Benedict the Moor, the scholarship has academic and scholastic requirements.

New Guide: It was announced on April 29 that a new edition of *The Catholic Funding Guide: A Directory of Resources for Catholic Activities* has been published by the Foundation and Donors Interested in Catholic Activities. This edition contains 100 new entries and includes Internet addresses. The addresses and principal contacts of grant-makers, special funding interests, giving patterns, and other details are also in the guide.

MAY 2003

Vatican

Pope in Spain: On May 3, Pope John Paul II met with 700,000 Spanish young people and shared his conviction that a life spent in the service of God and one's neighbor is the only type of life worth living. The assembled crowd chanted: "John Paul II, the world loves you." The Holy Father responded: "Of Spain, it's true...."

Canonizations: One million Spaniards attended the May 4 canonizations of five saints in Madrid. Pope John Paul II canonized the saints in Columbus Square, announcing that Spain continues a legacy of evangelization. Two of the new are priests, Pedro Poveda Castroverde (1874-1936), founder of the Teresian Association, martyred during the Spanish Civil War, and José María Rubio y Peralta (1864-1922), the Jesuit apostle to the poor. The other three saints are women religious: Genoveva Torres Morales (1870-1956), founder of the Angelicas; Angela de la Cruz (1846-1932), founder of the Sisters of the Company of the Cross; and María Maravillas de Jesus (1891-1974), a Discalced Carmelite.

Swiss Guard: On May 6, Pope John Paul II welcomed 32 new recruits for the Swiss Guards, the Vatican force that protects the popes. The ceremony of swearing in is held annually in St. Damaso's courtyard of the Vatican Apostolic Palace to commemorate the day in 1527 when 147 Swiss Guards gave their lives defending Pope Clement VII during the sack of Rome by the forces of Emperor Charles V. The Holy Father thanked the Guards for their commitment and for their daily labors in welcoming "with kindness" the thousands of pilgrims visiting the Vatican. Among the newly invested guards is Dhani Bachmann, a young man of Indian descent who was adopted as a child by a Swiss family.

Abominable Attack: Pope John Paul II condemned the May 5 slaying of 10 hostages by rebels in Colombia. The hostages, taken by the rebel movement known as FARC, included a former Colombian defense minister, a provincial governor, and soldiers.

Faith and Science: It was reported on May 6 that the Vatican, with the support of the John Templeton Foundation, launched academic programs to promote a scholarly dialogue between faith and science. Cardinal Paul Poupard, president of the Pontifical Council for Culture, heads the Vatican office coordinating the program, which is called, "Science, Theology and the Ontological Quest."

Woman President: It was announced on May 17 that Pope John Paul II had appointed Letizia Pani Ermini, an Italian specialist in medieval archaeology, as the president of the Pontifical Roman Academy of Archaeology. She is the first woman to hold a post at this level in the Vatican.

Anniversary: It was announced on May 8 that all the cardinals of the Church have been invited to celebrate Pope John Paul II's 25th anniversary of his pontificate on October 16. Cardinal Angelo Sodano, the Vatican Secretary of State, said: "It is a historic date, a date we are happy to celebrate."

Pontifical Aims: Pope John Paul II, addressing a congress convoked by the Lateran University, stated on May 9 that, "The Way of the Church is man, without any distinctions, to whom she proclaims the truth that makes him completely free, Christ." The Holy Father said that an important theme of his pontificate over the last almost 25 years has been trying to bring Christ's liberating message to people in all walks of life. The theme of the congress that will initiate celebrations is: "The Church at the Service of Man."

African Reconciliation: Pope John Paul II announced on May 15 that the future of Africa rests in the hands of Africans but the international community must support efforts to promote peace and development. The Holy Father made this observation while welcoming new ambassadors, including those from Zimbabwe, Burundi, and Ethiopia.

Mission Obligations: Pope John Paul II on May 16 said that despite economic problems, Catholics have an obligation to help the poor and to support the mission apostolate. There has been "a worrying decrease" in the financial donations to the Pontifical Missions, the Holy Father commented. Addressing the national directors of missionary organizations, he encouraged their efforts and told them to remind Catholics that cooperation with such evangelical ministries is a right and obligation of all the baptized.

New Dioceses: On May 17, Pope John Paul II established two new dioceses in Kazakstan. Kazakstan became an independent republic 12 years ago. The two dioceses will make possible an "orderly development" of the Catholic community. The apostolic administration in Astana will now be the archdiocese of Mary Most Holy. The other diocese was established in Almaty.

New Saints: On May 18, the 83rd birthday of Pope John Paul II, the Holy Father canonized four saints. The new saints were: Jozef Sebastian Pelczar (1842-1924), a Polish bishop; Urszula Ledochowska (1865-1939), Maria de Mattias (1805-66), and Virginia Centurione Bracelli (1587-1651), all of whom were founders of religious congregations. Some 50,000 pilgrims attended the ceremonies in St. Peter's Square in the Vatican.

Sacred Music: On May 19, Father Valenti Miserachs Grau, president of the Pontifical Institute of Sacred Music, called for a Vatican entity to preserve sacred music. At the present time, sacred music is not under the direction of any Vatican congregation or commission. Father Grau stated that sacred music is essential to the life of the Church. He also stressed the need to safeguard Gregorian Chant, calling it universal, "an instrument of Catholicity." The Pontifical Institute of Sacred Music is an academic institution designed to form and counsel students in Western liturgical music.

Updated Latin: It was reported on May 19 that the Vatican had published a new edition of their dictionary, *Lexicon*, that translated modern Italian into Latin. The new edition took almost 50 years to prepare and updates Latin phrases for modern language and linguistic trends.

Papal Primacy: Theologians from Orthodox Churches joined a symposium on May 21 for an academic discussion with Catholics concerning papal primacy. The meeting was hosted by the Vatican, and cardinal Walter Kasper, president of the Pontifical Council for Promoting Christian Unity, welcomed the guests. High ranking Orthodox leaders were present.

Rosary of Peace: It was announced on May 21 that the Vatican had published a book on the recitation of the Rosary for peace. Written by the Pontifical Council for Justice and Peace, the work contains comments on the mysteries of the Marian devotion. The rosary is considered a prayer that transforms the devout. Pope John Paul II entrusted the cause of peace to the Rosary in 2000.

World Jewry: Members of the World Jewish Congress visited Pope John Paul II on May 22, with delegates of the International Committee for Interreligious Consultations. The Jewish visitors heard the Holy Father urge them to work with Catholics for peace in a world threatened by violence. Some of the Jewish representatives have been researching the Vatican archives for details concerning the pontificate of Pope Pius XII.

Dress Code: Visitors to St. Peter's Basilica must dress according to the traditional code even during the hot summer months, it was announced on May 22. Such tourists wearing scanty or sheer clothing will be refused entrance into the basilica. Local merchants are now offering paper coats and pants to accommodate the visitors.

Pre-Vatican Rite: It was reported on May 23 that an English Benedictine priest had been given permission to celebrate the pre-Vatican II rite in St. Peter's Basilica. The Vatican is now allowing the "Old Mass" with conditions. Others have been given permission in the past but the celebration of the old rite was not especially welcomed.

Algerian Earthquake: On May 23, Pope John Paul II expressed his sorrow over the devastation of the Algerian earthquake, a disaster that killed more than 1,000 people. Some 7,000 were injured and thousands left homeless. The Holy Father's condolences were conveyed in a telegram sent by Cardinal Angelo Sodano, the Vatican Secretary of State, to the apostolic nuncio in Algeria.

Bishop's Role: On May 23, it was reported Cardinal Giovanni Battista Re described a bishop as a "man of his work, man of the Word, and man made word." The prefect of the Congregation of Bishops in Rome added that bishops must proclaim the Word of God with the courage and ardor of the early Church. Cardinal Re made these observations to the Italian Episcopal conference's General Assembly.

Tridentine Mass: On May 24, Cardinal Dario Castrillon Hoyos, prefect of the Congregation for Clergy, celebrated a Tridentine-rite Mass in the Basilica of St. Mary Major in Rome. The Mass was part of the ongoing promotion of reconciliation with members of Archbishop Marcel Lefebvre's Society of St. Pius X, who welcomed the news. Archbishop Lefebvre died in 1991.

Macedonian Invitation: On May 25, it was announced that Prime Minister Branko Crvenkovski of Macedonia had invited Pope John Paul II to visit his country. The Prime Minister visited Rome with a Macedonian delegation, including Orthodox. The Holy Father thanked the prime minister for the invitation and welcomed the delegation.

General Audience Topics
• John Paul II's address from April 23 audience (May 1)

• Pope evaluates his visit to Spain (May 7)
• Meditation on Psalm 107 (108) (May 28)

International

Spanish Changes: A new study of Spain reported on May 2 that just under 85 percent of Spaniards claimed to be Catholic in 1998. That percentage dropped to just under 80 percent in 2002. Only 18.1 percent attend Sunday Mass, and 70.5 percent send their children to Catholic schools.

Seminarians Slain: It was announced on May 5 that Muslim rebels had killed two seminarians in an attack on Siocon, a coastal town in the southern Philippines. The seminarians, attending Cor Jesu Seminary in Dipolog City, had been assigned to Holy Cross parish in Siocon as part of the summer pastoral program. Some 70 Moro Islamic Liberation Front guerillas staged the attack. Over 20 people died in that raid.

Caritas Iraq: A convoy of medical aid was reported having reached the warehouses of Caritas-Iraq on May 5. The Caritas International network in Iraq is distributing medicines and basic clinical equipment valued at $335,000. Precautions were taken to secure the shipment so that the Iraqi needy could be served. Mobile medical teams are also active in the country.

Nine Killed: On May 5, it was reported that the Catholic bishops in the Indian state of Kerala pleaded for peace after Hindu-Muslim violence claimed the lives of nine people in a southern fishing village. Cardinal Varkey Vithayathil, Major abp. of Ernakulam-Angamaly for Syro-Malabars, called the violence inhuman. Eight of the victims were Hindus.

Priest Slain: Father Raphael Ngona was slain in northwest Congo on the night of May 6-7, as withdrawing Ugandan troops went on a rampage killing Hema ethnics. The Ugandan troops were Lendu. Father Ngona was buried in the courtyard of the headquarters of the diocese of Buna because continued fighting made it impossible to go to the local cemetery. The priest was pastor of Drodro parish, where 300 Hema people were murdered in April.

Seminarians Increase: It was announced on May 11 that the number of Catholic seminarians is rising, even as the ranks of priests and Women religious continue to decline in the world. Father Vito Magno, of the vocations review, *Rogate*, detailed his study of the numbers, taken from 1978 to December 2001. The numbers of religious and diocesan priests was 420,000 in 1978 while at the end of 2001 the number was 405,067. Women religious numbered 990,768 in 1978 and totaled 792,317.at the end of 2001. Seminarian numbers almost doubled in the same time period, from 63,882 candidates to the priesthood in 1978 to 112,244 at the end of 2001.

Papal Meetings: The former archbishop of Canterbury, George Carey, announced on May 11 that Pope John Paul II should hold meetings with leaders of other Christian communities as he does with Catholic bishops. Archbishop Carey is addressing a seminar organized by the Lateran University on the Holy Father's approaching 25-year-old pontificate. Archbishop Carey praised the tradition of the ad limina visits of the world's Catholic bishops with the pope and recommended informal consultations with non-Catholic leaders.

Congolese Slaying It was reported on May 11 that

attacks by ethnic Lendu militias on the Catholic parish of Nyakasanza, Congo, killed 14, including two priests. 10 members of a tribal militia killed the victims and looted the parish because of rivalries between the Lendus and Hemas. Father François Xavier Mateso and his assistant, Father Aime Ndjabu, both Hemas, were mutilated.

Seminary Kidnappings: On May 11, members of a rebel army in northern Uganda kidnapped 41 boys from a minor seminary where they studied for the priesthood. Some 95 other seminarians managed to escape. A gunfight between the rebels and government troops lasted about two hours.

Mother Teresa: On May 13, it was announced that *Mother Teresa: The Musical* had proven a success throughout Italy. The stage production that combines song, dance, and a plot depicting the labors of Mother Teresa has drawn favorable reviews from many critics. Mother Teresa will be beatified in October by Pope John Paul II.

Polish Missionary: On May 14, a Polish missionary returned to his parish outside St. Petersburg, ending his exile from Russia since March. Father Bronislaw Czaplicki, 49, was allowed to return to his parish in the city of Pushkin and to his active ministry in Russia. Father Czaplicki also serves as program coordinator of the Catholic Newmartyrs of Russia Program, documenting Catholics who were killed by Soviet authorities and possibly eligible for beatification.

English Euthanasia: A poll reported on May 14 indicates that nearly 75% of British doctors would refuse to perform assisted suicide or euthanasia if the procedure were legal. Some 56% do not believe that safeguards would adequately limit the practice of euthanasia if legalized. Another recent survey demonstrates that 57% of British doctors are opposed to a change in the law to allow euthanasia.

Muslim Terrorism: On May 15, it was reported that Father Pierre Grech, the Secretary General of the Conference of Latin Bishops in the Arab Regions, stated that terrorist attacks on Western homes in Saudi Arabia suggest more an economic character than religious. Father Grech proposed a dialogue to understand the reasons for the hatred that spawn terrorism. He believes that terrorism is economically based, as there is suffering and poverty in the area.

Canadian Catholics: It was announced on May 15 that the number of Catholics in Canada had increased by almost 5% from 1991 to 2001. There are reportedly 12.8 million Catholics in Canada, many of them among the 1.8 million immigrants arriving during the period.

Social Deterioration: The Latin American bishops cited heavy foreign debt, widespread corruption and impunity for crimes by influential social groups as the primary causes for Latin American problems, it was reported on May 20. The region faces growing poverty, unemployment, and a lack of human dignity. The Latin American bishops' council, CELAM, also stated that inadequate housing, health and educational services add to the rapid decline evident in the region. The bishops urged new programs of evangelization to address the problems.

Daily Suicides: It was reported on May 20 that about 5,000 people commit suicide every day in Europe, with adolescent suicides increasing in Austria, Denmark, Finland, Germany, and Switzerland. The young people of these affluent societies appear unable to suffer pain. Such fragile personalities are unable to face spiritual emptiness and the lack of ideals. This data were highlighted at a congress conducted by the Camillianum International Institute of Pastoral and Health Theology in Rome, "Suicide: Option, Madness, or Mystery?" Father Arnaldo Pangrazzi, the institute's deputy director, covered the suicide statistics in an address.

Missionary Slain: Franciscan missionary Father Manus Patrick Campbell, 71, was murdered on May 20 in the parish church of Amanzimtoti, just outside of Durban, South Africa. Thieves broke into the church of Our Lady of Peace and reportedly strangled the mission veteran.

Polish Ale: The Cistercian monks of the Polish monastery at Szczyrzyc in the Beskidy Mountains, in southern Poland, were reported on May 21 as having found a 17th century recipe for ale. The monks plan to market the brew made from the 400-year-old recipe, with 5.3 million gallons to be available to Polish bars. The ale is described as dark and distinctive.

Accelerated Paganism: Four Cardinals of Europe were reported on May 25 as launching a series of international congresses to counter the rapid spread of paganism and to bolster the Christian response in their nations. The prelates involved are Cardinals Godfried Danneels of Malines-Brussels, Belgium, Jean-Marie Lustiger of Paris, Christoph Schönborn of Vienna, and José da Cruz Policarpo, patriarch of Lisbon.

Nun Murdered: A Polish nun was murdered in the Democratic Republic of the Congo, it was announced on May 29. Sacred Heart Sister Czeslawa Lorek, 65, was beaten to death by unknown assailants in Kinshasa, the capital. She had been serving as a missionary nun in the Congo since 1984.

National

Cause Possible: The cause of possible beatification and canonization of Mary Virginia Merrick was reported on May 1 as having been approved by authorities in Rome. Cardinal Theodore McCarrick of Washington was notified in April by the Vatican Congregation for the Causes of Saints that nothing stands in the way of the cause being officially opened. Confined to a bed or a wheelchair by partial paralysis, Merrick founded the Christ Child Society in 1887 to serve needy children. She was known as "Miss Mary" to the thousands of children that she aided during her lifetime. She died in 1955.

Codes of Conduct: Ethical conduct in any walk of life goes beyond just following the rules, Chief Justice Mary Ann McMorrow of the Illinois Supreme Court was reported as saying on May 2. Chief Justice McMorrow took part in the Christian Brothers' *Signum Fidei* ("Sign of Faith") lecture series at Lewis University at Romeoville, IL. She stated that modern codes of conduct provide at best, minimum standards, and they cannot replace a person's will to exhibit good character.

Lexington Diocese: On May 2, Fayette Circuit Court Judge Mary Noble removed the diocese of Lexington, KY, as a defendant in a sexual abuse lawsuit because the diocese did not exist at the time of the alleged abuse. Covington Diocese is still part of the lawsuit concerning seven eastern Kentucky priests.

Voices Clarified: On May 5, it was announced that Voices of the Faithful, the lay organization formed last year in response to the sex abuse crisis, is developing a statement of beliefs to clarify the group's loyalty. Voices of the Faithful leaders claim to "love and support" the Church, accepting the teaching authority and the traditional role of the bishops and the pope.

Cardinals Gather: It was reported on May 7 that Cardinals of the United States gathered in San Francisco for the annual American Cardinals' Dinner to benefit the Catholic University of America in Washington, DC. Archbishop William J. Levada of San Francisco hosted the dinner for the first time in his archdiocese. The Catholic University of America was founded by the U.S. Bishops in 1887. Archbishop Levada concelebrated Mass with six cardinals before the dinner.

Papal Display: It was announced on May 7 that the exhibit: "John Paul II A Passion for Peace," was offered by the Knights of Columbus Museum in New Haven, CN. The display explores the Holy Father's unceasing efforts to bring peace to the world through photos, art, religious objects, and texts. The early days of Pope John Paul II's pontificate and the events of his time as pope are also presented.

Catholic Online: A new Bakersfield, CA, based Catholic Internet service was reported on May 7. "Your Catholic Voice Foundation" was launched by Catholic Online to aid in inspiring Catholics to become more active in the political process and to motivate voters on pro-life issues. The president of the foundation is deacon Keith A. Fournier.

Oregon Suicide: On May 8 a panel of the 9th U.S. Circuit Court of Appeals heard oral arguments concerning Oregon's assisted suicide law. The federal government has contested the law on the basis that assisted suicide is not a "legitimate medical practice," thereby prohibiting the use of federally controlled drugs for lethal injections. Oregon filed suit after the ruling issued by the U.S. Attorney General John Ashcroft. In April 2002, a federal judge sided with Oregon. The appeal from the U.S. Department of Justice brought about the hearing in the 9th U.S. Circuit Court of Appeals.

Abandoned Priests: On May 9, it was reported that "many priests felt the bishops simply abandoned them." This announcement was made by Father Silva, president of the Chicago-based national Federation of Priests' Councils. Father Silva was addressing a gathering of about 230 priests from 78 dioceses who met in Kansas City for the 35th annual convention.

Sin's Presence: A recent Gallup poll, reported on May 9, indicates that 84% of American adults believe in sin, while 14% do not. Despite the presence of "postmodernism," which has resulted in the weakening of religious and cultural norms, the vast majority of Americans affirm a belief in the doctrine of sin. The number of non-believers, however, is the highest total recorded in 22 years.

Global Catholicism: It was announced on May 14 that a new book, *Global Catholicism*, was published by Orbis Books. Subtitled, "Portrait of a World Church," the book tracks the evolution of the Catholic Church from a predominately European institution into a world church. The book was prepared by the researchers at the Washington-based Center for Applied Research in the Apostoloate (CARA).

Florida Seminary: On May 15, it was reported that St. Vincent de Paul Regional Seminary in Boynton Beach, FL, celebrated 40 years of service to the Catholic Church in the area. The seminary has an increased enrollment, new facilities and a refurbished campus. St. Vincent de Paul Regional Seminary fosters a bilingual and multicultural environment that serves the growing Hispanic population.

National Shrine: The Mary, Mother of the Church Shrine, on the grounds of St. Patrick parish in Laurie, MO, has been designated a national shrine, it was announced on May 15. This is believed to be the first shrine in the world dedicated to Mary under the title of "Mother of the Church." There are now 16 national shrines in the United States. The U.S. Bishops' Administrative Committee voted unanimously in March to grant the national shrine status to Laurie.

St. Juan Diego: A relic of St. Juan Diego will visit Denver, CO, it was announced on May 21. Part of the Tilma of Tepeyac Tour, the relic, an actual piece of the cloth, is scheduled to visit other cities in the U.S. during the autumn. The image of Our Lady of Guadalupe, imprinted on the tilma, is seen by countless pilgrims in Mexico City each year. Also included in the tour are relics of St. Teresa of Ávila and St. Francis Xavier.

Bishops Absent: On May 23, Bishop Daniel P. Reilly of Worcester declined to attend the commencement at the College of the Holy Cross because author, television host, and commentator Chris Matthews was the guest speaker and the recipient of an honorary degree. The appearance of Chris Matthews at the University of Scranton caused Bishop James Timlin, then bishop of the Scranton diocese, to decline his invitation to the commencement ceremonies. Matthews, a best-selling author and host of MSNBC's *Hardball*, reportedly supports laws favoring abortion.

St. Columba's Voyage: It was announced on May 23 that the U.S. Archdiocese for the Military Services plans to commemorate the 1,440th anniversary of St. Columba's voyage from Northern Ireland to Southend, Scotland. That voyage will be duplicated by Americans, Irish, and Scots, who will propel the same craft as St. Columba and his companions did in 563 A.D.

JUNE 2003

Vatican

Media and Peace: On June 1, Pope John Paul II marked World Communications Day by stating that the mass media can serve the cause of peace in the world by promoting reconciliation, understanding and mutual respect. World Communications Day 2003 celebrated the theme of *Pacem in Terris*, the encyclical of Pope Blessed John XXIII, written in 1963.

Colin Powell: On June 2, Pope John Paul II met with U.S. Secretary of State Colin Powell and discussed plans for ending the Israeli-Palestinian conflict. At the end of the talks, the Holy Father sent his regards to President George W. Bush and closed the meeting by saying, "God bless America." Secretary of State Powell then met with Cardinal Angelo Sodano, the Vatican Secretary of State, and Archbishop Jean-Louis Tauran, the Vatican Foreign minister.

Menacing Threats: On June 3, Pope John Paul II met with the bishops of central and western India and urged them to defend their people against the menacing threats of unacceptable types of family planning. Such measures are being imposed on India and other Asian nations, targeting the unborn, especially girls. The Holy Father asked the bishops to fight the "culture of death" and its frightful programs.

Croatian Visit: Pope John Paul II arrived on June 5 in Croatia, planning a five day stay in the country. He announced at the arrival ceremony: "Christianity greatly contributed to Croatia's development in the past. It can also continue to make an effective contribution to Croatian President Stiepan Mesic welcomed the Holy Father and called him "an integral part of the history and daily life of our homeland."

Beatification: On June 6, Pope John Paul II beatified a Croatian nun, Sister Maria Petkovic, before a crowd of about 65,000 people in Dubrovnik, Croatia. During the ceremony, the Holy Father announced: "Perhaps more than in other periods of history, our time is in need of that genius which belongs to women and which can insure sensitivity for human beings in every circumstances."

Croatian Farewell: Some 100,000 Croatians sang: "Pope, we love you" as Pope John Paul II left their country on June 9. The gathering in the central coastal city of Zadar completed the Holy Father's five-day trip to Croatia. The crowd roared a response to every gesture of the pope. He urged them to draw on their Catholic faith as they rebuild their society.

Europe's Families: On June 13, Pope John Paul II saluted the reawakening of the defense of the family in Europe. Despite low birthrates and negative cultural stresses, the Holy Father proclaimed, "there are many families who remain faithful, despite the difficulties, to their human and Christian vocation." The pope was addressing the heads of the European bishops' communions for family and life. He also urged European legislators to assume their duties in defense of the family and promote a culture of life.

Holy Childhood: On June 14, Pope John Paul II met with 8,000 young people to celebrate the 160th anniversary of the founding of the Holy Childhood Association. This mission society asks Catholic children to help young people in need. The Holy Father announced: "In the South of the planet, the cry of millions of children condemned to die of hunger or

of diseases connected to poverty, has become more heartbreaking and is heard by all." He thanked the young people assembled for the celebration for responding to such cries.

Endless Vortex: On June 15, Pope John Paul II described the Israeli-Palestinian crisis as an "endless vortex of violence and reprisal" and urged efforts to make justice and forgiveness hallmarks of present negotiations. The Holy Father made these comments at the noon blessing from his apartment window above St. Peter's Square in Vatican City.

Pastoral Urgency: On June 16, Pope John Paul II urged leaders of the Order of Friars Minor" to "Hold to sanctity! Here is a real pastoral urgency for our time." Participants of the Order's General Chapter met with the Holy Father at the Francis of Assisi and asked the Franciscans to maintain the missionary commitment and filial adherence to the directives of the pastors of the Church.

Papal Foundation: On June 17 it was reported that Pope John Paul II appealed for support for the John Paul II Foundation for the Sahel, a foundation that trains workers to assist the Sahel, a semi-arid region south of Saharan Africa and visited in 1980 by the Holy Father. The conditions in the region inspired Pope John Paul II to create the foundation to aid the sub-Saharan people there in 1984. The foundation provides $4.1 million a year for projects in the region.

Bosnia Visit: On June 22, Pope John Paul II spent 10 hours in Bosnia-Herzegovina, visiting Banja Luka and beatifying a native born layman, Ivan Merz. The Holy Father urged the Serbian Orthodox, Croatian Catholics, and Bosnian Muslims to put the "suffering and bloodshed" of the past behind them and to begin "afresh" together. The Serb majority did not demonstrate enthusiasm for the papal visit.

The Wojtyla Files: It was reported on June 22 that a new book released in Poland documents the secret police surveillance of Pope John Paul II before his election in 1978. Then Cardinal Karol Wojtyla's activities were carefully documented by the Communist authorities, who understood clearly his opposition. The Wojtyla Files begins with a profile by the Communist Department for Religions, a document demonstrating Cardinal Wojtyla's confrontation with the Communists and his loyalty to the faith. The Polish publisher Pax has printed the work.

Vatican Museums: It was announced on June 24 that the Vatican Museum, one of the most popular and most visited museums in the world, can now be viewed on the Internet. The centuries-old collections and other displays can be viewed online. The website is www.vatican.va.

Vatican Web Site: On June 26, Bishops Claudio Maria Celli, secretary of the Administration of the Patrimony of the Holy See (APSA), provided details about the Vatican's official page at www.vatican.va, which was inaugurated at Christmas in 1995. The site receives 50 million hits a month from 150 countries.

Christians Persecuted: On June 27, the Aid to the Church in Need organization announced that 938 Christians died for the faith in 2002. Some 100,000 Christians were arrested as well, and 629 were injured. The information is included in the 2003 Report on Religious Liberty in the World. The most critical situations can be found in China, Cuba, Nigeria, and Sudan.

Ecclesia in Europa: Pope John Paul II published his new post-synodal apostolic exhortation, *Ecclesia in Europa*, "The Church in Europe," on June 29. The 135-page exhortation included 40 proposals presented by bishops at a special synod of the bishops in 1999. The Holy Father stressed the Christian religious patrimony in Europe, stating, "Europe needs a qualitative leap in awareness of its spiritual heritage…. The Gospel is not against you, but for you." (*See* **News in Depth**.)

Pallium **Conferred:** On June 29, Pope John Paul II conferred the *pallium* on 40 metropolitan archbishops from around the world. Among the recipients was one American, Archbishop Timothy M. Dolan of Milwaukee, WI. The *pallium* is a white woolen band embroidered with six black crosses, worn around the neck during solemn celebrations as a symbol of communion with the Holy See.

General Audience Topics
• Focus on the lesson of John XXIII, 40 years after his death (June 4)
• Highlights of apostolic trip to Croatia (June 11)
• Reflection on a canticle in Isaiah 61 and 62 (June 18)
• Remembering Paul VI 40 years after his election (June 25)

International

Church Assembly: On June 1, more than 200,000 Catholics and Protestants gathered at the German Parliament, the Reichstag, in closing services of the nation's first ecumenical church assembly. Cardinal Karl Lehmann of Mainz, the head of the German bishops' conference, was one of the Catholic Church leaders who welcomed participants in the assembly.

Nobel Nominee: It was reported on June 3 that Oswaldo Paya Sardinas was nominated for the Nobel Peace Prize. A dissident in Cuba, Paya Sardinas was saddened by the imprisonment of Cuban human rights activists, intellectuals, labor leaders, and poets. He is involved in the Christian Liberation Movement and the Varela Project, intent on reforming Cuban political and economic laws but describes himself as a Catholic and a man of peace. Paya Sardinas spent time in Cuba's labor camps when he was younger.

Mexican Rights: Mexican Church officials were reported on June 3 as having defended their rights to speak out on issues such as abortion and same-sex unions. Cardinal Norberto Rivera Carrera and Auxiliary Bishop Abelardo Alcantara, general secretary of the Mexican bishops' conference, urged the government to change a Mexican Constitution article that bans religious leaders from making political statement.

Auschwitz Pilgrimage: Melkite Archbishop Emile Shoufani was reported on June 5 as leading a group of 250 Israeli Arabs and Jews on a pilgrimage to Auschwitz concentration camp. The archbishop said that the visit created a "sense of revulsion" but also created a realization that "we are all united in the pain and suffering of the victims." Archbishop Shoufani is director of St. Joseph Seminary and High School in Nazareth, Israel.

Romanian Bishops: On June 6, Romanian bishops

from the Latin and Eastern Catholic Churches urged the government and society to take immediate steps to reverse a crisis in family life in Romania. The bishops are seeking ways in which Romanians can restore the "dignity, strength, and brilliance" that God endowed families with in His Divine Plan. Living conditions and models for the young are key elements in the restoration of an authentic Romanian culture.

Tiananmen Martyrs: Bishop Joseph Zen Ze-kiun of Hong Kong was reported on June 6 as using the word "martyrs" to describe the victims of Beijing's Tiananmen Square on June 4, 1989, while addressing a Catholic prayer meeting. He also made reference to the 120 canonized Chinese martyrs who died for the faith.

Euro Constitution: Archbishop Mario Conti of Glasgow, Scotland, announced on June 8 that the draft preamble of the new European Constitution represents "an act of cultural vandalism." This charge was based on the fact that there are no references to Christianity in the text. The exclusion of Christian references creates what the archbishop termed "a yawning historical and philosophical vacuum" that deprives Europeans of any references to Christian roots and culture.

Nights of Mercy: It was reported on June 9 that Cardinal Christoph Schönborn of Vienna had introduced "The Night of Mercy," an initiative to keep churches open around the clock to provide havens of silence and prayer. Working with the archbishops of Paris, Lisbon, and Brussels, Cardinal Schönborn is seeking to implement the International Congress for the New Evangelization and the Urban Mission, an initiative first developed by the Emmanuel charismatic community.

Nine Martyrs: The Oblates of Mary Immaculate were reported on June 9 as opening the research necessary to the cause of nine martyred faithful in Laos, from 1954-70. The Communist persecutions claimed the lives of the martyrs. Six were Oblate Missionaries, two were lay catechists, and one was a diocesan priest.

Congo Losses: It was reported on June 10 that the Catholic Church in the Congo is suffering losses as a result of the ongoing war in that nation. Priests have had to flee from their parishes since the war began in 1996, and two priests were slain with their parishioners. More than 430 people have died in the battle for the Congolese area of Bunia.

Canadian Marriages: The definition of marriage as a heterosexual union has been set aside by an Ontario, Canada, court, it was reported on June 10. Toronto City clerks have been ordered to issue marriage licenses to homosexual couples who ask for them. The federal government has not filed an appeal to this ruling and has not asked for a stay. An interfaith group in Canada has registered its disappointment.

Berlin Layoffs: It was announced on June 10 that the Archdiocese of Berlin, Germany, is laying off 400 employees and closing half of the archdiocese's parishes in order to pay off a debt of $107 million. One seminary will also be closed, and another will not be subsidized. The action is intended to provide the archdiocese with a balanced budget by 2008.

Chateaubriand Revived: It was reported on June 15 that Francois-René de Chateaubriand (1768-1848) is being honored in an exhibition in Rome for his defense of the Church after the French Revolution. Chateaubriand wrote "The Genius of Christianity or Beauties of the Christian Religion" in 1802. The Rome exhibition was held at the Primoli Foundation throughout the summer under the title, "Chateaubriand in Rome: 1803-2003." Chateaubriand served as ambassador to Rome in 1829.

Imam Removed: It was announced on June 16 that the Islamic Cultural Center of Rome had ousted Imama Abdel-Samie Mahmoud Ibrahim Moussa from the city's Great Mosque. The imam had urged Muslims to mobilize and to "ensure the victory of the nation of Islam everywhere in the world." A 32-year-old Egyptian, the imam was removed from the mosque, one of the largest in Europe, and was replaced by another Egyptian, as the grand imam of the mosque must be from Egypt. The mosque has a special relationship with the Islamic University of Al-Azhar in Cairo.

Kenya Apology: It was reported on June 17 that the Kenya Television Network apologized to the Archbishop of Nairobi, Archbishop Raphael Ndingi Mwana'a Nzeki, for a satirical skit involving the consecration at Mass. A program called *Redykyulass* (pronounced "Ridiculous") lampooned the archbishop, setting off a storm of protest. The cast members and crew declared that they intended no ridicule but will become more sensitive to religious and social beliefs in the future.

Iraqi Salesians: A children's summer camp will open again in Mosul, Iraq, it was announced by the Salesians on June 17. Three weeks of daily activities will be offered to about 400 young people in the morning and to 300 youngsters in the afternoon. The children come from seven Chaldean parishes in Mosul and from one Syrian-Catholic parish.

Forged Inscription: On June 18, the committee set up by the Israeli Antiquities Authority declared an inscription on a controversial ossuary box to be a fraud. The inscription on the so-called James Ossuary read, "James, son of Joseph, brother of Jesus." While the committee determined the box to be from antiquity, it dismissed as unlikely its presence in Jerusalem, as this particular type of box was consistent with Syrian and northern regions. More important, the careful examination of the inscription revealed it to be a modern forgery.

Melkite Eparchy: Basilian Salvatorian Father Ibrahim Ibrahim, a Melkite pastor in Brooklyn, OH, was appointed on June 19 by Pope John Paul II to head the Eparchy (Diocese) of Saint-Sauveur de Montreal in Canada. The 41-year-old bishop succeeded Bishop Sleiman Hajjar as the Melkite bishop for all of Canada; Bishop Hajjar drowned in 2002 while on vacation in Florida. When consecrated a bishop in August, Bishop Ibrahim was set to become the youngest bishop in the Melkite Catholic Church.

Monastic Ruins: On June 20, it was announced that Israeli archaeologists had uncovered a monastic complex believed to be used from the 5th to the 8th centuries. Several monasteries were found, and one site was definitely a convent. The convent contained an inscription honoring the mother superior and several female skeletons. The inscription was written in Greek.

Same-Sex Weddings: In a statement issued on June 23, Archbishop Marcel Gervais of Ottawa, Canada, announced that priests officiating at same-sex marriages will be suspended. The archbishop stated: "In the Catholic Church, an attempted marriage of two of the same sex would not be recognized and the person officiating would be suspended from their sacred duties." An Ontario Court of Appeals declared that the constitutional definition of marriage had to be changed to accommodate same-sex unions.

Abortion Ship: It was reported on June 29 that a Dutch ship operated by abortion activists left Polish water after being denounced by Catholic leaders. The *Langenort* sailed out of Wladyslawowo on the Baltic Sea after paying part of a $3,150 fine for entering the port without permission. The presence of the Langenort was viewed as a provocative interference in the legal order of the sovereign Polish State.

National

Dominican Sisters: It was reported on June 3 that the Dominican Sisters of St. Cecilia celebrated their growing numbers by holding a groundbreaking and blessing for an addition to the motherhouse in Nashville, TN. Included in the addition will be living quarters, a new chapel, dining facilities, and an infirmary. A fund-raising campaign has been conducted for these renovations.

Tilma Tour: It was reported on June 3 that 6,000 people attended services at the Cathedral of the Immaculate Conception in Denver to take part in the Tilma of Tepeyac Tour. The tilma was a cloak-like garment worn by Mexicans centuries ago, and St. Juan Diego had his on when Our Lady of Guadalupe appeared to him. A tiny piece of the tilma, which bears the image of the Blessed Virgin Mary and is enshrined in the Basilica of Our Lady of Guadalupe in Mexico City, is touring American dioceses. The last stop of the Tilma of Tepeyac Tour will be New York, where it will be on display until December.

Damien Miracle: A six-member tribunal convened by Honolulu Bishop Francis X. DiLorenzo has investigated an alleged healing attributed to the intercession of Blessed Damien de Veuster, S.S.C.C. The findings will be forwarded to Rome, and if the Holy See agrees with the tribunal of Hawaii, Blessed Damien could be declared a saint. Pope John Paul II beatified Blessed Damien, the Hero of Molokai, in 1995.

Marriage Definition: On June 5 it was reported that the Catholic dioceses of Massachusetts are urging state legislators to enact an amendment to the state constitution that would reaffirm the legal definition of marriage as the union between one man and one woman. The bishops sent a statement to all parishes urging Catholics to press for quick passage of the Marriage Affirmation and Protection Amendment.

Priests For Life: It was announced on June 6 that the Christian Coalition of America and the National Pro-Life Religious Council have started a series of voter registration Sundays with Priests for Life. Pastors are being encouraged to preach to their congregations about the responsibility of every citizen to register and vote on issues of great importance.

Abortion Poll: A *Newsweek* poll reported on June 9 indicated that nearly half of the country believes that human life begins at conception. The poll conducted by Princeton Survey Research Associates for

Newsweek also gave evidence that 56% of the Americans polled believed that prosecutors should be able in all cases to bring separate murder charges against someone who kills a fetus still in the womb.

Lay Ministry: A grant of $644,935 was reported on June 10 as being awarded by the Lilly Endowment to a new lay ministry program at the Benedictine Center in Maplewood in the St. Paul-Minneapolis Archdiocese. The Benedictine Center promotes pastoral excellence by nurturing good Church leadership.

Priestly Formation: A record enrollment was announced on June 10 for the Institute of Priestly Formation in Omaha, NE. Some 105 seminarians have enrolled in the 10-week summer program, representing 51 dioceses in 24 states, as well as Australia, Canada, and Vietnam. The Institute provides assistance in the spiritual formation of diocesan priests and is being used by bishops to strengthen their ongoing seminary programs.

Archdiocese Settles: The archdiocese of Louisville, KY, was reported on June 10 as agreeing to settle 243 sexual abuse lawsuits by 240 plaintiffs for $25.7 million. Archbishop Thomas C. Kelly of Louisville spoke at a news conference and apologized to the victims of the abuse.

Interfaith Conferences: On June 10, the case for giving patriarchal status to the Ukrainian Catholic Church was heard by participants in the *Orientale Lumen* ("Light of the East") conference sponsored by the Catholic University of America in Washington, DC. The conference examined aspects of expanding and adapting the patriarchal traditions of the Church. The Society of St. John Chrysostom, Eastern Christian Publications, and the university's school of religious studies co-sponsored the gathering.

Keating Resignation: It was reported on June 16 that National Review Board chairman Frank Keating would resign in the wake of remarks. The governor was quoted in the *Los Angeles Times* two days before as saying that some unnamed Catholic bishops were acting "like Cosa Nostra." He was accusing some prelates of fighting full disclosure to the board of the abuse data for their dioceses. Cardinal Roger M. Mahony, archbishop of Los Angeles, called Gov. Keating's remarks "irresponsible and uninformed."

Wisconsin Grant: The Catholic Foundation of the Diocese of Green Bay was reported on June 16 as receiving a grant of $1 million from Darlene and Donald J. Long, Sr., and their children. The funds will establish an initiative to analyze issues concerning low-income housing. The initiative will also develop a plan to form a comprehensive system of care.

Bishop O'Brien: Bishop Thomas J. O'Brien of Phoenix was arrested on June 16 on a felony charge of leaving the scene of a fatal collision. The hit-and-run case involved Jim L. Reed, who jaywalked after dark across a busy street and was struck by two vehicles. The other car was not found.

Vietnamese Bishop: It was reported on June 16 that Bishop Dominic Dinh Mai Luong, the first bishop of Vietnamese descent in the United States Church, was consecrated as the auxiliary bishop of the diocese of Orange, in California. Two Vietnamese bishops came to the United States to participate in the liturgy.

Bible Version: A version of the Bible published by Tyndale House Publishers does not have required Catholic approval, it was announced on June 17. The work is promoted as a "Catholic Reference Edition" but has not been approved by the U.S. bishops or the Vatican. A Tyndale spokesman said that the company is aware that the translation does not have Catholic approval but is continuing to sell the book, called "The Holy Bible: New Living Translation, Catholic Reference Edition."

Bishops Convene: It was reported on June 19 that the U.S. Bishops' meeting in St. Louis closed their afternoon session to reporters so that the national study of the sexual abuse matters could be discussed. At the request of Cardinal Francis E. George of Chicago, the U.S. bishops gave him their approval to submit to the Holy See the revised statutes of the International Commission of English in the Liturgy.

Nuncio's Warning: Archbishop Gabriel Montalvo, papal nuncio to the United States, warned America's bishops on June 19 that the Church faces a threat from those seeking to manipulate the current sexual abuse crisis to damage the Catholic faith. Speaking at the start of the Bishops' meeting in St. Louis, the nuncio commented, "some real problems within the Church have been magnified to discredit the moral authority of the Church." Addressing the 260 U.S. Bishops, Archbishop Montalvo urged those gathered to "stand together as men of faith."

Native Americans: On June 19, Bishop Donald E. Pelotte of Gallup diocese in New Mexico reported on Native American Catholics to the U.S. bishops gathered in St. Louis and marked the publication of a document entitled, "Native American Catholics at the Millennium." Bishop Pelotte cited the population figures for these Native Americans in the 2000 census. There are 4.1 million Native Americans, and more than half of these live in cities or towns where there are specific programs available. Bishop Pelotte also reminded the bishops that Catholicism among the Native American tribes spans centuries, as many such groups were converted by the earliest Catholic missionaries and stayed loyal to the faith.

Korean-Americans: It was reported on June 23 that the U.S. Catholic bishops have proclaimed Sept. 21 as Catholic Korean-American Day. The celebration will honor Korean-American contributions to the Church. This year marks the 100th anniversary of Korean immigration into the United States. Special observances will be held in the Basilica of the National Shrine of the Immaculate Conception in Washington, DC.

Opus Dei: On June 25, the eve of the feast day for the recently canonized founder of Opus Dei, St. Josemaria Escriva de Balaguer, members of the personal prelature that St. Josemaria had founded attended Mass in the Basilica of the National Shrine of the Immaculate Conception in Washington. Cardinal William H. Keeler of Baltimore was the chief celebrant of the Mass.

Sodomy Laws: On June 26, the U.S. Supreme Court struck down the sodomy laws of the state of Texas, declaring them an unconstitutional violation of privacy. In a 6-3 decision, the court declared that a Texas law was an unwarranted government intrusion into a person's home. (*See* **News in Depth**.)

JULY 2003

Vatican

International Conflicts: On July 1, Pope John Paul II received Abdulhafed Gaddur, the new ambassador from Libya, to the Vatican. The pontiff used the reception of the new ambassador's credentials to urge the world to promote courageous and tenacious dialogue as responses to existing tensions. The Holy Father added that recourse to armed conflict serves as "a defeat of reason and humanity."

Bond of Peace: Bartholomew I, the Orthodox patriarch of Constantinople, sent a letter on July 2 to Pope John Paul II. The patriarch remarked on the bond of love and peace that exists between the churches. The patriarch also extended his "sincere fraternal affection."

World Alliance: It was announced on July 2 that the Vatican has proposed a world alliance that would unite international groups, society, and governments. Archbishop Celestino Migliore, permanent observer of the Holy See before the U.N., presented the proposal to the U.N. Economic and Social Committee. The world alliance would focus on economic inequities and promote collective responsibility.

Liberian Tragedy: On July 2, Pope John Paul II appealed to the world community to aid in restoring peace and security to Liberia and to northern Uganda. He also expressed his closeness to the local churches, encouraging them to be strong and steadfast in hope. The Holy Father asked the international community to intervene in the deadly civil war in the region.

Christian Meaning: Pope John Paul II announced on July 3 that a theology that does not invite conversion to Christ, one that considers all religions equal, empties Christianity of all meaning. Addressing a group of bishops from Bangalore, Hyderabad and Visakhapatnam, the Holy Father added that any "theology of mission that omits the call to a radical conversion to Christ and denies the cultural transformation which such conversion will entail necessarily misrepresents the reality of our faith." He warned against the modern relativist explanation of religious pluralism that empties Christianity of its "defining Christological heart."

Korean Ambassador: On July 4, the new ambassador to the Vatican from South Korea, Ambassador Youm Seong, was welcomed by Pope John Paul II. The Holy Father expressed his satisfaction with the growth of the Catholic Church in South Korea. In his address, the Holy Father spoke Latin, reciprocating the use of Latin by the ambassador. The new ambassador earned a degree in theology from the Catholic University of Gwangju, South Korea, and a doctorate in classical literature from Rome's Salesian University.

Gypsy Council: It was announced on July 4 that the Pontifical Council for Migrants and Travelers has organized a world congress concerning modern gypsies. Called the "Children of the Wind," gypsies number about 18 million in Europe and India. The congress will discuss the discrimination and rejection suffered by gypsies and is being held in Budapest, Hungary. The gathering is an effort to offer gypsies solidarity with Catholics and a welcoming environment.

Summer Renewal: Pope John Paul II said that the summer vacation period is a good time to rediscover the authentic values of the spirit. The Holy Father added that the accelerated speed of life can make it difficult to cultivate this important dimension, and the vacation period can give new breath to the interior life.

Don Orione: A miracle attributed to the intercession of Blessed Luigi Orione, a beloved apostle of charity and the founder of the Small Work of Divine Providence and the Congregation of the Little Missionary Sisters of Charity, was approved by the Holy See on July 7. The decree recognizing the miracle marked formal approval by the Vatican's authorities in charge of the process of canonizations and meant as well that the last hurdle was passed for the anticipated canonization of Don Luigi Orione by the Holy Father.

Beatifications Approved: On July 7, in the presence of Pope John Paul II, decrees were issued concerning the beatifications of several Servants of God and martyrs. The approved candidates for beatification are: Joseph Marie Cassant (1878-1903), a French priest and Trappist monk; Laura of St. Catherine of Siena (1874-1944), a Colombian and founder of the Congregation of Missionary Sisters of Immaculate Mary and of St. Catherine of Siena; Anne Catherine Emmerich (1774-1824), a German nun; and Alberto Marvelli (1918-1946), an Italian layman. In addition, two Slovak martyrs were approved for beatification: Monsignor Basil Hopko (1904-1976), an auxiliary Greek-Catholic bishop of Presov, and Sister Zdenka (1916-1955) a member of the Congregation of the Sisters of Charity of the Holy Cross. It was speculated that they might be beatified during the planned visit of the Holy Father to Slovakia in Sept..

No Mongolia Trip: It was reported on July 7 that Pope John Paul II decided not to travel to Mongolia in the coming months because the timing was not yet right. He planned to reschedule the tour to that Asian country for next year. There are fewer than 200 Catholics in Mongolia, but the Holy Father wants to visit this historically rich nation. Complicating the trip was the pontiff's hope to stop in Moscow, a longstanding desire, and a journey long delayed by the position of the Russian Orthodox Church's leadership.

Swiss President: On July 8, the Swiss president Pascal Couchepin admitted that he had been so overwhelmed during his meeting with Pope John Paul II at the Vatican that he neglected to remember to invite the pope to visit Switzerland next June 5-6 so that he might attend a national meeting to prepare for World Youth Day 2005 in Germany. The bishops of the Swiss dioceses had invited the Holy Father, but any papal visit requires an official invitation from the Swiss Federal Council. President Couchepin declared after the audience, "Had I been able to, I would have stayed longer with him."

Peter's Pence: The Peter's Pence collection, the fund allocated to charitable works in the Third World and to aid populations injured by natural disasters or wars, was reported on July 9 as reaching $52.8 million. The exact amount collected and reported by the Holy See was $52,836,693.50. It was also reported that the Holy See in the year 2002 registered a deficit of 13.5 million euros (approximately $15.2 million). The Vatican City State (Stato della Città del Vaticano) also registered a deficit of 16 million euros (approximately $18.1 million). (*See* **News in Depth**.)

Castel Gandolfo: It was reported on July 11 that Pope John Paul II had embarked upon his annual summer holiday to Castel Gandolfo. The papal residence is situated approximately 13 miles from Rome in the Alban Hills on Lake Albano, on the ancient Appian Way. Castel Gandolfo is the traditional summer residence of the papacy, enjoying a position of extra-territoriality.

American Generosity: The Holy See expressed its gratitude to the Catholics of the United States on July 10 for the generosity of their donations to the Vatican in 2001. Despite the ongoing sexual abuse scandal, U.S. Catholics continued to donate the most of any region to the Vatican budget. Cardinal Sergio Sebastiani, president of the Prefecture of the Economic Affairs of the Holy See, reported that a deficit for the Holy See was the result of global economic difficulties and the expense of building new embassies in various parts of the world. The Holy See's income totaled 216,575,034 euros (approximately $245 million), while expenses totaled 230,081,756 euros (approximately $260 million), causing a deficit of 13,506,722 euros (approximately $15.3 million). After the U.S., the next two most generous countries were Germany and Italy. (*See* **News in Depth**.)

Cor Unum: The 2002 Report of the Pontifical Council *Cor Unum* was released on July 17, reflecting Pope John Paul II's increase of aid to suffering people. Donations have been made to those in need in Uganda, the Holy Land, the Ukraine, Afghanistan, Angola, Azerbaijan, Burundi, Ivory Coast, Lebanon, Libya, Nigeria, Pakistan, Papua New Guinea, the Central African Republic, the Republic of the Congo, Syria, the U.S., Tanzania, and Vietnam. A special donation was made through the Pope's Foundation for the Sahel, the desert region of Sub-Saharan Africa.

Communion Posture: Cardinal Francis Arinze, prefect of the Congregation for Divine Worship and the Sacraments was reported on July 17 as having pronounced that the Church's liturgical norms do not forbid Catholics from sitting or kneeling when they return to their place after Communion. The statement was published in the July issue of the newsletter of the U.S. Bishops' Committee on Liturgy and came in reply to a *dubium*, or formal question on law, from Cardinal Francis George of Chicago who, as head of the Bishops' Committee had received many inquiries from bishops concerning the norms established in the new General Instruction of the Roman Missal.

General Audience Topics:
• Meditation on Psalm 145 (146) (July 2)
• Meditation on Psalm 142 (143) (July 9)
• Meditation on canticle of Isiah 66:10-14 (July 16)
• God allows himself to be conquered by humility (July 23)
• Mercy, my God (July 30)

International

Bethlehem Relief: Bethlehem's Basilica of the Nativity is in the process of being relieved as Israeli troops withdrew, it was reported on July 1. The U.S. "Road Map" for peace has brought hope to the region about an economic recovery and the return of pilgrims to the Holy Land.

Malawi perils: It was reported on July 1 that a priest was stoned and a Catholic bishop had to be guarded by police during the recent Malawi riots. A mob was protesting the removal of five Muslims suspected of al-Qaeda ties and was threatening Catholic personnel. The priest was in his car when attacked and fled, and the rioters burned the vehicle. At least seven churches and a charity were looted and vandalized.

Fetal Rights: On July 3, it was reported that Archbishop Peter Smith of Cardiff, Wales, condemned the research being conducted in the British Isles to harvest eggs from aborted fetuses. "There is something deeply wrong with a society that can even contemplate harvesting eggs from the ovaries of aborted fetuses," he stated. The archbishop also asked, "How is it that we can recognize that the aborted fetus is human enough to become a biological parent and yet not human enough to have the right to life?"

Mosque Demolished: On July 3, it was reported that Israeli authorities had demolished the foundation of an unauthorized mosque in Nazareth. The mosque was being erected next to the Basilica of the Annunciation and would have blocked access to the main road. The foundation was replaced by an Italian-style plaza.

Douai Abbey: Cardinal Cormac Murphy-O'Connor, archbishop of Westminster, the Catholic primate of England and Wales, presided over a solemn Mass on July 3 to celebrate the first centenary of Douai Abbey. The Benedictines observe monastic tradition at the abbey at Woolhampton. Originally Douai Abbey was in Paris, where the English martyrs were trained for missionary duties in the British Isles. The community was re-founded nearly two centuries ago and in 1903 started again in Woolhampton. A history of Douai Abbey is available at www.douaiabbey.org.uk.

Greek Melkites: It was announced on July 3 that the bishops of the Catholic Church for the Greek-Melkite rite have offered their services to bring about a just peace in the Holy Land. The offer was the result of a synod of Melkites under the presidency of Gregory III Laham, the patriarch of Antioch of the Greek-Melkites. The Greek-Melkite Church has 1.5 million members.

Lahore Ordinations: The Lahore Archdiocese in Pakistan celebrated on July 3 the ordinations of five new priests, the largest class in its history. Archbishop Lawrence Saldhana ordained the priests in the Sacred Heart Cathedral, thanking the parents of the new priests and the Franciscans who are active in the archdiocesan training programs.

Myanmar Catholics: Archbishop Charles Maung Bo of Yangon was reported on July 4 as being pleased with the steady increase of the Catholic population in his country. According to the *Annuarium Statisticum Ecclesiae* for 2001, the Catholic population stands at 606,000 of Myanmar's total population of 47 million people. This marks a steady increase over the last years.

Mauritanian Mosques: It was reported on July 4 that the government of Mauritania had taken control of the nation's Islamic houses of worship in order to combat fundamentalism. A law was adopted to regulate religious activity, determining the function of the imam of each mosque and his assistants. A coup d'etat was attempted in June but failed, possibly a response to the government's efforts to control Islamic fundamentalists. Muslims represent the vast majority of Mauritania's 2.8 million people.

Veils in France: A debate on Muslim girls wearing veils in France was reported on July 6. So intense was the issue that a government panel was empowered to study the matter. Muslim girls attend school wearing veils, a custom that has caused considerable discussion and school directives. President Jacques Chirac is the author of the initiative prompting the government study.

Priest Slain: On July 6, it was reported that Father George Ibrahim had been killed in his residence in Renala Khurd in the Faisalabad Diocese in Pakistan. The 36-year-old priest was shot in the chest by a group of masked gunmen. The priest had received threats in the past, and his murder followed a massacre of 44 people in a Quetta Mosque when three suicide bombers attacked the Muslim holy place.

Chinese Arrested: Four priests and a Catholic deacon were arrested in Baoding City in Hebei province, China, it was reported on July 6. Fathers Chen Guozhen, Joseph Yin, Kang Fuliang, and Pang Guangzhao and Deacon Wang Lijun were arrested by Chinese police while on their way to visit a Father Lu Genjun. Father Genjun had just been released after three years in a Communist labor camp.

Fatima Status: It was announced on July 6 that the municipality of Fatima in Portugal would become an autonomous city on January 1, 2004. Fatima is the site of the apparition of the Virgin Mary in 1917 in the Cova da Iria. The city has grown to accommodate the vast numbers of pilgrims who visit each year.

More Same-Sex Rulings: The British Columbia Court of Appeal on July 8 allowed a second province of Canada to recognize same-sex marriages. The ruling regarded marriage as "the lawful union of two persons to the exclusion of all others" and decreed that this ruling would take effect immediately. The Ontario Court of Appeal led the way in this matter last month, and the Canadian government said that it would introduce legislation to allow same-sex marriages.

Mother Teresa: On July 9, the Missionaries of Charity applied for a copyright over Mother Teresa's name to prevent and halt growing exploitation by commercial interests. It was Mother Teresa's wish that her name not be used by individuals or organizations without her permission or the permission of her successors.

Bishop Fined: A Japanese bishop was ordered on July 11 to pay $6,800 in a defamation suit filed by two Catholics. Bishop Joseph Satoshi Fukahori of Takamatsu was ordered to pay $3,400 each to Takamitsu Kuribayashi and Genzo Morioka; the bishop had criticized the plaintiffs in a pastoral letter for publicly opposing the founding of a diocesan seminary.

Buddhist Attack: On July 13, around 100 Buddhists ransacked the church of Kok Pring in southeastern Cambodia during a Mass. Police stopped the destruction of the church, but there were injuries to worshippers. The rampage was linked by authorities to the presence of Montagnards and other Vietnamese Christians in the area.

World Youth Day: The organizers of World Youth Day 2005 launched a new website on July 15. The site includes a preliminary schedule of events for the celebration, from Aug. 16-21, 2005, in Cologne, Germany. The theme is, "We have come to worship him." The website is available at www.wyd2005.org.

Prayer Meetings: On July 15, the ecumenical community of Taizé announced plans for prayer gatherings for world peace in a variety of European cities. The organizers plan on holding peace prayers in Rome, London, and Paris, with schedules already set for certain Saturdays or Sundays each month. Large weekly meetings are also held in Taizé, France, by the community.

Archbishop Peacemaker: Archbishop Thomas Menamparampil of Guwahati, India, reported on July 17 that progress had been made in mediated talks between the Dimasa and Hmar tribes in the east Indian state of Assam. In 1996, the archbishop also settled a dispute between the Bodo and Adivisi and in 1997 pacified the Kuki and Paite in Manipur. The archbishop was invited to assist in the talks between the Dimasa and Hmar tribes after the Indian government failed repeatedly to resolve the regional crisis.

Open Communion: Father Gotthold Hasenhuettl, 69, of Trier in southwestern Germany, a professor emeritus at the University of Saarbruecken, was suspended by Bishop Reinhard Marx of Trier, it was announced on July 17. The priest had led an "open communion" service at a Lutheran church. He distributed communion to Catholics and non-Catholics alike. Father Hasenhuettl was forbidden to celebrate Mass and was deprived of his Church teaching permit, the mandatum. Hasenhuettl argued that the communion had been distributed during an ecumenical *Kirchentag*, or church assembly, and was thus within the parameters reiterated by Pope John Paul II in the new encyclical, *Ecclesia de Eucharistia*.

Archbishop Attacked: On July 17, Archbishop Silvestre Luís Scandian of Vitoria, Brazil, was attacked in his office. A 50-year-old teacher stabbed the archbishop after making an appointment and arriving at the prelate's office. The attacker was described as mentally disturbed. The archbishop was treated for stab wounds and released.

Guatemalan Laity: Guatemala lay missionaries are evangelizing entire rural communities, it was announced on July 18. The missionary effort has been in response to the Holy Year of Mission being celebrated in Central America in preparation for the Second American Mission Congress (CAM 2), planned for November 2003, in Guatemala. In one mission area alone, about 1,500 lay Indian missionaries prepared for three months to evangelize the Carcha and Chisec missions. Salesian priests assigned to northern Guatemala assist the over 400 communities of Qeqchi Indians and facilitate the training of lay missionaries, including women and the young.

Collector Arrested: Oded Golan, an Israeli antiquities collector who claimed to have the burial box, or ossuary, linked to the "brother" of Jesus, was arrested on July 23 by Israeli police on charges of fraud. The police uncovered a warehouse and laboratory with sophisticated forging equipment in Golan's home. The inscription on the ossuary stated that it contained the remains of the brother of Jesus. The Israeli antiquities authority, however, declared on June 18 that the inscription was a forgery.

National

Boston Archbishop: Bishop Sean Patrick O'Malley, 59, bishop of the Diocese of Palm Beach, FL, for less than a year, was named on July 1 the new archbishop of Boston by Pope John Paul II. Bishop O'Malley succeeded Cardinal Bernard F. Law, who resigned last December in the wake of a major crisis over his handling of priests who sexually abused children. As bishop in Palm Beach, O'Malley handled the problems of a diocese whose last two bishops resigned because of allegations of sexual misconduct. Bishop Gerald M. Barbarito, 53, of Ogdensburg, NY, was appointed O'Malley's successor in Palm Beach. The pope also named Auxiliary Bishop Thomas G. Wenski, 52, of Miami as coadjutor bishop of Orlando, FL

Charles Carroll: A new book, *Charles Carroll of Carrollton: Faithful Revolutionary*, was reported on July 3 as depicting the impact of the life of this Catholic co-signer of the Declaration of Independence. Charles Carroll was an apologist for the Catholic faith in an era of persecution of the Church in the American colonies.

Oblate Sisters: It was reported on July 3 that the Oblate Sisters of Providence, the first Catholic congregation of Black nuns, celebrated 175 years of service at their mother house in Baltimore. The Oblates were founded in 1829 by Mother Mary Elizabeth Lange and Sulpician Father James Nicholas Hector Joubert. These Black religious women began educating children of slaves and former slaves.

U.S. Catholics: It was announced on July 7 that the 2003 edition of the *Official Catholic Directory*, the *Kenedy Directory*, reported an increase in the Catholic population in 2002. The Catholic population was listed at 66,407,105, an increase of 1,136,661 for the year. As a percentage of the total population, Catholics comprise 22.8%. The increase is keeping pace with the general increase in the U.S. population. Also reported was a priestly population of 44,487, a decrease of 1,186, and a population of women religious of 74,698, a decrease of 802.

Multicultural Liturgy: On July 8, Cardinal Theodore McCarrick, archbishop of Washington, spoke at a meeting in Washington of the National Catholic Association of Diocesan Directors for Hispanic Ministry. "We need to look for the people we have lost. The number is growing. We are losing more than 10 percent," the cardinal declared. Speaking mostly in Spanish, the Cardinal urged the greater use of resources for Hispanic ministry. Members were encouraged by other speakers to work toward having multicultural parishes and dioceses unified by developing ethnic liturgies. The Hispanic ministry must include all ethnic groups because Catholics should celebrate together.

Kindness in Ministry: On July 9, Cardinal Theodore McCarrick spoke to a gathering of the North American Institute for Catholic Evangelization in Portland, OR. About 470 of the institute's members had gathered in Portland for a four-day conference on the importance of spreading the Gospel message. Cardinal McCarrick told the members, "Deep in my heart I believe that evangelization is intimately related to charity…. If we are unkind, if we are arrogant, if we are proud, we will never find people open to our message."

Bush Praised: Catholic Relief Services applauded President George W. Bush for his efforts to aid Africa

on July 11. CRS produced a television commercial lauding the Bush Administration's concerns for the welfare and stability of Africa. The Catholic charitable organization stressed, however, the ongoing crisis of starvation, draughts, and wars in the region.

Drug Prevention: On July 11, it was announced that Catholic leaders had joined with the National Youth anti-drug Media Campaign and the White House office of Faith-Based Community Initiatives in releasing resource materials for education on drugs and drug prevention. New programs and the expansion of proven methods are stressing awareness and activities.

Tough Mission: On July 12, Oblate Father Ronald Rolheiser was reported as categorizing the U.S. as the toughest mission territory in the world. Affluence and secularization have altered the way Americans and others view the Faith and their own commitments. Father Rolheiser made these remarks while addressing a gathering of the North American Institute for Catholic Evangelization in Portland, OR. "We're being asked to go back to the upper room," said Father Rolheiser. "What's the strategy? I don't know, and neither does anyone else."

Maronites Gather: Brooklyn was the site of a gathering of Maronite Catholics for the 40th annual convention of the National Apostolate of Maronites from July 9-13. About 1,000 attended the convention that was dedicated to study sessions on current issues and future ministries. The apostolate is an organization that includes the U.S. eparchies of St. Maron of Brooklyn and Our Lady of Lebanon.

New Archbishop: On July 15, Pope John Paul II accepted the resignation of Cardinal Anthony J. Bevilacqua of Philadelphia and named Archbishop Justin F. Rigali of St. Louis to succeed him. Cardinal Bevilacqua, who turned 80 in June, was archbishop since 1988 and for the past two-and-a-half years has been the oldest active U.S. bishop. Archbishop Rigali, 68, has served as archbishop of St. Louis since 1994. Prior to that appointment, he served for 30 years in Vatican service, including in the post of president of the Pontifical Ecclesiastical Academy in Rome, 1985-89, and secretary of the Vatican Congregation for Bishops, 1989-94.

Significant Church: It was announced on July 17 that the Vatican has recognized Los Angeles's new Cathedral of Our Lady of the Angels as one of the largest and most significant Christian churches in the world. The cathedral cost $200 million and has been honored by having its name added to the list of 29 other significant churches, along with St. Peter's Basilica. The Los Angeles Cathedral is the 17th longest church in the ranking.

Hurricane Claudette: Parishes in the dioceses of Corpus Christi and Victoria, TX, had only minimal damage as a result of Hurricane Claudette, it was reported on July 20. The area was called blessed, as the storm killed two and left thousands homeless or without power.

Bob Hope: On July 27, beloved actor and comedian Bob Hope died, at age 100. The entertainer passed away at his home in Toluca Lake outside Los Angeles. Hope had become a Catholic at the age of 93; his wife of nearly 70 years, Dolores, was a lifelong Catholic, and Hope had been honored for his many contributions to the Catholic Church and related organizations.

AUGUST 2003

Vatican

Mini-Catechisms: It was reported on August 1 that "little catechisms" are now available from the Institute of St. Clement I in Rome. Pope John Paul II asked Vatican officials to prepare a synthesized version of the *Catechism of the Catholic Church*, and the Institute provided a version of these small editions. The "little catechisms" focus on the sacraments of the Eucharist and Penance. They are available at low cost, and translations are free to poor countries. The volume on the Eucharist has been published in nine languages.

Cardinal Defense: On August 3, Cardinal Francis E. George of Chicago countered a newspaper headline that charged Pope John Paul II with launching a campaign against homosexuals. The charge was leveled against a 12-page document that called on legislators to defend marriage and the traditional family by opposing same-sex marriages. The document reiterated the traditional values involved with support of family life.

Sacred Sabbath: Pope John Paul II announced on August 3 that making Sunday a special day of prayer and rest allows Christians to give witness to Christ's victory over sin and death. Sunday also serves as a celebration of Christ's "commitment to the full liberation of each man and woman."

Christian Scouts: On August 4, Pope John Paul II sent a message to the 20,000 Italian girls and boys participating in scout camps. The Holy Father had been invited to attend one of the four national camps sponsored by the Italian Catholic Association of Guides and Scouts but was unable to accept the invitation. He sent a message, saying that they were in his prayers as he thought of the "thousands of you in the splendid scenery where you have pitched your tents."

Norms Invalid: The Vatican's 1962 norms for handling cases of priests accused of soliciting sex in the confessional have been declared invalid, it was announced on August 7. These norms have been superseded by the 1983 Code of Canon Law and new 2001 norms for dealing with serious crimes involving the sacraments. The 1962 norms were used by some lawyers for victims of clerical abuse to incriminate diocesan administrators.

Time and Infinity: On August 8, the Vatican announced that Pope John Paul II hosted a seminar at Castel Gandolfo for 11 Polish scholars representing theology, astronomy, philosophy, and physicians. The groups discussed relationships between faith and science in a search for truth. The seminar concerned "time, eternity, and infinity."

Prayers for Rain: On August 10, Pope John Paul II asked the pilgrims joining him at Catsel Gandolfo to pray for rain and to remember the victims of the fires burning out of control in Europe. The heat wave and draught has damaged the environment and has brought intense suffering in many countries. Fifteen people died in fires in Portugal and another 25 deaths in Europe were blamed on the heat wave.

Cloning a Crime It was reported on August 11 that Cardinal Alfonso Lopez Trujillo, the president of the Pontifical Council for the Family, stated that attempts to clone human beings should be banned internationally. The cardinal terms such cloning as a "crime against the human person" that assaults the human right to life and true individuality.

International

St. Juan Diego: A new study in Mexico was reported on August 1, reconfirming the existence of St. Juan Diego Cuauhtlataotzin. Mexico's National Library of Anthropology and History made the report public on the first anniversary of the canonization of the Aztec who was visited by the Blessed Virgin Mary as Our Lady of Guadalupe. The report also states that St. Juan was a noble Aztec.

Priest Hero: It was announced on August 1 that Father Stefano Gorzegno, a pastor in Boiano, Italy, died of a heart attack after helping to save seven of his parishioners from drowning on an Adriatic beach. Father Gorzegno saved five children and two adults from waves and then came out of the water. He asked if the children were safe and then stopped breathing.

"Road Map": On August 1, the Latin Patriarch of Jerusalem, Michel Sabbah, said that the "road map" for peace in the Middle East is the only practical way for an end to the Israeli-Palestinian conflict. He asked that it be "implemented now."

Comboni Mediator: Father Carlos Rodriguez, a Comboni missionary assisting in peace negotiations in Uganda, was reported on August 5 as facing a lack of commitment and concrete answers from the members of the rebel Lord's Resistance Army. Father Rodriguez recognized that the rebels negotiate only when they feel weakened or threatened. The rebels have been trying to overthrow the Ugandan government since 1987, torturing and mutilating civilians in northern Uganda. The Sudanese have supplied the Lord's Resistance Army with arms.

Terrorism Condemned: It was reported on August 7 that Christian and Muslim leaders condemned the bomb attack that killed at least 10 and injured about 150 outside a Jakarta, Indonesia, hotel. Protestant churches joined the Catholics and Muslims in deploring terrorism based on religious beliefs. All demanded swift legal action to halt the terrorism.

Ministry Imperiled: Bishop Tomas Mauro Muldoon of Juticalpo, Honduras was reported on August 7 as having suspended the work of 40 lay social ministry workers because of death threats. One lay worker was killed in July. Tension is high in the region because of activities by environmentalists. Priests and the actual church ministry are not involved in the suspension, although some priests have been placed on death lists and have to have police escorts.

Chinese Refusal: A U.S. government commission on religious freedom announced on August 8 that Chinese officials have refused to allow commission members to visit Hong Kong. The Chinese had originated the visit, and it was assumed that Hong Kong would be on the itinerary. The U.S. Commission on International Religious Freedom canceled the trip to China as a response to this refusal.

Ethnic Conference: On August 8 it was reported that Christian leaders in Nigeria are asking for peaceful coexistence of the nation's religious and ethnic societies. Archbishop Peter Yariyok Jatau of Kaduna, president of the northern Nigerian chapter of the

Christian Association of Nigeria, stated that all Christian faiths are united in seeking national unity and stability. Another factor addressed is the controlling efforts of Jamat Nasril Islam, the leading Muslim group in northern Nigeria.

Kenya Inquest: The Kenyan government officials have begun an inquest into the August 24, 2000, death of Mill Hill Father John Kaiser. It was reported on August 12 that the death was now being investigated. Originally, Father Kaiser was labeled a suicide. He had often denounced abuses under Kenya's former president. Religious and priests will attend the inquest.

National

Peace Movements: The peace movement in the U.S. was reported on Aug. 1 as standing at a crossroads. A consultation hosted by Pax Christi International and Pax Christi USA at St. John's University drew 200 Americans and some foreign representatives. No consensus was reached after a day of critiques of the American Church and political life. Latin-rite Patriarch Michel Sabbah of Jerusalem, president of Pax Christi International, attended the gathering.

Sisters Sentenced: Three Dominican Sisters told a gathering of supporters on Aug. 1 that they were not afraid to go to jail after being sentenced for obstructing national defense and causing more than $1,000 worth of damage to federal property. Sisters Ardeth Platte, 67, Carol Gilbert, 55, and Jackie Hudson, 68, had been charged after staging an unlawful protest at a missile silo in October 2002. U.S. District Judge Robert Blackburn sentenced Sister Platte to 41 months in prison, Sister Gilbert to 33 months, and Sister Hudson to 30 months. The judge did waive all fines, but he ordered that the sisters pay $3,080 to cover what the government estimated was the amount spent to fix a fence that was violated as they made their way to the silo.

Brake the Cycle: On Aug. 1, riders completed the last leg of a 3,832-mile cross country bicycle trip, an initiative of the U.S. Bishops' Campaign for Human Development, called the "Brake the Cycle of Poverty" tour. Bikers visited 12 states and 32 dioceses on their arduous journey.

African Clergy: On August 3 delegates concluded their annual conference for African clergy and religious serving in the United States. The conference from July 31-Aug. 3, was hosted by the Los Angeles Archdiocese and had the theme for this year of "Collaboration in Ministry." It was held at the Poverello of Assisi Retreat Center in San Fernando. Delegates met to share their experiences in the American communities. The majority of participants were native Nigerians, stationed in the U.S. parishes, and others were from Eritrea, Ethiopia, Tanzania, Kenya, Ghana, and the Republic of the Congo. They are laboring in Chicago, Houston, New Orleans, New York, Seattle, and Washington.

Anti-Catholicism: The Supreme Knight of the Knights of Columbus, Carl Anderson, warned on August 5 that a new wave of anti-Catholicism is being demonstrated in the United States. Citing the obdurate stand by Democrat Senators against William Pryor, a Catholic nominee for the 11th U.S. Circuit Court of Appeals, Anderson announced the rise of anti-Catholicism to the opening session of the Supreme Council of the Knights of Columbus in Washington.

Discrimination Charged: It was reported on August 6 that Democrats in the U.S. Senate are punishing Alabama Attorney General William Pryor for being loyal to his Catholic beliefs. Republicans made the charge when the Democrats repeatedly blocked Pryor's nomination to the 11th U.S. Circuit Court of Appeals. The Democrats' references to Pryor's "deeply held beliefs" on abortion and other issues brought about the charge.

Syro-Malankar Catholics: It was reported on August 8 that Syro-Malankara Catholics gathered in Melville, New York to celebrate their faith and their heritage. They came from all across the United States and Canada for the fifth Malankara Catholic Convention of North America. India's ambassador to the United Nations and Malankara and Latin-rite bishops were also present. The Malankara Catholic Church has about 300,000 members and was formed in 1930 when bishops from the Malankara Orthodox Syrian Church expressed their union with the Holy See.

Priesthood Sunday: It was announced on August 11 that the National Federation of Priests' Councils, joined by other Catholic groups, has designated October 26 as "Priesthood Sunday" in the United States. The observance is designed to celebrate the gifts and ministries of priests in the service of the American Catholics. Other groups taking part include Serra International, Pastor Summit, the Raskob Foundation, the National Association for Lay Ministry, and The Official Catholic Directory.

New Archbishop: It was announced on August 11 that Archbishop Sean O'Malley, recently appointed archbishop of Boston, has chosen to live in the rectory of the Cathedral of the Holy Cross instead of the official residence of his predecessors. The archbishop stated that he regretted his decision had become the cause of such media attention. He explained his decision that in previous years such trappings were helpful for immigrant Catholics, but such displays "now seem ambiguous at best and a contradiction of some of our Gospel values at worst."

Knights' Conventions: The Knights of Columbus held their annual convention in Washington on Aug. 7-8 with a two-day Eucharistic Congress at the Basilica of the National Shrine of the Immaculate Conception. Among the Catholic leaders who addressed the gathering of the Knights were Archbishop John P. Foley, president of the Pontifical Council for Social Communications and Bishop William E. Lori of Bridgeport, CT.

Episcopalian Vote: On Aug. 11, Bishop Stephen E. Blaire of Stockton, Calif., chairman of the Catholic Bishops' Committee on Ecumenical and Interreligious Affairs, said that the U.S. Episcopal Church's decision to confirm an openly gay bishop and recognize that some Episcopal communities bless same-sex unions has created "new ecumenical challenges" to Catholic-Anglican Dialogue. While reiterating the Catholic commitment to dialogue, Bishop Blaire stated that actions on the part of the Episcopalians "reflect a departure from the common understanding of the meaning and purpose of human sexuality and the morality of homosexual activity as found in sacred Scripture and the Christian tradition."

DEATHS
AUGUST 2002 TO AUGUST 2003

Berrigan, Philip, 79, Dec. 6, 2002, former Josephite priest and leader in the Catholic anti-war movement; born Oct. 5, 1923, in Two Harbors, MN, and served in the U.S. Army in Europe during World War II; he was ordained a Josephite priest in 1955; became active in the civil rights movement and then the Vietnam War protests; best known as the leader of the Catonsville Nine, a group of peace activists who burned 500 draft files using homemade napalm at a Selective Service office in Catonsville, MD, in May 1968; in 1969, he married Elizabeth McAlister, a former nun and fellow peace activist (the marriage was made public in 1973); frequently arrested, his last prison term ended in 2001.

Birkenhauer, Fr. Henry F., 89, June 13, 2003, Jesuit priest and president of John Carroll University in Cleveland from 1970 to 1980; born in Toledo, he entered the Society of Jesus in 1933 and was ordained. a priest in 1945; earned a doctorate in geophysics, with an emphasis on seismology, from St. Louis University; became known as the "polar priest" because he spent 15 months in the late 1950s as chief seismologist and chaplain with a team of scientists in Antarctica.

Bloom, David, 39, Apr. 6, 2003, adult convert and NBC News reporter who died of a pulmonary embolism while covering the war in Iraq; served as a reporter, White House correspondent for NBC, and co-anchor of NBC's "Weekend Today" program before covering the Iraq War; converted in 1989 while a reporter in Wichita, KS; his funeral Mass was celebrated at St. Patrick's Cathedral in New York by Cardinal Edward M. Egan; survived by his wife, Melanie, and their three daughters.

Branson, Sr. Serena, 90, July 8, 2003, Daughter of Charity and national Catholic Charities leader; a native of Washington, she entered the Daughters of Charity in 1931; in the 1950s, she founded centers for children with special needs; in 1974, she was appointed executive director of Catholic Charities in the Albany Diocese.

Breen, Bishop Vincent DePaul, 66, Mar. 30, 2003, bishop of Metuchen, NJ, 1997-2002; born in 1936 in Brooklyn, NY, he was ordained a priest in 1962; named bishop of Metuchen, July 8, 1997; as bishop, he was instrumental in gathering support for the Donna Santa Marie case — a class-action suit filed by New Jersey women who say they did not receive adequate information from their abortionists to make an informed decision about having an abortion.

Carter, Cardinal Gerald Emmett, 91, Apr. 6, 2003, archbishop of Toronto from 1978-90 and a participant in the Second Vatican Council; born in 1912 in Montreal, Canada, he was ordained a priest in 1937; ordained titular bishop of Altiburo and auxiliary bishop of London, ON in 1962; he then served as bishop of London, ON, 1964-78; from 1973 to 1975 vice pres. and from 1975-77 pres. of Canada's bishops conference; named archbishop. of Toronto in 1978 and cardinal in 1979 (titular church, St. Mary in Traspontina); one of his brothers also became a bishop and two of his sisters became nuns.

Carter, Archbishop Samuel, 83, Sept. 3, 2002, retired Jamaican archbishop, the first Jamaican-born bishop on the Caribbean island; born in Kingston, he joined the Jesuits in 1944 and was ordained 10 years later in Weston, MA; named an auxiliary bishop of Kingston in 1966 and archbishop in 1970; he was widely praised for his work for Christian unity.

Casserly, Fr. Patrick, 59, Jan. 2, 2003, Marist Father and an official at the Vatican's Pontifical Council for Social Communications; prior to his joining the Social Communications council's staff in 1992, he had served as a council consultor and as a Marist missionary in Papua New Guinea and Fiji; a native of Kells, Ireland, he had coordinated satellite links for international telecasts of papal liturgies and represented the Holy See to the International Catholic Union of the Press and at meetings of the Council of Europe on communications.

Clark, Sr. Mary Kathleen, 83, Feb. 21, 2003, Sister of St. Joseph of Carondelet who took $17 and a year's leave of absence to establish in 1973 Casa de Los Ninos in Tucson, AZ, which became the nation's largest crisis nursery; the house served as the prototype nationwide; since its opening it has provided shelter or services to 33,000 children.

Clinch, Bishop Harry, 94, Mar. 8, 2003, the first bishop of Monterey in California, from 1967-82 and the second oldest U.S. Catholic prelate; born Oct. 27, 1908, in San Anselmo, CA, he was ordained a priest on June 6, 1936; ordained titular bishop of Badiae and auxiliary bishop of Monterey-Fresno on Feb. 27, 1957, he was appointed the first bishop of Monterey, CA, Oct. 16, 1967; resigned Jan. 19, 1982; he was one of the last surviving bishops named by Pope Pius XII; he had been a priest for 66 years and a bishop for 46 years.

Colasuonno, Cardinal Francesco, 78, May 31, 2003, long-time Vatican diplomat, an expert in East European diplomacy, and cardinal; born Jan. 2, 1925, in Grumo Appulia, Italy, he was ordained a priest on Sept. 28, 1947; he entered diplomatic service in 1958 and served in the section for Extraordinary Ecclesiastical Affairs of the Secretariat of State and in nunciatures in U.S., India, and Taiwan; ordained titular archbishop of Truentum, Dec. 6, 1974, he was named the first apostolic delegate to Mozambique, 1974-81, apostolic delegate to Zimbabwe, 1981-85, and apostolic pro-nuncio to Yugoslavia, 1985-86; he headed the Holy See delegation for permanent working contacts with Poland, 1986-90, and was representative to the USSR, 1990-94; appointed nuncio to Italy in 1994 and San Marino in 1995, he became a cardinal on Feb. 21, 1998.

Costello, Fr. Les, 74, Dec. 10, 2002, a priest, former NHL player and co-founder of the Flying Fathers hockey team; best remembered as a man who gave up a promising career as a professional hockey player to enter the priesthood, he played for the Toronto Maple Leafs' Stanley Cup-winning team in 1948 and later for the Pittsburgh Hornets in the American Hockey League before retiring in 1950; ordained a priest in 1957; in 1962 he and Father Brian McKee of the Sault Ste. Marie Diocese founded the barnstorming charitable hockey team made up of priests; since their first game, the Flying Fathers have raised more than $2.5 million for various charities.

DeBusschere, Dave, 62, May 14, 2003, member of the National Basketball Hall of Fame; born in Detroit, he led Austin Catholic High School to a state championship in basketball in 1958 and later played basketball and baseball at the University of Detroit, pitched for the Chicago White Sox, and played and coached pro basketball for the Detroit Pistons and the New York Knicks; inducted into the Basketball Hall of Fame in 1983, he was also named in 1996 one of the greatest 50 players of all time in the National Basketball Association; he also served as a basketball executive and was commissioner of the old American Basketball Association (ABA).

Drahmann, Br. Theodore R., 76, Sept. 2, 2002, Christian Brother, former superintendent of schools for the Archdiocese of St. Paul-Minneapolis and president of Christian Brothers University in Memphis, TN from 1980 to 1993; born in Minnesota and entered the Christian Brothers in 1946; later served as director of education for the regional office of the Christian Brothers Conference in Landover, MD.

"Du" Burns, Clarence H., 84, Jan. 12, 2003, a convert to Catholicism, the first African-American Catholic to be mayor of Baltimore; born Sept. 13, 1918, in Baltimore; studied jazz at the Larry London Music School and was a staff sergeant in the U.S. Army at the end of World War II; Burns worked for 22 years as a locker room attendant at a high school; he began the Eastside Democratic Organization and in 1971 was elected to the Baltimore City Council and represented the city's 2nd District from 1971-86; the first black president of the council, he became mayor in 1987 after then-Mayor William Donald Schaefer took office as Maryland's governor; he served for 11 months before being defeated by Kurt L. Schmoke; Burns ran for mayor again in 1991 only to be defeated once more by Schmoke.

Foley, Laurence, 60, Oct. 28, 2002, U.S. diplomat in Amman, Jordan, killed by a lone gunman at close range as he walked outside his home; served as a probation officer in California in the 1970s and assistant director of the Peace Corps mission in the Philippines; also worked in Bolivia, Peru and Zimbabwe before transferring to Jordan, where he was responsible for the rehabilitation of medical clinics; in the embassy, he was executive administrator for the U.S. Agency for International Development; received an achievement award from the U.S. Embassy the day before he was shot; survived by his wife, Virginia; regularly attended Saturday evening Mass in the English-speaking Sweifieh parish in Amman and was a member of the choir.

Gallant, William, 48, Nov. 26, 2002, director of communications for the Archdiocese of Seattle from 2000; worked as a news anchor, reporter, and radio talk show host; hosted *The Bill Gallant Show* on KIRO radio from 1991 to 1996 and he appeared as a commentator on Chronicles from 1996 to 1998; moved to Northwest Cable News as executive producer in April 1998; survived by his wife, mother, sisters, and brother.

Grabowski, Fr. Fidelis, 85, Dec. 21, 2002; priest and former worldwide leader of the Congregation of the Marians of the Immaculate Conception; born in Evanston, IL, on Apr. 14, 1917, he was ordained to the priesthood in 1945; served as an official of several Marian seminaries and for 25 years was the province's novice master; he was elected to a six-year term as superior general in 1981, but resigned in 1984 because of poor health.

Gröer, Cardinal Hans Hermann, 83, Mar. 23, 2003, cardinal, archbishop of Vienna from 1986 to 1995, who reigned amidst charges of sexual misconduct; born in Vienna in 1919, he entered the minor seminary at the age of 14 and was ordained a diocesan priest in 1942; at the age of 61, he became a Benedictine monk and renamed himself after Blessed Hermann the Cripple, an 11th-century Benedictine monk; named archbishop of Vienna in 1986, he became a cardinal in 1988 (titular church, Sts. Joachim and Anne al Tuscolano); from late 1995 to early 1998 he was prior at the Benedictine monastery in Goettweig, Austria, then additional allegations surfaced; in April 1998 he relinquished all public ministry.

Ham, Bishop J. Richard, 81, Dec. 20, 2002, Maryknoll missionary to Central America who also served as auxiliary bishop in the Archdiocese of St. Paul-Minneapolis from 1980 until 1990; born in Chicago July 11, 1921, he was ordained a priest on June 12, 1948, following studies at Maryknoll Seminary in NY; a priest for 54 years, he spent 21 of those in Central America; he later became an auxiliary bishop of Guatemala City in November 1967 and ordained a bishop Jan. 6, 1968; in 1980, he was named auxiliary bishop and vicar for Hispanic affairs of St. Paul-Minneapolis.

Healy, Fr. Kilian, 90, May 18, 2003, former prior general of Carmelites; born John Lawrence Healy in Worcester, MA, on Nov. 15, 1912, he entered the Carmelite order at Mount Carmel College in Niagara Falls, ON, in 1929; sent to St. Albert's International College in Rome to study theology, he was ordained on July 11, 1937; he taught at Mount Carmel College, Whitefriars Hall in Washington and Marymount Junior College in Arlington, VA; he later served in Rome as assistant general for English-speaking Carmelites throughout the world and as professor of theology at St. Albert's International College.

Heim, Archbishop Bruno, 92, Mar. 18, 2003, papal diplomat and Vatican representative in England from 1973 to 1985; born in Switzerland in 1911; ordained a priest in 1938; during World War II he served as a chaplain to Italian prisoners, and he joined the Vatican's diplomatic corps in 1947; his career included a period in Paris as secretary to the papal nuncio, Archbishop Angelo Roncalli — later Pope John XXIII – and the two remained close friends until the pope's death in 1963; served in various European countries before being named an archbishop and apostolic delegate in Scandinavia in 1961; named nuncio to Finland in 1966 and Egypt in 1969; as nuncio to England, he became a friend of the Queen Mother and was responsible for advising Rome on the appointment of 19 bishops, including the late Cardinal George Basil Hume as archbishop of Westminster; he was also an expert on heraldry, he wrote three books on the subject, and designed coats of arms for the last four popes.

Hoffman, Bishop James R., 70, Feb. 8, 2003, bishop of Toledo from 1980; born June 12, 1932, in Fremont, OH, he was ordained a priest on July 28, 1957; appointed auxiliary bishop of Toledo in 1978, he was ordained titular bishop of Italica on June 23, 1978; named bishop of Toledo, on Dec. 16, 1980, he was the sixth bishop of Toledo and the longest serving of the diocese; among his contributions to the U.S. Conference of Catholic Bishops was his work as a member of the subcommittee on lay ministry of the U.S. Bishops' Committee on the Laity.

Hope, Bob, 100, July 27, 2003, beloved entertainer honored in 1999 as the top entertainment figure of the millennium in an ABC News telephone poll; he became a Catholic at 93 after retiring from show business, although he had long supported Catholic causes with his wife of nearly 70 years, Dolores, a life-long Catholic; born Leslie Townes Hope in Eltham, England, on May 29, 1903; his family moved to Cleveland in 1907; his career spanned radio, TV and movies; his relationship with NBC began in 1936 on NBC's radio network, a world record in entertainment; aside from hundreds of NBC specials, he starred in almost 50 movies, including the famed "Road" movies with Bing Crosby and Dorothy Lamour; he also visited troops stationed overseas, from World War II to the Persian Gulf War; received an honorary degree from Georgetown University; he served on the first honorary committee of Catholics in Media Associates and received countless honors.

Hoyt, Robert, 81, Apr. 10, 2003, founding editor of the *National Catholic Reporter*; born in Clinton, IA in 1922, he was orphaned at age 12, attended high school in Detroit and at St. Norbert High School and College in DePere, WI, graduating in 1942; he joined the Norbertine order at St. Norbert's in 1940 but left two years later; after service in the U.S. Army, he worked for the *Denver Catholic Register*; he went to Kansas City in 1949 at the invitation of Bishop (later Archbishop) Edwin V. O'Hara; at Bishop O'Hara's encouragement, the Hoyts and several colleagues published the *Sun-Herald* for six months; in 1957 Hoyt was made editor of *The Catholic Register*, the Kansas City edition of the national chain; in 1964, Hoyt, Michael J. Greene, and Father Vincent J. Lovett launched the *National Catholic Reporter*; Hoyt was also executive editor and then editor in chief, 1977-85, of *Christianity & Crisis*, and senior writer for *Commonweal* magazine from 1989 to 2001; in October 1968, Bishop Helmsing of Kansas City-St. Joseph issued a condemnation and demanded that the editors remove "Catholic" from the paper's name; Hoyt was fired in 1971; in 1999, he received the St. Francis de Sales Award.

Illich, Ivan, 76, Dec. 2, 2002, former Catholic priest and social critic who spoke against institutionalized religion and formal education; born in Vienna, Austria, he left school in 1941 under Nazi race laws due to his mother's Jewish ancestry; moved to the U.S. in 1951 and became a priest of the NY Archdiocese; later, he served as rector of the Catholic University of Puerto Rico; founded in 1961 the Intercultural Center of Documentation, which trained missionaries in Latin America; while at the center, his criticisms of institutionalized religion caused the protests of opponents; the Vatican banned priests and religious from attending the center in the late 1960s; the ban was lifted upon the condition that the then-Msgr. Illich leave the center; soon after, he announced his plans to leave the priesthood.

Lynch, Bishop George E., 86, May 25, 2003, retired auxiliary bishop of Raleigh; born Mar. 4, 1917, in New York City, he studied at Fordham, Mt. St. Mary's Seminary, and Catholic University of America and was ordained a priest on May 29, 1943; he served as chancellor of the Raleigh diocese and calmed down an angry mob in 1953 protesting Bishop Vincent Waters' decision to integrate black and white parishes in the rural town of Newton Grove; named ordained titular bishop of Satafi and auxiliary of Raleigh on Jan. 6, 1970, he retired on Apr. 16, 1985; after his retirement, he was very active in Pro-Life activities, working with Operation Rescue; he was arrested over 20 times over 18 years for violating the federal Freedom of Access to Clinic Entrances Act of 1994, known as FACE, by blocking access to an abortion clinic.

MacEoin, Gary, 94, July 9, 2003, Catholic writer, expert on Latin America, and advocate of poor; born Gary Johnson on June 12, 1909, in Curry, County Sligo, Ireland, he adopted the Gaelic form of his last name, MacEoin (son of John), years later; he entered the Redemptorist seminary at age 18, but was informed three weeks before ordination that he would not be ordained; he then became a writer and earned a doctorate in Spanish; the author of more than 25 books, he wrote on Latin America, the Church, and Northern Ireland; served as editor for the Port-of-Spain *Gazette* in Trinidad and a correspondent for Catholic News Service, *National Catholic Reporter*, *La Prensa*, and *La Hacienda*.

McClendon, Sarah, 92, Jan. 7, 2003, veteran Washington reporter who covered presidents from Franklin D. Roosevelt to the early days of the current Bush administration; born July 8, 1910, in Tyler, TX, her family were Episcopalian, but Sarah became a Catholic in 1930 while a student at the University of Missouri; after graduation from the University of Missouri School of Journalism in 1931, she spent 10 years working for various Texas newspapers; in 1942, she volunteered for the WAAC headquarters and the War Department Bureau of Public Relations. A graduate of Officer Candidate School, she first served in the public affairs office at the WAAC training center at Fort Oglethorpe, GA, and was later assigned to the Pentagon. During her time of WAAC service (later the Women's Army Corps), she married John T. O'Brien, but he abandoned her after only seven months, leaving her pregnant; discharged from the Army because of her pregnancy, she needed to find work to support herself and her child. In 1944, she returned to journalism as a correspondent for the Philadelphia *Daily News,* and in 1946 founded the McClendon News Service, providing stories for a number of media outlets. As a member of the Washington press corps, she was famed for her sharp questioning of U.S. presidents.

McSorley, Fr. Richard T., 88, Oct. 17, 2002, Jesuit a theologian, controversial peace activist, and author of eight books on social justice and pacifism; born in Philadelphia in 1914, he entered the Society of Jesus at 18, and was not ordained when he was sent to the Philippines to teach in southern Luzon; in 1941, a few days after the Japanese attacked Pearl Harbor, he and his fellow Jesuits were taken prisoner by the Japanese and held until 1945; ordained in 1946 after his return to the U.S.; from the time of his first parish assignment as a priest at a segregated southern Maryland parish, he was an activist for social justice;

marched with Rev. Martin Luther King Jr. in Alabama and Mississippi, and led protests against the Vietnam War and the production of nuclear weapons; served as vice president of the International Peace Bureau of Geneva and as a member of the national council of Pax Christi USA, a Catholic peace movement.

Moloney, Thomas F., 74, Mar. 1, 2003, photographer for *The Long Island Catholic*; a native of Long Island, he attended the New York Institute of Photography after graduation from Hempstead High School; after a stint in the U.S. Army in 1953-55, he worked for eight years as a cameraman before joining *The Long Island Catholic* in 1964; in his 38-year career as a news photographer, he won numerous awards from the Catholic Press Association and from the Press Photographers Association of Long Island, which he also served for six years as treasurer.

Moynihan, Sen. Daniel Patrick, 76, Mar. 26, 2003, Democratic U.S. senator from New York for 24 years who served four terms before retiring in 2001; born in Tulsa, OK, he moved with his parents to New York City as an infant; he attended public and Catholic schools and worked, including as a longshoreman, before enrolling in New York's City College in 1943; a year later, he enlisted in the Navy; upon his return from World War II, he went back to school, and earned a doctorate and a Fulbright Fellowship to study at the London School of Economics; he was assistant labor secretary in the Kennedy administration, assistant secretary for policy planning in the Johnson administration, and urban affairs advisor to President Nixon; in 1973, Moynihan was appointed ambassador to India; in 1975-76, he served as U.S. ambassador to the U.N.; he was also a professor at Harvard from 1966 until 1977; his votes as a senator were most often in favor of laws to make abortion more accessible; Moynihan was awarded the Presidential Medal of Freedom in 2000; he made a famous remark that anti-Catholicism is "the only bigotry that intellectuals tolerate."

Neves, Cardinal Lucas Moreira, O.P., 76, Sept. 8, 2002, Rome, prefect emeritus of the Congregation for Bishops and long-time Curia official; born Sept. 16, 1925, São Joao del Rei, Brazil; ordained a priest July 9, 1950; ordained titular bishop of Feradi maggiore and auxiliary of São Paulo, Aug. 26, 1967; assigned to Vatican, 1974, he became vice president of the Pontifical Commission for Laity, 1974-79; secretary of the Congregation for Bishops, 1979-87; archbishop of São Salvador da Bahia, 1987-98, he became a cardinal in 1988 (titular church, Sts. Boniface and Alexius); he helped organize a 1986 meeting involving Brazilian bishops, Vatican officials and the pope, an encounter that looked at liberation theology and other points of contention between the world's largest bishops' conference and the Vatican.

Nguyên Van Thuân, Cardinal François Xavier, 74, Sept. 16, 2002, Rome, Italy; Vietnamese cardinal, imprisoned for 13 years, and prefect of the Pontifical Council for Justice and Peace; born in Huê, Viet Nam; ordained a priest June 11, 1953; appointed bishop of Nha Trang, Apr. 13, 1967, and coadjutor archbishop of Saigon (now Ho Chi Minh City), Apr. 24, 1975; his uncle was South Vietnamese President Ngo Dinh Diem, a Catholic who was assassinated in 1963; Vietnam's communist regime jailed him in 1975; while never tried or sentenced, he spent nine of his 13 years of detention in solitary confinement; he fled to Rome in 1991; even after leaving Vietnam, he continued to wear a pectoral cross and chain he fashioned in prison out of wood and electrical wire and which he hid from guards in a bar of soap; after arriving in Rome, he was made vice president of the Vatican's justice and peace council in 1994 and its president four years later; named a cardinal Feb. 21, 2001, with the titular church Deaconry of St. Mary della Scala; he published several books about his detention.

O'Donnell, William, 88, May 4, 2003, the first layman to head the Catholic newspaper in Arkansas and one of the first lay editors in the U.S. Catholic press; born Dec. 6, 1914, in East Orange, NJ, and raised in Providence, RI, he began work in 1935 as a free-lance journalist for the *Boston Herald*, United Press International and *New York Daily News Record*; he was recruited from RI in 1954 to become managing editor of *The Guardian* newspaper in Little Rock (now called the *Arkansas Catholic*) and was named editor in 1959 by Bishop Albert Fletcher; at the time, there were only four other laymen leading Catholic papers around the country; under his direction, *The Guardian* earned six national awards for excellence.

O'Neill, James, 74, Sept. 4, 2002, Catholic journalist who covered Vatican II; born Jan. 15, 1928, in San Francisco and received a master's degree in journalism in 1951 from Columbia University in NY; he worked for the *Wall Street Journal* and United Press International before joining the Rome bureau of the National Catholic News Service, as Catholic News Service was then called, in 1957 and was bureau chief from 1964-75; covered all four sessions of the 1962-65 Second Vatican Council; began working in 1975 for Catholic Relief Services, overseas aid agency of the U.S. bishops, as a press officer; since 1982, he represented the International Catholic Union of the Press at the U.N. in NY; in 1979 he became a managing editor for the March of Dimes Foundation; co-authored the book *Pope John XXIII: An Authentic Biography* (1959); in 1964, he received the *Pro Ecclesia et Pontifice* medal; he is survived by his wife of 42 years, Rosaleen Doyle, three daughters and three grandchildren.

Ovian, Fr. Leo J., 78, Jan. 30, 2003, a founding member and first vicar general of the Society of the Missionaries of the Holy Apostles; born Apr. 2, 1925, and raised in Whitinsville, MA, he served in the Army Air Corps in World War II; after working for seven years as a public school teacher in Groton, CN, he entered the Catholic Church in 1959 and was ordained to the priesthood on Feb. 12, 1966; served for 22 years as president and rector of what was then Holy Apostles Seminary in Cromwell, CN, now known as Holy Apostles College and Seminary.

Peck, Gregory, 87, June 12, 2003, Academy Award-winning actor; born in La Jolla, CA, he began his career on the New York stage; his films included *The Gunfighter, The Keys of the Kingdom, Gentleman's Agreement, Cape Fear, Twelve O'Clock High, Captain Horatio Hornblower, Moby Dick,* and *MacArthur*; he won a Best Actor Academy Award for his part in *To Kill a Mockingbird*; promoted the "Family Theater" radio drama anthology in the 1940s and 1950s started by Father Patrick Peyton, the Holy Cross priest and advocate of the who also advocated the rosary for families; survived by his second wife of 49 years, Veronique, and by two children from his first marriage and two from his second.

Raphaël I Bidawid, Patriarch, 81, July 7, 2003, patriarch of Babylon of the Chaldeans from 1989-2003; born Apr. 17, 1922, he was ordained on Oct. 22, 1944; elected bishop of Amadya in 1957 at the age of 35 years of age, he was then the youngest bishop in the world; he attended every session of the 1962-65 Second Vatican Council; in 1966, he was transferred to the Chaldean diocese in Beirut where he remained until members of the Chaldean synod elected him patriarch in 1989.

Roach, Archbishop John R., 81, July 11, 2003, archbishop of St. Paul-Minneapolis from 1975-95 and president of the NCCB/USCC from 1980-83; born July 31, 1921, in Prior Lake, MN, he was ordained on June 18, 1946; ordained titular bishop of Cenae and auxiliary bishop of St. Paul-Minneapolis on Sept. 8, 1971, he was appointed, archbishop on May 28, 1975; while he was president, the NCCB published two of its most famous documents: "The Challenge of Peace: God's Promise and Our Response" (1983) and "Economic Justice for All: Catholic Social Teaching and the U.S. Economy" (1986); after his retirement in 1995, Archbishop Roach served as head of the bishops' national Task Force on Catholic Social Teaching and Catholic Education; the task force later secured publication of the 1998 statement "Sharing Catholic Social Teaching: Challenges and Directions."

Rotelle, Fr. John, 63, Sept. 1, 2002, Augustinian priest and liturgical translator; born Jan. 18, 1939, Ambler, PA; entered the Augustinian novitiate at New Hamburg, NY, professing first vows in 1957 and solemn vows in 1960; ordained at the International College of St. Monica in Rome on Feb. 20, 1965; served as executive secretary of the International Commission on English in the Liturgy, known as ICEL, from 1973 to 1980, and as associate director and then director of the U.S. Bishops' Secretariat for Liturgy from 1970 to 1978; known also for his efforts in translating and publishing the writings of St. Augustine and the Augustinian heritage.

Rusnak, Bishop Michael, 81, Jan. 16, 2003, Redemptorist priest, bishop, and head of Slovak Catholics in Canada; born Aug. 21, 1921, in Beaverdale, Pa., he was ordained in Presov, Slovakia, in 1949; shortly after his ordination, he was arrested and sent to a concentration camp with other Slovak Byzantine and Latin-rite Catholic priests; he escaped fourteen months later, made his way to the U.S. with his American passport, and arrived in 1951 in Canada, where he set up parishes in the Ontario cities of Toronto, Hamilton, Oshawa and Welland; appointed auxiliary bishop of the Ukrainian Eparchy of Toronto and apostolic visitor for Slovaks of the Byzantine rite in Canada in 1965; appointed the first eparch of the Eparchy of Sts. Cyril and Methodius in 1981; he was also a member of the Congregation for Eastern Churches from 1968 to 1975, and from 1973 to 1978 served on the commission that worked on the revisions to the Code of Canons of the Eastern Churches.

Sabattani, Cardinal Aurelio, 90, Apr. 19, 2003, Italian cardinal and expert in law; born in Casal Fiumanese, Italy, in 1912, he was ordained in 1935; jurist; in 1939, he entered the Vatican Secretariat of State; he then served in various assignments in his native diocese of Imola and as judge and later an official of the regional ecclesiastical tribunal of Bologna; called to Rome in 1955 as prelate auditor of the Roman Rota, he was ordained titular archbishop of Justinian Prima in 1965 and served as prelate of Loreto, 1965-71; he then served as secretary of the Supreme Tribunal of Apostolic Signatura and consultor of Secretariat of State, 1971, and pro-prefect of the Apostolic Signatura, 1982-83; named a cardinal deacon in 1983, he was transferred to the order of cardinal priests in 1993 (titular church, St. Apollinaris); prefect of Apostolic Signatura, 1983-88, archpriest of the Patriarchal Vatican Basilica, and president of the Fabric of St. Peter, 1983-91, he retired in 1991.

Salatka, Archbishop Charles A., 85, Mar. 17, 2003, bishop of Marquette from 1968-77 and archbishop of Oklahoma City from 1977-92; born Feb. 26, 1918, in Grand Rapids, MI, he was ordained in 1945 after studies in Rome; appointed auxiliary in Grand Rapids in 1962, he was ordained titular bishop of Cariana on Mar. 6, 1962; as archbishop, he founded the archdiocesan Office of Hispanic Ministry and acquired a working knowledge of Spanish at age 60; he also organized an evangelization office, a telecommunications office and a pastoral ministry program, and he ordained the archdiocese's first 50 deacons; in 1989, he was one of 35 U.S. bishops to meet with a group of 26 Vatican officials over four days to discuss U.S. church issues, focusing on evangelization in society and the role of bishops as teachers of faith.

Setian, Bishop Nerses Mikail, 83, Sept. 9, 2002, retired apostolic exarch for Armenian Catholics in the United States and Canada; born Oct. 18, 1918, Sebaste, Turkey; ordained on Apr. 13, 1941, after 19 years of pastoral assignments in Turkey, he returned to Rome in 1960 as rector of the Armenian College; in Rome, he also was in charge of the daily Armenian transmissions of Vatican Radio and was a consultor to the Pontifical Commission for the Revision of Eastern-Rite Canon Law; in 1981, he received appointment as titular bishop of Ancira of the Armenians and first exarch of the apostolic exarchate for Armenian Catholics in Canada and the United States, Dec. 5, 1981; retired Nov. 24, 1993.

Sheets, Bishop John R., S.J., 80, Apr. 16, 2003, auxiliary bishop of Fort Wayne-South Bend, IN, 1991-97; born in Omaha, NE, 1922; he joined Jesuits in 1940 and was ordained a priest in 1953 (with a final profession of vows as a Jesuit in 1957); ordained titular bishop of Murcona and auxiliary bishop of Fort Wayne-South Bend on June 25, 1991; he retired in 1997; he earned a doctorate in theology under the famed Jesuit theologian, Father Karl Rahner, from the University of Innsbruck, Austria; he taught theology at Marquette University and Creighton University; during a 1982 sabbatical in Africa, he did pastoral work in Rwanda, Kenya and Uganda, and the following year taught a semester at Sogang University in Seoul, South Korea; editor and chairman of the board of the English edition of the respected theological periodical *Communio: International Catholic Review*.

Smith, O.M.I., Bishop Philip F., 77, Sept. 30, 2002, Cotabato, Philippines, U.S.-born missionary bishop in the Philippines for fifty years; born in Lowell, MA, he joined the Oblates of Mary Immaculate and was ordained in 1950; he arrived in the Philippines in 1951;

named apostolic vicar of Jolo, Philippines in 1972 and appointed bishop later that year; as bishop of Jolo, he supported the establishment of housing projects to bring together Christians and Muslims after the burning of the town in 1974; appointed coadjutor bishop of Cotabato in 1979 and became archbishop a year later; in December 1986 he survived a plane crash near Cotabato City, but was badly injured after being thrown out the front window of the light plane.

Smith, Thomas J., 81, Nov. 27, 2002, longtime editor of the *Catholic Herald* newspaper in Milwaukee; after serving four years in World War II with the Army Signal Corps, he returned to Marquette and graduated in 1948 with a degree in journalism; he joined the *Waukesha Freeman*, rising to assistant managing editor in 14 years with the daily; he then joined the then-*Catholic Herald Citizen* in 1962; in 1967, he became the principal editorialist for the paper and encouraged its advocacy of the civil rights movement; subsequently, he served under two archbishops, William E. Cousins (1959-77) and Rembert G. Weakland (1977-2002).

Spalding, Br. Thomas W., 78, Jan. 28, 2003, Xaverian brother and a former teacher and historian; a Xaverian for 60 years, he graduated in 1942 from the former St. Joseph Prep School in Bardstown; he also attended the now-closed Xaverian College in Silver Spring, MD, Fordham University, Spalding University, and the Catholic University of America where he received his doctorate; he was the author of *The Premier See: A History of the Archdiocese of Baltimore*, published in 1989; a distant relative of Archbishop Martin John Spalding of Baltimore, whose biography he also wrote; he also co-edited and/ or co-authored other historical works, and wrote articles for the *American Historical Society, The Catholic Historical Review* and the *Filson Club Historical Quarterly*; he joined the Spalding University faculty in 1970 after several years as head of the history department at Xaverian College.

van Straaten, Fr. Werenfried, 90, Jan. 31, 2003, Norbertine founder of the international Catholic charity Aid to the Church in Need; born in the Netherlands, he entered the Norbertine Order at Tongerlo Abbey in 1934 and was ordained to the priesthood in 1940; in 1947, his efforts to collect food for homeless refugees in Germany after World War II earned him the nickname the "Bacon Priest"; his focus soon shifted to raising money and collecting religious literature for the Catholic communities suffering or outlawed under the communist regimes of Eastern Europe; over the decades, Father van Straaten and Aid to the Church in Need raised more than $3 billion in donations; since the early 1960s, the organization also has worked in Latin America, Africa and Asia, funding projects in 130 countries; he was also a tireless spokesman for Catholic communities forced into an underground life, in particular the Ukrainian Catholic Church.

Velasco García, S.D.B., Cardinal Ignacio Antonio, 74, July 6, 2003, cardinal and archbishop of Caracas, Venezuela from 1995; born Jan. 17, 1929, Acarigua, Venezuela; ordained priest for the Salesians Dec. 17, 1955; worked as a catechist and taught at the major Salesian seminary in Altamira; rector of various Salesian colleges and member of the Salesian General Council with responsibility for Latin America, Caribbean, and Pacific; appointed titular bishop of Utimmira and vicar apostolic of Puerto Ayacucho Oct. 23, 1989; consecrated by the pope on Jan. 6, 1990; appointed apostolic admin. ad nutum *Sanctae Sedis* of San Fernando de Apure; archbishop of Caracas May 27, 1995; cardinal priest Feb. 21, 2001; titular church, St. Maria Domenica Mazzarello.

Wu Cheng-chung, Cardinal John Baptist, 77, Sept. 23, 2002, Hong Kong, Bishop of Hong Kong from 1975 and cardinal from 1988; born Mar. 26, 1925, in Wuhua County in Guangdong, China; ordained a priest in Hong Kong in 1952; after serving in Hong Kong and the U.S., he spent the next 18 years in Hsinchu Diocese; ordained bishop of Hong Kong July 25, 1975; as bishop, he issued two letters to bishops and cardinals worldwide, the first asking support for Hong Kong in facing the 1997 handover to China and the other concerning the June 4, 1989, crackdown on the pro-democracy movement in Tiananmen Square in Beijing.

Zhang Wenbin, Bishop Lawrence, 87, Dec. 24, 2002, bishop of Weinan Diocese in Shaanxi, China; born into a Catholic family May 30, 1915, he was ordained in 1943 and named administrator of the diocese in 1952, three years after the communists took over China; he was sent to a prison labor camp at the start of the Cultural Revolution in 1966 and was freed 14 years later after being deemed "politically rehabilitated"; he was ordained bishop of Weinan in the government-approved church in 1981.

BISHOP JOSEPH R. CROWLEY

Bishop Joseph R. Crowley, retired auxiliary bishop of the Diocese of Fort Wayne-South Bend, and former longtime editor of *Our Sunday Visitor* newspaper, died on Feb. 4 at the age of 88.

Born in Fort Wayne on Jan. 12, 1915, to Irish immigrant parents, he served in the U.S. Army Air Corps from 1942-46 in England, Africa and Italy during WW II, reaching the rank of captain. After the war, he enrolled at St. Mary's College in St. Mary, KY, and St. Meinrad Seminary in St. Meinrad. He was ordained a priest of the Ft. Wayne-South Bend Diocese on May 1, 1953, at age 38. In 1958, he became an editor at *Our Sunday Visitor*, a post he held for a decade. Named a monsignor in 1960, during the Second Vatican Council, he was moderator of the U.S. bishops' press panel during the council's final session.

Bishop Crowley left *Our Sunday Visitor* to serve as pastor of his home parish, St. Joseph, in 1967. In 1969, he became rector of St. Matthew Cathedral, South Bend, a post he held until retirement. On Aug. 24, 1971, Crowley was ordained titular bishop of Maraguis and auxiliary bishop of Ft. Wayne-South Bend. From 1973-79, Bishop Crowley became chairman of the U.S. Bishops' Committee on Communications, a post he held for six years. He promoted an annual national collection to improve Catholic communications, what became the Catholic Communication Campaign. Crowley retired on May 8, 1990, both as auxiliary bishop and rector of St. Matthew Cathedral. In nearly 50 years in the priesthood, Bishop Crowley served as a pastor, vicar general, consultor, assistant chancellor, director of religious instruction, and auxiliary bishop.

News In Depth

POPE JOHN PAUL II 2002-2003

JOHN PAUL II'S PONTIFICATE — FOURTH LONGEST IN HISTORY

In 2003, Pope John Paul II became the fourth longest reigning pontiff in the history of the Church. The pontiff was elected to the papacy on Oct. 16, 1978, although the formal calculation of his pontificate is from the solemn inauguration of his papacy on Oct. 22, 1978. The Holy Father's pontificate surpassed Pope Pius VI (r.1775-1799), whose pontificate extended to 24 years, 6 months, and 8 days. The three longest-reigning popes are Leo XIII (1878-1903; 25 years, 5 months), Blessed Pius IX (1846-78; 31 years, 7 months, 21 days) and St. Peter (d. c. 64 or 67; precise dates unknown).

PAPAL TRIPS 2002-2003

SPAIN, MAY 3-4, 2003

Pope John Paul II, on the 99th foreign trip of his pontificate, visited Spain from May 3-4, 2003.

Itinerary

May 3 (Madrid)
Welcome Ceremony: Address of the Holy Father
Meeting with the President of Government
Meeting with youth: Greetings of the Holy Father; Address of the Holy Father

May 4 (Madrid)
Mass and Canonization; homily of the Holy Father
Recital of the Regina Caeli; address of the Holy Father
Meeting and lunch with the cardinals of Spain, the members of the Executive Committee of the Spanish Episcopal Conference and the cardinals and bishops of the papal entourage
Meeting with the royal majesties of Spain
Farewell ceremony

Overview

The Holy Father devoted his visit to two chief events. First, as he often does during his pastoral visits, the pope visited with youth. The gathering on May 3 was attended by over half a million youth, largely from Spain. The pontiff also used his apostolic visit to canonize five Spanish saints: Pedro Poveda Castroverde (1874-1936); José María Rubio y Peralta (1864-1929); Genoveva Torres Morales (1870-1956); Angela de la Cruz (1846-1932); María Maravillas de Jesus (1891-1974).

Excerpts of Addresses and Homilies

Madrid

May 3, 2003 – Arrival Ceremony, International Airport of Madrid-Barajas

With intense emotion, I arrive once again in Spain on my fifth Apostolic Journey to this noble and beloved nation. I greet everyone most cordially, those who are present here and all who are following this event on radio or television, addressing you with deep affection in the words of the risen Lord: "Peace be with you."

I wish for each one the peace that God alone, through Jesus Christ, can give to us; the peace that is a work of justice, of truth, of love and of solidarity; the peace that peoples only enjoy when they follow the dictates of God's law; the peace that makes itself felt to men and women, and to peoples who are brothers and sisters to one another.

Peace be with you, Spain! …

At this supremely important time for the consolidation of a united Europe, I would like to recall the words with which I took my leave from Santiago de Compostela at the end of my first Apostolic Trip on Spanish territory in November 1982. From there I encouraged Europe with a cry full of love, reminding it of its rich and fruitful Christian roots: "Europe, find yourself again. Be yourself... Revive your roots!" (Declaration to Europe, Santiago de Compostela, 9 November 1982, n. 4; ORE, 29 November 1982, p. 6). I am certain that Spain will contribute the rich cultural and historical legacy of its Catholic roots and its own values to the integration of a Europe which, in the plurality of its cultures and respecting the identity of its member States, seeks a unity based on criteria and principles in which the integral good of its citizens holds sway.

Madrid

May 3, 2003 – Youth Meeting, Air Base of Cuatro Vientos in Madrid

Led by the hand of the Virgin Mary and accompanied by the example and intercession of the new Saints, we have revisited in prayer several moments in the life of Jesus.

Indeed, in its simplicity and depth the Rosary is a true compendium of the Gospel and leads to the very heart of the Christian message: "God so loved the world that he gave his only Son, that whoever believes in him should not perish but have eternal life" (Jn. 3:16).

Mary, in addition to being our Mother who is close, discreet and understanding, is the best Teacher for achieving knowledge of the truth through contemplation. The drama of contemporary culture is the lack of interiority, the absence of contemplation. Without interiority culture has no content; it is like a body that has not yet found its soul. What can humanity do without interiority?

Unfortunately, we know the answer very well. When the contemplative spirit is missing, life is not protected and all that is human is denigrated. Without interiority, modern man puts his own integrity at risk....

Dear young people, I invite you to be part of the "School of the Virgin Mary." She is the incomparable model of contemplation and wonderful example of fruitful, joyful and enriching interiority. She will teach you never to separate action from contemplation, so as to contribute to making a great dream come true: the birth of the new Europe in the spirit. A Europe that is faithful to its Christian roots, not closed in on itself but open to dialogue and collaboration with the other peoples of the earth; a Europe aware that it is called to be the beacon of civilization and an incentive to progress for the world, determined to combine its efforts and its creativity to serve peace and solidarity among peoples.

I give you my own witness: I was ordained a priest when I was 26 years old. Fifty-six years have passed since then. So how old is the Pope? Almost 83! A young man of 83! Looking back and remembering those years of my life, I can assure you that it is worthwhile dedicating oneself to the cause of Christ and, out of love for him, devoting oneself to serving humanity. It is worthwhile to give one's life for the Gospel and for one's brothers and sisters! How many hours are there still to go until midnight? Three hours. Just three hours until midnight and then comes morning.

Madrid
May 4, 2003 – Canonization Mass, Homily of John Paul II, Plaza de Colón, Madrid

"You are witnesses of these things" (cf. Lk. 24: 46-48), Jesus said to his Apostles in the Gospel account just proclaimed. This was a difficult and demanding mission, entrusted to men who did not dare to show themselves in public for fear of being recognized as disciples of the Nazarene. Nevertheless, the first reading presented to us Peter who, once he received the Holy Spirit at Pentecost, has the courage to proclaim the Resurrection of Jesus to the people and urge them to repent and convert.

Since then the Church, with the power of the Holy Spirit, continues to announce this extraordinary news to all people of all times. And the Successor of Peter, a pilgrim on Spanish soil, repeats to you: Spain, following a past of courageous evangelization, continue today to be witnesses of the risen Christ! ...

The new Saints are presented to us today as true disciples of the Lord and witnesses of his Resurrection....

The new Saints have very concrete faces and their history is well known. What is their message? Their works, which we admire and for which we thank God,

are not due to their own efforts nor to human wisdom but to the mysterious action of the Holy Spirit who inspired in them an unshakeable adherence to the risen and crucified Christ and the decision to imitate him. Dear Catholic faithful of Spain: let yourselves be influenced by these marvelous examples!0...

In celebrating this Mass, I invoke upon you all the great gift of fidelity to your Christian commitments. May God the Father grant it to you through the intercession of the Most Holy Virgin, who is venerated in Spain under many titles, and of the Saints.

(For biographies of the new saints, see Saints.)

Madrid
May 4, 2003 – Regina Caeli, Plaza de Colón, Madrid

At the end of this celebration during which I canonized five new Saints, I would like to thank God who enabled me to make my fifth Apostolic Journey to your nation, a land of faithful children of the Church which has produced so many saints and missionaries. The theme of my first visit was: "Witness of hope," and this time it was "You will be my witnesses." Always remember that the badge of Christians is their authentic and courageous witness of Jesus Christ, who died and rose for our salvation....

Today Plaza de Colón has been transformed into a great church in order to accomodate this solemn celebration, during which we prayed with devotion and sang with enthusiasm.

We are meeting in the heart of Madrid, close to important museums, libraries and other centres of culture founded on the Christian faith, which Spain, as a part of Europe, was later able to offer to America with its evangelization and subsequently, to other parts of the world. Thus, the place evokes the vocation of Spanish Catholics to be builders of Europe in solidarity with the rest of the world.

Spain evangelized and evangelizing Spain, this is the way forward. Do not neglect this mission which ennobled your Country in the past and is the bold challenge for the future.

I thank the youth of Spain who came in such large numbers yesterday to show modern society that it is possible to be modern and profoundly faithful to Jesus Christ. They are the great hope of the future of Spain and of Christian Europe. The future belongs to them.... Adiós, Spain!

CROATIA, JUNE 5-9, 2003
Pope John Paul II, on the 100th foreign trip of his pontificate, visited Croatia from June 5-9, 2003.

Itinerary
June 5 (Rijeka/Krk)
Welcome ceremony: Address of the Holy Father.
Arrival at harbour of Rijeka
Meeting with the president of the Republic
June 6 (Rijeka/Krk)
Flight to Dubrovnik
June 6 (Dubrovnik)
Mass and Beatification of Sr. Marija Petkovic; homily of the Holy Father
Departure for Rijeka
June 7 (Rijeka/Krk)
Departure for Osijek
June 7 (Osiek/Èepin)

Sportive Airport of Osijek — Mass; homily of the Holy Father.

June 7 (Djakovo)

Cathedral of Djakovo — private visit

Departure for Rijeka

June 8 (Rijeka)

Rijeka Delta Mass; homily of the Holy Father

Recital of the Regina Caeli; address of the Holy Father

Meeting with the bishops of Croatia

Meeting with the prime minister

Shrine of Our Lady of Trsat in Rijeka — private visit

June 9 (Rijeka)

Archdiocesan Seminary of Rijeka — Mass in private

Departure for Zadar

June 9 (Zadar)

Forum of Zadar Liturgy of the Word; homily of the Holy Father

Airport of Zadar farewell ceremony; address of the Holy Father

Departure for Rome

Overview

On the 100th pastoral visit of his pontificate, Pope John Paul II journeyed to Croatia to deliver a message of peace and hope to a country still recovering from years of civil strife and social upheaval. The pope used the trip as an opportunity to beatify Maria of Jesus Crucified Petkovic (1892-1966), founded the *Congregation of the Daughters of Mercy of the Third Order Regular of Saint Francis*, and to deliver a powerful message in praise of the women of Croatia. Pope John Paul called them, "those who are wives and mothers, those whose lives were for ever changed by the grief of losing a family member in the cruel war of the 1990s or by other bitter troubles which they have endured." He also endured triple digits temperatures throughout his visit, receiving nevertheless, wildly enthusiastic greetings from the Croatian people and the many thousands of pilgrims who journeyed to Croatia to take part.

Excerpts of Addresses and Homilies

Rijeka/Krk

June 5 – Welcome Ceremony, International Airport Adrija Riviera Kvarner of Rijeka in the Island of Krk

With great joy I set foot for the third time on the beloved land of Croatia. I thank Almighty God for having allowed me to come back among you on this, my hundredth Pastoral Visit....

I have come among you in order to fulfill my mission as the Successor of Peter and to bring to all those living in this country greetings of peace and a heartfelt prayer for peace. In visiting the Dioceses of Dubrovnik, Djakovo-Srijem, Rijeka and Zadar I will be able to honor the ancient Christian roots of this land steeped in the blood of countless martyrs. I think of the martyrs of the first three centuries — and in particular of the Martyrs of Sirmium and of Roman Dalmatia as a whole – and I think of those of successive centuries, up to the last century and the heroic figure of Blessed Cardinal Alojzije Stepinac.

Christianity greatly contributed to Croatia's development in the past. It can also continue to make an effective contribution to Croatia's present and its future. For there are values – like the dignity of the human person, moral and intellectual integrity, religious freedom, the defense of the family, openness to and respect for life, solidarity, subsidiarity and participation, respect for minorities – which are inscribed in the nature of every human being, but which Christianity had the merit of clearly identifying and proclaiming. It is on these values that the stability and true greatness of a nation is based.

Croatia has recently asked to become an integral part, also from the political and economic point of view, of the great family of the European peoples. I can only express my hope that this aspiration will be happily realized: the rich tradition of Croatia will surely contribute to strengthening the Union as an administrative and territorial unit, and also as a cultural and spiritual reality.

This country, like several neighboring countries, still bears painful signs of a recent past: may those who exercise civil and religious authority never tire of trying to heal the wounds caused by a cruel war and of rectifying the consequences of a totalitarian system that for all too long attempted to impose an ideology opposed to man and his dignity.

For almost thirteen years Croatia has trod the path of liberty and democracy. As it looks to the future with confidence and hope, it now needs to consolidate, with the responsible and generous contribution of everyone, a social stability that will further promote steady employment, public assistance, an education system open to all young people and freedom from all forms of poverty and inequality, in a climate of cordial relations with neighboring countries.

May God bless this land and its people!

Dubrovnik

June 6 – Harbor Square in Dubrovnik, Mass and Beatification of Sr. Marija Petkovic

"Good Teacher, what must I do to inherit eternal life?" (Mk. 10:17). This was the question asked by the young man who met Jesus that day and knelt down before him.

Today, dear brothers and sisters, gathered in this liturgical assembly as disciples of the "Good Teacher," we too put this question to Jesus, for we wish to know *t*he path which leads to undying life.

Jesus' response is simple and immediate: "Keep the commandments!". It comes from the One who is the true source of truth and life. Gathered for this joyous celebration, the people of Dubrovnik, together with the pilgrims who have come from the rest of Croatia, from Bosnia-Hercegovina, from Montenegro and from other countries, accept with trepidation the invitation of the Good Teacher, and they implore his help and grace in order to be able to respond with generosity and conviction....

In the footsteps of my predecessor Pius IV who was Archbishop here, I have come with joy to this ancient and glorious city of Dubrovnik, a city proud of its history and its traditions of freedom, justice and the advancement of the common good. This is seen in the lapidary phrase inscribed on the fortress of Saint Lawrence: Non bene pro toto libertas venditur auro ("Freedom cannot be sold for all the money in the world") and above the door of the Council Hall in the Governor's Palace: Obliti privatorum, publica curate ("Forget all private interests, and tend to public concerns").

It is my hope that the patrimony of human and Christian values, accumulated down the centuries, will continue, with the help of God and of your Patron Saint Blase, to be the most precious treasure of the people of this country.

The figure of Blessed Marija Propetoga Isusa reminds me of all the women of Croatia, those who are wives and mothers, those whose lives were for ever changed by the grief of losing a family member in the cruel war of the 1990s or by other bitter troubles which they have endured.

I think of you, dear women, because by your sensitivity, generosity and strength, "you enrich the world's understanding and help to make human relations more honest and authentic" (*Letter to Women*, 2). In a special way God has entrusted children to your care, and thus you are called to become *an important support in the life of every person*, especially within the context of the family....

Women of Croatia, conscious of your lofty vocation as "wives" and "mothers," continue to see every person with the eyes of the heart. Continue to reach out to them and to stand beside them with the sensitivity born of your maternal instinct. Your presence is indispensable in the family, in society, and in the ecclesial community....

Be tireless in responding faithfully to the one Love of your life. For the consecrated life is not only a generous commitment on the part of a human being; it is first and foremost a response to a gift from on high which cries out to be accepted in complete openness. May the daily experience of God's freely-given love inspire you to give your lives unreservedly to the service of the Church and of your brothers and sisters commending all things, present and future, to his hands.

Osijek

June 7 — Sportive Airport of Osijek, Mass and Homily of the Holy Father

"I beg you to lead a life worthy of the calling to which you have been called" (Eph. 4:1). Saint Paul wrote these words to the Ephesians. His exhortation, dear brothers and sisters, resounds today in our assembly with particular timeliness.

But what is the vocation of a Christian? The answer is demanding, but clear: the vocation of Christian is holiness. It is a vocation which has its roots in Baptism and is proposed anew by the other sacraments, and principally by the Eucharist.

Dear brothers and sisters of the Dioceses of Djakovo and Srijem, the Bishop of Rome has come among you today in order to remind you, in the name of the Lord, that you are called to holiness in every season of life: in the spring of youth, in the summer of maturity, then in the autumn and winter of old age, and at last at the hour of death and even beyond death, in the final purification preordained by God's merciful love....

"I appointed you that you should go and bear fruit and that your fruit should abide" (Jn. 15:16). How can we not be grateful to God for the clearer awareness which, in the years following the Second Vatican Council, the lay faithful – men and women alike – have gained of the baptismal dignity that is theirs? Christ's followers can never cultivate sufficiently the awareness of their proper identity. This in fact is the model for their mission.

Consequently there are essential questions to which we continually need to respond: What have I done with my Baptism and my Confirmation? Is Christ truly the centre of my life? Do I give space to prayer during my day? Do I live my life as a vocation and a mission?

At the beginning of the third millennium God is calling believers, and the laity in particular, to a renewed missionary outreach. Mission is not "something added on" to the Christian vocation. Indeed, the Council states that the Christian vocation is by its very nature a vocation to the apostolate (cf. *Apostolicam Actuositatem*, 2).

Dear brothers and sisters, the Church in Slavonia and Srijem has need of you! After the trying times of the war, which has left the people of this region with deep wounds not yet completely healed, a commitment to reconciliation, solidarity and social justice calls for courage on the part of individuals inspired by faith, open to brotherly love and concerned for defending the dignity of the human person made in the image of God.

Dear lay faithful, men and women, you are called to assume generously your own share of responsibility for the life of the ecclesial communities to which you belong. The image which parishes present, as places of welcome and of mission, also depends upon you. As sharers in the priestly, prophetic and royal office of Christ (cf. *Lumen Gentium*, 34-36), enriched by the gifts of the Holy Spirit, you can make your contribution in the areas of liturgy and catechesis, and in the promotion of missionary and charitable initiatives of various kinds. No baptized person can remain idle!...

Rijeka

June 8 – Rijeka Delta Mass for Families, Homily of the Holy Father

In the final days of his earthly life, Jesus promises his disciples the gift of the Holy Spirit as his greatest legacy, the continuation of his own presence (cf. Jn. 14:16-17).

The Gospel just proclaimed has enabled us to relive the moment in which that promise became a reality: the Risen Lord enters the Upper Room, greets the disciples, breathes on them and says: "Receive the Holy Spirit" (Jn. 20:22). Pentecost, described in today's first reading from the Acts of the Apostles, is the event that made publicly evident, fifty days later, the gift which Jesus bestowed upon his disciples on the evening of Easter.

The Church of Christ is always, so to speak, in a situation of Pentecost: she is always gathered in the Upper Room in prayer, and at the same time, driven by the powerful wind of the Spirit, she is always on the streets preaching. The Church is kept ever young and alive, one, holy, catholic and apostolic, because the Spirit constantly descends upon her in order to remind her of all that the Lord has said to her (cf. Jn. 14:25) and to guide her into the fullness of truth (cf. Jn. 16:13).

Today I wish to greet with special affection that portion of the Church which makes its pilgrim way in the land of Croatia, gathered here around its Pastors and represented in its richness and variety by the faithful coming from different regions of the country....

Nowadays the family, also in Croatia, requires special consideration and concrete policies aimed at promoting and protecting its essential nature, its development and its stability. Among other things, I am thinking of the serious problems associated with housing and employment. It must not be forgotten that in helping the family we also help to resolve other important problems, such as providing assistance to the sick and the elderly, stopping the spread of crime, and finding a remedy to drug use.

It is your responsibility to provide for the human and Christian education of your children, trusting also in the expert assistance of committed and well-trained educators and catechists…. In carrying out your ministry as parents, do not tire of repeating the invocation that for centuries the citizens of Rijeka have confidently raised before the miraculous Crucifix venerated in their Cathedral: *"Pomogao nam sveti Kri•svetog Vida!"* (May the holy Cross of Saint Vitus come to our aid!)….

Christ's desire is that all people should be one in him, so that all may experience the fullness of his joy (cf. Jn. 15:11; 17:13). Today too he expresses this desire, for the Church which is ourselves. For this reason he, together with the Father, has sent us the Holy Spirit. The Spirit is tirelessly at work, overcoming every division and healing every wound.

Saint Paul has reminded us that "the fruit of the Spirit is love, joy, peace, patience, kindness, goodness, faithfulness, gentleness, self-control" (Gal. 5:22-23). Today the Pope invokes these gifts of the Spirit on all the Christian married couples of Croatia, that by their mutual gift of self, in fidelity to the duties of marriage and in service to the cause of the Gospel, they may be in the world a sign of God's love for humanity.

Rijeka
June 8 – Rijeka Delta, Recital of the *Regina Caeli*

At the conclusion of this solemn celebration, I particularly wish to greet the young people of Croatia. Dear friends, you already know one thing: the Pope looks to you with confidence and hope, and he asks you once more to be sentinels of the dawn and people of the Beatitudes, as I called you at the recent World Youth Day.

Through the family and professional life for which you are now preparing, you will take on great responsibilities for the good of society and the Church. I ask you to remember that human beings are of value for what they are more than what they do or what they possess; that superficial goals will never satisfy the thirst for happiness and fulfillment deep within your hearts; that the mission which Providence has assigned to each of you cannot be carried out by anyone else. Listen to Lord Jesus, follow him as the Teacher of life, make him your Companion along the way. (Greetings in various languages.)

Zadar
June 9 – Forum Square of Zadar, Liturgy of the Word and Homily of the Holy Father

As my Apostolic Journey to Croatia draws to an end, I am happy to join you, the faithful of the Archdiocese of Zadar and neighboring areas, here in Forum Square, in the shadow of the Cathedral of Saint Anastasia, the martyr from Sirmio. We are gathered here to celebrate Midday Prayer, the hour of Sext.

Our liturgical assembly takes place on the day after the Solemnity of Pentecost, the day on which Croatians celebrate the feast of Mary, Mother of the Church. The reading we have just heard portrays Mary in the Cenacle, surrounded by the early community. The small group, gathered in "the upper room" of the house (Acts 1:13), prays and waits. With the coming of the Holy Spirit the doors of the room will burst open and enable the Gospel proclamation to go out to the streets of Jerusalem, and then to set forth on the paths of the world.

As on the day of Pentecost, the Blessed Virgin has remained spiritually in the midst of the Christian faithful down the centuries, invoking the constant outpouring of the Spirit's gifts upon the Church as she faces the challenges which arise in different periods of her history.

Mary's words and example represent a sublime school of life, at which apostles are formed. Apostles in the past and apostles today. Mary continues to prepare them for mission by her assiduous prayer to the Father, by her closeness to her Son, and by her openness to the promptings of the Spirit.

It pleases me to know that this Archdiocese has witnessed in recent years the growth and expansion of different forms of lay engagement and apostolate. Dear brothers and sisters, learn from Mary how to be credible witnesses and generous apostles, as you make your own contribution to the great enterprise of the new evangelization. And never forget that a genuine apostolate demands as a prior condition a personal encounter with Jesus, the Living One, the Lord (cf. Rev, 1:17-18).

Mary Most Holy remains a model for all who hear the word of God and put it into practice (cf. Lk, 8:21). How then could there not be a profound spiritual understanding between all believers and the Virgin of the Magnificat? The poor and the humble in every age were not mistaken when they made Mary in silence their Advocate and Mary in service their Queen.

Let us too draw near to her and learn to imitate her docility and openness to God. Let us too, the pilgrims of the third millennium, commend ourselves to her intercession, so that by her prayers she may sustain our faith, nourish our hope and make fruitful our charity:

Holy Mary, Mother of God and our own Mother, look upon all your children
and come to our aid.
Guide us to Christ, the Way, and the Truth, and the Life;
from the Father implore for us the gifts of the Spirit, protection from every snare, and freedom from all evil.
Help us ever to bear witness
to the fruitfulness of love and the authentic meaning of life;
teach us to build with you the Kingdom of your Son the Kingdom of justice, love and peace.

BOSNIA-HERZEGOVINA, JUNE 22, 2003

Pope John Paul II, on the 101st foreign trip of his pontificate, visited Bosnia-Herzegovina on June 22.

Itinerary
June 22 (Banja Luka)

Arrival and welcome ceremony; address of the Holy Father

Mass with Beatification of Ivan Merz; homily of the Holy Father

Recital of the Angelus Domini; address of the Holy Father

Meeting with the bishops of Bosnia and Herzegovina and with the cardinals and bishops of the papal entourage

Courtesy visit of the president of the Serbian Republic and of the president of the Federation of Bosnia and Herzegovina

Catholic Cathedral of Banja Luka — private visit

Departure for Rome; farewell ceremony

Overview

In the first trip to Bosnia Herzegovina in six years, Pope John Paul II took as his central theme reconciliation, noting the severe suffering that the country has endured over the last years: "I know the long ordeal which you have endured, the burden of suffering which is daily a part of your lives, the temptations to discouragement and resignation which you experience." The Holy Father used the occasion of his 101st pastoral visit to beatify Blessed Ivan Merz, a Catholic intellectual and founder of the League of Young Croatian Catholics and the Croatian League of Eagles.

EXCERPTS OF ADDRESSES AND HOMILIES

Banja Luka International Airport – Welcome Ceremony Address

With gratitude for your invitation, I have returned after six years to Bosnia-Hercegovina. I give thanks to God for allowing me once again to meet peoples who have always been so close to my heart....

Knowing that I am entering your homes through radio and television, I greet and embrace all of you, dear people living in the different parts of Bosnia-Hercegovina. I know the long ordeal which you have endured, the burden of suffering which is daily a part of your lives, the temptations to discouragement and resignation which you experience. I stand beside you in asking the international community, which already has done so much, to continue to be close to you and to help you to reach quickly a situation of full security in justice and harmony.

You yourselves must be the primary builders of your future! The tenacity of your character and the rich human, cultural and religious traditions which distinguish you are your true wealth. Do not give up! Certainly starting afresh is not easy. It requires sacrifice and steadfastness; it requires knowing how to sow seeds and then to wait patiently. But you know that starting afresh is nevertheless possible. Trust in God's help, and trust too in human initiative.

Banja Luka — Mass and Beatification of Ivan Merz, plaza in front of the Most Holy Trinity Convent in Banja Luka: Homily

"You are the light of the world." Jesus today repeats these words for us, dear brothers and sisters, for our liturgical assembly. They are not simply a moral exhortation. They are a statement of fact which expresses an essential requirement flowing from the reception of Baptism.

By virtue of this sacrament human beings become members of the Mystical Body of Christ (cf. Rom. 6:3-5). The Apostle Paul states: "As many of you as were baptized into Christ have put on Christ" (Gal. 3:27). Saint Augustine rightly exclaimed: "Let us rejoice and give thanks: we have become not only Christians but Christ himself.... Marvel and rejoice, for we have become Christ" (In Ioann. Evang. Tract. 21:8, CCL 36:216).

Christ is "the true light that enlightens every man" (Jn. 1:9). Christians for their part are called to become a reflection of this Light by following and imitating Jesus. For this reason they will listen to and meditate on Christ's word, take conscious and active part in the Church's liturgical and sacramental life, and carry out the commandment of love by serving their brothers and sisters, especially the helpless, the poor and the suffering... .

From this city, marked in the course of history by so much suffering and bloodshed, I ask Almighty God to have mercy on the sins committed against humanity, human dignity and freedom also by children of the Catholic Church, and to foster in all the desire for mutual forgiveness. Only in a climate of true reconciliation will the memory of so many innocent victims and their sacrifice not be in vain, but encourage everyone to build new relationships of fraternity and understanding.

The future of this land depends also on you! Do not seek a more comfortable life elsewhere, do not flee from your responsibilities and expect others to resolve problems, but resolutely counter evil with the power of good.

PAPAL DOCUMENTS AND ANNOUNCEMENTS

ECCLESIA DE EUCHARISTIA

The fourteenth encyclical letter of Pope John Paul II, Ecclesia de Eucharistia *was promulgated on April 17, 2003, Holy Thursday, during the Mass of the Lord's Supper, within the liturgical setting of the beginning of the Paschal Triduum. It is intended to offer a theological reflection on the mystery of the Eucharist in its relationship with the Church.*

The encyclical is notable for being comparatively brief when compared with the pontiff's earlier encyclicals, although it contains several important theological, disciplinary, and pastoral aspects. Specifically, the pope uses the letter to reaffirm the traditional teaching of the Church on the real presence of Christ in the Eucharist, on the need for validly ordained ministers for its celebration, and on the importance of following the Church's liturgical norms. The encyclical is organized into five chapters and a conclusion, beginning with the declaration: "The Church draws her life from the Eucharist. This truth does not simply express a daily experience of faith, but recapitulates the heart of the mystery of the Church. In a variety of ways she joyfully experiences the constant fulfillment of the promise." The Eucharistic Sacrifice is thus truly "the source and summit of the Christian life," as the Second Vatican Council proclaimed, and contains the Church's entire spiritual wealth: Jesus Christ, who offers himself to the Father for the redemption of the world. In celebrating this "mystery of faith," the Church presents the Paschal Triduum in a contemporary way, for men and women in every age.

Chapter One, "The Mystery of Faith," describes the sacrificial nature of the Eucharist which, through the ministry of the priest, makes sacramentally present at each Mass the body "given up" and the blood "poured out" by Christ for the salvation of the world. In examining the Church's teachings on the Eucharist, the pontiff reminds the faithful that the celebration of the Eucharist is not a repetition of Christ's passover, nor its multiplication in time and in space. "It is, truly, the one sacrifice of the Cross, which is re-presented until the end of time. The sacramental re-presentation of Christ's sacrifice, crowned by the resurrection, in the Mass involves a most special presence which — in the words of Paul VI — 'is called "real" not as a way of excluding all other types of presence as if they were "not real", but because it is a presence in the fullest sense: a substantial presence whereby Christ, the God-Man, is wholly and entirely present.' "

Chapter Two, "The Eucharist Builds the Church," states that the Church "teaches that the celebration of the Eucharist is at the centre of the process of the Church's growth." When the faithful approach the sacred banquet, they receive Christ and are in turn received by Christ: "Eucharistic communion also confirms the Church in her unity as the body of Christ.... The gift of Christ and his Spirit which we receive in Eucharistic communion superabundantly fulfills the yearning for fraternal unity deeply rooted in the human heart; at the same time it elevates the experience of fraternity already present in our common sharing at the same Eucharistic table to a degree which far surpasses that of the simple human experience of sharing a meal." The pope stressed as well the value of eucharistic adoration, a worship "strictly linked to the celebration of the Eucharistic Sacrifice."

Chapter Three, "The Apostolicity of the Eucharist and of the Church," notes that just as the Church is apostolic so too is the Eucharist in three ways. First, "The Eucharist too has its foundation in the Apostles, not in the sense that it did not originate in Christ himself, but because it was entrusted by Jesus to the Apostles and has been handed down to us by them and by their successors. It is in continuity with the practice of the Apostles, in obedience to the Lord's command, that the Church has celebrated the Eucharist down the centuries." Second, "it is celebrated in conformity with the faith of the Apostles." Third, just as the full reality of Church does not exist without apostolic succession, so there is no true Eucharist without the Bishop. "The assembly gathered together for the celebration of the Eucharist, if it is to be a truly Eucharistic assembly, absolutely requires the presence of an ordained priest as its president. On the other hand, the community is by itself incapable of providing an ordained minister. This minister is a gift which the assembly receives through episcopal succession going back to the Apostles." It is thus the priest, acting *in persona Christi*, who brings about the Eucharistic Sacrifice, and, "For this reason, the Roman Missal prescribes that only the priest should recite the Eucharistic Prayer, while the people participate in faith and in silence."

Chapter Four, "The Eucharist and Ecclesial Communion," teaches that "the culmination of all the sacraments in perfecting our communion with God the Father by identification with his only-begotten Son through the working of the Holy Spirit." The Church, faithful to the teaching of the Apostles, united in the discipline of the sacraments, must also manifest in a visible manner her invisible unity. The Eucharist is also not some starting-point for communion. Rather, it presupposes that communion already exists, a communion that it seeks to consolidate and bring to perfection. In this context, the Eucharist has a vital role in the commitment to ecumenism. The Eucharist creates communion and builds communion, when it is celebrated truthfully.

Chapter Five, "The Dignity of the Eucharistic Celebration" is concerned with the truthful celebration of the Eucharist enunciated in the previous chapter: "We understand how the faith of the Church in the mystery of the Eucharist has found historical expression not only in the demand for an interior disposition of devotion, but also in outward forms meant to evoke and emphasize the grandeur of the event being celebrated.... It can be said that the Eucharist, while shaping the Church and her spirituality, has also powerfully affected 'culture,' and the arts in particular." The pope urges a careful fidelity to the norms of the Church regarding the liturgy. While praising how well local language, customs, and culture can be incorporated into the Mass, creativity has sometimes been overemphasized. He writes that norms must be respected: "These norms are a concrete expression of the authentically ecclesial nature of the Eucharist; this is their deepest meaning. Liturgy is never anyone's private property, be it of the celebrant or of the community in which the mysteries are celebrated.... Our time, too, calls for a renewed awareness and appreciation of liturgical norms as a reflection of, and a witness to, the one universal Church made present in every celebration of the Eucharist."

Chapter Six, "At the School of Mary, 'Woman of the Eucharist,' offers a reflection on the analogy between the Mother of God, and the Church. By bearing the body of Jesus in her womb, Mary became the first "tabernacle": "When, at the Visitation, she bore in her womb the Word made flesh, she became in some way a 'tabernacle'—the first 'tabernacle' in history—in which the Son of God, still invisible to our human gaze, allowed himself to be adored by Elizabeth, radiating his light as it were through the eyes and the voice of Mary." The Church offers to the world Christ's body and blood. At the same time, "the *Magnificat* expresses Mary's spirituality, and there is nothing greater than this spirituality for helping us to experience the mystery of the Eucharist. The Eucharist has been given to us so that our life, like that of Mary, may become completely a *Magnificat*!"

In his Conclusion, the pontiff quotes his Apostolic Letter *Novo Millennio Ineunte* in stating, "it is not a matter of inventing a 'new programme.' The programme already exists: it is the plan found in the Gospel and in the living Tradition; it is the same as ever." Clearly, the implementation of this process of a renewed impetus in Christian living passes through the Eucharist. He concludes, "In the humble signs of bread and wine, changed into his body and blood, Christ walks beside us as our strength and our food for the journey, and he enables us to become, for everyone, witnesses of hope."

ROSARIUM VIRGINIS MARIAE

On October 16, 2002, Pope John Paul II issued an apostolic letter, Rosarium Virginis Mariae (The Rosary of the Virgin Mary), *that sought a renewal of the Church's tradition of praying the rosary and that added five new mysteries dedicated to chapters from Jesus' public life.*

In his letter, the pope announced the start of a Year of the Rosary, from October 2002 to October 2003 with the aim of reviving the recitation of the rosary among all of the faithful, especially among families. He left to each ecclesial community the specifics of the celebration. The pope asked that the new mysteries be recited especially on Thursdays. The new mysteries, called the "Mysteries of Light," focused specifically on:

• Christ's baptism in the Jordan River.
• Christ's self-revelation at the marriage of Cana.
• Christ's announcement of the kingdom of God with the invitation to conversion.
• Christ's Transfiguration, when he revealed his glory to his Apostles.
• The institution of the Eucharist at the Last Supper as the sacramental expression of the paschal mystery.

The Holy Father discussed the new mysteries by declaring:

Certainly the whole mystery of Christ is a mystery of light. He is the "light of the world" (Jn. 8:12). Yet this truth emerges in a special way during the years of his public life, when he proclaims the Gospel of the Kingdom. In proposing to the Christian community five significant moments – "luminous" mysteries – during this phase of Christ's life, I think that the following can be fittingly singled out: (1) his Baptism in the Jordan, (2) his self-manifestation at the wedding of Cana, (3) his proclamation of the Kingdom of God, with his call to conversion, (4) his Transfiguration, and finally, (5) his institution of the Eucharist, as the sacramental expression of the Paschal Mystery.

Each of these mysteries is a revelation of the Kingdom now present in the very person of Jesus. The Baptism in the Jordan is first of all a mystery of light. Here, as Christ descends into the waters, the innocent one who became "sin" for our sake (cf. 2Cor. 5:21), the heavens open wide and the voice of the Father declares him the beloved Son (cf. Mt. 3:17 and parallels), while the Spirit descends on him to invest him with the mission which he is to carry out. Another mystery of light is the first of the signs, given at Cana (cf. Jn. 2:1- 12), when Christ changes water into wine and opens the hearts of the disciples to faith, thanks to the intervention of Mary, the first among believers. Another mystery of light is the preaching by which Jesus proclaims the coming of the Kingdom of God, calls to conversion (cf. Mk. 1:15) and forgives the sins of all who draw near to him in humble trust (cf. Mk. 2:3-13; Lk. 7:47- 48): the inauguration of that ministry of mercy which he continues to exercise until the end of the world, particularly through the Sacrament of Reconciliation which he has entrusted to his Church (cf. Jn. 20:22-23). The mystery of light par excellence is the Transfiguration, traditionally believed to have taken place on Mount Tabor. The glory of the Godhead shines forth from the face of Christ as the Father commands the astonished Apostles to

"listen to him" (cf. Lk. 9:35 and parallels) and to prepare to experience with him the agony of the Passion, so as to come with him to the joy of the Resurrection and a life transfigured by the Holy Spirit. A final mystery of light is the institution of the Eucharist, in which Christ offers his body and blood as food under the signs of bread and wine, and testifies "to the end" his love for humanity (Jn. 13:1), for whose salvation he will offer himself in sacrifice.

The Pope made clear that he respected the traditional form of the rosary and did not want to change it, but he recognized that the "Mysteries of Light" were particularly appropriate for the modern world. The letter thus provided a detailed recapitulation of the Church's practice of the Rosary:

The Rosary of the Virgin Mary, which gradually took form in the second millennium under the guidance of the Spirit of God, is a prayer loved by countless Saints and encouraged by the Magisterium. Simple yet profound, it still remains, at the dawn of this third millennium, a prayer of great significance, destined to bring forth a harvest of holiness.... The Rosary, though clearly Marian in character, is at heart a Christocentric prayer. In the sobriety of its elements, it has all the depth of the Gospel message in its entirety, of which it can be said to be a compendium. It is an echo of the prayer of Mary, her perennial Magnificat for the work of the redemptive Incarnation which began in her virginal womb. With the Rosary, the Christian people sits at the school of Mary and is led to contemplate the beauty on the face of Christ and to experience the depths of his love. Through the Rosary the faithful receive abundant grace, as though from the very hands of the Mother of the Redeemer.

The pontiff examined the Joyful, Sorrowful, and Glorious Mysteries, noting that together, "The cycles of meditation proposed by the Holy Rosary are by no means exhaustive, but they do bring to mind what is essential and they awaken in the soul a thirst for a knowledge of Christ continually nourished by the pure source of the Gospel. Every individual event in the life of Christ, as narrated by the Evangelists, is resplendent with the Mystery that surpasses all understanding (cf. Eph. 3:19): the Mystery of the Word made flesh, in whom 'all the fullness of God dwells bodily' (Col. 2:9)."

The Rosary, the pope stated, is an ideal instrument at a time when the world is experiencing a powerful demand for new forms of meditation. Such keen interest on the part of Catholics and Christians leads to the investigation of other religions: "Some Christians, limited in their knowledge of the Christian contemplative tradition, are attracted by those forms of prayer. While the latter contain many elements which are positive and at times compatible with Christian experience, they are often based on ultimately unacceptable premises. Much in vogue among these approaches are methods aimed at attaining a high level of spiritual concentration by using techniques of a psychophysical, repetitive and symbolic nature. The Rosary is situated within this broad gamut of religious phenomena, but it is distinguished by characteristics of its own which correspond to specifically Christian requirements.

Finally, the Holy Father examined the entire structure of reciting the Rosary, adding that the valid method of the rosary can, nevertheless, be improved. "The Rosary is simply a method of contemplation. As a method, it serves as a means to an end and cannot become an end in itself. All the same, as the fruit of centuries of experience, this method should not be undervalued. In its favour one could cite the experience of countless Saints. This is not to say, however, that the method cannot be improved. Such is the intent of the addition of the new series of *mysteria lucis* to the overall cycle of mysteries and of the few suggestions which I am proposing in this Letter regarding its manner of recitation. These suggestions, while respecting the well-established structure of this prayer, are intended to help the faithful to understand it in the richness of its symbolism and in harmony with the demands of daily life. Otherwise there is a risk that the Rosary would not only fail to produce the intended spiritual effects, but even that the beads, with which it is usually said, could come to be regarded as some kind of amulet or magic object, thereby radically distorting their meaning and function."

ECCLESIA IN EUROPA

On June 28, 2003, Pope John Paul II signed the apostolic exhortation Ecclesia in Europa, *the pontiff's response to the deliberations and proposals of European bishops who met for a special continental synod in October 1999.*

The Holy Father begin his exhortation by reiterating the central theme of the synod, Jesus Christ, alive in his Church, the source of hope for Europe. The pope writes, "This is a theme which I too wish to proclaim to all the Christians of Europe at the beginning of this third millennium, as I join my Brother Bishops in repeating the words of the First Letter of Saint Peter: 'Have no fear, nor be troubled, but in your hearts reverence Christ as Lord. Always be prepared to make a defence to any one who calls you to account for the hope that is in you' (3:14-15)."

The theme is an important one, for the pontiff acknowledges that Europe suffers from a "dimming of hope…. Many men and women seem disoriented, uncertain, without hope, and not a few Christians share these feelings. There are many troubling signs which at the beginning of the third millennium are clouding the horizon of the European continent." The pope focuses particularly on the loss of "Europe's Christian memory and heritage," accompanied by a fear for the future, existential fragmentation, and a weakening of interpersonal solidarity. At the root of this loss of hope is what John Paul describes as an effort "to promote a vision of man apart from God and apart from Christ."

Nevertheless, there are distinct signs of hope: the recovery of freedom of the Church in Eastern Europe; the labors of the Church in the areas of evangelization and her spiritual mission; the growing missionary awareness of all of the faithful; and the increasing role of women in the life of the Church. Similarly, signs of hope are visible in civil affairs throughout Europe, including efforts at reconciliation, improvement in the quality of life, the promotion of peace, and Europe's growing unity.

The pope stresses the witness to the faith provided by the martyrs, "that great sign of hope represented by the many witnesses to the Christian faith who lived in the last century, in both East and West. They found suitable ways to proclaim the Gospel amid situations of hostility and persecution, often even making the supreme sacrifice by shedding their blood." He notes also the activities of the faithful, the ecclesial movements, and ecumenism.

Pope John Paul then proclaims: "From the synodal Assembly there emerged the clear and passionate certainty that the Church has to offer Europe the most precious of all gifts, a gift which no one else can give: faith in Jesus Christ, the source of the hope that does not disappoint; a gift which is at the origin of the spiritual and cultural unity of the European peoples and which both today and tomorrow can make an essential contribution to their development and integration."

The heart of the exhortation is what the pontiff calls the Gospel of Hope, examining how it is entrusted to the Church and then how it must be proclaimed, celebrated, served, and made manifest to a "new Europe." The entire Church is sent on a mission of evangelization: "Whatever the charism and ministry of each individual, charity is the royal road prescribed for all and which all can travel: it is the road upon which the whole ecclesial community is called to journey in the footsteps of its Master."

In discussing the role of ordained ministers, the pope reiterates the place of celibacy, calling it "a priceless gift of God for his Church." He notes the need for new vocations and salutes the role of women in the Church, looking to them "for the life-giving contribution of a new wave of hope."

Finally, the pontiff discusses the Church for the new Europe, observing, "If it is to be 'new,' by analogy with what is said about the 'new city' of the Book of Revelation (cf. 21:2), it must open itself to the workings of God …. The Catholic Church in fact provides a model of essential unity in a diversity of cultural expressions, a consciousness of membership in a universal community which is rooted in but not confined to local communities, and a sense of what unites beyond all that divides."

POPE'S MESSAGE TO NEW ANGLICAN ARCHBISHOP OF CANTERBURY

On Feb. 13, 2003, Pope John Paul II sent the following message on the occasion of the enthronement of the new Anglican archbishop of Canterbury, Rowan Williams. The message was handed to the primate of All England and president of the Anglican Communion by Cardinal Walter Kasper, president of the Pontifical Council for Promoting Christian Unity:

I greet you in the name of the "one God and Father of us all," and of his Son, our Lord, Jesus Christ (cf. Eph. 4:5-6), and with sentiments of joy and cordial esteem I offer my prayerful best wishes on the occasion of your enthronement as Archbishop of Canterbury.

The liturgy of your enthronement will be an occa-

sion for you and for the Anglican Communion to celebrate the glory of God, contemplating Saint John's
vision of a multitude crying out, "Alleluia! Salvation
and glory and power belong to our God" (Rev. 19: 1).
You will ponder the mystery of God, who calls and
sends forth those who, like Isaiah, do not consider
themselves prepared (Is. 6:5-8).

You begin your ministry as Archbishop of Canterbury at a painful and tense moment in history, a moment nonetheless marked by hope and promise.
Marred by long-standing and seemingly relentless
conflicts, the world stands on the brink of yet another
war. The dignity of the human person is being threatened and undermined in various ways. Whole populations, especially the most vulnerable, are living
amidst fear and danger. At times the ardent and legitimate human longing for freedom and security
manifests itself through the wrong means, means
which themselves are violent and destructive. It is
precisely amidst these tensions and difficulties of our
world that we are called to serve.

We can sincerely rejoice in the fact that, in recent
decades, our predecessors have developed an increasingly close relationship, even bonds of affection,
through constructive dialogue and close communication. They set the Catholic Church and the Anglican

Communion on a path that they hoped would lead to
full communion. Despite disagreements and obstacles, we are still on that path, and irrevocably committed to it. Over the past decade, the various opportunities to meet Dr. George Carey have been particularly helpful and encouraging, signs of progress on
our ecumenical journey. The work of the Anglican-
Roman Catholic International Commission, and the
more recently formed International Commission for
Unity and Mission, continue to move us forward.

We are both aware that overcoming divisions is no
easy task, and that full communion will come as a
gift of the Holy Spirit. That same Spirit prods and
guides us even now to continue to seek a resolution
to remaining areas of doctrinal disagreement, and to
engage more profoundly in common witness and mission.

With renewed sentiments of fraternal regard, I invoke upon you the blessings of Almighty God as you
take up your lofty responsibilities. Amidst whatever
trials and tribulations you may encounter, may you
ever know the glory of the Father, the steady guidance of the Holy Spirit, and the merciful face of our
Lord Jesus Christ.

From the Vatican, 13 February 2003 -- IOANNES
PAULUS II

THE FINANCES OF THE HOLY SEE

On July 10, 2003, Cardinal Sergio Sebastiani, presi-
dent of the Prefecture for the Economic Affairs of the
Holy See, presented to international reporters the
Consolidated Financial Statement of the Holy See for
fiscal year 2002.

The Consolidated Financial Statement of the Holy
See for fiscal year 2002 was the first expressed using the euro (the new currency for the European
Union) and represented as an integrated whole all
the income and expense of the various Vatican administrations. Thus it included the Administration
of the Patrimony of the Holy See (APSA) – the most
important in that it provides for all the administrative operations of almost the totality of the Offices
and the Entities of the Curia Romana: the Congregation for the Evangelization of Peoples, the Apostolic Camera, Vatican Radio, the *L'Osservatore*
Romano/Vatican Printing Press (merged with regard
to administration), the Vatican Television Center, and
the Vatican Publishing House.

The report indicated that a deficit was incurred for
the fiscal year 2002, owing chiefly to a severe global
economic downturn. The result was that for 2002 the
Holy See registered a deficit of 13,506,722 euro

($15,290,960). Total income was 216,575,034 euro
($245,184,596) and total expenses were 230,081,756
euro ($260,475,556).

Several significant points were noted in the financial report:

• Despite the worldwide economic downturn, the
volume of donations given to the Holy See in 2002
showed a surprising increase, bringing the sum at the
end of the year to 85,385,000 euro.

• The 2002 consolidated financial statements for
Vatican City State revealed a deficit of 16,048,508
($18,215,057). The deficit is in contrast to the sur-
plus for 2001.

• Peter's Pence, the annual donation given by Catholics to the Holy See, amounted to $52,836,693 for
2002. The amount was used by the Holy Father entirely for charitable purposes, with particular focus
on assisting the Church communities in the Third
World and to help the victims of wars or natural ca-
lamities.

• Peter's Pence offerings by the faithful for 2002 increased by 1.8 percent over 2001. The United States
was also the largest contributor to Peter's Pence, followed by Germany and Italy.

SPECIAL REPORTS: INTERNATIONAL NEWS 2002-2003

WAR IN IRAQ

(*By Russell Shaw.*)

American Catholics were divided in their views on the morality of the war in Iraq. Leaders of the Church in the U.S. and elsewhere—notably including Pope John Paul II — generally were either skeptical or opposed, but other Catholics were split. Some held that the war was morally wrong while others supported it on moral grounds. For the most part, both sides in this debate argued from a just war perspective.

President George W. Bush frequently stated the case for the war in moral terms and used religious language about it. For instance, in his January 28 State of the Union Message to Congress, laying out the argument for disarming Iraq, by force if necessary, Bush declared: "The liberty we prize is not America's gift to the world; it is God's gift to humanity."

Rhetoric aside, many pointed out, the coalition forces in Iraq, primarily U.S. and British, attempted to conduct the conflict in light of just war criteria like proportionality (no more force than necessary) and discrimination (noncombatant immunity). The use of precision weapons and tactics intended to minimize civilian deaths was a notable feature of the campaign. Even so, many civilians died.

Pope John Paul for his part became increasingly vocal and active in opposing war, unless undertaken as a genuine last resort and with United Nations authorization.

In his annual address to the diplomatic corps accredited to the Holy See, January 13, the Pope said in part: "War is not always inevitable. It is always a defeat for humanity. International law, honest dialogue, solidarity between states, the noble exercise of diplomacy: these are methods worthy of resolving their differences."

And, with specific reference to Iraq: "As the Charter of the United Nations Organization and international law itself remind us, war cannot be decided upon, even when it is a matter of ensuring the common good, except as the very last option and in accordance with very strict conditions, without ignoring the consequences for the civilian population both during and after the military operations."

Other voices at the Vatican also chimed in on the subject of the war. Among those speaking out were included Cardinal Angelo Sodano, the Secretary of State, Cardinal Joseph Ratzinger, Prefect of the Congregation for the Doctrine of the Faith, Cardinal James Francis Stafford, President of the Pontifical Council for the Laity, Cardinal Roberto Tucci, S.J., former head of Vatican Radio, Archbishop Renato Martino, president of the Pontifical Council for Justice and Peace, and Archbishop Jean-Louis Tauran, the Secretary for Relations with States. While observers credited Pope John Paul with being careful to avoid anti-Americanism in his remarks, some discerned an anti-American tone in certain other comments from Rome.

The United States Conference of Catholic Bishops, in a statement adopted at its general meeting in November 2002, said that "a resort to war under present circumstances ... would not meet the strict conditions in Catholic teaching for overriding the strong presumption against the use of military force."

Four months later, on March 19, a statement by USCCB president Bishop Wilton D. Gregory of Belleville, IL, repeated the bishops' concerns while acknowledging that they expressed "prudential judgments." The statement said there were "no easy answers" to whether the war was just, and it expressed support for "those who have accepted the call to serve their country in a conscientious way in the armed services" and for those who objected to the war on conscientious grounds.

Except for the Southern Baptist Convention and evangelical and Pentecostal leaders who supported the war, most Christian bodies in the United States opposed it. Jewish leaders were divided.

In Great Britain, Cardinal Cormac Murphy-O'Connor of Westminster and the Archbishop of Canterbury, Rowan Williams, issued a joint statement in late February saying "doubts still persist about the moral legitimacy" of war with Iraq, as well as about "the unpredictable humanitarian and political consequences" it would have. But Archbishop Mario Conti of Glasgow, the ranking Catholic churchman in Scotland, expressed confidence in Prime Minister Tony Blair and said in a newspaper interview that "as a leader he has the right to take steps to ensure that [Iraqi President] Saddam Hussein is contained."

Some prominent American Catholics argued that the war did meet just war criteria. On February 10, speaking in Rome at the invitation of U.S. Ambassador to the Holy See James Nicholson as a guest of the U.S. State Department, theologian and social commentator Michael Novak, a resident scholar at the American Enterprise Institute, strongly defended this view.

"Under the original Catholic doctrine of *justum bellum*," Novak declared, "a limited and carefully conducted war to bring about a change of regime in Iraq is, as a last resort, morally obligatory. For public authorities to fail to conduct such a war would be to put their trust imprudently in the sanity and good will of Saddam Hussein."

Meanwhile, the pope continued to hammer home his views in addresses and in a series of meetings with world leaders like Prime Minister Blair, U.N. Secretary General Kofi Annan, and Iraqi Deputy Prime Minister Tariq Aziz.

In February, he dispatched Cardinal Roger Etchegaray, former President of the Vatican's Council for Justice and Peace, to Baghdad to meet with Saddam Hussein. The cardinal on February 15 urged the Iraqi leader to comply with U.N. Security Council Resolution 1441 calling for him to give up weapons of mass destruction or face "serious consequences."

In March Pope John Paul sent Cardinal Pio Laghi to Washington, where he had served as papal representative from 1980 to 1990, to meet with President Bush and relay the pope's plea for peace. The President received the cardinal on Ash Wednesday, March 5, in what was described as a cordial meeting, but he remained unmoved.

Cardinal Laghi later issued a statement in which, while calling on the Iraqi government to meet its obligations regarding human rights and disarmament under U.N. resolutions, repeated the view that a decision regarding the use of force could only rightly be taken a U.N. framework.

After the three-week war broke out, the pope made numerous appeals on behalf of the Iraq people and for speedy peace. With the fighting concluded, a Vati-

can statement on April 10 said the people of Iraq now had a significant opportunity to shape their own future and expressed hope for "an era of peace in the Middle East." On Easter Sunday, April 20, John Paul II prayed in his Easter message to the world the Iraqis would be "the protagonists of their collective rebuilding of their country" and that the world would be "free from the peril of a tragic clash between cultures and religions."

STATEMENTS BY CHURCH LEADERS AROUND THE WORLD

Pope John Paul II, Easter Message in St. Peter's Square, April 20, 2003:

Peace on earth, the profound aspiration of men and women of all times, can be firmly established and sustained only if the order established by God is firmly respected" (Encyclical *Pacem in Terris*, Introduction). These are the first words of the historic Encyclical, in which forty years ago Blessed Pope John XXIII indicated to the world the way of peace. These words remain as timely as ever at the dawn of the third millennium, tragically marred by acts of violence and conflicts.

Peace in Iraq! With the support of the international community, may the Iraqi people become the protagonists of the collective rebuilding of their country. Peace in other parts of the world, where forgotten wars and protracted hostilities are causing deaths and injuries amid silence and neglect on the part of considerable sectors of public opinion.

With profound grief I think of the wake of violence and bloodshed, with no sign of ceasing, in the Holy Land. I think of the tragic situation of many countries on the African continent, which cannot be abandoned to itself. I am well aware of the centers of tension and the attacks on people's freedom in the Caucasus, in Asia and in Latin America, areas of the world equally dear to me.

Let there be an end to the chain of hatred and terrorism, which threatens the orderly development of the human family. May God grant that we be free from the peril of a tragic clash between cultures and religions. May faith and love of God make the followers of every religion courageous builders of understanding and forgiveness, patient weavers of a fruitful inter-religious dialogue, capable of inaugurating a new era of justice and peace.

Pope John Paul II, Homily and Prayers of the Faithful during Palm Sunday Mass, April 13, 2003:

[Christ is the] King of truth, freedom, justice and love. These are the four pillars on which it is possible to construct the building of true peace, as Blessed John XXIII wrote 40 years ago in the encyclical *Pacem in Terris*.

I hand symbolically to you, young people of the whole world, this historic document, more important than ever. Read it, meditate on it, make every effort to put it into practice. Then you will be "blessed," because you will be real children of the God of peace.

Peace is a gift of Christ, which he obtained for us with the sacrifice of the cross.

Let us pray for all peoples and cultures of the world, for all those who seek God in different religious ways. May there always be dialogue among them, may in-

tolerance and contempt be extinguished, and together may they seek ways of concord and fraternity.

Most Reverend Wilton D. Gregory, President, United States Conference of Catholic Bishops, March 19, 2003:

Our nation is on the brink of war. We worked and prayed and hoped that war would be avoided. The task now is to work and pray and hope that war's deadly consequences will be limited, that civilian life will be protected, that weapons of mass destruction will be eliminated, and that the people of Iraq soon will enjoy a peace with freedom and justice.

A time for prayer and solidarity. In time of war, our first obligation is prayer and solidarity. We pray for all those most directly affected by this war: the men and women who risk their lives in the service of our nation, their families and loved ones who face such fear and anxiety at this time, and the chaplains who serve them; the long-suffering people of Iraq, and those who labor to provide for their humanitarian needs. All of us should do what we can to reach out in solidarity to all those who will suffer as a result of this war.

Iraq's obligation to disarm. Since the Gulf War, we have been clear in calling on the Iraqi leadership to abandon efforts to develop weapons of mass destruction and to meet its obligations to destroy such weapons. We have also been clear that the international community must ensure that Iraq complies with its obligations under UN resolutions. As the Holy Father said last Sunday, "the political leaders in Baghdad have an urgent duty to cooperate fully with the international community, to eliminate any motive for armed intervention."

Deep regret that war was not averted. Our nation's leaders have made the momentous decision to go to war to address the failure of the Iraqi government to comply completely with its obligations. We deeply regret that war was not averted. We stand by the statement of the full body of bishops last November. Our conference's moral concerns and questions, as well as the call of the Holy Father to find alternatives to war, are well known and reflect our prudential judgments about the application of traditional Catholic teaching on the use of force in this case. We have been particularly concerned about the precedents that could be set and the possible consequences of a major war of this type in perhaps the most volatile region of the world. Echoing the Holy Father's admonition that war "is always a defeat for humanity," we have prayed and urged that peaceful means be pursued to disarm Iraq under UN auspices.

The decisions being made about Iraq and the war on terrorism could have historic implications for the use of force, the legitimacy of international institutions, and the role of the United States in the world. The moral significance of these issues must continue to be assessed given their importance in shaping a more just and peaceful world.

The role of conscience. While we have warned of the potential moral dangers of embarking on this war, we have also been clear that there are no easy answers. War has serious consequences; so could the failure to act. People of good will may and do disagree on how to interpret just war teaching and how to apply just war norms to the controverted facts of this case. We understand and respect the difficult moral choices that must be made by our president and others who bear the responsibility of making these grave decisions involving our nation's and the world's security (#2309).

We affirm the words of the *Catechism*: "[t]hose who are sworn to serve their country in the armed forces are servants of the security and freedom of nations. If they carry out their duty honorably, they truly contribute to the common good of the nation and the maintenance of peace" (#2310). We also affirm that "[p]ublic authorities should make equitable provision for those who for reasons of conscience refuse to bear arms" (#2311). We support those who have accepted the call to serve their country in a conscientious way in the armed services and we reiterate our long-standing support for those who pursue conscientious objection and selective conscientious objection.

The moral conduct of war. Once the decision to use military force is taken, the moral and legal constraints on the conduct of war must be observed. The United States and its allies are at war with a regime that has shown, and we fear will continue to show, a disregard for civilian lives and traditional norms governing the use of force. All the more reason that our nation upholds and reinforces these values by its own actions. While we recognize and welcome the improved capability and commitment to avoid civilian casualties, every effort must be made to ensure that efforts to reduce the risk to U.S. forces are limited by careful judgments of military necessity and the duty to respect the lives and dignity of Iraqi civilians, who have suffered so much already from war, repression, and a debilitating embargo.

Any decision to defend against Iraq's weapons of mass destruction by using our own weapons of mass destruction would be clearly unjustified. The use of anti-personnel landmines, cluster bombs and other weapons that cannot distinguish between soldiers and civilians, or between times of war and times of peace, ought to be avoided. In all our actions in war, including assessments of whether "collateral damage" is proportionate, we must value the lives and livelihood of Iraqi civilians, as we would the lives and livelihood of our own families and our own citizens.

Humanitarian concerns and post-war obligations. An already vulnerable Iraqi population could face terrible new burdens during this war, and a region already full of conflict and refugees could see more conflict and many more displaced persons with nowhere to go. Even amidst the chaos of war, every effort must be made to prevent internal strife and to protect vulnerable groups. We are deeply concerned that adequate resources and effective plans be put in place to address the humanitarian crisis in Iraq, which,

at least in the short term, will be worsened by war. The United States, working with the United Nations, private relief organizations, and all interested parties, bears a heavy burden, during and after the war, of providing for POWs and the civilian population, especially refugees and displaced persons. Catholic relief agencies will continue to do all that they can to respond to the needs of the Iraqi people. The United States also must accept the long-term responsibility to help Iraqis build a just and enduring peace in their country, while also addressing the many serious unresolved issues in the Middle East, especially the Israeli-Palestinian conflict. War and reconstruction in Iraq must not result in an abandonment of our nation's responsibilities to the poor at home and abroad, or a diversion of essential resources from other humanitarian emergencies around the world.

At times like these, we turn to God and ask for wisdom and perseverance, courage and compassion, faith and hope. We Christians are called to be "sentinels of peace," the Holy Father reminds us. We join with him in urging Catholics to dedicate this Lenten season to reflection, prayer and fasting that the trials and tragedy of war will soon be replaced by a just and lasting peace.

Archbishop Renato Martino, president of the Pontifical Council for Justice and Peace, April 11, 2003:

The crisis situation of the U.N., caused by the war in Iraq, does not contradict but reinforces the appeal of *Pacem in Terris* for a world political authority.... [T]he common good is a qualitative moral concept that calls for an appropriate world political authority...[T]he U.N. in not a super-state or a super-court; rather, its essence lies in the participatory process of construction of this universal authority.... [It] is the obligatory path for modern civilization and world peace.... [I]t is time to undertake a constitutional engineering of humanity so that the United Nations can carry out its irreplaceable role.... [To achieve this objective,] it is necessary to favor multilateralism, not only at the diplomatic level, but also in the area of development plans.

[This requires] the desired revision of the very structure of the United Nations, so that all the member states will find sufficient guarantees of respect for their interests and — as *Pacem in Terris* underlines — of respect of the principle of dignity of all nations and peoples.... [T]he weakening of international organizations might imply a weakening of the consciousness of being one single family.

Cardinal Angelo Sodano, Vatican Secretary of State, interview with reporters in Rome, April 11, 2003:

We are a family of nations. We have to cooperate; this is the destiny of peoples....We pray that God's providence, which guides the destiny of peoples, will be able to draw good from evil.

Cardinal Angelo Sodano, Vatican Secretary of State, April 10, 2003:

The latest developments in Baghdad, which mark an important turning point in the Iraqi conflict and a significant opportunity for the future of the people, raises hopes that the military operations underway in the rest of the country will soon end, with the aim of sparing further victims, civilian or military, and further suffering for those populations. Given that the material, political and social reconstruction of the country are on the horizon, the Catholic Church is ready, through her social and charitable institutions, to lend the necessary assistance. The dioceses of Iraq are likewise available to offer their structures to contribute to an equitable distribution of humanitarian aid. The Secretariat of State hopes once again that, with the silencing of weapons, the Iraqis and the international community will know how to meet the compelling present challenge which is to definitively bring an era of peace to the Middle East.

Archbishop Diarmuid Martin, then Vatican representative to agencies of the United Nations in Geneva, statement at session of U.N. Human Rights Commission, April 8, 2003:

Religious leaders have a special responsibility to strongly reaffirm — whenever possible together — that attempts to use religious sentiments to generate division, or to use religion as an excuse for violence or terrorism, cannot be reconciled with any true religious spirit....There is no place in a culture of tolerance for gestures and declarations...which show disrespect for or are offensive to what is most sacred to the conscience of individual believers and their communities.

Archbishop John P. Foley, President of the Pontifical Council for Social Communications, Mass at the Basilica of St. Mary Major, March 12, 2003:

[A] just peace, involving also the effective disarmament of Iraq, is badly needed, not only for the poor, the innocent and the defenseless in the Middle East, but for the members of our own armed forces and

indeed for our own populations who risk being victimized again by horrible terrorism.

Commission of the Bishops' Conferences of the European Community, Statement March 27-28, 2003:

This is not a conflict between religions, and the name of God should never be invoked to justify the resort to war or the use of violence. We appeal to Christians, Jews and Muslims to work together in solidarity in order to bring an end to the current strife in the region and to promote harmonious relations in our own countries....We also strongly urge the European Union, with its partners in the international community, to redouble their efforts to help find a lasting solution to the conflict between Israelis and Palestinians....This situation reinforces our conviction that the world needs a system of global governance capable of promoting and sustaining peace and the common good, in which the United Nations must play the central role.

Catholic Bishops' Conference of England and Wales, Statement, March 18, 2003:

[I]t is important at this time of great fear and tension to look at what brings us together—our common humanity and our shared faith....We pray all those caught up in the horror of war, above all the innocent civilians of Iraq, will be touched by God's mercy. We pray for our leaders that they will recognize that reconciliation and justice are the only grounds for true and lasting peace. We must show our solidarity with those most affected by the consequences of military action, whether they be members of the armed forces and their families, or those groups in this country who might be the victims of prejudice....[I]n the midst of preparation for war we remember our true vocation is to be builders of peace.

CATHOLICS IN POLITICAL LIFE

On January 16, 2003, the Congregation for the Doctrine of the Faith made public a Doctrinal Note on Some Questions Regarding the Participation of Catholics in Political Life.

The *Note* was directed to "Bishops of the Catholic Church, Catholic politicians and all lay members of the faithful called to participate in the political life of democratic societies" and was reminder of those "principles proper to the Christian conscience, which inspire the social and political involvement of Catholics in democratic societies." The following is a synopsis developed as a resource by Staff of the United States Conference of Catholic Bishops (USCCB); it was reviewed by Bishop Donald W. Trautman, Chairman of the USCCB Committee on Doctrine, and approved by Msgr. William P. Fay, General Secretary of the USCCB. (*Courtesy USCCB.*)

What the document is: This "Doctrinal Note" has been issued by the Congregation for the Doctrine of the Faith to address authoritatively some ambiguous positions and questionable opinions on the relationship between ethics and politics. This Note was approved by Pope John Paul II who ordered its publication for the Universal Church.

To whom the document is addressed: This Doc-

trinal Note is addressed to three groups of people:

To the Bishops of the Catholic Church who have the responsibility of forming the consciences of the members of the Church;

To Catholic politicians who are active in political life by profession; and

To all lay members of the faithful whose Baptism calls them also to participate in the political life of democratic societies.

A Constant Teaching

(*Guided by a Christian conscience, Catholics are obliged to promote the common good by participating in public life.*)

Christians have a commitment [by reason of Baptism] to be active in the world. One way of being active is "involvement in political life." (I.1.1)

With the growth of democracies, more people are able to participate in political life to benefit the common good by "voting for lawmakers and government officials, and in other ways." (I.1.2)

The laity have a proper task of "infusing the temporal order with Christian values" while respecting "the nature and rightful autonomy of that order." The laity fulfill this task successfully when "guided by a Christian conscience." (I.1.3)

This *Note* seeks "only to recall some principles proper to the [well-formed] Christian conscience" on this issue, because of "ambiguities or questionable positions in recent times." (I.1.4)

Central points in the current cultural and political debate

(*The signs of the times.*)

Great strides have taken place in civil society today, but real dangers exist. (II.2.1)

There is a new relativism in our culture today that espouses "ethical pluralism" as "the very condition for democracy." This is the doctrine that every point of view is of equal value and truth and that there is "no moral law rooted in the nature of the human person, which must govern our understanding of man, the common good and the state." (II.2.2)

(*Legitimate political differences versus ethical relativism.*)

The relativism in question here "has nothing to do with the legitimate freedom of Catholic citizens to choose among the various political opinions [e.g. in economics, foreign policy, etc.] that are compatible with faith and the natural moral law." (II.3.1)

The legitimacy of the presence of a plurality of political parties to address the contingent dimensions of political life, in which Catholics can rightly participate, should not be confused with an ambiguous pluralism. [While it is the right and duty of Catholics to attend to the contingencies of the political order (e.g., economic theory, foreign policy), this activity must always be based moral principles and essential values.] (II.3.2)

Democracy is successful only when "it is based on a correct understanding of the human person." (II.3.3)

(*The obligation of all Catholics to Catholic Doctrine.*)

In the face of scientific progress and legislative proposals that violate human life, "Catholics ... have the right and the duty to recall society to a deeper understanding of human life and to the responsibility of everyone in this regard." Catholic politicians have a graver and clearer obligation here. (II.4.1)

There is "an integral unity" to the Catholic doctrine on faith and morals. Consequently, "A political commitment to a single isolated aspect of the Church's social doctrine does not exhaust one's responsibility towards the common good." [In short, a "well-formed Christian conscience" does not allow one to pick and choose particular elements of Catholic doctrine, exclusive of others, in promoting the common good.] (II.4.2)

The above is especially true "of fundamental and inalienable ethical demands" concerning "the integral good of the human person." This is the case with the person's (and the embryo's) right to life. "Analogously," this is also the case for the protection and promotion of the family, the parents' freedom to educate their children, society's right to protect minors, the right to religious freedom, the fostering of a just economy and the work of peace. (II.4.3)

Principles of Catholic doctrine on the autonomy of the temporal order and on pluralism.

(*The Divine versus the natural moral law.*)

The "ethical precepts" that form the moral teaching of the Catholic Church are "rooted in human nature itself and belong to the natural moral law." One does not have to profess the Catholic faith to know these truths; natural reason can and should discover them on its own. (III.5.1)

(*The rightful autonomy of the participation of lay Catholics in politics.*)

While there is a proper distinction between the "political or civil sphere" and "that of the Church," the exercise of one's conscience in recognizing moral truth and in promoting the common good is not "confessionalism" or an improper intrusion of the Church into the secular domain. [In short, it is false for a Catholic or anyone else to suggest that in promoting the ethical truths of the natural law one is promoting Catholicism in a "confessional" or denominational way.] (III.6.1)

The search for and defense of moral truths is the "right and duty" of all citizens. "The fact that some of these truths may also be taught by the Church does not lessen the political legitimacy or the rightful 'autonomy' of the contribution of those citizens who are committed to them." [The "autonomy" spoken of here refers to the human person's ability to know moral truth independently of religion.] (III.6.2)

The Church's teaching that there are natural moral truths that obligate does not "eliminate the freedom of opinion of Catholics regarding contingent questions." Neither is the social doctrine of the Church "an intrusion into the government of individual countries." (III.6.3)

Those who would deny Christians who exercise their conscience an active role in political life are "guilty of a form of intolerant *secularism*," opening themselves to the denial of "the possibility of natural ethics itself." Moral anarchy would result. (III.6.4)

Considerations regarding particular aspects

(*The urgency of reclaiming the Catholic tradition of moral thinking for political life.*)

In recent years, some Catholic organizations and periodicals in various countries have misunderstood the principles explicated here and have contradicted fundamental moral law or at least rendered it ambiguous "by misinterpreting the idea of political autonomy enjoyed by Catholics." (IV.7.1)

The Catholic Tradition has much to offer the societies of today in building and strengthening modern culture. The fulfillment of this task by Catholics in political life is urgent, and one in which Catholics should feel no inferiority. (IV.7.2)

Given a well-informed conscience, the Catholic contribution to the common good is reasoned (guided by truth) and not "utopian" (guided by imagined idealities). (IV.7.3)

There is no authentic freedom without the truth. Freedom without truth is license and destructive of society. (IV.7.4)

(*A clarification on freedom of conscience and religious freedom.*)

Freedom of conscience and religious freedom are based on "the ontological [the very nature of the] dignity of the human person and not on a non-existent equality among religions or cultural systems of human creation." (IV.8.1)

Conclusion

(*Catholics, by their participation in political life,*

bring faith to life and Gospel to culture, as directed by the Second Vatican Council.)

Though Christians know this world is transitory, the Council teaches clearly that Catholics have a right and duty to safeguard and promote the common good in society. (V.9.1)

CATHOLICS AND THE NEW AGE MOVEMENT

On Feb. 3, 2003, Cardinal Paul Poupard, president of the Pontifical Council for Culture, Archbishop Michael Fitzgerald, president of the Pontifical Council for Interreligious Dialogue, and members of their respective staffs published a 93-page reflection on the New Age movement, "Jesus Christ, Bearer of the Water of Life: A Christian Reflection on the New Age."

As the paper declares, "These reflections are offered primarily to those engaged in pastoral work so that they might be able to explain how the New Age movement differs from the Christian faith. This study invites readers to take account of the way that New Age religiosity addresses the spiritual hunger of contemporary men and women."

The report seeks to examine the attraction of the New Age movement for some Christians, which is due in part to the lack of serious attention in their own ecclesial communities in fostering the spiritual dimension of existence and their integration with the whole of life, the search for the meaning of life, and the connection between human beings and the rest of creation. There is thus a necessity to know and understand New Age "as a cultural current, as well as the need for Catholics to have an understanding of authentic Catholic doctrine and spirituality in order to properly assess New Age themes."

The timing of the paper is an ideal one, for, as the paper observes, the beginning of the Third Millennium arrives not only two thousand years after the birth of Christ, but also at a time that astrologers call the end of the Age of Pisces, considered by them to be synonymous with the Christian age. The new impending era is termed the astrological Age of Aquarius, and the New Age movement is successfully pervading contemporary (especially western) culture with its vision of what this period is supposed to entail. Given the pervasive quality of this movement's ideas, Christians are often challenged to recognize what is and what is not consistent with the Christian message.

The New Age movement responds, as the report notes, "to the legitimate spiritual longing of human nature … In Western culture in particular, the appeal of "alternative" approaches to spirituality is very strong. On the one hand, new forms of psychological affirmation of the individual have become very popular among Catholics, even in retreat houses, seminaries and institutes of formation for religious. At the same time there is increasing nostalgia and curiosity for the wisdom and ritual of long ago, which is one of the reasons for the remarkable growth in the popularity of esotericism and gnosticism."

In analyzing New Age thought, the thoughtful Christian can recognize that many positions underlying the seemingly harmless or ambiguous aspects of the movement (the music, incense, clothing, and writings) advance the age-old principles of the heresy of Gnosticism.

Pope John Paul II is quoted that the New Age "is only a new way of practising gnosticism – that attitude of the spirit that, in the name of a profound knowledge of God, results in distorting His Word and replacing it with purely human words" (*Crossing the Threshold of Hope*, Knopf 1994, p. 90). The success of the New Age thus offers the Church a challenge, for many people feel that the Christian religion no longer offers them what they need, and in searching for a deeper spirituality they are led instead to the positive tone of New Age philosophies.

The paper devotes its first two chapters to the present New Age movement as a multifaceted cultural tendency, noting the cultural background of New Age spirituality, including what the New Age claims to offer and the fundamental principles of its thinking. The "essential matrix" of the New Age thought is rooted in the esoteric-theosophical tradition that was fairly widely accepted in European intellectual circles in the 18th and 19th centuries. "People can be initiated into the mysteries of the cosmos, God and the self by means of a spiritual itinerary of transformation. The eventual goal is gnosis, the highest form of knowledge, the equivalent of salvation."

The succeeding chapters compare and contrast the Christian faith and New Age philosophy, concluding that the New Age replaces the Judeo-Christian profession of a personal God with a vague "impersonal energy, really a particular extension or component of the cosmos." The movement also denies the uniqueness of Jesus Christ, denies the existence of sin and evil, and promotes self-realization and self-redemption. Thus, it denies that salvation is a gift of God.

The paper concludes with a formulation of ideas concerning the New Age and a useful select glossary of New Age terms and key places.

The reflection paper was drafted by members of several congregations and offices in the Roman Curia, including the Pontifical Councils for Culture and for Interreligious Dialogue (the principal redactors for this project), the Congregation for the Evangelization of Peoples and the Pontifical Council for Promoting Christian Unity.

The text of the apostolic exhortation can be found online at: http://www.vatican.va/holy_father/ john_paul_ii/apost_exhortations.

SPECIAL REPORTS: NATIONAL NEWS 2002-2003

THE SEX-ABUSE SCANDAL IN THE U.S. CHURCH

The Catholic Church in the United States has been troubled profoundly in the last year by the severe crisis over the issue of sexual abuse of minors by members of the clergy. The following is a recapitulation of the events of the crisis over the last year, including the most significant documents and statements by Church authorities. Special thanks are offered to Russell Shaw for his kind assistance.

SEX ABUSE SCANDAL CONTINUES

As the crisis in U.S. Catholicism arising from the scandal of clergy sex abuse continued in 2003, several things became clear.

One was that most cases receiving attention in courts and the media had occurred a decade or more earlier—in some instances, 30 or 40 years in the past. It appeared possible, though hardly certain, that policies adopted in the early 1990s had largely put an end to the problem. In his book *The New Anti-Catholicism* (Oxford University Press, 2003), Philip Jenkins, a professor of history and religious studies at Pennsylvania State University, suggested as much. In recent years, Jenkins wrote, most dioceses did "a respectable job of acknowledging the problem and responding to it."

But something else also became clear as time passed. Many concerned parties — media, abuse victims, ordinary Catholics — not only were incensed over clergy sex abuse but held present Church leadership to blame.

The scandal mushroomed and came to involve many issues. These included questions of secrecy in ecclesiastical affairs, lay involvement, and the sexual mores of priests and Catholics generally. Suggestions for holding a new plenary council for the Church in the United States or a regional synod of bishops received serious attention from the bishops themselves.

The National Review Board and the Office for Child and Youth Protection set up in 2002 by the United States Conference of Catholic Bishops (USCCB) to oversee handling of the sex abuse problem continued their work amid occasional controversy. There was controversy, too, over the activities of an unofficial lay group called Voice of the Faithful that began in Boston and spread to other places.

In January, *The New York Times* reported that more than 1,200 priests had been accused of sexually abusing children since the scandal erupted the year before. This was 1.8% of all priests ordained between 1950 and 2001, the newspaper said. Allegations of abuse were made by 4,268 people and concerned incidents said to have occurred as far back as the 1930s, with the largest number occurring in the 1970s and 1980s.

By May 30, according to the Associated Press, about 1,000 people had made new claims against the Church in the year past. Dioceses where large numbers of claims were pending included Boston, Los Angeles, and others. New multi-million-dollar settlements were reached in Manchester, NH, and Louisville, KY, with the latter announcing payments of $25.7 million to 240 persons.

Further underscoring the financial dimensions of the crisis, the Diocese of San Bernardino, CA, took the unprecedented step of filing suit against the Archdiocese of Boston for damages resulting from failure to disclose that Father Paul R. Shanley, a Boston priest who moved to the California diocese in 1990, had a history of child molestation. The diocese later dropped the suit, however, in favor of efforts by the ordinaries of the two sees to work out an agreement.

In June it was announced that, in order to avoid prosecution, Bishop Thomas J. O'Brien of Phoenix, AZ, had admitted to hushing up abuse cases, paid $600,000 in diocesan funds to settle claims by victims, and separated himself from the handling of such cases in the future. Subsequently Bishop O'Brien was arrested for leaving the scene of an accident after the car he was driving struck and killed a pedestrian. Pope John Paul II then accepted his resignation, making him the sixth U.S. bishop to leave office amid scandal in a year and a half.

At mid-year, a comprehensive audit of diocesan policies was underway, conducted by the Gavin Group of Boston and commissioned by the Office for Child and Youth Protection. Findings were to be submitted to the National Review Board.

Another study, by the John Jay College of Criminal Justice in New York, was commissioned by the board to gather information on how many priests and deacons had abused minors, the number of victims, and how bishops and law enforcement agencies handled the cases. The study was to be completed later in 2003.

An uproar greeted remarks in June by former Oklahoma Gov. Frank Keating, chairman of the 13-member review board, who compared some bishops to the Mafia for refusing to answer certain questions on the questionnaire. The comment appeared aimed especially at the bishops of California. Cardinal Roger Mahony of Los Angeles called it "the last straw," and Keating resigned.

During the USCCB's semiannual spring meeting, June 19-21 in St. Louis, the bishops met in executive session with the board and child protection office to iron out differences. The John Jay College researchers agreed to modifications in their survey; the California bishops said they would cooperate.

Also during the meeting the bishops reviewed steps taken in the year past to carry out policies they had put in place, with Vatican approval, in 2002. "There is still a long road ahead of us," said Archbishop Harry J. Flynn of St. Paul-Minneapolis, chairman of the USCCB committee on sex abuse. But he insisted, "Our commitment has not wavered. We have made a pledge to our people and to the people of this nation and especially to the vulnerable ones, and we will keep that pledge."

In another, widely anticipated development, the *Boston Globe* in April received the 2003 Pulitzer Prize for public service in journalism for its coverage of clergy sex abuse.

The abuse problem first came to light in the media in the mid-1980s and was extensively covered in the years that followed. Beginning in January 2002, however, the *Globe* provided detailed information, largely based on heretofore, secret court documents, regarding cases in the Boston archdiocese. Besides enormously heightening media and public interest, this coverage helped bring about the December 2002 resignation as Archbishop of Boston of Cardinal Bernard Law. Bishop Sean O'Malley of Palm Beach was named Law's successor on July 1, 2003.

An editorial in *The Pilot*, Boston's archdiocesan newspaper, congratulated the *Globe* on its Pulitzer but added: "History may interpret their [*Globe* editors' and journalists'] work not as a public service effort, but as the convenient alliance between plaintiffs' lawyers and the press to pursue their own objectives: astronomical settlements for the plaintiffs and the advancement of a reputed anti-Catholic agenda by Boston's leading newspaper."

AMERICAN CATHOLICS IN POLITICAL LIFE

On January 16, 2003, the Congregation for the Doctrine of the Faith made public a Doctrinal Note on Some Questions Regarding the Participation of Catholics in Political Life.

The *Note* was directed to "Bishops of the Catholic Church, Catholic politicians and all lay members of the faithful called to participate in the political life of democratic societies" and was a reminder of those "principles proper to the Christian conscience, which inspire the social and political involvement of Catholics in democratic societies." (*See* **above** for details.)

The *Doctrinal Note* had immediate ramification for American politics when the number of United States political leaders who are Catholic and who, in some cases, hold positions contrary to the teachings of the Church, especially on the issue of abortion. The Note raises the significant question of whether a political leader is able to continue calling himself or herself a Catholic and still advance an agenda contrary to the teachings of the Church.

Bishop Wilton D. Gregory, President of the United States Conference of Catholic Bishops, issued a statement on the Doctrinal Note on January 16, 2003:

The Congregation for the Doctrine of the Faith has made public today a *Doctrinal Note on Some Questions Regarding the Participation of Catholics in Political Life*. That Note, which is directed to "Bishops of the Catholic Church, Catholic politicians and all lay members of the faithful called to participate in the political life of democratic societies" is a most timely reminder of "some of the principles proper to the Christian conscience, which inspire the social and political involvement of Catholics in democratic societies." I welcome this statement as it addresses some of the profound challenges faced by Catholic politicians and voters who are confronted with various moral and social issues in the context of a democratic society.

I am pleased that the Note has recalled the tradition of the Church that there exist various political opinions compatible with faith and the natural moral law written into the hearts of every man and woman. For this reason, Catholic men and women can make a great contribution to the political sphere by their participation, and by bringing to that process their properly formed convictions based in moral principles and essential values which are rooted in our nature as human beings and in our Catholic faith. Because, as the Note reminds us, there are "non-negotiable ethical principles which are the underpinning of life in society" Catholic politicians cannot subscribe to any notion which equates freedom or democracy with a moral relativism that denies these moral principles. Further, while acknowledging the differences between the political and religious orders, the values brought by Christians to the political process must not be muted or silenced by any intolerant secularism which would deny the legitimacy of moral values espoused by Christians who would speak or act according to their conscience.

The Catholic Bishops of the United States have a long tradition of adding their voices to the political and moral dialogue of our democratic process. We too have stressed the fundamental and inalienable ethical demands of our human nature which support the life of every human person, from conception until natural death. This respect for the human person extends to safeguarding the family, promoting education, protecting minors, defending religious freedom, assuring a just economy and fostering peace. Indeed Catholics involved in politics recognize that in these essential moral questions, our faith does not allow a commitment to support only one or some of these areas of responsibility for the common good.

The Catholic Church is rightly proud of the contribution of its members to the democratic process in this country. We owe a debt of gratitude to those Catholics involved in politics on all levels who work to enact policies which truly respect the most essential moral values of our human nature. I hope that this letter will serve as an encouragement to them and a reminder to all of the profound duty and obligation which Catholics involved in politics have to work without exception or reservation for all of the goods rooted in our human nature.

In the wake of the Doctrinal Note, several U.S. Bishops took steps to apply its provisions.

GENERAL INSTRUCTION OF THE ROMAN MISSAL

On November 12, 2002, the Latin Church members of the United States Conference of Catholic Bishops approved a translation of the Institutio Generalis Missalis Romani *prepared by the International Commission on English in the Liturgy.*

In spring 2001, Pope John Paul II had authorized the publication of an *editio typica tertia* of the *Missale Romanum*. The much anticipated revision included a new edition of the *Institutio Generalis Missalis Romani* (*General Instruction of the Roman Missal*).The translation was confirmed by the Congregation for Divine Worship and the Discipline of the Sacraments on March 17, 2003. This translation of the *General Instruction of the Roman Missal* is the sole translation of the *Institutio Generalis Missalis Romani, editio typica tertia* for use in the dioceses of the United States of America.

Concerning the new edition, Msgr. James P. Moroney, Executive Director of the USCCB Secretariat for the Liturgy, wrote in the Foreword:

"This revised *Institutio Generalis* possesses a unique role among all the documents on the liturgy. Like its preceding editions, it has been published in order to give life to a dream. It was the dream of reformers such as St. Hippolytus, St. Gregory, and St. Leo. It was the dream of Pope Paul VI and clearly remains the vision of Pope John Paul II, who calls us to 'an ever deeper grasp of the liturgy of the Church, celebrated according to the current books and lived above all as a reality in the spiritual order' (*Vicesimus Quintus Annus*, 1988, no. 14). Likewise, this dream is shared by the Bishops' Committee on the Liturgy and the United States Conference of Catholic Bishops that it serves. Finally, it is the vision of the Church itself: the dream of God's people joined to Christ in Baptism and made 'ever more holy by conscious, active, and fruitful participation in the mystery of the Eucharist' (*General Instruction of the Roman Missal*, no. 5)."

The following is the Foreword to the new edition Msgr. James P. Moroney, Executive Director, USCCB Secretariat for the Liturgy:

"The liturgical reforms of the Second Vatican Council have enjoyed great success in bringing many Catholics closer to the perfect sacrifice of praise that Christ the Lord offered from the wood of the Cross. Perhaps most of all, the reforms of the *Missale Romanum*, which regulates the celebration of the Eucharist as the 'source and summit of the Christian life' (*Sacrosanctum Concilium*, no. 47), have been the cause and witness of this great work.

"The first stages of the postconciliar reform of the Mass were marked by Pope Paul VI's apostolic constitution *Missale Romanum* (1969), which was quickly followed by the revised *Ordo Missae* (1970), including the first edition of the *Institutio Generalis Missalis Romani* (1970). This last document, which described the form for the new Order of Mass, was further revised in 1972 and yet more definitively as a part of the *editio typica altera* of the *Missale Romanum* in March 27, 1975.

"After many years of preparation, the publication of an *editio typica tertia* of the *Missale Romanum* was authorized by Pope John Paul II in the course of the Jubilee Year of our Redemption and was published in spring 2001. This long-awaited revision includes a new edition of the *Institutio Generalis Missalis Romani*. On November 12, 2002, the Latin Church members of the United States Conference of Catholic Bishops approved a translation of the *Institutio Generalis Missalis Romani* prepared by the International Commission on English in the Liturgy. The translation was confirmed by the Congregation for Divine Worship and the Discipline of the Sacraments on March 17, 2003 (Prot. N. 2235/02/L).

"The translation is published in this volume as a revision of the Bishops' Committee on the Liturgy's Liturgy Documentary Series 2, which first appeared in 1970 and was intended to aid a common understanding of the first edition of the *Missale Romanum*. With the publication of the third edition of the *Missale Romanum*, the Bishops' Committee on the Liturgy hopes that this edition will assist in that same goal in our present day.

"This revised *Institutio Generalis* possesses a unique role among all the documents on the liturgy. Like its preceding editions, it has been published in order to give life to a dream. It was the dream of reformers such as St. Hippolytus, St. Gregory, and St. Leo. It was the dream of Pope Paul VI and clearly remains the vision of Pope John Paul II, who calls us to 'an ever deeper grasp of the liturgy of the Church, celebrated according to the current books and lived above all as a reality in the spiritual order' (*Vicesimus Quintus Annus*, 1988, no. 14). Likewise, this dream is shared by the Bishops' Committee on the Liturgy and the United States Conference of Catholic Bishops that it serves. Finally, it is the vision of the Church itself: the dream of God's people joined to Christ in Baptism and made 'ever more holy by conscious, active, and fruitful participation in the mystery of the Eucharist' (*General Instruction of the Roman Missal*, no. 5)."

SUPREME COURT DECISION ON TEXAS LAW

(Courtesy United States Conference of Catholic Bishops.) On June 26, 2003, the United States Supreme Court struck down the Texas state anti-sodomy law by a vote of 6-3.

The decision on the case of Lawrence vs. Texas brought with it considerable moral ramifications for the United States, as well as Constitutional implications involving states rights. Bishop Wilton D. Gregory, president of the United States Conference of Catholic Bishops, issued the following statement about the ramifications of the Supreme Court's decision:

"In its decision, Lawrence vs. Texas, the Supreme Court has chosen to view homosexual behavior between consenting adults as a matter of privacy.

"However, human sexuality cannot be viewed this way. Sexual activity has profound social consequences which are not limited to those immediately engaged in sexual acts. For this reason, the larger society has always shown a concern about what is and is not acceptable in sexual behavior between individuals. The very fact that this case came before the Supreme Court is evidence of that concern.

"The Catholic Church teaches, in agreement with other faith traditions and with what were once the norms generally accepted by society, that sexual activity belongs to the marital relationship between one man and one woman in fidelity to each other. This relationship is the basis of the family which is the basic unit of society. Respect for the purpose of human sexuality and the family needs to be reaffirmed in our society; and anything which reduces respect for them – such as yesterday's Supreme Court decision – is to be deplored."

In an accompanying statement, Mark Chopko, General Counsel for the United States Catholic Conference, pointed out the legal limits of the decision:

"This case was decided on the narrowest grounds. Justice Kennedy took pains to insulate this case from broader conclusions. He points to laws against prostitution and rape to show that not every sexual act between adults is outside the reach of legislatures. He is equally careful to note that this case does not involve the question whether the government must formally recognize homosexual relationships."

BISHOPS' REPORT ON NATIVE AMERICAN CATHOLICS

(Courtesy United States Conference of Catholic Bishops.)

On June 19, 2003, the United States Conference of Catholic Bishops issued a report, "Native American Catholics at the Millennium," on the current state of Native American Catholics in the United States.

The report was prepared by the United States Conference of Catholic Bishops' (USCCB) Ad Hoc Committee on Native American Catholics and was presented to the bishops at their semi-annual meeting in St. Louis by Bishop Donald E. Pelotte, S.S.S., Bishop of Gallup, NM, and chair of the Ad Hoc Committee. The report was based on the findings of two national studies conducted with dioceses by Mary Beth Celio of the Archdiocese of Seattle between 1996 and 1999; the data were then correlated with 2000 U.S. Census data. "The purpose of the study," said Bishop Pelotte, "was to better understand the present state of the church's ministry to Native Americans and to project the need for personnel serving Native American ministry for the next ten years."

The report presents important statistical informa-tion on Native American Catholics:

• There are 4.1 million people who identify themselves as Native American, the majority of whom live in cities or small towns, according to the 2000 U.S. Census. Of these, 493,615 Native Americans, or 12 percent of the total population, are Catholic.

• There has been an extensive demographic shift among Native Americans to urban areas. As a consequence, the report found that large numbers of Native American Catholics remain uncounted in the population estimate.

• Presently, 51 dioceses offer liturgies integrating Native American symbols.

• There are currently 322 individuals currently engaged in Native American ministry.

• Currently 27 Native American priests, 8 Native American seminarians, 74 Native American deacons, 34 Native American women religious, and 65 Native American ecclesial ministers serve the Church.

• There are presently also two Native American bnishops in active service in the United States. They are: Archbishop Charles J. Chaput, O.F.M. Cap. of Denver and Bishop Donald Pelotte, S.S.S., of Gallup.

LIFE ISSUES 2002-2003

ABORTION

Pro-Life Protest Decision

On Feb. 26, 2003, the United States Supreme Court ruled that federal racketeering and extortion laws were improperly used to punish anti-abortion protesters, thereby lifting a nationwide injunction that barred people from interfering with the operations of abortion clinics. The 8-1 decision by the court applied not only to anti-abortion protesters but to protests of all kinds. The court's ruling was a significant victory for Operation Rescue, anti-abortion leader Joseph Scheidler and others who had been subject to various draconian laws, had been ordered to pay damages to abortion clinics, and had been barred from interfering with their businesses for ten years. The ruling ended the injunction, and Chief Justice William H. Rehnquist said their protest activity did not qualify as extortion.

Scheidler and other anti-abortion organizers had been sued in 1986 by abortion clinics in Delaware and Wisconsin and the National Organization for Women. It was argued that racketeering and extortion laws should protect businesses from violent protests that drive away clients. Specifically, they accused the protesters of blocking clinic entrances, threatening doctors, patients and clinic staff, and destroying equipment. Scheidler and others were charged under provisions of the 1970 Racketeer Influenced and Corrupt Organizations Act, known as RICO, and the Hobbs Act, a 1946 law that makes it a crime to take property from another with force; it was intended chiefly to curb the activities of organized crime. The demonstrators were ordered subsequently to pay around $258,000 in damages.

In the majority opinion, Rehnquist stated that as protesters do not "obtain" property, they are not subject to federal extortion laws. Further, there is no question that abortion protesters interfered with clinic operations and in some cases actually committed crimes. Nevertheless, "even when their acts of interference and disruption achieved their ultimate goal of 'shutting down' a clinic that performed abortions, such acts did not constitute extortion."

Justice John Paul Stevens was the only dissenting vote. He wrote, "The principal beneficiaries of the court's dramatic retreat from the position that federal prosecutors and federal courts have maintained throughout the history of this important statute will certainly be the class of professional criminals whose conduct persuaded Congress that the public needed federal protection from extortion."

PARTIAL-BIRTH ABORTION BAN

(Courtesy United States Conference of Catholic Bishops.)

On June 4, 2003, the United States House of Representatives voted 282-139 to ban the cruel procedure known as the partial-birth abortion.

Earlier, on March 26, 2003, the House Judiciary Committee voted 19 to 11 to pass H.R. 760, the Partial-Birth Abortion Ban Act, without amendment. The vote placed the bill in position for a vote on the House floor. The ban on partial-birth abortion was passed by the Senate earlier on March 13, 64-33, approving S. 3, the Partial-Birth Abortion Ban Act, the first time in seven years that the Senate has passed the ban without the threat of presidential veto. President Bush has vowed to sign it into law once the bill passes through the process of Conference Committee.

Cardinal Anthony Bevilacqua, Chairman of the Committee for Pro-Life Activities of the United States Conference of Catholic Bishops, made the following statement upon passage yesterday of the ban on partial-birth abortion by the House of Representatives:

"The Catholic Bishops of the United States are grateful and encouraged by the House of Representatives.

In voting to ban this procedure, one of the most heinous acts ever perpetrated upon an unborn child, Congress is in harmony with the vast majority of Americans who find this violent act intolerable and want it stopped.

We hope and expect that President George W. Bush will sign the Partial-Birth Abortion Ban Act into law as soon as possible.

Abortion advocates have said they intend to challenge the constitutionality of the Partial-Birth Abortion Ban Act in court. Nothing in our constitution demands that unborn children must be subjected to a procedure so violent and so painful. To allow the brutal killing of a child mere inches from being born is barbaric. To cloak the act in the Constitution is a national disgrace."

OTHER DEVELOPMENTS

Indiana Abortion Law

On Feb. 24, 2003, the United States Supreme Court upheld an Indiana state law that imposed various restrictions on abortions. The 1995 Indiana law required that women give what the state called "informed consent" before procuring an abortion. The law's provisions include: an 18-hour waiting period before a woman can procure an abortion; face-to-face counseling concerning the risks of an abortion and about alternatives to abortion and the availability of child support if the pregnancy proceeds; and photographs of what her fetus might look like.

The 7th U.S. Circuit Court of Appeals upheld the constitutionality of the law in 2002. A majority of a three-judge appeals court panel said the law did not create an excessive burden for women, adding that the law included a provision permitting the counseling requirement to be waived in medical emergencies.

When brought before the Supreme Court, the justices did not comment in rejecting the case and thus left in place the law. The law itself is similar in key ways to those of other states, including Utah, Wisconsin, and Louisiana. The Indiana law is especially remarkable in its requirement for abortion providers to give women information about the considerable risks of abortion.

Michigan Partial Birth Abortion Ban

On May 8, 2003, the Michigan House of Representatives voted to ban partial birth abortions by declaring a child to be legally born once any part of that child is delivered outside his or her mother. The 74-29 vote to approve House Bill 4603 followed an overwhelming vote by the Michigan Senate the previous week to approve an identical bill. The two chambers were then required to agree to send one of the two bills to the governor.

Overseas Abortions

On May 22 the United States Senate voted 51-48 to maintain the ban on elective abortions at military hospitals overseas, defeating an amendment to the FY 2004 National Defense Authorization Act that would

have permitted abortions on demand in such institutions. The U.S. House of Representatives also passed a defense authorization bill on May 22, defeating a similar amendment by a vote of 227-201. The existing ban contains exceptions for cases where the mother's life is endangered or where pregnancy occurred from rape or incest. Cardinal Anthony Bevilacqua, Archbishop of Philadelphia and Chairman of the Committee for Pro-Life Activities for the United States Conference of Catholic Bishops (USCCB), praised the votes in the House and Senate, stating, "I commend both bodies for this action which is so important to the defense of human life."

Cloning

(*Courtesy United States Conference of Catholic Bishops.*)

On Feb. 27, 2003, the United States House of Representatives passed the Human Cloning Prohibition Act (H.R. 534) by the vote of 244 to 151.

The act, sponsored by Congressmen Dave Weldon (R-Fla.) and Bart Stupak (D-Mich.), prohibits human cloning for any purpose, although it does explicitly permit biomedical research involving the cloning of DNA, genes, tissues, organs, plants, animals, and cells other than human embryos. A similar bill, S. 245, has been introduced in the Senate. The House also rejected a substitute amendment to authorize the mass-producing of human embryos with the sole purpose of destroying them for experimentation.

Cathy Cleaver, Esq., Director of Planning and Information for the Pro-Life Secretariat of the United States Conference of Catholic Bishops (USCCB) stated:

"This vote reflects America's rejection of the notion that human life is a commodity to be created for experimentation.... The impact of cloning on women was also considered. Allowing human cloning for 'therapeutic' or research purposes would require countless numbers of women to surrender their eggs by an extraction process that is both painful and dangerous. Making women into egg factories for this research is an utterly demeaning proposition."

UNITED STATES CONFERENCE OF CATHOLIC BISHOPS

MEETINGS OF U.S. BISHOPS 2002-2003

November 11-14, 2002

The meeting of the U.S. Bishops in Washington, DC, was dominated once again by the on-going crisis concerning the sexual abuse of minors by members of the clergy. The bishops also dealt with a variety of other issues, including a vote on a historic joint pastoral letter with the bishops of Mexico, extended discussion on the just-war ramifications of a possible conflict with Iraq, and action on such topics as domestic violence, poverty in the United States and abroad, abortion, Hispanic ministry, liturgical and canonical matters, stewardship, Catholic schools, and border concerns with Mexico. The chief concern of the fall assembly, however, was securing approval of the revised norms on clergy sex abuse that emerged from a joint Vatican-U.S. commission in October 2002.

Presidential Address: Bishop Wilton Gregory of Belleville, president of the USCCB, opened the annual bishops' meeting on November 11. The bishop declared:

My brother bishops, my sisters and brothers in Christ,

In a few short weeks during the season of Advent, we shall listen again to the opening words of the 40th chapter of the Book of Isaiah. The prophet is speaking in the name of God to the people of Israel who have long been in exile in Babylon. The Israelites are broken and afraid; they are dispirited and uncertain of their future. They needed a word of hope. Isaiah steps into their midst and declares in God's name: "Comfort, give comfort to my people, says your God."

The times in which we live are likewise characterized by fear and uncertainty, and there are many reasons for this anxiety. The signs of the times are painfully obvious:

•We live at a particular moment when our nation is faced with war, and terrorism has become an unwelcome guest.

•A weakened economy has many of us question if we will have enough to provide for ourselves and our loved ones.

•The scandal of poverty and disease is ever more prevalent in our country and around the world.

•In our own church, as well, we have had to face the criminal and sinful sexual abuse of children and the mismanagement of those violations by some church leaders.

Like the Israelites of old, we too need a word of hope. We need the word that God spoke through Isaiah: "Comfort, give comfort to my people, says your God." But we also need to know what we are seeking.

As teachers, we bishops are first evangelizers. We are to proclaim Jesus Christ to those who don't know him; we are to bring the fullness of Christ's truth to those who have been baptized in his name; and we are to help all men and women of good will to see that only the light of Christ can fully reveal the truth of the world in which we live. By bringing our sisters and brothers to Christ, the council tells us, we help them to recognize "the divinely revealed way to give glory to God and thus attain to everlasting happiness" (*Christus Dominus*, 12). What greater comfort could ever be proclaimed or received!

In a special way, following the example of the Divine Teacher, we bishops have an obligation to bring the Gospel of Christ and his comfort to the poorest and the most marginalized in our society, to those for whom anxiety and fear are only too familiar. Fulfilling that mission, thank God, has been a preoccupation of the work of our conference throughout our history. Last June we gave over the whole of our assembly to addressing the needs of those who, tragically, have been victims of sexual abuse in the church; and we put in place measures to ensure the greatest protection of our children in the church. With the help of the very fine work of the recently established mixed commission, we look forward to strengthening that work. As I have said repeatedly since our groundbreaking work in June, we will not step back from our compassion for those who have been harmed, or from our determination to put into place policies that will protect children….

As administrators of the church, the council exhorts us bishops to keep the model of the Good Shepherd always before us (*Lumen Gentium*, 27). Like the Good Shepherd, we are called to know and to love those entrusted to our care. The council tells us, moreover, that we are responsible not only for attending to the needs of the faithful, especially of those who are lost or marginalized; we are also responsible for recognizing the "duty and right" that other members of the church have "to collaborate actively in the building up of the body of Christ" (*Christus Dominus*, 16). The mission given us by the Lord is one in which all members of the church have a proper share. That is especially true of those who are related to us in ministry by sacred ordination. It is also true of the religious and laity.

When I think of those in my own diocese who assist me in fulfilling the mission that the Lord has given to me, my heart's eye turns toward all of my brother priests. The priestly vocation puts a man in contact with people in places where comfort is needed, at times when one of our brothers or sisters needs someone who can act "in persona Christi," in the person of Christ. The priest finds himself beside the hospital bed and at the graveside, in the office with the troubled married couple, in the confessional with the penitent weighed down by sin, and with those who face unexpected tragedy.

Priests were among those who quickly came to the scenes of torment that most of us saw only on television on Sept. 11. On that first terrible day and on the following days, there were many stories of the rescuers themselves — firefighters, police officers, emergency workers — gravitating to this priestly presence for prayers, words of consolation, or simply to shed tears with someone whose vocation personifies God's mercy and tenderness.

Each priest brings his own individual gifts and talents to the mission of making Christ present. Each excels at different and particular aspects of our multifaceted vocation. But every priest knows that being present for those in need is fundamental to acting "*in persona Christi*."

Priests today too often are being unfairly judged by the misdeeds of other priests, men often long departed from ministry or even deceased. One can hardly talk of the priesthood today without mentioning that some priests and bishops have seriously failed to live up to our vocation. Whenever I am listening to or reading a story about the good work of priests, I have gotten into the habit of anticipating the "but…," which will lead into some tale of malfeasance.

Well, this morning there is no "but." We need to pay more than lip service to the truth that the overwhelming majority of priests are faithful servants of the Lord.

At the direction of the Second Vatican Council, the permanent diaconate has been restored as a vital ministry in assisting us bishops in the mission of the church. By sacred ordination and their exercise of "the ministry of the liturgy, of the word, and of charity," deacons have a special relationship to us in fulfilling our responsibilities of bringing the knowledge and genuine comfort of Christ to the people of God.

As bishops, we need to attend, thoughtfully and constantly, to the way in which the council exhorted us to give both the religious and laity their rightful place and share in the mission of the church. Much of the council's intention has been identified and codified in church law. Religious and laity assist us well in our chanceries and tribunals, and on our diocesan financial and pastoral councils. We should continue to encourage our pastors to ensure that their gifts are well recognized and called forth in their parishes. The opportunities for the laity to assist us are great and we need to seize upon them in order to fulfill effectively the mission the Lord has given us.

As president of our conference during the past year, I have been particularly privileged to witness the extraordinary contribution of the religious and laity at the national level. I think first of the very talented lay men and women who serve us at the conference in Washington, Miami and New York. I include here my own faithful lay colleagues in the Diocese of Belleville. I also acknowledge the very gifted laity who serve at our Catholic national organizations in the areas of health, disabilities, education and social services. In a special way, I want to express my thanks to the members of our recently established National Review Board for the generosity and expertise that they bring in assisting us in the protection of our children….

My brother bishops, my brothers and sisters in Christ, with God's strength and encouragement let us embrace the hope that is put before us; let us walk together in our communion in Christ; and let us give ourselves completely to the mission that God has given us: "Comfort, give comfort to my people, says your God."

God bless each and every one of you!

Agenda:

The bishops attending their meeting in Washington, DC, acted on the following issues:

• Approved revised norms intended both to protect minors and protect bishops' relationships with their priests.

• Approved slight changes in the "Charter for the Protection of Children and Young People" to conform to the norms. The final vote on the norms was 246-7. In their statement on bishops' accountability, they apologized for past mistakes in dealing with sexually abusive priests and spelled out what they will do if a bishop engages in sexual misconduct.

• Approved by a vote of 243-1 a pastoral letter, *Strangers No Longer*, on migration, approved by the Mexican bishops; it is one of the first statements to be issued jointly by two national bishops' conferences,

• Voted overwhelmingly to urge the United States to "step back from the brink of war" with Iraq, arguing that circumstances did not justify the use of military force.

• Approved by a vote of 241-1 the statement, *A Place at the Table: A Catholic Recommitment to Overcome Poverty and Respect the Dignity of All God's Children*, recommitting themselves to fighting poverty here and abroad with the same urgency devoted to terrorism and other threats.

• Approved by a vote of 249-2 with one abstention, *When I Call for Help: A Pastoral Response to Domestic Violence Against Women*, an updated version of a 10-year-old pamphlet-sized document, with new statistics that reflect the scope of domestic violence against women and updated information on resources available to help them.

• Approved by a 250-0 vote, the brief statement, *A Matter of the Heart*, intended to mark the 30th anniversary of the Supreme Court's Roe v. Wade decision; the bishops pledged to continue working to overturn the decision, "no matter how long it make take, no matter the sacrifices required."

• Approved by a 254-1 vote *Encuentro and Mission: A Renewed Pastoral Framework for Hispanic Ministry*, outlining a new program to strengthen ministry among the 25 million Hispanic Catholics.

• Agreed to start a review process to assess the strengths and weaknesses of the 5-year-old Lectionary and approved for U.S. use two liturgical texts – the General Instruction of the Roman Missal and the Rites of Ordination of a Bishop, of Priests and of Deacons.

• Approved an updated preface for the 10th anniversary edition of the pastoral letter on stewardship and approved a pamphlet-sized statement intended for young people on the principles of stewardship.

• Ratified new national norms for church fund raising and the sale or lease of church-owned property, as well as a lengthy new handbook on diocesan financial concerns.

• Voted to authorize the bishops' Committee on Education to update a 1990 statement in support of Catholic elementary and secondary schools. The committee plans to bring a new statement on the topic to the bishops at their November 2004 meeting.

• Approved a $53.1 million USCCB budget for 2003; a 3.5 percent increase for 2004 in the assessment on dioceses to support the conference's work; 2003 plans for USCCB committees, offices and support units; goals and objectives for 2004-2006; and requests for budgetary exceptions in 2003. The exceptions included more than three million in spending from the bishops' General Reserve Fund for costs associated with the national Office for Child and Youth Protection, National Review Board and two studies mandated by the charter.

St. Louis, June 19-21, 2003

At their spring meeting in St. Louis, the U.S. bishops focused almost exclusively on the crisis of clergy sexual abuse of minors in the U.S. Church.

President's Address: Bishop Wilton D. Gregory of Belleville, IL, president of the USCCB, opened the Bishops' spring meeting on June 19 with a speech titled "A Catholic Response to Sexual Abuse: Confession, Contrition, Resolve."

Nuncio's Address: Archbishop Gabriel Montalvo, apostolic nuncio to the United States, addressed the bishops on June 19. Archbishop Montalvo stressed the need for bishops to stand united "as men of faith" during a period of genuine difficulty for the Church in the United States. He warned also that there are those in the United States willing to exploit the current crisis to damage the moral authority of the Church. Taking as the foundation of his address the words from the Book of Wisdom, "As gold in the furnace he proved them," the archbishop provided models in recent Church history for American Catholics, including several modern popes and holy women such as Mother Teresa of Calcutta and the American saints, St. Frances Cabrini and St. Katharine Drexel. "They show us, the archbishop declared, "that in the worst and most difficult of times they refused to sit idle or to retreat to a place of isolation or seclusion. Nor would they quit or give up the fight to which they had been called."

Agenda:

The gathering of bishops was marked by the decision to spend three of their five half-day sessions behind closed doors. One entire day of meetings behind closed doors was devoted to discussions of three of the highest-priority issues in the U.S. Church: the identity and spirituality of bishops and priests; declines in sacramental practice and the absence of adequate faith formation among U.S. Catholics; and challenges facing Catholic laity in today's culture. Following the closed-door meetings, reporters were briefed on the general nature and content of those sessions.

One of the objectives of the day of reflection was to implement a key first step in an on-going year and a half process launched last November to assess whether the bishops should convoke the first plenary council of the U.S. Church since 1884. During their closed meeting, the bishops also met with researchers and lay leaders appointed to watch over their efforts to combat sexual abuse of minors by clergy. The bishops also acted on the following issues:

• Approved by a voice vote Sept. 21 as Catholic Korean-American Day.

• Elected Bishop Thomas J. Tobin of Youngstown, OH, as chairman of the USCCB Committee on Pastoral Practices until November 2004.

• Granted approval for Cardinal Francis George, U.S. representative on the International Commission on English in the Liturgy, to vote in favor of sending revised ICEL statutes to the Holy See for approval when the episcopal board of ICEL holds its next meeting.

• Released a new study of the state of Catholic Native Americans. (*See* **Special Report**.)

• Heard a presentation on a 357-page *National Directory for Catechesis*, intended to replace the 1979 directory, *Sharing the Light of Faith*, taking into account many intervening developments, including the issuance of a new general directory on catechesis by the Holy See.

• Heard an opening presentation on a 217-page *National Directory for the Formation, Ministry and Life of Permanent Deacons in the United States*. Originally approved in 2000, the directives did not receive the required Vatican confirmation and have been revised to reflect the more than 200 Vatican observations on the earlier text. (Votes were taken on both directories, but as a number of bishops had left the meeting early, not enough votes were cast for an official decision. Bishops who did not cast a vote were then polled by mail to complete the balloting; passage of both documents was considered certain.)

• Voted to proceed with a pastoral letter on the theology of mission to promote mission awareness as an integral part of religious education in U.S. Catholic schools and parishes.

• Voted to proceed with a statement applying Catholic social teaching to agricultural issues in the face of emerging challenges of biotechnology, global trade, and the increasing concentration of agriculture in the hands of large corporations.

• Voted to proceed with a statement offering practical ways of improving collaboration between women and clergy in the Church.

• Voted to proceed with a "foundational document" on the formation and preparation of ecclesial lay ministers.

• Received a report from Archbishop Daniel M. Buechlein of Indianapolis on the chief concerns in the U.S. Church discussed by the bishops last November.

• Received a report from Auxiliary Bishop Joseph M. Sullivan of Brooklyn, NY, on the New Covenant initiative to foster greater collaboration among Catholic parishes, schools, health care institutions and social service agencies.

Doctrine of the Catholic Church

THE CATECHISM OF THE CATHOLIC CHURCH

(*By Russell Shaw.*)

"The Catechism of the Catholic Church ... is a statement of the Church's faith and of Catholic doctrine, attested to or illumined by Sacred Scripture, the Apostolic Tradition, and the Church's Magisterium. I declare it to be a sure norm for teaching the faith and thus a valid and legitimate instrument for ecclesial communion."

Thus Pope John Paul II in the Apostolic Constitution *Fidei Depositum* ("The Deposit of Faith") formally presented the first official catechism or compendium of doctrine for the universal Church to have been published since the 16th century.

Fidei Depositum is dated October 11, 1992, the 30th anniversary of the opening of the Second Vatican Council (1962-65), and that date is significant. The predecessor of the Catechism of the Catholic Church is the Roman Catechism or Catechism of the Council of Trent, which was published by Pope St. Pius V in 1566 following the great reforming council held from 1545 to 1563. As the Roman Catechism sets forth the doctrine of the Church in light of the Council of Trent, so the Catechism of the Catholic Church sets forth the Church's teaching against the background of Vatican Council II.

History of the Catechism

In development since 1986, the definitive text of the *Catechism of the Catholic Church* was officially approved by Pope John Paul on June 25, 1992, with December 8 the date of formal promulgation.

Nine separate drafts of the *Catechism* were prepared. The document was written in French. In November 1989, the commission of cardinals sent a draft text to all the bishops of the world asking for their comments and suggestions. Although this consultation produced a reaction generally favorable to the text, more than 24,000 individual amendments were submitted by the bishops, and these were reviewed by the commission, and helped to shape the further revision of the document.

The pope in *Fidei Depositum* described the *Catechism* as "a sure and authentic reference text" both for the teaching of Catholic doctrine and particularly for the preparation of local catechisms; he said the *Catechism* was presented to "all the Church's Pastors and the Christian faithful" with these ends in view. Other purposes mentioned included helping Catholics to deepen their knowledge of the faith, supporting ecumenical efforts by "showing carefully the content and wondrous harmony of the Catholic faith," and providing authoritative answers to anyone who wishes to know "what the Catholic Church believes."

Structure and Contents of the Catechism

The *Catechism* adopts the four-fold division of the *Roman Catechism*. The four parts or "pillars" deal with the Creed; the Sacred Liturgy, with special emphasis on the sacraments; the Christian way of life, analyzed according to the Ten Commandments; and prayer, considered in the framework of the petitions of the Our Father.

Describing this organizational scheme, Pope John Paul said: "The four parts are related one to another: the Christian mystery is the object of faith (first part); it is celebrated and communicated in liturgical actions (second part); it is present to enlighten and sustain the children of God in their actions (third part); it is the basis of our prayer, the privileged expression of which is the Our Father, and it represents the object of our supplication, our praise and our intercession (fourth part)."

The pope also stressed the Christocentric nature of Christian faith as it is presented in the *Catechism*. "In reading the *Catechism of the Catholic Church* we can perceive the wonderful unity of the mystery of God, his saving will, as well as the central place of Jesus Christ, the only-begotten Son of God, sent by the Father, made man in the womb of the Blessed Virgin Mary by the power of the Holy Spirit, to be our Savior. Having died and risen, Christ is always present in his Church, especially in the sacraments; he is the source of our faith, the model of Christian conduct, and the Teacher of our prayer."

The text of the *Catechism of the Catholic Church*, with extensive cross-references and sectional summaries, consists of 2,865 numbered paragraphs. Passages in large print set out its more substantive contents, while passages in small print provide background information and explanations; there are numerous cross-references in the margins directing readers to other passages that treat the same theme or related themes. Among the features of the *Catechism* are the "In Brief" sections found throughout, which sum up the teaching of the preceding unit.

Outline of the Catechism

Prologue (1-25). The nature of catechesis is described, along with the aim of the present *Catechism* and its intended readership, its structure, its use, and the desirability of adaptations for different cultures, age groups, etc.

Part One: The Profession of Faith (26-1065)

Section One discusses the nature of faith. "Faith is man's response to God, who reveals himself and gives himself to man, at the same time bringing man a superabundant light as he searches for the ultimate meaning of his life. Thus we shall consider first that search (Chapter One), then the divine Revelation by which God comes to meet man (Chapter Two), and finally the response of faith (Chapter Three)" (26). The topics discussed include knowledge of God; Divine Revelation and its transmission; Sacred Scripture; and faith as the human response to God. "We do not believe in formulas, but in those realities they express, which faith allows us to touch…. All the same, we do approach these realities with the help of formulations of the faith which permit us to express the faith and to hand it on, to celebrate it in community, to assimilate and live on it more and more" (170).

Section Two deals with the profession of Christian faith, with the treatment organized according to the articles of the Creed. The Creed used is the Apostles' Creed; its "great authority," says the *Catechism*, quoting St. Ambrose, arises from its being "the Creed of the Roman Church, the See of Peter, the first of the apostles" (194). Among the doctrines covered in the three chapters of this section are the Trinity, creation, the angels, the creation of man, original sin, the Incarnation, the virgin birth, redemption, the Resurrection of Christ, the work of the Holy Spirit, the Church, the hierarchical constitution of the Church, the communion of saints, the Virgin Mary as Mother of Christ and Mother of the Church, the resurrection of the dead, judgment, heaven, and hell. "[T]he Creed's final 'Amen' repeats and confirms its first words: 'I believe.' To believe is to say 'Amen' to God's words, promises and commandments; to entrust oneself completely to him who is the 'Amen' of infinite love and perfect faithfulness. The Christian's everyday life will then be the 'Amen' to the 'I believe' of our baptismal profession of faith" (1064).

Part Two: The Celebration of the Christian Mystery (1066-1690)

Section One considers the sacramental economy. It explains that in this present "age of the Church," begun on Pentecost, "Christ now lives and acts in his Church, in a new way appropriate to this new age. He acts through the sacraments in what the common Tradition of the East and the West calls 'the sacramental economy'… the communication (or 'dispensation') of the fruits of Christ's Paschal Mystery in the celebration of the Church's 'sacramental' liturgy" (1076). Topics treated here are the Paschal Mystery and its sacramental celebration.

Section Two covers the seven sacraments of the Church. "Christ instituted the sacraments of the new law…. The seven sacraments touch all the stages and all the important moments of Christian life: they give birth and increase, healing and mission to the Christian's life of faith. There is thus a certain resemblance between the stages of natural life and the stages of the spiritual life" (1210). The presentation is organized in four chapters. These are: the sacraments of

Christian initiation (Baptism, Confirmation, the Eucharist) in chapter one; the sacraments of healing (Penance and Reconciliation, the Anointing of the Sick) in chapter two; the "sacraments at the service of communion" (Holy Orders and Matrimony) in chapter three; and sacramentals and Christian funerals in chapter four.

Part Three: Life in Christ (1691-2557)

Section One is entitled "Man's Vocation: Life in the Spirit." Its three chapters discuss the dignity of the human person, the human community, and "God's Salvation: Law and Grace" (the moral law, grace and justification, the Church as teacher of moral truth). "Catechesis has to reveal in all clarity the joy and the demands of the way of Christ…. The first and last point of reference of this catechesis will always be Jesus Christ himself, who is 'they way, and the truth, and the life' " (1697-1698).

Section Two reflects on the contents of Christian moral life. The treatment is organized according to the Ten Commandments, with a chapter devoted to each commandment and its concrete applications. While the commandments admit of what is traditionally called light matter (venial sin), nevertheless, the text says: "Since they express man's fundamental duties towards God and towards his neighbor, the Ten Commandments reveal, in their primordial content, grave obligations. They are fundamentally immutable, and they oblige always and everywhere. No one can dispense from them. The Ten Commandments are engraved by God in the human heart" (2072).

Part Four: Christian Prayer (2558-2865)

Section One considers prayer in Christian life, underlining the relationship of this topic to the rest of the *Catechism*: "The Church professes this mystery [of faith] in the Apostles' Creed (Part One) and celebrates it in the sacramental liturgy (Part Two), so that the life of the faithful may be conformed to Christ in the Holy Spirit to the glory of God the Father (Part Three). This mystery, then, requires that the faithful believe in it, that they celebrate it, and that they live from it in a vital and personal relationship with the living and true God. This relationship is prayer" (2558). The section then discusses the "revelation of prayer" in the Old Testament and now in the age of the Church, the tradition of prayer, and the life of prayer (kinds of prayer, problems and perseverance in prayer).

Section Two presents an extended reflection on the Our Father, considered as the model of prayer. Quoting Tertullian, the *Catechism* says: "The Lord's Prayer 'is truly the summary of the whole Gospel.' 'Since the Lord … after handing over the practice of prayer, said elsewhere, 'Ask and you will receive,' and since everyone has petitions which are peculiar to his circumstances, the regular and appropriate prayer [the Lord's Prayer] is said first, as the foundation of further desires'" (2761).

Reception of the Catechism

Following the publication of the *Catechism of the Catholic Church*, Pope John Paul established an Interdicasterial Commission for the Catechism, under the chairmanship of Cardinal Ratzinger, responsible for overseeing translations of the volume and reviewing and approving suggested changes in the text. The commission approved the English translation of the *Catechism* in February 1994, and it was published on June 22 of that year — in the United States, under the auspices of the National Conference of Catholic Bishops.

Pope John Paul presented the *editio typica* or normative Latin version of the *Catechism* in a formal ceremony on September 8, 1997.

The following day, Cardinal Ratzinger presented the *editio typica* at a Vatican news conference. At the same time, he also introduced more than a hundred changes which had been approved for incorporation into the text. Most of the changes were of a minor, editorial nature. The most important was in paragraphs 2265-2267 of the *Catechism*, where the treatment of capi-

tal punishment had been strengthened to reflect the discussion of the same topic in Pope John Paul's 1995 encyclical letter *Evangelium Vitae* (*"The Gospel of Life"*).

In the United States, the National Conference of Catholic Bishops in 1994 established an Ad Hoc Committee to Oversee the Use of the Catechism. It has an office and staff at NCCB headquarters in Washington, D.C.. The committee reviews and approves materials that seek to make substantial direct use of the text of the *Catechism of the Catholic Church*, and also reviews catechetical series for their conformity with the *Catechism*. In addition, the committee was mandated to conduct a feasibility study of a national catechism or catechetical series for the United States.

DOGMATIC CONSTITUTION ON THE CHURCH — *LUMEN GENTIUM*

Following are excerpts from the first two chapters of the "Dogmatic Constitution on the Church" (*Lumen Gentium*) promulgated by the Second Vatican Council. They describe the relation of the Catholic Church to the Kingdom of God, the nature and foundation of the Church, the People of God, the necessity of membership and participation in the Church for salvation. Additional subjects in the constitution are treated in other Almanac entries.

I. MYSTERY OF THE CHURCH

By her relationship with Christ, the Church is a kind of sacrament or sign of intimate union with God, and of the unity of all mankind (No. 1).

He (the eternal Father) planned to assemble in the holy Church all those who would believe in Christ. Already from the beginning of the world the foreshadowing of the Church took place. She was prepared for in a remarkable way throughout the history of the people of Israel and by means of the Old Covenant. Established in the present era of time, the Church was made manifest by the outpouring of the Spirit. At the end of time she will achieve her glorious fulfillment. Then all just men from the time of Adam, "from Abel, the just one, to the last of the elect," will be gathered together with the Father in the universal Church (No. 2).

When the work which the Father had given the Son to do on earth (cf. Jn. 17:4) was accomplished, the Holy Spirit was sent on the day of Pentecost in order that he might forever sanctify the Church, and thus all believers would have access to the Father through Christ in the one Spirit (cf. Eph. 2:18).

The Spirit dwells in the Church and in the hearts of the faithful as in a temple (cf. 1 Cor. 3:16; 6:19)…. The Spirit guides the Church into the fullness of truth (cf. Jn. 16:13) and gives her a unity of fellowship and service. He furnishes and directs her with various gifts, both hierarchical and charismatic, and adorns her with the fruits of His grace (cf. Eph. 4:11-12; 1 Cor. 12:4; Gal. 5:22). By the power of the Gospel he makes the Church grow, perpetually renews her, and leads her to perfect union with her Spouse (No. 4).

Foundation of the Church

The mystery of the holy Church is manifest in her very foundation, for the Lord Jesus inaugurated her by preaching the Good News, that is, the coming of

God's Kingdom, which, for centuries, had been promised in the Scriptures…. In Christ's word, in his works, and in his presence this Kingdom reveals itself to men.

The miracles of Jesus also confirm that the Kingdom has already arrived on earth.

Before all things, however, the Kingdom is clearly visible in the very Person of Christ, Son of God and Son of Man.

When Jesus rose up again after suffering death on the cross for mankind, he manifested that he had been appointed Lord, Messiah, and Priest forever (cf. Acts 2:36; Heb. 5:6; 7:17-21), and he poured out on his disciples the Spirit promised by the Father (cf. Acts 2:33). The Church, consequently, equipped with the gifts of her Founder and faithfully guarding his precepts receives the mission to proclaim and to establish among all peoples the Kingdom of Christ and of God. She becomes on earth the initial budding forth of that Kingdom. While she slowly grows, the Church strains toward the consummation of the Kingdom and, with all her strength, hopes and desires to be united in glory with her King (No. 5).

Figures of the Church

In the Old Testament the revelation of the Kingdom had often been conveyed by figures of speech. In the same way the inner nature of the Church was now to be made known to us through various images.

The Church is a sheepfold … a flock … a tract of land to be cultivated, the field of God … his choice vineyard … the true vine is Christ … the edifice of God … the house of God … the holy temple (whose members are) living stones … this holy city … a bride … our Mother … the spotless spouse of the spotless Lamb … an exile (No. 6).

In the human nature which he united to himself, the Son of God redeemed man and transformed him into a new creation (cf. Gal. 6:15; 2 Cor. 5:17) by overcoming death through his own death and resurrection. By communicating his Spirit to his brothers, called together from all peoples, Christ made them mystically into his own body.

In that body, the life of Christ is poured into the believers, who, through the sacraments, are united in a hidden and real way to Christ who suffered and was glorified. Through baptism we are formed in the likeness of Christ.

Truly partaking of the body of the Lord in the breaking of the eucharistic bread, we are taken up into communion with him and with one another (No. 7).

One Body in Christ

As all the members of the human body, though they are many, form one body, so also are the faithful in Christ (cf. 1 Cor. 12:12). Also, in the building up of Christ's body there is a flourishing variety of members and functions. There is only one Spirit who distributes his different gifts for the welfare of the Church (cf. 1 Cor. 12:1-11). Among these gifts stands out the grace given to the apostles. To their authority, the Spirit himself subjected even those who were endowed with charisms (cf. 1 Cor. 14). The head of this body is Christ (No. 7).

Mystical Body of Christ

Christ, the one Mediator, established and ceaselessly sustains here on earth his holy Church, the community of faith, hope, and charity, as a visible structure. Through her he communicates truth and grace to all. But the society furnished with hierarchical agencies and the Mystical Body of Christ are not to be considered as two realities, nor are the visible assembly and the spiritual community, nor the earthly Church and the Church enriched with heavenly things. Rather they form one interlocked reality which is comprised of a divine and a human element. For this reason, this reality is compared to the mystery of the incarnate Word. Just as the assumed nature inseparably united to the divine Word serves him as a living instrument of salvation, so, in a similar way, does the communal structure of the Church serve Christ's Spirit, who vivifies it by way of building up the body (cf. Eph. 4:16).

This is the unique Church of Christ which in the Creed we avow as one, holy, catholic, and apostolic. After his Resurrection our Savior handed her over to Peter to be shepherded (Jn. 21:17), commissioning him and the other apostles to propagate and govern her (cf. Mt. 28:18, ff.). Her he erected for all ages as "the pillar and mainstay of the truth" (1 Tm. 3:15). This Church, constituted and organized in the world as a society, subsists in the Catholic Church, which is governed by the successor of Peter and by the bishops in union with that successor, although many elements of sanctification and of truth can be found outside of her visible structure. These elements, however, as gifts properly belonging to the Church of Christ, possess an inner dynamism toward Catholic unity.

The Church, embracing sinners in her bosom, is at the same time holy and always in need of being purified, and incessantly pursues the path of penance and renewal.

The Church, "like a pilgrim in a foreign land, presses forward, announcing the cross and death of the Lord until he comes" (cf. 1 Cor. 11:26) (No. 8).

II. THE PEOPLE OF GOD

At all times and among every people, God has given welcome to whosoever fears him and does what is right (cf. Acts 10:35). It has pleased God, however, to make men holy and save them not merely as individuals without any mutual bonds, but by making them into a single people, a people which acknowledges him in truth and serves him in holiness. He therefore chose the race of Israel as a people unto himself. With it he set up a covenant. Step by step he taught this people by manifesting in its history both himself and the decree of his will, and by making it holy unto himself. All these things, however, were done by way of preparation and as a figure of that new and perfect covenant which was to be ratified in Christ.

Christ instituted this New Covenant, that is to say, the New Testament, in his blood (cf. 1 Cor. 11:25), by calling together a people made up of Jew and Gentile, making them one, not according to the flesh but in the Spirit.

This was to be the new People of God ... reborn ... through the Word of the living God (cf. 1 Pt. 1:23). from water and the Holy Spirit (cf. Jn. 3:5-6) ... "a chosen race, a royal priesthood, a holy nation, a purchased people. You who in times past were not a people, but are now the People of God" (1 Pt. 2:9-10).

That messianic people has for its head Christ. Its law is the new commandment to love as Christ loved us (cf. Jn. 13:34). Its goal is the Kingdom of God, which has been begun by God himself on earth, and which is to be further extended until it is brought to perfection by him at the end of time.

This messianic people, although it does not actually include all men, and may more than once look like a small flock, is nonetheless a lasting and sure seed of unity, hope, and salvation for the whole human race. Established by Christ as a fellowship of life, charity, and truth, it is also used by him as an instrument for the redemption of all, and is sent forth into the whole world as the light of the world and the salt of the earth (cf. Mt. 5:13-16).

Israel according to the flesh ... was already called the Church of God (Neh. 13:1; cf. Nm. 20:4; Dt. 23:1, ff.). Likewise the new Israel ... is also called the Church of Christ (cf. Mt. 16:18). For he has bought it for himself with his blood (cf. Acts 20:28), has filled it with his Spirit, and provided it with those means which befit it as a visible and social unity. God has gathered together as one all those who in faith look upon Jesus as the author of salvation and the source of unity and peace, and has established them as the Church, that for each and all she may be the visible sacrament of this saving unity (No. 9).

Priesthood

The baptized, by regeneration and the anointing of the Holy Spirit, are consecrated into a holy priesthood.

[All members of the Church participate in the priesthood of Christ, through the common priesthood of the faithful. See **Priesthood of the Laity**.]

Though they differ from one another in essence and not only in degree, the common priesthood of the faithful and the ministerial or hierarchical priesthood are nonetheless interrelated. Each of them in its own special way is a participation in the one priesthood of Christ (No. 10).

It is through the sacraments and the exercise of the virtues that the sacred nature and organic structure of the priestly community is brought into operation (No. 11). (See Role of the Sacraments.)

Prophetic Office

The holy People of God shares also in Christ's prophetic office. It spreads abroad a living witness to him, especially by means of a life of faith and charity and by offering to God a sacrifice of praise…. The body of the faithful as a whole, anointed as they are by the Holy One (cf. Jn. 2:20, 27), cannot err in matters of belief. Thanks to a supernatural sense of faith which characterizes the People as a whole, it manifests this unerring quality when, "from the bishops down to the last member of the laity," it shows universal agreement in matters of faith and morals.

God's People accepts not the word of men but the very Word of God (cf. 1 Thes. 2:13). It clings without fail to the faith once delivered to the saints (cf. Jude 3), penetrates it more deeply by accurate insights, and applies it more thoroughly to life. All this it does under the lead of a sacred teaching authority to which it loyally defers.

It is not only through the sacraments and Church ministries that the same Holy Spirit sanctifies and leads the People of God…. He distributes special graces among the faithful of every rank. By these gifts he makes them fit and ready to undertake the various tasks or offices advantageous for the renewal and upbuilding of the Church. These charismatic gifts … are to be received with thanksgiving and consolation, for they are exceedingly suitable and useful for the needs of the Church.

Judgment as to their genuineness and proper use belongs to those who preside over the Church, and to whose special competence it belongs … to test all things and hold fast to that which is good (cf. 1 Thes. 5:12; 19-21) (No. 12).

All Are Called

All men are called to belong to the new People of God. Wherefore this People, while remaining one and unique, is to be spread throughout the whole world and must exist in all ages, so that the purpose of God's will may be fulfilled. In the beginning God made human nature one. After his children were scattered, he decreed that they should at length be united again (cf. Jn. 11:52). It was for this reason that God sent his Son…. that he might be Teacher, King, and Priest of all, the Head of the new and universal People of the sons of God. For this God finally sent his Son's Spirit as Lord and Lifegiver. He it is who, on behalf of the whole Church and each and every one of those who believe, is the principle of their coming together and remaining together in the teaching of the apostles and in fellowship, in the breaking of bread and in prayers (cf. Acts 2:42) (No. 13).

One People of God

It follows that among all the nations of earth there is but one People of God, which takes its citizens from every race, making them citizens of a Kingdom which is of a heavenly and not an earthly nature. For all the faithful scattered throughout the world are in communion with each other in the Holy Spirit…. the Church or People of God foster(s) and take(s) to herself, insofar as they are good, the ability, resources and customs of each people. Taking them to herself, she purifies, strengthens, and ennobles them…. This characteristic of universality which adorns the People of God is a gift from the Lord himself. By reason of it, the Catholic Church strives energetically and constantly to bring all humanity with all its riches back to Christ its Head in the unity of his Spirit.

In virtue of this catholicity each individual part of the Church contributes through its special gifts to the good of the other parts and of the whole Church. Thus through the common sharing of gifts. The whole and each of the parts receive increase.

All men are called to be part of this catholic unity of the People of God. And there belong to it or are related to it in various ways, the Catholic faithful as well as all who believe in Christ, and indeed the whole of mankind. For all men are called to salvation by the grace of God (No. 13).

The Catholic Church

This sacred Synod turns its attention first to the Catholic faithful. Basing itself upon sacred Scripture and tradition, it teaches that the Church is necessary for salvation. For Christ, made present to us in his Body, which is the Church, is the one Mediator and the unique Way of salvation. In explicit terms he himself affirmed the necessity of faith and baptism (cf. Mk. 16:16; Jn. 3:5) and thereby affirmed also the necessity of the Church, for through baptism as through a door men enter the Church. Whosoever, therefore, knowing that the Catholic Church was made necessary by God through Jesus Christ, would refuse to enter her or to remain in her could not be saved.

They are fully incorporated into the society of the Church who, possessing the Spirit of Christ, accept her entire system and all the means of salvation given to her, and through union with her visible structure are joined to Christ, who rules her through the Supreme Pontiff and the bishops. This joining is effected by the bonds of professed faith, of the sacraments, of ecclesiastical government, and of communion. He is not saved, however, who, though he is part of the body of the Church, does not persevere in charity. He remains indeed in the bosom of the Church, but only in a "bodily" manner and not "in his heart."

Catechumens who, moved by the Holy Spirit, seek with explicit intention to be incorporated into the Church, are by that very intention joined to her. Mother Church already embraces them as her own (No. 14).

Other Christians, The Unbaptized

The Church recognizes that in many ways she is linked with those who, being baptized, are honored with the name of Christian, though they do not profess the faith in its entirety or do not preserve unity of communion with the successor of Peter.

We can say that in some real way they are joined with us in the Holy Spirit, for to them also he gives his gifts and graces, and is thereby operative among them with his sanctifying power (No. 15).

Finally, those who have not yet received the Gospel are related in various ways to the People of God. In the first place there is the people to whom the covenants and the promises were given and from whom Christ was born according to the flesh (cf. Rom. 9:4-5). On account of their fathers, this people remains most dear to God, for God does not repent of the gifts he makes nor of the calls he issues (cf. Rom. 11:28-29).

But the plan of salvation also includes those who acknowledge the Creator. In the first place among these are the Moslems. Nor is God himself far distant from those who in shadows and images seek the unknown God.

Those also can attain to everlasting salvation who through no fault of their own do not know the Gospel of Christ or his Church, yet sincerely seek God and, moved by grace, strive by their deeds to do his will as it is known to them through the dictates of conscience. Nor does divine Providence deny the help necessary for salvation to those who, without blame on their part, have not yet arrived at an explicit knowledge of God, but who strive to live a good life, thanks to his grace. Whatever goodness or truth is found among them is looked upon by the Church as a preparation for the Gospel. She regards such qualities as given by him who enlightens all men so that they may finally have life. (No. 16).

THE POPE, TEACHING AUTHORITY, COLLEGIALITY

The Roman Pontiff — the successor of St. Peter as the bishop of Rome and head of the Church on earth — has full and supreme authority over the universal Church in matters pertaining to faith and morals (teaching authority), discipline and government (jurisdictional authority).

The primacy of the pope is real and supreme power. It is not merely a prerogative of honor — that is, of his being regarded as the first among equals. Neither does primacy imply that the pope is just the presiding officer of the collective body of bishops. The pope is the head of the Church.

Catholic belief in the primacy of the pope was stated in detail in the dogmatic constitution on the Church, *Pastor Aeternus*, approved in 1870 by the fourth session of the First Vatican Council. Some elaboration of the doctrine was made in the Dogmatic Constitution on the Church which was approved and promulgated by the Second Vatican Council Nov. 21, 1964. The entire body of teaching on the subject is based on Scripture and tradition and the centuries-long experience of the Church.

Infallibility

The essential points of doctrine concerning infallibility in the Church and the infallibility of the pope were stated by the Second Vatican Council in the Dogmatic Constitution on the Church, as follows:

"This infallibility with which the divine Redeemer willed his Church to be endowed in defining a doctrine of faith and morals extends as far as extends the deposit of divine revelation, which must be religiously guarded and faithfully expounded. This is the infallibility which the Roman Pontiff, the head of the college of bishops, enjoys in virtue of his office, when, as the supreme shepherd and teacher of all the faithful who confirms his brethren in their faith (cf. Lk. 22:32), he proclaims by a definitive act some doctrine of faith or morals. Therefore his definitions, of themselves, and not from the consent of the Church, are justly styled irreformable, for they are pronounced with the assistance of the Holy Spirit, an assistance promised to him in blessed Peter. Therefore they need no approval of others, nor do they allow an appeal to any other judgment. For then the Roman Pontiff is not pronouncing judgment as a private person. Rather, as the supreme teacher of the universal Church, as one in whom the charism of the infallibility of the Church herself is individually present, he is expounding or defending a doctrine of Catholic faith.

"The infallibility promised to the Church resides also in the body of bishops when that body exercises supreme teaching authority with the successor of Peter. To the resultant definitions the assent of the Church can never be wanting, on account of the activity of that same Holy Spirit, whereby the whole flock of Christ is preserved and progresses in unity of faith.

"But when either the Roman Pontiff or the body of bishops together with him defines a judgment, they pronounce it in accord with revelation itself. All are obliged to maintain and be ruled by this revelation, which, as written or preserved by tradition, is transmitted in its entirety through the legitimate succession of bishops and especially through the care of the Roman Pontiff himself.

"Under the guiding light of the Spirit of truth, revelation is thus religiously preserved and faithfully expounded in the Church. The Roman Pontiff and the bishops, in view of their office and of the importance of the matter, strive painstakingly and by appropriate means to inquire properly into that revelation and to give apt expression to its contents. But they do not allow that there could be any new public revelation pertaining to the divine deposit of faith" (No. 25).

Authentic Teaching

The pope rarely speaks *ex cathedra* — that is, "from the chair" of St. Peter — for the purpose of making an infallible pronouncement. More often and in various ways he states authentic teaching in line with Scripture, tradition, the living experience of the Church, and the whole analogy of faith. Of such teaching, the Second Vatican Council said in its Dogmatic Constitution on the Church (No. 25):

"Religious submission of will and of mind must be shown in a special way to the authentic teaching authority of the Roman Pontiff, even when he is not speaking *ex cathedra*. That is, it must be shown in such a way that his supreme magisterium is acknowledged with reverence, the judgments made by him are sincerely adhered to, according to his manifest mind and will. His mind and will in the matter may be known chiefly either from the character of the documents, from his frequent repetition of the same doctrine, or from his manner of speaking."

Bishops "are authentic teachers, that is, teachers endowed with the authority of Christ, who preach to the people committed to them the faith they must believe and put into practice. By the light of the Holy Spirit, they make that faith clear, bringing forth from the treasury of revelation new things and old (cf. Mt. 13:52), making faith bear fruit and vigilantly warding off any errors which threaten their flock (cf. 2 Tm. 4:1-4).

"Bishops, teaching in communion with the Roman Pontiff, are to be respected by all as witnesses to divine and Catholic truth. In matters of faith and morals, the bishops speak in the name of Christ and the faithful are to accept their teaching and adhere to it with a religious assent of soul."

Magisterium — Teaching Authority

Responsibility for teaching doctrine and judging

orthodoxy belongs to the official teaching authority of the Church.

This authority is personalized in the pope, the successor of St. Peter as head of the Church, and in the bishops together and in union with the pope, as it was originally committed to Peter and to the whole college of apostles under his leadership. They are the official teachers of the Church.

Others have auxiliary relationships with the magisterium: theologians, in the study and clarification of doctrine; teachers — priests, religious, lay persons — who cooperate with the pope and bishops in spreading knowledge of religious truth; the faithful, who by their sense of faith and personal witness contribute to the development of doctrine and the establishment of its relevance to life in the Church and the world.

The magisterium, Pope Paul VI noted in an address at a general audience Jan. 11, 1967, "is a subordinate and faithful echo and secure interpreter of the divine word." It does not reveal new truths, "nor is it superior to sacred Scripture." Its competence extends to the limits of divine revelation manifested in Scripture and tradition and the living experience of the Church, with respect to matters of faith and morals and related subjects. Official teaching in these areas is infallible when it is formally defined, for belief and acceptance by all members of the Church, by the pope, acting in the capacity of supreme shepherd of the flock of Christ; also, when doctrine is proposed and taught with moral unanimity of bishops with the pope in a solemn collegial manner, as in an ecumenical council, and/or in the ordinary course of events. Even when not infallibly defined, official teaching in the areas of faith and morals is authoritative and requires religious assent.

The teachings of the magisterium have been documented in creeds, formulas of faith, decrees and enactments of ecumenical and particular councils, various kinds of doctrinal statements, encyclical letters and other teaching instruments. They have also been incorporated into the liturgy, with the result that the law of prayer is said to be a law of belief.

Collegiality

The bishops of the Church, in union with the pope, have supreme teaching and pastoral authority over the whole Church in addition to the authority of office they have for their own dioceses.

This collegial authority is exercised in a solemn manner in an ecumenical council and can be exercised in other ways as well, "provided that the head of the college calls them to collegiate action, or at least so approves or freely accepts the united action of the dispersed bishops that it is made a true collegiate act."

This doctrine is grounded on the fact that: "Just as, by the Lord's will, St. Peter and the other apostles constituted one apostolic college, so in a similar way the Roman Pontiff as the successor of Peter, and the bishops as the successors of the apostles are joined together."

Doctrine on collegiality was stated by the Second Vatican Council in the Dogmatic Constitution on the Church (Nos. 22 and 23).

(For coverage of the *Role of Mary in the Mystery of Christ and the Church,* Chapter VIII, *Lumen Gentium,* see the section on the Blessed Virgin Mary.)

REVELATION

Following are excerpts from the "Dogmatic Constitution on Divine Revelation" (*Dei Verbum*) promulgated by the Second Vatican Council. They describe the nature and process of divine revelation, inspiration and interpretation of Scripture, the Old and New Testaments, and the role of Scripture in the life of the Church.

I. REVELATION ITSELF

God chose to reveal himself and to make known to us the hidden purpose of his will (cf. Eph. 1:9) by which through Christ, the Word made flesh, man has access to the Father in the Holy Spirit and comes to share in the divine nature (cf. Eph. 2:18; 2 Pt. 1:4). Through this revelation, therefore, the invisible God (cf. Col. 1:15; 1 Tm. 1:17). speaks to men as friends (cf. Ex. 33:11; Jn. 15:14-15) and lives among them (cf. Bar. 3:38) so that he may invite and take them into fellowship with himself. This plan of revelation is realized by deeds and words having an inner unity: the deeds wrought by God in the history of salvation manifest and confirm the teaching and realities signified by the words, while the words proclaim the deeds and clarify the mystery contained in them. By this revelation then, the deepest truth about God and the salvation of man is made clear to us in Christ, who is the Mediator and at the same time the fullness of all revelation (No. 2).

God from the start manifested himself to our first parents. Then after their fall his promise of redemption aroused in them the hope of being saved (cf. Gn. 3:15), and from that time on he ceaselessly kept the human race in his care, in order to give eternal life to those who perseveringly do good in search of salvation (cf. Rom. 2:6-7). He called Abraham in order to make of him a great nation (cf. Gn. 12:2). Through the patriarchs, and after them through Moses and the prophets, he taught this nation to acknowledge himself as the one living and true God and to wait for the Savior promised by him. In this manner he prepared the way for the Gospel down through the centuries (No. 3).

Revelation in Christ

Then, after speaking in many places and varied ways through the prophets, God "last of all in these days has spoken to us by his Son" (Heb. 1:1-2). Jesus perfected revelation by fulfilling it through his whole work of making himself present and manifesting himself: through his words and deeds, his signs and wonders, but especially through his death and glorious resurrection from the dead and final sending of the Spirit of truth. Moreover, he confirmed with divine testimony what revelation proclaimed: that God is with us to free us from the darkness of sin and death, and to raise us up to life eternal.

The Christian dispensation, therefore, as the new and definitive covenant, will never pass away, and we now await no further new public revelation before the glorious manifestation of our Lord Jesus Christ (cf. 1 Tm. 6:14; Ti. 2:13) (No. 4).

II. TRANSMISSION OF REVELATION

God has seen to it that what he had revealed for the salvation of all nations would abide perpetually in its full integrity and be handed on to all generations. Therefore Christ the Lord, in whom the full revelation of the supreme God is brought to completion (cf. 2 Cor. 1:20; 3:16; 4:6), commissioned the apostles to preach to all men that Gospel which is the source of all saving truth and moral teaching, and thus to impart to them divine gifts. This Gospel had been promised in former times through the prophets, and Christ himself fulfilled it and promulgated it with his own lips. This commission was faithfully fulfilled by the apostles who, by their oral preaching, by example, and by ordinances, handed on what they had received from Christ or what they had learned through the prompting of the Holy Spirit. The commission was fulfilled, too, by those apostles and apostolic men who under the inspiration of the same Holy Spirit committed the message of salvation to writing (No. 7).

Tradition

But in order to keep the Gospel forever whole and alive within the Church, the apostles left bishops as their successors, "handing over their own teaching role" to them. This sacred tradition, therefore, and sacred Scripture of both the Old and the New Testament are like a mirror in which the pilgrim Church on earth looks at God (No. 7).

The apostolic preaching, which is expressed in a special way in the inspired books, was to be preserved by a continuous succession of preachers until the end of time. Therefore the apostles, handing on what they themselves had received, warn the faithful to hold fast to the traditions which they have learned. Now what was handed on by the apostles includes everything which contributes to the holiness of life, and the increase in faith of the People of God; and so the Church, in her teaching, life, and worship, perpetuates and hands on to all generations all that she herself is, all that she believes (No. 8).

Development of Doctrine

This tradition which comes from the apostles develops in the Church with the help of the Holy Spirit. For there is a growth in the understanding of the realities and the words which have been handed down. This happens through the contemplation and study made by believers through the intimate understanding of spiritual things they experience, and through the preaching of those who have received through episcopal succession the sure gift of truth. For, as the centuries succeed one another, the Church constantly moves forward toward the fullness of divine truth until the words of God reach their complete fulfillment in her.

The words of the holy Fathers witness to the living presence of this tradition, whose wealth is poured into the practice and life of the believing and praying Church. Through the same tradition the Church's full canon of the sacred books is known, and the sacred writings themselves are more profoundly understood

and unceasingly made active in her; … and the Holy Spirit, through whom the living voice of the Gospel resounds in the Church, and through her, in the world, leads unto all truth those who believe and makes the word of Christ dwell abundantly in them (cf. Col. 3:16) (No. 8).

Tradition and Scripture

Hence there exist a close connection and communication between sacred tradition and sacred Scripture. For both of them, flowing from the same divine wellspring, in a certain way merge into a unity and tend toward the same end. For sacred Scripture is the word of God inasmuch as it is consigned to writing under the inspiration of the divine Spirit. To the successors of the apostles, sacred tradition hands on in its full purity God's word, which was entrusted to the apostles by Christ the Lord and the Holy Spirit. Thus, led by the light of the Spirit of truth, these successors can in their preaching preserve this word of God faithfully, explain it, and make it more widely known. Consequently, it is not from sacred Scripture alone that the Church draws her certainty about every thing which has been revealed. Therefore both sacred tradition and sacred Scripture are to be accepted and venerated with the same sense of devotion and reverence (No. 9).

Sacred tradition and sacred Scripture form one sacred deposit of the word of God, which is committed to the Church (No. 10).

Teaching Authority of Church

The task of authentically interpreting the word of God, whether written or handed on, has been entrusted exclusively to the living teaching office of the Church, whose authority is exercised in the name of Jesus Christ. This teaching office is not above the word of God, but serves it, teaching only what has been handed on … it draws from this one deposit of faith everything which it presents for belief as divinely revealed.

It is clear, therefore, that sacred tradition, sacred Scripture, and the teaching authority of the Church … are so linked and joined together that one cannot stand without the others, and that all together and each in its own way under the action of the one Holy Spirit contribute effectively to the salvation of souls (No. 10).

III. INSPIRATION, INTERPRETATION

Those revealed realities contained and presented in sacred Scripture have been committed to writing under the inspiration of the Holy Spirit. Holy Mother Church, relying on the belief of the apostles, holds that the books of both the Old and New Testament in their entirety, with all their parts, are sacred and canonical because, having been written under the inspiration of the Holy Spirit (cf. Jn. 20:31; 2 Tm. 3:16; 2 Pt. 1:19-21; 3:15-16) they have God as their author and have been handed on as such to the Church herself. In composing the sacred books, God chose men and, while employed by him, they made use of their powers and abilities, so that, with him acting in them and through them, they, as true authors, consigned to writing everything and only those things which he wanted (No. 11).

Inerrancy

Therefore, since everything asserted by the inspired authors or sacred writers must be held to be asserted by the Holy Spirit, it follows that the books of Scripture must be acknowledged as teaching firmly, faithfully, and without error that truth which God wanted put into the sacred writings for the sake of our salvation. Therefore "all Scripture is inspired by God and useful for teaching, for reproving, for correcting, for instruction in justice; that the man of God may be perfect, equipped for every good work" (2 Tm. 3:16-17) (No. 11).

Literary Forms

However, since God speaks in sacred Scripture through men in human fashion, the interpreter of sacred Scripture, in order to see clearly what God wanted to communicate to us, should carefully investigate what meaning the sacred writers really intended, and what God wanted to manifest by means of their words.

The interpreter must investigate what meaning the sacred writer intended to express and actually expressed in particular circumstances as he used contemporary literary forms in accordance with the situation of his own time and culture. For the correct understanding of what the sacred author wanted to assert, due attention must be paid to the customary and characteristic styles of perceiving, speaking, and narrating which prevailed at the time of the sacred writer, and to the customs men normally followed at that period in their everyday dealings with one another (No. 12).

Analogy of Faith

No less serious attention must be given to the content and unity of the whole of Scripture, if the meaning of the sacred texts is to be correctly brought to light. The living tradition of the whole Church must be taken into account along with the harmony which exists between elements of the faith. All of what has been said about the way of interpreting Scripture is subject finally to the judgment of the Church, which carries out the divine commission and ministry of guarding and interpreting the word of God (No. 12).

IV. THE OLD TESTAMENT

In carefully planning and preparing the salvation of the whole human race, the God of supreme love, by a special dispensation, chose for himself a people to whom he might entrust his promises. First he entered into a covenant with Abraham (cf. Gn. 15:18) and, through Moses, with the people of Israel (cf. Ex. 24:8). To this people which he had acquired for himself, he so manifested himself through words and deeds as the one true and living God that Israel came to know by experience the ways of God with men. The plan of salvation, foretold by the sacred authors, recounted and explained by them, is found as the true word of God in the books of the Old Testament: these books, therefore, written under divine inspiration, remain permanently valuable (No. 14).

Principal Purpose

The principal purpose to which the plan of the Old Covenant was directed was to prepare for the coming both of Christ, the universal Redeemer, and of the messianic Kingdom. Now the books of the Old Testament, in accordance with the state of mankind before the time of salvation established by Christ, reveal to all men the knowledge of God and of man and the ways in which God deals with men. These books show us true divine pedagogy (No. 15).

The books of the Old Testament with all their parts, caught up into the proclamation of the Gospel, acquire and show forth their full meaning in the New Testament (cf. Mt. 5:17; Lk. 24:27; Rom. 16:25-26; 2 Cor. 3:14-16) and in turn shed light on it and explain it (No. 16).

V. THE NEW TESTAMENT

The word of God is set forth and shows its power in a most excellent way in the writings of the New Testament. For when the fullness of time arrived (cf. Gal. 4:4), the Word was made flesh and dwelt among us in the fullness of grace and truth (cf. Jn. 12:32). This mystery had not been manifested to other generations as it was now revealed to his holy apostles and prophets in the Holy Spirit (cf. Eph. 3:4-6), so that they might preach the Gospel, stir up faith in Jesus, Christ and Lord, and gather the Church together. To these realities, the writings of the New Testament stand as a perpetual and divine witness (No. 17).

The Gospels and Other Writings

The Gospels have a special preeminence for they are the principal witness of the life and teaching of the incarnate Word, our Savior.

The Church has always and everywhere held and continues to hold that the four Gospels are of apostolic origin. For what the apostles preached afterwards they themselves and apostolic men, under the inspiration of the divine Spirit, handed on to us in writing: the foundation of faith, namely, the fourfold Gospel, according to Matthew, Mark, Luke, and John (No. 18).

The four Gospels ... whose historical character the Church unhesitatingly asserts, faithfully hand on what Jesus Christ, while living among men, really did and taught for their eternal salvation until the day he was taken up into heaven (see Acts 1:1-2). Indeed, after the ascension of the Lord the apostles handed on to their hearers what he had said and done. The sacred authors wrote the four Gospels, selecting some things from the many which had been handed on by word of mouth or in writing, reducing some of them to a synthesis, explicating some things in view of the situation of their churches, and preserving the form of proclamation but always in such fashion that they told us the honest truth about Jesus. For their intention in writing was that we might know "the truth" concerning those matters about which we have been instructed (cf. Lk. 1:2-4) (No. 19).

Besides the four Gospels, the canon of the New Testament also contains the Epistles of St. Paul and other apostolic writings, composed under the inspiration of the Holy Spirit. In these writings those matters which concern Christ the Lord are confirmed, his true teaching is more and more fully stated, the saving power of the divine work of Christ is preached, the story is told of the beginnings of the Church and her marvelous growth, and her glorious fulfillment is foretold (No. 20).

SCRIPTURE IN CHURCH LIFE

The Church has always venerated the divine Scriptures just as she venerates the body of the Lord. She has always regarded the Scriptures together with sacred tradition as the supreme rule of faith, and will ever do so. For, inspired by God and committed once and for all to writing, they impart the word of God himself without change, and make the voice of the Holy Spirit resound in the words of the prophets and apostles. Therefore, like the Christian religion itself, all the preaching of the Church must be nourished and ruled by sacred Scripture (No. 21).

Easy access to sacred Scripture should be provided for all the Christian faithful. That is why the Church from the very beginning accepted as her own that very ancient Greek translation of the Old Testament which is named after seventy men (the Septuagint); and she has always given a place of honor to other translations, Eastern and Latin, especially the one known as the Vulgate. But since the word of God should be available at all times, the Church with maternal concern sees to it that suitable and correct translations are made into different languages, especially from the original texts of the sacred books. And if, given the opportunity and the approval of Church authority, these translations are produced in cooperation with the separated brethren as well, all Christians will be able to use them (No. 22).

Biblical Studies, Theology

The constitution encouraged the development and progress of biblical studies "under the watchful care of the sacred teaching office of the Church."

It also noted: "Sacred theology rests on the written word of God, together with sacred tradition, as its primary and perpetual foundation," and that "the study of the sacred page is, as it were, the soul of sacred theology" (Nos. 23, 24).

(*See* separate article, **Interpretation of the Bible**.)

THE BIBLE

The Canon of the Bible is the Church's official list of sacred writings. These works, written by men under the inspiration of the Holy Spirit, contain divine revelation and, in conjunction with the tradition and teaching authority of the Church, constitute the rule of Catholic faith. The Canon was fixed and determined by the tradition and teaching authority of the Church.

The Catholic Canon

The Old Testament Canon of 46 books is as follows.
• **The Pentateuch**, the first five books: Genesis (Gn.), Exodus (Ex.), Leviticus (Lv.), Numbers (Nm.), Deuteronomy (Dt.).
• **Historical Books**: Joshua (Jos.), Judges (Jgs.), Ruth (Ru.) 1 and 2 Samuel (Sm.), 1 and 2 Kings (Kgs.), 1 and 2 Chronicles (Chr.), Ezra (Ezr.), Nehemiah (Neh.), Tobit (Tb.), Judith (Jdt.), Esther (Est.), 1 and 2 Maccabees (Mc.).
• **Wisdom Books**: Job (Jb.), Psalms (Ps.), Proverbs (Prv.), Ecclesiastes (Eccl.), Song of Songs (Song), Wisdom (Wis.), Sirach (Sir.).
• **The Prophets**: Isaiah (Is.), Jeremiah (Jer.), Lamentations (Lam.), Baruch (Bar.), Ezekiel (Ez.), Daniel (Dn.), Hosea (Hos.), Joel (Jl.), Amos (Am.), Obadiah (Ob.), Jonah (Jon.), Micah (Mi.), Nahum (Na.), Habakkuk (Hb.), Zephaniah (Zep.), Haggai (Hg.), Zechariah (Zec.) Malachi (Mal.).
The New Testament Canon of 27 books is as follows.
• **The Gospels**: Matthew (Mt.), Mark (Mk.), Luke (Lk.), John (Jn.).
• **The Acts of the Apostles** (Acts).
• **The Pauline Letters**: Romans (Rom.), 1 and 2 Corinthians (Cor.), Galatians (Gal.), Ephesians (Eph.), Philippians (Phil.), Colossians (Col.), 1 and 2 Thessalonians (Thes.) 1 and 2 Timothy (Tm.), Titus (Ti.), Philemon (Phlm.), Hebrews (Heb.).
• **The Catholic Letters**: James (Jas.), 1 and 2 Peter (Pt.), 1, 2, and 3 John (Jn.), Jude (Jude).
• **Revelation** (Rv.).

Developments

The Canon of the Old Testament was firm by the fifth century despite some questioning by scholars. It was stated by a council held at Rome in 382, by African councils held in Hippo in 393 and in Carthage in 397 and 419, and by Innocent I in 405.

All of the New Testament books were generally known and most of them were acknowledged as inspired by the end of the second century. The Muratorian Fragment, dating from about 200, listed most of the books recognized as canonical in later decrees. Prior to the end of the fourth century, however, there was controversy over the inspired character of several works — the Letter to the Hebrews, James, Jude, 2 Peter, 2 and 3 John and Revelation. Controversy ended in the fourth century and these books, along with those about which there was no dispute, were enumerated in the canon stated by the councils of Hippo and Carthage and affirmed by Innocent I in 405.

The Canon of the Bible was solemnly defined by the Council of Trent in the dogmatic decree *De Canonicis Scripturis*, Apr. 8, 1546.

Hebrew and Other Canons

The Hebrew Canon of sacred writings was fixed by tradition and the consensus of rabbis, probably by about 100 A.D. by the Synod or Council of Jamnia and certainly by the end of the second or early in the third century. It consists of the following works in three categories.
• **The Law** (Torah): the five books of Moses: Genesis, Exodus, Leviticus, Numbers, Deuteronomy.
• **The Prophets**: former prophets — Joshua, Judges, 1 and 2 Samuel, 1 and 2 Kings; latter prophets — Isaiah, Jeremiah, Ezekiel, and 12 minor prophets (Hosea, Joel, Amos, Obadiah, Jonah, Micah, Nahum, Habakkuk, Zephaniah, Haggai, Zechariah, Malachi).
• **The Writings**: 1 and 2 Chronicles, Ezra, Nehemiah, Job, Psalms, Proverbs, Ecclesiastes, Song of Songs, Ruth, Esther, Daniel.

This Canon, embodying the tradition and practice of the Palestine community, did not include a number of works contained in the Alexandrian version of sacred writings translated into Greek between 250 and 100 B.C. and in use by Greek-speaking Jews of the Dispersion (outside Palestine). The rejected works, called apocrypha and not regarded as sacred, are: Tobit, Judith, Wisdom, Sirach, Baruch, 1 and 2 Maccabees, the last six chapters of Esther and three passages of Daniel (3:24-90; 13; 14). These books have also been rejected from the Protestant Canon, although they are included in Bibles under the heading "Apocrypha."

The aforementioned books are held to be inspired and sacred by the Catholic Church. In Catholic usage, they are called deuterocanonical because they were under discussion for some time before questions about their canonicity were settled. Books regarded as canonical with little or no debate were called protocanonical. The status of both categories of books is the same in the Catholic Bible.

The Protestant Canon of the Old Testament is the same as the Hebrew.

The Old Testament Canon of some separated Eastern churches differs from the Catholic Canon. Christians are in agreement on the Canon of the New Testament.

Languages

Hebrew, Aramaic and Greek were the original languages of the Bible. Most of the Old Testament books were written in Hebrew. Portions of Daniel, Ezra, Jeremiah, Esther, and probably the books of Tobit and Judith were written in Aramaic. The Book of Wisdom, 2 Maccabees and all the books of the New Testament were written in Greek.

Manuscripts and Versions

The original writings of the inspired authors have been lost. The Bible has been transmitted through ancient copies called manuscripts and through translations or versions.

Authoritative Greek manuscripts include the Sinaitic and Vatican manuscripts of the fourth century and the Alexandrine of the fifth century A.D. The Septuagint and Vulgate translations are in a class by themselves.

The Septuagint version, a Greek translation of the Old Testament for Greek-speaking Jews, was begun about 250 and completed about 100 B.C. The work of several Jewish translators at Alexandria, it differed from the Hebrew Bible in the arrangement of books and included several, later called deuterocanonical, which were not acknowledged as sacred by the community in Palestine.

The Vulgate was a Latin version of the Old and New Testaments produced from the original languages by St. Jerome from about 383 to 404. It became the most widely used Latin text for centuries and was regarded as basic long before the Council of Trent designated it as authentic and suitable for use in public reading, controversy, preaching and teaching. Because of its authoritative character, it became the basis for many translations into other languages. A critical revision was completed by a pontifical commission in 1977.

Hebrew and Aramaic manuscripts of great antiquity and value have figured more significantly than before in recent scriptural work by Catholic scholars, especially since their use was strongly encouraged, if not mandated, in 1943 by Pius XII in the encyclical *Divino Afflante Spiritu.*

The English translation of the Bible in general use among Catholics until well into the 20th century was the Douay-Rheims, so-called because of the places where it was prepared and published, the New Testament at Rheims in 1582 and the Old Testament at Douay in 1609. The translation was made from the Vulgate text. As revised and issued by Bishop Richard Challoner in 1749 and 1750, it became the standard Catholic English version for about 200 years.

A revision of the Challoner New Testament, made on the basis of the Vulgate text by scholars of the Catholic Biblical Association of America, was published in 1941 in the United States under the sponsorship of the Episcopal Committee of the Confraternity of Christian Doctrine.

New American Bible

A new translation of the entire Bible, the first ever made directly into English from the original languages under Catholic auspices, was projected in 1944 and completed in the fall of 1970 with publication of the *New American Bible.* The Episcopal Committee of the Confraternity of Christian Doctrine sponsored the NAB. The translators were members of the Catholic Biblical Association of America and scholars of other faiths. The typical edition was produced by St. Anthony Guild Press, Paterson, N.J.

The *Jerusalem Bible,* published by Doubleday & Co., Inc., is an English translation of a French version based on the original languages.

Biblical translations approved for liturgical use by the National Conference of Catholic Bishops and the Holy See are the *New American Bible* (1970 edition), the *Revised Standard Version-Catholic Edition,* and the *Jerusalem Bible* (1966).

The Protestant counterpart of the *Douay-Rheims Bible* was the *King James Bible,* called the *Authorized Version* in England. Originally published in 1611 and in general use for more than three centuries, its several revisions include the *Revised Standard Version* and the *New Revised Standard Version.*

Biblical Federation

In November 1966, Pope Paul VI commissioned the Secretariat for Promoting Christian Unity to start work for the widest possible distribution of the Bible and to coordinate endeavors toward the production of Catholic-Protestant Bibles in all languages.

The World Catholic Federation for the Biblical Apostolate, established in 1969, sponsors a program designed to create greater awareness among Catholics of the Bible and its use in everyday life.

The U. S. Center for the Catholic Biblical Apostolate is related to the Secretariat for Pastoral Research and Practices, National Conference of Catholic Bishops, 3211 Fourth St. N.E., Washington, D.C. 20017.

APOCRYPHA

In Catholic usage, Apocrypha are books which have some resemblance to the canonical books in subject matter and title but which have not been recognized as canonical by the Church. They are characterized by a false claim to divine authority; extravagant accounts of events and miracles alleged to be supplemental revelation; material favoring heresy (especially in "New Testament" apocrypha); minimal, if any, historical value. Among examples of this type of literature itemized by J. McKenzie, S.J., in *Dictionary of the Bible* are: the Books of Adam and Eve, Martyrdom of Isaiah, Testament of the Patriarchs, Assumption of Moses, Sibylline Oracles; Gospel of James, Gospel of Thomas, Arabic Gospel of the Infancy, History of Joseph the Carpenter; Acts of John, Acts of

Paul, Acts of Peter, Acts of Andrew, and numerous epistles.

Books of this type are called "pseudepigrapha" by Protestants.

In Protestant usage, some books of the Catholic Bible (deuterocanonical) are called apocrypha because their inspired character is rejected.

DEAD SEA SCROLLS

The Qumran Scrolls, popularly called the Dead Sea Scrolls, are a collection of manuscripts, all but one of them in Hebrew, found since 1947 in caves in the Desert of Juda west of the Dead Sea.

Among the findings were a complete text of Isaiah dating from the second century, more or less extensive fragments of other Old Testament texts (including the deuterocanonical Tobit), and a commentary on Habakkuk. Until the discovery of these materials, the oldest known Hebrew manuscripts were from the 10th century A.D.

Also found were messianic and apocalyptic texts, and other writings describing the beliefs and practices of the Essenes, a rigoristic Jewish sect.

The scrolls, dating from about the first century before and after Christ, are important sources of information about Hebrew literature, Jewish history during the period between the Old and New Testaments, and the history of Old Testament texts. They established the fact that the Hebrew text of the Old Testament was fixed before the beginning of the Christian era and have had definite effects in recent critical studies and translations of the Old Testament. Together with other scrolls found at Masada, they are still the subject of intensive study.

BOOKS OF THE BIBLE

OLD TESTAMENT BOOKS

Pentateuch

The Pentateuch is the collective title of the first five books of the Bible. Substantially, they identify the Israelites as Yahweh's Chosen People, cover their history from Egypt to the threshold of the Promised Land, contain the Mosaic Law and Covenant, and disclose the promise of salvation to come. Principal themes concern the divine promise of salvation, Yahweh's fidelity and the Covenant. Work on the composition of the Pentateuch was completed in the sixth century.

Genesis: The book of origins, according to its title in the Septuagint. In two parts, covers: religious prehistory, including accounts of the origin of the world and man, the original state of innocence and the fall, the promise of salvation, patriarchs before and after the deluge, the Tower of Babel narrative, genealogies (first 11 chapters); the covenant with Abraham and patriarchal history from Abraham to Joseph (balance of the 50 chapters). Significant are the themes of Yahweh's universal sovereignty and mercy.

Exodus: Named with the Greek word for departure, is a religious epic which describes the oppression of the 12 tribes in Egypt and their departure, liberation or passover therefrom under the leadership of Moses; Yahweh's establishment of the covenant with them, making them his chosen people, through the mediation of Moses at Mt. Sinai; instructions concerning the tabernacle, the sanctuary and Ark of the Covenant; the institution of the priesthood. The book is significant because of its theology of liberation and redemption. In Christian interpretation, the Exodus is a figure of baptism.

Leviticus: Mainly legislative in theme and purpose, contains laws regarding sacrifices, ceremonies of ordination and the priesthood of Aaron, legal purity, the holiness code, atonement, the redemption of offerings and other subjects. Summarily, Levitical laws provided directives for all aspects of religious observance and for the manner in which the Israelites were to conduct themselves with respect to Yahweh and each other. Leviticus was the liturgical handbook of the priesthood.

Numbers: Taking its name from censuses recounted at the beginning and near the end, is a continuation of Exodus. It combines narrative of the Israelites' desert pilgrimage from Sinai to the border of Canaan with laws related to and expansive of those in Leviticus.

Deuteronomy: The concluding book of the Pentateuch, recapitulates, in the form of a testament of Moses, the Law and much of the desert history of the Israelites; enjoins fidelity to the Law as the key to good or bad fortune for the people; gives an account of the commissioning of Joshua as the successor of Moses. Notable themes concern the election of Israel by Yahweh, observance of the Law, prohibitions against the worship of foreign gods, worship of and confidence in Yahweh, the power of Yahweh in nature. The Deuteronomic Code or motif, embodying all of these elements, was the norm for interpreting Israelite history.

Joshua, Judges, Ruth

Joshua: Records the fulfillment of Yahweh's promise to the Israelites in their conquest, occupation and division of Canaan under the leadership of Joshua. It also contains an account of the return of Transjordanian Israelites and of a renewal of the Covenant. It was redacted in final form probably in the sixth century or later.

Judges: Records the actions of charismatic leaders, called judges, of the tribes of Israel between the death of Joshua and the time of Samuel, and a crisis of idolatry among the people. The basic themes are sin and punishment, repentance and deliverance; its purpose was in line with the Deuteronomic motif, that the fortunes of the Israelites were related to their observance or non-observance of the Law and the Covenant. It was redacted in final form probably in the sixth century.

Ruth: Named for the Gentile (Moabite) woman who, through marriage with Boaz, became an Israelite and an ancestress of David (her son, Obed, became his grandfather). Themes are filial piety, faith and trust in Yahweh, the universality of messianic salvation. Dates ranging from c. 950 to the seventh century have been assigned to the origin of the book, whose author is unknown.

Historical Books

These books, while they contain a great deal of factual material, are unique in their preoccupation with presenting and interpreting it, in the Deuteronomic manner, in primary relation to the Covenant on which the nation of Israel was founded and in accordance with which community and personal life were judged.

The books are: Samuel 1 and 2, from the end of Judges (c. 1020) to the end of David's reign (c. 961); Kings 1 and 2, from the last days of David to the start of the Babylonian exile and the destruction of the Temple (587); Chronicles 1 and 2, from the reign of Saul (c. 1020-1000) to the return of the people from the exile (538); Ezra and Nehemiah, covering the reorganization of the Jewish community after the exile (458-397); Maccabees 1 and 2, recounting the struggle against attempted suppression of Judaism (168-142).

Three of the books listed below — Tobit, Judith, and Esther — are categorized as religious novels.

Samuel 1 and 2: A single work in concept and contents, containing episodic history of the last two Judges, Eli and Samuel, the establishment and rule of the monarchy under Saul and David, and the political consequences of David's rule. The royal messianic dynasty of David was the subject of Nathan's oracle in 2 Sm. 7. The books were edited in final form probably late in the seventh century or during the exile.

Kings 1 and 2: Cover the last days of David and the career of Solomon, including the building of the Temple and the history of the kingdom during his reign; stories of the prophets Elijah and Elisha; the history of the divided kingdom to the fall of Israel in the North (721) and the fall of Judah in the South (587), the destruction of Jerusalem and the Temple. They reflect the Deuteronomic motif in attributing the downfall of the people to corruption of belief and practice in public and private life. They were completed probably in the sixth century.

Chronicles 1 and 2: A collection of historical traditions interpreted in such a way as to present an ideal picture of one people governed by divine law and united in one Temple worship of the one true God. Contents include genealogical tables from Adam to David, the careers of David and Solomon, coverage of the kingdom of Judah to the exile, and the decree of Cyrus permitting the return of the people and rebuilding of Jerusalem. Both are related to and were written about 400 by the same author, the Chronicler, who composed Ezra and Nehemiah.

Ezra and Nehemiah: A running account of the return of the people to their homeland after the exile and of practical efforts, under the leadership of Ezra and Nehemiah, to restore and reorganize the religious and political community on the basis of Israelite traditions, divine worship and observance of the Law. Events of great significance were the building of the second Temple, the building of a wall around Jerusalem and the proclamation of the Law by Ezra. This restored community was the start of Judaism. Both are related to and were written about 400 by the same author, the Chronicler, who composed Chronicles 1 and 2.

Tobit: Written in the literary form of a novel and having greater resemblance to wisdom than to historical literature, narrates the personal history of Tobit, a devout and charitable Jew in exile, and persons connected with him, viz., his son Tobiah, his kinsman Raguel and Raguel's daughter Sarah. Its purpose was to teach people how to be good Jews. One of its principal themes is patience under trial, with trust in divine Providence which is symbolized by the presence and action of the angel Raphael. It was written about 200.

Judith: Recounts, in the literary form of a historical novel or romance, the preservation of the Israelites from conquest and ruin through the action of Judith. The essential themes are trust in God for deliverance from danger and emphasis on observance of the Law. It was written probably during the Maccabean period.

Esther: Relates, in the literary form of a historical novel or romance, the manner in which Jews in Persia were saved from annihilation through the central role played by Esther, the Jewish wife of Ahasuerus; a fact commemorated by the Jewish feast of Purim. Like Judith, it has trust in Divine Providence as its theme and indicates that God's saving will is sometimes realized by persons acting in unlikely ways. It may have been written near the end of the fourth century.

Maccabees 1 and 2: While related to some extent because of common subject matter, are quite different from each other.

The first book recounts the background and events of the 40-year (175-135) struggle for religious and political freedom led by Judas Maccabaeus and his brothers against the Hellenist Seleucid kings and some Hellenophiles among the Jews. Victory was symbolized by the rededication of the Temple. Against the background of opposition between Jews and Gentiles, the author equated the survival of belief in the one true God with survival of the Jewish people, thus identifying religion with patriotism. It was written probably near the year 100.

The second book supplements the first to some extent, covering and giving a theological interpretation to events from 180 to 162. It explains the feast of the dedication of the Temple, a key event in the survival of Judaism which is commemorated in the feast of Hanukkah; stresses the primacy of God's action in the struggle for survival; and indicates belief in an afterlife and the resurrection of the body. It was completed probably about 124.

Wisdom Books

With the exceptions of Psalms and the Song of Songs, the titles listed under this heading are called "wisdom books" because their purpose was to formulate the fruits of human experience in the context of meditation on sacred Scripture and to present them as an aid toward understanding the problems of life. Hebrew wisdom literature was distinctive from pagan literature of the same type, but it had limitations; these were overcome in the New Testament, which added the dimensions of the New Covenant to those of the Old. Solomon was regarded as the archetype of the wise man.

Job: A dramatic, didactic poem consisting mainly of several dialogues between Job and his friends concerning the mystery involved in the coexistence of the just God, evil and the suffering of the just. It describes an innocent man's experience of suffering and conveys the truth that faith in and submission to God rather than complete understanding, which is impossible, make the experience bearable; also, that the justice of God cannot be defended by affirming that it is realized in this world. Of unknown authorship, it was composed between the seventh and fifth centuries.

Psalms: A collection of 150 religious songs or lyrics reflecting Israelite belief and piety dating from the time of the monarchy to the post-Exilic period, a span of well over 500 years. The psalms, which are a compendium of Old Testament theology, were used in the temple liturgy and for other occasions. They were of several types suitable for the king, hymns, lamentations, expressions of confidence and thanksgiving, prophecy, historical meditation and reflection, and the statement of wisdom. About one-half of them are attributed to David; many were composed by unknown authors.

Proverbs: The oldest book of the wisdom type in the Bible, consisting of collections of sayings attributed to Solomon and other persons regarding a wide variety of subjects including wisdom and its nature, rules of conduct, duties with respect to one's neighbor, the conduct of daily affairs. It reveals many details of Hebrew life. Its nucleus dates from the period before the exile. The extant form of the book dates probably from the end of the fifth century.

Ecclesiastes: A treatise about many subjects whose unifying theme is the vanity of strictly human efforts and accomplishments with respect to the achievement of lasting happiness; the only things which are not vain are fear of the Lord and observance of his commandments. The pessimistic tone of the book is due to the absence of a concept of afterlife. It was written by an unknown author probably in the third century.

Song of Songs: A collection of love lyrics reflecting various themes, including the love of God for Israel and the celebration of ideal love and fidelity between man and woman. It was written by an unknown author after the exile.

Wisdom: Deals with many subjects including the reward of justice; praise of wisdom, a gift of Yahweh proceeding from belief in him and the practice of his Law; the part played by him in the history of his people, especially in their liberation from Egypt; the folly and shame of idolatry. Its contents are taken from the whole sacred literature of the Jews and represent a distillation of its wisdom based on the law, beliefs and traditions of Israel. The last of the Old Testament books, it was written in the early part of the first century before Christ by a member of the Jewish community at Alexandria.

Sirach: Resembling Proverbs, is a collection of sayings handed on by a grandfather to his grandson. It contains a variety of moral instruction and eulogies of patriarchs and other figures in Israelite history. Its moral maxims apply to individuals, the family and community, relations with God, friendship, education, wealth, the Law, divine worship. Its theme is that true wisdom consists in the Law. (It was formerly called Ecclesiasticus, the Church Book, because of its extensive use by the Church for moral instruction.) It was written in Hebrew between 200 and 175, during a period of strong Hellenistic influence, and was translated into Greek after 132.

The Prophets

These books and the prophecies they contain "express judgments of the people's moral conduct, on the basis of the Mosaic alliance between God and Israel. They teach sublime truths and lofty morals. They contain exhortations, threats, announcements of punishment, promises of deliverance. In the affairs of men, their prime concern is the interests of God, especially in what pertains to the Chosen People through whom the Messiah is to come; hence their denunciations of idolatry and of that externalism in worship which exclude the interior spirit of religion. They are concerned also with the universal nature of the moral law, with personal responsibility, with the person and office of the Messiah, and with the conduct of foreign nations" (*The Holy Bible*, Prophetic Books, CCD Edition, 1961; Preface). There are four major (Isaiah, Jeremiah, Ezekiel, Daniel) and twelve minor prophets (distinguished by the length of books), Lamentations and Baruch. Earlier prophets, mentioned in historical books, include Samuel, Gad, Nathan, Elijah, and Elisha.

Before the exile, prophets were the intermediaries through whom God communicated revelation to the people. Afterwards, prophecy lapsed and the written word of the Law served this purpose.

Isaiah: Named for the greatest of the prophets whose career spanned the reigns of three Hebrew kings from 742 to the beginning of the seventh century, in a period of moral breakdown in Judah and threats of invasion by foreign enemies. It is an anthology of poems and oracles credited to him and a number of followers deeply influenced by him. Of special importance are the prophecies concerning Immanuel (6 to 12), including the prophecy of the virgin birth (7:14). Chapters 40 to 55, called Deutero-Isaiah, are attributed to an anonymous poet toward the end of the exile; this portion contains the Songs of the Servant. The concluding part of the book (56-66) contains oracles by later disciples. One of many themes in Isaiah concerned the saving mission of the remnant of Israel in the divine plan of salvation.

Jeremiah: Combines history, biography and prophecy in a setting of crisis caused by internal and external factors, viz., idolatry and general infidelity to the Law among the Israelites and external threats from the Assyrians, Egyptians and Babylonians. Jeremiah prophesied the promise of a new covenant as well as the destruction of Jerusalem and the Temple. His career began in 626 and ended some years after the beginning of the exile. The book, the longest in the Bible, was edited in final form after the exile.

Lamentations: A collection of five laments or elegies over the fall of Jerusalem and the fate of the people in exile, written by an unknown eyewitness. They convey the message that Yahweh struck the people because of their sins and reflect confidence in his love and power to restore his converted people.

Baruch: Against the background of the already-begun exile, it consists of an introduction and several parts: an exile's prayer of confession and petition for forgiveness and the restoration of Israel; a poem praising wisdom and the Law of Moses; a lament in which Jerusalem, personified, bewails the fate of her people and consoles them with the hope of blessings to come; and a polemic against idolatry. Although ascribed to Baruch, Jeremiah's secretary, it was written by several authors, probably in the second century.

Ezekiel: Named for the priest-prophet who prophesied in Babylon from 593 to 571, during the first phase of the exile. To prepare his fellow early exiles for the impending fall of Jerusalem, he reproached the Israelites for past sins and predicted woes to come upon them. After the destruction of the city, the burden of his message was hope and promise of restoration. Ezekiel had great influence on the religion of Israel after the exile.

Daniel: The protagonist is a young Jew, taken early to Babylon where he lived until about 538, who figured in a series of edifying stories which originated in Israelite tradition. The stories, whose characters are not purely legendary but rest on historical tradition, recount the trials and triumphs of Daniel and his three companions, and other episodes including those concerning Susannah, Bel, and the Dragon. The book is more apocalyptic than prophetic: it envisions Israel in glory to come and conveys the message that men of faith can resist temptation and overcome adversity. It states the prophetic themes of right conduct, divine control of men and events, and the final triumph of the kingdom. It was written by an unknown author in the 160s to give moral support to Jews during the persecutions of the Maccabean period.

Hosea: Consists of a prophetic parallel between Hosea's marriage and Yahweh's relations with his people. As the prophet was married to a faithless wife whom he would not give up, Yahweh was bound in Covenant with an idolatrous and unjust Israel whom he would not desert but would chastise for purification. Hosea belonged to the Northern Kingdom of Israel and began his career about the middle of the eighth century. He inaugurated the tradition of describing Yahweh's relation to Israel in terms of marriage.

Joel: Is apocalyptic and eschatological regarding divine judgment, the Day of the Lord, which is symbolized by a ravaging invasion of locusts, the judgment of the nations in the Valley of Josaphat and the outpouring of the Spirit in the messianic era to come. Its message is that God will vindicate and save Israel, in view of the prayer and repentance of the people, and will punish their enemies. It was composed about 400.

Amos: Consists of an indictment against foreign enemies of Israel; a strong denunciation of the people of Israel, whose infidelity, idolatry and injustice made them subject to divine judgment and punishment; and a messianic oracle regarding Israel's restoration. Amos prophesied in the Northern Kingdom of Israel, at Bethel, in the first half of the eighth century; chronologically, he was the first of the canonical prophets.

Obadiah: A 21-verse prophecy, the shortest and one of the sternest in the Bible, against the Edomites, invaders of southern Judah and enemies of those returning from the exile to their homeland. It was probably composed in the fifth century.

Jonah: A parable of divine mercy with the theme that Yahweh wills the salvation of all, not just a few, men who respond to his call. Its protagonist is a disobedient prophet; forced by circumstances beyond his control to preach penance among Gentiles, he is highly successful in his mission but baffled by the divine concern for those who do not belong to the Chosen People. It was written after the exile, probably in the fifth century.

Micah: Attacks the injustice and corruption of priests, false prophets, officials and people; announces judgment and punishment to come; foretells the restoration of Israel; refers to the saving remnant of Israel. Micah was a contemporary of Isaiah.

Nahum: Concerns the destruction of Nineveh in 612 and the overthrow of the Assyrian Empire by the Babylonians.

Habakkuk: Dating from about 605-597, concerns sufferings to be inflicted by oppressors on the people of Judah because of their infidelity to the Lord. It also sounds a note of confidence in the Lord, the Savior, and declares that the just will not perish.

Zephaniah: Exercising his ministry in the second half of the seventh century, during a time of widespread idolatry, superstition and religious degradation, he prophesied impending judgment and punishment for Jerusalem and its people. He prophesied too that a holy remnant of the people (*anawim*, mentioned also by Amos) would be spared. Zephaniah was a forerunner of Jeremiah.

Haggai: One of the first prophets after the exile, Haggai in 520 encouraged the returning exiles to reestablish their community and to complete the second Temple (dedicated in 515), for which he envisioned greater glory, in a messianic sense, than that enjoyed by the original Temple of Solomon.

Zechariah: A contemporary of Haggai, he prophesied in the same vein. A second part of the book, called Deutero-Zechariah and composed by one or more unknown authors, relates a vision of the coming of the Prince of Peace, the Messiah of the Poor.

Malachi: Written by an anonymous author, presents a picture of life in the post-Exilic community between 516 and the initiation of reforms by Ezra and Nehemiah about 432. Blame for the troubles of the community is placed mainly on priests for failure to carry out ritual worship and to instruct the people in the proper manner; other factors were religious indifference and the influence of doubters who were scandalized at the prosperity of the wicked. The vision of a universal sacrifice to be offered to Yahweh (1:11) is interpreted in Catholic theology as a prophecy of the sacrifice of the Mass. Malachi was the last of the minor prophets.

DATES OF THE OLD TESTAMENT

c. 1800 - c. 1600 B.C.: Period of the patriarchs (Abraham, Isaac, Jacob).

c. 1600: Israelites in Egypt.

c. 1250: Exodus of Israelites from Egypt.

c. 1210: Entrance of Israelites into Canaan.

c. 1210-c. 1020: Period of the Judges.

c. 1020-c. 1000: Reign of Saul, first king.

c. 1000-c. 961: Reign of David.

c. 961-922: Reign of Solomon. Temple built during his reign.

922: Division of the Kingdom into Israel (North) and Judah (South).

721: Conquest of Israel by Assyrians.

587-538: Conquest of Judah by Babylonians.

Babylonian Captivity and Exile. Destruction of Jerusalem and the Temple, 587. Captivity ended with the return of exiles, following the decree of Cyrus permitting the rebuilding of Jerusalem.

515: Dedication of the second Temple.

458-397: Restoration and reform of the Jewish religious and political community; building of the Jerusalem wall, 439. Leaders in the movement were Ezra and Nehemiah.

168-142: Period of the Maccabees; war against Syrians.

142: Independence granted to Jews by Demetrius II of Syria.
135-37: Period of the Hasmonean dynasty.
63: Beginning of Roman rule.
37-4: Period of Herod the Great.

NEW TESTAMENT BOOKS

Gospels

The term "Gospel" is derived from the Anglo-Saxon *god-spell* and the Greek *euangelion*, meaning good news, good tidings. In Christian use, it means the good news of salvation proclaimed by Christ and the Church, and handed on in written form in the Gospels of Matthew, Mark, Luke and John.

The initial proclamation of the coming of the kingdom of God was made by Jesus in and through his Person, teachings and actions, and especially through his Passion, death and resurrection. This proclamation became the center of Christian faith and the core of the oral Gospel tradition with which the Church spread the good news by apostolic preaching for some 30 years before it was committed to writing by the Evangelists.

Nature of the Gospels

The historical truth of the Gospels was the subject of an instruction issued by the Pontifical Commission for Biblical Studies Apr. 21, 1964.

• The sacred writers selected from the material at their disposal (the oral Gospel tradition, some written collections of sayings and deeds of Jesus, eyewitness accounts) those things which were particularly suitable to the various conditions (liturgical, catechetical, missionary) of the faithful and the aims they had in mind, and they narrated these things in such a way as to correspond with those circumstances and their aims.

• The life and teaching of Jesus were not simply reported in a biographical manner for the purpose of preserving their memory but were "preached" so as to offer the Church the basis of doctrine concerning faith and morals.

• In their works, the Evangelists presented the true sayings of Jesus and the events of his life in the light of the better understanding they had following their enlightenment by the Holy Spirit. They did not transform Christ into a "mythical" Person, nor did they distort his teaching. Passion narratives are the core of all the Gospels, covering the suffering, death and resurrection of Jesus as central events in bringing about and establishing the New Covenant. Leading up to them are accounts of the mission of John the Baptizer and the ministry of Jesus, especially in Galilee and finally in Jerusalem before the Passion. The infancy of Jesus is covered by Luke and Matthew with narratives inspired in part by appropriate Old Testament citations.

Matthew, Mark and Luke, while different in various respects, have so many similarities that they are called Synoptic; their relationships are the subject of the Synoptic Problem.

Matthew: Written probably between 80 and 100 for Jewish Christians with clear reference to Jewish background and identification of Jesus as the divine Messiah, the fulfillment of the Old Testament. Distinctive are the use of Old Testament citations regarding the Person, activity and teaching of Jesus, and the presentation of doctrine in sermons and discourses.

Mark: Most likely the first of the Gospels, dating from about 70. Written for Gentile Christians, it is noted for the realism and wealth of concrete details with which it reveals Jesus as Son of God and Savior more by his actions and miracles than by his discourses. Theologically, it is less refined than the other Gospels.

Luke: Written about 75 for Gentile Christians. It is noted for the universality of its address, the insight it provides into the Christian way of life, the place it gives to women, the manner in which it emphasizes Jesus' friendship with sinners and compassion for the suffering.

John: Edited and arranged in final form probably between 90 and 100, this is the most sublime and theological of the Gospels, and is different from the Synoptics in plan and treatment. Combining accounts of signs with longer discourses and reflections, it progressively reveals the Person and mission of Jesus — as Word, Way, Truth, Life, Light — in line with the purpose, "to help you believe that Jesus is the Messiah, the Son of God, so that through this faith you may have life in his name" (Jn. 20:31). There are questions about the authorship but no doubt about the Johannine authority and tradition behind the Gospel.

Acts of the Apostles

Written by Luke about 75 as a supplement to his Gospel. It describes the origin and spread of Christian communities through the action of the Holy Spirit from the resurrection of Christ to the time when Paul was placed in custody in Rome in the early 60s.

Letters (Epistles)

These letters, many of which antedated the Gospels, were written in response to existential needs of the early Christian communities for doctrinal and moral instruction, disciplinary action, practical advice, and exhortation to true Christian living.

Pauline Letters

These letters, which comprise approximately one-fourth of the New Testament, are primary and monumental sources of the development of Christian theology. Several of them may not have had Paul as their actual author, but evidence of the Pauline tradition behind them is strong. The letters to the Colossians, Philippians, Ephesians and Philemon have been called the "Captivity Letters" because of a tradition that they were written while Paul was under house arrest or another form of detention.

Romans: Written about 57, probably from Corinth, on the central significance of Christ and faith in him for salvation, and the relationship of Christianity to Judaism; the condition of mankind without Christ; justification and the Christian life; duties of Christians.

Corinthians 1: Written near the beginning of 57 from Ephesus to counteract factionalism and disorders, it covers community dissension, moral irregularities, marriage and celibacy, conduct at religious gatherings, the Eucharist, spiritual gifts (charisms) and their function in the Church, charity, the resurrection of the body.

Corinthians 2: Written later in the same year as 1

Cor., concerning Paul's defense of his apostolic ministry, and an appeal for a collection to aid poor Christians in Jerusalem.

Galatians: Written probably between 54 and 55 to counteract Judaizing opinions and efforts to undermine his authority, it asserts the divine origin of Paul's authority and doctrine, states that justification is not through Mosaic Law but through faith in Christ, insists on the practice of evangelical virtues, especially charity.

Ephesians: Written probably between 61 and 63, mainly on the Church as the Mystical Body of Christ.

Philippians: Written between 56 and 57 or 61 and 63 to warn the Philippians against enemies of their faith, to urge them to be faithful to their vocation and unity of belief, and to thank them for their kindness to him while he was being held in detention.

Colossians: Written probably while he was under house arrest in Rome from 61 to 63, to counteract the influence of self-appointed teachers who were watering down doctrine concerning Christ. It includes two highly important Christological passages, a warning against false teachers, and an instruction on the ideal Christian life.

Thessalonians 1 and 2: Written within a short time of each other probably in 51 from Corinth, mainly on doctrine concerning the *Parousia*, the second coming of Christ.

Timothy 1 and 2, Titus: Written between 65 and 67, or perhaps in the 70s, giving pastoral counsels to Timothy and Titus, who were in charge of churches in Ephesus and Crete, respectively. 1 Tm. emphasizes pastoral responsibility for preserving unity of doctrine; 2 Tm. describes Paul's imprisonment in Rome.

Philemon: A private letter written between 61 and 63 to a wealthy Colossian concerning a slave, Onesimus, who had escaped from him; Paul appealed for kind treatment of the man.

Hebrews: Dating from sometime between 70 and 96, a complex theological treatise on Christology, the priesthood and sacrifice of Christ, the New Covenant, and the pattern for Christian living. Critical opinion is divided as to whether it was addressed to Judaeo or Gentile Christians.

Catholic Letters

These seven letters have been called "catholic" because it was thought for some time, not altogether correctly, that they were not addressed to particular communities.

James: Written sometime before 62 in the spirit of Hebrew wisdom literature and the moralism of Tobit. An exhortation to practical Christian living, it is also noteworthy for the doctrine it states on good works and its citation regarding anointing of the sick.

Peter 1 and 2: The first letter may have been written between 64 and 67 or between 90 and 95; the second may date from 100 to 125. Addressed to Christians in Asia Minor, both are exhortations to perseverance in the life of faith despite trials and difficulties arising from pagan influences, isolation from other Christians and false teaching.

John 1: Written sometime in the 90s and addressed to Asian churches, its message is that God is made known to us in the Son and that fellowship with the Father is attained by living in the light, justice and love of the Son.

John 2: Written sometime in the 90s and addressed to a church in Asia, it commends the people for standing firm in the faith and urges them to perseverance.

John 3: Written sometime in the 90s, it appears to represent an effort to settle a jurisdictional dispute in one of the churches.

Jude: Written probably about 80, it is a brief treatise against erroneous teachings and practices opposed to law, authority and true Christian freedom.

Revelation

Written in the 90s along the lines of Johannine thought, it is a symbolic and apocalyptic treatment of things to come and of the struggle between the Church and evil combined with warning but hope and assurance to the Church regarding the coming of the Lord in glory.

INTERPRETATION OF THE BIBLE

According to the Dogmatic Constitution on Divine Revelation (*Dei Verbum*) issued by the Second Vatican Council, "the interpreter of Sacred Scripture, in order to see clearly what God wanted to communicate to us, should carefully investigate what meaning the sacred writers really intended, and what God wanted to manifest by means of their words" (No. 12).

Hermeneutics, Exegesis

This careful investigation proceeds in accordance with the rules of hermeneutics, the normative science of biblical interpretation and explanation. Hermeneutics in practice is called exegesis.

The principles of hermeneutics are derived from various disciplines and many factors which have to be considered in explaining the Bible and its parts. These include: the original languages and languages of translation of the sacred texts, through philology and linguistics; the quality of texts, through textual criticism; literary forms and genres, through literary and form criticism; cultural, historical, geographical and other conditions which influenced the writers, through related studies; facts and truths of salvation history; the truths and analogy of faith.

Distinctive to biblical hermeneutics, which differs in important respects from literary interpretation in general, is the premise that the Bible, though written by human authors, is the work of divine inspiration in which God reveals his plan for the salvation of men through historical events and persons, and especially through the Person and mission of Christ.

Textual, Form Criticism

Textual criticism is the study of biblical texts, which have been transmitted in copies several times removed from the original manuscripts, for the purpose of establishing the real state of the original texts. This purpose is served by comparison of existing copies; by application to the texts of the disciplines of philology and linguistics; by examination of related works of antiquity; by study of biblical citations in works of the Fathers of the Church and other authors; and by other means of literary study.

Since about 1920, the sayings of Christ have been a particular object of New Testament study, the purpose being to analyze the forms of expression used by the Evangelists in order to ascertain the words actually spoken by him.

Literary Criticism

Literary criticism aims to determine the origin and kinds of literary composition, called forms or genres, employed by the inspired authors. Such determinations are necessary for decision regarding the nature and purpose and, consequently, the meaning of biblical passages. Underlying these studies is the principle that the manner of writing was conditioned by the intention of the authors, the meaning they wanted to convey, and the then-contemporary literary style, mode or medium best adapted to carry their message — e.g., true history, quasi-historical narrative, poems, prayers, hymns, psalms, aphorisms, allegories, discourses. Understanding these media is necessary for the valid interpretation of their message.

Literal Sense

The key to all valid interpretation is the literal sense of biblical passages. Regarding this matter and the relevance to it of the studies and procedures described above, Pius XII wrote the following in the encyclical *Divino Afflante Spiritu:*

"What the literal sense of a passage is, is not always as obvious in the speeches and writings of ancient authors of the East as it is in the works of our own time. For what they wished to express is not to be determined by the rules of grammar and philology alone nor solely by the context; the interpreter must, as it were, go back wholly in spirit to those remote centuries of the East and with the aid of history, archeology, ethnology, and other sciences accurately determine what modes of writing, so to speak, the authors of that ancient period would be likely to use and in fact did use. In explaining the Sacred Scripture and in demonstrating and proving its immunity from all error [the Catholic interpreter] should make a prudent use of this means, determine to what extent the manner of expression or literary mode adopted by the sacred writer may lead to a correct and genuine interpretation; and let him be convinced that this part of his office cannot be neglected without serious detriment to Catholic exegesis."

The literal sense of the Bible is the meaning in the mind of and intended by the inspired writer of a book or passage of the Bible. This is determined by the application to texts of the rules of hermeneutics. It is not to be confused with word-for-word literalism.

Typological Sense

The typological sense is the meaning which a passage has not only in itself but also in reference to something else of which it is a type or foreshadowing. A clear example is the account of the Exodus of the Israelites: in its literal sense, it narrates the liberation of the Israelites from death and oppression in Egypt; in its typical sense, it foreshadowed the liberation of men from sin through the redemptive death and resurrection of Christ. The typical sense of this and other passages emerged in the working out of God's plan of salvation history. It did not have to be in the mind of the author of the original passage.

Accommodated Senses

Accommodated, allegorical and consequent senses are figurative and adaptive meanings given to books and passages of the Bible for moral and other purposes. Such interpretations involve the danger of stretching the literal sense beyond proper proportions. Hermeneutical principles require that interpretations like these respect the integrity of the literal sense of the passages in question.

In the Catholic view, the final word on questions of biblical interpretation belongs to the teaching authority of the Church. In other views, generally derived from basic principles stated by Martin Luther, John Calvin and other reformers, the primacy belongs to individual judgment acting in response to the inner testimony of the Holy Spirit, the edifying nature of biblical subject matter, the sublimity and simplicity of the message of salvation, the intensity with which Christ is proclaimed.

Biblical Studies

The first center for biblical studies, in some strict sense of the term, was the School of Alexandria, founded in the latter half of the second century. It was noted for allegorical exegesis. Literal interpretation was a hallmark of the School of Antioch.

St. Jerome, who produced the Vulgate, and St. Augustine, author of numerous commentaries, were the most important figures in biblical studies during the patristic period. By the time of the latter's death, the Old and New Testament canons had been stabilized. For some centuries afterwards, there was little or no progress in scriptural studies, although commentaries were written, collections were made of scriptural excerpts from the writings of the Fathers of the Church, and the systematic reading of Scripture became established as a feature of monastic life.

Advances were made in the 12th and 13th centuries with the introduction of new principles and methods of scriptural analysis stemming from renewed interest in Hebraic studies and the application of dialectics.

By the time of the Reformation, the Bible had become the first book set in movable type, and more than 100 vernacular editions were in use throughout Europe.

The Council of Trent

In the wake of the Reformation, the Council of Trent formally defined the Canon of the Bible; it also reasserted the authoritative role of tradition and the teaching authority of the Church as well as Scripture with respect to the rule of faith. In the heated atmosphere of the 16th and 17th centuries, the Bible was turned into a polemical weapon; Protestants used it to defend their doctrines, and Catholics countered with citations in support of the dogmas of the Church. One result of this state of affairs was a lack of substantial progress in biblical studies during the period.

Rationalists from the 18th century on and later Modernists denied the reality of the supernatural and doctrine concerning inspiration of the Bible, which they generally regarded as a strictly human production expressive of the religious sense and experience of mankind. In their hands, the tools of positive critical research became weapons for biblical subversion. The defensive Catholic reaction to their work had the temporary effect of alienating scholars of the Church from solid advances in archeology, philology, history, textual and literary criticism.

Catholic Developments

Major influences in bringing about a change in Catholic attitude toward use of these disciplines in biblical studies were two papal encyclicals and two institutes of special study, the *École Biblique*, founded in Jerusalem in 1890, and the Pontifical Biblical Institute established in Rome in 1909. The encyclical *Providentissimus Deus*, issued by Leo XIII in 1893, marked an important breakthrough; in addition to defending the concept of divine inspiration and the formal inspiration of the Scriptures, it encouraged the study of allied and ancillary sciences and techniques for a more fruitful understanding of the sacred writings. The encyclical *Divino Afflante Spiritu*, by Pope Pius XII 50 years later, gave encouragement for the use of various forms of criticism as tools of biblical research. A significant addition to documents on the subject is "The Interpretation of the Bible in the Church," published by the Pontifical Biblical Com-

mission in November, 1993. It presents an overview of approaches to the Bible and probes the question: "Which hermeneutical theory best enables a proper grasp of the profound reality of which Scripture speaks and its meaningful expression for people today?"

The documents encouraged the work of scholars and stimulated wide communication of the fruits of their study.

Great changes in the climate and direction of biblical studies have occurred in recent years. One of them has been an increase in cooperative effort among Catholic, Protestant, Orthodox and Jewish scholars. Their common investigation of the Dead Sea Scrolls is well-known. Also productive has been the collaboration of Catholics and Protestants in turning out various editions of the Bible.

The development and results of biblical studies in this century have directly and significantly affected all phases of the contemporary renewal movement in the Church. Their influence on theology, liturgy, catechetics, and preaching indicate the importance of their function in the life of the Church.

APOSTLES AND EVANGELISTS

The Apostles were the men selected, trained, and commissioned by Christ to preach the Gospel, to baptize, to establish, direct and care for his Church as servants of God and stewards of his mysteries. They were the first bishops of the Church.

St. Matthew's Gospel lists the Apostles in this order: Peter, Andrew, James the Greater, John, Philip, Bartholomew, Thomas, Matthew, James the Less, Jude, Simon, and Judas Iscariot. Matthias was elected to fill the place of Judas. Paul became an Apostle by a special call from Christ. Barnabas was called an Apostle.

Two of the Evangelists, John and Matthew, were Apostles. The other two, Luke and Mark, were closely associated with the apostolic college.

Andrew: Born in Bethsaida, brother of Peter, disciple of John the Baptist, a fisherman, the first Apostle called; according to legend, preached the Gospel in northern Greece, Epirus and Scythia, and was martyred at Patras about 70; in art, is represented with an X-shaped cross, called St. Andrew's Cross; is honored as the patron of Russia and Scotland; Nov. 30.

Barnabas: Originally called Joseph but named Barnabas by the Apostles, among whom he is ranked because of his collaboration with Paul; a Jew of the Diaspora, born in Cyprus; a cousin of Mark and member of the Christian community at Jerusalem, influenced the Apostles to accept Paul, with whom he became a pioneer missionary outside Palestine and Syria, to Antioch, Cyprus, and southern Asia Minor; legend says he was martyred in Cyprus during the Neronian persecution; June 11.

Bartholomew (Nathaniel): A friend of Philip; according to various traditions, preached the Gospel in Ethiopia, India, Persia, and Armenia, where he was martyred by being flayed and beheaded; in art, is depicted holding a knife, an instrument of his death; Aug. 24 (Roman Rite), Aug. 25 (Byzantine Rite).

James the Greater: A Galilean, son of Zebedee, brother of John (with whom he was called a "Son of Thunder"), a fisherman; with Peter and John, wit-

nessed the raising of Jairus's daughter to life, the transfiguration, the agony of Jesus in the Garden of Gethsemane; first of the Apostles to die, by the sword in 44 during the rule of Herod Agrippa; there is doubt about a journey legend says he made to Spain and also about the authenticity of relics said to be his at Santiago de Compostela; in art, is depicted carrying a pilgrim's bell; July 25 (Roman Rite), Apr. 30 (Byzantine Rite).

James the Less: Son of Alphaeus, called "Less" because he was younger in age or shorter in stature than James the Greater; one of the Catholic Epistles bears his name; was stoned to death in 62 or thrown from the top of the temple in Jerusalem and clubbed to death in 66; in art, is depicted with a club or heavy staff; May 3 (Roman Rite), Oct. 9 (Byzantine Rite).

John: A Galilean, son of Zebedee, brother of James the Greater (with whom he was called a "Son of Thunder"), a fisherman, probably a disciple of John the Baptist, one of the Evangelists, called the "Beloved Disciple"; with Peter and James the Greater, witnessed the raising of Jairus's daughter to life, the transfiguration, the agony of Jesus in the Garden of Gethsemane; Mary was commended to his special care by Christ; the fourth Gospel, three Catholic Epistles, and Revelation bear his name; according to various accounts, lived at Ephesus in Asia Minor for some time and died a natural death about 100; in art, is represented by an eagle, symbolic of the sublimity of the contents of his Gospel; Dec. 27 (Roman Rite), May 8 (Byzantine Rite).

Jude Thaddeus: One of the Catholic Epistles, the shortest, bears his name; various traditions say he preached the Gospel in Mesopotamia, Persia, and elsewhere, and was martyred; in art, is depicted with a halberd, the instrument of his death; Oct. 28 (Roman Rite), June 19 (Byzantine Rite).

Luke: A Greek convert to the Christian community, called "our most dear physician" by Paul, of whom he was a missionary companion; author of the third Gospel and Acts of the Apostles; the place — Achaia,

Bithynia, Egypt — and circumstances of his death are not certain; in art, is depicted as a man, a writer, or an ox (because his Gospel starts at the scene of temple sacrifice); Oct. 18.

Mark: A cousin of Barnabas and member of the first Christian community at Jerusalem; a missionary companion of Paul and Barnabas, then of Peter; author of the Gospel which bears his name; according to legend, founded the Church at Alexandria, was bishop there and was martyred in the streets of the city; in art, is depicted with his Gospel and a winged lion, symbolic of the voice of John the Baptist crying in the wilderness, at the beginning of his Gospel; Apr. 25.

Matthew: A Galilean, called Levi by Luke and John and the son of Alphaeus by Mark, a tax collector, one of the Evangelists; according to various accounts, preached the Gospel in Judea, Ethiopia, Persia and Parthia, and was martyred; in art, is depicted with a spear, the instrument of his death, and as a winged man in his role as Evangelist; Sept. 21 (Roman Rite), Nov. 16 (Byzantine Rite).

Matthias: A disciple of Jesus whom the faithful 11 Apostles chose to replace Judas before the Resurrection; uncertain traditions report that he preached the Gospel in Palestine, Cappadocia or Ethiopia; in art, is represented with a cross and a halberd, the instruments of his death as a martyr; May 14 (Roman Rite), Aug. 9 (Byzantine Rite).

Paul: Born at Tarsus, of the tribe of Benjamin, a Roman citizen; participated in the persecution of Christians until the time of his miraculous conversion on the way to Damascus; called by Christ, who revealed himself to him in a special way; became the Apostle of the Gentiles, among whom he did most of his preaching in the course of three major missionary journeys through areas north of Palestine, Cyprus, Asia Minor, and Greece; 14 epistles bear his name; two years of imprisonment at Rome, following initial arrest in Jerusalem and confinement at Caesarea, ended with martyrdom, by beheading, outside the walls of the city in 64 or 67 during the Neronian persecution; in art, is depicted in various ways with St. Peter, with a sword, in the scene of his conversion; June 29 (with St. Peter), Jan. 25 (Conversion).

Peter: Simon, son of Jonah, born in Bethsaida, brother of Andrew, a fisherman; called Cephas or Peter by Christ who made him the chief of the Apostles and head of the Church as his vicar; named first in the listings of Apostles in the Synoptic Gospels and the Acts of the Apostles; with James the Greater and John, witnessed the raising of Jairus's daughter to life, the transfiguration, the agony of Jesus in the Garden of Gethsemane; was the first to preach the Gospel in and around Jerusalem and was the leader of the first Christian community there; established a local church in Antioch; presided over the Council of Jerusalem in 51; wrote two Catholic Epistles to the Christians in Asia Minor; established his see in Rome where he spent his last years and was martyred by crucifixion in 64 or 65 during the Neronian persecution; in art, is depicted carrying two keys, symbolic of his primacy in the Church; June 29 (with St. Paul), Feb. 22 (Chair of Peter).

Philip: Born in Bethsaida; according to legend, preached the Gospel in Phrygia where he suffered martyrdom by crucifixion; May 3 (Roman Rite), Nov. 14 (Byzantine Rite).

Simon: Called the Cananean or the Zealot; according to legend, preached in various places in the Middle East and suffered martyrdom by being sawed in two; in art, is depicted with a saw, the instrument of his death, or a book, symbolic of his zeal for the Law; Oct. 28 (Roman Rite), May 10 (Byzantine Rite).

Thomas (Didymus): Notable for his initial incredulity regarding the Resurrection and his subsequent forthright confession of the divinity of Christ risen from the dead; according to legend, preached the Gospel in places from the Caspian Sea to the Persian Gulf and eventually reached India where he was martyred near Madras; Thomas Christians trace their origin to him; in art, is depicted kneeling before the risen Christ, or with a carpenter's rule and square; feast, July 3 (Roman Rite), Oct. 6 (Byzantine Rite).

Judas: The Gospels record only a few facts about Judas, the Apostle who betrayed Christ. The only non-Galilean among the Apostles, he was from Carioth, a town in southern Judah. He was keeper of the purse in the apostolic band. He was called a petty thief by John. He voiced dismay at the waste of money, which he said might have been spent for the poor, in connection with the anointing incident at Bethany. He took the initiative in arranging the betrayal of Christ. Afterwards, he confessed that he had betrayed an innocent man and cast into the Temple the money he had received for that action. Of his death, Matthew says that he hanged himself; the Acts of the Apostles states that he swelled up and burst open; both reports deal more with the meaning than the manner of his death — the misery of the death of a sinner.

The consensus of speculation over the reason why Judas acted as he did in betraying Christ focuses on disillusionment and unwillingness to accept the concept of a suffering Messiah and personal suffering of his own as an Apostle.

APOSTOLIC FATHERS, FATHERS, DOCTORS OF THE CHURCH

The writers listed below were outstanding and authoritative witnesses to authentic Christian belief and practice, and played significant roles in giving them expression.

Apostolic Fathers

The Apostolic Fathers were Christian writers of the first and second centuries whose writings echo genuine apostolic teaching. Chief in importance are: St. Clement (d. c. 97), bishop of Rome and third successor of St. Peter in the papacy; St. Ignatius (50-c. 107), bishop of Antioch and second successor of St. Peter in that see, reputed to be a disciple of St. John; St. Polycarp (69-155), bishop of Smyrna and a disciple of St. John. The authors of the Didache and the Epistle of Barnabas are also numbered among the Apostolic Fathers.

Other early ecclesiastical writers included: St. Justin, martyr (100-165), of Asia Minor and Rome, a layman and apologist; St. Irenaeus (130-202), bishop of Lyons, who opposed Gnosticism; and St. Cyprian (210-258), bishop of Carthage, who opposed Novatianism.

Fathers and Doctors

The Fathers of the Church were theologians and writers of the first eight centuries who were outstanding for sanctity and learning. They were such authoritative witnesses to the belief and teaching of the Church that their unanimous acceptance of doctrines as divinely revealed has been regarded as evidence that such doctrines were so received by the Church in line with apostolic tradition and Sacred Scripture. Their unanimous rejection of doctrines branded them as heretical. Their writings, however, were not necessarily free of error in all respects.

The greatest of these Fathers were: Sts. Ambrose, Augustine, Jerome, and Gregory the Great in the West; Sts. John Chrysostom, Basil the Great, Gregory of Nazianzus, and Athanasius in the East.

The Doctors of the Church were ecclesiastical writers of eminent learning and sanctity who have been given this title because of the great advantage the Church has derived from their work. Their writings, however, were not necessarily free of error in all respects.

Albert the Great, St. (c. 1200-1280): Born in Swabia, Germany; Dominican; bishop of Regensburg (1260-1262); wrote extensively on logic, natural sciences, ethics, metaphysics, Scripture, systematic theology; contributed to development of Scholasticism; teacher of St. Thomas Aquinas; canonized and proclaimed doctor, 1931; named patron of natural scientists, 1941; called *Doctor Universalis, Doctor Expertus*; Nov. 15.

Alphonsus Liguori, St. (1696-1787): Born near Naples, Italy; bishop of Saint Agatha of the Goths (1762-1775); founder of the Redemptorists; in addition to his principal work, *Theologia Moralis*, wrote on prayer, the spiritual life and doctrinal subjects in response to controversy; canonized, 1839; proclaimed doctor, 1871; named patron of confessors and moralists, 1950; Aug. 1.

Ambrose, St. (c. 340-397): Born in Trier, Germany; bishop of Milan (374-397); one of the strongest opponents of Arianism in the West; his homilies and other writings — on faith, the Holy Spirit, the Incarnation, the sacraments and other subjects — were pastoral and practical; influenced the development of a liturgy at Milan which was named for him; Father and Doctor of the Church; Dec. 7.

Anselm, St. (1033-1109): Born in Aosta, Piedmont, Italy; Benedictine; archbishop of Canterbury (1093-1109); in addition to his principal work, *Cur Deus Homo*, on the atonement and reconciliation of man with God through Christ, wrote about the existence and attributes of God and defended the *Filioque* explanation of the procession of the Holy Spirit from the Father and the Son; proclaimed doctor, 1720; called Father of Scholasticism; Apr. 21.

Anthony of Padua, St. (1195-1231): Born in Lisbon, Portugal; first theologian of the Franciscan Order; preacher; canonized, 1232; proclaimed doctor, 1946; called Evangelical Doctor; June 13.

Athanasius, St. (c. 297-373): Born in Alexandria, Egypt; bishop of Alexandria (328-373); participant in the Council of Nicaea I while still a deacon; dominant opponent of Arians whose errors regarding Christ he refuted in *Apology Against the Arians*, Discourses against the Arians and other works; Father and Doctor of the Church; called Father of Orthodoxy; May 2.

Augustine, St. (354-430): Born in Tagaste, North Africa; bishop of Hippo (395-430) after conversion from Manichaeism; works include the autobiographical and mystical *Confessions, City of God*, treatises on the Trinity, grace, passages of the Bible and doctrines called into question and denied by Manichaeans, Pelagians, and Donatists; had strong and lasting influence on Christian theology and philosophy; Father and Doctor of the Church; called Doctor of Grace; Aug. 28.

Basil the Great, St. (c. 329-379): Born in Caesarea, Cappadocia, Asia Minor; bishop of Caesarea (370-379); wrote three books; *Contra Eunomium,* in refutation of Arian errors; a treatise on the Holy Spirit; many homilies; and several rules for monastic life, on which he had lasting influence; Father and Doctor of the Church; called Father of Monasticism in the East; Jan. 2.

Bede the Venerable, St. (c. 673-735): Born in Northumberland, England; Benedictine; in addition to his principal work, *Ecclesiastical History* of the English Nation (covering the period 597-731), wrote scriptural commentaries; regarded as probably the most learned man in Western Europe of his time; called Father of English History; May 25.

Bernard of Clairvaux, St. (c. 1090-1153): Born near Dijon, France; abbot; monastic reformer, called the second founder of the Cistercian Order; mystical theologian with great influence on devotional life; opponent of the rationalism brought forward by Abélard and others; canonized, 1174; proclaimed doctor, 1830; called Mellifluous Doctor because of his eloquence; Aug. 20.

Bonaventure, St. (c. 1217-1274): Born near Viterbo, Italy; Franciscan; bishop of Albano (1273-1274); cardinal; wrote *Itinerarium Mentis in Deum, De Reductione Artium ad Theologiam, Breviloquium*, scriptural commentaries, additional mystical works affecting devotional life, and a life of St. Francis of Assisi; canonized, 1482; proclaimed doctor, 1588; called Seraphic Doctor; July 15.

Catherine of Siena, St. (c. 1347-1380): Born in Siena, Italy; member of the Third Order of St. Dominic; mystic; authored a long series of letters, mainly concerning spiritual instruction and encouragement, to associates, and *Dialogue*, a spiritual testament in four treatises; was active in support of a crusade against the Turks and efforts to end war between papal forces and the Florentine allies; had great influence in inducing Gregory XI to return himself and the Curia to Rome in 1377, to end the Avignon period of the papacy; canonized, 1461; proclaimed the second woman doctor, Oct. 4, 1970; Apr. 29; named a co-patroness of Europe, with St. Edith Stein and St. Bridget of Sweden, on Oct. 1, 1999.

Cyril of Alexandria, St. (c. 376-444): Born in Egypt; bishop of Alexandria (412-444); wrote treatises on the Trinity, the Incarnation and other subjects, mostly in refutation of Nestorian errors; made key contributions to the development of Christology; presided at the Council of Ephesus, 431; proclaimed doctor, 1882; June 27.

Cyril of Jerusalem, St. (c. 315-386): Bishop of Jerusalem from 350; vigorous opponent of Arianism; principal work, *Catecheses*, a pre-baptismal explanation of the creed of Jerusalem; proclaimed doctor, 1882; Mar. 18.

Ephraem, St. (c. 306-373): Born in Nisibis, Mesopotamia; counteracted the spread of Gnostic and Arian errors with poems and hymns of his own composition; wrote also on the Eucharist and Mary; proclaimed doctor, 1920; called Deacon of Edessa and Harp of the Holy Spirit; June 9.

Francis de Sales, St. (1567-1622): Born in Savoy; bishop of Geneva (1602-1622); spiritual writer with strong influence on devotional life through treatises such as *Introduction to a Devout Life*, and *The Love of God*; canonized, 1665; proclaimed doctor, 1877; patron of Catholic writers and the Catholic press; Jan. 24.

Gregory Nazianzen, St. (c. 330-c. 390): Born in Arianzus, Cappadocia, Asia Minor; bishop of Constantinople (381-390); vigorous opponent of Arianism; in addition to five theological discourses on the Nicene Creed and the Trinity for which he is best known, wrote letters and poetry; Father and Doctor of the Church; called the Christian Demosthenes because of his eloquence and, in the Eastern Church, the Theologian; Jan. 2.

Gregory I, the Great, St. (c. 540-604): Born in Rome; pope (590-604): wrote many scriptural commentaries, a compendium of theology in the *Book of Morals* based on Job, Dialogues concerning the lives of saints, the immortality of the soul, death, purgatory, heaven and hell, and fourteen books of letters; enforced papal supremacy and established the position of the pope vis-á-vis the emperor; worked for clerical and monastic reform and the observance of clerical celibacy; Father and Doctor of the Church; Sept. 3.

Hilary of Poitiers, St. (c. 315-368): Born in Poitiers, France; bishop of Poitiers (c. 353-368); wrote *De Synodis*, with the Arian controversy in mind, and *De Trinitate*, the first lengthy study of the doctrine in Latin; introduced Eastern theology to the West; contributed to the development of hymnology; proclaimed doctor, 1851; called the Athanasius of the West because of his vigorous defense of the divinity of Christ against Arians; Jan. 13.

Isidore of Seville, St. (c. 560-636): Born in Cartagena, Spain; bishop of Seville (c. 600-636); in addition to his principal work, *Etymologiae*, an encyclopedia of the knowledge of his day, wrote on theological and historical subjects; regarded as the most learned man of his time; proclaimed doctor, 1722; Apr. 4.

Jerome, St. (c. 343-420): Born in Stridon, Dalmatia; translated the Old Testament from Hebrew into Latin and revised the existing Latin translation of the New Testament to produce the Vulgate version of the Bible; wrote scriptural commentaries and treatises on matters of controversy; regarded as Father and Doctor of the Church from the eighth century; called Father of Biblical Science; Sept. 30.

John Chrysostom, St. (c. 347-407): Born in Antioch, Asia Minor; archbishop of Constantinople (398-407); wrote homilies, scriptural commentaries and letters of wide influence in addition to a classical treatise on the priesthood; proclaimed doctor by the Council of Chalcedon, 451; called the greatest of the Greek Fathers; named patron of preachers, 1909; called Golden-Mouthed because of his eloquence; Sept. 13.

John Damascene, St. (c. 675-c. 749): Born in Dam-

ascus, Syria; monk; wrote Fountain of Wisdom, a three-part work including a history of heresies and an exposition of the Christian faith, three discourses against the Iconoclasts, homilies on Mary, biblical commentaries, and treatises on moral subjects; proclaimed doctor, 1890; called Golden Speaker because of his eloquence; Dec. 4.

John of the Cross, St. (1542-1591): Born in Old Castile, Spain; Carmelite; founder of Discalced Carmelites; one of the greatest mystical theologians, wrote *The Ascent of Mt. Carmel*; *The Dark Night of the Soul*, *The Spiritual Canticle*, *The Living Flame of Love*; canonized, 1726; proclaimed doctor, 1926; called Doctor of Mystical Theology; Dec. 14.

Lawrence of Brindisi, St. (1559-1619): Born in Brindisi, Italy; Franciscan (Capuchin); vigorous preacher of strong influence in the post-Reformation period; 15 tomes of collected works include scriptural commentaries, sermons, homilies and doctrinal writings; canonized, 1881; proclaimed doctor, 1959; July 21.

Leo I, the Great, St. (c. 400-461): Born in Tuscany, Italy; pope (440-461); wrote the *Tome* of Leo, to explain doctrine concerning the two natures and one Person of Christ, against the background of the Nestorian and Monophysite heresies; other works included sermons, letters and writings against the errors of Manichaeism and Pelagianism; was instrumental in dissuading Attila from sacking Rome in 452; proclaimed doctor, 1574; Nov. 10.

Peter Canisius, St. (1521-1597): Born in Nijmegen, Holland; Jesuit; wrote popular expositions of the Catholic faith in several catechisms which were widely circulated in 20 editions in his lifetime alone; was one of the moving figures in the Counter-Reformation period, especially in southern and western Germany; canonized and proclaimed doctor, 1925; Dec. 21.

Peter Chrysologus, St. (c. 400-450): Born in Imola, Italy; served as archbishop of Ravenna (c. 433-450); his sermons and writings, many of which were designed to counteract Monophysitism, were pastoral and practical; proclaimed doctor, 1729; July 30.

Peter Damian, St. (1007-1072): Born in Ravenna, Italy; Benedictine; cardinal; his writings and sermons, many of which concerned ecclesiastical and clerical reform, were pastoral and practical; proclaimed doctor, 1828; Feb. 21.

Robert Bellarmine, St. (1542-1621): Born in Tuscany, Italy; Jesuit; archbishop of Capua (1602-1605); wrote *Controversies*, a three-volume exposition of doctrine under attack during and after the Reformation, two catechisms and the spiritual work, *The Art of Dying Well*; was an authority on ecclesiology and Church-state relations; canonized, 1930; proclaimed doctor, 1931; Sept. 17.

Teresa of Jesus (Ávila), St. (1515-1582): Born in Ávila, Spain; entered the Carmelite Order, 1535; in the early 1560s, initiated a primitive Carmelite reform which greatly influenced men and women religious, especially in Spain; wrote extensively on spiritual and mystical subjects; principal works included her *Autobiography*, *Way of Perfection*, *The Interior Castle*, *Meditations on the Canticle*, *The Foundations*, *Visitation of the Discalced Nuns*; canonized, 1622; proclaimed first woman doctor, Sept. 27, 1970; Oct. 15.

Thérèse of Lisieux, St. (1873-1897): Born in Alençon, Normandy, France; entered the Carmelites at Lisieux in 1888, lived for only nine more years, dying on September 30, 1897 from tuberculosis. Trusting completely in God, a path she described as the "little way," she lived a seemingly ordinary life of a nun, but her spiritual advancement was such that her superiors instructed her to write an autobiography in 1895 (*The Story of a Soul*). One of the most popular and respected saints throughout the twentieth century, she was canonized on May 17, 1925. Pope John Paul II declared her the third woman doctor on Oct. 20, 1997 in the letter *Divini amoris scientia*; her relics also toured the United States, attracting huge crowds; Oct. 1.

Thomas Aquinas, St. (1225-1274): Born near Naples, Italy; Dominican; teacher and writer on virtually the whole range of philosophy and theology; principal works were *Summa contra Gentiles*, a manual and systematic defense of Christian doctrine, and *Summa Theologiae*, a new (at that time) exposition of theology on philosophical principles; canonized, 1323; proclaimed doctor, 1567; called *Doctor Communis*, *Doctor Angelicus*, the Great Synthesizer because of the way in which he related faith and reason, theology and philosophy (especially that of Aristotle), and systematized the presentation of Christian doctrine; named patron of Catholic schools and education, 1880; Jan. 28.

CREEDS

Creeds are formal and official statements of Christian doctrine. As summaries of the principal truths of faith, they are standards of orthodoxy and are useful for instructional purposes, for actual profession of the faith and for expression of the faith in the liturgy.

The classical creeds are the Apostles' Creed and the Creed of Nicaea-Constantinople. Two others are the Athanasian Creed and the Creed of Pius IV.

Apostles' Creed

Text: *I believe in God, the Father almighty, Creator of heaven and earth.*

And in Jesus Christ, his only Son, our Lord; who was conceived by the Holy Spirit, born of the Virgin Mary, suffered under Pontius Pilate, was crucified, died, and was buried. He descended into hell; the third day he arose again from the dead; he ascended into heaven, sits at the right hand of God, the Father almighty; from thence he shall come to judge the living and the dead.

I believe in the Holy Spirit, the holy Catholic Church, the communion of saints, the forgiveness of sins, the resurrection of the body, and life everlasting. Amen.

Background: The Apostles' Creed reflects the teaching of the Apostles but is not of apostolic origin. It probably originated in the second century as a rudimentary formula of faith professed by catechumens before the reception of baptism. Baptismal creeds in fourth-century use at Rome and elsewhere in the West closely resembled the present text, which was quoted in a handbook of Christian doctrine written between 710 and 724. This text was in wide use throughout the West by the ninth century. The Apostles' Creed is common to all Christian confessional churches in the West, but is not used in Eastern Churches.

Nicene Creed

The following translation of the Latin text of the Creed was prepared by the International Committee on English in the Liturgy.

Text: *We believe in one God, the Father, the Almighty, maker of heaven and earth, of all that is seen and unseen.*

We believe in one Lord, Jesus Christ, the only Son of God, eternally begotten of the Father, God from God, Light from Light, true God from true God, begotten, not made, one in Being with the Father. Through him all things were made. For us men and for our salvation he came down from heaven: by the power of the Holy Spirit he was born of the Virgin

Mary, and became man. For our sake he was crucified under Pontius Pilate; he suffered, died, and was buried. On the third day he rose again in fulfillment of the Scriptures; he ascended into heaven and is seated at the right hand of the Father. He will come again in glory to judge the living and the dead, and his kingdom will have no end.

We believe in the Holy Spirit, the Lord, the giver of life, who proceeds from the Father and the Son. With the Father and the Son he is worshipped and glorified. He has spoken through the prophets.

We believe in one holy catholic and apostolic Church. We acknowledge one baptism for the forgiveness of sins. We look for the resurrection of the dead, and the life of the world to come. Amen.

Background: The Nicene Creed (Creed of Nicaea-Constantinople) consists of elements of doctrine contained in an early baptismal creed of Jerusalem and enactments of the Council of Nicaea (325) and the Council of Constantinople (381).

Its strong trinitarian content reflects the doctrinal errors, especially of Arianism, it served to counteract. Theologically, it is much more sophisticated than the Apostles' Creed.

Since late in the fifth century, the Nicene Creed has been the only creed in liturgical use in the Eastern Churches. The Western Church adopted it for liturgical use by the end of the eighth century.

The Athanasian Creed

The Athanasian Creed, which has a unique structure, is a two-part summary of doctrine concerning the Trinity and the Incarnation-Redemption bracketed at the beginning and end with the statement that belief in the cited truths is necessary for salvation; it also contains a number of anathemas or condemnatory clauses regarding doctrinal errors. Although attributed to St. Athanasius, it was probably written after his death, between 381 and 428, and may have been authored by St. Ambrose. It is not accepted in the East; in the West, it formerly had place in the Roman-Rite Liturgy of the Hours and in the liturgy for the Solemnity of the Holy Trinity.

Creed of Pius IV

The Creed of Pius IV, also called the Profession of Faith of the Council of Trent, was promulgated in the bull *Injunctum Nobis*, Nov. 13, 1564. It is a summary of doctrine defined by the council concerning: Scripture and tradition, original sin and justification, the

Mass and sacraments, veneration of the saints, indulgences, the primacy of the See of Rome. It was slightly modified in 1887 to include doctrinal formulations of the First Vatican Council.

CHRISTIAN MORALITY

(*By Fr. Alfred McBride, O.Praem.*)
"Incorporated into Christ by Baptism, Christians are 'dead to sin and alive in Christ Jesus ... ' " (Rom 6:11).

CHRISTIAN MORALITY IS LIFE IN CHRIST

The third part of the *Catechism* focuses on Christian morality. After the Creed as faith professed, and sacraments as faith celebrated, the *Catechism* turns our attention to the faith lived. It deals with this issue in two major sections. The first section establishes the context for Christian morality. The second section analyzes the ten commandments. This approach preserves the *Catechism's* resolute insistence on the primacy of God's initiative through Revelation, salvation, and grace followed by our human response in faith, celebration, and Christian witness. Hence morality does not begin with the rules but with the call to life in Christ and the Holy Spirit. Covenant love comes first, then the response of Christian affection in the life of the commandments. This saves us both from legalism and from piety without practical witness.

The following excerpt from the *Catechism of the Catholic Church* sets the vision for the Christian moral life:

LIFE IN CHRIST

1691 "Christian, recognize your dignity and, now that you share in God's own nature, do not return to your former base condition by sinning. Remember who is your head and of whose body you are a member. Never forget that you have been rescued from the power of darkness and brought into the light of the Kingdom of God."[1]

1692 The Symbol of the faith confesses the greatness of God's gifts to man in his work of creation, and even more in redemption and sanctification. What faith confesses, the sacraments communicate: by the sacraments of rebirth, Christians have become "children of God,"[2] "partakers of the divine nature."[3] Coming to see in the faith their new dignity, Christians are called to lead henceforth a life "worthy of the gospel of Christ."[4] They are made capable of doing so by the grace of Christ and the gifts of his Spirit, which they receive through the sacraments and through prayer.

1693 Christ Jesus always did what was pleasing to the Father,[5] and always lived in perfect communion with him. Likewise Christ's disciples are invited to live in the sight of the Father "who sees in secret,"[6] in order to become "perfect as your heavenly Father is perfect."[7]

1694 Incorporated into Christ by Baptism, Christians are "dead to sin and alive to God in Christ Jesus" and so participate in the life of the Risen Lord.[8] Following Christ and united with him,[9] Christians can strive to be "imitators of God as beloved children, and walk in love"[10] by conforming their thoughts, words and actions to the "mind ... which is yours in Christ Jesus,"[11] and by following his example.[12]

1695 "Justified in the name of the Lord Jesus Christ and in the Spirit of our God,"[13] "sanctified ... [and] called to be saints,"[14] Christians have become the temple of the Holy Spirit.[15] This "Spirit of the Son" teaches them to pray to the Father[16] and, having become their life, prompts them to act so as to bear "the fruit of the Spirit"[17] by charity in action. Healing the wounds of sin, the Holy Spirit renews us interiorly through a spiritual transformation.[18] He enlightens and strengthens us to live as "children of light" through "all that is good and right and true."[19]

1696 The way of Christ "leads to life"; a contrary way "leads to destruction."[20] The Gospel parable of the two ways remains ever present in the catechesis of the Church; it shows the importance of moral decisions for our salvation: "There are two ways, the one of life, the other of death; but between the two, there is a great difference."[21]

1697 Catechesis has to reveal in all clarity the joy and the demands of the way of Christ.[22] Catechesis for the "newness of life"[23] in him should be:

• a catechesis of the Holy Spirit, the interior Master of life according to Christ, a gentle guest and friend who inspires, guides, corrects, and strengthens this life;

• a catechesis of grace, for it is by grace that we are saved and again it is by grace that our works can bear fruit for eternal life;

• a catechesis of the beatitudes, for the way of Christ is summed up in the beatitudes, the only path that leads to the eternal beatitude for which the human heart longs;

• a catechesis of sin and forgiveness, for unless man acknowledges that he is a sinner he cannot know the truth about himself, which is a condition for acting justly; and without the offer of forgiveness he would not be able to bear this truth;

• a catechesis of the human virtues which causes one to grasp the beauty and attraction of right dispositions towards goodness;

• a catechesis of the Christian virtues of faith, hope, and charity, generously inspired by the example of the saints; a catechesis of the twofold commandment of charity set forth in the Decalogue;

• an ecclesial catechesis, for it is through the manifold exchanges of "spiritual goods" in the "communion of saints" that Christian life can grow, develop, and be communicated.

1698 The first and last point of reference of this catechesis will always be Jesus Christ himself, who is "the way, and the truth, and the life."[24] It is by looking to him in faith that Christ's faithful can hope that he himself fulfills his promises in them, and that, by loving him with the same love with which he has loved them, they may perform works in keeping with their dignity: "I ask you to consider that our Lord Jesus Christ is your true head, and that you are one of his members. He belongs to you as the head belongs to its members; all that is his is yours: his spirit, his heart, his body and soul, and all his faculties. You must make use of all these as of your own, to serve, praise, love, and glorify God. You belong to him, as members belong to their head. And so he longs for you to use all that is in you, as if it were his own, for the service and glory of the Father."[25] "For to me, to live is Christ."[26]

FOOTNOTES

1. St. Leo the Great, Sermo 22 in nat. Dom. 3: PL 54, 192C. 2. Jn. 1:12; 1 Jn. 3:1. 3. 2 Pet. 1:4. 4. Phil. 1:27. 5. Cf. Jn. 8:29. 6. Mt. 6:6. 7. Mt. 5:48. 8, Rom. 6:11 and cf. 6:5; cf. Col. 2:12. 9. Cf. Jn. 15:5. 10. Eph. 5:1-2. 11. Phil. 2:5. 12. Cf. Jn. 13:12-16. 13. 1 Cor 6:11. 14. 1 Cor .1:2. 15. Cf. 1 Cor. 6:19. 16. Cf. Gal. 4:6. 17. Gal. 5:22, 25. 18. Cf. Eph. 4:23. 19. Eph. 5:8, 9. 20. Mt. 7:13; cf. Dt. 30: 15-20. 21. Didache 1, 1: SCh 248, 140. 22 .Cf. John Paul II, CT 29. 23. Rom. 6:4. 24. Jn. 14:6. 25. St. John Eudes, Tract. de admirabili corde Jesu, 1, 5. 26. Phil. 1:21.

THE TEN COMMANDMENTS

Any discussions of the commandments should begin with the scene at Sinai where God gave them to us. Read Ex. 19:3-6; 20:1-17. The first event is a covenant experience. God tells Moses how much he had loved the Israelites, is delivering them from slavery by "raising them up on eagles' wings," and is bringing them to freedom. God then offers them a binding covenant of love. He will be their only God and they will be his chosen people. It's like a marriage experience, an exchange of vows between God and Israel.

The next section shows God telling them how to live out the love they have pledged. He gives them the Ten Commandments as the means to live the covenant, to express the love they have promised. The *Catechism* points out that the Ten Commandments are privileged expressions of the natural law, made known to us by reason as well as Divine Revelation. We are obliged in obedience to observe these laws of love, both in serious and light matters. Love is in the details as well as the large matters. We must remember that what God has commanded, he makes possible by his grace.

Jesus set the tone for understanding the importance of the commandments. When a rich young man came to him and asked him what he should do to enter eternal life, Jesus replied, "if you wish to enter into life, keep the commandments" (Mt. 19:17). In another case, someone asked him which were the greatest commandments, Jesus replied, "you shall love the Lord, your God, with all your heart, with all your soul, and with all your mind. This is the greatest and first commandment. The second is like it: You shall love your neighbor as yourself" (Mt. 22:37-39). The first three commandments deal with Christ's call to God with all our being. The last seven commandments show us how to love our neighbors as we love ourselves.

The following excerpt from the *Catechism of the Catholic Church* shows how Jesus taught the importance of the Ten Commandments:

"Teacher, what must I do . . .?"

2052 "Teacher, what good deed must I do, to have eternal life?" To the young man who asked this question, Jesus answers first by invoking the necessity to recognize God as the "One there is who is good," as the supreme Good and the source of all good. Then Jesus tells him: "If you would enter life, keep the commandments." And he cites for his questioner the precepts that concern love of neighbor: "You shall not kill, You shall not commit adultery, You shall not steal, You shall not bear false witness, Honor your father and mother." Finally Jesus sums up these commandments positively: "You shall love your neighbor as yourself."[1]

2053 To this first reply Jesus adds a second: "If you would be perfect, go, sell what you possess and give to the poor, and you will have treasure in heaven; and come, follow me."[2] This reply does not do away with the first: following Jesus Christ involves keeping the Commandments. The Law has not been abolished,[3] but rather man is invited to rediscover it in the person of his Master who is its perfect fulfillment. In the three synoptic Gospels, Jesus' call to the rich young man to follow him, in the obedience of a disciple and in the observance of the Commandments, is joined to the call to poverty and chastity.[4] The evangelical counsels are inseparable from the Commandments.

2054 Jesus acknowledged the Ten Commandments, but he also showed the power of the Spirit at work in their letter. He preached a "righteousness [which] exceeds that of the scribes and Pharisees"[5] as well as that of the Gentiles.[6] He unfolded all the demands of the Commandments. "You have heard that it was said to the men of old, 'You shall not kill.' ... But I say to you that every one who is angry with his brother shall be liable to judgment."[7]

2055 When someone asks him, "Which commandment in the Law is the greatest?"[8] Jesus replies: "You shall love the Lord your God with all your heart, and with all your soul, and with all your mind. This is the greatest and first commandment. And a second is like it: You shall love your neighbor as yourself. On these two commandments hang all the Law and the prophets."[9] The Decalogue must be interpreted in light of this twofold yet single commandment of love, the fullness of the Law: "The commandments: 'You shall not commit adultery, You shall not kill, You shall not steal, You shall not covet,' and any other commandment, are summed up in this sentence: 'You shall love your neighbor as yourself.' Love does no wrong to a neighbor; therefore love is the fulfilling of the law."[10]

FOOTNOTES

1. Mt. 19:16-19. 2. Mt. 19:21. 3. Cf. Mt. 5:17. 4. Cf. Mt. 19:6-12, 21, 23-29. 5. Mt. 5:20. 6.Cf. Mt. 5:46-47. 7. Mt. 5:21-22. 8. Mt. 22:36. 9. Mt. 22:37-40; cf. Dt. 6:5; Lv. 19:18. 10. Rom. 13:9-10.

In the traditional Catholic enumeration and according to Dt. 5:6-21, the Commandments are:

1. "I, the Lord, am your God You shall not have other gods besides me. You shall not carve idols."
2. "You shall not take the name of the Lord, your God, in vain."
3. "Take care to keep holy the Sabbath day."
4. "Honor your father and your mother."
5. "You shall not kill."
6. "You shall not commit adultery."

7. "You shall not steal."

8. "You shall not bear dishonest witness against your neighbor."

9. "You shall not covet your neighbor's wife."

10. "You shall not desire your neighbor's house or field, nor his male or female slave, nor his ox or ass, nor anything that belongs to him" (summarily, his goods).

Another version of the Commandments, substantially the same, is given in Ex. 20:1-17.

The traditional enumeration of the Commandments in Protestant usage differs from the above. Thus: two commandments are made of the first, as above; the third and fourth are equivalent to the second and third, as above, and so on; and the 10th includes the ninth and 10th, as above.

Love of God and Neighbor

The first three of the commandments deal directly with man's relations with God, viz.: acknowledgment of one true God and the rejection of false gods and idols; honor due to God and his name; observance of the Sabbath as the Lord's day.

The rest cover interpersonal relationships, viz.: the obedience due to parents and, logically, to other persons in authority, and the obligations of parents to children and of persons in authority to those under their care; respect for life and physical integrity; fidelity in marriage, and chastity; justice and rights; truth; internal respect for faithfulness in marriage, chastity, and the goods of others.

Perfection in Christian Life

The moral obligations of the Ten Commandments are complemented by others flowing from the twofold law of love, the whole substance and pattern of Christ's teaching, and everything implied in full and active membership and participation in the community of salvation formed by Christ in his Church. Some of these matters are covered in other sections of the *Almanac* under appropriate headings.

Precepts of the Church

The purpose of the precepts of the Church, according to the *Catechism of the Catholic Church*, is "to guarantee to the faithful the indispensable minimum in the spirit of prayer and moral effort, in the growth and love of God and neighbor" (No. 2041).

1. Attendance at Mass on Sundays and holy days of obligation. (Observance of Sundays and holy days of obligation involves refraining from work that hinders the worship due to God.)

2. Confession of sins at least once a year. (Not required by the precept in the absence of serious sin.)

3. Reception of the Eucharist at least during the Easter season (in the U.S., from the first Sunday of Lent to Trinity Sunday).

4. Keep holy the holy days of obligation.

5. Observance of specified days of fasting and abstinence.

There is also an obligation to provide for the material needs of the Church.

CATHOLIC MORAL TEACHINGS OF POPE JOHN PAUL II

On Aug. 6, 1993, Pope John Paul II published his tenth encyclical, Veritatis Splendor *("The Splendor of the Truth") regarding the fundamental truths of the Church's moral teachings. On Mar. 25, 1995, he published his eleventh encyclical,* Evangelium Vitae *("The Gospel of Life"), concerning the value and inviolability of human life. The following material is adapted from* The Encyclicals of John Paul II, *with the kind permission of Rev. J. Michael Miller, C.S.B.*

Veritatis Splendor ("The Splendor of the Truth")

On Aug. 6, 1993, John Paul II signed his tenth encyclical, *Veritatis Splendor,* regarding certain fundamental truths of the Church's moral teaching.[1] Undoubtedly it is the pope's most complex and most discussed document. Since its publication, the encyclical has generated a great deal of comment in the media and among theologians. This is not surprising, since *Veritatis Splendor* is the first-ever papal document on the theological and philosophical foundations of Catholic moral teaching. In this encyclical the pope affirms that divine revelation contains "a specific and determined moral content, universally valid and permanent" (§37.1), which the Magisterium has the competence to interpret and teach.

Six years before, in the apostolic letter *Spiritus Domini* (1987), John Paul had publicly announced his intention to publish a document that would treat "more fully and more deeply the issues regarding the very foundations of moral theology" (§5.1). For several reasons the encyclical's preparation took longer than was first anticipated. First, the pope widely consulted

bishops and theologians throughout the world, and various drafts were drawn up. Second, he thought that it was fitting for the encyclical "to be preceded by the *Catechism of the Catholic Church,* which contains a complete and systematic exposition of Christian moral teaching" (§5.3). The *Catechism,* published in 1992, gives a full presentation of the Church's moral doctrine, including that on particular questions, and expounds it in a positive way. *Veritatis Splendor,* on the other hand, limits itself to dealing with the fundamental principles underlying all moral teaching.

But why does John Paul think that an encyclical on moral issues will serve the Church and the world on the threshold of the third millennium? According to him, reflection on the ethical implications of Christian faith, lived from the beginning as the "way" (Acts 22:4), belongs to the full proclamation of the Gospel. Moreover, he is convinced that society is in the throes of a *"crisis of truth"* (§32.2). This crisis has the "most serious implications for the moral life of the faithful and for communion in the Church, as well as for a just and fraternal social life" (§5.2).

The dechristianization of many cultures involves not only a loss of faith but also *"a decline or obscuring of the moral sense"* (§106.2). This new moral situation brings with it "the *confusion between good and evil,* which makes it impossible to build up and to preserve the moral order" (§93.1). The ethical bewilderment of some Catholics has led to "the spread of numerous doubts and objections of a human and psychological, social and cultural, religious and even properly theological nature, with regard to the Church's moral teachings" (§4.2). In an increasingly secular world, believers are "making judgments and decisions [that] often appear extraneous or even contrary to those of the Gospel" (§88.2). Moreover, dissent from Catholic moral teaching often entails "an overall and systematic calling into question of traditional moral doctrine" (§4.2). Thus, as a service to the ethical and spiritual welfare of individuals and cultures, John Paul addresses the basic moral principles handed down by the Christian Tradition.

In order to meet his goal, the pope responds in a constructive way to the contemporary moral crisis by proclaiming "the splendor of the truth." When he announced the forthcoming publication of *Veritatis Splendor*, he described the encyclical's purpose: "It reaffirms the dignity of the human person, created in God's image, and proposes anew the genuine concept of human freedom, showing its essential and constitutive relationship with the truth in accordance with Christ's words: 'The truth will make you free!' (Jn 8:32)."[2] On another occasion, John Paul said that he intended the encyclical to be "a proclamation of truth and a hymn to freedom: values felt strongly by contemporary man and deeply respected by the Church."[3] His primary aim, then, is not to censure specific dissident moral opinions but to proclaim that Christ is "the true and final answer to the problem of morality" (§85).

John Paul sets several specific objectives for the encyclical. First, he wishes "*to reflect on the whole of the Church's moral teaching*, with the precise goal of recalling certain fundamental truths of Catholic doctrine which, in the present circumstances, risk being distorted or denied" (§4.2, cf. §30.1). Second, he aims to show the faithful "the inviting splendor of that truth which is Jesus Christ himself" (§83.2). Christ alone is the answer to humanity's questions, "the only response fully capable of satisfying the desire of the human heart" (§7.1). Third, if the present crisis is to be successfully resolved, the Magisterium must authoritatively discern "*interpretations of Christian morality which are not consistent with 'sound teaching'* (2 Tim 4:3)" (§29.4, cf. §27.4). This pastoral discernment of the pope and bishops is necessary as a way of assuring "*the right of the faithful* to receive Catholic doctrine in its purity and integrity" (§113.2).

The pope addresses *Veritatis Splendor* specifically to his brother bishops. He intends them to be the first, but not exclusive, recipients of the encyclical. John Paul reminds them of their responsibility to safeguard and find "ever new ways of speaking with love and mercy" about "*the path of the moral life*" (§3.1,2).

John Paul II's training in ethics and moral theology is clearly evident in *Veritatis Splendor*. The encyclical's exposition is sometimes highly technical, especially in its analyses and responses to opinions contrary to Church teaching. While some commentators have voiced disagreement about the accuracy of the pope's descriptions of the ethical positions with which he disagrees, they respect his desire to be fair-minded. As we shall see, whenever John Paul deals with an opinion he disagrees with, he first takes great pains to point out what is positive in the view. Only after doing this does he then examine its weaknesses. When unmasking theological and philosophical ideas incompatible with revealed truth, he scrupulously avoids imposing "any particular theological system, still less a philosophical one" (§29.4).

Throughout the encyclical the pope repeatedly draws inspiration from the Bible. Chapter one, structured around the encounter of Jesus with the rich young man (Mt 19:16-21), establishes a biblical foundation for fundamental moral principles. In this chapter the pope wishes to apply the theological method proposed by the Second Vatican Council: "Sacred Scripture remains the living and fruitful source of the Church's moral doctrine" (§28.2, cf. §5.3). Chapter two, on the other hand, uses Scripture chiefly to corroborate positions advanced on the basis of the natural moral law. The beginning of chapter three returns to a more biblical approach; it discusses discipleship in terms of the Paschal Mystery and of martyrdom as the supreme expression of following Christ.

More so than in his other encyclicals, in *Veritatis Splendor* John Paul relies considerably on the teaching of Saint Thomas Aquinas, referring to him directly at least 20 times, and on the teaching of Saint Augustine, citing him 16 times. The pope also mines extensively the documents of Vatican II, especially *Gaudium et Spes*, which he cites more than 25 times. Except for one reference to Saint Alphonsus Liguori and a single direct citation of John Henry Newman, the pope mentions no moral philosopher or theologian after the Middle Ages.

FOOTNOTES

1.*Acta Apostolicae Sedis*, 85 (1993), 1133-1228. 2. *Angelus*, October 3, 1993, *L'Osservatore Romano*, 40 (1993), 1. 3. *Angelus*, October 17, 1993, *L'Osservatore Romano*, 42 (1993), 1.

Evangelium Vitae ("The Gospel of Life")

"The *Gospel of life* is at the heart of Jesus' message" (§1.1). With these words Pope John Paul II begins his eleventh encyclical, *Evangelium Vitae*, published on March 25, 1995.[1] He aptly chose the feast of the Annunciation, which celebrates Mary's welcoming of the Son of God who took flesh in her womb, to issue a document dedicated to the value and inviolability of human life. By taking up the cause of the "great multitude of weak and defenseless human beings" (§5.4), especially unborn children and those at the end of life, the pope continues the defense of human dignity dealt with in his three social encyclicals. *Evangelium Vitae* is an anguished and vigorous response to "*scientifically and systematically programmed threats*" against life (§17.2), assaults which have repercussions on Church teaching, touching upon "the core of her faith in the redemptive Incarnation of the Son of God" (§3.1).

For Pope John Paul II, the cause of life is the cause of the Gospel entrusted to the Church, which is duty-bound to raise her voice in the defense of life. His encyclical is a "pressing appeal addressed to each and every person, in the name of God: *respect, protect, love and serve life, every human life*!" (§5.5).

Preparations for the encyclical began in April 1991, when the pope called a special meeting in Rome of the College of Cardinals to discuss current threats to human life. After their deliberations, the cardinals asked him "to reaffirm with the authority of the Successor of Peter the value of human life and its inviolability" (§5.1). As a first response to their request, the pope wrote a personal letter to every bishop, seeking contributions to the planned document. They replied with valuable suggestions, and he incorporated many of their proposals into the encyclical. *Evangelium Vitae,* then, is the fruit of genuine episcopal collegiality. By taking an active part in its preparation, the bishops "bore witness to their unanimous desire to share in the doctrinal and pastoral mission of the Church with regard to the *Gospel of life*" (§5.2).

Unlike *Veritatis Splendor,* which was directed primarily to bishops, John Paul intends *Evangelium Vitae* to be read also by the lay faithful, indeed by all people of good will. Concern for the sacredness of human life is not just a matter for Catholics. "The value at stake," writes the pope, "is one which every human being can grasp by the light of reason" (§101.2). The essential truths of the Gospel of life "are written in the heart of every man and woman," echoing in every human conscience "from the time of creation itself" (§29.3). He insists that anyone who is sincerely open to truth and goodness can discover "the sacred value of human life from its very beginning until its end, and can affirm the right of every human being to have this primary good respected to the highest degree" (§2.2).

The encyclical's style is typically Wojtylan. It intersperses rigorous analysis with prayers and exhortations. As can be seen from the more than three hundred biblical quotations and references, Scripture accompanies the pope's presentation from start to finish, giving *Evangelium Vitae* an inspirational tone and familiar style. He also relies heavily on the Church Fathers. The eighteen patristic quotations that appear in the encyclical reinforce the truths that God is the origin of life, that human beings share in divine life, and that Jesus gave his life so that others might live. As is customary, John Paul frequently cites the documents of the Second Vatican Council — here, more than 25 times. He also makes use of the *Catechism of the Catholic Church,* citing it on 10 occasions.

Of particular significance in *Evangelium Vitae* are the pope's three authoritative doctrinal pronouncements: on the direct and voluntary killing of innocent human life (cf. §57.4), on abortion (cf. §62.3), and on euthanasia (cf. §65.3). In each of these formal statements John Paul recalls, through his ordinary magisterium, that a specific proposition is taught infallibly by the ordinary and universal Magisterium of the College of Bishops in communion with the Successor of Peter. He does not, therefore, call upon the charism which belongs to the Petrine ministry to teach infallibly, as this was defined at the First Vatican Council (1870). Rather, the pope "confirms" or "declares" (as in the case of abortion) a doctrine already taught by the bishops as belonging to the Catholic faith. Thus, there is nothing "new" in the Pope's affirmations, but merely the reiteration of teaching about which a consensus exists in the Episcopal College.

FOOTNOTES

1. *Acta Apostolicae Sedis,* 87 (1995), 401-522.

CATHOLIC SOCIAL DOCTRINE

Nature of the Doctrine

Writing in *Christianity and Social Progress,* Pope John XXIII made the following statement about the nature and scope of the Church's social doctrine as stated in the encyclicals in particular and related writings in general:

"What the Catholic Church teaches and declares regarding the social life and relationships of men is beyond question for all time valid.

"The cardinal point of this teaching is that individual men are necessarily the foundation, cause, and end of all social institutions insofar as they are social by nature, and raised to an order of existence that transcends and subdues nature.

"Beginning with this very basic principle whereby the dignity of the human person is affirmed and defended, Holy Church — especially during the last century and with the assistance of learned priests and laymen, specialists in the field — has arrived at clear social teachings whereby the mutual relationships of men are ordered. Taking general norms into account, these principles are in accord with the nature of things and the changed conditions of man's social life, or with the special genius of our day. Moreover, these norms can be approved by all."

Background

While social concerns have always been a part of the Church's teachings, Catholic social doctrine has been the subject of much consideration since the end of the last century and has been formulated in a progressive manner in a number of authoritative documents starting with the encyclical *Rerum Novarum* ("On Capital and Labor") issued by Leo XIII in 1891. Owing to its significance, the encyclical was called by Pope John XXIII the *magna carta* of Catholic social doctrine.

Other outstanding examples are the encyclicals: *Quadragesimo Anno* ("On Reconstruction of the Social Order") by Pius XI in 1931; *Mater et Magistra* ("Christianity and Social Progress") and *Pacem in Terris* ("Peace on Earth"), by John XXIII in 1961 and 1963, respectively; *Populorum Progressio* ("Development of Peoples"), by Paul VI in 1967; *Laborem Exercens* ("On Human Work"), *Sollicitudo Rei Socialis* ("On Social Concerns") and *Centesimus Annus* ("The 100th Year") by John Paul II in 1981, 1987 and 1991, respectively. Among many other accomplishments of ideological importance in the social field, Pius XII made a distinctive contribution with his formulation of a plan for world peace and order in Christmas messages from 1939 to 1941, and in other documents.

Of particular significance to the contemporary application of social doctrine are the document *Gaudium et Spes* (Pastoral Constitution on the Church in the Modern World) issued by the Second Vatican Council and Pope John Paul II's encyclical letters, *Laborem Exercens* ("On Human Work"), *Sollicitudo Rei Socialis* ("On Social Concerns"), and *Centesimus Annus* ("The 100th Year").

These documents represent the most serious attempts in modern times to systematize the social implications of divine revelation as well as the socially relevant writings of the Fathers and Doctors of the Church. Their contents are theological penetrations into social life, with particular reference to human rights, the needs of the poor and those in underdeveloped countries, and humane conditions of life, freedom, justice and peace. In some respects, they read like juridical documents; essentially, however, they are Gospel-oriented and pastoral in intention.

Gaudium et Spes

Gaudium et Spes ("Pastoral Constitution on the Church in the Modern World") was the last document issued by Vatican Council II (Dec. 7, 1965). The document has as its purpose to search out the signs of God's presence and meaning in and through the events of this time in human history. Accordingly, it deals with the situation of men in present circumstances of profound change, challenge and crisis on all levels of life. It is evenly divided into two main parts: the Church's teaching on humanity in the modern era and urgent problems of the times.

Part One

The first part begins: "The joys and the hopes, the griefs and the anxieties of this age" (No. 1) — a clear indication that the Council Fathers were aware both of the positive nature of the modern world and its many dangers and travails. Further, the council places great emphasis throughout on the human existence, a stress that was quite innovative in its presentation: "According to the almost unanimous opinion of believers and unbelievers alike, all things on earth should be related to man as their center and crown" (No. 12). Having developed an analysis of humanity, the document then offered a thorough summary of traditional Church teaching on human life, complete with discussion of sin, the union of body and soul, and the moral conscience.

There is, as well, a genuinely realistic appraisal of contemporary society, noting the pervasiveness of atheism, adding that its spread can be attributed in part to the fault and carelessness of those within the Church whose actions and failures "must be said to conceal rather than reveal the authentic face of God and religion" (No. 19). Toward the fuller understanding of the place of the Church in the modern world, *Gaudium et Spes* emphasizes the harmony that should exist between the Catholic faith and scientific progress because "earthly matters and the concerns of faith derive from the same God" (No. 36). This does not mean, however, that there ought to be no qualifying elements or restraints to science; the Council Fathers

add to this positive statement the provision that such research, "within every branch of learning," must be "carried out in a genuinely scientific manner and in accord with moral norms" (No. 36). Finally, the first part makes an ecumenical gesture, noting that the Church "holds in high esteem the things which other Christian Churches or ecclesial communities have done…." (No. 40).

Part Two

Part Two offers the practical application of the Church's teaching and message enunciated in Part One. Most pressing is the council's concern for the family, and its treatment of family life and marriage is the most detailed and extensive in the history of the councils of the Church. This leads to study of the deeply troubling presence of contraception. The council reiterates Church instruction in an affirmation of opposition to contraception that would receive even fuller expression in three years in the encyclical *Humanae Vitae*. In the matter of abortion, the document states clearly: "… from the moment of its conception life must be guarded with the greatest care, while abortion and infanticide are unspeakable crimes" (No. 51). In its study of culture, in which the council reminds all humanity that culture and civilization are creations of man, it points out his responsibility over it and his duty to seek that which is above, which entails an "obligation to work with all men in constructing a more human world" (No. 57). Here we have a powerful preface or introduction to the next concerns voiced in *Gaudium et Spes*: the questions of economic life, political systems, and war. In building upon earlier social encyclicals, *Gaudium et Spes* discusses economics as vital to human progress and social development, striking the important balance (developed so masterfully in the later writings of Pope John Paul II) between the rights of an individual to possess goods and the obligation to aid the poor (Nos. 63-72). While declaring the autonomous and independent nature of the Church and politics, the Council Fathers do acknowledge: "There are, indeed, close links between earthly affairs and those aspects of man's condition which transcend this world. The Church herself employs the things of time to the degree that her own proper mission demands" (No. 76). The document goes on to state that "the arms race is an utterly treacherous trap for humanity" (No. 81) and "It is our clear duty, then, to strain every muscle as we work for the time when all war can be completely outlawed by international consent" (No. 82).

SOCIAL DOCTRINE UNDER POPE JOHN PAUL II

Background

Throughout his pontificate, Pope John Paul II has traveled the globe speaking out on all matters of the Church's social teachings and has written a number of important encyclicals that are reflective not only of the Church's traditions of social doctrine but that seek to utilize the teachings of the faith to offer specific points of reflection and solutions to the many pressing problems of the late 20th century. Rooted in Christian anthropol-

ogy and Tradition, Scripture, and Magisterium, John Paul's writings have encompassed economic ethics, the rights and dignity of the worker, the primacy of the human person, the place of the family in society and the Church, and the integrative teachings of the Church in the areas of moral and pastoral theology. The three main expressions of his social teachings have been the encyclicals: *Laborem Exercens* (1981); *Sollicitudo Rei Socialis* (1987); and *Centesimus Annus* (1991).

SOCIAL ENCYCLICALS OF POPE JOHN PAUL II

(The following material is adapted from The Encyclicals of John Paul II, *with the kind permission of the Rev. J. Michael Miller, C.S.B.)*

Laborem Exercens

Fascinated as he is by commemorative events, Pope John Paul II marked the ninetieth anniversary of Leo XIII's *Rerum Novarum* (1891) by publishing his first social encyclical, *Laborem Exercens,* on Sept. 14, 1981.[1] Before him, Pius XI in *Quadragesimo Anno* (1931), John XXIII in *Mater et Magistra* (1961), and Paul VI in *Octogesima Adveniens* (1971) had observed the anniversary of Leo's ground-breaking encyclical with documents of their own.

Laborem Exercens is a very personal document. The encyclical has solid roots in the pope's own experience as a worker. It reflects his familiarity with various worlds of work: in mines and factories, in artistic and literary production, in scholarship and pastoral ministry. More particularly, *Laborem Exercens* has its origins in the long debate carried on by the Archbishop of Kracow with Marxist intellectuals. The topics chosen, which include the struggle between capital and labor, ownership of the means of production, and solidarity, as well as the terminology of the encyclical, bear ample witness to this background of controversy. Here, however, he is less concerned with economic systems than with the human person as a "worker." Furthermore, John Paul intended his letter to encourage the Solidarity union movement, which in the early 1980s was the primary motor for effecting social and political change in a Poland under a totalitarian regime.

The style of encyclical is distinctively Wojtylan. It reveals the pope's preference for combining a phenomenological description of experience with philosophical-theological meditation. While he cites the Second Vatican Council's *Gaudium et Spes,* John Paul never directly quotes from any previous social encyclical, not even from *Rerum Novarum.* The encyclical's footnotes are almost entirely biblical, indicating that its primary inspiration is Sacred Scripture. As in his two previous encyclicals, *Redemptor Hominis* (1979) and *Dives in Misericordia* (1980), the pope relies heavily upon the plastic and descriptive language of the Bible, especially from the opening chapters of Genesis, to develop his theme. The encyclical unfolds the meaning of the human vocation to work in light of the biblical text on "subduing the earth" (cf. Gn 1:28). This call to exercise dominion is to be carried out by those created "in the image of God" (Gn 1:27) through their work, which the pope qualifies as *"one of the characteristics that distinguish* man from the rest of creatures" (preface).

Unlike earlier social encyclicals which dealt with a wide range of different questions, *Laborem Exercens* is sharply focused. John Paul chooses a very specific theme — the dignity and role of human work — and explores its many ramifications: "Through work man must earn his daily bread and contribute to the continual advance of science and technology and, above all, to elevating unceasingly the cultural and moral level of the society within which he lives in community with those who belong to the same family" (preface). At the present moment, he believes, the world is faced with important choices. It is "on the eve of new developments in technological, economic, and political conditions which, according to many experts, will influence the world of work and production no less than the industrial revolution of the last century" (§1.3).

A crisis in the meaning of human work is a crucial factor contributing to society's current plight. "Work, as human issue, is at the very center of the 'social question' " (§2.1). Moreover, the pope adds, "human work is *a key,* probably *the essential key,* to the whole social question" (§3.2). It is a problem with ramifications which extend beyond the so-called "working class"; the dimensions of the crisis are universal. Therefore he does not confine his encyclical to a reflection on the work only of industrial or agricultural workers. Instead, he extends it to encompass the work done by every sector of society: management, white-collar workers, scientists, intellectuals, artists, women in the home. "Each and every individual, to the proper extent and in an incalculable number of ways, takes part in the giant process whereby man 'subdues the earth' through his work" (§4.4). To use a favorite expression of the pope's, the world's "workbench" includes all those who labor for their daily bread — all men and women.

As in his two previous encyclicals, John Paul takes up the "way" of the human person, this time with regard to his fundamental activity of work. *Laborem Exercens* is yet another chapter in the pope's book on Christian anthropology. Moreover, since work is a great gift and good for humanity, his tone throughout the encyclical is constructive and exhortatory.

Footnote

1. *Acta Apostolicae Sedis,* 73 (1981), 577-647.

Sollicitudo Rei Socialis

Although signed on Dec. 30, 1987, Pope John Paul II's encyclical "on social concern" was not officially published until Feb. 19, 1988.[1] Like *Laborem Exercens* (1981), this second social encyclical commemorates a previous papal document. *Sollicitudo Rei Socialis* marks the twentieth anniversary of Paul VI's *Populorum Progressio* (1967). But more than merely recalling the relevance and doctrine of Pope Paul's encyclical, it highlights new themes and responds to the problems of development in the Third World which had emerged in the intervening twenty years.

John Paul writes as a teacher, explaining why the proclamation of the Church's social doctrine belongs to her evangelizing mission. He also writes as an informed witness to the increasing injustice and poverty in the world. Lastly, he writes as a defender of human dignity and inalienable rights, and of every person's transcendent vocation to communion with the Triune God.

In some ways *Sollicitudo Rei Socialis* echoes *Laborem Exercens* (1981). John Paul's use of Sacred Scripture, for example, is similar in that he frequently quotes from the opening chapters of Genesis. The differences between the two social encyclicals, however, are noteworthy. Whereas in *Laborem Exercens* (1981) the pope never directly cites *Rerum Novarum* (1891), the encyclical of Leo XIII which it commemorates, throughout *Sollicitudo Rei Socialis* John Paul quotes or refers to *Populorum Progressio* more than forty times. It is his constant point of reference. Second, to support his presentation, the pope marshals statements taken from earlier writings and discourses of his own pontificate, as well as the social teaching of the Second Vatican Council expressed in *Gaudium et Spes*. Third, more than in any other encyclical, John Paul makes use of documents published by the Roman Curia. Especially notable are his six references to the *Instruction on Christian Freedom and Liberation* (1986) issued by the Congregation for the Doctrine of the Faith. He also cites two publications of the Pontifical Commission "Iustitia et Pax": *At the Service of the Human Community: An Ethical Approach to the International Debt Question* (1986) and *The Church and the Housing Problem* (1987).

While *Sollicitudo Rei Socialis* perceptively analyzes the economic, political, social, and cultural dimensions of world development, its perspective is primarily ethical and theological. John Paul rereads *Populorum Progressio* through a moral-spiritual lens. His main concern is to form the consciences of individual men and women, to help them in their task of promoting authentic development "in the light of faith and of the Church's Tradition" (§41.7).

Footnote

1. *Acta Apostolicae Sedis,* 80 (1988), 513-586.

Centesimus Annus

Pope John Paul II issued his ninth encyclical, *Centesimus Annus,* on May 1, 1991.[1] Not surprisingly, the pope chose to mark the centenary of Leo XIII's *Rerum Novarum* (1891) with a document of his own. In the four years since the signing of *Sollicitudo Rei Socialis* (1987) the Berlin Wall had collapsed, and in the light of this event John Paul offers his "rereading" of *Rerum Novarum*. His purpose is twofold. He wishes to recall Leo's contribution to the development of the Church's social teaching and to honor the popes who drew upon the encyclical's "vital energies" in their social teaching.

Centesimus Annus has some interesting peculiarities. First, among all John Paul's encyclicals, it relies the least on citing Sacred Scripture. Its few biblical

references are primarily exhortatory or illustrative. For his sources the pope depends mostly on *Rerum Novarum* and on the social encyclicals of his predecessors, as well as on earlier documents and discourses of his own Magisterium. Second, much of the encyclical's content is conditioned by current geopolitical affairs. Indeed, the encyclical reads as if the pope had *Rerum Novarum* in one hand and a diary of the 1989 events sweeping eastern Europe in the other.

Despite the opinions of some commentators, John Paul's primary interest is not to pass judgment on either failed socialism or contemporary capitalism. Above all, in keeping with his desire to articulate a Christian anthropology, he recalls the need for Catholic social doctrine to have a "*correct view of the human person* and of his unique value" (§11.3). Without such a view, he believes, it is impossible to solve today's social, economic, and political problems. The Church's distinctive contribution to meeting these challenges is her vision of the transcendent dignity of the human person created in God's image and redeemed by Christ's blood.

The pope's rereading of Leo XIII encompasses three time frames: "looking back" at *Rerum Novarum* itself, "looking around" at the contemporary situation, and "looking to the future" (§3.1). In looking back, John Paul confirms the enduring principles of Leo's encyclical, principles that belong to the Church's doctrinal inheritance. His "pastoral solicitude" also impels the pope to analyze recent political events from the perspective of the Gospel "in order to discern the new requirements of evangelization" (§3.5).

Even more clearly than in his two previous social encyclicals, *Laborem Exercens* (1981) and *Sollicitudo Rei Socialis* (1987), John Paul clearly distinguishes the authentic doctrine contained in the Church's social teaching from the analysis of contingent historical events. This analysis, he states, "is not meant to pass definitive judgments, since this does not fall *per se* within the Magisterium's specific domain" (§3.5). Whatever comes within the doctrinal sphere, however, "pertains to the Church's evangelizing mission and is an essential part of the Christian message" (§5.5).

Footnote

1. *Acta Apostolicae Sedis,* 83 (1991), 793-867.

SOCIO-ECONOMIC STATEMENTS BY U.S. BISHOPS

Over a period of nearly 80 years, the bishops of the United States have issued a great number of socio-economic statements reflecting papal documents in a U.S. context.

One such statement, entitled "Economic Justice for All: Social Teaching and the U.S. Economy" was issued in November, 1986. It's contents are related in various ways with the subsequently issued encyclical letter, *Centesimus Annus*. Principles drawn from the bishops' document are given in the following excerpt entitled "A Catholic Framework for Economic Life." Another significant statement, entitled "The Harvest of Justice Is Sown in Peace" (1993) follows.

A Catholic Framework for Economic Life

As followers of Jesus Christ and participants in a powerful economy, Catholics in the United States, are called to work for greater economic justice in the face

of persistent poverty, growing income gaps and increasing discussion of economic issues in the United States and around the world. We urge Catholics to use the following ethical framework for economic life as principles for reflection, criteria for judgment and directions for action. These principles are drawn directly from Catholic teaching on economic life.

1. The economy exists for the person, not the person for the economy.

2. All economic life should be shaped by moral principles. Economic choices and institutions must be judged by how they protect or undermine the life and dignity of the human person, support the family and serve the common good.

3. A fundamental moral measure of an economy is how the poor and vulnerable are faring.

4. All people have a right to life and to secure the basic necessities of life (e.g., food, clothing, shelter,

education, health care, safe environment, economic security).

5. All people have the right to economic initiative, to productive work, to just wages and benefits, to decent working conditions as well as to organize and join unions or other associations.

6. All people, to the extent they are able, have a corresponding duty to work, a responsibility to provide for the needs of their families and an obligation to contribute to the broader society.

7. In economic life, free markets have both clear advantages and limits; government has essential responsibilities and limitations; voluntary groups have irreplaceable roles, but cannot substitute for the proper working of the market and the just policies of the state.

8. Society has a moral obligation, including governmental action where necessary, to assure opportunity, meet basic human needs and pursue justice in economic life.

9. Workers, owners, managers, stockholders and consumers are moral agents in economic life. By our choices, initiative, creativity and investment, we enhance or diminish economic opportunity, community life and social justice.

10. The global economy has moral dimensions and human consequences. Decisions on investment, trade, aid and development should protect human life and promote human rights, especially for those most in need wherever they might live on this globe.

The Harvest of Justice Is Sown in Peace

The National Conference of Catholic Bishops, at a meeting Nov. 17, 1993, issued a statement entitled "The Harvest of Justice Is Sown in Peace," marking the 10th anniversary of their earlier pastoral letter, "The Challenge of Peace: God's Promise and Our Response."

The Challenge of Peace

"The challenge of peace today is different, but no less urgent" than in 1983, and the threat of global nuclear war "may seem more remote than at any time in the nuclear age." Questions of peace and war, however, cannot be addressed "without acknowledging that the nuclear question remains of vital political and moral significance."

The statement outlines an agenda for action to guide future advocacy efforts of the bishops' national conference. It also urges that the cause of peace be reflected constantly in liturgical prayers of petition, preaching and Catholic education at all levels.

Confronting the temptation to isolationism in U.S. foreign policy is among "the major challenges peacemakers face in this new era."

Factors in a vision for peace include a commitment to the universal common good and recognition of the imperative of human solidarity.

Nonviolent revolutions in some countries "challenge us to find ways to take into full account the power of organized, active nonviolence."

With respect to just war criteria, the statement says that "important work needs to be done in refining, clarifying and applying the just war tradition to the choices facing our decision-makers in this still violent and dangerous world."

Subjects of concern include humanitarian intervention, deterrence, conscientious objection and the development of peoples.

Presumption against Force

"Our conference's approach, as outlined in 'The Challenge of Peace,' can be summarized in this way:

"1) In situations of conflict our constant commitment ought to be, as far as possible, to strive for justice through nonviolent means.

"2) But when sustained attempts at nonviolent action fail to protect the innocent against fundamental injustice, then legitimate political authorities are permitted as a last resort to employ limited force to rescue the innocent and establish justice."

Lethal Force

"Whether lethal force may be used is governed by the following criteria:

• "Just cause: Force may be used only to correct a grave, public evil, i.e., aggression or massive violation of the basic rights of whole populations.

• "Comparative justice: While there may be rights and wrongs on all sides of a conflict, to override the presumption against the use of force, the injustice suffered by one party must significantly outweigh that suffered by the other.

• "Legitimate authority: Only duly constituted public authorities may use deadly force or wage war.

• "Right intention: Force may be used only in a truly just cause and solely for that purpose.

• "Probability of Success: Arms may not be used in a futile cause or in a case where disproportionate measures are required to achieve success.

• "Proportionality: The overall destruction expected from the use of force must be outweighed by the good to be achieved.

• "Last Resort: Force may be used only after all peaceful alternatives have been seriously tried and exhausted.

"These criteria [of just war], taken as a whole, must be satisfied in order to override the strong presumption against the use of force."

Just War

"The just-war tradition seeks also to curb the violence of war through restraint on armed combat between the contending parties by imposing the following moral standards for the conduct of armed conflict:

• "Noncombatant Immunity: Civilians may not be the object of direct attack, and military personnel must take due care to avoid and minimize indirect harm to civilians.

• "Proportionality: In the conduct of hostilities, efforts must be made to attain military objectives with no more force than is militarily necessary and to avoid disproportionate collateral damage to civilian life and property.

• "Right Intention: Even in the midst of conflict, the aim of political and military leaders must be peace with justice so that acts of vengeance and indiscriminate violence, whether by individuals, military units or governments, are forbidden."

Structures for Justice and Peace

Quoting an address given by Pope John Paul in August, 1993, in Denver, the statement said:

" 'The international community ought to establish more effective structures for maintaining and promoting justice and peace. This implies that a concept of strategic interest should evolve which is based on the full development of peoples — out of poverty and toward a more dignified existence, out of injustice and exploitation toward fuller respect for the human person and the defense of universal rights.'

"As we consider a new vision of the international community, five areas deserve special attention: (1) strengthening global institutions; (2) securing human rights; (3) promoting human development; (4) restraining nationalism and eliminating religious violence; and (5) building cooperative security.'"

Humanitarian Intervention

"Pope John Paul, citing the 'conscience of humanity and international humanitarian law,' has been outspoken in urging that 'humanitarian intervention be obligatory where the survival of populations and entire ethnic groups is seriously compromised. This is a duty for nations and the international community.' He elaborated on this right and duty of humanitarian intervention in his 1993 annual address to the diplomatic corps (accredited to the Holy See):

" 'Once the possibilities afforded by diplomatic negotiations and the procedures provided for by international agreements and organizations have been put into effect, and that [sic], nevertheless, populations are succumbing to the attacks of an unjust aggressor, states no longer have a 'right to indifference.' It seems clear that their duty is to disarm this aggressor if all other means have proved ineffective. The principles of the sovereignty of states and of noninterference in their internal affairs — which retain all their value — cannot constitute a screen behind which torture and murder may be carried out.' "

(For the most recent Bishops' Statements concerning the Iraqi War, please see **News in Depth**.)

THE BLESSED VIRGIN MARY

ROLE OF MARY IN THE MYSTERY OF CHRIST AND THE CHURCH

The following excerpts are from Chapter VIII of the Second Vatican Council's "Constitution on the Church," Lumen Gentium.

Preface

Wishing in his supreme goodness and wisdom to effect the redemption of the world, "when the fullness of time came, God sent his Son, born of a woman, that we might receive the adoption of sons" (Gal. 4:4-5). "He for us men, and for our salvation, came down from heaven, and was incarnate by the Holy Spirit from the Virgin Mary." This divine mystery of salvation is revealed to us and continued in the Church, which the Lord established as his own body. In this Church, adhering to Christ the head and having communion with all his saints, the faithful must also venerate the memory "above all of the glorious and perpetual Virgin Mary. Mother of our God and Lord Jesus Christ." (52)

At the message of the angel, the Virgin Mary received the Word of God in her heart and in her body, and gave Life to the world. Hence, she is acknowledged and honored as being truly the Mother of God and Mother of the Redeemer. Redeemed in an especially sublime manner by reason of the merits of her Son, and united to him by a close and indissoluble tie, she is endowed with the supreme office and dignity of being the Mother of the Son of God. As a result, she is also the favorite daughter of the Father and the temple of the Holy Spirit. Because of this gift of sublime grace, she far surpasses all other creatures, both in heaven and on earth.

At the same time, however, because she belongs to the offspring of Adam, she is one with all human beings in their need for salvation. Indeed, she is "clearly the Mother of the members of Christ since she cooperated out of love so that there might be born in the Church the faithful, who are members of Christ their head. Therefore, she is also hailed as a pre-eminent and altogether singular member of the Church, and as the Church's model and excellent exemplar in faith and charity. Taught by the Holy Spirit, the Catholic Church honors her with filial affection and piety as a most beloved Mother. (53)

This sacred synod intends to describe with diligence the role of the Blessed Virgin in the mystery of the Incarnate Word and the Mystical Body. It also wishes to describe the duties of redeemed mankind toward the Mother of God, who is the Mother of Christ and Mother of men, particularly of the faithful.

The synod does not, however, have it in mind to give a complete doctrine on Mary, nor does it wish to decide those questions which have not yet been fully illuminated by the work of theologians. (54)

II. The Role of the Blessed Virgin in the Economy of Salvation

The Father of mercies willed that the consent of the predestined Mother should precede the Incarnation so that, just as a woman contributed to death, so also a woman should contribute to life. This contrast was verified in outstanding fashion by the Mother of Jesus. She gave to the world that very Life which renews all things, and she was enriched by God with gifts befitting such a role.

It is no wonder, then, that the usage prevailed among the holy Fathers whereby they called the Mother of God entirely holy and free from all stain of sin, fashioned by the Holy Spirit into a kind of new substance and new creature. Adorned from the first instant of her conception with the splendors of an entirely unique holiness, the Virgin of Nazareth is, on God's command, greeted by an angel messenger as "full of grace" (cf. Lk. 1:28). To the heavenly messenger she replies: "Behold the handmaid of the Lord; be it done to me according to thy word" (Lk. 1:38).

By thus consenting to the divine utterance, Mary, a daughter of Adam, became the Mother of Jesus. Embracing God's saving will with a full heart and impeded by no sin, she devoted herself totally as a handmaid of the Lord to the person and work of her Son. In subordination to him and along with him, by the grace of almighty God she served the mystery of redemption.

Rightly, therefore, the holy Fathers see her as used by God not merely in a passive way but as cooperating in the work of human salvation through free faith and obedience. (56)

This union of the Mother with the Son in the work of salvation was manifested from the time of Christ's virginal conception up to his death. It is shown first of all when Mary, arising in haste to go to visit Elizabeth, was greeted by her as blessed because of her belief in the promise of salvation, while the precursor leaped for joy in the womb of his mother (cf. Lk. 1:41-45). This association was shown also at the birth of our Lord, who did not diminish his Mother's virginal integrity but sanctified it, when the Mother of God joyfully showed her first-born Son to the shepherds and the Magi.

When she presented him to the Lord in the Temple, making the offering of the poor, she heard Simeon foretelling at the same time that her Son would be a sign of contradiction and that a sword would pierce the Mother's soul, that out of many hearts thoughts might be revealed (cf. Lk. 2:34-35). When the Child Jesus was lost and they had sought him sorrowing, his parents found him in the temple, taken up with things which were his Father's business. They did not understand the reply of the Son. But his Mother, to be sure, kept all these things to be pondered over in her heart (cf. Lk. 2:41-51). (57)

In the public life of Jesus, Mary made significant appearances. This was so even at the very beginning, when she was moved with pity at the marriage feast of Cana, and her intercession brought about the beginning of the miracles by Jesus the Messiah (Cf. Jn. 2:1-11). In the course of her Son's preaching, she received his praise when, in extolling a kingdom beyond the calculations and bonds of flesh and blood, he declared blessed (cf. Mk. 3:35 par.; Lk. 11:27-28) those who heard and kept the word of the Lord as she was faithfully doing (cf. Lk. 2:19, 51).

Thus, the Blessed Virgin advanced in her pilgrimage of faith and loyally persevered in her union with her Son unto the cross. There she stood, in keeping with the divine plan (cf. Jn. 19:25), suffering grievously with her only-begotten Son. There she united herself with a maternal heart to his sacrifice, and lovingly consented to the immolation of this Victim whom she herself had brought forth. Finally, the same Christ Jesus dying on the cross gave her as a mother to his disciple. This he did when he said: "Woman, behold your son" (Jn. 19:26-27). (58)

But since it pleased God not to manifest solemnly the mystery of the salvation of the human race until he poured forth the Spirit promised by Christ, we see the apostles before the day of Pentecost "continuing with one mind in prayer with the women and Mary, the Mother of Jesus, and with his brethren" (Acts 1:14). We see Mary prayerfully imploring the gift of the Spirit, who had already overshadowed her in the Annunciation.

Finally, preserved free from all guilt of original sin, the Immaculate Virgin was taken up body and soul into heavenly glory upon the completion of her earthly sojourn. She was exalted by the Lord as Queen of all, in order that she might be the more thoroughly conformed to her Son, the Lord of lords (cf. Rev. 19:16) and the conqueror of sin and death. (59)

III. The Blessed Virgin and the Church

We have but one Mediator, as we know from the words of the Apostle: "For there is one God, and one Mediator between God and men, himself man, Christ Jesus, who gave himself as a ransom for all" (1 Tim. 2:5-6). The maternal duty of Mary toward men in no way obscures or diminishes this unique mediation of Christ, but rather shows its power. For all the saving influences of the Blessed Virgin on men originate, not from some inner necessity, but from the divine pleasure. They flow forth from the superabundance of the merits of Christ, rest on his mediation, depend entirely on it, and draw all their power from it. In no way do they impede the immediate union of the faithful with Christ. Rather, they foster this union. (60)

In an utterly singular way, she (Mary) cooperated by her obedience, faith, hope and burning charity in the Savior's work of restoring supernatural life to souls. For this reason she is a mother to us in the order of grace. (61)

This maternity of Mary in the order of grace began with the consent which she gave in faith at the Annunciation and which she sustained without wavering beneath the cross. This maternity will last without interruption until the eternal fulfillment of all the elect. For, taken up to heaven, she did not lay aside this saving role, but by her manifold acts of intercession continues to win for us gifts of eternal salvation.

By her maternal charity, Mary cares for the brethren of her Son who still journey on earth surrounded by dangers and difficulties until they are led to their happy fatherland. Therefore, the Blessed Virgin is invoked by the Church under the titles of Advocate, Auxiliatrix, Adjutrix and Mediatrix. These, however, are to be so understood that they neither take away nor add anything to the dignity and efficacy of Christ the one Mediator.

For no creature could ever be classed with the Incarnate Word and Redeemer. But, just as the priesthood of Christ is shared in various ways both by sacred ministers and by the faithful; and as the one goodness of God is in reality communicated diversely to his creatures: so also the unique mediation of the Redeemer does not exclude but rather gives rise among creatures to a manifold cooperation which is but a sharing in this unique source.

The Church does not hesitate to profess this subordinate role of Mary. She experiences it continuously and commends it to the hearts of the faithful so that, encouraged by this maternal help, they may more closely adhere to the Mediator and Redeemer. (62)

Through the gift and role of divine maternity, Mary is united with her Son, the Redeemer, and with his singular graces and offices. By these, the Blessed Virgin is also intimately united with the Church. As St. Ambrose taught, the Mother of God is a model of the Church in the matter of faith, hope and charity, and perfect union with Christ. For in the mystery of the Church, herself rightly called Mother and Virgin, the Blessed Virgin stands out in eminent and singular fashion as exemplar of both virginity and motherhood. (63)

In the most holy Virgin, the Church has already reached that perfection whereby she exists without spot or wrinkle (cf. Eph. 5:27). Yet, the followers of Christ still strive to increase in holiness by conquering sin. And so they raise their eyes to Mary who shines forth to the whole community of the elect as a model of the virtues. Devotedly meditating on her and contemplating her in the light of the Word made man, the Church with reverence enters more intimately into the supreme mystery of the Incarnation and becomes ever increasingly like her Spouse. (64)

The Church in her apostolic work looks to her who brought forth Christ, conceived by the Holy Spirit and born of the Virgin, so that through the Church Christ may be born and grow in the hearts of the faithful also. The Virgin Mary in her own life lived as an example of that maternal love by which all should be fittingly animated who cooperate in the apostolic mission of the Church on behalf of the rebirth of men. (65)

IV. Devotion to the Blessed Virgin in the Church

Mary was involved in the mystery of Christ. As the most holy Mother of God she was, after her Son, exalted by divine grace above all angels and men. Hence, the Church appropriately honors her with special reverence. Indeed, from most ancient times the Blessed Virgin has been venerated under the title of "God-bearer." In all perils and needs, the faithful; have fled prayerfully to her protection. Especially after the Council of Ephesus the cult of the people of God toward Mary wonderfully increased in veneration and love, in invocation and imitation, according to her own prophetic words: "All generations shall call me blessed; because he who is mighty has done great things for me" (Lk. 1:48).

As it has always existed in the Church, this cult (of Mary) is altogether special, Still, it differs essentially from the cult of adoration which is offered to the Incarnate Word, as well as to the Father and the Holy Spirit. Yet, devotion to Mary is most favorable to this supreme cult. The Church has endorsed many forms of piety toward the Mother of God, provided that they were within the limits of sound and orthodox doctrine. These forms have varied according to the circumstances of time and place, and have reflected the diversity of native characteristics and temperament among the faithful. While honoring Christ's Mother, these devotions cause her Son to be rightly known, loved and glorified, and all his commands observed. Through him all things have their beginning (cf. Col. 1: 15-16) and in him "it has pleased (the eternal Father) that all his fullness should dwell" (Col. 1:19). (66)

This most holy synod deliberately teaches this Catholic doctrine. At the same time, it admonishes all the sons of the Church that the cult, especially the liturgical cult, of the Blessed Virgin, be generously fostered. It charges that practices and exercises of devotion toward her be treasured as recommended by the teaching authority of the Church in the course of centuries.

This synod earnestly exhorts theologians and preachers of the divine word that, in treating of the unique dignity of the Mother of God, they carefully and equally avoid the falsity of exaggeration on the one hand and the excess of narrow-mindedness on the other.

Let the faithful remember, moreover, that true devotion consists neither in fruitless and passing emotion, nor in a certain vain credulity. Rather, it proceeds from the true faith, by which we are led to know the excellence of the Mother of God, and are moved to a filial love toward our Mother and to the imitation of her virtues. (67)

REDEMPTORIS MATER

Redemptoris Mater (*Mother of the Redeemer*), Pope John Paul II's sixth encyclical letter, is a "reflection on the role of Mary in the mystery of Christ and on her active and exemplary presence in the life of the Church." The letter was published Mar. 25, 1987.

Central to consideration of Mary is the fact that she is the Mother of God (*Theotokos*), since by the power of the Holy Spirit she conceived in her virginal womb and brought into the world Jesus Christ, the Son of God, who is of one being with the Father and the Holy Spirit.

Mary was preserved from original sin in view of her calling to be the Mother of Jesus. She was gifted in grace beyond measure. She fulfilled her role in a unique pilgrimage of faith. She is the Mother of the Church and the spiritual mother of all people.

The following excerpts are from the English text provided by the Vatican and circulated by the CNS Documentary Service, *Origins*, Apr. 9, 1987 (Vol. 16, No. 43). Subheads have been added. Quotations are from pertinent documents of the Second Vatican Council.

Mary's Presence in the Church

Mary, through the same faith which made her blessed, especially from the moment of the Annunciation, is present in the Church's mission, present in the Church's work of introducing into the world the kingdom of her Son.

This presence of Mary finds as many different expressions in our day just as it did throughout the Church's history. It also has a wide field of action: through the faith and piety of individual believers; through the traditions of Christian families or "domestic churches," of parish and missionary communities, religious institutes and dioceses; through the radiance and attraction of the great shrines where not only individuals or local groups, but sometimes whole nations and societies, even whole continents, seek to meet the Mother of the Lord, the one who is blessed because she believed, is the first among believers, and therefore became the Mother of Emmanuel.

This is the message of the land of Palestine, the spiritual homeland of all Christians, because it was the homeland of the Savior of the world and of his Mother.

This is the message of the many churches in Rome and throughout the world which have been raised up in the course of the centuries by the faith of Christians. This is the message of centers like Guadalupe, Lourdes, Fátima and others situated in the various countries. Among them, how could I fail to mention the one in my own native land, Jasna Gora? One could perhaps speak of a specific "geography" of faith and Marian devotion which includes all of these special places of pilgrimage where the people of God seek to meet the Mother of God in order to find, within the radius of the maternal presence of her "who believed," a strengthening of their own faith.

Mary and Ecumenism

"In all of Christ's disciples the Spirit arouses the desire to be peacefully united, in the manner determined by Christ, as one flock under one shepherd." The journey of the Church, especially in our own time, is marked by the sign of ecumenism: Christians are seeking ways to restore that unity which Christ implored from the Father for his disciples on the day before his passion.

Christians must deepen in themselves and each of their communities that "obedience of faith" of which Mary is the first and brightest example.

Christians know that their unity will be truly rediscovered only if it is based on the unity of their faith. They must resolve considerable discrepancies of doctrine concerning the mystery and ministry of the Church, and sometimes also concerning the role of Mary in the work of salvation.

Mary, who is still the model of this pilgrimage, is to lead them to the unity which is willed by their one Lord, and which is so much desired by those who are attentively listening to what "the Spirit is saying to the churches" today.

A Hopeful Sign

Meanwhile, it is a hopeful sign that these churches and ecclesial communities are finding agreement with the Catholic Church on fundamental points of Christian belief, including matters relating to the Virgin Mary. For they recognize her as the Mother of the Lord and hold that this forms part of our faith in Christ, true God and true man. They look to her who at the foot of the cross accepted as her son the Beloved Disciple (John), the one who in his turn accepted her as his Mother.

On the other hand, I wish to emphasize how profoundly the Catholic Church, the Orthodox Church and the ancient churches of the East feel united by love and praise of the *Theotokos*. Not only "basic dogmas of the Christian faith concerning the Trinity and God's Word made flesh of the Virgin Mary were defined in ecumenical councils held in the East," but also in their liturgical worship "the Eastern Christians pay high tribute, in very beautiful hymns, to Mary ever-Virgin. God's most holy Mother."

The churches which profess the doctrine of Ephesus proclaim the Virgin as "true Mother of God" since "our Lord Jesus Christ, born of the Father before time began according to his divinity, in the last days he himself, for our sake and for our salvation, was begotten of Mary the Virgin Mother of God according to his humanity." The Greek Fathers and the Byzantine tradition, contemplating the Virgin in the light of the Word made flesh, have sought to penetrate the depth of that bond which unites Mary, as the Mother of God, to Christ and the Church. The Virgin is a permanent presence in the whole reality of the salvific mystery.

Marian Mediation

The Church knows and teaches with St. Paul that there is only one mediator: "For there is one God, and there is one mediator between God and men, the man Christ Jesus, who gave himself as a ransom for all" (1 Tm. 2:5-6). "The maternal role of Mary toward people in no way obscures or diminishes the unique mediation of Christ, but rather shows its power." It is mediation in Christ.

The Church knows and teaches that "all the saving influences of the Blessed Virgin on mankind originate from the divine pleasure. They flow forth from the superabundance of the merits of Christ, rest on his mediation, depend entirely on it and draw all their power from it. In no way do they impede the immediate union of the faithful with Christ. Rather, they foster this union." This saving influence is sustained by the Holy Spirit, who, just as he overshadowed the Virgin Mary when he began in her the divine motherhood, in a similar way constantly sustains her solicitude for the brothers and sisters of her Son.

Mediation and Motherhood

In effect, Mary's mediation is intimately linked with her motherhood. It possesses a specifically maternal character, which distinguishes it from the mediation of the other creatures who in various and always subordinate ways share in the one mediation of Christ, although her own mediation is also a shared mediation. In fact, while it is true that "no creature could ever be classed with the Incarnate Word and Redeemer," at the same time "the unique mediation of the Redeemer does not exclude but rather gives rise among creatures a manifold cooperation which is but a sharing in this unique source." Thus "the one goodness of God is in reality communicated diversely to his creatures."

Subordinate Mediation

The teaching of Vatican II presents the truth of Mary's mediation as "a sharing in the one unique source that is the mediation of Christ himself." Thus we read: "The Church does not hesitate to profess this subordinate role of Mary. She experiences it continuously and commends it to the hearts of the faithful so that, encouraged by this maternal help, they may more closely adhere to the Mediator and Redeemer."

This role is at the same time special and extraordinary. It flows from her divine motherhood and can be understood and lived in faith only on the basis of the full truth of this motherhood. Since by virtue of divine election Mary is the earthly Mother of the Father's consubstantial Son and his "generous companion" in the work of redemption, "she is a Mother to us in the order of grace." This role constitutes a real dimension of her presence in the saving mystery of Christ and the Church.

Mary is honored in the Church "with special reverence. Indeed, from most ancient times the Blessed Virgin Mary has been venerated under the title of 'God-bearer.' In all perils and needs, the faithful have fled prayerfully to her protection." This cult is altogether special; it bears in itself and expresses the profound link which exists between the Mother of Christ and the Church. As Virgin and Mother, Mary remains for the Church a "permanent model." It can therefore be said that, especially under this aspect, namely, as a model or rather as a "figure," Mary, present in the mystery of Christ, remains constantly present also in the mystery of the Church. For the Church too is "called mother and virgin," and these names have a profound biblical and theological justification.

Mary and Women

This Marian dimension of Christian life takes

on special importance in relation to women and their status. In fact, femininity has a unique relationship with the Mother of the Redeemer, a subject which can be studied in greater depth elsewhere.... The figure of Mary of Nazareth sheds light on womanhood as such by the very fact that God, in the sublime event of the incarnation of his Son, entrusted himself to the ministry, the free and active ministry, of a woman.

… Women, by looking to Mary, find in her the secret of living their femininity with dignity and of achieving their own true advancement. In the light of Mary, the Church sees in the face of women the reflection of a beauty which mirrors the loftiest sentiments of which the human heart is capable: the self-offering totality of love; the strength that is capable of bearing the greatest sorrows; limitless fidelity and tireless devotion to work; the ability to combine penetrating intuition with words of support and encouragement.

APPARITIONS OF THE BLESSED VIRGIN MARY

Seven of the best-known apparitions are described.

Banneux, near Liège, Belgium: Mary appeared eight times between Jan. 15 and Mar. 2, 1933, to an 11-year-old peasant girl, Mariette Beco, in a garden behind the family cottage in Banneux. She called herself the Virgin of the Poor, and has since been venerated as Our Lady of the Poor, the Sick, and the Indifferent. A small chapel was blessed Aug. 15, 1933. Approval of devotion to Our Lady of Banneux was given in 1949 by Bishop Louis J. Kerkhofs of Liège, and a statue of that title was solemnly crowned in 1956.

Beauraing, Belgium: Mary appeared 33 times between Nov. 29, 1932, and Jan. 3, 1933, to five children in the garden of a convent school in Beauraing. A chapel was erected on the spot. Reserved approval of devotion to Our Lady of Beauraing was given Feb. 2, 1943, and final approbation July 2, 1949, by Bishop Charue of Namur (d. 1977).

Fátima, Portugal: Mary appeared six times between May 13 and Oct. 13, 1917, to three children (Lucia dos Santos, 10, who is now a Carmelite nun; Francisco Marto, 9, who died in 1919; and his sister Jacinta, 7, who died in 1920; Jacinta and Francisco were beatified by Pope John Paul II in 2000) in a field called Cova da Iria near Fátima. She recommended frequent recitation of the Rosary; urged works of mortification for the conversion of sinners; called for devotion to herself under the title of her Immaculate Heart; asked that the people of Russia be consecrated to her under this title, and that the faithful make a Communion of reparation on the first Saturday of each month.

The apparitions were declared worthy of belief in October 1930, and devotion to Our Lady of Fátima was authorized under the title of Our Lady of the Rosary. In October, 1942, Pius XII consecrated the world to Mary under the title of her Immaculate Heart. Ten years later, in the first apostolic letter addressed directly to the peoples of Russia, he consecrated them in a special manner to Mary. For more on the Third Secret of Fátima, see below.

Guadalupe, Mexico: Mary appeared four times in 1531 to an Indian, Juan Diego (declared Blessed in 1990), on Tepeyac hill outside of Mexico City, and instructed him to tell Bishop Zumarraga of her wish that a church be built there. The bishop complied with the request about two years later, after being convinced of the genuineness of the apparition by the evidence of a miraculously painted life-size figure of the Virgin on the mantle of the Indian. The mantle bearing the picture has been preserved and is enshrined in the Basilica of Our Lady of Guadalupe. The shrine church, originally dedicated in 1709 and subsequently enlarged, has the title of basilica.

Benedict XIV, in a 1754 decree, authorized a Mass and Office under the title of Our Lady of Guadalupe for celebration on Dec. 12, and named Mary the patroness of New Spain. Our Lady of Guadalupe was designated patroness of Latin America by St. Pius X in 1910 and of the Americas by Pius XII in 1945.

La Salette, France: Mary appeared as a sorrowing and weeping figure Sept. 19, 1846, to two peasant children, Melanie Matthieu, 15, and Maximin Giraud, 11, at La Salette. The message she confided to them, regarding the necessity of penance, was communicated to Pius IX in 1851 and has since been known as the "secret" of La Salette. Bishop de Bruillard of Grenoble declared in 1851 that the apparition was credible, and devotion to Mary under the title of Our Lady of La Salette was authorized. A Mass and Office with this title were authorized in 1942. The shrine church was given the title of minor basilica in 1879.

Lourdes, France: Mary, identifying herself as the Immaculate Conception, appeared 18 times between Feb. 11 and July 16, 1858, to 14-year-old Bernadette Soubirous (canonized in 1933) at the grotto of Massabielle near Lourdes. Her message concerned the necessity of prayer and penance for the conversion of peoples. Mary's request that a chapel be built at the grotto and spring was fulfilled in 1862. Devotion under the title of Our Lady of Lourdes was authorized, and a Feb. 11 feast commemorating the apparitions was instituted by Leo XIII. St. Pius X extended this feast throughout the Church in 1907. The Church of Notre Dame was made a basilica in 1870, and the Church of the Rosary was built later. The underground Church of St. Pius X, with a capacity of 20,000 persons, was consecrated Mar. 25, 1958. Plans were announced in 1994 for renovation and reconstruction of the Lourdes sanctuary.

Our Lady of the Miraculous Medal, France: Mary appeared three times in 1830 to Catherine Labouré (canonized in 1947) in the chapel of the motherhouse of the Daughters of Charity of St. Vincent de Paul, Rue de Bac, Paris. She commissioned Catherine to have made the medal of the Immaculate Conception, now known as the Miraculous Medal, and to spread devotion to her under this title. In 1832, the medal was struck.

THE THIRD SECRET OF FÁTIMA

(*Courtesy Vatican Information Service.*)

On June 26, 2000, the Holy See Press Office issued the document "The Message Of Fátima" that had been prepared by the Congregation for the Doctrine of the Faith and carried the signatures of Cardinal Joseph Ratzinger and Archbishop Tarcisio Bertone S.D.B., respectively prefect and secretary of the congregation.

The document, which is over 40 pages long, was published in English, French, Italian, Spanish, German, Portuguese and Polish. It was made up of an introduction by Archbishop Bertone; the first and second parts of the "secret" of Fátima in Sr. Lucia's original text dated August 31, 1941, and addressed to the bishop of Leiria-Fátima, and a translation; the photostatic reproduction of the original manuscript of the third part of the "secret" and a translation; John Paul II's letter to Sr. Lucia dated April 19, 2000, and a translation; a summary of Sr. Lucia's conversation with Archbishop Bertone and Bishop Serafim de Sousa Ferreira e Silva of Leiria-Fátima which took place on April 27, 2000, in the Carmel Monastery of St. Teresa of Coimbra, Portugal; the words of Cardinal Secretary of State Angelo Sodano at the end of the beatification of Jacinta and Francisco on May 13, 2000; a theological commentary by Cardinal Ratzinger.

In his introduction, Archbishop Bertone affirms that "Fátima is undoubtedly the most prophetic of modern apparitions.... In 1917 no one could have imagined all this: the three '*pastorinhos*' of Fátima see, listen and remember, and Lucia, the surviving witness, commits it all to paper when ordered to do so by the Bishop of Leiria and with Our Lady's permission."

He continues: "The third part of the 'secret' was written ... on January 3, 1944. There is only one manuscript, which is here reproduced photostatically. The sealed envelope was initially in the custody of the Bishop of Leiria. To ensure better protection for the 'secret' the envelope was placed in the secret archives of the Holy Office on April 4, 1957. The Bishop of Leiria informed Sr. Lucia of this."

The secretary of the Congregation for the Doctrine of the Faith indicates that "according to the records of the Archives, the Commissary of the Holy Office, Fr.

Pierre Paul Philippe O.P., with the agreement of Cardinal Alfredo Ottaviani, brought the envelope containing the third part of the 'secret of Fátima' to Pope John XXIII on August 17, 1959. 'After some hesitation,' His Holiness said: 'We shall wait. I shall pray. I shall let you know what I decide.' In fact Pope John XXIII decided to return the sealed envelope to the Holy Office and not to reveal the third part of the 'secret.' Paul VI read the contents with the Substitute, Archbishop Angelo Dell'Acqua, on March 27, 1965, and returned the envelope to the Archives of the Holy Office, deciding not to publish the text. John Paul II, for his part, asked for the envelope containing the third part of the 'secret' following the assassination attempt on May 13, 1981," and this was given to Archbishop Eduardo Martinez Somalo, Substitute of the Secretariat of State, on July 18 of the same year. On August 11 it was returned to the Archives of the Holy Office.

"As is well known," added Archbishop Bertone, "Pope John Paul II immediately thought of consecrating the world to the Immaculate Heart of Mary and he himself composed a prayer for what he called an 'Act of Entrustment' which was to be celebrated in the Basilica of St. Mary Major on June 7 1981."

"In order to respond more fully to the requests of 'Our Lady,' the Holy Father desired to make more explicit during the Holy Year of the Redemption the Act of Entrustment of June 7, 1981, which had been repeated in Fátima on May 13, 1982."

"Sr. Lucia," continued the archbishop, "personally confirmed that this solemn and universal act of consecration corresponded to what Our Lady wished. Hence any further discussion or request is without basis."

Sr. Lucia had already hinted at the interpretation of the third part of the "secret" in a letter to the Holy Father dated May 12, 1982. That letter is also published in the document.

Finally, Archbishop Tarcisio Bertone indicates that "the decision of His Holiness Pope John Paul II to make public the third part of the 'secret' of Fátima brings to an end a period of history marked by tragic human lust for power and evil, yet pervaded by the merciful love of God and the watchful care of the Mother of Jesus and of the Church."

TRANSLATION OF THE THIRD SECRET OF FÁTIMA

On June 26, 2000, the Holy See issued the complete translation of the original Portuguese text of the third part of the secret of Fátima, revealed to the three shepherd children at Cova da Iria-Fátima on July 13, 1917, and committed to paper by Sr. Lucia on January 3, 1944:

"I write in obedience to you, my God, who command me to do so through his Excellency the Bishop of Leiria and through your Most Holy Mother and mine.

"After the two parts which I have already explained, at the left of Our Lady and a little above, we saw an Angel with a flaming sword in his left hand; flashing, it gave out flames that looked as though they would set the world on fire; but they died out in contact with the splendor that Our Lady radiated towards him from her right hand: pointing to the earth with his right

hand, the Angel cried out in a loud voice: 'Penance, Penance, Penance!'. And we saw in an immense light that is God: 'something similar to how people appear in a mirror when they pass in front of it' a Bishop dressed in White 'we had the impression that it was the Holy Father.' Other Bishops, Priests, men and women Religious going up a steep mountain, at the top of which there was a big Cross of rough-hewn trunks as of a cork-tree with the bark; before reaching there the Holy Father passed through a big city half in ruins and half trembling with halting step, afflicted with pain and sorrow, he prayed for the souls of the corpses he met on his way; having reached the top of the mountain, on his knees at the foot of the big Cross he was killed by a group of soldiers who fired bullets and arrows at him, and in the same way there died one after another the other Bishops, Priests, men and women Religious, and various lay people of different ranks and positions. Beneath the two arms of the Cross there were two Angels each with a crystal aspersorium in his hand, in which they gathered up the blood of the Martyrs and with it sprinkled the souls that were making their way to God."

EVENTS AT MEDJUGORJE

The alleged apparitions of the Blessed Virgin Mary to six young people of Medjugorje, Bosnia-Herzogovina, have been the source of interest and controversy since they were first reported in June 1981, initially in the neighboring hillside field, subsequently in the village church of St. James and even in places far removed from Medjugorje.

Reports say the alleged visionaries have seen, heard, and even touched Mary during visions, and that they have variously received several or all of 10 secret messages related to coming world events and urging a quest for peace through penance and personal conversion. An investigative commission appointed by former local Bishop Pavao Zanic of Mostar-Duvno reported in March 1984 that the authenticity of the apparitions had not been verified. He called the apparitions a case of "collective hallucination" exploited by local Franciscan priests at odds with him over control of a parish.

Former Archbishop Frane Franic of Split-Makarska, on the other hand, said in December 1985: "Speaking as a believer and not as a bishop, my personal conviction is that the events at Medjugorje are of supernatural inspiration." He based his conviction on the observations of spiritual benefits related to the reported events, such as the spiritual development of the six young people, the increases in Mass attendance and sacramental practice at the scene of the apparitions, and the incidence of reconciliation among people.

On Jan. 29, 1987, the bishops of Yugoslavia declared: "On the basis of research conducted so far, one cannot affirm that supernatural apparitions are involved" at Medjugorje. Currently, the events at Medjugorje are under on-going investigation by the Holy See to determine their authenticity. Nevertheless, the site of Medjugorje remains a popular destination for Catholic pilgrims from Europe and the United States.

THE CODE OF CANON LAW

Canon Law is the term that denotes the body of laws governing the Catholic Church. The name is derived from the Greek word *kanon* (rule, i.e., rule of practical direction), which, from the fourth century, was used to denote the ordinances and regulations promulgated by the various Church councils that were convened to discuss problems or important topics. The actual term "canon law" (*ius canonicum*) came into use in the 1100s and was intended to differentiate ecclesiastical law from civil law (*ius civile*).

History of Canon Law

In a practical sense, the laws and regulations began to take shape as early as apostolic times and were evident in their nascent form in the Didache, the Didscalia and the Apostolic Tradition. Owing to the persecution of the Church, however, there was little effort to gather laws together, and certainly less time was devoted to systematizing them.

The fourth century brought the Church freedom from persecution and the resulting rapid growth in membership that was a concomitant of the favors bestowed upon the faith by the rulers of the Roman Empire. New laws were naturally needed and desired. Local regulations were soon established through the decrees of the councils, although these most often had only a local authority and adherence. The general (or ecumenical) councils made laws for the whole Church, and the custom developed of carrying on the decrees of previous assemblies by having them read before the start of a new council. Collections of these laws or canons were then undertaken, but these did not bear the weight of being an official code as they were gathered under private authority.

The earliest efforts at collecting Church laws were centered around the private compilation of the decrees of the Eastern councils to which were added those of the Western Church. The councils of the African Church also made lasting contributions, the most significant coming out of the Seventeenth Council of Carthage (419), which accepted the book of canons later adopted into the canon law of both the Eastern and Western Churches. An official Code of Canon Law was recognized in the seventh century under the Isidorian Collection. Other important influences were the writings of monks in England and Ireland. The monks compiled lists of sins and various offenses to which confessors applied the proper fines or penances. The resulting books were called Penitentials, and they offer scholars an invaluable glimpse into the state of Church law in early medieval England and the development of moral theology.

The Carolingian Reforms of the Church under Charlemagne facilitated the enactment of much legislation that was beneficial to the faith, but it also signaled a long period of secular interference in ecclesiastical affairs. Two by-products of this lay intrusion were the creation of the forged but interesting False Decretals (collections of false canons and decrees of the popes used to falsify the Church's position) and the application of legal arguments by Churchmen that could protect the Church from abuse. Efforts at revitalization would become heightened under the Gregorian Reform, in particular with the reign of Pope St. Gregory VII (1073-1085). From that time, throughout the Middle Ages, laws from the Church would be centered in and produced by the papacy, assisted in running the administration of the Church by the Roman Curia.

Gradually, legal experts collected the decrees of popes, enactments of councils, and sources of older, ancient canons. To these were added glosses, or commentaries, to assist in the teaching of the details of the subject. Still, the study of canon law was severely handicapped by the sheer number of collections, the contradiction between many points of law, and the inability to find specific laws because of the chronological arrangements of the material. Thus can be seen the major significance of the *Decretum* of Gratian, published around 1148 in Bologna. Compiled by the legal expert Gratian, the *Decretum* (in full, *Concordantia discordantum canonum*) was not a formal collection of canons but sought to provide a juridical system for its readers. Toward this end, though, Gratian examined (and excerpted) virtually every canon ever published. The *Decretum* was quickly adopted as the textbook of canon law, despite the fact that it was a private collection and not codified.

Over the next centuries, the popes added to the body of laws by giving rulings to those questions posed to them by bishops from around the Church. These decretal letters were then brought together and, for purposes of comprehensiveness, added to the *Decretum Gratiani*. The most important of these was the *Liber extra*, the collection made by St. Raymond Peñafort for Pope Gregory IX. This received official approval and was to be a vital source for the *Corpus Juris Canonici*. Other remarkable contributors to canon law in the late Middle Ages were Zenzelinus de Cassanis, Jean Chappuis, Guido de Baysio, John the Teuton (or Joannes Teutonicus), Stephen of Tournai, and most of all, Joannes Andreae (d. 1348).

Considerable activity was initiated by the Council of Trent (1545-1563), which sought to reform and reinvigorate the Church in the wake of the Protestant Reformation. The same century brought the formation in 1588 of the Sacred Congregation of the Curia by Pope Sixtus V (r. 1585-1590), which became the main means of implementing new laws and examining facets of established ones.

The final decision to codify the laws of the Church was made by Pope St. Pius X who, in 1903, issued *Arduum*, the *motu proprio* ordering the complete reform and codification of all canon law. It was completed and promulgated in 1917 as the *Codex Juris Canonici*, the first official guide to the laws of the Catholic Church. A new Code of Canon Law was issued by Pope John Paul II in 1983, the final result of a call for a new code dating back to Pope John XXIII (r. 1958-1963) and continued by Pope Paul VI (r. 1963-1978).

The 1983 Code of Canon Law

Pope John Paul II promulgated a revised Code of Canon Law for the Latin Rite on January 25, 1983, with the apostolic constitution *Sacrae Disciplinae Legis* ("Of the Sacred Discipline of Law") and ordered it into effect as of the following November 27. Promulgation of the Code marked the completion of the last major reform in the Church stemming from the Second Vatican Council.

The 1983 Code of Canon Law replaced the one which had been in effect since 1918. The new Code incorporates into law the insights of Vatican Council II. These 1,752 canons focus on the People of God and the threefold ministries of sanctifying, teaching and governance. Also included are general norms, temporalities, sanctions and procedures.

Guiding Principles

When Pope John XXIII announced on January 25, 1959, that he was going to convoke the Second Vatican Council, he also called for a revision of the existing Code of Canon Law. His successor, Paul VI, appointed a commission for this purpose in 1963 and subsequently enlarged it. The commission, which began its work after the conclusion of the Council in 1965, was directed by the 1967 Synod of Bishops to direct its efforts in line with 10 guiding principles. The bishops said the revised Code should:

- be juridical in character, not just a set of broad moral principles;
- be intended primarily for the external forum (regarding determinable fact, as opposed to the internal forum of conscience);
- be clearly pastoral in spirit;
- incorporate most of the faculties bishops need in their ministry;
- provide for subsidiarity or decentralization;
- be sensitive to human rights;
- state clear procedures for administrative processes and tribunals;
- be based on the principle of territoriality;
- reduce the number of penalties for infraction of law;
- have a new structure.

The commission carried out its mandate with the collegial collaboration of bishops all over the world and in consultation and correspondence with individuals and experts in canon law, theology, and related disciplines. The group finished its work in 1981 and turned its final draft over to Pope John Paul II at its final plenary meeting in October of that year.

Features

The revised code is shorter (1,752 canons) than the one it replaced (2,414 canons) and has a number of important features:

It is more pastoral and flexible, as well as more theologically oriented than the former Code. It gives greater emphasis than its predecessor to a number of significant facets and concepts in church life.

In the apostolic constitution with which he promulgated the Code, Pope John Paul II called attention to its nature and some of its features, as follows:

Prime Legislative Document

"Since this is so, it seems clear enough that the Code in no way has its scope to substitute for faith, grace, the charisms, and especially charity in the life of the Church of the faithful. On the contrary, its end is rather to create such order in ecclesial society that, assigning primacy to love, grace and charisms, it at the same time renders more active their organic developments in the life both of the ecclesial society and of the individuals belonging to it. Inasmuch as it is the Church's prime legislative document, based on the juridical and legislative heritage of revelation and tradition, the Code must be regarded as the necessary instrument whereby due order is preserved in both individual and social life and in the Church's activity. Therefore, besides containing the fundamental elements of the hierarchical and organic structure of the Church, laid down by her divine Founder and founded on apostolic or at any rate most ancient tradition, and besides outstanding norms concerning the carrying out of the task mandated to the Church herself, the Code must also define a certain number of rules and norms of action."

Suits the Nature of the Church

"The instrument the Code is fully suits the Church's nature, for the Church is presented, especially through the magisterium of the Second Vatican Council, in her universal scope, and especially through the Council's ecclesiological teaching. In a certain sense, indeed, this new Code may be considered as a great effort to transfer that same ecclesiological or conciliar doctrine into canonical language. And, if it is impossible for the image of the Church described by the Council's teaching to be perfectly converted into canonical language, the Code nonetheless must always be referred to that very image, as the primary pattern whose outline the Code ought to express as well as it can by its own nature.

"From this derive a number of fundamental norms by which the whole of the new Code is ruled, of course within the limits proper to it as well as the limits of the very language befitting the material.

"It may rather be rightly affirmed that from this comes that note whereby the Code is regarded as a complement to the magisterium expounded by the Second Vatican Council.

"The following elements are most especially to be noted among those expressing a true and genuine image of the Church: the doctrine whereby the Church is proposed as the People of God and the hierarchical authority is propounded as service; in addition, the doctrine which shows the Church to be a 'communion' and from that lays down the mutual relationships which ought to exist between the particular and universal Church and between collegiality and primacy; likewise, the doctrine whereby all members of the People of God, each in the manner proper to him, share in Christ's threefold office of priest, prophet and king; to this doctrine is also connected that regarding the duties and rights of the Christian faithful, particularly the laity; then there is the effort which the Church has to make for ecumenism."

Code Necessary for the Church

"Indeed, the Code of Canon Law is extremely necessary for the Church ... The Church needs it for her hierarchichal and organic structure to be visible: so that exercise of the offices and tasks divinely entrusted to her, especially her sacred power and administration of the sacraments, should be rightly ordered; so that mutual relations of the Christian faithful may be carried out according to justice based on charity, with the rights of all being safeguarded and defined; so that we may then prepare and perform our common tasks, and that these, undertaken in order to live a Christian life more perfectly, may be fortified by means of the canonical laws.

"Thus, canonical laws need to be observed because of their very nature. Hence it is of the greatest importance that the norms be carefully expounded on the basis of solid juridical, canonical and theological foundations."

BOOKS OF THE CODE

Book I, General Norms (Canons 1-203):

Canons in this book cover Church laws, in general, custom and law, general decrees and instructions, administrative acts, statutes, physical and juridical persons, juridical acts, the power of governing, ecclesiastical offices, prescription (statutes of limitations), the reckoning of time.

Book II, The People of God (Canons 204-746):

Canons in Part I cover the obligations and rights of all the faithful, the obligations and rights of lay persons, sacred ministers and clerics, personal prelatures and associations of the faithful.

Canons in Part II cover the hierarchic constitution of the Church under the headings: the supreme authority of the Church and the college of bishops, diocesan churches and the authority constituted in them, councils of diocesan churches and the internal order of diocesan churches.

Canons in Part III cover institutes of consecrated life and societies of apostolic life.

Book III: The Teaching Office of the Church (Canons 747-833):

Canons under this heading cover: the ministry of the divine word, the missionary action of the Church, Catholic education, the instruments of social communication and books in particular, and the profession of faith.

Book IV, The Sanctifying Office of the Church (Canons 834-1252):

Canons under this heading cover each of the seven sacraments – baptism, confirmation, the Eucharist, penance, anointing of the sick, holy orders and matrimony; other acts of divine worship including sacramentals, the Liturgy of the Hours, ecclesiastical burial; the veneration of saints, sacred images and relics, vows and oaths.

Book V, Temporal Goods of the Church (Canons 1254-1310):

Canons under this heading cover: the acquisition and administration of goods, contracts, the alienation of goods, wills and pious foundations.

Book VI, Sanctions in the Church (Canons 1311-1399):

Canons in Part I cover crimes and penalties in general: the punishment of crimes in general, penal law and penal precept, persons subject to penal sanctions, penalties and other punishments, the application and cessation of penalties.

Canons in Part II cover penalties for particular crimes: crimes against religion and the unity of the Church; crimes against the authority of the Church and the liberty of the Church; the usurpation of Church offices and crimes in exercising office; false accusation of a confessor; crimes against special obligations; crimes against human life and liberty; a general norm regarding the punishment of external violations of divine law not specifically covered in the Code.

Book VII, Procedures (Canons 1400-1752):

Judicial proceedings are the principal subjects of canons under this heading: tribunals and their personnel, parties to proceedings, details regarding litigation and the manner in which it is conducted, special proceedings – with emphasis on matrimonial cases.

Glossary

A

Abbacy Nullius: A non-diocesan territory whose people are under the pastoral care of an abbot acting in general in the manner of a bishop.

Abbess: The female superior of a monastic community of nuns; e.g., Benedictines, Poor Clares, some others. Elected by members of the community, an abbess has general authority over her community but no sacramental jurisdiction.

Abbey: *See* **Monastery**.

Abbot: The male superior of a monastic community of men religious; e.g., Benedictines, Cistercians, some others. Elected by members of the community, an abbot has ordinary jurisdiction and general authority over his community. Eastern Rite equivalents of an abbot are a hegumen and an archimandrite. A regular abbot is the head of an abbey or monastery. An abbot general or archabbot is the head of a congregation consisting of several monasteries. An abbot primate is the head of the modern Benedictine Confederation.

Abiogenesis: The term used to describe the spontaneous generation of living matter from non-living matter.

Ablution: A term derived from Latin, meaning washing or cleansing and referring to the cleansing of the hands of a priest celebrating Mass, after the offering of gifts; and to the cleansing of the chalice with water and wine after Communion.

Abnegation: The spiritual practice of self-denial (or mortification), in order to atone for past sins or in order to join oneself to the passion of Christ. Mortification can be undertaken through fasting, abstinence, or refraining from legitimate pleasure.

Abortion: Abortion is not only "the ejection of an immature fetus" from the womb, but is "also the killing of the same fetus in whatever way at whatever time from the moment of conception it may be procured." (This clarification of Canon 1398, reported in the Dec. 5, 1988, edition of *L'Osservatore Romano*, was issued by the Pontifical Council for the Interpretation of Legislative Texts — in view of scientific developments regarding ways and means of procuring abortion.) Accidental expulsion, as in cases of miscarriage, is without moral fault. Direct abortion, in which a fetus is intentionally removed from the womb, constitutes a direct attack on an innocent human being, a violation of the Fifth Commandment. A person who procures a completed abortion is automatically excommunicated (Canon 1398 of the *Code of Canon Law*); also excommunicated are all persons involved in a deliberate and successful effort to bring about an abortion. Direct abortion is not justifiable for any reason, e.g.: therapeutic, for the physical and/or psychological welfare of the mother; preventive, to avoid the birth of a defective or unwanted child; social, in the interests of family and/or community. Indirect abortion, which occurs when a fetus is expelled during medical or other treatment of the mother for a reason other than procuring expulsion, is permissible under the principle of double effect for a proportionately serious reason; e.g., when a medical or surgical procedure is necessary to save the life of the mother. Such a procedure should not be confused with the purportedly "medical" procedure of the partial-birth abortion, a particularly cruel form of abortion.

Abrogation: The abolition or elimination of a law by some official action. In Canon Law, abrogation occurs through a direct decree of the Holy See or by the enactment of a later or subsequent law contrary to the former law.

Absolute: (1) A term in philosophy, first introduced at the end of the 18th century and used by Scholasticism, that signifies the "perfect being" (i.e., God), who relies upon no one for existence. Modern philosophical thought has added two new concepts: a) the Absolute is the sum of all being; b) the Absolute has no relationship with any other things; the Absolute is thus unknowable. These concepts are agnostic and contrary to Catholicism, which holds that God is the cause of all being (and hence not the sum) and is knowable by his creatures, at least in part. (2) Certain truths, revealed by God, which are unchanging.

Absolution, Sacramental: The act by which bishops and priests, acting as agents of Christ and ministers of the Church, grant forgiveness of sins in the sacrament of penance. The essential formula of absolution is: "I absolve you from your sins; in the name of the Father, and of the Son, and of the Holy Spirit. Amen." The power to absolve is given with ordination to the priesthood and episcopate. Priests exercise this power in virtue of authorization (faculties) granted by a bishop, a religious superior, or canon law. Authorization can be limited or restricted regarding certain sins and penalties or censures. In cases of necessity, and also in cases of the absence of their own confessors, Eastern and Latin Rite Catholics may ask for and receive sacramental absolution from an Eastern or Latin Rite priest; so may Polish National Catholics, according to a Vatican decision issued in May, 1993. Any priest can absolve a person in danger of death; in the absence of a priest with the usual faculties, this includes a laicized priest or a priest under censure. (*See additional entry under* **Sacraments**.)

Abstinence: 1. The deliberate deprivation by a person of meat or of foods prepared with meat on those days prescribed by the Church as penitential (Ash Wednesday, Good Friday and all Fridays of the year which are not solemnities — in the United States, not all Fridays of the year but only the Fridays of Lent). Those 14 years of age and above are bound by the discipline. (2) Sexual abstinence is the willing refrain from sexual intercourse; total abstinence is observed in obedience to the Sixth Commandment by single persons and couples whose marriages are not recognized by the Church as valid; periodic abstinence or periodic continence is observed by a married couple for regulating conception by natural means or for ascetical motives.

Adoration: The highest act and purpose of religious worship, which is directed in love and reverence to God alone in acknowledgment of his infinite perfection and goodness, and of his total dominion over creatures. Adoration, which is also called "latria," consists of internal and external elements, private and social prayer, liturgical acts and ceremonies, and especially sacrifice.

Adultery: Marital infidelity. Sexual intercourse between a married person and another to whom one is not married, a violation of the obligations of the marital covenant, chastity and justice; any sin of impurity (thought, desire, word, action) involving a married person who is not one's husband or wife has the nature of adultery.

Advent Wreath: A wreath of laurel, spruce, or similar foliage with four candles which are lighted successively in the weeks of Advent to symbolize the approaching celebration of the birth of Christ, the Light of the World, at Christmas. The wreath originated among German Protestants.

Agape: A Greek word, meaning love, love feast, designating the meal of fellowship eaten at some gatherings of early Christians. Although held in some places in connection with the Mass, the agape was not part of the Mass, nor was it of universal institution and observance. It was infrequently observed by the fifth century and disappeared altogether between the sixth and eighth centuries.

Age of Reason: (1) The time of life when one begins to distinguish between right and wrong, to understand an obligation and take on moral responsibility; seven years of age is the presumption in church law. (2) Historically, the 18th century period of Enlightenment in England and France, the age of the Encyclopedists and Deists. According to a basic thesis of the Enlightenment, human experience and reason are the only sources of certain knowledge of truth; consequently, faith and revelation are discounted as valid sources of knowledge, and the reality of supernatural truth is called into doubt and/or denied.

Aggiornamento: An Italian word having the general meaning of bringing up to date, renewal, revitalization, descriptive of the processes of spiritual renewal and institutional reform and change in the Church; fostered by the Second Vatican Council.

Agnosticism: A theory which holds that a person cannot have certain knowledge of immaterial reality, especially the existence of God and things pertaining to him. Immanuel Kant, one of the philosophical fathers of agnosticism, stood for the position that God,

as well as the human soul, is unknowable on speculative grounds; nevertheless, he found practical imperatives for acknowledging God's existence, a view shared by many agnostics. The First Vatican Council declared that the existence of God and some of his attributes can be known with certainty by human reason, even without divine revelation. The word agnosticism was first used, in the sense given here, by T. H. Huxley in 1869.

Agnus Dei: A Latin phrase, meaning Lamb of God. (1) A title given to Christ, the Lamb (victim) of the Sacrifice of the New Law (on Calvary and in Mass). (2) A prayer said at Mass before the reception of Holy Communion. (3) A sacramental. It is a round paschal-candle fragment blessed by the pope. On one side it bears the impression of a lamb, symbolic of Christ. On the reverse side, there may be any one of a number of impressions; e.g., the figure of a saint, the name and coat of arms of the reigning pope. The *agnus dei* may have originated at Rome in the fifth century. The first definite mention of it dates from about 820.

Akathist Hymn: The most profound and famous expression of Marian devotion in churches of the Byzantine Rite. It consists of 24 sections, 12 of which relate to the Gospel of the Infancy and 12 to the mysteries of the Incarnation and the virginal motherhood of Mary. In liturgical usage, it is sung in part in Byzantine churches on the first four Saturdays of Lent and in toto on the fifth Saturday; it is also recited in private devotion. It is of unknown origin prior to 626, when its popularity increased as a hymn of thanksgiving after the successful defense and liberation of Constantinople, which had been under siege by Persians and Avars. Akathist means "without sitting," indicating that the hymn is recited or sung while standing. Pope John Paul II, in a decree dated May 25, 1991, granted a plenary indulgence to the faithful of any rite who recite the hymn in a church or oratory, as a family, in a religious community or in a pious association — in conjunction with the usual conditions of freedom from attachment to sin, reception of the sacraments of penance and the Eucharist, and prayers for the intention of the pope (e.g., an Our Father, the Apostles' Creed and an aspiration). A partial indulgence can be gained for recitation of the hymn in other circumstances.

Alleluia: An exclamation of joy derived from Hebrew, "All hail to him who is, praise God," with various use in the liturgy and other expressions of worship.

Allocution: A formal type of papal address, as distinguished from an ordinary sermon or statement of views.

Alms: An act, gift, or service of compassion, motivated by love of God and neighbor, for the help of persons in need; an obligation of charity, which is measurable by the ability of one person to give assistance and by the degree of another's need. Almsgiving, along with prayer and fasting, is regarded as a work of penance as well as an exercise of charity. (*See* **Mercy, Works of.**)

Alpha and Omega: The first and last letters of the Greek alphabet, used to symbolize the eternity of God (Rv. 1:8) and the divinity and eternity of Christ, the beginning and end of all things (Rv. 21:6; 22:13). Use of the letters as a monogram of Christ originated in the fourth century or earlier.

Amen: A Hebrew word meaning truly, it is true. In the Gospels, Christ used the word to add a note of authority to his statements. In other New Testament writings, as in Hebrew usage, it was the concluding word to doxologies. As the concluding word of prayers, it expresses assent to and acceptance of God's will.

Anamnesis: A prayer recalling the saving mysteries of the death and resurrection of Jesus, following the consecration at Mass in the Latin Rite.

Anaphora: A Greek term for the Canon or Eucharistic Prayer of the Mass.

Anathema: A Greek word with the root meaning of cursed or separated and the adapted meaning of excommunication, used in church documents, especially the canons of ecumenical councils, for the condemnation of heretical doctrines and of practices opposed to proper discipline.

Anchorite: A kind of hermit living in complete isolation and devoting himself exclusively to exercises of religion and severe penance according to a rule and way of life of his own devising. In early Christian times, anchorites were the forerunners of the monastic life. The closest contemporary approach to the life of an anchorite is that of Carthusian and Camaldolese hermits.

Angels: Purely spiritual beings with intelligence and free will whose name indicates their mission as servants and messengers of God. They were created before the creation of the visible universe. Good angels enjoy the perfect good of the beatific vision. They can intercede for persons. The doctrine of guardian angels, although not explicitly defined as a matter of faith, is rooted in long-standing tradition. No authoritative declaration has ever been issued regarding choirs or various categories of angels: seraphim, cherubim, thrones, dominations, principalities, powers, virtues, archangels and angels. Archangels commemorated in the liturgy are: Michael, leader of the angelic host and protector of the synagogue; Raphael, guide of Tobiah and healer of his father; Gabriel, angel of the Incarnation. Fallen angels, the chief of whom is called the Devil or Satan, rejected the love of God and were therefore banished from heaven to hell. They can tempt persons to commit sin.

Angelus: A devotion which commemorates the Incarnation of Christ. It consists of three versicles, three Hail Marys and a special prayer, and recalls the announcement to Mary by the Archangel Gabriel that she was chosen to be the Mother of Christ, her acceptance of the divine will, and the Incarnation (Lk. 1:26-38). The Angelus is recited in the morning, at noon and in the evening. The practice of reciting the Hail Mary in honor of the Incarnation was introduced by the Franciscans in 1263. The *Regina Caeli*, commemorating the joy of Mary at Christ's Resurrection, replaces the Angelus during the Easter season.

Anger (Wrath): Passionate displeasure arising from some kind of offense suffered at the hands of another person, frustration or other cause, combined with a tendency to strike back at the cause of the displeasure; a violation of the Fifth Commandment and one of the capital sins if the displeasure is out of proportion to the cause and/or if the retaliation is unjust.

Anglican Orders: Holy orders conferred according to the rite of the Anglican Church, which Leo XIII declared null and void in the bull *Apostolicae Curae*,

Sept. 13, 1896. The orders were declared null because they were conferred according to a rite that was substantially defective in form and intent, and because of a break in apostolic succession that occurred when Matthew Parker became head of the Anglican hierarchy in 1559. In making his declaration, Pope Leo cited earlier arguments against validity made by Julius III in 1553 and 1554 and by Paul IV in 1555. He also noted related directives requiring absolute ordination, according to the Catholic ritual, of convert ministers who had been ordained according to the Anglican Ordinal.

Anglican-Use Parishes: In line with Vatican-approved developments since 1980, several Anglican-use parishes have been established in the United States with the right to continue using some elements of Anglican usage in their liturgical celebrations. A Vatican document dated Mar. 31, 1981, said: "In June 1980, the Holy See, through the Congregation for the Doctrine of the Faith, agreed to the request presented by the bishops of the United States of America in behalf of some clergy and laity formerly or actually belonging to the Episcopal (Anglican) Church for full communion with the Catholic Church. The Holy See's response to the initiative of these Episcopalians includes the possibility of a 'pastoral provision' which will provide, for those who desire it, a common identity reflecting certain elements of their own heritage."

Animals: Creatures of God, they are entrusted to human stewardship for appropriate care, use for human needs, as pets, for reasonable experimentation for the good of people. They should not be subject to cruel treatment.

Annulment: A decree issued by an appropriate Church authority or tribunal that a sacrament or ecclesiastical act is invalid and therefore lacking in all legal or canonical consequences.

Antichrist: The "deceitful one," the "antichrist" (2 Jn. 7), adversary of Christ and the kingdom of God, especially in the end time before the second coming of Christ. The term is also used in reference to anti-Christian persons and forces in the world.

Antiphon: (1) A short verse or text, generally from Scripture, recited in the Liturgy of the Hours before and after psalms and canticles. (2) Any verse sung or recited by one part of a choir or congregation in response to the other part, as in antiphonal or alternate chanting.

Anti-Semitism: A prejudice against Jews, and often accompanied by persecution. The prejudice has existed historically from the time of the ancient Persian Empire and survives even to the present day. It has been condemned consistently by the Church as being in opposition to scriptural principles and Christian charity.

Apologetics: The science and art of developing and presenting the case for the reasonableness of the Christian faith, by a wide variety of means including facts of experience, history, science, philosophy. The constant objective of apologetics, as well as of the total process of pre-evangelization, is preparation for response to God in faith; its ways and means, however, are subject to change in accordance with the various needs of people and different sets of circumstances.

Apostasy: (1) The total and obstinate repudiation of the Christian faith. An apostate automatically incurs a penalty of excommunication. (2) Apostasy from orders is the unlawful withdrawal from or rejection of the obligations of the clerical state by a man who has received major orders. An apostate from orders is subject to a canonical penalty. (3) Apostasy from the religious life occurs when a Religious with perpetual vows unlawfully leaves the community with the intention of not returning, or actually remains outside the community without permission. An apostate from religious life is subject to a canonical penalty.

Apostolate: The ministry or work of an apostle. In Catholic usage, the word is an umbrella-like term covering all kinds and areas of work and endeavor for the service of God and the Church and the good of people. Thus, the apostolate of bishops is to carry on the mission of the Apostles as pastors of the People of God: of priests, to preach the word of God and to carry out the sacramental and pastoral ministry for which they are ordained; of religious, to follow and do the work of Christ in conformity with the evangelical counsels and their rule of life; of lay persons, as individuals and/or in groups, to give witness to Christ and build up the kingdom of God through practice of their faith, professional competence and the performance of good works in the concrete circumstances of daily life. Apostolic works are not limited to those done within the Church or by specifically Catholic groups, although some apostolates are officially assigned to certain persons or groups and are under the direction of church authorities. Apostolate derives from the commitment and obligation of baptism, confirmation, holy orders, matrimony, the duties of one's state in life, etc.

Apostolic Succession: Bishops of the Church, who form a collective body or college, are successors to the Apostles by ordination and divine right; as such they carry on the mission entrusted by Christ to the Apostles as guardians and teachers of the deposit of faith, principal pastors and spiritual authorities of the faithful. The doctrine of apostolic succession is based on New Testament evidence and the constant teaching of the Church, reflected as early as the end of the first century in a letter of Pope St. Clement to the Corinthians. A significant facet of the doctrine is the role of the pope as the successor of St. Peter, the vicar of Christ and head of the college of bishops. The doctrine of apostolic succession means more than continuity of apostolic faith and doctrine; its basic requisite is ordination by the laying on of hands in apostolic succession.

Archives: Documentary records, and the place where they are kept, of the spiritual and temporal government and affairs of the Church, a diocese, church agencies like the departments of the Roman Curia, bodies like religious institutes, and individual parishes. The collection, cataloguing, preserving and use of these records are governed by norms stated in canon law and particular regulations. The strictest secrecy is always in effect for confidential records concerning matters of conscience, and documents of this kind are destroyed as soon as circumstances permit.

Ark of the Covenant: The sacred chest of the Israelites in which were placed and carried the tablets of stone inscribed with the Ten Commandments, the basic moral precepts of the Old Covenant (Ex. 25: 10-22; 37:1-9). The Ark was also a symbol of God's presence. The Ark was probably destroyed with the Temple in 586 B.C.

Asceticism: The practice of self-discipline. In the spiritual life, asceticism — by personal prayer, meditation, self-denial, works of mortification and outgoing interpersonal works — is motivated by love of God and contributes to growth in holiness.

Ashes: Religious significance has been associated with their use as symbolic of penance since Old Testament times. Thus, ashes of palm blessed on the previous Sunday of the Passion are placed on the foreheads of the faithful on Ash Wednesday to remind them to do works of penance, especially during the season of Lent, and that they are dust and unto dust will return. Ashes are a sacramental.

Aspergillum: A vessel or device used for sprinkling holy water. The ordinary type is a metallic rod with a bulbous tip which absorbs the water and discharges it at the motion of the user's hand.

Aspersory: A portable metallic vessel, similar to a pail, for carrying holy water.

Aspiration (Ejaculation): Short exclamatory prayer; e.g., My Jesus, mercy.

Atheism: Denial of the existence of God, finding expression in a system of thought (speculative atheism) or a manner of acting (practical atheism) as though there were no God. The Second Vatican Council, in its Pastoral Constitution on the Church in the Modern World (*Gaudium et Spes*, Nos. 19 to 21), noted that a profession of atheism may represent an explicit denial of God, the rejection of a wrong notion of God, an affirmation of man rather than of God, an extreme protest against evil. It said that such a profession might result from acceptance of such propositions as: there is no absolute truth; man can assert nothing, absolutely nothing, about God; everything can be explained by scientific reasoning alone; the whole question of God is devoid of meaning.

Atonement: The redemptive activity of Christ, who reconciled man with God through his Incarnation and entire life, and especially by his suffering and Resurrection. The word also applies to prayer and good works by which persons join themselves with and take part in Christ's work of reconciliation and reparation for sin.

Attributes of God: Perfections of God. God possesses — and is — all the perfections of being, without limitation. Because he is infinite, all of these perfections are one, perfectly united in him. Because of the limited power of human intelligence, divine perfections — such as omnipotence, truth, love, etc. — are viewed separately, as distinct characteristics, even though they are not actually distinct in God.

Authority, Ecclesiastical: The authority exercised by the Church, and particularly by the pope and the bishops; it is delegated by Jesus Christ to St. Peter. This authority extends to all those matters entrusted to the Apostles by Christ, including teaching of the Faith, the liturgy and sacraments, moral guidance, and the administration of discipline.

Avarice (Covetousness): A disorderly and unreasonable attachment to and desire for material things; called a capital sin because it involves preoccupation with material things to the neglect of spiritual goods and obligations of justice and charity.

Ave Maria: See **Hail Mary**.

B

Baldacchino: A canopy over an altar.

Baptism: *See* **Sacraments**.

Beatification: A preliminary step toward canonization of a saint. It begins with an investigation of the candidate's life, writings, and heroic practice of virtue, and, except in the case of martyrs, the certification of one miracle worked by God through his or her intercession. If the findings of the investigation so indicate, the pope decrees that the Servant of God may be called "Blessed" and may be honored locally or in a limited way in the liturgy. Additional procedures lead to canonization (*see* **separate entry**).

Beatific Vision: The intuitive, immediate and direct vision and experience of God enjoyed in the light of glory by all the blessed in heaven. The vision is a supernatural mystery.

Beatitude: A literary form of the Old and New Testaments in which blessings are promised to persons for various reasons. Beatitudes are mentioned 26 times in the Psalms, and in other books of the Old Testament. The best known Beatitudes — identifying blessedness with participation in the kingdom of God and his righteousness, and descriptive of the qualities of Christian perfection — are those recounted in Mt. 5:3-12 and Lk. 6:20-23. The Beatitudes are of central importance in the teaching of Jesus.

Benedictus: The canticle or hymn of Zechariah at the circumcision of St. John the Baptist (Lk. 1:68-79). It is an expression of praise and thanks to God for sending John as a precursor of the Messiah. The *Benedictus* is recited in the Liturgy of the Hours as part of the Morning Prayer.

Biglietto: A papal document of notification of appointment to the cardinalate.

Biretta: A stiff, square hat with three ridges on top worn by clerics in church and on other occasions.

Blasphemy: Any internal or external expression of hatred, reproach, insult, defiance, or contempt with respect to God and the use of his name, principally, and to the Church, saints and sacred things, secondarily; a serious sin, directly opposed to the second commandment. Blasphemy against the Spirit is the deliberate refusal to accept divine mercy, rejection of forgiveness of sins and of the promise of salvation. The sin that is unforgivable because a person refuses to seek or accept forgiveness.

Blessing: Invocation of God's favor, by official ministers of the Church or by private individuals. Blessings are recounted in the Old and New Testaments, and are common in the Christian tradition. Many types of blessings are listed in the *Book of Blessings* of the Roman Ritual. Private blessings, as well as those of an official kind, are efficacious. Blessings are imparted with the Sign of the Cross and appropriate prayer.

Bride of Christ: A metaphorical title that denotes the intimate union that Christ enjoys with his Church; the title is mentioned specifically in the NT (2 Cor. 11:2).

Brief, Apostolic: A papal letter, less formal than a bull, signed for the pope by a secretary and impressed with the seal of the Fisherman's Ring. Simple apostolic letters of this kind are issued for beatifications and with respect to other matters.

Bull, Apostolic: Apostolic letter, a solemn form of papal document, beginning with the name and title of the pope (e.g., John Paul II, Servant of the Servants of God), dealing with an important subject, sealed with a *bulla* or red-ink imprint of the device on the *bulla*. Bulls are issued to confer the titles of bishops and cardinals, to promulgate canonizations, to proclaim Holy Years, and for other purposes. A collection of bulls is called a *bullarium*.

Burial, Ecclesiastical: Interment with ecclesiastical rites, a right of the Christian faithful. The Church recommends burial of the bodies of the dead, but cremation is permissible if it does not involve reasons against church teaching. Ecclesiastical burial is in order for catechumens; for unbaptized children whose parents intended to have them baptized before death; and even, in the absence of their own ministers, for baptized non-Catholics unless it would be considered against their will.

Burse, Financial: A special fund maintained by a diocese, religious institute, or private foundation usually endowed by a private benefactor; it often has the purpose of making possible the education of candidates for the priesthood.

C

Calumny (Slander): Harming the name and good reputation of a person by lies; a violation of obligations of justice and truth. Restitution is due for calumny.

Calvary: A knoll about 15-feet high just outside the western wall of Jerusalem where Christ was crucified, so-called from the Latin *calvaria* (skull), which described its shape.

Canon: A Greek word meaning rule, norm, standard, measure. (1) The word designates the Canon of Sacred Scripture, which is the list of books recognized by the Church as inspired by the Holy Spirit. (2) The term also designates the canons (Eucharistic Prayers, anaphoras) of the Mass, the core of the eucharistic liturgy. (3) Certain dignitaries of the Church have the title of Canon, and some religious are known as Canons. (*See* Bible.)

Canonization: An infallible declaration by the pope that a person, who died as a martyr and/or practiced Christian virtue to a heroic degree, is now in heaven and is worthy of honor and imitation by all the faithful. Such a declaration is preceded by the process of beatification and another detailed investigation concerning the person's reputation for holiness, writings, and (except in the case of martyrs) a miracle ascribed to his or her intercession after death. The pope can dispense from some of the formalities ordinarily required in canonization procedures (equivalent canonization), as Pope John XXIII did in the canonization of St. Gregory Barbarigo on May 26, 1960. A saint is worthy of honor in liturgical worship throughout the universal Church. From its earliest years the Church has venerated saints. Public official honor always required the approval of the bishop of the place. Martyrs were the first to be honored. St. Martin of Tours, who died in 397, was an early non-martyr venerated as a saint. The earliest canonization by a pope with positive documentation was that of St. Ulrich (Uldaric) of Augsburg by John XV in 993. Alexander III reserved the process of canonization to the Holy See in 1171. In 1588 Sixtus V established the Sacred

Congregation of Rites for the principal purpose of handling causes for beatification and canonization: this function is now the work of the Congregation for the Causes of Saints. The official listing of saints and blessed is contained in the *Roman Martyrology* (revised, updated and published in 2002 by the Congregation for Divine Worship and the Discipline of the Sacraments) and related decrees issued after its last publication. Butler's unofficial *Lives of the Saints* (1956) contains 2,565 entries. The Church regards all persons in heaven as saints, not just those who have been officially canonized. (*See* **Beatification, Saints, Canonizations by Leo XIII and His Successors**.)

Canon Law: The Code of Canon Law (*Corpus Iuris Canonici*) enacted and promulgated by ecclesiastical authority for the orderly and pastoral administration and government of the Church. A revised Code for the Latin Rite, effective Nov. 27, 1983, consists of 1,752 canons in seven books under the titles of general norms, the people of God, the teaching mission of the Church, the sanctifying mission of the Church, temporal goods of the Church, penal law and procedural law. The antecedent of this Code was promulgated in 1917 and became effective in 1918; it consisted of 2,414 canons in five books covering general rules, ecclesiastical persons, sacred things, trials, crimes and punishments. There is a separate Code of the Canons of Eastern Churches, in effect since Oct. 1, 1991.

Canticle: A scriptural chant or prayer differing from the psalms. Three of the canticles prescribed for use in the Liturgy of the Hours are: the *Magnificat*, the Canticle of Mary (Lk. 1:46-55); the *Benedictus*, the Canticle of Zechariah (Lk. 1:68-79); and the *Nunc Dimittis*, the Canticle of Simeon (Lk. 2:29-32).

Capital Punishment: Punishment for crime by means of the death penalty. The political community, which has authority to provide for the common good, has the right to defend itself and its members against unjust aggression and may in extreme cases punish with the death penalty persons found guilty before the law of serious crimes against individuals and a just social order. Such punishment is essentially vindictive. Its value as a crime deterrent is a matter of perennial debate. The prudential judgment as to whether or not there should be capital punishment belongs to the civic community. The U.S. Supreme Court, in a series of decisions dating from June 29, 1972, ruled against the constitutionality of statutes on capital punishment except in specific cases and with appropriate consideration, with respect to sentence, of mitigating circumstances of the crime. Pope John Paul II, in his encyclical letter *Evangelium Vitae* ("The Gospel of Life"), wrote: "There is a growing tendency, both in the Church and in civil society, to demand that it (capital punishment) be applied in a very limited way or even that it be abolished completely."

Capital Sins: Sins which give rise to other sins: pride, avarice, lust, wrath (anger), gluttony, envy, sloth.

Cardinal Virtues: The four principal moral virtues are prudence, justice, temperance and fortitude.

Casuistry: In moral theology, the application of moral principles to specific cases. Casuistry can be of assistance because it takes the abstract and makes it practical in a particular situation. It has definite limitations and does not replace the conscience in the decision-making process; additionally, it must be aligned with the cardinal virtue of prudence.

Catacombs: Underground Christian cemeteries in various cities of the Roman Empire and Italy, especially in the vicinity of Rome; the burial sites of many martyrs and other Christians.

Catechesis: The whole complex of church efforts to make disciples of Christ, involving doctrinal instruction and spiritual formation through practice of the faith.

Catechism: A systematic presentation of the fundamentals of Catholic doctrine regarding faith and morals. Sources are Sacred Scripture, tradition, the magisterium (teaching authority of the Church), the writings of Fathers and Doctors of the Church, liturgy. The new *Catechism of the Catholic Church*, published Oct. 11, 1992, consists of four principal sections: the profession of faith (the Creed), the sacraments of faith, the life of faith (the Commandments), and the prayer of the believer (the Lord's Prayer). The 16th century Council of Trent mandated publication of the *Roman Catechism*. Catechisms such as these two are useful sources for other catechisms serving particular needs of the faithful and persons seeking admission to the Catholic Church.

Catechumen: A person preparing in a program (catechumenate) of instruction and spiritual formation for baptism and reception into the Church. The Church has a special relationship with catechumens. It invites them to lead the life of the Gospel, introduces them to the celebration of the sacred rites, and grants them various prerogatives that are proper to the faithful (one of which is the right to ecclesiastical burial). (*See* **Rite of Christian Initiation of Adults**, under **Baptism**.)

Cathedra: A Greek word for chair, designating the chair or seat of a bishop in the principal church of his diocese, which is therefore called a cathedral.

Cathedraticum: The tax paid to a bishop by all churches and benefices subject to him for the support of episcopal administration and for works of charity.

Catholic: A Greek word, meaning universal, first used in the title "Catholic Church" in a letter written by St. Ignatius of Antioch about 107 to the Christians of Smyrna.

Celebret: A Latin word, meaning "Let him celebrate," the name of a letter of recommendation issued by a bishop or other superior stating that a priest is in good standing and therefore eligible to celebrate Mass or perform other priestly functions.

Celibacy: The unmarried state of life, required in the Roman Church of candidates for holy orders and of men already ordained to holy orders, for the practice of perfect chastity and total dedication to the service of people in the ministry of the Church. Celibacy is enjoined as a condition for ordination by church discipline and law, not by dogmatic necessity. In the Roman Church, a consensus in favor of celibacy developed in the early centuries while the clergy included both celibates and men who had been married once. The first local legislation on the subject was enacted by a local council held in Elvira, Spain, about 306; it forbade bishops, priests, deacons and other ministers to have wives. Similar enactments were passed by other local councils from that time on, and by the 12th century particular laws regarded marriage by clerics in major orders to be not only unlawful but also null and void. The latter view was translated by the Second Lateran Council in 1139 into what seems to be the first written universal law making holy orders an invalidating impediment to marriage. In 1563, the Council of Trent ruled definitely on the matter and established the discipline in force in the Roman Church. Some exceptions to this discipline have been made in recent years. A number of married Protestant and Episcopalian (Anglican) clergymen who became converts and were subsequently ordained to the priesthood have been permitted to continue in marriage. Married men over the age of 35 can be ordained to the permanent diaconate. Eastern Church discipline on celibacy differs from that of the Roman Church. In line with legislation enacted by the Synod of Trullo in 692 and still in force, candidates for holy orders may marry before becoming deacons and may continue in marriage thereafter, but marriage after ordination is forbidden. Bishops of Eastern Catholic Churches in the U.S., however, do not ordain married candidates for the priesthood. Bishops of Eastern Catholic Churches are unmarried.

Cenacle: The upper room in Jerusalem where Christ ate the Last Supper with his Apostles.

Censer: A metal vessel with a perforated cover and suspended by chains, in which incense is burned. It is used at some masses, Benediction of the Blessed Sacrament, and other liturgical functions.

Censorship of Books: An exercise of vigilance by the Church for safeguarding authentic religious teaching. Pertinent legislation in a decree issued by the Congregation for the Doctrine of the Faith Apr. 9, 1975, is embodied in the Code of Canon Law (Book III, Title IV). The legislation deals with requirements for prepublication review and clearance of various types of writings on religious subjects. Permission to publish works of a religious character, together with the apparatus of reviewing them beforehand, falls under the authority of the bishop of the place where the writer lives or where the works are published. Clearance for publication is usually indicated by the terms *Nihil obstat* ("Nothing stands in the way") issued by the censor and *Imprimatur* ("Let it be printed") authorized by the bishop. The clearing of works for publication does not necessarily imply approval of an author's viewpoint or his manner of handling a subject.

Censures: Sanctions imposed by the Church on baptized Roman Catholics 18 years of age or older for committing certain serious offenses and for being or remaining obstinate therein: (1) excommunication (exclusion from the community of the faithful, barring a person from sacramental and other participation in the goods and offices of the community of the Church), (2) suspension (prohibition of a cleric to exercise orders) and (3) interdict (deprivation of the sacraments and liturgical activities). The intended purposes of censures are to correct and punish offenders; to deter persons from committing sins which, more seriously and openly than others, threaten the common good of the Church and its members; and to provide for the making of reparation for harm done to the community of the Church. Censures may be incurred automatically (*ipso facto*) on the commission of certain offenses for which fixed penalties have been laid down in church law (*latae sententiae*); or they may be inflicted by sentence of a judge (*ferendae sententiae*). Automatic excommunication is incurred for the offenses of abortion, apostasy, heresy and schism. Obstinacy in crime — also called contumacy, disregard of a penalty, defiance of church authority — is presumed by law in the commission of offenses for which automatic censures are decreed. The presence and degree of contumacy in other cases, for which judicial sentence is required, is subject to determination by a judge. Absolution can be obtained from any censure, provided the person repents and desists from obstinacy. Absolution may be reserved to the pope, the bishop of a place, or the major superior of an exempt clerical religious institute. In danger of death, any priest can absolve from all censures; in other cases, faculties to absolve from reserved censures can be exercised by competent authorities or given to other priests. The penal law of the Church is contained in Book VI of the Code of Canon Law.

Ceremonies, Master of: One who directs the proceedings of a rite or ceremony during the function.

Chamberlain (*Camerlengo*): (1) The Chamberlain of the Holy Roman Church is a cardinal with special responsibilities, especially during the time between the death of one pope and the election of his successor; among other things, he safeguards and administers the goods and revenues of the Holy See and heads particular congregations of cardinals for special purposes. (*See also* **Papal Election**.) (2) The Chamberlain of the College of Cardinals has charge of the property and revenues of the College and keeps the record of business transacted in consistories. (3) The Chamberlain of the Roman Clergy is the president of the secular clergy of Rome.

Chancellor: Notary of a diocese, who draws up written documents in the government of the diocese; takes care of, arranges, and indexes diocesan archives, records of dispensations and ecclesiastical trials.

Chancery: (1) A branch of church administration that handles written documents used in the government of a diocese. (2) The administrative office of a diocese, a bishop's office.

Chant: A type of sacred singing. It is either recitative in nature with a short two-to-six tones for an *accentus*, or melodic in one of three styles (syllabic, neumatic, or melismatic).

Chapel: A building or part of another building used for divine worship; a portion of a church set aside for the celebration of Mass or for some special devotion.

Chaplain: A priest — or, in some instances, a properly qualified religious or lay person — serving the pastoral needs of particular groups of people and institutions, such as hospitals, schools, correctional facilities, religious communities, the armed forces, etc.

Chaplet: A term, meaning "little crown," applied to a rosary or, more commonly, to a small string of beads used for devotional purposes; e.g., the Infant of Prague chaplet.

Chapter: A general meeting of delegates of religious orders for elections and the handling of other important affairs of their communities.

Charismatic Renewal: A movement which originated with a handful of Duquesne University students and faculty members in the 1966-67 academic year and spread from there to Notre Dame, Michigan State University, the University of Michigan, other campuses and cities throughout the U.S., and to well over 125 other countries. Scriptural keys to the renewal are: Christ's promise to send the Holy Spirit upon the Apostles; the description, in the Acts of the Apostles, of the effects of the coming of the Holy Spirit upon the Apostles on Pentecost; St. Paul's explanation, in the Letter to the Romans and 1 Corinthians, of the charismatic gifts (for the good of the Church and persons) the Holy Spirit would bestow on Christians; New Testament evidence concerning the effects of charismatic gifts in and through the early Church. The personal key to the renewal is baptism in the Holy Spirit. This is not a new sacrament but the personally experienced actualization of grace already sacramentally received, principally in baptism and confirmation. The experience of baptism in the Holy Spirit is often accompanied by the reception of one or more charismatic gifts. A characteristic form of the renewal is the weekly prayer meeting, a gathering which includes periods of spontaneous prayer, singing, sharing of experience and testimony, fellowship and teaching. (*See also* **Index**.)

Charisms: Gifts or graces given by God to persons for the good of others and the Church. Examples are special gifts for apostolic work, prophecy, healing, discernment of spirits, the life of evangelical poverty, here-and-now witness to faith in various circumstances of life. The Second Vatican Council made the following statement about charisms in the Dogmatic Constitution on the Church (No. 12): "It is not only through the sacraments and Church ministries that the same Holy Spirit sanctifies and leads the People of God and enriches it with virtues. Allotting his gifts 'to everyone according as he will' (1 Cor. 12:11), he distributes special graces among the faithful of every rank. By these gifts he makes them fit and ready to undertake the various tasks or offices advantageous for the renewal and upbuilding of the Church, according to the words of the Apostle: 'The manifestation of the Spirit is given to everyone for profit' (1 Cor. 12:7). These charismatic gifts, whether they be the most outstanding or the more simple and widely diffused, are to be received with thanksgiving and consolation, for they are exceedingly suitable and useful for the needs of the Church. Still, extraordinary gifts are not to be rashly sought after, nor are the fruits of apostolic labor to be presumptuously expected from them. In any case, judgment as to their genuineness and proper use belongs to those who preside over the Church, and to whose special competence it belongs, not indeed to extinguish the Spirit, but to test all things and hold fast to that which is good" (cf. 1 Thes. 5:12; 19-21).

Charity: Love of God above all things for his own sake, and love of one's neighbor as oneself because and as an expression of one's love for God; the greatest of the three theological virtues. The term is sometimes also used to designate sanctifying grace.

Chastity: Properly ordered behavior with respect to sex. In marriage, the exercise of the procreative power is integrated with the norms and purposes of marriage. Outside of marriage, the rule is self-denial of the voluntary exercise and enjoyment of the procreative faculty in thought, word or action. The vow of chastity, which reinforces the virtue of chastity with the virtue of religion, is one of the three vows professed publicly by members of institutes of consecrated life.

Chirograph or Autograph Letter: A letter written by a pope himself, in his own handwriting.

Chrism: A mixture of olive or other vegetable oil and balsam (or balm), that is consecrated by a bishop for use in liturgical anointings: baptism, confirmation, holy orders, the blessing of an altar.

Christ: The title of Jesus, derived from the Greek translation *Christos* of the Hebrew term "Messiah," meaning the anointed of God, the Savior and Deliverer of his people. Christian use of the title is a confession of belief that Jesus is the Savior.

Christianity: The sum total of things related to belief in Christ — the Christian religion, Christian churches, Christians themselves, society based on and expressive of Christian beliefs, culture reflecting Christian values.

Christians: The name first applied about the year 43 to followers of Christ at Antioch, the capital of Syria. It was used by the pagans as a contemptuous term. The word applies to persons who profess belief in the divinity and teachings of Christ and who give witness to him in life.

Circumcision: A ceremonial practice symbolic of initiation and participation in the covenant between God and Abraham.

Circumincession: The indwelling of each divine Person of the Holy Trinity in the others.

Clergy: Men ordained to holy orders and commissioned for sacred ministries and assigned to pastoral and other duties for the service of the people and the Church. (1) Diocesan or secular clergy are committed to pastoral ministry in parishes and in other capacities in a particular church (diocese) under the direction of their bishop, to whom they are bound by a promise of obedience. (2) Regular clergy belong to religious institutes (orders, congregations, societies — institutes of consecrated life) and are so called because they observe the rule (*regula*, in Latin) of their respective institutes. They are committed to the ways of life and apostolates of their institutes. In ordinary pastoral ministry, they are under the direction of local bishops as well as their own superiors.

Clericalism: A term generally used in a derogatory sense to mean action, influence and interference by the Church and the clergy in matters with which they allegedly should not be concerned. Anticlericalism is a reaction of antipathy, hostility, distrust and opposition to the Church and clergy arising from real and/or alleged faults of the clergy, over-extension of the role of the laity, or for other reasons.

Cloister: Part of a monastery, convent, or other house of religious reserved for use by members of the institute. Houses of contemplative religious have a strict enclosure.

Code: A digest of rules or regulations, such as the Code of Canon Law.

Code of Canon Law: *See* **Canon Law**.

Collegiality: A term in use especially since the Second Vatican Council to describe the authority exercised by the College of Bishops. The bishops of the Church, in union with and subordinate to the pope — who has full, supreme and universal power over the Church which he can always exercise independently — have supreme teaching and pastoral authority over the whole Church. In addition to their proper authority of office for the good of the faithful in their respective dioceses or other jurisdictions, the bishops have authority to act for the good of the universal

Church. This collegial authority is exercised in a solemn manner in an ecumenical council and can also be exercised in other ways sanctioned by the pope. Doctrine on collegiality was set forth by the Second Vatican Council in *Lumen Gentium* (the Dogmatic Constitution on the Church). (*See separate entry.*) By extension, the concept of collegiality is applied to other forms of participation and co-responsibility by members of a community.

Communicatio in Sacris: The reception of the Church's sacraments by non-members or the reception by Catholics of sacraments in non-Catholic Churches.

Communion of Saints: "The communion of all the faithful of Christ, those who are pilgrims on earth, the dead who are being purified, and the blessed in heaven, all together forming one Church; in this communion, the merciful love of God and his saints is always (attentive) to our prayers" (Paul VI, *Creed of the People of God*).

Communism: The substantive principles of modern communism, a theory and system of economics and social organization, were stated about the middle of the 19th century by Karl Marx, author of *The Communist Manifesto* and, with Friedrich Engels, *Das Kapital*. The elements of communist theory include: radical materialism; dialectical determinism; the inevitability of class struggle and conflict, which is to be furthered for the ultimate establishment of a worldwide, classless society; common ownership of productive and other goods; the subordination of all persons and institutions to the dictatorship of the collective; denial of the rights, dignity, and liberty of persons; militant atheism and hostility to religion; utilitarian morality. Communism in theory and practice has been the subject of many papal documents and statements. Pius IX condemned it in 1846. Leo XIII dealt with it at length in the encyclical letter *Quod Apostolici Muneris* in 1878 and *Rerum Novarum* in 1891. Pius XI wrote on the same subject in the encyclicals *Quadragesimo Anno* in 1931 and *Divini Redemptoris* in 1937. These writings have been updated and developed in new directions by Pius XII, John XXIII, Paul VI, and John Paul II.

Compline: The night prayer of the Church that completes the daily *cursus* (course) of the Liturgy of the Hours (Divine Office).

Concelebration: The liturgical act in which several priests, led by one member of the group, offer Mass together, all consecrating the bread and wine. Concelebration has always been common in churches of Eastern Rite. In the Roman Rite, it was long restricted, taking place only at the ordination of bishops and the ordination of priests. The Constitution on the Sacred Liturgy issued by the Second Vatican Council set new norms for concelebration, which is now relatively common in the Roman Rite.

Concordance, Biblical: An alphabetical, verbal index enabling a user knowing one or more words of a scriptural passage to locate the entire text.

Concordat: A church-state treaty with the force of law concerning matters of mutual concern — e.g., rights of the Church, arrangement of ecclesiastical jurisdictions, marriage laws, education. Approximately 150 agreements of this kind have been negotiated since the Concordat of Worms in 1122.

Concupiscence: Any tendency of the sensitive appetite. The term is most frequently used in reference to desires and tendencies for sinful sense pleasure.

Confession: Sacramental confession is the act by which a person tells or confesses his sins to a priest who is authorized to give absolution in the sacrament of penance.

Confessor: A priest who administers the sacrament of penance. The title of confessor, formerly given to a category of male saints, was suppressed with publication of the calendar reform of 1969.

Confraternity: An association whose members practice a particular form of religious devotion and/or are engaged in some kind of apostolic work.

Congregation: (1) The collective name for the people who form a parish. (2) One of the chief administrative departments of the Roman Curia. (3) An unofficial term for a group of men and women who belong to a religious community or institute of consecrated life.

Conscience: Practical judgment concerning the moral goodness or sinfulness of an action (thought, word, desire). In the Catholic view, this judgment is made by reference of the action, its attendant circumstances and the intentions of the person to the requirements of moral law as expressed in the Ten Commandments, the summary law of love for God and neighbor, the life and teaching of Christ, and the authoritative teaching and practice of the Church with respect to the total demands of divine Revelation. A person is obliged: (1) to obey a certain and correct conscience; (2) to obey a certain conscience even if it is inculpably erroneous; (3) not to obey, but to correct, a conscience known to be erroneous or lax; (4) to rectify a scrupulous conscience by following the advice of a confessor and by other measures; (5) to resolve doubts of conscience before acting. It is legitimate to act for solid and probable reasons when a question of moral responsibility admits of argument (*See* **Probabiliorism** and **Probabilism**).

Conscience, Examination of: Self-examination to determine one's spiritual state before God, regarding one's sins and faults. It is recommended as a regular practice and is practically necessary in preparing for the sacrament of penance. The particular examen is a regular examination to assist in overcoming specific faults and imperfections.

Consequentialism: A moral theory, closely associated with proportionalism and utilitarianism, that holds that the preferable action is one that brings about the best consequences. Preferred results, rather than the objective truth and intentionality, are the object of actions based on consequentialism. While traditional moral theology acknowledges that consequences are important in determining the rightness of an act, importance is also placed on the intrinsic morality of the act and the agent's intention.

Consistory: An assembly of cardinals presided over by the pope.

Constitution: (1) An apostolic or papal constitution is a document in which a pope enacts and promulgates law. (2) A formal and solemn document issued by an ecumenical council on a doctrinal or pastoral subject, with binding force in the whole Church; e.g., the four constitutions issued by the Second Vatican Council on the Church, liturgy, Revelation, and the Church in the modern world. (3) The constitutions of institutes of consecrated life and societies of apostolic life spell out details of and norms drawn from the various rules for the guidance and direction of the life and work of their members.

Consubstantiation: A theory which holds that the Body and Blood of Christ coexist with the substance of bread and wine in the Holy Eucharist. This theory, also called impanation, is incompatible with the doctrine of transubstantiation.

Contraception: Anything done by positive interference to prevent sexual intercourse from resulting in conception. Direct contraception is against the order of nature. Indirect contraception — as a secondary effect of medical treatment or other action having a necessary, good, non-contraceptive purpose — is permissible under the principle of the double effect. The practice of periodic continence is not contraception because it does not involve positive interference with the order of nature. (*See Humanae Vitae*, other entries.)

Contrition: Sorrow for sin coupled with a purpose of amendment. Contrition arising from a supernatural motive is necessary for the forgiveness of sin. (1) Perfect contrition is total sorrow for and renunciation of attachment to sin, arising from the motive of pure love of God. Perfect contrition, which implies the intention of doing all God wants done for the forgiveness of sin (including confession in a reasonable period of time), is sufficient for the forgiveness of serious sin and the remission of all temporal punishment due for sin. (The intention to receive the sacrament of penance is implicit — even if unrealized, as in the case of some persons — in perfect contrition.) (2) Imperfect contrition or attrition is sorrow arising from a quasi-selfish supernatural motive; e.g., the fear of losing heaven, suffering the pains of hell, etc. Imperfect contrition is sufficient for the forgiveness of serious sin when joined with absolution in confession, and sufficient for the forgiveness of venial sin even outside of confession.

Contumely: Personal insult, reviling a person in his presence by accusation of moral faults, by refusal of recognition or due respect; a violation of obligations of justice and charity.

Conversion: In a general sense, the turning away from someone or something and the moving toward another person or thing. In Christian belief, conversion is the embrace of Jesus Christ and a rejection of all that keeps one from God.

Corpus Iuris Canonici: See **Canon Law**.

Council: A formal meeting of Church leaders, summoned by a bishop or appropriate Church leader, with the general purpose of assisting the life of the Church through deliberations, decrees and promulgations. Different councils include: **diocesan** councils (synod), a gathering of the officials of an individual diocese; **provincial** councils, the meeting of the bishops of a province; **plenary** councils, the assembly of the bishops of a country; and **ecumenical** councils, a gathering of all the bishops in the world under the authority of the Bishop of Rome.

Counsels, Evangelical: Gospel counsels of perfection, especially voluntary poverty, perfect chastity and obedience, which were recommended by Christ to those who would devote themselves exclusively and completely to the immediate service of God. Religious (members of institutes of consecrated life) bind themselves by public vows to observe these counsels in a life of total consecration to God and service to people through various kinds of apostolic works.

Counter-Reformation: The period of approximately 100 years following the Council of Trent (1545-63), which witnessed a reform within the Church to stimulate genuine Catholic life and to counteract effects of the Reformation.

Covenant: A bond of relationship between parties pledged to each other. God-initiated covenants in the Old Testament included those with Noah, Abraham, Moses, Levi and David. The Mosaic (Sinai) covenant made Israel God's Chosen People on terms of fidelity to true faith, true worship and righteous conduct according to the Decalogue. The New Testament covenant, prefigured in the Old Testament, is the bond people have with God through Christ. All people are called to be parties to this perfect and everlasting covenant, which was mediated and ratified by Christ. The marriage covenant seals the closest possible relationship between a man and a woman.

Creation: The production by God of something out of nothing. The biblical account of creation is contained in the first two chapters of Genesis.

Creator: God, the supreme, self-existing Being, the absolute and infinite First Cause of all things.

Creature: Everything in the realm of being is a creature, except God.

Cremation: The reduction of a human corpse to ashes by means of fire. Cremation is not in line with Catholic tradition and practice, even though it is not opposed to any article of faith. The Congregation for the Doctrine of the Faith, under date of May 8, 1963, circulated among bishops an instruction which upheld the traditional practices of Christian burial but modified anti-cremation legislation. Cremation may be permitted for serious reasons, of a private as well as public nature, provided it does not involve any contempt of the Church or of religion, or any attempt to deny, question, or belittle the doctrine of the resurrection of the body. In a letter dated Mar. 21, 1997, and addressed to Bishop Anthony M. Pilla, president of the National Conference of Catholic Bishops, the Congregation for Divine Worship and the Discipline of the Sacraments granted "a particular permission to the diocesan bishops of the United States of America. By this, local Ordinaries (heads of dioceses) are authorized … to permit that the funeral liturgy, including where appropriate the celebration of the Eucharist, be celebrated in the presence of the cremated remains instead of the natural body." (*See* **Burial, Ecclesiastical**).

Crib: Also Crèche, a devotional representation of the birth of Jesus. The custom of erecting cribs is generally attributed to St. Francis of Assisi, who in 1223 obtained from Pope Honorius III permission to use a crib and figures of the Christ Child, Mary, St. Joseph and others, to represent the mystery of the Nativity.

Crosier: The bishop's staff, symbolic of his pastoral office, responsibility and authority; used at liturgical functions.

Crypt: An underground or partly underground chamber; e.g., the lower part of a church used for worship and/or burial.

Cura Animarum: A Latin phrase, meaning care of souls, designating the pastoral ministry and responsibility of bishops and priests.

Curia: The personnel and offices through which (1)

the pope administers the affairs of the universal Church, the Roman Curia (see p. 268), or (2) a bishop the affairs of a diocese, diocesan curia. The principal officials of a diocesan curia are the vicar general of the diocese, the chancellor, officials of the diocesan tribunal or court, examiners, consultors, auditors, notaries.

Custos: A religious superior who presides over a number of convents collectively called a "custody." In some institutes of consecrated life a custos may be the deputy of a higher superior.

D

Dean: (1) A priest with supervisory responsibility over a section of a diocese known as a deanery. The post-Vatican II counterpart of a dean is an episcopal vicar. (2) The senior or ranking member of a group.

Decision: A judgment or pronouncement on a cause or suit, given by a church tribunal or official with judicial authority. A decision has the force of law for concerned parties.

Declaration: (1) An ecclesiastical document which presents an interpretation of an existing law. (2) A position paper on a specific subject; e.g., the three declarations issued by the Second Vatican Council on religious freedom, non-Christian religions and Christian education.

Decree: An edict or ordinance issued by a pope and/or by an ecumenical council, with binding force in the whole Church; by a department of the Roman Curia, with binding force for concerned parties; by a territorial body of bishops, with binding force for persons in the area; by individual bishops, with binding force for concerned parties until revocation or the death of the bishop. The nine decrees issued by the Second Vatican Council were combinations of doctrinal and pastoral statements with executive orders for action and movement toward renewal and reform in the Church.

Dedication of a Church: The ceremony whereby a church is solemnly set apart for the worship of God. The custom of dedicating churches had an antecedent in Old Testament ceremonies for the dedication of the Temple, as in the times of Solomon and the Maccabees. The earliest extant record of the dedication of a Christian church dates from early in the fourth century, when it was done simply by the celebration of Mass. Other ceremonies developed later. A church can be dedicated by a simple blessing or a solemn consecration. The rite of consecration is generally performed by a bishop.

Deposit of the Faith: The body of saving truth, entrusted by Christ to the Apostles and handed on by them to the Church to be preserved and proclaimed. As embodied in Revelation and Tradition. the term is very nearly coextensive with objective revelation, in that it embraces the whole of Christ's teaching. But the term of deposit highlights particular features of the apostolic teaching implying that this teaching is an inexhaustible store that rewards and promotes reflection and study so that new insights and deeper penetration might be made into the mystery of the divine economy of salvation. Although our understanding of this teaching can develop, it can never be augmented in its substance; the teaching is a divine trust that cannot be altered, modified, or debased. The term *depositum fidei* first entered official Catholic teaching with the Council of Trent, but its substance is well-attested in the Scriptures and the Fathers.

Despair: Abandonment of hope for salvation arising from the conviction that God will not provide the necessary means for attaining it, that following God's way of life for salvation is impossible, or that one's sins are unforgivable; a serious sin against the Holy Spirit and the theological virtues of hope and faith, involving distrust in the mercy and goodness of God and a denial of the truths that God wills the salvation of all persons and provides sufficient grace for it. Real despair is distinguished from unreasonable fear with respect to the difficulties of attaining salvation, from morbid anxiety over the demands of divine justice, and from feelings of despair.

Detraction: Revelation of true but hidden faults of a person without sufficient and justifying reason; a violation of requirements of justice and charity, involving the obligation to make restitution when this is possible without doing more harm to the good name of the offended party. In some cases, e.g., to prevent evil, secret faults may and should be disclosed.

Devil: (1) Lucifer, Satan, chief of the fallen angels who sinned and were banished from heaven. Still possessing angelic powers, he can cause such diabolical phenomena as possession and obsession, and can tempt men to sin. (2) Any fallen angel.

Devotion: (1) Religious fervor, piety; dedication. (2) The consolation experienced at times during prayer; a reverent manner of praying.

Devotions: Pious practices of members of the Church include not only participation in various acts of the liturgy but also in other acts of worship generally called popular or private devotions. Concerning these, the Second Vatican Council said in the Constitution on the Sacred Liturgy (*Sacrosanctum Concilium*, No. 13): "Popular devotions of the Christian people are warmly commended, provided they accord with the laws and norms of the Church. Such is especially the case with devotions called for by the Apostolic See. Devotions proper to the individual churches also have a special dignity. These devotions should be so drawn up that they harmonize with the liturgical seasons, accord with the sacred liturgy, are in some fashion derived from it, and lead the people to it, since the liturgy by its very nature far surpasses any of them." Devotions of a liturgical type are Exposition of the Blessed Sacrament, recitation of Evening Prayer, and Night Prayer of the Liturgy of the Hours. Examples of para-liturgical devotion are a Bible service or vigil, and the Angelus, Rosary, and Stations of the Cross, which have a strong scriptural basis.

Diocese: A particular church, a fully organized ecclesiastical jurisdiction under the pastoral direction of a bishop as local Ordinary.

Discalced: Of Latin derivation and meaning without shoes, the word is applied to religious orders or congregations whose members go barefoot or wear sandals.

Disciple: A term used sometimes in reference to the Apostles, but more often to a larger number of followers (70 or 72) of Christ mentioned in Lk. 10:1.

Disciplina Arcani: A Latin phrase, meaning "discipline of the secret" and referring to a practice of the early Church, especially during the Roman persecutions, to: (1) conceal Christian truths from those who, it was feared, would misinterpret, ridicule and profane the teachings, and persecute Christians for believing them; (2) instruct catechumens in a gradual manner, withholding the teaching of certain doctrines until the catechumens proved themselves of good faith and sufficient understanding.

Dispensation: The relaxation of a law in a particular case. Laws made for the common good sometimes work undue hardship in particular cases. In such cases, where sufficient reasons are present, dispensations may be granted by proper authorities. Bishops, religious superiors and others may dispense from certain laws; the pope can dispense from all ecclesiastical laws. No one has authority to dispense from obligations of the divine law.

Divination: Attempting to foretell future or hidden things by means of things like dreams, necromancy, spiritism, examination of entrails, astrology, augury, omens, palmistry, drawing straws, dice, cards, etc. Practices like these attribute to created things a power which belongs to God alone and are violations of the First Commandment.

Divine Praises: Fourteen praises recited or sung at Benediction of the Blessed Sacrament in reparation for sins of sacrilege, blasphemy and profanity. Some of these praises date from the end of the 18th century: *Blessed be God. / Blessed be his holy Name. / Blessed be Jesus Christ, true God and true Man. / Blessed be the Name of Jesus. / Blessed be his most Sacred Heart. / Blessed be his most Precious Blood. / Blessed be Jesus in the most holy Sacrament of the Altar. / Blessed be the Holy Spirit, the Paraclete. / Blessed be the great Mother of God, Mary most holy. / Blessed be her holy and Immaculate Conception. / Blessed be her glorious Assumption. / Blessed be the name of Mary, Virgin and Mother. / Blessed be St. Joseph, her most chaste Spouse. / Blessed be God in his Angels and in his Saints.*

Double Effect Principle: Actions sometimes have two effects closely related to each other, one good and the other bad, and a difficult moral question can arise: Is it permissible to place an action from which two such results follow? It is permissible to place the action, if: the action is good in itself and is directly productive of the good effect; the circumstances are good; the intention of the person is good; the reason for placing the action is proportionately serious to the seriousness of the indirect bad effect.

Doxology: (1) The lesser doxology, or ascription of glory to the Trinity, is the Glory Be to the Father. The first part dates back to the third or fourth century, and came from the form of baptism. The concluding words, "As it was in the beginning," etc., are of later origin. (2) The greater doxology, Glory to God in the Highest, begins with the words of angelic praise at the birth of Christ recounted in the Infancy Narrative (Lk. 2:14). It is often recited at Mass. Of early Eastern origin, it is found in the Apostolic Constitutions in a form much like the present. (3) The formula of praise at the end of the Eucharistic Prayer at Mass, sung or said by the celebrant while he holds aloft the paten containing the consecrated host in one hand and the chalice containing the consecrated wine in the other.

Dulia: A Greek term meaning the veneration or homage, different in nature and degree from that given to God, paid to the saints. It includes honoring the saints and seeking their intercession with God.

Duty: A moral obligation deriving from the binding force of law, the exigencies of one's state in life, and other sources.

E

Easter Controversy: A three-phase controversy over the time for the celebration of Easter. Some early Christians in the Near East, called Quartodecimans, favored the observance of Easter on the 14th day of Nisan, the spring month of the Hebrew calendar, whenever it occurred. Against this practice, Pope St. Victor I, about 190, ordered a Sunday observance of the feast. The Council of Nicaea, in line with usages of the Church at Rome and Alexandria, decreed in 325 that Easter should be observed on the Sunday following the first full moon of spring. Uniformity of practice in the West was not achieved until several centuries later, when the British Isles, in delayed compliance with measures enacted by the Synod of Whitby in 664, accepted the Roman date of observance. Unrelated to the controversy is the fact that some Eastern Christians, in accordance with traditional calendar practices, celebrate Easter at a different time than the Roman and Eastern Churches.

Easter Duty: The serious obligation binding Catholics of Roman Rite, to receive the Eucharist during the Easter season (in the U.S., from the first Sunday of Lent to and including Trinity Sunday).

Easter Water: Holy water blessed with special ceremonies and distributed on the Easter Vigil; used during Easter Week for blessing the faithful and homes.

Ecclesiology: Study of the nature, constitution, members, mission, functions, etc., of the Church.

Ecology: The natural environment of the total range of creation — mineral, vegetable, animal, human — entrusted to people for respect, care and appropriate use, as well as conservation and development for the good of present and future generations.

Ecstasy: An extraordinary state of mystical experience in which a person is so absorbed in God that the activity of the exterior senses is suspended.

Economy, Divine: The fulfillment of God's plan of salvation. It was fully developed in his divine mind from eternity, and fully revealed in Jesus Christ. Before the Incarnation it was known only obscurely, but after the ascension of Christ and the coming of the Holy Spirit at Pentecost, it became the substance of apostolic preaching and is preserved in its integrity for each new generation.

Ecumenism: The movement of Christians and their churches toward the unity willed by Christ. The Second Vatican Council called the movement "those activities and enterprises which, according to various needs of the Church and opportune occasions, are started and organized for the fostering of unity among Christians" (Decree on Ecumenism, No. 4). Spiritual ecumenism, i.e., mutual prayer for unity, is the heart of the movement. The movement also involves scholarly and pew-level efforts for the development of mutual understanding and better interfaith relations in general, and collaboration by the churches and their members in the social area. (*See* **Index** for other entries.)

Elevation: The raising of the host after consecration at Mass for adoration by the faithful. The custom was introduced in the Diocese of Paris about the close of the 12th century to offset an erroneous teaching of the time which held that transubstantiation of the bread did not take place until after the consecration of the wine in the chalice. The elevation of the chalice following the consecration of the wine was introduced in the 15th century.

Encyclical: The highest form of papal teaching document. It is normally addressed to all the bishops and/or to all the faithful.

Envy: Sadness over another's good fortune because it is considered a loss to oneself or a detraction from one's own excellence; one of the seven capital sins, a violation of the obligations of charity.

Epiclesis: An invocation of the Holy Spirit, to bless the offerings consecrated at Mass; before the consecration in the Latin Rite, after the consecration in Eastern usage.

Epikeia: A Greek word meaning "reasonableness," and designating a moral theory and practice; a mild interpretation of the mind of a legislator who is prudently considered not to wish positive law to bind in certain circumstances.

Episcopate: (1) The office, dignity and sacramental powers bestowed upon a bishop at his ordination. (2) The body of bishops collectively.

Equivocation: (1) The use of words, phrases, or gestures having more than one meaning in order to conceal information which a questioner has no strict right to know. It is permissible to equivocate (have a broad mental reservation) in some circumstances. (2) A lie, i.e., a statement of untruth. Lying is intrinsically wrong. A lie told in joking, evident as such, is not wrong.

Eschatology: Doctrine concerning the last things: death, judgment, heaven and hell, and the final state of perfection of the people and kingdom of God at the end of time.

Eternity: The interminable, perfect possession of life in its totality without beginning or end; an attribute of God, who has no past or future, but always is. Man's existence has a beginning but no end and is, accordingly, called immortal.

Ethics: Moral philosophy, the science of the morality of human acts deriving from natural law, the natural end of man, and the powers of human reason. It includes all the spheres of human activity — personal, social, economic, political, etc. Ethics is distinct from, but can be related to, moral theology, whose primary principles are drawn from divine revelation.

Euthanasia: Mercy killing, the direct causing of death for the purpose of ending human suffering. Euthanasia is murder and is totally illicit, for the natural law forbids the direct taking of one's own life or that of an innocent person. The use of drugs to relieve suffering in serious cases, even when this results in a shortening of life as an indirect and secondary effect, is permissible under conditions of the double-effect principle. It is also permissible for a seriously ill person to refuse to follow — or for other responsible persons to refuse to permit — extraordinary medical procedures, even though the refusal might entail shortening of life.

Evangelization: Proclamation of the Gospel, the Good News of salvation in and through Christ, among those who have not yet known or received it; and efforts for the progressive development of the life of faith among those who have already received the Gospel and all that it entails. Evangelization is the primary mission of the Church, in which all members of the Church are called to participate.

Evolution: Scientific theory concerning the development of the physical universe from unorganized matter (inorganic evolution) and, especially, the development of existing forms of vegetable, animal and human life from earlier and more primitive organisms (organic evolution). Various ideas about evolution were advanced for some centuries before scientific evidence in support of the main-line theory of organic evolution, which has several formulations, was discovered and verified in the second half of the 19th century and afterwards. This evidence — from the findings of comparative anatomy and other sciences — confirmed evolution of species and cleared the way to further investigation of questions regarding the processes of its accomplishment. While a number of such questions remain open with respect to human evolution, a point of doctrine not open to question is the immediate creation of the human soul by God. For some time, theologians regarded the theory with hostility, considering it to be in opposition to the account of creation in the early chapters of Genesis and subversive of belief in such doctrines as creation, the early state of man in grace, and the fall of man from grace. This state of affairs and the tension it generated led to considerable controversy regarding an alleged conflict between religion and science. Gradually, however, the tension was diminished with the development of biblical studies from the latter part of the 19th century onwards, with clarification of the distinctive features of religious truth and scientific truth, and with the refinement of evolutionary concepts. So far as the Genesis account of creation is concerned, the Catholic view is that the writer(s) did not write as a scientist but as the communicator of religious truth in a manner adapted to the understanding of the people of his time. He used anthropomorphic language, the figure of days and other literary devices to state the salvation truths of creation, the fall of man from grace, and the promise of redemption. It was beyond the competency and purpose of the writer(s) to describe creation and related events in a scientific manner.

Excommunication: Severe ecclesiastical penalty imposed by the Church that excludes a member of the faithful from the wider community. Excommunication is today covered in its particulars by Canon 1331 of the new Code of Canon Law, promulgated in 1983. It exists in two contemporary forms, *ferendae sententiae* and *latae sententiae*. The former is a penalty imposed after a formal proceeding presided over by at least three judges. The latter is considered an automatic penalty for certain acts, including the procuring of a successful abortion (Canon 1398), the embrace of heresy (Canon 1364), violation of the Seal of Confession (Canon 1388), and the blasphemous and sacrilegious use of the Eucharist (Canon 1367). A person under the ban of excommunication is unable to take part in all ceremonies of public worship, especially the Eucharist, to receive or celebrate the sacraments, and to discharge any ecclesiastical offices, ministries, or functions. (*See* **Censures**).

Ex Opere Operantis: A term in sacramental theology meaning that the effectiveness of sacraments depends on the moral rectitude of the minister or participant. This term was applied to rites of the OT in contrast with those of the NT, when it was first advanced in the 13th century.

Ex Opere Operato: A term in sacramental theology meaning that sacraments are effective by means of the sacramental rite itself and not because of the worthiness of the minister or participant.

Exorcism: (1) Driving out evil spirits; a rite in which evil spirits are charged and commanded on the authority of God and with the prayer of the Church to depart from a person or to cease causing harm to a person suffering from diabolical possession or obsession. The sacramental is officially administered by a priest delegated for the purpose by the bishop of the place. Elements of the rite include the Litany of Saints; recitation of the Our Father, one or more creeds, and other prayers; specific prayers of exorcism; the reading of Gospel passages and use of the Sign of the Cross. On Jan. 26, 1999, the Congregation for Divine Worship and the Discipline of the Sacraments published a new rite of exorcism in the Roman Ritual. (*See* **Special Report** for additional details.) (2) Exorcisms which do not imply the conditions of either diabolical possession or obsession form part of the ceremony of baptism and are also included in formulas for various blessings; e.g., of water.

Exposition of the Blessed Sacrament: "In churches where the Eucharist is regularly reserved, it is recommended that solemn exposition of the Blessed Sacrament for an extended period of time should take place once a year, even though the period is not strictly continuous. Shorter expositions of the Eucharist (Benediction) are to be arranged in such a way that the blessing with the Eucharist is preceded by a reasonable time for readings of the word of God, songs, prayers and a period for silent prayer." So stated Vatican directives issued in 1973.

F

Faculties: Grants of jurisdiction or authority by the law of the Church or superiors (pope, bishop, religious superior) for exercise of the powers of holy orders; e.g., priests are given faculties to hear confessions, officiate at weddings; bishops are given faculties to grant dispensations, etc.

Faith: In religion, faith has several aspects. Catholic doctrine calls faith the assent of the mind to truths revealed by God, the assent being made with the help of grace and by command of the will on account of the authority and trustworthiness of God revealing. The term "faith" also refers to the truths that are believed (content of faith) and to the way in which a person, in response to Christ, gives witness to and expresses belief in daily life (living faith). All of these elements, and more, are included in the following statement: " 'The obedience of faith' (Rom. 16:26; 1:5; 2 Cor. 10:5-6) must be given to God who reveals, an obedience by which man entrusts his whole self freely to God, offering 'the full submission of intellect and will to God who reveals' (First Vatican Council, Dogmatic Constitution on the Catholic Faith, Chap. 3), and freely assenting to the truth revealed by him. If this faith is to be shown, the grace of God and the interior help of the Holy Spirit must precede and assist, moving the heart and turning it to God, opening the eyes of the mind, and giving 'joy and ease to everyone in assenting to the truth and believing it'" (Second Council of Orange, Canon 7) (Second Vatican Council, Constitution on Revelation, *Dei Verbum*, No. 5). Faith is necessary for salvation.

Faith, Rule of: The norm or standard of religious belief. The Catholic doctrine is that belief must be professed in the divinely revealed truths in the Bible and tradition as interpreted and proposed by the infallible teaching authority of the Church.

Fast, Eucharistic: Abstinence from food and drink, except water and medicine, is required for one hour before the reception of the Eucharist. Persons who are advanced in age or suffer from infirmity or illness, together with those who care for them, can receive Holy Communion even if they have not abstained from food and drink for an hour. A priest celebrating two or three Masses on the same day can eat and drink something before the second or third Mass without regard for the hour limit.

Father: A title of priests, who are regarded as spiritual fathers because they are the ordinary ministers of baptism, by which persons are born to supernatural life, and because of their pastoral service to people.

Fear: A mental state caused by the apprehension of present or future danger. Grave fear does not necessarily remove moral responsibility for an act, but may lessen it.

First Friday: A devotion consisting of the reception of Holy Communion on the first Friday of nine consecutive months in honor of the Sacred Heart of Jesus and in reparation for sin. (*See* **Sacred Heart, Promises**.)

First Saturday: A devotion tracing its origin to the apparitions of the Blessed Virgin Mary at Fátima in 1917. Those practicing the devotion go to confession and, on the first Saturday of five consecutive months, receive Holy Communion, recite five decades of the Rosary, and meditate on the mysteries for 15 minutes.

Fisherman's Ring: A signet ring (termed in Italian the *pescatorio*) engraved with the image of St. Peter fishing from a boat, and encircled with the name of the reigning pope. It is not worn by the pope. It is used to seal briefs, and is destroyed after each pope's death.

Forgiveness of Sin: Catholics believe that sins are forgiven by God through the mediation of Christ in view of the repentance of the sinner and by means of the sacrament of penance. (*See* **Penance, Contrition**).

Fortitude: Courage to face dangers or hardships for the sake of what is good; one of the four cardinal virtues and one of the seven gifts of the Holy Spirit.

Forty Hours Devotion: A Eucharistic observance consisting of solemn exposition of the Blessed Sacrament coupled with special Masses and forms of prayer, for the purposes of making reparation for sin and praying for God's blessings of grace and peace. The devotion was instituted in 1534 in Milan. St. John Neumann of Philadelphia was the first bishop in the U.S. to prescribe its observance in his diocese. For many years in this country, the observance was held annually on a rotating basis in all parishes of a diocese. Simplified and abbreviated Eucharistic observances have taken the place of the devotion in some places.

Forum: The sphere in which ecclesiastical authority or jurisdiction is exercised. (1) External: Authority is exercised in the external forum to deal with matters affecting the public welfare of the Church and its members. Those who have such authority because of their office (e.g., diocesan bishops) are called ordinaries. (2) Internal: Authority is exercised in the internal forum to deal with matters affecting the private spiritual good of individuals. The sacramental forum is the sphere in which the sacrament of penance is administered; other exercises of jurisdiction in the internal forum take place in the non-sacramental forum.

Freedom, Religious: The Second Vatican Council declared that the right to religious freedom in civil society "means that all men are to be immune from coercion on the part of individuals or of social groups and of any human power, in such wise that in matters religious no one is to be forced to act in a manner contrary to his own beliefs. Nor is anyone to be restrained from acting in accordance with his own beliefs, whether privately or publicly, whether alone or in association with others, within due limits" of requirements for the common good. The foundation of this right in civil society is the "very dignity of the human person" (Declaration on Religious Freedom, *Dignitatis Humanae*, No. 2). The conciliar statement did not deal with the subject of freedom within the Church. It noted the responsibility of the faithful "carefully to attend to the sacred and certain doctrine of the Church" (No. 14).

Freemasons: A fraternal order which originated in London in 1717 with the formation of the first Grand Lodge of Freemasons. From England, the order spread to Europe and elsewhere. Its principles and basic rituals embody a naturalistic religion, active participation in which is incompatible with Christian faith and practice. Grand Orient Freemasonry, developed in Latin countries, is atheistic, irreligious and anticlerical. In some places, Freemasonry has been regarded as subversive of the state; in Catholic quarters, it has been considered hostile to the Church and its doctrine. In the United States, Freemasonry has been widely regarded as a fraternal and philanthropic order. For serious doctrinal and pastoral reasons, Catholics were forbidden to join the Freemasons under penalty of excommunication, according to church law before 1983. Eight different popes in 17 different pronouncements, and at least six different local councils, condemned Freemasonry. The first condemnation was made by Clement XII in 1738. Eastern Orthodox and many Protestant bodies have also opposed the order. In the U.S., there was some easing of the ban against Masonic membership by Catholics in view of a letter written in 1974 by Cardinal Franjo Seper, prefect of the Congregation for the Doctrine of the Faith. The letter was interpreted to mean that Catholics might join Masonic lodges that were not anti-Catholic. This was called erroneous in a declaration issued by the Doctrinal Congregation Feb. 17, 1981. The prohibition against Masonic membership was restated in a declaration issued by the Doctrinal Congregation Nov. 26, 1983, with the approval of Pope John Paul II, as follows: "The Church's negative position on Masonic associations remains unaltered, since their principles have always been regarded as irreconcilable with the Church's doctrine. Hence, join-

ing them remains prohibited by the Church. Catholics enrolled in Masonic associations are involved in serious sin and may not approach Holy Communion. Local ecclesiastical authorities do not have the faculty to pronounce a judgment on the nature of Masonic associations which might include a diminution of the above-mentioned judgment." This latest declaration, like the revised Code of Canon Law, does not include a penalty of excommunication for Catholics who join the Masons. Local bishops are not authorized to grant dispensations from the prohibition. The foregoing strictures against Masonic membership by Catholics were reiterated in a report by the Committee for Pastoral Research and Practice, National Conference of Catholic Bishops, released through Catholic News Service June 7, 1985.

Free Will: The faculty or capability of making a reasonable choice among several alternatives. Freedom of will underlies the possibility and fact of moral responsibility.

Friar: Term applied to members of mendicant orders to distinguish them from members of monastic orders. (*See* **Mendicants**.)

Fruits of the Holy Spirit: Charity, joy, peace, patience, kindness, goodness, generosity, gentleness, faithfulness, modesty, self-control, chastity.

Fruits of the Mass: The spiritual and temporal blessings that result from the celebration of the Holy Sacrifice of the Mass. The general fruits are shared by all the faithful, living and departed, while the special fruits are applied to the priest who celebrates it, to those for whose intention it is offered, and to all those who participate in its celebration.

Fundamental Option: The orientation of one's life either to God by obedience or against Him through disobedience. Catholic Tradition acknowledges that one free and deliberate act with knowledge renders one at odds with God. A prevalent and vague moral theory today asserts that one act cannot change one's option to God — no matter how grave — unless the action comes from the person's "center." Pope John Paul II cautioned against this ambiguous position in the encyclical *Veritatis Splendor* (1993).

G

Gehenna: Greek form of a Jewish name, Gehinnom, for a valley near Jerusalem, the site of Moloch worship; used as a synonym for hell.

Genuflection: Bending of the knee, a natural sign of adoration or reverence, as when persons genuflect with the right knee in passing before the tabernacle to acknowledge the Eucharistic presence of Christ.

Gethsemani: A Hebrew word meaning oil press, designating the place on the Mount of Olives where Christ prayed and suffered in agony the night before he died.

Gifts of the Holy Spirit: Supernatural habits disposing a person to respond promptly to the inspiration of grace; promised by Christ and communicated through the Holy Spirit, especially in the sacrament of confirmation. They are: wisdom, understanding, counsel, knowledge, fortitude, piety and fear of the Lord.

Glorified Body: The definitive state of humanity in eternity. The risen Christ calls humanity to the glory of his resurrection; this is a theological premise that presupposes that, like Christ, all of his brothers and sisters will be transformed physically.

Gluttony: An unreasonable appetite for food and drink; one of the seven capital sins.

God: The infinitely perfect Supreme Being, uncaused and absolutely self-sufficient, eternal, the Creator and final end of all things. The one God subsists in three equal Persons, the Father and the Son and the Holy Spirit. God, although transcendent and distinct from the universe, is present and active in the world in realization of his plan for the salvation of human beings, principally through Revelation, the operations of the Holy Spirit, the life and ministry of Christ, and the continuation of Christ's ministry in the Church. The existence of God is an article of faith, clearly communicated in divine Revelation. Even without this Revelation, however, the Church teaches, in a declaration by the First Vatican Council, that human beings can acquire certain knowledge of the existence of God and some of his attributes. This can be done on the bases of principles of reason and reflection on human experience. Non-revealed arguments or demonstrations for the existence of God have been developed from the principle of causality; the contingency of human beings and the universe; the existence of design, change and movement in the universe; human awareness of moral responsibility; widespread human testimony to the existence of God.

Goods of Marriage: Three blessings — children, faithful companionship and permanence — that were first enumerated by St. Augustine in a work on marriage.

Grace: A free gift of God to persons (and angels), grace is a created sharing or participation in the life of God. It is given to persons through the merits of Christ and is communicated by the Holy Spirit. It is necessary for salvation. The principal means of grace are the sacraments (especially the Eucharist), prayer and good works. (1) **Sanctifying or habitual grace** makes persons holy and pleasing to God, adopted children of God, members of Christ, temples of the Holy Spirit, heirs of heaven capable of supernaturally meritorious acts. With grace, God gives persons the supernatural virtues and gifts of the Holy Spirit. The sacraments of baptism and penance were instituted to give grace to those who do not have it; the other sacraments, to increase it in those already in the state of grace. The means for growth in holiness, or the increase of grace, are prayer, the sacraments and good works. Sanctifying grace is lost by the commission of serious sin. Each sacrament confers sanctifying grace for the special purpose of the sacrament; in this context, grace is called sacramental grace. (2) **Actual grace** is a supernatural help of God which enlightens and strengthens a person to do good and to avoid evil. It is not a permanent quality, like sanctifying grace. It is necessary for the performance of supernatural acts. It can be resisted and refused. Persons in the state of serious sin are given actual grace to lead them to repentance.

Grace at Meals: Prayers said before meals, asking a blessing of God, and after meals, giving thanks to God. In addition to traditional prayers for these purposes, many variations suitable for different occasions are possible, at personal option.

Guilt: The condition of an individual who has committed some moral wrong and is liable to receive punishment.

H

Habit: (1) A disposition to do things easily, given with grace (and therefore supernatural) and/or acquired by repetition of similar acts. (2) The garb worn by Religious.

Hagiography: Writings or documents about saints and other holy persons.

Hail Mary: A prayer addressed to the Blessed Virgin Mary; also called the *Ave Maria* (Latin equivalent of Hail Mary) and the Angelic Salutation. In three parts, it consists of the words addressed to Mary by the Archangel Gabriel on the occasion of the Annunciation, in the Infancy Narrative (*Hail Mary, full of grace, the Lord is with you, blessed are you among women.*); the words addressed to Mary by her cousin Elizabeth on the occasion of the Visitation (*Blessed is the fruit of your womb.*); a concluding petition (*Holy Mary, Mother of God, pray for us sinners now and at the hour of our death. Amen.*). The first two salutations were joined in Eastern rite formulas by the sixth century, and were similarly used at Rome in the seventh century. Insertion of the name of Jesus at the conclusion of the salutations was probably made by Urban IV about 1262. The present form of the petition was incorporated into the breviary in 1514.

Heaven: The state of those who, having achieved salvation, are in glory with God and enjoy the beatific vision. The phrase, kingdom of heaven, refers to the order or kingdom of God, grace, salvation.

Hell: The state of persons who die in mortal sin, in a condition of self-alienation from God which will last forever.

Heresy: The obstinate post-baptismal denial or doubt by a Catholic of any truth which must be believed as a matter of divine and Catholic faith (Canon 751, of the Code of Canon Law). Formal heresy involves deliberate resistance to the authority of God who communicates revelation through Scripture and tradition and the teaching authority of the Church. Heretics automatically incur the penalty of excommunication (Canon 1364 of the Code of Canon Law). Heresies have been significant not only as disruptions of unity of faith but also as occasions for the clarification and development of doctrine. Heresies from the beginning of the Church to the 13th century are described in **Dates and Events in Church History**.

Hermeneutics: *See* **Interpretation of the Bible**.

Hermit: *See* **Anchorite**.

Heroic Act of Charity: The completely unselfish offering to God of one's good works and merits for the benefit of the souls in purgatory rather than for oneself. Thus a person may offer to God for the souls in purgatory all the good works he performs during life, all the indulgences he gains, and all the prayers and indulgences that will be offered for him after his death. The act is revocable at will, and is not a vow. Its actual ratification depends on the will of God.

Heroic Virtue: The exemplary practice of the four cardinal virtues and three theological virtues; such virtue is sought in persons considered for sainthood.

Heterodoxy: False doctrine teaching or belief; a departure from truth.

Hierarchy: The hierarchy of order who carry out the sacramental, teaching and pastoral ministry of the Church; the hierarchy consists of the pope, bishops, priests and deacons; the pope and the bishops give pastoral governance to the faithful.

Holy Father: A title used for the pope; it is a shortened translation of the Latin title *Beatissimus Pater*, "Most Blessed Father" and refers to his position as the spiritual father of all the Christian faithful.

Holy See: (1) The diocese of the pope, Rome. (2) The pope himself and/or the various officials and bodies of the Church's central administration at Vatican City — the Roman Curia — which act in the name and by authority of the pope.

Holy Spirit: God the Holy Spirit, third Person of the Holy Trinity, who proceeds from the Father and the Son and with whom he is equal in every respect; inspirer of the prophets and writers of sacred Scripture; promised by Christ to the Apostles as their advocate and strengthener; appeared in the form of a dove at the baptism of Christ and as tongues of fire at his descent upon the Apostles; soul of the Church and guarantor, by his abiding presence and action, of truth in doctrine; communicator of grace to human beings, for which reason he is called the sanctifier.

Holy Water: Water blessed by the Church and used as a sacramental, a practice which originated in apostolic times.

Holy Year: A year during which the pope grants the plenary Jubilee Indulgence to the faithful who fulfill certain conditions. For those who make a pilgrimage to Rome during the year, the conditions are reception of the sacraments of penance and the Eucharist, visits and prayer for the intention of the pope in the basilicas of St. Peter, St. John Lateran, St. Paul and St. Mary Major. For those who do not make a pilgrimage to Rome, the conditions are reception of the sacraments and prayer for the pope during a visit or community celebration in a church designated by the bishop of the locality. Pope Boniface VIII formally proclaimed the first Holy Year on Feb. 22, 1300, and the first three Holy Years were observed in 1300, 1350, and 1390. Subsequent ones were celebrated at 25-year intervals except in 1800 and 1850, when, respectively, the French invasion of Italy and political turmoil made observance impossible. Pope Paul II (1464-1471) set the 25-year timetable. In 1500, Pope Alexander VI prescribed the start and finish ceremonies — the opening and closing of the Holy Doors in the major basilicas on successive Christmas Eves. All but a few of the earlier Holy Years were classified as ordinary. Several — like those of 1933 and 1983-84 to commemorate the 1900th and 1950th anniversaries of the death and resurrection of Christ — were in the extraordinary category. Pope John Paul designated Jubilee Year 2000 to be a Holy Year ending the second and beginning the third millennium of Christianity.

Homosexuality: The condition of a person whose sexual orientation is toward persons of the same rather than the opposite sex. The condition is not sinful in itself. Homosexual acts are seriously sinful in themselves; subjective responsibility for such acts, however, may be conditioned and diminished by compulsion and related factors.

Hope: The theological virtue by which a person firmly trusts in God for the means and attainment salvation.

Hosanna: A Hebrew word, meaning *O Lord, save, we pray*.

Host, The Sacred: The bread under whose appearances Christ is and remains present in a unique manner after the consecration which takes place during Mass. (*See* **Transubstantiation**.)

Human Dignity: The inherent worth of all human persons as they are made in God's image and likeness and they alone — of all God's creatures on earth — have an immortal soul.

Humanism: A world view centered on man. Types of humanism which exclude the supernatural are related to secularism.

Humility: A virtue which induces a person to evaluate himself or herself at his or her true worth, to recognize his or her dependence on God, and to give glory to God for the good he or she has and can do.

Hyperdulia: The special veneration accorded the Blessed Virgin Mary because of her unique role in the mystery of Redemption, her exceptional gifts of grace from God, and her pre-eminence among the saints. *Hyperdulia* is not adoration; only God is adored.

Hypostatic Union: The union of the human and divine natures in the one divine Person of Christ.

I

Icons: Byzantine-style paintings or representations of Christ, the Blessed Virgin and other saints, venerated in the Eastern Churches where they take the place of statues.

Idolatry: Worship of any but the true God; a violation of the First Commandment.

IHS: In Greek, the first three letters of the name of Jesus — *Iota, Eta, Sigma*.

Immaculate Conception: The doctrine that affirms that "the Blessed Virgin Mary was preserved, in the first instant of her conception, by a singular grace and privilege of God omnipotent and because of the merits of Jesus Christ the Savior of the human race, free from all stain of Original Sin," as stated by Pope Pius IX in his declaration of the dogma, Dec. 8, 1854. Thus, Mary was conceived in the state of perfect justice, free from Original Sin and its consequences, in virtue of the redemption achieved by Christ on the cross.

Immortality: The survival and continuing existence of the human soul after death.

Imprimatur: *See* **Censorship of Books**.

Impurity: Unlawful indulgence in sexual pleasure. (*See* **Chastity**.)

Imputability: A canonical term for the moral responsibility of a person for an act that he or she has performed.

Incardination: The affiliation of a priest to his diocese. Every secular priest must belong to a certain diocese. Similarly, every priest of a religious community must belong to some jurisdiction of his community; this affiliation, however, is not called incardination.

Incarnation: (1) The coming-into-flesh or taking of human nature by the Second Person of the Trinity. He became human as the Son of Mary, being miraculously conceived by the power of the Holy Spirit, without ceasing to be divine. His divine Person hypostatically unites his divine and human natures. (2) The supernatural mystery coextensive with Christ from the moment of his human conception and continuing through his life on earth; his sufferings and death; his resurrection from the dead and ascension to glory with the Father; his sending, with the Father, of the Holy Spirit upon the Apostles and the Church; and his unending mediation with the Father for the salvation of human beings.

Incense: A granulated substance which, when burnt, emits an aromatic smoke. It symbolizes the zeal with which the faithful should be consumed, the good odor of Christian virtue, the ascent of prayer to God. An incense boat is a small vessel used to hold incense which is to be placed in the censer.

Incest: Sexual intercourse with relatives by blood or marriage; a sin of impurity and also a grave violation of the natural reverence due to relatives. Other sins of impurity desire, etc., concerning relatives have the nature of incest.

Inculturation: The correct and entirely appropriate adaptation of the Catholic liturgy and institutions to the culture, language and customs of an indigenous or local people among whom the Gospel is first proclaimed. Pope John Paul II Feb. 15, 1982, at a meeting in Lagos with the bishops of Nigeria proclaimed: "An important aspect of your own evangelizing role is the whole dimension of the inculturation of the Gospel into the lives of your people. The Church truly respects the culture of each people. In offering the Gospel message, the Church does not intend to destroy or to abolish what is good and beautiful. In fact, she recognizes many cultural values and, through the power of the Gospel, purifies and takes into Christian worship certain elements of a people's customs."

Index of Prohibited Books: A list of books which Catholics were formerly forbidden to read, possess or sell, under penalty of excommunication. The books were banned by the Holy See after publication because their treatment of matters of faith and morals and related subjects were judged to be erroneous or serious occasions of doctrinal error. Some books were listed in the Index by name; others were covered under general norms. The Congregation for the Doctrine of the Faith declared June 14, 1966, that the Index and its related penalties of excommunication no longer had the force of law in the Church. Persons are still obliged, however, to take normal precautions against occasions of doctrinal error.

Indifferentism: A theory that any one religion is as true and good — or as false — as any other religion, and that it makes no difference, objectively, what religion that one professes, if any. The theory is completely subjective, finding its justification entirely in personal choice without reference to or respect for objective validity. It is also self-contradictory, since it regards as equally acceptable — or unacceptable — the beliefs of all religions, which in fact are not only not all the same but are in some cases opposed to each other.

Indulgence: According to The Doctrine and Practice of Indulgences, an apostolic constitution issued by Paul VI Jan. 1, 1967, an indulgence is the remission before God of the temporal punishment due for sins already forgiven as far as their guilt is concerned, which a follower of Christ — with the proper dispositions and under certain determined conditions — acquires through the intervention of the Church. An indulgence is partial or plenary, depending on whether it does away with either part or all of the temporal punishment due for sin. Both types of indulgences can always be applied to the dead by way of suffrage; the actual disposition of indulgences applied to the dead rests with God. Only one plenary indulgence can be gained in a single day. The Apostolic Penitentiary issued a decree Dec. 14, 1985, granting diocesan bishops the right to impart — three times a year on solemn feasts of their choice — the papal blessing with a plenary indulgence to those who cannot be physically present but who follow the sacred rites at which the blessing is imparted by radio or television transmission. In July 1986, publication was announced of a new and simplified *Enchiridion Indulgentiarum*, in accord with provisions of the revised Code of Canon Law. A revised manual was issued by the Holy See on Sept. 17, 2000.

Indult: A favor or privilege granted by competent ecclesiastical authority, giving permission to do something not allowed by the common law of the Church.

Infallibility: (1) The inability of the Church to err in its teaching, in that she preserves and teaches the deposit of truth as revealed by Christ; (2) The inability of the Roman Pontiff to err when he teaches *ex cathedra* in matters of faith or morals, and indicates that the doctrine is to be believed by all the faithful; and (3) the inability of the college of bishops to err when speaking in union with the pope in matters of faith and morals, agreeing that a doctrine must be held by the universal Church, and the doctrine is promulgated by the Pontiff.

Infused Virtues: The theological virtues of faith, hope and charity; principles or capabilities of supernatural action, they are given with sanctifying grace by God rather than acquired by repeated acts of a person. They can be increased by practice; they are lost by contrary acts. Natural-acquired moral virtues, like the cardinal virtues of prudence, justice, temperance and fortitude, can be considered infused in a person whose state of grace gives them supernatural orientation.

Inquisition: A tribunal for dealing with heretics, authorized by Gregory IX in 1231 to search them out, hear, and judge them; sentence them to various forms of punishment; and in some cases, to hand them over to civil authorities for punishment. The Inquisition was a creature of its time when crimes against faith, which threatened the good of the Christian community, were regarded also as crimes against the state, and when heretical doctrines of such extremists as the Cathari and Albigensians threatened the very fabric of society. The institution, which was responsible for many excesses, was most active in the second half of the 13th century.

Inquisition, Spanish: An institution peculiar to Spain and the colonies in Spanish America. In 1478, at the urging of King Ferdinand, Pope Sixtus IV approved the establishment of the Inquisition for trying charges of heresy brought against Jewish (*Marranos*) and Moorish (*Moriscos*) converts. It acquired jurisdiction over other cases as well, however, and fell into disrepute because of irregularities in its functions, cruelty in its sentences, and the manner in which it served the interests of the Spanish crown more than the accused persons and the good of the Church. Protests by the Holy See failed to curb excesses of the Inquisition, which lingered in Spanish history until early in the 19th century.

I N R I: The first letters of words in the Latin inscription atop the cross on which Christ was crucified: *(I)esus (N)azaraenus, (R)ex (I)udaeorum* — Jesus of Nazareth, King of the Jews.

Insemination, Artificial: The implanting of human semen by some means other than consummation of natural marital intercourse. In view of the principle that procreation should result only from marital intercourse, donor insemination is not permissible.

In Sin: The condition of a person called spiritually dead because he or she does not possess sanctifying grace, the principle of supernatural life, action and merit. Such grace can be regained through repentance.

Instruction: A document containing doctrinal explanations, directive norms, rules, recommendations, admonitions, issued by the pope, a department of the Roman Curia, or other competent authority in the Church. To the extent that they so prescribe, instructions have the force of law.

Intercommunion, Eucharistic Sharing: The common celebration and reception of the Eucharist by members of different Christian churches; a pivotal issue in ecumenical theory and practice. Catholic participation and intercommunion in the Eucharistic liturgy of another church without a valid priesthood and with a variant Eucharistic belief is out of order. Under certain conditions, other Christians may receive the Eucharist in the Catholic Church. (*See* additional **Intercommunion** entry). Intercommunion is acceptable to some Protestant churches and unacceptable to others.

Interdict: A censure imposed on persons for certain violations of church law. Interdicted persons may not take part in certain liturgical services, administer, or receive certain sacraments.

Intinction: A method of administering Holy Communion under the dual appearances of bread and wine, in which the consecrated host is dipped in the consecrated wine before being given to the communicant. The administering of Holy Communion in this manner, which has been traditional in Eastern Rite liturgies, was authorized in the Roman Rite for various occasions by the Constitution on the Sacred Liturgy promulgated by the Second Vatican Council.

Irenicism: Peace-seeking, conciliation, as opposed to polemics; an important element in ecumenism, provided it furthers pursuit of the Christian unity willed by Christ without degenerating into a peace-at-any-price disregard for religious truth.

Irregularity: A permanent impediment to the lawful reception or exercise of holy orders. The Church instituted irregularities — which include apostasy, heresy, homicide, attempted suicide — out of reverence for the dignity of the sacraments.

J

Jehovah: The English equivalent of the Hebrew *Adonai* ("my Lord") used out of fear and reverence for the Holy Name of Yahweh. *Jehovah* uses the consonants YHWH and the vowels of *Adonai* (a, o, a). Scholars today maintain that *Jehovah* is a false derivation.

Jesus: The name of Jesus, meaning "God saves," expressing the identity and mission of the second Person of the Trinity become man; derived from the Aramaic and Hebrew "Yeshua" and "Joshua," meaning "Yahweh is salvation."

Jesus Prayer: A prayer of Eastern origin, dating back to the fifth century: *"Lord Jesus Christ, Son of God, have mercy on me (a sinner)."*

Judgment: (1) **Last or final judgment**: Final judgment by Christ, at the end of the world and the general resurrection. (2) **Particular judgment**: The judgment that takes place immediately after a person's death, followed by entrance into heaven, hell, or purgatory.

Jurisdiction: Right, power, authority to rule. Jurisdiction in the Church is of divine institution; has pastoral service for its purpose; includes legislative, judicial and executive authority; can be exercised only by persons with the power of orders. (1) Ordinary jurisdiction is attached to ecclesiastical offices by law; the officeholders, called Ordinaries, have authority over those who are subject to them. (2) Delegated jurisdiction is that which is granted to persons rather than attached to offices. Its extent depends on the terms of the delegation.

Justice: One of the four cardinal virtues by which a person gives to others what is due to them as a matter of right. (*See* **Cardinal Virtues**.)

Justification: The act by which God makes a person just, and the consequent change in the spiritual status of a person, from sin to grace; the remission of sin and the infusion of sanctifying grace through the merits of Christ and the action of the Holy Spirit.

K

Kenosis: A term from the Greek for "emptying" that denotes Christ's emptying of Himself in his free renunciation of his right to divine status, by reason of the Incarnation, particularly as celebrated in the kenotic hymn (Phil 2:6-11), where it is said that Christ "emptied himself," taking the form of a slave, born in the likeness of man totally integrated with his divinity.

Kerygma: Proclaiming the word of God, in the manner of the Apostles, as here and now effective for salvation. This method of preaching or instruction, centered on Christ and geared to the facts and themes of salvation history, is designed to dispose people to faith in Christ and/or to intensify the experience and practice of faith in those who have it.

Keys, Power of the: Spiritual authority and jurisdiction in the Church, symbolized by the keys of the kingdom of heaven. Christ promised the keys to St. Peter, as head-to-be of the Church (Mt. 16:19), and commissioned him with full pastoral responsibility to feed his lambs and sheep (Jn. 21:15-17), The pope, as the successor of St. Peter, has this power in a primary and supreme manner. The bishops of the Church also have the power, in union with and subordinate to the pope. Priests share in it through holy orders and the delegation of authority. Examples of the application of the Power of the Keys are the exercise of teaching and pastoral authority by the pope and bishops, the absolving of sins in the sacrament of penance, the granting of indulgences, the imposing of spiritual penalties on persons who commit certain serious sins.

Kingdom of God: God's sovereign lordship or rule over salvation history, leading to the eschatological goal of eternal life with God.

Koinonia: A term from the Greek word for "community, fellowship, or association" that was used by St. Luke for the fellowship of believers who worshipped together and held all their possessions in common (Acts 2:42-47); it is also used of fellowship with God (1 Jn. 1:3, 6), with the Son (1 Cor. 1:9), and with the Holy Spirit (2 Cor. 13:13; Phil. 2:1). St. Paul used *koinonia* to denote the intimate union of the believer with Christ and the community that exists among all the faithful themselves (Rom. 15:26; 2 Cor. 6:14).

L

Laicization: The process by which a man ordained to holy orders is relieved of the obligations of orders and the ministry and is returned to the status of a lay person.

Languages of the Church: The languages in which the Church's liturgy is celebrated. These include Ge'ez, Syriac, Greek, Arabic and Old Slavonic in the Eastern Churches. In the West, there is, of course, Latin and the various vernaculars. The Eastern Rites have always had the vernacular. The first language in church use, for divine worship and the conduct of ecclesiastical affairs, was Aramaic, the language of the first Christians in and around Jerusalem. As the Church spread westward, Greek was adopted and prevailed until the third century, when it was supplanted by Latin for official use in the West. In the Western Church, Latin prevailed as the general official language until the promulgation on Dec. 4, 1963, of the Constitution on the Sacred Liturgy (*Sacrosanctum Concilium*) by the second session of the Second Vatican Council. Since that time, vernacular languages have come into use in the Mass, administration of the sacraments, and the Liturgy of the Hours. Latin, however, remains the official language for documents of the Holy See, administrative and procedural matters.

Latria: Greek-rooted Latin term that refers to that form of praise due to God alone.

Law: An ordinance or rule governing the activity of things. (1) **Natural law**: Moral norms corresponding to man's nature by which he orders his conduct toward God, neighbor, society and himself. This law, which is rooted in human nature, is of divine origin, can be known by the use of reason, and binds all persons having the use of reason. The Ten Commandments are declarations and amplifications of natural law. The primary precepts of natural law, to do good and to avoid evil, are universally recognized, despite differences with respect to understanding and application resulting from different philosophies of good and evil. (2) **Divine positive law**: That which has been revealed by God. Among its essentials are the twin precepts of love of God and love of neighbor, and the Ten Commandments. (3) **Ecclesiastical law**: That which is established by the Church for the spiritual welfare of the faithful and the orderly conduct of ecclesiastical affairs. (*See* **Canon Law**.) (4) **Civil law**: That which is established by a sociopolitical community for the common good.

Liberalism: A multi-phased trend of thought and movement favoring liberty, independence and progress in moral, intellectual, religious, social, economic and political life. Traceable to the Renaissance, it developed through the Enlightenment, the rationalism of the 19th century and modernist- and existentialist-related theories of the 20th century. Evaluations of various kinds of liberalism depend on the validity of their underlying principles. Extremist positions — regarding subjectivism, libertinarianism, naturalist denials of the supernatural, and the alienation of individuals and society from God and the Church —

were condemned by Gregory XVI in the 1830s, Pius IX in 1864, Leo XIII in 1899 and St. Pius X in 1907. There is, however, nothing objectionable about forms of liberalism patterned according to sound principles of Christian doctrine.

Liberation Theology: Deals with the relevance of Christian faith and salvation — and, therefore, of the mission of the Church — to efforts for the promotion of human rights, social justice and human development. It originated in the religious, social, political and economic environment of Latin America, with its contemporary need for a theory and corresponding action by the Church, in the pattern of its overall mission, for human rights and integral personal and social development. Some versions of liberation theology are at variance with the body of church teaching because of their ideological concept of Christ as liberator, and also because they play down the primary spiritual nature and mission of the Church. Instructions from the Congregation for the Doctrine of the Faith — "On Certain Aspects of the Theology of Liberation" (Sept. 3, 1984) and "On Christian Freedom and Liberation" (Apr. 5, 1986) — contain warnings against translating sociology into theology and advocating violence in social activism.

Life in Outer Space: Whether rational life exists on other bodies in the universe besides earth, is a question for scientific investigation to settle. The possibility can be granted, without prejudice to the body of revealed truth.

Limbo: The limbo of the fathers was the state of rest and natural happiness after death enjoyed by the just of pre-Christian times until they were admitted to heaven following the Ascension of Christ.

Litany: A prayer in the form of responsive petition; e.g., St. Joseph, pray for us, etc. Examples are the litanies of Loreto (Litany of the Blessed Mother), the Holy Name, All Saints, the Sacred Heart, the Precious Blood, St. Joseph, Litany for the Dying.

Logos: A Greek term for "word, speech, or reason." It is most commonly identified with the title given to Jesus in John's Gospel, though not exclusive to that Gospel; In the NT, however, the term reflects more the influence of Hellenistic philosophy: St. Paul uses logos as interchangeable with *sophia*, wisdom (1 Cor. 1:24). The *Logos* is the Wisdom of God made manifest in the Son. As a name for the Second Person of the Trinity, the Incarnate Word, the term receives new meaning in the light of the life, death and resurrection of Jesus Christ.

Loreto, House of: A Marian shrine in Loreto, Italy, consisting of the home of the Holy Family which, according to an old tradition, was transported in a miraculous manner from Nazareth to Dalmatia and finally to Loreto between 1291 and 1294. Investigations conducted shortly after the appearance of the structure in Loreto revealed that its dimensions matched those of the house of the Holy Family missing from its place of enshrinement in a basilica at Nazareth. Among the many popes who regarded it with high honor was John XXIII, who went there on pilgrimage Oct. 4, 1962. The house of the Holy Family is enshrined in the Basilica of Our Lady.

Love: A devotion to a person or object that has been categorized by Greek philosophy into four types: *storge* (one loves persons and things close to him); *philia* (the love of friends); *eros* (sexual love and that of a spiritual nature); *agape* (a self-giving to one in need). Christian charity is love, but not all love is true charity.

Lust: A disorderly desire for sexual pleasure; one of the seven capital sins.

M

Magi: In the Infancy Narrative of St. Matthew's Gospel (2:1-12), three wise men from the East whose visit and homage to the Child Jesus at Bethlehem indicated Christ's manifestation of himself to non-Jewish people. The narrative teaches the universality of salvation. The traditional names of the Magi are Caspar, Melchior and Balthasar.

Magisterium: The Church's teaching authority, instituted by Christ and guided by the Holy Spirit, which seeks to safeguard and explain the truths of the faith. The Magisterium is exercised in two ways. The extraordinary Magisterium is exercised when the pope and ecumenical councils infallibly define a truth of faith or morals that is necessary for one's salvation and that has been constantly taught and held by the Church. Ordinary Magisterium is exercised when the Church infallibly defines truths of the Faith as taught universally and without dissent; which must be taught or the Magisterium would be failing in its duty; is connected with a grave matter of faith or morals; and which is taught authoritatively. Not everything taught by the Magisterium is done so infallibly; however, the exercise of the Magisterium is faithful to Christ and what He taught.

Magnificat: The canticle or hymn of the Virgin Mary on the occasion of her visitation to her cousin Elizabeth (Lk. 1:46-55). It is an expression of praise, thanksgiving and acknowledgment of the great blessings given by God to Mary, the Mother of the Second Person of the Blessed Trinity made Man. The *Magnificat* is recited in the Liturgy of the Hours as part of the Evening Prayer.

Martyr: A Greek word, meaning "witness," denoting one who voluntarily suffered death for the faith or some Christian virtue.

Martyrology: A catalogue of martyrs and other saints, arranged according to the calendar. The *Roman Martyrology* contains the official list of saints venerated by the Church. Additions to the list are made in beatification and canonization decrees of the Congregation for the Causes of Saints.

Mass for the People: On Sundays and certain feasts throughout the year pastors are required to offer Mass for the faithful entrusted to their care. If they cannot offer the Mass on these days, they must do so at a later date or provide that another priest offer the Mass.

Materialism: Theory that holds that matter is the only reality, and everything in existence is merely a manifestation of matter; there is no such thing as spirit, and the supernatural does not exist. Materialism is incompatible with Christian doctrine.

Meditation: Mental, as distinguished from vocal, prayer, in which thought, affections and resolutions of the will predominate. There is a meditative element to all forms of prayer, which always involves the raising of the heart and mind to God.

Mendicants: A term derived from Latin and meaning beggars, applied to members of religious orders without property rights; the members, accordingly, worked or begged for their support. The original mendicants were Franciscans and Dominicans in the early 13th century; later, the Carmelites, Augustinians, Servites and others were given the mendicant title and privileges, with respect to exemption from episcopal jurisdiction and wide faculties for preaching and administering the sacrament of penance. The practice of begging is limited at the present time, although it is still allowed with the permission of competent superiors and bishops. Mendicants are supported by free will offerings and income received for spiritual services and other work.

Mercy, Divine: The love and goodness of God, manifested particularly in a time of need.

Mercy, Works of: Works of corporal or spiritual assistance, motivated by love of God and neighbor, to persons in need. (1) **Corporal works**: feeding the hungry, giving drink to the thirsty, clothing the naked, visiting the imprisoned, sheltering the homeless, visiting the sick, burying the dead. (2) **Spiritual works**: counseling the doubtful, instructing the ignorant, admonishing sinners, comforting the afflicted, forgiving offenses, bearing wrongs patiently, praying for the living and the dead.

Merit: In religion, the right to a supernatural reward for good works freely done for a supernatural motive by a person in the state of and with the assistance of grace. The right to such reward is from God, who binds himself to give it. Accordingly, good works, as described above, are meritorious for salvation.

Metanoia: A term from the Greek *metanoein* ("to change one's mind, repent, be converted") that is used in the NT for conversion. It entails the repentance of sin and the subsequent turning toward the Lord. *Metanoia* is fundamental to the Christian life and is necessary for spiritual growth.

Metaphysics: The branch of philosophy (from the Greek *meta* — after + *physika* — physics) dealing with first things, including the nature of being (ontology), the origin and structure of the world (cosmology), and the study of the reality and attributes of God (natural theology). Metaphysics has long been examined by Catholic philosophers, most especially in the writings of St. Augustine and St. Thomas Aquinas.

Millennium: A thousand-year reign of Christ and the just upon earth before the end of the world. This belief of the Millenarians, Chiliasts and some sects of modern times is based on an erroneous interpretation of Rv. 20.

Miracles: Observable events or effects in the physical or moral order of things, with reference to salvation, which cannot be explained by the ordinary operation of laws of nature and which, therefore, are attributed to the direct action of God. They make known, in an unusual way, the concern and intervention of God in human affairs for the salvation of men.

Mission: (1) Strictly, it means being sent to perform a certain work, such as the mission of Christ to redeem mankind, the mission of the Apostles and the Church and its members to perpetuate the prophetic, priestly and royal mission of Christ. (2) A place where: the Gospel has not been proclaimed; the Church has not been firmly established; the Church, although established, is weak. (3) An ecclesiastical territory with the simplest kind of canonical organization, under the jurisdiction of the Congregation for the Evangelization of Peoples. (4) A church or chapel without a resident priest. (5) A special course of sermons and spiritual exercises conducted in parishes for the purpose of renewing and deepening the spiritual life of the faithful and for the conversion of lapsed Catholics.

Modernism: The "synthesis of all heresies," which appeared near the beginning of the 20th century. It undermines the objective validity of religious beliefs and practices which, it contends, are products of the subconscious developed by mankind under the stimulus of a religious sense. It holds that the existence of a personal God cannot be demonstrated, the Bible is not inspired, Christ is not divine, nor did he establish the Church or institute the sacraments. A special danger lies in modernism, which is still influential, because it uses Catholic terms with perverted meanings. St. Pius X condemned 65 propositions of modernism in 1907 in the decree *Lamentabili* and issued the encyclical *Pascendi* to explain and analyze its errors.

Monastery: The dwelling place, as well as the community thereof, of monks belonging to the Benedictine and Benedictine-related orders like the Cistercians and Carthusians; also, the Augustinians and Canons Regular. Distinctive of monasteries are: their separation from the world; the enclosure or cloister; the permanence or stability of attachment characteristic of their members; autonomous government in accordance with a monastic rule, like that of St. Benedict in the West or of St. Basil in the East; the special dedication of its members to the community celebration of the liturgy, as well as to work that is suitable to the surrounding area and the needs of its people. Monastic superiors of men have such titles as abbot and prior; of women, abbess and prioress. In most essentials, an abbey is the same as a monastery.

Monk: A member of a monastic order — e.g., the Benedictines, the Benedictine-related Cistercians and Carthusians and the Basilians, who bind themselves by religious profession to stable attachment to a monastery, the contemplative life and the work of their community. In popular use, the title is wrongly applied to many men religious who really are not monks.

Monotheism: Belief in and worship of one God.

Morality: Conformity or difformity of behavior to standards of right conduct. (*See* **Moral Obligations, Commandments of God, Precepts of the Church, Conscience, Law**.)

Mortification: Acts of self-discipline, including prayer, hardship, austerities and penances undertaken for the sake of progress in virtue.

Motu Proprio: A Latin phrase designating a document issued by a pope on his own initiative. Documents of this kind often concern administrative matters.

Mystagogy: Experience of the mystery of Christ, especially through participation in the liturgy and the sacraments.

Mysteries of Faith: Supernatural truths whose existence cannot be known without revelation by God and whose intrinsic truth, while not contrary to reason, can never be wholly understood even after revelation. These mysteries are above reason, not against reason. Among them are the divine mysteries of the Trinity, Incarnation and Eucharist. Some mysteries — e.g., concerning God's attributes — can be known by reason without revelation, although they cannot be fully understood.

N

Natural Law: *See* **Law**.

Natural Theology: The field of knowledge that relies upon human reason and the observation of nature, instead of revelation, to determine the existence and attributes of God.

Necromancy: Supposed communication with the dead; a form of divination.

Neo-Scholasticism: A movement begun in the late 19th century that had as its aim the restoration of Scholasticism for use in contemporary philosophy and theology. Great emphasis was placed upon the writings of such Scholastic masters as Peter Lombard, St. Albert the Great, St. Anselm, St. Bonaventure, Bl. John Duns Scotus and especially St. Thomas Aquinas. The movement began at the Catholic University of Louvain, in Belgium, and then found its way into theological centers in Italy, France and Germany. Particular attention was given to the philosophical and theological works of St. Thomas Aquinas, from which arose a particular school of neo-Thomism; the movement was strongly reinforced by Pope Leo XIII, who issued the encyclical *Aeterni Patris* (1879) mandating that Scholasticism, in particular Thomism, be the foundation for all Catholic philosophy and theology taught in Catholic seminaries, universities and colleges. Neo-Scholasticism was responsible for a true intellectual renaissance in 20th-century Catholic philosophy and theology. Among its foremost modern leaders were Jacques Maritain, Étienne Gilson, M. D. Chenu, Henri de Lubac and Paul Claudel.

Nihil Obstat: *See* **Censorship of Books**.

Non-Expedit: A Latin expression. It is not expedient (fitting, proper), used to state a prohibition or refusal of permission.

Novena: A term designating public or private devotional practices over a period of nine consecutive days; or, by extension, over a period of nine weeks, in which one day a week is set aside for the devotions.

Novice: A man or woman preparing, in a formal period of trial and formation called a novitiate, for membership in an institute of consecrated life. The novitiate lasts a minimum of 12 and a maximum of 24 months; at its conclusion, the novice professes temporary promises or vows of poverty, chastity and obedience. Norms require that certain periods of time be spent in the house of novitiate; periods of apostolic work are also required, to acquaint the novice with the apostolate(s) of the institute. A novice is not bound by the obligations of the professed members of the institute, is free to leave at any time, and may be discharged at the discretion of competent superiors. The superior of a novice is a master of novices or director of formation.

Nun: (1) Strictly, a member of a religious order of women with solemn vows (*moniales*). (2) In general, all women religious, even those in simple vows who are more properly called sisters.

Nunc Dimittis: The canticle or hymn of Simeon at the sight of Jesus at the Temple on the occasion of his presentation (Lk. 2:29-32). It is an expression of joy and thanksgiving for the blessing of having lived to see the Messiah. It is prescribed for use in the Night Prayer of the Liturgy of the Hours.

O

Oath: Calling upon God to witness the truth of a statement. Violating an oath, e.g., by perjury in court, or taking an oath without sufficient reason, is a violation of the honor due to God.

Obedience: Submission to one in authority. General obligations of obedience fall under the Fourth Commandment. The vow of obedience professed by religious is one of the evangelical counsels.

Obsession, Diabolical: The extraordinary state of one who is seriously molested by evil spirits in an external manner. Obsession is more than just temptation.

Occasion of Sin: A person, place or thing that is a temptation to sin. An occasion may be either a situation that always leads to sin or one that usually leads to sin.

Octave: A period of eight days given over to the celebration of a major feast such as Easter.

Oils, Holy: The oils blessed by a bishop at the Chrism Mass on Holy Thursday or another suitable day, or by a priest under certain conditions. (1) The oil of catechumens (olive or vegetable oil), used at baptism; also, poured with chrism into the baptismal water blessed in Easter Vigil ceremonies. (2) Oil of the sick (olive or vegetable oil) used in anointing the sick. (3) Chrism (olive or vegetable oil mixed with balm), which is ordinarily consecrated by a bishop, for use at baptism, in confirmation, at the ordination of a priest and bishop, in the dedication of churches and altars.

Ontologism: A philosophical theory (the name is taken from the Greek for being and study) that posits that knowledge of God is immediate and intuitive; it stipulates further that all other human knowledge is dependent upon this. It was condemned in 1861 by Pope Pius IX. (*See* **Ontology**.)

Ontology: A branch of metaphysics that studies the nature and relations of existence.

Oratory: A chapel.

Ordinariate: An ecclesiastical jurisdiction for special purposes and people. Examples are military ordinariates for armed services personnel (in accord with provisions of the apostolic constitution *Spirituali militum curae*, Apr. 21, 1986) and Eastern Rite ordinariates in places where Eastern Rite dioceses do not exist.

Ordination: The consecration of sacred ministers for divine worship and the service of people in things pertaining to God. The power of ordination comes from Christ and the Church, and must be conferred by a minister capable of communicating it.

Organ Transplants: The transplanting of organs from one person to another is permissible provided it is done with the consent of the concerned parties and does not result in the death or essential mutilation of the donor. Advances in methods and technology have increased the range of transplant possibilities in recent years.

Original Sin: The sin of Adam (Gn. 2:8-3:24), personal to him and passed on to all persons as a state of privation of grace. Despite this privation and the related wounding of human nature and weakening of natural powers, original sin leaves unchanged all that man himself is by nature. The scriptural basis of the doctrine was stated especially by St. Paul in 1 Cor. 15:21ff. and Rom. 5:12-21. Original sin is remitted by baptism and incorporation in Christ, through whom grace is given to persons. Pope John Paul II, while describing original sin during a general audience Oct. 1, 1986, called it "the absence of sanctifying grace in nature which has been diverted from its supernatural end."

O Salutaris Hostia: The first three Latin words, *O Saving Victim*, of a Benediction hymn.

Ostpolitik: Policy adopted by Pope Paul VI in an attempt to improve the situation of Eastern European Catholics through diplomatic negotiations with their governments.

Oxford Movement: A movement in the Church of England from 1833 to about 1845 which had for its objective a threefold defense of the Church as a divine institution, the apostolic succession of its bishops, and the *Book of Common Prayer* as the rule of faith. The movement took its name from Oxford University and involved a number of intellectuals who authored a series of influential "Tracts for Our Times." Some of its leading figures — e.g., F. W. Faber, John Henry Newman and Henry Edward Manning — became converts to the Catholic Church. In the Church of England, the movement affected the liturgy, historical and theological scholarship, the status of the ministry, and other areas of ecclesiastical life.

P

Paganism: A term referring to non-revealed religions, i.e., religions other than Christianity, Judaism and Islam.

Palms: Blessed palms are a sacramental. They are blessed and distributed on the Sunday of the Passion in commemoration of the triumphant entrance of Christ into Jerusalem. Ashes of the burnt palms are used on Ash Wednesday.

Pange Lingua: First Latin words, *Sing, my tongue*, of a hymn in honor of the Holy Eucharist, used particularly on Holy Thursday and in Eucharistic processions.

Pantheism: Theory that all things are part of God, divine, in the sense that God realizes himself as the ultimate reality of matter or spirit through being and/or becoming all things that have been, are, and will be. The theory leads to hopeless confusion of the Creator and the created realm of being, identifies evil with good, and involves many inherent contradictions.

Papal Election: See Conclave, under the section on the College of Cardinals.

Paraclete: A title of the Holy Spirit meaning, in Greek, Advocate, Consoler.

Parental Duties: All duties related to the obligation of parents to provide for the welfare of their children. These obligations fall under the Fourth Commandment.

Parish: A community of the faithful served by a pastor charged with responsibility for providing them with full pastoral service. Most parishes are territorial, embracing all of the faithful in a certain area of a diocese: some are personal or national, for certain classes of people, without strict regard for their places of residence.

Parousia: The coming, or saving presence, of Christ that will mark the completion of salvation history and the coming to perfection of God's kingdom at the end of the world.

Particular Church: A term used since Vatican II that denotes certain divisions of the Universal Church. Examples include dioceses, vicariates and prelatures.

Paschal Candle: A large candle, symbolic of the risen Christ, blessed and lighted during the Easter Vigil and placed at the altar until Pentecost. It is ornamented with five large grains of incense, representing the wounds of Christ, inserted in the form of a cross; the Greek letters Alpha and Omega, symbolizing Christ the beginning and end of all things, at the top and bottom of the shaft of the cross; and the figures of the current year of salvation in the quadrants formed by the cross.

Paschal Precept: Church law requiring reception of the Eucharist in the Easter season (*see* separate entry) unless, for a just cause, once-a-year reception takes place at another time.

Passion of Christ: Sufferings of Christ, recorded in the four Gospels.

Pastor: An ordained minister charged with responsibility for the doctrinal, sacramental and related service of people committed to his care; e.g., a bishop for the people in his diocese, a priest for the people of his parish.

Pater Noster: The initial Latin words, *Our Father*, of the Lord's Prayer.

Patriarch: (1) The leaders of the Israelite tribes and heads of prominent families who appear in Genesis from Adam to Joseph. Among the most significant patriarchs of the Old Testament are Abraham, Isaac and Jacob; the patriarchal narratives in Genesis associated with them constitute the prologue to Israel's salvation history, and the period during which they lived is known as the Age of the Patriarchs. It is noted that the title of patriarch that was used for David (Acts 2:29) was simply one of honor. (2) The head of a branch of the Eastern Church, corresponding to a province of the one-time Roman Empire. There are five official traditional patriarchal sees: Rome, Constantinople, Alexandria, Antioch and Jerusalem. Presently, the autocephalous churches of the Orthodox Church comprise several of these traditional patriarchates.

Peace, Sign of: A gesture of greeting — e.g., a handshake — exchanged by the ministers and participants at Mass.

Pectoral Cross: A cross worn on a chain about the neck and over the breast by bishops and abbots as a mark of their office.

Penance or Penitence: (1) The spiritual change or conversion of mind and heart by which a person turns away from sin, and all that it implies, toward God, through a personal renewal under the influence of the Holy Spirit. Penance involves sorrow and contrition for sin, together with other internal and external acts of atonement. It serves the purposes of reestablishing in one's life the order of God's love and commandments, and of making satisfaction to God for sin. (2) Penance is a virtue disposing a person to turn to God in sorrow for sin and to carry out works of amendment and atonement. (3) The sacrament of penance and sacramental penance.

People of God: A name for the Church in the sense that it is comprised by a people with Christ as its head, the Holy Spirit as the condition of its unity, the law of love as its rule, and the kingdom of God as its destiny. Although it is a scriptural term, it was given new emphasis by the Second Vatican Council's "Dogmatic Constitution on the Church" (*Lumen Gentium*).

Perjury: Taking a false oath, lying under oath, a violation of the honor due to God.

Persecution, Religious: A campaign waged against a church or other religious body by persons and governments intent on its destruction. The best-known campaigns of this type against the Christian Church were the Roman persecutions which occurred intermittently from about 54 to the promulgation of the Edict of Milan in 313. More Catholics have been persecuted in the 20th century than in any other period in history.

Personal Prelature: A special-purpose jurisdiction — for particular pastoral and missionary work, etc. — consisting of secular priests and deacons and open to lay persons willing to dedicate themselves to its apostolic works. The prelate in charge is an Ordinary, with the authority of office; he can establish a national or international seminary, incardinate its students, and promote them to holy orders under the title of service to the prelature. The prelature is constituted and governed according to statutes laid down by the Holy See. Statutes define its relationship and mode of operation with the bishops of territories in which members live and work. Opus Dei is a personal prelature.

Peter's Pence: A collection made each year among Catholics for the maintenance of the pope and his works of charity. It was originally a tax of a penny on each house, and was collected on St. Peter's day, whence the name. It originated in England in the 8th century.

Petition: One of the four purposes of prayer. In prayers of petition, persons ask of God the blessings they and others need.

Pharisees: Influential class among the Jews, referred to in the Gospels, noted for their self-righteousness, legalism, strict interpretation of the Law, acceptance of the traditions of the elders as well as the Law of Moses, and beliefs regarding angels and spirits, the resurrection of the dead and judgment. Most of them were laymen, and they were closely allied with the Scribes; their opposite numbers were the Sadducees. The Pharisaic and rabbinical traditions had a lasting influence on Judaism following the destruction of Jerusalem in 70 A.D.

Pious Fund: Property and money originally accumulated by the Jesuits to finance their missionary work in Lower California. When the Jesuits were expelled from the territory in 1767, the fund was appropriated by the Spanish Crown and used to support Dominican and Franciscan missionary work in Upper and Lower California. In 1842 the Mexican government took over administration of the fund, incorporated most of the revenue into the national treasury, and agreed to pay the Church interest of six percent a year on the capital so incorporated. From 1848 to 1967 the fund was the subject of lengthy negotiations between the U.S. and Mexican governments because of the latter's failure to make payments as agreed. A lump-sum settlement was made in 1967 with payment by Mexico to the U.S. government of more than $700,000, to be turned over to the Archdiocese of San Francisco.

Polytheism: Belief in and worship of many gods or divinities, especially prevalent in pre-Christian religions.

Poor Box: Alms-box; found in churches from the earliest days of Christianity.

Pope: A title from the Italian word *papa* (from Greek *pappas*, father) used for the Bishop of Rome, the Vicar of Christ, and successor of St. Peter, who exercises universal governance over the Church.

Portiuncula: (1) Meaning little portion (of land), the Portiuncula was the chapel of Our Lady of the Angels near Assisi, Italy, which the Benedictines gave to St. Francis early in the 13th century. He repaired the chapel and made it the first church of the Franciscan Order. It is now enshrined in the Basilica of St. Mary of the Angels in Assisi. (2) The plenary Portiuncula Indulgence, or Pardon of Assisi, was authorized by Honorius III. Originally, it could be gained for the souls in purgatory only in the chapel of Our Lady of the Angels; by later concessions, it could be gained also in other Franciscan and parish churches.

Positivism: The philosophy that teaches that the only reality is that which is perceived by the senses; the only truth is that which is empirically verified. It asserts that ideas about God, morality or anything else that cannot be scientifically tested are to be rejected as unknowable.

Possession, Diabolical: The extraordinary state of a person who is tormented from within by evil spirits who exercise strong influence over his powers of mind and body. (*See* **Exorcism**.)

Postulant: One of several names used to designate a candidate for membership in a religious institute during the period before novitiate.

Poverty: (1) The quality or state of being poor, in actual destitution and need, or being poor in spirit. In the latter sense, poverty means the state of mind and disposition of persons who regard material things in proper perspective as gifts of God for the support of life and its reasonable enrichment, and for the service of others in need. It means freedom from unreasonable attachment to material things as ends in themselves, even though they may be possessed in small or large measure. (2) One of the evangelical counsels professed as a public vow by members of an institute of consecrated life. It involves the voluntary renunciation of rights of ownership and of independent use and disposal of material goods; or, the right of independent use and disposal, but not of the radical right of ownership. Religious institutes provide their members with necessary and useful goods and services from common resources. The manner in which goods are received and/or handled by religious is determined by poverty of spirit and the rule and constitutions of their institute.

Pragmatism: Theory that the truth of ideas, concepts and values depends on their utility or capacity to serve a useful purpose rather than on their conformity with objective standards; also called utilitarianism.

Prayer: The raising of the mind and heart to God in adoration, thanksgiving, reparation and petition. Prayer, which is always mental because it involves thought and love of God, may be vocal, meditative, private and personal, social, and official. The official prayer of the Church as a worshipping community is called the liturgy.

Precepts: Commands or orders given to individuals or communities in particular cases; they establish law for concerned parties. Preceptive documents are issued by the pope, departments of the Roman Curia and other competent authority in the Church.

Presence of God: A devotional practice of increasing one's awareness of the presence and action of God in daily life.

Presumption: A sin against hope, by which a person striving for salvation (1) either relies too much on his own capabilities or (2) expects God to do things which he cannot do, in keeping with his divine attributes, or does not will to do, according to his divine plan. Presumption is the opposite of despair.

Preternatural Gifts: Exceptional gifts, beyond the exigencies and powers of human nature, enjoyed by Adam in the state of original justice: immunity from suffering and death, superior knowledge, integrity or perfect control of the passions. These gifts were lost as the result of original sin; their loss, however, implied no impairment of the integrity of human nature.

Pride: Unreasonable self-esteem; one of the seven capital sins.

Prie-Dieu: A French phrase, meaning "pray God," designating a kneeler or bench suitable for kneeling while at prayer.

Priesthood: (1) The common priesthood of the non-ordained faithful. In virtue of baptism and confirmation, the faithful are a priestly people who participate in the priesthood of Christ through acts of worship, witness to the faith in daily life, and efforts to foster the growth of God's kingdom. (2) The ordained priesthood, in virtue of the sacrament of orders, of bishops, priests and deacons, for service to the common priesthood.

Primary Option: The life-choice of a person for or against God which shapes the basic orientation of moral conduct. A primary option for God does not preclude the possibility of serious sin.

Prior: A superior or an assistant to an abbot in a monastery.

Privilege: A favor, an exemption from the obligation of a law. Privileges of various kinds, with respect to ecclesiastical laws, are granted by the pope, departments of the Roman Curia and other competent authority in the Church.

Probabiliorism: The moral system asserting that the more probable opinion of a varied set of acceptable positions regarding the binding character of a law should be accepted. If the reasons for being free from a law are more probably true, one is freed from the law's obligations. Probabiliorism, however, maintained that if it was probable that the law did not bind, one still had to follow it unless it was more probable that the law did not bind.

Probabilism: A moral system for use in cases of conscience which involve the obligation of doubtful laws. There is a general principle that a doubtful law does not bind. Probabilism, therefore, teaches that it is permissible to follow an opinion favoring liberty, provided the opinion is certainly and solidly probable. Probabilism may not be invoked when there is question of: a certain law or the certain obligation of a law; the certain right of another party; the validity of an action; something which is necessary for salvation.

Pro-Cathedral: A church used as a cathedral.

Promoter of the Faith (*Promotor fidei*): An official of the Congregation for the Causes of Saints, whose role in beatification and canonization procedures is to establish beyond reasonable doubt the validity of evidence regarding the holiness of prospective saints and miracles attributed to their intercession.

Prophecy: (1) The communication of divine revelation by inspired intermediaries, called prophets, between God and his people. Old Testament prophecy was unique in its origin and because of its ethical and religious content, which included disclosure of the saving will of Yahweh for the people, moral censures and warnings of divine punishment because of sin and violations of the Law and Covenant, in the form of promises, admonitions, reproaches and threats. Although Moses and other earlier figures are called prophets, the period of prophecy is generally dated from the early years of the monarchy to about 100 years after the Babylonian Exile. From that time on, the written Law and its interpreters supplanted the prophets as guides of the people. Old Testament prophets are cited in the New Testament, with awareness that God spoke through them and that some of their oracles were fulfilled in Christ. John the Baptist is the outstanding prophetic figure in the New Testament. Christ never claimed the title of prophet for himself, although some people thought he was one. There were prophets in the early Church, and St. Paul mentioned the charism of prophecy in 1 Cor. 14:1-5. Prophecy disappeared after New Testament times. Revelation is classified as the prophetic book of the New Testament. (2) In contemporary non-scriptural usage, the term is applied to the witness given by persons to the relevance of their beliefs in everyday life and action.

Proportionalism: The moral theory that asserts that an action is judged on whether the evils resulting are proportionate to the goods that result. If the evils outweigh the goods, the act is objectionable; if the opposite is true, the act is permissible. Proportionalism differs from consequentialism in that the former admits that the inherent morality of the act and the agent's intention must also be considered. Proportionalism is rejected by critics as it does not offer an objective criterion for determining when evils are proportionate or disproportionate. It also fails to consider the intrinsic nature of human acts and does nothing to assist Christians to grow in virtue.

Province: (1) A territory comprising one archdiocese called the metropolitan see and one or more dioceses called suffragan sees. The head of the archdiocese, an archbishop, has metropolitan rights and responsibilities over the province. (2) A division of a religious order under the jurisdiction of a provincial superior.

Prudence: Practical wisdom and judgment regarding the choice and use of the best ways and means of doing good; one of the four cardinal virtues.

Punishment Due for Sin: The punishment which is a consequence of sin. It is of two kinds: (1) Eternal punishment is the punishment of hell, to which one becomes subject by the commission of mortal sin. Such punishment is remitted when mortal sin is forgiven. (2) Temporal punishment is a consequence of venial sin and/or forgiven mortal sin; it is not everlasting and may be remitted in this life by means of penance. Temporal punishment unremitted during this life is remitted by suffering in purgatory.

Purgatory: The state or condition of those who have died in the state of grace but with some attachment to

sin, and are purified for a time before they are admitted to the glory and happiness of heaven. In this state and period of passive suffering, they are purified of unrepented venial sins, satisfy the demands of divine justice for temporal punishment due for sins, and are thus converted to a state of worthiness of the beatific vision.

Q

Quadragesima: From the Latin for "fortieth," the name given to the 40 penitential days of Lent.

Quinquennial Report: A report on the current state of a diocese that must be compiled and submitted by a bishop to the Holy See every five years in anticipation of the *ad liminal* visit.

Quinque Viae: From the Latin for the "five ways," the five proofs for the existence of God that were proposed by St. Thomas Aquinas in his *Summa Theologiae* (Part I, question 2, article 3). The five ways are: (1) all the motion in the world points to an unmoved Prime Mover; (2) the subordinate agents in the world imply the First Agent; (3) there must be a Cause Who is not perishable and Whose existence is underived; (4) the limited goodness in the world must be a reflection of Unlimited Goodness; (5) all things tend to become something, and that inclination must have proceeded from some Rational Planner.

R

Racism: A theory which holds that any one or several of the different races of the human family are inherently superior or inferior to any one or several of the others. The teaching denies the essential unity of the human race, the equality and dignity of all persons because of their common possession of the same human nature, and the participation of all in the divine plan of redemption. It is radically opposed to the virtue of justice and the precept of love of neighbor. Differences of superiority and inferiority which do exist are the result of accidental factors operating in a wide variety of circumstances, and are in no way due to essential defects in any one or several of the branches of the one human race. The theory of racism, together with practices related to it, is incompatible with Christian doctrine.

Rash Judgment: Attributing faults to another without sufficient reason; a violation of the obligations of justice and charity.

Rationalism: A theory which makes the mind the measure and arbiter of all things, including religious truth. A product of the Enlightenment, it rejects the supernatural, divine revelation and authoritative teaching by any church.

Recollection: Meditation, attitude of concentration or awareness of spiritual matters and things pertaining to salvation and the accomplishment of God's will.

Relativism: Theory which holds that all truth, including religious truth, is relative, i.e., not absolute, certain or unchanging; a product of agnosticism, indifferentism and an unwarranted extension of the notion of truth in positive science. Relativism is based on the tenet that certain knowledge of any and all truth is impossible. Therefore, no religion, philosophy, or science can be said to possess the real truth; consequently, all religions, philosophies and sciences may be considered to have as much or as little of truth as any of the others.

Relics: The physical remains and effects of saints, which are considered worthy of veneration inasmuch as they are representative of persons in glory with God. Catholic doctrine proscribes the view that relics are not worthy of veneration. In line with norms laid down by the Council of Trent and subsequent enactments, discipline concerning relics is subject to control by the Congregations for the Causes of Saints and for Divine Worship and the Discipline of the Sacraments.

Religion: The adoration and service of God as expressed in divine worship and in daily life. Religion is concerned with all of the relations existing between God and human beings, and between humans themselves because of the central significance of God. Objectively considered, religion consists of a body of truth that is believed, a code of morality for the guidance of conduct, and a form of divine worship. Subjectively, it is a person's total response, theoretically and practically, to the demands of faith; it is living faith, personal engagement, self-commitment to God. Thus, by creed, code and cult, a person orders and directs his or her life in reference to God and, through what the love and service of God implies, to all people and all things.

Reliquary: A vessel for the preservation and exposition of a relic; sometimes made like a small monstrance.

Reparation: The making of amends to God for sin committed; one of the four ends of prayer and the purpose of penance.

Requiem: A Mass offered for the repose of the soul of one who has died in Christ. Its name is derived from the first word of the Gregorian (Latin) entrance chant (or Introit) at Masses for the dead: *Requiem aeternam dona eis, Domine* ("Eternal rest grant unto them, O Lord"). The revised Rite for Funerals refers to the requiem as the Mass of Christian Burial; however, it would not be uncommon to hear people employ the former usage.

Rescript: A written reply by an ecclesiastical superior regarding a question or request; its provisions bind concerned parties only. Papal dispensations are issued in the form of rescripts.

Reserved Censure: A sin or censure, absolution from which is reserved to religious superiors, bishops, the pope, or confessors having special faculties. Reservations are made because of the serious nature and social effects of certain sins and censures.

Restitution: An act of reparation for an injury done to another. The injury may be caused by taking and/or retaining what belongs to another or by damaging either the property or reputation of another. The intention of making restitution, usually in kind, is required as a condition for the forgiveness of sins of injustice, even though actual restitution is not possible.

Ring: In the Church a ring is worn as part of the insignia of bishops, abbots, et al.; by sisters to denote their consecration to God and the Church. The wedding ring symbolizes the love and union of husband and wife.

Ritual: A book of prayers and ceremonies used in the administration of the sacraments and other ceremonial functions. In the Roman Rite, the standard book of this kind is the Roman Ritual.

Rogito: The official notarial act or document testifying to the burial of a pope.

Rosary: A form of mental and vocal prayer centered on mysteries or events in the lives of Jesus and Mary. Its essential elements are meditation on the mysteries and the recitation of a number of decades of Hail Marys, each beginning with the Lord's Prayer. Introductory prayers may include the Apostles' Creed, an initial Our Father, three Hail Marys and a Glory be to the Father; each decade is customarily concluded with a Glory be to the Father; at the end, it is customary to say the Hail, Holy Queen and a prayer from the liturgy for the feast of the Blessed Virgin Mary of the Rosary. Traditionally, the Mysteries of the Rosary, which are the subject of meditation, are: (1) *Joyful* — the Annunciation to Mary that she was to be the Mother of Christ, her visit to Elizabeth, the birth of Jesus, the presentation of Jesus in the Temple, the finding of Jesus in the Temple. (2) *Sorrowful* — Christ's agony in the Garden of Gethsemani, scourging at the pillar, crowning with thorns, carrying of the cross to Calvary, and crucifixion. (3) *Glorious* — the Resurrection and Ascension of Christ, the descent of the Holy Spirit upon the Apostles, Mary's Assumption into heaven and her crowning as Queen of angels and men.

The complete Rosary, called the Dominican Rosary, consists of 15 decades. In customary practice, only five decades are usually said at one time. Rosary beads are used to aid in counting the prayers without distraction. The Rosary originated through the coalescence of popular devotions to Jesus and Mary from the 12th century onward. Its present form dates from about the 15th century. Carthusians contributed greatly toward its development; Dominicans have been its greatest promoters. The fifteen mysteries were standardized by Pope Pius V in 1569.

In 2002, Pope John Paul II added five new mysteries dedicated to chapters from Jesus' public life. Titled the Mysteries of Light, or Luminous Mysteries, they are: Christ's baptism in the Jordan River; Christ's self-revelation at the marriage of Cana; Christ's announcement of the kingdom of God with the invitation to conversion; Christ's Transfiguration, when he revealed his glory to his Apostles; and the institution of the Eucharist at the Last Supper as the sacramental expression of the paschal mystery. The pope asked that the Mysteries of Light be recited especially on Thursdays. [*See* **News in Depth** for other details.]

S

Sabbath: The seventh day of the week, observed by Jews and Sabbatarians as the day for rest and religious observance.

Sacrarium: A basin with a drain leading directly into the ground; standard equipment of a sacristy.

Sacred Heart, Enthronement of the: An acknowledgment of the sovereignty of Jesus Christ over the Christian family, expressed by the installation of an image or picture of the Sacred Heart in a place of honor in the home, accompanied by an act of consecration.

Sacred Heart, Promises: Twelve promises to persons having devotion to the Sacred Heart of Jesus, which were communicated by Christ to St. Margaret Mary Alacoque in a private revelation in 1675: (1) *I* *will give them all the graces necessary in their state in life.* (2) *I will establish peace in their homes.* (3) *I will comfort them in all their afflictions.* (4) *I will be their secure refuge during life and, above all, in death.* (5) *I will bestow abundant blessing upon all their undertakings.* (6) *Sinners shall find in my Heart the source and the infinite ocean of mercy.* (7) *By devotion to my Heart tepid souls shall grow fervent.* (8) *Fervent souls shall quickly mount to high perfection.* (9) *I will bless every place where a picture of my Heart shall be set up and honored.* (10) *I will give to priests the gift of touching the most hardened hearts.* (11) *Those who promote this devotion shall have their names written in my Heart, never to be blotted out.* (12) *I will grant the grace of final penitence to those who communicate (receive Holy Communion) on the first Friday of nine consecutive months.*

Sacrilege: Violation of and irreverence toward a person, place or thing that is sacred because of public dedication to God; a sin against the virtue of religion. Personal sacrilege is violence of some kind against a cleric or religious, or a violation of chastity with a cleric or religious. Local sacrilege is the desecration of sacred places. Real sacrilege is irreverence with respect to sacred things, such as the sacraments and sacred vessels.

Sacristy: A utility room where vestments, church furnishings and sacred vessels are kept, and where the clergy vest for sacred functions.

Sadducees: The predominantly priestly party among the Jews in the time of Christ, noted for extreme conservatism, acceptance only of the Law of Moses, and rejection of the traditions of the elders. Their opposite numbers were the Pharisees.

Saints, Cult of: The veneration, called *dulia*, of holy persons who have died and are in glory with God in heaven; it includes honoring them and petitioning them for their intercession with God. Liturgical veneration is given only to saints officially recognized by the Church; private veneration may be given to anyone thought to be in heaven. The veneration of saints is essentially different from the adoration given to God alone; by its very nature, however, it terminates in the worship of God. (*See* also **Dulia** and **Latria**.)

Salvation: The liberation of persons from sin and its effects, reconciliation with God in and through Christ, the attainment of union with God forever in the glory of heaven as the supreme purpose of life, and as the God-given reward for fulfillment of his will on earth. Salvation-in-process begins and continues in this life through union with Christ in faith professed and in action; its final term is union with God and the whole community of the saved in the ultimate perfection of God'ss kingdom. The Church teaches that: God wills the salvation of all men; men are saved in and through Christ; membership in the Church established by Christ, known and understood as the community of salvation, is necessary for salvation; men with this knowledge and understanding who deliberately reject this Church, cannot be saved. The Catholic Church is the Church founded by Christ. (*See* **Salvation outside the Church**.)

Salvation History: The facts and the record of God's relations with human beings, in the past, present and future, for the purpose of leading them to live in accordance with his will for the eventual attainment after death of salvation, or everlasting happiness with him in heaven. The essentials of salvation history are: God's love for all human beings and will for their salvation; his intervention and action in the world to express this love and bring about their salvation; the revelation he made of himself and the covenant he established with the Israelites in the Old Testament; the perfecting of this revelation and the new covenant of grace through Christ in the New Testament; the continuing action-for-salvation carried on in and through the Church; the communication of saving grace to people through the merits of Christ and the operations of the Holy Spirit in the here-and-now circumstances of daily life and with the cooperation of people themselves.

Salvation outside the Church: The Second Vatican Council covered this subject summarily in the following manner: "Those also can attain to everlasting salvation who through no fault of their own do not know the Gospel of Christ or his Church, yet sincerely seek God and, moved by grace, strive by their deeds to do his will as it is known to them through the dictates of conscience. Nor does divine Providence deny the help necessary for salvation to those who, without blame on their part, have not yet arrived at an explicit knowledge of God, but who strive to live a good life, thanks to his grace. Whatever good or truth is found among them is looked upon by the Church as a preparation for the Gospel. She regards such qualities as given by him who enlightens all men so that they may finally have life" ("Dogmatic Constitution on the Church," *Lumen Gentium*, No. 16).

Sanctifying Grace: *See* **Grace**.

Satanism: Worship of the devil, a blasphemous inversion of the order of worship which is due to God alone.

Scandal: Conduct which is the occasion of sin to another person.

Scapular: (1) A part of the habit of some religious orders like the Benedictines and Dominicans; a nearly shoulder-wide strip of cloth worn over the tunic and reaching almost to the feet in front and behind. Originally a kind of apron, it came to symbolize the cross and yoke of Christ. (2) Scapulars worn by lay persons as a sign of association with religious orders and for devotional purposes are an adaptation of monastic scapulars. Approved by the Church as sacramentals, they consist of two small squares of woolen cloth joined by strings and are worn about the neck. They are given for wearing in a ceremony of investiture or enrollment. There are nearly 20 scapulars for devotional use: the five principal ones are generally understood to include those of Our Lady of Mt. Carmel (the brown Carmelite Scapular), the Holy Trinity, Our Lady of the Seven Dolors, the Passion, the Immaculate Conception.

Scapular Medal: A medallion with a representation of the Sacred Heart on one side and of the Blessed Virgin Mary on the other. Authorized by St. Pius X in 1910, it may be worn or carried in place of a scapular by persons already invested with a scapular.

Scapular Promise: According to a legend of the Carmelite Order, the Blessed Virgin Mary appeared to St. Simon Stock in 1251 at Cambridge, England, and declared that wearers of the brown Carmelite Scapular would be the beneficiaries of her special intercession. The scapular tradition has never been the subject of official decision by the Church. Essentially, it expresses belief in the intercession of Mary and the efficacy of sacramentals in the context of truly Christian life.

Schism: Derived from a Greek word meaning separation, the term designates formal and obstinate refusal by a baptized Catholic, called a schismatic, to be in communion with the pope and the Church. The canonical penalty is excommunication. One of the most disastrous schisms in history resulted in the definitive separation of the Church in the East from union with Rome about 1054.

Scholasticism: The term usually applied to the Catholic theology and philosophy which developed in the Middle Ages. (*See* **Neo-Scholasticism**.)

Scribes: Hebrew intellectuals noted for their knowledge of the Law of Moses, influential from the time of the Exile to about 70 A.D. Many of them were Pharisees. They were the antecedents of rabbis and their traditions, as well as those o the Pharisees, had a lasting influence on Judaism following the destruction of Jerusalem in 70 A.D.

Scruple: A morbid, unreasonable fear and anxiety that one's actions are sinful when they are not, or more seriously sinful than they actually are. Compulsive scrupulosity is quite different from the transient scrupulosity of persons of tender or highly sensitive conscience, or of persons with faulty moral judgment.

Seal of Confession: The obligation of secrecy which must be observed regarding knowledge of things learned in connection with the confession of sin in the sacrament of penance. The seal covers matters whose revelation would make the sacrament burdensome. Confessors are prohibited, under penalty of excommunication, from making any direct revelation of confessional matter; this prohibition holds, outside of confession, even with respect to the person who made the confession unless the person releases the priest from the obligation. Persons other than confessors are obliged to maintain secrecy, but not under penalty of excommunication. General, non-specific discussion of confessional matter does not violate the seal.

Secularism: A school of thought, a spirit and manner of action which ignores and/or repudiates the validity or influence of supernatural religion with respect to individual and social life.

See: Another name for diocese or archdiocese.

Seminary: A house of study and formation for men, called seminarians, preparing for the priesthood. Traditional seminaries date from the Council of Trent in the middle of the 16th century; before that time, candidates for the priesthood were variously trained in monastic schools, universities under church auspices, and in less formal ways.

Sermon on the Mount: A compilation of sayings of Our Lord in the form of an extended discourse in Matthew's Gospel (5:1 to 7:27) and, in a shorter discourse, in Luke (6:17-49). The passage in Matthew, called the "Constitution of the New Law," summarizes the living spirit of believers in Christ and members of the kingdom of God. Beginning with the Beatitudes and including the Lord's Prayer, it covers the perfect justice of the New Law, the fulfillment of the Old Law in the New Law of Christ, and the integrity of internal attitude and external conduct with respect to love of God and neighbor, justice, chastity, truth, trust and confidence in God.

Seven Last Words of Christ: The Seven Last Words of Christ on the Cross were: (1) *"Father, forgive them; for they do not know what they are doing."* (Lk. 23:34); (2) To the penitent thief: *"I assure you: today you will be with me in Paradise."* (Lk. 23:24); (3) To Mary and his Apostle John: *"Woman, behold thy son! ... Behold your mother."* (Jn. 19:26); (4) *"Eli Eli, lama sabacthani* [*"My God, my God, why have you forsaken me?"*] (Mt. 27:46; cf. Mk. 15:34); (5) *"I thirst."* (Jn. 19:28); (6) *"It is finished."* (Jn. 19:30); (7) *"Father, into thy hands I commend my spirit."*(Lk. 23:46).

Shrine, Crowned: A shrine approved by the Holy See as a place of pilgrimage. The approval permits public devotion at the shrine and implies that at least one miracle has resulted from devotion at the shrine. Among the best-known crowned shrines are those of the Virgin Mary at Lourdes and Fátima. Shrines with statues crowned by Pope John Paul II in 1985 in South America were those of Our Lady of Coromoto, patroness of Venezuela, in Caracas, and Our Lady of Carmen of Paucartambo in Cuzco, Peru.

Shroud of Turin: A strip of brownish linen cloth, 14 feet, three inches in length and three feet, seven inches in width, bearing the front and back imprint of a human body. A tradition dating from the 7th century, which has not been verified beyond doubt, claims that the shroud is the fine linen in which the body of Christ was wrapped for burial. The early history of the shroud is obscure. It was enshrined at Lirey, France, in 1354 and was transferred in 1578 to Turin, Italy, where it has been kept in the cathedral down to the present time. Scientific investigation, which began in 1898, seems to indicate that the markings on the shroud are those of a human body. The shroud, for the first time since 1933, was placed on public view from Aug. 27 to Oct. 8, 1978, and was seen by an estimated 3.3 million people. Scientists conducted intensive studies of it thereafter, finally determining that the material of the shroud dated from between 1260 and 1390. The shroud, which had been the possession of the House of Savoy, was willed to Pope John Paul II in 1983.

Sick Calls: When a person is confined at home by illness or other cause and is unable to go to church for reception of the sacraments, a parish priest should be informed and arrangements made for him to visit the person at home. Such visitations are common in pastoral practice, both for special needs and for providing persons with regular opportunities for receiving the sacraments. If a priest cannot make the visitation, arrangements can be made for a deacon or Eucharistic minister to bring Holy Communion to the homebound or bedridden person.

Sign of the Cross: A sign, ceremonial gesture, or movement in the form of a cross by which a person confesses faith in the Holy Trinity and Christ, and intercedes for the blessing of himself or herself, other persons, and things. In Roman Rite practice, a person making the sign touches the fingers of the right hand to forehead, below the breast, left shoulder, and right shoulder while saying: *"In the name of the Father, and of the Son, and of the Holy Spirit."* The sign is also made with the thumb on the forehead, the lips, and the breast. For the blessing of persons and objects, a large sign of the cross is made by movement of the right hand. In Eastern Rite practice, the sign is made with the thumb and first two fingers of the right hand joined together and touching the forehead, below the breast, the right shoulder and the left shoulder; the formula generally used is the doxology, *"O Holy God, O Holy Strong One, O Immortal One."* The Eastern manner of making the sign was general until the first half of the 13th century; by the 17th century, Western practice involved the whole right hand and the reversal of direction from shoulder to shoulder.

Signs of the Times: Contemporary events, trends, and features in culture and society, the needs and aspirations of people, all the factors that form the context in and through which the Church has to carry on its saving mission. The Second Vatican Council spoke on numerous occasions about these signs.

Simony: The deliberate intention and act of selling and/or buying spiritual goods or material things so connected with the spiritual that they cannot be separated therefrom; a violation of the virtue of religion, and a sacrilege, because it wrongfully puts a material price on spiritual things, which cannot be either sold or bought. In church law, actual sale or purchase is subject to censure in some cases. The term is derived from the name of Simon Magus, who attempted to buy from Sts. Peter and John the power to confirm people in the Holy Spirit (Acts 8:4-24).

Sin: (1) Actual sin is the free and deliberate violation of God's law by thought, word, or action. (a) Mortal sin — involving serious matter, sufficient reflection, and full consent — results in the loss of sanctifying grace and alienation from God, and renders a person incapable of performing meritorious supernatural acts and subject to everlasting punishment. (b) Venial sin — involving less serious matter, reflection, and consent — does not have such serious consequences. (2) Original sin is the sin of Adam, with consequences for all human beings. (*See* separate entry.)

Sins against the Holy Spirit: Despair of salvation, presumption of God's mercy, impugning the known truths of faith, envy at another's spiritual good, obstinacy in sin, final impenitence. Those guilty of such sins stubbornly resist the influence of grace and, as long as they do so, cannot be forgiven.

Sins, Occasions of: Circumstances (persons, places, things, etc.) which easily lead to sin. There is an obligation to avoid voluntary proximate occasions of sin, and to take precautions against the dangers of unavoidable occasions.

Sister: Any woman religious, in popular speech; strictly, the title applies only to women religious belonging to institutes whose members never professed solemn vows. Most of the institutes whose members are properly called Sisters were established during and since the 19th century. Women religious with solemn vows, or belonging to institutes whose members formerly professed solemn vows, are properly called nuns.

Sisterhood: A generic term referring to the whole institution of the life of women religious in the Church, or to a particular institute of women religious.

Situation Ethics: A subjective, individualistic ethical theory which denies the binding force of ethical principles as universal laws and preceptive norms of moral conduct, and proposes that morality is determined only by situational conditions and considerations and the intention of the person. It has been criticized for ignoring the principles of objective ethics.

(*See* **Consequentialism** and **Proportionalism**.)

Slander: Attributing to a person faults which he or she does not have; a violation of the obligations of justice and charity, for which restitution is due.

Sloth (Acedia): One of the seven capital sins; spiritual laziness, involving distaste and disgust for spiritual things; spiritual boredom, which saps the vigor of spiritual life. Physical laziness is a counterpart of spiritual sloth.

Sorcery: A kind of black magic in which evil is invoked by means of diabolical intervention; a violation of the virtue of religion.

Soteriology: The division of theology which treats of the mission and work of Christ as Redeemer.

Species, Sacred: The appearances of bread and wine (color, taste, smell, etc.) which remain after the substance has been changed at the Consecration of the Mass into the Body and Blood of Christ. (*See* **Transubstantiation**.)

Spiritism: Attempts to communicate with spirits and departed souls by means of seances, table tapping, ouija boards, and other methods; a violation of the virtue of religion. Spiritualistic practices are noted for fakery.

Stational Churches, Days: Churches, especially in Rome, where the clergy and lay people were accustomed to gather with their bishop on certain days for the celebration of the liturgy. The 25 early titular or parish churches of Rome, plus other churches, each had their turn as the site of divine worship in practices which may have started in the third century. The observances were rather well-developed toward the latter part of the fourth century, and by the fifth they included a Mass concelebrated by the pope and attendant priests. On some occasions, the stational liturgy was preceded by a procession from another church called a *collecta*. There were 42 Roman stational churches in the 8th century, and 89 stational services were scheduled annually in connection with the liturgical seasons. Stational observances fell into disuse toward the end of the Middle Ages. Some revival was begun by John XXIII in 1959 and continued by Paul VI and John Paul II.

Stations (Way) of the Cross: A form of devotion commemorating the Passion and death of Christ, consisting of a series of meditations (stations): (1) his condemnation to death, (2) taking up of the cross, (3) the first fall on the way to Calvary, (4) meeting his Mother, (5) being assisted by Simon of Cyrene and (6) by the woman Veronica who wiped his face, (7) the second fall, (8) meeting the women of Jerusalem, (9) the third fall, (10) being stripped and (11) nailed to the cross, (12) his death, (13) the removal of his body from the cross and (14) his burial. Depictions of these scenes are mounted in most churches, chapels, and in some other places, beneath small crosses. A person making the Way of the Cross passes before these stations, or stopping points, pausing at each for meditation. If the stations are made by a group of people, only the leader has to pass from station to station. A plenary indulgence is granted to the faithful who make the stations, under the usual conditions: freedom from all attachment to sin, reception of the sacraments of penance and the Eucharist, and prayers for the intentions of the pope. Those who are impeded from making the stations in the usual manner can gain the same indulgence if, along with the aforementioned conditions, they spend at least a half hour in spiritual reading and meditation on the passion and death of Christ. The stations originated remotely from the practice of Holy Land pilgrims who visited the actual scenes of incidents in the Passion of Christ. Representations elsewhere of at least some of these scenes were known as early as the 5th century. Later, the stations evolved in connection with and as a consequence of strong devotion to the Passion in the 12th and 13th centuries. Franciscans, who were given custody of the Holy Places in 1342, promoted the devotion widely; one of them, St. Leonard of Port Maurice, became known as the greatest preacher of the Way of the Cross in the 18th century. The general features of the devotion were fixed by Clement XII in 1731.

Statutes: Virtually the same as decrees (*see* separate entry), they almost always designate laws of a particular council or synod rather than pontifical laws.

Stigmata: Marks of the wounds suffered by Christ in his crucifixion, in hands and feet by nails, and side by the piercing of a lance. Some persons, called stigmatists, have been reported as recipients or sufferers of marks like these. The Church, however, has never issued any infallible declaration about their possession by anyone, even in the case of St. Francis of Assisi, whose stigmata seem to be the best substantiated and may be commemorated in the Roman Rite liturgy. Ninety percent of some 300 reputed stigmatists have been women. Judgment regarding the presence, significance, and manner of causation of stigmata would depend, among other things, on irrefutable experimental evidence.

Stipend, Mass: An offering given to a priest for applying the fruits of the Mass according to the intention of the donor. The offering is a contribution to the support of the priest. The disposition of the fruits of the sacrifice, in line with doctrine concerning the Mass in particular and prayer in general, is subject to the will of God. Mass offerings and intentions were the subjects of a decree approved by John Paul II and made public Mar. 22, 1991: (1) Normally, no more than one offering should be accepted for a Mass; the Mass should be offered in accord with the donor's intention; the priest who accepts the offering should celebrate the Mass himself or have another priest do so. (2) Several Mass intentions, for which offerings have been made, can be combined for a "collective" application of a single Mass only if the previous and explicit consent of the donors is obtained. Such Masses are an exception to the general rule.

Stole Fee: An offering given on certain occasions; e.g., at a baptism, wedding, funeral, for the support of the clergy who administer the sacraments and perform other sacred rites.

Stoup: A vessel used to contain holy water.

Suffragan See: Any diocese, except the archdiocese, within a province.

Suicide: The taking of one's own life; a violation of God's dominion over human life. Ecclesiastical burial is denied to persons while in full possession of their faculties; it is permitted in cases of doubt.

Supererogation: Actions which go beyond the obligations of duty and the requirements enjoined by God's law as necessary for salvation. Examples of these works are the profession and observance of the evangelical counsels of poverty, chastity, and obedience, and efforts to practice charity to the highest degree.

Supernatural: Above the natural; that which exceeds and is not due or owed to the essence, exigencies, requirements, powers, and merits of created nature. While human beings have no claim on supernatural things and do not need them in order to exist and act on a natural level, they do need them in order to exist and act in the higher order or economy of grace established by God for their salvation. God has freely given them certain things which are beyond the powers and rights of their human nature. Examples of the supernatural are: grace, a kind of participation by human beings in the divine life, by which they become capable of performing acts meritorious for salvation; divine revelation, by which God manifests himself to them and makes known truth that is inaccessible to human reason alone; faith, by which they believe divine truth because of the authority of God, who reveals it through Sacred Scripture and tradition and the teaching of his Church.

Suspension: A censure by which a cleric is forbidden to exercise some or all of his powers of orders and jurisdiction, or to accept the financial support of his benefices.

Syllabus, The: (1) When not qualified, the term refers to the list of 80 errors accompanying Pope Pius IX's encyclical *Quanta Cura*, issued in 1864. (2) The Syllabus of St. Pius X in the decree *Lamentabili*, issued by the Holy Office July 4, 1907, condemning 65 heretical propositions of modernism. This schedule of errors was followed shortly by that pope's encyclical *Pascendi*, the principal ecclesiastical document against modernism, issued Sept. 8, 1907.

Synod, Diocesan: Meeting of representative persons of a diocese — priests, religious, lay persons — with the bishop, called by him for the purpose of considering and taking action on matters affecting the life and mission of the Church in the diocese. Persons taking part in a synod have consultative status; the bishop alone is the legislator, with power to authorize synodal decrees. According to canon law, every diocese should have a synod every 10 years.

T

Tabernacle: The receptacle in which the Blessed Sacrament is reserved in churches, chapels, and oratories. It is to be immovable, solid, locked, and located in a prominent place.

Te Deum: The opening Latin words, *Thee, God*, of a hymn of praise and thanksgiving prescribed for use in the Office of Readings of the Liturgy of the Hours on many Sundays, solemnities, and feasts.

Temperance: Moderation, one of the four cardinal virtues.

Temptation: Any enticement to sin, from any source: the strivings of one's own faculties, the action of the devil, other persons, circumstances of life, etc. Temptation itself is not sin. Temptation can be avoided and overcome with the use of prudence and the help of grace.

Thanksgiving: An expression of gratitude to God for his goodness and the blessings he grants; one of the four ends of prayer.

Theism: A philosophy which admits the existence of God and the possibility of divine revelation; it is generally monotheistic and acknowledges God as transcendent and also active in the world. Because it is a philosophy rather than a system of theology derived from revelation, it does not include specifically Christian doctrines, like those concerning the Trinity, the Incarnation, and Redemption.

Theodicy: From the Greek for God (*theos*) and judgment (*dike*), the study of God as he can be known by natural reason, rather than from supernatural revelation. First used by Gottfried Leibniz (1646-1716), its primary objective is to make God's omnipotence compatible with the existence of evil.

Theological Virtues: The virtues which have God for their direct object: faith, or belief in God's infallible teaching; hope, or confidence in divine assistance; charity, or love of God. They are given to a person with grace in the first instance, through baptism and incorporation in Christ.

Theology: Knowledge of God and religion, deriving from and based on the data of divine Revelation, organized and systematized according to some kind of scientific method. It involves systematic study and presentation of the truths of divine Revelation in Sacred Scripture, tradition, and the teaching of the Church. Theology has been divided under various subject headings. Some of the major fields have been: dogmatic (systematic theology), moral, pastoral, historical, ascetical (the practice of virtue and means of attaining holiness and perfection), sacramental, and mystical (higher states of religious experience). Other subject headings include ecumenism (Christian unity, interfaith relations), ecclesiology (the nature and constitution of the Church), and Mariology (doctrine concerning the Blessed Virgin Mary), etc.

Theotokos: From the Greek for God-bearer, the preeminent title given to the Blessed Mother in the Oriental Church. This title has very ancient roots, stretching as far back as the third century but it did not became official in the Church until the Council of Ephesus in 431.

Thomism: The philosophy based on St. Thomas Aquinas (1224/5-1274), which is mandated to be the dominant philosophy used in Catholic educational institutions. (*See* **Neo-Scholasticism** and **Scholasticism**.)

Tithing: Contribution of a portion of one's income, originally one-tenth, for purposes of religion and charity. The practice is mentioned 46 times in the Bible. In early Christian times, tithing was adopted in continuance of Old Testament practices of the Jewish people, and the earliest positive church legislation on the subject was enacted in 567. Catholics are bound in conscience to contribute to the support of their church, but the manner in which they do so is not fixed by law. Tithing, which amounts to a pledged contribution of a portion of one's income, has aroused new attention in recent years in the United States.

Titular Sees: Dioceses where the Church once flourished but which now exist only in name or title. Bishops without a territorial or residential diocese of their own; e.g., auxiliary bishops, are given titular sees. There are more than 2,000 titular sees; 16 of them are in the United States.

Transfinalization, Transignification: Terms coined to express the sign value of consecrated bread and wine with respect to the presence and action of Christ in the Eucharistic sacrifice and the spiritually vivifying purpose of the Eucharistic banquet in Holy Communion. The theory behind the terms has strong undertones of existential and "sign" philosophy, and has been criticized for its openness to interpretation at variance with the doctrine of transubstantiation and the abiding presence of Christ under the appearances of bread and wine after the sacrifice of the Mass and Communion have been completed. The terms, if used as substitutes for transubstantiation, are unacceptable; if they presuppose transubstantiation, they are acceptable as clarifications of its meaning.

Transubstantiation: "The way Christ is made present in this sacrament (Holy Eucharist) is none other than by the change of the whole substance of the bread into his Body, and of the whole substance of the wine into his Blood (in the Consecration at Mass), this unique and wonderful change the Catholic Church rightly calls transubstantiation" (encyclical *Mysterium Fidei* of Paul VI, Sept. 3, 1965). The first official use of the term was made by the Fourth Council of the Lateran in 1215. Authoritative teaching on the subject was issued by the Council of Trent.

Treasury of the Church: The superabundant merits of Christ and the saints from which the Church draws to confer spiritual benefits, such as indulgences.

Triduum: A three-day series of public or private devotions.

U-Z

Ultramontanism: The movement, found primarily in France during the 19th century, which advocated a strong sense of devotion and service to the Holy See. Generally considered a reaction to the anti-papal tendencies of Gallicanism, its name was derived from the Latin for "over the mountains," a reference to the Alps, beyond which rested Rome and the Holy See.

Unction: From the Latin *ungere*, meaning to anoint or smear, a term used to denote the Sacrament of the Sick (or the Anointing of the Sick) and was more commonly termed Extreme Unction and was given as an anointing to a person just before death.

Universal Law: *See* **Law**.

Urbi et Orbi: A Latin phrase meaning "To the City and to the World" that is a blessing given by the Holy Father. Normally, the first *Urbi et Orbi* delivered by a pontiff is immediately after his election by the College of Cardinals. This is a blessing accompanied by a short address to the crowds in St. Peter's Square and to the world; frequently, as with Pope John Paul II in 1978, it is delivered in as many languages as possible. The pope also delivers an *Urbi et Orbi* each year at Christmas and at Easter.

Usury: Excessive interest charged for the loan and use of money; a violation of justice.

Vagi: A Latin word meaning wanderers that is used to describe any homeless person with no fixed residence.

Veni Creator Spiritus: A Latin phrase, meaning "Come, Creator Spirit" that is part of a hymn sung to the Holy Spirit. The hymn invokes the presence of the Holy Spirit and was perhaps first composed by Rabanus Maurus (776-856). The hymn is commonly sung as part of the Divine Office, papal elections, episcopal consecrations, ordinations, councils, synods, canonical elections, and confirmations.

Venial Sin: *See* under **Sin**.

Veronica: A word resulting from the combination of a Latin word for true, *vera*, and a Greek word for image, *eikon*, designating a likeness of the face of Christ, or the name of a woman said to have given him a cloth on which he caused an imprint of his face to appear. The veneration at Rome of a likeness depicted on cloth dates from about the end of the 10th century; it figured in a popular devotion during the Middle Ages, and in the Holy Face devotion practiced since the 19th century. A faint, indiscernible likeness said to be of this kind is preserved in St. Peter's Basilica. The origin of the likeness is uncertain, and the identity of the woman is unknown. Before the 14th century, there were no known artistic representations of an incident concerning a woman who wiped the face of Christ with a piece of cloth while he was carrying the cross to Calvary.

Vespers: From the Latin for evening, the evening service of the Divine Office, also known as Evening Prayer, or among Anglicans as Evensong.

Viaticum: Holy Communion given to those in danger of death. The word, derived from Latin, means provision for a journey through death to life hereafter.

Vicar Forane: A Latin term meaning "deputy outside" that is applied to the priest given authority by the local bishop over a certain area or region of the diocese.

Vicar General: A priest or bishop appointed by the bishop of a diocese to serve as his deputy, with ordinary executive power, in the administration of the diocese.

Vicar, Judicial: The title given to the chief judge and head of the tribunal of a diocese.

Virginity: Observance of perpetual sexual abstinence. The state of virginity, which is embraced for the love of God by religious with a public vow or by others with a private vow, was singled out for high praise by Christ (Mt. 19:10-12), and has always been so regarded by the Church. In the encyclical *Sacra Virginitas*, Pius XII stated: "Holy virginity and that perfect chastity which is consecrated to the service of God is without doubt among the most perfect treasures which the founder of the Church has left in heritage to the society which he established." Paul VI approved in 1970 a rite in which women can consecrate their virginity "to Christ and their brethren" without becoming members of a religious institute. The *Ordo Consecrationis Virginum*, a revision of a rite promulgated by Clement VII in 1596, is traceable to the Roman liturgy of about 50

Virtue: A habit or established capability for performing good actions. Virtues are natural (acquired and increased by repeating good acts) and/or supernatural (given with grace by God).

Visions: A charism by which a specially chosen individual is able to behold a person or something that is naturally invisible. A vision should not be confused with an illusion or hallucination. Like other charisms, a vision is granted for the good of people; it should be noted, however, that they are not essential for holiness or salvation. Many saints throughout history have beheld visions, among them St. Thomas Aquinas, St. Teresa of Ávila, St. John of the Cross and St. Francis of Assisi.

Vocation: A call to a way of life. Generally, the term applies to the common call of all persons, from God, to holiness and salvation. Specifically, it refers to particular states of life, each called a vocation, in which response is made to this universal call; *viz.*, marriage, the religious life and/or priesthood, the single state freely chosen or accepted for the accomplishment of God's will. The term also applies to the various occupations in which persons make a living. The Church supports the freedom of each individual in choosing a particular vocation, and reserves the right to pass on the acceptability of candidates for the priesthood and religious life. Signs or indicators of particular vocations are many, including a person's talents and interests, circumstances and obligations, invitations of grace and willingness to respond thereto.

Vow: A promise made to God with sufficient knowledge and freedom, which has as its object a moral good that is possible and better than its voluntary omission. A person who professes a vow binds himself or herself by the virtue of religion to fulfill the promise. The best known examples of vows are those of poverty, chastity and obedience professed by religious (*see* **Evangelical Counsels**, individual entries). Public vows are made before a competent person, acting as an agent of the Church, who accepts the profession in the name of the Church, thereby giving public recognition to the person's dedication and consecration to God and divine worship. Vows of this kind are either solemn, rendering all contrary acts invalid as well as unlawful; or simple, rendering contrary acts unlawful. Solemn vows are for life; simple vows are for a definite period of time or for life. Vows professed without public recognition by the Church are called private vows. The Church, which has authority to accept and give public recognition to vows, also has authority to dispense persons from their obligations for serious reasons.

Witness, Christian: Practical testimony or evidence given by Christians of their faith in all circumstances of life — by prayer and general conduct, through good example and good works, etc.; being and acting in accordance with Christian belief; actual practice of the Christian faith.

Zeal: The expression of charity that permits one to serve God and others fully with the objective of furthering the Mystical Body of Christ.

Zucchetto: A small skullcap worn by ecclesiastics, most notably prelates and derived from the popular Italian vernacular term *zucca*, meaning a pumpkin, and used as slang for head. The Holy Father wears a white zucchetto made of watered silk; cardinals use scarlet, and bishops use purple. Priests of the monsignorial rank may wear black with purple piping. All others may wear simple black.

The Church Calendar

The calendar of the Roman Church consists of an arrangement throughout the year of a series of liturgical seasons, commemorations of divine mysteries and commemorations of saints for purposes of worship.

The key to the calendar is the central celebration of the Easter Triduum, commemorating the supreme saving act of Jesus in his death and resurrection to which all other observances and acts of worship are related.

The purposes of this calendar were outlined in the Constitution on the Sacred Liturgy (*Sacrosanctum Concilium*, Nos. 102-105) promulgated by the Second Vatican Council.

"Within the cycle of a year … (the Church) unfolds the whole mystery of Christ, not only from his incarnation and birth until his ascension, but also as reflected in the day of Pentecost, and the expectation of a blessed, hoped-for return of the Lord.

"Recalling thus the mysteries of redemption, the Church opens to the faithful the riches of her Lord's powers and merits, so that these are in some way made present at all times, and the faithful are enabled to lay hold of them and become filled with saving grace (No. 102).

"In celebrating this annual cycle of Christ's mysteries, holy Church honors with special love the Blessed Mary, Mother of God" (No. 103).

"The Church has also included in the annual cycle days devoted to the memory of the martyrs and the other saints (who) sing God's perfect praise in heaven and offer prayers for us. By celebrating the passage of these saints from earth to heaven the Church proclaims the paschal mystery as achieved in the saints who have suffered and been glorified with Christ; she proposes them to the faithful as examples who draw all to the Father through Christ, and through their merits she pleads for God's favors (No. 104).

"In the various seasons of the year and according to her traditional discipline, the Church completes the formation of the faithful by means of pious practices for soul and body, by instruction, prayer, and works of penance and mercy (No. 105)."

The Roman Calander

Norms for a revised calendar for the Western Church as decreed by the Second Vatican Council were approved by Paul VI in the *motu proprio Mysterii Paschalis* dated Feb. 14, 1969. The revised calendar was promulgated a month later by a decree of the Congregation for Divine Worship and went into effect Jan. 1, 1970, with provisional modifications. Full imple-

mentation of all its parts was delayed in 1970 and 1971, pending the completion of work on related liturgical texts. The U.S. bishops ordered the calendar into effect for 1972.

The Seasons

Advent: The liturgical year begins with the first Sunday of Advent, which introduces a season of four weeks or slightly less duration with the theme of expectation of the coming of Christ. During the first two weeks, the final coming of Christ as Lord and Judge at the end of the world is the focus of attention. From Dec. 17 to 24, the emphasis shifts to anticipation of the celebration of his Nativity on the solemnity of Christmas.

Advent has four Sundays. Since the 10th century, the first Sunday has marked the beginning of the liturgical year in the Western Church. In the Middle Ages, a kind of pre-Christmas fast was in vogue during the season.

Christmas Season: The Christmas season begins with the vigil of Christmas and lasts until the Sunday after Jan. 6, inclusive.

The period between the end of the Christmas season and the beginning of Lent belongs to the ordinary time of the year. Of variable length, the pre-Lenten phase of this season includes what were formerly called the Sundays after Epiphany and the suppressed Sundays of Septuagesima, Sexagesima and Quinquagesima.

Lent: The penitential season of Lent begins on Ash Wednesday, which occurs between Feb. 4 and Mar. 11, depending on the date of Easter, and lasts until the Mass of the Lord's Supper (Holy Thursday). It has six Sundays. The sixth Sunday marks the beginning of Holy Week and is known as Passion (formerly called Palm) Sunday.

The origin of Lenten observances dates back to the fourth century or earlier.

Easter Triduum: The Easter Triduum begins with evening Mass of the Lord's Supper and ends with Evening Prayer on Easter Sunday.

Easter Season: The Easter season whose theme is resurrection from sin to the life of grace, lasts for 50 days, from Easter to Pentecost. Easter, the first Sunday after the first full moon following the vernal equinox, occurs between Mar. 22 and Apr. 25. The terminal phase of the Easter season, between the solemnities of the Ascension of the Lord and Pentecost, stresses anticipation of the coming and action of the Holy Spirit.

Ordinary Time: The season of Ordinary Time begins on Monday (or Tuesday if the feast of the Baptism of the Lord is celebrated on that Monday) after the Sunday following Jan. 6 and continues until the day before Ash Wednesday, inclusive. It begins again on the Monday after Pentecost and ends on the Saturday before the first Sunday of Advent. It consists of 33 or 34 weeks. The last Sunday is celebrated as the Solemnity of Christ the King. The overall purpose of the season is to elaborate the themes of salvation history.

The various liturgical seasons are characterized in part by the scriptural readings and Mass prayers assigned to each of them. During Advent, for example, the readings are messianic; during the Easter season, from the Acts of the Apostles, chronicling the Resurrection and the original proclamation of Christ by the Apostles, and from the Gospel of John; during Lent, baptismal and penitential passages. Mass prayers reflect the meaning and purpose of the various seasons.

Commemorations of Saints

The commemorations of saints are celebrated concurrently with the liturgical seasons and feasts of our Lord. Their purpose is to illustrate the paschal mysteries as reflected in the lives of saints, to honor them as heroes of holiness, and to appeal for their intercession.

In line with revised regulations, some former feasts were either abolished or relegated to observance in particular places by local option for one of two reasons: (1) lack of sufficient historical evidence for observance of the feasts; or, (2) lack of universal significance.

The commemoration of a saint, as a general rule, is observed on the day of death (*dies natalis*, day of birth to glory with God in heaven). Exceptions to this rule include the feasts of St. John the Baptist, who is honored on the day of his birth; Sts. Basil the Great and Gregory Nazianzen; and the brother Saints, Cyril and Methodius, who are commemorated in joint feasts. Application of this general rule in the revised calendar resulted in date changes of some observances.

Sundays and Other Holy Days

Sunday is the original Christian feast day and holy day of obligation because of the unusually significant events of salvation history which took place and are commemorated on the first day of the week viz., the Resurrection of Christ, the key event of his life and the fundamental fact of Christianity; and the descent of the Holy Spirit upon the Apostles on Pentecost, the birthday of the Church. The transfer of observance of the Lord's Day from the Sabbath to Sunday was made in apostolic times. The Mass and Liturgy of the Hours (Divine Office) of each Sunday reflect the themes and set the tones of the various liturgical seasons.

Holy days of obligation are special occasions on which Catholics who have reached the age of reason are seriously obliged, as on Sundays, to assist at Mass: they are also to refrain from work and involvement with business that impedes participation in divine worship and the enjoyment of appropriate rest and relaxation.

The holy days of obligation observed in the U.S. are: Christmas, the Nativity of Jesus, Dec. 25; Solemnity of Mary the Mother of God, Jan. 1; Ascension of the Lord; Assumption of Blessed Mary the Virgin, Aug. 15; All Saints' Day, Nov. 1; Immaculate Conception of Blessed Mary the Virgin, Dec. 8.

The precept to attend Mass is abrogated in the U.S. whenever the Solemnity of Mary, the Assumption, or All Saints falls on a Saturday or Monday (1991 decree of U.S. bishops; approved by Holy See July 4, 1992, and effective Jan. 1, 1993).

In addition to these, there are four other holy days of obligation prescribed in the general law of the Church which are not so observed in the U.S.: Epiphany, Jan. 6; St. Joseph, Mar. 19; Corpus Christi; Sts. Peter and Paul, June 29. The solemnities of Epiphany and Corpus Christi are transferred to a Sunday in countries where they are not observed as holy days of obligation.

Solemnities, Feasts, Memorials

Categories of observances according to dignity and manner of observance are: solemnities, principal days in the calendar (observance begins with Evening Prayer I of the preceding day; some have their own vigil Mass); feasts (celebrated within the limits of the natural day); obligatory memorials (celebrated throughout the Church); optional memorials (observable by choice).

Fixed observances are those that are regularly celebrated on the same calendar day each year.

Movable observances are those that are not observed on the same calendar day each year. Examples of these are Easter (the first Sunday after the first full moon following the vernal equinox), Ascension (40 days after Easter), Pentecost (50 days after Easter), Trinity Sunday (first after Pentecost), Christ the King (last Sunday of the liturgical year).

Weekdays, Days of Prayer

Weekdays are those on which no proper feast or vigil is celebrated in the Mass or Liturgy of the Hours (Divine Office). On such days, the Mass may be that of the preceding Sunday, which expresses the liturgical spirit of the season, an optional memorial, a votive Mass, or a Mass for the dead. Weekdays of Advent and Lent are in a special category of their own.

Days of Prayer: Dioceses, at times to be designated by local bishops, should observe "days or periods of prayer for the fruits of the earth, prayer for human rights and equality, prayer for world justice and peace, and penitential observance outside of Lent." So stated the Instruction on Particular Calendars (No. 331) issued by the Congregation for the Sacraments and Divine Worship June 24, 1970.

These days are contemporary equivalents of what were formerly called ember and rogation days.

Ember days originated at Rome about the fifth century, probably as Christian replacements for seasonal festivals of agrarian cults. They were observances of penance, thanksgiving, and petition for divine blessing on the various seasons; they also were occasions of special prayer for clergy to be ordained. These days were observed four times a year.

Rogation days originated in France about the fifth century. They were penitential in character and also occasions of prayer for a bountiful harvest and protection against evil.

Days and Times of Penance

Fridays throughout the year and the season of Lent are penitential times.

• **Abstinence:** Catholics in the U.S., from the age of 14 throughout life, are obliged to abstain from meat on Ash Wednesday, the Fridays of Lent and Good Friday. The law forbids the use of meat, but not of eggs, the products of milk or condiments made of animal fat. Permissible are soup flavored with meat, meat gravy and sauces. The obligation to abstain from meat is not in force on days celebrated as solemnities (e.g., Christmas, Sacred Heart).

• **Fasting:** Catholics in the U.S., from the day after their 18th birthday to the day after their 59th birthday, are also obliged to fast on Ash Wednesday and Good Friday. The law allows only one full meal a day, but does not prohibit the taking of some food in the morning and evening, observing as far as quantity and quality are concerned approved local custom. The order of meals is optional, i.e., the full meal may be taken in the evening instead of at midday. Also: (1) The combined quantity of food taken at the two lighter meals should not exceed the quantity taken at the full meal; (2) The drinking of ordinary liquids does not break the fast.

• **Obligation**: There is a general obligation to do penance for sins committed and for the remission of punishment resulting from sin. Substantial observance of fasting and abstinence, prescribed for the community of the Church, is a matter of serious obligation; it allows, however, for alternate ways of doing penance (e.g., works of charity, prayer and prayer-related practices, almsgiving).

Readings at Mass

Scriptural readings for Masses on Sundays and holy days are indicated under the appropriate dates in the calendar pages for the year 2003-04. The Year B cycle was prescribed for Sunday Masses in liturgical year 2003, beginning Dec. 1, 2002, to Nov. 23, 2003. The Year C cycle is prescribed for Masses on Sundays in liturgical year 2004, beginning Nov. 30, 2003, to Nov. 21, 2004. The Year Two cycle of weekday readings is prescribed for the year 2004.

Monthly Prayer Intentions

Intentions chosen and recommended by Pope John Paul II to the prayers of the faithful and circulated by the Apostleship of Prayer are given for each month of the calendar. He has expressed his desire that all Catholics make these intentions their own "in the certainty of being united with the Holy Father and praying according to his intentions and desires."

Celebrations in U.S. Particular Calendar

The General Norms for the Liturgical Year and the Calendar, issued in 1969 and published along with the General Roman Calendar for the Universal Church, noted that the calendar consists of the General Roman Calendar used by the entire Church and of particular calendars used in particular churches (nations or dioceses) or in families of religious.

The particular calendar for the U.S. contains the following celebrations. **January**: 4, Elizabeth Ann Seton; 5, John Neumann; 6, Bl. André Bessette. **March**: 3, Katharine Drexel. **May**: 10, Bl. Damien DeVeuster; 15, Isidore the Farmer. **July**: 1, Bl. Junípero Serra; 4, Independence Day; 14, Bl. Kateri Tekakwitha. **August**: 18, Jane Frances de Chantal. **September**: 9, Peter Claver. **October**: 6, Bl. Marie-Rose Durocher; 19, Isaac Jogues and John de Brébeuf and Companions; 20, Paul of the Cross. **November**: 13, Frances Xavier Cabrini; 18, Rose Philippine Duchesne; 23, Bl. Miguel Agustín Pro; fourth Thursday, Thanksgiving Day. **December**: 9, Juan Diego; 12, Our Lady of Guadalupe.

| | | | | | Weeks of Ordinary Time | | | | |
| | | | | | Before Lent | | After Pent. | | First Sunday of Advent |
Year	Ash Wed.	Easter	Ascension	Pentecost	Week	Ends	Week	Ends	
2003	Mar. 5	Apr. 20	May 29	June 8	8	Mar. 4	10	June 9	Nov. 30
2004	Feb. 25	Apr. 11	May 20	May 30	7	Feb. 24	9	May 31	Nov. 28
2005	Feb. 9	Mar. 27	May 5	May 15	5	Feb. 8	7	May 16	Nov. 27
2006	Mar. 1	Apr. 16	May 25	June 4	8	Feb. 28	9	June 5	Dec. 3
2007	Feb. 21	Apr. 8	May 17	May 27	7	Feb. 20	8	May 28	Dec. 2
2008	Feb. 6	Mar. 23	May 1	May 11	4	Feb. 5	6	May 12	Nov. 30
2009	Feb. 25	Apr. 12	May 21	May 31	7	Feb. 24	9	June 1	Nov. 29
2010	Feb. 17	Apr. 4	May 13	May 23	6	Feb. 16	8	May 24	Nov. 28
2011	Mar. 9	Apr. 24	June 2	June 12	9	Mar. 8	11	June 13	Nov. 27
2012	Feb. 22	Apr. 8	May 17	May 27	7	Feb. 21	8	May 28	Dec. 2
2013	Feb. 13	Mar. 31	May 9	May 19	5	Feb. 12	7	May 20	Dec. 1
2014	Mar. 5	Apr. 20	May 29	June 8	8	Mar. 4	10	June 9	Nov. 30
2015	Feb. 18	Apr. 5	May 14	May 24	6	Feb. 17	8	May 25	Nov. 29
2016	Feb. 10	Mar. 27	May 5	May 15	5	Feb. 9	7	May 16	Nov. 27
2017	Mar. 1	Apr. 16	May 25	June 4	8	Feb. 28	9	June 5	Dec. 3
2018	Feb. 14	Apr. 1	May 10	May 20	6	Feb. 13	7	May 21	Dec. 2
2019	Mar. 6	Apr. 21	May 30	June 9	8	Mar. 5	10	June 1	Dec. 1
2020	Feb. 26	Apr. 12	May 21	May 31	7	Feb. 25	9	June 1	Nov. 29
2021	Feb. 17	Apr. 4	May 13	May 23	6	Feb. 16	8	May 24	Nov. 28

2004 CALENDAR

January 2004

General: That all men and women may recognize that they are members of God's one family and end wars, injustice and discrimination among themselves.

Missionary: That every mission Church may engage itself in the training of apostolic personnel.

1 Thurs. Octave of Christmas; Solemnity of the Blessed Virgin Mary, Mother of God; holy day of obligation (Nm. 6: 22 -27; Gal. 4:4-7; Lk.2:16-21).
2 Fri. Sts. Basil the Great and Gregory Nazianzus, bishops and doctors of the Church; memorial.
3 Sat. Weekday; Vigil: Epiphany of the Lord
4 Sun. Epiphany of Our Lord; solemnity (Is. 60:1-6; Eph. 3:2-3a, 5-6; Mt. 2:1-12).
5 Mon. Weekday. St. John Neumann, bishop; memorial in the U.S.
6 Tues. Weekday. Bl. Andre Bessette, religious; optional memorial.
7 Wed. Weekday. St. Raymond of Penafort, priest; optional memorial.
8 Thurs. Weekday.
9 Fri. Weekday.
10 Sat. Weekday. Vigil: Baptism of the Lord
11 Sun. Baptism of the Lord; feast (Is. 42:1-4,6-7; Acts 10:34-38; Mk. 1:7-11).
12 Mon. Weekday. First week in ordinary time.
13 Tues. Weekday. St. Hilary, bishop-doctor; optional memorial.
14 Wed. Weekday.
15 Thurs. Weekday.
16 Fri. Weekday
17 Sat. St. Anthony, abbot; memorial.
18 Sun. Second Sunday in ordinary time (Is. 62, 1-5; 1 Cor. 12, 4-11; Jn 2, 1-11).
19 Mon. Weekday.
20 Tues. St. Fabian, pope-martyr; St. Sebastian, martyr; optional memorials.
21 Wed. Weekday. St. Agnes, virgin and martyr; memorial.
22 Thurs. St. Vincent, deacon-martyr; optional memorial
23 Fri. Weekday
24 Sat. St. Francis de Sales, bishop-doctor; memorial.
25 Sun. Third Sunday in ordinary time (Neh. 8, 2-4a, 5-6, 8-10; I Cor. 12, 12-30; Lk.1, 1-4;4, 14-21).
26 Mon. Weekday. Sts. Timothy and Titus, bishops; memorial.
27 Tues. St. Angela Merici, virgin; optional memorial.
28 Wed. St. Thomas Aquinas, priest-doctor; memorial.
29 Thurs. Weekday.
30 Fri. Weekday.
31 Sat. St. John Bosco, priest; memorial.

Observances: World Day of Peace, Jan. 1. Customary ordination of bishops by the pope on the Solemnity of the Epiphany, Jan. 6. Week of Prayer for Christian Unity, Jan. 18-25. National Prayer Vigil for Life and March for Life in Washington, DC., Jan. 21-22.

February 2004

General: For peaceful co-existence among Christians, Jews and Muslims in the Holy Land.

Missionary: That in Oceania priestly and religious vocations for evangelization in the local churches may receive special care.

1 Sun. Fourth Sunday in ordinary time (Jer. 1:4-5, 17-19).
2 Mon. Presentation of the Lord, feast (Mal. 3:1-4; Heb. 2:14-18; Lk.2:22-40).
3 Tues. St. Blase, bishop-martyr; St. Ansgar, bishop; optional memorial.
4 Wed. Weekday.
5 Thurs. St. Agatha, virgin-martyr; memorial.
6 Fri. St. Paul Miki, priest-martyr and companions, martyrs; memorial
7 Sat. Weekday. St. Jerome Emiliani, priest; optional memorial.
8 Sun. Fifth Sunday in ordinary time (Is. 6:1-2a, 3-8; 1 Cor. 15:1-11 or 15:3-8, 11; Lk. 5: 1-11).
9 Mon. Weekday.
10 Tue. St. Scholastica, virgin; memorial.
11 Wed. Our Lady of Lourdes; optional memorial.
12 Thurs. Weekday.
13 Fri. Weekday.
14 Sat. Sts. Cyril, monk and Methodius, bishop; memorial
15 Sun. Sixth Sunday in ordinary time (Jer. 17:5-8; 1 Cor. 15:12, 16-20; Lk. 6:20-26).
16 Mon. Weekday.
17 Tues. Weekday. Seven Holy Founders of the Order of Servites; optional memorial.
18 Wed. Weekday.
19 Thurs. Weekday.
20 Fri. Weekday
21 Sat. St. Peter Damian, bishop-doctor; memorial.
22 Sun. Seventh Sunday in ordinary time (1 Sm. 26:2, 7-9, 12-13, 22-23; 1 Cor. 15:45-49; Lk. 6:27-38).
23 Mon. Weekday.
24 Tue. Weekday.
25 Wed. Ash Wednesday (Jl. 2:12-18; 2 Cor. 5: 20-6:2; Mt. 6:1-6, 16-18). Fast and abstinence.
26 Thurs. Lenten Weekday.
27 Fri. Lenten Weekday.
28 Sat. Lenten Weekday.
29 Sun. First Sunday of Lent

Observances: The Presentation of the Child Jesus in the Temple, traditional day for the blessings of candles that will be used throughout the year. Optional memorial of St. Blase. Monday, Feb. 2, is World Day for Consecrated Life. Wed., Feb. 11, is the optional memorial of Our Lady of Lourdes and the World Day of the Sick.

The Lenten season begins with Ash Wednesday (Feb. 25), when ashes are blessed and imposed on the foreheads of the faithful to remind them of their obligation to do penance of sins, to seek spiritual renewal by means of prayer, fasting, good works and by bearing with patience and for God's purposes the trials and difficulties of everyday life.

March 2004

General: That the land, culture and all the rights of the indigenous populations of the world may be respected, so that true harmony between them and those among whom they live may be attained.

Missionary: That in Africa, cooperation between missionary Institutes and local Churches may grow, with respect for the variety of gifts.

1   Mon. Lenten Weekday.
2   Tues. Lenten Weekday.
3   Wed. Lenten Weekday. St. Katherine Drexel, virgin; optional memorial.
4   Thurs. Lenten Weekday. St. Casimir; optional memorial.
5   Fri. Lenten Weekday.
6   Sat. Lenten Weekday.
7   Sun. Second Sunday of Lent (Gn. 15:5-12, 17-18; Phil. 3:17-4:1; Lk. 9: 28b-36).
8   Mon. Lenten Weekday. St. John of God, religious; optional memorial.
9   Tues. Lenten Weekday. St. Frances of Rome, religious; optional memorial.
10 Wed. Lenten Weekday.
11 Thurs. Lenten Weekday.
12 Fri. Lenten Weekday. Abstinence.
13 Sat. Lenten Weekday.
14 Sun. Third Sunday of Lent (Ex. 3:1-8a, 13-15; 1 Cor. 10:1-6, 10-12; Lk. 13, 1-9).
15 Mon. Lenten Weekday.
16 Tues. Lenten Weekday.
17 Wed. Lenten Weekday. St. Patrick, bishop; optional memorial.
18 Thurs. Lenten Weekday. St. Cyril of Jerusalem, bishop-doctor; optional memorial.
19 Fri. Lenten Weekday. St. Joseph, husband of the Blessed Virgin Mary; solemnity, abstinence.
20 Sat. Lenten Weekday.
21 Sun. Fourth Sunday of Lent (Josh. 5:9a, 10-12; 2 Cor. 5:17-21; Lk. 15:1-3, 11-32).
22 Mon. Lenten Weekday.
23 Tues. Lenten Weekday. St. Toribio de Mogrovejo, bishop; optional memorial.
24 Wed. Lenten Weekday.
25 Thurs. Annunciation of the Lord; solemnity.
26 Fri. Lenten Weekday. Abstinence.
27 Sat. Lenten Weekday.
28 Sun. Fifth Sunday of Lent (Is. 43:16-21; Phil. 3:8-14; Jn. 8:1-11).
29 Mon. Lenten Weekday.
30 Tues. Lenten Weekday.
31 Wed. Lenten Weekday.

Observances: The Solemnity of St. Joseph, husband of Mary, is observed Mar. 19. The Solemnity of the Annunciation is observed Mar. 25.

April 2004

General: That solid preparation of the candidates for holy orders and permanent training of ordained ministers may be carefully provided for.

Missionary: That the missionary spirit of *Ad Gentes* may become a theme of reflection and a matter of constant commitment in the ordinary pastoral activity of the Christian community.

1   Thurs. Lenten Weekday.
2   Fri. Lenten Weekday. Abstinence. St. Francis of Paola, hermit; optional memorial.
3   Sat. Lenten Weekday.
4   Sun. Palm Sunday/The Lord's Passion (Lk. 19:28-40; Is. 50: 4-7; Phil. 2:6-11; Lk. 22:14-23 or 23:1-49).
5   Mon. Monday of Holy Week.
6   Tues. Tuesday of Holy Week.
7   Wed. Wednesday of Holy Week.
8   Thurs. Holy Thursday. Chrism Mass in the morning. The Easter Triduum begins with the evening Mass of the Lord's Supper.
9   Fri. Good Friday. The Lord's Passion. Fast and abstinence.
10 Sat. Holy Saturday. Easter Vigil.
11 Sun. Easter Sunday: Resurrection of the Lord; solemnity (Acts 10:34a, 37-43; Col. 3:1-4 or 1 Cor. 5:6-8; Jn. 20:1-9 or at an evening Mass, Lk. 24:13-56).
12 Mon. Easter Monday; solemnity
13 Tue. Easter Tuesday; solemnity.
14 Wed. Easter Wednesday; solemnity.
15 Thurs. Easter Thursday; solemnity
16 Fri. Easter Friday; solemnity.
17 Sat. Easter Saturday; solemnity.
18 Sun. Second Sunday of Easter/Divine Mercy Sunday (Acts 5:12-16; Rv. 1:9-11a, 12-13, 17-19; Jn. 20: 19-31).
19 Mon. Easter Weekday.
20 Tues. Easter Weekday.
21 Wed. Easter Weekday. St. Anselm, bishop and doctor; optional memorial.
22 Thurs. Easter Weekday.
23 Fri. Easter Weekday. St. George; optional memorial
24 Sat. Easter Weekday. St. Fidelis, priest and martyr; optional memorial.
25 Sun. Third Sunday of Easter (Acts 5: 27-32, 40b-41; Rv. 5:11-14; Jn. 21: -19 or 21:1-14).
26 Mon. Easter Weekday.
27 Tues. Easter Weekday
28 Wed. Easter Weekday. St. Peter Chanel, priest-martyr; St. Louis Mary de Montfort; optional memorials.
29 Thurs St. Catherine of Siena, virgin-doctor; memorial.
30 Fri. Easter Weekday. St. Pius V, pope; optional memorial.

Observances: Holy Week: Passion Sunday, or Palm Sunday, begins these most solemn and holy celebrations of the Church year. Mon., Tues., and Wed. of Holy Week are preparatory days leading to the Sacred Triduum. The morning of Holy Thursday is the celebration of the Mass of the Holy Chrism. During this Mass all priests renew their vows. Easter is the day when the Holy Father delivers the traditional *Urbi et Orbi* address. Divine Mercy Sunday is celebrated by the universal Church the second Sunday of Easter.

May 2004

General: That the family — founded on the marriage of a man and a woman — may be recognized as the basic cell of human society.

Missionary: That through the motherly intercession of Our Lady, Catholic people may come to regard the Eucharist as the heart and soul of the missionary activity.

1 Sat. Easter Weekday. St. Joseph the Worker; optional memorial.
2 Sun. Fourth Sunday of Easter (Acts 13:14, 43-52; Rv. 7:9, 14b-17; Jn. 10:27-30).
3 Mon. Sts. Philip and James, apostles; feast.
4 Tues. Easter Weekday.
5 Wed. Easter Weekday.
6 Thurs. Easter Weekday.
7 Fri. Easter Weekday.
8 Sat. Easter Weekday.
9 Sun. Fifth Sunday of Easter (Acts 14:21-27; Rv. 21:1-5a; Jn. 13:31-33a, 34-35).
10 Mon. Easter Weekday. Bl. Damien Joseph de Veuster of Molokai, priest; optional memorial.
11 Tues. Easter Weekday.
12 Wed. Easter Weekday. Sts. Nereus and Achilleus, martyrs; St. Pancras, martyr; optional memorials.
13 Thurs. Easter Weekday. Our Lady of Fatima; optional memorial.
14 Fri. St. Mathias, apostle; feast.
15 Sat. Easter Weekday. St. Isidore the farmer; optional memorial.
16 Sun. Sixth Sunday of Easter (Acts 15:1-2, 22-29; Rv. 21:10-14, 22-23; Jn. 14:23-29).
17 Mon. Easter Weekday.
18 Tues. Easter Weekday. St. John I, pope and martyr; optional memorial.
19 Wed. Easter Weekday.
20 Thurs. Ascension of Our Lord; solemnity. Holy day of obligation (Acts 1:1-11; Eph. 4:1-13; Mk. 16:15-20). If transferred: Easter Weekday. St. Bernardine of Siena, priest; optional memorial.
21 Fri. Easter Weekday. St. Christopher Magallanes, priest and companions, martyrs; optional memorial.
22 Sat. Easter Weekday. St. Rita Cascia, religious; optional memorial
23 Sun. Ascension of Our Lord; solemnity. Holy day of obligation (Acts 1:1-11; Eph. 4:1-13; Mk. 16:15-20). Or Seventh Sunday of Easter (Acts 7:55-60; Rv. 22:12-14, 16-17, 20; Jn. 17:20-26).
24 Mon. Easter Weekday.
25 Tues. Easter Weekday. St. Bede, doctor; St. Gregory VII, pope; St. Mary Magdalene de Pazzi, virgin; optional memorials.
26 Wed. St. Philip Neri, priest; memorial.
27 Thurs. Easter Weekday. St. Augustine of Canterbury, bishop; optional memorial.
28 Fri. Easter Weekday.
29 Sat. Easter Weekday.
30 Sun. Pentecost Sunday; solemnity (Acts 2:1-11; 1 Cor. 12:3b-7, 12-13; or Rom. 8:1-7; Jn. 20:19-23 or Jn. 14: 15-16, 23b-26).
31 Mon. Visitation of the Blessed Virgin Mary to Elizabeth; feast.

Observances: May is traditionally dedicated to our Blessed Mother.

June 2004

General: That all Christians may be constantly more aware of their personal and community responsibility to bear witness to God's love for humanity and for every man and woman.

Missionary: That religious freedom — a fundamental right of mankind — may meet with ever-growing respect in Asian countries.

1 Tues. St. Justin, martyr; memorial.
2 Wed. Weekday. Sts. Marcellinus and Peter, martyrs; optional memorial.
3 Thurs. St. Charles Lwanga, martyr, and companions, martyrs; memorial.
4 Fri. Weekday.
5 Sat. St. Boniface, bishop-martyr; memorial.
6 Sun. The Most Holy Trinity; solemnity (Prvb. 8:22-31; Rom. 5:1-5; Jn. 16:12-15).
7 Mon. Tenth Week in ordinary time.
8 Tues. Weekday.
9 Wed. Weekday. St. Ephrem, deacon-doctor; optional memorial.
10 Thurs. Weekday.
11 Fri. St. Barnabas, apostle; memorial.
12 Sat. Weekday.
13 Sun. Most Holy Body and Blood of Christ (Corpus Christi); solemnity (Gn. 14:18-20;1 Cor. 11:23-26; Lk. 9:11a-17).
14 Mon. Eleventh Week in ordinary time.
15 Tues. Weekday.
16 Wed. Weekday.
17 Thurs. Weekday.
18 Fri. Most Sacred Heart of Jesus; solemnity.
19 Sat. Weekday, Immaculate Heart of Mary; optional memorial.
20 Sun. Twelfth Sunday in ordinary time (Zec. 12:10-11, 13:1; Gal. 3:26-29; Lk. 9:18-24).
21 Mon. Weekday.
22 Tues. Weekday. St. Paulinus, bishop; Sts. John Fisher, bishop and St. Thomas More, martyrs; optional memorials.
23 Wed. Weekday.
24 Thurs. Nativity of St. John the Baptist; solemnity.
25 Fri. Weekday.
26 Sat. Weekday
27 Sun. Thirteenth Sunday in ordinary time (1 Kgs. 19:16b, 19-21; Gal. 5:1, 13-18; Lk. 9:51-62).
28 Mon. St. Irenaeus, bishop-martyr; memorial.
29 Tue. Sts. Peter and Paul, apostles; solemnity
30 Wed. Weekday. First Martyrs of the Church of Rome; optional memorial.

Observances: Feast of the Most Holy Trinity is June 6. The Feast of the Body and Blood of Christ (Corpus Christi) is June 13. It is the custom in certain dioceses to gather for a Corpus Christi procession to venerate the Body of Christ at special altars prepared near the cathedral church. The Feast of the Sacred Heart is June 18 followed by the Feast of the Immaculate Heart of Mary on June 19, and the Feast of Sts. Peter and Paul on June 29.

July 2004

General: That all those who are able to benefit from a holiday period during this time of the year may be helped during their vacation to rediscover in God their inner harmony and to open themselves to the love of human beings.

Missionary: That in the young churches the lay faithful may receive more attention and may be turned to greater account for evangelization.

1   Thurs. Weekday. Bl. Junipero Serra, priest; optional memorial.
2   Fri. Weekday.
3   Sat. St. Thomas, apostle; feast.
4   Sun. Fourteenth Sunday in ordinary time (Is. 66:10-14c; Gal. 6: 4-18; Lk. 10:1-13, 17-20).
5   Mon. Weekday. St. Anthony Maria Zaccaria, priest; optional memorial.
6   Tues. Weekday. St. Maria Goretti, virgin and martyr; optional memorial.
7   Wed. Weekday.
8   Thurs. Weekday.
9   Fri. Weekday.
10 Sat. Weekday.
11 Sun. Fifteenth Sunday in ordinary time (Dt. 30:10-14; Col. 1: 5-20; Lk. 10:25-37).
12 Mon. Weekday
13 Tues. Weekday
14 Wed. Weekday. Bl. Kateri Tekakwitha, virgin; memorial.
15 Thurs. Weekday. St. Bonaventure, bishop-doctor; memorial.
16 Fri. Weekday. Our Lady of Mount Carmel; optional memorial.
17 Sat. Weekday.
18 Sun. Sixteenth Sunday in ordinary time (Gn. 18:1-10a; Col. 1:4-28; Lk. 10:8-42).
19 Mon. Weekday.
20 Tues. Weekday. St. Apollinarius, bishop; optional memorial.
21 Wed. Weekday. St. Lawrence of Brandisi, priest-doctor; optional memorial.
22 Thurs. St. Mary Magdalene; memorial.
23 Fri. Weekday. St. Bridget of Sweden; optional memorial.
24 Sat. Weekday.
25 Sun. Seventeenth Sunday in ordinary time (Gn. 18:20-32; Col. 2:12-14; Lk. 11:1-13).
26 Mon. Sts. Joachim and Anne, parents of the Blessed Virgin Mary; memorial.
27 Tues. Weekday.
28 Wed. Weekday.
29 Thurs. St. Martha; memorial.
30 Fri. Weekday. St. Peter Chrysologus, bishop-doctor; optional memorial.
31 Sat. St. Ignatius of Loyola, priest; memorial.

Observances: Blessed Juniper Serra, whose optional memorial may be celebrated July 1, founder of the California Missions. St. Thomas the Apostle is observed on July 3; St. Maria Goretti, July 6; Blessed Kateri Tekakwitha, July 14; St. Bonaventure, called the second founder of the Franciscan Order, July 15; St. Ignatius Loyola, founder of the Society of Jesus, July 31. Because Independence Day, July 4, is on a Sunday the particular mass for the country may not be observed; however, it would be appropriate to offer prayers for the U.S. during the Prayers of the Faithful.

August 2004

General: That the European Union may know how to draw new nourishment from the Christian patrimony which has been an essential part of its culture and history.

Missionary: That unity and cooperation between the Institutes which actively work in the missions may grow.

1   Sun. Eighteenth Sunday in ordinary time (Eccl. 1:2; 2:21-23; Col. 3:1-5, 9-11; Lk. 12:13-21).
2   Mon. Weekday. St. Eusebius, bishop; St. Peter Eymard, priest; memorial.
3   Tues. Weekday.
4   Wed. St. John Mary Vianney, priest; memorial.
5   Thurs. Weekday. Dedication of the Basilica of St. Mary Major in Rome; optional memorial.
6   Fri. Transfiguration of the Lord; feast.
7   Sat. St. Sixtus II, pope-martyr, and companions, martyrs; St. Cajetan, priest; optional memorial.
8   Sun. Nineteenth Sunday in ordinary time (Wis. 18:6-9; Heb. 11:1-2, 8-19; Lk. 12:32-48).
9   Mon. St. Teresa Benedicta of the Cross, virgin and martyr; memorial.
10 Tues. St. Lawrence, deacon and martyr; memorial.
11 Wed. St. Clare, virgin; memorial.
12 Thurs. Weekday.
13 Fri. Weekday. St. Pontian, pope-martyr and St. Hippolytus, priest-martyr; optional memorials.
14 Sat. Weekday. St. Maximillian Mary Kolbe, priest-martyr; memorial
15 Sun. Assumption of the Blessed Virgin Mary; solemnity. (Rv. 11:19a; 12:1-6a, 10; 1 Cor. 15:20-27; Lk. 1:39-56).
16 Mon. Weekday. St. Stephen of Hungary; optional memorial.
17 Tues. Weekday.
18 Wed. Weekday. St. Jane Frances de Chantal, religious; optional memorial.
19 Thurs. Weekday. St. John Eudes, priest; optional memorial.
20 Fri. St. Bernard, abbot-doctor; memorial.
21 Sat. St. Pius X, pope; memorial.
22 Sun. Twenty-first Sunday in ordinary time (Is. 66:18-21; Heb. 12:5-7, 11-13; Lk. 13:22-30).
23 Mon. St. Rose of Lima, virgin; memorial.
24 Tues. St. Bartholomew; apostle; feast.
25 Wed. Weekday. St. Louis and St. Joseph Calasanz; optional memorials.
26 Thurs. Weekday
27 Fri. St. Monica; memorial.
28 Sat. St. Augustine, bishop-doctor; memorial.
29 Sun. Twenty-second Sunday of ordinary time (Sir. 3:17-18, 20, 28-29; Heb. 12:18-19, 22-24a; Lk. 14:1, 7-14).
30 Mon. Weekday.
31 Tues. Weekday.

Observances: The Feast of the Transfiguration of the Lord, Aug. 6; St. Clare, Aug. 11; The Feast of the Assumption of the Blessed Virgin Mary, Aug. 15; St. Augustine, Aug. 28.

September 2004

General: That old people may be considered an asset for the spiritual and human growth of society.

Missionary: That in Africa a true brotherly cooperation may develop among all those who work for the growth and development of ecclesial communities.

1 Wed. Weekday.
2 Thurs. Weekday.
3 Fri. St. Gregory the Great, pope-doctor; memorial.
4 Sat. Weekday.
5 Sun. Twenty-third Sunday in ordinary time (Wis 9: 3-18b; Phlm. 9-10, 12-17; Lk. 14:25-33).
6 Mon. Weekday.
7 Tues. Weekday.
8 Wed. Birth of the Blessed Virgin Mary; feast.
9 Thurs. St. Peter Claver, priest; memorial.
10 Fri. Weekday
11 Sat. Weekday
12 Sun. Twenty-fourth Sunday in ordinary time (Ex. 21:7-11; 13-14; 1 Tim. 1:12-17; Lk. 15:1-32).
13 Mon. St. John Chrysostom, bishop-doctor; memorial.
14 Tues. Exaltation of the Holy Cross; feast.
15 Wed. Our Lady of Sorrows; memorial.
16 Thurs. Sts. Cornelius, pope-martyr, and Cyprian, bishop-martyr; memorial.
17 Fri. Weekday. St. Robert Bellarmine, bishop-doctor; optional memorial.
18 Sat. Weekday.
19 Sun. Twenty-fifth Sunday in ordinary time (Amos 8:4-7; 1 Tim. 2:1-8; Lk. 16:1-13).
20 Mon. Sts. Andrew Kim Taegon, priest-martyr, Paul Chong Hasang, martyr, and companions, martyrs; memorial.
21 Tues. St. Matthew, apostle and evangelist; feast.
22 Wed. Weekday.
23 Thurs. Weekday.
24 Fri. Weekday.
25 Sat. Weekday
26 Sun. Twenty-sixth Sunday in ordinary time (Amos 6:1a, 4-7; 1 Tim. 6:11-16; Lk. 16:19-31).
27 Mon. St. Vincent de Paul, priest; memorial.
28 Tues. Weekday. St. Wenceslaus, martyr; St. Lawrence Ruiz and companions, martyrs; optional memorials.
29 Wed. Michael, Gabriel, and Raphael, archangels; feast.
30 Thurs. St. Jerome; memorial.

Observances: Birth of the Blessed Virgin Mary, Sept. 8; St. John Chrysostom, Doctor of the Church, Sept. 13; Exaltation of the Holy Cross, Sept. 14; Our Lady of Sorrows, Sept. 15; St. Robert Bellarmine, Doctor of the Church, Sept. 17; St. Matthew, apostle and evangelist, Sept. 21; St. Vincent de Paul, founder of the Vincentians and Daughters of Charity, Sept. 27; Sts. Michael, Gabriel, and Raphael, archangels, Sept. 29.

Labor Day is celebrated Sept. 6 with a special votive mass.

October 2004

General: That, firm in their faith, Christians may be eager to dialogue with those who belong to another religious tradition.

Missionary: That the presence of Catholics in the national life and the media of the Latin-American continent may increase.

1 Fri. St. Thérèse of the Child Jesus, virgin; memorial.
2 Sat. Guardian Angels; memorial.
3 Sun. Twenty-seventh of ordinary time (Heb. 1: 2-3; 2:2-4; 2 Tim. 1:6-8, 13-14; Lk. 17:5-10).
4 Mon. St. Francis of Assisi, religious; memorial.
5 Tues. Weekday. St. Bruno, priest, and Bl. Marie Rose Durocher, virgin; optional memorials.
6 Wed. Weekday.
7 Thurs. Our Lady of the Rosary; memorial.
8 Fri. Weekday.
9 Sat. Weekday. St. Denis, bishop-martyr; St. John Leonardi, priest; optional memorials.
10 Sun. Twenty-eighth Sunday in ordinary time (2 Kgs. 5:14-17; 2 Tim. 2:8-13; Lk. 17:11-19).
11 Mon. Weekday.
12 Tues. Weekday.
13 Wed. Weekday.
14 Thurs. Weekday. St. Callistus I, pope-martyr; optional memorial.
15 Fri. St. Theresa of Avila, virgin-doctor; St. Ignatius of Antioch, bishop-martyr; memorials.
16 Sat. Weekday. St. Hedwig, religious; St. Margaret Mary Alacoque, virgin; optional memorial.
17 Sun. Twenty-ninth Sunday in ordinary time (Ex. 17:8-13; 2 Tim. 3:14-4:2; Lk. 18:1-8).
18 Mon. St. Luke, evangelist; feast.
19 Tues. Sts. John de Brebeuf, Isaac Jogues and companions, martyrs; memorial.
20 Wed. Weekday. Weekday. St. Paul of the Cross; optional memorial.
21 Thurs. Weekday.
22 Fri. Weekday.
23 Sat. Weekday. St. John of Capistrano, priest; optional memorial.
24 Sun. Thirtieth Sunday in ordinary time (Sir. 35:12-14, 16-18; 2 Tim. 4:6-8, 16-18; Lk. 18:9-14).
25 Mon. Weekday.
26 Tues. Weekday.
27 Wed. Weekday.
28 Thurs. Sts. Simon and Jude, apostles; feast
29 Fri. Weekday.
30 Sat. Weekday.
31 Sun. Thirty-first Sunday in ordinary time (Wis. 11:22-12:2; 2 Thes. 1:11-22; Lk. 19:1-10).

Observances: St. Thérèse of the Child Jesus, Doctor of the Church, Oct.1; Guardian Angels, Oct. 2; St. Francis of Assisi, founder of the Franciscan Order, Oct. 4; St. Teresa of Jesus, doctor of the Church, reformer of the Carmelite Order, Oct. 15; the North American Martyrs, Oct. 19; St. Paul of the Cross, founder of the Congregation of the Passion, Oct. 20.

Sunday, Oct. 3, is Respect Life Sunday, the customary day for Life Chains in various dioceses. Sunday, Oct. 10, is Vocation Awareness Sunday, and Oct. 24 is Mission Sunday, with appeals for prayer and financial support for persons and projects involved in the ministry of evangelization at home and abroad.

November 2004

General: That Christian men and women, aware of the vocation which is theirs in the Church, may answer generously God's call to seek holiness in the midst of their lives.

Missionary: That all those who work in the missions may never forget that personal holiness and intimate union with Christ are the source of the efficacy of evangelization.

1 Mon. All Saints; solemnity.
2 Tues. Commemoration of All the Faithful Departed; All Souls' Day.
3 Wed. Weekday. St. Martin de Porres, religious; optional memorial.
4 Thurs. St. Charles Borromeo, bishop; memorial.
5 Fri. Weekday.
6 Sat. Weekday.
7 Sun. Thirty-second Sunday in ordinary time (2 Mc. 7:1-2, 9-14; 2 Thes. 2:16-3:5; Lk. 20:27-38).
8 Mon. Weekday.
9 Tues. Dedication of the Basilica of St. John Lateran in Rome; feast
10 Wed. St. Leo the Great, pope-doctor; memorial.
11 Thurs. St. Martin of Tours, bishop; memorial.
12 Fri. St. Josaphat, bishop-martyr; memorial.
13 Sat. Weekday. St. Frances Xavier Cabrini; memorial.
14 Sun. Thirty-third Sunday in ordinary time (Mal. 3:19-20a; 2 Thes. 3:7-12; Lk. 21:5-19).
15 Mon. St. Albert the Great, bishop-doctor; optional memorial.
16 Tues. Weekday. St. Margaret of Scotland, virgin; St. Gertrude, virgin; optional memorials.
17 Wed. St. Elizabeth of Hungary, religious; memorial.
18 Thurs. Weekday. St. Rose Philippine Duchesne, virgin; dedication of the Basilicas of St. Peter and St. Paul, apostles, in Rome; optional memorials.
19 Fri. Weekday.
20 Sat. Weekday.
21 Sun. Our Lord Jesus Christ the King; solemnity (2 Sm. 5:1-3; Col. 1:12-20; Lk. 23:35-43).
22 Mon. St. Cecilia, virgin-martyr; memorial.
23 Tues. Weekday. St. Clement, pope-martyr; St. Columban, abbot; Bl. Miguel Agustin Pro, priest-martyr; optional memorials.
24 Wed. St. Andrew Dung-Lac, priest-martyr and companions, martyrs; memorial.
25 Thurs. Weekday. St. Catherine of Alexandria, virgin-martyr; optional memorial. Thanksgiving Day; proper mass.
26 Fri. Weekday.
27 Sat. Weekday.
28 Sun. First Sunday of Advent (Is. 2: -5; Rom. 13:11-14; Mt. 24:37-44).
29 Mon. Advent Weekday.
30 Tues. Andrew, apostle; feast.

Observances: All Saints' Day, Nov. 1; All Souls' Day, Nov. 2; Frances Xavier Cabrini, Nov. 13; St. Albert the Great, Nov. 15; Christ the King, Nov. 21; Thanksgiving Day, Nov. 25; the beginning of the Church year, the first Sunday of Advent, Nov. 28. The annual fall meeting of the U.S. bishops takes place this month in Washington, DC. Its agenda covers a wide range of topics, including doctrinal, pastoral and educational issues that impact the life of the Church in the U.S.

December 2004

General: That children may be considered as precious gifts of God and may be given due respect, understanding and love.

Missionary: That Jesus Christ's Incarnation may be the model of genuine inculturation.

1 Wed. Advent Weekday.
2 Thurs. Advent Weekday.
3 Fri. St. Francis Xavier, priest; memorial.
4 Sat. Advent Weekday. St. John Damascene, priest-doctor; optional memorial.
5 Sun. Second Sunday of Advent (Is.11:1-10; Rom. 15:4-9; Mt. 3:1-12).
6 Mon. Advent Weekday. St. Nicholas, bishop; optional memorial.
7 Tues. St. Ambrose, bishop-doctor; memorial.
8 Wed. Immaculate Conception of the Blessed Virgin Mary; solemnity (Gn. 3:9-15, 20; Eph. 1:3-6, 11-12; Lk. 1:26-38). Holy day of obligation.
9 Thurs. Advent Weekday. St. Juan Diego; optional memorial.
10 Fri. Our Lady of Guadalupe; feast.
11 Sat. Advent Weekday. St. Damasus, pope; optional memorial.
12 Sun. Third Sunday of Advent (Is. 35:1-6a, 10; Jas. 5:7-10; Mt. 11:2-11).
13 Mon. St. Lucy, virgin-martyr; memorial.
14 Tues. St. John of the Cross, priest-doctor; memorial.
15 Wed. Advent Weekday.
16 Thurs. Advent Weekday.
17 Fri. Advent Weekday.
18 Sat. Advent Weekday.
19 Sun. Fourth Sunday of Advent (Is. 7:10-14; Rom. 1:1-7; Mt. 1:18-24).
20 Mon. Advent Weekday.
21 Tues. Advent Weekday. St. Peter Canisius, priest-doctor; optional memorial.
22 Wed. Advent Weekday.
23 Thurs. Advent Weekday. St. John of Kanty, priest; optional memorial.
24 Fri. Advent Weekday.
25 Sat. Nativity of the Lord, Christmas; solemnity; holy day of obligation. (Vigil Mass — Is. 62:1-5; Acts 13:16-17, 22-25; Mt. 1:1-25 or 1:18-25. Midnight Mass — Is. 9:1-6; Ti. 2:11-14; Lk. 2:1-14. Mass at dawn — Is. 62:11-12; Ti. 3:4-7; Lk. 2:15-20. Mass during the day — Is. 52:7-10; Heb. 1:1-6; Jn.1:1-18 or 1:1-5, 9-14).
26 Sun. Holy Family of Jesus, Mary, and Joseph (Sir. 3:2-7, 12-14; Col. 3:12-21; Lk. 2:22-40).
27 Mon. St. John, apostle-evangelist; feast.
28 Tues. The Holy Innocents, martyrs. Feast. Sixth Day in the Octave of Christmas.
29 Wed. Fifth Day in the Octave of Christmas. St. Thomas Becket, bishop-martyr; optional memorial.
30 Thurs. Sixth Day in the Octave of Christmas.
31 Fri. Seventh Day in the Octave of Christmas. St. Sylvester, pope; optional memorial.

Observances: St. Francis Xavier, missionary, Dec. 3; Sts. John of Damascus, Ambrose, John of the Cross, Peter Canisius, Doctors of the Church, Immaculate Conception, Dec. 8; St. Juan Diego, Dec. 9; Birth of Our Lord, Dec. 25; Holy Family, Dec. 26; St. John, apostle-evangelist, Dec. 27.

HOLY DAYS AND OTHER OBSERVANCES

The following list includes the six holy days of obligation observed in the U.S. and additional observances of devotional and historical significance. The dignity or rank of observances is indicated by the terms: **solemnity** (highest in rank); **feast**; **memorial** (for universal observance); **optional memorial** (for celebration by choice).

All Saints, Nov. 1, holy day of obligation, solemnity. Commemorates all the blessed in heaven, and is intended particularly to honor the blessed who have no special feasts. The background of the feast dates to the fourth century when groups of martyrs, and later other saints, were honored on a common day in various places. In 609 or 610, the Pantheon, a pagan temple at Rome, was consecrated as a Christian church for the honor of Our Lady and the martyrs (later all saints). In 835, Gregory IV fixed Nov. 1 as the date of observance.

All Souls, Commemoration of the Faithful Departed, Nov. 2. The dead were prayed for from the earliest days of Christianity. By the sixth century it was customary in Benedictine monasteries to hold a commemoration of deceased members of the order at Pentecost. A common commemoration of all the faithful departed on the day after All Saints was instituted in 998 by St. Odilo, of the Abbey of Cluny, and an observance of this kind was accepted in Rome in the 14th century.

Annunciation of the Lord (formerly, Annunciation of the Blessed Virgin Mary), Mar. 25, solemnity. A feast of the Incarnation which commemorates the announcement by the Archangel Gabriel to the Virgin Mary that she was to become the Mother of Christ (Lk. 1:26-38), and the miraculous conception of Christ by her. The feast was instituted about 430 in the East. The Roman observance dates from the seventh century, when celebration was said to be universal.

Ascension of the Lord, movable observance held 40 days after Easter, holy day of obligation, solemnity. Commemorates the Ascension of Christ into heaven 40 days after his Resurrection from the dead (Mk. 16:19; Lk. 24:51; Acts 1:2). The feast recalls the completion of Christ's mission on earth for the salvation of all people and his entry into heaven with glorified human nature. The Ascension is a pledge of the final glorification of all who achieve salvation. Documentary evidence of the feast dates from early in the fifth century, but it was observed long before that time in connection with Pentecost and Easter.

Ash Wednesday, movable observance, six and one-half weeks before Easter. It was set as the first day of Lent by Pope St. Gregory the Great (590-604) with the extension of an earlier and shorter penitential season to a total period including 40 weekdays of fasting before Easter. It is a day of fast and abstinence. Ashes, symbolic of penance, are blessed and distributed among the faithful during the day. They are used to mark the forehead with the Sign of the Cross, with the reminder: "Remember you are dust, and to dust you will return," or: "Turn away from sin and be faithful to the Gospel."

Assumption, Aug. 15, holy day of obligation, solemnity. Commemorates the taking into heaven of Mary, soul and body, at the end of her life on earth, a truth of faith that was proclaimed a dogma by Pius XII on Nov. 1, 1950. One of the oldest and most solemn feasts of Mary, it has a history dating back to at least the seventh century when its celebration was already established at Jerusalem and Rome.

Baptism of the Lord, movable, usually celebrated on the Sunday after January 6, feast. Recalls the baptism of Christ by John the Baptist (Mk. 1:9-11), an event associated with the liturgy of the Epiphany. This baptism was the occasion for Christ's manifestation of himself at the beginning of his public life.

Birth of Mary, Sept. 8, feast. This is a very old feast which originated in the East and found place in the Roman liturgy in the seventh century.

Candlemas Day, Feb. 2. See **Presentation of the Lord**.

Chair of Peter, Feb. 22, feast. The feast, which has been in the Roman calendar since 336, is a liturgical expression of belief in the episcopacy and hierarchy of the Church.

Christmas, Birth of Our Lord Jesus Christ, Dec. 25, holy day of obligation, solemnity. Commemorates the birth of Christ (Lk. 2:1-20). This event was originally commemorated in the East on the feast of Epiphany or Theophany. The Christmas feast itself originated in the West; by 354 it was certainly kept on Dec. 25. This date may have been set for the observance to offset pagan ceremonies held at about the same time to commemorate the birth of the sun at the winter solstice. There are texts for three Christmas Masses at midnight, dawn, and during the day.

Christ the King, movable, celebrated on the last Sunday of the liturgical year, solemnity. Commemorates the royal prerogatives of Christ and is equivalent to a declaration of his rights to the homage, service and fidelity of all people in all phases of individual and social life. Pius XI instituted the feast Dec. 11, 1925.

Conversion of St. Paul, Jan. 25, feast. An observance mentioned in some calendars from the 8th and 9th centuries. Pope Innocent III (1198-1216) ordered its observance with great solemnity.

Corpus Christi (The Body and Blood of Christ), movable, celebrated on the Thursday (or Sunday, as in the U.S.) following Trinity Sunday, solemnity. Commemorates the institution of the Holy Eucharist (Mt. 26:26-28). The feast originated at Liège in 1246 and was extended throughout the Church in the West by Urban IV in 1264. St. Thomas Aquinas composed the Liturgy of the Hours for the feast.

Cross, The Holy, Sept. 14, feast. Commemorates the finding of the Cross on which Christ was crucified, in 326 through the efforts of St. Helena, mother of Constantine; the consecration of the Basilica of the Holy Sepulchre nearly 10 years later: and the recovery in 628 or 629 by Emperor Heraclius of a major portion of the cross which had been removed by the Persians from its place of veneration at Jerusalem. The feast originated in Jerusalem and spread through the East before being adopted in the West. General adoption followed the building at Rome of the Basilica of the Holy Cross "in Jerusalem," so called because it was the place of enshrinement of a major portion of the cross of crucifixion.

Dedication of St. John Lateran, Nov. 9, feast. Commemorates the first public consecration of a church, that of the Basilica of the Most Holy Savior by Pope St. Sylvester about 324. The church, as well as the Lateran Palace, was the gift of Emperor Constantine. Since the 12th century it has been known as St. John Lateran, in honor of John the Baptist after whom the adjoining baptistery was named. It was rebuilt by Innocent X (1644-55), reconsecrated by Benedict XIII in 1726, and enlarged by Leo XIII (1878-1903). This basilica is regarded as the church of highest dignity in Rome and throughout the Roman rite.

Dedication of St. Mary Major, Aug. 5, optional memorial. Commemorates the rebuilding and dedication by Pope Sixtus III (432-40) of a church in honor of Blessed Mary the Virgin. This is the Basilica of St. Mary Major on the Esquiline Hill in Rome. An earlier building was erected during the pontificate of Liberius (352-66); according to legend, it was located on a site covered by a miraculous fall of snow seen by a nobleman favored with a vision of Mary.

Easter, movable celebration held on the first Sunday after the full moon following the vernal equinox (between Mar. 22 and Apr. 25), solemnity with an octave. Commemorates the Resurrection of Christ from the dead (Mk. 16:1-7). The observance of this mystery, kept since the first days of the Church, extends throughout the Easter season which lasts until the feast of Pentecost, a period of 50 days. Every Sunday in the year is regarded as a "little" Easter. The date of Easter determines the dates of movable feasts, such as Ascension and Pentecost, and the number of weeks before Lent and after Pentecost.

Easter Vigil, called by St. Augustine the "Mother of All Vigils," the night before Easter. Ceremonies are all related to the Resurrection and renewal-in-grace theme of Easter: blessing of the new fire, procession with the Easter Candle, singing of the Easter Proclamation (*Exsultet*), Liturgy of the Word with at least three Old Testament readings, the Litany of Saints, blessing of water, baptism of converts and infants, renewal of baptismal promises, Liturgy of the Eucharist. The vigil ceremonies are held after nightfall on Saturday.

Epiphany of the Lord, Jan. 6 or (in the U.S.) a Sunday between Jan. 2 and 8, solemnity. Commemorates the manifestations of the divinity of Christ. It is one of the oldest Christian feasts, with an Eastern origin traceable to the beginning of the third century and antedating the Western feast of Christmas. Originally, it commemorated the manifestations of Christ's divinity — or Theophany — in his birth, the homage of the Magi, and baptism by John the Baptist. Later, the first two of these commemorations were transferred to Christmas when the Eastern Church adopted that feast between 380 and 430. The central feature of the Eastern observance now is the manifestation or declaration of Christ's divinity in his baptism and at the beginning of his public life. The Epiphany was adopted by the Western Church during the same period in which the Eastern Church accepted Christmas. In the Roman rite, commemoration is made in the Mass of the homage of the wise men from the East (Mt. 2:1-12).

Good Friday, the Friday before Easter, the second day of the Easter Triduum. Liturgical elements of the observance are commemoration of the Passion and Death of Christ in the reading of the Passion (according to John), special prayers for the Church and people

of all ranks, the veneration of the Cross, and a Communion service. The celebration takes place in the afternoon, preferably at 3:00 p.m.

Guardian Angels, Oct. 2, memorial. Commemorates the angels who protect people from spiritual and physical dangers and assist them in doing good. A feast in their honor celebrated in Spain in the 16th century was placed in the Roman calendar in 1615 and Oct. 2 was set as the date of observance. Earlier, guardian angels were honored liturgically in conjunction with the feast of St. Michael.

Holy Family, movable observance on the Sunday after Christmas, feast. Commemorates the Holy Family of Jesus, Mary and Joseph as the model of domestic society, holiness and virtue. The devotional background of the feast was very strong in the 17th century. In the 18th century, in prayers composed for a special Mass, a Canadian bishop likened the Christian family to the Holy Family. Leo XIII consecrated families to the Holy Family. In 1921, Benedict XV extended the Divine Office and Mass of the feast to the whole Church.

Holy Innocents, Dec. 28, feast. Commemorates the infants who suffered death at the hands of Herod's soldiers seeking to kill the child Jesus (Mt. 2:13-18). A feast in their honor has been observed since the fifth century.

Holy Saturday, the day before Easter. The Sacrifice of the Mass is not celebrated, and Holy Communion may be given only as Viaticum. If possible the Easter fast should be observed until the Easter Vigil.

Holy Thursday, the Thursday before Easter. Commemorates the institution of the sacraments of the Eucharist and holy orders, and the washing of the feet of the Apostles by Jesus at the Last Supper. The Mass of the Lord's Supper in the evening marks the beginning of the Easter Triduum. Following the Mass, there is a procession of the Blessed Sacrament to a place of reposition for adoration by the faithful. Usually at an earlier Mass of Chrism, bishops bless oils (of catechumens, chrism, the sick) for use during the year. (For pastoral reasons, diocesan bishops may permit additional Masses, but these should not overshadow the principal Mass of the Lord's Supper.)

Immaculate Conception, Dec. 8, holy day of obligation, solemnity. Commemorates the fact that Mary, in view of her calling to be the Mother of Christ and in virtue of his merits, was preserved from the first moment of her conception from original sin and was filled with grace from the very beginning of her life. She was the only person so preserved from original sin. The present form of the feast dates from Dec. 8, 1854, when Pius IX defined the dogma of the Immaculate Conception An earlier feast of the Conception, which testified to long-existing belief in this truth, was observed in the East by the eighth century, in Ireland in the ninth, and subsequently in European countries. In 1846, Mary was proclaimed patroness of the U.S. under this title.

Immaculate Heart of Mary, Saturday following the second Sunday after Pentecost, memorial. On May 4, 1944, Pius XII ordered this feast observed throughout the Church in order to obtain Mary's intercession for "peace among nations, freedom for the Church, the conversion of sinners, the love of purity and the practice of virtue." Two years earlier, he consecrated the entire human race to Mary under this title. Devotion to Mary under the title of her Most Pure Heart originated during the Middle Ages. It was given great impetus in the 17th century by the preaching of St. John Eudes, who was the first to celebrate a Mass and Divine Office of Mary under this title. A feast, celebrated in various places and on different dates, was authorized in 1799.

Joachim and Ann, July 26, memorial. Commemorates the parents of Mary. A joint feast, celebrated Sept. 9, originated in the East near the end of the sixth century. Devotion to Ann, introduced in the eighth century at Rome, became widespread in Europe in the 14th century; her feast was extended throughout the Latin Church in 1584. A feast of Joachim was introduced in the West in the 15th century.

John the Baptist, Birth of, June 24, solemnity. The precursor of Christ, whose cousin he was, was commemorated universally in the liturgy by the fourth century. He is the only saint, except the Blessed Virgin Mary, whose birthday is observed as a feast. Another feast, on Aug. 29, commemorates his passion and death at the order of Herod (Mk. 6:14-29).

Joseph, Mar. 19, solemnity. Joseph is honored as the husband of the Blessed Virgin Mary, the patron and protector of the universal Church and workman. Devotion to him already existed in the eighth century in the East, and in the 11th in the West. Various feasts were celebrated before the 15th century when Mar. 19 was fixed for his commemoration; this feast was extended to the whole Church in 1621 by Gregory XV. In 1955, Pius XII instituted the feast of St. Joseph the Workman for observance May 1; this feast, which may be celebrated by local option, supplanted the Solemnity or Patronage of St. Joseph formerly observed on the third Wednesday after Easter. St. Joseph was proclaimed protector and patron of the universal Church in 1870 by Pius IX.

Michael, Gabriel and Raphael, Archangels, Sept. 29, feast. A feast bearing the title of Dedication of St. Michael the Archangel formerly commemorated on this date the consecration in 530 of a church near Rome in honor of Michael, the first angel given a liturgical feast. For a while, this feast was combined with a commemoration of the Guardian Angels. The separate feasts of Gabriel (Mar. 24) and Raphael (Oct. 24) were suppressed by the calendar in effect since 1970 and this joint feast of the three archangels was instituted.

Octave of Christmas, Jan. 1. See **Solemnity of Mary, Mother of God**.

Our Lady of Guadalupe, Dec. 12, feast (in the U.S.). Commemorates under this title the appearances of the Blessed Virgin Mary in 1531 to an Indian, Juan Diego, on Tepeyac hill outside Mexico City (see Apparitions of the Blessed Virgin Mary). The celebration, observed as a memorial in the U.S., was raised to the rank of feast at the request of the National Conference of Catholic Bishops. Approval was granted in a decree dated Jan. 8, 1988.

Our Lady of Sorrows, Sept. 15, memorial. Recalls the sorrows experienced by Mary in her association with Christ: the prophecy of Simeon (Lk. 2:34-35), the flight into Egypt (Mt. 2:13-21), the three-day separation from Jesus (Lk. 2:41-50), and four incidents connected with the Passion — her meeting with Christ on the way to Calvary, the crucifixion, the removal of

Christ's body from the cross, and his burial (Mt. 27:31-61; Mk. 15:20-47; Lk. 23:26-56; Jn. 19:17-42). A Mass and Divine Office of the feast were celebrated by the Servites, especially, in the 17th century, and in 1814 Pius VII extended the observance to the whole Church.

Our Lady of the Rosary, Oct. 7, memorial. Commemorates the Virgin Mary through recall of the mysteries of the Rosary which recapitulate events in her life and the life of Christ. The feast was instituted in 1573 to commemorate a Christian victory over invading the forces of the Ottoman Empire at Lepanto in 1571, and was extended throughout the Church by Clement XI in 1716.

Passion Sunday (formerly called Palm Sunday), the Sunday before Easter. Marks the start of Holy Week by recalling the triumphal entry of Christ into Jerusalem at the beginning of the last week of his life (Mt. 21:1-9). A procession and other ceremonies commemorating this event were held in Jerusalem from very early Christian times and were adopted in Rome by the ninth century, when the blessing of palm for the occasion was introduced. Full liturgical observance includes the blessing of palm and a procession before the principal Mass of the day. The Passion, by Matthew, Mark or Luke, is read during the Mass.

Pentecost, also called **Whitsunday**, movable celebration held 50 days after Easter, solemnity. Commemorates the descent of the Holy Spirit upon the Apostles, the preaching of Peter and the other Apostles to Jews in Jerusalem, the baptism and aggregation of some 3,000 persons to the Christian community (Acts 2:1-41). It is regarded as the birthday of the Catholic Church. The original observance of the feast antedated the earliest extant documentary evidence from the third century.

Peter and Paul, June 29, solemnity. Commemorates the martyrdoms of Peter by crucifixion and Paul by beheading during the Neronian persecution. This joint commemoration of the chief Apostles dates at least from 258 at Rome.

Presentation of the Lord (formerly called Purification of the Blessed Virgin Mary, also Candlemas), Feb. 2, feast. Commemorates the presentation of Jesus in the Temple — according to prescriptions of Mosaic Law (Lv. 12:2-8; Ex. 13:2; Lk. 2:22-32) — and the purification of Mary 40 days after his birth. In the East, where the feast antedated fourth century testimony regarding its existence, it was observed primarily as a feast of Our Lord; in the West, where it was adopted later, it was regarded more as a feast of Mary until the calendar in effect since 1970. Its date was set for Feb. 2 after the celebration of Christmas was fixed for Dec. 25, late in the fourth century. The blessing of candles, probably in commemoration of Christ who was the Light to enlighten the Gentiles, became common about the 11th century and gave the feast the secondary name of Candlemas.

Queenship of Mary, Aug. 22, memorial. Commemorates the high dignity of Mary as Queen of heaven, angels and men. Universal observance of the memorial was ordered by Pius XII in the encyclical *Ad Caeli Reginam*, Oct. 11, 1954, near the close of a Marian Year observed in connection with the centenary of the proclamation of the dogma of the Immaculate Conception and four years after the proclamation of the dogma of the Assumption. The original date of the memorial was May 31.

Resurrection. See **Easter**.

Sacred Heart of Jesus, movable observance held on the Friday after the second Sunday after Pentecost (Corpus Christi, in the U.S.), solemnity. The object of the devotion is the divine Person of Christ, whose heart is the symbol of his love for all people — for whom he accomplished the work of Redemption. The Mass and Office now used on the feast were prescribed by Pius XI in 1929. Devotion to the Sacred Heart was introduced into the liturgy in the 17th century through the efforts of St. John Eudes who composed an Office and Mass for the feast. It was furthered as the result of the revelations of St. Margaret Mary Alacoque after 1675 and by the work of St. Claude de la Colombière, S.J. In 1765, Clement XIII approved a Mass and Office for the feast, and in 1856 Pius IX extended the observance throughout the Roman rite.

Solemnity of Mary, Mother of God, Jan. 1, holy day of obligation, solemnity. The calendar in effect since 1970, in accord with Eastern tradition, reinstated the Marian character of this commemoration on the octave day of Christmas. The former feast of the Circumcision, dating at least from the first half of the sixth century, marked the initiation of Jesus (Lk. 2:21) in Judaism and by analogy focused attention on the initiation of persons in the Christian religion and their incorporation in Christ through baptism. The feast of the Solemnity supplants the former feast of the Maternity of Mary observed on Oct. 11.

Transfiguration of the Lord, Aug. 6, feast. Commemorates the revelation of his divinity by Christ to Peter, James and John on Mt. Tabor (Mt. 17:1-9). The feast, which is very old, was extended throughout the universal Church in 1457 by Callistus III.

Trinity, The Holy, movable observance held on the Sunday after Pentecost, solemnity. Commemorates the most sublime mystery of the Christian faith, i.e., that there are Three Divine Persons — Father, Son and Holy Spirit — in one God (Mt. 28:18-20). A votive Mass of the Most Holy Trinity dates from the seventh century; an Office was composed in the 10th century; in 1334, John XXII extended the feast to the universal Church.

Visitation, May 31, feast. Commemorates Mary's visit to her cousin Elizabeth after the Annunciation and before the birth of John the Baptist, the precursor of Christ (Lk. 1:39-47). The feast had a medieval origin and was observed in the Franciscan Order before being extended throughout the Church by Urban VI in 1389. It is one of the feasts of the Incarnation and is notable for its recall of the *Magnificat*, one of the few New Testament canticles, which acknowledges the unique gifts of God to Mary because of her role in the redemptive work of Christ. The canticle is recited at Evening Prayer in the Liturgy of the Hours.

Liturgical Life of the Church

The nature and purpose of the liturgy, along with norms for its revision, were the subject matter of *Sacrosanctum Concilium* (the Constitution on the Sacred Liturgy) promulgated by the Second Vatican Council. The principles and guidelines stated in this document, the first issued by the Council, are summarized here and/or are incorporated in other Almanac entries on liturgical subjects.

Nature and Purpose of Liturgy

The paragraphs under this and the following subhead are quoted directly from *Sacrosanctum Concilium* (Constitution on the Sacred Liturgy).

"It is through the liturgy, especially the divine Eucharistic Sacrifice, that 'the work of our redemption is exercised.' The liturgy is thus the outstanding means by which the faithful can express in their lives, and manifest to others, the mystery of Christ and the real nature of the true Church" (No. 2).

"The liturgy is considered as an exercise of the priestly office of Jesus Christ. In the liturgy the sanctification of man is manifested by signs perceptible to the senses, and is effected in a way which is proper to each of these signs; in the liturgy full public worship is performed by the Mystical Body of Jesus Christ, that is, by the Head and his members.

"From this it follows that every liturgical celebration, because it is an action of Christ the priest and of his Body the Church, is a sacred action surpassing all others. No other action of the Church can match its claim to efficacy, nor equal the degree of it" (No. 7).

"The liturgy is the summit toward which the activity of the Church is directed; at the same time it is the fountain from which all her power flows. For the goal of apostolic works is that all who are made sons of God by faith and baptism should come together to praise God in the midst of his Church, to take part in her sacrifice, and to eat the Lord's Supper.

"From the liturgy, therefore, and especially from the Eucharist, as from a fountain, grace is channeled into us; and the sanctification of men in Christ and the glorification of God, to which all other activities of the Church are directed as toward their goal, are most powerfully achieved" (No. 10).

Full Participation

"Mother Church earnestly desires that all the faithful be led to that full, conscious, and active participation in liturgical celebrations which is demanded by the very nature of the liturgy. Such participation by the Christian people as 'a chosen race, a royal priesthood, a holy nation, a purchased people' (1 Pt. 2:9; cf. 2:4-5), is their right and duty by reason of their baptism.

"In the restoration and promotion of the sacred liturgy, this full and active participation by all the people is the aim to be considered before all else; for it is the primary and indispensable source from which the faithful are to derive the true Christian spirit" (No. 14).

"In order that the Christian people may more securely derive an abundance of graces from the sacred liturgy, holy Mother Church desires to undertake with great care a general restoration of the liturgy itself. For the liturgy is made up of unchangeable elements divinely instituted, and elements subject to change. The latter not only may but ought to be changed with the passing of time if features have by chance crept in which are less harmonious with the intimate nature of the liturgy, or if existing elements have grown less functional.

"In this restoration, both texts and rites should be drawn up so that they express more clearly the holy things which they signify. Christian people, as far as possible, should be able to understand them with ease and to take part in them fully, actively, and as befits a community" (No. 21).

Norms

Norms regarding the reforms concern the greater use of Scripture; emphasis on the importance of the sermon or homily on biblical and liturgical subjects; use of vernacular languages for prayers of the Mass and for administration of the sacraments; provision for adaptation of rites to cultural patterns.

Approval for reforms of various kinds — in liturgical texts, rites, etc. — depends on the Holy See, regional conferences of bishops and individual bishops, according to provisions of law. No priest has authority to initiate reforms on his own. Reforms may not be introduced just for the sake of innovation, and any that are introduced in the light of present-day circumstances should embody sound tradition.

To assure the desired effect of liturgical reforms, training and instruction are necessary for the clergy, religious and the laity. The functions of diocesan and regional commissions for liturgy, music and art are to set standards and provide leadership for instruction and practical programs in their respective fields.

Most of the constitution's provisions regarding liturgical reforms have to do with the Roman rite. The document clearly respects the equal dignity of all rites, leaving to the Eastern Churches control over their ancient liturgies.

(For coverage of the Mystery of the Eucharist, *see* **The Mass**; other sacraments, *see* separate entries.)

Sacramentals

Sacramentals, instituted by the Church, "are sacred signs which bear a resemblance to the sacraments: they signify effects, particularly of a spiritual kind, which are obtained through the Church's intercession. By them men are disposed to receive the chief effect of the sacraments, and various occasions in life are rendered holy" (No. 60).

"Thus, for well-disposed members of the faithful, the liturgy of the sacraments and sacramentals sanctifies almost every event in their lives; they are given access to the stream of divine grace which flows from the paschal mystery of the passion, death, and resurrection of Christ, the fountain from which all sacraments and sacramentals draw their power. There is hardly any proper use of material things which cannot thus be directed toward the sanctification of men and the praise of God" (No. 61).

Some common sacramentals are priestly blessings, blessed palm, candles, holy water, medals, scapulars, prayers and ceremonies of the Roman Ritual.

Liturgy of the Hours

The Liturgy of the Hours (Divine Office) is the public prayer of the Church for praising God and sanctifying the day. Its daily celebration is required as a sacred obligation by men in holy orders and by men and women religious who have professed solemn vows. Its celebration by others is highly commended and is to be encouraged in the community of the faithful.

"By tradition going back to early Christian times, the Divine Office is arranged so that the whole course of the day and night is made holy by the praises of God. Therefore, when this wonderful song of praise is worthily rendered by priests and others who are deputed for this purpose by Church ordinance, or by the faithful praying together with the priest in an approved form, then it is truly the voice of the bride addressing her bridegroom; it is the very prayer which Christ himself, together with his Body, addresses to the Father" (No. 84).

"Hence all who perform this service are not only fulfilling a duty of the Church, but also are sharing in the greatest honor accorded to Christ's spouse, for by offering these praises to God they are standing before God's throne in the name of the Church their Mother" (No. 85).

Revised Hours

The Liturgy of the Hours, revised since 1965, was the subject of Pope Paul VI's apostolic constitution *Laudis Canticum*, dated Nov. 1, 1970. The master Latin text was published in 1971; its four volumes have been published in authorized English translation since May 1975.

One-volume, partial editions of the Liturgy of the Hours containing Morning and Evening Prayer and other elements, have been published in approved English translation.

The revised Liturgy of the Hours consists of:

• Office of Readings, for reflection on the word of God. The principal parts are three psalms, biblical and non-biblical readings.

• Morning and Evening Prayer, called the "hinges" of the Liturgy of the Hours. The principal parts are a hymn, two psalms, an Old or New Testament canticle, a brief biblical reading, Zechariah's canticle (the *Benedictus*, morning) or Mary's canticle (the *Magnificat*, evening), responsories, intercessions and a concluding prayer.

• Daytime Prayer. The principal parts are a hymn, three psalms, a biblical reading and one of three concluding prayers corresponding to the time of day.

• Night Prayer. The principal parts are one or two psalms, a brief biblical reading, Simeon's canticle (*Nunc Dimittis*), a concluding prayer and an antiphon in honor of Mary.

In the revised Liturgy of the Hours, the hours are shorter than they had been, with greater textual variety, meditation aids, and provision for intervals of silence and meditation. The psalms are distributed over a four-week period instead of a week; some psalms, entirely or in part, are not included. Additional canticles from the Old and New Testaments are assigned for Morning and Evening Prayer. Additional scriptural texts have been added and variously arranged for greater internal unity, correspondence to readings at Mass, and relevance to events and themes of salvation history. Readings include some of the best material from the Fathers of the Church and other authors, and improved selections on the lives of the saints.

The book used for recitation of the *Office is the Breviary*.

For coverage of the Liturgical Year, see **Church Calendar**.

Sacred Music

"The musical tradition of the universal Church is a treasure of immeasurable value, greater even than that of any other art. The main reason for this pre-eminence is that, as sacred melody united to words, it forms a necessary or integral part of the solemn liturgy.

"Sacred music increases in holiness to the degree that it is intimately linked with liturgical action, winningly expresses prayerfulness, promotes solidarity, and enriches sacred rites with heightened solemnity. The Church indeed approves of all forms of true art, and admits them into divine worship when they show appropriate qualities" (No. 112).

The constitution decreed:

• Vernacular languages for the people's parts of the liturgy, as well as Latin, may be used.

• Participation in sacred song by the whole body of the faithful, and not just by choirs, is to be encouraged and brought about.

• Provisions should be made for proper musical training for clergy, religious and lay persons.

• While Gregorian Chant has a unique dignity and relationship to the Latin liturgy, other kinds of music are acceptable.

• Native musical traditions should be used, especially in mission areas.

• Various instruments compatible with the dignity of worship may be used.

Gregorian Chant: A form and style of chant called Gregorian was the basis and most highly regarded standard of liturgical music for centuries. It originated probably during the formative period of the Roman liturgy and developed in conjunction with Gallican and other forms of chant. Pope St. Gregory I the

Great's connection with it is not clear, although it is known that he had great concern for and interest in church music. The earliest extant written versions of Gregorian Chant date from the ninth century. A thousand years later, the Benedictines of Solesmes, France, initiated a revival of chant which gave impetus to the modern liturgical movement.

Sacred Art and Furnishings

"Very rightly the fine arts are considered to rank among the noblest expressions of human genius. This judgment applies especially to religious art and to its highest achievement, which is sacred art. By their very nature both of the latter are related to God's boundless beauty, for this is the reality which these human efforts are trying to express in some way. To the extent that these works aim exclusively at turning men's thoughts to God persuasively and devoutly, they are dedicated to God and to the cause of his greater honor and glory" (No. 122).

The objective of sacred art is "that all things set apart for use in divine worship should be truly worthy, becoming, and beautiful, signs and symbols of heavenly realities. The Church has always reserved to herself the right to pass judgment upon the arts, deciding which of the works of artists are in accordance with faith, piety, and cherished traditional laws, and thereby suited to sacred purposes.

"Sacred furnishings should worthily and beautifully serve the dignity of worship" (No. 122).

According to the constitution:

• Contemporary art, as well as that of the past, shall "be given free scope in the Church, provided that it adorns the sacred buildings and holy rites with due honor and reverence" (No. 123).

• Noble beauty, not sumptuous display, should be sought in art, sacred vestments and ornaments.

• "Let bishops carefully exclude from the house of God and from other sacred places those works of artists which are repugnant to faith, morals, and Christian piety, and which offend true religious sense either by their distortion of forms or by lack of artistic worth, by mediocrity or by pretense.

• "When churches are to be built, let great care be taken that they be suitable for the celebration of liturgical services and for the active participation of the faithful" (No. 124).

• "The practice of placing sacred images in churches so that they may be venerated by the faithful is to be firmly maintained. Nevertheless, their number should be moderate and their relative location should reflect right order. Otherwise they may create confusion among the Christian people and promote a faulty sense of devotion" (No. 125).

• Artists should be trained and inspired in the spirit and for the purposes of the liturgy.

• The norms of sacred art should be revised. "These laws refer especially to the worthy and well-planned construction of sacred buildings, the shape and construction of altars, the nobility, location, and security of the Eucharistic tabernacle, the suitability and dignity of the baptistery, the proper use of sacred images, embellishments, and vestments" (No. 128).

RITES

Rites are the forms and ceremonial observances of liturgical worship coupled with the total expression of the theological, spiritual and disciplinary heritages of particular churches of the East and the West.

Different rites have evolved in the course of church history, giving to liturgical worship and church life in general forms and usages peculiar and proper to the nature of worship and the culture of the faithful in various circumstances of time and place. Thus, there has been development since apostolic times in the prayers and ceremonies of the Mass, in the celebration of the sacraments, sacramentals and the Liturgy of the Hours, and in observances of the liturgical calendar. The principal sources of rites in present use were practices within the patriarchates of Rome (for the West) and Antioch, Alexandria and Constantinople (for the East). Rites are identified as Eastern or Western on the basis of their geographical area of origin in the Roman Empire.

Eastern and Roman Rites

Eastern rites are proper to Eastern Catholic Churches (see separate entry). The principal rites are Byzantine, Alexandrian, Antiochene, Armenian and Chaldean.

The Latin or Roman rite prevails in the Western Church. It was derived from Roman practices and the use of Latin from the third century onward, and has been the rite in general use in the West since the eighth century. Other rites in limited use in the Western Church have been the Ambrosian (in the Archdiocese of Milan), the Mozarabic (in the Archdiocese of Toledo), the Lyonnais, the Braga, and rites peculiar to some religious orders like the Dominicans, Carmelites and Carthusians.

The purpose of the revision of rites in progress since the Second Vatican Council is to renew them, not to eliminate the rites of particular churches or to reduce all rites to uniformity. The Council reaffirmed the equal dignity and preservation of rites as follows.

"It is the mind of the Catholic Church that each individual church or rite retain its traditions whole and entire, while adjusting its way of life to various needs of time and place. Such individual churches, whether of the East or the West, although they differ somewhat among themselves in what are called rites (that is, in liturgy, ecclesiastical discipline and spiritual heritage), are, nevertheless, equally entrusted to the pastoral guidance of the Roman Pontiff, the divinely appointed successor of St. Peter in supreme government over the universal Church. They are, consequently, of equal dignity, so that none of them is superior to the others by reason of rite."

Determination of Rite

Determination of a person's rite is regulated by church law. Through baptism, a child becomes a member of the rite of his or her parents. If the parents are of different rites, the child's rite is decided by mutual consent of the parents; if there is lack of mutual consent, the child is baptized in the rite of the father. A candidate for baptism over the age of 14 can choose to be baptized in any approved rite. Catholics baptized in one rite may receive the sacraments in any of the approved ritual churches; they may transfer to another rite only with the permission of the Holy See and in accordance with other provisions of the Code of Canon Law.

MASS, EUCHARISTIC SACRIFICE AND BANQUET

Declarations of Vatican II

The Second Vatican Council made the following declarations among others with respect to the Mass:

"At the Last Supper, on the night when he was betrayed, our Savior instituted the Eucharistic Sacrifice of his Body and Blood. He did this in order to perpetuate the Sacrifice of the Cross throughout the centuries until he should come again, and so to entrust to his beloved spouse, the Church, a memorial of his death and resurrection: a sacrament of love, a sign of unity, a bond of charity, a paschal banquet in which Christ is consumed, the mind is filled with grace, and a pledge of future glory is given to us" (*Sacrosanctum Concilium*, Constitution on the Sacred Liturgy, No. 47).

"… As often as the Sacrifice of the Cross in which 'Christ, our Passover, has been sacrificed' (1 Cor. 5:7) is celebrated on an altar, the work of our redemption is carried on. At the same time, in the sacrament of the Eucharistic bread the unity of all believers who form one body in Christ (cf. 1 Cor. 10:17) is both expressed and brought about. All men are called to this union with Christ" (*Lumen Gentium*, Dogmatic Constitution on the Church, No. 3).

"… The ministerial priest, by the sacred power he enjoys, molds and rules the priestly people. Acting in the person of Christ, he brings about the Eucharistic Sacrifice, and offers it to God in the name of all the people. For their part, the faithful join in the offering of the Eucharist by virtue of their royal priesthood" (Ibid., No. 10).

Declarations of Trent

Among its decrees on the Holy Eucharist, the Council of Trent stated the following points of doctrine on the Mass.

1. There is in the Catholic Church a true sacrifice, the Mass instituted by Jesus Christ. It is the sacrifice of his Body and Blood, Soul and Divinity, himself, under the appearances of bread and wine.

2. This Sacrifice is identical with the Sacrifice of the Cross, inasmuch as Christ is the Priest and Victim in both. A difference lies in the manner of offering, which was bloody upon the Cross and is bloodless on the altar.

3. The Mass is a propitiatory Sacrifice, atoning for the sins of the living and dead for whom it is offered.

4. The efficacy of the Mass is derived from the Sacrifice of the Cross, whose superabundant merits it applies to men.

5. Although the Mass is offered to God alone, it may be celebrated in honor and memory of the saints.

6. Christ instituted the Mass at the Last Supper.

7. Christ ordained the Apostles priests, giving them power and the command to consecrate his Body and Blood to perpetuate and renew the Sacrifice.

ORDER OF THE MASS

The Mass consists of two principal divisions called the **Liturgy of the Word**, which features the proclamation of the Word of God, and the **Eucharistic Liturgy**, which focuses on the central act of sacrifice in the Consecration and on the Eucharistic Banquet in Holy Communion. (Formerly, these divisions were called, respectively, the **Mass of the Catechumens**

and the **Mass of the Faithful**.) In addition to these principal divisions, there are ancillary introductory and concluding rites.

The following description covers the Mass as celebrated with participation by the people. This Order of the Mass was approved by Pope Paul VI in the apostolic constitution *Missale Romanum* dated Apr. 3, 1969, and promulgated in a decree issued Apr. 6, 1969, by the Congregation for Divine Worship. The assigned effective date was Nov. 30, 1969.

Introductory Rites

Entrance: The introductory rites begin with the singing or recitation of an entrance song consisting of one or more scriptural verses stating the theme of the mystery, season or feast commemorated in the Mass.

Greeting: The priest and people make the Sign of the Cross together. The priest then greets them in one of several alternative ways and they reply in a corresponding manner.

Introductory Remarks: At this point, the priest or another of the ministers may introduce the theme of the Mass.

Penitential Rite: The priest and people together acknowledge their sins as a preliminary step toward worthy celebration of the sacred mysteries.

This rite includes a brief examination of conscience, a general confession of sin and plea for divine mercy in one of several ways, and a prayer for forgiveness by the priest.

Glory to God: A doxology, a hymn of praise to God, sung or said on festive occasions.

Opening Prayer: A prayer of petition offered by the priest on behalf of the worshiping community.

I. Liturgy of the Word

Readings: The featured elements of this liturgy are readings of passages from the Bible. If three readings are in order, the first is usually from the Old Testament, the second from the New Testament (Letters, Acts, Revelation), and the third from one of the Gospels; the final reading is always a selection from a Gospel. The first reading(s) is (are) concluded with the formula, "The Word of the Lord" (effective Feb. 28, 1993; optional before that date), to which the people respond, "Thanks be to God." The Gospel reading is concluded with the formula, "The Gospel of the Lord," (effective as above), to which the people respond, "Praise to you, Lord Jesus Christ." Between the readings, psalm verses are sung or recited. A Gospel acclamation is either sung or omitted.

Homily: An explanation, pertinent to the mystery being celebrated and the special needs of the listeners, of some point in either the readings from sacred Scripture or in another text from the Ordinary or Proper parts of the Mass; it is a proclamation of the Good News for a response of faith.

Creed: The Nicene profession of faith, by priest and people, on certain occasions.

Prayer of the Faithful: Litany-type prayers of petition, with participation by the people. Called general intercessions, they concern needs of the Church, the salvation of the world, public authorities, persons in need, the local community.

PRAYER TO OUR LADY OF THE MIRACULOUS MEDAL

Virgin Mother of God,
Mary Immaculate,
   I unite myself to you
under your title of Our Lady of the
   Miraculous Medal.
May this medal be for me
   a sure sign of your motherly
   affection for me
   and a constant reminder of my filial
   duties toward you.
While wearing it,
   may I be blessed by your loving
   protection
   and preserved in the grace of your
   Son.

Most powerful Virgin, Mother of our
Savior,
   keep me close to you every moment
   of my life,
   so that like you I may live and act
   according to the teaching and
   example of your Son. Amen.

NATIONAL SHRINE OF OUR LADY OF THE MIRACULOUS MEDAL
Perryville, Missouri

2004

	JANUARY					
S	M	T	W	T	F	S
				1	2	3
4	5	6	7	8	9	10
11	12	13	14	15	16	17
18	19	20	21	22	23	24
25	26	27	28	29	30	31

	FEBRUARY					
S	M	T	W	T	F	S
1	2	3	4	5	6	7
8	9	10	11	12	13	14
15	16	17	18	19	20	21
22	23	24	●	26	●	28
29						

	MARCH					
S	M	T	W	T	F	S
	1	2	3	4	5	●
7	8	9	10	●	●	13
14	15	16	17	18	19	20
21	22	23	24	25	●	27
28	29	30	31			

	APRIL					
S	M	T	W	T	F	S
				1	2	3
4	5	6	7	●	●	10
11	12	13	14	15	16	17
18	19	20	21	22	23	24
25	26	27	28	29	30	

	MAY					
S	M	T	W	T	F	S
						1
2	3	4	5	6	7	8
9	10	11	12	13	14	15
16	17	18	19	20	21	22
23	24	25	26	27	28	29
30	31					

	JUNE					
S	M	T	W	T	F	S
		1	2	3	4	5
6	7	8	9	10	11	12
13	14	15	16	17	18	19
20	21	22	23	24	25	26
27	28	29	30			

	JULY					
S	M	T	W	T	F	S
				1	2	3
4	5	6	7	8	9	10
11	12	13	14	15	16	17
18	19	20	21	22	23	24
25	26	27	28	29	30	31

	AUGUST					
S	M	T	W	T	F	S
1	2	3	4	5	6	7
8	9	10	11	12	13	14
15	16	17	18	19	20	21
22	23	24	25	26	27	28
29	30	31				

	SEPTEMBER					
S	M	T	W	T	F	S
			1	2	3	4
5	6	7	8	9	10	11
12	13	14	15	16	17	18
19	20	21	22	23	24	25
26	27	28	29	30		

	OCTOBER					
S	M	T	W	T	F	S
					1	2
3	4	5	6	7	8	9
10	11	12	13	14	15	16
17	18	19	20	21	22	23
24	25	26	27	28	29	30
31						

	NOVEMBER					
S	M	T	W	T	F	S
	1	2	3	4	5	6
7	8	9	10	11	12	13
14	15	16	17	18	19	20
21	22	23	24	25	26	27
28	29	30				

	DECEMBER					
S	M	T	W	T	F	S
			1	2	3	4
5	6	7	8	9	10	11
12	13	14	15	16	17	18
19	20	21	22	23	24	25
26	27	28	29	30	31	

Sundays and Holy Days of Obligation are printed in red.

● Days of Total Abstinence

Some of the spiritual benefits offered by the Association of the Miraculous Medal

Novenas for Promoters and Members:
January 15th to 23rd
February 3rd to 11th
March 17th to 25th
April 18th to 26th
May 16th to 24th
June 12th to 20th
July 2nd to 10th
August 7th to 15th
September 7th to 15th
October 7th to 15th
November 19th to 27th
December 8th to 16th

Rosary Novena: October 7th to 15th

Novena for Promoters:
November 29th to December 7th

Novena for Christmas Remembrance cards:
December 25th to January 2nd

Novena for donors and their intentions:
December 25th to January 2nd

Monthly Novenas for Promoters
beginning on the 6th of each month
Monthly Mass on the 1st of each month
for postage donors

Weekly Masses:
Monday for the Christmas Remembrance cards
In Kenya for Mission donors

II. Eucharistic Liturgy

Presentation and Preparation of Gifts: Presentation to the priest of the gifts of bread and wine, principally, by participating members of the congregation. Preparation of the gifts consists of the prayers and ceremonies with which the priest offers bread and wine as the elements of the sacrifice to take place during the Eucharistic Prayer and of the Lord's Supper to be shared in Holy Communion.

Washing of Hands: After offering the bread and wine, the priest cleanses his fingers with water in a brief ceremony of purification.

Pray, Brothers and Sisters: Prayer that the sacrifice to take place will be acceptable to God. The first part of the prayer is said by the priest; the second, by the people.

Prayer over the Gifts: A prayer of petition offered by the priest on behalf of the worshipping community.

Eucharistic Prayer

Preface: A hymn of praise, introducing the Eucharistic Prayer or Canon, sung or said by the priest following responses by the people. The Order of the Mass contains a variety of prefaces, for use on different occasions.

Holy, Holy, Holy; Blessed is He: Divine praises sung or said by the priest and people.

Eucharistic Prayer (Canon): Its central portion is the Consecration, when the essential act of sacrificial offering takes place with the changing of bread and wine into the Body and Blood of Christ. The various parts of the prayer, which are said by the celebrant only, commemorate principal mysteries of salvation history and include petitions for the Church, the living and dead, and remembrances of saints.

Doxology: A formula of divine praise sung or said by the priest while he holds aloft the chalice containing the consecrated wine in one hand and the paten containing the consecrated host in the other.

Communion Rite

Lord's Prayer: Sung or said by the priest and people.

Prayer for Deliverance from Evil: Called an embolism because it is a development of the final petition of the Lord's Prayer; said by the priest. It concludes with a memorial of the return of the Lord to which the people respond, "For the kingdom, the power, and the glory are yours, now and forever."

Prayer for Peace: Said by the priest, with corresponding responses by the people. The priest can, in accord with local custom, bid the people to exchange a greeting of peace with each other.

Lamb of God (*Agnus Dei*): A prayer for divine mercy sung or said while the priest breaks the consecrated host and places a piece of it into the consecrated wine in the chalice.

Communion: The priest, after saying a preparatory prayer, administers Holy Communion to himself and then to the people, thus completing the sacrifice-banquet of the Mass. (This completion is realized even if the celebrant alone receives the Eucharist.) On giving the Eucharist to each person under both species separately, the priest or eucharistic minister says, "The Body of Christ," "The Blood of Christ." The customary response is "Amen." If the Eucharist is given by intinction (in which the host is dipped into the consecrated wine), the priest says, "The Body and Blood of Christ."

Communion Song: Scriptural verses or a suitable hymn sung or said during the distribution of Holy Communion. After Holy Communion is received, some moments may be spent in silent meditation or in the chanting of a psalm or hymn of praise.

Prayer after Communion: A prayer of petition offered by the priest on behalf of the worshipping community.

Concluding Rite

Announcements: Brief announcements to the people are in order at this time.

Dismissal: Consists of a final greeting by the priest, a blessing, and a formula of dismissal. This rite is omitted if another liturgical action immediately follows the Mass; e.g., a procession, the blessing of the body during a funeral rite.

Some parts of the Mass are changeable with the liturgical season or feast, and are called the proper of the Mass. Other parts are said to be common because they always remain the same.

Additional Mass Notes

Catholics are seriously obliged to attend Mass in a worthy manner on Sundays and holy days of obligation. Failure to do so without a proportionately serious reason is gravely wrong.

It is the custom for priests to celebrate Mass daily whenever possible. To satisfy the needs of the faithful on Sundays and holy days of obligation, they are authorized to say Mass twice (**bination**) or even three times (**trination**). Bination is also permissible on weekdays to satisfy the needs of the faithful. On Christmas every priest may say three Masses.

The **fruits of the Mass**, which in itself is of infinite value, are: **general**, for all the faithful; **special (ministerial)**, for the intentions or persons specifically intended by the celebrant; **most special (personal)**, for the celebrant himself. On Sundays and certain other days pastors are obliged to offer Mass for their parishioners, or to have another priest do so. If a priest accepts a stipend or offering for a Mass, he is obliged in justice to apply the Mass for the intention of the donor. Mass may be applied for the living and the dead, or for any good intention.

Mass can be celebrated in several ways: e.g., with people present, without their presence (privately), with two or more priests as co-celebrants (concelebration), with greater or less solemnity.

Some of the various types of Masses are: **for the dead** (Funeral Mass or Mass of Christian Burial, Mass for the Dead — formerly called Requiem Mass); **ritual**, in connection with celebration of the sacraments, religious profession, etc.; **nuptial**, for married couples, with or after the wedding ceremony; **votive**, to honor a Person of the Trinity, a saint, or for some special intention.

Places, Altars for Mass

The ordinary place for celebrating the Eucharist is a church or other sacred place, at a fixed or movable altar.

The altar is a table at which the Eucharistic Sacrifice is celebrated.

A fixed altar is attached to the floor of the church. It should be of stone, preferably, and should be consecrated. The Code of Canon Law orders observance of the custom of placing under a fixed altar relics of martyrs or other saints.

A movable altar can be made of any solid and suitable material, and should be blessed or consecrated.

Outside of a sacred place, Mass may be celebrated in an appropriate place at a suitable table covered with a linen cloth and corporal. An altar stone containing the relics of saints, which was formerly prescribed, is not required by regulations in effect since the promulgation Apr. 6, 1969, of *Institutio Generalis Missalis Romani*.

LITURGICAL VESTMENTS

In the early years of the Church, vestments worn by the ministers at liturgical functions were the same as the garments in ordinary popular use. They became distinctive when their form was not altered to correspond with later variations in popular style. Liturgical vestments are symbolic of the sacred ministry and add appropriate decorum to divine worship.

Mass Vestments

Alb: A body-length tunic of white fabric; a vestment common to all ministers of divine worship.

Amice: A rectangular piece of white cloth worn about the shoulders, tucked into the collar and falling over the shoulders; prescribed for use when the alb does not completely cover the ordinary clothing at the neck.

Chasuble: Originally, a large mantle or cloak covering the body, it is the outer vestment of a priest celebrating Mass or carrying out other sacred actions connected with the Mass.

Chasuble-Alb: A vestment combining the features of the chasuble and alb; for use with a stole by concelebrants and, by way of exception, by celebrants in certain circumstances.

Cincture: A cord which serves the purpose of a belt, holding the alb close to the body.

Dalmatic: The outer vestment worn by a deacon in place of a chasuble.

Stole: A long, band-like vestment worn by a priest about the neck and falling to about the knees. A deacon wears a stole over the left shoulder, crossed and fastened at his right side.

The material, form and ornamentation of the aforementioned and other vestments are subject to variation and adaptation, according to norms and decisions of the Holy See and concerned conferences of bishops. The overriding norm is that they should be appropriate for use in divine worship. The customary ornamented vestments are the chasuble, dalmatic and stole.

The minimal vestments required for a priest celebrating Mass are the alb, stole, and chasuble.

Liturgical Colors

The colors of outer vestments vary with liturgical seasons, feasts and other circumstances. The colors and their use are:

Green: For the season of ordinary time; symbolic of hope and the vitality of the life of faith.

Violet (Purple): For Advent and Lent; may also be used in Masses for the dead; symbolic of penance. (See below, Violet for Advent.)

Red: For the Sunday of the Passion, Good Friday, Pentecost; feasts of the Passion of Our Lord, the Apostles and Evangelists, martyrs; symbolic of the supreme sacrifice of life for the love of God.

Rose: May be used in place of purple on the Third Sunday of Advent (formerly called Gaudete Sunday) and the Fourth Sunday of Lent (formerly called Laetare Sunday); symbolic of anticipatory joy during a time of penance.

White: For the seasons of Christmas and Easter; feasts and commemorations of Our Lord, except those of the Passion; feasts and commemorations of the Blessed Virgin Mary, angels, saints who are not martyrs, All Saints (Nov. 1), St. John the Baptist (June 24), St. John the Evangelist (Dec. 27), the Chair of St. Peter (Feb. 22), the Conversion of St. Paul (Jan. 25). White, symbolic of purity and integrity of the life of faith, may generally be substituted for other colors, and can be used for funeral and other Masses for the dead.

Options are provided regarding the color of vestments used in offices and Masses for the dead. The newsletter of the U.S. Bishops' Committee on the Liturgy, in line with No. 308 of the General Instruction of the Roman Missal, announced in July 1970: "In the dioceses of the U.S., white vestments may be used, in addition to violet (purple) and black, in offices and Masses for the dead."

On more solemn occasions, better than ordinary vestments may be used, even though their color (e.g., gold) does not match the requirements of the day.

Violet for Advent: Violet is the official liturgical color for the season of Advent, according to the September 1988 edition of the newsletter of the U.S. Bishops' Committee on the Liturgy. Blue was being proposed in order to distinguish between the Advent season and the specifically penitential season of Lent. The newsletter said, however, that "the same effect can be achieved by following the official color sequence of the Church, which requires the use of violet for Advent and Lent, while taking advantage of the varying shades which exist for violet. Light blue vestments are not authorized for use in the U.S."

Considerable freedom is permitted in the choice of colors of vestments worn for votive Masses.

Other Vestments

Cappa Magna: Flowing vestment with a train, worn by bishops and cardinals.

Cassock: A non-liturgical, full-length, close-fitting robe for use by priests and other clerics under liturgical vestments and in ordinary use; usually black for priests, purple for bishops and other prelates, red for cardinals, white for the pope. In place of a cassock, priests belonging to religious institutes wear the habit proper to their institute.

Cope: A mantle-like vestment open in front and fastened across the chest; worn by sacred ministers in processions and other ceremonies, as prescribed by appropriate directives.

Habit: The ordinary (non-liturgical) garb of members of religious institutes, analogous to the cassock of diocesan priests; the form of habits varies from institute to institute.

Humeral Veil: A rectangular vestment worn about the shoulders by a deacon or priest in Eucharistic processions and for other prescribed liturgical ceremonies.

Mitre: A headdress worn at some liturgical functions by bishops, abbots and, in certain cases, other ecclesiastics.

Pallium: A circular band of white wool about two inches wide, with front and back pendants, marked with six crosses, worn about the neck. It is a symbol of the fullness of the episcopal office. Pope Paul VI, in a document issued July 20, 1978, on his own initiative and entitled *Inter Eximia Episcopalis*, restricted its use to the pope and archbishops of metropolitan sees. In 1984, Pope John Paul II decreed that the pallium would ordinarily be conferred by the pope on the solemnity of Sts. Peter and Paul, June 29. The pallium is made from the wool of lambs blessed by the pope on the feast of St. Agnes (Jan. 21).

Rochet: A knee-length, white linen-lace garment of prelates worn under outer vestments.

Surplice: a loose, flowing vestment of white fabric with wide sleeves. For some functions, it is interchangeable with an alb.

Zucchetto: A skullcap worn by bishops and other prelates.

SACRED VESSELS, LINENS

Vessels

Paten and Chalice: The principal sacred vessels required for the celebration of Mass are the paten (plate) and chalice (cup) in which bread and wine, respectively, are offered, consecrated and consumed. Both should be made of solid and noble material which is not easily breakable or corruptible. Gold coating is required of the interior parts of sacred vessels subject to rust. The cup of a chalice should be made of non-absorbent material.

Vessels for containing consecrated hosts (see below) can be made of material other than solid and noble metal — e.g., ivory, more durable woods — provided the substitute material is locally regarded as noble or rather precious and is suitable for sacred use.

Sacred vessels should be blessed, according to prescribed requirements.

Vessels, in addition to the paten, for containing consecrated hosts are:

Ciborium: Used to hold hosts for distribution to the faithful and for reservation in the tabernacle.

Luna, Lunula, Lunette: A small receptacle which holds the sacred host in an upright position in the monstrance.

Monstrance, Ostensorium: A portable receptacle so made that the sacred host, when enclosed therein, may be clearly seen, as at Benediction or during extended exposition of the Blessed Sacrament.

Pyx: A watch-shaped vessel used in carrying the Eucharist to the sick.

Linens

Altar Cloth: A white cloth, usually of linen, covering the table of an altar. One cloth is sufficient. Three were used according to former requirements.

Burse: A square, stiff flat case, open at one end, in which the folded corporal can be placed; the outside is covered with material of the same kind and color as the outer vestments of the celebrant.

Corporal: A square piece of white linen spread on the altar cloth, on which rest the vessels holding the Sacred Species — the consecrated host(s) and wine

— during the Eucharistic Liturgy. The corporal is used whenever the Blessed Sacrament is removed from the tabernacle; e.g., during Benediction the vessel containing the Blessed Sacrament rests on a corporal.

Finger Towel: A white rectangular napkin used by the priest to dry his fingers after cleansing them following the offering of gifts at Mass.

Pall: A square piece of stiff material, usually covered with linen, which can be used to cover the chalice at Mass.

Purificator: A white rectangular napkin used for cleansing sacred vessels after the reception of Communion at Mass.

Veil: The chalice intended for use at Mass can be covered with a veil made of the same material as the outer vestments of the celebrant.

THE CHURCH BUILDING

A church is a building set aside and dedicated for purposes of divine worship, the place of assembly for a worshipping community.

A Catholic church is the ordinary place in which the faithful assemble for participation in the Eucharistic Liturgy and other forms of divine worship.

In the early years of Christianity, the first places of assembly for the Eucharistic Liturgy were private homes (Acts 2:46; Rom. 16:5; 1 Cor. 16:5; Col. 4:15) and, sometimes, catacombs. Church building began in the latter half of the second century during lulls in persecution and became widespread after enactment of the Edict of Milan in 313, when it finally became possible for the Church to emerge completely from the underground. The oldest and basic norms regarding church buildings date from about that time.

The essential principle underlying all norms for church building was reformulated by the Second Vatican Council, as follows: "When churches are to be built, let great care be taken that they be suitable for the celebration of liturgical services and for the active participation of the faithful" (*Sacrosanctum Concilium*, Constitution on the Sacred Liturgy, No. 124).

This principle was subsequently elaborated in detail by the Congregation for Divine Worship in a document entitled *Institutio Generalis Missalis Romani*, which was approved by Paul VI Apr. 3, 1969, and promulgated by a decree of the congregation dated Apr. 6, 1969. Coverage of the following items reflects the norms stated in Chapter V of the *Institutio*.

Main Features

Sanctuary: The part of the church where the altar of sacrifice is located, the place where the ministers of the liturgy lead the people in prayer, proclaim the word of God and celebrate the Eucharist. It is set off from the body of the church by a distinctive structural feature — e.g., elevation above the main floor — or by ornamentation. (The traditional communion rail, removed in recent years in many churches, served this purpose of demarcation.) The customary location of the sanctuary is at the front of the church; it may, however, be centrally located.

Altar: The main altar of sacrifice and table of the Lord is the focal feature of the sanctuary and entire church. It stands by itself, so that the ministers can move about it freely, and is so situated that they face the people during the liturgical action. In addition to this main altar, there may also be others; in new churches, these are ideally situated in side chapels or alcoves removed to some degree from the body of the church.

Adornment of the Altar: The altar table is covered with a suitable linen cloth. Required candelabra and a cross are placed upon or near the altar in plain sight of the people and are so arranged that they do not obscure their view of the liturgical action.

Seats of the Ministers: The seats of the ministers should be so arranged that they are part of the seating arrangement of the worshipping congregation and suitably placed for the performance of ministerial functions. The seat of the celebrant or chief concelebrant should be in a presiding position.

Ambo, Pulpit, Lectern: The stand at which scriptural lessons and psalm responses are read, the word of God preached, and the prayer of the faithful offered. It is so placed that the ministers can be easily seen and heard by the people.

Places for the People: Seats and kneeling benches (pews) and other accommodations for the people are so arranged that they can participate in the most appropriate way in the liturgical action and have freedom of movement for the reception of Holy Communion. Reserved seats are out of order.

Place for the Choir: Where it is located depends on the most suitable arrangement for maintaining the unity of the choir with the congregation and for providing its members maximum opportunity for carrying out their proper function and participating fully in the Mass.

Tabernacle: The best place for reserving the Blessed Sacrament is in a chapel suitable for the private devotion of the people. If this is not possible, reservation should be at a side altar or other appropriately adorned place. In either case, the Blessed Sacrament should be kept in a tabernacle, i.e., a safe-like, secure receptacle.

Statues: Images of the Lord, the Blessed Virgin Mary and the saints are legitimately proposed for the veneration of the faithful in churches. Their number and arrangement, however, should be ordered in such a way that they do not distract the people from the central celebration of the Eucharistic Liturgy. There should be only one statue of one and the same saint in a church.

General Adornment and Arrangement of Churches: Churches should be so adorned and fitted out that they serve the direct requirements of divine worship and the needs and reasonable convenience of the people.

Other Items

Ambry: A box containing the holy oils, attached to the wall of the sanctuary in some churches.

Baptistery: The place for administering baptism. Some churches have baptisteries adjoining or near the entrance, a position symbolizing the fact that persons are initiated in the Church and incorporated in Christ through this sacrament. Contemporary liturgical practice favors placement of the baptistery near the sanctuary and altar, or the use of a portable font in the same position, to emphasize the relationship of baptism to the Eucharist, the celebration in sacrifice and banquet of the death and resurrection of Christ.

Candles: Used more for symbolical than illuminative purposes, they represent Christ, the light and life of grace, at liturgical functions. They are made of beeswax. (See **Index: Paschal Candle**.)

Confessional, Reconciliation Room: A booth-like structure for the hearing of confessions, with separate compartments for the priest and penitents and a grating or screen between them. The use of confessionals became general in the Roman rite after the Council of Trent. Since the Second Vatican Council, there has been a trend in the U.S. to replace or supplement confessionals with small reconciliation rooms so arranged that priest and penitent can converse face-to-face.

Crucifix: A cross bearing the figure of the body of Christ, representative of the Sacrifice of the Cross.

Cruets: Vessels containing the wine and water used at Mass. They are placed on a credence table in the sanctuary.

Holy Water Fonts: Receptacles containing holy water, usually at church entrances, for the use of the faithful.

Sanctuary Lamp: A lamp which is kept burning continuously before a tabernacle in which the Blessed Sacrament is reserved, as a sign of the Real Presence of Christ.

LITURGICAL DEVELOPMENTS

The principal developments covered in this article are enactments of the Holy See and actions related to their implementation in the U.S.

Modern Movement

Origins of the modern movement for renewal in the liturgy date back to the 19th century. The key contributing factor was a revival of liturgical and scriptural studies. Of special significance was the work of the Benedictine monks of Solesmes, France, who aroused great interest in the liturgy through the restoration of Gregorian Chant. St. Pius X approved their work in a *motu proprio* of 1903 and gave additional encouragement to liturgical study and development.

St. Pius X did more than any other single pope to promote early first Communion and the practice of frequent Communion, started the research behind a

revised breviary, and appointed a group to investigate possible revisions in the Mass.

The movement attracted some attention in the 1920s and 30s but made little progress.

Significant pioneering developments in the U.S. during the 20s, however, were the establishment of the Liturgical Press, the beginning of publication of *Orate Fratres* (now **Worship**), and the inauguration of the League of the Divine Office by the Benedictines at St. John's Abbey, Collegeville, MN. Later events of influence were the establishment of the Pius X School of Liturgical Music at Manhattanville College of the Sacred Heart and the organization of a summer school of liturgical music at Mary Manse College by the Gregorian Institute of America. The turning point toward real renewal was reached during and after World War II.

Pius XII gave it impetus and direction, principally

through the background teaching in his encyclicals on the Mystical Body (*Mystici Corporis Christi*, 1943), Sacred Liturgy (*Mediator Dei*, 1947), and On Sacred Music (*Musicae sacrae*, 1955), and by means of specific measures affecting the liturgy itself. His work was continued during the pontificates of his successors. The Second Vatican Council, in virtue of *Sacrosanctum Concilium*, the Constitution on the Sacred Liturgy, inaugurated changes of the greatest significance.

Before and After Vatican II

The most significant liturgical changes made in the years immediately preceding the Second Vatican Council were the following:

1. Revision of the rites of Holy Week for universal observance from 1956.
2. Modification of the Eucharistic fast and permission for afternoon and evening Mass, in effect from 1953 and extended in 1957.
3. The Dialogue Mass, introduced in 1958.
4. Use of popular languages in administration of the sacraments.
5. Calendar-missal-breviary reform, in effect from Jan. 1, 1961.
6. Seven-step administration of baptism for adults, approved in 1962.

The Constitution on the Sacred Liturgy, *Sacrosanctum Concilium*, approved (2,174 to 4) and promulgated by the Second Vatican Council on Dec. 4, 1963, marked the beginning of a profound renewal in the Church's corporate worship. Implementation of some of its measures was ordered by Paul VI on Jan. 25, 1964, in the *motu proprio Sacram Liturgiam*. On Feb. 29, a special commission, the Consilium for Implementing the Constitution on the Sacred Liturgy, was formed to supervise the execution of the entire program of liturgical reform. Implementation of the program on local and regional levels was left to bishops acting through their own liturgical commissions and in concert with their fellow bishops in national conferences.

Liturgical reform in the U.S. has been carried out under the direction of the Liturgy Committee, National Conference of Catholic Bishops. Its secretariat, established early in 1965, is located at 3211 Fourth St. N.E., Washington, DC 20017.

Stages of Development

Liturgical development after the Second Vatican Council proceeded in several stages. It started with the formulation of guidelines and directives, and with the translation into vernacular languages of virtually unchanged Latin ritual texts. Then came structural changes in the Mass, the sacraments, the calendar, the Divine Office and other phases of the liturgy. These revisions were just about completed with the publication of a new order for the sacrament of penance in February 1974. A continuing phase of development, in progress from the beginning, involves efforts to deepen the liturgical sense of the faithful, to increase their participation in worship and to relate it to full Christian life.

RECENT DEVELOPMENTS

On Nov. 14, 2001, the U.S. Bishops, attending the annual fall meeting in Washington, approved revised U.S. adaptations in the liturgy by a vote of 207-7. The adaptations govern matters ranging from liturgical music and church furnishings to posture at Mass and how Communion is to be received.

The bishops had approved a complete set of adaptations at their spring meeting in June 2001, but the Vatican Congregation for Divine Worship and the Sacraments asked for modification of several of those and proposed a new approach that required editorial changes in all of them.

When completed, the U.S. adaptations are to be incorporated into the new General Instruction of the Roman Missal and have the same force of law in the U.S. as the rest of the general instruction.

New U.S. Norms for Distribution of Communion Under Both Species

New norms for the distribution and reception of Communion under the outward signs of both bread and wine by Catholics in the U.S. were approved by the U.S. bishops on June 15, 2001, and confirmed by the Holy See on Mar. 22, 2002; they were subsequently published by Bishop Wilton D. Gregory of Belleville, IL, president of the USCCB.

The norms, which replace the U.S. bishops' 1984 directory titled "This Holy and Living Sacrifice," give specific directives regarding liturgical roles, sacred vessels and the rites to be followed in distributing Communion under both kinds.

The first section of the new norms provides a theological summary of the church's teaching on Communion under both kinds, while the following section describes the authorized procedures by which such distribution can be accomplished at mass.

The U.S. adaptations are to be incorporated into the new General Instruction of the Roman Missal and have the same force of law in the U.S. as the rest of the general instruction. The General Instruction of the recently revised Roman Missal permits bishops' conferences to provide norms for the distribution of Communion under both kinds, meaning under the outward signs of both bread and wine.

Included among the norms is an indult — or exception to the general requirement — from the Vatican Congregation for Divine Worship and the Sacraments that provides for the cleansing of sacred vessels by special eucharistic ministers. The indult was promulgated as "particular law" for the dioceses of the U.S. at the same time as the norms and it became effective on Apr. 7, 2002.

However, the Vatican congregation declined to approve an indult authorizing special ministers to assist with the distribution of the consecrated blood to other chalices during the singing of the "Lamb of God."

In the letter confirming the norms, the congregation also made clear that special eucharistic ministers, or indeed any communicant, may assist in the consumption of what remains of the blood after distribution of Communion has been completed.

Texts and Translations

The master texts of all documents on liturgical reform are in Latin. Effective dates of their implementation have depended on the completion and approval of appropriate translations into vernacular languages. English translations were made by the International Committee for English in the Liturgy.

The principal features of liturgical changes and the effective dates of their introduction in the U.S. are covered below under topical headings. (For expanded coverage of various items, especially the sacraments, see additional entries.)

On May 7, 2001, the Congregation for Divine Worship and the Sacraments issued the new instruction, *Liturgiam Authenticam* ("The Authentic Liturgy"). The instruction set stricter rules for the translation of Latin liturgical texts into other languages and bears the subtitle, "On the Use of Vernacular Languages in the Publication of the Books of the Roman Liturgy." The instruction was welcomed by then-NCCB president, Bishop Joseph A. Fiorenza of Galveston-Houston, who said that it reflects long consultations between the Vatican and English-speaking bishops, adding that "It is now our hope and expectation that there will be a much quicker approval of liturgical texts" by the Vatican. The instruction was subsequently debated at the bishops' meeting in November 2001.

General Instruction of the Roman Missal

In spring 2001, Pope John Paul II authorized the publication of an *editio typica tertia* of the *Missale Romanum*. The much anticipated revision included a new edition of the *Institutio Generalis Missalis Romani* (*General Instruction of the Roman Missal*). On November 12, 2002, the Latin Church members of the United States Conference of Catholic Bishops approved a translation of the *Institutio Generalis Missalis Romani* prepared by the International Commission on English in the Liturgy. The translation was confirmed by the Congregation for Divine Worship and the Discipline of the Sacraments on March 17, 2003. This translation of the *General Instruction of the Roman Missal* is the sole translation of the *Institutio Generalis Missalis Romani, editio typica tertia* for use in the dioceses of the United States of America. Concerning the new edition, Msgr. James P. Moroney, Executive Director of the USCCB Secretariat for the Liturgy, wrote in the Foreword:

"This revised *Institutio Generalis* possesses a unique role among all the documents on the liturgy. Like its preceding editions, it has been published in order to give life to a dream. It was the dream of reformers such as St. Hippolytus, St. Gregory, and St. Leo. It was the dream of Pope Paul VI and clearly remains the vision of Pope John Paul II, who calls us to 'an ever deeper grasp of the liturgy of the Church, celebrated according to the current books and lived above all as a reality in the spiritual order' (*Vicesimus Quintus Annus*, 1988, no. 14). Likewise, this dream is shared by the Bishops' Committee on the Liturgy and the United States Conference of Catholic Bishops that it serves. Finally, it is the vision of the Church itself: the dream of God's people joined to Christ in Baptism and made 'ever more holy by conscious, active, and fruitful participation in the mystery of the Eucharist' (*General Instruction of the Roman Missal*, no. 5)." (*See* **News in Depth**.)

The Mass

A new Order of the Mass, supplanting the one authorized by the Council of Trent in the 16th century, was introduced in the U.S. Mar. 22, 1970. It had been approved by Paul VI in the apostolic constitution *Missale Romanum*, dated Apr. 3, 1969.

Preliminary and related to it were the following developments.

Mass in English: Introduced Nov. 29, 1964. In the same year, Psalm 42 was eliminated from the prayers at the foot of the altar.

Incidental Changes: The last Gospel (prologue of John) and vernacular prayers following Mass were eliminated Mar. 7, 1965. At the same time, provision was made for the celebrant to say aloud some prayers formerly said silently.

Rubrics: An instruction entitled *Tres Abhinc Annos*, dated May 4 and effective June 29, 1967, simplified directives for the celebration of Mass, approved the practice of saying the canon aloud, altered the Communion and dismissal rites, permitted purple instead of black vestments in Masses for the dead, discontinued wearing of the maniple, and approved in principle the use of vernacular languages for the canon, ordination rites, and lessons of the Divine Office when read in choir.

Eucharistic Prayers (Canons): The traditional Roman Canon in English was introduced Oct. 22, 1967. Three additional Eucharistic prayers, authorized May 23, 1968, were approved for use in English the following Aug. 15.

The customary Roman Canon, which dates at least from the beginning of the fifth century and has remained substantially unchanged since the seventh century, is the first in the order of listing of the Eucharistic prayers. It can be used at any time, but is the one of choice for most Sundays, some special feasts like Easter and Pentecost, and for feasts of the Apostles and other saints who are commemorated in the canon. Any preface can be used with it.

The second Eucharistic prayer, the shortest and simplest of all, is best suited for use on weekdays and various special circumstances. It has a preface of its own, but others may be used with it. This canon bears a close resemblance to the one framed by St. Hippolytus about 215.

The third Eucharistic prayer is suitable for use on Sundays and feasts as an alternative to the Roman Canon. It can be used with any preface and has a special formula for remembrance of the dead.

The fourth Eucharistic prayer, the most sophisticated of them all, presents a broad synthesis of salvation history. Based on the Eastern tradition of Antioch, it is best suited for use at Masses attended by persons versed in Sacred Scripture. It has an unchangeable preface.

Five additional Eucharistic prayers — three for Masses with children and two for Masses of reconciliation — were approved in 1974 and 1975, respectively, by the Congregation for the Sacraments and Divine Worship.

Use of the Eucharistic Prayers for Various Needs and Occasions, was approved by the U.S. bishops in 1994, confirmed by the appropriate Vatican congregations May 9, 1995, and ratified for use beginning Oct. 1, 1995.

Lectionary: A new compilation of scriptural readings and psalm responsories for Mass was published in 1969. The Lectionary contains a three-year cycle of readings for Sundays and solemn feasts, a two-year weekday cycle, and a one-year cycle for the feasts of saints, in addition to readings for a variety of votive Masses, ritual Masses and Masses for various needs. There are also responsorial psalms to follow the first readings and gospel or alleluia versicles.

A second edition of the Lectionary, substantially the same as the first, was published in 1981. New features included an expanded introduction, extensive scriptural references and additional readings for a number of solemnities and feasts.

Volume One of a new Lectionary for the Mass was decreed by Bishop Anthony Pilla of Cleveland, then president of the NCCB, as permissible for use as of the first Sunday of Advent, Nov. 29, 1998. The first new Lectionary since 1973, Volume One contains the readings for Sundays, solemnities and feasts of the Lord. Volume Two, containing the readings for weekdays, feasts of saints, and various other occasions, was given final approval on June 19, 1998, by the NCCB but still required confirmation by the Holy See.

Sacramentary (Missal): The Vatican Polyglot Press began distribution in June 1970, of the Latin text of a new Roman Missal, the first revision published in 400 years. The English translation was authorized for optional use beginning July 1, 1974; the mandatory date for use was Dec. 1, 1974.

The **Sacramentary** is the celebrant's Mass book of entrance songs, prayers, prefaces and Eucharistic prayers, including special common sets of texts for various commemorations and intentions — dedication of churches, Mary, the apostles, martyrs, doctors of the Church, virgins, holy men and women, the dead, other categories of holy persons, administration of certain sacraments, special intentions.

Study of the Mass: The Bishops' Committee on the Liturgy, following approval by the National Conference of Catholic Bishops in May 1979, began a study of the function and position of elements of the Mass, including the Gloria, the sign of peace, the penitential rite and the readings. Major phases of the study have been completed, and work is still under way toward completion of the project.

Mass for Special Groups: Reasons and norms for the celebration of Mass at special gatherings of the faithful were the subject of an instruction issued May 15, 1969. Two years earlier, the U.S. Bishops' Liturgy Committee went on record in support of the celebration of Mass in private homes under appropriate conditions.

Sunday Mass on Saturday: The Congregation for the Clergy, under date of Jan. 10, 1970, granted the request that the faithful, where bishops consider it pastorally necessary or useful, may satisfy the precept of participating in Mass in the late afternoon or evening hours of Saturdays and the days before holy days of obligation. This provision is stated in Canon 1248 of the Code of Canon Law.

Bination and Trination: Canon 905 of the Code of Canon Law provides that local ordinaries may permit priests to celebrate Mass twice a day (bination), for a just cause; in cases of pastoral need, they may permit priests to celebrate Mass three times a day (trination) on Sundays and holy days of obligation.

Mass in Latin: According to notices issued by the Congregation for Divine Worship June 1, 1971, and Oct. 28, 1974: (1) Bishops may permit the celebration of Mass in Latin for mixed-language groups; (2) bishops may permit the celebration of one or two Masses in Latin on weekdays or Sundays in any church, irrespective of mixed-language groups involved (1971); (3) priests may celebrate Mass in Latin

when people are not present; (4) the approved revised Order of the Mass is to be used in Latin as well as vernacular languages; (5) by way of exception, bishops may permit older and handicapped priests to use the Council of Trent's Order of the Mass in private celebration of the holy Sacrifice. (*See* Permission for **Tridentine Mass**.)

Mass Obligation Waived: The Congregation for Bishops approved July 4, 1992, a resolution of the U.S. bishops to waive the Mass attendance obligation for the holy days of Mary, the Mother of God (Jan. 1), the Assumption of Mary (Aug. 15) and All Saints (Nov. 1) when these solemnities fall on Saturday or Monday.

Inter-Ritual Concelebration: The Apostolic Delegation (now Nunciature) in Washington, DC, announced in June 1971 that it had received authorization to permit priests of Roman and Eastern rites to celebrate Mass together in the rite of the host church. It was understood that the inter-ritual concelebrations would always be "a manifestation of the unity of the Church and of communion among particular churches."

Ordo of the Sung Mass: In a decree dated June 24 and made public Aug. 24, 1972, the Congregation for Divine Worship issued a new *Ordo of the Sung Mass* — containing Gregorian chants in Latin — to replace the *Graduale Romanum*.

Mass for Children: Late in 1973, the Congregation for Divine Worship issued special guidelines for children's Masses, providing accommodations to the mentality and spiritual growth of pre-adolescents while retaining the principal parts and structures of the Mass. The Directory for Masses with Children was approved by Paul VI Oct. 22 and was dated Nov. 1, 1973. Three Eucharistic prayers for Masses with children were approved by the congregation in 1974; English versions were approved June 5, 1975. Their use, authorized originally for a limited period of experimentation, was extended indefinitely Dec. 15, 1980.

Lectionary for Children: A lectionary for Masses with children, with an announced publication date of September 1993, was authorized for use by choice beginning Nov. 28, 1993.

Sacraments

The general use of English in administration of the sacraments was approved for the U.S. Sept. 14, 1964. Structural changes of the rites were subsequently made and introduced in the U.S. as follows.

Pastoral Care of the Sick: Revised rites, covering also administration of the Eucharist to sick persons, were approved Nov. 30, 1972, and published Jan. 18, 1973. The effective date for use of the provisional English prayer formula was Dec. 1, 1974. The mandatory effective date for use of the ritual, Pastoral Care of the Sick in English, was Nov. 27, 1983.

Baptism: New rites for the baptism of infants, approved Mar. 19, 1969, were introduced June 1, 1970.

Rite of Christian Initiation of Adults: Revised rites were issued Jan. 6, 1972, for the Christian initiation of adults — affecting preparation for and reception of baptism, the Eucharist and confirmation; also, for the reception of already baptized adults into full communion with the Church. These rites, which were introduced in the U.S. on the completion of English translation, nullified a seven-step baptismal process approved in 1962. On Mar. 8, 1988, the National Conference of Catholic Bishops was notified that the Congregation for Divine Worship had approved the final English translation of the Rite of Christian Initiation of Adults. The mandatory date for putting the rite into effect was Sept. 1, 1988.

Confirmation: Revised rites, issued Aug. 15, 1971, became mandatory in the U.S. Jan. 1, 1973. The use of a stole by persons being confirmed should be avoided, according to an item in the December 1984 edition of the Newsletter of the Bishops' Committee on the Liturgy. The item said: "The distinction between the universal priesthood of all the baptized and the ministerial priesthood of the ordained is blurred when the distinctive garb (the stole) of ordained ministers is used in this manner."

A decree regarding the proper age for confirmation, approved by the U.S. bishops in June 1993 was ratified by the Congregation for Bishops Feb. 8, 1994. The decree reads: "In accord with prescriptions of canon 891, the National Conference of Catholic Bishops hereby decrees that the sacrament of confirmation in the Latin rite shall be conferred between the age of discretion, which is about the age of seven, and 18 years of age, within the limits determined by the diocesan bishop and with regard for the legitimate exceptions given in canon 891, namely, when there is danger of death or where, in the judgment of the minister, grave cause urges otherwise." The decree became effective July 1, 1994, and continued in effect until July 1, 1999.

Special Ministers of the Eucharist: The designation of lay men and women to serve as special ministers of the Eucharist was authorized by Paul VI in an "Instruction on Facilitating Communion in Particular Circumstances" (*Immensae Caritatis*), dated Jan. 29 and published by the Congregation for Divine Worship Mar. 29, 1973. Provisions concerning them are contained in Canons 230 and 910 of the Code of Canon Law.

Qualified laypersons may serve as special ministers for specific occasions or for extended periods in the absence of a sufficient number of priests and deacons to provide reasonable and appropriate service in the distribution of Holy Communion, during Mass and outside of Mass (to the sick and shut-ins). Appointments of ministers are made by priests with the approval of the appropriate bishop.

The Newsletter of the U.S. Bishops' Committee on the Liturgy stated in its February 1988 edition: "When ordinary ministers (bishops, priests, deacons) are present during a Eucharistic celebration, whether they are participating in it or not, and are not prevented from doing so, they are to assist in the distribution of Communion. Accordingly, if the ordinary ministers are in sufficient number, special ministers of the Eucharist are not allowed to distribute Communion at that Eucharistic celebration." Pope John Paul II approved this decision and ordered it published June 15, 1987.

Holy Orders: Revised ordination rites for deacons, priests and bishops, validated by prior experimental use, were approved in 1970. The sacrament of holy orders underwent further revision in 1972 with the elimination of the Church-instituted orders of porter, reader, exorcist, acolyte and subdeacon, and of the tonsure ceremony symbolic of entrance into the cleri-

cal state. The former minor orders of reader and acolyte were changed from orders to ministries.

Matrimony: A revised rite for the celebration of marriage was promulgated by the Congregation for Divine Worship and the Discipline of the Sacraments Mar. 19, 1969, and went into effect June 1, 1970. A second typical edition of the order of celebration, with revisions in accord with provisions of the Code of Canon Law promulgated in 1983, was approved and published in 1990 (*Notitiae*, Vol. 26, No.6). The date for implementation was reported to be dependent on the completion of required translations and appropriate formalities.

Penance: Ritual revision of the sacraments was completed with approval by Pope Paul VI on Dec. 2, 1973, of new directives for the sacrament of penance or reconciliation. The U.S. Bishops' Committee on the Liturgy set Feb. 27, 1977, as the mandatory date for use of the new rite. The committee also declared that it could be used from Mar. 7, 1976, after adequate preparation of priests and people. Earlier, authorization was given by the Holy See in 1968 for the omission of any reference to excommunication or other censures in the formula of absolution unless there was some indication that a censure had actually been incurred by a penitent.

Additional Developments

Music: An instruction on Music in the Liturgy, dated Mar. 5 and effective May 14, 1967, encouraged congregational singing during liturgical celebrations and attempted to clarify the role of choirs and trained singers. More significantly, the instruction indicated that a major development under way in the liturgy was a gradual erasure of the distinctive lines traditionally drawn between the sung liturgy and the spoken liturgy, between what had been called the high Mass and the low Mass.

In the same year, the U.S. Bishops' Liturgy Committee approved the use of contemporary music, as well as guitars and other suitable instruments, in the liturgy. The Holy See authorized in 1968 the use of musical instruments other than the organ in liturgical services, "provided they are played in a manner suitable to worship."

Calendar: A revised liturgical calendar approved by Paul VI Feb. 14 and made public May 9, 1969, went into effect in the U.S. in 1972. Since that time, memorials and feasts of beatified persons and saints have been added.

Communion in Hand: Since 1969, the Holy See has approved the practice of in-hand reception of the Eucharist in regions and countries where it had the approval of the appropriate episcopal conferences. The first grant of approval was to Belgium, in May 1969. Approval was granted the U.S. in June 1977.

Liturgy of the Hours: The background, contents, scope and purposes of the revised Divine Office, called the Liturgy of the Hours, were described by Paul VI in the apostolic constitution *Laudis Canticum*, dated Nov. 1, 1970. A provisional English version, incorporating basic features of the master Latin text, was published in 1971. The four complete volumes of the Hours in English have been published since May 1975. One-volume, partial editions have also been published in approved form. Nov. 27, 1977, was set by the Congregation for Divine Worship and the

National Conference of Catholic Bishops as the effective date for exclusive use in liturgical worship of the translation of the Latin text of the Liturgy of the Hours approved by the International Committee on English in the Liturgy.

Holy Week: The English version of revised Holy Week rites went into effect in 1971. They introduced concelebration of Mass, placed new emphasis on commemorating the institution of the priesthood on Holy Thursday, and modified Good Friday prayers for other Christians, Jews and other non-Christians.

In another action, the Congregation for Divine Worship released Feb. 20, 1988, a "Circular Letter concerning the Preparation and Celebration of the Easter Feasts." It called the feasts the "summit of the whole liturgical year," and criticized practices which dilute or change appropriate norms for their celebration. Singled out for blame or the abuse or ignorance of norms was the "inadequate formation given to the clergy and the faithful regarding the paschal mystery as the center of the liturgical year and of Christian life." The document set out the appropriate norms for the Lenten season, Holy Week, the Easter Triduum, Easter and the weeks following. It was particularly insistent on the proper celebration of the Easter Vigil, to take place after nightfall on Saturday and before dawn on Sunday.

Oils: The Congregation for Divine Worship issued a directive in 1971 permitting the use of other oils — from plants, seeds or coconuts — instead of the traditional olive oil in admini‚stering some of the sacraments. The directive also provided that oils could be blessed at other times than at the usual Mass of Chrism on Holy Thursday, and authorized bishops' conferences to permit priests to bless oils in cases of necessity.

Dancing and Worship: Dancing and worship was the subject of an essay which appeared in a 1975 edition of *Notitiae* (11, pp. 202-205), the official journal of the Congregation for the Sacraments and Divine Worship. The article was called a "qualified and authoritative sketch," and should be considered "an authoritative point of reference for every discussion of the matter."

The principal points of the essay were:

• "The dance has never been made an integral part of the official worship of the Latin Church."

• "If the proposal of the religious dance in the West is really to be made welcome, care will have to be taken that in its regard a place be found outside of the liturgy, in assembly areas which are not strictly liturgical. Moreover, the priests must always be excluded from the dance."

Mass for Deceased Non-Catholic Christians: The Congregation for the Doctrine of the Faith released a decree June 11, 1976, authorizing the celebration of public Mass for deceased non-Catholic Christians under certain conditions: "(1) The public celebration of the Masses must be explicitly requested by the relatives, friends, or subjects of the deceased person for a genuine religious motive. (2) In the Ordinary's judgment, there must be no scandal for the faithful."

Built of Living Stones: Art, Architecture, and Worship: At their November 2001 meeting in Washington, DC, the Bishops approved this document by the U.S. Bishops' Committee on the Liturgy; it replaces the document *Environment and Art in Catholic Worship* issued in March 1978.

Doxology: The bishops' committee called attention in August 1978, to the directive that the Doxology concluding the Eucharistic Prayer is said or sung by the celebrant (concelebrants) alone, to which the people respond, "Amen."

Churches, Altars, Chalices: The Newsletter of the U.S. Bishops' Committee on the Liturgy reported in November 1978, that the Congregation for Divine Worship had given provisional approval of a new English translation for the rite of dedicating churches and altars, and of a new form for the blessing of chalices.

Eucharistic Worship: This was the subject of two documents issued in 1980. *Dominicae Coenae* was a letter addressed by Pope John Paul to bishops throughout the world in connection with the celebration of Holy Thursday; it was dated Feb. 24 and released Mar.18, 1980. It was more doctrinal in content than the "Instruction on Certain Norms concerning Worship of the Eucharistic Mystery" (*Inaestimabile Donum*, "The Priceless Gift"), which was approved by the Pope Apr. 17 and published by the Congregation for the Sacraments and Divine Worship May 23. Its stated purpose was to reaffirm and clarify teaching on liturgical renewal contained in enactments of the Second Vatican Council and in several related implementing documents.

Tridentine Mass: The celebration of Mass according to the 1962 typical (master) edition of the Roman Missal — the so-called Tridentine Mass — was authorized by Pope John Paul II under certain conditions. So stated a letter from the Congregation for Divine Worship, dated Oct. 3, 1984. The letter said the pope wished to be responsive to priests and faithful who remained attached to the so-called Tridentine rite. The principal condition for the celebration was: "There must be unequivocal, even public, evidence that the priest and people petitioning have no ties with those who impugn the lawfulness and doctrinal soundness of the Roman Missal promulgated in 1970 by Pope Paul VI." (This, in particular, with reference to the followers of dissident Archbishop Marcel Lefebvre.)

Six guidelines for celebration of the Tridentine Mass were contained in the letter regarding its "wide and generous" use, for two purposes: to win back Lefebvre followers and to clear up misunderstandings about liberal permission for use of the Tridentine rite. The letter, from the Pontifical Commission *Ecclesia Dei*, said in part:

• The Tridentine Mass can be celebrated in a parish church, so long as it provides a pastoral service and is harmoniously integrated into the parish liturgical schedule.

• When requested, the Mass should be offered on a regular Sunday and holy day basis, "at a central location, at a convenient time" for a trial period of several months, with "adjustment" later if needed.

• Celebrants of the Mass should make it clear that they acknowledge the validity of the postconciliar liturgy.

• Although the commission has the authority to grant use of the Tridentine rite to all groups that request it, the commission "would much prefer that such faculties be granted by the Ordinary himself so that ecclesial communion can be strengthened."

• While the new Lectionary in the vernacular can be

used in the Tridentine Mass, as suggested by the Second Vatican Council, it should not be "imposed on congregations that decidedly wish to maintain the former liturgical tradition in its integrity."

• Older and retired priests who have asked permission to celebrate Mass according to the Tridentine rite should be given the chance to do so for groups that request it.

In March 2003, the Vatican Secretariat of State issued new rules allowing the old rite to be used under very strict conditions. These include:

• The Mass cannot be celebrated in the main body of St. Peter's Basilica. The celebrations will take place in the Hungarian Chapel in the grotto under the basilica.

• The Mass must be "private," in the sense that the public is not invited and photographs are not allowed, although the priest may have a small group of faithful with him.

• The priest celebrating must show a permission from the Pontifical Commission *Ecclesia Dei*, the Vatican office responsible for the pastoral care of Catholic faithful with a special attachment to the old liturgy.

The ban on the Mass in the main body of the church stemmed from respect for the fact that it was in St. Peter's Basilica that the world's bishops gathered for the Second Vatican Council and ordered the reform of the liturgy.

Spanish: In accord with decrees of the Congregation for Divine Worship, Spanish was approved as a liturgical language in the U.S. (Jan. 19, 1985). The *texto unico* of the Ordinary of the Mass became mandatory in the U.S. Dec. 3, 1989. Spanish translations of Proper-of-the-Mass texts proper to U.S. dioceses were approved Mar. 12, 1990. An approved Spanish version of the Rite for the Christian Initiation of Adults was published in 1991. The Institute of Hispanic Liturgy opened its national office June 1, 1995, on the campus of the Catholic University of America in Washington.

Funeral Rites: A revised Order of Christian Funerals became mandatory in the U.S. Nov. 2, 1989.

Permission for the presence of cremated human remains in the funeral liturgy, including the Eucharist, was granted in 1997 to local bishops in the U.S. by the Congregation for Divine Worship and the Discipline of the Sacraments. Adaptations to existing rites are under study.

Popular Piety and Liturgy: The relation of popular piety to the liturgy was the subject of remarks by Pope John Paul II at a meeting with a group of Italian bishops Apr. 24, 1986. He said, in part:

"An authentic liturgical ministry will never be able to neglect the riches of popular piety, the values proper to the culture of a people, so that such riches might be illuminated, purified and introduced into the liturgy as an offering of the people."

Extended Eucharistic Exposition: In response to queries, the Secretariat of the U.S. Bishops' Committee on the Liturgy issued an advisory stating that liturgical law permits and encourages in parish churches:

• Exposition of the Blessed Sacrament for an ex-

tended period of time once a year, with consent of the local Ordinary and only if suitable numbers of the faithful are expected to be present;

• Exposition ordered by the local Ordinary, for a grave and general necessity, for a more extended period of supplication when the faithful assemble in large numbers.

With regard to perpetual exposition, this form is generally permitted only in the case of those religious communities of men or women who have the general practice of perpetual Eucharistic adoration or adoration over extended periods of time.

The Secretariat's advisory appeared in the June-July 1986 edition of the Newsletter of the Bishops' Committee on the Liturgy.

Native American Languages: The Newsletter of the U.S. Bishops' Committee on the Liturgy reported in December 1986, and May 1987, respectively, that the Congregation for Divine Worship had authorized Mass translations in Navajo and Choctaw. Lakota was approved as a liturgical language in 1989.

Communion Guidelines: In 1986 and again in 1996, the U.S. bishops' approved the insertion of advisories in missalettes and similar publications, stating that: (1) The Eucharist is to be received by Catholics only, except in certain specific cases; (2) To receive Communion worthily, a person must be in the state of grace (i.e., free of serious sin) and observe the eucharistic fast (*See* separate entry).

Unauthorized Eucharistic Prayers: The May 1987 Newsletter of the U.S. Bishops' Committee on the Liturgy restated the standing prohibition against the use of any Eucharistic Prayers other than those contained in the Sacramentary. Specifically, the article referred to the 25 unauthorized prayers in a volume entitled Spoken Visions.

Homilist: According to the Pontifical Commission for the Authentic Interpretation of Canon Law, the diocesan bishop cannot dispense from the requirement of Canon 767, par. 1, that the homily in the liturgy be reserved to a priest or deacon. Pope John Paul approved this decision June 20, 1987.

Concerts in Churches: In a letter released Dec. 5, 1987, the Congregation for Divine Worship declared that churches might be used on a limited basis for concerts of sacred or religious music, but not for concerts featuring secular music.

Blessings: A revised *Book of Blessings* was ordered into use beginning Dec. 3, 1989.

Litany of the Blessed Virgin Mary: "Queen of Families," a new invocation, was reported by the U.S. bishops in 1996, for insertion between "Queen of the Rosary" and "Queen of Peace."

Inclusive Language: "Criteria for the Evaluation of Inclusive Language Translations of Scriptural Texts Proposed for Liturgical Use" was issued by the U.S. bishops in November 1990. The criteria distinguish between non-use of vertical inclusiveness in references to God and use of horizontal, gender-inclusive terms (he/she, man/woman and the like) where appropriate in references to persons.

The Sacraments of the Church

The sacraments are actions of Christ and his Church (itself a kind of sacrament) that signify grace, cause it in the act of signifying it, and confer it upon persons properly disposed to receive it. They perpetuate the redemptive activity of Christ, making it present and effective. They infallibly communicate the fruit of that activity — namely grace — to responsive persons with faith. Sacramental actions consist of the union of sensible signs (matter of the sacraments) with the words of the minister (form of the sacraments).

Christ himself instituted the seven sacraments of the New Law by determining their essence and the efficacy of their signs to produce the grace they signify.

Christ is the principal priest or minister of every sacrament; human agents — an ordained priest, baptized persons contracting marriage with each other, any person conferring emergency baptism in a proper manner — are secondary ministers. Sacraments have efficacy from Christ, not from the personal dispositions of their human ministers.

Each sacrament confers sanctifying grace for the special purpose of the sacrament; this is, accordingly, called sacramental grace. It involves a right to actual graces corresponding to the purposes of the respective sacraments.

Baptism, confirmation and the Eucharist are sacraments of initiation; penance (reconciliation) and anointing of the sick, sacraments of healing; order and matrimony, sacraments for service.

While sacraments infallibly produce the grace they signify, recipients benefit from them in proportion to their personal dispositions. One of these is the intention to receive sacraments as sacred signs of God's saving and grace-giving action. The state of grace is also necessary for fruitful reception of the Holy Eucharist, confirmation, matrimony, holy orders and anointing of the sick. Baptism is the sacrament in which grace is given in the first instance and original sin is remitted. Penance is the secondary sacrament of reconciliation, in which persons guilty of serious sin after baptism are reconciled with God and the Church, and in which persons already in the state of grace are strengthened in that state.

Role of Sacraments

The Second Vatican Council prefaced a description of the role of the sacraments with the following statement concerning participation by all the faithful in the priesthood of Christ and the exercise of that priesthood by receiving the sacraments (Dogmatic Constitution on the Church, *Lumen Gentium*, Nos. 10 and 11).

"The baptized by regeneration and the anointing of the Holy Spirit are consecrated into a spiritual house and a holy priesthood. Thus through all those works befitting Christian men they can offer spiritual sacrifice and proclaim the power of him who has called them out of darkness into his marvelous light (cf. 1 Pt. 2:4-10).

"Though they differ from one another in essence and not only in degree, the common priesthood of the faithful and the ministerial or hierarchical priesthood (of those ordained to holy orders) are nonetheless interrelated. Each of them in its own special way is a participation in the one priesthood of Christ. The ministerial priest, by the sacred power he enjoys, molds and rules the priestly people. Acting in the Person of Christ, he brings about the Eucharistic Sacrifice, and offers it to God in the name of all the people. For their part, the faithful join in the offering of the Eucharist by virtue of their royal priesthood. They likewise exercise that priesthood by receiving the sacraments, by prayer and thanksgiving, by the witness of a holy life, and by self-denial and active charity.

"It is through the sacraments and the exercise of the virtues that the sacred nature and organic structure of the priestly community is brought into operation."

Baptism: "Incorporated into the Church through baptism, the faithful are consecrated by the baptismal character to the exercise of the cult of the Christian religion. Reborn as sons of God, they must confess before men the faith which they have received from God through the Church."

Confirmation: "Bound more intimately to the Church by the sacrament of confirmation, they are endowed by the Holy Spirit with special strength. Hence they are more strictly obliged to spread and defend the faith both by word and by deed as true witnesses of Christ."

Eucharist: "Taking part in the Eucharistic Sacrifice, which is the fount and apex of the whole Christian life, they offer the divine Victim to God, and offer themselves along with It. Thus, both by the act of oblation and through holy Communion, all perform their proper part in this liturgical service, not, indeed. all in the same way but each in that way which is appropriate to himself. Strengthened anew at the holy table by the Body of Christ, they manifest in a practical way that unity of God's People which is suitably signified and wondrously brought about by this most awesome sacrament."

Penance: "Those who approach the sacrament of penance obtain pardon from the mercy of God for offenses committed against him. They are at the same time reconciled with the Church, which they have wounded by their sins, and which by charity, example, and prayer seeks their conversion."

Anointing of the Sick: "By the sacred anointing of the sick and the prayer of her priests, the whole Church commends those who are ill to the suffering and glorified Lord, asking that he may lighten their suffering and save them (cf. Jas. 5:14-16). She exhorts them, moreover, to contribute to the welfare of the whole People of God by associating themselves freely with the passion and death of Christ (cf. Rom. 8:17; Col. 1:24; 2 Tm. 2:11-12; 1 Pt. 4:13)."

Holy Orders: "Those of the faithful who are consecrated by holy orders are appointed to feed the Church in Christ's name with the Word and the grace of God."

Matrimony: "Christian spouses, in virtue of the sacrament of matrimony, signify and partake of the mystery of that unity and fruitful love which exists between Christ and his Church (cf. Eph. 5:32). The spouses thereby help each other to attain to holiness in their married life and by the rearing and education of their children. And so, in their state and way of life, they have their own special gift among the People of God (cf. 1 Cor. 7:7).

"For from the wedlock of Christians there comes the family, in which new citizens of human society are born. By the grace of the Holy Spirit received in baptism these are made children of God, thus perpetuating the People of God through the centuries. The family is, so to speak, the domestic Church. In it parents should, by their word and example, be the first preachers of the faith to their children. They should encourage them in the vocation which is proper to each of them, fostering with special care any religious vocation.

"Fortified by so many and such powerful means of salvation, all the faithful, whatever their condition or state, are called by the Lord, each in his own way, to that perfect holiness whereby the Father himself is perfect."

Baptism

Baptism is the sacrament of spiritual regeneration by which a person is incorporated in Christ and made a member of his Mystical Body, given grace, and cleansed of original sin. Actual sins and the punishment owed for them are remitted also if the person baptized was guilty of such sins (e.g., in the case of a person baptized after reaching the age of reason). The theological virtues of faith, hope and charity are given with grace. The sacrament confers a character on the soul and can be received only once.

The matter is the pouring of water. The form is: "I baptize you in the name of the Father and of the Son and of the Holy Spirit."

The minister of solemn baptism is a bishop, priest or deacon, but in case of emergency anyone, including a non-Catholic, can validly baptize. The minister pours water on the forehead of the person being baptized and says the words of the form while the water is flowing. The water used in solemn baptism is blessed during the rite.

Baptism is conferred in the Roman rite by immersion or infusion (pouring of water), depending on the directive of the appropriate conference of bishops, according to the Code of Canon Law. The Church recognizes as valid baptisms properly performed by non-Catholic ministers. The baptism of infants has always been considered valid and the general practice of infant baptism was well established by the fifth century. Baptism is conferred conditionally when there is doubt about the validity of a previous baptism.

Baptism is necessary for salvation. If a person cannot receive the baptism of water described above, this can be supplied by baptism of blood (martyrdom suffered for the Catholic faith or some Christian virtue) or by baptism of desire (perfect contrition joined with at least the implicit intention of doing whatever God wills that people should do for salvation).

A sponsor is required for the person being baptized. (*See* **Godparents**, below).

A person must be validly baptized before he or she can receive any of the other sacraments.

Christian Initiation of Infants: Infants should be solemnly baptized as soon after birth as conveniently possible. Anyone may baptize an infant in danger of death. If the child survives, the ceremonies of solemn baptism should be supplied.

The sacrament is ordinarily conferred by a priest or deacon of the parents' parish.

Catholics 16 years of age and over who have received the sacraments of confirmation and the Eucharist and are practicing their faith are eligible to be sponsors or godparents. Only one is required. Two, one of each sex, are permitted. A non-Catholic Christian cannot be a godparent for a Catholic child, but may serve as a witness to the baptism. A Catholic may not be a godparent for a child baptized in a non-Catholic religion, but may be a witness.

"Because of the close communion between the Catholic Church and the Eastern Orthodox churches," states the 1993 *Directory on Ecumenism*, "it is permissible for a just cause for an Eastern faithful to act as godparent together with a Catholic godparent at the baptism of a Catholic infant or adult, so long as there is provision for the Catholic education of the person being baptized and it is clear that the godparent is a suitable one.

"A Catholic is not forbidden to stand as godparent in an Eastern Orthodox Church if he/she is so invited. In this case, the duty of providing for the Christian education binds in the first place the godparent who belongs to the church in which the child is baptized."

The role of godparents in baptismal ceremonies is secondary to the role of the parents. They serve as representatives of the community of faith and with the parents request baptism for the child and perform other ritual functions. Their function after baptism is to serve as proxies for the parents if the parents should be unable or fail to provide for the religious training of the child.

At baptism every child should be given a name with Christian significance, usually the name of a saint, to symbolize newness of life in Christ.

Christian Initiation of Adults: According to the *Ordo Initiationis Christianae Adultorum* ("Rite of the Christian Initiation of Adults") issued by the Congregation for Divine Worship on Jan. 6, 1972, and put into effect in revised form Sept. 1, 1988, adults are prepared for baptism and reception into the Church in several stages:

• An initial period of inquiry, instruction and evangelization.

• The catechumenate, a period of at least a year of formal instruction and progressive formation in and familiarity with Christian life. It starts with a statement of purpose and includes a rite of election.

• Immediate preparation, called a period of purification and enlightenment, from the beginning of Lent to reception of the sacraments of initiation — baptism, confirmation, Holy Eucharist — during ceremonies of the Easter Vigil. The period is marked by scrutinies, formal giving of the creed and the Lord's Prayer, the choice of a Christian name, and a final statement of intention.

• A mystagogic phase whose objective is greater familiarity with Christian life in the Church through observances of the Easter season and association with the community of the faithful, and through extended formation for about a year.

National Statutes for the Catechumenate were approved by the National Conference of Catholic Bishops Nov. 11, 1986, and were subsequently ratified by the Vatican.

The priest who baptizes a catechumen can also administer the sacrament of confirmation.

A sponsor is required for the person being baptized.

The *Ordo* also provides a simple rite of initiation for adults in danger of death and for cases in which all stages of the initiation process are not necessary, and guidelines for: (1) the preparation of adults for the sacraments of confirmation and Holy Eucharist in cases where they have been baptized but have not received further formation in the Christian life; (2) the formation and initiation of children of catechetical age.

The Church recognizes the right of anyone over the age of seven to request baptism and to receive the sacrament after completing a course of instruction and giving evidence of good will. Practically, in the case of minors in a non-Catholic family or environment, the Church accepts them when other circumstances favor their ability to practice the faith — e.g., well-disposed family situation, the presence of another or several Catholics in the family. Those who are not in such favorable circumstances are prudently advised to defer reception of the sacrament until they attain the maturity necessary for independent practice of the faith.

Reception of Baptized Christians: Procedure for the reception of already baptized Christians into full communion with the Catholic Church is distinguished from the catechumenate, since they have received some Christian formation. Instruction and formation are provided as necessary, however; and conditional baptism is administered if there is reasonable doubt about the validity of the person's previous baptism.

In the rite of reception, the person is invited to join the community of the Church in professing the Nicene Creed and is asked to state: "I believe and profess all that the holy Catholic Church believes, teaches, and proclaims as revealed by God." The priest places his hand on the head of the person, states the formula of admission to full communion, confirms (in the absence of a bishop), gives a sign of peace, and administers Holy Communion during a Eucharistic Liturgy.

Confirmation

Confirmation is the sacrament by which a baptized person, through anointing with chrism and the imposition of hands, is endowed with the fullness of baptismal grace; is united more intimately to the Church; is enriched with the special power of the Holy Spirit; is committed to be an authentic witness to Christ in word and action. The sacrament confers a character on the soul and can be received only once.

According to the apostolic constitution *Divinae Consortium Naturae,* dated Aug. 15, 1971, in conjunction with the *Ordo Confirmationis* ("Rite of Confirmation"): "The sacrament of confirmation is conferred through the anointing with chrism on the forehead, which is done by the imposition of the hand (matter of the sacrament), and through the words: *'N., receive the seal of the Holy Spirit, the Gift of the Father'*" (form of the sacrament). On May 5, 1975, bishops' conferences in English-speaking countries were informed by the Congregation for Divine Worship that Pope Paul had approved this English version of the form of the sacrament: *"Be sealed with the gift of the Holy Spirit."*

The ordinary minister of confirmation in the Roman rite is a bishop. Priests may be delegated for the purpose. A pastor can confirm a parishioner in danger of death, and a priest can confirm in ceremonies of Christian initiation and at the reception of a baptized Christian into union with the Church.

Ideally, the sacrament is conferred during the Eucharistic Liturgy. Elements of the rite include renewal of the promises of baptism, which confirmation ratifies and completes, and the laying on of hands by the confirming bishop and priests participating in the ceremony.

"The entire rite," according to the *Ordo*, "has a two-fold meaning. The laying of hands upon the candidates, done by the bishop and the concelebrating priests, expresses the biblical gesture by which the gift of the Holy Spirit is invoked. The anointing with chrism and the accompanying words clearly signify the effect of the Holy Spirit. Signed with the perfumed oil by the bishop's hand, the baptized person receives the indelible character, the seal of the Lord, together with the Spirit who is given and who conforms the person more perfectly to Christ and gives him the grace of spreading the Lord's presence among men."

A sponsor is required for the person being confirmed. Eligible is any Catholic 16 years of age or older who has received the sacraments of confirmation and the Eucharist and is practicing the faith. The baptismal sponsor, preferably, can also be the sponsor for confirmation. Parents may present their children for confirmation but cannot be sponsors.

In the Roman rite, it has been customary for children to receive confirmation within a reasonable time after first Communion and confession. There is a trend, however, to defer confirmation until later when its significance for mature Christian living becomes more evident. In the Eastern rites, confirmation is administered at the same time as baptism.

Eucharist

The Holy Eucharist is a sacrifice (*see* **The Mass**) and the sacrament in which Christ is present and is received under the appearances of bread and wine.

The matter is bread of wheat, unleavened in the Roman rite and leavened in the Eastern rites, and wine of grape. The form consists of the words of consecration said by the priest at Mass: "This is my body. This is the cup of my blood" (according to the traditional usage of the Roman rite).

Only a priest can consecrate bread and wine so they become the body and blood of Christ. After consecration, however, the Eucharist can be administered by deacons and, for various reasons, by religious and lay persons.

Priests celebrating Mass receive the Eucharist under the species of bread and wine. In the Roman rite, others receive under the species of bread only, i.e., the consecrated host, though in some circumstances they may receive under the species of both bread and wine. In Eastern-rite practice, the faithful generally receive a piece of consecrated leavened bread which has been dipped into consecrated wine (i.e., by intinction).

Conditions for receiving the Eucharist, commonly called Holy Communion, are the state of grace, the right intention and observance of the Eucharistic fast.

The faithful of Roman rite are required by a precept of the Church to receive the Eucharist at least once a year, ordinarily during the Easter time.

(*See* **Eucharistic Fast, Mass, Transubstantiation, Viaticum**.)

First Communion and Confession: Children are to be prepared for and given opportunity for receiving both sacraments (Eucharist and reconciliation, or penance) on reaching the age of discretion, at which time they become subject to general norms concerning confession and Communion. This, together with a stated preference for first confession before first Communion, was the central theme of a document entitled *Sanctus Pontifex* and published May 24, 1973, by the Congregation for the Discipline of the Sacraments and the Congregation for the Clergy, with the approval of Pope Paul VI.

What the document prescribed was the observance of practices ordered by St. Pius X in the decree *Quam Singulari* of Aug. 8, 1910. Its purpose was to counteract pastoral and catechetical experiments virtually denying children the opportunity of receiving both sacraments at the same time. Termination of such experiments was ordered by the end of the 1972-73 school year.

At the time the document was issued, two- or three-year experiments of this kind — routinely deferring reception of the sacrament of penance until after the first reception of Holy Communion — were in effect in more than half of the dioceses of the U.S. They have remained in effect in many places, despite the advisory from the Vatican.

One reason stated in support of such experiments is the view that children are not capable of serious sin at the age of seven or eight, when Communion is generally received for the first time, and therefore prior reception of the sacrament of penance is not necessary. Another reason is the purpose of making the distinctive nature of the two sacraments clearer to children.

The Vatican view reflected convictions that the principle and practice of devotional reception of penance are as valid for children as they are for adults, and that sound catechetical programs can avoid misconceptions about the two sacraments.

A second letter on the same subject and in the same vein was released May 19, 1977, by the aforementioned congregations. It was issued in response to the question:

" 'Whether it is allowed after the declaration of May 24, 1973, to continue to have, as a general rule, the reception of first Communion precede the reception of the sacrament of penance in those parishes in which this practice developed in the past few years.'

"The Sacred Congregations for the Sacraments and Divine Worship and for the Clergy, with the approval of the Supreme Pontiff, reply: Negative, and according to the mind of the declaration.

"The mind of the declaration is that one year after the promulgation of the same declaration, all experiments of receiving first Communion without the sacrament of penance should cease so that the discipline of the Church might be restored, in the spirit of the decree, *Quam Singulari*."

The two letters from the Vatican congregations have not produced uniformity of practice in this country. Simultaneous preparation for both sacraments is provided in some dioceses where a child has the option of receiving either sacrament first, with the counsel of parents, priests and teachers. Programs in other dioceses are geared first to reception of Communion and later to reception of the Sacrament of Reconciliation.

Commentators on the letters note that: they are disciplinary rather than doctrinal in content; they are subject to pastoral interpretation by bishops; they cannot be interpreted to mean that a person who is not guilty of serious sin must be required to receive the sacrament of penance before (even first) Communion.

Canon 914 of the Code of Canon Law states that sacramental confession should precede first Communion.

Holy Communion under the Forms of Bread and Wine (by separate taking of the consecrated bread and wine or by intinction, the reception of the host dipped in the wine): Such reception is permitted under conditions stated in instructions issued by the Congregation for Divine Worship (May 25, 1967; June 29, 1970), the General Instruction on the Roman Missal (No. 242), and directives of bishops' conferences and individual bishops.

Accordingly, Communion can be administered in this way to: persons being baptized, received into communion with the Church, confirmed, receiving anointing of the sick; couples at their wedding or jubilee; religious at profession or renewal of profession; lay persons receiving an ecclesiastical assignment (e.g., lay missionaries); participants at concelebrated Masses, retreats, pastoral commission meetings, daily Masses and, in the U.S., Masses on Sundays and holy days of obligation.

A communicant has the option of receiving the Eucharist under the form of bread alone or under the forms of bread and wine. (*See* **New U.S. Norms** in the **Liturgy** section.)

Holy Communion More Than Once a Day: A person who has already received the Eucharist may receive it (only) once again on the same day only during a Eucharistic celebration in which the person participates. A person in danger of death who has already received the Eucharist once or twice is urged to receive Communion again as Viaticum. Pope John Paul approved this decision, in accord with Canon 917, and ordered it published July 11, 1984.

Holy Communion and Eucharistic Devotion outside of Mass: These were the subjects of an instruction (*De Sacra Communione et de Cultu Mysterii Eucharistici extra Missam*) dated June 21 and made public Oct. 18, 1973, by the Congregation for Divine Worship.

Holy Communion can be given outside of Mass to persons unable for a reasonable cause to receive it during Mass on a given day. The ceremonial rite is modeled on the structure of the Mass, consisting of a penitential act, a scriptural reading, the Lord's Prayer, a sign or gesture of peace, giving of the Eucharist, prayer and final blessing. Viaticum and Communion to the sick can be given by extraordinary ministers (authorized lay persons) with appropriate rites.

Forms of devotion outside of Mass are exposition of the Blessed Sacrament (by men or women religious, especially, or lay persons in the absence of a priest; but only a priest can give the blessing), processions and congresses with appropriate rites.

Intercommunion: Church policy on inter-communion was stated in an "Instruction on the Admission of Other Christians to the Eucharist," dated June 1 and made public July 8, 1972, against the background of the Decree on Ecumenism approved by the Second Vatican Council, and the Directory on Ecumenism issued by the Secretariat for Promoting Christian Unity in 1967, 1970 and 1993.

Basic principles related to intercommunion are:

• "There is an indissoluble link between the mystery of the Church and the mystery of the Eucharist, or between ecclesial and Eucharistic communion; the celebration of the Eucharist of itself signifies the fullness of profession of faith and ecclesial communion" (1972 Instruction).

• "Eucharistic communion practiced by those who are not in full ecclesial communion with each other cannot be the expression of that full unity which the Eucharist of its nature signifies and which in this case does not exist; for this reason such communion cannot be regarded as a means to be used to lead to full ecclesial communion" (1972 Instruction).

• The question of reciprocity "arises only with those churches which have preserved the substance of the Eucharist, the sacrament of orders and apostolic succession" (1967 Directory).

• "A Catholic cannot ask for the Eucharist except from a minister who has been validly ordained" (1967 Directory).

The policy distinguishes between separated Eastern Christians and other Christians.

With Separated Eastern Christians (e.g., Orthodox): These may be given the Eucharist (as well as penance and anointing of the sick) at their request. Catholics may receive these same sacraments from priests of separated Eastern churches if they experience genuine spiritual necessity, seek spiritual benefit, and access to a Catholic priest is morally or physically impossible. This policy (of reciprocity) derives from the facts that the separated Eastern churches have apostolic succession through their bishops, valid priests, and sacramental beliefs and practices in accord with those of the Catholic Church.

With Other Christians (e.g., members of Reformation-related churches, others): Admission to the Eucharist in the Catholic Church, according to the Directory on Ecumenism, "is confined to particular cases of those Christians who have a faith in the sacrament in conformity with that of the Church, who

experience a serious spiritual need for the Eucharistic sustenance, who for a prolonged period are unable to have recourse to a minister of their own community and who ask for the sacrament of their own accord; all this provided that they have proper dispositions and lead lives worthy of a Christian." The spiritual need is defined as "a need for an increase in spiritual life and a need for a deeper involvement in the mystery of the Church and its unity."

Circumstances under which Communion may be given to other properly disposed Christians are danger of death, imprisonment, persecution, grave spiritual necessity coupled with no chance of recourse to a minister of their own community.

Catholics cannot ask for the Eucharist from ministers of other Christian churches who have not been validly ordained to the priesthood.

(For other teachings concerning the Eucharist, please *see* **News in Depth** for coverage of Pope John Paul II's 2003 encyclical, *Ecclesia de Eucharistia*.)

Penance

Penance is the sacrament by which sins committed after baptism are forgiven and a person is reconciled with God and the Church.

Individual and integral confession and absolution are the only ordinary means for the forgiveness of serious sin and for reconciliation with God and the Church.

(Other than ordinary means are perfect contrition and general absolution without prior confession, both of which require the intention of subsequent confession and absolution.)

A revised ritual for the sacrament — *Ordo Paenitentiae*, published by the Congregation of Divine Worship Feb. 7, 1974, and made mandatory in the U.S. from the first Sunday of Lent, 1977 — reiterates standard doctrine concerning the sacrament; emphasizes the social (communal and ecclesial) aspects of sin and conversion, with due regard for personal aspects and individual reception of the sacrament; prescribes three forms for celebration of the sacrament; and presents models for community penitential services.

The basic elements of the sacrament are sorrow for sin because of a supernatural motive, confession (of previously unconfessed mortal or grave sins, required; of venial sins also, but not of necessity), and reparation (by means of prayer or other act enjoined by the confessor), all of which comprise the matter of the sacrament; and absolution, which is the form of the sacrament.

The traditional words of absolution — *"I absolve you from your sins in the name of the Father, and of the Son, and of the Holy Spirit"* — remain unchanged at the conclusion of a petition in the new rite that God may grant pardon and peace through the ministry of the Church.

The minister of the sacrament is an authorized priest — i.e., one who, besides having the power of orders to forgive sins, also has faculties of jurisdiction granted by an ecclesiastical superior and/or by canon law.

The sacrament can be celebrated in three ways:

• For individuals, the traditional manner remains acceptable but is enriched with additional elements including: reception of the penitent and making of the Sign of the Cross; an exhortation by the confessor to trust in God; a reading from Scripture; confession of sins; manifestation of repentance; petition for God's forgiveness through the ministry of the Church and the absolution of the priest; praise of God's mercy, and dismissal in peace. Some of these elements are optional.

• For several penitents, in the course of a community celebration including a Liturgy of the Word of God and prayers, individual confession and absolution, and an act of thanksgiving.

• For several penitents, in the course of a community celebration, with general confession and general absolution. In extraordinary cases, reconciliation may be attained by general absolution without prior individual confession as, for example, under these circumstances: (1) danger of death, when there is neither time nor priests available for hearing confessions; (2) grave necessity of a number of penitents who, because of a shortage of confessors, would be deprived of sacramental grace or Communion for a lengthy period of time through no fault of their own. Persons receiving general absolution are obliged to be properly disposed and resolved to make an individual confession of the grave sins from which they have been absolved; this confession should be made as soon as the opportunity to confess presents itself and before any second reception of general absolution.

Norms regarding general absolution, issued by the Congregation for the Doctrine of the Faith in 1972, are not intended to provide a basis for convoking large gatherings of the faithful for the purpose of imparting general absolution, in the absence of extraordinary circumstances. Judgment about circumstances that warrant general absolution belongs principally to the bishop of the place, with due regard for related decisions of appropriate episcopal conferences.

Communal celebrations of the sacrament are not held in connection with Mass.

The place of individual confession, as determined by episcopal conferences in accordance with given norms, can be the traditional confessional or another appropriate setting.

A precept of the Church obliges the faithful guilty of grave sin to confess at least once a year.

The Church favors more frequent reception of the sacrament not only for the reconciliation of persons guilty of serious sins but also for reasons of devotion. Devotional confession — in which venial sins or previously forgiven sins are confessed — serves the purpose of confirming persons in penance and conversion.

Penitential Celebrations: Communal penitential celebrations are designed to emphasize the social dimensions of Christian life — the community aspects and significance of penance and reconciliation.

Elements of such celebrations are community prayer, hymns and songs, scriptural and other readings, examination of conscience, general confession and expression of sorrow for sin, acts of penance and reconciliation, and a form of non-sacramental absolution resembling the one in the penitential rite of the Mass.

If the sacrament is celebrated during the service, there must be individual confession and absolution of sin.

Recent developments: On May 2, 2002, officials of the Roman Curia released a *motu proprio* by Pope

John Paul II, *Misericordia Dei* ("Mercy of God, On Certain Aspects of the Celebration of the Sacrament of Penance"). The 15-page document called for a "vigorous revitalization" of the sacrament and asked bishops to adopt stricter observance on Church law's "grave necessity" requirement as a condition for the use of general absolution. It also requested that bishops' conferences submit national norms for general absolution to the Holy See for approval "as soon as possible."

In February 2003, the Bishops' Committee on the Liturgy and the Subcommittee for the Jubilee Year 2000 of the USCCB issued a new booklet, *Celebrating the Sacrament of Penance: Questions and Answers*. The booklet provides answers to some of the frequently asked questions about the Sacrament of Penance, including "Why Do We Need the Sacrament of Penance?" "What Happens in the Sacrament of Penance?" and "What is 'General Absolution'?" The booklet is intended for use in parishes during preparation for the Sacrament of Penance, as a resource for reflection on the sacrament during particular seasons such as Lent, and as a practical tool to aid penitents as they go to confession.

(*See* **Absolution, Confession, Confessional, Confessor, Contrition, Faculties, Forgiveness of Sin, Power of the Keys, Seal of Confession, Sin.**)

Anointing of the Sick

This sacrament, promulgated by St. James the Apostle (Jas. 5:13-15), can be administered to the faithful after reaching the age of reason who are in danger because of illness or old age. By the anointing with blessed oil and the prayer of a priest, the sacrament confers on the person comforting grace; the remission of venial sins and inculpably unconfessed mortal sins, together with at least some of the temporal punishment due for sins; and, sometimes, results in an improved state of health.

The matter of this sacrament is the anointing with blessed oil (olive oil, or vegetable oil if necessary) of the forehead and hands; in cases of necessity, a single anointing of another portion of the body suffices. The form is: "Through this holy anointing and his most loving mercy, may the Lord assist you by the grace of the Holy Spirit so that, when you have been freed from your sins, he may save you and in his goodness raise you up."

Anointing of the sick, formerly called extreme unction, may be received more than once, e.g., in new or continuing stages of serious illness. Ideally, the sacrament should be administered while the recipient is conscious and in conjunction with the sacraments of penance and the Eucharist. It should be administered in cases of doubt as to whether the person has reached the age of reason, is dangerously ill or dead.

The sacrament can be administered during a communal celebration in some circumstances, as in a home for the aged.

Holy Orders

Order is the sacrament by which the mission given by Christ to the Apostles continues to be exercised in the Church until the end of time; it is the sacrament of apostolic mission. It has three grades: episcopacy, priesthood and diaconate. The sacrament confers a character on the soul and can be received only once.

The minister of the sacrament is a bishop.

Order, like matrimony but in a different way, is a social sacrament. As the Second Vatican Council declared in *Lumen Gentium*, the Dogmatic Constitution on the Church:

"For the nurturing and constant growth of the People of God, Christ the Lord instituted in his Church a variety of ministries, which work for the good of the whole body. For those ministers who are endowed with sacred power are servants of their brethren, so that all who are of the People of God, and therefore enjoy a true Christian dignity, can work toward a common goal freely and in an orderly way, and arrive at salvation" (No. 18).

Bishop: The fullness of the priesthood belongs to those who have received the order of bishop. Bishops, in hierarchical union with the pope and their fellow bishops, are the successors of the Apostles as pastors of the Church: they have individual responsibility for the care of the local churches they serve and collegial responsibility for the care of the universal Church (*see* **Collegiality**). In the ordination or consecration of bishops, the essential form is the imposition of hands by the consecrator(s) and the assigned prayer in the preface of the rite of ordination.

"With their helpers, the priests and deacons, bishops have taken up the service of the community presiding in place of God over the flock whose shepherds they are, as teachers of doctrine, priests of sacred worship, and officers of good order" (No. 20).

Priests: A priest is an ordained minister with the power to celebrate Mass, administer the sacraments, preach and teach the word of God, impart blessings, and perform additional pastoral functions, according to the mandate of his ecclesiastical superior.

Concerning priests, the Second Vatican Council stated in *Lumen Gentium* (No. 28):

"The divinely established ecclesiastical ministry is exercised on different levels by those who from antiquity have been called bishops, priests, and deacons. Although priests do not possess the highest degree of the priesthood, and although they are dependent on the bishops in the exercise of their power, they are nevertheless united with the bishops in sacerdotal dignity. By the power of the sacrament of orders, and in the image of Christ the eternal High Priest (Heb. 5:1-10; 7:24; 9:11-28), they are consecrated to preach the Gospel, shepherd the faithful, and celebrate divine worship as true priests of the New Testament.

"Priests, prudent cooperators with the episcopal order as well as its aides and instruments, are called to serve the People of God. They constitute one priesthood with their bishop, although that priesthood is comprised of different functions."

In the ordination of a priest of Roman rite, the essential matter is the imposition of hands on the heads of those being ordained by the ordaining bishop. The essential form is the accompanying prayer in the preface of the ordination ceremony. Other elements in the rite are the presentation of the implements of sacrifice — the chalice containing the wine and the paten containing a host — with accompanying prayers.

Deacon: There are two kinds of deacons: those who receive the order and remain in it permanently, and those who receive the order while advancing to priesthood. The following quotation — from Vatican II's Dogmatic Constitution on the Church (*Lumen Gen-*

tium, No. 29) — describes the nature and role of the diaconate, with emphasis on the permanent diaconate.

"At a lower level of the hierarchy are deacons, upon whom hands are imposed 'not unto the priesthood, but unto a ministry of service.' For strengthened by sacramental grace, in communion with the bishop and his group of priests, they serve the People of God in the ministry of the liturgy, of the word, and of charity. It is the duty of the deacon, to the extent that he has been authorized by competent authority, to administer baptism solemnly, to be custodian and dispenser of the Eucharist, to assist at and bless marriages in the name of the Church, to bring Viaticum to the dying, to read the sacred Scripture to the faithful, to instruct and exhort the people, to preside at the worship and prayer of the faithful, to administer sacramentals, and to officiate at funeral and burial services. (Deacons are) dedicated to duties of charity and administration.

"The diaconate can in the future be restored as a proper and permanent rank of the hierarchy. It pertains to the competent territorial bodies of bishops, of one kind or another, to decide, with the approval of the Supreme Pontiff, whether and where it is opportune for such deacons to be appointed for the care of souls. With the consent of the Roman Pontiff, this diaconate will be able to be conferred upon men of more mature age, even upon those living in the married state. It may also be conferred upon suitable young men. For them, however, the law of celibacy must remain intact" (No. 29).

The Apostles ordained the first seven deacons (Acts 6:1-6): Stephen, Philip, Prochorus, Nicanor, Timon, Parmenas, Nicholas.

Former Orders, Ministries: With the revision of the sacrament of order which began in 1971, the orders of subdeacon, acolyte, exorcist, lector and porter were abolished because they and their respective functions had fallen into disuse or did not require ordination. The Holy See started revision of the sacrament of order in 1971. By virtue of an indult of Oct. 5 of that year, the bishops of the U.S. were permitted to discontinue ordaining porters and exorcists. Another indult, dated three days later, permitted the use of revised rites for ordaining acolytes and lectors.

To complete the revision, Pope Paul VI abolished Sept. 14, 1972, the orders of porter, exorcist and subdeacon; decreed that laymen, as well as candidates for the diaconate and priesthood, can be installed (rather than ordained) in the ministries (rather than orders) of acolyte and lector; reconfirmed the suppression of tonsure and its replacement with a service of dedication to God and the Church; and stated that a man enters the clerical state on ordination to the diaconate.

The abolished orders were:

• Subdeacon, with specific duties in liturgical worship, especially at Mass. The order, whose first extant mention dates from about the middle of the third century, was regarded as minor until the 13th century; afterwards, it was called a major order in the West but not in the East.

• Acolyte, to serve in minor capacities in liturgical worship; a function now performed by Mass servers.

• Exorcist, to perform services of exorcism for expelling evil spirits; a function which came to be reserved to specially delegated priests.

• Lector, to read scriptural and other passages during liturgical worship; a function now generally performed by lay persons.

• Porter, to guard the entrance to an assembly of Christians and to ward off undesirables who tried to gain admittance; an order of early origin and utility but of present insignificance.

Permanent Diaconate

Restoration of the permanent diaconate in the Roman rite — making it possible for men to become deacons permanently, without going on to the priesthood — was promulgated by Pope Paul VI June 18, 1967, in a document entitled *Sacrum Diaconatus Ordinem* ("Sacred Order of the Diaconate").

The Pope's action implemented the desire expressed by the Second Vatican Council for reestablishment of the diaconate as an independent order in its own right not only to supply ministers for carrying on the work of the Church but also to complete the hierarchical structure of the Church of Roman rite.

Permanent deacons have been traditional in the Eastern Church. The Western Church, however, since the fourth or fifth century, generally followed the practice of conferring the diaconate only as a sacred order preliminary to the priesthood, and of restricting the ministry of deacons to liturgical functions.

The pope's document, issued on his own initiative, provided:

• Qualified unmarried men 25 years of age or older may be ordained deacons. They cannot marry after ordination.

• Qualified married men 35 years of age or older may be ordained deacons. The consent of the wife of a prospective deacon is required. A married deacon cannot remarry after the death of his wife.

• Preparation for the diaconate includes a course of study and formation over a period of at least three years.

• Candidates who are not members of religious institutes must be affiliated with a diocese. Reestablishment of the diaconate among religious is reserved to the Holy See.

• Deacons will practice their ministry under the direction of a bishop and with the priests with whom they will be associated. (For functions, *see* the description of deacon, under **Holy Orders**.)

Restoration of the permanent diaconate in the U.S. was approved by the Holy See in October 1968. Shortly afterwards the U.S. bishops established a committee for the permanent diaconate, which was chaired by Bishop Edward U. Kmiec of Nashville in 1997. The current head of the committee is Bishop Robert C. Morlino of Helena. The committee operates through a secretariat, with offices at 3211 Fourth St. N.E., Washington, DC 20017. Deacon John Pistone is executive director.

Status and Functions

The 2003 *Official Catholic Directory* reports that in the U.S. there were a total of 14,106 permanent deacons (the highest total by far for any single country), an increase of 342 from the previous year and an increase of 3,266 from 1993. Worldwide, there are currently 29,204 deacons, according to the 2001 edition of the *Statisticum Annuarium Ecclesiae* (the most recent edition).

Training programs of spiritual, theological and pas-

toral formation are based on guidelines emanating from the National Conference of Catholic Bishops.

Deacons have various functions, depending on the nature of their assignments. Liturgically, they can officiate at baptisms, weddings, wake services and funerals, can preach and distribute Holy Communion. Some are engaged in religious education work. All are intended to carry out works of charity and pastoral service of one kind or another.

The majority of deacons, the majority of whom are married, continue in their secular work. Their ministry of service is developing in three dimensions: of liturgy, of the word, and of charity. Depending on the individual deacon's abilities and preference, he is assigned by his bishop to either a parochial ministry or to another field of service. Deacons are active in a variety of ministries including those to prison inmates and their families, the sick in hospitals, nursing homes and homes for the aged, alienated youth, the elderly and the poor, and in various areas of legal service to the indigent, of education and campus ministry.

National Association of Diaconate Directors: Membership organization of directors, vicars and other staff personnel of diaconate programs. Established in 1977 to promote effective communication and facilitate the exchange of information and resources of members; to develop professional expertise and promote research, training and self evaluation; to foster accountability and seek ways to promote means of implementing solutions to problems. The association is governed by an executive board of elected officers. Officers include Deacons: Maurice Reed of Green Bay, pres., 1997-98; Peter D'Heilly of St.Paul-Minneapolis, president-elect; Thomas Welch, exec. dir. Office: 1337 W. Ohio St., Chicago, IL 60622.

Ordination of Women

The Catholic Church believes and teaches that, in fidelity to the will of Christ, it cannot ordain women to the priesthood. This position has been set out over the last quarter-century in a series of authoritative documents published by or with the authority of Pope Paul VI and Pope John Paul II.

The first of these, *Inter Insigniores* ("Among the Characteristics"), was issued by the Congregation for the Doctrine of the Faith in October 1976. Its central statement is: "The Sacred Congregation for the Doctrine of the Faith judges it necessary to recall that the Church, in fidelity to the example of the Lord, does not consider herself authorized to admit women to priestly ordination."

In support of this, the document cited the constant tradition of the Church, the fact that Christ called only men to be Apostles and the continuation of this practice by the Apostles themselves, and the sacramental appropriateness of a male priesthood acting *in persona Christi* — in the person of Christi.

In light of continuing discussion, Pope John Paul II returned to the subject in the apostolic letter *Ordinatio Sacerdotalis* ("Priestly Ordination"), issued May 29, 1994: "Wherefore, in order that all doubt may be removed regarding a matter of great importance, a matter which pertains to the Church's divine constitution itself, in virtue of my ministry of confirming the brethren (cf. Lk. 22.32) I declare that the Church has no authority whatsoever to confer priestly ordination on women and that this judgment is to be definitively held by all the Church's faithful."

The Congregation for the Doctrine of the Faith followed this on Oct. 28, 1995, with a response, published over the signature of its Prefect, Cardinal Joseph Ratzinger, to a bishop's inquiry concerning how "to be definitively held" should be understood. The response was:

"This teaching requires definitive assent, since, founded on the written Word of God and from the beginning constantly preserved and applied in the Tradition of the Church, it has been set forth infallibly by the ordinary and universal Magisterium (cf. Second Vatican Council, Dogmatic Constitution on the Church *Lumen Gentium*, 25, 2).

Concerning the possible ordination of women to the diaconate, the International Theological Commission in 2002 concluded that the permanent diaconate belongs to the sacrament of orders and thus is limited to men only.

MATRIMONY

Marriage Doctrine

The following excerpts, stating key points of doctrine on marriage, are from *Gaudium et Spes*, (Nos. 48 to 51) promulgated by the Second Vatican Council:

Conjugal Covenant

The intimate partnership of married life and love has been established by the Creator and qualified by his laws. It is rooted in the conjugal covenant of irrevocable personal consent.

God himself is the author of matrimony, endowed as it is with various benefits and purposes. All of these have a very decisive bearing on the continuation of the human race, on the personal development and eternal destiny of the individual members of a family, and on the dignity, stability, peace, and prosperity of the family itself and of human society as a whole. By their very nature, the institution of matrimony itself and conjugal love are ordained for the procreation and education of children, and find in them their ultimate crown.

Thus a man and a woman render mutual help and service to each other through an intimate union of their persons and of their actions. Through this union they experience the meaning of their oneness and attain to it with growing perfection day by day. As a mutual gift of two persons, this intimate union, as well as the good of the children, imposes total fidelity on the spouses and argues for an unbreakable oneness between them (No. 48).

Sacrament of Matrimony

Christ the Lord abundantly blessed this many-faceted love. The Savior of men and the Spouse of the Church comes into the lives of married Christians through the sacrament of matrimony. He abides with them thereafter so that, just as he loved the Church and handed himself over on her behalf, the spouses may love each other with perpetual fidelity through mutual self-bestowal.

Graced with the dignity and office of fatherhood and motherhood, parents will energetically acquit themselves of a duty which devolves primarily on them; namely, education, and especially religious education.

The Christian family, which springs from marriage as a reflection of the loving covenant uniting Christ with the Church, and as a participation in that covenant, will manifest to all men the Savior's living presence in the world, and the genuine nature of the Church (No. 48).

Conjugal Love

The biblical Word of God several times urges the betrothed and the married to nourish and develop their wedlock by pure conjugal love and undivided affection.

This love is an eminently human one since it is directed from one person to another through an affection of the will. It involves the good of the whole person. Therefore it can enrich the expressions of body and mind with a unique dignity, ennobling these expressions as special ingredients and signs of the friendship distinctive of marriage. This love the Lord has judged worthy of special gifts, healing, perfecting, and exalting gifts of grace and of charity.

Such love, merging the human with the divine, leads the spouses to a free and mutual gift of themselves, a gift proving itself by gentle affection and by deed. Such love pervades the whole of their lives. Indeed, by its generous activity it grows better and grows greater. Therefore it far excels mere erotic inclination, which, selfishly pursued, soon enough fades wretchedly away.

This love is uniquely expressed and perfected through the marital act. The actions within marriage by which the couple are united intimately and chastely are noble and worthy ones. Expressed in a manner which is truly human, these actions signify and promote that mutual self-giving by which spouses enrich each other with a joyful and a thankful will.

Sealed by mutual faithfulness and hallowed above all by Christ's sacrament, this love remains steadfastly true in body and in mind, in bright days or dark. It will never be profaned by adultery or divorce. Firmly established by the Lord, the unity of marriage will radiate from the equal personal dignity of wife and husband, a dignity acknowledged by mutual and total love.

The steady fulfillment of the duties of this Christian vocation demands notable virtue. For this reason, strengthened by grace for holiness of life, the couple will painstakingly cultivate and pray for constancy of love, largeheartedness, and the spirit of sacrifice (No. 49).

Fruitfulness of Marriage

Marriage and conjugal love are by their nature ordained toward the begetting and educating of children. Children are really the supreme gift of marriage and contribute very substantially to the welfare of their parents. God himself wished to share with man a certain special participation in his own creative work. Thus he blessed male and female, saying: "Increase and multiply" (Gn. 1:28).

Hence, while not making the other purposes of matrimony of less account, the true practice of conjugal love, and the whole meaning of the family life which results from it, have this aim: that the couple be ready with stout hearts to cooperate with the love of the Creator and the Savior, who through them will enlarge and enrich his own family day by day.

Parents should regard as their proper mission the task of transmitting human life and educating those to whom it has been transmitted. They should realize that they are thereby cooperators with the love of God the Creator, and are, so to speak, the interpreters of that love. Thus they will fulfill their task with human and Christian responsibility (No. 50).

Norms of Judgment

They will thoughtfully take into account both their own welfare and that of their children, those already born and those who may be foreseen. For this accounting they will reckon with both the material and the spiritual conditions of the times as well as of their state in life. Finally, they will consult the interests of the family group, of temporal society, and of the Church herself.

The parents themselves should ultimately make this judgment in the sight of God. But in their manner of acting, spouses should be aware that they cannot proceed arbitrarily. They must always be governed according to a conscience dutifully conformed to the divine law itself, and should be submissive toward the Church's teaching office, which authentically interprets that law in the light of the Gospel. That divine law reveals and protects the integral meaning of conjugal love, and impels it toward a truly human fulfillment.

Marriage, to be sure, is not instituted solely for procreation. Rather, its very nature as an unbreakable compact between persons, and the welfare of the children, both demand that the mutual love of the spouses, too, be embodied in a rightly ordered manner, that it grow and ripen. Therefore, marriage persists as a whole manner and communion of life, and maintains its value and indissolubility, even when offspring are lacking — despite, rather often, the very intense desire of the couple (No. 50).

Love and Life

This Council realizes that certain modern conditions often keep couples from arranging their married lives harmoniously, and that they find themselves in circumstances where at least temporarily the size of their families should not be increased. As a result, the faithful exercise of love and the full intimacy of their lives are hard to maintain. But where the intimacy of married life is broken off, it is not rare for its faithfulness to be imperiled and its quality of fruitfulness ruined. For then the upbringing of the children and the courage to accept new ones are both endangered.

To these problems there are those who presume to offer dishonorable solutions. Indeed, they do not recoil from the taking of life. But the Church issues the reminder that a true contradiction cannot exist between the divine laws pertaining to the transmission of life and those pertaining to the fostering of authentic conjugal love.

Church Teaching

For God, the Lord of Life, has conferred on men the surpassing ministry of safeguarding life — a ministry which must be fulfilled in a manner which is worthy of men. Therefore from the moment of its conception life must be guarded with the greatest care, while abortion and infanticide are unspeakable crimes. The sexual characteristics of man and the human faculty of reproduction wonderfully exceed the dispositions of lower forms of life. Hence the acts themselves which are proper to conjugal love and which are exercised in accord with genuine human dignity must be honored with great reverence (No. 51).

Therefore when there is question of harmonizing conjugal love with the responsible transmission of life, the moral aspect of any procedure does not depend solely on the sincere intentions or on an evaluation of motives. It must be determined by objective standards. These, based on the nature of the human person and his acts, preserve the full sense of mutual self-giving and human procreation in the context of true love. Such a goal cannot be achieved unless the virtue of conjugal chastity is sincerely practiced. Relying on these principles, sons of the Church may not undertake methods of regulating procreation which are found blameworthy by the teaching authority of the Church in its unfolding of the divine law.

Everyone should be persuaded that human life and the task of transmitting it are not realities bound up with this world alone. Hence they cannot be measured or perceived only in terms of it, but always have a bearing on the eternal destiny of men (No. 51).

HUMANAE VITAE

Marriage doctrine and morality were the subjects of the encyclical letter *Humanae Vitae* ("Of Human Life"), issued by Pope Paul VI, July 29, 1968. *Humanae Vitae* was given reaffirmation and its teaching restated and defended by Pope John Paul II in his encyclical *Evangelium Vitae* (*The Gospel of Life*, 1995). Following are a number of key excerpts from *Humanae Vitae*, which was framed in the pattern of traditional teaching and statements by the Second Vatican Council.

Each and every marriage act ("*quilibet matrimonii usus*") must remain open to the transmission of life (No. 11).

Indeed, by its intimate structure, the conjugal act, while most closely uniting husband and wife, capacitates them for the generation of new lives according to laws inscribed in the very being of man and woman. By safeguarding both these essential aspects, the unitive and the procreative, the conjugal act preserves in its fullness the sense of true mutual love and its ordination toward man's most high calling to parenthood (No. 12).

It is, in fact, justly observed that a conjugal act imposed upon one's partner without regard for his or her condition and lawful desires is not a true act of love, and therefore denies an exigency of right moral order in the relationships between husband and wife. Hence, one who reflects well must also recognize that a reciprocal act of love which jeopardizes the responsibility to transmit life — which God the Creator, according to particular laws, inserted therein — is in contradiction with the design constitutive of marriage and with the will of the Author of life. To use this divine gift, destroying, even if only partially, its meaning and its purpose, is to contradict the nature both of man and of woman and of their most intimate relationship, and therefore it is to contradict also the plan of God and his will (No. 13).

Forbidden Actions

The direct interruption of the generative process already begun, and, above all, directly willed and procured abortion, even if for therapeutic reasons, are to be absolutely excluded as licit means of regulating birth.

Equally to be excluded is direct sterilization, whether perpetual or temporary, whether of the man or of the woman. Similarly excluded is every action which, either in anticipation of the conjugal act, or in its accomplishment, or in the development of its natural consequences, proposes, whether as an end or as a means, to render procreation impossible.

To justify conjugal acts made intentionally infecund, one cannot invoke as valid reasons the lesser evil, or the fact that such acts would constitute a whole together with the fecund acts already performed or to follow later and hence would share in one and the same moral goodness. In truth, if it is sometimes licit to tolerate a lesser evil in order to avoid a greater evil or to promote a greater good, it is not licit, even for the gravest reasons, to do evil so that good may follow therefrom; that is, to make into the object of a positive act of the will something which is intrinsically disorder, and hence unworthy of the human person, even when the intention is to safeguard or promote individual, family or social well-being.

Consequently, it is an error to think that a conjugal act which is deliberately made infecund, and so is intrinsically dishonest, could be made honest and right by the ensemble of a fecund conjugal life (No. 14).

If, then, there are serious motives to space out births, which derive from the physical or psychological conditions of husband and wife, or from external conditions, the Church teaches that it is then licit to take into account the natural rhythms immanent in the generative functions, for the use of marriage in the infecund periods only, and in this way to regulate birth without offending earlier stated principles (No. 16).

Pastoral Concerns

We do not at all intend to hide the sometimes serious difficulties inherent in the life of Christian married persons; for them, as for everyone else, "the gate is narrow and the way is hard that leads to life." But the hope of that life must illuminate their way, as with courage they strive to live with wisdom, justice and piety in this present time, knowing that the figure of this world passes away.

Let married couples then, face up to the efforts needed, supported by the faith and hope which "do not disappoint because God's love has been poured into our hearts through the Holy Spirit, who has been given to us." Let them implore divine assistance by persevering prayer; above all, let them draw from the source of grace and charity in the Eucharist. And, if sin should still keep its hold over them, let them not be discouraged but rather have recourse with humble perseverance to the mercy of God, which is poured forth in the sacrament of penance (No. 25).

MARRIAGE LAWS

The Catholic Church claims jurisdiction over its members in matters pertaining to marriage. Church legislation on the subject is stated principally in 111 canons of the Code of Canon Law.

Marriage laws of the Church provide juridical norms in support of the marriage covenant. In 10 chapters, the revised Code covers: pastoral directives for preparing men and women for marriage; impediments in general and in particular; matrimonial consent; form for the celebration of marriage; mixed marriages; secret celebration of marriage; effects of marriage; separation of spouses; and convalidation of marriage.

Catholics are bound by all marriage laws of the Church. Non-Catholics, whether baptized or not, are not considered bound by these ecclesiastical laws except in cases of marriage with a Catholic. Certain natural laws, in the Catholic view, bind all men and women, irrespective of their religious beliefs; accordingly, marriage is prohibited before the time of puberty, without knowledge and free mutual consent, in the case of an already existing valid marriage bond, in the case of antecedent and perpetual impotence.

Formalities

These include, in addition to arrangements for the time and place of the marriage ceremony, doctrinal and moral instruction concerning marriage and the recording of data which verifies in documentary form the eligibility and freedom of the persons to marry. Records of this kind, which are confidential, are preserved in the archives of the church where the marriage takes place.

Premarital instructions are the subject matter of Pre-Cana Conferences.

Marital Consent

Matrimonial consent can be invalidated by an essential defect, substantial error, the strong influence of force and fear, the presence of a condition or intention against the nature of marriage.

Form of Marriage

A Catholic is required, for validity and lawfulness, to contract marriage — with another Catholic or with a non-Catholic — in the presence of a competent priest or deacon and two witnesses.

There are two exceptions to this law. A Roman-rite Catholic (since Mar. 25, 1967) or an Eastern-rite Catholic (since Nov. 21, 1964) can contract marriage validly in the presence of a priest of a separated Eastern-rite Church, provided other requirements of law are complied with. With permission of the competent Roman-rite or Eastern-rite bishop, this form of marriage is lawful, as well as valid. (See **Eastern-rite Laws**, below.)

With these two exceptions, and aside from cases covered by special permission, the Church does not regard as valid any marriages involving Catholics which take place before non-Catholic ministers of religion or civil officials.

(An excommunication formerly in force against Catholics who celebrated marriage before a non-Catholic minister was abrogated in a decree issued by the Sacred Congregation for the Doctrine of the Faith on Mar. 18, 1966.)

The ordinary place of marriage is the parish of either Catholic party or of the Catholic party in case of a mixed marriage.

Church law regarding the form of marriage does not affect non-Catholics in marriages among themselves.

The Church recognizes as valid the marriages of non-Catholics before ministers of religion and civil officials, unless they are rendered null and void on other grounds.

The canonical form is not to be observed in the case of a marriage between a non-Catholic and a baptized Catholic who has left the Church by a formal act.

Impediments

Diriment Impediments to marriage are factors that render a marriage invalid.

• Age, which obtains before completion of the 14th year for a woman and the 16th year for a man

• Impotency, if it is antecedent to the marriage and permanent (this differs from sterility, which is not an impediment)

• The bond of an existing valid marriage

• Disparity of worship, which obtains when one party is a Catholic and the other party is unbaptized

• Sacred orders

• Religious profession of the perpetual vow of chastity

• Abduction, which impedes the freedom of the person abducted

• Crime, variously involving elements of adultery, promise or attempt to marry, conspiracy to murder a husband or wife

• Blood relationship in the direct line (father-daughter, mother-son, etc.) and to the fourth degree inclusive of the collateral line (brother-sister, first cousins)

• Affinity, or relationship resulting from a valid marriage, in any degree of the direct line

• Public honesty, arising from an invalid marriage or from public or notorious concubinage; it renders either party incapable of marrying blood relatives of the other in the first degree of the direct line

• Legal relationship arising from adoption; it renders either party incapable of marrying relatives of the other in the direct line or in the second degree of the collateral line.

Dispensations from impediments: Persons hindered by impediments cannot marry unless they are dispensed therefrom in view of reasons recognized in canon law. Local bishops can dispense from the impediments most often encountered (e.g., disparity of worship) as well as others.

Decision regarding some dispensations is reserved to the Holy See.

Separation

A valid and consummated marriage of baptized persons cannot be dissolved by any human authority or any cause other than the death of one of the persons.

In other circumstances:

1. A valid but unconsummated marriage of baptized persons, or of a baptized and an unbaptized person, can be dissolved:

a. by the solemn religious profession of one of the persons, made with permission of the pope. In such a case, the bond is dissolved at the time of profession, and the other person is free to marry again.

b. by dispensation from the pope, requested for a grave reason by one or both of the persons. If the dispensation is granted, both persons are free to marry again.

Dispensations in these cases are granted for reasons connected with the spiritual welfare of the concerned persons.

2. A legitimate marriage, even consummated, of unbaptized persons can be dissolved in favor of one of them who subsequently receives the sacrament of baptism. This is the Pauline Privilege, so called because it was promulgated by St. Paul (1 Cor. 7:12-15) as a means of protecting the faith of converts. Requisites for granting the privilege are:

a. marriage prior to the baptism of either person;

b. reception of baptism by one person;

c. refusal of the unbaptized person to live in peace with the baptized person and without interfering with his or her freedom to practice the Christian faith. The privilege does not apply if the unbaptized person agrees to these conditions.

3. A legitimate and consummated marriage of a baptized and an unbaptized person can be dissolved by the pope in virtue of the Privilege of Faith, also called the Petrine Privilege.

Civil Divorce

Because of the unity and the indissolubility of marriage, the Church denies that civil divorce can break the bond of a valid marriage, whether the marriage involves two Catholics, a Catholic and a non-Catholic, or non-Catholics with each other.

In view of serious circumstances of marital distress, the Church permits an innocent and aggrieved party, whether wife or husband, to seek and obtain a civil divorce for the purpose of acquiring title and right to the civil effects of divorce, such as separate habitation and maintenance, and the custody of children. Permission for this kind of action should be obtained from proper church authority. The divorce, if obtained, does not break the bond of a valid marriage.

Under other circumstances — as would obtain if a marriage was invalid (see **Annulment**, below) — civil divorce is permitted for civil effects and as a civil ratification of the fact that the marriage bond really does not exist.

Annulment

This is a decision by a competent church authority — e.g., a bishop, a diocesan marriage tribunal, the Roman Rota — that an apparently valid marriage was actually invalid from the beginning because of the unknown or concealed existence, from the beginning, of a diriment impediment, an essential defect in consent, radical incapability for marriage, or a condition placed by one or both of the parties against the very nature of marriage.

Eastern-rite Laws

Marriage laws of the Eastern Church differ in several respects from the legislation of the Roman rite. The regulations in effect since May 2, 1949, were contained in the *motu proprio Crebre Allatae* issued by Pius XII the previous February.

According to both the Roman Code of Canon Law and the Oriental Code, marriages between Roman-rite Catholics and Eastern-rite Catholics ordinarily take place in the rite of the groom and have canonical effects in that rite.

Regarding the form for the celebration of marriages between Eastern Catholics and baptized Eastern non-Catholics, the Second Vatican Council declared:

"By way of preventing invalid marriages between Eastern Catholics and baptized Eastern non-Catholics, and in the interests of the permanence and sanctity of marriage and of domestic harmony, this sacred Synod decrees that the canonical 'form' for the celebration of such marriages obliges only for lawfulness. For their validity, the presence of a sacred minister suffices, as long as the other requirements of law are honored" (Decree on Eastern Catholic Churches, No. 18).

Marriages taking place in this manner are lawful, as well as valid, with permission of a competent Eastern-rite bishop.

The Rota

The Roman Rota is the ordinary court of appeal for marriage, and some other cases, which are appealed to the Holy See from lower church courts. Appeals are made to the Rota if decisions by diocesan and archdiocesan courts fail to settle the matter in dispute. Pope John Paul II, at annual meetings with Rota personnel, speaks about the importance of the court's actions in providing norms of practice for other tribunals.

MIXED MARRIAGES

"Mixed Marriages" (*Matrimonia Mixta*) was the subject of a letter issued under this title by Pope Paul VI, on Mar. 31, 1970, and also a statement, "Implementation of the Apostolic Letter on Mixed Marriages," approved by the National Conference of Catholic Bishops on Nov. 16, 1970.

One of the key points in the bishops' statement referred to the need for mutual pastoral care by ministers of different faiths for the sacredness of marriage and for appropriate preparation and continuing support of parties to a mixed marriage.

Pastoral experience, which the Catholic Church shares with other religious bodies, confirms the fact that marriages of persons of different beliefs involve special problems related to the continuing religious practice of the concerned persons and to the religious education and formation of their children.

Pastoral measures to minimize these problems include instruction of a non-Catholic party in essentials of the Catholic faith for purposes of understanding. Desirably, some instruction should also be given the Catholic party regarding his or her partner's beliefs.

Requirements

The Catholic party to a mixed marriage is required to declare his (her) intention of continuing practice of the Catholic faith and to promise to do all in his (her) power to share his (her) faith with children born of the marriage by having them baptized and raised as Catholics. No declarations or promises are required of the non-Catholic party, but he (she) must be informed of the declaration and promise made by the Catholic.

Notice of the Catholic's declaration and promise is an essential part of the application made to a bishop for permission to marry a baptized non-Catholic, or a dispensation to marry an unbaptized non-Catholic.

A mixed marriage can take place with a Nuptial Mass. (The bishops' statement added this caution: "To the extent that Eucharistic sharing is not permitted by the general discipline of the Church, this is to be considered when plans are being made to have the mixed marriage at Mass or not.")

The ordinary minister at a mixed marriage is an authorized priest or deacon, and the ordinary place is the parish church of the Catholic party. A non-Catholic minister may not only attend the marriage ceremony but may also address, pray with and bless the couple.

For appropriate pastoral reasons, a bishop can grant a dispensation from the Catholic form of marriage and can permit the marriage to take place in a non-Catholic church with a non-Catholic minister as the officiating minister. A priest may not only attend such a ceremony but may also address, pray with and bless the couple.

"It is not permitted," however, the bishops' statement declared, "to have two religious services or to have a single service in which both the Catholic marriage ritual and a non-Catholic marriage ritual are celebrated jointly or successively."

PASTORAL MINISTRY FOR DIVORCED AND REMARRIED

Ministry to divorced and remarried Catholics is a difficult field of pastoral endeavor, situated as it is in circumstances tantamount to the horns of a dilemma.

At Issue

On the one side is firm church teaching on the permanence of marriage and norms against reception of the Eucharist and full participation in the life of the Church by Catholics in irregular unions.

On the other side are men and women with broken unions followed by second and perhaps happier attempts at marriage which the Church does not recognize as valid and which may not be capable of being validated because of the existence of an earlier marriage bond.

Factors involved in these circumstances are those of the Church, upholding its doctrine and practice regarding the permanence of marriage, and those of many men and women in irregular second marriages who desire full participation in the life of the Church.

Sacramental participation is not possible for those whose first marriage was valid, although there is no bar to their attendance at Mass, to sharing in other activities of the Church, or to their efforts to have children baptized and raised in the Catholic faith.

An exception to this rule is the condition of a divorced and remarried couple living in a brother-sister relationship.

There is no ban against sacramental participation by separated or divorced persons who have not attempted a second marriage, provided the usual conditions for reception of the sacraments are in order.

Unverified estimates of the number of U.S. Catholics who are divorced and remarried vary between six and eight million.

Tribunal Action

What can the Church do for them and with them in pastoral ministry, is an old question charged with new urgency because of the rising number of divorced and remarried Catholics.

One way to help is through the agency of marriage tribunals charged with responsibility for investigating and settling questions concerning the validity or invalidity of a prior marriage. There are reasons in canon law justifying the Church in declaring a particular marriage null and void from the beginning, despite the short- or long-term existence of an apparently valid union.

Decrees of nullity (annulments) are not new in the history of the Church. If such a decree is issued, a man or woman is free to validate a second marriage and live in complete union with the Church.

The 2001 *Statistical Yearbook of the Church* (*Annuarium Statisticum Ecclesiae*, the most recent edition) reported in 2000 that U.S. tribunals issued 49,069 annulments (in ordinary and documentary processes). The canonical reasons were: invalid consent (38,441), impotence (107), other impediments (2,264), defect of form (10,311). Worldwide, 69,896 decrees or declarations of nullity were issued in 2000.

Reasons behind Decrees

Pastoral experience reveals that some married persons, a short or long time after contracting an apparently valid marriage, exhibit signs that point back to the existence, at the time of marriage, of latent and serious personal deficiencies which made them incapable of valid consent and sacramental commitment.

Such deficiencies might include gross immaturity and those affecting in a serious way the capacity to love, to have a true interpersonal and conjugal relationship, to fulfill marital obligations, or to accept the faith aspect of marriage.

Psychological and behavioral factors like these have been given greater attention by tribunals in recent years and have provided grounds for numerous decrees of nullity.

Decisions of this type do not indicate any softening of the Church's attitude regarding the permanence of marriage. They affirm, rather, that some persons who have married were really not capable of doing so.

Serious deficiencies in the capacity for real interpersonal relationship in marriage were the reasons behind a landmark decree of nullity issued in 1973 by the Roman Rota, the Vatican high court of appeals in marriage cases. Pope John Paul referred to such deficiencies — the "grave lack of discretionary judgment," incapability of assuming "essential matrimonial rights and obligations," for example — in an address Jan. 26, 1984, to personnel of the Rota.

The tribunal way to a decree of nullity regarding a previous marriage, however, is not open to many persons in second marriages — because grounds are either lacking or, if present, cannot be verified in tribunal process.

Unacceptable Solutions

One unacceptable solution of the problem, called "good conscience procedure," involves administration of the sacraments of penance and the Eucharist to divorced and remarried Catholics unable to obtain a decree of nullity for a first marriage who are living in a subsequent marriage "in good faith."

This procedure, despite the fact that it has no standing or recognition in church law, is being advocated and practiced by some priests and remarried Catholics.

This issue was addressed by the Congregation for the Doctrine of the Faith in a letter to bishops dated Oct. 14, 1994, and published with the approval of Pope John Paul II. The letter said in part:

"Pastoral solutions in this area have been suggested according to which divorced-and-remarried members of the faithful could approach holy Communion in specific cases when they considered themselves authorized according to a judgment of conscience to do so. This would be the case, for example, when they had been abandoned completely unjustly although they sincerely tried to save the previous marriage; or when they are convinced of the nullity of their previous marriage although (they are) unable to demonstrate it in the external forum; or when they have gone through a long period of reflection and penance; or also when for morally valid reasons they cannot satisfy the obligation to separate.

"In some places it has also been proposed that, in order objectively to examine their actual situation, the divorced-and-remarried would have to consult a prudent and experienced priest. This priest, however, would have to respect their eventual decision in conscience to approach holy Communion, without this implying an official authorization.

"In these and similar cases, it would be a matter of a tolerant and benevolent pastoral solution in order to do justice to the different situations of the divorced-and-remarried.

"Even if analogous solutions have been proposed by a few fathers of the Church and in some measure were practiced, nevertheless these never attained the consensus of the fathers and in no way came to constitute the common doctrine of the Church nor to determine her discipline. It falls to the universal magisterium, in fidelity to sacred Scripture and tradition, to teach and to interpret authentically the deposit of faith."

Conditions for Receiving Communion

Practically speaking, "when for serious reasons — for example, for the children's upbringing — a man and a woman cannot satisfy the obligation to separate," they may be admitted to Communion if "they take on themselves the duty to live in complete continence, that is, by abstinence from the acts proper to married couples. In such a case they may receive holy Communion as long as they respect the obligation to avoid giving scandal."

The teaching of the Church on this subject "does not mean that the Church does not take to heart the situation of those faithful who, moreover, are not excluded from ecclesial communion. She is concerned to accompany them pastorally and invite them to share in the life of the Church in the measure that is compatible with the dispositions of divine law, from which the Church has no power to dispense. On the other hand, it is necessary to instruct these faithful so that they do not think their participation in the life of the Church is reduced exclusively to the question of the reception of the Eucharist. The faithful are to be helped to deepen their understanding of the value of sharing in the sacrifice of Christ in the Mass, or spiritual communion, of prayer, of meditation on the word of God, and of works of charity and justice."

The Communion of Saints

SAINTS OF THE CHURCH

Biographical sketches of additional saints and blesseds are found in other Almanac entries. See **Index**, under the name of each saint for the apostles, evangelists, Doctors of the Church, and Fathers of the Church. For beatification and canonization procedures, see those entries in the **Glossary**.

An asterisk with a feast date indicates that the saint is listed in the General Roman Calendar or the proper calendar for U.S. dioceses. For rank of observances, see listing in calendar for current year on preceding pages.

Adalbert (956-997): Born in Bohemia; bishop of Prague; Benedictine; missionary in Poland, Prussia and Hungary; martyred by Prussians near Danzig; Apr. 23.*

Adjutor (d. 1131): Norman knight; fought in First Crusade; monk-recluse after his return; Apr. 30.

Agatha (d. c. 250): Sicilian virgin-martyr; her intercession credited in Sicily with stilling eruptions of Mt. Etna; patron of nurses; Feb. 5.*

Agnes (d. c. 304): Roman virgin-martyr; martyred at age of 10 or 12; patron of young girls; Jan. 21.*

Aloysius Gonzaga (1568-1591): Italian Jesuit; died while nursing plague-stricken; canonized 1726; patron of youth; June 21.*

Amand (d. c. 676): Apostle of Belgium; b. France; established monasteries throughout Belgium; Feb. 6.

Andre Bessette, Bl. (Bro. Andre) (1845-1937): Canadian Holy Cross Brother; prime mover in building of St. Joseph's Oratory, Montreal; beatified May 23, 1982; Jan. 6* (U.S.).

Andre Grasset de Saint Sauveur, Bl. (1758-1792): Canadian priest; martyred in France, Sept. 2, 1792, during the Revolution; one of a group called the Martyrs of Paris who were beatified in 1926; Sept. 2.

Andrew Bobola (1592-1657): Polish Jesuit; joined Jesuits at Vilna; worked for return of Orthodox to union with Rome; martyred; canonized 1938; May 16.

Andrew Corsini (1302-1373): Italian Carmelite; bishop of Fiesoli; mediator between quarrelsome Italian states; canonized 1629; Feb. 4.

Andrew Dung-Lac and Companions (d. 18th-19th c.): Martyrs of Vietnam. Total of 117 included 96 Vietnamese, 11 Spanish and 10 French missionaries (8 bishops; 50 priests, including Andrew Dung-Lac; 1 seminarian, 58 lay persons). Canonized June 19, 1988; inscribed in General Roman Calendar, 1989, as a memorial. Nov. 24.*

Andrew Fournet (1752-1834): French priest; co-founder with St. Jeanne Elizabeth Bichier des Anges of the Daughters of the Holy Cross of St. Andrew; canonized 1933; May 13.

Andrew Kim, Paul Chong and Companions (d. between 1839-1867): Korean martyrs (103) killed in persecutions of 1839, 1846, 1866, and 1867; among them were Andrew Kim, the first Korean priest, and Paul Chong, lay apostle; canonized May 6, 1984, during Pope John Paul II's visit to Korea. Sept. 20.*

Angela Merici (1474-1540): Italian secular Franciscan; foundress of Company of St. Ursula, 1535, the first teaching order of women Religious in the Church; canonized 1807; Jan. 27.*

Angelico, Bl. (Fra Angelico; John of Faesulis) (1387-1455): Dominican; Florentine painter of early Renaissance; proclaimed blessed by John Paul II, Feb. 3, 1982; patron of artists; Feb. 18.

Anne Marie Javouhey, Bl. (1779-1851): French virgin; foundress of Institute of St. Joseph of Cluny, 1812; beatified 1950; July 15.

Ansgar (801-865): Benedictine monk; b. near Amiens; archbishop of Hamburg; missionary in Denmark, Sweden, Norway and northern Germany; apostle of Scandinavia; Feb. 3.*

Anthony (c. 251-c. 354): Abbot; Egyptian hermit; patriarch of all monks; established communities for hermits which became models for monastic life, especially in the East; friend and supporter of St. Athanasius in the latter's struggle with the Arias; Jan. 17.*

Anthony Claret (1807-1870): Spanish bishop; founder of Missionary Sons of the Immaculate Heart of Mary (Claretians), 1849; archbishop of Santiago, Cuba, 1851-57; canonized 1950; Oct. 24.*

Anthony Gianelli (1789-1846): Italian bishop; founded the Daughters of Our Lady of the Garden, 1829; bishop of Bobbio, 1838; canonized 1951; June 7.

Anthony Zaccaria (1502-1539): Italian priest; founder of Barnabites (Clerks Regular of St. Paul), 1530; canonized 1897; July 5.*

Apollonia (d. 249): Deaconess of Alexandria; martyred during persecution of Decius; her patronage of dentists and those suffering from toothaches probably rests on tradition that her teeth were broken by her persecutors; Feb. 9.

Augustine of Canterbury (d. 604 or 605): Italian missionary; apostle of the English; sent by Pope Gregory I with 40 monks to evangelize England; arrived there 597; first archbishop of Canterbury; May 27.*

Bartolomea Capitania (1807-1833): Italian

foundress with Vincenza Gerosa of the Sisters of Charity of Lovere; canonized 1950; July 26.

Beatrice da Silva Meneses (1424-1490): Foundress, b. Portugal; founded Congregation of the Immaculate Conception, 1484, in Spain; canonized 1976; Sept. 1.

Benedict Joseph Labré (1748-1783): French layman; pilgrim-beggar; noted for his piety and love of prayer before the Blessed Sacrament; canonized 1883; Apr. 16.

Benedict of Nursia (c. 480-547): Abbot; founder of monasticism in Western Europe; established monastery at Monte Cassino; proclaimed patron of Europe by Paul VI in 1964; July 11.*

Benedict the Black *(il Moro)* (1526-1589): Sicilian Franciscan; born a slave; joined Franciscans as lay brother; appointed guardian and novice master; canonized 1807; Apr. 3.

Bernadette Soubirous (1844-1879): French peasant girl favored with series of visions of Blessed Virgin Mary at Lourdes (see Lourdes Apparitions); joined Institute of Sisters of Notre Dame at Nevers, 1866; canonized 1933; Apr. 16.

Bernard of Montjoux (or Menthon) (d. 1081): Augustinian canon; probably born in Italy; founded Alpine hospices near the two passes named for him; patron of mountaineers; May 28.

Bernardine of Feltre, Bl. (1439-1494): Italian Franciscan preacher; a founder of *montes pietatis*; Sept. 28.

Bernardine of Siena (1380-1444): Italian Franciscan; noted preacher and missioner; spread of devotion to Holy Name is attributed to him; represented in art holding to his breast the monogram IHS; canonized 1450; May 20.*

Blase (d. c. 316): Armenian bishop; martyr; the blessing of throats on his feast day derives from tradition that he miraculously saved the life of a boy who had half-swallowed a fish bone; Feb. 3.*

Boniface (Winfrid) (d. 754): English Benedictine; bishop; martyr; apostle of Germany; established monastery at Fulda which became center of missionary work in Germany; archbishop of Mainz; martyred near Dukkum in Holland; June 5.*

Brendan (c. 489-583): Irish abbot; founded monasteries; his patronage of sailors probably rests on a legend that he made a seven-year voyage in search of a fabled paradise; called Brendan the Navigator; May 16.

Bridget (Brigid) (c. 450-525): Irish nun; founded religious community at Kildare, the first in Ireland; patron, with Sts. Patrick and Columba, of Ireland; Feb. 1.

Bridget (Birgitta) (c. 1303-1373): Swedish mystic; widow; foundress of Order of Our Savior (Brigittines); canonized 1391; patroness of Sweden; July 23.*

Bruno (1030-1101): German monk; founded Carthusians, 1084, in France; Oct. 6.*

Bridget (Birgitta) (c. 1803-1373): Swedish mystic; widow; foundress of Order of Our Savior (Brigittines); canonized 1391; patroness of Sweden; named a co-patroness of Europe, with St. Edith Stein and St. Catherine of Siena, on Oct. 1, 1999; July 23.*

Cabrini, Mother: See **Frances Xavier Cabrini.**

Cajetan (Gaetano) **of Thiene** (1480-1547): Italian lawyer; religious reformer; a founder of Oratory of Divine Love, forerunner of the Theatines; canonized 1671; Aug. 7.*

Callistus I (d. 222): Pope, 217-222; martyr; condemned Sabellianism and other heresies; advocated a policy of mercy toward repentant sinners; Oct. 14.*

Camillus de Lellis (1550-1614): Italian priest; founder of Camillians (Ministers of the Sick); canonized 1746; patron of the sick and of nurses; July 14.*

Casimir (1458-1484): Polish prince; grand duke of Lithuania; noted for his piety; buried at cathedral in Vilna, Lithuania; canonized 1521; patron of Poland and Lithuania; Mar. 4.*

Cassian of Tangier (d. 298): Roman martyr; an official court stenographer who declared himself a Christian; patron of stenographers; Dec. 3.

Catherine Labouré (1806-1876): French Religious; favored with series of visions soon after she joined Sisters of Charity of St. Vincent de Paul in Paris in 1830; first Miraculous Medal (see Index) struck in 1832 in accord with one of the visions; canonized 1947; Nov. 28.

Catherine of Bologna (1413-1463): Italian Poor Clare; mystic, writer, artist canonized 1712; patron of artists; May 9.

Cecilia (2nd-3rd century): Roman virgin-martyr; traditional patroness of musicians; Nov. 22.*

Charles Borromeo (1538-1584): Italian cardinal; nephew of Pope Pius IV; cardinal bishop of Milan; influential figure in Church reform in Italy; promoted education of clergy; canonized 1610; Nov. 4.*

Charles Lwanga and Companions (d. between 1885 and 1887): Twenty-two Martyrs of Uganda, many of them pages of King Mwanga of Uganda, who were put to death because they denounced his corrupt lifestyle; canonized 1964; first martyrs of black Africa; June 3.*

Charles of Sezze (1616-1670): Italian Franciscan lay brother who served in humble capacities; canonized 1959; Jan. 6.

Christopher (3rd cent.): Early Christian martyr inscribed in Roman calendar about 1550; feast relegated to particular calendars because of legendary nature of accounts of his life; traditional patron of travelers; July 25.

Clare (1194-1253): Foundress of Poor Clares; b. at Assisi; was joined in religious life by her sisters, Agnes and Beatrice, and eventually her widowed mother Ortolana; canonized 1255; patroness of television; Aug. 11.*

Claude de la Colombiere (1641-1682): French Jesuit; spiritual director of St. Margaret Mary Alacoque; instrumental in spreading devotion to the Sacred Heart; beatified, 1929; canonized May 31, 1992; Feb. 15.

Clement Hofbauer (1751-1820): Redemptorist priest, missionary; born in Moravia; helped spread Redemptorists north of the Alps; canonized 1909; Mar. 15.

Clement I (d. c. 100): Pope, 88-97; third successor of St. Peter; wrote important letter to Church in Corinth settling disputes there; venerated as a martyr; Nov. 23.*

Columba (521-597): Irish monk; founded monasteries in Ireland; missionary in Scotland; established monastery at Iona which became the center for conversion of Picts, Scots, and Northern English; Scotland's most famous saint; patron saint of Ireland (with Sts. Patrick and Brigid); June 9.

Columban (545-615): Irish monk; scholar; founded monasteries in England and Brittany (famous abbey of Luxeuil), forced into exile because of his criticism of Frankish court; spent last years in northern Italy where he founded abbey at Bobbio; Nov. 23.*

Conrad of Parzham (1818-1894): Bavarian Capuchin lay brother; served as porter at the Marian shrine of Altotting in Upper Bavaria for 40 years; canonized 1934; Apr. 21.

Contardo Ferrini, Bl. (1859-1902): Italian secular Franciscan; model of the Catholic professor; beatified 1947; patron of universities; Oct. 20.

Cornelius (d. 253): Pope, 251-253; promoted a policy of mercy with respect to readmission of repentant Christians who had fallen away during the persecution of Decius (*lapsi*); banished from Rome during persecution of Gallus; regarded as a martyr; Sept. 16 (with Cyprian).*

Cosmas and Damian (d. c. 303): Arabian twin brothers, physicians; martyred during Diocletian persecution; patrons of physicians; Sept. 26.*

Crispin and Crispinian (3rd cent.): Early Christian martyrs; said to have met their deaths in Gaul; patrons of shoemakers, a trade they pursued; Oct. 25.

Crispin of Viterbo (1668-1750): Capuchin brother; canonized June 20, 1982; May 21.

Cyprian (d. 258): Early ecclesiastical writer; b. Africa; bishop of Carthage, 249-258; supported Pope St. Cornelius concerning the readmission of Christians who had apostatized in time of persecution; erred in his teaching that baptism administered by heretics and schismatics was invalid; wrote *De Unitate*; Sept. 16 (with St. Cornelius).*

Cyril and Methodius (9th century): Greek missionaries, bothers; venerated as apostles of the Slavs; Cyril (d. 869) and Methodius (d. 885) began their missionary work in Moravia in 863; developed a Slavonic alphabet; used the vernacular in the liturgy, a practice that was eventually approved; declared patrons of Europe with St. Benedict, Dec. 31, 1980; Feb. 14.*

Damasus I (d. 384): Pope, 366-384; opposed Arians and Apollinarians; commissioned St. Jerome to work on Bible translation; developed Roman liturgy; Dec. 11.*

Damian: *See* Cosmas and Damian.

Damien of Molokai (d. 1889): The so-called leper priest of Molokai; originally from Belgium, Damien devoted over twenty years to the care of the lepers in Hawaii, ultimately dying from the same disease. He was beatified by Pope John Paul II in 1996.

David (5th or 6th cent.): Nothing for certain known of his life; said to have founded monastery at Menevia; patron saint of Wales; Mar. 1.

Denis and Companions (d. 3rd cent.): Denis, bishop of Paris, and two companions identified by early writers as Rusticus, a priest, and Eleutherius, a deacon; martyred near Paris; Denis is popularly regarded as the apostle and a patron saint of France; Oct. 9.*

Dismas (1st cent.): Name given to repentant thief (Good Thief) to whom Jesus promised salvation (Lk. 23:40-43); regarded as patron of prisoners; Mar. 25 (observed on second Sunday of October in U.S. prison chapels).

Dominic (Dominic de Guzman) (1170-1221): Spanish priest; founded the Order of Preachers (Dominicans), 1215, in France; preached against the Albigensian heresy; a contemporary of St. Francis of Assisi; canonized 1234; Aug. 8.*

Dominic Savio (1842-1857): Italian youth; pupil of St. John Bosco; died before his 15th birthday; canonized 1954; patron of choir boys; May 6.

Duns Scotus, John (d. 1308): Scottish Franciscan; theologian; advanced theological arguments for doctrine of the Immaculate Conception; proclaimed blessed; cult solemnly confirmed by John Paul II, Mar. 20, 1993; Nov. 8.

Dunstan (c. 910-988): English monk; archbishop of Canterbury; initiated reforms in religious life; counselor to several kings; considered one of greatest Anglo-Saxon saints; patron of goldsmiths, locksmiths, jewelers (trades in which he is said to have excelled); May 19.

Dymphna (dates unknown): Nothing certain known of her life; according to legend, she was an Irish maiden murdered by her heathen father at Gheel near Antwerp, Belgium, where she had fled to escape his advances; her relics were discovered there in the 13th century; since that time cures of mental illness and epilepsy have been attributed to her intercession; patron of those suffering from mental illness; May 15.

Edith Stein, St. (1891-1942): German Carmelite (Teresa Benedicta of the Cross); born of Jewish parents; author and lecturer; baptized in Catholic Church, 1922; arrested with her sister Rosa in 1942 and put to death at Auschwitz; beatified 1987, by Pope John Paul II during his visit to West Germany. She was canonized by Pope John Paul II on Oct. 11, 1998 and named a co-patroness of Europe, with St. Bridget of Sweden and St. Catherine of Siena, on Oct. 1, 1999. Aug. 10.

Edmund Campion (1540-1581): English Jesuit; convert 1573; martyred at Tyburn; canonized 1970, one of the Forty English and Welsh Martyrs; Dec. 1.

Edward the Confessor (d. 1066): King of England, 1042-66; canonized 1161; Oct. 13.

Eligius (c. 590-660): Bishop; born in Gaul; founded monasteries and convents; bishop of Noyon and Tournai; famous worker in gold and silver; Dec. 1.

Elizabeth Ann Seton (1774-1821): American foundress; convert, 1805; founded Sisters of Charity in the U.S.; beatified 1963; canonized Sept. 14, 1975; the first American-born saint; Jan. 4 (U.S.).*

Elizabeth of Hungary (1207-1231): Became secular Franciscan after death of her husband in 1227; devoted life to poor and destitute; a patron of the Secular Franciscan Order; canonized 1235; Nov. 17.*

Elizabeth of Portugal (1271-1336): Queen of Portugal; b. Spain; retired to Poor Clare convent as a secular Franciscan after the death of her husband; canonized 1626; July 4.*

Emily de Rodat (1787-1852): French foundress of the Congregation of the Holy Family of Villefranche; canonized 1950; Sept. 19.

Emily de Vialar (1797-1856): French foundress of the Sisters of St. Joseph of the Apparition; canonized 1951; June 17.

Erasmus (Elmo) (d. 303): Life surrounded by legend; martyred during Diocletian persecution; patron of sailors; June 2.

Ethelbert (552-616): King of Kent, England; baptized by St. Augustine of Canterbury, 597; issued legal code; furthered spread of Christianity; Feb. 26.

Eusebius of Vercelli (283-370): Italian bishop; exiled from his see (Vercelli) for a time because of his opposition to Arianism; considered a martyr because of sufferings he endured; Aug. 2.*

Fabian (d. 250): Pope, 236-250; martyred under Decius; Jan. 20.*

Felicity: See **Perpetua and Felicity**.

Ferdinand III (1198-1252): King of Castile and Leon; waged successful crusade against Muhammadans in Spain; founded university at Salamanca; canonized 1671; May 30.

Fiacre (Fiachra) (d. c. 670): Irish hermit; patron of gardeners; Aug. 30.

Fidelis of Sigmaringen (Mark Rey) (1577-1622): German Capuchin; lawyer before he joined the Capuchins; missionary to Swiss Protestants; stabbed to death by peasants who were told he was agent of Austrian emperor; Apr. 24.*

Frances of Rome (1384-1440): Italian model for housewives and widows; happily married for 40 years; after death of her husband in 1436 joined community of Benedictine Oblates she had founded; canonized 1608; patron of motorists; Mar. 9.*

Frances Xavier Cabrini (Mother Cabrini) (1850-1917): American foundress; b. Italy; founded the Missionary Sisters of the Sacred Heart, 1877; settled in the U.S. 1889; became an American citizen at Seattle 1909; worked among Italian immigrants; canonized 1946, the first American citizen so honored; Nov. 13 (U.S.).*

Francis Borgia (1510-1572): Spanish Jesuit; joined Jesuits after death of his wife in 1546; became general of the Order, 1565; Oct. 10.

Francis Caracciolo (1563-1608): Italian priest; founder with Father Augustine Adorno of the Clerics Regular Minor (Adorno Fathers); canonized 1807; declared patron of Italian chefs, 1996; June 4.

Francis Fasani (1681-1742): Italian Conventual Franciscan; model of priestly ministry, especially in service to poor and imprisoned; canonized 1986; Nov. 27.

Francis of Assisi (Giovanni di Bernardone) (1181/82-1226): Founder of the Franciscans, 1209; received stigmata 1224; canonized 1228; one of best known and best loved saints; patron of Italy, Catholic Action and ecologists; Oct. 4.*

Francis of Paola (1416-1507): Italian hermit: founder of Minim Friars; Apr. 2.*

Francis Xavier (1506-1552): Spanish Jesuit; missionary to Far East; canonized 1602; patron of foreign missions; considered one of greatest Christian missionaries; Dec. 3.*

Francis Xavier Bianchi (1743-1815): Italian Barnabite; acclaimed apostle of Naples because of his work there among the poor and abandoned; canonized 1951; Jan. 31.

Gabriel of the Sorrowful Mother (Francis Possenti) (1838-1862): Italian Passionist; died while a scholastic; canonized 1920; Feb. 27.

Gaspar (Caspar) **del Bufalo** (1786-1836): Italian priest; founded Missionaries of the Precious Blood, 1815; canonized 1954; Jan. 2.

Gemma Galgani (1878-1903): Italian laywoman; visionary; subject of extraordinary religious experiences; canonized 1940; Apr. 11.

Genesius (d. c. 300): Roman actor; according to legend, was converted while performing a burlesque of Christian baptism and was subsequently martyred; patron of actors; Aug. 25.

Geneviève (422-500): French nun; a patroness and protectress of Paris; events of her life not authenticated; Jan. 3.

George (d.c. 300): Martyr, probably during Diocletian persecution in Palestine; all other incidents of his life, including story of the dragon, are legendary; patron of England; Apr. 23.*

Gerard Majella (1725-1755): Italian Redemptorist lay brother; noted for supernatural occurrences in his life including bilocation and reading of consciences; canonized 1904; patron of mothers; Oct. 16.

Gertrude (1256-1302): German mystic; writer; helped spread devotion to the Sacred Heart; Nov. 16.*

Gregory VII (Hildebrand) (1020?-1085): Pope, 1075-1085; Benedictine monk; adviser to several popes; as pope, strengthened interior life of Church and fought against lay investiture; driven from Rome by Henry IV; died in exile; canonized 1584; May 25.*

Gregory Barbarigo (1626-1697): Italian cardinal; noted for his efforts to bring about reunion of separated Christians; canonized 1960; June 18.

Gregory of Nyssa (c. 335-395): Bishop; theologian; younger brother of St. Basil the Great; Mar. 9.

Gregory Thaumaturgus (c. 213-268): Bishop of Neocaesarea; missionary, famed as wonder worker; Nov. 17.

Gregory the Illuminator (257-332): Martyr; bishop; apostle and patron saint of Armenia; helped free Armenia from the Persians; Sept. 30.

Hedwig (1174-1243): Moravian noblewoman; married duke of Silesia, head of Polish royal family; fostered religious life in country; canonized 1266; Oct. 16.*

Helena (250-330): Empress; mother of Constantine the Great; associated with discovery of the True Cross; Aug. 18.

Henry (972-1024): Bavarian emperor; cooperated with Benedictine abbeys in restoration of ecclesiastical and social discipline; canonized 1146; July 13.*

Herman Joseph (1150-1241): German Premonstratensian; his visions were the subjects of artists; writer; cult approved, 1958; Apr. 7.

Hippolytus (d. c. 236): Roman priest; opposed Pope St. Callistus I in his teaching about the readmission to the Church of repentant Christians who had apostatized during time of persecution; elected antipope; exiled to Sardinia; reconciled before his martyrdom; important ecclesiastical writer; Aug. 13* (with Pontian).

Hugh of Cluny (the Great) (1024-1109): Abbot of Benedictine foundation at Cluny; supported popes in efforts to reform ecclesiastical abuses; canonized 1120; Apr. 29.

Ignatius of Antioch (d. c. 107): Early ecclesiastical writer; martyr; bishop of Antioch in Syria for 40 years; Oct. 17.*

Ignatius of Laconi (1701-1781): Italian Capuchin lay brother whose 60 years of religious life were spent in Franciscan simplicity; canonized 1951; May 11.

Ignatius of Loyola (1491-1556): Spanish soldier; renounced military career after recovering from wounds received at siege of Pampeluna (Pamplona) in 1521; founded Society of Jesus (Jesuits), 1534, at Paris; wrote The Book of Spiritual Exercises; canonized 1622; July 31.*

Irenaeus of Lyons (130-202): Early ecclesiastical writer; opposed Gnosticism; bishop of Lyons; traditionally regarded as a martyr; June 28.*

Isidore the Farmer (d. 1170): Spanish layman; farmer; canonized 1622; patron of farmers; May 15 (U.S.).*

Jane Frances de Chantal (1572-1641): French widow; foundress, under guidance of St. Francis of Sales, of Order of the Visitation; canonized 1767; Dec. 12* (General Roman Calendar); Aug. 18* (U.S.).

Januarius (Gennaro) (d. 304): Bishop of Benevento; martyred during Diocletian persecution; fame rests on liquefaction of some of his blood preserved in a phial at Naples, an unexplained phenomenon which has occurred regularly several times each year for over 400 years; Sept. 19.*

Jeanne Delanoue (1666-1736): French foundress of Sisters of St. Anne of Providence, 1704; canonized 1982; Aug. 16.

Jeanne (Joan) **de Lestonnac** (1556-1640): French foundress; widowed in 1597; founded the Religious of Notre Dame 1607; canonized 1947; Feb. 2.

Jeanne de Valois (Jeanne of France) (1464-1505): French foundress; deformed daughter of King Louis XI; was married in 1476 to Duke Louis of Orleans who had the marriage annulled when he ascended the throne as Louis XII; Jeanne retired to life of prayer; founded contemplative Annonciades of Bourges, 1504; canonized 1950; Feb. 5.

Jeanne-Elizabeth Bichier des Ages (1773-1838): French Religious; co-founder with St. Andrew Fournet of Daughters of the Cross of St. Andrew, 1807; canonized 1947; Aug. 26.

Jeanne Jugan, Bl. (1792-1879): French Religious; foundress of Little Sisters of the Poor; beatified Oct. 3, 1982; Aug. 30.

Jerome Emiliani (1481-1537): Venetian priest; founded Somascan Fathers, 1532, for care of orphans; canonized 1767; patron of orphans and abandoned children; Feb. 8.*

Joan Antida Thouret (1765-1826): French Religious; founded, 1799, congregation now known as Sisters of Charity of St. Joan Antida; canonized 1934; Aug. 24.

Joan of Arc (1412-1431): French heroine, called The Maid of Orleans, La Pucelle; led French army in 1429 against English invaders besieging Orleans; captured by Burgundians the following year; turned over to ecclesiastical court on charge of heresy, found guilty and burned at the stake; her innocence was declared in 1456; canonized 1920; patroness of France; May 30.

Joaquina de Vedruna de Mas (1783-1854): Spanish foundress; widowed in 1816; after providing for her children, founded the Carmelite Sisters of Charity; canonized 1959; Aug. 28.

John I (d. 526): Pope, 523-526; martyr; May 18.*

John XXIII, Bl.: see under **Popes of the Twentieth Century** in **Papacy and the Holy See**.

John Baptist de la Salle (1651-1719): French priest; founder of Brothers of the Christian Schools, 1680; canonized 1900; patron of teachers; Apr. 7.*

John Berchmans (1599-1621): Belgian Jesuit scholastic; patron of Mass servers; canonized 1888; Aug. 13.

John (Don) Bosco (1815-1888): Italian priest; founded Salesians, 1859, for education of boys; co-founder of Daughters of Mary Help of Christians for education of girls; canonized 1934; Jan. 31.*

John Capistran (1386-1456): Italian Franciscan; preacher; papal diplomat; canonized 1690; declared patron of military chaplains, Feb. 10, 1984. Oct. 23.*

John de Ribera (1532-1611): Spanish bishop and statesman; archbishop of Valencia, 1568-1611, and viceroy of that province; canonized 1960; Jan. 6.

John Eudes (1601-1680): French priest; founder of Sisters of Our Lady of Charity of Refuge, 1642, and Congregation of Jesus-Mary (Eudists), 1643; canonized 1925; Aug. 19.*

John Fisher (1469-1535): English prelate; theologian; martyr; bishop of Rochester, cardinal; refused to recognize validity of Henry VIII's marriage to Anne Boleyn; upheld supremacy of the pope; beheaded for refusing to acknowledge Henry as head of the Church; canonized 1935; June 22 (with St. Thomas More).*

John Francis Regis (1597-1640): French Jesuit priest; preached missions among poor and unlettered; canonized 1737; patron of social workers, particularly medical social workers, because of his concern for poor and needy and sick in hospitals; July 2.

John Gualbert (d. 1073): Italian priest; founder of Benedictine congregation of Vallombrosians, 1039; canonized 1193; July 12.

John Kanty (Cantius) (1395-1473): Polish theologian; canonized 1767; Dec. 23.*

John Leonardi (1550-1609): Italian priest; worked among prisoners and the sick; founded Clerics Regular of the Mother of God; canonized 1938; Oct. 9.*

John Nepomucene (1345-1393): Bohemian priest; regarded as a martyr; canonized 1729; patron of Czechoslovakia; May 16.

John Nepomucene Neumann (1811-1860): American prelate; b. Bohemia; ordained in New York 1836; missionary among Germans near Niagara Falls before joining Redemptorists, 1840; bishop of Philadelphia, 1852; first bishop in U.S. to prescribe Forty Hours devotion in his diocese; beatified 1963; canonized June 19, 1977; Jan. 5 (U.S.).*

John of Ávila (1499-1569): Spanish priest; preacher; ascetical writer; spiritual adviser of St. Teresa of Jesus (Ávila); canonized 1970; May 10.

John of Britto (1647-1693): Portuguese Jesuit; missionary in India where he was martyred; canonized 1947; Feb. 4.

John of God (1495-1550): Portuguese founder; his work among the sick poor led to foundation of Brothers Hospitallers of St. John of God, 1540, in Spain; canonized 1690; patron of sick, nurses, hospitals; Mar. 8.*

John of Matha (1160-1213): French priest; founder of the Order of Most Holy Trinity, whose original purpose was the ransom of prisoners from the Muslims; Feb. 8.

John Ogilvie (1579-1615): Scottish Jesuit; martyr; canonized 1976, the first canonized Scottish saint since 1250 (Margaret of Scotland); Mar. 10.

John Vianney (Curé of Ars) (1786-1859): French parish priest; noted confessor, spent 16 to 18 hours a day in confessional; canonized 1925; patron of parish priests; Aug. 4.*

Josaphat Kuncevyc (1584-1623): Basilian monk; b. Poland; archbishop of Polotsk, Lithuania; worked for reunion of separated Eastern Christians with Rome; martyred by mob of schismatics; canonized 1867; Nov. 12.*

Josemaria Escrivá de Balaguer (1902-75) Priest and Founder of Opus Dei; the society was designed to promote holiness among individuals in the world; beatified in 1992 and canonized on Oct. 6, 2002; May 17.

Joseph Benedict Cottolengo (1786-1842): Italian priest; established Little Houses of Divine Providence (*Piccolo Casa*) for care of orphans and the sick; canonized 1934; Apr. 30.

Joseph Cafasso (1811-1860): Italian priest; renowned confessor; promoted devotion to Blessed Sacrament; canonized 1947; June 23.

Joseph Calasanz (1556-1648): Spanish priest; founder of Piarists (Order of Pious Schools); canonized 1767; Aug. 25.*

Joseph of Cupertino (1603-1663): Italian Franciscan; noted for remarkable incidents of levitation; canonized 1767; Sept. 18.

Joseph Pignatelli (1737-1811): Spanish Jesuit; left Spain when Jesuits were banished in 1767; worked for revival of the Order; named first superior when Jesuits were reestablished in Kingdom of Naples, 1804; canonized 1954; Nov. 28.

Juan Diego (16th cent.): Mexican Indian, convert; indigenous name according to tradition Cuauhtlatohuac ("The eagle who speaks"); favored with apparitions of Our Lady (see Index: Our Lady of Guadalupe) on Tepeyac hill; beatified, 1990; canonized July 30, 2002; Dec. 9* (U.S.).

Julia Billiart (1751-1816): French foundress; founded Sisters of Notre Dame de Namur, 1804; canonized 1969; Apr. 8.

Juliana Falconieri (1270-1341): Italian foundress of the Servite Nuns; the niece of St. Alexis Falconieri; canonized in 1737; June 19.

Justin de Jacobis (1800-1860): Italian Vincentian; bishop; missionary in Ethiopia; canonized 1975; July 31.

Justin Martyr (100-165): Early ecclesiastical writer; Apologies for the Christian Religion, Dialog with the Jew Tryphon; martyred at Rome; June 1.*

Kateri Tekakwitha, Bl. (1656-1680): "Lily of the Mohawks." Indian maiden born at Ossernenon (Auriesville), N.Y.; baptized Christian, Easter, 1676, by Jesuit missionary Father Jacques de Lambertville; lived life devoted to prayer, penitential practices and care of sick and aged in Christian village of Caughnawaga near Montreal where her relics are now enshrined; beatified June 22, 1980; July 14* (in U.S.).

Katharine Drexel, St. (1858-1955): Philadelphia-born heiress; devoted wealth to founding schools and missions for Indians and Blacks; foundress of Sisters of Blessed Sacrament for Indians and Colored People, 1891; beatified 1988; canonized on Oct. 1, 2000; Mar. 3* (U.S.).

Ladislaus (1040-1095): King of Hungary; supported Pope Gregory VII against Henry IV; canonized 1192; June 27.

Lawrence (d. 258): Widely venerated martyr who suffered death, according to a long-standing but unverifiable legend, by fire on a gridiron; Aug. 10.*

Lawrence (Lorenzo) **Ruiz and Companions** (d. 1630s): Martyred in or near the city of Nagasaki, Japan; Lawrence Ruiz, first Filipino saint, and 15 companions (nine Japanese, four Spaniards, one Italian and one Frenchman); canonized 1987; Sept. 28.*

Leonard Murialdo (1828-1900): Italian priest; educator; founder of Pious Society of St. Joseph of Turin, 1873; canonized 1970; Mar. 30.

Leonard of Port Maurice (1676-1751): Italian Franciscan; ascetical writer; preached missions throughout Italy; canonized 1867; patron of parish missions; Nov. 26.

Leopold Mandic (1866-1942): Croatian-born Franciscan priest, noted confessor; spent most of his priestly life in Padua, Italy; canonized 1983; July 30.

Louis IX (1215-1270): King of France, 1226-1270; participated in Sixth Crusade; patron of Secular Franciscan Order; canonized 1297; Aug. 25.*

Louis de Montfort (1673-1716): French priest; founder of Sisters of Divine Wisdom, 1703, and Missionaries of Company of Mary, 1715; wrote True Devotion to the Blessed Virgin; canonized 1947; Apr. 28.*

Louis Zepherin Moreau, Bl. (d. 1901): Canadian bishop; headed St. Hyacinthe, Que., diocese, 1876-1901; beatified 1987; May 24.

Louise de Marillac (1591-1660): French foundress, with St. Vincent de Paul, of the Sisters of Charity; canonized 1934; Mar. 15.

Lucy (d. 304): Sicilian maiden; martyred during Diocletian persecution; one of most widely venerated early virgin-martyrs; patron of Syracuse, Sicily; invoked by those suffering from eye diseases; Dec. 13.*

Lucy Filippini (1672-1732): Italian educator, helped improve status of women through education; considered a founder of the Religious Teachers Filippini, 1692; canonized 1930; Mar. 25.

Madeleine Sophie Barat (1779-1865): French foundress of the Society of the Sacred Heart of Jesus; canonized 1925; May 25.

Malachy (1095-1148): Irish bishop; instrumental in establishing first Cistercian house in Ireland, 1142; canonized 1190; Nov. 3 (See Index: Prophecies of St. Malachy).

Marcellinus and Peter (d.c. 304): Early Roman martyrs; June 2.*

Margaret Clitherow (1556-1586): English martyr; convert shortly after her marriage; one of Forty Martyrs of England and Wales; canonized 1970; Mar. 25.

Margaret Mary Alacoque (1647-1690): French Religious; spread devotion to Sacred Heart in accordance with revelations made to her in 1675 (see Sacred Heart); canonized 1920; Oct. 16.*

Margaret of Cortona (1247-1297): Secular Franciscan; reformed her life in 1273 following the violent death of her lover; canonized 1728; May 16.

Margaret of Hungary (1242-1270): Contemplative; daughter of King Bela IV of Hungary; lived a life of self-imposed penances; canonized 1943; Jan. 18.

Margaret of Scotland (1050-1093): Queen of Scotland; noted for solicitude for the poor and promotion of justice; canonized 1250; Nov. 16.*

Maria Goretti (1890-1902): Italian virgin-martyr; a model of purity; canonized 1950; July 6.*

Mariana Paredes of Jesus (1618-1645): South American recluse; Lily of Quito; canonized, 1950; May 28.

Marie-Leonie Paradis, Bl. (1840-1912): Canadian Religious; founded Little Sisters of the Holy Family, 1880; beatified 1984; May 4.

Marie-Rose Durocher, Bl. (1811-1849): Canadian Religious; foundress of Sisters of Holy Names of Jesus and Mary; beatified 1982; Oct. 6* (in U.S.).

Martha (1st cent.): Sister of Lazarus and Mary of

Bethany; Gospel accounts record her concern for homely details; patron of cooks; July 29.*

Martin I (d. 655): Pope, 649-55; banished from Rome by emperor in 653 because of his condemnation of Monothelites; considered a martyr; Apr. 13.*

Martin of Tours (316-397): Bishop of Tours; opposed Arianism and Priscillianism; pioneer of Western monasticism, before St. Benedict; Nov. 11.*

Mary Domenica Mazzarello (1837-1881): Italian foundress, with St. John Bosco, of the Daughters of Mary Help of Christians, 1872; canonized 1951; May 14.

Mary Josepha Rossello (1811-1881): Italian-born foundress of the Daughters of Our Lady of Mercy; canonized 1949; Dec. 7.

Mary Magdalen Postel (1756-1846): French foundress of the Sisters of Christian Schools of Mercy, 1807; canonized 1925; July 16.

Mary Magdalene (1st cent.): Gospels record her as devoted follower of Christ to whom he appeared after the Resurrection; her identification with Mary of Bethany (sister of Martha and Lazarus) and the woman sinner (Lk. 7:36-50) has been questioned; July 22.*

Mary Magdalene dei Pazzi (1566-1607): Italian Carmelite nun; recipient of mystical experiences; canonized 1669; May 25.*

Mary Michaeli Desmaisières (1809-1865): Spanish-born foundress of the Institute of the Handmaids of the Blessed Sacrament, 1848; canonized 1934; Aug. 24.

Maximilian Kolbe (1894-1941): Polish Conventual Franciscan; prisoner at Auschwitz who heroically offered his life in place of a fellow prisoner; beatified 1971, canonized 1982; Aug. 14.*

Methodius: *See* **Cyril and Methodius.**

Miguel Febres Cordero (1854-1910): Ecuadorean Christian Brother; educator; canonized 1984; Feb. 9.

Miguel Pro, Bl. (1891-1927): Mexican Jesuit; joined Jesuits, 1911; forced to flee because of religious persecution; ordained in Belgium, 1925; returned to Mexico, 1926, to minister to people despite government prohibition; unjustly accused of assassination plot against president; arrested and executed; beatified 1988. Nov. 23* (U.S.).

Monica (332-387): Mother of St. Augustine; model of a patient mother; her feast is observed in the Roman calendar the day before her son's; Aug. 27.*

Nereus and Achilleus (d. c. 100): Early Christian martyrs; soldiers who, according to legend, were baptized by St. Peter; May 12.*

Nicholas of Flüe (1417-1487): Swiss layman; at the age of 50, with the consent of his wife and 10 children, he retreated from the world to live as a hermit; called Brother Claus by the Swiss; canonized 1947; Mar. 21.

Nicholas of Myra (4th cent.): Bishop of Myra in Asia Minor; one of most popular saints in both East and West; most of the incidents of his life are based on legend; patron of Russia; Dec. 6.*

Nicholas of Tolentino (1245-1305): Italian hermit; famed preacher; canonized 1446; Sept. 10.

Nicholas Tavelic and Companions (Deodatus of Aquitaine, Peter of Narbonne, Stephen of Cuneo) (d. 1391): Franciscan missionaries; martyred by Muslims in the Holy Land; canonized 1970; Nov. 14.

Norbert (1080-1134): German bishop; founded Canons Regular of Premontre (Premonstratensians,

Norbertines), 1120; promoted reform of the clergy, devotion to Blessed Sacrament; canonized 1582; June 6.*

Odilia (d. c. 720): Benedictine abbess; according to legend she was born blind, abandoned by her family and adopted by a convent of nuns where her sight was miraculously restored; patroness of blind; Dec. 13.

Oliver Plunket (1629-1681): Irish martyr; theologian; archbishop of Armagh and primate of Ireland; beatified 1920; canonized, 1975; July 1.

Pancras (d. c. 304): Roman martyr; May 12.*

Paola Frassinetti (1809-1882): Italian Religious; foundress, 1834, of Sisters of St. Dorothy; canonized 1984; June 11.

Paschal Baylon (1540-1592): Spanish Franciscan lay brother; spent life as door-keeper in various Franciscan friaries; defended doctrine of Real Presence in Blessed Sacrament; canonized 1690; patron of all Eucharistic confraternities and congresses, 1897; May 17.

Patrick (389-461): Famous missionary of Ireland; began missionary work in Ireland about 432; organized the Church there and established it on a lasting foundation; patron of Ireland, with Sts. Bridget and Columba; Mar. 17.*

Paul Miki and Companions (d. 1597): Martyrs of Japan; Paul Miki, Jesuit, and twenty-five other priests and laymen were martyred at Nagasaki; canonized 1862, the first canonized martyrs of the Far East; Feb. 6.*

Paul of the Cross (1694-1775): Italian Religious; founder of the Passionists; canonized 1867; Oct 19* (Oct. 20, U.S.*).

Paulinus of Nola (d. 451): Bishop of Nola (Spain); writer; June 22.*

Peregrine (1260-1347): Italian Servite; invoked against cancer (he was miraculously cured of cancer of the foot after a vision); canonized 1726; May 1.

Perpetua and Felicity (d. 203): Martyrs; Perpetua was a young married woman; Felicity was a slave girl; Mar. 7.*

Peter Chanel (1803-1841): French Marist; missionary to Oceania, where he was martyred; canonized 1954; Apr. 28.*

Peter Fourier (1565-1640): French priest; cofounder with Alice LeClercq (Mother Teresa of Jesus) of the Augustinian Canonesses of Our Lady, 1598; canonized 1897; Dec. 9.

Peter Gonzalez (1190-1246): Spanish Dominican; worked among sailors; court chaplain and confessor of King St. Ferdinand of Castile; patron of sailors; Apr. 14.

Peter Julian Eymard (1811-1868): French priest; founder of the Congregation of the Blessed Sacrament (men), 1856, and Servants of the Blessed Sacrament (women), 1864; dedicated to Eucharistic apostolate; canonized 1962; Aug. 2.*

Peter Nolasco (c. 1189-1258): Born in Langueduc area of present-day France; founded the Mercedarians (Order of Our Lady of Mercy), 1218, in Spain; canonized 1628; Jan. 31.

Peter of Alcantara (1499-1562): Spanish Franciscan; mystic; initiated Franciscan reform; confessor of St. Teresa of Jesus (Ávila); canonized 1669; Oct. 22 (in U.S.).

Philip Benizi (1233-1285): Italian Servite; noted

preacher, peacemaker; canonized 1671; Aug. 23.

Philip Neri (1515-1595): Italian Religious; founded Congregation of the Oratory; considered a second apostle of Rome because of his mission activity there; canonized 1622; May 26.*

Philip of Jesus (1517-157): Mexican Franciscan; martyred at Nagasaki, Japan; canonized 1862; patron of Mexico City; Feb. 6.*

Pio, Padre (1887-1968): Pio da Pietrelcina (Francesco Forgione), and Italian Capuchin Franciscan, mystic and stigmatic; assisted souls from all over the world who came to him for counsel and guidance; canonized on June 16, 2002; Sept. 23.

Pius V (1504-1572): Pope, 1566-1572; enforced decrees of Council of Trent; organized expedition against Turks resulting in victory at Lepanto; canonized 1712; Apr. 30.*

Polycarp (2nd cent.): Bishop of Smyrna; ecclesiastical writer; martyr; Feb. 23.*

Pontian (d. c. 235): Pope, 230-235; exiled to Sardinia by the emperor; regarded as a martyr; Aug. 13 (with Hippolytus).*

Rafaela Maria Porras y Ayllon (1850-1925): Spanish Religious; founded the Handmaids of the Sacred Heart, 1877; canonized 1977; Jan. 6.

Raymond Nonnatus (d. 1240): Spanish Mercedarian; cardinal; devoted his life to ransoming captives from the Moors; Aug. 31.

Raymond of Peñafort (1175-1275): Spanish Dominican; confessor of Gregory IX; systematized and codified canon law, in effect until 1917; master general of Dominicans, 1238; canonized 1601; Jan. 7.*

Rita of Cascia (1381-1457): Widow; cloistered Augustinian Religious of Umbria; invoked in impossible and desperate cases; May 22.

Robert Southwell (1561-1595): English Jesuit; poet; martyred at Tyburn; canonized 1970, one of the Forty English and Welsh Martyrs; Feb. 21.

Roch (1350-1379): French layman; pilgrim; devoted life to care of plague-stricken; widely venerated; invoked against pestilence; Aug. 17.

Romuald (951-1027): Italian monk; founded Camaldolese Benedictines; June 19.*

Rose of Lima (1586-1617): Peruvian Dominican tertiary; first native-born saint of the New World; canonized 1671; Aug. 23.*

Scholastica (d. c. 559): Sister of St. Benedict; regarded as first nun of the Benedictine Order; Feb. 10.*

Sebastian (3rd cent.): Roman martyr; traditionally pictured as a handsome youth with arrows; martyred; patron of athletes, archers; Jan. 20.*

Seven Holy Founders of the Servants of Mary (Buonfiglio Monaldo, Alexis Falconieri, Benedict dell'Antello, Bartholomew Amidei, Ricovero Uguccione, Gerardino Sostegni, John Buonagiunta Monetti): Florentine youths who founded Servites, 1233, in obedience to a vision; canonized 1888; Feb. 17.*

Sharbel Makhlouf (1828-1898): Lebanese Maronite monk-hermit; canonized 1977; Dec. 24.

Sixtus II and Companions (d. 258): Sixtus, pope 257-258, and four deacons, martyrs; Aug. 7.*

Stanislaus (1030-1079): Polish bishop; martyr; canonized 1253; Apr. 11.*

Stephen (d. c. 33): First Christian martyr; chosen by the Apostles as the first of the seven deacons; stoned to death; Dec. 26.*

Stephen (975-1038): King; apostle of Hungary; welded Magyars into national unity; canonized 1083; Aug. 16.*

Sylvester I (d. 335): Pope 314-335; first ecumenical council held at Nicaea during his pontificate; Dec. 31.*

Tarcisius (d. 3rd cent.): Early martyr; according to tradition, was martyred while carrying the Blessed Sacrament to some Christians in prison; patron of first communicants; Aug. 15.

Teresa Margaret Redi (1747-1770): Italian Carmelite; lived life of prayer and austere penance; canonized 1934; Mar. 11.

Teresa of Jesus Jornet Ibars (1843-1897): Spanish Religious; founded the Little Sisters of the Abandoned Aged, 1873; canonized 1974; Aug. 26.

Thérèse Couderc (1805-1885): French Religious; foundress of the Religious of Our Lady of the Retreat in the Cenacle, 1827; canonized 1970; Sept. 26.

Thomas Becket (1118-1170): English martyr; archbishop of Canterbury; chancellor under Henry II; murdered for upholding rights of the Church; canonized 1173; Dec. 29.*

Thomas More (1478-1535): English martyr; statesman, chancellor under Henry VIII; author of Utopia; opposed Henry's divorce, refused to renounce authority of the papacy; beheaded; canonized 1935; Pope John Paul II declared him patron of politicians on Oct. 31, 2000; June 22 (with St. John Fisher).*

Timothy (d. c. 97): Bishop of Ephesus; disciple and companion of St. Paul; martyr; Jan. 26.*

Titus (d. c. 96): Bishop; companion of St. Paul; recipient of one of Paul's epistles; Jan. 26.*

Titus Brandsma, Bl. (1881-1942): Dutch Carmelite priest; professor, scholar, journalist; denounced Nazi persecution of Jews; arrested by Nazis, Jan. 19, 1942; executed by lethal injection at Dachau, July 26, 1942; beatified 1985; July 26.

Valentine (d. 269): Priest, physician; martyred at Rome; legendary patron of lovers; Feb. 14.

Vicenta Maria Lopez y Vicuna (1847-1896): Spanish foundress of the Daughters of Mary Immaculate for domestic service; canonized 1975; Dec. 26.

Vincent (d. 304): Spanish deacon; martyr; Jan. 22.*

Vincent de Paul (1581?-1660): French priest; founder of Congregation of the Mission (Vincentians, Lazarists) and co-founder of Sisters of Charity; declared patron of all charitable organizations and works by Leo XIII; canonized 1737; Sept. 27.*

Vincent Ferrer (1350-1418): Spanish Dominican; famed preacher; Apr. 5.*

Vincent Pallotti (1795-1850): Italian priest; founded Society of the Catholic Apostolate (Pallottines), 1835; Jan. 22.

Vincent Strambi (1745-1824): Italian Passionist; bishop; reformer; canonized 1950; Sept. 25.

Vitus (d.c. 300): Martyr; died in Lucania, southern Italy; regarded as protector of epileptics and those suffering from St. Vitus Dance (chorea); June 15.

Walburga (d. 779): English-born Benedictine Religious; belonged to group of nuns who established convents in Germany at the invitation of St. Boniface; abbess of Heidenheim; Feb. 25.

Wenceslaus (d. 935): Duke of Bohemia; martyr; patron of Bohemia; Sept. 28.*

Zita (1218-1278): Italian maid; noted for charity to poor; patron of domestics; Apr. 27.

SAINTS — PATRONS AND INTERCESSORS

A patron is a saint who is venerated as a special intercessor before God. Most patrons have been so designated as the result of popular devotion and long-standing custom. In many cases, the fact of existing patronal devotion is clear despite historical obscurity regarding its origin. The Church has made official designation of relatively few patrons; in such cases, the dates of designation are given in parentheses in the list below. The theological background of the patronage of saints includes the dogmas of the Mystical Body of Christ and the Communion of Saints. Listed are patron saints of occupations and professions, and saints whose intercession is sought for special needs.

Academics: Thomas Aquinas.
Accomodations: Gertrude of Nivelles.
Accountants: Matthew.
Actors: Genesius.
Adopted children: Clotilde; Thomas More.
Advertisers: Bernardine of Siena (May 20, 1960).
Alcoholics: John of God; Monica.
Alpinists: Bernard of Montjoux (or Menthon) (Aug. 20, 1923).
Altar servers: John Berchmans.
Anesthetists: René Goupil.
Animals: Francis of Assisi.
Archaeologists: Damasus.
Archers: Sebastian.
Architects: Thomas, Apostle.
Art: Catherine of Bologna.
Artists: Luke, Catherine of Bologna, Bl. Angelico (Feb. 21, 1984).
Astronauts: Joseph Cupertino.
Astronomers: Dominic.
Athletes: Sebastian.
Authors: Francis de Sales.
Aviators: Our Lady of Loreto (1920), Thérèse of Lisieux, Joseph of Cupertino.
Bakers: Elizabeth of Hungary, Nicholas.
Bankers: Matthew.
Barbers: Cosmas and Damian, Louis.
Barren women: Anthony of Padua, Felicity.
Basket-makers: Anthony, Abbot.
Bees: Ambrose.
Birth: Margaret.
Beggars: Martin of Tours.
Blacksmiths: Dunstan.
Blind: Odilia, Raphael.
Blood banks: Januarius.
Bodily ills: Our Lady of Lourdes.
Bookbinders: Peter Celestine.
Bookkeepers: Matthew.
Booksellers: John of God.
Boy Scouts: George.
Brewers: Augustine of Hippo, Luke, Nicholas of Myra.
Bricklayers: Stephen.
Brides: Nicholas of Myra.
Bridges: John of Nepomucene.
Broadcasters: Gabriel.
Brushmakers: Anthony, Abbot.
Builders: Vincent Ferrer.
Bus drivers: Christopher.
Butchers: Anthony (Abbot), Luke.
Butlers: Adelelm.

Cabdrivers: Fiacre.
Cabinetmakers: Anne.
Cancer patients: Peregrine.
Canonists: Raymond of Peñafort.
Carpenters: Joseph.
Catechists: Viator, Charles Borromeo, Robert Bellarmine.
Catholic Action: Francis of Assisi (1916).
Catholic Press: Francis de Sales.
Chandlers: Ambrose, Bernard of Clairvaux.
Chaplains: John of Capistrano.
Charitable societies: Vincent de Paul (May 12, 1885).
Chastity: Thomas Aquinas.
Childbirth: Raymond Nonnatus; Gerard Majella.
Children: Nicholas of Myra.
Children of Mary: Agnes, Maria Goretti.
Choirboys: Dominic Savio (June 8, 1956), Holy Innocents.
Church: Joseph (Dec. 8, 1870).
Circus people: Julian the Hospitaller.
Clerics: Gabriel of the Sorrowful Mother.
Colleges: Thomas Aquinas.
Comedians: Vitus.
Communications personnel: Bernardine.
Confessors: Alphonsus Liguori (Apr. 26, 1950), John Nepomucene.
Converts: Helena; Vladimir.
Convulsive children: Scholastica.
Cooks: Lawrence, Martha.
Coopers: Nicholas of Myra.
Coppersmiths: Maurus.
Dairy workers: Brigid.
Dancers: Vitus.
Deaf: Francis de Sales.
Dentists: Apollonia.
Desperate situations: Gregory of Neocaesarea, Jude Thaddeus, Rita of Cascia.
Dietitians (in hospitals): Martha.
Diplomats: Gabriel.
Divorce: Helena.
Drug addiction: Maximilian Kolbe.
Dyers: Maurice, Lydia.
Dying: Joseph.
Ecologists: Francis of Assisi (Nov. 29, 1979).
Ecumenists: Cyril and Methodius.
Editors: John Bosco.
Emigrants: Frances Xavier Cabrini (Sept. 8, 1950).
Endurance: Pantaleon.
Engineers: Ferdinand III.
Epilepsy, Motor Diseases: Vitus, Willibrord.
Eucharistic congresses and societies: Paschal Baylon (Nov. 28, 1897).
Expectant mothers: Raymond Nonnatus, Gerard Majella.
Eye diseases: Lucy.
Falsely accused: Raymond Nonnatus.
Farmers: George, Isidore.
Farriers: John the Baptist.
Firemen: Florian.
Fire prevention: Catherine of Siena.
First communicants: Tarcisius.
Fishermen: Andrew.
Florists: Thérèse of Lisieux.
Forest workers: John Gualbert.
Foundlings: Holy Innocents.

Friendship: John the Divine.
Fullers: Anastasius the Fuller, James the Less.
Funeral directors: Joseph of Arimathea, Dismas.
Gardeners: Adelard, Tryphon, Fiacre, Phocas.
Glassworkers: Luke.
Goldsmiths: Dunstan, Anastasius.
Gravediggers: Anthony, Abbot.
Greetings: Valentine.
Grocers: Michael.
Grooms: King Louis IX of France.
Hairdressers: Martin de Porres.
Happy meetings: Raphael.
Hatters: Severus of Ravenna, James the Less.
Headache sufferers: Teresa of Jesus (Ávila).
Heart patients: John of God.
Homeless: Margaret of Cortona; Benedict Joseph Labré.
Horses: Giles; Hippolytus.
Housekeepers: Zita.
Hospital administrators: Basil the Great, Frances X. Cabrini.
Hospitals: Camillus de Lellis and John of God (June 22, 1886), Jude Thaddeus.
Housewives: Anne.
Hunters: Hubert, Eustachius.
Infantrymen: Maurice.
Innkeepers: Amand, Martha, Julian the Hospitaller.
Innocence: Hallvard.
Invalids: Roch.
Janitors: Theobald.
Jewelers: Eligius, Dunstan.
Journalists: Francis de Sales (Apr. 26, 1923).
Jurists: John Capistran.
Laborers: Isidore, James, John Bosco.
Lawyers: Ivo (Yves Helory), Genesius, Thomas More.
Learning: Ambrose.
Librarians: Jerome.
Lighthouse keepers: Venerius (Mar. 10, 1961).
Linguists: Gottschalk.
Locksmiths: Dunstan.
Lost souls: Nicholas of Tolentino.
Lovers: Raphael; Valentine.
Lunatics: Christina.
Maids: Zita.
Marble workers: Clement I.
Mariners: Michael, Nicholas of Tolentino.
Medical record librarians: Raymond of Peñafort.
Medical social workers: John Regis.
Medical technicians: Albert the Great.
Mentally ill: Dymphna.
Merchants: Francis of Assisi, Nicholas of Myra.
Messengers: Gabriel.
Metal workers: Eligius.
Military chaplains: John Capistran (Feb. 10, 1984).
Millers: Arnulph, Victor.
Missions, foreign: Francis Xavier (Mar. 25, 1904), Thérèse of Lisieux (Dec. 14, 1927).
Missions, black: Peter Claver (1896, Leo XIII), Benedict the Black.
Missions, parish: Leonard of Port Maurice (Mar. 17, 1923).
Monks: Benedict of Nursia.
Mothers: Monica.
Motorcyclists: Our Lady of Grace.
Motorists: Christopher, Frances of Rome.
Mountaineers: Bernard of Montjoux (or Menthon).
Musicians: Gregory the Great, Cecilia, Dunstan.

Mystics: John of the Cross.
Notaries: Luke, Mark.
Nuns: Bridget.
Nurses: Camillus de Lellis and John of God (1930, Pius XI), Agatha, Raphael.
Nursing and nursing service: Elizabeth of Hungary, Catherine of Siena.
Orators: John Chrysostom (July 8, 1908).
Organ builders: Cecilia.
Orphans: Jerome Emiliani.
Painters: Luke.
Paratroopers: Michael.
Pawnbrokers: Nicholas.
Plumbers: Vincent Ferrer.
Pharmacists: Cosmas and Damian, James the Greater.
Pharmacists (in hospitals): Gemma Galgani.
Philosophers: Justin.
Physicians: Pantaleon, Cosmas and Damian, Luke, Raphael.
Pilgrims: James the Greater.
Plasterers: Bartholomew.
Poets: David, Cecilia.
Politicians: Thomas More
Poison sufferers: Benedict.
Policemen: Michael.
Poor: Lawrence, Anthony of Padua.
Poor souls: Nicholas of Tolentino.
Popes: Gregory I the Great.
Porters: Christopher.
Possessed: Bruno, Denis.
Postal employees: Gabriel.
Priests: Jean-Baptiste Vianney (Apr. 23, 1929).
Printers: John of God, Augustine of Hippo, Genesius.
Prisoners: Dismas, Joseph Cafasso.
Protector of crops: Ansovinus.
Public relations: Bernardine of Siena (May 20, 1960).
Public relations (of hospitals): Paul, Apostle.
Publishers: John the Divine.
Race relations: Martin de Porres.
Radiologists: Michael (Jan. 15, 1941).
Radio workers: Gabriel.
Refugees: Alban.
Retreats: Ignatius Loyola (July 25, 1922).
Rheumatism: James the Greater.
Saddlers: Crispin and Crispinian.
Sailors: Cuthbert, Brendan, Eulalia, Christopher, Peter Gonzalez, Erasmus, Nicholas.
Scholars: Bede the Venerable; Brigid.
Schools, Catholic: Thomas Aquinas (Aug. 4, 1880), Joseph Calasanz (Aug. 13, 1948).
Scientists: Albert (Aug. 13, 1948).
Sculptors: Four Crowned Martyrs.
Seamen: Francis of Paola.
Searchers of lost articles: Anthony of Padua.
Secretaries: Genesius.
Secular Franciscans: Louis of France, Elizabeth of Hungary.
Seminarians: Charles Borromeo.
Servants: Martha, Zita.
Shepherds: Drogo.
Shoemakers: Crispin and Crispinian.
Sick: Michael, John of God and Camillus de Lellis (June 22, 1886).
Silversmiths: Andronicus.
Singers: Gregory, Cecilia.
Single mothers: Margaret of Cortona.
Single women: Catherine of Alexandria.

Skaters: Lidwina.
Skiers: Bernard of Montjoux (or Menthon).
Social workers: Louise de Marillac (Feb. 12, 1960).
Soldiers: Hadrian, George, Ignatius, Sebastian, Martin of Tours, Joan of Arc.
Speleologists: Benedict.
Stamp collectors: Gabriel.
Stenographers: Genesius, Cassian.
Stonecutters: Clement.
Stonemasons: Stephen.
Stress: Walter of Portnoise.
Students: Thomas Aquinas.
Surgeons: Cosmas and Damian, Luke.
Swimmers: Adjutor.
Swordsmiths: Maurice.
Tailors: Homobonus.
Tanners: Crispin and Crispinian, Simon.
Tax collectors: Matthew.
Teachers: Gregory the Great, John Baptist de la Salle (May 15, 1950).
Telecommunications workers: Gabriel (Jan. 12, 1951).
Television: Clare of Assisi (Feb. 14, 1958).
Television workers: Gabriel.
Thieves: Dismas.
Theologians: Augustine, Alphonsus Liguori.
Throat ailments: Blase.
Torture victims: Alban; Eustachius; Regina; Vincent; Victor of Marseilles.
Toymakers: Claude.
Travelers: Anthony of Padua, Nicholas of Myra, Christopher, Raphael.
Travel hostesses: Bona (Mar. 2, 1962).
Truck drivers: Christopher.
Universities: Blessed Contardo Ferrini.
Veterinarians: Blaise.
Vocations: Alphonsus.
Whales: Brendan the Voyager.
Watchmen: Peter of Alcantara.
Weavers: Paul the Hermit, Anastasius the Fuller, Anastasia.
Wine merchants: Amand.
Wineries: Morand; Vincent.
Women in labor: Anne.
Workingmen: Joseph.
Writers: Francis de Sales (Apr. 26, 1923), Lucy.
Yachtsmen: Adjutor.
Young girls: Agnes.
Youth: Aloysius Gonzaga (1729, Benedict XIII; 1926, Pius XI), John Berchmans, Gabriel of the Sorrowful Mother.

Patron Saints of Places

Albania: Our Lady of Good Counsel.
Alsace: Odilia.
Americas: Our Lady of Guadalupe, Rose of Lima.
Angola: Immaculate Heart of Mary (Nov. 21, 1984).
Argentina: Our Lady of Lujan.
Armenia: Gregory Illuminator.
Asia Minor: John, Evangelist.
Australia: Our Lady Help of Christians.
Belgium: Joseph.
Bohemia: Wenceslaus, Ludmilla.
Bolivia: Our Lady of Copacabana *"Virgen de la Candelaria."*
Borneo: Francis Xavier.
Brazil: Nossa Señora de Aparecida, Immaculate Conception, Peter of Alcantara.

Canada: Joseph, Anne.
Chile: James the Greater, Our Lady of Mt. Carmel.
China: Joseph.
Colombia: Peter Claver, Louis Bertran.
Corsica: Immaculate Conception.
Cuba: Our Lady of Charity.
Czechoslovakia: Wenceslaus, John Nepomucene, Procopius.
Denmark: Ansgar, Canute.
Dominican Republic: Our Lady of High Grace, Dominic.
East Indies: Thomas, Apostle.
Ecuador: Sacred Heart.
El Salvador: Our Lady of Peace (Oct. 10, 1966).
England: George.
Equatorial Guinea: Immaculate Conception (May 25, 1986).
Europe: Benedict (1964), Cyril and Methodius, co-patrons (Dec. 31, 1980); Sts. Catherine of Siena, Bridget of Sweden, and Edith Stein, co-patronesses (Oct. 1, 1999).
Finland: Henry.
France: Our Lady of the Assumption, Joan of Arc, Thérèse (May 3, 1944).
Germany: Boniface, Michael.
Gibraltar: Blessed Virgin Mary under title, "Our Lady of Europe" (May 31, 1979).
Greece: Nicholas, Andrew.
Holland: Willibrord.
Hungary: Blessed Virgin, "Great Lady of Hungary," Stephen, King.
Iceland: Thorlac (Jan. 14, 1984).
India: Our Lady of Assumption.
Ireland: Patrick, Brigid and Columba.
Italy: Francis of Assisi, Catherine of Siena.
Japan: Peter Baptist.
Korea: Joseph and Mary, Mother of the Church.
Lesotho: Immaculate Heart of Mary.
Lithuania: Casimir, Bl. Cunegunda.
Luxembourg: Willibrord.
Malta: Paul, Our Lady of the Assumption.
Mexico: Our Lady of Guadalupe.
Monaco: Devota.
Moravia: Cyril and Methodius.
New Zealand: Our Lady Help of Christians.
Norway: Olaf.
Papua New Guinea (including northern Solomon Islands): Michael the Archangel (May 31, 1979).
Paraguay: Our Lady of Assumption (July 13, 1951).
Peru: Joseph (Mar. 19, 1957).
Philippines: Sacred Heart of Mary.
Poland: Casimir, Bl. Cunegunda, Stanislaus of Krakow, Our Lady of Czestochowa.
Portugal: Immaculate Conception, Francis Borgia, Anthony of Padua, Vincent of Saragossa, George.
Russia: Andrew, Nicholas of Myra, Thérèse of Lisieux.
Scandinavia: Ansgar.
Scotland: Andrew, Columba.
Silesia: Hedwig.
Slovakia: Our Lady of Sorrows.
South Africa: Our Lady of Assumption (Mar. 15, 1952).
South America: Rose of Lima.
Solomon Islands: BVM, under title Most Holy Name of Mary (Sept. 4, 1991).
Spain: James the Greater, Teresa.

Sri Lanka (Ceylon): Lawrence.
Sweden: Bridget, Eric.
Tanzania: Immaculate Conception (Dec. 8, 1964).
United States: Immaculate Conception (1846).
Uruguay: Blessed Virgin Mary under title *"La Virgen de los Treinte y Tres"* (Nov. 21, 1963).
Venezuela: Our Lady of Coromoto.
Wales: David.
West Indies: Gertrude.

Emblems, Portrayals of Saints

Agatha: Tongs, veil.
Agnes: Lamb.
Ambrose: Bees, dove, ox, pen.
Andrew: Transverse cross.
Anne, Mother of the Blessed Virgin: Door.
Anthony of Padua: Infant Jesus, bread, book, lily.
Augustine of Hippo: Dove, child, shell, pen.
Bartholomew: Knife, flayed and holding his skin.
Benedict: Broken cup, raven, bell, crosier, bush.
Bernard of Clairvaux: Pen, bees, instruments of the Passion.
Bernardine of Siena: Tablet or sun inscribed with IHS.
Blase: Wax, taper, iron comb.
Bonaventure: Communion, ciborium, cardinal's hat.
Boniface: Oak, ax, book, fox, scourge, fountain, raven, sword.
Bridget of Sweden: Book, pilgrim's staff.
Bridget of Kildare: Cross, flame over her head, candle.
Catherine of Ricci: Ring, crown, crucifix.
Catherine of Siena: Stigmata, cross, ring, lily.
Cecilia: Organ.
Charles Borromeo: Communion, coat of arms with word "Humilitas."
Christopher: Giant, torrent, tree, Child Jesus on his shoulders.
Clare of Assisi: Monstrance.
Cosmas and Damian: A phial, box of ointment.
Cyril of Alexandria: Blessed Virgin holding the Child Jesus, pen.
Cyril of Jerusalem: Purse, book.
Dominic: Rosary, star.
Edmund the Martyr: Arrow, sword.
Elizabeth of Hungary: Alms, flowers, bread, the poor, a pitcher.
Francis of Assisi: Wolf, birds, fish, skull, the Stigmata.
Francis Xavier: Crucifix, bell, vessel.
Genevieve: Bread, keys, herd, candle.
George: Dragon.
Gertrude: Crown, taper, lily.
Gervase and Protase: Scourge, club, sword.
Gregory I (the Great): Tiara, crosier, dove.
Helena: Cross.

Ignatius of Loyola: Communion, chasuble, book, apparition of Our Lord.
Isidore: Bees, pen.
James the Greater: Pilgrim's staff, shell, key, sword.
James the Less: Square rule, halberd, club.
Jerome: Lion.
John Berchmans: Rule of St. Ignatius, cross, rosary.
John Chrysostom: Bees, dove, pen.
John of God: Alms, a heart, crown of thorns.
John the Baptist: Lamb, head on platter, skin of an animal.
John the Evangelist: Eagle, chalice, kettle, armor.
Josaphat Kuncevyc: Chalice, crown, winged deacon.
Joseph, Spouse of the Blessed Virgin: Infant Jesus, lily, rod, plane, carpenter's square.
Jude: Sword, square rule, club.
Justin Martyr: Ax, sword.
Lawrence: Cross, book of the Gospels, gridiron.
Leander of Seville: A pen.
Liberius: Pebbles, peacock.
Longinus: In arms at foot of the cross.
Louis IX of France: Crown of thorns, nails.
Lucy: Cord, eyes on a dish.
Luke: Ox, book, brush, palette.
Mark: Lion, book.
Martha: Holy water sprinkler, dragon.
Mary Magdalene: Alabaster box of ointment.
Matilda: Purse, alms.
Matthew: Winged man, purse, lance.
Matthias: Lance.
Maurus: Scales, spade, crutch.
Meinrad: Two ravens.
Michael: Scales, banner, sword, dragon.
Monica: Girdle, tears.
Nicholas: Three purses or balls, anchor or boat, child.
Patrick: Cross, harp, serpent, baptismal font, demons, shamrock.
Paul: Sword, book or scroll.
Peter: Keys, boat, cock.
Philip, Apostle: Column.
Philip Neri: Altar, chasuble, vial.
Rita of Cascia: Rose, crucifix, thorn.
Roch: Angel, dog, bread.
Rose of Lima: Crown of thorns, anchor, city.
Sebastian: Arrows, crown.
Simon Stock: Scapular.
Teresa of Jesus (Ávila): Heart, arrow, book.
Thérèse of Lisieux: Roses entwining a crucifix.
Thomas, Apostle: Lance, ax.
Thomas Aquinas: Chalice, monstrance, dove, ox, person trampled under foot.
Vincent de Paul: Children.
Vincent Ferrer: Pulpit, cardinal's hat, trumpet, captives.

CANONIZATIONS AND BEATIFICATIONS 2002-03

Pope John Paul II beatified and canonized the following individuals from Sept. 2002 to Aug. 2003. Included are the dates of the beatifications and canonizations, as well as relevant biographical information.

Canonizations: 2002

Josemaria Escrivá de Balaguer (1902-75) Priest and founder of Opus Dei. Born in Barbastro, Spain, and ordained on Mar. 28, 1925, he established Opus Dei in 1921, a society designed to promote holiness among individuals in the world; Josemaria received inspiration to take Opus Dei to women as well as to men. In 1943, he founded the Priestly Society of the Holy Cross. When he died, Josemaria left more than 60,000 members of Opus Dei in 80 countries and 1,000 priests dedicated to the Opus Dei apostolate. Pope John Paul II beatified Josemaria on May 17, 1992, and canonized him on Oct. 6, 2002.

Canonizations: 2003

Angela de la Cruz (1846-1932) Virgin, foundress of the Sisters of the Company of the Cross. Called the "Little Angel," she was born in Seville, Spain, to a family of modest means, one of 14 children. She attempted to enter the Carmelite cloister in Seville, but obstacles and illness prevented her acceptance. In 1875, however, the Company of the Cross, which she had helped to start and which became the Sisters of the Cross, was officially launched as a religious congregation dedicated to the care of the sick and poor. Pope John Paul II beatified her in 1982 and canonized her on May 4, 2003.

Genoveva Torres Morales (1870-1956) Foundress of the Congregation of the Sisters of the Sacred Heart of Jesus and of the Holy Angels. Born in Almenara, Castile, Spain, she lost both parents and four of her brothers and sisters. At the age of 13 her left leg was amputated at the thigh because of an illness, forcing her to endure pain and the continual use of crutches. By 1885, Blessed Genoveva lived at the Mercy Home conducted by the Carmelites of Charity, sewing to aid in her support. She asked to enter the Carmelites of Charity, but her physical problems presented obstacles. She then left Mercy Home and joined two other women who supported themselves by their own skills. In 1911, she and her companions started a religious congregation dedicated to serving elderly women in the working class. Pope John Paul II beatified Genoveva in 1995 and canonized her on May 4, 2003.

José María Rubio y Peralta (1864-1929) Priest of the Society of Jesus, revered as the "Apostle of Madrid." Born in Dalias, in Almeria Province, southern Spain, he entered the seminary at age 12 and later became a doctor of canon law. Ordained a priest, he held various assignments until 1906, when he entered the Society of Jesus in Granada. He returned as a professed Jesuit to Madrid in 1911, went into the suburban areas of the city with lay helpers, and aided the needy and the sick. Joseph continued this apostolate until his death, when thousands mourned his passing. Pope John Paul II beatified him in 1985, with two other Jesuits, and canonized him on May 4, 2003.

María Maravillas de Jesús Pidal y Chico de Guzmán (1891-1974) Member of the Order of Discalced Carmelites. Born in Madrid, Spain, she was the daughter of a Spanish ambassador to the Vatican. She entered the Carmelite Monastery of El Escorial in 1920. Four years later, she and three other Carmelites founded a daughter convent in Cerro de los Angeles. In 1933, she founded another Carmel in Kottayam, India. When the Spanish Civil War began, María and her nuns found haven in an apartment in Madrid. She subsequently founded numerous Carmels and combined all of them into an association of St. Teresa in 1972. She said: "What happiness to die a Carmelite." Pope John Paul II beatified her in 1994 and canonized her on May 4, 2003.

Pedro Poveda Castroverde (1874-1936) Priest, martyr, and founder of the Teresian Association. Born in Linares, Spain, he was ordained on Apr. 17, 1897. He joined the Third Order Carmelites and in 1911 opened St. Teresa of Ávila Academy, which became the foundation of a secular institute, called the Teresians, in Madrid in 1911. The Teresian Institute received papal approval in 1924. Pope John Paul II beatified Pedro in 1993 and canonized him on May 4, 2003.

Jozef Sebastian Pelczar (1842-1924) Bishop and founder of the Congregation of the Servants of the Sacred Heart of Jesus. Called the "Shepherd of Souls," he was born in Korczyna, Poland, and was named titular bishop of Meletopolis in 1899 and bishop of Przemysl in 1901. He founded the Servants of the Most Sacred Heart of Jesus in 1894, dedicated to domestic work (the congregation arrived in the United States in 1959). After Russian troops entered Przemysl in March 1915 and burned churches, Bishop Josef led his clergy, nuns, and people in helping the wounded and oppressed. He also opened hospitals and clinics. Pope John Paul II beatified Josef on June 2, 1991, and canonized him on May 18, 2003.

Maria de Mattias (1805-1866) Virgin and foundress of the Congregation of the Adoring Sisters of the Blood of Christ (Italy). Born in Vallecorsa, the southernmost town of the then Papal States, she was raised in a devout atmosphere and underwent a powerful conversion around the age of 17, especially after hearing the preaching of St. Gaspar del Bufalo. Under the guidance of one of St. Gaspar's companions, Ven. Fr. Giovanni Merlini, she founded the Congregation of the Adoring Sisters of the Blood of Christ in Acuto (Frosinone) in 1834, at the age of 29. From this start, Maria de Mattias opened some 70 communities during her lifetime, including three in Germany and England. She died at Rome and was buried in a tomb chosen for her by Blessed Pius IX. She was beatified by Pope Pius XII on Oct. 1, 1950, and canonized by Pope John Paul II on May 18, 2003.

Ursula Ledochowska (1865-1939) Virgin and foundress of the Ursuline Sisters of the Sacred Heart of Jesus in Agony (Poland). Born in Loosdorr, Austria, she was the daughter of Count Anthony Ledochowska. In 1885, Ursula's father died of smallpox, and the family was aided by an uncle, Cardinal Lebo, who was in Rome. Ursula subsequently founded the Ursulines of the Sacred Heart, also called the Gray Ursulines, submitting the rule and constitutions of the congregation to Pope Benedict XV (r. 1914-22) for approval. Pope John Paul II beatified Ursula in Poznan, Poland, on June 20, 1983, and canonized her on May 18, 2003.

Virginia Centurione Bracelli (1587-1651) Widow and foundress of the Sisters of Our Lady of Refuge on Mount Calvary (Italy). Born the daughter of the doge of Genoa, she was raised in splendor and married the wealthy Gasparo Grimaldi Bracelli (d. 1625). Virginia opened a home called "St. Mary of the Refuge" for poor children in Genoa and formed a group of dedicated women for her apostolate, adopting a Franciscan rule for the foundation. Pope John Paul II beatified Virginia on Sept. 22, 1985, and canonized her on May 18, 2003.

Beatifications: 2002

Andrew Hyacinth Longhin (1863-1936) A Capuchin bishop of Treviso, who labored as a shepherd during a difficult time in Italy during the late 19th and early 20th centuries. Born in Fiumicello di Campodarsego near Padua to poor tenant farmers, he entered the novitiate of the Capuchin Order in 1916. Ordained in 1886, he served as a gifted spiritual director and was elected Provincial Minister of the Capuchins of Venice in 1902. Soon after his election as pontiff, Pope St. Pius X personally appointed Fr. Andrew as bishop of Treviso. He served as bishop throughout World War I and was much revered for his holiness; Pope Pius X was one of those who held him in great esteem. Pope John Paul II beatified him on Oct. 20, 2002.

Daudi Okelo (1902-c. 1918) Ugandan martyr, with Jildo Irwa. He was the son of pagan parents and was baptized by Fr. Cesare Gambaretto on June 1, 1916. He was confirmed on Oct. 15, 1916, and later enrolled as a catechist. Sent as a catechist to Paimol with Irwa as his assistant, he was murdered by a mob of local pagans, and his body was dragged to a nearby termite hill. The remains, collected in Feb. 1926, were later placed in the mission church of Kitgum, at the foot of the altar of the Sacred Heart. Pope John Paul II beatified him on Oct. 20, 2002.

Jildo Irwa (1906-c. 1918) Ugandan martyr, with Daudi Okelo. He was born around 1906 in the village of Bar-Kitoba, northwest of Kitgum, from pagan parents; his father later became a Christian. Baptized by Cesare Gambaretto on June 6, 1916, he was confirmed on Oct. 15, 1916. He soon assisted the older Daudi in his work as a catechist. With Daudi, he was attacked by a local pagan mob and was first stabbed, then struck in the head. Pope John Paul II beatified him on Oct. 20, 2002.

Marcantonio Durando (1801-80) Italian priest, promoter of the missions, and founder of the Nazarene Sisters. Marcantonio entered the Congregation of the Mission at the age of 15 and was ordained in 1824. Rather than going to China, as was his dream, he labored instead on behalf of the missions in Italy, supporting the work of the Propagation of the Faith. Concerned for the poor, he invited the Daughters of Charity into northern Italy, and in 1865 established the Nazarene Sisters. In 1837, at the age of 36, he was appointed Visitor (or major superior) of the Province of North Italy of the Vincentian Fathers, a position he held for 43 uninterrupted years, until his death. He was beatified by Pope John Paul II on Oct. 20, 2002.

Marie of the Passion (1839-1904) French missionary nun and founder of the Franciscan Missionaries of Mary. Born to a noble Christian family, Hélène Marie Philippine de Chappotin de Neuville entered the Poor Clares in 1860. After an illness, she joined the Society of Marie Reparatrice in 1864 and took the name of Mary of the Passion. In March 1865, while still a novice, she was sent to India, to the Apostolic Vicariate of Madurai, confided to the Society of Jesus. Because of her gifts and virtues, she was nominated local superior and then, in July 1867, she was named provincial superior of the three convents of the Reparatrice. After internal difficulties divided the community, Marie journeyed to Rome and received permission to found a new Institute, which became the Franciscan Missionaries of Mary. She was beatified by Pope John Paul II on Oct. 20, 2002.

Liduina Meneguzzi (1901-41) An Italian nun and missionary in Ethiopia. Born into a poor family of farmers, she entered Sisters Congregation of Saint Francesco of Sales in 1926. In 1937, she was sent to Dire-Dawa in Ethiopia as a missionary, working as a nurse in the Parini Civil Hospital. During World War II, she cared for wounded soldiers and was noted for her concern for patients regardless of race or religion. She thus earned the name "Sister Gudda" (the

Great). Liduina died from complications after stomach surgery in 1941 and was mourned by the city of Dire-Dawa. She was beatified by Pope John Paul II on Oct. 20, 2002.

Beatifications: 2003

Juana María Condesa Lluch (1862-1916) Foundress of the Congregation of the Handmaids of the Immaculate Conception, Protectress of Workers. She was born in Valencia, Spain, to a wealthy Christian family and grew up deeply imbued with the faith. She was especially sensitive to the plight of exploited factory workers, especially those forced to leave the countryside to seek work in the cities as a result of the Industrial Revolution. When she was only 18, she felt called by Christ to found a religious order that would be committed to helping them. The Archbishop of Valencia considered her too young to begin a Congregation, but after struggling for several years, in 1884 she received permission to open a shelter for oppressed workers. A few months later, Juana opened a school for the factory workers' children. In 1892, the Congregation of the Handmaids of the Immaculate Conception, Protectress of Workers, received diocesan approval; the Congregation received pontifical approval from Pope Pius XII in 1947. She was beatified by Pope John Paul II on Mar. 23, 2003.

László Batthyány-Strattmann (1870-1931) Hungarian layman, doctor, and father. Born into an ancient noble family of Hungary, he grew up determined to be a doctor to the poor. After graduating as a physician in 1900, he opened a private hospital in Kittsee in 1902, specializing as a surgeon and oculist. On the death of his uncle in 1915, Ladislaus inherited the family castle in Hungary and the title "Prince." He and his wife turned one wing of the castle into a hospital that specialized in ophthalmology. He was also known as a "doctor of the poor," treating them free of charge, save for the request that they recite an Our Father. He and his wife, Countess Maria Teresa Coreth, a deeply religious woman in her own right, raised 13 children. His lifelong motto was "In fidelity and charity." He was beatified by Pope John Paul II on Mar. 23, 2003.

María Dolores Rodríguez Sopeña (1848-1918) Born in Velez Rubio, Almería, Spain, she was drawn from an early age to a life of aiding others, including lepers and women in prison. Journeying with her family to Puerto Rico in 1872, she founded the Association of the Sodality of the Virgin Mary and schools for the disadvantaged, where she taught reading and writing, as well as catechism. She also founded the "Centers of Instruction" to teach catechism and general education and to provide medical assistance to those in need. Her family returned to Madrid in 1877, and she devoted her life to apostolic work: in 1885, she opened a social center for the poor, and in 1892 launched the Association of the Apostolic Laymen (known as the Sopeña Lay Movement). In 1907, Pope St. Pius X approved officially the Civil Association (known today as OSCUS, or Social and Cultural Work, and known as the "Sopeña Catechetical Institute"). She was beatified by Pope John Paul II on Mar. 23, 2003.

María Caridad Brader (1860-1943) Foundress of the Congregation of the Franciscan Sisters of Mary Immaculate. A native of Kaltbrunn, St. Gallen, Switzerland, she entered the enclosed Franciscan convent of Maria Hilf in 1880. Owing to her excellent education, she was designated to teach at the convent school. In 1888, Sr. Caritas and a group of companions set out for Ecuador and worked as a missionary. To assist evangelization, she founded the Congregation of the Franciscan Sisters of Mary Immaculate, at first made up of young Swiss girls who were soon joined by local vocations, including many from Colombia. She served as Superior General of the Congregation from 1893-1919 and from 1928-40. In 1933, she received pontifical approval of the Congregation. She was beatified by Pope John Paul II on Mar. 23, 2003.

Pierre Bonhomme (1803-61) Founder of the Congregation of the Sisters of Our Lady of Calvary. Born in Gramat, France, he was ordained a priest in 1827 and soon opened an elementary and middle school for boys, a school to prepare students for the major seminary, and the spiritual group "Children of Mary" for young girls. He also received permission to establish a home for the needy. From this ministry to the poor, he established the Congregation of the Sisters of Our Lady of Calvary in Gramat, dedicated to educating children and to providing assistance to the poor, sick, elderly, deaf-mutes and the seriously mentally and physically disabled. He was beatified by Pope John Paul II on Mar. 23, 2003.

Eugenia Ravasco (1845-1900) Foundress of the Sisters of the Sacred Hearts of Jesus and Mary. Born in Milan, Italy, she faced many hardships in her youth after the death of her parents and developed swiftly in the spiritual life. In 1868, she began her own congregation and in 1878 opened a school for girls. Diocesan approval was granted in 1882 and papal approval in 1909. Today, the congregation serves in schools, parishes, and missions in Europe, Central and South America, Africa, and the Philippines. She was beatified by Pope John Paul II on Apr. 27, 2003.

Giacomo Alberione (1884-1971) Founder of the Pauline Family. Born in San Lorenzo di Fossano, Italy, he entered the seminary at the age of 16 and was ordained in 1907. After years of pastoral service and study of contemporary culture, he established in 1914 the Pious Society of St. Paul to bring Christ to the world. The following year he worked with Teresa Merlo to found the Congregation of Daughters of St. Paul; in 1924, he founded a second congregation for women, the Pious Disciples of the Divine Master, and in 1938, the Sisters of Jesus the Good Shepherd. These were followed by secular institutes. Collectively, the apostolate was called the Pauline Family. He was beatified by Pope John Paul II on Apri. 27, 2003.

Giulia Salzano (1846-1929) Foundress of the Catechist Sisters of the Sacred Heart. Born in Santa Maria Capua Vetere, Italy, she was raised by the Sisters of Charity and became a teacher. Renowned for her teaching abilities, she devoted herself to catechetics, founding in 1905 the Congregation the Catechist Sisters of the Sacred Heart to teach parish catechesis in

pastoral training centers. She was beatified by Pope John Paul II on Apr. 27, 2003.

Marco d'Aviano (1631-99) Capuchin priest and preacher. Born in Aviano, Italy, Marco set out at the age of 16 to die as a martyr against the Ottoman Turks; he encountered Capuchin Franciscans, however, and was so inspired that he entered the order in 1648 and was ordained in 1655. He subsequently proved a brilliant preacher and spiritual advisor. Named a papal nuncio to Vienna by Pope Innocent XI, Marco proved a key figure in the defense of the city against the Turks in 1683 and assisted in the liberation of Buda (1686) and Budapest (1688). He was beatified by Pope John Paul II on Apr. 27, 2003.

Maria Cristina Brando (1856-1906) Foundress of the Sisters, Expiatory Victims of Jesus in the Blessed Sacrament. Born in Naples, Italy, she overcame various illnesses and unsuccessful efforts to join a religious order to found her own congregation, the Pious Institute of Perpetual Adoration of the Blessed Sacrament. The congregation received papal approval in 1903 under the name of Sisters, Expiatory Victims of Jesus in the Blessed Sacrament. She was beatified by Pope John Paul II on Apr. 27, 2003.

Maria Domenica Mantovani (1862-1934) Cofoundress of the Little Sisters of the Holy Family. Born in Castelletto di Brenzone, Italy, she spent much of her youth working in her parish assisting the sick and teaching the catechism. In 1892, she founded — with Fr. Giuseppe Nascimbeni — the Little Sisters of the Holy Family. She was beatified by Pope John Paul II on Apr. 27, 2003.

Marija of Jesus Crucified Petkovic (1892-1966) Croatian nun and founder of the Congregation of the Daughters of Mercy. She was born on the island of Korcula in Blato, Croatia, the sixth of 11 children. In 1919, Marija entered the convent of the Servants of Charity and soon opened a day-recovery center, a child-care facility, and an orphanage. The next year, she wrote the first Constitutions of a new order, the Congregation of the Daughters of Mercy. From 1920-52, Mother Marija was elected five times as the Superior General. Pope John Paul II beatified her on June 6, 2003, during his visit to Croatia.

Ivan Merz (1896-1928) Catholic intellectual and founder of the League of Young Croatian Catholics and the Croatian League of Eagles. Ivan was born in Banja Luka, Bosnia, and later studied at the University of Vienna. In 1916, he was enlisted in the army and shipped to the Italian front, where he witnessed the full horrors of war. He underwent a profound conversion. After the war, he taught philosophy and theology and was especially noted for his concerns for young people. He launched the League of Young Croatian Catholics and the Croatian League of Eagles within the Croatian Catholic Action Movement. He died at the age of 32 in Zagreb. Pope John Paul II beatified Ivan on June 22, 2003, during his visit to Bosnia-Herzegovina.

Dates and Events in Catholic History

FIRST CENTURY

c. 33: First Christian Pentecost; descent of the Holy Spirit upon the disciples; preaching of St. Peter in Jerusalem; conversion, baptism and aggregation of some 3,000 persons to the first Christian community.

St. Stephen, deacon, was stoned to death at Jerusalem; he is venerated as the first Christian martyr.

c. 34: St. Paul, formerly Saul the persecutor of Christians, was converted and baptized. After three years of solitude in the desert, he joined the college of the apostles; he made three major missionary journeys and became known as the Apostle to the Gentiles; he was imprisoned twice in Rome and was beheaded there between 64 and 67.

39: Cornelius (the Gentile) and his family were baptized by St. Peter; a significant event signaling the mission of the Church to all peoples.

42: Persecution of Christians in Palestine broke out during the rule of Herod Agrippa; St. James the Greater, the first apostle to die, was beheaded in 44; St. Peter was imprisoned for a short time; many Christians fled to Antioch, marking the beginning of the dispersion of Christians beyond the confines of Palestine. At Antioch, the followers of Christ were called Christians for the first time.

49: Christians at Rome, considered members of a Jewish sect, were adversely affected by a decree of Claudius which forbade Jewish worship there.

51: The Council of Jerusalem, in which all the apostles participated under the presidency of St. Peter, decreed that circumcision, dietary regulations, and various other prescriptions of Mosaic Law were not obligatory for Gentile converts to the Christian community. The crucial decree was issued in opposition to Judaizers who contended that observance of the Mosaic Law in its entirety was necessary for salvation.

64: Persecution broke out at Rome under Nero, the emperor said to have accused Christians of starting the fire which destroyed half of Rome.

64 or 67: Martyrdom of St. Peter at Rome during the Neronian persecution. He established his see and spent his last years there after preaching in and around Jerusalem, establishing a see at Antioch, and presiding at the Council of Jerusalem.

70: Destruction of Jerusalem by Titus.

88-97: Pontificate of St. Clement I, third successor of St. Peter as bishop of Rome, one of the Apostolic Fathers. The First Epistle of Clement to the Corinthians, with which he has been identified, was addressed by the Church of Rome to the Church at Corinth, the scene of irregularities and divisions in the Christian community.

95: Domitian persecuted Christians, principally at Rome.

c. 100: Death of St. John, apostle and evangelist, marking the end of the Age of the Apostles and the first generation of the Church.

By the end of the century, Antioch, Alexandria and Ephesus in the East and Rome in the West were established centers of Christian population and influence.

SECOND CENTURY

c. 107: St. Ignatius of Antioch was martyred at Rome. He was the first writer to use the expression, "the Catholic Church."

112: Emperor Trajan, in a rescript to Pliny the Younger, governor of Bithynia, instructed him not to search out Christians but to punish them if they were publicly denounced and refused to do homage to the Roman gods. This rescript set a pattern for Roman magistrates in dealing with Christians.

117-38: Persecution under Hadrian. Many Acts of Martyrs date from this period.

c. 125: Spread of Gnosticism, a combination of elements of Platonic philosophy and Eastern mystery religions. Its adherents claimed that its secret-knowledge principle provided a deeper insight into Christian doctrine than divine revelation and faith. One gnostic thesis denied the divinity of Christ; others denied the reality of his humanity, calling it mere appearance (Docetism, Phantasiasm).

c. 144: Excommunication of Marcion, bishop and heretic, who claimed that there was total opposition and no connection at all between the Old Testament and the New Testament, between the God of the Jews and the God of the Christians; and that the Canon (list of inspired writings) of the Bible consisted only of parts of St. Luke's Gospel and 10 letters of St. Paul. Marcionism was checked at Rome by 200 and was condemned by a council held there about 260, but the heresy persisted for several centuries in the East and had some adherents as late as the Middle Ages.

c. 155: St. Polycarp, bishop of Smyrna and disciple of St. John the Evangelist, was martyred.

c. 156: Beginning of Montanism, a form of religious extremism. Its principal tenets were the imminent second coming of Christ, denial of the divine nature of the Church and its power to forgive sin, and excessively rigorous morality. The heresy, preached by Montanus of Phrygia and others, was condemned by Pope St. Zephyrinus (199-217).

161-80: Reign of Marcus Aurelius. His persecution, launched in the wake of natural disasters, was more violent than those of his predecessors.

165: St. Justin, an important early Christian writer, was martyred at Rome.

c. 180: St. Irenaeus, bishop of Lyons and one of the great early theologians, wrote *Adversus Haereses*. He stated that the teaching and tradition of the Roman See was the standard for belief.

196: Easter Controversy, concerning the day of celebration — a Sunday, according to practice in the West, or the 14th of the month of Nisan (in the Hebrew calendar), no matter what day of the week, according to practice in the East. The controversy was not resolved at this time.

The *Didache*, whose extant form dates from the second century, is an important record of Christian belief, practice and governance in the first century.

Latin was introduced as a liturgical language in the West. Other liturgical languages were Aramaic and Greek.

The Catechetical School of Alexandria, founded about the middle of the century, gained increasing influence on doctrinal study and instruction, and interpretation of the Bible.

THIRD CENTURY

202: Persecution under Septimius Severus, who wanted to establish a simple common religion in the Empire.

206: Tertullian, a convert since 197 and the first great ecclesiastical writer in Latin, joined the heretical Montanists; he died in 230.

215: Death of Clement of Alexandria, teacher of Origen and a founding father of the School of Alexandria.

217-35: St. Hippolytus, the first antipope; he was reconciled to the Church while in prison during persecution in 235.

232-54: Origen established the School of Caesarea after being deposed in 231 as head of the School of Alexandria; he died in 254. A scholar and voluminous writer, he was one of the founders of systematic theology and exerted wide influence for many years.

c. 242: Manichaeism originated in Persia: a combination of errors based on the assumption that two supreme principles (good and evil) are operative in creation and life, and that the supreme objective of human endeavor is liberation from evil (matter). The heresy denied the humanity of Christ, the sacramental system, the authority of the Church (and state), and endorsed a moral code which threatened the fabric of society. In the 12th and 13th centuries, it took on the features of Albigensianism and Catharism.

249-51: Persecution under Decius. Many of those who denied the faith (*lapsi*) sought readmission to the Church at the end of the persecution in 251. Pope St. Cornelius agreed with St. Cyprian that *lapsi* were to be readmitted to the Church after satisfying the requirements of appropriate penance. Antipope Novatian, on the other hand, contended that persons who fell away from the Church under persecution and/or those guilty of serious sin after baptism could not be absolved and readmitted to communion with the Church. The heresy was condemned by a Roman synod in 251.

250-300: Neo-Platonism of Plotinus and Porphyry gained followers.

251: Novatian, an antipope, was condemned at Rome.

256: Pope St. Stephen I upheld the validity of baptism properly administered by heretics, in the Rebaptism Controversy.

257: Persecution under Valerian, who attempted to destroy the Church as a social structure.

258: St. Cyprian, bishop of Carthage, was martyred.

c. 260: St. Lucian founded the School of Antioch, a center of influence on biblical studies.

Pope St. Dionysius condemned Sabellianism, a form of modalism (like Monarchianism and Patripassianism). The heresy contended that the Father, Son and Holy Spirit are not distinct divine persons but are only three different modes of being and self-manifestations of the one God. St. Paul of Thebes became a hermit.

261: Gallienus issued an edict of toleration which ended general persecution for nearly 40 years.

c. 292: Diocletian divided the Roman Empire into East and West. The division emphasized political, cultural and other differences between the two parts of the Empire and influenced different developments in the Church in the East and West. The prestige of Rome began to decline.

FOURTH CENTURY

303: Persecution broke out under Diocletian; it was particularly violent in 304.

305: St. Anthony of Heracles established a foundation for hermits near the Red Sea in Egypt.

c. 306: The first local legislation on clerical celibacy was enacted by a council held at Elvira, Spain; bishops, priests, deacons and other ministers were forbidden to have wives.

311: An edict of toleration issued by Galerius at the urging of Constantine the Great and Licinius officially ended persecution in the West; some persecution continued in the East.

313: The Edict of Milan issued by Constantine and Licinius recognized Christianity as a lawful religion in the Roman Empire.

314: A council of Arles condemned Donatism, declaring that baptism properly administered by heretics is valid, in view of the principle that sacraments have their efficacy from Christ, not from the spiritual condition of their human ministers. The heresy was condemned again by a council of Carthage in 411.

318: St. Pachomius established the first foundation of the cenobitic (common) life, as compared with the solitary life of hermits in Upper Egypt.

325: Ecumenical Council of Nicaea (I). Its principal action was the condemnation of Arianism, the most devastating of the early heresies, which denied the divinity of Christ. The heresy was authored by Arius of Alexandria, a priest. Arians and several kinds of Semi-Arians propagandized their tenets widely, established their own hierarchies and churches, and raised havoc in the Church for several centuries. The council contributed to formulation of the Nicene Creed (Creed of Nicaea-Constantinople); fixed the date for the observance of Easter; passed regulations concerning clerical discipline; adopted the civil divisions of the Empire as the model for the jurisdictional organization of the Church.

326: With the support of St. Helena, the True Cross on which Christ was crucified was discovered.

337: Baptism and death of Constantine.

c. 342: Beginning of a 40-year persecution in Persia.

343-44: A council of Sardica reaffirmed doctrine formulated by Nicaea I and declared also that bishops had the right of appeal to the pope as the highest authority in the Church.

361-63: Emperor Julian the Apostate waged an unsuccessful campaign against the Church in an attempt to restore paganism as the religion of the Empire.

c. 365: Persecution of orthodox Christians under Emperor Valens in the East.

c. 376: Beginning of the barbarian invasion in the West.

379: Death of St. Basil, the Father of Monasticism in the East. His writings contributed greatly to the development of rules for the life of Religious.

381: Ecumenical Council of Constantinople (I). It condemned various brands of Arianism as well as Macedonianism, which denied the divinity of the Holy Spirit; contributed to formulation of the Nicene Creed; approved a canon acknowledging Constantinople as the second see after Rome in honor and dignity.

382: The Canon of Sacred Scripture, the official list of the inspired books of the Bible, was contained in the Decree of Pope St. Damasus and published by a regional council of Carthage in 397; the Canon was formally defined by the Council of Trent in the 16th century.

382-c. 406: St. Jerome translated the Old and New Testaments into Latin; his work is called the Vulgate version of the Bible.

396: St. Augustine became bishop of Hippo in North Africa.

FIFTH CENTURY

410: Visigoths under Alaric sacked Rome and the last Roman legions departed Britain. The decline of imperial Rome dates approximately from this time.

430: St. Augustine, bishop of Hippo for 35 years, died. He was a strong defender of orthodox doctrine against Manichaeism, Donatism and Pelagianism. The depth and range of his writings made him a dominant influence in Christian thought for centuries.

431: Ecumenical Council of Ephesus. It condemned Nestorianism, which denied the unity of the divine and human natures in the Person of Christ; defined *Theotokos* (Bearer of God) as the title of Mary, Mother of the Son of God made Man; condemned Pelagianism. The heresy of Pelagianism, proceeding from the assumption that Adam had a natural right to supernatural life, held that man could attain salvation through the efforts of his natural powers and free will; it involved errors concerning the nature of original sin, the meaning of grace and other matters. Related Semi-Pelagianism was condemned by a council of Orange in 529.

432: St. Patrick arrived in Ireland. By the time of his death in 461 most of the country had been converted, monasteries founded and the hierarchy established.

438: The Theodosian Code, a compilation of decrees for the Empire, was issued by Theodosius II; it had great influence on subsequent civil and ecclesiastical law.

451: Ecumenical Council of Chalcedon. Its principal action was the condemnation of Monophysitism (also called Eutychianism), which denied the humanity of Christ by holding that he had only one, the divine, nature.

452: Pope St. Leo the Great persuaded Attila the Hun to spare Rome.

455: Vandals under Geiseric sacked Rome.

484: Patriarch Acacius of Constantinople was excommunicated for signing the *Henoticon*, a document which capitulated to the Monophysite heresy. The excommunication triggered the Acacian Schism which lasted for 35 years.

494: Pope St. Gelasius I declared in a letter to Emperor Anastasius that the pope had power and authority over the emperor in spiritual matters.

496: Clovis, King of the Franks, was converted and became the defender of Christianity in the West. The Franks became a Catholic people.

SIXTH CENTURY

520: Irish monasteries flourished as centers for spiritual life, missionary training, and scholarly activity.

529: The Second Council of Orange condemned Semi-Pelagianism.

c. 529: St. Benedict founded the Monte Cassino Abbey. Some years before his death in 543 he wrote a monastic rule which exercised tremendous influence on the form and style of religious life. He is called the Father of Monasticism in the West.

533: John II became the first pope to change his name. The practice did not become general until the time of Sergius IV (1009).

533-34: Emperor Justinian promulgated the *Corpus Iuris Civilis* for the Roman world; like the Theodosian Code, it influenced subsequent civil and ecclesiastical law.

c. 545: Death of Dionysius Exiguus who was the first to date history from the birth of Christ, a practice which resulted in use of the B.C. and A.D. abbreviations. His calculations were at least four years late.

553: Ecumenical Council of Constantinople (II). It condemned the Three Chapters, Nestorian-tainted writings of Theodore of Mopsuestia, Theodoret of Cyrus and Ibas of Edessa.

585: St. Columban founded an influential monastic school at Luxeuil.

589: The most important of several councils of Toledo was held. The Visigoths renounced Arianism, and St. Leander began the organization of the Church in Spain.

590-604: Pontificate of Pope St. Gregory I the Great. He set the form and style of the papacy which prevailed throughout the Middle Ages; exerted great influence on doctrine and liturgy; was strong in support of monastic discipline and clerical celibacy; authored writings on many subjects. Gregorian Chant is named in his honor.

596: Pope St. Gregory I sent St. Augustine of Canterbury and 40 monks to do missionary work in England.

597: St. Columba died. He founded an important monastery at Iona, established schools and did notable missionary work in Scotland. By the end of the century, monasteries of nuns were common; Western monasticism was flourishing; monasticism in the East, under the influence of Monophysitism and other factors, was losing its vigor.

SEVENTH CENTURY

613: St. Columban established the influential monastery of Bobbio in northern Italy; he died there in 615.

622: The *Hegira* (flight) of Mohammed from Mecca to Medina signalled the beginning of Islam which, by the end of the century, claimed almost all of the southern Mediterranean area.

628: Heraclius, Eastern Emperor, recovered the True Cross from the Persians.

649: A Lateran council condemned two erroneous formulas (Ecthesis and Type) issued by emperors Heraclius and Constans II as means of reconciling Monophysites with the Church.

664: Actions of the Synod of Whitby advanced the adoption of Roman usages in England, especially regarding the date for the observance of Easter. (See Easter Controversy.)

680-81: Ecumenical Council of Constantinople (III). It condemned Monothelitism, which held that Christ had only one will, the divine; censured Pope Honorius I for a letter to Sergius, bishop of Constantinople, in which he made an ambiguous but not infallible statement about the unity of will and/or operation in Christ.

692: Trullan Synod. Eastern-Church discipline on clerical celibacy was settled, permitting marriage before ordination to the diaconate and continuation in marriage afterwards, but prohibiting marriage following the death of the wife thereafter. Anti-Roman canons contributed to East-West alienation.
During the century, the monastic influence of Ireland and England increased in Western Europe; schools and learning declined; regulations regarding clerical celibacy became more strict in the East.

EIGHTH CENTURY

711: Muslims began the conquest of Spain.

726: Emperor Leo III, the Isaurian, launched a campaign against the veneration of sacred images and relics; called Iconoclasm (image-breaking), it caused turmoil in the East until about 843.

731: Pope Gregory III and a synod at Rome condemned Iconoclasm, with a declaration that the veneration of sacred images was in accord with Catholic tradition.
Venerable Bede issued his *Ecclesiastical History of the English People*.

732: Charles Martel defeated the Muslims at Poitiers, halting their advance in the West.

744: The Monastery of Fulda was established by St. Sturmi, a disciple of St. Boniface; it was influential in the evangelization of Germany.

754: A council of more than 300 Byzantine bishops endorsed Iconoclast errors. This council and its actions were condemned by the Lateran synod of 769.
Stephen II (III) crowned Pepin ruler of the Franks. Pepin twice invaded Italy, in 754 and 756, to defend the pope against the Lombards. His land grants to the papacy, called the Donation of Pepin, were later extended by Charlemagne (773) and formed part of the States of the Church.

c. 755: St. Boniface (Winfrid) was martyred. He was called the Apostle of Germany for his missionary work and organization of the hierarchy there.

781: Alcuin was chosen by Charlemagne to organize a palace school, which became a center of intellectual leadership.

787: Ecumenical Council of Nicaea (II). It condemned Iconoclasm, which held that the use of images was idolatry, and Adoptionism, which claimed that Christ was not the Son of God by nature but only by adoption. This was the last council regarded as ecumenical by Orthodox Churches.

792: A council at Ratisbon condemned Adoptionism.
The famous *Book of Kells* ("The Great Gospel of Columcille") dates from the early eighth or late seventh century.

NINTH CENTURY

800: Charlemagne was crowned Emperor by Pope Leo III on Christmas Day.
Egbert became king of West Saxons; he unified England and strengthened the See of Canterbury.

813: Emperor Leo V, the Armenian, revived Iconoclasm, which persisted until about 843.

814: Charlemagne died.

843: The Treaty of Verdun split the Frankish kingdom among Charlemagne's three grandsons.

844: A Eucharistic controversy involving the writings of St. Paschasius Radbertus, Ratramnus and Rabanus Maurus occasioned the development of terminology regarding the doctrine of the Real Presence.

846: Muslims invaded Italy and attacked Rome.

847-52: Period of composition of the False Decretals, a collection of forged documents attributed to popes from St. Clement (88-97) to Gregory II (714-731). The Decretals, which strongly supported the autonomy and rights of bishops, were suspect for a long time before being repudiated entirely about 1628.

848: The Council of Mainz condemned Gottschalk for heretical teaching regarding predestination. He was also condemned by the Council of Quierzy in 853.

857: Photius displaced Ignatius as patriarch of Constantinople. This marked the beginning of the Photian Schism, a confused state of East-West relations which has not yet been cleared up by historical research. Photius, a man of exceptional ability, died in 891.

865: St. Ansgar, apostle of Scandinavia, died.

869: St. Cyril died and his brother, St. Methodius (d. 885), was ordained a bishop. The Apostles of the Slavs devised an alphabet and translated the Gospels and liturgy into the Slavonic language.

869-70: Ecumenical Council of Constantinople (IV). It issued a second condemnation of Iconoclasm, condemned and deposed Photius as patriarch of Constantinople and restored Ignatius to the patriarchate. This was the last ecumenical council held in the East. It was first called ecumenical by canonists toward the end of the 11th century.

871-c. 900: Reign of Alfred the Great, the only English king ever anointed by a pope at Rome.

TENTH CENTURY

910: William, duke of Aquitaine, founded the Benedictine Abbey of Cluny, which became a center of monastic and ecclesiastical reform, especially in France.

915: Pope John X played a leading role in the expulsion of Saracens from central and southern Italy.

955: St. Olga, of the Russian royal family, was baptized.

962: Otto I, the Great, crowned by Pope John XII, revived Charlemagne's kingdom, which became the Holy Roman Empire.

966: Mieszko, first of a royal line in Poland, was baptized; he brought Latin Christianity to Poland.

988: Conversion and baptism of St. Vladimir and the people of Kiev which subsequently became part of Russia.

993: John XV was the first pope to decree the official canonization of a saint — Bishop Ulrich (Uldaric) of Augsburg — for the universal Church.

997: St. Stephen became ruler of Hungary. He assisted in organizing the hierarchy and establishing Latin Christianity in that country.

999-1003: Pontificate of Sylvester II (Gerbert of Aquitaine), a Benedictine monk and the first French pope.

ELEVENTH CENTURY

1009: Beginning of lasting East-West Schism in the Church, marked by dropping of the name of Pope Sergius IV from the Byzantine diptychs (the listing of persons prayed for during the liturgy). The deletion was made by Patriarch Sergius II of Constantinople.

1012: St. Romuald founded the Camaldolese Hermits.

1025: The Council of Arras, and other councils later, condemned the Cathari (Neo-Manichaeans, Albigenses).

1027: The Council of Elne proclaimed the Truce of God as a means of stemming violence; it involved armistice periods of varying length, which were later extended.

1038: St. John Gualbert founded the Vallombrosians.

1043-59: Constantinople patriarchate of Michael Cerularius, the key figure in a controversy concerning the primacy of the papacy. His and the Byzantine synod's refusal to acknowledge this primacy in 1054 widened and hardened the East-West Schism in the Church.

1047: Pope Clement II died; he was the only pope ever buried in Germany.

1049-54: Pontificate of St. Leo IX, who inaugurated a movement of papal, diocesan, monastic and clerical reform.

1054: Start of the Great Schism between the Eastern and Western Churches; it marked the separation of Orthodox Churches from unity with the pope.

1055: Condemnation of the Eucharistic doctrine of Berengarius.

1059: A Lateran council issued new legislation regarding papal elections; voting power was entrusted to the Roman cardinals.

1066: Death of St. Edward the Confessor, king of England from 1042 and restorer of Westminster Abbey.

Defeat, at Hastings, of Harold by William, Duke of Normandy (later William I), who subsequently exerted strong influence on the life-style of the Church in England.

1073-85: Pontificate of St. Gregory VII (Hildebrand). A strong pope, he carried forward programs of clerical and general ecclesiastical reform and struggled against German King Henry IV and other rulers to end the evils of lay investiture. He introduced the Latin liturgy in Spain and set definite dates for the observance of ember days.

1077: Henry IV, excommunicated and suspended from the exercise of imperial powers by Gregory VII, sought absolution from the pope at Canossa. Henry later repudiated this action and in 1084 forced Gregory to leave Rome.

1079: The Council of Rome condemned Eucharistic errors (denial of the Real Presence of Christ under the appearances of bread and wine) of Berengarius, who retracted.

1084: St. Bruno founded the Carthusians.

1097-99: The first of several Crusades undertaken between this time and 1265. Recovery of the Holy Places and gaining free access to them for Christians were the original purposes, but these were diverted to less worthy objectives in various ways. Results included: a Latin Kingdom of Jerusalem, 1099-1187; a military and political misadventure in the form of a Latin Empire of Constantinople, 1204-1261; acquisition, by treaties, of visiting rights for Christians in the Holy Land. East-West economic and cultural relationships increased during the period. In the religious sphere, actions of the Crusaders had the effect of increasing the alienation of the East from the West.

1098: St. Robert founded the Cistercians.

TWELFTH CENTURY

1108: Beginnings of the influential Abbey and School of St. Victor in France.

1115: St. Bernard established the Abbey of Clairvaux and inaugurated the Cistercian Reform.

1118: Christian forces captured Saragossa, Spain; the beginning of the Muslim decline in that country.

1121: St. Norbert established the original monastery of the Praemonstratensians near Laon, France.

1122: The Concordat of Worms (*Pactum Callixtinum*) was formulated and approved by Pope Callistus II and Emperor Henry V to settle controversy concerning the investiture of prelates. The concordat provided that the emperor could invest prelates with symbols of temporal authority but had no right to invest them with spiritual authority, which came from the Church alone, and that the emperor was not to interfere in papal elections. This was the first concordat in history.

1123: Ecumenical Council of the Lateran (I), the first of its kind in the West. It endorsed provisions of the Concordat of Worms concerning the investiture of prelates and approved reform measures in 25 canons.

1139: Ecumenical Council of the Lateran (II). It adopted measures against a schism organized by antipope Anacletus and approved 30 canons related to discipline and other matters; one of the canons stated that holy orders is an invalidating impediment to marriage.

1140: St. Bernard met Abelard in debate at the Council of Sens. Abelard, whose rationalism in theology was condemned for the first time in 1121, died in 1142 at Cluny.

1148: The Synod of Rheims enacted strict disciplinary decrees for communities of women Religious.

1152: The Synod of Kells reorganized the Church in Ireland.

1160: Gratian, whose *Decretum* became a basic text of canon law, died.
Peter Lombard, compiler of the Four Books of Sentences, a standard theology text for nearly 200 years, died.

1170: St. Thomas Becket, archbishop of Canterbury, who clashed with Henry II over church-state relations, was murdered in his cathedral.

1171: Pope Alexander III reserved the process of canonization of saints to the Holy See.

1179: Ecumenical Council of the Lateran (III). It enacted measures against Waldensianism and Albigensianism (see year 242 regarding Manichaeism), approved reform decrees in 27 canons, provided that popes be elected by a two-thirds vote of the cardinals.

1184: Waldenses and other heretics were excommunicated by Pope Lucius III.

THIRTEENTH CENTURY

1198-1216: Pontificate of Innocent III, during which the papacy reached its medieval peak of authority, influence and prestige in the Church and in relations with civil rulers.

1208: Innocent III called for a crusade, the first in Christendom itself, against the Albigensians; their beliefs and practices threatened the fabric of society in southern France and northern Italy.

1209: Verbal approval was given by Innocent III to a rule of life for the Order of Friars Minor, started by St. Francis of Assisi.

1212: The Second Order of Franciscans, the Poor Clares, was founded.

1215: Ecumenical Council of the Lateran (IV). It ordered annual reception of the sacraments of penance and the Eucharist; defined and made the first official use of the term transubstantiation to explain the change of bread and wine into the body and blood of Christ; adopted additional measures to counteract teachings and practices of the Albigensians and Cathari; approved 70 canons.

1216: Formal papal approval was given to a rule of life for the Order of Preachers, started by St. Dominic.
The Portiuncula Indulgence was granted by the Holy See at the request of St. Francis of Assisi.

1221: Rule of the Third Order Secular of St. Francis (Secular Franciscan Order) approved verbally by Honorius III.

1226: Death of St. Francis of Assisi.

1231: Pope Gregory IX authorized establishment of the Papal Inquisition for dealing with heretics. It was a creature of its time, when crimes against faith and heretical doctrines of extremists like the Cathari and Albigenses threatened the good of the Christian community, the welfare of the state and the very fabric of society. The institution, which was responsible for excesses in punishment, was most active in the second half of the century in southern France, Italy and Germany.

1245: Ecumenical Council of Lyons (I). It confirmed the deposition of Emperor Frederick II and approved 22 canons.

1247: Preliminary approval was given by the Holy See to a Carmelite rule of life.

1270: St. Louis IX, king of France, died.
Beginning of papal decline.

1274: Ecumenical Council of Lyons (II). It accomplished a temporary reunion of separated Eastern Churches with the Roman Church; issued regulations concerning conclaves for papal elections; approved 31 canons.
Death of St. Thomas Aquinas, Doctor of the Church, of lasting influence.

1280: Pope Nicholas III, who made the Breviary the official prayer book for clergy of the Roman Church, died.

1281: The excommunication of Michael Palaeologus by Pope Martin IV ruptured the union effected with the Eastern Church in 1274.

FOURTEENTH CENTURY

1302: Pope Boniface VIII issued the bull *Unam Sanctam*, concerning the unity of the Church and the temporal power of princes, against the background of a struggle with Philip IV of France; it was the most famous medieval document on the subject.

1309-77: For a period of approximately 70 years, seven popes resided at Avignon because of unsettled conditions in Rome and other reasons; see separate entry.

1311-12: Ecumenical Council of Vienne. It suppressed the Knights Templar and enacted a number of reform decrees.

1321: Dante Alighieri died a year after completing the *Divine Comedy*.

1324: Marsilius of Padua completed *Defensor Pacis*, a work condemned by Pope John XXII as heretical because of its denial of papal primacy and the hierarchical structure of the Church, and for other reasons. It was a charter for conciliarism (an ecumenical council is superior to the pope in authority).

1337-1453: Period of the Hundred Years' War, a dynastic struggle between France and England.

1338: Four years after the death of Pope John XXII, who had opposed Louis IV of Bavaria in a years-long controversy, electoral princes declared at the Diet of Rhense that the emperor did not need papal confirmation of his title and right to rule. Charles IV later (1356) said the same thing in a *Golden Bull*, eliminating papal rights in the election of emperors.

1347-50: The Black Death swept across Europe, killing perhaps one-fourth to one-third of the total population; an estimated 40 per cent of the clergy succumbed.

1374: Petrarch, poet and humanist, died.

1377: Return of the papacy from Avignon to Rome. Beginning of the Western Schism; see separate entry.

FIFTEENTH CENTURY

1409: The Council of Pisa, without canonical authority, tried to end the Western Schism but succeeded only in complicating it by electing a third claimant to the papacy; see Western Schism.

1414-18: Ecumenical Council of Constance. It took successful action to end the Western Schism involving rival claimants to the papacy; rejected the teachings of Wycliff; condemned Hus as a heretic. One decree — passed in the earlier stages of the council but later rejected — asserted the superiority of an ecumenical council over the pope (conciliarism).

1431: St. Joan of Arc was burned at the stake.

1431-45: Ecumenical Council of Florence (also called Basle-Ferrara-Florence). It affirmed the primacy of the pope against the claims of conciliarists that an ecumenical council is superior to the pope. It also formulated and approved decrees of union with several separated Eastern Churches — Greek, Armenian, Jacobite — which failed to gain general or lasting acceptance.

1438: The Pragmatic Sanction of Bourges was enacted by Charles VII and the French Parliament to curtail papal authority over the Church in France, in the spirit of conciliarism. It found expression in Gallicanism and had effects lasting at least until the French Revolution.

1453: The fall of Constantinople to the Turks.

c. 1456: Gutenberg issued the first edition of the Bible printed from movable type, at Mainz, Germany.

1476: Pope Sixtus IV approved observance of the feast of the Immaculate Conception on Dec. 8 throughout the Church.

1478: Pope Sixtus IV, at the urging of King Ferdinand of Spain, approved establishment of the Spanish Inquisition for dealing with Jewish and Moorish converts accused of heresy. The institution, which was peculiar to Spain and its colonies in America, acquired jurisdiction over other cases as well and fell into disrepute because of its procedures, cruelty and the manner in which it served the Spanish crown, rather than the accused and the good of the Church. Protests by the Holy See failed to curb excesses of the Inquisition, which lingered in Spanish history until early in the 19th century.

1492: Columbus discovered the Americas.

1493: Pope Alexander VI issued a Bull of Demarcation which determined spheres of influence for the Spanish and Portuguese in the Americas.
The Renaissance, a humanistic movement which originated in Italy in the 14th century, spread to France, Germany, the Low Countries and England. A transitional period between the medieval world and the modern secular world, it introduced profound changes which affected literature and the other arts, general culture, politics and religion.

SIXTEENTH CENTURY

1512-17: Ecumenical Council of the Lateran (V). It stated the relation and position of the pope with respect to an ecumenical council; acted to counteract the Pragmatic Sanction of Bourges and exaggerated claims of liberty by the Church in France; condemned erroneous teachings concerning the nature of the human soul; stated doctrine concerning indulgences. The council reflected concern for abuses in the Church and the need for reforms but failed to take decisive action in the years immediately preceding the Reformation.

1517: Martin Luther signaled the beginning of the Reformation by posting 95 theses at Wittenberg. Subsequently, he broke completely from doctrinal orthodoxy in discourses and three published works (1519 and 1520); was excommunicated on more than 40 charges of heresy (1521); remained the dominant figure in the Reformation in Germany until his death in 1546.

1519: Zwingli triggered the Reformation in Zurich and became its leading proponent there until his death in combat in 1531.

1524: Luther's encouragement of German princes in putting down the two-year Peasants' Revolt gained political support for his cause.

1528: The Order of Friars Minor Capuchin was approved as an autonomous division of the Franciscan Order; like the Jesuits, the Capuchins became leaders in the Counter-Reformation.

1530: The Augsburg Confession of Lutheran faith was issued; it was later supplemented by the Smalkaldic Articles, approved in 1537.

1533: Henry VIII divorced Catherine of Aragon, married Anne Boleyn, was excommunicated. In 1534 he decreed the Act of Supremacy, making the sovereign the head of the Church in England, under which Sts. John Fisher and Thomas More were executed in 1535. Despite his rejection of papal primacy and actions against monastic life in England, he generally maintained doctrinal orthodoxy until his death in 1547.

1536: John Calvin, leader of the Reformation in Switzerland until his death in 1564, issued the first edition of Institutes of the Christian Religion, which became the classical text of Reformed (non-Lutheran) theology.

1540: The constitutions of the Society of Jesus (Jesuits), founded by St. Ignatius of Loyola, were approved.

1541: Start of the 11-year career of St. Francis Xavier as a missionary to the East Indies and Japan.

1545-63: Ecumenical Council of Trent. It issued a great number of decrees concerning doctrinal matters opposed by the Reformers, and mobilized the Counter-Reformation. Definitions covered the Canon of the Bible, the rule of faith, the nature of justification, grace, faith, original sin and its effects, the seven sacraments, the sacrificial nature of the Mass, the veneration of saints, use of sacred images, belief in purgatory, the doctrine of indulgences, the jurisdiction of the pope over the whole Church. It initiated many reforms for renewal in the liturgy and general discipline in the Church, the promotion of religious instruction, the education of the clergy through the foundation of seminaries, etc. Trent ranks with Vatican II as the greatest ecumenical council held in the West.

1549: The first Anglican Book of Common Prayer was issued by Edward VI. Revised editions were published in 1552, 1559 and 1662 and later.

1553: Start of the five-year reign of Mary Tudor who tried to counteract actions of Henry VIII against the Roman Church.

1555: Enactment of the Peace of Augsburg, an arrangement of religious territorialism rather than toleration, which recognized the existence of Catholicism and Lutheranism in the German Empire and provided that citizens should adopt the religion of their respective rulers.

1558: Beginning of the reign (to 1603) of Queen Elizabeth I of England and Ireland, during which the Church of England took on its definitive form.

1559: Establishment of the hierarchy of the Church of England, with the consecration of Matthew Parker as archbishop of Canterbury.

1563: The first text of the 39 Articles of the Church of England was issued. Also enacted were a new Act of Supremacy and Oath of Succession to the English throne.

1570: Elizabeth I was excommunicated. Penal measures against Catholics subsequently became more severe.

1571: Defeat of the Turkish armada at Lepanto staved off the invasion of Eastern Europe.

1577: The Formula of Concord, the classical statement of Lutheran faith, was issued; it was, generally, a Lutheran counterpart of the canons of the Council of Trent. In 1580, along with other formulas of doctrine, it was included in the Book of Concord.

1582: The Gregorian Calendar, named for Pope Gregory XIII, was put into effect and was eventually adopted in most countries: England delayed adoption until 1752.

SEVENTEENTH CENTURY

1605: The Gunpowder Plot, an attempt by Catholic fanatics to blow up James I of England and the houses of Parliament, resulted in an anti-Catholic Oath of Allegiance.

1610: Death of Matteo Ricci, outstanding Jesuit missionary to China, pioneer in cultural relations between China and Europe.
Founding of the first community of Visitation Nuns by Sts. Francis de Sales and Jane de Chantal.

1611: Founding of the Oratorians.

1613: Catholics were banned from Scandinavia.

1625: Founding of the Congregation of the Mission (Vincentians) by St. Vincent de Paul. He founded the Sisters of Charity in 1633.

1642: Death of Galileo, scientist, who was censured by the Congregation of the Holy Office for supporting the Copernican theory of the sun-centered planetary system. The case against him was closed in his favor in 1992.
Founding of the Sulpicians by Jacques Olier.

1643: Start of publication of the Bollandist *Acta Sanctorum*, a critical work on lives of the saints.

1648: Provisions in the Peace of Westphalia, ending the Thirty Years' War, extended terms of the Peace of Augsburg (1555) to Calvinists and gave equality to Catholics and Protestants in the 300 states of the Holy Roman Empire.

1649: Oliver Cromwell invaded Ireland and began a severe persecution of the Church there.

1653: Pope Innocent X condemned five propositions of Jansenism, a complex theory which distorted doctrine concerning the relations between divine grace and human freedom. Jansenism was also a rigoristic movement which seriously disturbed the Church in France, the Low Countries and Italy in this and the 18th century.

1673: The Test Act in England barred from public office Catholics who would not deny the doctrine of transubstantiation and receive Communion in the Church of England.

1678: Many English Catholics suffered death as a consequence of the Popish Plot, a false allegation by Titus Oates that Catholics planned to assassinate Charles II, land a French army in the country, burn London, and turn over the government to the Jesuits.

1682: The four Gallican articles, drawn up by Bossuet, asserted political and ecclesiastical immunities of France from papal control. The articles, which rejected the primacy of the pope, were declared null and void by Pope Alexander VIII in 1690.

1689: The Toleration Act granted a measure of freedom of worship to other English dissenters but not to Catholics.

EIGHTEENTH CENTURY

1704: Chinese Rites — involving the Christian adaptation of elements of Confucianism, veneration of ancestors and Chinese terminology in religion — were condemned by Clement XI.

1720: The Passionists were founded by St. Paul of the Cross.

1724: Persecution in China.

1732: The Redemptorists were founded by St. Alphonsus Liguori.

1738: Freemasonry was condemned by Clement XII and Catholics were forbidden to join, under penalty of excommunication; the prohibition was repeated by Benedict XIV in 1751 and by later popes.

1760s: Josephinism, a theory and system of state control of the Church, was initiated in Austria; it remained in force until about 1850.

1764: Febronianism, an unorthodox theory and practice regarding the constitution of the Church and relations between Church and state, was condemned for the first of several times. Proposed by an auxiliary bishop of Trier using the pseudonym Justinus Febronius, it had the effects of minimizing the office of the pope and supporting national churches under state control.

1773: Clement XIV issued a brief of suppression against the Jesuits, following their expulsion from Portugal in 1759, from France in 1764 and from Spain in 1767. Political intrigue and unsubstantiated accusations were principal factors in these developments. The ban, which crippled the society, contained no condemnation of the Jesuit constitutions, particular Jesuits or Jesuit teaching. The society was restored in 1814.

1778: Catholics in England were relieved of some civil disabilities dating back to the time of Henry VIII, by an act which permitted them to acquire, own and inherit property. Additional liberties were restored by the Roman Catholic Relief Act of 1791 and subsequent enactments of Parliament.

1789: Religious freedom in the United States was guaranteed under the First Amendment to the Constitution.

Beginning of the French Revolution which resulted in: the secularization of church property and the Civil Constitution of the Clergy in 1790; the persecution of priests, religious and lay persons loyal to papal authority; invasion of the Papal States by Napoleon in 1796; renewal of persecution from 1797-1799; attempts to dechristianize France and establish a new religion; the occupation of Rome by French troops and the forced removal of Pius VI to France in 1798.

This century is called the age of Enlightenment or Reason because of the predominating rational and scientific approach of its leading philosophers, scientists and writers with respect to religion, ethics and natural law. This approach downgraded the fact and significance of revealed religion. Also characteristic of the Enlightenment were subjectivism, secularism and optimism regarding human perfectibility.

NINETEENTH CENTURY

1801: Concordat between Napoleon and Pope Pius VII is signed. It is soon violated by the Organic Articles issued by Napoleon in 1802.

1804: Napoleon crowns himself Emperor of the French with Pope Pius in attendance.

1809: Pope Pius VII was made a captive by Napoleon and deported to France where he remained in exile until 1814. During this time he refused to cooperate with Napoleon who sought to bring the Church in France under his own control, and other leading cardinals were imprisoned. The turbulence in church-state relations in France at the beginning of the century recurred in connection with the Bourbon Restoration, the July Revolution, the second and third Republics, the Second Empire and the Dreyfus case.

1814: The Society of Jesus, suppressed since 1773, was restored.

1817: Reestablishment of the Congregation for the Propagation of the Faith (Propaganda) by Pius VII was an important factor in increasing missionary activity during the century.

1820: Year's-long persecution, during which thousands died for the faith, ended in China. Thereafter, communication with the West remained cut off until about 1834. Vigorous missionary work got under way in 1842.

1822: The Pontifical Society for the Propagation of the Faith, inaugurated in France by Pauline Jaricot for the support of missionary activity, was established.

1829: The Catholic Emancipation Act relieved Catholics in England and Ireland of most of the civil disabilities to which they had been subject from the time of Henry VIII.

1832: Gregory XVI, in the encyclical *Mirari vos*, condemned indifferentism, one of the many ideologies at odds with Christian doctrine which were proposed during the century.

1833: Start of the Oxford Movement which affected the Church of England and resulted in some notable conversions, including that of John Henry Newman in 1845, to the Catholic Church.

Bl. Frederic Ozanam founded the Society of St. Vincent de Paul in France. The society's objectives are works of charity.

1848: *The Communist Manifesto*, a revolutionary document symptomatic of socio-economic crisis, was issued.

1850: The hierarchy was reestablished in England and Nicholas Wiseman made the first archbishop of Westminster. He was succeeded in 1865 by Henry Manning, an Oxford convert and proponent of the rights of labor.

1853: The Catholic hierarchy was reestablished in Holland.

1854: Pius IX proclaimed the dogma of the Immaculate Conception in the bull *Ineffabilis Deus*.

1858: The Blessed Virgin Mary appeared to St. Bernadette at Lourdes, France.

1864: Pius IX issued the encyclical *Quanta cura* and the *Syllabus of Errors* in condemnation of some 80 propositions derived from the scientific mentality and rationalism of the century. The subjects in question had deep ramifications in many areas of thought and human endeavor; in religion, they explicitly and/or implicitly rejected divine revelation and the supernatural order.

1867: The first volume of *Das Kapital* was published. Together with the Communist First International, formed in the same year, it had great influence on the subsequent development of communism and socialism.

1869: The Anglican Church was disestablished in Ireland.

1869-70: Ecumenical Council of the Vatican (I). It defined papal primacy and infallibility in a dogmatic constitution on the Church; covered natural religion, revelation, faith, and the relations between faith and reason in a dogmatic constitution on the Catholic faith.

1870-71: Victor Emmanuel II of Sardinia, crowned king of Italy after defeating Austrian and papal forces, marched into Rome in 1870 and expropriated the Papal States after a plebiscite in which Catholics, at the order of Pius IX, did not vote. In 1871, Pius IX refused to accept a Law of Guarantees. Confiscation of church property and hindrance of ecclesiastical administration by the regime followed.

1871: The German Empire, a confederation of 26 states, was formed. Government policy launched a *Kulturkampf* whose May Laws of 1873 were designed to annul papal jurisdiction in Prussia and other states and to place the Church under imperial control. Resistance to the enactments and the persecution they legalized forced the government to modify its anti-Church policy by 1887.

1878: Beginning of the pontificate of Leo XIII, who was pope until his death in 1903. Leo is best known for the encyclical *Rerum novarum*, which greatly influenced the course of Christian social thought and the labor movement. His other accomplishments included promotion of Scholastic philosophy and the impetus he gave to scriptural studies.

1881: The first International Eucharistic Congress was held in Lille, France.

Alexander II of Russia was assassinated. His policies of Russification — as well as those of his two predecessors and a successor during the century — caused great suffering to Catholics, Jews and Protestants in Poland, Lithuania, the Ukraine and Bessarabia.

1882: Charles Darwin died. His theory of evolution by natural selection, one of several scientific highlights of the century, had extensive repercussions in the faith-and-science controversy.

1887: The Catholic University of America was founded in Washington, D.C.

1893: The U.S. apostolic delegation was set up in Washington, D.C.

TWENTIETH CENTURY

1901: Restrictive measures in France forced the Jesuits, Benedictines, Carmelites and other religious orders to leave the country. Subsequently, 14,000 schools were suppressed; religious orders and congregations were expelled; the concordat was renounced in 1905; church property was confiscated in 1906. For some years the Holy See, refusing to comply with government demands for the control of bishops' appointments, left some ecclesiastical offices vacant.

1903-14: Pontificate of St. Pius X. He initiated the codification of canon law, 1904; removed the ban against participation by Catholics in Italian national elections, 1905; issued decrees calling upon the faithful to receive Holy Communion frequently and daily, and stating that children should begin receiving the Eucharist at the age of seven, 1905 and 1910, respectively; ordered the establishment of the Confraternity of Christian Doctrine in all parishes throughout the world, 1905; condemned Modernism in the decree *Lamentabili* and the encyclical *Pascendi*, 1907.

1908: The United States and England, long under the jurisdiction of the Congregation for the Propagation of the Faith as mission territories, were removed from its control and placed under the common law of the Church.

1910: Laws of separation were enacted in Portugal, marking a point of departure in church-state relations.

1911: The Catholic Foreign Mission Society of America — Maryknoll, the first U.S.-founded society of its type — was established.

1914: Start of World War I, which lasted until 1918.

1914-22: Pontificate of Benedict XV. Much of his pontificate was devoted to seeking ways and means of minimizing the material and spiritual havoc of World War I. In 1917 he offered his services as a mediator to the belligerent nations, but his pleas for settlement of the conflict went unheeded.

1917: The Blessed Virgin Mary appeared to three children at Fatima, Portugal.

A new constitution, embodying repressive laws against the Church, was enacted in Mexico. Its implementation resulted in persecution in the 1920s and 1930s.

Bolsheviks seized power in Russia and set up a communist dictatorship. The event marked the rise of communism in Russian and world affairs. One of its immediate, and lasting, results was persecution of the Church, Jews and other segments of the population.

1918: The Code of Canon Law, in preparation for more than 10 years, went into effect in the Western Church.

1919: Benedict XV stimulated missionary work through the decree *Maximum Illud*, in which he urged the recruiting and training of native clergy in places where the Church was not firmly established.

1920-22: Ireland was partitioned by two enactments of the British government which (1) made the six counties of Northern Ireland part of the United Kingdom in 1920 and (2) gave dominion status to the Irish Free State in 1922. The Irish Free State became an independent republic in 1949.

1922-39: Pontificate of Pius XI. He subscribed to the Lateran Treaty, 1929, which settled the Roman Question created by the confiscation of the Papal States in 1871; issued the encyclical *Casti connubii*, 1930, an authoritative statement on Christian marriage; resisted the efforts of Benito Mussolini to control Catholic Action and the

Church, in the encyclical *Non abbiamo bisogno*, 1931; opposed various fascist policies; issued the encyclicals *Quadragesimo anno*, 1931, developing the social doctrine of Leo XIII's *Rerum novarum*, and *Divini Redemptoris*, 1937, calling for social justice and condemning atheistic communism; condemned anti-Semitism, 1937.

1926: The Catholic Relief Act repealed virtually all legal disabilities of Catholics in England.

1931: Leftists proclaimed Spain a republic and proceeded to disestablish the Church, confiscate church property, deny salaries to the clergy, expel the Jesuits and ban teaching of the Catholic faith. These actions were preludes to the civil war of 1936-1939.

1933: Emergence of Adolf Hitler to power in Germany. By 1935 two of his aims were clear, the elimination of the Jews and control of a single national church. Six million Jews were killed in the Holocaust. The Church was subject to repressive measures, which Pius XI protested futilely in the encyclical *Mit brennender sorge* in 1937.

1936-39: Civil war in Spain between the leftist Loyalist and the forces of rightist leader Francisco Franco The Loyalists were defeated and one-man, one-party rule was established. Many priests, religious and lay persons fell victim to Loyalist persecution and atrocities.

1939-45: World War II.

1939-58: Pontificate of Pius XII. He condemned communism, proclaimed the dogma of the Assumption of Mary in 1950, in various documents and other enactments provided ideological background for many of the accomplishments of the Second Vatican Council. (See Twentieth Century Popes.)

1940: Start of a decade of communist conquest in more than 13 countries, resulting in conditions of persecution for a minimum of 60 million Catholics as well as members of other faiths. Persecution diminished in Mexico because of non-enforcement of anti-religious laws still on record.

1950: Pius XII proclaimed the dogma of the Assumption of the Blessed Virgin Mary.

1957: The communist regime of China established the Patriotic Association of Chinese Catholics in opposition to the Church in union with the pope.

1958-63: Pontificate of Bl. John XXIII. His principal accomplishment was the convocation of the Second Vatican Council, the twenty-first ecumenical council in the history of the Church. (See Twentieth Century Popes.)

1962-65: Ecumenical Council of the Vatican (II). It formulated and promulgated 16 documents — two dogmatic and two pastoral constitutions, nine decrees and three declarations — reflecting pastoral orientation toward renewal and reform in the Church, and making explicit dimensions of doctrine and Christian life requiring emphasis for the full development of the Church and the better accomplishment of its mission in the contemporary world.

1963-78: Pontificate of Paul VI. His main purpose and effort was to give direction and provide guidance for the authentic trends of church renewal set in motion by the Second Vatican Council. (See Twentieth Century Popes.)

1978: The thirty-four-day pontificate of John Paul I. Start of the pontificate of John Paul II; see Index.

1983: The revised Code of Canon Law, embodying reforms enacted by the Second Vatican Council, went into effect in the Church of Roman Rite.

1985: Formal ratification of a Vatican-Italy concordat replacing the Lateran Treaty of 1929.

1989-91: Decline and fall of communist influence and control in Middle and Eastern Europe and the Soviet Union.

1991: The Code of Canon Law for Eastern Churches went into effect.

1992: Approval of the new *Catechism of the Catholic Church*.
  The Vatican officially closed the case against Galileo Galilei.

1994: Initiation of celebration preparations of the start of the third Christian millennium in the year 2000.

1997: Pope John Paul II issued an apology for any anti-Semitism by Catholics; a conference on anti-Semitism was also held in Rome and a number of Catholic leaders in Europe issued apologies for historical anti-Semitism.

1998: Pope John Paul II visited Cuba and secured the release of over 300 political prisoners.
  The Vatican issued a white paper on Anti-Semitism, entitled: *We Remember: A Reflection on the Shoah*.
  Twentieth anniversary of the pontificate of Pope John Paul II; he became the longest reigning pontiff elected in the 20th century.

TWENTY-FIRST CENTURY

2000: The Catholic Church celebrated the Holy Year 2000 and the Jubilee; commencement of the third Christian millennium.
  Pope John Paul II issued apology for the sinful actions of the Church's members in the past.
  Pope John Paul II traveled to the Holy Land in an historic visit.

2001: Pope John Paul II traveled to Greece and Syria. He also named 44 new members to the College of Cardinals in an unprecedented consistory.
  On September 11, the World Trade Center was destroyed and the Pentagon attacked by Islamic terrorists who hijacked several planes and used them as weapons of mass destruction. The attacks launched a global war on terror.

2003: Pope John Paul II appealed for a peaceful resolution to the Iraq War. A coalition headed by the U.S. removed Saddam Hussein.

ECUMENICAL COUNCILS

An ecumenical council is an assembly of the college of bishops, with and under the presidency of the pope, which has supreme authority over the Church in matters pertaining to faith, morals, worship and discipline.

The Second Vatican Council stated: "The supreme authority with which this college (of bishops) is empowered over the whole Church is exercised in a solemn way through an ecumenical council. A council is never ecumenical unless it is confirmed or at least accepted as such by the successor of Peter. It is the prerogative of the Roman Pontiff to convoke these councils, to preside over them, and to confirm them" (Dogmatic Constitution on the Church, *Lumen Gentium*, No. 22).

Pope Presides

The pope is the head of an ecumenical council; he presides over it either personally or through legates. Conciliar decrees and other actions have binding force only when confirmed and promulgated by him. If a pope dies during a council, it is suspended until reconvened by another pope. An ecumenical council is not superior to a pope; hence, there is no appeal from a pope to a council.

Collectively, the bishops with the pope represent the whole Church. They do this not as democratic representatives of the faithful in a kind of church parliament, but as the successors of the Apostles with divinely given authority, care and responsibility over the whole Church.

All and only bishops are council participants with deliberative vote. The supreme authority of the Church can invite others and determine the manner of their participation.

Basic legislation concerning ecumenical councils is contained in Canons 337-41 of the Code of Canon Law. Basic doctrinal considerations were stated by the Second Vatican Council in the Dogmatic Constitution on the Church.

Background

Ecumenical councils had their prototype in the Council of Jerusalem in 51, at which the Apostles under the leadership of St. Peter decided that converts to the Christian faith were not obliged to observe all the prescriptions of Old Testament law (Acts 15). As early as the second century, bishops got together in regional meetings, synods or councils to take common action for the doctrinal and pastoral good of their communities of faithful. The expansion of such limited assemblies to ecumenical councils was a logical and historical evolution, given the nature and needs of the Church.

Emperors Involved

Emperors were active in summoning or convoking the first eight councils, especially the first five and the eighth. Among reasons for intervention of this kind were the facts that the emperors regarded themselves as guardians of the faith; that the settlement of religious controversies, which had repercussions in political and social turmoil, served the cause of peace in the state; and that the emperors had at their disposal ways and means of facilitating gatherings of bishops. Imperial actions, however, did not account for the formally ecumenical nature of the councils.

Some councils were attended by relatively few bishops, and the ecumenical character of several was open to question for a time. However, confirmation and de facto recognition of their actions by popes and subsequent councils established them as ecumenical.

Role in History

The councils have played a highly significant role in the history of the Church by witnessing to and defining truths of revelation, by shaping forms of worship and discipline, and by promoting measures for the ever-necessary reform and renewal of Catholic life. In general, they have represented attempts of the Church to mobilize itself in times of crisis for self-preservation, self-purification and growth.

The first eight ecumenical councils were held in the East; the other 13, in the West. The majority of separated Eastern Churches — e.g., the Orthodox — recognize the ecumenical character of the first seven councils, which formulated a great deal of basic doctrine. Other separated Eastern Churches acknowledge only the first two or first three ecumenical councils.

The 21 Councils

The 21 ecumenical councils in the history of the Church are listed below, with indication of their names or titles (taken from the names of the places where they were held); the dates; the reigning and/or approving popes; the emperors who were instrumental in convoking the eight councils in the East; the number of bishops who attended, when available; the number of sessions. Significant actions of the first 20 councils are indicated under appropriate dates in Dates and Events in Church History.

Nicaea I, 325: St. Sylvester I (Emperor Constantine I); attended by approximately 300 bishops; sessions held between May 20 or June 19 to near the end of August.

Constantinople I, 381: St. Damasus I (Emperor Theodosius I); attended by approximately 150 bishops; sessions held from May to July.

Ephesus, 431: St. Celestine I (Emperor Theodosius II); attended by 150 to 200 bishops; five sessions held between June 22 and July 17.

Chalcedon, 451: St. Leo I (Emperor Marcian); attended by approximately 600 bishops; 17 sessions held between Oct. 8 and Nov. 1.

Constantinople II, 553: Vigilius (Emperor Justinian I); attended by 165 bishops; eight sessions held between May 5 and June 2.

Constantinople III, 680-681: St. Agatho, St. Leo II (Emperor Constantine IV); attended by approximately 170 bishops; 16 sessions held between Nov. 7, 680, and Sept. 6, 681.

Nicaea II, 787: Adrian I (Empress Irene); attended by approximately 300 bishops: eight sessions held between Sept. 24 and Oct. 23.

Constantinople IV, 869-870: Adrian II (Emperor Basil I); attended by 102 bishops; six sessions held between Oct. 5, 869, and Feb. 28, 870.

Lateran I, 1123: Callistus II; attended by approximately 300 bishops; sessions held between Mar. 8 and Apr. 6.

Lateran II, 1139: Innocent II; attended by 900 to 1,000 bishops and abbots; three sessions held in April.

Lateran III, 1179: Alexander III; attended by at least 300 bishops; three sessions held between Mar. 5 and 19.

Lateran IV, 1215: Innocent III; sessions held between Nov. 11 and 30.

Lyons I, 1245: Innocent IV; attended by approximately 150 bishops; three sessions held between June 28 and July 17.

Lyons II, 1274: Gregory X; attended by approximately 500 bishops; six sessions held between May 7 and July 17.

Vienne, 1311-1312: Clement V; attended by 132 bishops; three sessions held between Oct. 16, 1311, and May 6, 1312.

Constance, 1414-1418: Gregory XII, Martin V; attended by nearly 200 bishops, plus other prelates and many experts; 45 sessions held between Nov. 5, 1414, and Apr. 22, 1418.

Florence (also called Basel-Ferrara-Florence), 1431-c. 1445: Eugene IV; attended by many Latin-Rite and Eastern-Rite bishops; preliminary sessions were held at Basel and Ferrara before definitive work was accomplished at Florence.

Lateran V, 1512-1517: Julius II, Leo X; 12 sessions held between May 3, 1512, and Mar. 6, 1517.

Trent, 1545-1563: Paul III, Julius III, Pius IV; 25 sessions held between Dec. 13, 1545, and Dec. 4, 1563.

Vatican I, 1869-1870: Pius IX; attended by approximately 800 bishops and other prelates; four public sessions and 89 general meetings held between Dec. 8, 1869, and Sept. 1, 1870.

VATICAN II

The Second Vatican Council, which was forecast by Pope John XXIII Jan. 25, 1959, was held in four sessions in St. Peter's Basilica.

Pope John convoked it and opened the first session, which ran from Oct. 11 to Dec. 8, 1962. Following John's death June 3, 1963, Pope Paul VI reconvened the council for the other three sessions which ran from Sept. 29 to Dec. 4, 1963; Sept. 14 to Nov. 21, 1964; Sept. 14 to Dec. 8, 1965.

A total of 2,860 Fathers participated in council proceedings, and attendance at meetings varied between 2,000 and 2,500. For various reasons, including the denial of exit from Communist-dominated countries, 274 Fathers could not attend.

The council formulated and promulgated 16 documents — two dogmatic and two pastoral constitutions, nine decrees and three declarations — all of which reflect its basic pastoral orientation toward renewal

and reform in the Church. Given below are the Latin and English titles of the documents and their dates of promulgation.

Lumen Gentium (Dogmatic Constitution on the Church), Nov. 21, 1964.

Dei Verbum (Dogmatic Constitution on Divine Revelation), Nov. 18, 1965.

Sacrosanctum Concilium (Constitution on the Sacred Liturgy), Dec. 4, 1963.

Gaudium et Spes (Pastoral Constitution on the Church in the Modern World), Dec. 7, 1965.

Christus Dominus (Decree on the Bishops' Pastoral Office in the Church), Oct. 28, 1965.

Ad Gentes (Decree on the Church's Missionary Activity), Dec. 7, 1965.

Unitatis Redintegratio (Decree on Ecumenism), Nov. 21, 1964.

Orientalium Ecclesiarum (Decree on Eastern Catholic Churches), Nov. 21, 1964.

Presbyterorum Ordinis (Decree on the Ministry and Life of Priests), Dec. 7, 1965.

Optatam Totius (Decree on Priestly Formation), Oct. 28, 1965.

Perfectae Caritatis (Decree on the Appropriate Renewal of the Religious Life), Oct. 28, 1965.

Apostolicam Actuositatem (Decree on the Apostolate of the Laity), Nov. 18, 1965.

Inter Mirifica (Decree on the Instruments of Social Communication), Dec. 4, 1963.

Dignitatis Humanae (Declaration on Religious Freedom), Dec. 7, 1965.

Nostra Aetate (Declaration on the Relationship of the Church to Non-Christian Religions), Oct. 28, 1965.

Gravissimum Educationis (Declaration on Christian Education), Oct. 28, 1965.

The key documents were the four constitutions, which set the ideological basis for all the others. To date, the documents with the most visible effects are those on the liturgy, the Church, the Church in the world, ecumenism, the renewal of religious life, the life and ministry of priests, the lay apostolate.

The main business of the council was to explore and make explicit dimensions of doctrine and Christian life requiring emphasis for the full development of the Church and the better accomplishment of its mission in the contemporary world.

Enactments of the Second Vatican Council have been points of departure for a wide variety of developments in the internal life of the Church and its mission in the world at large. Much effort has been made in the pontificate of Pope John Paul II to provide the interpretation and implementation of the conciliar documents with a more uniform and universal structure.

The Papacy and the Holy See

POPE JOHN PAUL II

(*Update courtesy of Russell Shaw. See many related entries under **John Paul II** in the **Index**.*)

Cardinal Karol Wojtyla of Cracow was elected Bishop of Rome and 263rd successor of St. Peter as Supreme Pastor of the Universal Church on Oct. 16, 1978. He chose the name John Paul II in honor of his predecessor, Pope John Paul I, as well as Popes John XXIII and Paul VI. He was invested with the pallium, symbol of his office, on Oct. 22 in ceremonies attended by more than 250,000 people in St. Peter's Square.

From the start, Pope John Paul II has labored to keep the Church faithful to its tradition and to the teaching and spirit of Vatican Council II, while positioning it to meet the challenges of the Third Millennium. He is a staunch defender of the sanctity of human life — "from conception to natural death," he often says — and of marriage and the family. Opposition to totalitarianism and support for human rights make this activist, long-reigning pope a major figure on the world political scene.

He is the first non-Italian pope since Adrian VI (1522-23) and the first Polish pope ever. At his election, he was the youngest pope since Pius IX (1846-78). On May 24, 1998, he became the longest-reigning pope elected in the 20th century, surpassing the 19 years, seven months and seven days of Pius XII (1939-58). (Leo XIII, who died in 1903, was pope for 25 years.) John Paul II's pontificate is also the fourth longest in the history of the Church. Only three Roman pontiffs have now reigned longer: Leo XIII (25 years, 5 months), Bl. Pius IX (31 years, 7 months, 21 days) and St. Peter (precise dates unknown).

He is the most-traveled pope in history. Through Sept. 2003, he had covered over 750,000 miles during 101 pastoral visits outside Italy, over 140 within Italy, and over 300 to the parishes of Rome. In all, he has visited 133 countries and has held talks with 850 heads of state or government. Certainly he is the pope most prolific in literary output, having issued by his 83rd birthday (May 2003) 14 encyclicals, 14 apostolic exhortations, 11 apostolic constitutions, 42 apostolic letters and 28 *motu proprio*.

By July 2003 John Paul II had proclaimed 1,316 Blesseds in 140 ceremonies and had proclaimed 469 Saints in 48 liturgical celebrations; his 17 predecessors from Pope Clement VIII to Pope Paul VI canonized a total of 296 people. He has held eight consistories for the creation of cardinals and has named a total of 201 cardinals. The last consistory

was February 2001. As of May 2003, the Holy Father has presided at 16 synods: the Particular Synod of Bishops of the Netherlands in 1980; five ordinary synods (1980, 1983, 1987, 1990, 1994); one extraordinary (1985) and eight special (1980, 1991, 1994, 1995, 1997, two in 1998, and the second synod for Europe in October 1999); the most recent synod was held in October 2001.

Over the years the pope has held 1,083 weekly general audiences and has welcomed nearly 17 million faithful from every part of the world. Other audiences, including various groups and heads of state and government, total over 1,500.

He is also the first pope ever to visit a synagogue (Rome, April 1986); the first to visit a mosque (Omayyad Great Mosque of Damascus, May 2001); the first to call for a Day of Pardon (Jubilee Year 2000); and the first to add five new mysteries to the Rosary (October 2002).

Early Life

Karol Josef Wojtyla was born May 18, 1920, in Wadowice, an industrial town near Cracow. His parents were Karol Wojtyla, who had been an adminstrative officer in the Austrian army and was a lieutenant in the Polish army until his retirement in 1927, and Emilia Kaczorowska Wojtyla. His mother died in 1929 of kidney and heart failure. His sister died a few days after birth; his older brother Edmund, a physician, died in 1932, and his father in 1941.

He attended schools in Wadowice and in 1938 enrolled in the faculty of philosophy of the Jagiellonian University in Cracow, where he moved with his father. At the university he was active in the Studio 38 experimental theater group.

For young Wojtyla, as for countless others, life changed forever on Sept. 1, 1939, when World War II began. Nazi occupation forces closed the Jagiellonian University and the young man had to work in a quarry as a stone cutter and later in a chemical plant to avoid deportation to Germany. In Feb. 1940, he met Jan Tryanowski, a tailor who became his spiritual mentor and introduced him to the writings of St. John of the Cross and St. Teresa of Ávila. He also participated in underground theater groups, including the Rhapsodic Theater of Mieczyslaw Kotlarczyk.

In Oct. 1942, he began studies for the priesthood in the underground seminary maintained by Cardinal Adam Sapieha of Cracow. He was struck by an automobile Feb. 29, 1944, and hospitalized until Mar. 12.

In Aug. of that year Cardinal Sapieha transferred him and the other seminarians to the Archbishop's Residence, where they lived and studied until war's end. Ordained a priest by the Cardinal on Nov. 1, 1946, he left Poland Nov. 15 to begin advanced studies in Rome at the Angelicum University (the Pontifical University of St. Thomas Aquinas).

He subsequently earned doctorates in theology and philosophy and was a respected moral theologian and ethicist.

Bishop and Cardinal

On July 4, 1958, Pope Pius XII named him Auxiliary Bishop to Archbishop Eugeniusz Baziak, Apostolic Administrator of Cracow. His book *Love and Responsibility* was published in 1960. (Earlier, he had published poetry and several plays.) Following Archbishop Baziak's death in 1962, he became Vicar Capitular and then on Jan. 13, 1964, Archbishop of Cracow—the first residential head of the See permitted by the communist authorities since Cardinal Sapieha's death in 1951.

Archbishop Wojtyla attended all four sessions of the Second Vatican Council, from 1962 to 1965, and helped draft Schema XIII, which became *Gaudium et Spes*, the Pastoral Constitution on the Church in the Modern World. He also contributed to *Dignitatis Humanae* (the "Declaration on Religious Freedom") and on the theology of the laity.

Pope Paul VI created him a cardinal in the consistory of June 28, 1967, with the titular Roman church of S. Cesario in Palatio. Although scheduled to attend the first general assembly of the Synod of Bishops in Sept. and Oct. of that year, Cardinal Wojtyla did not go, as a sign of solidarity with Cardinal Stefan Wyszynski of Warsaw, Poland's primate, whom the communist government refused a passport. In Oct. 1969, however, he participated in the first extraordinary assembly of the synod. Earlier that year, with approval of the statutes of the Polish bishops' conference, he became its vice president.

In 1971 he took part in the second general assembly of the synod and was elected to the council of the secretary general. He continued to participate in synod assemblies and to serve on the synod council up to his election as pope. May 8, 1972, saw the opening of the archdiocesan of synod of Cracow, which he had convened and would see conclude during his visit to Poland as pope in 1979. Also in 1972 he published *Foundations of Renewal: A Study on the Implementation of the Second Vatican Council*.

Pope Paul died Aug. 6, 1978. Cardinal Wojtyla participated in the conclave that chose Cardinal Albino Luciani of Venice his successor on Aug. 26. When the new Pope, who had taken the name John Paul I, died unexpectedly on Sept. 28, Cardinal Wojtyla joined 110 other cardinals in that year's second conclave. He emerged on the second day of voting, Oct. 16, as Pope John Paul II.

Pontificate

Pope John Paul set out the major themes and program of his pontificate in his first encyclical, *Redemptor Hominis (The Redeemer of Man)*, dated Mar. 4, 1979, and published Mar. 15. "The Redeemer of Man, Jesus Christ, is the center of the universe and of history," he wrote. Throughout his pontificate he emphasized preparation for the year 2000—which he proclaimed a Jubilee Year—and for the Third Millennium of the Christian era, with the aim of fostering a renewed commitment to evangelization among Catholics. He also has produced a significant body of magisterial teaching in such areas as Christian anthropology, sexual morality, and social justice, while working for peace and human rights throughout the world.

His pontificate has been uncommonly active and filled with dramatic events. Among the most dramatic are those associated with the fall of communism in Eastern Europe. Many students of that complex event credit John Paul with a central role. His visits to his Polish homeland in 1979 (June 2-10) and 1983 (June 16-23) bolstered Polish Catholicism and kindled Polish resistance to communism, while his determined support for the Solidarity labor movement gave his countrymen a vehicle for their resistance. The result was a growing nonviolent liberation movement leading to the dramatic developments of 1989—the collapse of communist regimes, the emergence of democracy in Poland and other countries, the fall of the Berlin Wall, and, in time, to the breakup of the Soviet Union and the end of the Cold War.

Dramatic in a much different way was the 1981 attempt on the Pope's life. At 5:19 p.m. on May 13, as he greeted crowds in St. Peter's Square before his Wednesday general audience, a Turkish terrorist named Mehmet Ali Agca shot John Paul at close range. Whether the assassin acted alone or at the behest of others—and which others—remain unanswered questions. Following a six-hour operation, John Paul was hospitalized for 77 days at Gemelli Hospital. He visited Ali Agca in the Rebibbia prison on Dec. 27, 1983.

Although he resumed his activities vigorously after his recuperation, the pope's health and strength have declined over the years. In July 1992, he had colon surgery for the removal of a non-cancerous tumor; in Nov. 1993, his shoulder was dislocated in a fall; he suffered a broken femur in another fall in Apr. 1994; and in Oct. 1996, he had an appendectomy. For several years, too, the effects have been apparent of what the Vatican acknowledges to be a neurological condition (many observers take the ailment to be Parkinson's disease). John Paul nevertheless maintains what is by any standards a highly demanding schedule.

Foreign Pastoral Visits

As noted, his pastoral visits have been a striking feature of his pontificate. Many have been to nations in the Third World. His 101 trips outside Italy (through Sept. 2003) are as follows:

1979 Dominican Republic and Mexico, Jan. 5-Feb. 1; Poland, June 2-10; Ireland and the United States, Sept. 29-Oct. 7; Turkey, Nov. 28-30.

1980 Africa (Zaire, Congo Republic, Kenya, Ghana, Upper Volta, Ivory Coast), May 2-12; France, May 30-June 2; Brazil (13 cities), June 30-July 12; West Germany, Nov. 15-19.

1981 Philippines, Guam, and Japan, with stopovers in Pakistan and Alaska, Feb. 16-27.

1982 Africa (Nigeria, Benin, Gabon, Equatorial Guinea), Feb. 12-19; Portugal, May 12-15; Great Britain, May 28-June 2; Argentina, June 11-12; Switzerland, June 15; San Marino, Aug. 29; Spain, Oct. 31-Nov. 9.

1983 Central America (Costa Rica, Nicaragua, Panama, El Salvador, Guatemala, Belize, Honduras) and Haiti, Mar. 2-10; Poland, June 16-23; Lourdes, France, Aug. 14-15; Austria, Sept. 10-13.

1984 South Korea, Papua New Guinea, Solomon Islands, Thailand, May 12; Switzerland, June 12-17; Canada, Sept. 9-20; Spain, Dominican Republic, and Puerto Rico, Oct. 10-12.

1985 Venezuela, Ecuador, Peru, Trinidad and Tobago, Jan. 26-Feb. 6; Belgium, The Netherlands, and Luxembourg, May 11-21; Africa (Togo, Ivory Coast, Cameroon, Central African Republic, Zaire, Kenya, and Morocco), Aug. 8-19; Liechtenstein, Sept. 8.

1986 India, Feb. 1-10; Colombia and Saint Lucia, July 1-7; France, Oct. 4-7; Oceania (Australia, New Zealand, Bangladesh, Fiji, Singapore, and Seychelles), Nov. 18-Dec. 1.

1987 Uruguay, Chile, and Argentina, Mar. 31-Apr. 12; West Germany, Apr. 30-May 4; Poland, June 8-14; the United States and Canada, Sept. 10-19.

1988 Uruguay, Bolivia, Peru, and Paraguay, May 7-18; Austria, June 23-27; Africa (Zimbabwe, Botswana, Lesotho, Swaziland, and Mozambique), Sept. 10-19; France, Oct. 8-11.

1989 Madagascar, Reunion, Zambia, and Malawi, Apr. 28-May 6; Norway, Iceland, Finland, Denmark, and Sweden, June 1-10; Spain, Aug. 19-21; South Korea, Indonesia, East Timor, and Mauritius, Oct. 6-16.

1990 Africa (Cape Verde, Guinea Bissau, Mali, and Burkna Faso), Jan. 25-Feb. 1; Czechoslovakia, Apr. 21-22; Mexico and Curaçao, May 6-13; Malta, May 25-27; Africa (Tanzania, Burundi, Rwanda, and Ivory Coast), Sept. 1-10.

1991 Portugal, May 10-13; Poland, June 1-9; Poland and Hungary, Aug. 13-20; Brazil, Oct. 12-21.

1992 Africa (Senegal, The Gambia, Guinea), Feb. 10-26; Africa (Angola, São Tome, and Principe), June 4-10; Dominican Republic, Oct. 10-14.

1993 Africa (Benin, Uganda, Sudan), Feb. 2-10; Al-

bania, Apr. 25; Spain, June 12-17; Jamaica, Mexico, Denver (United States), Aug. 9-15; Lithuania, Latvia, Estonia, Sept. 4-10.

1994 Zagreb, Croatia, Sept. 10.

1995 Philippines, Papua New Guinea, Australia, Sri Lanka, Jan. 12-21; Czech Republic and Poland, May 20-22; Belgium, June 3-4; Slovakia, June 30-July 3; Africa (Cameroon, South Africa, Kenya), Sept. 14-20; United Nations and United States, Oct. 4-8.

1996 Central America (Guatemala, Nicaragua, El Salvador), Feb. 5-11; Tunisia, Apr. 17; Slovenia, May 17-19; Germany, June 21-23; Hungary, Sept. 6-7; France, Sept. 19-22.

1997 Sarajevo, Apr. 12-13; Czech Republic, Apr. 25-27; Lebanon, May 10-11; Poland, May 31-June 10; France, Aug. 21-24; Brazil, Oct. 2-5.

1998 Cuba, Jan. 21-25; Nigeria, Mar. 21-23; Austria, June 19-21; Croatia, Oct. 3-4.

1999 Mexico, Jan. 22-25; St. Louis, United States, Jan. 26-27; Romania, May 2-5; Poland June, 5-17; Slovenia, Sept. 19; India, Nov. 6-7; Georgia, Nov. 8-9.

2000 Egypt and Mount Sinai, Feb. 24-26; Holy Land, March 20-26; Fátima, May 12-13.

2001 Greece, Syria, and Malta, May 4-9; Ukraine, June 23-27; Kazakstan and Armenia, Sept. 22-27.

2002 Azerbaijan and Bulgaria, May 22-26; Toronto, Canada, July 23-28; Guatemala City, July 29-30; Mexico City, July 31-Aug. 2; Poland, Aug. 16-19.

2003 Spain, May 3-4; Croatia, June 5-9; Bosnia-Herzegovina, June 22.

(For details on the Holy Father's recent trips, please see the **Papal Trips** section under **Special Reports**.)

Notable among the pope's pastoral visits have been journeys to celebrate World Youth Day with young people, including the 2002 celebration in Toronto.

Encyclicals and Other Writings

As noted above, Pope John Paul's first encyclical, *Redemptor Hominis* (1979), set the tone for and in general terms indicated the subject matter of many of the documents to follow. These are infused with the pope's distinctive personalism, which emphasizes the dignity and rights of the human person, most truly understood in the light of Christ, as the norm and goal of human endeavor.

His other encyclical letters to date are: *Dives in Misericordia* ("On the Mercy of God"), 1980; *Laborem Exercens* ("On Human Work"), 1981; *Slavorum Apostoli* ("The Apostles of the Slavs", honoring Sts. Cyril and Methodius), 1985; *Dominum et Vivificantem* ("Lord and Giver of Life," on the Holy Spirit), 1986; *Redemptoris Mater* ("Mother of the Redeemer"), 1987; *Sollicitudo Rei Socialis* ("On Social Concerns"), 1988; *Redemptoris Missio* ("Mission of the Redeemer") and *Centesimus Annus* ("The Hundredth Year", on the anniversary of Leo XIII's *Rerum Novarum*), both 1991; *Veritatis Splendor* ("The Splendor of Truth"), 1993; *Evangelium Vitae* ("The Gospel of Life") and *Ut Unum Sint* ("That All May Be One"), 1995; *Fides et Ratio* ("Faith and Reason"), 1998; and *Ecclesia de Eucharistia* ("Church of the Eucharist"), 2003.

Among his other publications are: *Catechesi*

Tradendae, a post-synodal apostolic exhortation on catechesis, 1979; apostolic letter proclaiming Sts. Cyril and Methodius, together with St. Benedict, patrons of Europe, 1980; post-synodal apostolic exhortation *Familiaris Consortio*, on the family, 1981; apostolic letter *Caritatis Christi*, for the Church in China, 1982; letter for the 500th anniversary of the birth of Martin Luther, 1983; apostolic letter *Salvifici Doloris* ("On the Christian Meaning of Suffering"), apostolic exhortation *Redemptionis Donum*, to men and women religious, apostolic letters *Redemptionis Anno*, on Jerusalem, and *Les Grands Mysteres*, on Lebanon, and post-synodal apostolic exhortation *Reconciliatio et Poenitentia* ("Reconciliation and Penance"), all 1984.

Also: apostolic letter *Dilecti Amici*, on the occasion of the United Nations' International Year of Youth, 1985; apostolic letter *Euntes in Mundum*, for the millennium of Christianity in Kievan Rus', and apostolic letter *Mulieris Dignitatem* ("On the Dignity and Vocation of Women"), all 1988; post-synodal apostolic exhortation *Christifideles Laici* ("The Lay Members of Christ's Faithful People") and apostolic exhortation *Redemptoris Custos* ("On St. Joseph"), 1989; post-synodal apostolic exhortation *Pastores Dabo Vobis* ("I Give You Shepherds"), 1992; "Letter to Families," for the International Year of the Family, "Letter on the International Conference on Population and Development" in Cairo, apostolic letter *Ordinatio Sacerdotalis* ("On Reserving Priestly Ordination to Men Alone"), apostolic letter *Tertio Millennio Adveniente*, on preparation for the Jubilee Year 2000, and "Letter to Children in the Year of the Family," all 1994.

Also: apostolic letter *Orientale Lumen* ("The Light of the East"), on Catholic-Orthodox relations, "Letter to Women," post-synodal apostolic exhortations *Ecclesia in Africa*, *Ecclesia in Asia*, and *Ecclesia in Europa*, and apostolic letter for the fourth centenary of the Union of Brest, all 1995; apostolic constitution *Universi Dominici Gregis* ("On the Vacancy of the Apostolic See and the Election of the Roman Pontiff"), post-synodal apostolic exhortation *Vita Consecrata* ("On the Consecrated Life and Its Mission in the Church and in the World"), and apostolic letter on the 350th anniversary of the Union of Uzhorod, all 1996; post-synodal apostolic exhortation, "A New Hope for Lebanon," 1997; *Incarnationis Mysterium*, Bull of Indiction of the Great Jubilee of the Year 2000, 1998; and the apostolic letter *Misericordia Dei* ("On Certain Aspects of the Celebration of the Sacrament of Penance"), 2002.

In his years as pope he has published several books, including *Crossing the Threshold of Hope* (1994) and *Gift and Mystery: On the Fiftieth Anniversary of My Priestly Ordination* (1996).

Issues and Activities

Doctrinal Concerns: The integrity of Catholic doctrine has been a major concern of Pope John Paul. On Nov. 25, 1981, he appointed Archbishop—later, Cardinal—Joseph Ratzinger of Munich-Freising, a prominent theologian, Prefect of the Congregation for the Doctrine of the Faith. The congregation under Cardinal Ratzinger has published important documents on bioethics, liberation theology (1984 and 1986), and the Church's inability to ordain women as

priests, the latter affirming that the teaching on this matter has been "set forth infallibly" (1995).

Catechism: One of Pope John Paul's most important initiatives was the *Catechism of the Catholic Church*. The idea for this up-to-date compendium was broached at the extraordinary assembly of the Synod of Bishops held in 1985 to evaluate the implementation of Vatican Council II. The pope approved, and the project went forward under a commission of cardinals headed by Cardinal Ratzinger. Published in 1992 by authorization of John Paul II (the original was in French, with the English translation appearing in 1994 and the authoritative Latin *editio typica* in 1997), this first catechism for the universal Church in four centuries is crucial to the hoped-for renewal of catechesis.

Canon Law: John Paul oversaw the completion of the revision of the Code of Canon Law begun in 1959 at the direction of Pope John XXIII. He promulgated the new code on Jan. 25, 1983; it went into effect on Nov. 27 of that year. In *Sacrae Disciplinae Leges*, the apostolic constitution accompanying the revised code, the pope says it has "one and the same intention" as Vatican Council II — whose convening John XXIII announced at the same time — namely, "the renewal of Christian living."

On Apr. 18, 1990, John Paul promulgated the Code of Canons for the Eastern Churches. Although particular sections of the Eastern code appeared at various times dating back to 1949, this was the first time an integrated code of law for the Eastern Churches had been issued in its entirety.

Ecumenical and Interreligious Relations: Ecumenical and interreligious relations have received much attention from Pope John Paul II. Two of his major documents, the encyclical *Ut Unum Sint* and the apostolic letter *Orientale Lumen*, both published in 1995, deal with these matters. He has met frequently with representatives of other religious bodies, has spoken frequently about the quest for unity, and has called for Catholics and others to pray and work to this end.

Among the important actions in this area have been the signings of common declarations with the Ecumenical Patriarch of Constantinople His Holiness Dimitrios (Dec. 7, 1987) and his successor Bartholomew I (June 29, 1995), with the Archbishop of Canterbury and Primate of the Anglican Communion, Dr. Robert Runcie (May 29, 1982, in Canterbury Cathedral and again Oct. 2, 1989, in Rome) and his successor Dr. George Leonard Carey (Dec. 6, 1996), with the Supreme Patriarch and Catholicos of All Armenians, His Holiness Karekin I (Dec. 14, 1996), and with His Holiness Aram I Keshishian, Catholicos of Cilicia of the Armenians (Jan. 26, 1997). On Oct. 5, 1991, for the first time since the Reformation, two Lutheran bishops joined the Pope and the Catholic bishops of Stockholm and Helsinki in an ecumenical prayer service in St. Peter's Basilica marking the sixth centenary of the canonization of St. Bridget of Sweden.

Pope John Paul II has had Jewish friends since boyhood, and he has worked hard to strengthen Catholic-Jewish ties. The Holy See formally initiated diplomatic relations with the State of Israel at the level of apostolic nunciature and embassy on June 15, 1994. In Mar. 1998, the Commission for Religious Relations with the Jews published an important document on the roots of the World War II Jewish Holocaust entitled *We Remember: A Reflection on the Shoah.* In a letter dated Mar. 12 to the commission chairman, Cardinal Edward Idris Cassidy, the Pope expressed "fervent hope" that it would "help to heal the wounds of past misunderstandings and injustices."

On Sunday, March 12, 2000, Pope John Paul II presided over a day of pardon for those sins committed by members of the Church over the centuries. The Holy Father issued a formal apology for the misdeeds of the members of the Church in the past, including a renewed apology for all anti-Semitic actions by Catholics. This apology was given even greater depth by the Holy Father's trip to the Holy Land in Mar. 2000. During his historic visit to Israel, the pope placed a written apology to the Jewish people in the Wailing Wall in Jerusalem. He made further efforts at ecumenical dialogue with the Orthodox Churches during his visits to Greece, Syria, and Ukraine in 2001 and at the Day of Prayer for Peace at Assisi in Jan. 2002.

Women's Concerns: Pope John Paul's insistence that, in fidelity to the will of Christ, the Church is unable to ordain women as priests has put him at odds with some feminists, as has his opposition to abortion and contraception. But it is clear from his writings that he is unusually sensitive to women's issues, and he is a strong defender of women's dignity and rights, about which he often has spoken. In 1995 he appointed a woman, Professor Mary Ann Glendon of the Harvard University Law School, head of the Holy See's delegation to the fourth U.N. conference on women, held in Beijing Sept. 4-15, the first time a woman had been named to such a post.

World Affairs: At least since Jan. 1979, when he accepted a request for mediation in a border conflict between Argentina and Chile, John Paul II has worked for peace in many parts of the world. He has supported efforts to achieve reconciliation between conflicting parties in troubled areas like Lebanon, the Balkans, and the Persian Gulf, where he sought to avert the Gulf War of 1991. He has advocated religious liberty and human rights during pastoral visits to many countries, including Cuba and Nigeria in 1998. Among the notable ecumenical and interreligious events of the pontificate was the World Day of Prayer for Peace on Oct. 27, 1986, which he convoked

in Assisi and attended along with representatives of numerous other churches and religious groups.

In 1984 the Holy See and the U.S. established diplomatic relations. (The pope has met with Presidents Jimmy Carter, Ronald Reagan, George Bush, Bill Clinton, and George W. Bush.) Relations with Poland were re-established in 1989. Diplomatic relations were established with the Soviet Union in 1990 and with the Russian Federation in 1992. Relations also have been established with other Eastern European countries and countries that were part of the former Soviet Union, with Mexico, and with other nations including Jordan, South Africa, and Libya. Working contacts of a "permanent and official character" were begun with the Palestine Liberation Organization in 1994, leading to the signing of a formal Basic Agreement with the PLO on Feb. 15, 2000. The pope also attempted to prevent the outbreak of hostilities in Iraq in 2003.

Administration: Under Pope John Paul II the long-term financial problems of the Holy See have been addressed and brought under control. Finances were on the agenda at the first plenary assembly of the College of Cardinals, Nov. 5-9, 1979, and subsequent meetings of that body. A council of cardinals for the study of organizational and economic problems of the Holy See was established in 1981. In 1988, the Holy See's financial report (for 1986) was published for the first time, along with the 1988 budget. In Apr. 1991, a meeting of the presidents of episcopal conferences was held to discuss ways of increasing the Peter's Pence Collection taken in support of the Pope.

A reorganization of responsibilities of Vatican offices was carried out in 1984, and in 1988 an apostolic constitution, *Pastor Bonus*, on reform of the Roman Curia was issued. A Vatican labor office was instituted in 1989. Pope John Paul established a new Pontifical Academy of Social Sciences in 1994 and Pontifical Academy for Life in 1995. On Apr. 8, 1994, he celebrated Mass in the Sistine Chapel for the unveiling of the Michelangelo frescoes, which had been painstakingly cleaned and restored. The opening presentation of the Holy See's Internet site took place on Mar. 24, 1997.

As Bishop of Rome, John Paul presided over a diocesan synod that concluded May 29, 1993. He also has visited numerous Roman parishes — close to 300 out of 328 by the time of his 82nd birthday.

POPES OF THE ROMAN CATHOLIC CHURCH

Information includes the name of the pope, in many cases his name before becoming pope, his birthplace or country of origin, the date of accession to the papacy, and the date of the end of reign that, in all but a few cases, was the date of death. Double dates indicate date of election and date of solemn beginning of ministry as Pastor of the universal Church. *Source*: Annuario Pontificio.

St. Peter (Simon Bar-Jona): Bethsaida in Galilee; d. c. 64 or 67.
St. Linus: Tuscany; 67-76.
St. Anacletus (Cletus): Rome; 76-88.
St. Clement: Rome; 88-97.
St. Evaristus: Greece; 97-105.

St. Alexander I: Rome; 105-115.
St. Sixtus I: Rome; 115-125.
St. Telesphorus: Greece; 125-136.
St. Hyginus: Greece; 136-140.
St. Pius I: Aquileia; 140-155.
St. Anicetus: Syria; 155-166.
St. Soter: Campania; 166-175.
St. Eleutherius: Nicopolis in Epirus; 175-189.
   Up to the time of St. Eleutherius, the years indicated for the beginning and end of pontificates are not absolutely certain. Also, up to the middle of the 11th century, there are some doubts about the exact days and months given in chronological tables.

St. Victor I: Africa; 189-199.

St. Zephyrinus: Rome; 199-217.

St. Callistus I: Rome; 217-222.

St. Urban I: Rome; 222-230.

St. Pontian: Rome; July 21, 230, to Sept. 28, 235.

St. Anterus: Greece; Nov. 21, 235, to Jan. 3, 236.

St. Fabian: Rome; Jan. 10, 236, to Jan. 20, 250.

St. Cornelius: Rome; Mar. 251 to June 253.

St. Lucius I: Rome; June 25, 253, to Mar. 5, 254.

St. Stephen I: Rome; May 12, 254, to Aug. 2, 257.

St. Sixtus II: Greece; Aug. 30, 257, to Aug. 6, 258.

St. Dionysius: birthplace unknown; July 22, 259, to Dec. 26, 268.

St. Felix I: Rome; Jan. 5, 269, to Dec. 30, 274.

St. Eutychian: Luni; Jan. 4, 275, to Dec. 7, 283.

St. Caius: Dalmatia; Dec. 17, 283, to Apr. 22, 296.

St. Marcellinus: Rome; June 30, 296, to Oct. 25, 304.

St. Marcellus I: Rome; May 27, 308, or June 26, 308, to Jan. 16, 309.

St. Eusebius: Greece; Apr. 18, 309, to Aug. 17, 309 or 310.

St. Melchiades (Miltiades): Africa; July 2, 311, to Jan. 11, 314.

St. Sylvester I: Rome; Jan. 31, 314, to Dec. 31, 335. (Most popes before St. Sylvester I were martyrs.)

St. Marcus: Rome; Jan. 18, 336, to Oct. 7, 336.

St. Julius I: Rome; Feb. 6, 337, to Apr. 12, 352.

Liberius: Rome; May 17, 352, to Sept. 24, 366.

St. Damasus I: Spain; Oct. 1, 366, to Dec. 11, 384.

St. Siricius: Rome; Dec. 15, or 22 or 29, 384, to Nov. 26, 399.

St. Anastasius I: Rome; Nov. 27, 399, to Dec. 19, 401.

St. Innocent I: Albano; Dec. 22, 401, to Mar. 12, 417.

St. Zosimus: Greece; Mar. 18, 417, to Dec. 26, 418.

St. Boniface I: Rome; Dec. 28 or 29, 418, to Sept. 4, 422.

St. Celestine I: Campania; Sept. 10, 422, to July 27, 432.

St. Sixtus III: Rome; July 31, 432, to Aug. 19, 440.

St. Leo I (the Great): Tuscany; Sept. 29, 440, to Nov. 10, 461.

St. Hilary: Sardinia; Nov. 19, 461, to Feb. 29, 468.

St. Simplicius: Tivoli; Mar. 3, 468, to Mar. 10, 483.

St. Felix III (II): Rome; Mar. 13, 483, to Mar. 1, 492. He should be called Felix II, and his successors of the same name should be numbered accordingly. The discrepancy in the numerical designation of popes named Felix was caused by the erroneous insertion in some lists of the name of St. Felix of Rome, a martyr.

St. Gelasius I: Africa; Mar. 1, 492, to Nov. 21, 496.

Anastasius II: Rome; Nov. 24, 496, to Nov. 19, 498.

St. Symmachus: Sardinia; Nov. 22, 498, to July 19, 514.

St. Hormisdas: Frosinone; July 20, 514, to Aug. 6, 523.

St. John I, Martyr: Tuscany; Aug. 13, 523, to May 18, 526.

St. Felix IV (III): Samnium; July 12, 526, to Sept. 22, 530.

Boniface II: Rome; Sept. 22, 530, to Oct. 17, 532.

John II: Rome; Jan. 2, 533, to May 8, 535. John II was the first pope to change his name. His given name was Mercury.

St. Agapitus I: Rome; May 13, 535, to Apr. 22, 536.

St. Silverius, Martyr: Campania; June 1 or 8, 536, to Nov. 11, 537 (d. Dec. 2, 537).

St. Silverius was violently deposed in Mar. 537, and abdicated Nov. 11, 537. His successor, Vigilius, was not recognized as pope by all the Roman clergy until his abdication.

Vigilius: Rome; Mar. 29, 537, to June 7, 555.

Pelagius I: Rome; Apr. 16, 556, to Mar. 4, 561.

John III: Rome; July 17, 561, to July 13, 574.

Benedict I: Rome; June 2, 575, to July 30, 579.

Pelagius II: Rome; Nov. 26, 579, to Feb. 7, 590.

St. Gregory I (the Great): Rome; Sept. 3, 590, to Mar. 12, 604.

Sabinian: Blera in Tuscany; Sept. 13, 604, to Feb. 22, 606.

Boniface III: Rome; Feb. 19, 607, to Nov. 12, 607.

St. Boniface IV: Abruzzi; Aug. 25, 608, to May 8, 615.

St. Deusdedit (Adeodatus I): Rome; Oct. 19, 615, to Nov. 8, 618.

Boniface V: Naples; Dec. 23, 619, to Oct. 25, 625.

Honorius I: Campania; Oct. 27, 625, to Oct. 12, 638.

Severinus: Rome; May 28, 640, to Aug. 2, 640.

John IV: Dalmatia; Dec. 24, 640, to Oct. 12, 642.

Theodore I: Greece; Nov. 24, 642, to May 14, 649.

St. Martin I, Martyr: Todi; July, 649, to Sept. 16, 655 (in exile from June 17, 653).

St. Eugene I: Rome; Aug. 10, 654, to June 2, 657. St. Eugene I was elected during the exile of St. Martin I, who is believed to have endorsed him as pope.

St. Vitalian: Segni; July 30, 657, to Jan. 27, 672.

Adeodatus II: Rome; Apr. 11, 672, to June 17, 676.

Donus: Rome; Nov. 2, 676, to Apr. 11, 678.

St. Agatho: Sicily; June 27, 678, to Jan. 10, 681.

St. Leo II: Sicily; Aug. 17, 682, to July 3, 683.

St. Benedict II: Rome; June 26, 684, to May 8, 685.

John V: Syria; July 23, 685, to Aug. 2, 686.

Conon: birthplace unknown; Oct. 21, 686, to Sept. 21, 687.

St. Sergius I: Syria; Dec. 15, 687, to Sept. 8, 701.

John VI: Greece; Oct. 30, 701, to Jan. 11, 705.

John VII: Greece; Mar. 1, 705, to Oct. 18, 707.

Sisinnius: Syria; Jan. 15, 708, to Feb. 4, 708.

Constantine: Syria; Mar. 25, 708, to Apr. 9, 715.

St. Gregory II: Rome; May 19, 715, to Feb. 11, 731.

St. Gregory III: Syria; Mar. 18, 731, to Nov. 741.

St. Zachary: Greece; Dec. 10, 741, to Mar. 22, 752.

Stephen II (III): Rome; Mar. 26, 752, to Apr. 26, 757. After the death of St. Zachary, a Roman priest named Stephen was elected but died (four days later) before his consecration as bishop of Rome, which would have marked the beginning of his pontificate. Another Stephen was elected to succeed Zachary as Stephen II. (The first pope with this name was St. Stephen I, 254-57.) The ordinal III appears in parentheses after the name of Stephen II because the name of the earlier elected but deceased priest was included in some lists. Other Stephens have double numbers.

St. Paul I: Rome; Apr. (May 29), 757, to June 28, 767.

Stephen III (IV): Sicily; Aug. 1 (7), 768, to Jan. 24, 772.

Adrian I: Rome; Feb. 1 (9), 772, to Dec. 25, 795.

St. Leo III: Rome; Dec. 26 (27), 795, to June 12, 816.

Stephen IV (V): Rome; June 22, 816, to Jan. 24, 817.

St. Paschal I: Rome; Jan. 25, 817, to Feb. 11, 824.

Eugene II: Rome; Feb. (May) 824 to Aug. 827.

Valentine: Rome; Aug. 827, to Sept. 827.

Gregory IV: Rome; 827, to Jan. 844.

Sergius II: Rome; Jan. 844 to Jan. 27, 847.

St. Leo IV: Rome; Jan. (Apr. 10) 847, to July 17, 855.

Benedict III: Rome; July (Sept. 29), 855, to Apr. 17, 858.

St. Nicholas I (the Great): Rome; Apr. 24, 858, to Nov. 13, 867.

Adrian II: Rome; Dec. 14, 867, to Dec. 14, 872.

John VIII: Rome; Dec. 14, 872, to Dec. 16, 882.

Marinus I: Gallese; Dec. 16, 882, to May 15, 884.

St. Adrian III: Rome; May 17, 884, to Sept. 885. Cult confirmed June 2, 1891.

Stephen V (VI): Rome; Sept. 885, to Sept. 14, 891.

Formosus: Bishop of Porto; Oct. 6, 891, to Apr. 4, 896.

Boniface VI: Rome; Apr. 896 to Apr. 896.

Stephen VI (VII): Rome; May 896 to Aug. 897.

Romanus: Gallese; Aug. 897 to Nov. 897.

Theodore II: Rome; Dec. 897 to Dec. 897.

John IX: Tivoli; Jan. 898 to Jan. 900.

Benedict IV: Rome; Jan. (Feb.) 900 to July 903.

Leo V: Ardea; July 903 to Sept. 903.

Sergius III: Rome; Jan. 29, 904, to Apr. 14, 911.

Anastasius III: Rome; Apr. 911 to June 913.

Landus: Sabina; July 913 to Feb. 914.

John X: Tossignano (Imola); Mar. 914 to May 928.

Leo VI: Rome; May 928 to Dec. 928.

Stephen VII (VIII): Rome; Dec. 928 to Feb. 931.

John XI: Rome; Feb. (Mar.) 931 to Dec. 935.

Leo VII: Rome; Jan. 3, 936, to July 13, 939.

Stephen VIII (IX): Rome; July 14, 939, to Oct. 942.

Marinus II: Rome; Oct. 30, 942, to May 946.

Agapitus II: Rome; May 10, 946, to Dec. 955.

John XII (Octavius): Tusculum; Dec. 16, 955, to May 14, 964 (date of his death).

Leo VIII: Rome; Dec. 4 (6), 963, to Mar. 1, 965.

Benedict V: Rome; May 22, 964, to July 4, 966.

Confusion exists concerning the legitimacy of claims to the pontificate by Leo VIII and Benedict V. John XII was deposed Dec. 4, 963, by a Roman council. If this deposition was invalid, Leo was an antipope. If the deposition of John was valid, Leo was the legitimate pope and Benedict was an antipope.

John XIII: Rome; Oct. 1, 965, to Sept. 6, 972.

Benedict VI: Rome; Jan. 19, 973 to June 974.

Benedict VII: Rome; Oct. 974 to July 10, 983.

John XIV (Peter Campenora): Pavia; Dec., 983 to Aug. 20, 984.

John XV: Rome; Aug. 985 to Mar. 996.

Gregory V (Bruno of Carinthia): Saxony; May 3, 996, to Feb. 18, 999.

Sylvester II (Gerbert): Auvergne; Apr. 2, 999, to May 12, 1003.

John XVII (Siccone): Rome; June 1003 to Dec. 1003.

John XVIII (Phasianus): Rome; Jan. 1004, to July 1009.

Sergius IV (Peter): Rome; July 31, 1009, to May 12, 1012.

The custom of changing one's name on election to the papacy is generally considered to date from the time of Sergius IV. Before his time, several popes had changed their names. After his time, it became a regular practice, with few exceptions, e.g., Adrian VI and Marcellus II.

Benedict VIII (Theophylactus): Tusculum; May 18, 1012, to Apr. 9, 1024.

John XIX (Romanus): Tusculum; Apr. (May) 1024 to 1032.

Benedict IX (Theophylactus): Tusculum; 1032 to 1044.

Sylvester III (John): Rome; Jan. 20, 1045, to Feb. 10, 1045.

Sylvester III was an antipope if the forcible removal of Benedict IX in 1044 was not legitimate.

Benedict IX (second time): Apr. 10, 1045, to May 1, 1045.

Gregory VI (John Gratian): Rome; May 5, 1045, to Dec. 20, 1046.

Clement II (Suitger, Lord of Morsleben and Hornburg): Saxony; Dec. 24 (25), 1046 to Oct. 9, 1047.

If the resignation of Benedict IX in 1045 and his removal at the Dec. 1046, synod were not legitimate, Gregory VI and Clement II were antipopes.

Benedict IX (third time): Nov. 8, 1047, to July 17, 1048 (d. c. 1055).

Damasus II (Poppo): Bavaria; July 17, 1048, to Aug. 9, 1048.

St. Leo IX (Bruno): Alsace; Feb. 12, 1049, to Apr. 19, 1054.

Victor II (Gebhard): Swabia; Apr. 16, 1055, to July 28, 1057.

Stephen IX (X) (Frederick): Lorraine; Aug. 3, 1057, to Mar. 29, 1058.

Nicholas II (Gerard): Burgundy; Jan. 24, 1059, to July 27, 1061.

Alexander II (Anselmo da Baggio): Milan; Oct. 1, 1061, to Apr. 21, 1073.

St. Gregory VII (Hildebrand): Tuscany; Apr. 22 (June 30), 1073, to May 25, 1085.

Bl. Victor III (Dauferius; Desiderius): Benevento; May 24, 1086, to Sept. 16, 1087. Cult confirmed July 23, 1887.

Bl. Urban II (Otto di Lagery): France; Mar. 12, 1088, to July 29, 1099. Cult confirmed July 14, 1881.

Paschal II (Raniero): Ravenna; Aug. 13 (14), 1099, to Jan. 21, 1118.

Gelasius II (Giovanni Caetani): Gaeta; Jan. 24 (Mar. 10), 1118, to Jan. 28, 1119.

Callistus II (Guido of Burgundy): Burgundy; Feb. 2 (9), 1119, to Dec. 13, 1124.

Honorius II (Lamberto): Fiagnano (Imola); Dec. 15 (21), 1124, to Feb. 13, 1130.

Innocent II (Gregorio Papareschi): Rome; Feb. 14 (23), 1130, to Sept. 24, 1143.

Celestine II (Guido): Citta di Castello; Sept. 26 (Oct. 3), 1143, to Mar. 8, 1144.

Lucius II (Gerardo Caccianemici): Bologna: Mar. 12, 1144, to Feb. 15, 1145.

Bl. Eugene III (Bernardo Paganelli di Montemagno): Pisa; Feb. 15 (18), 1145, to July 8, 1153. Cult confirmed Oct. 3, 1872.

Anastasius IV (Corrado): Rome; July 12, 1153, to Dec, 3, 1154.

Adrian IV (Nicholas Breakspear): England; Dec. 4 (5), 1154, to Sept. 1, 1159.

Alexander III (Rolando Bandinelli): Siena; Sept. 7 (20), 1159, to Aug. 30, 1181.

Lucius III (Ubaldo Allucingoli): Lucca; Sept. 1 (6), 1181, to Sept. 25, 1185.

Urban III (Uberto Crivelli): Milan; Nov. 25 (Dec. 1), 1185, to Oct. 20, 1187.

Gregory VIII (Alberto de Morra): Benevento; Oct. 21 (25), 1187, to Dec. 17, 1187.

Clement III (Paolo Scolari): Rome; Dec. 19 (20), 1187, to Mar. 1191.

Celestine III (Giacinto Bobone): Rome; Mar. 30 (Apr. 14), 1191, to Jan. 8, 1198.

Innocent III (Lotario dei Conti di Segni); Anagni; Jan. 8 (Feb. 22), 1198, to July 16, 1216.

Honorius III (Cencio Savelli): Rome; July 18 (24), 1216, to Mar. 18, 1227.

Gregory IX (Ugolino, Count of Segni): Anagni; Mar. 19 (21), 1227, to Aug. 22, 1241.

Celestine IV (Goffredo Castiglioni): Milan; Oct. 25 (28), 1241, to Nov. 10, 1241.

Innocent IV (Sinibaldo Fieschi): Genoa; June 25 (28), 1243, to Dec. 7, 1254.

Alexander IV (Rinaldo, House of Ienne): Ienne (Rome); Dec. 12 (20), 1254, to May 25, 1261.

Urban IV (Jacques Pantal,on): Troyes; Aug. 29 (Sept. 4), 1261, to Oct. 2, 1264.

Clement IV (Guy Foulques or Guido le Gros): France; Feb. 5 (15), 1265, to Nov. 29, 1268.

Bl. Gregory X (Teobaldo Visconti): Piacenza; Sept. 1, 1271 (Mar. 27, 1272), to Jan. 10, 1276. Cult confirmed Sept. 12, 1713.

Bl. Innocent V (Peter of Tarentaise): Savoy; Jan. 21 (Feb. 22), 1276, to June 22, 1276. Cult confirmed Mar. 13, 1898.

Adrian V (Ottobono Fieschi): Genoa: July 11, 1276, to Aug. 18, 1276.

John XXI (Petrus Juliani or Petrus Hispanus): Portugal; Sept. 8 (20), 1276, to May 20, 1277.
There is confusion in the numerical designation of popes named John. The error dates back to the time of John XV.

Nicholas III (Giovanni Gaetano Orsini): Rome; Nov. 25 (Dec. 26), 1277, to Aug. 22, 1280.

Martin IV (Simon de Brie): France; Feb. 22 (Mar. 23), 1281, to Mar. 28, 1285.
The names of Marinus 1 (882-84) and Marinus II (942-46) were construed as Martin. In view of these two pontificates and the earlier reign of St. Martin I (649-55), this pope was called Martin IV.

Honorius IV (Giacomo Savelli): Rome; Apr. 2 (May 20), 1285, to Apr. 3, 1287.

Nicholas IV (Girolamo Masci): Ascoli; Feb. 22, 1288, to Apr. 4, 1292.

St. Celestine V (Pietro del Murrone): Isernia; July 5 (Aug. 29), 1294, to Dec. 13, 1294; d. May 19, 1296. Canonized May 5, 1313.

Boniface VIII (Benedetto Caetani): Anagni; Dec. 24, 1294 (Jan. 23, 1295), to Oct. 11, 1303.

Bl. Benedict XI (Niccolo Boccasini): Treviso; Oct. 22 (27), 1303, to July 7, 1304. Cult confirmed Apr. 24, 1736.

Clement V (Bertrand de Got): France; June 5 (Nov. 14), 1305, to Apr. 20, 1314.
First of Avignon popes.

John XXII (Jacques d'Euse): Cahors; Aug. 7 (Sept. 5), 1316, to Dec. 4, 1334.

Benedict XII (Jacques Fournier): France; Dec. 20, 1334 (Jan. 8, 1335), to Apr. 25, 1342.

Clement VI (Pierre Roger): France; May 7 (19), 1342, to Dec. 6, 1352.

Innocent VI (Etienne Aubert): France; Dec. 18 (30), 1352, to Sept. 12, 1362.

Bl. Urban V (Guillaume de Grimoard): France; Sept. 28 (Nov. 6), 1362, to Dec. 19, 1370. Cult confirmed Mar. 10, 1870.

Gregory XI (Pierre Roger de Beaufort): France; Dec. 30, 1370 (Jan. 5, 1371), to Mar. 26, 1378.
Last of Avignon popes.

Urban VI (Bartolomeo Prignano): Naples; Apr. 8 (18), 1378, to Oct. 15, 1389.

Boniface IX (Pietro Tomacelli): Naples; Nov. 2 (9), 1389, to Oct. 1, 1404.

Innocent VII (Cosma Migliorati): Sulmona; Oct. 17 (Nov. 11), 1404, to Nov. 6, 1406.

Gregory XII (Angelo Correr): Venice; Nov. 30 (Dec. 19), 1406, to July 4, 1415, when he voluntarily resigned from the papacy to permit the election of his successor. He died Oct. 18, 1417. (*See* **Western Schism**.)

Martin V (Oddone Colonna): Rome; Nov. 11 (21), 1417, to Feb. 20, 1431.

Eugene IV (Gabriele Condulmer): Venice; Mar. 3 (11), 1431, to Feb. 23, 1447.

Nicholas V (Tommaso Parentucelli): Sarzana; Mar. 6 (19), 1447, to Mar. 24, 1455.

Callistus III (Alfonso Borgia): Jativa (Valencia); Apr. 8 (20), 1455, to Aug. 6, 1458.

Pius II (Enea Silvio Piccolomini): Siena; Aug. 19 (Sept. 3), 1458, to Aug. 14, 1464.

Paul II (Pietro Barbo): Venice; Aug. 30 (Sept. 16), 1464, to July 26, 1471.

Sixtus IV (Francesco della Rovere): Savona; Aug. 9 (25), 1471, to Aug. 12, 1484.

Innocent VIII (Giovanni Battista Cibo): Genoa; Aug. 29 (Sept. 12), 1484, to July 25, 1492.

Alexander VI (Rodrigo Borgia): Jativa (Valencia); Aug. 11 (26), 1492, to Aug. 18, 1503.

Pius III (Francesco Todeschini-Piccolomini): Siena; Sept. 22 (Oct. 1, 8), 1503, to Oct. 18, 1503.

Julius II (Giuliano della Rovere): Savona; Oct. 31 (Nov. 26), 1503, to Feb. 21, 1513.

Leo X (Giovanni de' Medici): Florence; Mar. 9 (19), 1513, to Dec. 1, 1521.

Adrian VI (Adrian Florensz): Utrecht; Jan. 9 (Aug. 31), 1522, to Sept. 14, 1523.

Clement VII (Giulio de' Medici): Florence; Nov. 19 (26), 1523, to Sept. 25, 1534.

Paul III (Alessandro Farnese): Rome; Oct. 13 (Nov. 3), 1534, to Nov. 10, 1549.

Julius III (Giovanni Maria Ciocchi del Monte): Rome; Feb. 7 (22), 1550, to Mar. 23, 1555.

Marcellus II (Marcello Cervini): Montepulciano; Apr. 9 (10), 1555, to May 1, 1555.

Paul IV (Gian Pietro Carafa): Naples; May 23 (26), 1555, to Aug. 18, 1559.

Pius IV (Giovan Angelo de' Medici): Milan; Dec. 25, 1559 (Jan. 6, 1560), to Dec. 9, 1565.

St. Pius V (Antonio-Michele Ghislieri): Bosco (Alexandria); Jan. 7 (17), 1566, to May 1, 1572. Canonized May 22, 1712.

Gregory XIII (Ugo Buoncompagni): Bologna; May 13 (25), 1572, to Apr. 10, 1585.

Sixtus V (Felice Peretti): Grottammare (Ripatransone); Apr. 24 (May 1), 1585, to Aug. 27, 1590.

Urban VII (Giambattista Castagna): Rome; Sept. 15, 1590, to Sept. 27, 1590.

Gregory XIV (Niccolo Sfondrati): Cremona; Dec. 5 (8), 1590, to Oct. 16, 1591.

Innocent IX (Giovanni Antonio Facchinetti): Bologna; Oct. 29 (Nov. 3), 1591, to Dec. 30, 1591.

Clement VIII (Ippolito Aldobrandini): Florence; Jan. 30 (Feb. 9), 1592, to Mar. 3, 1605.

Leo XI (Alessandro de' Medici): Florence; Apr. 1 (10), 1605, to Apr. 27, 1605.

Paul V (Camillo Borghese): Rome; May 16 (29), 1605, to Jan. 28, 1621.

Gregory XV (Alessandro Ludovisi): Bologna; Feb. 9 (14), 1621, to July 8, 1623.

Urban VIII (Maffeo Barberini): Florence; Aug. 6 (Sept. 29), 1623, to July 29, 1644.

Innocent X (Giovanni Battista Pamfili): Rome; Sept. 15 (Oct. 4), 1644, to Jan. 7, 1655.

Alexander VII (Fabio Chigi): Siena; Apr. 7 (18), 1655, to May 22, 1667.

Clement IX (Giulio Rospigliosi): Pistoia; June 20 (26), 1667, to Dec. 9, 1669.

Clement X (Emilio Altieri): Rome; Apr. 29 (May 11), 1670, to July 22, 1676.

Bl. Innocent XI (Benedetto Odescalchi): Como; Sept. 21 (Oct. 4), 1676, to Aug. 12, 1689. Beatified Oct. 7, 1956.

Alexander VIII (Pietro Ottoboni): Venice; Oct. 6 (16), 1689, to Feb. 1, 1691.

Innocent XII (Antonio Pignatelli): Spinazzola (Venosa); July 12 (15), 1691, to Sept. 27, 1700.

Clement XI (Giovanni Francesco Albani): Urbino; Nov. 23, 30 (Dec. 8), 1700, to Mar. 19, 1721.

Innocent XIII (Michelangelo dei Conti): Rome; May 8 (18), 1721, to Mar. 7, 1724.

Benedict XIII (Pietro Francesco Vincenzo Maria Orsini): Gravina (Bari); May 29 (June 4), 1724, to Feb. 21, 1730.

Clement XII (Lorenzo Corsini): Florence; July 12 (16), 1730, to Feb. 6, 1740.

Benedict XIV (Prospero Lambertini): Bologna; Aug. 17 (22), 1740, to May 3, 1758.

Clement XIII (Carlo Rezzonico): Venice; July 6 (16), 1758, to Feb. 2, 1769.

Clement XIV (Giovanni Vincenzo Antonio Lorenzo Ganganelli): Rimini; May 19, 28 (June 4), 1769, to Sept. 22, 1774.

Pius VI (Giovanni Angelo Braschi): Cesena; Feb. 15 (22), 1775, to Aug. 29, 1799.

Pius VII (Barnaba Gregorio Chiaramonti): Cesena; Mar. 14 (21), 1800, to Aug. 20, 1823.

Leo XII (Annibale della Genga): Genga (Fabriano); Sept. 28 (Oct. 5), 1823, to Feb. 10, 1829.

Pius VIII (Francesco Saverio Castiglioni): Cingoli; Mar. 31 (Apr. 5), 1829, to Nov. 30, 1830.

Gregory XVI (Bartolomeo Alberto-Mauro-Cappellari): Belluno; Feb. 2 (6), 1831, to June 1, 1846.

Bl. Pius IX (Giovanni M. Mastai-Ferretti): Senigallia; June 16 (21), 1846, to Feb. 7, 1878.

Leo XIII (Gioacchino Pecci): Carpineto (Anagni); Feb. 20 (Mar. 3), 1878, to July 20, 1903.

St. Pius X (Giuseppe Sarto): Riese (Treviso); Aug. 4 (9), 1903, to Aug. 20, 1914. Canonized May 29, 1954.

Benedict XV (Giacomo della Chiesa): Genoa; Sept. 3 (6), 1914, to Jan. 22, 1922.

Pius XI (Achille Ratti): Desio (Milan); Feb. 6 (12), 1922, to Feb. 10, 1939.

Pius XII (Eugenio Pacelli): Rome; Mar. 2 (12), 1939, to Oct. 9, 1958.

Bl. John XXIII (Angelo Giuseppe Roncalli): Sotto il Monte (Bergamo); Oct. 28 (Nov. 4), 1958, to June 3, 1963.

Paul VI (Giovanni Battista Montini): Concessio (Brescia); June 21 (30), 1963, to Aug. 6, 1978.

John Paul I (Albino Luciani): Forno di Canale (Belluno); Aug. 26 (Sept. 3), 1978, to Sept. 28, 1978.

John Paul II (Karol Wojtyla): Wadowice, Poland; Oct. 16 (22), 1978.

ANTIPOPES

This list of men who claimed or exercised the papal office in an uncanonical manner includes names, birthplaces and dates of alleged reigns. *Source:* Annuario Pontificio.

St. Hippolytus: Rome; 217-235; was reconciled before his death.

Novatian: Rome; 251.

Felix II: Rome; 355 to Nov. 22, 365.

Ursinus: 366-367.

Eulalius: Dec. 27 or 29, 418, to 419.

Lawrence: 498; 501-505.

Dioscorus: Alexandria; Sept. 22, 530, to Oct. 14, 530.

Theodore: ended alleged reign, 687.

Paschal: ended alleged reign, 687.

Constantine: Nepi; June 28 (July 5), 767, to 769.

Philip: July 31, 768; retired to his monastery on the same day.

John: ended alleged reign, Jan. 844.

Anastasius: Aug. 855 to Sept. 855; d. 880.

Christopher: Rome; July or Sept. 903 to Jan. 904.

Boniface VII: Rome; June 974 to July 974; Aug. 984 to July 985.

John XVI: Rossano; Apr. 997 to Feb. 998.

Gregory: ended alleged reign, 1012.

Benedict X: Rome; Apr. 5, 1058, to Jan. 24, 1059.

Honorius II: Verona; Oct. 28, 1061, to 1072.

Clement III: Parma; June 25, 1080 (Mar. 24, 1084), to Sept. 8, 1100.

Theodoric: ended alleged reign, 1100; d. 1102.

Albert: ended alleged reign, 1102.

Sylvester IV: Rome; Nov. 18, 1105, to 1111.

Gregory VIII: France; Mar. 8, 1118, to 1121.

Celestine II: Rome; ended alleged reign, Dec. 1124.

Anacletus II: Rome; Feb. 14 (23), 1130, to Jan. 25, 1138.

Victor IV: Mar. 1138, to May 29, 1138; submitted to Pope Innocent II.

Victor IV: Montecelio; Sept. 7 (Oct. 4), 1159, to Apr. 20, 1164; he did not recognize his predecessor (Victor IV, above).

Paschal III: Apr. 22 (26), 1164, to Sept. 20, 1168.

Callistus III: Arezzo; Sept., 1168, to Aug. 29, 1178; submitted to Pope Alexander III.

Innocent III: Sezze; Sept. 29, 1179, to 1180.

Nicholas V: Corvaro (Rieti); May 12 (22), 1328, to Aug. 25, 1330; d. Oct. 16, 1333.

Four antipopes of the Western Schism:

Clement VII: Sept. 20 (Oct. 31), 1378, to Sept. 16, 1394.

Benedict XIII: Aragon; Sept. 28 (Oct. 11), 1394, to May 23, 1423.

Alexander V: Crete; June 26 (July 7), 1409, to May 3, 1410.

John XXIII: Naples; May 17 (25), 1410, to May 29, 1415. (Date of deposition by Council of Constance which ended the Western Schism; d. Nov. 22, 1419.)

Felix V: Savoy; Nov. 5, 1439 (July 24, 1440), to Apr. 7, 1449; d. 1451.

AVIGNON PAPACY

Avignon was the residence (1309-77) of a series of French popes (Clement V, John XXII, Benedict XII, Clement VI, Innocent VI, Urban V and Gregory XI). Prominent in the period were power struggles over the mixed interests of Church and state with the rulers of France (Philip IV, John II), Bavaria (Lewis IV), England (Edward III); factionalism of French and Italian churchmen; political as well as ecclesiastical turmoil in Italy, a factor of significance in prolonging the stay of popes in Avignon. Despite some positive achievements, the Avignon papacy was a prologue to the Western Schism that began in 1378.

GREAT WESTERN SCHISM

The Great Western Schism was a confused state of affairs that divided Christendom into two and then three papal obediences from 1378 to 1417.

It occurred some 50 years after Marsilius theorized that a general (not ecumenical) council of bishops and other persons was superior to a pope and nearly 30 years before the Council of Florence stated definitively that no kind of council had such authority.

It was a period of disaster preceding the even more disastrous period of the Reformation.

Urban VI, following the return of the papal residence to Rome after approximately 70 years at Avignon, was elected pope Apr. 8, 1378, and reigned until his death in 1389. He was succeeded by Boniface IX (1389-1404), Innocent VII (1404-1406) and Gregory XII (1406-1415). These four are considered the legitimate popes of the period.

Some of the cardinals who chose Urban pope, dissatisfied with his conduct of the office, declared that his election was invalid. They proceeded to elect Clement VII, who claimed the papacy from 1378 to 1394. He was succeeded by Benedict XIII.

Prelates seeking to end the state of divided papal loyalties convoked the Council of Pisa (1409) which, without authority, found Gregory XII and Benedict XIII guilty in absentia on 30-odd charges of schism and heresy, deposed them, and elected a third claimant to the papacy, Alexander V (1409-1410). He was succeeded by John XXIII (1410-1415).

The schism was ended by the Council of Constance (1414-1418). Although originally called into session in an irregular manner, the council, acquired authority after being convoked by Gregory XII in 1415. In its early irregular phase, it deposed John XXIII whose election to the papacy was uncanonical anyway. After being formally convoked, it accepted the abdication of Gregory in 1415 and dismissed the claims of Benedict XIII two years later, thus clearing the way for the election of Martin V on Nov. 11, 1417. The Council of Constance also rejected the theories of John Wycliff and condemned John Hus as a heretic.

POPES OF THE TWENTIETH CENTURY

LEO XIII

Leo XIII (Gioacchino Vincenzo Pecci) was born May 2, 1810, in Carpineto, Italy. Although all but three years of his life and pontificate were in the 19th century, his influence extended well into the 20th century.

He was educated at the Jesuit college in Viterbo, the Roman College, the Academy of Noble Ecclesiastics, and the University of the Sapienza. He was ordained to the priesthood in 1837.

He served as an apostolic delegate to two States of the Church, Benevento from 1838 to 1841 and Perugia in 1841 and 1842. Ordained titular archbishop of Damietta, he was papal nuncio to Belgium from Jan. 1843, until May 1846; in the post, he had controversial relations with the government over education issues and acquired his first significant experience of industrialized society.

He was archbishop of Perugia from 1846 to 1878. He became a cardinal in 1853 and chamberlain of the Roman Curia in 1877. He was elected to the papacy Feb. 20, 1878. He died July 20, 1903.

Canonizations: He canonized 18 saints and beatified a group of English martyrs.

Church Administration: He established 300 new dioceses and vicariates; restored the hierarchy in Scotland and set up an English, as contrasted with the Portuguese, hierarchy in India; approved the action of the Congregation for the Propagation of the Faith in reorganizing missions in China.

Encyclicals: He issued 86 encyclicals, on subjects ranging from devotional to social. In the former category were *Annum Sacrum*, on the Sacred Heart, in 1899, and 11 letters on Mary and the Rosary.

Social Questions: Much of Leo's influence stemmed from social doctrine stated in numerous encyclicals, concerning liberalism, liberty, the divine origin of authority; socialism, in *Quod Apostolici Muneris*, 1878; the Christian concept of the family, in *Arcanum*, 1880; socialism and economic liberalism, relations between capital and labor, in *Rerum Novarum*, 1891. Two of his social encyclicals were against the African slave trade.

Interfaith Relations: He was unsuccessful in unity overtures made to Orthodox and Slavic Churches. He declared Anglican orders invalid in the apostolic bull *Apostolicae Curae* Sept. 13, 1896.

International Relations: Leo was frustrated in seeking solutions to the Roman Question arising from the seizure of church lands by the Kingdom of Italy in 1870. He also faced anticlerical situations in Belgium and France and in the *Kulturkampf* policies of Bismarck in Germany.

Scholarship: In the encyclical *Aeterni Patris* of Aug. 4, 1879, he ordered a renewal of philosophical and theological studies in seminaries along scholastic, and especially Thomistic, lines, to counteract influential trends of liberalism and Modernism. He issued guidelines for biblical exegesis in *Providentissimus Deus* Nov. 18, 1893, and established the Pontifical Biblical Commission in 1902.

In other actions affecting scholarship and study, he opened the Vatican Archives to scholars in 1883 and established the Vatican Observatory.

United States: He authorized establishment of the apostolic delegation in Washington, DC, Jan. 24, 1893. He refused to issue a condemnation of the Knights of Labor. With a document entitled *Testem Benevolentiae*, he eased resolution of questions concerning what was called an American heresy in 1899.

ST. PIUS X

St. Pius X (Giuseppe Melchiorre Sarto) was born in 1835 in Riese, Italy. Educated at the college of Castelfranco and the seminary at Padua, he was ordained to the priesthood Sept. 18, 1858. He served as a curate in Trombolo for nine years before beginning an eight-year pastorate at Salzano. He was chancellor of the Treviso diocese from Nov. 1875, and bishop of Mantua from 1884 until 1893. He was cardinal-patriarch of Venice from that year until his election to the papacy by the conclave held from July 31 to Aug. 4, 1903.

Aims: Pius's principal objectives as pope were "to restore all things in Christ, in order that Christ may be all and in all," and "to teach (and defend) Christian truth and law."

Canonizations, Encyclicals: He canonized four saints and issued 16 encyclicals. One of the encyclicals was issued in commemoration of the 50th anniversary of the proclamation of the dogma of the Immaculate Conception of Mary.

Catechetics: He introduced a whole new era of religious instruction and formation with the encyclical *Acerbo Nimis* of Apr. 15, 1905, in which he called for vigor in establishing and conducting parochial programs of the Confraternity of Christian Doctrine.

Catholic Action: He outlined the role of official Catholic Action in two encyclicals in 1905 and 1906. Favoring organized action by Catholics themselves, he had serious reservations about interconfessional collaboration.

He stoutly maintained claims to papal rights in the anticlerical climate of Italy. He authorized bishops to relax prohibitions against participation by Catholics in some Italian elections.

Church Administration: With the *motu proprio Arduum Sane* of Mar. 19, 1904, he inaugurated the work that resulted in the Code of Canon Law; the code was completed in 1917 and went into effect in the following year. He reorganized and strengthened the Roman Curia with the apostolic constitution *Sapienti Consilio* of June 29, 1908.

While promoting the expansion of missionary work, he removed from the jurisdiction of the Congregation for the Propagation of the Faith the Church in the United States, Canada, Newfoundland, England, Ireland, Holland and Luxembourg.

International Relations: He ended traditional prerogatives of Catholic governments with respect to papal elections, in 1904. He opposed anti-Church and anticlerical actions in several countries: Bolivia in 1905, because of anti-religious legislation; France in 1906, for its 1901 action in annulling its concordat with the Holy See, and for the 1905 Law of Separation by which it decreed separation of Church and state, ordered the confiscation of church property, and blocked religious education and the activities of religious orders; Portugal in 1911, for the separation of Church and state and repressive measures that resulted in persecution later.

In 1912 he called on the bishops of Brazil to work for the improvement of conditions among Indians.

Liturgy: "The Pope of the Eucharist," he strongly recommended the frequent reception of Holy Communion in a decree dated Dec. 20, 1905; in another decree, *Quam Singulari*, of Aug. 8, 1910, he called for the early reception of the sacrament by children. He initiated measures for liturgical reform with new norms for sacred music and the start of work on revision of the Breviary for recitation of the Divine Office.

Modernism: Pius was a vigorous opponent of "the synthesis of all heresies," which threatened the integrity of doctrine through its influence in philosophy, theology and biblical exegesis. In opposition, he condemned 65 of its propositions as erroneous in the decree *Lamentabili*, July 3, 1907; issued the encyclical *Pascendi* in the same vein, Sept. 8, 1907; backed both of these with censures; and published the Oath against Modernism in Sept. 1910, to be taken by all the clergy. Ecclesiastical studies suffered to some extent from these actions, necessary as they were at the time.

Pius followed the lead of Leo XIII in promoting the study of scholastic philosophy. He established the Pontifical Biblical Institute May 7, 1909.

His death, Aug. 20, 1914, was hastened by the outbreak of World War I. He was beatified in 1951 and canonized May 29, 1954. His feast is observed Aug. 21.

BENEDICT XV

Benedict XV (Giacomo della Chiesa) was born Nov. 21, 1854, in Pegli, Italy.

He was educated at the Royal University of Genoa and Gregorian University in Rome. He was ordained to the priesthood Dec. 21, 1878.

He served in the papal diplomatic corps from 1882 to 1907, as secretary to the nuncio to Spain from 1882 to 1887, as secretary to the papal secretary of state from 1887, and as undersecretary from 1901.

He was ordained archbishop of Bologna Dec. 22, 1907, and spent four years completing a pastoral visitation there. He was made a cardinal just three months before being elected to the papacy Sept. 3, 1914. He died Jan. 22, 1922. Two key efforts of his pontificate were for peace and the relief of human suffering caused by World War I.

Canonizations: Benedict canonized three saints; one of them was Joan of Arc.

Canon Law: He published the Code of Canon Law, developed by the commission set up by St. Pius X, May 27, 1917; it went into effect the following year.

Curia: He made great changes in the personnel of the Curia. He established the Congregation for the Oriental Churches May 1, 1917, and founded the Pontifical Oriental Institute in Rome later in the year.

Encyclicals: He issued 12 encyclicals. Peace was the theme of three of them. In another, published two years after the cessation of hostilities, he wrote about child victims of the war. He followed the lead of Leo XIII in *Spiritus Paraclitus*, Sept. 15, 1920, on biblical studies.

International Relations: He was largely frustrated on the international level because of the events and attitudes of the war period, but the number of diplomats accredited to the Vatican nearly doubled, from

14 to 26, between the time of his accession to the papacy and his death.

Peace Efforts: Benedict's stance in the war was one of absolute impartiality but not of uninterested neutrality. Because he would not take sides, he was suspected by both the Allies and the Central Powers, and the seven-point peace plan he offered to all belligerents, Aug. 1, 1917, was turned down. The points of the plan were: recognition of the moral force of right; disarmament; acceptance of arbitration in cases of dispute; guarantee of freedom of the seas; renunciation of war indemnities; evacuation and restoration of occupied territories; examination of territorial claims in dispute.

Relief Efforts: Benedict assumed personal charge of Vatican relief efforts during the war. He set up an international missing persons bureau for contacts between prisoners and their families, but was forced to close it because of the suspicion of warring nations that it was a front for espionage operations. He persuaded the Swiss government to admit into the country military victims of tuberculosis.

Roman Question: Benedict prepared the way for the meetings and negotiations which led to settlement of the question in 1929.

PIUS XI

Pius XI (Ambrogio Damiano Achille Ratti) was born May 31, 1857, in Desio, Italy.

Educated at seminaries in Seviso and Milan, and at the Lombard College, Gregorian University and Academy of St. Thomas in Rome. He was ordained to the priesthood in 1879.

He taught at the major seminary of Milan from 1882 to 1888. Appointed to the staff of the Ambrosian Library in 1888, he remained there until 1911, acquiring a reputation for publishing works on paleography and serving as director from 1907 to 1911. He then moved to the Vatican Library, of which he was prefect from 1914 to 1918. In 1919, he was named apostolic visitor to Poland in Apr. nuncio in June, and was made titular archbishop of Lepanto Oct. 28. He was made archbishop of Milan and cardinal June 13, 1921, before being elected to the papacy Feb. 6, 1922. He died Feb. 10, 1939.

Aims: The objective of his pontificate, as stated in the encyclical *Ubi Arcano*, Dec. 23, 1922, was to establish the reign and peace of Christ in society.

Canonizations: He canonized 34 saints, including the Jesuit Martyrs of North America, and conferred the title of Doctor of the Church on Sts. Peter Canisius, John of the Cross, Robert Bellarmine and Albertus Magnus.

Eastern Churches: He called for better understanding of the Eastern Churches in the encyclical *Rerum Orientalium* of Sept. 8, 1928 and developed facilities for the training of Eastern-Rite priests. He inaugurated steps for the codification of Eastern Church law in 1929. In 1935 he made Syrian Patriarch Tappouni a cardinal.

Encyclicals: His first encyclical, *Ubi Arcano*, in addition to stating the aims of his pontificate, blueprinted Catholic Action and called for its development throughout the Church. In *Quas Primas*, Dec. 11, 1925, he established the feast of Christ the King for universal observance. Subjects of some of his other encyclicals were: Christian education, in

Rappresentanti in Terra, Dec. 31, 1929; Christian marriage, in *Casti Connubii*, Dec. 31, 1930; social conditions and pressure for social change in line with the teaching in *Rerum Novarum*, in *Quadragesimo Anno*, May 15, 1931; atheistic Communism, in *Divini Redemptoris*, Mar. 19, 1937; the priesthood, in *Ad Catholici Sacerdotii*, Dec. 20, 1935.

Missions: Following the lead of Benedict XV, Pius called for the training of native clergy in the pattern of their own respective cultures, and promoted missionary developments in various ways. He ordained six native bishops for China in 1926, one for Japan in 1927, and others for regions of Asia, China and India in 1933. He placed the first 40 mission dioceses under native bishops, saw the number of native priests increase from about 2,600 to more than 7,000, and the number of Catholics in missionary areas more than double from nine million.

In the apostolic constitution *Deus Scientiarum Dominus* of May 24, 1931, he ordered the introduction of missiology into theology courses.

Interfaith Relations: Pius was negative to the ecumenical movement among Protestants but approved the Malines Conversations, 1921 to 1926, between Anglicans and Catholics.

International Relations: Relations with the Mussolini government deteriorated from 1931 on, as indicated in the encyclical *Non Abbiamo Bisogno*, when the regime took steps to curb liberties and activities of the Church; they turned critical in 1938 with the emergence of racist policies. Relations deteriorated in Germany also from 1933 on, resulting finally in condemnation of the Nazis in the encyclical *Mit Brennender Sorge*, March, 1937. Pius sparked a revival of the Church in France by encouraging Catholics to work within the democratic framework of the Republic rather than foment trouble over restoration of a monarchy. Pius was powerless to influence developments related to the civil war that erupted in Spain in July 1936, sporadic persecution and repression by the Calles regime in Mexico, and systematic persecution of the Church in the Soviet Union. Many of the 10 concordats and two agreements reached with European countries after World War I became casualties of World War II.

Roman Question: Pius negotiated for two and a half years with the Italian government to settle the Roman Question by means of the Lateran Agreement of 1929. The agreement provided independent status for the State of Vatican City; made Catholicism the official religion of Italy, with pastoral and educational freedom and state recognition of Catholic marriages, religious orders and societies; and provided a financial payment to the Vatican for expropriation of the former States of the Church.

PIUS XII

Pius XII (Eugenio Maria Giovanni Pacelli) was born Mar. 2, 1876, in Rome.

Educated at the Gregorian University and the Lateran University, in Rome, he was ordained to the priesthood Apr. 2, 1899.

He entered the Vatican diplomatic service in 1901, worked on the codification of canon law, and was appointed secretary of the Congregation for Ecclesiastical Affairs in 1914. Three years later he was ordained titular archbishop of Sardis and made apostolic nuncio to Bavaria. He was nuncio to Germany from 1920 to 1929, when he was made a cardinal, and took office as papal secretary of state in the following year. His diplomatic negotiations resulted in concordats between the Vatican and Bavaria (1924), Prussia (1929), Baden (1932), Austria and the German Republic (1933). He took part in negotiations that led to settlement of the Roman Question in 1929.

He was elected to the papacy Mar. 2, 1939. He died Oct. 9, 1958, at Castel Gandolfo after the 12th longest pontificate in history.

Canonizations: He canonized 34 saints, including Mother Frances X. Cabrini, the first U.S. citizen-saint.

Cardinals: He raised 56 prelates to the rank of cardinal in two consistories held in 1946 and 1953. There were 57 cardinals at the time of his death.

Church Organization and Missions: He increased the number of dioceses from 1,696 to 2,048. He established native hierarchies in China (1946), Burma (1955) and parts of Africa, and extended the native structure of the Church in India. He ordained the first black bishop for Africa.

Communism: In addition to opposing and condemning Communism on numerous occasions, he decreed in 1949 the penalty of excommunication for all Catholics holding formal and willing allegiance to the Communist Party and its policies. During his reign the Church was persecuted in some 15 countries that fell under communist domination.

Doctrine and Liturgy: He proclaimed the dogma of the Assumption of the Blessed Virgin Mary, Nov. 1, 1950 (apostolic constitution, *Munificentissimus Deus*).

In various encyclicals and other enactments, he provided background for the *aggiornamento* introduced by his successor, John XXIII: by his formulations of doctrine and practice regarding the Mystical Body of Christ, the liturgy, sacred music and biblical studies; by the revision of the Rites of Holy Week; by initiation of the work which led to the calendar-missal-breviary reform ordered into effect Jan. 1, 1961; by the first of several modifications of the Eucharistic fast; by extending the time of Mass to the evening. He instituted the feasts of Mary, Queen, and of St. Joseph the Worker, and clarified teaching concerning devotion to the Sacred Heart.

His 41 encyclicals and nearly 1,000 public addresses made Pius one of the greatest teaching popes. His concern in all his communications was to deal with specific points at issue and to bring Christian principles to bear on contemporary world problems.

Peace Efforts: Before the start of World War II, he tried unsuccessfully to get the contending nations — Germany and Poland, France and Italy — to settle their differences peaceably. During the war, he offered his services to mediate the widened conflict, spoke out against the horrors of war and the suffering it caused, mobilized relief work for its victims, proposed a five-point program for peace in Christmas messages from 1939 to 1942, and secured a generally open status for the city of Rome. He has been criticized in some quarters for not doing enough to oppose the Holocaust. This is a matter of historical debate, but it is a fact that through his direct intercession many thousands of Jews in Rome and Italy were saved from certain death, and he resisted wherever possible the threat of Nazism to human rights. Such were his contributions to assisting Jews that the rabbi of Rome, Dr.

Abraham Zolli, was converted to Catholicism, and upon his death, Pius was praised by Golda Meir for his efforts. After the war, he endorsed the principles and intent of the U.N. and continued efforts for peace.

United States: Pius appointed more than 200 of the 265 American bishops resident in the U.S. and abroad in 1958, erected 27 dioceses in this country, and raised seven dioceses to archiepiscopal rank.

BL. JOHN XXIII

John XXIII (Angelo Roncalli) was born Nov. 25, 1881, at Sotte il Monte, Italy.

He was educated at the seminary of the Bergamo diocese and the Pontifical Seminary in Rome, where he was ordained to the priesthood Aug. 10, 1904.

He spent the first nine or 10 years of his priesthood as secretary to the bishop of Bergamo and as an instructor in the seminary there. He served as a medic and chaplain in the Italian army during World War I. Afterwards, he resumed duties in his own diocese until he was called to Rome in 1921 for work with the Society for the Propagation of the Faith.

He began diplomatic service in 1925 as titular archbishop of Areopolis and apostolic visitor to Bulgaria. A succession of offices followed: apostolic delegate to Bulgaria (1931-1935); titular archbishop of Mesembria, apostolic delegate to Turkey and Greece, administrator of the Latin vicariate apostolic of Istanbul (1935-1944); apostolic nuncio to France (1944-1953). On these missions, he was engaged in delicate negotiations involving Roman, Eastern Rite and Orthodox relations; the needs of people suffering from the consequences of World War II; and unsettling suspicions arising from wartime conditions.

He was made a cardinal Jan. 12, 1953, and three days later was appointed patriarch of Venice, the position he held until his election to the papacy Oct. 28, 1958. He died of stomach cancer June 3, 1963.

John was a strong and vigorous pope whose influence far outmeasured both his age and the shortness of his time in the papacy. He was beatified by Pope John Paul II on Sept. 3, 2000.

Second Vatican Council: John announced Jan. 25, 1959, his intention of convoking the 21st ecumenical council in history to renew life in the Church, to reform its structures and institutions, and to explore ways and means of promoting unity among Christians. Through the council, which completed its work two and a half years after his death, he ushered in a new era in the history of the Church.

Canon Law: He established a commission Mar. 28, 1963, for revision of the Code of Canon Law. The revised Code was promulgated in 1983.

Canonizations: He canonized 10 saints and beatified Mother Elizabeth Ann Seton, the first native of the U.S. ever so honored. He named St. Lawrence of Brindisi a Doctor of the Church.

Cardinals: He created 52 cardinals in five consistories, raising membership of the College of Cardinals above the traditional number of 70; at one time in 1962, the membership was 87. He made the college more international in representation than it had ever been, appointing the first cardinals from the Philippines, Japan and Africa. He ordered episcopal ordination for all cardinals. He relieved the suburban bishops of Rome of ordinary jurisdiction over their dioceses so they might devote all their time to business of the Roman Curia.

Eastern Rites: He made all Eastern Rite patriarchs members of the Congregation for the Oriental Churches.

Ecumenism: He assigned to the Second Vatican Council the task of finding ways and means of promoting unity among Christians. He established the Vatican Secretariat for Promoting Christian Unity June 5, 1960. He showed his desire for more cordial relations with the Orthodox by sending personal representatives to visit Patriarch Athenagoras I June 27, 1961; approved a mission of five delegates to the General Assembly of the World Council of Churches which met in New Delhi, India, in Nov. 1961; and removed a number of pejorative references to Jews in the Roman-Rite liturgy for Good Friday.

Encyclicals: Of the eight encyclicals he issued, the two outstanding ones were *Mater et Magistra* ("Christianity and Social Progress"), in which he recapitulated, updated and extended the social doctrine stated earlier by Leo XIII and Pius XI; and *Pacem in Terris* ("Peace on Earth"), the first encyclical ever addressed to all men of good will as well as to Catholics, on the natural law principles of peace.

Liturgy: In forwarding liturgical reforms already begun by Pius XII, he ordered a calendar-missal-breviary reform into effect Jan. 1, 1961. He authorized the use of vernacular languages in the administration of the sacraments and approved giving Holy Communion to the sick in afternoon hours. He selected the liturgy as the first topic of major discussion by the Second Vatican Council.

Missions: He issued an encyclical on the missionary activity of the Church; established native hierarchies in Indonesia, Vietnam and Korea; and called on North American superiors of religious institutes to have one-tenth of their members assigned to work in Latin America by 1971.

Peace: John spoke and used his moral influence for peace in 1961 when tension developed over Berlin, in 1962 during the Algerian revolt from France, and later the same year in the Cuban missile crisis. His efforts were singled out for honor by the Balzan Peace Foundation. In 1963, he was posthumously awarded the U.S. Presidential Medal of Freedom.

PAUL VI

Paul VI (Giovanni Battista Montini) was born Sept. 26, 1897, at Concesio in northern Italy. Educated at Brescia, he was ordained to the priesthood May 29, 1920. He pursued additional studies at the Pontifical Academy for Noble Ecclesiastics and the Pontifical Gregorian University. In 1924 he began 30 years of service in the Secretariat of State; as undersecretary from 1937 until 1954, he was closely associated with Pius XII and was heavily engaged in organizing informational and relief services during and after World War II. He declined the offer of the cardinalate by Pope Pius XII.

Ordained archbishop of Milan Dec. 12, 1954, he was inducted into the College of Cardinals Dec. 15, 1958, by Pope John XXIII. Trusted by John, he was a key figure in organizing the first session of Vatican Council II and was elected to the papacy June 21, 1963, two days after the conclave began. He died of a heart attack Aug. 6, 1978.

Second Vatican Council: He reconvened the Second Vatican Council after the death of John XXIII, presided over its second, third and fourth sessions, formally promulgated the 16 documents it produced, and devoted the whole of his pontificate to the task of putting them into effect throughout the Church. The main thrust of his pontificate — in a milieu of cultural and other changes in the Church and the world — was toward institutionalization and control of the authentic trends articulated and set in motion by the council.

Canonizations: He canonized 84 saints. They included groups of 22 Ugandan martyrs and 40 martyrs of England and Wales, as well as two Americans — Elizabeth Ann Bayley Seton and John Nepomucene Neumann.

Cardinals: He created 144 cardinals, and gave the Sacred College a more international complexion than it ever had before. He limited participation in papal elections to 120 cardinals under the age of 80.

Collegiality: He established the Synod of Bishops in 1965 and called it into session five times. He stimulated the formation and operation of regional conferences of bishops, and of consultative bodies on other levels.

Creed and Holy Year: On June 30, 1968, he issued a Creed of the People of God in conjunction with the celebration of a Year of Faith. He proclaimed and led the observance of a Holy Year from Christmas Eve of 1974 to Christmas Eve of 1975.

Diplomacy: He met with many world leaders, including Soviet President Nikolai Podgorny in 1967, Marshal Tito of Yugoslavia in 1971 and President Nicolai Ceausescu of Romania in 1973. He worked constantly to reduce tension between the Church and the intransigent regimes of Eastern European countries by means of a detente type of policy called *Ostpolitik*. He agreed to significant revisions of the Vatican's concordat with Spain and initiated efforts to revise the concordat with Italy. More than 40 countries established diplomatic relations with the Vatican during his pontificate.

Encyclicals: He issued seven encyclicals, three of which are the best known. In *Populorum Progressio* ("Development of Peoples") he appealed to wealthy countries to take "concrete action" to promote human development and to remedy imbalances between richer and poorer nations; this encyclical, coupled with other documents and related actions, launched the Church into a new depth of involvement as a public advocate for human rights and for humanizing social, political and economic policies. In *Sacerdotalis Caelibatus* ("Priestly Celibacy") he reaffirmed the strict observance of priestly celibacy throughout the Western Church. In *Humanae Vitae* ("Of Human Life") he condemned abortion, sterilization and artificial birth control, in line with traditional teaching and in "defense of life, the gift of God, the glory of the family, the strength of the people."

Interfaith Relations: He initiated formal consultation and informal dialogue on international and national levels between Catholics and non-Catholics — Orthodox, Anglicans, Protestants, Jews, Muslims, Buddhists, Hindus, and unbelievers. He and Greek Orthodox Patriarch Athenagoras I of Constantinople nullified in 1965 the mutual excommunications imposed by their respective churches in 1054.

Liturgy: He carried out the most extensive liturgical

reform in history, involving a new Order of the Mass effective in 1969, a revised church calendar in 1970, revisions and translations into vernacular languages of all sacramental rites and other liturgical texts.

Ministries: He authorized the restoration of the permanent diaconate in the Roman Rite and the establishment of new ministries of lay persons.

Peace: In 1968, he instituted the annual observance of a World Day of Peace on New Year's Day as a means of addressing a message of peace to all the world's political leaders and the peoples of all nations. The most dramatic of his many appeals for peace and efforts to ease international tensions was his plea for "No more war!" before the U.N., Oct. 4, 1965.

Pilgrimages: A "Pilgrim Pope," he made pastoral visits to the Holy Land and India in 1964, the U.N. and New York City in 1965, Portugal and Turkey in 1967, Colombia in 1968, Switzerland and Uganda in 1969, and Asia, Pacific islands and Australia in 1970. While in Manila in 1970, he was stabbed by a Bolivian artist.

Roman Curia: He reorganized the central administrative organs of the Church in line with provisions of the apostolic constitution, *Regimini Ecclesiae Universae*, streamlining procedures for more effective service and giving the agencies a more international perspective by drawing officials and consultors from all over the world. He also instituted a number of new commissions and other bodies. Coupled with curial reorganization was a simplification of papal ceremonies.

JOHN PAUL I

John Paul I (Albino Luciani) was born Oct. 17, 1912, in Forno di Canale (now Canale d'Agordo) in northern Italy. Educated at the minor seminary in Feltre and the major seminary of the Diocese of Belluno, he was ordained to the priesthood July 7, 1935. He pursued further studies at the Pontifical Gregorian University in Rome and was awarded a doctorate in theology. From 1937 to 1947 he was vice rector of the Belluno seminary, where he taught dogmatic and moral theology, canon law and sacred art. He was appointed vicar general of his diocese in 1947 and served as director of catechetics.

Ordained bishop of Vittorio Veneto Dec. 27, 1958, he attended all sessions of the Second Vatican Council, participated in three assemblies of the Synod of Bishops (1971, 1974 and 1977), and was vice president of the Italian Bishops' Conference from 1972 to 1975.

He was appointed archbishop and patriarch of Venice Dec. 15, 1969, and was inducted into the College of Cardinals Mar. 5, 1973.

He was elected to the papacy Aug. 26, 1978, on the fourth ballot cast by the 111 cardinals participating in the largest and one of the shortest conclaves in history. The quickness of his election was matched by the brevity of his pontificate of 33 days, during which he delivered 19 addresses. He died of a heart attack Sept. 28, 1978.

JOHN PAUL II

See separate entry.

PAPAL ENCYCLICALS — BENEDICT XIV (1740) TO JOHN PAUL II

(*Source:* The Papal Encyclicals *[5 vols.], Claudia Carlen, I.H.M.; Pieran Press, Ann Arbor, MI. Used with permission.*)

An encyclical letter is a pastoral letter addressed by a pope to the whole Church. In general, it concerns matters of doctrine, morals or discipline, or significant commemorations. Its formal title consists of the first few words of the official text. Some encyclicals, notably *Pacem in terris* by John XXIII, *Ecclesiam Suam* by Paul VI and several by John Paul II, have been addressed to people of good will in general as well as to bishops and the faithful in communion with the Church.

An encyclical epistle resembles an encyclical letter but is addressed only to part of the Church. The authority of encyclicals was stated by Pius XII in the encyclical *Humani generis* Aug. 12, 1950: "Nor must it be thought that what is contained in encyclical letters does not of itself demand assent, on the pretext that the popes do not exercise in them the supreme power of their teaching authority. Rather, such teachings belong to the ordinary magisterium, of which it is true to say: 'He who hears you, hears me' (Lk. 10:16); for the most part, too, what is expounded and inculcated in encyclical letters already appertains to Catholic doctrine for other reasons."

The Second Vatican Council declared: "Religious submission of will and of mind must be shown in a special way to the authentic teaching authority of the Roman Pontiff, even when he is not speaking *ex cathedra*. That is, it must be shown in such a way that his supreme magisterium is acknowledged with reverence, the judgments made by him are sincerely adhered to, according to his manifest mind and will. His mind and will in the matter may be known chiefly either from the character of the documents (one of which could be an encyclical), from his frequent repetition of the same doctrine, or from his manner of speaking" (Dogmatic Constitution on the Church, *Lumen Gentium*, No. 25).

The following list contains the titles and indicates the subject matter of encyclical letters and epistles. The latter are generally distinguishable by the limited scope of their titles or contents.

Benedict XIV

(1740-58)

1740: *Ubi primum* (On the duties of bishops), Dec. 3.

1741: *Quanta cura* (Forbidding traffic in alms), June 30.

1743: *Nimiam licentiam* (To the bishops of Poland, on validity of marriages), May 18.

1745: *Vix pervenit* (To the bishops of Italy, on usury and other dishonest profit), Nov. 1.

1748: Magnae Nobis (To the bishops of Poland, on marriage impediments and dispensations), June 29.

1749: *Peregrinantes* (To all the faithful, proclaiming a Holy Year for 1750), May 5.

Apostolica Constitutio (On preparation for the Holy Year), June 26.

1751: *A quo primum* (To the bishops of Poland, on Jews and Christians living in the same place), June 14.

1754: *Cum Religiosi* (To the bishops of the States of the Church, on catechesis), June 26.

Quod Provinciale (To the bishops of Albania, on Christians using Mohammedan names), Aug. 1.

1755: *Allatae sunt* (To missionaries of the Orient, on the observance of Oriental rites), July 26.

1756: *Ex quo primum* (To bishops of the Greek rite, on the Euchologion), Mar. 1.

Ex omnibus (To the bishops of France, on the apostolic constitution, *Unigenitus*), Oct. 16.

Clement XIII
(1758-69)

1758: *A quo die* (Unity among Christians), Sept. 13.

1759: *Cum primum* (On observing canonical sanctions), Sept. 17.

Appetente Sacro (On the spiritual advantages of fasting), Dec. 20.

1761: *In Dominico agro* (On instruction in the faith), June 14.

1766: *Christianae republicae* (On the dangers of anti-Christian writings), Nov. 25.

1768: *Summa quae* (To the bishops of Poland, on the Church in Poland), Jan. 6.

Clement XIV
(1769-74)

1769: *Decet quam maxime* (To the bishops of Sardinia, on abuses in taxes and benefices), Sept. 21.

Inscrutabili divinae sapientiae (To all Christians, proclaiming a universal jubilee), Dec.12.

Cum summi (Proclaiming a universal jubilee), Dec. 12.

1774: *Salutis nostra* (To all Christians, proclaiming a universal jubilee), Apr. 30.

Pius VI
(1775-99)

1775: *Inscrutabile* (On the problems of the pontificate), Dec. 25.

1791: *Charitas* (To the bishops of France, on the civil oath in France), Apr. 13.

Pius VII
(1800-1823)

1800: *Diu satis* (To the bishops of France, on a return to Gospel principles), May 15.

Leo XII
(1823-29)

1824: *Ubi primum* (To all bishops, on Leo XII's assuming the pontificate), May 5.

Quod hoc ineunte (Proclaiming a universal jubilee), May 24.

1825: *Charitate Christi* (Extending jubilee to the entire Church), Dec. 25.

Pius VIII
(1829-30)

1829: *Traditi humilitati* (On Pius VIII's program for the pontificate), May 24.

Gregory XVI
(1831-46)

1832: *Summo iugiter studio* (To the bishops of Bavaria, on mixed marriages), May 27.

Cum primum (To the bishops of Poland, on civil obedience), June 9.

Mirari vos (On liberalism and religious indifferentism), Aug. 15.

1833: *Quo graviora* (To the bishops of the Rhineland, on the "pragmatic Constitution"), Oct. 4.

1834: *Singulari Nos* (On the errors of Lammenais), June 25.

1835: *Commissum divinitus* (To clergy of Switzerland, on Church and State), May 17.

1840: *Probe nostis* (On the Propagation of the Faith), Sept. 18.

1841: *Quas vestro* (To the bishops of Hungary, on mixed marriages), Apr. 30.

1844: *Inter praecipuas* (On biblical societies), May 8.

Pius IX
(1846-78)

1846: *Qui pluribus* (On faith and religion), Nov. 9.

1847: *Praedecessores Nostros* (On aid for Ireland), Mar. 25.

Ubi primum (To religious superiors, on discipline for religious), June 17.

1849: *Ubi primum* (On the Immaculate Conception), Feb. 2.

Nostis et Nobiscum (To the bishops of Italy, on the Church in the Pontifical States), Dec. 8.

1851: *Exultavit cor Nostrum* (On the effects of jubilee), Nov. 21.

1852: *Nemo certe ignorat* (To the bishops of Ireland, on the discipline for clergy), Mar. 25.

Probe noscitis Venerabiles (To the bishops of Spain, on the discipline for clergy), May 17.

1853: *Inter multiplices* (To the bishops of France, pleading for unity of spirit), Mar. 21.

1854: *Neminem vestrum* (To clergy and faithful of Constantinople, on the persecution of Armenians), Feb. 2.

Optime noscitis (To the bishops of Ireland, on the proposed Catholic university for Ireland), Mar. 20.

Apostolicae Nostrae caritatis (Urging prayers for peace), Aug. 1.

1855: *Optime noscitis* (To the bishops of Austria, on episcopal meetings), Nov. 5.

1856: *Singulari quidem* (To the bishops of Austria, on the Church in Austria), Mar. 17.

1858: *Cum nuper* (To the bishops of the Kingdom of the Two Sicilies, on care for clerics), Jan. 20.

Amantissimi Redemptoris (On priests and the care of souls), May 3.

1859: *Cum sancta mater Ecclesia* (Pleading for public prayer), Apr. 27.

Qui nuper (On Pontifical States), June 18.

1860: *Nullis certe verbis* (On the need for civil sovereignty), Jan. 19.

1862: *Amantissimus* (To bishops of the Oriental rite, on the care of the churches), Apr. 8.

1863: *Quanto conficiamur moerore* (To the bishops of Italy, on promotion of false doctrines), Aug. 10.

Incredibili (To the bishops of Bogota, on persecution in New Granada), Sept. 17.

1864: *Maximae quidem* (To the bishops of Bavaria, on the Church in Bavaria), Aug. 18.

Quanta cura (Condemning current errors), Dec. 8.

1865: *Meridionali Americae* (To the bishops of South America, on the seminary for native clergy), Sept. 30.

1867: *Levate* (On the afflictions of the Church), Oct. 27.

1870: *Respicientes* (Protesting the taking of the Pontifical States), Nov. 1.

1871: *Ubi Nos* (To all bishops, on Pontifical States), May 15.

Beneficia Dei (On the 25th anniversary of his pontificate), June 4.

Saepe Venerabiles Fratres (On thanksgiving for 25 years of pontificate), Aug. 5.

1872: *Quae in Patriarchatu* (To bishops and people of Chaldea, on the Church in Chaldea), Nov. 16.

1873: *Quartus supra* (To bishops and people of the Armenian rite, on the Church in Armenia), Jan. 6.

Etsi multa (On the Church in Italy, Germany and Switzerland), Nov. 21.

1874: *Vix dum a Nobis* (To the bishops of Austria, on the Church in Austria), Mar. 7.

Gravibus Ecclesiae (To all bishops and faithful, proclaiming a jubilee for 1875), Dec. 24.

1875: *Quod nunquam* (To the bishops of Prussia, on the Church in Prussia), Feb. 5.

Graves ac diuturnae (To the bishops of Switzerland, on the Church in Switzerland), Mar. 23.

Leo XIII
(1878-1903)

1878: *Inscrutabili Dei consilio* (On the evils of society), Apr. 21.

Quod Apostolici muneris (On socialism), Dec. 28.

1879: *Aeterni Patris* (On the restoration of Christian philosophy), Aug. 4.

1880: *Arcanum* (On Christian marriage), Feb. 10.

Grande munus (On Sts. Cyril and Methodius), Sept. 30.

Sancta Dei civitas (On mission societies), Dec. 3.

1881: *Diuturnum* (On the origin of civil power), June 29.

Licet multa (To the bishops of Belgium, on Catholics in Belgium), Aug. 3.

1882: *Etsi Nos* (To the bishops of Italy, on conditions in Italy), Feb. 15.

Auspicato concessum (On St. Francis of Assisi), Sept. 17.

Cum multa (To the bishops of Spain, on conditions in Spain), Dec. 8.

1883: *Supremi Apostolatus officio* (On devotion to the Rosary), Sept. 1.

1884: *Nobilissima Gallorum gens* (To the bishops of France, on the religious question), Feb. 8.

Humanum genus (On Freemasonry), Apr. 20.

Superiore anno (On the recitation of the Rosary), Aug. 30.

1885: *Immortale Dei* (On the Christian constitution of states), Nov. 1.

Spectata fides (To the bishops of England, on Christian education), Nov. 27.

Quod auctoritate (Proclamation of extraordinary Jubilee), Dec. 22.

1886: *Iampridem* (To the bishops of Prussia, on Catholicism in Germany), Jan. 6.

Quod multum (To the bishops of Hungary, on the liberty of the Church), Aug. 22.

Pergrata (To the bishops of Portugal, on the Church in Portugal), Sept. 14.

1887: *Vieben noto* (To the bishops of Italy, on the Rosary and public life), Sept. 20.

Officio sanctissimo (To the bishops of Bavaria, on the Church in Bavaria), Dec. 22.

1888: *Quod anniversarius* (On his sacerdotal jubilee), Apr. 1.

In plurimis (To the bishops of Brazil, on the abolition of slavery), May 5.

Libertas (On the nature of human liberty), June 20.

Saepe Nos (To the bishops of Ireland, on boycotting in Ireland), June 24.

Paterna caritas (To the Patriarch of Cilicia and the archbishops and bishops of the Armenian people, on reunion with Rome), July 25.

Quam aerumnosa (To the bishops of America, on Italian immigrants), Dec. 10.

Etsi cunctas (To the bishops of Ireland, on the Church in Ireland), Dec. 21.

Exeunte iam anno (On the right ordering of Christian life), Dec. 25.

1889: *Magni Nobis* (To the bishops of the United States, on the Catholic University of America), Mar. 7.

Quamquam pluries (On devotion to St. Joseph), Aug. 15.

1890: *Sapientiae Christianae* (On Christians as citizens), Jan. 10.

Dall'alto Dell'Apostolico seggio (To the bishops and people of Italy, on Freemasonry in Italy), Oct. 15.

Catholicae Ecclesiae (On slavery in the missions), Nov. 20.

1891: *In ipso* (To the bishops of Austria, on episcopal reunions in Austria), Mar. 3.

Rerum novarum (On capital and labor), May 15.

Pastoralis (To the bishops of Portugal, on religious union), June 25.

Pastoralis officii (To the bishops of Germany and Austria, on the morality of dueling), Sept. 12.

Octobri mense (On the Rosary), Sept. 22.

1892: *Au milieu des sollicitudes* (To the bishops, clergy and faithful of France, on the Church and State in France), Feb. 16.

Quarto abeunte saeculo (To the bishops of Spain, Italy, and the two Americas, on the Columbus quadricentennial), July 16.

Magnae Dei Matris (On the Rosary), Sept. 8.

Inimica vis (To the bishops of Italy, on Freemasonry), Dec. 8.

Custodi di quella fede (To the Italian people, on Freemasonry), Dec. 8.

1893: *Ad extremas* (On seminaries for native clergy), June 24.

Constanti Hungarorum (To the bishops of Hungary, on the Church in Hungary), Sept. 2.

Laetitiae sanctae (Commending devotion to the Rosary), Sept. 8.

Non mediocri (To the bishops of Spain, on the Spanish College in Rome), Oct. 25.

Providentissimus Deus (On the study of Holy Scripture), Nov. 18.

1894: *Caritatis* (To the bishops of Poland, on the Church in Poland), Mar. 19.

Inter graves (To the bishops of Peru, on the Church in Peru), May 1.

Litteras a vobis (To the bishops of Brazil, on the clergy in Brazil), July 2.

Iucunda semper expectatione (On the Rosary), Sept. 8.

Christi nomen (On the propagation of the Faith and Eastern churches), Dec. 24.

1895: *Longinqua* (To the bishops of the United States, on Catholicism in the United States), Jan. 6.

Permoti Nos (To the bishops of Belgium, on social conditions in Belgium), July 10.

Adiutricem (On the Rosary), Sept. 5.

1896: *Insignes* (To the bishops of Hungary, on the Hungarian millennium), May 1.

Satis cognitum (On the unity of the Church), June 29.

Fidentem piumque animum (On the Rosary), Sept. 20.

1897: *Divinum illud munus* (On the Holy Spirit), May 9.

Militantis Ecclesiae (To the bishops of Austria, Germany, and Switzerland, on St. Peter Canisius), Aug. 1.

Augustissimae Virginis Mariae (On the Confraternity of the Holy Rosary), Sept. 12.

Affari vos (To the bishops of Canada, on the Manitoba school question), Dec. 8.

1898: *Caritatis studium* (To the bishops of Scotland, on the Church in Scotland), July 25.

Spesse volte (To the bishops, priests, and people of Italy, on the suppression of Catholic institutions), Aug. 5.

Quam religiosa (To the bishops of Peru, on civil marriage law), Aug. 16.

Diuturni temporis (On the Rosary), Sept. 5.

Quum diuturnum (To the bishops of Latin America, on Latin American bishops' plenary council), Dec. 25.

1899: *Annum Sacrum* (On consecration to the Sacred Heart), May 25.

Depuis le jour (To the archbishops, bishops, and clergy of France, on the education of the clergy), Sept. 8.

Paternae (To the bishops of Brazil, on the education of the clergy), Sept. 18.

1900: *Omnibus compertum* (To the Patriarch and bishops of the Greek-Melkite rite, on unity among the Greek Melkites), July 21.

Tametsi futura prospicientibus (On Jesus Christ the Redeemer), Nov. 1.

1901: *Graves de communi re* (On Christian democracy), Jan. 18.

Gravissimas (To the bishops of Portugal, on religious orders in Portugal), May 16.

Reputantibus (To the bishops of Bohemia and Moravia, on the language question in Bohemia), Aug. 20.

Urbanitatis Veteris (To the bishops of the Latin church in Greece, on the foundation of a seminary in Athens), Nov. 20.

1902: *In amplissimo* (To the bishops of the United States, on the Church in the United States), Apr. 15.

Quod votis (To the bishops of Austria, on the proposed Catholic University), Apr. 30.

Mirae caritatis (On the Holy Eucharist), May 28.

Quae ad Nos (To the bishops of Bohemia and Moravia, on the Church in Bohemia and Moravia), Nov. 22.

Fin dal principio (To the bishops of Italy, on the education of the clergy), Dec. 8.

Dum multa (To the bishops of Ecuador, on marriage legislation), Dec. 24.

St. Pius X

(1903-14)

1903: *E supremi* (On the restoration of all things in Christ), Oct. 4.

1904: *Ad diem illum laetissimum* (On the Immaculate Conception), Feb. 2.

Iucunda sane (On Pope Gregory the Great), Mar. 12.

1905: *Acerbo nimis* (On teaching Christian doctrine), Apr. 15.

Il fermo proposito (To the bishops of Italy, on Catholic Action in Italy), June 11.

1906: *Vehementer Nos* (To the bishops, clergy, and people of France, on the French Law of Separation), Feb. 11.

Tribus circiter (On the Mariavites or Mystic Priests of Poland), Apr. 5.

Pieni l'animo (To the bishops of Italy, on the clergy in Italy), July 28.

Gravissimo officio munere (To the bishops of France, on French associations of worship), Aug. 10.

1907: *Une fois encore* (To the bishops, clergy, and people of France, on the separation of Church and State), Jan. 6.

Pascendi dominici gregis (On the doctrines of the Modernists), Sept. 8.

1909: *Communium rerum* (On St. Anselm of Aosta), Apr. 21.

1910: *Editae saepe* (On St. Charles Borromeo), May 26.

1911: *Iamdudum* (On the Law of Separation in Portugal), May 24.

1912: *Lacrimabili statu* (To the bishops of Latin America, on the Indians of South America), June 7.

Singulari quadam (To the bishops of Germany, on labor organizations), Sept. 24.

Benedict XV

(1914-22)

1914: *Ad beatissimi Apostolorum* (Appeal for peace), Nov. 1.

1917: *Humani generis Redemptionem* (On preaching the Word of God), June 15.

1918: *Quod iam diu* (On the future peace conference), Dec. 1.

1919: *In hac tanta* (To the bishops of Germany, on St. Boniface), May 14.

Paterno iam diu (On children of central Europe), Nov. 24.

1920: *Pacem, Dei munus pulcherrimum* (On peace and Christian reconciliation), May 23.

Spiritus Paraclitus (On St. Jerome), Sept. 15.

Principi Apostolorum Petro (On St. Ephrem the Syrian), Oct. 5.

Annus iam plenus (On children of central Europe), Dec. 1.

1921: *Sacra propediem* (On the Third Order of St. Francis), Jan. 6.

In praeclara summorum (To professors and students of fine arts in Catholic institutions of learning, on Dante), Apr. 30.

Fausto appetente die (On St. Dominic), June 29.

Pius XI

(1922-39)

1922: *Ubi arcano Dei consilio* (On the peace of Christ in the Kingdom of Christ), Dec. 23.

1923: *Rerum omnium perturbationem* (On St. Francis de Sales), Jan. 26.

Studiorum Ducem (On St. Thomas Aquinas), June 29.

Ecclesiam Dei (On St. Josaphat), Nov. 12.

1924: *Maximam gravissimamque* (To the bishops, clergy, and people of France, on French diocesan associations), Jan. 18.

1925: *Quas primas* (On the feast of Christ the King), Dec. 11.

1926: *Rerum Ecclesiae* (On Catholic missions), Feb. 28.

Rite expiatis (On St. Francis of Assisi), Apr. 30.

Iniquis afflictisque (On the persecution of the Church in Mexico), Nov. 18.

1928: *Mortalium animos* (On religious unity), Jan. 6.

Miserentissimus Redemptor (On reparation to the Sacred Heart), May 8.

Rerum Orientalium (On the promotion of Oriental Studies), Sept. 8.

1929: *Mens Nostra* (On the promotion of Spiritual Exercises), Dec. 20.

Quinquagesimo ante (On his sacerdotal jubilee), Dec. 23.

Rappresentanti in terra (On Christian education), Dec. 31. [Latin text, *Divini illius magistri*, published several months later with minor changes.]

1930: *Ad salutem* (On St. Augustine), Apr. 20.

Casti connubii (On Christian Marriage), Dec. 31.

1931: *Quadragesimo anno* (Commemorating the fortieth anniversary of Leo XIII's *Rerum novarum*, on reconstruction of the soical order), May 15.

Non abbiamo bisogno (On Catholic Action in Italy), June 29.

Nova impendet (On the economic crisis), Oct. 2.

Lux veritatis (On the Council of Ephesus), Dec. 25.

1932: *Caritate Christi compulsi* (On the Sacred Heart), May 3.

Acerba animi (To the bishops of Mexico, on persecution of the Church in Mexico), Sept. 29.

1933: *Dilectissima Nobis* (To the bishops, clergy, and people of Spain, on oppression of the Church in Spain), June 3.

1935: *Ad Catholici sacerdotii* (On the Catholic priesthood), Dec. 20.

1936: *Vigilanti cura* (To the bishops of the United States, on motion pictures), June 29.

1937: *Mit brennender Sorge* (To the bishops of Germany, on the Church and the German Reich), Mar. 14.

Divini Redemptoris (On atheistic communism), Mar. 19.

Nos es muy conocida (To the bishops of Mexico: on the religious situation in Mexico), Mar. 28

Ingravescentibus malis (On the Rosary) Sept. 29.

Pius XII
(1939-58)

1939: *Summi Pontificatus* (On the unity of human society), Oct. 20.

Sertum laetitiae (To the bishops of the United States, on the 150th anniversary of the establishment of the hierarchy in the United States), Nov. 1.

1940: *Saeculo exeunte octavo* (To the bishops of Portugal and its colonies, on the eighth centenary of the independence of Portugal), June 13.

1943: *Mystici Corporis Christi* (On the Mystical Body of Christ), June 29.

Divino afflante Spiritu (On promoting biblical studies, commemorating the fiftieth anniversary of *Providentissimus Deus*), Sept. 30.

1944: *Orientalis Ecclesiae* (On St. Cyril, Patriarch of Alexandria), Apr. 9.

1945: *Communium interpretes dolorum* (To the bishops of the world, appealing for prayers for peace during May), Apr. 15.

Orientales omnes Ecclesias (On the 350th anniversary of the reunion of the Ruthenian Church with the Apostolic See), Dec. 23.

1946: *Quemadmodum* (Pleading for the care of the world's destitute children), Jan. 6.

Deiparae Virginis Mariae (To all bishops, on the possibility of defining the Assumption of the Blessed Virgin Mary as a dogma of faith), May 1.

1947: *Fulgens radiatur* (On St. Benedict), Mar. 21.

Mediator Dei (On the sacred liturgy), Nov. 20.

Optatissima pax (Prescribing public prayers for social and world peace), Dec. 18.

1948: *Auspicia quaedam* (On public prayers for world peace and solution of the problem of Palestine), May 1.

In multiplicibus curis (On prayers for peace in Palestine), Oct. 24.

1949: *Redemptoris nostri cruciatus* (On the holy places in Palestine), Apr. 15.

1950: *Anni Sacri* (On the program for combating atheistic propaganda throughout the world), Mar. 12.

Summi maeroris (On public prayers for peace), July 19.

Humani generis (Concerning some false opinions threatening to undermine the foundations of Catholic doctrine), Aug. 12.

Mirabile illud (On the crusade of prayers for peace), Dec. 6.

1951: *Evangelii praecones* (On the promotion of Catholic missions), June 2.

Sempiternus Rex Christus (On the Council of Chalcedon), Sept. 8.

Ingruentium malorum (On reciting the Rosary), Sept. 15.

1952: *Orientales Ecclesias* (On the persecuted Eastern Church), Dec. 15.

1953: *Doctor Mellifluus* (On St. Bernard of Clairvaux, the last of the fathers), May 24.

Fulgens corona (Proclaiming a Marian Year to commemorate the centenary of the definition of the dogma of the Immaculate Conception), Sept. 8.

1954: *Sacra virginitas* (On consecrated virginity), Mar. 25.

Ecclesiae fastos (To the bishops of Great Britain, Germany, Austria, France, Belgium, and Holland, on St. Boniface), June 5.

Ad Sinarum gentem (To the bishops, clergy, and people of China, on the supranationality of the Church), Oct. 7.

Ad Caeli Reginam (Proclaiming the Queenship of Mary), Oct. 11.

1955: *Musicae sacrae* (On sacred music), Dec. 25.

1956: *Haurietis aquas* (On devotion to the Sacred Heart), May 15.

Luctuosissimi eventus (Urging public prayers for peace and freedom for the people of Hungary), Oct. 28.

Laetamur admodum (Renewing exhortation for prayers for peace for Poland, Hungary, and especially for the Middle East), Nov. 1.

Datis nuperrime (Lamenting the sorrowful events in Hungary and condemning the ruthless use of force), Nov. 5.

1957: *Fidei donum* (On the present condition of the

Catholic missions, especially in Africa), Apr. 21.

Invicti athletae (On St. Andrew Bobola), May 16.

Le pelerinage de Lourdes (Warning against materialism on the centenary of the apparitions at Lourdes), July 2.

Miranda prorsus (On the communications field, motion picture, radio, television), Sept. 8.

1958: *Ad Apostolorum Principis* (To the bishops of China, on Communism and the Church in China), June 29.

Meminisse iuvat (On prayers for persecuted Church), July 14.

Bl. John XXIII
(1958-63)

1959: *Ad Petri Cathedram* (On truth, unity, and peace, in a spirit of charity), June 29.

Sacerdotii Nostri primordia (On St. John Vianney), Aug. 1.

Grata recordatio (On the Rosary, prayer for the Church, missions, international and social problems), Sept. 26.

Princeps Pastorum (On the missions, native clergy, lay participation), Nov. 28.

1961: *Mater et Magistra* (On Christianity and social progress), May 15.

Aeterna Dei sapientia (On the fifteenth centenary of the death of Pope St. Leo I, the see of Peter as the center of Christian unity), Nov. 11.

1962: *Paenitentiam agere* (On the need for the practice of interior and exterior penance), July 1.

1963: *Pacem in terris* (On establishing universal peace in truth, justice, charity, and liberty), Apr. 11.

Paul VI
(1963-78)

1964: *Ecclesiam Suam* (On the Church), Aug. 6.

1965: *Mense maio* (On prayers during May for the preservation of peace), Apr. 29.

Mysterium Fidei (On the Holy Eucharist), Sept. 3.

1966: *Christi Matri* (On prayers for peace during Oct.), Sept. 15.

1967: *Populorum progressio* (On the development of peoples), Mar. 26.

Sacerdotalis caelibatus (On the celibacy of the priest), June 24.

1968: *Humanae vitae* (On the regulation of birth), July 25.

John Paul II
(1978-)

1979: *Redemptor hominis* (On redemption and dignity of the human race), Mar. 4

1980: *Dives in misericordia* (On the mercy of God), Nov. 30.

1981: *Laborem exercens* (On human work), Sept. 14.

1985: *Slavorum Apostoli* (Commemorating Sts. Cyril and Methodius, on the eleventh centenary of the death of St. Methodius), June 2.

1986: *Dominum et Vivificantem* (On the Holy Spirit in the life of the Church and the world), May 18.

1987: *Redemptoris Mater* (On the role of Mary in the mystery of Christ and her active and exemplary presence in the life of the Church), Mar. 25.

Sollicitudo Rei Socialis (On social concerns, on the twentieth anniversary of *Populorum progressio*), Dec. 30.

1991: *Redemptoris missio* (On the permanent validity of the Church's missionary mandate), Jan. 22.

Centesimus annus (Commemorating the centenary of *Rerum novarum* and addressing the social question in a contemporary perspective), May 1.

1993: *Veritatis Splendor* (On fundamental questions on the Church's moral teaching), Aug. 6.

1995: *Evangelium Vitae* (On the value and inviolability of human life), Mar. 25.

Ut Unum Sint (On commitment to ecumenism), May 25.

1998: *Fides et Ratio* (On faith and reason), Oct. 1.

2003: *Ecclesia de Eucharistia* (Church of the Eucharist), April 17.

CANONIZATIONS BY LEO XIII AND HIS SUCCESSORS

"Canonization" (*see* **Glossary**) is an infallible declaration by the pope that a person who suffered martyrdom and/or practiced Christian virtue to a heroic degree is in glory with God in heaven and is worthy of public honor by the universal Church and of imitation by the faithful.

Biographies of some of the saints listed below are given elsewhere in the **Almanac**; *see* **Index**; for biographies of all new saints for 2002-03, *see* **Saints**.

Leo XIII
(1878-1903)

1881: Clare of Montefalco (d. 1308); John Baptist de Rossi (1698-1764); Lawrence of Brindisi (d. 1619).

1883: Benedict J. Labre (1748-83).

1888: Seven Holy Founders of the Servite Order; Peter Claver (1581-1654); John Berchmans (1599-1621); Alphonsus Rodriguez (1531-1617).

1897: Anthony M. Zaccaria (1502-39); Peter Fourier of Our Lady (1565-1640).

1900: John Baptist de La Salle (1651-1719); Rita of Cascia (1381-1457).

St. Pius X
(1903-14)

1904: Alexander Sauli (1534-93); Gerard Majella (1725-55).

1909: Joseph Oriol (1650-1702); Clement M. Hofbauer (1751-1820).

Benedict XV
(1914-22)

1920: Gabriel of the Sorrowful Mother (1838-62); Margaret Mary Alacoque (1647-90); Joan of Arc (1412-31).

Pius XI
(1922-39)

1925: Thérèse of Lisieux (1873-97); Peter Canisius (1521-97); Mary Magdalen Postel (1756-1846); Mary Magdalen Sophie Barat (1779-1865); John Eudes (1601-80); John Baptist Vianney (Curé of Ars) (1786-1859).

1930: Lucy Filippini (1672-1732); Catherine Tomas (1533-74); Jesuit North American Martyrs; Robert Bellarmine (1542-1621); Theophilus of Corte (1676-1740).

1931: Albert the Great (1206-80) (equivalent canonization).

1933: Andrew Fournet (1752-1834); Bernadette Soubirous (1844-79).

1934: Joan Antida Thouret (1765-1826); Mary Michaeli (1809-65); Louise de Marillac (1591-1660); Joseph Benedict Cottolengo (1786-1842); Pompilius M. Pirotti, priest (1710-56); Teresa Margaret Redi (1747-70); John Bosco (1815-88); Conrad of Parzham (1818-94).

1935: John Fisher (1469-1535); Thomas More (1478-1535).

1938: Andrew Bobola (1592-1657); John Leonardi (c. 1550-1609); Salvatore of Horta (1520-67).

Pius XII
(1939-58)

1940: Gemma Galgani (1878-1903); Mary Euphrasia Pelletier (1796-1868).

1943: Margaret of Hungary (d. 1270) (equivalent canonization).

1946: Frances Xavier Cabrini (1850-1917).

1947: Nicholas of Flüe (1417-87); John of Britto (1647-93); Bernard Realini (1530-1616); Joseph Cafasso (1811-60); Michael Garicoits (1797-1863); Jeanne Elizabeth des Ages (1773-1838); Louis Marie Grignon de Montfort (1673-1716); Catherine Labouré (1806-76).

1949: Jeanne de Lestonnac (1556-1640); Maria Josepha Rossello (1811-80).

1950: Emily de Rodat (1787-1852); Anthony Mary Claret (1807-70); Bartolomea Capitanio (1807-33); Vincenza Gerosa (1784-1847); Jeanne de Valois (1461-1504); Vincenzo M. Strambi (1745-1824); Maria Goretti (1890-1902); Mariana Paredes of Jesus (1618-45).

1951: Maria Domenica Mazzarello (1837-81); Emilie de Vialar (1797-1856); Anthony M. Gianelli (1789-1846); Ignatius of Laconi (1701-81); Francis Xavier Bianchi (1743-1815).

1954: Pope Pius X (1835-1914); Dominic Savio (1842-57); Maria Crocifissa di Rosa (1813-55); Peter Chanel (1803-41); Gaspar del Bufalo (1786-1837); Joseph M. Pignatelli (1737-1811).

1958: Herman Joseph, O. Praem. (1150-1241) (equivalent canonization).

Bl. John XXIII
(1958-63)

1959: Joaquina de Vedruna de Mas (1783-1854); Charles of Sezze (1613-70).

1960: Gregory Barbarigo (1625-97) (equivalent canonization); John de Ribera (1532-1611).

1961: Bertilla Boscardin (1888-1922).

1962: Martin de Porres (1579-1639); Peter Julian Eymard (1811-68); Anthony Pucci, priest (1819-92); Francis Mary of Camporosso (1804-66).

1963: Vincent Pallotti (1795-1850).

Paul VI
(1963-78)

1964: Charles Lwanga and Twenty-one Companions, Martyrs of Uganda (d. between 1885-87).

1967: Benilde Romacon (1805-62).

1969: Julia Billiart (1751-1816).

1970: Maria Della Dolorato Torres Acosta (1826-87); Leonard Murialdo (1828-1900); Therese Couderc

(1805-85); John of Ávila (1499-1569); Nicholas Tavelic, Deodatus of Aquitaine, Peter of Narbonne and Stephen of Cuneo, martyrs (d. 1391); Forty English and Welsh Martyrs (d. 16th cent.).

1974: Teresa of Jesus Jornet Ibars (1843-97).

1975: Vicenta Maria Lopez y Vicuna (1847-90); Elizabeth Bayley Seton (1774-1821); John Masias (1585-1645); Oliver Plunket (1629-81); Justin de Jacobis (1800-60); John Baptist of the Conception (1561-1613).

1976: Beatrice da Silva (1424 or 1426-90); John Ogilvie (1579-1615).

1977: Rafaela Maria Porras y Ayllon (1850-1925); John Nepomucene Neumann (1811-60); Sharbel Makhlouf (1828-98).

John Paul II
(1978-)

1982: Crispin of Viterbo (1668-1750); Maximilian Kolbe (1894-1941); Marguerite Bourgeoys (1620-1700); Jeanne Delanoue (1666-1736).

1983: Leopold Mandic (1866-1942).

1984: Paola Frassinetti (1809-92); 103 Korean Martyrs (d. between 1839-67); Miguel Febres Cordero (1854-1910).

1986: Francis Anthony Fasani (1681-1742); Giuseppe Maria Tomasi (1649-1713).

1987: Giuseppe Moscati (d. 1927); Lawrence (Lorenzo) Ruiz and Fifteen Companions, Martyrs of Japan (d. 1630s).

1988: Eustochia Calafato (1434-85); 117 Martyrs of Vietnam (96 Vietnamese, 11 Spanish, 10 French, included 8 bishops, 50 priests, 1 seminarian, 58 lay persons); Roque Gonzalez (1576-1628), Alfonso Rodriguez (1598-1628) and Juan de Castillo (1596-1628), Jesuit martyrs of Paraguay; Rose Philippine Duchesne (1796-1852); Simon de Rojas (1552-1624); Magdalen of Canossa (1774-1835); Maria Rosa Molas y Vollve (d. 1876).

1989: Clelia Barbieri (1847-70); Gaspar Bertoni (1777-1853); Richard Pampuri, religious (1897-1930); Agnes of Bohemia (1211-82); Albert Chmielowski (1845-1916); Mutien-Marie Wiaux (1841-1917).

1990: Marguerite D'Youville (1701-77).

1991: Raphael (Jozef) Kalinowski (1835-1907).

1992: Claude La Colombiere (1641-82); Ezequiel Moreno y Diaz (1848-1905).

1993: Marie of St. Ignatius (Claudine Thevenet) (1774-1837); Teresa "de los Andes" (Juana Fernandez Solar) (1900-20); Enrique de Ossó y Cervelló (1840-96).

1995: Jan Sarkander (1576-1620); Zdislava of Lemberk (d. 1252); Marek Krizin (1588-1619), Stefan Pongracz (1582-1619), Melichar Grodziecky (1584-1619), martyrs of Kosice; Eugene de Mazenod (1782-1861).

1996: Jean-Gabriel Perboyre (1802-40); Juan Grande Roman (1546-1600); Bro. Egidio Maria of St. Joseph (1729-1812).

1997: Hedwig (1371-99); John Dukla, O.F.M. (d. 1484).

1998: Edith Stein (d. 1942).

1999: Marcellin Joseph Benoit Champagnat (1789-1840); Giovanni Calabria (1873-1954); Agostina Livia Pietrantonio (1864-94); Sr. Kunegunda Kinga (1224-92); Cirilo Bertrán and Eight Companion

Brothers of the Christian Schools (d. Oct. 9, 1934); Inocencio de la Immaculada (d. Oct. 9, 1934); St. Jaime Hilario Barbal (1889-1937); Benedetto Menni (1841-1914); Tommaso da Cori (1655-1729).

2000: Mary Faustina Kowalska (1905-38); María Josefa of the Heart of Jesus Sancho de Guerra (1842-1912); Cristóbal Magallanes and 24 Companions (d. 1915-28); José Maria de Yermo y Parres (1851-1904); Maria de Jesús Sacramentado Venegas (1868-1959); 120 Martyrs of China (17th-20th centuries); Katherine Drexel (1858-1955); Josephine Bakhita (d. 1947).

2001: Luigi Scrosoppi (1804-84); Agostino Roscelli (1818-1902); Bernardo da Corleone (1605-67); Teresa Eustochio Verzeri (1801-52); Rafqa Petra Choboq Ar-Rayes (1832-1914); Giuseppe Marello (1844-95); Paula Montal Fornés de San José de Calasanz (1799-1889); Léonie Françoise de Sales

Aviat (1844-1914); Maria Crescentia Höss (1682-1744).

2002: Alonso de Orozco (1500-91); Ignazio da Santhia (Lorenzo Maurizio Belvisotti) (1686-1770); Umile da Bisignano (Luca Antonio Pirozzo) (1582-1637); Paulina do Coracao Agonizante de Jesus (Amabile Visintainer) (1865-1942); Benedetta Cambiagio Frassinello (1791-1858); Pio da Pietrelcina (Padre Pio, 1887-1968); Juan Diego Cuauhlatoatzin (16th century); Pedro de San Jose de Betancur (1619-67); Josemaria Escriva (1902-75).

2003: Pedro Poveda Castroverde (1874-1936); José María Rubio y Peralta (1864-1929); Genoveva Torres Morales (1870-1956); Angela de la Cruz (1846-1932); María Maravillas de Jesus (1891-1974); Jozef Sebastian Pelczar (1842-1924); Urszula Ledochowska (1865-1939); Maria de Mattias (1805-66); Virginia Centurione Bracelli (1587-1651).

BEATIFICATIONS BY POPE JOHN PAUL II, 1979-2003

For biographical details of all those beatified in 2002-03, please *see* under **Saints**.

1979: Margaret Ebner (Feb. 24); Francis Coll, O.P., Jacques Laval, S.S.Sp. (Apr. 29); Enrique de Ossó y Cervelló (Oct. 14).

1980: José de Anchieta, Pedro de San Jose Betancur, François de Montmorency Laval, Kateri Tekakwitha, Marie Guyart of the Incarnation (June 22); Don Luigi Orione, Bartolomea Longo, Maria Anna Sala (Oct. 26).

1981: Sixteen Martyrs of Japan (Lorenzo Ruiz and Companions) (Feb 18); Maria Repetto, Alan de Solminihac, Richard Pampuri, Claudine Thevenet, Aloysius (Luigi) Scrosoppi (Oct. 4).

1982: Peter Donders, C.SS.R., Marie Rose Durocher, Andre Bessette, C.S.C., Maria Angela Astorch, Marie Rivier (May 23); Fra Angelico (equivalent beatification) (July); Jeanne Jugan, Salvatore Lilli and 7 Armenian Companions (Oct. 3); Sr. Angela of the Cross (Nov. 5).

1983: Maria Gabriella Sagheddu (Jan. 25); Luigi Versiglia, Callisto Caravario (May 15); Ursula Ledochowska (June 20); Raphael (Jozef) Kalinowski, Bro. Albert (Adam Chmielowski), T.O.R. (June 22); Giacomo Cusmano, Jeremiah of Valachia, Domingo Iturrate Zubero (Oct. 30); Marie of Jesus Crucified (Marie Bouardy) (Nov. 13).

1984: Fr. William Repin and 98 Companions (Martyrs of Angers during French Revolution), Giovanni Mazzucconi (Feb. 19); Marie Leonie Paradis (Sept. 11); Federico Albert, Clemente Marchisio, Isidore of St. Joseph (Isidore de Loor), Rafaela Ybarra de Villalongo (Sept. 30); José Manyanet y Vives, Daniel Brottier, C.S.Sp., Sr. Elizabeth of the Trinity (Elizabeth Catez) (Nov. 25).

1985: Mercedes of Jesus (Feb. 1); Ana de los Angeles Monteagudo (Feb. 2); Pauline von Mallinckrodt, Catherine Troiani (Apr. 14); Benedict Menni, Peter Friedhofen (June 23); Anwarite Nangapeta (Aug. 15); Virginae Centurione Bracelli (Sept. 22); Diego Luis de San Vitores, S.J., Jose M. Rubio y Peralta, S.J., Francisco Garate, S.J. (Oct. 6); Titus Brandsma, O.Carm. (Nov. 3); Pio Campidelli, C.P., Marie Teresa of Jesus Gerhardinger, Rafqa Ar-

Rayes (Nov. 17).

1986: Alphonsa Mattathupandatu of the Immaculate Conception, Kuriakose Elias Chavara (Feb. 8); Antoine Chevrier (Oct. 4); Teresa Maria of the Cross Manetti (Oct. 19).

1987: Maria Pilar of St. Francis Borgia, Teresa of the Infant Jesus, Maria Angeles of St. Joseph, Cardinal Marcellis Spinola y Maestre, Emmanuel Domingo y Sol (Mar. 29); Teresa of Jesus "de los Andes" (Apr. 3); Edith Stein (Teresa Benedicta of the Cross) (May 1); Rupert Meyer, S.J. (May 3); Pierre-Francois Jamet, Cardinal Andrea Carlo Ferrari, Benedicta Cambiagio Frassinello, Louis Moreau (May 10); Carolina Kozka, Michal Kozal (June 10); George Matulaitis (Matulewicz) (June 28); Marcel Callo, Pierino Morosini, Antonia Mesina (Oct. 4); Blandina Marten, Ulricke Nische, Jules Reche (Bro. Arnold) (Nov. 1); 85 Martyrs (d. between 1584-1689) of England, Scotland and Wales (Nov. 22).

1988: John Calabria, Joseph Nascimbeni (Apr. 17); Pietro Bonilli, Kaspar Stangassinger, Francisco Palau y Quer, Savina Petrilli (Apr. 24), Laura Vicuna (Sept. 3); Joseph Gerard (Sept. 11); Miguel Pro, Giuseppe Benedetto Dusmet, Francisco Faa di Bruno, Junipero Serra, Frederick Jansoone, Josefa Naval Girbes (Sept. 25); Bernardo Maria Silvestrelli, Charles Houben, Honoratus Kozminski (Oct. 16); Niels Stensen (Nicolaus Steno) (Oct. 23); Katherine Drexel, 3 Missionary Martyrs of Ethiopia (Liberato Weiss, Samuel Marzorati, Michele Pio Fasoli) (Nov. 20).

1989: Martin of Saint Nicholas, Melchior of St. Augustine, Mary of Jesus of the Good Shepherd, Maria Margaret Caiani, Maria of Jesus Siedliska, Maria Catherine of St. Augustine (Apr. 23); Victoria Rasoamanarivo (Apr. 30); Bro. Scubilionis (John Bernard Rousseau) (May 2); Elizabeth Renzi, Antonio Lucci (June 17); Niceforo de Jesus y Maria (Vicente Diez Tejerina and 25 Companions, martyred in Spain), Lorenzo Salvi, Gertrude Caterina Comensoli, Francisca Ana Cirer Carbonell (Oct. 1); 7 Martyrs from Thailand (Philip Sipong, Sr. Agnes Phila, Sr. Lucia Khambang, Agatha Phutta,

Cecilia Butsi, Bibiana Khampai, Maria Phon), Timothy Giaccardo, Mother Maria of Jesus Deluil-Martiny (Oct. 22); Giuseppe Baldo (Oct. 31).

1990: 9 Martyrs of Asturias during Spanish Civil War (De la Salle Brothers Cyrill Bertran, Marciano Jose, Julian Alfredo, Victoriano Pio, Benjamin Julian, Augustino Andres, Benito de Jesus, Aniceto Adolfo; and Passionist priest Innocencio Inmaculada), Mercedes Prat, Manuel Barbal Cosan (Brother Jaime), Philip Rinaldi (Apr. 29); Juan Diego (confirmation of Apr. 9 decree), 3 Child Martyrs (Cristobal, Antonio and Juan), Fr. Jose Maria de Yermo y Parres (May 6); Pierre Giorgio Frassati (May 20); Hanibal Maria Di Francia, Joseph Allamano (Oct. 7); Marthe Aimee LeBouteiller, Louise Therese de Montaignac de Chauvance, Maria Schinina, Elisabeth Vendramini (Nov. 4).

1991: Annunciata Cocchetti, Marie Therese Haze, Clara Bosatta (Apr. 21); Jozef Sebastian Pelczar (June 2); Boleslava Lament (June 5); Rafael Chylinski (June 9); Angela Salawa (Aug. 13); Edoardo Giuseppe Rosaz (July 14, Susa, Italy); Pauline of the Heart of Jesus in Agony Visentainer (Oct. 18, Brazil); Adolph Kolping (Oct. 27).

1992: Josephine Bakhita, Josemaria Escriva de Balaguer (May 17); Francesco Spinelli (June 21, Caravaggio, Italy); 17 Irish Martyrs, Rafael Arnáiz Barón, Nazaria Ignacia March Mesa, Léonie Françoise de Sales Aviat, and Maria Josefa Sancho de Guerra (Sept. 27); 122 Martyrs of Spanish Civil War, Narcisa Martillo Morán (Oct. 25); Cristóbal Magellanes and 24 Companions, Mexican martyrs, Maria de Jesús Sacramentado Venegas (Nov. 22).

1993: Dina Belanger (Mar. 20); John Duns Scotus (Mar. 20, cult solemnly recognized); Mary Angela Truszkowska, Ludovico of Casoria, Faustina Kowalska, Paula Montal Fornés (Apr. 18); Stanislaus Kazimierczyk (Apr. 18, cult solemnly recognized); Maurice Tornay, Marie-Louise Trichet, Columba Gabriel and Florida Cevoli (May 16); Giuseppe Marello (Sept. 26); Eleven Martyrs of Almeria, Spain, during Spanish Civil War (2 bishops, 7 brothers, 1 priest, 1 lay person); Victoria Diez y Bustos de Molina, Maria Francesca (Anna Maria) Rubatto; Pedro Castroverde, Maria Crucified (Elisabetta Maria) Satellico (Oct. 10).

1994: Isidore Bakanja, Elizabeth Canori Mora, Dr. Gianna Beretta Molla (Apr. 24); Nicolas Roland, Alberto Hurtado Cruchaga, Maria Rafols, Petra of St. Joseph Perez Florida, Josephine Vannini (Oct. 16); Magdalena Caterina Morano (Nov. 5); Hyacinthe Marie Cormier, Marie Poussepin, Agnes de Jesus Galand, Eugenia Joubert, Claudio Granzotto (Nov. 20).

1995: Peter ToRot (Jan. 17); Mother Mary of the Cross MacKillop (Jan. 19); Joseph Vaz (Jan. 21); Rafael Guizar Valencia, Modestino of Jesus and Mary, Genoveva Torres Morales, Grimoaldo of the Purification (Jan. 29); Johann Nepomuk von Tschiderer (Apr. 30); Maria Helena Stollenwerk, Maria Alvarado Cordozo, Giuseppina Bonino, Maria Domenica Brun Barbantini, Agostino Roscelli (May 7); Damien de Veuster (June 4); 109 Martyrs (64 from French Revolution – Martyrs of La Rochelle – and 45 from Spanish Civil War), Anselm Polanco Fontecha, Felipe Ripoll Morata, Pietro

Casini (Oct. 1); Mary Theresa Scherer, Maria Bernarda Butler, Marguerite Bays (Oct. 29).

1996: Daniel Comboni and Guido Maria Conforti (Mar. 17); Cardinal Alfredo Ildefonso Schuster, O.S.B., Filippo Smaldone and Gennaro Sarnelli (priests) and Candida Maria de Jesus Cipitria y Barriola, Maria Raffaella Cimatti, Maria Antonia Bandres (religious) (May 12); Bernhard Lichtenberg, Karl Leisner (June 23), Wincenty Lewoniuk and 12 Companions, Edmund Rice, Maria Ana Mogas Fontcuberta, Marcelina Darowska (Oct 6); Otto Neururer, Jakob Gapp, Catherine Jarrige (Nov. 24).

1997: Bishop Florentino Asensio Barroso, Sr. Maria Encarnacion Rosal of the Sacred Heart, Fr. Gaetano Catanoso, Fr. Enrico Rebuschini, Ceferino Gimenez Malla, first gypsy beatified (May 4); Bernardina Maria Jablonska, Maria Karlowska (June 6); Frédéric Ozanam (Aug. 22); Bartholomew Mary Dal Monte (Sep. 27); Elías del Socorro Nieves, Domenico Lentini, Giovanni Piamarta, Emilie d'Hooghvorst, Maria Teresa Fasce (Oct. 12); John Baptist Scalabrini, Vilmos Apor, María Vicenta of St. Dorothy Chávez Orozco (Nov. 9).

1998: Bishop Vincent Bossilkov, María Sallés, Brigida of Jesus (Mar. 15); Fr. Cyprian Tansi (Mar. 22); Nimatullah al-Hardini, 11 Spanish nuns (May 10); Secondo Polla (May 23); Giovanni Maria Boccardo, Teresa Grillo Chavez, Teresa Bracco (May 24); Jakob Kern, Maria Restituta Kafka, Anton Schwartz (June 21); Giuseppe Tovini (Sept. 20); Cardinal Alojzije Stepinac (Oct. 3); Antônio de Sant'Anna Galvão, Faustino Miguez, Zeferino Agostini, Mother Theodore Guérin (Oct. 25).

1999: Vicente Soler, and six Augustinian Recollect Companions, Manuel Martin Sierra, Nicolas Barre, Anna Schaeffer (Mar. 7); Padre Pio (May 2); Fr. Stefan Wincenty Frelichowski (June 7); 108 Polish Martyrs, Regina Protmann, Edmund Bojanowski (June 13); Bishop Anton Slomsek (Sept. 19); Ferdinando Maria Baccilieri, Edward Maria Joannes Poppe, Arcangelo Tadini, Mariano da Roccacasale, Diego Oddi, Nicola da Gesturi (Oct. 3).

2000: André de Soveral, Ambrósio Francisco Ferro and 28 Companions, Nicolas Bunkerd Kitbamrung, Maria Stella Mardosewicz and 10 Companions, Pedro Calungsod and Andrew of Phú Yên (March 5); Mariano de Jesus Euse Hoyos, Francis Xavier Seelos, Anna Rosa Gattorno, Maria Elisabetta Hesselblad, Mariam Thresia Chiramel Mankidiyan (Apr. 9); Jacinta and Francisco Marto of Fatima (May 13); Pope Pius IX, Pope John XXIII, Tommaso Reggio, Guillaume-Joseph Chaminade, Columba Marmion (Sept. 3).

2001: José Aparicio Sanz and 232 Companions of the Spanish Civil War (Mar. 11); Manuel Gonzalez Garcia, Marie-Anne Blondin, Caterina Volpicelli, Caterina Cittadini, Carlos Manuel Cecilio Rodriguez Santiago (Apr. 29); George Preca, Ignatius Falzon, Maria Adeodata Pisani (May 9); Abp. Jósef Bilczewski, Fr. Sygmunt Gorazdowski (June 26), Ukrainian Martyrs, Teodor Romza, Omeljan Kovc, Josephata Michaelina Hordashevska (June 27); Ignatius Maloyan, Nikolaus Gross, Alfonso Maria Fusco, Tommaso Maria Fusco, Emilie Tavernier Gamelin, Eugenia

Picco, Maria Euthymia Uffing (Oct. 7); Luigi Beltrame Quattrocchi and Maria Corsini (Oct. 21); Pavol Peter Gojdic, Metod Dominik Trcka, Giovanni Antonio Farina, Bartolomeu Fernandes dos Mártires, Lụigi Tezza, Paolo Manna, Gaetana Sterni, Maria Pilar Izquierdo Albero (Nov. 4).

2002: Gaetano Errico, Lodovico Pavoni, Luigi Variara, Maria del Transito de Jesus Sacramentado, Artemide Zatti, Maria Romero Meneses (Apr. 14); Kamen Vitchev, Pavel Djidjov, Josaphat Chichkov (May 26); Juan Bautista and Jacinto de Los Angeles (Aug. 1); Zygmunt Szczęsny Feliński, Jan

Balicki, Jan Beyzym, Sancja Szymkowiak (Aug. 18); Daudi Okelo, Jildo Irwa, Andrea Giacinto Longhin, O.F.M. Cap., Marcantonio Durando, Marie de la Passion Hélène Marie de Chappotin de Neuville, Liduina Meneguzzi (Oct. 20).

2003: Pierre Bonhomme, María Dolores Rodríguez Sopeña, María Caridad Brader, Juana María Condesa Lluch, László Batthyány-Strattmann (Mar. 23); Eugenia Ravasco, Giacomo Alberione, Giulia Salzano, Marco d'Aviano, Maria Cristina Brando, Maria Domenica Mantovani (Apr. 27); Maria of Jesus Crucified Petkovic (June 6); Ivan Merz (June 22).

ROMAN CURIA

The Roman Curia is the Church's network of central administrative agencies (called dicasteries) serving the Vatican and the local churches, with authority granted by the Pope.

The Curia evolved gradually from advisory assemblies or synods of the Roman clergy with whose assistance the popes directed church affairs during the first 11 centuries. Its original office was the Apostolic Chancery, established in the fourth century to transmit documents. The antecedents of its permanently functioning agencies and offices were special commissions of cardinals and prelates. Its establishment in a form resembling what it is now dates from the second half of the 16th century.

Pope Paul VI initiated a four-year reorganization study in 1963 that resulted in the constitution *Regimini Ecclesiae Universae*. The document was published Aug. 18, 1967, and went into full effect in March 1968. Pope John Paul II, in the apostolic constitution *Pastor Bonus,* published June 28, 1988, and effective Mar. 1, 1989, ordered modifications of the Curia based on the broad outline of Paul VI's reorganization.

In accordance with Pope John Paul II's reform effective Mar. 1, 1989, and later revisions, the Curia consists of the Secretariat of State, nine congregations (governing agencies), three tribunals (judicial agencies), 11 councils (promotional agencies) and three offices (specialized service agencies). All have equal juridical status with authority granted by the pope.

SECRETARIAT OF STATE

The Secretariat of State, *Palazzo Apostolico Vaticano*, Vatican City. Cardinal Angelo Sodano, Secretary of State; Most Rev. Leonardo Sandri, Deputy for General Affairs; Most Rev. Jean-Louis Tauran, Secretary for Relations with States.

The Secretariat of State provides the pope with the closest possible assistance in the care of the universal Church. It consists of two sections:

• The Section for General Affairs assists the pope in expediting daily business of the Holy See. It coordinates curial operations, prepares drafts of documents entrusted to it by the pope, has supervisory duties over the *Acta Apostolicae Sedis, Annuario Pontificio,* the Vatican Press Office and the Central Statistics Office.

• The Section for Relations with States (formerly the Council for Public Affairs of the Church, a separate body) handles diplomatic and other relations with civil governments. Attached to it is a council of Cardinals and Bishops.

Background: Evolved gradually from secretarial offices (dating back to the 15th century) and the Congregation for Extraordinary Ecclesiastical Affairs (dating back to 1793; restructured as the Council for the Public Affairs of the Church by Paul VI in 1967). John Paul II gave it its present form in his June 28, 1988, reform of the Curia.

CONGREGATIONS

Congregation for the Doctrine of the Faith: Piazza del S. Uffizio 11, 00193 Rome, Italy. Cardinal Joseph Ratzinger, prefect; Most Rev. Angelo Amato, S.D.B., secretary.

Has responsibility to safeguard the doctrine of faith and morals. Accordingly, it examines doctrinal questions and promotes studies thereon; evaluates theological opinions and, when necessary and after prior consultation with concerned bishops, reproves those regarded as opposed to principles of the faith; examines books on doctrinal matters and can reprove such works, if the contents so warrant, after giving authors the opportunity to defend themselves. It examines matters pertaining to the Privilege of Faith (Petrine Privilege) in marriage cases, and safeguards the dignity of the sacrament of penance. Attached to the congregation are the Pontifical Biblical Commission and the Theological Commission.

Background: At the beginning of the 13th century, legates of Innocent III were commissioned as the Holy Office of the Inquisition to combat heresy; the same task was entrusted to the Dominican Order by Gregory IX in 1231 and to the Friars Minor by Innocent IV from 1243 to 1254. On July 21, 1542 (apostolic constitution *Licet*), Paul III instituted a permanent congregation of cardinals with supreme and universal competence over matters concerning heretics and those suspected of heresy. Pius IV, St. Pius V and Sixtus V further defined the work of the congregation. St. Pius X changed its name to the Congregation of the Holy Office. Paul VI (*motu proprio Integrae Servandae,* Dec. 7, 1965), began reorganization of the Curia with this body, to which he gave the new title, Congregation for the Doctrine of the Faith. Its orientation is not merely negative, in the condemnation of error, but positive, in the promotion of orthodox doctrine.

Congregation for the Oriental Churches: Palazzo del Bramante, Via della Conciliazione 34, 00193 Rome, Italy. Cardinal Ignace Moussa I Daoud, prefect; Most Rev. Antonio Maria Vegliò, secretary. Members include all patriarchs of the Eastern Catholic Churches and major archbishops.

Has competence in matters concerning the persons and discipline of Eastern Catholic Churches. It has jurisdiction over territories in which the majority of Christians belong to Eastern Churches (i.e., Egypt, the Sinai Peninsula, Eritrea, Northern Ethiopia, Southern Albania, Bulgaria, Cyprus, Greece, Iran, Iraq, Lebanon, Palestine, Syria, Jordan, Turkey, Afghanistan); also, over minority communities of Eastern Church members no matter where they live.

Background: Established by Pius IX Jan. 6, 1862 (apostolic constitution *Romani Pontifices*), and united with the Congregation for the Propagation of the Faith. The congregation was made autonomous by Benedict XV May 1, 1917 (*motu proprio Dei Providentis*), and given wider authority by Pius XI Mar. 25, 1938 (*motu proprio Sancta Dei Ecclesia*).

Congregation for Divine Worship and the Discipline of the Sacraments: Piazza Pio XII 10, 00193 Rome, Italy. Cardinal Francis Arinze, prefect; Most Rev. Domenico Sorrentino, secretary.

Supervises everything pertaining to the promotion and regulation of the liturgy, primarily the sacraments, without prejudice to the competencies of the Congregation for the Doctrine of the Faith. Attached to the congregation are special commissions treating causes of nullity of sacred ordinations and dispensations from obligations of sacred ordination of deacons and priests.

Background: Originally two separate congregations: the Congregation for Divine Worship (instituted by Paul VI, May 8, 1969) and the Congregation for the Discipline of the Sacraments (established by St. Pius X, June 29, 1908, to replace the Congregation of Rites instituted by Pope Sixtus V in 1588). They were united by Paul VI, July 11, 1975, as the Congregation for the Sacraments and Divine Worship; reestablished as separate congregations by John Paul II in an autograph letter of Apr. 5, 1984, and reunited anew by the same Pope, June 28, 1988 (apostolic constitution *Pastor Bonus*), as the Congregation for Divine Worship and the Discipline of the Sacraments.

Congregation for the Causes of Saints: Piazza Pio XII 10, 00193 Rome, Italy. Cardinal José Saraiva Martins, C.F.M., prefect; Most Rev. Edward Nowak, secretary.

Handles matters connected with beatification and canonization causes (in accordance with revised procedures decreed in 1983), and the preservation of relics.

Background: Established by Sixtus V in 1588 as the Congregation of Rites; affected by legislation of Pius XI in 1930; title changed and functions defined by Paul VI, 1969 (apostolic constitution *Sacra Rituum Congregatio*). It was restructured and canonization procedures were revised by John Paul II in 1983 (apostolic constitution *Divinus Perfectionis Magister*).

Congregation for Bishops: Piazza Pio XII 10, 00193 Rome, Italy. Cardinal Giovanni Battista Re, prefect; Most Rev. Francesco Monterisi, secretary.

Has functions related in one way or another to bishops and the jurisdictions in which they serve. It supervises the Pontifical Commission for Latin America. Attached to the congregation are a central coordinating office for Military Vicars (established Feb. 2, 1985) and an office for coordinating *ad limina* visits (established June 29, 1988).

Background: Established by Sixtus V Jan. 22, 1588 (apostolic constitution *Immensa*); given an extension of powers by St. Pius X June 20, 1908, and Pius XII Aug. 1, 1952 (apostolic constitution *Exsul Familia*); given present title (was known as Consistorial Congregation) by Paul VI (Aug. 1, 1967); competencies redefined by John Paul II, June 28, 1988.

Congregation for the Evangelization of Peoples: Piazza di Spagna 48, 00187 Rome, Italy. Cardinal Crescenzio Sepe, prefect; Most Rev. Robert Sarah, secretary; Most Rev. Don Albert Malcolm Ranjith Patabendige, adjunct secretary.

Directs and coordinates missionary work throughout the world. Accordingly, it has competence over those matters which concern all the missions established for the spread of Christ's kingdom without prejudice to the competence of other congregations. These include: fostering missionary vocations; assigning missionaries to fields of work; establishing ecclesiastical jurisdictions and proposing candidates to serve them as bishops and in other capacities; encouraging the recruitment and development of indigenous clergy; mobilizing spiritual and financial support for missionary activity.

To promote missionary cooperation, the congregation has a Supreme Council for the Direction of Pontifical Missionary Works composed of the Missionary Union of the Clergy and Religious, the Society for the Propagation of the Faith, the Society of St. Peter the Apostle for Native Clergy, the Society of the Holy Childhood, and the International Center of Missionary Animation.

Background: Originated as a commission of cardinals by St. Pius V and Gregory XII for missions in East and West Indies, Italo-Greeks and for ecclesiastical affairs in Protestant territories of Europe; Clement VIII instituted a Congregation of the Propagation of the Faith in 1599 which ceased to exist after several years. Erected as a stable congregation by Gregory XV June 22, 1622 (apostolic constitution *Inscrutabili Divinae*); its functions were redefined by John Paul II, June 28, 1988.

Congregation for the Clergy: Piazza Pio XII 3, 00193 Rome, Italy. Cardinal Darío Castrillón Hoyos, prefect; Most Rev. Csaba Ternyák, secretary.

Has three offices with competencies concerning the life, discipline, rights and duties of the clergy; the preaching of the Word, catechetics, norms for religious education of children and adults; preservation and administration of the temporal goods of the Church. Attached to it are the International Council for Catechetics (established in 1973 by Paul VI) and the Institute *Sacrum Ministerium* for the permanent formation of the clergy (established in line with John Paul II's 1992 apostolic exhortation *Pastores Dabo Vobis*).

Background: Established by Pius IV Aug. 2, 1564 (apostolic constitution *Alias Nos*), under the title Congregation of the Cardinals Interpreters of the Council of Trent; affected by legislation of Gregory XIII and Sixtus V; known as Congregation of the Council until Aug. 15, 1967, when Paul VI renamed it the Congregation for the Clergy and redefined its competency; John Paul II gave it added responsibilities June 28, 1988.

Congregation for Institutes of Consecrated Life and Societies of Apostolic Life: Piazza Pio XII 3, 00193 Rome, Italy. Cardinal Eduardo Martinez Somalo, prefect; Most. Rev. Piergiorgio Silvano Nesti, C.P., secretary.

Has competence over institutes of Religious, secular institutes, societies of the apostolic life and third (secular) orders. With two sections, the congregation has authority in matters related to the establishment, general direction and suppression of the various institutes; general discipline in line with their rules and constitutions; the movement toward renewal and adaptation of institutes in contemporary circumstances; the setting up and encouragement of councils and conferences of major religious superiors for intercommunication and other purposes.

Background: Founded by Sixtus V May 27, 1586, with the title, Congregation for Consultations of Regulars; confirmed by the apostolic constitution *Immensa* Jan. 22, 1588; made part of the Congregation for Consultations of Bishops and other Prelates in 1601; made autonomous by St. Pius X in 1908 as Congregation of Religious; title changed to Congregation for Religious and Secular Institutes by Paul VI in 1967; given present title by John Paul II, June 28, 1988.

Congregation for Catholic Education (for Seminaries and Institutes of Study): Piazza Pio XII 3, 00193 Rome, Italy. Cardinal Zenon Grocholewski, prefect; Most Rev. Giuseppe Pittau, S.J., secretary.

Has supervisory competence over institutions and works of Catholic education. It carries on its work through three offices. One office handles matters connected with the direction, discipline and temporal administration of seminaries, and with the education of diocesan clergy, religious and members of secular institutes. A second office oversees Catholic universities, faculties of study and other institutions of higher learning inasmuch as they depend on the authority of the Church; encourages cooperation and mutual assistance among Catholic institutions, and the establishment of Catholic hospices and centers on campuses of non-Catholic institutions. A third office is concerned in various ways with all Catholic schools below the college-university level, with general questions concerning education and studies, and with the cooperation of conferences of bishops and civil authorities in educational matters. The congregation supervises Pontifical Works for Priestly Vocations.

Background: The title (Congregation of Seminaries and Universities) and functions of the congregation were defined by Benedict XV Nov. 4, 1915; Pius XI, in 1931 and 1932, and Pius XII, in 1941 and 1949, extended its functions; Paul VI changed its title to Congregation for Catholic Education in 1967; given its present title by Pope John Paul II, June 28, 1988. Its work had previously been carried on by two other congregations erected by Sixtus V in 1588 and Leo XII in 1824.

Inter-Agency Curia Commissions

In accordance with provisions of the apostolic constitution *Pastor Bonus,* John Paul II established the following interdepartmental permanent commissions to handle matters when more than one agency of the Curia is involved in activities:

• For matters concerning appointments to local Churches and the setting up and alteration of them and their constitution (Mar. 22, 1989). Members include officials of the Secretariat of State and Congregation for Bishops. President, Cardinal Angelo Sodano, Secretary of State.

• For matters concerning members, individually or as a community, of Institutes of Consecrated Life founded or working in mission territories (Mar. 22, 1989). Members include officials of the Congregations for the Evangelization of Peoples and for Institutes of Consecrated Life and Societies of Apostolic Life. President, Cardinal Crescenzio Sepe, prefect of the Congregation for the Evangelization of Peoples.

• For the formation of candidates for Sacred Orders (Mar. 22, 1989). Members include officials of the Congregations for Catholic Education, for Institutes of Consecrated Life and Societies of Apostolic Life, for Evangelization of Peoples, for Oriental Churches. President, Cardinal Zenon Grocholewski, prefect of the Congregation for Catholic Education.

• For promoting a more equitable distribution of priests throughout the world (July 20, 1991). Members include secretaries of congregations for Evangelization of Peoples, for the Clergy, Catholic Education, for the Institutes of Consecrated Life and Societies of Apostolic Life; and vice-president of Commission for Latin America. President, Card. Zenon Grocholewski, Prefect of the Congregation for Catholic Education.

• For the Church in Eastern Europe (Jan. 15, 1993), replacing the Pontifical Commission for Russia which was terminated. The commission is concerned with both Latin and Eastern-rite churches in territories of the former Soviet Union and other nations affected by the historical circumstances resulting from atheistic communism. It is responsible for promoting the apostolic mission of the Church and fostering ecumenical dialogue with the Orthodox and other Churches of the Eastern tradition. Members, under presidency of Cardinal Secretary of State, include the secretary and undersecretary of the Section for Relations with States and secretaries of Congregations for the Oriental Churches, for the Clergy, for Institutes of Consecrated Life and Societies of Apostolic Life, secretary of the Pontifical Council for Promoting Christian Unity. President, Cardinal Angelo Sodano.

TRIBUNALS

Apostolic Penitentiary: Piazza della Cancelleria 1, 00186 Rome, Italy. Most Rev. Luigi de Magistris, major penitentiary; regent, Rev. P. Gianfranco Girotti, O.F.M. Conv.

Has jurisdiction for the internal forum only (sacramental and non-sacramental). It issues decisions on questions of conscience; grants absolutions, dispensations, commutations, sanations and condonations; has charge of non-doctrinal matters pertaining to indulgences.

Background: Origin dates back to the 12th century; affected by the legislation of many popes; radically reorganized by St. Pius V in 1569; jurisdiction limited to the internal forum by St. Pius X; Benedict XV annexed the Office of Indulgences to it Mar. 25, 1917.

Apostolic Signatura: Piazza della Cancelleria 1,

00186 Rome, Italy. Cardinal Mario Francesco Pompedda, prefect; Most Rev. Francesco Saverio Salerno, secretary.

The principal concerns of this supreme court of the Church are to resolve questions concerning juridical procedure and to supervise the observance of laws and rights at the highest level. It decides the jurisdictional competence of lower courts and has jurisdiction in cases involving personnel and decisions of the Rota. It is the supreme court of the State of Vatican City.

Background: A permanent office of the Signatura has existed since the time of Eugene IV in the 15th century; affected by the legislation of many popes; reorganized by St. Pius X in 1908 and made the supreme tribunal of the Church.

Roman Rota: Piazza della Cancelleria 1, 00186 Rome, Italy. Msgr. Raffaello Funghini, Dean.

The ordinary court of appeal for cases appealed to the Holy See. It is best known for its competence and decisions in cases involving the validity of marriage.

Background: Originated in the Apostolic Chancery; affected by the legislation of many popes; reorganized by St. Pius X in 1908; further revised by Pius XI in 1934; new norms approved and promulgated by John Paul II in 1982 and 1987.

PONTIFICAL COUNCILS

Pontifical Council for the Laity: Piazza S. Calisto 16, 00153 Rome, Italy. Cardinal James Francis Stafford, president; Most Rev. Stanislaw Rylko, secretary; Prof. Guzman Carriquiry, undersecretary.

Its competence covers the apostolate of the laity and their participation in the life and mission of the Church. Members are mostly lay people from different parts of the world and involved in different apostolates.

Background: Established on an experimental basis by Paul VI Jan. 6, 1967; given permanent status Dec. 10, 1976 (*motu proprio Apostolatus Peragendi*).

Pontifical Council for Promoting Christian Unity: Via dell' Erba 1, 00193 Rome, Italy. Cardinal Walter Kasper, president; Most Rev. Brian Farrell, L.C., secretary.

Handles relations with members of other Christian ecclesial communities; deals with the correct interpretation and execution of the principles of ecumenism; initiates or promotes Catholic ecumenical groups and coordinates on national and international levels the efforts of those promoting Christian unity; undertakes dialogue regarding ecumenical questions and activities with churches and ecclesial communities separated from the Apostolic See; sends Catholic observer-representatives to Christian gatherings, and invites to Catholic gatherings observers of other churches; orders into execution conciliar decrees dealing with ecumenical affairs. The **Commission for Religious Relations with the Jews** is attached to the secretariat.

Background: Established by John XXIII June 5, 1960, as a preparatory secretariat of the Second Vatican Council; raised to commission status during the first session of the council in the fall of 1962; status as a secretariat confirmed and functions defined by Paul VI in 1966 and 1967; made a pontifical council by John Paul II, June 28, 1988.

Pontifical Council for the Family: Piazza S. Calisto

16, 00153 Rome, Italy. Cardinal Alfonso López Trujillo, president; Most Rev. Karl Josef Romer, secretary.

Is concerned with promoting the pastoral care of families so they may carry out their educative, evangelizing and apostolic mission and make their influence felt in areas such as defense of human life and responsible procreation according to the teachings of the Church. Members, chosen by the Pope, are married couples and men and women from all parts of the world and representing different cultures. They meet in general assembly at least once a year.

Background: Instituted by John Paul II May 9, 1981, replacing the Committee for the Family established by Paul VI Jan. 11, 1973.

Pontifical Council for Justice and Peace: Piazza S. Calisto 16, 00153 Rome, Italy. Most Rev. Renato Raffaele Martino, president; Most Rev. Giampaolo Crepaldi, secretary.

Its primary competence is to promote justice and peace in the world according to the Gospels and social teaching of the Church.

Background: Instituted by Paul VI Jan. 6, 1967, on an experimental basis; reconstituted and made a permanent commission Dec. 10, 1976; its competence was redefined and it was made a pontifical council June 28, 1988, by John Paul II.

Pontifical Council "Cor Unum": Piazza S. Calisto 16, 00153 Rome, Italy. Most Rev. Paul Josef Cordes, president; secretary, Msgr. Karel Kasteel.

Its principal aims are to provide informational and coordinating services for Catholic aid and human development organizations and projects on a worldwide scale. Attached to the council are the John Paul II Foundation for the Sahel and *"Populorum Progressio."*

Background: Instituted by Paul VI July 15, 1971.

Pontifical Council for Pastoral Care of Migrants and Itinerant Peoples: Piazza S. Calisto 16, 00153 Rome, Italy. Most Rev. Stephen Fumio Hamao president; Most Rev. Agostino Marchetto, secretary.

Is concerned with pastoral assistance to migrants, nomads, tourists, sea, and air travelers.

Background: Instituted by Paul VI and placed under general supervision of Congregation for Bishops, Mar. 19, 1970; made autonomous as a pontifical council and renamed by John Paul II, June 28, 1988.

Pontifical Council for Pastoral Assistance to Health Care Workers: Via della Conciliazione 3, 00193 Rome, Italy. Most Rev. Javier Lozano Barragán, president; Most Rev. José Luis Redrado Marchite, O.H., secretary.

Its functions are to stimulate and foster the work of formation, study and action carried out by various international Catholic organizations in the health care field.

Background: Established in 1985 as a commission by John Paul II; made a council June 28, 1988.

Pontifical Council for the Interpretation of Legislative Texts: Piazza Pio XII 10, 00193 Rome, Italy. Most Rev. Julián Herranz, president; Most Rev. Bruno Bertagna, secretary.

Primary function is the authentic interpretation of the universal laws of the Church.

Background: Established by John Paul II, Jan. 2, 1984, as the Pontifical Commission for the Authentic Interpretation of the Code of Canon Law; name changed and given additional functions June 28, 1988.

Its competency was extended in 1991 to include interpretation of Code of Canon Law of Oriental Church that was promulgated in 1990.

Pontifical Council for Interreligious Dialogue: Via dell' Erba 1, 00193 Rome, Italy. Most Rev. Michael Louis Fitzgerald, M. Afr., president; Most Rev. Pier Luigi Celata, secretary.

Its function is to promote studies and dialogue for the purpose of increasing mutual understanding and respect between Christians and non-Christians. The Commission for Religious Relations with Muslims is attached to the council.

Background: Established by Paul VI May 19, 1964, as the Secretariat for Non-Christians; given present title and functions by John Paul II, June 28, 1988.

Pontifical Council for Culture: Piazza S. Calisto 16, 00153 Rome, Italy. Cardinal Paul Poupard, president; Very Rev. Bernard Ardura, O. Praem., secretary.

Its functions are to foster the Church's and the Holy See's relations with the world of culture and to establish dialogue with those who do not believe in God or who profess no religion provided these are open to sincere cooperation. It consists of two sections: (1) faith and culture; (2) dialogue with cultures. Attached to it is the **Coordinating Council for Pontifical Academies.**

Background: Present council with expanded functions was instituted by John Paul II (*motu proprio* of Mar. 25, 1993) through the merger of the Pontifical Council for Culture (established May 20, 1982, by John Paul II) and the Pontifical Council for Dialogue with Non-Believers (established by Paul VI Apr. 9, 1965, as the secretariat for Non-Believers).

Pontifical Council for Social Communications: Palazzo S. Carlo, 00120 Vatican City. Most Rev. John P. Foley, president; Most Rev. Pierfranco Pastore, secretary.

Engaged in matters pertaining to instruments of social communication so that through them the message of salvation and human progress is fostered and carried forward in civil culture and mores.

Background: Instituted on an experimental basis by Pius XII in 1948; reorganized three times in the 1950s; made permanent commission by John XXIII Feb. 22, 1959; established as council and functions restated by John Paul II June 28, l988.

OFFICES

Apostolic Camera: Palazzo Apostolico, 00120 Vatican City. Cardinal Eduardo Martinez Somalo, chamberlain of the Holy Roman Church; Most Rev. Ettore Cunial, vice-chamberlain.

Administers the temporal goods and rights of the Holy See between the death of one pope and the election of another (*sede vacante*), in accordance with special laws.

Background: Originated in the 11th century; reorganized by Pius XI in 1934; functions redefined (especially of *camerlengo*) by subsequent legislation in 1945, 1962 and 1975.

Administration of the Patrimony of the Apostolic See: Palazzo Apostolico, 00120 Vatican City. Most Rev. Attilio Nicora, president; Most Rev. Claudio Maria Celli, secretary.

Handles the estate of the Apostolic See under the direction of papal delegates acting ith ordinary or extraordinary authorization.

Background: Some of its functions date back to 1878; established by Paul VI Aug. 15, 1967.

Prefecture for the Economic Affairs of the Holy See: Largo del Colonnato 3, 00193 Rome, Italy. Cardinal Sergio Sebastiani, president; Most Rev. Franco Croci, secretary.

A financial office that coordinates and supervises administration of the temporalities of the Holy See. Membership includes Cardinal Roger M. Mahony and Cardinal Edward Egan.

Background: Established by Paul VI Aug. 15, 1967; functions redefined by John Paul II, June 28, 1988.

Other Curia Agencies

Prefecture of the Papal Household: Most Rev. James M. Harvey, prefect; Most Rev. Stanislaw Dziwisz, adjunct-prefect.

Oversees the papal chapel — which is at the service of the pope in his capacity as spiritual head of the Church, and the pontifical family — which is at the service of the pope as a sovereign. It arranges papal audiences, has charge of preparing non-liturgical elements of papal ceremonies, makes all necessary arrangements for papal visits and trips outside the Vatican, and settles questions of protocol connected with papal audiences and other formalities.

Background: Established by Paul VI Aug. 15, 1967, under the title Prefecture of the Apostolic Palace; it supplanted the Sacred Congregation for Ceremonies founded by Sixtus V Jan. 22, 1588. The office was updated and reorganized under the present title by Paul VI, Mar. 28, 1968.

Office for Liturgical Celebrations of the Supreme Pontiff: Palazzo Apostolico Vaticano, 00120 Vatican City. Most Rev. Piero Marini, Master of Ceremonies.

Prepares everything necessary for liturgical and other sacred celebrations by the Pope or in his name; directs everything in accordance with prescriptions of liturgical law.

Background: Evolved gradually from the early office of Apostolic Master of Ceremonies; affected by legislation of Pope Paul IV in 1563 and Benedict XV in 1917; restructured by Paul VI in 1967; given its present title (formerly known as Prefecture of Pontifical Ceremonies) and constituted as an autonomous agency of the Roman Curia by John Paul II, June 28, 1988.

Vatican Press Office: Via della Conciliazione 54, 00120 Vatican City. Joaquin Navarro-Valls, director.

Established Feb. 29, 1968, to replace service agencies formerly operated by *L'Osservatore Romano* and an office created for press coverage of the Second Vatican Council. New directives were issued in 1986.

Vatican Information Service (VIS): Via della Conciliazione 54, 00120 Vatican City.

Established Mar. 28, 1990, within the framework but distinct from the Vatican Press Office. Furnishes information, in English, French and Spanish, on pastoral and magisterial activity of the Pope through use of electronic mail and fax.

Central Statistics Office: Palazzo Apostolico, 00120 Vatican City.

Established by Paul VI Aug. 15, 1967; attached to the Secretariat of State. Compiles, systematizes and analyzes information on the status and condition of the Church.

COMMISSIONS AND COMMITTEES

Listed below are non-curial institutes that assist in the work of the Holy See. Some are attached to curial agencies, as indicated. Other institutes are listed elsewhere in the *Almanac*; see *Index*.

Pontifical Commission for the Cultural Heritage of the Church: Established by John Paul II, June 28, 1988, as Pontifical Commission for Preserving the Church's Patrimony of Art and History and attached to the Congregation for the Clergy; made autonomous and given present title Mar. 25, 1993. Most Rev. Francesco Marchisano, president.

Pontifical Commission for Sacred Archeology: Instituted by Pius IX Jan, 6, 1852. Most Rev. Francesco Marchisano, president.

Pontifical Biblical Commission: Instituted by Leo XIII Oct. 30, 1902; completely restructured by Paul VI June 27, 1971; attached to the Congregation for the Doctrine of the Faith. Cardinal Joseph Ratzinger, president.

Pontifical Commission for Latin America: Instituted by Pius XII Apr. 19, 1958; attached to the Congregation for Bishops July, 1969; restructured by John Paul II in 1988. Cardinal Giovanni Battista Re, president.

Pontifical Commission for the Revision and Emendation of the Vulgate: Established in 1984 by John Paul II to replace the Abbey of St. Jerome instituted by Pius XI in 1933. Rev. Jean Mallet, O.S.B., director.

Pontifical Commission "*Ecclesia Dei*": Established by John Paul II, July 2, 1988, to facilitate the return to full ecclesial communion of priests, seminarians and religious who belonged to the fraternity founded by Marcel Lefebvre. Cardinal Darío Castrillón Hoyos, president.

International Theological Commission: Instituted by Paul VI Apr. 11, 1969, as an advisory adjunct of no more than 30 theologians to the Congregation for the Doctrine of the Faith; definitive statutes promulgated by John Paul II, Aug. 6, 1982. Cardinal Joseph Ratzinger, president; Rev. Georges Cottier, O.P., general secretary.

Commission for Religious Relations with the Jews: Instituted by Paul VI, Oct. 22, 1974, to promote and foster relations of a religious nature between Jews and Christians; attached to the Council for Promoting Christian Unity. Cardinal Walter Kasper, president.

Commission for Religious Relations with Muslims: Instituted by Paul VI, Oct. 22, 1974, to promote, regulate and interpret relations between Catholics and Muslims; attached to the Council for Interreligious Dialogue. Most Rev. Michael Louis Fitzgerald, M.Afr., president.

Pontifical Committee for International Eucharistic Congresses: Instituted, 1879, by Pope Leo XIII; established as a pontifical committee with new statutes by John Paul II, Feb. 11, 1986. Card. Jozef Tomko, president.

Pontifical Committee for Historical Sciences: Instituted by Pius XII Apr. 7, 1954, as a continuation of a commission dating from 1883. Msgr. Walter Brandmüller, president.

Vatican II Archives: Preserves the documents of the Second Vatican Council.

Disciplinary Commission of the Roman Curia: Most Rev. Julián Herranz, president.

Commission for the Protection of the Historical and Artistic Monuments of the Holy See: Instituted by Pius XI in 1923, reorganized by Paul VI in 1963. Most Rev. Francesco Marchisano, president.

Institute for Works of Religion: Instituted by Pius XII June 27, 1942, to bank and administer funds for works of religion; replaced an earlier administration established by Leo XIII in 1887; reorganized by John Paul II (chirograph of Mar. 1, 1990). Headed by a commission of cardinals, including Cardinal Angelo Sodano and Cardinal Adam Maida.

Fabric of St. Peter: Administration, care and preservation of Vatican Basilica. Abp. Francesco Marchisano, Archpriest of the Patriarchal Vatican Basilica, president.

Office of Papal Charities (Apostolic Almoner): Distributes alms and aid to those in need in the name of the pope. Most Rev. Oscar Rizzato, almoner.

Labor Office of the Apostolic See (ULSA - *Ufficio del Lavoro della Sede Apostolica*): Has competence in regard to those who work for the Apostolic See; charged with settling labor issues. Instituted by John Paul II (*motu proprio* of Jan. 1, 1989); functions reaffirmed and definitive text of statutes approved by John Paul II (*motu proprio* of Sept. 30, 1994). Cardinal Jan Schotte, C.I.C.M., president.

Internationalization

As of May 15, 2003, principal officials of the Roman Curia were from the following countries: Italy (Cards. Antonetti, Cacciavillan, Cheli, Fagiolo, Felici, Laghi, Monduzzi, Nicora, Noè, Pompedda,Ré, Sebastiani, Sepe, Silvestrini, Sodano; Abps. Amato, Celli, Crepaldi, Cunial, de Magistris, Marchetto, Marchisano, Martino, Monterisi, Nesti, Pompedda, Salerno, Sandri, Tamburinno, Vegliò; Bps. Bertagna, Marini, Pastore); France (Cards. Etchegaray, Poupard, Abp. Tauran); United States (Cards. Baum, Stafford, Szoka, Abps. Foley, Bp. Harvey); Spain (Card. Martinez Somalo; Abps. Gil Hellín, Herranz, Redrado Marchite); Argentina (Card. Mejía); Germany (Cards. Kasper, Ratzinger, Bp. Cordes); Poland (Card. Grocholewski, Abps. Nowak, Rylko, Bp. Dziwisz); Belgium (Card. Schotte); Brazil (Abp. Agnelo, Romer); Chile (Card. Medina Estévez); Colombia (Cards. Castrillón Hoyos, Lopez Trujillo); England (Abp. Fitzgerald); French Guinea (Abp. Sarah); Hungary (Ternyák); Mexico (Abp. Lozano Barrágan); Nigeria (Card. Arinze); Portugal (Card. Saraiva Martins); Ireland (Abp. Farrell); Slovakia (Card. Tomko); Sri Lanka (Abp. Ranjith); Switzerland (Card. Agustoni); Syria (Card. Moussa I Daoud); Ukraine (Abp. Marusyn); Vietnam (Card. Nguyên Van Thuân); Japan (Abp. Hamao).

VATICAN CITY STATE

The State of Vatican City (*Stato della Città del Vaticano*) is the territorial seat of the papacy. The smallest sovereign state in the world, it is situated within the city of Rome, embraces an area of 108.7

acres, and includes within its limits the Vatican Palace, museums, art galleries, gardens, libraries, radio station, post office, bank, astronomical observatory, offices, apartments, service facilities, St. Peter's Basilica, and neighboring buildings between the Basilica and Viale Vaticano. The extraterritorial rights of Vatican City extend to more than 10 buildings in Rome, including the major basilicas and office buildings of various congregations of the Roman Curia, and to the papal villas at **Castel Gandolfo** 15 miles southeast of the City of Rome. Castel Gandolfo is the summer residence of the Holy Father.

The government of Vatican City is in the hands of the reigning pope, who has full executive, legislative and judicial power. The administration of affairs, however, is handled by the **Pontifical Commission for the State of Vatican City** under Cardinal Edmund Casimir Szoka. The legal system is based on Canon Law; in cases where this code does not obtain, the laws of the City of Rome apply. The City is an absolutely neutral state and enjoys all the rights and privileges of a sovereign power. The citizens of Vatican City, and they alone, owe allegiance to the pope as a temporal head of state. On November 26, 2000, Pope John Paul II promulgated the new Fundamental Law of the Vatican City State. The new law replaced that first established in 1929 by Pope Pius XI.

Cardinals of the Roman Curia residing outside Vatican City enjoy the privileges of extraterritoriality. The Secretary General for the Governatorate of the Vatican City State is Most. Rev. Gianni Danzi.

The normal population is approximately 1,000. While the greater percentage is made up of priests and religious, there are several hundred laypersons living in Vatican City. They are housed in their own apartments in the City and are engaged in secretarial, domestic, trade and service occupations. Approximately 3,400 laypersons are employed by the Vatican.

Services of honor and order are performed by the Swiss Guards, who have been charged with responsibility for the personal safety of popes since 1506. The current Captain of the Swiss Guards is Elmar Theodor Mäder, who was appointed on November 9, 2002. Additional police and ceremonial functions are under the supervision of a special office. These functions were formerly handled by the Papal Gendarmes, the Palatine Guard of Honor, and the Guard of Honor of the Pope (Pontifical Noble Guard); the units were disbanded by Pope Paul VI on Sept. 14, 1970.

The **Basilica of St. Peter**, built between 1506 and 1626, is the largest church in Christendom (with the exception of the Basilica of Our Lady Queen of Peace in Ivory Coast) and the site of most papal ceremonies. The pope's own patriarchal basilica, however, is St. John Lateran, whose origins date back to 324.

St. Ann's, staffed by Augustinian Fathers, is the parish church of Vatican City. Its pastor is appointed by the pope, following the recommendation of the prior general of the Augustinians and the archpriest of the Vatican Basilica.

The Church of **Santa Susanna** was designated as the national church for Americans in Rome by Pope Benedict XV Jan. 10, 1922, and entrusted to the Paulist Fathers, who have served there continuously since then except for several years during World War II.

Pastoral care in Vatican City State, which is separate from the diocese of Rome, is entrusted to the archpriest of St. Peter's Basilica, who is also vicar general for Vatican City and the papal villas at Castel Gandolfo (chirograph of Pope John Paul II, Jan. 14, 1991). Abp. Francesco Marchisano was appointed to the posts in April 2002. He succeeded Cardinal Virgilio Noè, who had held the posts since 1991.

The Vatican Library (00120 Vatican City; Rev. Raffaele Farina, S.D.B., prefect; Dr. Ambrogio Piazzoni, vice-prefect) has among its holdings 150,000 manuscripts, about 1,000,000 printed books, and 7,500 incunabula. The **Vatican Secret Archives** (00120 Vatican City; Rev. Sergio Pagano, prefect), opened to scholars by Leo XIII in 1881, contain central church documents dating back to the time of Innocent III (1198-1216). Cardinal Jorge María Mejía is librarian and archivist of the Holy Roman Church.

The independent temporal power of the pope, which is limited to the confines of Vatican City and small areas outside, was for many centuries more extensive than it is now. As late as the 19th century, the pope ruled 16,000 square miles of Papal States across the middle of Italy, with a population of over 3,000,000. In 1870 forces of the Kingdom of Italy occupied these lands that, with the exception of the small areas surrounding the Vatican and Lateran in Rome and the Villas of Castel Gandolfo, became part of the Kingdom by the Italian law of May 13, 1871.

The **Roman Question**, occasioned by this seizure and the voluntary confinement of the pope to the Vatican, was settled with ratification of the Lateran Agreement June 7, 1929, by the Italian government and Vatican City. The agreement recognized Catholicism as the religion of Italy and provided, among other things, a financial indemnity to the Vatican in return for the former Papal States; it became Article 7 of the Italian Constitution, Mar. 26, 1947. The Lateran Agreement was superseded by a new concordat given final approval by the Italian Chamber of Deputies Mar. 20 and formally ratified June 3, 1985.

Papal Flag

The papal flag consists of two equal vertical stripes of yellow and white, charged with the insignia of the papacy on the white stripe — triple crown or tiara over two crossed keys, one of gold and one of silver, tied with a red cord and two tassels. The divisions of the crown represent the teaching, sanctifying and ruling offices of the pope. The keys symbolize his jurisdictional authority.

The papal flag is a national flag inasmuch as it is the standard of the Supreme Pontiff as the sovereign of the state of Vatican City. It is also universally accepted by the faithful as a symbol of the supreme spiritual authority of the Holy Father.

Vatican Radio

The declared purpose of Vatican radio station HVJ is "that the voice of the Supreme Pastor may be heard throughout the world by means of the ether waves, for the glory of Christ and the salvation of souls." Designed by Guglielmo Marconi, the inventor of radio, and supervised by him until his death, the station was inaugurated by Pope Pius XI in 1931. The original purpose has been extended to a wide variety of programming.

Vatican Radio operates on international wave lengths, transmits programs in 37 languages, and serves as a channel of communication between the Vatican, church officials and listeners in general in many parts of the world. The station broadcasts about 400 hours a week throughout the world.

The daily English-language program for North America is broadcast on 6095, 7305, 9600 Khz as well as via satellite INTELSAT 325,5° East (Atlantic) — 4097.75 Mhz — LHCP polarization.

Frequencies, background information and audio files can be obtained at www.wrn.org/vatican-radio and www.vatican.va.

The staff of 415 broadcasters and technicians includes 30 Jesuits. Studios and offices are at Palazzo Pio, Piazza Pia, 3, 00193 Rome. The transmitters are situated at Santa Maria di Galeria, a short distance north of Rome. Cardinal Roberto Tucci, S.J., president; Rev. Pasquale Borgomeo, S.J., director-general.

2003 Vatican Stamps and Coins

The Vatican Philatelic and Numismatic Office (00120 Vatican City) scheduled the following issues of stamps and coins for the Year 2003:

Stamps

• 25th Year of the Pontificate of His Holiness John Paul II.
• The Masterpieces of Art in the Vatican City: the restored "Niccolina Chapel."
• Europa 2003: The Posters.
• Great Painters of the XIX century: Paul Gauguin and Vincent van Gogh.
• XVII Centenary of the Death of St. George (27-303).
• St. Josemaría Escrivá de Balaguer.
• The Animal Creatures of God: Their Presence in the Vatican Basilica.
• The Journeys of His Holiness Pope John Paul II in the World.
• Holy Christmas.

Postal Stationery

Aerogram
Postcards

Publications

Vaticano 2003

Coins

• Series for XXV year (2003) of the Pontificate of John Paul II; in eight values (1, 2, 5, 10, 20, 50 Eurocent, 1 Euro and 2 Euro). Minting: B.U. and Mirror Proof (with a Silver Medal).
• First Silver Celebrative Coin — 5 euro. Subject: Year of the Rosary.
• Second Silver Celebrative Coin — 10 euro. Subject: XXV Year of the Pontificate of His Holiness John Paul II.
• Two Celebrative Gold Coins. Subject: the Roots of the Faith. 20 euro — The Birth of Moses; 50 euro — Moses Receives the Ten Commandments.

Papal Audiences

General audiences are scheduled weekly, on Wednesday.

In Vatican City, they are held in the Audience Hall on the south side of St. Peter's Basilica or, weather permitting, in St. Peter's Square. The hall, which was opened in 1971, has a seating capacity of 6,800 and a total capacity of 12,000. Audiences have been held during the summer at Castel Gandolfo when the pope is there on a working vacation.

General audiences last from about 60 to 90 minutes, during which the pope gives a talk and his blessing. A résumé of the talk, which is usually in Italian, is given in several languages. Arrangements for papal audiences are handled by an office of the Prefecture of the Apostolic Household.

American visitors can obtain passes for general audiences by applying to the Bishops' Office for United States Visitors to the Vatican, Casa Santa Maria, Via dell'Umilita, 30, 00187 Rome. Private and group audiences are reserved for dignitaries of various categories and for special occasions.

Publications

Acta Apostolicae Sedis, 00120 Vatican City: The only "official commentary" of the Holy See, was established in 1908 for the publication of activities of the Holy See, laws, decrees and acts of congregations and tribunals of the Roman Curia. The first edition was published in Jan. 1909. St. Pius X made *AAS* an official organ in 1908. Laws promulgated for the Church ordinarily take effect three months after the date of their publication in this commentary. The publication, mostly in Latin, is printed by the Vatican Press. The immediate predecessor of this organ was *Acta Sanctae Sedis,* founded in 1865 and given official status by the Congregation for the Propagation of the Faith in 1904.

Annuario Pontificio, 00120 Vatican City: The yearbook of the Holy See. It is edited by the Central Statistics Office of the Church and is printed in Italian, with some portions in other languages, by the Vatican Press. It covers the worldwide organization of the Church, lists members of the hierarchy, and includes a wide range of statistical information. The publication of a statistical yearbook of the Holy See dates back to 1716, when a volume called *Notizie* appeared. Publication under the present title began in 1860, was suspended in 1870, and resumed again in 1872 under the title *Catholic Hierarchy*. This volume was printed privately at first, but has been issued by the Vatican Press since 1885. The title *Annuario Pontificio* was restored in 1912, and the yearbook was called an "official publication" until 1924.

L'Osservatore Romano, Via del Pellegrino, 00120 Vatican City: The daily newspaper of the Holy See. It began publication July 1, 1861, as an independent enterprise under the ownership and direction of four Catholic laymen headed by Marcantonio Pacelli, vice minister of the interior under Pope Pius IX and a grandfather of the late Pius XII. Leo XIII bought the publication in 1890, making it the "pope's" own newspaper.

The only official material in *L'Osservatore Romano* is what appears under the heading, *"Nostre Informazioni."* This includes notices of appointments by the Holy See, the texts of papal encyclicals and addresses by the Holy Father and others, various types of documents, accounts of decisions and rulings of administrative bodies, and similar items. Additional material includes news and comment on developments in the Church and the world. Italian is the language most used. The editorial board is directed by Prof. Mario Agnes. A staff of about 15 reporters covers Rome news sources. A corps of correspondents provides foreign coverage.

A weekly roundup edition in English was inaugurated in 1968 (Fr. Paul S. Quinter is editor). Other weekly editions are printed in French (1949), Italian (1950), Spanish (1969), Portuguese (1970) and German (1971). The Polish edition (1980) is published monthly. *L'Osservatore della Domenica* is published weekly as a supplement to the Sunday issue of the daily edition.

Vatican Television Center (*Centro Televisivo Vaticano*, CTV), Palazzo Belvedere, 00120 Vatican City: Instituted by John Paul II Oct. 23, 1983, with the rescript, *Ex Audentia*. Dr. Emilio Rossi is president of the administrative council.

Vatican Press, 00120 Vatican City: The official printing plant of the Vatican. The Vatican press was conceived by Marcellus II and Pius IV but was actually founded by Sixtus V on Apr. 27, 1587, to print the Vulgate and the writings of the Fathers of the Church and other authors. A Polyglot Press was established in 1626 by the Congregation for the Propagation of the Faith to serve the needs of the Oriental council. St. Pius X merged both presses under the title Vatican Polyglot Press. It was renamed Vatican Press July 1, 1991, by John Paul II following restructuring. The plant has facilities for the printing of a wide variety of material in about 30 languages. Dir., Rev. Elio Torrigiani, S.D.B.

Vatican Publishing House (*Libreria Editrice***

Vaticana), Piazza S. Pietro, 00120 Vatican City: Formerly an office of the Vatican Press to assist in the circulation of the liturgical and juridical publications of the Apostolic See, the congregations and later the *Acta Apostolicae Sedis*. In 1926, with the expansion of publishing activities and following the promulgation of the 1917 Code, the office was made an independent entity. An administrative council and editorial commission were instituted in 1983; in 1988 *Pastor Bonus* listed it among institutes joined to the Holy See; new statutes were approved by the Secretariat of State July 1, 1991. Chairman, Most Rev. Giovanni De Andrea.

Activities of the Holy See: An annual documentary volume covering the activities of the pope and of the congregations, commissions, tribunals and offices of the Roman Curia.

Statistical Yearbook of the Church (*Annuarium Statisticum Ecclesiae***)**: Issued by the Central Statistics Office of the Church, it contains principal data concerning the presence and work of the Church in the world. The first issue was published in 1972 under the title *Collection of Statistical Tables, 1969*. It is printed in corresponding columns of Italian, French, and Latin. Some of the introductory material is printed in other languages.

DIPLOMATIC ACTIVITIES OF THE HOLY SEE

REPRESENTATIVES OF THE HOLY SEE

Representatives of the Holy See and their functions were the subject of a document entitled *Sollicitudo Omnium Ecclesiarum* which Pope Paul VI issued on his own initiative under the date of June 24, 1969.

Delegates and Nuncios

Papal representatives "receive from the Roman Pontiff the charge of representing him in a fixed way in the various nations or regions of the world.

"When their legation is only to local churches, they are known as apostolic delegates. When to this legation, of a religious and ecclesial nature, there is added diplomatic legation to states and governments, they receive the title of nuncio, pro-nuncio, and internuncio." An apostolic nuncio has the diplomatic rank of ambassador extraordinary and plenipotentiary. Traditionally, because the diplomatic service of the Holy See has the longest uninterrupted history in the world, a nuncio has precedence among diplomats in the country to which he is accredited and serves as dean of the diplomatic corps on state occasions. Since 1965 pro-nuncios, also of ambassadorial rank, have been assigned to countries in which this prerogative is not recognized. In recent years, the Vatican has phased out the title of pro-nuncio. The title of nuncio (with an asterisk denoting he is not dean of the diplomatic corps) has been given to the majority of appointments of ambassadorial rank. *See* **Other Representatives**.

Service and Liaison

Representatives, while carrying out their general and

special duties, are bound to respect the autonomy of local churches and bishops. Their service and liaison responsibilities include the following:

- Nomination of Bishops: To play a key role in compiling, with the advice of ecclesiastics and lay persons, and submitting lists of names of likely candidates to the Holy See with their own recommendations.
- Bishops: To aid and counsel local bishops without interfering in the affairs of their jurisdictions.
- Episcopal Conferences: To maintain close relations with them and to assist them in every possible way. (Papal representatives do not belong to these conferences.)
- Religious Communities of Pontifical Rank: To advise and assist major superiors for the purpose of promoting and consolidating conferences of men and women religious and to coordinate their apostolic activities.
- Church-State Relations: The thrust in this area is toward the development of sound relations with civil governments and collaboration in work for peace and the total good of the whole human family. The mission of a papal representative begins with appointment and assignment by the pope and continues until termination of his mandate. He acts "under the guidance and according to the instructions of the cardinal secretary of state to whom he is directly responsible for the execution of the mandate entrusted to him by the Supreme Pontiff." Normally representatives are required to retire at age 75.

NUNCIOS AND DELEGATES

(*Sources:* Annuario Pontificio, L'Osservatore Romano, Acta Apostolicae Sedis, *Catholic News Service*.) *As of July 30, 2003. Country, rank of legation (corresponding to rank of legate unless otherwise noted), name of legate (archbishop unless otherwise noted) as available. An asterisk indicates a nuncio who is not presently dean of the diplomatic corps.*

Delegate for Papal Legations: Archbishop Carlo M. Viganò, titular archbishop of Ulpiana. The post was established in 1973 to coordinate papal diplomatic efforts throughout the world. The office entails responsibility for "following more closely through timely visits the activities of papal representatives … and encouraging their rapport with the central offices" of the Secretariat of State.

Albania: Tirana, Nunciature; Giovanni Bulaitis.*

Algeria: Algiers, Nunciature; Augustine Kasujja* (also Nuncio* to Tunisia).

Andorra: Nunciature; Manuel Monteiro de Castro (also Nuncio to Spain).

Angola: Luanda, Nunciature; Giovanni Angelo Becciu* (also Nuncio* to São Tome and Principe). (Diplomatic relations established in 1997.)

Antigua and Barbuda: Nunciature; Emil Paul Tscherrig* (resides in Port of Spain, Trinidad).

Antilles: Apostolic Delegation; Emil Paul Tscherrig (resides in Port of Spain, Trinidad).

Arabian Peninsula: Apostolic Delegation; Luigi Gatti (also Nuncio in Kuwait and Lebanon; resides in Lebanon).

Argentina: Buenos Aires, Nunciature; Adriano Bernardini.

Armenia: Nunciature; Claudio Gugerotti* (resides in Tbilisi, Georgia; also nuncio* to Georgia and Azerbaijan). (Diplomatic relations established in 1992.)

Australia: Canberra, Nunciature; Francesco Canalini.

Austria: Vienna, Nunciature; Giorgio Zur.

Azerbaijan: Nunciature; Claudio Gugerotti* (resides in Tbilisi, Georgia; also nuncio* to Georgia and Armenia). (Diplomatic relations established in 1992.)

Bahamas: Nunciature; Emil Paul Tscherrig* (resides in Port of Spain, Trinidad).

Bahrain: Manama; Nunciature; Giuseppe De Andrea. (Diplomatic relations established Jan. 12, 2000).

Bangladesh: Dhaka, Nunciature; Paul Tschang In-Nam.*

Barbados: Nunciature; Emil Paul Tscherrig* (resides in Port of Spain, Trinidad).

Belarus: Nunciature; Ivan Jurkovic.*

Belgium: Brussels, Nunciature; Karl-Josef Rauber (also Nuncio to Luxembourg).

Belize: Nunciature; Giacinto Berloco* (resides in Port of Spain, Trinidad).

Benin (formerly Dahomey): Nunciature; Pierre Nguyên Van Tot* (resides in Accra, Ghana).

Bolivia: La Paz, Nunciature; Ivo Scapolo.

Bosnia and Herzegovina: Sarajevo; Nunciature; Abril y Castelló Santos.*

Botswana: See **South Africa**.

Brazil: Brasilia, Nunciature; Lorenzo Baldisseri.

Brunei: See **Malaysia and Brunei**.

Bulgaria: Sofia, Nunciature (reestablished in 1990); Giuseppe Leanza.*

Burkina Faso: Ouagadougou, Nunciature; Mario Zenari*(resides in Abidjan, Côte d'Ivoire).

Burma: See **Myanmar**.

Burundi: Bujumbura, Nunciature; Michael Aidan Courtney.*

Cambodia: Nunciature; Vacant* (resides in Bangkok, Thailand). (Diplomatic relations established in 1994.)

Cameroon: Yaounde, Nunciature; Eliseo Antonio Ariotti (also Nuncio to Equatorial Guinea).

Canada: Ottawa, Nunciature; Luigi Ventura.*

Cape Verde, Republic of: Nunciature; Giuseppe Pinto* (resides in Dakar, Senegal).

Central African Republic: Bangui, Nunciature; Joseph Chennoth* (also Nuncio* to Chad).

Chad: Nunciature; Joseph Chennoth* (resides in Bangui, Central African Republic).

Chile: Santiago, Nunciature; Aldo Cavalli.

China, Republic of: Taipei (Taiwan), Nunciature; vacant.

Colombia: Bogota, Nunciature; Beniamino Stella.

Comoros: See **Madagascar**: (formerly Zaire)

Congo (formerly Zaire): Kinshasa-Gombe, Nunciature; Giovanni d'Aniello.*

Congo: Brazzaville, Nunciature; Roberto Cassari* (also Nuncio* to Gabon).

Costa Rica: San Jose, Nunciature; vacant.

Côte d'Ivoire (Ivory Coast): Abidjan, Nunciature; Mario Zenari (also Nuncio* to Niger and Burkina Faso).

Croatia: Zagreb, Nunciature; Franjo Zenko.

Cuba: Havana, Nunciature; Luiz Robles Díaz.*

Cyprus: Nicosia, Nunciature; Pietro Sambi (also Nuncio to Israel), Pro-Nuncio.

Czech Republic: Prague, Nunciature; Erwin Josef Ender.

Denmark: Copenhagen, Nunciature; Piero Biggio* (also Nuncio* to Finland, Iceland, Norway and Sweden).

Djibouti: Nunciature (established May 2000); Silvano Tomasi, C.S. (resides in Addis Ababa, Ethiopia).

Dominica: Nunciature; Emil Paul Tscherrig* (resides in Port-of-Spain, Trinidad).

Dominican Republic: Santo Domingo, Nunciature; Timothy P. Broglio (also serves as Apostolic Delegate to Puerto Rico).

East Timor: Dili, Nunciature (diplomatic relations established on May 20, 2002); Renzo Fratini (also Nuncio* to Indonesia).

Ecuador: Quito, Nunciature; Alain Lebeaupin.

Egypt: Cairo, Nunciature; Marco Dino Brogi, O.F.M. (also delegate to the Organization of the League of Arab States).*

El Salvador: San Salvador, Nunciature; Giacinto Berloco.

Equatorial Guinea: Santa Isabel, Nunciature; Eliseo Antonio Ariotti* (resides in Yaounde, Cameroon).

Eritrea: Nunciature: Silvano Tomasi, C.S.* (resides in Ethiopia). (Diplomatic relations established in 1995.)

Estonia: Nunciature; Peter Stephan Zurbriggen* (resides in Vilna, Lithuania).

Ethiopia: Addis Ababa, Nunciature; Silvano Tomasi, C.S.* (also Nuncio* to Eritrea and apostolic delegate to Djibouti).

European Community: Brussels, Belgium, Nunciature; Faustino Sainz Muñoz.

Fiji: Nunciature; Patrick Coveney* (resides in Wellington, New Zealand).

Finland: Helsinki, Nunciature; Piero Biggio * (resides in Denmark).

France: Paris, Nunciature; Fortunato Baldelli.

Gabon: Libreville, Nunciature; Roberto Cassari* (resides in Congo).

Gambia: Nunciature; Alberto Bottari de Castello* (resides in Freetown, Sierra Leone).

Georgia: Tbilisi, Nunciature; Claudio Gugerotti* (also Nuncio* to Armenia and Azerbaijan). (Diplomatic relations established in 1992.)

Germany: Bonn, Nunciature; Giovanni Lajolo.

Ghana: Accra, Nunciature; George Kocherry * (also Nuncio to Benin and Togo).

Great Britain: London, Nunciature; Pablo Puente* (also papal representative to Gibraltar).

Greece: Athens, Nunciature; Paul Fouad Tabet.*

Grenada: Nunciature; vacant* (resides in Port of Spain, Trinidad).

Guatemala: Guatemala City, Nunciature; Ramiro Moliner Inglés.

Guinea: Conakry, Nunciature; Alberto Bottari de Castello* (resides in Freetown, Sierra Leone).

Guinea Bissau: Nunciature; Giuseppe Pinto* (resides at Dakar, Senegal).

Guyana: Nunciature; Emil Paul Tscherrig (resides in Port of Spain, Trinidad).

Haiti: Port-au-Prince, Nunciature; Luigi Bonazzi.

Honduras: Tegucigalpa, Nunciature; Antonio Arcari.

Hungary: Budapest, Nunciature; Juliusz Janusz (also Nuncio* to Moldova).

Iceland: Nunciature; Piero Biggio * (resides in Denmark).

India: New Delhi, Nunciature; Pedro López Quintana* (also Nuncio* to Nepal).

Indonesia: Jakarta, Nunciature; Renzo Fratini.*

Iran: Teheran, Nunciature; Angelo Mottola.*

Iraq: Baghdad, Nunciature; Fernando Filoni* (also Nuncio to Jordan).

Ireland: Dublin, Nunciature; Giuseppe Lazzarotto.

Israel: Nunciature; Pietro Sambi (also Nuncio to Cyprus). (Diplomatic relations established June 1994.)

Italy: Rome, Nunciature; Paolo Romeo (also Nuncio to San Marino).

Ivory Coast: See **Côte d'Ivoire**.

Jamaica: Nunciature; Emil Paul Tscherrig, Pro-Nuncio (resides in Port of Spain, Trinidad).

Japan: Tokyo, Nunciature; Ambrose de Paoli*.

Jerusalem and Palestine: Apostolic Delegation (also Nuncio to Israel): Pietro Sambi.

Jordan: Nunciature; Fernando Filoni* (also Nuncio to Iraq).

Kazakstan: Almaty, Nunciature; Józef Wesolowski* (also Nuncio* to Kyrgyzstan, Tajikistan and Uzbekistan).

Kenya: Nairobi, Nunciature; Giovanni Tonucci.*

Kiribati: Nunciature; Patrick Coveney* (resides in Wellington, New Zealand).

Korea: Seoul, Nunciature; Giovanni Battista Morandini* (also Nuncio* to Mongolia).

Kuwait: Al Kuwait, Nunciature; Giuseppe De Andrea* (resides in Lebanon).

Kyrgyzstan: Nunciature; Józef Wesolowski * (resides in Kazakhstan; also Nuncio* to Kyrgyzstan, Tajikistan and Uzbekistan).

Laos: Apostolic Delegation; Vacant (resides in Bangkok, Thailand).

Latvia: Nunciature; Peter Stephan Zurbriggen* (resides in Vilna, Lithuania).

Lebanon: Beirut, Nunciature; Luigi Gatti (also Nuncio* to Kuwait and apostolic delegate to Arabian Peninsula).

Lesotho: Maseru, Nunciature; Blasco Francisco Collaço (also Nuncio to South Africa, Namibia, and Swaziland; resides in Pretoria, South Africa).

Liberia: Monrovia, Nunciature; Alberto Bottari de Castello* (resides in Freetown, Sierra Leone).

Libya: Nunciature; Félix del Blanco Prieto* (resides in Malta). (Diplomatic relations established in 1997.)

Liechtenstein: Nunciature; Pier Giacomo De Nicolò (resides in Bern, Switzerland).

Lithuania: Vilnius, Nunciature; Peter Stephan Zurbriggen* (also Nuncio to Estonia and Latvia.).

Luxembourg: Nunciature; Karl-Josef Rauber (resides in Brussels, Belgium).

Macedonia: Nunciature; Abril y Castelló Santos* (also Nuncio to Slovenia; resides in Slovenia).

Madagascar: Antananarivo, Nunciature; Bruno Musarò* (also Nuncio* to Seychelles, and Mauritius and Apostolic Delegate to Comoros and Reunion).

Malawi: Lilongwe, Nunciature; Orlando Antonini* (resides in Lusaka, Zambia).

Malaysia and Brunei: Apostolic Delegation; Vacant (resides in Bangkok, Thailand).

Mali: Nunciature; Giuseppe Pinto* (resides in Dakar, Senegal).

Malta: La Valletta, Nunciature; Félix del Blanco Prieto (also Nuncio* to Libya).

Marshall Islands: Nunciature; Patrick Coveney* (resides in Wellington, New Zealand).

Mauritania: Nouakchott, Apostolic Delegation; Giuseppe Pinto (resides in Dakar, Senegal).

Mauritius: Port Louis, Nunciature; Bruno Musarò* (resides in Antananarivo, Madagascar).

Mexico: Mexico City, Nunciature; Giuseppe Bertello.* (Diplomatic relations established in 1992).

Micronesia, Federated States of: Nunciature; Patrick Coveney* (resides in Wellington, New Zealand).

Moldova: Nunciature; Jean-Claude Périsset* (resides in Bucharest, Romania). (Diplomatic relations established in 1992.)

Mongolia: Nunciature; Giovanni Battista Morandini* (resides in Seoul, South Korea).

Morocco: Rabat, Nunciature; Antonio Sozzo.*

Mozambique: Maputo, nunciature; George Panikulam.* (Diplomatic relations established in 1995.)

Myanmar (formerly Burma): Apostolic Delegation; Vacant (resides in Bangkok, Thailand).

Namibia: Nunciature; Blasco Francisco Collaço* (resides in Pretoria, South Africa).

Nauru: Nunciature; Patrick Coveney* (resides in Wellington, New Zealand).

Nepal: Nunciature; Pedro López Quintana* (resides in New Delhi, India).

Netherlands: The Hague, Nunciature; François Bacqué.*

New Zealand: Wellington, Nunciature; Patrick Coveney* (also Nuncio* to Fiji, Kiribati, Marshall Islands, Federated States of Micronesia, Tonga, Vanuatu and Western Samoa; Apostolic Delegate to Pacific Islands).

Nicaragua: Managua, Nunciature; Jean-Paul Gobel.

Niger: Niamey, Nunciature; Mario Zenari* (resides in Abidjan, Côte d'Ivoire.)

Nigeria: Lagos, Nunciature; Osvaldo Padilla*.

Norway: Nunciature; Piero Biggio* (resides in Denmark).

Pacific Islands: Apostolic Delegation; Patrick Coveney (resides in Wellington, New Zealand).

Pakistan: Islamabad, Nunciature; Alessandro D'Errico.

Palau, Republic of: Palau, Nunciature; Patrick Coveney.*

Panama: Panama City, Nunciature; Giacomo Ottonello.

Papua New Guinea: Port Moresby; Nunciature; Adolfo Tito Yllana* (also Nuncio* to Solomon Islands).

Paraguay: Asuncion, Nunciature; Antonio Lucibello.

Peru: Lima, Nunciature; Rino Passigato.

Philippines: Manila, Nunciature; Antonio Franco.

Poland: Warsaw; Nunciature; Hanna Suchoka.

Portugal: Lisbon, Nunciature; Edoardo Rovida.

Puerto Rico: See **Dominican Republic**.

Qatar: Diplomatic relations established in Nov. 2002.

Reunion: See **Madagascar**.

Romania: Bucharest, Nunciature. Jean-Claude Périsset*

Russia (Federation of): Moscow, Nunciature; Antonio Mennini. Nuncio appointed Representative of the Holy See to Russian Federation, 1994.

Rwanda: Kigali, Nunciature. Salvatore Pennacchio.

Saint Vincent and the Grenadines: Nunciature; Emil Paul Tscherrig, Pro-Nuncio (resides in Port of Spain, Trinidad).

San Marino: Nunciature; Paolo Romeo.

Santa Lucia: Nunciature; Emil Paul Tscherrig* (resides in Port of Spain, Trinidad).

São Tome and Principe: Nunciat ure; Giovanni Angelo Becciu* (also Nuncio* to Angola, where he resides).

Senegal: Dakar, Nunciature; Giuseppe Pinto* (also Nuncio* to Cape Verde, Guinea-Bissau and Mali; Apostolic Delegate to Mauritania.)

Seychelles Islands: Nunciature; Bruno Musarò* (resides in Antananrivo, Madagascar).

Sierra Leone: Freetown, Nunciature (1996); Alberto Bottari de Castello* (also Nuncio* to Gambia, Guinea and Liberia).

Singapore: Nunciature; Vacant* (He is also Nuncio to Cambodia and Thailand and apostolic delegate to Laos, Malaysia and Brunei, and Myanmar.)

Slovakia: Nunciature; Henryk Jozef Nowacki.

Slovenia: Ljubljana, Nunciature; Abril y Castelló Santos (also Nuncio to Macedonia).

Solomon Islands: Nunciature; Adolfo Tito Yllana (resides in Port Moresby, Papua New Guinea).

Somalia: Apostolic Delegation (est. 1992); Dominique Mamberti (resides in Sudan).

South Africa: Pretoria, Nunciature; Blasco Francisco Collaço.* (also Nuncio* to Namibia and Swaziland and apostolic delegate to Botswana.)

Spain: Madrid, Nunciature; Manuel Monteiro de Castro.

Sri Lanka: Colombo, Nunciature; Thomas Yeh Sheng-nan*

Sudan: Khartoum, Nunciature; Dominique Mamberti* (also Apostolic Delegate to Somalia).

Suriname: Nunciature; vacant* (resides in Port of Spain, Trinidad).

Swaziland: Nunciature; Blasco Francisco Collaço* (resides in Pretoria, South Africa).

Sweden: Nunciature; Piero Biggio* (resides in Denmark).

Switzerland: Bern, Nunciature; Pier Giacomo De Nicolò (also Nuncio to Liechtenstein).

Syria: (Syrian Arab Republic): Damascus, Nunciature, Diego Causero.*

Tajikistan: Nunciature (1996); Józef Wesolowski* (resides in Kazakstan; also Nuncio* to Kyrgyzstan, Kazakstan, and Uzbekistan).

Tanzania: Dar-es-Salaam, Nunciature; Luigi Pezzuto.*

Thailand: Bangkok, Nunciature; vacant* (also Nuncio* to Cambodia and Singapore and Apostolic Delegate to Laos, Malaysia, Brunei, Myanmar).

Togo: Lome, Nunciature; Pierre Nguyên Van Tot* (resides in Accra, Ghana).

Tonga: Nunciature; Patrick Coveney* (resides in Wellington, New Zealand).

Trinidad and Tobago: Port of Spain, Trinidad, Nunciature; Emil Paul Tscherrig, Pro-Nuncio (also Pro-Nuncio to Antigua and Barbuda, Bahamas, Barbados, Belize, Dominica, Grenada, Jamaica, Saint Lucia, Saint Vincent and the Grenadines, Suriname and Apostolic Delegate to Antilles).

Tunisia: Tunis, Nunciature; Augustine Kasujja* (resides in Algiers, Algeria).

Turkey: Ankara, Nunciature; Edmond Farhat.*

Turkmenistan: Nunciature (1996); Edmond Farhat* (resides in Ankara, Turkey.)

Ukraine: Kiev, Nunciature; Nikola Eterovic.*

Uganda: Kampala, Nunciature; Pro-Nuncio, Christophe Pierre.

United States of America: Washington, DC, Nunciature; Gabriel Montalvo.*

Uruguay: Montevideo, Nunciature; Janusz Bolonek.

Uzbekistan: Nunciature; Józef Wesolowski* (resides in Kazakstan; also Nuncio* to Kazakstan, Kyrgyzstan, and Tajikistan).

Vanuatu: Nunciature; Patrick Coveney* (resides in Wellington, New Zealand).

Venezuela: Caracas, Nunciature; André Dupuy.

Vietnam: Apostolic Delegation; vacant.

Western Samoa: Nunciature; Patrick Coveney* (resides in Wellington, New Zealand).

Yemen: San'a, Nunciature; Giuseppe De Andrea* (relations established in 1998).

Yugoslavia: Belgrade, Nunciature; Eugenio Sbarbaro.

Zaire: See Congo: Lusaka, Nunciature; Giuseppe Leanza* (also Nuncio* to Malawi).

Zambia: Lusaka, Nunciature; Orlando Antonini* (also Nuncio* to Malawi).

Zimbabwe: Harare, Nunciature; Edward Joseph Adams.*

The Current Nuncio to the U.S.

The representative of the Pope to the Church in the United States is Archbishop Gabriel Montalvo, J.C.D. Archbishop Montalvo was born Jan. 27, 1930, in Bogota, Colombia. Ordained to the priesthood Jan. 18, 1953, he earned a doctorate in canon law and entered the Vatican diplomatic service in 1957, serving in nunciatures in Bolivia, Argentina, and El Salvador. From 1964 to 1974, Archbishop Montalvo served in the Secretariat of State, Vatican City, where he dealt with matters affecting the Churches in Eastern Europe. In 1974, he was named Apostolic Nuncio in Honduras and Nicaragua. He was named Titular Archbishop of Celene on June 30, 1974. In 1980, Archbishop Montalvo was named Pro-Nuncio in Algeria and Tunisia and Apostolic Delegate in Libya. In 1986, Archbishop Montalvo was named Apostolic Pro-Nuncio in Yugoslavia and subsequently Apostolic Nuncio in Belarus. In 1993 he was appointed President of the Pontifical Ecclesiastical Academy where diplomats in service to the Holy See are trained. On Dec. 7, 1998, Archbishop Montalvo was appointed nuncio to the United States and permanent observer to the Organization of American States, succeeding Archbishop Agostino Cacciavillan.

The U.S. Apostolic Nunciature is located at 3339 Massachusetts Ave., N.W., Washington, DC 20008-3687; (202) 333-7121.

A Nuncio represents the Holy Father to both the hierarchy and Church of a particular nation and to that nation's civil government.

From 1893 to 1984, papal representatives to the Church in the U.S. were apostolic delegates (all archbishops): Francesco Satolli (1893-96), Sebastiano Martinelli, O.S.A., (1896-1902), Diomede Falconio, O.F.M. (1902-1911), Giovanni Bonzano (1911-22), Pietro Fumasoni-Biondi (1922-33), Amleto Cicognani (1933-58), Egidio Vagnozzi (1958-67), Luigi Raimondi (1967-73), Jean Jadot (1973-80), and Pio Laghi (1980-90) who was the first to hold the title Pro-Nuncio, beginning in 1984 (*See* Index, **U.S.-Vatican Relations**). Archbishop (now Cardinal) Agostino Cacciavillan was Pro-Nuncio and permanent observer to the Organization of American States from 1990 to 1998.

Other Representatives

(*Sources:* Annuario Pontificio; *Catholic News Service.*)

The Holy See has representatives to or is a regular member of a number of quasi-governmental and international organizations. Most Rev. Ernesto Gallina was appointed delegate to International Governmental Organizations Jan. 12, 1991.

Governmental Organizations: U.N. (Abp. Celestino Migliore, permanent observer); U.N. Office in Geneva and Specialized Institutions (Abp. Silvano Maria Tomasi, permanent observer); International Atomic Energy Agency (Msgr. Leo Boccardi, permanent representative); U.N. Office at Vienna and U.N. Organization for Industrial Development (Msgr. Leo Boccardi, permanent observer); U.N. Food and Agriculture Organization (Msgr. Renato Volante, permanent observer); U.N. Educational, Scientific and Cultural Organization (Msgr. Francesco Follo, permanent observer); World Organization of Commerce (Abp. Silvano Maria Tomasi); Council of Europe (Msgr. Paul Richard Gallagher, special representative with function of permanent observer); Council for Cultural Cooperation of the Council of Europe (Msgr. Paul Richard Gallagher, delegate); Organization of American States (Abp. Gabriel Montalvo, permanent observer, with personal title of Apostolic Nuncio); Organization for Security and Cooperation in Europe (Msgr. Leo Boccardi, permanent representative); International Institute for the Unification of Private Law (Prof. Giuseppe dalla Torre del Tiempo di Sanguinetto Conte, delegate); International Committee of Military Medicine (Rev. Luc De Maere, delegate), World Organization of Tourism (Msgr. Piero Monni, permanent observer).

Non-Governmental Organizations: International Committee of Historical Sciences (Msgr. Walter Brandmüller); International Committee of the History of Art (Dr. Francesco Buranelli); International Committee of Anthropological and Ethnological Sciences; Committee for the Neutrality of Medicine; International Center of Study for the Preservation and Restoration of Cultural Goods (Dr. Francesco Buranelli); International Council of Monuments and Sites (Msgr. Francesco Follo, delegate); International Alliance on Tourism; World Association of Jurists (Abp. Gabriel Montalvo); International Commission of the Civil State (Msgr. Paul Richard Gallagher); International Astronomical Union; International Institute of Administrative Sciences; International Technical Committee for Prevention and Extinction of Fires; World Medical Association; International Archives Council; World Trade Organization.

DIPLOMATS TO THE HOLY SEE

(*Sources:* Annuario Pontificio, L'Osservatore Romano).

Listed below are countries maintaining diplomatic relations with the Holy See, dates of establishment (in some cases) and names of Ambassadors (as of Aug. 30, 2003). Leaders (. . . . .) indicate the post was vacant.

The senior member of the diplomatic corps at the Vatican is Jean Wagner of Luxembourg who was appointed in Nov. 7, 1981, and presented his credentials Jan. 18, 1982.

Albania (1991): Zef Bushati.
Algeria (1972): Mohamed-Salah Dembri.
Andorra (1995): Manuel Mas Ribó.
Angola (1997): José Bernardo Domingos Quiosa.
Antigua and Barbuda (1986): . . . . .
Argentina: Vicente Espeche Gil.
Armenia (1992): Edward Nalbandian.
Australia (1973): John Joseph Herron.
Austria: Walter Greinert.
Azerbaijan (1992): . . . . .
Bahamas (1979): . . . . .
Bahrain (2000): . . . .
Bangladesh (1972):Toufiq Ali.
Barbados (1979): Peter Patrick Kenneth Simmons.
Belarus (1992): Vladimir R. Korolev.
Belgium (1835): Benoît Cardon De Lichtbuer.
Belize (1983): . . . . .
Benin (formerly Dahomey) (1971): Euloge Hinvi.
Bolivia: Pedro José Rivera Saavedra.
Bosnia and Herzegovina (1992): Ivan Mišic.
Brazil: Oto Agripino Maia.
Bulgaria (1990): Nikolaev Vladimir Gradev. Check.
Burkina Faso (1973): Felipe Savadogo.
Burundi (1963): Térence Nsanze.
Cambodia (1994): . . . . .
Cameroon (1966): Jean Melaga.
Canada (1969): Wilfred-Guy Licari.
Cape Verde (1976): Teófilo de Figueiredo Almeida.
Central African Republic (1975): . . . . .
Chad (1988): Mahmoud Hissein Mahmoud.
Chile: Maximo Pacheco Gómez.

China, Republic of (Taiwan) (1966): Raymond R.M. Tai.

Colombia: Dr. Guillermo León Escobar-Herrán.

Congo (formerly Zaire) (1963): . . . . .

Congo (1977): Henri Marie Joseph Lopes.

Costa Rica: Javier Guerra Laspiur.

Côte d'Ivoire (Ivory Coast) (1971): Louis Esmel.

Croatia (1992): Dr. Marijan Sunjic.

Cuba: Isidro Gómez Santos.

Cyprus (1973): Georgios F. Poulides.

Czech Republic (1929-50, reestablished, 1990, with Czech and Slovak Federative Republic; reaffirmed, 1993): Pavel Jajtner.

Denmark (1982): Bjarne Bladbjerg.

Djibouti: (2000): Barkat Gourad Hamadou. (Diplomatic relations established May 20, 2000.)

Dominica (1981): . . . . .

Dominican Republic: Victor A.Hidlago Justo.

East Timor (2002): . . . . (Diplomatic relations established on May 20, 2002.)

Ecuador: Marcelo Fernández de Córdoba Ponce.

Egypt (1966): Farouk Hussein Raafat

El Salvador: Roberto José Simán Jacir.

Equatorial Guinea (1981): . . . . .

Eritrea (1995): Zemede Tekle Woldetatios.

Estonia (1991): Indrek Tarand.

Ethiopia (1969): Negash Kebret.

Fiji (1978): Emitat Lausiki Boladuadua.

Finland (1966): Antti Hynninen.

France: Alain Dejammet.

Gabon (1967): Désiré Koumba.

Gambia, The (1978): Gibril Seman Joof.

Georgia (1992): Alexander Chikvaidze.

Germany: Gerhard Westdickenberg.

Ghana (1976): Albert Owusu-Sarpong.

Great Britain (1982): Mark Pellew.

Greece (1980): Christos Botzios.

Grenada (1979): . . . . .

Guatemala: Aciscio Valladares Molina.

Guinea (1986): Abraham Doukouré.

Guinea-Bissau (1986): . . . . .

Guyana (Cooperative Republic of): Laleshwar Kumar Narayan Singh.

Haiti: Carl Henri Guiteau.

Honduras: Alejandro Emilio Valladares Lanza.

Hungary (1990): Gábor Erdödy.

Iceland (1976): Hördur H. Bjarnason.

India: Praveen Lal Goyal.

Indonesia (1965): Widodo Sutiyo.

Iran (1966): Mostafa Borujerdi.

Iraq (1966): Wissam Chawkat Al-Zahawi.

Ireland: Bernard Davenport.

Israel (1994): Oded Ben-Hur.

Italy: Raniero Avogardo.

Ivory Coast: See **Côte d'Ivoire**.

Jamaica (1979): Marcia Gilbert-Roberts.

Japan (1966): Gunkatsu Kano.

Jordan (1994): Dina Kawar.

Kazakhstan (1992): Nurlan Danenov.

Kenya (1965): Boaz Kidiga Mbaya.

Kiribati: Diplomatic relations established Apr. 1995.

Korea (1966): Youm Seong.

Kuwait (1969): Ahmad Abdulkarim Al-Ebrahim.

Kyrgyzstan (1992): Apas Dschumagulov

Latvia (1991): Atis Sjanits.

Lebanon (1966): Fouad Aoun.

Lesotho (1967): Seymour Rehaulele Kikine.

Liberia (1966): . . . . .

Libya: (1997): Abdulhafed Gaddur.

Liechtenstein (1985): Nikolaus de Liechtenstein.

Lithuania: Alberts Sarkanis.

Luxembourg (1955): Jean Wagner.

Macedonia (1994): Ivan Angelov.

Madagascar (1967): Jean-Pierre Razafy-Andriamihaingo.

Malawi (1966): Silas Samuel Ncozana.

Mali (1979): Moussa Coulibaly.

Malta (1965): James Farrugia.

Marshall Islands (1993): . . . . .

Mauritius: Mohunlall Goburdhun.

Mexico (personal representative, 1990; diplomatic relations, 1992): Fernando Estrada Sámano.

Micronesia, Federated States (1994): . . . . .

Moldova (1992): Mihail Laur.

Monaco: Jean- Claude Michel.

Mongolia (1992): Chuluuny Batjargal.

Morocco: Mohammed Sbihi.

Mozambique: Diplomatic relations established Dec. 1995.

Namibia: Diplomatic relations established Sept. 1995.

Nauru (1992): . . . . .

Nepal (1983): Balram Singh Malla.

Netherlands (1967): Baron Hendrik Volkier Bentinck van Schoonheten.

New Zealand (1973): Christine Heather Bogle.

Nicaragua: Luvy Salerni Navas.

Niger (1971): Amadou Touré.

Nigeria (1976): Samuel Otuyelu.

Norway (1982): Helga Hernes.

Order of Malta (see Index): Alberto Leoncini Bartoli.

Pakistan (1965): Fauzia Mufti Abbas.

Palau, Republic of (1998): . . . . .

Panama: Edda Victoria Martinelli de Dutari.

Papua New Guinea (1977): . . . . .

Paraguay: Blanca Elida Zuccolillo de Rodríguez Alcalá.

Peru: Alberto Montagne Vidal.

Philippines (1951): Francisco A. Alba

Poland (1989): Hanna Suchocka.

Portugal: Pedro José Ribeiro de Menezes.

Qatar: Diplomatic relations established Nov. 2002.

Romania (1920; broken off, 1948; reestablished, 1990): Mihail Dobre.

Rwanda (1964): Emmanuel Kayitana Imanza.

Saint Lucia (1984): Desmond Arthur McNamara.

Saint Vincent and the Grenadines (1990): . . . . .

San Marino (1986): Giovanni Galassi.

São Tome and Principe (1984): . . . . .

Senegal (1966): Henri Antoine Turpin.

Seychelles (1984): . . . . .

Sierra Leone: (Diplomatic relations established July 1996): Fode Maclean Dabor.

Singapore (1981): Ampalavanar Selverajah.

Slovak Republic (1993; when it became independent republic): Dr. Marián Servátka.

Slovenia (1992): Dagmar Babcanová.

Solomon Islands (1984): . . . . .

South Africa (1994): Patricia Nozipho January-Bardill.

Spain: Carlos Abella y Ramallo.

Sri Lanka (1975): Prasad Kariyawasam.

Sudan (1972): Abdelbasit Badawi Ali Elsanosi.

Suriname (1994): Evert G. Azimullah.

Swaziland (1992): H.R.H. Prince David M. Dlamini.
Sweden (1982): Fredrik Vahlquist.
Switzerland (1992): Hansrudolf Hoffmann, Ambassador with special mission to Holy See.
Syria (Arab Republic) (1966): Siba Nasser.
Tajikistan: Diplomatic relations established June 1996.
Tanzania (1968): Andrew Mhando Daraja.
Thailand (1969): Jullapong Nonsirchai.
Togo (1981): . . . . .
Tonga (1994): . . . . .
Trinidad and Tobago (1978): Leari E. Rousseau.
Tunisia (1972): Saïda Chtioui.
Turkey (1966): Filiz Dinçmen.
Turkmenistan: Diplomatic relations established July 1996.
Uganda (1966): Tibamanya Mwene Mushanga.
Ukraine (1992): Nina Kovalska.
United States (1984):James Nicholson.
Uruguay: Daniel Pérez del Castillo.
Uzbekistan (1992): . . . . .

Vanuatu (1994): Michel Rittié.
Venezuela: Ignacio Quintana.
Western Samoa (1994): . . . . .
Yemen: (1998): Mohy Al-Dhabbi.
Yugoslavia: Darko Tanaskovic.
Zaire: See Congo.
Zambia (1965): Silumelume Kufunduka Mubukwanu.
Zimbabwe (1980): Kelebert Nkomani.

Special Representatives

Russia (Federation of) (1989): Vitaly Litvin, Ambassador Extraordinary and Plenipotentiary.
United Nations (Center of Information of UN at the Holy See): Shalini Dewan, director.
Office of the League of Arab States: Mohammad Ali Mohammad.
United Nations High Commission for Refugees: Ana Liria-Franch, delegate.
Organization for the Liberation of Palestine: Afif E. Safieh, director.

U.S.-HOLY SEE RELATIONS

The U.S. and the Holy See announced Jan. 10, 1984, the establishment of full diplomatic relations, thus ending a period of 117 years in which there was no formal diplomatic relationship. The announcement followed action by the Congress in Nov. 1983 to end a prohibition on diplomatic relations enacted in 1867.

William A. Wilson, President Reagan's personal representative to the Holy See from 1981, was confirmed as the U.S. ambassador by the Senate, on Mar. 7, 1984. He presented his credentials to Pope John Paul II on Apr. 9, 1984, and served until May 1986, when he resigned. He was succeeded by Frank Shakespeare, 1986-89, and Thomas P. Melady, 1989-93. Raymond L. Flynn, Mayor of Boston, was appointed by Bill Clinton and confirmed by the Senate in July 1993. He served until 1997 when he was succeeded by Corinne Claiborne "Lindy" Boggs. She presented her credentials to Pope John Paul II on Dec. 16, 1997. The present U.S. Ambassador to the Holy See is James Nicholson.

Archbishop (now Cardinal) Pio Laghi, apostolic delegate to the U.S. since 1980, was named first pro-nuncio by the Pope on Mar. 26, 1984. He served until 1990, when he was named prefect of the Congregation for Catholic Education. Archbishop Agostino Cacciavillan was appointed pro-nuncio on June 13, 1990. He served until he was named president of the Administration of the Patrimony of the Apostolic See (APSA) and was succeeded on Dec. 7, 1998, by Archbishop Gabriel Montalvo, the present nuncio.

Nature of Relations

The nature of relations was described in nearly identical statements by John Hughes, a State Department spokesman, and the Holy See. Hughes said: "The United States of America and the Holy See, in the desire to further promote the existing mutual friendly relations, have decided by common agreement to establish diplomatic relations between them at the level of embassy on the part of the United States of America, and nunciature on the part of the Holy See, as of today, January 10, 1984."

The Holy See statement said: "The Holy See and the United States of America, desiring to develop the mutual friendly relations already existing, have decided by common accord to establish diplomatic relations at the level of apostolic nunciature on the side of the Holy See and of embassy on the side of the United States beginning today, January 10, 1984."

The establishment of relations was criticized as a violation of the separation-of-church-and-state principle by spokesmen for the National Council of Churches, the National Association of Evangelicals, the Baptist Joint Committee on Public Affairs, Seventh Day Adventists, Americans United for Separation of Church and State, and the American Jewish Congress.

Legal Challenge Dismissed

U.S. District Judge John P. Fullam, ruling May 7, 1985, in Philadelphia, dismissed a legal challenge to U.S.-Holy See relations brought by Americans United for Separation of Church and State. He stated that Americans United and its allies in the challenge lacked legal standing to sue, and that the courts did not have jurisdiction to intervene in foreign policy decisions of the executive branch of the U.S. government. Parties to the suit brought by Americans United were the National Association of Laity, the National Coalition of American Nuns and several Protestant church organizations. Bishop James W. Malone, president of the U.S. Catholic Conference, said in a statement: "This matter has been discussed at length for many years. It is not a religious issue but a public policy question which, happily, has now been settled in this context."

Russell Shaw, a conference spokesman, said the decision to send an ambassador to the Holy See was not a church-state issue and "confers no special privilege or status on the Church."

Earlier Relations

Official relations for trade and diplomatic purposes were maintained by the U.S. and the Papal States while the latter had the character of and acted like other sovereign powers in the international community.

Consular relations developed in the wake of an announcement, made by the papal nuncio in Paris to the American mission there Dec. 15, 1784, that the Papal States had agreed to open several Mediterranean ports to U.S. shipping.

U.S. consular representation in the Papal States began with the appointment of John B. Sartori, a native of Rome, in June 1797. Sartori's successors as consuls were: Felix Cicognani, also a Roman, and Americans George W. Greene, Nicholas Browne, William C. Sanders, Daniel LeRoy, Horatio V. Glentworth, W.J. Stillman, Edwin C. Cushman, David M. Armstrong.

Consular officials of the Papal States who served in the U.S. were: Count Ferdinand Lucchesi, 1826 to 1829, who resided in Washington; John B. Sartori, 1829 to 1841, who resided in Trenton, NJ; Daniel J. Desmond, 1841 to 1850, who resided in Philadelphia; Louis B. Binsse, 1850 to 1895, who resided in New York.

U.S. recognition of the consul of the Papal States did not cease when the states were absorbed into the Kingdom of Italy in 1871, despite pressure from Baron Blanc, the Italian minister. Binsse held the title until his death Mar. 28, 1895. No one was appointed to succeed him.

Diplomatic Relations

The U.S. Senate approved a recommendation, made by President James K. Polk in Dec. 1847 for the establishment of a diplomatic post in the Papal States. Jacob L. Martin, the first charge d'affaires, arrived in Rome Aug. 2, 1848, and presented his credentials to Pius IX Aug. 19. Martin, who died within a month, was succeeded by Lewis Cass, Jr. Cass became minister resident in 1854 and served in that capacity until his retirement in 1858.

John P. Stockton, who later became a U.S. Senator from New Jersey, was minister resident from 1858 to 1861. Rufus King was named to succeed him but, instead, accepted a commission as a brigadier general in the Army. Alexander W. Randall of Wisconsin took the appointment. He was succeeded in Aug. 1862 by Richard M. Blatchford who served until the following year. King was again nominated minister resident and served in that capacity until 1867 when the ministry was ended because of objections from some quarters in the U.S. and failure to appropriate funds for its continuation. J. C. Hooker, a secretary, remained in the Papal States until the end of March, 1868, closing the ministry and performing functions of courtesy.

Personal Envoys

Myron C. Taylor was appointed by President Franklin D. Roosevelt in 1939 to serve as his personal representative to Pope Pius XII and continued serving in that capacity during the presidency of Harry S. Truman until 1951. Henry Cabot Lodge was named to the post by President Richard M. Nixon in 1970, served also during the presidency of Gerald Ford, and represented President Carter at the canonization of St. John Neumann in 1977. Miami attorney David Walters served as the personal envoy of President Jimmy Carter to the Pope from July 1977 until his resignation Aug. 16, 1978. He was succeeded by Robert F. Wagner who served from Oct. 1978 to the end of the Carter presidency in Jan. 1981. William A. Wilson, appointed by President Ronald Reagan in Feb. 1981, served as his personal envoy until 1984 when he was named ambassador to the Holy See.

None of the personal envoys had diplomatic status. President Harry S. Truman nominated Gen. Mark Clark to be ambassador to the Holy See in 1951, but withdrew the nomination at Clark's request because of controversy over the appointment.

None of Truman's three immediate successors — Dwight D. Eisenhower, John F. Kennedy and Lyndon B. Johnson — had a personal representative to the pope.

PONTIFICAL ACADEMIES

PONTIFICAL ACADEMY OF SCIENCES

(Sources: Annuario Pontificio, Catholic News Service.)

The Pontifical Academy of Sciences was constituted in its present form by Pius XI Oct. 28, 1936, in virtue of In Multis Solaciis, a document issued on his own initiative.

The academy is the only supranational body of its kind in the world with a pope-selected, life-long membership of outstanding mathematicians and experimental scientists regardless of creed from many countries. The normal complement of 70 members was increased to 80 in 1985-86 by John Paul II. There are additional honorary and supernumerary members.

The academy traces its origin to the Linceorum Academia (Academy of the Lynxes, its symbol) founded in Rome Aug. 17, 1603. Pius IX reorganized this body and gave it a new name, Pontificia Accademia dei Nuovi Lincei, in 1847. It was taken over by the Italian state in 1870 and called the Accademia Nationale dei Lincei. Leo XIII reconstituted it with a new charter in 1887. Pius XI designated the Casina of Pope Pius IV in the Vatican Gardens as the site of academy headquarters in 1922 and gave it its present title and status in 1936. In 1940, Pius XII gave the title of Excellency to its members; John XXIII extended the privilege to honorary members in 1961.

Members in U.S.

Scientists in the U.S. who presently hold membership in the Academy are listed below according to year of appointment. Nobel prize-winners are indicated by an asterisk.

Franco Rasetti, professor emeritus of physics at Johns Hopkins University, Baltimore, MD (Oct 28, 1936); Christian de Duve,* professor of biochemistry at the International Institute of Cellular and Molecular Pathology at Brussels, Belgium, and Rockefeller University, NY (Apr. 10, 1970);

Marshall Warren Nirenberg,* director of Laboratory on genetics and biochemistry at the National Institutes of Health, Bethesda, MD (June 24, 1974).

George Palade,* professor of cellular biology at University of California, San Diego and Victor Weisskopf, professor of physics at the Massachusetts Institute of Technology, Cambridge, Mass. (Dec. 2, 1975); David Baltimore,* professor of biology at the Massachusetts Institute of Technology, Cambridge, MA; Har Gobind Khorana,* professor of biochemistry, and Alexander Rich, professor of biophysics, both at the Massachusetts Institute of Technology, Cambridge, MA (Apr. 17, 1978).

Charles Townes,* professor emeritus of physics at the University of California at Berkeley (Jan. 26, 1983); Beatrice Mintz, senior member of the Cancer Research Institute of Philadelphia and Maxine Singer, biochemist, president of Carnegie Institution, Washington, DC (June 9, 1986).

Roald Z. Sagdeev, professor of physics at University of Maryland, College Park and Peter Hamilton Raven, professor of biology at the Missouri Botanical Garden of St. Louis, MO (Oct 4, 1990); Luis Angel Caffarelli, professor of mathematics at New York University and Luigi Luca Cavalli-Sforza, professor of genetics at Stanford University (Aug. 2, 1994).

Joshua Lederberg, professor of genetics at Rockefeller University, NY (Mar. 4, 1996); Joseph Edward Murray, professor of plastic surgery at Harvard Medical School, Cambridge, MA; Paul Berg, professor of biochemistry at Stanford Univ. and Vera C. Rubin, professor of astronomy at Carnegie Institution of Washington (June 25, 1996); Gary S. Becker,* professor of economics at the University of Chicago (Mar. 3, 1997); Chen-ning Yang,* professor of physics and director of the Institute of Theoretical Physics at the State University of NY at Stony Brook (Apr. 18,1997); Frank Press, professor of geophysics and director of the Washington Advisory Group (Sept. 3, 1999); Ahmed Zewail, professor of Chemistry and Physics, California Institute of Technology, Pasadena (Sept. 3, 1999); Mario Jose Molina, professor of atmospheric chemistry at the Massachusetts Institute of Technology (Nov. 9, 2000); Günter Blobel,* professor of cellular biology of the Rockefeller University, NY (Sept. 28, 2001).

There are also two honorary members from the U.S.: Stanley L, Jaki, O.S.B., professor of physics, history and philosophy at Seton Hall University, NJ (Sept. 5, 1990); Robert J. White, professor of neurosurgery at Case Western Reserve University, Cleveland (Mar. 29, 1994).

Members in Other Countries

Listing includes place and date of selection. Nobel prize winners are indicated by an asterisk.
Argentina: Antonio M. Battro (Sept. 21, 2002).
Armenia: Rudolf M. Muradian (Oct. 16, 1994).
Austria: Hans Tuppy (Apr. 10, 1970); Walter Thirring (June 9, 1986).
Belgium: Paul Adriaan Jan Janssen (June 25, 1990); Thierry Boon-Falleur (April 9, 2002).
Brazil: Carlos Chagas, former president of the academy (Aug. 18, 1961); Johanna Döbereiner (Apr. 17, 1978); Crodowaldo Pavan (Apr. 17, 1978); Rudolf Muradian (Oct. 16, 1994).
Canada: John Charles Polanyi* (June 9, 1986).

Chile: Héctor Rezzio Croxatto (Dec. 2, 1975); Rafael Vicuna (Nov. 10, 2000).
Congo (formerly Zaire): Felix wa Kalengo Malu (Sept. 26, 1983).
Denmark: Aage Bohr* (Apr. 17, 1978).
France: André Blanc-LaPierre (Apr. 17, 1978); Paul Germain (June 9, 1986); Jacques-Louis Lions (Oct. 4, 1990); Jean-Marie Lehn (May 30, 1996); Claude Cohen-Tannoudji (May 17, 1999); Nicole M. Le Douarin (Sept. 3, 1999); Pierre Jean Léna (Jan. 18, 2001).
Germany: Rudolf L. Mössbauer* (Apr. 10, 1970); Manfred Eigen* (May 12, 1981); Wolf Joachim Singer (Sept. 18, 1992); Paul Joseph Crutzen (June 25, 1996); Yuri Ivanovich Manin (June 26, 1996); Jürgen Mittelstrass (Sept. 21, 2002).
Ghana: Daniel Adzei Bekoe (Sept. 26, 1983).
Great Britain: Hermann Alexander Brück (Apr. 5, 1955); George Porter* (June 24, 1974); Max Ferdinand Perutz* (May 12, 1981); Stephen William Hawking (Jan. 9, 1986); Martin John Rees (June 25, 1990); Sir Richard Southwood (Sept. 18, 1992); Raymond Hide (June 25, 1996).
India: Mambillikalathil Govind Kumar Menon (May 12, 1981); Chintamani N.R. Rao (June 25, 1990).
Israel: Michael Sela (Dec. 2, 1975).
Italy: Giampietro Puppi (Apr. 17, 1978); Nicola Cabibbo (June 9, 1986), President; Nicola Dallaporta (Oct. 5, 1989), honorary member; Bernardo Maria Colombo (Sept. 18, 1992); Antonino Zichichi (Nov. 9, 2000); Enrico Berti (Sept. 28, 2001).
Japan: Minoru Oda (Sept. 18, 1992).
Kenya: Thomas R. Odhiambo (May 12, 1981).
Mexico: Marcos Moshinsky (June 9, 1986).
Nigeria: Thomas Adeoye Lambo (June 24, 1974).
Poland: Stanislaw Lojasiewicz (Jan. 28, 1983); Czeslaw Olech (June 9, 1986); Michal Heller (Oct. 4, 1990); Andrzej Szezeklik (Oct. 16, 1994).
Russia: Vladimir Isaakovich Keilis-Borok (Oct. 16, 1994); Sergei Petrovich Novikov (June 25, 1996), also teaches at University of Maryland).
Spain: Manuel Lora-Tamayo (Sept. 24, 1964).
Sweden: Sune Bergström* (Dec. 14, 1985); Kai Siegbahn* (Dec. 14, 1985).
Switzerland: Werner Arber* (May 12, 1981); Carlo Rubbia* (Dec. 14, 1985); Albert Eschenmoser (June 9, 1986).
Taiwan: Te-tzu Chang (Apr. 18, 1997).
Vatican City State: Cottier, Rev. George, O.P. (Oct. 28, 1992; honorary member); Rev. Enrico do Rovasenda, O.P. (Nov. 13, 1968), honorary member.
Venezuela: Marcel Roche (Apr. 10, 1970).
Ex officio members: Rev. George V. Coyne, S.J., director of Vatican Observatory (Sept. 2, 1978); Very Rev. Raffaele Farina, S.D.B., prefect of the Vatican Library (May 24, 1997); Very Rev. Sergio B. Pagano, prefect of the Secret Vatican Archives (Jan. 7, 1997). President: Nicola Cabibbo, professor of theoretical physics at University of Rome (app. Apr. 6, 1993). Chancellor: Most Rev. Marcelo Sánchez Sorondo.
Honorary members: Cardinal Joseph Ratzinger, Prefect of the Congregation for the Doctrine of the Faith and Cardinal Carlo Maria Martini, Archbishop of Milan.

PONTIFICAL ACADEMY OF SOCIAL SCIENCES

Founded by John Paul II, Jan. 1, 1994 (*motu proprio Socialium scientiarum investigationes*), to promote the study and the progress of social sciences, to advise the Vatican on social concerns and to foster research aimed at improving society. The number of members is not less than 20 nor more than 40. Two of the 30 members of the Academy (as of Jan. 1, 2003) were from the United States: Kenneth J. Arrow of Stanford University and Mary Ann Glendon of Harvard University. President, Prof. Edmond Malinvaud of France; Chancellor, Most Rev. Marcelo Sánchez Sorondo. Address: Casino Pio IV, Vatican Gardens.

PONTIFICAL ACADEMY FOR LIFE

Established by John Paul II, Feb. 11, 1994 (*motu proprio Vitae Mysterium*), "to fulfill the specific task of study, information and formation on the principal problems of biomedicine and law relative to the promotion and defense of life, especially in the direct relationship they have with Christian morality and the directives of the Church's magisterium."

Members, appointed by the pope without regard to religion or nationality, represent the various branches of "the biomedical sciences and those that are most closely related to problems concerning the promotion and protection of life." Membership, as of Jan. 1, 2003, included seven from the United States:

Prof. Carl Anderson, Vice-President of the Pontifical John Paul II Institute for Studies of Marriage and the Family; Mrs. Mercedes Arzu-Wilson, founder and president of the Foundations Family of the Americas and founder and director of the Commission at the World Organization for the Family; Dr. Thomas Hilgers, founder and director of the Institute "Paul VI," Omaha, NB; Mrs. Christine de Vollmer, president of the World Organization for the Family; Dr. Denis Cavanaugh, professor of obstetrics and gynecology at the University of South Florida College of Medicine; Prof. John M. Finnis, professor of philosophy of law, University of Oxford and Notre Dame University; Dr. A.J. Luke Gormally, director emeritus of Linacre Centre for Health Care Ethics in England and research professor at Ave Maria School of Law; Prof. Edmund Pellegrino, director of the Center for Advanced Studies in Ethics at Georgetown University, honorary member. President: Prof. Juan de Dios Vial Correa, physician and biologist.

Hierarchy of the Catholic Church

ORGANIZATION AND GOVERNMENT

As a structured society, the Catholic Church is organized and governed along lines corresponding mainly to the jurisdictions of the pope and Bishops. The pope is the supreme head of the Church. He has primacy of jurisdiction as well as honor over the entire Church. Bishops, in union with and in subordination to the pope, are the successors of the Apostles for care of the Church and for the continuation of Christ's mission in the world. They serve the people of their own dioceses, or particular churches, with ordinary authority and jurisdiction. They also share, with the pope and each other, common concern and effort for the general welfare of the whole Church.

Bishops of exceptional status are patriarchs of Eastern Catholic Churches who, subject only to the pope, are heads of the faithful belonging to their rites throughout the world.

Subject to the Holy Father and directly responsible to him for the exercise of their ministry of service to people in various jurisdictions or divisions of the Church throughout the world are: resident archbishops and metropolitans (heads of archdioceses), diocesan bishops, vicars and prefects apostolic (heads of vicariates apostolic and prefectures apostolic), certain abbots and prelates, and apostolic administrators. Each of these, within his respective territory and according to the provisions of canon law, has ordinary jurisdiction over pastors (who are responsible for the administration of parishes), priests, religious and lay persons.

Also subject to the Holy Father are titular archbishops and bishops, religious orders and congregations of pontifical right, pontifical institutes and faculties, papal nuncios and apostolic delegates.

Assisting the pope and acting in his name in the central government and administration of the Church are cardinals and other officials of the Roman Curia.

THE HIERARCHY

The ministerial hierarchy is the orderly arrangement of the ranks and orders of the clergy to provide for the spiritual care of the faithful, the government of the Church, and the accomplishment of the Church's total mission in the world.

Persons belong to this hierarchy by virtue of ordination and canonical mission.

The term hierarchy is also used to designate an entire body or group of bishops; for example, the hierarchy of the Church, the hierarchy of the United States.

Hierarchy of Order: Consists of the pope, bishops, priests and deacons. Their purpose, for which they are ordained to holy orders, is to carry out the sacramental and pastoral ministry of the Church.

Hierarchy of Jurisdiction: Consists of the pope and bishops by divine institution, and other church officials by ecclesiastical institution and mandate, who have authority to govern and direct the faithful for spiritual ends.

The Pope

His Holiness the Pope is the Bishop of Rome, Vicar of Jesus Christ, successor of St. Peter, Prince of the Apostles, Supreme Pontiff of the Universal Church, Patriarch of the West, Primate of Italy, Archbishop and Metropolitan of the Roman Province, Sovereign of the State of Vatican City, Servant of the Servants of God.

Cardinals
(*See* **Index**)

Patriarchs

Patriarch, a term which had its origin in the Eastern Church, is the title of a bishop who, second only to the pope, has the highest rank in the hierarchy of jurisdiction. He is the incumbent of one of the sees listed below. Subject only to the pope, a patriarch of the Eastern Church is the head of the faithful belonging to his rite throughout the world. The patriarchal sees are so called because of their special status and dignity in the history of the Church.

The Council of Nicaea (325) recognized three patriarchs — the Bishops of Alexandria and Antioch in the East, and of Rome in the West. The First Council of Constantinople (381) added the bishop of Constantinople to the list of patriarchs and gave him rank second only to that of the pope, the bishop of Rome and patriarch of the West; this action was seconded by the Council of Chalcedon (451) and was given full recognition by the Fourth Lateran Council (1215). The Council of Chalcedon also acknowledged patriarchal rights of the bishop of Jerusalem.

Eastern patriarchs are as follows: one of Alexandria, for the Copts; three of Antioch, one each for the Syrians, Maronites and Greek Melkites (the latter also has the personal title of Greek Melkite patriarch of Alexandria and of Jerusalem). The patriarch of

Babylonia, for the Chaldeans, and the patriarch of Sis, or Cilicia, for the Armenians, should be called, more properly, *Katholikos* — that is, a prelate delegated for a universality of causes. These patriarchs are elected by bishops of their churches; they receive approval and the pallium, symbol of their office, from the pope.

Latin Rite patriarchates were established for Antioch, Jerusalem, Alexandria and Constantinople during the Crusades; afterwards, they became patriarchates in name only. Jerusalem, however, was reconstituted as a patriarchate by Pius IX, in virtue of the bull *Nulla Celebrior* of July 23, 1847. In 1964, the Latin titular patriarchates of Constantinople, Alexandria and Antioch, long a bone of contention in relations with Eastern Churches, were abolished.

As of Aug. 15, 2003, the patriarchs in the Church were:

The Pope, Bishop of Rome, Patriarch of the West; Cardinal Stephanos II Ghattas, C.M., of Alexandria, for the Copts; Ignace Pierre VIII Abdel-Ahad, of Antioch, for the Syrians; Gregory III Laham, of Antioch, for the Greek Melkites (the patriarch also has personal titles of Alexandria and Jerusalem for the Greek Melkites); Cardinal Nasrallah Pierre Sfeir, of Antioch, for the Maronites; Michael Sabbah, of Jerusalem, for the Latin Rite; Nerses Bedros XIX Tarmouni, of Cilicia, for the Armenians. (For biographical information on the patriarchs, *see* **Eastern Catholics**.)

The titular patriarchs (in name only) of the Latin Rite were: Cardinal José da Cruz Policarpo of Lisbon; Archbishop Angelo Scola, of Venice; Archbishop Raul Nicolau Gonsalves of the East Indies (archbishop of Goa and Damao, India); and Archbishop Michel Sabbah of Jerusalem. The patriarchate of the West Indies has been vacant since 1963.

Major Archbishops

A major archbishop has the prerogatives but not the title of a patriarch. As of May 15, 2003, there were two major archbishops: Cardinal Lubomyr Husar of the major archbishopric of Lviv of the Ukrainian Catholic Church (Ukraine) and Cardinal Varkey Vithayathil, C.SS.R. of the major archbishopric of Ernakulam-Angomaly of the Syro-Malabar Church (India).

Archbishops, Metropolitans

Archbishop: A bishop with the title of an archdiocese.

Coadjutor Archbishop: An assistant archbishop with right of succession.

Metropolitan: Archbishop of the principal see, an archdiocese, in an ecclesiastical province consisting of several dioceses. He has the full powers of bishop in his own archdiocese and limited supervisory jurisdiction and influence over the other (suffragan) dioceses in the province. The pallium, conferred by the pope, is the symbol of his status as a metropolitan.

Titular Archbishop: Has the title of an archdiocese that formerly existed in fact but now exists in title only. He does not have ordinary jurisdiction over an archdiocese. Examples are archbishops in the Roman Curia, papal nuncios, apostolic delegates.

Archbishop *ad personam*: A title of personal honor and distinction granted to some bishops. They do not have ordinary jurisdiction over an archdiocese.

Primate: A title of honor given to the ranking prelate of some countries or regions.

Bishops

Diocesan Bishop: A bishop in charge of a diocese.

Coadjutor Bishop: An assistant (auxiliary) bishop to a diocesan bishop, with right of succession to the see.

Titular Bishops: A bishop with the title of a diocese that formerly existed in fact but now exists in title only; an assistant (auxiliary) bishop to a diocesan bishop.

Episcopal Vicar: An assistant, who may or may not be a bishop, appointed by a residential bishop as his deputy for a certain part of a diocese, a determined type of apostolic work, or the faithful of a certain rite.

Eparch, Exarch: Titles of bishops of Eastern churches.

Nomination of Bishops: Nominees for episcopal ordination are selected in several ways. Final appointment and/or approval in all cases is subject to decision by the pope.

In the U.S., bishops periodically submit the names of candidates to the archbishop of their province. The name are then considered at a meeting of the bishops of the province, and those receiving a favorable vote are forwarded to the pro-nuncio for transmission to the Holy See. Normally, three names are submitted. Bishops are free to seek the counsel of priests, religious and lay persons with respect to nominees.

Eastern Catholic churches have their own procedures and synodal regulations for nominating and making final selection of candidates for episcopal ordination. Such selection is subject to approval by the pope. The Code of Canon Law concedes no rights or privileges to civil authorities with respect to the election, nomination, presentation or designation of candidates for the episcopate.

Ad Limina Visit: Diocesan bishops and apostolic vicars are obliged to make an ad limina visit ("to the threshold" of the Apostles) every five years to the tombs of Sts. Peter and Paul, have audience with the Holy Father and consult with appropriate Vatican officials. They are required to send a report on conditions in their jurisdiction to the Congregation for bishops approximately six — and not less than three — months in advance of the scheduled visit.

Others with Ordinary Jurisdiction

Ordinary: One who has the jurisdiction of an office: the pope, diocesan bishops, vicars general, prelates of missionary territories, vicars apostolic prefects apostolic, vicars capitular during the vacancy of a see, superiors general, abbots primate and other major superiors of men religious.

Some prelates and abbots, with jurisdiction like that of diocesan bishops, are pastors of the people of God in territories (prelatures and abbacies) not under the jurisdiction of diocesan bishops.

Vicar Apostolic: Usually a titular bishop who has ordinary jurisdiction over a mission territory.

Prefect Apostolic: Has ordinary jurisdiction over a mission territory.

Apostolic Administrator: Usually a bishop appointed to administer an ecclesiastical jurisdiction temporarily. Administrators of lesser rank are also appointed on occasion and have more restricted supervisory duties.

Vicar General: A bishop's deputy for the administration of a diocese; does not have to be a bishop.

Prelates Without Jurisdiction

The title of protonotary apostolic was originally given by the fourth century or earlier to clergy who collected accounts of martyrdom and other church documents, or who served the Church with distinction in other ways. Other titles — e.g., domestic prelate, papal chamberlain, prelate of honor — are titles of clergy in service to the pope and the papal household, or of clergy honored for particular reasons. All prelates without jurisdiction are appointed by the pope, and have designated ceremonial privileges and the title of Rev. Monsignor.

SYNOD OF BISHOPS

The Synod of Bishops was chartered by Pope Paul VI Sept. 15, 1965, in a document he issued on his own initiative under the title *Apostolica Sollicitudo*. Provisions of this *motu proprio* are contained in Canons 342 to 348 of the Code of Canon Law. According to major provisions of the Synod charter:

• The purposes of the Synod are "to encourage close union and valued assistance between the Sovereign Pontiff and the bishops of the entire world; to insure that direct and real information is provided on questions and situations touching upon the internal action of the Church and its necessary activity in the world of today; to facilitate agreement on essential points of doctrine and on methods of procedure in the life of the Church."

• The Synod is a central ecclesiastical institution, permanent by nature.

• The Synod is directly and immediately subject to the pope, who has authority to assign its agenda, to call it into session, and to give its members deliberative as well as advisory authority.

• In addition to a limited number of ex officio members and a few heads of male religious institutes, the majority of the members are elected by and representative of national or regional episcopal conferences. The pope reserved the right to appoint the general secretary, special secretaries and no more than 15 per cent of the total membership.

The pope is president of the Synod. The secretary general is Cardinal Jan Schotte, C.I.C.M., of Belgium. Address: Palazzo del Bramante, Via della Concilizione 34, 00193 Rome, Italy.

An advisory council of 15 members (12 elected, three appointed by the pope) provides the secretariat with adequate staff for carrying on liaison with episcopal conferences and for preparing the agenda of synodal assemblies. Cardinal William H, Keeler, archbishop of Baltimore, is a member of the secretariat.

Assemblies

1. First Assembly: The first assembly was held from Sept. 29 to Oct. 29, 1967. Its objectives, as stated by Pope Paul VI, were "the preservation and strengthening of the Catholic faith, its integrity, its force, its development, its doctrinal and historical coherence." One result was a recommendation for the establishment of an international commission of theologians to assist the Congregation for the Doctrine of the Faith and to broaden approaches to theological research. Pope Paul set up the commission in 1969.

2. Pope-Bishop Relations: The second assembly, held Oct. 11 to 28, 1969, was extraordinary in character. It opened the way toward greater participation by bishops with the pope and each other in the governance of the Church. Proceedings were oriented to three main points: (1) the nature and implications of collegiality; (2) the relationship of bishops and their conferences to the pope; (3) the relationships of bishops and their conferences to each other.

3. Priesthood and Justice: The ministerial priesthood and justice in the world were the principal topics under discussion at the second ordinary assembly, Sept. 30 to Nov. 6, 1971. In one report, the Synod emphasized the primary and permanent dedication of priests in the Church to the ministry of word, sacrament and pastoral service as a full-time vocation. In another report, the assembly stated: "Action on behalf of justice and participation in the transformation of the world fully appear to us as a constitutive dimension of the preaching of the Gospel; or, in other words, of the Church's mission for the redemption of the human race and its liberation from every oppressive situation."

4. Evangelization: The assembly of Sept. 27 to Oct. 26, 1974, produced a general statement on evangelization of the modern world, covering the need for it and its relationship to efforts for total human liberation from personal and social evil. The assembly observed: "The Church does not remain within merely political, social and economic limits (elements which she must certainly take into account) but leads towards freedom under all its forms — liberation from sin, from individual or collective selfishness — and to full communion with God and with men who are like brothers. In this way the Church, in her evangelical way, promotes the true and complete liberation of all men, groups and peoples."

5. Catechetics: The fourth ordinary assembly, Sept. 30 to Oct. 29, 1977, focused attention on catechetics, with special reference to children and young people. The participants issued a "Message to the People of God," the first synodal statement issued since inception of the body, and also presented a set of 34 related propositions and a number of suggestions to Pope Paul VI.

6. Family: "A Message to Christian Families in the Modern World" and a proposal for a "Charter of Family Rights" were produced by the assembly held Sept. 26 to Oct. 25, 1980. The assembly reaffirmed the indissolubility of marriage and the contents of the encyclical letter *Humanae Vitae* (see separate entry), and urged married couples who find it hard to live up to "the difficult but loving demands" of Christ not to be discouraged but to avail themselves of the aid of divine grace. In response to synodal recommendation, Pope John Paul II issued a charter of family rights late in 1983.

7. Reconciliation: Penance and reconciliation in the mission of the Church was the theme of the assembly held Sept. 29 to Oct. 29, 1983. Sixty-three propositions related to this theme were formulated on a wide variety of subjects, including: personal sin and so-called systemic or institutional sin; the nature of serious sin; the diminished sense of sin and of the need of redemption, related to decline in the administration and reception of the sacrament of penance; general absolution; individual and social reconciliation; violence and violations of human rights; reconciliation as the basis of peace and justice in society. In a statement issued Oct. 27, the Synod stressed the need of the world to become increasingly "a reconciled community of peoples," and said that "the Church, as sacrament of reconciliation to the world, has to be an effective sign of God's mercy."

8. Vatican II Review: The second extraordinary assembly was convened Nov. 24 to Dec. 8, 1985, for the purposes of: (1) recalling the Second Vatican Council; (2) evaluating the implementation of its enactments during the 20 years since its conclusion; (3) seeking ways and means of promoting renewal in the Church in accordance with the spirit and letter of the council. At the conclusion of the assembly the bishops issued two documents. (1) In "A Message to the People of God," they noted the need for greater appreciation of the enactments of Vatican II and for greater efforts to put them into effect, so that all members of the Church might discharge their responsibility of proclaiming the good news of salvation. (2) In a "Final Report," the first of its kind published by a synodal assembly, the bishops reflected on lights and shadows since Vatican II, stating that negative developments had come from partial and superficial interpretations of conciliar enactments and from incomplete or ineffective implementation. The report also covered a considerable number of subjects discussed during the assembly, including the mystery of the Church, inculturation, the preferential (but not exclusive) option for the poor, and a suggestion for the development of a new universal catechism of the Catholic faith.

9. Vocation and Mission of the Laity in the Church and in the World 20 years after the Second Vatican Council: The seventh ordinary assembly, Oct. 1 to 30, 1987, said in a "Message to the People of God": "The majority of the Christian laity live out their vocation as followers and disciples of Christ in all spheres of life which we call 'the world': the family, the field of work, the local community and the like. To permeate this day-to-day living with the spirit of Christ has always been the task of the lay faithful; and it should be with still greater force their challenge today. It is in this way that they sanctify the world and collaborate in the realization of the kingdom of God." The assembly produced a set of 54 propositions which were presented to the pope for consideration in the preparation of a document of his own on the theme of the assembly. He responded with

the apostolic exhortation, *Christifideles Laici,* "The Christian Faithful Laity," released by the Vatican Jan. 30, 1989.

10. Formation of Priests in Circumstances of the Present Day: The eighth general assembly, Sept. 30 to Oct. 28, 1990, dealt principally with the nature and mission of the priesthood; the identity, multi-faceted formation and spirituality of priests; and, in a "Message to the People of God," the need on all levels of the Church for the promotion of vocations to the priesthood. Forty-one proposals were presented to the Pope for his consideration in preparing a document of his own on the theme of the assembly. Pope John Paul issued an apostolic exhortation entitled *Pastores Dabo Vobis* ("I Will Give You Shepherds") Apr. 7, 1992.

11. The Consecrated Life and Its Role in the Church and in the World: The ninth general assembly was held Oct. 2 to 29, 1994. Pope John Paul's reflections on the proceedings of the assembly and the recommendations of the bishops were the subjects of his apostolic exhortation *Vita Consecrata* ("Consecrated Life"), issued Mar. 25, 1996. The document dealt with various forms of consecrated life: contemplative institutes, apostolic religious life, secular institutes, societies of apostolic life, mixed institutes and new forms of evangelical life.

12. The Bishop: Servant of the Gospel of Jesus Christ for the Hope of the World: The 10th ordinary general assembly was held from September 30 to October 27, 2001. Pope John Paul II's reflections on the proceedings of the assembly and the recommendations of the Bishops will be the subject of an apostolic exhortation.

Recent Special Assemblies of the Synod of Bishops: Special Synods have been held for Europe (Nov. 28 to Dec. 14, 1991, on the theme "So that we might be witnesses of Christ who has set us free"); for Africa (Apr. 10 to May 8, 1994, on the theme "The Church in Africa and Her Evangelizing Mission Towards the Year 2000: 'You Shall Be My Witnesses' (Acts 1:8)"); for Lebanon (Nov. 27 to Dec. 14, 1995, on the theme "Christ is Our Hope: Renewed by His Spirit, in Solidarity We Bear Witness to His Love"); the Americas (Nov. 16 to Dec. 12, 1997, on the theme, "Encounter with the Living Jesus Christ: Way to Conversion, Community and Solidarity"); for Asia (Apr. 19 to May 14, 1998, on the theme "Jesus Christ the Savior and His Mission of Love and Service in Asia: '...That They May Have Life, and Have it Abundantly' (Jn. 10:10)"; for Oceania (Nov. 12 to Dec. 12, 1998, on the theme "Jesus Christ and the Peoples of Oceania: Walking His Way, Telling His Truth, Living His Life"; and a special assembly for Europe (Oct. 1-23, 1999), on the theme "Jesus Christ, Alive in His Church, Source of Hope for Europe."

COLLEGE OF CARDINALS

Cardinals are chosen by the pope to serve as his principal assistants and advisers in the central administration of church affairs. Collectively, they form the College of Cardinals. Provisions regarding their selection, rank, roles and prerogatives are detailed in Canons 349 to 359 of the Code of Canon Law.

History of the College

The College of Cardinals was constituted in its present form and categories of membership in the 12th century. Before that time the pope had a body of advisers selected from among the bishops of dioceses neighboring Rome, priests and deacons of Rome. The college was given definite form in 1150, and in 1179 the selection of cardinals was reserved exclusively to the pope. Sixtus V fixed the number at 70, in 1586. John XXIII set aside this rule when he increased membership at the 1959 and subsequent consistories. The number was subsequently raised by Paul VI. The number of cardinals entitled to participate in papal elections was limited to 120 by Paul VI in 1973. The limit on the number of cardinals was set aside by Pope John Paul II twice, in 1998 and again in 2001. As of Aug. 15, 2003, 109 of the 166 cardinals were eligible to vote.

In 1567 the title of cardinal was reserved to members of the college; previously it had been used by priests attached to parish churches of Rome and by the leading clergy of other notable churches. The Code of Canon Law promulgated in 1918 decreed that all cardinals must be priests. Previously there had been cardinals who were not priests (e.g., Cardinal Giacomo Antonelli, d. 1876, Secretary of State to Pius IX, was a deacon). John XXIII provided in the *motu proprio Cum Gravissima* Apr. 15, 1962, that cardinals would henceforth be bishops; this provision is included in the revised Code of Canon Law.

Age Limits

Pope Paul VI placed age limits on the functions of cardinals in the apostolic letter *Ingravescentem Aetatem,* dated Nov. 21, 1970, and effective Jan. 1, 1971. At 80, they cease to be members of curial departments and offices, and become ineligible to take part in papal elections. They retain membership in the College of Cardinals, however, with relevant rights and privileges.

Three Categories

All cardinals except Eastern patriarchs are aggregated to the clergy of Rome. This aggregation is signified by the assignment to each cardinal, except the patriarchs, of a titular church in Rome. The three categories of members of the college are cardinal bishops, cardinal priests and cardinal deacons.

Cardinal bishops include the six titular bishops of the suburbicarian sees and Eastern patriarchs. First in rank are the titular bishops of the suburbicarian sees neighboring Rome: Ostia, Palestrina, Porto-Santa

Rufina, Albano, Velletri-Segni, Frascati, Sabina-Poggio Mirteto. The dean of the college holds the title of the See of Ostia as well as his other suburbicarian see. These cardinal bishops are engaged in full-time service in the central administration of church affairs in departments of the Roman Curia.

Full recognition is given in the revised Code of Canon Law to the position of Eastern patriarchs as the heads of sees of apostolic origin with ancient liturgies. They are assigned rank among the cardinals in order of seniority, following the suburbicarian titleholders.

Cardinal priests, who were formerly in charge of leading churches in Rome, are bishops whose dioceses are outside Rome.

Cardinal deacons, who were formerly chosen according to regional divisions of Rome, are titular bishops assigned to full-time service in the Roman Curia.

The dean and sub-dean of the college are elected by the cardinal bishops — subject to approval by the pope — from among their number. The dean, or the sub-dean in his absence, presides over the college as the first among equals. Cardinals Joseph Ratzinger and Angelo Sodano were elected dean and vice-dean, respectively, on Nov. 30, 2002. The Secretary to the College of Cardinals is Archbishop Francesco Monterisi.

Selection and Duties

Cardinals are selected by the pope and are inducted into the college in appropriate ceremonies. Cardinals under the age of 80 elect the pope when the Holy See becomes vacant (*see* **Index: Papal Election**); and are major administrators of church affairs, serving in one or more departments of the Roman Curia. Cardinals in charge of agencies of the Roman Curia and Vatican City are asked to submit their resignation from office to the pope on reaching the age of 75. All cardinals enjoy a number of special rights and privileges. Their title, while symbolic of high honor, does not signify any extension of the powers of holy orders. They are called princes of the Church.

A cardinal *in pectore (petto)* is one whose selection has been made by the pope but whose name has not been disclosed; he has no title, rights or duties until such disclosure is made, at which time he takes precedence from the time of the secret selection.

BIOGRAPHIES OF CARDINALS

Biographies of the cardinals, as of Aug. 15, 2003, are given below in alphabetical order. For historical notes, order of seniority and geographical distribution of cardinals, see separate entries. An asterisk indicates cardinals ineligible to take part in papal elections.

Agré, Bernard: b. Mar. 2, 1926, Monga, Côte d'Ivoire; ord., July 20, 1953; headmaster in Dabou; vicar general of Abidjan archdiocese; app. bp. of Man, June 8, 1968; app. first bp. of Yamoussoukro, March 6, 1992; app. abp. of Abidjan, Dec. 19, 1994; pres. of the Episcopal Conferences of Francophone West Africa (CERAO) and chair of the Pan-African Episcopal Committee for Social Communications (CEPACS); cardinal, Feb. 21, 2001; titular church, St. John Chrysostom in Monte Sacro Alto. Abp. of Abidjan. *Curial membership:* Evangelization of Peoples (congregation); Justice and Peace, Family, Social Communications (councils).

Agustoni,* Gilberto: b. July 26, 1922, Schaffhausen, Switzerland; ord., Apr. 20, 1946; called to Rome in 1950 to work under Cardinal Ottaviani in the Congregation for the Holy Office; a Prelate Auditor of the Roman Rota, 1970-86; ord. titular abp. of Caorle Jan. 6, 1987; sec. of the Congregation for the Clergy, 1986-92; pro-prefect of the Apostolic Signatura, 1992-94; cardinal Nov. 26, 1994; deacon Sts. Urban and Laurence at Prima Porta. Prefect of Supreme Tribunal of Apostolic Signatura, 1994-98. Prefect emeritus of Supreme Tribunal of Apostolic Signatura. *Curial membership:* Bishops, Education (congregations); Supreme Tribunal of the Apostolic Signatura (tribunal); Interpretation of Legislative Texts (council); APSA (office).

Álvarez Martínez, Francisco: b. July 14, 1925, Santa Eulalia de Ferroñes Llanera, Spain; ord., June 11, 1950; personal secretary to Abp. Lauzurica y

Torralba of Oviedo; chancellor and secretary of archdiocesan curia; chaplain of the university students at Teresian Institute; app. bp. of Tarazona, April 13, 1973; cons., June 3, 1973; bp. of Calahorra and La Calzada-Logroño, Dec. 20, 1976; transferred to Orihuela-Alicante, May 12, 1989; abp. of Toledo, 1995-2002; member of the Standing Committee and the Executive Committee of the Spanish Episcopal Conference; cardinal, Feb. 21, 2001; titular church, St. Mary *Regina Pacis* in Monte Verde. Abp. emeritus of Toledo. *Curial membership:* Christian Unity, Laity (councils).

Ambrozic, Aloysius M.: b. Jan. 27, 1930, Gabrje, Slovenia (emigrated to Austria, 1945, and Canada, 1948); ord., June 4, 1955; taught Scripture, St. Augustine's Seminary, 1960-67; taught NT exegesis, Toronto School of Theology, 1970-76; aux. bp. of Toronto, March 26, 1976; co-adjutor of Toronto, May 22, 1986; abp. of Toronto, March 17, 1990; cardinal, Feb. 21, 1998; titular church, Sts. Marcellinus and Peter. *Curial membership*: Oriental Churches, Sacraments, Clergy (congregation); Pastoral Care of Migrants and Itinerant People, Culture (councils).

Angelini,* Fiorenzo: b. Aug. 1, 1916, Rome, Italy; ord., Feb. 3, 1940; master of pontifical ceremonies, 1947-54; ord. bp. (titular see of Messene) July 29, 1956, and head of Rome Vicariate's section for apostolate to health care workers; abp, 1985; pres. of newly established Curia agency for health care workers; cardinal, June 28, 1991, deacon, Holy Spirit (in Sassio). President of Pontifical Council for Pastoral Assistance to Health Care Workers, 1989-96.

Antonetti,* Lorenzo: b. July 31, 1922, Romagnano Sesia, Italy; ord., May 26, 1945; entered diplomatic service and served in Lebanon, Venezuela, first section for Extraordinary Affairs of the Secretariat of State, U.S., and France; ord. titular abp. of Roselle, May 12, 1968; apostolic nuncio to Nicaragua and Honduras, 1968-1973, and Zaire, 1973-77; secretary of the Administration of the Patrimony of the Apostolic See (APSA), 1977-88; apostolic nuncio to France, 1988-95; pro-president Admin. of the Patrimony of the Apostolic See, 1995-1998; pres. Administration of the Patrimony of the Apostolic See (APSA)., Feb. 23, 1998; cardinal, Feb. 21, 1998; deaconry, St. Agnes in Agone. President emeritus Administration of the Patrimony of the Apostolic See.

Aponte Martínez,* Luis: b. Aug. 4, 1922, Lajas, Puerto Rico; ord., Apr. 10, 1950; parish priest at Ponce; ord. titular bp. of Lares and aux. of Ponce, Oct. 12, 1960; bp. of Ponce, 1963-64; abp. of San Juan, Nov. 4, 1964-99; cardinal, Mar. 5, 1973; titular church, St. Mary Mother of Providence (in Monte Verde). Abp. emeritus of San Juan.

Aramburu,* Juan Carlos: b. Feb. 11, 1912, Reduccion, Argentina; ord. in Rome, Oct. 28, 194; ord. titular bp. of Plataea and aux. of Tucuman, Argentina, Dec. 15, 1946; bp., 1953, and first abp., 1957, of Tucuman; titular abp. of Torri di Bizacena and coadj. abp. of Buenos Aires, June 14, 1967; abp. of Buenos Aires, Apr. 22, 1975 (resigned July 10, 1990); cardinal, May 24, 1976; titular church, St. John Baptist of the Florentines. Abp. emeritus of Buenos Aires.

Arinze, Francis: b. Nov. 1, 1932, Eziowelle, Nigeria; ord., Nov. 23, 1958; ord. titular bp. of Fissiana and aux. bp. of Onitsha, Aug. 29, 1965; abp. of Onitsha, 1967-84; pro-president of Secretariat for Non-Christians (now the Council for Interreligious Dialogue), 1984; cardinal, May 25, 1985; deacon, St. John (della Pigna); transferred to the order of cardinal priests, Jan. 29, 1996; President of Council for Interreligious Dialogue, 1985-2002; Prefect of the Congregation for Divine Worship and the Discipline of the Sacraments, Oct. 1, 2002. *Curial membership*: Doctrine of the Faith, Oriental Churches, Evangelization of Peoples, Causes of Saints (congregations); Laity, Christian Unity, Culture (councils); International Eucharistic Congresses (committee).

Arns,* O.F.M., Paulo Evaristo: b. Sept. 14, 1921, Forquilhinha, Brazil; ord., Nov. 30, 1945; held various teaching posts; director of *Sponsa Christi*, monthly review for religious, and of the Franciscan publication center in Brazil; ord. titular bp. of Respetta and aux. bp. of São Paulo, July 3, 1966; abp. of São Paulo, Oct. 22, 1970-98; cardinal, Mar. 5, 1973; titular church, St. Anthony of Padua (in Via Tuscolana). Abp. emeritus of São Paulo.

Backis, Audrys Juozas: b. Feb. 1, 1937, Kaunas, Lithuania; ord., March 18, 1961; entered Holy See diplomatic service in 1964 and posted to the Philippines, Costa Rica, Turkey, Nigeria, and the Council for the Public Affairs of the Church; underscretary to the Council for the Public Affairs of the Church, 1979-88; app. titular abp. of Meta and nuncio to the Netherlands, Aug. 5, 1988; app. abp. of Vilnius Dec. 24, 1991; pres. of the Lithuanian Bishops' Conference; cardinal, Feb. 21, 2001; titular church, Nativity of Our Lord Jesus Christ in Via Gallia. Abp. of Vilnius. *Curial membership*: Education (congregation); Social Communication (council); Cultural Heritage of the Church (commission).

Bafile,* Corrado: b. July 4, 1903, L'Aquila, Italy; practiced law in Rome for six years before beginning studies for priesthood; ord., Apr. 11, 1936; served in Vatican secretariat of state, 1939-59; ord. titular abp. of Antiochia in Pisidia, Mar. 19, 1960; apostolic nuncio to Germany, 1960-75; pro-prefect of Congregation for Causes of Saints, July 18, 1975; cardinal, May 24, 1976; deacon, S. Maria (in Portico); transferred to order of cardinal priests, June 22, 1987; prefect of Congregation for Causes of Saints, 1976-80.

Baum, William Wakefield: b. Nov. 21, 1926, Dallas, TX; moved to Kansas City, MO, at an early age; ord. (Kansas City-St. Joseph diocese), May 12, 1951; executive director of U.S. Bishops' Commission for Ecumenical and Interreligious Affairs, 1964-69; attended Second Vatican Council as *peritus* (expert adviser); ord. bp. of Springfield-Cape Girardeau, MO, Apr. 6, 1970; abp. of Washington, DC, 1973-80; cardinal, May 24, 1976; titular church, Holy Cross on the Via Flaminia; prefect of Congregation for Catholic Education (Seminaries and Institutes of Study), 1980-90. Major Penitentiary, 1990-2001; res., Nov. 22, 2001. *Curial membership*: Bishops, Oriental Churches, Consecrated Life and Societies of Apostolic Life, Evangelization of Peoples (congregations).

Bergoglio, S.J., Jorge Mario: b. Dec. 17, 1936, Buenos Aires, Argentina; ord., priest for the Jesuits, Dec. 13, 1969; novice master in the Theological Faculty of San Miguel; Jesuit provincial for Argentina, 1973-79; rector of the Philosophical and Theological Faculty of San Miguel, 1980-86; completed doctoral dissertation in Germany and served as confessor and spiritual director in Córdoba; app. titular bp. of Auca and aux. bp. of Buenos Aires, May 20, 1992; cons., June 27, 1992; app. coadj. abp. of Buenos Aires, June 3, 1997; succeeded as abp. of Buenos Aires, Feb. 28, 1998; also serves as Ordinary for Eastern-rite faithful in Argentina who lack their own ordinary and second vice-pres. of the Argentine Episcopal Conference; cardinal, Feb. 21, 2001; titular church, St. Robert Bellarmine. Abp. of Buenos Aires. *Curial membership*: Sacraments, Clergy, Institutes of Consecrated Life and Societies of Apostolic Life (congregations); Family (council).

Bevilacqua,* Anthony Joseph: b. June 17, 1923, Brooklyn NY; ord., (Brooklyn diocese), June 11, 1949; ord. titular bp. of Aquae Albae in Byzacena and aux. bp. of Brooklyn, Nov. 24, 1980; bp. of Pittsburgh, Oct. 7, 1983, installed, Dec. 12, 1983; abp. of Philadelphia, Feb. 11, 1988; cardinal, June 28, 1991; titular church, Most Holy Redeemer and St. Alphonsus (on Via Merulana); ret., July 15, 2003. Abp. emeritus of Philadelphia. *Curial membership*: Clergy, Causes of Saints (congregations); "Cor Unum," Migrants and Itinerant People (councils); Institute for Works of Religion (commission).

Biffi, Giacomo: b. June 13, 1928, Milan, Italy; ord., Dec. 23, 1950; ord. titular bp. of Fidene and aux. of Milan, Jan. 11, 1976; abp. of Bologna, Apr. 19, 1984; cardinal, May 25, 1985; titular church, Sts. John the Evangelist and Petronius. Archbp. of Bologna. *Curial membership*: Clergy, Catholic Education, Evangelization (congregations).

Cacciavillan, Agostino: b. Aug. 14, 1926, Novale de Valdagno (Vicenza), Italy; ord., June 26, 1949; attended Pont. Ecclesiastical Academy; entered Holy See diplomatic service; posted to the Philippines, Spain, Portugal, and Secretariat of State; pro-nuncio in Kenya and apostolic delegate to Seychelles, 1976; titular abp. of Amiternum, Feb. 28, 1976; nuncio to India, 1981; pro-nuncio to Nepal, 1985; nuncio to United States and permanent observer at the Org. of American States, 1990; pres., Admin. of the Patrimony of the Apostolic See (APSA), 1998-2002; cardinal, Feb. 21, 2001; titular church, Deaconry of the Holy Guardian Angels in Città Giardino. Pres. emeritus Admin. of the Patrimony of the Apostolic See. *Curial membership*: Bishops, Causes of Saints, Evangelization of Peoples, Oriental Churches (congregations); Texts, (council); Latin America, Vatican City State (commissions); Signatura (tribunal).

Canestri,* Giovanni: b. Sept. 30, 1918, Castelspina, Italy; ord., Apr. 12, 1941; spiritual director of Rome's seminary, 1959; ord. titular bp. of Tenedo and aux. to the cardinal vicar of Rome, July 30, 1961; bp. of Tortona, 1971-75; titular bp. of Monterano (personal title of abp.) and vice regent of Rome, 1975-84; abp. of Cagliari, 1984-87; abp. of Genoa, July 6, 1987-95; cardinal, June 28, 1988; titular church, St. Andrew of the Valley. Abp. emeritus of Genoa.

Caprio,* Giuseppe: b. Nov. 15, 1914, Lapio, Italy; ord., Dec. 17, 1938; served in diplomatic missions in China (1947-51, when Vatican diplomats were expelled by communists, Belgium (1951-54), and South Vietnam (1954-56); internuncio in China with residence at Taiwan, 1959-67; ord. titular abp. of Apollonia, Dec. 17, 1961; pro-nuncio in India, 1967-69; secretary, 1969-77, and president, 1979-81, of APSA; substitute secretary of state, 1977-79; car-

dinal deacon, June 30, 1979; transferred to order of cardinal priests, Nov. 1990; titular church, St. Mary of Victory; president of Prefecture of Economic Affairs of the Holy See, 1981-90. Grand Master of Equestrian Order of the Holy Sepulchre, 1988-95.

Carles Gordó, Ricardo Maria: b. Sept. 24, 1926, Valencia, Spain; ord., June 29, 1951; ord. bp. of Tortosa, Aug. 3, 1969; abp. of Barcelona, Mar. 23, 1990; cardinal, Nov. 26, 1994; titular church, St. Mary of Consolation in Tiburtino. Abp. of Barcelona. *Curial membership*: Catholic Education (congregation); Economic Affairs of the Holy See (office).

Cassidy, Edward Idris: b. July 5, 1924, Sydney, Australia; ord., July 23, 1949; entered Vatican diplomatic service in 1955; served in nunciatures in India, Ireland, El Salvador and Argentina; ord. titular bp. of Amantia with personal title of abp., Nov. 15, 1970; pro-nuncio to Republic of China (Taiwan), 1970-79 and pro-nuncio to Bangladesh and apostolic delegate in Burma, 1973-79; pro-nuncio to Lesotho and apostolic delegate to southern Africa, 1979-84; pro-nuncio to the Netherlands, 1984-88; substitute of the Secretary of State for General Affairs, 1988-89; pres. of Pontifical Council for Promoting Christian Unity, 1989-2001; cardinal, June 28, 1991; deacon, St. Mary (in via Lata). President emeritus of Pontifical Council for Promoting Christian Unity. *Curial membership*: Bishops, Divine Worship and Sacraments, Evangelization of Peoples, Oriental Churches (congregations); Interreligious Dialogue (councils).

Castillo Lara,* S.D.B., Rosalio José: b. Sept. 4, 1922, San Casimiro, Venezuela; ord., Sept. 4, 1949; ord. titular bp. of Precausa, May 24, 1973; coadj. bp. of Trujillo, 1973-76; abp., May 26, 1982; pro-pres. of Pontifical Commission for Revision of Code of Canon Law, 1982-84; pro-pres. of Commission for Authentic Interpretation of Code of Canon Law, 1984-85; cardinal, May 25, 1985; deacon, Our Lady of Coromoto (in St. John of God); transferred to order of cardinal priests, Jan. 29, 1996; pres. of Administration of Patrimony of the Holy See, 1989-95. President of the Pontifical Commission for the State of Vatican City State, 1990-97.

Castrillón Hoyos, Darío: b. July 4, 1929, Medellín, Colombia; ord., Oct. 26, 1952; served as curate in two parishes; dir. local Cursillo Movement; delegate for Catholic Action; taught canon law at the Free Civil University; gen. sec. of the Colombian Bishops' Conference; coadj. bp. of Pereira, June 2, 1971; bp. of Pereira, 1976-1992; gen. sec. of Latin American Episcopal Council (CELAM), 1983-87; pres. CELAM, 1987-91; abp. of Bucaramanga, 1992-96; pro-prefect Cong. for the Clergy, 1996-98; Pref. Cong. for the Clergy, 1998; cardinal, Feb. 21, 1998; deaconry, Holy Name of Mary on the Forum Traiani. Prefect of the Congregation for the Clergy. *Curial membership*: Bishops, Divine Worship and Sacraments, Education, Evangelization of Peoples (congregations); Social Communications, Texts (councils); APSA (office); Latin America (commission).

Cé, Marco: b. July 8, 1925, Izano, Italy; ord., Mar. 27, 1948; taught sacred scripture and dogmatic theology at seminary in his home diocese of Crema; rector of seminary, 1957; presided over diocesan liturgical commission, preached youth retreats; ord. titular bp. of Vulturia, May 17, 1970; aux. bp. of Bologna, 1970-76; gen. ecclesiastical assistant of Italian Catholic Action, 1976-78; patriarch of Venice, 1978-2001; ret., Jan. 5, 2002; cardinal, June 30, 1979; titular church, St. Mark. Patriarch emeritus of Venice.

Cheli,* Giovanni: b. Oct. 4, 1918, Turin, Italy; ord., June 21, 1942; entered Secretariat of State and diplomatic service; second secretary, apostolic nunciature in Guatemala, 1952-55; first secretary, apostolic nunciature in Madrid, Spain, 1955-62; counselor, nunciature in Rome, 1962-67; Council for Public Affairs of the Church, Vatican City, 1967-73; Permanent Observer of the Holy See to the U.N., 1973-86; ord. titular abp. of Santa Giusta, Sept. 16, 1978; pres. Pontifical Council for the Pastoral Care of Migrants and Itinerant People, 1986-98; cardinal, Feb. 21, 1998; deaconry, Sts. Cosmas and Damian. President Emeritus Pontifical Council for the Pastoral Care of Migrants and Itinerant People.

Cipriani Thorne, Juan Luis: b. Dec. 28, 1943, Lima, Peru; champion basketball player and student in industrial engineering, he joined Opus Dei in 1962; ord. for the prelature, Aug. 21, 1977; after a doctorate in theology at the University of Navarre and pastoral work in Lima, he taught moral theology at the Pontifical Faculty of Theology, Lima, and was regional vicar for Peru and vice-chancellor of the University of Piura; app. titular bp. of Turuzi and aux. bp. of Ayacucho, May 23, 1988; cons. July 3, 1988; app. abp. of Ayacucho, May 13, 1995; tried to negotiate a peaceful resolution to the siege of the Japanese ambassador's residence in Lima, December 1996-April 1997 and ministered to Japanese and Peruvian hostages; app. abp. of Lima, Jan. 9, 1999; cardinal priest, Feb. 21, 2001; titular church St. Camillus de Lellis. Abp. of Lima. *Curial membership*: Causes of Saints, Sacraments (congregation); Latin America (commission).

Clancy, Edward Bede: b. Dec. 13, 1923, Lithgow, New South Wales, Australia; ord., July 23, 1949; ord. titular bp. of Ard Carna and aux. of Sydney, Jan. 19, 1974; abp. of Canberra, 1978-83; abp. of Sydney, Feb. 12, 1983; res., Mar. 26, 2001; cardinal, June 28, 1988; titular church, Holy Mary of Vallicella. Abp. emeritus of Sydney.

Connell, Desmond: b. Mar. 24, 1926, Phibsboro, Ireland; ord., May 19, 1951; taught at University College Dublin, 1953-72; dean of the faculty of Philosophy and Sociology, 1983; awarded degree of D.Litt. by National University of Dublin, 1981; chaplain to the Poor Clares in Donnybrook and Carmelites in Drumcondra and Blackrock; app. abp. of Dublin, Jan. 21, 1988; cons., Mar. 6, 1988; cardinal, Feb. 21, 2001; titular church, St. Sylvester *in Capite*. Abp. of Dublin. *Curial membership*: Bishops, Doctrine of the Faith (congregations); Laity (council).

Corripio Ahumada,* Ernesto: b. June 29, 1919, Tampico, Mexico; ord., Oct. 25, 1942, in Rome, where he remained until almost the end of World War II; taught and held various positions in local seminary of Tampico, 1945-50; ord. titular bp. of Zapara and aux. bp. of Tampico, Mar. 19, 1953; bp. of Tampico, 1956-67; abp. of Antequera, 1967-76; abp. of Puebla de los Angeles, 1976-77; abp. of Mexico City and primate of Mexico, July 19, 1977-1994; cardinal, June 30, 1979; titular church, Mary Immaculate al Tiburtino. Abp. emeritus of Mexico City.

Daly,* Cahal Brendan: b. Oct. 1, 1917, Loughguile, Northern Ireland; ord., June 22, 1941; earned ad-

vanced degrees in philosophy and theology; 30 years of priestly life dedicated to teaching; attended Second Vatican Council as a theological adviser to members of Irish hierarchy; outspoken critic of violence in Northern Ireland; ord. bp. of Ardagh, July 16, 1967; bp. of Down and Connor, 1982-90; abp. of Armagh and primate of All Ireland, 1990-96; cardinal, June 28, 1991; titular church, St. Patrick. Abp. emeritus of Armagh.

Danneels, Godfried: b. June 4, 1933, Kanegem, Belgium; ord., Aug. 17, 1957; professor of liturgy and sacramental theology at Catholic University of Louvain, 1969-77; ord. bp. of Antwerp, Dec. 18, 1977; app. abp. of Mechelen-Brussel, Dec. 19, 1979; installed, Jan. 4, 1980; cardinal, Feb. 2, 1983; titular church, St. Anastasia. Abp. of Mechelen-Brussel, military ordinary of Belgium. *Curial membership*: Secretariat of State (second section); Divine Worship and Sacraments, Education, Evangelization of Peoples, Oriental Churches (congregations).

Darmaatmadja, S.J., Julius Riyadi: b. Dec. 20, 1934, Muntilan, Mageland, Central Java, Indonesia; entered Society of Jesus in 1957; ord.; Dec. 18, 1969; ord. abp. of Semarang, June 29, 1983 (transferred to Jakarta, Jan. 11, 1996); cardinal, Nov. 26, 1994; titular church, Sacred Heart of Mary. Abp. of Jakarta, military ordinary of Indonesia (1984). *Curial membership*: Evangelization of Peoples (congregation); Interreligious Dialogue (council).

de Giorgi, Salvatore: b. Sep. 6, 1930 Vernole, Italy; ord., June 28, 1953; diocesan chaplain to the Teachers' Movement of Catholic Action; dir. Diocesan Pastoral Office; app. titular bp. of Tulana and aux. bp. of Oria, Nov. 21, 1973; bp. of Oria, Mar. 17, 1978; abp. of Foggia, Apr. 4, 1981; abp. of Taranto, Oct. 10, 1987 (resigned, 1990); general president of Catholic Action, 1990-96; abp. of Palermo, Apr. 4, 1996; president of the Sicilian Episcopal Conference; cardinal, Feb. 21, 1998; titular church, St. Mary in Ara Caeli. Abp. of Palermo. *Curial membership*: Clergy (congregations); Laity, Family (councils).

Deskur, Andrzej Maria: b. Feb. 29, 1924, Sancygniow, Poland; ord., Aug. 20, 1950, in France; assigned to Vatican secretariat of state, 1952; undersecretary and later secretary of Pontifical Commission for Film, Radio and TV (Social Communications), 1954-73; ord. titular bp. of Tene, June 30, 1974; abp., 1980; president of Pontifical Commission for Social Communications, 1974-84; cardinal, May 25, 1985; deacon, St. Cesario (in Palatio); transferred to order of cardinal priests, Jan. 29, 1996. President emeritus of Council for Social Communications. *Curial membership*: Causes of Saints, Divine Worship and Sacraments (congregations); Health Care Workers (council); State of Vatican City (commission).

Dias, Ivan: b. April 14, 1936, Bandra, India; ord., Dec. 8, 1958; entered the Holy See diplomatic service and was posted to Indonesia, Madagascar, Reunion, the Comorros, Mauritius, and Secretariat of State; app. titular abp. of Rusubisir and pro-nuncio in Ghana, Togo and Benin, May 8, 1982; cons., June 19, 1982; nuncio in Korea, 1987-91; nuncio in Albania, 1991-97; app. abp. of Bombay, Jan. 22, 1997; cons., Mar. 13, 1997; cardinal, Feb. 21, 2001; titular church, Holy Spirit in Ferratella. Abp. of Bombay. *Curial membership*: Doctrine of the Faith, Sacraments, Education (congregations); Culture, Laity (councils); Economic Affairs (office); Cultural Heritage of the Church (commission).

do Nascimento, Alexandre: b. Mar. 1, 1925, Malanje, Angola; ord., Dec. 20, 1952, in Rome; professor of dogmatic theology in major seminary of Luanda, Angola; editor of *O Apostolada*, Catholic newspaper; forced into exile in Lisbon, Portugal, 1961-71; returned to Angola, 1971; active with student and refugee groups; professor at Pius XII Institute of Social Sciences; ord. bp. of Malanje, Aug. 31, 1975; abp. of Lubango and apostolic administrator of Onjiva, 1977-86; held hostage by Angolan guerrillas, Oct. 15 to Nov. 16, 1982; cardinal, Feb. 2, 1983; titular church, St. Mark in Agro Laurentino. Abp. of Luanda, 1986. *Curial membership*: Catholic Education (congregations).

Dulles,* S.J., Avery: b. Aug. 24, 1918, Auburn, NY; the son of U.S. Secretary of State John Foster Dulles; raised a Protestant, he converted to the Catholic faith while a student at Harvard; served in U.S. Navy and then entered the Jesuits; ord. priest for the Jesuits, June 16, 1956; earned a doctorate in theology at the Gregorian University, Rome; taught theology at Woodstock College, 1960-74, and Catholic University of America, 1974-88; visiting professor at numerous other institutions; author of 21 books and over 650 articles; pres. of the Catholic Theological Society of America; member of the International Theological Commission and the U.S. Lutheran/Roman Catholic Dialogue; consultor to the U.S. Bishops' Committee on Doctrine; currently the Laurence J. McGinley Professor of Religion and Society at Fordham University; cardinal, Feb. 21, 2001; titular church, Deaconry of the Most Holy Names of Jesus and Mary in Via Lata.

Egan, Edward Michael: b. Apr. 2, 1932, Oak Park, IL; ord., Dec. 15, 1957, in Rome; sec. to Cardinal Albert Meyer, 1958-60; assistant vice-rector of the North American College, 1960-64; vice-chancellor of the archdiocese of Chicago, 1964-68; co-chancellor for human relations and ecumenism, 1968-72; judge of Roman Rota, 1972-85; ord. titular bp. of Allegheny and aux. bp. of New York, May 22, 1985; app. bp. of Bridgeport, Nov. 5, 1988; abp. of New York, May 11, 2000, inst., June 19, 2000; cardinal, Feb. 21, 2001; titular church, St. John and Paul. Abp. of New York. *Curial membership*: Family (council); Signatura (tribunal); Economic Affairs (office); Cultural Heritage (commission).

Errázuriz Ossa, Francisco Javier: b. Sept. 5, 1933, Santiago, Chile; ord. for the Schönstatt Fathers, July 16, 1961; chaplain to students and professionals of the Schönstatt Movement and regional superior; elected superior general of the Schönstatt Fathers, 1974; app. titular abp. of Hólar and sec. of the Cong. For Institutes of Consecrated Life and Societies of Apostolic Life, Dec. 22, 1990; app. abp. of Valparaiso, Sept. 24, 1996; transferred to archdiocese of Santiago, April 24, 1998; pres. of the Episcopal Conference of Chile and first vice-pres. of CELAM; cardinal, Feb. 21, 2001; titular church, St. Mary of Peace. Abp. of Santiago. *Curial membership*: Consecrated Life and Societies of Apostolic Life (congregation); Family (council); Latin America (commission).

Etchegaray,* Roger: b. Sept. 25, 1922, Espelette, France; ord., July 13, 1947; deputy director, 1961-66,

and secretary general, 1966-70, of French Episcopal Conference; ord. titular bp. of Gemelle di Numidia and aux. of Paris, May 27, 1969; abp. of Marseilles, 1970-84; prelate of Mission de France, 1975-82; president of French Episcopal Conference, 1979-81; cardinal, June 30, 1979; titular church, St. Leo I. President of Council *Cor Unum*, 1984-95; president of Council for Justice and Peace (1984-98) and President of Central Committee for the Jubilee of the Holy Year 2000 (1994-98); transferred to order of cardinal bishops, June 24, 1998 (suburbicarian see of Porto-Santa Rufina). President of the Central Committee for the Jubilee of the Holy Year 2000.

Etsou-Nzabi-Bamungwabi, C.I.C.M., Frédéric: b. Dec. 3, 1930, Mazalonga, Zaire; ord., July 13, 1958; educ. Catholic Institute of Paris (degree in sociology) and "Lumen Vitae" in Belgium (degree in pastoral theology); ord. titular bp. of Menefessi and coadj. abp. of Mbandaka-Bikora, Nov. 7, 1976; abp. of Mbandaka-Bikora, 1977-1990; abp. of Kinshasa, July 7, 1990; cardinal, June 28, 1991; titular church, St. Lucy (a Piazza d'Armi). Abp. of Kinshasa. *Curial membership*: Evangelization of Peoples (congregation); Family (council).

Falcão, José Freire: b. Oct. 23, 1925, Erere, Brazil; ord., June 19, 1949; ord. titular bp. of Vardimissa and coadj. of Limoeiro do Norte, June 17, 1967; bp. of Limoeiro do Norte, Aug. 19, 1967; abp. of Teresina, Nov. 25, 1971; abp. of Brasilia, Feb. 15, 1984; cardinal, June 28, 1988; titlar church, St. Luke (Via Prenestina). Abp. of Brasilia. *Curial membership*: Health Care Workers (council).

Felici,* Angelo: b. July 26, 1919, Segni, Italy; ord., Apr. 4, 1942; in Vatican diplomatic service from 1945; ord. titular bp. of Cesariana, with personal title of abp., Sept. 24, 1967; nuncio to Netherlands, 1967-76, Portugal, 1976-79, France, 1979-88; cardinal, June 28, 1988; deacon, Sts. Blaise and Charles in Catinari, promoted to cardinal priest, Jan. 9, 1999. Prefect of Congregation for Causes of Saints, 1988-95. President of Pontifical Commission "Ecclesia Dei," 1995.

Fernandes de Araújo, Serafim: b. Aug. 13, 1924, Minas Novas, Brazil; ord., Mar. 12, 1949; taught canon law at provincial seminary of Diamantina; titular bp. of Verinopolis and aux. bp. of Belo Horizonte, Jan. 19, 1959; co-adjutor abp. of Belo Horizonte, 1982; abp. Belo Horizonte, Feb. 5, 1986; co-president of the Fourth General Conference of the Latin American Episcopate, 1992; cardinal, Feb. 21, 1998; titular church, St. Louis Marie Grignion de Montfort. Abp. of Belo Horizonte. *Curial membership*: Bishops (congregation); Latin America (commission), Justice and Peace (council).

Fresno Larraín,* Juan Francisco: b. July 26, 1914, Santiago, Chile; ord., Dec. 18, 1937; ord. bp. of Copiapo, Aug. 15, 1958; abp. of La Serena, 1967-83; abp. of Santiago, May 3, 1983-90; cardinal, May 25, 1985; titular church, St. Mary Immaculate of Lourdes (a Boccea). Abp. emeritus of Santiago.

Furno,* Carlo: b. Dec. 2, 1921, Bairo Canavese, Italy; ord., June 25, 1944; entered diplomatic service of the Holy See in the 1950s; served in Colombia, Ecuador and Jerusalem; worked in Secretariat of State for 11 years and taught at Pontifical Ecclesiastical Academy, 1966-73; ord. titular bp. of Abari with personal title of abp., Sept. 16, 1973; nuncio in Peru, 1973-78, Lebanon, 1978-82, Brazil, 1982-92, Italy,

1992-94; cardinal, Nov. 26, 1994; deacon, Sacred Heart of Christ the King. Grand Master of the Equestrian Order of the Holy Sepulchre, 1995; pontifical delegate for Patriarchal Basilica of St. Francis in Assisi, 1996; archpriest of the patriarchal basilica of Santa Maria Maggiore, Rome, 1998.

Gagnon,* P.S.S., Edouard: b. Jan. 15, 1918, Port Daniel, Que., Canada; ord., Aug. 15, 1940; ord. bp. of St. Paul in Alberta, Mar. 25, 1969 (resigned May 3, 1972); rector of Canadian College in Rome, 1972-77; vice president-secretary of Vatican Committee for the Family, 1973-80; titular abp. of Giustiniana Prima, July 7, 1983; pro-president of Pontifical Council for the Family, 1983; cardinal, May 25, 1985; deacon, St. Elena (fuori Porta Prenestina); transferred to order of cardinal priests, Jan. 29, 1996; titular church St. Marcellus. President of Pontifical Council for the Family, 1985-90; president of Pontifical Committee for International Eucharistic Congresses, 1991-2000.

Gantin,* Bernardin: b. May 8, 1922, Toffo, Dahomey (now Benin); ord., Jan. 14, 1951; ord. titular bp. of Tipasa di Mauritania and aux. bp. of Cotonou, Feb. 3, 1957; abp. of Cotonou, 1960-71; associate secretary (1971-73) and secretary (1973-75) of Congregation for Evangelization of Peoples; vice-president (1975) and president (1976-84) of Pontifical Commission for Justice and Peace; cardinal deacon, June 27, 1977; transferred to order of priests, June 25, 1984; titular church, Sacred Heart of Christ the King; titular bp. of suburbicarian see of Palestrina Sept. 29, 1986, when he entered the order of cardinal bishops, and of Ostia June 5, 1993 (res. Nov. 30, 2002), when he became dean of the college of cardinals. Prefect of Congregation for Bishops, 1984-98; president of commission for Latin America, 1984-98; dean of college of cardinals, 1993-2002.

George, O.M.I., Francis E.: b. Jan. 16, 1937, Chicago, IL; ord., Dec. 21, 1963; provincial of central region of Oblates of Mary Immaculate, 1973-74, vicar general, 1974-86; ord. bp. of Yakima, Sept. 21, 1990; abp. of Portland, OR, Apr. 30, 1996, installed, May 27, 1996; abp. of Chicago, Apr. 8, 1997, installed, May 7, 1997; cardinal, Feb. 21, 1998; titular church, St. Bartholomew on Tiber Island. Abp. of Chicago. *Curial membership*: Divine Worship and the Discipline of the Sacraments, Institutes of Consecrated Life and Societies of Apostolic Life, Oriental Churches, Evangelization (congregations); *Cor Unum* (council); Cultural Heritage of the Church (commission).

Giordano, Michele: b. Sept. 26, 1930, S. Arcangelo, Italy; ord., July 5, 1953; ord. titular bp. of Lari Castello and aux. of Matera, Feb. 5, 1972; abp. of Matera and Irsina, 1974-87; abp. of Naples, May 9, 1987; cardinal, June 28, 1988; titular church, St. Joachim. Abp. of Naples. *Curial membership*: Clergy (congregation); Health Care Workers (council).

Glemp, Józef: b. Dec. 18, 1929, Inowroclaw, Poland; assigned to forced labor on German farm in Rycerzow during Nazi occupation; ord., May 25, 1956; studied in Rome, 1958-64; received degree in Roman and canon law from Pontifical Lateran University; secretary of primatial major seminary at Gniezno on his return to Poland, 1964; spokesman for secretariat of primate of Poland and chaplain of primate for archdiocese of Gniezno, 1967; ord. bp. of Warmia, Apr. 21, 1979; abp. of Gniezno, 1981-92, with title of abp. of Warsaw and primate of Poland;

cardinal, Feb. 2, 1983; titular church, St. Mary in Trastevere. Abp. of Warsaw (Mar. 25, 1992), primate of Poland, ordinary for Eastern-rite faithful in Poland who do not have ordinaries of their own rites. *Curial membership*: Oriental Churches (congregation); Signatura (tribunal); Culture (council).

González Martín,* Marcelo: b. Jan. 16, 1918, Villanubla, Spain; ord., June 29, 1941; taught theology and sociology at Valladolid diocesan seminary; founded organization for construction of houses for poor; ord. bp. of Astorga, Mar. 5, 1961; titular abp. of Case Mediane and coadj. of Barcelona, Feb. 21, 1966; abp. of Barcelona, 1967-71; abp. of Toledo, 1971-95; cardinal, Mar. 5, 1973; titular church, St. Augustine. Abp. emeritus of Toledo.

González Zumárraga, Antonio José: b. Mar. 18, 1925, Pujilí (Cotopaxi), Ecuador; ord., June 29, 1951; taught at the Pontifical Catholic University of Ecuador; chancellor of the Curia, 1964; rector of Our Mother of Mercy College; app. titular bp. of Tagarata and aux. bp. of Quito; apostolic admin. of Machala, Mar. 1976; bp. of Machata, Jan. 30, 1978; coadj. abp. of Quito, June 28, 1980; abp. of Quito, June 1, 1985; served two terms as pres. of the Ecuadorean Episcopal Conference; cardinal priest, Feb. 21, 2001; titular church, St. Mary *in Via*. Abp. of Quito. *Curial membership*: Laity (council); Latin America (commission).

Grocholewski, Zenon: b. Oct. 11, 1939, Bródki, Poland; ord., May 26, 1963; earned a doctorate in canon law; served in the Supreme Tribunal of the Apostolic Signatura, 1972-1999; prefect of the Supreme Tribunal of the Apostolic Signatura; member of the commission studying the 1983 *Code of Canon Law*; titular bp. of Agropoli, Dec. 21, 1982; titular abp., Dec. 16, 1991; prefect of the Cong. for Catholic Education, Nov. 15, 1999; titular church, Deaconry of St. Nicholas *in Carcere*. Prefect of the Congregation for Catholic Education. *Curial membership*: Bishops, Doctrine of the Faith (congregations); Texts (council).

Gulbinowicz, Henryk Roman: b. Oct. 17, 1928, Szukiszki, Poland; ord., June 18, 1950; ord. titular bp. of Acci and apostolic administrator of Polish territory in Lithuanian archdiocese of Vilnius (Vilna), Feb. 8, 1970; abp. of Wroclaw, Poland, Jan. 3, 1976; cardinal, May 25, 1985; titular church, Immaculate Conception of Mary (a Grottarosa). Abp. of Wroclaw. *Curial membership*: Oriental Churches (congregations).

Hickey,* James A.: b. Oct. 11, 1920, Midland, MI; ord., (Saginaw diocese) June 15, 1946; ord. titular bp. of Taraqua and aux. of Saginaw, Apr. 14, 1967; rector of North American College, Rome, 1969-74; bp. of Cleveland, 1974-80; app. abp. of Washington, DC, June 17, 1980, installed, Aug. 5, 1980; cardinal, June 28, 1988; titular church, St. Mary Mother of the Redeemer; ret., Nov. 2000. Abp. emeritus of Washington, DC.

Honoré,* Jean: b. Aug. 13, 1920; ord., June 29, 1943; authored doctoral dissertation under the direction of Jean Daniélou at the *Institute Catholique*, Paris; taught at St. Vincent's College in Rennes and in Saint-Malo; worked for six years at the National Religious Education Centre (CNEC); rector of the Catholic University of Angers; app. bp. of Evreux, Oct. 24, 1972; cons., Dec. 17, 1972; app. abp. of Tours, Aug. 13, 1981; participated in the preparation of the

Catechism, following the 1985 Synod of Bishops; res. as abp. of Tours, July 22, 1997; cardinal, Feb. 21, 2001; titular church, St. Mary of Health in Primavalle. Abp. emeritus of Tours.

Hummes, O.F.M., Cláudio: b. Aug. 8, 1934, Montenegro, Brazil; ord., priest for the Franciscans, Aug. 3, 1958; specialist in ecumenism; taught philosophy at the Franciscan seminary in Garibaldi, at the major seminary of Viamão and the Pontifical Catholic University of Porto Alegre; adviser for ecumenical affairs to the National Bishops' Conference of Brazil; Provincial of Rio Grande do Sul, 1972-75; pres. of the Union of Latin American Conferences of Franciscans; app. coadj. bp. of Santo André, Mar. 22, 1975; cons., May 25, 1975; succeeded to see, Dec. 29, 1975; app. abp. of Fortaleza, July 21, 1996; transferred to São Paulo, May 23, 1998; cardinal, Feb. 21, 2001; titular church, St. Anthony of Padua in Via Merulana. Abp. of São Paulo. *Curial membership*: Bishops, Doctrine of the Faith, Sacraments (congregation); *Cor Unum*, Culture, Family, Interreligious Dialogue, Laity (councils); Latin America (commission).

Husar, M.S.U., Lubomyr: b. Feb. 26, 1933, Lviv, Ukraine; family fled to Austria because of the war and then to the U.S.; ord. for the eparchy of Stamford for Ukrainians, U.S., Mar. 30, 1958; entered the Studite Monks after completing a doctorate in theology in Rome; superior of the Studion in Grottaferrata, Italy; ord. bp. April 2, 1977; app. archimandrite of Studite Monks residing outside Ukraine; organized a new Studite monastery in Ternopil, Ukraine, 1994; elected exarch of Kyiv-Vyshorod, 1995; app. aux. bp. to major abp. of Lviv, 1996; elected major abp. of Lviv for Ukrainians, Jan. 25, 2001; cardinal, Feb. 21, 2001; titular church, Holy Wisdom in Via Boccea. Major Abp. of Lviv for Ukrainians. *Curial membership*: Oriental Churches (congregation); Christian Unity, Texts (councils).

Innocenti,* Antonio: b. Aug. 23, 1915, Poppi, Italy; ord., July 17, 1938; held curial and diplomatic positions; ord. titular bp. of Eclano with personal title of abp., Feb. 18, 1968; nuncio to Paraguay, 1967-73; secretary of Congregation for Causes of Saints, 1973-75; secretary of Congregation for Sacraments and Divine Worship, 1975-80; nuncio to Spain, 1980-85; cardinal deacon, May 25, 1985; transferred to order of cardinal priests, Jan. 29, 1996; titular church, St. Marie (in Aquiro); prefect of Congregation for the Clergy, 1986-91; president of Pontifical Commission for Preservation of Artistic Patrimony of the Church, 1988-91; president of Pontifical Commission "Ecclesia Dei," 1991-95.

Javierre Ortas,* S.D.B., Antonio María: b. Feb. 21, 1921, Sietamo, Spain; ord., Apr. 24, 1949; leading European writer on ecumenism; ord. titular bp. of Meta with personal title of abp., June 29, 1976; Secretary of Congregation for Catholic Education, 1976-88; cardinal, June 28, 1988; deacon (Santa Maria Liberatrice a Monte Testaccio), promoted to cardinal priest, Jan. 9, 1999 (Santa Maria Liberatrice a Monte Testaccio; raised to presbyteral title). Librarian and Archivist of the Holy Roman Church, 1988-92. Prefect of Congregation for Divine Worship and the Sacraments, 1992-96.

Jaworski, Marian: b. Aug. 21, 1926, Lwów, Poland (modern Lviv, Ukraine); ord., June 25, 1950;

taught at the Catholic Theological Academy of Warsaw and Pontifical Theological faculty of Kraków; first rector of the Pontifical Theological Academy, Kraków, 1981-87; app. titular bp. of Lambaesis and apostolic admin. of Lubaczów, May 21, 1984; cons., June 23, 1984; app. abp. of Lviv for Latins, Jan. 16, 1991; pres. of the Ukrainian Episcopal Conference, 1992; cardinal (*in pectore*), Feb. 21, 1998; titular church, St. Sixtus. Abp. of Lviv for Latins. *Curial membership*: Clergy (congregation); Family (council).

Kasper, Walter: b. Mar. 5, 1933, Heidenheim/ Brenz, Germany; ord., April 6, 1957; taught theology and was later dean of the theological faculty in Münster and Tübingen; app. bp. of Rottenburg-Stuttgart, April 17, 1989, cons., June 17, 1989; co-chair of the International Commission for Lutheran/ Catholic Dialogue, 1994; sec. of the Pontifical Council for Promoting Christian Unity, June 1, 1999; pres. Pontifical Council for Promoting Christian Unity, 2001; cardinal deacon, Feb. 21, 2001; titular church, Deaconry of All Saints in Via Appia Nuova. President of the Pontifical Council for Promoting Christian Unity. *Curial membership:* Doctrine of the Faith, Oriental Churches (congregations); Signatura (tribunal); Culture (council).

Keeler, William Henry: b. Mar. 4, 1931, San Antonio, TX; ord., (Harrisburg diocese) July 17, 1955; secretary to Bp. Leech at Vatican II, named *peritus* by Pope John XXIII; ord. titular bp. of Ulcinium and aux. bp. of Harrisburg, Sept. 21, 1979; bp. of Harrisburg, Nov. 10, 1983, installed, Jan. 4, 1984; abp. of Baltimore, Apr. 6, 1989; cardinal, Nov. 26, 1994; titular church, St. Mary of the Angels. Abp. of Baltimore. *Curial membership*: Oriental Churches (congregation); Christian Unity (council).

Kim Sou-hwan,* Stephen: b. May 8, 1922, Tae Gu, Korea; ord., Sept. 15, 1951; ord. bp. of Masan, May 31, 1966; abp. of Seoul, Apr. 9, 1968 (resigned May 29, 1998); cardinal, Apr. 28, 1969; titular church, St. Felix of Cantalice (Centocelle). Abp. emeritus of Seoul, apostolic administrator emeritus of Pyeong Yang.

Kitbunchu, Michael Michai: b. Jan. 25, 1929, Samphran, Thailand; ord., Dec. 20, 1959, in Rome; rector of metropolitan seminary in Bangkok, 1965-72; ord. abp. of Bangkok, June 3, 1973; cardinal, Feb. 2, 1983, the first from Thailand; titular church, St. Laurence in Panisperna. Abp. of Bangkok. *Curial membership*: Evangelization of Peoples, Sacraments (congregation).

König,* Franz: b. Aug. 3, 1905, Rabenstein, Lower Austria; ord., Oct. 29, 1933; ord. titular bp. of Livias and coadj. bp. of Sankt Poelten, Aug. 31, 1952; abp. of Vienna, May 10, 1956-85; cardinal, Dec. 15, 1958; titular church, St. Eusebius; president of Secretariat (now Council) for Dialogue with Non-Believers, 1965-80. Abp. emeritus of Vienna.

Korec, Ján Chryzostom, S.J.: b. Jan. 22, 1924, Bosany, Slovakia; entered Society of Jesus in 1939; ord., Oct. 1, 1950; ord. bp. secretly, Aug. 24, 1951; sentenced to 12 years in prison in 1960 for helping seminarians with their study and ordaining priests; paroled in 1968; appointed bp. of Nitra, Feb. 6, 1990; cardinal, June 28, 1991; titular church, Sts. Fabian and Venantius (a Villa Forelli). Bp. of Nitra. *Curial membership*: Clergy, Institutes of Consecrated Life and Societies of Apostolic Life (congregation); Culture (council).

Kozlowiecki,* S.J., Adam: b. Apr. 1, 1911, Huta Komorowska, Poland; ord., June 24, 1937; arrested by Nazi Gestapo with 24 fellow priests in Kraków in 1939 and sent to Auschwitz concentration camp; moved to Dachau six months later where he suffered throughout the war; sent to Rhodesia after the war and taught until 1950; appointed apostolic administrator of prefecture of Lusaka, 1950; appointed bp. and vicar apostolic, Sept. 11, 1955; appointed abp. of Lusaka, 1959; res., 1969, to allow a native African to receive the post; member Congregation for the Evangelization of People, 1970-91; cardinal, Feb. 21, 1998; titular church, St. Andrew on the Quirinal.

Laghi,* Pio: b. May 21, 1922, Castiglione, Italy; ord., Apr. 20, 1946; entered diplomatic service of the Holy See in 1952; served in Nicaragua, the U.S. (as secretary of the apostolic delegation, 1954-61) and India; recalled to Rome and served on Council for Public Affairs of the Church; ord. titular abp. of Mauriana, June 22, 1969; apostolic delegate to Jerusalem and Palestine, 1969-74; nuncio to Argentina, 1974-80; apostolic delegate, 1980-84, and first pro-nuncio, 1984-90 to the U.S.; pro-prefect of Congregation for Catholic Education, 1990-91; cardinal, June 28, 1991; deacon, St. Mary Auxiliatrix (in Via Tuscolana). Prefect of Congregation for Catholic Education, 1991-99. Grand chancellor of Pontifical Gregorian University. Patron of Sovereign Military Order of Malta, 1993. Protodeacon, 1999-2002.

Law, Bernard F.: b. Nov. 4, 1931, Torreon, Mexico, the son of U.S. Air Force colonel; ord., (Jackson diocese), May 21, 1961; editor of Natchez-Jackson, MS, diocesan paper, 1963-68; director of NCCB Committee on Ecumenical and Interreligious Affairs, 1968-71; ord. bp. of Springfield-Cape Girardeau, MO, Dec. 5, 1973; abp. of Boston, Jan. 11, 1984; cardinal, May 25, 1985; titular church, St. Susanna; res., Dec.13, 2002. Abp. emeritus of Boston. *Curial membership*: Bishops, Clergy, Consecrated Life and Societies of Apostolic Life, Divine Worship and Sacraments, Education, Evangelization of Peoples, Oriental Churches; (congregations); Culture, Family (councils).

Lehmann, Karl: b. May 16, 1936, Sigmaringen, Germany; ord., Oct. 10, 1963; earned doctorates in theology and philosophy; assistant to Fr. Karl Rahner at University of Münster; taught dogmatic theology at the Johannes Gutenberg University, Mainz; member of the Central Committee of German Catholics and the Jaeger-Stählin Ecumenical Circle; taught at the Albert Ludwig University, Freiburg im Breisgau; member of the International Theological Commission; edited the official publication of the documents of the Joint Synod of the Dioceses in the Federal Republic of Germany, Synod of Würzburg, 1971-75; app. bp. of Mainz, June 21, 1983; cons., Oct. 2, 1983; pres. of the German Bishops' Conference; cardinal, Feb. 21, 2001; titular church, St. Leo I. Bp. of Mainz. *Curial membership*: Bishops, Oriental Churches (congregations); Christian Unity (council); APSA (office).

López Rodriguez, Nicolás de Jesús: b. Oct. 31, 1936, Barranca, Dominican Republic; ord., Mar. 18, 1961; sent to Rome for advanced studies at the Angelicum and Gregorian Univ.; served in various diocesan offices after returning to his home diocese of La Vega; ord. first bp. of San Francisco de Macoris, Feb. 25, 1978; abp. of Santo Domingo, Nov. 15, 1981; cardinal, June 28, 1991; titular church, St. Pius X (alla Balduina). Abp. of Santo Domingo and Military Ordinary for Dominican Republic. *Curial membership*: Clergy, Institutes of Consecrated Life and Societies of Apostolic Life (congregations); Social Communications (council); Latin America (commission) .

López Trujillo, Alfonso: b. Nov. 8, 1935, Villahermosa, Colombia; ord., Nov. 13, 1960, in Rome; returned to Colombia, 1963; was pastoral coordinator for 1968 International Eucharistic Congress in Bogota; vicar general of Bogota, 1970-72; ord. titular bp. of Boseta, Mar. 25, 1971; aux. bp. of Bogota, 1971-72; secretary-general of CELAM, 1972-78; helped organize 1979 Puebla Conference in which Pope John Paul II participated; app. coadj. abp. of Medellin, May 22, 1978; abp. of Medellin, June 2, 1979 (res. Jan 9, 1991); president of CELAM, 1979-83; cardinal, Feb. 2, 1983; titular church, St. Prisca; promoted to cardinal bishop, Nov. 17, 2001; suburbicarian see, Frascati. Abp. emeritus of Medellin. President of the Pontifical Council for the Family, 1990. *Curial membership*: Bishops, Doctrine of the Faith, Causes of Saints, Evangelization of Peoples (congregations); Latin America (commission).

Lorscheider, O.F.M., Aloisio: b. Oct. 8, 1924, Estrela, Brazil; received in Franciscan Order, Feb. 1, 1942; ord., Aug. 22, 1948; professor of theology at the Antonianum, Rome, and director of Franciscan international house of studies; ord. bp. of Santo Angelo, Brazil, May 20, 1962; abp. of Fortaleza, 1973-95; president of CELAM, 1975-79; cardinal, May 24, 1976; titular church, S. Pietro (in Montorio). Abp. of Aparecida, July 12, 1995. *Curial membership*: Consecrated Life and Societies of Apostolic Life (congregation).

Lourdusamy, D. Simon: b. Feb. 5, 1924, Kalleri, India; ord., Dec. 21, 1951; ord. titular bp. of Sozusa and aux. of Bangalore, Aug. 22, 1962; titular abp. of Filippi and coadj. abp. of Bangalore, Nov. 9, 1964; abp. of Bangalore, 1968-71; associate secretary, 1971-73, and secretary, 1973-85, of Congregation for Evangelization of Peoples; cardinal, May 25, 1985; deacon, St. Mary of Grace; transferred to the order of cardinal priests, Jan. 29, 1996; prefect of Congregation for Oriental Churches, 1985-91. *Curial membership*: Causes of Saints, Evangelization of Peoples (congregations); Signatura (tribunal); Family, Interreligious Dialogue (councils); International Eucharistic Congresses (commission).

Lustiger, Jean-Marie: b. Sept. 17, 1926, Paris, France, of Polish-Jewish parents who emigrated to France after World War I; taken in by Catholic family in Orleans when his parents were deported during Nazi occupation (his mother died in 1943 at Auschwitz); convert to Catholicism, baptized Aug. 25, 1940; active in Young Christian Students during university days; ord., Apr. 17, 1954; ord. bp. of Orleans, Dec. 8, 1979; abp. of Paris, Jan. 31, 1981; cardinal, Feb. 2, 1983; titular church, St. Louis of France. Abp. of Paris, ordinary for Eastern-Rite faithful in France without ordinaries of their own. *Curial membership*: Secretariat of State (second section); Bishops, Clergy, Consecrated Life and Societies of Apostolic Life, Oriental Churches, (congregations); Culture (council).

McCarrick, Theodore E.: b. July 7, 1930, New York, NY; ord., May 31, 1958; dean of students Catholic Univ. of America, 1961-63; pres., Catholic Univ. of Puerto Rico, 1965-69; secretary to Cardinal Cooke, 1970; ord. titular bp. of Rusubisir and aux. bp. of New York, June 29, 1977; app. first bp. of Metuchen, NJ, Nov. 19, 1981, installed, Jan. 31, 1982; app. abp. of Newark, June 3, 1986, installed, July 25, 1986; abp. of Washington, Nov. 21, 2000; ins., Jan. 3, 2001, cardinal priest, Feb. 21, 2001; titular church, Sts. Nereus and Achilleus. Abp. of Washington. *Curial membership*: Justice and Peace (council); APSA.

Macharski, Franciszek: b. May 20, 1927, Kraków, Poland; ord., Apr. 2, 1950; engaged in pastoral work, 1950-56; continued theological studies in Fribourg, Switzerland, 1956-60; taught pastoral theology at the Faculty of Theology in Kraków; app. rector of archdiocesan seminary at Kraków, 1970; ord. abp. of Kraków, Jan. 6, 1979, by Pope John Paul II; cardinal priest, June 30, 1979; titular church, St. John at the Latin Gate. Abp. of Kraków. *Curial membership*: Secretariat of State (second section); Bishops, Clergy, Consecrated Life and Societies of Apostolic Life, Education, Evangelization of Peoples (congregations).

Mahony, Roger M.: b. Feb. 27, 1936, Hollywood, CA; ord., (Fresno diocese) May 1, 1962; ord. titular bp. of Tamascani and aux. bp. of Fresno, Mar. 19,1975; bp. of Stockton, Feb. 15, 1980, installed, Apr. 25, 1980; abp. of Los Angeles, July 16, 1985, installed, Sept. 5, 1985; cardinal, June 28, 1991; titular church, Four Crowned Saints. Abp. of Los Angeles. *Curial membership*: Social Communications (council); Economic Affairs (office).

Maida, Adam Joseph: b. Mar. 18, 1930, East Vandergrift, PA; ord., (Pittsburgh diocese), May 26, 1956; ord. bp. of Green Bay, Jan. 25, 1984; app. abp. of Detroit, Apr. 28, 1990, installed, June 12, 1990; cardinal, Nov. 26, 1994; titular church, Sts. Vitalis, Valeria, Gervase and Protase. Abp. of Detroit. *Curial membership*: Clergy, Education (congregations); Migrants and Itinerant Peoples (council); Institute for Works of Religion (commission).

Majella Agnelo, Geraldo: b. Oct. 19, 1933, Juiz de Fora, Brazil; ord. June 29, 1957; taught at the seminary of Aparecida, Immaculate Conception Seminary, and Pius XI Theological Institute; rector of Our Lady of the Assumption Seminary; bp. of Toledo, May 5, 1978; cons., Aug. 6, 1978; app. abp. of Londrina, Oct. 27, 1982; pres. of the Brazilian Bishops' Liturgical Commission; app. sec. of the Cong. For Divine Worship and the Discipline of Sacraments, Sept. 16, 1991; app. abp. of São Salvador da Bahia, Jan. 13, 1999; cardinal priest, Feb. 21, 2001; titular church, St. Gregory the Great in Magliana Nuova. Abp. of São Salvador da Bahia. *Curial membership*: Pastoral Care of Migrants and Itinerant People (council); Cultural Heritage of the Church (commission).

Margéot,* Jean: b. Feb. 3, 1916, Quatre-Bornes, Mauritius; ord., Dec. 17, 1938; ord. bp. of Port Louis, 1969-93; cardinal, June 28, 1988; titular church, St. Gabriel the Archangel all'Acqua Traversa. Bp. emeritus of Port Louis.

Martinez Somalo, Eduardo: b. Mar. 31, 1927, Baños de Rio Tobia, Spain; ord., Mar. 19, 1950; ord. titular bp. of Tagora with personal title of abp., Dec. 13, 1975; in secretariat of state from 1956; substitute (assistant) secretary of state, 1979-88; cardinal, June 28, 1988; deacon, Most Holy Name of Jesus (raised *pro hac vice* to presbyteral title); promoted to cardinal priest, Jan. 9, 1999; prefect of Congregation for Divine Worship and Sacraments, 1988-92. Prefect of Congregation for Institutes of Consecrated Life and Societies of Apostolic Life, Jan. 21, 1992; Chamberlain (Camerlengo) of the Holy Roman Church, Apr. 5, 1993; Protodeacon, 1996-99. *Curial membership*: Secretariat of State (second section); Bishops, Causes of Saints, Clergy, Divine Worship and Sacraments, Education, Evangelization of Peoples (congregations); Texts (council); Latin America, Institute for Works of Religion (commissions).

Martini, S.J., Carlo Maria: b. Feb. 15, 1927, Turin, Italy; entered Jesuits, Sept. 25, 1944; ord., July 13, 1952; biblical scholar; seminary professor, Chieri, Italy, 1958-61; professor and later rector, 1969-78, of Pontifical Biblical Institute; rector of Pontifical Gregorian University, 1978-79; author of theological, biblical and spiritual works; abp. of Milan, 1980-2002; cardinal, Feb. 2, 1983; titular church, St. Cecilia. Abp. emeritus of Milan. *Curial membership*: Consecrated Life and Societies of Apostolic Life, Education Oriental Churches (congregations); Culture (council); Cultural Heritage of the Church (commission).

Mayer,* O.S.B., Paul Augustin: b. May 23, 1911, Altötting, Germany; ord., Aug. 25, 1935; rector of St. Anselm's Univ., Rome, 1949-66; secretary of Congregation for Religious and Secular Institutes, 1972-84; ord. titular bp. of Satriano with personal title of abp., Feb. 13, 1972; pro-prefect of Congregations for Sacraments and Divine Worship, 1984; cardinal, May 25, 1985; deacon, St. Anselm; transferred to order of cardinal priests, Jan. 29, 1996. Prefect of Congregation for Divine Worship and Sacraments, 1985-88; president of Pontifical Commission "Ecclesia Dei," 1988-91.

Medina Estévez, Jorge Arturo: b. Dec. 23, 1926, Santiago, Chile; ord., June 12, 1954; ord. abp., Jan. 6, 1985, Santiago, Chile; appointed pro-Prefect, Congregation for Divine Worship and the Discipline of the Sacraments, 1996-98; prefect of the Congregation for Divine Worship and the Discipline of the Sacraments, 1998-2002; cardinal, Feb. 21, 1998; deaconry, St. Sabas. Prefect emeritus of the Congregation for Divine Worship and the Discipline of the Sacraments. *Curial membership*: Bishops, Clergy, Doctrine of the Faith (congregations); Family, Texts (councils); Latin America, *Ecclesia Dei* (commission).

Meisner, Joachim: b. Dec. 25, 1933, Breslau, Silesia, Germany (present-day Wroclaw, Poland); ord., Dec. 22, 1962; regional director of Caritas; ord. titular bp. of Vina and aux. of apostolic administration of Erfurt-Meiningen, E. Germany, May 17, 1975; bp. of Berlin, 1980-88; cardinal, Feb. 2, 1983; titular church, St. Prudenziana. Abp. of Cologne, Dec. 20, 1988. *Curial membership*: Bishops, Clergy, Divine Worship and Sacraments (congregations); Economic Affairs of Holy See (office).

Mejía,* Jorge María: b. Jan. 31, 1923, Buenos Aires, Argentina; ord., Sept. 22, 1945; prof. of Old Testament studies at Catholic University of Buenos Aires; *peritus* at Second Vatican Council; sec. of CELAM's Department of Ecumenism, 1967-77; sec.

of Pontifical Commission for Religious Relations with Jews, 1977-86; vice-president of the Pontifical Commission Justice and Peace and titular bp. of Apollonia, April 12, 1986; sec. of the Cong. for Bishops and titular abp., Mar. 1994; Archivist and Librarian of the Holy Roman Church, 1998; cardinal deacon, Feb. 21, 2001; titular church, Deaconry of St. Jerome *della Carità*. Archivist and Librarian of the Holy Roman Church. *Curial membership*: Causes of Saints (congregation); Culture, Justice and Peace, Interreligious Dialogue (councils); Cultural Heritage of the Church (commission).

Monduzzi,* Dino: b. Apr. 2, 1922, Brisighella, Italy; ord., July 22, 1945; director of Catholic Action in Calabria and Sardinia; served in Agrarian Reform Agency in Fucino; sec. in the Office of the Maestro di Camera, 1959-67; sec. and regent of the Apostolic Palace, 1967-86; ord. titular bp. of Capri,Jan. 6, 1987; prefect of the Papal Household 1986-1998; cardinal, Feb. 21, 1998; deaconry, St. Sebastian on the Palatine. *Curial membership*: Causes of Saints, Divine Worship and the Discipline of the Sacraments (congregations).

Moussa I Daoud, Ignace: b. Sept. 18, 1930, Meskaneh, Syria; ord., Oct. 17, 1954; elected July 2, 1977, bp. of Cairo, Egypt by Syrian Patriarchal Synod; cons., Sept. 18, 1977; member of the commission for the revision of the Eastern Code of Canon Law and chaired the commission that translated the Code of Canons of the Eastern Churches into Arabic; promoted abp. of Homs for Syrians, Syria, July 6, 1994; elected patriarch of Antioch for Syrians, Oct. 13, 1998; app. prefect of the Cong. for the Oriental Churches, Nov. 25, 2000; cardinal, Feb. 21, 2001 (as patriarch, he has no titular church). Prefect of the Congregation for the Oriental Churches. *Curial membership*: Doctrine of the Faith, Causes of Saints (congregations), Christian Unity, Legislative Texts (councils).

Murphy-O'Connor, Cormac: b. Aug. 24, 1932, Reading, Great Britain; ord., Oct. 28, 1956; dir. of vocations and secretary to the bp.; rector of the Venerable English College, Rome, 1971-77; app. bp. of Arundel and Brighton, Nov. 17, 1977; cons., Dec. 21, 1977; co-chairman of the Anglican-Roman Catholic International Commission (ARCIC), 1982-2000; chairman of several committees of the Bishop's Conference of England and Wales; app. abp. of Westminster, Feb. 15, 2000; cardinal, Feb. 21, 2001; titular church, St. Mary *sopra Minerva*. Abp. of Westminster. *Curial membership*: Sacraments (congregation); Christian Unity, Culture, Family (councils); APSA (office); Cultural Heritage (commission).

Napier, O.F.M., Wilfrid Fox: b. Mar. 8, 1941, Swartberg, South Africa; ord., for the Franciscans, July 25, 1970; app. apostolic admin. of Kokstad, 1978; app. bp. of Kokstad, Nov. 29, 1980; cons., Feb. 28, 1981; deeply involved in the mediation and negotiations surrounding the ending of apartheid in South Africa and subsequent South African politics; pres. of the Southern African Catholic Bishops' Conference, 1987-94; app. abp. of Durban, May 29, 1992; apostolic admin. *sede vacante et ad nutum Sanctae Sedis* of Umzimkulu, 1994; cardinal, Feb. 21, 2001; titular church, St. Francis of Assisi in Acilia. Abp. of Durban. *Curial membership*: Evangelization of Peoples, Institutes of Consecrated Life and Societies of Apostolic Life (congregations).

Noè,* Virgilio: b. Mar. 30, 1922, Zelata di Bereguardo, Italy; ord., Oct. 1, 1944; master of pontifical ceremonies and undersecretary of Congregation for Sacraments and Divine Worship, 1970-82; ord. titular bp. of Voncario with personal title of abp., Mar. 6, 1982; coadj. Archpriest of St. Peter's Basilica, 1989-2002; vicar general of Vatican City State, 1991-2002; cardinal, June 28, 1991; deacon, St. John Bosco (in Via Tuscolana). Archpriest emeritus of St. Peter's Basilica, Vicar General emeritus of Vatican City State and President emeritus of the Fabric of St. Peter, 1991. *Curial membership*: Causes of Saints, Divine Worship and Sacraments (congregations).

Obando Bravo, S.D.B., Miguel: b. Feb. 2, 1926, La Libertad, Nicaragua; ord., Aug. 10, 1958; ord. titular bp. of Puzia di Bizacena and aux. of Matagalpa, Mar. 31, 1968; abp. of Managua, Feb. 16, 1970; cardinal, May 25, 1985; titular church, St. John the Evangelist (a Spinaceta). Abp. of Managua. *Curial membership*: Clergy, Consecrated Life and Societies of Apostolic Life, Divine Worship and Sacraments, (congregations); Latin America (commission).

Ortega y Alamino, Jaime Lucas: b. Oct. 18, 1936, Jagüey Grande, Cuba; ord., Aug. 2, 1964 detained in work camps (UMAP), 1966-67; parish priest; ord. bp. of Pinar del Rio, Jan. 14, 1979; app. abp. of Havana, Nov. 20, 1981; cardinal, Nov. 26, 1994; titular church, Sts. Aquila and Priscilla. Abp. of Havana. *Curial membership*: Clergy (congregation); Health Care Workers (council); Latin America (commission).

Otunga,* Maurice Michael: b. Jan., 1923, Chebukwa, Kenya; son of pagan tribal chief; baptized 1935, at age of 12; ord., Oct. 3, 1950, at Rome; taught at Kisumu major seminary for three years; attaché in apostolic delegation at Mombasa, 1953-56; ord. titular bp. of Tacape and aux. of Kisumu, Feb. 25, 1957; bp. of Kisii, 1960-69; titular abp. of Bomarzo and coadj. of Nairobi, Nov. 15, 1969; abp. of Nairobi, Oct. 24, 1971 (res. May 14, 1997); cardinal Mar. 5, 1973; titular church, St. Gregory Barbarigo. Abp. emeritus of Nairobi, military ordinary of Kenya, 1981. *Curial membership*: Consecrated Life and Societies of Apostolic Life (congregations).

Pappalardo,* Salvatore: b. Sept. 23, 1918, Villafranca Sicula, Sicily; ord., Apr. 12, 1941; entered diplomatic service of secretariat of state, 1947; ord. titular abp. of Miletus, Jan. 16, 1966; pro-nuncio in Indonesia, 1966-69; president of Pontifical Ecclesiastical Academy, 1969-70; abp. of Palermo, Oct. 17, 1970-96; cardinal, Mar. 5, 1973; titular church, St. Mary Odigitria of the Sicilians. Abp. emeritus of Palermo.

Paskai, O.F.M., László: b. May 8, 1927, Szeged, Hungary; ord., Mar. 3, 1951; ord., titular bp. of Bavagaliana and apostolic administrator of Veszprem, Apr. 5, 1978; bp. of Veszprem, Mar. 31, 1979; coadj. abp. of Kalocsa, Apr. 5, 1982; abp. of Esztergom (renamed Esztergom-Budapest, 1993), 1987-2002; cardinal, June 28, 1988; titular church, St. Theresa (al Corso d'Italia). Abp. emeritus of Esztergom-Budapest. *Curial membership*: Consecrated Life and Societies of Apostolic Life, Oriental Churches (congregations); Texts (council).

Pengo, Polycarp: b. Aug. 5, 1944, Mwayze, Tanzania; ord., Aug. 5, 1971; taught moral theology at the major seminary in Kipalapala, Tanzania, 1977; rector of the major seminary in Segerea, 1978-83; ord.

bp. of Nachingwea, Jan. 6, 1984; bp. of Tunduru-Masasi 1986-90; co-adjutor abp. of Dar-es-Salaam, Jan. 22, 1990; abp. of Dar-es-Salaam, July 22,1992, in succession to Laurean Cardinal Rugambwa; cardinal, Feb. 21, 1998; titular church, Our Lady of La Salette. Abp. of Dar-es-Salaam. *Curial membership*: Doctrine of the Faith, Evangelization of Peoples (congregation); Interreligious Dialogue (council).

Pham Dinh Tung,* Paul Joseph: b. June 15, 1919, Binh-Hoa, Vietnam; ord., June 6, 1949; ord. bp. of Bac Ninh, Aug. 15, 1963; apostolic administrator of Hanoi, June 18, 1990; abp. of Hanoi, Mar. 23, 1994; cardinal, Nov. 26, 1994; titular church, St. Mary Queen of Peace in Ostia mare. Abp. of Hanoi.

Pimenta,* Simon Ignatius: b. Mar. 1, 1920, Marol, India; ord., Dec. 21, 1949; ord. titular bp. of Bocconia and aux. of Bombay, June 29, 1971; coadj. abp. of Bombay, Feb. 26, 1977; abp. of Bombay, Sept. 11, 1978; cardinal, June 28, 1988; titular church, Mary, Queen of the World (a Torre Spaccata). Abp. emeritus of Bombay (res. Nov. 8, 1996).

Piovanelli, Silvano: b. Feb. 21, 1924, Ronta di Mugello, Italy; ord., July 13, 1947; ord. titular bp. of Tubune di Mauretania and aux. of Florence, June 24, 1982; abp. of Florence, 1983-2001; cardinal, May 25, 1985; titular church, St. Mary of Graces (Via Trionfale). Abp. emeritus of Florence.

Poggi,* Luigi: b. Nov. 25, 1917, Piacenza, Italy; ord., July 28, 1940; studied diplomacy at the Pontifical Ecclesiastical Academy, 1944-46; started to work at Secretariat of State; ord. titular bp. of Forontoniana with personal title of abp., May 9, 1965; apostolic delegate for Central Africa, 1965; nuncio in Peru; recalled to Rome, 1973; negotiated with various Eastern bloc governments to improve situation of the Church; named head of Holy See's delegation for permanent contact with government of Poland, 1974; nuncio in Italy, 1986-92; pro-librarian and pro-archivist of the Holy Roman Church, 1992; cardinal, Nov. 26, 1994; protodeacon, Feb. 2002; titular church, Diaconate of St. Mary in Domnica. Archivist and librarian emeritus of the Holy Roman Church.

Poletto, Severino: b. Mar. 18, 1933, Salgareda (Treviso), Italy; ord., June 29, 1957; pref. of discipline at the diocesan seminary and vocation director; founded the Diocesan Centre for Family Ministry, 1973; coordinated the city mission for the 500th anniversary of the foundation of the diocese of Casale Monferrato; app. coadj. bp. of Fossano, April 3, 1980; cons., May 17, 1980; succeeded to see on Oct. 29, 1980; app. bp. of Asti, Mar. 16, 1989; app. abp. of Turin, June 19, 1999; cardinal, Feb. 21, 2001; titular church, St. Joseph in Via Trionfale. Abp. of Turin. *Curial membership*: Clergy (congregation); Economic Affairs of the Holy See (office); Cultural Heritage of the Church (commission).

Policarpo, José Da Cruz: b. Feb. 26, 1936, Alvorninha, Portugal; ord., priest, Aug. 15, 1961; dir. of the seminary in Penafirme, rector of the seminary in Olivais and dean of the Theological Faculty of the Portuguese Catholic University; served two terms as rector of the Portuguese Catholic University, 1988-96; app. titular bp. of Caliabria and aux. bp. of Lisbon, May 26, 1978; cons., June 29, 1978; app. coadj. abp. of Lisbon, Mar. 5, 1997; succeeded as patriarch of Lisbon, Mar. 24, 1998; grand chancellor of the Portuguese Catholic University, pres. of the Portuguese

Episcopal Conference; cardinal, Feb. 21, 2001; titular church, St. Anthony in Campo Formio. Patriarch of Lisbon. *Curial membership:* Education (congregation), Culture, Laity (councils).

Pompedda, Mario Francesco: b. April 18, 1929, Ozieri (Sardinia), Italy; ord., Dec. 23, 1951 for Vatican clergy; app. to Tribunal of the Roman Rota, 1955, and held a variety of posts, including Defender of the Bond, prelate auditor, 1969, and dean, 1993; pres. of the Appellate Court of Vatican City State; app. titular abp. of Bisarcio, Nov. 29, 1997 and ord. by Holy Father, Jan. 6, 1998; app. prefect of the Supreme Tribunal of the Apostolic Signatura and pres. of the Court of Cassation of Vatican City State; cardinal, Feb. 21, 2001; titular church, Deaconry of the Annunciation of the Blessed Virgin Mary in Via Ardeatina. Prefect of the Supreme Tribunal of the Apostolic Signatura and President of the Court of Cassation of Vatican City State. *Curial membership*: Doctrine of the Faith, Sacraments (congregation); Texts (council).

Poupard, Paul: b. Aug. 30, 1930, Bouzille, France; ord., Dec. 18, 1954; scholar; author of a number of works; ord. titular bp. of Usula and aux. of Paris, Apr. 6, 1979; title of abp. and pro-president of the Secretariat for Non-Believers, 1980; cardinal deacon, May 25, 1985; transferred to order of cardinal priests, Jan. 29, 1996; titular church, St. Praxedes; president of Pontifical Council for Dialogue with Non-Believers, 1985-93. President of Pontifical Council for Culture, 1988. *Curial membership*: Divine Worship and Sacraments, Education, Evangelization of Peoples (congregations); Interreligious Dialogue (council).

Primatesta,* Raúl Francisco: b. Apr. 14, 1919, Capilla del Senor, Argentina; ord., Oct. 25, 1942, at Rome; taught at minor and major seminaries of La Plata; contributed to several theology reviews; ord. titular bp. of Tanais and aux. of La Plata, Aug. 15, 1957; bp. of San Rafael, 1961-65; abp. of Cordoba, 1965-98; cardinal, Mar. 5, 1973; titular church, Blessed Mary Sorrowful Virgin. Abp. emeritus of Cordoba, Argentina.

Pujats, Janis: b. Nov. 14, 1930, the Rezekne district of Latvia; ord., Mar. 29, 1951; taught art history and liturgy at the catholic Theological Seminary, Riga; vicar general in the Metropolitan Curia, Riga, 1979-84; declared *persona non grata* by the KGB, 1984; app. abp. of Riga, May 8, 1991, cons., June 1, 1991; pres. of the Latvian Bishops' Conference; cardinal priest (*in pectore*), Feb. 21, 1998, titular church, St. Sylvia. Abp. of Riga. *Curial membership*: Causes of Saints (congregation).

Puljic, Vinko: b. Sept. 8, 1945, Prijecani, Bosnia-Herzegovina; ord., June 29, 1970; spiritual director of minor seminary of Zadar, 1978-87; parish priest; app. vice-rector of Sarajevo major seminary, 1990; ord. abp. of Vrhbosna (Sarajevo), Jan. 6, 1991, in Rome; cardinal, Nov. 26, 1994; titular church, St. Clare in Vigna Clara. Abp. of Sarajevo. *Curial membership*: Evangelization of Peoples (congregation); Interreligious Dialogue (council).

Ratzinger, Joseph: b. Apr. 16, 1927, Marktl am Inn, Germany; ord., June 29, 1951; professor of dogmatic theology at University of Regensburg, 1969-77; member of International Theological Commission, 1969-80; ord. abp. of Munich-Freising, May 28, 1977 (res. Feb. 15, 1982); cardinal, June 27, 1977; titular church, St. Mary of Consolation (in Tiburtina); transferred to order of cardinal bishops as titular bp. of suburbicarian see of Velletri-Segni, Apr. 5, 1993 and of Ostia, Nov. 30, 2002, when he became dean of the college of cardinals. Prefect of Congregation for Doctrine of the Faith, 1981; president of Biblical and Theological Commissions; vice-dean 1998-2002, and Dean of the Sacred College of Cardinals (elected, Nov. 30, 2002). *Curial membership*: Secretariat of State (second section); Bishops, Divine Worship and Sacraments, Education, Evangelization of Peoples, Oriental Churches (congregations); Christian Unity, Culture (councils); *Ecclesia Dei*, Latin America (commissions).

Razafindratandra, Armand Gaétan: b. Aug. 7, 1925, Ambohimalaza, Madagascar; ord., July 27, 1954; ord. bp. of Mahajanga, July 2, 1978; app. abp. of Antananarivo, Feb. 3, 1994; installed, May 15, 1994; cardinal, Nov. 26, 1994; titular church, Sts. Sylvester and Martin ai Monti. Abp. of Antananarivo and apostolic administrator of Miarinarivo. *Curial membership*: Evangelization of Peoples (congregation); Laity (council).

Re, Giovanni Battista: b. Jan. 30, 1934, Borno (Brescia), Italy; ord., Mar. 3, 1957; earned doctorate in canon law and taught in the Brescia Seminary; entered Holy See diplomatic service, served in Panama and Iran; recalled for service in Secretariat of State; sec. for Cong. for Bishops, 1987; titular abp., Nov. 7, 1987; *sostituto* for Secretariat of State, 1989; prefect of the Cong. of Bishops and pres. of the Pont. Comm. for Latin America, Sept. 16, 2000; cardinal, Feb. 21, 2001; titular church, Twelve Holy Apostles; transferred to order of cardinal bishops as titular bp. of suburbicarian see of Sabina-Poggio Mirteto; Prefect of the Cong. of Bishops. *Curial membership*: Secretariat of State (second section); Doctrine of the Faith (congregation); Vatican City State (commission).

Rivera Carrera, Norberto: b. June 6, 1942, La Purísima, Mexico; ord., July 3, 1966; taught dogmatic theology at the major seminary of Mexico City; professor of ecclesiology at Pontifical University of Mexico; bp. of Tehuacán, Nov. 5, 1985; abp. of Mexico City, June 13,1995; cardinal, Feb. 21, 1998; titular church, St. Francis of Assisi at *Ripa Grande*. Abp. of Mexico City. *Curial membership*: Clergy, Divine Worship and the Discipline of Sacraments (congregation); Family (council); Latin America (commission).

Rodríguez Maradiaga, S.D.B., Oscar Andrés: b. Dec. 29, 1942, Tegucigalpa, Honduras; ord., for the Salesians June 28, 1870; taught in various Salesian colleges in El Salvador, Honduras and Guatemala; prof. at the Salesian Theological Institute, Guatemala, and rector of the Salesian Philosophical Institute, Guatemala; app. titular bp. of Pudentiana and aux. bp. of Tegucigalpa, Oct. 28, 1978; app. abp. of Tegucigalpa, Jan. 8, 1993; pres. of CELAM, 1995-99; pres. of the Episcopal Conference of Honduras; cardinal priest, Feb. 21, 2001; titular church, St. Mary of Hope. Abp. of Tegucigalpa. *Curial membership*: Clergy (congregation); Justice and Peace, Social Communication (councils); Latin America (commission).

Rossi,* Opilio: b. May 14, 1910, New York, NY; holds Italian citizenship; ord., for diocese of Piacenza (now Piacenza-Bobbio), Italy, Mar. 11, 1933; served in nunciatures in Belgium, The Netherlands, and

Germany, 1938-53; ord. titular abp. of Ancyra, Dec. 27, 1953; nuncio in Ecuador, 1953-59, Chile, 1959-61, Austria 1961-76; cardinal deacon, May 24, 1976; transferred to order of cardinal priests, June 22, 1987; titular church, St. Lawrence (in Lucina); president of Pontifical Committee for International Eucharistic Congresses, 1983-90; president of Commission for the Sanctuaries of Pompeii, Loreto and Bari, 1984-93.

Rouco Varela, Antonio María: b. Aug. 24, 1936, Villalba, Spain; ord., Mar. 28, 1959; taught fundamental theology and canon law at the Mondoñedo seminary; adjunct professor at the Univ. of Munich; taught ecclesiastical law at Pontifical Univ. of Salamanca; vice-rector of Pontifical Univ. of Salamanca; titular bp. of Gergis and aux. bp. of Santiago de Compostela, Sep. 17, 1976; abp. of Santiago de Compostela, May 9,1984; abp. of Madrid June 29, 1994; cardinal, Feb. 21, 1998, titular church, St. Laurence in Damaso. Abp. of Madrid. *Curial membership*: Bishops, Clergy, Education (congregations); "Cor Unum," Culture, Texts (councils).

Rubiano Sáenz, Pedro: b. Sept. 13, 1932, Cartago, Colombia; ord., July 8, 1956; chaplain to Marco Fidel Suárez Air Force Academy, St. Liberata National College, and Our Lady of Remedies Clinic; app. bp. of Cúcuta, June 2, 1971; cons., June 11, 1971; app. coadj. abp. of Cali, March 26, 1983; abp. of Cali Feb. 7, 1985; apost. admin. of Popayán; pres. of the Episcopal Conference of Colombia; app., December 27, 1994; cardinal priest, Feb. 21, 2001; titular church, Transfiguration of Our Lord Jesus Christ. Abp. of Bogotá. *Curial membership*: Education (congregation); Pastoral Care of Migrants and Itinerant Peoples (council).

Ruini, Camillo: b. Feb. 19, 1931, Sassuolo, Italy; ord., Dec. 8, 1954; taught at seminaries in central Italy; ord. titular bp. of Nepte and aux. bp. of Reggio Emilia and Guastella, June 29, 1983; secretary general of Italian Bishops' Conference, 1986-91; abp. Jan. 17, 1991 and pro-vicar general of the Pope for the Rome diocese; pro-Archpriest of Patriarchal Lateran Archbasilica; cardinal, June 28, 1991; titular church, St. Agnes outside the Wall. Vicar General of the Pope for the Diocese of Rome and Archpriest of Patriarchal Lateran Basilica, July 1, 1991; Grand Chancellor of Pontifical Lateran University; President of the Peregrinatio ad Petri Sedem, 1992-96. *Curial membership*: Bishops (congregation); APSA (office).

Saldarini, Giovanni: b. Dec. 11, 1924, Cantu, Italy; ord., May 31, 1947; respected scripture scholar; taught scripture at Milan archdiocesan seminary, 1952-67; ord. titular bp. of Guadiaba and aux. bp. of Milan, Dec. 7, 1984; abp. of Turin Jan. 31, 1989; cardinal, June 28, 1991 (resigned, June 19, 1999); titular church, Sacred Heart of Jesus (a Castro Pretorio). Abp. emeritus of Turin.

Sales,* Eugênio de Araújo: b. Nov. 8, 1920, Acari, Brazil; ord., Nov. 21, 1943; ord. titular bp. of Tibica and aux. bp. of Natal, Aug. 15, 1954; abp. of São Salvador, 1968-71; cardinal, Apr. 28, 1969; titular church, St. Gregory VII. Abp. of Rio de Janeiro (1971), ordinary for Eastern Rite Catholics in Brazil without ordinaries of their own rites.

Sánchez,* José T.: b. Mar. 17, 1920, Pandan, Philippines; ord., May 12, 1946; ord. titular bp. of Lesvi and coadj. bp. of Lucena, May 12, 1968; bp. of Lucena, 1976-82; abp. of Nueva Segovia, Jan. 12, 1982 (res Mar. 22, 1986); secretary of Congregation for Evangelization of Peoples, 1985-91; cardinal, June 28, 1991; deacon, St. Pius V (a Villa Carpegna); president of Commission for Preservation of Artistic and Historic Patrimony of the Holy See, 1991-93. Prefect of Congr. for the Clergy, 1991-96.

Sandoval Íñiguez, Juan: b. Mar. 28, 1933, Yahualica, Mexico; ord., Oct. 27, 1957; ord. coadj. bp. of Ciudad Juárez, Apr. 30, 1988; bp. of Ciudad Juarez, July 11, 1992; app. abp. of Guadalajara, Apr. 21, 1994; cardinal, Nov. 26, 1994; titular church, Our Lady of Guadalupe and St. Philip the Martyr on Via Aurelia. Abp. of Guadalajara. *Curial membership*: Institutes of Consecrated Life and Societies of Apostolic Life, Catholic Education (congregations); Latin America (commission); Economic Affairs of the Holy See (office); Laity, Latin America (councils); Works of Religion (commission).

Santos, O.F.M., Alexandre José Maria dos: b. Mar. 18, 1924, Zavala, Mozambique; ord., July 25, 1953; first Mozambican black priest; ord. abp. of Maputo, Mar. 9, 1975; cardinal, June 28, 1988; titular church, St. Frumentius (ai Prati Fiscali). Abp. of Maputo. *Curial membership*: Sacraments (congregation).

Saraiva Martins, C.M.F., José: b. Jan. 6, 1932, Gagos do Jarmelo, Portugal; ord., for the Claretians, Mar. 16, 1957; taught at Claretian seminary in Marino, Italy; taught at Claretianum, Rome; taught at the Pontifical Urbanian University and served as rector, 1977-80, 1980-83, 1986-88; sec. of the Cong. for Catholic Education and titular abp. of Thuburnica, May 26, 1988; cons. abp., July 2, 1988; pref. of Cong. for the Causes of Saints, May 30, 1998; cardinal, Feb. 21, 2001; titular church, Deaconry of Our Lady of the Sacred Heart. Prefect of the Congregation for the Causes of Saints. *Curial membership*: Bishops, Sacraments (congregations); Health Care (council).

Scheffczyk,* Leo: b. Feb. 21, 1920, Beuthen (modern Bytom), Poland; ord., June 29, 1947; named vice-rector of the seminary in Königstein (Taunus) for seminarians from then East Germany; studied under Michael Schmaus; taught at Tübingen University and was professor of dogmatic theology at the Ludwig Maximilian University of Münich, 1965-85; author of over 80 books, 500 papers, 400 book reviews, and countless articles; edited the *Münchener Theologisches Zeitschrift*, 1966-84; consultor to the Pontifical Council for the Family and the Commission on Faith of the German Bishops' Conference; cardinal, Feb. 21, 2001; titular church, Deaconry of St. Francis Xavier in Garbatella. Theologian.

Schönborn, O.P., Christoph: b. Jan. 22, 1945, Skalsko, Bohemia (fled to Austria in Sept. 1945); entered Dominican Order in 1963; ord., 1970; student pastor in Graz University, 1973-75; associate professor of dogma in the University of Fribourg, 1976; professor for theology, 1978; professor for dogmatic theology, 1981-91; member of the Orthodox-Roman Catholic Dialogue Commission of Switzerland, 1980-87; member of the International Theological Commission, 1980-; member of the foundation, "Pro Oriente" since 1984; Secretary for the Draft-Commission of the *Catechism of the Catholic Church*, 1987-1992; ord. aux. bp. (Sutri) of Vienna, Sept. 29, 1991; co-adjutor of Vienna, Apr. 13, 1995; abp. of Vienna, Sept. 14, 1995; cardinal, Feb. 21, 1998; titular church, Jesus the Divine Worker. Abp. of Vienna. *Curial membership*: Doctrine of the Faith, Education, Oriental Churches (congregations); Culture (council); Cultural Heritage of the Church (commission).

Schotte, C.I.C.M., Jan Pieter: b. Apr. 29, 1928, Beveren-Leie, Belgium; entered Congregation of the Immaculate Heart of Mary (Scheut Missionaries) in 1946; ord., Aug. 3, 1952; taught canon law at Louvain and was rector of community's seminary in Washington, DC; general secretary of Congregation of the Immaculate Heart of Mary in Rome, 1967-72; secretary (1980) and vice-president (1983) of the Pontifical Commission of Justice and Peace; ord. titular bp. of Silli, Jan. 6, 1984; promoted to titular abp., Apr. 24, 1985; cardinal, Nov. 26, 1994; deacon St. Julian of the Flemings. Secretary general of the Synod of Bishops since 1985; president of the Labor Office of the Holy See, 1989. *Curial membership*: Bishops, Causes of Saints, Evangelization of Peoples (congregations); Signatura (tribunal); Latin America (commission); APSA (office).

Schwery, Henri: b. June 14, 1932, Saint-Leonard, Switzerland; ord., July 7, 1957; director of minor seminary and later rector of the College in Sion; ord. bp. of Sion, Sept. 17, 1977; cardinal, June 28, 1991; titular church, Protomartyrs (a via Aurelia Antica). Bp. emeritus of Sion (ret. Apr. 1, 1995). *Curial membership*: Causes of Saints (congregation).

Sebastiani, Sergio: b. April 11, 1931, Montemonaco (Ascoli Piceno), Italy; ord., 1956; studied at Lateran University and Pontifical Ecclesiastical Academy; entered Holy See diplomatic service and posted to Peru, Brazil, and Chile; recalled to Secretariat of State; app. titular abp. of Caesarea in Mauretania and pro-nuncio in Madagascar and Mauritius and apostolic delegate to Reunion and Comorros; nuncio to Turkey, 1985; sec. to Central Committee for the Great Jubilee of the Year 2000, 1994; pres. Prefecture for the Economic Affairs of the Holy See, Nov. 3, 1997; card., Feb. 21, 2001; titular church, Deaconry of St. Eustace. President of the Prefecture for the Economic Affairs of the Holy See. *Curial membership*: Bishops, Causes of Saints, Clergy (congregations); Christian Unity, Interreligious Dialogue (councils); Signatura (tribunal).

Sepe, Crescenzio: b. June 2, 1943, Carinaro (Caserta), Italy; ord., March 12, 1967; taught at Lateran and Urbanian Universities; studied at Pontifical Ecclesiastical Academy; entered Holy See diplomatic service and posted to Brazil; recalled to Secretariat of State, 1987; pres. of Commission for Vatican Telecommunications; app. titular abp. of Grado and sec. of the Cong. for the Clergy, April 2, 1992; cons. April 26, 1992; General Secretary of the Central Committee for the Great Jubilee of the Year 2000, 1997-2001; Pref. Cong. for the Evangelization of Peoples, April 9, 2001; cardinal deacon, Feb. 21, 2001; titular church, Deaconry of God the Merciful Father. Prefect of the Cong. for the Evangelization of Peoples. *Curial membership*: Clergy, Doctrine of the Faith (congregation); Christian Unity, Interreligious Dialogue, Social Communication (council); Latin America (commission).

Sfeir,* Nasrallah Pierre: b. May 15, 1920, Reyfoun, in Maronite diocese of Sarba, Lebanon; ord., May 7, 1950; secretary of Maronite patriarchate, 1956-61;

taught Arabic literature and philosophy at Marist Fathers College, Jounieh, 1951-61; ord. titular bp. of Tarsus for the Maronites, July 16, 1961; elected Patriarch of Antioch for Maronites, Apr. 19, 1986; granted ecclesial communion by John Paul II May 7, 1986; cardinal, Nov. 26, 1994. Patriarch of Antioch for Maronites. *Curial membership*: Oriental Churches (congregation); Health Care (council).

Shan Kuo-hsi, S.J., Paul: b. Dec. 2, 1923, Puyang, China; ord., Mar. 18, 1955; director of the Chinese section of the Sacred Heart School in Cebu; socius of the novice master in Thu-duc, Vietnam; novice master and rector of Manresa House, Chanhua, Taiwan; rector of St. Ignatius High School, Taipei, Taiwan; bp. of Hualien, Nov. 15, 1979; bp. of Kaohsiung, Taiwan, 1991; cardinal, Feb. 21, 1998; titular church, St. Chrysogonus. Bp. of Kaohsiung. *Curial membership*: Evangelization of Peoples (congregation); Interreligious Dialogue, Social Communications (councils).

Shirayanagi, Peter Seiichi: b. June 17, 1928, Hachioji City, Japan; ord., Dec. 21, 1954; ord. titular bp. of Atenia and aux. bp. of Tokyo, May 8, 1966; titular abp. of Castro and coadj. abp. of Tokyo, Nov. 15, 1969; succeeded to see, Feb. 21, 1970; cardinal, Nov. 26, 1994; titular church, St. Emerentiana in Tor Fiorenza; res. June 12, 2000. Abp. emeritus of Tokyo.

Silvestrini, Achille: b. Oct. 25, 1923, Brisighella, Italy; ord., July 13, 1946; official in Secretariat of State from 1953; ord. titular bp. of Novaliciana with personal title of abp., May 27, 1979; undersecretary, 1973-79, and secretary, 1979-88, of the Council for Public Affairs of the Church (now the second section of the Secretariat of State); cardinal, June 28, 1988; deacon, St. Benedict Outside St. Paul's Gate, promoted to cardinal priest, Jan. 9, 1999; prefect of Apostolic Signatura, 1988-91. Prefect of Congregation for Oriental Churches, 1991-2001; Grand Chancellor of Pontifical Oriental Institute. Prefect emeritus of Congregation for Oriental Churches. *Curial membership*: Secretariat of State (second section); Bishops, Causes of Saints, Doctrine of the Faith, Education, Evangelization of Peoples (congregations); Christian Unity, Texts, Interreligious Dialogue (councils).

Simonis, Adrianus J.: b. Nov. 26, 1931, Lisse, Netherlands; ord., June 15, 1957; ord. bp. of Rotterdam, Mar. 20, 1971; coadj. abp. of Utrecht, June 27, 1983; abp. of Utrecht, Dec. 3, 1983; cardinal, May 25, 1985; titular church, St. Clement. Abp. of Utrecht. *Curial membership*: Consecrated Life and Societies of Apostolic Life, Education (congregations); Christian Unity (council).

Sin, Jaime L.: b. Aug. 31, 1928, New Washington, Philippines; ord., Apr. 3, 1954; diocesan missionary in Capiz, 1954-57; app. first rector of the St. Pius X Seminary, Roxas City, 1957; ord. titular bp. of Obba and aux. bp. of Jaro, Mar. 18, 1967; apostolic administrator of archdiocese of Jaro, June 20, 1970; titular abp. of Massa Lubrense and coadj. abp. of Jaro, Jan. 15, 1972; abp. of Jaro, 1972-74; abp. of Manila, Jan. 21, 1974; cardinal, May 24, 1976; titular church, S. Maria (ai Monti). Abp. of Manila. *Curial membership*: Clergy, Consecrated Life and Societies of Apostolic Life, Divine Worship and Sacraments (congregations).

Sodano, Angelo: b. Nov. 23, 1927, Isola d'Asti, Italy; ord., Sept. 23, 1950; entered diplomatic service of the Holy See in 1959; served in Ecuador and Uruguay; ord. titular abp. of Nova di Cesare, Jan. 15, 1978; nuncio to Chile, 1978-88; secretary of the Council for Relations with States, 1988-90; pro-Secretary of State, 1990-1991; cardinal June 28, 1991; titular church, S. Maria Nuova; transferred to order of cardinal bishops, Jan 10, 1994, as titular bp. of suburbicarian see of Albano (while retaining title to S. Maria Nuova). Secretary of State, June 29, 1991; Vice-dean of the Sacred College of Cardinals (elected, Nov. 30, 2002). *Curial membership*: Bishops, Doctrine of the Faith, Oriental Churches (congregations); Vatican City State, Institute for Works of Religion (commission).

Stafford, James Francis: b. July 26, 1932, Baltimore, MD; ord., (Baltimore*) Dec. 15, 1957; ord. titular bp. of Respetta and aux. bp. of Baltimore, Feb. 29, 1976; app. bp. of Memphis, Nov. 17, 1982; app. abp. of Denver, June 3, 1986, installed July 30, 1986; app. President of Pontifical Council for the Laity, Aug. 20, 1996; cardinal, Feb. 21, 1998; titular church, the church of Jesus, the Good Shepherd at Montagnola. President of Pontifical Council for the Laity. *Curial membership*: Bishops, Doctrine of the Faith, Causes of Saints (congregations); Texts (council).

Stéphanos II Ghattas, C.M.*: b. Jan. 16, 1920, Sheikh Zein-el-Dine, Egypt; ord., Mar. 25, 1944; taught philosophy and dogmatic theology at the major seminary in Tahta; joined Congregation of the Mission, 1952; worked in Lebanon and served as Vincentian econome and superior in Alexandria; elected by the Coptic Catholic Synod bp. of Thebes-Luxor, May 8, 1967; named apostolic admin. of the patriarchate to substitute for the ailing Patriarch Stéphanos I Sidarous; elected unanimously by the Coptic Catholic Synod patriarch of Alexandria for Copts; changed name from Andraos Ghattas to Stéphanos II in honor of his predecessor; cardinal, Feb. 21, 2001; as a patriarch, he did not receive a titular church. Patriarch emeritus of Alexandria for Copts. *Curial membership:* Oriental Churches (congregation).

Sterzinsky, Georg Maximilian: b. Feb. 9, 1936, Warlack, Germany; ord., June 29, 1960; vicar general to the apostolic administrator of Erfurt-Meiningen, 1981-89; ord. bp. of Berlin, Sept. 9, 1989; cardinal, June 28, 1991; titular church, St. Joseph (all'Aurelio). Abp. of Berlin (June 27, 1994). *Curial membership*: Catholic Education (congregation); Migrants and Itinerant People (council).

Stickler,* S.D.B., Alfons: b. Aug. 23, 1910, Neunkirchen, Austria; ord., Mar. 27, 1937; director of the Vatican Library, 1971; ord. titular bp. of Bolsena, Nov. 1, 1983, with personal title of abp.; Pro-Librarian and Pro-Archivist, 1984; cardinal, May 25, 1985; deacon, St. George (in Velabo); transferred to order of cardinal priests, Jan. 29, 1996. Librarian and Archivist of the Holy Roman Church, 1985-88.

Suárez Rivera, Adolfo Antonio: b. Jan. 9, 1927, San Cristobal, Mexico; ord., Mar. 8, 1952; ord. bp. of Tepic, Aug. 15, 1971; bp. of Tlalnepantla, May 8, 1980; app. abp. of Monterrey, Nov. 8, 1983, res., Jan. 25, 2002; cardinal, Nov. 26, 1994; titular church, Our Lady of Guadalupe on Monte Mario. Abp. emeritus of Monterrey. *Curial membership*: Clergy (congregation).

Suquía Goicoechea,* Angel: b. Oct. 2, 1916, Zaldivia, Spain; ord., July 7, 1940; ord. bp. of Almeria, July 16, 1966; bp. of Malaga, 1969-73; abp. of Santiago de Compostela, 1973-83; abp. of Madrid, Apr. 12, 1983-94; cardinal, May 25, 1985; titular church, Great Mother of God. Abp. emeritus of Madrid.

Swiàtek,* Kazimierz: b. Oct. 21, 1914, Walga, in apostolic administration of Estonia; ord., (of Pinsk, Belarus, clergy) Apr. 8, 1939; arrested by KGB Apr. 21, 1941, and imprisoned on death row until June 22, when he escaped during confusion of German invasion and returned to his parish; arrested again by KGB and imprisoned in Minsk until 1945; sentenced to 10 years of hard labor in concentration camps; released June 16, 1954; resumed pastoral work in cathedral parish in Pinsk; ord. abp. of Minsk-Mohilev, Belarus, May 21, 1991, and also appointed apostolic administrator of Pinsk; cardinal, Nov. 26, 1994; titular church, St. Gerard Majella. Abp. of Minsk-Mohilev; apostolic administrator of Pinsk.

Szoka, Edmund C.: b. Sept. 14, 1927, Grand Rapids, MI; ord., (Marquette diocese), June 5, 1954; ord. first bp. of Gaylord, MI, July 20, 1971; abp. of Detroit, 1981-90; cardinal, June 28, 1988; titular church, Sts. Andrew and Gregory (al Monte Celio). President of Prefecture for Economic Affairs of the Holy See, 1990-97. Pres. Pont. Comm. for Vatican City State, 1997. *Curial membership*: Secretariat of State (second section); Bishops, Causes of Saints, Clergy, Evangelization of Peoples, Consecrated Life and Societies of Apostolic Life (congregations).

Taofinu'u, S.M., Pio: b. Dec. 9, 1923, Falealupo, W. Samoa; ord., Dec. 8, 1954; joined Society of Mary, 1955; ord. bp. of Apia (Samoa and Tokelau), May 29, 1968, the first Polynesian bp.; cardinal, Mar. 5, 1973; titular church, St. Humphrey. Abp. of Samoa-Apia and Tokelau, Sept. 10, 1982 (title of see changed to Samoa-Apia, June 26, 1992); ret., November 16, 2002. Abp. emeritus of Samoa-Apia.

Terrazas Sandoval, C.SS.R., Julio: b. Mar. 7, 1936, Vallegrande, Bolivia; ord., for the Redemptorists July 29, 1962; superior of the Redemptorist community in Vallegrande and vicar forane; app. aux. bp. of La Paz and cons., April 15, 1978; transferred to the see of Oruro, Jan. 9, 1982; pres. of the Bolivian Episcopal Conference in 1985 and 1988; app. abp. of Santa Cruz, Feb. 6, 1991; cardinal priest, Feb. 21, 2001; titular church, St. John Baptist Rossi. Abp. of Santa Cruz. *Curial membership*: Laity (council); Latin America (commission).

Tettamanzi, Dionigi: b. Mar. 14, 1934, Renate, Italy; ord., June 28, 1957; taught fundamental theology at the major seminary of Lower Venegono, pastoral theology at the Priestly Institute of Mary Immaculate and the Lombard Regional Institute of Pastoral Ministry, Milan; rector of the Pontifical Lombard Seminary, Rome; abp. of Ancona-Osimo, July 1,1989 (resigned 1991); general secretary of the Italian Episcopal Conference, 1991-95; Vice-President of the Italian Episcopal Conference, May 25, 1995; abp. of Genoa Apr. 20, 1995; cardinal, Feb. 21, 1998; titular church, Sts. Ambrose and Charles. Abp. of Genoa; app. abp. of Milan, July 11, 2002. *Curial membership*: Clergy, Doctrine of the Faith, Education, Oriental Churches (congregations); Social Communications (council); Economic Affairs of the Holy See (office).

Thiandoum,* Hyacinthe: b. Feb. 2, 1921, Poponguine, Senegal; ord., Apr. 18, 1949; studied at Gregorian University, Rome, 1951-53; returned to Senegal, 1953; ord. abp. of Dakar, May 20, 1962, res., June 16, 2000; cardinal, May 24, 1976; titular church, S. Maria (del Popolo). Abp. emeritus of Dakar.

Tomko, Jozef: b. Mar. 11, 1924, Udavske, Slovakia; ord., Mar. 12, 1949; ord. titular abp. of Doclea, Sept, 15, 1979; secretary-general of the Synod of Bishops, 1979-85; cardinal deacon, May 25, 1985; transferred to order of cardinal priests, Jan. 29, 1996; titular church, St. Sabina. Prefect of the Congregation for the Evangelization of Peoples, 1985-2001; Grand Chancellor of Pontifical Urban University. President of Pontifical Committee for International Eucharistic Congresses, 2001. *Curial membership*: Secretariat of State (second section); Bishops, Clergy, Consecrated Life and Societies of Apostolic Life, Culture, Divine Worship and Sacraments, Doctrine of the Faith, Education (congregations); Interreligious Dialogue, Texts (councils); Latin America, State of Vatican City, Works of Religion (commissions).

Tonini,* Ersilio: b. July 20, 1914, Centovera di San Giorgio Piacentino, Italy; ord., Apr. 18, 1937; vice-rector and later rector of the Piacenza seminary; taught Italian, Latin and Greek; editor of diocesan weekly; ord. bp. of Macerata-Tolentino, June 2, 1969; abp. of Ravenna-Cervia, Nov. 22, 1975-90; cardinal, Nov. 26, 1994; titular church, Most Holy Redeemer in Val Melaina. Abp. emeritus of Ravenna-Cervia.

Tucci,* S.J., Roberto: b. April 19, 1921, Naples, Italy; ord., for the Jesuits, Aug. 24, 1950; editor of *La Civiltà Cattolica*; member of the Preparatory Commission on the *Apostolate of the Laity* for Vatican II and *peritus* involved in drafting *Ad Gentes* and *Gaudium et Spes*; consultor to the Pontifical Council for Social Communications, 1965-89; member of the editorial committee for the Pastoral Instruction *Communio et Progressio*; vice-pres. of the Italian Catholic Union of the Press, 1961-82; general sec. of the Italian Province of the Jesuits, 1967-69; app. general manager of Vatican Radio, 1973; since 1982, he has been responsible for all papal visits outside Italy; app. chairman of the Administrative Committee of Vatican Radio, 1986; cardinal, Feb. 21, 2001; titular church, Deaconry of St. Ignatius Loyola in Campo Marzio. Chairman of the Administrative Committee of Vatican Radio.

Tumi, Christian Wiyghan: b. Oct. 15, 1930, Kikaikelaki, Cameroon; ord., Apr. 17, 1966; ord. bp. of Yagoua, Jan. 6, 1980; coadj. abp. of Garoua, Nov. 19, 1982; abp. of Garoua, 1984-91; cardinal, June 28, 1988; titular church, Martyrs of Uganda (a Poggio Ameno). Abp. of Douala, Aug. 31, 1991. *Curial membership*: Education, Evangelization of Peoples (congregations); *Cor Unum*, Culture (councils).

Turcotte, Jean-Claude: b. June 26, 1936, Montreal, Canada; ord., May 24, 1959; ord. titular bp. of Suas and aux. of Montreal, June 29, 1982; abp. of Montreal, Mar. 17, 1990; cardinal, Nov. 26, 1994; titular church, Our Lady of the Blessed Sacrament and the Holy Canadian Martyrs. Abp. of Montreal. *Curial membership*: Causes of Saints (congregation); Social Communications (council).

Tzadua*, Paulos: b. Aug. 25, 1921, Addifini, Ethiopia; ord., Mar. 12, 1944; ord. titular bp. of Abila di Palestina and aux. of Addis Ababa, May 20, 1973;

abp. of Addis Ababa, Feb. 24, 1977-98; cardinal, May 25, 1985; titular church, Most Holy Name of Mary (a Via Latina). Abp. emeritus of Addis Ababa.

Ursi,* Corrado: b. July 26, 1908, Andria, Italy; ord., July 25, 1931; vice-rector and later rector of the Pontifical Regional Seminary of Molfetta, 1931-51; ord. bp. of Nardo, Sept. 30, 1951; abp. of Acerenza, Nov. 30, 1961; abp. of Naples, May 23, 1966-87; cardinal, June 26, 1967; titular church, St. Callistus. Abp. emeritus of Naples.

Vachon,* Louis-Albert: b. Feb. 4, 1912, Saint-Frederic-de-Beauce, Que., Canada; ord., June 11, 1938; ord. titular bp. of Mesarfelta and aux. of Quebec, May 14, 1977; abp. of Quebec, Mar. 20, 1981 (res. Mar. 17, 1990); cardinal, May 25, 1985; titular church, St. Paul of the Cross (a Corviale). Abp. emeritus of Quebec.

Vidal, Ricardo J.: b. Feb. 6, 1931, Mogpoc, Philippines; ord., Mar. 17, 1956; ord. titular bp. of Claterna and coadj. of Melalos, Nov. 30, 1971; abp. of Lipa, 1973-81; coadj. abp. of Cebu, Apr. 13, 1981; abp. of Cebu, Aug. 24, 1982; cardinal, May 25, 1985; titular church, Sts. Peter and Paul (in Via Ostiensi). Abp. of Cebu. *Curial membership*: Education, Evangelization of Peoples (congregations); Family, Health Care Workers (councils).

Vithayathil, C.SS.R., Varkey: b. May 29, 1927, North Paravur, India; ord., for the Redemptorists June 12, 1954; taught canon law for 25 years at the Redemptorist major seminary in Bangalore; served as provincial for Redemptorists in India and Sri Lanka, 1978-84; pres. of the Conference of Religious, India, 1984-85; apostolic administrator of the Asirvanum Benedictine Monastery, Bangalore, 1990-96; app. titular abp. of Ohrid and apostolic administrator of the vacant see of Ernakulam-Angamaly for Syro-Malabars; cons. by the pope, Jan. 6, 1997; app. major abp. of Ernakulam-Angamaly for Syro-Malabars, Dec. 18, 1999; cardinal, Feb. 21, 2001; titular church, St. Bernard at the Baths. Major abp. of Ernakulam-Angamaly for Syro-Malabars. *Curial membership:* Oriental Churches (congregation); Christian Unity, Texts (council).

Vlk, Miloslav: b. May 17, 1932, Lisnice, Czech Republic; during communist persecution when theological studies were impossible he studied archival science at Charles University and worked in various archives in Bohemia; ord., June 23, 1968, during "Prague Spring"; sent to isolated parishes in Bohe-

mian Forest by State authorities in 1971; state authorization to exercise his priestly ministry was cancelled in 1978; from then until 1986 he worked as a window-washer in Prague, carrying out his priestly ministry secretly among small groups. In 1989, he was permitted to exercise his priestly ministry for a "trial" year; the situation changed with the "velvet revolution"; ord. bp. of Ceske Budejovice, Mar. 31, 1990; abp. of Prague, Mar. 27, 1991; cardinal, Nov. 26, 1994; titular church, Holy Cross in Jerusalem. Abp. of Prague, President of the Council of European Episcopal Conferences, 1993-. *Curial membership*: Oriental Churches (congregation); Social Communications (council).

Wamala, Emmanuel: b. Dec. 15, 1926, Kamaggwa, Uganda; ord., Dec. 21, 1957; ord. bp. of Kiyinda-Mityana, Nov. 22, 1981; coadj. abp. of Kampala, June 21, 1988; abp. of Kampala, Feb. 8, 1990; cardinal, Nov. 26, 1994; titular church, St. Hugh. Abp. of Kampala. *Curial membership*: Evangelization of Peoples (congregation); *Cor Unum* (council).

Wetter, Friedrich: b. Feb. 20, 1928, Landau, Germany; ord., Oct. 10, 1953; ord. bp. of Speyer, June 29, 1968; abp. of Munich and Freising, Oct. 28, 1982; cardinal, May 25, 1985; titular church, St. Stephen (al Monte Celio). Abp. of Munich and Freising. *Curial membership*: Education, Evangelization of Peoples (congregations).

Willebrands,* Johannes: b. Sept. 4, 1909, Bovenkarspel, The Netherlands; ord., May 26, 1934; ord. titular bp. of Mauriana, June 28, 1964; secretary of Secretariat for Christian Unity, 1960-69; cardinal, Apr. 28, 1969; titular church, St. Sebastian (alle Catacombe); abp. of Utrecht, 1975-83; president of Council for Christian Unity, 1969-89. President emeritus of the Council for Promoting Christian Unity.

Williams, Thomas Stafford: b. Mar. 20, 1930, Wellington, New Zealand; ord., Dec. 20, 1959, in Rome; studied in Ireland after ordination, receiving degree in social sciences; served in various pastoral assignments on his return to New Zealand; missionary in Western Samoa to 1976; ord. abp. of Wellington, New Zealand, Dec. 20, 1979; cardinal, Feb. 2, 1983; titular church, Jesus the Divine Teacher (at Pineda Sacchetti). Abp. of Wellington; Military Ordinary for New Zealand (1995). *Curial membership*: Evangelization of Peoples (congregation).

CATEGORIES OF CARDINALS

(As of Aug. 20, 2003.)

Information below includes categories of cardinals and dates of consistories at which they were created. Seniority or precedence usually depends on order of elevation.

One of these 166 cardinals one was named by John XXIII (consistory of Dec. 15, 1958); 20 by Paul VI (consistories of June 26, 1967, Apr. 28, 1969, Mar. 5, 1973, May 24, 1976, and June 27, 1977); 145 by John Paul II (consistories of June 30, 1979, Feb. 2, 1983, May 25, 1985, June 28, 1988, June 28, 1991, Nov. 26, 1994, Feb. 21, 1998, and Feb. 21, 2001).

Order of Bishops

Titular Bishops of Suburbicarian Sees: Joseph

Ratzinger, dean (June 27, 1977, Ostia and Velletri-Segni); Angelo Sodano vice-dean (June 28, 1991, Albano); Bernardin Gantin, (June 27, 1977, Palestrina); Roger Etchegaray (June 24, 1998, Porto-Santa Rufina); Giovanni Battista Re (Oct. 1, 2002, Sabina-Poggio Mirteto); Alfonso López Trujillo (Nov. 17, 2001, Frascati). Eastern Rite Patriarchs: Nasrallah Pierre Sfeir (Nov. 26, 1994); Ignace Moussa I Daoud (Feb. 21, 2001); Stephanos II Ghattas, (Feb. 21, 2001).

Order of Priests

1958 (Dec. 15): Franz König.

1967 (June 26): Corrado Ursi.

1969 (Apr. 28): Stephen Sou-hwan Kim, Eugênio de Araújo Sales, Johannes Willebrands.

1973 (Mar. 5): Luis Aponte Martinez, Raúl Francisco Primatesta, Salvatore Pappalardo, Marcelo González Martin, Maurice Otunga, Paulo Evaristo Arns, O.F.M., Pio Taofinu'u.

1976 (May 24): Opilio Rossi, Juan Carlos Aramburu, Corrado Bafile, Hyacinthe Thiandoum, Jaime L. Sin, William W. Baum, Aloisio Lorscheider.

1979 (June 30): Giuseppe Caprio, Marco Cé, Ernesto Corripio Ahumada, Gerald Emmett, Franciszek Macharski.

1983 (Feb. 2): Michael Michai Kitbunchu, Alexandre do Nascimento, Alfonso López Trujillo (promoted to cardinal-bishop on Nov. 17, 2001), Godfried Danneels, Thomas Stafford Williams, Carlo Maria Martini, Jean-Marie Lustiger, Józef Glemp, Joachim Meisner.

1985 (May 25): Juan Francisco Fresno Larraín, Miguel Obando Bravo, S.D.B., Angel Suquía Goicoechea, Ricardo Vidal, Henryk Roman Gulbinowicz, Paulus Tzadua, Louis-Albert Vachon, Friedrich Wetter, Silvano Piovanelli, Adrianus J. Simonis, Bernard F. Law, Giacomo Biffi, Simon D. Lourdusamy, Francis A. Arinze, Antonio Innocenti, Paul Augustine Mayer, Jozef Tomko, Andrzej Maria Deskur, Paul Poupard, Rosalio José Castillo Lara, S.D.B., Edouard Gagnon, P.S.S., Alfons Stickler, S.D.B.

1988 (June 28): José Freire Falcão, Michele Giordano, Alexandre José Maria dos Santos, O.F.M., Giovanni Canestri, Simon Ignatius Pimenta, Edward Bede Clancy, James Aloysius Hickey, Edmund C. Szoka, László Paskai, O.F.M., Christian Wiyghan Tumi, Jean Margéot.

1991 (June 28): Frédéric Etsou-Nzabi-Bamungwabi, C.I.C.M., Nicolás de Jesús López Rodriguez, Roger Mahony, Anthony J. Bevilacqua, Giovanni Saldarini, Cahal Brendan Daly, Camillo Ruini, Ján Chryzostom Korec, S.J., Henri Schwery, Georg Sterzinsky.

1994 (Nov. 26): Miloslav Vlk, Peter Seiichi Shirayanagi, Adolfo Antonio Suárez Rivera, Jaime Lucas Ortega y Alamino, Julius Riyadi Darmaatmadja, S.J., Emmanuel Wamala, William Henry Keeler, Jean-Claude Turcotte, Ricardo Maria Carles Gordó, Adam Joseph Maida, Vinko Puljic, Armand Gaétan Razafindratandra, Paul Joseph Pham Dính Tung, Juan Sandoval Íñiguez, Kazimierz Swiàtek, Ersilio Tonino.

1998 (Feb. 21): Aloysius Ambrozic, Salvatore de Giorgi, Serafim Fernandes de Araújo, Francis George, O.M.I., Adam Kozlowiecki, S.J., Paul Shan Kuo-hsi, S.J., Marian Jaworski, Polycarp Pengo, Janis Pujats, Norberto Rivera Carrera, Antonio Maria Rouco Varela, Christoph Schönborn, O.P., Dionigi Tettamanzi.

2001 (Feb. 21): Bernard Agré, Francisco Álvarez Martínez, Audrys Juozas Backis, Jorge Mario Bergoglio, S.J., Desmond Connell, Ivan Dias, Edward Michael Egan, Francisco Javier Errázuriz Ossa, Antonio Jose Gonzalez Zumarraga, Jean Honoré, Cláudio Hummes, O.F.M., Lubomyr Husar, Karl Lehmann, Theodore E. McCarrick, Geraldo Majella Agnelo, Cormac Murphy-O'Connor, Wilfrid Fox Napier, O.F.M., José Da Cruz Policarpo, Severino Poletto, Oscar Andres Rodríguez Maradiaga, S.D.B., Pedro Rubiano Sáenz, Juan Julio Terrazas Sandoval, C.SS.R., Luis Cipriani Thorne, Varkey Vithayathil, C.SS.R.

Order of Deacons

1988 (June 28): Eduardo Martinez Somalo, Achille Silvestrini, Angelo Felici, Antonio Maria Javierre Ortas, S.D.B.

1991 (June 28): Pio Laghi, Edward I. Cassidy, José T. Sánchez, Virgilio Noè, Fiorenzo Angelini.

1994 (Nov. 26): Carlo Furno, Jan Pieter Schotte, C.I.C.M., Gilberto Agustoni.

1998 (Feb. 21): Lorenzo Antonetti, Darío Castrillón Hoyos, Giovanni Cheli, Francesco Jorge Medina Estévez, Dino Monduzzi, James Francis Stafford.

2001 (Feb. 21): Agostino Cacciavillan, Avery Dulles, S.J., Zenon Grocholewski, Walter Kasper, Jorge María Mejía, Mario Francesco Pompedda, José Saraiva Martins, C.M.F., Leo Scheffczyk, Sergio Sebastiani, Crescenzio Sepe, Roberto Tucci, S.J.

DISTRIBUTION OF CARDINALS

As of Aug. 15, 2003, there were 166 cardinals from more than 60 countries or areas. Listed below are areas, countries, number and last names.

Europe — 84

Italy (35): Angelini, Antonetti, Bafile, Biffi, Cacciavillan, Canestri, Caprio, Cé, Cheli, de Giorgi, Felici, Furno, Giordano, Innocenti, Laghi, Martini, Monduzzi, Noè, Pappalardo, Piovanelli, Poggi, Poletto, Pompedda, Re, Rossi, Ruini, Saldarini, Sebastiani, Sepe, Silvestrini, Sodano, Tettamanzi, Tonini, Tucci, Ursi.

Germany (8): Kasper, Lehmann, Mayer, Meisner, Ratzinger, Scheffczyk, Sterzinsky, Wetter.

Spain (7): Alvarez Martinez, Carles Gordó, Gonzalez Martin, Javierre Ortas, Martinez Somalo, RoucoVarela, Suquia Goicoechea.

Poland (6): Deskur, Glemp, Grocholewski, Gulbinowicz, Kozlowiecki, Macharski.

France (4): Etchegaray, Honoré, Lustiger, Poupard.

Austria (3): König, Schönborn, Stickler.

Belgium (2): Danneels, Schotte.

Ireland (2): Connell, Daly.

Lithuania (2): Backis, Pujats.

Netherlands (2): Simonis, Willebrands.

Portugal (2): Policarpo, Saraiva Martins.

Slovakia (2): Korec, Tomko.

Switzerland (2): Agustoni, Schwery.

Ukraine (2): Husar, Jaworski

One from each of the following countries: Belarus, Swiatek; Bosnia-Herzegovina, Puljic; Czech Republic, Vlk; England, Murphy-O'Connor; Hungary, Paskai.

Asia — 15

India (4): Dias, Lourdusamy, Pimenta, Vithayathil.

Philippines (3): Sánchez, Sin, Vidal.

One from each of the following countries: Indonesia, Darmaatmadja; Japan, Shirayanagi; Korea, Kim; Lebanon, Sfeir; Syria, Moussa I Daoud; Taiwan, Shan Kuo-hsi; Thailand, Kitbunchu; Vietnam, Pham Dinh Tung.

Oceania — 4

Australia (2): Cassidy, Clancy.

One each from: New Zealand, Williams; Pacific Islands (Samoa), Taofinu'u.

Africa — 16

One from each of the following countries: Angola,

do Nascimento; Benin, Gantin; Cameroon, Tumi; Congo (formerly Zaire), Etsou-Nzabi-Bamungwabi; Egypt, Stephanos II Ghattas; Ethiopia, Tzadua; Ivory Coast, Agre; Kenya, Otunga; Madagascar, Razafindratandra; Mauritius, Margeot; Mozambique, Santos; Nigeria, Arinze; Senegal, Thiandoum; South Africa, Napier; Tanzania, Pengo; Uganda, Wamala.

North America – 22

United States (13): Baum, Bevilacqua, Dulles, Egan, George, Hickey, Keeler, Law, McCarrick, Mahony, Maida, Stafford, Szoka.

Canada (4): Ambrozic, Gagnon, Turcotte, Vachon.

Mexico (4): Corripio Ahumada, Rivera Carrera, Sandoval Iñiguez, Suárez Rivera.

Puerto Rico (1): Aponte Martinez.

Central and South America – 25

Brazil (7): Arns, Falcão, Fernandes de Araújo, Hummes, Lorscheider, Majella Agnelo, Sales.

Argentina (4): Aramburu, Bergoglio, Mejia, Primatesta.

Chile (3): Errazuriz Ossa, Fresno Larraín, Medina Estévez.

Colombia (3): Castrillón Hoyos, Lopez Trujillo, Rubiano Saenz.

One each from the following countries: Bolivia, Sandoval; Cuba, Ortega y Alamino; Dominican Republic, Lopez Rodriguez; Ecuador, Gonzalez Zumarraga; Honduras, Rodriguez Maradiaga; Nicaragua, Obando Bravo; Peru, Thorne; Venezuela, Castillo Lara.

Ineligible to Vote

As of Sept. 15, 2003, 57 of the 166 cardinals were ineligible to take part in a papal election in line with the apostolic letter *Ingravescentem Aetetem* effective Jan. 1, 1971, which limited the functions of cardinals after completion of their 80th year.

Cardinals affected are: Agustoni, Angelini, Antonetti, Aponte Martínez, Aramburu, Arns, Bafile, Bevilacqua, Canestri, Caprio, Castillo Lara, Cheli, Corripio Ahumada, Daly, Dulles, Etchegaray, Felici, Fresno Larrain, Furno, Gagnon, Gantin, González Martin, Hickey, Honoré, Innocenti, Javierre Ortas, Kim Sou-hwan, König, Kozlowiecki, Laghi, Margéot, Mayer, Mejia, Monduzzi, Noè, Otunga, Pappalardo, Pham Dinh Tung, Pimenta, Poggi, Primatesta, Rossi, Sales, Sánchez, Scheffczyk, Sfeir, Stephanos II Ghattas, Stickler, Suguía Goicoechea, Swiatek, Thiandoum, Tonini, Tucci, Tzadua, Ursi, Vachon,

Willebrands. Cardinals who complete their 80th year in 2003 and who become ineligible to vote: Clancy, Shan Kuo-hsi, Silvestrini, Taofinu'u.

Cardinals of the United States

As of Aug. 15, 2003, the following cardinals were in service, according to their years of elevation (for biographies, *see* **College of Cardinals**):

1976: **William W. Baum** (major penitentiary emeritus); 1985: **Bernard F. Law** (abp. emeritus of Boston); 1988: **James A. Hickey** (abp. emeritus of Washington), **Edmund C. Szoka** (governor of the Vatican City State); 1991: **Roger M. Mahony** (abp. of Los Angeles), **Anthony M. Bevilacqua** (abp. emeritus of Philadelphia); 1994: **William H. Keeler** (abp. of Baltimore), **Adam J. Maida** (abp. of Detroit); 1998: **Francis E. George, O.M.I.** (abp. of Chicago), **James F. Stafford** (president of the Pontifical Council for the Laity); 2001: **Edward M. Egan** (abp. of New York), **Theodore McCarrick** (abp. of Washington), **Avery Dulles, S.J.** (theologian). **Cardinal Lubomyr Husar, M.S.U.**, major abp. of Lviv for Ukrainians, is also an American citizen.

U.S. Cardinals of the Past (according to year of elevation; for biographical data, *see* **American Catholics of the Past** at www.catholicalmanac.com): 1875: John McCloskey; 1886: James Gibbons; 1911: John Farley, William O'Connell; 1921: Dennis Dougherty; 1924: Patrick Hayes, George Mundelein; 1946: John Glennon, Edward Mooney, Francis Spellman, Samuel Stritch; 1953: James F. McIntyre; 1958: John O'Hara, C.S.C., Richard Cushing; 1959: Albert Meyer, Aloysius Muench; 1961: Joseph Ritter; 1965: Lawrence J. Shehan; 1967: Francis Brennan, John P. Cody, Patrick A. O'Boyle, John J. Krol; 1969: John J. Wright, Terence J. Cooke, John F. Dearden, John J. Carberry; 1973: Humberto S. Medeiros, Timothy Manning; 1983: Joseph L. Bernardin; 1985: John J. O'Connor. [Myroslav Lubachivsky, major abp. of Lviv of the Ukrainians (Ukraine), was made a cardinal in 1985. He was a citizen of the United States and metropolitan of the Philadelphia Ukrainian Rite Archeparchy, from 1979-81.]

Prelates who became cardinals after returning to their native countries: John Lefebvre de Chevrus, first bp. of Boston (1808-23) and apostolic administrator of New York (1810-15), elevated to the cardinalate, 1836, in France. Ignatius Persico, O.F.M. Cap., bp. of Savannah (1870-72), elevated to the cardinalate, 1893, in Italy; Diomede Falconio, O.F.M. ord. a priest in Buffalo, NY, missionary in U.S., apostolic delegate to the U.S. (1902-11), elevated to cardinalate, 1911, in Italy.

SPECIAL SUPPLEMENT:
NEW CARDINALS APPOINTED BY POPE JOHN PAUL II

On Sept. 28, 2003, Pope John Paul II announced the names of the 30 prelates and clerics who were to be elevated to the cardinalate in a consistory to be held on Oct. 21, 2003. The pope also announced that he was reserving *in pectore* one cardinal. As of Oct. 21, 2003, the total number of members of the College of Cardinals was 194, not counting the one reserved *in pectore*, and the electors numbered 135. Following are the new cardinals:

Antonelli, Ennio, b. Nov. 18, 1936, Todi, Italy; abp. of Florence, Mar. 21, 2001.

Barbarin, Philippe, b. Oct. 17, 1950, Rabat, Morocco; abp. of Lyon, July 16, 2002.

Bertone, Tarcisio, b. Dec. 2, 1934, Romano Canavese, Italy; abp. of Genoa, Dec. 10, 2002.

Bozanic, Josip, b. Mar. 20, 1949, Rijeka, Yugoslavia; abp. of Zagreb, Croatia, July 5, 1997.

Hamao, Stephen Fumio, b. Mar. 9, 1930, Tokyo, Japan; pres. of Pontifical Council for Pastoral Care of Migrants and Itinerants, June 15, 1998.

Erdő, Peter, b. June 25, 1952, Budapest, Hungary; abp. of Esztergom-Budapest, Dec. 7, 2002.

Herranz, Julián, b. Mar. 31, 1930, Baena, Spain; pres. of the Pontifical Council for the Interpretation of the Legislative Texts, Dec. 19, 1994; pres. of the Disciplinary Commission of the Roman Curia, Dec. 3, 1999.

Lozano Barragán, Javier, b. Jan. 26, 1933, Toluca, Mexico; pres. of Pontifical Council for Health Care Workers, 1996.

Marchisano, Francesco, b. June 25, 1929, Racconigi, Italy; pres. of the Pontifical Commission of Sacred Archeology, 1991; pres. of the Pontifical Commission for the Cultural Patrimony of the Church, 1993; archpriest of the Patriarchal Vatican Basilica, vicar general for the State of Vatican City, and pres. of the Fabric of St. Peter, Apr. 24, 2002; pres. of the Permanent Commission for the Care of the Historical and Artistic Monuments of the Holy See, Mar. 8, 2003.

Martino, Renato, b. Nov. 23, 1932, Salerno, Italy; pres. of the Pontifical Council Justice and Peace, Oct. 2002.

Nicora, Attilio, b. Mar. 16, 1937, Varese, Italy; pres. of the Administration of the Patrimony of the Apostolic See, Sept. 2002.

O'Brien, Keith Michael Patrick, b. Mar. 17, 1938, Ballycastle, Ireland; abp. of Saint Andrews and Edinburgh, May 30, 1985.

Okogie, Anthony Olubunmi, b. June 16, 1935, Lagos, Nigeria; abp. of Lagos, Apr. 13, 1973.

Ouellet, Marc P.S.S., b. June 8, 1944, Lamotte, Canada; abp. of Québec, Nov. 15, 2002.

Panafieu, Bernard, b. Jan. 26, 1931, Châtellerault, France; abp. of Marseilles, Apr. 22, 1995.

Pell, George, b. Apr. 8, 1941, Ballarat, Australia; abp. of Sydney, Mar. 26, 2001.

Pham Minh Man, Jean Baptiste, b. 1934, Ca Mau, Vietnam; abp. of Thàn-Phô Hô Chi Minh, Mar. 1, 1998.

Quezada Toruño, Rodolfo, b. Mar. 8, 1932, Ciudad de Guatemala, Guatemala; abp. of Guatemala, June 19, 2001.

Rigali, Justin Francis, b. Apr. 19, 1935, Los Angeles, United States; abp. of Philadelphia, July 15, 2003.

Scheid, Eusebio Oscar, b. Dec. 8, 1932, Luzerna, Brazil; abp. of São Sebastião do Rio de Janeiro, July 25, 2001.

Scola, Angelo, b. Nov. 7, 1941, Malgrate, Italy; patriarch of Venice, Jan. 5, 2002.

Tauran, Jean-Louis, b. Apr. 3, 1943, Bordeaux, France; secretary of the Secretariat of State for the Relations with the States, 1990.

Toppo, Telesphore Placidus, b. Oct. 15, 1939, Chainpur, India; abp. of Ranchi, Aug. 7, 1985.

Turkson, Peter Kodwo Appiah, b. Oct. 11, 1948, Wassaw Nsuta, Ghana; abp. of Cape Coast, Jan. 6, 1992.

Vallejo, Carlos Amigo, b. Aug. 23, 1934, Medina de Rioseco, Spain; abp. of Seville, May 22, 1984.

Wako, Gabriel Zubeir, b. Feb. 27, 1941, Mboro, Sudan; abp. of Khartoum, Oct. 10, 1981.

Four priests were also named in recognition of their outstanding service to the Church:

Father Georges Cottier, O.P., Swiss Papal Household theologian and secretary general of the International Theological Commission.

Monsignor Gustaaf Joos, canon of the Diocese of Gand, Belgium;

Father Thomas Spidlik, S.J., a Czech theologian and Jesuit.

Father Stanislas Nagy, a Polish priest of the Sacred Heart of Jesus.

ELECTING THE POPE: THE CONCLAVE

One of the primary duties of the Cardinals of the Catholic Church is the election of the Bishop of Rome, who becomes thereby the Supreme Pontiff of the Church. The election is held in what is termed the conclave. The name is derived from the Latin *cum* (with) and *clavis* (key), and implies the fact that the cardinals are locked together in a room until a new pontiff has been chosen. This form of papal election began in 1274 and is considered the third period in the historical evolution of choosing the successor to St. Peter. Central to the full understanding of the conclave is the firm belief that the entire process of election is guided by the Holy Spirit.

New legislation regarding papal elections and church government during a vacancy of the Holy See was promulgated by Pope John Paul II on Feb. 23, 1996, in the apostolic constitution *Universi Dominici Gregis* ("Shepherd of the Lord's Whole Flock"). Among the changes that were introduced was the call for heightened security in preventing electronic surveillance and the provision that after a set number of unsuccessful ballots, the cardinals may elect the new pope by a simple majority vote.

[For the entire article on the conclave, please visit www.catholicalmanac.com. We have moved it online to make room for the new cardinals, named just as the **Almanac** was going to press.]

The Universal Church

THE CHURCH IN COUNTRIES THROUGHOUT THE WORLD

(Principal sources for statistics: Annuarium Statisticum Ecclesiae, Statistical Yearbook of the Church, 2001 — *the most recent edition;* Annuario Pontificio, *2003; and* Agenzia Internazionale FIDES. *Figures are as of Jan. 1, 2003, except for cardinals [as of Aug. 30, 2003] and others which are indicated. For 2003 developments, see* **Index** *entries for individual countries.)*

An asterisk indicates that the country has full diplomatic relations with the Holy See *(see* **Diplomats to the Holy See** in the **Holy See** section).

Abbreviations (in order in which they appear): archd. – archdiocese; dioc. – diocese; ap. ex. – apostolic exarchate; prel. – prelature; abb. – abbacy; v.a. – apostolic vicariate; p.a. – apostolic prefecture; a.a. – apostolic administration; mil. ord. – military ordinariate; card. – cardinal; abp. – archbishops; bp. – bishops (diocesan and titular); priests (dioc. – diocesan or secular priests; rel. – those belonging to religious orders); p.d. – permanent deacons; sem. – major seminarians, diocesan and religious; bros. – brothers; srs. – sisters; bap. – baptisms; Caths. – Catholic population; tot. pop. – total population; (AD) – apostolic delegate *(see* **Index**: **Papal Representatives**).

Afghanistan

Republic in south-central Asia; capital, Kabul. Christianity antedated Muslim conquest in the seventh century but was overcome by it. All inhabitants are subject to the law of Islam. Under Afghan's Taliban regime, religious freedom was severely restricted, and proselytizing was forbidden. In January 2002, Italian and English chaplains celebrated the first public Mass in nearly 10 years in Kabul, at the Italian Embassy.

Albania*

Archd., 2; dioc., 4; a.a., 1; abp., 3; bp., 3; parishes, 123; priests, 133 (43 dioc., 90 rel.); p.d.,1; sem., 45; bros., 18; srs., 406; bap., 5,415; Caths., 495,000 (15.7%); tot. pop., 3,150,000.

Republic in the Balkans, bordering the Adriatic Sea; capital, Tirana. Christianity was introduced in apostolic times. The northern part of the country remained faithful to Rome while the South broke from unity following the schism of 1054. A large percentage of the population was to become Muslim following the invasion (15th century) and long centuries of occupation by the Ottoman Turks. Many Catholics fled to southern Italy, Sicily and Greece. In 1945, at the time of the communist takeover, an estimated 68 percent of the population was Muslim; 19 percent was Orthodox and 13 percent Roman Catholic. The Catholic Church prevailed in the north. During 45 years of communist dictatorship, the Church fell victim, as did all religions, to systematic persecution.

In 1967, the government, declaring it had eliminated all religion in the country, proclaimed itself the first atheist state in the world. The right to practice religion was restored in late 1990. In March 1991, a delegation from the Vatican was allowed to go to Albania; later in the year diplomatic relations were established with the Holy See at the request of the Albanian prime minister. Pope John Paul II made a one-day visit to the country April 25, 1993, during which he ordained four bishops appointed by him in December 1992 to fill long-vacant sees. Restoration of the Church is a slow and difficult process. The first Albanian cardinal was named in November 1994.

Although Catholics are a minority, they are well respected, including for their work in the education and health fields. Albanians welcomed hundreds of thousands of ethnic Albanians from Kosovo during Yugoslav persecution in 1999.

Algeria*

Archd., 1; dioc., 3; abp., 2; bp., 3; parishes, 40; priests, 102 (38 dioc., 64 rel.); p.d., 1; sem., 3; bros., 29; srs., 192; bap., 21; Caths., 4,000 (.01%); tot. pop., 30,840,000.

Republic in northwest Africa; capital, Algiers. Christianity, introduced at an early date, succumbed to Vandal devastation in the fifth century and Muslim conquest in 709, but survived for centuries in small communities into the 12th century. Missionary work was unsuccessful except in service to traders, military personnel and captives along the coast. Church organization was established after the French gained control of the territory in the 1830s. A large number of Catholics were among the estimated million Europ-eans who left the country after it secured independence from France July 5, 1962. Islam is the state religion.

Armed Islamic militants and guerrillas have caused terror and unrest in Algeria since 1992. Among the more than 80,000 people killed were seven Trappist monks and the Catholic bishop of Oran, all in 1996.

Andorra*

Parishes, 7; priests, 18 (13 dioc., 5 rel.); brs., 5; srs., 19; bap., 398; Caths., 64,000 (94%); tot. pop., 68,000.

Parliamentary state (1993) in the Pyrenees; capital,

Andorra la Vella. From 1278-1993, it was a co-principality under the rule of the French head of state and the bishop of Urgel, Spain, who retain their titles. Christianity was introduced at an early date. Catholicism is the state religion. Ecclesiastical jurisdiction is under the Spanish Diocese of Urgel. The constitution calls for freedom of religion, but also guarantees "the Roman Catholic Church free and public exercise of its activities and the preservation of the relations of special cooperation with the state."

Angola*

Archd., 3; dioc., 13; card., 1; abp., 6; bp., 16; parishes, 232; priests, 567 (281 dioc., 286 rel.); sem., 1,227; bros., p.d., 1; 123; srs., 1,636; catechists, 28,024; bap., 188,712; Caths., 7,973,000 (58.9%); tot. pop., 13,530,000.

Republic in southwest Africa; capital, Luanda. Evangelization by Catholic missionaries from Portugal, dating from 1491, reached high points in the 17th and 18th centuries. Independence from Portugal in 1975 and the long civil war that followed (peace accord signed in 1991) left the Church with a heavy loss of personnel resulting from the departure of about half the foreign missionaries and the persecution and martyrdom experienced by the Church during the war. Renewed fighting following elections in late 1992 brought repeated appeals for peace from the nation's bishops and religious in 1993 and 1994.

Despite another peace accord signed by the rebels and the government in late 1994, conditions have remained unsettled. One effect of the fighting was to cut off Church leaders from large groups of the faithful. In an attempt to encourage peace efforts, the Vatican established diplomatic relations with Angola in 1997. Attacks on Church workers, however, continued in 1998 and 1999. In 2000 Church leaders began an active peace movement, holding national and diocesan congresses and beginning a consultation with Angolan political leaders. Government and rebel representatives signed a peace agreement in 2002, after the government killed rebel leader Jonas Savimbi, and the Church offered humanitarian aid and helped to rebuild the country.

Antigua and Barbuda*

Dioc., 1; bp., 1; parishes, 2; priests, 8 (2 dioc., 6 rel.); p.d., 4; sem., 1; bros., 3; srs., 8; bap., 105; Caths., 8,000 (12.5%); tot. pop., 64,000.

Independent (1981) Caribbean island nation; capital, St. John's, Antigua. The Diocese of St. John's-Basseterre includes Antigua and Barbuda, St. Kitts and Nevis, Anguilla, the British Virgin Islands and Montserrat.

Argentina*

Archd., 14; dioc., 50; prel., 3; ap. ex., 3 (for Armenians of Latin America); mil. ord., 1; card., 4; abp., 23; bp., 78; parishes, 2,713; priests, 5,772 (3,612 dioc., 2,160 rel.); p.d., 556; sem., 1,949; bros., 791; srs., 9,887; bap., 536,618; catechists, 85,552; Caths., 33,402,000 (92%); tot. pop., 36,220,000

Republic in southeast South America, bordering on the Atlantic; capital, Buenos Aires. Priests were with the Magellan exploration party and the first Mass in the country was celebrated April 1, 1519. Missionary work began in the 1530s, diocesan organization in

the late 1540s, and effective evangelization about 1570. Independence from Spain was proclaimed in 1816. Since its establishment in the country, the Church has been influenced by Spanish cultural and institutional forces, antagonistic liberalism, government interference and opposition; the latter reached a climax during the last five years of the first presidency of Juan Peron (1946-55).

Widespread human rights violations, including the disappearance of thousands of people, marked the "Dirty War," the period of military rule from 1976 to December 1983, when an elected civilian government took over. In 1996 the Argentine bishops said they did not do enough to stop human rights violations during the "Dirty War." In the late 1990s, the bishops spoke out against government corruption and a severe government economic program.

Armenia*

Ord., 1 (for Catholic Armenians of Eastern Europe, with seat in Armenia); parishes, 18; abp., 2; priests, 4 (rel.); sem., 10; bros., 1; srs., 23; bap., 794; Caths., 150,000 (4%); tot. pop., 3,460,000.

Republic in Asia Minor; capital Yerevan. Part of the USSR from 1920 until it declared its sovereignty in September 1991. Ancient Armenia, which also included territory annexed by Turkey in 1920, was Christianized in the fourth century. Diplomatic relations were established with the Holy See May 23, 1992. Pope John Paul II visited Armenia in late September 2001 to help mark the 1,700th anniversary of Christianity in the nation. The small Catholic community in Armenia has good relations with the predominant Armenian Apostolic Church, an Oriental Orthodox Church.

Australia*

Archd., 7; dioc., 24; mil. ord., 1; card., 2; abp., 11; bp., 45; parishes, 1,395; priests, 3,148 (1,857 dioc., 1,291 rel.); p.d., 51; sem., 253; bros., 1,143; srs., 7,998; catechists, 5,045; bap., 65,813; Caths., 5,448,000 (28%); tot. pop. 19,490,000.

Commonwealth; island continent southeast of Asia; capital, Canberra. The first Catholics in the country were Irish under penal sentence, 1795-1804; the first public Mass was celebrated May 15, 1803. Official organization of the Church dates from 1820. The country was officially removed from mission status in March 1976.

As the 20th century neared its end, the Church in Australia was rocked by allegations of sexual abuse from previous decades. In 1996 the Australian bishops published a plan for dealing with such cases. In 1998 the bishops also apologized to aboriginal children, saying their support of government policy in the 1970s might have contributed to separation of the children from their families.

In an unusual move, in mid-November 1998, just before the Synod of Bishops for Oceania at the Vatican and after the Australian bishops' "ad limina" visits, Vatican officials met with Church leaders from Australia to discuss doctrinal and pastoral issues. In December 1998, the Vatican and representatives of Australian Church leaders signed a document, later endorsed by the Australian bishops' conference, that spoke of a "crisis of faith" in the Catholic Church on the continent.

Austria*

Archd., 2; dioc., 7; abb., 1; ord., 1; mil. ord., 1; card., 3; abp., 4; bp., 16; parishes, 3,046; priests, 4,478 (2,685 dioc., 1,793 rel.); p.d., 509; sem., 366; bros., 515; srs., 5,772; catechists, 2,976; bap., 55,453; Caths., 6,012,000 (74.4%); tot. pop., 8,080,000.

Republic in central Europe; capital, Vienna. Christianity was introduced by the end of the third century, strengthened considerably by conversion of the Bavarians from about 600, and firmly established in the second half of the eighth century. Catholicism survived and grew stronger as the principal religion in the country in the post-Reformation period, but suffered from Josephinism in the 18th century. Although liberated from much government harassment in the aftermath of the Revolution of 1848, the Church came under pressure again some 20 years later in the *Kulturkampf*. The Church faced strong opposition from Socialists after World War I and suffered persecution from 1938 to 1945 during the Nazi regime. Some Church-state matters are regulated by a concordat originally concluded in 1934.

Late in the 20th century, the Church in Austria was beset by internal difficulties, including the launch of a global movement seeking more lay participation in Church decision-making and changes in Church policy on ordination of women and priestly celibacy. In 1995, Cardinal Hans Hermann Gröer resigned as archbishop of Vienna amid charges of sexual misconduct. His successor, Cardinal Christoph Schönborn, worked to restore a sense of unity to the Church.

Azerbaijan*

Independent republic (1991) on the Caspian Sea; formerly part of the USSR; capital, Baku. Islam is the prevailing religion. Soviet rulers destroyed Baku's one Catholic church in the late 1930s. A small Catholic community of Polish and Armenian origin near the capital is ministered to by two missionaries. Latin-rite Catholics are under the apostolic administration of Caucasus (seat in Georgia), established in December 1993.

Bahamas*

Dioc., 1; bp., 1; parishes, 28; priests, 31 (13 dioc., 18 rel.); p.d., 14; sem., 4; srs., 28; catechists, 230; bap., 591; Caths., 48,000 (15%); tot. pop., 310,000.

Independent (July 10, 1973) island group consisting of some 700 (30 inhabited) small islands southeast of Florida and north of Cuba; capital, Nassau. On Oct. 12, 1492, Columbus landed on one of these islands, where the first Mass was celebrated in the New World. Organization of the Catholic Church in the Bahamas dates from about the middle of the 19th century.

Bahrain*

Parish, 1; priests, 4 (2 dioc., 2 rel.); srs., 6; bap., 172; Caths., 30,000 (4.3%); tot. pop., 690,000. (AD)

Island state in Persian Gulf; capital, Manama. Population is Muslim; Catholics are foreign workers, under ecclesiastical jurisdiction of Arabia apostolic vicariate. Diplomatic relations were established between Bahrain and the Holy See in January 2000.

Bangladesh*

Archd., 1; dioc., 5; abp., 2; bp., 7; parishes, 78; priests, 265 (124 dioc., 141 rel.); sem., 143; bros., 63; srs., 1,002; catechists, 1,443; bap., 7,017; Caths., 266,000 (.20%); tot. pop. 140,370,000.

Formerly the eastern portion of Pakistan. Officially constituted as a separate nation Dec. 16, 1971; capital, Dhaka. Jesuit, Dominican and Augustinian missionaries were in the area in the 16th century. An apostolic vicariate (of Bengali) was established in 1834; the hierarchy was erected in 1950. Islam, the principal religion, was declared the state religion in 1988; freedom of religion is granted. Church-run humanitarian and development agencies have been instrumental in responding to natural disasters, such as flooding. The bishops have emphasized inculturation and Church social doctrine.

Barbados*

Dioc., 1; bp., 2; parishes, 6; priests, 9 (4 dioc., 5 rel.); p.d., 1; srs., 11; bap., 173; sem., 3; Caths., 11,000 (3.8%); tot. pop., 269,000.

Parliamentary democracy (independent since 1966), easternmost of the Caribbean islands; capital, Bridgetown. About 70 percent of the population are Anglican.

Belarus*

Archd., 1; dioc., 3; card., 1; abp., 1; bp., 5; parishes, 382; priests, 339 (182 dioc., 157 rel.); sem., 196; bros., 10; srs., 335; bap., 7,064; Caths., 1,037,000 (10%); tot. pop., 9,970,000.

Independent republic (1991) in eastern Europe; former Soviet republic (Byelorussia); capital, Minsk. Slow recovery of the Church was reported after years of repression in the Soviet Union, although in the mid-1990s under the authoritarian rule of President Alexander Lukashenka, the Church encountered tensions, especially in refusal of permits for foreign religious workers. In December 2000, the nation's bishops asked forgiveness for the "human weaknesses" of Church members throughout the centuries and said the Church forgave acts of Soviet-era persecution. In October 2002, Belarus adopted one of the most restrictive religion laws in the former Soviet Union, but by April 2003 government officials had granted the Catholic Church full legal status.

Belgium*

Archd., l; dioc., 7; mil. ord., 1; card., 2; abp., 3; bp., 18; parishes, 3,949; priests, 7,794 (4,794 dioc., 3,000 rel.); p.d., 559; sem., 236; bros., 1,186; srs., 15,315; catechists, 8,118; bap., 75,708; Caths., 8,105,000 (79%); tot. pop., 10,250,000.

Constitutional monarchy in northwestern Europe; capital, Brussels. Christianity was introduced about the first quarter of the fourth century and major evangelization was completed about 730. During the rest of the medieval period the Church had firm diocesan and parochial organization, generally vigorous monastic life and influential monastic and cathedral schools. Lutherans and Calvinists made some gains during the Reformation period but there was a strong Catholic restoration in the first half of the 17th century, when the country was under Spanish rule. Jansenism disturbed the Church from about 1640 into the 18th century. Josephinism, imposed by an Austrian regime, hampered the Church late in the same century. Repressive and persecutory measures were enforced during the Napoleonic conquest. Freedom came with separation of Church and state in the wake of the Revolution of 1830, which ended the reign of William I. Thereafter, the Church encountered serious problems with philosophical liberalism and political socialism.

Catholics have long been engaged in strong educational, social and political movements. In 1990, in an unprecedented political maneuver, King Baudouin temporarily gave up his throne, saying his Catholic conscience would not allow him to sign a law legalizing abortion. In the mid- and late-1990s, Church leaders expressed concern that the Church was characterized by indifference toward the papacy and dissent from Church teachings. Therapeutic in vitro fertilization for stable married couples continued at a leading Belgian Catholic hospital despite Vatican objections.

Belize*

Dioc., 1; bp., 2; parishes, 13; priests, 40 (18 dioc., 22 rel.); p.d., 3; sem., 2; bros., 8; srs., 63; catechists, 611; bap., 2,840; Caths., 133,000 (52%); tot. pop., 250,000.

Independent (Sept. 21, 1981) republic on eastern coast of Central America; capital, Belmopan. Its history has points in common with Guatemala, where evangelization began in the 16th century. The Church in Belize worked with refugees during the decades of Central American civil wars.

Benin*

Archd., 2; dioc., 8; card., 1; abp., 2; bp., 9; parishes, 186; priests, 446 (340 dioc., 106 rel.); sem., 426; bros., 89; srs., 803; catechists, 10,210; bap., 51,497; Caths., 1,565,000 (24%); tot. pop., 6,420,000.

Democratic republic in West Africa, bordering on the Atlantic; capital, Porto Novo. Missionary work was very limited from the 16th to the 18th centuries. Effective evangelization dates from 1861. The hierarchy was established in 1955. In the 1970s, Benin's Marxist-Leninist government nationalized Catholic schools, expelled foreign missionaries and jailed some priests. After the government dropped the one-party system in 1989, Archbishop Isidore de Souza of Cotonou presided over the 1990 national conference that drew up a new constitution and prepared the way for elections. One challenge facing the Church as it entered the 21st century was maintaining peace with people of other faiths.

Bermuda

Dioc., 1; bp., 1; parishes, 6; priests, 6 (rel.); sem., 1; srs., 3; bap., 122; Caths., 9,000 (16%); tot. pop., 62,000. (AD)

British dependency, consisting of 360 islands (20 of them inhabited), nearly 600 miles east of Cape Hatteras; capital, Hamilton. Catholics were not permitted until about 1800. Occasional pastoral care was provided the few Catholics there by visiting priests during the 19th century. Early in the 1900s priests from Nova Scotia began serving the area. An apostolic prefecture was set up in 1953. The first bishop assumed jurisdiction in 1956, when it was made an apostolic vicariate; diocese established, 1967.

Bhutan

Parish; catechist, 1; bap., 4; Caths., 400 (approx.); tot. pop., 2,090,000.

Kingdom in the Himalayas, northeast of India; capital, Thimphu. Buddhism is the state religion; citizens of other faiths have freedom of worship but may not proselytize. Jesuits (1963) and Salesians (1965) were invited to the country to direct schools. Salesians were expelled in February 1982, on disputed charges of proselytism. The only Catholic missionary allowed to stay in the country was Canadian Jesuit Father William Mackey, who served Catholics there from 1963 until his death in 1995. Ecclesiastical jurisdiction is under the Darjeeling (India) Diocese, which ordained the first indigenous Bhutanese priest in 1995.

Bolivia*

Archd., 4; dioc., 6; prel., 2; mil. ord., 1; v.a., 5; card., 1; abp., 7; bp., 27; parishes, 596; priests, 1,115 (480 dioc., 635 rel.); p.d., 70; sem., 711; bros., 184; srs., 2,537; catechists, 12,614; bap., 117,519; Caths., 7,358,000 (89%); tot. pop., 8,270,000.

Republic in central South America; capital, Sucre; seat of government, La Paz. Catholicism, the official religion, was introduced in the 1530s, and the first diocese was established in 1552. Effective evangelization among the Indians, slow to start, reached high points in the middle of the 18th and the beginning of the 19th centuries and was resumed about 1840. Independence from Spain was proclaimed in 1825, at the end of a campaign that started in 1809. Church-state relations are regulated by a 1951 concordat with the Holy See. Catholics have worked against social poverty and corruption. In 1996, Pope John Paul II urged Bolivia to put its drug-trafficking "merchants of death" out of business.

Bosnia and Herzegovina*

Archd., 1; dioc., 2; card., 1; abp., 1; bp., 3; parishes, 282; priests, 582 (237 dioc., 346 rel.); sem., 116; bros., 15; srs., 508; bap., 5,824; Caths., 461,000 (12%); tot. pop., 4,070,000.

Independent republic (1992) in southeastern Europe; formerly part of Yugoslavia; capital, Sarajevo. During the three years of fighting that erupted after Bosnia-Herzegovina declared its independence, some 450,000 Catholics were driven from their homes; many fled to Croatia or southern Bosnia. Sarajevo Cardinal Vinko Puljic, named a cardinal in 1994, has led the bishops in calls for the safe return of all refugees from the war and acknowledged that in some areas Croatian Catholics were responsible for atrocities. In 1999 the Vatican and Franciscan officials formally agreed to the handover of seven parishes in the Diocese of Mostar, but the agreement was greeted in some areas with violence, and Church officials said many local people did not immediately accept the situation. The parish in Medjugorje, site of alleged Marian apparitions in 1981, remained the responsibility of the Franciscans.

Botswana

Dioc., 1; v.a., 1; bp., 2; parishes, 31; priests, 54 (18 dioc., 36 rel.); p.d., 1; sem., 8; bros., 5; srs., 73; catechists, 263; bap., 1,447; Caths., 79,000 (5.1%); tot. pop., 1,550,000.

Republic (independent since 1966) in southern Africa; capital, Gaborone. The first Catholic mission was opened in 1928 near Gaborone; earlier attempts at evangelization dating from 1879 were unsuccessful. The Church in Botswana gave strong support to tens of thousands of South African refugees from apartheid. As Botswana's diamond industry grew, Church leaders worked to minimize the effects of social changes such as pockets of unemployment and competition for jobs.

Brazil*

Archd., 41; dioc., 209; prel., 13; abb., 2; exarch., 1; mil. ord., 1; card., 7; abp., 54; bp., 354; parishes, 8,966; priests, 16,829 (9,462 dioc., 7,367 rel.); p.d., 1,251; sem., 9,610; bros., 2,588; srs., 35,300; catechists, 553,085; bap., 2,000,520; Caths., 147,440,000 (85%); tot. pop., 172,390,000.

Federal republic in northeastern South America; capital, Brasilia. One of several priests with the discovery party celebrated the first Mass in the country April 26, 1500. Evangelization began some years later, and the first diocese was erected in 1551. During the colonial period, which lasted until 1822, evangelization made some notable progress – especially in the Amazon region between 1680 and 1750 – but was seriously hindered by government policy and the attitude of colonists regarding Amazon Indians the missionaries tried to protect from exploitation and slavery. The Jesuits were suppressed in 1782 and other missionaries expelled as well. Liberal anti-Church influence grew in strength. The government exercised maximum control over the Church. After the proclamation of independence from Portugal in 1822 and throughout the regency, government control was tightened and the Church suffered greatly from dissident actions of ecclesiastical brotherhoods, Masonic anticlericalism and general decline in religious life. Church and state were separated by the constitution of 1891, proclaimed two years after the end of the empire.

The Church carried into the 20th century problems associated with increasingly difficult political, economic and social conditions affecting the majority of the population. Many Afro-Brazilians indiscriminately mixed African-based rites such as candomble with Catholic rituals. In the second half of the 20th century, the bishops became known for their liberal stances on social and some theological issues. In the 1980s, Vatican officials had a series of meetings with Brazilian bishops to discuss liberation theology and other issues. The Brazilian bishops' conference took the lead in advocating for land reform in the country. Members of the Church's Pastoral Land Commission often faced threats, harassment and murder. The Church-founded Indigenous Missionary Council worked for the rights of the country's Indians. Each year, the bishops' Lenten campaign targets a social issue, such as women's rights or economic reform.

Brunei

P.a., 1; parishes, 3; priests, 4 (3 dioc., 1 rel); sem., 3; srs. 2; bap., 163; Caths., 2,100 (0.6%); tot. pop., 331,000.

Independent state (1984) on the northern coast of Borneo; formal name, Brunei Darussalam; capital, Bandar Seri Begawan. Islam is the official religion; other religions are allowed with some restrictions. Most of the Catholics are technicians and skilled workers from other countries who are not permanent residents; under ecclesiastical jurisdiction of Miri Diocese, Malaysia.

Bulgaria*

Dioc., 2; ap. ex., 1; abp., 2; bp., 3; parishes, 44; priests, 47 (15 dioc., 32 rel.); sem., 9; bros., 2; srs., 85; bap., 333; Caths., 80,000 (1%), tot. pop., 7,870,000.

Republic in southeastern Europe on the eastern part of the Balkan peninsula; capital, Sofia. Most of the population is Orthodox. Christianity was introduced before 343 but disappeared with the migration of Slavs into the territory. The baptism of Boris I about 865 ushered in a new period of Christianity, which soon became involved in switches of loyalty between Constantinople and Rome. Through it all the Byzantine, and later Orthodox, element remained stronger and survived under the rule of Ottoman Turks into the 19th century. The Byzantines are products of a reunion movement of the 19th century.

In 1947 the constitution of the new republic decreed the separation of Church and state. Catholic schools and institutions were abolished and foreign religious banished in 1948. A year later the apostolic delegate was expelled. Ivan Romanoff, vicar general of Plovdiv, died in prison in 1952. Bishop Eugene Bossilkoff, imprisoned in 1948, was sentenced to death in 1952; his fate remained unknown until 1975, when the Bulgarian government informed the Vatican that he had died in prison shortly after being sentenced. He was beatified in 1998. Latin- and Eastern-rite apostolic vicars were permitted to attend the Second Vatican Council. All Church activity was under surveillance and/or control by the government, which professed to be atheistic. Pastoral and related activities were strictly limited. There was some improvement in Bulgarian-Vatican relations in 1975. In 1979, the Sofia-Plovdiv apostolic vicariate was raised to a diocese, and a bishop was appointed for the vacant see of Nicopoli.

Diplomatic relations with the Holy See were established in 1990. In the late 1990s, the government instituted religion classes in state schools, but Church leaders complained they had no input into the curriculum and that teachers were predominantly Orthodox. In 2002, Pope John Paul II visited Bulgaria, one of several trips to predominantly Orthodox Soviet-bloc countries, and said Catholics and Orthodox should work for closer relations.

Burkina Faso*

Archd., 3; dioc., 9; abps., 2; bp., 13; parishes, 129; priests, 643 (504 dioc., 139 rel.); sem., 370; bros., 190; srs., 1,162; catechists, 9,875; bap., 63,463; Caths., 1,450,000 (12.2%); tot. pop., 11,860,000.

Republic inland in West Africa; capital, Ouagadougou. Missionaries of Africa started the first missions in 1900 and 1901. Their sisters began work in 1911. A minor and a major seminary were established in 1926 and 1942, respectively. The first indigenous bishop in modern times from West Africa was ordained in 1956 and the first cardinal created in 1965. The hierarchy was established in 1955. In 1980 and 1990, Pope John Paul II's visits to the country were used to launch appeals for an end to desertification of sub-Saharan Africa and an end to poverty in the region. In later years, the pope encouraged increased evangelization and interreligious harmony.

Burma (See Myanmar)

Burundi*

Archd., 1; dioc., 6; abp., 3; bp., 8; parishes, 131; priests, 410 (323 dioc., 87 rel.); sem., 427; bros., 153; srs., 1,028; catechists, 4,765; bap., 143,155; Caths., 4,040,000 (62 %); tot. pop., 6,500,000.

Republic (1966), near the equator in east-central Africa; capital, Bujumbura. The first permanent Catholic mission station was established late in the 19th century. Large numbers were received into the Church following the ordination of the first Burundian priests in 1925. The first indigenous bishop was appointed in 1959.

In 1972-73, the country was torn by tribal warfare between the Tutsis, the ruling minority, and the Hutus. In 1979, the government began expelling foreign missionaries, and in 1986, seminaries were nationalized. A gradual resumption of Church activity since 1987 has been hampered by continuing ethnic violence, which began in 1993 and left more than 150,000 Burundians dead. The bishops repeatedly have called for peace and for an end to sanctions imposed by the Organization of African Unity in 1996. Missionaries continued to be the target of violent attacks.

Cambodia*

V.a., 1; p.a., 2; bp., 2; parishes, 34 (there were also 20 mission stations without resident priests); priests, 39 (7 dioc., 32 rel.); p.d., 1; sem., 8; bros., 5; srs., 74; catechists, 181; baptisms, 463; Caths., 20,000 (.15%); tot. pop., 13,310,000.

Republic in Southeast Asia; capital, Phnom Penh. Evangelization dating from the second half of the 16th century had limited results, more among Vietnamese than Khmers. Thousands of Catholics of Vietnamese origin were forced to flee in 1970 because of Khmer hostility. Most indigenous priests and nuns were killed under the 1975-79 Pol Pot regime. During those years, the Vietnamese invasion in 1979 and the long civil war that followed, foreign missionaries were expelled, local clergy and religious were sent to work the land and a general persecution followed. Religious freedom was re-established in 1990. Diplomatic relations with the Holy See were established in March 1994. Despite a lack of vocations, many Catholics maintain their faith through basic Christian communities led by lay catechists.

Cameroon*

Archd., 5; dioc., 18; card., 1; abp., 6; bp., 22; parishes, 680; priests, 1,369 (885 dioc., 484 rel.); p.d., 21; sem., 1,120; bros., 198; srs., 1,749; catechists, 16,028; bap., 88,674; Caths., 3,956,000 (26%); tot. pop., 15,200,000.

Republic in West Africa; capital, Yaounde. Effective evangelization began in 1890, although Catholics had been in the country long before that time. In the 40-year period from 1920 to 1960, the number of Catholics increased from 60,000 to 700,000. The first black priests were ordained in 1935. Twenty years later the first indigenous bishops were ordained and the hierarchy established. The first Cameroonian cardinal (Christian Wiyghan Tumi) was named in 1988. Around that same time, unknown people began persecuting Church personnel. Among those murdered was Archbishop Yves Plumy of Garoua in 1991. Some felt the government did not do enough to investigate.

Canada* (See **Catholic Church in Canada**; see also **Statistics of the Church in Canada**)

Cape Verde*

Dioc., 1; bp., 1; parishes, 31; priests, 48 (13 dioc., 35 rel.); sem., 25; bros., 6; srs., 123; catechists, 3,420; bap., 13,477; Caths., 488,000 (93%); tot. pop., 452,000.

Independent (July 5, 1975) island group in the Atlantic 300 miles west of Senegal; formerly a Portuguese overseas province; capital, Praia, São Tiago Island. Evangelization began some years before the establishment of a diocese in 1532. The Church languished from the 17th to the 19th centuries, and for two long periods there was no resident bishop. Portugal's anti-clerical government closed the only minor seminary in 1910. Missionaries returned in the 1940s. Cape Verde has faced massive emigration of youth because of perennial drought and a weak economy.

Central African Republic*

Archd., 1; dioc., 7; abp., 2; bp., 9; parishes, 122; priests, 262 (130 dioc., 132 rel.); sem., 201; bros., 64; srs., 371; catechists, 4,073; bap., 21,494; Caths., 811,000 (21%); tot. pop., 3,780,000.

Former French colony (independent since 1960) in central Africa; capital, Bangui. Effective evangelization dates from 1894. The region was organized as a mission territory in 1909. The first indigenous priest was ordained in 1938. The hierarchy was organized in 1955. Pope John Paul II has urged the country's bishops to give hope to a people ruled by corrupt dictatorships and the military. The Church in the country also has expressed concern about the growing number of sects.

Chad*

Archd., 1; dioc., 6; p.a., 1; abp., 1; bp., 7; parishes, 114; priests, 224 (114 dioc., 110 rel.); sem., 120; bros., 33; srs., 346; catechists, 8,908; bap., 19,068; Caths., 832,000 (10.2%); tot. pop., 8,140,000.

Republic (independent since 1960) in north-central Africa; former French possession; capital, N'Djamena. Evangelization began in 1929, leading to firm organization in 1947 and establishment of the hierarchy in 1955. Many catechists, who often were local community leaders, were killed during Chad's 1982-87 civil war. The Vatican established diplomatic relations with Chad in 1988. After the government established more freedoms in the early 1990s, the Church worked to teach people, including Catholics, that solidarity must extend across religious, ethnic and regional boundaries.

Chile*

Archd., 5; dioc., 18; prel., 2; v.a., 1; mil. ord., 1; card., 3; abp., 8; bp., 38; parishes, 920; priests, 2,343 (1,156 dioc., 1,188 rel.); p.d., 604; sem., 767; bros., 357; srs., 5,559; catechists, 50,705; bap., 157,479; Caths., 11,613,000 (75.4%); tot. pop., 15,400,000.

Republic on the southwest coast of South America; capital, Santiago. Priests were with the Spanish on their entrance into the territory early in the 16th century. The first parish was established in 1547 and the first diocese in 1561. Overall organization of the Church took place later in the century. By 1650, most of the peaceful Indians in the central and northern areas were evangelized. Missionary work was more difficult in the southern region. Church activity was hampered during the campaign for independence, 1810-18, and through the first years of the new government, to 1830. Later, Church activity increased but was hampered by shortages of indigenous personnel and attempts by the government to control Church administration through the patronage system. Separation of Church and state was decreed in the constitution of 1925.

Church-state relations were strained during the regime of Marxist President Salvador Allende (1970-73). In the mid-1970s, the Archdiocese of Santiago established the Vicariate of Solidarity to counter human-rights abuses under the rule of Gen. Augusto Pinochet. The Chilean bishops issued numerous statements strongly critical of human rights abuses by the military dictator, who remained in power until 1990, when an elected president took office. The Church was praised for its role in educating and registering voters in the 1988 plebiscite that rejected another term for Pinochet. In 1999, when a British court ruled that Pinochet could be extradited from Britain to Spain to face trial for torture and murder, some Chilean bishops said the ruling damaged the Chilean democracy they had fought so hard to get.

China, People's Republic of

Archd., 20; dioc., 92; p.a., 29. No Roman Catholic statistics are available. In 1949 there were between 3,500,000-4,000,000 Catholics, about .7 per cent of the total population; current total is unknown. Tot. pop. 1,275,724,000. **Hong Kong**: Dioc., 1; bps., 2; parishes, 54; priests, 320 (66 dioc., 254 rel.); p.d., 4; sem., 17; bros., 60; srs., 525; catechists, 1,211; bap., 3,903; Caths., 355,000 (5.2%); tot. pop., 6,720,000.

People's republic in eastern part of Asia; capital, Beijing. Christianity was introduced by Nestorians who had some influence on part of the area from 635 to 845 and again from the 11th century until 1368. John of Monte Corvino started a Franciscan mission in 1294; he was ordained an archbishop about 1307. Missionary activity involving more priests increased for a while thereafter, but the Franciscan mission ended in 1368. Jesuit Matteo Ricci initiated a remarkable period of activity in the 1580s. The Chinese-rites controversy, concerning the adaptation of rituals and other matters related to Chinese traditions and practices, ran throughout the 17th century, ending in a negative decision by mission authorities in Rome. Francis de Capillas, the Dominican protomartyr of China, was killed in 1648. Persecution occurred several times in the 18th century and resulted in the departure of most missionaries from the country.

The Chinese door swung open again in the 1840s, and progress in evangelization increased with an extension of legal and social tolerance. At the turn of the 20th century, however, Christian missionary activity helped provoke the Boxer Rebellion.

Missionary work in the 1900s reached a new high. The hierarchy was instituted by Pope Pius XII, April 11, 1946 (Apostolic Constitution *Quotidie Nos*). Then followed persecution initiated by communists, before and especially after they established the republic in 1949. The government began a savage persecution as soon as it came into power. Among its results were outlawed missionary work and pastoral activity; the expulsion of more than 5,000 foreign missionaries, 510 of whom were American; the arrest, imprisonment and harassment of Chinese Church officials; the forced closing of more than 4,000 schools, institutions and homes; denial of the free exercise of religion; the detention of hundreds of priests, religious and lay people in jail and their employment in slave labor; the proscription of Catholic movements for "counterrevolutionary activities" and "crimes against the new China."

The government formally established the Chinese Catholic Patriotic Association, independent of the Holy See, in July 1957. Relatively few priests and lay people joined the organization, which was condemned by Pius XII in 1958. The government formed the nucleus of what it hoped might become the hierarchy of a schismatic Chinese Church in 1958 by "electing" 26 bishops and having them consecrated validly but illicitly between April 13, 1958, and Nov. 15, 1959, without the permission or approval of the Holy See. Additional bishops were subsequently ordained. Officially, members of the Patriotic Association spurn ties with the Vatican.

Hong Kong Church leaders say more than two-thirds of the government-approved bishops in the Patriotic Association have secretly reconciled with the Vatican, and that the Vatican often approves the ordination of government-appointed bishops as long as the ordinations are conducted by the reconciled bishops. After China insisted on ordaining bishops Jan. 6, 2000, the same day the pope ordained bishops at the Vatican, bishops and clergy of the Patriotic Association began trying to distance themselves from the government.

Growth of the underground church has been reported for several years, despite sometimes intense persecution. The underground church's most senior leader, Cardinal Ignatius Kung Pin-mei, died March 12, 2000, in Stamford, CT, where, because of failing health, he had lived for years with his nephew.

In the early 21st century, Hong Kong Church leaders were outspoken against and took the lead in some protests about the region's new security law. The Vatican's diplomatic relations with Taiwan remain one of the biggest stumbling blocks to Sino-Vatican ties.

Colombia*

Archd., 12; dioc., 48; v.a., 10; mil. ord., 1; card., 3; abp., 18; bp., 87; parishes, 3,685; priests, 7,848 (5,514 dioc., 2,334 rel.); p.d., 218; sem., 4,690; bros., 1,022 srs., 17,413; catechists, 41,208; bap., 673,311; Caths., 38,639,000 (90%); tot. pop., 42,800,000.

Republic in northwest South America; capital, Bogotá. Evangelization began in 1508. The first two dioceses were established in 1534. Vigorous development of the Church was reported by the middle of the 17th century despite obstacles posed by the multiplicity of Indian languages, government interference through patronage rights, rivalry among religious orders and the small number of native American priests among the predominantly Spanish clergy. Some persecution, including the confiscation of property, followed in the wake of the proclamation of independence from Spain in 1819. Guerrilla warfare aimed at Marxist-oriented radical social reform and redistribution of land, along with violence related to drug traffic, has plagued the country since the 1960s, posing problems for the Church, which backed reforms but rejected actions of radical groups. In the late 20th and early 21st centuries, the Church worked as a mediator between the government and guerrillas, but Church leaders suffered threats, attacks, and sometimes death, including from paramilitaries. For example, on March 16, 2002, Abp. Isaias Duarte Cancino of Cali was shot to death for speaking out about the political situation; he was one of at least 10 church workers killed in 2002.

Comoros

A.a., 1; parishes, 2; missions, 4; priests, 4 (1 dioc., 3 rel.); srs., 4; catechists, 12; bap., 24; Caths., 2,000 (.02%); tot. pop., 722,000. (AD)

Consists of main islands of Grande Comore, Anjouan and Moheli in Indian Ocean off southeast coast of Africa; capital, Moroni, Grande Comore Island. Former French territory; independent (July 6, 1975). The majority of the population is Muslim. An apostolic administration was established in 1975.

Congo, Democratic Republic of *

Archd., 6; dioc., 41; card., 1; abp., 8; bp., 54; parishes, 1,254; priests, 3,902 (2,647 dioc., 1,255 rel.); p.d., 10; sem., 2,687; bros., 1,346; srs., 6,405; catechists, 73,024; bap., 426,111; Caths., 28,420,000 (54%); tot. pop., 52,520,000.

Republic in south central Africa; capital, Kinshasa. Christianity was introduced in 1484 and evangelization began about 1490. The first bishop from black Africa was ordained in 1518. Subsequent missionary work was hindered by factors including 18th- and 19th-century anticlericalism. Modern evangelization started in the second half of the 19th century. The hierarchy was established in 1959. In the civil disorders that followed independence in 1960, some missions and other Church installations were abandoned, thousands of people reverted to tribal religions and many priests and religious were killed.

Church-state tensions developed in the late 1980s and 1990s because of the Church's criticism of President Mobutu Sese Seko, who called a 1990 bishops' pastoral letter seditious. In 1992, after troops fired on thousands of protesters and killed 13, the government blamed priests who organized the march. In 1992, Archbishop Laurent Monswengo Pasinya was named president of a council charged with drafting a new constitution and overseeing a transition to democracy, but Mobutu supporters blocked effective change, and the archbishop resigned in 1994. As government and rebel forces battled in the Bukavu region of the country in 1996, Archbishop Christophe Munzihirwa Mwene Ngabo was killed in unclear circumstances. In the ensuing years of civil war, in which neighboring countries became involved, Church personnel worked to meet humanitarian needs and to promote peace through dialogue, but often were targeted for their work. Rebels forced one bishop into exile and house arrest for seven months.

Congo, Republic of *

Archd., 1; dioc., 5; p.a., 1; abp., 3; bp., 6; parishes, 143; priests, 288 (193 dioc., 95 rel.); sem., 300; bros., 36; srs., 225; catechists, 3,264; bap., 41,252; Caths., 1,556,000 (50%); tot. pop., 3,110,000.

Republic (independent since 1960) in west central Africa; former French possession; capital, Brazzaville. Small-scale missionary work with little effect preceded modern evangelization dating from the 1880s. The work of the Church has been affected by political instability, communist influence, tribalism and hostility to foreigners. The hierarchy was established in 1955. In 1992 Bishop Ernest Kombo of Owando was appointed chief organizer of the country's parliamentary elections. In 1994, the Church canceled independence day celebrations after more than 142 Catholics, mostly children, were crushed or suffocated in a rain-induced stampede at a Catholic church in Brazzaville. During renewed violence in the late 1990s, the bishops appealed for peace and stability.

Costa Rica*

Archd., 1; dioc., 6; abp., 2; bp., 8; parishes, 265; priests, 755 (534 dioc., 221 rel.); sem., 276; p.d., 2; bros., 47; srs., 850; catechists, 17,782; bap., 54,182; Caths., 3,371,000 (87%); tot. pop., 3,870,000.

Republic in Central America; capital, San José. Evangelization began about 1520 and proceeded by degrees to real development and organization of the Church in the 17th and 18th centuries. The republic became independent in 1838. Twelve years later Church jurisdiction also became independent with the establishment of a diocese in the present capital.

Côte d'Ivoire (Ivory Coast)*

Archd., 4; dioc., 10; card., 1; abp., 4; bp., 12; parishes, 281; priests, 813 (530 dioc., 283 rel.); p.d., 6; sem., 659; bros., 324; srs., 948; catechists, 13,979; bap., 46,227; Caths., 2,880,000 (17%); tot. pop., 16,940,000.

Republic in western Africa; capital, Abidjan. The Holy Ghost Fathers began systematic evangelization in 1895. The first priests from the area were ordained in 1934. The hierarchy was set up in 1955; the first indigenous cardinal (Bernard Yago) was named in 1983. In 1990 Pope John Paul II consecrated the continent's biggest, most costly and most controversial cathedral in Yamoussoukro. The pope only agreed to accept the cathedral after convincing the country's president to build an adjacent hospital and youth center.

Croatia*

Archd., 4; dioc., 10; mil. ord., 1; abp., 9; bp., 18; parishes, 1,554; priests, 2,259 (1,444 dioc., 816 rel.); p.d., 2; sem., 383; bros., 84; srs., 3,436; catechists, 1,610; bap., 41,402; Caths., 3,772,000 (81%); tot. pop., 4,660,000.

Independent (1991) republic in southeastern Europe; capital Zagreb; formerly a constituent republic of Yugoslavia. Christianity was introduced in the seventh century. On-again, off-again fighting from 1991 to 1995 pitted mostly Catholic Croats against mostly Orthodox Serbs. In 1995, Croatian bishops issued guidelines for rebuilding the nation including suppressing feelings of vengeance toward Serbs. However, in 1996 the head of Croatia's Helsinki human rights committee criticized the bishops for taking a weak stance on Croat abuses after the 1995 Croatian recapture of the Serb-occupied Krajina region. Pope John Paul II's 1998 beatification of Croatian Cardinal Alojzije Stepinac generated controversy among some Serb and Jewish leaders, who considered the cardinal a Nazi sympathizer.

Cuba*

Archd., 3; dioc., 8; card., 1; abp., 3; bp., 12; parishes, 266; priests, 303 (169 dioc., 134 rel.); p.d., 52; sem., 108; bros., 28; srs., 546; catechists, 5,024; bap., 67,485; Caths. 6,205,000 (55.2%); tot. pop., 11,230,000.

Republic under Communist dictatorship, south of Florida; capital, Havana. Effective evangelization began about 1514, leading eventually to the predominance of Catholicism on the island. Vocations to the priesthood and religious life were unusually numerous in the 18th century but declined in the 19th. The island became independent of Spain in 1902 following the Spanish-American War.

Fidel Castro took control of the government Jan. 1, 1959. In 1961, after Cuba was officially declared a socialist state, the University of Villanueva was closed, 350 Catholic schools were nationalized and 136 priests expelled. A greater number of foreign priests and religious had already left the country. Freedom of worship and religious instruction were limited to Church premises and no social action was permitted by the Church, which survived under surveillance. A new constitution approved in 1976 guaranteed freedom of conscience but restricted its exercise. Small improvements in Church-state relations occurred in the late 1980s and early 1990s. In December 1997, just before Pope John Paul II's historic visit, the government allowed public celebration of Christmas, banned for 30 years. Although the pope's January 1998 visit was seen as a new dawn for the Church on the islands, Cuban Catholics say change has come slowly.

Cyprus*

Archd., 1 (Maronite); abp., 1; parishes, 13; priests, 23 (12 dioc., 11 rel.); sem., 1; bros., 7; srs., 43; bap., 78; Caths., 17,000 (2.2%); tot. pop., 783,000.

Republic in the eastern Mediterranean; capital, Nicosia. Christianity was preached on the island in apostolic times and has a continuous history from the fourth century. Latin and Eastern rites were established but the latter prevailed and became Orthodox after the schism of 1054. Christians have suffered under many governments, particularly during the period of Turkish dominion from late in the 16th century to late in the 19th centuries, and from differences between the 80 percent Greek majority and the Turkish minority. About 80 percent of the population are Orthodox. Catholics are under the jurisdiction of the Maronite Archdiocese of Cipro, based in Nicosia.

Czech Republic*

Archd., 2; dioc., 6; ap. ex., 1; card., 1; abp., 2; bp., 13; parishes, 3,138; priests, 1,930 (1,335 dioc., 595 rel.); p.d., 144; sem., 315; bros., 107; srs., 2,246; catechists, 1,381; bap., 25,057; Caths., 4,003,000 (39%); tot. pop., 10,290,000.

Independent state (Jan. 1, 1993); formerly part of Czechoslovakia; capital, Prague. The martyrdom of Prince Wenceslaus in 929 triggered the spread of Christianity. Prague has had a continuous history as a diocese since 973. A parish system was organized about the 13th century in Bohemia and Moravia.

Mendicant orders strengthened relations with the Latin rite in the 13th century. In the next century the teachings of John Hus in Bohemia brought trouble to the Church in the forms of schism and heresy and initiated a series of religious wars that continued for decades following his death at the stake in 1415. So many of the faithful joined the Bohemian Brethren that Catholics became a minority.

In the 1560s, a Counter-Reformation got under way and led to a gradual restoration through the thickets of Josephinism, the Enlightenment, liberalism and troubled politics. St. Jan Sarkander was a priest killed by Protestants in 1620, accused of helping an invading Polish army. (His 1995 canonization caused strains with the Protestant community.)

In 1920, two years after the establishment of the Republic of Czechoslovakia, the schismatic Czechoslovak Church was proclaimed at Prague, resulting in numerous defections from the Catholic Church in the Czech region. Following the accession of the Gottwald regime to power early in 1948, persecution began in the Czech part of Czechoslovakia. A number of theatrical trials of bishops and priests were staged in 1950. Pressure was applied on Eastern Catholics in Slovakia to join the Orthodox Church. Diplomatic relations with the Holy See were terminated in 1950. In the following decade, thousands of priests were arrested and hundreds were deported, and attempts were made to force government-approved "peace priests" on the people. Pope Pius XII granted the Czech Church emergency powers to appoint clergy during the communist persecution.

From January to October 1968, Church-state relations improved to some extent under the Dubcek regime: a number of bishops were reinstated; some priests were still barred from priestly work; the "peace priests" organization was disbanded. The Eastern Catholic Church was re-established. In 1969, rehabilitation trials for priests and religious ended, but there was no wholesale restoration of priests and religious to their proper ways of life and work. Government restrictions continued to hamper the work of priests and nuns. Signatories of the human rights declaration Charter 77 were particular objects of government repression and retribution.

In December 1983, the Czechoslovakian foreign minister met with the pope at Vatican City; it was the first meeting of a high Czech official with a pope since the country had been under communist rule. In 1988, three new bishops were ordained in Czechoslovakia, the first since 1973. The communist government fell in late 1989. In 1990, bishops were appointed to fill vacant sees; diplomatic relations between the Holy See and Czechoslovakia were re-established, and Pope John Paul II visited the country. In 1997 the issue of married Czech priests secretly ordained under communist rule was resolved when they began work in the country's new Eastern Catholic jurisdiction. Under a 1949 communist decree declaring priests Culture Ministry employees, Czech priests were still paid by the state. A Church spokesman said confiscation of Church property under communist rule left priests still financially dependent on the state.

Denmark*

Dioc., 1; abp., 1; bp., 2; parishes, 49; priests, 99 (42 dioc., 47 rel.); sem., 13; bros., 4; srs., 223; bap.,

642; Caths., 35,000 (.6%); tot. pop., 5,330,000.

Includes the Faroe Islands and Greenland. Constitutional monarchy in northwestern Europe; capital, Copenhagen. Christianity was introduced in the ninth century and the first diocese for the area was established in 831. Intensive evangelization and full-scale organization of the Church occurred from the second half of the 10th century and ushered in a period of great development and influence in the 12th and 13th centuries. Decline followed, resulting in almost total loss to the Church during the Reformation, when Lutheranism became the national religion. A few Catholic families practiced the faith secretly until religious freedom was legally assured in the mid-1800s. Since then, immigration has increased the number of Catholics. About 95 percent of the population are Evangelical Lutherans.

Catholicism was introduced in Greenland, a Danish island province northeast of North America, about 1000. The first diocese was established in 1124 and a line of bishops dated from then until 1537. The first known churches in the Western Hemisphere, dating from about the 11th century, were on Greenland. The departure of Scandinavians and spread of the Reformation reduced the Church to nothing. The Moravian Brethren evangelized the Inuit from the 1720s to 1901. By 1930 the Danish Church — Evangelical Lutheran — was in full possession. Since 1930, priests have been in Greenland, which is part of the Copenhagen Diocese.

Djibouti*

Dioc., 1; bp., 2; parishes, 6; priests, 6 (3 dioc., 3 rel.); sem., 1; bros., 5; srs., 24; catechists, 16; bap., 14; Caths., 7,000 (1%); tot. pop., 640,000. (AD)

Independent (1977) republic in East Africa; capital, Djibouti. Christianity in the area, formerly part of Ethiopia, antedated but was overcome by the Arab invasion of 1200. Modern evangelization, begun in the latter part of the 19th century, had meager results. The hierarchy was established in 1955. Formal diplomatic relations with the Holy See were established in May 2000.

Dominica*

Dioc., 1; parishes, 15; priests, 47 (6 dioc., 41 rel.); sem., 11; bros., 8; srs., 23; catechists, 465; bap., 822; Caths., 60,000 (79%); tot. pop., 75,000.

Independent (Nov. 3, 1978) state in Caribbean; capital, Roseau. Evangelization began in 1642.

Dominican Republic*

Archd., 2; dioc., 9; mil. ord., 1; card., 1; abp., 2; bp., 17; parishes, 519; priests, 815 (386 dioc., 429 rel.); p.d., 253; sem., 548; bros., 81; srs., 1,691; catechists, 25,636; bap., 114,250; Caths., 7,668,000 (90%); tot. pop., 8,530,000.

Caribbean republic on the eastern two-thirds of the island of Hispaniola, bordering on Haiti; capital, Santo Domingo. Evangelization began shortly after discovery by Columbus in 1492 and Church organization, the first in America, was established by 1510. Catholicism is the state religion. Pope John Paul II visited the country in 1992 to mark the quincentennial celebrations of Columbus's discovery. The pope also opened the Fourth General conference of the Latin American Episcopate there. Church leaders worked to end social injustices, including the plight of mistreated sugar cane workers.

East Timor

Dioc., 2; bp., 2; parishes, 37; priests, 115 (44 dioc., 71 rel.); sem., 177; p.d., 1; bros., 21; srs., 303; catechists, 1,390; bap., 30,207; Caths., 767,000 (93%); tot. pop., 824,000.

Independent (May 2002) state; capital, Dili. Predominantly Catholic former Portuguese colony invaded by Indonesia in 1975 and annexed the following year. Most countries did not recognize the annexation. The Catholic Church worked to bring peace between the Indonesian government and guerrilla forces seeking independence. Bishop Carlos Filipe Ximenes Belo, apostolic administrator of Dili, was a co-winner of the 1996 Nobel Peace Prize for his peace efforts. In 1999, dozens of civilians were killed — including more than two dozen at a Catholic church — during a terror campaign waged by pro-Indonesia paramilitaries in the run-up to an August vote on independence for East Timor. Indonesian troops withdrew, and in August 2001 East Timor held elections for a transitional government. The church has worked on peace and reconciliation issues and at raising awareness of social issues.

Ecuador*

Archd., 4; dioc., 11; v.a., 7; p.a., 1; mil. ord., 1; card., 1; abp., 5; bp., 29; parishes, 1,157; priests, 1,910 (1,096 dioc., 814 rel.); p.d., 66; sem., 719; bros., 358; srs., 4,949; catechists, 39,107; bap., 252,709; Caths., 11,834,000 (92%); tot. pop., 12,880,000.

Republic on the west coast of South America, includes Galápagos Islands; capital, Quito. Evangelization began in the 1530s. The first diocese was established in 1545. Multi-phased missionary work, spreading from the coastal and mountain regions into the Amazon, made the Church highly influential during the colonial period. The Church was practically enslaved by the constitution enacted in 1824, two years after Ecuador, as part of Colombia, gained independence from Spain. Some change for the better took place later in the century, but from 1891 until the 1930s the Church labored under serious liabilities imposed by liberal governments. Foreign missionaries were barred from the country for some time; the property of religious orders was confiscated; education was taken over by the state; traditional state support was refused; legal standing was denied; attempts to control Church offices were made through insistence on rights of patronage. A period of harmony and independence for the Church began after agreement was reached on Church-state relations in 1937. In 1998, the Church was actively involved in peace talks that ended a border dispute of some 170 years with Peru. As the 20th century came to a close, Ecuador's bishops were working to fight social turmoil and the results of severe economic austerity measures.

Egypt*

Patriarchates, 2 (Alexandria for the Copts and for the Melkites); dioc., 10; v.a., 1; ex., 1; patriarch, 1; card., 1; abp., 2; bp., 12; parishes, 209; priests, 485

(206 dioc., 279 rel.); p.d., 15; sem., 124; bros., 71; srs., 1,296; catechists, 1,510; bap., 3,160; Caths., 240,000 (.35%); tot. pop., 67,890,000.

Arab Republic in northeastern Africa; capital, Cairo. Alexandria was the influential hub of a Christian community established by the end of the second century; it became a patriarchate and the center of the Coptic Church and had great influence on the spread of Christianity in various parts of Africa. Monasticism developed from desert communities of hermits in the third and fourth centuries. Arianism was first preached in Egypt in the 320s. In the fifth century, the Coptic Church went Monophysite through failure to accept doctrine formulated by the Council of Chalcedon in 451 with respect to the two natures of Christ. The country was thoroughly Arabized after 640 and was under the rule of Ottoman Turks from 1517 to 1798.

Islam, the religion of some 90 percent of the population, is the state religion. The tiny Catholic minority has a dialogue with the Muslims, but sometimes each side treats the other warily and with mistrust. Pope John Paul II's visit to Cairo and Mount Sinai in 2000 was considered to have given impetus to interreligious dialogue.

El Salvador*

Archd., 1; dioc., 7; mil. ord., 1; abp., 2; bp., 9; parishes, 383; priests, 673 (438 dioc., 235 rel.); p.d., 3; sem., 472; bros., 75; srs., 1,555; catechists, 7,688; bap., 96,019; Cath., 4,974,000 (79%); tot. pop., 6,400,000.

Republic in Central America; capital, San Salvador. Evangelization affecting the whole territory followed Spanish occupation in the 1520s. The country was administered by the captaincy general of Guatemala until 1821, when independence from Spain was declared and it was annexed to Mexico. El Salvador joined the Central American Federation in 1825, declared independence in 1841 and became a republic formally in 1856.

During the country's 1980-92 civil war, Church leaders worked to achieve social justice. The San Salvador Archdiocese's human rights office, *Tutela Legal*, documented abuses and political killings and offered legal support to victims, despite Church persecution. Archbishop Oscar Romero of San Salvador, peace advocate and outspoken champion of human rights, was murdered March 24, 1980, while celebrating Mass. Four U.S. Church women were murdered the same year. Six Jesuits and two lay women were assassinated Nov. 16, 1989, at Central American University in El Salvador. Church leaders, particularly Archbishop Romero's successor, Archbishop Arturo Rivera Damas, were active in the peace process. In the 1990s, Church-government relations cooled. Church leaders often urged the U.S. government not to deport the hundreds of thousands of Salvadoran refugees who lived, often illegally, in the United States, and sent money to their families in El Salvador. The situation worsened after the destruction caused by Hurricane Mitch in 1999.

England

Archd., 4; dioc., 15; ap. ex., 1; mil. ord. (Great Britain), 1; card., 1; abp., 4; bp., 31; parishes, 2,437; priests, 5,010 (3,592 dioc., 1,418 rel.); p.d., 473; sem., 211; bros., 1,943; srs., 6,382; bap., 62,913; Caths.,

3,780,140 (8.3%); tot. pop., 45,354,912 (tot. pop. for Great Britain: 53,364,542). *Note:* England and Wales share a joint Episcopal Conference; *see* also **Scotland** and **Wales**.

Center of the United Kingdom of Great Britain (England, Scotland, Wales) and Northern Ireland, off the northwestern coast of Europe; capital, London. The arrival of St. Augustine of Canterbury and a band of monks in 597 marked the beginning of evangelization. Real organization of the Church took place some years after the Synod of Whitby, held in 663. Heavy losses were sustained in the wake of the Danish invasion in the 780s, but recovery starting from the time of Alfred the Great and dating especially from the middle of the 10th century led to Christianization of the whole country and close Church-state relations. The Norman Conquest of 1066 opened the Church in England to European influence. The Church began to decline in numbers in the 13th century. In the 14th century, John Wycliff presaged the Protestant Reformation.

Henry VIII, failing in 1529 to gain annulment of his marriage to Catherine of Aragon, refused to acknowledge papal authority over the Church in England, had himself proclaimed its head, suppressed all houses of religious, and persecuted people — Sts. Thomas More and John Fisher, among others — for not subscribing to the Oath of Supremacy and Act of Succession. He held the line on other-than-papal doctrine, however, until his death in 1547. Doctrinal aberrations were introduced during the reign of Edward VI (1547-53), through the Order of Communion, two books of Common Prayer, and the Articles of the Established Church. Mary Tudor's attempted Catholic restoration (1553-58) was a disaster, resulting in the deaths of more than 300 Protestants. Elizabeth (1558-1603) firmed up the established Church with the aid of Matthew Parker, archbishop of Canterbury, with formation of a hierarchy, legal enactments and multiphased persecution. More than 100 priests and 62 lay persons were among the casualties of persecution during the underground Catholic revival that followed the return to England of missionary priests from France and the Lowlands.

Several periods of comparative tolerance ensued after Elizabeth's death. The first of several apostolic vicariates was established in 1685; this form of Church government was maintained until the restoration of the hierarchy and diocesan organization in 1850. The revolution of 1688 and subsequent developments to about 1781 subjected Catholics to a wide variety of penal laws and disabilities in religious, civic and social life. The situation began to improve in 1791, and from 1801 Parliament frequently considered proposals for the repeal of penal laws against Catholics.

The Act of Emancipation restored citizenship rights to Catholics in 1829. Restrictions remained in force for some time afterward, however, on public religious worship and activity. The hierarchy was restored in 1850. Since then the Catholic Church, existing side by side with the established Churches of England and Scotland, has followed a general pattern of growth and development. After the Church of England began ordaining women priests in 1994, more than 200 Anglican priests and four Anglican bishops were received into the Catholic Church, although many said ordination of women was not their primary reason for leaving. In the late 20th and early 21st centuries, the Church was active in the prolife movement and was outspoken on bioethical issues. (*See* also **Ireland, Northern**)

Equatorial Guinea*

Archd., 1; dioc., 2; abp., 1; bp., 2; parishes, 70; priests, 111 (64 dioc., 47 rel.); p.d. 2; sem., 56; bros., 28; srs., 236; catechists, 1,934; bap., 10,310; Caths., 389,000 (83%); tot. pop., 470,000.

Republic on the west coast of Africa, consisting of Rio Muni on the mainland and the islands of Bioko and Annobon in the Gulf of Guinea: capital, Malabo. Evangelization began in 1841. The country became independent of Spain in 1968. The Church was severely repressed during the 11-year rule of President Macias Nguema. Developments since his overthrow in 1979 indicated some measure of improvement. An ecclesiastical province was established in October 1982.

In the 1990s, bishops worked to educate Catholics about the need for social justice and respect for human rights. In mid-1998, the government expelled three foreign missionaries involved in development programs partially funded by the United States.

Eritrea*

Dioc., 3; bp., 5; parishes, 175; priests, 290 (60 dioc., 230 rel); sem., 110; bros., 38; srs., 542; catechists, 165; bap., 3,430; Caths., 137,000 (3.6%); tot. pop., 3,820,000.

Independent state (May 24, 1993) in northeast Africa; formerly a province of Ethiopia. Christianity was introduced in the fourth century. Population is evenly divided between Christians and Muslims. Catholics form a small minority; most of the population is Orthodox or Muslim. In 1995, two new dioceses were established, but because of three decades of civil war, the dioceses had no facilities and little staffing. In 1998 the government announced plans to take over private schools and health clinics, most of which were run by the Church. Eritrean bishops form an episcopal conference with Ethiopia, and the bishops of the two countries frequently appealed for peace during their governments' border war.

Estonia*

A.a., 1; abp., 1 (nuncio is apostolic administrator); parishes, 5; priests, 12 (6 dioc., 6 rel); sem., 3; srs., 19; bap., 79; Caths., 6,000 (.43%); tot. pop., 1,380,000.

Independent (1991) Baltic republic; capital, Tallinn. (Forcibly absorbed by the USSR in 1940, it regained independence in 1991.) Catholicism was introduced in the 11th and 12th centuries. Jurisdiction over the area was made directly subject to the Holy See in 1215. Lutheran penetration was general in the Reformation period, and Russian Orthodox influence was strong from early in the 18th century until 1917, when independence was attained. The first of several apostolic administrators was appointed in 1924. The small Catholic community was hard-hit during the 1940-91 Soviet occupation (not recognized by the Holy See or the United States). Since its independence, the small Catholic community in Estonia has worked to re-establish Catholic theology and education. In 1999 the Holy See and government of Estonia reached agree-

ment on a number of issues, including guarantees that the Church could name its own bishops and that priests from abroad would be able to continue to work in the country.

Ethiopia*

Archd., 1; dioc., 1; v.a., 5; p.a., 2; card., 1; abp., 2; bp., 8; parishes, 228; priests, 457 (174 dioc., 283 rel.); p.d., 1; sem., 268; bros., 63; srs., 688; catechists, 1,924; bap., 23,313; Caths., 465,000 (.7%); tot. pop., 65,370,000.

People's republic in northeast Africa; capital, Addis Ababa. The country was evangelized by missionaries from Egypt in the fourth century and had a bishop by about 340. Following the lead of its parent body, the Egyptian (Coptic) Church, the Church in the area succumbed to the Monophysite heresy in the sixth century. An apostolic delegation was set up in Addis Ababa in 1937 and several jurisdictions were organized, some under Vatican congregations. The northern Church jurisdictions follow the Alexandrian rite, while the southern part of the country is Latin rite. The small Church has good relations with Orthodox and Protestant Churches, all of which face the task of helping people move from a rural society to a more modern society without losing Christian identity. Although the constitution calls for religious freedom, treatment of the churches can vary in different localities. The bishops share an episcopal conference with the Eritrean bishops, and the bishops of the two countries frequently appealed for peace during their governments' border war.

Falkland Islands

P.a., 1; parish, 1; priests, 2 (rel.); bros., 1; srs., 1; bap., 3; Caths., 200 (approx.) (10%); tot. pop., 2,000 (approx).

British colony off the southern tip of South America; capital, Port Stanley. The islands are called Islas Malvinas by Argentina, which also claims sovereignty.

Fiji*

Archd., 1; abp., 1; parishes, 35; priests, 126 (27 dioc., 99 rel.); sem., 48; bros., 48; srs., 150; bap., 1,859; catechists, 466; Caths., 84,000 (10%); tot. pop., 824,000.

Independent island group (100 inhabited) in the southwest Pacific; capital, Suva. Marist missionaries began work in 1844 after Methodism had been firmly established. An apostolic prefecture was organized in 1863. The hierarchy was established in 1966.

Finland*

Dioc., 1; bp., 1; parishes, 7; priests, 19 (6 dioc., 13 rel.); p.d., 2; sem., 3; srs., 52; bap., 169; Caths., 8,000 (.01%); tot. pop., 5,190,000.

Republic in northern Europe; capital, Helsinki. Swedes evangelized the country in the 12th century. The Reformation swept the country, resulting in the prohibition of Catholicism in 1595, general reorganization of ecclesiastical life and affairs, and dominance of the Evangelical Lutheran Church. Catholics were given religious liberty in 1781 but missionaries and conversions were forbidden by law. The first Finnish priest since the Reformation was ordained in 1903 in Paris. An apostolic vicariate for Finland was erected in 1920 (made a diocese in 1955). A law on religious liberty, enacted in 1923, banned the foundation of monasteries.

France*

Archd., 23; dioc., 71; prel., 1; ap. ex., 2; mil. ord., 1; card., 4; abp., 31; bp., 138; parishes, 19,835; priests, 24,251 (18,528 dioc., 5,723 rel.); p.d., 1,684; sem., 1,428; bros., 3,167; srs., 46,565; catechists, 78,377; bap., 391,665; Caths., 46,434,000 (79%); tot. pop., 59,190,000.

Republic in western Europe; capital, Paris. Christianity was known around Lyons by the middle of the second century. By 250 there were 30 dioceses. The hierarchy reached a fair degree of organization by the end of the fourth century. Vandals and Franks subsequently invaded the territory and caused barbarian turmoil and doctrinal problems because of their Arianism. The Frankish nation was converted following the baptism of Clovis about 496. Christianization was complete by some time in the seventh century. From then on the Church, its leaders and people, figured in virtually every important development — religious, cultural, political and social — through the periods of the Carolingians, feudalism, the Middle Ages and monarchies to the end of the 18th century. The University of Paris became one of the intellectual centers of the 13th century. Churchmen and secular rulers were involved with developments surrounding the Avignon residence of the popes and curia from 1309 until near the end of the 14th century and with the disastrous Western Schism that followed.

Strong currents of Gallicanism and conciliarism ran through ecclesiastical and secular circles in France; the former was an ideology and movement to restrict papal control of the Church in the country, the latter sought to make the pope subservient to a general council. Calvinism entered the country about the middle of the 16th century and won a strong body of converts. Jansenism appeared in the next century, to be followed by the highly influential Enlightenment. The Revolution, which started in 1789 and was succeeded by the Napoleonic period, completely changed the status of the Church, taking a toll of numbers by persecution and defection and disenfranchising the Church in practically every way. Throughout the 19th century the Church was caught up in the whirl of imperial and republican developments and was made the victim of official hostility, popular indifference and liberal opposition.

In the 20th century, the Church struggled with problems involving the heritage of the Revolution and its aftermath, the alienation of intellectuals, liberalism, the estrangement of the working classes because of the Church's former identification with the ruling class, and the massive needs of contemporary society. In the 1990s, French bishops fought a racist backlash that resulted from large-scale immigration to Africa.

Gabon*

Archd., 1; dioc., 3; abp., 2; bp., 4; parishes, 72; priests, 112 (48 dioc., 64 rel.); p.d., 2; sem., 117; bros., 52; srs., 180; catechists, 1,017; bap., 6,500; Caths., 788,000 (63%); tot. pop., 1,240,000.

Republic on the west coast of central Africa; capital Libreville. Sporadic missionary effort took place before 1881 when effective evangelization began. The hierarchy was established in 1955. In 1993, Gabon's president defeated a Catholic priest in presidential elections. In the late 1990s, the government and the Holy See signed an agreement setting out the rights of the Church in society.

Gambia*

Dioc., 1; bp., 1; parishes, 56; priests, 25 (13 dioc., 12 rel.); sem., 5; bros., 11; srs., 54; bap., 2,290; Caths., 33,000 (2%); tot. pop., 1,420,000.

Republic (1970) on the northwestern coast of Africa; capital, Banjui. Christianity was introduced by Portuguese explorers in the 15th century; effective evangelization began in 1822. The country was under the jurisdiction of an apostolic vicariate until 1931. The hierarchy was established in 1957. Pope John Paul II has encouraged Catholics to dialogue with the majority Muslims.

Georgia*

A.a., 1; parishes, 27; abp., 1; bp., 1; priests, 16 (3 dioc., 13 rel); sem., 12; srs., 29; bap, 64; Caths., 100,000 (1.9%); tot. pop., 5,240,000

Independent (1991) state in the Caucasus; former Soviet republic; capital, Tbilisi. Christianity came to the area under Roman influence and, according to tradition, was spread through the efforts of St. Nino (or Christiana), a maiden who was brought as a captive to the country and is venerated as its apostle. The apostolic administration of the Caucasus (with seat in Georgia) was established in December 1993 for Latin-rite Catholics of Armenia, Azerbaijan and Georgia. Chaldean- and Armenian-rite Catholics also are present. Differences between Catholicism and Orthodoxy often are blurred on the parish level. The Catholic Church and the Armenian Orthodox Church have been unable to secure the return of Churches closed during the Soviet period, many of which were later given to the Georgian Orthodox Church. Early in the 21st century, many denominations, including Catholics, reported attacks and harassment from Orthodox mobs.

Germany*

Archd., 7; dioc., 20; ap. ex., 1; mil. ord., 1; card., 8; abp., 5; bp., 90; parishes, 12,466; priests, 19,263 (14,694 dioc., 4,569 rel.); p.d., 2,369; sem., 1,249; bros., 1,662; srs., 37,465; catechists, 21,971; bap., 218,120; Caths., 27,398,000 (33.2%); tot. pop., 82,360,000.

Country in northern Europe; capital, Berlin. From 1949-90 it was partitioned into the Communist German Democratic Republic in the East (capital, East Berlin) and the German Federal Republic in the West (capital, Bonn). Christianity was introduced in the third century, if not earlier. Trier, which became a center for missionary activity, had a bishop by 400. Visigoth invaders introduced Arianism in the fifth century but were converted in the seventh century by the East Franks, Celtic and other missionaries. St. Boniface, the apostle of Germany, established real ecclesiastical organization in the eighth century.

Beginning in the Carolingian period, bishops began to act in dual roles as pastors and rulers, a state of affairs that inevitably led to confusion and conflict in Church-state relations and perplexing problems of investiture. The Church developed strength and vitality through the Middle Ages but succumbed to abuses that antedated and prepared the ground for the Reformation. Martin Luther's actions from 1517 made Germany a confessional battleground. Religious strife continued until the conclusion of the Peace of Westphalia at the end of the Thirty Years' War in 1648. Nearly a century earlier the Peace of Augsburg (1555) had been designed, without success, to assure a degree of tranquility by recognizing the legitimacy of different religious confessions in different states, depending on the decisions of princes. The implicit principle that princes should control the churches emerged in practice into the absolutism and Josephinism of subsequent years. St. Peter Canisius and his fellow Jesuits spearheaded a Counter Reformation in the second half of the 16th century. Before the end of the century, however, 70 percent of the population of north and central Germany were Lutheran. Calvinism also had established a strong presence.

The Church suffered some impoverishment as a result of shifting boundaries and the secularization of property shortly after 1800. It came under direct attack in the *Kulturkampf* of the 1870s but helped to generate the opposition that resulted in a dampening of the campaign of Bismarck against it. Despite action by Catholics on the social front and other developments, discrimination against the Church spilled over into the 20th century and lasted beyond World War I. Catholics in politics struggled with others to pull the country through numerous postwar crises. The dissolution of the Center Party, agreed to by the bishops in 1933 without awareness of the ultimate consequences, contributed in part to the rise of Hitler to supreme power. Church officials protested the Nazi anti-Church and anti-Semitic actions, but to no avail.

After World War II East Germany, compelled to communism under Soviet domination, initiated a program of control and repression of the Church. The regime eliminated religious schools, curtailed freedom for religious instruction and formation, and restricted the religious press. Beginning in the mid-1950s, the communists substituted youth initiation and Communist ceremonies for many sacraments. Bishops were generally forbidden to travel outside the Republic. The number of priests decreased, partly because of reduced seminary enrollments ordered by the East German government.

The official reunification of Germany took place Oct. 3, 1990, and the separate episcopal conferences were merged to form one conference in November. During the 1990s, the united German bishops fought against introduction of the former East Germany's more liberal abortion law. When a high-court decision allowed a woman to obtain an abortion after visiting a state-approved counseling center and obtaining proof she had been counseled, German church leaders searched for a compromise position, since they ran more than 250 such centers. In 1999, Pope John Paul II asked the German bishops to include a line on the proof-of-counseling certificate that said it could not be used for abortion, but some German states said they would not consider the line valid. Eventually, most of the bishops withdrew from the system. As the 20th century came to an end, German Church leaders also spoke on behalf of immigrants, refugees and asylum seekers and against a surge in racist and anti-Semitic attacks.

Ghana*

Archd., 4; dioc., 14; abp., 4; bp., 15; parishes, 332; priests, 983 (801 dioc., 182 rel.); p.d., 3; sem., 644; bros., 164; srs., 798; catechists, 5,968; bap., 59,527; Caths., 2,356,000 (12%); tot. pop., 19,730,000.

Republic on the western coast of Africa; capital, Accra. Priests visited the country in 1482, 11 years after discovery by the Portuguese, but missionary effort, hindered by the slave trade and other factors, was slight until 1880 when systematic evangelization began. An apostolic prefecture was set up in 1879. The hierarchy was established in 1950.

In 1985, the government shut down the Church's newspaper, *The Catholic Standard*, for criticizing the government; in 1989 the government ordered religious bodies to register. However, in 1992 the paper resumed publication, and five new dioceses were established in 1995. In 1997 the bishops issued a pastoral letter urging an end to political corruption and ethnic tension.

Gibraltar

Dioc., 1; bp., 2; parishes, 5; priests, 17 (16 dioc., 1 rel.); sem., 1; srs., 5; bap., 322; Caths., 23,000 (85%); tot. pop., 27,000.

British dependency on the tip of the Spanish Peninsula on the Mediterranean. Evangelization took place after the Moors were driven out near the end of the 15th century. The Church was hindered by the British, who acquired the colony in 1713. Most of the Catholics were, and are, Spanish and Italian immigrants and their descendants. An apostolic vicariate was organized in 1817. The diocese was erected in 1910.

Great Britain (*See* separate entries for **England**, **Scotland**, **Wales**, **Northern Ireland**)

Greece*

Archd., 4; dioc., 4; v.a., 1; ap. ex., 2; abp., 6; bp., 3; parishes, 87; priests, 91 (51 dioc., 40 rel.); p.d., 2; sem., 3; bros., 34; srs., 130; bap., 636; Caths., 56,000 (.6%); tot. pop., 10,020,000.

Republic in southeastern Europe on the Balkan Peninsula; capital, Athens. St. Paul preached the Gospel at Athens and Corinth on his second missionary journey and visited the country again on his third tour. Other Apostles may have passed through. Two bishops from Greece attended the First Council of Nicaea. After the division of the Roman Empire, the Church remained Eastern in rite and later broke ties with Rome as a result of the schism of 1054. A Latin-rite jurisdiction was set up during the period of the Latin Empire of Constantinople, 1204-1261, but crumbled afterward. Unity efforts of the Council of Florence had poor results and failed to save the Byzantine Empire from conquest by the Ottoman Empire in 1453. The country now has Latin, Byzantine and Armenian rites. The Greek Orthodox Church is predominant. The Catholic Church continues to work to obtain full legal rights. In May 2001, during the first papal visit to Greece since the eighth century, Pope John Paul II apologized for past wrongs against the Orthodox, including the 13th-century sack of Constantinople.

Greenland (Statistics for **Greenland** are included in **Denmark**)

Grenada*

Dioc., 1; bp., 1; parishes, 20; priests, 22 (3 dioc., 19 rel.); p.d., 5; sem., 5; bros., 3; srs., 30; catechists, 123; bap., 563; Caths., 56,000 (54%); tot. pop., 103,000.

Independent island state in the West Indies; capital, St. George's.

Guam

Archd., 1; abp., 1; parishes, 24; priests, 48 (33 dioc., 15 rel.); p.d., 9; sem., 22; bro., 1; srs., 120; bap., 2,205; catechists, 471; Caths., 125,000 (80%); tot. pop., 155,000.

Outlying area of U.S. in the southwest Pacific; capital, Agana. The first Mass was offered in the Mariana Islands in 1521. The islands were evangelized by the Jesuits, from 1668, and other missionaries. The first Micronesian bishop was ordained in 1970. The Agana Diocese, which had been a suffragan of San Francisco, was made a metropolitan see in 1984.

Guatemala*

Archd., 2; dioc., 10; prel., 1; v.a., 2; abp., 4; bp., 17; parishes, 443; priests, 890 (369 dioc., 521 rel.); p.d., 7; sem., 464; bros., 211; srs., 2,660; catechists, 40,382; bap., 207,884; Caths. 9,594,000 (82%); tot. pop. 11,680,000.

Republic in Central America; capital, Guatemala City. Evangelization dates from the beginning of Spanish occupation in 1524. The first diocese, for all Central American territories administered by the captaincy general of Guatemala, was established in 1534. The country became independent in 1839, following annexation to Mexico in 1821, secession in 1823 and membership in the Central American Federation from 1825. In 1870, a government installed by a liberal revolution repudiated the concordat of 1853 and took active measures against the Church. Separation of Church and state was decreed; religious orders were suppressed and their property seized; priests and religious were exiled; schools were secularized. Full freedom was subsequently granted.

During the nation's 36-year civil war, which ended in 1996, Church officials spoke out against atrocities and illegal drafting of youths and often were persecuted. The Guatemala City archbishop's human rights office, established after decades of war, was one of the few agencies able to document abuses. Bishops participated in the country's peace process, at times withdrawing in an effort to force government and guerrilla leaders back to the table.

After the war, the archbishop's human rights office began an extensive project to help document abuses during the war. Two days after the report was released in April 1998, Auxiliary Bishop Juan Gerardi Conedera of Guatemala City, who headed the project, was murdered. In 2001, a priest who lived with the bishop and three military officers were convicted of involvement in the murder, but said they would appeal the decision. One of the three officers was killed in a Guatemala City prison riot in 2003.

Guinea*

Archd., 1; dioc., 2; bp., 3; parishes, 54; priests, 96 (73 dioc., 23 rel.); sem., 28; bros., 23; srs., 103; catechists, 572; bap., 4,262; Caths., 178,000 (2.1%); tot. pop., 8,270,000.

Republic on the west coast of Africa; capital,

Conakry. Occasional missionary work followed exploration by the Portuguese about the middle of the 15th century; organized effort dates from 1877. The hierarchy was established in 1955. Following independence from France in 1958, Catholic schools were nationalized, youth organizations banned and missionaries restricted. Foreign missionaries were expelled in 1967. Archbishop Raymond-Marie Tchidimbo of Conakry, sentenced to life imprisonment in 1971 on a charge of conspiring to overthrow the government, was released in August 1979; he resigned his see. Private schools, suppressed by the government for more than 20 years, again were authorized in 1984.

Guinea-Bissau*

Dioc., 2; bp., 2; parishes, 24; priests, 78 (17 dioc., 61 rel.); sem., 20; bros., 11; srs., 135; bap., 2,357; catechists, 825; Caths., 142,000 (11.5%); tot. pop., 1,230,000.

Independent state on the west coast of Africa; capital, Bissau. Catholicism was introduced in the second half of the 15th century but limited missionary work, hampered by the slave trade, had meager results. Missionary work in the 20th century began in 1933. An apostolic prefecture was made a diocese in 1977. In 1998, Bishop Settimio Ferrazzetta of Bissau worked to mediate a crisis between the government and military leaders.

Guyana

Dioc., 1; bp., 1; parishes, 24; priests, 46 (5 dioc., 41 rel.); sem., 5; bros., 6; srs., 47; catechists, 571; bap., 1,302; Caths., 88,000 (10.2%); tot. pop., 800,000.

Republic on the north coast of South America; capital, Georgetown. In 1899 the Catholic Church and other churches were given equal status with the Church of England and the Church of Scotland. Most of the Catholics are Portuguese. The Georgetown Diocese was established in 1956, 10 years before Guyana became independent of England. The first indigenous bishop was appointed in 1971. Schools were nationalized in 1976. In the late 1970s and in the 1980s, *The Catholic Standard* newspaper was cited by the Inter-American Press Association as the "sole independent voice" in Guyana.

Haiti*

Archd., 2; dioc., 7; abp., 4; bp., 11; parishes, 273; priests, 653 (373 dioc., 280 rel.); p.d., 4; sem., 399; bros., 301; srs., 1,046; catechists, 4,950; bap., 107,339; Caths., 6,654,000 (82%); tot. pop., 8,130,000.

Caribbean republic on the western third of Hispaniola adjacent to the Dominican Republic; capital, Port-au-Prince. Evangelization followed discovery by Columbus in 1492. Capuchins and Jesuits did most of the missionary work in the 18th century. From 1804, when independence was declared, until 1860, the country was in schism. Relations were regularized by a concordat concluded in 1860, when an archdiocese and four dioceses were established.

In the second half of the 20th century, the Church worked to develop the small nation, considered among the poorest in the Western Hemisphere. In the 1980s and 1990s, priests and religious often were targets of political violence, which resulted in a series of coups. The Church was sometimes seen as the lone voice for the people and, at times, was seen as backing the government. A Salesian priest, Father Jean-Bertrand Aristide, known for his fiery, anti-government sermons, won the December 1990 president election, considered the first genuinely democratic vote in Haitian history. A 1991 military coup forced him into exile for three years and resulted in an international trade embargo against Haiti. Aristide was laicized by the Vatican and married in January 1996. In the late 1990s, the Church continued its service in the social field through programs in basic literacy and operation of schools and health facilities. Early in the 21st century, church workers often decried worsening poverty and social injustices.

Honduras*

Archd., 1; dioc., 6; card., 1; abp., 2; bp., 8; parishes, 174; priests, 408 (185 dioc., 223 rel.); p.d., 1; sem., 140; bros., 34; srs., 590; catechists, 11,657; bap., 66,304; Caths., 5,335,000 (81%); tot. pop., 6,580,000.

Republic in Central America; capital, Tegucigalpa. Evangelization preceded establishment of the first diocese in the 16th century. Under Spanish rule and after independence from 1823, the Church held a favored position until 1880, when equal legal status was given to all religions. Harassment of priests and nuns working among indigenous peasants and Salvadoran refugees was reported during the years of Central American civil unrest in the late 20th century. In 1998 Hurricane Mitch killed more than 6,000 Hondurans and forced more than 2 million in the country to evacuate their homes. The Church took a lead role in post-hurricane relief and development efforts.

Hungary*

Archd., 4; dioc., 9; abb., 1; ap. ex., 1; mil. ord. 1; card., 1; abp., 6; bp., 21; parishes, 2,189; priests, 2,438 (1,910 dioc., 528 rel.); p.d., 50; sem., 477; bros., 71; srs., 1,470; catechists, 2,914; bap., 51,084; Caths., 6,266,000 (63%); tot. pop., 9,920,000.

Republic in east central Europe; capital, Budapest. The early origins of Christianity in the country, whose territory was subject to a great deal of change, is not known. Magyars accepted Christianity about the end of the 10th century. St. Stephen I promoted its spread and helped to organize some of its historical dioceses. Bishops became influential in politics as well as in the Church.

For centuries the country served as a buffer for the Christian West against barbarians from the East, notably the Mongols in the 13th century. Hussites and Waldensians prepared the way for the Reformation, which struck at almost the same time as the Turks. The Reformation made considerable progress after 1526, resulting in the conversion of large numbers to Lutheranism and Calvinism by the end of the century. Most of them or their descendants returned to the Church later, but many Magyars remained staunch Calvinists. Turks repressed the Churches, Protestant as well as Catholic, during a reign of 150 years, but they managed to survive. Domination of the Church was one of the objectives of government policy during the reigns of Maria Theresa and Joseph II in the second half of the 18th century; their Josephinism affected Church-state relations until World War I.

Secularization increased in the second half of the 19th century, which also witnessed the birth of many new Catholic organizations and movements. Catholics were involved in the social chaos and anti-religious atmosphere of the years following World War I, struggling with their compatriots for religious as well as political survival.

After World War II, the communist campaign against the Church started with the disbanding of Catholic organizations in 1946. In 1948, Caritas, the Catholic charitable organization, was taken over, and all Catholic institutions were suppressed. Interference in Church administration and attempts to split the bishops preceded the arrest of Cardinal Jozsef Mindszenty Dec. 26, 1948, and his sentence to life imprisonment in 1949. (He was free for a few days during the unsuccessful uprising of 1956. He then took up residence at the U.S. Embassy in Budapest, where he remained until September 1971, when he was permitted to leave the country. He died in 1975 in Vienna.)

In 1950, religious orders and congregations were suppressed and 10,000 religious were interned. Several dozen priests and monks were assassinated, jailed or deported. About 4,000 priests and religious were confined in jail or concentration camps. The government sponsored a national "Progressive Catholic" Church and captive organizations for priests. Despite a 1964 agreement with the Holy See regarding episcopal appointments, bishops remained subject to government surveillance and harassment.

On Feb. 9, 1990, an accord was signed between the Holy See and Hungary re-establishing diplomatic relations. Pope John Paul II reorganized the ecclesiastical structure of the country in May 1993. In 1997, the Vatican and Hungary signed an agreement that restored some Church property confiscated under communism and provided some sources of funding for Church activities. Hungary's bishops have said social conflicts, political changes and economic strains have put new pressures on the Church.

Iceland*

Dioc., 1; bp., 1; parishes, 4; priests, 10 (6 dioc., 4 rel.); srs., 36; bap., 97; Caths., 5,000 (1.4%); tot. pop., 286,000.

Island republic between Norway and Greenland; capital, Rekjavik. Irish hermits were there in the eighth century. Missionaries subsequently evangelized the island and Christianity was officially accepted about 1000. The first bishop was ordained in 1056. The Black Death had dire effects, and spiritual decline set in during the 15th century. Lutheranism was introduced from Denmark between 1537 and 1552 and made the official religion. Some Catholic missionary work was done in the 19th century. Religious freedom was granted to the few Catholics in 1874. A vicariate was erected in 1929 and was made a diocese in 1968.

India*

Patriarchate, 1 (titular of East Indies); major archbishopric (Syro-Malabar), 1; archd., 27; dioc., 120; card., 4; patr., 1; abp., 31; bp., 155; parishes, 8,333; priests, 19,811 (11,227 dioc., 8,584 rel.); p.d., 20; sem., 11,303; bros., 2,761; srs., 83,186; catechists, 60,144; bap., 356,470; Caths., 16,770,000 (1.6%); tot. pop. 1,017,540,000.

Republic on the subcontinent of south central Asia;

capital, New Delhi. Long-standing tradition credits the Apostle Thomas with the introduction of Christianity in the Kerala area. Evangelization followed the establishment of Portuguese posts and the conquest of Goa in 1510. Jesuits, Franciscans, Dominicans, Augustinians and members of other religious orders figured in the early missionary history. An archdiocese for Goa, with two suffragan sees, was set up in 1558.

Missionaries had some difficulties with the British East India Co., which exercised virtual government control from 1757 to 1858. They also had trouble because of a conflict that developed between policies of the Portuguese government, which pressed its rights of patronage in episcopal and clerical appointments, and the Vatican Congregation for the Propagation of the Faith, which sought greater freedom of action in the same appointments. This struggle resulted in the schism of Goa between 1838 and 1857. In 1886, when the number of Catholics was estimated to be 1 million, the hierarchy for India and Ceylon was restored.

Jesuits contributed greatly to the development of Catholic education from the second half of the 19th century. A large percentage of the Catholic population is located around Goa and Kerala and farther south. The country is predominantly Hindu. Anti-conversion laws in effect in several states have had a restrictive effect on pastoral ministry and social service.

Recent years have seen tensions within the Syro-Malabar rite over liturgy and tradition. In addition, there have been tensions between the Latin-rite and Eastern-rite Catholic churches in India over the care of Catholics outside the traditional boundaries of their rites. The Vatican has investigated several Jesuits in India for teaching relativism, which refrains from proclaiming Christ as the world's savior out of respect for other religions. From 1998 to mid-2001 more than 150 cases of anti-Christian violence were recorded in western India. An independent commission probing the violence said right-wing Hindus were responsible.

Indonesia*

Archd., 8; dioc., 27; mil. ord. 1; card., 1; abp., 9; bps., 33; parishes, 1,057; priests, 3,039 (1,230 dioc., 1,809 rel.); p.d., 15; sem., 2,818; bros., 955; srs., 7,148; catechists, 22,556; bap., 192,064; Caths., 6,440,000 (3%); tot. pop., 214,840,000. Note: East Timor was granted independence in May, 2002. *See* under **Timor, East,** for statistical details.

Republic in the Malay Archipelago, consisting of some 3,000 islands; capital, Jakarta. Evangelization by the Portuguese began about 1511. St. Francis Xavier spent some 14 months in the area. Christianity was strongly rooted in some parts of the islands by 1600. Islam's rise to dominance began at this time. The Dutch East Indies Co., which gained effective control in the 17th century, banned evangelization by Catholic missionaries for some time, but Dutch secular and religious priests managed to resume the work. A vicariate of Batavia for all the Dutch East Indies was set up in 1841. About 90 percent of the population is Muslim. The hierarchy was established in 1961.

From 1981 to about 1996, Catholics and Protestants clashed more than 40 times over what Catholics perceived as Communion host desecration. At least three Protestants died from beatings by Catholics after the incidents.

In the late 1990s, as the Indonesian economy took a nose-dive, Muslim-Christian violence increased, especially in the Molucca Islands. Church leaders continued to urge calm and dialogue, and at one point a bishop sought U.N. intervention to prevent what he saw as a potential genocide of Christians. A militant Muslim group charged with inciting much of the violence disbanded in late 2002, and church leaders expressed hope for peace.

Iran*

Archd., 4; dioc., 2; abp., 4; bp., 2; parishes, 18; priests, 17 (7 dioc., 10 rel.); p.d., 5; sem., 1; srs., 30; bap., 54; Caths., 25,000 (.02%); tot. pop., 64,530,000.

Islamic republic (Persia until 1935) in southwestern Asia; capital, Teheran. Some of the earliest Christian communities were established in this area outside the Roman Empire. They suffered persecution in the fourth century and were then cut off from the outside world. Nestorianism was generally professed in the late fifth century. Islam became dominant after 640. Some later missionary work was attempted but without success. Religious liberty was granted in 1834, but Catholics were the victims of a massacre in 1918. Islam is the religion of perhaps 98 percent of the population. Catholics belong to the Latin, Armenian and Chaldean rites.

After Iran nationalized many Church-run social institutions in 1980, about 75 Catholic missionaries left the country, by force or by choice. In recent years, however, Iranian authorities have shown more cooperation regarding entry visas for Church personnel. Although freedom of worship is guaranteed in Iran, Church sources said Catholic activities are monitored carefully by authorities. Since Pope John Paul II and Iranian President Mohammed Khatami met in 1999, the Holy See and Iran have had several high-level diplomatic exchanges.

Iraq*

Patriarchate, 1; archd., 9; dioc., 5; ap. ex., 2; patriarch, 1; abp., 10; bp., 8; parishes, 100; priests, 164 (139 dioc., 25 rel.); p.d., 5; sem., 74; bros., 8; srs., 301; catechists, 1,024; bap., 3,323; Caths., 280,000 (1%); tot. pop., 23,580,000.

Republic in southwestern Asia; capital, Baghdad. Some of the earliest Christian communities were established in the area, whose history resembles that of Iran. Catholics belong to the Armenian, Chaldean, Latin and Syrian rites; Chaldeans are most numerous. Islam is the religion of some 90 percent of the population. Iraq's Chaldean Catholic patriarch was outspoken against the international embargo against Iraq, saying it especially hurt children and the sick. In February 2003, Vatican officials met with Iraqi leaders in an effort to prevent the U.S.-led war; the Vatican embassy in Baghdad remained open throughout the conflict, and church aid agencies treated wounded. Catholic aid organizations geared up relief efforts after the war but were frustrated by lawlessness and looting.

Ireland*

Archd., 4; dioc., 22; card., 2; abp., 7; bp., 41; parishes, 1,367; priests, 5,440 (3,245 dioc., 2,195 rel.); p.d., 3; sem., 214; bros., 904; srs., 9,096; bap., 50,336 (preceding figures include Northern Ireland); Caths., 4,727,000 (76%); tot. 6,201,000 (population numbers include Northern Ireland; in Republic of Ireland, Catholics comprise 95% of the population).

Republic in the British Isles; capital, Dublin. St. Patrick, who is venerated as the apostle of Ireland, evangelized parts of the island for some years after the middle of the fifth century. Conversion of the island was not accomplished, however, until the seventh century or later. Celtic monks were the principal missionaries. The Church was organized along monastic lines at first, but a movement developed in the 11th century for the establishment of jurisdiction along episcopal lines. By that time many Roman usages had been adopted. The Church gathered strength during the period from the Norman Conquest of England to the reign of Henry VIII despite a wide variety of rivalries, wars, and other disturbances.

Henry introduced an age of repression of the faith, which continued for many years under several of his successors. The Irish suffered from proscription of the Catholic faith, economic and social disabilities, subjection to absentee landlords and a plantation system designed to keep them from owning property, and actual persecution which took an uncertain toll of lives up until about 1714. Some penal laws remained in force until emancipation in 1829. Nearly 100 years later Ireland was divided in two, making Northern Ireland, consisting of six counties, part of the United Kingdom (1920) and giving dominion status to the Irish Free State, made up of the other 26 counties (1922). This state (Eire, in Gaelic) was proclaimed the Republic of Ireland in 1949. The Catholic Church predominates but religious freedom is guaranteed for all. The Irish Republic and Northern Ireland share a bishops' conference, which has worked for peace in Northern Ireland. Recent years have witnessed a decrease in vocations and growing turmoil over issues such as priestly pedophilia, divorce, and abortion.

Ireland, Northern

Tot. pop., 1,610,000; Catholics comprise more than one third. (Other statistics are included in **Ireland**).

Part of the United Kingdom, it consists of six of the nine counties of Ulster in the northeast corner of Ireland; capital, Belfast. Early history is given under **Ireland**.

Nationalist-unionist tensions fall primarily along Catholic-Protestant lines, with nationalists, mainly Catholics, advocating an end to British rule. Violence and terrorism began in the late 1960s and, by the late 1990s, more than 3,000 people had been killed. Catholic-Protestant tensions are highlighted each year during the Protestant marching season, when members of the Protestant Orange Order parade through Catholic neighborhoods, culminating in a march to commemorate the 1690 Battle of the Boyne, when Protestant King William of Orange defeated Catholic King James II. Catholics see the marches as signs of triumphalism.

On April 10, 1998, the governments of the Irish Republic and Great Britain and the political parties of Northern Ireland reached an agreement known as the Good Friday agreement. Irish bishops supported it, and it was endorsed by the voters in Ireland and Northern Ireland. However, the agreement or the coalition government established as a result of the agreement were suspended several times, and Northern Ireland's bishops spoke out in support of continuing democratic structures.

For years, Catholics claimed discrimination in the workplace and harassment from the Royal Ulster Constabulary, Northern Ireland's police force that was disbanded and reformed as the Police Service of Northern Ireland. In 2002 some 40 percent of the new force was Catholic, compared to 8 percent in 2001.

Israel*

Patriarchates, 2 (Jerusalem for Latins; patriarchal vicariate for Greek-Melkites); archd., 2; ap.ex., 5; patriarch, 1; abp., 4; bp., 3; parishes, 81; priests, 373 (80 dioc., 293 rel.); p.d., 8; sem., 118; bros., 167; srs., 1,035; bap., 1,579; Caths., 113,000 (1.7%); tot. pop., 6,450,000.

Parliamentary democracy in the Middle East; capitals, Jerusalem and Tel Aviv (diplomatic). Israel was the birthplace of Christianity, the site of the first Christian communities. Some persecution was suffered in the early Christian era and again during the several hundred years of Roman control. Muslims conquered the territory in the seventh century and, except for the period of the Kingdom of Jerusalem established by Crusaders, remained in control most of the time up until World War I. The Church survived in the area, sometimes just barely, but it did not prosper greatly or show any notable increase in numbers. The British took over the protectorate of the area after World War I.

Partition into Israel for the Jews and Palestine for the Arabs was approved by the United Nations in 1947. War broke out a year later with the proclamation of the Republic of Israel. The Israelis won the war and 50 percent more territory than they had originally been ceded. War broke out again for six days in June 1967, and in October 1973, resulting in a Middle East crisis.

Judaism is the faith professed by about 85 percent of the inhabitants; approximately one-third of them are considered observant. Israeli-Holy See relations improved in 1994 with the implementation of full diplomatic relations, and the Church gained legal status in 1997.

The Holy See repeatedly has asked for an internationally guaranteed statute to protect the sacred nature of Jerusalem, which is holy to Christians, Muslims and Jews. It has underlined that this means more than access to specific holy places and that the political and religious dimensions of Jerusalem are interrelated. During the Palestinian intifada, the Vatican and Holy Land church leaders defended Israeli rights to live without the threat of terrorism and the Palestinians' right to a homeland, saying both would only be achieved through a negotiated settlement.

Italy*

Patriarchate, 1 (Venice); archd. 60 (40 are metropolitan sees); dioc., 156; prel., 3; abb., 7; mil. ord. 1; pat., 1 (Venice); card., 35; abp., 161; bps., 275 (hierarchy includes 220 residential, 25 coadjutors or auxiliaries, 124 in Curia offices, remainder in other offices or retired); parishes, 25,807; priests, 54,743 (36,133 dioc., 18,610 rel.); p.d., 2,640; sem., 6,205; bros., 3,798; srs., 111,032; catechists, 163,706; bap., 461,807; Caths., 56,285,000 (97%); tot. pop., 57,950,000.

Republic in southern Europe; capital, Rome. A Christian community was formed early in Rome, probably by the middle of the first century. St. Peter established his see there. He and St. Paul suffered death for the faith in the 60s. The early Christians were persecuted at various times, as in other parts of the empire, but the Church developed in numbers and influence, gradually spreading out from towns and cities in the center and south to rural areas and the north.

Church organization, in the process of formation in the second century, developed greatly between the fifth and eighth centuries. By the latter date the Church had already come to grips with serious problems, including doctrinal and disciplinary disputes that threatened the unity of faith, barbarian invasions, and the need for the pope and bishops to take over civil responsibilities because of imperial default. The Church has been at the center of life on the peninsula throughout the centuries. It emerged from underground in 313, with the Edict of Milan, and rose to a position of prestige and lasting influence. It educated and converted the barbarians, preserved culture through the early Middle Ages and passed it on to later times, suffered periods of decline and gained strength through recurring reforms, engaged in military combat for political reasons and intellectual combat for the preservation and development of doctrine, saw and patronized the development of the arts, and experienced all human strengths and weaknesses in its members.

From the fourth to the 19th centuries, the Church was a temporal as well as spiritual power. In the 1870s, the Papal States were annexed by the Kingdom of Italy. The 1929 Lateran Pacts included a treaty recognizing the Vatican as an independent state, a financial agreement by which Italy agreed to compensate the Vatican for loss of the papal states, and a concordat regulating Church-state relations. In 1984 the Vatican and Italy signed a revised concordat, reducing some of the Church's privileges and removing Catholicism as the state religion.

The Church strongly opposed Italy's abortion law in 1978 and forced a 1981 referendum on the issue. Abortion remained legal, and the Italian Church has taken a more low-profile stance. The Church has been active in social issues, including helping unprecedented numbers of illegal immigrants in the late 1990s. Church leaders have expressed concern about Italy's low birth rate.

In 1997, a double earthquake destroyed a large section of the ceiling of the Basilica of St. Francis in Assisi, killing four people. Restoration experts began work almost immediately on the basilica, one of the Italian Church's largest tourism sites. The upper basilica was reopened in November 1999.

Jamaica*

Archd., 1; dioc., 2; abp., 2; bp., 2; parishes, 89; priests, 93 (57 dioc., 36 rel.); p.d., 36; sem., 18; bros., 63; srs., 166; catechists, 494; bap., 1,054; Caths., 113,000 (4.3%); tot. pop., 2,600,000.

Republic in the West Indies; capital, Kingston. Franciscans and Dominicans evangelized the island from about 1512 until 1655. Missionary work was interrupted after the English took possession but was resumed by Jesuits about the turn of the 19th century. An apostolic vicariate was organized in 1837. The hierarchy was established in 1967. In the late 1990s,

Church leaders spoke out against violence; more than 800 people were murdered in Jamaica in 1997 alone.

Japan*

Archd., 3; dioc., 13; p.a., 1; card., 1; abp., 5; bp., 20; parishes, 865; priests, 1,686 (510 dioc., 1,176 rel.); p.d., 8; sem., 185; bros., 237; srs., 6,437; catechists, 1,733; bap., 8,733; Caths., 514,000 (.4%); tot. pop., 127,340,000.

Archipelago in the northwest Pacific; capital, Tokyo. Jesuits began evangelization in the middle of the 16th century and about 300,000 converts, most of them in Kyushu, were reported at the end of the century. The Nagasaki Martyrs were victims of persecution in 1597. Another persecution took some 4,000 lives between 1614 and 1651. Missionaries, banned for two centuries, returned about the middle of the 19th century and found Christian communities still surviving in Nagasaki and other places in Kyushu. A vicariate was organized in 1866. Religious freedom was guaranteed in 1889. The hierarchy was established in 1891. Several Japanese bishops at the 1998 Synod of Bishops for Asia said Catholicism has grown slowly in the region because the Church is too Western.

Since the 1980s, on several occasions Church leaders have apologized and asked forgiveness for the Church's complicity in the nation's aggression during the 1930s and 1940s. At the end of the 20th century, bishops and religious superiors suggested that during the 21st century the Japanese Church focus on pastoral care for migrant workers, concern for the environment and interreligious dialogue.

Jordan*

Archd., 1; ex. pat., 1; abp., 2; bp., 1; parishes, 62; priests, 76 (60 dioc., 16 rel.); sem., 3; bros., 9; srs., 239; bap., 1,099; Caths., 68,000 (1%); tot. pop., 5,050,000.

Constitutional monarchy in the Middle East; capital, Amman. Christianity there dates from apostolic times. Survival of the faith was threatened many times under the rule of Muslims from 636 and Ottoman Turks from 1517 to 1918, and in the Islamic Emirate of Trans-Jordan from 1918 to 1949. In the years following the creation of Israel, some 500,000 Palestinian refugees, including Christians, moved to Jordan. In the 1990s, Jordan cared for some 130,000 Iraqi refugees, including about 30,000 Chaldean Catholics. Islam is the state religion, but religious freedom is guaranteed for all. The Greek Melkite Archdiocese of Petra and Filadelfia is located in Jordan. Latin-rite Catholics are under the jurisdiction of the Latin Patriarchate of Jerusalem. Jordan established diplomatic relations with the Holy See in 1994.

Kazakstan*

Archd. 1, Dioc., 1; a.a., 2; abp., 1; bp., 3; parishes, 40, priests, 63 (36 dioc., 27 rel.); sem., 14; bros., 8; srs., 66; bap., 1,198; Caths., 178,000 (1.2%); tot. pop., 14,830,000.

Independent republic (1991); formerly part of USSR; capital, Astana. About 47 percent of the population is Muslim, and about 44 percent is Orthodox. The Catholic population is mainly of German, Polish and Ukrainian origin, descendants of those deported during the Stalin regime. A Latin-rite apostolic administration was established in 1991. In 1998, the

Vatican and the Kazak government signed an agreement guaranteeing the Church legal rights. Diocesan structure was established in 1999, and the Vatican created the first archdiocese and diocese in 2003. Pope John Paul II visited the country in 2001, saying he believed the post-communist era offered an evangelizing opportunity for the Catholic Church.

Kenya*

Archd. 4; dioc., 19; v.a., 1; mil. ord., 1; card., 1; abp. 5; bp., 25; parishes, 653; priests, 1,936 (1,014 dioc., 922 rel.); p.d., 1; sem., 1,476; bros., 714; srs., 3,916; catechists, 9,605; bap., 252,626; Caths., 7,532,000 (24%); tot. pop., 31,290,000.

Republic in East Africa on the Indian Ocean; capital, Nairobi. Systematic evangelization by the Holy Ghost Missionaries began in 1889, nearly 40 years after the start of work by Protestant missionaries. The hierarchy was established in 1953. Three metropolitan sees were established in 1990. Kenyan Catholics were in the forefront of ministering to victims of the 1998 explosion at the U.S. Embassy in Nairobi. The Kenyan bishops have been outspoken against ethnic violence, poverty, government corruption and mismanagement, and the need for a constitutional review.

Kiribati*

Dioc., 1; bp., 1; parishes, 23; priests, 31 (14 dioc., 17 rel.); p.d. 4; sem., 19; bros., 22; srs., 90; catechists, 222; bap., 1,591; Caths., 46,000 (54.2%); tot. pop., 83,000.

Former British colony (Gilbert Islands) in Oceania; became independent July 12, 1979; capital, Bairiki on Tarawa. French Missionaries of the Sacred Heart began work in the islands in 1888. A vicariate for the islands was organized in 1897. The hierarchy was established in 1966.

Korea, North

Tot. pop., 22,270,000. No recent Catholic statistics available; there were an estimated 100,000 Catholics reported in 1969.

Northern part of peninsula in eastern Asia; formal name Democratic People's Republic of Korea (May 1, 1948); capital, Pyongyang. *See* **South Korea** for history before country was divided. After liberation from Japan in 1945, the Soviet regime in the North systematically punished all religions. After the 1950-53 Korean war, Christian worship was not allowed outside of homes until 1988, when the country's one Catholic Church was built in Pyongyang. A 1999 South Korean government report said North Korea clearly restricts religious practices, and churches in the North exist only for show.

Korea, South*

Archd., 3; dioc., 11; mil. ord. 1; card., 1; abp., 5; bp., 23; parishes, 1,258; priests, 2,845 (2,400 dioc., 445 rel.); sem., 1,750; bros., 585; srs., 8,443; catechists, 12,035; bap., 155,805; Caths., 4,187,000 (8.8%); tot. pop., 47,340,000.

Southern part of peninsula in eastern Asia; formal name, Republic of Korea (1948); capital, Seoul. Some Catholics may have been in Korea before it became a "hermit kingdom" toward the end of the 16th century and closed its borders to foreigners. The modern introduction to Catholicism came in 1784 through lay converts. A priest arriving in the country in 1794 found 4,000 Catholics there who had never seen a priest. A vicariate was erected in 1831 but was not manned for several years thereafter. There were 15,000 Catholics by 1857. Four persecutions in the 19th century took a terrible toll; several thousand died in the last one, 1866-69. (Pope John Paul II canonized 103 martyrs of this period during his 1984 visit to South Korea.) Freedom of religion was granted in 1883, when Korea opened its borders. During World War II, most foreign priests were arrested and expelled, seminaries were closed and churches were taken over. After liberation from Japan in 1945, the Church in the South had religious freedom. Since the 1950-53 Korean war, the Church in South Korea has flourished. Church leaders in the South have worked at reconciliation with the North and to alleviate famine in the North.

Kuwait*

V.a., 1; pat. ex., 1; abp., 1; bp., 1; parishes, 5; priests, 9 (3 dioc., 6 rel.); p.d., 1; bros., 13; bap., 551; Caths., 155,000 (.8%); tot. pop., 1,970,000.

Constitutional monarchy (sultanate or sheikdom) in southwest Asia bordering on the Persian Gulf. Remote Christian origins probably date to apostolic times. Islam is the predominant and official religion. Catholics are mostly foreign workers; the Church enjoys religious freedom.

Kyrgyzstan*

Mission, 1; parishes, 11; priests, 8 (1 dioc., 7 rel.); bros., 1; srs., 4; bap., 27; Caths., 30,000; tot. pop., 4,950,000.

Independent republic bordering China; former Soviet republic; capital, Bishkek (former name, Frunze). Most of the people are Sunni Muslim. Established diplomatic relations with the Holy See in August 1992.

Laos

V.a., 4; bp., 3; parishes, 123; priests, 15 (13 dioc., 2 rel.); p.d., 1; sem., 15; srs., 76; catechists, 295; bap., 1,293; Caths., 37,000 (.6%); tot. pop., 5,400,000. (AD)

People's republic in southeast Asia; capital, Vientiane. Systematic evangelization by French missionaries started about 1881; earlier efforts ended in 1688. The first mission was established in 1885 by Father Xavier Guégo. An apostolic vicariate was organized in 1899. Most of the foreign missionaries were expelled following the communist takeover in 1975. Catholic schools remain banned, and the government lets foreign missionaries into the country only as "social workers." A Laotian bishop at the 1998 Synod of Bishops for Asia said religious practice was nearly normal in two of the country's four apostolic vicariates, but elsewhere was more controlled and sometimes difficult. Buddhism is the state religion.

Latvia*

Archd., 1; dioc., 3; bp., 5; parishes, 252; priests, 124 (100 dioc., 24 rel.); p.d., 1; sem., 50; brs., 1; srs., 87; catechist, 284; bap., 5,630; Caths., 415,000 (17.5%); tot. pop., 2,360,000.

Independent (1991) Baltic republic; capital, Riga. (Forcibly absorbed by the USSR in 1940; it regained independence in 1991). Catholicism was introduced late in the 12th century. Lutheranism became the dominant religion after 1530. Catholics were free to practice their faith during the long period of Russian control and during independence from 1918 to 1940. The relatively small Catholic community in Latvia was repressed during the 1940-91 Soviet takeover, which was not recognized by the Holy See or the United States. After Latvia declared its independence, the Church began to flourish, including among people who described themselves as nonreligious. In the late 1990s, one archbishop urged the Russian government not to interfere in disputes over citizenship for the country's ethnic Russians, who make up about one-third of the country's population.

Lebanon*

Patriarchates, 3; achd., 12 (1 Armenian, 4 Maronite, 7 Greek Melkite); dioc., 8 (1 Chaldean, 6 Maronite); v.a., 1 (Latin); card., 1 (patriarch of the Maronites); patriarchs, 3 (patriarchs of Antioch of the Maronites, Antioch of the Syrians and Cilicia of the Armenians who reside in Lebanon); abp., 25; bp., 17; parishes, 1,033; priests, 1,386 (752 dioc., 634 rel.); p.d., 3; sem., 481; bros., 196; srs., 2,685; catechists, 585; bap., 12,072; Caths., 1,859,000 (52%); tot. pop., 3,560,000.

Republic in the Middle East; capital, Beirut. Christianity, introduced in apostolic times, was firmly established by the end of the fourth century and has remained so despite heavy Muslim influence since early in the seventh century. The country is the center of the Maronite rite. In the 1980s, the country was torn by violence and often heavy fighting among rival political-religious factions drawn along Christian-Muslim lines. Pope John Paul II convened a synod of bishops for Lebanon in 1995 to urge Lebanese to forgive and forget the wounds of the war. Synod members provoked controversy by directly criticizing Israeli occupation of southern Lebanon and Syria's continued deployment of troops in the area. In 1999, Lebanon was the site of a historic meeting of Mideast and North African Church leaders, who discussed the future of the Catholic Church in the Arab world.

Lesotho*

Archd., 1; dioc., 3; abp., 1; bp., 3; parishes, 87; priests, 151 (63 dioc., 88 rel.); sem., 87; bros., 31; srs., 660; catechists, 1,640; bap., 24,277; Caths., 906,000 (41%); tot. pop., 2,190,000.

Constitutional monarchy, an enclave in the southeastern part of South Africa; capital, Maseru. Oblates of Mary Immaculate, the first Catholic missionaries in the area, started evangelization in 1862. Father Joseph Gerard, whom Pope John Paul II beatified in 1988, worked 10 years before he made his first conversion. An apostolic prefecture was organized in 1894. The hierarchy was established in 1951. Under the military government of the late 1980s, Lesotho's Catholics pressed for democratic reforms. In the 1990s, they gave special pastoral care to families whose breadwinners had to travel to South Africa to work, often for weeks at a time.

Liberia*

Archd., 1; dioc., 2; abp., 1; bp., 1; parishes, 48; priests, 40 (28 dioc., 12 rel.); p.d., 2; sem., 46; bros., 17; srs., 46; catechists, 593; bap. 9,148; Caths., 150,000 (4.8%); tot. pop., 3,110,000.

Republic in West Africa; capital, Monrovia. Missionary work and influence, dating intermittently from the 16th century, were slight before the Society of African Missions undertook evangelization in 1906. The hierarchy was established in 1982. Fighting within the country, which began in 1989, culminated in 1996 and resulted in the evacuation of most Church workers and the archbishop of Monrovia. The war claimed the lives of 150,000 and made refugees of or displaced another million. Most Church institutions in Monrovia were destroyed. Monrovia Archbishop Michael Francis was among leaders calling for U.S.-led intervention to quell chaos in the country in mid-2003.

Libya*

V.a., 3; p.a., 1; abp., 1; bp., 2; parishes, 6; priests, 13 (5 dioc., 8 rel.); sem. 2; srs., 67; bap., 65; Caths., 74,000 (1.5%); tot. pop., 5,410,000.

Arab state in North Africa; capital, Tripoli. Christianity was probably preached in the area at an early date but was overcome by the spread of Islam from the 630s. Islamization was complete by 1067, and there has been no Christian influence since then. Almost all Catholics are foreign workers. Islam is the state religion. After implementation of a U.N. embargo against the country in 1992, the government removed most limitations on entry of Catholic religious orders, especially health care workers. Libya established diplomatic relations with the Holy See in 1997.

Liechtenstein*

Archd. 1; abp., 1; parishes, 10; priests, 31 (19 dioc., 12 rel); sem., 14; srs., 66; bap., 314; Caths., 25,000 (80%); tot. pop., 33,000.

Constitutional monarchy in central Europe; capital, Vaduz. Christianity in the country dates from the fourth century; the area has been under the jurisdiction of Chur, Switzerland, since about that time. The Reformation had hardly any influence in the country. Catholicism is the state religion, but religious freedom for all is guaranteed by law.

Lithuania*

Archd., 2; dioc., 5; mil. ord., 1; card., 2; abp., 2; bp., 11; parishes, 677; priests, 782 (678 dioc., 104 rel.); p.d., 3; sem., 229; bros., 45; srs., 758; catechists, 2,235; bap., 27,689; Caths., 2,880,000 (82%); tot. pop., 3,490,000.

Baltic republic forcibly absorbed and under Soviet domination from 1940; regained independence, 1991; capital, Vilnius. Catholicism was introduced in 1251 and a short-lived diocese was established by 1260. Effective evangelization took place between 1387 and 1417, when Catholicism became the state religion. Losses to Lutheranism in the 16th century were overcome. Efforts of czars to "russify" the Church between 1795 and 1918 were strongly resisted. Concordat relations with the Vatican were established in 1927, nine years after independence from Russia and 13 years before Russia annexed Lithuania. The Russians closed convents and seminaries; in Kaunas, men needed government approval to attend the seminary. Priests were restricted in pastoral ministry and subject to appointment by government officials; no religious services were allowed outside churches; religious press and instruction were banned. Some bishops and hundreds of priests and laity were imprisoned or detained in Siberia between 1945 and 1955. Two bishops — Vincentas Sladkevicius and Julijonas Steponavicius — were forbidden to act as bishops and relegated to remote parishes in 1957 and 1961, respectively. Despite such conditions, a vigorous underground Church flourished in Lithuania.

In the 1980s, government pressure eased, and some bishops were allowed to return to their dioceses. In 1989 Pope John Paul II appointed bishops in all six Lithuanian dioceses. The Church strongly supported the 1990 independence movement, and Lithuanian independence leaders urged young men to desert the Russian army and seek sanctuary in churches. However, communist rule nearly destroyed the Church's infrastructure. In 2000 the Church and government signed a series of agreements regularizing the Church's position.

Luxembourg*

Archd., 1; abp., 2; parishes, 275; priests, 268 (196 dioc., 72 rel.); p.d., 7; sem., 4; bros., 12; srs., 619; catechism, 460; bap., 3,085; Caths. 380,000 (89%); tot. pop., 441,000.

Constitutional monarchy in western Europe; capital, Luxembourg. Christianity, introduced in the fifth and sixth centuries, was firmly established by the end of the eighth century. A full-scale parish system was in existence in the ninth century. Monastic influence was strong until the Reformation, which had minimal influence in the country. The Church experienced some adverse influence from the currents of the French Revolution. In recent years, the Church has restructured its adult formation program to involve more lay workers.

Macau

Dioc., 1; bp., 2; parishes, 8; priests, 70 (27 dioc., 43 rel.); sem., 1; bros., 18; srs., 183; bap., 418; catechists, 5,273; Caths., 20,000; tot. pop., 435,000.

Former Portuguese-administered territory in southeast Asia across the Pearl River estuary from Hong Kong; reverted to Chinese control Dec. 20, 1999. Christianity was introduced by the Jesuits in 1557. Diocese was established in 1576. Macau served as a base for missionary work in Japan and China. Portuguese and Chinese Catholics remained somewhat segregated throughout the more than 400 years of Portuguese rule. Bishop Domingos Lam Ka Tseung became the first Chinese bishop of Macau in 1988 and launched a lay formation plan that included Chinese and Portuguese language training. The Church has been prominent in education. A Catholic priest was among three religious leaders named to the committee to prepare for the enclave's return to Chinese rule in December 1999. Church leaders said the transition proceeded smoothly.

Macedonia*

Dioc., 1; bp., 2; parishes, 7; priests, 12 (10 dioc., 2 rel.); sem., 28; srs., 31; bap., 80; Caths., 15,000 (.9%); tot. pop., 2,040,000.

Former Yugoslav Republic of Macedonia; declared independence in 1992; capital, Skopje. The Diocese of Skopje-Prizren includes the Yugoslav province of Kosovo, so the Macedonian Church was intimately involved with ethnic Albanians during the period of

ethnic cleansing by Serb forces and retaliatory NATO air strikes.

Madagascar*

Archd., 3; dioc., 17; card., 1; abp., 4; bp., 23; parishes, 314; priests, 1,075 (450 dioc., 625 rel.); p.d., 4; sem., 862; bros., 486; srs., 3,602; catechists, 16,784; bap., 150,109; Caths., 4,440,000 (27%); tot. pop. 16,440,000.

Republic (Malagasy Republic) off the eastern coast of Africa; capital, Antananarivo. Missionary efforts were generally fruitless from early in the 16th century until the Jesuits were permitted to start open evangelization about 1845. An apostolic prefecture was set up in 1850 and an apostolic vicariate in the North was placed in charge of the Holy Ghost Fathers in 1898. There were 100,000 Catholics by 1900. The first native bishop was ordained in 1936. The hierarchy was established in 1955. In the late 1980s and early 1990s, the Church joined opposition calls for renewal of social institutions. Today, the Church in Madagascar runs hundreds of schools and dozens of orphanages and is active in the island's social justice concerns; some consider it the largest landowner, after the government.

Malawi*

Archd., 1; dioc., 6; abp., 2; bp., 7; parishes, 153; priests, 468 (277 dioc., 191 rel.); sem., 267; bros., 76; srs., 751; catechists, 7,664; bap., 115,893; Caths., 2,804,000 (25%); tot. pop., 11,400,000.

Republic in the interior of East Africa; capital, Lilongwe. Missionary work, begun by Jesuits in the late 16th and early 17th centuries, was generally ineffective until the end of the 19th century. The Missionaries of Africa (White Fathers) arrived in 1889 and later were joined by others. A vicariate was set up in 1897. The hierarchy was established in 1959. In the late 1980s, the Church in Malawi helped hundreds of thousands of refugees from the war in Mozambique. Malawi's churches, especially the Catholic Church, were instrumental in bringing about the downfall of President Hastings Kamuzu Banda, who ruled for 30 years. A 1992 bishops' pastoral letter criticized Banda's rule and the nation's poverty and galvanized Malawians into pro-democracy protests. Banda responded by summoning the country's bishops, seizing copies of the letter and expelling an Irish member of the Malawi hierarchy. Western donors called off aid, and in 1994 Banda was forced to call multi-party elections, which he lost. In 2002, church officials were outspoken against plans by Banda's successor, President Bakili Muluzi, to seek a third term of office; church officials said they were threatened and attacked for that criticism.

Malaysia

Archd., 2; dioc., 6; abp., 3; bp., 13; parishes, 139; priests, 237 (183 dioc., 54 rel.); p.d., 1; sem., 56; bros., 62; srs., 545; catechists, 2,306; bap., 21,891; Caths., 770,000 (3%); tot. pop., 22,630,000. (AD)

Parliamentary democracy in southeast Asia; capital, Kuala Lumpur. Christianity, introduced by Portuguese colonists about 1511, was confined almost exclusively to Malacca until late in the 18th century. The effectiveness of evangelization increased from then on because of the recruitment and training of indigenous clergy. Singapore (see separate entry), founded in 1819, became a center for missionary work. Effective evangelization in Sabah and Sarawak began in the second half of the 19th century. The hierarchy was established in 1973. In accordance with government wishes for Bahasa Malaysia to be the national language, the Church has tried to introduce it into its liturgies. For more than a decade, Church leaders campaigned against the Internal Security Act, which allows renewable 30-day detentions without trial. Proselytizing Muslims is illegal, but the government allows conversions from other religions.

Maldives

Republic, an archipelago 400 miles southwest of India and Ceylon; capital, Male. No serious attempt was ever made to evangelize the area, which is completely Muslim. Population, 290,000.

Mali*

Archd., 1; dioc., 5; abp., 1; bp., 5; parishes, 35; priests, 154 (74 dioc., 80 rel.); sem., 35; bros., 22; srs., 264; catechists, 958; bap., 3,795; Caths., 217,000 (.2%); tot. pop., 10,400,000.

Republic, inland in western Africa; capital, Bamako. Catholicism was introduced late in the second half of the 19th century. Missionary work made little progress in the midst of the predominantly Muslim population. A vicariate was set up in 1921. The hierarchy was established in 1955. In recent years, the Church has promoted the role of women in society. Catholics have cordial relations with Muslims.

Malta*

Archd., 1; dioc., 1; abp., 3; bp., 2; parishes, 79; priests, 941 (487 dioc., 454 rel.); sem., 94; bros., 84; srs., 1,241; catechists, 1,220; bap., 4,014; Caths., 367,000 (96%); tot. pop., 383,000.

Republic south of Sicily; capital, Valletta. Early catacombs and inscriptions are evidence of the early introduction of Christianity. St. Paul was shipwrecked on Malta in 60. Saracens controlled the islands from 870 to 1090, a period of difficulty for the Church. The line of bishops extends from 1090 to the present. Church-state conflict developed in recent years over passage of government-sponsored legislation affecting Catholic schools and Church-owned property. An agreement reached in 1985 ended the dispute and established a joint commission to study other Church-state problems.

Marshall Islands*

P.a., 1; parishes, 4; priests, 6 (rel.); p.d., 1; sem., 2; brs., 2; srs., 20; bap., 108; Caths., 5,000 (12.5%); tot. pop., 51,000.

Island republic in central Pacific Ocean; capital, Majura. Formerly administered by United States as part of U.N. Trust Territory of the Pacific; independent nation, 1991. An apostolic prefecture was erected May 25, 1993 (formerly part of Carolines-Marshall Diocese), with U.S. Jesuit Rev. James Gould as first apostolic prefect.

Mauritania*

Dioc., 1; bp., 1; parishes, 6; priests, 11 (1 dioc., 10 rel.); srs., 32; bap., 36; Caths., 5,000 (.2%); tot. pop., 2,750,000. (AD)

Islamic republic on the northwest coast of Africa; capital, Nouakchott. With few exceptions, the Catholics in the country are foreign workers. At the 1994 Synod of Bishops for Africa, a bishop from Mauritania reported increasing problems with fundamentalist Muslims, but cautioned Church leaders against generalizing about Muslims.

Mauritius*

Dioc., 1; v.a., 1; card., 1; bp., 1; parishes, 49; priests, 104 (62 dioc., 42 rel.); sem., 11; bros., 25; srs., 264; catechists, 807; bap., 6,107; Caths., 278,000 (23%); tot. pop., 1,200,000.

Island republic in the Indian Ocean; capital, Port Louis. Catholicism was introduced by Vincentians in 1722. Port Louis, made a vicariate in 1819 and a diocese in 1847, was a jumping-off point for missionaries to Australia, Madagascar and South Africa. During a 1989 visit to Mauritius, Pope John Paul II warned against sins that accompanied its rapid economic development and booming tourism industry.

Mexico* (*See* **Catholic Church in Mexico**; *see* also **Statistics of the Church in Mexico**)

Micronesia*

Dioc., 1; bp., 1; parishes, 24; priests, 23 (11 dioc., 12 rel.); p.d., 39; sem., 10; bros., 1; srs., 53; catechists, 525; bap., 1,920; Caths., 67,000 (53%); tot. pop., 117,000.

Federated States of Micronesia (Caroline archipelago) in southwest Pacific; capital, Palikir; former U.N. trust territory under U.S. administration; became independent nation September 1991. Effective evangelization began in the late 1880s. The government established diplomatic relations with the Holy See in 1994.

Moldova*

Dioc., 2; bp., 1; parishes, 11; priests, 18 (10 dioc., 8 rel.); p.d., 1; sem., 13; bros., 2; srs., 33; bap., 86; Caths., 20,000 (.46%); tot. pop., 4,290,000.

Independent republic, former constituent republic of the USSR; capital, Kishinev. The majority of people belong to the Orthodox Church. Catholics are mostly of Polish or German descent.

Monaco*

Archd., 1; abp., 1; parishes, 6; priests, 22 (13 dioc., 8 rel.); p.d., 1; sem., 1; srs., 15; bap., 184; Caths., 29,000 (90%); tot. pop., 32,000.

Constitutional monarchy, an enclave on the Mediterranean coast of France; capital, Monaco-Ville. Christianity was introduced before 1000. Catholicism is the official religion but religious freedom is guaranteed for all.

Mongolia*

Parish; priests, 9 (2 dioc., 7 rel.); sem., 5; bros., 5; srs., 19; bap., 20; Caths., 1,000 (.04%); tot. pop., 2,420,000.

Republic in north central Asia; formerly under communist control; capital, Ulan Bator. Christianity was introduced by Oriental Orthodox. Some Franciscans were in the country in the 13th and 14th centuries, en route to China. Freedom of worship is guaranteed under the new constitution, which went into effect in

1992. The government established relations with the Holy See in 1992 and indicated that missionaries would be welcome to help rebuild the country. The first Catholic parish was established in 1994, and by 1997 the Church had extended its work beyond the capital.

Morocco*

Archd., 2; abp., 3; parishes, 35; priests, 66 (25 dioc., 41 rel.); bros., 15; srs., 262; bap., 59; Caths., 24,000 (.08%); tot. pop., 29,170,000.

Constitutional monarchy in North Africa; capital, Rabat. Christianity was known in the area by the end of the third century. Bishops from Morocco attended a council at Carthage in 484. Catholic life survived under Visigoth and, from 700, Arab rule; later it became subject to influence from the Spanish, Portuguese and French. Islam is the state religion. The hierarchy was established in 1955. Pope John Paul II visited in 1985.

Mozambique

Archd., 3; dioc., 9; card., 1; abp. 4; bp., 11; parishes, 271; priests, 530 (155 dioc., 375 rel.); sem., 366; bros., 91; srs., 1,011; catechists, 36,096; bap., 119,808; Caths., 4,192,000 (24%); tot. pop., 17,660,000. (AD)

Republic in southeast Africa; capital, Maputo. Christianity was introduced by Portuguese Jesuits about the middle of the 16th century. Evangelization continued from then until the 18th century, when it went into decline largely because of the Portuguese government's expulsion of the Jesuits. Conditions worsened in the 1830s, improved after 1881, but deteriorated again during the anticlerical period from 1910 to 1925. Conditions improved in 1940, the year Portugal concluded a new concordat with the Holy See and the hierarchy was established. Missionaries' outspoken criticism of Portuguese policies in Mozambique resulted in Church-state tensions in the years immediately preceding independence. The first two indigenous bishops were ordained March 9, 1975. Two ecclesiastical provinces were established in 1984. Mozambican bishops and members of the Rome-based Sant' Egidio Community were official mediators in the talks that ended 16 years of civil war in 1992. Since then, Church participation has flourished, with high attendance at Mass, a boom in vocations and active catechists at the parish level.

Myanmar

Archd., 3; dioc., 9; abp., 3; bp., 12; parishes, 271; priests, 498 (476 dioc., 22 rel.); sem., 384; bros., 98; srs., 1,349; catechists, 3,098; bap., 25,456; Caths., 606,000 (1.2%); tot. pop., 48,360,000. (AD)

Socialist republic in southeast Asia, formerly Burma; name changed to Myanmar in 1989; capital, Yangon (Rangoon). Christianity was introduced about 1500. Small-scale evangelization had limited results from the middle of the 16th century until the 1850s, when effective organization of the Church began. The hierarchy was established in 1955. Buddhism was declared the state religion in 1961, but the state is now officially secular. In 1965, Church schools and hospitals were nationalized. In 1966, all foreign missionaries who had entered the country for the first time after 1948 were forced to leave when the government refused to renew their work permits. The Church is involved primarily in pastoral and social activities.

Namibia*

Archd., 1; dioc., 1; v.a., 1; abp., 1; bp., 3; parishes, 97; priests, 81 (19 dioc., 62 rel.); p.d., 46; sem., 32; bros., 24; srs., 281; catechists, 1,124; bap., 5,705; Caths., 360,000 (20%); tot. pop., 1,790,000. (AD)

Independent (March 21, 1990) state in southern Africa; capital, Windhoek. The area shares the history of South Africa. The hierarchy was established in 1994. The Church is hindered by a lack of priests.

Nauru*

Parish; priest, 1 (rel) p.d., 2; srs., 3; bap., 95; Caths., 3,000 (37%); tot. pop., 8,000.

Independent republic in western Pacific; capital, Yaren. Forms part of the Tarawa and Nauru Diocese (Kiribati). Established diplomatic relations with the Holy See in 1992.

Nepal*

P.a., 1; parishes, 35; priests, 52 (12 dioc.; 40 rel.); sem., 31; bros., 1; srs., 104; bap., 143; Caths., 6,000 (.2%); tot. pop., 23,590,000.

Constitutional monarchy, the only Hindu kingdom in the world, in central Asia; capital, Katmandu. Little is known of the country before the 15th century. Some Jesuits passed through from 1628 and some sections were evangelized in the 18th century, with minimal results, before the country was closed to foreigners. Conversions from Hinduism, the state religion, are not recognized in law and are punishable by imprisonment.

Netherlands*

Archd., 1; dioc., 6; mil ord., 1; card., 2; abp., 1; bp., 19; parishes, 1,599; priests 3,671 (1,470 dioc., 2,201 rel.); p.d., 298; sem., 173; bros., 1,333; srs., 10,694; bap., 41,734; Caths., 4,987,000 (31%); tot. pop., 16,040,000.

Constitutional monarchy in northwestern Europe; capital, Amsterdam (seat of government, The Hague). Evangelization, begun about the turn of the sixth century by Irish, Anglo-Saxon and Frankish missionaries, resulted in Christianization of the country by 800 and subsequent strong influence on the Lowlands. Invasion by French Calvinists in 572 brought serious losses to the Catholic Church and made the Reformed Church dominant. Catholics suffered a practical persecution of official repression and social handicap in the 17th century. The schism of Utrecht occurred in 1724. Only one-third of the population was Catholic in 1726. The Church had only a skeletal organization from 1702 to 1853, when the hierarchy was reestablished.

Despite this upturn, cultural isolation was the experience of Catholics until about 1914. From then on new vigor came into the life of the Church, and a whole new climate of interfaith relations began to develop. Before and for some years following the Second Vatican Council, the thrust and variety of thought and practice in the Dutch Church moved it to the vanguard position of "progressive" renewal. A synod of Dutch bishops held at the Vatican in January 1980 discussed ideological differences among Catholics with the aim of fostering unity and restoring some discipline within the nation's Church. However, even into the 1990s Church leaders spoke of a polarization among Catholics over issues such as sexual morality, ministries for women and priestly celibacy. The bishops also spoke out against permissive laws on euthanasia and assisted suicide.

New Zealand*

Archd., 1; dioc., 5; mil. ord., 1; card., 1; abp., 1; bp., 10; parishes, 270; priests, 534 (324 dioc., 210 rel.); p.d., 3; sem., 31; bros., 184; srs., 1,071; bap., 7,264; Caths. 471,000 (12%); tot. pop., 3,905,000.

Parliamentary democracy in southwestern Pacific Ocean; capital, Wellington. Protestant missionaries were the first evangelizers. On North Island, Catholic missionaries started work before the establishment of two dioceses in 1848; their work among the Maoris was not organized until about 1881. On South Island, whose first resident priest arrived in 1840, a diocese was established in 1869. These three jurisdictions were joined in a province in 1896. The Marists were the predominant Catholic missionaries in the area. The first Maori bishop was named in 1988. In 1998, Pope John Paul II urged New Zealand's bishops not to allow the Church to fall prey to the practices and values of prevailing culture. However, the president of the bishops' conference used the same occasion to express the bishops' concern to the pope about inconsistency in the way the Vatican exercises its authority.

Nicaragua*

Archd., 1; dioc., 6; v.a., 1; card., 1; abp., 1; bp., 10; parishes, 247; priests, 429 (257 dioc., 172 rel.); p.d., 29; sem., 253; bros., 48; srs., 1,001; catechists, 14,961; bap., 81,768; Caths., 4,643,000 (89%); tot. pop., 5,210,000.

Republic in Central America: capital, Managua. Evangelization began shortly after the Spanish conquest, about 1524, and eight years later the first bishop took over jurisdiction of the Church in the country. Jesuits were leaders in missionary work during the colonial period, which lasted until the 1820s. Evangelization endeavor increased after establishment of the republic in 1838. In this century it was extended to the Atlantic coastal area, where Protestant missionaries began work about the middle of the 1900s.

Many Church leaders, clerical and lay, supported the aims but not necessarily all the methods of the revolution, which forced the resignation and flight July 17, 1979, of Anastasio Somoza, whose family had controlled the government since the early 1930s. During the Sandinista period that followed, four priests accepted government posts. Some Nicaraguan Catholics threw their energies behind the Sandinista program of land reform and socialism, forming what some called a "popular church" based on liberation theology, while others strongly opposed the government. Managua Cardinal Miguel Obando Bravo helped mediate cease-fire talks during the war between the Sandinistas and U.S.-backed guerrillas. Land distribution, exacerbated by a wide gap in incomes, continued to be an issue, and in the late 1990s the Nicaraguan bishops continued to call for compromise between the government and former government officials. Despite an influx of aid after Hurricane Mitch killed more than 2,500 Nicaraguans and forced 900,000 to evacuate, Church leaders predicted an increase in poverty for the nation.

Niger*

Dioc., 2; bp., 3; parishes, 16; priests, 41 (16 dioc., 25 rel.); sem., 14; bros., 6; srs., 77; catechists, 269; bap., 341; Caths., 12,000 (.1%); tot. pop., 11,230,000.

Republic in west central Africa; capital, Niamey. The first mission was set up in 1831. An apostolic prefecture was organized in 1942, and the first diocese was established in 1961. The country is predominantly Muslim. The Church is active in the fields of health and education.

Nigeria*

Archd., 9; dioc., 37; v.a., 3; card., 1; abp., 11; bp., 43; parishes, 1,808; priests, 3,783 (3,136 dioc., 647 rel.); p.d., 5; sem., 4,388; bros., 425; srs., 3,507; catechists, 25,788; bap., 572,821; Caths., 17,414,000 (14.8%); tot. pop., 116,930,000.

Republic in West Africa; capital, Lagos. The Portuguese introduced Catholicism to the coastal region in the 15th century. Capuchins did some evangelization in the 17th century but systematic missionary work did not get under way along the coast until about 1840. A vicariate for this area was organized in 1870. A prefecture was set up in 1911 for missions in the northern part of the country, where Islam was strongly entrenched. From 1967, when Biafra seceded, until early in 1970 the country was torn by civil war. The hierarchy was established in 1950. Six dioceses were made metropolitan sees in 1994; four new dioceses were established as in 1995. Under the 1993-99 rule of Gen. Sani Abacha, Church leaders spoke out on behalf of human rights and democracy. After Abacha announced elections, the bishops said the country needed "new leading actors and fresh vision." As the 21st century began, bishops spoke out against imposition of Islamic law in individual states within the country.

Norway*

Dioc., 1; prel., 2; bp., 3; parishes, 32; priests, 66 (30 dioc., 36 rel.); p.d., 3; sem., 10; bros., 3; srs., 174; bap., 762; Caths., 54,000 (1%); tot. pop., 4,510,000.

Constitutional monarchy in northern Europe; capital, Oslo. Evangelization begun in the ninth century by missionaries from England and Ireland put the Church on a firm footing about the turn of the 11th century. The first diocese was set up in 1153 and development of the Church progressed until the Black Death in 1349 inflicted losses from which it never recovered. Lutheranism, introduced from outside in 1537 and furthered cautiously, gained general acceptance by about 1600 and was made the state religion. Legal and other measures crippled the Church, forcing priests to flee the country and completely disrupting normal activity. Changes for the better came in the 19th century, with the granting of religious liberty in 1845 and the repeal of many legal disabilities in 1897. Norway was administered as a single apostolic vicariate from 1892 to 1932, when it was divided into three jurisdictions.

Oman

Parishes, 4; priests, 8 (1 dioc., 7 rel.); bap., 192; Caths., 65,000 (2.6%); tot. pop., 2,450,000.

Independent monarchy in eastern corner of Arabian

Peninsula; capital, Muscat. Under ecclesiastical jurisdiction of Arabia apostolic vicariate.

Pakistan*

Archd., 2; dioc., 4; p.a., 1; abp., 2; bp., 6; parishes, 117; priests, 282 (142 dioc., 140 rel.); sem., 116; p.d., 2; bros., 44; srs., 703; catechists, 547; bap., 17,136; Caths., 1,255,000 (.09%); tot. pop., 144,970,000.

Islamic republic in southwest Asia; capital, Islamabad. Islam, firmly established in the eighth century, is the state religion. Christian evangelization of the native population began about the middle of the 19th century, years after earlier scattered attempts. The hierarchy was established in 1950. A series of death sentences against Christians accused of blasphemy resulted in acquittals during appeal processes, but in 1998 Bishop John Joseph of Faisalabad committed suicide to protest the strict blasphemy laws, which continued to be used as reasons for Christian arrests. In early 2002, the government did away with the system under which religious minorities, such as Catholics, could only vote n elections for members of their religious group. Pakistani Christians, including Catholics, have been the target of several terrorist incidents since the United States attacked Afghanistan in October 2001.

Palau*

Parishes, 6; priests, 4 (2 dioc., 2 rel.); p.d., 1; bros., 2; srs., 6; bap., 130; Caths., 9,000 (42%); tot. pop., 20,000.

Independent (1994) nation in western Pacific; capital, Koror; part of Caroline chain of Islands. Under ecclesiastical jurisdiction of diocese of Caroline Islands, Federated States of Micronesia.

Panama*

Archd., 1; dioc., 5; prel., 1; v.a., 1; abp., 2; bp., 8; parishes, 180; priests, 411 (196 dioc., 215 rel.); p.d., 69; sem., 120; bros., 63; srs., 439; catechists, 5,483; bap., 25,320; Caths., 2,414,000 (84%); tot. pop., 2,860,000.

Republic in Central America; capital, Panama City. Catholicism was introduced by Franciscan missionaries and evangelization started in 1514. The Panama Diocese, oldest in the Americas, was set up at the same time. The Catholic Church has favored status and state aid for missions, charities and parochial schools, but freedom is guaranteed to all religions. In May 1989, Panama's bishops accused the government of thwarting the presidential elections and of attempting to intimidate the Church. The elections' legitimate leader, Guillermo Endara, temporarily sought refuge at the Vatican Embassy in Panama City. After increasing unrest and violence, on Dec. 24, 1989, the country's dictator, Gen. Manuel Noriega, sought refuge at the Vatican Embassy. Ten days later, after U.S. troops spent days blasting the embassy with loud rock music and after meetings with Church diplomatic officials, Noriega surrendered.

Papua New Guinea*

Archd., 4; dioc., 14; abp., 6; bp., 24; parishes, 324; priests, 516 (170 dioc., 346 rel.); p.d., 9; sem., 357; bros., 227; srs., 860; catechists, 2,946; bap., 30,617; Caths., 1,625,000 (33%); tot. pop., 4,920,000.

Independent (Sept. 16, 1975) republic in southwest Pacific; capital, Port Moresby. Marists began evangelization about 1844 but were handicapped by many factors, including "spheres of influence" laid out for Catholic and Protestant missionaries. An apostolic prefecture was set up in 1896 and placed in charge of the Divine Word Missionaries. The territory suffered greatly during World War II. Hierarchy was established for New Guinea and adjacent islands in 1966. A decade-long war that began in the Bougainville area in the late 1980s left many churches, schools and health centers destroyed. At the end of the century, the Church fought social disintegration marked by violence, poverty and corruption.

Paraguay*

Archd., 1; dioc., 11; v.a., 2; mil. ord. 1; abp., 3; bp., 18; parishes, 386; priests, 797 (355 dioc., 442 rel.); p.d., 124; sem., 354; bros., 115; srs., 2,197; bap., 92,416; catechists, 80,607; Caths., 4,828,000 (86%); tot. pop., 5,640,000.

Republic in central South America; capital, Asunción. Catholicism was introduced in 1542, evangelization began almost immediately. A diocese erected in 1547 was occupied for the first time in 1556. On many occasions thereafter, dioceses in the country were left unoccupied because of political and other reasons. Jesuits who came into the country after 1609 devised the reductions system for evangelizing the Indians, teaching them agriculture, husbandry, trades and other arts, and giving them experience in property use and community life. The reductions were communes of Indians only, and had an average population of 3,000-4,000, under the direction of the missionaries. At their peak, some 30 reductions had a population of 100,000. Political officials regarded the reductions with disfavor because they did not control them and feared that the Indians trained in them might foment revolt and upset the established colonial system under Spanish control. The reductions lasted until about 1768, when the Jesuits were expelled.

Church-state relations following independence from Spain in 1811 were often tense because of government efforts to control the Church through continued exercise of Spanish patronage rights and by other means. The Church as well as the whole country suffered during the War of the Triple Alliance from 1865-70. After that time, the Church had the same kind of experience in Paraguay as in the rest of Latin America, with forces of liberalism, anticlericalism, massive educational needs, poverty, and a shortage of priests and other personnel.

In the 1980s, Church-state tensions increased as Catholic leaders spoke out against President Alfredo Stroessner's decades of one-man rule. A 1988 papal visit seemed to increase the Church's confidence, as bishops repeatedly spoke out against him. The army general who overthrew Stroessner in 1989 said he did so in part to defend the Catholic Church.

Peru*

Archd., 7; dioc., 18; prel., 11; v.a., 8; mil. ord. 1; card., 1; abp., 12; bp., 53; parishes, 1,429; priests, 2,749 (1,443 dioc., 1,306 rel.); p.d., 56; sem., 1,786; bros., 711; srs., 5,662; catechists, 44,566; bap., 340,065; Caths., 23,452,000 (89%); tot. pop., 26,350,000.

Republic on the west coast of South America; capital, Lima. An effective diocese became operational in 1537, five years after the Spanish conquest. Evangelization, already under way, developed for some time after 1570 but deteriorated before the end of the colonial period in the 1820s. The first American saint of the new world was a Peruvian, Rose of Lima, a Dominican tertiary who died in 1617 and was canonized in 1671.

In the new republic founded after the wars of independence the Church experienced problems of adjustment, government efforts to control it through continuation of the patronage rights of the Spanish crown; suppression of houses of religious and expropriation of Church property; religious indifference and outright hostility. In the 20th century, liberation theology was born in Peru under the leadership of Father Gustavo Gutierrez. In the 1980s and early 1990s, the Maoist Sendero Luminoso guerrillas often targeted Church workers, who also found themselves prone to false charges of terrorism. A Peruvian cardinal was credited with much of the success of an early 1990s government effort to win the surrender of the rebels. When the government initiated a drastic economic program in 1990, Peruvian Church leaders worked to help feed and clothe the poor. In the late '90s, the Church successfully fought a government program of sterilization.

Philippines*

Archd., 16; dioc., 53; prel., 6; v.a., 8; mil. ord. 1; card., 3; abp., 17; bp., 99; parishes, 2,792; priests, 7,614 (5,122 dioc., 2,492 rel.); p.d., 8; sem., 6,755; bros., 627; srs., 11,044; catechists, 99,567; bap., 1,624,994; Caths., 63,694,000 (83%); tot. pop., 77,130,000.

Republic, an archipelago of 7,000 islands off the southeast coast of Asia; capital, Manila. Systematic evangelization was begun in 1564 and resulted in firm establishment of the Church by the 19th century. During the period of Spanish rule, which lasted from the discovery of the islands by Magellan in 1521 to 1898, the Church experienced difficulties with the patronage system under which the Spanish crown tried to control ecclesiastical affairs through episcopal and other appointments. This system ended in 1898 when the United States gained possession of the islands and instituted a policy of separation of Church and state. Anticlericalism flared late in the 19th century. The Aglipayan schism, an attempt to set up a nationalist Church, occurred in 1902.

Church leaders and human rights groups constantly criticized abuses under former president and dictator Ferdinand Marcos. Church newspapers were among those censored or closed after he declared martial law, and religious and lay people were arrested and held without formal charges for long periods of time. After Marcos declared himself the victor in the 1986 elections and international observers declared his win a fraud, the Philippine bishops' call for a nonviolent struggle for justice was seen as the catalyst for the nation's "people power" revolution. Corazon Aquino, Marcos's successor, took refuge with Carmelite nuns during the revolution. At the turn of the century, Church workers often found themselves unintentional victims of violence spurred by Muslim separatists' fight for autonomy in the southern Philippines. Church social action focused on the poor, overseas workers, ecology and a fight against the death penalty.

Poland*

Archd., 15; dioc., 26; mil. ord., 1; ordinariate, 1; cards., 6; abps., 17; bps., 98; parishes, 10,036; priests, 27,635 (21,462 dioc., 6,173 rel.); p.d., 8; sem., 6,767; bros., 1,309; srs., 23,954; catechists, 15,515; bap., 367,765; Caths., 37,030,000 (96%); tot. pop., 38,640,000.

Republic in eastern Europe; capital, Warsaw. The first traces of Christianity date from the second half of the ninth century. Its spread was accelerated by the union of the Slavs in the 10th century. The first diocese was set up in 968. Some tensions with the Orthodox were experienced. The Reformation, supported mainly by city dwellers and the upper classes, peaked from about the middle of the 16th century, resulting in numerous conversions to Lutheranism, the Reformed Church and the Bohemian Brethren. A successful Counter-Reformation, with the Jesuits in a position of leadership, was completed by about 1632. The movement served a nationalist as well as religious purpose; in restoring religious unity to a large degree, it united the country against potential invaders, the Swedes, Russians and Turks. The Counter-Reformation had bad side effects, leading to the repression of Protestants long after it was over and to prejudice against Orthodox who returned to allegiance with Rome in 1596 and later. The Church, in the same manner as the entire country, was adversely affected by the partitions of the 18th and 19th centuries. Russification hurt the Eastern- and Latin-rite Catholics.

In the republic established after World War I the Church reorganized itself, continued to serve as a vital force in national life, and enjoyed generally harmonious relations with the state. Progressive growth was strong until 1939, when German and Russian forces invaded and World War II began. In 1945, seven years before the adoption of a Soviet-type of constitution, the communist-controlled government initiated a policy that included a constant program of atheistic propaganda; a strong campaign against the hierarchy and clergy; the imprisonment in 1948 of 700 priests and even more religious; rigid limitation on the activities of the Catholic press and religious movements.

Regular contacts on a working level were initiated by the Vatican and Poland in 1974; regular diplomatic relations were established in 1989. Cardinal Karol Wojtyla of Krakow was elected to the papacy in 1978. Church and papal support was strong for the independent labor movement, Solidarity, which was recognized by the government in August 1980 but outlawed in December 1981, when martial law was imposed (martial law was suspended in 1982). In May 1989, following recognition of Solidarity and a series of political changes, the Catholic Church was given legal status for the first time since the communists took control of the government in 1944. In 1990, a new constitution was adopted, declaring Poland a democratic state. In 1992, the pope restructured the Church in Poland, adding 13 new dioceses. A new concordat between the Polish government and the Holy See was signed in 1993.

Since the end of communist rule, Poland's Church

has struggled with anti-Semitism among some clergy. A dispute over a Carmelite convent outside the former Nazi death camp at Auschwitz resulted in the convent's removal, but several years later the Church was forced to speak against Catholic protesters who posted hundreds of crosses outside the camp. A nearly eight-year national synod process concluded in 1999 with calls for priests to live less luxurious lifestyles and to keep parishes finances open. The Polish Church continued to be a source of missionary priests in more than 90 countries.

Portugal*

Patriarchate (Lisbon), 1; archd., 2; dioc., 17; mil. ord., 1; patriarch, 1; card., 2; abp., 6; bp., 43; parishes, 4,364; priests, 4,188 (3,119 dioc., 1,069 rel.); p.d., 143; sem., 535; bros., 327; srs., 6,329; catechists, 53,314; bap., 100,256; Caths., 9,348,000 (93%); tot. pop., 10,020,000.

Republic in the western part of the Iberian peninsula; capital, Lisbon. Christianity was introduced before the fourth century. From the fifth century to early in the eighth century the Church experienced difficulties from the physical invasion of barbarians and the intellectual invasion of doctrinal errors in the forms of Arianism, Priscillianism and Pelagianism. The Church survived under the rule of Arabs from about 711 and of the Moors until 1249. Ecclesiastical life was fairly vigorous from 1080 to 1185, and monastic influence became strong. A decline set in about 1450. Several decades later Portugal became the jumping-off place for many missionaries to newly discovered colonies. The Reformation had little effect in the country.

In the early 1700s, King John V broke relations with Rome and required royal approval of papal acts. His successor, Joseph I, expelled the Jesuits from Portugal and the colonies. Liberal revolutionaries with anti-Church policies made the 19th century a difficult one for the Church. Similar policies prevailed in Church-state relations in the 20th century until the accession of Premier Antonio de Oliveira Salazar to power in 1928; the hierarchy was seen as closely aligned with him. In 1940 Salazar concluded a concordat with the Holy See that regularized Church-state relations but still left the Church in a subservient condition.

In 1930, after lengthy investigation, the Church authorized devotion to Our Lady of Fátima, who appeared to three Portuguese children in 1917. In 1971 several priests were tried for subversion for speaking out against colonialism and for taking part in guerrilla activities in Angola. A military coup April 25, 1974, ended the dictatorship and led to democratic socialism. Pope John Paul II, who credited Our Lady of Fátima with saving his life during a 1981 assassination attempt on her feast day, visited Portugal several times, including in May 2000 to beatify two of the Fátima visionaries. At that time, he had his Secretary of State, Cardinal Angelo Sodano, announce that the so-called third secret of Fátima would be published and that he believed part of it was a direct reference to the assassination attempt.

Puerto Rico

Archd., 1; dioc., 4; card., 1; abp., 1; bp., 7; parishes, 355; priests, 731 (356 dioc., 375 rel.); p.d., 407; sem., 101; bros., 62; srs., 1,212; catechists, 9,209; bap.,

34,926; Caths., 3,099,000 (78%); tot. pop., 3,950,000. (AD)

A U.S. commonwealth, the smallest of the Greater Antilles, 885 miles southeast of the southern coast of Florida; capital, San Juan. Following its discovery by Columbus in 1493, the island was evangelized by Spanish missionaries and remained under Spanish ecclesiastical as well as political control until 1898, when it became a possession of the United States. The original diocese, San Juan, was erected in 1511. The present hierarchy was established in 1960.

Qatar

Parish; priest, 3 (2 dioc., 1 rel.); p.d., 2; bap., 126; Caths., 65,000 (11.8%); tot. pop., 550,000.

Independent state in the Persian Gulf; capital, Doha. Under ecclesiastical jurisdiction of Arabia apostolic vicariate.

Réunion

Dioc., 1; bp., 1; parishes, 75; priests, 109 (57 dioc., 52 rel.); p.d., 13; sem., 19; bros., 28; srs., 505; catechists, 500; bap., 11,157; Caths., 595,000 (85.5%); tot. pop., 645,000. (AD)

French overseas department, 450 miles east of Madagascar; capital, Saint-Denis. Catholicism was introduced in 1667 and some intermittent missionary work was done through the rest of the century. An apostolic prefecture was organized in 1712. Vincentians began work there in 1817 and were joined later by Holy Ghost Fathers. In 1998 the bishops joined their counterparts in Guadeloupe, French Guiana and Martinique to call slavery "an immense collective sin."

Romania*

Archd., 3; dioc., 8; ord., 1; ex., 1; abp., 7; bp., 11; parishes, 1,415; priests, 1,749 (1,545 dioc., 204 rel.); p.d., 3; sem., 935; bros., 172; srs., 1,259; catechists, 522; bap., 11,991; Caths., 2,005,000 (8.9%); tot. pop., 22,410,000.

Republic in southeastern Europe; capital, Bucharest. Latin Christianity, introduced in the third century, all but disappeared during the barbarian invasions. The Byzantine rite was introduced by the Bulgars about the beginning of the eighth century and established firm roots. It eventually became Orthodox, but a large number of its adherents returned later to union with Rome.

Communists took over the government following World War II, forced the abdication of Michael I in 1947, and enacted a Soviet type of constitution in 1952. By that time a campaign against religion was already in progress. In 1948 the government denounced a concordat concluded in 1929, nationalized all schools and passed a law on religions that resulted in the disorganization of Church administration. The 1.5 million-member Romanian Byzantine-rite Church, by government decree, was incorporated into the Romanian Orthodox Church, and Catholic properties were given to the Orthodox. Five of the six Latin-rite bishops were immediately disposed of by the government, and the last was sentenced to 18 years' imprisonment in 1951. Religious orders were suppressed in 1949.

Some change for the better in Church-state relations was reported after the middle of the summer of 1964, although restrictions were still in effect. The Eastern Church regained liberty in 1990 with the change of government. The hierarchy was restored and diplomatic relations with the Holy See were re-established. Today, most Latin-rite Catholics are ethnic Hungarians residing in Transylvania.

Pope John Paul II visited Romania May 7-9, 1999, but remained in Bucharest; he split time between visits with Catholics and Orthodox and did not visit Transylvania, despite an invitation from the region's bishops. To facilitate the visit, Eastern Catholics gave up their demands for the return of all former Church properties and agreed to work on committees with Orthodox to discuss each case individually. Church leaders said the historic visit led to a deeper openness and understanding between Catholics and Orthodox.

Russia*

Archd., 1; dioc. 5 (1 for European Russia, 4 for Siberia); ap. ex., 1; abp., 2; bp., 4; parish, 300; priests, 290 (115 dioc., 175 rel.); p.d., 9; sem., 94; bros., 17; srs, 307; bap., 1,603; Caths., 804,000 (.05%); tot. pop., 144,440,000.

Federation in Europe and Asia; capital, Moscow. The Orthodox Church has been predominant in Russian history. It developed from the Byzantine Church before 1064. Some of its members subsequently established communion with Rome as the result of reunion movements, but most remained Orthodox. The government has always retained some kind of general or particular control of this Church.

From the beginning of the Communist government in 1917, all churches of whatever kind became the targets of official campaigns designed to negate their influence on society and/or to eliminate them entirely. An accurate assessment of the situation of the Catholic Church in Russia was difficult to make. Research by a Polish priest, reported in 1998, documented the arrests , trials and fabricated confessions of priests in the 1920s and 1930s. A report by a team of research specialists made public by the Judiciary Committee of the U.S. House of Representatives in 1964 said: "The fate of the Catholic Church in the USSR and countries occupied by the Russians from 1917 to 1959 shows the following: (a) the number killed: 55 bishops; 12,800 priests and monks; 2.5 million Catholic believers; (b) imprisoned or deported: 199 bishops; 32,000 priests and 10 million believers; (c) 15,700 priests were forced to abandon their priesthood and accept other jobs; and (d) a large number of seminaries and religious communities were dissolved. Despite repression, Lithuania and Ukraine remained strongholds of Catholicism.

During his 1985-91 presidency, Soviet President Mikhail Gorbachev met twice with Pope John Paul II — meetings later credited with the return of religious freedom in the Soviet Union. In 1991, the pope established two Latin-rite apostolic administrations in the Russian Republic: one in Moscow and one based in Novosibirsk, Siberia.

Catholic communities in Europe and the United States have been instrumental in helping to rebuild the Church in Russia. Under a 1997 religion law, every religious organization in Russia had to register on a national level, then re-register each parish by the end of 1999 to enjoy full legal benefits such as owning property and publishing religious literature. The apostolic administrations registered with no problems, but after the Russian government rejected the Jesuits' registration application, they were forced to take the matter to the country's constitutional court, which ruled that they qualified.

The Vatican's upgrading of Russia's four apostolic administrations to dioceses in early 2002 provoked new tensions with the Orthodox, who accused the Catholic Church of trying to convert its members. Russian authorities refused to readmit five prominent Church leaders, including one bishop, after they left the country. The Vatican eventually appointed a new bishop for the vacant Russian diocese and transferred the expelled bishop.

Rwanda*

Archd., 1; dioc., 8; abp., 2; bp., 9; parishes, 134; priests, 511 (393 dioc., 118 rel.); sem., 369; p.d., 2; bros., 155; srs., 1,269; catechists, 3,560; bap., 108,262; Caths., 3,849,000 (48%); tot. pop., 7,950,000.

Republic in east central Africa; capital, Kigali. Catholicism was introduced about the turn of the 20th century. The hierarchy was established in 1959. Intertribal warfare between the ruling Hutus (90 percent of the population) and the Tutsis (formerly the ruling aristocracy) plagued the country for a number of years. In April 1994, the deaths of the presidents of Rwanda and Burundi in a suspicious plane crash sparked the outbreak of a ferocious civil war. Among the thousands of victims — mostly Tutsis — were three bishops and about 25 percent of the clergy. Many more thousands fled the country.

Although in 1996 Pope John Paul II said that all members of the Church who participated in the genocide must face the consequences, in 1997 the Vatican donated $50,000 to help ensure that certain people — including priests and religious — received fair trials. Two nuns accused of participating in the genocide were sent to prison in Belgium, but a bishop was acquitted after a nine-month trial in Rwanda. The bishop later said Marian apparitions in his diocese in the 1980s foretold the genocide.

Saint Lucia*

Archd., 1; abp., 1; parishes, 22; priests, 29 (16 dioc., 13 rel.); sem., 3; p.d., 8; bros., 6; srs., 42; catechists, 400; bap., 1,639; Caths., 100,000 (63%); tot. pop., 158,000.

Independent (Feb. 22, 1979) island state in West Indies; capital, Castries.

Saint Vincent and the Grenadines*

Dioc., 1; bp., 1; parishes, 6; priests, 6 (3 dioc., 3 rel.); srs., 14; catechists, 62; bap., 149; Caths., 10,000 (9%); tot. pop., 107,000.

Independent state (1979) in West Indies; capital, Kingstown. The Kingstown diocese (St. Vincent) was established in 1989; it was formerly part of Bridgetown-Kingstown Diocese with see in Barbados. The Vatican established diplomatic relations with St. Vincent and the Grenadines in 1990. The Church is recognized for its role in education and health care.

Samoa, American

Dioc., 1; bp., 1; parishes, 13; priests, 13 (8 dioc., 5

rel.); p.d., 17; sem., 11; srs., 12; bap., 265; Caths., 12,000 (21%); tot. pop., 57,000.

Unincorporated U.S. territory in southwestern Pacific, consisting of six small islands; seat of government, Pago Pago on the Island of Tutuila. Samoa-Pago Pago Diocese established in 1982.

Samoa, Western*

Archd., 1; card., 1; parishes, 29; priests, 47 (27 dioc., 20 rel.); p.d., 24; sem., 23; bros., 21; srs., 72; catechists, 129; bap., 1,191; Caths., 31,000 (16%); tot. pop., 181,000.

Independent state in the southwestern Pacific; capital, Apia. Catholic missionary work began in 1845. Most of the missions now in operation were established by 1870 when the Catholic population numbered about 5,000. Additional progress was made in missionary work from 1896. The first Samoan priest was ordained in 1892. A diocese was established in 1966; elevated to a metropolitan see in 1982.

San Marino

Parishes, 12; priests, 29 (10 dioc., 19 rel.); p.d. 1; bro. 11; srs, 20; bap, 258; Caths., 27,000 (99%); tot, pop., 28,000.

Republic, a 24-square-mile enclave in northeastern Italy; capital, San Marino. The date of initial evangelization is not known, but a diocese was established by the end of the third century. Ecclesiastically, it forms part of the Diocese of San Marino-Montefeltro in Italy.

São Tome and Principe*

Dioc., 1; bp., 1; parishes, 12; priests, 10 (rel.); sem. 9; bros., 2; srs., 39; catechists, 455; bap., 3,040; Caths., 118,000 (88%); tot. pop., 133,000.

Independent republic (July 12, 1975), consisting of two islands off the western coast of Africa in the Gulf of Guinea; former Portuguese territory; capital, São Tome. Evangelization was begun by the Portuguese who discovered the islands in 1471-72. The São Tome Diocese was established in 1534. In a 1992 visit to São Tome, a major transport center for slaves until the mid-1800s, Pope John Paul II condemned slavery as "a cruel offense" to African dignity.

Saudi Arabia

Parishes, 5; priests, 5 (1 dioc., 4 rel.); p.d., 1; srs., 16.; bap., 556; Caths., 800,000; total pop., 21,030,000.

Monarchy occupying four-fifths of Arabian peninsula; capital, Riyadh. Population is Muslim; all other religions are banned. Christians in the area are workers from other countries. The Church falls under the ecclesiastical jurisdiction of the Arabian apostolic vicariate. In May 1999, Pope John Paul II met with the crown prince of Saudi Arabia at the Vatican.

Scotland

Archd., 2; dioc., 6; abp., 2; bp., 7; parishes, 471; priests, 779 (624 dioc., 155 rel.); p.d., 25; sem., 36; bros., 234; srs., 616; bap., 8,312; Caths., 693,247 (14%); tot. pop., 4,919,380.

Part of the United Kingdom, in the northern British Isles; capital, Edinburgh. Christianity was introduced by the early years of the fifth century. St. Ninian's arrival in 397 marked the beginning of Christianity in Scotland. The arrival of St. Columba and his monks in 563 inaugurated a new era of evangelization that reached into remote areas by the end of the sixth century. He was extremely influential in determining the character of the Church, which was tribal, monastic, and in union with Rome. Considerable disruption of Church activity resulted from Scandinavian invasions in the late eighth and ninth centuries. By 1153 the Scottish Church took a turn away from its insularity and was drawn into closer contact with the European community. Anglo-Saxon religious and political relations, complicated by rivalries between princes and ecclesiastical superiors, were not always the happiest.

From shortly after the Norman Conquest of England to 1560 the Church suffered adverse effects from the Hundred Years' War, the Black Death, the Western Schism and other developments. In 1560 Parliament abrogated papal supremacy over the Church in Scotland and committed the country to Protestantism in 1567. The Catholic Church was proscribed, to remain that way for more than 200 years, and the hierarchy was disbanded. Defections made the Church a minority religion from that time on. Presbyterian Church government was ratified in 1690. Priests launched the Scottish Mission in 1653, incorporating themselves as a mission body under an apostolic prefecture and working underground to serve the faithful in much the same way their confreres did in England. Catholics got some relief from legal disabilities in 1793 and more relief later. Many left the country about that time. Some of their numbers were filled subsequently by immigrants from Ireland. About 100 heather priests, trained in clandestine places in the heather country, were ordained by the early 19th century. The hierarchy was restored in 1878. Scotland, though predominantly Protestant, has a better record for tolerance than Northern Ireland. In a 1997 message to celebrations marking 1,600 years of Christianity in Scotland, Pope John Paul II urged Catholics to make new efforts at evangelization and ecumenism.

Senegal*

Archd., 1; dioc., 6; card., 1; abp., 2; bp., 7; parishes, 101; priests, 387 (253 dioc., 134 rel.); p.d., 1; sem., 147; bros., 184; srs., 711; catechists, 2,488; bap., 9,399; Caths., 527,000 (5%); tot. pop., 9,660,000.

Republic in West Africa; capital, Dakar. The country had its first contact with Catholicism through the Portuguese some time after 1460. Some incidental missionary work was done by Jesuits and Capuchins in the 16th and 17th centuries. A vicariate for the area was placed in charge of the Holy Ghost Fathers in 1779. More effective evangelization efforts were accomplished after the Senegambia vicariate was erected in 1863; the hierarchy was established in 1955. During a 1992 trip to the predominantly Muslim country, Pope John Paul II praised the small Catholic community for its contributions, especially in the areas of health care and education.

Serbia and Montenegro*

Archd., 2; dioc., 3; a.a., 1; abp., 5; bp., 4; parishes, 284; priests, 275 (231 dioc., 44 rel.); p.d., 7; sem., 60; bros., 9; srs., 352; bap., 4,886; Caths., 541,000 (5%); tot. pop., 10,650,000.

Federation in southeastern Europe formed in 2003

from the former Yugoslav republics of Serbia and Montenegro; capital, Belgrade.

Christianity was introduced from the seventh to ninth centuries in the regions combined to form Yugoslavia after World War I. Since these regions straddled the original line of demarcation for the Western and Eastern Empires (and churches), and since the Reformation had little lasting effect, the Christians are nearly all either Latin- or Eastern-rite Catholics or Orthodox. Yugoslavia was proclaimed a Socialist republic in 1945, and persecution of the church began.. In an agreement signed June 25, 1966, the government recognized the Holy See's spiritual jurisdiction over the Church in the country and guaranteed to bishops the possibility of maintaining contact with Rome in ecclesiastical and religious matters. During early 1990s the split of the Yugoslav republic, Catholic leaders joined Orthodox and, in some cases, Muslim leaders in calling for peace.

Seychelles*

Dioc., 1; bp., 2; parishes, 17; priests, 14 (9 dioc., 5 rel.); p.d., 1; sem., 4; srs., 58; catechists, 365; bap., 1,245; Caths., 69,000 (85%); tot. pop., 81,000.

Independent (1976) group of 92 islands in the Indian Ocean; capital, Victoria. Catholicism was introduced in the 18th century. An apostolic vicariate was organized in 1852. All education in the islands was conducted under Catholic auspices until 1954. In 1991, Bishop Felix Paul of Port Victoria said the country's one-party socialist government was an affront to the rights and dignity of its people, but President France-Albert René continued to lead the government into the 21st century. Pope John Paul II has warned Seychelles to beware of the dark side of tourism, a main industry in the country.

Sierra Leone*

Archd., 1; dioc., 2; abp., 2; bp., 2; parishes, 38; priests, 130 (54 dioc., 76 rel.); sem., 48; bros., 30; srs., 23; catechists, 355; bap., 3,670; Caths., 148,000 (3%); tot. pop., 4,590,000.

Republic on the west coast of Africa; capital, Freetown. Catholicism was introduced in 1858. Members of the African Missions Society, the first Catholic missionaries in the area, were joined by Holy Ghost Fathers in 1864. Protestant missionaries were active in the area before their Catholic counterparts. Educational work had a major part in Catholic endeavor. The hierarchy was established in 1950. Most of the inhabitants are followers of traditional African religions.

Church leaders suffered at the hands of rebel soldiers in the late 1990s, when a military coup ousted the country's democratically elected government. Although some Church workers fled to neighboring Guinea, some remained. Rebels kidnapped several foreign missionaries and, shortly before West African intervention forces ousted them from power in 1998, rebels forced the archbishop of Freetown to strip naked while they plundered his office. As the war lessened and later ended, the Church worked for reconciliation, to rehabilitate child soldiers and to rebuild damaged church property.

Singapore*

Archd., 1; abp., 2; parishes, 30; priests, 133 (69 dioc., 64 rel.); sem., 14; bros., 53; srs., 221; catechists, 1,373; bap., 3,882; Caths., 156,000 (3.7%); tot. pop., 4,130,000.

Independent island republic off the southern tip of the Malay Peninsula; capital, Singapore. Christianity was introduced in the area by Portuguese colonists about 1511. Singapore was founded in 1819; the first parish Church was built in 1846. Freedom of religion is generally respected, although in the late 1980s nearly a dozen people involved in Catholic social work were arrested and detained without trial under the Internal Security Act.

Slovakia*

Archd., 2; dioc., 5; ap. ex., 1; card., 2; abp., 3; bp., 15; parishes, 1,490; priests, 2,474 (1,893 dioc., 581 rel.); p.d., 21; sem., 867; bros., 243; srs., 2,832; catechists, 1,931 bap., 42,323; Caths., 4,034,000 (74%); tot. pop., 5,400,000.

Independent state (Jan. 1, 1993); formerly part of Czechoslovakia; capital, Bratislava. Christianity was introduced in Slovakia in the eighth century by Irish and German missionaries, and the area was under the jurisdiction of German bishops. In 863, Sts. Cyril and Methodius began pastoral and missionary work in the region, ministering to the people in their own language. A diocese established at Nitra in 880 had a continuous history (except for one century ending in 1024). The Church in Slovakia was severely tested by the Reformation and political upheavals. After World War I, when it became part of the Republic of Czechoslovakia, it was 75 percent Catholic.

Vigorous persecution of the Church began in Slovakia in 1944, when communists mounted an offensive against bishops, priests and religious. Msgr. Josef Tiso, a Catholic priest who served as president of the Slovak Republic from 1939-45, was tried for "treason" in December 1946 and was executed the following April.

In 1972, the government ordered the removal of nuns from visible but limited apostolates to farms and mental hospitals. In 1973, the government allowed the ordination of three bishops in the Slovak region.

When Slovakia split from Czechoslovakia in 1993, the country slid into economic difficulties. Church-state tensions increased, and the Slovakian government eventually apologized to Bishop Rudolf Balaz of Banska Bystrica, whose house had been raided in a government investigation of stolen art. In an attempt to fight the effects of decades of communism, in 1996 the bishops said all adult Catholics who had not received confirmation undergo a special two-year catechism course. In 2000, the government and Vatican signed an accord establishing the Church's legal status.

Slovenia*

Archd., 1; dioc., 2; abp., 3; bp., 9; parishes, 805; priests, 1,140 (844 dioc., 296 rel.); p.d., 10; sem., 137; bros., 41; srs., 801; catechists, 441; bap., 14,115; Caths., 1,644,000 (82.6%); tot. pop., 1,990,000.

Independent republic (1991) in southeastern Europe; formerly part of Yugoslavia; capital, Ljubljana. Established diplomatic relations with the Holy See in 1992. After independence, Church leaders found themselves in repeated skirmishes with Slovenia's governing coalition over religious education, restitution of Church property and the Church's proper social role.

Solomon Islands*

Archd., 1; dioc., 2; abp., 1; bp., 4; parishes, 25; priests, 54 (29 dioc., 25 rel.); sem., 38; bros., 14; srs., 80; catechists, 1,090; bap., 2,763; Caths., 88,000 (19%); tot. pop., 423,000.

Independent (July 7, 1978) island group in Oceania; capital, Honiara, on Guadalcanal. After violence interrupted the Marists' evangelization of the Southern Solomons, they resumed their work in 1898. An apostolic vicariate was organized in 1912. A similar jurisdiction was set up for the Western Solomons in 1959. World War II caused a great deal of damage to mission installations.

Somalia

Dioc., 1; parish, 1; priests, 4 (1 dioc., 3 rel.); bros., 1; srs., 3; Caths., 100; tot. pop., 9,160,000. (AD)

Republic on the eastern coast of Africa; capital, Mogadishu. The country has been Muslim for centuries. Pastoral activity has been confined to immigrants. Schools and hospitals were nationalized in 1972, resulting in the departure of some foreign missionaries.

South Africa*

Archd., 4; dioc., 21; v.a., 1; mil. ord., 1; card., 1; abp., 6; bp., 30; parishes, 769; priests, 1,091 (409 dioc., 682 rel.); p.d., 213; sem., 577; bros., 202; srs., 2,629; catechists, 12,516; bap., 53,460; Caths., 3,094,000 (7%); tot. pop., 44,330,000.

Republic in the southern part of Africa; capitals, Cape Town (legislative), Pretoria (administrative) and Bloemfontein (judicial). Christianity was introduced by the Portuguese who discovered the Cape of Good Hope in 1488. Boers, who founded Cape Town in 1652, expelled Catholics from the region. There was no Catholic missionary activity from that time until the 19th century. After a period of British opposition, a bishop established residence in 1837, and evangelization got under way thereafter among the Bantus and white immigrants. The hierarchy was established in 1951.

Under South Africa's apartheid regime, the Church found itself the victim of attacks, from the parish level to the headquarters of the bishops' conference in Pretoria. Some Church leaders were detained, tortured and deported, particularly in the 1970s and 1980s. However, in a 1997 statement to South Africa's Truth Commission, the Catholic Church said the complicity of some Catholics with apartheid was in "acts of omission rather than commission." Since the end of apartheid, Catholic leaders have spoken out against an increase in violence and anti-Muslim sentiment and have worked to combat the growing AIDS problem. Reports of clergy sexual abuse became public in 2003.

Spain*

Archd., 14; dioc., 53; mil. ord., 1; card., 7; abp., 19; bp., 95; parishes, 22,672; priests, 27,180 (18,257 dioc., 8,923 rel.); p.d., 232; sem., 2,732; bros., 5,040; srs., 59,218; catechists, 99,765; bap., 319,111; Caths., 37,883,000 (94%); tot. pop., 40,270,000.

Constitutional monarchy on the Iberian peninsula in southwestern Europe; capital, Madrid. Christians were on the peninsula by 200; some of them suffered martyrdom during persecutions of the third century.

A council held in Elvira about 305 enacted the first legislation on clerical celibacy in the West. Vandals invaded the peninsula in the fifth century, bringing with them an Arian brand of Christianity that they retained until their conversion following the baptism of their king, Reccared, in 589.

In the seventh century, Toledo was established as the primatial see. The Visigoth kingdom lasted to the time of the Arab invasion, 711-14. The Church survived under Muslim rule but experienced some doctrinal and disciplinary irregularities as well as harassment. Reconquest of most of the peninsula was accomplished by 1248; unification was achieved during the reign of Ferdinand and Isabella. The discoveries of Columbus and other explorers ushered in an era of colonial expansion in which Spain became one of the greatest mission-sending countries in history. In 1492, in repetition of anti-Semitic actions of 694, the expulsion of unbaptized Jews was decreed, leading to mass baptisms but a questionable number of real conversions in 1502. Activity by the Inquisition followed. Spain was not seriously affected by the Reformation. Ecclesiastical decline set in about 1650.

Anti-Church actions authorized by a constitution enacted in 1812 resulted in the suppression of religious and other encroachments on the leaders, people and goods of the Church. Political, religious and cultural turmoil recurred during the 19th century and into the 20th. A revolutionary republic was proclaimed in 1931, triggering a series of developments that led to civil war from 1936 to 1939. During the conflict, which pitted leftist Loyalists against the forces of Francisco Franco, more than 6,600 priests and religious and an unknown number of lay people were massacred. One-man, one-party rule, established after the civil war and with rigid control policies with respect to personal liberties and social and economic issues, continued for more than 35 years before giving way after the death of Franco to democratic reforms. Since the 1970s, the Catholic Church has not been the established religion; the constitution guarantees freedom for other religions as well. In the late 20th century, Spanish Church leaders fought a growing feeling of indifference among many Catholics.

Sri Lanka*

Archd., 1; dioc., 10; abp., 2; bp., 13; parishes, 380; priests, 948 (615 dioc., 333 rel.); sem., 486; bros., 236; srs., 2,333; catechists, 8,682; bap., 26,306; Caths., 1,354,000 (7%); tot. pop., 19,100,000.

Independent socialist republic, island southeast of India; capital, Colombo. The Portuguese began evangelizing in the 16th century. In 1638, the Dutch began forcing Portuguese from the coastal areas. The Dutch outlawed Catholicism, banished priests and confiscated buildings, forcing people to become Calvinists. Blessed Joseph Vaz, an Oratorian priest, is credited with almost single-handedly reviving the Catholic Church toward the end of the 17th century. Anti-Catholic laws were repealed by the British in 1806. The hierarchy was established in 1886; the country gained independence in 1948. Sri Lankan bishops repeatedly called for reconciliation in the nearly two-decade war between the Liberation Tigers of Tamil Eelam and the Sinhalese-dominated government; a cease-fire was signed in early 2002. In an unusual move in January 1998, Archbishop Nicholas

M. Fernando of Colombo, authorized by the Vatican Congregation for the Doctrine of the Faith, lifted the excommunication of a prominent Sri Lankan theologian, Oblate Father Tissa Balasuriya.

Sudan*

Archd., 2; dioc., 7; ap. ex., 1; abp., 3; bp., 11; parishes, 165; priests, 348 (234 dioc., 114 rel.); p.d., 4; sem., 269; bros., 80; srs., 327; catechists, 3,695; bap., 47,194; Caths., 3,836,000 (12%); tot. pop., 31,810,000.

Republic in northeastern Africa, the largest country on the continent; capital Khartoum. Christianity was introduced from Egypt and gained acceptance in the sixth century. Under Arab rule, it was eliminated in the northern region. No Christians were in the country in 1600.

Evangelization attempts begun in the 19th century in the south yielded hard-won results. By 1931 there were nearly 40,000 Catholics there, and considerable progress was made by missionaries after that time. In 1957, a year after the republic was established, Catholic schools were nationalized. An act restrictive of religious freedom went into effect in 1962, resulting in the harassment and expulsion of foreign missionaries. By 1964 all but a few Sudanese missionaries had been forced out of the southern region. The northern area, where Islam predominates, is impervious to Christian influence.

Late in 1971 some missionaries were allowed to return to work in the South. The hierarchy was established in 1974. The most recent fighting, which began in 1983, originally pitted the mostly Arab and Muslim North against the mostly black African Christian and animist South, but it has since evolved into a nationwide conflict fuelled by religion, ethnicity, oil and ideology. The imposition of Islamic penal codes in 1984 was a cause of concern to all Christian Churches. Recent government policies have denied Christians the right to places of worship and authorization to gather for prayer. Bishops from the South have condemned human rights violations — aggravated by famine and war — in their area. They have said they want peace but cannot accept an Islamic state.

Surinam*

Dioc., 1; bp., 1; parishes, 31; priests, 24 (7 dioc., 17 rel.); sem., 1; bros., 7; srs., 16; bap., 1,760; Caths., 104,000 (23%); tot. pop., 450,000.

Independent (Nov. 25, 1975) state in northern South America; capital, Paramaribo, Catholicism was introduced in 1683. Evangelization began in 1817.

Swaziland*

Dioc., 1; bp., 1; parishes, 15; priests, 40 (12 dioc., 28 rel.); sem., 6; bros., 6; srs., 55; bap., 762; Caths., 54,000 (5.4%); tot. pop., 990,000.

Monarchy in southern Africa; almost totally surrounded by South Africa; capital, Mbabane. Missionary work was entrusted to the Servites in 1913. An apostolic prefecture was organized in 1923. The hierarchy was established in 1951. Swaziland established diplomatic relations with the Holy See in 1992. In the 1990s, Swazi Catholics worked to help transform the country to a democracy but to retain the traditions of the people.

Sweden*

Dioc., 1; bp., 3; parishes, 40; priests, 147 (71 dioc., 76 rel.); p.d., 14; sem., 15; bros., 11; srs., 227; catechists, 384; bap., 1,091; Caths., 145,000 (1.6%); tot. pop., 8,830,000.

Constitutional monarchy in northwestern Europe; capital, Stockholm. Christianity was introduced by St. Ansgar, a Frankish monk, in 829-830. The Church became well-established in the 12th century and was a major influence at the end of the Middle Ages. Political and other factors favored the introduction and spread of the Lutheran Church, which became the state religion in 1560. The Augsburg Confession of 1530 was accepted by the government; all relations with Rome were severed; monasteries were suppressed; the very presence of Catholics in the country was forbidden in 1617. A decree of tolerance for foreign Catholics was issued about 1781. Two years later an apostolic vicariate was organized for the country. In 1873 Swedes were given the legal right to leave the Lutheran Church and join another Christian Church. Membership in the Lutheran Church is presumed by law unless notice is given of membership in another church.

Since 1952 Catholics have enjoyed almost complete religious freedom. The hierarchy was re-established in 1953. Hindrances to growth of the Church are the strongly entrenched established church, limited resources, a clergy shortage and the size of the country. In the 1960s, an influx of guest workers increased the number of Catholics, and in the 1970s and 1980s, refugees helped increase Church numbers. In 1998, the pope named the first Swedish bishop in more than 400 years. Reforms due to be implemented by the year 2004 will give the Church and other minority faiths the right to operate as legal entities, including owning property.

Switzerland*

Dioc., 6; abb., 2; card., 2; abp., 4; bp., 19; parishes, 1,662; priests, 3,091 (1,817 dioc., 1,274 rel.); p.d., 151; sem., 220; bros., 437; srs., 5,877; catechists, 1,877; bap., 31,122; Caths., 3,144,000 (44%); tot. pop., 7,230,000.

Confederation in central Europe; capital, Bern. Christianity was introduced in the fourth century or earlier and was established on a firm footing before the barbarian invasions of the sixth century. Constance, established as a diocese in the seventh century, was a stronghold of the faith against the pagan Alamanni, in particular, who were not converted until some time in the ninth century. During this period of struggle with the barbarians, a number of monasteries of great influence were established.

The Reformation in Switzerland was triggered by Zwingli in 1519 and furthered by him at Zurich until his death in battle against the Catholic cantons in 1531. Calvin set in motion the forces that made Geneva the international capital of the Reformation and transformed it into a theocracy. Catholics mobilized a Counter-Reformation in 1570, six years after Calvin's death. Struggle between Protestant and Catholic cantons was a fact of Swiss life for several hundred years. The Helvetic Constitution enacted at the turn of the 19th century embodied anti-Catholic measures and consequences, among them the dissolution of 130 monasteries. The Church was reorganized later in the century to meet the threats of liberalism, radicalism and the *Kulturkampf*. In the process, the Church, even though on the defensive, gained the strength and cohesion that characterizes it to the present time. In 1973, constitutional articles banning Jesuits from the country and prohibiting the establishment of convents and monasteries were repealed. In the 1990s, Swiss bishops battled internal divisions and sought forgiveness for any anti-Semitism on behalf of the Church.

Syria*

Patriarchates, 1 (Greek Melkites; patriarchs of Antioch of Maronites and Syrians reside in Lebanon); archd., 12 (1 Armenian, 2 Maronite, 5 Greek Melkite, 4 Syrian); dioc., 3 (Armenian, Chaldean, Maronite); v.a., 1 (Latin); ap.ex., 1; patriarch, 1; card., 1; abp., 18; bp., 5; parishes, 203; priests, 247 (176 dioc., 71 rel.); p.d., 12; sem., 81; bros., 12; srs., 381; catechists, 2,358; bap., 2,507; Caths., 350,000 (2%); tot. pop., 16,720,000.

Arab socialist republic in southwest Asia; capital, Damascus. Christian communities were formed in apostolic times. It is believed that St. Peter established a see at Antioch before going to Rome. Damascus became a center of influence. The area was the place of great men and great events in the early history of the Church. Monasticism developed there in the fourth century; so did the Monophysite and Monothelite heresies to which a portion of the Church succumbed. Byzantine Syrians who remained in communion with Rome were given the name Melkites. Christians of various persuasions — Jacobites, Orthodox and Melkites — were subject to various degrees of harassment from the Arabs who took over in 638 and from the Ottoman Turks who isolated the country and remained in control from 1516 to the end of World War II.

Syrian Catholics are members of the Armenian, Chaldean, Greek-Melkite, Latin, Maronite and Syrian rites. During a visit to Syria in May 2001, Pope John Paul II became the first pontiff in history to enter a mosque.

Taiwan

Archd., 1; dioc., 7; card., 1; abp., 3; bp., 11; parishes, 456; priests, 729 (266 dioc., 463 rel.); p.d., 2; sem., 113; bros., 105; srs., 1,040; catechists, 723; bap., 3,302; Caths., 309,000 (1.3%); tot. pop., 22,076,000.

Democratic island state, 100 miles off the southern coast of mainland China; capital, Taipei. Attempts to introduce Christianity in the 17th century were unsuccessful. Evangelization in the 19th century resulted in some 1,300 converts in 1895. Missionary endeavor was hampered by the Japanese, who occupied the island following the Sino-Japanese war of 1894-95. Great progress was made in missionary endeavor among the Chinese who emigrated to the island (seat of the Nationalist Government of the Republic of China) following the Communist takeover of the mainland in 1949. The hierarchy was established in 1952. Many Taiwanese Catholics have worked to form a bridge to Catholics in mainland China. China has said the Vatican's diplomatic relations with Taiwan form the biggest stumbling block to Sino-Vatican relations.

Tajikistan*

Mission, 3; parishes, 2; priests, 4 (1 dioc., 3 rel.); srs., 4; bap., 65; Cath., 2000; tot. pop. 6,290,000.

Independent republic (1992) in Asia; formerly part of the USSR; capital, Dushanbe. The majority of the population is Sunni Muslim. When the Vatican established diplomatic relations in 1996, Church officials estimated most of the country's Catholics had fled. In 1997, the Vatican decided to establish a mission in the country.

Tanzania*

Archd., 5; dioc., 25; card., 1; abp., 5; bp., 33; parishes, 813; priests, 2,080 (1,382 dioc., 698 rel.); p.d. 1; sem., 1,164; bros., 653; srs., 7,105; catechists, 12,292; bap., 272,767; Caths., 10,326,000 (29%); tot. pop., 35,970,000.

Republic on and off the eastern coast of Africa; capital, Dar es Salaam. The first Catholic mission in the former Tanganyikan portion of the republic was manned by Holy Ghost Fathers in 1868. The hierarchy was established there in 1953. Zanzibar was the landing place of Augustinians with the Portuguese in 1499. Some evangelization was attempted between then and 1698 when the Arabs expelled all priests from the territory. There was no Catholic missionary activity from then until the 1860s. The Holy Ghost Fathers arrived in 1863 and were entrusted with the mission in 1872. Zanzibar was important as a point of departure for missionaries to Tanganyika, Kenya and other places in East Africa. A vicariate for Zanzibar was set up in 1906.

In the late 20th century the Church in Tanzania saw an increase in vocations and an active Church life. The bishops assisted hundreds of thousands of refugees from Rwanda, Burundi and Mozambique.

Thailand*

Archd., 2; dioc., 8; card., 1; abp., 2; bp., 10; parishes, 354; priests, 652 (405 dioc., 247 rel.); sem., 257; bros., 124; srs., 1,422; catechists, 1,847; bap., 5,914; Caths., 279,000 (.04%); tot. pop., 62,910,000.

Constitutional monarchy in southeast Asia; capital, Bangkok. The first Christians in the region were Portuguese traders who arrived early in the 16th century. A number of missionaries began arriving in the mid-1500s, but pastoral care was confined mostly to the Portuguese until the 1660s, when evangelization began. A seminary was organized in 1665, a vicariate was set up four years later, and a point of departure was established for China. Persecution and death for some of the missionaries ended evangelization efforts in 1688. It was resumed, however, and made progress from 1824 onward. In 1881 missionaries were sent from Siam to neighboring Laos. The hierarchy was established in 1965. Archbishop Michael Michai Kitbunchu was named the first Thai cardinal in 1983. The Church is recognized for its social justice efforts, including work with refugees.

Togo*

Archd., 1; dioc., 6; abp., 1; bp., 6; parishes, 139; priests, 384 (259 dioc., 125 rel.); sem., 281; bros., 187; srs., 692; catechists, 4,329; bap., 38,595; Caths., 1,301,000 (28%); tot. pop., 4,660,000.

Republic on the west coast of Africa; capital, Lome. The first Catholic missionaries in the area, where slave raiders operated for nearly 200 years, were members of the African Missions Society who arrived in 1563.

They were followed by Divine Word Missionaries in 1914, when an apostolic prefecture was organized. At that time the Catholic population numbered about 19,000. The African Missionaries returned after their German predecessors were deported following World War I. The first indigenous priest was ordained in 1922. The hierarchy was established in 1955. In the early 1990s, Archbishop Philippe Fanoko Kossi Kpodzro of Lome served as president of the transitional legislative assembly.

Tonga*

Dioc., 1; bp., 1; parishes, 10; priests, 22 (12 dioc., 10 rel.); sem., 38; bros., 6; srs., 49; bap., 455; Caths., 16,000 (14.5%); tot. pop., 96,000.

Polynesian monarchy in the southwestern Pacific, consisting of about 150 islands; capital, Nuku'alofa. Marists started missionary work in 1842, some years after Protestants had begun evangelization. By 1880 the Catholic population numbered about 1,700. A vicariate was organized in 1937. The hierarchy was established in 1966. Tonga established diplomatic relations with the Holy See in 1994.

Trinidad and Tobago*

Archd., 1; abp., 1; bp., 2; parishes, 61; priests, 112 (42 dioc., 70 rel.); sem., 25; bros., 9; srs., 149; catechists, 311; bap., 4,414; Caths., 383,000 (30%); tot. pop., 1,278,000.

Independent nation, consisting of two islands in the Caribbean; capital, Port-of-Spain. The first Catholic Church in Trinidad was built in 1591, years after several missionary ventures had been launched and a number of missionaries killed. Capuchins were there from 1618 until about 1802. Missionary work continued after the British gained control early in the 19th century. Cordial relations have existed between the Church and state, both of which have manifested their desire for the development of indigenous clergy. In 1999, Church leaders protested reinstatement of the death penalty.

Tunisia*

Dioc., 1; abp., 1; parishes, 12; priests, 30 (11 dioc., 19 rel.); bros., 7; sem., 2; srs., 153; bap., 18; Caths., 22,000 (.02%); tot. pop., 9,670,000.

Republic on the northern coast of Africa; capital, Tunis. Ancient Carthage, now a site outside the capital city of Tunis, hosted early Church councils and was home to Church fathers like St. Augustine. Carthage was devastated by Vandals in the fifth century and invaded by Muslims in the seventh century, after which it had few Christians until the 19th century. An apostolic vicariate was organized in 1843, and the Carthage Archdiocese was established in 1884. The Catholic population in 1892 consisted of most of the approximately 50,000 Europeans in the country. When Tunis became a republic in 1956, most of the Europeans left the country. A 1964 agreement with the Vatican and Holy See suppressed the Archdiocese of Carthage and replaced it with the Territorial Prelature of Tunis. In 1995 the prelature was made a diocese.

Today Tunisia's Catholics are predominantly foreign nationals. The Church's social presence is seen in schools, hospitals and institutions for the disabled.

Turkey*

Archd., 3; v.a., 2; ord., 1; ap. ex., 1; abp., 4; bp., 2; parishes, 51; priests, 63 (15 dioc., 48 rel.); p.d., 3; sem., 13; bros., 13; srs., 115; bap., 95; Caths., 32,000 (.05%); tot. pop., 68,610,000.

Republic in Asia Minor and southeastern Europe; capital, Ankara. Christian communities were established in apostolic times, as attested in the Acts of the Apostles, some of the Letters of St. Paul and Revelation. The territory was the scene of heresies and ecumenical councils, the place of residence of Fathers of the Church, the area in which ecclesiastical organization reached the dimensions of more than 450 sees in the middle of the seventh century. The region remained generally Byzantine except for the period of the Latin occupation of Constantinople from 1204 to 1261, but was conquered by the Ottoman Turks in 1453 and remained under their domination until establishment of the republic in 1923. Christians, always a minority, numbered more Orthodox than Catholics; they all were under some restrictions during the Ottoman period. They suffered persecution in the 19th and 20th centuries, the Armenians being the most numerous victims. Turkey is overwhelmingly Muslim. Catholics are tolerated to a degree.

Turkmenistan*

Mission, 1; parish, 1; priests, 3 (rel.); bap., 10; Caths., 1,000; tot. pop., 4,840,000.

Former constituent republic of USSR; independent, 1991; capital, Ashgabat. Almost all the population is Sunni Muslim. The Vatican established diplomatic relations with the country in 1996 and set up a mission in 1997.

Tuvalu

Mission, 1; parish, 1; priest, 1 (rel.); bap., 2; Caths., 100; tot. pop., 10,000.

Independent state (1978) in Oceania, consisting of 9 islands; capital, Funafuti.

Uganda*

Archd., 4; dioc., 15; mil. ord., 1; card., 1; abp., 3; bp., 23; parishes, 430; priests, 1,569 (1,264 dioc., 305 rel.); p.d., 1; sem., 805; bros., 467; srs., 2,756; catechists, 11,885; bap., 316,130; Caths., 10,403,000 (46%); tot. pop., 22,790,000.

Republic in East Africa; capital, Kampala. The Missionaries of Africa (White Fathers) were the first Catholic missionaries, starting in 1879. Persecution broke out from 1885 to 1887, taking a toll of 22 Catholic martyrs, who were canonized in 1964, and a number of Anglican victims. (Pope Paul VI honored all those who died for the faith during a visit to Kampala in 1969.) By 1888, there were more than 8,000 Catholics. Evangelization was resumed in 1894, after being interrupted by war, and proceeded thereafter. The first African bishop was ordained in 1939. The hierarchy was established in 1953.

The Church was suppressed during the erratic regime of President Idi Amin, who was deposed in the spring of 1979. Guerrilla activity in northern and southwestern Uganda has hampered Church workers, and Church leaders have called for peace. The Church has devoted much of its resources to caring for the many victims of HIV/AIDS in the country.

Ukraine*

Major archbishopric, 1 (Ukrainian); archd., 3 (Metropolitans); dioc., 14; pat. ex., 2; card., 2; abp., 1; bp., 20; parishes, 3,746; priests, 2,629 (2,222 dioc., 407 rel.); p.d., 12; sem., 1,227; bros., 98; srs., 987; catechists, 1,076; bap., 28,182; Caths., 4,804,000 (10%); tot. pop., 49,110,000.

Independent republic bordering on the Black Sea; former USSR republic; capital, Kiev. The baptism of Vladimir and his people in 988 marked the beginning of Christianity in the territory of Kievan Rus, which is included in today's Ukraine. The 1596 Union of Brest brought the Ukrainian Byzantine-rite community back into communion with Rome. The Eastern Catholic Church was officially suppressed and underground in the USSR from the late 1940s; all of its bishops were killed or imprisoned and its property seized by the government and given to the Orthodox. Some Catholic priests continued to minister clandestinely under communist rule.

As the Eastern Church regained its legal status under Soviet President Mikhail Gorbachev, serious tensions arose with the Orthodox over ownership of property and the allegiance of priests and lay people. Latin-rite dioceses were re-established in 1991. In the late 1990s, rising inflation and weakening currency, aggravated by the government's and some companies' failure to pay wages, led Ukrainian Church leaders to fight homelessness and hunger. Despite opposition from Ukraine's largest Orthodox Church, Pope John Paul II visited Ukraine in June 2001. He challenged Ukrainians to talk to each other and focus on unity, despite religious, ethnic and political tensions.

United Arab Emirates

V.a, 1; bp., 1; parishes, 6; priests, 21 (3 dioc., 18 rel.); srs., 34; bap., 1,443; Caths., 336,000 (.8%); tot. pop., 2,650,000.

Independent state along Persian Gulf; capital, Abu Dhabi. The apostolic vicariate of Arabia has its seat in Abu Dhabi. It includes the states of Bahrain, Oman, Qatar, Saudi Arabia and Yemen (see separate entries) as well as United Arab Emirates.

United States* (See Catholic Church in the United States; see also Catholic History in the United States and Statistics of the Church in the United States)

Uruguay*

Archd., 1; dioc., 9; abp., 3; bp., 11; parishes, 228; priests, 489 (208 dioc., 281 rel.); p.d., 65; sem., 98; bros., 94; srs., 1,208; catechists, 2,643; bap., 30,682; Caths., 2,530,000 (75%); tot. pop., 3,360,000.

Republic on the southeast coast of South America; capital, Montevideo. The Spanish established a settlement in 1624 and evangelization followed. Missionaries followed the reduction pattern to reach the Indians, form them in the faith and train them in agriculture, husbandry, other arts, and the experience of managing property and living in community. Montevideo was made a diocese in 1878. The constitution of 1830 made Catholicism the religion of the state and subsidized some of its activities, principally the missions to the Indians. Separation of Church and state was provided for in the constitution of 1917. In 1997, despite a court decision halting further investi-

gations, the Church pledged to make one last effort to help search for people who remained missing from the 1973-85 military dictatorship.

Uzbekistan*

Mission, 1; parishes, 5; priests, 10 (2 dioc., 8 rel.); bros., 2; srs., 9; bap., 22 Caths. 3,000; tot. pop. 25,070,000.

Former republic of USSR; independent, 1991; capital, Tashkent. The majority of the population is Sunni Muslim. A small number of Catholics live in Tashkent. The Vatican established a mission in 1997.

Vanuatu*

Dioc., 1; bp., 1; parishes, 21; priests, 28 (15 dioc., 13 rel.); p.d., 1; sem., 15; bros., 22; srs., 60; catechists, 161; bap., 550; Caths., 29,000 (16%); tot. pop., 190,000.

Independent (July 29, 1980) island group in the southwest Pacific; capital, Vila. Effective, though slow, evangelization by Catholic missionaries began about 1887. An apostolic vicariate was set up in 1904. The hierarchy was established in 1966.

Vatican City State (See separate entry)

Venezuela*

Archd., 9; dioc., 22; ord.; v.a., 4; ap. ex., 2; mil. ord. 1; card., 2; abp., 11; bp., 42; parishes, 1,217; priests, 2,302 (1,364 dioc., 938 rel.); p.d., 106; sem., 1,121; bros., 291; srs., 3,946; catechists, 32,387; bap., 382,035; Caths., 21,821,000 (89%); tot. pop., 24,630,000.

Republic in northern South America; capital, Caracas. Evangelization began in 1513-14 and involved members of a number of religious orders who worked in assigned territories, developing missions into pueblos or villages of Indian converts. Nearly 350 towns originated as missions. The first diocese was established in 1531.

Fifty-four missionaries met death by violence from the start of missionary work until 1817. Missionary work was seriously hindered during the wars of independence in the second decade of the 19th century and continued in decline through the rest of the century as dictator followed dictator in a period of political turbulence. Restoration of the missions got under way in 1922. In the 1990s, the Church worked at reconciliation in the country but condemned government corruption and violent crime. Church leaders also called for respect for human rights.

Vietnam

Archd., 3; dioc., 22; card., 2; abp., 2; bp., 34; parishes, 2,559; priests, 2,501 (2,027 dioc., 474 rel.); p.d., 10; sem., 1,844; bros., 1,487; srs., 9,548; catechists, 49,862; bap., 152,830; Caths., 5,412,000 (6.8%); tot. pop., 79,180,000.

Country in southeast Asia, reunited officially July 2, 1976, as the Socialist Republic of Vietnam; capital, Hanoi.

Catholicism was introduced in 1533, but missionary work was intermittent until 1615, when Jesuits arrived to stay. Two vicariates were organized in 1659. A seminary was set up in 1666, and two Vietnamese priests were ordained two years later. A congregation of native women religious formed in 1670 is still active. Severe persecution broke out in 1698, three times in the 18th century, and again in the 19th. Up to 300,000 people suffered in some way from persecution during the 50 years before 1883, when the French moved in to secure religious liberty for the Catholics. Most of the 117 beatified Martyrs of Vietnam were killed during this 50-year period. After the French were forced out of Vietnam in 1954, the country was partitioned at the 17th parallel. The North became Communist and the Viet Cong, joined by North Vietnamese regular army troops in 1964, fought to gain control of the South. In 1954 there were approximately 1.1 million Catholics in the North and 480,000 in the South. More than 650,000 fled to the South to avoid the government repression. In South Vietnam, the Church continued to develop during the war years.

After the end of the war in 1975, the government exercised control over virtually all aspects of Church life. In the late 1980s, bishops noted some softening of the government's hard line. In the 1990s, the Vatican and Vietnam held intermittent talks on Church-state issues, with sporadic progress reported, but in 1997, the government censored the section of the "Catechism of the Catholic Church" that dealt with human rights. Although at times the Vatican was forced to wait years for government approval of bishops' appointments, in July 2001, just one month after Vatican officials visited Vietnam, Pope John Paul II named three new bishops.

Virgin Islands (U.S.)

Dioc., 1 (St. Thomas, suffragan of Washington, D.C.); bp., 2; parishes, 8; priests, 16 (9 dioc., 7 rel.); p.d., 18; sem., 11; bros., 11; srs., 17; bap., 336; Caths., 30,000 (29%); tot. pop., 102,000.

Organized unincorporated U.S. territory in Atlantic Ocean; capital, Charlotte Amalie on St. Thomas (one of the three principal islands). The islands were discovered by Columbus in 1493 and named for St. Ursula and her virgin companions. Missionaries began evangelization in the 16th century. A church on St. Croix dates from about 1660; another, on St. Thomas, from 1774. The Baltimore Archdiocese had jurisdiction over the islands from 1804 to 1820, when it was passed on to the first of several places in the Caribbean area. Some trouble arose over a pastoral appointment in the 19th century, resulting in a small schism. The Redemptorists took over pastoral care in 1858; normal conditions have prevailed since.

Wales

Archd., 1; dioc., 2; abp., 2; bp., 3; parishes, 183; priests, 251 (142 dioc., 109 rel.); p.d., 11; sem., 7; bros., 120; srs., 428; bap, 1,966; Caths., 139,215 (.5%); tot. pop., 3,090,250.

Part of the United Kingdom, on the western part of the island of Great Britain. Celtic missionaries completed evangelization by the end of the sixth century, the climax of what has been called the age of saints. Welsh Christianity received its distinctive Celtic character at this time. Some conflict developed when attempts were made — and proved successful later — to place the Welsh Church under the jurisdiction of Canterbury; the Welsh opted for direct contact with Rome.

The Church made progress despite the depredations of Norsemen in the eighth and ninth centuries.

Norman infiltration occurred near the middle of the 12th century, resulting in a century-long effort to establish territorial dioceses and parishes to replace the Celtic organizational plan of monastic centers and satellite churches. The Western Schism produced split views and allegiances. Actions of Henry VIII in breaking away from Rome had serious repercussions. Proscription and penal laws crippled the Church, resulted in heavy defections and touched off a 150-year period of repression. Methodism prevailed by 1750. Modern Catholicism came to Wales with Irish immigrants in the 19th century, when the number of Welsh Catholics was negligible. Catholic emancipation was granted in 1829. The hierarchy was restored in 1850. Wales shares a bishops' conference with England.

Yemen*

Parishes, 4; priests, 5 (rel.); srs., 28; bap., 6; Caths., 4,000; tot. pop., 19,110,000.

Republic on southern coast of Arabian peninsula; capital, San'a. Formerly North Yemen (Arab Republic of Yemen) and South Yemen (People's Republic of Yemen); formally reunited in 1990. Christians perished in the first quarter of the sixth century. Muslims have been in control since the seventh century. The state religion is Islam; the Church is under the ecclesiastical jurisdiction of Arabia apostolic vicariate. In the early 1990s, Salesians reported some harassment of Church workers in the South. In early 1998, three Missionaries of Charity nuns were murdered. The Vatican established diplomatic relations with Yemen in October 1998.

Yugoslavia* (See Serbia and Montenegro)

Zambia*

Archd., 2; dioc., 8; abp., 4; bp., 7; parishes, 245; priests, 616 (271 dioc., 345 rel.); p.d., 2; sem., 391; bros., 153; srs., 1,505; catechists, 20,011; bap., 92,025; Caths., 3,042,000 (28%); tot. pop., 10,650,000.

Republic in central Africa; capital, Lusaka. Portuguese priests did some evangelizing in the 16th and 17th centuries but no results of their work remained in the 19th century. Jesuits began work in the South in the 1880s and White Fathers in the North and East in 1895. Evangelization of the western region began for the first time in 1931. The number of Catholics doubled in the 20 years following World War II.

Zambian Catholics have welcomed tens of thousands of refugees from the region. During a 1989 visit, Pope John Paul II praised Zambians for their generosity and offered encouragement as they faced poverty. In the 1990s, Zambian Church leaders worked caring for victims of HIV/AIDS and spoke out against foreign debt.

Zimbabwe*

Archd., 2; dioc., 6; abp., 4; bp., 7; parishes, 197; priests, 441 (177 dioc., 264 rel.); p.d., 12; sem., 350; bros., 100; srs., 1,003; catechists, 4,164; bap., 34,301; Caths., 1,113,000 (8.5%); tot. pop., 12,960,000.

Independent republic (1980) in south central Africa; capital, Harare. Earlier unsuccessful missionary ventures preceded the introduction of Catholicism in 1879. Missionaries began to make progress after 1893. The hierarchy was established in 1955; the first black bishop was ordained in 1973.

CATHOLIC WORLD STATISTICS

(*Principal sources:* Statistical Yearbook of the Church, 2001 (*the latest edition*); *figures are as of Jan. 1, 2002, unless indicated otherwise.*)

	Africa	North America[1]	South America	Asia	Europe	Oceania	WORLD TOTALS
Patriarchates[2]	2	-	-	8	2	-	12
Archdioceses	85	86	98	117	174	18	578
Dioceses	380	357	406	321	505	54	2,023
Prelatures	-	7	31	6	6	-	50
Abbacies	-	-	2	-	11	-	13
Exarchates/Ords.	-	1	6	1	16	-	24
Military Ords.	3	4	9	3	13	2	34
Vicariates Apostolic	17	5	37	19	1	-	79
Prefectures	6	-	2	7	-	1	16
Apostolic Admin.	1	-	1	3	4	-	9
Independent Missions	1	2	-	5	1	2	11
Cardinals[3]	16	22	25	15	84	4	166
Patriarchs[2]	-	-	-	7	1	-	8
Archbishops	116	128	143	157	331	24	899[4]
Bishops	485	691	740	488	1,062	98	3,564[4]
Priests	27,988	78,989	42,258	44,446	206,761	4,725	405,067
Diocesan	17,582	51,057	24,709	26,309	144,215	2,576	266,448
Religious	10,406	27,932	17,549	18,137	62,546	2,149	138,619
Perm.Deacons	372	15,979	3,121	115	9,425	192	29,204
Brothers	7,256	10,208	6,526	7,972	21,258	1,757	54,970
Sisters	52,695	141,254	88,795	140,826	357,840	10,907	792,317
Maj. Seminarians	20,383	15,421	20,971	26,006	26,879	923	110,583
Sec. Inst. Mbrs. (Men)	24	24	127	36	413	1	625
Sec. Inst. Mbrs. (Women)	384	1,663	3,972	1,370	21,767	65	29,221
Lay Missionaries	1,488	5,811	128,127	1,684	1,927	41	139,078
Catechists	368,075	720,320	943,782	278,766	490,286	12,023	2,813,252
Parishes	11,355	33,720	21,376	20,811	127,120	2,354	216,736[5]
Kindergartens	10,738	9,160	6,816	12,196	23,171	821	62,902
Students	939,320	541,412	1,109,980	1,401,232	1,722,962	51,591	5,766,497
Elem./PrimarySchools	30,009	14,910	10,871	14,845	17,318	2,685	90,638
Students	11,901,780	3,894,944	4,015,083	4,839,090	3,004,295	611,551	28,266,743
Secondary Schools	7,488	3,957	6,073	8,345	9,897	665	36,425
Students	2,488,721	1,529,933	2,329,693	4,665,214	3,408,473	378,919	14,800,953
Students in Higher Insts.[6]	24,849	349,042	164,444	804,764	238,920	8,539	1,590,558
Social Service Facilities	14,144	16,319	22,719	20,378	31,403	1,628	106,591
Hospitals	849	1,055	876	1,059	1,288	178	5,304
Dispensaries	4,736	2,774	2,750	3,417	2,366	181	16,224
Leprosariums	354	19	47	315	4	1	740
Homes for Aged/Handic.	625	1,887	1,908	1,632	8,125	360	14,537
Orphanages	776	1,072	1,430	3,025	2,499	60	8,862
Nurseries	1,930	1,194	2,978	2,959	1,821	87	10,969
Matrimonial Advice Ctrs.	1,499	2,015	2,324	987	4,391	252	11,468
Social Educ.Ctrs.	2,049	4,751	7,334	5,860	9,302	329	29,625
Other Institutions	1,327	1,552	3,072	1,124	1,607	180	8,862
Baptisms	3,472,601	4,037,470	4,583,360	2,664,331	2,471,665	121,216	17,355,643
Under Age 7	2,218,491	3,742,213	4,048,151	2,236,511	2,390,439	110,338	14,746,143
Over Age 7	1,254,110	295,257	540,209	427,820	81,226	10,878	2,609,500
Marriages	325,079	759,738	668,030	618,813	967,050	23,970	3,362,680
Between Catholics	286,649	671,019	651,951	558,873	898,323	14,552	3,081,367
Mixed Marriages	38,430	88,719	16,079	59,940	68,727	9,418	281,313
Catholic Pop.[7]	135,660,000	224,844,000	303,259,000	108,168,000	280,589,000	8,320,000	1,060,840,000
World Population	809,105,000	492,762,000	349,392,000	3,747,739,000	702,115,000	31,077,000	6,132,190,000

1. Includes Central America. 2. For listing and description, *see* **Index**. 3. As of Aug. 30, 2003. 4. Figures for the hierarchy (cardinals, archbishops and bishops) included 2,670 ordinaries, 638 coadjutors or auxiliaries, 263 with offices in the Roman Curia, 31 in other offices, 1,047 retired. 5. 162,234 have parish priests; 49,861 are administered by other priests; 510 are entrusted to permanent deacons; 305 to brothers; 894 to women religious; 1,648 to lay people; 1,284 vacant. 6. There are also approximately 230,423 in universities for ecclesiastical studies and 2,746,323 other university students. 7. Percentages of Catholics in world population: Africa, 16.7; North America (Catholics 77,128,000; tot. pop., 316,004,000), 24.4; Central America (Catholics, 147,716,000; tot. pop., 176,758,000), 83.5; South America, 86.7; Asia, 2.8; Europe, 39.9; Oceania, 26.7; world, 17.3 (Catholic totals do not include those in areas that could not be surveyed, estimated to be approx. 7 million).

In 1969, four years after the government of Ian Smith made a unilateral declaration of independence from England, a new constitution was enacted for the purpose of assuring continued white supremacy over the black majority. Catholic and Protestant prelates in the country criticized. The Smith regime was ousted in 1979 after seven years of civil war in which at least 25,000 people were killed.

In 1997, the bishops published a report detailing more than 7,000 cases of killings, torture and human rights abuses by government troops in western Zimbabwe from 1981-87. As the Church entered the 21st century, it was devoting tremendous resources toward palliative care of AIDS victims and work with AIDS orphans. However, the Church was sometimes criticized for not doing enough to prevent the spread of AIDS, which Church and health-care workers said was exacerbated by poverty and cultural beliefs. Some lay church leaders were outspoken against a government-backed campaign of violence against white landowners; Bishop Pius Ncube of Bulawayo was targeted for speaking against government abuses.

EPISCOPAL CONFERENCES

(*Principal sources:* Annuario Pontificio *and* Catholic Almanac *survey*.)

Episcopal conferences, organized and operating under general norms and particular statutes approved by the Holy See, are official bodies in and through which the bishops of a given country or territory act together as pastors of the Church.

Listed below according to countries or regions are titles and addresses of conferences, telephone numbers (where possible), and names and sees of presidents.

Africa, Northern: *Conference Episcopale Regionale du Nord de l'Afrique* (CERNA), 13 rue Khelifa-Boukhalfa, 16000 Algiers, Algeria; (02) 64-53-88. Abp. Henri Teissier (Algiers).

Africa, Southern: Southern African Catholic Bishops' Conference (SACBC), 140 Visagie St., P.O. Box 941, Pretoria 0001, S. Africa; (021) 65-35-62. Cardinal Wilfrid Napier, O.F.M. (Durban, South Africa).

Albania: *Conferenza Episcopale dell'Albania*, Tirane, Rruga Don Bosco 1, Kulia Postare 2950; (042) 47-159. Abp. Angelo Massafra, O.F.M. (Shkodre, Albania).

Angola and São Tome: *Conferencia Episcopal de Angola e HR Tome* (CEAST), C.P. 3579 Luanda, Angola; (02) 44-36-86. Archbishop Zacarias Kamwenho (Lubango).

Antilles: Antilles Episcopal Conference (AEC), P.O. Box 3086, St. James (Trinidad and Tobago), W.I.; (868) 622-2932. Abp. Roland Clarke Edgerton (Kingston).

Arab Countries: *Conférence des Evêques Latins dans les Régions Arabes* (CELRA), Latin Patriarchate, P.O. Box 14152, Jerusalem (Old City); (02) 628-85-54. Patriarch Michel Sabbah (Jerusalem).

Argentina: *Conferencia Episcopal Argentina* (CEA), C1008AAV, Calle Suipacha 1034, 1008 Buenos Aires; (011) 4328-09-93. Abp. Eduardo Vicente Mirás (Rosario).

Australia: Australian Catholic Bishops' Conference, 63 Currong St., Braddon, A.C.T. 2601; (02) 6201-9845; www.catholic.org.au. Abp. Francis Patrick Carroll (Canberra, Australia).

Austria: *Österreichische Bischofskonferenz*, Wollzeile 2, A-1010 Vienna; 01-516-11-32. Cardinal Christoph Schönborn, O.P. (Vienna).

Bangladesh: Catholic Bishops' Conference of Bangladesh (CBCB), P.O. Box 3, Dhaka-1000; (02) 40-88-79. Abp. Michael Rozario (Dhaka).

Belgium: *Bisschoppenconferentie van België* — *Conférence Episcopale de Belgique*, Rue Guimard 1, B-1040 Brussel; (32) 2-509-96-93; www.catho.be; www.kerknet.be. Card. Godfried Danneels (Mechelen-Brussel).

Belarus: *Conferentia Episcoporum Catholicorum*, 220030 Minsk, pl. Swobody 9; (017) 26.61.27. Card. Kazimierz Swiàtek (Minsk-Mohilev).

Benin: *Conférence Episcopale du Bénin*, Cotonou, 01 B.P. 491; 30.01.45. Abp. Nestor Assogba (Dhaka).

Bolivia: *Conferencia Episcopal Boliviana* (CEB), Casilla 2309, Calle Potosi 814, La Paz; (02) 40-67-98. Card. Julio Terrazas Sandoval, C.SS.R. (Santa Cruz de la Sierra).

Bosnia and Herzegovina: *Biskupska Konferencija Bosne i Hercegovine* (B.K. B.i.H.), *Nadbiskupski Ordinariat*, Kaptol 7, 71000 Sarajevo; (071) 47-21-78. Bp. Franjo Komarica (Banja Luka).

Brazil: *Conferência Nacional dos Bispos do Brasil* (CNBB), C.P. 02067, SE/Sul Quadra 801, Conjunto "B," 70259-970 Brasilia, D.F.; (061) 313-8300. Bishop Jayme Henrique Chemello (Pelotas).

Bulgaria: *Mejduritual Episcopska Konferenzia vâv Bâlgaria*, Ul. Liulin Planina 5, 1606 Sofia; (0) 540-406. Bp. Christo Proykov (Briula, titular see).

Burkina Faso and Niger: *Conférence des Evêques de Burkina Faso et du Niger*, B.P. 1195, Ouagadougou, Burkina Faso; 30-60-26. Bp. Philippe Ouédraogo (Ouahigouya).

Burma: See **Myanmar**.

Burundi: *Conférence des Evêques catholiques du Burundi* (C.E.CA.B.), B. P. 1390, 5 Blvd. de l'Uprona, Bujumbura; 223-263. Archbishop Simon Ntamwana (Gitega).

Cameroon: *Conférence Episcopale Nationale du Cameroun* (CENC), BP 1963, Yaoundé; 231-15-92. Bp. Cornelius Fontem Esua (Kumbo).

Canada: *See* **Canadian Conference of Catholic Bishops** in the section on the **Catholic Church in Canada**.

Central African Republic: *Conférence Episcopale Centrafricaine* (CECA), B.P. 1518, Bangui; 50-24-84. Bp. Paulin Pomodimo (Bossangoa).

Chad: *Conférence Episcopale du Tchad*, B.P. 456, N'Djaména; (235) 51-74-44. Bp. Jean-Claude Bouchard, O.M.I. (Pala).

Chile: *Conferencia Episcopal de Chile* (CECH), Casilla 517-V, Correo 21, Cienfuegas 47, Santiago; (02) 671-77-33. Card. Francisco Javier Erráruiz Ossa (Santiago de Chile).

China: Chinese Regional Episcopal Conference, 34 Lane 32, Kuang-Fu South Rd., Taipeh 10552, Taiwan; (02) 578-2355. Card. Paul Shan Kuo-hsi, S.J. (Kaohsiung).

Colombia: *Conferencia Episcopal de Colombia*, Apartado 7448, Carrera 8ª 47, N. 84-85, Santafé de Bogotá D.E.; (91) 311-42-77. Card. Pedro Rubiano Saenz (Bogota).

Congo: *Conférence Episcopale du Congo*, B.P. 200, Brazzaville; (83) 06-29. Abp. Anatole Milandou (Brazzaville).

Congo, Democratic Republic (formerly Zaire): *Conférence Episcopale du Zaïre* (CEZ), B.P. 3258, Kinshasa-Gombe; 012-33-992. Card. Frédéric Etsou-Nzabi-Bamungwabi C.I.C.M. (Kinshasa).

Costa Rica: *Conferencia Episcopal de Costa Rica* (CECOR), Apartado 497, 1000 San Jose; 221-30-53. Bp. José Francisco Ulloa Rojas (Limon).

Côte d'Ivoire: *Conference Episcopale de la Côte d'Ivoire*, B.P. 1287, Abidjan 01. Abp. Vital Komenan Yao (Bouaké).

Croatia: *Hrvatska Biskupska Konferencija*, Kaptol 22, HR-10000 Zagreb; 385-01-481-18-93; www.hbk.hr. Abp. Josip Bozanic (Zagreb).

Cuba: *Conferencia de Obispos Católicos de Cuba* (COCC), Apartado 594, Calle 26 n. 314 Miramar, 10100 Havana 1; (07) 22-3868. Card. Jaime Lucas Ortega y Alamino (Havana).

Czech Republic: *Ceská Biskupská Konference*, Sekretariat, Thakurova 3, 160 00 Praha (Prague) 6; (02) 33-15-421. Bp. Jan Graubner (Olomouc).

Dominican Republic: *Conferencia del Episcopado Dominicano* (CED), Apartado 186, Santo Domingo; (809) 685-3141. Bp. Ramon Benito de la Rosa y Carpio (Nuestra Señora de la Altagracia en Higuey).

Ecuador: *Conferencia Episcopal Ecuatoriana*, Apartado 1081, Avenida América 1805 y Lagasca, Quito; (02) 23-82-21. Abp. Vicente Rodrigo Cisneros Duran (Cuenca).

El Salvador: *Conferencia Episcopal de El Salvador* (CEDES). 15 Av. Norte 1420, Col. Layco, Apartado 1310, San Salvador; 25-8997. Abp. Fernando Sáenz Lacalle (San Salvador).

Equatorial Guinea: *Conferencia Episcopal de Guinea Ecuatorial*, Apartado 106, Malabo. Abp. Ildefonso Obama Obono (Malabo).

Ethiopia: Ethiopian Episcopal Conference, P.O. Box 21322, Addis Ababa; (01) 55-03-00. Abp. Berhane-Yesus Demerew Souraphiel, C.M. (Addis Ababa).

France: *Conférence des Evêques de France*, 106 rue du Bac, 75341 Paris CEDEX 07; 33-01-45-49-69-70; www.cef.fr. Abp. Jean-Pierre Ricard (Bordeaux).

Gabon: *Conférence Episcopale du Gabon*, B.P. 2146, Libreville; 72-20-73. Bp. Basile Mvé Engone, S.D.B. (Oyem).

Gambia, Liberia and Sierra Leone: Inter-Territorial Catholic Bishops' Conference of the Gambia, Liberia and Sierra Leone (ITCABIC), Santanno House, P.O. Box 893, Freetown, Sierra Leone; (022) 22-82-40. Abp. Joseph Henry Ganda (Freetown).

Germany: *Deutsche Bischofskonferenz*, Postfach 2962, Kaiserstrasse 163, D-53019 Bonn; (0049) 228-103-290. Card. Karl Lehmann (Mainz).

Ghana: Ghana Bishops' Conference, National Catholic Secretariat, P.O. Box 9712 Airport, Accra; (021) 500-491. Bp. Peter Kodwo Appiah Turkson (Cape Coast).

Great Britain: Bishops' Conference of England and Wales, General Secretariat, 39 Eccleston Square, London, SWIV IBX; (020) 7630-8220. Card. Cormac Murphy-O'Connor (Westminster).

Greece: *Conferentia Episcopalis Graeciae*, Odos Homirou 9, 106 72 Athens; (01) 3642-311. Abp. Nikólaos Fóscolos (Athens).

Guatemala: *Conferencia Episcopal de Guatemala* (CEG), Apartado 1698, 01901 Ciudad de Guatemala; 543-18-27/8. Abp. Victor Hugo Martinez Contreras (Los Altos, Quetzaltenango-Totonicapán).

Guinea: *Conférence Episcopale de la Guinée*, B.P. 1006 bis, Conkary. Conakry. Bp. Philippe Kourouma (N'Zerekore).

Guinea-Bissau: See **Senegal**.

Haiti: *Conférence Episcopale de Haïti* (CEH). B.P. 1572, Angle rues Piquant et Lammarre, Port-au-Prince; 222-5194. Bp. Hubert Constant, O.M.I. (Fort-Liberté).

Honduras: *Conferencia Episcopal de Honduras* (CEH), Apartado 847, Blvd. Estadio Suyapa, Tegucigalpa; (504) 32-40-43. Abp. Oscar Andrés Rodríguez Maradiaga (Tegucigalpa).

Hungary: *Magyar Katolikus Püspöki Konferencia*, H-1071 Budapest VII, Városligeti fasor 45; 1-342-69-59. Abp. István Seregély (Eger).

India: Catholic Bishops' Conference of India (CBCI), CBCI Centre, Ashok Place, Goldakkhana, New Delhi-110001; (011) 334-44-70; Abp. Cyril Baseolios Malancharuvil, O.I.C. (Trivandrum). Conference of Catholic Bishops of India – Latin Rite (CCBI - L.R.), Divya Deepti Sadan, Second Floor, P.B. 680, 9-10 Bhai Vir Singh Marg; (011) 336-42-22; Abp. Placidius Toppo Telesphore (Ranchi).

Indian Ocean: *Conférence Episcopale de l'Océan Indien* (CEDOI) (includes Islands of Mauritius, Seychelles, Comore and La Réunion), 13 rue Msgr. Gonin, Port Louis, Mauritius; (230) 208-3068. Bp. Maurice Piat, C.S.Sp. (Port Louis).

Indonesia: *Konperensi Waligereja Indonesia* (KWI), Jl. Cut Mutiah 10, Tromolpos 3044, Jakarta 10002; (021) 33-64-22. Card. Julius Riyadi Darmaatmadja, S.J. (Jakarta).

Ireland: Irish Episcopal Conference, *"Ara Coeli,"* Armagh BT61 7QY; 028-3752-2045. Abp. Sean B. Brady (Armagh).

Italy: *Conferenza Episcopale Italiana* (CEI), Circonvallazione Aurelia, 50, 00165 Rome; 06-663-981. Card. Camillo Ruini (Vicar General, Rome).

Ivory Coast: See **Côte d'Ivoire**.

Japan: Catholic Bishops' Conference of Japan, Shiomi 2-10-10, Koto-Ku, Tokyo, 135; (03) 56324411. Bp. Augustinus Junichi Nomura (Nagoya).

Kenya: Kenya Episcopal Conference (KEC), The Kenya Catholic Secretariat, P.O. Box 13475, Nairobi; (02) 44-31-33. Bp. John Njue (Embu).

Korea: Catholic Bishops' Conference of Korea, Box 16, Seoul 100-600; (02) 466-3417. Abp. Andreas Choi Chang-mou (Kwangju).

Laos and Cambodia: *Conférence Episcopale du Laos et du Cambodge*, c/o Msgr. Pierre Bach, Paris Foreign Missions, 254 Silom Rd., Bangkok 10500; (02) 234-1714. Bp. Jean Khamsé Vithavong, O.M.I. (Moglena).

Latvia: *Latvijas Biskapu Konference*, Maza Pils iela 2/a, LV-1050, Riga; (7) 22-72-66. Card. Janis Pujats (Riga).

Lesotho: Lesotho Catholic Bishops' Conference, Catholic Secretariat, P.O. Box 200, Maseru 100; (0501) 31-25-25. Bp. Evaristus Thatho Bitsoane (Qacha's Nek).

Liberia: Catholic Bishops' Conference of Liberia, 1000 Monrovia 10, P.O. Box 10-2078; 227-245. Abp. Francis Michael Kpakala (Monrovia).

Lithuania: *Conferentia Episcopalis Lituaniae*, Sventaragio, 4, 2001 Vilnius; (5) 212-54-55. Card. Audrys Backia (Vilnius).

Madagascar: *Conférence Episcopale de Madagascar*, 102 bis Av. Maréchal Joffre, Antanimena, B. P 667, Antananarivo; (02) 2220-478. Bp. Fulgence Rabeony, S.J. (Toliara).

Malawi: Episcopal Conference of Malawi, Catholic Secretariat of Malawi, P.O. Box 30384, Lilongwe 3; 782-066. Bp. Tarcisius Gervazio Ziyaye (Blantyre).

Malaysia-Singapore-Brunei: Catholic Bishops' Conference of Malaysia, Singapore and Brunei (BCMSB), Xavier Selangor Darul Ehsan, 46000 Petaling Jaya, Malaysia; (03) 758-1371. Abp. Anthony Soter Fernandez (Kuala Lampur).

Mali: *Conférence Episcopale du Mali*, B.P. 298, Bamako; 225-499. Bp. Jean-Gabriel Diarra.

Malta: *Konferenza Episkopali Maltija*, Archbishop's Curia, Floriana; (356) 234317; www.malta church.org.mt. Abp. Joseph Mercieca (Malta).

Mexico: *See* the *Conferencia del Episcopado Mexicano* (CEM), under the section on the **Catholic Church in Mexico**.

Mozambique: *Conferência Episcopal de Moçambique* (CEM), Av. Paulo Samuel Kankhomba 188/RC, C.P. 286; (01) 49-07-66. Bp. Jaime Pedro Gonçalves (Beira).

Myanmar: Myanmar Catholic Bishops' Conference (MCBC), 292 Pyi Rd., P.O. Box 1080, Yangon; (01) 23-71-98. Bp. Bo Charles Maung, S.D.B. (Pathein).

Namibia: Namibian Catholic Bishops' Conference (NCBC). P.O. Box 11525 W., Windhoek; (061) 22-47-98. Vacant.

Netherlands: *Nederlandse Bisschoppenconferentie*, Postbus 13049, NL-3507 LA, Utrecht; (31)-30-232-69-00; www.omroep.nl/rkk. Card. Adrianus J. Simonis (Utrecht).

New Zealand: New Zealand Catholic Bishops Conference, P.O. Box 1937, Wellington 6015; (04) 496-1747. Bp. Peter James Culliname (Palmerston North).

Nicaragua: *Conferencia Episcopal de Nicaragua* (CEN), Apartado Postal 2407, de Ferretería Lang 1 cuadro al Norte y 1 cuadro al Este, Managua; (02) 666-292. Cardinal Miguel Odando Bravo, S.D.B. (Managua).

Niger: *See* **Burkina Faso**.

Nigeria: Catholic Bishops Conference of Nigeria, P.O. Box 951, 6 Force Rd., Lagos; (01) 263-58-49. Abp. John Olorunfemi Onaiyekan (Abuja).

Pacific: *Conferentia Episcopalis Pacifici* (CE PAC), P.O. Box 289, Suva (Fiji); 300-340. Abp. Michel Marie Bernard Calvet, S.M. (Noumea, New Caledonia).

Pakistan: Pakistan Episcopal Conference, P.O. Box 909, Lahore 54000; (042) 6366-137. Abp. Lawrence J. Saldanha (Lahore).

Panama: *Conferencia Episcopal de Panamá* (CEP), Apartado 870033, Panama 7; 223-0075. Abp. José Luis Lacunza Maestrojuán, O.A.R. (David).

Papua New Guinea and Solomon Islands: Catholic Bishops' Conference of Papua New Guinea and Solomon Islands, P.O. Box 398, Waigani, N.C.D., Papua New Guinea; 25-9577. Abp. Karl Hesse, M.S.C. (Rabaul).

Paraguay: *Conferencia Episcopal Paraguaya* (CEP), Alberdi 782, Casilla Correo 1436, Asunción; (021) 490-920. Bp. Claudio Catalino Gimenez Medina (Caacupe).

Peru: *Conferencia Episcopal Peruana*, Apartado 310, Rio de Janeiro 488, Lima 100; (01) 463-10-10. Bp. Luis Armando Bambarén Gastelumendi, S.J. (Chimbote).

Philippines: Catholic Bishops' Conference of the Philippines (CBCP), P.O. Box 3601, 470 General Luna St., 1099 Manila; (02) 527-4054. Abp. Orlando Quevedo, O.M.I. (Cotabato).

Poland: *Konferencja Episkopatu Polski*, Skwer Kardynala Stefana Wyszynskiego 6, 01-015 Warsaw; (022) 838-92-51. Card. Józef Glemp (Warsaw).

Portugal: *Conferência Episcopal Portuguesa*, Campo dos Mártires da Pátria, 43-1 Esq., 1100 Lisbon; 21-885-21-23. Abp. José da Cruz Policarpo (Lisbon).

Puerto Rico: *Conferencia Episcopal Puertorriqueña* (CEP), P.O. Box 40682, Estacion Minillas, San Juan 00940-0682; (787) 728-1650. Abp. Roberto Octavio Gonzalez Nieves, O.F.M. (San Juan de Puerto Rico).

Romania: *Conferinte Episcopala România*, Via Popa Tatu 58, Bucharest; (01) 311-12-89. Abp. Ioan Robu (Bucharest).

Russian Federation: Conference of Catholic Bishops of the Russian Federation (C.V.C.F.R.), 101031 Moskva, Via Pietrovka, d. 19 str., 5Kv. 35; (095) 923-16-97. Abp. Tadeusz Kondrusiewicz (Archdiocese of the Mother of God).

Rwanda: *Conférence Episcopale du Rwanda* (C.Ep.R.), B.P. 357, Kigali; 75439. Abp. Thadée Ntihinyurwa (Kigali).

Scandinavia: *Conferentia Episcopalis Scandiae*, Trollbärsvägen 16, S-426 55 Västra Frölunda (Sweden); (031) 709-64-87. Bp. Gerhard Schwenzer, S.S.C.C. (Oslo).

Scotland: Bishops' Conference of Scotland, 64 Aitken St., Airdrie, ML6; 44-1236-764-061. Keith Michael Patrick O'Brien (St. Andrews and Edinburgh).

Senegal, Mauritania, Cape Verde and Guinea Bissau: *Conférence des Evêques du Sénégal, de la Mauritanie, du Cap-Vert et de Guinée-Bissau*, B.P. 941, Dakar, Senegal. Abp. Théodore-Adrien Sarr (Dakar).

Sierra Leone: *See* **Gambia, Liberia and Sierra Leone**.

Slovakia: *Biskupská Konferencia Slovenska*, Kapitulská 11, 81521 Bratislava; (07) 733-54-50. Bp. Frantisek Tondra (Spis).

Slovenia: *Slovenska Skofovska Konferenca*, Ciril-Metodov trg 4, p.p.1990, 1001 Ljubljana; (386) 1-2342612. Abp. Franc Rodé, C.M. (Ljubljana).

Spain: *Conferencia Episcopal Española*, Apartado 29075, Calle Añastro 1, 28080 Madrid; 91-343-96-15. Cardinal Antonio María Rouco Varela (Madrid).

Sri Lanka: Catholic Bishops' Conference of Sri Lanka, 19 Balcombe Place, Cotta Rd., Borella, Colombo 8; (01) 95-091; 59-70-62. Bp. Oswald Thomas Colman Gomis (Anuradhapura).

Sudan: Sudan Catholic Bishops' Conference (SCBC), P.O. Box 6011, Khartoum; (011) 225-075-9. Abp. Paulino Lukudu Loro, M.C.C.I. (Juba).

Switzerland: *Conférence des Evêques Suisses*, Secretariat, C.P. 22, av. Moléson 21, CH-1706 Fribourg; (026) 322-47-94; www.kath.ch. Bp. Amédée Grab, O.S.B. (Chur).

Tanzania: Tanzania Episcopal Conference (TEC), P.O. Box 2133, Mansfield St., Dar-es-Salaam; (022) 51-075. Bp. Severine Niwemugizi (Rulenge).

Thailand: Bishops' Conference of Thailand, 122-6-7 Soi Naaksuwan, Nonsi Road, Yannawa, Bangkok; 02-6815361-8. Card. Michael Michai Kitbunchu (Bangkok).

Togo: *Conférence Episcopale du Togo*, B.P. 348, Lomé; 21-22-72. Abp. Philippe Fanoko Kossi Kpodzro (Lomé).

Turkey: Turkish Episcopal Conference, Ölçek Sokak 83, Harbiye, 80230 Istanbul; (212) 248-07-75. Bp. Ruggero Franceschini, O.F.M. Cap. (Sicilibba).

Uganda: Uganda Episcopal Conference, P.O. Box 2886, Kampala; (041) 510-398. Abp. Paul K. Bakyenga (Mbarara).

Ukraine: Ukraine Episcopal Conference, 79008 Lviv, Mytropolycha Kuria Latynskoho Obriadu, Pl. Katedralna 1; (0322) 76-94-15. Card. Marian Jaworski (Lviv of Latins).

United States: *See* **National Conference of Catholic Bishops**.

Uruguay: *Conferencia Episcopal Uruguaya* (CEU), Avenida Uruguay 1319, 11100 Montevideo; (02) 900-26-42. Bp. Carlos Maria Collazzi Irazábal, S.D.B. (Mercedes).

Venezuela: *Conferencia Episcopal de Venezuela* (CEV), Apartado 4897, Torre a Madrices, Edificio Juan XXIII, Piso 4, Caracas 1010-A; (0212) 4432-23-65. Abp. Baltazar Porras Cardozo (Mérida).

Vietnam: *Conferenza Episcopale del Viêt Nam*, Nha Trang, Khán Hoà, 22 Tran Phu; (058) 822-842. Bp. Paul Nguyen Van Hòa (Nha Trang).

Yugoslavia: *Biskupska Konferencija Savezne Republike Jugoslavije*, 11000 Beograd, Visegradska 23; (011) 642-280. Abp. Stanislav Hocevar, S.D.B. (Beograd).

Zambia: Zambia Episcopal Conference, P.O. Box 31965, 20201 Lusaka; [01] 212-070. Bp. Telesphore George Mpundu (Mpika).

Zimbabwe: Zimbabwe Catholic Bishops' Conference (ZCBC), Causeway, P.O. Box 8135, Harare; (14) 705-368. Bp. Michael Dixon Bhasera (Masvingo).

Regional Conferences

(*Sources:* Almanac *survey;* Annuario Pontificio.)

Africa: Symposium of Episcopal Conferences of Africa and Madagascar (SECAM) (*Symposium des Conférences Episcopales d'Afrique et de Madagascar*, SCEAM): Abp. Laurent Monsengwo Pasinya, abp. of Kisangani, president. Address: Secretariat, P.O. Box 9156 Airport, Accra, Ghana.

Association of Episcopal Conferences of Central Africa (*Association des Conférences Episcopales de l'Afrique Centrale*, ACEAC): Comprises Burundi, Rwanda and Zaire. Bp. Nicolas Djomo Lolo, bp. of Tshumbe, president. Address: B.P. 20511, Kinshasa, Democratic Republic of Congo.

Association of Episcopal Conferences of the Region of Central Africa (*Association des Conférences Episcopales de la Région de l'Afrique Central*, ACERAC): Comprises Cameroon, Chad, Congo, Equatorial Guinea, Central African Republic and Gabon. Bp. Jean-Claude Bouchard, O.M.I., bp. of Pala, president. Address: Secretariat, B.P. 200, Brazzaville, Republic of the Congo.

Association of Episcopal Conferences of

Anglophone West Africa (AECAWA): Comprises Gambia, Ghana, Liberia, Nigeria and Sierra Leone. Bp. John Olorunfemi Onaiyekan, abp. of Abuja, president. Address: P.O. Box 11, Santasi, Ghana.

Association of Member Episcopal Conferences in Eastern Africa (AMECEA): Represents Eritrea, Ethiopia, Kenya, Malawi, Sudan, Tanzania, Uganda and Zambia. Affiliate members: Seychelles (1979), Somalia (1994). Bp. Josaphat L. Lebulu, bp. of Arusha, president. Address: P.O. Box 21191, Nairobi, Kenya.

Regional Episcopal Conference of French-Speaking West Africa (*Conférence Episcopale Régionale de l'Afrique de l'Ouest Francophone*, CERAO): Comprises Benin, Burkina Faso, Cape Verde, Côte d'Ivoire, Guinea, Guinea-Bissau, Mali, Mauritania, Niger, Senegal and Togo. President: vacant. Address: Secretariat General, B.P.470 CIDEX 1, Abidjan — Côte d'Ivoire.

Inter-Regional Meeting of Bishops of Southern Africa (IMBISA): Bishops of Angola, Botswana, Lesotho, Mozambique, Namibia, São Tome e Principe, South Africa, Swaziland and Zimbabwe. Bp. Louis Ncamiso Ndlovu, O.S.M., bp. of Manzini, president. Address: 88 Broadlands Rd. Avondale Harare, Zimbabwe.

Asia: Federation of Asian Bishops' Conferences (FABC): Represents 14 Asian episcopal conferences and four independent jurisdictions (Hong Kong, Macau, Nepal, Mongolia) as regular members (excluding the Middle East). Established in 1970; statutes approved experimentally Dec. 6, 1972. Abp. Oswald Thomas Colman Gomis, bp. of Anuradhapura, secretary general. Address: 16 Caine Road, Hong Kong; 25258021; www.fabc.org.ph.

Oceania: Federation of Catholic Bishops' Conferences of Oceania (FCBCO). Statutes approved Dec. 25, 1997. Bp. Denis George Browne, bp. of Hamilton in New Zealand, president. Address: P.O. Box 1937, 22-30 Hill St., Wellington, New Zealand 6015.

Europe: Council of European Bishops' Conferences (*Consilium Conferentiarum Episcoporum Europae*, CCEE): Amédé Grab, bp. of Chur, president. Address of secretariat: Gallusstrasse 24, CH-9000 Sankt Gallen, Switzerland; (0041) 71-227-33-74; www.kath.ch/ccee. Reorganized in 1993 in accordance with suggestions made during the 1991 Synod of Bishops on Europe.

Commission of the Episcopates of the European Community (*Commissio Episcopatuum Com-munitatis Europaeae*, COMECE): Established in 1980; represents episcopates of states belonging to European Community. Bp. Josef Homeyer, bp. of Hildesheim, Germany, president. Address of secretariat: 42, Rue Stévin, B-1000 Brussels, Belgium; (02) 230-73-16.

Central and South America: Latin American Bishops' Conference (*Consejo Episcopal Latino-Americano*, CELAM): Established in 1956; statutes approved Nov. 9, 1974. Represents 22 Latin American national bishops' conferences. Bp. Jorge Enrique Jiménez Carvajal, C.I.M., president. Address of the secretariat: Carrera 5 No. 118-31, Usaquén, Bogotá, Colombia; (91) 612-16-20.

Episcopal Secretariat of Central America and Panama (*Secretariado Episcopal de America Central y Panama*, SEDAC): Statutes approved experimentally Sept. 26, 1970. Bp. Leonel Ramazzini Imeri Alvaro, bp. of San Marcos, president. Address of secretary general: Calle 20 y Av Mexico 24-45, Apartado 6386, Panama 5, Panama; 262-7802.

INTERNATIONAL CATHOLIC ORGANIZATIONS

(Principal sources: Sr. Dorothy Farley, Executive Director, ICO Information Center; Pontifical Council for the Laity; Catholic Almanac survey.)

Guidelines

International organizations wanting to call themselves "Catholic" are required to meet standards set by the Vatican's Council for the Laity and to register with and get the approval of the Papal Secretariat of State, according to guidelines dated Dec. 3 and published in *Acta Apostolicae Sedis* under the date of Dec. 23, 1971.

Among conditions for the right of organizations to "bear the name Catholic" are:

• leaders "will always be Catholics," and candidates for office will be approved by the Secretariat of State

• adherence by the organization to the Catholic Church, its teaching authority and the teachings of the Gospel

• evidence that the organization is really international with a universal outlook and that it fulfills its mission through its own management, meetings and accomplishments.

The guidelines also stated that leaders of the organizations "will take care to maintain necessary reserve as regards taking a stand or engaging in public activity in the field of politics or trade unionism. Abstention in these fields will normally be the best attitude for them to adopt during their term of office."

The guidelines were in line with a provision stated by the Second Vatican Council: "No project may claim the name 'Catholic' unless it has obtained the consent of the lawful Church authority."

They made it clear that all organizations are not obliged to apply for recognition, but that the Church "reserves the right to recognize as linked with her mission and her aims those organizations or movements which see fit to ask for such recognition."

CONFERENCE OF INTERNATIONAL CATHOLIC ORGANIZATIONS

A permanent body for collaboration among various organizations the conference seeks to promote the development of international life along the lines of Christian principles. Eleven international Catholic organizations participated in its foundation and first meeting in 1927 at Fribourg, Switzerland. In 1951, the conference established its general secretariat and adopted governing statutes that were approved by the Vatican Secretariat of State in 1953.

The permanent secretariat is located at 37-39 rue de Vermont, CH-1202 Geneva, Switzerland. Other office addresses are: 1 rue Varembe, CH-1211 Geneva 20, Switzerland (International Catholic Center of Geneva); 9, rue Cler, F-75007 Paris, France (International Catholic Center for UNESCO); ICO Information Center, 323 East 47th St., New York, NY 10017.

Charter

According to its charter (adopted in November 1997), the conference "responds to the challenge of *Christifideles Laici:* Open to the saving power of Christ the frontiers of States, economic and political systems, the vast domains of culture, civilization and development (no. 34)."

In a universal vision of those problems, these organizations have the following responsibilities to their members:

• to make them increasingly aware of the compexities of the situations in which they live and work

• to help them to grow in discernment and critical analysis

• to facilitate the search for solutions to concrete difficulties.

The Conference is open to any organization which is acting and is involved recognizably Catholic in its work in the international world, which accepts the present Charter, respects its principles in practice and adheres to its Statutes. The Conference witnesses to the organized presence of Catholics in the international world.

Fundamental Convictions

• Their desire to announce Jesus Christ to the women and men of our time, and their vocation to serve the world, are indivisible; faith calls for action

• Their wish to contribute to the building of the Kingdom of God is demonstrated by solidarity with all women and men of good will

• Their desire for participation in decision-making in the Church in areas which concern their competence and in which they are involved.

A unique spirituality

In its desire to live fully its faith in Jesus Christ, the Cnference stresses:

• The need to be rooted in reality, through a relationship with God lived out in the world

• An experience of community nourished by group sharing and exchange

• Openness to the international dimension, validated by experiences at local level to which it gives meaning

• Adaptation to different human groups and to different sensibilities

• The witness of Christian freedom to initiate, as well as willingness to live in "solid and strong communion" with the Church

• Desire to serve the universal Church through insertion in the local Churches by respecting diverse pastoral programmes, but also to participate in major events in the life of the universal Church.

Members

Members of the Conference of International Catholic Organizations are listed below. Information includes name, date and place of establishment (when available), address of general secretariat. Approximately 30 of the organizations have consultative status with other international or regional non-governmental agencies.

Caritas Internationalis (1951, Rome, Italy): Piazza San Calisto 16, I-00153, Rome, Italy. Coordinates and represents its 146 national member organizations (in 194 countries) operating in the fields of development, emergency aid, social action.

Catholic International Education Office (1952): 60, rue des Eburons, B-1000 Brussels, Belgium.

Catholic International Union for Social Service (1925, Milan, Italy): rue de la Poste 111, B-1210 Brussels, Belgium (general secretariat).

Christian Life Community (CVX) (1953): Borgo

Santo Spirito 8, C.P. 6139, I-00195 Rome, Italy. First Sodality of Our Lady founded in 1563.

International Ascent, The: 84, rue Charles Michels, F-93206 Saint Denis Cedex, France. Member of ICO.

International Association of Charities (1617, Chatillon les Dombes, France): Rue Joseph Brand, 118, B-1030 Brussels, Belgium.

International Catholic Child Bureau (1948, in Paris): 63, rue de Lausanne, CH-1202 Geneva, Switzerland.

International Catholic Committee of Nurses and Medico-Social Assistants (ICCN) (1933): Square Vergote, 43, B-1040 Brussels, Belgium.

International Catholic Conference of Scouting (1948): Piazza Pasquale Paoli, 18, I-00186 Rome, Italy.

International Catholic Migration Commission (1951): 37-39 rue de Vermont, C.P. 96, CH-1211 Geneva 20, Switzerland. Coordinates activities worldwide on behalf of refugees and migrants, both administering programs directly and supporting the efforts of national affiliated agencies.

International Catholic Organization for Cinema and Audiovisual (1928, The Hague, The Netherlands): Rue du Saphir, 15, B-1040 Brussels, Belgium (general secretariat). Federation of National Catholic film offices.

International Catholic Society for Girls (1897): 37-39, rue de Vermont, CH-1202 Geneva, Switzerland.

International Catholic Union of the Press: 37-39 rue de Vermont, Case Postale 197, CH-1211 Geneva 20 CIC, Switzerland. Coordinates and represents at the international level the activities of Catholics and Catholic federations or associations in the field of press and information. Has seven specialized branches: International Federation of Catholic Journalists; International Federation of Dailies; International Federation of Periodicals; International Federation of Catholic News Agencies; International Catholic Federation of Teachers and Researchers in the Science and Techniques of Information; International Federation of Church Press Associations; and International Federation of Book Publishers.

International Conference of Catholic Guiding (1965): c/o Mlle Francoise Parmentier, rue de la Tour 64, 75016 Paris. Founded by member bodies of interdenominational World Association of Guides and Girl Scouts.

International Coordination of Young Christian Workers (YCYCW): via dei Barbieri 22, I00186 Rome, Italy.

International Council of Catholic Men (ICCM) (**Unum Omnes**) (1948): Wahringer Str. 2-4, A.1090 Vienna IX, Austria.

International Federation of Catholic Medical Associations (1954): Palazzo San Calisto, I-00120 Vatican City.

International Federation of Catholic Parochial Youth Communities (1962, Rome, Italy): St. Kariliquai 12, 6000 Lucerne 5, Switzerland.

International Federation of Catholic Pharmacists (1954): Bosdorf 180, 9190 Stekene, Belgium.

International Federation of Rural Adult Catholic Movements (1964, Lisbon, Portugal): Rue Jaumain 15, B-5330 Assesse, Belgium.

International Federation of Catholic Universities

(1949): 21, rue d'Assas, F-75270 Paris 06, France.

International Federation of the Catholic Associations of the Blind: Avenue Dailly 90, B-1030 Brussels, Belgium. Coordinates actions of Catholic groups and associations for the blind and develops their apostolate.

International Independent Christian Youth (IICY): 11, rue Martin Bernard, 75013 Paris, France.

International Military Apostolate (1967): Breite Strasse 25. D-53111 Bonn, Germany. Comprised of organizations of military men.

International Movement of Apostolate of Children (1929, France): 24, rue Paul Rivet, F-92350 Le Plessis Robinson, France.

International Movement of Apostolate in the Independent Social Milieux (MIAMSI) (1963): Piazza San Calisto 16, 00153 Rome, Italy.

International Movement of Catholic Agricultural and Rural Youth (1954, Annevoie, Belgium): 53, rue J. Coosemans, B-1030 Brussels, Belgium (permanent secretariat).

International Young Catholic Students (1946, Fribourg, Switzerland; present name, 1954): 171 rue de Rennes, F-75006 Paris, France.

Pax Romana (1921, Fribourg, Switzerland, divided into two branches, 1947): **Pax Romana - IMCS (International Movement of Catholic Students)** (1921): 171, rue de Rennes, F-75006, Paris, France, for undergraduates; **Pax Romana - ICMICA (International Catholic Movement for Intellectual and Cultural Affairs)** (1947): rue du Grand Bureau 15, CH-1227 Geneva, Switzerland, for Catholic intellectuals and professionals.

Society of St. Vincent de Paul (1833, Paris): 5, rue du Pré-aux-Clercs, F-75007 Paris, France.

Unda: International Catholic Association for Radio and Television (1928, Cologne, Germany): rue de l'Orme, 12, B-1040 Brussels, Belgium.

World Movement of Christian Workers (1961): Blvd. du Jubilé 124, 1080 Brussels, Belgium.

World Organization of Former Pupils of Catholic Education (1967, Rome): 48, rue de Richelieu, F-75001 Paris, France.

World Union of Catholic Teachers (1951): Piazza San Calisto 16, 00153 Rome, Italy.

World Union of Catholic Women's Organizations (1910): 18, rue Notre Dame des Champs, F-75006 Paris, France.

Other Catholic Organizations

Apostleship of Prayer (1849): Borgo Santo Spirito 5, I-00193 Rome, Italy. National secretariat in most countries.

Apostolatus Maris (Apostleship of the Sea) (1922, Glasgow, Scotland): Pontifical Council for Migrants and Itinerant People, Piazza San Calisto 16, 00153 Rome, Italy. (*See* **Index**.)

L'Arche Communities: B.P. 35, 60350 Cuise Lamotte, France.

Associationes Juventutis Salesianae (Associations of Salesian Youth) (1847): Via della Pisana, 1111, 00163 Rome, Italy.

Blue Army of Our Lady of Fatima: P.O. Box 976, Washington, NJ, 07882.

Catholic International Federation for Physical and Sports Education (1911; present name, 1957): 5, rue Cernuschi, 75017 Paris, France.

Christian Fraternity of the Sick and Handicapped: 9, Avenue de la Gare, CH-1630, Bulle, Switzerland.

"Communione e Liberazione" Fraternity (1955, Milan, Italy): Via Marcello Malpighi 2, 00161 Rome, Italy. Catholic renewal movement.

"Focolare Movement" (Work of Mary) (1943, Trent, Italy): Via di Frascati, 306, I-00040 Rocca di Papa (Rome), Italy.

Foi et Lumiere: 8 rue Serret, 75015 Paris, France.

Franciscans International: 345 E. 47th St., New York, NY 10017. A non-governmental organization at the UN.

Inter Cultural Association (ICA, 1937, Belgium) and **Association Fraternelle Internationale** (AFI): 91, rue de la Servette, CH-1202 Geneva, Switzerland.

International Association of Children of Mary (1847): 67 rue de Sèvres, F-75006 Paris, France.

International Catholic Rural Association (1962, Rome): Piazza San Calisto, 00153 Rome, Italy. International body for agricultural and rural organizations. Invited member of ICO.

International Catholic Union of Esperanto: Via Berni 9, 00185 Rome, Italy.

International Centre for Studies in Religious Education LUMEN VITAE (1934-35, Louvain, Belgium, under name Catechetical Documentary Centre; present name, 1956): 184, rue Washington, B-1050 Brussels, Belgium. Also referred to as Lumen Vitae Centre; concerned with all aspects of religious formation.

International Young Christian Workers (1925, Belgium): 11, rue Plantin, B-1070 Brussels, Belgium. Associate member of ICO.

Legion of Mary (1921, Dublin, Ireland): De Montfort House, North Brunswick St., Dublin, Ireland. (*See* Index.)

Medicus Mundi Internationalis (1964, Bensberg, Germany FR): P.O. Box 1547, 6501 BM Nijmegen, Netherlands. To promote health and medico-social services, particularly in developing countries; recruit essential health and medical personnel for developing countries; contribute to training of medical and auxiliary personnel; undertake research in the field of health.

NOVALIS, Marriage Preparation Center: University of St. Paul, 1 rue Stewart, Ottawa 2, ON, Canada.

Our Lady's Teams (Equipes Notre-Dame) (1937, France): 49, rue de la Glacière, 75013 Paris, France. Movement for spiritual formation of couples.

Pax Christi International (1950): rue du Vieux Marché aux grains 21, B-1000 Brussels, Belgium. International Catholic peace movement. Originated in Lourdes, France, in 1948 by French and German Catholics to reconcile enemies from World War II; spread to Italy and Poland and acquired its international title when it merged with the English organization Pax. Associate member of ICO.

Pro Sanctity Movement: Piazza S. Andrea della Valle 3, 00166 Rome, Italy.

St. Joan's International Alliance (1911, in England, as Catholic Women's Suffrage Society): Quai Churchill 19, Boite 061, B-4020 Liège, Belgium. Associate member of ICO.

Salesian Cooperators (1876, Turin, Italy): **Salesian Cooperators**: Founded by St. John Bosco; for lay men and women and diocesan clergy. A public association of the faithful, members commit themselves to apostolates in the local Church, especially on behalf of the young, in the Salesian spirit and style. Address: 174 Filors Lane, Stony Point, NY 10980-2645; (845) 947-2200.

Secular Franciscan Order (1221, first Rule approved): Via Piemonte, 70, 00187, Rome, Italy.

Secular Fraternity of Charles de Foucauld: Katharinenweg 4, B4700 Eupen, Belgium.

Serra International (1953, in U.S.): 65 E. Wacker Pl. Suite 1210, Chicago, IL 60601.

Unio Internationalis Laicorum in Servitio Ecclesiae (1965, Aachen, Germany): Postfach 990125, Am Kielshof 2, 5000 Cologne, Germany 91. Consists of national and diocesan associations of persons who give professional services to the Church.

Union of Adorers of the Blessed Sacrament (1937): Largo dei Monti Parioli 3, I-00197, Rome, Italy.

World Catholic Federation for the Biblical Apostolate (1969, Rome): Mittelstrasse, 12, P.O. Box 601, D-7000, Stuttgart 1, Germany.

Regional Organizations

European Federation for Catholic Adult Education (1963, Lucerne, Switzerland): Hirschengraben 13, P.B. 2069, CH-6002 Lucerne, Switzerland.

European Forum of National Committees of the Laity (1968): 169, Booterstown Av., Blackrock, Co. Dublin, Ireland.

Movimiento Familiar Cristiano (1949-50, Montevideo and Buenos Aires): Carrera 17 n. 4671, Bogotá, D.E., Colombia. Christian Family Movement of Latin America.

Eastern Catholic Churches

(Sources: Rev. Ronald Roberson, C.S.P., Associate Director, Ecumenical and Interreligious Affairs, USCCB.; Annuario Pontificio; Official Catholic Directory.)

The Second Vatican Council, in its Decree on Eastern Catholic Churches (Orientalium Ecclesiarum), stated the following points regarding Eastern heritage, patriarchs, sacraments and worship.

Venerable Churches: The Catholic Church holds in high esteem the institutions of the Eastern Churches, their liturgical rites, ecclesiastical traditions, and Christian way of life. For, distinguished as they are by their venerable antiquity, they are bright with that tradition which was handed down from the Apostles through the Fathers, and which forms part of the divinely revealed and undivided heritage of the universal Church (No. 1). That Church, Holy and Catholic, which is the Mystical Body of Christ, is made up of the faithful who are organically united in the Holy Spirit through the same faith, the same sacraments, and the same government and who, combining into various groups held together by a hierarchy, form separate Churches or rites. It is the mind of the Catholic Church that each individual Church or rite retain its traditions whole and entire, while adjusting its way of life to the various needs of time and place (No. 2).

Such individual Churches, whether of the East or of the West, although they differ somewhat among themselves in what are called rites (that is, in liturgy, ecclesiastical discipline, and spiritual heritage) are, nevertheless, equally entrusted to the pastoral guidance of the Roman Pontiff, the divinely appointed successor of St. Peter in supreme government over the universal Church. They are consequently of equal dignity, so that none of them is superior to the others by reason of rite (No. 3).

Eastern Heritage: Each and every Catholic, as also the baptized of every non-Catholic Church or community who enters into the fullness of Catholic communion, should everywhere retain his proper rite, cherish it, and observe it to the best of his ability (No. 4). The Churches of the East, as much as those of the West, fully enjoy the right, and are in duty bound, to rule themselves. Each should do so according to its proper and individual procedures (No. 5). All Eastern rite members should know and be convinced that they can and should always preserve their lawful liturgical rites and their established way of life, and that these should not be altered except by way of an appropriate and organic development (No. 6)

Patriarchs: The institution of the patriarchate has existed in the Church from the earliest times and was recognized by the first ecumenical Synods. By the name Eastern Patriarch is meant the bishop who has jurisdiction over all bishops (including metropolitans), clergy, and people of his own territory or rite, in accordance with the norms of law and without prejudice to the primacy of the Roman Pontiff (No. 7). Though some of the patriarchates of the Eastern Churches are of later origin than others, all are equal in patriarchal dignity. Still the honorary and lawfully established order of precedence among them is to be preserved (No. 8). In keeping with the most ancient tradition of the Church, the Patriarchs of the Eastern Churches are to be accorded exceptional respect, since each presides over his patriarchate as father and head.

This sacred Synod, therefore, decrees that their rights and privileges should be re-established in accord with the ancient traditions of each Church and the decrees of the ecumenical Synods. The rights and privileges in question are those which flourished when East and West were in union, though they should be somewhat adapted to modern conditions.

The Patriarchs with their synods constitute the superior authority for all affairs of the patriarchate, including the right to establish new eparchies and to nominate bishops of their rite within the territorial bounds of the patriarchate, without prejudice to the inalienable right of the Roman Pontiff to intervene in individual cases (No. 9).

What has been said of Patriarchs applies as well, under the norm of law, to major archbishops, who preside over the whole of some individual Church or rite (No. 10).

Sacraments: This sacred Ecumenical Synod endorses and lauds the ancient discipline of the sacraments existing in the Eastern Churches, as also the practices connected with their celebration and administration (No. 12).

With respect to the minister of holy chrism (confirmation), let that practice be fully restored which existed among Easterners in most ancient times. Priests, therefore, can validly confer this sacrament, provided they use chrism blessed by a Patriarch or bishop (No. 13).

In conjunction with baptism or otherwise, all Eastern-Rite priests can confer this sacrament validly on all the faithful of any rite, including the Latin; licitly, however, only if the regulations of both common and particular law are observed. Priests of the Latin rite, to the extent of the faculties they enjoy for administering this sacrament, can confer it also on the faithful of Eastern Churches, without prejudice to rite.

They do so licitly if the regulations of both common and particular law are observed (No. 14).

The faithful are bound on Sundays and feast days to attend the divine liturgy or, according to the regulations or custom of their own rite, the celebration of the Divine Praises. That the faithful may be able to satisfy their obligation more easily, it is decreed that this obligation can be fulfilled from the Vespers of the vigil to the end of the Sunday or the feast day (No. 15). Because of the everyday intermingling of the communicants of diverse Eastern Churches in the same Eastern region or territory, the faculty for hearing confession, duly and unrestrictedly granted by his proper bishop to a priest of any rite, is applicable to the entire territory of the grantor, also to the places and the faithful belonging to any other rite in the same territory, unless an Ordinary of the place explicitly decides otherwise with respect to the places pertaining to his rite (No. 16).

This sacred Synod ardently desires that where it has fallen into disuse the office of the permanent diaconate be restored. The legislative authority of each individual church should decide about the subdiaconate and the minor orders (No. 17).

By way of preventing invalid marriages between Eastern Catholics and baptized Eastern non-Catholics, and in the interests of the permanence and sanctity of marriage and of domestic harmony, this sacred Synod decrees that the canonical 'form' for the celebration of such marriages obliges only for lawfulness. For their validity, the presence of a sacred minister suffices, as long as the other requirements of law are honored (No. 18).

Worship: Henceforth, it will be the exclusive right of an ecumenical Synod or the Apostolic See to establish, transfer, or suppress feast days common to all the Eastern Churches. To establish, transfer, or suppress feast days for any of the individual Churches is within the competence not only of the Apostolic See but also of a patriarchal or archiepiscopal synod, provided due consideration is given to the entire region and to other individual Churches (No. 19). Until such time as all Christians desirably concur on a fixed day for the celebration of Easter, and with a view meantime to promoting unity among the Christians of a given area or nation, it is left to the Patriarchs or supreme authorities of a place to reach a unanimous agreement, after ascertaining the views of all concerned, on a single Sunday for the observance of Easter (No. 20). With respect to rules concerning sacred seasons, individual faithful dwelling outside the area or territory of their own rite may conform completely to the established custom of the place where they live. When members of a family belong to different rites, they are all permitted to observe sacred seasons according to the rules of any one of these rites (No. 21). From ancient times the Divine Praises have been held in high esteem among all Eastern Churches. Eastern clerics and religious should celebrate these Praises as the laws and customs of their own traditions require. To the extent they can, the faithful too should follow the example of their forebears by assisting devoutly at the Divine Praises (No. 22).

Restoration of Ancient Practices

An "Instruction for the Application of the Liturgical Prescriptions of the Code of Canons of the Eastern Churches" was published in Italian by the Congregation for Eastern-Rite Churches in January, 1996. Msgr. Alan Detscher, executive director of the U.S. bishops' Secretariat for the Liturgy, said it was the first instruction on liturgical renewal of the Eastern Catholic Churches since the Second Vatican Council (1962-65).

JURISDICTIONS AND FAITHFUL OF THE EASTERN CATHOLIC CHURCHES

Introduction

The Church originated in Palestine, whence it spread to other regions of the world where certain places became key centers of Christian life with great influence on the local churches in their respective areas. These centers developed into the ancient patriarchates of Constantinople, Alexandria, Antioch and Jerusalem in the East, and Rome in the West. The main lines of Eastern Church patriarchal organization and usages were drawn before the Roman Empire became two empires, East (Byzantine) and West (Roman), in 292. Other churches with distinctive traditions grew up beyond the boundaries of the Roman Empire in Persia, Armenia, Syria, Egypt, Ethiopia, and India. The "nestorian" church in Persia, known today as the Assyrian Church of the East, broke communion with the rest of the church in the wake of the Council of Ephesus (431) whose teachings it did not accept. The "monophysite" churches of Armenia, Syria, Egypt, Ethiopia, Eritrea and India (known today as the Oriental Orthodox Churches) did not accept the christological teachings of the Council of Chalcedon (451) and so broke away from the church within the Roman Empire. And finally, in the wake of the mutual excommunications of 1054 between the Patriarch of Constantinople and the papal legate, the church within the empire divided into what would become the Catholic Church in the West and the Orthodox Church in the East. This was a lengthy process of estrangement that culminated only in 1204 and the sack of Constantinople by the Latin Crusaders.

In the following centuries, attempts to overcome these divisions took place, most notably at the Second Council of Lyons in 1274 and the Council of Ferrara-Florence in 1438-39. Both failed. Subsequently, the Catholic Church began to send missionaries to work with separated Eastern Christians, and some groups within those churches spontaneously asked to enter into full communion with Rome. Thus began the formation of the Eastern Catholic Churches, which retained most of the liturgical, canonical, spiritual and theological patrimony of their non-Catholic counterparts.

The Code of Canons of the Eastern Churches groups these churches today into four categories: patriarchal, major archepiscopal, metropolitan, and other churches *sui iuris*. In common usage, an eparchy is equivalent to a diocese in the Latin rite.

STATISTICS

(Principal source: Annuario Pontificio.)

The following statistics are the sum of those reported

for Eastern Catholic jurisdictions only, and do not include Eastern Catholics under the jurisdiction of Latin bishops. Some of the figures reported are only approximate. The churches are grouped according to their liturgical traditions.

PATRIARCHS

The current Patriarchs of the Eastern Catholic Churches (as of Aug. 15, 2003) are as follows:

Abdel-Ahad, Ignatius Peter VIII: b. June 28, 1930; ord. Oct. 17, 1954; cons. bp. June 21, 1997; Patriarch of Antioch of the Syrians, Feb. 16, 2001; granted "ecclesiastical communion" with Pope John Paul II, Feb. 20, 2001.

Ghattas, Stéphanos II, C.M.: Patriarch of Alexandria; for details, see under Cardinals, College of.

Laham, Gregory III: b. Dec. 15, 1933; ord. Feb. 15, 1959; cons. bp., Nov. 27, 1981; patriarch of Greek Melkites, Nov. 29, 2000; granted "ecclesiastical communion" with Pope John Paul II, Dec. 5, 2000.

Sfeir, Nasrallah Pierre: Patriarch of Antioch of the Maronites; for details, *see* Cardinals, College of.

Tarmouni, Nerses XIX Bedros: b. Jan. 17, 1940, in Cairo, Egypt; ord. Aug. 15, 1965; patriarch of Cilicia of the Armenians, Oct. 7, 1999; granted "ecclesiastical communion" with the Pope John Paul II, Oct. 13, 1999.

Patriarch Raphaël I Bidawid, patriarch of Babylon of the Chaldeans from 1989, died on July 7, 2003.

ALEXANDRIAN

The liturgical tradition of Egypt, in particular that of the early Greek Patriarchate of Alexandria. In the Egyptian desert monasteries the rite evolved in a distinctive way and eventually became that of the Coptic Orthodox Church. The Greek Patriarchate of Alexandria adopted the Byzantine rite by the 12th century. The Coptic rite, with its Alexandrian origins, spread to Ethiopia in the 4th century where it underwent substantial modifications under strong Syrian influence. The Catholic Churches in this group are:

The Coptic Catholic Church (Patriarchate): Six eparchies in Egypt, 216,990.

Catholic missionaries were present since the 17th century. The Patriarchate was established first in 1824 and renewed in 1895. Liturgical languages are Coptic and Arabic.

The Ethiopian Catholic Church (Metropolitanate): Two eparchies in Ethiopia and three in Eritrea; 205,999. Catholic missionary activity began in the 19th century, and the present ecclesiastical structure dates from 1961. The liturgical languages are Ge'ez and Amharic.

ANTIOCHIAN

The liturgical tradition of Antioch, one of the great centers of the early Christian world, also known as West Syrian. In Syria it developed under strong influence of Jerusalem, especially the Liturgy of St. James, into the form used by today's Syrian Orthodox and Catholics in the Middle East and India. The Maronites of Lebanon developed their own liturgical traditions under the influence of both the Antiochian and Chaldean rites.

The Catholic Churches of this group are:

The Syro-Malankara Catholic Church (Metropolitanate): Four eparchies in India; 395,476.

Began in 1930 when two bishops, a priest, a deacon and a layman of the Malankara Orthodox Church were received into full communion with Rome. The liturgical language is Malayalam.

The Maronite Catholic Church (Patriarchate): Ten eparchies in Lebanon, three in Syria, two in the United States, and one each in Cyprus, Egypt, Argentina, Brazil, Australia, Canada, and Mexico, plus patriarchal exarchates in Jordan and Jerusalem; 3,083,754.

Founded by St. Maron in the 4th century, the Maronites claim to have always been in communion with Rome. They have no counterpart among the separated Eastern churches. The patriarchate dates to the 8th century, and was confirmed by Pope Innocent III in 1216. Liturgical language is Arabic.

The Syrian Catholic Church (Patriarchate): Four eparchies in Syria, two in Iraq, and one each in Lebanon, Egypt, and North America, and patriarchal exarchates in Turkey and Iraq/Kuwait; 112,849.

Catholic missionary activity among the Syrian Orthodox began in the 17th century, and there has been an uninterrupted series of Catholic patriarchs since 1783. The liturgical languages are Syriac/Aramaic and Arabic.

ARMENIAN

The liturgical tradition of the Armenian Apostolic and Catholic Churches. It contains elements of the Syriac, Jerusalem, and Byzantine rites. From the 5th to the 7th centuries there was strong influence from Syria and Jerusalem. More Byzantine usages were adopted later, and in the Middle Ages elements of the Latin tradition were added.

The Armenian Catholic Church (Patriarchate): Two eparchies in Syria, one each in Lebanon, Iran, Iraq, Egypt, Turkey, Ukraine, France and Argentina. Apostolic Exarchate for the United States, and Ordinariates in Greece, Romania, and Eastern Europe (Armenia); 369,297.

Catholic missionaries had been working among the Armenians since the 14th century, and an Armenian Catholic patriarchate was established in Lebanon in 1742. The liturgical language is classical Armenian. His Beatitude Nerses Bedros XIX Tarmouni, canonically elected as patriarch of Cilicia of the Armenians, by the Synod of Bishops of the Armenian Catholic Church was approved by Pope John Paul II on October 18, 1999.

BYZANTINE

The tradition of the Eastern Orthodox and Byzantine Catholic Churches which originated in the Orthodox Patriarchate of Constantinople (Byzantium). Its present form is a synthesis of Constantinopolitan and Palestinian elements that took place in the monasteries between the 9th and 14th centuries. It is by far the most widely used Eastern liturgical tradition. The Catholic Churches of this group are:

Albanians: One apostolic administration in southern Albania; 2,800. Very small groups of Albanian Orthodox became Catholic in 1628 and again in 1900; liturgical language is Albanian.

Belarusans (formerly Byelorussian, also known as White Russian): No hierarchy, Apostolic Visitator. Most Belarusan Orthodox became Catholic with the Union of Brest in 1595-6, but this union was short lived. A modest revival has taken place since the end of communism. The liturgical language is Belarusan.

The Bulgarian Catholic Church: One apostolic exarchate in Bulgaria; 15,000. Originated with a group of Bulgarian Orthodox who became Catholic in 1861; liturgical language is Old Slavonic.

Eparchy of Krizevci: One eparchy located in Zagreb with jurisdiction over Slovenia, Croatia, Bosnia-Herzegovina, Serbia and Montenegro; Apostolic Exarchate in Macedonia; 48,174. A bishop for former Serbian Orthodox living in Catholic Croatia was first appointed in 1611; liturgical languages are Old Slavonic and Croatian.

The Greek Catholic Church: Apostolic exarchates in Greece and Turkey; 2,345. Catholic missionaries in Constantinople formed a small group of Byzantine Catholics there in the mid-19th century. Most of them moved to Greece in the 1920s. The liturgical language is Greek.

The Hungarian Catholic Church: One eparchy and one apostolic exarchate in Hungary; 278,000.

Descendants of groups of Orthodox in Hungary who became Catholic in the 17th century and after. The liturgical language is Hungarian.

The Italo-Albanian Catholic Church: Two eparchies, one territorial abbey in Italy; 60,548.

Descended mostly from Albanian Orthodox who came to southern Italy and Sicily in the 15th century and eventually became Catholic; liturgical languages are Greek and Italian.

The Melkite Greek Catholic Church (Patriarchate): Five eparchies in Syria, seven in Lebanon, one each in Jordan, Israel, Brazil, US, Canada, Mexico, and Australia. Apostolic Exarchates in Venezuela and Argentina, and patriarchal exarchates in Iraq and Kuwait; 1,295,061.

Catholic missionaries began work within the Greek Orthodox Patriarchate of Antioch in the mid-17th century. In 1724 it split into Catholic and Orthodox counterparts, the Catholics becoming known popularly as Melkites. Liturgical languages are Greek and Arabic.

The Romanian Greek Catholic Church (Metropolitanate): Five eparchies in Romania and one in the US; 752,500.

Romanian Orthodox in Transylvania formally entered into union with Rome in 1700; the liturgical language is Romanian.

Russians: No hierarchy. An apostolic exarchate was established for Russia in 1917 and for Russians in China in 1928, but neither is functioning today. Five parishes exist in the diaspora.

The Ruthenian Catholic Church (Metropolitanate in the United States): One eparchy in Ukraine, four in the United States, and an apostolic exarchate in the Czech Republic. Originated with the reception of 63 Orthodox priests into the Catholic Church at the Union of Uzhhorod in 1646. Liturgical languages are Old Slavonic and English; 610,688.

The Slovak Catholic Church: One eparchy and one apostolic exarchate in Slovakia, and one eparchy in Canada; 221,331.

Also originated with the Union of Uzhhorod in 1646; eparchy of Presov was established for them in 1818. Liturgical languages are Old Slavonic and Slovak.

The Ukrainian Greek Catholic Church (Major Archbishopric): Eight eparchies and two archepiscopal exarchates in Ukraine, two eparchies in Poland, five eparchies in Canada, four in the United States, one each in Australia, Brazil and Argentina, apostolic exarchates in Great Britain, Germany, and France; 4,366,131.

Originated with the Union of Brest between the Orthodox Metropolitanate of Kiev and the Catholic Church in 1595-6. Liturgical languages are Old Slavonic and Ukrainian.

CHALDEAN

Also called East Syrian, the liturgical tradition of the Chaldean Catholic and Syro-Malabar Catholic Churches as well as the Assyrian Church of the East. Descends from the ancient rite of the church of Mesopotamia in the Persian Empire. It is celebrated in the eastern dialect of classical Syriac. The Catholic Churches of this tradition are:

The Chaldean Catholic Church (Patriarchate): Ten eparchies in Iraq, three in Iran, two in the U.S., one each in Lebanon, Egypt, Syria, and Turkey; 343,501.

A group of disaffected members of the ("Nestorian") Assyrian Church of the East asked for union with Rome in 1553. In that year Pope Julius III ordained their leader a bishop and named him Patriarch; liturgical languages are Syriac, Arabic.

The Syro-Malabar Catholic Church (Major Archbishopric): 22 eparchies in India, one in the U.S.; 3,588,172.

Descended from Thomas Christians of India who became Catholic in the wake of Portuguese colonization; the diocese of Ernakulam-Angamaly was raised to Major Archepiscopal status in 1993; the liturgical language is Malayalam.

EASTERN JURISDICTIONS

For centuries Eastern Churches were identifiable with a limited number of nationality and language groups in certain countries of the Middle East, Eastern Europe, Asia and Africa. The persecution of religion in the former Soviet Union since 1917 and in communist-controlled countries for more than 40 years following World War II — in addition to decimating and destroying the Church in those places — resulted in the emigration of many Eastern Catholics from their homelands. This forced emigration, together with voluntary emigration, has led to the spread of Eastern Churches to many other countries.

Europe

(Bishop Krikor Ghabroyan, of the Armenian Eparchy of Sainte-Croix-de-Paris, France, is apostolic visitator for Armenian Catholics in Western Europe who do not have their own bishop. Bishop Youssef Ibrahim Sarraf of Cairo of the Chaldeans is apostolic visitator for Chaldeans in Europe. Bishop Samis Mazloum is apostolic visitator for Maronites in Western and Northern Europe. Archimandrite Jan Sergiusz Gajek is Apostolic Visitator for Greek Catholics in Belarus.)

Albania: Byzantine apostolic administration.
Austria: Byzantine ordinariate.
Bulgaria: Bulgarian apostolic exarchate
Croatia: Eparchy of Krizevci.

Czech Republic: Ruthenian apostolic exarchate.

France: Ukrainian apostolic exarchate. Armenian eparchy (1986). Ordinariate for all other Eastern Catholics.

Germany: Ukrainian apostolic exarchate.

Great Britain: Ukrainian apostolic exarchate.

Greece: Byzantine apostolic exarchate. Armenian ordinariate.

Hungary: Hungarian Byzantine eparchy, apostolic exarchate

Italy: Two Italo-Albanian eparchies, one abbacy.

Macedonia: One apostolic exarchate.

Poland: Ukrainian metropolitan see (1996), one eparchy. Ordinariate for all other Eastern Catholics.

Romania: Romanian Byzantine metropolitan, four eparchies; Armenian ordinariate.

Russia: Russian apostolic exarchate (for Byzantine Catholics in Moscow).

Slovakia: Slovak Byzantine eparchy, one apostolic exarchate.

Ukraine: Armenian archeparchy; Ruthenian eparchy; Ukrainian major archbishopric, seven eparchies.

Asia

Armenia: Armenian ordinariate (for Armenians of Eastern Europe).

China: Russian Byzantine apostolic exarchate.

Cyprus: Maronite archeparchy.

India: Syro-Malankara metropolitan see, three eparchies.
Syro-Malabar major archbishopric (1993), three metropolitan sees (1995), 18 eparchies.

Iran: Two Chaldean metropolitan sees, one archeparchy, one eparchy; Armenian eparchy.

Iraq: Two Syrian archeparchies; Melkite patriarchal exarchate; Chaldean patriarchate, two metropolitan sees, three archeparchies and five eparchies; Armenian archeparchy.

Israel (including Jerusalem): Syrians patriarchal exarchate; Maronite archeparchy; Melkite archeparchy, patriarchal exarchate; Chaldean patriarchal exarchate; Armenian patriarchal exarchate.

Jordan: Melkite archeparchy.

Kuwait: Melkite patriarchal exarchate; Syrian patriarchate exarchate.

Syria: Two Maronite archeparchies, one eparchy; two Syrian metropolitan and two archeparchal sees; Melkite patriarchate, four metropolitan sees, one archeparchy; Chaldean eparchy; Armenian archeparchy, one eparchy .

Turkey: Syrian patriarchal exarchate; Greek apostolic exarchate; Chaldean archeparchy; Armenian archeparchy.

Oceania

Australia: Ukrainian eparchy; Melkite eparchy (1987); Maronite eparchy.

Africa

Egypt: Coptic patriarchate, five eparchies; Maronite eparchy; Syrian eparchy; Melkite patriarchal dependency; Chaldean eparchy; Armenian eparchy.

Eritrea: Three Ethiopian eparchies.

Ethiopia: Ethiopian metropolitan see, one eparchy.

Sudan: Melkite patriarchal dependency.

North America

Canada: One Ukrainian metropolitan, four eparchies; Slovak eparchy; Melkite eparchy; Armenian apostolic exarchate for Canada and the U.S. (New York is see city); Maronite eparchy.

United States: Two Maronite eparchies; Syrian eparchy (1995); one Ukrainian metropolitan see, three eparchies; one Ruthenian metropolitan see, three eparchies; Melkite eparchy; Romanian eparchy; a new Syro-Malabar eparchy based in Chicago; Belarusan apostolic visitator; Armenian apostolic exarchate for Canada and U.S. (New York is see city); two Chaldean eparchies; other Eastern Catholics are under the jurisdiction of local Latin bishops. (*See* **Eastern Catholics in the United States.**)

Mexico: Melkite eparchy; Maronite eparchy (1995).

South America

Armenian Catholics in Latin America (including Mexico and excluding Argentina) are under the jurisdiction of an apostolic exarchate (see city, Buenos Aires, Argentina).

Argentina: Ukrainian eparchy; Maronite eparchy; Armenian eparchy; Melkite apostolic exarchate; ordinariate for all other Eastern Catholics.

Brazil: Maronite eparchy; Melkite eparchy; Ukrainian eparchy; ordinariate for all other Eastern Catholics.

Venezuela: Melkite apostolic exarchate.

Synods, Assemblies

These assemblies are collegial bodies that have pastoral authority over members of the Eastern Catholic Churches. (Canons 102-113, 152-153, 322 of Oriental Code of Canon Law.)

Patriarchal Synods:

Synod of the Coptic Catholic Church: Stephanos II Ghattas, C.M., patriarch of Alexandria of the Copts.

Synod of the Greek-Melkite Catholic Church: Gregory III Laham, patriarch of Antioch of the Greek Catholics-Melkites.

Synod of the Syrian Catholic Church: Ignatius Peter VIII, patriarch of Antioch of the Syrians.

Synod of the Maronite Church: Cardinal Nasrallah Pierre Sfeir, patriarch of Antioch of the Maronites.

Synod of the Chaldean Church: Raphaël I Bidawid, patriarch of Babylonia of the Chaldeans.

Synod of the Armenian Catholic Church: Nerses Bedros XIX Tarmouni, patriarch of Cilicia of the Armenians.

Major Archiepiscopal Synods:

The Synod of the Ukrainian Catholic Church (raised to major archiepiscopal status Dec. 23, 1963): Cardinal Lubomir Husar, major archbishop of Lviv of the Ukrainians, president.

The Synod of the Syro-Malabar Church (raised to major archiepiscopal status, Jan. 29, 1993): Cardinal Varkey Vithayathil, C.SS.R., major archbishop of Ernakulam-Angamaly of the Syro-Malabars, president.

Councils, Assemblies, Conferences

Council of Ethiopian Churches: Most Rev. Berhane-Yesus Demerew Souraphiel, C.M. of Addis Ababa, president.

Council of Romanian Churches: Abp. Lucian Muresan of Fagaras and Alba Julia, president.

Council of Ruthenian Churches, U.S.A.: Metropolitan of Pittsburgh of the Byzantines, presently vacant, president.

Council of Syro-Malankarese Churches: Abp. Cyril Baselios Malancharuvil, O.I.C., of Trivandrum of the Syro-Malankarese, president.

Assembly of the Catholic Hierarchy of Egypt (Dec. 5, 1983): Cardinal Stéphanos II Ghattas, C.M., patriarch of Alexandria of the Copts, president.

Assembly of Catholic Patriarchs and Bishops of Lebanon: Cardinal Nasrallah Pierre Sfeir, patriarch of Antioch of the Maronites, president.

Assembly of Ordinaries of the Syrian Arab Republic: Maximos V Hakim, patriarch of Antioch of the Greek Catholics-Melkites, president.

Assembly of Catholic Ordinaries of the Holy Land (Jan. 27, 1992): Michel Sabbah, patriarch of Jerusalem of the Latins, president.

Interritual Union of the Bishops of Iraq: Raphaël I Bidawid, patriarch of Babylonia of the Chaldeans, president.

Iranian Episcopal Conference (Aug. 11, 1977): Most Rev. Vartan Tékéyan, bishop of Ispahan of the Armenians of the Armenians, president.

Episcopal Conference of Turkey (Nov. 30, 1987): Most Rev. Louis A. Pelâtre, A.A., vicar apostolic of Istanbul, president.

EASTERN CATHOLIC CHURCHES IN THE U.S.

(Statistics, from the 2003 Annuario Pontificio unless noted otherwise, are membership figures reported by Eastern jurisdictions. Additional Eastern Catholics are included in statistics for Latin dioceses.)

Byzantine Tradition

Ukrainians: There were 105,074 reported in four jurisdictions in the U.S.: the metropolitan see of Philadelphia (1924, metropolitan 1958) and the suffragan sees of Stamford, Conn. (1956), St. Nicholas of Chicago (1961) and St. Josaphat in Parma (1983).

Ruthenians: There were 100,688 reported in four jurisdictions in the U.S.: the metropolitan see of Pittsburgh (est. 1924 at Pittsburgh; metropolitan and transferred to Munhall, 1969; transferred to Pittsburgh, 1977) and the suffragan sees of Passaic, N.J. (1963), Parma, Ohio (1969) and Van Nuys, Calif. (1981). Hungarian and Croatian Byzantine Catholics in the U.S. are also under the jurisdiction of Ruthenian bishops.

Melkites: There were 28,026 reported under the jurisdiction of the Melkite eparchy of Newton, Mass. (established as an exarchate, 1965; eparchy, 1976).

Romanians: There were 5,000 reported in 15 Romanian Catholic Byzantine Rite parishes in the U.S., under the jurisdiction of the Romanian eparchy of St. George Martyr, Canton, Ohio (established as an exarchate, 1982; eparchy, 1987).

Belarusans: Have one parish in the U.S. — Christ the Redeemer, Chicago, IL.

Russians: Have parishes in California (St. Andrew, El Segundo, and Our Lady of Fatima Center, San Francisco); New York (St. Michael's Chapel of St. Patrick's Old Cathedral). They are under the jurisdiction of local Latin bishops.

Alexandrian Tradition

Copts: Have a Catholic Chapel—Resurrection, in Brooklyn, N.Y., and St. Mary's Coptic Catholic parish, Los Angeles, CA.

Antiochian Tradition

Maronites: There were 56,133 reported in two jurisdictions in the U.S.: the eparchy of St. Maron, Brooklyn (established at Detroit as an exarchate, 1966; eparchy, 1972; transferred to Brooklyn, 1977) and the eparchy of Our Lady of Lebanon of Los Angeles (resident in St. Louis, MO, established Mar. 1, 1994).

Syrians: The eparchy of Our Lady of the Deliverance of Newark with 12,390 faithful (see city, Newark, N.J.) was established in 1995 for Syrian Catholics of the U.S. and Canada.

Malankarese: Have a mission in Chicago.

Armenian Tradition

An apostolic exarchate for Canada and the United States (see city, New York) was established July 3, 1981; 36,000 in the two countries.

Chaldean Tradition

Chaldeans: There were 90,000 reported under the jurisdictions of the eparchy of St. Thomas the Apostle of Detroit (established as an exarchate, 1982; eparchy, 1986) and the eparchy of St. Peter the Apostle of San Diego (established on May 21, 2002).

Syro-Malabarese (Malabar): Have an eparchy based in Chicago with five parishes around the country. Estimated 112,000 faithful with 18 diocesan and 13 religious order priests.

Eastern Catholic Associates

Eastern Catholic Associates is the association of all Eastern Catholic bishops and their equivalents in law in the United States, representing the Armenian, Chaldean, Maronite, Melkite, Syriac, Romanian, Ruthenian and Ukrainian churches. The Syro-Malabar and Russian churches are also represented even though they do not have bishops in the U.S. President: Bishop Robert M. Moskal, Eparch of St. Josaphat, P.O. Box 347180, Parma, OH 44134. The Vice President is Bishop Basil Schott, OFM, metropolitan abp. of Pittsburgh.

The association meets at the same time as the United States Conference of Catholic Bishops in the fall of each year.

BYZANTINE DIVINE LITURGY

The Divine Liturgy in all rites is based on the consecration of bread and wine by the narration-reactualization of the actions of Christ at the Last Supper, and the calling down of the Holy Spirit. Aside from this fundamental usage, there are differences between the Roman (Latin) Rite and Eastern Rites, and among the Eastern Rites themselves. Following is a general description of the Byzantine Divine Liturgy which is in widest use in the Eastern Churches.

In the Byzantine, as in all Eastern Rites, the bread

and wine are prepared at the start of the Liturgy. The priest does this in a little niche or at a table in the sanctuary. Taking a round loaf of leavened bread stamped with religious symbols, he cuts out a square host and other particles while reciting verses expressing the symbolism of the action. When the bread and wine are ready, he says a prayer of offering and incenses the oblations, the altar, the icons and the people.

Liturgy of the Catechumens: At the altar a litany for all classes of people is sung by the priest. The congregation answers, "Lord, have mercy." The Little Entrance comes next. In procession, the priest leaves the sanctuary carrying the Book of the Gospels, and then returns. He sings prayers especially selected for the day and the feast. These are followed by the solemn singing of the prayer, "Holy God, Holy Mighty One, Holy Immortal One." The Epistle follows. The Gospel is sung or read by the priest facing the people at the middle door of the sanctuary.

An interruption after the Liturgy of the Catechumens, formerly an instructional period for those learning the faith, is clearly marked. Catechumens, if present, are dismissed with a prayer. Following this are a prayer and litany for the faithful.

Great Entrance: The Great Entrance or solemn Offertory Procession then takes place. The priest first says a long silent prayer for himself, in preparation for the great act to come. Again he incenses the oblations, the altar, the icons and people. He goes to the table on the Gospel side for the veil-covered paten and chalice. When he arrives back at the sanctuary door, he announces the intention of the Mass in the prayer: "May the Lord God remember all of you in his kingdom, now and forever." After another litany, the congregation recites the Nicene Creed.

Consecration: The most solemn portion of the sacrifice is introduced by the preface, which is very much like the preface of the Roman Rite. At the beginning of the last phrase, the priest raises his voice to introduce the singing of the Sanctus. During the singing he reads the introduction to the words of consecration. The words of consecration are sung aloud, and the people sing "Amen" to both consecrations. As the priest raises the Sacred Species in solemn offering, he sings: "Thine of Thine Own we offer unto Thee in behalf of all and for all." A prayer to the Holy Spirit is followed by the commemorations, in which special mention is made of the all-holy, most blessed and glorious Lady, the Mother of God and ever-Virgin Mary. The dead are remembered and then the living.

Holy Communion: A final litany for spiritual gifts precedes the Our Father. The Sacred Body and Blood are elevated with the words, "Holy Things for the Holy." The Host is then broken and commingled with the Precious Blood. The priest recites preparatory prayers for Holy Communion, consumes the Sacred Species, and distributes Holy Communion to the people under the forms of both bread and wine. During this time the choir or congregation sings a communion verse.

The Liturgy closes quickly after this. The consecrated Species of bread and wine are removed to the side table to be consumed later by the priest. A prayer of thanksgiving is recited, a prayer for all the people is said in front of the icon of Christ, a blessing is invoked upon all, and the people are dismissed.

BYZANTINE CALENDAR

The Byzantine calendar has many distinctive features of its own, although it shares common elements with the Roman calendar — e.g., general purpose, commemoration of the mysteries of faith and of the saints, identical dates for some feasts. Among the distinctive things are the following. The liturgical year begins on Sept. 1, the Day of Indiction, in contrast with the Latin or Roman start on the First Sunday of Advent late in November or early in December. The Advent season begins on Dec. 10.

Cycles of the Year

As in the Roman usage, the dating of feasts follows the Gregorian Calendar. Formerly, until well into this century, the Julian Calendar was used. (The Julian Calendar, which is now about 13 days late, is still used by some Eastern Churches.) The year has several cycles, which include proper seasons, the feasts of saints, and series of New Testament readings. All of these elements of worship are contained in liturgical books of the rite. The ecclesiastical calendar, called the *Menologion,* explains the nature of feasts, other observances and matters pertaining to the liturgy for each day of the year. In some cases, its contents include the lives of saints and the history and meaning of feasts.

The Divine Liturgy (Mass) and Divine Office for the proper of the saints, fixed feasts, and the Christmas season are contained in the *Menaion*. The *Triodion* covers the pre-Lenten season of preparation for Easter; Lent begins two days before the Ash Wednesday observance of the Roman Rite. The Pentecostarion contains the liturgical services from Easter to the Sunday of All Saints, the first after Pentecost. The *Evangelion* and *Apostolos* are books in which the Gospels, and Acts of the Apostles and the Epistles, respectively, are arranged according to the order of their reading in the Divine Liturgy and Divine Office throughout the year.

The cyclic progression of liturgical music throughout the year, in successive and repetitive periods of eight weeks, is governed by the *Oktoechos*, the *Book of Eight Tones*.

Sunday Names

Many Sundays are named after the subject of the Gospel read in the Mass of the day or after the name of a feast falling on the day — e.g., Sunday of the Publican and Pharisee, of the Prodigal Son, of the Samaritan Woman, of St. Thomas the Apostle, of the Fore-Fathers (Old Testament Patriarchs).

Other Sundays are named in the same manner as in the Roman calendar e.g., numbered Sundays of Lent and after Pentecost.

Holy Days

The calendar lists about 28 holy days. Many of the major holy days coincide with those of the Roman calendar, but the feast of the Immaculate Conception is observed on Dec. 9 instead of Dec. 8, and the feast of All Saints falls on the Sunday after Pentecost rather than on Nov. 1. Instead of a single All Souls' Day, there are five All Souls' Saturdays. According to regulations in effect in the Byzantine (Ruthenian) Archeparchy of Pittsburgh and its suffragan sees of Passaic, Parma and Van Nuys, holy days are obligatory, solemn and simple, and attendance at the Divine Liturgy is required on five obligatory days — the feasts of the Epiphany, the Ascension, Sts. Peter and Paul, the Assumption of the Blessed Virgin Mary, and Christmas. Although attendance at the liturgy is not obligatory on 15 solemn and seven simple holy days, it is recommended. In the Byzantine (Ukrainian) Archeparchy of Philadelphia and its suffragan sees of St. Josaphat in Parma, St. Nicholas (Chicago) and Stamford, the obligatory feasts are the Epiphany, Annunciation, Ascension, SS. Peter & Paul, Dormition, and Christmas.

Lent

The first day of Lent — the Monday before Ash Wednesday of the Roman Rite — and Good Friday are days of strict abstinence for persons in the age bracket of obligation. No meat, eggs, or dairy products may be eaten on these days. All persons over the age of 14 must abstain from meat on Fridays during Lent, Holy Saturday, and the vigils of the feasts of Christmas and Epiphany; abstinence is urged, but is not obligatory, on Wednesdays of Lent. The abstinence obligation is not in force on certain "free" or "privileged" Fridays.

Synaxis

An observance without a counterpart in the Roman calendar is the synaxis. This is a commemoration, on the day following a feast, of persons involved with the occasion for the feast — e.g., Sept. 9, the day following the feast of the Nativity of the Blessed Virgin Mary, is the Synaxis of Joachim and Anna, her parents.

Holy Week

In the Byzantine Rite, Lent is liturgically concluded with the Saturday of Lazarus, the day before Palm Sunday, which commemorates the raising of Lazarus from the dead. On the following Monday, Tuesday and Wednesday, the Liturgy of the Presanctified is prescribed.

On Holy Thursday, the Liturgy of St. Basil the Great is celebrated together with Vespers.

The Divine Liturgy is not celebrated on Good Friday. On Holy Saturday, the Liturgy of St. Basil the Great is celebrated along with Vespers.

BYZANTINE FEATURES

Art: Named for the empire in which it developed, Byzantine art is a unique blend of imperial Roman and classic Hellenic culture with Christian inspiration. The art of the Greek Middle Ages, it reached a peak of development in the 10th or 11th century. Characteristic of its products, particularly in mosaic and painting, are majesty, dignity, refinement and grace. Its sacred paintings, called icons, are reverenced highly in all the Eastern Churches of the Byzantine tradition.

Church Building: The classical model of Byzantine church architecture is the Church of the Holy Wisdom (*Hagia Sophia*), built in Constantinople in the first half of the sixth century and still standing. The square structure, extended in some cases in the form of a cross, is topped by a distinctive onion-shaped dome and surmounted by a triple-bar cross. The altar is at the eastern end of building, where the wall bellies out to form an apse. The altar and sanctuary are separated from the body of the church by a fixed or movable screen, the iconostas, to which icons or sacred pictures are attached (see below).

Clergy: The Byzantine Churches have married as well as celibate priests. In places other than the U.S., where married candidates have not been accepted for ordination since about 1929, men already married can be ordained to the diaconate and priesthood and can continue in marriage after ordination. Celibate deacons and priests cannot marry after ordination; neither can a married priest remarry after the death of his wife. Bishops must be unmarried.

Iconostasis: A large screen decorated with sacred pictures or icons that separates the sanctuary from the nave of a church; its equivalent in the Roman Rite, for thus separating the sanctuary from the nave, is an altar rail. An iconostas has three doors through which the sacred ministers enter the sanctuary during the Divine Liturgy: smaller (north and south) Deacons' Doors and a large central Royal Door. The Deacons' Doors usually feature the icons of Sts. Gabriel and Michael; the Royal Door, the icons of the Evangelists—Matthew, Mark, Luke and John. To the right and left of the Royal Door are the icons of Christ the Teacher and of the Blessed Virgin Mary with the Infant Jesus. To the extreme right and left are the icons of the patron of the church and St. John the Baptist (or St. Nicholas of Myra). Immediately above the Royal Door is a picture of the Last Supper. To the right are six icons depicting the major feasts of Christ, and to the left are six icons portraying the major feasts of the Blessed Virgin Mary. Above the picture of the Last Supper is a large icon of Christ the King. Some icon screens also have pictures of the 12 Apostles and the major Old Testament prophets surmounted by a crucifixion scene.

Liturgical Language: In line with Eastern tradition, Byzantine practice has favored the use of the language of the people in the liturgy. Two great advocates of the practice were Sts. Cyril and Methodius, apostles of the Slavs, who devised the Cyrillic alphabet and pioneered the adoption of Slavonic in the liturgy.

Sacraments: Baptism is administered by immersion, and confirmation (Chrismation) is conferred at the same time. The Eucharist is administered by intinction, i.e., by giving the communicant a piece of consecrated leavened bread that has been dipped into the consecrated wine. When giving absolution in the sacrament of penance, the priest holds his stole over the head of the penitent. Distinctive marriage ceremonies include the crowning of the bride and groom. Ceremonies for anointing the sick closely resemble those of the Roman Rite. Holy orders are conferred by a bishop.

Sign of the Cross: The sign of the cross in conjunction with a deep bow expresses reverence for the presence of Christ in the Blessed Sacrament. (See also entry in Glossary.)

VESTMENTS, APPURTENANCES

Antimension: A silk or linen cloth laid on the altar for the Liturgy; it may be decorated with a picture of the burial of Christ and the instruments of his passion; the relics of martyrs are sewn into the front border.

Asteriskos: Made of two curved bands of gold or silver which cross each other to form a double arch; a star depends from the junction, which forms a cross; it is placed over the *diskos* holding the consecrated bread and is covered with a veil.

Diskos: A shallow plate, which may be elevated on a small stand, corresponding to the Roman-Rite paten.

Eileton: A linen cloth that corresponds to the Roman-Rite corporal.

Epimanikia: Ornamental cuffs; the right cuff symbolizing strength, the left, patience and good will.

Epitrachelion: A stole with ends sewn together, having a loop through which the head is passed; its several crosses symbolize priestly duties.

Lance: A metal knife used for cutting up the bread to be consecrated during the Liturgy.

Phelonion: An ample cape, long in the back and sides and cut away in front; symbolic of the higher gifts of the Holy Spirit.

Poterion: A chalice or cup that holds the wine and Precious Blood.

Spoon: Used in administering Holy Communion by intinction; consecrated leavened bread is dipped into consecrated wine and spooned onto the tongue of the communicant.

Sticharion: A long white garment of linen or silk with wide sleeves and decorated with embroidery; formerly the vestment for clerics in minor orders, acolytes, lectors, chanters, and subdeacons; symbolic of purity.

Veils: Three are used, one to cover the *poterion*, the second to cover the *diskos*, and the third to cover both.

Zone: A narrow clasped belt made of the same material as the *epitrachelion*; symbolic of the wisdom of the priest, his strength against enemies of the Church and his willingness to perform holy duties.

CODE OF CANONS OF THE EASTERN CHURCHES

Just as the Latin Catholics are governed by a specific set of universal laws, so too are the Eastern Catholics. The Code of Canons of the Eastern Churches serves as the legal corpus for the Eastern Churches, providing the legal principles for the preservation of the rich heritage of these Churches. The overarching theological structure for the Code was enunciated by the Second Vatican Council in its declaration in *Orientalium Ecclesiarum* (3):

These individual Churches, whether of the East or the West, although they differ somewhat among themselves in rite (to use the current phrase), that is, in liturgy, ecclesiastical discipline, and spiritual heritage, are, nevertheless, each as much as the others, entrusted to the pastoral government of the Roman Pontiff, the divinely appointed successor of St. Peter in primacy over the universal Church. They are consequently of equal dignity, so that none of them is superior to the others as regards rite and they enjoy the same rights and are under the same obligations, also in respect of preaching the Gospel to the whole world (cf. Mark 16:15) under the guidance of the Roman Pontiff.

Background

The creation and promulgation of the Code for the Eastern Churches began during the pontificate of Pope Pius XI (1922-39) when he established a commission of cardinals in 1929 to examine the requirements for a code. This preparatory commission was succeeded in 1935 by a new commission with the task of undertaking the actual composition of the Code. What followed was a gradual process of promulgations. Pope Pius XII (1939-58) issued a series of apostolic letters as different elements of the Eastern Code were completed. This method of promulgation continued until 1972 when Pope Paul VI (1963-78) established the Pontifical Commission for the Revision of the Code of Eastern Canon Law.

The commission approached the initial stages of its work quite deliberately. Extensive consultation was made with canonists as well as many bishops of the Eastern Churches. These efforts culminated in November 1988 with the unanimous vote of the commission's members accepting the draft of the new Code. On October 18, 1990, Pope John Paul II officially promulgated the Code of Canons of the Eastern Churches. The Code became effective on October 1, 1991. As the decree makes clear, in accordance with this universal legislation, each Eastern Catholic Church is to develop its own particular law. This stands in contrast to the Code of Canon Law that applies only to the single Latin Church.

Contents and Structure

The Code of Canons of the Eastern Churches marked a significant milestone in the history of Church law. It represented the long process in the development of Canon Law for the Eastern Churches throughout the 20th century and was an eloquent means of both respecting and preserving the proper discipline of those Churches. It was noted from the start that the Code for the Eastern Catholics was organized differently in comparison with the Code of Canon Law for the Latin Rite. There are different elements to Eastern Law, and the Code presents the independence of these laws from the Latin Rite, save, of course, for those canons that give reference to the Pope. Nevertheless, while safeguarding the centuries' old traditions and heritage of the Eastern Catholic Churches, the differences are not disruptive to the unity of the Church. Rather, the Code is an instrument in moving toward appropriate unity. As the 1996 document, "Applying the Liturgical Prescriptions of the Code of Canons of the Eastern Catholic Churches" (9), by the Congregation for the Eastern Churches states:

The Code of Canons of the Eastern Churches, in can. 28 § 1 which refers to *Lumen Gentium*, n. 23, and *Orientalium Ecclesiarum*, n. 3, elucidates the important areas which articulate the heritage of each of the Churches *sui iuris*: liturgy, theology, spirituality and discipline. It is necessary to note that these particular fields penetrate and condition one another in turn inside a global vision of divine revelation which pervades all life and which culminates in the praise of the most holy Trinity. Such articulations imply the idea of a history, of a culture, of conceptions and uses specific to each Church, and likewise constitute the rays originating in the one Lord, the sun of justice which illumines every man (cf. Jn 1:9) and brings him to live in communion with him. Every one of these rays, received by each individual Church *sui iuris*, has value and infinite dynamism and constitutes a part of the universal heritage of the Church.

The Catholic Church in the United States

CHRONOLOGY OF U.S. CATHOLIC HISTORY

The following are key dates in U.S. Catholic History. Reprinted from **Our Sunday Visitor's Encyclopedia of American Catholic History**.

1492 Christopher Columbus sailed to the New World and reached San Salvador (probably Watlings Island in the Bahamas). He subsequently made three voyages and established a Spanish presence on Santo Domingo (Hispaniola).

1497 John Cabot, a Genoese sailing under the English flag, reached the coasts of Labrador and Newfoundland.

1499 Alonso de Ojeda and Amerigo Vespucci reached Venezuela and explored the South American coast.

1500 Pedro Cabral reached Brazil.

1511 Diocese of Puerto Rico established as suffragan of Seville, Spain. Bishop Alonso Manso, sailing from Spain in 1512, became first bishop to take up residence in New World.

1513 Juan Ponce de León reached Florida and sailed as far north as the Carolinas.

1519 Hernando Cortes began the conquest of Mexico; by the next year, the Aztec Empire had been conquered and the Spanish rule over Mexico was established.

1521 Missionaries accompanying Ponce de León and other explorers probably said first Masses within present limits of U.S.

1526 Lucas Vázquez de Ayllón attempted to establish a colony in South Carolina; it later failed.

1534-36 Jacques Cartier explored the Newfoundland area and sailed up the St. Lawrence River.

1539 Hernando de Soto journeyed through Florida and as far north as Arkansas.

1540 Francisco Coronado set out to find the Seven Cities of Gold, journeying through Texas, Kansas and New Mexico. Franciscans Juan de Padilla and Marcos de Niza accompanied Coronado expedition through the territory. They celebrated the first Mass within territory of 13 original colonies.

c. 1540 Juan de Padilla, the first martyr of the United States, was murdered on the plains of Kansas by local Indians.

1565 City of St. Augustine, oldest in U.S., founded by Pedro Menendez de Aviles, who was accompanied by four secular priests. America's oldest mission, Nombre de Dios, was established. Fr. Martin Francisco Lopez de Mendoza Grajales became the first parish priest of St. Augustine, where the first parish in the U.S. was established.

1602 Carmelite Anthony of the Ascension offered first recorded Mass in Calif. on shore of San Diego Bay.

1608 Samuel de Champlain established the first permanent French colony at Québec.

1606 Bishop Juan de las Cabeyas de Altamirano, O.P., conducted the first episcopal visitation in the U.S.

1609 Henry Hudson entered New York Bay and sailed up the Hudson River. Santa Fe established as a mission in New Mexico. It later served as a headquarters for missionary efforts in the American Southwest.

1611 Pierre Biard, S.J., and Ennémond Massé, S.J., began missionary labors among the Indians of Maine.

1612 First Franciscan province in U.S. erected under title of Santa Elena; it included Georgia, South Carolina and Florida.

1613 Four Jesuits attempted to establish permanent French settlement near mouth of Kennebec River, Maine.

1619 French Franciscans began work among settlers and Indians. They were driven out by English in 1628.

1620 The Mayflower Compact drawn up by the Pilgrims. The chapel of *Nombre de Dios* was dedicated to *Nuestra Senora de la Leche y Buen Parto* (Our Nursing Mother of the Happy Delivery) in Florida; oldest shrine to the Blessed Mother in the U.S.

1622 Pope Gregory XV established the Congregation de Propaganda Fide to oversee all mission territories. The Catholics of America remained under its jurisdiction until 1908.

1630 New England made a prefecture apostolic in charge of French Capuchins.

1634 Ark and Dove reached Maryland with the first settlers. Maryland established by Lord Calvert; two Jesuits were among first colonists. First Mass offered on Island of St. Clement in Lower Potomac by Jesuit Fr. Andrew White.

1638 Jean Nicolet discovered the water route to the Mississippi.

1642 Jesuits Isaac Jogues and René Goupil were mutilated by Mohawks; Goupil was killed shortly afterwards. Dutch Calvinists rescued Fr. Jogues. The colony of Virginia outlawed priests and disenfranchised Catholics.

1646 Jesuit Isaac Jogues and John Lalande were martyred by Iroquois at Ossernenon, now Auriesville.

1647 Massachusetts Bay Company enacted an anti-priest law.

1649 The General Assembly of Maryland passed an act of religious toleration for the colony.

1653 Jesuits opened a school at Newton Manor, the first school in the American English colonies.

1654 Following the English Civil War and the deposition of King Charles I, the installed Puritan regime in Maryland repealed the act of religious toleration in Maryland.

1656 Church of St. Mary erected on Onondaga Lake, in first French settlement within the state. Kateri Tekakwitha, "Lily of the Mohawks," was born at Ossernenon, now Auriesville (d. in Canada, 1680). She was beatified in 1980.

1660 Jesuit René Menard opened first regular mission in Lake Superior region.

1668 Fr. Marquette founded Sainte Marie Mission at Sault Sainte Marie.

1671 Sieur de Lusson and Claude Allouez, S.J., arrived at Mackinac Island and claimed possession of the western country in the name of France.

1673 Louis Joliet and Jacques Marquette, S.J., began their expedition down the Mississippi River.

1674 Fr. Marquette set up a cabin for saying Mass in what later became the city of Chicago.

1675 Fr. Marquette established Mission of the Immaculate Conception among Kaskaskia Indians, near present site of Utica; transferred to Kaskaskia, 1703.

1678 Franciscan Recollect Louis Hennepin, first white man to describe Niagara Falls, celebrated Mass there.

1680 Louis Hennepin followed the Mississippi to its source. The missions of New Mexico destroyed by a local Indian uprising.

1682 Mission Corpus Christi de Isleta (Ysleta) founded by Franciscans near El Paso, first mission in present-day Texas.

1682 Religious toleration extended to members of all faiths in Pennsylvania.

1683 The New York colony passed the Charter of Liberties providing for religious freedom for believers in Christ.

1687 Eusebio Kino, S.J., launched the missions in Arizona at Pimería Alta.

1688 Maryland became royal colony as a result of the so-called Glorious Revolution in England; Anglican Church became the official religion (1692). Toleration Act repealed; Catholics disenfranchised and persecuted until 1776. Hanging of Ann Glover, an elderly Irish-Catholic widow, who refused to renounce her Catholic religion.

1689 Jesuit Claude Allouez died after 32 years of missionary activity among Indians of midwest; he had evangelized Indians of 20 different tribes. Jesuit Jacques Gravier succeeded Allouez as vicar general of Illinois.

1690 Mission San Francisco de los Tejas founded in east Texas.

1692 The Church of England officially established in Maryland. New Mexico re-subjugated by the Spanish and the missions re-opened.

1697 Religious liberty granted to all except "papists" in South Carolina.

1700 Jesuit Eusebio Kino, who first visited the area in 1692, established mission at San Xavier del Bac, near Tucson. In 1783, under Franciscan administration, construction was begun of the Mission Church of San Xavier del Bac near the site of the original mission; it is still in use as a parish church. Although the New York Assembly enacted a bill calling for religious toleration for all Christians in 1683, other penal laws were now enforced against Catholics; all priests were ordered out of the province.

1701 Tolerance granted to all except "papists" in New Jersey.

1703 Mission San Francisco de Solano founded on Rio Grande; rebuilt in 1718 as San Antonio de Valero, or the Alamo.

1704 Destruction of Florida's northern missions by English and Indian troops led by Governor James Moore of South Carolina. Franciscans Juan de Parga, Dominic Criodo, Tiburcio de Osorio, Augustine Ponze de León, Marcos Delgado and two Indians, Anthony Enixa and Amador Cuipa Feliciano, were slain by the invaders.

1709 French Jesuit missionaries obliged to give up their central New York missions.

1716 Antonio de Margil, O.F.M., began his missionary labors in Texas.

1718 The Catholics in Maryland officially disenfranchised. City of New Orleans founded by Jean Baptiste Le Moyne de Bienville.

1727 Ursuline Nuns founded convent in New Orleans, oldest convent in what is now U.S.; they conducted a school, hospital and orphan asylum.

1735 Bishop Francis Martinez de Tejadu Diaz de Velasco, auxiliary of Santiago, was the first bishop to take up residence in U.S., at St. Augustine.

1740s The First Great Awakening among Protestants.

1741 Because of an alleged popish plot to burn the city of New York, four whites were hanged and 11 blacks burned at the stake.

1744 Mission church of the Alamo built in San Antonio.

1751 First Catholic settlement founded among Huron Indians near Sandusky, Ohio, by Jesuit Fr. de la Richardie.

1754-63 The French and Indian War (The Seven Years War in Europe), the first world war; the conflict ended with the defeat of France and the loss of their American colonies.

1755 Fifty-six Catholics of Acadia expelled to the American colonies; those landing in Boston were denied the services of a Catholic priest.

1763 The Jesuits banished from the territories of Louisiana and Illinois Spain ceded Florida to England. The English also gained control of all French territories east of the Mississippi following the cessation of the French and Indian War.

1765 The Quartering Act imposed on the colonies by the British as a means of paying the cost of colonial defense. It was followed by the Stamp Act, sparking the rise of the Sons of Liberty and the convening of the Stamp Act Congress.

1767 Jesuits expelled from Spanish territory. Spanish Crown confiscated their property, including the Pious Fund for Missions. Upper California missions entrusted to Franciscans.

1769 Franciscan Junípero Serra, missionary in Mexico for 20 years, began establishment of Franciscan missions in California, in present San Diego. He was beatified in 1988.

1770 The Boston Massacre resulted in the deaths of five colonists in Boston.

1773 The Tea Act sparked the Boston Tea Party. The British responded with the Intolerable Acts in 1774. Charles Carroll of Carrollton published the "First Citizen" letter in defense of the Church and Catholics against Daniel Dulany and the royal colonial government in Maryland.

1774 Elizabeth Bayley Seton, foundress of the American Sisters of Charity, was born in New York City on Aug. 28. She was canonized in 1975. The British Parliament passed the Quebec Act granting the French in the region the right to their own religion, language and customs. The first Continental Congress is convened.

1775-1781 The American Revolution, in which Catholics played a major role. In 1790, newly elected President George Washington wrote to American Catholics to thank them for their instrumental role in the war for American freedom.

1775 The Continental Congress denounced the rampant anti-Catholicism of the colonies to King George III. General Washington discouraged Guy Fawkes Day procession, in which pope was carried in effigy.

1776 Charles Carroll received appointment with Samuel Chase and Benjamin Franklin to a commission of the Continental Congress seeking aid from Canada; Fr. John Carroll accompanied them on their mission. Virginia became the first state to vote for full religious freedom in the new state's bill of rights. Similar provisions were passed by Maryland and Pennsylvania. The Continental Congress passed the Declaration of Independence (Charles Carroll was also the longest surviving signer). The New Jersey State Constitution tacitly excluded Catholics from office.

1777 The New York State Constitution gave religious liberty, but the naturalization law required an oath to renounce allegiance to any foreign ruler, ecclesiastical as well as civil.

1778 Fr. Gibault aided George Rogers Clark in campaign against British in conquest of Northwest Territory.

1780 The Massachusetts State Constitution granted religious liberty, but required a religious test to hold public office and provided for tax to support Protestant teachers of piety, religion and morality.

1781 Expedition from San Gabriel Mission founded present city of Los Angeles, Pueblo "de Nuestra Senora de los Angeles." British General Cornwallis surrendered at Yorktown, ending the Revolutionary War.

1783 The Treaty of Paris ended the American Revolution; Great Britain recognized the independence of the United States.

1784 The Vatican appointed Fr. John Carroll to the post of superior of the American Catholic missions. The State Constitution of New Hampshire included a religious test that barred Catholics from public office; local support was provided for public Protestant teachers of religion.

1787 Daniel Carroll of Maryland and Thomas FitzSimons of Pennsylvania signed the Constitution of the United States.

1788 First public Mass said in Boston on Nov. 2 by Abbé de la Poterie, first resident priest.

1789 Pope Pius VI erected the first United States diocese, Baltimore; John Carroll is named the first bishop.

1790 Catholics given right to vote in South Carolina.

1791 French Sulpicians opened the first seminary in the United States, St. Mary's in Baltimore. Georgetown Academy is established and begins holding classes. Bishop Carroll convoked the first synod of the clergy of the diocese. The Bill of Rights ratified by the Congress. Pierre Charles L'Enfant designed the Federal City of Washington. His plans were not fully implemented until the early 1900s.

1792 James Hoban designed the White House.

1793 Rev. Stephen T. Badin first priest ordained by Bishop Carroll; he soon began missionary work in Kentucky.

1799 Prince Demetrius Gallitzin (Fr. Augustine Smith) arrived in the Allegheny Mountains. He labored there for the next 40 years and established the Church in western Pennsylvania, at Loretto.

1800 Jesuit Leonard Neale became first bishop consecrated in present limits of U.S.

1801 Start of the Second Great Awakening among Protestants.

1802 First mayor of Washington, appointed by President Jefferson, was Catholic Judge Robert Brent.

1803 The Louisiana Purchase resulted in the acquisition by the United States of all French lands from the Mississippi River to the Rocky Mountains for $15 million.

1804-06 President Jefferson sponsored the expedition of Lewis and Clark into the Louisiana Territory.

1806 New York anti-Catholic 1777 Test Oath for naturalization repealed.

1808 Pope Pius VII declared Baltimore the first metropolitan see of the United States, erecting at the same time the new dioceses of Bardstown (KY), Boston, New York, and Philadelphia as suffragans.

1809 Mother Elizabeth Ann Seton established the first native American congregation of sisters, at Emmitsburg, Maryland.

1810 The United States annexed West Florida under the pretext that it was included in the Louisiana Purchase.

1811 Catholic Canadian trappers and traders with John J. Astor expedition founded first American settlement, Astoria. Rev. Guy I. Chabrat becomes first priest ordained west of the Allegheny Mountains.

1812 The War of 1812; it was ended by the Treaty of Ghent in 1814.

1814 St. Joseph's Orphanage, Philadelphia, opened, the first Catholic asylum for children in the United States.

1818 Religious freedom established by new constitution in Connecticut, although the Congregational Church remained, in practice, the state church. Bishop Dubourg arrived at St. Louis, with Vincentians Joseph Rosati and Felix de Andreis. Rose Philippine Duchesne arrived at St. Charles; founded first American convent of the Society of the Sacred Heart. She was beatified in 1940 and canonized in 1988.

1822 Bishop John England founded the *United States Catholic Miscellany*, the first Catholic newspaper in the country of a strictly religious nature. The

Society for the Propagation of the Faith is founded in France; it sent missionaries throughout the world. Vicariate Apostolic of Mississippi and Alabama established.

1823 President Monroe proposed the Monroe Doctrine of foreign policy. Fr. Gabriel Richard elected delegate to Congress from Michigan territory; he was the first priest elected to the House of Representatives.

1828 New York State Legislature enacted a law upholding sanctity of seal of confession. The first hospital opened west of the Mississippi in St. Louis, staffed by the Sisters of Charity from Emmitsburg, Maryland.

1829 The First Provincial Council of Baltimore convoked. The Oblate Sisters of Providence, the first African-American congregation of women religious in the United States was established in Baltimore.

1831 Xavier University founded.

1833 Fr. Frederic Baraga celebrated first Mass in present Grand Rapids.

1834 First native New Yorker to become a secular priest, Rev. John McCloskey, was ordained. Indian missions in Northwest entrusted to Jesuits by Holy See. A mob of Nativists attacked and burned down the Ursuline Convent at Charlestown, Massachusetts.

1835 Samuel F.B. Morse published *The Foreign Conspiracy Against the Liberties of the United States.*

1836 Texans under Stephen F. Austin declared their independence from Mexico; the Battle of the Alamo in San Antonio resulted in the deaths of 188 Texans, including the commander William B. Travis and perhaps Davy Crockett. Texas soon won its independence and was annexed in 1845. John Nepomucene Neumann arrived from Bohemia and was ordained a priest in Old St. Patrick's Cathedral, New York City. He was canonized in 1977. The infamous work of Maria Monk's *Awful Disclosures of the Hotel Dieu Nunnery of Montreal*, detailing supposed scandals of Catholic religious, was published. President Jackson nominated Roger Brooke Taney as chief justice of the Supreme Court.

1838 Fathers Blanchet and Demers, "Apostles of the Northwest," sent to territory by Abp. of Québec.

1839 Pope Gregory XVI condemned the slave trade in his decree *In Supremo Apostolatus.*

1840 Mother Theodore Guérin founded the Sisters of Providence of St.-Mary-of-the-Woods in Indiana.

1842 Fr. Augustine Ravoux began ministrations to French and Indians at Fort Pierre, Vermilion and Prairie du Chien; printed devotional book in Sioux language the following year. Henriette Delille and Juliette Gaudin began the Sisters of the Holy Family in New Orleans, the second African-American community of women religious. University of Notre Dame founded by Holy Cross Fr. Edward Sorin and Brothers of St. Joseph on land given the diocese of Vincennes by Fr. Stephen Badin.

1844 Thirteen persons killed, two churches and a school burned in Know-Nothing riots at Philadelphia. Orestes Brownson received into the Church; he subsequently founded *Brownson's Quarterly Review.*

1845 Nativists opposed to Catholics and Irish

immigration, established the Native American Party. Issac Hecker received into the Church. The potato famine began in Ireland, causing in part the mass migration of Irish to the United States. The St. Vincent de Paul Society founded in the United States.

1846-48 The Mexican-American War was caused by a border dispute between the United States and Mexico. Catholic chaplains were appointed to the army, to minister to Mexican Catholics.

1846 Peter H. Burnett, who became first governor of California in 1849, received into Catholic Church. First Benedictine Abbey in New World founded near Latrobe by Fr. Boniface Wimmer.

1847 The Bishops of the United States requested Pope Pius IX to name the Immaculate Conception patron of the United States.

1848 The first permanent American Trappist foundation established, in Kentucky. Jacob L. Martin named the first American representative to the Vatican.

1852 The First Plenary Council of Baltimore held. Redemptorist John Nepomucene Neumann became fourth bishop of Philadelphia. He was beatified in 1963 and canonized in 1977.

1853 Calling for the exclusion of Catholics and foreigners from office and a 21-year residence requirement, the American Party was founded, known also as the Know-Nothing Party.

1854 Members of the Benedictine Swiss-American congregation established a community at St. Meinrad in southern Indiana.

1855 The German Catholic Central Verein founded. The "Bloody Monday" Riots in Louisville, Kentucky, leave 20 dead.

1857 The Supreme Court issued the Dred Scott Decision; Chief Justice Roger Taney stated that Congress could not exclude slavery from the territories since, according to the Constitution, slaves were property and could be transported anywhere. The American College at Louvain opened.

1858 Jesuit Fr. De Smet accompanied General Harney as chaplain on expedition sent to settle troubles between Mormons and U.S. government. The Paulists, the first native religious community for men, established. Cornerstone of second (present) St. Patrick's Cathedral, New York City, was laid; the cathedral was completed in 1879.

1859 The North American College founded in Rome as a training center for American seminarians.

1860 South Carolina seceded from the Union.

1861-65 The American Civil War. Catholics participated in large numbers on both sides. There were approximately 40 Catholic chaplains in the Union army and 28 in the Confederate army. More than 500 Catholic nuns ministered to the sick and wounded. Over 20 generals in the Union army and 11 generals in the Confederate army were Catholics.

1861 The Confederacy was formed after 11 states seceded from the Union. Jefferson Davis was elected president of the Confederacy.

1865 *Catholic World* founded. A Test Oath law passed by state legislature (called Drake Convention) to crush Catholicism in Missouri. Law law declared unconstitutional by Supreme Court in 1866. Rev.

H. H. Spalding, a Protestant missionary, published the Whitman Myth to hinder work of Catholic missionaries in Oregon. President Lincoln was assassinated. The murder sparked anti-Catholicism, including charges that Jesuits orchestrated his death. Congress passed the Thirteenth Amendment abolishing slavery.

1866 The Second Plenary Council of Baltimore.

1867 Reconstruction launched in the South; the presence of Federal troops did not end until 1877. The Ku Klux Klan founded to defeat Reconstruction, oppose Catholicism, and establish white supremacy in the post-war South. The U.S. purchased Alaska for $7.2 million; organized by Secretary of State William Seward, the purchase was called "Seward's Folly."

1869-70 The Fist Vatican Council convoked. Most of the bishops of the United States took part in the deliberations of the council.

1869 The Transcontinental Railroad completed, with the two tracks meeting at Promontory, near Ogden, Utah. The Knights of Labor founded.

1870 The Holy Name Society organized in the U.S.

1873 Blessed Fr. Damien de Veuster of the Sacred Hearts Fathers arrived in Molokai and spent the remainder of his life working among lepers. He was beatified in 1995.

1875 James A. Healy, first bishop of Negro blood consecrated in U.S., became second Bishop of Portland. Archbishop John McCloskey of New York became the first American prelate to be elevated to the College of Cardinals.

1876 George Armstrong Custer killed at the Battle of Little Bighorn (in the Second Sioux War) in Montana. *The American Catholic Quarterly Review* is established. James Gibbons publishes *Faith of Our Fathers*.

1878 Franciscan Sisters of Allegany becomes first native American community to send members to foreign missions.

1880 William R. Grace becomes the first Catholic mayor of New York City.

1882 Knights of Columbus founded by Fr. Michael J. McGivney.

1884 The Third Plenary Council of Baltimore held. John Gilmary Shea began the U.S. Catholic Historical Society.

1886 Abp. Charles J. Seghers, "Apostle of Alaska," was murdered by a guide; he had surveyed southern and northwest Alaska in 1873 and 1877. Archbishop James Gibbons of Baltimore is named the second American cardinal. Augustus Tolton is ordained the first African-American priest for the United States. The Knights of St. John was established.

1887 The American Protective Association (APA) was established to resist the growth of immigration. The Dawes Act was passed, dissolving all Indian tribes and distributing their lands among their former members, who were not permitted to dispose of their property for 25 years.

1889 The Catholic University of America opened. The first African-American Lay Congress was held in Washington, DC; subsequent congresses held in Cincinnati (1890), Philadelphia (1892), Chicago (1893), and Baltimore (1894). Mother Frances Xavier Cabrini arrived in New York City to begin work among Italian immigrants. She was canonized in 1946. *American Ecclesiastical Review* begun.

1890 Archbishop Ireland delivered an address on public and private schools at the gathering of the National Education Association in St. Paul, Minnesota.

1891 Vicariate Apostolic of Oklahoma and Indian Territory was established. Katharine Drexel founded Sisters of Blessed Sacrament for Indians and Colored Peoples. She was canonized in 2000. The Rosary Society organized.

1893 The Apostolic Delegation under Archbishop Francesco Satolli established in Washington, DC; it became an Apostolic Nunciature in 1984 with the establishment of full diplomatic relations between the U.S. and the Holy See. The first Catholic college for women in the United States, College of Notre Dame of Maryland, was established. *St. Anthony Messenger* launched.

1898 Puerto Rico ceded to U.S. (became self-governing Commonwealth in 1952); inhabitants granted U.S. citizenship in 1917. The United States annexed Hawaii; the monarchy had been overthrown in 1897.

1898 The Spanish-American War.

1899 Pope Leo XIII issued *Testem Benevolentiae*.

1901 President McKinley assassinated.

1904 The National Catholic Education Association (NCEA) founded. First publication of the *Catholic Almanac*.

1905 The Catholic Church Extension Society for home missions established.

1907 The first volume of the *Catholic Encyclopedia* was published by the Catholic University of America.

1908 Pope St. Pius X published *Pascendi Domini Gregis* against Modernism. Pope Pius issued the bull *Sapienti Consilio*, by which the Church in the U.S. was removed from mission status and the jurisdiction of the Congregation de Propaganda Fide. First American Missionary Congress held in Chicago.

1909 The Holy Name Society was established. *America* Magazine founded by the Jesuits.

1911 The Catholic Foreign Mission Society of America (Maryknoll) founded. Katharine Drexel founded the Sisters of the Blessed Sacrament.

1912 *Our Sunday Visitor* founded.

1914-18 World War I.

1917 The United States entered the First World War. The National Catholic War Council was founded. Over one million Catholics served in the Armed Forces (over 20% of the total U.S. military).

1919 The Bishops' *Program of Social Reconstruction* published. The National Catholic Welfare Council was founded. Peter Guilday began the American Catholic Historical Association.

1920 The National Catholic News Service (NC, now the Catholic News Service, CNS) was established.

1924 The Federated Colored Catholics of the United States was established. *Commonweal* Magazine was founded by Michael Williams.

1925 The Supreme Court declares the Oregon school law unconstitutional. The Scopes Trial, also called the Dayton Monkey Trial, took place in Dayton, Ohio.

1926 The Twenty-Eighth International Eucharistic Congress was held in Chicago.

1928 Alfred E. Smith of New York nominated for president by the Democratic Party; he was the first Catholic ever chosen to head a major-party national ticket. He was defeated by Herbert Hoover, in part because of his opposition to Prohibition and his faith.

1929 The stockmarket crash signaled the start of the Great Depression. The Catholic Church devoted enormous resources to alleviating the suffering of those afflicted by the global Depression.

1932 Franklin Delano Roosevelt was elected president, launching the New Deal period (1933-45).

1933 The Catholic Worker Movement was established by Dorothy Day and Peter Maurin.

1934 John LaFarge, S.J., begins the first Catholic Interracial Council in New York.

1937 The Association of Catholic Trade Unionists (ACTU) established.

1939 Myron C. Taylor named personal representative of President Roosevelt to Pope Pius XII.

1939-45 World War II.

1941 Pearl Harbor was attacked by Japan; the U.S. entered World War II. Catholics comprised over 25% of the Armed Forces.

1945 End of World War II. Delegates from 50 nations established the Charter of the United Nations.

1947 The Christian Family Movement was begun by Pat and Patty Crowley. The Supreme Court issued the decision *Everson v. Board of Education* approving the use of public school buses to carry Catholic students to parochial schools.

1948 Protestants and Other Americans for Separation of Church and State (POAU) founded.

1951 President Truman nominates General Mark Clark as Ambassador to Vatican City. The nomination later withdrawn in the face of anti-Catholic protests.

1954 The Sisters Formation Conference was founded. The Supreme Court decided *Brown v. Board of Education of Topeka*; the decision declared that segregation in the public schools was unconstitutional.

1955 John Tracy Ellis published *American Catholics and the Intellectual Life.*

1956 Leadership Conference of Women Religious and Conference of Major Superiors of Men was founded.

1957 The Civil Rights Act was passed, the first since 1875.

1958 Christopher Dawson was named the first holder of the Chauney Stillman Chair of Roman Catholic Studies at the Harvard Divinity School.

1959 Pope John XXIII announced his intention to convoke the Second Vatican Council.

1960 John F. Kennedy elected president of the United States; he was the first Catholic president.

1962-65 The Second Vatican Council.

1962 Gustave Weigel, S.J., appointed by the Vatican to be one of the five Catholic observers at the third general assembly of the World Council of Churches at New Delhi. Archbishop Joseph Rummel of New Orleans announced the integration of archdiocesan Catholic schools.

1963 The Catholic University of America prohibited Hans Küng, John Courtney Murray, S.J., Gustave Weigel, S.J., and Godfrey Diekmann, O.S.B., from speaking at the school. Elizabeth Ann Seton, the first American to be beatified. President Kennedy assassinated in Dallas.

1964 The Civil Rights Act passed.

1965 Pope Paul VI visited the United Nations, the first pope to visit the U.S. Gommar A. De Pauw organizes the Catholic Traditionalist movement.

1966 The National Conference of Catholic Bishops and the United States Catholic Conference were organized. Harold Perry, S.V.D., became the second African-American to be named a bishop.

1967 The Land O' Lakes Statement issued. The Catholic Charismatic Movement began. The Catholic Committee on Urban Ministry (CCUM) was established.

1968 Pope Paul VI issued *Humanae Vitae*. The National Black Catholic Clergy Caucus, the National Black Sisters' Conference, the National Black Catholic Seminarians Association, and the National Federation of Priests' Council were formed. Catholics United for the Faith established.

1969 The Organization of Priests Associated for Religious, Educational, and Social Rights (PADRES) established. The Campaign for Human Development established.

1970 Patricio Flores, the first modern Latino bishop, ordained.

1971 The Leadership Conference of Women Religious established.

1972 Religious Brothers Conference established.

1973 Roe v. Wade Decision handed down by the Supreme Court, legalizing abortion.

1975 Pope Paul VI canonized the first American saint, Elizabeth Ann Seton.

1976 The U.S. celebrated the Bicentennial.

1977 Fellowship of Catholic Scholars established.

1979 Pope John Paul II visited the U.S.

1983 The NCCB issued the *Challenge of Peace*.

1986 The NCCB issued *Economic Justice for All*. The Vatican and Catholic University of America removed Fr. Charles Curran from teaching theology at the university.

1987 Pope John Paul II visited the U.S. for the second time. The National Black Catholic Congress convoked in Washington, DC.

1991 The U.S. played a major role in the Gulf War.

1992 Council of Major Superiors of Women Religious founded.

1993 World Youth Day held in Denver.

1995 Pope John Paul II visited the United Nations, Baltimore, and New York.

1997 U.S. Bishops took part in a special assembly of the Synod of Bishops on the Church in the Americas.

1999 Pope John Paul II visited St. Louis.

2001 The U.S. attacked on Sept. 11. The NCCB and USSC merged to form the United States Conference of Catholic Bishops (USCCB); Bishop Wilton Gregory of Belleville was elected its black president of the USCCB.

2002 The pedophilia crisis erupted across the country; the USCCB passed a series of protective norms.

2003 The U.S. launched the Iraq War to topple Saddam Hussein.

U.S. CATHOLIC HISTORY

(Courtesy Rev. Clyde Crews, Ph.D.)

The starting point of the mainstream of Catholic history in the U.S. was in Baltimore at the end of the Revolutionary War. Long before that time, however, Catholic explorers had traversed much of the country and missionaries had done considerable work among Indians in the Southeast, Northeast and Southwest. (See Index, Chronology of Church in U.S.)

Spanish and French Missions

Missionaries from Spain evangelized Indians in Florida (which included a large area of the Southeast), New Mexico, Texas and California. Franciscan Juan de Padilla, killed in 1542 in what is now central Kansas, was the first of numerous martyrs among the early missionaries. The city of St. Augustine, settled by the Spanish in 1565, was the first permanent settlement in the United States and also the site of the first parish, established the same year with secular Fr. Martin Francisco Lopez de Mendoza Grajales as pastor. Italian Jesuit Eusebio Kino (1645-1711) established Spanish missions in lower California and southern Arizona, where he founded San Xavier del Bac mission in 1700. Bl. Junípero Serra (1713-84), who established nine of the famous chain of 21 Franciscan missions in California, was perhaps the most noted of the Spanish missionaries. He was beatified in 1988.

French missionary efforts originated in Canada and extended to parts of Maine, New York and areas around the Great Lakes and along the Mississippi River as far south as Louisiana. Sts. Isaac Jogues, René Goupil and John de Brébeuf, three of eight Jesuit missionaries of New France martyred between 1642 and 1649 (canonized in 1930), met their deaths near Auriesville, New York. Jesuit explorer Jacques Marquette (1637-75), who founded St. Ignace Mission at the Straits of Mackinac in 1671, left maps and a diary of his exploratory trip down the Mississippi River with Louis Joliet in 1673. Claude Allouez (1622-89), another French Jesuit, worked for 32 years among Indians in the Midwest, baptizing an estimated 10,000. French Catholics founded the colony in Louisiana in 1699. In 1727, Ursuline nuns from France founded a convent in New Orleans, the oldest in the United States.

English Settlements

Catholics were excluded by penal law from English settlements along the Atlantic coast.

The only colony established under Catholic leadership was Maryland, granted to George Calvert (Lord Baltimore) as a proprietary colony in 1632; its first settlement at St. Mary's City was established in 1634 by a contingent of Catholic and Protestant colonists who had arrived from England on the Ark and the Dove. Jesuits Andrew White and John Altham, who later evangelized Indians of the area, accompanied the settlers. The principle of religious freedom on which the colony was founded was enacted into law in 1649 as the Act of Toleration. It was the first such measure passed in the colonies and, except for a four-year period of Puritan control, remained in effect until 1688, when Maryland became a royal colony and the Anglican Church was made the official religion in 1692. Catholics were disenfranchised and perse-

cuted until 1776.

The only other colony where Catholics were assured some degree of freedom was Pennsylvania, founded by the Quaker William Penn in 1681.

One of the earliest permanent Catholic establishments in the English colonies was St. Francis Xavier Mission, Old Bohemia, in northern Maryland, founded by the Jesuits in 1704 to serve Catholics of Delaware, Maryland and southeastern Pennsylvania. Its Bohemia Academy, established in the 1740s, was attended by sons of prominent Catholic families in the area.

Catholics and the Revolution

Despite their small number, which accounted for about one percent of the population, Catholics made significant contributions to the cause for independence from England.

Fr. John Carroll (1735-1815), who would later become the first bishop of the American hierarchy, and his cousin, Charles Carroll (1737-1832), a signer of the Declaration of Independence, were chosen by the Continental Congress to accompany Benjamin Franklin and Samuel Chase to Canada to try to secure that country's neutrality. Fr. Pierre Gibault (1737-1804) gave important aid in preserving the Northwest Territory for the revolutionaries. Thomas FitzSimons (1741-1811) of Philadelphia gave financial support to the Continental Army, served in a number of campaigns and later, with Daniel Carroll of Maryland, became one of the two Catholic signers of the Constitution. John Barry (1745-1803), commander of the Lexington, the first ship commissioned by Congress, served valiantly and is considered a founder of the U.S. Navy. There is no record of the number of Catholics who served in Washington's armies, although 38 to 50 percent had Irish surnames.

Casimir Pulaski (1748-79) and Thaddeus Kosciusko (1746-1817) of Poland served the cause of the Revolution. Assisting also were the Catholic nations of France, with a military and naval force, and Spain, with money and the neutrality of its colonies.

Acknowledgment of Catholic aid in the war and the founding of the Republic was made by General Washington in his reply to a letter from prominent Catholics seeking justice and equal rights: "I presume your fellow citizens of all denominations will not forget the patriotic part which you took in the accomplishment of our Revolution and the establishment of our government or the important assistance which they received from a nation [France] in which the Roman Catholic faith is professed."

In 1789, religious freedom was guaranteed under the First Amendment to the Constitution. Discriminatory laws against Catholics remained in force in many of the states, however, until well into the 19th century.

Beginning of Organization

Fr. John Carroll's appointment as superior of the American missions on June 9, 1784, was the first step toward organization of the Church in this country. According to a report he made to Rome the following year, there were 24 priests and approximately 25,000 Catholics, mostly in Maryland and Pennsylvania, in a general population of four million. Many of them had been in the Colonies for several generations. For the most part, however, they were an unknown minority laboring under legal and social handicaps.

Establishment of the Hierarchy

Fr. Carroll was named the first American bishop in 1789 and placed in charge of the Diocese of Baltimore, whose boundaries were coextensive with those of the United States. He was ordained in England on Aug. 15, 1790, and installed in his see the following Dec. 12.

Ten years later, Fr. Leonard Neale became his coadjutor and the first bishop ordained in the U.S. Bishop Carroll became an archbishop in 1808 when Baltimore was designated a metropolitan see and the new dioceses of Boston, New York, Philadelphia and Bardstown (now Louisville) were established. These jurisdictions were later subdivided, and by 1840 there were, in addition to Baltimore, 15 dioceses, 500 priests and 663,000 Catholics in the general population of 17 million.

Priests and First Seminaries

The original number of 24 priests noted in Bishop Carroll's 1785 report was gradually augmented with the arrival of others from France and other countries. Among arrivals from France after the Civil Constitution of the Clergy went into effect in 1790 were Jean Louis Lefebvre de Cheverus and Sulpicians Ambrose Maréchal, Benedict Flaget and William Dubourg, who later became bishops.

The first seminary in the country was St. Mary's, established in 1791 in Baltimore, and placed under the direction of the Sulpicians. French seminarian Stephen T. Badin (1768-1853), who fled to the U.S. in 1792 and became a pioneer missionary in Kentucky, Ohio and Michigan, was the first priest ordained (1793) in the U.S. Demetrius Gallitzin (1770-1840), a Russian prince and convert to Catholicism who did pioneer missionary work in western Pennsylvania, was ordained to the priesthood in 1795; he was the first to receive all his orders in the U.S. By 1815, St. Mary's Seminary had 30 ordained alumni.

Two additional seminaries, Mt. St. Mary's at Emmitsburg, Maryland, and St. Thomas at Bardstown, Kentucky, were established in 1809 and 1811, respectively. These and similar institutions founded later played key roles in the development and growth of the American clergy.

Early Schools

Early educational enterprises included the establishment in 1791 of a school at Georgetown that later became the first Catholic university in the U.S.; the opening of a secondary school for girls, conducted by Visitation Nuns, in 1799 at Georgetown; and the start of a similar school in the first decade of the 19th century at Emmitsburg, Maryland, by St. Elizabeth Ann Seton.

By the 1840s, which saw the beginnings of the present public school system, more than 200 Catholic elementary schools, half of them west of the Alleghenies, were in operation. From this start, the Church subsequently built the greatest private system of education in the world.

Sisterhoods

Institutes of women Religious were largely responsible for the development of educational and charitable institutions. Among them were Ursuline Nuns in Louisiana from 1727 and Visitation Nuns at Georgetown in the 1790s.

The first contemplative foundation in the country was established in 1790 at Fort Tobacco, Maryland, by three American-born Carmelites trained at an English convent in Belgium.

The first community of American origin was the Sisters of Charity of St. Joseph, founded in 1808 at Emmitsburg, Maryland, by Mother Elizabeth Ann Bayley Seton (canonized in 1975). Other early American communities were the Sisters of Loretto and the Sisters of Charity of Nazareth, both founded in 1812 in Kentucky, and the Oblate Sisters of Providence, a black community founded in 1829 in Baltimore by Mother Mary Elizabeth Lange.

Among pioneer U.S. foundresses of European communities were Mother Rose Philippine Duchesne (canonized in 1980), who established the Religious of the Sacred Heart in Missouri in 1818, and Mother Theodore Guérin, who founded the Sisters of Providence of St.-Mary-of-the-Woods in Indiana in 1840.

The number of sisters' communities, most of them branches of European institutes, increased apace with needs for their missions in education, charitable service and spiritual life.

Trusteeism

The initial lack of organization in ecclesiastical affairs, nationalistic feeling among Catholics and the independent action of some priests were factors involved in several early crises.

In Philadelphia, some German Catholics, with the reluctant consent of Bishop Carroll, founded Holy Trinity, the first national parish in the U.S. They refused to accept the pastor appointed by the bishop and elected their own. This and other abuses led to formal schism in 1796, a condition that existed until 1802, when they returned to canonical jurisdiction. Philadelphia was also the scene of the Hogan Schism, which developed in the 1820s when Fr. William Hogan, with the aid of lay trustees, seized control of St. Mary's Cathedral. His movement, for churches and parishes controlled by other than canonical procedures and run in extralegal ways, was nullified by a decision of the Pennsylvania Supreme Court in 1822.

Similar troubles seriously disturbed the peace of the Church in other places, principally New York, Baltimore, Buffalo, Charleston and New Orleans.

Dangers arising from the exploitation of lay control were gradually diminished with the extension and enforcement of canonical procedures and with changes in civil law about the middle of the century.

Anti-Catholicism

Bigotry against Catholics waxed and waned during the 19th century and into the 20th. The first major campaign of this kind, which developed in the wake of the panic of 1819 and lasted for about 25 years, was mounted in 1830 when the number of Catholic immigrants began to increase to a noticeable degree. Nativist anti-Catholicism generated a great deal of violence, represented by loss of life and property in Charlestown, Massachusetts, in 1834, and in Philadelphia 10 years later. Later bigotry was fomented by the Know-Nothings, in the 1850s; the Ku Klux Klan, from 1866; the American Protective Association, from 1887; and the Guardians of Liberty. Perhaps the last eruption of virulently overt anti-Catholicism occurred during the campaign of Alfred E. Smith for the presidency in 1928. Observers feel the issue was muted to a considerable extent in the political area with the election of John F. Kennedy to the presidency in 1960.

The Catholic periodical press had its beginnings in response to the attacks of bigots. The *U.S. Catholic Miscellany* (1822-61), the first Catholic newspaper in the U.S., was founded by Bishop John England of Charleston to answer critics of the Church. This remained the character of most of the periodicals published in the 19th and into the 20th century.

Growth and Immigration

Between 1830 and 1900, the combined factors of natural increase, immigration and conversion raised the Catholic population to 12 million. A large percentage of the growth figure represented immigrants: some 2.7 million, largely from Ireland, Germany and France, between 1830 and 1880; and another 1.25 million during the 1880s when Eastern and Southern Europeans came in increasing numbers. By the 1860s the Catholic Church, with most of its members concentrated in urban areas, was probably the largest religious body in the country.

The efforts of progressive bishops to hasten the acculturation of Catholic immigrants occasioned a number of controversies, which generally centered around questions concerning national or foreign-language parishes. One of them, called Cahenslyism, arose from complaints that German Catholic immigrants were not being given adequate pastoral care.

Eastern Rite Catholics

The immigration of the 1890s included large numbers of Eastern Rite Catholics with their own liturgies and tradition of a married clergy, but without their own bishops. The treatment of their clergy and people by some of the U.S. (Latin Rite) hierarchy and the prejudices they encountered resulted in the defection of thousands from the Catholic Church.

In 1907, Basilian monk Stephen Ortynsky was ordained the first bishop of Byzantine Rite Catholics in the U.S. Eventually jurisdictions were established for most Byzantine and other Eastern Rite Catholics in the country.

Councils of Baltimore

The bishops of the growing U.S. dioceses met at Baltimore for seven provincial councils between 1829 and 1849.

In 1846, they proclaimed the Blessed Virgin Mary patroness of the United States under the title of the Immaculate Conception, eight years before the dogma was proclaimed in Rome.

After the establishment of the Archdiocese of Oregon City in 1846 and the elevation to metropolitan status of St. Louis, New Orleans, Cincinnati and New York, the first of the three plenary councils of Baltimore was held.

The first plenary assembly was convoked on May 9, 1852, with Abp. Francis P. Kenrick of Baltimore as papal legate. The bishops drew up regulations concerning parochial life, matters of church ritual and ceremonies, the administration of church funds and the teaching of Christian doctrine.

The second plenary council, meeting from Oct. 7 to 21, 1866, under the presidency of Abp. Martin J. Spalding, formulated a condemnation of several current doctrinal errors and established norms affecting the organization of dioceses, the education and conduct of the clergy, the management of ecclesiastical property, parochial duties and general education.

Abp. (later Cardinal) James Gibbons called into session the third plenary council which lasted from Nov. 9 to Dec. 7, 1884. Among highly significant results of actions taken by this assembly were the preparation of the line of Baltimore catechisms that became a basic means of religious instruction in this country; legislation that fixed the pattern of Catholic education by requiring the building of elementary schools in all parishes; the establishment of the Catholic University of America in Washington, DC, in 1889; and the determination of six holy days of obligation for observance in this country.

The enactments of the three plenary councils have had the force of particular law for the Church in the U.S.

The Holy See established the Apostolic Delegation in Washington, DC, on Jan. 24, 1893.

Slavery

In the Civil War period, as before, Catholics reflected attitudes of the general population with respect to the issue of slavery. Some supported it, some opposed it, but none were prominent in the Abolition Movement. Pope Gregory XVI had condemned the slave trade in 1839, but no contemporary pope or American bishop published an official document on slavery itself. The issue did not split Catholics in schism as it did Baptists, Methodists and Presbyterians.

Catholics fought on both sides in the Civil War. Five hundred members of 20 or more sisterhoods served the wounded of both sides.

One hundred thousand of the four million slaves emancipated in 1863 were Catholics; the highest concentrations were in Louisiana, about 60,000, and Maryland, 16,000. Three years later, their pastoral care was one of the subjects covered in nine decrees issued by the Second Plenary Council of Baltimore. The measures had little practical effect with respect to integration of the total Catholic community, predicated as they were on the proposition that individual bishops should handle questions regarding segregation in churches and related matters as best they could in the pattern of local customs.

Long-entrenched segregation practices continued in force through the rest of the 19th century and well into the 20th. The first effective efforts to alter them were initiated by Cardinal Joseph Ritter of St. Louis in 1947, Cardinal (then Abp.) Patrick O'Boyle of Washington in 1948, and Bishop Vincent Waters of Raleigh in 1953.

Friend of Labor

The Church became known during the 19th century as a friend and ally of labor in seeking justice for the working man. Cardinal Gibbons journeyed to Rome in 1887, for example, to defend and prevent a condemnation of the Knights of Labor by Leo XIII. The encyclical *Rerum Novarum* (1891) was hailed by many American bishops as a confirmation, if not vindication, of their own theories. Catholics have always formed a large percentage of union membership, and some have served unions in positions of leadership.

Americanism

Near the end of the century some controversy developed over what was characterized as Americanism or the phantom heresy. It was alleged that Americans were discounting the importance of contemplative virtues, exalting the practical virtues, and watering down the purity of Catholic doctrine for the sake of facilitating convert work.

The French translation of Fr. Walter Elliott's *Life of Isaac Hecker*, which fired the controversy, was one of many factors that led to the issuance of Leo XIII's *Testem Benevolentiae* in January 1899, in an attempt to end the matter. It was the first time the orthodoxy of the Church in the U.S. was called into question.

Schism

In the 1890s, serious friction developed between Poles and Irish in Scranton, Buffalo and Chicago, resulting in schism and the establishment of the Polish National Catholic Church. A central figure in the affair was Fr. Francis Hodur, who was excommunicated by Bishop William O'Hara of Scranton in 1898. Nine years later, his ordination by an Old Catholic Abp. of Utrecht gave the new church its first bishop.

Another schism of the period led to formation of the American Carpatho-Russian Orthodox Greek Catholic Church.

Coming of Age

In 1900, there were 12 million Catholics in the total U.S. population of 76 million, 82 dioceses in 14 provinces, and 12,000 priests and members of about 40 communities of men Religious. Many sisterhoods, most of them of European origin and some of American foundation, were engaged in Catholic educational and hospital work, two of their traditional apostolates.

The Church in the U.S. was removed from mission status with promulgation of the apostolic constitution *Sapienti Consilio* by Pope St. Pius X on June 29, 1908.

Before that time, and even into the early 1920s, the Church in this country received financial assistance from mission-aid societies in France, Bavaria and Austria. Already, however, it was making increasing contributions of its own. At the present time, it is one of the major national contributors to the worldwide Society for the Propagation of the Faith.

American foreign missionary personnel increased from 14 or less in 1906 to an all-time high in 1968 of 9,655 priests, brothers, sisters, seminarians, and lay persons. The first missionary seminary in the U.S. was in operation at Techny, Illinois, in 1909, under the auspices of the Society of the Divine Word. Maryknoll, the first American missionary society, was established in 1911 and sent its first priests to China in 1918. Despite these contributions, the Church in the U.S. has not matched the missionary commitment of some other nations.

Bishops' Conference

A highly important apparatus for mobilizing the Church's resources was established in 1917 under the title of the National Catholic War Council. Its name was changed to National Catholic Welfare Conference several years later, but its objectives remained the same: to serve as an advisory and coordinating agency of the American bishops for advancing works of the Church in fields of social significance and impact — education, communications, immigration, social action, legislation, youth and lay organizations.

The forward thrust of the bishops' social thinking was evidenced in a program of social reconstruction they recommended in 1919. By 1945, all but one of their 12 points had been enacted into legislation — including many later social security programs.

The NCWC was renamed the United States Catholic Conference (USCC) in November 1966, when the hierarchy also organized itself as a territorial conference with pastoral-juridical authority under the title, National Conference of Catholic Bishops. The USCC carried on the functions of the former NCWC until July 2001, when it merged with the National Conference of Catholic Bishops to create the USCCB.

Catholic Press

The establishment of the National Catholic News Service (NC) — now the Catholic News Service (CNS) — in 1920 was an important event in the development of the Catholic press, which had its beginnings about 100 years earlier. Early in the 20th century there were 63 weekly newspapers. The *2003 Catholic Press Directory*, published by the Catholic Press Association, reported a total of 626 periodicals in North America, with a circulation of 26,87 million. The figures included 215 newspapers, 242 magazines, 125 newsletters, and 44 other-language periodicals (newspapers and magazines).

Lay Organizations

A burst of lay organizational growth occurred from the 1930s onwards with the appearance of Catholic Action types of movements and other groups and associations devoted to special causes, social service and assistance for the poor and needy. Several special apostolates developed under the aegis of the National Catholic Welfare Conference (now the U.S. Catholic Conference); the outstanding one was the Confraternity of Christian Doctrine.

Nineteenth-century organizations of great influence included: The St. Vincent de Paul Society, whose first U.S. office was set up in 1845 in St. Louis; the Catholic Central Union (*Verein*), dating from 1855; the Knights of Columbus, founded in 1882; the Holy Name Society, organized in the U.S. in 1870; the Rosary Society (1891); and scores of chapters of the Sodality of the Blessed Virgin Mary.

Pastoral Concerns

The potential for growth of the Church in this country by immigration was sharply reduced but not entirely curtailed after 1921 with the passage of restrictive federal legislation. As a result, the Catholic population became more stabilized and, to a certain extent and for many reasons, began to acquire an identity of its own.

Some increase from outside has taken place in the

past 50 years, however, from Canada, from Central and Eastern European countries, and from Puerto Rico and Latin American countries since World War II. This influx, while not as great as that of the 19th century and early 20th, has enriched the Church here with a sizable body of Eastern Rite Catholics for whom 12 ecclesiastical jurisdictions have been established. It has also created a challenge for pastoral care of millions of Hispanics in urban centers and in agricultural areas where migrant workers are employed.

The Church continues to grapple with serious pastoral problems in rural areas, where about 600 counties have no priests in ministry. The National Catholic Rural Life Conference was established in 1922 in an attempt to make the Catholic presence felt on the land, and the Glenmary Society since its foundation in 1939 has devoted itself to this single apostolate. Religious communities and diocesan priests are similarly engaged.

Other challenges lie in the cities and suburbs, where 75 percent of the Catholic population lives. Conditions peculiar to each segment of the metropolitan area have developed in recent years as the flight to the suburbs has not only altered some traditional aspects of parish life but has also, in combination with many other factors, left behind a complex of special problems in inner city areas.

A Post-War World

In the years after the Second World War, Catholics increasingly assumed a mainline role in American life. This was evidenced especially in the 1960 election of John F. Kennedy as the nation's first Catholic president. Catholic writers and thinkers were making a greater impact in the nation's life. One example of this was Trappist Thomas Merton's runaway best-selling book of 1948, *The Seven Storey Mountain*; another was the early television success of Bishop Fulton Sheen's "Life is Worth Living" series, begun in 1952. Meanwhile, lay leader Dorothy Day, founder of the Catholic Worker movement, continued to challenge American society with her views on pacifism and evangelical poverty.

A Post-Conciliar World

Catholic life in the United States was profoundly affected by the Second Vatican Council (1962-65). In the post-conciliar generation, American Catholicism grew both in numbers and complexity. Lay ministry and participation expanded; extensive liturgical changes (including the use of English) were implemented; and the numbers of priests, vowed religious and seminarians declined.

The Church has taken a high profile in many social issues. This has ranged from opposition to abortion, capital punishments and euthanasia to support for civil rights, economic justice and international peace and cooperation. Meanwhile Catholics have been deeply involved in inter-faith and ecumenical relationships. The bishops have issued landmark pastoral statements, including "The Challenge of Peace" (1983) and "Economic Justice for All" (1986).

In these years after the Council, the Catholics in America have known something of alienation, dissent and polarity. They also found new intensity and maturity. New U.S. saints have been declared by the universal church, such as Elizabeth Ann Seton (1975),

John Nepomucene Neumann (1977), and Rose Philippine Duchesne (1988). Especially at the time of visits to America by Pope John Paul II (e.g., in 1979, 1987, 1993, 1995, and 1999), U.S. Catholics have given evidence – in their personal and corporate lives – of the ongoing power of faith, liturgy and the primal call of the Gospel in its many dimensions.

Modern U.S. Catholicism

In the decades after Vatican Council II, the American Church confronted a variety of challenges, including the increasing age of American religious, especially in the Religious Institutes of Women; the decline in vocations; the presence of nominally Catholic organizations that nevertheless seek to counter or alter Catholic teaching on such issues as abortion, contraception, papal supremacy, collegiality, women's ordination, clerical celibacy, and homosexuality; the societal decay precipitated by a proliferation of an abortion culture; the weakening of the family structure and the destructive effects of unrestrained materialism and secular humanism; the spread of religious apathy and indifferentism; the needs of Catholic immigrants; and the lamentable state of American education. The varied difficulties, however, were overshadowed from late 2001 by the sexual scandal involving child molestation by a small number of priests in the country and the resulting legal cases, lawsuits, and media frenzy. While perpetrated by only a few hundred priests over nearly 40 years, the cases of child molestation (the vast majority of cases involved teenage boys) created the most severe scandal faced by the Church in the U.S. in the previous century. Compounding the legal and financial problems caused by the actions of the priests was the failure on the part of many bishops to recognize the severity of the scandal and the willingness of some bishops to move pedophile priests from one pastoral assignment to another.

At the summer meeting of the USCCB, the American bishops drafted a series of documents to insure the safety of children and to improve oversight of the situation. The bishops approved a Charter for the Protection of Children and Young People and Essential Norms for Diocesan/Eparchial Policies Dealing With Allegations of Sexual Abuse of Minors by Priests, Deacons, or Other Church Personnel. Officials of the Holy See rejected initially certain elements of canonical details of the norms, but the subsequent changes made by the bishops were given full Vatican approval. Nevertheless, the scandal created crushing financial difficulties for many dioceses facing a host of lawsuits, as well as a crisis of confidence among American Catholics.

Even in the face of these problems, there are a number of positive developments that give reason for guarded optimism: the progress in ecumenism; the rise of new religious congregations; the increase in conversions (over 400,000 a year); the marked sophistication of Catholic communications, centered in the USCCB; the Church's active role in social issues (human rights, poverty, health care, race relations, abortion and economic justice); and the greater involvement of the laity – especially women – in the life of the Church. Today, the membership in the U.S. is approximately 23 percent (66 million) of the U.S. population.

MISSIONARIES TO THE AMERICAS

An asterisk with a feast date indicates that the saint or blessed is listed in the General Roman Calendar or the proper calendar for U.S. dioceses.

Allouez, Claude Jean (1622-89): French Jesuit; missionary in Canada and midwestern U.S.; preached to 20 different tribes of Indians and baptized over 10,000; vicar general of Northwest.

Altham, John (1589-1640): English Jesuit; missionary among Indians in Maryland.

Amadeus of the Heart of Jesus (1846-1920): Provincial Superior of the Ursulines in the United States and missionary in Montana, Wyoming, and Alaska; founded 12 Ursuline missions for the Native Americans.

Anchieta, José de, Bl. (1534-97): Portuguese Jesuit, born Canary Islands; missionary in Brazil; writer; beatified 1980; feast, June 9.

Andreis, Felix de (1778-1820): Italian Vincentian; missionary and educator in western U.S.

Aparicio, Sebastian, Bl. (1502-1600): Franciscan brother; born Spain; settled in Mexico, c. 1533; worked as road builder and farmer before becoming Franciscan at about the age of 70; beatified, 1787; feast, Feb. 25.

Badin, Stephen T. (1768-1853): French missioner; came to U.S., 1792, when Sulpician seminary in Paris was closed; ordained, 1793, Baltimore, the first priest ordained in U.S.; missionary in Kentucky, Ohio and Michigan; bought land on which Notre Dame University now stands; buried on its campus.

Baraga, Frederic (1797-1868): Slovenian missionary bishop in U.S.; studied at Ljubljana and Vienna, ordained, 1823; came to U.S., 1830; missionary to Indians of Upper Michigan; first bishop of Marquette, 1857-1868; wrote Chippewa grammar, dictionary, prayer book and other works.

Bauer, Benedicta (1803-65): Missionary Dominican sister who helped establish convents and schools for German-speaking immigrants in New Jersey, California, Missouri, Washington and Kansas.

Bertran, Louis, St. (1526-81): Spanish Dominican; missionary in Colombia and Caribbean, 1562-69; canonized, 1671; feast, Oct. 9.

Betancur, Pedro de San José, Bl. (1626-67): Secular Franciscan, born Canary Islands; arrived in Guatemala, 1651; established hospital, school and homes for poor; beatified 1980; feast, Apr. 25.

Bourgeoys, Marguerite, St. (1620-1700): French foundress, missionary; settled in Canada, 1653; founded Congregation of Notre Dame, 1658; beatified, 1950; canonized 1982; feast, Jan. 12.

Brébeuf, Jean de, St. (1593-1649): French Jesuit; missionary among Huron Indians in Canada; martyred by Iroquois, Mar. 16, 1649; canonized, 1930; one of Jesuit North American martyrs; feast, Oct. 19* (U.S.).

Cancer de Barbastro, Louis (1500-49): Spanish Dominican; began missionary work in Middle America, 1533; killed at Tampa Bay, Florida.

Castillo, John de, St. (1596-1628): Spanish Jesuit; worked in Paraguay Indian mission settlements (reductions); martyred; beatified, 1934; canonized, 1988; feast, Nov. 16.

Catala, Magin (1761-1830): Spanish Franciscan; worked in California mission of Santa Clara for 36 years.

Chabanel, Noel, St. (1613-49): French Jesuit; missionary among Huron Indians in Canada; murdered by renegade Huron, Dec. 8, 1649; canonized, 1930; one of Jesuit North American martyrs; feast, Oct. 19* (U.S.).

Chaumonot, Pierre Joseph (1611-93): French Jesuit; missionary among Indians in Canada.

Clarke, Mary Frances (1803-87): Founder of the Sisters of Charity of the Blessed Virgin Mary; went to Iowa to start schools for children of white farmers and Native Americans; in Iowa Women's Hall of Fame.

Claver, Peter, St. (1581-1654): Spanish Jesuit; missionary among Negroes of South America and West Indies; canonized, 1888; patron of Catholic missions among black people; feast, Sept. 9*.

Cope, Marianne (1838-1918): German-born immigrant; entered Sisters of St. Francis; led sisters to Hawaii to take over a hospital and then to Molokai to care for lepers, including Bl. Damien de Veuster; she cared for women and young girls with the disease; her cause has been opened.

Daniel, Anthony, St. (1601-48): French Jesuit; missionary among Huron Indians in Canada; martyred by Iroquois, July 4, 1648; canonized, 1930; one of Jesuit North American martyrs; feast, Oct. 19* (U.S.).

De Smet, Pierre Jean (1801-73): Belgian-born Jesuit; missionary among Indians of northwestern U.S.; served as intermediary between Indians and U.S. government; wrote on Indian culture.

Duchesne, Rose Philippine, St. (1769-1852): French nun; educator and missionary in the U.S.; established first convent of the Society of the Sacred Heart in the U.S., at St. Charles, Missouri; founded schools for girls; did missionary work among Indians; beatified, 1940; canonized, 1988; feast, Nov. 18* (U.S.).

Farmer, Ferdinand (family name, Steinmeyer) (1720-86): German Jesuit; missionary in Philadelphia, where he died; one of the first missionaries in New Jersey.

Flaget, Benedict J. (1763-1850): French Sulpician bishop; came to U.S., 1792; missionary and educator in U.S.; first bishop of Bardstown, Kentucky (now Louisville), 1810-32; 1833-50.

Frances Xavier Cabrini: *See* under **Saints**.

Friess, Caroline (1824-92): Mother Superior of the School Sisters of Notre Dame in America from 1850-92; through her labors, the sisters opened 265 parochial schools in 29 diocese and four institutes of higher education for women.

Gallitzin, Demetrius (1770-1840): Russian prince, born The Hague; convert, 1787; ordained priest at Baltimore, 1795; frontier missionary, known as Fr. Smith; Gallitzin, PA, named for him.

Garnier, Charles, St. (c. 1606-49): French Jesuit; missionary among Hurons in Canada; martyred by Iroquois, Dec. 7, 1649; canonized, 1930; one of Jesuit North American martyrs; feast, Oct. 19* (U.S.).

Gibault, Pierre (1737-1804): Canadian missionary in Illinois and Indiana; aided in securing states of Ohio, Indiana, Illinois, Michigan and Wisconsin for the Americans during Revolution.

Gonzalez, Roch, St. (1576-1628): Paraguayan Jesuit; worked in Paraguay Indian mission settlements (reductions); martyred; beatified, 1934; canonized, 1988; feast, Nov. 16.

Goupil, René, St. (1607-42): French lay missionary; had studied surgery at Orleans, France; missionary companion of St. Isaac Jogues among the Hurons; martyred, Sept. 29, 1642; canonized, 1930; one of Jesuit North American martyrs; feast, Oct. 19* (U.S.).

Gravier, Jacques (1651-1708): French Jesuit; missionary among Indians of Canada and midwestern U.S.

Guérin, Theodore (1798-1856): Pioneer educator and Sister of Providence; arrived in U.S. in 1830 and founded St. Mary-of the-Woods in Vincennes, Indiana.

Hennepin, Louis (d. c. 1701): Belgian-born Franciscan missionary and explorer of Great Lakes region and Upper Mississippi, 1675-81, when he returned to Europe.

Ireland, Seraphine (1842-1930): Mother Superior of the Sisters of St. Joseph in the upper Midwest; opened 30 schools, five hospitals, and the College of St. Catherine, the second Catholic college for women in the U.S.

Jesuit North American Martyrs: Isaac Jogues, Anthony Daniel, John de Brébeuf, Gabriel Lalemant, Charles Garnier, Noel Chabanel (Jesuit priests), and René Goupil and John Lalande (lay missionaries) who were martyred between Sept. 29, 1642, and Dec. 9, 1649, in the missions of New France; canonized June 29, 1930; feast, Oct. 19* (U.S.). See separate entries.

Jogues, Isaac, St. (1607-46): French Jesuit; missionary among Indians in Canada; martyred near present site of Auriesville, NY, by Mohawks, Oct. 18, 1646; canonized, 1930; one of Jesuit North American Martyrs; feast, Oct. 19* (U.S.).

Kino, Eusebio (1645-1711): Italian Jesuit; missionary and explorer in U.S.; arrived Southwest, 1681; established 25 Indian missions, took part in 14 exploring expeditions in northern Mexico, Arizona and southern California; helped develop livestock raising and farming in the area. He was selected in 1965 to represent Arizona in Statuary Hall.

Lalande, John, St. (d. 1646): French lay missionary, companion of Isaac Jogues; martyred by Mohawks at Auriesville, NY, Oct. 19, 1646; canonized, 1930; one of Jesuit North American Martyrs; feast, Oct. 19* (U.S.).

Lalemant, Gabriel, St. (1610-49): French Jesuit; missionary among the Hurons in Canada; martyred by the Iroquois, Mar. 17, 1649; canonized, 1930; one of Jesuit North American Martyrs; feast, Oct. 19* (U.S.).

Lalor, Teresa (d. 1846): Co-founder, with Bp. Neale of Baltimore, of the Visitation Order in the U.S.; helped establish houses in Mobile, Kaskaskia, and Baltimore.

Lamy, Jean Baptiste (1814-88): French prelate; came to U.S., 1839; missionary in Ohio and Kentucky; bishop in Southwest from 1850; first bishop (later Abp.) of Santa Fe, 1850-85. He was nominated in 1951 to represent New Mexico in Statuary Hall.

Las Casas, Bartolome (1474-1566): Spanish Dominican; missionary in Haiti, Jamaica and Venezuela; reformer of abuses against Indians and black people; bishop of Chalapas, Mexico, 1544-47; historian.

Laval, Françoise de Montmorency, Bl. (1623-1708): French-born missionary bishop in Canada; named vicar apostolic of Canada, 1658; first bishop

of Québec, 1674; jurisdiction extended over all French-claimed territory in New World; beatified 1980; feast, May 6.

Manogue, Patrick (1831-95): Missionary bishop in U.S., born Ireland; migrated to U.S.; miner in California; studied for priesthood at St. Mary's of the Lake, Chicago, and St. Sulpice, Paris; ordained, 1861; missionary among Indians of California and Nevada; coadj. bishop, 1881-84, and bishop, 1884-86, of Grass Valley; first bishop of Sacramento, 1886-95, when see was transferred there.

Margil, Antonio, Ven. (1657-1726): Spanish Franciscan; missionary in Middle America; apostle of Guatemala; established missions in Texas.

Marie of the Incarnation, St. (Marie Guyard Martin) (1599-1672): French widow; joined Ursuline Nuns; arrived in Canada, 1639; first superior of Ursulines in Québec; missionary to Indians; writer; beatified 1980; feast, Apr. 30.

Marquette, Jacques (1637-75): French Jesuit; missionary and explorer in America; sent to New France, 1666; began missionary work among Ottawa Indians on Lake Superior, 1668; accompanied Joliet down the Mississippi to mouth of the Arkansas, 1673, and returned to Lake Michigan by way of Illinois River; made a second trip over the same route; his diary and map are of historical significance. He was selected in 1895 to represent Wisconsin in Statuary Hall.

Massias (Macias), John de, St. (1585-1645): Dominican brother, a native of Spain; entered Dominican Friary at Lima, Peru, 1622; served as doorkeeper until his death; beatified, 1837; canonized 1975; feast, Sept. 16.

Mazzuchelli, Samuel C. (1806-64): Italian Dominican; missionary in midwestern U.S.; called builder of the West; writer. A decree advancing his beatification cause was promulgated July 6, 1993.

Membre, Zenobius (1645-87): French Franciscan; missionary among Indians of Illinois; accompanied LaSalle expedition down the Mississippi (1681-82) and Louisiana colonizing expedition (1684) that landed in Texas; murdered by Indians.

Mozcygemba, Leopold (1824-91): Polish Franciscan priest and missionary, the patriarch of American Polonia; labored as a missionary in Texas and 11 other states for nearly 40 years; co-founded the Polish seminary of Sts. Cyril and Methodius in Detroit (1885) and served as confessor at Vatican Council I.

Nerinckx, Charles (1761-1824): Belgian priest; missionary in Kentucky; founded Sisters of Loretto at the Foot of the Cross.

Nobrega, Manoel (1517-70): Portuguese Jesuit; leader of first Jesuit missionaries to Brazil, 1549.

Padilla, Juan de (d. 1542): Spanish Franciscan; missionary among Indians of Mexico and southwestern U.S.; killed by Indians in Kansas; proto-martyr of the U.S.

Palou, Francisco (c. 1722-89): Spanish Franciscan; accompanied Junípero Serra to Mexico, 1749; founded Mission Dolores in San Francisco; wrote history of the Franciscans in California.

Pariseau, Mary Joseph (1833-1902): Canadian Sister of Charity of Providence; missionary in state of Washington from 1856; founded first hospitals in northwest territory; artisan and architect. Represents Washington in National Statuary Hall.

Peter of Ghent (d. 1572): Belgian Franciscan brother; missionary in Mexico for 49 years.

Porres, Martin de, St. (1579-1639): Peruvian Dominican oblate; his father was a Spanish soldier and his mother a black freedwoman from Panama; called wonder worker of Peru; beatified, 1837; canonized, 1962; feast, Nov. 3*.

Quiroga, Vasco de (1470-1565): Spanish missionary in Mexico; founded hospitals; bishop of Michoacan, 1537.

Ravalli, Antonio (1811-84): Italian Jesuit; missionary in far-western U.S., mostly Montana, for 40 years.

Raymbaut, Charles (1602-43): French Jesuit; missionary among Indians of Canada and northern U.S.

Richard, Gabriel (1767-1832): French Sulpician; missionary in Illinois and Michigan; a founder of University of Michigan; elected delegate to Congress from Michigan, 1823; first priest to hold seat in the House of Representatives.

Riepp, Benedicta (1825-62): Founder of the first Benedictine community of nuns in the U.S.; by the time of her death, the order had founded convents in Illinois, Kentucky, Minnesota, and New Jersey.

Rodriguez, Alfonso, St. (1598-1628): Spanish Jesuit; missionary in Paraguay; martyred; beatified, 1934; canonized, 1988; feast, Nov. 16.

Rosati, Joseph (1789-1843): Italian Vincentian; missionary bishop in U.S. (vicar apostolic of Mississippi and Alabama, 1822; coadj. of Louisiana and the Two Floridas, 1823-26; administrator of New Orleans, 1826-29; first bishop of St. Louis, 1826-1843).

Russell, Mary Baptist (1829-98): Mother Superior of the Sisters of Mercy in San Francisco from 1854-98; founded St. Mary's Hospital in 1857, schools, and homes the aged and former prostitutes.

Sahagun, Bernardino de (c. 1500-90): Spanish Franciscan; missionary in Mexico for over 60 years; expert on Aztec archaeology.

Seelos, Francis X. (1819-67): Redemptorist missionary, born Bavaria; ordained, 1844, at Baltimore; missionary in Pittsburgh and New Orleans.

Seghers, Charles J. (1839-86): Belgian missionary bishop in North America; Apostle of Alaska; Abp. of Oregon City (now Portland), 1880-84; murdered by berserk companion while on missionary journey.

Serra, Junípero, Bl. (1713-84): Spanish Franciscan, born Majorca; missionary in America; arrived Mexico, 1749, where he did missionary work for 20 years; began work in Upper California in 1769 and established nine of the 21 Franciscan missions along the Pacific coast; baptized some 6,000 Indians and confirmed almost 5,000; a cultural pioneer of California Represents California in Statuary Hall. He was declared venerable May 9, 1985, and was beatified Sept. 25, 1988; feast, July 1* (U.S.).

Solanus, Francis, St. (1549-1610): Spanish Franciscan; missionary in Paraguay, Argentina and Peru; wonder worker of the New World; canonized, 1726; feast, July 14.

Sorin, Edward F. (1814-93): French priest; member of Congregation of Holy Cross; sent to U.S. in 1841; founder and first president of the University of Notre Dame; missionary in Indiana and Michigan.

Todadilla, Anthony de (1704-46): Spanish Capuchin; missionary to Indians of Venezuela; killed by Motilones.

Turibius de Mogrovejo, St. (1538-1606): Spanish Abp. of Lima, Peru, c. 1580-1606; canonized 1726; feast, Mar. 23*.

Twelve Apostles of Mexico (early 16th century): Franciscan priests who arrived in Mexico, 1524: Fathers Martin de Valencia (leader), Francisco de Soto, Martin de la Coruna, Juan Suares, Antonio de Ciudad Rodrigo, Toribio de Benevente, Garcia de Cisneros, Luis de Fuensalida, Juan de Ribas, Francisco Ximenes; Brothers Andres de Coroboda, and Juan de Palos.

Valdivia, Luis de (1561-1641): Spanish Jesuit; defender of Indians in Peru and Chile.

Vasques de Espiñosa, Antonio (early 17th century): Spanish Carmelite; missionary and explorer in Mexico, Panama and western coast of South America.

Vieira, Antonio (1608-87): Portuguese Jesuit; preacher; missionary in Peru and Chile; protector of Indians against exploitation by slave owners and traders; considered foremost prose writer of 17th-century Portugal.

Ward, Mary Francis Xavier (1810-84): Established the Sisters of Mercy in U.S.; arrived in Pittsburgh in 1843; founded convents in 10 states to care for the sick and poor and provide education.

White, Andrew (1579-1656): English Jesuit; missionary among Indians in Maryland.

Wimmer, Boniface (1809-87): German Benedictine; missionary among German immigrants in the U.S.

Youville, Marie Marguerite d', St. (1701-71): Canadian widow; foundress of Sisters of Charity (Grey Nuns), 1737, at Montréal: beatified, 1959; canonized 1990, first native Canadian saint; feast, Dec. 23.

Zumarraga, Juan de (1468-1548): Spanish Franciscan; missionary; first bishop of Mexico; introduced first printing press in New World, published first book in America, a catechism for Aztec Indians; extended missions in Mexico and Central America; vigorous opponent of exploitation of Indians; approved of devotions at Guadalupe; leading figure in early church history in Mexico.

FRANCISCAN MISSIONS

The 21 Franciscan missions of Upper California were established during the 54-year period from 1769 to 1822. Located along the old El Camino Real, or King's Highway, they extended from San Diego to San Francisco and were the centers of Indian civilization, Christianity and industry in the early history of the state.

Junípero Serra (beatified 1988) was the great pioneer of the missions of Upper California He and his successor as superior of the work, Fermin Lasuen, each directed the establishment of nine missions. One hundred and 46 priests of the Order of Friars Minor, most of them Spaniards, labored in the region from 1769 to 1845; 67 of them died at their posts, two as martyrs. The regular time of mission service was 10 years.

The missions were secularized by the Mexican government in the 1830s but were subsequently restored to the Church by the U.S. government. They are now variously used as the sites of parish churches, a university, houses of study and museums.

The names of the missions and the order of their establishment were as follows:

San Diego de Alcala, San Carlos Borromeo (El Carmelo), San Antonio de Padua, San Gabriel Arcangel, San Luis Obispo de Tolosa, San Francisco de Asis (Dolores), San Juan Capistrano; Santa Clara de Asis, San Buenaventura, Santa Barbara, La Purisima Concepcion de Maria Santisima, Santa Cruz, Nuestra Señora de la Soledad, San José de Guadalupe, San Juan Bautista, San Miguel Arcangel, San Fernando Rey de España, San Luis Rey de Francia, Santa Ines, San Rafael Arcangel, San Francisco Solano de Sonoma (Sonoma).

Find more material at: www.CatholicAlmanac.com.

CHURCH-STATE RELATIONS IN THE UNITED STATES

CHURCH-STATE DECISIONS OF THE SUPREME COURT

Among sources of this selected listing of U.S. Supreme Court decisions was *The Supreme Court on Church and State*, Joseph Tussman, editor; Oxford University Press, New York, 1962.

Watson v. Jones, 13 Wallace 679 (1872): The Court declared that a member of a religious organization may not appeal to secular courts against a decision made by a church tribunal within the area of its competence.

Reynolds v. United States, 98 US 145 (1879): Davis v. Beason, 133 US 333 (1890); Church of Latter-Day Saints v. United States, 136 US 1 (1890). The Mormon practice of polygamy was at issue in three decisions and was declared unconstitutional.

Bradfield v. Roberts, 175 US 291 (1899): The Court denied that an appropriation of government funds for an institution (Providence Hospital, Washington, DC) run by Roman Catholic sisters violated the No Establishment Clause of the First Amendment.

Pierce v. Society of Sisters, 268 US 510 (1925): The Court denied that a state can require children to attend public schools only. The Court held that the liberty of the Constitution forbids standardization by such compulsion, and that the parochial schools involved had claims to protection under the Fourteenth Amendment.

Cochran v. Board of Education, 281 US 370 (1930): The Court upheld a Louisiana statute providing textbooks at public expense for children attending public or parochial schools. The Court held that the children and state were beneficiaries of the appropriations, with incidental secondary benefit going to the schools.

United States v. MacIntosh, 283 US 605 (1931): The Court denied that anyone can place allegiance to the will of God above his allegiance to the government since such a person could make his own interpretation of God's will the decisive test as to whether he would or would not obey the nation's law. The Court stated that the nation, which has a duty to survive, can require citizens to bear arms in its defense.

Everson v. Board of Education, 330 US 1 (1947): The Court upheld the constitutionality of a New Jersey statute authorizing free school bus transportation for parochial as well as public school students. The Court expressed the opinion that the benefits of public welfare legislation, included under such bus transportation, do not run contrary to the concept of separation of Church and State.

McCollum v. Board of Education, 333 US 203 (1948): The Court declared unconstitutional a program for releasing children, with parental consent, from public school classes so they could receive religious instruction on public school premises from representatives of their own faiths.

Zorach v. Clauson, 343 US 306 (1952): The Court upheld the constitutionality of a New York statute permitting, on a voluntary basis, the release during school time of students from public school classes for religious instruction given off public school premises.

Torcaso v. Watkins, 367 US 488 (1961): The Court declared unconstitutional a Maryland requirement that one must make a declarati on of belief in the existence of God as part of the oath of office for notaries public.

McGowan v. Maryland, 81 Sp Ct 1101; Two Guys from Harrison v. McGinley, 81 Sp Ct 1135; Gallagher v. Crown Kosher Super Market, 81 Sp Ct 1128; Braunfield v. Brown, 81 Sp Ct 1144 (1961): The Court ruled that Sunday closing laws do not violate the No Establishment of Religion Clause of the First Amendment, even though the laws were religious in their inception and still have some religious overtones. The Court held that, "as presently written and administered, most of them, at least, are of a secular rather than of a religious character, and that presently they bear no relationship to establishment of religion as those words are used in the Constitution of the United States."

Engel v. Vitale, 370 US 42 (1962): The Court declared that the voluntary recitation in public schools of a prayer composed by the New York State Board of Regents is unconstitutional on the ground that it violates the No Establishment of Religion Clause of the First Amendment.

Abington Township School District v. Schempp and Murray v. Curlett, 83 Sp Ct 1560 (1963): The Court ruled that Bible reading and recitation of the Lord's Prayer in public schools, with voluntary participation by students, are unconstitutional on the ground that they violate the No Establishment of Religion Clause of the First Amendment.

Chamberlin v. Dade County, 83 Sp Ct 1864 (1964): The Court reversed a decision of the Florida Supreme Court concerning the constitutionality of prayer and devotional Bible reading in public schools during the school day, as sanctioned by a state statute which specifically related the practices to a sound public purpose.

Board of Education v. Allen, No. 660 (1968): The Court declared constitutional the New York schoolbook-loan law that requires local school boards to purchase books with state funds and lend them to parochial and private school students.

Walz v. Tax Commission of New York (1970): The Court upheld the constitutionality of a New York statute exempting church-owned property from taxation.

Earle v. DiCenso, Robinson v. DiCenso, Lemon v. Kurtzman, Tilton v. Richardson (1971): In Earle v. DiCenso and Robinson v. DiCenso, the Court ruled unconstitutional a 1969 Rhode Island statute that provided salary supplements to teachers of secular subjects in parochial schools; in Lemon v. Kurtzman, the Court ruled unconstitutional a 1968 Pennsylvania statute that authorized the state to purchase services for the teaching of secular subjects in nonpublic schools. The principal argument against constitutionality in these cases was that the statutes and programs at issue entailed excessive entanglement of government with religion. In Tilton v. Richardson, the Court held that this argument did not apply to a prohibitive degree with respect to federal grants, under the Higher Education Facilities Act of 1963, for the construction of facilities for nonreligious purposes by four church-related institutions of higher learning, three of which were Catholic, in Connecticut.

Yoder, Miller and Yutzy (1972): In a case appealed on behalf of Yoder, Miller and Yutzy, the Court ruled that Amish parents were exempt from a Wisconsin statute requiring them to send their children to school until the age of 16. The Court said in its decision that secondary schooling exposed Amish children to attitudes, goals and values contrary to their beliefs, and substantially hindered "the religious development of the Amish child and his integration into the way of life of the Amish faith-community at the crucial adolescent state of development."

Committee for Public Education and Religious Liberty, et al., v. Nyquist, et al., No. 72-694 (1973): The Court ruled that provisions of a 1972 New York statute were unconstitutional on the grounds that they were violative of the No Establishment Clause of the First Amendment and had the "impermissible effect" of advancing the sectarian activities of church-affiliated schools. The programs ruled unconstitutional concerned: (1) maintenance and repair grants, for facilities and equipment, to ensure the health, welfare and safety of students in nonpublic, nonprofit elementary and secondary schools serving a high concentration of students from low income families; (2) tuition reimbursement ($50 per grade school child, $100 per high school student) for parents (with income less than $5,000) of children attending nonpublic elementary or secondary schools; tax deduction from adjusted gross income for parents failing to qualify under the above reimbursement plan, for each child attending a nonpublic school.

Sloan, Treasurer of Pennsylvania, et al., v. Lemon, et al., No. 72-459 (1973): The Court ruled unconstitutional a Pennsylvania Parent Reimbursement Act for Nonpublic Education which provided funds to reimburse parents (to a maximum of $150) for a portion of tuition expenses incurred in sending their children to nonpublic schools. The Court held that there was no significant difference between this and the New York tuition reimbursement program (above), and declared that the Equal Protection Clause of the Fourteenth Amendment cannot be relied upon to sustain a program held to be violative of the No Establishment Clause.

Levitt, et al., v. Committee for Public Education and Religious Liberty, et al., No. 72-269 (1973): The Court ruled unconstitutional the Mandated Services Act of 1970 under which New York provided $28 million ($27 per pupil from first to seventh grade, $45 per pupil from seventh to 12th grade) to reimburse nonpublic schools for testing, recording and reporting services required by the state. The Court

declared that the act provided "impermissible aid" to religion in contravention of the No Establishment Clause.

In related decisions handed down June 25, 1973, the Court: (1) affirmed a lower-court decision against the constitutionality of an Ohio tax credit law benefiting parents with children in nonpublic schools; (2) reinstated an injunction against a parent reimbursement program in New Jersey; (3) affirmed South Carolina's right to grant construction loans to church-affiliated colleges, and (4) dismissed an appeal contesting its right to provide loans to students attending church-affiliated colleges (Hunt v. McNair, Durham v. McLeod).

Wheeler v. Barrera (1974): The Court ruled that nonpublic school students in Missouri must share in federal funds for educationally deprived students on a comparable basis with public school students under Title I of the Elementary and Secondary Education Act of 1965.

Norwood v. Harrison 93 S. Ct. 2804: The Court ruled that public assistance that avoids the prohibitions of the "effect" and "entanglement" tests (and which therefore does not substantially promote the religious mission of sectarian schools) may be confined to the secular functions of such schools.

Wiest v. Mt. Lebanon School District (1974): The Court upheld a lower court ruling that invocation and benediction prayers at public high school commencement ceremonies do not violate the principle of separation of Church and State.

Meek v. Pittenger (1975): The Court ruled unconstitutional portions of a Pennsylvania law providing auxiliary services for students of nonpublic schools; at the same time, it ruled in favor of provisions of the law permitting textbook loans to students of such schools. In denying the constitutionality of auxiliary services, the Court held that they had the "primary effect of establishing religion" and involved "excessive entanglement" of Church and state officials with respect to supervision; objection was also made against providing such services only on the premises of nonpublic schools and only at the request of such schools.

TWA, Inc., v. Hardison, 75-1126; International Association of Machinists and Aero Space Workers v. Hardison, 75-1385 (1977): The Court ruled that federal civil-rights legislation does not require employers to make more than minimal efforts to accommodate employees who want a particular working day off as their religion's Sabbath Day, and that an employer cannot accommodate such an employee by violating seniority systems determined by a union collective bargaining agreement. The Court noted that its ruling was not a constitutional judgment but an interpretation of existing law.

Wolman v. Walter (1977): The Court ruled constitutional portions of an Ohio statute providing tax-paid textbook loans and some auxiliary services (standardized and diagnostic testing, therapeutic and remedial services, off school premises) for nonpublic school students. It decided that other portions of the law, providing state funds for nonpublic school field trips and instructional materials (audio-visual equipment, maps, tape recorders), were unconstitutional.

Byrne v. Public Funds for Public Schools (1979): The Court decided against the constitutionality of a

1976 New Jersey law providing state income tax deductions for tuition paid by parents of students attending parochial and other private schools.

Student Bus Transportation (1979): The Court upheld a Pennsylvania law providing bus transportation at public expense for students to nonpublic schools up to 10 miles away from the boundaries of the public school districts in which they lived.

Reimbursement (1980): The Court upheld the constitutionality of a 1974 New York law providing direct cash payment to nonpublic schools for the costs of state-mandated testing and record-keeping.

Ten Commandments (1980): The Court struck down a 1978 Kentucky law requiring the posting of the Ten Commandments in public school classrooms in the state.

Widmar v. Vincent (1981): The Court ruled that the University of Missouri at Kansas City could not deny student religious groups the use of campus facilities for worship services. The Court also, in Brandon v. Board of Education of Guilderland Schools, declined without comment to hear an appeal for reversal of lower court decisions denying a group of New York high school students the right to meet for prayer on public school property before the beginning of the school day.

Lubbock v. Lubbock Civil Liberties Union (1983): By refusing to hear an appeal in this case, the Court upheld a lower court ruling against a public policy of permitting student religious groups to meet on public school property before and after school hours.

Mueller v. Allen (1983): The Court upheld a Minnesota law allowing parents of students in public and nonpublic (including parochial) schools to take a tax deduction for the expenses of tuition, textbooks and transportation. Maximum allowable deductions were $500 per child in elementary school and $700 per child in grades seven through 12.

Lynch v. Donnelly (1984): The Court ruled 5-to-4 that the First Amendment does not mandate "complete separation of church and state," and that, therefore, the sponsorship of a Christmas nativity scene by the City of Pawtucket, RI, was not unconstitutional. The case involved a scene included in a display of Christmas symbols sponsored by the city in a park owned by a non-profit group. The majority opinion said "the Constitution (does not) require complete separation of church and state; it affirmatively mandates accommodation, not merely tolerance, of all religions and forbids hostility toward any. Anything less" would entail callous indifference not intended by the Constitution. Moreover, "such hostility would bring us into 'war with our national tradition as embodied in the First Amendment's guaranty of the free exercise of religion.' " (The additional quotation was from the 1948 decision in McCollum v. Board of Education.)

Christmas Nativity Scene (1985): The Court upheld a lower court ruling that the Village of Scarsdale, NY, must make public space available for the display of privately sponsored nativity scenes.

Wallace v. Jaffree, No. 83-812 (1985): The Court ruled against the constitutionality of a 1981 Alabama law calling for a public-school moment of silence that specifically included optional prayer.

Grand Rapids v. Ball, No. 83-990, and **Aguilar v. Felton, No. 84-237** (1985): The Court ruled against the constitutionality of programs in Grand Rapids and New York City allowing public school teachers to teach remedial entitlement subjects (under the Elementary and Secondary Education Act of 1965) in private schools, many of which were Catholic.

Bender v. Williamsport Area School District (1986): The Court let stand a lower federal-court decision allowing a public high school Bible study group the same "equal access" to school facilities as that enjoyed by other extracurricular clubs. A similar decision was handed down in 1990 in Board of Education v. Mergens, involving Westside High School in Omaha.

County of Allegheny v. American Civil Liberties Union (1989): The Court ruled (1) that the display of a Christmas nativity scene in the Allegheny County Courthouse in Pittsburgh, PA, violated the principle of separation of church and state because it appeared to be a government-sponsored endorsement of Christian belief; (2) and that the display of a Hanukkah menorah outside the Pittsburgh-Allegheny city-county building was constitutional because of its "particular physical setting" with secular symbols.

Unemployment Division v. Smith (1990): The Court ruled that religious use of the hallucinogenic cactus peyote is not covered by the First Amendment protection of religious freedom.

Lee v. Weisman (1992): The Court banned officially organized prayer at public school graduation ceremonies.

Lamb's Chapel v. Center Moriches Union School District (1993): The Court reversed a ruling by the 3rd U.S. Circuit Court of Appeals, declaring that the school district was wrong in prohibiting the congregation of Lamb's Chapel from using public school meeting space after hours to show a film series addressing family problems from a religious perspective. In view of the variety of organizations permitted to use school property after school hours, said the Court's opinion: "There would have been no realistic danger that the community would think that the district was endorsing religion or any particular creed, and any benefit to religion or to the church would have been no more than incidental."

5th U.S. Circuit Court of Appeals (1993): The Court let stand a ruling by the 5th U.S. Circuit Court of Appeals, permitting students in Texas, Mississippi and Louisiana to include student-organized and student-led prayers in graduation exercises.

Church of Lukumi Babalu Aye v. City of Hialeah (1993): The Court ruled that municipal laws that effectively prohibit a single church from performing its religious rituals are unconstitutional. The ordinances at issue singled out one religion, Santeria, for the purpose of restricting its members from the practice of ritual animal sacrifices.

Zobrest v. Catalina Foothills School District (1993): The Court ruled that a public school district may provide a sign-language interpreter for a deaf student attending a Catholic school without violating constitutional separation of church and state. The majority opinion said: "Handicapped children, not sectarian schools are the primary beneficiaries of the Disabilities Education Act; to the extent sectarian schools benefit at all from (the act), they are only incidental beneficiaries."

Fairfax County, Va., school district (1994): The

Court upheld lower court rulings against a Fairfax County, VA, school district's practice of charging churches more rent than other entities for the use of school buildings.

Board of Education of Kiryas Joel Village School District v. Grumet (1994): The Court ruled in 1994 that a school district created to meet the special education needs of an Hasidic Jewish community violated the Establishment Clause of the Constitution. The Court said the New York Legislature effectively endorsed a particular religion when it established a public school district for the Satmar Hasidic Village of Kiryas Joel.

Agostino v. Felton (1997): The court reversed, 5 to 4, its 1985 Aguilar v. Felton ruling, which had declared it unconstitutional for teachers employed by public school districts to hold Title I remedial programs for low-income students on the property of church-related schools.

Boerne v. Flores (1997): The court ruled, 6 to 3, that the Religious Freedom Restoration Act (1993) was unconstitutional because Congress overstepped its constitutional authority in enacting the law. Congress "has been given the power to 'enforce,' not the power to determine what constitutes a constitutional violation," said the majority opinion.

Mitchell v. Helms (2000): The court ruled, 6 to 3, that a Louisiana parish can distribute money for instructional equipment — including computers, books, maps, and film strip projectors — to private schools as long as it is done in a "secular, neutral and non-ideological" way. The court's decision overturns two previous Supreme Court bans on giving public materials to parochial schools.

Santa Fe Independent School District v. Doe (2000): The court affirmed a lower court ruling that said prayer in public schools must be private and that such prayers at high school football games violate the constitutionally required separation of church and state. At issue in the Santa Fe case was a Texas school policy which permitted students selected by their peers to deliver an inspirational message of their own design at football games and the graduation ceremony. In 1999, the Santa Fe policy was struck down by the U.S. Court of Appeals for the Fifth Circuit. The Court of Appeals held that the policy violated the Establishment Clause of the First Amendment, even though the government played no role in creating the message or selecting the messenger.

Chandler v. Siegelman (2001): The court let stand a lower court ruling that students may participate in group prayers at school functions such as football games or graduations.

The Good News Club v. Milford Central Schools (2001): The court ruled that if the Boy Scouts and 4-H can use a public school as a meeting hall, a children's Bible study class can also.

Brown v. Gilmore (2001): The court declined to hear a challenge to Virginia's mandatory minute of silence in schools.

Children's Health Care is a Legal Duty Inc. v. McMullan (2001): The court turned down an appeal that claimed Medicare and Medicaid payments to church-run health centers violate the constitutional separation of church and state.

Gentala v. Tucson (2001): The court ordered a federal appeals court to take another look at a case that asked whether taxpayers must cover $340 in expenses from a prayer rally in a city park, saying it should be reconsidered in light of the high court's earlier ruling that a Bible club cannot be excluded from meeting at a public school so long as other groups with a moral viewpoint are allowed to gather there.

RELIGION IN PUBLIC SCHOOLS

(Based on a Catholic News Service article by Carol Zimmermann.)

A diverse group of religious and civil rights organizations issued a joint statement Apr. 13, 1995, in an effort to clarify the confusing issue of prayer and religious observances or discussions in public schools. Their six-page statement outlines what is and what is not currently permissible in expressing religious beliefs in public schools.

The statement says, for example: "Students have the right to pray individually or in groups, or to discuss their religious views with their peers so long as they are not disruptive." But, the statement specifies that such prayers or discussions do not include "the right to have a captive audience listen or to compel other students to participate."

Prayer at Graduations

Regarding prayer at graduation ceremonies, the document says school officials may not mandate or organize prayer, but fails to set the record straight about student-led prayer at these services.

"The courts have reached conflicting conclusions under the federal Constitution" in this area, says the statement, recommending that schools consult their lawyers for the rules that apply to them, "until the issue is authoritatively resolved."

Since the Supreme Court's 1992 Lee v. Weisman opinion prohibited school authorities from even arranging for a speaker to present a prayer, lower courts in different states have made various rulings about student-led prayer at commencement exercises.

In Virginia, the state's Attorney General and the Board of Education proposed guidelines in mid-April to allow student-led prayer at graduations, despite a 1994 ruling by a U.S. district judge banning all prayer at graduations.

Religion in the Classroom

"It is both permissible and desirable to teach objectively about the role of religion in the history of the United States and other countries," but public school teachers may not specifically teach religion.

The same rules apply to the recurring controversy surrounding theories of evolution. Teachers may discuss explanations of the beginnings of life, but only within the confines of classes on religion or social studies. Public school teachers are required, according to the statement, to teach only scientific explanations of life's beginnings in science classes. And, just as teachers may not advance a religious view, they should not ridicule a student's religious belief.

Constitutional Protection

The statement says that students' expressions of religious beliefs in reports, homework or artwork are constitutionally protected. Likewise, students have the right to speak to and attempt to persuade their peers on religious topics. "But school officials should intercede to stop student religious speech if it turns into religious harassment aimed at a student or a small group of students."

The statement also says:

• Students have the right to distribute religious literature to their schoolmates, subject to reasonable restrictions for any non-school literature.

• Student religious clubs in secondary schools "must be permitted to meet and to have equal access" to school media for announcing their events.

• Religious messages on T-shirts and the like cannot be singled out for suppression.

• Schools can use discretion about dismissing students for off-site religious instruction.

The 35 organizations that endorsed the statement included the National Association of Evangelicals, the American Jewish Congress, the Christian Legal Society, the National Council of Churches, the Baptist Joint Committee on Public Affairs, the American Muslim Council, the Presbyterian Church (USA) and the American Civil Liberties Union.

Purpose of the Statement

"By making this document available," said Phil Baum, executive director of the American Jewish Congress, "the organizations are attempting to clarify what has become one of the most divisive issues of our time: religion in the public schools."

He said the document attempts to "ensure that the rights of all students are respected in the public schools."

Baum noted that the American Jewish Congress, which initiated the effort to draft the statement, had a long-standing commitment to ensuring that public schools are themselves religiously neutral.

"We believe, however, that it is inconsistent with that historic commitment to ask the public schools to root out private expressions of religious faith."

CHURCH TAX EXEMPTION

The exemption of church-owned property was ruled constitutional by the U.S. Supreme Court May 4, 1970, in the case of Walz v. The Tax Commission of New York.

Suit in the case was brought by Frederick Walz, who purchased in June 1967, a 22-by-29-foot plot of ground in Staten Island valued at $100 and taxable at $5.24 a year. Shortly after making the purchase, Walz instituted a suit in New York State, contending that the exemption of church property from taxation authorized by state law increased his own tax rate and forced him indirectly to support churches in violation of his constitutional right to freedom of religion under the First Amendment. Three New York courts dismissed the suit, which had been instituted by mail. The Supreme Court, judging that it had probable jurisdiction, then took the case.

In a 7-1 decision affecting Church-state relations in every state in the nation, the Court upheld the New York law under challenge.

For and Against

Chief Justice Warren E. Burger, who wrote the majority opinion, said that Congress from its earliest days had viewed the religion clauses of the Constitution as authorizing statutory real estate tax exemption to religious bodies. He declared: "Nothing in this national attitude toward religious tolerance and two centuries of uninterrupted freedom from taxation has given the remotest sign of leading to an established church or religion, and on the contrary it has operated affirmatively to help guarantee the free exercise of all forms of religious beliefs."

Justice William O. Douglas wrote in dissent that the involvement of government in religion as typified in tax exemption may seem inconsequential but: "It is, I fear, a long step down the establishment path. Perhaps I have been misinformed. But, as I read the Constitution and the philosophy, I gathered that independence was the price of liberty."

Burger rejected Douglas' "establishment" fears. If tax exemption is the first step toward establishment, he said, "the second step has been long in coming."

The basic issue centered on the following question: Is there a contradiction between federal constitutional provisions against the establishment of religion, or the use of public funds for religious purposes, and state statutes exempting church property from taxation? In the Walz decision, the Supreme Court ruled that there is no contradiction.

Legal Background

The U.S. Constitution makes no reference to tax exemption. There was no discussion of the issue in the Constitutional Convention nor in debates on the Bill of Rights.

In the Colonial and post-Revolutionary years, some churches had established status and were state-supported. This changed with enactment of the First Amendment, which laid down no-establishment as the federal norm. This norm was adopted by the states which, however, exempted churches from tax liabilities.

No establishment, no hindrance, was the early American view of Church-State relationships.

This view, reflected in custom law, was not generally formulated in statute law until the second half of the 19th century, although specific tax exemption was provided for churches in Maryland in 1798, in Virginia in 1800, and in North Carolina in 1806.

The first major challenge to church property exemption was initiated by the Liberal League in the 1870s. It reached the point that President Grant included the recommendation in a State of the Union address in 1875, stating that church property should bear its own proportion of taxes. The plea fell on deaf ears in Congress, but there was some support for the idea at state levels. The exemption, however, continued to survive various challenges.

About 36 state constitutions contain either mandatory or permissive provisions for exemption. Statutes provide for exemption in all other states.

There has been considerable litigation challenging this exemption, but most of it focused on whether a particular property satisfied statutory requirements. Few cases before Walz focused on the strictly constitutional question, whether directly under the First Amendment or indirectly under the Fourteenth.

Objections

Objectors to the tax exempt status of churches feel that churches should share, through taxation, in the cost of the ordinary benefits of public services they enjoy, and/or that the amount of "aid" enjoyed through exemption should be proportionate to the amount of social good they do.

According to one opinion, exemption is said to weaken the independence of churches from the political system that benefits them by exemption.

In another view, exemption is said to involve the government in decisions regarding what is and what is not religion.

The Wall of Separation

Thomas Jefferson, in a letter written to the Danbury (Connecticut) Baptist Association Jan. 1, 1802, coined the metaphor, "a wall of separation between Church and State," to express a theory concerning interpretation of the religion clauses of the First Amendment: "Congress shall make no law respecting an establishment of religion or prohibiting the free exercise thereof."

The metaphor was cited for the first time in judicial proceedings in 1879, in the opinion by Chief Justice Waite in Reynolds v. United States. It did not, however, figure substantially in the decision.

Accepted as Rule

In 1947 the wall of separation gained acceptance as a constitutional rule, in the decision handed down in Everson v. Board of Education. Associate Justice Black, in describing the principles involved in the No Establishment Clause, wrote:

"Neither a state nor the Federal Government can set up a church. Neither can pass laws which aid one religion, aid all religions, or prefer one religion over another. Neither can force nor influence a person to go to or to remain away from church against his will or force him to profess a belief or disbelief in any religion. No person can be punished for entertaining or professing religious beliefs or disbeliefs, for church attendance or non-attendance. No tax in any amount, large or small, can be levied to support any religious activities or institutions, whatever they may be called, or whatever form they may adopt to teach or practice religion. Neither a state nor the Federal Government can, openly or secretly, participate in the affairs of any religious organizations or groups and vice versa. In the words of Jefferson, the clause against establishment of religion by law was intended to erect 'a wall of separation between Church and State.' "

Mr. Black's associates agreed with his statement of principles, which were framed without reference to the Freedom of Exercise Clause. They disagreed, however, with respect to application of the principles, as the split decision in the case indicated. Five members of the Court held that the benefits of public welfare legislation — in this case, free bus transportation to school for parochial as well as public school students — did not run contrary to the concept of separation of Church and State embodied in the First Amendment.

(For coverage of the recent Supreme Court decision pertaining to vouchers, see **Education**.)

CATHOLICS IN THE U.S. GOVERNMENT

CATHOLICS IN PRESIDENTS' CABINETS

From 1789 to 1940, nine Catholics were appointed to cabinet posts by six of 32 presidents. The first was Roger Brooke Taney (later named first Catholic Supreme Court Justice) who was appointed in 1831 by Andrew Jackson. Catholics have been appointed to cabinet posts from the time of Franklin D. Roosevelt to the present.

Listed below in chronological order are presidents, Catholic cabinet officials, posts held, dates.

Andrew Jackson: Roger B. Taney, Attorney General, 1831-33, Secretary of Treasury, 1833-34.

Franklin Pierce: James Campbell, Postmaster General, 1853-57.

James Buchanan: John B. Floyd, Secretary of War, 1857-61.

William McKinley: Joseph McKenna, Attorney General, 1897-98.

Theodore Roosevelt: Robert J. Wynne, Postmaster General, 1904-05; Charles Bonaparte, Secretary of Navy, 1905-06, Attorney General, 1906-09.

Franklin D. Roosevelt: James A. Farley, Postmaster General, 1933-40; Frank Murphy, Attorney General, 1939-40; Frank C. Walker, Postmaster General, 1940-45.

Harry S. Truman: Robert E. Hannegan, Postmaster General, 1945-47; J. Howard McGrath, Attorney General, 1949-52; Maurice J. Tobin, Secretary of Labor, 1948-53; James P. McGranery, Attorney General, 1952-53.

Dwight D. Eisenhower: Martin P. Durkin, Secretary of Labor, 1953; James P. Mitchell, Secretary of Labor, 1953-61.

John F. Kennedy: Robert F. Kennedy, Attorney General, 1961-63; Anthony Celebrezze, Secretary of Health, Education and Welfare, 1962-63; John S. Gronouski, Postmaster General, 1963.

Lyndon B. Johnson: Robert F. Kennedy, 1963-64, Anthony Celebrezze, 1963-65, and John S. Gronouski, 1963-65, reappointed to posts held in Kennedy Cabinet; John T. Connor, Secretary of Commerce, 1965-67; Lawrence O'Brien, Postmaster General, 1965-68.

Richard M. Nixon: Walter J. Hickel, Secretary of Interior, 1969-71; John A. Volpe, Secretary of Transportation, 1969-72; Maurice H. Stans, Secretary of Commerce, 1969-72; Peter J. Brennan, Secretary of Labor, 1973-74; William E. Simon, Secretary of Treasury, 1974.

Gerald R. Ford: Peter J. Brennan, 1974-75, and William E. Simon, 1974-76, reappointed to posts held above.

Jimmy Carter: Joseph Califano, Jr., Secretary of Health, Education and Welfare, 1977-79; Benjamin Civiletti, Attorney General, 1979-81; Moon Landrieu, Secretary of Housing and Urban Development, 1979-81; Edmund S. Muskie, Secretary of State, 1980-81.

Ronald Reagan: Alexander M. Haig, Secretary of State, 1981-82; Raymond J. Donovan, Secretary of Labor, 1981-84; Margaret M. Heckler, Secretary of Health and Human Services, 1983-85; William J. Bennett, Secretary of Education, 1985-88; Ann Dore McLaughlin, Secretary of Labor, 1988-89; Lauro F. Cavazos, Secretary of Education, 1988-89; Nicholas F. Brady, Secretary of Treasury, 1988-89.

George Bush: Lauro F. Cavazos (reappointed), Secretary of Education, 1989-90; Nicholas F. Brady (reappointed), Secretary of Treasury, 1989-93; James D. Watkins, Secretary of Energy, 1989-93; Manuel Lujan, Jr., Secretary of Interior, 1989-93; Edward J. Derwinski, Secretary of Veteran Affairs, 1989-92; Lynn Martin, Secretary of Labor, 1990-93; Edward Madigan, Secretary of Agriculture, 1991-93; William P. Barr, Attorney General, 1991-93.

Bill Clinton: Henry G. Cisneros, Secretary of Housing and Urban Development, 1993-97; Federico F. Peña, Secretary of Transportation, 1993-97; Donna Shalala, Secretary of Health and Human Services, 1993-2001; William M. Daley, Secretary of Commerce, 1997-2000; Andrew Cuomo, Secretary of Housing and Urban Development, 1997-2001; Alexis H. Herman, Secretary of Labor, 1997-2001.

George W. Bush: Paul O'Neill, Secretary of the Treasury, 2001-03; Tommy Thompson, Secretary of Health and Human Services, 2001-; Mel Martinez, Secretary of Housing and Urban Development, 2001-; Anthony Principi, Secretary of Veterans Affairs, 2001-.

Cabinet members who became Catholics after leaving their posts were: Thomas Ewing, Secretary of Treasury under William A. Harrison and Secretary of Interior under Zachary Taylor; Luke E. Wright, Secretary of War under Theodore Roosevelt; Albert B. Fall, Secretary of Interior under Warren G. Harding.

Catholics in the 107th Congress

As of the start of the 107th Congress in 2001 (the last year with an accounting), there were 152 Catholic members. There are presently 128 Catholics in the House and 24 Catholics in the Senate, a difference of one fewer senator from the 106th Congress and a decline by one from two years ago. The number of Catholics is distributed essentially the same as it was for the 106th Congress, with 93 Democrats and 59 Republicans this term. There are two fewer Democrats and one more Republican than two years ago.

CATHOLIC SUPREME COURT JUSTICES

Roger B. Taney, Chief Justice 1836-64; app. by Andrew Jackson.

Edward D. White, Associate Justice 1894-1910, app. by Grover Cleveland; Chief Justice 1910-21; app. by William H. Taft.

Joseph McKenna, Associate Justice 1898-1925; app. by William McKinley.

Pierce Butler, Associate Justice 1923-39; app. by Warren G. Harding.

Frank Murphy, Associate Justice 1940-49; app. by Franklin D. Roosevelt.

William Brennan, Associate Justice 1956-90; app. by Dwight D. Eisenhower.

Antonin Scalia, Associate Justice 1986-; app. by Ronald Reagan.

Anthony M. Kennedy, Associate Justice 1988-; app. by Ronald Reagan.

Clarence Thomas, Associate Justice 1991-; app. by George Bush.

Sherman Minton, Associate Justice from 1949 to 1956; became a Catholic several years before his death in 1965.

CATHOLICS IN STATUARY HALL

Statues of 13 Catholics deemed worthy of national commemoration are among those enshrined in National Statuary Hall and other places in the U.S. Capitol. The Hall, formerly the chamber of the House of Representatives, was erected by Act of Congress July 2, 1864.

Donating states, names and years of placement are listed.

Arizona: Rev. Eusebio Kino, S. J., missionary, 1965.

California: Rev. Junípero Serra, O. F. M. missionary, 1931. (Beatified 1988.)

Hawaii: Fr. Damien, missionary, 1969. (Beatified 1995.)

Illinois: Gen. James Shields, statesman, 1893.

Louisiana: Edward D. White, Justice of the U.S. Supreme Court (1894-1921), 1955.

Maryland: Charles Carroll, statesman, 1901.

Nevada: Patrick A. McCarran, statesman, 1960.

New Mexico: Dennis Chavez, statesman, 1966. (Abp. Jean B. Lamy, pioneer prelate of Santa Fe, was nominated for Hall honor in 1951.)

North Dakota: John Burke, U.S. treasurer, 1963.

Oregon: Dr. John McLoughlin, pioneer, 1953.

Washington: Mother Mary Joseph Pariseau, pioneer missionary and humanitarian.

West Virginia: John E. Kenna, statesman, 1901.

Wisconsin: Rev. Jacques Marquette, S.J., missionary, explorer, 1895.

United States Hierarchy

U.S. CATHOLIC JURISDICTIONS, HIERARCHY, STATISTICS

The organizational structure of the Catholic Church in the United States consists of 33 provinces with as many archdioceses (metropolitan sees); 152 suffragan sees (dioceses); five Eastern Church jurisdictions immediately subject to the Holy See — the eparchies of St. Maron and Our Lady of Lebanon of Los Angeles (Maronites), Newton (Melkites), St. Thomas Apostle of Detroit (Chaldeans), St. Thomas of Chicago (Syro-Malabars, created on March 13, 2001) and St. George Martyr of Canton, OH (Romanians); and the Military Services Archdiocese. The current number of suffragan sees reflects the creation of the new diocese of Laredo, TX, on July 3, 2000, and the eparchy of Saint Peter the Apostle of San Diego of the Chaldeans on May 21, 2002. The eparchy of Our Lady of Deliverance of Newark for Syrian-rite Catholics in the U.S. and Canada has its seat in Newark, NJ. An Armenian apostolic exarchate for the United States and Canada has its seat in New York. Each of these jurisdictions is under the direction of an archbishop or bishop, called an ordinary, who has apostolic responsibility and authority for the pastoral service of the people in his care.

The structure includes the territorial episcopal conference known as the United States Conference of Catholic Bishops (USCCB). In and through this body, which is an amalgamation of the National Conference of Catholic Bishops (NCCB) and the United States Catholic Conference (USCC), the bishops exercise their collegiate pastorate over the Church in the entire country (*see* **Index**).

The representative of the Holy See to the Church in the United States is an Apostolic Nuncio (presently Archbishop Gabriel Montalvo, J.C.D.).

ECCLESIASTICAL PROVINCES

(Sources: The Official Catholic Directory, *Catholic News Service.)*

The 33 ecclesiastical provinces bear the names of archdioceses, i.e., of metropolitan sees.

Anchorage: Archdiocese of Anchorage and suffragan sees of Fairbanks, Juneau. Geographical area: Alaska.

Atlanta: Archdiocese of Atlanta (GA) and suffragan sees of Savannah (GA); Charlotte and Raleigh (NC), Charleston (SC). Geographical area: Georgia, North Carolina, South Carolina.

Baltimore: Archdiocese of Baltimore (MD) and suffragan sees of Wilmington (DE); Arlington and Richmond (VA); Wheeling-Charleston (WV). Geographical area: Maryland (except five counties), Delaware, Virginia, West Virginia.

Boston: Archdiocese of Boston (MA) and suffragan sees of Fall River, Springfield and Worcester (MA); Portland (ME); Manchester (NH); Burlington (VT). Geographical area: Massachusetts, Maine, New Hampshire, Vermont.

Chicago: Archdiocese of Chicago and suffragan sees of Belleville, Joliet, Peoria, Rockford, Springfield. Geographical area: Illinois.

Cincinnati: Archdiocese of Cincinnati and suffragan sees of Cleveland, Columbus, Steubenville, Toledo, Youngstown. Geographical area: Ohio.

Denver: Archdiocese of Denver (CO) and suffragan sees of Colorado Springs and Pueblo (CO); Cheyenne (WY). Geographical area: Colorado, Wyoming.

Detroit: Archdiocese of Detroit and suffragan sees of Gaylord, Grand Rapids, Kalamazoo, Lansing, Marquette, Saginaw. Geographical area: Michigan.

Dubuque: Archdiocese of Dubuque and suffragan sees of Davenport, Des Moines, Sioux City. Geographical area: Iowa.

Hartford: Archdiocese of Hartford (CT) and suffragan sees of Bridgeport and Norwich (CT); Providence (RI). Geographical area: Connecticut, Rhode Island.

Indianapolis: Archdiocese of Indianapolis and suffragan sees of Evansville, Fort Wayne-South Bend, Gary, Lafayette. Geographical area: Indiana.

Kansas City (KS): Archdiocese of Kansas City and suffragan sees of Dodge City, Salina, Wichita. Geographical area: Kansas.

Los Angeles: Archdiocese of Los Angeles and suffragan sees of Fresno, Monterey, Orange, San Bernardino, San Diego. Geographical area: Southern and Central California.

Louisville: Archdiocese of Louisville (KY) and suffragan sees of Covington, Lexington and Owensboro (KY); Knoxville, Memphis and Nashville (TN). Geographical area: Kentucky, Tennessee.

Miami: Archdiocese of Miami and suffragan sees of Orlando, Palm Beach, Pensacola-Tallahassee, St. Augustine, St. Petersburg, Venice. Geographical area: Florida.

Milwaukee: Archdiocese of Milwaukee and suffragan sees of Green Bay, La Crosse, Madison, Superior. Geographical area: Wisconsin.

Mobile: Archdiocese of Mobile, AL, and suffragan sees of Birmingham (AL); Biloxi and Jackson (MS). Geographical area: Alabama, Mississippi.

Newark: Archdiocese of Newark and suffragan sees of Camden, Metuchen, Paterson, Trenton. Geographical area: New Jersey.

New Orleans: Archdiocese of New Orleans and suffragan sees of Alexandria, Baton Rouge, Houma-Thibodaux, Lafayette, Lake Charles and Shreveport. Geographical area: Louisiana.

New York: Archdiocese of New York and suffragan sees of Albany, Brooklyn, Buffalo, Ogdensburg, Rochester, Rockville Centre, Syracuse. Geographical area: New York.

Oklahoma City: Archdiocese of Oklahoma City (OK) and suffragan sees of Tulsa (OK) and Little Rock (AR). Geographical area: Oklahoma, Arkansas.

Omaha: Archdiocese of Omaha and suffragan sees of Grand Island, Lincoln. Geographical area: Nebraska.

Philadelphia: Archdiocese of Philadelphia and suffragan sees of Allentown, Altoona-Johnstown, Erie, Greensburg, Harrisburg, Pittsburgh, Scranton. Geographical area: Pennsylvania.

Philadelphia (Byzantine, Ukrainians): Metropolitan See of Philadelphia (Byzantine) and Eparchies of St. Josaphat in Parma (OH), St. Nicholas of the Ukrainians in Chicago and Stamford, CT The jurisdiction extends to all Ukrainian Catholics in the U.S. from the ecclesiastical province of Galicia in the Ukraine.

Pittsburgh (Byzantine, Ruthenians): Metropolitan See of Pittsburgh, PA and Eparchies of Passaic (NJ), Parma (OH), Van Nuys (CA).

Portland: Archdiocese of Portland (OR) and suffragan sees of Baker (OR); Boise (ID); Great Falls-Billings and Helena (MT). Geographical area: Oregon, Idaho, Montana.

St. Louis: Archdiocese of St. Louis and suffragan sees of Jefferson City, Kansas City-St. Joseph, Springfield-Cape Girardeau. Geographical area: Missouri.

St. Paul and Minneapolis: Archdiocese of St. Paul and Minneapolis (MN) and suffragan sees of Crookston, Duluth, New Ulm, St. Cloud and Winona (MN); Bismarck and Fargo (ND); Rapid City and Sioux Falls (SD). Geographical area: Minnesota, North Dakota, South Dakota.

San Antonio: Archdiocese of San Antonio (TX) and suffragan sees of Amarillo, Austin, Beaumont, Brownsville, Corpus Christi, Dallas, El Paso, Fort Worth, Galveston-Houston, Laredo, Lubbock, San Angelo, Tyler and Victoria (TX). Geographical area: Texas.

San Francisco: Archdiocese of San Francisco (CA) and suffragan sees of Oakland, Sacramento, San Jose, Santa Rosa and Stockton (CA); Honolulu (HI); Reno (NV); Las Vegas (NV); Salt Lake City (UT). Geographical area: Northern California, Nevada, Utah, Hawaii.

Santa Fe: Archdiocese of Santa Fe (NM) and suffragan sees of Gallup and Las Cruces (NM); Phoenix and Tucson (AZ). Geographical area: New Mexico, Arizona.

Seattle: Archdiocese of Seattle and suffragan sees of Spokane, Yakima. Geographical area: Washington.

Washington: Archdiocese of Washington, DC, and suffragan see of St. Thomas (VI). Geographical area: District of Columbia, five counties of Maryland, Virgin Islands.

ARCHDIOCESES, DIOCESES, ARCHBISHOPS, BISHOPS

(Sources: *Official Catholic Directory*; Catholic News Service; *L'Osservatore Romano*. As of Aug. 20, 2003.)

Information includes name of diocese, year of foundation (as it appears on the official document erecting the see), present ordinaries (year of installation), auxiliaries and former ordinaries (for biographies, *see* **Index**).

Archdioceses are indicated by an asterisk.

Albany, NY (1847): Howard J. Hubbard, bishop, 1977.

Former bishops: John McCloskey, 1847-64; John J. Conroy, 1865-77; Francis McNeirny, 1877-94; Thomas M. Burke, 1894-1915; Thomas F. Cusack, 1915-18; Edmund F. Gibbons, 1919-54; William A. Scully, 1954-69; Edwin B. Broderick, 1969-76.

Alexandria, LA (1853): Vacant.

Established at Natchitoches, transferred to Alexandria, 1910; title changed to Alexandria-Shreveport, 1977; redesignated Alexandria, 1986, when Shreveport was made a diocese.

Former bishops: Augustus M. Martin, 1853-75; Francis X. Leray, 1877-79, administrator, 1879-83; Anthony Durier, 1885-1904; Cornelius Van de Ven, 1904-32; Daniel F. Desmond, 1933-45; Charles P. Greco, 1946-73; Lawrence P. Graves, 1973-82; William B. Friend, 1983-86; John C. Favalora, 1986-89; Sam G. Jacobs, 1989-2003.

Allentown, PA (1961): Edward P. Cullen, 1997.

Former bishop: Joseph McShea, 1961-83; Thomas J. Welsh, 1983-97.

Altoona-Johnstown, PA (1901): Joseph V. Adamec, bishop, 1987.

Established as Altoona, name changed, 1957.

Former bishops: Eugene A. Garvey, 1901-20; John J. McCort, 1920-36; Richard T. Guilfoyle, 1936-57; Howard J. Carroll, 1958-60; J. Carroll McCormick, 1960-66; James J. Hogan, 1966-86.

Amarillo, TX (1926): John W. Yanta, bishop, 1997.

Former bishops: Rudolph A. Gerken, 1927-33; Robert E. Lucey, 1934-41; Laurence J. Fitzsimon, 1941-58; John L. Morkovsky, 1958-63; Lawrence M. De Falco, 1963-79; Leroy T. Matthiesen, 1980-97.

Anchorage,* Alaska (1966): Roger Lawrence Schwietz O.M.I., archbishop, 2001.

Former archbishop: Joseph T. Ryan, 1966-75; Francis T. Hurley, 1976-2001.

Arlington, VA (1974): Paul S. Loverde, bishop, 1999.

Former bishop: Thomas J. Welsh, 1974-83; John R. Keating, 1983-98.

Atlanta,* GA (1956; archdiocese, 1962): John F. Donoghue, archbishop, 1993.

Former ordinaries: Francis E. Hyland, 1956-61; Paul J. Hallinan, first archbishop, 1962-68; Thomas A. Donnellan, 1968-87; Eugene A. Marino, S.S.J., 1988-90; James P. Lyke, 1991-92.

Austin, TX (1947): Gregory Michael Aymond, bishop, 2001.

Former bishops: Louis J. Reicher, 1947-71; Vincent M. Harris, 1971-86; John E. McCarthy, 1986-2001.

Baker, OR (1903): Robert Francis Vasa, bishop, 2000.

Established as Baker City, name changed, 1952.

Former bishops: Charles J. O'Reilly, 1903-18; Joseph F. McGrath, 1919-50; Francis P. Leipzig, 1950-71; Thomas J. Connolly, 1971-99.

Baltimore,* MD (1789; archdiocese, 1808): Cardinal William H. Keeler, archbishop, 1989. Gordon D. Bennett, S.J., P. Francis Murphy, William C. Newman, W. Francis Malooly, auxiliaries.

Former ordinaries: John Carroll, 1789-1815, first archbishop; Leonard Neale, 1815-17; Ambrose Marechal, S.S., 1817-28; James Whitfield, 1828-34; Samuel Eccleston, S.S., 1834-51; Francis P. Kenrick, 1851-63; Martin J. Spalding, 1864-72; James R. Bayley, 1872-77; Cardinal James Gibbons, 1877-1921; Michael J. Curley, 1921-47; Francis P. Keough, 1947-61; Cardinal Lawrence J. Shehan, 1961-74; William D. Borders, 1974-89.

Baton Rouge, LA (1961): Robert W. Muench, bishop, 2001.

Former bishops: Robert E. Tracy, 1961-74; Joseph V. Sullivan, 1974-82; Stanley J. Ott, 1983-93; Alfred C. Hughes, 1993-2001.

Beaumont, TX (1966): Curtis J. Guillory, S.V.D., bishop, 2000.

Former bishops: Vincent M. Harris, 1966-71; Warren L. Boudreaux, 1971-77; Bernard J. Ganter, 1977-93; Joseph A. Galante, 1994-2000.

Belleville, IL (1887): Wilton D. Gregory, bishop, 1994.

Former bishops: John Janssen, 1888-1913; Henry Althoff, 1914-47; Albert R. Zuroweste, 1948-76; William M. Cosgrove, 1976-81; John N. Wurm, 1981-84; James P. Keleher, 1984-93.

Biloxi, MS (1977): Thomas John Rodi, bishop, 2001.

Former bishop: Joseph Lawson Howze, 1977-2001.

Birmingham, AL (1969): David E. Foley, bishop, 1994.

Former bishops: Joseph G. Vath, 1969-87; Raymond J. Boland, 1988-93.

Bismarck, ND (1909): Paul A. Zipfel, bishop, 1996.

Former bishops: Vincent Wehrle, O.S.B., 1910-39; Vincent J. Ryan, 1940-51; Lambert A. Hoch, 1952-56; Hilary B. Hacker, 1957-82; John F. Kinney, 1982-95.

Boise, ID (1893): Michael P. Driscoll, 1999.

Former bishops: Alphonse J. Glorieux, 1893-1917; Daniel M. Gorman, 1918-27; Edward J. Kelly, 1928-56; James J. Byrne, 1956-62; Sylvester Treinen, 1962-88; Tod David Brown, 1989-98.

Boston,* MA (1808; archdiocese, 1875): Sean O'Malley, O.F.M. Cap., 2003. John P. Boles, William

F. Murphy, John B. McCormack, Francis Xavier Irwin, Emilio Allué, S.D.B., Richard Joseph Malone, Walter James Edyvean, Richard Gerard Lennon, auxiliaries.

Former ordinaries: John L. de Cheverus, 1810-23; Benedict J. Fenwick, S.J., 1825-46; John B. Fitzpatrick, 1846-66; John J. Williams, 1866-1907, first archbishop; Cardinal William O'Connell, 1907-44; Cardinal Richard Cushing, 1944-70; Cardinal Humberto Medeiros, 1970-83; Cardinal Bernard F. Law, 1984-2002.

Bridgeport, CT (1953): William Edward Lori, 2001.

Former bishops: Lawrence J. Shehan, 1953-61; Walter W. Curtis, 1961-88; Edward M. Egan, 1988-2000.

Brooklyn, NY (1853): Nicholas A. DiMarzio, 2003. Joseph M. Sullivan, Rene A. Valero, Ignatius Catanello, auxiliaries.

Former bishops: John Loughlin, 1853-91; Charles E. McDonnell, 1892-1921; Thomas E. Molloy, 1921-56; Bryan J. McEntegart, 1957-68; Francis J. Mugavero, 1968-90; Thomas V. Daily, 1990-2003.

Brownsville, TX (1965): Raymundo J. Peña, bishop, 1995.

Former bishops: Adolph Marx, 1965; Humberto S. Medeiros, 1966-70; John J. Fitzpatrick, 1971-91; Enrique San Pedro, S.J., 1991-94.

Buffalo, NY (1847): Henry J. Mansell, bishop, 1995. Edward M. Grosz, auxiliary.

Former bishops: John Timon, C.M., 1847-67; Stephen V. Ryan, C.M., 1868-96; James E. Quigley, 1897-1903; Charles H. Colton, 1903-15; Dennis J. Dougherty, 1915-18; William Turner, 1919-36; John A. Duffy, 1937-44; John F. O'Hara, C.S.C., 1945-51; Joseph A. Burke, 1952-62; James McNulty, 1963-72; Edward D. Head, 1973-95.

Burlington, VT (1853): Kenneth A. Angell, bishop, 1992.

Former bishops: Louis De Goesbriand, 1853-99; John S. Michaud, 1899-1908; Joseph J. Rice, 1910-38; Matthew F. Brady, 1938-44; Edward F. Ryan, 1945-56; Robert F. Joyce, 1957-71; John A. Marshall, 1972-91.

Camden, NJ (1937): Vacant.

Former bishops: Bartholomew J. Eustace, 1938-56; Justin J. McCarthy, 1957-59; Celestine J. Damiano, 1960-67; George H. Guilfoyle, 1968-89; James T. McHugh, 1989-98; Nicholas A. DiMarzio, 1999-2003.

Charleston, SC (1820): Robert J. Baker, bishop, 1999.

Former bishops: John England, 1820-42; Ignatius W. Reynolds, 1844-55; Patrick N. Lynch, 1858-82; Henry P. Northrop, 1883-1916; William T. Russell, 1917-27; Emmet M. Walsh, 1927-49; John J. Russell, 1950-58; Paul J. Hallinan, 1958-62; Francis F. Reh, 1962-64; Ernest L. Unterkoefler, 1964-90; David B. Thompson, 1990-99.

Charlotte, NC (1971): Peter J. Jugis, 2003.

Former bishops: Michael J. Begley, 1972-84; John F. Donoghue, 1984-93; William G. Curlin, 1994-2002.

Cheyenne, WY (1887): David Laurin Ricken, bishop, 2001.

Former bishops: Maurice F. Burke, 1887-93; Thomas M. Lenihan, 1897-1901; James J. Keane, 1902-11; Patrick A. McGovern, 1912-51; Hubert M. Newell, 1951-78; Joseph Hart, 1978-2001.

Chicago,* IL (1843; archdiocese, 1880): Cardinal Francis E. George, archbishop, 1997. Edwin M.

Conway, John R. Manz, Joseph N. Perry, Jerome E. Listecki, Francis J. Kane, Thomas J. Paprocki, Gustavo Garcia-Siller, M.Sp.S., auxiliaries.

Former ordinaries: William Quarter, 1844-48; James O. Van de Velde, S.J., 1849-53; Anthony O'Regan, 1854-58; James Duggan, 1859-70; Thomas P. Foley, administrator, 1870-79; Patrick A. Feehan, 1880-1902, first archbishop; James E. Quigley, 1903-15; Cardinal George Mundelein, 1915-39; Cardinal Samuel Stritch, 1939-58; Cardinal Albert Meyer, 1958-65; Cardinal John Cody, 1965-82; Cardinal Joseph L. Bernardin, 1982-96.

Cincinnati,* OH (1821; archdiocese, 1850): Daniel E. Pilarczyk, archbishop, 1982. Carl K. Moeddel, auxiliary.

Former ordinaries: Edward D. Fenwick, O.P., 1822-32; John B. Purcell, 1833-83, first archbishop; William H. Elder, 1883-1904; Henry Moeller, 1904-1925; John T. McNicholas, O.P., 1925-50; Karl J. Alter, 1950-69; Paul F. Leibold, 1969-72; Joseph L. Bernardin, 1972-82.

Cleveland, OH (1847): Anthony M. Pilla, bishop, 1980. A. James Quinn, Roger W. Gries, O.S.B., Martin John Amos, auxiliaries.

Former ordinaries: L. Amadeus Rappe, 1847-70; Richard Gilmour, 1872-91; Ignatius F. Horstmann, 1892-1908; John P. Farrelly, 1909-21; Joseph Schrembs, 1921-45; Edward F. Hoban, 1945-66; Clarence G. Issenmann, 1966-74; James A. Hickey, 1974-80.

Colorado Springs, CO (1983): Michael J. Sheridan, bishop, 2003.

Former ordinaries: Richard C. Hanifen, 1984-2003.

Columbus, OH (1868): James A. Griffin, bishop, 1983.

Former bishops: Sylvester H. Rosecrans, 1868-78; John A. Watterson, 1880-99; Henry Moeller, 1900-03; James J. Hartley, 1904-44; Michael J. Ready, 1944-57; Clarence Issenmann, 1957-64; John J. Carberry, 1965-68; Clarence E. Elwell, 1968-73; Edward J. Herrmann, 1973-82.

Corpus Christi, TX (1912): Edmond Carmody, bishop, 2000.

Former bishops: Paul J. Nussbaum, C.P., 1913-20; Emmanuel B. Ledvina, 1921-49; Mariano S. Garriga, 1949-65; Thomas J. Drury, 1965-83; Rene H. Gracida, 1983-97. Roberto O. Gonzalez, O.F.M., 1997-99.

Covington, KY (1853): Roger J. Foys, bishop, 2002.

Former bishops: George A. Carrell, S.J., 1853-68; Augustus M. Toebbe, 1870-84; Camillus P. Maes, 1885-1914; Ferdinand Brossart, 1916-23; Francis W. Howard, 1923-44; William T. Mulloy, 1945-59; Richard Ackerman, C.S.Sp., 1960-78; William A. Hughes, 1979-95; Robert W. Muench, 1996-2001.

Crookston, MN (1909): Victor H. Balke, bishop, 1976.

Former bishops: Timothy Corbett, 1910-38; John H. Peschges, 1938-44; Francis J. Schenk, 1945-60; Laurence A. Glenn, 1960-70; Kenneth J. Povish, 1970-75.

Dallas, TX (1890): Charles V. Grahmann, bishop, 1990; Joseph Galante, coadjutor, 2000.

Established 1890, as Dallas, title changed to Dallas-Ft. Worth, 1953; redesignated Dallas, 1969, when Ft. Worth was made a diocese.

Former bishops: Thomas F. Brennan, 1891-92; Edward J. Dunne, 1893-1910; Joseph P. Lynch, 1911-54;

Thomas K. Gorman, 1954-69; Thomas Tschoepe, 1969-90.

Davenport, IA (1881): William E. Franklin, bishop, 1993.

Former bishops: John McMullen, 1881-83; Henry Cosgrove, 1884-1906; James Davis, 1906-26; Henry P. Rohlman, 1927-44; Ralph L. Hayes, 1944-66; Gerald F. O'Keefe, 1966-93.

Denver,* CO (1887; archdiocese, 1941): Charles J. Chaput, O.F.M. Cap., archbishop, 1997. José H. Gomez, auxiliary.

Former ordinaries: Joseph P. Machebeuf, 1887-89; Nicholas C. Matz, 1889-1917; J. Henry Tihen, 1917-31; Urban J. Vehr, 1931-67, first archbishop; James V. Casey, 1967-86; J. Francis Stafford, 1986-96.

Des Moines, IA (1911): Joseph L. Charron, C.PP.S., bishop, 1993.

Former bishops: Austin Dowling, 1912-19; Thomas W. Drumm, 1919-33; Gerald T. Bergan, 1934-48; Edward C. Daly, O.P., 1948-64; George J. Biskup, 1965-67; Maurice J. Dingman, 1968-86; William H. Bullock, 1987-93.

Detroit,* MI (1833; archdiocese, 1937): Cardinal Adam J. Maida, archbishop, 1990. Thomas J. Gumbleton, Moses B. Anderson, S.S.E., Leonard P. Blair, Earl Boyea, Walter A. Hurley, John M. Quinn, Francis R. Reiss, auxiliaries.

Former ordinaries: Frederic Rese, 1833-71; Peter P. Lefevere, administrator, 1841-69; Caspar H. Borgess, 1871-88; John S. Foley, 1888-1918; Michael J. Gallagher, 1918-37; Cardinal Edward Mooney, 1937-58, first archbishop; Cardinal John F. Dearden, 1958-80; Cardinal Edmund C. Szoka, 1981-90.

Dodge City, KS (1951): Ronald M. Gilmore, bishop, 1998.

Former bishops: John B. Franz, 1951-59; Marion F. Forst, 1960-76; Eugene J. Gerber, 1976-82; Stanley G. Schlarman, bishop, 1983-98.

Dubuque,* Iowa (1837; archdiocese, 1893): Jerome Hanus, O.S.B., archbishop, 1995.

Former ordinaries: Mathias Loras, 1837-58; Clement Smyth, O.C.S.O., 1858-65; John Hennessy, 1866-1900, first archbishop; John J. Keane, 1900-11; James J. Keane, 1911-29; Francis J. Beckman, 1930-46; Henry P. Rohlman, 1946-54; Leo Binz, 1954-61; James J. Byrne, 1962-83; Daniel W. Kucera, O.S.B., 1984-95.

Duluth, MN (1889): Dennis M. Schnurr, 2001.

Former bishops: James McGolrick, 1889-1918; John T. McNicholas, O.P., 1918-25; Thomas A. Welch, 1926-59; Francis J. Schenk, 1960-69; Paul F. Anderson, 1969-82; Robert H. Brom, 1983-89; Roger L. Schwietz, O.M.I., 1990-2000.

El Paso, TX (1914): Armando X. Ochoa, bishop, 1996.

Former bishops: Anthony J. Schuler, S.J., 1915-42; Sidney M. Metzger, 1942-78; Patrick F. Flores, 1978-79; Raymundo J. Pena, 1980-95.

Erie, PA (1853): Donald W. Trautman, bishop, 1990.

Former bishops: Michael O'Connor, 1853-54; Josue M. Young, 1854-66; Tobias Mullen, 1868-99; John E. Fitzmaurice, 1899-1920; John M. Gannon, 1920-66; John F. Whealon, 1966-69; Alfred M. Watson, 1969-82; Michael J. Murphy, 1982-90.

Evansville, IN (1944): Gerald A. Gettelfinger, bishop, 1989.

Former bishops: Henry J. Grimmelsman, 1944-65; Paul F. Leibold, 1966-69; Francis R. Shea, 1970-89.

Fairbanks, Alaska (1962): Donald Kettler, bishop, 2002.

Former bishops: Francis D. Gleeson, S.J., 1962-68; Robert L. Whelan, S.J., 1968-85; Michael J. Kaniecki, S.J., 1985-2000.

Fall River, MA (1904): George William Coleman, 2003.

Former bishops: William Stang, 1904-07; Daniel F. Feehan, 1907-34; James E. Cassidy, 1934-51; James L. Connolly, 1951-70; Daniel A. Cronin, 1970-91; Sean O'Malley, O.F.M. Cap., 1992-2002.

Fargo, ND (1889): Samuel J. Aquila, bishop, 2002.

Established at Jamestown, transferred, 1897.

Former bishops: John Shanley, 1889-1909; James O'Reilly, 1910-34; Aloysius J. Muench, 1935-59; Leo F. Dworschak, 1960-70; Justin A. Driscoll, 1970-84; James S. Sullivan, bishop, 1985-2002.

Fort Wayne-South Bend, IN (1857): John M. D'Arcy, bishop, 1985.

Established as Fort Wayne, name changed, 1960.

Former bishops: John H. Luers, 1858-71; Joseph Dwenger, C.Pp. S., 1872-93; Joseph Rademacher, 1893-1900; Herman J. Alerding, 1900-24; John F. Noll, 1925-56; Leo A. Pursley, 1957-76; William E. McManus, 1976-85.

Fort Worth, TX (1969): Joseph P. Delaney, bishop, 1981.

Former bishop: John J. Cassata, 1969-80.

Fresno, CA (1967): John T. Steinbock, bishop, 1991. Formerly Monterey-Fresno, 1922.

Former bishops (Monterey-Fresno): John J. Cantwell, administrator, 1922-24; John B. MacGinley, first bishop, 1924-32; Philip G. Sher, 1933-53; Aloysius J. Willinger, 1953-67.

Former bishops (Fresno): Timothy Manning, 1967-69; Hugh A. Donohoe, 1969-80; Joseph J. Madera, M.Pp.S., 1980-91.

Gallup, NM (1939): Donald Pelotte, S.S.S., bishop, 1990.

Former bishops: Bernard T. Espelage, O.F.M., 1940-69; Jerome J. Hastrich, bishop, 1969-90.

Galveston-Houston, TX (1847): Joseph A. Fiorenza, bishop, 1985. Vincent M. Rizzotto, José S. Vasquez, auxiliaries.

Established as Galveston, name changed, 1959.

Former bishops: John M. Odin, C.M., 1847-61; Claude M. Dubuis, 1862-92; Nicholas A. Gallagher, 1892-1918; Christopher E. Byrne, 1918-50; Wendelin J. Nold, 1950-75; John L. Morkovsky, 1975-84.

Gary, IN (1956): Dale J. Melczek, bishop, 1996.

Former bishops: Andrew G. Grutka, 1957-84; Norbert F. Gaughan, 1984-96.

Gaylord, MI (1971): Patrick R. Cooney, bishop, 1989, installed 1990.

Former bishops: Edmund C. Szoka, 1971-81; Robert J. Rose, 1981-89.

Grand Island, NE (1912): Lawrence J. McNamara, bishop, 1978.

Established at Kearney, transferred, 1917.

Former bishops: James A. Duffy, 1913-31; Stanislaus V. Bona, 1932-44; Edward J. Hunkeler, 1945-51; John L. Paschang, 1951-72; John J. Sullivan, 1972-77.

Grand Rapids, MI (1882): Robert J. Rose, bishop, 1989; Kevin M. Britt, coadjutor, 2002.

Former bishops: Henry J. Richter, 1883-1916; Michael J. Gallagher, 1916-18; Edward D. Kelly,

1919-26; Joseph G. Pinten, 1926-40; Joseph C. Plagens, 1941-43; Francis J. Haas, 1943-53; Allen J. Babcock, 1954-69; Joseph M. Breitenbeck, 1969-89.

Great Falls-Billings, MT (1904): Anthony M. Milone, bishop, 1988.

Established as Great Falls, name changed, 1980.

Former bishops: Mathias C. Lenihan, 1904-30; Edwin V. O'Hara, 1930-39; William J. Condon, 1939-67; Eldon B. Schuster, 1968-77; Thomas J. Murphy, 1978-87.

Green Bay, WI (1868): Robert J. Banks, bishop, 1990. Robert F. Morneau, auxiliary.

Former bishops: Joseph Melcher, 1868-73; Francis X. Krautbauer, 1875-85; Frederick X. Katzer, 1886-91; Sebastian G. Messmer, 1892-1903; Joseph J. Fox, 1904-14; Paul P. Rhode, 1915-45; Stanislaus V. Bona, 1945-67; Aloysius J. Wycislo, 1968-83; Adam J. Maida, 1984-90.

Greensburg, PA (1951): Anthony G. Bosco, bishop, 1987.

Former bishops: Hugh L. Lamb, 1951-59; Willam G. Connare, 1960-87.

Harrisburg, PA (1868): Nicholas C. Dattilo, bishop, 1990.

Former bishops: Jeremiah F. Shanahan, 1868-86; Thomas McGovern, 1888-98; John W. Shanahan, 1899-1916; Philip R. McDevitt, 1916-35; George L. Leech, 1935-71; Joseph T. Daley, 1971-83; William H. Keeler, 1984-89.

Hartford,* CT (1843; archdiocese, 1953): Daniel A. Cronin, archbishop, 1991, installed, 1992. Peter A. Rosazza, Christie A. Macaluso, auxiliaries.

Former ordinaries: William Tyler, 1844-49; Bernard O'Reilly, 1850-56; F. P. MacFarland, 1858-74; Thomas Galberry, O.S.A., 1876-78; Lawrence S. McMahon, 1879-93; Michael Tierney, 1894-1908; John J. Nilan, 1910-34; Maurice F. McAuliffe, 1934-44; Henry J. O'Brien, 1945-68, first archbishop; John F. Whealon, 1969-91.

Helena, MT (1884): Vacant.

Former bishops: John B. Brondel, 1884-1903; John P. Carroll, 1904-25; George J. Finnigan, C.S.C., 1927-32; Ralph L. Hayes, 1933-35; Joseph M. Gilmore, 1936-62; Raymond Hunthausen, 1962-75; Elden F. Curtiss, 1976-93; Alexander J. Brunett, 1994-97; Robert C. Morlino, 1999-2003.

Honolulu, HI (1941): Francis X. DiLorenzo (apostolic administrator, 1993), bishop, 1994.

Former bishops: James J. Sweeney, 1941-68; John J. Scanlan, 1968-81; Joseph A. Ferrario, 1982-93.

Houma-Thibodaux, LA (1977): Sam G. Jacobs, 2003.

Former bishop: Warren L. Boudreaux, 1977-92; C. Michael Jarrell, 1993-2002.

Indianapolis,* IN (1834; archdiocese, 1944): Daniel M. Buechlein, O.S.B., archbishop, 1992.

Established at Vincennes, transferred, 1898.

Former ordinaries: Simon G. Bruté, 1834-39; Celestine de la Hailandiere, 1839-47; John S. Bazin, 1847-48; Maurice de St. Palais, 1849-77; Francis S. Chatard, 1878-1918; Joseph Chartrand, 1918-33; Joseph E. Ritter, 1934-46, first archbishop; Paul C. Schulte, 1946-70; George J. Biskup, 1970-79; Edward T. O'Meara, 1980-92.

Jackson, MS (1837): Joseph Latino, bishop, 2003. Established at Natchez, title changed to Natchez-Jackson, 1956; transferred to Jackson, 1977 (Natchez made titular see).

Former bishops: John J. Chanche, S.S., 1841-52; James Van de Velde, S.J., 1853-55; William H. Elder, 1857-80; Francis A. Janssens, 1881-88; Thomas Heslin, 1889-1911; John E. Gunn, S.M., 1911-24; Richard O. Gerow, 1924-67; Joseph B. Brunini, 1968-84; William R. Houck, 1984-2003.

Jefferson City, MO (1956): John R. Gaydos, bishop, 1997.

Former bishops: Joseph Marling, C.Pp.S., 1956-69; Michael F. McAuliffe, 1969-97.

Joliet, IL (1948): Joseph L. Imesch, bishop, 1979. Former bishops: Martin D. McNamara, 1949-66; Romeo Blanchette, 1966-79.

Juneau, Alaska (1951): Michael W. Warfel, bishop, 1996.

Former bishops: Dermot O'Flanagan, 1951-68; Joseph T. Ryan, administrator, 1968-71; Francis T. Hurley, 1971-76, administrator, 1976-79; Michael H. Kenny, 1979-95.

Kalamazoo, MI (1971): James A. Murray, bishop, 1997.

Former bishops: Paul V. Donovan, 1971-94; Alfred J. Markiewicz, 1995-97.

Kansas City,* KS (1877; archdiocese, 1952): James P. Keleher, archbishop, 1993.

Established as vicariate apostolic, 1850, became Diocese of Leavenworth, 1877, transferred to Kansas City, 1947.

Former ordinaries: J. B. Miege, vicar apostolic, 1851-74; Louis M. Fink, O.S.B., vicar apostolic, 1874-77, first bishop, 1877-1904; Thomas F. Lillis, 1904-10; John Ward, 1910-29; Francis Johannes, 1929-37; Paul C. Schulte, 1937-46; George J. Donnelly, 1946-50; Edward Hunkeler, 1951-69, first archbishop; Ignatius J. Strecker, 1969-93.

Kansas City-St. Joseph, MO (Kansas City, 1880, St. Joseph, 1868, united 1956): Raymond J. Boland, bishop, 1993.

Former bishops: John J. Hogan, 1880-1913; Thomas F. Lillis, 1913-38; Edwin V. O'Hara, 1939-56; John P. Cody, 1956-61; Charles H. Helmsing, 1962-77; John J. Sullivan, 1977-93.

Former bishops (St. Joseph): John J. Hogan, 1868-80, administrator, 1880-93; Maurice F. Burke, 1893-1923; Francis Gilfillan, 1923-33; Charles H. Le Blond, 1933-56.

Knoxville, TN (1988): Joseph E. Kurtz, 1999. Former bishops: Anthony J. O'Connell, bishop, 1988-98.

La Crosse, WI (1868): Raymond L. Burke, bishop, 1995.

Former bishops: Michael Heiss, 1868-80; Kilian C. Flasch, 1881-91; James Schwebach, 1892-1921; Alexander J. McGavick, 1921-48; John P. Treacy, 1948-64; Frederick W. Freking, 1965-83; John J. Paul, 1983-94.

Lafayette, IN (1944): William L. Higi, bishop, 1984. Former bishops: John G. Bennett, 1944-57; John J. Carberry, 1957-65; Raymond J. Gallagher, 1965-82; George A. Fulcher, 1983-84.

Lafayette, LA (1918): C. Michael Jarrell, bishop, 2002. Former bishops: Jules B. Jeanmard, 1918-56; Maurice Schexnayder, 1956-72; Gerard L. Frey, 1973-89; Harry J. Flynn, 1989-94; Edward J. O'Donnell, 1994-2002

Lake Charles, LA (1980): Edward Braxton, bishop, 2000.

Former bishop: Jude Speyrer, 1980-2000.

Lansing, MI (1937): Carl F. Mengeling, bishop, 1995; installed 1996.

Former bishops: Joseph H. Albers, 1937-65; Alexander Zaleski, 1965-75; Kenneth J. Povish, 1975-95.

Laredo, Tx. (2000): James A. Tamayo, bishop, 2000.

Las Cruces, NM (1982): Ricardo Ramirez, C.S.B., bishop, 1982.

Las Vegas, NV (1995): Joseph Pepe, 2001.

Formerly Reno-Las Vegas, 1976; made separate diocese 1995.

Former bishops: Daniel F. Walsh, 1995-2000.

Lexington, KY (1988): Ronald William Gainer, bishop, 2002.

Former bishops: James Kendrick Williams, 1988-2002.

Lincoln, NE (1887): Fabian W. Bruskewitz, bishop, 1992.

Former bishops: Thomas Bonacum, 1887-1911; J. Henry Tihen, 1911-17; Charles J. O'Reilly, 1918-23; Francis J. Beckman, 1924-30; Louis B. Kucera, 1930-57; James V. Casey, 1957-67; Glennon P. Flavin, 1967-92.

Little Rock, AR (1843): James Peter Sartain, bishop, 2000.

Former bishops: Andrew Byrne, 1844-62; Edward Fitzgerald, 1867-1907; John Morris, 1907-46; Albert L. Fletcher, 1946-72; Andrew J. McDonald, 1972-2000.

Los Angeles,* CA (1840; archdiocese, 1936): Cardinal Roger M. Mahony, archbishop, 1985. Thomas J. Curry, Gerald E. Wilkerson, Gabino Zavala, Edward William Clark, auxiliaries.

Founded as diocese of Two Californias, 1840; became Monterey diocese, 1850; Baja California detached from Monterey diocese, 1852; title changed to Monterey-Los Angeles, 1859, Los Angeles-San Diego, 1922; became archdiocese under present title, 1936 (San Diego became separate see).

Former ordinaries: Francisco Garcia Diego y Moreno, O.F.M., 1840-46; Joseph S. Alemany, O.P., 1850-53; Thaddeus Amat, C.M., 1854-78; Francis Mora, 1878-96; George T. Montgomery, 1896-1903; Thomas J. Conaty, 1903-15; John J. Cantwell, 1917-47, first archbishop; Cardinal James McIntyre, 1948-70; Cardinal Timothy Manning, 1970-85.

Louisville,* KY (1808; archdiocese, 1937): Thomas C. Kelly, O.P., archbishop, 1982.

Established at Bardstown, transferred, 1841.

Former ordinaries: Benedict J. Flaget, S.S., 1810-32; John B. David, S.S., 1832-33; Benedict J. Flaget, S.S., 1833-50; Martin J. Spalding, 1850-64; Peter J. Lavialle, 1865-67; William G. McCloskey, 1868-1909; Denis O'Donaghue, 1910-24; John A. Floersh, 1924-67, first archbishop; Thomas J. McDonough, 1967-81.

Lubbock, TX (1983): Placido Rodriguez, C.M.F., bishop, 1994.

Former bishop: Michael J. Sheehan, 1983-93.

Madison, WI (1946): Robert C. Morlino, bishop, 2003. George O. Wirz, auxiliary.

Former bishops: William P. O'Connor, 1946-67; Cletus F. O'Donnell, 1967-92, William H. Bullock, 1993-2003.

Manchester, NH (1884): John B. McCormack, bishop, 1998; Francis J. Christian, auxiliary.

Former bishops: Denis M. Bradley, 1884-1903; John

B. Delany, 1904-06; George A. Guertin, 1907-32; John B. Peterson, 1932-44; Matthew F. Brady, 1944-59; Ernest J. Primeau, 1960-74; Odore J. Gendron, 1975-90; Leo E. O'Neil, 1990-97.

Marquette, MI (1857): James H. Garland, bishop, 1992.

Founded as Sault Ste. Marie and Marquette; changed to Marquette, 1937.

Former bishops: Frederic Baraga, 1857-68; Ignatius Mrak, 1869-78; John Vertin, 1879-99; Frederick Eis, 1899-1922; Paul J. Nussbaum, C.P., 1922-35; Joseph C. Plagens, 1935-40; Francis Magner, 1941-47; Thomas L. Noa, 1947-68; Charles A. Salatka, 1968-77; Mark F. Schmitt, 1978-92.

Memphis, TN (1970): J. Terry Steib, S.V.D., bishop, 1993.

Former bishops: Carroll T. Dozier, 1971-82; J. Francis Stafford, 1982-86; Daniel M. Buechlein, O.S.B.,1987-92.

Metuchen, NJ (1981): Paul G. Bootkoski, bishop, 2002.

Former bishops: Theodore E. McCarrick, 1981-86; Edward T. Hughes, 1987-97; Vincent DePaul Breen, 1997-2002.

Miami,* FL (1958; archdiocese, 1968): John C. Favalora, archbishop, 1994.

Former ordinaries: Coleman F. Carroll, 1958-77, first archbishop; Edward A. McCarthy, 1977-94.

Milwaukee,* WI (1843; archdiocese, 1875): Timothy M. Dolan, archbishop, 2002. Richard J. Sklba, auxiliary.

Former ordinaries: John M. Henni, 1844-81, first archbishop; Michael Heiss, 1881-90; Frederick X. Katzer, 1891-1903; Sebastian G. Messmer, 1903-30; Samuel A. Stritch, 1930-39; Moses E. Kiley, 1940-53; Albert G. Meyer, 1953-58; William E. Cousins, 1959-77; Rembert G. Weakland, O.S.B., 1977-2002.

Mobile,* AL (1829; archdiocese, 1980): Oscar H. Lipscomb, first archbishop, 1980.

Founded as Mobile, 1829, title changed to Mobile-Birmingham, 1954; redesignated Mobile, 1969.

Former bishops: Michael Portier, 1829-59; John Quinlan, 1859-83; Dominic Manucy, 1884; Jeremiah O'Sullivan, 1885-96; Edward P. Allen, 1897-1926; Thomas J. Toolen, 1927-69; John L. May, 1969-80.

Monterey in California (1967): Sylvester D. Ryan, bishop, 1992.

Formerly Monterey-Fresno, 1922. (Originally established in 1850, see Los Angeles listing.)

Former bishops (Monterey-Fresno): John J. Cantwell, administrator, 1922-24; John B. MacGinley, first bishop, 1924-32; Philip G. Sher, 1933-53; Aloysius J. Willinger, 1953-67.

Former bishops (Monterey): Harry A. Clinch, 1967-82; Thaddeus A. Shubsda, 1982-91.

Nashville, TN (1837): Edward U. Kmiec, bishop, 1992.

Former bishops: Richard P. Miles, O.P., 1838-60; James Whelan, O.P., 1860-64; Patrick A. Feehan, 1865-80; Joseph Rademacher, 1883-93; Thomas S. Byrne, 1894-1923; Alphonse J. Smith, 1924-35; William L. Adrian, 1936-69; Joseph A. Durick, 1969-75; James D. Niedergeses, 1975-92.

Newark,* NJ (1853; archdiocese, 1937): John J. Myers, 2001. David Arias, O.A.R., Charles J. McDonnell, Arthur J. Serratelli, Edgar M. da Cunha, auxiliaries.

Former ordinaries: James R. Bayley, 1853-72; Michael A. Corrigan, 1873-80; Winand M. Wigger, 1881-1901; John J. O'Connor, 1901-27; Thomas J. Walsh, 1928-52, first archbishop; Thomas A. Boland, 1953-74; Peter L. Gerety, 1974-86; Theodore E. McCarrick, 1986-2000.

New Orleans,* LA (1793; archdiocese, 1850): Alfred Hughes, 2002. Dominic Carmon, S.V.D., Roger Paul Morin, auxiliaries.

Former ordinaries: Luis Penalver y Cardenas, 1793-1801; John Carroll, administrator, 1805-15; W. Louis Dubourg, S.S., 1815-25; Joseph Rosati, C.M., administrator, 1826-29; Leo De Neckere, C.M., 1829-33; Anthony Blanc, 1835-60, first archbishop; Jean Marie Odin, C.M., 1861-70; Napoleon J. Perche, 1870-83; Francis X. Leray, 1883-87; Francis A. Janssens, 1888-97; Placide L. Chapelle, 1897-1905; James H. Blenk, S.M., 1906-17; John W. Shaw, 1918-34; Joseph F. Rummel, 1935-64; John P. Cody, 1964-65; Philip M. Hannan, 1965-88; Francis B. Schulte, 1988-2002.

Newton, MA (Melkite) (1966; eparchy, 1976): John A. Elya, B.S.O., eparch, 1993, installed, 1994. Nicholas Samra, auxiliary.

Former ordinaries: Justin Najmy, exarch, 1966-68; Joseph Tawil, exarch, 1969-76, first eparch, 1976-89; Ignatius Ghattas, B.S.O., 1990-92.

New Ulm, MN (1957): John Clayton Nienstedt, bishop, 2001.

Former bishop: Alphonse J. Schladweiler, 1958-75; Raymond A. Lucker, 1975-2000.

New York,* NY (1808; archdiocese, 1850): Cardinal Edward M. Egan, archbishop, 2000. Robert A. Brucato, Robert J. Iriondo, Dominick J. Lagonegro, Timothy A. McDonnell, auxiliaries.

Former ordinaries: Richard L. Concanen, O.P., 1808-10; John Connolly, O.P., 1814-25; John Dubois, S.S., 1826-42; John J. Hughes, 1842-64, first archbishop; Cardinal John McCloskey, 1864-85; Michael A. Corrigan, 1885-1902; Cardinal John Farley, 1902-18; Cardinal Patrick Hayes, 1919-38; Cardinal Francis Spellman, 1939-67; Cardinal Terence J. Cooke, 1968-83; Cardinal John J. O'Connor, 1984-2000.

Norwich, CT (1953): Michael R. Cote, bishop, 2003.

Former bishops: Bernard J. Flanagan, 1953-59; Vincent J. Hines, 1960-75; Daniel P. Reilly, 1975-94; Daniel A. Hart, 1995-2003.

Oakland, CA (1962): John S. Cummins, bishop, 1977; Allen H. Vigneron, coadjutor bishop, 2003.

Former bishop: Floyd L. Begin, 1962-77.

Ogdensburg, NY (1872): Vacant.

Former bishops: Edgar P. Wadhams, 1872-91; Henry Gabriels, 1892-1921; Joseph H. Conroy, 1921-39; Francis J. Monaghan, 1939-42; Bryan J. McEntegart, 1943-53; Walter P. Kellenberg, 1954-57; James J. Navagh, 1957-63; Leo R. Smith, 1963; Thomas A. Donnellan, 1964-68; Stanislaus J. Brzana, 1968-93; Paul S. Loverde, 1993-99; Gerald M. Barbarito, 1999-2003.

Oklahoma City,* OK (1905; archdiocese, 1972): Eusebius J. Beltran, archbishop, 1993.

Former ordinaries: Theophile Meerschaert, 1905-24; Francis C. Kelley, 1924-48; Eugene J. McGuinness, 1948-57; Victor J. Reed, 1958-71; John R. Quinn, 1971-77, first archbishop; Charles A. Salatka, 1977-92.

Omaha,* NE (1885; archdiocese, 1945): Elden F. Curtiss, archbishop, 1993.

Former ordinaries: James O'Gorman, O.C.S.O., 1859-74, vicar apostolic; James O'Connor, vicar apostolic, 1876-85, first bishop, 1885-90; Richard Scannell, 1891-1916; Jeremiah J. Harty, 1916-27; Francis Beckman, administrator, 1926-28; Joseph F. Rummel, 1928-35; James H. Ryan, 1935-47, first archbishop; Gerald T. Bergan, 1948-69; Daniel E. Sheehan, 1969-93.

Orange, CA (1976): Tod D. Brown, bishop, 1998; Jaime Soto, Dominic Mai Luong, auxiliaries.

Former bishop: William R. Johnson, 1976-86; Norman F. McFarland, 1986-98.

Orlando, FL (1968): Norbert M. Dorsey, C.P., bishop, 1990; Thomas G. Wenski, coadjutor bishop.

Former bishops: William Borders, 1968-74; Thomas J. Grady, 1974-89.

Our Lady of Deliverance of Newark (for Syrian-rite Catholics of the U.S. and Canada) (1995): Joseph Younan, bishop, 1996.

Our Lady of Lebanon of Los Angeles, CA (Maronite) (1994): Robert J. Shaheen, 2000.

Former eparch: John G. Chedid, 1994-2000.

Owensboro, KY (1937): John J. McRaith, bishop, 1982.

Former bishops: Francis R. Cotton, 1938-60; Henry J. Soenneker, 1961-82.

Palm Beach, FL (1984): Gerald Michael Barbarito, 2003.

Former bishop: Thomas V. Daily, 1984-90; J. Keith Symons, 1990-98; Anthony J. O'Connell, 1998-2002; Sean O'Malley, O.F.M. Cap., 2002-2003.

Parma, OH (Byzantine, Ruthenian) (1969): John Kudrick, bishop, 2002.

Former bishops: Emil Mihalik, 1969-84; Andrew Pataki, 1984-95; Basil Schott, O.F.M., 1996-2002.

Passaic, NJ (Byzantine, Ruthenian) (1963): Andrew Pataki, eparch, 1996.

Former bishops: Stephen Kocisko, 1963-68; Michael J. Dudick, 1968-95.

Paterson, NJ (1937): Frank J. Rodimer, bishop, 1978.

Former bishops: Thomas H. McLaughlin, 1937-47; Thomas A. Boland, 1947-52; James A. McNulty, 1953-63; James J. Navagh, 1963-65; Lawrence B. Casey, 1966-77.

Pensacola-Tallahassee, FL (1975): John H.Ricard, S.S.J., bishop, 1997.

Former bishops: Rene H. Gracida, 1975-83; J. Keith Symons, 1983-90; John M. Smith, 1991-95.

Peoria, IL (1877): Daniel R. Jenky, C.S.C., bishop, 2002.

Former bishops: John L. Spalding, 1877-1908; Edmund M. Dunne, 1909-29; Joseph H. Schlarman, 1930-51; William E. Cousins, 1952-58; John B. Franz, 1959-71; Edward W. O'Rourke, 1971- 90; John J. Myers, 1990-2001.

Philadelphia,* PA (1808; archdiocese, 1875): Justin F. Rigali, archbishop, 2003. Edward P. Cullen, Robert P. Maginnis, Michael F. Burbidge, auxiliaries.

Former ordinaries: Michael Egan, O.F.M., 1810-14; Henry Conwell, 1820-42; Francis P. Kenrick, 1842-51; John N. Neumann, C.SS.R., 1852-60; James F. Wood, 1860-83, first archbishop; Patrick J. Ryan, 1884-1911; Edmond F. Prendergast, 1911-18; Cardinal Dennis Dougherty, 1918-51; Cardinal John O'Hara, C.S.C.,

1951-60; Cardinal John Krol, 1961-88; Cardinal Anthony J. Bevilacqua, 1988-2003.

Philadelphia,* PA (Byzantine, Ukrainian) (1924; metropolitan, 1958): Stephen Soroka, archbishop, 2001.

Former ordinaries: Stephen Ortynsky, O.S.B.M., 1907-16; Constantine Bohachevsky, 1924-61; Ambrose Senyshyn, O.S.B.M., 1961-76; Joseph Schmondiuk, 1977-78; Myroslav J. Lubachivsky, 1979-80, apostolic administrator, 1980-81; Stephen Sulyk, 1981-2000.

Phoenix, AZ (1969): Vacant.

Former bishops: Edward A. McCarthy, 1969-76; James S. Rausch, 1977-81; Thomas J. O'Brien, 1982-2003.

Pittsburgh,* PA (Byzantine, Ruthenian) (1924; metropolitan, 1969): Basil Schott, O.F.M., archbishop, 2002.

Former ordinaries: Basil Takach 1924-48; Daniel Ivancho, 1948-54; Nicholas T. Elko, 1955-67; Stephen J. Kocisko, 1968-91, first metropolitan; Thomas V. Dolinay, 1991-93; Judson M. Procyk, 1995-2001.

Pittsburgh, PA (1843): Donald W. Wuerl, bishop, 1988. William J. Winter, David A. Zubic, auxiliaries.

Former bishops: Michael O'Connor, 1843-53, 1854-60; Michael Domenec, C.M., 1860-76; J. Tuigg, 1876-89; Richard Phelan, 1889-1904; J.F. Regis Canevin, 1904-20; Hugh C. Boyle, 1921-50; John F. Dearden, 1950-58; John J. Wright, 1959-69; Vincent M. Leonard, 1969-83; Anthony J. Bevilacqua, 1983-88.

Portland, ME (1853): Joseph J. Gerry, O.S.B., bishop, 1989.

Former bishops: David W. Bacon, 1855-74; James A. Healy, 1875-1900; William H. O'Connell, 1901-06; Louis S. Walsh, 1906-24; John G. Murray, 1925-31; Joseph E. McCarthy, 1932-55; Daniel J. Feeney, 1955-69; Peter L. Gerety, 1969-74; Edward C. O'Leary, 1974-88.

Portland,* OR (1846): John G. Vlazny, archbishop, 1997. Kenneth D. Steiner, auxiliary.

Established as Oregon City, name changed, 1928.

Former ordinaries: Francis N. Blanchet, 1846-80 vicar apostolic, first archbishop; Charles J. Seghers, 1880-84; William H. Gross, C.SS.R., 1885-98; Alexander Christie, 1899-1925; Edward D. Howard, 1926-66; Robert J. Dwyer, 1966-74; Cornelius M. Power, 1974-86; William J. Levada, 1986-95; Francis E. George, 1996-97.

Providence, RI (1872): Robert E. Mulvee, bishop, 1997. Robert McManus, auxiliary.

Former bishops: Thomas F. Hendricken, 1872-86; Matthew Harkins, 1887-1921; William A. Hickey, 1921-33; Francis P. Keough, 1934-47; Russell J. McVinney, 1948-71; Louis E. Gelineau, 1972-97.

Pueblo, CO (1941): Arthur N. Tafoya, bishop, 1980. Former bishops: Joseph C. Willging, 1942-59; Charles A. Buswell, 1959-79.

Raleigh, NC (1924): F. Joseph Gossman, bishop, 1975.

Former bishops: William J. Hafey, 1925-37; Eugene J. McGuinness, 1937-44; Vincent S. Waters, 1945-75.

Rapid City, SD (1902): Blase Cupich, bishop, 1998. Established at Lead, transferred, 1930.

Former bishops: John Stariha, 1902-09; Joseph F. Busch, 1910-15; John J. Lawler, 1916-48; William T. McCarty, C.SS.R., 1948-69; Harold J. Dimmerling, 1969-87; Charles J. Chaput, O.F.M., Cap., 1988-97.

Reno, NV (1931): Phillip F. Straling, bishop, 1995.

Established at Reno, 1931; title changed to Reno-Las Vegas, 1976, redesignated Reno, 1995, when Las Vegas was made a separate diocese.

Former bishops (Reno/Reno-Las Vegas): Thomas K. Gorman, 1931-52; Robert J. Dwyer, 1952-66; Joseph Green, 1967-74; Norman F. McFarland, 1976-86; Daniel F. Walsh, 1987-95.

Richmond, VA (1820): Walter F. Sullivan, bishop, 1974.

Former bishops: Patrick Kelly, 1820-22; Ambrose Marechal, S.S., administrator, 1822-28; James Whitfield, administrator, 1828-34; Samuel Eccleston, S.S., administrator, 1834-40; Richard V. Whelan, 1841-50; John McGill, 1850-72; James Gibbons, 1872-77; John J. Keane, 1878-88; Augustine Van de Vyver, 1889-1911; Denis J. O'Connell, 1912-26; Andrew J. Brennan, 1926-45; Peter L. Ireton, 1945-58; John J. Russell, 1958-73.

Rochester, NY (1868): Matthew H. Clark, bishop, 1979.

Former bishops: Bernard J. McQuaid, 1868-1909; Thomas F. Hickey, 1909-28; John F. O'Hern, 1929-33; Edward F. Mooney, 1933-37; James E. Kearney, 1937-66; Fulton J. Sheen, 1966-69; Joseph L. Hogan, 1969-78.

Rockford, IL (1908): Thomas G. Doran, bishop, 1994.

Former bishops: Peter J. Muldoon, 1908-27; Edward F. Hoban, 1928-42; John J. Boylan, 1943-53; Raymond P. Hillinger, 1953-56; Loras T. Lane, 1956-68; Arthur J. O'Neill, 1968-94.

Rockville Centre, NY (1957): William Francis Murphy, bishop, 2001. John C. Dunne, Emil A. Wcela, Paul H. Walsh, auxiliaries.

Former bishop: Walter P. Kellenberg, 1957-76; John R. McGann, 1976-2000; James McHugh, 2000.

Sacramento, CA (1886): William K. Weigand, bishop, 1993, installed, 1994. Richard J. Garcia, auxiliary.

Former bishops: Patrick Manogue, 1886-95; Thomas Grace, 1896-1921; Patrick J. Keane, 1922-28; Robert J. Armstrong, 1929-57; Joseph T. McGucken, 1957-62; Alden J. Bell, 1962-79; Francis A. Quinn, 1979-93.

Saginaw, MI (1938): Kenneth E. Untener, bishop, 1980.

Former bishops: William F. Murphy, 1938-50; Stephen S. Woznicki, 1950-68; Francis F. Reh, 1969-80.

St. Augustine, FL (1870): Victor Benito Galeone, bishop, 2001.

Former bishops: Augustin Verot, S.S., 1870-76; John Moore, 1877-1901; William J. Kenny, 1902-13; Michael J. Curley, 1914-21; Patrick J. Barry, 1922-40; Joseph P. Hurley, 1940-67; Paul F. Tanner, 1968-79; John J. Snyder, 1979-2000.

St. Cloud, MN (1889): John F. Kinney, bishop, 1995.

Former bishops: Otto Zardetti, 1889-94; Martin Marty, O.S.B., 1895-96; James Trobec, 1897-1914; Joseph F. Busch, 1915-53; Peter Bartholome, 1953-68; George H. Speltz, 1968-87; Jerome Hanus, O.S.B.,1987-94.

St. George's in Canton, OH (Byzantine, Romanian) (1982; eparchy, 1987): John Michael Botean, bishop, 1996.

Former bishop: Vasile Louis Puscas, 1983-93.

St. Josaphat in Parma, OH (Byzantine, Ukrainians) (1983): Robert M. Moskal, bishop, 1984.

St. Louis,* MO (1826; archdiocese, 1847): Vacant. Joseph F. Naumann, Robert J. Hermann, auxiliaries.

Former ordinaries: Joseph Rosati, C.M., 1827-43; Peter R. Kenrick, 1843-95, first archbishop; John J. Kain, 1895-1903; Cardinal John Glennon, 1903-46; Cardinal Joseph Ritter, 1946-67; Cardinal John J. Carberry, 1968-79; John L. May, 1980-92; Justin F. Rigali, 1994-2003.

St. Maron, Brooklyn, NY (Maronite) (1966; diocese, 1971): Hector Y. Doueihi, eparch, 1997.

Established at Detroit, transferred to Brooklyn, 1977.

Former eparch: Francis Zayek, exarch 1966-72, first eparch 1972-97

St. Nicholas in Chicago (Byzantine Eparchy of St. Nicholas of the Ukrainians) (1961): Richard Stephen Seminack, 2003.

Former bishops: Jaroslav Gabro, 1961-80; Innocent H. Lotocky, O.S.B.M., 1981-93; Michael Wiwchar, C.SS.R., 1993-2000.

St. Paul and Minneapolis,* MN (1850; archdiocese, 1888): Harry J. Flynn, archbishop, 1995. Frederick F. Campbell, Richard Edmund Pates, auxiliaries.

Former ordinaries: Joseph Cretin, 1851-57; Thomas L. Grace, O.P., 1859-84; John Ireland, 1884-1918, first archbishop; Austin Dowling, 1919-30; John G. Murray, 1931-56; William O. Brady, 1956-61; Leo Binz, 1962-75; John R. Roach, 1975-95.

St. Peter the Apostle of San Diego (Chaldean) (2002, eparchy): Sarhad Jammo, first eparch, 2002.

St. Petersburg, FL (1968): Robert N. Lynch, bishop, 1996.

Former bishops: Charles McLaughlin, 1968-78; W. Thomas Larkin, 1979-88; John C. Favalora, 1989-94.

St. Thomas the Apostle of Detroit (Chaldean) (1982; eparchy, 1985): Ibrahim N. Ibrahim, exarch, 1982; first eparch, 1985.

St. Thomas of the Syro-Malabars of Chicago (Syro-Malabars) (2001, eparchy): Jacob Angadiath, first eparch, 2001.

Salina, KS (1887): George K. Fitzsimons, bishop, 1984.

Established at Concordia, transferred, 1944.

Former bishops: Richard Scannell, 1887-91; John J. Hennessy, administrator, 1891-98; John F. Cunningham, 1898-1919; Francis J. Tief, 1921-38; Frank A. Thill, 1938-57; Frederick W. Freking, 1957-64; Cyril J. Vogel, 1965-79; Daniel W. Kucera, O.S.B., 1980-84.

Salt Lake City, UT (1891): George H. Niederauer, bishop, 1995.

Former bishops: Lawrence Scanlan, 1891-1915; Joseph S. Glass, C.M., 1915-26; John J. Mitty, 1926-32; James E. Kearney, 1932-37; Duane G. Hunt, 1937-60; J. Lennox Federal, 1960-80; William K. Weigand, 1980-93.

San Angelo, TX (1961): Michael D. Pfeifer, O.M.I., bishop, 1985.

Former bishops: Thomas J. Drury, 1962-65; Thomas Tschoepe, 1966-69; Stephen A. Leven, 1969-79; Joseph A. Fiorenza, 1979-84.

San Antonio,* TX (1874; archdiocese, 1926): Patrick F. Flores, archbishop, 1979. Thomas J.

Flanagan, Patrick J. Zurek, auxiliaries.

Former ordinaries: Anthony D. Pellicer, 1874-80; John C. Neraz, 1881-94; John A. Forest, 1895-1911; John W. Shaw, 1911-18; Arthur Jerome Drossaerts, 1918-40, first archbishop; Robert E. Lucey, 1941-69; Francis Furey, 1969-79.

San Bernardino, CA (1978): Gerald R. Barnes, bishop, 1995. Dennis P. O'Neil, auxiliary.

Former bishop: Phillip F. Straling, 1978-95.

San Diego, CA (1936): Robert H. Brom, bishop, 1990. Gilbert Espinoza Chavez, Salvatore Cordileone, auxiliaries.

Former bishops: Charles F. Buddy, 1936-66; Francis J. Furey, 1966-69; Leo T. Maher, 1969-90.

San Francisco,* CA (1853): William J. Levada, archbishop, 1995. John C. Wester, Ignatius Wang, auxiliaries.

Former ordinaries: Joseph S. Alemany, O.P., 1853-84; Patrick W. Riordan, 1884-1914; Edward J. Hanna, 1915-35; John Mitty, 1935-61; Joseph T. McGucken, 1962-77; John R. Quinn, 1977-95.

San Jose, CA (1981): Patrick J. McGrath, bishop, 1999.

Former ordinaries: R. Pierre DuMaine, 1981-98.

Santa Fe*, NM (1850; archdiocese, 1875): Michael J. Sheehan, archbishop, 1993.

Former ordinaries: John B. Lamy, 1850-85; first archbishop; John B. Salpointe, 1885-94; Placide L. Chapelle, 1894-97; Peter Bourgade, 1899-1908; John B. Pitaval, 1909-18; Albert T. Daeger, O.F.M., 1919-32; Rudolph A. Gerken, 1933-43; Edwin V. Byrne, 1943-63; James P. Davis, 1964-74; Robert F. Sanchez, 1974-93.

Santa Rosa, CA (1962): Daniel Walsh, 2000.

Former bishops: Leo T. Maher, 1962-69; Mark J. Hurley, 1969-86; John T. Steinbock, 1987-91; G. Patrick Ziemann, 1992-99.

Savannah, GA (1850): John Kevin Boland, bishop, 1995.

Former bishops: Francis X. Gartland, 1850-54; John Barry, 1857-59; Augustin Verot, S.S., 1861-70; Ignatius Persico, O.F.M. Cap., 1870-72; William H. Gross, C.SS.R., 1873-85; Thomas A. Becker, 1886-99; Benjamin J. Keiley, 1900-22; Michael Keyes, S.M., 1922-35; Gerard P. O'Hara, 1935-59; Thomas J. McDonough, 1960-67; Gerard L. Frey, 1967-72; Raymond W. Lessard, 1973-95.

Scranton, PA (1868): Joseph F. Martino, bishop, 2003. John M. Dougherty, auxiliary.

Former bishops: William O'Hara, 1868-99; Michael J. Hoban, 1899-1926; Thomas C. O'Reilly, 1928-38; William J. Hafey, 1938-54; Jerome D. Hannan, 1954-65; J. Carroll McCormick, 1966-83; John J. O'Connor, 1983-84; James C. Timlin, 1984-2003.

Seattle,* WA (1850; archdiocese, 1951): Alexander J. Brunett, archbishop, 1997. George L. Thomas, auxiliary.

Established as Nesqually, name changed, 1907.

Former ordinaries; Augustin M. Blanchet, 1850-79; Aegidius Junger, 1879-95; Edward J. O'Dea, 1896-1932; Gerald Shaughnessy, S.M., 1933-50; Thomas A. Connolly, first archbishop, 1950-75; Raymond G. Hunthausen, 1975-91; Thomas J. Murphy, 1991-97.

Shreveport, LA (1986): William B. Friend, bishop, 1986.

Sioux City, IA (1902): Daniel N. DiNardo, bishop, 1998.

Former bishops: Philip J. Garrigan, 1902-19; Edmond Heelan, 1919-48; Joseph M. Mueller, 1948-70; Frank H. Greteman, 1970-83; Lawrence D. Soens, 1983-98.

Sioux Falls, SD (1889): Robert J. Carlson, bishop, 1995.

Former bishops: Martin Marty, O.S.B., 1889-94; Thomas O'Gorman, 1896-1921; Bernard J. Mahoney, 1922-39; William O. Brady, 1939-56; Lambert A. Hoch, 1956-78; Paul V. Dudley, 1978-95.

Spokane, WA (1913): William S. Skylstad, bishop, 1990.

Former bishops: Augustine F. Schinner, 1914-25; Charles D. White, 1927-55; Bernard J. Topel, 1955-78; Lawrence H. Welsh, 1978-90.

Springfield, IL (1853): George J. Lucas, 1999.

Established at Quincy, transferred to Alton, 1857; transferred to Springfield, 1923.

Former bishops: Henry D. Juncker, 1857-68; Peter J. Baltes, 1870-86; James Ryan, 1888-1923; James A. Griffin, 1924-48; William A. O'Connor, 1949-75; Joseph A. McNicholas, 1975-83; Daniel L. Ryan, bishop, 1984-99.

Springfield, MA (1870): Thomas L. Dupre, bishop, 1995.

Former bishops: Patrick T. O'Reilly, 1870-92; Thomas D. Beaven, 1892-1920; Thomas M. O'Leary, 1921-49; Christopher J. Weldon, 1950-77; Joseph F. Maguire, 1977-91; John A. Marshall, 1991-94.

Springfield-Cape Girardeau, MO (1956): John J. Leibrecht, bishop, 1984.

Former bishops: Charles Helmsing, 1956-62; Ignatius J. Strecker, 1962-69; William Baum, 1970-73; Bernard F. Law, 1973-84.

Stamford, CT (Byzantine, Ukrainian) (1956): Basil Losten, eparch, 1977.

Former eparchs: Ambrose Senyshyn, O.S.B.M., 1956-61; Joseph Schmondiuk, 1961-77.

Steubenville, OH (1944): Robert Daniel Conlon, 2002.

Former bishops: John K. Mussio, 1945-77; Albert H. Ottenweller, 1977-92; Gilbert I. Sheldon, 1992-2002.

Stockton, CA (1962): Stephen E. Blaire, bishop, 1999.

Former bishops: Hugh A. Donohoe, 1962-69; Merlin J. Guilfoyle, 1969-79; Roger M. Mahony, 1980-85; Donald W. Montrose, 1986-99.

Superior, WI (1905): Raphael M. Fliss, bishop, 1985.

Former bishops: Augustine F. Schinner, 1905-13; Joseph M. Koudelka, 1913-21; Joseph G. Pinten, 1922-26; Theodore M. Reverman, 1926-41; William P. O'Connor, 1942-46; Albert G. Meyer, 1946-53; Joseph Annabring, 1954-59; George A. Hammes, 1960-85.

Syracuse, NY (1886): James M. Moynihan, bishop, 1995. Thomas J. Costello, auxiliary.

Former bishops: Patrick A. Ludden, 1887-1912; John Grimes, 1912-22; Daniel J. Curley, 1923-32; John A. Duffy, 1933-37; Walter A. Foery, 1937-70; David F. Cunningham, 1970-76; Frank J. Harrison, 1976-87; Joseph T. O'Keefe, 1987-95.

Toledo, OH (1910): Vacant, Robert W. Donnelly, auxiliary.

Former bishops: Joseph Schrembs, 1911-21; Samuel A. Stritch, 1921-30; Karl J. Alter, 1931-50; George J.

Rehring, 1950-67; John A. Donovan, 1967-80; James R. Hoffman, 1980-2003.

Trenton, NJ (1881): John M. Smith, bishop, 1997. Former bishops: Michael J. O'Farrell, 1881-94; James A. McFaul, 1894-1917; Thomas J. Walsh, 1918-28; John J. McMahon, 1928-32; Moses E. Kiley, 1934-40; William A. Griffin, 1940-50; George W. Ahr, 1950-79; John C. Reiss, 1980 -97.

Tucson, AZ (1897): Gerald F. Kicanas, bishop, 2003. Former bishops: Peter Bourgade, 1897-99; Henry Granjon, 1900-22; Daniel J. Gercke, 1923-60; Francis J. Green, 1960-81; Manuel D. Moreno, 1982-2003.

Tulsa, OK (1972): Edward J. Slattery, bishop, 1993. Former bishops: Bernard J. Ganter, 1973-77; Eusebius J. Beltran, 1978-92.

Tyler, TX (1986): Alvaro Corrada del Rio, S.J., 2000. Former bishop: Charles E. Herzig, 1987-91; Edmond Carmody, 1992-2000.

Van Nuys, CA (Byzantine, Ruthenian) (1981): William C. Skurla, 2002.

Former bishop: Thomas V. Dolinay, 1982-90; George M. Kuzma, 1991-2000.

Venice, FL (1984): John J. Nevins, bishop, 1984.

Victoria, TX (1982): David E. Fellhauer, bishop, 1990.

Former bishop: Charles V. Grahmann, 1982-89.

Washington,* DC (1939): Cardinal Theodore E. McCarrick, archbishop, 2000. Leonard Olivier, S.V.D., Kevin J. Farrell, Francisco González Valer, S.F., auxiliaries.

Former ordinaries: Michael J. Curley, 1939-47; Cardinal Patrick O'Boyle, 1948-73; Cardinal William Baum, 1973-80; Cardinal James A. Hickey, 1980-2000.

Wheeling-Charleston, WV (1850): Bernard W. Schmitt, bishop, 1989.

Established as Wheeling, name changed, 1974.

Former bishops: Richard V. Whelan, 1850-74; John J. Kain, 1875-93; Patrick J. Donahue, 1894-1922; John J. Swint, 1922-62; Joseph H. Hodges, 1962-85; Francis B. Schulte, 1985-88.

Wichita, KS (1887): Thomas J. Olmsted, bishop, 2001. Former bishops: John J. Hennessy, 1888-1920; Augustus J. Schwertner, 1921-39; Christian H. Winkelmann, 1940-46; Mark K. Carroll, 1947-67; David M. Maloney, 1967-82; Eugene J. Gerber, 1982-2001.

Wilmington, DE (1868): Michael A. Saltarelli, bishop, 1995.

Former bishops: Thomas A. Becker, 1868-86; Alfred A. Curtis, 1886-96; John J. Monaghan, 1897-1925; Edmond Fitzmaurice, 1925-60; Michael Hyle, 1960-67; Thomas J. Mardaga, 1968-84; Robert E. Mulvee, 1985-95.

Winona, MN (1889): Bernard J. Harrington, 1998. Former bishops: Joseph B. Cotter, 1889-1909; Patrick R. Heffron, 1910-27; Francis M. Kelly, 1928-49; Edward A. Fitzgerald, 1949-69; Loras J. Watters, 1969-86; John G. Vlazny, 1987-97.

Worcester, MA (1950): Daniel P. Reilly, bishop, 1994. George E. Rueger, auxiliary.

Former bishops: John J. Wright, 1950-59; Bernard J. Flanagan, 1959-83; Timothy J. Harrington, 1983-94.

Yakima, WA (1951): Carlos A. Sevilla, S.J., bishop, 1996.

Former bishops: Joseph P. Dougherty, 1951-69; Cornelius M. Power, 1969-74; Nicolas E. Walsh, 1974-76; William S. Skylstad, 1977-90; Francis E. George, O.M.I., 1990-96.

Youngstown, OH (1943): Thomas J. Tobin, bishop, 1995, installed 1996. Former bishops: James A. McFadden, 1943-52; Emmet M. Walsh, 1952-68; James W. Malone, 1968-95.

Apostolic Exarchate for Armenian Catholics in the United States and Canada, New York, NY (1981): Manuel Batakian, exarch, 2000.

Former exarchs: Nerses Mikael Setian, 1981-93; Hovhannes Tertzakian, O.M. Ven., 1995-2000.

Archdiocese for the Military Ordinariate, U.S.A., Washington, DC (1957; restructured, 1985): Archbishop Edwin F. O'Brien, military ordinary, 1997. Francis X. Roque, Joseph J. Madera, M.Pp.S., John J. Kaising, auxiliaries.

Military vicar appointed, 1917; canonically established, 1957, as U.S. Military Vicariate under jurisdiction of New York archbishop; name changed, restructured as independent jurisdiction, 1985.

Former military vicars: Cardinal Patrick Hayes, 1917-38; Cardinal Francis Spellman, 1939-67; Cardinal Terence J. Cooke, 1968-83; Cardinal John J. O'Connor, apostolic administrator, 1984-85.

Former military ordinaries: Archbishop Joseph T. Ryan, 1985-91; Joseph T. Dimino, 1991-97.

(Note: For coverage of **Missionary Bishops**, *see* under **Missionary Activity of the Church in the U.S.**)

CHANCERY OFFICES OF U.S. ARCHDIOCESES AND DIOCESES

A chancery office, under this or another title, is the central administrative office of an archdiocese or diocese. (Archdioceses are indicated by asterisk.)

Albany, NY: Pastoral Center, 40 N. Main Ave., 12203. (518) 453-6611; www.rcda.org.

Alexandria, LA: The Chancery Office, P.O. Box 7417, 71306. (318) 445-2401; www.diocesealex.org.

Allentown, PA: The Chancery Office, P.O. Box F, 18105-1538. (610) 437-0755.

Altoona-Johnstown, PA: The Chancery, 126 Logan Blvd., Hollidaysburg, 16648. (814) 695-5579; www.diocesealtjtn.org.

Amarillo, TX: Pastoral Center, 1800 N. Spring St., P.O. Box 5644, 79117-5644. (806) 383-2243.

Anchorage,* AK: The Chancery Office, 225

Cordova St., 99501. (907) 297-7700; www.archdioceseofanchorage.org

Arlington, VA: The Chancery Office, Suite 914, 200 N. Glebe Rd., 22203. (703) 841-2500.

Atlanta,* GA: Catholic Center, 680 W. Peachtree St. N.W., 30308. (404) 888-7802; www.archatl.com.

Austin, TX: The Chancery Office, 1600 N. Congress Ave., P.O. Box 13327, 78711. (512) 476-4888; www.austindiocese.org.

Baker, OR: Diocesan Pastoral Office, P.O. Box 5999, Bend, 97708. (541) 388-4004; users bendnet.com/dioceseofbakr/.

Baltimore,* MD: The Chancery Office, 320 Cathedral St., 21201. (410) 547-5446; www.archbalt.org.

Baton Rouge, LA: Catholic Life Center, P.O. Box

2028. 70821-2028. (225) 387-0561; www.diobr.org.

Beaumont, TX: Diocesan Pastoral Office, 703 Archie St., P.O. Box 3948, 77704-3948. (409) 838-0451.

Belleville, IL: The Chancery, 222 S. Third St. 62220-1985, (618) 277-8181; www.diobelle.org.

Biloxi, MS: Administration Offices, P.O. Box 6489, 39522-6489. (228) 702-2100; www.biloxidiocese.org.

Birmingham, AL: Catholic Life Center, P.O. Box 12047, 35202-2047. (205) 838-8322.

Bismarck, ND: The Chancery Office, 420 Raymond St., Box 1575, 58502-1575. (701) 223-1347.

Boise, ID: The Chancery Office, 303 Federal Way, 83705-5925. (208) 342-1311

Boston,* MA: The Chancery Office, 2121 Commonwealth Ave., Brighton, 02135. (617) 254-0100; www.rcab.org

Bridgeport, CT: The Catholic Center, 238 Jewett Ave., 06606-2892. (203) 372-4301

Brooklyn, NY: The Chancery Office, 75 Greene Ave., P.O. Box C, 11238. (718) 399-5970.

Brownsville, TX: The Catholic Pastoral Center, P.O. Box 2279, 1910 E. Elizabeth St., 78522-2279. (956) 542-2501; www.cdob.org.

Buffalo, NY: The Chancery Office, 795 Main St., 14203. (716) 847-5500; www.buffalodiocese.org

Burlington, VT: The Chancery Office, 351 North Ave., P.O. Box 526, 05401-0526. (802) 658-6110; www.vermontcatholic.org.

Camden, NJ: Camden Diocesan Center, 631 Market St., P.O. Box 708, 08101. (609) 756-7900.

Charleston, SC: The Chancery Office, 119 Broad St., P.O. Box 818, 29402. (843) 723-3488; www.catholic-doc.org.

Charlotte, NC: The Pastoral Center, P.O. Box 36776, 28236. (704) 370-6299; www.charlotte diocese.org.

Cheyenne, WY: The Chancery Office, Box 1468, 82003-0426. (307) 638-1530.

Chicago,* IL: Pastoral Center, P.O. Box 1979, 60690. (312) 751-7999; www.archdiocese-chgo.org

Cincinnati,* OH: The Chancery Office, 100 E. 8th St. 45202. (513) 421-3131; www.archdiocese-cinti.org.

Cleveland, OH: The Chancery Office, 1027 Superior Ave., 44114. (216) 696-6525; www.cle-dioc.org

Colorado Springs, CO: The Chancery Office, 29 W. Kiowa, 80903-1498. (719) 636-2345.

Columbus, OH: The Chancery Office, 198 E. Broad St., 43215-3766. (614) 224-2251.

Corpus Christi, TX: The Chancery Office, 620 Lipan St. P.O. Box 2620, 78403-2620. (512) 882-6191; www.diocesecc.org.

Covington, KY: The Catholic Center, P.O. Box 18548, Erlanger, 41018-0548. (859) 283-6200; www.dioofcovky.org.

Crookston, MN: The Chancery Office, 1200 Memorial Dr., P.O. Box 610, 56716. (218) 281-4533; www.crookston.org.

Dallas, TX: The Chancery Office, 3725 Blackburn, P.O. Box 190507, 75219. (214) 528-2240; www.cathdal.org.

Davenport, IA: The Chancery Office, St. Vincent Center, 2706 N. Gaines St., 52804-1998. (319) 324-1911; www.davenportdiocese.org.

Denver,* CO: Catholic Pastoral Center, 1300 South Steele St., 80210. (303) 715-2000; www.archden.org/archden.

Des Moines, IA: The Chancery Office, P.O. Box 1816, 50306. (515) 243-7653; www.dmdiocese.org.

Detroit,* MI: The Chancery Office, 1234 Washington Blvd., 48226. (313) 237-5816.

Dodge City, KS: The Chancery Office, 910 Central Ave., P.O. Box 137, 67801-0137. (316) 227-1500; www.dcdiocese.org.

Dubuque,* IA: The Chancery Office, P.O.Box 479, 52004-0479. (319) 556-2580; www.archdiocese.dbq.pvt.k12.ia.us.

Duluth, MN: Pastoral Center, 2830 E. 4th St., 55812. (218) 724-9111; www.dioceseduluth.org.

El Paso, TX: The Chancery Office, 499 St. Matthews St., 79907. (915) 595-5000; www.elpaso diocese.org.

Erie, PA: St. Mark Catholic Center, P.O. Box 10397, 16514-0397. (814) 824-1111; www.eriecd.org.

Evansville, IN: The Chancery Office, P.O. Box 4169, 47724-0169. (812) 424-5536; www.evansville-diocese.org.

Fairbanks, AK: The Chancery Office, 1316 Peger Rd., 99709. (907) 474-0753; www.cbna.org.

Fall River, MA: The Chancery Office, Box 2577, 02722. (508) 675-1311.

Fargo, ND: The Chancery Office, 1310 Broadway, Box 1750, 58107. (701) 235-6429; www.fargo diocese.org.

Fort Wayne-South Bend, IN: The Chancery Office, P.O. Box 390, Fort Wayne, 46801. (260) 422-4611; www.diocesefwsb.org.

Fort Worth, TX: Catholic Center, 800 W. Loop 820 South, 76108. (817) 560-3300; www.fwdioc.org.

Fresno, CA: The Chancery Office, 1550 N. Fresno St., 93703-3788. (559) 488-7400.

Gallup, NM: The Chancery Office, 711 S. Puerco Dr., P.O. Box 1338, 87305. (505) 863-4406.

Galveston-Houston, TX: The Chancery Office, P.O. Box 907, 77001. (713) 659-5461.

Gary, IN: The Chancery Office, 9292 Broadway, Merrillville, 46410. (219) 769-9292; www.chancery @dcgary.org.

Gaylord, MI: Diocesan Pastoral Center, 611 North St., 49735. (517) 732-5147.

Grand Island, NE: The Chancery Office, 311 W. 17th St., P.O. Box 996, 68802. (308) 382-6565.

Grand Rapids, MI: The Chancery Office, 660 Burton St., S.E., 49507. (616) 243-0491; www.diocese ofgrandrapids.org.

Great Falls-Billings, MT: The Chancery Office, P.O. Box 1399, Great Falls, 59401. (406) 727-6683; www.mcn.net/~dioceseofgfb.

Green Bay, WI: The Chancery Office, P.O. Box 23825, 54305-3825. (920) 437-7531; www.gb dioc.org.

Greensburg, PA: The Chancery Office, 723 E. Pittsburgh St., 15601. (724) 837-0901; www.catholic gbg.org.

Harrisburg, PA: The Chancery Office, P.O. Box 2153, 17105-2153. (717) 657-4804; www.hbg diocese.org.

Hartford,* CT: The Chancery Office, 134 Farmington Ave., 06105-3784. (860) 541-6491; www.archdiocese-hartford.org.

Helena, MT: The Chancery Office, 515 North Ewing, P.O. Box 1729, 59624-1729. (406) 442-5820.

Honolulu, HI: The Chancery Office, 1184 Bishop St., 96813. (808) 585-3342; www.pono.net.

Houma-Thibodaux, LA: The Chancery Office, P.O. Box 505, Schriever, 70395. (504) 868-7720; www.htdiocese.org.

Indianapolis,* IN: The Archbishop Edward T. O'Meara Catholic Center, 1400 N. Meridian St., 46206. (317) 236-1403; www.archindy.org.

Jackson, MS: The Chancery Office, 237 E. Amite St., P.O. Box 2248, 39225-2248. (601) 969-1880; www.jacksondiocese.org.

Jefferson City, MO: Chancery Office, 605 Clark Ave., P.O. Box 417, 65102-0417. (573) 635-9127; www.diojeffcity.org.

Joliet, IL: The Chancery Office, 425 Summit St., 60435. (815) 722-6606.

Juneau, AK: The Chancery Office, 419 6th St., No. 200, 99801. (907) 586-2227; www.juneau-diocese.addr.com.

Kalamazoo, MI: The Chancery Office, 215 N. Westnedge Ave., 49007-3760. (616) 349-8714.

Kansas City,* KS: The Chancery Office, 12615 Parallel Pkwy., 66109. (913) 721-1570; www.archkck.org.

Kansas City-St. Joseph, MO: The Chancery Office, P.O. Box 419037, Kansas City, 64141-6037. (816) 756-1850; www.diocese-kcsj.org.

Knoxville, TN: The Chancery Office, 805 Northshore Dr., P.O. Box 11127, 37939-1127. (865) 584-3307.

La Crosse, WI: The Chancery Office, 3710 East Ave. S., Box 4004, 54602-4004. (608) 788-7700; www.dioceseoflacrosse.com

Lafayette, IN: The Bishop's Office, P.O. Box 260, 47902-0260. (765) 742-0275; www.diocese oflafayette.org.

Lafayette, LA: The Chancery Office, 1408 Carmel Ave., 70501. (337) 261-5614; www.dol-louisiana.org.

Lake Charles, LA: The Chancery Office, P.O. Box 3223, 70602. (318) 439-7400; lcdiocese.laol.net

Lansing, MI: The Chancery Office, 300 W. Ottawa St., 48933-1577. (517) 342-2440.

Laredo, Tx.: Diocesan Pastoral Center, P.O. Box 2247, 78044. (956) 727-2140.

Las Cruces, NM: The Chancery Office, 1280 Med Park Dr., 88005. (505) 523-7577; www.zianet.com/diocese.

Las Vegas, NV: Chancery Office, P.O. Box 18316. 89114-8316. (702) 735-3500.

Lexington, KY: Catholic Center, 1310 Main St., 40508-2040. (606) 253-1993; www.cdlex.org.

Lincoln, NE: The Chancery Office, P.O. Box 80328, 68501-0328. (402) 488-0921.

Little Rock, AR: The Chancery Office, 2415 N. Tyler St., P.O. Box 7239. 72217. (501) 664-0340.

Los Angeles,* CA: Archdiocesan Catholic Center, 3424 Wilshire Blvd., 90010-2241. (213) 637-7000; www.LA-Archdiocese.org.

Louisville,* KY: Chancery Office, 212 E. College St., P.O. Box 1073, 40201-1073. (502) 585-3291; www.archlou.org.

Lubbock, TX: The Catholic Center, P.O. Box 98700, 79499. (806) 792-3943; www.catholiclubbock.org.

Madison, WI: Bishop O'Connor Catholic Pastoral Center, P.O. Box 44983, 3577 High Point Rd., 53744-4983. (608) 821-3000; www.madisondiocese.org.

Manchester, NH: The Chancery Office, 153 Ash St., P.O. Box 310, 03105-0310. (603) 669-3100; www.diocesemanch.org.

Marquette, MI: The Chancery Office, 444 S. Fourth St., P.O. Box 550. 49855. (906) 225-1141.

Memphis, TN: The Catholic Center, 5825 Shelby Oaks Dr., P.O. Box 341669, 38184-1669. (901) 373-1200; www.cdom.org.

Metuchen, NJ: The Chancery Office, P.O. Box 191, 08840. (732) 283-3800; www.diometuchen.org.

Miami,* FL: The Chancery Office, 9401 Biscayne Blvd., Miami Shores, 33138. (305) 757-6241; www.archdioceseofmiami.org.

Milwaukee,* WI: The Chancery Office, P.O. Box 07912, 53207-0912. (414) 769-3340; www.archmil.org.

Mobile,* AL: The Chancery Office, 400 Government St., P.O. Box 1966, 36633. (334) 434-1585

Monterey, CA: The Chancery Office, P.O. Box 2048, 93942-2048. (831) 373-4345; www.diocese ofmonterey.org.

Nashville, TN: The Chancery Office, 2400 21st Ave. S., 37212-5387. (615) 383-6393; www.serve.com/DIOCNASH/.

Newark,* NJ: Chancery Office, P.O. Box 9500, 07104-0500. (973) 497-4000; www.rcan.org.

New Orleans,* LA: The Chancery Office, 7887 Walmsley Ave., 70125. (504) 861-9521; www.catholic.org/neworleans/.

Newton, MA (Melkite): The Chancery Office, 158 Pleasant St., Brookline, 02446. (617) 566-4511; www.melkite.org.

New Ulm, MN: Catholic Pastoral Center, 1400 Sixth St. N., 56073-2099. (507) 359-2966; www.dnu.org.

New York,* NY: The Chancery Office, 1011 First Ave., 10022-4134. (212) 371-1000; www.ny-archdiocese.org.

Norwich, CT: The Chancery Office, 201 Broadway, P.O. Box 587. 06360-0587. (860) 887-9294; www.norwichdiocese.org.

Oakland, CA: The Chancery Office, 2900 Lakeshore Ave., 94610. (510) 893-4711.

Ogdensburg, NY: The Chancery Office, 604 Washington St., P.O. Box 369, 13669. (315) 393-2920.

Oklahoma City,* OK: The Chancery Office, P.O. Box 32180, 73123. (405) 721-5651.

Omaha,* NE: The Chancery Office, 100 N. 62nd St., 68132-2795. (402) 558-3100; www.oarch.org.

Orange, CA: The Chancery Office, 2811 E. Villa Real Dr., P.O. Box 14195, 92863-1595. (714) 282-3000; www.rcbo.org.

Orlando, FL: The Chancery Office, P.O. Box 1800, 32802-1800. (407) 246-4800; www.orlando diocese.org.

Our Lady of Deliverance of Newark, for Syrian rite Catholics of the U.S. and Canada: P.O. Box 8366, Union City, NJ, 07087-8262. (201) 583-1067; www.syriac-catholic.org.

Our Lady of Lebanon of Los Angeles, CA (Maronite): The Chancery Office, P.O. Box 16397, Beverly Hills, 90209. (310) 247-8322; www.eparchyla.org.

Owensboro, KY: The Catholic Pastoral Center, 600 Locust St., 42301-2130. (502) 683-1545; www.owens borodio.org.

Palm Beach, FL: Pastoral Center, P.O. Box 109650, Palm Beach Gardens, 33410-9650. (561) 775-9500; www.diocese.maco.net.

Parma, OH (Byzantine): The Chancery Office, 1900 Carlton Rd., 44134-3129. (216) 741-8773; www.parma.com.

Passaic, NJ (Byzantine): The Chancery Office, 445 Lackawanna Ave., W. Paterson, 07424. (973) 890-7777; members.aol.com/byzruth/index/htm.

Paterson, NJ: Diocesan Pastoral Center, 777 Valley Rd., Clifton, 07013. (973) 777-8818; www.patersondiocese.org.

Pensacola-Tallahassee, FL: Pastoral Center, P.O. Drawer 17329, Pensacola, 32522. (904) 432-1515; www.cfi.net/ptdiocese/pt.html.

Peoria, IL: The Chancery Office, 607 N.E. Madison Ave., P.O. Box 1406, 61655. (309) 671-1550.

Philadelphia,* PA: The Chancery Office, 222 N. 17th St., 19103. (215) 587-4538; www.archdiocese-phl.org.

Philadelphia,* PA (Byzantine): The Chancery Office, 827 N. Franklin St., 19123-2097. (215) 627-0143.

Phoenix, AZ: The Chancery Office, 400 E. Monroe St., 85004-2376. (602) 257-0030; www.catholicsun.org.

Pittsburgh,* PA (Byzantine): The Chancery Office, 66 Riverview Ave. ,15214-2253. (412) 231-4000.

Pittsburgh, PA: Pastoral Center, 111 Blvd. of the Allies, 15222-1618. (412) 456-3000; www.diopitt.org.

Portland, ME: The Chancery Office, 510 Ocean Ave., P.O. Box 11559. 04104-7559. (207) 773-6471.

Portland, OR*: Pastoral Center, 2838 E. Burnside St., 97214. (503) 234-5334; www.archdpdx.org/.

Providence, RI: The Chancery Office, One Cathedral Sq., 02903-3695. (401) 278-4500; www.dioceseofprovidence.com.

Pueblo, CO: Catholic Pastoral Center, 1001 N. Grand Ave., 81003-2948. (719) 544-9861; www.pueblo-diocese.com.

Raleigh, NC: Catholic Center, 715 Nazareth St., 27606-2187. (919) 821-9700; www.raldioc.org.

Rapid City, SD: The Chancery Office, 606 Cathedral Dr., P.O. Box 678, 57709. (605) 343-3541.

Reno, NV: Pastoral Center, P.O. Box 1211, 89504-1211. (775) 329-9274; www.catholicreno.com.

Richmond, VA: The Chancery Office, 811 Cathedral Pl., 23220-4801. (804) 359-5661; www.diocric.org.

Rochester, NY: The Pastoral Center, 1150 Buffalo Rd., 14624. (716) 328-3210; www.dor.org.

Rockford, IL: The Chancery Office, 1245 N. Court St., P.O. Box 7044, 61126-7044. (815) 962-3709; www.rockforddiocese.org.

Rockville Centre, NY: The Chancery Office, 50 N. Park Ave., 11570-4184. (516) 678-5800; www.drvc.org.

Sacramento, CA: Pastoral Center, 2110 Broadway, 95818-2541. (916) 733-0100; www.diocese-sacramento.org.

Saginaw, MI: The Chancery Office, 5800 Weiss St., 48603-2799. (517) 799-7910; www.dioceseofsaginaw.org.

St. Augustine, FL: Catholic Center, P.O. Box 24000, Jacksonville, 32241-4000. (904) 262-3200; staugustine.ml.org/diocese.

St. Cloud, MN: The Chancery Office, P.O. Box 1248, 56302. (320) 251-2340; www.stcdio.org.

St. George's in Canton, OH (Byzantine, Romanian): The Chancery Office, 1121 44th St. N.E., 44714-1297. (330) 492-4086; www.Romanian Catholic.org.

St. Josaphat in Parma, OH (Byzantine): The Chancery Office, P.O. Box 347180, 44134-7180. (440) 888-1522.

St. Louis,* MO: The Catholic Center, 4445 Lindell

Blvd., 63108-2497. (314) 633-2222; www.archstl.org.

St. Maron of Brooklyn (Maronite): The Pastoral Center, 294 Howard Ave., Staten Island, NY, 10301-4409. (718) 815-0436.

St. Nicholas in Chicago (Byzantine): The Chancery Office, 2245 W. Rice St., 60622. (312) 276-5080.

St. Paul and Minneapolis,* MN: The Chancery Office, 226 Summit Ave., St. Paul, 55102-2197. (651) 291-4400; www.mtn.org/archcom/.

St. Peter the Apostle of San Diego (Chaldean): Chancery Office, 1627 Jamacha Way, El Cajon, CA 92019. (619) 579-7913.

St. Petersburg, FL: The Chancery Office, P.O. Box 40200, 33743-0200. (727) 344-1611; www.dioceseofstpete.org.

St. Thomas of Chicago (Syro-Malabar): Diocesan Office, 717 N. Eastland, Elmhurst, IL 60126. (630) 530-8399.

St. Thomas the Apostle of Detroit (Chaldean Catholic Diocese – USA): The Chancery Office, 25603 Berg Rd., Southfield, MI 48034. (248) 351-0440.

Salina, KS: The Chancery Office, P.O. Box 980, 67402-0980. (785) 827-8746.

Salt Lake City, UT: The Chancery Office, 27 C St., 84103-2397. (801) 328-8641; www.utahcatholicdiocese.org.

San Angelo, TX: The Chancery Office, P.O. Box 1829, 76902-1829. (915) 651-7500; www.san-angelodiocese.org.

San Antonio,* TX: The Chancery Office, P.O. Box 28410, 78228-0410. (210) 734-2620; www.archdiosa.org.

San Bernardino, CA: The Chancery Office, 1201 E. Highland Ave., 92404. (909) 475-5300; www.sbdiocese.org.

San Diego, CA: Pastoral Center, P.O. Box 85728. 92186-5728, (619) 490-8200; www.diocese-sdiego.org.

San Francisco,* CA: The Chancery Office, 445 Church St., 94114. (415) 565-3609; www.sfarchdiocese.org.

San Jose, CA: The Chancery Office, 900 Lafayette St., Suite 301, Santa Clara, 95050-4966. (408) 983-0100; www.dsj.org.

Santa Fe,* NM: Catholic Center, 4000 St. Joseph's Pl. N.W., Albuquerque, 87120. (505) 831-8100.

Santa Rosa, CA: The Chancery Office, P.O. Box 1297, 95402-1297. (707) 545-7610; www.santarosacatholic.org.

Savannah, GA: Catholic Pastoral Center, 601 E. Liberty St., 31401-5196. (912) 238-2320; www.dioceseofsavannah.org.

Scranton, PA: The Chancery Office, 300 Wyoming Ave., 18503-1279. (570) 207-2216; www.dioceseofscranton.org.

Seattle,* WA: The Chancery Office, 910 Marion St., 98104-1299. (206) 382-4560; www.seattlearch.org.

Shreveport, LA: Catholic Center, 3500 Fairfield Ave. 71104. (318) 868-4441; www.dioshpt.org.

Sioux City, IA: The Chancery Office, P.O. Box 3379, 51102-3379. (712) 255-7933; www.scdiocese.org.

Sioux Falls, SD: Catholic Pastoral Center, 523 N. Duluth Ave., 57104-2714. (605) 334-9861; Diocese-of-Sioux-Falls.org.

Spokane, WA: Catholic Pastoral Center, Catholic Diocese of Spokane, P.O. Box 1453, 99210-1453. (509) 358-7300; www.dioceseofspokane.org.

Springfield, IL: Catholic Pastoral Center, 1615 West Washington, P.O. Box 3187, 62708-3187. (217) 698-8500.

Springfield, MA: The Chancery Office, P.O. Box 1730, 01101. (413) 732-3175; www.diospringfield.org.

Springfield-Cape Girardeau, MO: The Catholic Center, 601 S. Jefferson Ave., Springfield. 65806-3143. (417) 866-0841; www.diocspfdcape.org.

Stamford, CT (Byzantine): The Chancery Office, 14 Peveril Rd., 06902-3019. (203) 324-7698

Steubenville, OH: The Chancery Office, P.O. Box 969, 43952. (740) 282-3631; www.diosteub.org.

Stockton, CA: The Chancery Office, 1125 N. Lincoln St., 95203. (209) 466-0636.

Superior, WI: The Chancery Office, 1201 Hughitt Ave., Box 969, 54880. (715) 392-2937.

Syracuse, NY: The Chancery Office, P.O. Box 511, 13201-0511. (315) 422-7203; wwwsyrdioc.org.

Toledo, OH: The Chancery Office, P.O. Box 985, 43697-0895. (419) 244-6711; www.toledodiocese.org.

Trenton, NJ: Chancery Office, 701 Lawrenceville Rd., P.O. Box 5147, 08638. (609) 406-7400.

Tucson, AZ: The Chancery Office, 192 S. Stone Ave., Box 31. 85702. (520) 792-3410; www.azstarnet.com/~rccdot.

Tulsa, OK: The Chancery Office, P.O. Box 690240, 74169. (918) 294-1904.

Tyler, TX: The Chancery Office, 1015 E.S.E. Loop 323, 75701-9663. (903) 534-1077.

Van Nuys, CA (Byzantine): The Chancery Office, 8131 N. 16th St., Phoenix, AZ 85020. (602) 861-9778; eparchy-of-van-nuys.org.

Venice, FL: The Catholic Center, P.O. Box 2006, 34284. (941) 484-9543; www.dioceseofvenice.org.

Victoria, TX: The Chancery Office, P.O. Box 4070, 77903. (361) 573-0828.

Washington,* DC: Archdiocesan Pastoral Center, P.O. Box 29260, 20017. (301) 853-4500.

Wheeling-Charleston, WV: The Chancery Office, 1300 Byron St., P.O. Box 230, Wheeling, 26003. (304) 233-0880; www.dwc.org.

Wichita, KS: The Chancery Office, 424 N. Broadway, 67202. (316) 269-3900.

Wilmington, DE: The Chancery Office, P.O. Box 2030, 19899-2030. (302) 573-3100; www.cdow.org.

Winona, MN: The Chancery Office, P.O. Box 588, 55987. (507) 454-4643; www.dow.org.

Worcester, MA: The Chancery Office, 49 Elm St., 01609-2597. (508) 791-7171; www.worcester diocese.org.

Yakima, WA: The Chancery Office, 5301-A Tieton Dr., 98908. (509) 965-7117.

Youngstown, OH: The Chancery Office, 144 W. Wood St., 44503. (330) 744-8451; www.doy.org.

Military Archdiocese: P.O. Box 4469, Washington, DC 20017-0469; 3311 Toledo Terrace, Suite A201, Hyattsville, MD 20782-4135. (301) 853-0400; www.milarch.org.

Armenian Apostolic Exarchate for the United States and Canada: 110 E. 12th St., New York, NY 10003. (212) 477-2030.

CATHEDRALS, BASILICAS, AND SHRINES IN THE U.S.

CATHEDRALS IN THE UNITED STATES

A cathedral is the principal church in a diocese, the one in which the bishop has his seat (cathedra). He is the actual pastor, although many functions of the church, which usually serves a parish, are the responsibility of a priest serving as the rector. Because of the dignity of a cathedral, the dates of its dedication and its patronal feast are observed throughout a diocese. The pope's cathedral, the Basilica of St. John Lateran, is the highest-ranking church in the world. (Archdioceses are indicated by asterisk.)

Albany, NY: Immaculate Conception.
Alexandria, LA: St. Francis Xavier.
Allentown, PA: St. Catherine of Siena.
Altoona-Johnstown, PA: Blessed Sacrament (Altoona); St. John Gualbert (Johnstown).
Amarillo, TX: St. Laurence.
Anchorage,* AK: Holy Family.
Arlington, Va: St. Thomas More.
Atlanta,* GA: Christ the King.
Austin, TX: St. Mary (Immaculate Conception).
Baker, OR: St. Francis de Sales.
Baltimore,* MD: Mary Our Queen; Basilica of the National Shrine of the Assumption of the Blessed Virgin Mary (Co-Cathedral).
Baton Rouge, LA: St. Joseph.
Beaumont, TX: St. Anthony (of Padua).
Belleville, IL: St. Peter.
Biloxi, MS: Nativity of the Blessed Virgin Mary.

Birmingham, AL: St. Paul.
Bismarck, N.D.: Holy Spirit.
Boise, Id.: St. John the Evangelist.
Boston,* MA: Holy Cross.
Bridgeport, CT: St. Augustine.
Brooklyn, NY: St. James (Minor Basilica).
Brownsville, TX: Immaculate Conception.
Buffalo, NY: St. Joseph.
Burlington, VT: Immaculate Conception; St. Joseph (Co-Cathedral).
Camden, NJ: Immaculate Conception.
Charleston, SC: St. John the Baptist.
Charlotte, NC: St. Patrick.
Cheyenne, WY: St. Mary.
Chicago,* IL: Holy Name (of Jesus).
Cincinnati,* OH: St. Peter in Chains.
Cleveland, OH: St. John the Evangelist.
Colorado Springs, Colo: St. Mary.
Columbus, OH: St. Joseph.
Corpus Christi, TX: Corpus Christi.
Covington, KY: Basilica of the Assumption.
Crookston, MN: Immaculate Conception.
Dallas, TX: Cathedral-Santuario de Guadalupe.
Davenport, IA: Sacred Heart.
Denver,* CO: Immaculate Conception (Minor Basilica).
Des Moines, IA: St. Ambrose.
Detroit,* MI: Most Blessed Sacrament.

Dodge City, KS: Our Lady of Guadalupe.
Dubuque,* IA: St. Raphael.
Duluth, MN: Our Lady of the Rosary.
El Paso, TX: St. Patrick.
Erie, PA: St. Peter.
Evansville, IN: Most Holy Trinity (Pro-Cathedral).
Fairbanks, AK: Sacred Heart.
Fall River, MA: St. Mary of the Assumption.
Fargo, N.D.: St. Mary.
Fort Wayne-S. Bend, IN: Immaculate Conception (Fort Wayne); St. Matthew (South Bend).
Fort Worth, TX: St. Patrick.
Fresno, CA: St. John (the Baptist).
Gallup, NM: Sacred Heart.
Galveston-Houston, TX: St. Mary (Minor Basilica, Galveston); Sacred Heart Co-Cathedral (Houston).
Gary, IN: Holy Angels.
Gaylord, MI: St. Mary, Our Lady of Mt. Carmel.
Grand Island, NE: Nativity of Blessed Virgin Mary.
Grand Rapids, MI: St. Andrew.
Great Falls-Billings, MT: St. Ann (Great Falls); St. Patrick Co-Cathedral (Billings).
Green Bay, WI: St. Francis Xavier.
Greensburg, PA: Blessed Sacrament.
Harrisburg, PA: St. Patrick.
Hartford,* CT: St. Joseph.
Helena, MT: St. Helena.
Honolulu, HI: Our Lady of Peace; St. Theresa of the Child Jesus (Co-Cathedral).
Houma-Thibodaux, LA: St. Francis de Sales (Houma); St. Joseph Co-Cathedral (Thibodaux).
Indianapolis,* IN: Sts. Peter and Paul.
Jackson, MS: St. Peter.
Jefferson City, MO: St. Joseph.
Joliet, IL: St. Raymond Nonnatus.
Juneau, AK: Nativity of the Blessed Virgin Mary.
Kalamazoo, MI: St. Augustine.
Kansas City,* KS: St. Peter the Apostle.
Kansas City-St. Joseph, MO: Immaculate Conception (Kansas City); St. Joseph Co-Cathedral (St. Joseph).
Knoxville, TN: Sacred Heart of Jesus.
La Crosse, WI: St. Joseph the Workman.
Lafayette, IN: St. Mary.
Lafayette, LA: St. John the Evangelist.
Lake Charles, LA: Immaculate Conception.
Lansing, MI: St. Mary.
Laredo, TX: San Augustin.
Las Cruces, NM: Immaculate Heart of Mary.
Las Vegas, NV: Guardian Angel.
Lexington, KY: Christ the King.
Lincoln, NE: Cathedral of the Risen Christ.
Little Rock, AR: St. Andrew.
Los Angeles,* CA: Cathedral of Our Lady of the Angels of Los Angeles (opened in 2002).
Louisville,* KY: Assumption.
Lubbock, TX: Christ the King.
Madison, WI: St. Raphael.
Manchester, NH: St. Joseph.
Marquette, MI: St. Peter.
Memphis, TN: Immaculate Conception.
Metuchen, NJ: St. Francis (of Assisi).
Miami,* FL: St. Mary (Immaculate Conception).
Milwaukee,* WI: St. John.
Mobile,* AL: Immaculate Conception (Minor Basilica).
Monterey, CA: San Carlos Borromeo.
Nashville, TN: Incarnation.

Newark,* NJ: Sacred Heart (Minor Basilica).
New Orleans,* LA: St. Louis. (Minor Basilica)
Newton, MA (Melkite): Our Lady of the Annunciation (Boston).
New Ulm, MN: Holy Trinity.
New York,* NY: St. Patrick.
Norwich, CT: St. Patrick.
Oakland, CA: St. Francis de Sales.
Ogdensburg, NY: St. Mary (Immaculate Conception).
Oklahoma City,* OK: Our Lady of Perpetual Help.
Omaha,* NE: St. Cecilia.
Orange, CA: Holy Family.
Orlando, FL: St. James.
Our Lady of Deliverance of Newark, New Jersey for Syrian Rite Catholics in the U.S. and Canada: Our Lady of Deliverance.
Our Lady of Lebanon of Los Angeles, CA (Maronite): Our Lady of Mt. Lebanon-St. Peter.
Owensboro, KY: St. Stephen.
Palm Beach, FL: St. Ignatius Loyola, Palm Beach Gardens.
Parma, OH (Byzantine): St. John the Baptist.
Passaic, NJ (Byzantine): St. Michael.
Paterson, NJ: St. John the Baptist.
Pensacola-Tallahassee, FL: Sacred Heart (Pensacola); Co-Cathedral of St. Thomas More (Tallahassee).
Peoria, IL: St. Mary.
Philadelphia,* PA: Sts. Peter and Paul (Minor Basilica).
Philadelphia,* PA (Byzantine): Immaculate Conception of Blessed Virgin Mary.
Phoenix, AZ: Sts. Simon and Jude.
Pittsburgh,* PA (Byzantine): St. John the Baptist, Munhall.
Pittsburgh, PA: St. Paul.
Portland, ME: Immaculate Conception.
Portland,* OR: Immaculate Conception.
Providence, RI: Sts. Peter and Paul.
Pueblo, CO: Sacred Heart.
Raleigh, NC: Sacred Heart.
Rapid City, SD: Our Lady of Perpetual Help.
Reno, NV: St. Thomas Aquinas.
Richmond, VA: Sacred Heart.
Rochester, NY: Sacred Heart.
Rockford, IL: St. Peter.
Rockville Centre, NY: St. Agnes.
Sacramento, CA: Blessed Sacrament.
Saginaw, MI: St. Mary.
St. Augustine, FL: St. Augustine (Minor Basilica).
St. Cloud, MN: St. Mary.
St. George's in Canton, OH (Byzantine, Romanian): St. George.
St. Josaphat in Parma, OH (Byzantine): St. Josaphat.
St. Louis,* MO: St. Louis.
St. Maron, Brooklyn, NY (Maronite): Our Lady of Lebanon.
St. Nicholas in Chicago (Byzantine): St. Nicholas.
St. Paul and Minneapolis,* MN: St. Paul (St. Paul); Basilica of St. Mary Co-Cathedral (Minneapolis).
St. Petersburg, FL: St. Jude the Apostle.
St. Thomas the Apostle of Detroit (Chaldean): Our Lady of Chaldeans Cathedral (Mother of God Church), Southfield, MI
St. Thomas of Chicago (Syro-Malabar): Mar Thoma Shleeha Church.
Salina, KS: Sacred Heart.

Salt Lake City, UT: The Madeleine.
San Angelo, TX: Sacred Heart.
San Antonio,* TX: San Fernando.
San Bernardino, CA: Our Lady of the Rosary.
San Diego, CA: St. Joseph.
San Francisco,* CA: St. Mary (Assumption).
San Jose, CA: St. Joseph (Minor Basilica); St. Patrick, Proto-Cathedral.
Santa Fe,* NM: San Francisco de Asis.
Santa Rosa, CA: St. Eugene.
Savannah, GA: St. John the Baptist.
Scranton, PA: St. Peter.
Seattle,* WA: St. James.
Shreveport, LA: St. John Berchmans.
Sioux City, IA: Epiphany.
Sioux Falls, SD: St. Joseph.
Spokane, WA: Our Lady of Lourdes.
Springfield, IL: Immaculate Conception.
Springfield, MA: St. Michael.
Springfield-Cape Girardeau, MO: St. Agnes (Springfield): St. Mary (Cape Girardeau).
Stamford, CT (Byzantine): St. Vladimir.
Steubenville, OH: Holy Name.
Stockton, CA: Annunciation.

Superior, WI: Christ the King.
Syracuse, NY: Immaculate Conception.
Toledo, OH: Queen of the Most Holy Rosary.
Trenton, NJ: St. Mary (Assumption).
Tucson, AZ: St. Augustine.
Tulsa, OK: Holy Family.
Tyler, TX: Immaculate Conception.
Van Nuys, CA (Byzantine): St. Mary (Patronage of the Mother of God), Van Nuys; St. Stephen's (Pro-Cathedral), Phoenix, AZ
Venice, Fla: Epiphany.
Victoria, TX: Our Lady of Victory.
Washington,* DC: St. Matthew.
Wheeling-Charleston, WV: St. Joseph (Wheeling); Sacred Heart (Charleston).
Wichita, KS: Immaculate Conception.
Wilmington, DE: St. Peter.
Winona, MN: Sacred Heart.
Worcester, MA: St. Paul.
Yakima, WA: St. Paul.
Youngstown, OH: St. Columba.
Apostolic Exarchate for Armenian Catholics in the U.S. and Canada: St. Ann (110 E. 12th St., New York, NY 10003).

BASILICAS IN THE UNITED STATES

Basilica is a title assigned to certain churches because of their antiquity, dignity, historical importance or significance as centers of worship. Major basilicas have the papal altar and holy door, which is opened at the beginning of a Jubilee Year; minor basilicas enjoy certain ceremonial privileges.

Among the major basilicas are the patriarchal basilicas of St. John Lateran, St. Peter, St. Paul Outside the Walls and St. Mary Major in Rome; St. Francis and St. Mary of the Angels in Assisi, Italy. The patriarchal basilica of St. Lawrence, Rome, is a minor basilica. The dates in the listings below indicate when the churches were designated as basilicas.

Minor Basilicas in U.S., Puerto Rico, Guam

Alabama: Mobile, Cathedral of the Immaculate Conception (Mar. 10, 1962).

Arizona: Phoenix, St. Mary's (Immaculate Conception) (Sept. 11, 1985).

California: San Francisco, Mission Dolores (Feb. 8, 1952); Carmel, Old Mission of San Carlos (Feb. 5, 1960); Alameda, St. Joseph (Jan. 21, 1972); San Diego, Mission San Diego de Alcala (Nov. 17, 1975); San Jose, St. Joseph (Jan. 28, 1997).

Colorado: Denver, Cathedral of the Immaculate Conception (Nov. 3, 1979).

District of Columbia: National Shrine of the Immaculate Conception (Oct. 12, 1990).

Florida: St. Augustine, Cathedral of St. Augustine (Dec. 4, 1976).

Illinois: Chicago, Our Lady of Sorrows (May 4, 1956); Queen of All Saints (Mar. 26, 1962).

Indiana: Vincennes, Old Cathedral (Mar. 14, 1970); Notre Dame, Parish Church of Most Sacred Heart, Univ. of Notre Dame (Nov. 23, 1991).

Iowa: Dyersville, St. Francis Xavier (May 11, 1956); Des Moines, St. John the Apostle (Oct. 4, 1989).

Kentucky: Trappist, Our Lady of Gethsemani (May 3, 1949); Covington, Cathedral of Assumption (Dec. 8, 1953).

Louisiana: New Orleans, St. Louis King of France (Dec. 9, 1964).

Maryland: Baltimore, Assumption of the Blessed Virgin Mary (Sept. 1, 1937; designated national shrine, 1993); Emmitsburg, Shrine of St. Elizabeth Ann Seton (Feb. 13, 1991).

Massachusetts: Roxbury, Perpetual Help ("Mission Church") (Sept. 8, 1954); Chicopee, St. Stanislaus (June 25, 1991); Webster, St. Joseph (Oct. 1998).

Michigan: Grand Rapids, St. Adalbert (Aug. 22, 1979).

Minnesota: Minneapolis. St. Mary (Feb. 1, 1926).

Missouri: Conception, Basilica of Immaculate Conception (Sept. 14, 1940); St. Louis, St. Louis King of France (Jan. 27, 1961).

New Jersey: Newark, Cathedral Basilica of the Sacred Heart (Dec. 22, 1995).

New York: Brooklyn, Our Lady of Perpetual Help (Sept. 5, 1969), Cathedral-Basilica of St. James (June 22, 1982); Lackawanna, Our Lady of Victory (1926); Youngstown, Blessed Virgin Mary of the Rosary of Fatima (Oct. 7, 1975).

North Carolina: Asheville, St. Lawrence (Apr. 6, 1993; ceremonies, Sept. 5, 1993); Belmont, Our Lady Help of Christians (July 27, 1998).

North Dakota: Jamestown, St. James (Oct. 26, 1988).

Ohio: Carey, Shrine of Our Lady of Consolation (Oct. 21, 1971).

Pennsylvania: Latrobe, St. Vincent Basilica, Benedictine Archabbey (Aug. 22, 1955); Conewago, Basilica of the Sacred Heart (June 30, 1962); Philadelphia, Sts. Peter and Paul (Sept. 27, 1976); Danville, Sts. Cyril and Methodius (chapel at the motherhouse of the Sisters of Sts. Cyril and Methodius) (June 30, 1989); Loretto, St. Michael the Archangel (September 9, 1996); Scranton, National Shrine of St. Ann (Oct. 18, 1997).

Texas: Galveston, St. Mary Cathedral (Aug. 11, 1979); San Antonio, Basilica of the National Shrine of the Little Flower (Sept. 27, 1931); Basilica of Our Lady of San Juan del Valle-National Shrine (May 2, 1954).

Virginia: Norfolk, St. Mary of the Immaculate Conception (July 9, 1991).

Wisconsin: Milwaukee, St. Josaphat (Mar. 10, 1929).

Puerto Rico: San Juan, Cathedral of San Juan (Jan. 25, 1978).

Guam: Agana, Cathedral of Dulce Nombre de Maria (Sweet Name of Mary) (1985).

BASILICA OF THE NATIONAL SHRINE OF THE IMMACULATE CONCEPTION

The Basilica of the National Shrine of the Immaculate Conception is dedicated to the honor of the Blessed Virgin Mary, declared patroness of the United States under this title in 1846, eight years before the proclamation of the dogma of the Immaculate Conception. The church was designated a minor basilica by Pope John Paul II Oct. 12, 1990. The church is the eighth largest religious building in the world and the largest Catholic church in the Western Hemisphere, with numerous special chapels and with normal seating and standing accommodations for 6,000 people. Open daily, it is adjacent to The Catholic University of America, at Michigan Ave. and Fourth St. N.E., Washington, DC 20017; (202) 526-8300; www.nationalshrine.com. Rev. Msgr. Michael J. Bransfield is the rector.

SHRINES AND PLACES OF HISTORIC INTEREST IN THE U.S.

(Principal source: Catholic Almanac *survey.)*

Listed below, according to state, are shrines, other centers of devotion and some places of historic interest with special significance for Catholics. The list is necessarily incomplete because of space limitations.

Information includes, where possible: name and location of shrine or place of interest, date of foundation, sponsoring agency or group, and address for more information.

Alabama: Our Lady of the Angels, Hanceville; Birmingham Diocese. Address: Our Lady of the Angels Monastery, 3222 County Road 548, Hanceville, 35077; (256) 352-6267.

• St. Jude Church of the City of St. Jude, Montgomery (1934; dedicated, 1938); Mobile Archdiocese. Address: 2048 W. Fairview Ave., Montgomery, 36108; (334) 265-1390.

• Shrine of the Most Blessed Trinity, Holy Trinity (1924); Missionary Servants of the Most Blessed Trinity. Address: Holy Trinity, 36859.

Arizona: Chapel of the Holy Cross, Sedona (1956); Phoenix Diocese: P.O. Box 1043, W. Sedona 86339.

• Mission San Xavier del Bac, near Tucson (1692); National Historic Landmark; Franciscan Friars and Tucson Diocese; Address: 1950 W. San Xavier Rd., Tucson, 85746-7409; (520) 294-2624.

• Shrine of St. Joseph of the Mountains, Yarnell (1939); erected by Catholic Action League; currently maintained by Board of Directors. Address: P.O. Box 267, Yarnell, 85362.

California: Mission San Diego de Alcala (July 16, 1769); first of the 21 Franciscan missions of Upper California; Minor Basilica; National Historic Landmark; San Diego Diocese. Address: 10818 San Diego Mission Rd., San Diego, 92108; (619) 283-7319.

• Carmel Mission Basilica (Mission San Carlos Borromeo del Rio Carmelo), Carmel by the Sea (June 3, 1770); Monterey Diocese. Address: 3080 Rio Rd., Carmel, 93923; (831) 624-1271.

• Old Mission San Luis Obispo de Tolosa, San Luis Obispo (Sept. 1, 1772); Monterey Diocese (Parish Church). Address: Old Mission Church, 751 Palm St., San Luis Obispo, 93401.

• San Gabriel Mission, San Gabriel (Sept. 8, 1771); Los Angeles Archdiocese (Parish Church, staffed by Claretians). Address: 537 W. Mission, San Gabriel, 91776.

• Mission San Francisco de Asis (Oct. 9, 1776) and Mission Dolores Basilica (1860s); San Francisco Archdiocese. Address: 3321 Sixteenth St., San Francisco, 94114.

• Old Mission San Juan Capistrano, San Juan Capistrano (Nov. 1, 1776); Orange Diocese. Address: P.O. Box 697, San Juan Capistrano, 92693; (949) 248-2026; www.missionsjc.com.

• Old Mission Santa Barbara, Santa Barbara (Dec. 4, 1786); National Historic Landmark; Parish Church, staffed by Franciscan Friars. Address: 2201 Laguna St., Santa Barbara, 93105; (805) 682-4713.

• Old Mission San Juan Bautista, San Juan Bautista (June 24, 1797); National Historic Landmark; Monterey Diocese (Parish Church). Address: P.O. Box 400, San Juan Bautista, 95045.

• Mission San Miguel, San Miguel (July 25, 1797); Parish Church, Monterey diocese; Franciscan Friars. Address: P.O. Box 69, San Miguel, 93451; (805) 467-3256.

• Old Mission Santa Inés, Solvang (1804); Historic Landmark; Los Angeles Archdiocese (Parish Church, staffed by Capuchin Franciscan Friars). Address: P.O. Box 408, Solvang, 93464; (805) 688-4815; www.missionsantaines.org.

Franciscan Friars founded 21 missions in California. (*See* Index: **Franciscan Missions**.)

• Shrine of Our Lady of Sorrows, Sycamore (1883); Sacramento Diocese. Address: c/o Our Lady of Lourdes Church, 745 Ware Ave., Colusa, 95932.

Colorado: Mother Cabrini Shrine, Golden; Missionary Sisters of the Sacred Heart. Address: 20189 Cabrini Blvd., Golden, 80401.

Connecticut: Shrine of Our Lady of Lourdes, Litchfield (1958); Montfort Missionaries. Address: P.O. Box 667, Litchfield, 06759.

• Shrine of the Infant of Prague, New Haven (1945); Dominican Friars. Address: P.O. Box 1202, 5 Hillhouse Ave., New Haven, 06505.

District of Columbia: Mount St. Sepulchre, Franciscan Monastery of the Holy Land (1897; church dedicated, 1899); Order of Friars Minor. Address: 1400 Quincy St. N.E., Washington, DC 20017.

• Basilica of the National Shrine of the Immaculate Conception. See Index for separate entry.

Florida: Mary, Queen of the Universe Shrine, Orlando (1986, temporary facilities; new shrine dedicated, 1993); Orlando diocese. Address: 8300 Vineland Ave., Orlando, 32821; (407) 239-6600; www.maryqueenoftheuniverse.org.

• Our Lady of La Leche Shrine (Patroness of Mothers and Mothers-to-be) and Mission of Nombre de Dios, Saint Augustine (1565); Angelus Crusade Headquarters; St. Augustine Diocese. Address: 30 Ocean Ave., St. Augustine 32084.

Illinois: Holy Family Log Church, Cahokia (1799; original log church erected 1699); Belleville Diocese (Parish Church). Address: 116 Church St., Cahokia, 62206; (618) 337-4548.

• Marytown/Shrine of St. Maximilian Kolbe and Retreat Center, Libertyville; Our Lady of the Blessed Sacrament Sanctuary of Perpetual Eucharistic Adoration (1930) and Archdiocesan Shrine to St. Maximilian Kolbe (1989), conducted by Conventual Franciscan Friars, 1600 West Park Ave., Libertyville, 60048; (847) 367-7800.

• National Shrine of Our Lady of the Snows, Belleville (1958); Missionary Oblates of Mary Immaculate. Address: 442 S. De Mazenod Dr., Belleville, 62223.

• National Shrine of St. Jude, Chicago (1929); located in Our Lady of Guadalupe Church, founded and staffed by Claretians. Address: 3200 E. 91st St., Chicago, 60617; (312) 236-7782.

• National Shrine of St. Therese and Museum, Darien (1930), at St. Clara's Church, Chicago; new shrine, 1987, after original destroyed by fire); Carmelites of Most Pure Heart of Mary Province. Address: Carmelite Visitor Center, 8501 Bailey Rd., Darien, 60561; (630) 969-3311; www.saint-therese.org.

• Shrine of St. Jude Thaddeus, Chicago (1929) located in St. Pius V Church; staffed by Dominicans, Central Province. Address: 1909 S. Ashland Ave., Chicago, 60608; (312) 226-0020; www.op.org/domcentral/places/stjude.

Indiana: Our Lady of Monte Cassino Shrine, St. Meinrad (1870); Benedictines. Address: Saint Meinrad Archabbey, Highway 62, St. Meinrad, 47577; (812) 357-6585; www.saintmeinrad.edu/abbey/shrine.

• Old Cathedral (Basilica of St. Francis Xavier), Vincennes (1826, parish records go back to 1749); Evansville Diocese. Minor Basilica, 1970. Address: 205 Church St., Vincennes, 47591; (812) 882-5638.

Iowa: Grotto of the Redemption, West Bend (1912); Sioux City Diocese. Life of Christ in stone. Mailing address: P.O. Box 376, West Bend, 50597; (515) 887-2371; www.aw-cybermail.com/grotto.htm.

Louisiana: National Votive Shrine of Our Lady of Prompt Succor, New Orleans (1810); located in the Chapel of the Ursuline Convent (a National Historic Landmark). Address: 2635 State St., New Orleans, 70118.

• Shrine of St. Ann. Mailing address: 4920 Loveland St., Metaire, 70006; (504) 455-7071.

• Shrine of St. Roch, New Orleans (1876); located in St. Roch's Campo Santo (Cemetery); New Orleans Archdiocese. Address: 1725 St. Roch Ave., New Orleans, 70117.

Maryland: Basilica of the National Shrine of the Assumption of the Blessed Virgin Mary, Baltimore (1806). Mother Church of Roman Catholicism in the U.S. and the first metropolitan cathedral. Designed by Benjamin Henry Latrobe (architect of the Capitol) it is considered one of the finest examples of neoclassical architecture in the world. The church hosted many of the events and personalities central to the growth of Roman Catholicism in the U.S. Address:

Cathedral and Mulberry Sts., Baltimore, MD 21201.

• National Shrine Grotto of Our Lady of Lourdes, Emmitsburg (1809, Grotto of Our Lady; 1875, National Shrine Grotto of Lourdes); public oratory, Archdiocese of Baltimore. Address: Mount St. Mary's College and Seminary, Emmitsburg, 21727; (301) 447-5318; www.msmary.edu/grotto/.

• National Shrine of St. Elizabeth Ann Seton, Emmitsburg. Foundation of Sisters of Charity (1809); first parochial school in America (1810); dedicated as Minor Basilica (1991). Address: 333 South Seton Ave., Emmitsburg, 21727; (301) 447-6606; www.setonshrine.org.

• St. Francis Xavier Shrine, "Old Bohemia," near Warwick (1704); located in Wilmington Diocese; restoration under aupices of Old Bohemia Historical Society, Inc. Address: P.O. Box 61, Warwick, 21912.

• St. Jude Shrine (1873), Archdiocese of Baltimore. Address: 308 N. Paca St., P.O. Box 1455, Baltimore, 21203.

Massachusetts: National Shrine of Our Lady of La Salette, Ipswich (1945); Missionaries of Our Lady of La Salette. Address: 251 Topsfield Rd., Ipswich, 01938.

• Our Lady of Fatima Shrine, Holliston (1950); Xaverian Missionaries. Address: 101 Summer St., Holliston, 01746; (508) 429-2144.

• St. Anthony Shrine, Boston (1947); downtown Service Church with shrine; Boston Archdiocese and Franciscans of Holy Name Province. Address: 100 Arch St., Boston, 02107.

• Saint Clement's Eucharistic Shrine, Boston (1945); Boston Archdiocese, staffed by Oblates of the Virgin Mary. Address: 1105 Boylston St., Boston, 02215.

• National Shrine of The Divine Mercy, Stockbridge (1960); Congregation of Marians. Address: National Shrine of The Divine Mercy, Eden Hill, Stockbridge, 01262.

Michigan: Cross in the Woods-Parish, Indian River (1947); Gaylord diocese; staffed by Franciscan Friars of Sacred Heart Province, St. Louis. Address: 7078 M-68, Indian River, 49749; (231) 238-8973; www.rc.net/gaylord/crossinwoods.

• Shrine of the Little Flower, Royal Oak (c. 1929, by Father Coughlin); Detroit archdiocese. Address: 2123 Roseland, Royal Oak, 48073.

Minnesota: National Shrine of St. Odilia; St. Cloud Diocese. Address: P.O. Box 500, Onamia, 56359.

Missouri: Memorial Shrine of St. Rose Philippine Duchesne, St. Charles; Religious of the Sacred Heart of Jesus. Address: 619 N. Second St., St. Charles, 63301; (314) 946-6127..

• National Shrine of Our Lady of the Miraculous Medal, Perryville; located in St. Mary of the Barrens Church (1837); Vincentians. Address: 1811 W. St. Joseph St., Perryville, 63775; (573) 547-8343; www.amm.org.

• Old St. Ferdinand's Shrine, Florissant (1819, Sacred Heart Convent; 1821, St. Ferdinand's Church); Friends of Old St. Ferdinand's, Inc. Address: No. 1 Rue St. Francois, Florissant, 63031.

• Shrine of Our Lady of Sorrows, Starkenburg (1888; shrine building, 1910); Jefferson City Diocese. Address: c/o Church of the Risen Savior, 605 Bluff St., Rhineland, 65069; (573) 236-4390.

Nebraska: The Eucharistic Shrine of Christ the King (1973); Lincoln Diocese and Holy Spirit Adoration

Sisters. Address: 1040 South Cotner Blvd., Lincoln, 68510; (402) 489-0765.

New Hampshire: Shrine of Our Lady of Grace, Colebrook (1948); Missionary Oblates of Mary Immaculate. Address: R.R. 1, Box 521, Colebrook, 03576-9535; (603) 237-5511.

• Shrine of Our Lady of La Salette, Enfield (1951); Missionaries of Our Lady of La Salette. Address: Rt. 4A, P.O. Box 420, Enfield, 03748.

New Jersey: Blue Army Shrine of the Immaculate Heart of Mary (1978); National Center of the Blue Army of Our Lady of Fatima, USA, Inc. Address: Mountain View Rd. (P.O. Box 976), Washington, 07882-0976; (908) 689-1701; www.bluearmy.com

• Shrine of St. Joseph, Stirling (1924); Missionary Servants of the Most Holy Trinity. Address: 1050 Long Hill Rd., Stirling, 07980; (908) 647-0208; www.STShrine.org.

New Mexico: St. Augustine Mission, Isleta (1613); Santa Fe Archdiocese. Address: P.O. Box 463, Isleta, Pueblo, 87022.

• Santuario de Nuestro Senor de Esquipulas, Chimayo (1816); Santa Fe archdiocese, Sons of the Holy Family; National Historic Landmark, 1970. Address: Santuario de Chimayo, P.O. Box 235; Chimayo, 87522.

New York: National Shrine of Bl. Kateri Tekakwitha, Fonda (1938); Order of Friars Minor Conventual. Address: P.O. Box 627, Fonda, 12068.

• Marian Shrine (National Shrine of Mary Help of Christians), West Haverstraw (1953); Salesians of St. John Bosco. Address: 174 Filors Lane, Stony Point, NY 10980-2645; (845) 947-2200; www.Marian Shrine.org.

• National Shrine Basilica of Our Lady of Fatima, Youngstown (1954); designated a national shrine in 1994; Barnabite Fathers. Address: 1023 Swann Rd., Youngstown, 14174; (716) 754-7489.

• Original Shrine of St. Ann in New York City (1892); located in St. Jean Baptiste Church; Blessed Sacrament Fathers. Address: 184 E. 76th St., NY 10021; (212) 288-5082.

• Our Lady of Victory National Shrine, Lackawanna (1926); Minor Basilica. Address: 767 Ridge Rd., Lackawanna, 14218.

• Shrine Church of Our Lady of Mt. Carmel, Brooklyn (1887); Brooklyn Diocese (Parish Church). Address: 275 N. 8th St., Brooklyn, 11211; (718) 384-0223.

• Shrine of Our Lady of Martyrs, Auriesville (1885); Society of Jesus. Address: Auriesville, 12016; (518) 853-3033; www.klink.net/~jesuit.

• Shrine of Our Lady of the Island, Eastport (1975); Montfort Missionaries. Address: Box 26, Eastport, 11941; (516) 325-0661.

• Shrine of St. Elizabeth Ann Seton, New York City (1975); located in Our Lady of the Rosary Church. Address: 7 State St., NY 10004.

• Shrine of St. Frances Xavier Cabrini, New York (1938; new shrine dedicated 1960); Missionary Sisters of the Sacred Heart. Address: 701 Fort Washington Ave., 10040; (212) 923-3536; www.cabrini shrineny.org

Ohio: Basilica and National Shrine of Our Lady of Consolation, Carey (1867); Minor Basilica; Toledo Diocese; staffed by Conventual Franciscan Friars. Address: 315 Clay St., Carey, 43316; (419) 396-7107.

• National Shrine of Our Lady of Lebanon, North Jackson (1965); Eparchy of Our Lady of Lebanon of Los Angeles. Address: 2759 N. Lipkey Rd., N. Jackson, 44451; (330) 538-3351; www.nationalshrine.org.

• National Shrine and Grotto of Our Lady of Lourdes, Euclid (1926); Sisters of the Most Holy Trinity. Address: 21281 Chardon Rd., Euclid, 44117-2112; (216) 481-8232.

• National Shrine of St. Dymphna, Massillon (1938), Youngstown diocese. Address: 3000 Erie St. S., Massillon, 44648-0004.

• Our Lady of Czestochowa Shrine, Garfield Heights (1939); Sisters of St. Joseph, Third Order of St. Francis. Address: 12215 Granger Rd., Garfield Hts., 44125; (216) 581-3535.

• Our Lady of Fatima, Ironton (1954); Address: Old Rt. 52, Haverhill, OH. Mailing address: St. Joseph Church, P.O. Box 499, Ironton, 45638-0499; (740) 429-2144.

• St. Anthony Shrine, Cincinnati (1888); Franciscan Friars, St. John Baptist Province. Address: 5000 Colerain Ave., Cincinnati, 45223.

• Shrine and Oratory of the Weeping Madonna of Mariapoch, Burton (1956); Social Mission Sisters. Parma Diocese (Byzantine). Address: 17486 Mumford Rd., Burton, 44021.

• Shrine of the Holy Relics (1892); Sisters of the Precious Blood. Address: 2291 St. Johns Rd., Maria Stein, 45860; (419) 925-4532.

• Sorrowful Mother Shrine, Bellevue (1850); Society of the Precious Blood. Address: 4106 State Rt. 269, Bellevue, 44811; (419) 483-3435.

Oklahoma: National Shrine of the Infant Jesus of Prague, Prague (1949); Oklahoma City Archdiocese. Address: P.O. Box 488, Prague ,74864.

Oregon: The Grotto (National Sanctuary of Our Sorrowful Mother), Portland (1924); Servite Friars. Address: P.O. Box 20008, Portland, 97294; www.thegrotto.com.

Pennsylvania: Basilica of the Sacred Heart of Jesus, Conewago Township (1741; present church, 1787); Minor Basilica; Harrisburg Diocese. Address: 30 Basilica Dr., Hanover, 17331.

• National Shrine Center of Our Lady of Guadalupe, Allentown (1974); located in Immaculate Conception Church; Allentown Diocese. Address: 501 Ridge Ave., Allentown, 18102; (610) 433-4404.

• National Shrine of Our Lady of Czestochowa (1955); Order of St. Paul the Hermit (Pauline Fathers). Address: P.O. Box 2049, Doylestown, 18901.

• National Shrine of St. John Neumann, Philadelphia (1860); Redemptorist Fathers, St. Peter's Church. Address: 1019 N. 5th St., Philadelphia, 19123.

• National Shrine of the Sacred Heart, Harleigh (1975); Scranton Diocese. Address: P.O. Box 500, Harleigh (Hazleton), 18225; (570) 455-1162.

• Old St. Joseph's National Shrine, Philadelphia (1733); Philadelphia Archdiocese (Parish Church). Address: 321 Willings Alley, Philadelphia, 19106; (215) 923-1733; www.oldstjoseph.org.

• St. Ann's Basilica Shrine, Scranton (1902); Passionist Community. Designated a minor basilica Aug. 29, 1996. Address: 1230 St. Ann's St., Scranton, 18504; (570) 347-5691.

• St. Anthony's Chapel, Pittsburgh (1883); Pittsburgh Diocese. Address: 1700 Harpster St., Pittsburgh, 15212.

• Shrine of St. Walburga, Greensburg (1974); Sisters of St. Benedict. Address: 1001 Harvey Ave., Greensburg, 15601; (724) 834-3060.

South Dakota: Fatima Family Shrine, Alexandria; St. Cloud Diocese. Address: St. Mary of Mercy Church, Box 158, Alexandria, 57311.

Texas: Mission Espiritu Santo de Zuniga, Goliad (1749). Victoria Diocese.

• Mission Nuestra Senora de la Purisma Concepcion, San Antonio. San Antonio Archdiocese. Address: 807 Mission Rd., 78210.

• Mission San Francisco de la Espada, San Antonio (1731); San Antonio Archdiocese. Address: 10040 Espada Rd., 78214; (210) 627-2064.

• Mission San Jose y San Miguel de Aguayo, San Antonio (1720); San Antonio Archdiocese. Address: 701 E. Pyron Ave., 78214; (210) 922-0543.

• Mission San Juan Capistrano, San Antonio (1731); San Antonio Archdiocese. Address: 9101 Graf Rd., 78214.

• National Shrine of Our Lady of San Juan Del Valle, San Juan (1949); Brownsville Diocese; staffed by Oblates of Mary Immaculate. Address: P.O. Box 747, San Juan, 78589; (956) 787-0033.

• Nuestra Senora de la Concepcion del Socorro, Socorro, El Paso (1692).

• Oblate Lourdes Grotto Shrine of the Southwest,

Tepeyac de San Antonio, San Antonio Archdiocese. Address: P.O. Box 96, San Antonio, 78291-0096; (210) 342-9864; www.oblatemissions.org.

• Old Mission San Francisco de los Tejas, Weches (1690); San Antonio Archdiocese.

• Presidio La Bahia, Goliad (1749); Victoria Diocese. Address: P.O. Box 57, Goliad, 77963; (361) 645-3752.

• San Elizario Presidio Chapel, El Paso (1789); El Paso Diocese. Address: El Paso Co., San Elceario, P.O. Box 398, 79855.

• Ysleta Mission (Nuestra Senora del Carmen), Ysleta, El Paso (1744). El Paso Diocese.

Vermont: St. Anne's Shrine, Isle La Motte (1666); Burlington Diocese, conducted by Edmundites. Address: West Shore Rd., Isle La Motte, 05463; (802) 928-3362.

Wisconsin: Holy Hill — National Shrine of Mary, Help of Christians (1857); Discalced Carmelite Friars. Address: 1525 Carmel Rd., Hubertus, 53033.

• National Shrine of St. Joseph, De Pere (1889); Norbertine Fathers. Address: 1016 N. Broadway, De Pere, 54115.

• Shrine of Mary, Mother Thrice Admirable Queen and Victress of Schoenstatt (1965), Address: W284 N698 Cherry Lane, Waukesha, 53188-9402; (414) 547-7733.

THE CATHEDRAL OF OUR LADY OF THE ANGELS

On Sept. 2, 2002, the Cathedral of Our Lady of the Angels was dedicated and opened for the archdiocese of Los Angeles. Cardinal Roger M. Mahony, archbishop of Los Angeles, was the chief celebrant in a dedication liturgy that was attended by most of the cardinals in the United States, dozens of bishops, hundreds of clergy, and several thousand people. Also present was Cardinal James Francis Stafford, prefect of the Pontifical Council for the Laity in Rome, the official representative of Pope John Paul II.

The cathedral took six years to build and cost over $190 million. It is three times larger than the former cathedral, St. Vibiana's, torn down because of earthquake damage. Cardinal Mahony broke ground with a ceremonial shovel in 1999, starting the lengthy and sometimes controversial process of building Our Lady of the Angels. The designs for the cathedral and its extensive plaza were conceived by Spanish architect José Rafael Moneo; construction was undertaken by contractor Morley Builders. Moneo is noted for his style of combining classic architectural themes with modern designs. The square, 11-story cathedral thus utilizes an asymmetrical design and a lack of right angles, with a heavy emphasis on lighting and making the liturgy the central focus of the interior. The sandstone-colored walls are intended to evoke California's history of Spanish missions. At 58,000 square feet, the cathedral is 1,000 square feet smaller than Notre Dame in Paris but one foot longer that St. Patrick's in New York. Cardinal Stafford read a message from the pontiff that declared: "May this cathedral always remain an eloquent symbol of communion and fraternity, of mutual respect and understanding; may it be an enduring monument to Christian faith, hope and love, to Christian holiness…. May those who enter this house of prayer reflect on Mary's example and holiness and treasure in their hearts the

Mystery of Salvation and God's boundless love for all people."

Following are excerpts from Cardinal Roger M. Mahony's homily:

"A Cathedral achieves its destiny when the mystery of the Church is fully lived out: in the gathering of God's People; in the celebration of the Eucharist and the sacramental life of the Church. Every Eucharist is both a gathering and a sending, and both are only possible by the prior action of God….

"It is the same Spirit who is stirring now in our hearts as we ready to make the Profession of Faith for the first time in the Cathedral, our voices rising in proclamation of a living faith from the time of the apostolic church until now, at this time and in this place. Let our proclamation echo to the ends of the earth: We believe in one, holy, catholic and apostolic Church. We stand amidst that blessed communion of saints, women and men, young and old, heroic and humble, sung and unsung, as we prepare to invoke their names in litany. Hallowing the altar with the relics of Saints and Blesseds we are unceasingly reminded of the faith of those who have gone before us, leading us onward, interceding for us and strengthening us in our call to holiness.

And as we lift up our hearts in the prayer of dedication of the Cathedral altar, we enter more fully into the mystery of Christ's Church, a Church fruitful, holy, favored, and exalted. For the Church is the very Body of Christ — member for member — a living sacrifice of praise to the glory of God the Father. Transformed by the Word, strengthened by the celebration of the Sacraments, we, the Body, become a spiritual house, a living temple of the Lord, more radiant still than the hallowed ground on which we stand, and even more resplendent than the grandeur which today we behold."

Biographies of American Bishops

(*Sources:* Catholic Almanac *survey,* The Official Catholic Directory, Annuario Pontificio, *Catholic News Service. As of Aug. 20, 2003. For notable former bishops of the U.S., see* **American Catholics of the Past** at www.CatholicAlmanac.com.)

Information includes: date and place of birth; educational institutions attended; date of ordination to the priesthood with, where applicable, name of archdiocese (*) or diocese in parentheses; date of episcopal ordination; episcopal appointments; date of resignation/retirement.

A

Adamec, Joseph V.: b. Aug. 13, 1935, Bannister, MI; educ. Michigan State Univ. (East Lansing), Nepomucene College and Lateran Univ. (Rome); ord. priest (for Nitra diocese, Slovakia), July 3, 1960; served in Saginaw diocese; ord. bp. of Altoona-Johnstown, May 20, 1987.

Adams, Edward J.: b. Aug. 24, 1944, Philadelphia, PA; educ. St. Charles Borromeo Seminary (Philadelphia), Pontifical Ecclesiastical Academy (Rome); ord. priest (Philadelphia*), May 16, 1970; in Vatican diplomatic service from 1976; ord. titular abp. of Scala, Oct. 23, 1996; papal nuncio to Bangladesh.

Ahern, Patrick V.: b. Mar. 8, 1919, New York, NY; educ. Manhattan College and Cathedral College (New York City), St. Joseph's Seminary (Yonkers, NY), St. Louis Univ. (St. Louis, MO), Notre Dame Univ. (Notre Dame, IN); ord. priest (New York*), Jan. 27, 1945; ord. titular bp. of Naiera and aux. bp. of New York, Mar. 19, 1970; ret., Apr. 26, 1994.

Allué, Emilio S., S.D.B.: b. Feb. 18, 1935, Huesca, Spain; educ. Salesain schools (Huesca, Spain) Don Bosco College/Seminary (Newton, NJ); Salesian Pontifical Univ. (Rome), Fordham Univ. (New York); ord. priest Dec. 22, 1966, in Rome; ord. titular bp. of Croe and aux. bp. of Boston, Sept. 17, 1996.

Amos, Martin J.: b. Dec. 8, 1941, Cleveland; educ. St. Mary Seminary Cleveland; ord. priest (Cleveland), May 25, 1968; app. aux. bp. of Cleveland April 3, 2001, ord., June 7, 2001.

Anderson, Moses B., S.S.E.: b. Sept. 9, 1928, Selma, AL; educ. St. Michael's College (Winooski, VT), St. Edmund Seminary (Burlington, VT), Univ. of Legon (Ghana); ord. priest, May 30, 1958; ord. titular bp. of Vatarba and aux. bp. of Detroit, Jan. 27, 1983.

Angadiath, Jacob: b. Oct. 26, 1945, Periappuram, Kerala, India; educ. St. Thomas Apostolic Seminary, Vadavathoor, Kottayam, India, Univ. of Kerala, India, Univ. of Dallas (U.S.); ord. priest (Palai, Kerala) Jan. 5, 1972; Director, Syro-Malabar Catholic Mission, Archdiocese of Chicago, 1999-2001; app. bp. of Eparchy of St. Thomas of Chicago of the Syro-Malabarians and Permanent Apostolic Visitator in Canada, March 13, 2001; inst., July 1, 2001.

Angell, Kenneth A.: b. Aug. 3, 1930, Providence, RI; educ. St. Mary's Seminary (Baltimore, MD); ord. priest (Providence) May 26, 1956; ord. titular bp. of Septimunicia and aux. bp. of Providence, RI, Oct. 7, 1974; bp. of Burlington, Oct. 6, 1992; inst., Nov. 9, 1992.

Apuron, Anthony Sablan, O.F.M. Cap.: b. Nov. 1, 1945, Agana, Guam; educ. St. Anthony College and Capuchin Seminary (Hudson, NH), Capuchin Seminary (Garrison, NY), Maryknoll Seminary (New York), Notre Dame Univ. (Notre Dame, IN); ord. priest, Aug. 26, 1972, in Guam; ord. titular bp. of Muzuca in Proconsulari and aux. bp. of Agana, Guam (unicorporated U.S. territory), Feb. 19, 1984; abp. of Agana, Mar. 10, 1986.

Aquila, Samuel J.: b. Sept. 24, 1950, Burbank, CA; educ. St. Thomas Seminary, Denver, San Anselmo (Rome); ord. priest (Denver*), June 5, 1976; rector, St. John Vianney Seminary (Denver), 1999-2001; app. coadjutor bp. of Fargo, June 12, 2001; ord., Aug. 24, 2001; bp. of Fargo, March 19, 2002.

Arias, David, O.A.R.: b. July 22, 1929, Leon, Spain; educ. St. Rita's College (San Sebastian, Spain), Our Lady of Good Counsel Theologate (Granada, Spain), Teresianum Institute (Rome, Italy); ord. priest, May 31, 1952; ord. titular bp. of Badie and aux. bp. of Newark, Apr. 7, 1983; episcopal vicar for Hispanic affairs.

Arzube, Juan A.: b. June 1, 1918, Guayaquil, Ecuador; educ. Rensselaer Polytechnic Institute (Troy, NY), St. John's Seminary (Camarillo, CA); ord. priest, (Los Angeles*), May 5, 1954; ord. titular bp. of Civitate and aux. bp. of Los Angeles, Mar. 25, 1971; ret., Sept 7, 1993.

Aymond, Gregory M.: b. Nov. 12, 1949, New Orleans, LA; educ. St. Joseph Seminary College, Notre Dame Seminary (New Orleans, LA); ord. priest (New Orleans*), May 10, 1975; ord. titular bp. of Acolla and aux. bp. of New Orleans, Jan. 10, 1997; co-adjutor bp. of Austin, June 2, 2000, ins., Aug. 3, 2000; bp. of Austin, Jan. 2, 2001.

B

Baker, Robert J.: b. June 4, 1944, Fostoria, OH; educ. Pontifical College Josephinum, Columbus, OH, Gregorian Univ., Rome; ord. (St. Augustine), March 21, 1970; app. bp of Charleston, July 13, 1999; ord., Sept. 29, 1999.

Balke, Victor H.: b. Sept. 29, 1931, Meppen, IL; educ. St. Mary of the Lake Seminary (Mundelein, IL), St. Louis Univ. (St. Louis, MO); ord. priest (Springfield, IL), May 24, 1958; ord. bp. of Crookston, Sept. 2, 1976.

Baltakis, Paul Antanas, O.F.M.: b. Jan. 1, 1925, Troskunai, Lithuania; educ. seminaries of the Franciscan Province of St. Joseph (Belgium); ord. priest, Aug. 24, 1952, in Belgium; served in U.S. as director of Lithuanian Cultural Center, New York, and among Lithuanian youth; head of U.S. Lithuanian Franciscan Vicariate, Kennebunkport, ME, from 1979; ord. titular bp. of Egara, Sept. 24, 1984; assigned to pastoral assistance to Lithuanian Catholics living outside Lithuania (resides in Brooklyn).

Banks, Robert J.: b. Feb. 26, 1928, Winthrop, MA; educ. St. John's Seminary (Brighton, MA), Gregorian Univ., Lateran Univ. (Rome); ord. priest (Boston*), Dec. 20, 1952, in Rome; rector of St. John's Seminary, Brighton, MA, 1971-81; vicar general of Boston archdiocese, 1984; ord. titular bp. of Taraqua and aux. bp. of Boston, Sept. 19, 1985; bp. of Green Bay, Oct. 16, 1990, inst., Dec. 5, 1990.

Barbarito, Gerald M.: b. Jan. 4, 1950, Brooklyn, NY; educ. Cathedral College (Douglaston, NY), Immaculate Conception Seminary (Huntington, NY), Catholic University (Washington, DC); ord. priest (Brooklyn), Jan. 31, 1976; ord. titular bp. of Gisipa and aux. bp. of Brooklyn, Aug. 22, 1994; bp. of Ogdensburg, Oct. 27, 1999; inst., Jan. 7, 2000; app. bp. of Palm Beach, July 1, 2003.

Barnes, Gerald R.: b. June 22, 1945, Phoenix, AZ, of Mexican descent; educ. St. Leonard Seminary (Dayton, OH), Assumption-St. John's Seminary (San Antonio, TX); ord. priest (San Antonio*), Dec. 20, 1975; ord. titular bp. of Montefiascone and aux. bp. of San Bernardino, Mar. 18, 1992; bp. of San Bernardino, Dec. 28, 1995.

Batakian, Manuel: b. Nov. 5, 1929, Greece; moved with his family to Lebanon during World War II; educ. philosophy and theology studies in Rome; ord. priest (as a member of the Institute of the Clergy of Bzommar, an Armenian patriarchal religious order), Dec. 8, 1954; patriarchal vicar of the Institute and superior of its motherhouse in Bzommar, 1978-84; pastor of the Armenian Catholic Cathedral, Paris, 1984-90; rector of the Armenian Pontifical College, Rome, 1990-94; elected auxiliary of the patriarchate, Dec. 8, 1994, ordained bishop, March 12, 1995.

Baum, William W.: (*See* **Cardinals, Biographies.**)

Beltran, Eusebius J.: b. Aug. 31, 1934, Ashley, PA; educ. St. Charles Seminary (Philadelphia, PA); ord. priest (Atlanta*), May 14, 1960; ord. bp. of Tulsa, Apr. 20, 1978; app. abp. of Oklahoma City, Nov. 24, 1992; inst., Jan 22, 1993.

Bennett, Gordon D., S.J.: b. Oct. 21, 1946, Denver; educ. Mount St. Michael's (Spokane, WA), Jesuit School of Theology (Berkeley, CA), Fordham Univ. (NY); entered Society of Jesus, 1966; ord priest, June 14, 1975; app. titular bp. of Nesqually and aux. bp. of Baltimore, Dec. 23, 1997, ord. Mar 3, 1998.

Bevilacqua, Anthony J.: (*See* **Cardinals, Biographies.**)

Blair, Leonard P.: b. Dec. 12, 1949, Detroit; educ. Sacred Heart Seminary, Detroit, MI; Pontifical North American College, Gregorian University, and the Angelicum, Rome; ord. priest (Detroit*), June 26,

1976; at Vatican Secretariat of State, 1986-1991; Secretary to the President of the Prefecture for the Economic Affairs of the Holy See, 1994-1997; app. aux. of Detroit, July 9, 1999, ord., Aug. 24, 1999.

Blaire, Stephen E.: b. Dec. 22, 1941, Los Angeles, CA; educ. St. John's Seminary (Camarillo, CA); ord. priest (Los Angeles*), Apr. 29, 1967; ord. titular bp. of Lamzella and aux. of Los Angeles, May 31, 1990; app. bp. of Stockton, Jan. 19, 1999, inst., March 16, 1999.

Boland, Ernest B., O.P.: b. July 10, 1925, Providence, RI; educ. Providence College (RI), Dominican Houses of Study (Somerset, OH; Washington, DC); ord. priest, June 9, 1955; ord. bp. of Multan, Pakistan, July 25, 1966; res., Oct. 20, 1984.

Boland, J.(John) Kevin: b. Apr. 25, 1935, Cork, Ireland (brother of Bp. Raymond J. Boland); educ. Christian Brothers School (Cork), All Hallows Seminary (Dublin); ord. priest (Savannah), June 14, 1959; ord. bp. of Savannah, Apr. 18, 1995.

Boland, Raymond J.: b. Feb. 8, 1932, Tipperary, Ireland; educ. National Univ. of Ireland and All Hallows Seminary (Dublin); ord. priest (Washington*), June 16, 1957, in Dublin; vicar general and chancellor of Washington archdiocese; ord. bp. of Birmingham, Mar. 25, 1988; app. bp. of Kansas City-St. Joseph, June 22, 1993.

Boles, John P.: b. Jan. 21, 1930, Boston, MA; educ. St. John Seminary, Boston College (Boston, MA); ord. priest (Boston*), Feb. 2, 1955; ord. titular bp. of Nova Sparsa and aux. bp. of Boston, May 21, 1992.

Bootkoski, Paul G: b. July 4, 1940, Newark, NJ; educ. Seton Hall Univ. (South Orange, NJ), Immaculate Conception Seminary (Darlington, NJ); ord. priest, (Newark*), May 29, 1966; ord. titular bp. of Zarna and aux. bp. of Newark, Sept. 5, 1997; app. bp. of Metuchen, Jan. 4, 2002.

Borders, William D.: b. Oct. 9, 1913, Washington, IN; educ. St. Meinrad Seminary (St. Meinrad, IN), Notre Dame Seminary (New Orleans, LA), Notre Dame Univ. (Notre Dame, IN); ord. priest (New Orleans*), May 18, 1940; ord. first bp. of Orlando, June 14, 1968; app. abp. of Baltimore, Apr. 2, 1974, inst., June 26, 1974; ret., Apr. 11, 1989.

Bosco, Anthony G.: b. Aug. 1, 1927, New Castle, PA; educ. St. Vincent Seminary (Latrobe, PA), Lateran Univ. (Rome); ord. priest (Pittsburgh), June 7, 1952; ord. titular bp. of Labicum and aux. of Pittsburgh, June 30, 1970; app. bp. of Greensburg, Apr. 14, 1987, inst., June 30, 1987.

Botean, John Michael: b. July 9, 1955, Canton, OH; educ. St. Fidelis Seminary (Herman, PA), Catholic University of America (Washington, DC), St. Gregory Melkite Seminary (Newton Centre, MA), Catholic Theological Union (Chicago, IL); ord. priest (Romanian rite St. George's in Canton), May 18, 1986; ord. bp. of Saint George's in Canton for Romanians, Aug. 24, 1996.

Boyea, Earl: b. April 10, 1951, Pontiac, Mich.; educ. Sacred Heart Seminary (Detroit), North American College and Pontifical Gregorian University (Rome), Wayne State University (Detroit), Catholic University of America (Washington, DC); ord., May 20, 1978 (Detroit*); rector and president of the Pontifical College *Josephinum* (Columbus, Ohio), 2000-2002; app. titular bp. of Siccenna and aux. bp. of Detroit, July 22, 2002, ord., Sept. 13, 2002.

Boyle, Paul M., C.P.: b. May 28, 1926, Detroit, MI; educ. Passionist houses of study, Lateran Univ. (Rome); professed in Congregation of the Passion July 9, 1946; ord. priest, May 30, 1953; president of Conference of Major Superiors of Men, 1969-74; superior general of Passionists, 1976-88; ord. titular bp. of Canapium and first vicar apostolic of Mandeville, Jamaica, July 9, 1991.

Braxton, Edward K.: b. June 28, 1944, Chicago, IL; educ. Loyola Univ. of Chicago, Univ. of St. Mary of the Lake and Mundelein Seminary (Chicago), Louvain Univ. (Belgium); ord. priest (Chicago*), May 13, 1970; ord. titular bp. of Macomades rusticiana and aux. bp. of St. Louis, May 17, 1995; app. bp. of Lake Charles, Dec. 11, 2000; inst., Feb. 22, 2001.

Breitenbeck, Joseph M.: b. Aug. 3, 1914, Detroit, MI; educ. University of Detroit, Sacred Heart Seminary (Detroit, MI), North American College and Lateran Univ. (Rome), Catholic Univ. (Washington, DC); ord. priest (Detroit*), May 30, 1942; ord. titular bp. of Tepelta and aux. bp. of Detroit, Dec. 20, 1965; app. bp. of Grand Rapids, Oct. 15, 1969, inst., Dec. 2, 1969; ret., July 11, 1989.

Britt, Kevin Michael: b. Nov. 19, 1944, Detroit, MI; educ. Sacred Heart Seminary, St. John Provincial Seminary, Universtiy of Detroit Mercy (Detroit, MI), Lateran Univ. (Rome); ord. priest (Detroit*), June 28, 1970; ord. titular bp. of Esco and aux. of Detroit, Jan. 6, 1994; app. coadjutor bp. of Grand Rapids, Dec. 10, 2002.

Broderick, Edwin B.: b. Jan. 16, 1917, New York, NY; educ. Cathedral College (Douglaston, NY), St. Joseph's Seminary (Yonkers, NY), Fordham Univ. (New York City); ord. priest (New York*), May 30, 1942; ord. titular bp. of Tizica and aux. of New York, Apr. 21, 1967; bp. of Albany, 1969-76; executive director of Catholic Relief Services, 1976-82. Bp. emeritus of Albany.

Broglio, Timothy M.: b. Dec. 22, 1951, Cleveland, OH; educ. Boston College (Boston, MA), North American College and Gregorian Univ. (Rome); ord. May 19, 1977; graduate of the Pontifical Ecclesiastical Academy; entered the diplomatic corps in 1983; chief of staff to the Vatican Secretary of State; app. titular abp. (Amiternum) and papal nuncio to the Dominican Republic and apostolic delegate to Puerto Rico, Feb. 27, 2001; ord., Mar. 19, 2001.

Brom, Robert H.: b. Sept. 18, 1938, Arcadia, WI; educ. St. Mary's College (Winona, MN), Gregorian Univ. (Rome); ord. priest (Winona), Dec. 18, 1963, in Rome; ord. bp. of Duluth, May 23, 1983; coadjutor bp. of San Diego, May, 1989; bp. of San Diego, July 10, 1990.

Brown, Tod D.: b. Nov. 15, 1936, San Francisco, CA; educ. St. John's Seminary (Camarillo, CA), North American College (Rome); ord. priest (Monterey-Fresno), May 1, 1963; ord. bp. of Boise, Apr. 3, 1989; app. bp. of Orange, June 30, 1998.

Brucato, Robert A.: b. Aug. 14, 1931, New York, NY; educ. Cathedral College (Douglaston, NY), St. Joseph's Seminary (Dunwoodie, NY), Univ. of Our Lady of the Lake (San Antonio, TX); ord. priest (New York*), June 1, 1957; air force chaplain for 22 years; ord. titular bp. of Temuniana and aux. of New York, Aug. 25, 1997.

Brunett, Alexander J.: b. Jan. 17, 1934, Detroit, MI; educ. Gregorian Univ. (Rome), Sacred Heart Seminary, University of Detroit (Detroit, MI), Marquette Univ. (Milwaukee, WI); ord. priest (Detroit*), July 13, 1958; ord. bp. of Helena, July 6, 1994; app. abp. of Seattle, Oct. 28, 1997, inst., Dec. 18, 1997.

Bruskewitz, Fabian W.: b. Sept. 6, 1935, Milwaukee, WI; educ. North American College, Gregorian Univ. (Rome); ord. priest (Milwaukee*), July 17, 1960; ord. bp. of Lincoln, May 13, 1992.

Buechlein, Daniel M., O.S.B.: b. Apr. 20, 1938; educ. St. Meinrad College and Seminary (St. Meinrad, IN), St. Anselm Univ. (Rome); solemn profession as Benedictine monk, Aug. 15, 1963; ord. priest (St. Meinrad Archabbey) May 3, 1964; ord. bp. of Memphis, Mar. 2, 1987; app. abp. of Indianapolis, July 14, 1992; inst., Sept. 9, 1992.

Bukovsky, John, S.V.D.: b. Jan. 18, 1924, Cerova, Slovakia; educ. Slovakia, Divine Word Seminary (Techny, IL), Catholic Univ. (Washington, DC), Univ. of Chicago, Gregorian Univ. (Rome); ord. priest, Dec. 3, 1950; became U.S. citizen, 1958; worked at East European desk of Secretariat of State; ord. titular abp. of Tabalta, Oct. 13, 1990; nuncio to Romania, 1990-94; app. papal representative to Russia, Dec. 20, 1994-99.

Bullock, William H.: b. Apr. 13, 1927, Maple Lake, MN; educ. St. Thomas College and St. Paul Seminary (St. Paul, MN), Notre Dame Univ. (Notre Dame, IN); ord. priest (St. Paul-Minneapolis*), June 7, 1952; ord. titular bp. of Natchez and aux. bp. of St. Paul and Minneapolis, Aug. 12, 1980; app. bp. of Des Moines, Feb. 10, 1987; app. bp. of Madison, WI, Apr. 13, 1993; ret., May 23, 2003.

Burbidge, Michael F.: b. June 16, 1957, Philadelphia; educ. St. Charles Borromeo Seminary; ord. priest (Philadelphia*), May 19, 1984; app. titular bp. of Cluain Iraird and aux. bp. of Philadelphia, June 21, 2002, ord., Sept. 5, 2002.

Burke, John J., O.F.M.: b. Mar. 16, 1935, River Edge, NJ; educ. St. Joseph Seminary (Callicoon, NY), St. Bonaventure Univ. (St. Bonaventure, NY), Holy Name College (Washington, DC); solemnly professed in Franciscan Order, Aug. 20, 1958; ord. priest, Feb. 25, 1961; missionary in Brazil from 1964; ord. coadjutor bp. of Miracema do Tocantins, Brazil, Mar. 25, 1995; bp. of Miracema do Tocantins, Feb. 14, 1996.

Burke, Raymond L.: b. June 30, 1948, Richland Center, WI; educ. Holy Cross Seminary (La Crosse, WI), Catholic Univ. (Washington, DC), North American College and Gregorian Univ. (Rome); ord. priest (La Crosse), June 29, 1975; ord. bp. of La Crosse, Jan. 6, 1995, inst., Feb. 22, 1995.

Buswell, Charles A.: b. Oct. 15, 1913, Homestead, OK; educ. St. Louis Preparatory Seminary (St. Louis, MO), Kenrick Seminary (Webster Groves, MO), American College, Univ. of Louvain (Belgium); ord. priest (Oklahoma City*), July 9, 1939; ord. bp. of Pueblo, Sept. 30, 1959; resigned, Sept. 18, 1979.

C

Camacho, Tomas Aguon: b. Sept. 18, 1933, Chalon Kanoa, Saipan; educ. St. Patrick's Seminary (Menlo Park, CA); ord. priest, June 14, 1961; ord. first bp. of Chalan Kanoa, Northern Marianas (U.S. Commonwealth), Jan. 13, 1985.

Campbell, Frederick F.: b. Aug. 5, 1943, Elmira, NY; educ. Ohio State Univ., St. Paul Seminary, St.

Paul, MN; ord. priest (St. Paul and Minneapolis*), May 31, 1980; app. titular bp. of Afufenia and aux. bp. of St. Paul and Minneapolis, March 2, 1999, ord., May 14, 1999.

Carlson, Robert J.: b. June 30, 1944, Minneapolis, MN; educ. Nazareth Hall and St. Paul Seminary (St. Paul, MN), Catholic Univ. (Washington, DC): ord. priest (St. Paul-Minneapolis*), May 23, 1970; ord. titular bp. of Avioccala and aux. bp. of St. Paul and Minneapolis, Jan. 11, 1984; app. coadjutor bp. of Sioux Falls, Jan. 13, 1994; succeeded as bp. of Sioux Falls, Mar. 21, 1995.

Carmody, Edmond: b. Jan. 12, 1934, Ahalena, Kerry, Ireland; educ. St. Brendan's College (Killarney), St. Patrick Seminary (Carlow); ord. priest (San Antonio*), June 8, 1957; missionary in Peru 1984-89; ord. titular bp. of Mortlach and aux. bp. of San Antonio, Dec. 15, 1988; app. bp. of Tyler, 1992-2000; app. bp. of Corpus Christi, Feb. 3, 2000; inst., March 17, 2000.

Carmon, Dominic, S.V.D.: b. Dec. 13, 1930, Opelousas, LA; entered Society of Divine Word, 1946; ord. priest, Feb. 2, 1960; missionary in Papua-New Guinea, 1961-68; ord. titular bp. of Rusicade and aux. bp. of New Orleans, Feb. 11, 1993.

Casey, Luis Morgan: b. June 23, 1935, Portageville, MO; ord. priest (St. Louis*), Apr. 7, 1962; missionary in Bolivia from 1965; ord. titular bp. of Mibiarca and aux. of La Paz, Jan. 28, 1984; vicar apostolic of Pando, Bolivia, Jan. 18, 1988, and apostolic administrator (1995) of La Paz.

Catanello, Ignatius A.: b. July 23, 1938, Brooklyn, NY; educ. Cathedral Preparatory Seminary and St. Francis College (Brooklyn, NY), Catholic Univ. (Washington, DC); St. John's University (Jamaica, NY), New York University; ord. priest (Brooklyn), May 28, 1966; ord. titular bp. of Deulto and aux. bp. of Brooklyn, Aug. 22, 1994.

Chaput, Charles J., O.F.M. Cap.: b. Sept. 26, 1944, Concordia, KS; educ. St. Fidelis College (Herman, PA), Capuchin College and Catholic Univ. (Washington, DC), Univ. of San Francisco; solemn vows as Capuchin, July 14, 1968; ord. priest, Aug. 29, 1970; ord. bp. of Rapid City, SD, July 26, 1988, the second priest of Native American ancestry (member of Prairie Band Potawatomi Tribe) ordained a bp. in the U.S.; app abp. of Denver, inst., Apr. 7, 1997.

Charron, Joseph L., C.PP.S.: b. Dec. 30, 1939, Redfield, SD; educ. St. John's Seminary (Collegeville, MN); ord. priest, June 3, 1967; ord. titular bp. of Bencenna and aux. bp. of St. Paul and Minneapolis, Jan. 25, 1990; app. bp. of Des Moines, Nov. 12, 1993.

Chavez, Gilbert Espinoza: b. May 9, 1932, Ontario, CA; educ. St. Francis Seminary (El Cajon, CA), Immaculate Heart Seminary (San Diego), Univ. of CA; ord. priest (San Diego). Mar. 19, 1960; ord. titular bp. of Magarmel and aux. of San Diego, June 21, 1974.

Chedid, John: b. July 4, 1923, Eddid, Lebanon; educ. seminaries in Lebanon and Pontifical Urban College (Rome); ord. priest, Dec. 21, 1951, in Rome; ord. titular bp. of Callinico and aux. bp. of St. Maron of Brooklyn for the Maronites, Jan. 25, 1981; app. first bp. of Eparchy of Our Lady of Lebanon of Los Angeles for the Maronites, Mar. 1, 1994; res., Dec. 5, 2000.

Christian, Francis J.: b. Oct. 8, 1942, Peterborough, NH; educ. St. Anselm College (Manchester, NH), St.

Paul Seminary (Ottawa), American College in Louvain (Belgium); ord. priest (Manchester), June 29, 1968; ord titular bp. of Quincy and aux. of Manchester, May 14, 1996.

Clark, Edward W.: b. Nov. 30, 1946, Minneapolis; educ. Our Lady Queen of Angels Seminary (San Fernando, CA), St. John's Seminary College (Camarillo, CA), Gregorian University (Rome); ord. priest (Los Angeles*), May 9, 1972; President/Rector, St. John's Seminary College (Camarillo, CA), 1994-2001; app. titular bp. of Gardar and aux. bp. of Los Angeles, Jan. 16, 2001, ord., Mar. 26, 2001.

Clark, Matthew H.: b. July 15, 1937, Troy, NY; educ. St. Bernard's Seminary (Rochester, NY), Gregorian Univ. (Rome); ord. priest (Albany) Dec. 19, 1962; ord. bp. of Rochester, May 27, 1979; inst., June 26, 1979.

Coleman, George W.: b. Feb. 1, 1939, Fall River, MA; educ. Holy Cross College (Worcester, MA), Fall River, Saint John's Seminary (Boston, MA), North American College and Gregorian Univ. (Rome), Brown University (Providence, RI); ord. priest, Dec. 16, 1964; app. bp. of Fall River, April 30, 2003; ord. bp., July 22, 2003.

Conlon, Robert D.: b. Dec. 4, 1948, Cincinnati; educ. Mount St. Mary's Seminary of the West, University of St. Paul, Ottawa; ord. priest (Cincinnati*), Jan. 15, 1977; app. bp. of Steubenville, May 31, 2002.

Connolly, Thomas J.: b. July 18, 1922, Tonopah, NV; educ. St. Patrick's Seminary (Menlo Park, CA), Catholic Univ. (Washington, DC), Lateran Univ. (Rome); ord. priest (Reno-Las Vegas), Apr. 8, 1947; ord. bp. of Baker, June 30, 1971; res., Nov. 19, 1999.

Connors, Ronald G., C.SS.R.: b. Nov. 1, 1915, Brooklyn, NY; ord. priest, June 22, 1941; ord. titular bp. of Equizetum and coadjutor bp. of San Juan de la Maguana, Dominican Republic, July 20, 1976; succeeded as bp. of San Juan de la Maguana, July 20, 1977; ret., Feb. 20, 1991.

Conway, Edwin M.: b. Mar. 6, 1934, Chicago, IL; educ. St. Mary of the Lake Seminary (Chicago), Loyola in Chicago; ord. priest (Chicago*), May 3, 1960; ord. titular bp. of Auguro and aux. of Chicago, Mar. 20, 1995.

Cooney, Patrick R.: b. Mar. 10, 1934, Detroit, MI; educ. Sacred Heart Seminary (Detroit), Gregorian Univ. (Rome), Notre Dame Univ. (Notre Dame, IN); ord. priest (Detroit*), Dec. 20, 1959; ord. titular bp. of Hodelm and aux. bp. of Detroit, Jan. 27, 1983; app. bp. of Gaylord, Nov. 6, 1989; inst., Jan. 28, 1990.

Cordileone, Salvatore: b. June 5, 1956, San Diego, Calif.; educ. Saint Francis Seminary (San Diego), University of San Diego (San Diego), North American College (Rome), Pontifical Gregorian University (Rome); ord. July 9, 1982; official of the Supreme Tribunal of the Apostolic Signatura in Roma, 1995-2002 and vice-director of Villa Stritch in Rome; app. titular bp. of Natchez and aux. bp. of San Diego, July 5, 2002, ord., Aug. 21, 2002.

Corrada del Rio, Alvaro, S.J.: b. May 13, 1942, Santurce, Puerto Rico; entered Society of Jesus, 1960, at novitiate of St. Andrew-on-Hudson (Poughkeepsie, NY); educ. Jesuit seminaries, Fordham Univ. (New York), Institut Catholique (Paris); ord. priest, July 6, 1974, in Puerto Rico; pastoral coordinator of Northeast Catholic Hispanic Center, New York, 1982-85; ord. titular bp. of Rusticiana and aux. bp. of Washington, DC, Aug. 4, 1985; app. apostolic administrator of Caguas, Puerto Rico, Aug. 5, 1997 (retained his title as aux. bp. of Washington); app. bp. of Tyler, Dec. 5, 2000; inst., Jan. 30, 2001.

Coscia, Benedict Dominic, O.F.M.: b. Aug. 10, 1922, Brooklyn, NY; educ. St. Francis College (Brooklyn, NY), Holy Name College (Washington, DC); ord. priest June 11, 1949; ord. bp. of Jataí, Brazil, Sept. 21, 1961.

Costello, Thomas J.: b. Feb. 23, 1929, Camden, NY; educ. Niagara Univ. (Niagara Falls, NY), St. Bernard's Seminary (Rochester, NY), Catholic Univ. (Washington, DC); ord. priest (Syracuse), June 5, 1954; ord. titular bp. of Perdices and aux. bp. of Syracuse, Mar. 13, 1978.

Cote, Michael R.: b. June 19, 1949, Sanford, ME; educ. Our Lady of Lourdes Seminary (Cassadaga, NY), St. Mary's Seminary College (Baltimore, MD); Gregorian Univ. (Rome), Catholic Univ. (Washington, DC); ord. priest (Portland, ME), June 29, 1975, by Pope Paul VI in Rome; secretary, 1989-94 at apostolic nunciature, Washington; ord. titular bp. of Cebarades and aux. of Portland, ME, July 27, 1995; app. bp. of Norwich, March 11, 2003; inst., May 13, 2003.

Cotey, Arnold R., S.D.S.: b. June 15, 1921, Milwaukee, WI; educ. Divine Savior Seminary (Lanham, MD), Marquette Univ. (Milwaukee, WI); ord. priest, June 7, 1949; ord. first bp. of Nachingwea (now Lindi), Tanzania, Oct. 20, 1963; ret., Nov. 11, 1983.

Cronin, Daniel A.: b. Nov. 14, 1927, Newton, MA; educ. St. John's Seminary (Boston, MA), North American College and Gregorian Univ. (Rome); ord. priest (Boston*), Dec. 20, 1952; attaché apostolic nunciature (Addis Ababa), 1957-61; served in papal Secretariat of State, 1961-68; ord. titular bp. of Egnatia and aux. bp. of Boston, Sept. 12, 1968; bp. of Fall River, Dec. 16, 1970; abp. of Hartford, Dec. 10, 1991.

Cullen, Edward P.: b. Mar. 15, 1933, Philadelphia, PA; educ. St. Charles Borromeo Seminary (Overbrook, PA), Univ. of Pennsylvania and LaSalle Univ. (Philadelphia), Harvard Graduate School of Business; ord. priest (Philadelphia*), May 19, 1962; ord. titular bp. of Paria in Proconsolare and aux. of Philadelphia, Feb. 8, 1994; app. bp. of Allentown, Dec. 16, 1997, ord., Feb. 9, 1998.

Cummins, John S.: b. Mar. 3, 1928, Oakland, CA; educ. St. Patrick's Seminary (Menlo Park, CA), Catholic Univ. (Washington, DC), Univ. of CA; ord. priest (San Francisco*), Jan. 24, 1953; executive director of the CA Catholic Conference 1971-76; ord. titular bp. of Lambaesis and aux. bp. of Sacramento, May 16, 1974; app. bp. of Oakland, inst., June 30, 1977.

Cupich, Blase: b. Mar. 19, 1949, Omaha, NE; educ. College of St. Thomas (St. Paul, MN), Gregorian Univ. (Rome), Catholic University of America (Washington, DC); ord. priest (Omaha*), Aug. 16, 1975; service at the apostolic nunciature, Washington, DC, 1981-87; rector, Pontifical College Josephinum (Columbus, OH), 1989-97; app. bp. of Rapid City, SD, July 7, 1998; inst., Sept. 21, 1998.

Curlin, William G.: b. Aug. 30, 1927, Portsmouth, VA; educ. Georgetown Univ. (Washington, DC), St. Mary's Seminary (Baltimore, MD); ord. priest (Washington*), May 25, 1957; ord. titular bp. of Rosemarkie and aux. bp. of Washington, Dec. 20, 1988; app. bp. of Charlotte, Feb. 22, 1994, ret., Sept. 16, 2002.

Curry, Thomas J.: b. Jan. 17, 1943, Drumgoon,

Ireland; educ. Patrician College (Ballyfin), All Hallows Seminary (Dublin); ord. priest (Los Angeles*), June 17, 1967; ord. titular bp. of Ceanannus Mór and aux. of Los Angeles, Mar. 19, 1994.

Curtiss, Elden F.: b. June 16, 1932, Baker, OR; educ. St. Edward Seminary College and St. Thomas Seminary (Kenmore, WA); ord. priest (Baker), May 24, 1958; ord. bp. of Helena, MT, Apr. 28, 1976; app. abp. of Omaha, NE, May 4, 1993.

D

Da Cunha, Edgar M., S.D.V.: b. Aug. 21, 1953, Riachão do Jacuípe Bahia, Brazil; educ. Catholic University of Salvador (Brazil), Immaculate Conception Seminary (Newark, NJ); professed perpetual vows, Feb. 11, 1979, and ord., priest March 27, 1982; app. titular bp. of Ucres and aux. of Newark, June 27, 2003.

Daily, Thomas V.: b. Sept. 23, 1927, Belmont, MA; educ. Boston College, St. John's Seminary (Brighton, MA); ord. priest (Boston*), Jan. 10, 1952; missionary in Peru for five years as a member of the Society of St. James the Apostle; ord. titular bp. of Bladia and aux. bp. of Boston, Feb. 11, 1975; app. first bp. of Palm Beach, FL, July 17, 1984; app. bp. of Brooklyn, Feb. 20, 1990; inst., Apr. 18, 1990; ret., Aug. 1, 2003.

Daly, James: b. Aug. 14, 1921, New York, NY; educ. Cathedral College (Brooklyn, NY), Immaculate Conception Seminary (Huntington, L.I.); ord. priest (Brooklyn), May 22, 1948; ord. titular bp. of Castra Nova and aux. bp. of Rockville Centre, May 9, 1977; ret., July 1, 1996.

D'Antonio, Nicholas, O.F.M.: b. July 10, 1916, Rochester, NY; educ. St. Anthony's Friary (Catskill, NY); ord. priest, June 7, 1942; ord. titular bp. of Giufi Salaria and prelate of Olancho, Honduras, July 25, 1966; resigned, 1977; vicar general of New Orleans archdiocese and episcopal vicar for Spanish Speaking, 1977-91.

D'Arcy, John M.: b. Aug. 18, 1932, Brighton, MA; educ. St. John's Seminary (Brighton, MA), Angelicum Univ. (Rome); ord. priest (Boston*), Feb. 2, 1957; spiritual director of St. John's Seminary; ord. titular bp. of Mediana and aux. bp. of Boston, Feb. 11, 1975; app. bp. of Fort Wayne-South Bend, Feb. 26, 1985, inst., May 1, 1985.

Dattilo, Nicholas C.: b. Mar. 8, 1932, Mahoningtown, PA; educ. St. Vincent Seminary (Latrobe, PA), St. Charles Borromeo Seminary (Philadelphia, PA); ord. priest (Pittsburgh), May 31, 1958; ord. bp. of Harrisburg, Jan. 26, 1990.

Delaney, Joseph P.: b. Aug. 29, 1934, Fall River, MA; educ. Cardinal O'Connell Seminary (Boston, MA), Theological College (Washington, DC), North American College (Rome), Rhode Island College (Providence, RI); ord. priest (Fall River), Dec. 18, 1960; ord. bp. of Fort Worth, TX, Sept. 13, 1981.

De Palma, Joseph A., S.C.J.: b. Sept. 4, 1913, Walton, NY; ord. priest, May 20, 1944; superior general of Congregation of Priests of the Sacred Heart, 1959-67; ord. first bp. of De Aar, South Africa, July 19, 1967; ret., Nov. 18, 1987.

De Paoli, Ambrose: b. Aug. 19, 1934, Jeannette, PA, moved to Miami at age of nine; educ. St. Joseph Seminary (Bloomfield, CT), St. Mary of the West Seminary (Cincinnati, OH), North American College and Lateran Univ. (Rome); ord. priest (Miami*), Dec. 18, 1960, in Rome; served in diplomatic posts in

Canada, Turkey, Africa and Venezuela; ord. titular abp. of Lares, Nov. 20, 1983, in Miami; apostolic pro-nuncio to Sri Lanka, 1983-88; apostolic delegate in southern Africa and pro-nuncio to Lesotho, 1988; first apostolic nuncio to South Africa, 1994; apostolic nuncio to Japan.

De Simone, Louis A.: b. Feb. 21, 1922, Philadelphia, PA; educ. Villanova Univ. (Villanova, PA), St. Charles Borromeo Seminary (Overbrook, PA); ord. priest (Philadelphia*), May 10, 1952; ord. titular bp. of Cillium and aux. bp. of Philadelphia, Aug. 12, 1981; ret., Apr. 5, 1997.

Di Lorenzo, Francis X.: b. Apr. 15, 1942, Philadelphia, PA; educ. St. Charles Borromeo Seminary (Philadelphia), Univ. of St. Thomas (Rome); ord. priest (Philadelphia*), May 18, 1968; ord. titular bp. of Tigia and aux. bp. of Scranton, Mar. 8, 1988; app. apostolic administrator of Honolulu, Oct. 12, 1993; bp. of Honolulu, Nov. 29, 1994.

DiMarzio, Nicholas: b. June 16, 1944, Newark, NJ; educ. Seton Hall University (South Orange, NJ), Immaculate Conception Seminary (Darlington, NJ), Catholic Univ. (Washington, DC), Fordham Univ. (New York), Rutgers Univ. (New Brunswick, NJ); ord. priest (Newark*), May 30, 1970; ord. titular bp. of Mauriana and aux. bp. of Newark, Oct. 31, 1996, app. Bishop of Camden, June 8, 1999, inst., July 22, 1999; app. bp. of Brooklyn, Aug. 1, 2003.

Dimino, Joseph T.: b. Jan. 7, 1923, New York, NY; educ. Cathedral College (Douglaston, NY), St. Joseph's Seminary (Yonkers, NY), Catholic Univ. (Washington, DC); ord. priest (New York*), June 4, 1949; ord. titular bp. of Carini and aux. bp. of the Military Services archdiocese, May 10, 1983; app. ordinary of Military Services archdiocese, May 14, 1991; ret., Aug. 12, 1997.

DiNardo, Daniel N.: b. May 23, 1949, Steubenville, OH; educ. Catholic Univ. of America (Washington, DC) North American College, (Rome), Gregorian Univ. (Rome); ord. priest (Pittsburgh), July 16, 1977; app. Coadjutor Bp. of Sioux City, Aug. 19, 1997, ord., Oct. 7, 1997, Bp. of Sioux City, Nov. 28, 1998.

Dion, George E., O.M.I.: b. Sept. 25, 1911, Central Falls, RI; educ. Holy Cross College (Worcester, MA), Oblate Juniorate (Colebrook, NH), Oblate Scholasticates (Natick, MA, and Ottawa, Ont.); ord. priest, June 24, 1936; ord. titular bp. of Arpaia and vicar apostolic of Jolo, Philippines Apr. 23, 1980; ret., Oct. 11, 1991; titular bp. of Arpaia.

Dolan, Timothy M.: b. Feb. 6, 1950, St. Louis; educ. St. Louis Preparatory Seminary, Cardinal Glennon College, North American College, Pontifical Univ. of St. Thomas (Rome), Catholic University of America (Washington, DC); ord. priest (St. Louis*), June 19, 1976; served on staff of Apostolic Nunciature, (Washington); rector, North American College (Rome), 1994-2001; app. titular bp. of Natchez and aux. bp. of St. Louis, June 19, 2001; ord., Aug. 15, 2001; app. abp. of Milwaukee, June 25, 2002; inst., Aug. 28, 2002.

Donnelly, Robert William: b. Mar. 22, 1931, Toledo, OH; educ. St. Meinrad Seminary College (St. Meinrad, IN), Mount St. Mary's in the West Seminary (Norwood, OH); ord. priest (Toledo), May 25, 1957; ord. titular bp. of Garba and aux. bp. of Toledo, May 3, 1984.

Donoghue, John F.: b. Aug. 9, 1928, Washington,

DC; educ. St. Mary's Seminary (Baltimore, MD); Catholic Univ. (Washington, DC); ord. priest (Washington*), June 4, 1955; chancellor and vicar general of Washington archdiocese, 1973-84; ord. bp. of Charlotte, Dec. 18, 1984; app. abp. of Atlanta, June 22, 1993; inst., Aug. 19, 1993.

Donovan, Paul V.: b. Sept. 1, 1924, Bernard, IA; educ. St. Gregory's Seminary (Cincinnati, OH), Mt. St. Mary's Seminary (Norwood, OH), Lateran Univ. (Rome); ord. priest (Lansing), May 20, 1950; ord. first bp. of Kalamazoo, July 21, 1971; ret., Nov. 22, 1994.

Doran, Thomas George: b. Feb. 20, 1936, Rockford, IL; educ. Loras College (Dubuque, IA), Gregorian Univ. (Rome), Rockford College (Rockford, IL); ord. priest (Rockford), Dec. 20, 1961; ord. bp. of Rockford, June 24, 1994.

Dorsey, Norbert M., C.P.: b. Dec. 14, 1929, Springfield, MA; educ. Passionist seminaries (eastern U.S. province), Pontifical Institute of Sacred Music and Gregorian Univ. (Rome, Italy); professed in Passionists, Aug. 15, 1949; ord. priest, Apr. 28, 1956; assistant general of Passionists, 1976-86; ord. titular bp. of Mactaris and aux. bp. of Miami, Mar. 19, 1986; app. bp. of Orlando, Mar. 20, 1990, inst., May 25, 1990.

Doueihi, Stephen Hector: b. June 25, 1927, Zghorta, Lebanon; educ. University of St. Joseph (Beirut, Lebanon), Propaganda Fide, Gregorian Univ. and Institute of Oriental Study (Rome); ord. priest, Aug. 14, 1955; came to U.S. in 1973; ord. eparch of Eparchy of St. Maron of Brooklyn, Jan 11, 1997

Dougherty, John Martin: b. Apr. 29, 1932, Scranton, PA; educ. St. Charles College (Catonsville, MD), St. Mary's Seminary (Baltimore), Univ. of Notre Dame (South Bend); ord. priest (Scranton), June 15, 1957; ord. titular bp. of Sufetula and aux. bp. of Scranton, Mar. 7, 1995.

Driscoll, Michael P.: b. Aug. 8, 1939, Long Beach, CA; educ. St. John Seminary (Camarillo, CA), Univ. of Southern CA; ord. priest (Los Angeles*), May 1, 1965; ord. titular bp. of Massita and aux. bp. of Orange, Mar. 6, 1990; app. bp. of Boise, Jan. 19, 1999, inst., Mar. 18, 1999.

Dudick, Michael J.: b. Feb. 24, 1916, St. Clair, PA; educ. St. Procopius College and Seminary (Lisle, IL); ord. priest (Passaic, Byzantine Rite), Nov. 13, 1945; ord. bp. of Byzantine Eparchy of Passaic, Oct. 24, 1968; ret., Nov. 6, 1995.

Dudley, Paul V.: b. Nov. 27, 1926, Northfield, MN; educ. Nazareth College and St. Paul Seminary (St. Paul, MN); ord. priest (St. Paul-Minneapolis*), June 2, 1951; ord. titular bp. of Ursona and aux. bp. of St. Paul and Minneapolis, Jan. 25, 1977; app. bp. of Sioux Falls, inst., Dec. 13, 1978; ret., Mar. 21, 1995.

Duffy, Paul, O.M.I.: b. July 25, 1932, Norwood, MA; educ Oblate houses of study in Canada and Washington, DC; ord. priest, 1962; missionary in Zambia from 1984; app. first bp. of Mongu, Zambia, July 1, 1997.

Duhart, Clarence James, C.SS.R.: b. Mar. 23, 1912, New Orleans, LA; ord. priest, June 29, 1937; ord. bp. of Udon Thani, Thailand, Apr. 21, 1966; resigned, Oct. 2, 1975.

DuMaine, (Roland) Pierre: b. Aug. 2, 1931, Paducah, KY; educ. St. Joseph's College (Mountain View, CA), St. Patrick's College and Seminary (Menlo Park, CA), Univ. of CA (Berkeley), Catholic Univ. (Washington, DC); ord. priest (San Francisco) June

15, 1957; ord. titular bp. of Sarda and aux. bp. of San Francisco, June 29, 1978; app. first bp. of San Jose, Jan. 27, 1981; inst., Mar. 18, 1981; res., Nov. 27, 1999.

Dunne, John C.: b. Oct. 30, 1937, Brooklyn, NY; educ. Cathedral College (Brooklyn, NY). Immaculate Conception Seminary (Huntington, NY), Manhattan College (New York); ord. priest (Rockville Centre), June 1, 1963; ord. titular bp. of Abercorn and aux. bp. of Rockville Centre, Dec. 13, 1988. Vicar for Central Vicariate.

Dupre, Thomas L.: b. Nov. 10, 1933, South Hadley Falls, MA; educ. College de Montreal, Assumption College (Worcester, MA), Catholic Univ. (Washington, DC), ord. priest (Springfield, MA), May 23, 1959; ord. titular bp. of Hodelm and aux. bp. of Springfield, MA, May 31, 1990; bp. of Springfield, Mar. 14, 1995.

Durning, Dennis V., C.S.Sp.: b. May 18, 1923, Germantown, PA; educ. St. Mary's Seminary (Ferndale, CT); ord. priest, June 3, 1949; ord. first bp. of Arusha, Tanzania, May 28, 1963; resigned, Mar. 6, 1989.

E

Edyvean, Walter J.: b. Oct. 18, 1938, Medford, MA; educ. Boston College, St. John's Seminary (Brighton, MA), the North American College and the Gregorian Univ. (Rome); ord. priest (Boston*), Dec. 16, 1964; served on staff of Congregation for Catholic Education, 1990-2001; app. titular bp. of Elie and aux. bp. of Boston, June 29, 2001, ord., Sept. 14, 2001

Egan, Edward M.: (*See* **Cardinals, Biographies.**)

Elya, John A., B.S.O.: b. Sept. 16, 1928, Maghdouche, Lebanon; educ. diocesan monastery (Sidon, Lebanon), Gregorian Univ. (Rome, Italy); professed as member of Basilian Salvatorian Order, 1949; ord. priest, Feb. 17, 1952, in Rome; came to U.S., 1958; ord. titular bp. of Abilene of Syria and aux. bp. of Melkite diocese of Newton, MA, June 29, 1986; app. bp. of Newton (Melkites), Nov. 25, 1993.

F

Farrell, Kevin J.: b. Dublin, Ireland, Sept. 2, 1947; educ. University of Salamanca (Spain), Gregorian University and University of St. Thomas Aquinas (Rome), University of Notre Dame (South Bend, IN); ord. priest (of the Legionaries of Christ), Dec. 24, 1978; incardinated into Archdiocese of Washington, 1984; app. titular bp. of Rusuccuru and aux. bp. of Washington, Dec. 28, 2001.

Favalora, John C.: b. Dec. 5, 1935, New Orleans, LA; educ. St. Joseph Seminary (St. Benedict, LA), Notre Dame Seminary (New Orleans, LA), Gregorian Univ. (Rome), Catholic Univ. of America (Washington, DC), Xavier Univ. and Tulane Univ. (New Orleans); ord. priest (New Orleans*), Dec. 20, 1961; ord. bp. of Alexandria, LA, July 29, 1986; bp. of St. Petersburg, Mar. 14, 1989; app. abp. of Miami, inst., Dec. 20, 1994.

Fellhauer, David E.: b. Aug. 19, 1939, Kansas City, MO; educ. Pontifical College Josephinum (Worthington, OH), St. Paul Univ. (Ottawa); ord. priest (Dallas), May 29, 1965; ord. bp. of Victoria, May 28, 1990.

Fernandez, Gilberto: b. Feb. 13, 1935, Havana, Cuba; educ. El Buen Pastor Seminary (Havana); ord. priest (Havana*), May 15, 1959; came to US, 1967; app. titular bp. of Irina and aux. of Miami, June 24, 1997; ret., Dec. 10, 2002.

Ferrario, Joseph A.: b. Mar. 3, 1926, Scranton, PA; educ. St. Charles College (Catonsville, MD), St. Mary's Seminary (Baltimore, MD), Catholic Univ. (Washington, DC); Univ. of Scranton; ord. priest (Honolulu), May 19, 1951; ord. titular bp. of Cuse and aux. bp. of Honolulu, Jan. 13, 1978; bp. of Honolulu, May 13, 1982; ret., Oct. 12, 1993.

Fiorenza, Joseph A.: b. Jan. 25, 1931, Beaumont, TX; educ. St. Mary's Seminary (LaPorte, TX); ord. priest (Galveston-Houston), May 29, 1954; ord. bp. of San Angelo, Oct. 25, 1979; app. bp. of Galveston-Houston, Dec. 18, 1984, inst., Feb. 18, 1985; vice president, NCCB/USCC, 1995-1998; President, 1998-2001.

Fitzgerald, James: b. Dec. 30, 1938, Chicago; educ. Conception Seminary, Conception, MO; app. titular bp. of Walla Walla and aux. bp. of Joliet, Jan. 11, 2002, ord., March 19, 2002; res., June 5, 2003.

Fitzpatrick, John J.: b. Oct. 12, 1918, Trenton, ON, Canada; educ. Urban Univ. (Rome), Our Lady of the Angels Seminary (Niagara Falls, NY); ord. priest (Buffalo), Dec. 13, 1942; ord. titular bp. of Cenae and aux. bp. of Miami, Aug. 28, 1968; bp. of Brownsville, TX, May 28, 1971; ret., Nov. 30, 1991.

Fitzsimons, George K.: b. Sept. 4, 1928, Kansas City, MO; educ. Rockhurst College (Kansas City, MO), Immaculate Conception Seminary (Conception, MO); ord. priest (Kansas City-St. Joseph), Mar. 18, 1961; ord. titular bp. of Pertusa and aux. bp. of Kansas City-St. Joseph, July 3, 1975; app. bp. of Salina, Mar. 28, 1984, inst., May 29, 1984.

Flanagan, Thomas Joseph: b: Oct. 23, 1930, Rathmore, Ireland; educ. St. Patrick's College, Thurles, Ireland; ord priest (San Antonio*), June 10, 1956; app. titular bp. of Bavagaliana and aux. bp. of San Antonio, Jan. 5, 1998, ord., Feb. 16, 1998.

Fliss, Raphael M.: b. Oct. 25, 1930, Milwaukee, WI; educ. St. Francis Seminary (Milwaukee, WI), Catholic University (Washington, DC), Pontifical Lateran Univ. (Rome); ord. priest (Milwaukee*), May 26, 1956; ord. coadjutor bp. of Superior with right of succession, Dec. 20, 1979; bp. of Superior, June 27, 1985.

Flores, Patrick F.: b. July 26, 1929, Ganado, TX; educ. St. Mary's Seminary (Houston, TX); ord. priest (Galveston-Houston), May 26, 1956; ord. titular bp. of Itolica and aux. bp. of San Antonio, May 5, 1970 (first Mexican-American bp.); app. bp. of El Paso, Apr. 4, 1978, inst., May 29, 1978; app. abp. of San Antonio, 1979; inst., Oct. 13, 1979.

Flynn, Harry J.: b. May 2, 1933, Schenectady, NY; educ. Siena College (Loudonville, NY), Mt. St. Mary's College (Emmitsburg, MD); ord. priest (Albany), May 28, 1960; ord. coadjutor bp. of Lafayette, LA, June 24, 1986; bp. of Lafayette, LA, May 15, 1989; app. coadjutor abp. of St. Paul and Minneapolis, Feb. 24, 1994, inst., Apr. 27, 1994; abp. of St. Paul and Minneapolis, Sept. 8, 1995.

Foley, David E.: b. Feb. 3, 1930, Worcester, MA; educ. St. Charles College (Catonsville, MD), St. Mary's Seminary (Baltimore, MD); ord. priest (Washington*), May 26, 1952; ord. titular bp. of Octaba and aux. bp. of Richmond, June 27, 1986; app. bp. of Birmingham, Mar. 22, 1994.

Foley, John Patrick: b. Nov. 11, 1935, Sharon Hill, PA; educ. St. Joseph's Preparatory School (Philadelphia, PA), St. Joseph's College (now University) (Philadelphia, PA), St. Charles Borromeo Seminary

(Overbrook, PA), St. Thomas Univ. (Rome), Columbia School of Journalism (New York); ord. priest (Philadelphia*), May 19, 1962; assistant editor (1967-70) and editor (1970-84) of *The Catholic Standard and Times*, Philadelphia archdiocesan paper; ord. titular abp. of Neapolis in Proconsulari, May 8, 1984, in Philadelphia; app. president of the Pontifical Council for Social Communications, Apr. 5, 1984.

Forst, Marion F.: b. Sept. 3, 1910, St. Louis, MO; educ. St. Louis Preparatory Seminary (St. Louis, MO), Kenrick Seminary (Webster Groves, MO); ord. priest (St. Louis*), June 10, 1934; ord. bp. of Dodge City, Mar. 24, 1960; app. titular bp. of Scala and aux. bp. of Kansas City, KS, Oct. 16, 1976; ret., Dec. 23, 1986; titular bp. of Leavenworth.

Foys, Roger J.: b. July 27, 1945, Chicago; educ. University of Steubenville, St. John Vianney Seminary, (Bloomingdale, OH), the Catholic University of America, Washington, DC; ord. priest (Steubenville), May 16, 1973; Knight Commander of the Equestrian Order of the Holy Sepulchre of Jerusalem, 1986; app. bp. of Covington, May 31, 2002.

Franklin, William Edwin: b. May 3, 1930, Parnell, IA; educ. Loras College and Mt. St. Bernard Seminry (Dubuque, IA); ord. priest (Dubuque*), Feb. 4, 1956; ord. titular bp. of Surista and aux. bp. of Dubuque, Apr. 1, 1987; app. bp. of Davenport, Nov. 12, 1993, inst., Jan. 20, 1994.

Franzetta, Benedict C.: b. Aug. 1, 1921, East Liverpool, OH; educ. St. Charles College (Catonsville, MD), St. Mary Seminary (Cleveland, OH); ord. priest (Youngstown), Apr. 29, 1950; ord. titular bp. of Oderzo and aux. bp. of Youngstown, Sept. 4, 1980; ret., Sept. 4, 1996.

Frey, Gerard L.: b. May 10, 1914, New Orleans, LA; educ. Notre Dame Seminary (New Orleans, LA); ord. priest (New Orleans*), Apr. 2, 1938; ord. bp. of Savannah, Aug. 8, 1967; app. bp. of Lafayette, LA, Nov. 7, 1972, inst., Jan, 7, 1973; ret., May 15, 1989.

Friend, William B.: b. Oct. 22, 1931, Miami, FL; educ. St. Mary's College (St. Mary, KY), Mt. St. Mary Seminary (Emmitsburg, MD), Catholic Univ. (Washington, DC), Notre Dame Univ. (Notre Dame, IN); ord. priest (Mobile*), May 7, 1959; ord. titular bp. of Pomaria and aux. bp. of Alexandria-Shreveport, LA, Oct. 30, 1979; app. bp. of Alexandria-Shreveport, Nov. 17, 1982, inst., Jan 11, 1983; app. first bp. of Shreveport, June, 1986; inst., July 30, 1986.

G

Gainer, Ronald W.: b. Aug. 24, 1947, Pottsville, PA; educ. St. Charles Borromeo Seminary (Philadelphia), Gregorian Univ. (Rome); ord. priest (Allentown), May 19, 1973; app. bp. of Lexington, KY, ord. bp., Feb. 22, 2003.

Galante, Joseph A.: b. July 2, 1938, Philadelphia, PA; educ. St. Joseph Preparatory School, St. Charles Seminary (Philadelphia, PA); Lateran Univ., Angelicum, North American College (Rome); ord. priest (Philadelphia*), May 16, 1964; on loan to diocese of Brownsville, TX, 1968-72, where he served in various diocesan posts; returned to Philadelphia, 1972; assistant vicar (1972-79) and vicar (1979-87) for religious; undersecretary of Congregation for Institutes of Consecrated Life and Societies of Apostolic Life (Rome), 1987-92; ord. titular bp. of

Equilium and aux. bp. of San Antonio, Dec. 11, 1992; app. bp. of Beaumont, Apr. 5, 1994; app. co-adjutor bp. of Dallas, Nov. 23, 1999.

Galeone, Victor Benito: b. Sept. 13, 1935, Philadelphia; educ. St. Charles College (Baltimore), North American College, Pontifical Gregorian University (Rome), ord. priest (Baltimore*), Dec. 18, 1960; served as missionary in Peru, 1970-75, 1978-85; app. bp. of St. Augustine, June 25, 2001, ord., Aug. 21, 2001.

Garcia, Richard J.: b. Apr. 24, 1947, San Francisco; educ. St. Patrick's Seminary (Menlo Park, CA); ord priest (San Francisco*), May 13, 1973; app. Titular bp. of Bapara and aux. bp. of Sacramento, Nov. 25, 1997, ord., Jan. 28, 1998.

Garcia-Siller, Gustavo, M.Sp.S.: b. Dec. 21, 1956, San Luis Potosi, Mexico, educ. St. John's Seminary (Camarillo, Calif.), Western Jesuit University (Guadalajara, Mexico), Gregorian University (Rome); ord. priest, June 22, 1984; app. aux. bp of Chicago and titular bp. of Esco, Jan. 24, 2003; ord., March 19, 2003.

Garland, James H.: b. Dec. 13, 1931, Wilmington, OH; educ. Wilmington College (OH), Ohio State Univ. (Columbus, OH); Mt. St. Mary's Seminary (Cincinnati, OH), Catholic Univ. (Washington, DC); ord. priest (Cincinnati*), Aug. 15, 1959; ord. titular bp. of Garriana and aux. bp. of Cincinnati, July 25, 1984; app. bp. of Marquette, Oct. 6, 1992; inst., Nov. 11, 1992.

Garmendia, Francisco: b. Nov. 6, 1924, Lozcano, Spain; ord. priest, June 29, 1947, in Spain; came to New York in 1964; became naturalized citizen; ord. titular bp. of Limisa and aux. bp. of New York, June 29, 1977. Vicar for Spanish pastoral development in New York archdiocese; res., Oct. 31, 2001.

Garmo, George: b. Dec. 8, 1921, Telkaif, Iraq; educ. St. Peter Chaldean Patriarchal Seminary (Mossul, Iraq), Pontifical Urban Univ. (Rome); ord. priest, Dec. 8, 1945; pastor of Chaldean parish in Detroit archdiocese, 1960-64, 1966-80; ord. abp. of Chaldean archdiocese of Mosul, Iraq, Sept. 14, 1980.

Gaydos, John R.: b. Aug. 14, 1943, St. Louis, MO; educ Cardinal Glennon College (St. Louis, MO), North American College, Gregorian Univ. (Rome); ord. priest (St. Louis*), Dec. 20, 1968; ord. bp. of Jefferson City, Aug. 27, 1997.

Gelineau, Louis E.: b. May 3, 1928, Burlington, VT; educ. St. Michael's College (Winooski, VT), St. Paul's Univ. Seminary (Ottawa), Catholic Univ. (Washington, DC); ord. priest (Burlington), June 5, 1954; ord. bp. of Providence, RI, Jan. 26, 1972; ret., June 11, 1997.

Gendron, Odore J.: b. Sept. 13, 1921, Manchester, NH; educ. St. Charles Borromeo Seminary (Sherbrooke, QC), Univ. of Ottawa, St. Paul Univ. Seminary (Ottawa, Ont., Canada); ord. priest (Manchester), May 31, 1947; ord. bp. of Manchester, Feb. 3, 1975; res., June 12, 1990.

George, Cardinal Francis E., O.M.I.: (*See* **Cardinals, Biographies**).

Gerber, Eugene J.: b. Apr. 30, 1931, Kingman, KS; educ. St. Thomas Seminary (Denver, CO), Wichita State Univ.; Catholic Univ. (Washington, DC), Angelicum (Rome); ord. priest (Wichita), May 19, 1959; ord. bp. of Dodge City, Dec. 14, 1976; app. bp. of Wichita, Nov. 17, 1982, inst., Feb. 9, 1983; res. Oct. 4, 2001.

Gerety, Peter L.: b. July 19, 1912, Shelton, CT;

educ. Sulpician Seminary (Paris, France); ord. priest, (Hartford*), June 29, 1939; ord. titular bp. of Crepedula and coadjutor bp. of Portland, ME, with right of succession, June 1, 1966; app. apostolic administrator of Portland, 1967; bp. of Portland, ME, Sept. 15, 1969; app. abp. of Newark, Apr. 2, 1974; inst., June 28, 1974; ret., June 3, 1986.

Gerry, Joseph J., O.S.B.: b. Sept. 12, 1928, Millinocket, ME; educ. St. Anselm Abbey Seminary (Manchester, NH), Univ. of Toronto (Canada), Fordham Univ. (New York); ord. priest, June 12, 1954; abbot of St. Anselm Abbey, Manchester, NH, 1972; ord. titular bp. of Praecausa and aux. of Manchester, Apr. 21, 1986; bp. of Portland, ME, Dec. 27, 1988, inst., Feb. 21, 1989.

Gettelfinger, Gerald A.: b. Oct. 20, 1935, Ramsey, IN; educ. St. Meinrad Seminary (St. Meinrad, IN), Butler Univ. (Indianapolis, IN); ord. priest (Indianapolis*), May 7, 1961; ord. bp. of Evansville, Apr. 11, 1989.

Gilbert, Edward J., C.SS.R.: b. Dec. 26, 1936, Brooklyn, NY; educ. Mt. St. Alphonsus Seminary (Esopus, NY), Catholic Univ. (Washington, DC); ord. priest (Redemptorists, Baltimore Province), June 21, 1964; ord. bp. of Roseau, Dominica, Sept. 7, 1994.

Gilmore, Ronald W.: b. Apr. 23, 1942, Wichita, KS; educ. University Seminary (Ottawa), St. Paul University (Ottawa); ord. priest (Wichita), June 7, 1969; app. Bp. of Dodge City, May 11, 1998, ord., July 16, 1998.

Glynn, John J.: b. Aug. 6, 1926, Boston, MA; educ. St. John's Seminary (Brighton, MA); ord. priest (Boston*), Apr. 11, 1951; Navy chaplain, 1960-85; ord. titular bp. of Monteverde and aux. bp. of Military Services archdiocese, Jan. 6, 1992; res., Aug. 13, 2002.

Goedert, Raymond E.: b. Oct. 15, 1927, Oak Park, IL; educ. Quigley Preparatory Seminary (Chicago, IL), St. Mary of the Lake Seminary and Loyola Univ. (Chicago, IL), Gregorian Univ. (Rome); ord. priest (Chicago*), May 1, 1952; ord. titular bp. of Tamazeni and aux. bp. of Chicago, Aug. 29, 1991; ret., Jan. 24, 2003.

Gomez, José H.: b. Dec. 26, 1951, Monterrey, Mexico (became U.S. citizen 1995); educ. National University, Mexico, University of Navarre (Spain); ord. priest of the Prelature of Opus Dei, Aug. 15, 1978; Vicar of Opus Dei for State of Texas, 1999-2001; app. titular bp. of Belali and aux. bp of Denver, Jan. 23, 2001, ord., Mar. 26, 2001.

Gonzalez, Roberto O., O.F.M., b. June 2, 1950, Elizabeth, NJ; educ. St. Joseph Seminary (Callicoon, NY), Siena College, (Loudonville, NY), Washington Theological Union (Silver Spring, MD), Fordham Univ. (New York, NY); solemnly professed in Franciscan Order, 1976; ord. priest, May 8, 1977; ord. titular bp. of Ursona and aux. bp. of Boston, Oct. 3, 1988; app. coadjutor bp. of Corpus Christi, May 16, 1995; bishop of Corpus Christi, Apr. 1, 1997; app. abp. of San Juan de Puerto Rico, Mar. 26, 1999, ord., May 8, 1999.

Gonzalez Valer, S.F., Francisco: b. Arcos de Jalon, Spain, May 22, 1939; educ. Missionary Seminary of the Holy Family, Barcelona (Spain), Catholic University of America (Washington, DC); ord. priest (of the Congregation of the Sons of the Holy Family), May 1, 1964; Episcopal Vicar for Hispanic Catholics, Archdiocese of Washington, 1997; app. titular bp. of Lamfua and aux. bp. of Washington, Dec. 28, 2001.

Gorman, John R.: b. Dec. 11, 1925, Chicago, IL; educ. St. Mary of the Lake Seminary (Mundelein, IL),

Loyola Univ. (Chicago, IL); ord. priest (Chicago*), May 1, 1956; ord. titular bp. of Catula and aux. bp. of Chicago, Apr. 11, 1988; ret., Jan. 24, 2003.

Gossman, F. Joseph: b. Apr. 1, 1930, Baltimore, MD; educ. St. Charles College (Catonsville, MD), St. Mary's Seminary (Baltimore, MD), North American College (Rome), Catholic Univ. (Washington, DC); ord. priest (Baltimore*), Dec. 17, 1955; ord. titular bp. of Agunto and aux. bp. of Baltimore, Sept. 11, 1968; app. bp. of Raleigh, Apr. 8, 1975.

Gracida, Rene H.: b. June 9, 1923, New Orleans, LA; educ. Rice Univ. and Univ. of Houston (Houston, TX), Univ. of Fribourg (Switzerland); ord. priest (Miami*), May 23, 1959; ord. titular bp. of Masuccaba and aux. bp. of Miami, Jan. 25, 1972; app. first bp. of Pensacola-Tallahassee, Oct. 1, 1975, inst., Nov. 6, 1975; app. bp. of Corpus Christi, May 24, 1983, inst., July 11, 1983; ret., Apr. 1, 1997.

Grahmann, Charles V.: b. July 15, 1931, Halletsville, TX; educ. The Assumption-St. John's Seminary (San Antonio, TX); ord. priest (San Antonio*), Mar. 17, 1956; ord. titular bp. of Equilium and aux. bp. of San Antonio, Aug. 20, 1981; app. first bp. of Victoria, TX, Apr. 13, 1982; app. coadjutor bp. of Dallas, Dec. 9, 1989; bp. of Dallas, July 14, 1990.

Gregory, Wilton D.: b. Dec. 7, 1947, Chicago, IL; educ. Quigley Preparatory Seminary South, Niles College of Loyola Univ. (Chicago, IL), St. Mary of the Lake Seminary (Mundelein, IL), Pontifical Liturgical Institute, Sant'Anselmo (Rome); ord. priest, (Chicago*), May 9, 1973; ord. titular bp. of Oliva and aux. bp. of Chicago, Dec. 13, 1983; app. bp. of Belleville, Dec. 29, 1993; inst., Feb. 10, 1994 vice president, NCCB/USCC, 1998-2001; president, USCCB, 2001-.

Gries, Roger W., O.S.B.: b. Mar. 26, 1937, Cleveland; educ. St. John Univ., (Collegeville, MN), St. Joseph's Seminary, Cleveland, Loyola Univ., Chicago; ord. priest (Order of St. Benedict), May 16, 1963; Abbot, St. Andrew Abbey, Cleveland, 1981-2001; app. aux. bp. of Cleveland, April 3, 2001, ord., June 7, 2001.

Griffin, James A.: b. June 13, 1934, Fairview Park, OH; educ. St. Charles College (Baltimore, MD), Borromeo College (Wicklife, OH); St Mary Seminary (Cleveland, OH); Lateran Univ. (Rome); Cleveland State Univ.; ord. priest (Cleveland), May 28, 1960; ord. titular bp. of Holar and aux. bp. of Cleveland, Aug. 1, 1979; app. bp. of Columbus, Feb. 8, 1983.

Grosz, Edward M.: b. Feb. 16, 1945, Buffalo, NY; educ. St. John Vianney Seminary (East Aurora, NY), Notre Dame Univ. (Notre Dame, IN); ord. priest (Buffalo), May 29, 1971; ord. titular bp. of Morosbisdus and aux. bp. of Buffalo, Feb. 2, 1990.

Guillory, Curtis J., S.V.D.: b. Sept. 1, 1943, Mallet, LA; educ. Divine Word College (Epworth, IA), Chicago Theological Union (Chicago), Creighton Univ. (Omaha, NE); ord. priest, Dec. 16, 1972; ord. titular bp. of Stagno and aux. bp. of Galveston-Houston, Feb. 19, 1988; bp. of Beaumont, June 2, 2000, inst., July 28, 2000.

Gumbleton, Thomas J.: b. Jan. 26, 1930, Detroit, MI; educ. St. John Provincial Seminary (Detroit, MI), Pontifical Lateran Univ. (Rome); ord. priest (Detroit*), June 2, 1956; ord. titular bp. of Ululi and aux. bp. of Detroit, May 1, 1968.

H

Ham, J. Richard, M.M.: b. July 11, 1921, Chicago, IL; educ. Maryknoll Seminary (NY); ord. priest June 12, 1948; missionary to Guatemala, 1958; ord. titular bp. of Puzia di Numidia and aux. bp. of Guatemala, Jan. 6, 1968; resigned see 1979; aux. bp. of St. Paul and Minneapolis, Oct., 1980; ret., Oct. 29, 1990.

Hanifen, Richard C.: b. June 15, 1931, Denver, CO; educ. Regis College and St. Thomas Seminary (Denver, CO), Catholic Univ. (Washington, DC), Lateran Univ. (Rome); ord. priest (Denver*), June 6, 1959; ord. titular bp. of Abercorn and aux. bp. of Denver, Sept. 20, 1974; app. first bp. of Colorado Springs, Nov. 10, 1983; inst., Jan. 30, 1984; ret., Jan. 30, 2003.(Died Dec. 20, 2002.)

Hannan, Philip M.: b. May 20, 1913, Washington, DC; educ. St. Charles College (Catonsville, MD), Catholic Univ. (Washington, DC), North American College (Rome); ord. priest (Washington*), Dec. 8, 1939; ord. titular bp. of Hieropolis and aux. bp. of Washington, DC, Aug. 28, 1956; app. abp. of New Orleans, inst., Oct. 13, 1965; ret., Dec. 6, 1988.

Hanus, Jerome George, O.S.B.: b. May 25, 1940, Brainard, NE; educ. Conception Seminary (Conception, MO), St. Anselm Univ. (Rome), Princeton Theological Seminary (Princeton, NJ); ord. priest (Conception Abbey, MO), July 30, 1966; abbot of Conception Abbey, 1977-87; president of Swiss American Benedictine Congregation, 1984-87; ord. bp. of St. Cloud, Aug. 24, 1987; app. coadjutor abp. of Dubuque, Aug. 23, 1994; abp. of Dubuque, Oct. 16, 1995.

Harrington, Bernard J.: b. Sept. 6, 1933, Detroit, MI; educ. Sacred Heart Seminary (Detroit), St. John's Provincial Seminary (Plymouth, MI), Catholic Univ. of America (Washington, DC), University of Detroit; ord. priest (Detroit*), June 6, 1959; ord. titular bp. of Uzali and aux. bp. of Detroit, Jan. 6, 1994; app. Bp. of Winona, Nov. 5, 1998, ord., Jan. 6, 1999.

Harrison, Frank J.: b. Aug. 12, 1912; Syracuse, NY; educ. Notre Dame Univ. (Notre Dame, IN), St. Bernard's Seminary (Rochester, NY), ord. priest (Syracuse), June 4, 1937; ord. titular bp. of Aquae in Numidia and aux. of Syracuse, Apr. 22, 1971; app. bp. of Syracuse, Nov. 9, 1976, inst., Feb. 6, 1977; ret., June 16, 1987.

Hart, Daniel A.: b. Aug. 24, 1927, Lawrence, MA; educ. St. John's Seminary (Brighton, MA); ord. priest (Boston*), Feb. 2, 1953; ord. titular bp. of Tepelta and aux. bp. of Boston, Oct. 18, 1976; bp. of Norwich, Sept. 12, 1995; ret. March 11, 2003.

Hart, Joseph: b. Sept. 26, 1931, Kansas City, MO; educ. St. John Seminary (Kansas City, MO), St. Meinrad Seminary (Indianapolis, IN); ord. priest (Kansas City-St. Joseph), May 1, 1956; ord. titular bp. of Thimida Regia and aux. bp. of Cheyenne, WY, Aug. 31, 1976; app. bp. of Cheyenne, inst., June 12, 1978; ret., Sept. 26, 2001.

Harvey, James M.: b. Oct. 20, 1949, Milwaukee, WI; educ. De Sales Preparatory Seminary and St. Francis De Sales College, Milwaukee, North American College and Gregorian Univ. (Rome); ord. priest (Milwaukee*), June 29, 1975; entered Vatican diplomatic service, 1980; Apostolic Nunciature, Dominican Republic, 1980-82; transferred to the Vatican Secretariat of State, 1982; named assessor of the Secretariat, 1997; named titular bp. of Memphis and prefect of the papal household, Feb. 7, 1998; ordained bp., Mar. 19, 1998.

Head, Edward D.: b. Aug. 5, 1919, White Plains, NY; educ. Cathedral College, St. Joseph's Seminary, Columbia Univ. (New York City); ord. priest (New York*), Jan. 27, 1945; director of New York Catholic Charities; ord. titular bp. of Ardsratha and aux. bp. of New York, Mar. 19, 1970; app. bp. of Buffalo, Jan. 23, 1973, inst., Mar. 19, 1973; ret., Apr. 18, 1995.

Heim, Capistran F., O.F.M.: b. Jan. 21, 1934, Catskill, NY; educ. Franciscan Houses of Study; ord. priest, Dec. 18, 1965; missionary in Brazil; ord. first bp. of prelature of Itaituba, Brazil, Sept. 17, 1988; inst., Oct. 2, 1988.

Hermann, Robert J.: b. Aug. 12, 1934, Weingarten, Mo.; educ. Cardinal Glennon College (Shrewsbury, MO.), St. Louis Univ.; ord. priest (St. Louis), March 30, 1963; aux. bp. St. Louis and tit. bp. of Zerta, Oct. 16, 2002; ord., Dec. 12, 2002.

Hermes, Herbert, O.S.B.: b. May 25, 1933, Scott City, KS; ord. priest (St. Benedict Abbey, Atchison, KS), May 26, 1960; missionary in Brazil; ord. bp. of territorial prelature of Cristalandia, Brazil, Sept. 2, 1990.

Hickey, James A.: (*See* **Cardinals, Biographies**.)

Higi, William L.: b. Aug. 29, 1933, Anderson, IN; educ. Our Lady of the Lakes Preparatory Seminary (Wawasee, IN), Mt. St. Mary of the West Seminary and Xavier Univ. (Cincinnati, OH); ord. priest, (Lafayette, IN) May 30, 1959; ord. bp. of Lafayette, IN, June 6, 1984.

Hogan, James J.: b. Oct. 17, 1911, Philadelphia, PA; educ. St. Charles College (Catonsville, MD), St. Mary's Seminary (Baltimore), Gregorian Univ. (Rome), Catholic Univ. (Washington, DC); ord. priest (Trenton), Dec. 8, 1937; ord. titular bp. of Philomelium and aux. bp. of Trenton, Feb. 25, 1960; app. bp. of Altoona-Johnstown, inst., July 6, 1966; ret., Nov. 4, 1986.

Houck, William Russell: b. June 26, 1926, Mobile, AL; educ. St. Bernard Junior College (Cullman, AL), St. Mary's Seminary College and St. Mary's Seminary (Baltimore, MD), Catholic Univ. (Washington, DC); ord. priest (Mobile*), May 19, 1951; ord. titular bp. of Alessano and aux. bp. of Jackson, MS, May 27, 1979, by Pope John Paul II; app. bp. of Jackson, Apr. 11, 1984, inst., June 5, 1984; ret., Jan. 3, 2003.

Howze, Joseph Lawson: b. Aug. 30, 1923, Daphne, AL; convert to Catholicism, 1948; educ. St. Bonaventure Univ. (St. Bonaventure, NY); ord. priest (Raleigh), May 7, 1959; ord. titular bp. of Massita and aux. bp. of Natchez-Jackson, Jan. 28, 1973; app. first bp. of Biloxi, Mar. 8, 1977; inst., June 6, 1977; res. May 15, 2001.

Hubbard, Howard J.: b. Oct. 31, 1938, Troy, NY; educ. St. Joseph's Seminary (Dunwoodie, NY); North American College and Gregorian Univ. (Rome), Catholic Univ. (Washington, DC); ord. priest (Albany), Dec. 18, 1963; ord. bp. of Albany, Mar. 27, 1977.

Hughes, Alfred C.: b. Dec. 2, 1932, Boston, MA; educ. St. John Seminary (Brighton, MA), Gregorian Univ. (Rome); ord. priest (Boston*), Dec. 15, 1957, in Rome; ord. titular bp. of Maximiana in Byzacena and aux. bp. of Boston, Sept. 14, 1981; app. bp. of Baton Rouge, Sept. 7, 1993; co-adj. abp. of New Orleans, Feb. 16, 2001; abp. of New Orleans, Jan. 3, 2002.

Hughes, Edward T.: b. Nov. 13, 1920, Lansdowne, PA; educ. St. Charles Seminary, Univ. of Pennsylvania (Philadelphia); ord. priest (Philadelphia*), May

31, 1947; ord. titular bp. of Segia and aux. bp. of Philadelphia, July 21, 1976; app. bp. of Metuchen, Dec. 11, 1986, inst., Feb. 5, 1987; ret., July 8, 1997.

Hughes, William A.: b. Sept. 23, 1921, Youngstown, OH; educ. St. Charles College (Catonsville, MD), St. Mary's Seminary (Cleveland, OH), Notre Dame Univ. (Notre Dame, IN); ord. priest (Youngstown), Apr. 6, 1946; ord. titular bp. of Inis Cathaig and aux. bp. of Youngstown, Sept. 12, 1974; app. bp. of Covington, inst., May 8, 1979; ret., July 4, 1995.

Hunthausen, Raymond G.: b. Aug. 21, 1921, Anaconda, MT; educ. Carroll College (Helena, MT), St. Edward's Seminary (Kenmore, WA), St. Louis Univ. (St. Louis, MO), Catholic Univ. (Washington, DC), Fordham Univ. (New York City), Notre Dame Univ. (Notre Dame, IN); ord. priest (Helena), June 1, 1946; ord. bp. of Helena, Aug. 30, 1962; app. abp. of Seattle, Feb. 25, 1975; ret., Aug. 21, 1991.

Hurley, Francis T.: b. Jan. 12, 1927, San Francisco, CA; educ. St. Patrick's Seminary (Menlo Park, CA), Catholic Univ. (Washington, DC); ord. priest (San Francisco*), June 16, 1951; assigned to NCWC in Washington, DC, 1957; assistant (1958) and later (1968) associate secretary of NCCB and USCC; ord. titular bp. of Daimlaig and aux. bp. of Juneau, AK, Mar. 19, 1970; app. bp. of Juneau, July 20, 1971, inst., Sept. 8, 1971; app. abp. of Anchorage, May 4, 1976, inst., July 8, 1976; res., March 3, 2001.

Hurley, Walter A.: b. May 30, 1937, Fredericton, New Brunswick; educ. Sacred Heart Seminary, St. John Provincial Seminary, The Catholic University of America; ord. priest, June 5, 1965 (Detroit); app. aux. bp. of Detroit and titular bishop of Cunavia, July 7, 2003.

I-J

Ibrahim, Ibrahim N.: b. Oct. 1, 1937, Telkaif, Mosul, Iraq.; educ. Patriarchal Seminary (Mosul, Iraq), St. Sulpice Seminary (Paris, France); ord. priest, Dec. 30, 1962, in Baghdad, Iraq; ord. titular bp. of Anbar and apostolic exarch for Chaldean Catholics in the United States, Mar. 8, 1982, in Baghdad; inst., in Detroit, Apr. 18, 1982; app. first eparch, Aug. 3, 1985, when exarchate was raised to eparchy of St. Thomas Apostle of Detroit.

Imesch, Joseph L.: b. June 21, 1931, Detroit, MI; educ. Sacred Heart Seminary (Detroit, MI), North American College, Gregorian Univ. (Rome); ord. priest (Detroit*), Dec. 16, 1956; ord. titular bp. of Pomaria and aux. bp. of Detroit, Apr. 3, 1973; app. bp. of Joliet, June 30, 1979.

Iriondo, Robert J.: b. Dec. 19, 1938, Legazti, Spain; educ. Collegio San Vittore and Pontifical Gregorian University, Rome; ord. priest (of the Canons Regular of the Lateran), Dec. 22, 1962; incardinated into Archdiocese of New York, 1996; Vicar for Hispanics, 1997; ord. titular bp. of Alton and aux. of New York, Dec. 12, 2001.

Irwin, Francis X.: b. Jan 9, 1934, Medford, MA; educ. Boston College High School, Boston College, St. John's Seminary (Brighton, MA), Boston College School of Social Service; ord. priest (Boston*), Feb. 2, 1960; ord. titular bp. of Ubaza and aux. bp. of Boston, Sept. 17, 1996.

Jacobs, Sam Gallip: b. Mar. 4, 1938, Greenwood, MS; educ. Immaculata Seminary (Lafayette, LA),

Catholic Univ. (Washington, DC); ord. priest (Lafayette), June 6, 1964; became priest of Lake Charles diocese, 1980, when that see was established; ord. bp. of Alexandria, LA, Aug. 24, 1989; app. bp. of Houma-Thibodaux, Aug. 1, 2003.

Jakubowski, Thad J.: b. Apr. 5, 1924, Chicago, IL; educ. Mundelein Seminary, St. Mary of the Lake Univ., Loyola Univ. (Chicago); ord priest (Chicago*), May 3, 1950; ord. titular bp. of Plestia and aux. bp. of Chicago, Apr. 11, 1988; ret., Jan. 24, 2003.

Jammo, Sarhad: b. March 14, 1941, Baghdad, Iraq; educ. Patriarchal Seminary of Mosul, Urban College of the Propaganda Fide Pontifical Oriental Institute (Rome); ord. priest (Baghdad*), Dec. 19, 1964; rector, Chaldean Seminary, Baghdad; after service in Iraq, transferred in 1977 to the Eparchy of Saint Thomas the Apostle of Detroit for Chaldeans; app. first eparch of the eparchy of St. Peter the Apostle of San Diego (Chaldean), May 21, 2002.

Jarrell, C. Michael: b. May 15, 1940, Opelousas, LA; educ. Immaculata Minor Seminary (Lafayette, LA); Catholic Univ. (Washington, DC); ord. priest (Lafayette, LA), June 3, 1967; ord. bp. of Houma-Thibodaux, Mar. 4, 1993; app. bp. of Lafayette, Nov. 8, 2002.

Jenky, Daniel R.: b. Mar. 3, 1947, Chicago; educ. University of Notre Dame; ord. priest, Apr. 6, 1974; Religious Superior of the Holy Cross religious at Notre Dame, 1985-1990; app. Titular Bp. of Amanzia and Aux. of Fort Wayne-South Bend, Oct. 21, 1997; ord., Dec. 16, 1997, bp. of Peoria, Feb. 12, 2002, inst. Apr. 10, 2002.

Jugis, Peter J.: b. March 3, 1957, Charlotte, NC; educ. University of North Carolina, North American College and Gregorian Univ. (Rome), Catholic University of America (Washington, DC); ord. priest, June 12, 1983; app. bp. of Charlotte, Aug. 1, 2003.

K

Kaffer, Roger L.: b. Aug. 14, 1927, Joliet, IL; educ. Quigley Preparatory Seminary (Chicago, IL), St. Mary of the Lake Seminary (Mundelein, IL), Gregorian Univ. (Rome); ord. priest (Joliet), May 1, 1954; ord. titular bp. of Dusa and aux. bp. of Joliet, June 26, 1985; res., Aug. 15, 2002, ret., Sept. 1, 2002.

Kaising, John. J.: b. March 3, 1936, Cincinnati; educ. Seminary of Cincinnati, Xavier University; ord. priest (Cincinnati*), Dec. 22, 1962; military chaplain in the Army 1970-1998, exec. assist. to the Chief of Chaplains of the Army, 1994-1998; app. titular bp. of Orreacelia and aux. bp. of the Archdiocese for the Military Services, Feb. 21, 2000, ord., April 11, 2000.

Kalisz, Raymond P., S.V.D.: b. Sept. 25, 1927, Melvindale, MI; educ. St. Mary's Seminary (Techny, IL); ord. priest, Aug. 15, 1954; ord. bp. of Wewak, Papua New Guinea, Aug. 15, 1980.

Kane, Francis Joseph: b. Oct. 30, 1942, Chicago, IL; educ. Quigley Preparatory Seminary (Chicago, IL), Niles College Seminary (Chicago, IL), Saint Mary of the Lake Seminary (Chicago, IL); ord. priest, May 14, 1969 (Chicago*); app. aux. bp. of Chicago and titular bp. of Sault Sainte Marie in Michigan Jan. 24, 2003; ord., March 19, 2003.

Keeler, Cardinal William Henry: (*See* **Cardinals, Biographies.**)

Keleher, James P.: b. July 31, 1931, Chicago, IL; educ. Quigley Preparatory Seminary (Chicago, IL), St.

Mary of the Lake Seminary (Mundelein, IL); ord. priest (Chicago*), Apr. 12, 1958; ord. bp. of Belleville, Dec. 11, 1984; app. abp. of Kansas City, KS, June 28, 1993.

Kelly, Thomas C., O.P.: b. July 14, 1931, Rochester, NY; educ. Providence College (Providence, RI), Immaculate Conception College (Washington, DC), Angelicum (Rome); professed in Dominicans, Aug. 26, 1952; secretary, apostolic delegation, Washington, DC, 1965-71; associate general secretary, 1971-77, and general secretary, 1977-81, NCCB/USCC; ord. titular bp. of Tusurus and aux. bp. of Washington, DC, Aug. 15, 1977; app. abp. of Louisville, Dec. 28, 1981, inst., Feb. 18, 1982.

Kettler, Donald J.: b. Nov. 26, 1944, Minneapolis: educ. St. John's Seminary Collegeville, Minnesota; ord. priest (Sioux Falls), May 29, 1970; app. bp. of Fairbanks, Alaska, June 7, 2002, ord., Aug. 22, 2002.

Kicanas, Gerald F.: b. Aug. 18, 1941, Chicago, IL; educ. Quigley Preparatory Seminary, St. Mary of the Lake Seminary and Loyola University in Chicago; ord. priest (Chicago*), Apr. 27, 1967; ord. titular bp. of Bela and aux. of Chicago, Mar. 20, 1995; app. coadj. bp. of Tucson, Oct. 30, 2001; inst. as coadj. bp. of Tuscon, Jan. 17, 2002; bp. of Tucson, March 7, 2003.

Kinney, John F.: b. June 11, 1937, Oelwein, IA; educ. Nazareth Hall and St. Paul Seminaries (St. Paul, MN); Pontifical Lateran University (Rome); ord. priest (St. Paul-Minneapolis*), Feb. 2, 1963; ord. titular bp. of Caorle and aux. bp. of St. Paul and Minneapolis, Jan. 25, 1977; app. bp. of Bismarck June 30, 1982; app. bp. of St. Cloud, May 9, 1995.

Kmiec, Edward U.: b. June 4, 1936, Trenton, NJ; educ. St. Charles College (Catonsville, MD), St. Mary's Seminary (Baltimore, MD), Gregorian Univ. (Rome); ord. priest (Trenton), Dec. 20, 1961; ord. titular bp. of Simidicca and aux. bp. of Trenton, Nov. 3, 1982; app. bp. of Nashville, Oct. 13, 1992; inst., Dec. 3, 1992.

Kucera, Daniel W., O.S.B.: b. May 7, 1923, Chicago, IL; educ. St. Procopius College (Lisle, IL), Catholic Univ. (Washington, DC); professed in Order of St. Benedict, June 16, 1944; ord. priest, May 26, 1949; abbot, St. Procopius Abbey, 1964-71; pres. Illinois Benedictine College, 1959-65 and 1971-76; ord. titular bp. of Natchez and aux. bp. of Joliet, July 21, 1977; app. bp. of Salina, Mar. 5, 1980; app. abp. of Dubuque, inst., Feb. 23, 1984; ret., Oct. 16, 1995.

Kuchmiak, Michael, C.SsR.: b. Feb. 5, 1923, Obertyn, Horodenka, Western Ukraine; left during World War II; educ. St. Josaphat Ukrainian Seminary (Rome, Italy), St. Mary's Seminary (Meadowvale, Ont., Canada); ord. priest, May 13, 1956; in the U.S. from 1967; ord. titular bp. of Agathopolis and aux. bp. of Ukrainian metropolitan of Philadelphia, Apr. 27, 1988; exarch of apostolic exarchate for Ukrainian Catholics in Great Britain, June 24, 1989.

Kudrick, John M.: b. Dec. 23, 1947, Lloydell, PA; educ. Third Order Regular of St. Francis, 1967; ord. priest, May 3, 1975; granted bi-ritual faculties for service in the Byzantine Rite, 1978; app. bp. of Parma, May 3, 2002.

Kupfer, William F., M.M.: b. Jan. 28, 1909, Brooklyn, NY; educ. Cathedral College (Brooklyn, NY), Maryknoll Seminary (Maryknoll, NY); ord. priest, June 11, 1933; missionary in China; app. prefect apostolic of Taichung, Taiwan, 1951; ord. first bp. of Taichung, July 25, 1962; ret., Sept. 3, 1986.

Kurtz, Joseph E.: b. Aug. 18, 1946, Shenandoah, PA.; educ. St. Charles Borromeo Seminary, Philadelphia, Marywood College, Scranton; ord. priest (Allentown), Mar. 18, 1972; app. bishop of Knoxville, Oct. 26, 1999, ord., Dec. 8, 1999.

Kurtz, Robert, C.R.: b. July 25, 1939, Chicago, IL; ord. priest, Mar. 11, 1967; ord. bp. of Hamilton, Bermuda, Sept. 15, 1995.

Kuzma, George M.: b. July 24, 1925, Windber, PA; educ. St. Francis Seminary (Loretto, PA), St. Procopius College (Lisle, IL), Sts. Cyril and Methodius Byzantine Catholic Seminary, Duquesne Univ. (Pittsburgh, PA); ord. priest (Pittsburgh*, Byzantine Rite), May 5, 1955; ord. titular bp. of Telmisso and aux. bp. of Byzantine eparchy of Passaic, 1987; app. bp. of Byzantine diocese of Van Nuys, CA, Oct. 23, 1990, inst., Jan. 15, 1991; res., Dec. 5, 2000.

L

Lagonegro, Dominick J.: b. Mar. 6, 1943, White Plains, NY; educ. Cathedral College, (Douglaston), St. Joseph Seminary, Yonkers; ord. priest (New York*), May 31, 1969; ord. titular bp. of Modrus and aux. of New York, Dec. 12, 2001.

Lambert, Francis, S.M.: b. Feb. 7, 1921, Lawrence, MA; educ. Marist Seminary (Framingham, MA); ord. priest, June 29, 1946; served in Marist missions in Oceania; provincial of Marist Oceania province, 1971; ord. bp. of Port Vila, Vanuatu (New Hebrides), Mar. 20, 1977; ret., Nov. 30, 1996.

Larkin, W. Thomas: b. Mar. 31, 1923, Mt. Morris, NY; educ. St. Andrew Seminary and St. Bernard Seminary (Rochester, NY); Angelicum Univ. (Rome); ord. priest (St. Augustine), May 15, 1947; ord. bp. of St. Petersburg, May 27, 1979; ret., Nov. 29, 1988.

Latino, Joseph: b. Oct. 21, 1937, New Orleans, LA; educ. Saint Joseph College Seminary (Covington, LA), Notre Dame Seminary (New Orleans, LA); ord. priest, May 25, 1963; app. bp. Jackson, Jan. 3, 2003; ord., March 7, 2003.

Law, Bernard F.: (*See* **Cardinals, Biographies**.)

Leibrecht, John J.: b. Aug. 30, 1930, Overland, MO; educ. Catholic Univ. (Washington, DC); ord. priest (St. Louis*), Mar. 17, 1956; superintendent of schools of St. Louis archdiocese, 1962-1981; ord. bp. of Springfield-Cape Girardeau, MO, Dec. 12, 1984.

Lennon, Richard G.: b. Mar. 26, 1947, Arlington, (MA); educ. St. John's Seminary, Brighton; ord. priest (Boston*), May 19, 1973; rector, St. John's Seminary 1999-2001; app. titular bp. of Sufes and aux. bp. of Boston, June 29, 2001, ord., Sept. 14, 2001; apost. admin. of Boston, 2002-03.

Lessard, Raymond W.: b. Dec. 21, 1930, Grafton, N.D.; educ. St. Paul Seminary (St. Paul, MN), North American College (Rome); ord. priest (Fargo), Dec. 16, 1956; served on staff of the Congregation for Bps. in the Roman Curia, 1964-73; ord. bp. of Savannah, Apr. 27, 1973; ret., Feb. 7, 1995.

Levada, William J.: b. June 15, 1936, Long Beach, CA; educ. St. John's College (Camarillo, CA), Gregorian Univ. (Rome); ord. priest (Los Angeles*), Dec. 20, 1961; ord. titular bp. of Capri and aux. bp. of Los Angeles, May 12, 1983; app. abp. of Portland, OR, July 3, 1986; coadj. abp. of San Francisco, Aug. 17, 1995; abp. of San Francisco, Dec. 27, 1995.

Lipscomb, Oscar H.: b. Sept. 21, 1931, Mobile,

AL; educ. McGill Institute, St. Bernard College (Cullman, AL), North American College and Gregorian Univ. (Rome), Catholic Univ. (Washington, DC); ord. priest (Mobile*), July 15, 1956; ord. first abp. of Mobile, Nov. 16, 1980.

Listecki, Jerome E.: b. March 12, 1949, Chicago; educ. Loyola University and St. Mary of the Lake Seminary, Mundelein, IL, De Paul University College of Law, University of St. Thomas Aquinas and Pontifical Gregorian University, Rome; ord. priest (Chicago*), June 1, 1975, app. titular bp. of Nara and aux bp. of Chicago, Nov. 7, 2000, ord., Jan. 8, 2001.

Lohmuller, Martin N.: b. Aug. 21, 1919, Philadelphia, PA; educ. St. Charles Borromeo Seminary (Philadelphia, PA), Catholic Univ. (Washington, DC); ord. priest (Philadelphia*), June 3, 1944; ord. titular bp. of Ramsbury and aux. bp. of Philadelphia, Apr. 2, 1970; ret., Oct. 11, 1994.

Lori, William E.: b. May 6, 1951, Louisville, KY; educ. St. Pius X College (Covington, KY), Mount St. Mary's Seminary (Emmitsburg, MD), Catholic Univ. (Washington, DC); ord. priest (Washington*), May 14, 1977; ord. titular bp. of Bulla and aux. bp. of Washington, DC, Apr. 20, 1995; app. bp. of Bridgeport, Jan. 23, 2001; inst., Mar. 19, 2001.

Losten, Basil: b. May 11, 1930, Chesapeake City, MD; educ. St. Basil's College (Stamford, CT), Catholic University (Washington, DC); ord. priest (Philadelphia* Ukrainian Byzantine), June 10, 1957; ord. titular bp. of Arcadiopolis in Asia and aux. bp. of Ukrainian archeparchy of Philadelphia, May 25, 1971; app. apostolic administrator of archeparchy, 1976; app. bp. of Ukrainian eparchy of Stamford, Sept. 20, 1977.

Lotocky, Innocent Hilarius, O.S.B.M.: b. Nov. 3, 1915, Petlykiwci, Ukraine; educ. seminaries in Ukraine, Czechoslovakia and Austria; ord. priest, Nov. 24, 1940; ord. bp. of St. Nicholas of Chicago for the Ukrainians, Mar. 1, 1981; ret., July 15, 1993.

Loverde, Paul S.: b. Sept. 3, 1940, Framingham, MA; educ. St. Thomas Seminary (Bloomfield, CT), St. Bernard Seminary (Rochester, NY), Gregorian Univ. (Rome), Catholic Univ. (Washington, DC); ord. priest (Norwich), Dec. 18, 1965; ord. titular bp. of Ottabia and aux. bp. of Hartford, Apr. 12, 1988; app. bp. of Ogdensburg, Nov. 11, 1993; inst., Jan. 17, 1994; app. bp. of Arlington, Jan. 25, 1999, inst., Mar. 25, 1999.

Lucas, George J.: b. June 12, 1949, St. Louis, MO; educ. Major Seminary of St. Louis, Univ. of St. Louis; ord. priest (St. Louis*), May 24, 1975; rector, Kenrick-Glennon Seminary, 1995-1999; app. bishop of Springfield in Illinois, Oct. 19, 1999, ord., Dec. 14, 1999.

Luong, Dominic Dinh Mai: b: Dec. 20, 1940, Minh Cuong, Vietnam; educ. seminary (Buffalo, N.Y.), and St. Bernard Seminary (Rochester, N.Y.), Canisius College (Buffalo); ord. priest in Buffalo for Diocese of Danang, Vietnam, May 21, 1966; incardinated into New Orleans 1986; named aux. bp. of Orange, CA, and titular bp. of Cebarades, April 25, 2003; ord., June 11, 2003.

Lynch, Robert N.: b. May 27, 1941, Charleston, WV; educ. Pontifical College Josephinum (Columbus, OH); John XXIII National Seminary (Weston, MA); ord. priest (Miami*), May 13, 1978; associate general secretary (1984-89) and general secretary (1989-95) of the NCCB/USCC; app. bp. of St. Petersburg, Dec. 5,

1995; ord. and inst., Jan. 26, 1996; app. apostolic administrator of Palm Beach (while continuing as bp. of St. Petersburg), June 2, 1998.

Lyne, Timothy J.: b. Mar. 21, 1919, Chicago, IL; educ. Quigley Preparatory Seminary, St. Mary of the Lake Seminary (Mundelein, IL); ord. priest (Chicago*), May 1, 1943; ord. titular bp. of Vamalla and aux. bp. of Chicago, Dec. 13, 1983; ret., Jan. 24, 1995.

M

Macaluso, Christie Albert: b. June 12, 1945, Hartford, CT; educ. St. Thomas Seminary (Bloomfield, CT), St. Mary's Seminary (Baltimore, Md), Trinity College (Hartford, CT), New York University; ord. priest (Hartford*), May 21, 1971; ord. titular bp. of Grass Valley and aux. bp. of Hartford, June 10, 1997.

McAuliffe, Michael F.: b. Nov. 22, 1920, Kansas City, MO; educ. St. Louis Preparatory Seminary (St. Louis, MO), Catholic Univ. (Washington, DC); ord. priest (Kansas City-St. Joseph), May 31, 1945; ord. bp. of Jefferson City, Aug. 18, 1969; ret., June, 1997.

McCarrick, Theodore E.: (*See* **Cardinals, Biographies.**)

McCarthy, Edward A.: b. Apr. 10, 1918, Cincinnati, OH; educ. Mt. St. Mary Seminary (Norwood, OH), Catholic Univ. (Washington, DC), Lateran and Angelicum (Rome); ord. priest (Cincinnati*), May 29, 1943; ord. titular bp. of Tamascani and aux. bp. of Cincinnati, June 15, 1965; first bp. of Phoenix, AZ, Dec. 2, 1969; app. coadjutor abp. of Miami, FL, July 7, 1976; succeeded as abp. of Miami, July 26, 1977; ret., Nov. 3, 1994.

McCarthy, James F.: b. July 9, 1942, Mount Kisco, NY; educ. Cathedral College and St. Joseph's Seminary, New York; ord. priest (New York*), June 1, 1968; app. titular bp. of Veronna and aux. bp. of New York, May 11, 1999, inst., June 29, 1999; res., June 12, 2002.

McCarthy, John E.: b. June 21, 1930, Houston, TX; educ. Univ. of St. Thomas (Houston, TX); ord. priest (Galveston-Houston), May 26, 1956; assistant director Social Action Dept. USCC, 1967-69; executive director Texas Catholic Conference; ord. titular bp. of Pedena and aux. bp. of Galveston-Houston, Mar. 14, 1979; app. bp. of Austin, Dec. 19, 1985, inst., Feb. 25, 1986; res., Jan. 2, 2001.

McCormack, John B.: b Aug. 12, 1935, Winthrop, MA; educ. St. John Seminary College and St. John Seminary Theologate (Boston, MA); ord. priest (Boston*), Feb. 2, 1960; ord. titular bp. of Cerbali and aux. bp. of Boston, Dec. 27, 1995; app. bp. of Manchester, NH, July 21, 1998, inst., Sept. 22, 1998.

McCormack, William J.: b. Jan. 24, 1924, New York, NY; educ. Christ the King Seminary, St. Bonaventure Univ. (St. Bonaventure, NY); ord. priest (New York*), Feb. 21, 1959; national director of Society for the Propagation of the Faith, 1980; ord. titular bp. of Nicives and aux. bp. of New York, Jan. 6, 1987; res., Oct. 31, 2001.

McDonald, Andrew J.: b. Oct. 24, 1923, Savannah, GA; educ. St. Mary's Seminary (Baltimore, MD), Catholic Univ. (Washington, DC), Lateran Univ. (Rome); ord. priest (Savannah), May 8, 1948; ord. bp. of Little Rock, Sept. 5, 1972; res., Jan. 4, 2000.

McDonnell, Charles J.: b. July 7, 1928, Brooklyn, NY; educ. Seton Hall Univ. (South Orange, NJ), Immaculate Conception Seminary (Darlington, NJ), Long Island Univ. (Brooklyn, NY); ord. priest (Newark*), May 29, 1954; U.S. Army Chaplain, 1965-89; ret., from active duty with rank of Brigadier General; ord. titular bp. of Pocofelto and aux. bp. of Newark, May 12, 1994.

McDonnell, Timothy A.: b. Dec. 23, 1937, New York City; educ. St. Joseph Seminary, Yonkers, Iona College, New Rochelle; ord. priest (New York*), June 1, 1963; ord. titular bp. of Semina and aux. bp. of New York, Dec. 12, 2001.

McDowell, John B.: b. July 17, 1921, New Castle, PA; educ. St. Vincent College, St. Vincent Theological Seminary (Latrobe, PA), Catholic Univ. (Washington, DC); ord. priest (Pittsburgh), Nov. 4, 1945; superintendent of schools, Pittsburgh diocese, 1955-70; ord. titular bp. of Tamazuca, and aux. bp. of Pittsburgh, Sept. 8, 1966; ret., Sept. 9, 1996.

McFarland, Norman F.: b. Feb. 21, 1922, Martinez, CA; educ. St. Patrick's Seminary (Menlo Park, CA), Catholic Univ. (Washington, DC); ord. priest (San Francisco*), June 15, 1946; ord. titular bp. of Bida and aux. bp. of San Francisco, Sept. 8, 1970; apostolic adminstrator of Reno, 1974; app. bp. of Reno, Feb. 10, 1976, inst., Mar. 31, 1976; title of see changed to Reno-Las Vegas; app. bp. of Orange, CA, Dec. 29, 1986; inst., Mar. 31, 1976; res., June 30, 1998.

McGarry, Urban, T.O.R.: b. Nov. 11, 1911, Warren, PA; ord. priest, Oct. 3, 1942, in India; prefect apostolic of Bhagalpur, Aug. 7, 1956; ord. first bp. of Bhagalpur, India, May 10, 1965; res., Nov. 30, 1987.

McGrath, Patrick J.: b. July 11, 1945, Dublin, Ire.; educ. St. John's College Seminary (Waterford), Lateran Univ. (Rome, Italy); ord. priest in Ireland, June 7, 1970; came to U.S. same year and became San Francisco archdiocesan priest; ord. titular bp. of Allegheny and aux. bp. of San Francisco, Jan. 25, 1989; app. coadj. bp. of San Jose, June 30, 1998; bp. of San Jose, Nov. 29, 1999.

McKinney, Joseph C.: b. Sept. 10, 1928, Grand Rapids, MI: educ. St. Joseph's Seminary (Grand Rapids, MI), Seminaire de Philosophie (Montreal, Canada), Urban Univ. (Rome, Italy); ord. priest (Grand Rapids), Dec. 20, 1953; ord. titular bp. of Lentini and aux. bp. of Grand Rapids, Sept. 26, 1968; res., Oct. 2, 2001.

McLaughlin, Bernard J.: b. Nov. 19, 1912, Buffalo, NY; educ. Urban Univ. (Rome, Italy); ord. priest (Buffalo), Dec. 21, 1935, at Rome; ord. titular bp. of Mottola and aux. bp. of Buffalo, Jan. 6, 1969; res., Jan. 5, 1988.

McManus, Robert J.: b. July 5, 1951, Warwick, RI; educ. Our Lady of Providence Seminary, Catholic Univ. (Washington, DC), Seminary of Toronto, Canada, Pontifical Gregorian Univ. (Rome); ord. priest (Providence), May 27, 1978; diocesan Vicar for Education and Rector of Our Lady of Providence; app. titular bp. of Allegheny and aux. of Providence, Dec. 1, 1998, ord., Feb. 22, 1999.

McNabb, John C., O.S.A.: b. Dec. 11, 1925, Beloit, WI; educ. Villanova Univ. (Villanova, PA), Augustinian College and Catholic Univ. (Washington, DC), De Paul Univ. (Chicago, IL); ord. priest, May 24, 1952; ord. titular bp. of Saia Maggiore, June 17, 1967 (resigned titular see, Dec. 27, 1977); prelate of Chulucanas, Peru, 1967; first bp. of Chulucanas, Dec. 12, 1988.

McNamara, Lawrence J.: b. Aug. 5, 1928, Chicago, IL; educ. St. Paul Seminary (St. Paul, MN),

Catholic Univ. (Washington, DC); ord. priest (Kansas City-St. Joseph), May 30, 1953; executive director of Campaign for Human Development 1973-77; ord. bp. of Grand Island, NE, Mar. 28, 1978.

McNaughton, William J., M.M.: b. Dec. 7, 1926, Lawrence, MA; educ. Maryknoll Seminary (Maryknoll, NY); ord. priest, June 13, 1953; ord. titular bp. of Thuburbo Minus and vicar apostolic of Inchon, Korea, Aug. 24, 1961; first bp. of Inchon, Mar. 10, 1962, when vicariate was raised to diocese.

McRaith, John Jeremiah: b. Dec. 6, 1934, Hutchinson, MN; educ. St. John Preparatory School (Collegeville, MN), Loras College, St. Bernard Seminary (Dubuque, IA); ord. priest (New Ulm), Feb. 21, 1960; exec. dir. of Catholic Rural Life Conference, 1971-78; ord. bp. of Owensboro, KY, Dec. 15, 1982.

Madera, Joseph J., M.Sp.S.: b. Nov. 27, 1927, San Francisco, CA; educ. Domus Studiorum of the Missionaries of the Holy Spirit (Coyoacan, D.F. Mexico); ord. priest, June 15, 1957; ord. coadjutor bp. of Fresno, Mar. 4, 1980; bp. of Fresno, July 1, 1980; app. titular bp. of Orte and aux. of Military Services archdiocese, June 30, 1991.

Maginnis, Robert P.: b. Dec. 22, 1933, Philadelphia, PA; educ. St. Charles Borromeo Seminary (Overbrook, PA); ord. priest (Philadelphia*), May 13, 1961; ord. titular bp. of Siminina and aux. bp. of Philadelphia, Mar. 11, 1996.

Maguire, Joseph F.: b. Sept. 4, 1919, Boston, MA; educ. Boston College, St. John's Seminary (Boston, MA); ord. priest (Boston*), June 29, 1945; ord. titular bp. of Macteris and aux. bp. of Boston, Feb. 2, 1972; app. coadjutor bp. of Springfield, MA, Apr. 13, 1976; succeeded as bp. of Springfield, MA, Oct. 15, 1977; ret., Dec. 27, 1991.

Mahony, Roger M.: (*See* **Cardinals, Biographies**.)

Maida, Adam J.: (*See* **Cardinals, Biographies**.)

Malone, Richard J.: b. March 19, 1946, Salem, MA; educ. St. John's Seminary, Brighton, Boston University, ord. priest (Boston*), May 20, 1972; app. titular bp. of Aptuca and aux. bp. of Boston, Jan. 27, 2000, ord., March 1, 2000.

Maloney, Charles G.: b. Sept. 9, 1912, Louisville, KY; educ. St. Joseph's College (Rensselaer, IN), North American College (Rome); ord. priest (Louisville*), Dec. 8, 1937; ord. titular bp. of Capsa and aux. bp. of Louisville, Feb. 2, 1955; res., Jan. 8, 1988; transferred to Bardstown, 1995, when it was reestablished as a titular see.

Malooly, W.(William) Francis: b. Jan. 18, 1944, Baltimore; educ. St. Charles Minor Seminary, St. Mary's Seminary (Baltimore); ord priest (Baltimore*), May 7, 1970, app. titular bp. of Flumenzer and aux. bp. of Baltimore, Dec. 12, 2000, ord., March 1, 2001.

Manning, Elias (James), O.F.M. Conv.: b. Apr. 14, 1938, Troy, NY; educ. Sao José Seminary (Rio de Janeiro, Brazil); ord. priest, Oct. 30, 1965, in New York; ord. bp. of Valenca, Brazil, May 13, 1990.

Manning, Thomas R., O.F.M.: b. Aug. 29, 1922, Baltimore, MD; educ. Duns Scotus College (Southfield, MI), Holy Name College (Washington, DC); ord. priest, June 5, 1948; ord. titular bp. of Arsamosata, July 14, 1959 (res. titular see, Dec. 30, 1977); prelate of Coroico, Bolivia, July 14, 1959; became first bp., 1983, when prelature was raised to diocese; ret., Oct. 9, 1996.

Mansell, Henry J.: b. Oct. 10, 1937, New York, NY; educ. Cathedral College, St. Joseph's Seminary and College (New York); North American College, Gregorian Univ. (Rome); ord. priest (New York*), Dec. 19, 1962; ord. titular bp. of Marazane and aux. bp. of New York, Jan. 6, 1993, by John Paul II in Vatican City; app. bp. of Buffalo, Apr. 18, 1995; inst., June 12, 1995.

Manz, John R.: b. Nov. 14, 1945, Chicago, IL; educ. Niles College Seminary (Niles, IL), Univ. of St. Mary of the Lake-Mundelein Seminary (Chicago); ord. priest (Chicago*), May 12, 1971; ord. titular bp. of Mulia and aux. bp. of Chicago, Mar. 5, 1996.

Marcinkus, Paul C.: b. Jan. 15, 1922, Cicero, IL; ord. priest (Chicago*), May 3, 1947; served in Vatican secretariat from 1952; ord. titular bp. of Orta, Jan. 6, 1969; secretary (1968-71) and president (1971-89) of Institute for Works of Religion (Vatican Bank); titular abp., Sept. 26, 1981; former pro-president of Pontifical Commission for the State of Vatican City; res. in 1990.

Marconi, Dominic A.: b. Mar. 13, 1927, Newark, NJ; educ. Seton Hall Univ. (S. Orange, NJ), Immaculate Conception Seminary (Darlington, NJ), Catholic Univ. (Washington, DC); ord. priest (Newark*), May 30, 1953; ord. titular bp. of Bure and aux. bp. of Newark, June 25, 1976; res., July 1, 2002.

Martino, Joseph F.: b. May 1, 1946, Philadelphia, PA; educ. St. Charles Borromeo Seminary (Overbrook, PA), Gregorian Univ. (Rome); ord. priest (Philadelphia*), Dec. 18, 1970; ord. titular bp. of Cellae in Mauretania and aux. bp. of Philadelphia, Mar. 11, 1996; app. bp. of Scranton, July 25, 2003.

Matthiesen, Leroy Theodore: b. June 11, 1921, Olfen, TX; educ. Josephinum College (Columbus, OH), Catholic Univ. (Washington, DC), Register School of Journalism; ord. priest (Amarillo), Mar. 10, 1946; ord. bp. of Amarillo, May 30, 1980; ret., Jan. 21, 1997.

Melczek, Dale J.: b. Nov. 9, 1938, Detroit, MI; educ. St. Mary's College (Orchard Lake, MI), St. John's Provincial Seminary (Plymouth, MI), Univ. of Detroit; ord. priest (Detroit*), June 6, 1964; ord. titular bp. of Trau and aux. bp. of Detroit, Jan. 27, 1983; apostolic administrator of Gary, Aug. 19, 1992; coadjutor bp. of Gary, Oct. 28, 1995; bp. of Gary, June 1, 1996.

Mengeling, Carl F.: b. Oct. 22, 1930, Hammond, IN; educ. St. Meinrad College and Seminary (St. Meinrad, IN), Alphonsianum Univ. (Rome); ord. priest (Gary), May 25, 1957; ord. bp. of Lansing, Jan. 25, 1996.

Mestice, Anthony F.: b. Dec. 6, 1923, New York, NY; educ. St. Joseph Seminary (Yonkers, NY); ord. priest (New York*), June 4, 1949; ord. titular bp. of Villa Nova and aux. bp. of New York, Apr. 27, 1973; ret., Oct. 31, 2001.

Michaels, James E., S.S.C.: b. May 30, 1926, Chicago, IL; educ. Columban Seminary (St. Columban, NE), Gregorian Univ. (Rome); ord. priest, Dec. 21, 1951; ord. titular bp. of Verbe and aux. bp. of Kwang Ju, Korea, Apr. 14, 1966; app. aux. bp. of Wheeling, Apr. 3, 1973 (title of see changed to Wheeling-Charleston, 1974); res., Sept. 22, 1987.

Milone, Anthony M.: b. Sept. 24, 1932, Omaha, NE; educ. North American College (Rome); ord. priest (Omaha*), Dec. 15, 1957, in Rome; ord. titular bp. of Plestia and aux. bp. of Omaha, Jan. 6, 1982;

app. bp. of Great Falls-Billings, Dec. 14, 1987, inst., Feb. 23, 1988.

Minder, John, O.S.F.S.: b. Nov. 1, 1923, Philadelphia, PA; educ. Catholic Univ. (Washington, DC); ord. priest, June 3, 1950; ord. bp. of Keimos (renamed Keimos-Upington, 1985), South Africa, Jan. 10, 1968.

Moeddel, Carl K.: b. Dec. 28, 1937, Cincinnati, OH; educ. Athenaeum of Ohio, Mt. St. Mary's Seminary (Cincinnati); ord. priest (Cincinnati*), Aug. 15, 1962; ord. titular bp. of Bistue and aux. bp. of Cincinnati, Aug. 24, 1993.

Montrose, Donald W.: b. May 13, 1923, Denver, CO; educ. St. John's Seminary (Camarillo, CA); ord. priest (Los Angeles*), May 7, 1949; ord. titular bp. of Forum Novum and aux. bp. of Los Angeles, May 12, 1983; app. bp. of Stockton, Dec. 17, 1985, inst., Feb. 20, 1986; res., Jan. 19, 1999.

Moreno, Manuel D.: b. Nov. 27, 1930, Placentia, CA; educ. Univ. of CA (Los Angeles), Our Lady Queen of Angels (San Fernando, CA), St. John's Seminary (Camarillo, CA); ord. priest (Los Angeles*), Apr. 25, 1961; ord. titular bp. of Tanagra and aux. bp. of Los Angeles, Feb. 19, 1977; bp. of Tucson, Jan. 12, 1982, inst., Mar. 11, 1982; res., March 7, 2003.

Morin, Roger Paul: b. March 7, 1941, Lowell, MA; educ. Notre Dame Seminary (New Orleans, LA), Tulane University (New Orleans, LA); ord. priest, April 15, 1971 (New Orleans*); app. aux. bp. of New Orleans and titular bishop of Aulona, Feb. 11, 2003; ord., April 22, 2003.

Morlino, Robert C.: b. Dec. 31, 1946, Scranton, PA; educ. Fordham Univ., University of Notre Dame, Weston School of Theology, Cambridge, MA, Gregorian University, Rome; ord. priest for the Society of Jesus, Maryland Province, June 1, 1974, incardinated into the Diocese of Kalamazoo, MI, Oct. 26, 1983, app. bp. of Helena, July 6, 1999, inst,. Sept. 21, 1999; app. bp. of Madison, May 23, 2003.

Morneau, Robert F.: b. Sept. 10, 1938, New London, WI; educ. St. Norbert's College (De Pere, WI), Sacred Heart Seminary (Oneida, WI), Catholic Univ. (Washington, DC); ord. priest (Green Bay), May 28, 1966; ord. titular bp. of Massa Lubrense and aux. bp. of Green Bay, Feb. 22, 1979.

Moskal, Robert M.: b. Oct. 24, 1937, Carnegie, PA; educ. St. Basil Minor Seminary (Stamford, CT), St. Josaphat Seminary and Catholic Univ. (Washington, DC); ord. priest (Philadelphia*, Byzantine Ukrainian), Mar. 25, 1963; ord. titular bp. of Agatopoli and aux. bp. of the Ukrainian archeparchy of Philadelphia, Oct. 13, 1981; app. first bp. of St. Josaphat in Parma, Dec. 5, 1983.

Moynihan, James M.: b. July 16, 1932, Rochester, NY; educ. St. Bernard's Seminary (Rochester, NY), North American College and Gregorian Univ. (Rome); ord. priest (Rochester), Dec. 15, 1957, in Rome; ord. bp. of Syracuse, May 29, 1995.

Muench Robert W.: b. Dec. 28, 1942, Louisville, KY; educ. St. Joseph Seminary and Notre Dame Seminary (New Orleans, LA), Catholic Univ. (Washington, DC); ord. priest (New Orleans*), June 18, 1968; ord. titular bp. of Mactaris and aux. bp. of New Orleans, June 29, 1990; app. bp. of Covington Jan., 1996; inst., Mar. 19, 1996; app. bp. of Baton Rouge, Dec. 15, 2001.

Mulvee, Robert E.: b. Feb. 15, 1930, Boston, MA; educ. St. Thomas Seminary (Bloomfield, CT), University Seminary (Ottawa, ON), American College

(Louvain, Belgium), Lateran Univ. (Rome); ord. priest (Manchester), June 30, 1957; ord. titular bp. of Summa and aux. bp. of Manchester, NH, Apr. 14, 1977; app. bp. of Wilmington, Del., Feb. 19, 1985; app. coadjutor bp. of Providence, Feb. 9, 1995; bp. of Providence, June 11, 1997.

Mundo, Miguel P.: b. July 25, 1937, New York, NY; educ. Fordham Univ. (Bronx, NY), St. Jerome's College (Kitchener, ON), St Francis Seminary (Loretto, PA); ord. priest (Camden), May 19, 1962; missionary in Brazil from 1963; ord. titular bp. of Blanda Julia and aux. bp. of Jatai, Brazil, June 2, 1978.

Murphy, Michael J.: b. July 1, 1915, Cleveland, OH; educ. Niagara Univ. (Niagara Falls, NY); North American College (Rome), Catholic Univ. (Washington, DC); ord. priest (Cleveland), Feb. 28, 1942; ord. titular bp. of Ariendela and aux. bp. of Cleveland, June 11, 1976; app. coadjutor bp. of Erie, Nov. 20, 1978; bp. of Erie, July 16, 1982; ret., June 12, 1990.

Murphy, William F.: b. May 14, 1940, Boston MA; educ. Boston Latin School (Boston), Harvard College, St. John's Seminary (Boston), Gregorian Univ. (Rome); ord. priest (Boston*), Dec. 16, 1964; ord. titular bp. of Saia Maggiore and aux. bp. of Boston, Dec. 27, 1995; app. bp. of Rockville Centre, June 25, 2001, and., Sept. 5, 2001.

Murray, James A.: b. July 5, 1932, Jackson, MI; educ. Sacred Heart Seminary Detroit, St. John Provincial Seminary (Plymouth, MI), Catholic Univ. of America; ord. priest (Lansing), June 7, 1958; app. bp. of Kalamazoo, Nov. 18, 1997, ord., Jan. 27, 1998.

Murry, George V., S.J.: b. Dec. 28, 1948, Camden, NJ; educ. St. Joseph's College (Philadelphia, PA), St. Thomas Seminary (Bloomfield, CT), St. Mary Seminary (Baltimore, MD), Jesuit School of Theology (Berkeley, CA), George Washington Univ. (Washington, DC); entered Jesuits 1972; ord. priest, June 9, 1979; ord. titular bp. of Fuerteventura and aux. bp. of Chicago, Mar. 20, 1995; app. co-adjutor of St. Thomas in the Virgin Islands, May 5, 1998; bp. of St. Thomas in the Virgin Islands, June 30, 1999.

Myers, John Joseph: b. July 26, 1941, Ottawa, IL; educ. Loras College (Dubuque, IA), North American College and Gregorian Univ. (Rome), Catholic Univ. of America (Washington, DC); ord. priest (Peoria), Dec. 17, 1966, in Rome; ord. coadjutor bp. of Peoria, Sept. 3, 1987; bp. of Peoria, Jan. 23, 1990; app. abp. of Newark, July 24, 2001.

N

Naumann, Joseph F.: b. June 4, 1949, St. Louis, MO; educ. Cardinal Glennon Seminary College and Kenrick Seminary (St. Louis, MO); ord. priest (St. Louis*), 1975; app. titular bp. of Caput Cilla and aux. bp. of St. Louis, July 9, 1997.

Nevins, John J.: b. Jan. 19, 1932, New Rochelle, NY; educ. Iona College (New Rochelle, NY), Catholic Univ. (Washington, DC); ord. priest (Miami*), June 6, 1959; ord. titular bp. of Rusticana and aux. bp. of Miami, Mar. 24, 1979; app. first bp. of Venice, FL, July 17, 1984; inst., Oct. 25, 1984.

Newman, William C.: b. Aug. 16, 1928, Baltimore, MD; educ. St. Mary Seminary (Baltimore, MD), Catholic Univ. (Washington, DC), Loyola College (Baltimore, MD); ord. priest (Baltimore*), May 29, 1954; ord. titular bp. of Numluli and aux. bp. of Baltimore, July 2, 1984.

Neylon, Martin J., S.J.: b. Feb. 13, 1920, Buffalo, NY; ord. priest, June 18, 1950; ord. titular bp. of Libertina and coadjutor vicar apostolic of the Caroline and Marshall Islands, Feb. 2, 1970; vicar apostolic of Caroline and Marshall Is., Sept. 20, 1971; first bp. of Carolines-Marshalls when vicariate apostolic was raised to diocese, 1979 (title of see changed to Caroline Islands, Apr. 23, 1993); ret., Mar. 25, 1995.

Niederauer, George H.: b. June 14, 1936, Los Angeles, CA; educ. St. John's Seminary (Camarillo, CA), Catholic Univ. (Washington, DC), Loyola Univ. of Los Angeles, Univ. of Southern CA, Loretta Heights College (Denver, CO); ord. priest (Los Angeles*), Apr. 30, 1962; app. bp. of Salt Lake City, Nov. 3, 1994, ord., Jan. 25, 1995.

Niedergeses, James D.: b. Feb. 2, 1917, Lawrenceburg, TN; educ. St. Bernard College (St. Bernard, AL), St. Ambrose College (Davenport, IA), Mt. St. Mary Seminary of the West and Athenaeum (Cincinnati, OH); ord. priest (Nashville), May 20, 1944; ord. bp. of Nashville, May 20, 1975; ret., Oct. 13, 1992.

Nienstedt, John C.: b. Mar. 18, 1947, Detroit, MI; educ. Sacred Heart Seminary (Detroit), North American College, Gregorian Univ., Alphonsianum (Rome); ord. priest (Detroit*), July 27, 1974; served in Vatican Secretariat of State, 1980-86; rector of Sacred Heart Seminary (Detroit), 1988-94; pastor of the Shrine of the Little Flower (Royal Oak, MI), 1994; ord. titular bp. of Alton and aux. bp. of Detroit, July 9, 1996; app. bp. of New Ulm, June 12, 2001, inst., Aug. 6, 2001.

Novak, Alfred, C.SS.R.: b. June 2, 1930, Dwight, NE; educ. Immaculate Conception Seminary (Oconomowoc, WI); ord. priest, July 2, 1956; ord. titular bp. of Vardimissa and aux. bp. of Sao Paulo, Brazil, May 25, 1979; bp. of Paranagua, Brazil, Mar. 14, 1989.

O

O'Brien, Edwin F.: b. Apr. 8, 1939, Bronx, NY; educ. St. Joseph's Seminary (Yonkers, NY), Angelicum (Rome); ord. priest (New York*), May 29, 1965; ord. titular bp. of Tizica and aux. bp. of New York, Mar. 25, 1996; app. coadjutor abp. for Military Services Archdiocese, Apr. 8, 1997; abp. of Military Services Archdiocese, Aug. 12, 1997.

O'Brien, Thomas Joseph: b. Nov. 29, 1935, Indianapolis, IN; educ. St. Meinrad High School Seminary, St. Meinrad College Seminary (St. Meinrad, IN); ord. priest (Tucson), May 7, 1961; ord. bp. of Phoenix, Jan. 6, 1982; res., June 18, 2003.

Ochoa, Armando: b. Apr. 3, 1943, Oxnard, CA; educ. Ventura College (Ventura, CA), St. John's College and St. John's Seminary (Camarillo, CA); ord. priest (Los Angeles*), May 23, 1970; ord. titular bp. of Sitifi and aux. bp. of Los Angeles, Feb. 23, 1987; app. bp. of El Paso, Apr. 1, 1996; inst., June 26, 1996.

O'Connell, Anthony J.: b. May 10, 1938, Lisheen, Co. Clare, Ireland; came to U.S. at age 20; educ. Mt. St. Joseph College (Cork), Mungret College (Limerick), Kenrick Seminary (St. Louis); ord. priest (Jefferson City), Mar. 30, 1963; ord. First Bp. of Knoxville, TN, Sept. 8, 1988; app. bp. of Palm Beach, Nov. 12, 1998, ord., Jan. 14, 1999; res., March 8, 2002.

O'Donnell, Edward J.: b. July 4, 1931, St. Louis, MO; educ. St. Louis Preparatory Seminary and Kenrick

Seminary (St. Louis, MO); ord. priest (St. Louis*), Apr. 6, 1957; ord. titular bp. of Britania and aux. bp. of St. Louis, Feb. 10, 1984; app. bp. of Lafayette, LA, inst., Dec. 16, 1994; ret. Nov. 8, 2002.

Olivier, Leonard J., S.V.D.: b. Oct. 12, 1923, Lake Charles, LA; educ. St. Augustine Major Seminary (Bay St. Louis, MS), Catholic Univ. (Washington, DC), Loyola Univ. (New Orleans, LA); ord. priest, June 29, 1951; ord. titular bp. of Leges in Numidia and aux. bp. of Washington, Dec. 20, 1988.

Olmsted, Thomas J.: b. Jan. 21, 1947, Oketo, Kansas; educ. St. Thomas Seminary (Denver), North American College and Pontifical Gregorian University (Rome); ord. priest (Lincoln), July 2, 1973; served in Vatican Secretariat of State, 1979-1988; Dean of Formation, Pontifical College Josephinum, Columbus, OH, 1993, President and Rector, Pontifical College, Josephinum, 1997; app. coadjutor bp. of Wichita, Feb. 16, 1999, ord., Apr. 20, 1999; bp. of Wichita, Oct. 4, 2001.

O'Malley, Sean, O.F.M.Cap.: b. June 29, 1944, Lakewood, OH; educ. St. Fidelis Seminary (Herman, PA), Capuchin College and Catholic Univ. (Washington, DC); ord. priest, Aug. 29, 1970; episcopal vicar of priests serving Spanish speaking in Washington archdiocese, 1974-84; executive director of Spanish Catholic Center, Washington, from 1973; ord. coadjutor bp. of St. Thomas, Virgin Islands, Aug. 2, 1984; bp. of St. Thomas, Oct. 16, 1985; app. bp. of Fall River, June 16, 1992; app. bp. of Palm Beach, Sept. 3, 2002; app. abp. of Boston, July 1, 2003.

O'Neil, Dennis P.: b. Jan. 16, 1940, Fremont, NE; educ. St. John's Seminary College (Camarillo, CA.); ord. priest (Los Angeles*), 1966; on assignment in Diocese of Juneau (AK), 1979-1984; app. titular bp. of Macon and aux. bp. of San Bernardino, Jan. 16, 2001, ord., Mar. 27, 2001.

O'Neill, Arthur J.: b. Dec. 14, 1917, East Dubuque, IL; educ. Loras Collge (Dubuque, IA), St. Mary's Seminary (Baltimore, MD); ord. priest (Rockford), Mar. 27, 1943; ord. bp. of Rockford, Oct. 11, 1968; ret., Apr. 19, 1994.

Ottenweller, Albert H.: b. Apr. 5, 1916, Stanford, MT; educ. St. Joseph's Seminary (Rensselaer, IN), Catholic Univ. (Washington, DC); ord. priest (Toledo), June 19, 1943; ord. titular bp. of Perdices and aux. bp. of Toledo, May 29, 1974; app. bp. of Steubenville, OH, Oct. 11, 1977, inst., Nov. 22, 1977; ret., Jan. 28, 1992.

P

Paprocki, Thomas J.: b. Aug. 5, 1952, Chicago, IL; educ. Niles College of Loyola (Chicago, IL), Saint Mary of the Lake Seminary (Chicago, IL), DePaul University College of Law (Chicago, IL), Gregorian University (Rome); ord. priest, May 10, 1978 (Chicago); app. aux. bp. of Chicago and titular bishop of Vulturara, Jan. 24, 2003; ord., March 19, 2003.

Paska, Walter: b. Nov. 29, 1923, Elizabeth, NJ; educ. St. Charles Seminary (Catonsville, MD), Catholic Univ. (Washington, DC), Fordham Univ. (New York); ord. priest (Philadelphia of Ukrainians*), June 2, 1947; ord. titular bp. of Tigilava and aux. of Ukrainian archdiocese of Philadelphia, Mar. 19, 1992; res., Nov. 29, 2000.

Pataki, Andrew: b. Aug. 30, 1927, Palmerton, PA; educ. St. Vincent College (Latrobe, PA), St. Procopius

College, St. Procopius Seminary (Lisle, IL), Sts. Cyril and Methodius Byzantine Catholic Seminary (Pittsburgh, PA), Gregorian Univ. and Oriental Pontifical Institute (Rome, Italy); ord. priest (Pittsburgh.* Ruthenian Byzantine), Feb. 24, 1952; ord. titular bp. of Telmisso and aux. bp. of Byzantine diocese of Passaic, Aug. 23, 1983; app. bp. of Ruthenian Byzantine diocese of Parma, July 3, 1984; app. bp. of Ruthenian Byzantine diocese of Passaic, Nov. 6, 1995; inst., Feb. 8, 1996.

Pates, Richard E.: b. Feb. 12, 1943, St. Paul; educ. St. Paul Seminary, North American College (Rome); ord. priest (St. Paul and Minneapolis*), Dec. 20, 1968; staff, Apostolic Nunciature, Washington, 1975-81; app. titular bp. of Suacia and aux. bp. of St. Paul and Minneapolis, Dec. 22, 2000, ord., March 26, 2001.

Paul, John J.: b. Aug. 17, 1918, La Crosse, WI; educ. Loras College (Dubuque, IA), St. Mary's Seminary (Baltimore, MD), Marquette Univ. (Milwaukee, WI), ord. priest (Lincoln), Jan. 24, 1943; ord. titular bp. of Lambaesis and aux. bp. of La Crosse, Aug. 4, 1977; app. bp. of La Crosse, Oct. 18, 1983, inst., Dec. 5, 1983; ret., Dec. 10, 1994.

Pearce, George H., S.M.: b. Jan. 9, 1921, Brighton, MA; educ. Marist College and Seminary (Framington, MA); ord. priest, Feb. 2, 1947; ord. titular bp. of Attalea in Pamphylia and vicar apostolic of the Samoa and Tokelau Islands, June 29, 1956; title changed to bp. of Apia, June 21, 1966; app. abp. of Suva, Fiji Islands, June 22, 1967; res., Apr. 10, 1976.

Pelotte, Donald E., S.S.S.: b. Apr. 13, 1945, Waterville, ME; educ. Eymard Seminary and Junior College (Hyde Park, NY), John Carroll Univ. (Cleveland, OH), Fordham Univ. (Bronx, NY); ord. priest, Sept. 2, 1972; ord. coadjutor bp. of Gallup, May 6, 1986 (first priest of Native American ancestry to be named U.S. bp.); bp. of Gallup, Mar. 20, 1990.

Peña, Raymundo J.: b. Feb. 19, 1934, Robstown, TX; educ. Assumption Seminary (San Antonio, TX); ord. priest (Corpus Christi), May 25, 1957; ord. titular bp. of Trisipa and aux. bp. of San Antonio, Dec. 13, 1976; app. bp. of El Paso, Apr. 29, 1980; app. bp. of Brownsville, May 23, 1995.

Pepe, Joseph A.: : b. June 18, 1942, Philadelphia; educ. St. Charles Borromeo Seminary, University of St. Thomas (Rome); ord. priest (Philadelphia*), May 16, 1970; app. bp. of Las Vegas, April 6, 2001, ord., May 31, 2001.

Perry, Joseph N.: b. Apr. 18, 1948, Chicago, IL; educ. Capuchin Seminary of St. Lawrence, (Milwaukee), St. Mary Capuchin Seminary, Crown Point, (Indiana), St. Francis Seminary (Milwaukee), Catholic Univ. of America (Washington, DC); ord. priest (Milwaukee*), May 24, 1975; app. titular bp. of Lead and aux. bp. of Chicago, May 5, 1998; ord., June 29, 1998.

Pevec, A. Edward: b. Apr. 16, 1925, Cleveland, OH; educ. St. Mary's Seminary, John Carroll Univ. (Cleveland, OH); ord. priest (Cleveland), Apr. 29, 1950; ord. titular bp. of Mercia and aux. bp. of Cleveland, July 2, 1982; res., Apr. 3, 2001.

Pfeifer, Michael, O.M.I.: b. May 18, 1937, Alamo, TX; educ. Oblate school of theology (San Antonio, TX); ord. priest, Dec. 21, 1964; provincial of southern province of Oblates of Mary Immaculate, 1981; ord. bp. of San Angelo, July 26, 1985.

Pilarczyk, Daniel E.: b. Aug. 12, 1934, Dayton, OH; educ. St. Gregory's Seminary (Cincinnati, OH), Urban Univ. (Rome), Xavier Univ. and Univ. of Cincinnati (Cincinnati, OH); ord. priest (Cincinnati*), Dec. 20, 1959; ord. titular bp. of Hodelm and aux. bp. of Cincinnati, Dec. 20, 1974; app. abp. of Cincinnati, Oct. 30, 1982; inst., Dec. 20, 1982; president of NCCB/USCC, 1989-92.

Pilla, Anthony M.: b. Nov. 12, 1932, Cleveland, OH; educ. St. Gregory College Seminary (Cincinnati, OH), Borromeo College Seminary (Wickliffe, OH), St. Mary Seminary and John Carroll Univ. (Cleveland, OH); ord. priest (Cleveland), May 23, 1959; ord. titular bp. of Scardona and aux. bp. of Cleveland, Aug. 1, 1979; app. apostolic administrator of Cleveland, 1980; bp. of Cleveland, Nov. 13, 1980. President of NCCB/USCC, 1995-98.

Popp, Bernard F.: b. Dec. 6, 1917, Nada, TX; educ. St. John's Seminary and St. Mary's Univ. (San Antonio, TX); ord. priest (San Antonio*), Feb. 24, 1943; ord. titular bp. of Capsus and aux. bp. of San Antonio, July 25, 1983; ret., Mar. 23, 1993.

Potocnak, Joseph J., S.C.J.: b. May 13, 1933, Berwick, PA; educ. Dehon Seminary (Great Barrington, MA), Kilroe Seminary (Honesdale, PA), Sacred Heart (Hales Corners, WI); ord. priest, Sept 21, 1966; missionary in South Africa from 1973; ord. bp. of De Aar, South Africa, May 1, 1992.

Povish, Kenneth J.: b. Apr. 19, 1924, Alpena, MI; educ. St. Joseph's Seminary (Grand Rapids, MI), Sacred Heart Seminary (Detroit, MI), Catholic Univ. (Washington, DC); ord. priest (Saginaw), June 3, 1950; ord. bp. of Crookston, Sept. 29, 1970; app. bp. of Lansing, Oct. 8, 1975, inst., Dec. 11, 1975; ret., Nov. 7, 1995.

Puscas, Vasile Louis: b. Sept. 13, 1915, Aurora, IL; educ. Quigley Preparatory Seminary (Chicago, IL), seminary in Oradea-Mare (Romania), Propaganda Fide Seminary (Rome), Illinois Benedictine College (Lisle, IL); ord. priest (Erie), May 14, 1942; ord. titular bp. of Leuce and first exarch of apostolic exarchate for Byzantine Romanians in the U.S., June 26, 1983 (seat of the exarchate, Canton, OH); app. first eparch, Apr. 11, 1987, when exarchate was raised to eparchy of St. George's in Canton; ret., July 15, 1993.

Q

Quinn, Alexander James: b. Apr. 8, 1932, Cleveland, OH; educ. St. Charles College (Catonsville, MD), St. Mary Seminary (Cleveland, OH), Lateran Univ. (Rome), Cleveland State Univ.; ord. priest (Cleveland), May 24, 1958; ord. titular bp. of Socia and aux. bp. of Cleveland, Dec. 5, 1983.

Quinn, Francis A.: b. Sept. 11, 1921, Los Angeles, CA; educ. St. Joseph's College (Mountain View, CA), St. Patrick's Seminary (Menlo Park, CA), Catholic Univ. (Washington, DC); Univ. of CA (Berkeley); ord. priest (San Francisco*), June 15, 1946; ord. titular bp. of Numana and aux. bp. of San Francisco, June 29, 1978; app. bp. of Sacramento, Dec. 18, 1979; ret., Nov. 30, 1993.

Quinn, John M.: b. Dec. 17, 1945, Detroit; educ. Sacred Heart Seminary, St. John Provincial Seminary, University of Detroit and the Catholic University of America (Washington, D.C.); ord. priest, March 17, 1972; app. aux. bp. of Detroit and titular bishop of Ressiana, July 7, 2003.

Quinn, John R.: b. Mar. 28, 1929, Riverside, CA; educ. St. Francis Seminary (El Cajon, CA), North

American College (Rome); ord. priest (San Diego), July 19, 1953; ord. titular bp. of Thisiduo and aux. bp. of San Diego, Dec. 12, 1967; bp. of Oklahoma City and Tulsa, Nov. 30, 1971; first abp. of Oklahoma City, Dec. 19, 1972; app. abp. of San Francisco, Feb. 22, 1977, inst., Apr. 26, 1977; president NCCB/USCC, 1977-80; res., see Dec. 27, 1995.

R

Ramirez, Ricardo, C.S.B.: b. Sept. 12, 1936, Bay City, TX; educ. Univ. of St. Thomas (Houston, TX), Univ. of Detroit (Detroit, MI), St. Basil's Seminary (Toronto, ON), Seminario Concilium (Mexico City, Mexico), East Asian Pastoral Institute (Manila, Philippines); ord. priest, Dec. 10, 1966; ord titular bp. of Vatarba and aux. of San Antonio, Dec. 6, 1981; app. first bp. of Las Cruces, NM, Aug. 17, 1982; inst., Oct. 18, 1982.

Raya, Joseph M.: b. July 20, 1917, Zahle, Lebanon; educ. St. Louis College (Paris, France), St. Anne's Seminary (Jerusalem); ord. priest, July 20, 1941; came to U.S., 1949, became U.S. citizen; ord. abp. of Acre, Israel, of the Melkites, Oct. 20, 1968; res., Aug. 20, 1974; assigned titular metropolitan see of Scytopolis (resides in Canada).

Reichert, Stephen J., O.F.M. Cap.: b. May 14, 1943, Leoville, KS; educ. Capuchin minor seminary (Victoria, KS), St. Fidelis College (Hermann, PA), Capuchin College (Washington, DC); ord. priest, Sept. 27, 1969; missionary in Papua New Guinea since 1970; ord. bp. of Mendi, Papua New Guinea, May 7, 1995.

Reilly, Daniel P.: b. May 12, 1928, Providence, RI; educ. Our Lady of Providence Seminary (Warwick, RI), St. Brieuc Major Seminary (Cotes du Nord, France); ord. priest (Providence), May 30, 1953; ord. bp. of Norwich, Aug. 6, 1975; app. bp. of Worcester, Oct. 27, 1994, inst., Nov. 8, 1994.

Reiss, Francis R.: b. Nov. 11, 1940, Detroit; educ. Sacred Heart Seminary, St. John Provincial Seminary, University of Detroit, Gregorian University; ord. priest, June 4, 1966; app. aux. bp. of Detroit and titular bishop of Remesiana, July 7, 2003.

Reiss, John C.: b. May 13, 1922, Red Bank, NJ; educ. Catholic Univ. (Washington, DC), Immaculate Conception Seminary (Darlington, NJ); ord. priest (Trenton), May 31, 1947; ord. titular bp. of Simidicca and aux. bp. of Trenton, Dec. 12, 1967; app. bp. of Trenton, Mar. 11, 1980; ret., July 1, 1997.

Riashi, Georges, B.C.O.: b. Nov. 25, 1933, Kaa-el-Rim, Lebanon; ord. priest, Apr. 4, 1965; parish priest of Our Lady of Redemption Parish, Warren, MI (Newton Greek-Catholic Melkite eparchy); U.S. citizen; ord. first bp. of eparchy of St. Michael's of Sydney (Australia) for Greek-Catholic Melkites, July 19, 1987; app. abp. of archeparchy of Tripoli of Lebanon for Greek-Melkites, Aug. 5, 1995.

Ricard, John H., S.S.J.: b. Feb. 29, 1940, Baton Rouge, LA; educ. St. Joseph's Seminary (Washington, DC), Tulane Univ. (New Orleans, LA); ord. priest, May 25, 1968; ord. titular bp. of Rucuma and aux. of Baltimore, July 2, 1984; urban vicar, Baltimore; app. bp. of Pensacola-Tallahassee, Jan 21, 1997.

Ricken, David L.: b. Nov. 9, 1952, Dodge City, Kansas; educ. Conception Seminary College, MO, Univ. of Louvain (Belgium), Pontifical Gregorian Univ., Rome; ord. priest (Pueblo), Sept. 12, 1980; official of the Congregation for the Clergy, 1996-1999;

app. Coadjutor Bishop of Cheyenne, Dec. 14, 1999, ord. bp. by Pope John Paul II at the Vatican, Jan. 6, 2000; bp. of Cheyenne, Sept. 26, 2001.

Rigali, Justin F.: b. Apr. 19, 1935, Los Angeles, CA; educ. St. John's Seminary (Camarillo, CA); ord. priest (Los Angeles*), Apr. 25, 1961; in Vatican diplomatic service from 1964; ord. titular abp. of Bolsena, Sept. 14, 1985, by Pope John Paul II; president of the Pontifical Ecclesiastical Academy, 1985-89; secretary of Congregation for Bps., 1989-94, and the College of Cardinals, 1990-94; app. abp. of St. Louis, Jan. 25, 1994, inst., Mar. 16, 1994; app. abp. of Philadelphia, July 15, 2003.

Rizzotto, Vincent M.: b. Sept. 9, 1931, Houston; educ. St. Mary Seminary (Houston), the Catholic University of America (Washington, D.C.), ord. priest, (Galveston, now Galveston-Houston) May 26, 1956; Vicar General of Galveston-Houston, 1994; app. titular bp. of Lamasba and aux. bp. of Galveston-Houston June 22, 2001, ord., July 31, 2001.

Rodi, Thomas J: b. March 27, 1949, New Orleans; educ. Georgetown University (Washington, D.C.), Tulane University School of Law (New Orleans), Notre Dame Seminary (New Orleans); ord. priest, (New Orleans*), May 20, 1978; app. bp. of Biloxi, May 15, 2001, ord., July 2, 2001.

Rodimer, Frank J.: b. Oct. 25, 1927, Rockaway, NJ; educ. Seton Hall Prep (South Orange, NJ), St. Charles College (Catonsville, MD), St. Mary's Seminary (Baltimore, MD), Immaculate Conception Seminary (Darlington, NJ), Catholic Univ. (Washington, DC); ord. priest (Paterson), May 19, 1951; ord. bp. of Paterson, Feb. 28, 1978.

Rodriguez, Migúel, C.SS.R.: b. Apr. 18, 1931, Mayaguez, P.R.; educ. St. Mary's Minor Seminary (North East, PA), Mt. St. Alphonsus Major Seminary (Esopus, NY); ord. priest, June 22, 1958; ord. bp. of Arecibo, P.R., Mar. 23, 1974; res., Mar. 20, 1990.

Rodriguez, Placido, C.M.F.: b. Oct. 11, 1940, Celaya, Guanajuato, Mexico; educ. Claretian Novitate (Los Angeles, CA), Claretville Seminary College (Calabasas, CA), Catholic Univ. (Washington, DC), Loyola Univ. (Chicago, IL); ord. priest, May 23, 1968; ord. titular bp. of Fuerteventura and aux. bp. of Chicago, Dec. 13, 1983; app. bp. of Lubbock, TX, Apr. 5, 1994.

Roman, Agustin A.: b. May 5, 1928, San Antonio de los Banos, Havana, Cuba; educ. San Alberto Magno Seminary (Matanzas, Cuba), Missions Etrangeres (Montreal, Canada), Barry College (Miami, FL); ord. priest, July 5, 1959, Cuba; vicar for Spanish speaking in Miami archdiocese, 1976; ord. titular bp. of Sertei and aux. bp. of Miami, Mar. 24, 1979; ret., June 7, 2003.

Roque, Francis X.: b. Oct. 9, 1928, Providence RI; educ. St. John's Seminary (Brighton, MA); ord. priest, (Providence) Sept. 19, 1953; became chaplain in U.S. Army 1961; ord. titular bp. of Bagai and aux. bp. of Military Services archdiocese, May 10, 1983.

Rosazza, Peter Anthony: b. Feb. 13, 1935, New Haven, CT; educ. St. Thomas Seminary (Bloomfield, CT), Dartmouth College (Hanover, NH), St. Bernard's Seminary (Rochester, NY), St. Sulpice (Issy, France); ord. priest (Hartford*), June 29, 1961; ord. titular bp. of Oppido Nuovo and aux. bp. of Hartford, June 24, 1978.

Rose, Robert John: b. Feb. 28, 1930, Grand Rap-

ids, MI; educ. St. Joseph's Seminary (Grand Rapids, MI), Seminaire de Philosophie (Montreal, Canada), Urban University (Rome), Univ. of Michigan (Ann Arbor); ord. priest (Grand Rapids), Dec. 21, 1955; ord. bp. of Gaylord, Dec. 6, 1981; app. bp. of Grand Rapids, inst., Aug. 30, 1989.

Rueger, George E.: b. Sept. 3, 1933, Framingham, Mass; educ. Holy Cross College (Worcester, MA), St. John's Seminary (Brighton), Harvard University (Cambridge, MA); ord. priest (Worcester), Jan. 6, 1958; ord. titular bp. of Maronana and aux. bp. of Worcester, Feb. 25, 1987.

Ryan, Daniel L.: b. Sept. 28, 1930, Mankato, MN; educ. St. Procopius Seminary (Lisle, IL), Lateran Univ. (Rome); ord. priest (Joliet), May 3, 1956; ord. titular bp. of Surista and aux. bp. of Joliet, Sept. 30, 1981; app. bp. of Springfield, IL, Nov. 22, 1983, inst., Jan. 18, 1984; res. Oct. ,19, 1999.

Ryan, Sylvester D.: b. May 3, 1930, Catalina Is., CA; educ. St. John's Seminary (Camarillo, CA); ord. priest (Los Angeles*), May 3, 1957; ord. titular bp. of Remesiana and aux. bp. of Los Angeles, May 31, 1990; app. bp. of Monterey, Jan. 28, 1992.

S

Saltarelli, Michael A.: b. Jan. 17, 1932, Jersey City, NJ; educ. Seton Hall College and Immaculate Conception Seminary (S. Orange, NJ); ord. priest (Newark*), May 28, 1960; ord. titular bp. of Mesarfelta and aux. bp. of Newark, July 30, 1990; app. bp. of Wilmington, Nov. 21, 1995; inst., Jan. 23, 1996.

Samra, Nicholas J.: b. Aug. 15, 1944, Paterson, NJ; educ. St. Anselm College (Manchester, NH), St. Basil Seminary (Methuen, MA), St. John Seminary (Brighton, MA); ord. priest (Newton) May 10, 1970; ord. titular bp. of Gerasa and aux. bp. of Melkite diocese of Newton, July 6, 1989.

Sanchez, Robert F.: b. Mar. 20, 1934, Socorro, NM; educ. Immaculate Heart Seminary (Santa Fe, NM), Gregorian Univ. (Rome), Catholic Univ. (Washington, DC); ord. priest (Santa Fe*), Dec 20, 1959; ord. abp. of Santa Fe, NM, July 25, 1974; res., Apr. 6, 1993.

Sartain, James P.: b. June 6, 1952, Memphis, TN; educ. St. Meinrad Seminary, (Indiana), North American College, (Rome), Pontifical University of St. Thomas (the Angelicum), Pontifical Institute of St. Anselm (Rome); ord. priest (Memphis), July 15, 1978; app. bp. of Little Rock, Jan. 4, 2000, ord., March 6, 2000.

Sartoris, Joseph M.: b. July 1, 1927, Los Angeles, CA; educ. St. John's Seminary (Camarillo, CA); ord. priest (Los Angeles*), May 30, 1953; ord. titular bp. of Oliva and aux. bp. of Los Angeles, Mar. 19, 1994; ret., Dec. 31, 2002.

Scarpone Caporale, Gerald, O.F.M.: b. Oct. 1, 1928, Watertown, MA; ord. priest, June 24, 1956; ord. coadjutor bp. of Comayagua, Honduras, Feb. 21, 1979; succeeded as bp. of Comayagua, May 30, 1979.

Schlarman, Stanley Gerard: b. July 27, 1933, Belleville, IL; educ. St. Henry Prep Seminary (Belleville, IL), Gregorian Univ. (Rome), St. Louis Univ. (St. Louis, MO); ord. priest (Belleville), July 13, 1958, Rome; ord. titular bp. of Capri and aux. bp. of Belleville, May 14, 1979; app. bp. of Dodge City, Mar. 1, 1983; res., May 12, 1998.

Schleck, Charles A., C.S.C.: b. July 5, 1925, Milwaukee, WI; educ. Univ. of Notre Dame (IN), Pontifical Univ. of St. Thomas (Rome); ord. priest, Dec. 22, 1951; ord. titular abp. of Africa (Mehdia), Apr. 1, 1995; adjunct secretary of Congregation for Evangelization of Peoples; president of the superior council of the Pontifical Mission Societies.

Schmidt, Firmin M., O.F.M. Cap.: b. Oct. 12, 1918, Catherine, KS; educ. Catholic Univ. (Washington, DC); ord. priest, June 2, 1946; app. prefect apostolic of Mendi, Papua New Guinea, Apr. 3, 1959; ord. titular bp. of Conana and first vicar apostolic of Mendi, Dec.15, 1965; became first bp. of Mendi when vicariate apostolic was raised to a diocese, Nov. 15, 1966; ret., Feb. 22, 1995.

Schmitt, Bernard W.: b. Aug. 17, 1928, Wheeling, WV; educ. St. Joseph College (Catonsville, MD), St. Mary's Seminary (Baltimore), Ohio Univ. (Athens, OH); ord. priest (Wheeling-Charleston), May 28, 1955; ord. titular bp. of Walla Walla and bp. of Wheeling-Charleston, Aug. 1, 1988; bp. of Wheeling-Charleston, Mar. 29, 1989.

Schmitt, Mark F.: b. Feb. 14, 1923, Algoma, WI; educ. Salvatorian Seminary (St. Nazianz, WI), St. John's Seminary (Collegeville, MN); ord. priest (Green Bay), May 22, 1948; ord. titular bp. of Ceanannus Mor and aux. bp. of Green Bay, June 24, 1970; app. bp. of Marquette, Mar. 21, 1978, inst., May 8, 1978; ret., Oct. 6, 1992.

Schmitz Simon, Paul, O.F.M. Cap.: b. Dec. 4, 1943, Fond du Lac, WI; ord. priest, Sept. 3, 1970; missionary in Nicaragua from 1970; superior of vice province of Capuchins in Central America (headquartered in Managua), 1982-84; ord. titular bp. of Elepla and aux. of the vicariate apostolic of Bluefields, Nicaragua, Sept. 17, 1984; app. bp. of vicariate apostolic of Bluefields, Aug. 17, 1994.

Schnurr, Dennis M.: b. June 21, 1948, Sheldon, Iowa; educ. Loras College (Dubuque), Gregorian University (Rome), Catholic University of America (Washington, DC); ord. priest (Sioux City), July 20, 1974; Staff, Apostolic Nunciature, Washington, DC, 1985-1989; Associate General Secretary, National Conference of Catholic Bishops/United States Catholic Conference (NCCB/USCC), 1989-1995; National Executive Director, World Youth Day 1993, Denver, 1991-1993; General Secretary, NCCB/USCC, 1995-2001; app. bp. of Duluth, Jan. 18, 2001, ord., Apr. 2, 2001.

Schoenherr, Walter J.: b. Feb. 28, 1920, Detroit, MI; educ. Sacred Heart Seminary (Detroit, MI), Mt. St. Mary Seminary (Norwood, OH); ord. priest (Detroit*), Oct. 27, 1945; ord. titular bp. of Timidana and aux. bp. of Detroit, May 1, 1968; ret., Mar. 7, 1995.

Schott, Basil, O.F.M.: b. July 21, 1939, Freeland, PA; entered Byzantine Franciscans, professed Aug. 4, 1959; educ. Immaculate Conception College (Troy, NY), St. Mary's Seminary (Norwalk, CT) and Post Graduate Center (New York, NY); ord. priest, Aug. 29, 1965; ord. bp. of Byzantine eparchy of Parma, July 11, 1996; app. metropolitan abp. of Pittsburgh (Byzantine Ruthenian), May 3, 2002.

Schulte, Francis B.: b. Dec. 23, 1926, Philadelphia, PA; educ. St. Charles Borromeo Seminary (Overbrook, PA); ord. priest (Philadelphia*), May 10, 1952; ord. titular bp. of Afufenia and aux. bp. of Philadelphia, Aug. 12, 1981; app. bp. of Wheeling-Charleston, June 4, 1985; abp. of New Orleans, Dec. 6, 1988, inst., Feb. 14, 1989; ret., Jan. 3, 2002.

Schwietz, Roger L., O.M.I.: b. July 3, 1940, St. Paul, MN; educ. Univ. of Ottawa (Canada), Gregorian Univ. (Rome); ord. priest, Dec. 20, 1967; ord. bp. of Duluth Feb. 2, 1990; bp. of Duluth, 1990-2000; coadj. abp. of Anchorage, Jan. 18, 2000; abp. of Anchorage, March 3, 2001.

Seminack, Richard: b. March 3, 1942, Philadelphia; educ. St. Basil Seminary College (Stamford, Conn.), St. Josaphat Major Seminary and Catholic University of America (Washington), Oriental Institute (Rome); ord. priest, May 25, 1967 (archeparchy of Philadelphia); incard. Eparchy of St. Josaphat (Parma) 1983; app. bp. of St. Nicholas of Chicago for Ukrainians, March 25, 2003; ord., June 4, 2003.

Serratelli, Arthur J.: b. April 18, 1944, Newark, NJ; educ. Seton Preparatory School (NJ), Seton Hall University (NJ), North American College and Gregorian University (Rome), Pontifical Biblical Institute (Rome); ord. priest (Newark*), Dec. 20, 1968; prof. of Sacred Scripture, Immaculate Conception Seminary; rector of the College Seminary, Seton Hall University; prelate of honor, 1998; app. titular bp. of Enera and aux. bp. of Newark, July 3, 2000.

Sevilla, Carlos A., S.J.: b. Aug. 9, 1935, San Francisco, CA; entered Jesuits Aug. 14, 1953; educ. Gonzaga Univ. (Spokane, WA), Santa Clara Univ. (Santa Clara, CA), Jesuitenkolleg (Innsbruck, Austria), Catholic Institute of Paris (France); ord. priest, June 3, 1966; ord. titular bp. of Mina and aux. bp. of San Francisco, Jan. 25, 1989; bp. of Yakima, Dec. 31, 1996.

Shaheen, Robert J.: b. June 3, 1937, Danbury, Conn.; ord., May 2, 1964; elected eparch of Our Lady of Lebanon of Los Angeles of the Maronites (U.S.A.), Dec. 5, 2000.

Sheehan, Michael J.: b. July 9, 1939, Wichita, KS; educ. Assumption Seminary (San Antonio, TX), Gregorian Univ. and Lateran Univ. (Rome); ord. priest (Dallas), July 12, 1964; ord. first bp. of Lubbock, TX, June 17, 1983; apostolic administrator of Santa Fe, Apr. 6, 1993; app. abp. of Santa Fe, Aug. 17, 1993.

Sheldon, Gilbert I.: b. Sept. 20, 1926, Cleveland, OH; educ. John Carroll Univ. and St. Mary Seminary (Cleveland, OH); ord. priest (Cleveland), Feb. 28, 1953; ord. titular bp. of Taparura and aux. bp. of Cleveland, June 11, 1976; app. bp. of Steubenville, Jan. 28, 1992, ret., May 31, 2002.

Sheridan, Michael J.: b. Mar. 4, 1945, St. Louis, MO; educ. Glennon College, Kenrick Seminary (St. Louis, MO), Angelicum (Rome); ord. priest (St. Louis*), 1971; app. titular bp. of Thibiuca and aux. bp. of St. Louis, July 9, 1997; co-adjutor bp. of Colorado Springs, Dec. 4, 2001; bp. of Colorado Springs, Jan. 30, 2003.

Sheridan, Patrick J.: b. Mar. 10, 1922, New York, NY; educ. St. Joseph's Seminary (Yonkers, NY), University of Chicago; ord. priest (New York*), Mar. 1, 1947; ord. titular bp. of Curzola and aux. bp. of New York, Dec. 12, 1990; res., Jan.15, 2001.

Sklba, Richard J.: b. Sept. 11, 1935, Racine, WI; educ. Old St. Francis Minor Seminary (Milwaukee, WI), North American College, Gregorian Univ., Pontifical Biblical Institute, Angelicum (Rome); ord. priest (Milwaukee*), Dec. 20, 1959; ord. titular bp. of Castra and aux. bp. of Milwaukee, Dec. 19, 1979.

Skurla, William C.: b. June 1, 1956, Duluth; educ. Columbia Univ., New York, Mary Immaculate Seminary, Northhampton, PA; ord. priest (Franciscan), 1987; incardinated into Eparchy of Van Nuys, 1996; app. bp. of Van Nuys Byzantine Catholic Eparchy in California, Feb. 19, 2002.

Skylstad, William S.: b. Mar. 2, 1934, Omak, WA; educ. Pontifical College Josephinum (Worthington, OH), Washington State Univ. (Pullman, WA), Gonzaga Univ. (Spokane, WA); ord. priest (Spokane), May 21, 1960; ord. bp. of Yakima, May 12, 1977; app. bp. of Spokane, Apr. 17, 1990; vice-pres. of USCCB, 2001-.

Slattery, Edward J.: b. Aug. 11, 1940, Chicago, IL; educ. Quigley Preparatory, St. Mary of the Lake Seminary (Mundelein, IL), Loyola Univ. (Chicago); ord. priest (Chicago*), Apr. 26, 1966; vice president, 1971-76, and president, 1976-94, of the Catholic Church Extension Society; ord. bp. of Tulsa, Jan. 6, 1994.

Smith, John M.: b. June 23, 1935, Orange, NJ; educ. Immaculate Conception Seminary (Darlington, NJ), Seton Hall Univ. (South Orange, NJ), Catholic Univ. (Washington, DC); ord. priest (Newark*), May 27, 1961; ord. titular bp. of Tre Taverne and aux. bp. of Newark, Jan. 25, 1988; app. bp. of Pensacola-Tallahassee, FL, June 25, 1991; app. coadjutor bp. of Trenton, Nov. 21, 1995; bp. of Trenton, July 1, 1997.

Snyder, John J.: b. Oct. 25, 1925, New York, NY; educ. Cathedral College (Brooklyn, NY), Immaculate Conception Seminary (Huntington, NY); ord. priest (Brooklyn), June 9, 1951; ord. titular bp. of Forlimpopli and aux. bp. of Brooklyn, Feb. 2, 1973; app. bp. of St. Aug.ine, inst., Dec. 5, 1979; res., Dec. 11, 2000.

Soens, Lawrence D.: b. Aug. 26, 1926, Iowa City, IA; educ. Loras College (Dubuque, IA), St. Ambrose College (Davenport, IA), Kenrick Seminary (St. Louis, MO), Univ. of Iowa; ord. priest (Davenport), May 6, 1950; ord. bp. of Sioux City, Aug. 17, 1983, res., Nov. 28, 1998.

Soroka, Stephen: b. Nov. 13, 1951, Winnipeg, Manitoba; educ. Univ. of Manitoba, Ukrainian Seminary, Washington, DC, Catholic Univ. of America, ordained (Ukrainian Archdiocese of Winnipeg*), June 13, 1982; Chancellor and financial administrator of the Winnipeg archdiocese, 1994, auxiliary bishop, Winnipeg, 1996; metropolitan abp. of Philadelphia for the Ukrainians, Nov. 29, 2000; inst., Feb. 27, 2001.

Soto, Jaime: b. Dec. 31, 1955, Inglewood, CA; educ. St. John's Seminary, Camarillo, CA, Columbia University School of Social Work, New York; ord. priest (Orange), June 12, 1982; Episcopal Vicar for Hispanic Ministry, 1989; app. titular bp. of Segia and aux. bp. of Orange, Mar. 23, 2000, ord., May 31, 2000.

Sowada, Alphonse A., O.S.C.: b. June 23, 1933, Avon, MN; educ. Holy Cross Scholasticate (Fort Wayne, IN), Catholic Univ. (Washington, DC), ord. priest, May 31, 1958; missionary in Indonesia from 1958; ord. bp. of Agats, Indonesia, Nov. 23, 1969.

Speltz, George H.: b. May 29, 1912, Altura, MN; educ. St. Mary's College, St. Paul's Seminary (St. Paul, MN), Catholic Univ. (Washington, DC); ord. priest (St. Cloud), June 2, 1940; ord. titular bp. of Claneus and aux. bp. of Winona, Mar. 25, 1963; app. coadjutor bp. of St. Cloud, Apr. 4, 1966; bp. of St. Cloud, Jan. 31, 1968; ret., Jan. 13, 1987.

Speyrer, Jude: b. Apr. 14, 1929, Leonville, LA; educ. St. Joseph Seminary (Covington, LA), Notre Dame Seminary (New Orleans, LA), Gregorian Univ. (Rome), Univ. of Fribourg (Switzerland); ord. priest (Lafayette, LA), July 25, 1953; ord. first bp. of Lake Charles, LA, Apr. 25, 1980; res., Dec. 11, 2000.

Stafford, James Francis: (*See* **Cardinals, Biographies**).

Steib, J. (James) Terry, S.V.D.: b. May 17, 1940, Vacherie, LA; educ. Divine Word seminaries (Bay St. Louis, MS, Conesus, NY, Techny, IL), Xavier Univ. (New Orleans, LA); ord. priest, Jan. 6, 1967; ord. titular bp. of Fallaba and aux. bp. of St. Louis, Feb. 10, 1984; app. bp. of Memphis, Mar. 24, 1993.

Steinbock, John T.: b. July 16, 1937, Los Angeles, CA; educ. Los Angeles archdiocesan seminaries; ord. priest (Los Angeles*), May 1, 1963; ord. titular bp. of Midila and aux. bp. of Orange, CA, July 14, 1984; app. bp. of Santa Rosa, Jan. 27, 1987; app. bp. of Fresno, Oct. 15, 1991.

Steiner, Kenneth Donald: b. Nov. 25, 1936, David City, NE; educ. Mt. Angel Seminary (St. Benedict, OR), St. Thomas Seminary (Seattle, Wash); ord. priest (Portland,* OR), May 19, 1962; ord. titular bp. of Avensa and aux. bp. of Portland, OR, Mar. 2, 1978.

Straling, Phillip F.: b. Apr. 25, 1933, San Bernardino, CA; educ. Immaculate Heart Seminary, St. Francis Seminary, Univ. of San Diego and San Diego State University (San Diego, CA), North American College (Rome); ord. priest (San Diego), Mar. 19, 1959; ord. first bp. of San Bernardino, Nov. 6, 1978; app. first bp. of Reno, Mar. 21, 1995, when Reno-Las Vegas diocese was made two separate dioceses.

Strecker, Ignatius J.: b. Nov. 23, 1917, Spearville, KS; educ. St. Benedict's College (Atchison, KS), Kenrick Seminary (Webster Groves, MO), Catholic Univ. (Washington, DC); ord. priest (Wichita), Dec. 19, 1942; ord. bp. of Springfield-Cape Girardeau, MO, June 20, 1962; abp. of Kansas City, KS, Oct. 28, 1969; ret., June 28, 1993.

Sullivan, James S.: b. July 23, 1929, Kalamazoo, MI; educ. Sacred Heart Seminary (Detroit, MI), St. John Provincial Seminary (Plymouth, MI); ord. priest (Lansing), June 4, 1955; ord. titular bp. of Siccessi and aux. bp. of Lansing, Sept. 21, 1972; app. bp. of Fargo, Apr. 2, 1985; inst., May 30, 1985; ret., March 19, 2002.

Sullivan, Joseph M.: b. Mar. 23, 1930, Brooklyn, NY; educ. Immaculate Conception Seminary (Huntington, NY), Fordham Univ. (New York); ord. priest (Brooklyn), June 2, 1956; ord. titular bp. of Suliana and aux. bp. of Brooklyn, Nov. 24, 1980.

Sullivan, Walter F.: b. June 10, 1928, Washington, DC; educ. St. Mary's Seminary (Baltimore, MD), Catholic Univ. (Washington, DC); ord. priest (Richmond), May 9, 1953; ord. titular bp. of Selsea and aux. bp. of Richmond, VA, Dec. 1, 1970; app. bp. of Richmond, June 4, 1974.

Sulyk, Stephen: b. Oct. 2, 1924, Balnycia, Western Ukraine; migrated to U.S. 1948; educ. Ukrainian Catholic Seminary of the Holy Spirit (Hirschberg, Germany), St. Josaphat's Seminary and Catholic Univ. (Washington, DC); ord. priest (Philadelphia,* Byzantine), June 14, 1952; ord. abp. of the Ukrainian archeparchy of Philadelphia, Mar. 1, 1981; res., Nov. 29, 2000.

Symons, J. Keith: b. Oct. 14, 1932, Champion, MI; educ. St. Thomas Seminary (Bloomfield, CT), St. Mary Seminary (Baltimore, MD); ord. priest (St.

Augustine), May 18, 1958; ord. titular bp. of Siguitanus and aux. bp. of St. Petersburg, Mar. 19, 1981; app. bp. of Pensacola-Tallahassee, Oct. 4, 1983, inst., Nov. 8, 1983; app. bp. of Palm Beach, June 12, 1990; res., June 2, 1998.

Szoka, Edmund C.: (*See* **Cardinals, Biographies.**)

T

Tafoya, Arthur N.: b. Mar. 2, 1933, Alameda, NM; educ. St. Thomas Seminary (Denver, CO), Conception Seminary (Conception, MO); ord. priest (Santa Fe*), May 12, 1962; ord. bp. of Pueblo, Sept. 10, 1980.

Tamayo, James A.: b. Oct. 23, 1949, Brownsville, TX; educ. Del Mar College (Corpus Christi, TX), Univ. of St. Thomas and Univ. of St. Thomas School of Theology (Houston); ord. priest (Corpus Christi), June 11, 1976; ord. titular bp. of Ita and aux. bp. of Galveston-Houston, Mar. 10, 1993; app. first bp. of Laredo, TX, July 3, 2000, ins., Aug. 9, 2000.

Thomas, Elliott G.: b. July 15, 1926, Pittsburgh, PA; educ. Howard Univ. (Washington, DC), Gannon Univ. (Erie, PA), St. Vincent de Paul Seminary (Boynton Beach, FL); ord. priest (St. Thomas, Virgin Islands), June 6, 1986; ord. bp. of St. Thomas in the Virgin Islands, Dec. 12, 1993; res., June 30, 1999.

Thomas, George L.: b. May 19, 1950, Anaconda, MT, educ. St. Thomas Seminary, Seattle, Univ. of Washington, Seattle; ord. priest (Seattle*), May 22, 1976; chancellor and vicar general, 1988-1999, diocesan administrator of Seattle, 1996-1997; app. titular bp. of Vagrauta and aux. bp. of Seattle, Nov. 19, 1999, inst., Jan. 28, 2000.

Thompson, David B.: b. May 29, 1923, Philadelphia, PA; educ. St. Charles Seminary (Overbrook, PA), Catholic Univ. (Washington, DC); ord. priest (Philadelphia*), May 27, 1950; ord. coadjutor bp. of Charleston, May 24, 1989; bp. of Charleston, Feb. 22, 1990; res., July 13, 1999

Timlin, James C.: b. Aug. 5, 1927, Scranton, PA; educ. St. Charles College (Catonville, MD), St. Mary's Seminary (Baltimore, MD), North American College (Rome); ord. priest (Scranton), July 16, 1951; ord. titular bp. of Gunugo and aux. bp. of Scranton, Sept. 21, 1976; app. bp. of Scranton, Apr. 24, 1984; ret., July 25, 2003.

Tobin, Thomas J.: b. Apr. 1, 1948, Pittsburgh, PA; educ. St. Mark Seminary High School, Gannon Univ. (Erie, PA), St. Francis College (Loretto, PA), North American College (Rome); ord. priest (Pittsburgh), July 21, 1973; ord. titular bp. of Novica and aux. bp. of Pittsburgh, Dec. 27, 1992; app. bp. of Youngstown Dec. 5, 1995; inst., Feb. 2, 1996.

Trautman, Donald W.: b. June 24, 1936, Buffalo, NY; educ. Our Lady of Angels Seminary (Niagara Falls, NY), Theology Faculty (Innsbruck, Austria), Pontifical Biblical Institute (Rome), Catholic Univ. (Washington, DC); ord. priest (Buffalo), Apr. 7, 1962, in Innsbruck; ord. titular bp. of Sassura and aux. of Buffalo, Apr. 16, 1985; app. bp. of Erie, June 12, 1990.

Tschoepe, Thomas: b. Dec. 17, 1915, Pilot Point, TX; educ. Pontifical College Josephinum (Worthington, OH); ord. priest (Dallas), May 30, 1943; ord. bp. of San Angelo, TX, Mar. 9, 1966; app. bp. of Dallas, TX, Aug. 27, 1969; ret., July 14, 1990.

Turley Murphy, Daniel T., O.S.A.: b. Jan. 25, 1943, Chicago, IL; ord. priest, Dec. 21, 1961; ord. coadjutor bp. of Chulucanas, Peru, Aug. 17, 1996.

U-V

Untener, Kenneth E.: b. Aug. 3, 1937, Detroit, MI; educ. Sacred Heart Seminary (Detroit, MI), St. John's Provincial Seminary (Plymouth, MI), Gregorian Univ. (Rome); ord. priest (Detroit*), June 1, 1963; ord. bp. of Saginaw, Nov. 24, 1980.

Valero, René A.: b. Aug. 15, 1930, New York, NY; educ. Cathedral College, Immaculate Conception Seminary (Huntington, NY), Fordham Univ. (New York); ord. priest (Brooklyn), June 2, 1956; ord. titular bp. of Turris Vicus and aux. bp. of Brooklyn, Nov. 24, 1980.

Vasa, Robert F.: b. May 7, 1951, Lincoln, NE, educ. St. Thomas Seminary, Denver, Holy Trinity Seminary, Dallas, Pontifical Gregorian Univ. (Rome, Italy); ord. priest (Lincoln), May 22,1976; Vicar General and Moderator of the Curia, 1996; app. bp. of Baker, OR Nov. 19, 1999, inst., Jan. 26, 2000.

Vasquez, José S.: b. July 9, 1957, Stamford, Texas; educ. St. Mary Seminary, Houston, University of St. Thomas, North American College and Pontifical Gregorian University (Rome); ord. priest (San Angelo), June 30, 1984; app. titular bp. of Cova and aux. of Galveston-Houston, Nov. 30, 2001, ord., Jan. 23, 2002.

Veigle, Adrian J.M., T.O.R.: b. Sept. 15, 1912, Lilly, PA; educ. St. Francis College (Loretto, PA), Pennsylvania State College; ord. priest, May 22, 1937; ord. titular bp. of Gigthi, June 9, 1966 (res., titular see May 26, 1978); prelate of Borba, Brazil, 1966; ret., July 6, 1988.

Vigneron, Allen H.: b. Oct. 21, 1948, Detroit, MI; educ. Sacred Heart Seminary (Detroit, MI), North American College, Gregorian Univ. (Rome), Catholic Univ.(Washington, DC); ord. priest (Detroit*), July 26, 1975; served in Vatican Secretariat of State, 1991-94; rector of Sacred Heart Seminary (Detroit), 1994; ord. titular bp. of Sault Sainte Marie and aux. bp. of Detroit, July 9, 1996; app. coadjutor bp. of Oakland, Jan. 10, 2003.

Vlazny, John G.: b. Feb. 22, 1937, Chicago, IL; educ. Quigley Preparatory Seminary (Chicago, IL), St. Mary of the Lake Seminary (Mundelein, IL), Gregorian Univ. (Rome), Univ. of Michigan, Loyola Univ. (Chicago, IL); ord. priest (Chicago*), Dec. 20, 1961; ord. titular bp. of Stagno and aux. bp. of Chicago, Dec. 13, 1983; app. bp. of Winona, MN, May 19, 1987; app. abp. of Portland in Oregon, Oct. 28, 1997, inst., Dec. 19, 1997.

W

Walsh, Daniel Francis: b. Oct. 2, 1937, San Francisco, CA; educ. St. Joseph Seminary (Mountain View, CA), St. Patrick Seminary (Menlo Park, CA) Catholic Univ. (Washington, DC); ord. priest (San Francisco*), Mar. 30, 1963; ord. titular bp. of Tigia and aux. bp. of San Francisco, Sept. 24, 1981; app. bp. of Reno-Las Vegas, June 9, 1987; app. first bp. of Las Vegas, Mar. 21, 1995, when the Reno-Las Vegas diocese was made two separate dioceses; app. bp. Santa Rosa, Apr. 11, 2000.

Walsh, Paul H.: b. Aug. 17, 1937, Brooklyn; educ. Providence College (R.I.), St. Stephen's College (Dover, MA), Dominican House of Studies (Washington); ord. Dominican, June 9, 1966; incard. Rockville Centre Dec. 13, 1984; app. aux. bp. of Rockville Centre and titular bishop of Abtugni, April 3, 2003; ord. bp., May 29, 2003.

Wang, Ignatius: b. Feb. 27, 1934, Beijing, China; educ. Urbanian Univ. and Gregorian Univ. (Rome); ord. priest (for apostolic vicariate in southern China) July 4, 1959; unable to return home, he served in the Antilles and transferred to San Francisco in 1974; auxiliary bishop of San Francisco and titular bishop of Sitipa, Dec. 13, 2002; ord., Jan. 30, 2003.

Ward, John J.: b. Sept. 28, 1920, Los Angeles, CA; educ. St. John's Seminary (Camarillo, CA), Catholic Univ. (Washington, DC); ord. priest (Los Angeles*), May 4, 1946; ord. titular bp. of Bria and aux. of Los Angeles, Dec. 12, 1963; ret., May 7, 1996; titular bp. of CA.

Warfel, Michael William: b. Sept 16, 1948, Elkhart, IN; educ. Indiana Univ, St. Gregory's College Seminary, Mt. St. Mary's Seminary of the West (Cincinnati, OH); ord. priest, Apr. 26, 1980; ord. bp. of Juneau, Dec. 17, 1996.

Watters, Loras J.: b. Oct. 14, 1915, Dubuque, IA; educ. Loras College (Dubuque, IA), Gregorian Univ. (Rome), Catholic Univ. (Washington, DC); ord. priest (Dubuque*), June 7, 1941; ord. titular bp. of Fidoloma and aux. bp. of Dubuque, Aug. 26, 1965; bp. of Winona, inst., Mar. 13, 1969; ret., Oct. 14, 1986.

Watty Urquidi, Ricardo, M.Sp.S.: b. July 16, 1938, San Diego, CA; ord. priest, June 8, 1968; ord. titular bp. of Macomedes and aux. bp. of Mexico City, July 19, 1980; app. first bp. of Nuevo Laredo, Mexico, Nov. 6, 1989.

Wcela, Emil A.: b. May 1, 1931, Bohemia, NY; educ. St. Francis College (Brooklyn, NY), Immaculate Conception Seminary (Huntington, NY), Catholic Univ. (Washington, DC), Pontifical Biblical Institute (Rome, Italy); ord. priest (Brooklyn), June 2, 1956; ord. titular bp. of Filaca and aux. bp. of Rockville Centre, Dec. 13, 1988.

Weakland, Rembert G., O.S.B.: b. Apr. 2, 1927, Patton, PA; joined Benedictines, 1945; ord. priest, June 24, 1951; abbot-primate of Benedictine Confederation, 1967-77; ord. abp. of Milwaukee, Nov. 8, 1977; res., May 24, 2002.

Weigand, William K.: b. May 23, 1937, Bend, OR; educ. Mt. Angel Seminary (St. Benedict, OR), St. Edward's Seminary and St. Thomas Seminary (Kenmore, WA); ord. priest (Boise), May 25, 1963; ord. bp. of Salt Lake City, Nov. 17, 1980; app. bp. of Sacramento, Nov. 30, 1993, inst., Jan. 27, 1994.

Weitzel, John Quinn, M.M.: b. May 10, 1928, Chicago, IL; educ. Maryknoll Seminary (Maryknoll, NY); ord. priest, Nov. 5, 1955; missionary to Samoa, 1979; ord. bp. of Samoa-Pago Pago, American Samoa, Dec. 29, 1986.

Welsh, Thomas J.: b. Dec. 20, 1921, Weatherly, PA; educ. St. Charles Borromeo Seminary (Philadelphia, PA), Catholic Univ. (Washington, DC); ord. priest (Philadelphia*), May 30, 1946; ord. titular bp. of Scattery Island and aux. bp. of Philadelphia, Apr. 2, 1970; app. first bp. of Arlington, VA, June 4, 1974; app. bp. of Allentown, Feb. 8, 1983, inst., Mar. 21, 1983; ret.,: Dec. 16, 1997.

Wenski, Thomas G.: b. Oct. 18, 1950, West Palm Beach, FL; educ. St. John Vianney College Seminary, St. Vincent de Paul Regional Seminary, Fordham Univ.; ord. priest (Miami*), May 15, 1976; director of Miami Haitian Apostolate; app. titular bp. of Kearney and aux. of Miami, June 24, 1997; app. coadjutor bp. of Orlando, July 1, 2003.

Wester, John Charles: b. Nov. 5, 1950, San Francisco; educ. St. John's Seminary, Camarillo, CA, St. Patrick's Seminary, Menlo Park, CA, Univ. of San Francisco; ord. priest (San Francisco*), May 15, 1976; app. titular bp. of Lamiggiga and aux. bp. of San Francisco, June 30, 1998.

Wilkerson, Gerald E.: b. Oct. 21, 1939, Des Moines, IA; educ. St. John's Seminary (Camarillo, CA); ord. priest (Los Angeles*), Jan. 5, 1965; app. Titular Bp. of Vincennes and aux. bp. of Los Angeles, Nov. 5, 1997, ord., Jan. 21, 1998.

Williams, James Kendrick: b. Sept. 5, 1936, Athertonville, KY; educ. St. Mary's College (St. Mary's, KY), St. Maur's School of Theology (South Union, KY); ord. priest (Louisville*), May 25, 1963; ord. titular bp. of Catula and aux. bp. of Covington, June 19, 1984; first bp. of Lexington, KY, inst., Mar. 2, 1988; res., June 11, 2002.

Winter, William J.: b. May 20, 1930, Pittsburgh, PA; educ. St. Vincent College and Seminary (Latrobe, PA), Gregorian Univ. (Rome, Italy); ord. priest (Pittsburgh), Dec. 17, 1955; ord. titular bp. of Uthina and aux. bp. of Pittsburgh, Feb. 13, 1989.

Wirz, George O.: b. Jan. 17, 1929, Monroe, WI; educ. St. Francis Seminary and Marquette Univ. (Milwaukee, WI); Cath. Univ. (Washington, DC); ord. priest (Madison), May 31, 1952; ord. titular bp. of Municipa and aux. bp. of Madison, Mar. 9, 1978.

Wiwchar, Michael, C.SS.R.: b. May 9, 1932, Komarno, Manitoba, Can.; educ. Redemptorist Seminary (Windsor, Ontario); made solemn vows as Redemptorist, 1956; ord. priest, June 28, 1959; pastor St. John the Baptist Parish, Newark, NJ, 1990-93; ord. bp. of St. Nicholas of Chicago for the Ukrainians, Sept. 28, 1993; bp. of Saskatoon of Ukrainians, Nov. 29, 2000.

Wuerl, Donald W.: b. Nov. 12, 1940, Pittsburgh, PA; educ. Catholic Univ. (Washington, DC), North American College, Angelicum (Rome); ord. priest (Pittsburgh), Dec. 17, 1966, in Rome; ord. titular bp. of Rosemarkie Jan. 6, 1986, in Rome; aux. bp. of Seattle, 1986-87; app. bp. of Pittsburgh, Feb. 11, 1988, inst., Mar. 25, 1988.

Wycislo, Aloysius John: b. June 17, 1908, Chicago, IL; educ. St. Mary's Seminary (Mundelein, IL), Catholic Univ. (Washington, DC); ord. priest (Chicago*), Apr. 4, 1934; ord. titular bp. of Stadia and aux. bp. of Chicago, Dec. 21, 1960; app. bp. of Green Bay, inst., Apr. 16, 1968; res., May 10, 1983.

Y-Z

Yanta, John W.: b. Oct. 2, 1931, Runge, TX; educ. St. John's Preparatory Seminary and Assumption Seminary (San Antonio); ord. priest (San Antonio*), Mar. 17, 1956; ord. titular bp. of Naratcata and aux. bp. of San Antonio, Dec. 30, 1994; app. bp. of Amarillo, Jan. 21,1997, inst., Mar. 17, 1997.

Younan, Joseph: b. Nov. 15, 1944, Hassakeh, Syria; educ. Our Lady of Deliverance Seminary (Charfet, Lebanon), Pontifical College of the Propagation of the Faith (Rome); ord. priest, Sept. 12, 1971; came to U.S., 1986; served Syrian Catholics in U.S.; ord. first bp. Our Lady of Deliverance of Newark for Syrian Catholics in the U.S. and Canada, Jan. 7, 1996, in Kamisly, Syria.

Zavala, Gabino: b. Sept. 7, 1951, Guerrero, Mexico; became U.S. citizen, 1976; educ. St. John's Seminary

(Los Angeles), Catholic Univ. (Washington, DC); ord. priest (Los Angeles*), May 28, 1977; ord. titular bp. of Tamascani and aux. bp. of Los Angeles, Mar. 19, 1994.

Zayek, Francis: b. Oct. 18, 1920, Manzanillo, Cuba; ord. priest, Mar. 17, 1946; ord. titular bp. of Callinicum and aux. bp. for Maronites in Brazil, Aug. 5, 1962; named apostolic exarch for Maronites in U.S., with headquarters in Detroit; inst., June 11. 1966; first eparch of St. Maron of Detroit, Mar. 25, 1972; see transferred to Brooklyn, June 27, 1977; given personal title of abp., Dec. 22, 1982; ret., Nov. 23, 1996.

Ziemann, G. Patrick: b. Sept. 13, 1941, Pasadena, CA; educ. St. John's College Seminary and St. John's Seminary (Camarillo, CA), Mt. St. Mary's College (Los Angeles, CA); ord. priest (Los Angeles*), Apr. 29, 1967; ord. titular bp. of Obba and aux. bp. of Los Angeles, Feb. 23, 1987; app. bp. of Santa Rosa, July 14, 1992; res., July 22, 1999.

Zipfel, Paul A.: b. Sept. 22, 1935, St. Louis, MO; educ. Cardinal Glennon College, Kenrick Seminary (St. Louis, MO), Catholic Univ. (Washington, DC), St. Louis Univ. (St. Louis, MO); ord. priest (St. Louis*), Mar. 18, 1961; ord. titular bp. of Walla Walla and aux. bp. of St. Louis, June 29, 1989; app. bp. of Bismarck, Dec. 31, 1996.

Zubic, David A.: b. Sept. 4, 1949, Sewickley, PA; educ. St. Paul Seminary-Duquesne Univ. (Pittsburgh), St. Mary's Seminary (Baltimore), Duquesne Univ. (Pittsburgh); ord. priest (Pittsburgh), May 3, 1975; ord. titular bp. of Jamestown and aux. of Pittsburgh, Apr. 6, 1997.

Zurek, Patrick J.: b. Aug. 17, 1948, Wallis, TX; educ. Univ.of St. Thomas (Houston), Angelicum and Alphonsian Academy (Rome); ord priest (Austin), June 29, 1975; app. titular bp. of Tamugadi and aux. bp. of San Antonio, Jan. 5, 1998, ord., Feb. 16, 1998.

BISHOP-BROTHERS

(The asterisk indicates brothers who were bishops at the same time.)

There have been 10 pairs of brother-bishops in the history of the U.S. hierarchy.

Living: Francis T. Hurley,* abp. of Anchorage and Mark J. Hurley,* bp. emeritus of Santa Rosa. Raymond J. Boland,* bp. of Kansas City-St. Joseph, MO and John Kevin Boland,* bp. of Savannah.

Deceased: Francis Blanchet* of Oregon City (Portland) and Augustine Blanchet* of Walla Walla; John S. Foley of Detroit and Thomas P. Foley of Chicago; Francis P. Kenrick,* apostolic administrator of Philadelphia, bp. of Philadelphia and Baltimore, and Peter R. Kenrick* of St. Louis; Matthias C. Lenihan of Great Falls and Thomas M. Lenihan of Cheyenne; James O'Connor, vicar apostolic of Nebraska and bp. of Omaha, and Michael O'Connor of Pittsburgh and Erie; Jeremiah F. and John W. Shanahan, both of Harrisburg; Sylvester J. Espelage, O.F.M.* of Wuchang, China, who died 10 days after the ordination of his brother, Bernard T. Espelage, O.F.M.* of Gallup; Coleman F. Carroll* of Miami and Howard Carroll* of Altoona-Johnstown.

U.S. BISHOPS OVERSEAS

Cardinal William W. Baum, major penitentiary emeritus; Cardinal Edmund C. Szoka, President, Pontifical Commission for Vatican City State; Cardinal James Francis Stafford, president of the Pontifical Council for the Laity; Abp. John P. Foley, president of Pontifical Commission for Social Communications; Abp. Ambrose de Paoli, apostolic nuncio to Japan; Abp. Charles A. Schleck, C.S.C., former adjunct secretary of the Congregation for the Evangelization of Peoples; Abp. Edward Joseph Adams, nuncio in Bangladesh; Abp. Timothy P. Broglio, apostolic nuncio to the Dominican Republic and apostolic delegate to Puerto Rico; Abp. George Riashi, B.C.O., abp. of archeparchy of Tripoli of Lebanon (Lebanon) for Greek-Catholic Melkites; Abp. John Bukovsky, S.V.D. (naturalized U.S. citizen), former papal representative to Russia;

Bp. James M. Harvey, prefect of the Papal Household; Bp. Michael R. Kuchmiak, exarch of apostolic exarchate emeritus of Great Britain for Ukrainian Catholics; Bp. Joseph Pelletier, M.S., bp. of Morondava, Madagascar; Bp. Paul Simon Schmitz, O.F.M.Cap., bp. of Bluefields, Nicaragua; Bp. Ambrose Ravasi, I.M.C., bp. of Marsabit, Kenya; Bp. Caesar Mazzolari, M.C.C.J., bp. of Rumbek, Kenya; Bp. George Biguzzi, S.X., bp. of Makeni, Sierra Leone; Bp. John B. Minder, O.S.F.S., bp. of Keimoes-Upington, South Africa; Bp. Joseph J. Potocnak, S.C.J., bp. of De Aar, South Africa; Bp. Paul Duffy, O.M.I., bp. of Mongu, Zambia; Bp. Henry Howaniec, O.F.M., apostolic admin. of Almaty, Kazakstan; Bp. William J. McNaughton, M.M. bp. of Inchon., Korea; Bp. Gerald Scarpone Caporale, O.F.M., bp. of: Comayagua, Honduras; Bp. Thomas Maurus Muldoon, O.F.M., bp. of Juticalpa, Honduras; Bp. Paul M. Boyle, C.P., bp. of Mandeville, Jamaica; Bp. Edward J. Gilbert, C.SS.R., bp. of Port of Spain, Trinidad and Tobago; Bp. George Murry, S.J., bp. of St. Thomas, Virgin Islands; Bp. Robert Kurtz, C.R., bp. of Hamilton, Bermuda; Bp. Ricardo Watty Urquidi, M.Sp.S., bp. of Nuevo Laredo, Mexico; Bp. John Quinn Weitzel, M.M., bp. of Samoa-Pago Pago, American Samoa; Bp. Stephen J. Reichert, O.F.M.Cap., bp. of Mendi, Papua New Guinea; Bp. Raymond P. Kalisz, S.V.D., bp. of Wewak Papua New Guinea; Bp. Christopher Cardone, O.P., Gizo, Solomon Islands; Bp. Luis Morgan Casey, vicar apostolic of Pando, Bolivia; Bp. Herbert Hermes, O.S.B., prelate of Cristalandia, Brazil; Bp. Capistran Heim, O.F.M., prelate of Itaituba, Brazil; Bp. John J. Burke, O.F.M., bp. of Miracema do Tocantins Brazil; Bp. Alfred Novak, C.Ss.R., bp. of Paranagua, Brazil; Bp. Elias James Manning, O.F.M. Conv., bp. of Valença, Brazil; Bp. John C. McNabb, O.S.A., bp. of Chulucanas, Peru; Bp. Daniel Thomas Turley Murphy, O.S.A., coadjutor bp. of Chulucanas, Peru; Bp. Michael La Fay Bardi, O.Carm. prelate of Sicuani, Peru. (*See* **Missionary Bishops.**)

RETIRED/RESIGNED U.S. PRELATES

Information, as of Aug. 20, 2003, includes name of the prelate and see held at the time of retirement or resignation; abps. are indicated by an asterisk. Most of the prelates listed below resigned their sees because of age in accordance with church law. See **Index: Biographies, U.S. Bishops.**

Forms of address of retired residential prelates (unless they have a titular see): Abp. or Bp. Emeritus of (last see held); Former Abp. or Bp. of (last see held).

Patrick V. Ahern (New York, aux.), Juan Arzube (Los

Angeles, aux.), Cardinal Anthony J. Bevilacqua* (Philadelphia), Ernest B. Boland, O.P. (Multan, Pakistan), William D. Borders* (Baltimore), Joseph M. Breitenbeck (Grand Rapids), Edwin B. Broderick (Albany), William H. Bullock (Madison), Charles A. Buswell (Pueblo).

John Chedid (Our Lady of Lebanon), John W. Comber, M.M. (Foratiano, titular see), Thomas Connolly (Baker), Ronald G. Connors, C.SS.R. (San Juan de la Maguana, Dominican Republic), Arnold R. Cotey, S.D.S. (Nachingwea, now Lindi, Tanzania), William G. Curlin (Charlotte), James J. Daly (Rockville Centre, aux.), Thomas V. Daily (Brooklyn), Nicholas D'Antonio, O.F.M. (Olancho, Honduras).

Joseph A. DePalma, S.C.J. (DeAar, South Africa), Louis A. DeSimone (Philadelphia, aux.), Joseph T. Dimino* (Military Services archdiocese), George Dion, O.M.I. (titular see, Arpaia), Paul V. Donovan (Kalamazoo), Michael J. Dudick (Passaic, Byzantine rite), Paul V. Dudley (Sioux Falls), Roland Pierre DuMaine (San Jose), Dennis V. Durning, C.S.Sp. (Arusha, Tanzania), J. Lennox Federal (Salt Lake City), Gilberto Fernandez (Miami, aux.), Joseph A. Ferrario (Honolulu), James Fitzgerald (Joliet, aux.), John J. Fitzpatrick (Brownsville), Marion F. Forst (Dodge City), Benedict C. Franzetta (Youngstown, aux.), Gerard L. Frey (Lafayette, LA).

Francisco Garmendia (New York, aux.), Louis E. Gelineau (Providence), Odore Gendron (Manchester), Peter L. Gerety* (Newark), John J. Glynn (Military Services archdiocese), Raymond E. Goedert (Chicago, aux.), John R. Gorman (Chicago, aux.), Rene H. Gracida (Corpus Christi), Richard C. Hanifen (Colorado Springs), Philip M. Hannan* (New Orleans), Frank J. Harrison (Syracuse), Daniel A. Hart (Norwich), Edward D. Head (Buffalo), Joseph Hart (Cheyenne), Cardinal James A. Hickey* (Washington, D.C.).

James J. Hogan (Altoona-Johnstown), Joseph L. Hogan (Rochester), William Russell Houck (Jackson), Joseph Lawson Howze (Biloxi), Edward T. Hughes (Metuchen), William A. Hughes (Covington), Raymond G. Hunthausen* (Seattle), Thad J. Jakubowski (Chicago, aux.) Roger L. Kaffer (Joliet, aux.), Daniel W. Kucera, O.S.B.* (Dubuque), William F. Kupfer, M.M. (Taichung, Taiwan), George Kuzma (Van Nuys), Francis Lambert, S.M. (Port Vila, Vanuatu), W. Thomas Larkin (St. Petersburg), Bernard Cardinal Law* (Boston), Raymond W. Lessard (Savannah), Martin N. Lohmuller (Philadelphia, aux.), Innocent Hilarius Lotocky, O.S.B.M. (St. Nicholas of Chicago for Ukrainians), Timothy J. Lyne (Chicago, aux.).

Michael F. McAuliffe (Jefferson City), Edward A. McCarthy* (Miami), James F. McCarthy (New York, aux.) John McCarthy (Austin), William J. McCormack (New York, aux.), Andrew McDonald (Little Rock), John B. McDowell (Pittsburgh, aux.), Norman McFarland (Orange, CA), Urban McGarry, T.O.R. (Bhagalpur, India), Bernard J. McLaughlin (Buffalo, aux.), Joseph F. Maguire (Springfield, MA), Charles G. Maloney (Louisville, aux.), Thomas R. Manning, O.F.M. (Coroico, Bolivia), Paul C. Marcinkus* (titular see of Orta), Dominic Anthony Marconi (Newark, aux.), Leroy T. Matthiesen (Amarillo), Anthony F. Mestice (New York, aux.), James E. Michaels (Wheeling-Charleston, aux.), Donald W. Montrose (Stockton), Manuel D. Moreno (Tucson), Michael J. Murphy (Erie), Martin J. Neylon, S.J. (Caroline Islands), James D. Niedergeses (Nashville), Thomas Joseph O'Brien (Phoenix), Anthony J. O'Connell (Palm Beach), Edward J. O'Donnell (Lafayette, LA), Arthur J. O'Neill (Rockford).

Albert H. Ottenweller (Steubenville), Walter Paska (Philadelphia, Ukrainians, aux.), John J. Paul (La Crosse), George H. Pearce, S.M.* (Suva, Fiji Islands), Edward Pevec (Cleveland, aux.), Bernard F. Popp (San Antonio, aux.), Kenneth J. Povish (Lansing), Vasile Louis Puscas (St. George's in Canton of the Romanians), Francis A. Quinn (Sacramento), John R. Quinn* (San Francisco), Joseph M. Raya* (Acre), John C. Reiss (Trenton), Agustin Roman (Miami, aux.), Daniel Ryan (Springfield, IL).

Robert F. Sanchez* (Santa Fe), Joseph Sartoris (Los Angeles, aux.), Stanley G. Schlarman (Dodge City), Firmin M. Schmidt, O.F.M. Cap. (Mendi, Papua New Guinea), Mark Schmitt (Marquette), Walter J. Schoenherr (Detroit, aux.), Francis B. Schulte* (New Orleans), Daniel E. Sheehan* (Omaha), Gilbert I. Sheldon (Steubenville), Patrick Sheridan (New York, aux.), John Snyder (St. Augustine), Jude Speyrer (Lake Charles), George H. Speltz (St. Cloud), Ignatius J. Strecker* (Kansas City, KS), Stephen Sulyk* (Philadelphia, Ukrainians).

Elliott Thomas (Virgin Islands), David B. Thompson (Charleston), Thomas Tschoepe (Dallas), James C. Timlin (Scranton), Adrian Veigle, T.O.R. (Borba, Brazil, Prelate), John J. Ward (Los Angeles, aux.), Loras J. Watters (Winona), Rembert G. Weakland, O.S.B.* (Milwaukee), Thomas J. Welsh (Allentown), James Kendrick Williams (Lexington), Aloysius J. Wycislo (Green Bay), Francis Zayek (St. Maron of Brooklyn); G. Patrick Ziemann (Santa Rosa).

American Bishops of the Past: For coverage of the deceased bishops who served in the United States, please visit www.CatholicAlmanac.com.

The United States Conference of Catholic Bishops

(*Courtesy USCCB.*)

When the Bishops merged their two national organizations into the United States Conference of Catholic Bishops (USCCB) on July 1, 2001, it marked the latest chapter in the evolution of the bishops' national structure, which was established 82 years ago in the aftermath of the First World War. Like its immediate predecessors — the National Conference of Catholic Bishops (NCCB) and United States Catholic Conference (USCC) – the USCCB is an organization staffed by lay people, priests, and members of religious orders, but whose members are the bishops of the United States, and it is the bishops who direct its activities.

The concept of the Bishops acting together on matters of mutual interest can be traced back to 1919 when, in their first national meeting since 1884, they agreed to meet annually and to form the National Catholic Welfare Council (NCWC) to serve as their organized voice on the national scene. The word "Council" was replaced by the word "Conference" in 1922.

In 1966, following the Second Vatican Council, NCWC was reorganized into two parallel conferences. The National Conference of Catholic Bishops – sometimes referred to as the canonical arm – would deal with matters connected to the internal life of the Church, such as liturgy and priestly life and ministry. The U.S. Catholic Conference – in effect the civil arm – would represent the bishops as they related to the "secular" world, in areas such as social concerns, education, communications and public affairs. During the period from 1992 to 1996, a Conference committee on mission and structure, headed by the late Cardinal Joseph L. Bernardin of Chicago, led the bishops in extensive consultation on restructuring. A primary purpose of this undertaking was to provide more of the nation's approximately 300 bishops with an opportunity to be directly involved in the work of the Conference, which operates primarily through a committee structure.

In 1997 the bishops voted to combine NCCB-USCC into one conference, to be called the U.S. Conference of Catholic Bishops. They decided that in the future only bishops would be voting members of committees, and non-bishops could serve on some committees as consultants or advisers. A new committee on statutes and bylaws, headed by Archbishop Daniel E. Pilarczyk of Cincinnati, which was formed to lead the rest of the reorganization process, completed its work last year. The new statutes and bylaws were subsequently approved by the Holy See.

It is unlikely that persons outside the Bishops' Conference will notice any immediate difference in the new structure. Many of the same concerns that motivated the Bishops in 1919 – like the welfare of immigrants, communicating through the Catholic press, and defending the legal rights of the Church – are still pressing today, as evidenced in the departments which carry out these functions, though many others have been added as well. In a May 23, 2001, letter sent to organizations which have dealings with the Conference, its General Secretary, Monsignor William P. Fay, said the renaming "will not affect any change in the activities or programs of the Conference but simply how the Conference is identified."

Mission Statement

The United States Conference of Catholic Bishops is a permanent institute composed of Catholic Bishops of the United States of America in and through which the bishops exercise in a communal or collegial manner the pastoral mission entrusted to them by the Lord Jesus of sanctification, teaching, and leadership, especially by devising forms and methods of the apostolate suitably adapted to the circumstances of the times. Such exercise is intended to offer appropriate assistance to each bishop in fulfilling his particular ministry in the local Church, to effect a commonality of ministry addressed to the people of the United States of America, and to foster and express communion with the Church in other nations within the Church universal, under the leadership of its chief pastor, the pope.

Administration

The principal officers of the conference are: Wilton D. Gregory, president; William S. Skylstad, vice president; Archbishop James P. Keleher, treasurer; Bishop William B. Friend, secretary; Msgr. William Fay, Ph.D., general secretary. Headquarters of the conferences are located at 3211 Fourth St. N.E., Washington, DC 20017; (202) 541-3000; www.usccb.org.

USCCB REGIONS

I. Maine, Vermont, New Hampshire, Massachusetts, Rhode Island, Connecticut. II. New York. III. New Jersey, Pennsylvania. IV. Delaware, District of Columbia, Florida, Georgia, Maryland, North Carolina, South Carolina, Virgin Islands, Virginia, West Virginia. V. Alabama, Kentucky, Louisiana, Mississippi, Tennessee. VI. Michigan, Ohio. VII. Illinois, Indiana, Wisconsin. VIII. Minnesota, North Dakota, South Dakota. IX. Iowa, Kansas, Missouri, Nebraska. X. Arkansas, Oklahoma, Texas. XI. California, Hawaii, Nevada. XII.

Idaho, Montana, Alaska, Washington, Oregon. XIII. Utah, Arizona, New Mexico, Colorado, Wyoming.

Pastoral Council

The conference, one of many similar territorial conferences envisioned in the conciliar Decree on the Pastoral Office of Bishops in the Church (No. 38), is "a council in which the bishops of a given nation or territory [in this case, the United States] jointly exercise their pastoral office to promote the greater good which the Church offers mankind, especially through the forms and methods of the apostolate fittingly adapted to the circumstances of the age."

Its decisions, "provided they have been approved legitimately and by the votes of at least two-thirds of the prelates who have a deliberative vote in the conference, and have been recognized by the Apostolic See, are to have juridically binding force only in those cases prescribed by the common law or determined by a special mandate of the Apostolic See, given either spontaneously or in response to a petition of the conference itself."

All bishops who serve the Church in the U.S., its territories and possessions, have membership and voting rights in the USCCB. Retired bishops cannot be elected to conference offices nor can they vote on matters that by law are binding by two-thirds of the membership. Only diocesan bishops can vote on diocesan quotas, assessments or special collections.

Officers, Committees

The conference operates through a number of bishops' committees with functions in specific areas of work and concern. Their basic assignments are to prepare materials on the basis of which the bishops, assembled as a conference, make decisions, and to put suitable action plans into effect.

The officers, with several other bishops, hold positions on executive-level committees — Executive Committee, the Committee on Budget and Finance, the Committee on Personnel, and the Committee on Priorities and Plans. They also, with other bishops, serve on the USCCB Administrative Committee.

The standing committees and their chairmen (Cardinals, Archbishops, and Bishops) are as follows:

African American Catholics: Gordon D. Bennett
American Bishops' Overseas Appeal: Wilton D. Gregory
American College, Louvain: Edward K. Braxton
Bishops' Welfare Emergency Relief: Joseph Fiorenza
Boundaries of Dioceses and Provinces: Joseph Fiorenza
Canonical Affairs: Thomas G. Doran
Catechesis: Donald W. Wuerl
Campaign for Human Development: George V. Murry, S.J.
Communications: Joseph A. Galante
Consecrated Life: Sean P. O'Malley, O.F.M. Cap.
Diaconate: Robert C. Morlino
Doctrine: Donald W. Trautmann
Domestic Policy: Theodore E. Cardinal McCarrick
Ecumenical and Interreligious Affairs: Stephen E. Blaire
Education: Bernard J. Harrington
Evangelization: Edward J. Slattery
Hispanic Affairs: James A. Tamayo

Home Missions: Paul A. Zipfel
International Policy: John H. Ricard, S.S.J.
Laity: Dale J. Melczek
Latin America: Edmond Carmody
Lay Ministry, Subcommittee: Gerald Kicanas
Lay Ministry, Subcommittee on Youth: Dennis Schnurr
Liturgy: Francis E. Cardinal George, O.M.I.
Marriage and Family Life: J. Kevin Boland
Migration: Thomas G. Wenski
North American College, Rome: Edwin F. O'Brien
Pastoral Practices: Thomas J. Tobin
Priestly Formation: John C. Nienstedt
Priestly Life and Ministry: John R. Gaydos
Pro-Life Activities: Anthony J. Cardinal Bevilacqua
Relationship between Eastern and Latin Catholic Churches: Basil Schott
Science and Human Values: Francis X. DiLorenzo
Selection of Bishops: Wilton D. Gregory
Vocations: Kevin M. Britt
Women in Society and in the Church: Edward P. Cullen
World Missions: Gregory M. Aymond

Ad hoc committees and their chairmen:
Agricultural Issues: Ronald Gilmore
Aid to the Church in Central and Eastern Europe: Adam Cardinal Maida
Bishops Life and Ministry: Robert H. Brom
Catechism, Oversee the Use of the: Alfred C. Hughes
Catholic Charismatic Renewal: Sam G. Jacobs
Diocesan Audits: Joseph P. Delaney
Economic Concerns of the Holy See: John G. Vlazny
Forum on the Principles of Translation: Jerome G. Hanus, O.S.B.
Health Care Issues and the Church: Robert C. Morlino
Mandatum: Daniel E. Pilarczyk
Native American Catholics: Donald E. Pelotte, S.S.S.
Nomination of Conference Officers: Daniel E. Pilarczyk
Plenary Council Varium: Daniel M. Buechlein, O.S.B.
Review of Scripture Translations: Arthur J. Serratelli
Sexual Abuse: Harry J. Flynn
Shrines: James P. Keleher
Stewardship: Sylvester D. Ryan

STATE CATHOLIC CONFERENCES

These conferences are agencies of bishops and dioceses in the various states. Their general purposes are to develop and sponsor cooperative programs designed to cope with pastoral and common-welfare needs, and to represent the dioceses before governmental bodies, the public, and in private sectors. Their membership consists of representatives from the dioceses in the states — bishops, clergy and lay persons in various capacities.

The National Association of State Catholic Conference Directors maintains liaison with the general secretariat of the United States Conference of Catholic Bishops. President: Robert J. Castagna, executive director of Oregon Catholic Conference.

Alaska Catholic Conference, 225 Cordova, Anchorage. AK 99501; (907) 297-7738; Contact Person, Robert Flint.

Arizona Catholic Conference, 400 E. Monroe St., Phoenix, AZ 85004-2376; (602) 257-5597; Exec. Dir., Rev. Msgr. Edward J. Ryle.

California Catholic Conference, 1119 K St., 2nd Floor, Sacramento, CA 95814; (916) 443-4851; Exec. Dir., Edward Dolejsi.

Colorado Catholic Conference, 1535 Logan St., Denver, CO 80203; (303) 894-8808.

Connecticut Catholic Conference, 134 Farmington Ave., Hartford, CT 06105; (860) 524-7882; Exec. Dir., Dr. Marie T. Hilliard, Ph.D., R.N.

Florida Catholic Conference, 313 S.Calhoun St., Tallahassee, FL 32301; (850) 222-3803; Exec. Dir., D. Michael McCarron, Ph.D.

Georgia Catholic Conference, Office Bldg., 3200 Deans Bridge Rd., Augusta, GA 30906; (706) 798-1719; Exec. Dir., Francis J. Mulcahy, Esq.

Hawaii Catholic Conference, St. Stephen Diocesan Center, 6301 Pali Hwy., Kaneohe, HI 96744; (808) 263-8844; Exec. Dir., Errol J. Christian.

Illinois, Catholic Conference of, 65 E. Wacker Pl., Ste. 1620, Chicago, IL 60601; (312) 368-1066. 108 E. Cook, Springfield, IL 62701; (217) 528-9200; Acting Dir., Robert Gilligan.

Indiana Catholic Conference, 1400 N. Meridian St., P.O. Box 1410, Indianapolis, IN 46206; (317) 236-1455; Exec. Dir., M. Desmond Ryan, Ph.D.

Iowa Catholic Conference, 505 Fifth Ave., Suite No. 818, Des Moines, IA 50309-2393; (515) 243-6256; Exec. Dir., Dr. Thomas Feld.

Kansas Catholic Conference, 6301 Antioch, Merriam, KS 66202; (913) 722-6633; Exec. Dir., Michael P. Farmer.

Kentucky, Catholic Conference of, 1042 Burlington Lane, Frankfort, KY 40601; (502) 875-4345; Exec. Dir., Jane J. Chiles.

Louisiana Catholic Conference, 3423 Hundred Oaks Ave., Baton Rouge, LA 70808; (225) 344-7120; Exec. Dir., Daniel J. Loar.

Maryland Catholic Conference, 188 Duke of Gloucester St., Annapolis, MD 21401; (410) 269-1155; Exec. Dir., Richard J. Dowling, Esq.

Massachusetts Catholic Conference, 150 Staniford St., West End Pl., Boston, MA 02114-2511; (617) 367-6060; Exec. Dir., Gerald D. D'Avolio, Esq.

Michigan Catholic Conference, 510 N. Capitol Ave., Lansing, MI 48933; (517) 372-9310; President and CEO, Sr. Monica Kostielney, R.S.M.

Minnesota Catholic Conference, 475 University Ave. W., St. Paul, MN 55103; (651) 227-8777; Interim Exec. Dir., Christopher Leifeld.

Missouri Catholic Conference, P.O. Box 1022, 600 Clark Ave., Jefferson City, MO 65102; (573) 635-7239; Exec. Dir., Lawrence A. Weber.

Montana Catholic Conference, P.O. Box 1708, Helena, MT 59624; (406) 442-5761; www.mt.net/~mcc; Exec. Dir., Sr. Mary Jo McDonald, S.C.L.

Nebraska Catholic Conference, 215 Centennial Mall South, Suite 410, Lincoln, NE 68508-1890; (402) 477-7517; Exec. Dir., James R. Cunningham.

Nevada Catholic Conference, 290 South Arlington Ave., Ste. 200, Reno, NV 89501-1713; (775) 326-9416; Exec. Dir., Robert Payant.

New Jersey Catholic Conference, 211 N. Warren St., Trenton, NJ 08618; (609) 599-2110; Exec. Dir., William F. Bolan, Jr., J.D.

New York State Catholic Conference, 465 State St., Albany, NY 12203; (518) 434-6195; www.nys catholicconference.org; Interim Exec. Dir., Richard E. Barnes.

North Dakota Catholic Conference, 227 West Broadway, Suite No. 2, Bismarck, ND 58501; (701) 223-2519; www.ndcatholic.org; Exec. Dir., Christopher T. Dodson.

Ohio, Catholic Conference of, 9 E. Long St., Suite 201, Columbus, OH 43215; (614) 224-7147; Exec. Dir., Timothy V. Luckhaupt.

Oregon Catholic Conference, 2838 E. Burnside, Portland, OR 97214; (503) 233-8387; General Counsel and Exec. Dir., Robert J. Castagna.

Pennsylvania Catholic Conference, 223 North St., Box 2835, Harrisburg, PA 17105; (717) 238-9613; (717) 238-9613; Exec. Dir., Robert J. O'Hara, Jr.

Texas Catholic Conference, 1625 Rutherford Lane, Bldg. D, Austin, TX 78754; (512) 339-9882; Exec. Dir., Bro. Richard Daly, C.S.C.

Washington State Catholic Conference, 508 2nd Ave. West, Seattle, WA 98119-3928; (206) 301-0556; Exec. Dir., Sr. Sharon Park, O.P.

West Virginia State Catholic Conference, P.O. Box 230, Wheeling, WV 26003; (304) 233-0880; Dir., Very Rev. John R. Gallagher.

Wisconsin Catholic Conference, 30 W. Mifflin St., Suite 302, Madison, WI 53703; (608) 257-0004; Exec. Dir., John A. Huebscher.

Background

The National Conference of Catholic Bishops (NCCB), was established by action of the U.S. hierarchy Nov. 14, 1966, as a strictly ecclesiastical body with defined juridical authority over the Church in this country. It was set up with the approval of the Holy See and in line with directives from the Second Vatican Council. Its constitution was formally ratified during the November 1967 meeting of the U.S. hierarchy. The NCCB was a development from the Annual Meeting of the Bishops of the United States, whose pastoral character was originally approved by Pope Benedict XV, Apr. 10, 1919.

The USCC, as of Jan. 1, 1967, took over the general organization and operations of the former National Catholic Welfare Conference, Inc., whose origins dated back to the National Catholic War Council of 1917. The council underwent some change after World War I and was established on a permanent basis on Sept. 24, 1919, as the National Catholic Welfare Council to serve as a central agency for organizing and coordinating the efforts of U.S. Catholics in carrying out the social mission of the Church in this country. In 1923, its name was changed to National Catholic Welfare Conference, Inc., and clarification was made of its nature as a service agency of the bishops and the Church rather than as a conference of bishops with real juridical authority in ecclesiastical affairs.

The Official Catholic Directory stated that the USCC assisted "the bishops in their service to the Church in this country by uniting the people of God where voluntary collective action on a broad interdiocesan level is needed. The USCC provided an organizational structure and the resources needed to insure coordination, cooperation, and assistance in the public, educational and social concerns of the Church at the national, regional, state and, as appropriate, diocesan levels."

CATHOLIC RELIEF SERVICES

Catholic Relief Services is the official overseas aid and development agency of U.S. Catholics; it is a separately incorporated organization of the U.S. Conference of Catholic Bishops.

CRS was founded in 1943 by the bishops of the United States to help civilians in Europe and North Africa caught in the disruption and devastation of World War II. As conditions in Europe improved in the late 1940s and early 1950s, the works conducted

by CRS spread to other continents and areas — Asia, Africa and Latin America.

Although best known for its record of disaster response, compassionate aid to refugees and commitment to reconstruction and rehabilitation, CRS places primary focus on long-term development projects designed to help people to help themselves and to determine their own future. Administrative funding for CRS comes largely from the American Bishops' Overseas Appeal (ABOA). Major support is derived from private, individual donors and through a program of sacrificial giving called Operation Rice Bowl.

Kenneth F. Hackett is Executive Director. CRS headquarters are located at 209 W. Fayette St., Baltimore, MD 21201; (410) 625-2220.

REPORT OF THE NATIONAL REVIEW BOARD

(*Courtesy of the USCCB Office of Communications.*)
On July 29, 2003, the National Review Board established by the USCCB to assist the efforts of the Bishops of the United States in addressing the clergy abuse scandal issued their first anniversary report. Following are excerpts:

To the Catholic Faithful of the United States:

One year ago we met for the first time as the National Review Board to assist the U.S. Conference of Catholic Bishops in addressing the clerical sex abuse scandal. Acting in the midst of a crisis without precedent in the history of the Church in America, the bishops had established the board as part of the charter they adopted in Dallas in June 2002 to protect children and young people from any repetition of the horrors then coming to light. We convened as strangers, diverse in backgrounds and experience, but united in a love for the Church and determined to do our part in safeguarding her and her young.

In the beginning we spent endless hours educating ourselves in order to achieve an adequate understanding of the sources of the trouble, of the tragic toll it had exacted from the innocent young and their families, and of the frequently dismaying history of the Church's responses. Only then were we able to establish a program of work that would fulfill the role envisioned for us in the Dallas charter. In drawing this blueprint, we first resolved that in order to establish credibility for our actions we had to operate with independence and transparency. We could not be seen as mere window dressing or a public relations response to a gnawing embarrassment. Indeed we believed that to be a source of healing and reform, we had to produce promptly a plan for meaningful and robust measures directed against the sin and crime devastating the Church.

Given these ambitious goals, we have spent the past 12 months immersing ourselves in this work. At least monthly we have gathered as a board in various parts of the country but we have met far more frequently in subcommittees to tackle specific tasks. Of equal importance, we have read numerous books, documents and articles to educate ourselves on the complexities

of the crisis and have conducted meetings and interviews with scores of knowledgeable observers. What began as a volunteer assignment has become an almost full-time endeavor that frequently crowds out other duties from busy schedules.

Now, as we observe the first anniversary of our founding, we want to make an accounting of our stewardship to our fellow Catholics and others of good will. We know that much of our agenda has yet to be accomplished. But we believe that for real change, our prescriptions must go to the root of the troubles if their effects are to be lasting. Change is never easy for either individuals or organizations and the inevitable obstacles which block one's way can be formidable to overcome. But we are united in an unshakeable resolve to help the Church mend itself and reassure its members. For us to succeed, we need your patience and your prayers.

(To read the complete status reports for each of the following areas, read the complete document on the USCCB web site at www.nccbuscc.org/comm/reviewboard.htm.)

- Establish an Office for Child and Youth Protection
- Establish Safe Environment Standards
- Audit the Nation's Dioceses/Eparchies to Determine Compliance with the Dallas Charter
- Commission a Descriptive Study of the "Nature and Scope" of the Crisis
- Commission a Comprehensive Study of the Causes and Context of the Crisis
- Causes and Context Phase I — A task force headed by Robert Bennett, an experienced Washington lawyer and a member of this board, has undertaken the initial phase of an inquiry, which, when completed, will render the board's consensus view of the causes of the crisis
- Causes and Context Phase II — Once the "nature and scope" findings are available and the board's own Phase I research has been accomplished, the foundation will have been laid for a further and more detailed study into the causes and context, particularly on those issues which require broad-based statistical data and analysis before conclusions can be firmly reached.

Hispanic, African-American, and Native-American Catholics

HISPANIC CATHOLICS IN THE UNITED STATES

The nation's Hispanic population totaled 35.3 million in 2000, according to figures reported by the U.S. Census Bureau. It is estimated that 73 percent of the Hispanics were baptized Catholics. It was estimated that perhaps 100,000 Catholic Hispanics a year were being lost, principally to fundamentalist and pentecostal sects.

Pastoral Patterns

Pastoral ministry to Hispanics varies, depending on differences among the people and the availability of personnel to carry it out. The pattern in cities with large numbers of Spanish-speaking people is built around special and bilingual churches, centers or other agencies where pastoral and additional forms of service are provided in a manner suited to the needs, language and culture of the people. Services in some places are extensive and include legal advice, job placement, language instruction, recreational and social assistance, specialized counseling, replacement services. In many places, however, even where there are special ministries, the needs are generally greater than the means available to meet them.

Some urban dwellers have been absorbed into established parishes and routines of church life and activity. Many Spanish-speaking communities remain in need of special ministries. An itinerant form of ministry best meets the needs of the thousands of Hispanic migrant workers who follow the crops.

Pastoral ministry to Hispanics was the central concern of three national meetings, Encuentros, held in 1972, 1977 and 1985.

The third National Encuentro in 1985 produced a master pastoral plan for ministry which the National Conference of Catholic Bishops approved in 1987. Its four keys are collaborative ministry; evangelization; a missionary option regarding the poor, the marginalized, the family, women and youth; and the formation of lay leadership. A National Encuentro was held in 2000. In 2002, the Secretariat published *Encuentro and Mission: A New Pastoral Framework for Hispanic Ministry*. (*See* **News in Depth** for details.)

The U.S. bishops, at their annual meeting in November 1983, approved and subsequently published a pastoral letter on Hispanic Ministry under the title, "The Hispanic Presence: Challenge and Commitment." (For text, see pp. 46-49 of the 1985 *Catholic Almanac*.)

Bishops

As of Aug. 1, 2003, there were 31 (23 active) bishops of Hispanic origin in the United States; all were named since 1970 (for biographies, *see* **Index**). Eleven were heads of archdioceses or dioceses: Archbishop Patrick F. Flores (San Antonio); Bishops Raymundo J Peña (Brownsville), James A. Tamayo (Laredo), Ricardo Ramirez, C.S.B. (Las Cruces), Alvaro Corrada del Rio, S.J. (Tyler), Arthur N. Tafoya (Pueblo), Placido Rodriguez, C.M.F. (Lubbock), Gerald R. Barnes (San Bernardino), Armando Ochoa (El Paso), Carlos A. Sevilla, S.J. (Yakima), and Victor Benito Galeone (St. Augustine). Twelve were auxiliary bishops: Gabino Zavala (Los Angeles), José H. Gomez (Denver), Gilbert Espinoza Chavez (San Diego), Joseph J. Madera (Military Services), Rene Valero (Brooklyn), David Arias, O.A.R. (Newark), Dominick J. Lagonegro (New York), Emilio Simeon Allué (Boston), Richard J. Garcia (Sacramento), Francisco Gonzalez Valer, S.F. (Washington, DC), José S. Vasquez (Galveston-Houston), and Gustavo Garcia-Siller, M.Sp.S. (Chicago). Resigned/retired prelates: Archbishop Robert F. Sanchez (Santa Fe), Bishop Juan Arzube (Los Angeles, auxiliary), Bishop Rene H. Gracida (Corpus Christi), Manuel D. Moreno (Tucson), Bishop Francisco Garmendia (New York), Bishop Agustin Roman (Miami), Bishop Gilberto Fernandez (Miami). Bishop Roberto O. Gonzalez, O.F.M. (Corpus Christi), was appointed archbishop of San Juan de Puerto Rico on Mar. 26, 1999, by Pope John Paul II.

Hispanic priests and nuns in the U.S. number about 1,600 and 2,900, respectively, according to an estimate made in June 1988 by Father Gary Riebe Estrella, S.V.D., director of a Hispanic vocational recruitment program and recent estimates by the U.S. Census.

Secretariat for Hispanic Affairs

The national secretariat was established by the U.S.

Catholic Conference for service promoting and co-ordinating pastoral ministry to the Spanish-speaking. Its basic orientation is toward integral evangelization, combining religious ministry with development efforts in programs geared to the culture and needs of Hispanics. Its concerns are urban and migrant Spanish-speaking people; communications and publications in line with secretariat purposes and the service of people; bilingual and bicultural religious and general education; liaison for and representation of Hispanics with church, civic and governmental agencies.

The Secretariat states that its mission is:

"To assist the Catholic Church in its efforts to serve the large Catholic Hispanic/Latino population in the United States and in the New Evangelization as we approach the Great Jubilee of the Year 2000.

"To coordinate Hispanic ministry efforts in the Catholic Church through regional and diocesan offices, pastoral institutes, secular and ecclesial organizations, and apostolic movements.

"To promote the implementation of the National Pastoral Plan for Hispanic Ministry, *Ecclesia in America, Many Faces in God's House: A Catholic Vision for the Third Millennium*, and other church documents, as well as the development of small ecclesial communities.

"To integrate the Hispanic presence into the life of the Catholic Church and society."

The secretariat publishes a newsletter, *En Marcha*, available to interested parties.

Ronaldo M. Cruz is executive director of the national office at 3211 Fourth St. N.E., Washington, DC, 20017, (202) 541-3000, www.usccb.org.

The secretariat works in collaboration with regional and diocesan offices and pastoral institutes throughout the country.

The Northeast Regional Office, officially the Northeast Hispanic Catholic Center, was established in 1976 under the auspices of the bishops in 12 states from Maine to Virginia. It has established the Conference of Diocesan Directors of the Hispanic Apostolate, the Association of Hispanic Deacons, a Regional Youth Task Force and a Regional Committee of Diocesan Coordinators of Religious Educators for the Hispanics. The office is the official publishing house for the Hispanic Lectionary approved by the National Conference of Catholic Bishops for the United States. The center has liturgical, evangelization and youth ministry departments and an office of cultural affairs. Mario J. Paredes is executive director. The center is located at 1011 First Ave., New York, NY 10022, (212) 751-7045.

The Southeast Regional Office serves 26 dioceses in Tennessee, North and South Carolina, Florida, Georgia, Mississippi, Alabama and Louisiana. Father Mario Vizcaino, Sch. P., is director of the region and institute. The office is located at 7700 S.W. 56 St., Miami, FL 33155, (305) 279-2333. The Southeast Pastoral Institute serves as the educational arm of the regional office by providing formation programs for the development of leadership skills focused on ministry among Hispanics, at the Miami site and in the various dioceses of the region.

In the Southwest, the Mexican American Cultural Center serves as convener of diocesan directors and representatives of Hispanic ministry in Arkansas, Oklahoma and Texas.

A regional office serving the Mountain States (Arizona, New Mexico, Utah, Colorado and Wyoming) is under the coordination of Deacon Germán Toro, 27 C St., Salt Lake City, UT 84103.

The Northwest Regional Office for Hispanic Affairs serves 11 dioceses in Alaska, Montana, Washington, Oregon and Idaho. Father Heliodoro Lucatero is president. The office is located at 2838 Burnside, Portland, OR 97214. It serves as convener for regional workshops, retreats, formation programs and social advocacy.

The National Pastoral Plan for Hispanic Ministry

The National Pastoral Plan for Hispanic Ministry was approved by the NCCB in November 1987. This plan is addressed to the entire Church in the United States. It focuses on the pastoral needs of the Hispanic Catholic, but it challenges all Catholics as members of the Body of Christ.

General Objective: To live and promote by means of a *Pastoral de Conjunto*, a model of Church that is: communitarian, evangelizing, and missionary, incarnate in the reality of the Hispanic people and open to the diversity of cultures, a promoter and example of justice … that develops leadership through integral education … that is leaven for the Kingdom of God in society.

Specific Dimensions: *Pastoral de Conjunto*: To develop a *Pastoral de Conjunto*, which through pastoral agents and structures, manifests communion in integration, coordination in servicing, and communication of the Church's pastoral action, in keeping with the general objective of this plan. Evangelization: To recognize, develop, accompany and support small ecclesial communities and other church groups (e.g., *Cursillos de Cristiandad, Movimiento Familiar Cristiano*, RENEW, Charismatic Movement, prayer groups, etc.) which in union with the bishop are effective instruments of evangelization for the Hispanic people. These small ecclesial communities and other groups within the parish framework promote experiences of faith and conversion, prayer life, missionary outreach and evangelization, interpersonal relations and fraternal love, and prophetic questioning and actions for justice. They are a prophetic challenge for the renewal of our Church and humanization of our society. Missionary Option: To promote faith and effective participation in Church and societal structures on the part of these priority groups (the poor, women, families, youth) so that they may be agents of their own destiny (self-determination) and capable of progressing and becoming organized. Formation: To provide leadership formation adapted to the Hispanic culture in the United States that will help people to live and promote a style of Church that will be leaven of the Kingdom of God in society.

National Hispanic Priests Association

The National Association of Hispanic Priests of the USA (ANSH — *La Asociación Nacional de Sacerdotes Hispanos*, EE. UU.) was established in September 1989 with a representation of about 2,400 Hispanic priests residing and ministering in the U.S. The association came into its present form after a 20-year process of organization by different groups of Hispanic priests around the country.

By 1985, the first National Convention of Hispanic Priests was organized in New York City, and in 1989 the Association was established in Miami, Florida, as a non-profit Corporation for priestly fraternity and support for Hispanic priests in the United States. Among the multiple objectives are: to help members develop their priestly identity in the United States and encourage a genuine spirituality; to provide a national forum of Hispanic priests to help solve the problems that arise in the Hispanic community; to promote vocations to the priesthood among Hispanics; to pray and ask for more Hispanic bishops in the U.S., for the growing needs of the Catholic Hispanic community; and to cooperate with the Bishops and the laity in implementing the National Pastoral Plan for Hispanic Ministry. The Association publishes a quarterly newsletter and holds an annual national convention. The president is Rev. José H. Gomez, S.T.D. 2472 Bolsover, Suite 442, Houston, TX 77005, (713) 528-6517.

National Catholic Council for Hispanic Ministry (NCCHM)

The council is a volunteer federation of Roman Catholic organizations, agencies and movements committed to the development of Hispanics/Latinos in Church and society. It was established June 17, 1990, at a gathering at Mundelein College, Chicago; its by-laws were adopted in January 1991 at Mercy Center, Burlingame, CA. The council convokes a national gathering every three years called *Raices y Alas* (Roots and Wings). With funding from foundations NCCHM has designed and piloted a leadership development program that links contemporary understandings of leadership with experiences and insights from faith and Hispanic cultures. NCCHM has 53 member organizations. It publishes *Puentes*, a newsletter. Exec. Dir., Rosa Maria Sanchez, 2025 Chickasaw Ave., Los Angeles, CA 90041, (213) 344-9153.

Mexican American Cultural Center

This national center, specializing in pastoral studies and language education, was founded in 1972 to provide programs focused on ministry among Hispanics and personnel working with Hispanics in the U.S. Courses — developed according to the see-judge-act methodology — include culture, faith development, Scripture, theology, and praxis; some are offered in Spanish, others in English. Intensive language classes are offered in Spanish, with emphasis on pastoral usage.

The center also conducts workshops for the development of leadership skills and for a better understanding of Hispanic communities. Faculty members serve as resource personnel for pastoral centers, dioceses and parishes throughout the U.S. The center offers master's-degree programs in pastoral ministry in cooperation with Incarnate Word College, Boston College, the Oblate School of Theology, St. Mary's University and Loyola University, New Orleans, and other educational institutions.

The center is a distribution agency for the circulation of bilingual pastoral materials in the U.S. and Latin America. Sister Maria Elena Gonzalez, R.S.M., is president of the center, which is located at 3019 W. French Place, San Antonio, TX 78228.

Institute of Hispanic Liturgy

Spanish-speaking communities in the U.S. are served by the Institute of Hispanic Liturgy, a national organization of liturgists, musicians, artists and pastoral agents, funded in part by the U.S. bishops. The institute promotes the study of liturgical texts, art, music and popular religiosity in an effort to develop liturgical spirituality among Hispanics. It works closely with the U.S. Bishops' Committee on the Liturgy, and has published liturgical materials. Rev. Heliodoro Lucatero, is the president; Sr. Doris Mary Turek, S.S.N.D., is executive director. Address: P.O. Box 29387, Washington, DC, 20017, (202) 319-6450.

Statistics

(*Courtesy, Secretariat for Hispanic Affairs, USCCB.*)

The official 2000 Census estimates a population of 35.3 million Hispanics, or about 12.5 percent of the total population. Since 1990, the Hispanic population has increased 58 percent, up from a total of 22.4 million.

The nation's Hispanic Catholic population (not including Puerto Rico) has increased by 71 percent since 1960. The total Hispanic Catholic population as a percentage of the U.S. Catholic population is 39 percent. Of these Hispanic Catholics, 64 percent attend church services regularly.

According to the most recent statistics based on the 2000 Census, there are 4,000 U.S. parishes with Hispanic ministry; 20.6 percent of U.S. parishes have a majority Hispanic presence. There are approximately 2,900 Hispanic priests and 25 active Hispanic bishops (see above).

The 10 metropolitan areas with the largest Hispanic populations are: Los Angeles, New York, Chicago, Miami, Houston, Riverside-San Bernardino, Orange County, Phoenix, San Antonio, and Dallas. Seven states in 2000 had more than one million Hispanic residents: Arizona, California, Florida, Illinois, New Jersey, New York, and Texas. Approximately one half of the Hispanic population lived in just two states: California and Texas. In New Mexico, Hispanics made up 42 percent of the state's total population, the highest for any state.

Current U.S. Census figures reveal that the Hispanic population increased by 13 million between 1990 and 2000. Hispanics also accounted for 40 percent of the nation's increase in population over the decade. The Hispanic population more than tripled between 1990 and 2000 in Alabama, Arkansas, Georgia, Nevada, North Carolina, South Carolina, and Tennessee.

Data demonstrate that the Hispanic population in the U.S. is young. In 2000, 35.7 percent of Hispanics were less than 18 years old, compared with 23.5 percent of non-Hispanic whites. Only 5.3 percent of Hispanics are older than 65.

The poverty rate in the general population in 1999 was 7.7 percent among non-Hispanic whites; the poverty rate among Hispanics was 21.2 percent or 7.2 million people. This is a record low matching that of the 1970s.

It is projected that in 2020, the Hispanic population will be approximately 52.7 million; by 2040, the population will be about 80.2 million; by 2050 the population will be 96.5 million, comprising approximately 24.5 percent of the entire U.S. population.

AFRICAN-AMERICAN CATHOLICS IN THE UNITED STATES

Secretariat for African-American Catholics

(*Courtesy, Secretariat for African-American Catholics, USCCB.*)

The Secretariat for African-American Catholics is the officially recognized voice of the African-American Catholic community as it articulates the needs and aspirations regarding ministry, evangelization, social justice issues, and worship.

The USCCB *Secretariat for African-American Catholics* supports the Bishops' Committee for African-American Catholics through identification and communication of the socio-cultural dimension of the African-American Community. The vastness of this dimension encompasses historical, social and cultural elements at work within African-American communities. The Secretariat's role is consultative. It is often the voice of conscience, as we, a people of faith, grow toward a truly universal church.

The Secretariat for African-American Catholics serves as the chief advisor to the National Conference of Catholic Bishops and the United States Catholic Conference in fulfilling its ministry to African-American Catholics in the United States. The Secretariat has as its function the coordination of responses regarding ministry, evangelization, and worship in the African-American Community on the national level. The work of the Secretariat is guided by the Bishop's Committee on African-American Catholics whose primary mission is to encourage the development and assist in the implementation of pastoral programs in relation to evangelization and incorporation into the local church of racial, ethnic, cultural and language groups within the National Conference of Catholic Bishops.

It also serves as a liaison to the National Black Catholic Clergy Caucus, the National Black Catholic Seminarians Association, the National Black Sisters' Conference, National Black Catholic Administrators, Knights of St. Peter Claver and Ladies Auxiliary, the National Black Catholic Congress, and the National Black Catholic Theological Society. The Secretariat for African-American Catholics is under the executive direction of Beverly Carroll. The committee and secretariat have offices at 3211 Fourth St. N.E., Washington, DC, 20017, (202) 541-3000; www. usccb.org/saac.

USCCB Committee

The Committee on African-American Catholics, established by the National Conference of Catholic Bishops in 1987, is chaired by Bishop George V. Murry, S.J., auxiliary of Chicago. The purpose of the committee is to assist the bishops in their evangelization efforts to the African-American community by initiating, encouraging and supporting programs which recognize and respect African-American genius and values. Priorities of the Committee include implementation of the National Black Catholic Pastoral Plan of 1987, inculturation of liturgy and ministry, and increasing lay leadership and vocations.

The Secretariat for African-American Catholics was established as a service agency to the committee.

National Office for Black Catholics

The National Office for Black Catholics, organized in July 1970 is a central agency with the general purposes of promoting active and full participation by black Catholics in the Church and of making more effective the presence and ministry of the Church in the black community.

Its operations are in support of the aspirations and calls of black Catholics for a number of objectives, including the following:

• representation and voice for blacks among bishops and others with leadership and decision-making positions in the Church

• promoting vocations to the priesthood and religious life

• sponsoring programs of evangelization, pastoral ministry, education and liturgy on a national level

• recognition of the black heritage in liturgy, community life, theology and education.

Walter T. Hubbard is executive director of the NOBC. The NOBC office is located at 3025 Fourth St. N.E., Washington, DC, 20017, (202) 635-1778.

National Black Catholic Clergy Caucus

The National Black Catholic Clergy Caucus, founded in 1968 in Detroit, is a fraternity of several hundred black priests, permanent deacons and brothers pledged to mutual support in their vocations and ministries.

The Caucus develops programs of spiritual, theological, educational and ministerial growth for its members, to counteract the effects of institutionalized racism within the Church and American society. A bimonthly newsletter is published. The NBCCC office is located at 321 N. Walnut St., P.O. Box 1088, Opelousas, LA 70571, (318) 942-2392. Other peer and support groups are the National Black Sisters' Conference and the National Black Catholic Seminarians Association.

National Black Catholic Congress

The National Black Catholic Congress, Inc., was formed in 1985 exclusively to assist in the development of the Roman Catholic Church in the African-American community and to devise effective means of evangelization of African-American peoples in the United States. Its fundamental purpose is the formation and development of concrete approaches toward the evangelization of African-Americans through revitalization of African-American Catholic life.

The Congress is under the sponsorship of the African-American Roman Catholic bishops of the United States, the National Black Catholic Clergy Caucus, the National Black Sisters' Conference, the National Association of Black Catholic Administrators and the Knights of Peter Claver and the Ladies Auxiliary Knights of Peter Claver. The Congress is also in consultation with African-American clergy and vowed religious women communities. The Congress sponsors "Pastoring in African-American Parishes," an annual workshop first held in 1988 and an African-American Catholic Ministries Program, a week-long curriculum presented twice a year, usually in January and June.

The National Black Catholic Congress sponsored the seventh assembly of African-American Catholics and those serving in African-American communities,

July 9 to 12, 1992, in New Orleans. The most recent National Congress convened in Baltimore, Aug. 27 to 31, 1997. The Congress is sponsoring construction of "Our Mother of Africa Chapel" at the Basilica of the National Shrine of the Immaculate Conception in Washington, DC. The office of the Congress is located at the Archdiocese of Baltimore Catholic Center, 309 Cathedral St., 3rd Floor, Baltimore, MD 21201, (410) 547-8496, www.nbccongress.org. The executive director is Dr. Hilbert D. Stanley

Josephite Pastoral Center

The Josephite Pastoral Center was established in September 1968 as an educational and pastoral service agency for the Josephites in their mission work, specifically in the black community, subsequently to all those who minister in the African-American community. St. Joseph's Society of the Sacred Heart, the sponsoring body, has about 134 priests and 11 brothers in 64 mostly southern parishes in 17 dioceses. The staff of the center includes Father John G. Harfmann, S.S.J., director, and Maria M. Lannon, administrator. Address: Josephite Pastoral Center 1200 Varnum St. N.E., Washington, DC, 20017, (202) 526-9270.

African-American Evangelization

The National Black Catholic Pastoral Plan adopted by the National Black Catholic Congress in May 1987 was approved and recommended for implementation by the National Conference of Catholic Bishops in November 1989.

Following is an account of several points in the bishops' statement, based on coverage by the CNS Documentary Service, *Origins*, Dec. 28, 1989 (Vol. 19, No. 30).

"Evangelization," wrote the bishops, "would not be complete if it did not take account of the unceasing interplay of the Gospel and of man's concrete life, both personal and social. Evangelization involves an explicit message, adapted to the different situations constantly being realized, about the rights and duties of every human being, about family life, without which personal growth and development are hardly possible, about life in society, about international life, peace, justice and development — a message especially energetic today about liberation."

Three Areas

The pastoral plan "embraces three broad areas: 1) the Catholic identity of African-American Catholics; 2) ministry and leadership within the African-American community; and 3) the responsibility of this community to reach out to the broader society. Within these areas are such issues as culture, family, youth, spirituality, liturgy, ministry, lay leadership, parishes, education, social action and community development."

Reflecting a recommendation of the plan, the bishops encourage African-American Catholics to "discover their past" since "possession of one's history is the first step in an appreciation of one's culture."

Bishops

There were 13 (11 active) black bishops as of Sept. 1, 2003. Six were heads of dioceses: Bishops Wilton D. Gregory (Belleville, President of the USCCB), Curtis J. Guillory, S.V.D. (Beaumont), George V. Murry, S.J. (St. Thomas, Virgin Islands), John H. Ricard, S.S.J. (Pensacola-Tallahassee), Edward K. Braxton (Lake Charles), J. Terry Steib, S.V.D. (Memphis). Five were auxiliary bishops: Moses Anderson, S.S.E. (Detroit), Gordon D. Bennett, S.J. (Baltimore), Dominic Carmon, S.V.D. (New Orleans), Leonard J. Olivier, S.V.D. (Washington), Joseph N. Perry (Chicago). Elliott G. Thomas, of St. Thomas, Virgin Islands, res., June 30, 1999, and Joseph L. Howze of Biloxi, res., May 15, 2001. Bishop Wilton Gregory was elected president of the USCCB in November 2001.

African-American Bishops of the Past: James August Healy (1830-1900); Joseph A. Francis, S.V.D. (1923-1997); Eugene A. Marino, S.S.J. (1934-2000); Raymond Rodly Caeser, S.V.D. (1932-1987); James Lyke, O.F.M. (1939-1992); Carl A. Fisher, S.S.J. (1945-1993); Emerson J. Moore (1938-1995); Harold R. Perry, S.V.D. (1916-1991).

Statistics

The Secretariat for African-American Catholics reports that there are presently approximately 2.3 million African-American Catholics in the United States. They are served by 1300 parishes and 75 African-American pastors. There are approximately 250 African-American priests, 300 African-American sisters, and 380 African-American deacons.

NATIVE-AMERICAN CATHOLICS IN THE UNITED STATES

The Kateri Tekakwitha Conference is so named in honor of Blessed Kateri Tekakwitha, "Lily of the Mohawks," who was born in 1656 at Ossernenon (Auriesville), NY, in 1656, baptized in 1676, lived near Montreal, died in 1680, and was beatified in 1980.

The conference was established in 1939 as a missionary-priest advisory group in the Diocese of Fargo. It was a missionary-priest support group from 1946 to 1977. Since 1977 it has been a gathering of Catholic Native peoples and the men and women — clerical, religious and lay persons — who minister to Native Catholic communities.

The primary focus of conference concern and activity is evangelization, with specific emphasis on development of Native ministry and leadership. Other priorities include catechesis, liturgy, family life, social justice ministry, chemical dependency, youth

ministry, spirituality and Native Catholic dialogue. Conferences and local Kateri Circles serve as occasions for the exchange of ideas, prayer and mutual support. Since 1980, the national center has promoted and registered 130 Kateri Circles in the U.S. and Canada. Publications include a quarterly newsletter.

The conference has a board of 12 directors, the majority of whom are Native people. Archbishop Charles Chaput, O.F.M. Cap., is the episcopal moderator. Address: Tekakwitha Conference National Center, P.O. Box 6768, Great Falls, MT, 59406, (406) 727-0147.

STATISTICS

On June 19, 2003, the United States Conference of Catholic Bishops issued a report, "Native American Catholics at the Millennium," on the current state of Native American Catholics in the United

States. There are 4.1 million people who identify themselves as Native American. Of these, 493,615 Native Americans, or 12 percent of the total population, are considered Catholic. Other details are available in **News in Depth.**

Bishops

There are presently two Native American Bishops in active service in the United States. They are: Archbishop Charles J. Chaput, O.F.M. Cap. of Denver and Bishop Donald Pelotte, S.S.S., of Gallup.

MISSIONARY ACTIVITY OF THE U.S. CHURCH

Sources: U.S. Catholic Mission Handbook 2002: Mission Inventory 2000-2001 *(the most recent issue), reproduced with permission of the United States Catholic Mission Council, 3029 Fourth St. N.E., Washington, DC.*

OVERSEAS MISSIONS

Field Distribution, 2000-2001

Africa: 704 (376 men; 328 women). Largest numbers in Kenya, 184; Tanzania, 93; Ghana, 56; Zambia, 53; South Africa, 53; Uganda, 51; Nigeria, 51.

Asia: 734 (490 men; 244 women). Largest numbers in Philippines, 165; Japan, 142; Taiwan, 101; China PRC-Hong Kong SAR, 73; India, 62; Korea, 44; Thailand, 44. (Those present in China were there for professional services.)

Caribbean: 342 (195 men; 147 women). Largest numbers in Puerto Rico, 95; Haiti, 52; Belize, 50; Dominican Republic 48; Jamaica, 40.

Eurasia (Kazakhstan, Russia, Siberia): 147 (14 men; 0 women). Largest group, Russia, 12.

Europe: 167 (81 men; 86 women). Largest numbers in Italy, 57; Ireland, 22; England, 16; Spain, 11; France, 10.

Latin America: 1,247 (622 men; 625 women). Largest numbers in Peru, 231; Mexico, 211; Brazil, 191; Guatemala, 113; Bolivia, 113; Chile, 102.

Middle East: 35 (30 men; 5 women). Largest numbers in Israel, 25; Jordan, 4; Lebanon, 4.

North America (Canada and United States): 2,682 (809 men; 1,872 women). Largest number in the United States, 2,625.

Oceania: 175 (111 men; 64 women). Largest numbers in Papua New Guinea, 65; Micronesia, 37; Australia, 16; Guam, 15; Marshall Island, 12.

TOTAL: 6,108 (2,726 men; 3,382 women).

Missionary Personnel, 2000-2001

Bishops: See below.

Religious Priests: 65 mission-sending groups had 1,784 priests in overseas assignments. Listed below are those with 15 or more members abroad.

Jesuits, 353; Maryknoll Fathers and Brothers, 223; Franciscans (O.F.M.), 130; Oblates of Mary Immaculate, 124; Redemptorists, 93; Society of Divine Word, 88; Franciscans (O.F.M. Cap), 59; Holy Cross Fathers, 57; Dominicans, 52; Vincentians, 37; Columbans, 36; Passionists, 22; Oblates of St. Francis de Sales, 22; Comboni Missionaries, 20; Congregation of Sacred Heart, 18; LaSalette Fathers, 17; Marianists, 17; Spiritans, 16; Legionaries of Christ, 15; Carmelites, 16; Xaverian Missionaries, 15.

Diocesan Priests: There were 153 priests from 57 dioceses. The majority were in Latin American countries.

Religious Brothers: 48 mission-sending groups had 349 brothers in overseas assignments. Those with 15 or more members:

Christian Brothers: (Brothers of the Christian Schools), 85; Marianists, 31; Holy Cross Brothers, 29; Franciscans (O.F.M.), 28; Christian Brothers, 24; Maryknoll Priests and Brothers, 20.

Religious Sisters: 172 mission-sending communities of women Religious had 2,589 sisters in overseas missions. Those with 15 or more members:

Maryknoll Mission Sisters, 276; School Sisters of Notre Dame, 150; Blessed Sacrament Sisters, 115; Dominicans,102; Franciscan Missionaries of Mary, 99; Sisters of Mercy (various communities), 81; Missionaries of Charity, 75; Sisters of Notre Dame de Namur, 69; Medical Mission Sisters, 57; Society of the Sacred Heart, 60; Marist Missionary Sisters, 52; Sisters of Charity, BVM, 52; Congregation of Sisters of St. Agnes, 49; St. Joseph Sisters, 44; Presentation Sisters, 38; Sisters of St. Joseph of Carondelet, 38; Ursulines, 37; Providence, Sisters, 36; Holy Cross, Cong. of Sisters, 35; Daughters of Charity, 32; Cong. of St. Joseph, 29; Franciscan Sisters of Atonement, 27; Sacred Heart of Jesus Sisters, 27; Medical Missionaries of Mary, 26; Franciscan Sisters of Philadelphia, 25; IIHM Sisters of Immaculata, 25; Franciscan Sisters of Little Falls, 23; Little Sisters of the Poor, 21; Mission Sisters of the Immaculate Heart of Mary, 21; Benedictine Sisters, 20; Franciscan Sisters of Charity, 20; School Sisters of St. Francis, 20; Sisters of Charity of Cincinnati, 20; Franciscan Sisters, 18; Immaculate Heart of Mary Sisters of Monroe, 18; Apostles of the Sacred Heart, 17; Good Shepherd Sisters, 15; St. Columban Sisters, 15.

Lay Persons: 83 mission sending groups had 1,191 members in overseas missions. Those with 15 or more members:

Jesuit Volunteer Corps, 379; Maryknoll Mission Associates, 124; Jesuit Volunteers International, 62; Our Lady of the Most Holy Trinity, 54; Vincentian Service Corps, 50; Holy Cross Assoc., 44; Mercy Corps, 33; Urban Catholic Teacher Corps, 23; Salesian Lay Missionaries, 22; Comboni Lay Missionaries, 17.

Seminarians: There were 15 from 7 groups.

Maryknoll, 4; Holy Cross Fathers, 3; Legionaries of Christ, 3; Jesuits, 2; Annunciation House, 1; Glenmary Home Missioners, 1; Dominicans, 1.

MISSIONARY BISHOPS

The following is a list of missionary bishops in active service around the world. This last does not include retired bishops.

Africa

Kenya: Marsabit (diocese), Ambrose Ravasi, I.M.C.; Rumbek (diocese), Caesar Mazzolari, M.C.C.J.

Madagascar: Morondava (diocese), Donald Pelletier, M.S.

Sierra Leone: Makeni (diocese), George Biguzzi, S.X.

South Africa: Keimoes-Upington (diocese), John B. Minder, O.S.F.S.; De Aar (diocese), Joseph J. Potocnak, S.C.J.

Zambia: Mongu (diocese), Paul Duffy, O.M.I.

Asia

Kazakstan: Almaty (apostolic admin.), Henry Howaniec, O.F.M.

Korea: Inchon (diocese), William J. McNaughton, M.M.

Central America, West Indies

Honduras: Comayagua (diocese), Gerald Scarpone Caporale, O.F.M.; Juticalpa (diocese), Thomas Maurus Muldoon, O.F.M.

Jamaica: Mandeville (diocese), Paul M. Boyle, C.P.

Nicaragua: Bluefields (vicariate apostolic), Paul Simon Schmitz, O.F.M.Cap.

Trinidad and Tobago: Port of Spain (archdiocese), Edward J. Gilbert, C.SS.R.

Virgin Islands: St. Thomas (diocese), George Murry, S.J.

North America

Bermuda: Hamilton (diocese), Robert Kurtz, C.R.

Mexico: Nuevo Laredo (diocese), Ricardo Watty Urquidi, M.Sp.S., first bishop.

Oceania

American Samoa: Samoa-Pago Pago (diocese), John Quinn Weitzel, M.M.

Papua New Guinea: Mendi (diocese), Stephen J. Reichert, O.F.M.Cap.; Wewak (diocese), Raymond P. Kalisz, S.V.D.

Solomon Islands: Gizo (diocese), Christopher Cardone, O.P., aux. bp

South America

Bolivia: Pando (vicariate apostolic), Luis Morgan Casey.

Brazil: Cristalandia (prelacy), Herbert Hermes, O.S.B.; Itaituba (prelacy), Capistran Heim, O.F.M.; Miracema do Tocantins (diocese), John J. Burke, O.F.M.; Paranagua (diocese), Alfred Novak, C.Ss.R.; Valença (diocese), Elias James Manning, O.F.M. Conv.

Peru: Chulucanas (diocese), John C. McNabb, O.S.A.; Daniel Thomas Turley Murphy, O.S.A., co-adjutor; Sicuani (prelacy), Michael La Fay Bardi, O.Carm.

U.S. CATHOLIC MISSION ASSOCIATION

This is a voluntary association of individuals and organizations for whom the missionary presence of the universal Church is of central importance. It is a nonprofit religious, educational and charitable organization which exists to promote global missions. Its primary emphasis is on cross-cultural evangelization and the promotion of international justice and peace. The association is also responsible for gathering and publishing annual statistical data on U.S. missionary personnel overseas. President: William J. Morton, S.S.C.; Executive Director, Sister Rosanne Rustemeyer, S.S.N.D. Address: 3029 Fourth St. N.E., Washington, DC, 20017, (202) 832-3112, www.uscatholicmission.org.

Mission Statement

In its 1996-97 handbook, the association included the following in a mission statement.

"In the Church, our understanding of the mission of evangelization is evolving to embrace dialogue, community building, struggles for justice, efforts to model justice and faith in our lifestyles, activities and structures, in addition to the teaching/preaching/witnessing role traditionally at the heart of the mission enterprise. Still, the contemporary 'identity-confusion' about 'mission' stands forth as a major challenge for USCMA as we move toward the 21st century.

"The larger context of mission is the Spirit moving in the Signs of our Times: the liberation movements, the women's movements, the economy movements, the rising awareness and celebration of cultural diversity, the search for ways to live peacefully and creatively with great pluralism, rapid technological change, the emergence of the global economy, the steady increase in poverty and injustice, the realigning of the global political order - and the many ripples radiating out from each of these."

Home Missions

The expression "home missions" is applied to places in the U.S. where the local church does not have its own resources, human and otherwise, which are needed to begin or, if begun, to survive and grow. These areas share the name "missions" with their counterparts in foreign lands because they too need outside help to provide the personnel and means for making the Church present and active there in carrying out its mission for the salvation of people.

Dioceses in the Southeast, the Southwest, and the far West are most urgently in need of outside help to carry on the work of the Church. Millions of persons live in counties in which there are no resident priests. Many others live in rural areas beyond the reach and influence of a Catholic center. According to recent statistics compiled by the Glenmary Research Center, there are more than 500 priestless counties in the United States.

Mission Workers

A number of forces are at work to meet the pastoral needs of these missionary areas and to establish permanent churches and operating institutions where they are required. In many dioceses, one or more missions and stations are attended from established parishes and are gradually growing to independent status. Priests, brothers and sisters belonging to scores of religious institutes are engaged full-time in the home missions. Lay persons, some of them in affiliation with special groups and movements, are also involved.

The Society for the Propagation of the Faith, which conducts an annual collection for mission support in all parishes of the U.S., allocates 40 per cent of this sum for disbursement to home missions through the American Board of Catholic Missions.

Various mission-aid societies frequently undertake projects on behalf of the home missions.

The Glenmary Home Missioners, founded by Father W. Howard Bishop in 1939, is the only home mission society established for the sole purpose of carrying out the pastoral ministry in small towns and rural districts of the United States. Glenmary serves in many areas where at least 20 per cent of the people live in poverty and less than one per cent are Catholic. With 61 priests and 19 professed brothers as of January 1998 the Glenmary Missioners had missions in the archdioceses of Atlanta and Cincinnati, and in the dioceses of Birmingham, Charlotte, Covington, Jackson, Lexington, Little Rock, Nashville,

Owensboro, Richmond, Savannah, Tulsa, Tyler and Wheeling-Charleston. National headquarters are located at 4119 Glenmary Trace, Fairfield, OH. The mailing address is P.O. Box 465618, Cincinnati, OH, 45246; (513) 874-8900.

Organizations

Black and Indian Mission Office (The Commission for Catholic Missions among the Colored People and the Indians): Organized officially in 1885 by decree of the Third Plenary Council of Baltimore. Provides financial support for religious works among Blacks and Native Americans in 133 archdioceses and dioceses through funds raised by an annual collection in all parishes of the U.S. on the first Sunday of Lent, the designated Sunday. In 2002, $8,733,168 was raised; disbursements amounted to $9,487,585 for African-American missions and for Native American evangelization programs.

Bureau of Catholic Indian Missions (1874): Established as the representative of Catholic Indian missions before the federal government and the public; made permanent organization in 1884 by Third Plenary Council of Baltimore. After a remarkable history of rendering important services to the Indian people, the bureau continues to represent the Catholic Church in the U.S. in her apostolate to the American Indian. Concerns are evangelization, catechesis, liturgy, family life, education, advocacy. Address: 2021 H Street N.W., Washington, DC, 20006-4207, (202) 331-8542.

Catholic Negro-American Mission Board (1907): Supports priests and sisters in southern states and provides monthly support to sisters and lay teachers in the poorest Black schools.

Board of Directors of the three organizations above are: Cardinal Anthony Bevilacqua, president; Cardinal William Keeler; Msgr. Paul A. Lenz, secretary-treasurer; Patricia L. O'Rourke, D.St.G.G., assistant secretary/treasurer. Address: 2021 H Street N.W., Washington, DC, 20006-4207, (202) 331-8542.

The Catholic Church Extension Society (1905): Established with papal approval for the purpose of preserving and extending the Church in rural and isolated parts of the U.S. and its dependencies through the collection and disbursement of funds for home mission work. Since the time of its founding, more than $300 million has been received and distributed for this purpose. Works of the society are supervised by a 14-member board of governors: Cardinal Francis George of Chicago, chancellor; Rev. Msgr. Kenneth Velo, president; three archbishops, three bishops and six lay people. Headquarters: 150 S. Wacker Drive, 20th Floor, Chicago, IL, 60601, (312) 236-7240.

National Catholic Rural Life Conference: Founded in 1923 through the efforts of Bishop Edwin V. O'Hara. Applies the Gospel message to rural issues through focus on rural parishes and the provision of services including distribution of educational materials development of prayer and worship resources, advocacy for strong rural communities. Bishop Raymond L. Burke of LaCrosse, president; Brother David G. Andrews C.S.C., exec. dir. National headquarters: 4625 Beaver Ave., Des Moines, IA, 50310, (515) 270-2634; www.ncrle.com.

U.S. Catholic Statistics

U.S. STATISTICAL SUMMARY

(Principal sources: The Official Catholic Directory, *2003; Bill Ryan, USCC Dept. of Communications. Comparisons, where given, are with figures reported in the previous edition of the* Directory. *Totals below do not include statistics for Outlying Areas of U.S. These are given in tables on the preceding pages and elsewhere in the* Catholic Almanac; *see Index.)*

Catholic Population: 66,407,105; increase, 1,136,661. Percent of total population: 22.8%.

Jurisdictions: 34 archdioceses (includes 33 metropolitan sees and the Military Archdiocese), 152 dioceses (includes St. Thomas, Virgin Islands, and the eparchy of Our Lady of Deliverance of Newark for Syrians of the U.S. and Canada), 1 apostolic exarchate (New York-based Armenian exarchate for U.S. and Canada). The current number of dioceses reflects the creation on July 3, 2000, of the new diocese of Laredo. There are also the eparchies of St. Maron and Our Lady of Lebanon of Los Angeles (Maronites), Newton (Melkites), St. Thomas Apostle of Detroit (Chaldeans), St. George Martyr of Canton, Ohio (Romanians), St. Thomas of Chicago (Syro-Malabars) which was created on March 13, 2001, and the Eparchy of St. Peter the Apostle of San Diego which was created on May 21, 2002. The eparchy of Our Lady of Deliverance of Newark has its seat in Newark, NJ. The Armenian apostolic exarchate for the United States and Canada has its seat in New York. Vacant jurisdictions (as of Aug. 15, 2003): Alexandria, Camden, Helena, Ogdensburg, Phoenix, St. Louis, Toledo.

Cardinals: 14 (8 head archiepiscopal sees in U.S.; 2 are Roman Curia officials; three are retired, including Puerto Rico, one is a theologian). As of July 10, 2003.

Archbishops: 49. Diocesan, in U.S., 34 (does not include 8 cardinals and military archbishop); retired, 17; there are also 9 archbishops serving outside U.S. As of July 10, 2003.

Bishops: 373. Diocesan, in U.S. (and Virgin Islands), 155; auxiliaries, 90; coadjutors, 3; retired, 88; there are also 25 bishops serving outside U.S. As of July 10, 2003.

Priests: 44,487; decrease, 1,186. Diocesan, 29,715 (decrease, 714); religious order priests (does not include those assigned overseas), 14,772 (decrease, 472). There were 449 newly ordained priests; decrease, 30.

Permanent Deacons: 14,106; increase, 342.

Brothers: 5,568; increase, 122.

Sisters: 74,698; decrease, 802.

Seminarians: 4,522. Diocesan seminarians, 3,251; religious order seminarians, 1,271.

Receptions into Church: 1,168,795. Includes 1,005,490 infant baptisms; 81,013 adult baptisms and 82,292 already baptized persons received into full communion with the Church.

First Communions: 897,635.

Confirmations: 637,705.

Marriages: 241,727.

Deaths: 477,702.

Parishes: 19,484.

Seminaries, Diocesan: 70.

Religious Seminaries: 143.

Colleges and Universities: 237. Students, 749,512.

High Schools: 1,376. Students, 686,651.

Elementary Schools: 7,142. Students, 1,873,217.

Non-Residential Schools for Handicapped: 85. Students, 18,535.

Teachers: 171,814 (priests, 1,596; brothers, 1,021; scholastics, 33; sisters, 7,389; laity, 161,775).

Public School Students in Religious Instruction Programs: 4,350,682. High school students, 767,739; elementary school students, 3,582,943.

Hospitals: 585; patients treated, 83,921,898.

Health Care Centers: 477; patients treated, 5,249,083.

Specialized Homes: 1,534; patients assisted, 778,623.

Residential Care of Children (Orphanages): 226; children assisted, 714,253.

Day Care and Extended Day Care Centers: 1,117; children assisted, 136,000.

Special Centers for Social Services: 3,044; assisted annually, 20,032,104.

PERCENTAGE OF CATHOLICS IN TOTAL POPULATION IN U.S.

(*Source:* The Official Catholic Directory, *2003; figures are as of Jan. 1, 2003. Total general population figures at the end of the table are U.S. Census Bureau estimates for Jan. 1 of the respective years. Archdioceses are indicated by an asterisk; for dioceses marked +, see Dioceses with Interstate Lines.*)

State Diocese	Catholic Pop.	Total Pop.	Cath. Pct.	State Diocese	Catholic Pop.	Total Pop.	Cath. Pct.
Alabama	**153,336**	**4,459,745**	**3.4**	**Illinois, cont.**			
*Mobile	64,821	1,640,683	3.9	Springfield	152,985	1,106,124	13.8
Birmingham	88,515	2,819,062	3.1	**Indiana**	**770,377**	**6,041,872**	**12.7**
Alaska	**57,419**	**630,218**	**9.1**	*Indianapolis	229,482	2,430,606	9.4
*Anchorage	32,170	401,610	8.0	Evansville	89,464	490,986	18.2
Fairbanks	18,931	156,500	12.1	Ft.Wayne-S.Bend	166,816	1,178,520	14.1
Juneau	6,318	72,108	8.7	Gary	186,200	765,024	24.3
Arizona	**808,643**	**5,173,860**	**17.0**	Lafayette	98,415	1,176,736	8.3
Phoenix	530,541	3,650,009	14.5	**Iowa**	**510,640**	**2,865,948**	**17.8**
Tucson	350,120	1,523,851	22.9	*Dubuque	212,619	927,161	22.9
Arkansas				Davenport	102,716	728,048	14.1
Little Rock	103,069	2,692,090	3.8	Des Moines	100,825	742,190	13.5
California	**10,057,197**	**32,732,862**	**28.9**	Sioux City	94,480	468,549	20.1
*Los Angeles	4,206,875	11,012,763	38.1	**Kansas**	**419,057**	**2,690,424**	**15.5**
*San Francisco	247,493	1,731,161	14.2	*Kansas City	200,012	1,193,425	16.7
Fresno	375,000	2,410,600	15.5	Dodge City	55,053	222,502	24.7
Monterey	319,437	967,992	32.9	Salina	48,510	325,112	14.9
Oakland	432,890	2,433,952	17.7	Wichita	115,482	949,385	12.1
Orange	1,127,736	2,890,444	39.0	**Kentucky**	**384,127**	**4,013,653**	**9.5**
Sacramento	510,099	3,169,750	16.0	*Louisville	197,285	1,220,070	16.1
San Bernardino	1,000,000	3,402,125	34.0	Covington	88,612	464,629	19.1
San Diego	919,195	3,116,335	29.4	Lexington	46,183	1,492,79	23.0
San Jose	584,000	1,688,309	35.0	Owensboro	52,047	836,162	6.2
Santa Rosa	151,218	753,893	20.0	**Louisiana**	**1,326,072**	**4,432,840**	**29.9**
Stockton	183,254	1,175,538	15.5	*New Orleans	488,584	1,355,542	36.0
Colorado	**603,196**	**4,293,890**	**14.0**	Alexandria	48,050	389,970	12.3
*Denver	367,996	2,907,890	12.6	Baton Rouge	221,424	856,734	25.8
Colo. Springs	125,000	785,000	15.9	Houma-			
Pueblo	110,200	601,000	18.3	Thibodaux	126,000	202,000	62.3
Connecticut	**1,270,093**	**3,428,965**	**37.0**	Lafayette	331,186	568,154	58.2
*Hartford	698,655	1,873,983	37.2	Lake Charles	71,772	277,849	25.8
Bridgeport	343,992	885,368	38.8	Shreveport	39,056	782,591	4.9
Norwich+	227,446	669,614	33.9	**Maine**			
Delaware+				Portland	217,705	1,274,923	17.0
Wilmington	220,000	1,199,701	18.3	**Maryland**			
District of Columbia				*Baltimore	500,178	2,972,083	16.8
*Washington+	556,851	2,571,359	21.6	**Massachusetts**	**3,071,921**	**6,327,819**	**48.5**
Florida	**2,295,307**	**16,345,291**	**14.0**	*Boston	2,083,899	3,951,377	52.7
*Miami	844,685	3,955,969	21.3	Fall River	346,054	824,235	41.9
Orlando	352,909	3,466,422	10.2	Springfield	251,311	790,000	31.8
Palm Beach	268,350	1,648,253	16.2	Worcester	390,657	762,207	51.2
Pensacola-				**Michigan**	**2,236,163**	**9,962,404**	**22.4**
Tallahassee	62,553	1,267,077	4.9	*Detroit	1,432,734	4,441,551	32.2
St. Augustine	158,792	1,717,530	9.2	Gaylord	80,165	497,120	16.1
St. Petersburg	391,422	2,609,480	15.0	Grand Rapids	162,670	1,283,717	12.6
Venice	216,596	1,680,560	12.8	Kalamazoo	118,452	940,352	12.5
Georgia	**446,005**	**8,382,376**	**5.3**	Lansing	232,818	1,757,906	13.2
*Atlanta	367,472	5,752,854	6.3	Marquette	69,500	317,616	21.8
Savannah	78,533	2,629,53	22.9	Saginaw	139,824	724,142	19.3
Hawaii				**Minnesota**	**1,248,381**	**4,903,424**	**25.4**
Honolulu	232,935	1,211,537	19.2	*St. Paul and			
Idaho				Minneapolis	786,149	2,940,382	26.7
Boise	133,950	1,302,100	10.2	Crookston	41,080	246,667	16.6
Illinois	**3,939,250**	**12,611,719**	**31.2**	Duluth	71,853	430,900	16.6
*Chicago	2,446,000	6,047,000	40.4	New Ulm	70,406	287,090	24.5
Belleville	107,041	845,906	12.6	St. Cloud	148,466	440,701	33.6
Joliet	620,363	1,694,173	36.6	Winona	130,427	557,684	23.3
Peoria	193,970	1,452,688	13.3	**Mississippi**	**124,633**	**2,758,281**	**4.5**
Rockford	418,891	1,465,828	28.5	Biloxi	73,286	778,256	9.4

State Diocese	Catholic Pop.	Total Cath. Pop.	Pct.	State Diocese	Catholic Pop.	Total Cath. Pop.	Pct.
Mississippi, cont.				**Pennsylvania, cont.**			
Jackson	51,347	1,980,025	2.6	Erie	225,197	874,057	25.7
Missouri	856,561	5,582,694	15.3	Greensburg	183,034	681,720	26.8
*St. Louis	555,000	2,118,721	26.1	Harrisburg	247,861	2,027,835	12.2
Jefferson City	86,336	843,840	10.2	Pittsburgh	812,078	1,967,494	41.2
Kansas City-				Scranton	355,422	1,069,367	33.2
St. Joseph	151,900	1,394,054	10.8	**Rhode Island**			
Springfield-				Providence	639,962	1,048,319	61.0
C. Girardeau	63,325	1,226,079	5.1	**South Carolina**			
Montana	**124,837**	**900,799**	**13.8**	Charleston	148,116	4,027,012	3.6
Great Falls-				**South Dakota**	**155,222**	**2,796,364**	**5.5**
Billings	57,144	391,360	14.6	Rapid City	29,940	272,211	13.1
Helena	67,693	509,439	13.3	Sioux Falls	125,282	524,153	23.9
Nebraska	**366,899**	**1,687,824**	**21.7**	**Tennessee**	**183,459**	**5,694,788**	**3.2**
*Omaha	222,938	853,300	26.1	Knoxville	47,057	2,141,075	2.2
Grand Island	54,549	295,176	18.4	Memphis	65,779	1,455,808	4.5
Lincoln	89,412	539,348	16.5	Nashville	70,623	2,097,905	3.3
Nevada	**571,767**	**2,193,268**	**26.0**	**Texas**	**5,665,053**	**21,074,207**	**26.8**
Las Vegas	494,353	1,594,690	31.0	*San Antonio	644,357	1,959,950	32.8
Reno	77,414	598,578	12.9	Amarillo	49,128	406,672	12.0
New Hampshire				Austin	401,541	2,178,507	18.3
Manchester	336,803	1,235,786	27.2	Beaumont	94,780	596,992	15.8
New Jersey	**3,468,014**	**7,921,192**	**43.7**	Brownsville	831,614	978,369	85.0
*Newark	1,319,558	2,809,267	46.9	Corpus Christi	328,447	547,411	60.0
Camden	445,017	1,329,206	33.4	Dallas	853,961	3,247,837	26.2
Metuchen	548,000	1,304,764	41.9	El Paso+	656,035	811,739	80.8
Paterson	415,082	1,110,607	37.3	Fort Worth	400,078	2,698,443	14.8
Trenton	740,357	1,367,348	54.1	Galveston			
New Mexico	**488,825**	**2,072,708**	**23.5**	-Houston	1,006,425	4,704,532	21.3
*Santa Fe	302,436	1,111,071	27.2	Laredo	89,550	294,776	30.3
Gallup	53,743	477,000	11.2	Lubbock	55,701	451,995	12.3
Las Cruces	132,646	484,637	27.3	San Angelo	89,372	682,945	13.0
New York	**7,813,438**	**19,099,261**	**40.9**	Tyler	56,127	1,302,043	4.3
*New York	2,488,146	5,529,214	44.9	Victoria	107,937	211,996	50.9
Albany	400,000	1,342,461	29.7	**Utah**			
Brooklyn	1,824,642	4,689,802	38.9	Salt Lake City	125,000	2,295,971	5.4
Buffalo	709,258	1,581,686	44.8	**Vermont**			
Ogdensburg	143,700	462,000	31.1	Burlington	149,048	608,827	24.4
Rochester	341,500	1,489,576	22.9	**Virginia**	**596,102**	**7,131,178**	**8.3**
Rockville Ctr.	1,560,456	2,829,635	55.1	Arlington	382,574	2,403,540	15.9
Syracuse	345,736	1,174,887	29.4	Richmond	213,528	4,727,638	4.5
North Carolina	**314,891**	**8,103,159**	**3.8**	**Washington**	**680,497**	**5,852,497**	**11.6**
Charlotte	135,398	4,168,955	3.2	*Seattle	548,900	4,711,700	11.6
Raleigh	179,493	3,934,204	4.5	Spokane	66,274	679,105	9.7
North Dakota	**149,108**	**629,395**	**23.6**	Yakima	65,323	461,600	14.1
Bismarck	61,378	254,426	24.1	**West Virginia**			
Fargo	87,730	374,969	23.3	Wheeling-			
Ohio	**2,159,410**	**11,396,147**	**18.9**	Charleston	69,614	1,806,926	3.8
*Cincinnati	514,928	2,932,047	17.5	**Wisconsin**	**1,643,656**	**5,387,346**	**30.5**
Cleveland	814,791	2,852,331	28.5	*Milwaukee	694,508	2,248,785	30.8
Columbus	236,402	2,383,015	9.9	Green Bay	381,472	930,419	41.0
Steubenville	40,562	515,672	7.8	La Crosse	215,573	848,455	25.4
Toledo	312,767	1,489,769	20.9	Madison	268,123	938,308	28.5
Youngstown	239,960	1,223,313	19.5	Superior	83,980	421,379	20.0
Oklahoma	**162,683**	**3,963,963**	**4.1**	**Wyoming**			
*Oklahoma City	102,683	2,403,280	4.3	Cheyenne	49,000	494,423	9.9
Tulsa	60,000	1,560,683	3.8				
Oregon	**394,427**	**3,450,300**	**11.4**	**East. Churches**	551,867	-	-
*Portland	356,037	3,010,800	11.8	**Military Arch.**('99)	1,194,000	-	-
Baker	38,390	439,500	8.7	**Outlying Areas**	**3,134,901**	**4,423,566**	**70.8**
Pennsylvania	**3,699,440**	**12,289,321**	**30.0**				
*Philadelphia	1,494,883	3,861,648	38.7	**Total 2003**	**66,407,105**	**290,446,533**	**22.8**
Allentown	270,843	1,161,932	23.3	**Total 2002**	**65,270,444**	**284,972,437**	**22.9**
Altoona-J'town	110,122	645,268	17.0	**Total 1993**	**59,220,723**	**256,042,585**	**23.1**

CATHOLIC POPULATION OF THE UNITED STATES

(*Source:* The Official Catholic Directory, *2003; figures as of Jan. 1, 2003. Archdioceses are indicated by an asterisk; for dioceses marked +, see Dioceses with Interstate Lines.*)

State Diocese	Cath. Pop.	Dioc. Priests	Rel. Priests	Total Priests	Perm. Deac.	Bros.	Sisters	Par- ishes
Alabama	**153,336**	**185**	**71**	**256**	**108**	**38**	**294**	**133**
*Mobile	64,821	111	38	149	63	12	170	76
Birmingham	88,515	74	33	107	45	26	124	57
Alaska	**57,419**	**35**	**29**	**64**	**60**	**6**	**66**	**72**
*Anchorage	32,170	16	10	26	18	3	43	20
Fairbanks	18,931	8	17	25	37	3	19	41
Juneau	6,318	11	2	13	5	-	4	11
Arizona	**880,643**	**248**	**169**	**417**	**331**	**25**	**463**	**160**
Phoenix	530,541	134	102	236	211	15	220	89
Tucson	350,102	114	67	181	120	10	243	71
Arkansas, Little Rock	**103,069**	**75**	**53**	**128**	**96**	**31**	**276**	**88**
California	**10,057,197**	**2,111**	**1,516**	**3,627**	**831**	**490**	**4,749**	**1,071**
*Los Angeles	4,206,875	549	592	1,141	219	161	1,800	288
*San Francisco	247,493	223	168	391	67	58	807	93
Fresno	375,000	116	30	146	5	4	131	86
Monterey	319,437	82	22	104	3	33	112	46
Oakland	432,890	204	99	303	92	56	354	87
Orange	1,127,736	179	108	287	61	13	344	56
Sacramento	510,099	168	67	235	110	24	170	98
San Bernardino	1,000,000	134	103	237	92	17	155	97
San Diego	919,195	180	97	277	104	20	351	98
San Jose	584,000	122	204	326	7	65	393	48
Santa Rosa	151,218	87	12	99	38	36	66	42
Stockton	183,254	67	14	81	33	3	66	32
Colorado	**603,196**	**261**	**182**	**443**	**200**	**29**	**625**	**203**
*Denver	367,996	153	123	276	143	22	404	118
Colo. Springs	125,000	36	27	63	28	2	125	33
Pueblo	110,200	72	32	104	29	5	96	52
Connecticut	**1,270,093**	**763**	**239**	**1,002**	**442**	**84**	**1,559**	**381**
*Hartford	698,655	357	133	490	290	60	883	216
Bridgeport	343,992	268	44	312	93	-	439	87
Norwich+	227,446	138	62	200	59	24	237	78
Delaware, Wilmington+	**220,000**	**119**	**87**	**206**	**77**	**29**	**259**	**57**
D.C.,*Washington+	**556,851**	**309**	**603**	**912**	**243**	**139**	**749**	**140**
Florida	**2,295,307**	**876**	**425**	**1,301**	**572**	**164**	**1,207**	**459**
*Miami	844,685	258	116	374	137	60	329	111
Orlando	352,909	125	42	167	138	15	114	72
Palm Beach	268,350	105	33	138	40	3	154	49
Pensacola-Tallahassee	62,553	73	9	82	54	6	52	49
St. Augustine	158,792	90	25	115	32	3	118	51
St. Petersburg	391,422	128	129	257	100	49	332	73
Venice	216,596	97	71	168	71	28	108	54
Georgia	**446,005**	**234**	**89**	**323**	**195**	**14**	**227**	**127**
*Atlanta	367,472	166	65	231	150	2	113	75
Savannah	78,533	68	24	92	45	12	114	52
Hawaii, Honolulu	**232,935**	**74**	**81**	**155**	**52**	**49**	**168**	**66**
Idaho, Boise	**133,950**	**81**	**12**	**93**	**50**	**7**	**93**	**55**
Illinois	**3,939,250**	**1,748**	**1,196**	**2,944**	**1,055**	**515**	**4,811**	**1,050**
*Chicago	2,446,000	854	886	1,740	624	360	2,806	374
Belleville	107,041	134	39	173	30	13	233	124
Joliet	620,363	195	120	315	171	86	652	122
Peoria	193,970	221	47	268	111	11	244	165
Rockford	418,891	212	48	260	112	17	250	105
Springfield	152,985	132	56	188	7	28	626	160
Indiana	**770,377**	**574**	**338**	**912**	**88**	**189**	**1,818**	**432**
*Indianapolis	229,482	162	106	268	-	41	725	139
Evansville	89,464	92	7	99	21	2	282	70
Ft. Wayne-South Bend	166,816	89	164	253	22	128	622	87
Gary	186,200	117	42	159	39	16	110	74
Lafayette	98,415	114	19	133	6	2	79	62

State Diocese	Cath. Pop.	Dioc. Priests	Rel. Priests	Total Priests	Perm. Deac.	Bros.	Sisters	Par- ishes
Iowa	**510,640**	**614**	**52**	**666**	**224**	**32**	**1,227**	**493**
*Dubuque	212,619	232	35	267	69	28	841	201
Davenport	102,716	129	2	131	47	1	210	85
Des Moines	100,825	97	11	108	72	3	91	83
Sioux City	94,480	156	4	160	36	-	85	124
Kansas	**419,057**	**325**	**84**	**409**	**11**	**17**	**1,282**	**351**
*Kansas City	200,012	96	57	153	-	15	652	119
Dodge City	55,053	36	9	45	9	-	96	49
Salina	48,510	65	14	79	-	1	205	92
Wichita	115,482	128	4	132	3	2	329	91
Kentucky	**384,127**	**401**	**110**	**511**	**172**	**94**	**1,669**	**297**
*Louisville	197,285	172	59	231	111	77	944	111
Covington	88,612	95	2	97	24	9	379	47
Lexington	46,183	52	21	73	37	4	141	60
Owensboro	52,047	82	28	110	-	4	205	79
Louisiana	**1,317,072**	**662**	**321**	**983**	**369**	**153**	**1,159**	**490**
*New Orleans	488,584	222	185	407	186	104	763	142
Alexandria	48,050	56	13	69	5	4	48	48
Baton Rouge	221,424	76	37	113	40	12	101	70
Houma-Thibodaux	126,000	67	9	76	28	5	29	39
Lafayette	331,186	149	55	204	71	23	130	121
Lake Charles	71,772	51	9	60	33	1	26	38
Shreveport	39,056	41	13	54	6	4	62	32
Maine, Portland	**217,705**	**170**	**48**	**218**	**24**	**29**	**390**	**135**
Maryland, *Baltimore	**500,178**	**261**	**234**	**495**	**171**	**74**	**1,131**	**154**
Massachusetts	**3,071,921**	**1,483**	**997**	**2,480**	**470**	**253**	**4,108**	**713**
*Boston	2,083,899	887	715	1,602	246	147	2,763	360
Fall River	346,054	173	141	314	90	16	295	101
Springfield	251,311	179	30	209	58	9	580	126
Worcester	390,657	244	111	355	76	81	470	126
Michigan	**2,236,163**	**1,058**	**398**	**1,456**	**326**	**134**	**3,008**	**802**
*Detroit	1,432,734	475	293	768	145	119	1,871	308
Gaylord	80,165	65	13	78	12	2	45	81
Grand Rapids	162,670	114	21	135	26	1	279	90
Kalamazoo	118,452	58	11	69	28	2	175	46
Lansing	232,818	149	36	185	76	9	460	95
Marquette	69,500	90	11	101	25	-	58	74
Saginaw	139,824	107	13	120	14	-	120	108
Minnesota	**1,248,381**	**796**	**307**	**1,103**	**300**	**144**	**2,358**	**719**
*St.Paul & Minneapolis	786,149	341	172	513	207	47	936	221
Crookston	41,080	51	2	53	10	1	133	69
Duluth	71,853	75	10	85	33	1	160	93
New Ulm	70,406	80	1	81	3	-	85	80
St. Cloud	148,466	131	114	245	40	74	609	138
Winona	130,427	118	8	126	7	21	435	118
Mississippi	**124,633**	**119**	**56**	**175**	**33**	**32**	**275**	**119**
Biloxi	73,286	54	28	82	27	18	47	45
Jackson	51,347	65	28	93	6	14	228	74
Missouri	**856,561**	**692**	**498**	**1,190**	**381**	**239**	**2,482**	**462**
*St. Louis	555,000	401	337	738	246	139	2,013	217
Jefferson City	86,336	101	7	108	67	2	83	95
Kansas City-St. Joseph	151,900	116	97	213	60	30	289	85
Springfield-Cape Girardeau	63,325	74	57	131	8	68	97	65
Montana	**124,837**	**160**	**21**	**181**	**38**	**2**	**117**	**124**
Great Falls-Billings	57,144	69	14	83	4	1	74	66
Helena	67,693	91	7	98	34	1	43	58
Nebraska	**366,899**	**446**	**103**	**549**	**165**	**22**	**206**	**313**
*Omaha	222,938	220	96	316	163	21	-	138
Grand Island	54,549	76	-	76	-	-	73	39
Lincoln	89,412	150	7	157	9	2	133	136
Nevada	**571,767**	**54**	**32**	**86**	**15**	**7**	**61**	**52**
Las Vegas	494,353	32	23	55	6	3	22	24
Reno	77,414	22	9	31	9	4	39	28
New Hampshire								
Manchester	**336,803**	**215**	**62**	**277**	**49**	**32**	**652**	**131**

State / Diocese	Cath. Pop.	Dioc. Priests	Rel. Priests	Total Priests	Perm. Deac.	Bros.	Sisters	Par- ishes
New Jersey	**3,468,014**	**1,747**	**553**	**2,300**	**903**	**236**	**3,274**	**705**
*Newark	1,319,558	721	227	948	198	98	1,318	234
Camden	445,017	313	47	360	114	17	315	126
Metuchen	548,000	228	54	282	141	14	385	108
Paterson	415,082	246	182	428	174	32	823	111
Trenton	740,357	239	43	282	276	72	433	126
New Mexico	**488,825**	**196**	**147**	**343**	**197**	**99**	**404**	**190**
*Santa Fe	302,436	117	85	202	143	86	235	92
Gallup	55,743	48	23	71	29	10	123	54
Las Cruces	132,646	31	39	70	25	3	46	44
New York	**7,813,438**	**3,000**	**1,477**	**4,777**	**1,227**	**918**	**9,211**	**1,655**
*New York	2,488,146	734	856	1,590	356	435	3,269	412
Albany	400,000	267	105	372	101	94	910	181
Brooklyn	1,824,642	548	191	739	165	187	1,153	217
Buffalo	709,258	400	163	563	103	47	1,272	265
Ogdensburg	143,700	143	9	152	57	12	153	119
Rochester	341,500	246	62	308	135	38	651	158
Rockville Centre	1,560,456	391	23	414	233	89	1,398	134
Syracuse	345,736	271	68	339	77	16	405	169
North Carolina	**314,891**	**197**	**113**	**310**	**105**	**15**	**180**	**146**
Charlotte	135,398	105	58	163	76	7	108	68
Raleigh	179,493	92	55	147	29	8	72	78
North Dakota	**149,108**	**229**	**36**	**265**	**96**	**26**	**355**	**222**
Bismarck	61,378	70	27	97	66	26	138	62
Fargo	87,730	159	9	169	30	-	217	160
Ohio	**2,159,410**	**1,403**	**519**	**1,922**	**663**	**149**	**3,893**	**928**
*Cincinnati	514,928	301	242	543	142	157	1,150	237
Cleveland	814,791	442	133	575	182	53	1,384	234
Columbus	236,402	183	38	221	70	2	356	107
Steubenville	40,562	99	27	126	6	9	82	73
Toledo	312,767	197	55	252	195	6	684	161
Youngstown	239,960	181	24	205	68	22	237	116
Oklahoma	**162,683**	**175**	**44**	**219**	**117**	**16**	**237**	**151**
*Oklahoma City	102,683	99	241	23	60	11	142	71
Tulsa	60,000	76	20	96	57	5	95	80
Oregon	**394,427**	**187**	**183**	**370**	**43**	**87**	**531**	**161**
*Portland	356,037	149	178	327	30	86	506	125
Baker	38,390	38	5	43	13	1	25	36
Pennsylvania	**3,699,440**	**2,428**	**726**	**3,154**	**511**	**220**	**7,387**	**1,262**
*Philadelphia	1,494,883	736	366	1,102	211	128	3,428	282
Allentown	270,843	230	-	230	98	-	470	153
Altoona-Johnstown	110,122	150	56	206	30	8	107	99
Erie	225,197	223	9	232	25	-	438	126
Greensburg	183,034	142	79	221	-	31	295	103
Harrisburg	242,861	157	32	189	47	-	464	89
Pittsburgh	812,078	467	121	588	50	35	1,483	215
Scranton	355,422	323	63	386	50	18	702	195
Rhode Island								
Providence	**639,962**	**306**	**105**	**411**	**96**	**129**	**655**	**157**
South Carolina								
Charleston	**148,116**	**87**	**44**	**131**	**103**	**31**	**140**	**93**
South Dakota	**155,222**	**173**	**59**	**232**	**54**	**16**	**441**	**248**
Rapid City	29,940	44	27	71	27	6	63	97
Sioux Falls	125,282	129	32	161	27	10	378	151
Tennessee	**182,459**	**169**	**55**	**224**	**127**	**57**	**294**	**137**
Knoxville	47,057	53	15	68	23	13	35	44
Memphis	65,779	69	15	84	51	43	78	42
Nashville	70,623	47	25	72	53	1	181	51
Texas	**5,665,053**	**1,190**	**821**	**2,011**	**1,377**	**169**	**2,738**	**1,025**
*San Antonio	644,357	146	196	342	312	41	834	139
Amarillo	49,128	57	9	66	51	1	130	35
Austin	401,541	136	48	184	173	46	99	101
Beaumont	94,780	47	23	70	30	1	48	44
Brownsville	831,614	58	41	99	67	17	118	65
Corpus Christi	328,447	115	41	156	62	5	199	65

State Diocese	Cath. Pop.	Dioc. Priests	Rel. Priests	Total Priests	Perm. Deac.	Bros.	Sisters	Par-ishes
Texas, cont.								
Dallas	853,961	103	74	177	158	4	147	67
El Paso	656,035	80	36	116	10	13	254	58
Fort Worth	400,078	60	64	124	62	12	93	88
Galveston-Houston	1,006,000	197	222	419	250	12	482	150
Laredo	89,550	21	23	44	27	10	88	32
Lubbock	55,701	35	7	42	49	-	28	34
San Angelo	89,372	35	16	51	36	-	30	49
Tyler	56,127	42	13	55	65	7	67	48
Victoria	107,937	58	8	66	25	-	121	50
Utah, Salt Lake City	**125,000**	**57**	**29**	**86**	**47**	**14**	**54**	**47**
Vermont, Burlington	**149,048**	**127**	**47**	**174**	**39**	**18**	**182**	**83**
Virginia	**596,102**	**313**	**111**	**424**	**75**	**35**	**348**	**209**
Arlington	382,574	157	78	235	42	20	148	66
Richmond	213,528	156	33	189	33	15	200	143
Washington	**680,497**	**336**	**185**	**521**	**142**	**37**	**774**	**263**
*Seattle	548,900	183	105	288	70	24	473	139
Spokane	66,274	84	69	153	48	9	255	83
Yakima	65,323	69	11	80	24	4	46	41
West Virginia								
Wheeling-Charleston	**69,614**	**119**	**68**	**187**	**32**	**19**	**240**	**112**
Wisconsin	**1,643,656**	**1,048**	**481**	**1,529**	**368**	**98**	**4,103**	**822**
*Milwaukee	694,508	422	301	723	179	56	2,601	224
Green Bay	381,472	212	130	342	104	34	603	185
La Crosse	215,573	191	21	212	31	4	483	166
Madison	268,123	150	14	164	2	3	315	135
Superior	83,980	73	15	88	52	1	101	112
Wyoming, Cheyenne+	**49,000**	**46**	**10**	**56**	**15**	**1**	**25**	**36**
EASTERN CHURCHES	**551,867**	**588**	**118**	**706**	**121**	**33**	**344**	**572**
*Philadelphia	60,290	65	9	74	-		4	98	85
St. Nicholas	10,000	20	13	33	12	-	2	36
Stamford	16,500	62	16	78	9	3	32	52
St. Josaphat (Parma)	11,162	41	1	42	5	10	7	38
*Pittsburgh	60,686	64	9	73	-	4	102	86
Parma	12,417	37	2	39	6	-	14	31
Passaic	24,265	81	10	91	16	2	14	90
Van Nuys	3,071	18	5	23	3	7	4	19
St. Maron (Maronites)	30,000	59	12	71	13	7	2	33
Our Lady of Lebanon (Maronites)	27,870	24	6	30	9	-	7	30
Newton (Melkites)	29,323	47	16	63	37	-	3	35
St. Peter the Apostle of San Diego	35,000	8	9	17	-	-	-	7
St. Thomas Apostle of Detroit (Chaldean)	70,000	14		14	-	-	-	7
St. Thomas (Syro-Malabrs)	112,000	22	5	27	-	62	5	33
St. George Martyr (Romanian)	5,000	15	2	17	-	-	-	15
Our Lady of Deliverance (Syrians, U.S.-Canada)	12,610	12	-	12	4	-	-	8
Armenian Ex.(U.S.-Canada)	25,000	5	6	11	1	-	15	7
Military Archd. ('99)[1]	**1,194,000**	**-**	**-**	**-**	**-**	**-**	**-**	**-**
Outlying Areas								
Puerto Rico	2,791,000	357	380	737	402	66	1,225	325
Samoa-Pago Pago	12,000	10	5	15	16	-	12	13
Caroline Islands	72,940	13	18	31	43	1	33	26
Chalan Kanoa (N. Mariana Is.)	43,000	15	2	17	1	-	-	11
Guam, *Agana	131,430	35	13	48	7	2	101	24
Marshall Islands	4,531	5	5	10	2	-	11	4
Virgin Islands, St. Thomas	30,000	14	6	20	20	4	17	8
TOTAL 2003	**66,407,105**	**29,715**	**14,772**	**44,487**	**14,106**	**5,568**	**74,698**	**19,484**
TOTAL 2002	**65,270,444**	**30,429**	**15,244**	**45,713**	**13,764**	**5,690**	**75,500**	**19,496**
TOTAL 1993	**59,220,723**	**33,476**	**17,576**	**50,907**	**10,840**	**6,260**	**94,022**	**19,863**

[1]892 diocesan and 193 religious-order chaplains are on loan to the miliary (2003 *Annuario Pontificio*).

RECEPTIONS INTO THE CHURCH IN THE UNITED STATES

(Source: The Official Catholic Directory, *2003; figures as of Jan. 1, 2003. Archdioceses are indicated by an asterisk; for dioceses marked +, see Dioceses with Interstate Lines. Information includes infant and adult baptisms and those received into full communion.)*

State Diocese	Infant Baptisms	Adult Bapts.	Rec'd into Full Com.	State Diocese	Infant Baptisms	Adult Bapts.	Rec'd into Full Com.
Alabama	2,831	450	872	**Indiana, cont.**			
*Mobile	1,085	243	380	Gary	2,063	158	283
Birmingham	1,746	207	492	Lafayette	2,084	322	481
Alaska	932	107	119	**Iowa**	8,918	762	1,276
*Anchorage	444	61	84	*Dubuque	3,185	188	443
Fairbanks	371	31	14	Davenport	1,722	247	151
Juneau	117	15	21	Des Moines	2,279	239	417
Arizona	19,337	852	1,932	Sioux City	1,732	88	265
Phoenix	12,288	532	1,146	**Kansas**	8,334	1,070	1,453
Tucson	7,049	320	786	*Kansas City	4,179	470	719
Arkansas, Lit. Rock	2,452	290	510	Dodge City	990	70	98
California	196,198	10,117	12,216	Salina	906	101	159
*Los Angeles	88,172	2,305	4,095	Wichita	2,259	429	477
*San Francisco	6,730	538	617	**Kentucky**	5,906	1,198	1,089
Fresno	16,320	719	842	*Louisville	2,855	456	566
Monterey	6,223	242	511	Covington	1,368	444	139
Oakland	9,373	610	428	Lexington	675	167	147
Orange	16,263	676	821	Owensboro	1,008	131	237
Sacramento	9,022	638	1,205	**Louisiana**	18,316	1,094	1,620
San Bernardino	10,545	902	1,185	*New Orleans	6,498	341	292
San Diego	14,645	2,424	1,024	Alexandria	716	68	117
San Jose	9,235	650	498	Baton Rouge	2,598	269	373
Santa Rosa	3,282	149	165	Houma-Thibodaux	1,584	42	70
Stockton	6,388	264	825	Lafayette	5,059	145	380
Colorado	15,161	1,084	1,811	Lake Charles	1,343	144	215
*Denver	11,501	746	1,291	Shreveport	518	85	173
Colorado Springs	1,640	167	199	**Maine,** Portland	2,743	283	336
Pueblo	2,020	171	321	**Maryland,***Baltimore	7,115	574	958
Connecticut	18,015	514	640	**Massachusetts**	36,736	3,388	1,165
*Hartford	9,183	234	272	*Boston	24,097	3,031	403
Bridgeport	5,789	98	106	Fall River	4,585	90	168
Norwich+	3,043	182	262	Springfield	3,535	138	281
Delaware, Wilm.+	3,014	169	321	Worcester	4,519	129	313
D.C., *Washington+	6,921	982	721	**Michigan**	27,136	2,949	3,499
Florida	40,693	3,076	4,230	*Detroit	15,139	1,261	1,714
*Miami	17,767	817	868	Gaylord	993	123	170
Orlando	6,197	484	598	Grand Rapids	2,841	344	-
Palm Beach	4,507	284	427	Kalamazoo	1,634	201	208
Pensacola-				Lansing	3,830	695	1,051
Tallahassee	1,116	224	301	Marquette	907	79	100
St. Augustine	2,523	368	642	Saginaw	1,792	246	256
St. Petersburg	4,899	658	550	**Minnesota**	17,995	845	2,267
Venice	3,684	241	844	*St. Paul and			
Georgia	12,543	1,004	1,880	Minneapolis	11,040	524	1,471
*Atlanta	10,684	739	1,450	Crookston	651	24	92
Savannah	1,859	265	430	Duluth	1,025	60	140
Hawaii, Honolulu	3,225	348	322	New Ulm	967	78	119
Idaho, Boise	2,503	390	232	St. Cloud	2,367	88	196
Illinois	63,179	4,070	4,156	Winona	1,945	71	249
*Chicago	39,785	2,328	1,739	**Mississippi**	1,838	634	568
Belleville	1,374	334	314	Biloxi	923	506	265
Joliet	10,354	385	662	Jackson	915	128	303
Peoria	2,971	419	552	**Missouri**	12,135	2,389	1,913
Rockford	6,455	245	438	*St. Louis	7,566	927	1,031
Springfield	2,240	359	451	Jefferson City	1,441	304	278
Indiana	12,804	1,871	2,348	Ks. City-St. Joe	2,411	584	326
*Indianapolis	4,542	780	879	Springfield-			
Evansville	1,339	144	200	Cape Girardeau	717	574	278
Ft.Wayne-S. Bend	2,776	467	505	**Montana**	1,522	358	206

State Diocese	Infant Baptisms	Adult Bapts.	Rec'd into Full Com.
Montana, cont.			
Great Falls-Billings	807	94	103
Helena	715	264	103
Nebraska	6,561	720	962
*Omaha	4,115424	579	
Grand Island	1,049	125	176
Lincoln	1,397	171	207
Nevada	6,911	380	361
Las Vegas	5,177	208	188
Reno	1,734	172	173
New Hampshire			
Manchester	4,423	353	-
New Jersey	49,185	2,242	2,117
*Newark	16,980	449	555
Camden	6,553	1,001	511
Metuchen	6,596	238	276
Paterson	8,630	163	330
Trenton	10,446	391	445
New Mexico	9,107	786	833
*Santa Fe	6,126	388	609
Gallup	905	252	139
Las Cruces	2,076	146	85
New York	91,389	3,962	4,200
*New York	30,489	1,069	1,181
Albany	4,650	150	259
Brooklyn	17,670	670	662
Buffalo	6,432	588	501
Ogdensburg	1,281	155	95
Rochester	4,962	330	660
Rockville Centre	20,983	744	442
Syracuse	4,919	256	400
North Carolina	9,201	604	1,152
Charlotte	4,494	319	692
Raleigh	4,707	285	460
North Dakota	2,104	139	248
Bismarck	882	84	87
Fargo	1,222	55	161
Ohio	28,521	3,821	4,128
*Cincinnati	7,660	961	983
Cleveland	9,885	1,066	947
Columbus	3,938	505	971
Steubenville	625	183	109
Toledo	3,521	789	563
Youngstown	2,892	317	555
Oklahoma	3,640	577	889
*Okla. City	2,290	414	554
Tulsa	1,350	163	335
Oregon	6,787	956	707
*Portland	5,911	802	631
Baker	876	154	76
Pennsylvania	41,176	3,546	2,835
*Philadelphia	17,149	1,165	618
Allentown	3,635	189	-
Altoona-Johnstn.	1,419	108	160
Erie	1,986	477	230
Greensburg	1,930	160	282
Harrisburg	3,088	441	481
Pittsburgh	7,787	368	737
Scranton	4,182	638	327
Rhode Island			
Providence	5,398	201	312
South Carolina			
Charleston	2,491	321	637
South Dakota	2,313	137	355
Rapid City	574	77	92

State Diocese	Infant Baptisms	Adult Bapts.	Rec'd into Full Com.
South Dakota, cont.			
Sioux Falls	1,739	60	263
Tennessee	3,305	876	934
Knoxville	852	202	292
Memphis	869	462	294
Nashville	1,584	212	348
Texas	91,906	9,989	6,103
*San Antonio	12,211	546	645
Amarillo	1,250	96	109
Austin	8,147	638	1,027
Beaumont	1,333	106	234
Brownsville	4,290	4,622	597
Corpus Christi	3,408	257	426
Dallas	15,105	800	634
El Paso	9,538	144	288
Fort Worth	6,633	485	568
Galv.-Houston	19,630	1,616	922
Laredo	3,307	113	41
Lubbock	1,629	157	217
San Angelo	1,990	168	158
Tyler	1,903	180	140
Victoria	1,532	61	97
Utah, Salt Lake City	3,467	476	337
Vermont, Burlington	1,514	113	158
Virginia	11,282	937	1,657
Arlington	7,477	863	518
Richmond	3,805	74	1,139
Washington	11,500	1,604	792
*Seattle	7,122	1,253	667
Spokane	1,530	211	-
Yakima	2,848	140	125
West Virginia			
Wheeling-Chas.	985	224	278
Wisconsin	21,112	986	1,823
*Milwaukee	9,315	398	687
Green Bay	4,656	213	375
La Crosse	2,858	125	287
Madison	3,274	131	327
Superior	1,009	119	147
Wyoming, Chey.+	860	162	133
Eastern Churches	4,010	183	322
*Philadelphia	216	20	18
St. Nicholas	255	5	7
Stamford	179	1	-
St. Josaphat (Parma)	89	5	3
*Pittsburgh	234	29	89
Parma	109	12	29
Passaic	244	16	24
Van Nuys	78	8	15
St. Maron (Maronites)	428	12	5
Our Lady of Lebanon (Maronites)	494	24	-
Newton (Melkites)	373	21	25
St. Peter the Apostle	220	2	-
St. Thomas Apostle of Detroit (Chaldeans)	863	16	—
St. Thomas (Syro-Malabar)	48		32
St. George Martyr (Romanian)	19	-	16
Our Lady of Deliverance (Syrians, U.S.-Can.)	82	4	4
Armenian Ex. (U.S.-Can.)	79	5	84
Military Archd.	3,762	779	373
Outlying Areas	34,709	5,071	952
Total 2003	**1,005,490**	**81,013**	**82,292**

The Catholic Church in Canada

Background

The first date in the remote background of the Catholic history of Canada is July 7, 1534, when a priest in the exploration company of Jacques Cartier celebrated Mass on the Gaspe Peninsula.

Successful colonization and the significant beginnings of the Catholic history of the country date from the foundation of Québec in 1608 by Samuel de Champlain and French settlers. Montréal was established in 1642.

The earliest missionaries were Franciscan Récollets (Recollects) and Jesuits who arrived in 1615 and 1625, respectively. They provided some pastoral care for the settlers but worked mainly among the 100,000 Indians — Algonquins, Hurons and Iroquois — in the interior and in the Lake Ontario region. Eight of the Jesuit missionaries, killed in the 1640s, were canonized in 1930. (*See* **Index: Jesuit North American Martyrs.**) Sulpician Fathers, who arrived in Canada late in the 1640s, played a part in the great missionary period, which ended about 1700.

Kateri Tekakwitha, "Lily of the Mohawks," who was baptized in 1676 and died in 1680, was declared "Blessed" on June 22, 1980.

The communities of women religious with the longest histories in Canada are the Canonesses of St. Augustine and the Ursulines, since 1639; and the Hospitallers of St. Joseph, since 1642. Communities of Canadian origin are the Congregation of Notre Dame, founded by St. Marguerite Bourgeoys in 1658, and the Grey Nuns, formed by St. Marie Marguerite d'Youville in 1737.

Mother Marie (Guyard) of the Incarnation, an Ursuline nun, was one of the first three women missionaries to New France; called "Mother of the Church in Canada," she was declared "Blessed" on June 22, 1980.

Start of Church Organization

Ecclesiastical organization began with the appointment in 1658 of François De Montmorency-Laval, "Father of the Church in Canada," as vicar apostolic of New France. He was the first bishop of Québec from 1674 to 1688, with jurisdiction over all French-claimed territory in North America. He was declared "Blessed" on June 22, 1980.

In 1713, the French Canadian population numbered 18,000. In the same year, the Treaty of Utrecht ceded Acadia, Newfoundland and the Hudson Bay Territory to England. The Acadians were scattered among the American colonies in 1755.

The English acquired possession of Canada and its 70,000 French-speaking inhabitants by virtue of the Treaty of Paris in 1763. Anglo-French and Anglican-Catholic differences and tensions developed. The pro-British government at first refused to recognize the titles of church officials, hindered the clergy in their work and tried to install a non-Catholic educational system. Laws were passed that guaranteed religious liberties to Catholics (Québec Act of 1774, Constitutional Act of 1791, legislation approved by Queen Victoria in 1851), but it took some time before actual respect for these liberties matched the legal enactments. The initial moderation of government antipathy toward the Church was caused partly by the loyalty of Catholics to the Crown during the American Revolution and the War of 1812.

Growth

The 15 years following the passage in 1840 of the Act of Union, which joined Upper and Lower Canada, were significant. New communities of men and women religious joined those already in the country. The Oblates of Mary Immaculate, missionaries par excellence in Canada, advanced the penetration of the West that had been started in 1818 by Abbé Provencher. New jurisdictions were established, and Québec became a metropolitan see in 1844. The first Council of Québec was held in 1851. The established Catholic school system enjoyed a period of growth.

Laval University was inaugurated in 1854 and canonically established in 1876.

Archbishop Elzear-Alexandre Taschereau of Québec was named Canada's first cardinal in 1886.

The apostolic delegation to Canada was set up in 1899. It became a nunciature October 16, 1969, with the establishment of diplomatic relations with the Vatican. The present Apostolic Nuncio is Archbishop Luigi Ventura, appointed on June 22, 2001.

Early in this century, Canada had eight ecclesiastical provinces, 23 dioceses, three vicariates apostolic, 3,500 priests, 2 million Catholics, about 30 communities of men religious, and 70 or more communities of women religious. The Church in Canada was phased out of mission status and removed from the jurisdiction of the Congregation for the Propagation of the Faith in 1908.

Diverse Population

The greatest concentration of Catholics is in the eastern portion of the country. In the northern and western portions, outside metropolitan centers, there are some of the most difficult parish and mission areas in the world. Bilingual (English-French) differences in the general population are reflected in the Church; for example, in the parallel structures of the Canadian Conference of Catholic Bishops, which was established in 1943. Québec is the center of French cultural influence. Many language groups are represented among Catholics, who include more than 257,000 members of Eastern Rites in one metropolitan see, seven eparchies and an apostolic exarchate.

Education, a past source of friction between the Church and the government, is administered by the civil provinces in a variety of arrangements authorized by the Canadian Constitution. Denominational schools have tax support in one way in Québec and Newfoundland, and in another way in Alberta, Ontario and Saskatchewan. Several provinces provide tax support only for public schools, making private financing necessary for separate church-related schools.

ECCLESIASTICAL JURISDICTIONS OF CANADA

Provinces

Names of ecclesiastical provinces and metropolitan sees in bold face; suffragan sees in parentheses.

Edmonton (Calgary, St. Paul).

Gatineau-Hull (Amos, Mont-Laurier, Rouyn Noranda).

Grouard-McLennan (Mackenzie-Ft. Smith, Prince George, Whitehorse).

Halifax (Antigonish, Charlottetown, Yarmouth).

Keewatin-LePas (Churchill-Hudson Bay, Labrador-Schefferville, Moosonee).

Kingston (Alexandria-Cornwall, Peterborough, Sault Ste. Marie).

Moncton (Bathurst, Edmundston, St. John).

Montréal (Joliette, St. Jean-Longueuil, St. Jerome, Valleyfield).

Ottawa (Hearst, Pembroke, Timmins).

Québec (Chicoutimi, Ste.-Anne-de-la-Pocatiere,

Trois Rivieres).

Regina (Prince Albert, Saskatoon, Abbey of St. Peter).

Rimouski (Baie-Comeau, Gaspe).

St. Boniface (no suffragan).

St. John's (Grand Falls, St. George).

Sherbrooke (Nicolet, St. Hyacinthe).

Toronto (Hamilton, London, St. Catharines, Thunder Bay).

Vancouver (Kamloops, Nelson, Victoria).

Winnipeg-Ukrainian (Edmonton, New Westminster, Saskatoon, Toronto).

Jurisdictions immediately subject to the Holy See: Roman-Rite Archdiocese of Winnipeg, Byzantine Eparchy of Sts. Cyril and Methodius for Slovaks, Byzantine Eparchy of St. Sauveur de Montréal for Greek Melkites; Antiochene Eparchy of St. Maron of Montréal for Maronites.

JURISDICTIONS, HIERARCHY

(Principal sources: Information office, Canadian Conference of Catholic Bishops; Rev. Mr. William Kokesch, Dir., Communications Service, Canadian Conference of Catholic Bishops; Annuaire, Conférence des Évêques Catholiques du Canada; Catholic Almanac survey; Annuario Pontificio; L'Osservatore Romano; Catholic News Service. As of June 1, 2003.)

Information includes names of archdioceses (indicated by asterisk) and dioceses, date of foundation, present ordinaries and auxiliaries; addresses of chancery office/bishop's residence; cathedral.

Alexandria-Cornwall, ON (1890 as Alexandria; name changed to Alexandria-Cornwall, 1976): Paul-André Durocher, bishop, 2002.

Diocesan Center: 220, chemin Montréal, C.P. 1388, Cornwall, ON K6H 5V4; (613) 938-1138; www.diocese-alex-cnwl.on.ca/. Cathedral: St. Finnans (Alexandria); Nativity Co-Cathedral (Cornwall).

Amos, QC (1938): Gérard Drainville, bishop, 1978.

Bishop's Residence: 450, rue Principale Nord, Amos, QC J9T 2M1; (819) 732-6515; www.cableamos.com/dioceseamos. Cathedral: St. Teresa of Ávila.

Antigonish, NS (Arichat, 1844; transferred, 1886): Raymond A. Lahey, bishop, 2003.

Chancery Office: 168 Hawthorne St., P.O. Box 1330, Antigonish, NS B2G 2L7; (902) 863-3335; www.antigonishdiocese.com/title.htm. Cathedral: St. Ninian.

Baie-Comeau, QC (p.a., 1882; v.a., 1905; diocese Gulf of St. Lawrence, 1945; name changed to Hauterive, 1960; present title, 1986): Pierre Morissette, bishop, 1990.

Bishop's Residence: 639, rue de Bretagne,

Baie-Comeau, QC G5C 1X2; (418) 589-5744; www.diocese-bc.org. Cathedral: Paroisse St. Jean-Eudes.

Bathurst, NB (Chatham, 1860; transferred, 1938): Valéry Vienneau, bishop, 2002.

Bishop's Residence: 645, avenue Murray, C.P. 460, Bathurst, NB E2A 3Z4; (506) 546-1420. Cathedral: Sacred Heart of Jesus.

Calgary, AB (1912): Frederick Henry, bishop, 1997.

Address: Room 290, The Iona Building, 120 17 Ave. SW, Calgary, AB T2S 2T2; (403) 218-5526; www.rcdiocese-calgary.ab.ca. Cathedral: St. Mary.

Charlottetown, PEI (1829): Joseph Vernon Fougere, bishop, 1992.

Bishop's Residence: P.O. Box 907, Charlottetown, PEI C1A 7L9; (902) 368-8005; www.dioceseof charlottetown.com. Cathedral: St. Dunstan's.

Chicoutimi, QC (1878): Jean-Guy Couture, bishop, 1979. Roch Pedneault, aux.

Bishop's Residence: 602, Racine Est, Chicoutimi, QC G7H 6J6; (418) 543-0783; www.evechede chicoutimi.qc.ca. Cathedral: St. Francois-Xavier.

Churchill-Hudson Bay, MB (p.a., 1925; v.a. Hudson Bay, 1931; diocese of Churchill, 1967; present title, 1968): Reynald Rouleau, O.M.I., bishop, 1987.

Diocesan Office: P.O. Box 10, Churchill, MB R0B 0E0; (204) 675-2252. Cathedral: Holy Canadian Martyrs.

Edmonton,* AB (St. Albert, 1871; archdiocese, transferred Edmonton, 1912): Thomas C. Collins, archbishop, 1999.

Archdiocesan Office: 8421-101 Avenue, Edmonton, Alta. T6A 0L1; (780) 469-1010; www.edmonton catholic-church.com. Cathedral: Basilica of St. Joseph.

Edmonton, AB (Ukrainian Byzantine) (ap. ex. of western Canada, 1948; eparchy, 1956): Lawrence Daniel Huculak, O.S.B.M., eparch, 1997.

Eparch's Residence: 9645 108th Ave., Edmonton, Alta. T5H 1A3; (780) 424-5496. Cathedral: St. Josaphat.

Edmundston, NB (1944): François Thibodeau, C.J.M., bishop, 1994.

Diocesan Center: 60, rue Bouchard, Edmundston, NB E3V 3K1; (506) 735-5578; www.diocese-edmunston.ca. Cathedral: Immaculate Conception.

Gaspé, QC (1922): Jean Gagnon, bishop, 2002.

Bishop's House: 172, rue Jacques-Cartier, Gaspé, QC G4X 1M9; (418) 368-2274; www.gaspesie.net/diocesegaspe. Cathedral: Christ the King.

Gatineau-Hull,* QC (1963, as Hull; name changed, 1982; archdiocese, 1990): Roger Ébacher, bishop, 1988; first archbishop, Oct. 31, 1990.

Diocesan Center: 180 Boulevard Mont-Bleu, Hull, QC J8Z 3J5; (819) 771-8391; www.diocesegatineau-hull.qc.ca.

Grand Falls, NL (Harbour Grace, 1856; present title, 1964): Martin W. Currie, bishop, 2000.

Chancery Office: 8A Church Rd., P.O. Box 771, Grand Falls-Windsor, NL A2A 2M4; (709) 489-2778; home.thezone.net/~rcecgf/. Cathedral: Immaculate Conception.

Grouard-McLennan,* AB (v.a. Athabaska-Mackenzie, 1862; Grouard, 1927; archdiocese Grouard-McLennan, 1967); Arthé Guimond, archbishop, 2000.

Archbishop's Residence: 210-1 Street West, C.P. 388, McLennan, AB T0H 2L0; (780) 324-3820. Cathedral: St. Jean-Baptiste (McLennan).

Halifax,* NS (1842; archdiocese, 1852): Terrence Prendergast, S.J., archbishop, 1998. Claude Champagne, auxiliary.

Chancery Office: 1531 Grafton St., P.O. Box 1527, Halifax, NS B3J 2Y3; (902) 429-9800; www.catholichalifax.org.

Hamilton, ON (1856): Anthony Tonnos, bishop, 1984. Matthew Ustrzycki, auxiliary.

Chancery Office: 700 King St. West, Hamilton, ON L8P 1C7; (905) 528-7988; www.hamilton diocese.com/. Cathedral: Christ the King.

Hearst, ON (p.a., 1918; v.a., 1920; diocese, 1938): André Vallée, P.M.É., bishop, 1996.

Bishop's Residence: 76 7e rue, C.P. 1330, Hearst, ON P0L 1N0; (705) 362-4903; www.diocesehearst.com. Cathedral: Notre Dame de la Assumption.

Joliette, QC (1904): Gilles Lussier, bishop, 1991.

Bishop's Residence: 2 rue Saint-Charles-Borromée Nord, C.P. 470, Joliette, QC J6E 6H6; (450) 753-7596; www.diocesedejoliette.org. Cathedral: St. Charles Borromeo.

Kamloops, BC (1945): David Monroe, bishop, 2002.

Bishop's Residence: 635-A Tranquille Rd., Kamloops, BC V2B 3H5; (250) 376-3351. Cathedral: Sacred Heart.

Keewatin-Le Pas,* MB (v.a., 1910; archdiocese, 1967): Peter-Alfred Sutton, O.M.I., archbishop, 1986.

Archbishop's Residence: 76 1st St. W., P.O. Box 270, The Pas, MB R9A 1K4; (204) 623-6152. Cathedral: Our Lady of the Sacred Heart.

Kingston,* ON (1826; archdiocese, 1889): Anthony Meagher, archbishop, 2002.

Chancery Office: 390 Palace Rd., Kingston, ON K7L 4T3; (613) 548-4461; www.roman catholic.kingston.on.ca. Cathedral: St. Mary of the Immaculate Conception.

Labrador City-Schefferville, QC (v.a. Labrador, 1946; diocese, 1967): Douglas Crosby, O.M.I., bishop, 1997.

Bishop's Residence: Sutton House, 320 avenue Elizabeth, C.P. 545, Labrador City, Labrador, NL A2V 2L3; (709) 944-2046. Cathedral: Our Lady of Perpetual Help.

London, ON (1855; transferred Sandwich, 1859; London, 1869): Ronald P. Fabbro, C.S.B., bishop, 2002.

Bishop's Residence: 1070 Waterloo St., London, ON N6A 3Y2; (519) 433-0658; www.rcec.lon don.on.ca. Cathedral: St. Peter's Cathedral Basilica.

Mackenzie-Fort Smith, NT (v.a. Mackenzie, 1902; diocese Mackenzie-Fort Smith, 1967): Denis Croteau, O.M.I., bishop, 1986.

Diocesan Office: 5117-52nd St., Yellowknife, NT X1A 1T7; (867) 920-2129. Cathedral: St. Joseph (Ft. Smith).

Moncton,* NB (1936): Ernest Léger, archbishop, 1997.

Archbishop's Residence: 452, rue Amirault, Dieppe, NB E1A 1G3; (506) 857-9531. Cathedral: Our Lady of the Assumption.

Mont-Laurier, QC (1913): Vital Massé, bishop, 2001.

Bishop's Residence: 435, rue de la Madone, Mont-Laurier, QC J9L 1S1; (819) 623-5530. Cathedral: Notre Dame de Fourvières.

Montréal,* QC (1836; archdiocese, 1886): Cardinal Jean-Claude Turcotte, archbishop, 1990. Anthony Mancini, Louis Dicaire, Jude Saint-Antoine, André Rivest, auxiliaries.

Archbishop's Residence: 2000, rue Sherbrooke Ouest, Montréal, QC H3H 1G4; (514) 931-7311; www.archeveche-mtl.qc.ca. Cathedral: Basilica of Mary Queen of the World and Saint James.

Montréal, QC (Sauveur de Montréal, Eparchy of Greek Melkites) (ap. ex. 1980; eparchy, 1984): Vacant.

Address: 34 rue Maplewood, Montréal, QC H2V 2MI; (514) 272-6430.

Montréal, QC (St. Maron of Montréal, Maronites) (1982): Joseph Khoury, eparch, 1996.

Chancery Office: 12 475 rue Grenet, Montréal, QC H4J 2K4; (514) 331-2807. Cathedral: St. Maron.

Moosonee, ON (v.a. James Bay, 1938; diocese Moosonee, 1967): Vincent Cadieux, O.M.I., bishop, 1992.

Bishop's Residence: 6 Bay Rd., C.P. 40, Moosonee, ON P0L 1Y0; (705) 336-2908. Cathedral: Christ the King.

Nelson, BC (1936): Eugene J. Cooney, bishop, 1996.

Bishop's Residence: 402 West Richards St., Nelson, BC VIL 3K3; (250) 354-4740; www.diocese.nel son.bc.ca/. Cathedral: Mary Immaculate.

New Westminster, BC (Ukrainian Byzantine) (1974): Severian Stephen Yakymyshyn, O.S.B.M., eparch, 1995.

Eparch's address: 502 5th Ave., New Westminster, BC V3L 1S2; (604) 524-8824; www.vcn.bc.ca/ucepnw.

Nicolet, QC (1885): Raymond Saint-Gelais, bishop, 1989.

Bishop's Residence: 49, rue Mgr Brunault, Nicolet, QC J3T 1X7; (819) 293-4696. Cathedral: St. Jean-Baptiste.

Ottawa,* ON (Bytown, 1847, name changed, 1854; archdiocese, 1886): Marcel A.J. Gervais, archbishop, 1989.

Archbishop's Residence: 1247 Place Kilborn, Ottawa, ON K1H 6K9; (613) 738-5025; www.ecclesia-ottawa.org. Cathedral: Basilica of Notre Dame-of-Ottawa.

Pembroke, ON (v.a. 1882; diocese, 1898): Richard Smith, bishop, 2002.

Bishop's Residence: 188 Renfrew St., P.O. Box 7, Pembroke, ON K8A 6X1; (613) 732-7933; www3.simpatico.ca/recpembroke. Cathedral: St. Columbkille.

Peterborough, ON (1882): Nicola De Angelis, C.F.I.C., bishop, 2002.

Bishop's Residence: 350 Hunter St. West, P.O. Box 175, Peterborough, ON K9J 6Y8; (705) 745-5123; www.peterboroughdiocese.org. Cathedral: St. Peter-in-Chains.

Prince Albert, SK (v.a., 1890; diocese, 1907): Blaise Morand, bishop, 1983.

Address: 1415 4th Ave. West, Prince Albert, SK S6V 5H1; (306) 922-4747; www.padiocese.sk.ca. Cathedral: Sacred Heart.

Prince George, BC (p.a., 1908; v.a. Yukon and Prince Rupert, 1944; diocese Prince George, 1967): Gerald Wiesner, O.M.I., bishop, 1993.

Chancery Office: 6500 Southbridge Ave., P.O. Box 7000, Prince George, BC V2N 3Z2; (250) 964-4424; www.pgdiocese.bc.ca. Cathedral: Sacred Heart.

Québec,* QC (v.a., 1658; diocese, 1674; archdiocese, 1819; metropolitan, 1844; primatial see, 1956): Marc Ouellet, P.S.S., archbishop, 2002. Jean Pierre Blais, Eugène Tremblay, auxiliaries.

Chancery Office: 1073, boul. René-Lévesque ouest, Québec, QC G1S 4R5; (418) 688-1211; www.diocese quebec.qc.ca/. Cathedral: Notre-Dame- de-Québec (Basilica).

Regina,* SK (1910; archdiocese, 1915): Peter Mallon, archbishop, 1995.

Chancery Office: 445 Broad St. North, Regina, SK S4R 2X8; (306) 352-1651; www.archregina.sk.ca. Cathedral: Our Lady of the Most Holy Rosary.

Rimouski,* QC (1867; archdiocese, 1946): Bertrand Blanchet, archbishop, 1992.

Archbishop's Residence: 34, rue de l'Évêché Ouest, C.P. 730, Rimouski, QC G5L 7C7; (418) 723-3320; www.dioceserimouski.com.

Rouyn-Noranda, QC (1973): Dorylas Moreau, bishop, 2001.

Bishop's Residence: 515, avenue Cuddihy, C.P. 1060, Rouyn-Noranda, QC J9X 4C5; (819) 764-4660; www.dioc-cath-rouyn-noranda.org. Cathedral: St. Michael the Archangel.

Saint-Boniface,* MB (1847; archdiocese, 1871): Émilius Goulet, P.S.S..

Archbishop's Residence: 151, avenue de la Cathédrale, Saint-Boniface, MB R2H 0H6; (204) 237-9851. Cathedral: Basilica of St. Boniface.

St. Catharine's, ON (1958): James M. Wingle, bishop, 2001.

Bishop's Residence: P.O. Box 875, St. Catharines, ON L2R 6Y3; (905) 684-0154; www.roman catholic.niagara.on.ca. Cathedral: St. Catherine of Alexandria.

St. George's, NL (p.a., 1870; v.a., 1890; diocese, 1904): Douglas Crosby, O.M.I., bishop, 2003 (also bp. of Labrador City-Shefferville).

Bishop's Residence: 13 Mount Bernard, Corner Brook, NL A2H 6K6; (709) 639-7073; www.rcchurch.com. Cathedral: Most Holy Redeemer and Immaculate Conception.

Saint-Hyacinthe, QC (1852): François Lapierre, P.M.E., bishop, 1998.

Bishop's Residence: 1900, rue Girouard Ouest, C.P. 190, Saint-Hyacinthe, QC J2S 7B4; (450) 773-8581; www.diocese-st-hyacinthe.qc.ca. Cathedral: St. Hyacinthe the Confessor.

Saint-Jean-Longueuil, QC (1933 as St.-Jean-de-Québec; named changed, 1982): Jacques Berthelet, C.S.V., bishop, 1996.

Bishop's Residence: 740, boulevard Sainte-Foy, C.P. 40, Longueuil, QC J4K 4X8; (450) 679-1100; www.diocese-st-jean-longueuil.org. Cathedral: St. John the Evangelist.

St. Jérôme, QC (1951): Gilles Cazabon, O.M.I., bishop, 1998; Donald Lapointe, auxiliary.

Bishop's Residence: 355, rue Saint-Georges, Saint-Jerome, QC J7Z 5A9; (450) 432-9742; www.diocese-stjerome.qc.ca. Cathedral: St. Jerome.

Saint John, NB (1842): Joseph Faber MacDonald, bishop, 1998.

Chancery Office: 1 Bayard Dr., Saint John, NB E2L 3L5; (506) 653-6800; www.dioceseofsaintjohn.org. Cathedral: Immaculate Conception.

St. John's,* NL (p.a., 1784; v.a., 1796; diocese, 1847; archdiocese, 1904): Brendan Michael O'Brien, archbishop, 2000.

Chancery Office: P.O. Box 37, St. John's, NL. A1C 5N5; (709) 726-3660; www.stjohnsarchdiocese.nf.ca. Cathedral: St. John the Baptist.

St. Paul in AB (1948): Joseph Luc André Bouchard, bishop, 2001.

Bishop's Residence: 4410, 51e avenue, Saint Paul, AB T0A 3A2; (780) 645-3277. Cathedral: St. Paul.

Sainte-Anne-de-la-Pocatière, QC (1951): Clément Fecteau, bishop, 1996.

Bishop's Residence: 1200, 4e avenue, C.P. 430, La Pocatière, QC G0R 1Z0; (418) 856-1811. Cathedral: St. Anne.

Saskatoon, SK (1933): Albert LeGatt, 2001.

Chancery Office: 100-5th Ave. North, Saskatoon, SK S7K 2N7; (306) 242-1500; www.rc diocesesktn.sk.ca. Cathedral: St. Paul.

Saskatoon, SK (Ukrainian Byzantine) (ap. ex., 1951; diocese, 1956): Michael Wiwchar, CSsR, 2000.

Address: 866 Saskatchewan Crescent East, Saskatoon, SK S7N 0L4; (306) 653-0138.

Sault Ste. Marie, ON (1904): Jean-Louis Plouffe, bishop, 1990; Robert Harris, auxiliary.

Chancery Office: 30, chemin Ste. Anne, Sudbury, ON P3C 5E1, (705) 674-2727; www.isys.ca/cathcom.htm. Cathedral: Pro-Cathedral of the Assumption, North Bay.

Sherbrooke,* QC (1874; archdiocese, 1951): André Gaumond, archbishop, 1996.

Archbishop's Residence: 130, rue de la Cathédrale, C.P. 430, Sherbrooke, QC J1H 5K1; (819) 563-9934; www.diosher.org. Cathedral: St. Michel.

Thunder Bay, ON (Ft. William, 1952; transferred, 1970): Frederick J. Colli, bishop, 1999.

Bishop's Office: 1222 Reaume St., P.O. Box 10400,

Thunder Bay, ON P7B 6T8; (807) 343-9313; www.dotb.baynet.net. Cathedral: St. Patrick.

Timmins, ON (v.a. Temiskaming, 1908; diocese Haileybury, 1915; present title, 1938): Paul Marchand, S.M.M., bishop, 1999.

Address: 65, Ave. Jubilee Est, Timmins, ON P4N 5W4; www.nt.net/~dioctims/. Cathedral: St. Anthony of Padua.

Toronto,* ON (1841; archdiocese, 1870): Cardinal Aloysius M. Ambrozic, archbishop, 1990. John A. Boissonneau, Richard Grecco, Daniel Bohan, auxiliaries.

Chancery Office: Catholic Pastoral Centre, 1155 Yonge St., Toronto, ON M4T 1W2; (416) 934-0606; www.archtoronto.org. Cathedral: St. Michael.

Toronto, ON (Eparchy for Slovakian Byzantine) (1980): John Pazak, C.SS.R., 2000.

Eparch's Residence: 223 Carlton Rd., Unionville, ON L3R 3M2; (905) 477-4867.

Toronto, ON (Eparchy for Ukrainian Byzantine) (ap. ex., 1948; eparchy, 1956): Isidore Borecky (exarch 1948-56), first eparch, 1956. Stephen Victor Chmilar eparch, 2003.

Chancery Office: 3100-A Weston Rd., Weston, ON M9M 2S7; (416) 746-0154; www.ucet.ca. Cathedral: St. Josaphat.

Trois-Rivières, QC (1852): Martin Veillette, bishop, 1996.

Bishop's Residence: 362, rue Bonaventure, C.P. 879, Trois-Rivières, QC G9A 5J9; (819) 374-9847; www.diocese-tr.qc.ca/. Cathedral: The Assumption.

Valleyfield, QC (1892): Luc Cyr, bishop, 2001.

Bishop's Residence: 11, rue de l'Eglise, Salaberry-de-Valleyfield, QC J6T 1J5; (450) 373-8122; www.rocler.qc.ca/diocese-valleyfield/. Cathedral: St. Cecilia.

Vancouver,* BC (v.a. British Columbia, 1863; diocese New Westminster, 1890; archdiocese Vancouver, 1908): Adam Exner, O.M.I., archbishop, 1991.

Chancery Office: 150 Robson St., Vancouver, BC V6B 2A7; (604) 683-0281; www.rcav.bc.ca. Cathedral: Holy Rosary.

Victoria, BC (diocese Vancouver Is., 1846; archdiocese, 1903; diocese Victoria, 1908): Raymond Roussin, S.M., bishop, 1999.

Chancery Office: Diocesan Pastoral Centre, #1-4044 Nelthorpe St., Victoria, BC V8X 2A1; (250) 479-1331; www.rcdvictoria.org. Cathedral: St. Andrew.

Whitehorse, YT (v.a., 1944; diocese 1967): Vacant.

Chancery Office: 5119 5th Ave., Whitehorse, YT Y1A 1L5; (867) 667-2052. Cathedral: Sacred Heart.

Winnipeg,* MB (1915): James V. Weisberger, archbishop, 2000.

Chancery Office: Catholic Centre, 1495 Pembina Highway, Winnipeg, MB R3T 2C6; (204) 452-2227; www.archwinnipeg.ca. Cathedral: St. Mary.

Winnipeg,* MB (Ukrainian Byzantine) (Ordinariate of Canada, 1912; ap. ex. Central Canada, 1948; ap. ex. Manitoba, 1951; archeparchy Winnipeg, 1956): Michael Bzdel, C.Ss.R., archeparch, 1993; David Motiuk, auxiliary.

Archeparchy Office: 233 Scotia St., Winnipeg, MB R2V 1V7; (204) 338-7801; www.archeparchy.ca. Cathedral: Sts. Vladimir and Olga.

Yarmouth, NS (1953): Vacant.

Address: C.P. 278, Yarmouth, NS B5A 4B2; (902) 742-7163; www.dioceseyarmouth.org Cathedral: St. Ambrose.

Military Ordinariate of Canada (1951):Donald J. Thériault, bishop, 1998.

Address: Canadian Forces Support Unit (Ottawa), Uplands Site – Bldg. 469, Ottawa, ON K1A 0K2; (613) 998-8747.

An Apostolic Exarchate for Armenian-Rite Catholics in Canada and the United States was established in July 1981 with headquarters in New York City (110 E. 12th St., New York, NY 10003); (212) 477-2030. Manuel Batakian, exarch, 1995.

The Eparchy of Our Lady of Deliverance of Newark for Syrian-rite Catholics in the United States and Canada was established Nov. 6, 1995. Address: 502 Palisade Ave., Union City, NJ 08087-5213; (201) 583-1067; www.Syriac-Catholic.org. Joseph Younan, bishop.

Hungarian Emigrants throughout the world, resides in Canada: Most Rev. Attila Mikloshazy, S.J., titular bishop of Cast`el Minore. Address: 2661 Kingston Rd., Scarborough, ON M1M 1M3; (416) 261-7207.

Note: The diocese of Gravelbourg, in Saskatchewan, was dissolved in September 1998 as part of a reorganization of Canadian dioceses. The regions under the jurisdiction of Gravelbourg were integrated into the neighboring dioceses of Regina and Saskatoon. The Territorial Abbacy of St. Peter, Muenster, SK, was also dissolved.

Dioceses with Interprovincial Lines

The following dioceses, indicated by + in the table, have interprovincial lines.

Churchill-Hudson Bay includes part of Northwest Territories.

Keewatin-LePas includes part of Manitoba and Saskatchewan provinces.

Labrador City-Schefferville includes the Labrador region of Newfoundland and the northern part of Québec province.

Mackenzie-Fort Smith, Northwest Territories, includes part of Alberta and Saskatchewan provinces.

Moosonee, Ontario, includes part of Québec province.

Pembroke, Ontario, includes one county of Québec province.

Whitehorse, Yukon Territory, includes part of British Columbia.

CANADIAN CONFERENCE OF CATHOLIC BISHOPS

The Canadian Conference of Catholic Bishops was established Oct. 12, 1943, as a permanent voluntary association of the bishops of Canada, was given official approval by the Holy See in 1948, and acquired the status of an episcopal conference after the Second Vatican Council.

The CCCB acts in two ways: (1) as a strictly ecclesiastical body through which the bishops act together with pastoral authority and responsibility for the Church throughout the country; (2) as an operational secretariat through which the bishops act on a wider scale for the good of the Church and society.

At the top of the CCCB organizational table are the president, an executive committee, a permanent council and a plenary assembly. The membership consists of all the bishops of Canada.

Departments and Offices

The CCCB's work is planned and coordinated by the Programmes and Priorities Committee composed of the six chairmen of the national episcopal commissions and the two general secretaries. It is chaired by the vice-president of the CCCB.

The CCCB's 12 episcopal commissions undertake study and projects in special areas of pastoral work. Six serve nationally (social affairs; canon law/inter-rite; relations with associations of clergy, consecrated life and laity; evangelization of peoples; ecumenism; theology); three relate to French sectors (*communications sociale, éducation Chrétienne, liturgie*); and three relate to corresponding English sectors (social communications, Christian education, liturgy).

The general secretariat consists of a general secretary and assistants and directors of public relations. The current general secretary is Msgr. Peter Schonenbach, P.H.

Administrative services for purchasing, archives and library, accounting, personnel, publications, printing and distribution are supervised by directors who relate to the general secretaries.

Various advisory councils and committees with mixed memberships of lay persons, religious, priests and bishops also serve the CCCB on a variety of topics.

Operations

Meetings for the transaction of business are held at least once a year by the plenary assembly, six times a year by the executive committee, and four times a year by the permanent council.

Bishop Jacques Berthelet, C.S.V. of Saint-Jean-Longueuil, is president of the CCCB and Bishop Brendan O'Brien, of Saint John's, is vice president, for the 2002-2003 term.

The Conference headquarters is located at 2500 Don Reid Dr., Ottawa, K1N 2J2, Canada; (613) 241-9461; www.cccb.ca.

CANADIAN SHRINES

Our Lady of the Cape (Cap de la Madeleine), Queen of the Most Holy Rosary: The Three Rivers, Québec, parish church, built in 1714 and considered the oldest stone church on the North American continent preserved in its original state, was rededicated June 22, 1888, as a shrine of the Queen of the Most Holy Rosary. The site increased in importance as a pilgrimage and devotional center, and in 1904 St. Pius X decreed the crowning of a statue of the Blessed Virgin which had been donated 50 years earlier to commemorate the dogma of the Immaculate Conception. In 1909, the First Plenary Council of Québec declared the church a shrine of national pilgrimage. In 1964, the church at the shrine was given the status and title of minor basilica.

St. Anne de Beaupre: The devotional history of this shrine in Québec began with the reported cure of a cripple, Louis Guimont, on Mar. 16, 1658, the starting date of construction work on a small chapel of St. Anne. The original building was successively enlarged and replaced by a stone church, which was given the rank of minor basilica in 1888. The present structure, a Romanesque-Gothic basilica, houses the shrine proper in its north transept, including an eight-foot-high oaken statue and a relic of St. Anne, and a portion of her forearm.

St. Joseph's Oratory: The massive oratory basilica standing on the western side of Mount Royal and overlooking the city of Montréal had its origin in a primitive chapel erected there by Blessed André Bessette, C.S.C., in 1904. Eleven years later, a large crypt was built to accommodate an increasing number of pilgrims, and in 1924 construction work was begun on the large church. A belfry, housing a 60-bell carillon and standing on the site of the original chapel, was dedicated May 15, 1955, as the first major event of the jubilee year observed after the oratory was given the rank of minor basilica.

Martyrs' Shrine: A shrine commemorating several of the Jesuit Martyrs of North America who were killed between 1642 and 1649 in the Ontario and northern New York area is located on the former site of old Fort Sainte Marie. Before its location was fixed near Midland, ON, in 1925, a small chapel had been erected in 1907 at old Mission St. Ignace to mark the martyrdom of Fathers Jean de Brebeuf and Gabriel Lalemant. This sanctuary has a U.S. counterpart in the Shrine of the North American Martyrs near Auriesville, NY, under the care of the Jesuits.

Others

In Québec City: Basilica of Notre Dame (1650), once the cathedral of a diocese stretching from Canada to Mexico; Notre Dame des Victoires (1690); the Ursuline Convent (1720), on du Parloir St.

Near Montréal: Hermitage of St. Anthony, La Bouchette; Ste. Anne de Micmacs, Restigouche; Chapel of Atonement, Pointe aux Trembles; Our Lady of Lourdes, Rigaud; St. Benoît du Lac, near Magog.

In Montréal: Notre Dame Basilica (1829).

Near Montréal: Chapel of St. Marie Marguerite d'Youville, foundress of the Grey Nuns; Notre Dame de Lourdes, at Rigaud.

STATISTICAL SUMMARY OF THE CATHOLIC CHURCH IN CANADA

(*Principal source:* 2003 Directory of the Canadian Conference of Catholic Bishops; *figures as of Jan. 2003.*) Catholic population statistics are those reported in the 1991 Canadian Census. Archdioceses are indicated by an asterisk. For dioceses marked +, *see* **Canadian Dioceses with Interprovincial Lines**.

Canada's 10 civil provinces and two territories are divided into 18 ecclesiastical provinces consisting of 18 metropolitan sees (archdioceses) and 45 suffragan sees; there are also eight Oriental Rite dioceses, one archdiocese and three eparchies immediately subject to the Holy See, and the Military Ordinariate.

This table presents a regional breakdown of Catholic statistics. In some cases, the totals are approximate because diocesan boundaries fall within several civil provinces.

Civil Province Diocese	Cath. Pop.	Dioc. Priests	Rel. Priests	Total Priests	Perm. Deacs.	Bro- thers	Sis- ters	Lay Assts.	Par- ishes[1]
Newfoundland	213,055	97	22	119	3	14	301	31	227
St. John's*	119,260	35	10	45	-	11	218	2	73
Grand Falls	41,940	33	-	33	-	-	35	5	73
Labrador- Schefferville+	13,550	1	11	12	2	2	23	21	25
St. George's	38,305	28	1	29	1	1	25	3	56
Prince Edward Island									
Charlottetown	60,625	52	2	53	1	-	147	3	58
Nova Scotia	331,010	228	40	268	27	4	612	31	237
Halifax*	152,515	65	28	93	25	2	268	8	76
Antigonish	138,990	137	12	149	1	2	319	14	122
Yarmouth	39,505	26	0	26	1	-	25	9	39
New Brunswick	386,480	219	57	276	4	28	794	180	250
Moncton*	105,775	56	28	84	1	22	298	84	60
Bathurst	115,560	56	6	62	1	4	212	11	63
Edmundston	52,435	37	9	46	-	1	117	17	32
St. John	112,710	70	14	84	2	1	167	68	95
Québec	5,945,275	2,703	1,740	4,443	404	1,546	13,956	1,243	1,768
Gatineau-Hull*	216,725	55	38	93	2	5	212	55	61
Montréal*	1,566,410	554	740	1,294	104	485	4,972	134	259
Québec*	902,545	498	351	849	89	251	3,766	200	229
Rimouski*	152,565	123	17	140	9	38	667	34	114
Sherbrooke*	235,145	204	110	314	19	89	1,068	42	116
Amos	103,890	24	21	45	-	11	105	52	60
Baie Comeau	86,786	43	16	59	8	9	65	25	45
Chicoutimi	275,580	188	40	228	38	34	626	73	95
Gaspé	94,645	60	6	66	3	5	166	25	66
Joliette	177,103	85	52	137	6	107	248	50	57
Mont Laurier	72,755	33	9	42	-	12	65	38	58
Montréal, St. Maron (Maronites)	80,000	9	6	15	1	-	3	-	13
Montréal, St. Sauveur (Greek-Melkites)	38,000	5	8	13	1	-	-	-	8
Nicolet	177,620	153	21	174	21	25	489	46	85
Rouyn-Noranda	56,475	26	9	35	1	1	85	21	44
Ste-Anne-de-la- Pocatière	87,865	111	-	111	6	-	172	15	58
St.-Hyacinthe	330,515	151	77	228	34	184	840	102	108
St.-Jean-Longueuil	524,150	106	44	150	3	115	291	160	90
St. Jérôme	338,121	87	82	169	18	79	183	84	69
Trois Rivières	243,085	113	69	182	30	73	593	53	70
Valleyfield	185,295	75	24	99	11	23	96	34	63
Ontario	3,575,065	1,472	834	2,306	377	144	3,354	194	1,267
Kingston*	102,650	67	9	76	9	6	186	-	72
Ottawa*	364,285	160	100	260	55	12	888	4	114
Toronto*	1,420,395	398	443	841	106	77	753	-	223
Alexandria-Corn	56,020	43	7	50	16	4	56	5	34
Hamilton	480,695	132	97	229	2	14	322	66	149

Civil Province Diocese	Cath. Pop.	Dioc. Priests	Rel. Priests	Total Priests	Perm. Deacs.	Bro- thers	Sis- ters	Lay Assts.	Par- ishes[1]
Ontario, cont.									
Hearst	34,840	31	-	31	-	4	15	24	29
London	414,285	160	72	232	2	6	473	51	169
Moosonee+	3,905	-	3	3	2	3	3	3	18
Pembroke+	64,925	69	2	71	7	3	165	7	67
Peterborough	83,680	107	7	114	12	-	119	5	70
St. Catharine's	145,850	59	37	96	1	4	46	13	48
Sault Ste. Marie	218,850	102	32	134	108	4	253	2	117
Thunder Bay	78,480	29	13	42	32	-	19	-	42
Timmins	55,195	26	3	29	6	5	29	13	32
Toronto (Ukrainians)	41,010	89	9	98	19	2	27	1	76
Toronto (Slovaks, Sts. Cyril and Methodius)	10,000	4	3	7	-	-	-	-	7
Manitoba	346,180	194	111	305	48	16	512	34	396
Keewatin-Le Pas*+	35,195	5	12	17	-	1	11	13	49
St. Boniface*	101,920	86	57	185	17	12	329	9	105
Winnipeg*	170,590	64	28	92	16	3	142	4	91
Winnepeg (Ukrainians)*	33,490	39	9	48	15	-	28	-	134
Churchill-Hudson Bay+	4,985	-	5	5	-	-	2	8	17
Saskatchewan+	301,335	174	87	261	11	22	479	25	454
Regina*#	138,965	79	11	90	3	5	150	10	167
Prince-Albert	57,580	33	9	42	2	-	87	4	85
Saskatoon#	84,710	42	57	99	-	15	224	11	105
Saskatoon (Ukrainians)	20,080	20	10	30	6	2	18	-	97
Alberta	665,870	194	196	390	30	43	581	73	436
Edmonton*	294,935	74	110	184	-	31	404	52	144
Grouard-McLennan*	40,715	5	19	24	2	-	22	14	67
Calgary	250,605	71	48	119	19	12	102	-	81
Edmonton (Ukrainians)	26,250	24	15	39	8	-	35	-	87
St. Paul	53,365	20	4	24	1	-	18	7	57
British Columbia	600,175	184	132	316	5	26	274	248	303
Vancouver*	340,775	89	87	176	1	16	129	-	94
Kamloops	47,010	13	11	24	1	3	15	-	71
Nelson	63,570	31	4	35	-	-	18	-	53
New Westminster (Ukrainians)	7,555	10	2	12	2	-	2	-	16
Prince Geo	51,200	12	8	20	1	4	21	248	40
Victoria	90,065	29	20	49	-	3	89	-	29
Yukon Territory									
Whitehorse+	8,235	3	8	11	2	1	8	18	20
Northwest Territories									
MacKenzie-Ft. Smith+	19,745	3	4	7	2	-	15	21	40
Military Ordinariate	41,853	35*	3**	38	1	-	-	36	24**
TOTALS	12,494,903[2]	5,562	3,239	8,801	920	1,895	21,789	2,137	5,480

1. Denotes both parishes and missions.
2. Catholics comprise about 43% of the total population. According to the 2001 *Annuarium Statisticum Ecclesiae* (the most recent edition), there were 132,479 baptisms and 31,705 marriages.
* The Canadian Military Ordinariate does not incardinate clerics.
** Not included in the total.

The Catholic Church in Mexico

BACKGROUND

Start of Church Organization

The history of the Catholic Church in Mexico began in 1519 with the capture of Mexico's native civilization, the Aztec Empire, by the Spanish *conquistadores* under Hernándo Cortés. The Spanish army besieged the Aztec capital of Tenochtitlan, massacred most of the inhabitants, strangled the Aztec emperor Montezuma, and crushed the rest of the empire. Mexico City became the chief city of New Spain and the cultural and religious center of colonial Mexico; it was declared a diocese in 1530.

The record of Colonial Spanish treatment of the native peoples of Mexico is a grim one. The Indians suffered exploitation, slavery, and rapid depletion of their population from disease; they were forced to labor in inhuman conditions in mines and endured servitude in the *encomienda* system.

In sharp contrast to the treatment of the natives by the government was the effort to evangelize Mexico by the religious orders, who followed the command of Pope Alexander VI in the 1494 Treaty of Tordesillas to convert all peoples who would be encountered in the coming age of exploration. A papal bull, dated Apr. 25, 1521, gave the Franciscans the permission of the Holy See to preach in New Spain. They were joined by the Dominicans and, later, by the Jesuits. The missionary orders soon distinguished themselves by their resistance to the brutal enslavement of the Indians, their mastery of native languages, and their willingness to endure enormous hardships in bringing the faith to the distant corners of Mexico.

As the Church became more established, however, the missionary priests and friars came increasingly into conflict with the secular clergy, who desired full control over ecclesiastical affairs, resented the extensive powers of religious orders, and normally identified closely with the interests of the crown. The government thus decreed that the missionaries were to have 10 years in which to convert the Indians, after which control would pass to the diocesan clergy. This was protested by the missionary orders, and the conflict was resolved in favor of the diocesan priests in 1640 thanks to the efforts of Bishop Juan de Palafox de Mendoza of Puebla.

The alliance of the secular clergy with the government was a reflection of the control enjoyed by the Spanish Crown over the Church in Mexico. The Holy See had granted to the kings of Spain royal patronage over the Church in Mexico, and the practice of the *Patronato Real* meant that the king nominated all Church officials in New Spain and held authority over the Church's temporal concerns. A major element in this policy was the forced conversion of the local peoples. Coerced into adopting the faith, many Indians were insincere or hesitant to embrace the faith. To insure the full embrace of the faith, Spanish authorities received permission from King Philip II in 1569 to introduce the Inquisition to Mexico. Indians who had survived the mines, diseases, and brutality of the colonial rulers were now subjected to tribunals to test their faith. This practice was eventually ended when authorities decided that the natives were not culpable because of limited intelligence. Nevertheless, the close identification of the diocesan clergy with the interests and policies of the Spanish crown created a hostility toward the Church in Mexico by the lower classes that endures today.

On the positive side, the Church did much through its missionaries to save many Indians from death and enslavement and to preserve vital portions of Mesoamerican culture, art, and history. Friars also traveled to northern Mexico and beyond, bringing the faith into California, Texas, and New Mexico.

The native peoples were given a profound encouragement to embrace the Catholic faith in 1531 by the appearance of Our Lady of Guadalupe to the farmer Juan Diego (beatified in 1990 by Pope John Paul II) on the Tepeyac hill just outside of Mexico City. The shrine built in her honor remains the most important religious site in Mexico. Enshrined within it is the mantle brought by Juan Diego to Bishop Zumaragga to convince him of the genuine nature of the apparition. Miraculously emblazoned upon it is the life-size image of the Virgin Mary.

MEXICAN INDEPENDENCE

The Spanish domination of Mexico endured for nearly three centuries, deteriorating gradually throughout the 1700s as the gulf widened between the Spanish ruling class and the native classes that were joined by the *mestizos* and *creoles* (descendants of Native Americans and Europeans). Unrest broke out into a full-scale rebellion in 1810 with the uprising of many priests led by Father Miguel Hidalgo y Costilla and, after his execution, by Father José María Morelos y Pavón. While suppressed in 1816 by the colonial regime with the support of the upper classes and most of the diocesan clergy, it proved only the first of several revolts, culminating in the 1821 declaration of Mexican independence. By the terms of the independence, the Church received a special status and had enormous sway in political life.

A republic was proclaimed in 1834 and various liberal regimes came to power. Anticlericalism became commonplace, made even more strident by the lingering hostility over the Church's activities with Spanish colonial government. Much influenced by the ideals of the European revolutions then taking place, the Mexican republican movements were strongly anti-Catholic. For more than a decade, power was in the hands of Antonio López de Santa Anna (also known for his victory at the Alamo) and Valentin Gómez Farías. After the Mexican-American War (1846-1848), the political instability led to the dictatorship of Santa Anna.

Santa Anna was toppled in 1855 by a liberal regime whose anti-Church legislation sparked an armed struggle called the War of the Reform (1858-1861). The laws issued by the government included the *Ley Juárez*, abolishing all ecclesiastical courts, and the *Ley Lerdo*, forcing the Church to sell all of its lands. Deprived of its properties, the Church lost control of education and schools, and Mexico's educational system became often bitterly anti-Catholic.

While the liberal forces won the War of the Reform, the conflict had so debilitated Mexico that the French were able to intervene in 1861 and install their puppet, the Austrian duke Maximilian, on the Mexican throne. As the United States was embroiled in its own civil war from 1861-1865, it was unable to respond to French imperialist ambitions in Mexico. Maximilian initially enjoyed the support of the conservative elements and the Church, but his liberal reforms alienated the mistrustful conservatives and he soon clung to power only with French support. When France finally withdrew its troops in 1867, Maximilian was deposed by republican forces and executed.

MODERN MEXICO

The fall of Emperor Maximilian signaled a restoration of the anticlerical constitution of 1857 and the elevation of Benito Juárez – the republican leader long recognized by the United States – as president. His successor, Sebastián Lerdo de Tijada, was toppled in 1876 by Porfirio Diáz, who remained dictator for thirty-four years. A civil war ended his regime, and more bloodshed ensued. Finally, a constitution was issued in 1917 that placed severe restrictions on the Church: there could be no criticism of the government, only Mexicans could be clergy, the Church was not permitted to own property, and any privileges were stripped away.

The situation became worse after 1923, when the papal legate was expelled. The administration of Plutarco Calles (1924-1928) launched a wave of persecution that sparked a popular but ultimately unsuccessful uprising called the Cristero Rebellion. Coupled with the repressive measures of local governments, the Calles regime and its successors forced the Church into very difficult circumstances, with only a few priests remaining in the country. The tragedy was deepened by the execution of dozens of priests and nuns by republican forces for assorted and imaginary crimes or for speaking out on behalf of the poor or oppressed Catholics. A number of the executed clergy have been beatified and canonized since the tragedy, most so during the pontificate of Pope John Paul II. The persecution prompted Pope Pius XI to issue the encyclicals *Iniquis afflictisque* (1926) and *Acerba animi* (1932).

An easing of the situation began in 1940 as the rigid anticlerical laws ceased to be enforced with enthusiasm. A rapprochement was visible in the 1958 elections, when the Church received conciliatory gestures from the ruling Revolutionary Party and its presidential candidate Adolfo López Mateos. The Church continued to exist under numerous legal disabilities and was oppressed in a number of the Mexican states.

Gradual improvement in relations between Mexico and the Holy See led to the exchange in 1990 of personal representatives between the Mexican president and Pope John Paul II. The Holy Father's efforts to build a further diplomatic bridge culminated in the establishment of full diplomatic ties in 1992. This was followed by the final easing of many of the handicaps under which the Church had long suffered.

The faith of the Mexican people is profoundly deep, as was seen in the nearly frenzied greeting given to Pope John Paul II in 1979, 1990, 1993, and 1999. However, social unrest, poverty, economic challenges, the violence of drug cartels, and corruption still plague the country. Church leaders — especially religious orders — have been outspoken in their criticism of government human rights abuses and corruption. During the mid-1990s, the Jesuits said they were the target of a "campaign of intimidation" because of their human rights work.

On May 24, 1993, Cardinal Juan Jesus Posadas Ocampo of Guadalajara was killed during a supposed shoot-out among rival drug cartels. The murder remained unsolved, although Cardinal Posadas' successor, Cardinal Juan Sandoval Íñiguez, continued to claim that high-ranking officials, including the Mexican attorney general at the time, lied to protect others involved in a plot. In 2001 Cardinal Sandoval said he would seek a reopening of the case because he had new evidence contradicting the findings of the official investigation; he also claimed he had been almost fatally poisoned in 1999 during a dinner with federal officials angry with his insistence that the murder was not accidental.

In the 1970s and 1980s, one of Mexico's most prominent proponents of liberation theology was Bishop Samuel Ruiz Garcia of San Cristobal de Las Casas. In the early 1990s the Vatican began investigating his views, but because he had the trust of indigenous peasants, in 1994 he was thrown into the role of mediator between the government and the mostly native Zapatista National Liberation Army in Chiapas. He continued that role until 1998, when he resigned after accusing the government of "dismantling any possible means or effort to solve the crisis in Chiapas." Mexico's bishops said at that time that they would provide support to the peace process but would not seek to mediate the conflict.

On July 2, 2000, Vicente Fox Quesada, head of the National Action Party and a practicing Catholic, won the Mexican presidential election, marking the first time since 1929 that the country was not ruled by the Institutional Revolutionary Party. Mexico City Cardinal Norberto Rivera Carrera told reporters the election was "not a miracle, as some have suggested, but it is an extraordinary act." Church officials emphasized that they expected no special privileges from the new government, but the general climate was one of optimism for an improvement in church-state relations.

Within weeks, Fox – with news cameras flashing – received Communion in his hometown parish. However, in July 2001, the Vatican said he failed to have his first marriage annulled before marrying his spokeswoman in a civil ceremony; thus, he would be prohibited from receiving the sacraments. In June 2001, federal and state officials participated in a public Mass at the Basilica of Our Lady of Guadalupe, breaking a taboo on government officials publicly practicing their religion.

On July 31, 2002 during his fifth pastoral visit to Mexico, Pope John Paul II proclaimed Juan Diego a saint. The pope declared at the canonization: " 'The Guadalupe Event,' as the Mexican Episcopate has pointed out, 'meant the beginning of evangelization with a vitality that surpassed all expectations. Christ's message, through his Mother, took up the central elements of the indigenous culture, purified them and gave them the definitive sense of salvation."

ORGANIZATION

Presently, the Church in Mexico is organized into 14 provinces. There are 14 archdioceses, 66 dioceses (including the 2000 creation of two new suffragan dioceses of the archdiocese of Xalapa, a suffragan diocese of Monterrey in 2002, and suffragan dioceses of Monterrey and Tlalnepantla in 2003), 5 prelacies, and 2 eparchs, for the Greek Melkites and Maronites. As of August 15, 2003, there were four Mexican members of the College of Cardinals: Ernesto Corripio Ahumada, Norberto Rivera Carrera, Juan Sandoval Íñiguez, and Adolfo Antonio Suárez Rivera. (For statistical information on the Church in Mexico, see below.)

The current apostolic delegation to Mexico was set up in 1992 as a nunciature with the establishment of renewed formal diplomatic relations with the Vatican. The present Apostolic Nuncio is Archbishop Giuseppe Bertolli, appointed in December 2000.

ECCLESIASTICAL JURISDICTIONS OF MEXICO
Provinces
Names of ecclesiastical provinces and metropolitan sees in bold face: suffragan sees in parentheses.

Acapulco (Ciudad Lázaro Cárdenas, Chilpancingo-Chilapa, Ciudad Altamirano, Tlapa).

Chihuahua (Ciudad Juárez, Cuauhtémoc-Madera, Parral, Tarahumara).

Durango (Culiacán, Mazatlán, Torreón, El Salto,).

Guadalajara (Aguascalientes, Autlán, Ciudad Guzmán, Colima, San Juan de los Lagos, Tepic, Zacatecas; Prelature of Jesús Maria del Nayar).

Hermosillo (Ciudad Obregón, La Paz, Mexicali, Tijuana).

México (Atlacomulco, Cuernavaca, Toluca, Tula, Tulancingo).

Monterrey (Ciudad Valles, Ciudad Victoria, Linares, Matamoros, Nuevo Laredo, Piedras Negras, Saltillo, Tampico, Nuevo Casas Grandes).

Morelia (Apatzingán, Tacámbaro, Zamora).

Oaxaca, Antequera (San Cristóbal de las Casas, Tapachula, Tehuantepec, Tuxtla Gutiérrez, Tuxtepec; Prelacies of Mixes and Huautla).

Puebla de los Angeles (Huajuapan de León, Huejutla, Tehuacán, Tlaxcala).

San Luis Potosi (Celaya, León, Querétaro, Matehuala).

Tlalnepantla (Texcoco, Cuautitlán, Netzahualcóyotl, Ecatepec, Valle de Chalco).

Xalapa (Papantla, San Andrés Tuxtla, Coatzacoalcos, Tuxpan, Veracruz, Orizaba, Córdoba).

Yucatán (Campeche, Tabasco, Prelacy of Cancún-Chetumal; Eparchy of Nuestra Señora del Paraiso).

Jurisdictions, Hierarchy
(Principal sources: Information office, Mexican Conference of Catholic Bishops; Catholic Almanac *survey;* Annuario Pontificio; L'Osservatore Romano; *Catholic News Service. As of July 1, 2003. Addresses and phone numbers are provided by the* Annuario Pontificio.*)*

Information includes names of archdioceses (indicated by asterisk) and dioceses, date of foundation, present ordinaries and auxiliaries; addresses of chancery office/bishop's residence.

Acapulco* (1958; promoted to archdiocese, 1983): Felipe Aguirre Franco, archbishop, 2001.

Diocesan Address: Apartado Postal 201, Quebrada 16, 39850 Acapulco, Guerrero; (748) 2-07-63.

Aguascalientes (1899): Ramón Godinez Flores, bishop, 1998.

Diocesan Address: Apartado 167, Galeana 105 Norte, 20000 Aquascalientes, Aguascalientes; (449) 9-15-32-61.

Apatzingán (1962): Miguel Patiño Velázquez, M.S.F., bishop, 1981.

Diocesan Address: Calle Esteban Vaca Calderón 100, 60600 Apatzingán, Mich.; (453) 5-34-17-87.

Atlacomulco (1984): Constancio Miranda Weckmann, bishop, 1998.

Diocesan Address: Hidalgo Sur 1, Apartado 22, 50450 Atlacomulco, Méx.; (712) 1-22-05-53.

Autlán (1961): Lázaro Pérez Jiménez, bishop, 1991.

Diocesan Address: Apartado 8, Hidalgo 74, 48900 Autlán, Jal., Mex.; (317) 3-82-12-28.

Campeche (1895): José Luis Amezcua Melgoza, bishop, 1995.

Diocesan Address: Calle 53 # 1-B Entre 8 y 10 Centro Apdo. Postal # 12724000 - Campeche, Camp.; (981) 8-16-25-24.

Cancún-Chetumal, Prelacy of (1970, as Chetumal; name changed in 1996): Jorge Bernal Vargas, bishop, 1978.

Diocesan Address: Apartado Postal 165, Othón P. Blanco 150, 77000 Chetumal, Quintana Roo; (983) 2-06-38.

Celaya (1973): Jesús Humberto Velázquez Garay, bishop, 1988.

Diocesan Address: Curia Diocesana, Apartado 207, Manuel Doblado 110, 38000 Celaya, Gto.; (461) 6-12-48-35.

Chihuahua* (1891; promoted to archdiocese, 1958): José Fernández Arteaga, archbishop, 1991.

Diocesan Address: Av. Cuauhtémoc # 1828 Col. Cuauhtémoc, Apartado Postal 7, 31000 Chihuahua, Chihuahua; (614) 4-10-32-02.

Chilpancingo-Chilapa (1863 as Chilpancingo; name changed to Chilpancingo-Chilapa, 1989): Efrén Ramos Salazar, bishop, 1990.

Diocesan Address: Abasolo e Hidalgo, Apartado Postal #185, 39000 Chilpancingo, Gro.; (747) 4-71-05-92.

Ciudad Altamirano (1964): Vacant.

Diocesan Address: Juárez 18 Oriente, Centro, Apdo 17, 40680 Ciudad Altamirano, Gro.; (767) 6-72-17-74.

Ciudad Guzmán (1972): Braulio Rafael León Villegas, bishop, 1999.

Diocesan Address: Ramón Corona 26, Apartado 86, 49000 Ciudad Guzman, Jal.; (341) 4-12-19-94.

Ciudad Juárez (1957): Renato Ascencio León, bishop, 1994.

Diocesan Address: Apartado Postal 188, 32000 Cuidad Juárez, Chih.; (16) 15-09-22.

Ciudad Lázaro Cárdenas (1985): Salvador Flores Huerta, bishop, 1993.

Diocesan Address: Apartado 500, Andador Ciudad del Carmen #4, Fideicomiso 2° Sector, 60950 Lázaro Cardenas, Mich.; (753) 5-41-64-07.

Ciudad Obregón (1959): Vicente Garcia Bernal, bishop, 1988.

Diocesan Address: Apartado 402, Sonora 161 Norte, 85000 Ciudad Obregón, Son.; (644) 4-13-20-98.

Ciudad Valles (1960): Roberto Octavio Balmori Cinta, M.J., bishop, 2002.

Diocesan Address: 16 de Septiembre 726, Apartado 170, 79000 Ciudad Valles, S.L.P.; (138) 2-25-97

Ciudad Victoria (1964): Antonio González Sánchez, bishop, 1995.

Diocesan Address: 15 Hidalgo y Juárez, Centro, Apartado Postal #335, 87000 Ciudad Victoria, Tamps.; (834) 3-12-87-16.

Coatzacoalcos (1984): Rutilo Muñoz Zamora, bishop, 2002.

Diocesan Address: Apartado 513 y 513, Aldama 502, 96400 Coatzacoalcos, Ver.; (921) 2-12-23-99.

Colima (1881): Gilberto Valbuena Sánchez, bishop, 1989.

Diocesan Address: Hidalgo 135, Apartado 1, 28000 Colima, Colima; (312) 3-12-02-62.

Cordoba (2000): Eduardo Porfirio Patiño Leal, bishop, 2000.

Diocesan Address: Avenida 11-1300, Esquina con Calle 13, Apartado 154, Zona Centro, 94500 Cordoba, Ver., Mexico; (271) 7-14-91-56.

Cuauhtémoc-Madera (1966): Juan Guillermo López Soto, bishop, 1995.

Diocesan Address: Reforma y 4ª # 479, Apartado Postal 209, 31500 Cuauhtemoc, Chih.; (625) 5-81-57-22.

Cuautitlán (1979): Manuel Samaniego Barriga, bishop, 1979.

Diocesan Address: Apartado 14-21, Sor Juana Inés de la Cruz 208, Anexo a Catedral, 54800 Cuautitlán de Romero Rubio; (55) 58-72-19-96.

Cuernavaca (1891): Florencio Olvera Ochoa, bishop, 2002.

Diocesan Address: Apartado 13, Hidalgo #17, 62000 Cuernavaca, Mor.; (777) 3-18-45-90.

Culiacán (1883 as Sinaloa; name changed 1959): Benjamín Jiménez Hernández, bishop, 1993.

Diocesan Address: Apartado Postal 666, Av. Las Palmas #26 Oriente, 80220 Culiacán, Sinaloa; (667) 7-12-32-72.

Durango* (1620, promoted to archdiocese, 1891): Hector González Martínez, archbishop, 2003; Juan de Dios Caballero Reyes, aux.

Diocesan Address: Apartado Postal 116, 34000 Durango, Durango; (618) 8-11-42-42

Ecatepec (1995): Onésimo Cepeda Silva, bishop, 1995.

Diocesan Address: Plaza Principal s/n, San Cristóbal Centro, Apartado Postal 95, 55000 Ecatepec de Morelos; (5) 116-09-76.

El Salto, Prelacy of (1968): Manuel Mireles Vaquera, bishop, 1988.

Prelature Address: Mons. Francisco Medina s/n, Apartado Postal 58, 34950 El Salto, Durango; (675) 8-76-00-70.

Guadalajara* (1548; promoted to archdiocese, 1863): Cardinal Juan Sandoval Íñiguez, archbishop, 1994; José Trinidad González Rodriguez, Miguel Romano Gómez, Rafael Martínez Sainz, José María De la Torre Martín, auxiliaries.

Diocesan Address: Arzobispado, Apartado Postal 1-331, Calle Liceo 17, 44100 Guadalajara, Jal.; (33) 36-14-55-04; www.arquidiocesisgdl.org.mx.

Hermosillo* (1779, as Sonora, promoted to an archdiocese, 1963): José Ulises Macias Salcedo, archbishop, 1996.

Diocesan Address: Apartado 1, Dr. Paliza 81, 83260 Hermosillo, Son.; (662) 2-13-21-38.

Huajuapan de Leon (1903): Teodoro Enrique Pino Miranda, 2000.

Diocesan Address: Apartado 43, Anexos de Catedral, 69000 Huajuapan de León, Oax.; (953) 5-32-07-97.

Huautla, Prelacy of (1972): Hermengildo Ramirez Sánchez, M.J., bishop, 1978.

Diocesan Address: Casa Prelaticia Calle 5 de Feb. # 15, Apartado 2, 68500 Huautla de Jiménez, Oaxaca; (236) 3-78-00-19.

Huejutla (1922): Salvador Martínez Pérez, bishop, 1994.

Diocesan Address: Obispado, Apartado 8, Ave. Corona del Rosal s/n, Col. Tecoluco, 43000 Huejutla, Hgo.; (789) 8-96-01-85.

Jesús María of Nayar, Prelature of (1962): José Antonio Pérez Sánchez, O.F.M., bishop, 1992.

Diocesan Address: Curia Prelaticia de Jesús María, Belén #24, Apartado 33-B, 63150 Tepic, Nayar; (311) 2-13-88-80.

La Paz en la Baja California Sur (1988): Miguel Angel Alba Díaz, 2001.

Diocesan Address: Apartado 25, Revolución y 5 de Mayo, 23000 La Paz, B.C.S.; (112) 2-25-96.

León (1863): José Guadalupe Martin Rábago, bishop, 1995.

Diocesan Address: Pedro Moreno #312, Apartado 108, 37000 León, Gto.; (477) 7-13-27-47; www.diocesisleon.org.mx.

Linares (1962): Ramón Calderón Batres, bishop, 1988.

Diocesan Address: Morelos y Zaragoza s/n, Apartado 70, 67700 Linares, N.L.; (821) 2-00-54.

Matamoros (1958): Francisco Javier Chavolla Ramos, bishop, 1991.

Diocesan Address: Apartado 70, Calle 5 y Morelos, 87351 Matamoros, Tamps.; (88) 13-55-11; www.communion.org.mx.

Matehuala (1997): Rodrigo Aguilar Martínez, bishop, 1997.

Diocesan Address: Rayón #200 Centro, Apartado 40, 78700 Matehuala, S.L.P.; (01) 488-2-51-42.

Mazatlán (1958): Rafael Barraza Sánchez, bishop, 1981.

Diocesan Address: Apartado Postal 1, Canizales y Benito Juárez s/n, 82000 Mazatlán, Sin.; (69) 81-33-52.

Mexicali (1966): José Isidro Guerrero Macías, bishop, 1997.

Diocesan Address: Av. Morelos #192, Col. Primera sección, Apartado 3-547, 21100 Mexicali, B.C. Norte; (686) 5-52-40-09.

México* (1530, promoted to an archdiocese, 1546): Cardinal Norberto Rivera Carrera, archbishop, 1995; Abelardo Alvarado Alcántara, José de Jesús Martinez Zepeda, Marcelino Hernández Rodríguez, Luis Fletes Santana, Rodrigo Guillermo Ortiz Mondragón, Felipe Tejeda Garcia, M.Sp.S., Francisco Clavel Gil, Rogelio Esquivel Medina, Jonás Guerrero Corona, auxiliaries.

Diocesan Address: Curia Arzobispal, Apartado Postal 24-433, Durango 90, Col. Roma, 06700 - México, D. F.; (55) 55-25-11-10; www.arzobispadomexico.org.mx.

Mixes, Prelacy of (1964): Braulio Sánchez Fuentes, S.D.B., bishop, 1978.

Diocesan Address: Casa del Señor Obispo, 70283, Ayutla, Mixes, Oax.; (951) 5-58-20-98.

Monterrey* (1777, as Linares o Nuevo León, promoted to an archdiocese, 1891; name changed 1922): Francisco Robles Ortega, archbishop, 2003; José Lizares Estrada, Gustavo Rodríguez Vega, auxiliaries.

Diocesan Address: Apartado 7, Zuazua 1110 Sur con Ocampo, 64000 Monterrey, N.L.; (81) 83-45-24-66; www.pixel.com.mx/info-gral/info-nl/religion/catolica/arqui.html.

Morelia* (1536, as Michoacan, promoted to an archdiocese 1863, name changed in 1924): Alberto Suárez Inda, archbishop, 1995; Leopoldo González González, Enrique Díaz Díaz, auxiliaries.

Diocesan Address: Apartado 17, 58000 Morelia, Mich.; (443) 3-12-05-23.

Netzahualcóyotl (1979): Carlos Garfias Merlos, bishop, 2003.

Diocesan Address: Apartado 89, 4 Avenida esq. Bellas Artes, Col. Evolución, 57700 Ciudad Netzahualcóyotl; (55) 57-97-61-32.

Nuestra Señora de los Mártires del Libano, Eparchy of (Maronites, 1995): Georges M. Saad Abi Younes, O.L.M., eparch, 2003.

Diocesan address: Ntra. Sra. de Balvarena Correo Mayor # 65, 06060 — México, D. F.; (55) 55-21-20-11.

Nuestra Señora del Paraiso, Eparchy of (Greek Melkites, 1988): vacant.

Diocesan Address: Matías Romero 1014, Dpto. 601, Col. Del Valle, 3100 Mexico, D.F.; (5) 542-0225.

Nuevo Casas Grandes (1977): Hilario Chávez Joya, M.N.M., bishop, 2000.

Diocesan Address: Apartado Postal 198, Av. Hidalgo #105, 31700 Nuevo Casas Grandes, Chih.; (636) 6-94-05-20.

Nuevo Laredo (1989): Ricardo Watty Urquidi, M.Sp.S., bishop, 1989.

Diocesan Address: Saltillo 206, Apartado Postal #20-B, Col. México, 88280 Nuevo Laredo, Tamps.; (867) 7-15-29-28.

Oaxaca* (Also Antequara, 1535, promoted to arch-diocese, 1891): Vacant, archbishop; Miguel Ángel Alba Díaz, aux.

Diocesan Address: Apartado Postal # 31, Garcia Vigil #600, 68000 Oaxaca, Oax.; (951) 6-20-49.

Orizaba (2000): Hipolito Reyes Larios, bishop,

2000. Diocesan Address: Templo de Ntra. Sra. del Carmen, Sur 9 # 142 esq. Oriente 4, Apdo. Postal # 151, 94300 - Orizaba, Ver.; (272) 7-24-17-33.

Papantla (1922): Lorenzo Cárdenas Aregullin, bishop, 1980.

Diocesan Address: Apartado 27, Juárez 1102, 73800 Teziutlán, Pue.; (231) 3-24-30.

Parral (1992): José Andrés Corral Arredondo, bishop, 1992.

Diocesan Address: Apartado Postal 313, Fray Bartolomé de las Casas #13, 33800 Parral, Chih.; (152) 2-03-71.

Piedras Negras (2003): Alonso Gerardo Garza Treviño, first bishop, 2003. Diocesan address: Hidalgo Sur # 404 Centro 26000 - Piedras Negras, Coah.; (878) 7-82-94-80.

Puebla de los Angeles* (1525, as Tlaxcala, renamed in 1903): Rosendo Huesca Pacheco, archbishop, 1977.

Diocesan Address: Apartado 235, Av. 2, Sur N. 305, 72000 Puebla, Pue.; (222) 2-32-62-12.

Querétaro (1863): Mario de Gasperín Gasperín, bishop, 1989.

Diocesan Address: Apartado Postal 49, Reforma #48, 76000 Querétaro, Qro.; (42) 12-10-33.

Saltillo (1891): Raul Vera López, O.P., bishop, 1999.

Diocesan Address: Hidalgo Sur 166, Apartado 25, 25000 Saltillo, Coah.; (844) 4-12-37-84.

San Andrés Tuxtla (1959): Guillermo Ranzahuer González, bishop, 1969.

Diocesan Address: Constitución y Morelos, 95700 San Andrés Tuxtla, Ver.; (294) 9-42-03-74.

San Cristóbal de las Casas (1539, as Chiapas, renamed in 1964): Felipe Arizmendi Esquivel, bishop, 2000.

Diocesan Address: 5 de Feb. y 20 de Nov. # 1 Centro 29200 — San Cristóbal las Casas, Chis; (967) 6-78-00-53; www.laneta.apc.org/curiasc.

San Juan de los Lagos (1972): Javier Navarro Rodríguez, bishop, 1999.

Diocesan Address: Morelos 30, Apartado #1, 47000 San Juan de los Lagos, Jal.; (395) 7-85-05-70; www.redial.com.mx/obispado/index.htm.

San Luis Potosí* (1854, promoted to an archdiocese, 1988): Luis Morales Reyes, archbishop, 1999.

Diocesan Address: Madero # 300, Apartado N. 1, 78000 - San Luis Potosí, S.L.P.; (444) 8-12-45-55.

Tabasco (1880): Benjamin Castillo Plascencia, bishop, 2003.

Diocesan Address: Apartado Postal 97, Fidencia 502, 86000 Villahermosa, Tab.; (93) 12-13-97.

Tacámbaro (1913): Luis Castro Medellín, M.S.F., 2002.

Diocesan Address: Apartado 4, Professor Enrique Aguilar 49, 61650 Tacámbaro, Mich.; (459) 6-00-44.

Tampico (1870, as Ciudad Victoria o Tamaulipas, renamed in 1958): Rafael Gallardo Garcia, bishop, 1987.

Diocesan Address: Apartado 545, Altamira 116 Oriente, 89000 Tampico, Tamps.; (12) 12-28-02.

Tapachula (1957): Rogelio Cabrera López, 2001.

Diocesan Address: Apartado 70, Av. Primera Sur 1, 30700 Tapachula, Chiapas; (962) 6-15-03; www.diocesis-tapachula.org.mx.

Tarahumara (1958, as a vicariate apostolic, promoted to diocese, 1993): José Luis Dibildox Martinez, bishop, 1994.

Diocesan Address: Apartado Postal 11, Av. López Mateos #7, 33190 Guachochi, Chih.; (649) 5-43-02-23.

Tehuacán (1962): Mario Espinosa Contreras, bishop, 1996.
Diocesan Address: Apartado Postal 137, Agustin A. Cacho 107, 75700 Tehuacán, Pue.; (238) 3-83-14-68.

Tehuantepec (1891): Felipe Padilla Cardona, bishop, 2000.
Diocesan Address: Apartado Postal 93, Mina s/n. Anexos de Catedral, 70760 Tehuantepec, Oax.; (971) 7-15-00-60.

Tepic (1891): Alfonso Humberto Robles Cota, bishop, 1981.
Diocesan Address: Apartado 15, Av. de las Flores 10, Fraccionamiento Residencial La Loma, 63137 Tepic, Nay.; (311) 2-14-46-45.

Texcoco (1960): Carlos Aguiar Retes, bishop, 1997; Juan Manuel Mancilla Sanchez, auxiliary.
Diocesan Address: Apartado Postal 35, Fray Pedro de Gante 2, 56100 Texcoco, Méx.; (595) 4-08-69.

Tijuana (1963): Rafael Romo Muñoz, bishop, 1996.
Diocesan Address: Apartado 226, Calle 10ª y Av. Ocampo # 1049, 22000 Tijuana, B.C.N.; (664) 6-84-84-11 y 12; www.iglesiatijuana.org.

Tlalnepantla* (1964, promoted to archdiocese, 1989): Ricardo Guizar Díaz, archbishop, 1996; Francisco Ramírez Navarro, auxiliary.
Diocesan Address: Apartado 268 y 270, Av. Juárez 42, 54000 Tlalnepantla, Méx.; (55) 55-65-39-44.

Tlapa (1992): Alejo Zavala Castro, bishop, 1992.
Diocesan Address: Anexo Catedral, Centro, 41300 Tlapa de Comonfort, Gro.; (757) 4-76-08-35.

Tlaxcala (1959): Jacinto Guerrero Torres bishop, 2001.
Diocesan Address: Apartado 84, Lardizábal 45, 90000 Tlaxcala, Tlax.; (246) 4-62-32-43.

Toluca (1950): Vacant.
Diocesan Address: Apartado 82, Portal Reforma Norte 104, 50000 Toluca, Méx.; (72) 15-25-35; www.diocesistoluca.org.mx.

Torreón (1957): Vacant.
Diocesan Address: Apartado Postal 430, Av. Morelos 46 Poniente, 27000 Torreón, Coah.; (871) 7-12-30-43.

Tula (1961): Octavio Villegas Aguilar, bishop, 1994.
Diocesan Address: 5 de Mayo, #5, Apartado 31, 42800 Tula de Allende, Hgo.; (773) 7-32-02-75.

Tulancingo (1863): Pedro Aranda Díaz-Muñoz, bishop, 1975.
Diocesan Address: Apartado #14, Plaza de la Constitución, 43600 Tulancingo, Hgo.; (775) 3-10-10.

Tuxpan (1962): Domingo Díaz Martínez, bishop, 2002.
Diocesan Address: Independencia #56, 92870 Tuxpan, Ver.; (783) 4-16-36.

Tuxtepec (1979): José de Jesús Castillo Rentería, M.N.M., bishop, 1979.
Diocesan Address: Bonfil # 597, entre Juárez y Villa Col. Santa Fe Apartado Postal 9, 68320 — Tuxtepec, Oax.; (287) 5-00-42.

Tuxtla Gutiérrez (1964): José Luis Chávez Botello, 2001.
Diocesan Address: Uruguay # 500 A Col. El Retiro Apdo. Postal # 36529040 - Tuxtla Gutiérrez, Chis.; (961) 6-04-06-44; www.chisnet.com.mx/~cosi/obispado.

Valle de Chalco (2003): Luis Artemio Flores Calzada, first bishop, 2003.
Diocesan Address: N/A.

Veracruz (1962): Luis Gabriel Cuara Méndez, bishop, 2000.
Diocesan Address: Insurgentes Veracruzanos #470, Paseo del Malecón, 91700 Veracruz, Ver.; (229) 9-31-24-13.

Xalapa* (1962; originally Veracruz and Xalapa, 1863; promoted to archdiocese, 1951): Sergio Obeso Rivera, archbishop, 1979.
Diocesan Address: Apartado 359, Av. Manuel Avila Camacho #73, 91000 Xalapa, Ver.; (228) 8-12-05-79.

Yucatán* (1561, promoted to archdiocese, 1906): Emilio Carlos Berlie Belaunzarán, archbishop, 1995.
Diocesan Address: Calle 58 N. 501, 97000 Mérida, Yuc.; (99) 23-79-83; www.geocities.com/SoHo/207/principa.html.

Zacatecas (1863): Fernando Chávez Ruvalcaba, bishop, 1999.
Diocesan Address: Apartado #1, Miguel Auza #219, 98000 Zacatecas, Zacatecas; (492) 9-22-02-32; www.logicnet.com.mx/obispado.

Zamora (1863): Carlos Suárez Cázares, bishop, 1994.
Diocesan Address: Altos de Catedral (Calle Hidalgo), Apartado Postal #18, 59600 Zamora, Mich.; (351) 5-12-12-08.

CONFERENCIA DEL EPISCOPADO MEXICANO

(*Sources: Annuario Pontificio; Pbro. Jorge Fco. Vázquez M., Secretario Adjunto, Conferencia del Episcopado Mexicano; Conferencia del Episcopado Mexicano, Directorio, 2001-2003; translation courtesy Suzanne Lea.)*

STRUCTURE

The Mexican Conference of Bishops (CEM, *Conferencia del Episcopado Mexicano*) is the permanent body of Mexican bishops. The bishops adhere to the guidelines of the conference in specific fulfillment of their pastoral labors. They do this in order to obtain the greatest good for the people that the church can achieve. The conference proposes:

1) To study the problems that occur in pastoral work, and to seek solutions. 2) To initiate, with a common end in mind and a common course of action, the forms and methods of preaching that best suit the needs of the country. 3) In regard to the collective salvific mission of the church: To look for and to teach the best way in which the respective activities of the deacons, priests, religious, and lay person will be most efficient. 4) To facilitate relations with the civil authority and with other organizations in specific cases. 5) To write to the Episcopal commission regarding patrimonial and proprietary matters, and give counsel on determined financial or labor related points.

All those elected to the body of the CEM will have three years of service and will not be reelected to the same position after two three-year sessions have been completed consecutively.

The address of the conference headquarters is:

Prolongación Misterios No. 26, Col. Tepeyac Insurgentes, 07020 México, D.F. Tels. (01-55) 5577-5401; www.cem.org.mx.

Permanent Assembly

The Permanent Assembly is the representative arm of the bishops belonging to the CEM. Its function is to ensure the continuation of the works of the conference and the fulfillment of its accords.

The Permanent Assembly is comprised of the Presidential Assembly and the Assembly of Pastoral Regions. It meets four times per year in ordinary session. It meets in extraordinary sessions whenever the majority of its members or those of the Presidential Assembly determine it to be necessary.

A session is valid if two-thirds of the members are present.

Officers

President: Bishop Luis Morales Reyes of San Luis Potosí.

Vice-President: Bishop José Guadalupe Martin Rábago of Léon.

Secretary General: Bishop Abelardo Alvarado Alcántara, aux. of Mexico.

General Treasurer: Bishop José Guadalupe Galván Galindo of Ciudad Valles.

Vocals: Bishop Ricardo Watty Urquidi, M.Sp.S. of

Nuevo Laredo; Bishop Javier Navarro Rodríguez of San Juan de los Lagos.

Commissions, Section One:
Biblical Studies: Bishop Rogelio Cabrera López.
Doctrine: Bishop Lázaro Pérez Jiménez.
Culture: Archbishop Rosenda Huesca Pacheco.
Education: Bishop Ramón Godínez Flores.
Evangelization: Bishop José Luis Chávez Botello.
Liturgy: Bishop Mario de Gasperín Gasperín.
Missions: Archbishop Ricardo Guizar Díaz.
Pastoral Sanctuaries: Bishop Efren Ramos Salazar.
Social Communications: Bishop Rodrigo Guillermo Ortiz Mondragón.
Social Justice: Bishop Jacinto Guerreo Torres.

Commissions, Section Two:
Clergy: Bishop José Ulises Macías Salcedo.
Consecrated Life: Bishop Felipe Tejeda García, M.Sp.S.
Lay Apostolates: Bishop Carlos Talavera Ramírez.
Lay Ministry and Diaconate: Bishop José de Jesus Martinez Zepeda.
Military Chaplains: Bishop Hilario Chávez Joya.
Priestly Formation: Bishop Benjamin Jiménez Hernández.
Seminaries and Vocations: Bishop Carlos Suárez Cázares.

CANONIZATION OF ST. JUAN DIEGO CUAUHTLATOATZIN

On July 31, 2002, during his pastoral visit to Mexico, Pope John Paul II canonized St. Juan Diego. The pontiff was on his fifth visit to the country and received another boisterous welcome from the Mexican people. The canonization was celebrated in the Basilica of Our Lady of Guadalupe in Mexico City. Juan Diego is the first indigenous saint of the American continent.

The Life of Juan Diego

A figure of considerable historical mystery and interest, Juan Diego was born probably in 1474 with the name "Cuauhtlatoatzin" ("the talking eagle") in Cuautlitlán, today part of Mexico City, Mexico. He was a member of the Chichimeca people, one of the indigenous communities that resided in the Anáhuac Valley. Little is known about his life prior to conversion, but when he was 50 years old he received baptism by a Franciscan priest, Fr Peter da Gand, one of the first Franciscan missionaries in Mexico.

On December 9, 1531, Juan Diego was on his way to morning Mass when the Blessed Mother appeared to him on Tepeyac Hill. She asked him to go to the bishop and request in her name that a shrine be built at Tepeyac. There, she promised, she would pour out her grace upon those who invoked her. The bishop, not surprisingly, did not believe Juan Diego, and demanded some kind of proof that the apparition was true. On December 12, Juan Diego returned to Tepeyac. The Blessed Mother appeared again and instructed him to climb the hill and to pick the flowers that he would find there. Juan Diego obeyed, and although it was winter, he found magnificent roses in bloom. He gathered up the flowers and carried them to Our Lady. She placed them in his mantle and told him to take them to the Bishop as the proof that had been demanded.

Juan Diego went back to the skeptical bishop with

the roses hidden in his mantle. When he opened his mantle, the flowers fell on the ground. Even more remarkable was the mantle, for where the flowers had been wrapped there was now impressed an image of the Blessed Mother.

The bishop accepted without question the claim of Juan Diego, granting permission for Juan Diego to live the rest of his life as a hermit in a small hut near the chapel where the bishop had commanded the miraculous image to be preserved. Juan Diego devoted his remaining life to the care for the church and the many pilgrims who came to visit and pray to Our Lady.

Juan Diego died in 1548 and was buried in the first chapel dedicated to the Virgin of Guadalupe. He was beatified on May 6, 1990, by Pope John Paul II in the Basilica of Our Lady of Guadalupe.

Homily of Pope John Paul II

Following are excerpts from the homily of the Holy Father for the canonization on July 31:

." 'The Guadalupe Event,' as the Mexican Episcopate has pointed out, 'meant the beginning of an evangelization with a vitality that surpassed all expectations. Christ's message, through his Mother, took up the central elements of the indigenous culture, purified them and gave them the definitive sense of salvation" (May 14, 2002, No. 8). Consequently Guadalupe and Juan Diego have a deep ecclesial and missionary meaning and are a model of perfectly inculturated evangelization....

"The noble task of building a better Mexico, with greater justice and solidarity, demands the cooperation of all. In particular, it is necessary today to support the indigenous peoples in their legitimate aspirations, respecting and defending the authentic values of each ethnic group...."

STATISTICAL SUMMARY OF THE CATHOLIC CHURCH IN MEXICO

(Principal sources: Annuario Pontificio, *2003;* Conferencia del Espicopado Mexicano, Directorio, 2001-2003; *figures as of January 2003. Catholic population statistics are those reported in the most recent* Annuario *population estimates. Archdioceses are indicated by an asterisk.)*

Includes 14 provinces: 14 archdioceses, 60 dioceses, 6 prelacies, and one vicariate apostolic. The Catholic population of Mexico comprises approximately 92% of the `overall Mexican population of 135,379,786 (in 2002 there were 1,930,298 baptisms and 368,383 marriages). This table presents a provincial breakdown of Catholic statistics. In some cases, the totals are approximate because diocesan estimates are often considered unreliable owing to difficulties in adequate assessment of demographics and population distribution.

Province Diocese	Cath. Pop.	Dioc. Priests	Rel. Priests	Total Priests	Perm. Deacs.	Bro- thers	Sis- ters	Par- ishes
Acapulco	**5,306,135**	**323**	**71**	**394**	**22**	**74**	**220**	**349**
Acapulco*	2,836,000	90	18	108	20	20	204	84
Chilpancingo-Chilapa	825,000	116	21	137	1	21	12 82	
Ciudad Lázaro Cárdenas	683,600	27	13	40	1	14	71	23
Ciudad Altamirano	538,535	58	5	63	-	5	91	25
Tlapa	423,000	32	14	46	-	14	26	24
Chihuahua	**4,596,795**	**261**	**122**	**383**	**18**	**167**	**635**	**195**
Chihuahua*	992,973	85	32	117	8	45	188	62
Ciudad Juárez	2,370,000	82	37	119	10	50	170	63
Cuauhtémoc-Madera	315,807	23	14	37	-	17	71	25
Nuevo Casas Grandes	128,000	25	8	33	-	8	27	14
Parral	522,200	34	9	43	-	12	71	17
Tarahumara	267,815	12	22	34	-	35	108	14
Durango	**6,837,180**	**517**	**70**	**587**	**4**	**113**	**1,003**	**272**
Durango*	2,157,812	199	19	218	-	46	387	105
Culiacán	2,238,368	130	5	135	4	10	296	68
El Salto	296,000	18	-	18	-	-	22	13
Mazatlán	692,000	77	7	84	-	8	147	40
Torreón	1,453,000	93	39	132	-	49	151	46
Guadalajara	**11,905,968**	**2,200**	**403**	**2,603**	**5**	**1,060**	**5,617**	**854**
Guadalajara*	5,715,000	982	288	1,270	2	832	3,387	385
Aguascalientes	1,503,500	216	47	263	-	82	635	89
Autlán	297,083	97	-	97	2	-	179	43
Ciudad Guzmán	471,500	107	14	121	-	18	179	54
Colima	633,636	123	9	132	-	14	211	52
San Juan los Lagos	799,578	261	17	278	-	61	375	65
Tepic	1,068,671	215	7	222	-	7	271	65
Zacatecas	1,300,000	190	5	195	-	26	380	101
Jesús Maria of Nayar[1]	117,000	9	16	25	1	20	6	15
Hermosillo	**5,980,488**	**480**	**157**	**637**	**15**	**250**	**1,153**	**282**
Hermosillo*	955,567	99	14	113	1	18	150	57
Ciudad Obregón	830,000	104	17	121	1	27	138	56
La Paz	381,637	36	24	60	-	24	189	27
Mexicali	1,181,907	101	27	128	1	45	156	49
Tijuana	2,631,377	140	75	215	12	136	520	93
Mexico	**15,537,071**	**1,354**	**760**	**2,114**	**83**	**1,796**	**5,610**	**833**
Mexico*	6,999,402	698	635	1,333	81	1,643	4,744	426
Atlacomulco	836,853	77	8	85	1	12	77	41
Cuernavaca	1,829,341	128	53	181	1	50	139	115
Toluca	2,878,775	237	50	287	-	68	415	125
Tula	1,052,700	59	12	71	-	13	85	43
Tulancingo	1,940,000	155	2	157	-	10	150	83
Monterrey	**10,844,515**	**824**	**230**	**1,054**	**19**	**367**	**1,706**	**477**
Monterrey*	4,470,807	333	122	455	18	217	775	166
Ciudad Valles	875,500	48	12	60	-	12	121	41

Province Diocese	Cath. Pop.	Dioc. Priests	Rel. Priests	Total Priests	Perm. Deacs.	Bro- thers	Sis- ters	Par- ishes
Monterrey, cont.								
Ciudad Victoria	370,770	37	16	53	-	22	79	33
Linares	222,431	34	2	36	-	2	55	21
Matamoros	1,656,044	89	10	99	-	11	86	47
Nuevo Laredo	791,000	38	17	55	1	19	94	34
Saltillo	1,347,343	148	37	185	-	64	338	77
Tampico	1,110,620	97	14	111	-	20	158	58
Morelia	**5,431,935**	**888**	**157**	**1,045**	**-**	**334**	**2,231**	**433**
Morelia*	2,825,654	482	127	609	-	245	1,107	253
Apatzingán	630,000	55	3	58	-	3	130	26
Tacámbaro	357,435	74	2	76	-	2	150	33
Zamora	1,618,846	277	25	302	-	84	844	121
Oaxaca	**6,747,011**	**446**	**142**	**588**	**397**	**202**	**1,078**	**348**
Oaxaca*	1,365,439	152	39	191	21	59	290	141
San Cristobal	995,322	37	36	73	342	55	209	46
Tapachula	1,271,750	62	8	70	-	8	112	38
Tehuantepec	1,145,000	53	8	61	-	9	122	33
Tuxtepec	630,000	26	10	36	17	10	24	27
Tuxtla Gutiérrez	1,026,000	101	12	113	-	25	274	39
Huautla[1]	123,500	9	4	13	-	7	3	7
Mixes[1]	190,000	6	25	31	17	29	44	17
Puebla de los Angeles	**6,466,636**	**798**	**136**	**934**	**1**	**253**	**1,922**	**471**
Puebla de los Angeles*	3,567,489	407	100	507	-	210	1,206	243
Huajuapan de León	620,300	108	-	108	-	-	136	71
Huejutla	512,140	73	9	82	-	9	76	38
Tehuacán	919,830	85	12	97	-	13	144	57
Tlaxcala	846,877	125	15	140	1	21	360	62
San Luis Potosi	**7,795,262**	**793**	**350**	**1,143**	**10**	**560**	**4,151**	**371**
San Luis Potosi*	1,700,000	192	50	242	9	72	650	82
Celaya	1,130,882	153	57	210	1	125	541	62
León	3,081,802	252	137	389	-	145	1,443	119
Matehuala	267,355	31	6	37	-	6	37	17
Querétaro	1,615,223	165	100	265	-	212	1,480	91
Tlalnepantla	**21,916,385**	**857**	**211**	**1,068**	**51**	**428**	**1,287**	**565**
Tlalnepantla*	3,207,022	255	78	333	8	138	355	193
Cuautitlan	3,350,000	176	58	234	-	168	330	82
Ecatepec	3,500,000	98	10	108	19	18	136	82
Netzahualcóyotl	8,891,872	192	41	233	-	56	167	131
Texcoco	2,967,491	136	24	160	24	48	299	77
Xalapa	**8,634,648**	**600**	**55**	**655**	**47**	**66**	**1,166**	**365**
Xalapa*	1,009,128	130	5	135	-	9	301	61
Coatzacoalcos	857,408	42	6	48	4	13	74	24
Cordoba	605,555	68	-	68	-	-	98	40
Orizaba	490,000	49	7	56	-	7	185	35
Papantla	1,336,419	82	1	83	1	1	151	43
San Andrés Tuxtla	921,138	66	2	68	31	2	106	45
Tuxpan	1,380,000	78	-	78	3	-	68	48
Veracruz	2,035,000	85	34	119	8	34	183	69
Yucatán	**4,211,230**	**305**	**119**	**424**	**22**	**177**	**917**	**220**
Yucatán*	1,517,252	155	45	200	16	80	505	95
Campeche	592,908	44	12	56	1	30	135	35
Tabasco	1,056,570	97	15	112	-	17	185	52
Cancún-Chetumal[1]	890,000	4	42	46	2	48	92	34
Nuestra Sra. de los Mártires[2]								
	150,000	4	3	7	3	-	-	3
Nuestra Sra. del Paraiso[2]	4,500	1	2	3	-	2	-	1
Totals:	**122,211,269**	**10,646**	**2,983**	**13,629**	**694**	**6,442**	**28,696**	**6,035**

Note: The statistics do not reflect the creation of the dioceses of Piedras Negras and Valle de Chalco in 2003. 1. Prelacy 2. Eparchy

Consecrated Life

INSTITUTES OF CONSECRATED LIFE

Religious institutes and congregations are special societies in the Church — institutes of consecrated life — whose members, called Religious, commit themselves by public vows to observance of the evangelical counsels of poverty, chastity and obedience in a community kind of life in accordance with rules and constitutions approved by church authority.

Secular institutes (covered in their own *Almanac* entries) are also institutes of consecrated life.

The particular goal of each institute and the means of realizing it in practice are stated in the rule and constitutions proper to the institute. Local bishops can give approval for rules and constitutions of institutes of diocesan rank. Pontifical rank belongs to institutes approved by the Holy See. General jurisdiction over all Religious is exercised by the Congregation for Institutes of Consecrated Life and Societies of Apostolic Life. General legislation concerning Religious is contained in Canons 573 to 709 in Book II, Part III, of the Code of Canon Law.

All institutes of consecrated life are commonly called religious orders, despite the fact that there are differences between orders and congregations. The best known orders include the Benedictines, Trappists, Franciscans, Dominicans, Carmelites and Augustinians, for men; and the Carmelites, Benedictines, Poor Clares, Dominicans of the Second Order and Visitation Nuns, for women. The orders are older than the congregations, which did not appear until the 16th century.

Contemplative institutes are oriented to divine worship and service within the confines of their communities, by prayer, penitential practices, other spiritual activities and self-supporting work. Examples are the Trappists and Carthusians, the Carmelite and Poor Clare nuns. Active institutes are geared for pastoral ministry and various kinds of apostolic work. Mixed institutes combine elements of the contemplative and active ways of life. While most institutes of men and women can be classified as active, all of them have contemplative aspects.

Clerical communities of men are those whose membership is predominantly composed of priests.

Non-clerical or lay institutes of men are the various brotherhoods.

"The Consecrated Life and Its Role in the Church and in the World", was the topic of the ninth general assembly of the Synod of Bishops held Oct. 2 to 29, 1994.

Societies of Apostolic Life

Some of the institutes listed below have a special kind of status because their members, while living a common life like that which is characteristic of Religious, do not profess the vows of Religious. Examples are the Maryknoll Fathers, the Oratorians of St. Philip Neri, the Paulists and Sulpicians. They are called societies of apostolic life and are the subject of Canons 731 to 746 of the Code of Canon Law.

RELIGIOUS INSTITUTES OF MEN IN THE UNITED STATES

(*Sources:* Annuario Pontificio, The Official Catholic Directory; Catholic Almanac *survey. As of June 1, 2003.*)

Africa, Missionaries of, M. Afr.: Founded 1868 at Algiers by Cardinal Charles M. Lavigerie; known as White Fathers until 1984. U.S. headquarters, 1624 21st St. N.W., Washington, DC 20009, (202) 232-5154. Missionary work in Africa.

African Missions, Society of, S.M.A.: Founded 1856, at Lyons, France, by Bishop Melchior de Marion Brésillac. Generalate, Rome, Italy; American province (1941), 23 Bliss Ave., Tenafly, NJ 07670, (201) 567-9085. Missionary work.

Alexian Brothers, C.F.A.: Founded 14th century in western Germany and Belgium during the Black Plague. Motherhouse, Aachen, Germany; generalate, 198 James Blvd., Signal Mountain, TN 37377, (423) 886-0380. Hospital and general health work.

Assumptionists (Augustinians of the Assumption), A.A.: Founded 1845, at Nimes, France, by Rev. Emmanuel d'Alzon; in U.S., 1946. General house, Rome, Italy; U.S. province, 330 Market St., Brighton, MA 02135, (617) 783-0400, www.assumptionists.com. Educational, parochial, ecumenical, retreat, foreign mission work.

Atonement, Franciscan Friars of the, S.A.: Founded as an Anglican Franciscan community in 1898 at Garrison, NY, by Rev. Paul Wattson. Community corporately received into the Catholic Church in 1909. Generalate, St. Paul's Friary, Graymoor, Rte. 9, P.O. Box 300, Garrison, NY 10524, (914) 424-2113.

Ecumenical, mission, retreat and charitable works.

Augustinian Recollects, O.A.R.: Founded 1588; in U.S., 1944. General motherhouse, Rome, Italy. Monastery of St. Cloud (formerly St. Augustine Province, 1944), 29 Ridgeway Ave., W. Orange, NJ 07052-3297, (973) 731-0616, www.augustinianrecollects.org. St. Nicholas of Tolentino Province (U.S. Delegation), St. Anselm's Church, 685 Tinton Ave., Bronx, NY, 10455, (718) 585-8666. Missionary, parochial, education work.

Augustinians (Order of St. Augustine), O.S.A.: Established canonically in 1256 by Pope Alexander IV; in U.S., 1796. General motherhouse, Rome, Italy. 214 Ashwood Rd. P.O. Box 340, Villanova, PA 19085-0338, (610) 527-3330, www.augustinians.org., (1796); Our Mother of Good Counsel Province (1941), Tolentine Center, 20300 Governors Hwy., Olympia Fields, IL 60461-1081, (708) 748-9500, www.midweststaugustinians.org. St. Augustine, Province of (1969), 1605 28th St., San Diego, CA 92102-1417, (619) 235-0247.

Barnabites (Clerics Regular of St. Paul), C.R.S.P.: Founded 1530, in Milan, Italy, by St. Anthony M. Zaccaria; approved 1533; in U.S., 1952. Historical motherhouse, Church of St. Barnabas (Milan). Generalate, Rome, Italy; North American province, 981 Swann Rd, P.O. Box 167, Youngstown, NY 14174, (716) 754-7489, www.catholicchurch.org/barnabites. Parochial, educational, mission work.

Basil the Great, Order of St. (Basilian Order of St. Josaphat), O.S.B.M.: General motherhouse, Rome, Italy; U.S. province, 31-12 30th St., Long Island City, NY 11106, (718) 278-6626. Parochial work among Byzantine Ukrainian Rite Catholics.

Basilian Fathers (Congregation of the Priests of St. Basil), C.S.B.: Founded 1822, at Annonay, France. General motherhouse, Toronto, ON, Canada. U.S. address: 1910 W. Alabama, Houston, TX 77098, (713) 522-1736. Educational, parochial work.

Basilian Salvatorian Fathers, B.S.O.: Founded 1684, at Saida, Lebanon, by Eftimios Saifi; in U.S., 1953. General motherhouse, Saida, Lebanon; American headquarters, 30 East St., Methuen, MA 01844. Educational, parochial work among Eastern Rite peoples.

Benedictine Monks (Order of St. Benedict), O.S.B.: Founded 529, in Italy, by St. Benedict of Nursia; in U.S., 1846.

• **American Cassinese Congregation (1855).** Pres., Rt. Rev. Melvin J. Valvano, O.S.B., Newark Abbey, 528 Dr. Martin Luther King Blvd., Newark, NJ 07102, (973) 733-2822. Abbeys and priories belonging to the congregation:

St. Vincent Archabbey, 300 Fraser Purchase Rd., Latrobe, PA 15650, (724) 539-9761, www.benedictine.stvincent.edu. Saint John's Abbey, P.O. Box 2015, Collegeville, MN 56321, (320) 363-2548, www.saintjohnsabbey.org. St. Benedict's Abbey, 1020 North Second St., Atchison, KS 66002, (913) 367-7853, www.benedictine.edu/abbey/index.html. St. Mary's Abbey, 230 Mendham Rd., Morristown, NJ 07960, (973) 538-3231, www.osbmonks.org. Newark Abbey, 528 Dr. Martin Luther King, Jr., Blvd., Newark, NJ 07102, (973) 643-4800. Belmont Abbey, 100 Belmont-Mt. Holly Rd., Belmont, NC 28012, (704) 825-6675, www.bac.edu/monastery. St. Bernard Abbey, Cullman, AL 35055, (256) 734-8291. St.

Procopius Abbey, 5601 College Rd., Lisle, IL 60532, (630) 969-6410, www.procopius.org. St. Gregory's Abbey, 1900 W. MacArthur, Shawnee, OK 74804, (405) 878-5491, www.sgc.edu. St. Leo Abbey, St. Leo, FL 33574, (352) 588-8626, www.saintleoabbey.org. Assumption Abbey, P.O. Box A, Richardton, ND 58652, (701) 974-3315. St. Bede Abbey, Peru, IL 61354, (815) 223-3140, www.theramp.net/stbede/index.html. St. Martin's Abbey, 5300 Pacific Ave. S.E., Lacey, WA 98503-1297, (360) 438-4440, www.stmartin.edu. Holy Cross Abbey, P.O. Box 1510, Canon City, CO 81215, (719) 275-8631, www.holycrossabbey.org. St. Anselm's Abbey, 100 St. Anselm Dr., Manchester, NH 03102, (603) 641-7285, www.anselm.edu. St. Andrew Abbey, 10510 Buckeye Rd., Cleveland, OH 44104-3725, (216) 721-5300, www.bocohio.org. Holy Trinity Priory, P.O. Box 990, Butler, PA 16003, (724) 287-4461. Benedictine Priory, 6502 Seawright Dr., Savannah, GA 31406, (912) 356-3520, www.bcsav.net. Woodside Priory, 302 Portola Rd., Portola Valley, CA 94028, (415) 851-8220. Mary Mother of the Church Abbey, 12829 River Rd., Richmond, VA 23233, (804) 784-3508, www.richmondmonks.org. Abadia de San Antonio Abad, P.O. Box 729, Humacao, PR 00792, (787) 852-1616.

• **Swiss-American Congregation (1870).** Abbeys and priory belonging to the congregation:

St. Meinrad Archabbey, 100 Hill Dr., St. Meinrad, IN 47577-1003, (812) 357-6514, www.saintmeinrad.edu. Conception Abbey, 37174 State Hwy., VV, Conception, MO 64433-0501, (660) 944-3100, www.conceptionabbey.org. Mt. Michael Abbey, 22520 Mt. Michael Rd., Elkhorn, NE 68022-3400, (402) 289-2541, www.mountmichael.org. Subiaco Abbey, Subiaco, AR 72865, (479) 934-1000, www.subi.org. St. Joseph's Abbey, St. Benedict, LA 70457, (504) 892-1800. Mt. Angel Abbey, St. Benedict, OR 97373, (503) 845-3030. Marmion Abbey, 850 Butterfield Rd., Aurora, IL 60504, (630) 897-7215.

St. Benedict's Abbey, 12605 224th Ave., Benet Lake, WI 53102, (888) 482-1044, www.benetlake.org. Glastonbury Abbey, 16 Hull St., Hingham, MA 02043, (781) 749-2155, www.glastonburyabbey.org. Blue Cloud Abbey, Marvin, SD 57251-0098, (605) 398-9200, www.bluecloud.org. Corpus Christi Abbey, 101 South Vista Dr., Sandia, TX 78383, (361) 547-3257, www.geocities.com/Athens/styx/8125/ccabbey.html. Prince of Peace Abbey, 650 Benet Hill Rd., Oceanside, CA 92054, (760) 430-1305. St. Benedict Abbey, 254 Still River Rd., PO Box 22, Still River (Harvard), MA 01467, (978) 456-8017.

• **Congregation of St. Ottilien for Foreign Missions:** St. Paul's Abbey, P.O. Box 7, 289 Rt. 206 South, Newton, NJ 07860, (973) 383-2470. Christ the King Priory, P.O. Box 528, Schuyler, NE 68661, (402) 352-2177, www.megavision.net/benedict.

• **Congregation of the Annunciation,** St. Andrew Abbey, P.O. Box 40, Valyermo, CA 93563-0040, (661) 944-2178, www.valyermo.com.

• **English Benedictine Congregation**: St. Anselm's Abbey, 4501 S. Dakota Ave. N.E., Washington, DC 20017, (202) 269-2300; Abbey of St. Gregory the Great, Cory's Lane, Portsmouth, RI 02871-1352, (401) 683-2000; Abbey of St. Mary and St. Louis, 500 S. Mason Rd., St. Louis, MO 63141-8500, (314) 434-2557, www.priory.org, www.stlouisabbey.org.

• **Houses not in Congregations**: Mount Saviour Monastery, 231 Monastery Rd., Pine City, NY 14871-9787, (607) 734-1688, www.servtech.com/~msaviour; Weston Priory, 58 Priory Hill Rd., Weston, VT 05161-6400, (802) 824-5409, www.weston priory.org.

Benedictines, Camaldolese Hermits of America, O.S.B. Cam.: Founded 1012, at Camaldoli, near Arezzo, Italy, by St. Romuald; in U.S., 1958. General motherhouse, Arezzo, Italy; U.S. foundation, New Camaldoli Hermitage, 62475 Highway 1, Big Sur, CA 93920, (831) 667-2456, www.contemplation.org.

Benedictines, Olivetan, O.S.B.: General motherhouse, Siena, Italy. U.S. monasteries, Our Lady of Guadalupe Abbey, P.O. Box 1080, Pecos, NM 87552, (505) 757-6600, www.pecosabbey.org; Holy Trinity Monastery, P.O. Box 298, St. David, AZ 85630-0298, (520) 720-4642, www.holytrinitymonas tery.org; Monastery of the Risen Christ, P.O. Box 3931, San Luis Obispo, CA 93403-3931, (805) 544-1810; Benedictine Monastery of Hawaii, P.O. Box 490, Waialua, HI 96791, (808) 637-7887, www.catholichawaii.com/religious/benedictine.

Benedictines, Subiaco Congregation, O.S.B.: Independent priory, 1983. Monastery of Christ in the Desert, Abiquiu, NM 87510, (505) 470-4515; St. Mary's Priory, P.O. Box 345, Petersham, MA 01366, (978) 724-3350.

Benedictines, Sylvestrine, O.S.B.: Founded 1231, in Italy, by Sylvester Gozzolini. General motherhouse, Rome, Italy; U.S. foundations: 17320 Rosemont Rd., Detroit, MI 48219, (313) 532-6064; 2711 E. Drahner Rd., Oxford, MI 48051, (248) 628-2249; 1697 State Highway 3, Clifton, NJ 07012, (201) 778-1177.

Blessed Sacrament, Congregation of the, S.S.S.: Founded 1856, at Paris, France, by St. Pierre Julien Eymard; in U.S., 1900. General motherhouse, Rome, Italy; U.S. province, 5384 Wilson Mills Rd., Cleveland, OH 44143-3092, (440) 442-6311, www.blessed sacrament.com. Eucharistic apostolate.

Brigittine Monks (Order of the Most Holy Savior), O.Ss.S.: Monastery of Our Lady of Consolation, 23300 Walker Lane, Amity, OR 97101, (503) 835-8080, www.brigittine.org.

Camaldolese Hermits of the Congregation of Monte Corona, Er. Cam.: Founded 1520, from Camaldoli, Italy, by Bl. Paul Giustiniani. General motherhouse, Frascati (Rome), Italy; U.S. foundation, Holy Family Hermitage, 1501 Fairplay Rd., Bloomingdale, OH 43910-7971, (740) 765-4511.

Camillian Fathers and Brothers (Order of St. Camillus; Order of Servants of the Sick), O.S.Cam.: Founded 1582, at Rome, by St. Camillus de Lellis; in U.S., 1923. General motherhouse, Rome, Italy; North American province, 10101 W. Wisconsin Ave., Wauwatosa, WI 53226, (414) 481-3696.

Carmelites (Order of Our Lady of Mt. Carmel), O. Carm.: General motherhouse, Rome, Italy. Most Pure Heart of Mary Province (1864), 1317 Frontage Rd., Darien, IL 60559, (630) 971-0050. North American Province of St. Elias (1931), P.O. Box 3079, Middletown, NY 10940-0890, (845) 344-2225. Mt. Carmel Hermitage, Pineland, R.R. 1, Box 330 C, Bolivar, PA, 15923, (724) 238-0423. Educational, charitable work.

Carmelites, Order of Discalced, O.C.D.: Established 1562, a Reform Order of Our Lady of Mt. Carmel; in U.S., 1924. Generalate, Rome, Italy. Western Province (1983), 926 E. Highland Ave., P.O. Box 2178, Redlands, CA 92373, (909) 793-0424. Province of St. Thérèse (Oklahoma,1935), 515 Marylake Dr., Little Rock AR 72206, (501) 888-5827. Immaculate Heart of Mary Province (1947), 1233 S. 45th St., Milwaukee, WI 53214, (414) 672-7212. Our Lady of Mt. Carmel Monastery, 1628 Ridge Rd., Munster, IN 46321, (219) 838-7111. Spiritual direction, retreat, parochial work.

Carmelites of Mary Immaculate, C.M.I.: Founded 1831, in India, by Bl. Kuriakose Elias Chavara and two other Syro-Malabar priests; canonically established, 1855. Generalate, Kerala, India; North American headquarters, Holy Family Church, 21 Nassau Ave., Brooklyn, NY 11222, (718) 388-4866.

Carthusians, Order of, O. Cart.: Founded 1084, in France, by St. Bruno; in U.S., 1951. General motherhouse, St. Pierre de Chartreuse, France; U.S., Charterhouse of the Transfiguration, Carthusian Monastery, 1800 Beartown Rd., Arlington, VT 05250, (802) 362-2550, www.chartreux.org. Cloistered contemplatives; semi-eremitic.

Charity, Brothers of, F.C.: Founded 1807, in Belgium, by Canon Peter J. Triest. General motherhouse, Rome, Italy; American District (1963), 7720 Doe Lane, Laverock, PA 19038.

Charity, Servants of (Guanellians), S.C.: Founded 1908, in Italy, by Bl. Luigi Guanella. General motherhouse, Rome, Italy; U.S. headquarters, St. Louis School, 16195 Old U.S. 12, Chelsea, MI 48118, (734) 475-8430, www.stlouiscenter.org.

Christ, Society of, S.Ch.: Founded 1932. General Motherhouse, Poznan, Poland; U.S.-Canadian Province, 3000 Eighteen Mile Rd., Sterling Heights, MI 48311.

Christian Brothers, Congregation of, C.F.C. (formerly Christian Brothers of Ireland): Founded 1802 at Waterford, Ireland, by Bl. Edmund Ignatius Rice; in U.S., 1906. General motherhouse, Rome, Italy; American Province, Eastern U.S. (1916), 33 Pryer Terr., New Rochelle, NY 10804, (914) 636-6194; Brother Rice Province, Western U.S. (1966), 958 Western Ave., Joliet, IL 60435, (815) 723-5464. Educational work.

Christian Instruction, Brothers of (La Mennais Brothers), F.I.C.: Founded 1817, at Ploermel, France, by Abbe Jean Marie de la Mennais and Abbe Gabriel Deshayes. General motherhouse, Rome, Italy; American province, Notre Dame Institute, P.O. Box 159, Alfred, ME 04002, (207) 324-6612.

Christian Schools, Brothers of the (Christian Brothers), F.S.C.: Founded 1680, at Reims, France, by St. Jean Baptiste de la Salle. General motherhouse, Rome, Italy; U.S. Conference, 4351 Garden City Dr., Suite 200, Landover, MD 20785, (301) 459-9410, www.cbconf.org. Baltimore Province (1845), Box 29, Adamstown, MD 21710-0029, (301) 874-5188, www.fscbaltimore.org. Brothers of the Christian Schools (Midwest Province) (1995), 7650 S. County Line Rd., Burr Ridge, IL 60527-4718, (630) 323-3725, www.cbmidwest.org. New York Province (1848), 800 Newman Springs Rd., Lincroft, NJ 07738, (732) 842-7420. Long Island-New England Province (1957), Christian Brothers Center, 635 Ocean Rd., Narragansett, RI 02882-1314, (401) 789-0244. San Francisco Province (1868), P.O. Box 3720, Napa, CA 94558, (707) 252-0222. New Orleans-Santa Fe Province (1921), De La Salle Christian Brothers, 1522 Carmel Dr., Lafayette, LA 70501, (337) 234-1973. Educational, charitable work.

Cistercians, Order of, O.Cist.: Founded 1098, by St. Robert. Headquarters, Rome, Italy. Our Lady of Spring Bank Abbey, 17304 Havenwood Rd., Sparta, WI 54656-8177, (608) 269-8138. Our Lady of Dallas Monastery, 1 Cistercian Rd., Irving, TX 75039, (972) 438-2044. Cistercian Monastery of Our Lady of Fatima, 564 Walton Ave., Mt. Laurel, NJ 08054, (856) 235-1330. Cistercian Conventual Priory, St. Mary's Priory, R.D. 1, Box 206, New Ringgold, PA 17960, (717) 943-2645.

Cistercians of the Strict Observance, Order of (Trappists), O.C.S.O.: Founded 1098, in France, by St. Robert; in U.S., 1848. Generalate, Rome, Italy.

Our Lady of Gethsemani Abbey (1848), Trappist, KY 40051, (502) 549-3117. Our Lady of New Melleray Abbey (1849), 6500 Melleray Circle, Peosta, IA 52068, (319) 588-2319. St. Joseph's Abbey (1825), Spencer, MA 01562, (508) 885-8700. Holy Spirit Monastery (1944), 2625 Hwy. 212 S.W., Conyers, GA 30094-4044, (770) 483-8705 (fax), www.trappist.net. Our Lady of Guadalupe Abbey (1947), P.O. Box 97, Lafayette, OR 97127, (503) 852-7174, www.trappistabbey.org. Our Lady of the Holy Trinity Abbey (1947), 1250 South 9500 East, Huntsville, UT 84317, (801) 745-3784, www.xmission.com~hta. Abbey of the Genesee (1951), P.O. Box 900, Piffard, NY 14533, (585) 243-0660, www.geneseeabbey.org. Mepkin Abbey (1949), 1098 Mepkin Abbey Rd., Moncks Corner, SC 29461-4796, (843) 761-8509, www.mepkin abbey.org. Our Lady of the Holy Cross Abbey (1950), 901 Cool Spring Lane, Berryville, VA 22611-2900, (540) 955-5277, www.holycrossabbeybrryville.org. Assumption Abbey (1950), Rt. 5, Box 1056, Ava, MO 65608-9142, (417) 683-5110. Abbey of New Clairvaux (1955), Vina, CA 96092, (530) 839-2161, www.maxinet.com/trappist. St. Benedict's Monastery (1956), 1012 Monastery Rd., Snowmass, CO 81654, (970) 927-3311.

Claretians (Missionary Sons of the Immaculate Heart of Mary), C.M.F.: Founded 1849, at Vich, Spain, by St. Anthony Mary Claret. General headquarters, Rome, Italy. Western Province, 1119 Westchester Pl., Los Angeles, CA 90019-3523, (323) 734-1824. Eastern Province, 400 N. Euclid Ave. Oak Park, IL 60302, (708) 848-2076. Missionary, parochial, educational, retreat work.

Clerics Regular Minor (Adorno Fathers) C.R.M.: Founded 1588, at Naples, Italy, by Ven. Augustine Adorno and St. Francis Caracciolo. General motherhouse, Rome, Italy; U.S. address, 575 Darlington Ave., Ramsey, NJ 07446, (201) 327-7375, members.tripod.com/~adornofathers.

Columban, Society of St. (St. Columban Foreign Mission Society), S.S.C.: Founded 1918. General headquarters, Dublin, Ireland; U.S. headquarters., P.O. Box 10, St. Columbans, NE 68056, (402) 291-1920, www.columban.org. Foreign mission work.

Comboni Missionaries of the Heart of Jesus (Verona Fathers), M.C.C.J.: Founded 1867, in Italy by Bl. Daniel Comboni; in U.S., 1939. General motherhouse, Rome, Italy; North American headquarters, Comboni Mission Center, 8108 Beechmont Ave., Cincinnati, OH 45255, (513) 474-4997. Mission work in Africa and the Americas.

Consolata Missionaries, I.M.C.: Founded 1901, at Turin, Italy, by Bl. Joseph Allamano. General motherhouse, Rome, Italy; U.S. headquarters, P.O. Box 5550, 2301 Rt. 27, Somerset, NJ 08875, (732) 297-9191.

Crosier Fathers (Canons Regular of the Order of the Holy Cross), O.S.C.: Founded 1210, in Belgium by Bl. Theodore De Celles. Generalate, Rome, Italy; U.S. Province of St. Odilia, 3510 Vivian Ave., Shoreview, MN 55126-3852, (651) 486-7456, www.crosier.org. Mission, retreat, educational work.

Cross, Brothers of the Congregation of Holy, C.S.C.: Founded 1837, in France, by Rev. Basil Moreau; U.S. province, 1841. Generalate, Rome, Italy.

Midwest Province (1841), Box 460, Notre Dame, IN 46556-0460, (219) 631-2912, www.hcc-nd.edu/mwp/. Southwest Province (1956), 1101 St. Edward's Dr., Austin, TX 78704-6512, (512) 442-7856, www.holycross-sw.org/. Eastern Province (1956), 85 Overlook Circle, New Rochelle, NY 10804, (914) 632-4468, www.holycrossbrothers.org. Educational, social work, missions.

Cross, Congregation of Holy, C.S.C.: Founded 1837, in France; in U.S., 1841. Generalate, Rome, Italy. Indiana Province (1841), 54515 State Rd. 933, North, P.O. Box 1064, Notre Dame, IN 46556-1064, (574) 631-6196. Eastern Province (1952), 835 Clinton Ave., Bridgeport, CT 06604-2393, (203) 367-7252, www.holycross.org. Southern Province (1968), 2111 Brackenridge St., Austin, TX 78704, (512) 443-3886, www.southerncsc.org. Educational and pastoral work; home missions and retreats; foreign missions; social services and apostolate of the press.

Divine Word, Society of the, S.V.D.: Founded 1875, in Holland, by Bl. Arnold Janssen. General motherhouse, Rome, Italy. North American Province founded 1897 with headquarters in Techny, IL. Province of Bl. Joseph Freinademetz (Chicago Province) (1985, from merger of Eastern and Northern provinces), 1985 Waukegan Rd., Techny, IL 60082, (847) 272-2700. St. Augustine (Southern Province) (1940), 201 Ruella Ave., Bay St. Louis, MS 39520, (228) 467-4322, www.svdsouth.com. St. Therese of the Child Jesus (Western Province) (1964), 2737 Pleasant St., Riverside, CA 92507, (323) 735-8130.

Dominicans (Order of Friars Preachers), O.P.: Founded early 13th century by St. Dominic de Guzman. General headquarters, Santa Sabina, Rome, Italy. Eastern Province of St. Joseph (1805), 869 Lexington Ave., New York, NY 10021-6680, (212) 737-5757, www.op-stjoseph.org. Most Holy Name of Jesus (Western) Province (1912), 5877 Birch Ct., Oakland, CA 94618-1626, (510) 658-8722, www.op west.org. St. Albert the Great (Central) Province (1939), 1909 S. Ashland Ave., Chicago, IL 60608, (312) 666-3244, www.op.org/doccentral. St. Martin de Porres Province (1979), 1421 N. Causeway Blvd., Suite 200, Metairie, LA 70001-4144, (504) 837-2129, www.opsouth.org. Spanish Province, U.S. foundation (1926), P.O. Box 279, San Diego, TX 78384, (512) 279-3596. Preaching, teaching, missions, research, parishes.

Edmund, Society of St., S.S.E.: Founded 1843, in France, by Fr. Jean Baptiste Muard. General motherhouse, Edmundite Generalate, 270 Winooski Park, Colchester, VT 05439-0270, (802) 654-3400, www.sse.org. Educational, missionary work.

Eudists (Congregation of Jesus and Mary), C.J.M.: Founded 1643, in France, by St. John Eudes. General motherhouse, Rome, Italy; North American province, 6125 Premiere Ave., Charlesbourg, QC G1H 2V9, Canada, (418) 626-6494; U.S. community, 36 Flohr Ave., W. Seneca, N.Y. 14224, (716) 825-4475. Parochial, educational, pastoral, missionary work.

Francis, Brothers of Poor of St., C.F.P.: Founded 1857. Motherhouse, Aachen, Germany; U.S. province, P.O. Box 35, Wever, IA 52658-0035, (319) 752-4000, www.brothersofthepoorofstfrancis.org. Educational work, especially with poor and neglected youth.

Francis, Third Order Regular of St., T.O.R.: Founded 1221, in Italy; in U.S., 1910. General motherhouse, Rome, Italy. Most Sacred Heart of Jesus Province (1910), 128 Woodshire Dr., Pittsburgh, PA 15215-1714, (412) 781-8333. Immaculate Conception Province (1925), 3811 Emerson Ave. N., Minneapolis, MN 55412, (612) 529-7779, www.franciscanfriarstor.com. Franciscan Commissariat of the Spanish Province (1924), 301 Jefferson Ave., Waco, TX 76701-1419, (254) 752-8434. Educational, parochial, missionary work.

Francis de Sales, Oblates of St., O.S.F.S.: Founded 1871, by Fr. Louis Brisson. General motherhouse, Rome, Italy. Wilmington-Philadelphia Province (1906), 2200 Kentmere Parkway, Wilmington, DE 19806, (302) 656-8529, www.oblates.org. Toledo-Detroit Province (1966), 2056 Parkwood Ave. N., Toledo, OH 43620, (419) 243-5105. Educational, missionary, parochial work.

Francis Xavier, Brothers of St. (Xaverian Brothers), C.F.X.: Founded 1839, in Belgium, by Theodore J. Ryken. Generalate, Twickenham, Middlesex, England. Generalate, 4409 Frederick Ave., Baltimore, MD, 21229, (410) 644-0034. Educational work.

Franciscan Brothers of Brooklyn, O.S.F.: Founded in Ireland; established at Brooklyn, 1858. Generalate, 135 Remsen St., Brooklyn, NY 11201, (718) 858-8217, www.franciscanbros.org. Educational work.

Franciscan Brothers of Christ the King, O.S.F.: Founded 1961. General motherhouse, 7329 E. Eastwood Ave., Indianapolis, IN 46239, (317) 862-9211.

Franciscan Brothers of the Holy Cross, F.F.S.C.: Founded 1862, in Germany. Generalate, Hausen, Linz Rhein, Germany; U.S. region, 2500 St. James Rd., Springfield, IL 62707, (217) 747-5947. Educational work.

Franciscan Brothers of the Third Order Regular, O.S.F.: Generalate, Mountbellew, Ireland; U.S. region, 2117 Spyglass Trail W., Oxnard, CA 93030, (805) 485-5002. (Mailing address: 4522 Gainsborough Ave., Los Angeles, CA 90029.)

Franciscan Friars of the Immaculate, F.F.I: Founded 1990, Italy. General motherhouse, Benevento, Italy. U.S. addresses, 600 Pleasant St., New Bedford, MA. 02740; 22 School Hill Rd., Baltic, CT 06330, (508) 996-8274.

Franciscan Friars of the Renewal, C.F.R.: Community established under jurisdiction of the archbishop of New York. Central House, St. Crispin Friary, 420 E. 156th St., Bronx, NY 10455, (718) 665-2441.

Franciscan Missionary Brothers of the Sacred Heart of Jesus, O.S.F.: Founded 1927, in the St. Louis archdiocese. Motherhouse, St. Joseph Rd., Eureka, MO 63025, (314) 587-3661. Care of aged, infirm, homeless men and boys.

Franciscans (Order of Friars Minor), O.F.M.: A family of the First Order of St. Francis (of Assisi) founded in 1209 and established as a separate jurisdiction in 1517; in U.S., 1844. General headquarters, Rome, Italy. English-speaking conference: 1615 Vine St., Cincinnati, OH 45210-1200, (513) 721-4700.

Immaculate Conception Province (1855), 125 Thompson St., New York, NY 10012, (212) 674-4388. Sacred Heart Province, Franciscan Missionary Union (1858), 3140 Meramec St., St. Louis, MO 63118-4339, (314) 353-7729. Assumption of the Blessed Virgin Mary Province (1887), P.O. Box 100, 165 East Pulaski St., Pulaski, WI 54162-0100. Most Holy Name of Jesus Province (1901), 126 W. 32nd St., New York, NY 10001, (212) 967-6300, www.hnp.org. St. Barbara Province (1915), 1500 34th Ave., Oakland, CA 94601, (510) 536-3722.

Our Lady of Guadalupe Province (1985), 1350 Lakeview Rd. S.W., Albuquerque, NM 87105, (505) 877-5425. Commissariat of the Holy Cross (1912), P.O. Box 608, Lemont, IL 60439-0608, (630) 257-2494. Mt. Alverna Friary, 517 S. Belle Vista Ave., Youngstown, OH 44509, (330) 799-1888. Holy Family Croatian Custody (1926), 4851 S. Drexel Blvd., Chicago, IL 60615-1703, (773) 536-0552.

St. Casimir Lithuanian Vice-Province, P.O. Box 980, Kennebunkport, ME 04046, (207) 967-2011. Holy Gospel Province (Mexico), U.S. foundation, 2400 Marr St., El Paso, TX 79903, (915) 565-2921. Commissariat of the Holy Land, Mt. St. Sepulchre, 1400 Quincy St. N.E., Washington, DC 20017, (202) 269-5430. Holy Dormition Friary, Byzantine Slavonic Rite, P.O. Box 270, Rt. 93, Sybertsville, PA 18251, (570) 788-1212, www.holydorm.com; Academy of American Franciscan History, 1712 Euclid Ave., Berkeley, CA 94709. Preaching, missionary, educational, parochial, charitable work.

Franciscans (Order of Friars Minor Capuchin), O.F.M. Cap.: A family of the First Order of St. Francis (of Assisi) founded in 1209 and established as a separate jurisdiction in 1528. St. Joseph Province/St. Bonaventure Monastery (1857), 1740 Mt. Elliott Ave., Detroit, MI 48207-3427, (313) 579-2100. Province of St. Augustine (1873), 220 37th St., Pittsburgh, PA 15201, (412) 682-6011, www.capuchin.com. St. Mary Province (1952), 30 Gedney Park Dr., White Plains, NY 10605, (914) 761-3008. Province of the Stigmata of St. Francis (1918), P.O. Box 809, Union City, NJ 07087-0809, (201) 865-0611. Western American Capuchin Province, Our Lady of the Angels, 1345 Cortez Ave., Burlingame, CA 94010, (650) 342-1489, www.beafriar.com.

St. Stanislaus Friary (1948), 2 Manor Dr., Oak Ridge, NJ 07438, (973) 697-7757. Province of Mid-America (1977), 3553 Wyandot St., Denver, CO 80211, (303) 477-5436, www.midamcaps.org. Vice-Province of Texas, 604 Bernal Dr., Dallas, TX 75212, (214) 631-1937. St. John the Baptist Vice-Province, P.O. Box 21350, Rio Piedras, Puerto Rico 00928-1350, (787) 764-3090. General motherhouse, Rome, Italy. Missionary, parochial work, chaplaincies.

Franciscans (Order of Friars Minor Conventual), O.F.M. Conv.: A family of the First Order of St. Francis (of Assisi) founded in 1209 and established as a separate jurisdiction in 1517; first U.S. foundation, 1852. General curia, Rome, Italy. Immaculate Conception Province (1852), Immaculate Conception Friary, P.O. Box 629, Rensselaer, NY 12144, (518) 472-1000, www.franciscanseast. St. Anthony of Padua Province (1906), 12300 Folly Quarter Rd., Ellicott City, MD 21042, (410) 531-9200, www.stanthony province.org. St. Bonaventure Province (1939), 6107 Kenmore Ave., Chicago, IL 60660, (773) 274-7681. Our Lady of Consolation Province (1926), 101 St. Anthony Dr., Mt. St. Francis, IN 47146, (812) 923-8444. St. Joseph of Cupertino Province (1981), P.O. Box 820, Arroyo Grande, CA 93421-0820, (805) 489-1012. Missionary, educational, parochial work.

Glenmary Missioners (The Home Missioners of America): Founded 1939, in U.S., general headquarters, P.O. Box 465618, Cincinnati, OH 45246, (513) 874-8900, www.glenmary.org. Home mission work.

Good Shepherd, Little Brothers of the, B.G.S.: Founded 1951, by Bro. Mathias Barrett. Foundation House, P.O. Box 389, Albuquerque, NM 87103, (505) 243-4238. General headquarters, Hamilton, ON, Canada. Operate shelters and refuges for aged and homeless; homes for handicapped men and boys, alcoholic rehabilitation center.

Holy Eucharist, Brothers of the, F.S.E.: Founded in U.S., 1957. Generalate, P.O. Box 25, Plaucheville, LA 71362, (318) 922-3630. Teaching, social, clerical, nursing work.

Holy Family, Congregation of the Missionaries of the, M.S.F.: Founded 1895, in Holland, by Rev. John P. Berthier. General motherhouse, Rome, Italy; U.S. provincialate, 3014 Oregon Ave., St. Louis, MO, 63118-1498, (314) 577-6300. Belated vocations for the missions.

Holy Family, Sons of the, S.F.: Founded 1864, at Barcelona, Spain, by Bl. Jose Mañanet y Vives; in U.S., 1920. General motherhouse, Barcelona, Spain; U.S. address, 401 Randolph Rd., P.O. Box 4138, Silver Spring, MD 20914-4138, (301) 622-1184, www.hometown.aol.com/holyfamsem/index.htm.

Holy Ghost Fathers, C.S.Sp.: Founded 1703, in Paris, France, by Claude Francois Poullart des Places; in U.S., 1872. Generalate, Rome, Italy. Eastern Province (1872), 6230 Brush Run Rd., Bethel Park, PA 15102, (412) 831-0302, www.spiritans.org.Western Province (1964), 1700 W. Alabama St., Houston, TX 77098-2808, (713) 522-2882, www.spiritans.org. Missions, education.

Holy Ghost Fathers of Ireland: Founded 1971. U.S. delegates: 4849 37th St., Long Island City, NY 11101 (East); St. Dunstan's Church, 1133 Broadway, Mill Brae, CA 94030 (West).

Holy Spirit, Missionaries of the, M.Sp.S.: Founded 1914, at Mexico City, Mexico, by Felix Rougier. General motherhouse, Mexico City; U.S. headquarters, 9792 OMA Place, Garden Grove, CA 92841, (714) 534-5476. Missionary work.

Immaculate Heart of Mary, Brothers of the, I.H.M.: Founded 1948, at Steubenville, Ohio, by Bishop John K. Mussio. Villa Maria Generalate, 609 N. 7th St., Steubenville, OH 43952, (740) 283-2462. Educational, charitable work.

Jesuits (Society of Jesus), S.J.: Founded 1534, in France, by St. Ignatius of Loyola; received papal approval, 1540; suppressed in 1773 and revived in 1814 by Pope Pius VII; first U.S. province, 1833. The Jesuits remain the largest single order in the Church.

Generalate, Rome, Italy; U.S. national office, Jesuit Conference, 1616 P Street, N.W., Suite 300, Washington, DC 20036-1420, (202) 462-0400, www.jesuit.org. Maryland Province (1833), 5704 Roland Ave., Baltimore, MD 21210, (410) 532-1400, www.marprovjesuits.org. New York Province (1943), 39 East 83rd St., New York, NY 10028, (212) 774-5500, www.nysj.org. Missouri Province (1863), 4511 W. Pine Blvd., St. Louis, MO 63108-2191, (314) 361-7765, www.jesuits-mis.org. New Orleans Province (1907), 500 S. Jefferson Davis Pkwy., New Orleans, LA 70119, (504) 821-0334.

California Province (1909), 300 College Ave., P.O. Box 519, Los Gatos, CA 95031, (408) 884-1600, www.calprov.org. New England Province (1926), 771 Harrison Ave., Boston, MA 02118, (617) 266-7233. Chicago Province (1928), 2050 N. Clark St., Chicago, IL 60614, (773) 975-6363, www.jesuits-chi.org. Oregon Province (1932), 2222 N.W. Hoyt, Portland, OR 97210, (503) 226-6977. Detroit Province (1955), 7303 W. Seven Mile Rd., Detroit, MI 48221-2121, (313) 861-7500, www.jesuitdet.org. Wisconsin Province (1955), PO Box 080288, Milwaukee, WI 53208-0288, (414) 937-6949, www.jesuitwisprov.org. Province of the Antilles (1947), U.S. address, 12725 S.W. 6th St., Miami, FL 33184, (305) 559-9044. Missionary, educational, literary work.

John of God, Brothers of the Hospitaller Order of St., O.H.: Founded 1537, in Spain. General motherhouse, Rome, Italy; American province, 2425 S. Western Ave., Los Angeles, CA 90018, (323) 731-0233, www.hospitallers.org. Nursing and related fields.

Joseph, Congregation of St., C.S.J.: General motherhouse, Rome, Italy; U.S. vice-province, 338 North Grand Ave., San Pedro, CA 90731-2006, (310) 831-5360. Parochial, missionary, educational work.

Joseph, Oblates of St., O.S.J.: Founded 1878, in Italy, by Bl. Joseph Marello; in U.S., 1929. General motherhouse, Rome, Italy. Our Lady of Sorrows Province, 1880 Hwy 315, Pittston, PA 18640, (570) 654-7542. California Province, 544 W. Cliff Dr., Santa Cruz, CA 95060, (831) 457-1868. Parochial, educational work.

Josephite Fathers, C.J.: General motherhouse, Ghent, Belgium; U.S. foundation, 180 Patterson Rd., Santa Maria, CA 93455, (805) 937-5378.

Josephites (St. Joseph's Society of the Sacred Heart), S.S.J.: Established 1893, in U.S. as American congregation (originally established in U.S., in 1871 by Mill Hill Josephites from England). General motherhouse, 1130 N. Calvert St., Baltimore, MD 21202-3802, (410) 727-3386, www.josephite.com. Evangelization in African-American community.

LaSalette, Missionaries of Our Lady of: Province of Mary, Mother of the Americas, 915 Maple Ave., Hartford, CT 06114-2330, (860) 956-8870; Mary Queen of Our Lady of LaSalette, P.O. Box 777, Twin Lakes, WI 53181.

Lateran, Canons Regular of the, C.R.L.: General house, Rome, Italy; U.S. address: 2317 Washington Ave., Bronx, NY 10458, (212) 295-9600.

Legionaries of Christ, L.C.: Founded 1941, in Mexico, by Rev. Marcial Maciel; in U.S., 1965. General headquarters, Rome, Italy; U.S. headquarters, 393 Derby Ave., Orange, CT 06477, (203) 795-2800, novitiate, 475 Oak Ave., Cheshire, CT 06410, (203) 271-0805, www.legionofchrist.org.

Little Brothers of St. Francis, L.B.S.F.: Founded 1970 in Archdiocese of Boston by Bro. James Curran. General fraternity, 785-789 Parker St., Boston, MA 02120-3021, (617) 442-2556. Combine contemplative life with evangelical street ministry.

Mariannhill, Congregation of the Missionaries of, C.M.M.: Trappist monastery, begun in 1882 by Abbot Francis Pfanner in Natal, South Africa, became an independent modern congregation in 1909; in U.S., 1920. Generalate, Rome, Italy; U.S.-Canadian province (1938), Our Lady of Grace Monastery, 23715 Ann Arbor Trail, Dearborn Hts., MI 48127-1449, (313) 561-7140, www.rc.net/detroit/marianhill. Foreign mission work.

Marians of the Immaculate Conception, Congregation of, M.I.C.: Founded 1673; U.S. foundation, 1913. General motherhouse, Rome, Italy. St. Casimir Province (1913), 6336 S. Kilbourn Ave., Chicago, IL 60629-5588, (773) 582-8191, www.marians.org. St. Stanislaus Kostka Province (1948), Eden Hill, Stockbridge, MA 01262, (413) 298-1100. Educational, parochial, mission, publication work.

Marist Brothers, F.M.S.: Co-founded 1817, in France, by St. Marcellin Champagnat. Generalate, Rome, Italy. Esopus Province, 1241 Kennedy Blvd., Bayonne, NJ 07002, (201) 823-1115. Poughkeepsie Province, 26 First Ave., Pelham, NY 10803, (914) 738-0740. Educational, social, catechetical work.

Marist Fathers (Society of Mary), S.M.: Founded 1816, at Lyons, France, by Jean Claude Colin; in U.S., 1863. General motherhouse, Rome, Italy. Atlanta Province, P.O. Box 81144, Atlanta, GA 30366-1144, (770) 458-1435, www.maristsociety.org. Boston Province (1924), 27 Isabella St., Boston, MA 02116, (508) 879-7223. Educational, foreign mission, pastoral work.

Maronite Lebanese Missionaries, Congregation of, C.M.L.M.: Founded in Lebanon 1865; established in the U.S., 1991. U.S. foundation, Our Lady of the Cedars Maronite Mission, 11935 Bellfort Village, Houston, TX 77031, (281) 568-6800.

Mary, Society of (Marianist Fathers and Brothers; Brothers of Mary), S.M.: Founded 1817, at Bordeaux, France, by Rev. William-Joseph Chaminade; in U.S., 1849. General motherhouse, Rome, Italy. Marianist Province of the U.S., 4425 W. Pine Blvd., St. Louis, MO 63108, (314) 533-1207, www.marianists.org. The Marianist provinces of Cincinnati, St. Louis, Pacific, and New York have merged to form one province. Educational work.

Mary Immaculate, Missionary Oblates of, O.M.I.: Founded 1816, in France, by St. Charles Joseph Eugene de Mazenod; in U.S., 1849. General house, Rome, Italy. U.S. Province: 391 Michigan Ave., N.E., Washington, DC, 20017, (202) 281-1608; Southwest Area, 327 Oblate Dr., San Antonio, TX 78216-6602, (210) 349-1475, www.omiusa.org. Parochial, foreign mission, educational work, ministry to marginal.

Maryknoll (Catholic Foreign Mission Society of America), M.M.: Founded 1911, in U.S., by Frs. Thomas F. Price and James A. Walsh. General Center, Maryknoll, NY 10545, (914) 941-7590.

Mercedarians (Order of Our Lady of Mercy), O. de M.: Founded 1218, in Spain, by St. Peter Nolasco. General motherhouse, Rome, Italy; U.S. headquarters, 7758 E. Main Rd., LeRoy, NY, 14482, (716) 768-7110.

Mercy, Brothers of, F.M.M.: Founded 1856, in Germany. General motherhouse, Montabaur, Germany. American headquarters, 4520 Ransom Rd., Clarence, NY 14031, (716) 759-8341. Hospital work.

Mercy, Brothers of Our Lady, Mother of, C.F.M.M.: Founded 1844, in The Netherlands by Abp. Jan Zwijsen. Generalate, Tilburg, The Netherlands; U.S. region, 7140 Ramsgate Ave., Los Angeles, CA 90045, (310) 338-5954, www.inter.nl.net/users.gbcmm.

Mercy, Congregation of Priests of (Fathers of Mercy), C.P.M.: Founded 1808, in France, by Rev. Jean Baptiste Rauzan; in U.S., 1839. General mission house, South Union, KY 42283, (502) 542-4164. Mission work.

Mill Hill Missionaries (St. Joseph's Society for Foreign Missions), M.H.M.: Founded 1866, in England, by Cardinal Vaughan; in U.S., 1951. International headquarters, London, England; American headquarters, 222 W. Hartsdale Ave., Hartsdale, NY 10530, (914) 682-0645.

Minim Fathers, O.M.: General motherhouse, Rome, Italy. North American delegation (1970), 3431 Portola Ave., Los Angeles, CA 90032, (213) 223-1101.

Missionaries of St. Charles, Congregation of the (Scalabrinians), C.S.: Founded 1887, at Piacenza, Italy, by Bl. John Baptist Scalabrini. General motherhouse, Rome, Italy. St. Charles Borromeo Province (1888), 27 Carmine St., New York, NY 10014, (212) 675-3993. St. John Baptist Province (1903), 546 N. East Ave., Oak Park, IL 60302, (708) 386-4430.

Missionaries of the Holy Apostles, M.Ss.A.: Founded 1962, Washington, DC, by Very Rev. Eusebe M. Menard. North American headquarters, 24 Prospect Hill Rd., Cromwell, CT 06416, (860) 632-3039.

Missionary Servants of Christ, M.S.C.: Founded 1979 in U.S. by Bro. Edwin Baker. Headquarters, P.O. Box 270, 305 S. Lake St., Aurora, IL 60507-0270, (630) 892-2371, www.misacor-usa.org.

Missionhurst-CICM (Congregation of the Immaculate Heart of Mary): Founded 1862, at Scheut, Brussels, Belgium, by Very Rev. Theophile Verbist. General motherhouse, Rome, Italy; U.S. province, 4651 N. 25th St., Arlington, VA 22207, (703) 528-3800, www.missionhurst.org. Home and foreign mission work.

Montfort Missionaries (Missionaries of the Company of Mary), S.M.M.: Founded 1715, by St. Louis Marie Grignon de Montfort; in U.S., 1948. General motherhouse, Rome, Italy; U.S. province, 101-18 104th St., Ozone Park, NY 11416, (718) 849-5885. Mission work.

Mother Co-Redemptrix, Congregation of, C.M.C.: Founded 1953 at Lein-Thuy, Vietnam (North), by Fr. Dominic Mary Tran Dinh Thu; in U.S., 1975. General house, Hochiminhville, Vietnam; U.S. provincial house, 1900 Grand Ave., Carthage, MO 64836, (417) 358-7787, www.dongcong.net. Work among Vietnamese Catholics in U.S.

Oblates of the Virgin Mary, O.M.V.: Founded 1815, in Italy; in U.S., 1976; Generalate, Rome, Italy; U.S. provincialate: 2 Ipswich St., Boston, MA 02215, (617) 536-4141.

Oratorians (Congregation of the Oratory of St. Philip Neri), C.O.: Founded 1575, at Rome, by St. Philip Neri. A confederation of autonomous houses.

U.S. addresses: P.O. Box 11586, Rock Hill, SC 29731, (803) 327-2097, www.rockhilloratory.org; P.O. Box 1688, Monterey, CA 93940, (831) 373-0476; 4450 Bayard St., Pittsburgh, PA 15213, (412) 681-3181; P.O. Drawer II, Pharr, TX 78577, (956) 843-8217; 109 Willoughby St., Brooklyn, NY 11201, (718) 875-2096.

Pallottines (Society of the Catholic Apostolate), S.A.C.: Founded 1835, at Rome, by St. Vincent Pallotti. Generalate, Rome, Italy. Immaculate Conception Province (1953), P.O. Box 979, South Orange, NJ 07079, (201) 762-2926. Mother of God Province (1946), 5424 W. Blue Mound Rd., Milwaukee, WI 53208, (414) 259-0688. Irish Province (1909), U.S. address: 3352 4th St., Wyandotte, MI 48192. Queen of Apostles Province (1909), 448 E. 116th St., New York, NY 10029, (212) 534-0681. Christ the King Province, 3452 Niagara Falls, Blvd., N. Tonawanda, NY 14120, (716) 694-4313. Charitable, educational, parochial, mission work.

Paraclete, Servants of the, s.P.: Founded 1947, Santa Fe, N.M., archdiocese. Generalate and U.S. motherhouse, 18161 State Hwy. 4, Jemez Springs, NM 87025-0010, (505) 829-3586. Devoted to care of priests.

Paris Foreign Missions Society, M.E.P.: Founded 1662, at Paris, France. Headquarters, Paris, France; U.S. establishment, 930 Ashbury St., San Francisco, CA 94117, (415) 664-6747. Mission work and training of native clergy.

Passionists (Congregation of the Passion), C.P.: Founded 1720, in Italy, by St. Paul of the Cross. General motherhouse, Rome, Italy. St. Paul of the Cross Province (Eastern Province) (1852), 80 David St., South River, NJ 08882, (732) 257-7177. Holy Cross Province (Western Province), 5700 N. Harlem Ave., Chicago, IL 60631, (773) 631-6336.

Patrician Brothers (Brothers of St. Patrick), F.S.P.: Founded 1808, in Ireland, by Bishop Daniel Delaney; U.S. novitiate, 7820 Bolsa Ave., Midway City, CA 92655, (714) 897-8181. Educational work.

Patrick's Missionary Society, St., S.P.S.: Founded 1932, at Wicklow, Ireland, by Msgr. Patrick Whitney; in U.S., 1953. International headquarters, Kiltegan Co., Wicklow, Ireland. U.S. foundations: 70 Edgewater Rd., Cliffside Park, NJ 07010, (201) 943-6575; 19536 Eric Dr., Saratoga, CA 95070, (408) 253-3135; 1347 W. Granville Ave., Chicago, IL 60660, (773) 973-3737.

Pauline Fathers (Order of St. Paul the First Hermit), O.S.P.P.E.: Founded 1215; established in U.S., 1955. General motherhouse, Czestochowa, Jasna Gora, Poland; U.S. province, P.O. Box 2049, Doylestown, PA 18901, (215) 345-0607.

Pauline Fathers and Brothers (Society of St. Paul for the Apostolate of Communications), S.S.P.: Founded 1914, by Very Rev. James Alberione; in U.S., 1932. Motherhouse, Rome, Italy; New York province (1932), P.O. Box 139, Ellsworth, OH 44416-0139, (330) 533-7427. Social communications work.

Paulists (Missionary Society of St. Paul the Apostle), C.S.P.: Founded 1858, in New York, by Fr. Isaac Thomas Hecker. Motherhouse: 86-11 Midland Pkwy, Jamaica Estates, N.Y. 11432, (718) 291-5995, www.paulist.org. Missionary, ecumenical, pastoral work.

Piarists (Order of the Pious Schools), Sch.P.:

Founded 1617, at Rome, Italy, by St. Joseph Calasanctius. General motherhouse, Rome, Italy. U.S. province, 363 Valley Forge Rd., Devon, PA 19333, (610) 688-7337. New York-Puerto Rico vice-province (Calasanzian Fathers), P.O. Box 118, Playa Sta., Ponce, PR 00734, (809) 840-0610. California vice province, 3940 Perry St., Los Angeles, CA 90063, (323) 261-1386. Educational work.

Pius X, Brothers of St., C.S.P.X.: Founded 1952, at La Crosse, WI, by Bishop John P. Treacy. Motherhouse, P.O. Box 217, De Soto, WI 54624. Education.

Pontifical Institute for Foreign Missions, P.I.M.E.: Founded 1850, in Italy, at request of Pope Pius IX. General motherhouse, Rome, Italy; U.S. province, 17330 Quincy Ave., Detroit, MI 48221, (313) 342-4066, www.pimeusa.org work.

Precious Blood, Society of, C.P.P.S.: Founded 1815, in Italy, by St. Gaspar del Bufalo. General motherhouse, Rome, Italy. Cincinnati Province, 431 E. Second St., Dayton, OH 45402, (937) 228-9263, www.cpps-preciousblood.org. Kansas City Province, P.O. Box 339, Liberty, MO 64068-0339, (816) 781-4344. Pacific Province, 2337 134th Ave. W., San Leandro, CA 94577, (510) 357-4982. Atlantic Province, 13313 Niagara Pkwy, Niagara Falls, ON L2E 6S6, Canada, (905) 382-1118, www.preciousblood.org.

Premonstratensians (Order of the Canons Regular of Premontre; Norbertines), O. Praem.: Founded 1120, at Premontre, France, by St. Norbert; in U.S., 1893. Generalate, Rome, Italy. St. Norbert Abbey, 1016 N. Broadway, DePere, WI 54114, (920) 337-4300, www.snc.edu/norbertines. Daylesford Abbey, 220 S. Valley Rd., Paoli, PA 19301, (610) 647-2530, www.daylesford.org. St. Michael's Abbey, 19292 El Toro Rd., Silverado, CA 92676, (949) 858-0222. Immaculate Conception Priory (1997), 3600 Philadelphia Pike, Claymont, DE 19703, (302) 792-2791. Educational, parish work.

Priestly Fraternity of St. Peter, F.S.S.P.: Founded and approved Oct. 18, 1988; first foundation in U.S., 1991. U.S. headquarters, St. Peter's House, Griffin Rd., P.O. Box 196, Elmhurst, PA 18416, (570) 842-4000, www.fssp.com. Pastoral and sacramental ministry using the 1962 liturgical books.

Providence, Sons of Divine, F.D.P.: Founded 1893, at Tortona, Italy, by Bl. Luigi Orione; in U.S., 1933. General motherhouse, Rome, Italy; U.S. address, 111 Orient Ave., E. Boston, MA 02128, (617) 569-2100.

Redemptorist Fathers and Brothers (Congregation of the Most Holy Redeemer), C.SS.R.: Founded 1732, in Italy, by St. Alphonsus Mary Liguori. Generalate, Rome, Italy. Baltimore Province (1850), 7509 Shore Rd., Brooklyn, NY 11209, (718) 833-1900. Redemptorist-Denver Province (1875), Box 300399, Denver, CO 80203-0399, (303) 370-0035, www.redemptorists-denver.org. New Orleans Vice-Province, 5354 Plank Rd., P.O. Box 53900, Baton Rouge, LA 70892, (225) 355-2600. Richmond Vice-Province (1942), 313 Hillman St., P.O. Box 1529, New Smyrna Beach, FL 32170, (904) 427-3094. Mission work.

Resurrectionists (Congregation of the Resurrection), C.R.: Founded 1836, in France, under direction of Bogdan Janski. Motherhouse, Rome, Italy. U.S. Province, 7050 N. Oakley Ave., Chicago, IL 60645-

3426, (773) 465-8320, www.resurrectionists.com. Ontario Kentucky Province, U.S. address, 338 N. 25th St., Louisville, KY 40212, (502) 772-3694.

Rogationist Fathers, R.C.J.: Founded by Bl. Annibale (Hannibal) di Francia, 1887. General motherhouse, Rome, Italy. U.S. delegation: 2688 S. Newmark Ave., Sanger, CA 91343, (209) 875-5808. Charitable work.

Rosary, Brothers of Our Lady of the Holy, F.S.R.: Founded 1956, in U.S. Motherhouse and novitiate, 232 Sunnyside Dr., Reno, NV 89503-3510, (775) 747-4441.

Rosminians (Institute of Charity), I.C.: Founded 1828, in Italy, by Antonio Rosmini-Serbati. General motherhouse, Rome, Italy; U.S. address, 2327 W. Heading Ave., Peoria, IL 61604, (309) 676-6341. Charitable work.

Sacred Heart, Brothers of the, S.C.: Founded 1821, in France, by Rev. Andre Coindre. General motherhouse, Rome, Italy. New Orleans Province (1847), 4540 Elysian Fields Ave., New Orleans, LA 70122, (504) 282-5693. New England Province (1945), 159 Earle St., Woonsocket, RI 02895, (401) 769-0313, www.brothersofthesacredheart.org. New York Province (1960), 141-11 123 Ave., South Ozone Park, NY 11436-1426, (718) 322-3309. Educational work.

Sacred Heart, Missionaries of the, M.S.C.: Founded 1854, by Rev. Jules Chevelier. General motherhouse, Rome, Italy; U.S. province, 305 S. Lake St., Aurora, IL 60507-0271, (630) 892-8400.

Sacred Heart of Jesus, Congregation of the (Sacred Heart Fathers and Brothers), S.C.J.: Founded 1877, in France. General motherhouse, Rome, Italy; U.S. provincial office, P.O. Box 289, Hales Corners, WI 53130-0289, (414) 425-6910, www.scj.org. Educational, preaching, mission work.

Sacred Hearts of Jesus and Mary, Congregation of (Picpus Fathers), SS.CC.: Founded 1805, in France, by Fr. Coudrin. General motherhouse, Rome, Italy. Eastern Province (1946), 77 Adams St. (Box 111), Fairhaven, MA 02719, (508) 993-2442, www.sscc.org. Western Province (1970), 2150 Damien Ave., La Verne, CA 91750, (909) 593-5441. Hawaii Province, Box 797, Kaneohe, Oahu, HI 96744, (808) 247-5035. Mission, educational work.

Sacred Hearts of Jesus and Mary, Missionaries of the, M.SS.CC.: Founded 1833, in Naples, Italy, by Cajetan Errico. General motherhouse, Rome, Italy; U.S. headquarters, 2249 Shore Rd., Linwood, NJ 08221, (609) 927-5600.

Salesians of St. John Bosco (Society of St. Francis de Sales), S.D.B.: Founded 1859, by St. John (Don) Bosco. Generalate, Rome, Italy. St. Philip the Apostle Province (1902), 148 Main St., P.O. Box 639, New Rochelle, NY 10802-0639, (914) 636-4225. San Francisco Province (1926), 1100 Franklin St., San Francisco, CA 94109, (415) 441-7144.

Salvatorians (Society of the Divine Savior), S.D.S.: Founded 1881, in Rome, by Fr. Francis Jordan; in U.S., 1896. General headquarters, Rome, Italy; U.S. province, 1735 N. Hi-Mount Blvd., Milwaukee, WI 53208-1720, (414) 258-1735, www.salvatorians.com. Educational, parochial, mission work; campus ministries, chaplaincies.

Scalabrinians: See **Missionaries of St. Charles**.

Servites (Order of Friar Servants of Mary),

O.S.M.: Founded 1233, at Florence, Italy, by Seven Holy Founders. Generalate, Rome, Italy. United States Province (1967), 3121 W. Jackson Blvd., Chicago, IL 60612, (773) 533-0360. General apostolic ministry.

Somascan Fathers, C.R.S.: Founded 1534, at Somasca, Italy, by St. Jerome Emiliani. General motherhouse, Rome, Italy; U.S. address, Pine Haven Boys Center, River Rd., P.O. Box 162, Suncook, NH 03275, (603) 485-7141, www.somascans.org.

Society of Our Lady of the Most Holy Trinity, S.O.L.T.: Headquarters, Casa San Jose, 109 W. Avenue F, P.O. Box 152, Robstown, TX 78380, (512) 387-2754.

Sons of Mary Missionary Society (Sons of Mary, Health of the Sick), F.M.S.I.: Founded 1952, in the Boston archdiocese, by Rev. Edward F. Garesche, S.J. Headquarters, 567 Salem End Rd., Framingham, MA 01702-5599, (617) 879-2541, www.sonsofmary.com.

Stigmatine Fathers and Brothers (Congregation of the Sacred Stigmata), C.S.S.: Founded 1816, by St. Gaspar Bertoni. General motherhouse, Rome, Italy; North American Province, 554 Lexington St., Waltham, MA 02452-3097, (781) 209-3100, www.stigmatines.com. Parish work.

Sulpicians (Society of Priests of St. Sulpice), S.S.: Founded 1641, in Paris, by Rev. Jean Jacques Olier. General motherhouse, Paris, France; U.S. province, 5408 Roland Ave., Baltimore, MD 21210, (410) 323-5070, www.sulpicians.org. Education of seminarians and priests.

Theatines (Congregation of Clerics Regular), C.R.: Founded 1524, in Rome, by St. Cajetan. General motherhouse, Rome, Italy; U.S. headquarters, 1050 S. Birch St., Denver, CO 80246, (303) 756-5522.

Trappists: See **Cistercians of the Strict Observance.**

Trinitarians (Order of the Most Holy Trinity), O.SS.T.: Founded 1198, by St. John of Matha; in U.S., 1911. General motherhouse, Rome, Italy; U.S. headquarters, P.O. Box 5742, Baltimore, MD 21282, (410) 486-5171.

Trinity Missions (Missionary Servants of the Most Holy Trinity), S.T.: Founded 1929, by Fr. Thomas Augustine Judge. Generalate, P.O. Box 7130, Silver Springs, MD 20907-7130, (301) 434-6761, www.trinitymissions.org. Home mission work.

Viatorian Fathers (Clerics of St. Viator), C.S.V.: Founded 1831, in France, by Fr. Louis Joseph Querbes. General motherhouse, Rome, Italy. Province of Chicago (1882), 1212 E. Euclid St., Arlington Hts., IL 60004, (847) 398-1354. Educational work.

Vincentians (Congregation of the Mission; Lazarists), C.M.: Founded 1625, in Paris, by St. Vincent de Paul; in U.S., 1818. General motherhouse, Rome, Italy. Eastern Province (1867), 500 E. Chelten Ave., Philadelphia, PA 19144, (215) 848-1985. Midwest Province (1888), 13663 Rider Trail North, Earth City, MO 63045, (314) 344-1184. New England Province (1975), 234 Keeney St., Manchester, CT 06040-7048, (860) 643-2828. American Italian Branch, Our Lady of Pompei Church, 3600 Claremont St., Baltimore, MD 21224, (410) 675-7790. American Spanish Branch (Barcelona, Spain), 118 Congress St., Brooklyn, NY 11201-6045, (718) 624-5670. American Spanish Branch (Zaragoza, Spain), Holy Agony Church, 1834 3rd Ave., New York, NY 10029, (212) 289-5589.

Western Province (1975), 420 Date St., Montebello, CA 90640, (323) 721-5486. Southern Province (1975), 3826 Gilbert Ave., Dallas, TX 75219, (214) 526-0234, www.cmsouth.org. Educational work.

Vocationist Fathers (Society of Divine Vocations), S.D.V.: Founded 1920, in Italy; in U.S., 1962. Generalate, Rome, Italy; U.S. headquarters, 90 Brooklake Rd., Florham Park, NJ 07932, (973) 966-6262, www.vocationist.org.

Xaverian Missionary Fathers, S.X.: Founded 1895, by Bl. Guido Conforti, at Parma, Italy. General motherhouse, Rome, Italy; U.S. province, 12 Helene Ct., Wayne, NJ 07470, (973) 942-2975, www.xavier missionaries.org. Foreign mission work.

MEMBERSHIP OF RELIGIOUS INSTITUTES OF MEN

(*Principal source:* Annuario Pontificio. *Statistics as of Jan. 1, 2003, unless indicated otherwise.*) *Listed below are world membership statistics of institutes of men of pontifical right with 500 or more members; the number of priests is in parentheses. Also listed are institutes with less than 500 members with houses in the U.S.*

Jesuits (14,623)	20,743
Salesians (11,180)	16,911
Franciscans (Friars Minor) (11,116)	16,642
Franciscans (Capuchins) (7,208)	11,465
Benedictines (4,484)	7,967
Dominicans (4,663)	6,314
Brothers of Christian Schools	6,273
Society of the Divine Word (3,800)	6,075
Redemptorists (4,185)	5,701
Marist Brothers	4,802
Oblates of Mary Immaculate (3,391)	4,696
Franciscans (Conventuals) (2,848)	4,553
Vincentians (3,160)	4,002
Discalced Carmelites (O.C.D.) (2,550)	3,962
Holy Spirit (Holy Ghost), Vincentians Congregation of (2,191)	3,052
Claretians (2,050)	3,043
Augustinians (2,140)	2,911
Priests of the Sacred Heart (1,666)	2,393
Passionists (1,783)	2,351
Pallottines (1,587)	2,348
Trappists (1,012)	2,325
Combonian Missionaries of the Heart of Jesus (1,316)	2,250
Missionaries of the Sacred Heart of Jesus (1,473)	2,134
Carmelites of BVM (1,309)	2,106
Carmelites (O.Carm.) (1,376)	2,044
Missionaries of Africa (1,693)	2,013
Legionaries of Christ (511)	1,758
Holy Cross, Congregation of (787)	1,682
Christian Brothers	1,603
Marianists (485)	1,546
Piarists (1,059)	1,466
Cistercians (Common Observance) (735)	1,457
Hospitallers of St. John of God (142)	1,420
Premonstratensians (930)	1,310
Brothers of the Sacred Heart (42)	1,281
Brothers of Christian Instruction of St. Gabriel (28)	1,281
Marists (1,043)	1,251
Augustinians (Recollects) (981)	1,243
Salvatorians (793)	1,206
Congregation of the Immaculate Heart of Mary (Missionhurst; Scheut Missionaries) (941)	1,190
Missionaries of St. Francis de Sales of Annecy (631)	1,183
Society of St. Paul (569)	1,118
Brothers of Christian Instruction of Ploërmel	1,112
Little Workers of Divine Providence (727)	1,105
Ministers of the Sick (Camillians) (695)	1,087
Sacred Hearts, Congregation (Picpus) (830)	1,042
Society of African Missions (870)	1,007
Montfort Missionaries (721)	1,005
Consolata Missionaries (777)	993
Blessed Sacrament, Congregation of (683)	973
Missionaries of the Holy Family (676)	952
LaSalette Missionaries (668)	952
Assumptionists (623)	944
Servants of Mary (698)	929
Xaverian Missionaries (682)	881
Franciscans (Third Order Regular) (567)	838
Scalabrinians (614)	781
Canons Regular of St. Augustine (625)	762
Mercedarians (514)	730
Most Precious Blood (451) 726	
Viatorians (299)	694
Order of St. Basil the Great (Basilians of St. Josaphat) (308)	691
Missionaries of the Mill Hill (481)	651
Congregation of St. Joseph (506)	651
Oblates of St. Francis de Sales (492)	630
Columbans (578)	625
Maryknollers (495)	604
Oratorians (417)	569
Pontifical Institute for Foreign Missions (504)	564
Trinitarians (390)	548
Brothers of Charity (Ghent)	543
Marian Fathers and Brothers (356)	539
Eudists (406)	523
Oblates of St. Joseph (329)	512
Somascans (360)	509
Society of Christ (384)	491
Order of St. Paul the First Hermit (280)	472
Servants of Charity (322)	462
Crosiers (Order of the Holy Cross) (311)	458
Stigmatine Fathers and Brothers (316)	419
Resurrection, Congregation of the (339)	412
Missionaries of the Holy Spirit (261)	404
Mariannhill Missionaries (210)	397
St. Patrick's Mission Society (333)	382
Barnabites (303)	381
Rogationists (226)	365
Maronite Order of Lebanon (1998) (267)	357
Vocationist Fathers (152)	357
Priestly Fraternity of St. Peter (125)	357
Sulpicians (355)	355
Carthusians (163)	349
Little Brothers of Jesus (69)	243
Discalced Augustinians (89)	242

RELIGIOUS INSTITUTES OF WOMEN IN THE UNITED STATES

(Sources: The Official Catholic Directory*;* Catholic Almanac *survey. As of June 1, 2003.)*

Adorers of the Blood of Christ, A.S.C.: Founded 1834, in Italy; in U.S., 1870. General motherhouse, Rome, Italy. U.S. provinces: 721 Emerson Rd., #685, St. Louis, MO 63141, (314) 991-5400, www.adorers.org. Education, retreats, social services, pastoral ministry.

Africa, Missionary Sisters of Our Lady of (Sisters of Africa), M.S.O.L.A.: Founded 1869, at Algiers, Algeria, by Cardinal Lavigerie; in U.S., 1929. General motherhouse, Rome, Italy; U.S. headquarters, 47 W. Spring St., Winooski, VT 05404-1397, (802) 655-4003. Medical, educational, catechetical and social work in Africa.

Agnes, Sisters of St., C.S.A.: Founded 1858, in U.S., by Rev. Caspar Rehrl. General motherhouse, 320 County Rd., Fond du Lac, WI 54935, (920) 907-2321, www.csasisters.org. Education, health care, social services.

Ann, Sisters of St., S.S.A.: Founded 1834, in Italy; in U.S., 1952. General motherhouse, Rome, Italy; U.S. headquarters, Mount St. Ann, Ebensburg, PA 15931, (814) 472-9354.

Anne, Sisters of St., S.S.A.: Founded 1850, at Vaudreuil, QC, Canada; in U.S., 1866. General motherhouse, Lachine, QC, Canada; U.S. address, 720 Boston Post Rd., Marlboro, MA 01752, (508) 481-4934, www.sistersofsaintanne.org. Retreat work, pastoral ministry, religious education.

Anthony, Missionary Servants of St., M.S.S.A.: Founded 1929, in U.S., by Rev. Peter BaQC General motherhouse, 100 Peter Baque Rd., San Antonio, TX 78209, (210) 824-4553. Social work.

Antonine Maronite Sisters: Founded in Beirut, Lebanon; motherhouse, Couvent Mar-Doumith, Roumieh, El-Metn, B.P. 84, Borumana, Lebanon; U.S. house, 2691 North Lipkey Rd., North Jackson, OH 44451, (330) 538-9822.

Assumption, Little Sisters of the, L.S.A.: Founded 1865, in France; in U.S., 1891. General motherhouse, Paris, France; U.S. provincialate, 100 Gladstone Ave., Walden, NY 12586, (914) 778-0667. Social work, nursing, family life education.

Assumption, Religious of the, R.A.: Founded 1839, in France; in U.S., 1919. Generalate, Paris, France; North American province, 11 Old English Rd., Worcester, MA 01609, (508) 793-1954.

Assumption of the Blessed Virgin, Sisters of the, S.A.S.V.: Founded 1853, in Canada; in U.S., 1891. General motherhouse, Nicolet, QC, Canada; U.S. province, 316 Lincoln St., Worcester, MA 01605, (508) 856-9450. Education, mission, pastoral ministry.

Augustinian Nuns of Contemplative Life, O.S.A.: Established in Spain in 13th century; U.S. foundation, Convent of Our Mother of Good Counsel, 440 Marley Rd., New Lenox, IL, 60451, (815) 463-9662.

Augustinian Sisters, Servants of Jesus and Mary, Congregation of, O.S.A.: Generalate, Rome, Italy; U.S. foundation, St. John School, 513 E. Broadway, Brandenburg, KY 40108, (270) 422-2088, www.st johnonline.org.

Basil the Great, Sisters of the Order of St. (Byzantine Rite), O.S.B.M.: Founded fourth century, in Cappadocia, by St. Basil the Great and his sister, St. Macrina; in U.S., 1911. Generalate, Rome, Italy; U.S. motherhouses: Philadelphia Ukrainian Byzantine Rite, 710 Fox Chase Rd., Philadelphia, PA 19046-4198, (215) 342-4222, www.basilianfoxchase.org; Pittsburgh Ruthenian Byzantine Rite, Mount St. Macrina, P.O. Box 878, Uniontown, PA 15401, (724) 438-8644. Education, health care.

Benedict, Sisters of the Order of St., O.S.B.: Our Lady of Mount Caritas Monastery (founded 1979, Ashford, CT), 54 Seckar Rd., Ashford, CT 06278, (860) 429-7457. Contemplative.

Benedictine Nuns, O.S.B.: St. Scholastica Priory, Box 606, Petersham, MA 01366, (978) 724-3213. Cloistered.

Benedictine Nuns of the Congregation of Solesmes, O.S.B.: U.S. establishment, 1981, in Burlington diocese. Monastery of the Immaculate Heart of Mary, 4103 Vt. Rte 100, Westfield, VT 05874, (802) 744-6525. Cloistered, papal enclosure.

Benedictine Nuns of the Primitive Observance, O.S.B.: Founded c. 529, in Italy; in U.S., 1948. Abbey of Regina Laudis, Flanders Rd., Bethlehem, CT 06751, (203) 266-7727, www.abbeyofreginalaudis.com. Cloistered.

Benedictine Sisters, O.S.B.: Founded c. 529, in Italy; in U.S., 1852. General motherhouse, Eichstatt, Bavaria, Germany. U.S. addresses: St. Emma Monastery, motherhouse and novitiate, 1001 Harvey Ave., Greensburg, PA 15601, (724) 834-3060, www.stem ma.org; Abbey of St. Walburga, 32109 N. U.S. Highway 287, Virginia Dale, CO 80536, (970) 472-0612, www.walburga.org.

Benedictine Sisters (Regina Pacis), O.S.B.: Founded 1627, in Lithuania as cloistered community; reformed 1918 as active community; established in U.S. 1957, by Mother M. Raphaela Simonis. Regina Pacis, 333 Wallace Rd., Bedford, NH 03102, (603) 472-3239.

Benedictine Sisters, Missionary, O.S.B.: Founded 1885. Generalate, Rome, Italy; U.S. motherhouse, 300 N. 18th St., Norfolk, NE 68701-3687, (402) 371-3438, www.norfolkosb.org.

Benedictine Sisters, Olivetan, O.S.B.: Founded 1887, in U.S. General motherhouse, Holy Angels Convent, P.O. Drawer 130, Jonesboro, AR 72403-0130, (870) 935-5810, www.olivben.org. Educational, hospital work.

Benedictine Sisters of Perpetual Adoration of Pontifical Jurisdiction, Congregation of the, O.S.B.: Founded in U.S., 1874, from Maria Rickenbach, Switzerland. General motherhouse, 8300 Morganford Rd., St. Louis, MO 63123, (314) 638-6427.

Benedictine Sisters of Pontifical Jurisdiction, O.S.B.: Founded c. 529, in Italy. No general motherhouse in U.S. Three federations:

• **Federation of St. Scholastica** (1922). Pres., Sister Esther Fangman, O.S.B., 3741 Forest Ave., Kansas City, MO 64109, (816) 753-2514. Motherhouses belonging to the federation:

Mount St. Scholastica, 801 S. 8th St., Atchison, Kans. 66002, (913) 360-6200, www.mountosb.org. Benedictine Sisters of Elk Co., St. Joseph's Monastery, St. Mary's, PA 15857, (814) 834-2267. Benedictine Sisters of Erie, 6101 E. Lake Rd., Erie, PA 16511, (814) 899-0614, www.eriebene dictines.org. Benedictine Sisters of Chicago, St. Scholastica Priory, 7430 N. Ridge Blvd., Chicago, IL 60645, (773) 764-2413, www.benedictine-sisters.org. Benedictine Sisters of the Sacred Heart, 1910 Maple Ave., Lisle, IL 60532-2164, (630) 969-7040, www.shmlisle.org. Benedictine Sisters of Elizabeth, St. Walburga Monastery, 851 N. Broad St., Elizabeth, NJ 07208-2593, (201) 352-4278, www.catholicforum.com/bensisnj. Benedictine Sisters of Pittsburgh, 4530 Perrysville Ave., Pittsburgh, PA 15229, (412) 931-2844, www.osbpgh.org.

Red Plains Monastery, 728 Richland Rd. S.W., Piedmont, OK 73078, (405) 373-4565, www.geo cities.com/redplains. St. Joseph's Monastery, 2200 S. Lewis, Tulsa, OK 74114, (918) 742-4989, www.tulsaosb.org. St. Gertrude's Monastery, 14259 Benedictine Lane, Ridgely, MD 21660, (410) 634-2497. St. Walburga Monastery, 2500 Amsterdam Rd., Villa Hills, KY 41017, (606) 331-6324. Sacred Heart Monastery, P.O. Box 2040, Cullman, AL 35056, (256) 734-4622, www.shmon.org. Benedictine Sisters of Virginia, 9535 Linton Hall Rd., Bristow, VA 20136-

1217, (703) 361-0106, www.osbva.org. St. Scholastica Monastery, 416 W. Highland Dr., Boerne, TX 78006, (830) 816-8504, www.boerne benedictines.com. St. Lucy's Priory, 19045 E. Sierra Madre Ave., Glendora, CA 91741, (626) 335-1682. Benedictine Sisters of Florida, Holy Name Monastery, P.O. Box 2450, St. Leo, FL 33574-2450, (352) 588-8320, www.floridabenedictines.com. Benet Hill Monastery, 2555 N. Chelton Rd., Colorado Springs, CO 80909, (719) 633-0655, www.benethill monastery.org. Queen of Heaven Monastery (Byzantine Rite), 8640 Squires Lane N.E., Warren, OH 44484, (330) 856-1813, www.benedictine byzantine.org. Queen of Angels Monastery, 23615 N.E. 100th St., Liberty, MO 64068, (816) 750-4618.

• **Federation of St. Gertrude the Great** (1937). Office: St. Benedict of Ferdinand, Indiana, 802 E. 10th St., Ferdinand, IN 47532, (812) 367-1411, www.thedome.org. Pres., Sister Kathryn Huber, O.S.B. Motherhouses belonging to the federation:

Mother of God Monastery, 110 28th Ave., S.E., Watertown, SD 57201, (605) 882-6633, www.water townbenedictines.org. Sacred Heart Monastery, 1005 W. 8th St., Yankton, SD 57078-3389, (605) 668-6000, www.yanktonbenedictines.org. Mt. St. Benedict Monastery, 620 E. Summit Ave., Crookston, MN 56716, (218) 281-3441. Sacred Heart Monastery, P.O. Box 364, Richardton, ND 58652, (701) 974-2121, www.sacredheartmonastery.com. St. Martin Monastery, 2110-C St. Martin's Dr., Rapid City, SD 57702-9660, (605) 343-8011, www.blackhillsbenedic tine.com. Monastery of Immaculate Conception, 802 E. 10th St., Ferdinand, IN 47532, (812) 367-2313. Monastery of St. Gertrude, HC3, Box 121, Cottonwood, ID 83522-9408, (208) 962-3224, www.st gertrudes.org.

Monastery of St. Benedict Center, Box 5070, Madison, WI 53705-0070, (608) 836-1631, www.sb center.org. Queen of Angels Monastery, 840 S. Main St., Mt. Angel, OR 97362, (503) 845-6141, www.benedictine-srs.org. St. Scholastica Monastery, P.O. Box 3489, Fort Smith, AR 72913-3489, (479) 783-4147, www.scholasticafortsmith.org. Our Lady of Peace Monastery, 3710 W. Broadway, Columbia, MO 65203, (573) 446-2300, www.benedictine sister.org. Queen of Peace Monastery, Box 370, Belcourt, ND 58316, (701) 477-6167. Our Lady of Grace Monastery, 1402 Southern Ave., Beech Grove, IN 46107, (317) 787-3287, www.benedictine.com. Holy Spirit Monastery, 22791 Pico St., Grand Terrace, CA 92324, (909) 783-4446. Spirit of Life Monastery, 10760 W. Glennon Dr., Lakewood, CO 80226, (303) 986-9234. St. Benedict's Monastery 225 Masters Ave., Winnipeg, MB, R4A 2A1, Canada, (204) 338-4601, www.mts.net/~stbens. The Dwelling Place Monastery, 150 Mt. Tabor Rd., Martin, KY 41649, (606) 886-9624.

• **Federation of St. Benedict** (1947). Pres., Sister Colleen Haggerty, O.S.B., St. Benedict Convent, 104 Chapel Lane, St. Joseph, MN 56374-0220, (320) 363-7100, www.sbm.osb.org. Motherhouses in U.S. belonging to the federation:

St. Benedict's Convent, St. Joseph, MN 56374, (320) 363-7100. St. Scholastica Monasstery, 1001 Kenwood Ave., Duluth, MN 55811-2300, (218) 723-7001, www.duluthbenedictines.org. St. Bede Monastery, 1190 Priory Rd., Eau Claire, WI 54702, (715) 834-

3176, www.saintbede.org. St. Mary Monastery, 2200 88th Ave. W., Rock Island, IL 61201-7649, (309) 283-2100. Annunciation Monastery, 7520 University Dr., Bismarck, ND 58504, (701) 255-1520, www.annunciationmonastery.org. St. Paul's Monastery, 2675 Larpenteur Ave. E., St. Paul, MN 55109, (651) 777-8181, www.osb.org/spm. St. Placid Priory, 500 College St. N.E., Lacey, WA 98516, (360) 438-1771, www.stplacid.org. Mount Benedict Monastery, 6000 South 1075 East, Ogden, UT 84405-4945, (801) 479-6030, www.mbutah.org.

Bethany, Sisters of, C.V.D.: Founded 1928, in El Salvador; in U.S. 1949. General motherhouse, Santa Tecla, El Salvador; U.S. address: 850 N. Hobart Blvd., Los Angeles, CA 90029, (213) 669-9411.

Bethlemita Sisters, Daughters of the Sacred Heart of Jesus (Beth.): Founded 1861, in Guatemala. Motherhouse, Bogota, Colombia; U.S. address, St. Joseph Residence, 330 W. Pembroke St., Dallas, TX 75208, (214) 948-3597.

Bon Secours, Congregation of, C.B.S.: Founded 1824, in France; in U.S., 1881. Generalate, Rome, Italy; U.S. provincial house, 1525 Marriottsville Rd., Marriottsville, MD 21104, (410) 442-1333, www.bonsecours.org. Hospital work.

Brigid, Congregation of St., C.S.B.: Founded 1807, in Ireland; in U.S., 1953. U.S. regional house, 5118 Loma Linda Dr., San Antonio, TX 78201, (210) 733-0701.

Brigittine Sisters (Order of the Most Holy Savior), O.SS.S.: Founded 1344, at Vadstena, Sweden, by St. Bridget; in U.S., 1957. General motherhouse, Rome, Italy; U.S. address, Vikingsborg, 4 Runkenhage Rd., Darien, CT 06820, (203) 655-1068.

Canossian Daughters of Charity (Fd.C.C.): Founded 1808 in Verona, Italy, by St. Magdalen of Canossa. General motherhouse, Rome, Italy; U.S. provincial house, 5625 Isleta Blvd. S.W., Albuquerque, NM 87105, (505) 873-2854, www.fdcc.org.

Carmel, Congregation of Our Lady of Mount, O. Carm.: Founded 1825, in France; in U.S., 1833. Generalate, P.O. Box 476, Lacombe, LA 70445, (504) 882-7577, www.mountcarmel.home.minsdpring.com. Education, social services, pastoral ministry, retreat work.

Carmel, Institute of Our Lady of Mount, O. Carm.: Founded 1854, in Italy; in U.S., 1947. General motherhouse, Rome, Italy; U.S. novitiate, 5 Wheatland St., Peabody, MA 01960, (978) 531-4733. Apostolic work.

Carmelite Community of the Word, C.C.W.: Motherhouse and novitiate, 394 Bem Rd., Gallitzin, PA 16641, (814) 886-4098 (fax).

Carmelite Nuns, Discalced, O.C.D.: Founded 1562, Spain. First foundation in U.S. in 1790, at Charles County, MD; this monastery was moved to Baltimore. Monasteries in U.S. are listed below by state.

Alabama: 716 Dauphin Island Pkwy., Mobile 36606, (334) 471-3991. Arkansas: 7201 W. 32nd St., Little Rock 72204, (501) 565-5121, www.aristotle.net/~carmelitenunslr.org. California: 215 E. Alhambra Rd., Alhambra 91801, (626) 282-2387, www.carmelites.org/teresacarmel; 27601 Highway 1, Carmel 93923, (831) 624-3043; 68 Rincon Rd., Kensington 94707; 6981 Teresian Way, Georgetown 95634, (530) 333-1617; 5158 Hawley Blvd., San Diego 92116, (619) 280-5424, www.carmelsandiego.com; 721 Parker Ave., San Francisco 94118; 530 Blackstone Dr., San Rafael 94903, (415) 479-6872; 1000 Lincoln St., Santa Clara 95050-5285, (408) 296-8412, www.members.aol.com/santaclaracarmel.

Colorado: 6138 S. Gallup St., Littleton 80120, (303) 798-4176. Georgia: Coffee Bluff, 11 W. Back St., Savannah 31419, (912) 925-8505. Hawaii: 6301 Pali Hwy., Kaneohe 96744, (808) 261-6542; Illinois: 1101 N. River Rd., Des Plaines 60016, (847) 298-4241. Indiana: 2500 Cold Spring Rd., Indianapolis 46222-2323, (317) 926-5654, www.praythenews.com; 59 Allendale Pl., Terre Haute 47802, (812) 299-1410. Iowa: 17937 250th St., Eldridge 52748, (319) 285-8387; 2901 S. Cecilia St., Sioux City 51106, (712) 276-1680. Kentucky: 1740 Newburg Rd., Louisville 40205, (502) 451-6796. Louisiana: 1250 Carmel Ave., Lafayette 70501, (337) 232-4651; 73530 River Rd., Covington 70435.

Maryland: 1318 Dulaney Valley Rd., Towson, Baltimore 21286, (410) 823-7415, www.geocities.com/baltimorecarmel; 5678 Mt. Carmel Rd., La Plata, 20646, (301) 934-1654. Massachusetts: 61 Mt. Pleasant Ave., Roxbury, Boston 02119, (617) 442-1411, www.carmelitesofboston.org; 15 Mt. Carmel Rd., Danvers 01923, (978) 774-3008. Michigan: 4300 Mt. Carmel Dr. NE, Ada 49301, (616) 691-8538; 35750 Moravian Dr., Clinton Township 48035, (586) 790-7255, www.rc.net/detroit/carmelite; U.S. 2 Highway, P.O. Box 397, Iron Mountain 49801, (906) 774-0561; 3501 Silver Lake Rd., Traverse City 49684, (231) 946-4960. Minnesota: 8251 De Montreville Trail N., Lake Elmo 55042-9547, (651) 777-3882. Mississippi: 2155 Terry Rd., Jackson 39204, (601) 373-1460.

Missouri: 2201 W. Main St., Jefferson City 65101, (573) 636-3364; 9150 Clayton Rd., Ladue, St. Louis Co. 63124, (314) 993-3494, www.stormpages.com/mtcarmel; 424 E. Monastery Rd., Springfield 65807, (417) 881-2115. Nevada: 1950 La Fond Dr., Reno 89509-3099, (775) 323-3236. New Hampshire: 275 Pleasant St., Concord, 03301-2590, (603) 225-5791. New Jersey: 26 Harmony School Rd., Flemington 08822-2606, www.carmelitehermitage.com/flemingtoncarmel.htm; 189 Madison Ave., Morristown 07960, (973) 538-2886. New Mexico: 49 Mt. Carmel Rd., Santa Fe 87505-0352, (505) 983-7232. New York: c/o Chancery Office, Diocese of Brooklyn, 75 Greene Ave., Brooklyn 11238, (718) 399-5990; 89 Hiddenbrook Dr., Beacon, 12508, (914) 831-5572; 75 Carmel Rd., Buffalo 14214, (716) 837-6499; 1931 W. Jefferson Rd., Pittsford 14534, (716) 427-7094; 428 Duane Ave., Schenectady 12304.

Ohio: 3176 Fairmount Blvd., Cleveland Heights 44118, (216) 321-6568. Oklahoma: 20,000 N. County Line Rd., Piedmont 73078, (405) 348-3947. Oregon: 87609 Green Hill Rd., Eugene 97402, (541) 345-8649. Pennsylvania: 70 Monastery Rd., Elysburg 17824-9697, (570) 672-2935, www.carmelelysburg.org; 510 E. Gore Rd., Erie 16509-3799, (814) 825-0846; R.D. 6, Box 28, Center Dr., Latrobe 15650, (724) 539-1056; P.O. Box 57, Loretto 15940-0057, (814) 472-8620; Byzantine Rite, 403 West County Rd., Sugarloaf 18249-9998, (570) 788-1205; 66th and Old York Rd., Philadelphia 19126, (215) 424-6143. Rhode Island: 25 Watson Ave., Barrington 02806, (401) 245-3421. South Dakota: 221 5th St., W., Alexandria, 57311, (605) 239-4382.

Texas: 600 Flowers Ave., Dallas 75211; 5801 Mt.

Carmel Dr., Arlington 76017, (817) 468-1781; 1100 Parthenon Pl., Roman Forest, New Caney 77357-3039, (281) 399-0270, www.icansurf.com/ocdnewcaney; 6301 Culebra and St. Joseph Way, San Antonio 78238-4909, (210) 680-1834, www.carmels anantonio.org. Utah: 5714 Holladay Blvd., Salt Lake City 84121, (801) 277-6075, www.carmelslc.org. Vermont: 94 Main St., Montpelier, 05601, (914) 831-5572. Washington, DC: 2215 N.E. 147th St., Shoreline 98155, (206) 365-7335 (fax). Wisconsin: W267 N2517 Meadowbrook Rd., Pewaukee 53072, (262) 691-0336, www.geocities.com/pewaukeecarmel.org; 6100 Pepper Rd., Denmark, WI 54208.

Carmelite Nuns of the Ancient Observance (Calced Carmelites), O. Carm.: Founded 1452, in The Netherlands; in U.S., 1930, from Naples, Italy, convent (founded 1856). U.S. monasteries: Carmelite Monastery of St. Therese, 3551 Lanark Rd., Coopersburg, PA 18036; Carmel of Mary, Wahpeton, ND 58075; Our Lady of Grace Monastery, 6200 CR 339 Via Maria, Christoval, TX 76935, (325) 853-1722; Carmel of the Sacred Heart, 430 Laurel Ave., Hudson, WI 54016, (715) 862-2156, www.pres senter.com~carmelit. Papal enclosure.

Carmelite Sisters (Corpus Christi), O. Carm.: Founded 1908, in England; in U.S., 1920. General motherhouse, Tunapuna, Trinidad, W.I. U.S. address: Mt. Carmel Home, 412 W. 18th St., Kearney, NE 68847, (308) 237-2287. Home and foreign mission work.

Carmelite Sisters for the Aged and Infirm, O. Carm.: Founded 1929, at New York, by Mother M. Angeline Teresa, O. Carm. Motherhouse, 600 Woods Rd., Avila-on-Hudson, Germantown, NY 12526, (518) 537-5000. Social work, nursing and educating in the field of gerontology.

Carmelite Sisters of Charity, C.a.Ch.: Founded 1826 at Vich, Spain, by St. Joaquina de Vedruna. Generalate, Rome, Italy; U.S. address, 701 Beacon Rd., Silver Spring, MD 20903, (301) 434-6344.

Carmelite Sisters of St. Therese of the Infant Jesus, C.S.T.: Founded 1917, in U.S. General motherhouse, 1300 Classen Dr., Oklahoma City, OK 73103, (405) 232-7926. Educational work.

Carmelite Sisters of the Divine Heart of Jesus, Carmel D.C.J.: Founded 1891, in Germany; in U.S., 1912. General motherhouse, Sittard Netherlands. U.S. provincial houses: Northern Province, 1230 Kavanaugh Pl., Milwaukee, WI 52313 (414) 453-4040, www.carmelitedcjnorth.org; Central Province, 10341 Manchester Rd., St. Louis, MO 63122, (314) 965-7616, www.carmelitesdcj.org; South Western Province, 8585 La Mesa Blvd., La Mesa, CA 91941-3901, (619) 466-3163. Social services, mission work.

Carmelite Sisters of the Most Sacred Heart of Los Angeles, O.C.D.: Founded 1904, in Mexico. General motherhouse and novitiate, 920 E. Alhambra Rd., Alhambra, CA 91801-2799, (626) 289-1353, wwwcarmelgeneralate.homestead.com. Social services, retreat and educational work.

Carmelites, Calced, O. Carm.: Founded 1856 in Naples, Italy. U.S. address: Carmelite Monastery of St. Therese, 3551 Lanark Rd., Coopersburg, PA 18036.

Carmelites of St. Theresa, Congregation of Missionary, C.M.S.T.: Founded 1903, in Mexico. General motherhouse, Mexico City, Mexico; U.S. foun-

dation, 9548 Deer Trail Dr., Houston, TX 77038, (281) 445-5520.

Casimir, Sisters of St., S.S.C.: Founded 1907, in U.S., by Mother Maria Kaupas. General motherhouse, 2601 W. Marquette Rd., Chicago, IL 60629, (773) 776-1324. Education, missions, social services.

Cenacle, Congregation of Our Lady of the Retreat in the, R.C.: Founded 1826, in France; in U.S., 1892. Generalate, Rome, Italy. Eastern Province, Cenacle Rd., Lake Ronkonkoma, NY 11779, (516) 471-6270; Midwestern Province, 513 Fullerton Pkwy., Chicago, IL 60614-5999, (773) 528-6300, www.cenaclesisters.org.

Charity, Daughters of Divine, F.D.C.: Founded 1868, at Vienna, Austria; in U.S., 1913. General motherhouse, Rome, Italy; U.S. province: 205 Major Ave., Staten Island, NY 10305, (718) 720-4377, www.godslovefdc.org. Education, social services.

Charity, Missionaries of, M.C.: Founded 1950, in Calcutta, India, by Mother Teresa; first U.S. foundation, 1971. General motherhouse, 54A Lower Circular Road, Calcutta 700016, India. U.S. address, 335 E. 145th St., Bronx, NY 10451, (718) 292-0019. Service of the poor.

Charity, Religious Sisters of, R.S.C.: Founded 1815, in Ireland; in U.S., 1953. Motherhouse, Dublin, Ireland; U.S. headquarters, 206 N. Edgemont St., Los Angeles, CA 90029, (310) 559-0176.

Charity, Sisters of (of Seton Hill), S.C.: Founded 1870, at Altoona, PA, from Cincinnati foundation. Generalate, De Paul Center, 463 Mt. Thor Rd., Greensburg, PA 15601, (724) 836-0406, www.scsh.org. Educational, hospital, social, foreign mission work.

Charity, Sisters of (Grey Nuns of Montréal), S.G.M.: Founded 1737, in Canada, by St. Marie Marguerite d'Youville; in U.S., 1855. General administration, Montréal, QC H2Y 2L7, Canada; U.S. provincial house, 10 Pelham Rd., Ste. 1000, Lexington, MA 02421, (781) 862-4700, www.sqmlex.org.

Charity, Sisters of (of Leavenworth), S.C.L.: Founded 1858, in U.S. Motherhouse, 4200 S. 4th St., Leavenworth, KS 66048, (913) 758-6508, www.scls.org/

Charity, Sisters of (of Nazareth), S.C.N.: Founded 1812, in U.S. General motherhouse, SCN Center, P.O. Box 172, Nazareth, KY 40048, (502) 348-1568, www.scnazareth.org. Education, health services.

Charity, Sisters of (of St. Augustine), C.S.A.: Founded 1851, at Cleveland, Ohio. Motherhouse, 5232 Broadview Rd., Richfield, OH 44286, (330) 659-5100, www.srsofcharity.org.

Charity, Sisters of Christian, S.C.C.: Founded 1849, in Paderborn, Germany, by Bl. Pauline von Mallinckrodt; in U.S., 1873. Generalate, Rome, Italy. U.S. provinces: Mallinckrodt Convent, 350 Bernardsville Rd., Mendham, NJ 07945, (973) 543-6528, www.scceast.org; 2041 Elmwood Ave., Wilmette, IL 60091-1431, (847) 920-9341, www.sccwilmette.org. Education, health services, other apostolic work.

Charity, Vincentian Sisters of, V.S.C.: Founded 1835, in Austria; in U.S., 1902. General motherhouse, 8200 McKnight Rd., Pittsburgh, PA 15237, (412) 364-3000, www.vincentiansrspgh.org.

Charity, Vincentian Sisters of, V.S.C.: Founded 1928, at Bedford, Ohio. General motherhouse, 1160 Broadway, Bedford, OH 44146, (440) 232-4755.

Charity of Cincinnati, Ohio, Sisters of, S.C.: Founded 1809; became independent community, 1852. General motherhouse, 5900 Delhi Rd., Mt. St. Joseph, OH 45051, (513) 347-5200, www.sr charitycinti.org. Educational, hospital, social work.

Charity of Ottawa, Sisters of (Grey Nuns of the Cross), S.C.O.: Founded 1845, at Ottawa, Canada; in U.S., 1857. General motherhouse, Ottawa, Canada; U.S. provincial house, 559 Fletcher St., Lowell, MA 01854, (978) 453-4993. Educational, hospital work, extended health care.

Charity of Our Lady, Mother of Mercy, Sisters of, S.C.M.M.: Founded 1832, in Holland; in U.S., 1874. General motherhouse, Den Bosch, The Netherlands; U.S. provincialate, 520 Thompson Ave., East Haven, CT 06512, (203) 469-7872.

Charity of Our Lady, Mother of the Church, S.C.M.C: U.S. foundation, 1970. General motherhouse, 520 Thompson Ave., East Haven, CT 06512, (203) 469-7872.

Charity of Our Lady of Mercy, Sisters of, O.L.M.: Founded 1829, in Charleston, SC. Generalate and motherhouse, 424 Fort Johnson Rd., P. O. Box 12410, Charleston, SC 29422, (843) 795-6083. Education, campus ministry, social services.

Charity of Quebec, Sisters of (Grey Nuns), S.C.Q.: Founded 1849, at QC; in U.S., 1890. General motherhouse, 2655 Le Pelletier St., Beauport, QC GIC 3X7, Canada; U.S. address, 359 Summer St., New Bedford, MA 02740, (508) 996-6751. Social work.

Charity of St. Elizabeth, Sisters of (Convent Station, N.J.), S.C.: Founded 1859, at Newark, NJ. General motherhouse, P.O. Box 476, Convent Station, NJ 07961-0476, (973) 290-5335. Education, pastoral ministry, social services.

Charity of St. Hyacinthe, Sisters of (Grey Nuns), S.C.S.H.: Founded 1840, at St. Hyacinthe, Canada; in U.S., 1878. General motherhouse, 16470 Avenue Bourdages, SUD, St. Hyacinthe, QC J2T 4J8, Canada; U.S. regional house, 98 Campus Ave., Lewiston, ME 04240, (207) 797-8607.

Charity of St. Joan Antida, Sisters of, S.C.S.J.A.: Founded 1799, in France; in U.S., 1932. General motherhouse, Rome, Italy; U.S. provincial house, 8560 N. 76th Pl., Milwaukee, WI 53223, (414) 354-9233, www.scsja.org.

Charity of St. Louis, Sisters of, S.C.S.L.: Founded 1803, in France; in U.S., 1910. Generalate, Rome, Italy; U.S. provincialate, 4907 S. Catherine St., Plattsburgh, NY 12901, (518) 563-0383.

Charity of St. Vincent de Paul, Daughters of, D.C.: Founded 1633, in France; in U.S., 1809, at Emmitsburg, MD, by St. Elizabeth Ann Seton. General motherhouse, Paris, France. U.S. provinces: 333 South Seton Ave., Emmitsburg, MD 21727, (301) 447-2900, www.daughtersofcharity-emmitsburg.org; 7800 Natural Bridge Rd., St. Louis, MO 63121, (314) 382-2800; 9400 New Harmony Rd., Evansville, IN 47720-8912, (812) 963-3341, www.doc-ecp.org; 96 Menands Rd., Albany, NY 12204; 26000 Altamont Rd., Los Altos Hills, CA 94022, (650) 949-8865.

Charity of St. Vincent de Paul, Sisters of, V.Z.: Founded 1845, in Croatia; in U.S., 1955. General motherhouse, Zagreb, Croatia; U.S. foundation, 171 Knox Ave., West Seneca, NY 14224, (716) 825-5859.

Charity of St. Vincent de Paul, Sisters of, Halifax, S.C.: Founded 1856, at Halifax, NS, from Emmitsburg foundation. Generalate, Mt. St. Vincent, Halifax, NS, Canada. U.S. addresses: Commonwealth of Massachusetts, 125 Oakland St., Wellesley Hills, MA 02481-5338, (781) 997-1165, www.schalifax.ca; Boston Province, 26 Phipps St., Quincy, MA 02169, (617) 773-6085; New York Province, 84-32 63rd Ave., Middle Village, NY 11379, (718) 651-1685. Educational, hospital, social work.

Charity of St. Vincent de Paul, Sisters of, New York, SC.: Founded 1817, from Emmitsburg foundation. General motherhouse, Mt. St. Vincent on Hudson, 6301 Riverdale Ave., Bronx, NY 10471, (718) 549-9200, www.scny.org. Educational, hospital work.

Charity of the Blessed Virgin Mary, Sisters of, B.V.M.: Founded 1833, in U.S. by Mary Frances Clarke. General motherhouse, BVM Center, 1100 Carmel Dr., Dubuque, IA 52003, (563) 588-2351, www.bvmcong.com. Education, pastoral ministry, social services.

Charity of the Immaculate Conception of Ivrea, Sisters of, S.C.I.C.: Founded 18th century, in Italy; in U.S., 1961. General motherhouse, Rome, Italy; U.S. address, Immaculate Virgin of Miracles Convent, Box 348, Mt. Pleasant, PA 15666, (724) 887-6753.

Charity of the Incarnate Word, Congregation of the Sisters of, C.C.V.I.: Founded 1869, at San Antonio, TX, by Bishop C. M. Dubuis. Generalate, 4709 Broadway, San Antonio, TX 78209, (210) 828-0020.

Charity of the Incarnate Word, Congregation of the Sisters of (Houston, TX), C.C.V.I.: Founded 1866, in U.S., by Bishop C. M. Dubuis. General motherhouse, P.O. Box 230969, Houston, TX 77223, (713) 928-6053. Educational, hospital, social work.

Charity of the Sacred Heart, Daughters of, F.C.S.C.J.: Founded 1823, at La Salle de Vihiers, France; in U.S., 1905. General motherhouse, La Salle de Vihiers, France; U.S. address, Sacred Heart Province, Grove St., P.O. Box 642, Littleton, NH 03561, (603) 444-5346.

Charles Borromeo, Missionary Sisters of St. (Scalabrini Srs.): Founded 1895, in Italy; in U.S., 1941. American novitiate, 3800 Lottsford Vista Rd., Mitchellville, MD 20721, (301) 459-4700.

Child Jesus, Sisters of the Poor, P.C.J.: Founded 1844, at Aix-la-Chapelle, Germany; in U.S., 1924. General motherhouse, Simpelveld, The Netherlands; American provincialate, 4567 Olentangy River Rd., Columbus, OH 43214, (614) 451-3900.

Chretienne, Sisters of Ste., S.S.Ch.: Founded 1807, in France; in U.S., 1903. General motherhouse, Metz, France; U.S. provincial house, 297 Arnold St., Wrentham, MA 02093, (508) 384-8066, www.sisters ofstchretienne.org. Educational, hospital, mission work.

Christ the King, Missionary Sisters of, M.S.C.K.: Founded 1959 in Poland; in U.S., 1978. General motherhouse, Poznan, Poland; U.S. address, 3000 18-Mile Rd., Sterling Heights, MI 48314.

Christ the King, Sister Servants of, S.S.C.K.: Founded 1936, in U.S. General motherhouse, Loretto Convent, N8114 Calvary St., Mt. Calvary, WI 53057, (920) 753-3211. Social services.

Christian Doctrine, Sisters of Our Lady of, R.C.D.: Founded 1910, in New York. Central office, 23 Haskell Ave., Suffern, NY 10901, (914) 357-0046.

Christian Education, Religious of, R.C.E.:

Founded 1817, in France; in U.S., 1905. General motherhouse, France; U.S. provincial residence, 55 Parkwood Dr., Milton, MA 02186, (617) 696-7732.

Cistercian Nuns, O. Cist.: Headquarters, Rome, Italy; U.S. address, Valley of Our Lady Monastery, E. 11096 Yanke Dr., Prairie du Sac, WI 53578, (608) 643-3520, www.cistercianorder.org.

Cistercian Nuns of the Strict Observance, Order of, O.C.S.O.: Founded 1125, in France, by St. Stephen Harding; in U.S., 1949. U.S. addresses: Mt. St. Mary's Abbey, 300 Arnold St., Wrentham, MA 02093, (508) 528-1282; HC 1, Box 929, Sonoita, AZ 85637, (520) 455-5595, www.santaritabbey.org; Our Lady of the Redwoods Abbey, 18104 Briceland Thorn Rd., Whitethorn, CA 95589, (707) 986-7419, www.redwoodsabbey.org. Our Lady of the Mississippi Abbey, 8400 Abbey Hill Rd., Dubuque, IA 52003, (563) 582-2595, www.mississippiabbey.org/; Our Lady of the Angels Monastery, 3365 Monastery Dr., Crozet, VA 22932, (434) 823-1452, www.ola monastery.org.

Clare, Sisters of St., O.S.C.: General motherhouse, Dublin, Ireland; U.S. foundation, St. Francis Convent, 1974 Cherrywood St., Vista, CA 92083, (760) 945-8040.

Claretian Missionary Sisters (Religious of Mary Immaculate), R.M.I.: Founded 1855, in Cuba; in U.S., 1956. Generalate, Rome, Italy; U.S. address, 9600 W. Atlantic Ave., Delray Beach, FL 33446.

Clergy, Congregation of Our Lady, Help of the, C.L.H.C.: Founded 1961, in U.S. Motherhouse, Maryvale Convent, 2522 June Bug Rd., Vale, NC 28168, (704) 276-2626.

Clergy, Servants of Our Lady Queen of the, S.R.C.: Founded 1929, in Canada; in U.S., 1934. General motherhouse, 57 Jules A. Brillant, Rimouski, QC G5L 1X1 Canada, (418) 724-0508. Domestic work.

Colettines: *See* Franciscan Poor Clare Nuns.

Columban, Missionary Sisters of St., S.S.C.: Founded 1922, in Ireland; in U.S., 1930. General motherhouse, Wicklow, Ireland; U.S. region, 73 Mapleton St., Brighton, MA 02135, (617) 782-5683.

Comboni Missionary Sisters (Missionary Sisters of Verona), C.M.S.: Founded 1872, in Italy; in U.S., 1950. U.S. address, 5405 Loch-Raven Blvd., Baltimore, MD 21239, (410) 323-1469, www.combonisrs.com.

Consolata Missionary Sisters, M.C.: Founded 1910, in Italy, by Bl. Giuseppe Allamano; in U.S., 1954. General motherhouse, Turin, Italy; U.S. headquarters, 6801 Belmont Rd., P.O. Box 97, Belmont, MI 49306 (616) 361-9609, www.consolatasisters.org.

Cross, Daughters of the, D.C.: Founded 1640, in France; in U.S., 1855. General motherhouse, 411 E. Flournoy-Lucas Rd., Shreveport, LA 71115, (318) 797-0887. Educational work.

Cross, Daughters of, of Liege, F.C.: Founded 1833, in Liege, Belgium; in U.S., 1958. U.S. address, 165 W. Eaton Ave., Tracy, CA 95376.

Cross, Sisters of the Holy, C.S.C.: Founded 1841, at Le Mans, France; established in Canada, 1847; in U.S., 1881. General motherhouse, St. Laurent, Montreal, QC, Canada; U.S. regional office, 377 Island Pond Rd., Manchester, NH 03109, (603) 622-9504. Educational work.

Cross, Sisters of the Holy, Congregation of, C.S.C.: Founded 1841, at Le Mans, France; in U.S., 1843. General motherhouse, 100 Lourdes Hall-Saint Mary's, Notre Dame, IN 46556, (574) 284-5572, www.cscsisters.org. Education, health care, social services, pastoral ministry.

Cross and Passion, Sisters of the (Passionist Sisters), C.P.: Founded 1852; in U.S., 1924. Generalate, Northampton, England; U.S. address: Holy Family Convent, One Wright Lane, N. Kingstown, RI 02852, (401) 294-3554.

Cyril and Methodius, Sisters of Sts., SS.C.M.: Founded 1909, in U.S., by Rev. Matthew Jankola. General motherhouse, Villa Sacred Heart, Danville, PA 17821, (570) 275-3581, www.sscm.org. Education, care of aged.

Disciples of the Lord Jesus Christ, D.L.J.C.: Founded 1972; canonically erected 1991. Address, P.O. Box 17, Channing, TX 79018, (806) 534-2312, www.dljc.org.

Divine Compassion, Sisters of, R.D.C.: Founded 1886, in U.S. General motherhouse, 52 N. Broadway, White Plains, NY 10603, (914) 949-2950. Education, other ministries.

Divine Love, Daughters of, D.D.L.: Founded 1969, in Nigeria; in U.S., 1990. General house, Enugu, Nigeria; U.S. regional house, 140 North Ave., Highwood, IL 60040, (847) 432-4946.

Divine Spirit, Congregation of the, C.D.S.: Founded 1956, in U.S., by Archbishop John M. Gannon. Motherhouse, 409 W. 6th St., Erie, PA 16507, (814) 455-3590. Education, social services.

Divine Zeal, Daughters of, F.D.Z.: Founded 1887 in Italy by Bl. Hannibal Maria DiFrancia; in U.S., 1951. Generalate, Rome; U.S. headquarters, Hannibal House Spiritual Center, 1526 Hill Rd., Reading, PA 19602, (610) 375-1738.

DOMINCANS

Dominican Nuns: Nuns of the Order of Preachers, O.P.: Founded 1206 by St. Dominic at Prouille, France. Cloistered, contemplative. Two branches in the United States:

• **Dominican Nuns having Perpetual Adoration.** First monastery established 1880, in Newark, NJ, from Oullins, France, foundation (1868). Autonomous monasteries:

Monastery of St. Dominic, 375 13th Ave., Newark, NJ 07103-2124, (973) 622-6622; Corpus Christi Monastery, 1230 Lafayette Ave., Bronx, NY 10474, (718) 328-6996; Blessed Sacrament, 29575 Middlebelt Rd., Farmington Hills, MI 48334-2311, (248) 626-8321; Monastery of the Angels, 1977 Carmen Ave., Los Angeles, CA 90068-4098, (323) 466-2186, www.op-stjoseph.org/nuns/angels/; Corpus Christi Monastery, 215 Oak Grove Ave., Menlo Park, CA 94025-3272, (650) 322-1801, www.op.org/nunsmenlo; Infant Jesus, 1501 Lotus Lane, Lufkin, TX 75904-2699, (936) 634-4233.

Dominican Nuns devoted to the Perpetual Rosary. First monastery established 1891, in Union City, NJ, from Calais, France, foundation (1880). Autonomous monasteries (some also observe Perpetual Adoration):

Dominican Nuns of Perpetual Rosary, 14th and West Sts., Union City, NJ 07087; 217 N. 68th St., Milwaukee, WI 53213, (414) 258-0579, www.dsopr.home. mindspring.com. Perpetual Rosary, 1500 Haddon Ave., Camden, NJ 08103. Our Lady of the Rosary, 335 Doat St., Buffalo, NY 14211. Our Lady of the Rosary, 543 Spingfield Ave., Summit, NJ 07901, (908) 273-1228, www.op.org/nunsopsummit. Monastery of the Mother of God, 1430 Riverdale St., W. Springfield, MA 01089-4698, (413) 736-3639, www.op-stjoseph.org/nuns/ws. Dominican Monastery of the Perpetual Rosary, 802 Court St., Syracuse, NY 13208-1766. Monastery of the Immaculate Heart of Mary, 1834 Lititz Pike, Lancaster, PA 17601-6585, (717) 569-2104. Mary the Queen, 1310 W. Church St., Elmira, NY 14905, (607) 734-9506, www.oporg/maryqueen. St. Jude, Marbury, AL 36051-0170, (205) 755-1322. Our Lady of Grace Monastery, 11 Race Hill Rd., North Guilford, CT 06437, (203) 345-0599, www.op-stjoseph.org/nuns/olgrace/olgrace.htm. St. Dominic's Monastery, 4901 16th St. N.W., Washington, DC 20011, (202) 726-2107.

Dominican Sisters of Charity of the Presentation, O.P.: Founded 1696, in France; in U.S., 1906. General motherhouse, Tours, France; U.S. headquarters, 3012 Elm St., Dighton, MA 02715, (508) 669-5425, www.dominicansistersofthepresentation.org. Hospital work.

Dominican Sisters of Hope, O.P.: Formed 1995 through merger of Dominican Sisters of the Most Holy Rosary, Newburgh, NY, Dominican Sisters of the Sick Poor, Ossining, NY, and Dominican Sisters of St. Catherine of Siena, Fall River, MA. General Offices: 229 N. Highland Ave., Ossining, NY 10562, (914) 941-4420, www.ophope.org.

Dominican Sisters of Our Lady of the Rosary and of St. Catherine of Siena (Cabra): Founded 1644 in Ireland. General motherhouse, Cabra, Dublin, Ireland. U.S. regional house, 1930 Robert E. Lee Rd., New Orleans, LA 70122, (504) 288-1593.

Dominican Sisters of the Perpetual Rosary, O.P.: 217 N. 68th St., Milwaukee, WI 53213. Cloistered, contemplative.

Dominican Sisters of the Roman Congregation of St. Dominic, O.P.: Founded 1621, in France; in U.S., 1904. General motherhouse, Rome, Italy; U.S. province, 18 Tampa St., Lewiston, ME 04240, (207) 782-7480. Educational work.

Eucharistic Missionaries of St. Dominic, O.P.: Founded 1927, in Louisiana. General motherhouse, 3801 Canal St., Suite 400, New Orleans, LA 70119, (504) 486-1133, www.emdsisters.org. Parish work, social services.

Religious Missionaries of St. Dominic, O.P.: General motherhouse, Rome, Italy. U.S. address (Spanish province), 2237 Waldron Rd., Corpus Christi, TX 78418, (361) 939-8102.

Sisters of St. Dominic, O.P.: Names of congregations are given below, followed by the date of foundation, and location of motherhouse. St. Catherine of Siena, 1822. 2645 Bardstown Rd., St. Catharine, KY 40061, (606) 336-9303, www.opkentucky.org. St. Mary of the Springs, 1830. 2320 Airport Dr., Columbus, OH 43219-2098, (614) 416-1038. Most Holy Rosary, 1847. Sinsinawa, WI 53824, (608) 748-4411. Most Holy Name of Jesus, 1850. 1520 Grand Ave., San Rafael, CA 94901, (415) 453-8303, www.sanrafaelop.org. Holy Cross, 1853. 555 Albany Ave., Amityville, NY 11701, (631) 842-6000, www.amityvilleop.org. St. Cecilia, 1860. 801 Dominican Dr., Nashville, TN 37228, (615) 256-5486, www.nashvilledominican.org.

St. Mary, 1860. 7300 St. Charles Ave., New Orleans, LA 70118, (504) 861-8183. St. Catherine of Siena, 1862. 5635 Erie St., Racine, WI 53402, (262) 639-

4100, www.racinedominicans.org. Sacred Heart Convent, 1873. 1237 W. Monroe St., Springfield, IL 62704, (217) 787-0481, www.springfieldop.org. Sisters of Our Lady of the Rosary, Dominican Convent, 175 Route 340, Sparkill, NY 10976, (845) 359-6400, www.sparkill.org, 1876. Queen of the Holy Rosary, 1876. P.O. Box 3908, Mission San Jose, CA 94539, (510) 657-2468, www.msjdominicans.org. Most Holy Rosary, 1892. 1257 Siena Heights Dr., Adrian, MI 49221, (517) 266-3570.

Our Lady of the Sacred Heart, 1877. 2025 E. Fulton St., Grand Rapids, MI 49503, (616) 459-2910. St. Dominic, 1878. 496 Western Hwy., Blauvelt, NY 10913, (845) 359-0696, www.opblauvelt.org. St. Catherine de Ricci, 1880. 750 Ashbourne Rd., Elkins Park, PA 19027, (215) 635-6027. Sisters of St. Dominic, 1881. 1 Ryerson Ave., Caldwell, NJ 07006, (973) 403-3331. Dominican Sisters of Houston, 1882. 6501 Almeda Rd., Houston, TX 77021-2095, (713) 747-3310, www.op.org/houstonop. Tacoma Dominican Center, 1888. 935 Fawcett Ave., Tacoma, WA 98402, (253) 272-9688. Holy Cross, 1890. P.O. Box 280, Edmonds, WA 98020, (206) 542-3212, www.opedmonds.org.

St. Rose of Lima (Servants of Relief for Incurable Cancer) 1896. 600 Linda Ave., Hawthorne, NY 10532, (914) 769-0114, www.hawthorne-dominicans.org. Dominican Sisters of Great Bend, 1902. 3600 Broadway, Great Bend, KS 67530, (316) 792-1232, www.ksdom.org. Mission Center, 1911. Box 1288, Kenosha, WI 53141, (262) 694-2067. St. Rose of Lima, 1923. 775 Drahner Rd., #204, Oxford, MI 48371, (248) 628-2872, www.op.org/oxford. Immaculate Conception, 1929. 9000 W. 81st St., Justice, IL 60458, (708) 458-3040. Immaculate Heart of Mary, 1929. 1230 W. Market St., Akron, OH 44313-7108, (330) 836-4908, www.akronop.org. Dominican Sisters of Oakford (St. Catherine of Siena), 1889. Motherhouse, Oakford, Natal, South Africa; U.S. regional house, 1965. 980 Woodland Ave., San Leandro, CA 94577, (510) 638-2822.

(**End of listing for Dominicans**.)

Dorothy, Institute of the Sisters of St., S.S.D.: Founded 1834, in Italy, by St. Paola Frassinetti; in U.S., 1911. General motherhouse, Rome, Italy; U.S. provincialate, Mt. St. Joseph, 13 Monkeywrench Lane, Bristol, RI 02809-2916, (401) 253-7835.

Eucharist, Religious of the, R.E.: Founded 1857, in Belgium; in U.S., 1900. General motherhouse, Belgium; U.S. foundation, 2907 Ellicott Terr., N.W., Washington, DC 20008, (202) 966-3111.

Felix, Congregation of the Sisters of St. (Felician Sisters), C.S.S.F.: Founded 1855, in Poland by Bl. Mary Angela Truszkowska; in U.S., 1874. General motherhouse, Rome, Italy. U.S. provinces: 36800 Schoolcraft Rd., Livonia, MI 48150, (734) 591-1730; 600 Doat St., Buffalo, NY 14211, (716) 892-4141; 3800 W. Peterson Ave., Chicago, IL 60659-3116, (773) 463-3020, www.felicianchicago.org; 260 South Main St., Lodi, NJ 07644, (973) 473-7447, www.felician.edu/cssf.htm; 1500 Woodcrest Ave., Coraopolis, PA 15108, (412) 264-2890; 1315 Enfield St., Enfield, CT 06082, (860) 745-7791; 4210 Meadowlark Lane, S.E., Rio Rancho, NM 87124-1021, (505) 892-8862.

Filippini, Religious Teachers, M.P.F.: Founded

1692, in Italy; in U.S., 1910. General motherhouse, Rome, Italy; U.S. provinces: St. Lucy Filippini Province, Villa Walsh, Morristown, NJ 07960, (973) 538-2886; Queen of Apostles Province, 474 East Rd., Bristol, CT 06010, (860) 584-2138, www.queenofapostles.com. Educational work.

Francis de Sales, Oblate Sisters of St., O.S.F.S.: Founded 1866, in France; in U.S., 1951. General motherhouse, Troyes, France; U.S. headquarters, Villa Aviat Convent, 399 Childs Rd., MD 21916, (410) 398-3699. Educational, social work.

FRANCISCANS

Bernardine Sisters of the Third Order of St. Francis, O.S.F.: Founded 1457, at Cracow, Poland; in U.S., 1894. Generalate, 403 Allendale Rd., King of Prussia, PA 19406, (610) 337-3864. Educational, hospital, social work.

Capuchin Poor Clares, O.S.C. Cap: U.S. establishment, 1981, Amarillo diocese. Convent of the Blessed Sacrament and Our Lady of Guadalupe, 4201 N.E. 18th St., Amarillo, TX 79107, (806) 383-9877. Cloistered.

Congregation of the Servants of the Holy Child Jesus, O.S.F.: Founded 1855, in Germany; in U.S., 1929. General motherhouse, Würzburg, Germany; American motherhouse, Villa Maria, 641 Somerset St., North Plainfield, NJ 07060-4909, (908) 757-3050.

Congregation of the Third Order of St. Francis of Mary Immaculate, O.S.F.: Founded 1865, in U.S., by Fr. Pamphilus da Magliano, O.F.M. General motherhouse, 520 Plainfield Ave., Joliet, IL 60435, (815) 727-3686. Educational and pastoral work.

Daughters of St. Francis of Assisi, D.S.F.: Founded 1894, in Hungary; in U.S., 1946. Provincial motherhouse, 507 N. Prairie St., Lacon, IL 61540, (309) 246-2175. Nursing, CCD work.

Eucharistic Franciscan Missionary Sisters, E.F.M.S.: Founded 1943, in Mexico. Motherhouse, 943 S. Soto St., Los Angeles, CA 90023, (323) 264-6556.

Franciscan Handmaids of the Most Pure Heart of Mary, F.H.M.: Founded 1916, in U.S. General motherhouse, 15 W. 124th St., New York, NY 10027-5634, (212) 289-5655. Educational, social work.

Franciscan Hospitaller Sisters of the Immaculate Conception, F.H.I.C.: Founded 1876, in Portugal; in U.S., 1960. General motherhouse, Lisbon, Portugal; U.S. novitiate, 300 S. 17th St., San Jose, CA 95112, (408) 998-3407.

Franciscan Missionaries of Mary, F.M.M.: Founded 1877, in India; in U.S., 1904. General motherhouse, Rome, Italy; U.S. provincialate, 3305 Wallace Ave., Bronx, NY 10467, (718) 547-4693, www.fmmusa.org. Mission work.

Franciscan Missionaries of Our Lady, O.S.F.: Founded 1854, at Calais, France; in U.S., 1913. General motherhouse, Desvres, France; U.S. provincial house, 4200 Essen Lane, Baton Rouge, LA 70809, (225) 926-1627. Hospital work.

Franciscan Missionaries of St. Joseph (Mill Hill Sisters), F.M.S.J.: Founded 1883, at Rochdale, Lancashire, England; in U.S., 1952. Generalate, Manchester, England; U.S. headquarters, Franciscan House, 1006 Madison Ave., Albany, NY 12208, (518) 482-1991.

Franciscan Missionary Sisters for Africa, O.S.F.: American foundation, 1953. Generalate, Ireland; U.S. headquarters, 172 Foster St., Brighton, MA 02135, (617) 254-4343.

Franciscan Missionary Sisters of Assisi, F.M.S.A.: First foundation in U.S., 1961. General motherhouse, Assisi, Italy; U.S. address, St. Francis Convent, 1039 Northampton St., Holyoke, MA 01040, (413) 536-0853.

Franciscan Missionary Sisters of Our Lady of Sorrows, O.S.F.: Founded 1939, in China, by Bishop Rafael Palazzi, O.F.M.; in U.S., 1949. U.S. address, 3600 S.W. 170th Ave., Beaverton, OR 97006, (503) 649-7127. Educational, social, domestic, retreat and foreign mission work.

Franciscan Missionary Sisters of the Divine Child, F.M.D.C.: Founded 1927, at Buffalo, NY, by Bishop William Turner. General motherhouse, 6380 Main St., Williamsville, NY 14221, (716) 632-3144. Educational, social work.

Franciscan Missionary Sisters of the Infant Jesus, F.M.I.J.: Founded 1879, in Italy; in U.S., 1961. Generalate, Rome, Italy; U.S. provincialate, 1215 Kresson Rd., Cherry Hill, NJ 08003, (609) 428-7930.

Franciscan Missionary Sisters of the Sacred Heart, F.M.S.C.: Founded 1860, in Italy; in U.S., 1865. Generalate, Rome, Italy; U.S. provincialate, 250 South St., Peekskill, NY 10566-4419, (914) 737-5409. Educational and social welfare apostolates.

Franciscan Poor Clare Nuns (Poor Clares, Order of St. Clare, Poor Clares of St. Colette), P.C., O.S.C., P.C.C.: Founded 1212, at Assisi, Italy, by St. Francis of Assisi; in U.S., 1875. Proto-monastery, Assisi, Italy. Addresses of autonomous motherhouses in U.S. are listed below.

8650 Russell Ave., S., Minneapolis, MN 55431, (952) 881-4766, www.poorclare.com. 3626 N. 65th Ave., Omaha, NE 68104-3299, (402) 558-4916, www.poorclare.org/omaha. 720 Henry Clay Ave., New Orleans, LA 70118-5891, (504) 895-2019, www.poorclarenuns.com. 6825 Nurrenbern Rd., Evansville, IN 47712-8518, (812) 425-4396, www.poorclare.org/evansville. 1310 Dellwood Ave., Memphis, TN 38127-6399, (901) 357-6662, www.poorclare.org/memphis. 920 Centre St., Jamaica Plain, MA 02130-3099, (617) 524-1760, www.stanthonyshrine.org/poorclares. 327 S. Broad St., Trenton, NJ 08608, (609) 392-7673. 1271 Langhorne-Newtown Rd., Langhorne, PA 19047-1297, (215) 968-5775. 4419 N. Hawthorne St., Spokane, WA 99205, (509) 327-4479. 86 Mayflower Ave., New Rochelle, NY, 10801-1615, (914) 632-5227. 421 S. 4th St., Sauk Rapids, MN 56379-1898, (612) 251-3556. 3501 Rocky River Dr., Cleveland, OH 44111, (216) 941-2820.

1671 Pleasant Valley Rd., Aptos, CA 95001, (831) 761-9659. 2111 S. Main St., Rockford, IL 61102, (815) 963-7343. 215 E. Los Olivos St., Santa Barbara, CA 93105-3605, (805) 682-7670. 445 River Rd., Andover, MA 01810, (978) 683-7599. 809 E. 19th St., Roswell, NM 88201-7514, (505) 622-0868. 28210 Natoma Rd., Los Altos Hills, CA 94022, (650) 948-2947. 1916 N. Pleasantburg Dr., Greenville, SC 29609-4080, (864) 244-4514. 28 Harpersville Rd., Newport News, VA 23601, (804) 596-5942. 1171 N. 300 W., Kokomo, IN 46901-1799, (765) 457-5743. 3900 Sherwood Blvd., Delray Beach, FL 33445, (561) 498-3294. 200 Marycrest Dr., St. Louis, MO 63129,

(314) 846-2618. 6029 Estero Blvd., Fort Myers Beach, FL 33931, (239) 463-5599, www.poorclares-fmb.org. 9300 Hwy 105, Brenham, TX 77833, (409) 836-2444.

Franciscan Sisters, Daughters of the Sacred Hearts of Jesus and Mary, O.S.F.: Founded 1860, in Germany; in U.S., 1872. Generalate, Rome, Italy; U.S. motherhouse, P.O. Box 667, Wheaton, IL 60189-0667, (630) 462-7422, www.wheatonfranciscan.org. Educational, hospital, foreign mission, social work.

Franciscan Sisters Daughters of Mercy, F.H.M.: Founded 1856, in Spain; in U.S., 1962. General motherhouse, Palma de Mallorca, Spain; U.S. address, 612 N. 3rd St., Waco, TX 76701, (254) 753-5565.

Franciscan Sisters of Allegany, O.S.F.: Founded 1859, at Allegany, NY, by Fr. Pamphilus da Magliano, O.F.M. General motherhouse, P.O. Box W, 115 East Main St., Allegany, NY 14706, (716) 373-0200, www.fsalleg.org. Educational, hospital, foreign mission work.

Franciscan Sisters of Baltimore, O.S.F.: Founded 1868, in England; in U.S., 1881. General motherhouse, 3725 Ellerslie Ave., Baltimore, MD 21218, (410) 235-0139. Educational work; social services.

Franciscan Sisters of Chicago, O.S.F.: Founded 1894, in U.S., by Mother Mary Therese (Josephine Dudzik). General motherhouse, 11500 Theresa Dr., Lemont, IL 60439, (630) 243-3558. Educational work, social services.

Franciscan Sisters of Christian Charity, O.S.F.: Founded 1869, in U.S. Motherhouse, Holy Family Convent, 2409 S. Alverno Rd., Manitowoc, WI 54220, (920) 682-7728, www.sl.edu/fscc; Hospital work.

Franciscan Sisters of Little Falls, MN, O.S.F.: Founded 1891, in U.S. General motherhouse, 116 8th Ave., S.E., Little Falls, MN 56345, (320) 632-0612, www.fslf.org. Health, education, social services, pastoral ministry, mission work.

Franciscan Sisters of Mary, F.S.M.: Established, 1987, through unification of the Sisters of St. Mary of the Third Order of St. Francis (founded 1872, St. Louis) and the Sisters of St. Francis of Maryville, MO (founded 1894). Address of general superior: 1100 Bellevue Ave., St. Louis, MO 63117-1883, (314) 768-1833. Health care, social services.

Franciscan Sisters of Mary Immaculate of the Third Order of St. Francis of Assisi, F.M.I.: Founded 16th century, in Switzerland; in U.S., 1932. General motherhouse, Bogota, Colombia; U.S. provincial house, 4301 N.E. 18th Ave., Amarillo, TX 79107-7220, (806) 383-5769. Education.

Franciscan Sisters of Our Lady of Perpetual Help, O.S.F.: Founded 1901, in U.S., from Joliet, IL, foundation. General motherhouse, 335 South Kirkwood Rd., St. Louis, MO 63122, (314) 965-3700, www.franciscansisters-olph.org. Educational, hospital work.

Franciscan Sisters of Peace, F.S.P.: Established 1986, in U.S., as archdiocesan community, from Franciscan Missionary Sisters of the Sacred Heart. Congregation Center, 20 Ridge St., Haverstraw, NY 10927, (845) 942-2527, www.fspnet.org.

Franciscan Sisters of Ringwood, F.S.R.: Founded 1927, at Passaic, NJ. General motherhouse, Mt. St. Francis, 474 Sloatsburg Rd., Ringwood, NJ 07456, (973) 962-7411. Educational work.

Franciscan Sisters of St. Elizabeth, F.S.S.E.: Founded 1866, at Naples, Italy, by Bl. Ludovico of Casorio; in U.S., 1919. General motherhouse, Rome, Italy; U.S. delegate house, 499 Park Rd., Parsippany, NJ 07054, (973) 539-3797, www.franciscan sisters.com. Educational work, social services.

Franciscan Sisters of St. Joseph, F.S.S.J.: Founded 1897, in U.S. General motherhouse, 5286 S. Park Ave., Hamburg, NY 14075, (716) 649-1205. Educational, hospital work.

Franciscan Sisters of St. Joseph (of Mexico): U.S. foundation, St. Paul College, 3015 4th St. N.E., Washington, DC 20017, (202) 832-6262.

Franciscan Sisters of the Atonement (Graymoor Sisters), S.A.: Founded 1898, in U.S., as Anglican community; entered Church, 1909. General motherhouse, St. Francis Convent-Graymoor, 41 Old Highland Turnpike, Garrison, NY 10524, (914) 424-3624. Mission work.

Franciscan Sisters of St. Paul, MN, O.S.F.: Founded 1863, at Neuwied, Germany (Franciscan Sisters of the Blessed Virgin Mary of the Holy Angels); in U.S., 1923. General motherhouse, Rhine, Germany; U.S. motherhouse, 1388 Prior Ave. S., St. Paul, MN 55116, (516) 690-1501. Educational, hospital, social work.

Franciscan Sisters of the Immaculate Conception, O.S.F.: Founded in Germany; in U.S., 1928. General motherhouse, Kloster, Bonlanden, Germany; U.S. province, 291 North St., Buffalo, NY 14201, (716) 881-2323.

Franciscan Sisters of the Immaculate Conception, O.S.F.: Founded 1874, in Mexico; in U.S., 1926. U.S. provincial house, 11306 Laurel Canyon Blvd., San Fernando, CA 91340, (818) 365-2582.

Franciscan Sisters of the Immaculate Conception, Missionary, M.F.I.C.: Founded 1873, in U.S. General motherhouse, Rome, Italy; U.S. address, 790 Centre St., Newton, MA 02158, (617) 527-1004. Educational work.

Franciscan Sisters of the Immaculate Conception and St. Joseph for the Dying, O.S.F.: Founded 1919, in U.S. General motherhouse, 1249 Joselyn Canyon Rd., Monterey, CA 93940, (408) 372-3579.

Franciscan Sisters of the Poor, S.F.P.: Founded 1845, at Aachen, Germany, by Bl. Frances Schervier; in U.S., 1858. Congregational office, 133 Remsen St., Brooklyn, NY 11201, (718) 643-1919, www.fran ciscansisters.org. Hospital, social work and foreign missions.

Franciscan Sisters of the Sacred Heart, O.S.F.: Founded 1866, in Germany; in U.S., 1876. General motherhouse, St. Francis Woods, 9201 W. St. Francis Rd., Frankfort, IL 60423-8335, (815) 469-4895, www.fssh.com. Education, health care, other service ministries.

Hospital Sisters of the Third Order of St. Francis, O.S.F.: Founded 1844, in Germany; in U.S., 1875. General motherhouse, Muenster, Germany; U.S. motherhouse, 4849 La Verna Rd., Springfield, IL 62707, (217) 522-3386, www.springfieldfran ciscans.org. Hospital work.

Institute of the Franciscan Sisters of the Eucharist, F.S.E.: Founded 1973. Motherhouse, 405 Allen Ave., Meriden, CT 06450, (203) 237-0841.

Little Franciscans of Mary, P.F.M.: Founded 1889, in U.S. General motherhouse, Baie St. Paul, QC,

Canada; U.S. region, 55 Moore Ave., Worcester, MA 01602, (508) 755-0878. Educational, hospital, social work.

Missionary Sisters of the Immaculate Conception of the Mother of God, S.M.I.C.: Founded 1910, in Brazil; in U.S., 1922. U.S. provincialate, P.O. Box 3026, Paterson, NJ 07509, (973) 279-3790, www.smic-missionarysisters.com. Mission, educational, health work, social services.

Mothers of the Helpless, M.D.: Founded 1873, in Spain; in U.S., 1916. General motherhouse, Valencia, Spain; U.S. address, Sacred Heart Residence, 432 W. 20th St., New York, NY 10011, (212) 929-5790.

Poor Clares of Perpetual Adoration, P.C.P.A.: Founded 1854, at Paris, France; in U.S., 1921, at Cleveland, OH. U.S. monasteries: 4200 N. Market Ave., Canton, OH 44714; 2311 Stockham Lane, Portsmouth, OH 45662-3049, (740) 353-4713; 4108 Euclid Ave., Cleveland, OH 44103, (216) 361-0783; 3900 13th St. N.E., Washington, DC 20017, (202) 526-6808; 5817 Old Leeds Rd., Birmingham, AL 35210, (205) 271-2917. Contemplative, cloistered, perpetual adoration.

St. Francis Mission Community, O.S.F.: Autonomous province of Franciscan Sisters of Mary Immaculate. Address: 4305 54th St., Lubbock, TX 79413, (806) 793-9859.

School Sisters of St. Francis, O.S.F.: Founded 1874, in U.S. General motherhouse, 1501 S. Layton Blvd., Milwaukee, WI 53215, (414) 384-4105.

School Sisters of St. Francis, (Pittsburgh, PA), O.S.F.: Established 1913, in U.S. Motherhouse, Mt. Assisi Convent, 934 Forest Ave., Pittsburgh, PA 15202-1199, (412) 761-2855, www.franciscansisters-pa.org. Education, health care services and related ministries.

School Sisters of the Third Order of St. Francis (Bethlehem, PA), O.S.F.: Founded in Austria, 1843; in U.S., 1913. General motherhouse, Rome, Italy; U.S. province, 395 Bridle Path Rd., Bethlehem, PA 18017, (610) 866-2597. Educational, mission work.

School Sisters of the Third Order of St. Francis (Panhandle, TX), O.S.F.: Established 1931, in U.S., from Vienna, Austria, foundation (1845). General motherhouse, Vienna, Austria; U.S. center and novitiate, P.O. Box 906, Panhandle, TX 79068, (806) 537-3182, www.members.amaonline.com/schsrspan handle. Educational, social work.

Sisters of Mercy of the Holy Cross, S.C.S.C.: Founded 1856, in Switzerland; in U.S. 1912. General motherhouse, Ingenbohl, Switzerland; U.S. provincial residence, 501 S. Center Ave., Merrill, WI 54452, (715) 539-5000, www.holycrosssisters.org.

Sisters of Our Lady of Mercy (Mercedarians), S.O.L.M.: General motherhouse, Rome, Italy; U.S. address: Most Precious Blood, 133 27th Ave., Brooklyn, NY 11214.

Sisters of St. Francis (Clinton, IA), O.S.F.: Founded 1868, in U.S. General motherhouse, 588 N. Bluff Blvd., Clinton, IA 57232-3953, (563) 242-7611, www.clintonfranciscans.com. Educational, hospital, social work.

Sisters of St. Francis (Millvale, PA), O.S.F.: Founded 1865, Pittsburgh. General motherhouse, 146 Hawthorne Rd., Millvale P.O., Pittsburgh, PA 15209, (412) 821-2200. Educational, hospital work.

Sisters of St. Francis (Hastings-on-Hudson),

O.S.F.: Founded 1893, in New York. General motherhouse, 49 Jackson Ave., Hastings-on-Hudson, NY 10706-3217, (914) 478-3932. Education, parish ministry, social services.

Sisters of St. Francis of Assisi, O.S.F.: Founded 1849, in U.S. General motherhouse, 3221 S. Lake Dr., St. Francis, WI 53235-3799, (414) 744-3150, www.lakeosfs.org. Education, other ministries.

Sisters of St. Francis of Christ the King, O.S.F.: Founded 1864, in Austria; in U.S., 1909. General motherhouse, Rome, Italy; U.S. provincial house, 13900 Main St., Lemont, IL 60439, (630) 257-7495. Educational work, home for aged.

Sisters of St. Francis of Penance and Christian Charity, O.S.F.: Founded 1835, in Holland; in U.S., 1874. General motherhouse, Rome, Italy. U.S. provinces: 4421 Lower River Rd., Stella Niagara, NY 14144-1001, (716) 754-2193, www.franciscans-stella-niagara.org; 2851 W. 52nd Ave., Denver, CO 80221, (303) 458-6270; 3910 Bret Harte Dr., P.O. Box 1028, Redwood City, CA 94064, (650) 369-1725.

Sisters of St. Francis of Philadelphia, O.S.F.: Founded 1855, at Philadelphia, by Mother Mary Francis Bachmann and St. John N. Neumann. General motherhouse, Convent of Our Lady of the Angels, Aston, PA 19014, (610) 558-7701, www.osfphila.org. Education, health care, social services.

Sisters of St. Francis of Savannah, MO, O.S.F.: Founded 1850, in Austria; in U.S., 1922. Provincial house, La Verna Heights, Box 488, 104 E. Park, Savannah, MO 64485-0488, (816) 324-3179. Educational, hospital work.

Sisters of St. Francis of the Congregation of Our Lady of Lourdes, O.S.F.: Founded 1916, in U.S. General motherhouse, 6832 Convent Blvd., Sylvania, OH 43560-2897, (419) 824-3606, www.sistersosf.org. Education, health care, social services, pastoral ministry.

Sisters of St. Francis of the Holy Cross, O.S.F.: Founded 1881, in U.S., by Rev. Edward Daems, O.S.C. General motherhouse, 3025 Bay Settlement Rd., Green Bay, WI 54311, (920) 884-2700, www.gbfranciscansisters.org. Educational, nursing work, pastoral ministry, foreign missions.

Sisters of St. Francis of the Holy Eucharist, O.S.F.: Founded 1378, in Switzerland; in U.S., 1893. General motherhouse, 2100 N. Noland Rd., Independence, MO 64050, (816) 252-1673. Education, health care, social services, foreign missions.

Sisters of St. Francis of the Holy Family, O.S.F.: U.S. foundation, 1875. Motherhouse, Mt. St. Francis, 3390 Windsor Ave., Dubuque, IA 52001, (563) 583-9786, www.osfdbq.org. Varied apostolates.

Sisters of St. Francis of the Immaculate Conception, O.S.F.: Founded 1890, in U.S. General motherhouse, 2408 W. Heading Ave., West Peoria, IL 61604-5096, (309) 674-6168, www.osfsistersw peoria.org. Education, care of aging, pastoral ministry.

Sisters of St. Francis of the Immaculate Heart of Mary, O.S.F.: Founded 1241, in Bavaria; in U.S., 1913. General motherhouse, Rome, Italy; U.S. motherhouse, 102 6th St., S.E., Hankinson, ND 58041, (701) 242-7195, www.fargodiocese.org/sfc/index.htm. Education, social services.

Sisters of St. Francis of the Martyr St. George, O.S.F.: Founded 1859, in Germany; in U.S., 1923.

General motherhouse, Thuine, Germany; U.S. provincial house, St. Francis Convent, 2120 Central Ave., Alton, IL 62002, (618) 463-2750, www.sa hc.org/sisters. Education, social services, foreign mission work.

Sisters of St. Francis of the Perpetual Adoration, O.S.F.: Founded 1863, in Germany; in U.S., 1875. General motherhouse, Olpe, Germany. U.S. provinces: Box 766, Mishawaka, IN 46546-0766, (574) 259-5427, www.ssfpa.org; 7665 Assisi Heights, Colorado Springs, CO 80919, (719) 598-5486, www.st francis.org.

Sisters of St. Francis of the Providence of God, O.S.F.: Founded 1922, in U.S., by Msgr. M. L. Krusas. General motherhouse, 3603 McRoberts Rd., Pittsburgh, PA 15234, (412) 885-7407. Education, varied apostolates.

Sisters of St. Joseph of the Third Order of St. Francis, S.S.J.: Founded 1901, in U.S. Administrative office, P.O. Box 305, Stevens Pt., WI 54481-0305, (715) 341-8457, www.ssj-tosf.org. Education, health care, social services.

Sisters of the Infant Jesus, I.J.: Founded 1662, at Rouen, France; in U.S., 1950. Motherhouse, Paris, France. Generalate, Rome, Italy. U.S. address: 20 Reiner St., Colma, CA 94014.

Sisters of the Sorrowful Mother (Third Order of St. Francis), S.S.M.: Founded 1883, in Italy; in U.S., 1889. General motherhouse, Rome, Italy; U.S. address: 17600 E. 51st St., Broken Arrow, OK 74012, (918) 355-1148, www.ssmfranciscans.org. Educational, hospital work.

Sisters of the Third Franciscan Order, O.S.F.: Founded 1860, at Syracuse, N.Y. Generalate offices, 2500 Grant Blvd., Syracuse, NY 13208, (315) 425-0115.

Sisters of the Third Order of St. Francis, O.S.F.: Founded 1877, in U.S., by Bishop John L. Spalding. Motherhouse, 1175 St. Francis Lane, E. Peoria, IL 61611-1299, (309) 699-7215. Hospital work.

Sisters of the Third Order of St. Francis (Oldenburg, IN), O.S.F.: Founded 1851, in U.S. General motherhouse, Sisters of St. Francis, P.O. Box 100, Oldenburg, IN 47036-0100, (812) 934-2475, oldenburgfranciscans.org. Education, social services, pastoral ministry, foreign missions.

Sisters of the Third Order of St. Francis of Penance and Charity, O.S.F.: Founded 1869, in U.S., by Rev. Joseph Bihn. Motherhouse, 200 St. Francis Ave., Tiffin, OH 44883, (419) 447-0435, www.tiffin ohio.com/stfrancis. Education, social services.

Sisters of the Third Order of St. Francis of the Perpetual Adoration, F.S.P.A.: Founded 1849, in U.S. Generalate, 912 Market St., La Crosse, WI 54601, (608) 782-5610, www.fspa.org. Education, health care.

Sisters of the Third Order Regular of St. Francis of the Congregation of Our Lady of Lourdes, O.S.F.: Founded 1877, in U.S. General motherhouse, Assisi Heights, Rochester, MN 55901, (507) 282-7441. Education, health care, social services.

(End of listing for Franciscans.)

Good Shepherd Sisters (Servants of the Immaculate Heart of Mary), S.C.I.M.: Founded 1850, in Canada; in U.S., 1882. General motherhouse, QC, Canada; in U.S., Provincial House, Bay View, 313 Seaside Ave., Saco, Maine 04072, (207) 284-6429. Educational, social work.

Good Shepherd, Sisters of Our Lady of Charity of the, R.G.S.: Founded 1835, in France, by St. Mary Euphrasia Pelletier; in U.S., 1843. Generalate, Rome, Italy. U.S. provinces: 2108 Hatmaker St., Cincinnati, OH 45204, (513) 921-5923; 82-31 Doncaster Pl., Jamaica, NY 11432, (718) 380-3270, www.good shepherdsistersna.org; 504 Hexton Hill Rd., Silver Spring, MD 20904, (301) 384-1169; 7654 Natural Bridge Rd., St. Louis, MO 63121, (314) 381-3400, www.goodshepherdsisters.org; 5100 Hodgson Rd., St. Paul, MN 55112, (651) 482-5251. Active and contemplative (Contemplative Sisters of the Good Shepherd, C.G.S.).

Graymoor Sisters: *See* **Franciscan Sisters of the Atonement.**

Grey Nuns of the Sacred Heart, G.N.S.H.: Founded 1921, in U.S. General motherhouse, 1750 Quarry Rd., Yardley, PA 19067-3998, (215) 968-4236, www.greynun.org.

Guadalupan Missionaries of the Holy Spirit, M.G.Sp.S.: Founded 1930 in Mexico by Rev. Felix de Jesus Rougier, M.Sp.S. General motherhouse, Mexico; U.S. delegation: 2483 S.W. 4th St. Miami, FL 33135-2907, (305) 642-9544.

Guardian Angel, Sisters of the, S.A.C.: Founded 1839, in France. General motherhouse, Madrid, Spain; U.S. foundation, 1245 S. Van Ness, Los Angeles, CA 90019, (213) 732-7881.

Handmaids of the Precious Blood, Congregation of, H.P.B.: Founded 1947, at Jemez Springs, NM. Motherhouse and novitiate, Cor Jesu Monastery, P.O. Box 90, Jemez Springs, NM 87025, (505) 829-3906.

Helpers, Society of, H.H.S.: Founded 1856, in France; in U.S., 1892. General motherhouse, Paris, France; American province, 3206 S. Aberdeen, Chicago, IL 60657, (773) 523-8638.

Hermanas Catequistas Guadalupanas, H.C.G.: Founded 1923, in Mexico; in U.S., 1950. General motherhouse, Mexico; U.S. addresses: 4110 S. Flores, San Antonio, TX 78214, (210) 533-9344.

Hermanas Josefinas, H.J.: General motherhouse, Mexico; U.S. foundation, Assumption Seminary, 2600 W. Woodlawn Ave., P.O. Box 28240, San Antonio, TX 78284, (210) 734-0039. Domestic work.

Holy Child Jesus, Society of the, S.H.C.J.: Founded 1846, in England; in U.S., 1862. General motherhouse, Rome, Italy; U.S. province, 460 Shadeland Ave., Drexel Hill, PA 19026, (610) 626-1400, www.shcj.org.

Holy Faith, Congregation of the Sisters of the, C.H.F.: Founded 1856, in Ireland; in U.S., 1953. General motherhouse, Dublin, Ireland; U.S. province, 12322 S. Paramount Blvd., Downey, CA 90242, (562) 869-6092.

Holy Family, Congregation of the Sisters of the, S.S.F.: Founded 1842, in Louisiana, by Henriette Delille and Juliette Gaudin. General motherhouse, 6901 Chef Menteur Hwy., New Orleans, LA 70126, (504) 242-8315, www.sistersoftheholyfamily.org. hospital work.

Holy Family, Little Sisters of the, P.S.S.F.: Founded 1880, in Canada; in U.S., 1900. General motherhouse, Sherbrooke, QC, Canada. U.S. novitiate, 285 Andover St., Lowell, MA 01852, (508) 454-7481.

Holy Family, Sisters of the, S.H.F.: Founded 1872,

in U.S. General motherhouse, P.O. Box 3248, Fremont, CA 94539, (510) 624-4596, www.holyfamily sisters.com. Educational, social work.

Holy Family of Nazareth, Sisters of the, C.S.F.N.: Founded 1875, in Italy; in U.S., 1885. General motherhouse, Rome, Italy; U.S. provinces: Sacred Heart, 310 N. River Rd., Des Plaines, IL 60016-1211, (847) 298-6760; Immaculate Conception BVM, 4001 Grant Ave., Philadelphia, PA 19114, (215) 268-1035, www.phila-csfn.org; St. Joseph, 285 Bellevue Rd., Pittsburgh, PA 15229-2195, (412) 931-4778, www.csfn.org; Immaculate Heart of Mary, Marian Heights, 1428 Monroe Turnpike, Monroe, CT 04648, (203) 268-7646; Bl. Frances Siedliska Provincialate, 1814 Egyptian Way, Box 530959, Grand Prairie, TX 75053, (972) 641-4496, www.csfn.org.

Holy Heart of Mary, Servants of the, S.S.C.M.: Founded 1860, in France; in U.S., 1889. General motherhouse, Montreal, QC, Canada; U.S. province, 485 W. Merchant St., Kankakee, IL 60901, (815) 937-2380, www.inil.com/users/hatton. Educational, hospital, social work.

Holy Names of Jesus and Mary, Sisters of the, S.N.J.M.: Founded 1843, in Canada by Bl. Marie Rose Durocher; in U.S., 1859. Generalate, Longueuil, QC, Canada. U.S. addresses: Oregon Province, Box 25, Marylhurst, OR 97036, (503) 675-2449; California Province, P.O. Box 907, Los Gatos, CA 95031, (408) 395-5150, www.holynames.net; New York Province, 1061 New Scotland Rd., Albany, NY 12208, (518) 489-5469, www.snjm.org; Washington Province, 2911 W. Ft. Wright Dr., Spokane, WA 99224, (509) 328-7470, www.snjm.org, www.holynames.net.

Holy Spirit, Community of the, C.H.S.: Founded 1970 in San Diego, CA. Address: 6151 Rancho Mission Rd., No. 205, San Diego, CA 92108, (619) 584-0809.

Holy Spirit, Daughters of the, D.H.S.: Founded 1706, in France; in U.S., 1902. Generalate, Bretagne, France; U.S. motherhouse, 72 Church St., Putnam, CT 06260-1817, (860) 928-0891. Educational work, district nursing, pastoral ministry.

Holy Spirit, Mission Sisters of the, M.S.Sp.: Founded 1932, at Cleveland, OH. Motherhouse, 1030 N. River Rd., Saginaw, MI 48603, (517) 781-0934.

Holy Spirit, Missionary Sisters, Servants of the: Founded 1889, in Holland; in U.S., 1901. Generalate, Rome, Italy; U.S. motherhouse, Convent of the Holy Spirit, P.O. Box 6026, Techny, IL 60082-6026, (847) 441-0126, www.ssps-usa.org. International congregation for the spread of the Gospel *ad gentes*.

Holy Spirit, Sisters of the, C.S.Sp.: Founded 1890, in Rome, Italy; in U.S. as independent diocesan community, 1929. General motherhouse, 10102 Granger Rd., Garfield Hts., OH 44125. Educational, social, nursing work.

Holy Spirit, Sisters of the, S.H.S.: Founded 1913, in U.S., by Most Rev. J. F. Regis Canevin. General motherhouse, 5246 Clarwin Ave., Ross Township, Pittsburgh, PA 15229-2208, (412) 931-1917. Educational, nursing work, care of aged.

Holy Spirit and Mary Immaculate, Sisters of, S.H.Sp.: Founded 1893, in U.S. Motherhouse, 301 Yucca St., San Antonio, TX 78203, (210) 533-5149. Education, hospital work.

Holy Spirit of Perpetual Adoration, Sister Servants of the, S.Sp.S.deA.P.: Founded 1896, in Holland; in U.S., 1915. Generalate, Bad Driburg, Germany; U.S. novitiate, 2212 Green St., Philadelphia, PA 19130, (215) 567-0123, www.adorationsisters.org.

Holy Union Sisters, S.U.S.C.: Founded 1826, in France; in U.S., 1886. Generalate, Rome, Italy. U.S. provinces: P.O. Box 410, Milton, MA 02186-0006, (617) 696-8765; Box 993, Main St., Groton, MA 01450, (978) 448-6049. Varied ministries.

Home Mission Sisters of America (Glenmary Sisters), G.H.M.S.: Founded 1952, in U.S. Glenmary Center, P.O. Box 22264, Owensboro, KY 42304-2264, (270) 686-8401.

Home Visitors of Mary, Sisters, H.V.M.: Founded 1949, in Detroit, MI. Motherhouse, 121 E. Boston Blvd., Detroit, MI 48202, (313) 869-2160.

Humility of Mary, Congregation of, C.H.M.: Founded 1854, in France; in U.S., 1864. U.S. address, Humility of Mary Center, Davenport IA, 52804, (319) 323-9466, www.chmiowa.org.

Humility of Mary, Sisters of the, H.M.: Founded 1854, in France; in U.S., 1864. U.S. address, Villa Maria Community Center, Villa Maria, PA 16155, (724) 964-8861.

Immaculate Conception, Little Servant Sisters of the, L.S.I.C.: Founded 1850, in Poland; in U.S., 1926. General motherhouse, Poland; U.S. provincial house, 1000 Cropwell Rd., Cherry Hill, NJ 08003, (609) 424-1962. Education, social services, African missions.

Immaculate Conception, Sisters of the, R.C.M.: Founded 1892, in Spain; in U.S., 1962. General motherhouse, Madrid, Spain; U.S. address, 2230 Franklin, San Francisco, CA 94109, (415) 474-0159.

Immaculate Conception, Sisters of the, C.I.C.: Founded 1874, in U.S. General motherhouse, P.O. Box 50426, New Orleans, LA 70185, (504) 486-7426.

Immaculate Conception of the Blessed Virgin Mary, Sisters of the (Lithuanian): Founded 1918, at Mariampole, Lithuania; in U.S., 1936. U.S. headquarters, Immaculate Conception Convent, 600 Liberty Hwy., Putnam, CT 06260, (860) 928-7955.

Immaculate Heart of Mary, Missionary Sisters, I.C.M.: Founded 1897, in India; in U.S., 1919. Generalate, Rome, Italy; U.S. province, 283 E. 15th St., New York, NY 10003, (212) 254-0658. Educational social, foreign mission work.

Immaculate Heart of Mary, Sisters of the, I.H.M.: Founded 1848, in Spain; in U.S., 1878. General motherhouse, Rome, Italy; U.S. province, 3820 Sabino Canyon Rd., Tucson, AZ 85750, (520) 886-4273. Educational work.

Immaculate Heart of Mary, Sisters, Servants of the, I.H.M.: Founded 1845. SSIHM Leadership Council, 610 W. Elm, Monroe, MI 48162, (734) 340-9700, www.sistersihm.org.

Immaculate Heart of Mary, Sisters, Servants of the, I.H.M.: Founded 1845; established in Scranton, PA, 1871. General motherhouse, 2300 Adams Ave., Scranton, PA 18509, (570) 346-5404, ihm.mary wood.edu.

Immaculate Heart of Mary, Sisters Servants of the, I.H.M.: Founded 1845; established in West Chester, PA, 1872. General motherhouse, Villa Maria, Immaculata, PA 19345, (610) 647-2160.

Immaculate Heart of Mary of Wichita, Sisters of, I.H.M.: Established at Wichita, KS. 1979. Address: 605 N. Woodchuck, Wichita, KS 67212, (316) 722-9316, www.sistersofwichita.org.

Incarnate Word, Religious of, C.V.I.: General motherhouse, Mexico City, Mexico; U.S. address, 153 Rainier Ct., Chula Vista, CA 92011, (619) 420-0231.

Incarnate Word and Blessed Sacrament, Congregation of, C.V.I.: Founded 1625, in France; in U.S., 1853. Incarnate Word Convent, 3400 Bradford Pl., Houston, TX 77025, (713) 668-0423.

Incarnate Word and Blessed Sacrament, Congregation of the, I.W.B.S.: Motherhouse, 1101 Northeast Water St., Victoria, TX 77901, (361) 575-2266, www.catholic-forum.com/iwbsvictoria.

Incarnate Word and Blessed Sacrament, Congregation of the, I.W.B.S.: Motherhouse, 2930 S. Alameda, Corpus Christi, TX 78404, (361) 882-5413, www.iwbscc.org.

Incarnate Word and Blessed Sacrament, Sisters of the, S.I.W.: Founded 1625, in France; in U.S. 1853. Motherhouse, 6618 Pearl Rd., Parma Heights, Cleveland, OH 44130, (216) 886-6440, wwwincarnate wordorder.org.

Infant Jesus, Congregation of the (Nursing Sisters of the Sick Poor), C.I.J.: Founded 1835, in France; in U.S., 1905. General motherhouse, 310 Prospect Park W., Brooklyn, NY 11215, (718) 965-7300.

Institute of the Blessed Virgin Mary (Loretto Sisters), I.B.V.M.: Founded 17th century in Belgium; in U.S., 1954. Motherhouse, Rathfarnham, Dublin, Ireland; U.S. address: 2521 W. Maryland Ave., Phoenix, AZ 85017, (602) 242-2544.

Institute of the Blessed Virgin Mary (Loretto Sisters), I.B.V.M.: Founded 1609, in Belgium; in U.S., 1880. U.S. address, Loretto Convent, Box 508, Wheaton, IL 60189, (630) 665-3814. Educational work.

Jesus, Daughters of (*Filles de Jesus*), F.J.: Founded 1834, in France; in U.S., 1904. General motherhouse, Kermaria, Locmine, France; U.S. address, 4209 3rd Ave. S., Great Falls, MT 59405, (406) 452-7231. Educational, hospital, parish and social work.

Jesus, Little Sisters of, L.S.J.: Founded 1939, in Sahara; in U.S., 1952. General motherhouse, Rome, Italy; U.S. headquarters, 400 N. Streeper St., Baltimore, MD 21224, www.rc.net/org/littlesisters.

Jesus, Society of the Sisters, Faithful Companions of, F.C.J.: Founded 1820, in France; in U.S., 1896. General motherhouse, Kent, England; U.S. province, St. Philomena Convent, Cory's Lane, Portsmouth, RI 02871, (401) 683-2000, www.ports mouthabbey.org.

Jesus and Mary, Little Sisters of, L.S.J.M.: Founded 1974 in U.S. Address: Joseph House, P.O. Box 1755, Salisbury, MD 21802, (410) 543-1645.

Jesus and Mary, Religious of, R.J.M.: Founded 1818, at Lyons, France; in U.S., 1877. General motherhouse, Rome, Italy; U.S. province, 3706 Rhode Island Ave., Mt. Ranier, MD 20712, (301) 277-3594. Educational work.

Jesus Crucified, Congregation of: Founded 1930, in France; in U.S., 1955. General motherhouse, Brou, France; U.S. foundation: Benedictines of Jesus Crucified, Monastery of the Glorious Cross, 61 Burban Dr., Branford, CT 06405-4003, (203) 315-9964.

Jesus Crucified and the Sorrowful Mother, Poor Sisters of, C.J.C.: Founded 1924, in U.S., by Rev. Alphonsus Maria, C.P. Motherhouse, 261 Thatcher St., Brockton, MA 02402. Education, nursing homes, catechetical centers.

Jesus, Mary and Joseph, Missionaries of, M.J.M.J.: Founded 1942, in Spain; in U.S., 1956. General motherhouse, Madrid, Spain; U.S. regional house, 12940 Leopard St., Corpus Christi, TX 78410, (361) 241-1955.

John the Baptist, Sisters of St., C.S.J.B.: Founded 1878, in Italy; in U.S., 1906. General motherhouse, Rome, Italy; U.S. provincialate, 3308 Campbell Dr., Bronx, NY 10465, (718) 518-7820, www.home.att.net /~baptistines. Education, parish and retreat work; social services.

Joseph, Poor Sisters of St., P.S.S.J.: Founded 1880, in Argentina. General motherhouse, Muniz, Buenos Aires, Argentina; U.S. addresses: Casa Belen, 305 E. 4th St., Bethlehem, PA 78015, (610) 867-4030; Casa Nazareth, 5321 Spruce St., Reading, PA 19602, (610) 378-1947; St. Gabriel Convent, 4319 Sano St., Alexandria, VA 22312, (703) 354-0395 .

Joseph, Religious Daughters of St., F.S.J.: Founded 1875, in Spain. General motherhouse, Spain; U.S. foundation, 319 N. Humphreys Ave., Los Angeles, CA 90022.

Joseph, Servants of St., S.S.J.: Founded 1874, in Spain; in U.S., 1957. General motherhouse, Salamanca, Spain; U.S. address, 203 N. Spring St., Falls Church, VA 22046, (703) 533-8441.

Joseph, Sisters of St., C.S.J. or S.S.J.: Founded 1650, in France; in U.S., 1836, at St. Louis. Independent motherhouses in U.S.: 637 Cambridge St., Brighton, MA 02135, (617) 783-9090. 1515 W. Ogden Ave., La Grange Park, IL, 60526, (708) 354-9200, www.ministryofthearts.org. 480 S. Batavia St., Orange, CA 92868, (714) 633-8121. St. Joseph Convent, 1725 Brentwood Rd., Brentwood, NY 11717-5587, (516) 273-4531. 23 Agassiz Circle, Buffalo, NY 14214, (716) 838-4400. 7 Clement Rd., Rutland, VT 05701, (802) 775-0665. 3430 Rocky River Dr., Cleveland, OH 44111, (216) 252-0440. 1440 W. Division Rd., Tipton, IN 46072, (765) 675-6203, www.sistersstjo-tipton.org. Motherhouse and novitiate, Nazareth, MI 49074, (616) 381-6290. 1425 Washington St., Watertown, NY 13601, (315) 782-3460. 1020 State St., Baden, PA 15005-1342, (724) 869-2151, www.stjoseph-baden.org. 5031 W. Ridge Rd., Erie, PA 16506, (814) 838-4100. 4095 East Ave., Rochester, NY 14618, (585) 641-8119, www.ssjvolunteers. Mont Marie, 34 Lower Westfield Rd. Ste. 1, Holyoke, MA 01040, (413) 536-0853. Pogue Run Rd., Wheeling, WV 26003, (304) 232-8160, www.ssjwhg.org. 3700 E. Lincoln St., Wichita, KS 67218, (316) 686-7171, www.csjwichita.org.

Joseph, Sisters of St. (Lyons, France), C.S.J.: Founded 1650, in France; in U.S., 1906. General motherhouse, Lyons, France; U.S. provincialate, 93 Halifax St., Winslow, ME 04901, (207) 873-4512, www.e-livingwater.org. Educational, hospital work.

Joseph, Sisters of St., of Peace, C.S.J.P.: Founded 1884, in England; in U.S. 1885. Generalate, 3043 Fourth St., N.E., Washington, DC 20017, (202) 832-5333. Educational, hospital, social service work.

Joseph of Carondelet, Sisters of St., C.S.J.: Founded 1650, in France; in U.S., 1836, at St. Louis, MO. U.S. headquarters, 2311 S. Lindbergh Blvd., St. Louis, MO 63131, (314) 966-4048, www.csj congregation.org.

Joseph of Chambery, Sisters of St.: Founded 1650,

in France; in U.S., 1885. Generalate, Rome, Italy; U.S. provincial house, 27 Park Rd., West Hartford, CT 06119, (860) 233-5126. Educational, hospital, social work.

Joseph of Chestnut Hill, Sisters of St., S.S.J.: Founded 1650; Philadelphia foundation, 1847. Motherhouse, Mt. St. Joseph Convent, 9701 Germantown Ave., Chestnut Hill, PA 19118, (215) 248-7200, www.ssjphila.org.

Joseph of Cluny, Sisters of St., S.J.C.: Founded 1807, in France. Generalate, Paris, France; U.S. provincial house, Brenton Rd., Newport, RI 02840, (401) 846-4757.

Joseph of Medaille, Sisters of, C.S.J.: Founded 1650, in France; in U.S., 1855. Became an American congregation Nov. 30, 1977. Central office, 1821 Summit Rd., Suite 210, Cincinnati, OH 45237, (513) 761-2888.

Joseph of St. Augustine, Florida, Sisters of St., S.S.J.: General motherhouse, 241 St. George St., P.O. Box 3506, St. Augustine, FL 32085, (904) 824-1752. Educational, hospital, pastoral, social work.

Joseph of St. Mark, Sisters of St., S.J.S.M.: Founded 1845, in France; in U.S., 1937. General motherhouse, 21800 Chardon Rd., Euclid, Cleveland, OH 44117, (216) 531-7426. Nursing homes.

Joseph the Worker, Sisters of St., S.J.W.: General motherhouse, St. William Convent, 1 St. Joseph Lane, Walton, KY 41094, (859) 485-4256.

Lamb of God, Sisters of the, A.D.: Founded 1945, in France; in U.S., 1958. General motherhouse, France; U.S. address, 2063 Wyandotte Ave., Owensboro KY 42301, (502) 281-5450.

Life, Sisters of, S.V. (*Sorer Vitae*): Founded by Cardinal John J. O'Connor, 1991, to protect life. Address: St. Frances de Chantal Convent, 198 Hollywood Ave., Bronx, NY 10465, (718) 863-2264; Our Lady of New York, 1955 Needham Ave., Bronx, NY, 10466, (718) 881-8008; Sacred Heart Convent, 450 W. 51st St., New York, NY, (212) 397-1386.

Little Sisters of the Gospel, L.S.G.: Founded 1963 in France by Rev. Rene Voillaume; in U.S., 1972. U.S. address, Box 305, Mott Haven Sta., Bronx, NY 10454, (718) 292-2867.

Little Workers of the Sacred Hearts, P.O.S.C.: Founded 1892, in Italy; in U.S., 1948. General house, Rome, Italy; U.S. address, Our Lady of Grace Convent, 635 Glenbrook Rd., Stamford, CT 06906, (203) 348-5531.

Living Word, Sisters of the, S.L.W.: Founded 1975, in U.S. Motherhouse, Living Word Center, 800 N. Fernandez Ave. B, Arlington Heights, IL 60004-5316, (847) 577-5972, www.slw.org. Education, hospital, parish ministry work.

Loretto at the Foot of the Cross, Sisters of, S.L.: Founded 1812 in U.S., by Rev. Charles Nerinckx. General motherhouse, 300 E. Hampden Ave., Ste. 400, Englewood, CO 80110-2661, (303) 783-0450, www.lorettocommunity.org. Educational work.

Louis, Juilly-Monaghan, Congregation of Sisters of St., S.S.L.: Founded 1842, in France; in U.S., 1949. General motherhouse, Monaghan, Ireland; U.S. regional house, 22300 Mulholland Dr., Woodland Hills, CA 91364, (818) 883-1678. Educational, medical, parish, foreign mission work.

Lovers of the Holy Cross Sisters (Phat Diem), L.H.C.: Founded 1670, in Vietnam; in U.S. 1976. U.S.

address, Holy Cross Convent, 14700 South Van Ness Ave., Gardena, CA 90249, (310) 516-0271.

Mantellate Sisters, Servants of Mary, of Blue Island, O.S.M.: Founded 1861, in Italy; in U.S., 1916. Generalate, Rome, Italy; U.S. motherhouse, 13811 S. Western Ave., Blue Island, IL 60406, (708) 385-2103. Educational work.

Mantellate Sisters Servants of Mary, of Plainfield, O.S.M.: Founded 1861 in Italy; in U.S., 1916. Address: 16949 S. Drauden Rd., Plainfield, IL 60544, (815) 436-5796.

Marian Sisters of the Diocese of Lincoln: Founded 1954. Marycrest Motherhouse, 6905 N. 112th St., Waverly, NE 68462-9690, (402) 786-2750.

Marianites of Holy Cross, Congregation of the Sisters, M.S.C.: Founded 1841, in France; in U.S., 1843. Motherhouse, Le Mans, Sarthe, France. North American headquarters, 1011 Gallier St., New Orleans, LA 70117-6111, (504) 945-1620, www.marianites.org.

Marist Sisters, Congregation of Mary, S.M.: Founded 1824, in France. General motherhouse, Rome, Italy; U.S. foundation: 810 Peach, Abilene, TX 79602, (915) 675-5806.

Mary, Company of, O.D.N.: Founded 1607, in France; in U.S., 1926. General motherhouse, Rome, Italy; U.S. motherhouse, 16791 E. Main St., Tustin, CA 92680-4034, (714) 541-3125, www.company ofmary.com.

Mary, Daughters of the Heart of, D.H.M.: Founded 1790, in France; in U.S., 1851. Generalate, Paris, France; U.S. provincialate, 1339 Northampton St., Holyoke, MA 01040, (413) 532-7406. Education, retreat work.

Mary, Missionary Sisters of the Society of (Marist Sisters), S.M.S.M.: Founded 1845, at St. Brieuc, France; in U.S., 1922. General motherhouse, Rome, Italy; U.S. provincial house, 349 Grove St., Waltham, MA 02543, (781) 893-0149. Foreign missions.

Mary, Servants of, O.S.M.: Founded 13th century, in Italy; in U.S., 1893. General motherhouse, England; U.S. provincial motherhouse, 7400 Military Ave., Omaha, NE 68134, (402) 571-2547.

Mary, Servants of (Servite Sisters), O.S.M.: Founded 13th century, in Italy; in U.S., 1912. General motherhouse, Servants of Mary Convent, 1000 College Ave., Ladysmith, WI 54848, (715) 532-3364.

Mary, Sisters of St., of Oregon, S.S.M.O.: Founded 1886, in Oregon, by Bishop William H. Gross, C.Ss.R. General motherhouse, 4440 S.W. 148th Ave., Beaverton, OR 97007, (503) 644-9181, www.ss mo.org. Educational, nursing work.

Mary, Sisters of the Little Company of, L.C.M.: Founded 1877, in England; in U.S., 1893. Generalate, London, England; U.S. provincial house, 9350 S. California Ave., Evergreen Park, IL 60805, (708) 229-5490.

Mary, Sisters Servants of (Trained Nurses), S.M.: Founded 1851, at Madrid, Spain; in U.S., 1914. General motherhouse, Rome, Italy; U.S. motherhouse, 800 N. 18th St., Kansas City, KS 66102, (913) 371-3423. Home nursing.

Mary and Joseph, Daughters of, D.M.J.: Founded 1817, in Belgium; in U.S., 1926. Generalate, Rome, Italy; American provincialate, 5300 Crest Rd., Rancho Palos Verdes, CA 90274, (310) 541-8194.

Mary Help of Christians, Daughters of (Salesian Sisters of St. John Bosco), F.M.A.: Founded 1872, in Italy, by St. John Bosco and St. Mary Dominic Mazzarello; in U.S., 1908. General motherhouse, Rome, Italy; U.S. provinces, 655 Belmont Ave., Haledon, NJ 07508, (937) 790-7963; 6019 Buena Vista St., San Antonio, TX 78237, (210) 432-0090. Education, youth work.

Mary Immaculate, Daughters of (Marianist Sisters), F.M.I.: Founded 1816, in France, by Very Rev. William-Joseph Chaminade. General motherhouse, Rome, Italy; U.S. foundation, 251 W. Ligustrum Dr., San Antonio, TX 78228-4092, (210) 433-5501, www.marianistsisters.org. Educational work.

Mary Immaculate, Religious of, R.M.I.: Founded 1876, in Spain; in U.S., 1954. Generalate, Rome, Italy; U.S. foundation, 719 Augusta St., San Antonio, TX 78215, (210) 226-0025.

Mary Immaculate, Sisters Minor of, S.M.M.I.: Established in U.S., 1989. Address: 138 Brushy Hill Rd., Danbury, CT 06818, (203) 744-8041.

Mary Immaculate, Sisters of, S.M.I.: Founded 1948, in India, by Bishop Louis LaRavoire Morrow; in U.S., 1981. General motherhouse, Bengal, India; U.S. address, R.D. 5, Box 1231, Leechburg, PA 15656, (724) 845-2828.

Mary Immaculate, Sisters Servants of, S.S.M.I.: Founded 1878 in Poland. General motherhouse, Mariowka-Opoczynska, Poland; American provincialate, 1220 Tugwell Dr., Catonsville, MD 21228, (410) 747-1353.

Mary Immaculate, Sisters Servants of, S.S.M.I Founded 1892, in Ukraine; in U.S., 1935. General motherhouse, Rome, Italy; U.S. address, 9 Emmanuel Dr., P.O. Box 9, Sloatsburg, NY 10974-0009, (845) 753-2840. Educational, hospital work.

Mary of Namur, Sisters of St., S.S.M.N.: Founded 1819, at Namur, Belgium; in U.S., 1863. General motherhouse, Namur, Belgium. U.S. provinces: 241 Lafayette Ave., Buffalo, NY 14213-1453, (716) 884-8221, www.ssmn.org; 909 West Shaw St., Ft. Worth, TX 76110, (817) 923-8393.

Mary of Providence, Daughters of St., D.S.M.P.: Founded 1872, at Como, Italy; in U.S., 1913. General motherhouse, Rome, Italy; U.S. provincial house, 4200 N. Austin Ave., Chicago, IL 60634, (773) 545-8300. Special education for mentally handicapped.

Mary of the Immaculate Conception, Daughters of, D.M.: Founded 1904, in U.S., by Msgr. Lucian Bojnowski. General motherhouse, 314 Osgood Ave., New Britain, CT 06053, (860) 225-9406. Educational, hospital work.

Mary Queen, Congregation of, C.M.R.: Founded in Vietnam; established in U.S., 1979. U.S. region, 625 S. Jefferson, Springfield, MO 65806.

Mary Reparatrix, Society of, S.M.R.: Founded 1857, in France; in U.S., 1908. Generalate, Rome, Italy. U.S. province, 225 E. 234th St., Bronx NY 10470.

Maryknoll Sisters, M.M.: Founded in 1912 in U.S. by Mother Mary Joseph. General motherhouse: P.O. Box 311, Maryknoll, NY 10545-0311, (914) 941-7575, www.maryknoll.org.

Medical Mission Sisters (Society of Catholic Medical Missionaries, Inc.), M.M.S.: Founded 1925, in U.S., by Mother Anna Dengel. Generalate, London, England; U.S. headquarters, 8400 Pine Rd., Philadelphia, PA 19111, (215) 742-6100, www.med icalmissionsisters.org. Medical work, health educa-

tion, especially in mission areas.

Medical Missionaries of Mary, M.M.M.: Founded 1937, in Ireland, by Mother Mary Martin; in U.S., 1950. General motherhouse, Dublin, Ireland; U.S. headquarters, 563 Minneford Ave., City Island, Bronx, NY 10464, (718) 885-0945. Medical aid in missions.

Medical Sisters of St. Joseph, M.S.J.: Founded 1946, in India; first U.S. foundation, 1985. General motherhouse, Kerala, S. India; U.S. address, 3435 E. Funston, Wichita, KS 67218, (316) 689-5360. Health care apostolate.

Mercedarian Sisters of the Blessed Sacrament, H.M.S.S.: Founded 1910, in Mexico; first U.S. foundation, 1926. Regional House, 222 W. Cevallos St., San Antonio, TX 78204, (210) 223-5013.

Mercy, Daughters of Our Lady of, D.M.: Founded 1837, in Italy, by St. Mary Joseph Rossello; in U.S., 1919. General motherhouse, Savona, Italy; U.S. motherhouse, Villa Rossello, 1009 Main Rd., Newfield, NJ 08344, (609) 697-2983. Educational, hospital work.

Mercy, Missionary Sisters of Our Lady of, M.O.M.: Founded 1938, in Brazil; in U.S., 1955. General motherhouse, Brazil; U.S. address, 388 Franklin St., Buffalo, NY 14202, (716) 854-5198.

Mercy, Religious Sisters of, R.S.M.: Founded 1973 in U.S. Motherhouse, 1835 Michigan Ave., Alma, MI 48801, (517) 463-6035.

Mercy, Sisters of, of the Americas: Formed in July, 1991, through union of 9 provinces and 16 regional communities of Sisters of Mercy which previously were independent motherhouses or houses which formed the Sisters of Mercy of the Union. Mother Mary Catherine McAuley founded the Sisters of Mercy in Dublin, Ireland, in 1831; first established in the U.S., 1843, in Pittsburgh. Address of administrative office: 8300 Colesville Rd., No. 300, Silver Spring, MD 20910, (301) 587-0423. Pres., Sr. Marie Chin, R.S.M. Total in congregation 5,840.

Mill Hill Sisters: *See* **Franciscan Missionaries of St. Joseph**.

Minim Daughters of Mary Immaculate, C.F.M.M.: Founded 1886, in Mexico; in U.S., 1926. General motherhouse, Leon, Guanajuato, Mexico; U.S. address, 555 Patagonia Hwy., Nogales, AZ 85628, (520) 287-3377.

Misericordia Sisters, S.M.: Founded 1848, in Canada; in U.S., 1887. General motherhouse, 12435 Ave. Misericorde, Montreal, QC H4J 2G3, Canada; U.S. address, 225 Carol Ave., Pelham, NY 10803. Social work with unwed mothers and their children; hospital work.

Mission Helpers of the Sacred Heart, M.H.S.H.: Founded 1890, in U.S. General motherhouse, 1001 W. Joppa Rd., Baltimore, MD 21204, (410) 823-8585. Religious education, evangelization.

Missionary Catechists of the Sacred Hearts of Jesus and Mary (Violetas), M.C.S.H.: Founded 1918, in Mexico; in U.S., 1943. Motherhouse, Tlalpan, Mexico; U.S. address, 805 Liberty St., Victoria, TX 77901, (512) 578-9302.

Missionary Daughters of the Most Pure Virgin Mary, M.D.P.V.M.: Founded in Mexico; in U.S., 1916. Address: 919 N. 9th St., Kingsville, TX 78363, (512) 595-1087.

Mother of God, Missionary Sisters of the,

M.S.M.G.: Byzantine, Ukrainian Rite, Stamford. Motherhouse, 711 N. Franklin St., Philadelphia, PA 19123, (215) 627-7808.

Mother of God, Sisters Poor Servants of the, S.M.G.: Founded 1869, in London, England; in U.S., 1947. General motherhouse, Maryfield, Roehampton, London. U.S. address: Maryfield Nursing Home, Greensboro Rd., High Point, NC 27260, (336) 886-2444, www.greensboro.com/mnh. Hospital, educational work.

Nazareth, Poor Sisters of, P.S.N.: Founded in England; U.S. foundation, 1924. General motherhouse, Hammersmith, London, England; U.S. novitiate, 3333 Manning Ave., Los Angeles, CA 90064, (310) 839-2361. Social services, education.

Notre Dame, School Sisters of, S.S.N.D.: Founded 1833, in Germany; in U.S., 1847. General motherhouse, Rome, Italy. U.S. provinces: 13105 Watertown Plank Rd., Elm Grove, WI 53122-2291, (262) 782-9850; 6401 N. Charles St., Baltimore, MD 21212, (410) 377-7774, www.ssndba.org; 320 E. Ripa Ave., St. Louis, MO 63125, (314) 633-7000, www.ssnd.org; 170 Good Counsel Dr., Mankato, MN 56001-3138, (507) 389-4210, www.ssndmankato.org; 345 Belden Hill Rd., Wilton, CT 06897, (203) 762-1220; P.O. Box 227275, Dallas, TX 75222, (214) 330-9152, www.ssnd.org; 1431 Euclid Ave., Berwyn, IL 60402, (708) 749-1390.

Notre Dame, Sisters of, S.N.D.: Founded 1850, at Coesfeld, Germany; in U.S., 1874. General motherhouse, Rome, Italy. U.S. provinces: 13000 Auburn Rd., Chardon, OH 44024, (440) 286-7101; 1601 Dixie Highway, Covington, KY 41011, (606) 291-2040; 3837 Secor Rd., Toledo, OH 43623, (419) 474-5485; 1776 Hendrix Ave., Thousand Oaks, CA 91360, (805) 496-3243.

Notre Dame, Sisters of the Congregation of, C.N.D.: Founded 1658, in Canada, by St. Marguerite Bourgeoys; in U.S., 1860. General motherhouse, Montréal, QC, Canada; U.S. province, 223 West Mountain Rd., Ridgefield, CT 06877-3627, (203) 438-3115, www.cnd-m.com. Education.

Notre Dame de Namur, Sisters of, S.N.D.deN.: Founded 1804, in France; in U.S., 1840. General motherhouse, Rome, Italy. U.S. provinces: 351 Broadway, Everett, MA 02149, (617) 387-2500, www.SNDdeN.org; 30 Jeffrey's Neck Rd., Ipswich, MA 01938, (978) 356-4381; 468 Poquonock Ave., Windsor, CT 06095-2473, (860) 688-1832, www.sndden.org; 1531 Greenspring Valley Rd., Stevenson, MD 21153, (410) 486-5599; 305 Cable St., Baltimore, MD 21210, (410) 243-1993, www.sndden.org; 701 E. Columbia Ave., Cincinnati, OH 45215, (513) 761-7636; 1520 Ragston Ave., Belmont, CA 94002-1908, (650) 593-2045; SND Base Communities, 3037 Fourth St. N.E., Washington, DC 20017, (202) 832-8770. Educational work.

Notre Dame de Sion, Congregation of, N.D.S.: Founded 1850, in France; in U.S., 1892. Generalate, Rome, Italy; U.S. province, 3823 Locust St., Kansas City, MO 64109, (816) 531-1374. Creation of better understanding between Christians and Jews.

Notre Dame Sisters: Founded 1853, in Czechoslovakia; in U.S., 1910. General motherhouse, Javornik, Czech Republic; U.S. motherhouse, 3501 State St., Omaha, NE 68112, (402) 455-2994, www.notre damesisters.org. Educational work.

Oblates of the Mother of Orphans, O.M.O: Founded 1945, in Italy. General motherhouse, Milan, Italy; U.S. address, 20 E. 72nd St., New York, NY 10021.

Our Lady of Charity, North American Union of Sisters of, Eudist Sisters (Sisters of Our Lady of Charity of the Refuge), N.A.U.-O.L.C.: Founded 1641, in Caen, France, by St. John Eudes; in U.S., 1855. Autonomous houses were federated in 1944 and in March 1979 the North American Union of the Sisters of Our Lady of Charity was established. General motherhouse and administrative center, 154 Edgington Ln., Wheeling, WV 26003, (304) 242-0042. Primarily devoted to re-education and rehabilitation of women and girls in residential and non-residential settings.

Independent houses: 1125 Malvern Ave., Hot Springs, AR 71901, (501) 623-9651, www.light ofmary.org; 4500 W. Davis St., Dallas, TX 75211, (214) 331-1754.

Our Lady of Sorrows, Sisters of, O.L.S.: Founded 1839, in Italy; in U.S., 1947. General motherhouse, Rome, Italy; U.S. headquarters, 9894 Norris Ferry Rd., Shreveport, LA 71106.

Our Lady of the Holy Rosary, Daughters of, F.M.S.R. (Filiae Mariae Sacri Rosarii): Founded 1946, in North Vietnam; foundation in U.S., 1968. General Motherhouse, Saigon, Vietnam; U.S. Province, 1492 Moss St., New Orleans, LA 70119, (504) 486-0039.

Our Lady of Victory Missionary Sisters, O.L.V.M.: Founded 1922, in U.S. Motherhouse, Victory Noll, 1900 W. Park Dr., P.O. Box 109, Huntington, IN 46750, (260) 356-0628, www.olv.org. Educational, social work.

Pallottine Missionary Sisters (Missionary Sisters of the Catholic Apostolate), S.A.C.: Founded in Rome, 1838; in U.S., 1912. Generalate, Rome, Italy; U.S. provincialate, 15270 Old Halls Ferry Rd., Florissant, MO 63034, (314) 837-7100, www.geveities.com/pallottinerenewal.org.

Pallottine Sisters of the Catholic Apostolate, C.S.A.C.: Founded 1843, at Rome, Italy; in U.S., 1889. General motherhouse, Rome; U.S. motherhouse, St. Patrick's Villa, Harriman Heights, Harriman, NY 10926, (914) 783-9007. Educational work.

Parish Visitors of Mary Immaculate, P.V.M.I.: Founded 1920, in New York. General motherhouse, Box 658, Monroe, NY 10950, (845) 783-2251. Mission work.

Passion of Jesus Christ, Religious of (Passionist Nuns), C.P.: Founded 1771, in Italy, by St. Paul of the Cross; in U.S., 1910. U.S. convents: 2715 Churchview Ave., Pittsburgh, PA 15227-2141, (412) 881-1155; 631 Griffin Pond Rd., Clarks Summit, PA 18411-8899, (570) 586-2791, www.intiques.net/cpnuns; 8564 Crisp Rd., Whitesville, KY 42378-9729, (270) 233-4571, www.passionistnuns.org; 1151 Donaldson Hwy., Erlanger, KY 41018, (859) 371-8568; 15700 Clayton Rd., Ellisville, MO 63011, (314) 227-5275. Contemplatives.

Passionist Sisters: See **Cross and Passion, Sisters of the Paul, Daughters of St. (Missionary Sisters of the Media of Communication), D.S.P.**: Founded 1915, at Alba, Piedmont, Italy; in U.S., 1932. General motherhouse, Rome, Italy; U.S. provincial house,

50 St. Paul's Ave., Boston, MA 02130-3491, (617) 522-8911, www.pauline.org. Apostolate of the communications arts.

Paul of Chartres, Sisters of St., S.P.C.: Founded 1696, in France. General house, Rome, Italy; U.S. address, 1300 County Rd. 492, Marquette, MI 49855, (906) 226-3932, members.aol.com/spcmqt/index.htm.

Perpetual Adoration of Guadalupe, Sisters of, A.P.G.: U.S. foundation, 2403 W. Travis, San Antonio, TX 78207, (210) 227-7785.

Peter Claver, Missionary Sisters of St., S.S.P.C.: Founded 1894 in Austria by Bl. Maria Teresa Ledochowska; in U.S., 1914. General motherhouse, Rome, Italy; U.S. address, 667 Woods Mill Rd. S., Chesterfield, MO 63006, (314) 434-8084.

Pious Disciples of the Divine Master, P.D.D.M.: Founded 1924 in Italy; in U.S., 1948. General motherhouse, Rome, Italy; U.S. headquarters, 60 Sunset Ave., Staten Island, NY 10314, (718) 494-8597.

Pious Schools, Sisters of the, Sch. P.: Founded 1829 in Spain; in U.S., 1954. General motherhouse, Rome, Italy; U.S. headquarters, 17601 Nordhoff St., Northridge, CA 91325, (818) 882-6265.

Poor, Little Sisters of the, L.S.P.: Founded 1839, in France, by Bl. Jeanne Jugan; in U.S., 1868. General motherhouse, St. Pern, France. U.S. provinces: 110-30 221st St., Queens Village, NY 11429, (718) 464-1800; 601 Maiden Choice Lane, Baltimore, MD 21228, (410) 744-9367; 80 W. Northwest Hwy., Palatine, IL 60067, (847) 358-5700. Care of aged.

Poor Clare Missionary Sisters (Misioneras Clarisas), M.C.: Founded in Mexico. General motherhouse, Rome, Italy; U.S. novitiate, 1019 N. Newhope, Santa Ana, CA 92703-1534, (714) 554-8850.

Poor Clare Nuns: *See* **Franciscan Poor Clare Nuns.**

Poor Handmaids of Jesus Christ (Ancilla Domini Sisters), P.H.J.C.: Founded 1851, in Germany by Bl. Mary Kasper; in U.S., 1868. General motherhouse, Dernbach, Westerwald, Germany; U.S. motherhouse, Ancilla Domini Convent, Donaldson, IN 46513, (219) 936-9936. Educational, hospital work, social services.

Precious Blood, Daughters of Charity of the Most, D.C.P.B.: Founded 1872, at Pagani, Italy; in U.S., 1908. General motherhouse, Rome, Italy; U.S. convent, 1482 North Ave., Bridgeport, CT 06604, (203) 334-7000.

Precious Blood, Missionary Sisters of the, C.P.S.: Founded 1885, at Mariannhill, South Africa; in U.S., 1925. Generalate, Rome, Italy; U.S. novitiate, P.O. Box 97, Reading, PA 19607, (610) 777-1624. Home and foreign mission work.

Precious Blood, Sisters Adorers of the, A.P.B.: Founded 1861, in Canada; in U.S., 1890. General motherhouse, Canada. U.S. autonomous monasteries: 54th St. and Fort Hamilton Pkwy., Brooklyn, NY 11219, (718) 438-6371; 700 Bridge St., Manchester, NH 03104-5495, (603) 623-4264; 166 State St., Portland, ME 04101; 1106 State St., Lafayette, IN 47905, (765) 742-8227, www.members.aol.com/saotproc/index.htm; 400 Pratt St., Watertown, NY 13601, (315) 788-1669. Cloistered, contemplative.

Precious Blood, Sisters of the, C.PP.S.: Founded 1834, in Switzerland; in U.S., 1844. Generalate, 4000 Denlinger Rd., Dayton, OH 45426, (937) 837-3302. Education, health care, other ministries.

Precious Blood, Sisters of the Most, C.PP.S.: Founded 1845, in Steinerberg, Switzerland; in U.S., 1870. General motherhouse, 204 N. Main St., O'Fallon, MO 63366-2203, (636) 240-3420. Education, other ministries.

Presentation, Sisters of Mary of the, S.M.P.: Founded 1829, in France; in U.S., 1903. General motherhouse, Broons, Côtes-du-Nord, France. U.S. address, Maryvale Novitiate, 11550 River Rd., Valley City, ND 58072, (701) 845-2864, www.sistersofmarypresenattion.com. Hospital work.

Presentation of Mary, Sisters of the, P.M.: Founded 1796, in France by Bl. Marie Rivier; in U.S., 1873. General motherhouse, Castel Gandolfo, Italy. U.S. provincial houses: 495 Mammoth Rd., Manchester, NH 03104, (603) 669-1080, www.presentationofmary.com; 209 Lawrence St., Methuen, MA 01844, (978) 687-1369, www.presmarymethuen.org.

Presentation of the B.V.M., Sisters of the, P.B.V.M.: Founded 1775, in Ireland; in U.S., 1854, in San Francisco. U.S. motherhouses: 2360 Carter Rd., Dubuque, IA 52001, (563) 588-2008, www.dubuquepresentations.org; 880 Jackson Ave., New Windsor, NY 12553, (914) 564-0513; 281 Masonic Ave., San Francisco, CA 94118, (415) 422-5013, www.presentationsistersf.org; St. Colman's Convent, Watervliet, NY 12189, (518) 273-4911; 1101 32nd Ave., S., Fargo ND 58103, (701) 237-4857; Presentation Convent, Aberdeen, SD 57401, (605) 229-8419, www.sistersonline.org; Leominster, MA 01453; 419 Woodrow Rd., Staten Island, NY 10312, (718) 356-2121.

Presentation of the Blessed Virgin Mary, Sisters of, of Union: Founded in Ireland, 1775; union established in Ireland, 1976; first U.S. vice province, 1979. Generalate, Kildare, Ireland; U.S. provincialate, 729 W. Wilshire Dr., Phoenix, AZ 85007, (602) 271-9687.

Providence, Daughters of Divine, F.D.P.: Founded 1832, Italy; in U.S., 1964. General motherhouse, Rome, Italy; U.S. address, 3100 Mumphrey Rd., Chalmette, LA 70043, (504) 279-4617.

Providence, Missionary Catechists of Divine, M.C.D.P.: Administrative house, 2318 Castroville Rd., San Antonio, TX 78237, (210) 432-0113.

Providence, Oblate Sisters of, O.S.P.: Founded 1829, in U.S., by Mother Mary Elizabeth Lange and Father James Joubert, S.S. First order of black nuns in U.S. General motherhouse, 701 Gun Rd., Baltimore, MD 21227, (410) 242-8500. Educational work.

Providence, Sisters of, S.P.: Founded 1861, in Canada; in U.S., 1873. General motherhouse, Our Lady of Victory Convent, 5 Gamelin St., Holyoke, MA 01040, (413) 536-7511, wwwsisofprov.org.

Providence, Sisters of, S.P.: Founded 1843, in Canada; in U.S., 1854. General motherhouse, Montreal, QC, Canada; U.S. province, Mother Joseph Province, 506 Second Ave., #1200, Seattle, WA 98104, (206) 464-3394, www.sistersofprovidence.net.

Providence, Sisters of (of St. Mary-of-the-Woods), S.P.: Founded 1806, in France; in U.S., 1 Sisters of Providence, St. Mary-of-the-Woods, IN 47876, (812) 535-3131, www.sistersofprovidence.org.

Providence, Sisters of Divine, C.D.P.: Founded 1762, in France; in U.S., 1866. Generalate, Box 197, Helotes, TX 78023, (210) 695-8721. Educational, hospital work.

Providence, Sisters of Divine, C.D.P.: Founded 1851, in Germany; in U.S., 1876. Generalate, Rome,

Italy. U.S. provinces: 9000 Babcock Blvd., Allison Park, PA 15101-2793, (412) 931-5241, www.sistersofdivprovidence.org; 3415 Bridgeland Dr., Bridgetown, MO 63044, (314) 524-3803. Educational, hospital work.

Providence, Sisters of Divine (of Kentucky), C.D.P.: Founded 1762, in France; in U.S., 1889. General motherhouse, Fenetrange, France; U.S. province, 1000 St. Anne Dr., Melbourne, KY 41059, (859) 441-0700, www.cdpkentucky.org. Education, social services, other ministries.

Redeemer, Oblates of the Most Holy, O.SS.R.: Founded 1864, in Spain. General motherhouse, Spain; U.S. foundation, 60-80 Pond St., Jamaica Plain, MA 02130, (617) 524-1640.

Redeemer, Order of the Most Holy, O.SS.R.: Founded 1731, by Ven. Mother Marie Celeste Crostarosa, with the help of St. Alphonsus Liguori; in U.S., 1957. U.S. addresses: Mother of Perpetual Help Monastery, P.O. Box 220, Esopus, NY 12429, (914) 384-6533; Monastery of St. Alphonsus, 200 Ligouri Dr. Liguori, MO 63057, (636) 464-1093.

Redeemer, Sisters of the Divine, S.D.R.: Founded 1849, in Niederbronn, France; in U.S., 1912. General motherhouse, Rome, Italy; U.S. province, 999 Rock Run Road, Elizabeth, PA 15037, (412) 751-8600. Educational, hospital work; care of the aged.

Redeemer, Sisters of the Holy, C.S.R.: Founded 1849, in Alsace; in U.S., 1924. General motherhouse, Wurzburg, Germany; U.S. provincial house, 521 Moredon Rd., Huntingdon Valley, PA 19006, (215) 914-4100. Personalized medical care in hospitals, homes for aged, private homes; retreat work.

Reparation of the Congregation of Mary, Sisters of, S.R.C.M.: Founded 1903, in U.S. Motherhouse, St. Zita's Villa, Monsey, NY 10952, (914) 356-2011.

Reparation of the Sacred Wounds of Jesus, Sisters of, S.R.: Founded 1959 in U.S. General motherhouse, 2120 S.E. 24th Ave., Portland, OR 97214-5504, (503) 236-4207.

Resurrection, Sisters of the, C.R.: Founded 1891, in Italy; in U.S., 1900. General motherhouse, Rome, Italy. U.S. provinces: 7432 Talcott Ave., Chicago, IL 60631, (773) 792-6363; Mt. St. Joseph, 35 Boltwood Ave., Castleton-on-Hudson, NY 12033, (518) 732-2226, www.resurrectionsisters.org. Education, nursing.

Rita, Sisters of St., O.S.A.: General motherhouse, Wurzburg, Germany. U.S. foundation, St. Monica's Convent, 3920 Green Bay Rd., Racine, WI 53404, (262) 639-5050, www.geocities.com/sistersofstrita.

Rosary, Congregation of Our Lady of the Holy, R.S.R.: Founded 1874, in Canada; in U.S., 1899. General motherhouse, Rimouski, QC, Canada; U.S. regional house, 20 Thomas St., Portland, ME 04102-3638, (207) 774-3756, www.soeursdusaintrasaire.org/. Educational work.

Rosary, Missionary Sisters of the Holy, M.S.H.R.: Founded 1924, in Ireland; in U.S., 1954. Motherhouse, Dublin, Ireland; in U.S., 741 Polo Rd., Bryn Mawr, PA 19010, (610) 520-1974, www.mshr.org. African missions.

Sacrament, Missionary Sisters of the Most Blessed, M.SS.S.: General motherhouse, Madrid, Spain; U.S. foundation, 1111 Wordin Ave., Bridgeport, CT 06605.

Sacrament, Nuns of the Perpetual Adoration of the Blessed, A.P.: Founded 1807 in Rome, Italy; in U.S., 1925. U.S. monasteries: 145 N. Cotton Ave., El Paso, TX 79901, (915) 533-5323; 771 Ashbury St., San Francisco, CA 94117, (415) 566-2743.

Sacrament, Oblate Sisters of the Blessed, O.S.B.S.: Founded 1935, in U.S. Motherhouse, St. Sylvester Convent, P.O. Box 217, Marty, SD 57361, (605) 384-3305. Care of American Indians.

Sacrament, Servants of the Blessed, S.S.S.: Founded 1858, in France, by St. Pierre Julien Eymard; in U.S., 1947. General motherhouse, Rome, Italy; American provincial house, St. Charles Borromeo Parish, 1818 Coal Pl. SE, Albuquerque, NM 87106, (505) 242-3692. Contemplative.

Sacrament, Sisters of the Blessed, for Indians and Colored People, S.B.S.: Founded 1891, in U.S., by St. Katharine Drexel. General motherhouse, 1663 Bristol Pike, P.O. Box 8502, Bensalem, PA 19020, (215) 244-9900, www.katharinedrexel.org.

Sacrament, Sisters of the Most Holy, M.H.S.: Founded 1851, in France; in U.S., 1872. Generalate, 313 Corona Dr. (P.O. Box 90037), Lafayette, LA 70509, (337) 981-8475.

Sacrament, Sisters Servants of the Blessed, S.J.S.: Founded 1904, in Mexico; in U.S., 1926. General motherhouse, Mexico; U.S. address, 215 Lomita St., El Segundo, CA 90245, (310) 615-0766.

Sacramentine Nuns (Religious of the Order of the Blessed Sacrament and Our Lady), O.SS.: Founded 1639, in France; in U.S., 1912. U.S. monasteries: 235 Bellvale Lakes Rd., Warwick NY 10990; 2798 US 31 N, P.O. Box 86, Conway, MI 49722, (231) 347-0447. Perpetual adoration of the Holy Eucharist.

Sacred Heart, Daughters of Our Lady of the, F.D.N.S.C.: Founded 1882, in France; in U.S., 1955. General motherhouse, Rome, Italy; U.S. address, 424 E. Browning Rd., Bellmawr, NJ 08031, (609) 931-8973. Educational work.

Sacred Heart, Missionary Sisters of the (Cabrini Sisters), M.S.C.: Founded 1880, in Italy, by St. Frances Xavier Cabrini; in U.S., 1889. General motherhouse, Rome, Italy; U.S. provincial office, 222 E. 19th St., 5B, New York, NY 10003. Educational, health, social and catechetical work.

Sacred Heart, Society Devoted to the, S.D.S.H.: Founded 1940, in Hungary; in U.S., 1956. U.S. motherhouse, 9814 Sylvia Ave., Northridge, CA 91324, (818) 831-9710. Educational work.

Sacred Heart, Society of the, R.S.C.J.: Founded 1800, in France; in U.S., 1818. Generalate, Rome, Italy. U.S. provincial house, 4389 W. Pine Blvd., St. Louis, MO 63108, (314) 652-1500, www.rscj.org. Educational work.

Sacred Heart of Jesus, Apostles of, A.S.C.J.: Founded 1894, in Italy; in U.S., 1902. General motherhouse, Rome, Italy; U.S. motherhouse, 265 Benham St., Hamden, CT 06514, (203) 248-4225, www.ascjus.org. Educational, social work.

Sacred Heart of Jesus, Handmaids of the, A.C.J.: Founded 1877, in Spain. General motherhouse, Rome, Italy; U.S. province, 1242 S. Broad St., Philadelphia, PA 19146, (214) 468-6368. Educational, retreat work.

Sacred Heart of Jesus, Missionary Sisters of the Most (Hiltrup), M.S.C.: Founded 1899, in Germany; in U.S., 1908. General motherhouse, Rome, Italy; U.S. province, 51 Seminary Ave., Reading, PA 19605,

(610) 929-5751. Education, health care, pastoral ministry.

Sacred Heart of Jesus, Oblate Sisters of the, O.S.H.J.: Founded 1894; in U.S., 1949. General motherhouse, Rome, Italy; U.S. headquarters, 50 Warner Rd., Hubbard, OH 44425, (330) 759-9329, www.oblatesister.com. Educational, social work.

Sacred Heart of Jesus, Servants of the Most, S.S.C.J.: Founded 1894, in Poland; in U.S., 1959. General motherhouse, Cracow, Poland; U.S. address, 866 Cambria St., Cresson, PA 16630, (814) 886-4223, www.nb.net/~sscjusa. Education, health care, social services.

Sacred Heart of Jesus, Sisters of the, S.S.C.J.: Founded 1816, in France; in U.S., 1903. General motherhouse, St. Jacut, Brittany, France; U.S. provincial house, 11931 Radium St., San Antonio, TX 78216, (210) 344-7203. Educational, hospital, domestic work.

Sacred Heart of Jesus and of the Poor, Servants of the (Mexican), S.S.H.J.P.: Founded 1885, in Mexico; in U.S., 1907. General motherhouse, Apartado 92, Puebla, Mexico; U.S. address, 3310 S. Zapata Hwy, Laredo, TX 78043, (956) 723-3343.

Sacred Heart of Jesus and Our Lady of Guadalupe, Missionaries of the, M.S.C.Gpe.: U.S. address, 1212 E. Euclid Ave., Arlington Heights, IL 60004, (708) 398-1350.

Sacred Heart of Jesus for Reparation, Congregation of the Handmaids of the, A.R.: Founded 1918, in Italy; in U.S., 1958. U.S. address, 36 Villa Dr., Steubenville, OH 43953, (740) 282-3801.

Sacred Heart of Mary, Religious of the, R.S.H.M.: Founded 1848, in France; in U.S., 1877. Generalate, Rome, Italy. U.S. provinces; 50 Wilson Park Dr., Tarrytown, NY 10591, (914) 631-8872, www.rshm.org; 441 N. Garfield Ave., Montebello, CA 90640, (323) 887-8821, www.rshm.org.

Sacred Hearts and of Perpetual Adoration, Sisters of the, SS.CC.: Founded 1797, in France; in U.S., 1908. General motherhouse, Rome, Italy; U.S. provinces: 1120 Fifth Ave., Honolulu, Hawaii 96816, (808) 737-5822 (Pacific); 35 Huttleston Ave., Fairhaven, MA 02719, (508) 994-9341 (East Coast). Varied ministries.

Sacred Hearts of Jesus and Mary, Sisters of the, S.H.J.M.: Established 1953, in U.S. General motherhouse, Essex, England; U.S. address, 2150 Lake Shore Ave., Oakland CA 94606, (510) 832-2935.

Savior, Company of the, C.S.: Founded 1952, in Spain; in U.S., 1962. General motherhouse, Madrid, Spain; U.S. foundation, 820 Clinton Ave., Bridgeport, CT 06604, (203) 368-1875.

Savior, Sisters of the Divine, S.D.S.: Founded 1888, in Italy; in U.S., 1895. General motherhouse, Rome, Italy; U.S. province, 4311 N. 100th St., Milwaukee, WI 53222, (414) 466-0810. Educational, hospital work.

Social Service, Sisters of, S.S.S.: Founded in Hungary, 1923, by Sr. Margaret Slachta. U.S. generalate, 296 Summit Ave., Buffalo, NY 14214, (716) 834-0197. Social work.

Social Service, Sisters of, of Los Angeles, S.S.S.: Founded 1908, in Hungary; in U.S., 1926. General motherhouse, 2303 S. Figueroa Way, Los Angeles, CA 90007, (213) 746-2117.

Teresa of Jesus, Society of St., S.T.J.: Founded

1876, in Spain; in U.S., 1910. General motherhouse, Rome, Italy; U.S. provincial house, 18080 St. Joseph's Way, Covington, LA 70435, (985) 893-1470, www.teresians.org.

Thomas of Villanova, Congregation of Sisters of St., S.S.T.V.: Founded 1661, in France; in U.S., 1948. General motherhouse, Neuilly-sur-Seine, France; U.S. foundation, W. Rocks Rd., Norwalk, CT 06851, (203) 847-2885.

Trinity, Missionary Servants of the Most Blessed, M.S.B.T.: Founded 1912, in U.S., by Very Rev. Thomas A. Judge. General motherhouse, 3501 Solly Ave., Philadelphia, PA 19136, (215) 335-7550, www.msbt.org. Educational, social work, health services.

Trinity, Sisters Oblates to the Blessed, O.B.T.: Founded 1923, in Italy. U.S. novitiate, Beekman Rd., P.O. Box 98, Hopewell Junction, NY 12533, (914) 226-5671.

Trinity, Sisters of the Most Holy, O.Ss.T.: Founded 1198, in Rome; in U.S., 1920. General motherhouse, Rome, Italy; U.S. address, Immaculate Conception Province, 21281 Chardon Rd., Euclid, OH 44117, (216) 481-8232, www.srstrinity.org. Educational work.

Trinity, Society of Our Lady of the Most Holy, S.O.L.T.: Motherhouse, P.O. Box 189 Skidmore, TX 78389, (361) 287-3256.

Ursula of the Blessed Virgin, Society of the Sisters of St., S.U.: Founded 1606, in France; in U.S., 1902. General motherhouse, France; U.S. novitiate, 50 Linnwood Rd., Rhinebeck, NY 12572, (845) 876-2557, www.sistersofstursula.com. Educational work.

Ursuline Nuns (Roman Union), O.S.U.: Founded 1535, in Italy; in U.S., 1727. Generalate, Rome, Italy. U.S. provinces: 323 E. 198th St., Bronx, NY 10458, (718) 365-7410; 210 Glennon Heights Rd., Crystal City, MO 63019, (636) 937-6206, www.osu central.org; 639 Angela Dr., Santa Rosa, CA 95401, (707) 545-6811; 45 Lowder St., Dedham, MA 02026, (781) 326-6219.

Ursuline Sisters of Mount Saint Joseph, O.S.U.: Founded 1535, in Italy; in U.S., 1727, in New Orleans. U.S. motherhouses: 20860 St, Rte. 251, St. Martin, OH 45118-9705, (513) 875-2020; 901 E. Miami St., Paola, KS 66071, (913) 557-2349; 3105 Lexington Rd., Louisville, KY 40206, (502) 896-3914, www.ursulineslou.org; 2600 Lander Rd., Cleveland, OH. 44124, (440) 449-1200, www.ursuline sisters.org; 8001 Cummings Rd., Maple Mount, KY 42356-9999, (270) 229-4103, www.ursulinesmsj.org; 4045 Indian Rd., Toledo, OH 43606, (419) 536-9587, www.toledoursulines.org; 4250 Shields Rd., Canfield, OH 44406, (330) 792-7636; 1339 E. McMillan St., Cincinnati, OH 45206, (513) 961-3410.

Ursuline Sisters of the Congregation of Tildonk, Belgium, O.S.U.: Founded 1535, in Italy; Tildonk congregation, 1832; in U.S., 1924. Generalate, Brussels, Belgium; U.S. address, 81-15 Utopia Parkway, Jamaica, NY 11432, (718) 591-0681, www.tres sy.tripod.com. Educational, foreign mission work.

Ursuline Sisters of Belleville, O.S.U.: Founded 1535, in Italy; in U.S., 1910; established as diocesan community, 1983. Central house, 1026 N. Douglas Ave., Belleville, IL 62220, (618) 235-3444. Educational work.

Venerini Sisters, Religious, M.P.V.: Founded 1685,

in Italy; in U.S., 1909. General motherhouse, Rome, Italy; U.S. provincialate; 23 Edward St., Worcester, MA 01605, (508) 754-1020, www.venerinisisters.org.

Vietnamese Adorers of the Holy Cross, M.T.G.: Founded 1670 in Vietnam; in U.S. 1976. General motherhouse 7408 S.E. Adler, Portland, OR 97215, (503) 254-3284.

Vincent de Paul, Sisters: *See* **Charity of St. Vincent de Paul, Sisters of.**

Visitation Nuns, V.H.M.: Founded 1610, in France; in U.S. (Georgetown, DC), 1799. Contemplative, educational work. Two federations in U.S.

• First Federation of North America. Major pontifical enclosure. Pres., Mother Mary Jozefa Kowalewski, Monastery of the Visitation, 2055 Ridgedale Dr., Snellville, GA 30078, (770) 972-1060. Addresses of monasteries belonging to the federation: 2300 Springhill Ave., Mobile, AL 36607, (251) 473-2321; Beach Rd., Tyringham, MA 01264, (413) 243-3995; 12221 Bievenue Rd, Rockville, VA 23146, (804) 749-4885; 5820 City Ave., Philadelphia, PA 19131, (215) 473-5888; 1745 Parkside Blvd., Toledo, OH 43607, (419) 536-1343; 2055 Ridgedale Dr., Snellville, GA 30078-2443, (770) 972-1060.

• Second Federation of North America. Constitutional enclosure. Pres., Sr. Anne Madeleine Godefroy, Monastery of the Visitation, 3020 N. Ballas Rd., St. Louis, MO 63131, (314) 432-5353, www.visitation monastery.org/stlouis. Addresses of monasteries belonging to the federation: 1500 35th St., Washington, DC 20007, (202) 337-0305; 3020 N. Ballas Rd., St. Louis, MO 63131, (314) 432-5353; 200 E. Second St., Frederick, MD 21701, (301) 622-3322; Mt. de Chantal Monastery of the Visitation, 410 Washington Ave., Wheeling, WV 26003, (304) 232-1283; 8902 Ridge Blvd., Brooklyn, NY 11209, (718) 745-5151, www.visitationsisters.org; 2455 Visitation Dr., Mendota Heights, MN 55120, (651) 683-1700.

Visitation of the Congregation of the Immaculate Heart of Mary, Sisters of the, S.V.M.: Founded 1952, in U.S. Motherhouse, 2950 Kaufmann Ave., Dubuque, IA 52001, (319) 556-2440. Educational work, parish ministry.

Vocationist Sisters (Sisters of the Divine Vocations), S.V.D.: Founded 1921, in Italy; in U.S., 1967 General motherhouse, Naples, Italy; U.S. foundation, Perpetual Help Nursery, 172 Broad St., Newark, NJ 07104, (973) 484-3535.

Wisdom, Daughters of, D.W.: Founded 1703, in France, by St. Louis Marie Grignion de Montfort; in U.S., 1904. General motherhouse, Vendee, France; U.S. province, 385 Ocean Ave., Islip, NY 11751, (631) 277-2660. Education, health care, parish ministry, social services.

Xaverian Missionary Society of Mary, Inc., X.M.M.: Founded 1945, in Italy; in U.S., 1954. General motherhouse, Parma, Italy; U.S. address, 242 Salisbury St., Worcester, MA 01609, (508) 757-0514.

MEMBERSHIP OF RELIGIOUS INSTITUTES OF WOMEN

(Principal source: Annuario Pontificio. Statistics as of Jan. 1, 2003, unless indicated otherwise.) Listed below are world membership statistics of institutes of women with 500 or more members. Numbers in parentheses reflect the number of houses. For statistical information of institutes in the United States, see Statistics.

Salesian Srs. (1,559)	15,703
Calced Carmelites (870)	12,037
Claretians (566)	8,063
Franciscan Mission. of Mary (826)	7,555
Franciscan Clarist Congr. (605)	6,792
Carmel, Srs. of the Mother of (576)	6,275
Mercy of the Americas, Srs. of (2,221)	5,208
Benedictine Nuns (245)	4,778
Charity, Mission of (673)	4,690
Holy Cross, Srs. of Mercy of the (455)	4,524
Notre Dame, School Srs. of (654)	4,495
Ador. of the Bl. Sacrament. (427)	4,272
Paul of Chartres, Srs. of St. (543)	3,981
Holy Spirit, Mission Servants of the (405)	3,678
Dominicans (225)	3,567
Sacred Heart Congregation. (389)	3,409
Sacred Heart of Jesus "Sophie Barat," Society of the (446)	3,394
Charity of St. Joan Antida, Srs. of (440)	3,330
Canossian Daught. of Charity (363)	3,311
Srs. of Mercy, Cong. of the (552)	3,068
Joseph, Srs. of St. (Cluny) (419)	3,060
Dominicans of the Presentation of the Virgin (419)	3,005
Ancianos Desamparados, Hermanitas de los (209)	2,632
Paul, Daught. of St. (256)	2,628
Anne, Srs. of Charity of St.	2,568
Ursulines of the Roman Union (259)	2,559
Notre Dame, Srs. of (288)	2,542
Visitandine Nuns (146)	2,494
Holy Family, Srs. of the (Bordeaux) (337)	2,405
Joseph Benedetto, Srs. of St. (151)	2,319
Claretian Capuchins (157)	2,301
Carmelites of Charity of Vedruna (307)	2,275
Wisdom, Daught. of (317)	2,256
Cross, Srs. of the (Swiss) (276)	2,250
Felician Srs. (262)	2,190
B.V.M., Inst. of the (English) (241)	2,188
Concezioniste (Franciscan Concessionists) (162)	2,121
Joseph, Srs. of St. (Chambéry) (337)	2,107
Franciscans of the Penance and Christian Charity (253)	2,058
Holy Savior, Srs. of the (215)	2,013
Notre Dame de Namur, Srs. of (287)	1,975
Joseph, Srs. of St. (Carondolet) (691)	1,970
Mission. Carmelites (265)	1,896
Mary, Minister of the Infirm, Servants of (121)	1,886
Adorers of the Blood of Christ (359)	1,882
Elizabeth, Srs. of St. (236)	1,859
Mercy of Australia, Inst. of Srs. (487)	1,820
Mary Our Lady, Company of (221)	1,814

Comboni Missionary Srs. (228) 1,803
Teresa of Jesus, Society of St. (217) 1,742
Holy Family Srs. (198) 1,730
Heart of Mary, Soc. of Daught. of (148) 1,730
Franciscan Hospitallers
    of the Immaculate Conception (188) 1,660
Dorothy, Srs. of St. (179) 1,657
Cistercian Nuns (Strict Observance) (65) 1,655
Anne, Daught. of Saint (257) 1,639
Jesus and Mary, Religious of (216) 1,632
Holy Family of Nazareth, Srs. of (155) 1,611
Holy Spirit, Daught. of the (216) 1,606
Holy Names of Jesus and Mary,
    Srs. of the (164) 1,581
Sacred Heart of Jesus, Apostles of (207) 1,581
Presentation of Mary, Srs. of the (196) 1,570
Notre Dame, Srs. of the Cong. of (173) 1,560
Franciscans of George the Martyr (174) 1,558
Divine Providence,
    Srs. of (St. Maurice) (252) 1,557
Jesus, Daught. of
    (St. Joseph of Kermaria) (220) 1,483
Divine Master, Pious Disciples of (175) 1,469
Adorers of the Blessed
    Sacrament and Charity (169) 1,457
Mary Immaculate, Religious of 1,452
Sacred Heart of Jesus, Ancelle (141) 1,436
Immaculate Conception,
    Little Srs. of the (239) 1,423
Capuchin Tertiaries of the
    Holy Family (229) 1,407
Jesus, Mary, and Joseph, Society of (143) ... 1,402
Infirm of St. Francis, Srs. of (138) 1,393
Cross, Srs. of the (193) 1,357
Charity of Jesus and Mary, Srs. of (177) 1,351
School Srs. of St. Francis
    of Milwaukee (201) 1,316
Destitute, Srs. of the (185) 1,299
Assumption, Religious of (175) 1,284
Anne, Srs. of Saint (164) 1,283
Salesian Missionaries
    of Mary Immaculate (155) 1,274
Dorothy of Frassinetti, Srs. of St. (165) 1,248
Hospitallers of the
    Sacred Heart of Jesus (118) 1,238
Joseph, Srs. of St. (Philadelphia) (157) 1,201
Claretian (Urban) (88) 1,201
Jesus, Daught. of (Salamanca) (153) 1,197
Little Flower of Bethany, Srs. of the (133) 1,197
Franciscans of the
    Immaculate Conception (144) 1,194
Franciscans of the Family of Mary (147) 1,190
Assumption, Little Srs. of the (175) 1,183
Immaculate Heart of Mary (105) 1,180
Teresian Carmelites of Verapoly (128) 1,176
Sacred Heart of Jesus,
    Daught. of Charity of the (189) 1,165
Joseph, Inst. of Srs. of St. (253) 1,152
Elizabethan Francsicans (127) 1,151
Providence, Srs. of (118) 1,129
Caritas Srs. of Miyazaki (177) 1,117
Immaculate Conception,
    Srs. of Charity (129) 1,094
Our Lady of Africa, Mission. Srs. of (157) 1,093
Joseph of the Sacred Heart of Jesus,
    Srs. of St. (317) 1,079
Servants of Mary,

Srs. of Our Lady of Sorrows (146) 1,062
Mary, Mother of Mercy, Daught. of (173) ... 1,050
Our Lady of Mercy, Daught. of (142) 1,049
Benedictine Srs.,
    Fed. of St. Scholastica (22) 1,047
Franciscan Srs. of Dillingen (100) 1,042
Dominican Srs. of the Rosary (276) 1,031
Cistercian Nuns, O. Cist. (25) 1,028
Benedictine Srs., Federation of
    St. Gertrude the Great (18) 1,025
Sacramentines (Perp. Ador. of the Blessed
    Sacrament) (62) 1,012
Holy Family, Little Srs. of the (148) 1,008
Sacred Heart of Mary Virgin Immaculate,
    Srs. of the (153) 1,004
Joseph, Srs. of St. (Lyon) (160) 1,004
Cross and Passion,
    Srs. of the (Passionist Srs.) (147) 996
Joseph of the Apparition, Srs. of St. (160) 988
Sacred Heart of Jesus, Mission. Srs. (144) 981
Mary Immaculate of Catherine of Siena (162) .. 980
Vincent de Paul, Srs. of Charity of (125) 972
Franciscan Srs. (Pondicherry) (171) 970
Precious Blood, Mission. Srs. of the (95) 952
Our Lady of the Missions, Srs. of (235) 952
Poor of the Inst. Palazzolo, Srs. of the (124) .. 949
Sacramentine Srs. (117) 928
Immaculate Heart
    of Mary, Mission. Srs. (131) 927
Mary Immaculate of the B.V.M. (136) 925
B.V.M., Institute of the
    (Dame Inglesi, Irlandesi) (136) 923
Holy Cross and Seven Dolors, Srs. of the (67) .. 918
Jesus Crucified, Missionary Srs. of (173) 911
Cross, Daught. of, of Liege (108) 910
Mary Reparatrix, Society of (107) 909
Love of God, Srs. of the (124) 909
Our Lady of the Apostles,
    Missionary Srs. of (130) 897
Consolata Missionary Srs. (135) 894
Baptistine Srs., Srs.
    of St. John the Baptist (110) 889
Immaculate, Mission. of (103) 884
Ursulines of Tildonk (100) 882
Benedictine Srs., Fed. of St. Benedict (12) 877
Charity, Little Mission. Srs. of (117) 877
Ursulines of the Sacred Heart of Jesus (99) ... 871
Mary Immaculate, Srs. of the B.V.M. (166) 868
Franciscans Third Order Regular (56) 866
Clarist Franciscan Mission. (133) 863
Anne, Daught. of Saint (Ranchi) (111) 859
Carmelite Srs. of St. Teresa (112) 859
Maria Santissima dell'Orto, Figlie (129) 857
Charles Borromeo, Srs. of Charity of (95) 842
Enfant-Jesus, Soeurs de l' (163) 838
Immaculate Heart of Mary,
    Mother of Christ (116) 836
Anne de Lachine, Srs. of Saint (76) 830
Sacred Heart
    of Jesus and Mary, Srs. of (137) 830
Jesus Christ, Poor Srs. of (107) 819
Immaculate Conception of the B.V.M. (117) 817
Franciscan Mission. of Mary, Auxiliatrix (121) ... 815
Mary Help of Christians, Mission. Srs. (122) 814
Franciscan Mission. of Baby Jesus (102) 808
Christian Charity of the B.V.M,
    Srs. of (Paderborn) (85) 802

ORGANIZATIONS OF RELIGIOUS

Conferences

Conferences of major superiors of religious institutes, dating from the 1950s, are encouraged by the Code of Canon Law (Code 708) "so that joining forces they can work toward the achievement of the purpose of their individual institutes more fully, transact common business and foster suitable coordination and cooperation with conferences of bishops and also with individual bishops." Statutes of the conferences must be approved by the Holy See "by which alone they are erected" (Canon 709). Conferences have been established in 24 countries of Europe, 14 in North and Central America, 10 in South America, 35 in Africa and 19 in Asia and Oceania.

Listed below are U.S. and international conferences.

Conference of Major Superiors of Men: Founded in 1956; canonically established Sept. 12, 1957. Membership, 269 major superiors representing institutes with a combined membership of approximately 24,000. Pres., Fr. Canice Connors, O.F.M. Conv.; executive director, Rev. Ted Keating, S.M. National office: 8808 Cameron St., Silver Spring, MD 20910, (301) 588-4030.

Leadership Conference of Women Religious: Founded in 1956; canonically established Dec. 12, 1959. Membership, nearly 1,000 (Dec. 31, 1996), representing approximately 400 religious institutes. Pres., Sr. Mary Ann Zollman, B.V.M.; Constance Phelps, SCL vice president/president elect; executive director, Sister Carole Shinnick, SSND. National office: 8808 Cameron St., Silver Spring, MD 20910, (301) 588-4955, www.lcwr.org.

Council of Major Superiors of Women Religious: Canonically erected June 13, 1992. Membership, 141 superiors of 103 religious congregations. Chairperson, Sister Mary McGreevy, R.S.M. National office: P.O. Box 4467, Washington, DC 20017-0467, (202) 832-2575, www.cmswr.org.

International Union of Superiors General (Women): Established Dec. 8, 1965; approved, 1967. General secretary, Sister Rita Burley, A.C.I. Address: Piazza Ponte S. Angelo, 28, 00186, Rome, Italy, 06-684-00-20.

Union of Superiors General (Men): Established in 1957. President, Father Alvaro Echeverria, F.S.C.; general secretary, Bro. Lino Da Campo, F.S.F. Address: Via dei Penitenzieri 19, 00193 Rome, Italy, 06-686-82-29.

Latin American Confederation of Religious (Confederacion Latinoamericana de Religiosos — CLAR): Established in 1959; statutes reformed in 1984. President, Sr. Margarita Fagot Carmen, R.S.C.J.; secretary general, Sr. Lurdes Cascho, C.F. Address: Calle 64 No 10-45, Piso 5°, Apartado Aéreo 56804, Santafé de Bogotá, D.C., Colombia, (91) 31-00-481-21-57-774, www.clar.org.

Union of European Conferences of Major Superiors (UCESM): Established Dec. 25, 1983. Permanent secretary, P. Jesús Maria Lecea Sainz, S.P. Rue de Pascal 4, B-1040, Bruxelles, Belgium, 02-230-86-22.

Other Organizations

Institute on Religious Life (1974). To foster more effective understanding and implementation of teachings of the Church on religious life, promote vocations to religious life and the priesthood, and promote growth in sanctity of all the faithful according to their state in life. Pres., Bishop Thomas Doran. National office, P.O. Box 410007, Chicago, IL 60641, (773) 267-1195, www.religiouslife.com. Publishes *Religious Life* magazine and *Consecrated Life* periodical.

Religious Brothers Conference (1972): To publicize the unique vocations of brothers, to further communication among brothers and provide liaison with various organizations of the Church. Executive secretary, Br. Kenneth Pfister, F.S.C. National office, 1337 West Ohio, Chicago, IL 60622, (312) 829-8525, www.brothersonline.org.

National Black Sisters' Conference (1968): Black Catholic women religious and associates networking to provide support through prayer, study, solidarity and programs. President, Sr. Patricia Chappell, SNDdeN. Address: 3027 4th Street, N.E., Washington, DC 20017, (202) 529-9250.

National Conference of Vicars for Religious (1967): National organization of diocesan officials concerned with relations between their respective dioceses and religious communities engaged therein. President, Sr. Therese Sullivan, S.P., 9292 Broadway, Merrillville, IN 46410; secretary, Eymard Flood, O.S.C. Address: 2811 East Villareal Dr., P.O. Box 14195, Orange, CA, 92863-1595.

National Religious Vocation Conference (NRVC) (1988, with merger of National Sisters Vocation Conference and National Conference of Religious Vocation Directors.) Service organization of men and women committed to the fostering and discernment of vocations. Executive director, Paul Bednarczyk, C.S.C. Address: 5420 S. Cornell, #105, Chicago, IL 60615, (773) 363-5454, www.nrvc.net.

Religious Formation Conference (1953): Originally the Sister Formation Conference; membership includes women and men Religious and non-canonical groups. Facilitates the ministry of formation, both initial and ongoing, in religious communities. Executive director, Sister Janet Mock, C.S.J. National office: 8820 Cameron St., Silver Spring, MD 20910-4152, (301) 588-4938, www.relforcon.org.

SECULAR INSTITUTES

(*Sources*: Catholic Almanac *survey; United States Conference of Secular Institutes*; Annuario Pontificio.)

Secular institutes are societies of men and women living in the world who dedicate themselves to observe the evangelical counsels and to carry on apostolic works suitable to their talents and opportunities in the areas of their everyday life.

"Secular institutes are not religious communities but they carry with them in the world a profession of evangelical counsels which is genuine and complete, and recognized as such by the Church. This profession confers a consecration on men and women, laity and clergy, who reside in the world. For this reason they should chiefly strive for total self-dedication to God, one inspired by perfect charity. These institutes should preserve their proper and particular character, a secular one, so that they may everywhere measure up successfully to that apostolate which they were designed to exercise, and which is both in the world and, in a sense, of the world" ("Decree on the Appropriate Renewal of Religious Life," No. 11; Second Vatican Council).

Secular institutes are under the jurisdiction of the Congregation for Institutes of Consecrated Life and Societies of Apostolic Life. General legislation concerning them is contained in Canons 710 to 730 of the Code of Canon Law.

A secular institute reaches maturity in several stages. It begins as an association of the faithful, technically called a pious union, with the approval of a local bishop. Once it has proved its viability, he can give it the status of an institute of diocesan right, in accordance with norms and permission emanating from the Congregation for Institutes of Consecrated Life and Societies of Apostolic Life. On issuance of a separate decree from this congregation, an institute of diocesan right becomes an institute of pontifical right.

Secular institutes, which originated in the latter part of the 18th century, were given full recognition and approval by Pius XII Feb. 2, 1947, in the apostolic constitution *Provida Mater Ecclesia*. On Mar. 25 of the same year a special commission for secular institutes was set up within the Congregation for Religious. Institutes were commended and confirmed by Pius XII in a *motu proprio* of Mar. 12, 1948, and were the subject of a special instruction issued a week later, Mar. 19, 1948.

The World Conference of Secular Institutes (CMIS) was approved by the Vatican May 23, 1974. Address: Via Tullio Levi-Civita 5, 00146 Rome, Italy.

The United States Conference of Secular Institutes (USCSI) was established following the organization of the World Conference of Secular Institutes in Rome. Its membership is open to all canonically erected secular institutes with members living in the United States. The conference was organized to offer secular institutes an opportunity to exchange experiences, to do research in order to help the Church carry out its mission, and to search for ways and means to make known the existence of secular institutes in the U.S. Address: P.O. Box 4556, 12th St. N.E., Washington, DC 20017, (262) 547-7733, www.secularinstitutes.org. Pres., Carol Winkler.

Institutes in the U.S.

Apostolic Oblates: Founded in Rome, Italy, 1947; established in the U.S., 1962; for women. Approved as a secular institute of pontifical right Dec. 8, 1994. Addresses: 2125 W. Walnut Ave., Fullerton, CA 92633; 6762 Western Ave., Omaha, NE 68132, (402) 553-4418; 730 E. 87th St., Brooklyn, NY 11236-3621, (718) 649-0324, www.prosanctity.org.

Apostolic Sodales: Founded in Rome, Italy, 1992 by Bp. Guglielmo; for priests. Established to promote a spirit of fraternity among diocesan priests gathered around their bishop in docile availability in the two-fold universal vocation — the call to holiness and brotherhood. Address: Rev. Michael F. Murphy, 655 C. Ave. Coronado, CA 92118-2299, (619) 435-3167.

Caritas Christi: Originated in Marseilles, 1937; for women. Established as a secular institute of pontifical right Mar. 19, 1955. Address: P.O. Box 5162, River Forest, IL 60305. International membership.

Catechists of the Heart of Jesus (Ukrainian): Founded in Parana, Brazil, 1940, by Christoforo Myaskiv, OSBM; approved as Secular Institute of Pontifical Right, 1971; for women. Established for religious instruction, to assist clerics in missionary work, to help the Church, and to maintain the Ukrainian rite and culture. Address: 161 Glenbrook Rd., Stamford, CT 06902.

Company of St. Paul: Originated in Milan, Italy, 1920; for lay people and priests. Approved as a secular institute of pontifical right June 30, 1950. Address: Rev. Stuart Sandberg, 52 Davis Ave., White Plains, NY 10605.

Crusaders of St. Mary: Founded 1947 in Madrid, Spain; approved as a secular institute of diocesan right, 1988; for men. Address: 2001 Great Falls St., McLean, VA 22101, (703) 536-3546.

Diocesan Laborer Priests: Founded 1885 in Spain; approved as a secular institute of pontifical right, 1952. The specific aim of the institute is the promotion, sustenance and cultivation of apostolic, religious and priestly vocations. Address: Rev. Rutilio J. del Riego, 3706 15th St. N.E., Washington, DC 20017, (202) 832-4217.

Don Bosco Volunteers: Founded 1917 by Bl. Philip Rinaldi; for women. Approved as a secular institute of pontifical right Aug. 5, 1978. Follow spirituality and charism of St. John Bosco. Address: Cathy Sylvester, Don Bosco Volunteers, P.O. Box 588, Hawthorne, NJ 07507, www.secularinstitutes.org/dby.html.

Don Bosco Institute: Founded in Rome on Sept. 12, 1994, by Fr. Egidio Viganó, rector major of the Salesians of Don Bosco, for celibate men. Recognized as public association of the faithful on May 24, 1998, by Cardinal Ignacio Velasco Garcia, Abp. of Caracas, Venezuela. The association, which follows the spirit and charism of St. John Bosco, intends to become established juridically as a secular institute. Address: P.O. Box 639, New Rochelle, NY 10802-0639, www.secularinstitutes.org/a-dbi.htm.

Family of Mary of the Visitation: Founded in Vietnam, 1976. Approved as a Secular Institute of Diocesan Right; intended to promote faith-filled vowed women, to help people protect their faith and to meet social needs. Address: Therese Chan Ngo, P.O. Box 441, Westminster, CA 92684.

Fr. Kolbe Missionaries of the Immaculata: Founded in Bologna, Italy, in 1954, by Fr. Luigi Faccenda, O.F.M. Conv.; for women. Approved as a secular institute of pontifical right Mar. 25, 1992. Live the fullness of baptismal consecration, strive for perfect charity and promote the knowledge and veneration of Mary. Address: 531 E. Merced Ave., West Covina, CA 91790, (626) 917-0040.

Handmaids of Divine Mercy: Founded in Bari, Italy, 1951; for women. Approved as an institute of pontifical right 1972. Address: 2410 Hughes Ave., Bronx, NY 10458, (718) 295-3770.

Holy Family Institute (aggregated to the Society of St. Paul): Founded by Fr. James Alberione in 1963 for married couples who wish to commit themselves to seeking evangelical perfection in marriage; definitively approved by the Holy See, 1993. First Americans professed, 1988. Address: 9531 Akron-Canfield Rd., Box 498, Canfield, OH 44406.

Institute of Secular Missionaries: Founded in Vitoria, Spain, 1939; for women. Approved as a secular institute, 1955. Address: 2710 Ruberg Ave., Cincinnati, OH 45211. Attn.: E. Dilger.

Institute of the Heart of Jesus (Men): Originated in France Feb. 2, 1791; restored Oct. 29, 1918; for diocesan priests and laity. Received final approval from the Holy See as a secular institute of pontifical right Feb. 2, 1952. U.S. address, Rev. William S. Whelan, Conception Seminary College, Conception, MO 64433, (660) 944-3100.

Institute of the Heart of Jesus (Women): Foundation stems from the Institute of the Heart of Jesus which originated in France Feb. 2, 1791. Established to help lay women live the Gospel radically in the modern world by means of the evangelical counsels, to engage in group discernment and various forms of prayer. Address, Diana Bland, 417 N. Buena Vista St., Burbank, CA 91505-3208.

Jesu Caritas Fraternity: Founded in France, 1952. Approved as a Secular Institute of Diocesan Right, 1996. Established to form members in the contemplative tradition of Brother Charles de Foucauld, bringing God's love especially to his most neglected children; members strive in their daily life to live the Gospel message. Address: Mary D. Christensen, P.O. Box 92, Yonkers, N.Y. 10704.

Mission of Our Lady of Bethany: Founded in France, 1948; for women. Approved as a secular institute of diocesan right, 1965. Address: Estelle Nichols, 109 Rollins Rd., Nottingham, NH 03290; P.O. Box 807, Boston, MA 02130.

Missionaries of the Kingship of Christ the King: Under this title are included three distinct and juridically separate institutes founded by Agostino Gemelli, O.F.M. (1878-1959) and Armida Barelli (1882-1952). Two are active in the U.S.

• **Women Missionaries of the Kingship of Christ**: Founded in 1919, in Italy; definitively approved as an institute of pontifical right 1953. U.S. branch established 1950.

• **Men Missionaries of the Kingship of Christ**: Founded 1928, in Italy, as an institute of diocesan right. U.S. branch established 1962.

Addresses: Rev. Dominic Monti, O.F.M., Spiritual Assistant, 10400 Lorain Ave., Silver Spring, MD 20901 (for Men Missionaries); Rev. Dominic Monti, O.F.M., 10400 Lorain Ave., Silver Spring, MD, 20901 (for Women Missionaries); (301) 593-4479, www.simkc.org.

Nuestra Señora de la Altagracia: Founded in Dominican Republic, 1956; approved as a secular institute of diocesan right, 1964; for women. Address: Ms. Christiana Perez, 129 Van Siclen Ave., Brooklyn, NY 11207.

Oblate Missionaries of Mary Immaculate: Founded, 1952; approved as a secular institute of pontifical right 1984; for women. Address: Oblate Missionaries of Mary Immaculate, P.O. Box 764, Lowell, MA 01853, www.ommi-is.org.

Opus Spiritus Sancti: Originated in West Germany, 1952; for diocesan priests and unmarried permanent deacons. Formally acknowledged by Rome as a secular institute of diocesan right, 1977. Address: Rev. James McCormick, 421 E. Bluff St., Carroll, IA 51401-3099, (712) 792-4386.

Schoenstatt Sisters of Mary: Originated in Schoenstatt, Germany, 1926; for women. Established as a secular institute of diocesan right May 20, 1948; of pontifical right Oct. 18, 1948. Addresses: W. 284 N. 404 Cherry Lane, Waukesha, WI 53188, (262) 542-4384; House Schoenstatt, 134 Front St., Rockport, TX 78382, (361) 729-2019.

Secular Institute of Pius X: Originated in Manchester, NH, 1940; for priests and laymen. Approved as a secular institute, 1959. Also admits married couples and unmarried men as associate members. Addresses: C.P. 7731, Charlesbourg, QC G1G 5W6, Canada, (418) 626-5881.

Secular Institute of Schoenstatt Fathers: Founded in Germany by Fr. Joseph Kentenich in 1965; for priests serving the International Schoenstatt Movement in over 20 countries. Approved as a secular institute of pontifical right, June 24, 1988. Address: W. 284 N. 746 Cherry Lane, Waukesha, WI 53188, (262) 548-9061.

Secular Institute of St. Francis de Sales: Founded in Vienna, Austria, 1940; for women. Pontifical right, 1964. Address: Thérèse Keyes, Dir., 87 Gerrish Ave., T2, East Haven, CT 06512, (203) 469-3277, www.secularinstitutes.org/sfs.ht.

Society of Our Lady of the Way: Originated, 1936; for women. Approved as a secular institute of pontifical right Jan. 3, 1953. Address: 2339 N. Catalina, Los Angeles, CA 90027, (323) 665-0333, www.execpc.com/uscsi/index.html.

Voluntas Dei Institute: Originated in Canada, 1958, by Father L. M. Parent; for secular priests and laymen (with married couples as associates). Approved as a secular institute of pontifical right, July 12, 1987. Established in 21 countries. Address: Rev. George Hazler, 615 Palm Ave., Los Altos, CA 94022-3953; (650) 917-4519, www.voluntasdeiusa.org.

The *Annuario Pontificio* lists the following secular institutes of pontifical right that are not established in the U.S.:

For men: Christ the King; Institute of Our Lady of Life; Institute of Prado; Priests of the Sacred Heart of Jesus.

For women: Alliance in Jesus through Mary; Apostles of the Sacred Heart; Catechists of Mary, Virgin and Mother; Company of St. Ursula, Cordimarian Filiation; Daughters of the Nativity of Mary; Daughters of the Queen of the Apostles; Daughters of the Sacred Heart; Evangelical Crusade; Faithful Servants of Jesus; Handmaids of Our Mother of Mercy; Institute of Notre Dame du Travail; Institute of Our Lady of Life; Institute of St. Boniface; Little Apostles of Charity.

Life and Peace in Christ Jesus; Missionaries of Royal Priesthood; Missionaries of the Sick; Oblates of Christ the King; Oblates of the Sacred Heart of Jesus; Servants of Jesus the Priest; Servite Secular Institute; Union of the Daughters of God; Workers of Divine Love; Workers of the Cross; Handmaids of Holy Church; Augustinian Auxiliary Missionaries; Heart of Jesus; Apostolic Missionaries of Charity; Combonian Secular Missionaries; Missionaries of the Gospel; Secular Servants of Jesus Christ Priest; Women of Schoenstatt; Missionaries of Infinite Love.

Associations

Association of Mary Help of Christians: Founded by St. John Bosco in Turin, Italy, in 1869, for men and women. Public association of the faithful. Members encourage participation in the liturgical life of the Church, emphasizing frequent reception of the Eucharist and the Sacrament of Reconciliation. They also live and spread devotion to Mary Help of Christians according to the spirit of St. John Bosco. Address: 174 Filors Lane, Stony Point, NY 10980-2645, (845) 947-2200.

Caritas: Originated in New Orleans, 1950; for women. Follow guidelines of secular institutes. Small self-supporting groups who live and work among the poor and oppressed; in Louisiana and Guatemala. Address: Box 308, Abita Springs, LA 70420, (985) 892-4345.

Daughters of Our Lady of Fatima: Originated in Lansdowne, PA, 1949; for women. Received diocesan approval, Jan. 1952. Address: Fatima House, Rolling Hills Rd., Ottsville, PA 18942, (215) 795-0924.

Focolare Movement: Founded in Trent, Italy, in 1943, by Chiara Lubich; for men and women. Approved as an association of the faithful, 1962. It is not a secular institute by statute; however, vows are observed by its totally dedicated core membership of 4,000 who live in small communities called Focolare (Italian word for "hearth") centers. There are 17 resident centers in the U.S. and four in Canada. GEN (New Generation) is the youth organization of the movement. An estimated 75,000 are affiliated with the movement in the U.S. and Canada, 2,000,000 worldwide. Publications include *Living City*, monthly; *GEN II* and *GEN III* for young people and children. Five week-long summer conventions, called "Mariapolis" ("City of Mary"), are held annually. Address for information: 204 Cardinal Rd., Hyde Park, NY 12538, (845) 229-0230 (men's or women's branch), www.rc.net/focolare.

Jesus-Caritas Fraternity of Priests: An international association of diocesan priests who strive to combine an active life with a contemplative calling by their membership in small fraternities. U.S. address for information: Rev. Greg Pawloski, St. Patrick's Church, P.O. Box 96, 126 E. 7th St., Imperial, NE 69033-0096, (308) 882-4995, www.rc.net/org/jesuscaritas.

Franciscan Missionaries of Jesus Crucified: Founded in New York in 1987; separate communities for women and men. Approved as an association of the faithful Jan. 7, 1992. To provide an opportunity for persons with disabilities to live a life of total consecration in the pursuit of holiness in the apostolate of service to the Church and to those who suffer in any way. Address: Louise D. Principe, F.M.J.C., 400 Central Ave., Apt. 3D, Albany, NY 12206, (518) 438-5887.

Madonna House Apostolate: Originated in Toronto, Canada, 1930; for priests and lay persons. Public association of the Christian faithful. Address: Madonna House, Combermere, ON, Canada K0J 1L0, (613) 756-3713, www.madonnahouse.org. Directors General: Jean Fox (women), Albert Osterberger (men), Fr. Robert Pelton (priests). International membership and missions.

Opus Spiritus Sancti: Originated in Germany; for women. An association of the faithful. Address: 20 Washington St., West Warwick, RI 02893, (401) 821-

7661. Attn.: Rev. Msgr. Jacques Plante, Regional Coord., (401) 278-4515.

Pax Christi: Lay institute of men and women dedicated to witnessing to Christ, with special emphasis on service to the poor in Mississippi. Addresses: St. Francis Center, 708 Ave. I, Greenwood, MS 38930; LaVerna House, 2108 Altawoods Blvd., Jackson, MS 39204, (601) 373-4463.

Rural Parish Workers of Christ the King: Founded in 1942; for women. A secular institute of the Archdiocese of St. Louis. Dedicated to the glory of God in service of neighbor, especially in rural areas. Address: Rt. 1, Box 1667, Cadet, MO 63630, (636) 586-5171, www.web.jcn.net/rpwck.

Salesian Cooperators: Founded by St. John Bosco in Turin, Italy, in 1876; for lay men and women and diocesan clergy. A public association of the faithful, members commit themselves to apostolates in the local Church, especially on behalf of the young, in the Salesian spirit and style. Address: P.O. Box 639, New Rochelle, NY 10802-0639. Provincial Coordinator: Lucille Hahn.

Teresian Institute: Founded in Spain 1911 by Pedro Poveda. Approved as an association of the faithful of pontifical right, Jan. 11, 1924. Mailing Address: 3400 S. W. 99th Ave., Miami, FL 33165, (305) 553-8567.

THIRD ORDERS

Third orders (commonly called secular orders) are societies of the faithful living in the world who seek to deepen their Christian life and apostolic commitment in association with and according to the spirit of various religious institutes. The orders are called "third" because their foundation usually followed the establishment of the first and second religious orders with which they are associated.

In addition to the recognized third orders, there are other groups of lay persons with strong ties to religious orders. Relationships of this kind serve the spiritual good of the faithful and also enrich the religious orders in a complementary fashion, with the mutual vitality of prayer in the cloister or convent and action in the marketplace.

Augustine, Third Order Secular of St.: Founded 13th century; approved Nov. 9, 1400.

Carmelites, Lay (Third Order of Our Lady of Mt. Carmel): Rule for laity approved by Pope Nicholas V, Oct. 7, 1452; new statutes, January 1991. Addresses: 8501 Bailey Rd., Darien, IL 60561; P.O. Box 613, Williamston, MA 01267; P.O. Box 27, Tappan, NY 10983-0027, (845) 359-0535. Approximately 270 communities and 10,000 members in the U.S. and Canada.

Carmelites, The Secular Order of Discalced (formerly the Third Order Secular of the Blessed Virgin Mary of Mt Carmel and of St. Teresa of Jesus): Rule based on the Carmelite reform established by St. Teresa and St. John of the Cross, 16th century; approved Mar. 23, 1594. Revised rule approved May 10, 1979. Office of National Secretariat, U.S.A.: P.O. Box 3079, San Jose, CA 95156-3079, (408) 251-1361. Approximately 24,445 members throughout the world; 130 groups/communities and 5,200 members in the U.S. and Canada.

Dominican Laity (formerly known as Third Order of St. Dominic): Founded in the 13th century. Addresses of provincial promoters in the United States: Central Province, 1909 South Ashland Ave.,

Chicago, IL 60608-2994, (312) 666-3244, www.op.org/domcentral; Eastern Province, 487 Michigan Ave., N.E., Washington, DC, 20017, (202) 529-5300; Priory of St. Martin de Porres, P.O. Box 12927, Raleigh, NC 27605, (919) 833-1893; Western Province, 2005 Berryman St., Berkeley, CA 94709, (510) 526-4811.

Franciscan Order, Secular (SFO): Founded 1209 by St. Francis of Assisi; approved Aug. 30, 1221. Vocation Director, 37430 Stonegate Circle, Clinton Township, MI 48036, (800) FRANCIS, www.NAFRA-SFO.org. International Secretariate, Via Pomponia Grecina, 31, 00145 Rome. *Tau USA*, quarterly. Approximately 780,000 throughout the world; 18,000 in U.S.

Mary, Third Order of (Marist Laity): Founded, Dec. 8, 1850; rule approved by the Holy See, 1857. Addresses of provincial directors: Marist Laity Center, 1706 Jackson Ave., New Orleans, LA 70113-1510, (504) 524-5192, www.maristsociety.org; Marist Fathers, 27 Isabella St., Boston, MA 02116, (617) 426-4448; Marist Fathers, 2335 Warring St., Berkeley, CA 94704. Approximately 14,000 in world, 5,600 in U.S.

Mary, Secular Order of Servants of (Servite): Founded 1233; approved 1304. Revised rule approved 1995. Address: National Assistant for the Secular Order, 3121 W. Jackson Blvd., Chicago, IL 60612-2729, (773) 638-5800.

Mercy, Secular Third Order of Our Lady of (Mercedarian): Founded 1219 by St. Peter Nolasco; approved the same year.

Norbert, Third Order of St.: Founded 1122 by St. Norbert; approved by Pope Honorius II in 1126.

Oblates of St. Benedict: Lay persons affiliated with a Benedictine abbey or monastery who strive to direct their lives, as circumstances permit, according to the spirit and Rule of St. Benedict.

Trinity, Third Order Secular of the Most: Founded 1198; approved 1219.

Apostolates and Ministries

RIGHTS AND OBLIGATIONS OF ALL THE FAITHFUL

The following rights are listed in Canons 208-223 of the revised Code of Canon Law; additional rights are specified in other canons.
- Because of their baptism and regeneration, there is equality regarding dignity and action for the building up of the Body of Christ.
- They are bound always to preserve communion with the Church.
- According to their condition and circumstances, they should strive to lead a holy life and promote the growth and holiness of the Church.
- They have the right and duty to work for the spread of the divine message of salvation to all peoples of all times and places.
- They are bound to follow with Christian obedience those things which the bishops, as they represent Christ, declare as teachers of the faith or establish as rulers of the Church.
- They have the right to make known their needs, especially their spiritual needs, to pastors of the Church.
- They have the right, and sometimes the duty, of making known to pastors and others of the faithful their opinions about things pertaining to the good of the Church.
- They have the right to receive help from their pastors, from the spiritual goods of the Church and especially from the word of God and the sacraments.
- They have the right to divine worship performed according to prescribed rules of their rite, and to follow their own form of spiritual life in line with the doctrine of the Church.

- They have the right to freely establish and control associations for good and charitable purposes, to foster the Christian vocation in the world, and to hold meetings related to the accomplishment of these purposes.
- They have the right to promote and support apostolic action but may not call it "Catholic" unless they have the consent of competent authority.
- They have a right to a Christian education.
- They have a right to freedom of inquiry in sacred studies, in accordance with the teaching authority of the Church.
- They have a right to freedom in the choice of their state of life.
- No one has the right to harm the good name of another person or to violate his or her right to maintain personal privacy.
- They have the right to vindicate the rights they enjoy in the Church, and to defend themselves in a competent ecclesiastical forum.
- They have the obligation to provide for the needs of the Church, with respect to things pertaining to divine worship, apostolic and charitable works, and the reasonable support of ministers of the Church.
- They have the obligation to promote social justice and to help the poor from their own resources.
- In exercising their rights, the faithful should have regard for the common good of the Church and for the rights and duties of others.
- Church authority has the right to monitor the exercise of rights proper to the faithful, with the common good in view.

RIGHTS AND OBLIGATIONS OF LAY PERSONS

In addition to rights and obligations common to all the faithful and those stated in other canons, lay persons are bound by the obligations and enjoy the rights specified in these canons (224-231).
- Lay persons, like all the faithful, are called by God to the apostolate in virtue of their baptism and confirmation. They have the obligation and right, individually or together in associations, to work for the spread and acceptance of the divine message of salvation among people everywhere; this obligation is more urgent in those circumstances in which people can hear the Gospel and get to know Christ only through them (lay persons).
- They are bound to bring an evangelical spirit to bear on the order of temporal things and to give

Christian witness in carrying out their secular pursuits.
- Married couples are obliged to work for the building up of the people of God through their marital and family life.
- Parents have the most serious obligation to provide for the Christian education of their children according to the doctrine handed down by the Church.
- Lay persons have the same civil liberty as other citizens. In the use of this liberty, they should take care that their actions be imbued with an evangelical spirit. They should attend to the doctrine proposed by the magisterium of the Church but should take care that, in questions of opinion, they

do not propose their own opinion as the doctrine of the Church.

- Qualified lay persons are eligible to hold and perform the duties of ecclesiastical offices open to them in accord with the provisions of law.
- Properly qualified lay persons can assist pastors of the Church as experts and counselors.
- Lay persons have the obligation and enjoy the right to acquire knowledge of doctrine commensurate with their capacity and condition.
- They have the right to pursue studies in the sacred sciences in pontifical universities or facilities and in institutes of religious sciences, and to obtain academic degrees.
- If qualified, they are eligible to receive from ecclesiastical authority a mandate to teach sacred sciences.
- Laymen can be invested by liturgical rite and in a stable manner in the ministries of lector and acolyte.

- Lay persons, by temporary assignment, can fulfill the office of lector in liturgical actions; likewise, all lay persons can perform the duties of commentator or cantor.
- In cases of necessity and in the absence of the usual ministers, lay persons — even if not lectors or acolytes — can exercise the ministry of the word, lead liturgical prayers, confer baptism and distribute Communion, according to the prescripts of law.
- Lay persons who devote themselves permanently or temporarily to the service of the Church are obliged to acquire the formation necessary for carrying out their duties in a proper manner.
- They have a right to remuneration for their service which is just and adequate to provide for their own needs and those of their families; they also have a right to insurance, social security and health insurance.

(*See* **Canon Law** for details on the **Code**.)

DIRECTORY OF LAY GROUPS

In February 2003, the U.S. Conference of Catholic Bishops' Secretariat for Family, Laity, Women and Youth released its 2002-2003 Directory of Lay Movements, Organizations, and Professional Associations. The directory contains listings for more than 100 national lay movements, professional associations, and organizations. Each listing includes a brief description of the group and the name, address, phone number of a contact person, and web/email information if available. The groups listed are national in scope, but

not all are solely lay. Some are included because their work affects the life and mission of the laity and/or because their membership has a significant lay component. The secretariat acknowledges that the listing is a partial one and welcomes suggestions for groups to be included in future editions. Copies are $5.00 each (including postage) and may be ordered from the USCCB Secretariat for Family, Laity, Women, and Youth, 3211 4th St., N.E., Washington, DC 20017; (202) 541-3040 (phone); (202) 541-3176 (fax).

SPECIAL APOSTOLATES AND GROUPS

Apostleship of the Sea (1920, Glasgow, Scotland; 1947 in U.S.): 3211 Fourth St. N.E., Washington, DC 20017 (national office); (202) 541-3226; www.aos-usa.org. An international Catholic organization for the moral, social and spiritual welfare of seafarers and those involved in the maritime industry. Formally instituted by the Holy See in 1952 (apostolic constitution *Exul Familia*), it is a sector of the Pontifical Council for Migrants and Itinerant Peoples. Its norms were updated by Pope John Paul II in a *motu proprio* dated Jan. 31, 1997. The U.S. unit, an affiliate of the USCCB, serves port chaplains in 63 U.S. ports. Nat. Dir., Rev. Fr. John A. Jamnicky.

Apostleship of the Sea of the United States of America (formerly, National Catholic Conference for Seafarers); affiliated with the Apostleship of the Sea in the U.S.: Apostleship of the Sea, 1500 Jefferson Dr., Pt. Arthur, TX 77642; (409) 985-5111. The membership organization of the Roman Catholic ministry to the people of the sea. Inspired by Pope John Paul II's apostolic letter, *Stella Maris*, AOSUSA brings together chaplains, clergy, religious, laity, and mariners in the common interest of promoting the spiritual and social life of the people of the sea. The people of the sea include fishermen, their families, U.S. and foreign mariners, cadets and trainees and those who have retired from sea service. Pres., Fr. Sinclair Oubre, J.C.L.

Auxiliaries of Our Lady of the Cenacle (1878, France): 18 Sycamore Meadow Rd., Sunderland, MA 01375; www.cenaclesisters.org. An association of consecrated Catholic laywomen, under the direction

of the Congregation of Our Lady of the Cenacle. They profess annually the evangelical counsels of celibacy, poverty and obedience and serve God through their own professions and life styles and pursue individual apostolates. Reg. Dir., Dr. Carolyn Jacobs.

Catholic Central Union of America (1855): 3835 Westminster Pl., St. Louis, MO 63108; (314) 371-1653; *Social Justice Review*, bimonthly. One of the oldest Catholic lay organizations in the U.S. and the first given an official mandate for Catholic Action by a committee of the American bishops (1936).

Catholic Medical Mission Board (1928): 10 W. 17th Street, New York, NY 10011-5765; (212) 242-7757; www.cmmb.org. A charitable, non-profit organization dedicated to providing health care supplies and support for the medically disadvantaged in developing and transitional countries. CMMB depends upon the financial generosity of over 25,000 individual donors and through product contributions by major pharmaceutical corporations. In 2002, CMMB delivered more than $97 million in medicines, volunteer medical servies and healthcare programming to 59 countries and responded to emergencies across the globe. New programs include Born to Live, an international effort to prevent mother-to-child transmission of HIV, especially in Africa. The CMMB also placed long and short term volunteers in various countries and provided training of local health care workers. CMMB's medical program includes a placement service for health care specialists who volunteer at Catholic medical facilities in developing countries. Pres., John F. Galbraith.

Catholic Movement for Intellectual and Cultural Affairs: 3025 Fourth St., N.E., Washington, DC, 20017; (202) 269-6672. The U.S. affiliate of *Pax Romana*-ICMICA (*see* **International Catholic Organizations**); *The Notebook*, quarterly. Pres., Joseph Kirchner.

Catholic Network of Volunteer Service (1963; formerly, International Liaison of Lay Volunteers in Mission): 1410 Q. St., N.W., Washington, DC 20009-3808; (202) 332-6000; www.cnvs.org. Membership organization of 235 faith-based volunteer programs, placing persons in all fifty states and 120 countries; *The Response*, annual directory. Exec. Dir., James Lindsay.

Catholic Volunteers in Florida (1983): P.O. Box 536476, Orlando, FL 32853-6476; (407) 660-8800; www.cvif.org. Co-sponsored by the bishops of Florida to promote values of social justice by direct service to farm workers, homeless, hungry, low-income people, single mothers and others in need. Volunteers, 20 years of age and older, serve for a one-year period in urban and rural settings. Exec. Dir., Richard Galentino.

Center for Applied Research in the Apostolate (CARA): Georgetown University, Washington, DC 20057-1233; (202) 687-8080; www.cara.george town.edu. A non-profit research center serving the planning needs of the Catholic Church. CARA gathers empirical data for use by bishops, diocesan agencies, parishes, congregations of men and women religious and Catholic organizations. The *CARA Report*, quarterly; *CARA Catholic Ministry Formation Directory*, annually. Exec. Dir., Bryan Froehle, Ph.D.

Christian Family Movement (CFM) (1947): National office, Box 272, Ames, IA 50010. Originated in Chicago to Christianize family life and create communities conducive to Christian family life. Since 1968, CFM in the U.S. has included couples from all Christian churches.

Christian Life Communities (1971, promulgation of revised norms by Pope Paul VI; originated, 1563, as Sodalities of Our Lady, at the Jesuit College in Rome): 3601 Lindell Blvd., Room 202, St. Louis, MO 63108 (national office); (314) 977-7370; www.clc-usa.org; the world CLC office is in Rome. Small communities of primarily lay persons who come together to form committed individuals for service to the world and the Church.

Cursillo Movement (1949, in Spain; in U.S., 1957): National Cursillo Center, P.O. Box 210226, Dallas, TX 75211. An instrument of Christian renewal designed to form and stimulate persons to engage in evangelizing their everyday environments.

Franciscan Mission Service of North America, an Overseas Lay Ministry Program (1990): P.O. Box 29034, Washington, DC 20017; (202) 832-1762; www.franciscanmissionservice.catholic.edu. Lay missioners work with Franciscan sisters, brothers and priests for a minimum of three years in underdeveloped countries. Co-Dir. Joseph Nangle, O.F.M. and Megeen White.

Grail, The (1921, in The Netherlands, by Rev. Jacques van Ginneken, S.J.; 1940, in U.S.): Grailville, 932 O'Bannonville Rd., Loveland, Ohio 45140 (U. S. headquarters); (513) 683-2340; www.grailville.org; Duisburger Strasse 442, 45478 Mulheim, Germany; international secretariat). An international movement of women concerned about the full development of all peoples, working in education, religious, social, cultural and ecological areas.

Jesuit Volunteer Corps (1956): 18th and Thompson Sts., Philadelphia, PA 19121 (address for information); (215) 232-0300; www.jesuitvolunteers.org. Sponsored by the Society of Jesus in the U.S. Men and women volunteers work throughout the U.S. serving the poor directly and working for structural change.

LAMP Ministries (Lay Apostolic Ministries with the Poor): 2704 Schurz Ave., Bronx, NY 10465; (718) 409-5062; www.lampministries.org. Missionary service of evangelization with the materially poor and homeless in the larger metropolitan New York-New Jersey area. Newsletter, two times a year. Directors, Drs. Tom and Lyn Scheuring.

Lay Mission-Helpers Association (1955): 3424 Wilshire Blvd., Los Angeles, CA 90010. Trains and assigns men and women for work in overseas apostolates for periods of two to three years. Approximately 700 members of the association have served in overseas assignments since its founding. Director, Msgr. Michael Meyers. **The Mission Doctors Association** (same address; (213) 637-7499; www.mission doctors.org) recruits, trains and sends Catholic physicians and their families to mission hospitals and clinics throughout the world for tours of two to three years. Additionally, MDA has a short-term program for volunteer physicians with a term of service of 1-2 months. Program Dir., Elise Frederick.

Legion of Mary (1921, in Dublin, Ireland, by Frank Duff): Maria Center, 326 E. Ripa, St. Louis, MO 63125 (U.S. address); (314) 631-3447; De Montfort House, Dublin 7, Ireland (headquarters). Membership: active Catholics of all ages, under the direction of local bishops and priests, for the work of conversion, conservation and consolation. Pres., Mary T. Budde.

***Movimiento Familiar Cristiano*-USA (MFC)** (1969): 700 Waverly, San Antonio, TX 78201; (210) 736-5228. Movement of Catholic Hispanic families united in their efforts to promote the human and Christian virtues of the family so that it may become a force that forms persons, transmits the faith and contributes to the total development of the community. Rev. Clemente Barron, C.P., national spiritual director.

***Pax Christi* USA** (1972): 532 W. 8th St., Erie, PA 16502; (814) 453-4955. Pax Christi (see International Catholic Organizations). Founded to establish peacemaking as a priority for the American Catholic Church. *Pax Christi USA*, quarterly; membership.

Schoenstatt Lay Movement (1914): International Schoenstatt Center, W284 N 698 Cherry Lane, Waukesha, WI 53188; (262) 547-7733. Lay movement founded in Germany by Fr. Joseph Kentenich. A Marian and apostolic way of life, Schoenstatt is present on all continents and includes people of all ages and walks of life, men and women, young and old, priests and laity. The Schoenstatt Shrine, dedicated to Mary, Mother Thrice Admirable, Queen and Victress of Schoenstatt, is an integral part of the spirituality of Schoenstatt. There are over 160 shrines around the world, 6 of them in the U.S., in Minnesota, New York, Texas, and Wisconsin.

Volunteer Missionary Movement (1969): 5980 W. Loomis Rd., Milwaukee, WI 53129; www.vm

musa.org. *Bridges*, quarterly. Independent lay international mission organization with origins in the Catholic tradition but ecumenical and open to all Christian denominations.

Volunteers for Educational and Social Services (VESS): 1625 Rutherford Lane, Bldg. D, Austin, TX 78754; (512) 339-7123. A program of the Texas Catholic Conference. Volunteers offer their services for a year at mission-sites throughout Texas as teachers, social workers, counselors, ESL instructors, immigration and refugee assistants, parish, youth and campus ministers, health care workers and nurses. The experience offers individuals the opportunity to acquire professional experience by ministering to the needs of parishes, agencies and schools that are economically disadvataged. Dir., Michael G. Guerra.

CATHOLIC YOUTH ORGANIZATIONS

Camp Fire Boys and Girls: 4601 Madison Ave., Kansas City, MO 64112; (816) 756-1950; www.campfireusa.org. The National Catholic Committee for Girl Scouts and Camp Fire, a standing committee of the National Federation for Catholic Youth Ministry, cooperates with Camp Fire Boys and Girls.

Catholic Forester Youth Program, Catholic Order of Foresters: Naperville, IL 60566; (800) 552-0145. To develop Christian leadership and promote the moral, intellectual, social and physical growth of its youth members. Catholic Forester. Membership: youth up to 16 years of age; over 19,046 in 610 local courts in U.S. High Chief Ranger-Pres., Robert Ciesla.

Catholic Youth Organization (CYO): Name of parish-centered diocesan Catholic youth programs throughout the country. CYO promotes a program of spiritual, social and physical activities. The original CYO was organized in 1930 by Archbishop Bernard Sheil, auxiliary bishop of Chicago.

Columbian Squires (1925): 1 Columbus Plaza, New Haven, CT 06510-3326; (203) 752-4402; www.kofc.org; *Squires Newsletter*, monthly. The official youth organization of the Knights of Columbus. To train and develop leadership through active participation in a well-organized program of spiritual, service, social, cultural and athletic activities. Membership: Catholic young men, 12-18 years old. More than 25,000 in over 1,000 circles (local units) active in the U.S., Canada, Puerto Rico, Philippines, Mexico, the Bahamas, Virgin Islands and Guam.

Girl Scouts: 830 Third Ave., New York, NY 10022. Girls from archdioceses and dioceses in the U.S. and its possessions participate in Girl Scouting through the collaboration of Girl Scouts of the U.S.A., with the National Catholic Committee for Girl Scouts and Camp Fire, a standing committee of the National Federation for Catholic Youth Ministry.

Holy Childhood Association (Pontifical Association of the Holy Childhood) (1843): 266 Fifth Ave., New York, NY 10001; (212) 563-8700; www.world missions-catholicchurch.org. The official children's mission-awareness society of the Church. Provides mission awareness for elementary-grade students in parochial schools and religious education programs and financial assistance to children in more than 100 developing countries. Publishes *It's Our World*, three times a year, in two grade levels. Nat. Dir., Rev. Francis W. Wright, C.S.Sp.

The National Catholic Committee on Scouting: P.O. Box 152079, Irving, TX 75015-2079; (972) 580-2114; www.catholic-church.org/catholicscouting; www.nccs-bsa.org Works with the Boy Scouts of America in developing the character and spiritual life of members in units chartered to Catholic and non-Catholic organizations. National Committee Chairman, Robert Runnels of Leawood, KS. Admin. Sec., Barbara Nestel.

National Catholic Forensic League (1952): 21 Nancy Rd., Milford, MA 01757; (508) 473-0431. To develop articulate Catholic leaders through an interdiocesan program of speech and debate activities. Newsletter, quarterly. Membership: 925 schools; membership open to Catholic, private and public schools through the local diocesan league. Exec. Sec.-Treas., Richard Gaudette.

National Catholic Young Adult Ministry Association (1982): P.O. Box 32253, Washington, DC 20007; (888) NCYAMA1; www.ncyama.org. A response to the needs of young adults, an invitation to share their gifts with the larger community and a challenge to live gospel values in the world. A national network for single and married young adults. Exec. Dir., Michelle M. Miller.

National Federation for Catholic Youth Ministry, Inc. (1981): 415 Michigan Ave., N.E., Washington, DC 20017; (202) 636-3825; www.nfcym.org. To foster the development of youth ministry in the United States. Exec. Dir., Robert McCarty.

Young Christian Students: 19646 W. Dunlap Rd., Dennison, IL 62423; (217) 826-5708. A student movement for Christian personal and social change.

CAMPUS MINISTRY

Campus ministry is an expression of the Church's special desire to be present to all who are involved in higher education and to further dialogue between the Church and the academic community. In the words of the U.S. bishops' 1985 pastoral letter entitled "Empowered by the Spirit," this ministry is "the public presence and service through which properly prepared baptized persons are empowered by the Spirit to use their talents and gifts on behalf of the Church in order to be sign and instrument of the Kingdom in the academic world."

Campus ministry, carried on by lay, Religious and ordained ministers, gathers members of the Church on campus to form the faith community, appropriate the faith, form Christian consciences, educate for justice and facilitate religious development.

The dimensions and challenge of this ministry are evident from, among other things, the numbers involved: approximately 550,000 Catholics on more than 230 Catholic college and university campuses; about four million in several thousand non-Catholic private and public institutions; 1,200 or more campus ministers. In many dioceses, the activities of ministers are coordinated by a local diocesan director. Two professional organizations serve the ministry on the national level:

The National Association of Diocesan Directors of Campus Ministry, Ms. Krista Bajoka (contact), 305 Michigan Ave., Detroit, MI 48226; (313) 237-5962.

The Catholic Campus Ministry Association, 1,200 members, 300 College Park, Dayton, OH 45469-2515; (937) 229-4648; www.ccmanet.org. Exec. Dir., Edmund Franchi.

COLLEGE SOCIETIES

Alpha Sigma Nu (1915): Marquette University, Brooks 201, P.O. Box 1881, Milwaukee, WI 53201-1881 (national headquarters); (414) 288-7542; www.alphasigmanu.org. National honor society of the 30 Jesuit institutions of higher education in the U.S. and a chapter at Sogany University in Korea; members chosen on the basis of scholarship, loyalty and service; 1,575 student and 38,000 alumni members. Member, Association of College Honor Societies. Gamma Pi Epsilon (1925) merged with Alpha Sigma Nu in 1973 to form society for men and women. Exec. Dir., Peg Fennig.

Delta Epsilon Sigma (1939): Barry University, 11300 NE Second Ave., Miami Shores, FL 33161; (305) 899-3020; www.socrates.barry.edu\des. National scholastic honor society for students, faculty and alumni of colleges and universities with a Catholic tradition. *Delta Epsilon Sigma Journal*, three times a year. Membership: 60,000 in 116 chapters. Sec., Dr. J. Patrick Lee.

Kappa Gamma Pi (1926): KGP National Office, 10215 Chardon Rd., Chardon, OH, 44024-9700; (440) 286-3764; www.kappagammapi.org. A national Catholic college honor society for graduates who, in addition to academic excellence, have shown outstanding leadership in extra-curricular activities. *Kappa Gamma Pi News*, five times a year. Membership: more than 37,000 in 139 colleges; 20 alumnae chapters in metropolitan areas. Nat. Exec. Sec., Christine Walick.

Phi Kappa Theta: 3901 W. 86th St., Suite 425, Indianapolis, IN 46268. National social fraternity with a Catholic heritage. Merger (1959) of Phi Kappa Fraternity, founded at Brown University in 1889, and Theta Kappa Phi Fraternity, founded at Lehigh University in 1919. *The Temple Magazine*, semi-annually, and newsletters. Membership: 2,800 undergraduate and 50,500 alumni in 63 collegiate and 40 alumni chapters. Exec. Dir., Mark T. McSweeney.

National Catholic Student Coalition (1988); 45 Lovett Ave., Newark, DE 19717; www.catholicstudent.org. National coalition of Catholic campus ministry groups at public and private institutions of higher education. Formed after National Newman Club Federation and the National Federation of Catholic College Students dissolved in the 1960s. The U.S. affiliate of Pax Romana-IMCS (see International Catholic Organizations). *The Catholic Collegian*, four times a year. Membership: 200 campus groups. Exec. Dir., Jamie Williams; contact, Kim Zitzner.

ASSOCIATIONS, MOVEMENTS, SOCIETIES IN THE U.S.

(*Principal source*: Catholic Almanac *survey*.)

Academy of American Franciscan History (1944): 1712 Euclid Ave., Berkeley, CA 94709; (510) 548-1755; www.aafh.org. To encourage the study of the Franciscan Order in the New World. Dir., Dr. Jeffrey M. Burns.

Adoremus-Society for the Renewal of the Sacred Liturgy (1995): P.O. Box 3286, St. Louis, MO 63130; (314) 863-8385; www.adoremus.org. Promotes authentic renewal of Catholic liturgy in accordance with the Second vatican Council's Constitution of the sacred Liturgy, *Sacrosanctum Concilium*. Publishes *Adoremus Bulletin,* 10 times a year; editor, Helen Hull Hitchcock.

Aid to the Church in Need (1947): U.S. office, 378 Broome St., 3rd Floor, New York, NY 10013-3706,; (212) 334-5340; www.aidtothechurchinneed.org. Assists the pastoral activities of the church in Third World countries, Eastern Europe and the former Soviet Union. *Mirror,* newsletter, 9 times a year. Pres./Exec. Dir., Joseph Donnelly.

Albanian Catholic Institute "Daniel Dajani, S.J." (1992): University of San Francisco, Xavier Hall, 650 Parker Ave., San Francisco, CA 94118; (415) 422-6966. To assist the rebuilding of the Catholic Church in Albania and to promote the dissemination of knowledge of Albania's national, religious and cultural heritage. Founder, Gjon Sinishta (1930-95) in memory of the martyr Daniel Dajani (d. 1946). Exec. Dir., Raymond Frost; Jesuit Community Liaison, Paul Bernardicou, S.J.

American Benedictine Academy (1947): Saint Meinrad Archabbey, Guest House, 100 Hill Dr. Saint Meinrad, IN, 47577; (800) 581-6905. To promote Benedictine values in contemporary culture. Pres., Eugene Hensell, O.S.B.

American Catholic Correctional Chaplains Association (1952): 701 Lawrenceville Rd., P.O. Box 1547, Trenton, NJ. 08638; (609) 406-7400. Pres., Rev. Robert R. Schulze.

American Catholic Historical Association (1919): The Catholic University of America, Washington, DC 20064; (202) 319-5079; www.research.cua.edu/acha; *The Catholic Historical Review*, quarterly. Sec.-Treas., Rev. Msgr. Robert Trisco.

American Catholic Philosophical Association (1926): Administration Building, Fordham University, 441 E. Fordham Rd., Bronx, NY, 10458; (718) 817-3295; www.acpa-main.org; *American Catholic Philosophical Quarterly*; *Proceedings*, annually.

American Committee on Italian Migration (1952): 352 W. 44th St., New York, NY 10036; (212) 5419; www.acimny.org; *ACIM Newsletter* and *ACIM Nuova Via*, 6 times a year.

American Friends of the Vatican Library (1981): 581 E. Fourteen Mile Rd., Clawson, 48017-2175; (248) 589-7305; *AMICI*, newsletter. Pres., Rev. Charles G. Kosanke. Sponsored by the Catholic Library Association. To assist in supporting the Vatican Library.

American Life League, Inc. (1979), P.O. Box 1350, Stafford, VA 22555; (540) 659-4171; www.all.org;

publishes *Celebrate Life*, six times a year, and the *ABAC Quarterly*, for the American Bioethics Advisory Commission. Pres., Judie Brown.

Ancient Order of Hibernians in America, Inc. (1836): 31 Logan St., Auburn, NY 13021; *National Hibernian Digest*, bimonthly. 120,000 members. Nat. Sec., Thomas McNabb.

Apostleship of Prayer (1844, France; 1861, U.S.): 3 Stephen Ave., New Hyde Park, NY 11040. Promotes Daily Offering and Sacred Heart devotion. Nat. Dir., Rev. John H. Rainaldo, S.J.

Apostolate for Family Consecration (1975): 3375 County Rd. 36, Bloomingdale, OH 43910; (740) 765-5500; www.familyland.org. Pope John Paul II Holy Family Center, known as Catholic Familyland, Pres., Jerome F. Coniker. To transform families and parishes and nourish families through the Catholic faith.

Archconfraternity of Christian Mothers (Christian Mothers) (1881): 220 37th St., Pittsburgh, PA 15201; (412) 683-2400; www.capuchin.com; over 3,500 branches. Dir., Rev. Bertin Roll, O.F.M. Cap.

Archconfraternity of the Holy Ghost (1912): Holy Ghost Fathers, 6230 Brush Run Rd., Bethel Park, PA 15102, (412) 831-0970, www.spiritans.org (U.S. headquarters).

Archdiocese for the Military Services Seminary Education Fund (1988): P.O. Box 4469, Washington, D.C., 20017-0469; (202) 269-9100; www.milarch.org.

Association for Spiritual, Ethical, and Religious Values in Counseling (ASERVIC): Dept. of Educational Psychology and Special Education, Southern Illinois University at Carbondale, Carbondale, IL 62901; *Counseling and Values*, 3 times a year. Division of the American Counseling Association.

Association for Social Economics (formerly the Catholic Economic Association) (1941): Marquette University, Milwaukee, WI 53233. 1,300 members. *Review of Social Economy*, quarterly.

Association of Catholic Diocesan Archivists (1979): 711 W. Monroe, Chicago, IL 60661; (312) 831-0711. To work for establishment of an archival program in every American diocese. *ACDA Bulletin*, quarterly. Treas. John J. Treanor.

Association of Marian Helpers (1944): Eden Hill, 2 Prospect Rd., Stockbridge, MA 01263; (413) 298-3691; www.marian.org; *Marian Helpers Bulletin*, quarterly. 900,000 members, mostly in U.S. To promote vocations to Church service and support worldwide apostolates of Marians of the Immaculate Conception. Exec. Dir., Rev. Joseph, M.I.C.

Assumption Guild — Mass Cards: 330 Market St., Brighton, MA 02135; (617) 783-0495; www.mass cardsaa.com.

Beginning Experience (1974): International Ministry Center, 1247 171st Plc., Hammond, IN 46324; (219) 989-8915. Adult and youth programs to help divorced, widowed and separated start a new beginning in their lives. Pres., Kathleen Murphy.

The Blue Army of Our Lady of Fatima, USA (1947): P.O. Box 976, Washington, NJ 07882-0976; (908) 689-1701; www.bluearmy.com; *Soul*, bimonthly; *Hearts Aflame*, quarterly. U.S. branch of the World Apostolate of Fatima. Promote the Fatima Message. Fatima shrine. Nat. Pres., Most Rev. James S. Sullivan.

Calix Society (1947): 2555 Hazelwood St., St. Paul, MN 55109; www.calixsociety.org. Association of Catholic alcoholics maintaining their sobriety through 12-step program. Sec. Jim Billigmeier

Canon Law Society of America (1939): Catholic University, Caldwell Hall, 431, Washington, DC 20064; (202) 269-3491; www.clsa.org. To further research and study in canon law; 1,600 members. Exec. Coord., Arthur J. Espelage, O.F.M.

Cardinal Mindszenty Foundation (CMF) (1958): P.O. Box 11321, St. Louis, MO 63105-0121; (314) 727-6279; www.mindszenty.org; *The Mindszenty Report*, monthly. To uphold and defend the Catholic Church, family life and freedom for all under God. Pres., Eleanor Schlafly.

Catholic Aid Association (1878): 3499 N. Lexington Ave. North, St. Paul, MN 55126; (651) 490-0170; *Catholic Aid News*, monthly. www.catholicaid.com. Fraternal life insurance society. Chairman of the Board and CEO, Michael McGovern.

Catholic Alumni Clubs International (1957): P.O. Box 2412, Youngstown, OH 44509. 7,500 members in 48 clubs in U.S. To advance social, cultural and spiritual well-being of members. Membership limited to single Catholics with professional education. Pres., Sue Gentile.

Catholic Answers (1982): 2020 Gillespie Way, El Cajon, CA 92020; (619) 387-7200; www.catholic.com; *This Rock*, monthly. Apologetics and evangelization organization. Founder and dir., Karl Keating.

Catholic Biblical Association of America (1936): The Catholic University of America, Washington, DC 20064; (202) 319-5519; www.cba.cua.edu; *The Catholic Biblical Quarterly*, *Old Testament Abstracts*, *CBQ* monograph series. Exec. Sec., Joseph Jensen, O.S.B.

Catholic Book Publishers Association, Inc. (1987): 8404 Jamesport Dr., Rockford, IL 61108; (815) 332-3245; www.cbpa.org. Exec. Dir., Terry Wessels.

Catholic Coalition on Preaching: Madonna University, 36600 Schoolcraft Rd. Livonia, MI 48150-1173; (734) 432-5538. Pres., Rev. Francis Tebbe, O.F.M.

Catholic Committee of Appalachia (1970): P.O. Box 62, Wittensville, KY 41274; (606) 297-8792. Exec. Coord., Sr. Robbie Pentecost, O.S.F.

Catholic Daughters of the Americas (1903): 10 W. 71st St., New York, NY 10023; (212) 877-3041; www.catholicdaughters.org; *Share Magazine*. 125,000 members. Nat. Regent, Eunice Riles.

Catholic Familyland (1975): 3375 County Rd. 36, Bloomingdale, OH 43910; (740) 765-5500; www.familyland.org. Canonically named the John Paul II Holy Family Center; functions under the auspices of the Apostolate for Family Consecration. Pres., Jerome F. Coniker.

Catholic Golden Age (1975): P.O. Box 3658, Scranton, PA 18505-0658; (800) 836-5699; *CGA World*, quarterly. For Catholics over 50 years of age.

Catholic Guardian Society (1913): 1011 First Ave., New York, NY 10022; (212) 371-1000. Exec. Dir., John J. Frein.

Catholic Home Bureau (1899): 1011 First Ave., New York, NY 10022; (212) 371-1000; www.catholic homebureau.com. Exec. Dir., Philip Georgini.

Catholic Home Study Service (1936): P.O. Box 363, Perryville, MO 63775-0363; (573) 547-4084;

www.amm.org/chss.htm. Provides instruction in the Catholic faith by mail free of charge. Dir., Rev. Oscar Lukefahr, C.M.

Catholic Interracial Council of New York, Inc. (1934): 899 Tenth Ave., New York, NY 10019; (212) 237-8600; www.amm.org/chss.htm. To promote racial and social justice.

Catholic Knights of America (1877): Publication Office, 1850 Dalton St., Cincinnati, OH 45214; *C K of A Journal*, monthly. 7,800 members. Fraternal insurance society.

Catholic Knights of Ohio (1891): 22005 Mastick Rd., Fairview Park, OH 44126; (440) 777-5355; The *Messenger*, monthly. 8000 members in Ohio and Kentucky. Fraternal insurance society. Mr. Tom Welsh, General Secretary.

Catholic Kolping Society of America (1849): 9 East 8th St., Clifton, NJ 07011-1101; *Kolping Banner*, monthly. International society concerned with spiritual and educational development of members. Nat. Admin., Edward Farkas.

Catholic Lawyers' Guild: Organization usually on a diocesan basis, under different titles.

Catholic League for Religious Assistance to Poland (1943): 6002 W. Berteau Ave., Chicago, IL 60634-1630; (773) 202-7720. Exec. Dir., Most Rev. Thad Jakubowski.

Catholic League for Religious and Civil Rights (1973): 450 Seventh Ave., 34th Floor, New York, NY 10123; (212) 371-3191; www.catholicleague.org; *Catalyst*, league journal. Local chapters throughout U.S. Serves Catholic community as an anti-defamation and civil rights agency. Pres., William A. Donohue, Ph.D.

Catholic Library Association (1921): 100 North St., Suite 224, Pittsfield, MA 01201-5109; (413) 442-2252; www.cathla.org; *Catholic Library World*, *Catholic Periodical* and *Literature Index*, quarterlies. Exec.Dir., Jean R. Bostley, S.S.J.

Catholic Marketing Network (1955): 111 Ferguson Court, #102, Irving, TX 75062; (800) 506-6333; www.catholicmarketing.com; *Catholic Marketing Network*, quarterly. A trade associaton founded to encourage the most effective production and distribution of Catholic goods and provide a common forum for mutual interchange of ideas. Exec. Dir., Cherylann Tucker.

Catholic Near East Welfare Association (1926): 1011 First Ave., Suite 1552, New York, NY 10022; (212) 826-1480; www.cnewa.org. A papal agency for humanitarian and pastoral support serving the churches and peoples of the Middle East, Northeast Africa, India and Eastern Europe, with offices in New York, Vatican City, Addis Ababa, Amman, Jerusalem and Beirut. Pres., Cardinal Edward Egan; Sec. Gen., Msgr. Robert L. Stern.

Catholic Order of Foresters (1883): 355 Shuman Blvd., P.O. Box 3012, Naperville, IL 60566; (630) 983-4900; www.catholicforester.com; *The Catholic Forester*, bimonthly. 136,685 members. Fraternal insurance society. High Chief Ranger, Robert Ciesla.

Catholic Press Association of the U.S. and Canada, Inc. (1911): 3555 Veterans Memorial Highway, Unit O, Ronkonkoma, NY 11779; (631) 471-4730; www.catholicpress.org; *The Catholic Journalist*, monthly; *Catholic Press Directory*, annually. Exec. Dir., Owen P. McGovern.

Catholic Theological Society of America (1946), John Carroll University, 20700 North Park Blvd., University Hgts., OH, 44118, (216) 397-1631, www.bc.edu/ctsa; *Proceedings*, annually. Exec. Sec., Dolores Christie.

Catholic Union of Texas, The K.J.T. (1889): 214 E. Colorado St., La Grange, TX 78945-0297; (979) 968-5877; www.kjtnet.org; *Nasinec*, weekly, and *K. J. T. News*, monthly. 18,226 members. Fraternal and insurance society. Pres., Elo J. Goerig.

Catholic War Veterans (1935): 441 N. Lee St., Alexandria, VA 22314; (703) 549-3622; www.cwv.org; *Catholic War Veteran*, bimonthly. 500 posts.

Catholic Worker Movement (1933): 36 E. 1st St., New York, NY 10003; *The Catholic Worker*, 8 times a year. Lay apostolate founded by Peter Maurin and Dorothy Day; has Houses of Hospitality in over 60 U.S. cities and several communal farms in various parts of the country. Promotes the practice of the works of mercy, nonviolence, personalism, voluntary poverty.

Catholic Workman (*Katolicky Delnik***)** (1891): 111 West Main St., New Prague, MN 56071; (612) 758-2229; *Catholic Workman*, monthly. 16,405 members. Fraternal and insurance society.

Catholics Against Capital Punishment (1992), P.O. Box 5706, Bethesda, MD 20824-5706; (301) 652-1125; www.cacp.org; *CACP News Notes*, bimonthly. Promotes greater awareness of papal and episcopal statements against the death penalty. Nat. Coord., Frank McNeirney.

Catholics United for the Faith (1968): 827 N. Fourth St., Steubenville, OH 43952; (800) 693-2484; www.cuf.org; *Lay Witness*, monthly. 23,000 members worldwide. Lay apostolic group concerned with spiritual and doctrinal formation of members. Mike Sullivan, Dir. of Communications.

Center of Concern (1971): 1225 Otis St., N.E., Washington, DC 20017; (202) 635-2757; www.coc.org. Exec. Dir., James E. Hug.

Central Association of the Miraculous Medal (1915): 475 E. Chelten Ave., Philadelphia, PA 19144; (800) 523-3674; www.cammonline.org; *Miraculous Medal*, quarterly. Dir., Rev. William J. O'Brien, C.M.

Chaplains' Aid Association, Inc. (1917): 3311 Toledo Terrace, Hyattsville, MD 20780. To receive and administer funds toward education of seminarians to become priest-chaplains in military services.

Christian Foundation for Children and Aging: One Elmwood Ave., Kansas City, KS 66103; (913) 384-6500; www.cfcausa.org. Grassroots movement dedicated to improving through sponsorship the lives of children and aging at Catholic mission sites around the world. Exec. Dir., Paco Wertin.

Christophers, Inc., The (1945): 12 E. 48th St., New York, NY 10017; (212) 759-4050; www.christophers.org. Founded by Rev. James Keller, M.M. The Christophers stimulate personal initiative and responsible action in line with Judeo-Christian principles through broadcast of Christopher radio and TV programs; free distribution of *Christopher News Notes*, ten times a year; publication of a weekly Christopher column in over 200 newspapers; Spanish literature; annual media awards; youth outreach. Pres., Dennis W. Heaney.

Citizens for Educational Freedom (1959): 921 S. Walter Reed Dr., Suite 1, Arlington, VA 22204. Nonsectarian group concerned with parents' right to educational choice by means of tuition tax credits and vouchers. Exec. Dir., Patrick J. Reilly.

Confraternity of Bl. Junipero Serra (1989): P.O. Box 7125, Mission Hills, CA 91346. 3,500 members in U.S. and foreign countries. Founded in Monterey (CA) diocese to help promote process of canonization of Bl. Junipero Serra and increase spiritual development of members. Dir., Rev. Thomas L. Davis, Jr.; Spiritual Dir., Rev. Noel F. Moholy, O.F.M.

Confraternity of Catholic Clergy (1976): 4445 W. 64th St., Chicago, IL 60629, (773) 581-8904. Association of priests pledged to pursuit of personal holiness, loyalty to the pope, theological study and adherence to authentic teachings of the Catholic faith. Sec., Rev. L. Dudley Day, O.S.A.

Confraternity of Christian Doctrine, Inc.: 3211 Fourth St., N.E., Washington, DC 20017; (202) 541-3098; www.usccb.org/nab. A distinct entity, separately incorporated and directed by a Board of Trustees from the United States Catholic Conference of Bishops. Its purpose is to foster and promote the teaching of Christ as understood and handed down by the Roman Catholic Church. To this end it licenses use of the Lectionary for Mass and the *New American Bible* (NAB), the Revised Psalms of the NAB and the Revised New Testament of the NAB, translations made from the original languages in accordance with the papal encyclical *Divino Afflante Spiritu* (1943) of Pope Pius XII.

Confraternity of the Immaculate Conception of Our Lady of Lourdes (1874): Box 561, Notre Dame, IN 46556. Distributors of Lourdes water.

Confraternity of the Most Holy Rosary: *See* **Dominican Rosary Apostolate**.

Couple to Couple League (1971), P.O. Box 111184, Cincinnati, OH 45211; (513) 471-2000; www.ccli.org. Founded to teach and promote marital chastity through Natural Family Planning. Exec. Dir., Mark Hayden.

Courage (1980): c/o St. John the Baptist Church and Friary, 210 West 31st St., New York, NY 10001; (212) 268-1010; www.couragerc.org. Ministry to men and women who experience same-sex attractions and desire to live Christian chastity in accordance with the teachings of the Catholic Church. Newsletter, 4 times a year. Nat. Dir., Rev. John F. Harvey, O.S.F.S.

CUSA (Catholics United for Spiritual Action, Inc.) — An Apostolate of the Sick or Disabled (1947): 176 W. 8th St., Bayonne, NJ, 07002-1227; (201) 437-0412; www.cusan.org. A group-correspondence apostolate for the disabled and chronically ill. Admin. Ms. Anna Marie Sopko.

Damien-Dutton Society for Leprosy Aid, Inc. (1944): 616 Bedford Ave., Bellmore, NY 11710; (516) 221-5829; www.damienleprosysociety.org; *Damien Dutton Call*, quarterly. 25,000 members. Provides medicine, rehabilitation and research for conquest of leprosy. Pres., Howard E. Crouch; Vice Pres., Elizabeth Campbell.

Daughters of Isabella (1897): P.O. Box 9585, New Haven, CT 06535. 100,000 members. To unite Catholic women into a fraternal order for spiritual benefits and to promote higher ideals within society.

Disaster Response Office (1990): Catholic Charities USA, 1731 King St., Suite 200, Alexandria, VA 22314; (703) 549-1390; www.catholiccharities usa.org. Promotes and facilitates Catholic disaster response in the U.S. Dir., Jane A. Gallagher.

Dominican Rosary Apostolate (1806): 141 E. 65th St., New York, NY 10021. Dir., Rev. Edward L. Martin, O.P.

Edith Stein Guild, Inc. (1955): Church of St. John the Baptist, 210 W. 31st St., New York, NY 10001-2876, (212) 567-8230. Assists and encourages Jewish Catholics; fosters among Catholics a better understanding of their Jewish heritage; promotes spread of knowledge of life and writings of St. Edith Stein; fosters better understanding between Jews and Christians and supports the Church's spirit of ecumenism. Pres., Sr. Marie Goldstein, R.S.H.M.

Enthronement of the Sacred Heart in the Home (1907): P.O. Box 111, Fairhaven, MA 02719; (508) 999-2680.

Federation of Diocesan Liturgical Commissions (FDLC) (1969): P.O. Box 29039, Washington, DC 20017; (202) 635-6990; www.fdlc.org. Voluntary association of personnel from diocesan liturgical commissions and worship offices. The main purpose is promotion of the liturgy as the heart of Christian life, especially in the parish community. Exec. Dir., Rev. Michael J. Spillane.

Federation of Seminary Spiritual Directors (1972): Cardinal Muench Seminary, 100 35th Ave., N.E., Fargo, ND 58102; (701) 232-8969. Responsible for priestly spiritual formation in high school and college seminaries, novitiates, theologates and houses of formation in the U.S. Pres., Dan Trapp.

Fellowship of Catholic Scholars (1977): Ave Maria School of Law, 3475 Plymouth Rd., Ann Arbor, Michigan 48105; (734) 827-8043. 1,000 members. Interdisciplinary research and publications of Catholic scholars in accord with the magisterium of the Catholic Church. Acting Pres., Bernard Dobranski.

First Catholic Slovak Ladies' Association, USA (1892): 24950 Chagrin Blvd., Beachwood, OH 44122; (800) 464-4642; www.fcsla.com; *Fraternally Yours*, monthly. 102,000 members. Fraternal insurance society. Pres., Mary Ann Johanek.

First Catholic Slovak Union (Jednota) (1890): FCSU Corporate Center, 6611 Rockside Rd., Independence, OH 44131; (216) 642-9406; www.fcsu.com; *Jednota*, biweekly. 96,206 members. Nat. Sec., Kenneth A. Arendt.

Foundation for the Family (1986): P.O. Box 111184, Cincinnati, OH 45211; (513) 471-2000; www.ccli.org. Established by Couple to Couple League (see entry above) to provide materials for family not relating to Natural Family Planning, Exec. Dir., Mark Hayden.

Foundations and Donors Interested in Catholic Activities, Inc. (FADICA): 1350 Connecticut Ave. N.W., Suite 303, Washington, DC 20036; (202) 223-3550; www.FADICA.org. A consortium of private foundations providing continuing education and research to members to make church-related philanthropy more effective. Pres., Francis J. Butler.

Franciscan Apostolate of the Way of the Cross (1949): P.O. Box 23, Boston, MA 02112; (617) 542-6659. Distributes religious materials to the sick and shut-in. Dir., Rev. Robert Lynch, O.F.M.

Free The Fathers (1983): 845 Oak St. Chattanooga,

TN 37403; (423) 756-9660; www.ftf.org. To work for the freedom of bishops and priests imprisoned in China. Pres., John M. Davies.

Friends of the Holy Land, Inc. (1974): 347 Mile Square Rd., Yonkers, NY 10701; *Friends of the Holy Land Newsletter*. 300 members. To provide spiritual and material support for the Christian communities in the Holy Land. Gen. Dir., Ernest F. Russo.

Gabriel Richard Institute (1949): 3641 Estates Dr., Troy, MI 48084; (248) 643-8887. Conducts Christopher Leadership Course. Exec. Dir., Dolores Ammar.

Guard of Honor of the Immaculate Heart of Mary (1932): 135 West 31st St., New York, NY 10001; (212) 924-1994; www.hnp.org. An archconfraternity approved by the Holy See whose members cultivate devotion to the Blessed Virgin Mary, particularly through a daily Guard Hour of Prayer. Dir., Rev. Cassian A. Miles, O.F.M.

Holy Cross Family Ministries (formerly The Family Rosary, Inc.) (1942): 518 Washington St., North Easton, MA, 02356-1200; (508) 238-4095; www.hcfm.org. Founded by Father Patrick Peyton, C.S.C. Encourages family prayer, especially the Rosary. Pres., Rev. John Phalen, C.S.C.

Holy Name Society: Founded in 1274 by Blessed John Vercelli, master general of the Dominicans, to promote reverence for the Holy Name of Jesus; this is still the principal purpose of the society, which also develops lay apostolic programs in line with directives of the Second Vatican Council. Introduced in the U.S. in 1870-71 by Dominican Father Charles H. McKenna, the society has about 5 million members on diocesan and parochial levels. With approval of the local bishop and pastor, women as well as men may be members.

Holy Name Society, National Association (NAHNS) (1970): P.O. Box 12012, Baltimore, MD 21281; (410) 276-1166; www.members.aol.com/nahns; *Holy Name Newsletter*, monthly. Association of diocesan and parochial Holy Name Societies.

Hungarian Catholic League of America, Inc. (1945): One Cathedral Sq., Providence, RI 02903-3695; (401) 278-4520. Chair., Rev. Msgr. William I. Varsanyi.

International Catholic Stewardship Council (1962): 1275 K St. N.W., Suite 980, Washington, DC 20005-4006; (202) 289-1093; www.catholicstewardship.org. A professional association which fosters an environment in which stewardship is understood, accepted and practiced throughout the church. Nat. Dir., Matthew R. Paratore.

International Catholic Charismatic Renewal Services: Palazzo della Cancelleria, 00120 Vatican City; 39 06 698 87538; www.iccrs.org. The ICCRS provides leadership and vision to the Catholic Charismatic Renewal throughout the world in harmony with the Pontifical Council for the Laity which has established ICCRS as a Private Association of the Faithful. *See* **National Catholic Charismatic Renewal Services**.

Italian Catholic Federation (1924): 675 Hegenberger Rd., #230, Oakland, CA 94621; (888) 423-1924; www.icf.org.19,000 members. Fraternal organization of Italian-American Catholics.

John Carroll Society, The (1951): P.O. Box 50188, Washington, DC 20091; (703) 573-3043; www.johncarrollsociety.org. Exec. Asst., Mary Ann Dmochowski, Ph.D.

Judean Society, Inc., The (1966): 1075 Space Park Way No. 336, Mt. View, CA 94043.

Knights of Peter Claver (1909), and **Knights of Peter Claver, Ladies Auxiliary** (1926): 1825 Orleans Ave., New Orleans, LA 70116; (504) 821-4225; www.knightsofpeterclaver.com; *The Claverite*, biannually. Fraternal and aid society. National Chaplain, Most Rev. Curtis J. Guillory, S.V.D.

Knights of St. John, International Supreme Commandery (1886): 89 So. Pine Ave., Albany, N.Y. 12208; (518) 453-5675; www.members.tripod.com/ksji/knights/ksji.html. Supreme Sec., Maj. Gen. Joseph Hauser, Jr.

Ladies of Charity of the United States of America (1960): P.O. Box 31697, St. Louis, MO 63131; (314) 821-1296. 25,000 members in U.S.; 250,000 worldwide. International Association founded by St. Vincent de Paul in 1617.

Latin Liturgy Association (1975): 34 Dumont Ave., Staten Island, NY 10305-1450; (718) 979-6685; www.latinliturgy.com; quarterly journal. 850 members. To promote the use of the Latin language and music in the approved rites of the Church. Pres., William J. Leininger.

Legatus (1987): 30 Frank Lloyd Wright Dr., P.O. Box 997, Ann Arbor, MI 48106; (734) 930-3854; *Legatus Newsletter*, monthly. To apply Church's moral teaching in business and personal lives of members.

Lithuanian Groups: Ateitininkai, members of **Lithuanian Catholic Federation Ateitis** (1910), 1209 Country Lane, Lemont, IL 60439; *Ateitis*, bimonthly. Pres., Juozas Polikaitis. **Knights of Lithuania** (1913): Roman Catholic educational-fraternal organization. *Vytis*, monthly. Pres., Evelyn Ozelis, 2533 W. 45th St., Chicago, IL 60632.

Lithuanian Catholic Alliance (1886), 71-73 S. Washington St., Wilkes-Barre, PA 18701. Fraternal insurance organization. Pres., Thomas E. Mack.

Lithuanian Roman Catholic Federation of America (1906): 4545 W. 63rd St., Chicago, IL 60629; (312) 585-9500; *The Observer*, bimonthly. Umbrella organization for Lithuanian parishes and organizations. Pres., Saulius Kuprys.

Lithuanian Roman Catholic Priests' League (1909): P.O. Box 1025, Humarock, MA 02047-1025; (781) 834-4079. Religious-professional association. Pres., Rev. Albert Contons.

Lithuanian Catholic Religious Aid, Inc. (1961): 351 Highland Blvd., Brooklyn, NY 11207; (718) 827-7932. To assist Catholics in Lithuania. Chairman and Pres., Most Rev. Paul Baltakis, O.F.M.

Little Flower Mission League (1957), P.O. Box 25, Plaucheville, LA 71362; (318) 922-3630. Sponsored by the Brothers of the Holy Eucharist. Dir., Bro. André M. Lucia, F.S.E.

Little Flower Society (1923): 1313 Frontage Rd. Darien, IL 60561. 200,000 members. Nat. Dir., Rev. Robert E. Colaresi, O. Carm.

Liturgical Conference, The: 415 Michigan Ave., NE, #65, Washington, DC 20017; (202) 832-6520; www.litconf.org. Liturgy, homily service. Education, research and publication programs for renewing and enriching Christian liturgical life. Ecumenical.

Loyal Christian Benefit Association (1890): P.O. Box 13005, Erie, PA 16514; (814) 453-4331; www.lcba.com; *The Fraternal Leader*, quarterly. Fraternal benefit and insurance society. Pres., Jackie Sobania-Robison.

Marian Movement of Priests (1972): P.O. Box 8, St. Francis, ME 04774-0008 (U.S.); (207) 398-3375; www.mmp-usa.net. International headquarters, Via Mercalli, 23, 20122 Milan, Italy. 4,000 clergy members, 53,000 religious and laity (U.S.). Spiritual renewal through consecration to the Immaculate Heart of Mary. Nat. Dir., Rev. Albert G. Roux.

Mariological Society of America (1949): Marian Library, Box 1390, University of Dayton, Dayton, OH 45469; (937) 229-4294; *Marian Studies*, annually. Founded by Rev. Juniper B. Carol, O.F.M., to promote greater appreciation of and scientific research in Marian theology. Sec., Rev. Thomas A. Thompson, S.M.

Marriage Encounter, National: 4704 Jamerson Pl., Orlando, FL 32807. The national office of Worldwide Marriage Encounter is located at 2210 East Highland Ave., #106, San Bernardino, CA 92404; (909) 863-9963. Brings couples together for a weekend program of events directed by a team of several couples and a priest, to develop their abilities to communicate with each other as husband and wife.

Maryheart Crusaders, The (1964): 22 Button St., Meriden, CT 06450; (203) 239-5979; www.maryheart crusaders.org. Pres., Louise D'Angelo.

Men of the Sacred Heart (1964): National Shrine of the Sacred Heart, P.O. Box 500, Harleigh, PA 18225; (570) 455-1162. Promotes enthronement of Sacred Heart.

Militia Immaculate National Center — Marytown (1917): 1600 W. Park Ave., Libertyville, IL 60048; (847) 367-7800, www.consecration.com. Canonically established with international headquarters in Rome. A pious association to promote total consecration to Mary in the spirit of St. Mximilian Kolbe. Pres., Fr. Patrick Greenough, O.F.M. Conv.

Missionary Association of Catholic Women (1916): 3501 S. Lake Dr., P.O. Box 07212, Milwaukee, WI 53207-0912; (414) 769-3406.

Missionary Vehicle Association, Inc. (MIVA America) (1971): 1400 Michigan Ave., N.E., Washington, DC 20017-7234; (202) 635-3444; www.MIVA.org. To raise funds and distribute them annually as vehicle grants to missionaries working with the poor in Third World countries. Nat. Dir., Rev. Philip De Rea, M.S.C.; Exec. Dir., Rev. Anthony F. Krisak.

Morality in Media, Inc. (1962): 475 Riverside Dr., New York, NY 10115; (212) 870-3222; www.morality inmedia.org; Newsletter, bimonthly. Interfaith national organization. Works by constitutional means to curb the explosive growth of hard-core pornography and to turn back the tide of grossly offensive, indecent media. A major project is the National Obscenity Law Center which provides legal information for prosecutors and other attorneys. Pres., Robert W. Peters.

National Assembly of Religious Women (NARW): 529 S. Wabash Ave., Suite 404, Chicago, IL 60605;

(312) 663-1980. Founded as the National Assembly of Women Religious, 1970; title changed, 1980. A movement of feminist women committed to prophetic tasks of giving witness, raising awareness and engaging in public action and advocacy for justice in church and society.

National Association for Lay Ministry (1977): 5420 S. Cornell Ave., Chicago, IL 60615; (773) 241-6050; www.nalm.org. Acts as advocate and support for lay people who respond to a call to ministry in the Church.

National Association of Catholic Family Life Ministers: 300 College Park, Dayton, OH 45469; (937) 229-3324; www.nacflm.org. Strives to be a voice and advocate for families and family ministry in Church and society. Exec. Dir., David Abele.

National Association of Catholic Home Educators (1993): 6102 Saints Hill Lane, Broad Run, VA 20137; (540) 349-4314; www.nache.com; *The Catholic Home Educator*, quarterly. Promotion of homeschooling.

National Association of Church Personnel Administrators (1971): 100 E. 8th St., Cincinnati, OH 45202; (513) 421-3134; www.nacpa.org. Association for human resource and personnel directors dedicated to promotion and development of just personnel practices for all church employees. Exec. Dir., Sr. Ellen Doyle, O.S.U.

National Association of Diaconate Directors: 1204 N. Church St., Rockford, IL 61103; (815) 965-0075. Deacon Thomas C. Welch, Exec. Dir.

National Association of Diocesan Ecumenical Officers: 7800 Kenrick Rd., St. Louis, MO 63119; (314) 961-4320. Network of Catholics involved in ecumenical and interreligious work. Pres., Vincent A. Heier.

National Association of Pastoral Musicians (1976): 962 Wayne Ave., Suite 210, Silver Spring, MD 20910; (240) 247-3000; www.npm.org; *Pastoral Music*, six times a year. 9,000 members. Dedicated to fostering the art of musical liturgy. Exec. Dir., Dr. J. Michael McMahon.

National Association of Priest Pilots (1964): 481 N. Shore Dr., Apt. 301, Clear Lake IA 50428-1368; (641) 435-2070. Pres., Rev. John Hemann.

National Catholic AIDS Network: P.O. Box 422984, San Francisco, CA 94142; (707) 874-3031; www.ncan.org. Exec. dir., Rev. Rodney DeMartini; Board Pres., Rev. Robert J. Vitillo.

National Catholic Band Association (1953): 3334 N. Normandy, Chicago, IL 60634; (773) 282-9153; www.thencba.org.

National Catholic Cemetery Conference (1949): 710 N. River Rd., Des Plaines, IL 60016; (847) 824-8131. Exec. Dir., Irene K. Pesce.

National Catholic Conference for Interracial Justice (NCCIJ) (1960): 1200 Varnum St. N.E., Washington, DC 20017; (202) 529-6480. Exec. Dir., Rev. Mr. Joseph M. Conrad, Jr.

National Catholic Conference for Seafarers: 4219 Constance St., New Orleans, LA 70115; (504) 891-6677. Association of chaplains and laity serving in the pastoral care of seafarers.

National Catholic Council on Alcoholism and Related Drug Problems, Inc.: 1550 Hendrickson St., Brooklyn, NY 11234-3514; (718) 951-7177; P.O. Box 248, Lafayette, IN 47902-0248; (765) 420-0129, www.nccatoday.com. An affiliate of the USCCB. Committed to assisting members in a greater awareness of alcoholism, other chemical addictions and prevention issues. Exec. Dir., Thomas A. Russell.

National Catholic Development Conference (1968): 86 Front St., Hempstead, NY 11550; (516) 481-6000. Professional association of organizations and individuals engaged in raising funds for Catholic charitable activities. Pres., Sr. Georgette Lehmuth, O.S.F.

National Catholic Ministry to the Bereaved (NCMB) (1990): 28700 Euclid Ave., Wickliffe, OH, 44092-2527; (440) 943-3480; www.griefwork.org. Offers ongoing education, resources and assistance to dioceses, parishes and caregivers in their ministry to the bereaved. Pres., Sr. Maureen O'Brien, O.P.

National Catholic Pharmacists Guild of the United States (1962): 1012 Surrey Hills Dr., St. Louis, MO 63117; (314) 645-0085; *The Catholic Pharmacist*. Co-Pres., Exec. Dir. and Editor, John P. Winkelmann.

National Catholic Society of Foresters (1891): 320 S. School St., Mt. Prospect, IL 60056; (847) 342-4500; www.ncsf@enteract.com; *National Catholic Forester*, quarterly. A fraternal insurance society. Pres. and CEO, Sue Koleczek.

National Catholic Women's Union (1916): 3835 Westminster Pl., St. Louis, MO 63108; (314) 371-1653; www.socialjustice.org. 7,000 members.

National Center for the Laity (1977): P.O. Box 291102, Chicago, IL 60629; (708) 974-5221; *Initiatives*, six times a year. To promote and implement the vision of Vatican II: That the laity are the Church in the modern world as they attend to their occupational, family and neighborhood responsibilities.

National Center for Urban Ethnic Affairs (1971): P.O. Box 20, Cardinal Station, Washington, DC 20064; (202) 319-6188. Research and action related to the Church's concern for cultural pluralism and urban neighborhoods. An affiliate of the USCCB. Pres., Dr. John A. Kromkowski.

National Christ Child Society Inc. (1887): 6900 Wisconsin Ave. N.W., Suite 604, Bethesda, MD 20815; (800) 814-2149; www.NationalChristChildSoc.org. Founder, Mary V. Merrick. A non-profit Catholic association of volunteers of all denominations dedicated to the service of needy children and youth regardless of race or creed. Approximately 7,000 adult members in 37 chapters in U.S. Exec. Dir., Margaret Saffell.

National Committee of Catholic Laymen, The (1977): 215 Lexington Ave., Fourth Floor, New York, NY 10016; (212) 685-6666; *Catholic Eye*, monthly. Lobbying and publishing organization representing "orthodox" Catholics who strongly support Pope John Paul II. Editor, Catholic Eye, Mrs. Anne Conlon.

National Conference of Catechetical Leadership (formerly, National Conference of Diocesan Directors of Religious Education) (1936): 3021 4th St. N.E., Washington, DC 20017; (202) 636-3826. 1,300 members. To promote catechetical ministry at the national diocesan and parish levels. Exec. Dir., Neil A. Parent.

National Conference of Catholic Airport Chaplains (1986): P.O. Box 66353, Chicago, IL 60666; (773) 686-2636. Provides support and communication for Catholics performing pastoral ministry to airport and airline workers and Catholic travelers; affiliated with Bishops' Committee on Migration,

USCCB. Episcopal liaison, Most Rev. James C. Timlin. Pres., Deacon James A. O'Malley.

National Conference of Diocesan Vocation Directors (NCDVD) (1961): P.O. Box 1570, Little River, SC 29566; (843) 280-7191. Professional organization for diocesan vocation personnel providing resources and on-going education in their promoting, assessing and forming of candidates for the diocesan priesthood.

National Council for Catholic Evangelization (1983): 415 Michigan Ave, NE, Suite 90, Washington, DC, DC 20017; 1-800-786-NCCE; www.catholicevangelization.org. To promote evangelization as the "primary and essential mission of the Church," in accordance with *Evangelii Nuntiandi*, the 1975 apostolic exhortation of Pope Paul VI. Exec. Dir., Sr. Priscilla Lemire, R.J.M.

National Council of Catholic Men: 5664 Midforest Ln., Cincinnati, OH 45329. A federation of Catholic organizations through which Catholic men may be heard nationally on matters of common interest. NCCM is a constituent of the National Council of Catholic Laity.

National Council of Catholic Women (1920): 1275 K St. N.W., Suite 975, Washington, DC 20005; (202) 682-0334; www.nccw.org; *Catholic Woman*, bi-monthly. A federation of some 7,000 organizations of Catholic women in the U.S. NCCW unites Catholic organizations and individual Catholic women of the U.S., develops their leadership potential, assists them to act upon current issues in the Church and society, provides a medium through which Catholic women may speak and act upon matters of common interest, and relates to other national and international organizations in the solution of present-day problems. It is an affiliate of the World Union of Catholic Women's Organizations. Exec. Dir., Susan T. Muskett.

National Evangelization Teams (NET): 110 Crusader Ave., West St. Paul, MN 55118-4427; (651) 450-6833. Trains Catholic young adults to be evangelists to peers and high school/junior high youth through traveling retreat teams.

National Federation of Catholic Physicians' Guilds) (1927): P.O. Box 757, Pewaukee, WI 53072; (262) 523-6201; www.cathmed.com; *Linacre Quarterly*. Exec. Dir., Robert H. Herzog.

National Federation of Priests' Councils (1968): 1337 West Ohio, Chicago, IL 60622-6490; (312) 226-3334; www.nfpc.org; *Touchstone*, quarterly. To give priests' councils a representative voice in matters of presbyteral, pastoral and ministerial concern to the U.S. and the universal Church. Pres., Rev. Donald J. Wolf; Exec. Dir., Bro. Bernard Stratman, S.M.

National Institute for the Word of God (1972): 487 Michigan Ave. N.E., Washington, DC 20017; (202) 529-0001; www.niwg.op.org/niwg. For renewed biblical preaching, Bible sharing and evangelization. Dir., Rev. John Burke, O.P.

National Life Center, Inc.: 686 N. Broad St., Woodbury, NJ 08096; (856) 848-1819, (800) 848-LOVE; www.nationallifecenter.com. Interdenominational guidance and referral service organization offering pregnant women alternatives to abortion. Pres., Denise F. Cocciolone.

National Organization for Continuing Education of Roman Catholic Clergy, Inc. (1973): 1337 W. Ohio St., Chicago, IL 60622; (312) 226-1890. Membership: 152 dioceses, 66 religious provinces, 46 institutions, 49 individuals in U.S., 18 associates outside U.S. Pres., Rev. Francis S. Tebbe, O.F.M.

National Pastoral Life Center: 18 Bleecker St., New York, NY 10012-2404; (212) 431-7825; www.nplc.org; *Church*, quarterly. Dir., Msgr. Philip Murnion.

National Service Committee of the Catholic Charismatic Renewal: Chariscenter USA, P.O. Box 628, Locust Grove, VA 22508; (540) 972-0225; www.nsc-chariscenter.org, www.iccrs.org. The mission of the National Service Committee is "to stir into flame the grace of Pentecost within and beyond the Church, to broaden and deepen the understanding that baptism in the Holy Spirit is the Christian inheritance of all, and to strengthen the Catholic Charismatic Renewal."

NETWORK, A Catholic Social Justice Lobby (1971): 801 Pennsylvania Ave. S.E., Suite 460, Washington, DC 20003; (202) 547-5556; www.network lobby.org; *NETWORK Connection*, bimonthly. A national Catholic social justice lobby. Nat. Coord., Kathy Thornton, R.S.M.

Nocturnal Adoration Society of the United States (1882): 184 E. 76th St., New York, NY 10021; (212) 288-5082. Nat. Dir., Rev. Mario Marzocchi, S.S.S.

North American Academy of Liturgy: c/o CSSR Executive Office, Valparaiso University, Valparaiso, IN 46383; *Proceedings*, annually. Foster ecumenical and interreligious liturgical research, publication and dialogue on a scholarly level. Pres., Alan Barthel.

North American Conference of Separated and Divorced Catholics (1972): P.O. Box 360, Richland, OR 97870; (541) 893-6089; www.nacsdc.com. Exec. Dir., Irene Varley.

North American Forum on the Catechumenate: 3033 Fourth St. NE, Washington, DC 20017; (202) 529-9493; www.naforum.org. An international network committed to the implementation of the Order of Christian Initiation of Adults. Exec. Dir., James Schellman.

Order of the Alhambra (1904): 4200 Leeds Ave., Baltimore, MD 21229; (410) 242-0660; www.Order Alhambra.org. 7,000 members in U.S. and Canada. Fraternal society dedicated to assisting developmentally disabled and handicapped children. Supreme Commander, Angelo Miele.

Our Lady's Rosary Makers (1949): 4611 Poplar Level Rd., Louisville, KY 40233. 23,000 members. To supply missionaries with free rosaries for distribution throughout the world. *News Bulletin*, monthly. Pres., Michael Ford.

Paulist National Catholic Evangelization Association (1977): 3031 Fourth St., N.E., Washington, DC 20017-1102; (202) 832-5022; www.pncea.org; *Share the Word*, bimonthly magazine; *Evangelization Update*, bimonthly newsletter. To work with unchurched and alienated Catholics; to develop, test and document contemporary ways in which Catholic parishes and dioceses can evangelize the unchurched and inactive Catholics. Dir., Rev. Kenneth Boyack, C.S.P.

Philangeli (Friends of the Angels) (1949 in England; 1956 in U.S.): Viatorian Fathers, 1115 E. Euclid St., Arlington Heights, IL 60004.

Pious Union of Prayer (1898): St. Joseph's Home,

P.O. Box 288, Jersey City, NJ 07303; (201) 798-4141; *St. Joseph's Messenger* and *Advocate of the Blind*, quarterly.

Polish Roman Catholic Union of America (1887): 984 N. Milwaukee Ave., Chicago, IL 60622; (773) 728-2600; www.prcua.org; *Narod Polski*, bimonthly. Fraternal benefit society.

Pontifical Mission for Palestine (1949): 1011 First Ave., New York, NY 10022-4195; (212) 826-1480; www.cnewa.org. A papal relief and development agency of the Holy See for the Middle East, with offices in New York, Vatican City, Amman, Beirut and Jerusalem. Pres., Msgr. Archim. Robert L. Stern, J.C.D.

Pontifical Missionary Union (1916): 366 Fifth Ave., New York, NY 10001; (212) 563-8700; www.worldmissions-catholicchurch.org. To promote mission awareness among clergy, religious, candidates to priestly and religious life, and others engaged in pastoral ministry of the Church. Nat. Dir., Most Rev. William J. McCormack; Nat. Sec., Rev. Eugene LaVerdiere, S.S.S.

Population Research Institute (1989): 1190 Progress Drive, Suite 2D, P.O. Box 1559, Front Royal, VA 22630; (540) 622-5240; www.pop.org; *PRI Review*, a bimonthly newsletter, which reports on population news of interest from around the world. Nonprofit research and educational organization dedicated to objectively presenting the truth about population-related issues. Pres., Steven W. Mosher.

Priests' Eucharistic League (1887): Hampton House-Apt. 91, 5300 South Shore Dr., Chicago, IL 60615-5708; *Emmanuel*, 10 issues a year. Nat. Dir., Rev. Anthony Schueller, S.S.S.

Pro Ecclesia Foundation (1970): 350 Fifth Ave., New York, NY 10118; *Pro Ecclesia Magazine*. Pres., Dr. Timothy A. Mitchell.

Pro Maria Committee (1952): 112 Norris Rd. Tyngsboro, MA 01879; (978) 649-1813. Promotes devotion to Our Lady of Beauraing (*See* **Index**).

Pro Sanctity Movement: Pro Sanctity Spirituality Center, 205 S. Pine Dr., Fullerton, CA 92833; (714) 956-1020. 730 E. 87th St., Brooklyn, NY 11236, (718) 649-0324; www.prosanctity.org. 6762 Western Ave., Omaha, NE 68132; (402) 553-4418; www.pro sanctity.org. 1102 N. 204 St. Elkhorn, NE 68022; (402) 289-2670; www.prosanctity.org. Organized to spread God's call of all persons to holiness.

Project Children (1975): P.O. Box 933, Greenwood Lake, NY 10925; (845) 477-3472; www.inter webinc.com/children/. Nonsectarian volunteer group; provides children of Northern Ireland with a six-week summer vacation with host families in the U.S.

The Providence Association of the Ukrainian Catholics in America (Ukrainian Catholic Fraternal Benefit Society) (1912): 817 N. Franklin St., Philadelphia, PA 19123; (215) 627-4984.

Queen of the Americas Guild, Inc. (1979): P.O. Box 851, St. Charles, IL 60174; (630) 584-1822; www.queenoftheamericasguild.org. 7,000 members. To build English information center and retreat center near Basilica in Mexico City and spread the message of Guadalupe. Nat. Coord. Rebecca Nichols.

Raskob Foundation for Catholic Activities, Inc. (1945): P.O. Box 4019, Wilmington, DE 19807-0019; (302) 655-4440; www.rfca.org. Exec. Pres., Frederick Perella, Jr.

Reparation Society of the Immaculate Heart of Mary, Inc. (1946): 100 E. 20th St., Baltimore, MD 21218; *Fatima Findings*, monthly.

Retrouvaille: P.O.Box 25, Kelton, PA 19346. A minstry to hurting marriages, Retrouvaille consists of a weekend experience with follow-up sessions designed to provide couples with ways and means of healing and reconciling. Emphasis is placed on communication, enabling husband and wife to rediscover each other and to examine their lives in a new and positive way. The ministry is neither a retreat nor a sensitivity group, nor does it include group dynamics or discussions. The program is conducted by trained couples and priests, with programs offered under the auspices of diocesan family life agencies. International Coordinating Team: Bill and Peg Swaan.

Sacred Heart League: 6050 Hwy 61 N, P.O. Box 190, Walls, MS 38680. Pres., Rev. Robert Hess, S.C.J.

St. Ansgar's Scandinavian Catholic League (1910): 3 East 28th St., New York, NY 10016; (212) 675-0400; *St. Ansgar's Bulletin*, annually. 1,000 members. Prayers and financial support for Church in Scandinavia. Pres., Astrid M. O'Brien.

St. Anthony's Guild (1924): P.O. 2948, Paterson, NJ 07509-2948; (973) 777-3737; *The Anthonian*, quarterly. Promotes devotion to St. Anthony of Padua and support for formation programs, infirm friars and ministries of the Franciscans of Holy Name Province. Dir., Fr. Joseph Hertel, O.F.M.

St. Bernadette Institute of Sacred Art (1993): P.O. Box 8249, Albuquerque, NM 87198-8249; (505) 265-9126; www.nmia.com/~paulos. To promote, initiate, encourage interest and sustain projects and persons engaged in sacred art.

St. Gregory Foundation for Latin Liturgy (1989): Newman House, 5401 S. 33rd St., Omaha, NE 68107; (402) 733-2423. To promote within the Church in the U.S. the use of the Latin language in the Mass in accordance with the teachings of Vatican II. Founder and Pres., Rev. Peter M.J. Stravinskas, Ph.D., S.T.D.

St. Jude League (1929): 205 W. Monroe St., Chicago, IL 60606; (312) 236-7782; www.stjude league.org. Promotes devotion to St. Jude; supports work of Claretian Missionaries throughout the world. Dir., Rev. Mark J. Brummel, C.M.F.

St. Margaret of Scotland Guild, Inc. (1938): Graymoor, P.O. Box 300, Garrison, NY 10524-0300; (845) 424-3671. Moderator, Bro. Pius MacIsaac.

St. Martin de Porres Guild (1935): 141 E. 65th St., New York, NY 10021; (212) 744-2410; www.op-stjoseph.org. Dir., Rev. Raymond F. Halligan, O.P.

Serra International (1934): 220 S. State St., Suite 1703, Chicago, IL 60604; (312) 588-0700; www.serrainternational.org; *Serran*, bimonthly. 21,000 members in 673 clubs in 35 countries. Fosters vocations to the priesthood, and religious life, trains Catholic lay leadership. Formally aggregated to the Pontifical Society for Priestly Vocations, 1951. Exec. Dir., John W. Woodward.

Slovak Catholic Federation (1911): 408 North Main St., Taylor, PA 18517-1108; (570) 562-1341; www.slovakcatholicfederation.org. Founded by Rev. Joseph Murgas to promote and coordinate religious activities among Slovak Catholic fraternal societies, religious communities and Slovak ethnic parishes in their effort to address themselves to the special needs of Slovak Catholics in the U.S. and Canada. Pres., Rev. Philip A. Altavilla.

Slovak Catholic Sokol (1905): 205 Madison St., Passaic, NJ 07055; (973) 777-2606; www.slovak catholicsokol.org; *Slovak Catholic Falcon*, weekly. 38,000 members. Fraternal benefit society.

Society for the Propagation of the Faith (1822): 366 Fifth Ave., New York, NY 10001; (212) 563-8725 (fax); www.propfaith.org; *Mission*, 4 times a year; *Director's Newsletter*, monthly. Established in all dioceses. Church's principal instrument for promoting mission awareness and generating financial support for the missions. General fund for ordinary and extraordinary subsidies for all mission dioceses. Is subject to Congregation for the Evangelization of Peoples. Nat. Dir., Rev. John Kozar.

Society of St. Monica (1986): 215 Falls Ave., Cuyahoga Falls, OH 44221. More than 10,000 members worldwide. Confident, daily prayer for the return of inactive Catholics and Catholics who have left the Church. Founder and Spir. Dir., Rev. Dennis M. McNeil.

Society of St. Peter Apostle (1889): 366 Fifth Ave., New York, NY 10001; (212) 563-8700; www.prop faith.org; all dioceses. Church's central fund for support of seminaries, seminarians and novices in all mission dioceses. Nat. Dir., Rev. John Kozar.

Society of the Divine Attributes (1974): 2905 Castlegate Ave., Pittsburgh, PA 15226; (412) 456-3114. 3,000 members worldwide (lay, clerical and religious). Contemplative prayer society. Spir. Dir. Rev. Ronald D. Lawler, O.F.M. Cap.

Spiritual Life Institute of America (1960): Box 219, Crestone, CO 81131; (719) 256-4778; www.spirituallifeinstitute.org. Forefront, seasonal. An eremetical movement to foster the contemplative spirit in America. Founder, Rev. William McNamara, O.C.D. Second foundation: Nova Nada, Primitive Wilderness Hermitage, Kemptville, Nova Scotia, Canada B0W 1Y0. Third foundation, Holy Hill Hermitage, Skreen, Co. Sligo, Ireland.

Support Our Aging Religious (SOAR) (1986): 1400 Spring St., Suite 320, Silver Spring, MD 20910-2755; (301) 589-9811; www.soar-usa.org. Laity-led campaign to raise funds for retired religious. Pres., Timothy P. Hamer.

Theresians of the United States (1961): 1237 W. Monroe St., Springfield, IL 62704; (217) 726-5484, www.theresians.org. Spiritual, educational and ministerial organization of Christian women. Exec. Dir., Victoria S. Schmidt. International division: Theresian World Ministry (1971), same address.

United Societies of U.S.A. (1903): 613 Sinclair St., McKeesport, PA 15132; *Prosvita-Enlightenment*, bimonthly newspaper.3,755 members.

United States Catholic Historical Society (1884): St. Joseph's Seminary, 201 Seminary Ave., Yonkers, NY 10704; (914) 337-8381; www.uschs.com. Exec. Vice-Pres., John T. Gildea.

Western Catholic Union (1877): 510 Maine St., Quincy, IL 62301; (800) 223-4928; www.wcu life.com; *Western Catholic Union Record*, quarterly. 19,000 members. A fraternal benefit society. Pres., Mark A. Wiewel.

Women for Faith and Family (1984): P.O. Box 8326, St. Louis, MO 63132; (314) 863-8385; www.wf-f.org; *Voices*, quarterly. 60,000 signers worldwide of the Affirmation for Catholic Women. An international movement to promote Catholic teachings especially on all issues involving the family and roles for women. Members sign an eight-point statement of fidelity to the Church.Dir., Helen Hull Hitchcock.

Young Ladies' Institute (1887): 1111 Gough St., San Francisco, CA 94109-6606; (415) 346-4367; *Voice of YLI*, bimonthly. 13,000 members. Grand Sec., Frances Ridley.

Young Men's Institute (1883): 1625 "C" Palmetto Ave., Pacifica, CA 94044; (650) 738-3007; www.ymi usa.org; *Institute Journal*, bimonthly. 4,500 members. Grand Sec., Clifford C. Smethurst.

PERSONAL PRELATURE OF THE HOLY SEE: OPUS DEI

Founded in Madrid in 1928 by Msgr. Josemaría Escrivá de Balaguer (beatified in 1992 and canonized in October 2002), Opus Dei has the aim of spreading throughout all sectors of society a profound awareness of the universal call to holiness and apostolate (of Christian witness and action) in the ordinary circumstances of life, and, more specifically, through one's professional work. On Nov. 28, 1982, Pope John Paul II established Opus Dei as a personal prelature with the full title, Prelature of the Holy Cross and Opus Dei. The 2003 edition of the *Annuario Pontificio* reported that the prelature had 1,819 priests (37 newly ordained) and 366 major seminarians. Also, there were 82,765 lay persons – men and women, married and single, of every class and social condition — of about 80 nationalities, as well as 1,727 churches and pastoral centers.

Further, the prelature operates the Pontifical University of the Holy Cross in Rome; it was established in 1985 and received approval as a pontifical institution in 1995. Courses of study include theology, philosophy, canon law, and the recently established School of Social Communications.

In the United States, members of Opus Dei, along with cooperators and friends, conduct apostolic works corporately in major cities in the East and Midwest, Texas and on the West Coast. Elsewhere, corporate works include universities, vocational institutes, training schools for farmers and numerous other apostolic initiatives. Opus Dei information offices are located at: 99 Overlook Cir., New Rochelle, NY 10804; (914) 235-6128 (office of the New York chaplain); and 655 Levering Ave., Los Angeles, CA 90024; (310) 208-0941; www.opusdei.org.

KNIGHTS OF COLUMBUS

The Knights of Columbus, a fraternal benefit society of Catholic men, is a family service organization founded by Fr. Michael J. McGivney and chartered by the General Assembly of Connecticut on Mar. 29, 1882.

Currently, there are over 1.6 million Knights of Columbus - more than ever before in the Order's history. Together with their families, the Knights are nearly 6 million strong. In addition, from the first local council in New Haven, the Order has grown to more than 12,000 councils in the United States, Canada, Mexico, the Philippines, Puerto Rico, Cuba, the Dominican Republic, Panama, the Virgin Islands, Guatemala, Guam and Saipan.

In keeping with their general purpose to be of service to the Church, the Knights and their families are active in many apostolic works and community programs. The Knights cooperate with the U.S. bishops in Pro-Life activities and are engaged in other apostolic endeavors as well.

According to the organization's 2002 Survey of Fraternal Activity the Knights raised and donated a record $128.5 million to charity and volunteered a record 60.8 million hours of service. The totals are all-time highs for the Knights. Approximately 73 percent of the organization's 11,700 state and local units responded to the survey. Of the $128.5 million raised and donated in 2002, $106 million was raised locally and donated directly to charities chosen by K of C units raising the funds; the remaining $22.3 million

was given by the Knights of Columbus Supreme Council and its designated charities from its headquarters.

In 2001, members raised and contributed to charity more than $125.6 million and volunteered more than 58.9 million hours of service. In 2000, the Knights raised and donated $116 million and 55.3 million volunteer hours. Twenty years ago, the Knights reported raising and donating to charity $52 million and volunteering 13.4 million hours of service. In the decade of the 1990s, the Knights donated nearly $1 billion to numerous charitable causes and nearly 400 million hours of volunteer service.

The programmatic activities of the Knights remain much the same from one year to the next. The K of C funded the restoration of the Maderno Atrium of St. Peter's Basilica in Rome, named for the architect, Carlo Maderno (1556-1629). The atrium is the big "front porch" through which every visitor to St. Peter's passes. This is one of a series of projects for the restoration of St. Peter's funded by the Knights over the years: renovation of the roof of the Blessed Sacrament Chapel (1993); renovation of the Room of the Architects and Room of the Window Panes (1987-88); restoration of the facade (1985-86); construction of chapels in the grottoes (1981-82).

The Knights of Columbus headquarters address is One Columbus Plaza, New Haven, CT 06510-3326; (203) 752-4350; www.kofc.org. The Grand Knight is Carl Anderson.

Catholic Social Services

Catholic Charities USA (formerly National Conference of Catholic Charities): 1731 King St., Suite 200, Alexandria, VA 22314; (703) 549-1390; www.catholiccharitiesusa.org. Founded in 1910 by Most Rev. Thomas J. Shahan and Rt. Rev. Msgr. William J. Kerby in cooperation with lay leaders of the Society of St. Vincent de Paul to help advance and promote the charitable programs and activities of Catholic community and social service agencies in the United States. As the central and national organization for this purpose, it services a network of more than 1,400 agencies and institutions by consultation, information and assistance in planning and evaluating social service programs under Catholic auspices.

Diocesan member agencies provide shelter, food, counseling, services to children, teen parents and the elderly, and a variety of other services to people in need — without regard to religion, gender, age or national origin. Each year millions of people receive help from Catholic Charities; in 1995 (latest statistics available), more than 10 million turned to Catholic Charities agencies for help. In addition, Catholic Charities is an advocate for persons and families in need.

Catholic Charities USA serves members through national and regional meetings, training programs, literature and social policy advocacy on the national level. It is charged by the U.S. bishops with responding to disasters in this country. Catholic Charities USA's president represents North America before *Caritas Internationalis*, the international conference of Catholic Charities, and thus maintains contact with the Catholic Charities movement throughout the world. Publications include *Charities USA*, a quarterly membership magazine, and a directory of U.S. Catholic Charities agencies and institutions. Pres., Rev. J. Bryan Hehir, S.J.

Society of St. Vincent de Paul, Council of the United States (originally called the Conference of Charity): National Council, 58 Progress Parkway, St. Louis, MO 63043; (314) 576-3993; www.svdpuscouncil.org. An association of Catholic lay men and women devoted to personal service to the poor through the spiritual and corporal works of mercy. The first conference was formed at Paris in 1833 by Bl. Frederic Ozanam and his associates.

The first conference in the U.S. was organized in 1845 at St. Louis. There are now approximately 4,400 units of the society in this country, with a membership of more than 60,000. The society operates world wide in more than 130 countries and has more than 800,000 members.

Besides person-to-person assistance, increasing emphasis is being given to stores and rehabilitation workshops of the society through which persons with marginal income can purchase refurbished goods at minimal cost. Handicapped persons are employed in renovating goods and store operations. The society also operates food centers, shelters, criminal justice and other programs. Publications include *The Ozanam News*, a biannual membership magazine, and *The United States Councilor*, a quarterly newsletter. Nat. Pres., Eugene Smith; Exec. Dir., Richard Hennicke.

Catholic Health Association of the United States (CHA): National Headquarters, 4455 Woodson Road, St. Louis, MO 63134; (314) 427-2500; www.chusa.org. Represents more than 1,200 Catholic-sponsored facilities and organizations, works with its members to promote justice and compassion in healthcare, influence public policy, shape a continuum of care through integraated delivery, and strengthen ministry presence and influence in the U.S. healthcare system. CHA supports and strengthens the Catholic health ministry by being a catalyst through research and development (leading edge tools for sustaining a faith-based ministry in price competitive markets), education and facilitation (annual assembly, conferences, and other methods for engaging the ministry), and advocacy (a united ministry voice for public policy). CHA members make up the nation's largest group of not-for-profit healthcare facilities under a single form of sponsorship. Pres., Rev. Michael D. Place, S.T.D.

National Association of Catholic Chaplains: 3501 S. Lake Dr., Milwaukee, WI 53207; (414) 483-4898. Founded in 1965. Membership is over 3,500.

SOCIAL SERVICE ORGANIZATIONS

(*See* separate article for a listing of facilities for the handicapped.)

The Carroll Center for the Blind (formerly the Catholic Guild for All the Blind): 770 Centre St., Newton, MA 02158. The center conducts diagnostic evaluation and rehabilitation programs for blind people over 16 years of age, and provides computer training and other services. Pres., Rachel Rosenbaum.

International Catholic Deaf Association: 8002 S. Sawyer Rd., Darian, IL 60561; TTY (630) 887-9472. Established by deaf adults in Toronto, Canada, in 1949, the association has more than 8,000 members in 130 chapters, mostly in the U.S. It is the only international lay association founded and controlled by deaf Catholic adults. The ICDA publishes *The Deaf Catholic*, bimonthly, sponsors regional conferences, workshops and an annual convention. Pres., Kathleen Kush.

National Apostolate for Inclusion Ministry (NAfIM): P.O. Box 218, Riverdale, MD, 20738; (800) 736-1280; www.nafim.org. Formerly known as the National Apostolate for Persons with Mental Retardation (NAPMR). Established in 1968 to promote the full participation by persons with mental retardation in the life of the Church. Exec. Dir., Barbara Lampe.

National Catholic Office for the Deaf: 7202 Buchanan St., Landover Hills, MD 20784; (301) 577-1684; www.ncod.org. Formally established in 1971, at Washington, DC, to provide pastoral service to those who teach deaf children and adults, to the parents of deaf children, to pastors of deaf persons, and to organizations of the deaf. Exec.Dir., Arvilla Rank.

National Catholic Office for Persons with Disabilities (NCPD): 415 Michigan Ave., N.E., Washington, DC 20017; (202) 529-2933; www.ncpd.org. NCPD's mission is to provide resources and consultation to a national network of diocesan directors who oversee access and inclusion at the parish level; to collaborate with other national Catholic organizations, advocating for inclusion within all their programs and initiatives and to work with Catholic organizations addressing the concerns and needs of those with various disabilities. Established in 1982 as a result of the 1978 Pastoral Statement of the U.S. Catholic Bishops on People with Disabilities., the office continues to press for words and actions which promote meaningful participation and inclusion at all levels of the Church.

Xavier Society for the Blind: 154 E. 23rd St., New York, NY 10010-4595; (212) 473-7800. Founded in 1900 by Rev. Joseph Stadelman, S.J., it is a center for publications for the blind and partially sighted. Exec. Dir., Rev. Alfred E. Caruana, S.J.

OTHER SOCIAL SERVICES

Cancer Hospitals or Homes: The following homes or hospitals specialize in the care of cancer patients. Capacities are in parentheses.

Our Lady of Perpetual Help Home, Servants of Relief for Incurable Cancer, 760 Pollard Blvd., S.W., Atlanta, GA 30315; (404) 688-9515 (52).

Rose Hawthorne Lathrop Home, Servants of Relief for Incurable Cancer, 1600 Bay St., Fall River, MA 02724; (508) 673-2322 (35).

Our Lady of Good Counsel Home, Servants of Relief for Incurable Cancer, 2076 St. Anthony Ave., St. Paul, MN 55104; (651) 646-2797.

Calvary Hospital, Inc., 1740 Eastchester Rd., Bronx, NY 10461; (718) 863-6900 (200). Operated in connection with Catholic Charities, Department of Health and Hospitals, Archdiocese of New York.

St. Rose's Home, Servants of Relief for Incurable Cancer, 71 Jackson St., New York, NY 10002; (212) 677-8132 (60).

Rosary Hill Home, Servants of Relief for Incurable Cancer, 600 Linda Ave., Hawthorne, NY 10532; (914) 769-0114 (72).

Holy Family Home, Servants of Relief for Incurable Cancer, 6753 State Rd., Parma, OH 44134; (440) 845-7700; www.cle-dioc.org (50).

Sacred Heart Free Home for Incurable Cancer, Servants of Relief for Incurable Cancer, 1315 W. Hunting Park Ave., Philadelphia, PA 19140; (215) 329-3222 (45).

Substance Abuse: Facilities for substance abuse (alcohol and other drugs) include:

Daytop Village, Inc., 54 W. 40th St., New York, NY 10018; (212) 354-6000; www.daytop.org. Msgr. William B. O'Brien, president. Twenty-eight residential and ambulatory sites in New York, New Jersey, Pennsylvania, Florida, Texas and California.

Good Shepherd Gracenter, Convent of the Good Shepherd, 1310 Bacon St., San Francisco, CA 94134; (415) 586-2822. Residential program for chemically dependent women.

New Hope Manor, 35 Hillside Rd., Barryville, NY 12719; fax (914) 557-6603. Residential substance abuse treatment center for teen-age girls and women ages 13-40. Residential; half-way house and aftercare program totaling 6 months or more.

St. Joseph's Hospital, L.E. Phillips Libertas Center for the Chemically Dependent, 2661 County Road, Hwy. I, Chippewa Falls, WI 54729; (715) 723-1811 (46). Residential and outpatient. Adult and adolescent programs. Hospital Sisters of the Third Order of St. Francis.

St. Joseph's Hospital (Chippewa Falls, WI) Libertas Center for the Treatment of Chemical Dependency, 1701 Dousman St., Green Bay, WI 54302 (23). Residental and outpatient adolescent programs. Hospital Sisters of the Third Order of St. Francis.

St. Luke's Addiction Recovery Services, 7707 NW 2nd Ave., Miami, FL 33150; (305) 795-0077; www.catholiccharitiesadm.org/stluke. A program of Catholic Community Services, Miami. Adult residential and family outpatient recovery services for drug, alcohol addiction and DUI.

Miami Substance Abuse Prevention Programs, 7707 N.W. Second Ave., Miami, FL 33150; (305) 795-0077; www.catholiccharitiesadm.org/stluke. Trains parents, youth, priests and teachers as prevention volunteers in the area of substance abuse.

Transitus House, 1830 Wheaton St., Chippewa Falls, WI 54729; (715) 723-1155. Two programs for chemically dependent: adult intensive residential (15 beds, women); adolescent intensive residential (5 beds, girls 15-18 yrs.). Hospital Sisters of the Third Order of St. Francis.

Matt Talbot Inn, 2270 Professor Ave., Cleveland, OH 44113; (216) 781-0288. Two programs: Chemical dependency Residential Treatment/Halfway House (capacity 27) and outpatient treatment/aftercare. Serves male clients 18 years and over.

Sacred Heart Rehabilitation Center, Inc., 2203 St. Antoine, Detroit, MI 48201 (admissions/assessment, outpatient). 400 Stoddard Rd., P.O. Box 41038, Memphis, MI 48041 (12 beds, detoxification; 70 beds residential treatment). 28573 Schoenherr, Warren, MI 48093 (outpatient). All facilities serve male and female clients 18 and over.

Straight and Narrow, Inc., 396 Straight St., Paterson, NJ 07501. Facilities and services include (at various locations): Straight and Narrow Hospital (Mount Carmel Guild), substance abuse, detoxification (20 beds); Alpha House for Drug and Alcohol Rehabilitation (women; 30 beds — 25 adults, 5 children), Dismas House for Drug and Alcohol Rehabilitation (men; 78 beds); The Guild for Drug and Alcohol Rehabilitation (men, 56 beds); juvenile residential units; outpatient services and facility; three halfway houses; counseling services; employment assistance; intoxicated driver's resource center; medical day care center (available to HIV infected persons and persons diagnosed with AIDS); methadone clinic.

The National Catholic Council on Alcoholism and Related Drug Problems, Inc., 1550 Hendrickson St., Brooklyn, NY 11234, offers educational material to those involved in pastoral ministry on ways of dealing with problems related to alcoholism and medication dependency.

Convicts: Priests serve as full- or part-time chaplains in penal and correctional institutions throughout the country. Limited efforts have been made to assist in the rehabilitation of released prisoners in Halfway House establishments.

Dining Rooms: Facilities for homeless: Representative of places where meals are provided, and in some cases lodging and other services as well, are:

St. Anthony Foundation, 121 Golden Gate Ave., San Francisco, CA 94102; (415) 241-2600; www.stanthonyfdn.org. Founded in 1950 by the Franciscan Friars. Multi-program social service agency serving people who are poor and homeless. Dining room serves up to 2,100 meals daily; more than 25 million since its founding. Other services include free clothing and furniture; free medical clinic; residential drug and alcohol rehabilitation programs; employment program; emergency shelter, housing and daytime facility for homeless women; residence for low-income senior women; free hygiene services; case management for seniors; social services.

St. Vincent de Paul Free Dining Room, 675 23rd St., Oakland, CA 94612; (510) 451-7676. Administered by Daughters of Charity of St. Vincent de Paul, under sponsorship of St. Vincent de Paul Society. Hot meals served at lunch time 7 days a week. Also provides counseling, referral/information services.

St. Vincent's Dining Room, P.O. Box 5099, Reno, NV 89513; (775) 329-5363.

St. Vincent Dining Room, 1501 Las Vegas Blvd., Las Vegas, NV 89101. Structured program for 275 men in which job development office works with homeless to enable them to find employment. For non-residents, there is a hot meal every day at noon. Emergency overnight shelter facility for families, women and men.

Good Shepherd Center, Little Brothers of the Good Shepherd, 218 Iron St. S.W., P.O. Box 749, Albuquerque, NM 87103; (505) 243-2527.

Holy Name Centre for Homeless Men, Inc., 18 Bleecker St., New York, NY 10012. A shelter for alcoholic, homeless men. Provides social services and aid to transients and those in need. Affiliated with New York Catholic Charities.

St. Francis Inn, 2441 Kensington Ave., Philadelphia, PA 19125. Serves hot meals. Temporary shelter for men. Day center for women. Thrift shop.

St. John's Hospice for Men, staffed by Little Brothers of the Good Shepherd, 1221 Race St., Philadelphia, PA 19107. Hot meals served daily; 36-bed shelter; clothing distribution, showers, mail distribution, drug/alcohol rehabilitation and work programs. Good Shepherd Program of St. John's Hospice, 1225 Race St., Philadelphia, PA 19107. Ten-bed facility for homeless men with AIDS.

Camillus House, Little Brothers of the Good Shepherd, P.O. Box 11829, Miami, FL 33101; (305) 374-1065; www.camillus.org. Free comprehensive services for the poor and homeless including daily dinner; night

lodging for 70; clothing distribution; showers; mail distribution; drug/alcohol rehabilitation program. Forty-eight units of single-room housing for employed formerly homeless women and men who have completed drug and alcohol rehabilitation programs.

Camillus Health Concern, P.O. Box 12408, Miami, FL 33101; (305) 577-4840. Free comprehensive medical and social services for the homeless.

Shelters: Facilities for runaways, the abused, exploited and homeless include:

Anthony House, supported by St. Anthony's Guild (*see* Index). 38 E. Roosevelt Ave., Roosevelt, NY 11575 (with St. Vincent de Paul Society — for homeless men), 128 W. 112th St., New York, NY 10026 (emergency food and clothing), 6215 Holly St., P.O. Box 880, Zellwood, FL 32798 (for migrant workers and their families).

Good Shepherd Shelter-Convent of the Good Shepherd. Office, 2561 W. Venice Blvd., Los Angeles, CA 90019; (323) 737-6111. Non-emergency long-term shelter for battered women and their children.

Covenant House, 346 W. 17th St., New York, NY 10011; (212) 727-4973. President, Sister Mary Rose McGeady, D.C. Provides crisis care — food, shelter, clothing, medical treatment, job placement and counseling — for homeless youth without regard to race, creed, color and national origin. Locations: New York, New Jersey (Newark, Atlantic City), Houston, Ft. Lauderdale, New Orleans, Anchorage, Los Angeles, Detroit, Orlando, Washington, DC; Toronto (Canada), Tegucigalpa (Honduras), Guatemala City (Guatemala), Mexico City (Mexico).

Crescent House, 1000 Howard Ave., Suite 1200, New Orleans, LA 70113. Provides temporary shelter, counseling and advocacy for battered women and their children.

The Dwelling Place, 409 W. 40th St., New York, NY 10018; (212) 564-7887. For homeless women 30 years of age and over.

Gift of Hope, Missionaries of Charity, 724 N.W. 17th St., Miami, FL 33136; (305) 326-0032. Shelter for women and children; soup kitchen for men.

House of the Good Shepherd, 1114 W. Grace St., Chicago, IL 60613; (773) 935-3434. For abused women with children.

Mercy Hospice, 334 S. 13th St., Philadelphia, PA 19107; (215) 545-5153. Temporary shelter and relocation assistance for homeless women and children.

Mt. Carmel House, Carmelite Sisters, 471 G Pl., N.W., Washington, DC 20001. For homeless women.

Ozanam Inn, 843 Camp St., New Orleans, LA 70130. Under sponsorship of the St. Vincent de Paul Society. Hospice for homeless men.

St. Christopher Inn, P.O. Box 150, Graymoor, Garrison, NY 10524; (845) 424-3616; www.atonementfriars.org. Temporary shelter (21 days) for alcohol- and drug-free homeless and needy men.

Siena-Francis House, Inc., P.O. Box 217 D.T.S., Omaha, NE 68102. Two units, both at 1702 Nicholas St., Omaha, NE 68101; (402) 341-1821. Siena House (for homeless and abused women or women with children; provides 24-hour assistance and advocacy services); and Francis House (temporary shelter for homeless men). Also at this location: a 50-bed residential substance abuse program.

Unwed Mothers: Residential and care services for unwed mothers are available in many dioceses.

FACILITIES FOR RETIRED AND AGED PERSONS

(*Sources:* Almanac *survey,* The Official Catholic Directory.)

This list covers residence, health care and other facilities for the retired and aged under Catholic auspices. Information includes name, type of facility if not evident from the title, address, and total capacity (in parentheses); unless noted otherwise, facilities are for both men and women. Many facilities for the aged offer intermediate nursing care.

Alabama: Allen Memorial Home (Skilled Nursing), 735 S. Washington Ave., Mobile 36603; (334) 433-2642 (119).

Cathedral Place Apartments (Retirement Complex), 351 Conti St., Mobile 36602; (334) 434-1590 (184).

Mercy Medical (Acute Rehabilitation Hospital, Skilled and Post-Acute Nursing, Hospice, Home Health and Assisted and Independent Living), P.O. Box 1090, Daphne 36526; (334) 626-2694 (162). Not restricted to elderly.

Sacred Heart Residence Little Sisters of the Poor, 1655 McGill Ave., Mobile 36604; (334) 476-6335 (84).

Seton Haven (Retirement Complex), 3721 Wares Ferry Rd., Montgomery 36193; (334) 272-4000 (114).

Arizona: Guadalupe Senior Village, 222 W. Thomas Rd., Ste. 214, Phoenix, 85103; (602) 406-6218.

California: Alexis Apartments of St. Patrick's Parish, 756 Mission St. 94103; 390 Clementina St., San Francisco 94103; (415) 495-3690 (240).

Casa Manana Inn, 3700 N. Sutter St., Stockton 95204; (209) 466-4046 (162). Non-profit housing for low-income elderly over 62.

Cathedral Plaza, 1551 Third Ave., San Diego 92101; (619) 234-0093 (222 apartments).

Guadalupe Plaza, 4142 42nd St., San Diego 92105; (619) 584-2414 (147 apartments).

Jeanne d'Arc Manor, 85 S. Fifth St., San Jose 95112; (408) 288-7421 (145). For low income elderly and handicapped.

La Paz Villas, P.O. Box 1962, Palm Desert 92261; (760) 772-1382 (24 units).

Little Flower Haven (Residential Care Facility for Retired), 8585 La Mesa Blvd., La Mesa 91941; (619) 466-3163 (85).

Little Sisters of the Poor, St. Anne's Home, 300 Lake St., San Francisco 94118; (415) 751-6510 (90).

Little Sisters of the Poor, Jeanne Jugan Residence, 2100 South Western Ave., San Pedro 90732; (310) 548-0625 (100).

Madonna Senior Center and Residence, St. Anthony Foundation, 350 Golden Gate Ave., San Francisco 94102; (415) 592-2864; www.stanthonysf.org (37).

Marian Residence (Retirement Home), 124 S. College Dr., Santa Maria 93454; (805) 922-7731 (32).

Mercy McMahon Terrace (Residential Care Facility), 3865 J St., Sacramento 95816; (916) 733-6510; www.mercysacramento.org (118 units).

Mercy Retirement and Care Center, 3431 Foothill Blvd., Oakland 94601; (510) 534-8540; www.mercy retirementcenter.com (59).

Mother Gertrude Home for Senior Citizens, 11320 Laurel Canyon Blvd., San Fernando 91340; (818) 898-

1546 (98).

Nazareth House (Residential and Skilled Care), 2121 N. 1st St., Fresno 93703; (559) 237-2257 (65 residential; 39 skilled nursing).

Nazareth House (Residential and Skilled Nursing), 3333 Manning Ave., Los Angeles 90064; (310) 839-2361 (123).

Nazareth House (Retirement Home), 245 Nova Albion Way, San Rafael 94903; (415) 479-8282 (151).

Nazareth House Retirement Home, 6333 Rancho Mission Rd., San Diego 92108; (619) 563-0480 (354).

O'Connor Woods, 3400 Wagner Heights Rd., Stockton 95209; (209) 956-3400; www.oconnorwoods.org, (48).

Our Lady of Fatima Villa (Skilled Nursing Facility), 20400 Saratoga-Los Gatos Rd., Saratoga 95070; (408) 741-2950 (85).

St. Bernardine Plaza (Retirement Home), 550 W. 5th St., San Bernardino 92401; (909) 888-0153 (150 units).

St. John of God (Retirement and Care Center), 2468 S. St. Andrew Place, Los Angeles 90018; (323) 731-0641; www.hospitallers.org, (215).

Vigil Light Apartments, 1945 Long Dr., Santa Rosa 95405; (707) 544-2810 (54).

Villa Scalabrini (Retirement Center and Skilled Nursing Care), 10631 Vinedale St., Sun Valley 91352; (818) 768-6500; www.villascalabrini.com (130 residence; 58 skilled nursing).

Villa Siena (Residence and Skilled Nursing Care), 1855 Miramonte Ave., Mountain View 94040; (650) 961-6484; www.vsiena.org (56, residence; 20, skilled nursing care).

Colorado: Francis Heights, Inc., 2626 Osceola St., Denver 80212; (303) 433-6268 (384 units; 411 residents).

Gardens at St. Elizabeth (Congregate Housing and Assisted Living), 2835 W. 32nd Ave., Denver 80211; (303) 964-2005 (320).

Little Sisters of the Poor, 3629 W. 29th Ave., Denver 80211; (303) 433-7221 (70).

Connecticut: Augustana Homes (Residence), Simeon Rd., Bethel 06801; (203) 743-2508.

Carmel Ridge, 6454 Main St., Trumbull 06611; (203) 261-2229.

Holy Family Home and Shelter, Inc., 88 Jackson St., P.O. Box 884, Willimantic 06226; (860) 423-7719 (155).

Monsignor Bojnowski Manor, Inc. (Skilled Nursing Facility), 50 Pulaski St., New Britain 06053; (860) 229-0336 (60).

Notre Dame Convalescent Home, 76 West Rocks Rd., Norwalk 06851; (203) 847-5893 (60).

St. Joseph Living Center, 14 Club Rd., Windham 06280; (860) 456-1107 (120).

St. Joseph's Manor (Health Care Facility; Home for Aged), Carmelite Srs. for Aged and Infirm, 6448 Main St., Trumbull 06611; (203) 268-6204; www.st josephmanor.org; (297).

St. Joseph's Residence, Little Sisters of the Poor, 1365 Enfield St., Enfield 06082; (860) 741-0791 (84).

St. Lucian's Home for the Aged, 532 Burritt St., New Britain 06053; (860) 223-2123 (42).

St. Mary's Home (Residence and Health Care Facility) 2021 Albany Ave., W. Hartford 06117; (860) 570-8200 (26).

Delaware: The Antonian, 1701 W. 10th St., Wilmington 19805; (302) 421-3758 (136 apartments).

Jeanne Jugan Residence, Little Sisters of the Poor, 185 Salem Church Rd., Newark 19713; (302) 368-5886 (80).

Marydale Retirement Village, 135 Jeandell Dr., Newark 19713; (302) 368-2784 (118 apartments).

St. Patrick's House, Inc., 115 E. 14th St., Wilmington 19801; (302) 654-6908 (12).

District of Columbia: Jeanne Jugan Residence-St. Joseph Villa, Little Sisters of the Poor, 4200 Harewood Rd., N.E., Washington 20017; (202) 269-1831 (73).

Florida: All Saints Home, 5888 Blanding Blvd., Jacksonville 32246; (904) 772-1220; www.all saints.org (118).

Casa Calderon, Inc. (Retirement Apartments), 800 W. Virginia St., Tallahassee 32304; (850) 222-4026 (111).

Haven of Our Lady of Peace (Assisted Living and Nursing Home), 5203 N. 9th Ave., Pensacola 32504; (850) 477-0531 (89).

Palmer House, Inc., 1225 S.W. 107th Ave., Miami 33174; (305) 221-9566 (120 apartments).

St. Andrew Towers (Retirement Apartments), 2700 N.W. 99th Ave., Coral Springs 33065 (432).

St. Catherine Laboure (Skilled and Intermediate Care), 1750 Stockton St., Jacksonville 32204; (904) 308-4700 (239).

St. Dominic Gardens (Retirement Apartments), 5849 N.W. 7th St., Miami 33126 (149 apartments).

St. Elizabeth Gardens, Inc. (Retirement Apartments), 801 N.E. 33rd St., Pompano Beach 33064 (150).

St. John's Rehabilitation Hospital and Nursing Center, Inc., 3075 N.W. 35th Ave., Lauderdale Lakes 33311.

Stella Maris House, Inc., 8636 Harding Ave., Miami Beach 33141 (136 apartments).

Illinois: Addolorata Villa (Sheltered Intermediate, Skilled Care Facility; Apartments), 555 McHenry Rd., Wheeling 60090; (847) 808-6168 (100 apartments).

Alvernia Manor (Sheltered Care), 13950 Main St., Lemont 60439; (630) 257-7721 (50).

Carlyle Healthcare Center, 501 Clinton St., Carlyle 62231; (618) 594-3112 (131).

Carmelite Carefree Village, 8419 Bailey Rd., Darien 60561; (630) 960-4060 (98).

Cortland Manor Retirement Home, 1900 N. Karlov, Chicago 60639; (773) 235-3670 (48).

Holy Family Health Center, 2380 Dempster, Des Plaines 60016; (847) 296-3335 (362).

Holy Family Villa (Intermediate Care Facility), 12395 McCarthy Rd., Lemont 60439; (630) 257-7721 (50).

Jugan Terrace, Little Sisters of the Poor, 2300 N. Racine, Chicago 60614; (773) 935-9600 (50 apartments).

Little Sisters of the Poor, St. Joseph's Home for the Elderly, 80 W. Northwest Hwy., Palatine 60067; (847) 358-5700 (61).

Little Sisters of the Poor Center for the Aging, 2325 N. Lakewood Ave., Chicago 60614; (773) 935-9600 (71).

Maria Care Center (Skilled Intermediary Facility), 350 W. S. First St., Red Bud 62278; (618) 282-3891 (115).

Marian Heights Apartments (Elderly, Handicapped), 20 Marian Heights Dr., Alton 62002; (618) 462-0363 (130).

Marian Park, Inc., 26 W. 171 Roosevelt Rd., Wheaton 60187; (630) 665-9100 (470).

Maryhaven, Inc. (Skilled and Intermediate Care Facility), 1700 E. Lake Ave., Glenview 60025; (847) 729-1300 (138).

Mayslake Village (Retirement Apartments), 1801 35th St., Oak Brook 60521; (630) 850-8232; www.mayslake.com (630 apartments).

Mercy Residence at Tolentine Center, 20300 Governors Hwy., Olympia Fields 60461; (708) 748-9500 (48).

Meredith Memorial Home, 16 S. Illinois St., Belleville 62220; (618) 233-8780 (86).

Merkle-Knipprath Countryside (Apartments and Nursing Facility), 1190 E. 2900 N. Rd., Clifton 60927; (815) 694-2306 (130).

Mother Theresa Home (Skilled, Intermediate and Sheltered Care), 1270 Franciscan Dr., Lemont 60439; (630) 257-5801; www.franciscancommunities.com; (150).

Nazarethville (Intermediate and Sheltered Care), 300 N. River Rd., Des Plaines 60016; (847) 297-5900; (83).

Our Lady of Angels Retirement Home, 1201 Wyoming, Joliet 60435; (815) 725-6631; (101).

Our Lady of the Snows, Apartment Community, 9500 West Illinois Highway 15, Belleville 62223; (618) 397-6700 (201).

Our Lady of Victory Nursing Home (Intermediate and Skilled Care), 20 Briarcliff Lane, Bourbonnais 60914; (815) 937-2022 (107).

Pope John Paul Apartments (Elderly and Handicapped), 1 Pope John Paul Plaza, Springfield 62703; (217) 528-1771; www.dio.org (160).

Provena Cor Mariae Center (Assisted Living and Nursing Home), 3330 Maria Linden Dr., Rockford 61107; (815) 877-7416 (146).

Provena St. Anne Center (Nursing Home), 4405 Highcrest Rd., Rockford 61107; (815) 229-1999 (179).

Provena St. Joseph's Home for the Aged, 659 E. Jefferson St., Freeport 61032; (815) 232-6181 (120).

Provena Villa Franciscan (Skilled Care), 210 N. Springfield, Joliet 60435; (815) 725-3400, www.provenahealth.com.

Queen of Peace Center, 1910 Maple Ave., Lisle 60532; (630) 852-5360; www.Qopc.net (32).

Resurrection Nursing Pavilion (Skilled Care), 1001 N. Greenwood, Park Ridge 60068; (847) 692-5600 (295).

Resurrection Retirement Community, 7262 W. Peterson Ave., Chicago, 60631; (773) 792-7930 (472 apartments).

Rosary Hill Home (Women), 9000 W. 81st St., Justice 60458; (708) 458-3040 (48).

St. Andrew Life Center (Retirement Residence), 7000 N. Newark Ave., Niles 60714; (847) 647-8332 (99).

St. Anne Place (Retirement Apartments), 4444 Brendenwood Rd., Rockford 61107; (815) 399-6167 (120).

St. Benedict Home, 6930 W. Touhy Ave., Niles 60714; (847) 647-0003; (99).

St. Elizabeth Home (Residence), 704 W. Marion St., Joliet 60436; (815) 727-0125 (11). Group living for Senior women.

St. James Manor, 1251 East Richton Rd., Crete 60417; (708) 672-6700 (110).

St. Joseph's Home (Sheltered and Intermediate Care), 3306 S. 6th St. Rd., Springfield 62703; (217) 529-5596 (110).

St. Joseph's Home (Sheltered and Intermediate Care), 2223 W. Heading Ave., Peoria 61604; (309) 673-7425; www.stjhome.org, (200).

St. Joseph Home of Chicago, Inc. (Skilled Care), 2650 N. Ridgeway Ave., Chicago 60647; (773) 235-8600 (173).

St. Patrick's Residence, 1400 Brookdale Rd., Naperville 60563-2125; (630) 416-6565, www.stpat ricksresidence.org

Villa Scalabrini (Sheltered, Intermediate and Skilled), 480 N. Wolf Rd., Northlake 60164; (708) 562-0040 (259).

Indiana: Albertine Home, 1501 Hoffman St., Hammond 46327; (219) 937-0575 (35).

Our Lady of Holy Cross Care Center (Comprehensive Nursing), 7520 S. US Hwy 421, San Pierre 46374; (219) 828-4111 (200).

Provena LaVerna Terrace, 517 N. Main St., Avilla 46710; (260) 897-2093 (51).

Provena Sacred Heart Home (Comprehensive Nursing), 515 N. Main St., Avilla 46710; (219) 897-2841, (133).

Regina Continuing Care Center (Intermediate Care Facility), 3900 Washington Ave., Evansville 47714; (812) 485-4226; www.stmarys.org (137).

St. Anne Home (Residential and Comprehensive Nursing), 1900 Randallia Dr., Ft. Wayne 46805; (219) 484-5555 (254).

St. Anthony Home, Inc., 203 Franciscan Rd., Crown Point 46307; (219) 661-5100 (219).

St. Augustine Home for the Aged, Little Sisters of the Poor, 2345 W. 86th St., Indianapolis 46260; (317) 872-6420; (92).

St. John's Home for the Aged, Little Sisters of the Poor, 1236 Lincoln Ave., Evansville 47714; (812) 464-3607 (70).

St. Paul Hermitage (Residential and Intermediate Care Nursing), 501 N. 17th Ave., Beech Grove 46107; (317) 786-2261 (100).

Iowa: The Alverno Health Care Facility (Nursing Care), 849 13th Ave. N., Clinton 52732; (319) 242-1521 (194).

Bishop Drumm Retirement Center, 5837 Winwood Dr., Johnston 50131; (515) 270-1100 (64).

Hallmar-Mercy Medical Center, 701 Tenth St. S.E., Cedar Rapids 52403, (319) 369-4638 (57).

Holy Spirit Retirement Home (Intermediate Care), 1701 W. 25th St., Sioux City 51103; (712) 252-2726 (95).

Kahl Home for the Aged and Infirm (Skilled and Intermediate Care Facility), 1101 W. 9th St., Davenport 52804; (319) 324-1621 (135).

The Marian Home, 2400 6th Ave. North, Fort Dodge 50501; (515) 576-1138 (110).

St. Anthony Nursing Home (Intermediate Care), 406 E. Anthony St., Carroll 51401; (712) 792-3581 (79).

St. Francis Continuation Care and Nursing Home Center, Burlington 52601; (319) 752-4564 (170).

Stonehill Adult Center (Day Care), 3485 Windsor, Dubuque 52001; (319) 557-7180 (35).

Kansas: Catholic Care Center (Skilled and Intermediate Care Facility), 6700 E. 45th St, Wichita 67226; (316) 744-2020 (294).

Mt. Joseph Senior Community (Intermediate Care Facility), 1110 W. 11, Concordia 66901; (785) 243-1347 (16 apartments).

St. John Rest Home (Nursing Facility), 701 Seventh St., Victoria 67671; (785) 735-2208 (90).

St. John's New Horizons, 2225 Canterbury, Hays 67601; (785) 628-8742 (43).

Villa Maria, Inc. (Intermediate Care Facility), 116 S. Central, Mulvane 67110; (316) 777-1129 (99).

Kentucky: Bishop Soenneker Personal Care Home, 9545 Ky. 144, Knottsville, KY 42366; (270) 281-4881 (55).

Carmel Home (Residence, Adult Day Care, Respite Care and Nursing Care), 2501 Old Hartford Rd., Owensboro 42303; (270) 683-0227 (101).

Carmel Manor (Skilled, Intermediate and Personal Care Home), 100 Carmel Manor Rd., Ft. Thomas, 41075; (859) 781-5111; (145).

Madonna Manor Nursing Home, 2344 Amsterdam Rd., Villa Hills 41017; (606) 341-3981 (60).

Marian Home, 3105 Lexington Rd., Louisville 40206; (502) 893-0121 (69).

Nazareth Home, 2000 Newburg Rd., Louisville 40205; (502) 459-9681 (168).

St. Charles Care Center and Village, 500 Farrell Dr., Covington 41011 (606) 331-3224; www.stcharles care.org (149). Nursing home; adult day health program. Independent living cottages (44); assisted living (60); independent living apartments (12).

Louisiana: Annunciation Inn, 1220 Spain St., New Orleans 70117; (504) 944-0512 (111).

Bethany M.H.S. Health Care Center (Women), P.O. Box 2308, Lafayette 70502; (337) 234-2459; (200).

Château de Notre Dame (Residence and Nursing Home), 2832 Burdette St., New Orleans 70125; (504) 866-2741 (103).

Christopher Inn Apartments, 2110 Royal St., New Orleans 70116; (504) 949-0312 (144).

Christus St. Joseph's Home (Nursing Home), 2301 Sterlington Rd., Monroe 71211; (318) 323-3426 (150).

Consolata Home (Nursing Home), 2319 E. Main St., New Iberia 70560; (337) 365-8226 (114).

Haydel Heights Apartments, 4402 Reynes St., New Orleans 70126; (504) 242-4438 (65 units).

Lafon Nursing Home of the Holy Family, 6900 Chef Menteur Hwy., New Orleans 70126; (504) 246-1100 (171).

Mary-Joseph Residence for the Elderly, 4201 Woodland Dr., New Orleans 70131-7339; (504) 394-2200 (127).

Metairie Manor, 4929 York St., Metairie 70001; (504) 456-1467 (287).

Nazareth Inn, 9630 Hayne Blvd., New Orleans 70127; (504) 241-9630 (158).

Ollie Steele Burden Manor (Nursing Home), 4250 Essen Lane, Baton Rouge 70809; (225) 926-0091 (184).

Our Lady of Prompt Succor Home, 954 East Prudhomme St., Opelousas 70570; (337) 948-3634 (80).

Our Lady's Manor, Inc., 402 Monroe St., Alexandria 71301; (318) 473-2560 (114).

Place Dubourg, 201 Rue Dubourg, LaPlace 70068; (504) 652-1981 (115).

Rouquette Lodge, 4300 Hwy 22, Mandeville 70471; (504) 626-5217 (51).

St. John Berchmans Manor, 3400 St. Anthony Ave., New Orleans 70122; (504) 943-9342 (157).

St. Margaret's Daughters Home (Nursing Home), 6220 Chartres St., New Orleans 70117; (504) 279-6414 (139).

St. Martin Manor, 1501 N. Johnson St., New Orleans 70116; (504) 945-7728 (145).

Villa St. Maurice 500 St. Maurice Ave., New Orleans 70117; (504) 277-8477 (193).

Villa St. Maurice II, 6101 Douglas St., New Orleans 70117; (504) 277-8731 (80).

Village du Lac, Inc., 1404 Carmel Ave., Lafayette 70501; (337) 234-5106 (200).

Wynhoven Apartments and Wynhoven II (Residence for Senior Citizens), 4600-10th St., Marrero; (504) 347-8442 (375).

Maine: Deering Pavilion (Apartments for Senior Citizens), 880 Forest Ave., Portland 04103; (207) 797-8777 (232 units).

Maison Marcotte (Independent Living Community), 100 Campus Ave., Lewiston 04240; (207) 786-0062 (128 apartments).

Mt. St. Joseph Holistic Care Community, Highwood St., Waterville 04901; (207) 873-0705 (138).

St. Andre Health Care Facility, Inc. (Nursing Facility), 407 Pool St., Biddeford 04005; (207) 282-5171 (96).

St. Joseph's Manor (Nursing Care Facility), 1133 Washington Ave., Portland 04103; (207) 797-0600; www.saintjosephsmanor.org; (200).

St. Marguerite D'Youville Pavilion, 102 Campus Ave., Lewiston 04240; (207) 777-4200 (280).

St. Xavier's Home (Apartments), 199 Somerset St., Bangor 04401; (207) 942-4815 (19 units).

Seton Village, Inc., 1 Carver St., Waterville 04901; (207) 873-0178 (140 housing units).

Maryland: Little Sisters of the Poor, St. Martin's Home (for the Aged), 601 Maiden Choice Lane, Baltimore 21228; (410) 744-9367 (104).

Sacred Heart Home, 5805 Queens Chapel Rd., Hyattsville 20782; (301) 277-6500 (102).

St. Joseph Nursing Home, 1222 Tugwell Dr., Baltimore 21228; (410) 747-0026 (51).

Villa Rosa Nursing Home, 3800 Lottsford Vista Rd., Mitchellville 20721; (301) 459-4700 (100).

Massachusetts: Catholic Memorial Home (Nursing Home), 2446 Highland Ave., Fall River 02720; (508) 679-0011 (300).

Don Orione Nursing Home, 111 Orient Ave., East Boston 02128; (617) 569-2100 (185).

D'Youville Manor (Nursing Home), 981 Varnum Ave., Lowell 01854; (978) 454-5681; www.dyouville.com (203).

Jeanne Jugan Pavilion, 190 Highland Ave., Somerville 02143; (617) 776-4420 (30).

Jeanne Jugan Residence, Little Sisters of the Poor (Home for the Elderly), 186 Highland Ave., Somerville 02143; (617) 776-4420 (84).

Madonna Manor (Nursing Home), 85 N. Washington St., N. Attleboro 02760; (508) 699-2740 (129).

Marian Manor, for the Aged and Infirm (Nursing Home), 130 Dorchester St., S. Boston, 02127; (617) 268-3333; www.marianmanor.org (366).

Marian Manor of Taunton (Nursing Home), 33 Summer St., Taunton 02780; (508) 822-4885 (184).

Maristhill Nursing Home, 66 Newton St., Waltham 02154; (781) 893-0240 (154).

MI Nursing/Restorative Center, Zero Bennington St., Lawrence 01841; (508) 685-6321 (335).

MI Residential Community, 189 Maple St., Lawrence 01841; (978) 682-7575; www.mihcs.com, (35).

Our Lady's Haven (Nursing Home), 71 Center St., Fairhaven 02719; (508) 999-4561; www.dhfo.org (158).

Sacred Heart Home (Nursing Home), 359 Summer St., New Bedford 02740 (508) 996-6751; www.dhfo.org (217).

St. Joseph Manor Health Care, Inc., 215 Thatcher St., Brockton 02302; (508) 583-5834 (118).

St. Joseph's Nursing Care Center, 321 Centre St., Dorchester, Boston 02122; (617) 825-6320 (191).

St. Patrick's Manor (Nursing Home), 863 Central St., Framingham 01701 (508) 879-8000, www.stpatricksmanor.org (460).

Michigan: Bishop Noa Home for Senior Citizens (Nursing Home and Residence), 2900 3rd Ave. S., Escanaba 49829; (906) 786-5810 (123).

Lourdes Nursing Home (Skilled Facility), 2300 Watkins Lake Rd., Waterford 48328; (248) 674-2241; www.lourdescampus.com (108).

Marycrest Manor (Skilled Nursing Facility), 15475 Middlebelt Rd., Livonia 48154; (313) 427-9175; (55).

Ryan Senior Residences of the Archdiocese of Detroit: Casa Maria, 600 Maple Vista, Imlay City 48444; (810) 724-6300 (84). Kundig Center, 3300 Jeffries Freeway, Detroit 48208; (313) 894-0555 (160). Lourdes Assisted Living Home, Inc., (Residence), 2450 Watkins Lake Rd., Waterford 48328; (248) 618-6361, www.lourdescampus.com (6). Marian-Oakland West, 29250 W. Ten Mile Rd., Farmington Hills 48336; (248) 474-7204 (87). Marian Place, 408 W. Front St., Monroe 48161; (734) 241-2414 (53). Marydale Center, 3147 Tenth Ave., Port Huron 48060; (810) 985-9683 (56). Maryhaven, 11350 Reeck Rd., Southgate 48195; (734) 287-2111 (90). Mercy Madonna Villa 17825 Fifteen Mile Rd., Clinton Twp. 48035; (810) 792-0358 (86). Stapleton Center, 9341 Agnes St., Detroit 48214; (313) 822-0397 (59). Villa Marie, 15131 Newburgh Rd., Livonia 48154; (734) 464-9494 (86). St. Ann's Home, (Residence and Nursing Home), 2161 Leonard St. N.W., Grand Rapids 49504; (616) 453-7715 (140). St. Catherine House, 1641 Webb Ave., Detroit 48206; (313) 868-4505 (12). St. Elizabeth Briarbank (Women, Residence), 1315 N. Woodward Ave., Bloomfield Hills 48304; (248) 644-1011 (44).

St. Francis Home (Nursing Home), 915 N. River Rd., Saginaw 48609, (517) 781-3150 (100).

St. Joseph's Home, 4800 Cadieux Rd., Detroit 48224; (313) 882-3800 (104).

Minnesota: Alverna Apartments, 300 8th Ave. S.E., Little Falls 56345; (320) 632-1246; (68).

Assumption Home, 715 North First St., Cold Spring 56320; (320) 685-4110 (34)

Divine Providence Community Home (Skilled Nursing Care) and Lake Villa Maria Senior Housing, 702 Third Ave. N.W., Sleepy Eye 56085; (507) 794-5333 (58).

Franciscan Health Community, 1925 Norfolk Ave., St. Paul 55116; (651) 696-8400 (223).

John Paul Apartments, 200 8th Ave. N., Cold Spring 56320; (320) 685-4429 (61).

Little Sisters of the Poor, Holy Family Residence (Skilled Nursing and Intermediate Care), 330 S. Exchange St., St. Paul 55102; (651) 227-0336 (73). Independent living apartments (32).

Madonna Towers (Retirement Apartments and Nursing Home), 4001 19th Ave. N.W., Rochester 55901; (507) 288-3911 (184).

Mary Rondorf Retirement Home of Sacred Heart Parish, Inc., 222 5th St., N.E., Staples 56479; (218) 894-2124 (45). Board and lodging with special services.

Mother of Mercy Nursing Home and Retirement Center, 230 Church Ave., Box 676, Albany 56307; (320) 845-2195 (114).

Regina Nursing Home and Retirement Residence Center, 1175 Nininger Rd., Hastings 55033; (651) 480-6836; www.reginamedical.com. Nursing home (61); retirement home (43); boarding care (32). Admin., Juliane M. Saxon.

Sacred Heart Hospice (Skilled Nursing Home, Adult Day Care, Home Health Care) 1200 Twelfth St. S.W., Austin 55912; (507) 433-1808 (59).

St. Ann's Residence, 330 E. 3rd St., Duluth 55805; (218) 727-8831; www.stanns.com (185).

St. Anne of Winona (Skilled Nursing Home), 1347 W. Broadway, Winona 55987; (507) 454-3621, www.saintannehosp.homestead.com (74).

St. Benedict's Center, 1810 Minnesota Blvd. S.E., St. Cloud 56304; (320) 252-0010 (198 bed skilled nursing care; adult day care, respite care). Benedict Village (Retirement Apartments), 2000 15th Ave. S.E., St. Cloud 56304; (320) 252-0010, www.centra care.com. Benedict Homes (Alzheimer Residential Care) and Benedict Court (Assisted Living), 1980 15th Ave. S.E., St. Cloud 56304; (320) 252-0010.

St. Elizabeth's Health Care Center, 1200 Grant Blvd., Wabasha 55981; (651) 565-4531; www.steliz abethswabasha.org, (106).

St. Elizabeth's Medical Center, 626 Shields Ave., Wabasha, MN 55981; (651) 565-4581; www.steliz abethswabasha.org.

St. Francis Home, 501 Oak St., Breckenridge 56520; (218) 643-7661; www.sfcare.org (124).

St. Mary's Regional Health Center, 1027 Washington Ave., Detroit Lakes 56501; (218) 847-5611 (100).

St. Otto's Care Center (Nursing Home), 920 S.E. 4th St., Little Falls 56345; (320) 632-9281 (150).

St. William's Nursing Home, P.O. Box 30, Parkers Prairie 56361; (218) 338-4671 (90).

Villa of St. Francis Nursing Home, 1001 Scott Ave., Morris 56267; (320) 589-1133 (128).

Villa St. Vincent (Skilled Nursing Home and Residence), 516 Walsh St., Crookston 56716; (218) 281-3424. Skilled Nursing home (80), special care unit (24), apartments (27), board and care (34).

Westwood Senior Apartments, 925 Kenwood Ave., Duluth 55811; (218) 733-2238; www.westwood duluth.org (70).

Mississippi: Notre Dame de la Mer Retirement Apartments, 292 Hwy. 90, Bay St. Louis 39520; (228) 467-2885 (61).

Santa Maria Retirement Apartments, 674 Beach Blvd., Biloxi, 39530; (228) 432-1289 (223).

Villa Maria Retirement Apartments, 921 Porter Ave., Ocean Springs 39564; (228) 875-8811 (225).

Missouri: Cathedral Square Towers, 444 W. 12th St., Kansas City 64105; (816) 471-6555 (167).

Chariton Apartments (Retirement Apartments), 4249 Michigan Ave., St. Louis 63111; (314) 352-7600 (122 units; 143 residents).

LaVerna Heights Retirement Home (Women), 104 E. Park Ave., Savannah 64485; (816) 324-3185; www.sistersofstfrancis.org (57).

LaVerna Village Nursing Home, 904 Hall Ave., Savannah 64485; (816) 324-3185 (133).

Little Sisters of the Poor (Home for Aged), 3225 N. Florissant Ave., St. Louis 63107; (314) 421-6022 (114).

Mary, Queen and Mother Center (Nursing Care), 7601 Watson Rd., St. Louis 63119; (314) 961-8000; www.cardinalcarberry.org, (230).

Mother of Good Counsel Home (Skilled Nursing, Women), 6825 Natural Bridge Rd., Northwoods, 63121; (314) 383-4765 (114).

Our Lady of Mercy Country Home, 2205 Hughes Rd., Liberty 64068; (816) 781-5711 (105).

Price Memorial Skilled Nursing Facility, Forby Rd., P.O. Box 476, Eureka 63025; (636) 587-3200 (120).

St. Agnes Home for the Elderly, 10341 Manchester Rd., Kirkwood 63122; (314) 965-7616 (124).

St. Joseph Hill Infirmary, Inc., (Nursing Care Facility, Men), St. Joseph Road, Eureka 63025; (636) 587-3661 (120).

St. Joseph's Home (Residential and Intermediate Care), 723 First Capitol Dr., St. Charles 63301; (314) 946-4140; (110).

St. Joseph's Home (Residential and Intermediate Care Facility), 1306 W. Main St., Jefferson City 65109; (573) 635-0166 (90).

Nebraska: Madonna Rehabilitation Hospital, 5401 South St., Lincoln 68506; (402) 489-7102; www.ma donna.org (252).

Mercy Care Center (Skilled Nursing Facility for Chronic, Complex and Subacute Levels of Care and Rehabilitation), 1870 S. 75th St., Omaha 68124; (402) 343-8500 (246).

Mercy Villa, 1845 S. 72nd St., Omaha 68124; (402) 391-6224.

Mt. Carmel Home, Keens Memorial (Nursing Home), 412 W. 18th St., Kearney 68847; (308) 237-2287 (75).

New Cassel Retirement Center, 900 N. 90th St., Omaha 68114; (402) 393-2277; www.newcassel.org (165).

St. Joseph's Nursing Home, 401 N. 18th St., Norfolk 68701; (402) 644-7375 (99).

St. Joseph's Retirement Community, 320 E. Decatur St., West Point 68788; (402) 372-3477 (90).

St. Joseph's Villa (Nursing Home), 927 7th St., David City 68632; (402) 367-3045 (65).

New Hampshire: Mount Carmel Healthcare Center, 235 Myrtle St., Manchester 03104; (603) 627-3811 (120).

St. Ann Home (Nursing Home), 195 Dover Point Rd., Dover 03820; (603) 742-2612 (54).

St. Francis Home (Nursing Home), 406 Court St., Laconia 03246; (603) 524-0466 (51).

St. Teresa Healthcare Center (Nursing Home), 519 Bridge St., Manchester 03104; (603) 668-2373 (5).

St. Vincent de Paul Healthcare Center, 29 Providence Ave., Berlin 03570; (603) 752-1820 (80).

New Jersey: McCarrick Care Center, 15 Dellwood Lane, Somerset 08873; (732) 545-4200 (142).

Mater Dei Nursing Home, 176 Rt. 40, Newfield 08344; (856) 358-2061 (64).

Morris Hall (St. Joseph Skilled Nursing Center, St. Mary Residence), 1 Bishops' Dr., Lawrenceville 08648; (609) 896-0006; www.morrishall.org (100).

Mount St. Andrew Villa (Residence), 55 W. Midland Ave., Paramus 07652; (201) 261-5950 (55).

Our Lady's Residence (Nursing Home), 1100 Clematis Ave., Pleasantville 08232; (609) 646-2450 (236).

St. Ann's Home for the Aged (Skilled and Intermediate Nursing Care Home, Women), 198 Old Bergen Rd., Jersey City 07305; (201) 433-0950 (106).

St. Francis Health Resort (Residence), Denville 07834; (973) 625-9245 (150).

St. Joseph's Home for the Elderly, Little Sisters of the Poor, 140 Shepherd Lane, Totowa 07512; (973) 942-0300 (134).

St. Joseph's Rest Home for Aged Women, 46 Preakness Ave., Paterson 07522; (973) 956-1921 (35).

St. Joseph's Senior Residence (Sheltered Care), 1 St. Joseph Terr., Woodbridge, 07095; (732) 634-0004 (60).

St. Mary's Nursing Home, 210 St. Mary's Dr., Cherry Hill 08003; (856) 424-9521 (215). The Manor at St. Mary's, 220 St. Mary's Dr., Cherry Hill 08003; (856) 424-3817 (739).

St. Vincent's Nursing Home, 45 Elm St., Montclair 07042; (973) 754-4800 (220).

Villa Maria (Residence and Infirmary, Women), 641 Somerset St., N. Plainfield 07061; (908) 757-3050 (86).

New Mexico: Good Shepherd Manor (Residential Care for Aged Persons), Little Brothers of the Good Shepherd, P.O. Box 10248, Albuquerque 87184; (505) 898-0177 (40).

New York: Bernardine Apartments, 417 Churchill Ave., Syracuse 13205; (315) 469-7786.

Brothers of Mercy Sacred Heart Home (Residence) 4520 Ransom Rd., Clarence 14031; (716) 759-2644 (80). Brothers of Mercy Nursing Home, 10570 Bergtold Rd., Clarence 14031; (716) 759-6985; www.brothersofmercy.org (240). Brothers of Mercy Housing Co., Inc. (Apartments), 10500 Bergtold Rd., Clarence 14031; (716) 759-2122 (110).

Carmel Richmond Nursing Home, 88 Old Town Rd., Staten Island 10304; (718) 979-5000 (300).

Ferncliff Nursing Home, 21 Ferncliff Dr., Rhinebeck 12572; (845) 876-2011 (328).

Franciscan Health System of New York, 2975 Independence Ave., Bronx 10463; (718) 548-1700.

Good Samaritan Nursing Home (Skilled Nursing), 101 Elm St., Sayville 11782; (631) 244-2400 (100).

The Heritage (Apartments with Skilled Nursing Care), 1450 Portland Ave., Rochester 14621; (716) 342-1700; www.stannsrochester.org (237)

Holy Family Home, 1740-84th St., Brooklyn 11214; (718) 232-3666 (200).

Holy Family Home (Adult Home), 410 Mill St., Williamsville 14221; (716) 634-5400 (85).

Kateri Residence (Skilled Nursing), 150 Riverside Dr., New York 10024; (212) 769-0744; www.catholic healthcaresystem.org/kateri (610).

Little Sisters of the Poor, Jeanne Jugan Residence (Skilled Nursing and Health Related; Adult Care), 3200 Baychester Ave., Bronx 10475; (718) 671-2120 (60).

Little Sisters of the Poor, Queen of Peace Residence, 110-30 221st St., Queens Village 11429; (718) 464-1800.

Mary Manning Walsh Home (Nursing Home), 1339 York Ave., New York 10021; (212) 628-2800 (362).

Mercy Healthcare Center (Skilled Nursing Facility), 114 Wawbeek Ave., Tupper Lake 12986; (518) 359-3355; www.muhc.org (80).

Mt. Loretto Nursing Home, (Skilled Nursing Home), Sisters of the Resurrection, 302 Swart Hill Rd., Amsterdam 12010; (518) 842-6790 (120).

Nazareth Nursing Home (Women), 291 W. North St., Buffalo 14201; (716) 881-2323 (125).

Our Lady of Consolation Nursing and Rehabilitation Care Center (Skilled Nursing) 111 Beach Dr., West Islip 11795; www.olcny.org; (631) 587-1600 (450).

Our Lady of Hope Residence (Home for the Aged), Little Sisters of the Poor, 1 Jeanne Jugan Lane, Latham 12210; (518) 785-4551 (117).

Ozanam Hall of Queens Nursing Home, Inc., 42-41 201st St., Bayside 11361; (718) 423-2000 (432).

Providence Rest, 3304 Waterbury Ave., Bronx 10465; (718) 931-30000; www.chcn.org/providence (242).

Resurrection Nursing Home (Skilled Nursing Facility), Castleton 12033; (518) 732-7617 (80).

St. Ann's Community (Skilled Nursing Facility), 1500 Portland Ave., Rochester 14621; (716) 342-1216; www.stannscommunity.com (354).

St. Cabrini Nursing Home, 115 Broadway, Dobbs Ferry 10522; (914) 693-6800 (304).

St. Clare Manor (Nursing Home), 543 Locust St., Lockport 14094; (716) 434-4718 (28).

St. Columban's on the Lake (Retirement Home), 2546 Lake Rd., Silver Creek 14136; (716) 934-4515 (50).

St. Elizabeth Home (Adult Home), 5539 Broadway, Lancaster 14086; (716) 683-5150 (117).

St. Francis Home (Skilled Nursing Facility), 147 Reist St., Williamsville 14221; (716) 633-5400 (142).

St. Joseph Manor (Nursing Home), 2211 W. State St., Olean 14760; (716) 372-7810 (22).

St. Joseph Nursing Home, 2535 Genesee St., Utica 13501; (315) 797-1230; www.stjosephnh.org.

St. Joseph's Guest Home, Missionary Sisters of St. Benedict, 350 Cuba Hill Rd., Huntington 11743; (631) 368-9528.

St. Joseph's Home (Nursing Home), 420 Lafayette St., Ogdensburg 13669; (315) 393-3780; www.stjh.org (117).

St. Joseph's Villa (Adult Home), 38 Prospect Ave., Catskill 12414; (518) 943-5701.

St. Luke Manor, 17 Wiard St., Batavia 14020; (585) 343-8806 (20).

St. Mary's Manor, 515 Sixth St., Niagara Falls 14301; (716) 285-3236 (165).

St. Patrick's Home for the Aged and Infirm, 66 Van Cortlandt Park S., Bronx NY 10463; (718) 519-2800; www.hometown.aol.com/stpatshome/stp/ (264).

St. Teresa Nursing Home, 120 Highland Ave., Middletown 10940; (914) 342-1033; (98).

St. Vincent's Home for the Aged, 319 Washington Ave., Dunkirk 14048; (716) 366-2066 (40).

Terence Cardinal Cooke Health Care Center (Skilled Nursing), 1249 Fifth Ave., New York 10029; (212) 360-1000 (523).

Teresian House, 200 Washington Ave. Extension, Albany 12203; (518) 456-2000; www.teresianhouse.com (300).

Uihlein Mercy Center (Nursing Home), 420 Old Military Rd., Lake Placid 12946; (518) 523-2464 (220).

North Carolina: Maryfield Nursing Home, 1315 Greensboro Rd., High Point 27260; (336) 886-2444 (115).

North Dakota: Manor St. Joseph (Basic Care Facility), 404 Fourth Ave., Edgeley 58433; (701) 493-2477 (40).

Marillac Manor Retirement Center, 1016 28th St., Bismarck 58501-3139; (701) 258-8702 (78 apartments).

St. Anne's Guest Home, 524 N. 17th St., Grand Forks 58203; (701) 746-9401 (86)

St. Vincent's Care Center (Nursing Facility), 1021 N. 26th St., Bismarck 58501; (701) 223-6888 (101).

Ohio: Archbishop Leibold Home for the Aged, Little Sisters of the Poor, 476 Riddle Rd., Cincinnati 45220; (513) 281-8001 (100).

The Assumption Village, 9800 Market St., North Lima 44452; (330) 549-0740 (120).

Center for Older Adults (Nursing Care), 10204 Granger Rd., Cleveland 44125; (216) 581-2900; www.jenningscenter.org (150).

Francesca Residence (Retirement), 39 N. Portage Path, Akron 44303; (330) 867-6334; (40).

House of Loreto (Nursing Home), 2812 Harvard Ave. N.W., Canton 44709; (330) 453-8137 (76).

Little Sisters of the Poor, Sacred Heart Home, 4900 Navarre Ave., Oregon 43616; (419) 698-4331 (81).

Little Sisters of the Poor, Sts. Mary and Joseph Home for Aged, 4291 Richmond Rd., Cleveland 44122; (216) 464-1222 (125).

The Maria-Joseph Living Care Center, 4830 Salem Ave., Dayton 45416; (937) 278-2692; www.mariajoseph.org (440).

Mercy Franciscan Terrace, 100 Compton Rd., Cincinnati 45215; (513) 761-9036 (148).

Mercy St. Theresa Center, 7010 Rowan Hill Dr., Cincinnati 45227; (513) 271-7010, www.e-mercy.com (157).

Mercy Siena Retirement Community, 6125 N. Main St., Dayton 45415; (937) 278-8211 (99).

Mount Alverna (Intermediate Care Nursing Facility), 6765 State Rd., Cleveland 44134; (440) 843-7800; www.franciscanservices.com/facilities/ (203).

Mt. St. Joseph (Skilled Nursing Facility, Dual Certified), 21800 Chardon Rd., Euclid 44117; (216) 531-7426 (100).

Nazareth Towers, 300 E. Rich St., Columbus 43215; (614) 464-4780 (229).

St. Augustine Manor (Skilled Nursing Facility), 7801 Detroit Ave., Cleveland 44102; (216) 634-7400 (248).

St. Francis Health Care Centre, 401 N. Broadway St., Green Springs 44836; (419) 639-2626, www.sfhcc.org (186).

St. Francis Home, Inc. (Residence and Nursing Care), 182 St. Francis Ave., Tiffin 44883; (419) 447-2723 (173).

St. Joseph's Care Center, 2308 Reno Dr., Louisville 44641; (330) 875-5562 (100, nursing home; 40 assisted living).

St. Margaret Hall (Rest Home and Nursing Facility), Carmelite Sisters for the Aged and Infirm, 1960 Madison Rd., Cincinnati 45206; (513) 751-5880 (133).

St. Raphael Home (Nursing Home), 1550 Roxbury Rd., Columbus 43212; (614) 486-0436 (78).

St. Rita's Home (Skilled Nursing Home), 880 Greenlawn Ave., Columbus 43223; (614) 443-9433 (100).

Schroder Manor Retirement Community (Residential Care, Skilled Nursing Care and Independent Living Units), Franciscan Sisters of the Poor, 1302 Millville Ave., Hamilton 45013; (513) 867-1300 (125).

The Villa Sancta Anna Home for the Aged, Inc., 25000 Chagrin Blvd., Beachwood 44122; (216) 464-9250 (68).

The Village at St. Edward (Apartments, Nursing Care and Assisted Living), 3131 Smith Rd., Fairlawn 44333; (330) 666-1183; www.vased.org (160).

Oklahoma: St. Ann's Home, 9400 St. Ann's Dr., Oklahoma City 73162; (405) 728-7888 (120).

Westminster Village, Inc. (Residence), 1601 Academy, Ponca City 74604; (580) 762-0927 (131).

Oregon: Benedictine Nursing Center, 540 S. Main St., Mt. Angel 97362; (503) 845-6841 (75). Home Health Agency, Outpatient Therapies. Benedictine Institute for Long Term Care. Child Development Center.

Evergreen Court Retirement Apartments, 451 O'Connell St., North Bend 97459; (541) 756-4466.

Maryville Nursing Home, 14645 S.W. Farmington, Beaverton 97007; (503) 643-8626 (156).

Mt. St. Joseph, 3060 S.E. Stark St., Portland 97214; (503) 535-4700 (347).

St. Catherine's Residence and Nursing Center, 3959 Sheridan Ave., North Bend 97459; (541) 756-4151 (200).

Pennsylvania: Antonian Towers, 2405 Hillside Ave., Easton 18042; (610) 258-2033 (50).

Ascension Manor I (Senior Citizen Housing), 911 N. Franklin St., Philadelphia 19123; (215) 922-1116.

Ascension Manor II (Senior Citizen Housing), 970 N. 7th St., Philadelphia 19123; (215) 922-1116.

Benetwood Apartments, Benedictine Sisters of Erie, 641 Troupe Rd., Harborcreek 16421; (814) 899-0088 (80).

Bethlehem Retirement Village, 100 W. Wissahickon Ave., Flourtown 19031; (215) 233-0998.

Christ the King Manor, 1100 W. Long Ave., Du Bois 15801; (814) 371-3180 (160).

D'Youville Manor (Residential Care Facility), 1750 Quarry Rd., Yardley 19067; (215) 579-1750 (49).

Garvey Manor and Our Lady of the Allegheny Residence (Nursing Home), 128 Logan Blvd., Hollidaysburg 16648-2693; (814) 695-5571; www.garveymanor.org (150).

Grace Mansion (Personal Care Facility), Holy Family Residential Services, 1200 Spring St., Bethlehem; (610) 865-6748 (33).

Holy Family Apartments, 1318 Spring St., Bethlehem 18018; (610) 865-3963; hfmanor.com/html/independent_living.html (50).

Holy Family Home, Little Sisters of the Poor, 5300 Chester Ave., Philadelphia 19143; (215) 729-5153 (105).

Holy Family Manor (Skilled and Intermediate Nursing Facility), 1200 Spring St., Bethlehem 18018; (610) 865-5595; www.hfmanor.com (208).

Holy Family Residence (Personal Care Facility), 900 W. Market St., Orwigsburg 17961; (570) 366-2912 (85).

Immaculate Mary Home (Nursing Care Facility), 2990 Holme Ave., Philadelphia 19136; (215) 335-2100 (296).

John XXIII Home (Skilled, Intermediate and Personal Care), 2250 Shenango Freeway, Hermitage 16148; (724) 981-3200; www.johnxxiiihome.org; (196).

Little Flower Manor (Residence, Women), 1215 Springfield Rd., Darby 19023; (610) 534-6000 (180).

Little Flower Manor Nursing Home (Skilled Nursing), 1201 Springfield Rd., Darby 19023; (610) 534-6000 (185).

Little Flower Manor of Diocese of Scranton, (Long-Term Skilled Nursing Care Facility), 200 S. Meade St., Wilkes-Barre 18702; (570) 823-6131.

Little Sisters of the Poor, 1028 Benton Ave., Pittsburgh 15212; (412) 761-5373, (40).

Little Sisters of the Poor, Holy Family Residence, 2500 Adams Ave., Scranton 18509; (570) 343-4065 (58).

Maria Joseph Manor (Skilled Nursing, Personal Care Facility and Independent Living Cottages), 875 Montour Blvd., Danville 17821; (570) 275-4221 (135).

Marian Hall Home for the Aged (Women), 934 Forest Ave., Pittsburgh 15202; (412) 761-1999 (49).

Marian Manor (Intermediate Care), 2695 Winchester Dr., Pittsburgh 15220; (412) 563-6866 (194).

Mount Macrina Manor (Skilled Nursing Facility), 520 W. Main St., Uniontown 15401; (724) 437-1400 (141).

Neumann Apartments (Low Income), 25 N. Nichols St., St. Clair 17970; (570) 429-0699 (25).

Queen of Angels Apartments, 22 Rothermel St., Hyde Park, Reading 19605; (610) 921-3115 (45 units).

Queen of Peace Apartments (Low Income), 777 Water St., Pottsville 17901; (570) 628-4504 (65).

Redeemer Village II, 1551 Huntingdon Pike, Huntingdon Valley 19006; (215) 947-8168; www.holyredeemer.com (151

Sacred Heart Manor (Nursing Home and Independent Living), 6445 Germantown Ave., Philadelphia 19119; (215) 438-5268 (171 nursing home; 48 personal care; 48 independent living).

St. Anne's Home and Village, 3952 Columbia Ave., Columbia 17512; (717) 285-5443 (121).

St. Anne Home (Nursing Facility), 685 Angela Dr., Greensburg 15601; (724) 837-6070 (125).

St. Ignatius Nursing Home, 4401 Haverford Ave., Philadelphia 19104; (215) 349-8800 (176).

St. John Neumann Nursing Home, 10400 Roosevelt Blvd., Philadelphia 19116; (215) 248-7200 (107).

St. Joseph Home for the Aged (Residential and Skilled Nursing Facility), 1182 Holland Rd., Holland 18966; (215) 357-5511 (76).

St. Joseph Nursing and Health Care Center (Skilled Nursing Facility), 5324 Penn Ave., Pittsburgh 15224; (412) 665-5100 (153).

St. Leonard's Home Inc. (Personal Care Facility), 601 N. Montgomery St., Hollidaysburg 16648; (814) 695-9581 (30).

St. Mary of Providence Center, R.D. 2, Box 145, Elverson 19520; (610) 942-4166 (52).

Saint Mary's East, 607 E. 26th St., Erie 16504-2813; (814) 459-0621; www.stmaryshome.org (131).

Saint Mary's at Asbury Ridge, 4855 West Ridge Rd., Erie, PA 16506; (814) 836-5300.

Saint Mary's Manor (Residential, Personal Care, Short-Term Rehabilitation and Nursing Care), 701 Lansdale Ave., Lansdale 19446; (215) 368-0900 (200).

St. Mary's Villa Nursing Home, 675 St. Mary's Villa Rd., Moscow 18444; (570) 842-7621; (176).

Trexler Pavilion (Personal Care Facility), 1220 Prospect Ave., Bethlehem 18018; (610) 868-7776 (30).

Villa Teresa (Nursing Home), 1051 Avila Rd., Harrisburg 17109; (717) 652-5900 (184).

Vincentian de Marillac Nursing Home, 5300 Stanton Ave., Pittsburgh 15206; (412) 361-2833 (52).

Vincentian Home (Nursing Facility), 111 Perrymont Rd., Pittsburgh 15237; (412) 366-5600 (217).

Rhode Island: Jeanne Jugan Residence of the Little Sisters of the Poor, 964 Main St., Pawtucket 02860; (401) 723-4314 (95).

Saint Antoine Residence (Skilled Nursing Facility), 10 Rhodes Ave., North Smithfield 02896; (401) 767-3500; www.stantoine.net (416).

St. Clare Home (Nursing Facility), 309 Spring St., Newport 02840; (401) 849-3204 (47).

St. Francis House, 167 Blackstone St., Woonsocket 02895; (401) 762-5255 (59).

Scalabrini Villa (Convalescent, Rest-Nursing Home). 860 N. Quidnessett Rd., North Kingstown 02852; (401) 884-1802; www.freeyellow.com/members3/scalabrini/ (175).

South Carolina: Carter-May Home, 1660 Ingram Rd., Charleston 29407; (843) 556-8314 (15).

South Dakota: Avera Brady Memorial Home (Skilled Nursing Facility), 500 S. Ohlman St., Mitchell 57301; (605) 966-7701 (83).

Mother Joseph Manor (Skilled Nursing Facility), 1002 North Jay St., Aberdeen 57401; (605) 622-5850 (81).

Prince of Peace Retirement Community, 4500 Prince of Peace Pl., Sioux Falls 57103; (605) 322-5600 (204).

St. William's Home for the Aged (Intermediate Care, 60), and Angela Hall (Assisted Living Center for Developmentally Handicapped Women, 22), 901 E. Virgil, Box 432, Milbank 57252; (605) 432-4538.

Tekakwitha Nursing Home (Skilled and Intermediate Care), 6 E. Chestnut St., Sisseton 57262; (605) 698-7693 (101).

Tennessee: Alexian Village of Tennessee, 100 James Blvd., Signal Mountain 37377; (423) 886-0100 (277).

St. Mary Manor, 1771 Highway 45 Bypass, Jackson 38305; (731) 668-5633.

St. Peter Manor (Retirement Community), 108 N. Auburndale, Memphis 38104; (901) 278-8200.

St. Peter Villa (Intermediate and Skilled Care), 141 N. McLean, Memphis 38104; (901) 276-2021.

Villa Maria Manor, 32 White Bridge Rd., Nashville 37205; (615) 352-3084 (230).

Texas: Casa, Inc., Housing for Elderly and Handicapped, 3201 Sondra Dr., Fort Worth 76107; (817) 332-7276 (200).

Casa Brendan Housing for the Elderly and Handicapped (56 apartments) and Casa II, Inc. (30 apartments), 1300 Hyman St., Stephenville 76401; (254) 965-6964 (83).

John Paul II Nursing Home (Intermediate Care and Personal Care), 209 S. 3rd St., Kenedy 78119; (830) 583-9841.

Mother of Perpetual Help Home (Intermediate Care Facility), 519 E. Madison Ave., Brownsville 78520; (956) 546-6745; (38).

Mt. Carmel Home (Personal Care Home), 4130 S. Alameda St., Corpus Christi 78411; (512) 855-6243 (92).

Nuestro Hogar Housing for Elderly and Handicapped, 709 Magnolia St., Arlington 76012; (817) 261-0608 (63).

St. Ann's Nursing Home, P.O. Box 1179, Panhandle 79068; (806) 537-3194 (56).

St. Dominic Residence Hall, 2401 Holcombe Blvd., Houston 77021; (713) 741-8700 (149).

St. Francis Nursing Home (Intermediate Care Facility), 630 W. Woodlawn, San Antonio 78212; (210) 736-3177 (152).

St. Francis Village, Inc. (Retired and Elderly), 1 Chapel Plaza, Crowley 76036; (817) 292-5786 (420).

San Juan Nursing Home, Inc. (Skilled and Intermediate Care Facility), P.O. Box 1238, San Juan, 78589; (956) 787-1771 (127).

Villa Maria (Home for Aged Women-Men), 920 S. Oregon St., El Paso 79901; (915) 533-5152 (17 units).

Villa Maria, Inc. (Apartment Complex), 3146 Saratoga Blvd., Corpus Christi 78415; (361) 857-6171 (59).

Utah: Christus Health Utah (Christus St. Joseph Villa and Christus Marian Center), 451 Bishop Federal Lane, Salt Lake City 84115; www.stjosephvilla.com; (801) 487-7557 (300).

Vermont: Loretto Home for Aged, 59 Meadow St., Rutland 05701; (802) 773-8840 (57).

Michaud Memorial Manor (Residential Home for Elderly), Derby Line 05830; (802) 873-3152 (34).

St. Joseph's Home for Aged, 243 N. Prospect St., Burlington 05401; (802) 864-0264 (32).

Virginia: Madonna Home (Home for Aged), 814 W. 37th St., Norfolk 23508; (757) 623-6662 (16).

Marian Manor (Assisted Living, Nursing Care), 5345 Marian Lane, Virginia Beach 23462; (757) 456-5018 (100).

Marywood Apartments, 1261 Marywood Lane, Richmond 23229; (804) 740-5567 (126).

McGurk House Apartments, 2425 Tate Springs Rd., Lynchburg 24501; (434) 846-2425 (89).

Our Lady of the Valley Retirement Community, 650 N. Jefferson St., Roanoke 24016; (540) 345-5111.

Russell House Apartments, 900 First Colonial Rd., Virginia Beach 23454; (757) 481-0770 (126).

St. Francis Home, 2511 Wise St., Richmond 23225; (804) 231-1043 (34).

St. Joseph's Home for the Aged, Little Sisters of the Poor, 1503 Michael Rd., Richmond 23229; (804) 288-6245 (72).

St. Mary's Woods (Independent and Assisted Living Apartments), 1257 Marywood Lane, Richmond 23229; (804) 741-8624; www.stmaryswood.com (118 apartments).

Seton Manor (Apartments), 215 Marcella Rd., Hampton 23666; (757) 827-6512 (112).

Washington: Cathedral Plaza Apartments (Retirement Apartments), W. 1120 Sprague Ave., Spokane 99204 (150).

Chancery Place (Retirement Apartments), 910 Marion, Seattle 98104; (206) 343-9415.

The Delaney, W. 242 Riverside Ave., Spokane 99201, (509) 747-5081 (83).

Elbert House, 16000 N.E. 8th St., Bellevue 98008; (206) 747-5111.

Emma McRedmond Manor, 7960-169th N.E., Redmond 98052; (206) 869-2424 (31).

Fahy Garden Apartments, W. 1403-11 Dean Ave., Spokane 99201 (31).

Fahy West Apartments, W. 1523 Dean Ave., Spokane 99201 (55).

The Franciscan (Apartments), 15237-21stAve. S.W., Seattle 98166; (206) 431-8001.

Providence Mt. St. Vincent (Nursing Center and Retirement Apartments), 4831 35th Ave. S.W., Seattle 98126; (206) 937-3700 (174).

Tumwater Apartments, 5701-6th Ave. S.W., Tumwater 98501; (360) 352-4321.

West Virginia: Welty Home for the Aged, 21 Washington Ave., Wheeling 26003; (304) 242-5233 (46).

Wisconsin: Alexian Village of Milwaukee (Retirement Community/Skilled Nursing Home), 9301 N. 76th St., Milwaukee 53223; (414) 355-9300; www.alexianvillage.org (327).

Bethany-St. Joseph Health Care Center, 2501 Shelby Rd., La Crosse 54601; (608) 788-5700 (226).

Clement Manor (Retirement Community and Skilled Nursing), 3939 S. 92nd St., Greenfield 53228; (414) 321-1800 (162).

Divine Savior Nursing Home, 715 W. Pleasant St., Portage 53901; (608) 742-4131 (124).

Felician Village (Independent Living), 1700 S. 18th St., Manitowoc 54020; (920) 683-8811 (134 apartments).

Franciscan Care Center, 2915 North Meade St., Appleton 54911; (920) 831-8700 (215).

Franciscan Skemp Healthcare, Mayo Health System: Arcadia Campus Nursing Home, 464 S. St. Joseph Ave., Arcadia 54612; (608) 323-3341 (75).

McCormick Memorial Home, 212 Iroquois St., Green Bay 54301; (920) 437-0883 (60).

Marian Catholic Home (Skilled Care Nursing Home), 3333 W. Highland Blvd., Milwaukee 53208; (414) 344-8100 (215).

Marian Franciscan Center, 9632 W. Appleton Ave., Milwaukee 53225; (414) 461-8850 (310).

Marian Housing Center (Independent Living), 4105 Spring St., Racine 53405; (262) 633-5807 (40).

Maryhill Manor Nursing Home (Skilled Nursing Facility), 501 Madison Ave., Niagara 54151; (715) 251-3178 (75).

Milwaukee Catholic Home (Continuing Care Retirement Community), 2462 N. Prospect Ave., Milwaukee 53211-4462; (414) 224-9700; www.milwau keecatholichome.org (131).

Nazareth House (Skilled Nursing Facility), 814 Jackson St., Stoughton 53589; (608) 873-6448 (99).

St. Ann Rest Home (Intermediate Care Facility, Women), 2020 S. Muskego Ave., Milwaukee 53204; (414) 383-2630 (50).

St. Anne's Home for the Elderly, 3800 N. 92nd St., Milwaukee 53222; (414) 463-7570; www.wahsa.org/ st.anne/index.html (106).

St. Camillus Campus (Continuing Care Retirement Community), 10100 West Blue Mound Road, Wauwatosa 53226; (414) 258-1814; www.stcam.com (386).

St. Elizabeth Nursing Home, 502 St. Lawrence Ave., Janesville 53545; (608) 752-6709 (43).

St. Francis Home (Skilled Nursing Facility), 1416 Cumming Ave., Superior 54880; (715) 394-5591.

St. Francis Home (Skilled Nursing), 33 Everett St., Fond du Lac 54935; (920) 923-7980 (106).

St. Joseph's Home, 9244 29th Ave., Kenosha 53143; (262) 694-0080; www.sjosephs.com (93).

St. Joseph's Rehabilitation Center, 2902 East Ave. S., La Crosse 54601; (608) 788-9870; www.crs inc.org; (80).

St. Joseph's Nursing Home of St. Joseph Community Health Services, Inc. P.O. Box 527, Hillsboro 54634; (608) 489-8000.

St. Joseph Residence, Inc. (Nursing Home), 107 E. Beckert Rd., New London 54961; (920) 982-5354; (107).

St. Mary's Home for the Aged (Skilled Nursing, Alzheimer's Unit, Respite Care), 2005 Division St., Manitowoc 54220; (920) 684-7171; www.felician community.com; (266).

St. Mary's Nursing Home, 3515 W. Hadley St., Milwaukee 53210; (414) 873-9250 (88).

St. Monica's Senior Citizens Home, 3920 N. Green Bay Rd., Racine 53404; (262) 639-5050 (110).

St. Paul Home, Inc. (Intermediate and Skilled Nursing Home), 1211 Oakridge Ave., Kaukauna 54130; (920) 766-6020 (129).

Villa Loretto Nursing Home, N8114 Calvary St., Mount Calvary 53057; (920) 753-3211; (52).

Villa St. Francis, Inc., 1910 W. Ohio Ave., Milwaukee 53215; (414) 649-2888; (142).

FACILITIES FOR CHILDREN AND ADULTS WITH DISABILITIES

(*Sources:* Catholic Almanac *survey;* The Official Catholic Directory.)

This listing covers facilities and programs with educational and training orientation. Information about other services for the handicapped can generally be obtained from the Catholic Charities Office or its equivalent (c/o Chancery Office) in any diocese. (See Index for listing of addresses of chancery offices in the U.S.)

Abbreviation code: b, boys; c, coeducational; d, day; g, girls; r, residential. Other information includes age for admission. The number in parentheses at the end of an entry indicates total capacity or enrollment.

Deaf and Hearing Impaired

California: St. Joseph's Center for Deaf and Hard of Hearing, 3880 Smith St., Union City 94587.

Louisiana: Chinchuba Institute (d,c; birth through 18 yrs.), 1131 Barataria Blvd., Marrero 70072.

Missouri: St. Joseph Institute for the Deaf (r,d,c; birth to 14 years), 1809 Clarkson Rd., Chesterfield, MO 63017; (314) 532-3211 (Voice/TDD).

New York: Cleary School for the Deaf (d,c; infancy through 21), 301 Smithtown Blvd., Nesconset, NY 11767-2077; (516) 588-0530, www.clearyschool.org, (70).

St. Francis de Sales School for the Deaf (d,c; infant through elementary grades), 260 Eastern Parkway, Brooklyn 11225; (718) 636-4573 (150).

St. Joseph's School for the Deaf (d,c; parent-infant through 14 yrs.), 1000 Hutchinson River Pkwy, Bronx 10465; (718) 828-9000 (140).

Ohio: St. Rita School for the Deaf (r,d,c; birth to 12th grade), 1720 Glendale-Milford Rd., Cincinnati 45215; (513) 771-7600; www.srsdeaf.org (130).

Pennsylvania: Archbishop Ryan School for Hearing Impaired Children (d,c; parent-infant programs through 8th grade), 233 Mohawk Ave., Norwood, PA 19074; (610) 586-7044 (49).

De Paul Institute (d,c; birth through 21 yrs.), 2904 Castlegate Ave., Pittsburgh 15226; (412) 561-4848 (77).

Emotionally and/or Socially Maladjusted

This listing includes facilities for abused, abandoned and neglected as well as emotionally disturbed children and youth.

Alabama: St. Mary's Home for Children (r,c; referred from agencies), 4350 Moffat Rd., Mobile 36618; (334) 344-7733.

California: Hanna Boys Center (r,b; 10-15 yrs. at intake; school, 4th to 10th grade), Box 100, Sonoma 95476; (707)996-6767 (107). Treatment center and therapeutic special school for boys with emotional problems, behavior disorders, learning disabilities.

Rancho San Antonio (r,b; 13-17 yrs.), 21000 Plummer St., Chatsworth 91311; (818) 882-6400.

St. Vincent's (r,d,g; 12-17 yrs.), 4200 Calle Real, Santa Barbara 93110-1454; (805) 683-6381.

Colorado: Mt. St. Vincent Home (r,c; 5-13 yrs.), 4159 Lowell Blvd., Denver 80211; (303) 458-7220; www.nahse.org/member/st.vincent.

Connecticut: St. Francis Home for Children (r,d,c; 4-17 yrs.), 651 Prospect St., New Haven 06511; (203) 777-5513. Exec. Dir., Peter Salerno.

Mt. St. John Home and School for Boys (r,b; 11-16 yrs.), 135 Kirtland St., Deep River 06417; (860) 526-5391, www.mtstjohn.org (77).

Delaware: Our Lady of Grace Home for Children (r,d,c; 6-12 yrs.), 487 E. Chestnut Hill Rd., Newark 19713; (302) 738-4658.

Seton Villa, Siena Hall and Children's Home (r,c; group home; 12-18 yrs,; mothers and their children), c/o 2307 Kentmere Pkwy, Wilmington 19806; (302) 656-2183.

Florida: Boystown of Florida (r,b; 12-16 yrs.; group home), 11400 S.W. 137th Ave., Miami 33186.

Georgia: Village of St. Joseph (r,c; 6-16 yrs.), 1961 Druid Hills Rd., Ste. 205-B, 30329; (404) 321-2900.

Illinois: Guardian Angel Home (d,c; r,b), 1550 Plainfield Rd., Joliet 60435; (815) 729-0930 (35).

Maryville Academy (r,c; 6-18 yrs.), 1150 North River Rd., Des Plaines 60016; (708) 824-6126.

Mission of Our Lady of Mercy, Mercy Home for Boys and Girls (r,d,c; 15-18 yrs.), 1140 W. Jackson Blvd., Chicago 60607; (312) 738-7560; www.mercyhome.org.

St. Joseph's Carondelet Child Center (r,b, 5-21 yrs.; d.c.,5-18 yrs., 739 E. 35th St., Chicago 60616; (773) 624-7443, www.stjccc.org.

Indiana: Gibault School for Boys (r; 10-18 yrs.), 6301 South U.S. Highway 41, P.O. Box 2316, Terre Haute 47802; (812) 299-1156.

Hoosier Boys Town (r; 10-18 yrs.), 7403 Cline Ave., Schererville 46375; (219) 322-8614.

Kentucky: Boys' Haven (r; 12-18 yrs.), 2301 Goldsmith Lane, Louisville 40218; (502) 458-1171, www.boyshaven.org.

Louisiana: Hope Haven Center (r,c; 5-18 yrs.), 1101 Barataria Blvd., Marrero 70072; (504) 347-5581.

Maryland: Good Shepherd Center (r,g; 13-18 yrs.), 4100 Maple Ave., Baltimore, 21227; (410) 247-2770; www.goodshepherdcenter.com.

Massachusetts: The Brightside for Families and Children (r,d,c; 6-16 yrs.), 2112 Riverdale St., W. Springfield 01089; (413) 827-4255; www.mercy cares.com; Vice-Pres. James Bastien.

McAuley Nazareth Home for Boys (r; 6-13 yrs.), 77 Mulberry St., Leicester 01524; (508) 892-4886 (16). Residential treatment center.

St. Vincent Home (r,c 5-22 yrs.), 2425 Highland Ave., Fall River 02720; (508) 679-8511.

Michigan: Don Bosco Hall (r,b; 13-17 years.), 10001 Petoskey Ave., Detroit 48204; (313) 834-8677.

Holy Cross Children's Services, (r,d,c; 13-17 yrs.), 8759 Clinton-Macon Rd., Clinton 49236; (517) 423-7451 (650). Facilities located throughout the state and northern Ohio.

Vista Maria (r,g; 11-18 yrs.), 20651 W. Warren Ave., Dearborn Heights 48127; (313) 271-6250; www.com munity.milive.com/cc/girls.

Minnesota: St. Cloud Children's Home (r,c; 8-18 yrs.), RTC Campus, Bld. 4-D, P.O. Box 1006, Fergus Falls, MN 56538; (218) 739-9325. Day Treatment Program (d,c; 7-14 yrs.), same address.

St. Elizabeth Home (r,c; 18 yrs. and older), 306 15th Ave. N., St. Cloud 56301; (320) 252-8350.

Missouri: Child Center of Our Lady (r,d,c; 5-14 yrs.), 7900 Natural Bridge Rd., St. Louis 63121; (314) 383-0200.

Marygrove (r,d,c; 6-21 yrs.) (97); intense treatment unit (r,b; 13-18 yrs) (13); overnight crises care (r,d,c; birth to 18 yrs.) (8), 2705 Mullanphy Lane, Florissant,

63031; (314) 837-1702; www.marygroveonline.org.

St. Joseph's Home for Boys (r,d,b; 6-14 yrs.), 4753 S. Grand Blvd., St. Louis 63111; (314) 481-9121.

Montana: Big Sky Ranch (r,g; 12-18 yrs.), P.O. Box 1128, Glendive 59330; (406) 687-3839.

Nebraska: Father Flanagan's Boys' Home (r,c; 10-16 yrs.), 14100 Crawford St., Boys Town 68010; (402) 498-1000; www.boystown.org (556). Boys Town National Research Hospital (r,d,c; 1-18 yrs.), 555 N. 30th St., Omaha 68131; (402) 498-6511; www.boys townhospital.org. Center for Abused Handicapped Children; diagnosis of speech, language and hearing problems in children. Boys Town also has various facilities or programs in Brooklyn, NY; Portsmouth, RI; Philadelphia, PA; Washington, DC; Tallahassee, Orlando and Delray Beach, FL; Atlanta, GA; New Orleans, LA; San Antonio, TX; Las Vegas, NV; and southern California.

New Jersey: Catholic Community Services/Mt. Carmel Guild, 1160 Raymond Blvd., Newark 07102; (973) 596-4084.

Collier High School (d,c; 13-18 yrs.), 160 Conover Rd., Wickatunk 07765; (732) 946-4771; www.collier services.com.

Collier Group Home, 180 Spirng St., Red Bank, NJ 07701; (732) 842-8337.

Mt. St. Joseph Children's Center (r,d,b; 6-14 yrs.), 124 Shepherd Lane, Totowa 07512; (973) 595-5720.

New York: The Astor Home for Children (r,d,c; 5-12 yrs.), 6339 Mill St., P.O. Box 5005, Rhinebeck 12572-5005; (845) 871-1000; www.astorservices.org. Child Guidance Clinics/Day Treatment (Rhinebeck, Poughkeepsie, Beacon, Bronx). Head Start - Day Care (Poughkeepsie, Beacon, Red Hook, Dover, Millerton).

Baker Victory Services, 780 Ridge Rd. Lackawanna 14218; (716) 828-9500; www.ourladyofvictory.org.

Good Shepherd Services (r,d,c), 305 Seventh Ave., New York, NY 10001; (212) 243-7070; www.good shepherds.org. City-wide residential programs or adolescents (12-21 yrs.); foster care and adoption services (infant-21 yrs.); training institute for human services workers; day treatment program (13-18 yrs.); community-based neighborhood family services in South Brooklyn Community (infant-adult),

LaSalle School (r,d,b; 12-18 yrs.), 391 Western Ave., Albany 12203; (518) 242-4731.

Madonna Heights Services (r,d,g; 12-18 yrs.), 151 Burrs Lane, Dix Hills 11746; (631) 643-8800; www.scony.org (110). Also conducts group homes on Long Island and outpatient programs.

Saint Anne Institute (r,d,g; 12-18 yrs.), 160 N. Main Ave., Albany 12206; (518) 437-6500.

St. Catherine's Center for Children (r,d,c; birth through 12 yrs.), 40 N. Main Ave., Albany 12203; (518) 453-6700; www.st-cath.org.

St. John's of Rockaway Beach (r,b; 9-21 yrs.), 144 Beach 111th St., Rockaway Park 11694; (718) 945-2800. Programs include diagnostic centers and independent living programs.

North Dakota: Home on the Range (r,c; 10-18 yrs.), 16351 I-94, Sentinel Butte 58654; (701) 872-3745; www.gohotr.org (79). Residential and emergency shelter therapeutic programs.

Home on the Range-Red River Victory Ranch (r,b; 10-18 yrs.), P.O. Box 9615, Fargo 58106; (701) 293-6321; www.hotr.org (12). Residential chemical addictions program.

Ohio: St. Vincent Family Centers (d,c; preschool) Outpatient counseling program (c; 2-18 yrs.), 1490 East Main St., Columbus 43205; (614) 252-0731; www.svfc.org.

Marycrest (r,g; 13-18 yrs.), 7800 Brookside Rd., Independence 44131.

Catholic Charities Services/Parmadale (r,c; 12-18 yrs.), 6753 State Rd., Parma 44134; (440) 845-7700.

Rosemont (r,g;d,c; 11-18 yrs.), 2440 Dawnlight Ave., Columbus 43211; (614) 471-2626.

Oregon: St. Mary's Home for Boys (r; 10-18 yrs.), 16535 S.W. Tualatin Valley Highway, Beaverton 97006; (503) 649-5651.

Pennsylvania: Auberle (r,c; 7-18 yrs.), 1101 Hartman St., McKeesport 15132-1500; (412) 673-5800; www.auberle.org, (181). Residential treatment for boys; emergency shelter care, foster care, group home for girls and family preservation program.

De LaSalle in Towne (d,b; 14-17 yrs.), 25 S. Van Pelt St., Philadelphia 19103; (215) 567-5500.

De LaSalle Vocational Day Treatment (b; 15-18 yrs.), P.O. Box 344, Bensalem 19020; (215) 464-0344.

Gannondale (r,g; 12-17 yrs.), 4635 E. Lake Rd., Erie 16511; (814) 899-7659.

Harborcreek Youth Services (r,d,c; 10-17 yrs.), 5712 Iroquois Ave., Harborcreek 16421; (814) 899-7664; www.hys-erie.org.

Holy Family Institute (r,d,c; 0-18 yrs.), 8235 Ohio River Blvd., Emsworth 15202, (412) 766-4030; www.hfi-pgh.org.

Lourdesmont Good Shepherd Youth and Family Services (r,g;d,c; 12-17 yrs.), 537 Venard Rd., Clarks Summit 18411; (507) 587-4741; www.lourdes mont.com. Sponsored by the Sisters of the Good Shepherd. John A. Antognoli.

St. Gabriel's Hall (r,b; 10-18 yrs.), P.O. Box 7280, Audubon 19407; (215) 247-2776.

St. Michael's School (r,b; d,c; 12-17 yrs.), Box 370, Tuckhannock 18657; (570) 388-6155.

Texas: St. Joseph Adolescent and Family Counseling Center (c; 13-17 yrs.), 5415 Maple Ave., #320, Dallas 75235; (214) 631-TEEN.

Washington: Morning Star Boys Ranch (Spokane Boys' Ranch, Inc.), (r,b; 10-18 yrs.), Box 8087, Spokane 99203-0087; (509) 448-1411; www.morning starboysranch.org. Dir. Joseph M. Weitensteiner.

Wisconsin: North American Union Sisters of Our Lady of Charity Center (r,c; 10-17 yrs.), 154 Edgington Lane, Wheeling, WV 26003-1535; (304) 242-0042.

St. Charles Youth and Family Services (r,d,b; 12-18 yrs.), 151 S. 84th St., Milwaukee 53214; (414) 476-3710; www.stcharlesinc.org.

Wyoming: St. Joseph's Children's Home (r,c; 6-18 yrs.), P.O. Box 1117, Torrington 82240; (307) 532-4197.

Developmentally Challenged

This listing includes facilities for children, youth, and adults with learning disabilities.

Alabama: Father Purcell Memorial Exceptional Children's Center (r, c; birth to 10 yrs.), 2048 W. Fairview Ave., Montgomery 36108; (334) 834-5590.

Father Walter Memorial Child Care Center (r,c; birth-12 yrs.), 2815 Forbes Dr., Montgomery 36110; (334) 262-6421.

California: Child Study Center of St. John's Hos-

pital (d,c; birth-18 yrs.), 1339-20th St., Santa Monica 90404; (310) 829-8921.

St. Madeleine Sophie's Center (d,c; 18 yrs. and older), 2111 E. Madison Ave., El Cajon 92019.

Tierra del Sol Foundation (d,c; 18 yrs. and older), 9919 Sunland Blvd., Sunland 91040; (818) 352-1419. 14547 Gilmore St., Van Nuys 91411; (818) 904-9164.

Connecticut: Gengras Center (d,c; 3-21 yrs.), St. Joseph College, 1678 Asylum Ave., W. Hartford 06117.

Villa Maria Education Center (d,c; 6-14 yrs.), 161 Sky Meadow Dr., Stamford 06903-3400; (203) 322-5886; www.villamariaedcenter.org.

District of Columbia: Lt. Joseph P. Kennedy, Jr., Institute (d,c; 6 weeks to 5 yrs. for Kennedy Institute for Child Development Center; 6-21 yrs. for Kennedy School; 18 yrs. and older for training and employment, therapeutic and residential services). Founded in 1959 for people of all ages with developmental disabilities and their families in the Washington archdiocese. Heaquarters: 801 Buchanan St. N.E., Washington 20017; (202) 529-7600; www.kennedy institute.org. Other locations in D.C. and Maryland. No enrollment limit.

Florida: L'Arche Harbor House, (c; 20 yrs. and older; community home), 700 Arlington Rd., Jacksonville 32211; (904) 721-5992.

Marian Center Services for Developmentally Handicapped and Mentally Retarded (r,d,c; 2-21 yrs.), 15701 Northwest 37th Ave., Opa Locka 33054; (305) 625-8354; www.mariancenterschool.org. Pre-school, school, workshop residence services.

Morning Star School (d,c; 4-16 yrs.), 725 Mickler Rd., Jacksonville 32211; (904) 421-2144.

Morning Star School (d,c; school age), 954 Leigh Ave., Orlando 32804.

Morning Star School (d,c; 6-14 yrs.), 4661-80th Ave. N., Pinellas Park 33781; (727) 544-6036; www.morn ingstarschool.org.

Morning Star School (d,c; 6-16 yrs.), 210 E. Linebaugh Ave., Tampa 33612; (813) 935-0232; www.tampa-morningstar.org..

Georgia: St. Mary's Home (r,c), 2170 E. Victory Dr., Savannah 31404; (912) 236-7164.

Illinois: Bartlett Learning Center (r,d,c; 3-21 yrs.), 801 W. Bartlett Rd., Bartlett 60103; (630) 289-4221.

Brother James Court (r, men over 18 yrs.), 2500 St. James Rd., Springfield 62707; (217) 544-4876.

Good Shepherd Manor (men; 18 yrs. and older), Little Brothers of the Good Shepherd, P.O. Box 260, Momence 60954; (815) 472-6492; www.good shepherdmanor.org. Resident care for developmentally disabled men.

Misericordia Home South (r,c), 2916 W. 47th St., Chicago 60632; (773) 254-9595. For severely and profoundly impaired children.

Misericordia Home — Heart of Mercy Village (r,c; 6-45 yrs.), 6300 North Ridge, Chicago 60660; (773) 973-6300; www.misericordia.com.

Mt. St. Joseph (developmentally disabled women; over age 21), 24955 N. Highway 12, Lake Zurich 60047; (847) 438-5050.

St. Coletta's of Illinois (r,d,; 6 to adult), 123rd and Wolf Rd., Palos Park 60464; (708) 448-6520.

St. Mary of Providence (r,women; 18 yrs. and older), 4200 N. Austin Ave., Chicago 60634; (773) 545-8300.

St. Vincent Community Living Facility (r,c; adults,

over 18 yrs.) (20), and St. Vincent Supported Living Arrangement (r,c; adults, over 18 yrs.) (20), 659 E. Jefferson St., Freeport 61032; (815) 232-6181.

Springfield Developmental Center (m; 21 yrs. and over), 4595 Laverna Rd., Springfield 62707; (217) 525-8271; www.ffsc.net.

Massachusetts: Cardinal Cushing Centers (d,c; 3-22 yrs.), 85 Washington St., Braintree 02184; (781) 848-6250.

Vocational Training

Indiana: Marian Day School (d,c; 6-16 yrs.), 700 Herndon Dr., Evansville 47711; (812) 422-5346.

Kansas: Lakemary Center, Inc. (r,d,c), 100 Lakemary Dr., Paola 66071; (913) 557-4000.

Kentucky: Pitt Academy (d,c), 4605 Poplar Level Rd., Louisville 40213; (502) 966-6979; www.pitt.com.

Louisiana: Department of Special Education, Archdiocese of New Orleans, St. Michael Special School (d,c; 6-21 yrs.), 1522 Chippewa St., New Orleans 70130.

Holy Angels Residential Facility (r,c; teenage, 14 yrs. and older), 10450 Ellerbe Rd., Shreveport 71106; (318) 797-8500.

Ocean Avenue Community Home, 361 Ocean Ave., Gretna 70053; (504) 361-0674.

Padua Community Services (r,c; birth-25 yrs.), 200 Beta St., Belle Chasse 70037.

St. Jude the Apostle, 1430 Claire Ave., Gretna 70053; (504) 361-8457.

St. Mary's Residential Training School (r,c: 3-22 yrs.), P.O. Drawer 7768, Alexandria 71306; (318) 445-6443.

St. Peter the Fisherman, 62269 Airport Dr., Slidell 70458; (504) 641-4914.

St. Rosalie (r; men 18 and up), 119 Kass St., Gretna 70056; (504) 361-8320.

Sts. Mary and Elizabeth, 720 N. Elm St., Metairie 70003; (504) 738-6959.

Maryland: The Benedictine School for Exceptional Children (r,c; 6-21 yrs.), 14299 Benedictine Lane, Ridgely 21660; (410) 634-2112; www.benschool.com.

Francis X. Gallagher Services (r), 2520 Pot Spring Rd., Timonium 21093.

St. Elizabeth School and Habilitation Center (d,c; 11-21 yrs.), 801 Argonne Dr., Baltimore 21218; (410) 889-5054; www.stelizabeth-school.org.

Massachusetts: Cardinal Cushing School and Training Center (r,d,c; 16-22 yrs.), Hanover 02339 (116 r; 28 d).

Mercy Centre (d,c; 3-22 yrs. and over), 25 West Chester St., Worcester 01605-1136; (508) 852-7165; www.mercycentre.com.

Michigan: Our Lady of Providence Center (r,g; 11-30 yrs., d,c; 26 yrs. and older), 16115 Beck Rd., Northville 48118; (734) 453-1300.

St. Louis Center and School (r,d,b; 6-18 yrs. child care; 18-36 yrs. adult foster care), 16195 Old U.S. 12, Chelsea 48118-9646; (734) 475-8430; www.st louiscenter.org.

Minnesota: Mother Teresa Home (r,c; 18 yrs. and older), 101-10th Ave. N., Cold Spring 56320.

St. Francis Home (r,c; 18 yrs. and older), P.O. Box 326, Waite Park 56387; (320) 251-7630.

St. Luke's Home (r; 18 yrs. and older), 411 8th Ave. N., Cold Springs 56320.

Missouri: Department of Special Education, Archdiocese of St. Louis, 4472 Lindell Blvd., St. Louis. 63108; (314) 533-3454. Serves children with developmental disabilities, mental retardation or learning disabilities; services include special ungraded day classes in 8 parish schools.

Good Shepherd Homes (residential for developmentally disabled men; 18 yrs. and up), The Community of the Good Shepherd, 10101 James A. Reed Rd., Kansas City 64134; (816) 767-8090.

St.Mary's Special School (r,c; 5-21 yrs.), 1724 Redman, St. Louis 63138; (314) 261-8533. St. Mary's Supported Living (r,c) (24); suprvised homes for adolescents or adults. St. Mary's Early Intervention (d,c) (30); early intervention for toddlers.

Nebraska: Madonna School for Exceptional Children (d,c; 5-21 yrs.), 2537 N. 62nd St., Omaha 68104; (402) 556-1883; www.madonnaschool.org. Children with learning problems.

Villa Marie School and Home for Exceptional Children (r,d,c; 6-18 yrs.), P.O. Box 80328, Lincoln 68501; (402) 488-2040.

New Jersey: Archbishop Damiano School (d,c; 3-21 yrs.), 1145 Delsea Dr., Westville Grove 08093.

Catholic Community Services, Archdiocese of Newark, 1160 Raymond Blvd., Newark 07102.

Department of Special Education, Diocese of Camden, 5609 Westfield Ave., Pennsauken, NJ 08110-1836; (609) 488-7123; www.catholiccharities.org. Services include: Archbishop Damiano School (above), and full time programs (d,c; 6-21 yrs.) at 4 elementary (96) and 2 high schools (60) and some religious education programs.

Department for Persons with Disabilities, Diocese of Paterson, 1049 Weldon Rd., Oak Ridge, N.J. 07438; (973) 697-4394; www.dpd.org. Services include 8 residential programs for adults, one adult training center, family support services.

Felician School for Exceptional Children (d,c; 5-21 yrs.), 260 S. Main St., Lodi 07644; (201) 777-0725.

McAuley School for Exceptional Children (d,c; 5-21 yrs.), 1633 Rt. 22 at Terrill Rd., Watchung 07060.

Mt. Carmel Guild Special Education School (d,c ; 6-21 yrs.), 60 Kingsland Ave., Kearny 07032; (201) 995-3280.

St. Anthony's Special Education School (d,c), 25 N. 7th St., Belleville 07109; (973) 844-3700.

Sister Georgine School (d,c; 6-17 yrs.), 544 Chestnut Ave., Trenton 08611; (609) 396-5444.

St. Patrick's Special Education School (d,c), 72 Central Ave., Newark 07102.

New York: Baker Victory Services (r), 780 Ridge Rd., Lackawanna, N.Y. 14218; (716) 828-9500. Residential care for handicapped and retarded children; nursery school program for emotionally disturbed preschool children.

Bishop Patrick V. Ahern High School (d,c; 15-21 yrs.), 100 Merrill Ave., Staten Island 10314.

Cantalician Center for Learning (d,c; birth-21 yrs.), 3233 Main St., Buffalo 14214; (716) 833-5353; www.cantalician.org. Infant and pre-school; elementary and secondary; workshop (426). Three group homes. Rehabilitation, day treatment and senior rehabilitation programs.

Catholic Charities Residential Services, Rockville Center Diocese, 269 W. Main St., Bay Shore 11706. Residences for developmentally disabled adults (88).

Cobb Memorial School (r,d,c; 5-21 yrs.), 100-300 Mt. Presentation Way, Altamont 12009; (518) 861-6446.

Joan Ann Kennedy Memorial Preschool (d,c; 3-5 yrs.), 26 Sharpe Ave., Staten Island 10302.

L'Arche Syracuse (r, adults), 1232 Teall Ave., Syracuse 13206-3468; (315) 479-8088; www.larche syracuse.com (12). Homes where assistants and persons with developmental disabilities share life, following the philosophy of Jean Vanier. Member of International L'Arche Federation, Exec. Dir., Frank Woolever.

Maryhaven Center of Hope (r,d,c; school age to adult), 1010 Route 112, Port Jefferson 11776; (631) 474-4120; www.maryhaven.org.

Mercy Home for Children (r,c), 243 Prospect Park West, Brooklyn 11215; (718) 832-1075. Residences for adolescents and young adults who are developmentally disabled: Visitation, Warren, Vincent Haire, Santulli and Littlejohn residences (Brooklyn), Kevin Keating Residence (Queens).

Office for Disabled Persons, Catholic Charities, Diocese of Brooklyn, 191 Joralemon St., Brooklyn 11201; (718) 722-6000; www.ccbg.org. Services include: adult day treatment center; community residences for mentally retarded adults; special events for disabled children (from age 3) and adults.

Office for Disabled Persons, Archdiocese of New York, 1011 First Ave., New York 10022; (212) 371-1000. Services include consultation and referral, variety of services for deaf, blind, mentally retarded, mentally ill.

School of the Holy Childhood (d,c; 5-21 yrs.), 100 Groton Parkway, Rochester 14623.

Seton Foundation for Learning (d,c; 5-15 yrs.), 104 Gordon St., Staten Island 10304; (718) 447-1750.

North Carolina: Holy Angels (r,c; birth to adult), 6600 Wilkinson Blvd., P.O. Box 710, Belmont 28012; (704) 825-4161; www.holyangelsnc.org.

North Dakota: Friendship, Inc. (r,d,c; all ages), 3004 11th St. South, Fargo 58103; (701) 235-8217.

Ohio: Julie Billiart School (d,c; 6-12 yrs.), 4982 Clubside Rd., Cleveland 44124; (216) 381-1191.

Mary Immaculate School (d,c; 6-14 yrs.), 3837 Secor Rd., Toledo 43623; (419) 474-1688; www.maryimmaculatetoledo.org

OLA/St. Joseph Center (d,c; 6-16 yrs.), 2346 W. 14th St., Cleveland 44113; (216) 621-3451.

Rose Mary, The Johanna Graselli Rehabilitation and Education Center (r,c; 5 yrs. and older), 19350 Euclid Ave., Cleveland 44117.

St. John's Villa (r,c; continued care and training, 15 yrs. and over), P.O. Box 457, Carrollton 44615; (330) 627-9789.

Oregon: Providence Montessori School Early Intervention Program (d,c; 3-5 yrs.), 830 N.E. 47th Ave., Portland 97213; (503) 215-2409.

Pennsylvania: Clelian Heights School for Exceptional Children (r,d,c; 5-21 yrs.), R.D. 9, Box 607, Greensburg 15601; (724) 837-8120; (95). Also conducts re-socialization program (r,d,c; young adults).

Divine Providence Village (adults), 686 Old Marple Rd., Springfield 19064; (610) 328-7730. Admin., Sr. Esther Leroux.

Don Guanella Village: Don Guanella School (r,d,b; 6-21 yrs.) and Cardinal Krol Center (r; adults, post-school age), 1797 S. Sproul Rd., Springfield 19602; (610) 543-3380; Admin. Rev. Dennis Weber, S.C.

John Paul II, Center for Special Learning (d,c; 3-21 yrs.), 1092 Welsh Rd., Shillington, PA 19607; (610) 777-0605; www.jp2center.org.

McGuire Memorial (r,d,c; 18 mos. to adult.), 2119 Mercer Rd., New Brighton 15066; (724) 843-3400; Exec. Dir., Sr. Mary Thaddeus Markelewicz.

Mercy Special Learning Center (d,c; 3-21 yrs. and early intervention), 830 S. Woodward St., Allentown 18103; (610) 797-8242.

Our Lady of Confidence Day School (d,c; 4½-21 yrs.), 10th and Lycoming Sts., Philadelphia 19140.

Queen of the Universe Day Center (d,c; 4½-16 yrs.), 2443 Trenton Rd., Levittown 19056; (215) 945-6090; www.qudaycenter.org.

St. Anthony School Programs (d,c; 5-21 yrs.), 2718 Custer Ave., Pittsburgh 15227; (412) 882-1333.

St. Joseph Center for Special Learning (d,c; 4-21 yrs.), 2075 W. Norwegian St., Pottsville 17901; (570) 622-4638; www.pottsville.com/stjosephctr.

St. Joseph's Center (r,d,c; birth-10 yrs.), 2010 Adams Ave., Scranton 18509; (570) 342-8379; www.st josephcenter.org. Pres. ,Therese O'Rourke, I.H.M.

St. Katherine Day School (d,c; 4½-21 yrs.), 930 Bowman Ave., Wynnewood 19096; (610) 667-3958.

Tennessee: Madonna Learning Center, Inc., for Retarded Children (d,c; 5-16 yrs.), 7007 Poplar Ave., Germantown 38138.

Texas: Notre Dame of Dallas School (d,c; 3-21 yrs.), 2018 Allen St., Dallas 75204; (214) 720-3911.

Virginia: St. Coletta School (d,c; 5-22 yrs.), 207 S. Peyton St., Alexandria, 22314; (703) 683-3686. For developmentally disabled. Services include: occupational, physical and language therapy; vocational program with job search, placement, training and follow-up services.

St. Mary's Infant Home (r,c; birth to 14 yrs.), 317 Chapel St., Norfolk 23504; (757) 622-2208. For multiple handicapped.

Wisconsin: St Coletta of Wisconsin, W4955 Hwy 18, Jefferson 53549; (920) 674-4330; www.st colettawi.org. Year-round special education programs for adolescents and adults; pre-vocational and vocational skills training; residential living alternatives. Young adult population. Employment opportunities for those who qualify.

St. Coletta Day School (c; 8-17 yrs.), 1740 N. 55th St., Milwaukee. 53208; (414) 453-1850.

Orthopedically/Physically Challenged

Pennsylvania: St. Edmond's Home for Children (r,c; 1-21 yrs.)., 320 S. Roberts Rd., Rosemont 19010; (610) 525-8800.

Virginia: St. Joseph Villa Housing Corp. (adults), 8000 Brook Rd., Richmond 23227; (804) 553-3283.

Visually Challenged

Maine: Educational Services for Blind and Visually Impaired Children (Catholic Charities, Maine), 1066 Kenduskeag Ave., Bangor 04401. 66 Western Ave., Fairfield 04937. 15 Westminster St., Lewiston 04240. P.O. Box 378, Fairfield, ME 04937; (800) 660-5231. Itinerant teachers, instructional materials center.

New Jersey: St. Joseph's School for the Blind (r,d,c; 3-21 yrs.), 257 Baldwin Ave., Jersey City 07306; (201) 653-0578; www.sjsb.net.

New York: Lavelle School for the Blind (d,c; 3-21

yrs.), East 221st St. and Paulding Ave., Bronx 10469; (718) 882-1212. For visually impaired, multiple handicapped.

Pennsylvania: St. Lucy Day School (d,c; pre-K to 8th grade), 130 Hampden Rd., Upper Darby 19082; (610) 352-4550; www.stlucydayschool.org. For children with visual impairments.

There is great variety in retreat and renewal programs, with orientations ranging from the traditional to teen encounters. Central to all of them are celebration of the liturgy and deepening of a person's commitment to faith and witness in life.

Features of many of the forms are as follows.

Traditional Retreats: Centered around conferences and the direction of a retreat master; oriented to the personal needs of the retreatants; including such standard practices as participation in Mass, reception of the sacraments, private and group prayer, silence and meditation, discussions.

Team Retreat: Conducted by a team of several leaders or directors (priests, religious, lay persons) with division of subject matter and activities according to their special skills and the nature and needs of the group.

Closed Retreat: Involving withdrawal for a period of time — overnight, several days, a weekend — from everyday occupations and activities.

Open Retreat: Made without total disengagement from everyday involvements, on a part-time basis.

Private Retreat: By one person, on a kind of do-it-yourself basis with the one-to-one assistance of a director.

Special Groups: With formats and activities geared to particular groups; e.g., members of Alcoholics Anonymous, vocational groups and apostolic groups.

Marriage Encounters: Usually weekend periods of husband-wife reflection and dialogue; introduced into the U.S. from Spain in 1967.

Charismatic Renewal: Featuring elements of the movement of the same name; "Spirit-oriented," communitarian and flexible, with spontaneous and shared prayer, personal testimonies of faith and witness.

Christian Community: Characterized by strong community thrust.

Teens Encounter Christ (TEC), SEARCH: Formats adapted to the mentality and needs of youth, involving experience of Christian faith and commitment in a community setting.

Christian Maturity Seminars: Similar to teen encounters in basic concept but different to suit persons of greater maturity.

RENEW International: Spiritual renewal process involving the entire parish. Office, 1232 George St., Plainfield, NJ 07062; (908) 769-5400. Director, Msgr. Thomas A. Kleissler.

Cursillo: *see* separate entry.

Conference

Retreats International Inc.: National Office, Box 1067, Notre Dame, IN 46556; (219) 631-5320. An organization for promoting retreats in the U.S. was started in 1904 in New York. Its initial efforts and the gradual growth of the movement led to the formation in 1927 of the National Catholic Laymen's Retreat Conference, the forerunner of the men's division of Retreats International. The women's division developed from the National Laywomen's Retreat Movement which was founded in Chicago in 1936. The men's and women's divisions merged July 9, 1977. The services of the organization include an annual summer institute for retreat and pastoral ministry, regional conferences for retreat center leadership and area meetings of directors and key leadership in the retreat movement. The officers are: Episcopal advisor, Auxiliary Bishop Robert Morneau of Green Bay; pres., Sr. Mary Elizabeth Imler, O.S.F.; exec. dir., Anne M. Luther.

HOUSES OF RETREAT AND RENEWAL

(*Principal sources:* Catholic Almanac *survey;* The Official Catholic Directory.)

Abbreviation code: m, men; w, women; mc, married couples; y, youth. Houses and centers without code generally offer facilities to most groups. An asterisk after an abbreviation indicates that the facility is primarily for the group designated but that special groups are also accommodated. Houses furnish information concerning the types of programs they offer.

Alabama: Blessed Trinity Shrine Retreat and Cenacle, 107 Holy Trinity Rd., Holy Trinity 36859, (334) 855-4474; Visitation Sacred Heart Retreat House, 2300 Spring Hill Ave., Mobile 36607, (334) 473-2321.

Alaska: Holy Spirit Center, 10980 Hillside Dr., Anchorage 99507, (907) 346-2343, home.gci.net/~hsrh.

Arizona: Franciscan Renewal Center, 5802 E. Lincoln Dr., Scottsdale 85253, (480) 948-7460; Holy Trinity Monastery, P.O. Box 298, St. David 85630, Benedictine community, self-directed/Spirit-directed monastic retreat, (520) 720-4642; Mount Claret Retreat Center, 4633 N. 54th St., Phoenix 85018, (602) 840-5066; Our Lady of Solitude House of Prayer, P.O. Box 1140, Black Canyon City 85324, (623) 374-9204; Redemptorist Picture Rocks Retreat House, 7101 W. Picture Rocks Rd., Tucson 85743, (520) 744-3400, www.desertrenewal.org.

Arkansas: Brothers and Sisters of Charity, Little Portion Hermitage, 350 C R 048, Barryville, 72616-8505, (479) 253-7710, www.johnmichaeltalbot.com; Little Portion Retreat and Training Center, Rt. 4, Box 430, Eureka Springs 72632, (501) 253-7379; St. Scholastica Retreat Center, P.O. Box 3489, Ft. Smith 72913, (501) 783-1135, www.catholic-church.org/scholastica; Hesychia House of Prayer, 204 St. Scholastica Rd., New Blaine, Shoal Creek, 72851, (501) 938-7375.

California: Angela Center, 535 Angela Dr., Santa Rosa 95403, (707) 528-8578; Christ the King Retreat Center, 6520 Van Maren Lane, Citrus Heights 95621, (916) 969-4706, www.passionist.org; Claretian Retreat Center, 1119 Westchester Pl., Los Angeles 90019, (323) 737-8464; De Paul Center, 1105 Bluff Rd., Montebello 90640, (323) 721-6060; El Carmelo Retreat House, P.O. Box 446, Redlands 92373, (909) 792-1047; Heart of Jesus Retreat Center, 2927 S. Greenville St., Santa Ana 92704, (714) 557-4538; Holy Spirit Retreat Center, 4316 Lanai Rd., Encino

91436, (818) 784-4515; Holy Transfiguration Monastery (m*), Monks of Mt. Tabor (Byzantine Ukrainian), 17001 Tomki Rd., P.O. Box 217, Redwood Valley 95470, (707) 485-8959; Jesuit Retreat House, 300 Manresa Way, Los Altos 94022, (650) 948-4491, www.elretiro.org; Madonna of Peace Renewal Center (y), P.O. Box 71, Copperopolis 95228, (209) 785-2157; Marian Retreat Center, 535 Sacramento St., Auburn 95603, (916) 887-2019; Mary and Joseph Retreat Center, 5300 Crest Rd., Rancho Palos Verdes 90275, (310) 377-4867, www.maryjoseph.org.

Marywood Retreat Center, 2811 E. Villa Real Dr., Orange 92863-1595, (714) 282-2300, www.rcbo.org; Mater Dolorosa Retreat Center, 700 N. Sunnyside Ave., Sierra Madre 91024, (626) 355-7188, www.passionist.org; Mercy Center, 2300 Adeline Dr., Burlingame 94010, (650) 340-7474, www.mercy-center.org; Mission San Luis Rey Retreat, 4070 Mission Ave., Oceanside, 92057-6402, (760) 757-3659, www.sanluisrey.org; Mount Alverno Retreat and Conference Center, 3910 Bret Harte Dr., Redwood City 94061, (650) 369-0798, www.mountalverno.com; New Camaldoli Hermitage, Big Sur 93920, (831) 667-2456, www.contemplation.com; Our Lady of the Oaks Villa, P.O. Box 128, Applegate 95703, (530) 878-2776.

Poverello of Assisi Retreat House, 1519 Woodworth St., San Fernando 91340, (818) 365-1071; Presentation Education and Retreat Center, 19480 Bear Creek Rd., Los Gatos 95033, (408) 354-2346, www.prescenter.org; Prince of Peace Abbey, 650 Benet Hill Rd., Oceanside 92054, (760) 430-1305; Pro Sanctity Spirituality Center, 205 S. Pine St., Fullerton 92633 (for day use); Sacred Heart Retreat House (w*), 920 E. Alhambra Rd., Alhambra 91801, (626) 289-1353; St. Andrew's Abbey Retreat House, P.O. Box 40, Valyermo 93563, (661) 944-2178, www.valyermo.com; St. Anthony's Retreat House, P.O. Box 249, Three Rivers 93271, (559) 561-4595, www.stanthonyretreat.org; St. Clare's Retreat, 2381 Laurel Glen Rd., Soquel 95073, (831) 423-8093, www.infoteam.com/nonprofit/stclaresretreat/index.html; St. Francis Retreat, P.O. Box 970, San Juan Bautista 95045, (831) 623-4234, www.stfrancis retreat.com; St. Francis Youth Center (y), 2400 E. Lake Ave., Watsonville 95076; St. Joseph's Salesian Youth Center, P.O. Box 1639, 8301 Arroyo Dr., Rosemead 91770, (626) 280-8622; St. Mary's Seminary and Retreat House, 1964 Las Canoas Rd., Santa Barbara 93105, (805) 966-4829; San Damiano Retreat, P.O. Box 767, Danville 94526, (925) 837-9141, www.sandamiano.org.

San Miguel Retreat House, P.O. Box 69, San Miguel 93451, (805) 467-3256; Santa Sabina Center, 25 Magnolia Ave., San Rafael 94901, (415) 457-7727; Serra Retreat, 3401 S. Serra Rd., Box 127, Malibu 90265, (310) 456-6631, www.sbfranciscans.org; Starcross Community, 34500 Annapolis Rd., Annapolis 95412, (707) 886-1919, www.starcross.org; Villa Maria del Mar, Santa Cruz, 2-1918 E. Cliff Dr., Santa Cruz 95062, (831) 475-1236; Villa Maria – House of Prayer (w), 1252 N. Citrus Dr., La Habra 90631, (562) 691-5838.

Colorado: Benet Pines Retreat Center, 15880 Highway 83, Colorado Springs 80921, (719) 495-4469 (fax), www.geocities.com; Camp St. Malo Religious Retreat and Conference Center, 10758, Hwy. 7,

Allenspark 80510, (303) 747-2892; Sacred Heart Retreat House, Box 185, Sedalia 80135, (303) 688-4198, www.gabrielmedia.org/shjrh; Spiritual Life Institute (individuals only), Nada Hermitage, P.O. Box 219, Crestone 81131, (719) 256-4778., www.spiritual lifeinstitute.org.

Connecticut: St. Edmund's Retreat, P.O. Box 399, Mystic 06355, (860) 536-0565, www.sse.org/enders; Emmaus Spiritual Life Center, 24 Maple Ave., Uncasville 06382, (860) 848-3427; Holy Family Retreat, 303 Tunxis Rd., Farmington 06107, (860) 521-0440; Immaculata Retreat House, P.O. Box 55, Willimantic 06226, (860) 423-8484, www.ntplx.net/~omict; Mercy Center at Madison, P.O. Box 191, 167 Neck Rd., Madison 06443, (203) 245-0401, www.mercyctmadison.com; My Father's House, Box 22, 39 North Moodus Rd., Moodus 06469, (860) 873-1906, www.myfathershouse.com; Our Lady of Calvary Retreat (w*), 31 Colton St., Farmington 06032, (860) 677-8519; Trinita Retreat Center, 595 Town Hill Rd., Rt. 219, New Hartford 06057, (860) 379-4329; Villa Maria Retreat House, 161 Sky Meadow Dr., Stamford 06903, (203) 322-5886; Wisdom House Retreat Center, 229 E. Litchfield Rd., 06759, (860) 567-3163, www.wisdomhouse.org.

Delaware: St. Francis Renewal Center, 1901 Prior Rd., Wilmington 19809, (302) 798-3360.

District of Columbia: Washington Retreat House, 4000 Harewood Rd. N.E., Washington 20017, (202) 529-1111.

Florida: Cenacle Retreat House, 1400 S. Dixie Highway, Lantana 33462-5492, (561) 582-2534, www.cenaclesisters.org; Dominican Retreat House, Inc., 7275 S.W. 124th St., Miami 33156-5324, (305) 238-2711; Franciscan Center, 3010 Perry Ave., Tampa 33603, (813) 229-2695, www.fsalleh.org/franciscancenter.htm; John Paul II Retreat House, 720 N.E. 27th St., Miami 33137, (305) 576-2748, www.acu-adsum.org; Our Lady of Divine Providence, 702 S. Bayview Ave., Clearwater, 33759, (727) 797-7412, www.divineprovidence.org; Our Lady of Perpetual Help Retreat and Spirituality Center, 3989 S. Moon Dr., Venice 34292, (941) 486-1524, www.olph retreat.org; Saint John Neumann Renewal Center, 685 Miccosukee Rd., Tallahassee 32308, (850) 224-2971; St. Leo Abbey Retreat Center, P.O. Box 2350, St. Leo 33574, (352) 588-2009.

Georgia: Ignatius House, 6700 Riverside Dr. N.W., Atlanta 30328, (404) 255-0503.

Idaho: Nazareth Retreat Center, 4450 N. Five Mile Rd., Boise 83704, (208) 375-2932.

Illinois: Bellarmine Jesuit Retreat House (mc), 175 W. County Line Rd, Barrington 60010, (847) 381-1261, www.bellarminehall.org; Bishop Lane Retreat House, 7708 E. McGregor Rd., Rockford 61102, (815) 965-5011; Cabrini Retreat Center, 9430 Golf Rd., Des Plaines 60016, (847) 297-6530; Carmelite Spiritual Center, 8433 Bailey Rd., Darien 60561, (630) 969-4141; Cenacle Retreat House, 513 Fullerton Parkway, Chicago 60614, (773) 528-6300; Cenacle Retreat House, P.O. Box 797, Warrenville 60555, (630) 393-1231, www.cenacle.org; King's House of Retreats, Henry 61537, (309) 364-3084, www.cdop.org.

La Salle Manor, Christian Brothers Retreat House, 12480 Galena Rd., Plano 60545, (630) 552-3224; Retreat and Renewal Center, 700 N. 66th St., Belleville

62223-3949, (618) 397-0584; St. Mary's Retreat House, P.O. Box 608, 14230 Main St., Lemont 60439, (630) 257-5102; Tolentine Center, 20300 Governors Highway, Olympia Fields 60461, (708) 748-9500.

Indiana: Archabbey Guest House, St. Meinrad Archabbey, St. Meinrad 47577, (800) 581-6905; Benedict Inn Retreat and Conference Center, 1402 Southern Ave., Beech Grove 46107, (317) 788-7581, www.benedictinn.org; Bethany Retreat House, 2202 Lituanica Ave., 46312, (219) 398-5047; Fatima Retreat House, 5353 E. 56th St., Indianapolis 46226-1486, (317) 545-7681, www.archindy.org; John XXIII Center, 407 W. McDonald St., Hartford City 47348, (765) 348-4008, www.netusa1.net/~john23rd; Kordes Retreat Center, 841 E. 14th St., Ferdinand 47532, (812) 367-2777, www.thedome.org/kordes.

Lindenwood, PHJC Ministry Center, P.O. Box 1, Donaldson 46513, (574) 935-1780; Mary's Solitude, St.Mary's, 100 Lourdes Hall, Notre Dame 46556, (219) 284-5599; Mount Saint Francis Retreat Center and Friary, 101 St. Anthony Dr., Mount Saint Francis 47146, (812) 923-8817, www.cris.com/~mtstfran; Our Lady of Fatima Retreat Center, P.O. Box 929, Notre Dame 46556, (219) 631-8288, www.nd.edu/~fatima; Sarto Retreat House, 4200 N. Kentucky Ave., Evansville 47714, (812) 424-5536.

Iowa: American Martyrs Retreat House, 2209 N. Union Rd., P.O. Box 605, Cedar Falls 50613-0605, (319) 266-3543; Emmanuel House of Prayer Country Retreat and Solitude Center, 4427 Kotts Rd. N.E., Iowa City 52240; New Melleray Guest House, 6500 Melleray Circle, Dubuque 52068, (319) 588-2319; Shalom Retreat Center, 1001 Davis Ave., Dubuque 52001, (319) 582-3592, members.aol.com/dbqshalom.

Kansas: Heartland Center for Spirituality, 3600 Broadway, Great Bend 67530, (316) 792-1232; Manna House of Prayer, 323 East 5th St., Box 675, Concordia 66901, (785) 243-4428; Spiritual Life Center, 7100 E. 45th St., N. Wichita 67226, (316) 744-0167, www.feist.com/~spiritlife/index.html.

Kentucky: Bethany Spring, 115 Dee Head Rd., New Haven, 40051, (502) 549-8277; Catherine Spalding Center, P.O. Box 24, Nazareth 40048, (502) 348-1516, www.scnazarethky.org/csc; Flaget Center, 1935 Lewiston Dr., Louisville 40216, (502) 448-8581; Marydale Retreat Center, 945 Donaldson Hwy., Erlanger 41018, (606) 371-4224; Mt. St. Joseph Retreat Center, 8001 Cummings Rd., Maple Mount 42356-9999, (502) 229-0200, www.msjcenter.org. Our Lady of Gethsemani (m, w, private), The Guestmaster, Abbey of Gethsemani, Trappist, 40051; Passionist Nuns, 8564 Crisp Rd, Whitesville 42378, (270) 233-4571.

Louisiana: Abbey Christian Life Center, St. Joseph's Abbey, St. Benedict 70457, (504) 892-3473; Ave Maria Retreat House, 8089 Barataria Blvd., Crown Point, 70072, (504) 689-3837; Cenacle Retreat House (w*), 5500 St. Mary St., P.O. Box 8115, Metairie 70011, (504) 887-1420, www.cenaclesisters.org/metairie.htm; Jesuit Spirituality Center (m,w; directed), P.O. Box C, Grand Coteau 70541-1003, (337) 662-5251, members.aol.com/jespiritcen; Lumen Christi Retreat Center, 100 Lumen Christi Lane, Hwy. 311, Schriever 70395, (504) 868-1523; Magnificat Center of the Holy Spirit, 23629 Faith Rd., Ponchatoula 70454, (504) 362-4356.

Manresa House of Retreats (m), P.O. Box 89, Convent 70723, (225) 562-3596; Maryhill Renewal Center, 600 Maryhill Rd., Pineville 71360, (318) 640-1378, www.diocesealex.org; Our Lady of the Oaks Retreat House, P.O. Box D, 214 Church St., Grand Coteau 70541, (318) 662-5410; Regina Coeli Retreat Center, 17225 Regina Coeli Rd., Covington 70433, (504) 892-4110; Sophie Barat House, 1719 Napoleon Ave., New Orleans 70115, (504) 899-6027.

Maine: Bay View Villa, 187 Bay View Rd., Saco 04072, (207) 286-8762; Marie Joseph Spiritual Center, RFD 2, Biddeford 04005, (207) 284-5671; Mother of the Good Shepherd Monastery by the Sea, 235 Pleasant Ave., Peaks Island 04108, (207) 766-2717; Notre Dame Retreat & Spiritual Center, P.O. Box 159, Alfred 04002, (207) 324-6160; St. Paul Retreat and Cursillo Center, 136 State St., Augusta 04330, (207) 622-6235.

Maryland: Bon Secours Spiritual Center, Marriottsville 21104, (410) 442-1320, www.bonsecours.org/bssc; Christian Brothers Spiritual Center (m,w,y), P.O. Box 29, 2535 Buckeyestown Pike, Adamstown 21710, (301) 874-5180; Loyola on the Potomac Retreat House, Faulkner 20632, (301) 870-3515, www.loyolaretreat.org; Msgr. Clare J. O'Dwyer Retreat House (y*), 15523 York Rd., P.O. Box 310, Sparks 21152, (410) 666-2400; Our Lady of Mattaponi Youth Retreat and Conference Center, 11000 Mattaponi Rd., Upper Marlboro 20772, (301) 952-9074; Seton Retreat Center, 333 S. Seton Ave., Emmitsburg 21727, (301) 447-6021.

Massachusetts: Boston Cenacle Society, 25 Avery St., Dedham 02026; Calvary Retreat Center, 59 South St., P.O. Box 219, Shrewsbury 01545, (508) 842-8821, www.calvaryretreat.org; Campion Renewal Center, 319 Concord Rd., Weston 02193, (781) 788-6810; Community of teresian Carmelites, 30 Chrome St., 01613, (508) 752-5734; Don Orione Center, P.O. Box 205, Old Groveland Rd., Bradford 01835, (508) 373-0461; Eastern Point Retreat House, Gonzaga Hall, 37 Niles Pond Rd., Gloucester 01930, (978) 283-0013; Espousal Center, 554 Lexington St., Waltham 02452, (781) 209-3101; Esther House of Spiritual Renewal, Sisters of St. Anne, 1015 Pleasant St., Worcester 01602-1338

Franciscan Center - Retreat House, 459 River Rd., Andover 01810, (978) 851-3391, www.franrcent.org; Genesis Spiritual Life Center, 53 Mill St., Westfield 01085, (413) 562-3627; Glastonbury Abbey (Benedictine Monks), 16 Hull St., Hingham 02043, (701) 749-2155, www.glastonburyabbey.org; Holy Cross Fathers Retreat House, 490 Washington St., N. Easton 02356, (508) 238-2051; La Salette Center for Christian Living, 947 Park St., Attleboro 02703, (508) 222-8530, www.ultranet.com/~lasalett; Marian Center, 1365 Northampton St., Holyoke 01040-1913, (413) 534-4502 (day and evening programs); Marist House, 518 Pleasant St., 01701, (508) 879-1620; Miramar Retreat Center, P.O. Box M, Duxbury, 02331-0614, (781) 585-2460; Mt. Carmel Christian Life Center, Oblong Rd., Box 613, Williamstown 01267, (413) 458-3164.

Sacred Heart Retreat Center, Salesians of St. John Bosco, P.O. Box 567, Ipswich 01938; St. Benedict Abbey (Benedictine Monks), 252 Still River Rd., P.O. Box 67, Still River 01467, (978) 456-3221; St. Joseph Villa Retreat Center, Sisters of St. Joseph, 339

Jerusalem Rd., Cohasset 02025, (781) 383-6024; St. Joseph's Abbey Retreat House (m) (Trappist Monks), 167 North Spencer Rd., Spencer 01562, (508) 885-8710, www.spencerabbey.org; St. Stephen Priory Spiritual Life Center (Dominican), 20 Glen St., Box 370, Dover 02030, (508) 785-0124, www.ststephen priory.org.

Michigan: Augustine Center, 2798 U.S. 31 North, Box 84, Conway 49722, (231) 347-3657, www.dioceseofgaylord.org; Capuchin Retreat, 62460 Mt. Vernon, Box 396, Washington 48094, (248) 651-4826; Colombiere Conference and Retreat Center, Box 139, 9075 Big Lake Rd., Clarkston 48347-0139, (248) 620-2534, www.colombiere.com; Manresa Jesuit Retreat House, 1390 Quarton Rd., Bloomfield Hills 48304, (313) 564-6455; Marygrove Retreat Center, Garden 49835, (906) 644-2771; Queen of Angels Retreat, 3400 S. Washington Rd., P.O. Box 2026, Saginaw 48605, (517) 755-2149, www.rc.net/ saginaw/retreat.

St. Francis Retreat Center, 703 E. Main St., De Witt 48820-9499, (517) 669-8321, www.stfrancis.ws; St. Lazare Retreat House, 18600 W. Spring Lake Rd., P.O. Box 462, Spring Lake 49456, (616) 842-3370; St. Mary's Retreat House (w*), 775 W. Drahner Rd., Oxford 48371, (248) 628-3894, www.op.org/oxford; St. Paul of the Cross Retreat Center (m*), 23333 Schoolcraft, Detroit 48223, (313) 535-9563; Weber Retreat Center, 1257 Siena Hghts. Dr., Adrian 49221, (517) 266-4000.

Minnesota: Benedictine Center, St. Paul's Monastery, 2675 Larpenteur Ave. East, St. Paul 55109, (651) 777-7251, www.osb.org/spm; The Cenacle, 1221 Wayzata Blvd., Wayzata 55391; Center for Spiritual Development, 211 Tenth St. S., P.O. Box 538, Bird Island 55310, (320) 365-3644, www.centerbi.com; Christ the King Retreat Center, 621 First Ave. S., Buffalo 55313, (763) 682-1394; Dunrovin Christian Brothers Retreat Center, 15525 St. Croix Trail North, Marine-on-St. Croix 55047, (651) 433-2486, www.dunrovin.org.

Franciscan Retreats, Conventual Franciscan Friars, 16385 St. Francis Lane, Prior Lake 55372, (952) 447-2182, www.franciscanretreats.net; Holy Spirit Retreat House, 3864 420th Ave., Janesville, 56048, (507) 234-5712; Jesuit Retreat House (m), 8243 DeMontreville Trail North, Lake Elmo 55042, (651) 777-1311; Maryhill (m,w*), 1988 Summit Ave., St. Paul 55105, (651) 696-2970, www.sdhm.net; Villa Maria Center, Villa Maria Center, 29847 County 2 Blvd., Frontenac 55026, (651) 345-4582.

Missouri: Assumption Abbey, Rte. 5, Box 1056, Ava 65608, (417) 683-5110, www.assump tionabbey.org; The Cenacle, 3393 McKelvey Rd., Apt. 211, Bridgeton, 63044-2544, (314) 387-2211; Cordis House, 648 S. Assisi Way, Republic 65738, (417) 732-6684; *Il Ritiro* - The Little Retreat, P.O. Box 38, Eime Rd., Dittmer 63023, (636) 285-3759; La Salle Institute, 2101 Rue de la Salle, Wildwood 63038, (636) 938-5374; Maria Fonte Solitude (private; individual hermitages), P.O. Box 322, High Ridge 63049, (314) 677-3235.

Marianist Retreat and Conference Center, P.O. Box 718, Eureka 63025-0718, (636) 938-5390; Mercy Center, 2039 N. Geyer Rd., St. Louis 63131, (314) 966-4686; Our Lady of Assumption Abbey (m,w), Trappists, Rt. 5, Box 1056, Ava 65608-9142;

Pallottine Renewal Center, 15270 Old Halls Ferry Rd., Florissant 63034, (314) 837-7100, members.aol.com/ prcrenewal/home.html; Society of Opur Mother of Peace (private, individual hermitages), 12494 Hwy. T, Marionville 65705, (417) 744-2011; White House Retreat, 3601 Lindell Blvd., St. Louis 63108, (314) 846-2575, www.whretreat.org; Windridge Solitude, 1932 W. Linda Lane, Lonedell 63060.

Montana: Sacred Heart Retreat Center, 26 Wyoming Ave., P.O. Box 153, Billings 59103, (406) 252-0322; Ursuline Retreat Centre, 2300 Central Ave., Great Falls 59401, (406) 452-8585.

Nebraska: Our Lady of Good Counsel retreat House, R.R. 1, Box 110, 7303 N. 112th St., Waverly 68462, (402) 786-2705.

New Hampshire: Epiphany Monastery, 96 Scobie Rd., P.O. Box 60, New Boston 03070; La Salette Shrine (private and small groups), 410 NH, Route 4A, P.O. Box 420, Enfield 03748, (603) 632-7087.

New Jersey: Bethany Ridge, P.O. Box 241, Little York 08834, (908) 995-9758; Bethlehem Hermitage, 82 Pleasant Hill Rd., Chester 07930-2135, (908) 879-7059; Carmel Retreat House, 1071 Ramapo Valley Rd., Mahwah 07430, (201) 327-7090, www.carmel retreat.com; Cenacle Retreat House, 411 River Rd., Highland Park 08904, (732) 249-8100, www.cena cle.sisters.org; Emmaus House, 101 Center St., Perth Amboy 08861, (732) 442-7688; Father Judge Apostolic Center (young adults), 1292 Long Hill Rd., Stirling 07980; Felician Retreat House, 35 Windemere Ave., Mt. Arlington 07856, (973) 398-9806; John Paul II Retreat Center, 414 S. 8th St., Vineland 08360; Loyola House of Retreats, 161 James St., Morristown 07960, (973) 539-0740, www.loyola.org.

Marianist Family Retreat Center (families*), 417 Yale Ave., Box 488, Cape May Point 08212-0488; Maris Stella (Retreat and Vacation Center), 7201 Long Beach Blvd., P.O. Box 3135, Harvey Cedars 08008, (609) 361-8863; Mount Paul Retreat Center, 243 Mt. Paul Rd., Oak Ridge 07438, (973) 697-6341; Mt. St. Francis Retreat House, 474 Sloatsburg Rd., Ringwood 07456-1978, (973) 962-9778; Queen of Peace Retreat House, St. Paul's Abbey, P.O. Box 7, Newton 07860, (973) 383-2470; Sacred Heart Renewal Center, P.O. Box 68, Belvidere 07823, (908) 475-4694; Sacred Heart Retreat Center (y*, m,w), 20 Old Swartswood Rd., Newton 07860, (973) 383-2620; St. Joseph by the Sea Retreat House, 400 Rte. 35 N., South Mantoloking 08738-1309 (732) 892-8494, www.filippiniusa.org.

St. Pius X Spiritual Life Center, P.O. Box 216, Blackwood 08012, (856) 227-1436; San Alfonso Retreat House, P.O. Box 3098, 755 Ocean Ave., Long Beach 07740, (732) 222-2731, www.sanalfonso retreats.org; Sanctuary of Mary, Pilgrimage Place, Branchville 07826, (973) 875-7625; Stella Maris Retreat House, 981 Ocean Ave., Elberon 07740, (732) 229-0602, www.stellamarisretreatcenter.org; Villa Pauline Retreat House, 350 Bernardsville Rd., Mendham 07945, (973) 543-9058; Vincentian Renewal Center, 75 Mapleton Rd., P.O. Box 757, Plainsboro 08536, (609) 520-9626; Vocationist Fathers Retreat, 90 Brooklake Rd., Florham Park 07932, (973) 966-6262, www.vocationist.org; Xavier Retreat and Conference Center, P.O. Box 211, Convent Station 07961, (973) 290-5121.

New Mexico: Holy Cross Retreat, Conventual

Franciscan Friars, P.O. Box 158, Mesilla Park 88047, (505) 524-3688, www.zianet.com/franciscan; Immaculate Heart of Mary Retreat and Conference Center, Mt. Carmel Rd., Santa Fe 87501, (505) 988-1975; Madonna Retreat Center, Inc., 4040 St. Joseph Pl., N.W., 87120, (505) 831-8196; Pecos Benedictine Abbey, Pecos 87552, (505) 757-6415, www.pecos abbey.org; Spiritual Renewal Center, 2348 Pajarito Rd., S.W., Albuquerque 87105, (505) 877-4211, www.christdesert.org/dominican; Sacred Heart Retreat, P.O. Box 1989, Gallup 87301.

New York: Bethany Retreat House, County Road 105, Box 1003, Highland Mills 10930, (845) 928-2213, www.rcnet/newyork/bethany; Bethlehem Retreat House, Abbey of the Genesee, Piffard 14533; Bishop Molloy Retreat House, 86-45 Edgerton Blvd., Jamaica 11432, (718) 739-1229; Blessed Kateri Retreat House, National Kateri Shrine, P.O. Box 627, Fonda 11432, (518) 853-3646; Cardinal Spellman Retreat House, Passionist Community, 5801 Palisade Ave., Bronx (Riverdale) 10471, (718) 549-6500, www.passionists.org; Cenacle Center for Spiritual Renewal, 310 Cenacle Rd., Ronkonkoma 11779-2203, (631) 588-8366, www.cenaclesisters.org.

Cenacle Retreat House, State Rd., P.O. Box 467, Bedford Village 10506, (914) 234-3344; Christ the King Retreat and Conference Center, 500 Brookford Rd., Syracuse 13224, (315) 446-2680; Cormaria Retreat House, Sag Harbor, L.I. 11963, (631) 725-4206; Dominican Spiritual Life Center, 1945 Union St., Niskayuma 12309, (518) 393-4169; Don Bosco Retreat Center, 174 Filors Lane, Stony Point, 10980-2645, (845) 947-2200, www.marianshrine.org; Graymoor Spiritual Life Center, Graymoor, Route 9, P.O. Box 300, Garrison 10524; Jesuit Retreat House, Auriesville, (518) 853-3033; Monastery of the Precious Blood (w), Ft. Hamilton Parkway and 54th St., Brooklyn 11219 (single day retreats); Mount Alvernia Retreat Center, Box 858, Wappingers Falls 12590, (845) 297-5706, www.mtalvernia.org.

Mount Irenaeus Franciscan Mountain Retreat, Holy Peace Friary, P.O. Box 100, West Clarksville, NY 14786, (716) 973-2470; Mount Manresa Retreat House, 239 Fingerboard Rd., Staten Island 10305, (718) 727-3844; Mt. St. Alphonsus Redemptorist Retreat Ministry, P.O. Box 219, Esopus 12429, (845) 384-8000, www.msaretreat.com; Notre Dame Retreat House, Box 342, 5151 Foster Rd., Canandaigua 14424, (585) 394-5700, www.notredameretreat house.org; Our Lady of Hope Center, 434 River Rd., Newburgh 12550, (914) 568-0780; Regina Maria Retreat House, 77 Brinkerhoff St., Plattsburgh 12901-2701, (518) 561-3421; St. Andrew's House, 257 St. Andrew's Rd., Walden 12586, (914) 778-5941; St. Columban Center, Diocese of Buffalo, 6892 Lake Shore Rd., P.O. Box 816, Derby 14047, (716) 947-4708, www.stcolumbacenter.org.

St. Francis Retreat, 1 Pryer Manor Rd., Larchmont 10538, (914) 235-6839; St. Francis Center for Spirituality, 500 Todt Hill Rd., Staten Island, N.Y. 10304, (718) 981-3131, www.st-francis-center-for-spirituality.org; St. Gabriel's Spiritual Center for Youth (y, mc), 64 Burns Rd., P.O. Box 3015, Shelter Island Heights 11965, (631) 749-3154 (fax); St. Ignatius Retreat House, 251 Searingtown Rd., Manhasset 11030, (516) 621-8300, www.inisfada.net; St. Josaphat's Retreat House, Basilian Monastery, East

Beach Rd., Glen Cove 11542; St. Joseph Center (Spanish Center), 275 W. 230th St., Bronx 10463, (718) 796-4340; St. Mary's Villa, 150 Sisters Servants Lane, P.O. Box 9, Sloatsburg 10974-0009, (914) 753-5100; St. Paul Center, 21-35 Crescent St., Astoria 11105, (718) 932-0752; St. Ursula Retreat Center, 186 Middle Rd., Blue Point 11715, (631) 363-2422; Stella Maris Retreat Center, 130 E. Genesee St., Skaneateles 13152, (315) 685-6836; Tagaste Monastery, 220 Lafayette Ave., Suffern 10901; Trinity Retreat, 1 Pryer Manor Rd., Larchmont 10538, (914) 235-6839.

North Carolina: Avila Retreat Center, 711 Mason Rd., Durham 27712, (919) 477-1285; Madonna House, 424 Rose Ln., Raleigh 27610.

North Dakota: Presentation Prayer Center, 1101 32nd Ave. S., Fargo 58103, (701) 237-4857; Queen of Peace Retreat, 1310 Broadway, Fargo 58102, (701) 293-9286.

Ohio: Bergamo Center for Lifelong Learning, 4400 Shakertown Rd., Dayton 45430, (937) 426-2363, www.bergamocenter.org; Franciscan Renewal Center, Pilgrim House, 321 Clay St., Carey 43316, (419) 396-7970, www.olcshrine.com; Friarhurst Retreat House, 8136 Wooster Pike, Cincinnati 45227, (513) 561-2270; Jesuit Retreat House, 5629 State Rd., Cleveland 44134-2292, (440) 884-9300; Loyola of the Lakes, 700 Killinger Rd., Clinton 44216-9653, (330) 896-2315, www.loyolaofthelakes..com; Maria Stein Center, 2365 St. Johns Rd., Maria Stein 45860, (419) 925-7625, www.spiritualcenter.net; Milford Spiritual Center, 5361 S. Milford Rd., Milford 45150, (513) 248-3500, www.milfordspiritualcenter.org; Our Lady of the Pines, 1250 Tiffin St., Fremont 43420, (419) 332-6522, www.nwonline.net/thepines.

Sacred Heart Retreat and Renewal Center, 3128 Logan Ave., P.O. Box 6074, Youngstown 44501, (330) 759-9539; St. Joseph Christian Life Center, 18485 Lake Shore Blvd., Cleveland 44119, (216) 531-7370, www.stjosephchristianlife.com; St. Francis Spirituality Center, 200 St. Francis Ave., Tiffin 44883, (419) 443-1485, www.tiffinohio.com/sfscretreat; St. Therese Retreat Center, 5277 E. Broad St., Columbus, OH 43213, (614) 866-1611, www.cathedral-bookshop.com.

Oklahoma: St. Gregory's Abbey, 1900 W. MacArthut, Shawnee 74804, (405) 878-5491, www.sgc.edu.

Oregon: The Jesuit Spirituality Center, 424 S.W. Mill St., Portland 97201, (503) 242-1973; Mount Angel Abbey Retreat House, 1 Abbey Dr., St. Benedict 97373, (503) 845-3027, www.mtangel.edu; Our Lady of Peace Retreat, 3600 S. W. 170th Ave., Beaverton 97006, (503) 649-7127, www.geocities.com/ ourladyofpeaceretreat; St. Rita Retreat Center, P.O. Box 310, Gold Hill 97525, (541) 855-1333; Shalom Prayer Center, Benedictine Sisters, 840 S. Main St., Mt. Angel 97362-9527, (503) 845-6773, www.open.org/shalom; St. Benedict Lodge, 56630 North Bank Rd., McKenzie Bridge 97413, (541) 822-3572; Trappist Abbey Guesthouse (m,w), 9200 N.E. Abbey Rd., Lafayette 97127, (503) 852-0107.

Pennsylvania: Avila Retreat Center, 61 E. High St., Union City 16438, (814) 438-7020; Dominican Retreat House, 750 Ashbourne Rd., Elkins Park 19027, (215) 782-8520; Ecclesia Center, 9101 Ridge Rd., Erie 16417, (814) 774-9691; Fatima Renewal Center, 1000 Seminary Rd., Dalton 18414, (570) 563-

8500; Franciscan Spirit and Life Center, 3605 McRoberts Rd., Pittsburgh 15234, (412) 881-9207; Gilmary Diocesan Center, 601 Flaugherty Run Rd., Coraopolis 15108-3899, (412) 264-8400, www.diopitt.org.

Jesuit Center for Spiritual Growth, Box 223, Church Rd., Wernersville 19656, (610) 670-3642, www.jesuitspiritualcenter.org; Kearns Spirituality Center, 9000 Babcock Blvd., Allison Park 15101, (412) 366-1124, www.sistersofdivprovidence.org; Mariawald Renewal Center, P.O. Box 97 (1094 Welsh Rd.), Reading 19607, (610) 777-0135, www.hometown.aol.com/mariawald/index.html; Martina Spiritual Renewal Center, 5244 Clarwin Ave., Pittsburgh 15229, (412) 931-9766; St. Emma Retreat House, 1001 Harvey Ave., Greensburg 15601-1494, (724) 834-7483, www.stemm.org; St. Francis Retreat Center (y*), c/o Dept. of Youth Ministry, 900 W. Market St., Orwigsburg 17961, (570) 366-1016; St. Francis Center for Renewal, Monocacy Manor, 395 Bridle Path Rd., Bethlehem 18017, (610) 867-8890, www.catholic-church.org/stfrancis-cfn; St. Francis Retreat House, 3918 Chipman Rd., Easton 18045, (610) 258-3053; St. Gabriel's Retreat House, 631 Griffin Pond Rd., Clarks Summit 18411-8899, (570) 586-4957, www.intiques.com/cpnuns/.

St. Joseph's in the Hills, 315 S. Warren Ave., Malvern 19355-0315, (610) 644-0400, www.malvernretreat.com; St. Paul of the Cross Retreat Center, 148 Monastery Ave., Pittsburgh 15203, (412) 381-7676, www.trfn.clpgh.org/stpaulrc/; Saint Raphaela Center, 616 Coopertown Rd., Haverford 19041, (610) 642-5715; St. Vincent Summer Retreat Program (m,w,mc; summers only), Latrobe 15650, (724) 805-2139; Urban House of Prayer, 1919 Cambridge St., Philadelphia 19130, (215) 236-8328; Villa of Our Lady Retreat Center (w, mc, y), HCR No. 1, Box 41, Mt. Pocono 18344, (570) 839-7217.

Rhode Island: Bethany Renewal Center, 397 Fruit Hill Ave., N. Providence 02911, (401) 353-5860; Father Marot CYO Center (y), 53 Federal St., Woonsocket 02895, (401) 762-3252; Our Lady of Peace Spiritual Life Center, 333 Ocean Rd., Box 507, Narragansett 02882, (401) 884-7676; St. Paul Priory Guest House, 61 Narrangansett Ave., 02840, (401) 847-2423.

South Carolina: Sea of Peace House of Prayer, 59 Palmetto Pointe Rd., Edisto Island 29438, (843) 869-0513; Springbank Center for Eco-Spirituality and the Arts, 1345 Springbank Rd., Kingstree 29556, (800) 671-0361, www.springbankspirit.org.

South Dakota: St. Martin's Community Center, 2110C St. Martin's Dr., Rapid City 57702, (605) 343-8011; Sioux Spiritual Center, 20100 Center Rd., Howes, SD 57748, (605) 985-5906.

Tennessee: Carmelites of Mary Immaculate Center of Spirituality, 610 Bluff Rd., Liberty 37095, (615) 536-5177.

Texas: Benedictine Retreat Center, HC#2, Box 6300, Sandia 78383; Bishop DeFalco Retreat Center, 2100 N. Spring, Amarillo 79107-7274, (806) 383-1811, www.bdrc.org; Bishop Rene H. Gracida Retreat Center, 3036 Saratoga Blvd., Corpus Christi 78415, (512) 851-1443; Catholic Renewal Center of North Texas, 4503 Bridge St., Ft. Worth 76103, (817) 429-2920; Cenacle Retreat House, 420 N. Kirkwood, Houston 77079, (281) 497-3131, www.cenacleretreathouse.org; Christian Renewal Center (Centro de Renovacion Cristiana), Oblates of Mary Immacu-

late, P.O. Box 699, Dickinson 77539, (281) 337-1312; www.retreatcentercrc.org.

Holy Family Retreat Center, 9920 N. Major Dr., Beaumont 77713-7618, (409) 899-5617, www.dioceseofbmt.org/hfrc.htm; Holy Name Retreat Center, 430 Bunker Hill Rd., Houston 77024, (713) 464-0211; Holy Spirit Retreat and Conference Center, 501 Century Dr. S., Laredo 78040, (956) 726-4352, www.stjean.com/laredo/hsrc/holy.htm; Lebh Shomea House of Prayer, La Parra Ranch, P.O. Box 9, Sarita 78385; Montserrat Retreat House, P.O. Box 398, Lake Dallas 75065, (940) 321-6020, www.montserratretreat.org; Moye Center, 600 London, Castroville 78009, (830) 931-2233, www.moyecenter.org; Oblate Renewal Center, 5700 Blanco Rd., San Antonio 78216, (210) 349-4173.

Omega Retreat Center, 216 W. Highland Dr., Boerne 78006, (830) 816-8471; Our Lady of Mercy Retreat Center, P.O. Box 744, 19th & Division, Slaton 79364, (806) 828-6428; Prayer Town Emmanuel Retreat House, P.O. Box 17, Channing 79018, (806) 534-2312; San Juan Retreat House (St. Eugene de Mazenod Retreat Center), P.O. Box 747, San Juan 78589, (956) 787-0033.

Utah: Abbey of Our Lady of the Holy Trinity (m), 1250 S 9500 E, Huntsville 84317, (801) 745-3784, www.xmission.com/~hta; Our Lady of the Mountains, 1794 Lake St., Ogden 84401, (801) 392-9231.

Virginia: Benedictine Retreat and Conf. Center, Mary Mother of the Church Abbey, 12829 River Rd., 23233, (804) 784-3508; Dominican Retreat, 7103 Old Dominion Dr., McLean 22101-2799, (703) 356-4243, www.dominicanretreat.org; The Dwelling Place, 601 Holly Grove Ln., Richmond 23235, (804) 323-3360; Holy Family Retreat House, The Redemptorists, P.O. 3151, 1414 N. Mallory St., Hampton 23663, (757) 722-3997; Madonna House, 828 Campbell Ave., S.W., Roanoke 24016, (540) 343-8464; Missionhurst Mission Center, 4651 N. 25th St., Arlington 22207, (703) 525-6557, www.missionhurst.org.

Retreat House, Holy Cross Abbey, Rt. 2, Box 3870, Berryville 22611, (540) 955-3124; Shalom House, P.O. Box 196, Montpelier 23192, (804) 883-6149; Tabor Retreat Center, 2125 Langhorne Rd., Lynchburg 24501, (804) 846-6475; The Well, 18047 Quiet Way, Smithfield 23430, (757) 255-2366, www.thewellretreatcenter.org.

Washington: Immaculate Heart Retreat Center, 6910 S. Ben Burr Rd., Spokane 99223, (509) 448-1224, www.ihrc.net; House of the Lord Retreat Center, P.O. Box 1034, Tum Tum 99034, (509) 276-2219; KAIROS House of Prayer, 1714 W. Stearns Rd., Spokane 99208, (509) 466-2187; Palisades Retreat House, 4700 SW Dash Point Rd., #100, Federal Way 98063, (206) 748-7991; St. Peter Retreat Center, 15880 Summitview Rd., Cowiche 98923, (509) 678-4935.

West Virginia: Bishop Hodges Pastoral Center, Rt. 1, Box 9D, Huttonsville, 26273, (304) 335-2165; Good Counsel Friary, 493 Tyrone Rd., Morgantown 26508, (304) 594-1714; John XXIII Pastoral Center, 100 Hodges Rd., Charleston 25314, (304) 342-0507; Paul VI Pastoral Center, 667 Stone and Shannon Rd., Wheeling 26003, (304) 277-3300; Priest Field Pastoral Center, Rt. 51, Box 133, Kearneysville 25430, (304) 725-1435; West Virginia Institute for Spirituality, 1414 Virginia St. E., Charleston, WV 25301, (304) 345-0926, www.wvis.ws.

Wisconsin: Archdiocesan Retreat Center, 3501 S. Lake Dr., P.O. Box 07912, Milwaukee 53207, (414) 769-3491, www.archmil.org; The Dwelling Place, 528 N. 31st St., Milwaukee 53208, (414) 933-1100; Franciscan Spirituality Center, 920 Market St., La Crosse 54601, (608) 791-5295, www.fspa.org; Holy Name Retreat House, Chambers Island, mailing address: 1825 Riverside Drive, P.O. Box 23825, Green Bay 54305, (920) 437-7531; Jesuit Retreat House, 4800 Fahrnwald Rd., Oshkosh 54902, (920) 231-9060, www.jesuitretreathouse.org; Marywood Franciscan Spirituality Center (FSPA), 3560 Hwy. 51 N., Arbor Vitae 54568, (715) 385-3750, www.fspa.org.

Monte Alverno Retreat Center, 1000 N. Ballard Rd., Appleton 54911, (920) 733-8526; Mount Carmel Hermitage, 897 U.S. Hwy. 8, 54001, (715) 268-9313; Mount Tabor, 522 2 St., Menasha 54952, (920) 722-8918; Norbertine Center for Spirituality, St. Norbert Abbey, 1016 N. Broadway, De Pere 54115, (920) 337-4315, www.norbertines.org; Redemptorist Retreat Center, 1800 N. Timber Trail Lane, Oconomowoc 53066-4897, (262) 567-6900, www.redemptoristretreat.org; St. Anthony Retreat Center, 300 E. 4th St., Marathon 54448, (715) 443-2236, www.sarcenter.com.

St. Bede Retreat and Conference Center, 1190 Priory Rd., P.O. Box 66, Eau Claire 54702, (715) 834-8642; Saint Benedict Center (monastery and ecumenical retreat and conference center), P.O. Box 5070, Madison 53705-0070, (608) 836-1631, www.sbcenter.org; St. Clare Center for Spirituality, 7381 Church St., Custer 54423, (715) 592-4099; St. Joseph's Retreat Center, 3035 O'Brien Rd., Bailey's Harbor 54202, (920) 839-2391; St. Vincent Pallotti Center, N6409 Bowers Rd., Elkhorn 53121, (262) 723-2108, (877) 220-3306, www.elknet.net/vpallelk; Schoenstatt Center, W. 284 N. 698 Cherry Lane, Waukesha 53188, (414) 547-7733.

MESSAGE OF POPE JOHN PAUL II FOR THE 18TH WORLD YOUTH DAY

On April 13, 2003, Pope John Paul II issued his message for the 18th annual World Youth Day. Following are excerpts from the papal statement:

"Behold, your mother!" (Jn.19:27)

My dear young people!

It always gives me great joy to address a special message to you on the occasion of World Youth Day. It is also a way to show you the extent of my affection for you. The vivid recollection of my experiences during our World Youth Day meetings is impressed on my memory: young people and the Pope together, and a large gathering of bishops and priests, all with our gaze on Christ, light of the world, invoking him and proclaiming him to the entire human family. While I give thanks to God for the witness of faith that you have given once again recently in Toronto, I renew the invitation I made to you on the banks of Lake Ontario: "the Church today looks to you with confidence and expects you to be the people of the Beatitudes!" (Exhibition Place, 25 July 2002; ORE, 31 July 2002, p. 6).

For the 18th World Youth Day that will be celebrated in dioceses all over the world, I have chosen a theme related to the Year of the Rosary: "Behold, your mother!" (Jn.19:27). Before his death, Jesus entrusted to the apostle John what was most precious to him: his Mother, Mary. These are the final words of the Redeemer, and therefore they take on a solemn nature and could be regarded as his spiritual testimony.

... The Son upon the Cross can pour out his suffering into his Mother's heart. Every child who suffers experiences that need. You too, my dear young people, are faced with suffering: loneliness, failures and disappointments in your personal lives; difficulties in inserting yourselves in the adult world and in professional life: the separations and losses in your families; the violence of war and the death of the innocent. Know, however, that in difficult times, when everyone experiences, you are not alone: like John at the foot of the Cross, Jesus also gives his Mother to you so that she will comfort you with her tenderness.

It says in the Gospel that "from that hour the disciple took her to his own home (Jn.19:27). This statement, the subject of many commentaries since early Christian times, does not simply point out the place where John lived. Beyond the material aspect, it evokes the spiritual dimension of this welcome and of the new bond established between Mary and John.

My dear young people, you are more or less the same age as John and you have the same desire to be with Jesus. Today, it is you whom Jesus expressly asks to receive Mary "into your home" and to welcome her "as one of yours"; to learn from her the one who "kept all these things, pondering them in her heart" (Lk. 2:19) that inner disposition to listen and the attitude of humility and generosity that singled her out as God's first collaborator in the work of salvation. She will discharge her ministry as a mother and train you and mould you until Christ is fully formed in you (cf. *Rosarium Virginis Mariae*, n.15).

This is why I now wish to repeat the motto of my episcopal and pontifical service: *Totus tuus*. Throughout my life I have experienced the loving and forceful presence of the Mother of Our Lord. Mary accompanies me every day in the fulfillment of my mission as Successor of Peter.

... My dear young people, only Jesus knows what is in your hearts and your deepest desires. Only He, who has loved you to the end (cf. Jn.13:1), can fulfill your aspirations. His are words of eternal life, words that give meaning to life. No one apart from Christ can give you true happiness. By following the example of Mary, you should know how to give Him your unconditional "yes." There is no place in your lives for selfishness or laziness. Now more than ever it is crucial that you be "watchers of the dawn," the lookouts who announce the light of dawn and the new springtime of the Gospel of which the buds can already be seen. Humanity is in urgent need of the witness of free and courageous young people who dare to go against the tide and proclaim with vigor and enthusiasm their personal faith in God, Lord and Savior.

... True disciples of Christ are conscious of their own weakness. For this reason they put all their trust in the grace of God and they accept it with undivided hearts, convinced that without Him they can do nothing (cf. Jn.15:5)....

Catholic Education

LEGAL STATUS OF CATHOLIC EDUCATION

The right of private schools to exist and operate in the United States is recognized in law. It was confirmed by the U.S. Supreme Court in 1925 when the tribunal ruled (Pierce v. Society of Sisters, see Church-State Decisions of the Supreme Court) that an Oregon state law requiring all children to attend public schools was unconstitutional.

Private schools are obliged to comply with the education laws in force in the various states regarding such matters as required basic curricula, periods of attendance, and standards for proper accreditation.

The special curricula and standards of private schools are determined by the schools themselves. Thus, in Catholic schools, the curricula include not only the subject matter required by state educational laws but also other fields of study, principally, education in the Catholic faith.

The Supreme Court has ruled that the First Amendment to the U.S. Constitution, in accordance with the No Establishment of Religion Clause of the First Amendment, prohibits direct federal and state aid from public funds to church-affiliated schools. (*See* several cases in **Church-State Decisions of the Supreme Court.**)

Public Aid

This prohibition does not extend to all child-benefit and public-purpose programs of aid to students of non-public elementary and secondary schools.

Statutes authorizing such programs have been ruled constitutional on the grounds that they:
• have a "secular legislative purpose"
• neither inhibit nor advance religion as a "principal or primary effect"
• do not foster "excessive government entanglement with religion."

Aid programs considered constitutional have provided bus transportation, textbook loans, school lunches and health services, and "secular, neutral or non-ideological services, facilities and materials provided in common to all school children," public and non-public.

The first major aid to education program in U.S. history containing provisions benefiting non-public school students was enacted by the 89th Congress and signed into law by President Lyndon B. Johnson on Apr. 11, 1965. The Elementary and Secondary Education Act was designed to avoid the separation of Church and state impasse which had blocked all earlier aid proposals pertaining to non-public, and especially church-affiliated, schools. The objective of the program, under public control, is to serve the public purpose by aiding disadvantaged pupils in non-public as well as public schools.

With respect to college and university education in church-affiliated institutions, the Supreme Court has upheld the constitutionality of statutes providing student loans and, under the Federal Higher Education Facilities Act of 1963, construction loans and grants for secular-purpose facilities.

Catholic schools are exempt from real estate taxation in all of the states. Since Jan. 1, 1959, nonprofit parochial and private schools have also been exempt from several federal excise taxes.

NCEA

The National Catholic Educational Association, founded in 1904, is a voluntary organization of educational institutions and individuals concerned with Catholic education in the U.S. Its objectives are to promote and encourage the principles and ideals of Christian education and formation by suitable service and other activities. The NCEA serves approximately 200,000 Catholic educators at all levels from pre-K through university. Its official publication is *Momentum*. Numerous service publications are issued to members. Bishop Gregory M. Aymond of Austin, chairman of the Board of Directors; Michael Guerra, president. Address: 1077 30th St. N.W., Washington, DC 20007; (202) 337-6232.

EDUCATIONAL VOUCHERS

Although 41 educational voucher programs funded by private philanthropy were operating in the United States by 1998-99, discussion of vouchers as a political, legal, and educational issue primarily concerns publicly-funded plans allowing parents to send their children to the school of their choice. At present there are three educational voucher programs of this kind — in Milwaukee, Cleveland, and the state of Florida.

The Vouchers Debate

Proponents of vouchers argue that they are not merely consistent with parental rights but an appropriate, even necessary, practical means of realizing them. In particular, it is said, they enable low-income parents to exercise a choice about schools. Another pro-vouchers argument is that they create an incentive for self-improvement by public schools that is lacking when they enjoy a near monopoly.

Arguments against vouchers are that they take funds away from public schools and encourage highly motivated parents and competent students to abandon failing public institutions in favor of private ones. Using vouchers at church-related schools also is said to violate the First Amendment ban on an establishment of religion. The chief opponents of educational vouchers are teacher unions — the National Education Association, the American Federation of Teachers, and their affiliates — and other public school groups, church-state separationists, and some mainline African-American organizations. Phi Delta Kappa/Gallup polls in 1998 and 1999 found 51% of the respondents, including 60% of public school parents in the latter year, were in favor of total or partial government-paid tuition for children in private or church-related schools, although support declined when vouchers were specified.

Recent Developments

On June 27, 2002, the U.S. Supreme Court upheld the Cleveland voucher program in a 5-4 ruling, saying it is "entirely neutral with respect to religion." The majority opinion, written by Chief Justice William Rehnquist, said the program is therefore "a program of true private choice" and does not violate the Establishment Clause of the First Amendment.

Cleveland established the voucher program in 1995 to help address problems in what was considered one of the worst public school systems in the country. The state Legislature created the system after a federal judge declared the schools were being mismanaged and put them under the authority of the state superintendent of public instruction. The program provides for vouchers of up to $4,000 annually for children in low-income families to attend other public or private schools or pay for tutors. The vast majority of participants use their vouchers to pay tuition at church-affiliated schools, nearly all of them Catholic.

The case came to the Supreme Court after the 6th U.S. Circuit Court of Appeals ruled in 2000 that the program was unconstitutional because the vouchers are primarily used at religious schools. The U.S. Conference of Catholic Bishops in a friend-of-the-court brief argued that the program should not be considered unconstitutional because most voucher recipients choose to attend church schools.

Opponents of the program who filed briefs included the National Association for the Advancement of Colored People, an association of Ohio school boards and several groups of public schools from around the country. Opponents call vouchers a fraud meant to siphon tax money from struggling public schools. The Ohio school boards argued that the state has ignored its responsibility to provide a good education and is merely shifting the burden to religious schools.

Central to the court's reasoning was that children in the Cleveland program have a theoretical choice of attending religious schools, secular private academies, suburban public schools, or charter schools run by parents or others outside the education establishment. The fact that only a handful of secular schools and no suburban public schools have signed up to accept voucher students is not the fault of the program itself, Ohio authorities say. "We believe that the program challenged here is a program of true private choice," Chief Justice William H. Rehnquist wrote for himself and Justices Sandra Day O'Connor, Antonin Scalia, Anthony M. Kennedy and Clarence Thomas.

The Cleveland program goes too far toward state-sponsored religion, the dissenting justices said. It does not treat religion neutrally, as Rehnquist contended, wrote Justice David H. Souter. The majority is also wrong about the question of whether parents have a true choice among schools, Souter wrote for himself and Justices John Paul Stevens, Ruth Bader Ginsburg and Stephen Breyer. "There is, in any case, no way to interpret the 96.6 percent of current voucher money going to religious schools as reflecting a free and genuine choice by the families that apply for vouchers," Souter wrote.

President George W. Bush has been a staunch advocate of school vouchers, and emphasized the issue in his campaign for the White House. Congress last year shelved that effort, but Bush resurrected the idea, proposing in his 2003 budget to give families up to $2,500 per child in tax credits if they choose a private school rather than a failing neighborhood public school. Following the court's hearing on arguments in February 2002, Education Secretary Rod Paige said he would continue advocating on behalf of both improved public schools and school choice. Republican lawmakers in Congress agreed with Bush's stance. The Bush administration sided with Ohio, arguing that the program is constitutional because parents control where the money goes. In Cleveland, the public money flows to parents, not directly to the church-run schools, the program's supporters noted.

EX CORDE ECCLESIAE

On November 17, 1999, the Catholic Bishops of the Unites States approved *The Application of Ex corde Ecclesiae for the United States*, implementing the Apostolic Constitution *Ex corde Ecclesiae*. This action received the *recognitio* from the Congregation for Bishops on May 3, 2000. Bishop Joseph Fiorenza, President of the National Conference of Catholic Bishops, decreed that the application would have the force of particular law for the United States on May 3, 2001. Guidelines concerning the Academic *Mandatum* in Catholic Universities were subsequently issued, based on Canon 812. The following is the furst guidelines.

Pope John Paul II's Constitution *Ex corde Ecclesiae* of 1990 fostered a productive dialogue between the Bishops of the United States and the leaders of our Catholic colleges and universities. It is anticipated that this recently approved *Application of Ex corde Ecclesiae for the United States* would further that dialogue and build a community of trust between bishops and theologians. Both bishops and theologians are engaged in a necessary though complementary service to the Church that requires ongoing and mutually respectful conversation.

Article 4, 4, e, iv of the *Application* states that "a detailed procedure will be developed outlining the process of requesting and granting (or withdrawing) the *mandatum*." These guidelines are intended to explain and serve as a resource for the conferral of the *mandatum*. Only those guidelines herein which repeat a norm of the *Application* have the force of particular law. They were approved for distribution to the members of NCCB by the Conference's general membership.

Nature of the *mandatum*.

• The *mandatum* is fundamentally an acknowledgment by Church authority that a Catholic professor of a theological discipline is a teacher within the full communion of the Catholic Church (*Application*: Article 4,4,e,i).

• The *mandatum*, therefore, recognizes the professor's commitment and responsibility to teach authentic Catholic doctrine and to refrain from putting forth as Catholic teaching anything contrary to the Church's magisterium (cf. *Application*: Article 4,4,e, iii).

• The *mandatum* should not be construed as an appointment, authorization, delegation or approbation of one's teaching by Church authorities. Those who have received a *mandatum* teach in their own name in virtue of their baptism and their academic and professional competence, not in the name of the bishop or of the Church's magisterium (*Application*: Article 4,4,e,ii).

SUMMARY OF SCHOOL STATISTICS

Status and figures (as of Jan. 1, 2003) reported by The Official Catholic Directory.

Colleges and Universities: 237 (U.S., 232; outlying areas, 5).

College and University Students: 749,512 (U.S., 721,540; outlying areas, 27,972).

High Schools: 1,376 (824 diocesan and parochial; 552 private). U.S., 1,239 (732 diocesan and parochial; 507 private). Outlying areas, 137 (92 diocesan and parochial; 45 private).

High School Students: 686,651 (386,764 diocesan and parochial; 299,887 private). U.S., 655,894 (368,960 diocesan and parochial; 286,934 private). Outlying areas, 30,757 (17,804 diocesan and parochial; 12,953 private).

Public High School Students Receiving Religious Instruction: 767,739 (U.S., 744,542; outlying areas, 23,197).

Elementary Schools: 7,142 (6,773 diocesan and parochial; 369 private). U.S., 6,986 (6,679 diocesan and parochial; 307 private). Outlying areas, 156 (94 diocesan and parochial; 62 private).

Elementary School Students: 1,971,394 (1,872,848 diocesan and parochial; 98,546 private). U.S., 1,919,242 (1,844,698 diocesan and parochial; 74,544 private). Outlying areas, 52,152 (28,150 diocesan and parochial; 24,002 private).

Public Elementary School Students Receiving Religious Instruction: **3,582,943** (U.S., 3,555,191; outlying areas, 27,752).

Non-Residential Schools for Handicapped: **84** (U.S.). Students: 18,397 (U.S.).

Teachers: 171,814 U.S., 166,740 (lay persons 157,076; sisters, 7,123; priests, 1,503; brothers, 1,011; scholastics, 27). Outlying areas, 5,074 (lay persons, 4,699; sisters, 266; priests, 93; brothers, 10; scholastics, 6).

Seminaries: 213 (70 diocesan; 143 religious). U.S.: 196 (66 diocesan; 130 religious). Outlying areas: 17 (4 diocesan; 13 religious).

Seminarians: 4,522 (3,251 diocesan; 1,271 religious). U.S.: 4,444 (3,221 diocesan; 1,223 religious). Outlying areas: 78 (30 diocesan; 48 religious).

CATHOLIC SCHOOLS AND STUDENTS IN THE UNITED STATES

(Source: Official Catholic Directory, *2003; figures as of Jan. 1, 2003. Archdioceses are indicated by an asterisk.)*

State Diocese	Universities/ Colleges	Students	High Schools	Students	Elem. Schools	Students
Alabama	1	1,050	9	3,040	38	10,204
*Mobile	1	1,050	3	1,460	19	5,100
Birmingham	-	-	6	1,580	19	5,104
Alaska	-	-	3	329	5	866
*Anchorage	-	-	2	104	3	407
Fairbanks	-	-	1	225	1	295
Juneau	-	-	-	-	1	164
Arizona	-	-	10	6,125	51	15,384
Phoenix	-	-	6	4,359	27	9,229
Tucson	-	-	4	1,766	24	6,155
Arkansas						
Little Rock	-	-	6	1,778	31	6,563
California	13	41,959	113	69,396	597	176,368
*Los Angeles	5	11,023	50	30,060	225	66,920
*San Francisco	3	11,420	14	6,249	66	20,004
Fresno	-	-	2	1,369	23	5,301
Monterey	-	-	5	1,697	13	3,856
Oakland	3	5,050	9	5,659	51	14,190
Orange	-	-	6	5,637	38	14,406
Sacramento	-	-	7	4,498	47	12,512
San Bernardino	-	-	2	903	35	8,033
San Diego	1	7,098	5	3,690	44	14,177
San Jose	1	7,368	6	6,151	30	10,755
Santa Rosa	-	-	5	1,951	13	2,941
Stockton	-	-	2	1,532	12	3,273
Colorado	1	12,400	7	3,683	48	13,879
*Denver	1	12,400	5	3,203	38	11,443
Colorado Springs	-	-	1	386	5	1,558
Pueblo	-	-	1	94	5	878
Connecticut	5	17,462	23	14,377	129	31,619
*Hartford	2	5,945	9	8,368	71	17,621
Bridgeport	3	11,517	8	3,792	35	9,674
Norwich	-	-	6	2,217	23	4,324
Delaware, Wilmington	-	-	8	4,737	30	10,659
District of Columbia						
*Wash., DC	3	20,183	17	9,310	86	23,729
Florida	3	23,154	34	28,356	185	66,285
*Miami	2	12,433	13	12,567	58	25,539
Orlando	-	-	5	2,612	31	12,930
Palm Beach	-	-	3	2,287	16	6,124
Pensacola-Tallahassee	-	-	2	654	9	2,413
St. Augustine	-	-	2	1,918	27	8,320
St. Petersburg	1	10,721	5	2,954	35	10,959
Venice	-	-	3	1,653	9	3,711
Georgia	-	-	9	5,437	37	13,706
*Atlanta	-	-	4	2,943	21	9,029
Savannah	-	-	5	2,494	16	4,677
Hawaii, Honolulu	1	1,054	7	3,433	35	8,025
Idaho, Boise	-	-	1	695	13	2,503
Illinois	12	54,190	74	46,805	478	147,672
*Chicago	5	43,995	41	29,902	247	86,876
Belleville	-	-	3	1,672	36	6,541
Joliet	3	8,517	8	5,894	56	19,177
Peoria	1	150	7	2,630	45	11,802
Rockford	1	82	8	4,106	41	11,847
Springfield	2	1,446	7	2,601	53	11,429
Indiana	11	27,383	22	12,085	179	50,216
*Indianapolis	2	3,052	10	5,512	63	19,772
Evansville	-	-	4	1,621	24	6,129

State Diocese	Universities/ Colleges	Students	High Schools	Students	Elem. Schools	Students
Indiana, cont.						
Ft.Wayne-S. Bend	5	15,267	4	3,093	41	12,252
Gary	1	1,141	3	1,499	28	7,026
Lafayette	3	7,923	1	360	23	5,037
Iowa	7	9,827	24	7,691	113	27,196
*Dubuque	3	4,307	7	2,782	53	13,037
Davenport	2	3,995	7	1,563	18	4,187
Des Moines	1	552	2	1,393	16	4,910
Sioux City	1	973	8	1,980	26	5,062
Kansas	4	4,837	16	6,803	96	23,096
*Kansas City	3	2,908	7	3,573	44	11,791
Dodge City	-	-	-	-	9	1,211
Salina	-	-	5	919	12	1,987
Wichita	1	1,929	4	2,311	32	8,132
Kentucky	5	7,117	23	11,638	121	33,873
*Louisville	3	4,735	9	6,444	59	17,776
Covington	1	1,555	9	3,286	29	8,935
Lexington	-	-	2	905	15	3,288
Owensboro	1	827	3	1,003	18	3,874
Louisiana	4	12,648	50	28,659	167	67,770
*New Orleans	3	11,227	23	16,527	81	34,085
Alexandria	-	-	3	592	8	2,386
Baton Rouge	1	1,421	8	4,486	24	12,321
Houma-Thib.	-	-	3	1,937	10	4,067
Lafayette	-	-	10	3,810	31	11,162
Lake Charles	-	-	1	531	7	2,125
Shreveport	-	-	2	776	6	1,624
Maine, Portland	1	4,197	3	1,090	18	3,995
Maryland,*Baltimore	4	11,537	20	10,831	72	25,989
Massachusetts	12	31,937	50	26,684	200	61,582
*Boston	7	21,700	34	17,833	127	42,430
Fall River	1	2,550	4	2,871	24	5,864
Springfield	1	866	4	1,675	25	6,981
Worcester	3	6,821	8	4,305	24	6,307
Michigan	8	25,579	53	20,139	277	71,325
*Detroit	4	20,545	33	13,415	120	40,897
Gaylord	-	-	4	688	16	2,668
Grand Rapids	1	2,579	4	1,899	39	6,772
Kalamazoo	-	-	3	775	22	3,711
Lansing	3	2,455	6	2,478	44	10,012
Marquette	-	-	-	-	10	1,473
Saginaw	-	-	3	884	26	3,792
Minnesota	7	24,944	23	11,130	193	44,909
*St.Paul and Minn.	3	16,906	13	8,337	96	28,545
Crookston	-	-	1	169	9	1,414
Duluth	1	2,518	-	-	12	2,015
New Ulm	-	-	3	494	18	2,595
St. Cloud	2	4,144	2	906	31	5,189
Winona	1	1,376	4	1,224	27	5,151
Mississippi	1	45	9	2,539	29	7,323
Biloxi	-	-	5	1,770	14	3,251
Jackson	1	45	4	769	15	4,072
Missouri	4	19,176	42	20,695	250	63,435
*St.Louis	2	13,618	30	15,284	243	60,590
Jefferson City	-	-	2	1,028	37	6,365
Kansas City-St. Joseph	2	5,558	7	3,458	35	9,464
Springfield-Cape Girar.	-	-	3	925	22	3,732
Montana	2	2,207	5	973	16	3,015
Great Falls-Billings	1	825	3	578	12	2,201
Helena	1	1,382	2	395	4	814
Nebraska	2	7,270	27	8,285	97	22,521
*Omaha	2	7,270	17	5,710	65	16,397
Grand Island	-	-	4	876	7	696
Lincoln	-	-	6	1,699	25	5,428

State Diocese	Universities/ Colleges	Students	High Schools	Students	Elem. Schools	Students
Nevada	-	-	2	1,431	11	3,860
Las Vegas	-	-	1	882	7	2,753
Reno	-	-	1	549	4	1,107
New Hampshire						
Manchester	5	5,513	5	2,575	37	7,777
New Jersey	7	22,245	76	39,130	345	111,226
*Newark	4	18,208	37	16,555	134	38,418
Camden	-	-	13	7,598	57	14,736
Metuchen	-	-	6	3,601	42	13,601
Paterson	2	1,797	9	3,765	60	16,386
Trenton	1	2,420	11	7,611	52	28,085
New Mexico	1	1,588	4	2,003	30	5,941
*Santa Fe	1	1,588	2	1,750	16	3,991
Gallup	-	-	2	253	10	1,470
Las Cruces	-	-	-	-	4	480
New York	29	121,147	124	74,895	679	210,821
*New York	12	65,934	54	28,966	229	82,356
Albany	4	5,000	7	3,061	38	8,211
Brooklyn	3	22,899	20	17,576	154	51,400
Buffalo	7	15,838	17	6,107	92	20,327
Ogdensburg	-	-	2	650	22	3,192
Rochester	-	-	7	3,493	54	11,307
Rockville Centre	2	8,347	11	11,665	62	27,932
Syracuse	1	3,129	6	3,377	29	6,096
North Carolina	2	883	3	2,353	46	12,876
Charlotte	2	883	2	1,438	15	5,680
Raleigh	-	-	1	915	31	7,196
North Dakota	1	2,546	4	1,376	25	3,480
Bismarck	1	2,546	3	1,097	12	1,350
Fargo	-	-	1	279	13	2,130
Ohio	12	24,899	78	44,878	445	136,109
*Cincinnati	4	10,248	21	15,767	113	40,653
Cleveland	3	6,916	23	14,162	140	48,517
Columbus	1	2,317	11	5,026	46	14,076
Steubenville	1	2,253	3	747	17	2,212
Toledo	2	1,761	14	6,382	84	20,300
Youngstown	1	1,404	6	2,794	45	10,402
Oklahoma	1	730	4	2,489	31	7,517
*Oklahoma City	1	730	2	962	20	4,196
Tulsa	-	-	2	1,527	11	3,321
Oregon	2	4,813	10	4,967	45	9,681
*Portland	2	4,813	10	4,967	42	9,026
Baker	-	-	-	-	3	655
Pennsylvania	26	81,747	87	51,663	564	159,714
*Philadelphia	11	34,345	37	30,571	230	81,041
Allentown	2	3,894	9	4,184	52	13,884
Altoona-Johnstown	2	4,449	3	1,255	24	4,169
Erie	2	6,761	7	2,935	41	9,417
Greensburg	2	4,871	2	788	23	4,928
Harrisburg	-	-	7	3,816	40	10,444
Pittsburgh	3	13,631	11	4,000	108	25,232
Scranton	4	13,796	11	4,114	46	10,599
Rhode Island, Providence	2	7,557	12	6,021	53	13,204
South Carolina						
Charleston	-	-	4	1,555	25	6,341
South Dakota	2	1,694	5	1,261	27	5,124
Rapid City	-	-	2	379	2	700
Sioux Falls	2	1,694	3	882	25	4,424
Tennessee	2	3,007	11	6,198	47	10,309
Knoxville	-	-	2	1,081	8	2,640
Memphis	1	2,030	6	3,615	20	3,338
Nashville	1	977	3	1,502	19	4,331
Texas	8	27,368	47	16,614	229	67,816
*San Antonio	4	12,095	10	3,735	39	11,499

State Diocese	Univs. Colleges	Students	High Schools	Students	Elem. Schools	Students
Texas, cont.						
Amarillo	-	-	1	123	6	760
Austin	1	4,267	4	842	16	3,930
Beaumont	-	-	1	487	6	1,407
Brownsville	-	-	2	807	10	3,045
Corpus Christi	1	44	1	254	16	2,525
Dallas	1	3,788	7	3,703	33	11,118
El Paso	-	-	3	921	12	4,428
Fort Worth	-	-	4	1,463	15	7,061
Galveston-Houston	1	7,174	8	2,895	49	16,090
Laredo	-	-	1	650	6	1,662
Lubbock	-	-	-	-	2	388
San Angelo	-	-	-	-	3	801
Tyler	-	-	1	213	4	903
Victoria	-	-	3	521	12	2,199
Utah, Salt Lake City	-	-	3	1,725	10	3,686
Vermont, Burlington	3	3,112	2	659	15	2,710
Virginia	4	5,286	14	6,395	63	22,368
Arlington	4	5,286	6	4,249	35	13,570
Richmond	-	-	8	2,146	28	8,798
Washington	3	12,452	13	6,869	79	20,912
*Seattle	2	7,937	9	5,624	57	15,965
Spokane	1	4,515	3	1,085	16	3,202
Yakima	-	-	1	160	7	1,745
West Virginia, Wheeling-Charleston	1	1,515	8	1,678	26	5,059
Wisconsin	9	32,052	27	11,779	334	59,181
*Milwaukee	5	22,613	13	7,424	123	29,493
Green Bay	2	5,014	6	2,205	72	11,040
La Crosse	1	2,167	7	1,537	77	8,791
Madison	1	2,258	1	613	45	7,084
Superior	-	-	-	-	17	2,773
Wyoming, Cheyenne	-	-	1	17	7	965
EASTERN CHURCHES	1	1,050	7	620	23	3,678
*Philadelphia	1	1,050	1	364	7	1,057
St. Nicholas (Chicago)	-	-	1	76	2	380
Stamford	-	-	5	180	3	245
St. Josaphat (Parma)	-	-	-	-	2	265
*Pittsburgh	-	-	-	-	2	335
Parma	-	-	-	-	2	296
Passaic	-	-	-	-	1	124
Van Nuys	-	-	-	-	-	-
St. Maron (Maronites)	-	-	-	-	-	-
Our Lady of Deliverance (Syriacs)	-	-	-	-	-	-
Our Lady of Lebanon (Maronites)	-	-	-	-	-	-
Newton (Melkites)	-	-	-	-	-	-
St. George Martyr (Romanians)	-	-	-	-	-	-
St. Peter the Apostle (Chaldeans)	-	-	-	-	-	-
St. Thomas Apostle of Detroit (Chaldeans)	-	-	-	-	-	-
St. Thomas (Syro-Malabars)	-	-	-	-	-	-
Armenians (Ap. Ex.)	-	-	-	-	4	976
SCHOOLS AND STUDENTS IN OUTLYING AREAS						
American Samoa	-	-	1	154	2	383
Caroline Islands	-	-	4	798	5	1,309
Guam	-	-	3	994	7	2,107
Marshall Islands	-	-	2	367	5	962
Marianas	-	-	1	195	3	389
Puerto Rico	5	27,972	124	28,013	131	46,411
Virgin Islands	-	-	2	236	3	591
TOTAL 2003	237	749,512	1,376	686,651	7,142	1,971,394
TOTAL 2002	238	724,065	1,344	691,456	6,949	2,005,573
TOTAL 1993	231	660,787	1,377	635,740	7,346	2,007,299

CATHOLIC UNIVERSITIES AND COLLEGES IN THE UNITED STATES

(*Sources:* Catholic Almanac *survey;* The Official Catholic Directory.)

Listed below are institutions of higher learning established under Catholic auspices. Some of them are now independent.

Information includes: name of each institution; indication of male (m), female (w), coeducational (c) student body; name of founding group or group with which the institution is affiliated; year of foundation; total number of students, in parentheses.

Albertus Magnus College (c): 700 Prospect St., New Haven, CT 06511; (203) 773-8550; www.albert us.edu. Dominican Sisters; 1925; independent (2,065).

Alvernia College (c): 400 Saint Bernardine St., Reading, PA 19607; (610) 796-8200; www.alve rnia.edu. Bernardine Sisters; 1958 (2,457).

Alverno College (w): 3400 S. 43th St., P.O. Box 343922, Milwaukee, WI 53234; (414) 382-6000; www.alverno.edu. School Sisters of St. Francis; 1887; independent (2,000).

Anna Maria College (c): 50 Sunset Lane, Paxton, MA 01612; (508) 849-3300; www.annamaria.edu. Sisters of St. Anne;1946; independent (1,244).

Aquinas College (c): 1607 Robinson Rd. S.E., Grand Rapids, MI 49506; (616) 459-8281. Sisters of St. Dominic; 1922; independent (2,571).

Aquinas College (c): 4210 Harding Rd., Nashville, TN 37205; (615) 297-7545; www.aquinas-tn.edu. Dominican Sisters; 1961 (506).

Aquinas Institute of Theology (c): 3642 Lindell Boulevard, St. Louis, MO 63108; (314) 977-3869; www.op.org/aquinas. Dominicans, 1961; graduate theology; offers distance learning program in pastoral studies and specializations in preaching (200).

Assumption College (c): 500 Salisbury St., Worcester, MA 01615-0005; (508) 767-7000; www.assump tion.edu. Assumptionist Religious; 1904 (2,766).

Ave Maria School of Law (c): 3475 Plymouth Rd., Ann Arbor, MI 48105; (734) 930-4408.

Avila University (c): 11901 Wornall Rd., Kansas City, MO 64145-1698; (816) 942-8400; www.avila.edu. Sisters of St. Joseph of Carondelet; 1916 (2,658).

Barry University (c): 11300 N.E. 2nd Ave., Miami Shores, FL 33161; (305) 899-3000; www.barry.edu. Dominican Sisters (Adrian, MI); 1940 (8,691).

Bellarmine College (c): 2001 Newburg Rd., Louisville, KY 40205; (502) 452-8211; www.bellar mine.edu. Louisville archdiocese; independent (2,323).

Belmont Abbey College (c): 100 Belmont-Mt. Holly Rd., Belmont, NC 28012; (704) 825-6700; www.belmontabbeycollege.edu. Benedictine Fathers; 1876 (883).

Benedictine College (c): 1020 N. Second St., Atchison, KS 66002; (913) 367-5340; www.bene dictine.edu. Benedictines; 1859; independent (1,375).

Benedictine University (formerly Illinois Benedictine College) (c): 5700 College Rd., Lisle, IL 60532-0900; (630) 829-600 0; www.ben.edu. Benedictine Monks of St. Procopius Abbey; 1887 (2,809).

Boston College (University status) (c): Chestnut Hill, MA 02167; (617) 552-8000; www.bc.edu. Jesuit Fathers; 1863 (14,297).

Brescia University (c): 717 Frederica St., Owensboro, KY 42301; (270) 685-3131; www.brescia.edu. Ursuline Sisters; 1950 (820).

Briar Cliff College (c): 3303 Rebecca St., Sioux City, IA 51104; (712) 279-5405; www.briarcliff.edu. Sisters of St. Francis of the Holy Family; 1930 (994).

Cabrini College (c): 610 King of Prussia Rd., Radnor, PA 19087; (610) 902-8100; www.cabrini.edu. Missionary Srs. of Sacred Heart; 1957; private (2,669).

Caldwell College (c): 9 Ryerson Ave., Caldwell, NJ 07006; (973) 618-3000; www.caldwell.edu. Dominican Sisters; 1939 (2,270).

Calumet College of St. Joseph (c): 2400 New York Ave., Whiting, IN 46394; (219) 473-7770; www.cc sj.edu. Society of the Precious Blood, 1951 (1,141).

Canisius College (c): 2001 Main St., Buffalo, NY 14208; (716) 883-7000; www.canisius.edu. Jesuit Fathers; 1870; independent (4,995).

Cardinal Stritch University (c): 6801 N. Yates Rd., Milwaukee, WI 53217; (414) 410-4000; www.stritch.edu. Sisters of St. Francis of Assisi; 1937 (5,855).

Carlow College (w): 3333 5th Ave., Pittsburgh, PA 15213; (412) 578-6059; www.carlow.edu. Sisters of Mercy; 1929 (2,199).

Carroll College (c): 1601 N. Benton Ave., Helena, MT 59625; (406) 447-4300. Diocesan; 1909 (1,400).

Catholic Distance University (c): 120 East Colonial Highway, Hamilton, VA 20158-9012; www.cdu.edu. Offers External Degree programs, including Masters degrees in Religious Studies (7,000).

Catholic Theological Union (c): 5401 South Cornell Ave., Chicago, IL 60615; (773) 324-8000; www.ctu.edu (348). Offers Graduate theological programs, including M.Div., M.A., M.A.P.S., and D.Min.

Catholic University of America, The (c): Michigan Ave. & Fourth St., NE, Washington, DC 20064; (202) 319-5000; www.cua.edu. Hierarchy of the United States; 1887. Pontifical University (5,777).

Chaminade University of Honolulu (c): 3140 Waialae Ave., Honolulu, HI 96816; (808) 735-4711; www.chaminade.edu. Marianists; 1955 (2,788).

Chestnut Hill College (w): 9601 Germantown Ave., Philadelphia, PA 19118; (215) 248-7000; www.chc.edu. Sisters of St. Joseph; 1924 (1,645).

Christendom College (c): 134 Christendom Dr., Front Royal, VA 22630; (540) 636-2900. Independent, 1977 (477).

Christian Brothers University (c): 650 E. Parkway S., Memphis, TN 38104; (901) 321-3000. Brothers of the Christian Schools; 1871 (2,027).

Clarke College (c): 1550 Clarke Dr., Dubuque, IA 52001; (563) 588-6300; www.clarke.edu. Sisters of Charity, BVM; 1843; independent (1,126).

Creighton University (c): 2500 California Plaza, Omaha, NE 68178; (402) 280-2700; www.creight on.edu. Jesuit Fathers; 1878; independent (6,297).

Dallas, University of (c): 1845 E. Northgate, Irving, TX 75062; (972) 721-5000. Dallas diocese; 1956; independent (3,518).

Dayton, University of (c): 300 College Park, Dayton, OH 45469-1660; (937) 229-1000; www.udayton.edu. Marianists; 1850 (10,248).

DePaul University (c): One E. Jackson Blvd., Chicago, IL 60604; (312) 362-8000; www.depaul.edu. Vincentians; 1898 (23,174).

De Sales University (c): 2755 Station Ave., Center Valley, PA 18034; (610) 282-1100; www.desales.edu. Oblates of St. Francis de Sales; 1965 (1,339).

Detroit Mercy, University of (c): 4001 W. McNichols Rd., Detroit, MI, 48221; 8200 W. Outer Dr., Detroit MI 48219; (313) 993-1000. Society of Jesus and Sisters of Mercy; 1877; independent (5,843).

Dominican College (c): 470 Western Hwy., Orangeburg, NY 10962; (845) 359-7800; www.dc.edu. Dominican Sisters; 1952; independent (1,700).

Dominican University of California (c): 50 Acacia Ave., San Rafael, CA 94901-2298; (415) 457-4440; www.dominican.edu. Dominican Sisters; 1890; independent (1,578).

Dominican University (formerly Rosary College) (c): 7900 W. Division St., River Forest, IL 60305; (708) 366-2490; www.dom.edu. Sinsinawa Dominican Sisters; 1901 (**2,533).**

Duquesne University (c): 600 Forbes Ave., Pittsburgh, PA 15282; (412) 396-6000; www.duq.edu. Congregation of the Holy Ghost; 1878 (9,600).

D'Youville College (c): 320 Porter Ave., Buffalo, NY 14201; (716) 881-3200; www.dyc.edu. Grey Nuns of the Sacred Heart; 1908; independent (2,453).

Edgewood College (c): 1000 Edgewood College Dr., Madison, WI 53711; (608) 663-4861. Sinsinawa Dominican Sisters; 1927 (2,258).

Emmanuel College (w): 400 The Fenway, Boston, MA 02115; (617) 735-9715; www.emmanuel.edu. Sisters of Notre Dame de Namur; 1919; independent (1,549).

Fairfield University (c): 1073 North Benson Rd., Fairfield, CT 06430; (203) 254-4000; www.fairfield.edu. Jesuits; 1942 (6,001).

Felician College (c): 262 S. Main St., Lodi, NJ 07644; (201) 559-6000; www.felician.edu. Felician Sisters; 1942; independent (1,400).

Fontbonne University (c): 6800 Wydown Blvd., St. Louis, MO 63105; (314) 862-3456; www.fontbonne.edu. Sisters of St. Joseph of Carondelet; 1917; independent (2,344).

Fordham University (c): Fordham Rd. and Third Ave., New York, NY 10458; (718) 817-3040. Society of Jesus (Jesuits); 1841; independent (13,800).

Franciscan University of Steubenville (c): 1235 University Blvd., Steubenville, OH 43952; (740) 283-3771; www.franuniv.edu. Franciscan TOR Friars; 1946 (2,208). Also offers distance learning programs.

Gannon University (c): 109 University Square, Erie, PA 16541-0001; (814) 871-7000; www.gannon.edu. Diocese of Erie; 1933 (3,404).

Georgetown University (c): 37th and O Sts. N.W., Washington, DC 20057; (202) 687-0100; www.georgetown.edu. Jesuit Fathers; 1789 (12,688).

Georgian Court College (w/c): 900 Lakewood Ave., Lakewood, NJ 08701; (732) 364-2200; www.georgian.edu. Sisters of Mercy; 1908 (3,561).

Gonzaga University (c): E. 502 Boone Ave., Spokane, WA 99258; (509) 328-4220. Jesuit Fathers; 1887 (4,515).

Graduate School of Theology (c): 5890 Birch Ct., Oakland, CA 94618; (510) 652-1651; www.satgtu.org. Affiliate of the Graduate Theological Union.

Great Falls, University of (c): 1301 20th St. S., Great Falls, MT 59405; (406) 761-8210; www.ugf.edu. Sisters of Providence; 1932; independent (825).

Gwynedd-Mercy College (c): Gwynedd Valley, PA 19437; (215) 646-7300; www.gmc.edu. Sisters of Mercy; 1948; independent (2,198).

Hilbert College (c): 5200 S. Park Ave., Hamburg, NY 14075; (716) 649-7900; www.hilbert.edu. Franciscan Sisters of St. Joseph; 1957; independent (970).

Holy Cross, College of the (c): Worcester, MA 01610; (508) 793-2011; www.holycross.edu. Jesuits; 1843 (2,811).

Holy Family College (c): Grant and Frankford Aves., Philadelphia, PA 19114 and One Campus Dr., Newtown, PA 18940; (215) 637-7700; www.hfc.edu. Sisters of Holy Family of Nazareth; 1954; independent (2,559).

Holy Names College (c): 3500 Mountain Blvd., Oakland, CA 94619; (510) 436-1000; www.hnc.edu. Sisters of the Holy Names of Jesus and Mary; 1868; independent (947).

Immaculata College (w): Immaculata, PA 19345; (610) 647-4400; www.immaculata.edu. Sisters, Servants of the Immaculate Heart of Mary; 1920 (3,062).

Incarnate Word, University of the (c): 4301 Broadway, San Antonio, TX 78209; (210) 829-6000; www.uiw.edu. Sisters of Charity of the Incarnate Word; 1881 (4,264).

Iona College (c): 715 North Ave., New Rochelle, NY 10801; (914) 633-2000; www.iona.edu. Congregation of Christian Brothers; 1940; independent (4,897).

John Carroll University (c): 20700 N. Park Blvd., Cleveland, OH 44118; (216) 397-1886; www.jcu.edu. Jesuits; 1886 (4,294).

King's College (c): 133 North River St., Wilkes-Barre, PA 18711; (570) 208-5900; www.kings.edu. Holy Cross Fathers; 1946 (2,178).

La Roche College (c): 9000 Babcock Blvd., Pittsburgh, PA 15237; (412) 367-9300; www.laroche.edu. Sisters of Divine Providence; 1963 (1,981).

La Salle University (c): 1900 W. Olney Ave., Philadelphia, PA 19141; (215) 951-1000. Christian Brothers; 1863 (5,567).

Le Moyne College (c): 1419 Salt Springs Rd., Syracuse, NY 13214; (315) 445-4100; www.lemoyne.edu. Jesuit Fathers; 1946; independent (approx. 3,129, full-time, part-time, graduate)

Lewis University (c): Romeoville, IL 60446; (815) 838-0500; www.lewisu.edu. Christian Brothers; 1932 (4,348).

Loras College (c): 1450 Alta Vista St., Dubuque, IA 52004; (563) 588-7100. Archdiocese of Dubuque; 1839 (1,736).

Lourdes College (c): 6832 Convent Blvd., Sylvania, OH 43560; (419) 885-3211; www.lourdes.edu. Sisters of St. Francis; 1958 (1,356).

Loyola College (c): 4501 N. Charles St., Baltimore, MD 21210; (410) 617-2000; www.loyola.edu. Jesuits; 1852; combined with Mt. St. Agnes College, 1971 (6,144).

Loyola Marymount University (c): 7900 Loyola Blvd., Los Angeles, CA 90045-2699; (310) 338-2700;

www.lmu.edu. Society of Jesus; Religious of Sacred Heart of Mary, Sisters of St. Joseph of Orange, 1911 (6,591).

Loyola University (c): 6363 St. Charles Ave., New Orleans, LA 70118; (504) 865-2011. Jesuit Fathers; 1912 (5,842).

Loyola University Chicago (c): 820 N. Michigan Ave., Chicago, IL 60611; (312) 915-6000; www.luc.edu. Society of Jesus; 1870 (12,604).

Madonna University (c): 36600 Schoolcraft Rd., Livonia, MI 48150; (734) 432-5300. Felician Sisters; 1947 (3,979).

Magdalen College (c): 511 Kearsarge Mountain Rd., Warner, NH 03278; (603) 456-2656; www.mag dalen.edu. Magdalen College Corporation; 1973 (81).

Manhattan College (c): Manhattan College Pkwy., Bronx, NY 11201; (718) 862-7200; www.man hattan.edu. De La Salle Christian Brothers; 1835; independent (2,744). Cooperative program with College of Mt. St. Vincent.

Marian College of Fond du Lac (c): 45 S. National Ave., Fond du Lac, WI 54935; (920) 923-7600; www.mariancollege.edu. Sisters of St. Agnes; 1936 (2,558).

Marian College (c): 3200 Cold Spring Rd., Indianapolis, IN 46222; (317) 955-6000; www.marian.edu. Sisters of St. Francis (Oldenburg, IN); 1851; independent (1,425).

Marquette University (c): P.O. Box 1881, Milwaukee, WI 53201-1881; (414) 288-7250; www.mar quette.edu. Jesuit Fathers; 1881; independent (10,832).

Mary, University of (c): 7500 University Dr., Bismarck, ND 58504; (701) 255-7500; www.umary.edu. Benedictine Sisters; 1959 (2,546).

Marygrove College (c): 8425 W. McNichols Rd., Detroit, MI 48221; (313) 927-1200. Sisters, Servants of the Immaculate Heart of Mary; 1905; independent (6,459).

Marylhurst College (c): P.O. Box 261, Marylhurst, OR 97036-0261; (503) 636-8141; www.maryl hurst.edu. Sisters of Holy Names of Jesus and Mary; 1893; independent (1,579).

Marymount College (w): Tarrytown, NY 10591; (914) 631-3200; www.marymt.edu. Religious of the Sacred Heart of Mary; 1907; independent (842). Coed in weekend degree programs.

Marymount Manhattan College (w): 221 E. 71st St., New York, NY 10021; (212) 517-0400; www.cm sv.edu. Religious of the Sacred Heart of Mary; 1936; independent (2,330).

Marymount University (c): 2807 N. Glebe Rd., Arlington, VA 22207; (703) 522-5600; www.mary mount.edu. Religious of the Sacred Heart of Mary; 1950; independent (3,672).

Marywood College (c): Scranton, PA 18509; (570) 348-6211; www.marywood.edu. Sisters, Servants of the Immaculate Heart of Mary; 1915; independent (3,087).

Mercy College of Health Sciences (c): 928-6th Ave., Des Moines, IA 50309-1239; (515) 643-3180; www.mchs.edu. Sisters of Mercy of the Americas (552).

Mercyhurst College (c): 501 E. 38th St., Erie, PA 16546; (814) 824-2000; www.mercyhurst.edu. Sisters of Mercy; 1926 (3,404).

Merrimack College (c): North Andover, MA 01845; (978) 837-5000; www.merrimack.edu. Augustinians;1947 (2,108).

Misericordia (College Misericordia) (c): 301 Lake St., Dallas, PA 18612-1098; (570) 674-6400; www.miseri.edu. Religious Sisters of Mercy of the Union; 1924 (1,983).

Molloy College (c): 1000 Hempstead Ave., P.O. Box 5002, Rockville Centre, NY 11570-5002; (516) 678-5000. Dominican Sisters; 1955; independent (2,500).

Mount Aloysius College (c): 7373 Admiral Peary Hwy., Cresson, PA 16630; (814) 886-4131; www.mtaloy.edu. Sisters of Mercy; 1939 (2,000).

Mount Marty College (c): 1105 W. 8th St., Yankton, SD 57078; (800) 658-4552; www.mtmc.edu. Benedictine Sisters; 1936 (1,168).

Mount Mary College (w): 2900 N. Menomonee River Pkwy., Milwaukee, WI 53222; (414) 258-4810. School Sisters of Notre Dame; 1913 (1,368).

Mount Mercy College (c): 1330 Elmhurst Dr. N.E., Cedar Rapids, IA 52402; (319) 363-8213; www.mt mercy.edu. Sisters of Mercy; 1928; independent (1,432).

Mount St. Clare College (c): 400 N. Bluff Blvd., Clinton, IA 52732; (319) 242-4023; www.clare.edu. Sisters of St. Francis of Clinton, Iowa; 1918 (appr. 497).

Mount St. Joseph, College of (c): 5701 Delhi Rd., Cincinnati, OH 45233-1670; (513) 244-4200; www.msj.edu. Sisters of Charity; 1920 (5,527).

Mount Saint Mary College (c): Newburgh, NY 12550; (914) 561-0800; www.msmc.edu.. Dominican Sisters; 1954; independent (2,541).

Mount St. Mary's College (c): Emmitsburg, MD 21727; (301) 447-6122; www.msmary.edu. Founded by Fr. John DuBois, 1808; independent (1,821).

Mount St. Mary's College (w/c): 12001 Chalon Rd., Los Angeles, CA 90049 and 10 Chester Pl., Los Angeles, CA 90007 (Doheny Campus); (310) 954-4010; www.msmc.la.edu. Sisters of St. Joseph of Carondelet; 1925. Coed in music, nursing and graduate programs (1,965).

Mount Saint Vincent, College of (c): 6301 Riverdale Ave., New York, NY 10471; (718) 405-3200; www.cmsv.edu. Sisters of Charity; 1847; independent (1,515). Cooperative program with Manhattan College.

Neumann College (c): One Neumann Dr., Aston, PA 19014; (610) 459-0905; www.neumann.edu. Sisters of St. Francis; 1965; independent (2,221).

Newman University (c): 3100 McCormick Ave., Wichita, KS 67213; (316) 942-4291; www.new manu.edu. Sisters Adorers of the Blood of Christ; 1933 (1,929).

New Rochelle, College of (w/c): 29 Castle Pl., New Rochelle, NY 10805 (main campus); (914) 654-5000; www.cnr.edu. Ursuline Order; 1904; independent (6,084). Coed in nursing, graduate, new resources divisions.

Niagara University (c): Lewiston Rd. Niagara Univ., NY 14109-2015; (716) 285-1212; www.nia gara.edu. Vincentian Fathers and Brothers; 1856 (3,446).

Notre Dame de Namur University (c): 1500 Ralston Ave., Belmont, CA 94002; (650) 593-1601; www.cnd.edu. Sisters of Notre Dame de Namur; 1851; independent (1,799).

Notre Dame, University of (c): (University of Notre

Dame du Lac) Notre Dame, IN 46556; (219) 631-5000; www.nd.edu. Congregation of Holy Cross; 1842 (11,054).

Notre Dame College of Ohio (w): 4545 College Rd., Cleveland, OH 44121; (216) 381-1680; www.ndc.edu. Sisters of Notre Dame; 1922 (1,093).

Notre Dame of Maryland, College of (w): 4701 N. Charles St., Baltimore, MD 21210; (410) 435-0100; www.ndm.edu. School Sisters of Notre Dame; 1873 (3,077).

Oblate School of Theology (c): 285 Oblate Dr., San Antonio, TX 78216-6693; (210) 341-1366; www.ost.edu. Oblates of Mary Immaculate; 1903 (264). Graduate theology programs.

Ohio Dominican College (c): 1216 Sunbury Rd., Columbus, OH 43219-2099; (614) 253-2741; www.odc.edu. Dominican Sisters of St. Mary of the Springs; 1911 (2,300).

Our Lady of Holy Cross College (c): 4123 Woodland Dr., New Orleans, LA 70131; (504) 394-7744; www.olhcc.edu. Congregation of Sisters Marianites of Holy Cross; 1916 (3,994).

Our Lady of the Elms, College of (w): Chicopee, MA 01013; (413) 594-2761; www.elms.edu. Sisters of St. Joseph; 1928 (866).

Our Lady of the Lake College (c): 5345 Brittany Dr., Baton Rouge, LA 70808-4398; (225) 768-1710; www.ololcollege. Independent (1,421).

Our Lady of the Lake University (c): 411 S.W. 24th St., San Antonio, TX 78207; (210) 434-6711; www.ollusa.edu. Sisters of Divine Providence; 1895 (3,324).

Pontifical Catholic University of Puerto Rico (c): 2250 Avenida de las Americas, Ponce, PR 00717-0777; (787) 841-2000; www.pucpr.edu. Hierarchy of Puerto Rico; 1948; Pontifical University (9,912).

Portland, University of (c): 5000 N. Willamette Blvd., Portland, OR 97203; (503) 943-7911; www.up.edu. Holy Cross Fathers; 1901; independent (3,234).

Presentation College (c): Aberdeen, SD 7401; (605) 225-1634. Sisters of the Presentation; 1951 (615).

Providence College (c): 549 River Ave., Providence, RI 02918; (401) 865-1000; www.providence.edu. Dominican Friars; 1917 (5,742, day, evening, and graduate).

Queen of the Holy Rosary College (c): P.O. Box 3908, Mission San Jose, CA 94539; (510) 657-2468. Dominican Sisters of Mission San Jose, independent (200).

Quincy University (c): 1800 College Ave., Quincy, IL 62301; (217) 222-8020; www.quincy.edu. Franciscan Friars; 1860 (1,146).

Regis College (w): 235 Wellesley St., Weston, MA 02493-1571; (781) 768-7000; www.regiscollege.edu. Sisters of St. Joseph; 1927; independent (1,300).

Regis University (c): 3333 Regis Blvd. Denver, CO 80221; (303) 458-4100. Jesuits; 1887 (11,240).

Rivier College (c): Nashua, NH 03060; (603) 888-1311; www.rivier.edu. Sisters of the Presentation of Mary; 1933; independent (2,572).

Rockhurst College (c): 1100 Rockhurst Rd., Kansas City, MO 64110; (816) 501-4000; www.rockhurst.edu. Jesuit Fathers; 1910 (3,536).

Rosemont College of the Holy Child Jesus (w): Rosemont, PA 19010-1699; (610) 526-2984; www.rosemont.edu. Society of the Holy Child Jesus; 1921 (1,210).

Sacred Heart University (c): 5151 Park Ave., Fairfield, CT 06432; (203) 371-7999; www.sacredheart.edu. Diocese of Bridgeport; 1963; independent (6,001).

St. Ambrose University (c): Davenport, IA 52803; (319) 333-6300; www.sau.edu. Diocese of Davenport; 1882 (3,500).

Saint Anselm College (c): Manchester NH 03102-1030; (603) 641-7000; www.anselm.edu. Benedictines; 1889 (1,985).

St. Basil College (m): 195 Glenbrook Rd., Stamford, CT 06902; (203) 324-4578; UkrCathSem@aol.com. The Ukrainian Catholic Diocese of Stamford.

Saint Benedict, College of (w): 37 S. College Ave., St. Joseph, MN 56374; (320) 363-5407; www.csbsju.edu. Benedictine Sisters; 1913 (2,072). Sister college of St. John's University, Collegeville

St. Bonaventure University (c): St. Bonaventure, NY 14778; (716) 375-2000; www.sbu.edu. Franciscan Friars; 1858; independent (2,719).

St. Catherine, College of (w): St. Paul: 2004 Randolph Ave., St. Paul, MN 55105; (651) 690-6000; Minneapolis; www.stkate.edu. Sisters of St. Joseph of Carondelet; 1905 (4,622).

St. Edward's University (c): 3001 S. Congress Ave., Austin, TX 78704; (512) 448-8400; www.stedwards.edu. Holy Cross Brothers; 1881; independent (4,267).

Saint Elizabeth, College of (w): 2 Convent Rd., Morristown, NJ 07960-6989; (973) 290-4000; www.st-elizabeth.edu. Sisters of Charity; 1899; independent (1,766). Coed in adult undergraduate and graduate programs.

St. Francis College (c): 180 Remsen St., Brooklyn Heights, NY 11201; (718) 489-5200. Franciscan Brothers; 1884; private, independent in the Franciscan tradition (2,505).

St. Francis University (c): P.O. Box 600, Loretto, PA 15940-0600; (814) 472-3000; www.sfcpa.edu. Franciscan Friars; 1847; independent (2,012).

St. Francis, University of (c): 500 N. Wilcox, Joliet, IL 60435; (815) 740-3360; www.stfrancis.edu. Sisters of St. Francis of Mary Immaculate (3,920).

St. Francis, University of (c): 2701 Spring St., Fort Wayne, IN 46808-3994; (219) 434-3100; www.sf.edu. Sisters of St. Francis; 1890 (1,740).

St. Gregory's University (c): 1900 W. MacArthur, Shawnee, OK 74801; (405) 878-5100; www.sgc.edu. Benedictine Monks; 1876 (805).

St. John's University (c): 8000 Utopia Pkwy., Jamaica, NY 11439 (Queens Campus); 300 Howard Ave., Staten Island, NY 10301 (Staten Island Campus); (718) 990-6161; www.stjohns.edu. Vincentians; 1870 (18,523).

St. John's University (m): Collegeville, MN 56321; (320) 363-2011; www.csbsju.edu. Benedictines; 1857 (2,072). All classes and programs are coeducational with College of St. Benedict.

St. Joseph in Vermont, College of (c): 71 Clement Rd., Rutland, VT 05701; (802) 773-5900; www.csj.edu. Sisters of St. Joseph; 1950; independent (482).

Saint Joseph College (w/c): 1678 Asylum Ave., West Hartford, CT 06117-2700; (860) 232-4571; www.sjc.edu. Sisters of Mercy; 1932 (1,965). Women's college in undergraduate liberal arts. Coed in graduate school and Weekend College.

Saint Joseph's College (c): 278 Whites Bridge Rd., Standish, ME 04084-5263; (207) 893-7711; www.sjcme.edu. Sisters of Mercy; 1912 (4,197 total; 1,609 graduate). Offers extensive distance education programs.

Saint Joseph's College (c): P.O. Box 909, Rensselaer, IN 47978; (219) 866-6000; www.st joe.edu. Society of the Precious Blood; 1891 (1,101).

St. Joseph's College (c): 245 Clinton Ave., Brooklyn, NY 11205; (718) 636-6800 and 155 W. Roe Blvd., Patchogue, NY 11772; (631) 447-3200; www.sjc ny.edu. Sisters of St. Joseph; 1916; independent (3,444).

St. Joseph's University (c): 5600 City Ave., Philadelphia, PA 19131; (610) 660-1000; www.sju.edu. Jesuit Fathers; 1851 (6,850).

Saint Leo University (c): P.O. Box 6665, MC 2186, Saint Leo, FL 33574; (352) 588-8200; www.saint leo.edu. Order of St. Benedict; 1889; independent (9,931).

Saint Louis University (c): 221 N. Grand Blvd., St. Louis, MO 63103; (314) 977-2222; www.slu.edu. Society of Jesus; 1818; independent (11,274).

Saint Martin's College (c): 5300 Pacific Ave. SE, Lacey, WA 98503-1297; (360) 438-4311; www.s tmartin.edu. Benedictine Monks; 1895 (1,474 main and extension campuses).

Saint Mary, College of (w): 1901 S. 72nd St., Omaha, NE 68124; (402) 399-2400; www.csm.edu. Sisters of Mercy; 1923; independent (981).

Saint Mary College (c): Leavenworth, KS 66048; (913) 682-5151. Sisters of Charity of Leavenworth; 1923 (888).

Saint Mary-of-the-Woods College (w): St. Mary-of-the-Woods, IN 47876; (812) 535-5151; www.sm wc.edu. Sisters of Providence; 1840 (1,510).

Saint Mary's College (w): Notre Dame, IN 46556; (219) 284-4556; www.saintmarys.edu. Sisters of the Holy Cross; 1844 (1,473).

Saint Mary's College (c): 3535 Indian Trail, Orchard Lake, MI 48324; (248) 683-0521; www.st marys-avemaria.edu. 1885 (510).

St. Mary's College (c): Moraga, CA 94575; (510) 631-4000. Brothers of the Christian Schools; 1863 (4,127).

Saint Mary's University of Minnesota (c): 700 Terrace Heights, Winona, MN 55987-1399; (507) 452-4430; www.smumn.edu. Brothers of the Christian Schools; 1912 (1,376).

St. Mary's University of San Antonio (c): One Camino Santa Maria, San Antonio, TX 78228-8607; (210) 436-3011; www.stmarytx.edu. Society of Mary (Marianists). 1852 (4,264).

Saint Meinrad School of Theology (c): 200 Hill Dr., St. Meinrad, IN 47577; (812) 357-6611; www.saintmeinrad.edu. Benedictines (91 full- and part-time lay students.) Graduate-level theological studies.

St. Michael's College (c): Winooski Park, Colchester, VT 05439; (802) 654-2211; www.sm cvt.edu. Society of St. Edmund; 1904 (2,630).

St. Norbert College (c): De Pere, WI 54115; (920) 403-3181; www.snc.edu. Norbertine Fathers; 1898; independent (2,045).

Saint Peter's College (c): 2641 Kennedy Blvd., Jersey City, NJ 07306; (201) 915-9000; www.spc.edu. Society of Jesus; 1872; independent (4,201).

Saint Rose, College of (c): 432 Western Ave., Al-

bany, NY 12203; (518) 454-5111. Sisters of St. Joseph of Carondelet; 1920; independent (4,441).

St. Scholastica, The College of (c): 1200 Kenwood Ave., Duluth, MN 55811; (218) 723-6000. Benedictine Sisters; 1912; independent (2,518).

St. Thomas, University of (c): 2115 Summit Ave., St. Paul, MN 55105; (651) 962-5000; www.st thomas.edu. Archdiocese of St. Paul and Minneapolis; 1885 (11,366).

St. Thomas, University of (c): 3800 Montrose Blvd., Houston, TX 77006-4696; (713) 522-7911; www.stthom.edu. Basilian Fathers; 1947 (7,174).

St. Thomas Aquinas College (c): Sparkill, NY 10976; (914) 398-4000; www.stac.edu. Dominican Sisters of Sparkill; 1952; independent, corporate board of trustees (2,200).

St. Thomas University (c): 16400 N.W. 32nd Ave., Miami, FL 33054; (305) 625-6000; www.stu.edu. Archdiocese of Miami; 1962 (3,677).

Saint Vincent College (c): 300 Fraser Purchase Rd., Latrobe, PA 15650-2690; (724) 539-9761; www.benedictine.stvincent.edu/seminary. Benedictine Fathers; 1846 (1,222).

Saint Vincent's College (c): 2800 Main St., Bridgeport, CT 06606; (203) 576-5235; www.stvincents college.edu. (345).

St. Xavier University (c): 3700 W. 103rd St., Chicago, IL 60655; (773) 298-3000. Sisters of Mercy; chartered 1847 (4,100).

Salve Regina University (c): Ochre Point Ave., Newport, RI 02840-4192; (401) 847-6650; www.salve.edu. Sisters of Mercy; 1934 (1,542). Offers distance learning programs in graduate studies.

San Diego, University of (c): 5998 Alcala Park, San Diego, CA 92110; (619) 260-4600. San Diego diocese and Religious of the Sacred Heart; 1949; independent (7,062).

San Francisco, University of (c): 2130 Fulton St., San Francisco, CA 94117; (415) 422-5555. Jesuit Fathers; 1855 (8,130).

Santa Clara University (c): 500 El Camino Real, Santa Clara, CA 95053; (408) 554-4000; www.scu.edu. Jesuit Fathers; 1851; independent (7,368).

Santa Fe, College of (c): 1600 St. Michael's Dr., Santa Fe, NM 87505; (505) 473-6011. Brothers of the Christian Schools; 1947 (1,588).

Scranton, University of (c): Scranton, PA 18510; (570) 941-7533; www.uofs.edu. Society of Jesus; 1888; independent (4,728).

Seattle University (c): 900 Broadway, Seattle, WA 98122; (206) 296-6000; www.seattleu.edu. Society of Jesus; 1891 (6,337).

Seton Hall University (c): 400 South Orange Ave., South Orange, NJ 07079; (973) 761-9000. Diocesan Clergy; 1856 (9,760).

Seton Hill College (w): Seton Hill Dr., Greensburg, PA 15601-1599; (724) 834-2200; www.setonhill.edu. Sisters of Charity of Seton Hill; 1883 (1,521).

Siena College (c): 515 Loudon Rd., Loudonville, NY 12211; (518) 783-2300; www.siena.edu. Franciscan Friars; 1937 (3,379).

Siena Heights University (c): 1247 E. Siena Heights Dr., Adrian, MI 49221; (517) 263-0731; www.sienahts.edu. Adrian Dominican Sisters; 1919 (2,124).

Silver Lake College of the Holy Family (c): 2406 S. Alverno Rd., Manitowoc, WI 54220-9319; (920)

684-6691. Franciscan Sisters of Christian Charity; 1935 (2,969).

Spalding University (c): 851 S. 4th Ave., Louisville, KY 40203; (502) 585-9911; www.spalding.edu. Sisters of Charity of Nazareth; 1814; independent (1,670).

Spring Hill College (c): 4000 Dauphin St., Mobile, AL 36608; (334) 380-4000; www.shc.edu. Jesuit Fathers; 1830 (1,050).

Stonehill College (c): North Easton, MA 02357; (508) 565-1000; www.stonehill.edu. Holy Cross Fathers; 1948; independent (2,550).

Thomas Aquinas College (c): 10000 N. Ojai Rd., Santa Paula, CA 93060; (805) 525-4417; www.thomasaquinas.edu. Founded 1971 (331).

Thomas More College (c): 333 Thomas More Pkwy., Crestview Hills, Covington, KY 41017; (859) 341-5800; www.thomasmore.edu. Diocese of Covington; 1921 (1,555).

Trinity College of Vermont (w): 208 Colchester Ave., Burlington, VT 05401; (802) 658-0337; www.trinityvt.edu. Sisters of Mercy; 1925 (200).

Trinity College (w): 125 Michigan Ave. NE, Washington, DC 20017; (202) 939-5000. Sisters of Notre Dame de Namur; 1897 (1,600). Coed graduate school.

Ursuline College (w): 2550 Lander Rd., Pepper Pike, OH 44124; (440) 449-4200; www.ursuline.edu. Ursuline Nuns; 1871 (1,319).

Villanova University (c): Villanova, PA 19085; (610) 519-7499; www.villanova.edu. Order of St. Augustine; 1842 (10,396).

Viterbo College (c): 815 S. 9th, La Crosse, WI 54601; (608) 796-3000; www.viterbo.org. Franciscan Sisters of Perpetual Adoration; 1890 (2,200).

Walsh University (c): 2020 Easton St. N.W., North Canton, Ohio 44720-3396; (330) 490-7090; www.walsh.edu. Brothers of Christian Instruction; 1958 (1,648).

Washington Theological Union (c): 6896 Laurel Street N.W., Washington, DC 20012-2016; (202) 726-8800; www.wtu.edu. Coalition of Religious Seminaries; 1968 (263).

Wheeling Jesuit University (c): 316 Washington Ave., Wheeling, WV 26003-6295; (304) 243-2000; www.wju.edu. Jesuit Fathers; 1954 (1,703).

Xavier University (c): 3800 Victory Pkwy., Cincinnati, OH 45207; (513) 745-3000; www.xu.edu.

Jesuit Fathers; 1831 (2,631).

Xavier University of Louisiana (c): 1 Drexel Dr., New Orleans, LA 70125; (504) 486-7411; www.xula.edu. Sisters of Blessed Sacrament; 1925 (3,787).

Catholic Two-Year Colleges

Ancilla Domini College (c): P.O. Box 1, Donaldson, IN 46513; (219) 936-8898; www.ancilla.edu. Ancilla Domini Sisters; 1937 (546).

Assumption College for Sisters: Mendham, NJ 07945; (973) 543-6528. Sisters of Christian Charity; 1953 (24).

Chatfield College (c): St. Martin, OH 45118; (937) 875-3344; www.chatfield.edu. Ursulines; 1971 (273).

The College of St. Catherine-Minneapolis (c): 601 25th Ave. S., Minneapolis, MN 55454; (651) 690-7702. Sisters of St. Joseph of Carondelet (918).

Donnelly College (c): 608 N. 18th St., Kansas City, KS 66102; (913) 621-6070; www.donnelly.cc.ks.us. Archdiocesan College; 1949 (645).

Don Bosco Technical Institute (m): 1151 San Gabriel Blvd., Rosemead, CA 91770; (626) 307-6500; www.boscotech.tec.ca.us. Salesians; 1969 (994).

Holy Cross College (c): 54515 State Rd., 933 N., Notre Dame, IN 46556-0308; (219) 239-8400; www.hcc-nd.edu. Brothers of Holy Cross; 1966 (503).

Manor College (c): 700 Fox Chase Road, Jenkintown, PA 19046; (215) 885-2360; www.manor.edu. Sisters of St. Basil the Great; 1947.

Maria College (c): 700 New Scotland Ave., Albany, NY 12208. Sisters of Mercy; 1963 (1,048).

Marymount College Palos Verdes (c): 30800 Palos Verdes Dr., E., Rancho Palos Verdes, CA 90275-6299; (310) 377-5501; www.marymountpv.edu. Religious of the Sacred Heart of Mary; independent (840).

St. Catharine College (c): 2735 Bardstown Rd., St. Catharine, KY 40061; (859) 336-5082. Dominican Sisters; 1931 (742).

Springfield College in Illinois (c): 1500 N. Fifth St., Springfield, IL 62702-2694; (217) 525-1420; www.sci.edu. Ursuline Sisters; 1929 (300).

Trocaire College (c): 360 Choate Ave., Buffalo, NY 14220; (716) 827-2423; www.trocaire.edu. Sisters of Mercy; 1958; independent (780).

Villa Maria College of Buffalo (c): 240 Pine Ridge Rd., Buffalo, NY 14225; (716) 896-0700; www.villa.edu. Felician Sisters 1960; independent (475).

DIOCESAN AND INTERDIOCESAN SEMINARIES

(Sources: Catholic Almanac *survey;* The Official Catholic Directory; *Catholic News Service.)*

Information, according to states, includes names of archdioceses and dioceses, and names and addresses of seminaries. Types of seminaries, when not clear from titles, are indicated in most cases. Interdiocesan seminaries are generally conducted by religious orders for candidates for the priesthood from several dioceses. The list does not include houses of study reserved for members of religious communities. Archdioceses are indicated by an asterisk.

California: Los Angeles* — St. John's Seminary (major), 5118 Seminary Rd., Camarillo 93012-2599; (805) 482-2755; www.stjohnsem.edu.

San Diego — St. Francis Seminary (college and pre-theology formation program), 1667 Santa Paula Dr., 92111; (619) 291-7446.

San Francisco* — St. Patrick's Seminary (major), 320 Middlefield Rd., Menlo Park 94025; (650) 325-5621; www.stpatricksseminary.org..

Colorado: Denver* — St. John Vianney Theological Seminary (college and pre-theology formation program), 1300 S. Steele St., 80210; (303) 282-3427.

Connecticut: Hartford* — St. Thomas Seminary (college formation program), 467 Bloomfield Ave., Bloomfield 06002-2999; (860) 242-5573.

Norwich — Holy Apostles College and Seminary (adult vocations; minor and major), 33 Prospect Hill

Rd., Cromwell 06416; (860) 632-3000; www.holy apostles.edu.

Stamford — Byzantine Rite: Ukrainian Catholic Seminary: St. Basil College Seminary (minor), 195 Glenbrook Rd., Stamford 06902-3099; (203) 324-4578.

District of Columbia: Washington, DC* — Theological College (national, major), The Catholic University of America, 401 Michigan Ave., N.E., 20017; (202) 756-4900; www.theologicalcollege.org.

St. Josaphat's Seminary, 201 Taylor St. N.E., 20017; (202) 529-1177. (Major house of formation serving the four Ukrainian Byzantine-rite dioceses in the U.S.)

Florida: Miami* — St. John Vianney College Seminary, 2900 S.W. 87th Ave., 33165; (305) 223-4561.

Palm Beach — St. Vincent de Paul Regional Seminary (major), 10701 S. Military Trail, Boynton Beach 33436; (561) 732-4424; www.svdp.edu.

Illinois: Chicago* — Archbishop Quigley Preparatory Seminary (high school), 103 East Chestnut St., Chicago 60611; (312) 787-9343; www.quigley.org. St. Joseph Seminary (college), 6551 N. Sheridan Rd., Chicago 60626; (773) 973-9700; www.stjoseph.luc.edu. University of St. Mary of the Lake Mundelein Seminary (School of Theology), 1000 E. Maple Ave., Mundelein 60060; (847) 566-6401; www.vocations.org.

Indiana: Indianapolis* — Saint Meinrad Seminary, College and School of Theology (interdiocesan), St. Meinrad 47577; (812) 357-6611; www.saintmeinrad.edu.

Iowa: Davenport — St. Ambrose University Seminary (interdiocesn), 518 W. Locust St., 52803; (319) 333-6151; www.davenportdiocese.org.

Dubuque* — Seminary of St. Pius X (interdiocesan), Loras College, 52004-0178; (319) 588-7782.

Louisiana: New Orleans* — Notre Dame Seminary Graduate School of Theology, 2901 S. Carrollton Ave., 70118; (504) 866-7426; St. Joseph Seminary College (interdiocesan), St. Benedict 70457-9999; (504) 892-1800; www.stjosephabbey.org.

Maryland: Baltimore* — Mount St. Mary's Seminary and University, 5400 Roland Ave., 21210; (410) 864-4000; www.stmarys.edu. Mount St. Mary's Seminary, Emmitsburg 21727-7797; (301) 447-5295; www.msmary.edu.

Massachusetts: Boston* — St. John's Seminary, School of Theology, 127 Lake St., Brighton 02135; (617) 254-2610. St. John's Seminary, College of Liberal Arts, 127 Lake St., Brighton 02135; (617) 746-5450. Pope John XXIII National Seminary (for ages 30-60), 558 South Ave., Weston 02943; (781) 899-5500; www.blessedjohnXXIII.org.

Newton — Melkite Greek Catholic: St. Gregory the Theologian Seminary, 3 VFW Parkway, Roslindale, MA 02131; (617) 323-9922. Seminary of St. Basil the Great, 30 East St., 01844; (978) 683-2471.

Michigan: Detroit* — Sacred Heart Major Seminary (college/theologate and institute for ministry), 2701 Chicago Blvd., Detroit 48206; (313) 883-8500. Sts. Cyril and Methodius Seminary, St. Mary's College (theologate and college) independent, primarily serving Polish-American community, 3535 Indian Trail, Orchard Lake 48324; (248) 683-0311.

Grand Rapids — Christopher House, 723 Rosewood Ave., S.E., East Grand Rapids 49506; (616) 243-6538.

Minnesota: St. John's School of Theology and Seminary, St. John's University, P.O. Box 7288, Collegeville 56321-7288; (320) 363-2100; www.csbsju.edu/sot.

St. Paul and Minneapolis* — St. Paul Seminary School of Divinity, University of St. Thomas, St. Paul 55101; (612) 962-5050; www.stthomas.edu. St. John Vianney Seminary (college residence), 2115 Summit Ave., St. Paul 55105; (651) 962-6825; www.st thomas.edu/sjv.

Winona — Immaculate Heart of Mary Seminary, St. Mary's University, No. 43, 700 Terrace Heights, 55987; (507) 457-7373; www.ihmseminary.org.

Missouri: St. Louis* — Kenrick — Glennon Seminary (St. Louis Roman Catholic Theological Seminary). Kenrick School of Theology and Cardinal Glennon College, 5200 Glennon Dr., 63119; (314) 792-6100.

Nebraska: Seward — St. Gregory the Great Seminary (pre-theology), 1301 280th Rd., 68434; (402) 643-4052, www.stgregoryseminary.org. Our Lady of Guadalupe Seminary, P.O. Box 147, Denton, NE 68339; (402) 797-7700.

New Jersey: Newark* — Immaculate Conception Seminary — college seminary; major seminary; graduate school — Seton Hall University, 400 South Orange Ave., South Orange 07079; (973) 761-9575; www.shu.edu. Redemptoris Mater, Archdiocesan Missionary Seminary, 672 Passaic Ave., 07032; (201) 997-3220.

New York: Brooklyn — Cathedral Seminary Residence of the Immaculate Conception (college and pre-theology), 7200 Douglaston Parkway, Douglaston 11362; (718) 229-8001. Cathedral Preparatory Seminary, 56-25 92nd St., Elmhurst 11373; (718) 592-6800. St. Alphonsus Formation Residence, 22-04 Parsons Blvd., 11357-3440; (718) 321-1096.

Buffalo — Christ the King Seminary (interdiocese theologate), P.O. Box 607, 711 Knox Rd., East Aurora 14052; (716) 652-8900. Pope John Paul II Residence, 217 Winston Rd., 14216; (716) 836-5526.

New York* — St. Joseph's Seminary (major), 201 Seminary Ave., Dunwoodie, Yonkers 10704; (914) 968-6200. St. John Neumann Residence (college and pre-theology), 201 Seminary Ave., Yonkers, N.Y., 10704-1896; (914) 964-3025. Cathedral Preparatory Seminary, 946 Boston Post Rd., Rye 10580; (914) 968-6200; www.cathedralprep.com.

Rockville Centre — Seminary of the Immaculate Conception (major), 440 West Neck Rd., Huntington, 11743; (631) 423-2346.

St. Maron Eparchy, Brooklyn — Our Lady of Lebanon Maronite Seminary, 7164 Alaska Ave. N.W., Washington, DC 20012; (202) 723-8831; www.maroniteseminary.org.

North Dakota: Fargo — Cardinal Muench Seminary (interdiocesan high school, college and pre-theology), 100 35th Ave. N.E., Fargo 58102; (701) 232-8969; www.cardinalmuench.org.

Ohio: Cincinnati* — Mt. St. Mary's Seminary of the West (division of the Athenaeum of Ohio), 6616 Beechmont Ave., 45230; (513) 231-2223; www.mtsm.org..

Cleveland — St. Mary Seminary and Graduate School of Theology, 28700 Euclid Ave. Wickliffe 44092; (440) 943-7600. Borromeo Seminary, 28700 Euclid Ave., 44092-2585; (440) 943-7600; www.a-full-life.com.

Columbus — Pontifical College Josephinum (national), theologate and college, 7625 North High St., 43235-1498; (614) 885-5585; www.pcj.edu.

Oregon: Portland* — Mount Angel Seminary (interdiocesan, college, pre-theology program, graduate school of theology), 1 Abbey Dr., St. Benedict 97373; (503) 845-3951. Felix Rougier House of Studies, 585 E. College St., 97362. Jesuit Novitiate of St. Francis Xavier, 3301 S.E. 45th Ave., 97206.

Pennsylvania: Erie — St. Mark Seminary, P.O. Box 10397, Erie 16514; (814) 824-1200.

Greensburg — St. Vincent Seminary (interdiocesan; pre-theology program; theologate; graduate programs in theology; religious education), 300 Fraser Purchase Rd., Latrobe 15650-2690; (724) 539-9761; www.stvincent.edu.

Philadelphia* — Theological Seminary of St. Charles Borromeo (College, pre-theology program, spirituality year pogram, theologate), 100 East Wynnewood Rd., Wynnewood 19096; (610) 667-3394; www.scs.edu.

Pittsburgh* (Byzantine-Ruthenian) — Byzantine Catholic Seminary of Sts. Cyril and Methodius (college, pre-theology program, theologate), 3605 Perrysville Ave., 15214; (412) 321-8383; www.byzcath.org/seminary.

Pittsburgh — St. Paul Seminary (interdiocesan, college and pre-theology), 2900 Noblestown Rd., 15205; (412) 921-5800; www.diopitt.org.

Scranton — St. Pius X Seminary (college and pre-theology formation; interdiocesan), 1000 Seminary Rd., Dalton 18414; (570) 563-1131. Affiliated with the University of Scranton.

Rhode Island: Providence — Seminary of Our Lady of Providence (House of Formation; college students and pre-theology), 485 Mount Pleasant Ave., 02908; (401) 331-1316; www.catholicpriest.com.

Texas: Dallas — Holy Trinity Seminary (college and pre-theology; English proficiency and academic foundation programs), P.O. Box 140309, Irving 75014; (972) 438-2212.

El Paso — St. Charles Seminary College, P.O. Box 17548, 79917; (915) 591-9821.

Galveston-Houston — St. Mary's Seminary (theologate), 9845 Memorial Dr., Houston 77024; (713) 686-4345.

San Antonio* — Assumption Seminary (theologate and pre-theology, Hispanic ministry emphasis), 2600 W. Woodlawn Ave., 78228; (210) 734-2324.

Washington: Spokane — Bishop White Seminary, College Formation Program, E. 429 Sharp Ave., 99202; (509) 326-3255; www.bishopwhiteseminary.org.

Wisconsin: Milwaukee* — St. Francis Seminary, 3257 S. Lake Dr., St. Francis 53235; (414) 747-6400; www.sfs.edu. College Program, 2497 N. Murray Ave., Milwaukee, 53211; (414) 964-6982. Sacred Heart School of Theology (interdiocesan seminary for second-career vocations), P.O. Box 429, Hales Corners, 53130-0429; (414) 425-8300.

North American College

Founded by the U.S. Bishops in 1859, the North American College serves as a residence and house of formation for U.S. seminarians and graduate students in Rome. The first ordination of an alumnus took place June 14, 1862. Pontifical status was granted the college by Pope Leo XIII Oct. 25, 1884. Students pursue theological and related studies principally at the Pontifical Gregorian University and at the Pontifical University of Saint Thomas Aquinas (the Angelicum). The current rector is Msgr. Kevin McCoy, S.T.D. Address: 00120 Città del Vaticano; 011-39-06-684-931.

American College of Louvain

Founded by U.S. Bishops in 1857, the American College of Louvain, Belgium, is a seminary for U.S. students. It also serves as a community for English-speaking graduate-student priests and religious priests pursuing studies at the Catholic University of Louvain (*Université Catholique de Louvain*, founded 1425). The college is administered by an American rector and faculty, and operates under the auspices of a committee of the national Conference of Catholic Bishops. The rector is Rev. Kevin A. Codd. Address: The American College, Catholic University of Louvain, Naamsestraat 100, B-3000, Leuven, Belgium; 32-16-32-00-11.

WORLD AND U.S. SEMINARY STATISTICS

The 2001 Statistical Yearbook of the Church (*the most recent edition*) *reports the following comparative statistics for the years 1990 to 2001 of candidates in Philosophy and Theology (major seminarians). World totals are given first; U.S. statistics are given in parentheses.*

Year	Total Major Seminarians	Diocesan	Religious
1990	96,155 (5,552)	64,629 (3,676)	31,526 (1,876)
1991	99,668 (5,487)	66,305 (3,777)	33,363 (1,710)
1992	102,000 (5,380)	67,960 (3,645)	34,040 (1,735)
1993	103,709 (5,123)	68,829 (3,505)	34,880 (1,618)
1994	105,075 (5,100)	69,613 (3,526)	35,462 (1,574)
1995	106,346 (4,831)	69,777 (3,234)	36,569 (1,597)
1996	105,870 (4,785)	70,034 (3,268)	35,836 (1,517)
1997	108,517 (4,729)	70,534 (3,311)	37,983 (1,418)
1998	109,171 (4,830)	70,564 (3,436)	38,607 (1,394)
1999	110,021 (5,024)	70,989 (3,428)	39,032 (1,596)
2000	110,583 (5,109)	71,756 (3,479)	38,827 (1,630)
2001	112,244 (5,080)	72,241 (3,404)	40,003 (1,676)

PONTIFICAL UNIVERSITIES

(*Principal source:* Annuario Pontificio.)

These universities, listed according to country of location, have been canonically erected and authorized by the Congregation for Catholic Education to award degrees in stated fields of study. New laws and norms governing ecclesiastical universities and faculties were promulgated in the apostolic constitution *Sapientia Christiana*, issued Apr. 15, 1979. Phone numbers are listed where possible.

Argentina: Pontifical Catholic University of S. Maria of Buenos Aires (June 16, 1960): Av. Alicia Moreau de Justo 1400, 1107 Buenos Aires.

Belgium: Catholic University of Louvain (founded Dec. 9, 1425; canonically erected, 1834), with autonomous institutions for French- (Louvain) and Flemish-(Leuven) speaking: Place de l'Universite I, B-1348 Louvain-La-Neuve (French); Naamsestraat 22/b, B-3000 Leuven (Flemish).

Brazil: Pontifical Catholic University of Rio de Janeiro (Jan. 20, 1947): Rua Marquês de São Vicente 225, 22451-000 Rio de Janeiro, RJ.

Pontifical Catholic University of Minas Gerais (June 5, 1983): Av. Dom José Gaspar 500, C.P. 2686, 30161-000 Belo Horizonte, MG.; (031) 319-1127.

Pontifical Catholic University of Parana (Aug. 6, 1985): Rua Imaculada Conceição, 1155, Prado Velho, C.P. 670, 80001-000 Curitiba, PR; (041) 223-0922.

Pontifical Catholic University of Rio Grande do Sul (Nov. 1, 1950): Av. Ipiranga 6681, C.P.1429,90001-000 Porto Alegre, RS.

Pontifical Catholic University of São Paulo (Jan. 25, 1947): Rua Monte Alegre 984, 05014-901 São Paulo SP.

Pontifical University of Campinas (Sept. 8, 1956): Rua Marechal Deodoro 1099, 13020-000 Campinas, SP.; (0192) 27-001.

Canada: Laval University (Mar. 15, 1876): Case Postale 460, QC G1K 7P4.

St. Paul University (formerly University of Ottawa) (Feb. 5, 1889): 223 Rue Main, Ottawa, ON K1S 1C4;

University of Sherbrooke (Nov. 21, 1957): Chemin Ste.-Catherine, 2500, boulevard de l'Université, Sherbrooke, QC J1K 12R1.

Chile: Pontifical Catholic University of Chile (June 21, 1888): Avenida Bernardo O'Higgins, 340, Casilla 114D, Santiago.

Catholic University of Valparaíso (Nov. 1, 1961): Avenida Brasil 2950, Casilla 4059, Valparaíso.

Colombia: Bolivarian Pontifical Catholic University (Aug. 16, 1945): Circular 1a, N.70-01, Apartado 56006, Medellín.

Pontifical Xaverian University (July 31, 1937): Carrera 7, N. 40-62, Apartado 56710, Santafé de Bogota D.C.; Apartado 26239, Calle 18, N. 118-250, Cali (Cali campus).

Cuba: Catholic University of St. Thomas of Villanueva (May 4, 1957): Avenida Quenta 16,660, Marianao.

Dominican Republic: Pontifical Catholic University "Mother and Teacher" (Sept. 9, 1987): Apartado 822, Santiago de Los Caballeros.

Ecuador: Pontifical Catholic University of Ecuador (July 16, 1954): Doce de Octubre, N. 1076, Apartado 17-01-2184, Quito.

France: Catholic University of Lille (Nov. 18, 1875): Boulevard Vauban 60, 59016 Lille.

Catholic Faculties of Lyon (Nov. 22, 1875): 25, Rue du Plat, 69288 Lyon 02.

Catholic Institute of Paris (Aug. 11, 1875): 21, Rue d'Assas, 75270 Paris 06.

Catholic Institute of Toulouse (Nov. 15, 1877): Rue de la Fonderie 31, 31068 Toulouse.

Catholic University of the West (Sept. 16, 1875): 3, Place André Leroy, B.P. 808, 49005 Angers; 2-41-81-66-00.

Germany: Catholic University Eichstätt (Apr. 1, 1980): Ostenstrasse 26, D-85072, Eichstätt, Federal Republic of Germany; (08421) 201.

Guatemala: Rafael Landívar University (Oct. 18, 1961): Vista Hermosa III, Zona 16, Guatemala; (02) 69-21-51.

Hungary: Catholic University Pázmány Péter (March 25, 1999): Papnövelde Utea 7, H-1053 Budapest, Hungary; (01) 11-73-701.

Ireland: St. Patrick's College (Mar. 29, 1896): Maynooth, Co. Kildare.

Italy: Catholic University of the Sacred Heart (Dec. 25, 1920): Largo Gemelli 1, 20123 Milan.

Libera University Mary of the Assumption (Oct. 26, 1939): Via della Transpontina 21, 00193 Rome, Italy.

Japan: Jochi Daigaku (Sophia University) (Mar. 29, 1913): Chiyoda-Ku, Kioi-cho 7, Tokyo 102.

Lebanon: St. Joseph University of Beirut (Mar. 25, 1881): Rue de l'Université St.-Joseph, Boite Postale 293, Beyrouth (Beirut), Liban; (01) 42-64-56.

Netherlands: Catholic University of Nijmegen (June 29, 1923): P.B. 9102, Comeniuslaam 4, 6500 HC, Nijmegen.

Panama: University of S. Maria La Antigua (May 27, 1965): Apartado 6-1696, Panama 6.

Paraguay: Catholic University of Our Lady of the Assumption (Feb. 2, 1965): Independencia Nacional y Comuneros, Casilla 1718, Asunción; (021) 44-10-44.

Peru: Pontifical Catholic University of Peru (Sept. 30, 1942): Av. Universitaria, s/n. San Miguel, Apartado 1761, Lima 100.

Philippines: Pontifical University of Santo Tomás (Nov. 20, 1645): España Street, 1008 Manila.

Poland: Catholic University of Lublin (July 25, 1920): Aleje Racùawickie 14, Skr. Poczt. 129, 20-950, Lublin.

Catholic Theological Academy (June 29, 1989): Ul. Dewajtis 5, 01-815, Warsaw.

Pontifical Academy of Theology of Krakow (Dec. 8, 1981): Ul. Kanonicza, 25, 31-002 Kraków; (014) 22-33-31.

Portugal: Portuguese Catholic University (Nov. 1, 1967): Palma de Cima, 1 600 Lisbon.

Puerto Rico: Pontifical Catholic University of Puerto Rico (Aug. 15, 1972): 2250 Ave. Las Américas Suite 523, Ponce, Puerto Rico 00731-6382.

Spain: Catholic University of Navarra (Aug. 6, 1960): Campus Universitario, E-31080 Pamplona.

Pontifical University "Comillas" (Mar. 29, 1904): Campus de Cantoblanco, 28049 Madrid.

Pontifical University of Salamanca (Sept. 25, 1940): Compañía 5, 37002 Salamanca.

University of Deusto (Aug. 10, 1963): Avenida de las Universidades, 28, 48007 Bilbao o Apartado 1, 48080 Bilbao; 94-445-31-00.

Taiwan (China): Fu Jen Catholic University (Nov. 15, 1923, at Peking; reconstituted at Taipeh, Sept. 8, 1961): Hsinchuang, Taipeh Hsien 24205.

United States: The Catholic University of America (Mar. 7, 1889): 620 Michigan Ave. N.E., Washington, DC 20064.

Georgetown University (Mar. 30, 1833): 37th and O Sts. N.W., Washington, DC 20057.

Niagara University (June 21, 1956): Lewiston Rd., Niagara Falls, NY 14109.

Uruguay: Catholic University of Uruguay "Dámaso Antonio Larrañaga" (Jan. 25, 1985): Avda. 8 de Octubre 2738, 11.600 Montevideo.

Venezuela: Catholic University "Andrés Bello" (Sept. 29, 1963): Esquina Jesuitas, Apartado 29068, Caracas 1021; (02) 442-21-20.

ECCLESIASTICAL FACULTIES

(*Principal source:* Annuario Pontificio.)

These faculties in Catholic seminaries and universities, listed according to country of location, have been canonically erected and authorized by the Congregation for Catholic Education to award degrees in stated fields of study.

Argentina: Faculties of Philosophy and Theology, San Miguel (Sept. 8, 1932).

Australia: Catholic Institute of Sydney, Sydney (Feb. 2, 1954).

Austria: Theological Faculty, Linz (Dec. 25, 1978).

International Theological Institute for Family Studies (Oct. 1, 1996).

Brazil: Philosophical and Theological Faculties of the Company of Jesus, Belo Horizonte (July 15, 1941 and Mar. 12, 1949).

Ecclesiastical Faculty of Philosophy "John Paul II," Rio de Janeiro (Aug. 6, 1981).

Cameroon: Catholic Institute of Yaoundé (Nov. 15, 1991).

Canada: College of Immaculate Conception — Montréal Section of Jesuit Faculties in Canada (Sept. 8, 1932). Suspended.

Pontifical Institute of Medieval Studies, Toronto (Oct. 18, 1939).

Dominican Faculty of Theology of Canada, Ottawa (1965; Nov. 15, 1975).

Regis College, Toronto Section of the Jesuit Faculty of Theology in Canada, Toronto (Feb. 17, 1956; Dec. 25, 1977).

Congo (formerly Zaire): Catholic Faculties of Kinshasa, Kinshasa (theology, Apr. 25, 1957; philosophy, Nov. 25, 1987).

Côte d'Ivoire (Ivory Coast): Catholic Institute of West Africa, Abidjan (Aug. 12, 1975).

Croatia: Philosophical Faculty, Zagreb (July 31, 1989).

France: Centre Sèvres, Faculties of Theology and Philosophy of the Jesuits, Paris (Sept. 8, 1932).

Germany: Theological Faculty of the Major Episcopal Seminary, Trier (Sept. 8, 1955).

Theological Faculty, Paderborn (June 11, 1966).

Theological-Philosophical Faculty, Frankfurt (1932; June 7, 1971).

Philosophical Faculty, Munich (1932; Oct. 25, 1971).

Theological Faculty, Fulda (Dec. 22, 1978).

Philosophical-Theological School of Salesians, Benediktbeuern (May 24, 1992).

Philosphical-Theological School, Vallendar (Oct. 7, 1993).

Great Britain: Heythrop College, University of London, London (Nov. 1, 1964). Theology, philosophy.

Hungary: Faculty of Theology (1635), Institute on Canon Law (Nov. 30, 1996), Budapest.

India: *Jnana Deepa Vidyapeeth* (Pontifical Athenaeum), Institute of Philosophy and Religion, Poona (July 27, 1926).

Vidyajyoti, Institute of Religious Studies, Faculty of Theology, Delhi (1932; Dec. 9, 1974).

Satya Nilayam, Institute of Philosophy and Culture. Faculty of Philosophy, Madras (Sept. 8, 1932; Dec. 15, 1976).

Pontifical Institute of Theology and Philosophy at the Pontifical Interritual Seminary of St. Joseph, Alwaye, Kerala (Feb. 24, 1972).

Dharmaram Vidya Kshetram, Pontifical Athenaeum of Theology and Philosophy, Bangalore (theology, Jan. 6, 1976; philosophy, Dec. 8, 1983).

Pontifical Oriental Institute of Religious Studies, Kottayam (July 3, 1982).

Faculty of Theology, Ranchi (Aug. 15, 1982).

St. Peter's Pontifical Institute of Theology, Bangalore (Jan. 6, 1985).

Indonesia: Wedabhakti Pontifical Faculty of Theology, Yogyakarta (Nov. 1, 1984).

Ireland: The Milltown Institute of Theology and Philosophy, Dublin (1932).

Israel: French Biblical and Archeological School, Jerusalem (founded 1890; approved Sept. 17, 1892; canonically approved to confer Doctorate in Biblical Science, June 29, 1983).

Italy: Theological Faculty of Southern Italy, Naples. Two sections: St. Louis Posillipo (Mar. 16, 1918) and St. Thomas Aquinas Capodimonte (Oct. 31, 1941).

Pontifical Theological Faculty of Sardinia, Cagliari, (Aug. 5, 1927).

Interregional Theological Faculty, Milan (Aug. 8, 1935; restructured 1969).

Faculty of Philosophy "Aloisianum," Gallarate (1937; Mar. 20, 1974).

Pontifical Ambrosian Institute of Sacred Music, Milan (Mar. 12, 1940).

Theological Faculty of Sicily, Palermo (Dec. 8, 1980).

Theological Institute Pugliese, Molfetta (June 24, 1992).

Theological Institute Calabro, Catanzaro (Jan. 28, 1993).

Theological Faculty of Central Italy, Florence (Sep. 9, 1997).

Japan: Faculty of Theology, Nagoya (May 25, 1984).

Kenya: Catholic Higher Institute of Eastern Africa, Nairobi (May 2, 1984).

Lebanon: Faculty of Theology, University of the Holy Spirit, Kaslik (May 30, 1982).

Madagascar: Superior Institute of Theology and Philosophy, at the Regional Seminary of Antananarivo, Ambatoroka-Antananarivo (Apr. 21, 1960).

Malta: Faculty of Theology, Tal-Virtù (Nov. 22, 1769), with Institute of Philosophy and Human Studies (Sept. 8, 1984).

Mexico: Theological Faculty of Mexico (June 29, 1982) and Philosophy (Jan. 6, 1986), Institute of Canon Law (Sept. 4, 1995), Mexico City.

Nigeria: Catholic Institute of West Africa, Port Harcourt (May 9, 1994).

Peru: Pontifical and Civil Faculty of Theology, Lima (July 25, 1571).

Poland: Pontifical Theological Faculty, Warsaw (May 3, 1988) with two sections: St. John Baptist (1837, 1920, Nov. 8, 1962) at the Metropolitan Seminary Duchowne, and St. Andrew Bobola – Bobolanum (Sept. 8, 1932).

Philosophical Faculty, Krakow (1932; Sept. 20, 1984).

Theological Faculty, Poznan (1969; pontifical designation, June 2, 1974).

Spain: Theological Faculty, Granada (1940; July 31, 1973).

Theological Faculty of San Esteban, Salamanca (1947; Oct. 4, 1972).

Theological Faculty of the North, of the Metropolitan Seminary of Burgos and the Diocesan Seminary of Vitoria (Feb. 6, 1967).

Theological Faculty of Catalunya, (Mar. 7, 1968), with the Institutes of Fundamental Theology (Dec. 28, 1984), Liturgy (Aug. 15, 1986) and Philosophy (July 26, 1988), Barcelona.

Theological Faculty "San Vicente Ferrer" (two sections), Valencia (Jan. 23, 1974).

Theological Faculty "San Damaso" (Sept. 19, 1996), Madrid.

Switzerland: Theological Faculty, Lucerne (Dec. 25, 1973).

Theological Faculty, Chur (Jan. 1, 1974).

Theological Faculty, Lugano (Nov. 20, 1993).

United States: St. Mary's Seminary and University, School of Theology, Baltimore (May 1, 1822).

St. Mary of the Lake Faculty of Theology, Mundelein, IL (Sept. 30, 1929).

Weston Jesuit School of Theology, Cambridge, MA (Oct. 18, 1932).

The Jesuit School of Theology, Berkeley, CA (Feb. 2, 1934, as "Alma College," Los Gatos, CA).

Faculty of Philosophy and Letters, St. Louis, MO (Feb. 2, 1934).

St. Michael's Institute, Jesuit School of Philosophy and Letters, Spokane, WA (Feb. 2, 1934).

Pontifical Faculty of Theology of the Immaculate Conception, Dominican House of Studies, Washington, DC (Nov. 15, 1941).

Also located in the **United States** are:

The Marian Library/International Marian Research Institute (IMRI), U.S. branch of Pontifical Theological Faculty "Marianum," University of Dayton, Dayton, OH 45469 (affil. 1976, inc. 1983).

John Paul II Institute for Studies on Marriage and the Family, U.S. section of Pontifical John Paul II Institute for Studies on Marriage and Family at the Pontifical Lateran University, 487 Michigan Ave. N.E., Washington, DC 20017 (Aug. 22, 1988).

Pontifical College Josephinum (Theologate and College) at Columbus, OH, is a national pontifical seminary. Established Sept. 1, 1888, it is directly under the auspices of the Vatican through the Apostolic Pro-Nuncio to the U.S., who serves as the seminary's chancellor.

Vietnam: Theological Faculty of the Pontifical National Seminary of St. Pius X, Dalat (July 31, 1965). Activities suppressed.

In addition to those listed above, there are other faculties of theology or philosophy in state universities and for members of certain religious orders only. These include:

Austria: Katholisch-Theologische Fakultät (1619), Universitätsstrasse, 1, A-5010 Salzburg, Österreich.

Katholisch-Theologische Fakultät (1365), Dr. Karl-Lueger-Ring, 1, A-1010 Wien, Österreich.

Theologische Fakultät (1586), Karl-Franzens-Universität, Universitätsplatz, 3, A-8010 Graz, Österreich.

Theologische Fakultät (1669), Leopold-Franzens-Universität, Karl-Rahner-Platz 1, A-6020 Innsbruck, Österreich.

Canada: Faculté de Theologie et Institut Supérieur de Science Religieuses (1878), University of Montreal, 3034, Bd. Edouard-Montpetit, C.P. 6128, Montral, QC H3C 3J7, Canada.

Croatia: Facolta di Teologia Cattolica nell'Università Statale de Split (1999), Zrinsko-Frankopanska, 19, 21000 Split, Hrvatska.

Katolicki Bogoslovni Fakultet u Zagrebu (1669), Vlaska 38, 10000 Zagreb, Hrvatska.

Czech Republic: Cyrilometodejska teologicka fakulta (1570), Univerzitni 22, 771-11 Olomouc, Ceska Republika.

Katolicka teologicka fakulta University Karlovy (1347), Thakurova 3, 160 00 Praha 6/Dejvice, Ceska Republika.

France: Faculté de Theologie Catholique (1567), 9, Place de l'Université, 67084 Strasbourg, France.

Germany: Katholisch-Theologische Fakultät, Universität Augsburg (1970), Universitätsstrasse 10, D-86159 Augsburg, Bundesrepublik Deutschland.

Katholisch-Theologische Fakultät, Universität Bamberg (1972), An der Universität 2, D-96045 Bamberg, Bundesrepublik Deutschland.

Katholisch-Theologische Fakultät (1965), Universität Ruhr, Universitätsstrasse 150, Postfach 102148, D-44801 Bochum, Bundesrepublik Deutschland.

Katholisch-Theologische Fakultät Universität Bonn (1818), Am Hof 1, D-53113 Bonn, Bundesrepublik Deutschland.

Theologische Fakultät (1657), Albert-Ludwigs Universität, Erbprinzstrasse 13, D-79098 Freiburg im Breisgau, Bundesrepublik Deutschland.

Fachbereich Katholische Theologie (1946), Johannes Gutenberg-Universität, Saarstrasse 21, D-55122, Mainz, Bundesrepublik Deutschland.

Katholisch-Theologische Fakultät (1472), Ludwig-Maximilians-Universität, Geschw.-Scholl-Platz 1, D-80539, München, Bundesrepublik Deutschland.

Katholisch-Theologische Fakultät (1780), WestfälischeWilhelms-Universität, Johannisstrasse 8-10, D-48143, Münster, Bundesrepublik Deutschland.

Katholisch-Theologische Fakultät (1978), Michaeligasse 13, D-94032, Passau, Bundesrepublik Deutschland.

Fachbereich Katholische Theologie (1962), Universitätsstrasse 31, D-93053 Regensburg, Bundesrepublik Deutschland.

Katholisch-Theologische Fakultät (1477), Eberhard-Karls-Universität Tübingen, Libermeisterstr., 18, D-72076 Tübingen, Bundesrepublik Deutschland.

Katholisch-Theologische Fakultät (1402), Bayerische Julius-Maximilians-Universität, Sanderring 2, D-97070 Würzburg, Bundesrepublik Deutschland.

Lithuania: Kataliku Teologijos Fakultetas (1922), Vilniaus 29, LT-3000 Kaunas, Lietuva.

Poland: Wydzial Teologiczny, Wydzial Prawa Kanonicznego, Wydzial Filozofii Chrzescijanskiej (1999), ul. Dewajtis, 5, 01-815 Warszawa, Polska.

Wydzial Teologiczny Uniwersytetu Slaskiego w Katowicach (2000), ul. Wita Stwosza 17 A, 40-042 Katowice, Polska.

Wydzial Teologii Uniwersytetu Warminsko-Mazurskiego w Olsztynie (1999), ul. Stanislawa Kard. Hozjusza, 15, 11-041 Olsztyn, Polska.

Wydzial Teologiczny (1994), ul. Drzymaly, 1/a, 45-342 Opole, Polska.

Wydzial Teologiczny Uniwersytetu Mikolaja Kopernika w. Toruniu (2001), pl. Bl. Ks. S. Frelichowskiego 1, 87-100, Torun, Polska.

Slovakia: Rimskokatolicka cyrilo-metodska bohoslovecka fakulta (1919), Archdiocese of Bratislava-Trnava, Kapitulska 26, 814-58 Bratislava, Slovenska Republika.

Slovenia: Teoloska Fakulteta v. Ljublana (1920), p.p. 2007, 1001 Ljubljana, Slovenia.

Switzerland: Theologische Fakultät (1889), University of Fribourg, Misericorde, CH-1700 Fribourg, Switzerland.

PONTIFICAL UNIVERSITIES AND INSTITUTES IN ROME

(*Source*: Annuario Pontificio.)

Pontifical Gregorian University (*Gregorian*) (1552): Piazza della Pilotta, 4, 00187 Rome. Associated with the university are: **Pontifical Biblical Institute** (May 7, 1909): Via della Pilotta, 25, 00187 Rome; **Pontifical Institute of Oriental Studies** (Oct. 15, 1917): Piazza S. Maria Maggiore, 7, 00185 Rome.

Pontifical Lateran University (1773): Piazza S. Giovanni in Laterano, 4, 00184 Rome. Attached to the university is the **Pontifical Institute of Studies of Marriage and the Family**, erected by Pope John Paul II, Oct 7, 1982; a section of the Institute was established at the Dominican House of Studies, Washington, DC, by a decree dated Aug. 22, 1988; sections were opened in Mexico in 1992 and Valencia, Spain, in 1994.

Pontifical Urbaniana University (1627): Via Urbano VIII, 16, 00165 Rome.

Pontifical University of St. Thomas Aquinas (*Angelicum*) (1580), of the Order of Preachers: Largo Angelicum, 1, 00184 Rome.

Pontifical University Salesianum (May 3, 1940; university designation May 24, 1973), of the Salesians of Don Bosco: Piazza dell'Ateneo Salesiano, 1, 00139 Rome. Associated with the university is the **Pontifical Institute of Higher Latin Studies**, known as the Faculty of Christian and Classical Letters (June 4, 1971).

Pontifical University della Santa Croce (of the Holy Cross) (Jan. 9, 1985), of the Personal Prelature of Opus Dei: Piazza S. Apollinare, 49, 00186 Rome.

Pontifical Athenaeum of St. Anselm (1687) of the Benedictines: Piazza Cavalieri di Malta, 5, 00153 Rome.

Pontifical Athenaeum Antonianum (of St. Anthony) (May 17, 1933), of the Order of Friars Minor: Via Merulana, 124, 00185 Rome.

Athenaeum Regina Apostolorum (Queen of the Apostles), of the Legionaries of Christ: Via Aurelia Antica, 460, 00165 Rome.

Pontifical Institute of Sacred Music (1911; May 24, 1931): Via di Torre Rossa, 21, 00165 Rome.

Pontifical Institute of Christian Archeology (Dec. 11, 1925): Via Napoleone III, 1, 00185 Rome.

Pontifical Theological Faculty St. Bonaventure (Dec. 18, 1587), of the Order of Friars Minor Conventual: Via del Serafico, 1, 00142 Rome.

Pontifical Theological Faculty, Pontifical Institute of Spirituality Teresianum (1935), of the Discalced Carmelites: Piazza San Pancrazio, 5-A, 00152 Rome.

Pontifical Theological Faculty Marianum (1398), of the Servants of Mary: Viale Trente Aprile, 6, 00153 Rome. Attached to the university is **The Marian Library/International Marian Research Institute** (IMRI), U.S. branch of Pontifical Theological Faculty *Marianum*, University of Dayton, Dayton, OH, 45469 (affil. 1976, inc. 1983).

Pontifical Institute of Arabic and Islamic Studies (1926), of the Missionaries of Africa: Viale di Trastevere, 89, 00153 Rome.

Pontifical Faculty of Educational Science Auxilium (June 27, 1970), of the Daughters of Mary, Help of Christians: Via Cremolino, 141, 00166 Rome.

Catholic Communications

CATHOLIC PRESS

Statistics

The *2003 Catholic Press Directory*, published by the Catholic Press Association, reported a total of 626 periodicals in North America, with a circulation of 26,874,009. The figures included 215 newspapers, with a circulation of 6,673,207; 242 magazines, with a circulation of 14,469,227; 125 newsletters, with a circulation of 4,564,597; and 44 other-language periodicals (newspapers and magazines), with a circulation of 1,166,978.

Newspapers in the U.S.

There were 203 newspapers in the United States, with a circulation 6,516,407. Six of these had national circulation totaling 219,616; 167 were diocesan newspapers with a total circulation of 5,984,534; 13 were Eastern Catholic Church publications with a total circulation of 80,261. Seventeen other publications were recently reclassified by the CPA from magazine to newspaper status to classify them correctly based on their actual format; they had a total circulation of 231,996.

National papers included: **National Catholic Register**, founded 1900; **Our Sunday Visitor**, founded 1912; **National Catholic Reporter**, founded 1964; **The Wanderer**, founded 1867; **The Adoremus Bulletin**, founded 1995; and the English-language weekly edition of *L'Osservatore Romano*, established in the U.S. in 1998.

The oldest U.S. Catholic newspaper is **The Pilot** of Boston, established in 1829 (under a different title).

Other diocesan newspapers: There were three other diocesan newspapers located outside continental North America (Samoa, U.S. Virgin Islands, West Indies), with a circulation of 21,500.

Magazines in U.S.

The *Catholic Press Directory* reported 229 magazines in the U.S., with a circulation of 13,688,952. In addition, there were 124 newsletters, with a circulation of 4,557,097.

America and **Commonweal** are the only weekly and biweekly magazines, respectively, of general interest. The monthly magazines with the largest circulation are **Columbia** (1,497,206), the official organ of the Knights of Columbus, **Catholic Digest** (400,000) and **St. Anthony's Messenger** (332,000).

Other-language publications: There were an additional 30 publications (newspapers and magazines) in the U.S. in languages other than English, with a circulation of 915,778.

Canadian Statistics

There were nine newspapers in Canada with a circulation of 135,300. These included three national newspapers (**The Catholic Register**, founded 1893; **Restoration**, founded 1947; and **Catholic New Times**, founded 1976) and six diocesan. There were 13 magazines, with a circulation of 780,275; one newsletter, with a circulation of 7,500; and 14 publications in languages other than English, with a circulation of 251,200.

CATHOLIC NEWSPAPERS, MAGAZINES, AND NEWSLETTERS IN THE U.S.

(*Sources:* Catholic Press Directory; The Catholic Journalist; Catholic Almanac *survey; Catholic News Service.*) *Abbreviation code: a, annual; bm, bimonthly; m, monthly; q, quarterly; w, weekly; bw, bi-weekly.*

Newspapers

Acadiana Catholic, m; 1408 Carmel Ave., Lafayette, LA 70501; (337) 261-5511; Lafayette diocese.

A.D. Times, bw; P.O. Box F, Allentown, PA 18105-1538; (610) 871-5200; Allentown diocese.

Adoremus Bulletin, The, 10 times a year; P.O. Box 3286, St. Louis, MO 63130; (314) 863-8385; www.adoremus.org; national liturgical journal.

Agua Viva, m; 1280 Med Park Dr., Las Cruces, NM 88005-3239; (505) 523-7577; www.dioceseof lascruces.org; Las Cruces diocese.

Alaskan Shepherd, bm; 1312 Peger Rd., Fairbanks, AK 99709; (904) 474-0753; www.cbna.org; Fairbanks diocese.

America (Ukrainian-English), 2 times a week; 817 N. Franklin St., Philadelphia, PA 19123; (215) 627-4519; Providence Association of Ukrainian Catholics in America.

Anchor, The, w; P.O. Box 7, Fall River, MA 02722; (508) 675-7151; Fall River diocese.

Arkansas Catholic, w; P.O. Box 7417, Little Rock, AR 72217; (501) 664-0125; Little Rock diocese.

Arlington Catholic Herald, w; 200 N. Glebe Rd., Suite 607, Arlington, VA 22203; (703) 841-2590; www.catholicherald.com; Arlington diocese.

Atchison Benedictines, q; Mt. St. Scholastica Convent, 801 S. 8th St., Atchison, KS 66002; (913) 360-6200.

Bayou Catholic, The, w; P.O. Box 505, Schriever, LA 70395; (985) 850-3132; Houma-Thibodaux diocese.

Beacon, The, w; P.O. Box 1887, Clifton, NJ 07015-1887; (973) 279-8845; www.patersondiocese.org; Paterson diocese.

Bishop's Bulletin, m; 523 N. Duluth Ave., Sioux Falls, SD 57104-2714; (605) 988-3791; www.sfcatholic.org; Sioux Falls diocese.

Bolletino, m; 675 Hegenberger Rd., Suite 110, Oakland, CA 94621; (510) 633-9058; www.icf.org; Italian Catholic Federation.

Byzantine Catholic World, bw; 66 Riverview Ave., Pittsburgh, PA 15214; (412) 231-4000; Pittsburgh Byzantine archdiocese.

Catholic Accent, 40 times a year; 725 E. Pittsburgh St., Greensburg, PA 15601; (724) 834-4010; www.dioceseofgreensburg.org; Greensburg diocese.

Catholic Advance, The, w; 424 N. Broadway, Wichita, KS 67202-2377; (316) 269-3965; www.cdowk.org; Wichita diocese.

Catholic Advocate, The, w; 171 Clifton Ave., Newark, NJ 07104-9500; (973) 497-4200; www.catholic advocate@rcan.org; Newark archdiocese.

Catholic Aid News, m; 3499 N. Lexington Ave., St. Paul, MN 55126; (651) 490-0170; www.catholic aid.com.

Catholic Anchor, w; 225 Cordova St., Anchorage, AK 99501; (907) 297-7708; Anchorage diocese.

Catholic Calendar, semi-monthly; 411 Iris St., Lake Charles, LA 70601; (337) 439-7426; www.lcdiocese.org; one page in local newspaper twice a month; Lake Charles diocese.

Catholic Chronicle, bw; P.O. Box 1866, Toledo, OH 43603-1866; (419) 244-6711; www.catholic chronicle.org; Toledo diocese.

Catholic Commentator, The, bw; P.O. Box 14746, Baton Rouge, LA 70898-4746; (225) 387-0983; www.diobr.com; Baton Rouge diocese.

Catholic Connector, The, m; 660 Burton, SE, Grand Rapids, MI 49507; (616) 243-0491; www.dio ceseofgrandrapids.org; Grand Rapids diocese.

Catholic Courier, w; P.O. Box 24379, Rochester, NY 14624-0379; (585) 529-9530; www.catholic courier.com; Rochester diocese.

Catholic East Texas, bw; 1015 ESE Loop 323, Tyler, TX 75701-9663; (903) 534-1077; Tyler diocese.

Catholic Explorer, w (bw July, Aug.); 402 S. Independence Blvd., Romeoville, IL 60446-2264; (815) 838-6475; www.dioceseofjoliet.org/explorer; Joliet diocese.

Catholic Exponent, bw; P.O. Box 6787, Youngstown, OH 44501-6787; (330) 744-5251; www.doy.org; Youngstown diocese.

Catholic Free Press, w; 51 Elm St., Worcester, MA 01609; (508) 757-6387; www.catholicfreepress.org; Worcester diocese.

Catholic Health World, semi-monthly; 4455 Woodson Rd., St. Louis, MO 63134-3797; (314) 427-2500; www.chausa.org; Catholic Health Association.

Catholic Herald, The, m; 29 W. Kiowa St., Colorado Springs, CO 80903; (719) 685-5202; Colorado Springs diocese.

Catholic Herald, w; P.O. Box 070913, Milwaukee, WI 53207-0913; (414) 769-3500; www.execpc.com/~chn; Milwaukee archdiocese; also publishes editions for Madison and Superior dioceses.

Catholic Herald: Madison Edition, w; P.O. Box 44985, Madison, WI 53744-4985; (608) 821-3070; www.madisoncatholicherald.org; Madison diocese.

Catholic Herald: Superior Edition, w; P.O. Box 969, Superior, WI 54880; (715) 392-8268; www.catholic herald.org; Superior diocese.

Catholic Herald, bw; 5890 Newman Ct., Sacramento, CA 95819; (916) 452-3344; Sacramento diocese.

Catholic Islander, m; P.O. Box 301825, St. Thomas, USVI, 00803-1825; (340) 774-3166; Virgin Islands diocese.

Catholic Journalist, The, m; 3555 Veterans Highway, Unit O, Ronkonkoma, NY 11779; (631) 471-4730; www.catholicpress.org; Catholic Press Association.

Catholic Key, 44 times a year; P.O. Box 419037, Kansas City, MO 64141-6037; (816) 756-1850; www.catholickey.org; Kansas City-St. Joseph diocese.

Catholic Light, bw; 300 Wyoming Ave., Scranton, PA 18503; (570) 207-2229; www.dioceseof scranton.org; Scranton diocese.

Catholic Lighthouse, m; P.O. Box 4070, Victoria, TX 77903; (361) 573-0828; Victoria diocese.

Catholic Messenger, w; P.O. Box 460, Davenport, IA 52805; (563) 323-9959; Davenport diocese.

Catholic Mirror The, m; 601 Grand Ave., Des Moines, IA 50309; (515) 244-6234; www.dmdio cese.org; Des Moines diocese.

Catholic Missourian, w; P.O. Box 1107, Jefferson City, MO 65102-1107; (573) 635-9127; Jefferson City diocese.

Catholic Moment, The, w; P.O. Box 1603, Lafayette, IN 47902; (765) 742-2050; www.dioceseof lafayette.org; Lafayette diocese.

Catholic New World, The, w; 721 N. La Salle St., Chicago, IL 60610; (312) 655-7777; www.catholic newworld.com; Chicago archdiocese.

Catholic New York, w; 1011 First Ave., New York, NY 10022; (212) 688-2399; www.cny.org; New York archdiocese.

Catholic News, w; P.O. Box 85, Independence Square, Port-of-Spain, Trinidad, West Indies; (868) 623-6093; www.catholicnews-tt.net.

Catholic News and Herald, The, w; P.O. Box 37267, Charlotte, NC 28237; (704) 370-3333; www.charlottediocese.org; Charlotte diocese.

Catholic Northwest Progress, The, w; 910 Marion St., Seattle, WA 98104; (206) 382-4850; www.seattleearch.org; Seattle archdiocese.

Catholic Observer, bw; Box 1730, Springfield, MA 01101-1730; (413) 737-4744; Springfield diocese.

Catholic Peace Voice, q.; 532 W. Eighth St., Erie, PA 16502-1343; (814) 453-4955; www.paxchristi usa.org; published by Pax Christi.

Catholic Post, The, w; P.O. Box 1722, Peoria, IL 61656; (309) 673-3603; www.cdop.org/post; Peoria diocese.

Catholic Register, bw; P.O. Box 413, Hollidaysburg, PA 16648; (814) 695-7563; Altoona-Johnstown diocese.

Catholic Review, w; P.O. Box 777, Baltimore, MD 21203; (443) 524-3150; www.catholicreview.org; Baltimore archdiocese.

Catholic San Francisco, bw; One Peter Yorke Way, San Francisco, CA 94109; (415) 614-5630; San Francisco archdiocese.

Catholic Sentinel, w; P.O. Box 18030, Portland, OR 97218-0030; (503) 281-1191; www.sentinel.org; Portland archdiocese, Baker diocese.

Catholic Spirit, The, w; 244 Dayton Ave., Ste. 2, St. Paul, MN 55102-1893; (651) 291-4444; www.thecatholicspirit.com; St. Paul and Minneapolis archdiocese.

Catholic Spirit, The, w; P.O. Box 191, Metuchen, NJ 08840-0969; (732) 562-1990; www.catholic spirit.com; Metuchen diocese.

Catholic Spirit, The, m; P.O. Box 13327, Austin, TX 78711; (512) 476-4888; www.austindiocese.org; Austin diocese.

Catholic Spirit, The, m; P.O. Box 951, Wheeling, WV 26003-0119; (304) 233-0880; www.dwc.org; Wheeling-Charleston diocese.

Catholic Standard, w; P.O. Box 4464, Washington, DC, 20017; (202) 281-2410; www.cathstan.org; Washington archdiocese.

Catholic Standard and Times, w; 222 N. 17th St., Philadelphia, PA 19103; (215) 587-3660; www.archdiocese-phl.org/cs&t; Philadelphia archdiocese.

Catholic Star Herald, w; 15 North 7th St., Camden, NJ 08102; (856) 756-7900; Camden diocese.

Catholic Sun, The, semi-monthly; P.O. Box 13549, Phoenix, AZ 85002; (602) 257-5565; www.catholic sun.org; Phoenix diocese.

Catholic Sun, The, w; 421 S. Warren St., Syracuse, NY 13202; (315) 422-8153; Syracuse diocese.

Catholic Telegraph, w; 100 E. 8th St., Cincinnati, OH 45202; (513) 421-3131; www.catholic cincinnati.org; Cincinnati archdiocese.

Catholic Times, w; 197 E. Gay St., Columbus, OH 43215-3229; (614) 224-5195; www.ctonline.org; Columbus diocese.

Catholic Times, The, w; P.O. Box 4248, Flint, MI 48504; (810) 659-4670; Lansing diocese.

Catholic Times, The, w; P.O. Box 4004, La Crosse, WI 54602-4004; (608) 788-1524; www.diocese oflacrosse.com; La Crosse diocese.

Catholic Times, w; P.O. Box 3187, Springfield, IL 62708-3187; (217) 698-8500; Springfield diocese.

Catholic Transcript, w; 467 Bloomfield Ave., Bloomfield, CT 06002; (860) 286-2828; Hartford archdiocese; Bridgeport and Norwich dioceses.

Catholic Universe Bulletin, bw; 1027 Superior Ave. NE, Cleveland, OH 44114-2556; (216) 696-6525; www.catholicuniversebulletin.org; Cleveland diocese.

Catholic Virginian, bw; Box 26843, Richmond, VA 23220; (804) 359-5654; www.catholicvirginia.org; Richmond diocese.

Catholic Vision, m.; P.O. Box 31, Tucson, AZ 85702; (520) 792-3410; www.catholicvision.org; Tuscon diocese.

Catholic Voice, The, bw; 3014 Lakeshore Ave., Oakland, CA 94610; (510) 893-5339; Oakland diocese.

Catholic Voice, The, bw; P.O. Box 4010, Omaha, NE 68104-0010; (402) 558-6611; www.tcv omaha.com; Omaha archdiocese.

Catholic War Veteran, bm; 441 N. Lee St., Alexandria, VA 22314-2344; (703) 549-3622; www.cwv.org.

Catholic Week, The, w; P.O. Box 349, Mobile, AL 36601; (334) 432-3529; Mobile archdiocese.

Catholic Weekly, The, w; 1520 Court St., Saginaw, MI 48602; (989) 793-7661; Saginaw diocese.

Catholic Weekly, The, w; P.O. Box 1405, Saginaw, MI 48602; (989) 793-7661; Gaylord diocese.

Catholic Witness, The, bw; P.O. Box 2555, Harrisburg, PA 17105; (717) 657-4804; Harrisburg diocese.

Catholic Women's Network, bm; 877 Spinosa Dr., Sunnyvale, CA 94087; (408) 245-8663; www.catholic womensnet.org.

Catholic Workman, m; P.O. Box 47, New Prague, MN 56071; (952) 758-2229; www.catholic workman.com.

Catolico de Texas, El (Spanish), m; P.O. Box 190347, Dallas, TX 75219; (214) 528-8792; Dallas diocese.

Centinela, El (Spanish), m; P.O.Box 18030, Portland, OR 97218-0300; (503) 281-1191.

Central Washington Catholic, bm; 5301-A Tieton Dr., Yakima, WA 98908; (509) 965-7117; Yakima diocese.

Chicago Catolico (Spanish), m; 721 N. La Salle St., 4th Floor, Chicago, IL 60610; (312) 655-7880; Chicago archdiocese.

Christian Renewal News, q; P.O. Box 547, Fillmore, CA 93016-0547; (805) 524-5890; www.theservantsandhandmaids.com; Apostolate of Christian Renewal.

Chronicle of Catholic Life, bm; 1001 North Grand Ave., Pueblo, CO 81003; (719) 685-5202; www.diocesenet.com; Pueblo diocese.

Church Today, twice a month; P.O. Box 7417, Alexandria, LA 71306-0417; (318) 445-2401; www.diocesealex.org, Alexandria diocese.

Church World, The, w; P.O. Box 11559, Portland, ME 04104; (207) 773-6471; Portland diocese.

Clarion Herald, bw; P.O. Box 53247, New Orleans, LA 70153; (504) 596-3035; www.clarionherald,org; New Orleans archdiocese.

Compass, The, w; P.O. Box 23825, Green Bay, WI 54305-3825; (920) 437-7531; www.gbdioc.org; Green Bay diocese.

Courier, The, m; 55 W. Sanborn St., P.O. Box 949, Winona, MN 55987-0949; (507) 454-4643; www.dow.org; Winona diocese.

Credo, bw; P.O.Box 504, Ann Arbor, MI 48106; (734) 930-3100.

Criterion, The, w; P.O. Box 1717, Indianapolis, IN 46206; (317) 236-1570; www.archindy.org/criterion; Indianapolis archdiocese.

Cross Roads, bw; 1310 W. Main St., Lexington, KY 40508-2040; (859) 253-1993; Lexington diocese.

Dakota Catholic Action, m (except July); P.O. Box 1137, Bismarck, ND 58502-1137; (701) 222-3035; www.bismarckdiocese.com; Bismarck diocese.

Denver Catholic Register, w; 1300 S. Steele St., Denver, CO 80210-2599; (303) 715-3215; www.archden.org; Denver archdiocese.

Dialog, The, w; P.O. Box 2208, Wilmington, DE 19899; (302) 573-3109; www.edow.org/dialog.html; Wilmington diocese.

East Tennessee Catholic, The, bw; P.O. Box 11127, Knoxville, TN 37939-1127; (865) 584-3307; www.etcatholic.com; Knoxville diocese.

East Texas Catholic, semi-monthly; P.O. Box 3948, Beaumont, TX 77704-3948; (409) 832-3944; Beaumont diocese.

Eastern Catholic Life, bw; 445 Lackawanna Ave.,

W. Paterson, NJ 07424; (201) 890-7794; Passaic Byzantine eparchy.

Eastern Oklahoma Catholic, bw; Box 690240, Tulsa, OK 74169-0240; (918) 294-1904; www.dioceseoftulsa.org; Tulsa diocese.

Eternal Flame (Armenian-English), 110 E. 12th St., New York, NY 10003; (212) 477-2030; Armenian exarchate.

Evangelist, The, w; 40 N. Main Ave., Albany, NY 12203; (518) 453-6688; www.evangelist.org; Albany diocese.

Fairfield County Catholic, m; 238 Jewett Ave., Bridgeport, CT 06606; (203) 372-4301; www.bridgeportdiocese.org; Bridgeport diocese.

Florida Catholic, The, w; P.O. Box 609512, Orlando, FL 32860-9512; (407) 660-9141; www.the floridacatholic.org, Orlando diocese; publishes editions for Miami archdiocese and Palm Beach, Pensacola-Tallahassee, St. Petersburg and Venice dioceses.

Florida Catholic: Miami Edition, w; 9401 Biscayne Blvd., Miami, FL 33138; (305) 762-1131; www.thefloridacatholic.org.

Florida Catholic: Palm Beach Edition, w; P.O. Box 109650, Palm Beach Gardens, FL 33410-9650; (561) 775-9528; www.thefloridacatholic.org, Palm Beach diocese.

Florida Catholic: Pensacola-Tallahassee Edition, w; P.O. Drawer 17329, Pensacola, FL 32522; (904) 432-5215; www.thefloridacatholic.org.

Florida Catholic: St. Petersburg Edition, w; P.O. Box 43022, St. Petersburg, FL 33743; (727) 345-3338.

Florida Catholic: Venice Edition, w; 1000 Pinebrook Rd., Venice, FL 34292; (941) 484-9543; www.thefloridacatholic.org.

Four County Catholic, m; 1595 Norwich New London Turnpike, Uncasville, CT 06382; (860) 848-2237; www.norwichdiocese.org; Norwich diocese.

Georgia Bulletin, w; 680 W. Peachtree St. NW, Atlanta, GA 30308; (404) 877-5500; www.archatl.com; Atlanta archdiocese.

Glasilo KSKJ Amerikanski Slovenec (Slovenian), bw; 708 E. 159th, Cleveland, OH 44110; (216) 541-7243; American Slovenian Catholic Union.

Globe, The, w; P.O. Box 5079, Sioux City, IA 51102; (712) 255-2550; Sioux City diocese.

Good News for the Diocese of Kalamazoo, The, m; 215 N. Westnedge, Kalamazoo, MI 49007-3760; (616) 349-8714; www.dioceseofkalamazoo.org; Kalamazoo diocese.

Gulf Pine Catholic, w; P.O. Box 1189, Biloxi, MS 39533-1189; (228) 702-2127; Biloxi diocese.

Harvest, The, 121 23rd St. South, Great Falls, MT 59405; (406) 727-6683; www.dioceseofgfb.org; Great Falls diocese.

Hawaii Catholic Herald, bw; 1184 Bishop St., Honolulu, HI 96813; (808) 533-1791; Honolulu diocese.

Heraldo Catolico, El (Spanish), bw; 5890 Newman Ct., Sacramento, CA 95819; (916) 733-0680; Sacramento diocese.

Hlas Naroda (Voice of the Nation) (Czech-English), bw; 2340 61st Ave., Cicero, IL 60650; (708) 656-1050.

Holy Smoke: Our Lady of the Hills Church, six

times a year; 2700 Ashland Rd., Columbia, SC 29210; (803) 772-7400.

Horizons, twice a month; 1900 Carlton Rd., Parma, OH 44134-3129; (216) 741-3312; www.parma.org; Parma Byzantine eparchy.

Idaho Catholic Register, twice a month; 303 Federal Way, Boise, ID 83705; (208) 342-1311; www.catholicidaho.org/icr.cfm; Boise diocese.

Inland Register, every 3 weeks; P.O. Box 48, Spokane, WA 99210; (509) 358-7340; www.diocese ofspokane.org; Spokane diocese.

Inside Passage, bw; 415 6th St., Juneau, AK 99801; (907) 586-2237; www.dioceseofjuneau.org, Juneau diocese.

Intermountain Catholic, w; P.O. Box 2489, Salt Lake City, UT 84110-2489; (801) 328-8641; www.icnp.com; Salt Lake City diocese.

Jednota (Slovak-Eng.), w; 6611 Rockside Rd., Independence, OH 44131; (216) 642-9406; First Catholic Slovak Union.

Lake Shore Visitor, w; P.O. Box 10668, Erie, PA 16514-0668; (814) 824-1160; www.eriecd.org; Erie diocese.

Leaven, The, w; 12615 Parallel Parkway, Kansas City, KS 66109; (913) 721-1570; www.the leaven.com; Kansas City archdiocese.

Long Island Catholic, The, w; P.O. Box 9000, Rockville Centre, NY 11575-9000; (516) 594-1000; www.licatholic.org; Rockville Centre diocese.

L'Osservatore Romano, w; P.O. Box 777, The Cathedral Foundation, Baltimore, MD, 21203; (443) 263-0248; www.catholicreview.org; English edition of the Vatican newspaper.

Maronites Today, m; 1320 East 51st St., Austin, TX 78723; (512) 458-3693; www.eparchyla.org; Maronite Epachy of Our Lady of Lebanon of Los Angeles.

Maronite Voice, The, m; 4611 Sadler Rd., Glen Allen, VA 23060; (804) 270-7234; www.stmaron.org; Eparchy of St. Maron of Brooklyn.

Message, The, w; P.O. Box 4169, Evansville, IN 47724-0169; (812) 424-5536; Evansville diocese.

Messenger, The, w; 2620 Lebanon Ave., Belleville, IL 62221; (618) 233-8670; www.belleville messenger.org; Belleville diocese.

Messenger, The, 45 times a year; P.O. Box 18068, Erlanger, KY 41018; (859) 283-6270; www.coving tondiocese.org; Covington diocese.

Michigan Catholic, The, w; 305 Michigan Ave., 4th Floor, Detroit, MI 48226; (313) 224-8000; Detroit archdiocese.

Mirror, The, w; 601 S. Jefferson Ave., Springfield, MO 65806-3143; (417) 866-0841; www.the mirror.org; Springfield-Cape Girardeau diocese.

Mississippi Catholic, w; 237 E. Amite St., P.O. Box 2130, Jackson, MS 39225-2130; (601) 969-1880; www.mississippicatholic.com; Jackson diocese.

Monitor, The, w; P.O. Box 5147, Trenton, NJ 08638-0147; (609) 406-7404; www.dioceseoftrenton.org; Trenton diocese.

Montana Catholic, The, 16 times a year; P.O. Box 1729, Helena, MT 59624; (406) 442-5820; www.diocesehelena.org; Helena diocese.

Narod Polski (Polish Nation) (Polish-Eng.) semi-monthly; 984 Milwaukee Ave., Chicago, IL 60622-4101; (773) 782-2600; www.prcua.com; Polish Roman Catholic Union of America.

National Catholic Register, w; 432 Washington Ave., North Haven, CT 06473; (203) 230-3800; www.ncregister.com; national.

National Catholic Reporter, w; P.O. Box 419281, Kansas City, MO 64141; (816) 531-0538; www.natcath.org; national.

National Jesuit News, m; 1616 P St. NW, Suite 300, Washington, DC 20036; (202) 462-0400; www.jesuit.org.

New Catholic Miscellany, The, w; 119 Broad St., Charleston, SC 29401; (843) 724-8375; www.catholic-doc.org; Charleston diocese.

New Earth, The, m; 244 Dayton Ave., Suite 2, St. Paul, MN 55102; (651) 291-4444; www.thecatholicspirit.com; Fargo diocese.

New Star, The, every 3 weeks; 2208 W. Chicago Ave., Chicago, IL 60622; (312) 772-1919; St. Nicholas of Chicago Ukrainian diocese.

NC Catholic, bw; 715 Nazareth St., Raleigh, NC 27606; (919) 821-9736; www.nccatholic.org; Raleigh diocese.

North Country Catholic, w; P.O. Box 326, Ogdensburg, NY 13669; (315) 393-2540; www.northcountrycatholic.org; Ogdensburg diocese.

North Texas Catholic, w; 800 West Loop 820 South, Fort Worth, TX 76108; (817) 560-3300; Fort Worth diocese.

Northern Nevada Catholic, m; 290 S. Arlington Ave., #200, Reno, NV 89501; (775) 826-1010; Reno diocese.

Northwest Indiana Catholic, w; 9292 Broadway, Merrillville, IN 46410-7088; (219) 769-9292; www.nwic@dcgary.org; Gary diocese.

Northwestern Kansas Register, w; P.O. Box 1038, Salina, KS 67402; (785) 827-8746; www.salinadiocese.org; Salina diocese.

Oblate World, The and Voice of Hope, twice a month; P.O. Box 680, Tewksbury, MA 01876; (978) 851-7258; www.omiusa.org; published by the Missionary Oblates of Mary Immaculate.

Observer, The, m; P.O. Box 2079, Monterey, CA 93942; (831) 373-2919; www.dioceseofmonterey.org. Monterey diocese.

Observer, The, m; 4545 W. 63rd St., Chicago, IL 60629; (312) 585-9500; Lithuanian Roman Catholic Federation of America.

Observer, The, twice a month; P.O. Box 7044, Rockford, IL 61126; (815) 399-4300; Rockford diocese.

One Voice, w; P.O. Box 10822, Birmingham, AL 35202; (205) 838-8305; Birmingham diocese.

Orange County Catholic, m.; P.O. Box 14195, Orange, CA 92863-1595; (714) 282-3023; Orange diocese.

Our Northland Diocese, semi-monthly; 1200 Memorial Dr., P.O. Box 610, Crookston, MN 56716; (218) 281-4553; www.crookston.org; Crookston diocese.

Our Sunday Visitor, w; 200 Noll Plaza, Huntington, IN 46750; (219) 356-8400; www.osv.com; national.

People of God, m; 4000 St. Joseph Pl. NW, Albu-querque, NM 87120; (505) 831-8188; Santa Fe archdiocese.

Pilot, The, w; 2121 Commonwealth Ave., Brighton, MA 02135-3193; (617) 746-5889; www.rcab.org; Boston archdiocese.

Pittsburgh Catholic, w; 135 First Ave., Suite 200, Pittsburgh, PA 15222-1506; (412) 471-1252; www.pittsburghcatholic.org; Pittsburgh diocese.

Prairie Catholic, m; 1400 6th St. North, New Ulm, MN 56073-2099; (507) 359-2966; www.dnu.org; New Ulm diocese.

Praxis Press, 10 times a year; P.O. Box 508, San Jose, CA 95103; (408) 370-4748.

Pregonero, El (Spanish), w; P.O. Box 4464, Washington, DC 20017; (202) 281-2440; www.elpreg.org; Washington archdiocese.

Providence Visitor, The, w; 184 Broad St., Providence, RI 02903; (401) 272-1010; www.providence visitor.com; Providence diocese.

Record, The, w; Maloney Center, 1200 S. Shelby St., Louisville, KY 40203-2600; (502) 636-0296; Louisville archdiocese.

Redwood Crozier, The, m; P.O. Box 1297, Santa Rosa, CA 95402; (707) 459-5710; Santa Rosa diocese.

Rio Grande Catholic, The, m; 499 St. Matthews St., El Paso, TX 79907; (915) 872-8414; El Paso diocese.

Saint Cloud Visitor, The, w; P. O. Box 1068, St. Cloud, MN 56302-1066; (320) 251-3022; www.stclouddiocese.org/visitor; St. Cloud diocese.

St. Louis Review, w; 20 Archbishop May Dr., St. Louis, MO 63119; (314) 792-7500; www.stlouisreview.com; St. Louis archdiocese.

Seasons, q; 5800 Weiss St., Saginaw, MI 48603-2799; (989) 797-6666; www.dioceseofsaginaw.org; Saginaw diocese.

Slovak Catholic Falcon (Slovak-English), w; 205 Madison St., P.O.Box 899, Passaic, NJ 07055; (973) 777-4010; Slovak Catholic Sokol.

Sooner Catholic, The, bw; P.O. Box 32180, Oklahoma City, OK 73123; (405) 721-1810; www.catharchdioceseok.org; Oklahoma City archdiocese.

Sophia, q; 200 E. North Ave., Northlake, IL 60164; (708) 865-7050; Newton Melkite eparchy.

South Plains Catholic, twice a month; P.O. Box 98700, Lubbock, TX 79499-8700; (806) 792-3943; www.catholiclubbock.org; Lubbock diocese.

South Texas Catholic, twice a month; P.O. Box 2620, Corpus Christi, TX 78403-2620; (361) 882-6191; www.goccn.org; Corpus Christi diocese.

Southern Cross, semi-monthly; P.O. Box 81869, San Diego, CA 92138; (858) 490-8266; www.thesoutherncross.org; San Diego diocese.

Southern Cross, The, w; 601 E. Liberty Street, Savannah, GA 31401-5196; (912) 201-4100; www.diosav.org; Savannah diocese.

Southern Nebraska Register, w; P.O. Box 80329, Lincoln, NE 68501; (402) 488-0090; Lincoln diocese.

Southwest Catholic, The, m; P.O. 411 Iris St., Lake Charles, LA 70601; (337) 439-7426; www.lcdiocese.org; Lake Charles diocese.

Southwest Kansas Register, bw; P.O. Box 137, Dodge City, KS 67801; (620) 227-1519; www.dcdiocese.org/swkregister; Dodge City diocese.

Sower (Ukrainian and English), bw; 14 Peveril Rd., Stamford, CT 06902; (203) 324-7698; www.the sower@adcus.com; Stamford Ukrainian diocese.

Spinnaker, 5 times a year; 610 W. Elm, Monroe, MI 48161; (313) 241-3660; IHM Sisters.

Star of Chaldeans (Arabic and English), bm; 25585 Berg Rd., Southfield, MI 48034; St. Thomas the Apostle Chaldean diocese.

Steubenville Register, bw; P.O. Box 160, Steubenville, OH 43952; (740) 282-3631; www.diosteub.org; Steubenville diocese.

Tablet, The, w; 310 Prospect Park West, Brooklyn, NY 11215-6214; (718) 965-7333; www.diocese ofbrooklyn.org/tablet; Brooklyn diocese.

Tautai, bw; P.O. Box 532, Feiloaimauso Hall, Apia, Samoa; Samoa-Apia archdiocese.

Tennessee Register, The, bw; 2400 21st Ave. S., Nashville, TN 37212; (615) 783-0770; Nashville diocese.

Texas Catholic, The, bw; P.O. Box 190346, Dallas, TX 75219; (214) 528-8792; Dallas diocese.

Texas Catholic Herald, The, twice a month; 1700 San Jacinto St., Houston, TX 77001-0907; (713) 659-5461; Galveston-Houston diocese.

Tidings, 11 times a year; 153 Ash St., Manchester, NH 03105-0310; (603) 669-3100; www.catholic churchnh.org; Manchester diocese.

Tidings, The, w; 3424 Wilshire Blvd, Los Angeles, CA 90010; (213) 637-7360; www.the-tidings.com; Los Angeles archdiocese.

Today's Catholic, w; P.O. Box 11169, Fort Wayne, IN 46856; (260) 456-2824; www.diocesefwsb.org; Fort Wayne-South Bend diocese.

Today's Catholic, bw; P.O. Box 28410, San Antonio, TX 78228-0410; (210) 734-2620; tcpaper@arch diosa.org; San Antonio archdiocese.

UNIREA (The Union) (Romanian) 10 times a year; P.O. Box 7189, Canton, OH 44714-0189; (330) 492-4086; Romanian diocese of Canton.

U. P. Catholic, The, semi-monthly; P.O. Box 548, Marquette, MI 49855; (906) 227-9131; www.up catholic.org; Marquette diocese.

Valley Catholic, m; 900 Lafayette St., Suite 301, Santa Clara, CA 95050-4966; (408) 983-0260; www.dsj.org/vc/valley; San Jose diocese.

Verelk (Armenian-English), bm; 1237 Pleasant Ave., Los Angeles, CA 90033; (213) 267-1740.

Vermont Catholic Tribune, bw; P.O. Box 489, Burlington, VT 05402; (802) 658-6110; www.vermon tcatholic.org; Burlington diocese.

Visitante, El (Spanish), w; Apartado 41305 – Est Minillas, San Juan, PR 00940-1305; (787) 728-3710; www.elvisitante.com; Puerto Rican Catholic Conference.

Voice of the Southwest, m; 414 N. Allen, Farmington, NM 87401; (505) 325-9743; Gallup diocese.

Voz Catolica, La (Spanish); m; 9401 Biscayne Blvd., Miami, FL 33138; (305) 762-1201; www.vozcat.com; Miami archdiocese.

Wanderer, The, w; 201 Ohio St., St. Paul, MN 55107; (651) 224-5733; national.

Way, The (Ukrainian-Eng.), bw; 827 N. Franklin St., Philadelphia, PA 19123; (215) 922-5231; Philadelphia archeparchy.

West Nebraska Register, w; P.O. Box 608, Grand Island, NE 68802; (308) 382-4660; Grand Island diocese.

West River Catholic, m; P.O. Box 678, Rapid City, SD 57709; (605) 343-3541; Rapid City diocese.

West Tennessee Catholic, w; P.O. Box 341669, Memphis, TN 38184-1669; (901) 373-1213; www.cdom.org; Memphis diocese.

West Texas Angelus, m; P.O. Box 1829, San Angelo, TX 76902; (915) 651-7500; www.san-angelo-diocese.org; San Angelo diocese.

West Texas Catholic, bw; P.O. Box 5644, Amarillo, TX 79117-5644; (806) 383-2243; www.amarillo diocese.org; Amarillo diocese.

Western Kentucky Catholic, m; 600 Locust St., Owensboro, KY 42301; (270) 683-1545; Owensboro diocese.

Western New York Catholic, m; 795 Main St., Buffalo, NY 14203-1250; (716) 847-8727; www.wny catholic.org; Buffalo diocese.

Witness, The, w; P.O. Box 917, Dubuque, IA 52004-0917; (319) 588-0556; Dubuque archdiocese.

Wyoming Catholic Register, m; P.O. Box 1468, Cheyenne, WY 82003; (307) 638-1530; Cheyenne diocese.

Magazines

Abbey Banner, The, 3 times a year; Saint John's Abbey, Collegeville, MN 56321; (320) 363-3875; www.sja.osb/abbeybanner.

AIM: Liturgy Resources, q; 3825 N. Willow Rd., Schiller Park, IL 60176-2309; (800) 566-6150.

America, w; 106 W. 56th St., New York, NY 10019; (212) 581-4640; www.americamagazine.org; Jesuits of U.S. and Canada.

American Benedictine Review, q; Assumption Abbey, Box A, Richardton, ND 58652; (701) 974-3315.

American Catholic Philosophical Quarterly (formerly **The New Scholasticism**), Fordham University, Bronx, NY 10458; (718) 817-4081; www.acpa-main.org; American Catholic Philosophical Assn.

American Catholic Studies; Villanova University, 800 Lancaster Ave., Villanova, PA 19085; (610) 519-5470.

The Annals of St. Anne de Beaupre, m; P.O. Box 1000, St. Anne de Beaupre, Quebec, GOA 3CO; (418) 827-4538.

Anthonian, The, q; c/o St. Anthony's Guild, Paterson, NJ 07509; (201) 777-3737; www.hnp.org/publications; St. Anthony's Guild.

Apostolate of the Little Flower, bm; P.O. Box 5280, San Antonio, TX 78201-0280; (210) 736-3889; Discalced Carmelite Fathers.

Barry Magazine, 2 times a year; 11300 NE 2nd Ave., Miami Shores, FL 33161; (305) 899-3188; Barry University.

Be Magazine, 6 times a year; 2020 Gillespie Way, El Cajon, CA 92020; (619) 387-7200; www.catholic.com.

Benedictines, m., 44 N. Mill St., Kansas City, KS 66101; (913) 342-0938; www.mountosb.com.

Bible Today, The, bm; Liturgical Press, Collegeville, MN 56321-7500; (320) 363-2213; www.litpress.org.

Bright Ideas; P.O. Box 510817, New Berlin, WI, 53151-0817; (800) 876-4574; www.4lpi.com.

Carmelite Digest, q; P.O. Box 2178, Relands, CA

92373-0701; (909) 793-0424; www.carmelite digest.org.

Carmelite Review, twice a month; 6725 Reed Rd., Houston, TX 77087-6830; (713) 644-8400; www.carmelnet.org/publications.htm; published by the Province of the Most Pure Heart of Mary of the Carmelite Order.

Catechist, The, 7 times a year; 2621 Dryden Rd., Dayton, OH 45439; (937) 293-1415; www.pflaum.com.

Catechumenate: A Journal of Christian Initiation, bm; 1800 N. Hermitage Ave., Chicago, IL 60622-1101; (773) 486-8970; www.ltp.org.

Catholic Answer, The, bm; 200 Noll Plaza, Huntington, IN 46750; (260) 356-8400; www.osv.com; Our Sunday Visitor, Inc.

Catholic Biblical Quarterly; Catholic University of America, Washington, DC 20064; (202) 319-5519; www.cba.cua.edu; Catholic Biblical Assn.

Catholic Cemetery, The, m; 710 N. River Rd., Des Plaines, IL 60016; (847) 824-8131; National Catholic Cemetery Conference.

Catholic Connection, The, m.; 3500 Fairfield Ave., Shreveport, LA 71104; (318) 868-4441; www.dioshpt.org; diocese of Shreveport.

Catholic Digest, m; 185 Willow St., Mystic, CT 06355; (860) 536-2611; www.catholicdigest.org.

Catholic Dossier, bm; P.O. Box 591120, San Francisco, CA 94159; (415) 387-2324; www.ignatius.com.

Catholic Faith, The, bm; P.O. Box 591090, San Francisco, CA 94159-1090; (415) 387-2324; www.ignatius.com.

Catholic Family News, m.; MPO Box 743, Niagara Falls, NY 14302; (905) 871-6292.

Catholic Historical Review, q; 620 Michigan Ave. N.E., Washington, DC 20064; (202) 319-5079; research.cua.edu/acha.

Catholic International, m; Cathedral Foundation, P.O. Box 777, Baltimore, MD 21203; (443) 524-3150; www.catholicreview.org.

Catholic Knights of America Journal, m; 1850 Dalton St., Cincinnati, OH 45214; (513) 721-0781; Catholic Knights of America.

Catholic Lawyer, q; St. John's University, 8000 Utopia Parkway, Jamaica, NY 11439; (718) 990-6655; St. Thomas More Institute for Legal Research.

Catholic Library World, q; 100 North St., #224, Pittsfield, MA 01201-5109; (413) 443-2252; www.cathla.org; Catholic Library Association.

Catholic Near East Magazine, bm; 1011 First Ave., New York, NY 10022; (212) 826-1480; www.cnewa.org; Catholic Near East Welfare Assn.

Catholic Outlook, m; 2830 E. 4th St., Duluth, MN 55812; (218) 724-9111; www.dioceseduluth.org; Duluth diocese.

Catholic Parent, bm; 200 Noll Plaza, Huntington, IN 46750; (260) 356-8400; www.osv.com; Our Sunday Visitor, Inc.

Catholic Pharmacist, q; 1012 Surrey Hills Dr., St. Louis, MO 63117-1438; (314) 645-0085; National Catholic Pharmacists Guild.

Catholic Press Directory, a; 3555 Veterans Highway, Unit O, Ronkonkoma, NY 11779; (631) 471-4730; www.catholicpress.com; Catholic Press Assn.

Catholic Quote, m; Valparaiso, NE 68065.

Catholic Review (Braille, tape, large print), bm; 154 E. 23rd St., New York, NY 10010; (212) 473-7800; Xavier Society for the Blind.

Catholic Southwest: A Journal of History and Culture, a; 1625 Rutherford Lane, Bldg. D, Austin, TX, 78754-5105; (512) 339-9882.

Catholic Telephone Guide, a. 210 North Ave., New Rochelle, NY 10801; (914) 632-1220; www.catholicguides.com; published by the Catholic New Publishing Co.

Catholic Woman, bm; 1275 K St. N.W., Suite 975, Washington, DC 20005; (202) 682-0334; www.nccw.org; National Council of Catholic Women.

Catholic Worker, 7 times a year; 36 E. First St., New York, NY 10003; (212) 677-8627; Catholic Worker Movement.

Catholic World Report, The, 11 times a year; P.O. Box 1328, Dedham, MA 02027 (editorial office); Ignatius Press.

Celebration, m; 115 E. Armour Blvd., Kansas City, MO 64111; (816) 968-2266; National Catholic Reporter Publishing Co.

Charities USA, q; 1731 King St., Suite 200, Alexandria, VA 22314; (703) 549-1390; www.catholiccharitiesusa.org.

Chesterton Review, The, q; Seton Hall University, 400 South Orange Ave., South Orange, NJ 07079; (973) 275-2430; G.K. Chesterton Society.

Chicago Studies, 3 times a year; 1800 N. Hermitage Ave., Chicago, IL 60622-1101; (800) 933-1800.

Christian Renewal News, q.; P.O. Box 547, Fillmore, CA 93016-0547; (805) 524-5890; www.theservantsandhandmaids.net; published by The Servants and Handmaids of the Sacred Heart of Jesus.

Christianity and the Arts, q; P.O. Box 118088, Chicago, IL 60611; (312) 642-8606; www.christianarts.net.

Church, q; 18 Bleeker St., New York, NY 10012; (212) 431-7825; www.nplc.org; National Pastoral Life Center.

CNEWA World, bm; 1011 First Ave., New York, NY 10022; (212) 826-1480; www.cnewa.org; Catholic Near East Welfare.

Columban Mission, 8 times a year; St. Columbans, NE 68056; (402) 291-1920; www.st.columban.org; Columban Fathers.

Columbia, m; One Columbus Plaza, New Haven, CT 06510; (203) 752-4398; www.kofc.org; Knights of Columbus.

Commonweal, bw; 475 Riverside Dr., Room 405, New York, NY 10115; (212) 662-4200; www.commonwealmagazine.org.

Communio: International Catholic Review, q; P.O. Box 4557, Washington, DC 20017-0557; (202) 526-0251; www.communio-icr.org.

Company, q; P.O. Box 60790, Chicago, IL 60660-0790; (773) 760-9432; www.companymagazine.com; Jesuit magazine.

Consecrated Life, semi-annually; P.O. Box 41007, Chicago, IL 60641; (773) 267-1195; www.religiouslife.com; Institute on Religious Life. English edition of *Informationes,* official publication of Congregation for Institutes of Consecrated Life and Societies of Apostolic Life.

Consolata Missionaries, bm; P.O. Box 5550, Somerset, NJ 08875-5550; (732) 297-9191; www.consolata.org.

Cord, The, m; Franciscan Institute, St. Bonaventure University, St. Bonaventure, NY 14778; (716) 375-

2160; www.franinst@sbu.edu; Franciscan Institute.

Counseling and Values, 3 times a year; College of Educational, Southern Illinois University, Carbondale, IL 62901; (618) 537-7791.

Crescat, 3 times a year; Belmont Abbey, Belmont, NC 28012; (704) 825-6707; Benedictine Monks.

Crisis, 11 times a year; 1814½ N St., N.W., Washington, DC 20036; (202) 861-7790; www.crisis magazine.com; journal of lay Catholic opinion.

Cross Currents, q; College of New Rochelle, New Rochelle, NY 10805; (914) 235-1439; www.aril.org; interreligious; Assn. for Religion and Intellectual Life.

Crusade Magazine, bm; P.O. Box 341, Hanover, PA 17331; (717) 225-9177; Foundation for a Christian Civilization, Inc.

CUA Magazine, 3 times a year; 620 Michigan Ave. N.E., Washington, DC 20064; (202) 319-5600; www.cua.edu; Catholic University of America.

Darbininkas (The Worker) (Lithuanian), w; 341 Highland Blvd., Brooklyn, NY 11207; (718) 827-1352; Lithuanian Franciscans.

Desert Call, q.; P.O. Box 219, Crestone, CO 81131-0219; (719) 256-4778; www.spirituallifeinstitute.org; published by the Spiritual Life Institute.

Desert Clarion, 10 times a year; 4519 Simmons St., North Las Vegas, NV 89031; (702) 657-0200; Las Vegas diocese.

Diakonia, 3 times a year; University of Scranton, Scranton, PA 18510-4643; (717) 941-6116; www.nyssa.cecs.uofs.edu/diaktoc.html; Center for Eastern Christian Studies.

Divine Word Missionaries, q; P.O. Box 6099, Techny, IL 60082-6099; (847) 272-7600; www.svd missions.org.

Don Bosco Alive/The Salesian Bulletin; 148 Main Street, New Rochelle, NY 10802-0639; (914) 636-4225; www.salesians.org.

Ecumenical Trends, m (except Aug.); Graymoor, Route 9, P.O. Box 306, Garrison, NY 10524-0306; (845) 424-2109; www.atonementfriars.org; Graymoor Ecumenical Institute.

Eglute (The Little Fir Tree) (Lithuanian), m; 13648 Kikapoo Trail, Lockport, IL 60441; (708) 301-6410; for children ages 5-10.

Emmanuel, 10 times a year; 5384 Wilson Mills Rd., Cleveland, OH 44143; (440) 449-2103; www.blessed sacrament.com; Congregation of Blessed Sacrament.

Envoy, bm; P.O. Box 585, Granville, OH 43023; (740) 587-2292; www.envoymagazine.com; journal of Catholic apologetics and evangelization.

Extension, m; 150 S. Wacker Dr., 20th Floor, Chicago, IL 60606; (312) 236-7240; www.catholic-extension.org; Catholic Church Extension Society.

Faith, 300 W. Ottawa St., Lansing, MI 48933-1577; (517) 342-2595.

Faith and Family, bm; 432 Washington Ave., North Haven, CT 06473; (203) 230-3800; formerly *Catholic Twin Circle*.

Faith and Reason, q; 134 Christendom Dr., Front Royal, VA 22630; (540) 636-2900.

Family Digest, The, bm; P.O. Box 40137, Fort Wayne, IN 46804 (editorial address); (952) 929-6765.

Family Friend, q; P.O. Box 11563, Milwaukee, WI 53211; (414) 961-0500; www.cfli.org; Catholic Family Life Insurance.

Fidelity, m; 206 Marquette Ave., South Bend, IN 46617; (219) 289-9786.

F.M.A. Focus, q; P.O. Box 598, Mt. Vernon, NY 10551; (914) 664-5604; Franciscan Mission Associates.

Forum Focus, q.; P.O. Box 542, Hudson, WI 54016-0542; (651) 276-1429; www.wandererforum.org.

Franciscan Studies, a; Franciscan Institute, St. Bonaventure, NY 14778; (716) 375-2105; www.franinst.sbu.edu; Franciscan Institute.

Franciscan Way, q; 1235 University Blvd., Steubenville, OH 43952; (740) 283-6450; www.fran univ.edu.

Fraternal Leader, q; P.O. Box 13005; Erie, PA 16514-1302; (814) 453-4331; Loyal Christian Benefit Association.

Fraternally Yours (Engish-Slovak), m; 24950 Chagrin Blvd., Beachwood, OH 44122; (216) 464-8015; First Catholic Slovak Ladies Assn.

Fuente de Misericordia, q; Eden Hill, Stockbridge, MA 01263; (413) 298-3691; www.marian.org; Congregation of Marians of the Immaculate Conception.

Glenmary Challenge, The, q; P.O. Box 465618, Cincinnati, OH 45246-5618; (513) 874-8900; www.glenmary.org; Glenmary Home Missioners.

God's Word Today, m; 2115 Summit Ave., St. Paul, MN 55105-1982; (651) 962-6738; www.godsword today.org; University of St. Thomas.

Good News, m; P.O. Box 432, Milwaukee, WI 53201-0432; (800) 876-4574; www.execpc.com/~lpi; Liturgical Publications.

Good News for Children, 32 times during school year; 2621 Dryden Rd., Suite 300, Dayton, OH 45439; (937) 293-1415; www.pflaum.com.

Good Shepherd (Dobry Pastier) (Slovak-English), a; 8200 McKnight Rd., Pittsburgh, PA 15237; (412) 364-3000.

Greyfriars Review, 3 times a year; Franciscan Institute, St. Bonventure University, St. Bonaventure, NY 14778; (716) 375-2105; www.franinst.sbu.edu; Franciscan Institute.

Growing with the Gospel, w; Publications Division, P.O. Box 432, Wisconsin, WI, 53201-0432; (800) 876-4574; www.execpc.com/~lpi.

Guide to Religious Ministries, A, a; 210 North Ave., New Rochelle, NY 10801; (914) 632-1220; www.catholicguides.com.

Guide to Religious Ministries for Catholic Men and Women, A, a; 210 North Ave., New Rochelle, NY 10801; (914) 632-1220; www.catholicguides.com.

Health Progress, bm; 4455 Woodson Rd., St. Louis, MO 63134-3797; (314) 427-2500; www.chausa.org; Catholic Health Association.

Hearts Aflame, q; P.O. Box 976, Washington, NJ 07882; (210) 689-1700; www.ewtn.com/Bluearmy/; for youth ages 13-23.

Homiletic and Pastoral Review, m; P.O. Box 591810, San Francisco, CA 94159-1810; (415) 387-2324.

Horizon, q; 5420 S. Cornell Ave., #105, Chicago, IL 60615-5604; (773) 363-5454.

Horizons, 2 times a year; Villanova University, Villanova, PA 19085; (610) 519-7302; College Theology Society.

Human Development, q; 5401 South Cornell Ave., Chicago, IL 60615-5698; (773) 684-8146; www.ctu.edu/cishs.html.

ICSC Resource; 1275 K St. N.W., Suite 980, Washington, DC, 20005-4006; (202) 289-1093; www.catholicstewardship.org; published by International Catholic Stewardship Council.

Immaculata, bm; 1600 W. Park Ave., Libertyville, IL 60048; (847) 367-7800; www.marytown.com.

Immaculate Heart Messenger, q; P.O. Box 158, Alexandria, SD 57311-0158; (800) 271-6279; www.fatimafamily.org.

In a Word, m; 199 Seminary Dr., Bay Saint Louis, MS 39520-4626; (601) 467-1097; www.inaword.com; Society of the Divine Word.

Jesuit Bulletin, 3 times a year; 3601 Lindell Blvd., St. Louis, MO 63108; (314) 977-7363; www.jesuitsmis.org; Jesuit Seminary Aid Association.

Jesuit Journeys, 3 times a year; 3400 W. Wisconsin Ave., Milwaukee, WI 53208-0288; (414) 937-6949; www.jesuitswisprov.org.

Josephinum Journal of Theology, twice a year; 7625 N. High St., Columbus, OH 43235; (614) 985-2278; www.pcj.edu.

Josephite Harvest, The, q; 1130 N. Calvert St., Baltimore, MD 21202-3802; (410) 727-2233; www.josephite.com; Josephite Missionaries.

Jurist, The, semi-annually; Catholic University of America, Washington, DC 20064; (202) 319-5439; Department of Canon Law.

Kinship, q; P.O. Box 22264, Owensboro, KY 42304; (270) 686-8401; www.glenmarysisters.org; Glenmary Sisters.

Knights of St. John International, q; 89 South Pine Ave., Albany, NY 12208; (518) 453-5675; www.members.tripod.com/ksji/knights/ksji.html.

Law Briefs, m; 3211 Fourth St. N.E., Washington DC 20017; (202) 541-3300; Office of General Counsel, USCCB.

Lay Witness, m; 827 North Fourth St., Steubenville, OH, 43952; (740) 283-2484; www.cuf.org; Catholics United for the Faith.

Leaflet Missal, 16565 South State St., S. Holland, IL 60473; (708) 331-5485; www.leafletmissal.com.

Leaves, bm; P.O. Box 87, Dearborn, MI 48121-0087; (313) 561-2330; www.rc.net/detroit/marianhill/leaves.htm; Mariannhill Mission Society.

Liguorian, m; 1 Liguori Dr., Liguori, MO 63057; (636) 464-2500; www.liguori.org; Redemptorists.

Linacre Quarterly; P.O. Box 757, Pewaukee, WI 53072; (262) 523-6201; Catholic Medical Association (National Federation of Catholic Physicians Guilds).

Liturgia y Cancion (Spanish and English), q; 5536 NE Hassalo, Portland, OR 97213; (800) 548-8749; Oregon Catholic Press.

Liturgical Catechesis, 6 times a year; 160 E. Virginia St., #290, San Jose, CA 95112; (408) 286-8505; www.rpinet.com/lc.

Liturgy Planner, The, semi-annual; P.O. Box 13071, Portland, OR 97213; (503) 331-2965.

Living City, m; P.O. Box 837, Bronx, NY 10465; (718) 828-2932; www.rc.net/focolare.org; Focolare Movement.

Living Faith: Daily Catholic Devotions, q; 1564 Fencorp Dr., Fenton, MO 63026-2942; (636) 305-9777; www.livingfaith.com.

Living Light, The, q; 3211 Fourth St. N.E., Washington, DC 20017; (202) 541-3453; www.usccb.org/education/catechetics/livinglt.htm; Department of Education, USCCB.

Magnificat, m.; Dunwoodie, 201 Seminary Ave., Yonkers, NY 10704; (914) 377-8513; www.magnificat.net.

Marian Helper, q.; Eden Hill, Stockbridge, MA 01263; (413) 298-3691; www.marian.org.

Marriage, bm; 955 Lake Dr., St. Paul, MN 55120; (651) 454-7947; www.marriagemagazine; International Marriage Encounter.

Mary's Shrine, 2 times a year; 400 Michigan Ave. N.E., Washington, DC 20017-1566; (202) 526-8300; www.nationalshrine.com; Basilica of National Shrine of the Immaculate Conception.

Maryknoll, m; Maryknoll, NY 10545-0308; (914) 941-7590; www.maryknoll.org; Catholic Foreign Mission Society.

Matrimony, q; 215 Santa Rosa Pl., Santa Barbara, CA 93109; (805) 965-9541; Worldwide Marriage Encounter.

Medical Mission News, q; 10 W. 17th St., New York, NY 10011; (212) 242-7757; www.cmmb.org; Catholic Medical Mission Board, Inc.

Medjugorje Magazine, q; 317 W. Ogden Ave., Westmont, IL 60559; (630) 968-4684; www.medjugor.com.

Migration World, 5 times a year; 209 Flagg Pl., Staten Island, NY 10304; (718) 351-8800; www.cmsny.org; Center for Migration Studies.

Ministry & Liturgy, m.; 160 E. Virginia St., #290, San Jose, CA 95112; (408) 286-8505; www.rpinet.com.

Miraculous Medal, q; 475 E. Chelten Ave., Philadelphia, PA 19144; (215) 848-1010; www.cmphila.org/camm; Central Association of the Miraculous Medal.

Mission, q; 1663 Bristol Pike, Bensalem, PA 19020-8502; (215) 244-9900; www.katharinedrexel.org; Sisters of the Blessed Sacrament.

MISSION Magazine, q; 366 Fifth Ave., New York, NY 10001; (212) 563-8700; www.propfaith.org; Society for Propagation of the Faith.

Mission Helper, The, q; 1001 W. Joppa Rd., Baltimore, MD 21204-3787; (410) 823-8585; Mission Helpers of the Sacred Heart.

Missionhurst, bm; 4651 N. 25th St., Arlington, VA 22207; (703) 528-3804; www.missionhurst.org.

Modern Schoolman, The, q; St. Louis University, P.O. Box 56907, St. Louis, MO 63156; (314) 997-3149; St. Louis University Philosophy Department.

Momento Catolico, El; 205 W. Monroe St., Chicago, IL, 60606; (312) 236-7782; www.hmrc.claretianpubs.org.

Momentum, q; Suite 100, 1077 30th St. N.W., Washington, DC 20007-3852; (202) 337-6232; www.ncea.org; National Catholic Educational Association.

Mountain Spirit, The, bm; P.O. Box 459, Hagerhill, KY 41222; (606) 789-9791; www.chrisapp.org; Christian Appalachian Project.

My Daily Visitor, bm; 200 Noll Plaza, Huntington, IN 46750; (260) 356-8400; www.osv.com; Our Sunday Visitor, Inc.

My Friend – The Catholic Magazine for Kids, 10 times a year; 50 St. Paul's Ave., Jamaica Plain, Boston, MA 02130; (617) 522-8911; www.myfriend magazine.org; for children ages 6-12.

National Apostolate for Inclusion Ministry, q; P.O. Box 218, Riverdale, MD, 20738-0218; (301) 699-9500; www.nafim.org.

National Catholic Forester, q; 320 S. School St., Mt. Prospect, IL 60056; (847) 342-4500; www.ncsf.com.

National Catholic Rural Life, bi-annual; 4625 Beaver Ave., Des Moines, IA 50310; (515) 270-2634; www.ncrlc.com.

NETWORK Connection, bm; 801 Pennsylvania Ave. S.E., #460, Washington, DC 20003; (202) 547-5556; www.networklobby.org; Network.

New Oxford Review, 10 issues a year; 1069 Kains Ave., Berkeley, CA 94706; (510) 526-5374; www.newoxfordreview.org.

Notebook, The, q; CMICA-USA, 3049 4 St. N.E., Washington, DC 20017; (202) 269-6672; www.pax romana.org; Catholic Movement for Intellectual and Cultural Affairs.

Notre Dame Magazine, q; Notre Dame University, Notre Dame, IN 46556; (574) 631-5335; www.nd.edu /~mdmag.

Nova-Voice of Ministry, bm; P.O. Box 432, Milwaukee, WI 53201; (800) 876-4574; www.exec pc.com/~lpi; Liturgical Publications.

Old Testament Abstracts, 3 times a year; 320 Caldwell Hall, Catholic University of America, Washington, DC 20064; (202) 319-5519.

Origins, 48 times a year; 3211 4th St. NE, Washington, DC 20017; (202) 541-3284; documentary service.

Ozanam News, The, twice a year; 58 Progress Parkway, St. Louis, MO 63043-3706; (314) 576-3993; www.svdpuscouncil.org; Society of St. Vincent de Paul.

Palabra Entre Nosotros, La, bm; 9639 Dr. Perry Rd., Unit 126N, Jamesville, MD, 21754; (301) 831-1262; www.wau.org.

Parish Liturgy, q; 16565 S. State St., S. Holland, IL 60473; (708) 331-5485; www.parishliturgy.com.

Partners Magazine: Chicago Province of the Society of Jesus, 3 times a year; 2059 N. Sedgwick St., Chicago, IL 60614; (773) 975-8181; www.jesuits-chi.org.

Passionists' Compassion, The, q; 526 Monastery Pl., Union City, NJ 07087; (201) 864-0018; www.cptryon.org.

Pastoral Life, m; Box 595, Canfield, OH 44406; (216) 533-5503; www.albahouse.org; Society of St. Paul.

Pastoral Music, bm; 962 Wayne Ave., Suite 210, Silver Spring, MD 20910-4433; (240) 247-3000; www.npm.org; National Association of Pastoral Musicians.

Pax Romana/CMICA-USA, q; 3049 4th St., N.E., Washington, DC 20017; (202) 269-6672; www.pax romana.org.

Philosophy Today, q; De Paul University, 2219 N. Kenmore Ave., Chicago, IL 60614-3504; (773) 325-7267; Philosophy Department.

PIME World, m (except July-Aug.); 17330 Quincy St., Detroit, MI 48221; (313) 342-4066; www.pime ysa.org; PIME Missionaries.

Pope Speaks, The: Church Documents Bimonthly; 200 Noll Plaza, Huntington, IN 46750; (260) 356-8400; www.osv.com; Our Sunday Visitor, Inc.

Poverello, The, 10 times a year; 6832 Convent Blvd., Sylvania, OH 43560; (419) 824-3627; www.sisters osf; Sisters of St. Francis of Sylvania.

Prayers for Worship, q; P.O. Box 432, Milwaukee, WI 53201-0432; (800) 876-4574; www.execpc.com/ ~lpi.

Priest, The, m; 200 Noll Plaza, Huntington, IN 46750; (260) 356-8400; www.osv.com; Our Sunday Visitor, Inc.

Proceedings, a; Fordham University, Adm. Bldg., Bronx, NY 10458; (718) 817-4081; www.acpa-main.org; Journal of the American Catholic Philosophical Association.

Promise, 32 times a year; 2621 Dryden Rd., Suite 300, Dayton, OH 45439; (937) 293-1415; www.pflaum.com.

Queen of All Hearts, bm; 26 S. Saxon Ave., Bay Shore, NY 11706; (631) 665-0726; www.montfort missionaries.com; Montfort Missionaries.

Reign of the Sacred Heart, q; 6889 S. Lovers Lane, Hales Corners, WI 53130; (414) 425-3383.

Religion Teacher's Journal, m (Sept.-May); P.O. Box 180, Mystic, CT 06355; (860) 536-2611; www.twentythirdpublications.com.

Religious Life, bm., P.O. Box 41007, Chicago, IL 60641; (773) 267-1195; www.religiouslife.com.

Renascence, q; P.O. Box 1881, Marquette University, Milwaukee, WI 53201-1881; (414) 288-6725.

Report on U.S. Catholic Overseas Mission, bi-annually; 3029 Fourth St. N.E., Washington, DC 20017; (202) 832-3112; www.catholicmission.org; United States Catholic Mission Association.

Response: Directory of Volunteer Opportunities, a; 1410 Q St. N.W., Washington, DC 20009-3808; (202) 332-6000; www.cnvs.org; Catholic Network of Volunteer Service.

Review for Religious, bm; Room 428, 3601 Lindell Blvd., St. Louis, MO 63108; (314) 977-7363; www.reviewforreligious.org.

Review of Politics, q; Box B, Notre Dame, IN 46556; (574) 631-6623; www.nd.edu/~rop.

Review of Social Economy, q; Marquette University, Milwaukee, WI 53233; (414) 288-5438; Association for Social Economics.

Revista Maryknoll (Spanish-English), m; Maryknoll, NY 10545; (914) 941-7590; www.maryknoll.org; Catholic Foreign Mission Society of America.

RITE, 8 times a year; 1800 North Hermitage Ave., Chicago, IL 60622-1101; (773) 486-8970; www.ltp.org.

Roze Maryi (Polish), m; Eden Hill, Stockbridge, MA 01263; (413) 298-3691; www.marian.org; Marian Helpers Center.

Sacred Music, q; 134 Christendom Dr., c/o K. Poterack, Front Royal, VA 22630; (540) 636-2900.

St. Anthony Messenger, m; 28 W. Liberty St., Cincinnati, OH 45210-1298; (513) 241-5615; www.americancatholic.org; Franciscan Friars.

St. Augustine Catholic, bm (Sept-May); P.O. Box 24000, Jacksonville, FL 32241-4000; (904)

262-3200; www.staugcatholic.org; St. Augustine diocese.

St. Joseph's Messenger and Advocate of the Blind, bi-annually; St. Joseph Home, 537 Pavonia Ave., Jersey City, NJ 07303; (201) 798-4141.

St. Paul's Family Magazine, q; 14780 W. 159th St., Olathe, KS 66062; (913) 780-0405.

Salesian Directory, q; 148 Main St., P.O. Box 639, New Rochelle, NY 10802; (914) 636-4225; Salesians of Don Bosco.

Salesian Missions of St. John Bosco, q; 2 Lefevre Lane, New Rochelle, NY 10801-5710; (914) 633-8344; www.salesianmissions.org; Salesians of Don Bosco.

SALT/Sisters of Charity, BVM, q; 1100 Carmel Dr., Dubuque, IA 52001; (563) 588-2351; www.bvmcong.org.

Scalabrinians, q; 209 Flagg Pl., Staten Island, NY 10304; (718) 351-0257.

School Guide, a; 210 North Ave., New Rochelle, NY 10801; (914) 632-7771; www.schoolguides.com.

SCN Journey, bm; SCN Office of Communications, P.O. Box 9, Nazareth, KY 40048; (502) 348-1564; www.scnazarethky.org; Sisters of Charity of Nazareth.

Seeds, 32 times a year; 2621 Dryden Rd., Dayton, OH 45439; (937) 293-1415; www.pflaum.com.

Serenity, q; 601 Maiden Choice Lane, Baltimore, MD 21228; (410) 744-9367; Little Sisters of the Poor.

Serran, The, bm; 65 E. Wacker Pl., #802, Chicago, IL 60601-7203; (312) 201-6549; www.serraus.org; Serra International.

Share Magazine, q; 10 W. 71st St., New York, NY 10023; (212) 877-3041; www.catholicdaughters.com; Catholic Daughters of the Americas.

Share the Word, bm; 3031 Fourth St. N.E., Washington, DC 20017-1102; (202) 832-5022; www.sharetheword.net; Paulist Catholic Evangelization Association.

Silent Advocate, q; St. Rita School for the Deaf, 1720 Glendale-Milford Rd., Cincinnati, OH 45215; (513) 771-7600; www.srsdeaf.org.

Social Justice Review, bm; 3835 Westminster Pl., St. Louis, MO 63108-3409; (314) 371-1653; www.socialjusticereview.com; Catholic Central Union of America.

SOUL Magazine, bm; P.O. Box 976, Washington, NJ 07882; (908) 213-2223; www.bluearmy.com; The Blue Army of Our Lady of Fatima, USA, Inc.

Spirit, w; 1884 Randolph Ave., St. Paul, MN 55105; (612) 690-7012; www.goodgroundpress.com; for teens.

Spirit, bi-annually; Seton Hall University, South Orange, NJ 07079; (201) 761-9000.

Spirit & Life, bm; 800 N. Country Club Rd., Tucson, AZ 85716; (520) 325-6401; www.benedictinesisters.org; Benedictine Srs. of Perpetual Adoration.

Spiritual Life, q; 2131 Lincoln Rd. N.E., Washington, DC 20002; (800) 832-8489; Discalced Carmelite Friars.

Star, 10 times a year; 22 W. Kiowa, Colorado Springs, CO 80903.

Studies in the Spirituality of Jesuits, 5 times a year; 3601 Lindell Blvd., St. Louis, MO 63108; (314) 977-7257.

Sunday by Sunday, w; 1884 Randolph Ave., St. Paul, MN 55105; (651) 690-7012; www.goodground press.com.

Sword Magazine, 2 times a year; 2097 Town Hall Terrace, #3, Grand Island, NY 14072-1737; (716) 773-0992; Carmelite Fathers.

Theological Studies, q; Marquette University, 100 Coughlin Hall, Milwaukee, WI 53201-1881; (414) 288-3164; www.ts.mu.edu.

Theology Digest, q; P.O. Box 56907, St. Louis, MO 63156-0907; (314) 977-3410; St. Louis University.

This Rock Magazine, 10 times a year; 2020 Gillespie Way, El Cajon, CA 92020; (619) 387-7200; www.catholic.com.

Thomist, The, q; 487 Michigan Ave. N.E., Washington, DC 20017; (202) 529-5300; www.thomist.org; Dominican Fathers.

Today's Catholic Teacher, m (Sept.-April); 2621 Dryden Rd., Dayton, OH 45439; (937) 293-1415; www.catholicteacher.com.

Today's Liturgy, q; 5536 NE Hassalo, Portland, OR 97213; (800) 548-8749.

Today's Parish, m (Sept.-May); P.O. Box 180, Mystic, CT 06355; (860) 536-2611; www.twentythird publications.com

Together in the Word, bi-annual; Box 577, Techny, IL 60082-0577; (708) 272-2700; www.divine word.org; Chicago province, Society of Divine Word.

The Tower, w; The Catholic University of America, University Center, W. Michigan Ave., Ste. 400A, Washington, DC 20064; (202) 319-5778.

Tracings, q; 5 Gamelin St., Holyoke, MA 01040; (413) 536-7511; www.sisofprov.org; Sisters of Providence.

Turnaround, The, five times a year; Cardinal Newman Society, 207 Park Ave., Ste. B-2, Falls Church, VA 22046; (703) 536-9585; www.cardinal newmansociety.org.

TV Prayer Guide, 19 Second Ave., P.O. Box 440, Pelham, NY 10803-0440; (914) 738-3344; www.thesundaymass.org.

Ultreya Magazine, bm; 4500 W. Davis St., P.O. Box 210226, Dallas, TX 75211; (214) 339-6321; Cursillo Movement.

L'Union (French and English), q; P.O. Box F, Woonsocket, RI 02895; (401) 769-0520.

Universitas, q; 221 N. Grand, Room 39, St. Louis, MO 63103; (314) 977-2537; www.slu.edu; St. Louis University.

U.S. Catholic, m; 205 W. Monroe St., Chicago, IL 60606; (312) 236-7782; www.uscatholic.org; Claretians.

Venture, 32 times during school year; 2621 Dryden Rd., Suite 300, Dayton, OH 45439; (937) 293-1415; www.pflaum.com; intermediate grades.

Vida Catolica, La, m.; 40 Green St., Lynn, MA 01902; (781) 586-0197; www.la-vida.org/catolica; Boston archdiocese Hispanic community.

Vincentian Heritage, twice a year; 2233 N. Kenmore Ave., Chicago, IL 60614; (773) 325-7348; www.depaul.edu/~vstudies.

Vision, a, 205 W. Monroe St., Chicago, IL 60606; (312) 236-7782; www.visionguide.org; Claretian Publications in conjunction with National Religious Vocation Conference.

Vision, 3 times a year; 7202 Buchanan St., Landover Hills, MD 20784; (301) 577-1684; www.ncod.org; National Catholic Office for the Deaf.

Vision (Spanish-English), P.O. Box 28185, San Antonio, TX 78228; (210) 732-2156; www.maccsa.org; Mexican American Cultural Center.

Visions, 32 times during school year; 2621 Dryden Rd., Suite 300, Dayton, OH 45439; (937) 293-1415; www.pflaum.com; for students in grades 7 to 9.

Vocations and Prayer, q; 6635 Tobias Ave., Van Nuys, CA 91405; (818) 782-1765; www.rcj.org; Rogationist Fathers.

Voice Crying in the Wilderness, A, q; 4425 Schneider Rd., Filmore, NY 14735; (716) 567-4433; Most Holy Family Monastery.

Waif's Messenger, q; 1140 W. Jackson Blvd., Chicago, IL 60607; (312) 738-7565; Mission of Our Lady of Mercy.

Way of St. Francis, bm; 1500 34th Ave., Oakland, CA 94601; (916) 443-5717; www.sbfranciscans.org; Franciscan Friars of California, Inc.

Wheeling Jesuit University Chronicle, 3 times a year; 316 Washington Ave., Wheeling, WV 26003; (304) 243-2295.

Word Among Us, The, m; 9639 Dr. Perry Rd., No. 126N, Jamesville, MD 21754; (301) 831-1262; www.wau.org.

Word and Witness, P.O. Box 510817, Wisconsin, WI, 53151-0817; (800) 876-4574; www.4lpi.com.

World Lithuanian Catholic Directory, P.O. Box 1025, Humarock , MA 02407; (781) 834-4079.

Worship, bm; St. John's Abbey, Collegeville, MN 56321; (612) 363-3883.

YOU! Magazine, 10 times a year; 29963 Mulholland Highway, Agoura Hills, CA 91301; (818) 991-1813; www.youmagazine.com; Catholic youth magazine.

Newsletters

ACT, 10 times a year; Box 925, Evansville, IN 47706-0925; (812) 962-5508; www.cfm.org; Christian Family Movement.

Action News, q; Pro-Life Action League, 6160 N. Cicero Ave., Chicago, IL 60646; (773) 777-2900; www.prolifeaction.org.

Annual Report, The, 2021 H St. N.W., Washington, DC 20006; (202) 331-8542; Black and Indian Mission Office.

Archdiocesan Bulletin, bm; 827 N. Franklin St., Philadelphia, PA 19123; (215) 627-0143; Philadelphia archeparchy.

At Home with Our Faith, 10 times a year; 205 W. Monroe St., Chicago, IL 60606; (312) 236-7782; www.homefaith.com; Claretians.

Baraga Bulletin, The, q; P.O. Box 550, Marquette, MI 49855; (906) 227-9117; www.dioceseof marquette.org; Bishop Baraga Association.

Benedictine Orient, twice a year; 2400 Maple Ave., Lisle, IL 60532; (630) 968-4264.

Brothers' Voice, 5420 South Cornell Ave., #205, Chicago, IL 60615-5604; (773) 493-2306.

Campaign Update, bm; 1513 Sixteenth St. N.W., Ste. 400, Washington, DC 20036; (202) 833-4999; www.cathcamp.org; Catholic Campaign for America.

Capuchin Chronicle, q.; P.O. Box 15099, Pittsburgh, PA 15237-0099; (412) 367-2222; www.capu chin.org.

CARA Report, The, bm; Georgetown University, Washington, DC 20057-1203; (202) 687-8080; www.cara.georgetown.edu; Center for Applied Research in the Apostolate.

Caring Community, The, m; 115 E. Armour Blvd., Kansas City, MO 64111; (816) 968-2278; www.ncr pub.com.

Catalyst, 10 times a year; 450 Seventh Ave., New York, NY, 10123; (212) 371-3191; www.catholic league.org; Catholic League for Civil and Religious Rights.

Catechist's Connection, The, 10 times a year; 115 E. Armour Blvd., Kansas City, MO 64111; (816) 968-2278; www.ncrpub.com.

Catholic Communicator, The, q; 120 East Colonial Hgwy., Hamilton, VA 20158-9012; (540) 338-2700; Catholic Distance University Newsletter.

Catholic Trends, bw; 3211 Fourth St. N.E., Washington, DC 20017; (202) 541-3290; Catholic News Service.

Catholic Update, m; 28 W. Liberty St., Cincinnati, OH 45202-6498; (513) 241-5615; www.american catholic.org.

CCHD News, q; 3211 Fourth St. N.E., Washington, DC 20017-1194; (202) 541-3210; www.poverty usa.org; Catholic Campaign for Human Development.

Celebration, Sisters of Charity of Seaton Hill, q; DePaul Center, 463 Mount Thor Rd., Greensburg, PA 15601; (724) 836-0406; www.scsh.org.

C.F.C. Newsletter, 5 times a year; 145 Huguenot Ave., Suite 402, New Rochelle, NY 10801; (914) 712-7580; Christian Brothers.

Christ the King Seminary Newsletter, 3 times a year; 711 Knox Rd., Box 607, E. Aurora, NY 14052; (716) 652-8900.

Christian Response Newsletter, P.O. Box 125, Staples, MN 56479-0125; (218) 894-1165.

Christopher News Notes, 10 times a year; 12 E. 48th St., New York, NY 10017; (212) 759-4050; www.christophers.org; The Christophers.

Clarion, The, 5 times a year; Box 159, Alfred, ME 04002-0159; (207) 324-0067; Brothers of Christian Instruction.

CMSM Bulletin, m; 8808 Cameron St., Silver Spring, MD 20910; (301) 588-4030; www.cmsm.org.

Comboni Mission Newsletter, q; 1318 Nagel Rd., Cincinnati, OH 45255-3194; (513) 474-4997; www.combonimissionaries.org.

Commentary, bm; 1119 K St., Second Floor, Sacramento, CA 95814; (916) 443-4851; California Catholic Conference

Context, 22 issues a year; 205 W. Monroe St., Chicago, IL 60606; (312) 236-7782; www.context online.org; Claretians.

CPN Newsletter, twice a month; 1318 Nagel Rd., Cincinnati, OH, 45255-3120; (513) 474-4997; www.combonimissionaries.org.

Cross and Feathers (Tekakwitha Conference Newsletter), q; P.O. Box 6768, Great Falls, MT 59406; (406) 727-0147; www.tekconf.org; Tekakwitha Conference.

Crossroads, 8 times a year; 1118 Pendleton St., #300, Cincinnati, OH 45202; (888) 714-6631; www.ccmanet.org; Catholic Campus Ministry Association.

CRUX of the News, w; P.O. Box 758, Latham, NY 12110-0758; (518) 783-0058.

Cycles of Faith, P.O. Box 432, Milwaukee, WI 53201-0432; (800) 876-4574; www.execpcl.com/~lpi.

Damien-Dutton Call, q; 616 Bedford Ave., Bellmore, NY 11710.

Dimensions, m; 86 Front St., Hempstead, NY 11550; (516) 481-6000; www.ncdc.org; National Catholic Development Conference.

Diocesan Dialogue, two times a year; 16565 South State St., South Holland, IL 60473; (708) 331-5485; www.acpress.org.

Diocesan Newsletter, The, m; P.O. Box 2147, Harlingen, TX 78551; (956) 421-4111; www.cdob.org; Brownsville diocese.

Environment and Art Letter, m; 1800 N. Hermitage Ave., Chicago, IL 60622-1101; (773) 486-8970; www.ltp.org; Liturgy Training Publications.

E-Proclaim, 10 times a year; 3211 Fourth St., N.E., Washington, DC, 20017-1194; (202) 541-3204; www.usccb.org/ccc.

Ethics and Medics, m; 159 Washington St., Boston, MA 02135; (617) 787-1900; www.ncbcenter.org; National Catholic Bioethics Center.

Eucharistic Minister, m; 115 E. Armour, Kansas City, MO 64111; (816) 968-2278; www.ncrpub.com.

Every Day Catholic, m; 28 W. Liberty St., Cincinnati, OH 45202-6498; (513) 241-5615; www.everydaycatholic.org; St. Anthony Messenger Press.

EWTN Family Newsletter, 13 times a year; 5817 Leeds Rd., Irondale, AL 35210; (205) 271-2900; www.ewtn.com; Eternal Word Television Network.

Explorations, q; American Interfaith Institute, 321 Chestnut St., Philadelphia, PA, 19106; (215) 238-5345.

Family Connection, The, bm; 3753 MacBeth Dr., San Jose, CA 95127; (408) 258-8534.

Father Flood, q; P.O. Box 51087, New Berlin, WI 53151-0817; (800) 876-4574; www.4lpi.org; Liturgical Publications.

Fellowship of Catholic Scholars Newsletter Quarterly, De Sales Univ., 2755 Station Ave., Center Valley, PA 18034-9568; www.catholicscholars.org.

Fonda Tekakwitha News, P.O. Box 627, Fonda, NY 12068; (518) 853-3636; www.katerishrine.com; Order Minor Conventuals.

Food for the Poor, 3 times a year; 550 SW 12th Ave., Deerfield Beach, FL 33442; (954) 427-2222; www.foodforthepoor.org.

Foundations Newsletter for Newly Married Couples, bm; P.O. Box 1632, Portland, ME, 04104-1632; (207) 775-4757.

Franciscan Reporter, a; 3140 Meramec St., St. Louis, MO 63118-4399; (314) 353-3132; www.thefriars.org; Franciscan Friars of Sacred Heart Province.

Franciscan World Care, q; P.O. Box 29034, Washington, DC 20017; (202) 832-1762; www.franciscanmissionsservice.catholic.edu; Franciscan Mission Service.

Frontline Report, bm; 23 Bliss Ave., Tenafly, NJ 07670; (201) 567-0450; www.smafathers.org; Society of African Missions.

Graymoor Today, m; P.O. Box 301, Garrison, NY 10524-0301; (845) 424-3671; www.atonementfriars.org.

Happiness, q; 567 Salem End Rd., Framingham, MA 01702-5599; (508) 879-2541; www.sonsofmary.com; Sons of Mary, Health of the Sick.

Harmony, 3 times a year; 800 N. Country Club Rd., Tucson, AZ 85716; (520) 325-6401; Benedictine Srs. of Perpetual Adoration.

Healing & Hope, 9480 North De Mazenod Dr., Belleville, IL 62223-1160; (618) 398-4848; www.snows.org.

Heart Beats, 169 Cummins Hwy., Roslindale, MA 02131; (617) 325-3322.

HLI Reports, m; 4 Family Life, Front Royal, VA 22630; Human Life International.

HN People, bm; 127 W. 31st St., New York, NY 10001-3403; (212) 594-6224; www.hnp.org/publications; Franciscans of Holy Name Province.

HNP Today, w; 127 W. 31st St., New York, NY 10011-3403; (212) 594-6224; www.friars.com; Franciscans of Holy Name Province.

ICSC Commitment, 1275 K St. N.W., Suite 980, Washington, DC 20005-4006; (202) 289-1093; www.catholicstewardship.org.

Immaculate Heart of Mary Shrine Bulletin, 3 times a year; Mountain View Road, P.O. Box 976, Washington, NJ 07882-0976; (908) 689-1700; www.ewtn.com/bluearmy.

Initiatives, bm; P.O. Box 291102, Chicago, IL 60629; (773) 776-9036; www.centerforlaity.org; National Center for the Laity.

Interchange, Assisi Heights, 1001 14 St., NW, #100, Rochester, MN 55901-2525; (507) 529-3523; www.rochesterfranciscan.org; Rochester Franciscan Sisters.

It's Our World, 4 times during school year; 366 Fifth Ave., New York, NY 10001; (212) 563-8700; www.holychildhoodusa.org; Young Catholics in Mission.

Journey, The, q; 210 W. 31st St., New York, NY 10001-2876; (212) 714-0950; www.capuchin.org; Province of St. Mary of Capuchin Order.

Joyful Noiseletter, The, m; P.O. Box 895, Portage, MI 49081-0895; (616) 324-0990; www.joyfulnoiseletter.com; Fellowship of Merry Christians.

Knightline, 18 times a year; 1 Columbus Plaza, New Haven, CT 06510-3326; (203) 772-2130; www.kofc.org; Knights of Columbus Supreme Council.

Laity and Family Life Updates, bm; 7800 Kenrick Rd., St. Louis, MO, 63119; (314) 961-4320.

Land of Cotton, q; 2048 W. Fairview Ave., Montgomery, AL 39196; (205) 265-6791; City of St. Jude.

Law Reports, q; 4455 Woodson Rd., St. Louis, MO 63134; (314) 427-2500; Catholic Health Association.

LCWR Update, m; 8808 Cameron St., Silver Spring, MD 20910; (301) 588-4955; www.lcwr.org; Leadership Conference of Women Religious.

Legatus, m; 24 Frank Lloyd Wright Dr., Ann Arbor, MI 48105; (734) 930-3854; www.legatus.org; Legatus.

Let's Talk! (English edition), **Hablemos!** (Spanish edition), bm; 3031 Fourth St. N.E., Washington, DC 20017-1102; (202) 832-5022; www.prisonministry.org; prison ministries of Paulist National Catholic Evangelization Assn.

Letter to the Seven Churches, bm; 1516 Jerome St., Lansing, MI 48912; (517) 372-6222; Catholic Charismatics.

Life at Risk, 10 times a year; 3211 Fourth St. N.E., Washington, DC 20017; (202) 541-3070; Pro-Life Activities Committee, USCCB.

Life Insight, m; 3211 Fourth St. N.E., Washington, DC 20017; (202) 541-3070; Committee for Pro-Life Activities, USCCB.

Liturgical Images, m; P.O. Box 2225, Hickory, NC 28603; (828) 327-3225.

Loyola World, 22 times a year; 820 North Michigan Ave., Chicago, IL, 60611; (312) 915-6157; www.luc.edu.

Magnificat, three times a year; Star Route 1, Box 226, Eagle Harbor, MI, 49950; (906) 289-4388 (fax); www.societystjohn.com.

Malvern Retreat House, q; Malvern, PA 19355-0315; (610) 644-0400; www.malvernretreat.org; Laymen's Retreat League.

Maronites Today, m; P.O. Box 1891, Austin, TX 78767-1891; (512) 458-3693; www.eparchyla.org; Eparchy of Our Lady of Los Angeles.

Medical Mission Sisters News, q; 8400 Pine Road, Philadelphia, PA 19111; (215) 742-6100; www.medicalmissionsisters.org.

Messenger of St. Joseph's Union, The, 3 times a year; 108 Bedell St., Staten Island, NY 10309; (718) 984-9296.

Mission, The, three times a year; 90 Cherry Lane, Hicksville, NY 11801-6299; (516) 733-7042; www.catholiccharities.cc; Catholic Charities.

Mission Messenger, The, q; P.O. Box 610, Thoreau, NM, 87323; (505) 862-7847; www.sbms.k12.nm.us; St. Bonaventure Indian Mission and School.

Missionaries of Africa Report, q; 1624 21st St. N.W., Washington, DC 20009; (202) 232-5154; Society of Missionaries of Africa (White Fathers).

Mission Update, bm; 3029 Fourth St. N.E., Washington, DC 20017; (202) 832-3112; www.uscatholicmission.org.

Mountain View, q.; 8501 Bailey Rd., Darien, IL 60561; (630) 969-5050; Lay Carmelite Headquarters.

National Holy Name Newsletter, bm; 53 Laux Street, Buffalo, NY 14206-2218; (716) 847-6419; www.members.aol.com/nahns.

NCPD National Update, q; 415 Michigan Ave. N.E., #240, Washington, DC 20017; (202) 529-2933; www.ncpd.org; National Catholic Office for Persons with Disabilities.

Neighbors, Committee on Home Missions, q.; 3211 Fourth St. N.E., Washington, D.C. 20017; (202) 541-5400; Bishops' Committee on Home Missions.

News and Ideas, q.; 9480 North De Mazenod Dr., Belleville, IL 62223; (618) 398-4848; www.snows.org; Missionary Oblates of Mary Immaculate.

News and Views, q; 3900 Westminster Pl., St. Louis, MO 63108; (314) 533-0320; www.sacredheartprogram.org; Sacred Heart Program.

Newsletter of the Bureau of Catholic Indian Missions, 10 times a year; 2021 H St. N.W., Washington, DC 20006; (202) 331-8542.

North Coast Catholic, bi-monthly; P.O. Box 1297, Santa Rosa, CA 95402; (707) 566-3302; www.santarosacatholic.org; Santa Rosa diocese.

Nuestra Parroquia (Spanish-English), m; 205 W. Monroe St., Chicago, IL 60606; (312) 236-7782; www.hmrc.claretianpubs.org; Claretians.

Oblates, six times a year; 9480 North De Mazenod Dr., Belleville, IL 62223-1160; (618) 398-4848; www.snows.org; Missionary Oblates of Mary Immaculate.

Origins, 48 times a year; 3211 Fourth St. N.E., Washington, DC 20017; (202) 541-3284; Catholic News Service.

Overview, m; 205 W. Monroe St., 6th Floor, Chicago, IL 60606; (312) 609-8880; Thomas More Assn.

Pacer, m; P.O. Box 34008, Seattle, WA 98124; (206) 320-2402; Providence Medical Center.

Paulist, Today, q; 415 W. 59th St., New York, NY 10019; (212) 265-0730; www.paulist.org.

Peace Times, 3-4 times a year; P.O. Box 248, Bellevue, WA 98009-0248; (425) 451-1770.

Pentecost Today, q; P.O. Box 628, Locust Grove, VA 22508-0628; (540) 972-0628; www.nsc-charis center.org.

Perspectives, q; 912 Market St., La Crosse, WI 54601; (608) 791-5289; www.fspa.org.

Pilgrim, The, q; 136 Shrine Rd., Auriesville, NY 12016; (518) 853-3033; Shrine of North American Martyrs.

Priests for Life, bm; P.O. Box 141172, Staten Island, NY 10314; (718) 980-4400; www.priestsforlife.org.

Proclaim, 10 times a year; 3211 Fourth St. N.E., Washington, DC 20017-1194; (202) 541-3237; www.usccb.org.

Quarterly, The, q; 209 W. Fayette St., Baltimore, MD 21201; (410) 951-7455; www.catholicrelief.org; Catholic Relief Services.

Religious Life, m (bm, May-Aug.); P.O. Box 41007, Chicago, IL 60641; (312) 267-1195; www.ewtn.com/religious life; Institute on Religious Life.

RSCJ Newsletter, m; 1235 Otis St. N.E., Washington, DC 20017-2516; (202) 526-6258; www.rscj.org; Religious of Sacred Heart.

St. Anthony's Newsletter, m; 103 St. Francis Blvd., Mt. St. Francis, IN 47146; (812) 923-5250; Conventual Franciscans.

St. Joseph's Parish Life Quarterly, q; 1382 Highland Ave., Needham, MA 02192; (617) 444-0245.

Sacred Ground, three times a year; 1 Elmwood Ave., Kansas City, KS 66103-3719; (913) 384-6500; www.cfcusa.org; Christian Foundation for Children.

San Francisco Charismatics, m; 2555 17th Ave., San Francisco, CA 94116; (415) 664-8481; www.sfspirit.com.

SCJ News, 9 times a year; P.O. Box 289, Hales Corners, WI 53130-0289; (414) 427-4266; Sacred Heart Fathers and Brothers.

SCRC Spirit, The, bm; 9795 Cabrini Dr., #105, Burbank, CA, 91504-1739; (818) 771-1361; www.scrc.org.

Scripture from Scratch, m.; 28 W. Liberty St., Cincinnati, OH 45202-6498; (513) 241-5615; www.americancathoilic.org; understanding the Bible.

Spirit & The Bide, The, m; 8300 Morganford Rd., St. Louis, MO 63123; (314) 792-7070; www.stlcharismatic.org.

Spiritual Book Associates, 8 times a year; Notre Dame, IN 46556-0428; (219) 287-2838; www.spiritualbookassoc.org.

Squires Newsletter, m; One Columbus Plaza, New Haven, CT 06510-3326; (203) 772-2130; Columbian Squires.

SSpS Mission, q; P.O. Box 6026, Techny, IL 60082-6026; (847) 441-0126; Holy Spirit Missionary Sisters.

Tidings, Washington Theological Union, 3 times a year; 6896 Laurel St. N.W., Washington, DC 20012; (202) 726-8800; www.wtu.edu.

Touchstone, q; NFPC Office, 1337 W. Ohio St., Chicago, IL 60622; (312) 226-3334; www.nfpc.org; National Federation of Priests' Councils.

Trinity Missions Report, q; 9001 New Hampshire Ave., Silver Spring, MD 20903; (301) 434-6761.

Triumph of the Past, m.; P.O. Box 29535, Columbus, OH 43229; (614) 261-1300.

Unda USA Newsletter, q; 901 Irving Ave., Dayton, OH 45409-2316; (937) 229-2303; www.undausa.org.

Vision: National Association of Catholic Chaplains, 10 times a year; P.O. Box 070473, Milwaukee, WI 53207-0473; (414) 483-4898; www.nacc.org.

Voices, 2 times a year; 1625 Rutherford Lane, Bldg. D, Austin, TX 78754-5105; (512) 339-7123; Volunteers for Educational and Social Services.

Voices in Mission and Ministry, q.; 1257 E. Siena Heights Dr., Adrian, MI 49221; (517) 266-3400; www.adriansisters.org; Adrian Dominicans.

Woodstock Report, q; Georgetown University, Box 571137, Washington, DC 20057; (202) 687-3532; www.georgetown.edu/centers/woodstock; Woodstock Theological Center.

Word One, 5 times a year; 205 W. Monroe St., Chicago, IL 60606; (312) 236-7782; www.wordone.org; Claretians.

Xaverian Missions Newsletter, bm; 101 Summer St., P.O. Box 5857, Holliston, MA 01746; (508) 429-2144; Xaverian Missionary Fathers.

Your Edmundite Missions Newsletter, bm; 1428 Broad St., Selma, AL 36701; (334) 872-2359; www.edmunditemissions.com; Southern Missions of Society of St. Edmund.

Youth Update, m; 28 W. Liberty St., Cincinnati, OH 45210; (513) 241-5615; www.americancatholic.org.

Zeal Newsletter, 3 times a year; P.O. Box 86, Allegany, NY 14706; (716) 373-1130; www.fsalleg.org/sem.htm; Franciscan Sisters of Allegany.

BOOKS

The Catholic Almanac, a; Our Sunday Visitor, Inc., 200 Noll Plaza, Huntington, IN 46750, publisher; editorial offices, 2017 Scenic Sunrise Dr., Las Vegas, NV 89117; (702) 254-2678; www.osv.com; first edition, 1904.

The Official Catholic Directory, a; P.J. Kenedy & Sons in association with R.R. Bowker, a Reed Reference Publishing Company, 121 Chanlon Rd., New Providence, NJ 07974; (847) 966-8278; first edition, 1817.

BOOK CLUBS

Catholic Book Club (1928), 106 W. 56th St., New York, NY 10019; (212) 581-4640; www.americapress.org/cbc.htm; sponsors the Campion Award.

Catholic Digest Book Club (1954), 2115 Summit Ave., St. Paul, MN 55105-1081; (651) 962-6748.

Spiritual Book Associates (1934), Ave Maria Press Building, P.O. Box 428, Notre Dame, IN 46556; (219) 287-2838.

Thomas More Book Club (1939), Thomas More Association, 205 W. Monroe St., Sixth Floor, Chicago, IL 60606; (312) 609-8880.

GENERAL PUBLISHERS

(*Source:* Catholic Press Directory, Almanac *Survey.*)

Our Sunday Visitor Publishing: 200 Noll Plaza, Huntington IN 46750; (800) 348-2440, (260) 356-8400; e-mail: booksed@osv.com.

Ave Maria Press, Inc.: PO Box 428, Notre Dame IN 46556; (800) 282-1865, (219) 287-2831; e-mail: avemariapress.1@nd.edu.

Catholic News Service: 3211 Fourth St N.E., Washington DC 20017; (202) 541-3250; e-mail: cns@catholicnews.com.

Catholic Relief Services: 209 West Fayette St., Baltimore MD 21201; (410) 625-2220.

The Christophers: 12 East 48th St., New York NY 10017; (212) 759-4050; e-mail: mail@christophers.org.

Claretian Publications: 205 West Monroe St., Chicago IL 60606; (800) 328-6515, (312) 236-7782; e-mail: editors@uscatholic.org.

Clarity Publishing, Inc.: PO Box 758, Latham NY 12110-3510; (518) 783-0058.

Franciscan Mission Associates: PO Box 598, Mount Vernon NY 10551-0598; (914) 664-5604.

Ignatius Press: P.O. Box 1339, Ft. Collins, CO 80522; (800) 651-1531.

Liguori Publications: One Liguori Drive, Liguori MO 63057; (636) 464-2500.

Loyola Press: 3441 North Ashland Avenue, Chicago, IL 60657; (800) 621-1008; e-mail: editorial@loyolapress.com.

Missionary Oblates of Mary Immaculate: 9480 North De Mazenod Dr., Belleville, IL 62223-1160; (888) 330-6264; e-mail: mami@oblatesusa.org.

National Catholic Bioethics Center (NCBC): 159 Washington Street, Boston MA 02135; (617) 787-1900; e-mail: ChadM@ncbcenter.org.

Pauline Books & Media: 50 St. Paul's Avenue, Boston MA 02130; (617) 522-8911; e-mail: editorial@pauline.org.

Paulist National Catholic Evangelization Association: 3031 Fourth Street N.E., Washington DC 20017; (800) 237-5515, (202) 832-5022; e-mail: pncea@pncea.org.

Pontifical Mission Societies in the United States: 366 Fifth Ave., New York NY 10001; (800) 431-2222, (212) 563-8700; e-mail: propfaith@aol.com.

St. Anthony Messenger Press: 28 W Liberty St, Cincinnati OH 45210; (513) 241-5615; e-mail: stanthony@americancatholic.org.

CANADIAN CATHOLIC PUBLICATIONS

(*Principal source*: 2003 Catholic Press Directory.)

Newspapers

Atlantic Catholic, The, bw; 88 College Street, Antigonish, NS B2G 2L7; (902) 863-4370.

B. C. Catholic, The, w; 150 Robson St., Vancouver, BC V6B 2A7; (604) 683-0281; www.rcav.bc.ca.

Casket, The, w; 88 College St., Antigonish, NS B2G 2L7; (902) 863-4370.

Catholic New Times (national), bw; 80 Sackville St., Toronto, ON M5A 3E5; (416) 361-0761; www.catholicnewtimes.org.

Catholic Register, The (national), w; 1155 Younge St., Suite 401, Toronto, ON M4T 1W2; (416) 934-3410; www.catholicregister.org; lay edited.

Catholic Times, 10 times a year; 2005 St. Marc St., Montreal, QC H3H 2G8; (514) 937-2301.

Monitor, The, m; P.O. Box 986, St. John's, NF A1C 5M3; (709) 739-6553; www.stjohnsarchdiocese.nf.ca.

New Freeman, The, w; 1 Bayard Dr., St. John, NB E2L 3L5; (506) 653-6806.

Prairie Messenger, w; Box 190, Muenster, SK S0K 2Y0; (306) 682-1772; www.stpeters.sk.ca/prairie_messenger.

Restoration, 10 times a year; Madonna House, Combemere, ON K0J 1L0; (613) 756-3713; www.madonnahouse.org.

St. Vladimir's College Gazette, q; Box 789, Roblin, MB, R0L 1PO; (204) 937-2173.

Teviskes Ziburiai (**The Lights of the Homeland**) (Lithuanian), w; 2185 Stavebank Rd., Mississauga, ON L5C 1T3; (905) 275-4672.

Vida Nueva; 3424 Wilshire Blvd., Los Angeles, CA 90010-2241; (213) 637-7310.

Western Catholic Reporter, w.; 8421 101 Ave. NW, Edmonton, AB T6A 0L1; (780) 465-8030; www.wcr.ab.ca.

Magazines, Other Periodicals

L'Almanach Populaire Catholique, a; P.O. Box 1000, St. Anne de Beaupre, QC G0A3C0; (418) 827-4538.

ANNALS of St. Anne de Beaupre, The, m; Box 1000, Ste. Anne de Beaupre, QC G0A 3C0; (418) 827-4538; Basilica of St. Anne.

Apostolat, bm; 8844 Notre-Dame Est, Montréal, QC H1L 3M4; (514) 351-9310; Oblates of Mary Immaculate, CMO (*Centre Missionnaire Oblat*).

Bread of Life, The, bm; P.O. Box 395, Hamilton, ON L8N 3H8; (905) 529-4496; www.breadoflife.ca.

Canadian Catholic Review, The, St. Joseph's College, University of Alberta, Edmonton, AB T6G 2J5; (403) 492-7681.

Canadian League, The, q; 1-160 Murray Park Rd., Winnipeg, MB R3J 3X5; (204) 927-2310; www.cwl.ca; Catholic Women's League of Canada.

Caravan, q; 90 Parent Ave., Ottawa, ON K1N 7B1; (613) 241-9461; www.cccb.ca; Canadian Conference of Catholic Bishops.

Celebrate! (Novalis), bm; St. Paul University, 223 Main St., Ottawa, ON K1S 1C4; (780) 451-2228.

Companion Magazine, m; 695 Coxwell Ave., Suite 600, Toronto, ON M4C 5R6; (416) 690-5611; www.franciscan.on.ca; Conventual Franciscan Fathers.

Compass — A Jesuit Journal, bm (Jan.-Nov.); Box 400, Stn. F, 50 Charles St. East, Toronto, ON M4Y 2L8; (416) 921-0653; www.io.org/ngvanv/compass/com-phome.html.

CRC Bulletin (French-English), q; 219 Argyle Ave., Ottawa, ON K2P 2H4; (613) 236-0824; www.crcn.ca; Canadian Religious Conference.

L'Église Canadienne (French), 11 times a year; 6255 rue Hutchison, Bureau 103, Montreal, QC H2V 4C7; (514) 278-3020; www.novalis.ca.

Fatima Crusader, q; P.O. Box 602, Fort Erie, ON L2A 4M7; (905) 871-7607; www.fatima.org.

Global Village Voice, The, q; 10 St. Mary St., Suite 420, Toronto, ON M4Y 1P9; (416) 922-1592; Canadian Organization for Development and Peace.

Kateri (English-French), q; P.O. Box 70, Kahnawake, QC J0L 1B0; (450) 638-1546.

Le Messager de Saint Antoine (French), 10 times a year; Lac-Bouchette, QC G0W 1V0; (418) 348-6344.

Messenger of the Sacred Heart, m; 661 Greenwood Ave., Toronto, ON M4J 4B3; (416) 466-1195; Apostleship of Prayer.

Mission Canada, q; 201-1155 Younge St., Toronto, ON M4T 1W2; (416) 934-3424; www.missioncanada.ca.

Missions Étrangères (French), bm; 180 Place Juge-Desnoyers, Laval, QC H7G 1A4; (450) 667-4190; www.smelaval.org.

Nouvel Informateur Catholiqué, Le, semi-monthly; 6550 Rte 125, Rawdon, QC J0K 1S0; (450) 834-8503.

Oratory, bm; 3800 Ch. Queen Mary, Montreal, QC H3V 1H6; (514) 733-8211; www.saint-joseph.org.

Our Family, m; P.O. Box 249, Battleford, SK; S0M 0E0; (306) 937-7771; www.ourfamilymagazine.com; Oblates of Mary Immaculate.

Prêtre et Pasteur (French), m; 4450 St. Hubert St., #500, Montreal, QC H2J 2W9; (514) 525-6210.

Prieres Missionaires, m; Missionaires de la Consolata, 2505 Boulevard Gouin ouest, Montréal, QC H3M 1B5; (514) 334-1910; www.consolata.org.

Relations (French), 10 times a year; 25 Rue Jarry Ouest, Montreal, QC H2P 1S6; (514) 387-2541.

Reveil Missionaire, bm; Missionaire de la Consolata, 2505 Boulevard Gouin ouest, Montréal, QC H3M 1B5; (514) 334-1910; www.consolata.org.

La Revue d'Sainte Anne de Beaupre (French), m; P.O. Box 1000, Ste. Anne de Beaupre, Québec G0A 3C0; (418) 827-4538.

Scarboro Missions, 9 times a year; 2685 Kingston Rd., Scarboro, ON M1M 1M4; (416) 261-7135; www.web.net/~sfms.

Spiritan Missionary News, q; 121 Victoria Park Ave., Toronto, ON M4E 3S2; (416) 698-2003; www.spiritans.com.

Unity, q; 308 Young St., Montréal, QC H3C 2G2; (514) 937-5973.

INTERNATIONAL CATHOLIC PERIODICALS

(Principal source: Catholic Almanac *survey. Included are English-language Catholic periodicals published outside the U.S.)*

African Ecclesial Review (AFER), bm; Gaba Publications, P.O. Box 4002, Eldoret, Kenya.

Australasian Catholic Record, q; 99 Albert Rd., Strathfield 2135, New South Wales, Australia.

Christ to the World, 5 times a year; Via di Propaganda 1-C, 00187, Rome, Italy.

Christian Orient, q; P.B. 1 Vadavathoor, Kottayam 686010, Kerala, India.

Doctrine and Life, m; Dominican Publications, 42 Parnell Sq., Dublin 1, Ireland.

Downside Review, q; Downside Abbey, Stratton on the Fosse, Bath, BA3 4RH, England.

East Asian Pastoral Review, q; East Asian Pastoral Institute, P.O. Box 221 U.P. Campus, 1101 Quezon City, Philippines.

Furrow, The, m; St. Patrick's College, Maynooth, Ireland.

Heythrop Journal, q; Heythrop College, Kensington Sq., London W8 5HQ, England (editorial office); published by Blackwell Publishers, 108 Cowley Rd., Oxford, OX4 1JF, England.

Holy Land Magazine, q; P.O. Box 186, 91001 Jerusalem, Israel; illustrated.

Inside the Vatican, 10 times a year; Rome office: Via della Mura Aurelio 7c, 00165 Rome, Italy; U.S. office: St. Martin de Porres Lay Dominican Community, 3050 Gap Knob Rd., New Hope, KY 40052; (270) 325-5499; www.insidethevatican.com. The only current journal that focuses exclusively on Rome, the impact of the papacy worldwide, and the functioning, travels, and activities of the Holy Father and the Roman Curia.

Irish Biblical Studies, The, q; Union Theological College, 108 Botanic Ave., Belfast BT7 1JT, N. Ireland.

Irish Journal of Sociology, The, a; St. Patrick's College, Maynooth, Ireland.

Irish Theological Quarterly, q; St. Patrick's College, Maynooth, Ireland.

L'Osservatore Romano, w; Vatican City. (*See above* under **U.S. Newspapers**.)

Louvain Studies, q; Peeters Publishers, Bondgenotenlaan 153, B-3000, Leuven, Belgium.

Lumen Vitae (French, with English summaries), q; International Center for Studies in Religious Education, 186, rue Washington, B-1050 Brussels, Belgium.

Mediaeval Studies, a; Pontifical Institute of Mediaeval Studies, 59 Queen's Park Crescent East, Toronto, ON M5S 2C4, Canada.

Month, m; 114 Mount St., London WIY 6AH, England.

Music and Liturgy, bm; The Editor, 33 Brockenhurst Rd., Addiscombe Croydan, Surrey CRO 7DR, England.

New Blackfriars, m; edited by English Dominicans, Blackfriars, Oxford OX1 3LY, England.

Omnis Terra (English Edition), m; Pontifical Missionary Union, Congregation for the Evangelization of Peoples, Via di Propaganda 1/c, 00187 Rome, Italy.

One in Christ, q; Edited at Turvey Abbey, Turvey, Bedfordshire MK43 8DE, England.

Priests & People (formerly **The Clergy Review**), 11 times a year; Blackfriars, Buckingham Rd., Cambridge CB3 0DD, England.

Recusant History, bi-annual; Catholic Record Society, 12 Melbourne Pl., Wolsingham, Durham DL13 3EH, England.

Religious Life Review, bm; Dominican Publications, 42 Parnell Sq., Dublin 1, Ireland.

Scripture in Church, q; Dominican Publications, 42 Parnell Sq., Dublin 1, Ireland.

Southwark Liturgy Bulletin, q; The Editor, 10 Claremont Rd., Maidstone, Kent ME14 5L2, England.

Spearhead, 5 times a year; Gaba Publications, P.O. Box 4002, Eldoret, Kenya.

Spirituality, bm; Dominican Publications, 42 Parnell Sq., Dublin 1, Ireland.

Tablet, The, w; 1 King Street Cloisters, Clifton Walk, London W60QZ, England; 44(0)-20-8748-8484.

Way, The, q; 114 Mount St., London W1Y6AN, England.

CATHOLIC NEWS AGENCIES

(*Sources: International Catholic Union of the Press, Geneva; Catholic Press Association, U.S.*)

Argentina: *Agencia Informativa Catolica Argentina* (AICA), av. Rivadavia, 413, 40 Casilla de Correo Central 2886, 1020 Buenos Aires.

Austria: *Katholische Presse-Agentur* (Kathpress), Singerstrasse 7/6/2, 1010 Vienna 1.

Belgium: *Centre d'Information de Presse* (CIP), 35 Chausée de Haecht, 1030 Brussels.

Bolivia: *Agencia Noticias Fides*, ANF, Casilla 5782, La Paz.

ERBOL, Casilla 5946, La Paz.

Chile: *Agencia informativa y de comunicaciones* (AIC Chile), Brasil 94, Santiago.

Croatia: *Christian Information Service*, Marulicev 14, PP 434, 410001 Zagreb.

Germany: *Katholische Nachrichten Agentur* (KNA), Adenauer Allee 134, 5300 Bonn 1.

Greece: *Agence TYPOS*, Rue Acharnon 246, Athens 815.

Hong Kong: *UCA-News*, P.O. Box 69626, Kwun Tong (Hong Kong).

Hungary: *Magyar Kurir*, Milkszath ter 1, 1088, Budapest.

India: *South Asian Religious News* (SAR-News), PB 6236, Mazagaon, Bombay 400 010.

Italy: *Servizio Informazioni Religiosa* (SIR), Via di Porta Cavalleggeri 143, I-00165 Roma.

Centrum Informationis Catolicae (CIC-Roma), via Delmonte de la Farina, 30/4, 00186 Roma.

Peru: ACI-PRENSA, A.P. 040062, Lima.

Switzerland: *Katholische Internationale Presse-Agentur* (KIPA), Case Postale 1054 CH 1701, Fribourg.

Centre International de Reportages et d'Information Culturelle (CIRIC), Chemin Clochetons 8, P.O. Box 1000, Lausanne.

United States of America: *Catholic News Service* (CNS), 3211 Fourth St. N.E., Washington, DC 20017; (202) 541-3250; www.catholicnews.com.

U.S. PRESS SERVICES

Catholic News Service (CNS), established in 1920 (NC News Service), provides a worldwide daily news report by satellite throughout the U.S. and Canada and by wire and computer links into several foreign countries, and by mail to other clients, serving Catholic periodicals and broadcasters including Vatican Radio in about 40 countries. CNS also provides feature and photo services and a weekly religious education package, "Faith Alive!" It publishes "Origins," a weekly documentary service, and *Catholic Trends*, a fortnightly newsletter, the weekly *TV and Movie Guide* and *Movie Guide Monthly*. CNS maintains a full-time bureau in Rome. It is a division of the United States Catholic Conference, with offices at 3211 Fourth

St. N.E., Washington, DC 20017; (202) 541-3250; www.catholicnews.com. The director and editor-in-chief is Thomas N. Lorsung.

Spanish-Language Service: A weekly news summary provided by Catholic News Service, used by a number of Catholic newspapers. Some papers carry features of their own in Spanish.

Religion News Service (RNS) provides coverage of all religions as well as ethics, spirituality and moral issues. Founded in 1934 (as the Religious News Service) by the National Conference of Christian and Jews as an independent agency, RNS became an editorially independent subsidiary of the United Methodist Reporter, an interfaith publishing company, in 1983. It was acquired by Newhouse News Service in 1994. Address: 1101 Connecticut Ave. N.W., Suite 350, Washington, DC 20036.

RADIO, TELEVISION, THEATER

(The following listings are as of June 1, 2003; sources, Catholic Almanac survey, William Ryan, Communications, USCCB. Telephone and web addresses are listed as available.)

Radio Stations and Networks

Catholic Family Radio (Catholic Radio Network): 8910 University Center Lane, Suite 130, San Diego, CA 92122-1016; (619) 784-6900; www.catholicfamilyradio.com; rapidly expanding network founded by Fr. Joseph Fessio and Nick Healy; launched in 1999.

Vatican Radio: *See* under **Vatican City State**.

WEWN Radio Network: Part of the Eternal Word Television Network (EWTN): 5817 Old Leeds Rd., Birmingham, AL 35210; (205) 271-2900; www.ewtn.com; the first 24-hour U.S. Catholic radio network; launched in 1996.

Programs

Catholic Views Broadcasts, Inc.: 10 Audrey Place, Fairfield, NJ 07004; (973) 882-8700. Produces weekly 15-minute program "Views of the News." Also operates Catholic community TV stations in Chicago and Minneapolis.

Christopher Radio Program: 14-minute interview series, "Christopher Closeup" weekly and "Christopher Minutes" daily, on 400 stations. Address: 12 E. 48th St., New York, NY 10017; (212) 759-4050; www.christophers.org.

Father Justin Rosary Hour (radio): P.O. Box 454, Athol Springs, NY 14010; (716) 627-3861; www.franciszkanie.com/rosary.hour. Founded in 1931. Polish Catechetical Radio Network. Rev. Marion M. Tolczyk, O.F.M. Conv., director.

Journeys Thru Rock (radio): Produced in cooperation with the Department of Communication, USCCB. A 15-minute weekly program currently employing a youth-oriented music and commentary format (ABC).

Radio Maria (Italian): Italian Catholic radio station founded in 1992, 352 W. 44th St., New York, NY 10036. Rev. Mariano Cisco, C.S., executive director.

Television and Communications Services

Catholic Communication Campaign (CCC): A U.S. Catholic bishops' program that produces, distributes and supports Catholic media projects, including a weekly television talk show, "Personally Speaking," television documentaries and public service messages. Ellen McCloskey, 3211 4th Street N.E., Washington, DC 20017; (202) 541-3204; www.usccb.org/ccc.

Catholic Communications Foundation (CCF): A foundation established by the Catholic Fraternal Benefit Societies in 1966 to lend support and assistance to development of the communications apostolate of the Church. The CCF promotes diocesan communications capabilities and funds a scholarship program at the Annual Institute for Religious Communications. CCF officers include Bishop Anthony G. Bosco, chairman of the board; 303 W. Lancaster Ave., PMB 333, Wayne, PA 19087.

Christopher TV Series, "Christopher Closeup": Originated in 1952. Half-hour interviews, weekly, on commercial TV and numerous cable outlets; 12 E. 48th St., New York, NY 10017; (212) 759-4050; www.christophers.org.

Clemons Productions, Inc.: Produces "That's the Spirit," a family show for television; "Thoughts for the Week," on the ABC Satellite Network, and "Spirituality for Today" on the internet. Available to dioceses, organizations or channels; P.O. Box 7466, Greenwich, CT 06830; www.spirituality.org.

Eternal Word Television Network (EWTN): 5817 Old Leeds Rd., Irondale, AL 35210; (205) 271-2900; www.ewtn.com. America's largest religious cable network; features 24 hours of spiritual-growth programming for the entire family. Offers documentaries, weekly teaching series and talk shows, including the award-winning "Mother Angelica Live." Also features live Church events from around the world and devotional programs such as "The Holy Rosary." Mother M. Angelica, P.C.P.A., foundress.

Family Theater Productions: Founded by Father Peyton. Videocassettes, films for TV; 7201 Sunset Blvd., Hollywood, CA 90046; (323) 874-6633; www.familytheater.org. Nat. Dir., Rev. Wilfred J. Raymond, C.S.C.

Franciscan Communications: Producer of video and print resources for pastoral ministry; St. Anthony Messenger Press, 28 W. Liberty St., Cincinnati, OH 45210; (513) 241-5615; www.AmericanCatholic.org.

Hispanic Telecommunications Network, Inc. (HTN): Produces "Nuestra Familia," a national weekly Spanish-language TV series; 1405 N. Main, Suite 240, San Antonio, TX 78212.

Mary Productions: Originated in 1950. Offers royalty-free scripts for stage, film, radio and tape production. Audio and video tapes of lives of the saints and historical characters. Traveling theater company; Mary Productions, 212 Oakdale Dr., Tomaso Plaza, Middletown, NJ 07748; (732) 617-8144.

National Interfaith Cable Coalition: A 28-member consortium representing 64 faith groups from Roman Catholic, Jewish, Protestant and Eastern Orthodox traditions; works with faith groups to present programming on the Faith and Values Media; 74 Trinity Place, Suite 1550, New York, NY 10006; (212) 406-4121; www.faithandvalues.com.

Oblate Media and Communication Corporation: Producers, Broadcast syndicators and distributors of Catholic and value-centered video programming; 7315 Manchester Rd., St. Louis, MO 63143.

Passionist Communications, Inc.: Presents Sunday Mass on TV seen in U.S. and available to dioceses and channels; publishes "TV Prayer Guide," semi-annually; P.O. Box 440, Pelham, NY 10803-0440.

Paulist Media Works: Full service audio production in syndication to dioceses, religious communities and church groups; 3055 4th St. N.E., Washington, DC 20017. Pres., Sue Donovan.

Paulist Productions: Producers and distributors of the INSIGHT Film Series (available for TV) and educational film series; 17575 Pacific Coast Hwy., Pacific Palisades, CA 90272; (310) 454-0688; www.paulistproductions.org.

Sacred Heart Program, Inc.: Produces and distributes free of charge the weekly "CONTACT" program in 30-, 15-, and 5-minute formats to more than 300 stations in North America; 3900 Westminster Pl., St. Louis, MO 63108; (341) 533-0320; www.sacredheartprogram.org/www.contactradio.org. Exec. Dir., Gary Kolarcik.

Telecare: Instructional TV operations or broadcasts of Masses have been established in the following archdioceses and dioceses; www.telecaretv.org. Archdioceses are indicated by an asterisk.

Boston,* MA: Rev. Francis McFarland, Director, P.O. Box 9109, Newton, 02160; (617) 965-0050.

Brooklyn, NY: Rev. Msgr. Michael J. Dempsey, Director, 1712 10th Ave., 11215.

Chicago, *IL: Mr. Joseph Loughlin, Director, Radio/TV Office, Archdiocese of Chicago, 155 E. Superior, 60611.

Corpus Christi, TX: Mr. Martin L. Wind, 1200 Lantana St., 78407.

Dallas, TX: Mr. Michael McGee, 3725 Blackburn, P.O. Box 190507, 75219.

Detroit,* MI: Mr. Ned McGrath, Director, 305 Michigan Ave., 48226.

Los Angeles,* CA: Mr. David Moore, 3424 Wilshire

Blvd., 90010; (213) 637-7312; www.la-archdiocese.org.

New York,* NY: Mr. Michael Lavery, Director, 215 Seminary Ave., Yonkers, 10704; (914) 968-7800.

Oakland, San Jose, San Francisco,* CA: Shirley Connolly, Director, 324 Middlefield Rd., Menlo Park, 94025; (650) 326-4605 (fax); www.ctnba.org.

Orlando, FL: Rev. Robert Hoeffner. Director, P.O. Box 1800, 32802.

Rockville Centre, NY: Rev. Msgr. Thomas Hartman, Director, 1200 Glen Curtiss Blvd., Uniondale, 11553; (516) 538-4108.

San Bernardino, CA: Caritas Telecommunications, Clare Colella, Director, 1201 E. Highland Ave., 92404; (909) 475-5350; www.sbdiocese.org or www.caritastelecommunications.org.

Youngstown, OH: Rev. James Korda, P.O. Box 430, Canfield, 44406.

Unda-USA: A national professional Catholic association for broadcasters and other allied communicators in church ministry; organized in 1972. It succeeded the Catholic Broadcasters Association of America that in 1948 had replaced the Catholic Forum of the Air organized in 1938. It is a member of Unda-International, the international Catholic association for radio and television (Unda is the Latin word for "wave," symbolic of air waves of communication). In addition to providing support and network opportunities in church communications the organization works to encourage the secular media to produce value-oriented programs and stories. Unda-USA sponsors an annual general assembly and presents the Gabriel Awards annually for excellence in broadcasting. It publishes six newsletters for its membership. President, Frank Morock. Unda-USA, 901 Irving Ave., Dayton, OH 45409; (937) 229-2303; www.UNDAUSA.org.

Theater

Catholic Actors' Guild of America, Inc.: Established in 1914 to provide material and spiritual assistance to people in the theater. Has more than 500 members; publishes *The Call Board*; 1501 Broadway, Suite 510, New York, NY 10036; (212) 398-1868 (fax).

FILM

Best Films Of 2002

(*Courtesy, U.S. Bishops' Office of Film and Broadcasting, OFB*). The U.S. Bishops' Office of Film and Broadcasting (OFB) announced its 2002 Ten Best Films List. The following are the best films, in alphabetical order: *About Schmidt*; *Antwone Fisher*; *The Emperor's Club*; *Evelyn*; *The Lord of the Rings: The Two Towers*; *My Big Fat Greek Wedding*; *Nicholas Nickleby*; *Road to Perdition*; *The Rookie*; *Spirit: Stallion of the Cimmaron*.

The Office for Film and Broadcasting (OFB) has the responsibility of reviewing and rating theatrical motion pictures, previewing and evaluating television programming, and providing the Catholic public with information about the role of the entertainment and news media in influencing societal and personal values. The Office is supported by the U.S. Bishops' Catholic Communication Campaign (CCC). Weekly movie reviews, brief capsules, and film classifications of new film releases can be heard on the office's toll-free

movieline at 1-800-311-4222, sponsored by the CCC. Movie reviews are available online at www.usccb.org/movies.

Vatican List of the Greatest Films of the 20th Century

On the occasion of the 100th anniversary of cinema in 1995, the Vatican compiled this list of "great films." The 45 movies are divided into three categories: "Religion," "Values," and "Art."

Religion

Andrei Rublev (1969); **Babette's Feast** (1988); **Ben-Hur** (1959); **The Flowers of St. Francis** (1950); **Francesco** (1989); **The Gospel According to St. Matthew** (1966); **La Passion de Notre Seigneur Jesus-Christ** (1905); **A Man for All Seasons** (1966); **The Mission** (1986); **Monsieur Vincent** (1947); **Nazarin** (1958); **Ordet** (1954); **The Passion of Joan of Arc** (1928); **The Sacrifice** (1986); **Thérèse** (1986).

Values

Au Revoir les Enfants (1988); The Bicycle Thief (1949); The Burmese Harp (1956); Chariots of Fire (1981); Decalogue (1988); Dersu Uzala (1978); Gandhi (1982); Intolerance (1916); It's a Wonderful Life (1946); On the Waterfront (1954); Open City (1945); Schindler's List (1993); The Seventh Seal (1956); The Tree of Wooden Clogs (1978); Wild Strawberries (1958).

Art

Citizen Kane (1941); 8-1/2 (1963); Fantasia (1940); Grand Illusion (1937); La Strada (1956); The Lavender Hill Mob (1951); The Leopard (1963); Little Women (1933); Metropolis (1926); Modern Times (1936); Napoleon (1927); Nosferatu (1922); Stagecoach (1939); 2001: A Space Odyssey (1968); The Wizard of Oz (1939).

CATHOLIC INTERNET SITES

Web site addresses change periodically. Find this list online at www.CatholicAlmanac.com. Visit Our Sunday Visitor's web site at www.osv.com.

Holy See Sites

Vatican: www.vatican.va
L'Osservatore Romano: www.vatican.va/ news_services/or/or_eng/index.html
Vatican Radio: www.vatican.va/news_services/ radio/index.htm

Catholic Megasites, Directories and Links

Biblical Evidence for Catholicism: http://ic.net/ ~erasmus/erasmus.htm
Catholic Almanac: www.CatholicAlmanac.com
Catholic Canada: www.catholicanada.com
Catholic Community Forum: www:catholic-forum.com
Catholic Goldmine!: www.catholicgoldmine.com
Catholic Hotlinks: www.cathinsight.com
Catholic Information Center on the Internet: www.catholic.net/
Catholic Information Network: www.cin.org
Catholic Internet Directory: www.catholic-church.org/cid
Catholic Internet Yellow Pages: www.monksofadoration.org/directory.html
Catholic Life: www.diocese.net
Catholic Kiosk: www.aquinas-multimedia.com/ arch/index.html
Catholic.Net Periodicals: www.catholic.net/RCC/ Periodicals/index.html
Catholic Pages: www.catholic-pages.com
Catholic Press Association: www.catholicpress.org
Catholic Web: www.catholicweb.com
Catholicity Internet Directory: www.catholicity.com/airport
DioceseNet: www.diocesenet.com/index.html
Catholic Exchange: www.e3mil.com
Ecclesia Web Service for Catholics: www.catholic-church.org/
El Directorio Catolico en Internet: www.iglesia.org/
New Advent: www.newadvent.org
Our Sunday Visitor: www.OSV.com
Our Sunday Visitor Links Page: www.osvpublishing.com/links/view-links.asp
PetersNet: www.petersnet.net/
RCNet: www.rc.net
St. Jane's: www.stjane.org
The Internet Padre: www.internetpadre.com
Thelogy Library Search Engines: www.shc.edu/ theolibrary/engines.htm
Totally Catholic Link Directory: www.tcld.net/

Catholic Internet Service Providers

Catholic Families Network: www.catholicfamilies.net
Catholic Online: www.catholiconline.com
FamiLink (ISP for the family): www.familink.com

Catholic Movements and Organizations

Adoremus: www.adoremus.org
Catholic Charismatic Center: www.garg.com/ccc
Catholic Doctrinal Concordance: www.infpage.com/concordance
Catholic Family and Human Rights Institute: www.c-fam.org/
Catholic Health Association USA: www.chausa.org/CHAHOME.ASP
Catholic League: www.catholicleague.org
Focolare Movement: www.rc.net/focolare
Friendship House: www.friendshiphouse.org/
Madonna House: www.madonnahouse.org
Nat'l Bioethics Center: www.ncbcenter.org
Opus Dei: www.opusdei.org/
Pax Christi International: www.paxchristi.net/
Pax Christi USA: www.paxchristiusa.org/
Saints Alive: www.ichrusa.com/saintsalive/
Schoenstatt (information): www.catholiclinks.org/ schoenstattunitedstates.htm
Seton Home Study School: www.setonhome.org/

Catholic Newspapers and Magazines

Catholic Digest: www.catholicdigest.org
Catholic New York Online: www.cny.org
Catholic Worker: www.catholicworker.org
First Things: www.firstthings.com
Houston Catholic Worker: www.cjd.org
Our Sunday Visitor: www.osv.com
The Tablet, U.K.: www.thetablet.co.uk
The Universe, U.K.: www.totalcatholic.com/
The Wanderer: www.thewandererpress.com

Religious Orders and Apostolates

Apostolates/Orders: www.catholic-forum.com/ links/pages/Religious_Orders/
EWTN: www.ewtn.com
RCNet-Apostolates: www.rc.net/org

Colleges and Universities (Links To)

Colleges: www.shc.edu/theolibrary/edu.htm
Assocation of Catholic Colleges and Universities: www.accunet.org
Useful and Informative Sites
Mass Times: www.masstimes.org
Mass in Transit: www.massintransit.com
Christworld: www.christworld.com
Catholic Web: www.catholicweb.com

Catholic-Pages: www.catholic-pages.com
Catholic U.S.A.: www.catholic-usa.com
PetersVoice: www.petersvoice.com
Rosary Center: www.rosary-center.org
Daily E-pistle (e-newsletter) Signup Page:
www.catholic-forum.com/e-pistle.html
Grace In Action Stewardship:
www.GraceInAction.org

For Kids and Families
Catholic Kids Net: www.catholickidsnet.org/
Global Schoolhouse: www.gsn.org/

My Friend: www.myfriendmagazine.com
Teaching Catholic Kids:
www.TeachingCatholicKids.com
Apostolate for Family Consecration:
www.familyland.org
Catholic Family and Human Rights Institute:
www.c-fam.org
Catholic Fathers: www.dads.org
Catholic Parent Magazine:
www.CatholicParent.com
CatholiCity Men: www.catholicmen.com/
Natural Family Planning: www.ccli.org
Domestic Church: www.domestic-church.com/

DEVELOPMENTS IN COMMUNICATIONS 2002-2003

The following are significant developments in the field of Catholic communications in 2002-2003.

MESSAGE OF THE HOLY FATHER FOR THE 37TH WORLD COMMUNICATIONS DAY

On June 1, 2003, Pope John Paul II issued his annual message for World Communications Day. His theme was: "The Communications Media at the Service of Authentic Peace in the Light of 'Pacem in Terris.'"

Dear Brothers and Sisters,

1. In the dark days of the Cold War, Blessed Pope John XXIII's Encyclical Letter *Pacem in Terris* came as a beacon of hope to men and women of good will. Declaring that authentic peace requires "diligent observance of the divinely established order" (*Pacem in Terris*, 1), the Holy Father pointed to truth, justice, charity and freedom as the pillars of a peaceful society (ibid., 37).

The emergence of the power of modern social communications formed an important part of the Encyclical's background. Pope John XXIII had the media especially in mind when he called for "fairness and impartiality" in the use of "instruments for the promotion and spread of mutual understanding between nations" afforded by science and technology; he decried "ways of disseminating information which violate the principles of truth and justice, and injure the reputation of another nation" (ibid., 90).

2. Today, as we observe the fortieth anniversary of *Pacem in Terris*, the division of peoples into opposing blocs is mostly a painful memory, but peace, justice and social stability are still lacking in many parts of the world. Terrorism, conflict in the Middle East and other regions, threats and counter-threats, injustice, exploitation, and assaults upon the dignity and sanctity of human life both before and after birth are dismaying realities of our times.

Meanwhile, the power of the media to shape human relationships and influence political and social life, both for good and for ill, has enormously increased. Hence the timeliness of the theme chosen for the Thirty-seventh World Day of Communications: "The Communications Media at the Service of Authentic Peace in the Light of *Pacem in Terris*." The world and the media still have much to learn from the message of Blessed Pope John XXIII.

3. Media and Truth. The fundamental moral requirement of all communication is respect for and service of the truth. Freedom to seek and speak what is true is essential to human communication, not only in relation to facts and information but also, and especially, regarding the nature and destiny of the human person, regarding society and the common good, regarding our relationship with God. The mass media have an inescapable responsibility in this sense, since they constitute the modern arena in which ideas are shared and people can grow in mutual understanding and solidarity.

4. Media and Justice. Blessed Pope John XXIII spoke eloquently in *Pacem in Terris* of the universal human good — "the good, that is, of the whole human family" (No.132) — in which every individual and all peoples have a right to share.

The global outreach of the media carries with it special responsibilities in this regard. While it is true that the media often belong to particular interest groups, private and public, the very nature of their impact on life requires that they must not serve to set one group against another - for example, in the name of class conflict, exaggerated nationalism, racial supremacy, ethnic cleansing, and the like. Setting some against others in the name of religion is a particularly serious failure against truth and justice, as is discriminatory treatment of religious beliefs, since these belong to the deepest realm of the human person's dignity and freedom.

5. Media and Freedom. Freedom is a precondition of true peace as well as one of its most precious fruits. The media serve freedom by serving truth: they obstruct freedom to the extent that they depart from what is true by disseminating falsehoods or creating a climate of unsound emotional reaction to events. Only when people have free access to true and sufficient information can they pursue the common good and hold public authority accountable.

6. Media and Love. "The anger of man does not work the righteousness of God" (James 1:20). At the height of the Cold War, Blessed Pope John XXIII expressed this simple but profound thought on what the path to peace entailed: "The preservation of peace will have to be dependent on a radically different principle from the one which is operative at the present time. True peace among nations must depend not on the possession of an equal supply of weapons, but

solely upon mutual trust" (*Pacem in Terris*, 113).

The communications media are key actors in today's world, and they have an immense role to play in building that trust. Their power is such that in a few short days they can create the positive or negative public reaction to events which suits their purposes. Reasonable people will realize that such enormous power calls for the highest standards of commitment to truth and goodness.

Challenging as all this is, it is by no means asking too much of the men and women of the media. For by vocation as well as by profession they are called to be agents of truth, justice, freedom, and love, contributing by their important work to a social order "founded on truth, built up on justice, nurtured and animated by charity, and brought into effect under the auspices of freedom" (*Pacem in Terris*, 167). My prayer therefore on this year's World Communications Day is that the men and women of the media will ever more wholly live up to the challenge of their calling: service of the universal common good. Their personal fulfillment and the peace and happiness of the world depend greatly on this. May God bless them with light and courage.

HONORS AND AWARDS

Pontifical Orders

The Pontifical Orders of Knighthood are secular orders of merit whose membership depends directly on the pope.

Supreme Order of Christ (Militia of Our Lord Jesus Christ): The highest of the five pontifical orders of knighthood, the Supreme Order of Christ was approved Mar. 14, 1319, by John XXII as a continuation in Portugal of the suppressed Order of Templars. Members were religious with vows and a rule of life until the order lost its religious character toward the end of the 15th century. Since that time it has existed as an order of merit. Paul VI, in 1966, restricted awards of the order to Christian heads of state.

Order of the Golden Spur (Golden Militia): Although the original founder is not certainly known, this order is one of the oldest knighthoods. Indiscriminate bestowal and inheritance diminished its prestige, however, and in 1841 Gregory XVI replaced it with the Order of St. Sylvester and gave it the title of Golden Militia. In 1905 St. Pius X restored the Order of the Golden Spur in its own right, separating it from the Order of St. Sylvester. Paul VI, in 1966, restricted awards of the order to Christian heads of state.

Order of Pius IX: Founded by Pius IX June 17, 1847, the order is awarded for outstanding services for the Church and society, and may be given to non-Catholics as well as Catholics. The title to nobility formerly attached to membership was abolished by Pius XII in 1939. In 1957 Pius XII instituted the Class of the Grand Collar as the highest category of the order; in 1966, Paul VI restricted this award to heads of state "in solemn circumstances." The other three classes are of Knights of the Grand Cross, Knight Commanders with and without emblem, and Knights. The new class was created to avoid difficulties in presenting papal honors to Christian or non-Christian leaders of high merit.

Order of St. Gregory the Great: First established by Gregory XVI in 1831 to honor citizens of the Papal States, the order is conferred on persons who are distinguished for personal character and reputation, and for notable accomplishment. The order has civil and military divisions, and three classes of knights.

Order of St. Sylvester: Instituted Oct. 31, 1841, by Gregory XVI to absorb the Order of the Golden Spur, this order was divided into two by St. Pius X in 1905, one retaining the name of St. Sylvester and the other assuming the title of Golden Militia. Membership consists of three degrees: Knights of the Grand Cross, Knight Commanders with and without emblem, and Knights.

Papal Medals

Pro Ecclesia et Pontifice: This decoration ("For the Church and the Pontiff") had its origin in 1888 as a token of the golden sacerdotal jubilee of Leo XIII; he bestowed it on those who had assisted in the observance of his jubilee and on persons responsible for the success of the Vatican Exposition. The medal, cruciform in shape, bears the likenesses of Sts. Peter and Paul, the tiara and the papal keys, the words *Pro Ecclesia et Pontifice*, and the name of the present pontiff, all on the same side; it is attached to a ribbon of yellow and white, the papal colors. Originally, the medal was issued in gold, silver or bronze. It is awarded in recognition of service to the Church and the papacy.

Benemerenti: Several medals ("To a well-deserving person") have been conferred by popes for exceptional accomplishment and service. The medals, which are made of gold, silver or bronze, bear the likeness and name of the reigning pope on one side; on the other, a laurel crown and the letter "B." These two medals may be given by the pope to both men and women. Their bestowal does not convey any title or honor of knighthood.

Ecclesiastical Orders

Equestrian Order of the Holy Sepulchre of Jerusalem

The order traces its origin to Godfrey de Bouillon who instituted it in 1099. It took its name from the Basilica of the Holy Sepulchre where its members were knighted. After the fall of the Latin Kingdom of Jerusalem and the consequent departure of the knights from the Holy Land, national divisions were established in various countries.

The order was re-organized by Pius IX in 1847 when he reestablished the Latin Patriarchate of Jerusalem and placed the order under the jurisdiction of its patriarch. In 1888, Leo XIII confirmed permission to admit women — Ladies of the Holy Sepulchre — to all degrees of rank. Pius X reserved the office of grand master to himself in 1907; Pius XII gave the order a cardinal patron in 1940 and, in 1949, transferred the office of grand master from the pope to the cardinal patron. Pope John XXIII approved updated constitutions in 1962; the latest statutes were approved by Paul VI in 1977.

The purposes of the order are strictly religious and charitable. Members are committed to sustain and aid the charitable, cultural and social works of the Catholic Church in the Holy Land, particularly in the Latin Patriarchate of Jerusalem.

The order is composed of knights and ladies grouped in three classes: class of Knights of the Collar and Ladies of the Collar; Class of Knights (in four grades); Class of Ladies (in four grades). Members are appointed by the cardinal grand master according to procedures outlined in the constitution.

Under the present constitution the order is divided into national lieutenancies, largely autonomous, with international headquarters in Rome. Cardinal Carlo Furno is the grand master of the order.

There are nine lieutenancies of the order in the United States and one in Puerto Rico. Vice Governor General: F. Russell Kendall, 309 Knipp Rd., Houston, TX 77024; (713) 468-5602.

Order of Malta

The Sovereign Military Hospitaller Order of St. John of Jerusalem and of Rhodes and of Malta traces its origin to a group of men who maintained a Christian hospital in the Holy Land in the 11th century. The group was approved as a religious order — the Hospitallers of St. John — by Paschal II in 1113.

The order, while continuing its service to the poor, principally in hospital work, assumed military duties in the 12th century and included knights, chaplains and sergeants-at-arms among its members. All the knights were professed monks with the vows of poverty, chastity and obedience. Headquarters were located in the Holy Land until the last decade of the 13th century and on Rhodes after 1308 (whence the title, Knights of Rhodes).

After establishing itself on Rhodes, the order became a sovereign power like the sea republics of Italy and the Hanseatic cities of Germany, flying its own flag, coining its own money, floating its own navy, and maintaining diplomatic relations with many nations.

The order was forced to abandon Rhodes in 1522 after the third siege of the island by the Turks under Sultan Suleyman I. Eight years later, the Knights were given the island of Malta, where they remained as a bastion of Christianity until near the end of the 18th century. Headquarters have been located in Rome since 1834.

The title of Grand Master of the Order, in abeyance for some time, was restored by Leo XIII in 1879. A more precise definition of both the religious and the sovereign status of the order was embodied in a new constitution of 1961 and a code issued in 1966.

The four main classifications of members are: Knights of Justice, who are religious with the vows of poverty, chastity and obedience; Knights of Obedience, who make a solemn promise to strive for Christian perfection; Knights of Honor and Devotion and of Grace and Devotion, all of noble lineage; and Knights of Magistral Grace. There are also chaplains, Dames and Donats of the order.

The order, with six grand priories, three sub-priories and 40 national associations, is devoted to hospital and charitable works of all kinds in some 100 countries.

Under the provisions of international law, the order maintains full diplomatic relations with the Holy See — on which, in its double nature, it depends as a religious Order, but of which, as a sovereign Order of Knighthood, it is independent — and 68 countries throughout the world.

The Grand Master, who is the head of the order, has the title of Most Eminent Highness with the rank of Cardinal. He must be of noble lineage and under solemn vows for a minimum period of 10 years, if under 50.

The present Grand Master is Fra' Andrew Willoughby Ninian Bertie, member of the British aristocracy, who was elected for life Apr. 8, 1988, by the Council of State. His election was approved by the pope.

On Dec. 6, 1999, John Paul Reiner, an attorney from Manhattan, was elected the new president of the American Association of the Knights of Malta.

The address of headquarters of the order is Via Condotti, 68, Palazzo Malta, 00187 Rome, Italy; (011) 3906-679-8851. U.S. addresses: American Association, 1011 First Ave., New York, NY 10022; Western Association of U.S.A., 465 California St., Suite 524, San Francisco, CA 94104; Federal Association of U.S.A., 1730 M St. N.W., Suite 403, Washington, D.C. 20036; (202) 331-2494; www.smom.org.

Order of St. George

The Sacred Military Constantinian Order of St. George was established by Pope Clement XI in 1718. The purposes of the order are to work for the preaching and defense of the Catholic faith and to promote the spiritual and physical welfare of sick, disabled, homeless and other unfortunate persons. The principal officer is Prince Carlo of Bourbon-Two Sicilies, duke of Calabria. Addresses: Via Sistina 121, 00187 Rome, Italy; Via Duomo 149, 80138 Naples, Italy; American Delegation, 302 Gessner Rd., Houston, TX 77024; (713) 888-0242.

2003 CATHOLIC PRESS ASSOCIATION AWARDS

Catholic Press Association Awards for material published in 2002 were presented on May 30, 2003, during the annual Catholic Press Association Convention in Atlanta. Awards included:

Newspapers — General Excellence

National Newspapers: *National Catholic Reporter*, First Place; *The Catholic Register,* Second Place; *Our Sunday Visitor*, Third Place.

Diocesan Newspapers, 40,001+ Circulation: *The Tidings* (Los Angeles, CA), First Place; *The*

Catholic Review (Baltimore, MD), Second Place; *Western New York Catholic* (Buffalo, NY), Third Place.

Diocesan Newspapers, 17,001-40,000: *Today's Catholic* (Fort Wayne, IN), First Place; *The Catholic Herald* (Milwaukee, WI), Second Place; *The Catholic Sun* (Syracuse, NY), Third Place.

Diocesan Newspapers, 1-17,000: *Hawaii Catholic Herald* (Honolulu, HI), First Place; *Catholic Anchor* (Anchorage, AK), Second Place; *Idaho Catholic Register* (Boise, ID), Third Place.

Magazines — General Excellence

General Interest: *Faith and Family* (North Haven, CT), First Place; *U.S. Catholic* (Chicago, IL), Second Place; St. Anthony Messenger (Cincinnati, OH), Third Place; *Catholic Parent* (Huntington, IN) and *St. Augustine Catholic* (Jacksonville, FL), Honorable Mention.

Mission Magazines: *Mission* (New York, NY), First Place; *CNEWA World* (New York, NY), Second Place; *Maryknoll Magazine* (Maryknoll, NY), Third Place; *EXTENSION Magazine* (Chicago, IL), *Columban Mission* (St. Columbans, NE), Honorable Mention.

Religious Order: *Roze Maryi* (Stockbridge, MA), First Place; *Marian Helper* (Stockbridge, MA), Second Place; *The Anthonian* (Paterson, NJ), Third Place; *The Abbey Banner*, Honorable Mention.

Professional/Special Interest: *Faith Magazine* (Lansing, MI), First Place; *Church Magazine* (New York, NY), Second Place; *CUA Magazine* (Washington, DC), Third Place; *My Friend* (Boston, MA), *Review for Religious* (St. Louis, MO), *The Priest* (Huntington, IN), and *Today's Catholic Teacher* (Dayton, OH), Honorable Mention.

Scholarly: *National Catholic Bioethics Quarterly* (Boston, MA), First Place; *Horizons* (Villanova, PA), Second Place; *American Catholic Studies* (Villanova, PA), Third Place; *Catholic Southwest: A Journal of History & Culture* (Azle, TX), Honorable Mention.

Prayer and Spirituality: *Desert Call* (Crestone, CO), First Place; *Magnificat* (Yonkers, NY), Second Place; *Spiritual Life* (Washington, DC), Third Place; *Queen of All Hearts* (Bay Shore, NY), *The Bible Today* (Collegeville, MN), Honorable Mention.

Newsletters

General Interest: *The CARA Report* (Washington, DC), First Place; *Youth Update* (Cincinnati, OH), Second Place; *Every Day Catholic* (Cincinnati, OH), Third Place; *Christopher News Notes* (New York, NY), Honorable Mention.

Special Interest: *Call to Action*, First Place; *At Home with our Faith* (Chicago, IL), Second Place; *Mission – Friendship Club News* (Belleville, IL),

Third Place; *Scripture from Scratch* (Cincinnati, OH), Honorable Mention.

Books — First Place Awards

Popular Presentation of the Catholic Faith: Viking Compass Books, *Thirty Days*, Paul Mariani.

Spirituality, Softcover: Crossroad, *The Jesus Meditations*, Michael Kennedy with Martin Sheen. **Hardcover**: Orbis, *The Cosmic Dance*, Joyce Rupp and Mary Southard; St. Anthony Messenger, *Healing Plants of the Bible*, Vincenzina Krymow.

Theology: Paulist Press, *Original Sin*, Tatha Wiley.

Scripture: Orbis, *Lamentations and the Tears of the World*, Kathleen M. O'Connor.

Liturgy: Liturgy Training Publications, *The Weekday Lectionary: Ritual Edition*, Bishops' Committee on the Liturgy, USCCB.

Pastoral Ministry: Liturgical Press, *Sacred Silence: Denial and the Crisis in the Church*, Donald Cozzens.

Professional Books:: Liturgical Press, *Hearing the Word of God*, John R. Donhaue.

Educational Books: Orbis, *Reading the Bible from the Margins*, Miguel A. De La Torre.

Design and Production: Loyola, *God in the Garden*, Maureen Gilmer.

Children's Books: Pauline Books and Media, *God is Here: When Bad Things Happen*, Mary Martha Moss, FSP.

First Time Author of a Book: Orbis Books, *The Blindfold's Eyes*, Sister Dianna Ortiz and Patricia Davis.

Family Life: Ave Maria Press, *Daddyhood*, Daniel W. Driscoll.

History/Biography: Orbis Books, *The Blindfold's Eyes*, Sister Dianna Ortiz and Patricia Davis.

Gender Issues: Crossroad, *The Church Women Want*, Elizabeth Johnson.

Spanish Language Titles: Liturgy Training Publications, *La Iniciacion Cristiana: Un Recurso Basico*, Miguel Arias, Walter Fircowycz, Richard E. McCarron, Arturo J. Perez-Rodriguez, Tim Piasecki, Juan J. Sosa, Richard Vega.

Reference: Orbis Books, *The Thomas Merton Encyclopedia*, William H. Shannon, Christine M. Bochen, Patrick F. O'Connell.

2003 CHRISTOPHER AWARDS

Christopher Awards are given each year to recognize the creative writers, producers and directors who have achieved artistic excellence in films, books and television specials affirming the highest values of the human spirit. The 2003 awards were presented Feb. 27, 2003, in New York.

Books: *Five Past Midnight in Bhopal* by Dominique Lapierre and Javier Moro; *Standing on Holy Ground* by Sandra E. Johnson; *The Day the World Came to Town* by Jim DeFede; *Choosing Naia* by Mitchell Zuckoff; *Fatal Passage* by Ken McGoogan; and *Jim's Last Summer* by Teresa Rhodes McGee.

Books for Young People: *Mole and the Baby Bird* by Marjorie Newman and illustrated by Patrick Benson, preschool; *Dear Mrs. LaRue: Letters From Obedience School* by Mark Teague, ages 6-8; *The Ugly*

Princess and the Wise Fool by Margaret Gray and illustrated by Randy Cecil, ages 8-10; *Pictures of Hollis Woods* by Patricia Reilly Giff, ages 10-12; and *Left for Dead* by Peter Nelson, young adult.

Television Specials: CBS's "The Rosa Parks Story," PBS's *The Rise and Fall of Jim Crow*; HBO's "Murder on a Sunday Morning"; PBS's *Frontline* documentary "Faith and Doubt at Ground Zero"; CBS's "9/11"; ABC reality miniseries "ICU: Arkansas Children's Hospital"; Cinemax pay-cable Holocaust documentary miniseries "Broken Silence"; and the TNT cable movie *Door to Door*.

Films: *Signs About a Boy*; *Antwone Fisher*; *Evelyn*; *Rabbit-Proof Fence*; *Spirited Away*.

James Keller Award: Mystery novelist Mary Higgins Clark was named winner of The Christophers' lifetime achievement award.

"THE CHURCH AND INTERNET" AND "ETHICS IN INTERNET"

On Feb. 28, 2002, the Pontifical Council for Social Communications under Abp. John P. Foley issued two documents encouraging the Church to embrace the technology of the Internet and to help utilize it for the benefit of all humanity.

The two 27-page documents, "Ethics in Internet" and "The Church and Internet," provide assessments of the ethical demands of the Internet and the online pastoral opportunities of the World Wide Web. Russell Shaw, a U.S. journalist who serves as a consultor on the council, headed the drafting process. Here are excerpts:

"The Church and Internet"

The Church's interest in the Internet is a particular expression of her longstanding interest in the media of social communication. Seeing the media as an outcome of the historical scientific process by which humankind "advances further and further in the discovery of the resources and values contained in the whole of creation," the Church often has declared her conviction that they are, in the words of the Second Vatican Council, "marvellous technical inventions" that already do much to meet human needs and may yet do even more....

The Church has a two-fold aim in regard to the media. One aspect is to encourage their right development and right use for the sake of human development, justice, and peace — for the upbuilding of society at the local, national, and community levels in light of the common good and in a spirit of solidarity. Considering the great importance of social communications, the Church seeks "honest and respectful dialogue with those responsible for the communications media"—a dialogue that relates primarily to the shaping of media policy....

... We offer words of encouragement to several groups in particular — Church leaders, pastoral personnel, educators, parents, and especially young people.

To Church leaders. People in leadership positions in all sectors of the Church need to understand the media, apply this understanding in formulating pastoral plans for social communications together with concrete policies and programs in this area, and make appropriate use of media....

To pastoral personnel. Priests, deacons, religious, and lay pastoral workers should have media education to increase their understanding of the impact of social communications on individuals and society and help them acquire a manner of communicating that speaks to the sensibilities and interests of people in a media culture....

To educators and catechists. The Pastoral Instruction *Communio et Progressio* spoke of the "urgent duty" of Catholic schools to train communicators and recipients of social communications in relevant Christian principles. The same message has been repeated many times. In the age of the Internet, with its enormous outreach and impact, the need is more urgent than ever.

To parents. ... As far as the Internet is concerned, children and young people often are more familiar with it than their parents are, but parents still are seriously obliged to guide and supervise their children in its use If this means learning more about the Internet than they have up to now, that will be all to good.

To children and young people. The Internet is a door opening on a glamorous and exciting world with a powerful formative influence; but not everything on the other side of the door is safe and wholesome and true.... The Internet places in the grasp of young people at an unusually early age an immense capacity for doing good and doing harm, to themselves and others. It can enrich their lives beyond the dreams of earlier generations and empower them to enrich others' lives in turn. It also can plunge them into consumerism, pornographic and violent fantasy, and pathological isolation.

To all persons of good will. Finally, then, we would suggest some virtues that need to be cultivated by everyone who wants to make good use of the Internet; their exercise should be based upon and guided by a realistic appraisal of its contents.

"Ethics in Internet"

... The Internet has a number of striking features. It is instantaneous, immediate, worldwide, decentralized, interactive, endlessly expandable in contents and outreach, flexible and adaptable to a remarkable degree. It is egalitarian, in the sense that anyone with the necessary equipment and modest technical skill can be an active presence in cyberspace, declare his or her message to the world, and demand a hearing. It allows individuals to indulge in anonymity, role-playing, and fantasizing and also to enter into community with others and engage in sharing....

One of the most important [concerns] involves what today is called the digital divide — a form of discrimination dividing the rich from the poor, both within and among nations, on the basis of access, or lack of access, to the new information technology. In this sense it is an updated version of an older gap between the "information rich" and "information poor".... We are particularly concerned about the cultural dimensions of what is now taking place.... Cultures have much to learn from one another, and merely imposing the world view, values, and even language of one culture upon another is not dialogue but cultural imperialism. Cultural domination is an especially serious problem when a dominant culture carries false values inimical to the true good of individuals and groups. As matters stand, the Internet, along with the other media of social communication, is transmitting the value-laden message of Western secular culture to people and societies in many cases ill-prepared to evaluate and cope with it....

It also can help men and women in their age-old search for self-understanding. In every age, including our own, people ask the same fundamental questions: "Who am I? Where have I come from and where am I going? Why is there evil? What is there after this life?" The Church cannot impose answers, but she can—and must—proclaim to the world the answers she has received; and today, as always, she offers the one ultimately satisfying answer to the deepest questions of life—Jesus Christ, who "fully reveals man to himself and brings to light his most high calling". Like today's world itself, the world of media, including the Internet, has been brought by Christ, inchoately yet truly, within the boundaries of the kingdom of God and placed in service to the word of salvation.

Ecumenism and Interreligious Dialogue

ECUMENISM

(*Sources: Brother Jeffrey Gros, F.S.C. and Rev. Ronald Roberson, C.S.P., associate directors, Secretariat for Ecumenical and Interreligious Affairs, USCCB.*)

The modern ecumenical movement, with roots in nineteenth-century scholars and individuals began its institutional life in 1910 among Protestants and Orthodox and led to formation of the World Council of Churches in 1948, developed outside the mainstream of Catholic interest for many years. It has now become for Catholics as well one of the great religious facts of our time.

The *magna carta* of ecumenism for Catholics is a complex of several documents which include, in the first place, *Unitatis Redintegratio*, the "Decree on Ecumenism," promulgated by the Second Vatican Council Nov. 21, 1964. Other enactments underlying and expanding this decree are *Lumen Gentium* ("Dogmatic Constitution on the Church"), *Orientalium Ecclesiarum* ("Decree on Eastern Catholic Churches"), and *Gaudium et Spes* ("Pastoral Constitution on the Church in the Modern World").

The Holy See has more recently brought together Catholic ecumenical priorities in *Directory for the Application of Principles and Norms on Ecumenism* (1993) and *The Ecumenical Dimension in the Formation of Pastoral Workers* (1998). These, in addition to Pope John Paul II's encyclical letter, *Ut Unum Sint* (1995), provide a guide for Catholic ecumenical initiatives.

VATICAN II DECREE

The following excerpts from Unitatis Redintegratio *cover the broad theological background and principles and indicate the thrust of the Church's commitment to ecumenism.*

Men who believe in Christ and have been properly baptized are brought into a certain, though imperfect, communion with the Catholic Church. Undoubtedly, the differences that exist in varying degrees between them and the Catholic Church — whether in doctrine and sometimes in discipline, or concerning the structure of the Church — do indeed create many and sometimes serious obstacles to full ecclesiastical communion. These the ecumenical movement is striving to overcome (No. 3).

Elements Common to Christians

Moreover some, even very many, of the most significant elements or endowments which together go to build up and give life to the Church herself can exist outside the visible boundaries of the Catholic Church: the written word of God; the life of grace; faith, hope, and charity, along with other interior gifts of the Holy Spirit and visible elements. All of these, which come from Christ and lead back to Him, belong by right to the one Church of Christ (No. 3).

[In a later passage, the decree singled out a number of elements which the Catholic Church and other churches have in common but not in complete agreement: confession of Christ as Lord and God and as mediator between God and man; belief in the Trinity; reverence for Scripture as the revealed word of God; baptism and the Lord's Supper; Christian life and worship; faith in action; concern with moral questions.]

The brethren divided from us also carry out many of the sacred actions of the Christian religion. Undoubtedly, in ways that vary according to the condition of each church or community, these actions can truly engender a life of grace, and can be rightly described as capable of providing access to the community of salvation.

It follows that these separated Churches and Communities, though we believe they suffer from defects already mentioned, have by no means been deprived of significance and importance in the mystery of salvation. For the Spirit of Christ has not refrained from using them as means of salvation which derive their efficacy from the very fullness of grace and truth entrusted to the Catholic Church (No. 3).

Unity Lacking

Nevertheless, our separated brethren, whether considered as individuals or as Communities and Churches, are not blessed with that unity which Jesus Christ wished to bestow on all those whom he has regenerated and vivified into one body and newness of life - that unity which the holy Scriptures and the revered tradition of the Church proclaim. For it is through Christ's Catholic Church alone, which is the all-embracing means of salvation, that the fullness of the means of salvation can be obtained. It was to the apostolic college alone, of which Peter is the head, that we believe our Lord entrusted all the blessings of the New Covenant, in order to establish on earth the one Body of Christ into which all those should be fully incorporated who already belong in any way to God's People (No. 3).

What the Movement Involves

Today, in many parts of the world, under the inspiring grace of the Holy Spirit, multiple efforts are being expended through prayer, word, and action to attain that fullness of unity which Jesus Christ desires. This sacred Synod, therefore, exhorts all the Catholic faithful to recognize the signs of the times and to participate skillfully in the work of ecumenism.

The "ecumenical movement" means those activities and enterprises which, according to various needs of the Church and opportune occasions, are started and organized for the fostering of unity among Christians. These are:

• First, every effort to eliminate words, judgments, and actions which do not respond to the condition of separated brethren with truth and fairness and so make mutual relations between them more difficult.

• Then, "dialogue" between competent experts from different Churches and Communities [scholarly ecumenism].

• In addition, these Communions cooperate more closely in whatever projects a Christian conscience demands for the common good [social ecumenism].

• They also come together for common prayer, where this is permitted [spiritual ecumenism].

• Finally, all are led to examine their own faithfulness to Christ's will for the Church and, wherever necessary, undertake with vigor the task of renewal and reform.

It is evident that the work of preparing and reconciling those individuals who wish for full Catholic communion is of its nature distinct from ecumenical action. But there is no opposition between the two, since both proceed from the wondrous providence of God (No. 4).

Primary Duty of Catholics

In ecumenical work, Catholics must assuredly be concerned for their separated brethren, praying for them, keeping them informed about the Church, making the first approaches toward them. But their primary duty is to make an honest and careful appraisal of whatever needs to be renewed and achieved in the Catholic household itself, in order that its life may bear witness more loyally and luminously to the teachings and ordinances which have been handed down from Christ through the Apostles.

Every Catholic must aim at Christian perfection (cf. Jas. 1:4; Rom. 12:1-2) and, each according to his station, play his part so that the Church may daily be more purified and renewed, against the day when Christ will present her to himself in all her glory, without spot or wrinkle (cf. Eph. 5:27).

Catholics must joyfully acknowledge and esteem the truly Christian endowments from our common heritage which are to be found among our separated brethren.

Nor should we forget that whatever is wrought by the grace of the Holy Spirit in the hearts of our separated brethren can contribute to our own edification. Whatever is truly Christian never conflicts with the genuine interests of the faith; indeed, it can always result in a more ample realization of the very mystery of Christ and the Church (No. 4).

Participation in Worship

Norms concerning participation by Catholics in the worship of other Christian Churches were sketched in this conciliar decree and elaborated in a number of other documents such as: the Decree on Eastern Catholic Churches, promulgated by the Second Vatican Council in 1964; Interim Guidelines for Prayer in Common, issued June 18, 1965, by the U.S. Bishops' Committee for Ecumenical and Interreligious Affairs; a Directory on Ecumenism, published in 1967, 1970 and 1993 by the Pontifical Council for Promoting Christian Unity; additional communications from the U.S. Bishops' Committee, and numerous sets of guidelines issued locally by and for dioceses throughout the U.S.

The norms encourage common prayer services for Christian unity and other intentions. Beyond that, they draw a distinction between separated churches of the Reformation tradition and of the Anglican Communion, and separated Eastern churches, in view of doctrine and practice the Catholic Church has in common with the separated Eastern churches concerning the apostolic succession of bishops, holy orders, liturgy and other credal matters.

Full participation by Catholics in official Protestant liturgies is prohibited, because it implies profession of the faith expressed in the liturgy. Intercommunion by Catholics at Protestant liturgies is prohibited. Under certain conditions, Protestants may be given Holy Communion in the Catholic Church (*see* **Intercommunion**). A Catholic may stand as a witness, but not as a sponsor, in baptism, and as a witness in the marriage of separated Christians. Similarly, a Protestant may stand as a witness, but not as a sponsor, in a Catholic baptism, and as a witness in the marriage of Catholics.

The principal norms regarding liturgical participations with separated Eastern Churches are included under Eastern Ecumenism.

DIRECTORY ON ECUMENISM

A Directory for the Application of the Principles and Norms of Ecumenism *was approved by Pope John Paul II on Mar. 25, 1993, and published early in June. The Pontifical Council for Promoting Christian Unity said on release of the document that revision of Directories issued in 1967 and 1970 was necessary in view of subsequent developments. These included promulgation of the Code of Canon Law for the Latin Church in 1983 and of the Code of Canons of the Eastern Churches in 1990; publication of the* Catechism of the Catholic Church *in 1992; additional documents and the results of theological dialogues.*

In 1998, The Ecumenical Dimension in the Formation of Pastoral Workers *was published by the Holy See to give practical and detailed guidance in the implementation of Chapter 3 of the* Directory.

The following excerpts are from the text published in the June 16, 1993, English edition of L'Osservatore Romano.

Address and Purpose

"The Directory is addressed to the pastors of the Catholic Church, but it also concerns all the faithful, who are called to pray and work for the unity of Christians, under the direction of their bishops."

"At the same time, it is hoped that the Directory will also be useful to members of churches and ecclesial communities that are not in full communion with the Catholic Church."

"The new edition of the Directory is meant to be an instrument at the service of the whole Church, and especially of those who are directly engaged in ecumenical activity in the Catholic Church. The Directory intends to motivate, enlighten and guide this activity, and in some particular cases also to give binding directives in accordance with the proper competence of the Pontifical Council for Promoting Christian Unity."

Outline

Principles and norms of the document are covered in five chapters.

"I. The Search for Christian Unity. The ecumenical commitment of the Catholic Church based on the doctrinal principles of the Second Vatican Council.

"II. Organization in the Catholic Church at the Service of Christian Unity. Persons and structures involved in promoting ecumenism at all levels, and the norms that direct their activity.

"III. Ecumenical Formation in the Catholic Church. Categories of people to be formed, those responsible for formation; the aims and methods of formation; its doctrinal and practical aspects.

"IV. Communion in Life and Spiritual Activity among the Baptized. The communion that exists with other Christians on the basis of the sacramental bond of baptism, and the norms for sharing in prayer and other spiritual activities, including, in particular cases, sacramental sharing.

"V. Ecumenical Cooperation, Dialogue and Common Witness. Principles, different forms and norms for cooperation between Christians with a view to dialogue and common witness in the world."

ECUMENICAL AGENCIES

Pontifical Council

The top-level agency for Catholic ecumenical efforts is the Pontifical Council for Promoting Christian Unity (formerly the Secretariat for Promoting Christian Unity), which originated in 1960 as a preparatory commission for the Second Vatican Council. Its purposes are to provide guidance and, where necessary, coordination for ecumenical endeavor by Catholics, and to establish and maintain relations with representatives of other Christian Churches for ecumenical dialogue and action.

The council, under the direction of Cardinal Walter Kasper (successor to Cardinal Edward I. Cassidy), has established firm working relations with representative agencies of other churches and the World Council of Churches. It has joined in dialogue with Orthodox Churches, the Anglican Communion, the Lutheran World Federation, the World Alliance of Reformed Churches, the World Methodist Council, Baptist World Alliance, World Evangelical Alliance, the Pentecostals, Mennonites and other religious bodies. In the past several years, staff members and representatives of the council have been involved in one way or another in nearly every significant ecumenical enterprise and meeting held throughout the world.

While the council and its counterparts in other churches have focused primary attention on theological and other related problems of Christian unity, they have also begun, and in increasing measure, to emphasize the responsibilities of the churches for greater unity of witness and effort in areas of humanitarian need.

Bishops' Committee

The U.S. Bishops' Committee for Ecumenical and Interreligious Affairs was established by the American hierarchy in 1964. Its purposes are to maintain relationships with other Christian churches and other religious communities at the national level, to help other offices of the Conference do their work ecumenically, to advise and assist dioceses in developing and applying ecumenical policies, and to maintain liaison with corresponding Vatican offices — the Pontifical Councils for Christian Unity and for Interreligious Dialogue.

This standing committee of the National Conference of Catholic Bishops is chaired by Bishop Stephen E. Blaire of Stockton. Operationally, the committee is assisted with Rev. Arthur L. Kennedy, executive director; Dr. Eugene J. Fisher, executive secretary for Catholic-Jewish Relations; Dr. John Borelli, executive secretary for Interreligious Relations, the Rev. Ronald Roberson, C.S.P., and Brother Jeffrey Gros, F.S.C., associate directors.

The committee co-sponsors several national consultations with other churches and confessional families. These bring together Catholic representatives and their counterparts from the Episcopal Church, Evangelical Lutheran Church in America, the Polish National Catholic Church, the United Methodist Church, the Orthodox Churches, the Oriental Orthodox Churches, the Alliance of Reformed Churches: the United Church of Christ, the Presbyterian Church and Reformed Church in America. (See Ecumenical Dialogues.)

The committee relates with the National Council of Churches of Christ, through membership in the Faith and Order Commission and through observer relationship with the Commission on Ecumenical Networks, and has sponsored a joint study committee investigating the possibility of Roman Catholic membership in that body in the 1970's. Collaboration in multiple areas of Church life have proved to be more fruitful than membership given the disparity of numbers and diversity of program priorities of the Bishop's Conference and the Council.

The USCCB in currently considering membership in a new ecumenical entity, The Christian Churches Together in the USA. If this body comes into existence, it will include at least representatives from the Evangelical and Pentecostal churches, the Orthodox churches, the African American and ethnic churches, the Catholic Church and historic Protestant churches.

Advisory and other services are provided by the committee to ecumenical commissions and agencies in dioceses throughout the world.

Through its Section for Catholic-Jewish Relations, the committee is in contact with several national Jewish agencies and bodies. Issues of mutual interest and shared concern are reviewed for the purpose of furthering deeper understanding between the Catholic and Jewish communities.

Through its Section for Interreligious Relations, the committee promotes activity in wider areas of dialogue with other religions, notably, with Muslims, Buddhists and Hindus. Offices of the committee are located at 3211 Fourth St. N.E., Washington, DC 20017; www.usccb.org/seia/index.htm.

World Council of Churches

The World Council of Churches is a fellowship of churches which acknowledge "Jesus Christ as Lord and Savior." It is a permanent organization providing constituent members — 330 churches with some 450 million communicants in 100 countries — with opportunities for meeting, consultation and cooperative action with respect to doctrine, worship, practice, social mission, evangelism and missionary work, and other matters of mutual concern.

The WCC was formally established Aug. 23, 1948, in Amsterdam with ratification of a constitution by 147 communions. This action merged two previously existing movements — Life and Work (social mission), Faith and Order (doctrine) — which had initiated practical steps toward founding a fellowship of Christian churches at meetings held in Oxford, Edinburgh and Utrecht in 1937 and 1938. A third movement for cooperative missionary work, which originated about 1910 and, remotely, led to formation of the WCC, was incorporated into the council in 1971 under the title of the International Missionary Council.

Additional general assemblies of the council have been held since the charter meeting of 1948: in Evanston, Ill. (1954), New Delhi, India (1961), Uppsala, Sweden (1968), Nairobi, Kenya (1975), Vancouver, British Columbia, Canada (1983) and Canberra, Australia (1991). The 1998 general assembly was held in Harare, Zimbabwe, with the regular Catholic delegation in attendance, led by Bishop Mario Conti from St. Andrew's, Scotland.

The council continues the work of the International Missionary Council, the Commission on Faith and Order, and the Commission on Church and Society. The work of the council is carried out through four program units: unity and renewal; mission, education and witness; justice, peace and creation; sharing and service.

Liaison between the council and the Vatican has been maintained since 1966 through a joint working group. Roman Catholic membership in the WCC is a question officially on the agenda of this body. The Joint Commission on Society, Development and Peace (SODEPAX) was an agency of the council and the Pontifical Commission for Justice and Peace from 1968 to Dec. 31, 1980, after which another working group was formed. Roman Catholics serve individually as full members of the Commission on Faith and Order and in various capacities on other program committees of the council.

WCC headquarters are located in Geneva, Switzerland. The United States Conference for the World Council of Churches at 475 Riverside Drive, Room 915, New York, NY 10115, provides liaison between the U.S. churches and Geneva, a communications office for secular and church media relations, and a publications office. The WCC also maintains frater-

nal relations with regional, national and local councils of churches throughout the world. Web site: http://www.wcc-coe.org/wcc/english.html.

National Council of Churches

The National Council of the Churches of Christ in the U.S.A., the largest ecumenical body in the United States, is an organization of 36 Protestant, Orthodox and Anglican communions, with an aggregate membership of about 50 million in 140,000 congregations.

The NCC, established by the churches in 1950, was structured through the merger of 12 separate cooperative agencies. Presently, the NCC carries on work in behalf of member churches in overseas ministries, Christian education, domestic social action, communications, disaster relief, refugee assistance, rehabilitation and development, biblical translation, international affairs, theological dialogue, interfaith activities, worship and evangelism, and other areas.

Policies of the NCC are determined by a general board of approximately 270 members appointed by the constituent churches. The board meets once a year. NCC president: Elenie K. Huszagh, President in 2002-2003; Bishop Thomas L. Hoyt, Jr., President Elect in 2004-2005. General Secretary: Rev. Dr. Robert W. Edgar. NCC headquarters are located at 475 Riverside Drive, New York, NY 10115; (212) 870-2141; www.ncccusa.org.

Consultation on Church Union

(Courtesy of Rev. David W.A. Taylor, General Secretary.)

The Consultation on Church Union, officially begun in 1962, is a venture of American churches seeking a united church "truly catholic, truly evangelical, and truly reformed." The churches engaged in this process, representing 25 million Christians, are the African Methodist Episcopal Church, the African Methodist Episcopal Zion Church, the Christian Church (Disciples of Christ), the Christian Methodist Episcopal Church, the Episcopal Church, the Presbyterian Church (U.S.A.); the United Church of Christ, the United Methodist Church and the International Council of Community Churches.

At a plenary assembly of COCU in December 1988, a plan of church unity was unanimously approved for submission to member churches for their action. The plan is contained in a 102-page document entitled "Churches in Covenant Communion: The Church of Christ Uniting." It proposes the formation of a covenant communion of the churches which, while remaining institutionally autonomous, would embrace together eight elements of ecclesial communion: claiming unity in faith, commitment to seek unity with wholeness, mutual recognition of members in one baptism, mutual recognition of each other as churches, mutual recognition and reconciliation of ordained ministries, celebrating the Eucharist together, engaging together in Christ's mission, and the formation together of covenanting councils at each level (national, regional, and local). At its January 1999 plenary in St. Louis, the churches proposed a 2002 decision to come into full communion as the Churches Uniting in Christ. This new step was celebrated in Memphis, during the week of prayer, in Jan. 2002.

General Secretary: Rev. Dr. Bertrice Wood.

Churches Uniting in Christ, 700 Prospect Avenue East, Cleveland, OH 44115; (216) 736-3295, fax: 216-736-2120.

Graymoor Institute

The Graymoor Ecumenical and Interreligious Institute is a forum where issues that confront the Christian Churches are addressed, the spiritual dimensions of ecumenism are fostered, and information, documentation and developments within the ecumenical movement are published through *Ecumenical Trends*, a monthly journal.

Director: The Rev. James Lougran. Address: 475 Riverside Dr., Rm. 1960, New York, NY 10115-1999.

INTERNATIONAL BILATERAL COMMISSIONS

Anglican-Roman Catholic International Commission, sponsored by the Pontifical Council for Promoting Christian Unity and the Lambeth Conference, from 1970 to 1981; succeeded by a **Second Anglican-Roman Catholic International Commission**, called into being by the Common Declaration of Pope John Paul and the Archbishop of Canterbury in 1982.

The International Theological Colloquium between Baptists and Catholics, established in 1984 by the Pontifical Council for Promoting Christian Unity and the Commission for Faith and Interchurch Cooperation of the Baptist World Alliance.

The Disciples of Christ-Roman Catholic Dialogue, organized by the Council of Christian Unity of the Christian Church (Disciples of Christ) and the U.S. Bishops' Committee for Ecumenical and Interreligious Affairs, along with participation by the Disciples' Ecumenical Consultative Council and the Unity Council; since 1977.

The Evangelical-Roman Catholic Dialogue on Mission, organized by Evangelicals and the Pontifical Council for Promoting Christian Unity; from 1977. This dialogue is now sponsored by the World Evangelical Alliance, on the evangelical side.

The Lutheran-Roman Catholic Commission on Unity, established by the Pontifical Council for Promoting Christian Unity and the Lutheran World Federation; from 1967.

The Joint International Commission for Theological Dialogue between the Orthodox Church and the Catholic Church, established by the Holy See and 14 autocephalous Orthodox Churches, began its work at a first session held at Patmos/Rhodes in 1980. Subsequent sessions have been held at Munich (1982), Crete (1984), Bari (1987), Valamo (1988), Freising (1990), Balamand (1993), and Emmitsburg, Maryland (2000).

Pentecostal-Roman Catholic Conversations, since 1966.

The Reformed-Roman Catholic Conversations, inaugurated in 1970 by the Pontifical Council for Promoting Christian Unity and the World Alliance of Reformed Churches.

The International Joint Commission between the Catholic Church and the Coptic Orthodox Church, since 1974. Established officially in the Common Declaration signed by Pope Paul VI and Coptic Pope Shenouda III in Rome in 1973.

The Joint International Commission between the Roman Catholic Church and the Malankara Orthodox Syrian Church, since 1989.

The Joint Commission between the Catholic Church and the Malankara Jacobite Syrian Orthodox Church, since 1990.

The Assyrian Church of the East-Roman Catholic Dialogue, officially established in the Common Declaration signed by Pope John Paul II and Mar Dinkha IV in November 1994. Has been meeting annually since 1995.

A new Catholic Church-Oriental Orthodox Churches International Joint Commission for Dialogue was planned at a Preparatory Meeting held in Rome in January 2003. The first meeting of the Joint Commission was foreseen for the end of January 2004.

U.S. ECUMENICAL DIALOGUES

Representatives of the Bishops' Committee for Ecumenical and Interreligious Affairs, National Conference of Catholic Bishops, have met in dialogue with representatives of other churches since the 1960s, for discussion of a wide variety of subjects related to the quest for unity among Christians. Following is a list of dialogue groups and the years in which dialogue began.

Anglican-Roman Catholic Consultation, 1965; North American Orthodox-Catholic Theological Consultation, 1965; Joint Committee of Orthodox and Catholic Bishops, 1981; Lutheran Consultation, 1965; Oriental Orthodox Consultation (with Armenian, Coptic, Ethiopian, Indian Malabar and Syrian Orthodox Churches), 1978; Polish National-Catholic Consultation, 1984; Presbyterian/Reformed Consultation, 1965; Southern Baptist Conversations, 1969; United Methodist Consultation, 1966; Faith and Order National Council of Churches, 1968.

COMMON DECLARATIONS OF POPES, OTHER CHURCH LEADERS

(*Source: Secretariat of the Bishops' Committee for Ecumenical and Interreligious Affairs, United States Conference of Catholic Bishops.*)

The following Common Declarations, issued by several popes and heads, carry the authority given them by their signators.

Paul VI and Orthodox Ecumenical Patriarch Athenagoras I, First Common Declaration, Dec. 7, 1965: They hoped the differences between the churches would be overcome with the help of the Holy Spirit, and that their "full communion of faith, brotherly concord and sacramental life" would be restored.

Paul VI and Anglican Archbishop Michael Ramsey of Canterbury, Mar. 24, 1966: They stated their intention "to inaugurate between the Roman

Catholic Church and the Anglican Communion a serious dialogue which, founded on the Gospels and on the ancient common traditions, may lead to that unity in truth for which Christ prayed."

Paul VI and Patriarch Athenagoras I, Second Common Declaration, Oct. 27, 1967: They wished "to emphasize their conviction that the restoration of full communion (between the churches) is to be found within the framework of the renewal of the Church and of Christians in fidelity to the traditions of the Fathers and to the inspirations of the Holy Spirit who remains always with the Church."

Paul VI and Vasken I, Orthodox Catholicos-Patriarch of All Armenians, May 12, 1970: They called for closer collaboration "in all domains of Christian life…. This collaboration must be based on the mutual recognition of the common Christian faith and the sacramental life, on the mutual respect of persons and their churches."

Paul VI and Mar Ignatius Jacob III, Syrian Orthodox Patriarch of Antioch, Oct. 27, 1971: They declared themselves to be "in agreement that there is no difference in the faith they profess concerning the mystery of the Word of God made flesh and become really man, even if over the centuries difficulties have arisen out of the different theological expressions by which this faith was expressed."

Paul VI and Shenouda III, Coptic Orthodox Pope of Alexandria, May 10, 1973: Their common declaration recalls the common elements of the Catholic and Coptic Orthodox faith in the Trinity, the divinity and humanity of Christ, the seven sacraments, the Virgin Mary, the Church founded upon the Apostles, and the Second Coming of Christ. It recognizes that the two churches "are not able to give more perfect witness to this new life in Christ because of existing divisions which have behind them centuries of difficult history" dating back to the year 451 A.D. In spite of these difficulties, they expressed "determination and confidence in the Lord to achieve the fullness and perfection of that unity which is his gift."

Paul VI and Anglican Archbishop Donald Coggan of Canterbury, Apr. 29, 1977: They stated many points on which Anglicans and Roman Catholics hold the faith in common and called for greater cooperation between Anglicans and Roman Catholics.

John Paul II and Orthodox Ecumenical Patriarch Dimitrios I, First Common Declaration, Nov. 30, 1979: "Purification of the collective memory of our churches is an important fruit of the dialogue of charity and an indispensable condition of future progress." They announced the establishment of the Catholic-Orthodox Theological Commission.

John Paul II and Anglican Archbishop Robert Runcie of Canterbury, May 29, 1982: They agreed to establish a new Anglican-Roman Catholic commission with the task of continuing work already begun toward the eventual resolution of doctrinal differences.

John Paul II and Ignatius Zakka I, Syrian Orthodox Patriarch of Antioch, June 23, 1984: They recalled and solemnly reaffirmed the common profession of faith made by their predecessors, Paul VI and Mar Ignatius Jacob III, in 1971. They said: "The confusions and the schisms that occurred between the churches, they realize today, in no way affect or touch the substance of their faith, since these arose only because of differences in terminology and culture, and in the various formulae adopted by different theological schools to express the same matter. Accordingly, we find today no real basis for the sad divisions which arose between us concerning the doctrine of the Incarnation." On the pastoral level, they declared: "It is not rare for our faithful to find access to a priest of their own church materially or morally impossible. Anxious to meet their needs and with their spiritual benefit in mind, we authorize them in such cases to ask for the sacraments of penance, Eucharist and anointing of the sick from lawful priests of either of our two sister churches, when they need them."

John Paul II and Orthodox Ecumenical Patriarch Dimitrios I, Second Common Declaration, Dec. 7, 1987: Dialogue conducted since 1979 indicated that the churches can already profess together as common faith about the mystery of the Church and the connection between faith and the sacraments. They also stated that, "when unity of faith is assured, a certain diversity of expressions does not create obstacles to unity, but enriches the life of the Church and the understanding, always imperfect, of the revealed mystery.

John Paul II and Anglican Archbishop Robert Runcie of Canterbury, Oct. 2, 1989: They said: "We solemnly re-commit ourselves and those we represent to the restoration of visible unity and full ecclesial communion in the confidence that to seek anything less would be to betray our Lord's intention for the unity of his people."

John Paul II and His Holiness Mar Dinkha IV, Catholicos-Patriarch of the Assyrian Church of the East, Nov. 11, 1994: Following is the text of the "Common Christological Declaration" between the Catholic Church and the Assyrian Church of the East, signed Nov. 11, 1994, by Pope John Paul II and His Holiness Mar Dinkha IV, Catholicos-Patriarch of the Assyrian Church of the East. The declaration acknowledges that, despite past differences, both churches profess the same faith in the real union of divine and human natures in the divine Person of Christ. Providing background to the declaration was the Assyrian Church's adherence to the teaching of Nestorius who, in the fifth century, denied the real unity of divine and human natures in the single divine Person of Christ.

Pope John Paul II with Ecumenical Orthodox Patriarch Bartholomew I, June 29, 1995: Pope John Paul and Ecumenical Orthodox Patriarch Bartholomew I, after several days of meetings, signed a common declaration June 29, 1995, declaring: "Our meeting has followed other important events which have seen our Churches declare their desire to relegate the excommunications of the past to oblivion and to set out on the way to establishing full communion. "Our new-found brotherhood in the name of the Lord has led us to frank discussion, a dialogue that seeks understanding and unity. This dialogue — through the Joint International (Catholic-Orthodox) Commission — has proved fruitful and has made substantial progress.

Pope John Paul II with Anglican Archbishop George Carey, Common Ecumenical Declaration, Dec. 5, 1996: The pontiff and archbishop praised the work of the Anglican-Roman Catholic International Commission and stated that "In many parts of the world Anglicans and Catholics attempt to witness together in the face of growing secularism, religious apathy and moral confusion."

Pope John Paul II with Karekin I, Catholicos of All Armenians, Dec. 13, 1996.

Pope John Paul and His Holiness Karekin I, Supreme Patriarch and Catholicos of All Armenians, signed Dec. 13, 1996, signed a common declaration in which they said in part: "Pope John Paul II and Catholicos Karekin I recognize the deep spiritual communion which already unites them and the bishops and clergy and lay faithful of their churches. It is a communion which finds its roots in the common faith in the holy and life-giving Trinity proclaimed by the Apostles and transmitted down the centuries. . . . They rejoice in the fact that recent developments of ecumenical relations and theological discussions . . . have dispelled many misunderstandings inherited from the controversies and dissensions of the past. Such dialogues and encounters have prepared a healthy situation of mutual understanding and recovery of the deeper spiritual communion based on the common faith in the holy Trinity that they have been given through the Gospel of Christ and in the holy tradition of the Church.

Pope John Paul II with Aram I, Armenian Catholicos of Cilicia, Jan. 25, 1997: The common declaration stated, "the two spiritual leaders stress the vital importance of sincere dialogue¼. The Catholic Church and the Catholicate of Cilicia also have an immense field of constructive cooperation before them."

Cardinal Edward Cassidy with Bishop Christian Krause, President of the Lutheran World Federation, October 31, 1999: "Joint Declaration on Justification by Faith." (*See* **Special Section**.)

Pope John Paul II with Karekin II, Catholicos of All Armenians, Nov. 10, 2000 in Rome: His Holiness Pope John Paul II, Bishop of Rome, and His Holiness Karekin II, Supreme Patriarch and Catholicos of All Armenians, give thanks to the Lord and Savior Jesus Christ, for enabling them to meet together on the occasion of the Jubilee of the Year 2000 and on the threshold of the 1700th anniversary of the proclamation of Christianity as the state religion of Armenia.

Pope John Paul II with Christodoulos, Archbishop of Athens, May 4, 2001:

We, Pope John Paul II, Bishop of Rome, and Christodoulos, Archbishop of Athens and All Greece, standing before the bema of the Areopagus, from which Saint Paul, the Great Apostle to the Nations, "called to be an Apostle, set apart for the Gospel of God" (Rom 1:1), preached to the Athenians the One True God, Father, Son and Holy Spirit, and called them unto faith and repentance, do hereby declare:

We give thanks to the Lord for our meeting and communication with one another, here in the illustrious City of Athens, the Primatial See of the Apostolic Orthodox Church of Greece.

We repeat with one voice and one heart the words of the Apostle to the Nations: "I appeal to you, brethren, by the name of our Lord Jesus Christ, that all of you agree and that there be no schisms among you, but that you be united in the same mind and the same judgment"(1 Cor 1:10).

We are anguished to see that wars, massacres, tor-

ture and martyrdom constitute a terrible daily reality for millions of our brothers. We commit ourselves to struggle for the prevailing of peace throughout the whole world, for the respect of life and human dignity, and for solidarity towards all who are in need. We are pleased to add our voice to the many voices around the world which have expressed the hope that, on the occasion of the Olympic Games to be held in Greece in 2004, the ancient Greek tradition of the Olympic Truce will be revived, according to which all wars had to stop, and terrorism and violence had to cease.

We follow carefully and with unease what is referred to as globalization. We hope that it will bear good fruit. However, we wish to point out that its fruits will be harmful if what could be termed the "globalization of brotherhood" in Christ is not achieved in all sincerity and efficacy.

We rejoice at the success and progress of the European Union. The union of the European world in one civil entity, without her people losing their national self-awareness, traditions and identity, has been the vision of its pioneers. However, the emerging tendency to transform certain European countries into secular states without any reference to religion constitutes a retraction and a denial of their spiritual legacy. We are called to intensify our efforts so that the unification of Europe may be accomplished. We shall do everything in our power, so that the Christian roots of Europe and its Christian soul may be preserved inviolate.

John Paul II and Karekin II, Catholicos of All Armenians, Sept. 27, 2001, in Etchmiadzin, Armenia:

The celebration of the 1700th anniversary of the proclamation of Christianity as the religion of Armenia has brought us together — John Paul II, Bishop of Rome and Pastor of the Catholic Church, and Karekin II, the Supreme Patriarch and Catholicos of All Armenians — and we thank God for giving us this joyous opportunity to join again in common prayer, in praise of his all-holy Name. Blessed be the Holy Trinity — Father, Son and Holy Spirit — now and for ever.

Pope John Paul II and Ecumenical Patriarch Bartholomew I signed a Common Declaration on Environmental Ethics, June 10, 2002: We are gathered here today in the spirit of peace for the good of all human beings and for the care of creation. At this moment in history, at the beginning of the third millennium, we are saddened to see the daily suffering of a great number of people from violence, starvation, poverty and disease. We are also concerned about the negative consequences for humanity and for all creation resulting from the degradation of some basic natural resources such as water, air and land, brought about by an economic and technological progress which does not recognize and take into account its limits.

Almighty God envisioned a world of beauty and harmony, and He created it, making every part an expression of His freedom, wisdom and love (cf. Gen 1:1-25).

At the centre of the whole of creation, He placed us, human beings, with our inalienable human dignity. Although we share many features with the rest of the living beings, Almighty God went further with us and gave us an immortal soul, the source of self-awareness and freedom, endowments that make us in His image and likeness (cf. Gen 1:26-31;2:7). Marked with that resemblance, we have been placed by God in the world in order to cooperate with Him in realizing more and more fully the divine purpose for creation.

What is required is an act of repentance on our part and a renewed attempt to view ourselves, one another, and the world around us within the perspective of the divine design for creation. The problem is not simply economic and technological; it is moral and spiritual. A solution at the economic and technological level can be found only if we undergo, in the most radical way, an inner change of heart, which can lead to a change in lifestyle and of unsustainable patterns of consumption and production. A genuine conversion in Christ will enable us to change the way we think and act.

First, we must regain humility and recognize the limits of our powers, and most importantly, the limits of our knowledge and judgement. We have been making decisions, taking actions and assigning values that are leading us away from the world as it should be, away from the design of God for creation, away from all that is essential for a healthy planet and a healthy commonwealth of people. A new approach and a new culture are needed, based on the centrality of the human person within creation and inspired by environmentally ethical behavior stemming from our triple relationship to God, to self and to creation. Such an ethics fosters interdependence and stresses the principles of universal solidarity, social justice and responsibility, in order to promote a true culture of life.

Secondly, we must frankly admit that humankind is entitled to something better than what we see around us. We and, much more, our children and future generations are entitled to a better world, a world free from degradation, violence and bloodshed, a world of generosity and love.

Thirdly, aware of the value of prayer, we must implore God the Creator to enlighten people everywhere regarding the duty to respect and carefully guard creation.

We therefore invite all men and women of good will to ponder the importance of the following ethical goals:

1. To think of the world's children when we reflect on and evaluate our options for action.

2. To be open to study the true values based on the natural law that sustain every human culture.

3. To use science and technology in a full and constructive way, while recognizing that the findings of science have always to be evaluated in the light of the centrality of the human person, of the common good and of the inner purpose of creation. Science may help us to correct the mistakes of the past, in order to enhance the spiritual and material well-being of the present and future generations. It is love for our children that will show us the path that we must follow into the future.

4. To be humble regarding the idea of ownership and to be open to the demands of solidarity. Our mortality and our weakness of judgement together warn us not to take irreversible actions with what we choose to regard as our property during our brief stay on this earth. We have not been entrusted with unlimited power over creation, we are only stewards of the common heritage.

5. To acknowledge the diversity of situations and responsibilities in the work for a better world environment. We do not expect every person and every institution to assume the same burden. Everyone has a part to play, but for the demands of justice and charity to be respected the most affluent societies must carry the greater burden, and from them is demanded a sacrifice greater than can be offered by the poor. Religions, governments and institutions are faced by many different situations; but on the basis of the principle of subsidiarity all of them can take on some tasks, some part of the shared effort.

6. To promote a peaceful approach to disagreement about how to live on this earth, about how to share it and use it, about what to change and what to leave unchanged. It is not our desire to evade controversy about the environment, for we trust in the capacity of human reason and the path of dialogue to reach agreement. We commit ourselves to respect the views of all who disagree with us, seeking solutions through open exchange, without resorting to oppression and domination.

It is not too late. God's world has incredible healing powers. Within a single generation, we could steer the earth toward our children's future. Let that generation start now, with God's help and blessing.

Rome — Venice, 10 June 2002

Joint Declaration

Pope John Paul II and Patriarch Teoctist of the Romanian Orthodox Church signed a **Joint Declaration** in Rome on October 12, 2002: "The glory which you have given me I have given to them, that they may be one even as we are one, I in them and you in me, that they may become perfectly one, so that the world may know that you have sent me and have loved them even as you have loved me" (Jn. 17:22-23).

In the deep joy of being together again in the city of Rome, close to the tombs of the holy Apostles Peter and Paul, we exchange the kiss of peace under the gaze of the One who watches over his Church and guides our steps; and we meditate anew on these words, which the Evangelist John transmitted to us and which constitute Christ's heartfelt prayer on the eve of his Passion.

1. Our meeting takes place in continuity with the embrace we exchanged in Bucharest in May 1999, while still resounding in our hearts is the moving appeal "Unitate, unitate! Unity, unity!", that a great crowd of faithful spontaneously raised on that occasion when they saw us. This appeal is the echo of our Lord's prayer that "they may all be one" (Jn 17,21).

Today's meeting reinforces our dedication to pray and to work to achieve the full and visible unity of all the disciples of Christ. Our aim and our ardent desire is full communion, which is not absorption but communion in truth and love. It is an irreversible journey for which there is no alternative: it is the path of the Church.

2. Still marked by the sad historical period during which people denied the Name and Lordship of the Redeemer, even today Christian communities in Romania often have difficulty in surmounting the negative effects those years have had on the practice of fraternity and sharing, and on the quest for commun-

ion. Our meeting must be taken as an example: brothers must meet to be reconciled, to reflect together, to find the means to achieve mutual understanding, to expound and to explain each other's differences. We therefore urge those who are called to live side by side in the same land of Romania, to find solutions of justice and charity. By means of a sincere dialogue, we must overcome the conflicts, misunderstandings and suspicions coming from the past so that in this decisive period of their history Christians in Romania can be witnesses of peace and reconciliation.

3. Our relations must reflect the real and profound communion in Christ, that already exists between us, even if it is not yet full. In fact, we recognize with joy that we possess together the tradition of the undivided Church centered on the mystery of the Eucharist, to which the saints we have in common in our calendars bear witness. Moreover, the many witnesses of the faith who showed their fidelity to Christ in the times of oppression and persecution in the last century are a seed of hope in our present difficulties.

In order to promote the quest for full communion, even with the doctrinal differences that still remain, it is appropriate to find concrete means by setting up regular consultations, with the conviction that no difficult situation is destined to remain beyond redress, and that thanks to the attitude of listening and dialogue and the regular exchange of information, satisfactory solutions can be found to straighten out points of friction and reach equitable solutions for concrete problems. We should reinforce this process so that the full truth of the faith becomes a common patrimony, shared by both sides, that can give birth to a truly peaceful conviviality, rooted in and founded in charity.

We know well how to behave to establish the orientations that must guide the work of evangelization so necessary after the sombre period of State atheism. We agree to recognize the religious and cultural traditions of each people, and religious freedom as well.

Evangelization cannot be based on a spirit of competition, but on reciprocal respect and' cooperation which recognize the freedom of each person to live according to his own convictions in respect for his religious belonging.

4. In the development of our contacts, starting with the Pan Orthodox Conferences and the Second Vatican Council, we have been the witnesses of a promising reconciliation between East and West, based on prayer and on a dialogue of charity and of truth, which has had many moments of profound communion. This is why we look with concern at the current difficulties that beset the Joint International Commission for Theological Dialogue between the Catholic Church and the Orthodox Church and, on the occasion of our meeting, we desire to express the hope that no initiative will be neglected that can reactivate the theological dialogue and re-launch the activity of the commission. We have the duty to do so, for. theological dialogue makes stronger the affirmation of our shared will for communion over against the present situation of division.

5. The Church is not a reality closed in on herself: she is sent to the world and she is open to the world. The new possibilities that are being created in an already united Europe that is in the process of extending its frontiers to associate the peoples and cultures of the Central and Eastern parts of the continent, are a challenge that the Christians of East and West must face together. The more the latter are united in their witness to the one Lord, the more they will contribute to giving voice, consistency and space to the Christian soul of Europe, to respect for life, to the dignity and the fundamental rights of the human person, to justice and to solidarity, to peace, to reconciliation, to the values of the family and to the protection of creation. Europe in its entirety needs the cultural richness forged by Christianity.

The Orthodox Church of Romania, the centre of contacts and exchanges between the fruitful Slav and Byzantine traditions of the East, and the Church of Rome who in her Latin element, evokes the Western voice of the one Church of Christ, must contribute together to a task that belongs to the third millennium. In accord with the traditional beautiful expression, the particular Churches like to call one another "Sister Churches". To be open to this dimension means collaborating to restore to Europe its deepest ethos and its truly human face.

With these perspectives and these dispositions, together we entrust ourselves to the Lord, imploring him to make us worthy of building the Body of Christ, "until we all attain to the unity of the faith and of the knowledge of the Son of God, to mature manhood, to the measure of the stature of the fullness of Christ" (Eph 4:13).

ECUMENICAL STATEMENTS

The ecumenical statements listed below, and others like them, reflect the views of participants in the dialogues which produced them. They have not been formally accepted by the respective churches as formulations of doctrine or points of departure for practical changes in discipline. (For other titles, see U.S. Ecumenical Dialogues, Ecumenical Reports.)

• The "Windsor Statement" on Eucharistic doctrine, published Dec. 31, 1971, by the Anglican-Roman Catholic International Commission of theologians. (For text, see pages 132-33 of the 1973 *Catholic Almanac*.)

• The "Canterbury Statement" on ministry and ordination, published Dec. 13, 1973, by the same commission. (For excerpts, see pages 127-30 of the 1975 *Catholic Almanac*.)

• "Papal Primacy/Converging Viewpoints," published Mar. 4, 1974, by the dialogue group sanctioned by the U.S.A. National Convention of the World Lutheran Federation and the U.S. Bishops' Committee for Ecumenical and Interreligious Affairs. (For excerpts, see pages 130-31 of the 1975 *Catholic Almanac*.)

• An "Agreed Statement on the Purpose of the Church," published Oct. 31, 1975, by the Anglican-Roman Catholic Consultation in the U.S.

• "Christian Unity and Women's Ordination," published Nov. 7, 1975, by the same consultation, in which it was said that the ordination of women (approved in principle by the Anglican Communion but not by the Catholic Church) would "introduce a new element" in dialogue but would not mean the end of consultation nor the abandonment of its declared goal of full communion and organic unity.

• "Holiness and Spirituality of the Ordained Ministry," issued early in 1976 by theologians of the Catholic Church and the United Methodist Church; the first statement resulting from dialogue begun in 1966.

• "Mixed Marriages," published in the spring of 1976 by the Anglican-Roman Catholic Consultation in the U.S.

• "Bishops and Presbyters," published in July, 1976, by the Orthodox-Roman Catholic Consultation in the U.S. on the following points of common understanding: (1) Ordination in apostolic succession is required for pastoral office in the Church. (2) Presiding at the Eucharistic Celebration is a task belonging to those ordained to pastoral service. (3) The offices of bishop and presbyter are different realizations of the sacrament of order. (4) Those ordained are claimed permanently for the service of the Church.

• "The Principle of Economy," published by the body named above at the same time, concerning God's plan and activities in human history for salvation.

• "Venice Statement" on authority in the Church, published Jan. 20, 1977, by the Anglican-Roman Catholic International Commission of theologians.

• "Response to the Venice Statement," issued Jan. 4, 1978, by the Anglican-Roman Catholic Consultation in the U.S.A., citing additional questions.

• "An Ecumenical Approach to Marriage," published in January, 1978, by representatives of the Catholic Church, the Lutheran World Federation and the World Alliance of Reformed Churches.

• "Teaching Authority and Infallibility in the Church," released in October, 1978, by the Catholic-Lutheran dialogue group in the U.S.

• "The Eucharist," reported early in 1979, in which the Roman Catholic-Lutheran Commission indicated developing convergence of views.

• "The Holy Spirit," issued Feb. 12, 1979, by the International Catholic-Methodist Commission.

• A statement on "Ministry in the Church," published in March, 1981, by the International Roman Catholic-Lutheran Joint Commission, regarding possible mutual recognition of ministries.

• The Final Report of the Anglican-Roman Catholic International Commission, 1982, on the results of 12 years of dialogue.

• "The Mystery of the Church and of the Eucharist in the Light of the Mystery of the Holy Trinity," issued by the Mixed International Commission for Theological Dialogue between the Catholic Church and the Orthodox Church at Munich, Germany, in July 1982.

• The Final Report of the Anglican-Roman Catholic International Commission, 1982, on the results of 12 years of dialogue.

• "Justification by Faith," issued Sept. 30, 1983, by the U.S. Lutheran-Roman Catholic dialogue group, claiming a "fundamental consensus on the Gospel."

• "Images of God: Reflections on Christian Anthropology," released Dec. 22, 1983, by the Anglican-Roman Catholic Dialogue in the United States.

• "The Journeying Together in Christ — The Report of the Polish National Catholic-Roman Catholic Dialogue (1984-89)."

• "Salvation and the Church," issued Jan. 22, 1987, by the Second Anglican-Roman Catholic International Commission.

• "Faith, Sacraments and the Unity of the Church,"

issued by the Mixed International Commission for Theological Dialogue between the Catholic Church and the Orthodox Churches in June, 1987.

• "The Sacrament of Order in the Sacramental Structure of the Church, with Particular Reference to the Importance of Apostolic Succession for the Sanctification and Unity of the People of God," issued by the Mixed International Commission for Theological Dialogue between the Catholic Church and the Orthodox Church in Valamo, Finland, in 1988.

• "The Presence of Christ in Church and World" and "Toward a Common Understanding of the Church" (developed between 1984 and 1990), by the Reformed-Roman Catholic Conversations, under the auspices of the Pontifical Council for Promoting Christian Unity and the World Alliance of Reformed Churches.

• "The Church as Communion," issued by the Second Anglican-Roman Catholic International Commission, 1991.

• "Uniatism, Method of Union of the Past, and the Present Search for Full Communion," issued by the Mixed International Commission for Theological Dialogue between the Catholic Church and the Orthodox Church at Balamand, Lebanon, in 1993.

• "Life in Christ: Morals, Communion and the Church," issued by the Second Anglican-Roman Catholic International Commission, 1994.

• "Common Response to the Aleppo Statement on the Date of Easter/Pacha," issued by the North American Orthodox-Catholic Theological Consultation in Washington, D.C., Oct. 31, 1998.

• "The Gift of Authority," issued by the Second Anglican-Roman Catholic International Commission, May 12, 1999.

• "Baptism and 'Sacramental Economy'," issued by the North American Orthodox-Catholic Theological Consultation at Crestwood, New York, in June 1999.

• "Guidelines Concerning the Pastoral Care of Oriental Orthodox Students in Catholic Schools," issued by the Oriental Orthodox-Roman Catholic Theological Consultation in the United States at New Rochelle, New York, in June 1999.

• "Joint Declaration of the Catholic Church and the Lutheran World Federation on the Doctrine of Justification," issued July 8, 1999 by the International Roman Catholic-Lutheran Joint Commission.

• "Agreed Report on the Local/Universal Church," issued by the United States Anglican-Roman Catholic Consultation, November 12, 1999.

• "Communion in Mission" and "Action Plan to Implement 'Communion in Mission,'" issued by a special consultation of Anglican and Roman Catholic bishops in Mississauga, Ontario, Canada, May 19, 2000.

• "Sharing the Ministry of Reconciliation: A Statement on the Orthodox-Catholic Dialogue and the Ecumenical Movement," issued June 1, 2000, by the North American Orthodox-Catholic Theological Consultation in Brookline, Massachusetts.

• "Doing the Truth in Charity," issued in July 2001 by the World Methodist Council and the Pontifical Council for Promoting Unity's Methodist-Catholic International Commission.

• "Interchurch Families: Resources for Ecumenical Hope," issued by the Catholic/Reformed Dialogue in the United States in 2002.

ANGLICAN-ROMAN CATHOLIC FINAL REPORT

The Anglican-Roman Catholic International Commission issued a Final Report in 1982 on 12 years of dialogue on major issues of concern, especially the Eucharist and ordained ministry.

In 1988 the Lambeth Conference called parts of the report on these two subjects "consonant in substance with the faith of Anglicans." In 1991 the Congregation for the Doctrine of the Faith and the Pontifical Council for Promoting Christian Unity called the Report a significant milestone not only in relations between the Catholic Church and the Anglican Communion but in the ecumenical movement as a whole. They said, however, that it was not yet possible to state that substantial agreement had been reached on all the questions studied by the commission, and that important differences still remained with respect to essential matters of Catholic doctrine regarding the Eucharist, ordination and other subjects. Clarifications were requested.

The Anglican-Roman Catholic Commission II responded in 1994, saying that its members were in agreement regarding:

• the substantial and sacramental presence of Christ in the Eucharist;

• the propitiatory nature of the Eucharistic Sacrifice, which can also be applied to the deceased;

• institution of the sacrament of order from Christ;

• the character of priestly ordination, implying configuration to the priesthood of Christ.

In 1994 Cardinal Edward I. Cassidy, president of the Pontifical Council for Interreligious Dialogue addressed a letter to the Catholic and Anglican co-chairmen of the commission, responding to the clarifications, stating that "no further work" seems to be necessary at this time on Eucharist and ministry. Questions still remained to be answered about a number of subjects, including the authority in the Church, ordination of women, infallibility and Marian doctrine.

JOINT DECLARATION ON JUSTIFICATION

(By Russell Shaw.)

Hailed by Pope John Paul II as a "milestone" on the road to Christian unity, a Lutheran-Catholic Joint Declaration on the Doctrine of Justification was signed October 31, 1999, in Augsburg, Germany, by representatives of the Catholic Church and the Lutheran World Federation.

"This document represents a sound basis for continuing the ecumenical theological research and for addressing the remaining problems with a better founded hope of resolving them in the future," Pope John Paul said the same day in Rome in a talk accompanying the recitation of the Angelus. "It is also a valuable contribution to the purification of historical memory and to our common witness."

The Joint Declaration states a "consensus" shared by the signers regarding the doctrine of justification. The key passage formulating this consensus says:

"In faith we together hold the conviction that justification is the work of the triune God. The Father sent his Son into the world to save sinners. The foundation and presupposition of justification is the incarnation, death, and resurrection of Christ. Justification thus means that Christ himself is our righteousness, in which we share through the Holy Spirit in accord with the will of the Father.

"Together we confess: By grace alone, in faith in Christ's saving work and not because of any merit on our part, we are accepted by God and receive the Holy Spirit, who renews our hearts while equipping and calling us to good works."

The signers of the Joint Declaration were Cardinal Edward I. Cassidy, President of the Vatican's Pontifical Council for Promoting Christian Unity, and Bishop Christian Krause, President of the Lutheran World Federation, which represents 58 million of the world's 61 million Lutherans. Most, but not all, of the churches within the federation have accepted the Joint Declaration.

Both the date and the place of the signing had symbolic significance. October 31 is observed by Protestants as Reformation Day, commemorating Martin Luther's nailing of his Ninety-five Theses on the castle church door in Wittenberg on that date in 1517. The city of Augsburg is associated with the Augsburg Confession, a document authored in 1530 by the Protestant Reformer Philipp Melancthon in an attempt to bring about a reconciliation between Lutherans and Catholics.

From a theological perspective, the doctrine of justification was of central importance in the Reformation and in the mutual condemnations exchanged by Catholics and Lutherans in the 16th century via the Council of Trent and the Lutheran Confessions.

The Joint Declaration stresses that the churches "neither take the condemnations lightly nor do they disavow their own past." But, it insists, as a result of ecumenical dialogue during the last 30 years, they have come to "new insights" that transcend the mutual polemics of the Reformation era and make it clear that neither party's understanding of justification, as it is expressed in the Joint Declaration, now merits condemnation by the other, while the differences about the doctrine that continue to exist between them "are acceptable."

The Council for Promoting Christian Unity and the Lutheran World Federation reached basic agreement on the document in June, 1998, but further clarifications were required on both sides before official approval was forthcoming. These clarifications are embodied in an "Annex" to the text.

Despite the harmonious tone of the document and the various statements that accompanied its signing, the Joint Declaration has been, and to some extent remains, a controversial document. Some Lutheran bodies, including the Lutheran churches of several countries, have not accepted it. Nor has an unknown number of individual Lutherans, theologians among them.

On the Catholic side, there has been criticism that the document does not go far enough in coming to terms with Lutheranism and, on the other hand, that it goes too far in papering-over serious theological differences. According to the theologian Father Avery Dulles, S.J., it is "a bold statement, difficult to defend" to claim that the differing views still held by

Catholics and Lutherans on various questions relating to the doctrine of justification really do "escape the condemnations" pronounced by each side on the other in the 16th century.

"But notwithstanding all the theological reservations on both sides," Father Dulles added in an October, 1999, lecture at Fordham University, New York, reprinted in the magazine *First Things*, the signing of the Joint Declaration "can be a powerful symbolic event."

"It says clearly to a world that hovers on the brink of unbelief that the two churches that split Western Christendom on the issue of justification nearly five centuries ago are still united on truths of the highest import," he said.

The Joint Declaration has been hailed as the fruit of some 30 years of ecumenical dialogue between Lutherans and Catholics. The doctrine of justification was an issue in these conversations from the start. The 1972 report of the international Lutheran-Catholic dialogue included five paragraphs on the topic, and observed that "today...a far-reaching consensus is developing." This emerging consensus also was noted in 1980 and 1981 reports by the international dialogue.

The doctrine of justification was considered in reports from national Lutheran-Catholic dialogues in the United States ("Justification by Faith," 1985) and Germany ("The Condemnations of the Reformation Era. Do They Still Divide?", 1986). These reports from national dialogues contributed to a lengthy report developed by the third phase of the international dialogue and published in 1993 as "Church and Justification: Understanding the Church in the Light of the Doctrine of Justification." In 1993, at the request of the Lutheran World Federation and the Council for Promoting Christian Unity, a small Lutheran-Catholic working group was formed to begin work on what became the Joint Declaration.

While the document first of all marks a significant new stage in Lutheran-Catholic relations, it also has broader ecumenical significance, Cardinal Cassidy said in an article published in the Vatican newspaper *L'Osservatore Romano*.

"What has been achieved in this mutual agreement of the Joint Declaration surely is an historic development of particular importance in the history of Western Christianity, and indeed for the whole ecumenical movement as well, since it illustrates that ecumenical progress can be made on questions that are of central importance, and have long been seen as church-dividing issues," he wrote.

Cardinal Cassidy listed "three basic truths" that he said were central to the doctrine of justification and to the Lutheran-Catholic consensus expressed in the Joint Declaration. They are:

"Firstly, justification is a free gift bestowed by the Trinitarian God and centers on the person of Christ who became incarnate, died and rose. In being related to the person of Christ through the work of the Holy Spirit, we enter into a condition of righteousness....

"Secondly, we receive this salvation in faith....[T]he reality of justification is linked to faith, but not simply as an intellectual assent of the mind. Rather the believer is to give him/herself over to Christ in the renewal of life.

"Thirdly, justification points to the heart of the Gospel message, but must be seen in an organic unity with all the other truths of faith: Trinity, Christology, Ecclesiology and Sacraments."

The Joint Declaration begins with a Preamble that includes this statement of the document's intention: "...to show that on the basis of their dialogue the subscribing Lutheran churches and the Roman Catholic Church are now able to articulate a common understanding of our justification by God's grace through faith in Christ. It does not cover all that either church teaches about justification; it does encompass a consensus on basic truths of the doctrine of justification and shows that the remaining differences in its explication are no longer the occasion for doctrinal condemnations."

Following an overview of significant scriptural passages on the doctrine (section one), the document notes that, historically, justification has been an ecumenical problem between the Catholic Church and the Reformation churches and that differences focusing on it were the "principal cause" of their division and mutual condemnations in the 16th century. But in the ecumenical dialogue since the Second Vatican Council (1962-1965), it says, a "notable convergence" has emerged (section two).

The Joint Declaration then states the "consensus" on the basic truths of the doctrine, quoted above (section three). Justification is said to be "more than just one part of Christian doctrine. It stands in an essential relation with all truths of faith, which are to be seen as internally related to each other."

The fourth section of the Declaration ("Explicating the Common Understanding of Justification") is the document's longest section. It identifies, one by one, seven particular questions relating to the doctrine, states the consensus shared by Lutherans and Catholics regarding these seven questions, and then sets out distinctive Catholic and Lutheran perspectives on each.

The seven topics treated in this manner are: "Human Powerlessness and Sin in Relation to Justification," "Justification as Forgiveness of Sins and Making Righteous," "Justification by Faith and through Grace," "The Justified as Sinner," "Law and Gospel," "Assurance of Salvation," and "The Good Works of the Justified."

The Joint Declaration closes by once again underlining the "consensus in basic truths" regarding justification and stating its "significance and scope" (section five):

"In light of this consensus the remaining differences of language, theological elaboration, and emphasis in the understanding described in paras. 18 to 39 [section four] are acceptable. Therefore the Lutheran and Catholic explications of justification are in their difference open to one another and do not destroy the consensus regarding the basic truths.

"Thus the doctrinal condemnations of the 16th century, in so far as they relate to the doctrine of justification, appear in a new light. The teaching of the Lutheran churches presented in this Declaration does not fall under the condemnations from the Council of Trent. The condemnations of the Lutheran Confessions do not apply to the teaching of the Roman Catholic Church presented in this Declaration."

The document lists a number of other questions between Catholics and Lutherans that need clarification: the relationship between the Word of God and church doctrine, ecclesiology, ecclesial authority, church unity, ministry, the sacraments, and the relation between justification and social ethics. "We are confident that the consensus we have reached offers a solid basis for this clarification," it says.

An "Official Common Statement" of the Lutheran World Federation and the Catholic Church, issued at the time of the signing in Augsburg, commits both to continued ecumenical dialogue on outstanding questions regarding justification as well as the matters just mentioned. Such dialogue is necessary, it says, "in order to reach full church communion, a unity in diversity, in which remaining differences would be 'reconciled' and no longer have a divisive force."

In his article in *L'Osservatore Romano*, Cardinal Cassidy linked the signing of the *Joint Declaration* to the preparations for the third millennium of Christianity and the Great Jubilee of the Year 2000. In his 1994 Apostolic Letter *Tertio Millennio Adveniente* ("On the Coming of the Third Millennium"), he pointed out, Pope John Paul spoke of the scandal of Christian divi-

sion and the need to work for unity in the new millennium. The Lutheran-Catholic accord marks important progress toward this goal, he suggested.

At the same time, the Cardinal acknowledged "the limits of our achievement" as represented in the Joint Declaration: "The declaration brings the Catholic Church and the member churches of the Lutheran World Federation which affirmed it a clear step closer to unity. They have not yet, however, achieved the goal of full, visible unity."

In particular, he said, "Catholics are not able to share the Eucharist with their Lutheran brothers and sisters....Our common participation in the Eucharist awaits the full ecclesial communion which we seek."

Nevertheless, Cardinal Cassidy added, the limitations of what has been accomplished in reaching this agreement should not cause it to be underestimated. "Serious difficulties remain, but they are secondary to what we hold in common. No longer may we look upon our different expressions of faith as being like two huge cannons drawn up in battle line and facing each other....We need, above all, to give thanks to God for this achievement."

THE RELATIONSHIP BETWEEN ANGLICANS AND ROMAN CATHOLICS

(By Dr. John Borelli, associate director, Secretariat for Ecumenical and Interreligious Affairs, National Conference of Catholic Bishops.)

A special consultation of Roman Catholic and Anglican bishops from thirteen regions around the world met in Mississauga, Ontario, May 14-20, 2000 to review and evaluate the accomplishment of thirty years of dialogue between the two traditions and to reflect on how the special relationship has been developing in various parts of the world. Bishops attended from New Zealand, Canada, England, United States, Ireland, India, Nigeria, Papua New Guinea, Southern Africa, Uganda, Australia, Brazil and the West Indies.

The meeting was convened by His Eminence Edward Cardinal Cassidy, then President of the Pontifical Council Promoting Christian Unity, and His Grace Archbishop George Carey of Canterbury. Also participating were the two recently appointed co-chairman for the Anglican-Roman Catholic International Commission: the Most Rev. Frank T. Griswold, Presiding Bishop of the Episcopal Church (U. S.) and Most Rev. Alexander J. Brunett, Archbishop of Seattle.

The meeting grew out of the visit of Archbishop Carey with Pope John Paul II in Advent 1996 and was suggested in their Common Declaration of December 5, 1996, "it may be opportune at this stage in our journey to consult further about how the relationship between the Anglican Communion and the Catholic Church is to progress." With consensus yet to be achieved on authority in the church and with the new situation created by ordination of women as priests and bishops in some provinces of the Anglican Communion becoming increasingly evident, a certain amount of risk was involved in calling for a special consultation. The meeting could end in a stand-off on certain issues and might even conclude with a simple acknowledgment of past achievements, current good will, and hope that the future will be brighter. These scenarios would be viewed as evidence that the dialogue is deadlocked or, at best, lost in a maze of seemingly endless study of details and dif-

ferences and no certain direction towards reconciliation. Over three years were spent in preparations for the special consultation. Independent provinces of the Anglican Communion and national conferences of Catholic bishops were asked twice in the course of the planning to advise on agenda and other aspects of the proposed meeting. It was postponed once from May 1999 to May 2000 so that careful reflection and thorough preparation could take place first, and conveniently the meeting did not coincide other developments related to restoration of unity between Anglicans and Catholics.

In the mean time, the Lambeth Conference met in July 1998. The Lambeth Conference is a meeting of Anglican bishops, currently from 36 provinces and other churches in the communion worldwide, and one of its actions in 1998 was to receive "the Virginia Report," prepared by the Inter-Anglican Theological and Doctrinal Commission. This study is a response to the particular need recognized by the Lambeth Conference of 1988 for exploration of the meaning and nature of communion and how the Anglican Communion makes authoritative decisions while maintaining unity and interdependence among the independent provinces. The Lambeth Conference of 1998 recommended the report for study throughout the Communion. Also, in May 1999, the Anglican-Roman Catholic International Commission released its third agreed statement on authority in the Church, "The Gift of Authority," which among other suggestions lists eleven advances points of consensus on authority (See page 102 of the 2000 Catholic Almanac.) In a dramatic gesture of unity, on January 18, 2000, Archbishop Carey assisted Pope John Paul II in opening the holy door at St. Paul-Outside-the-Walls Basilica. Thus there was a certain momentum building up to the Mississauga meeting.

On May 20, 2000, Cardinal Cassidy and Archbishop Carey released two short documents resulting from the meeting and a press release: "Communion in Mission" and "Action Plan to Implement 'Communion in Mission.'" They reported that the bishops had spent a week in prayer together, worship, and reflection. They focused on the relationship between their communions which the Second Vatican Council said "occupies a special place" (*Decree on Ecumenism* 13). They also reported how the participants came to see that the relationship is no longer to be viewed in minimal terms but has reached a significant new place. The texts acknowledge unresolved differences and challenges, but they felt that these did not compare with all that Anglicans and Catholics hold in common. They also list the essentials of the faith and common practices to which the faithful hold fast and noted areas of theological convergence that have been achieved. They also express a common vision of full and visible unity.

The strength of the texts resulting from the special consultation lies in the recommendations. First, as a sign of the new stage in relations, they recommend the signing and celebration of a Joint Declaration of Agreement. This may turn out to be something on the scale of the joint declaration between Catholics and Lutherans on the doctrine of justification. To prepare the joint declaration and promote and monitor the reception of theological agreements, they recommend the formation of a Joint Unity Commission. They go into some detail how the bishops at the meeting believed the membership, accountability and mandate of the commission should be defined as well as how the participants themselves and how the Anglican-Roman Catholic International Commission for dialogue might follow up to this meeting.

Some of the specific recommendations have been seen before in previous reports. For example, "the Malta Report" (1968) of the Joint Preparatory Commission, established by Pope Paul VI and Archbishop Michael Ramsey of Canterbury to work out the steps towards a formal theological dialogue, made several of recommendations that were repeated, in some way or another, in the Mississauga texts. The Anglican-Roman Catholic Consultation in the U.S. produced a twelve-year report in 1977 that contained similar recommendations. Also in 1981, a U.S. Anglican/Roman Catholic Leaders Conference proposed, on a smaller scale, that a Joint Commission be established to deal with specific areas, like pastoral ministry for Anglican-Catholic couples, and other recommendations requiring joint efforts and liaison. At best, these various recommendations were implemented sporadically. The difference with the steps taken at the Mississauga meeting is that accountability and responsibility for the implementation of these excellent recommendations lies with the Holy See's Pontifical Council for Promoting Christian Unity and the Inter-Anglican Standing Commission on Ecumenical Relations, a body established at the Lambeth Conference of 1998. The proposed Joint Unity Commission will report to these two high offices.

Much has been achieved in thirty five years of dialogue both on the international commission and on various national Anglican-Roman Catholic commissions, but now a special effort will be made to incorporate these theological agreements into the lives of the churches. Also, in more formal ways, Anglicans and Catholics will be encouraged to spend more time together in prayer, study, consultation, teaching, preparation of educational and liturgical materials, marriage preparation, and common action.

SEPARATED EASTERN CHURCHES

THE ORTHODOX CHURCH

This is a group of Eastern churches of the Byzantine tradition that were in full communion with Rome during the first millennium, and which all recognize the Patriarch of Constantinople as the first Orthodox bishop. In spite of the division between Catholics and Orthodox, often symbolized by the mutual excommunications of 1054, the Catholic Church considers itself to be in almost full communion with the Orthodox Churches. According to Vatican II, they "are still joined to us in closest intimacy" in various ways, especially in the priesthood and Eucharist. The Orthodox Churches recognize the first seven ecumenical councils as normative for their faith, along with the Scriptures and other local councils that took place in later centuries.

The Orthodox Churches are organized in approximately 15 autocephalous (independent) churches that correspond in most cases to nations or ethnic groups. The Ecumenical Patriarch of Constantinople (modern Istanbul) has a primacy of honor among the patriarchs, but his actual jurisdiction is limited to his own patriarchate. As the spiritual head of worldwide Orthodoxy, he serves as a point of unity, and has the right to call Pan-Orthodox assemblies.

Top-level relations between the Churches have improved in recent years through the efforts of Ecumenical Patriarch Athenagoras I, Bl. John XXIII, Paul VI and Patriarch Dimitrios I. Pope Paul met with Athenagoras three times before the latter's death in 1972. The most significant action of both spiritual leaders was their mutual nullification of excommunications imposed by the two Churches on each other in 1054. Development of better relations with the Orthodox has been a priority of John Paul II since the beginning of his pontificate. Both he and Orthodox Ecumenical Patriarch Bartholomew have made known their commitment to better relations, despite contentions between Eastern Catholic and Orthodox Churches over charges of proselytism and rival property claims in places liberated from anti-religious communist control in the recent past.

The largest Orthodox body in the United States is the Greek Orthodox Archdiocese of America consisting of nine dioceses; it has an estimated membership of 1.9 million. The second largest is the Orthodox Church in America, with more than one million members; it was given autocephalous status by the Patriarchate of Moscow May 18, 1970, without the consent of the Patriarchate of Constantinople. An additional 650,000 or more Orthodox belong to smaller national and language jurisdictions. Heads of orthodox jurisdictions in this hemisphere hold membership in the Standing Conference of Canonical Orthodox Bishops in the Americas.

JURISDICTIONS

The Autocephalous Orthodox Churches

Patriarchate of Constantinople (Ecumenical Patriarchate), with jurisdiction in Turkey, Crete, the Dodecanese, and Greeks in the rest of the world outside Greece and Africa. Autonomous churches linked to the Ecumenical Patriarchate exist in Finland and Estonia. Several other jurisdictions of various ethnicities in the diaspora are also directly under the Patriarchate.

Patriarchate of Alexandria, with jurisdiction in Egypt and the rest of Africa; it includes a native African Orthodox Church centered in Kenya and Uganda.

Patriarchate of Antioch, with jurisdiction in Syria, Lebanon, Iraq, Australia, the Americas.

Patriarchate of Jerusalem, with jurisdiction in Israel and Jordan. The autonomous church of Mount Sinai is linked to the Jerusalem Patriarchate.

Russian Orthodox Church, the Patriarchate of Moscow with jurisdiction over most of the former Soviet Union. Autonomous churches in Japan and China are linked to the Moscow Patriarchate, and since the breakup of the Soviet Union, a certain autonomy has been granted to the Orthodox churches in the newly independent republics of Ukraine, Belarus, Estonia, Moldova and Latvia.

The Serbian Orthodox Church, a patriarchate with jurisdiction in all of former Yugoslavia, Western Europe, North America and Australia.

The Romanian Orthodox Church, a patriarchate with jurisdiction in Romania, Western Europe and North America.

The Bulgarian Orthodox Church, a patriarchate with jurisdiction in Bulgaria, Western Europe and North America.

The Georgian Orthodox Church, a patriarchate with jurisdiction in the republic of Georgia.

The Orthodox Church of Cyprus, an archbishopric with jurisdiction in Cyprus.

The Orthodox Church of Greece, an archbishopric with jurisdiction in most of Greece.

The Orthodox Church of Poland, a metropolitanate with jurisdiction in Poland.

The Orthodox Church of Albania, an archbishopric with jurisdiction in Albania.

The Orthodox Church in the Czech and Slovak Republics, a metropolitanate with jurisdiction in the Czech and Slovak Republics. Its autocephalous status was granted by Moscow in 1951 but by Constantinople only in 1998.

The Orthodox Church in America, a metropolitanate with jurisdiction in North America and a few parishes in Latin America and Australia. Its autocephalous status was granted by Moscow in 1970; Constantinople and most other Orthodox churches have not recognized this.

Population

The Division of Archives and Statistics of the Eastern Orthodox World Foundation reported a 1970 estimate of more than 200 million Orthodox Church members throughout the world. A contemporary estimate put the number close to 220 million. Many Orthodox today claim a total membership of about 300 million.

Standing Conference of Orthodox Bishops

The Standing Conference of Canonical Orthodox Bishops in the Americas was established in 1960 to achieve cooperation among the various Orthodox jurisdictions in the Americas. Office: 8-10 East 79th St., New York, NY 10021.

Member churches are the: Albanian Orthodox Diocese of America (Ecumenical Patriarchate), American Carpatho-Russian Orthodox Greek Catholic Diocese in the U.S.A. (Ecumenical Patriarchate), Antiochian Orthodox Christian Archdiocese of North America, Bulgarian Eastern Orthodox Church, Greek Orthodox Archdiocese of America (Ecumenical Patriarchate), Orthodox Church in America, Romanian Orthodox Archdiocese in America and Canada, Serbian Orthodox Church in the United States and Canada, Ukrainian Orthodox Church in the United States (Ecumenical Patriarchate), Ukrainian Orthodox Church of Canada (Ecumenical Patriarchate).

ANCIENT CHURCHES OF THE EAST

The Ancient Eastern Churches, which are distinct from the Orthodox Churches, were the subject of an article by Gerard Daucourt published in the Feb. 16, 1987, English edition of *L'Osservatore Romano*. Following is an adaptation:

By Ancient Eastern Churches one means: the Assyrian Church of the East (formerly called Nestorian), the Armenian Apostolic Church, the Coptic Orthodox Church, the Ethiopian Orthodox Church, the Syrian Orthodox Church (sometimes called Jacobite) and the Malankara Orthodox Syrian Church of India.

After the Council of Ephesus (431), the Assyrian Church of the East did not maintain communion with the rest of the Christian world. For reasons as much and perhaps more political than doctrinal, it did not accept the Council's teaching (that Mary is the Mother of God, in opposition to the opinion of Nestorius; see Nestorianism. For this reason, the Assyrian Church of the East came to be called Nestorian.) It is well known that in the 16th century a great segment of the faithful of this Church entered into communion with the See of Rome and constitutes today, among the Eastern Catholic Churches, the Chaldean Patriarchate. The Patriarch of the Assyrian Church of the East, His Holiness Mar Dinkha IV, in the course of his visit to the Holy Father and to the Church of Rome of 7 to 9 November, 1984, requested that people stop using the term "Nestorian" to designate his Church and expressed the desire that a declaration made jointly by the Pope of Rome and himself may one day serve to express the common faith of the two Churches in Jesus Christ, Son of God incarnate, born of the Virgin Mary. The labors of Catholic historians and theologians have, moreover, already contributed to showing that such a declaration would be possible.

The other Ancient Churches of the East (today known as the Oriental Orthodox Churches) for a long time have been designated by the term "Monophysite Churches" (*see* **Monophysitism**). It is regrettable to find this name still employed sometimes in certain publications, since already in 1951, in the encyclical Sempiternus Rex, on the occasion of the 15th centenary of the Council of Chalcedon, Pius XII declared with regard to the Christians of these Churches: "They depart from the right way only in terminology, when they expound the doctrine of the Incarnation of the Lord. This may be deduced from their liturgical and theological books."

In this same encyclical, Pius XII expressed the view that the separation at the doctrinal level came about "above all, through a certain ambiguity of terminology that occurred at the beginning." Since then, two important declarations have been arrived at in line with the ecumenical stance taken by the Church at the Second Vatican Council and the labors of the theologians (particularly in the framework of the Foundation "Pro Oriente" of Vienna). One was signed by Pope Paul VI and Coptic Patriarch Shenouda III on 10 May, 1973, and the other by Pope John Paul II and the Syrian Patriarch Ignatius Zakka II was, on 23 June, 1984. In both of these texts, the hierarchies of the respective Churches confess one and the same faith in the mystery of the Word Incarnate. After such declarations, it is no longer possible to speak in general terms of the "Monophysite" Churches. The Armenian Apostolic Church has communicants in the former Soviet Union, the Middle and Far East, the Americas. The Coptic Orthodox Church is centered in Egypt and has a growing diaspora overseas. The Syrian Orthodox Church has communicants in the Middle East, the Americas, and India. Members of the Assyrian Church of the East are scattered throughout the world, and the Patriarch now resides near Chicago, Illinois.

It is estimated that there are approximately 10 million or more members of these other Eastern Churches throughout the world. For various reasons, a more accurate determination is not possible.

EASTERN ECUMENISM

The Second Vatican Council, in *Orientalium Ecclesiarum*, the "Decree on Eastern Catholic Churches," pointed out the special role they have to play "in promoting the unity of all Christians." The document also stated in part as follows.

The Eastern Churches in communion with the Apostolic See of Rome have a special role to play in promoting the unity of all Christians, particularly Easterners, according to the principles of this sacred Synod's Decree on Ecumenism first of all by prayer, then by the example of their lives, by religious fidelity to ancient Eastern traditions, by greater mutual knowledge, by collaboration, and by a brotherly regard for objects and attitudes (No. 24).

If any separated Eastern Christian should, under the guidance of grace of the Holy Spirit, join himself to Catholic unity, no more should be required of him than what a simple profession of the Catholic faith demands. A valid priesthood is preserved among Eastern clerics. Hence, upon joining themselves to the unity of the Catholic Church, Eastern clerics are permitted to exercise the orders they possess, in accordance with the regulations established by the competent authority (No. 25).

Divine Law forbids any common worship (*communicatio in sacris*) that would damage the unity of the Church, or involve formal acceptance of falsehood or the danger of deviation in the faith, of scandal, or of indifferentism. At the same time, pastoral experience clearly shows that with respect to our Eastern brethren there should and can be taken into consideration various circumstances affecting individuals, wherein the unity of the Church is not jeopardized nor are intolerable risks involved, but in which salvation itself and the spiritual profit of souls are urgently at issue.

Hence, in view of special circumstances of time, place, and personage, the Catholic Church has often adopted and now adopts a milder policy, offering to all the means of salvation and an example of charity among Christians through participation in the sacraments and in other sacred functions and objects. With these considerations in mind, and "lest because of the harshness of our judgment we prove an obstacle to those seeking salvation," and in order to promote closer union with the Eastern Churches separated from us, this sacred Synod lays down the following policy:

In view of the principles recalled above, Eastern Christians who are separated in good faith from the Catholic Church, if they ask of their own accord and have the right dispositions, may be granted the sacraments of penance, the Eucharist, and the anointing of the sick. Furthermore, Catholics may ask for these same sacraments from those non-Catholic ministers whose Churches possess valid sacraments, as often as necessity or a genuine spiritual benefit recommends such a course of action, and when access to a Catholic priest is physically or morally impossible (Nos. 26, 27).

Again, in view of these very same principles, Catholics may for a just cause join with their separated Eastern brethren in sacred functions, things, and places (No. 28). Bishops decide when and if to follow this policy.

RECENT DOCUMENTS

Two recent documents of importance with respect to relations between the Catholic and separated Eastern Churches are the apostolic letter, *Orientale Lumen*, issued May 5, 1995; and the encyclical letter, *Ut Unum Sint*, issued May 30, 1995, especially paragraphs 50-63.

In addition, the Pontifical Council for Promoting Christian Unity issued the following *Guidelines for Admission to the Eucharist between the Chaldean Church and the Assyrian Church of the East* on July 20, 2001, and made public on October 25, 2001:

Given the great distress of many Chaldean and Assyrian faithful, in their motherland and in the diaspora, impeding for many of them a normal sacramental life according to their own tradition, and in the ecumenical context of the bilateral dialogue between the Catholic Church and the Assyrian Church of the East, the request has been made to provide for admission to the Eucharist between the Chaldean Church and the Assyrian Church of the East. This request has first been studied by the Joint Committee for Theological Dialogue between the Catholic Church and the Assyrian Church of the East. The present guidelines subsequently have been elaborated by the Pontifical Council for Promoting Christian Unity, in agreement with the Congregation for the Doctrine of Faith and the Congregation for the Oriental Churches.

1. Pastoral necessity

The request for admission to the Eucharist between the Chaldean Church and the Assyrian Church of the East is connected with the particular geographical and social situation in which their faithful are actually living. Due to various and sometimes dramatic circumstances, many Assyrian and Chaldean faithful left their motherlands and moved to the Middle East, Scandinavia, Western Europe, Australia and Northern America. As there cannot be a priest for every local community in such a widespread diaspora, numerous Chaldean and Assyrian faithful are confronted with a situation of pastoral necessity with regard to the administration of sacraments. Official documents of the Catholic Church provide special regulations for such situations, namely the Code of Canons of the Eastern Churches, can. 671, §2-§3 and the Directory for the Application of Principles and Norms of Ecumenism, n. 123.

2. Ecumenical rapprochement

The request is also connected with the ongoing process of ecumenical rapprochement between the Catholic Church and the Assyrian Church of the East. With the 'Common Christological Declaration', signed in 1994 by Pope John Paul II and Patriarch Mar Dinkha IV, the main dogmatic problem between the Catholic Church and the Assyrian Church has been resolved. As a consequence, the ecumenical rapprochement between the Chaldean Church and the Assyrian Church of the East also entered a further phase of development. On 29 November 1996 Patriarch Mar Raphaël Bidawid and Patriarch Mar Dinkha IV signed a list of common proposals with a view to the re-establishment of full ecclesial unity among both historical heirs of the ancient Church of the East. On 15 August 1997 this program was approved by their respective Synods and confirmed in a 'Joint Synodal Decree'. Supported by their respective Synods, both Patriarchs approved a further series of initiatives to foster the progressive restoration of their ecclesial unity. Both the Congregation for the Oriental Churches and the Pontifical Council for the Promotion of Christian Unity support this process.

3. The Anaphora of Addai and Mari

The principal issue for the Catholic Church in agreeing to this request, related to the question of the validity of the Eucharist celebrated with the Anaphora of Addai and Mari, one of the three Anaphoras traditionally used by the Assyrian Church of the East. The Anaphora of Addai and Mari is notable because, from time immemorial, it has been used without a recitation of the Institution Narrative. As the Catholic Church considers the words of the Eucharistic Institution a constitutive and therefore indispensable part of the Anaphora or Eucharistic Prayer, a long and careful study was undertaken of the Anaphora of Addai and Mari, from a historical, liturgical and theological perspective, at the end of which the Congregation for the Doctrine of Faith on January 17th, 2001 concluded that this Anaphora can be considered valid. H.H. Pope John Paul II has approved this decision. This conclusion rests on three major arguments.

In the first place, the Anaphora of Addai and Mari is one of the most ancient Anaphoras, dating back to the time of the very early Church; it was composed and used with the clear intention of celebrating the Eucharist in full continuity with the Last Supper and according to the intention of the Church; its validity was never officially contested, neither in the Christian East nor in the Christian West.

Secondly, the Catholic Church recognises the Assyrian Church of the East as a true particular Church, built upon orthodox faith and apostolic succession. The Assyrian Church of the East has also preserved full Eucharistic faith in the presence of our Lord under the species of bread and wine and in the sacrificial character of the Eucharist. In the Assyrian Church of the East, though not in full communion with the Catholic Church, are thus to be found "true sacraments, and above all, by apostolic succession, the priesthood and the Eucharist" (U.R., n. 15). Secondly, the Catholic Church recognises the Assyrian Church of the East as a true particular Church, built upon orthodox faith and apostolic succession. The Assyrian Church of the East has also preserved full Eucharistic faith in the presence of our Lord under the species of bread and wine and in the sacrificial character of the Eucharist. In the Assyrian Church of the East, though not in full communion with the Catholic Church, are thus to be found "true sacraments, and above all, by apostolic succession, the priesthood and the Eucharist" (U.R., n. 15).

Finally, the words of *Eucharistic Institution* are indeed present in the *Anaphora of Addai and Mari*, not in a coherent narrative way and ad litteram, but rather in a dispersed euchological way, that is, integrated in successive prayers of thanksgiving, praise and intercession.

4. Guidelines for admission to the Eucharist

Considering the liturgical tradition of the Assyrian Church of the East, the doctrinal clarification regarding the validity of the Anaphora of Addai and Mari, the contemporary context in which both Assyrian and Chaldean faithful are living, the appropriate regulations which are foreseen in official documents of the Catholic Church, and the process of rapprochement between the Chaldean Church and the Assyrian Church of the East, the following provision is made:

1. When necessity requires, Assyrian faithful are permitted to participate and to receive Holy Communion in a Chaldean celebration of the Holy Eucharist; in the same way, Chaldean faithful for whom it is physically or morally impossible to approach a Catholic minister, are permitted to participate and to receive Holy Communion in an Assyrian celebration of the Holy Eucharist.

2. In both cases, Assyrian and Chaldean ministers celebrate the Holy Eucharist according to the liturgical prescriptions and customs of their own tradition.

3. When Chaldean faithful are participating in an Assyrian celebration of the Holy Eucharist, the Assyrian minister is warmly invited to insert the words of the Institution in the Anaphora of Addai and Mari, as allowed by the Holy Synod of the Assyrian Church of the East.

4. The above considerations on the use of the Anaphora of Addai and Mari and the present guidelines for admission to the Eucharist, are intended exclusively in relation to the Eucharistic celebration and admission to the Eucharist of the faithful from the Chaldean Church and the Assyrian Church of the East, in view of the pastoral necessity and ecumenical context mentioned above.

CRISIS IN RELATIONS WITH THE MOSCOW PATRIARCHATE

On February 11, 2002, it was made public that Pope John Paul II had elevated the four Apostolic Administrations in Russia to the status of dioceses. This precipitated a crisis in relations with the Moscow Patriarchate. On February 12, 2002, Patriarch Aleksy II of Moscow and All Russia and the Holy Synod of the Russian Orthodox Church released the following statement:

It was announced on February 11 in the Vatican that the Pope John Paul II of Rome decided to elevate the status of the administrative structures of the Roman Catholic Church in the territory of Russia to the level of dioceses. From now on the Vatican in its documents will name the territory of our country a "church province" led by a metropolitan.

The Russian Orthodox Church has been presented with a fait accompli, whereas such matters, in our opinion, require a preliminary discussion. We see this step as unfriendly and undermining the prospects for better relations between the two Churches.

Historically the Catholic Church in the territory of our country took pastoral care of the flock that traditionally belonged to it - Poles, Lithuanians, Germans, etc. Precisely for this reason the territory of Russia was not divided into Catholic dioceses and the Catholic ethnic parishes were part of the dioceses of Mogilev and Tiraspol. The establishment of a "church province," a "metropolitanate," means in fact the establishment of a national Catholic Church in Russia having its center in Moscow and claiming the Russian people, who are the flock of the Russian Orthodox Church culturally, spiritually and historically, as its flock.

The formation of such a church in Russia means in fact a challenge to Orthodoxy which has been rooted in the country for centuries. Nothing of this sort has ever happen in the history of our country. Moreover, this form of the organization of Catholic church life is atypical even of Catholic countries where there are no church provinces or dioceses governed actually by a metropolitan.

The fact should be pointed out that in taking care of its faithful in Catholic countries, the Russian Orthodox Church has never tried to establish church institutions parallel to Catholic ones. Our dioceses are established to take care of the Russian-speaking Orthodox diaspora, that is the children of the Russian Church who are far from their Motherland, not to carry out missionary work among the local population. If the Catholic Church worked in Russia with the same tact and good will as we do in Catholic countries, then no difficulties would arise in our relations.

We see as absolutely wrongful the references made by representatives of the Roman Catholic Church to the Catholic structures which existed in Russia before the 1917 Revolution and which they say they restore. Almost all the Roman Catholic dioceses that existed in the Russian empire by the early 20th century were in the territory of what today are Poland, Lithuania, Ukraine and Belorussia and did not have one center in the Russian capital city or any other city. The boundaries of our country as well as the ethnic and confessional composition of its population have considerably changed since. The number of Catholics in the present-day Russia is incomparably smaller than it was in the Russian Empire of the 20th

century.

We are convinced that to take care of the Catholics who are not so many in our country it was not necessary to elevate the status of the already existing Catholic church structures, the more so to establish a special church division. Such actions of the Roman Catholic Church, not conditioned by any real pastoral needs, expose the missionary purposes of the changes made. This is corroborated by numerous facts of missionary work carried out by Catholic clergy among the Russian population. This is the activity we call proselytic and keep pointing to as one of the basic obstacles for improving relations between our two Churches.

It is especially regretful that the Vatican has taken this decision just before the next round of official talks between our Churches to take place in the end of this February. As a result, a serious threat has emerged for the fragile negotiation process, which in its turn will make extremely difficult the settlement of problems and perplexities existing between us.

The leadership of the Roman Catholic Church is now responsible before God and history for a sharp aggravation of our relations, for the frustration of the hope for their normalization that has just begun to shape. The Vatican's action has put in jeorpady the ability of the Catholic West and the Orthodox East to cooperate as two great civilizations for the benefit of Europe and the world. The opportunity for common Christian witness before divided humanity has been sacrificed for momentary benefits.

The question arises: Does the Vatican still regard its relations with the Orthodox Church as those of dialogue and cooperation, as it has continually stated, or it sees Orthodoxy as an undesirable rival? If the latter is the case, any agreement between us is out of question.

Nevertheless, we continue to remind the Vatican that at a time when the confused world expects the Orthodox and the Catholics to take common public action, we should work together rather than be at enmity. We still have good relations with dioceses, parishes and monasteries of the Catholic Church and cooperation with Catholic humanitarian organizations and educational institutions. These examples make it possible to hope that, whatever difficulties provoked by the Vatican's mistaken policy towards the Russian Orthodox Church, relations between the Orthodox and the Catholics will develop to become an important factor in the preservation of Christian values in the life of Europe and the world.

Addressing our flock, we call them to be faithful to Holy Orthodoxy. Let us respond calmly and peacefully but firmly to any attempts to divide our people spiritually. "Stand therefore, having your loins girt about with truth, and having on the breastplate of righteousness; and your feet shod with the preparation of the gospel of peace" (Eph. 6:14-15). Moscow Patriarchate Press Release, Feb. 12.

Archbishop Tadeusz Kondrusiewicz of the newly-created Archdiocese of the Mother of God in Moscow, issued the following statement on February 13:

1. We want to express our bewilderment and serious concern at the interference in the internal affairs of the Catholic Church in Russia which in the past

few days has become more glaring. We would like to make our statement in the light of the following points:

§religious groups have the right to self government in accordance with their own hierarchical and organizational structure;

§it is the duty of the Apostolic Representation and the bishops of the Catholic Church to create normal conditions for the pastoral care of the faithful;

§according to Canon Law the normal structures of the Catholic Church are dioceses and metropolitan sees (ecclesiastical provinces);

§the setting up of temporary Russian Apostolic Administrations as regular dioceses which took place on 11th February 2002, does not contravene present Russian law;

§this essential step for Russian Catholics was carried out with notification to the government and ecclesiastical authorities of the Russian Orthodox Church in accordance with generally accepted international practice;

Furthermore we are convinced that the Catholics of the Russian Federation have the same rights as citizens professing other religions and that the lawful exercise of those rights must not in any way give rise to suspicion or be held subject to political speculation.

2. Moreover, we consider it our duty to publicly reject the unfounded assertions contained in the public Statement of the Patriarch of Moscow and of all Russia, Aleksy II, and of the Holy Synod of the Russian Orthodox Church dated 12th February 2002.

3. In that Statement it is alleged that "a form of Catholic Church life" has been founded in Russia which is "untypical even for Catholic countries where ecclesiastical provinces do not usually exist - that is dioceses administered by a Metropolitan."

This assertion is not correct. The Code of the Church's Canon Law states that for proper collegiate pastoral activity in different neighboring dioceses and for the proper collaboration between diocesan bishops and different neighboring dioceses, higher ecclesiastical authority is invested in ecclesiastical provinces, that is in metropolitan sees. (cf Canon 431)

The head of a metropolitan see is a metropolitan bishop, who is always a resident archbishop in the archdiocese governed by him. This authority is bound to an episcopal see which is created by the Roman Pontiff. Metropolitan sees exist for example, in Paris, Washington, Prague, Milan and Warsaw. (In Poland alone there are thirteen metropolitan sees.) At present they also exist in countries of the former Soviet Union, the metropolitan sees of Riga, Minsk-Mogiliev, Vilnius, Kaunas and Lvov.

Other dioceses within an ecclesiastical province are called "suffragan" sees. Canon law defines the authority of the metropolitan bishop in their regard:

§to assure the fullness of the faith and ecclesiastical discipline and to bring abuse to the attention of the Roman Pontiff (Canon 436 sect. 1)

§to conduct canonical visitation with the approval of the Apostolic See in the case of a suffragan bishop not administering his diocese (Canon 436 sect. 1)

§to appoint an administrator to a vacant episcopal see within eight days of its falling vacant (Canon 436 sect 1)

A metropolitan does not have any other authority in his suffragan dioceses (Canon 436 sect.3)

4. In its Statement the ruling authorities of the Russian Orthodox Church state that "Russian territory was never divided into Catholic dioceses."

We must call to mind the following facts;

§Episcopal structures of the Catholic Church already existed in the south of Russia in the XIV-XV centuries.

§St Petersburg, the capital of the Russian Empire, was the center of the Mogiliev metropolitan diocese. Saratov was the seat of the Tiraspolis diocese. Besides this the diocese of Vladivostok was erected in 1922. The Archbishop of Mogiliev had the title of Metropolitan of all the Catholic churches in the Russian Empire.

§from the founding of the Metropolitan See of Mogiliev to its extinction at the expulsion from the country of its last occupant, Metropolitan Ian Tsepliak, the see of St Petersburg was occupied by twenty-seven bishops.

Therefore Catholic dioceses and metropolitan sees with their metropolitan and suffragan bishops have in fact existed within the present day boundaries of the Russian Federation.

5. Taking the above into consideration, we hold that the changes in the status of the Catholic Church in Russia and the erection of an ecclesiastical province cannot be described as establishing "a new Catholic structure, parallel to the Russian Orthodox Church." We would also like to make the following points:

Firstly, the dioceses do not take their names from the cities where they have their centers. There is no Metropolitan of Moscow or of Russia, instead there is a Metropolitan in Moscow.

Secondly, in the Russian Orthodox Church, there exists, for example, the Metropolitan of Vilnius and Lithuania and the Archbishop of Brussels and Belgium, of Berlin and Germany, and no-one in the Catholic Church is against these, since these metropolitan titles are the internal affair of the Russian Orthodox Church which names archbishops according to its needs:

Thirdly, a metropolitan does not have any real authority in different dioceses for they are autonomous and are governed by their own bishops.

6. In the Statement referred to above, mention is made in turn of multiple examples of missionary activity by Catholic clergy among the Russian population. "In fact, we describe this activity as "proselytism" and continually indicate this as one of the outstanding reasons working against the improvement of relations between our two Churches" it is said in the document.

For our part we have repeatedly invited over a period of eleven years the leaders of the Russian Orthodox Church to discuss concrete details and to give hard facts of proselytism by Catholics in Russia. We want to know the facts of exactly who is involved or has been involved in proselytism, in what places, at what times and in what circumstances.

Unfortunately, we have not yet received any answer, neither have we received any response to our invitation "to sit at a round table to arrive at an agreement of the meaning of the term "proselytism."

7. Despite the deterioration in the already strained situation in relations between the Catholic and Russian Orthodox Churches, I hope and pray to God that the dialogue will continue and be fruitful. I am con-

vinced that the Catholic and Orthodox Churches can together respond to the calls of our age for the good of mankind and of civilization.

Statement distributed by the Information Center of the Conference of Catholic Bishops of the Russian Federation.

RECENT DEVELOPMENTS

On May 13, 2003, Pope John Paul II established a new Catholic church structure in Kazakhstan with four dioceses and one apostolic administration. In response, the Communication Service of the Department for External Church Relations of the Moscow Patriarchate issued the following statement on May 19, 2003:

The Vatican has officially announced its decision to establish two new Catholic dioceses in Kazakhstan. Accordingly, the Apostolic Administrations in Astana and Alma-Ata become respectively "The Archdiocese of the Most Holy Virgin Mary in Astana" and the "Diocese of the Most Holy Trinity in Alma-Ata". Previously there was only one diocese of the Roman Catholic Church in the country, that of Karaganda. By the Vatican's decision, the Catholic dioceses in Alma-Ata and Karaganda and the Apostolic Administration in Atyrau are now subjects to the newly establish "Archdiocese of the Most Holy Virgin Mary in Astana". Thus, a centralized administrative structure of the Catholic Church has been established in Kazakhstan.

This decision has been made without any consultation with the Russian Orthodox Church in spite of the fact that the overwhelming majority of Christians in Kazakhstan belong to precisely her canonical jurisdiction and has belonged to her traditionally, in accordance with their historical choice. The action taken by the Catholic side has conclusively confirmed the reluctance of the present leadership of the Vatican to hold consultations on matters of concern for the both Churches and signifies an actual refusal to be in dialogue for working out constructive decisions together.

The establishment of new dioceses in Kazakhstan, united in a single centralized structure, testifies to the invariability of the course taken by the Vatican to engage in expansion throughout the former Soviet Union. Against this background, the declarations made by Catholic hierarchs on the need for dialogue between the two Churches appear insincere.

The Russian Orthodox Church categorically rejects the decision to establish new Catholic dioceses in Kazakhstan and considers this step to be another serious blow on the entire complex of Orthodox-Catholic relations. Responsibility for its consequences, ruinous for the relations between the two Churches, lies wholly on the side that has taken it.

REFORMATION CHURCHES

LEADERS AND DOCTRINES OF THE REFORMATION

Some of the leading figures, doctrines and churches of the Reformation are covered below. A companion article covers Major Protestant Churches in the United States.

LEADERS

John Wycliff (c. 1320-1384): English priest and scholar who advanced one of the leading Reformation ideas nearly 200 years before Martin Luther — that the Bible alone is the sufficient rule of faith — but had only an indirect influence on the 16th century Reformers. Supporting belief in an inward and practical religion, he denied the divinely commissioned authority of the pope and bishops of the Church; he also denied the Real Presence of Christ in the Holy Eucharist, and wrote against the sacrament of penance and the doctrine of indulgences. Nearly 20 of his propositions were condemned by Gregory XI in 1377; his writings were proscribed more extensively by the Council of Constance in 1415. His influence was strongest in Bohemia and Central Europe.

John Hus (c. 1369-1415): A Bohemian priest and preacher of reform who authored 30 propositions condemned by the Council of Constance. Excommunicated in 1411 or 1412, he was burned at the stake in 1415. His principal errors concerned the nature of the Church and the origin of papal authority. He spread some of the ideas of Wycliff but did not subscribe to his views regarding faith alone as the condition for justification and salvation, the sole sufficiency of Scripture as the rule of faith, the Real Presence of Christ in the Eucharist, and the sacramental system. In 1457 some of his followers founded the Church of the Brotherhood which later became known as the United Brethren or Moravian Church and is considered the earliest independent Protestant body.

Martin Luther (1483-1546): An Augustinian friar, priest and doctor of theology, the key figure in the Reformation. In 1517, as a special indulgence was being preached in Germany, and in view of needed reforms within the Church, he published at Wittenberg 95 theses concerning matters of Catholic belief and practice. Leo X condemned 41 statements from Luther's writings in 1520. Luther, refusing to recant, was excommunicated the following year. His teachings strongly influenced subsequent Lutheran theology; its statements of faith are found in the Book of Concord (1580).

Luther's doctrines included the following: The sin of Adam, which corrupted human nature radically (but not substantially), has affected every aspect of man's being. Justification, understood as the forgiveness of sins and the state of righteousness, is by grace for Christ's sake through faith. Faith involves not merely intellectual assent but an act of confidence by the will. Good works are indispensably necessary concomitants of faith, but do not merit salvation. Of the sacraments, Luther retained baptism, penance and the Holy Communion as effective vehicles of the grace of the Holy Spirit; he held that in the Holy Communion the consecrated bread and wine are the Body and Blood of Christ. The rule of faith is the divine revelation in the Sacred Scriptures. He rejected purgatory, indulgences and the invocation of the saints, and held that prayers for the dead have no efficacy. Catholics clarified their positions at the Council of Trent. The 1999 Joint Declaration indicates that the condemnations of doctrine by the Council of Trent and the Book of Concord do not apply to present day Catholic and Lutheran teaching respectively.

Ulrich Zwingli (1484-1531): A priest who triggered the Reformation in Switzerland with a series of New Testament lectures in 1519, later disputations and by other actions. He held the Gospel to be the only basis of truth; rejected the Mass (which he suppressed in 1525 at Zurich), penance and other sacraments; denied papal primacy and doctrine concerning purgatory and the invocation of saints; rejected celibacy, monasticism and many traditional practices of piety. His symbolic view of the Eucharist, which was at odds with Catholic doctrine, caused an irreconcilable controversy with Luther and his followers. Zwingli was killed in a battle between the forces of Protestant and Catholic cantons in Switzerland.

John Calvin (1509-1564): French leader of the Reformation in Switzerland, whose key tenet was absolute predestination of some persons to heaven and others to hell. He rejected Catholic doctrine in 1533 after becoming convinced of a personal mission to reform the Church. In 1536 he published the first edition of Institutes of the Christian Religion, a systematic exposition of his doctrine which became the classic textbook of Reformed — as distinguished from Lutheran — theology. To Luther's principal theses — regarding Scripture as the sole rule of faith, the radical corruption of human nature, and justification by faith alone — he added absolute predestination, certitude of salvation for the elect, and the incapability of the elect to lose grace. Calvin's Eucharist teaching, while affirming Christ's true presence, was not able to find agreement with that of Luther. However, in our own time, agreement has been reached between Lutherans and Reformed (Calvinists), and considerable progress has been made with Catholics and Orthodox toward a common understanding of Christ's presence in Communion.

CHURCHES AND MOVEMENTS

Adventists: Members of several Christian groups whose doctrines are dominated by belief in a more or less imminent second advent or coming of Christ upon earth for a glorious 1,000-year reign of righteousness. This reign, following victory by the forces of good over evil in a final Battle of Armageddon, will begin with the resurrection of the chosen and will end with the resurrection of all others and the annihilation of the wicked. Thereafter, the just will live forever in a renewed heaven and earth. A sleep of the soul takes place between the time of death and the day of judgment. There is no hell. The Bible, in literalist interpretation, is regarded as the only rule of faith and practice. About six churches have developed in the course of the Adventist movement which originated with William Miller (1782-1849) in the United States. Miller, on the basis of calculations made from the Book of Daniel, predicted that the second advent of Christ would occur between 1843 and 1844. After the prophecy went unfulfilled, divisions occurred in the movement and the Seventh Day Adventists, whose actual formation dates from 1860, emerged as the largest single body. The observance of Saturday instead of Sunday as the Lord's Day dates from 1844.

Anabaptism: Originated in Saxony in the first quarter of the 16th century and spread rapidly through southern Germany. Its doctrine included several key Lutheran tenets but was not regarded with favor by Luther, Calvin or Zwingli. Anabaptists believed that baptism is for adults only and that infant baptism is invalid. Their doctrine of the Inner Light, concerning the direct influence of the Holy Spirit on the believer, implied rejection of Catholic doctrine concerning the sacraments and the nature of the Church. Eighteen articles of faith were formulated in 1632 in Holland. Mennonites are Anabaptists.

Arminianism: A modification of the rigid predestinationism of Calvin, set forth by Jacob Arminius (1560-1609) and formally stated in the Remonstrance of 1610. Arminianism influenced some Calvinist bodies.

Baptists: So called because of their doctrine concerning baptism. They reject infant baptism and consider only baptism by immersion as valid. Leaders in the formation of the church were John Smyth (d. 1612) in England and Roger Williams (d. 1683) in America.

Congregationalists: Evangelical in spirit and seeking a return to forms of the primitive church, they uphold individual freedom in religious matters, do not require the acceptance of a creed as a condition for communion, and regard each congregation as autonomous. Robert Browne influenced the beginnings of Congregationalism.

Disciples: From a nineteenth century revival movement and desire for the unity of the Christian churches, a network of congregations developed which desired to be called simply "Christian churches." These churches opened their communion and membership to all, celebrated the Eucharist each Sunday and baptized only adults. From this movement the Christian Church/Disciples of Christ, the Churches of Christ and the independent Christian Churches emerged.

Methodists: A group who broke away from the Anglican Communion under the leadership of John Wesley (1703-1791), although some Anglican beliefs were retained. Doctrines include the witness of the Spirit to the individual and personal assurance of salvation. The largest Methodist body in the United States is the United Methodist Church. There are three Black Methodist bodies: African Methodist Episcopal, African Methodist Episcopal Zion, and Christian Methodist Episcopal Churches. There are also several Holiness Churches in the Wesleyan tradition: i.e., Nazarene, Free Methodist, Wesleyan Church.

Pentecostals: Churches that grew up after the 1906 enthusiastic revival, accompanied by the phenomena of speaking in foreign tongues and the experience of baptism in the Holy Spirit. From this revival churches of a Methodist or Baptist theological emphasis emerged, such as the Church of God in Christ or the Assemblies of God. In the mid-twentieth century, the charismatic experience began to be shared by some members of the classical churches, including Roman Catholic.

Puritans: Congregationalists who sought church reform along Calvinist lines in severe simplicity. (Use of the term was generally discontinued after 1660.)

Presbyterians: Basically Calvinistic, called Presbyterian because church polity centers around assemblies of presbyters or elders. John Knox (c. 1513-1572) established the church in Scotland.

Quakers: Their key belief is in internal divine illumination, the inner light of the living Christ, as the only source of truth and inspiration. George Fox (1624-1691) was one of their leaders in England. Called the Society of Friends, the Quakers are noted for their pacifism.

Unitarianism: A 16th century doctrine which rejected the Trinity and the divinity of Christ in favor of a uni-personal God. It claimed scriptural support for a long time but became generally rationalistic with respect to "revealed" doctrine as well as in ethics and its world-view. One of its principal early proponents was Faustus Socinus (1539-1604), a leader of the Polish Brethren. A variety of communions developed in England in the Reformation and post-Reformation periods.

Universalism: A product of 18th-century liberal Protestantism in England. The doctrine is not Trinitarian and includes a tenet that all men will ultimately be saved.

Anglican Communion: This communion, which regards itself as the same apostolic Church as that which was established by early Christians in England, derived not from Reformation influences but from the renunciation of papal jurisdiction by Henry VIII (1491-1547). His Act of Supremacy in 1534 called Christ's Church an assembly of local churches subject to the prince, who was vested with fullness of authority and jurisdiction. In spite of Henry's denial of papal authority, this Act did not reject substantially other principal articles of faith. Notable changes, proposed and adopted for the reformation of the church, took place in the subsequent reigns of Edward VI and Elizabeth, with respect to such matters as Scripture as the rule of faith, the sacraments, the nature of the Mass, and the constitution of the hierarchy. There are 27 provinces in the Anglican Communion. (See Episcopal Church, Anglican Orders, Anglican-Catholic Final Report.)

MAJOR PROTESTANT CHURCHES IN THE UNITED STATES

There are more than 250 Protestant church bodies in the U.S.

The majority of U.S. Protestants belong to the following denominations: Baptist, Methodist, Lutheran, Presbyterian, Protestant Episcopal, the United Church of Christ, the Christian Church (Disciples of Christ), Evangelicals.

See **Ecumenical Dialogues, Reports** and related entries for coverage of relations between the Catholic Church and other Christian churches.

Baptist Churches

Baptist churches, comprising the largest of all American Protestant denominations, were first established by John Smyth near the beginning of the 17th century in England. The first Baptist church in America was founded at Providence by Roger Williams in 1639.

Largest of the nearly 30 Baptist bodies in the U.S. are:

The Southern Baptist Convention, 901 Commerce St., Suite 750, Nashville, TN 37203, with 15.7 million members.

The National Baptist Convention, U.S.A., Inc., 915 Spain St., Baton Rouge, LA 70802, with 8 million members;

The National Baptist Convention of America, Inc., 1320 Pierre Ave., Shreveport, LA 71103, with 4.5 million members.

The American Baptist Churches in the U.S.A., P.O. Box 851, Valley Forge, PA 19482, with 1.5 million members.

The total number of U.S. Baptists is more than 29 million. The world total is 33 million.

Proper to Baptists is their doctrine on baptism. Called an "ordinance" rather than a sacrament, baptism by immersion is a sign that one has experienced and decided in favor of the salvation offered by Christ. It is administered only to persons who are able to make a responsible decision. Baptism is not administered to infants.

Baptists do not have a formal creed but generally subscribe to two professions of faith formulated in 1689 and 1832 and are in general agreement with classical Protestant theology regarding Scripture as the sole rule of faith, original sin, justification through faith in Christ, and the nature of the Church. Their local churches are autonomous.

Worship services differ in form from one congregation to another. Usual elements are the reading of Scripture, a sermon, hymns, vocal and silent prayer. The Lord's Supper, called an "ordinance," is celebrated at various times.

Christian Church (Disciples of Christ)

The Christian Church (Disciples of Christ) originated early in the 1800s from two movements against rigid denominationalism led by Presbyterians Thomas and Alexander Campbell in western Pennsylvania and Barton W. Stone in Kentucky. The two movements developed separately for about 25 years before being merged in 1832.

The church, which identifies itself with the Protestant mainstream, has nearly one million members in almost 4,000 congregations in the U.S. and Canada. The greatest concentration of members in the U.S. is located roughly along the old frontier line, in an arc sweeping from Ohio and Kentucky through the Midwest and down into Oklahoma and Texas.

The general offices of the church are located at 130 E. Washington St., Indianapolis, IN 46204. The church's persistent concern for Christian unity is based on a conviction expressed in a basic document, Declaration and Address, dating from its founding. The document states: "The church of Christ upon earth is essentially, intentionally and constitutionally one."

The Disciples have no official doctrine or dogma. Their worship practices vary widely from more common informal services to what could almost be described as "high church" services. Membership is granted after a simple statement of belief in Jesus Christ and baptism by immersion; most congregations admit un-immersed transfers from other denominations. The Lord's Supper or Eucharist, generally called Communion, is always open to Christians of all persuasions. Lay men and women routinely preside over the Lord's Supper, which is celebrated each Sunday; they often preach and perform other pastoral functions as well. Distinction between ordained and non-ordained members is blurred somewhat because of the Disciples' emphasis on all members of the church as ministers.

The Christian Church is oriented to congregational government, and has a unique structure in which three sections of polity (general, regional and congregational) operate as equals rather than in a pyramid of authority. At the national or international level, it is governed by a general assembly which has voting representation direct from congregations and regions as well as all ordained and licensed clergy.

Episcopal Church

The Episcopal Church, which includes 100 dioceses in the United States, Central and South America, and elsewhere overseas, regards itself as part of the same apostolic church which was established by early Christians in England. Established in this country during the colonial period, it became independent of the jurisdiction of the Church of England when a new constitution and Prayer Book were adopted at a general convention held in 1789. It has approximately 2.5 million members worldwide.

Offices of the presiding bishop and the executive council are located at 815 Second Ave., New York, NY 10017.

The presiding bishop is chief pastor and primate; he is elected by the House of Bishops and confirmed by the House of Deputies for a term of nine years.

The Episcopal Church, which is a part of the Anglican Communion, regards the Archbishop of Canterbury as the "First among Equals," though not under his authority.

The Anglican Communion, worldwide, has 70 million members in 36 self-governing churches.

Official statements of belief and practice are found in the Book of Common Prayer. Scripture has primary importance with respect to the rule of faith, and authority is also attached to tradition.

An episcopal system of church government prevails, but presbyters, deacons and lay persons also have an active voice in church affairs. The levels of government are the general convention, and executive council, dioceses, and local parishes. At the parish level, the congregation has the right to select its own rector, with the consent of the bishop.

Liturgical worship is according to the Book of Common Prayer as adopted in 1979, but details of ceremonial practice vary from one congregation to another.

Lutheran Churches

The origin of Lutheranism is generally traced to Oct. 31, 1517, when Martin Luther — Augustinian friar, priest, doctor of theology — tacked "95 Theses" to the door of the castle church in Wittenberg, Germany. This call to debate on the subject of indulgences and related concerns has come to symbolize the beginning of the Reformation. Luther and his supporters intended to reform the Church they knew. Though Lutheranism has come to be visible in separate denominations and national churches, at its heart it professes itself to be a confessional movement within the one, holy, catholic and apostolic Church.

The world's 61 million Lutherans form the third largest grouping of Christians, after Roman Catholics and Orthodox. About 57 million of them belong to church bodies which make up the Lutheran World Federation, headquartered in Geneva.

There are about 8.5 million Lutherans in the United States, making them the fourth largest Christian grouping, after Roman Catholics, Baptists and Methodists. Although there are nearly 20 U.S. Lutheran church bodies, all but 100,000 Lutherans belong to either the Evangelical Lutheran Church in America (with 5.2 million members and headquarters at 8765 W. Higgins Rd., Chicago, IL 60631), The Lutheran Church-Missouri Synod (with 2.61 million members and headquarters at 1333 S. Kirkwood Rd., St. Louis, MO 63122), or the Wisconsin Evangelical Lutheran Synod (with 420,000 members and headquarters at 2929 N. Mayfair Rd., Milwaukee, WI 53222).

The Evangelical Lutheran Church in America and the Lutheran Church-Missouri Synod carry out some work together through inter-Lutheran agencies such as Lutheran World Relief and Lutheran Immigration and Refugee Services; both agencies have offices at 390 Park Ave. South, New York, NY 10010.

The statements of faith which have shaped the confessional life of Lutheranism are found in the *Book of Concord*. This 1580 collection includes the three ancient ecumenical creeds (Apostles', Nicene and Athanasian), Luther's Large and Small Catechisms (1529), the Augsburg Confession (1530) and the Apology in defense of it (1531), the Smalkald Articles (including the "Treatise on the Power and Primacy of the Pope") (1537), and the Formula of Concord (1577).

The central Lutheran doctrinal proposition is that Christians "receive forgiveness of sins and become righteous before God by grace, for Christ's sake." Baptism and the Lord's Supper (Holy Communion, the Eucharist) are universally celebrated among Lutherans as sacramental means of grace. Lutherans also treasure the Word proclaimed in the reading of the Scriptures, preaching and absolution.

In the ELCA, the bishop is the minister of ordination. Much of Lutheranism continues what it understands as the historic succession of bishops (though without considering the historic episcopate essential for the church). All of Lutheranism is concerned to preserve apostolic succession in life and doctrine. Lutheran churches in Scandinavia and the Baltics, in the U.S., and in Canada have moved into full communion with their Anglican counterparts.

Lutheran jurisdictions corresponding to dioceses are called districts or synods in North America. There are more than 100 of them; each of them is headed by a bishop or president. The Evangelical Lutheran Church in America moved into full communion with the three Reformed Churches (Presbyterian Church, United Church of Christ and Reformed Church in America) in 1997, and in 2000 into full communion with the Episcopal Church, all of its bishops being ordained by bishops including those in the apostolic succession as understood by Anglicans.

Methodist Churches

John Wesley (1703-1791), an Anglican clergyman, was the founder of Methodism. In 1738, following a period of missionary work in America and strongly influenced by the Moravians, he experienced a new conversion to Christ and shortly thereafter became a leader in a religious awakening in England. By the end of the 18th century, Methodism was strongly rooted also in America.

The United Methodist Church, formed in 1968 by a merger of the Methodist Church and the Evangelical United Brethren Church, is the second largest Protestant denomination in the U.S., with more than nine million members; its principal agencies are located in New York, Evanston, IL, Nashville, TN, Washington, DC, Dayton, OH, and Lake Junaluska, NC (World Methodist Council, P.O. Box 518 28745). The second largest body, with just under two million communicants, is the African Methodist Episcopal Church. Four other major churches in the U.S. are the African Methodist Episcopal Zion, Christian Methodist Episcopal, Free Methodist Church and the Wesleyan Church. The total Methodist membership in the U.S. is about 15.5 million.

Worldwide, there are more than 73 autonomous Methodist/Wesleyan churches in 107 countries, with a membership of more than 33 million. All of them participate in the World Methodist Council, which gives global unity to the witness of Methodist communicants.

Methodism rejects absolute predestination and maintains that Christ offers grace freely to all men, not just to a select elite. Wesley's distinctive doctrine was the "witness of the Spirit" to the individual soul and personal assurance of salvation. He also emphasized the central themes of conversion and holiness. Methodists are in general agreement with classical Protestant theology regarding Scripture as the sole rule of faith, original sin, justification through faith in Christ, the nature of the Church, and the sacraments of baptism and the Lord's Supper. Church polity is structured along episcopal lines in America, with ministers being appointed to local churches by a bishop; churches stemming from British Methodism do not have bishops but vest appointive powers within an appropriate conference. Congregations are free to choose various forms of worship services; typical elements are readings from Scripture, sermons, hymns and prayers.

Presbyterian Churches

Presbyterians are so called because of their tradition of governing the church through a system of representative bodies composed of elders (presbyters).

Presbyterianism is a part of the Reformed Family of Churches that grew out of the theological work of John Calvin following the Lutheran Reformation, to which it is heavily indebted. Countries in which it acquired early strength and influence were Switzerland, France, Holland, Scotland and England.

Presbyterianism spread widely in this country in the latter part of the 18th century and afterwards. Presently, it has approximately 4.5 million communicants in nine bodies.

The two largest Presbyterian bodies in the country — the United Presbyterian Church in the U.S.A. and the Presbyterian Church in the United States — were reunited in June 1983, to form the Presbyterian Church (U.S.A.), with a membership of 2.7 million. Its national offices are located at 100 Witherspoon St., Louisville, KY 40202.

These churches, now merged, are closely allied with the Reformed Church in America, the United Church

of Christ, the Cumberland Presbyterian Churches, the Korean Presbyterian Church in America and the Associate Reformed Presbyterian Church.

In Presbyterian doctrine, baptism and the Lord's Supper, viewed as seals of the covenant of grace, are regarded as sacraments. Baptism, which is not necessary for salvation, is conferred on infants and adults The Lord's Supper is celebrated as a covenant of the Sacrifice of Christ. In both sacraments, a doctrine of the real presence of Christ is considered the central theological principle.

The Church is twofold, being invisible and also visible; it consists of all of the elect and all those Christians who are united in Christ as their immediate head.

Presbyterians are in general agreement with classical Protestant theology regarding Scripture as the sole rule of faith and practice, salvation by grace, and justification through faith in Christ.

Presbyterian congregations are governed by a session composed of elders elected by the communicant membership. On higher levels there are presbyteries, synods and a general assembly with various degrees of authority over local bodies; all such representative bodies are composed of elected elders and ministers in approximately equal numbers. The church annually elects a moderator who presides at the General Assembly and travels throughout the church to speak to and hear from the members.

Worship services, simple and dignified, include sermons, prayer, reading of the Scriptures and hymns. The Lord's Supper is celebrated at intervals.

Doctrinal developments of the past several years included approval in May, 1967, by the General Assembly of the United Presbyterian Church of a contemporary confession of faith to supplement the historic Westminster Confession. A statement entitled "The Declaration of Faith" was approved in 1977 by the Presbyterian Church in the U.S. for teaching and liturgical use.

The reunited church adopted "A Brief Statement of Reformed Faith" in 1991 regarding urgent concerns of the church. The Presbyterian Church, USA, has moved into full communion with the Evangelical Lutheran Church in America in 1997.

United Church of Christ

The 1,501,310-member (in 1994) United Church of Christ was formed in 1957 by a union of the Congregational Christian and the Evangelical and Reformed Churches. The former was originally established by the Pilgrims and the Puritans of the Massachusetts Bay Colony, while the latter was founded in Pennsylvania in the early 1700s by settlers from Central Europe. The denomination had 6,362 congregations throughout the United States in 1988.

It considers itself "a united and uniting church" and keeps itself open to all ecumenical options. Its headquarters are located at 700 Prospect, Cleveland, OH 44115.

Its statement of faith recognizes Jesus Christ as "our crucified and risen Lord (who) shared our common lot, conquering sin and death and reconciling the world to himself." It believes in the life after death, and the fact that God "judges men and nations by his righteous will declared through prophets and apostles."

The United Church further believes that Christ calls its members to share in his baptism "and eat at his table, to join him in his passion and victory." Each local church is free to adopt its own methods of worship and to formulate its own covenants and confessions of faith. Some celebrate communion weekly; others, monthly or on another periodical basis. Like other Calvinistic bodies, it believes that Christ is spiritually present in the sacrament.

The United Church is governed along congregational lines, and each local church is autonomous. However, the actions of its biennial General Synod are taken with great seriousness by congregations. Between synods, a 44-member executive council oversees the work of the church. In 1989 the UCC moved into full communion with the Christian Church (Disciples of Christ) and in 1997 with the Evangelical Lutheran Church in America.

Evangelicalism

Evangelicalism, dating from 1735 in England (the Evangelical Revival) and after 1740 in the United States (the Great Awakening), has had and continues to have widespread influence in Protestant churches. It has been estimated that about 45 millon American Protestants — communicants of both large denominations and small bodies — are evangelicals.

The Bible is their rule of faith and religious practice. Being born again in a life-changing experience through faith in Christ is the promise of salvation. Missionary work for the spread of the Gospel is a normal and necessary activity.

Additional matters of belief and practice are generally of a conservative character. Fundamentalists, numbering perhaps 4.5 million, comprise an extreme right-wing subculture of evangelicalism. They are distinguished mainly by militant biblicism, belief in the absolute inerrancy of the Bible and emphasis on the Second Coming of Christ. Fundamentalism developed early in the 20th century in reaction against liberal theology and secularizing trends in mainstream and other Protestant denominations.

The Holiness or Perfectionist wing of evangelicalism evolved from Methodist efforts to preserve, against a contrary trend, the personal-piety and inner-religion concepts of John Wesley. There are at least 30 Holiness bodies in the U.S.

Pentecostals, probably the most demonstrative of evangelicals, are noted for speaking in tongues and the stress they place on healing, prophecy and personal testimony to the practice and power of evangelical faith. There are strong charismatic movements within many of the historic Protestant churches and Roman Catholicism.

The evangelical communities have national and international ecumenical bodies. Black and white Pentecostal churches belong to the Pentecostal and Charismatic Fellowship of North America. Over forty Pentecostal, Holiness and evangelical churches belong to the US National Association of Evangelicals. Internationally, these national evangelical associations collaborate in the World Evangelical Alliance.

Assemblies of God

Assemblies (Churches) of God form the largest body (more than 2 million members) in the Pentecostal Movement which developed from (1) the Holiness Revival in the Methodist Church after the Civil War and (2) the Apostolic Faith Movement at the beginning of the 20th century. Members share with other Pentecostals belief in the religious experience of conversion and in the baptism by the Holy Spirit that sanctifies. Distinctive is the emphasis placed on the charismatic gifts of the apostolic church, healing and speaking in tongues, which are signs of the "second blessing" of the Holy Spirit.

The Assemblies are conservative and biblicist in theology; are loosely organized in various districts, with democratic procedures; are vigorously evangelistic. The moral code is rigid.

INTERRELIGIOUS DIALOGUE

JUDAISM

Judaism is the religion of the Hebrew Bible and of contemporary Jews. Divinely revealed and with a patriarchal background (Abraham and Sarah, Isaac and Jacob), it originated with the Mosaic Covenant, was identified with the Israelites, and achieved distinctive form and character as the religion of the Torah (Law, "The Teaching") from this Covenant and reforms initiated by Ezra and Nehemiah after the Babylonian Exile.

Judaism does not have a formal creed but its principal points of belief are clear. Basic is belief in one transcendent God who reveals himself through the Torah, the prophets, the life of his people and events of history. The fatherhood of God involves the brotherhood of all humanity. Religious faith and practice are equated with just living according to God's Law. Moral conviction and practice are regarded as more important than precise doctrinal formulation and profession. Formal worship, whose principal act was sacrifice from the Exodus times to 70 A.D., is by prayer, reading and meditating upon the sacred writings, and observance of the Sabbath and festivals.

Judaism has messianic expectations of the complete fulfillment of the Covenant, the coming of God's kingdom, the ingathering of his people, and final judgment and retribution for all. Views differ regarding the manner in which these expectations will be realized — through a person, the community of God's people, an evolution of historical events, an eschatological act of God himself. Individual salvation expectations also differ, depending on views about the nature of immortality, punishment and reward, and related matters.

Sacred Books

The sacred books are the 24 books of the Masoretic Hebrew Text of The Law, the Prophets and the Writings (see The Bible). Together, they contain the basic instruction or norms for just living. In some contexts, the term Law or Torah refers only to the Pentateuch (Genesis, Exodus, Leviticus, Numbers, Deuteronomy); in others, it denotes all the sacred books and/or the whole complex of written and oral tradition.

Also of great authority are two Talmuds, which were composed in Palestine and Babylon in the fourth and fifth centuries A.D., respectively. They consist of the

Mishna, a compilation of oral laws, and the Gemara, a collection of rabbinical commentary on the Mishna. Midrash are collections of scriptural comments and moral counsels.

Priests were the principal religious leaders during the period of sacrificial and temple worship. Rabbis were originally teachers; today they share with cantors the function of leaders of prayer. The synagogue is the place of community worship. The family and home are focal points of many aspects of Jewish worship and practice.

Of the various categories of Jews, Orthodox are the most conservative in adherence to strict religious traditions. Others — Reformed, Conservative, Reconstructionist — are liberal in comparison with the Orthodox. They favor greater or less modification of religious practices in accommodation to contemporary culture and living conditions.

Principal events in Jewish life include the circumcision of males, according to prescriptions of the Covenant; the bar and bat mitzvah that marks the coming-of-age of boys and girls in Judaism at age 13; marriage; and observance of the Sabbath and festivals.

Observances of the Sabbath and festivals begin at sundown of the previous calendar day and continue until the following sundown.

Sabbath: Saturday, the weekly day of rest prescribed in the Decalogue.

Sukkoth (Tabernacles): A seven-to-nine-day festival in the month of Tishri (Sept.-Oct.), marked by some Jews with Covenant-renewal and reading of The Law. It originated as an agricultural feast at the end of the harvest and got its name from the temporary shelters used by workers in the fields.

Hanukkah (The Festival of Lights, the Feast of Consecration and of the Maccabees): Commemorates the dedication of the new altar in the Temple at Jerusalem by Judas Maccabeus in 165 B.C. The eight-day festival, during which candles in an eight-branch candelabra are lighted in succession, one each day, occurs near the winter solstice, close to Christmas time.

Pesach (Passover): A seven-day festival commemorating the liberation of the Israelites from Egypt. The narrative of the Exodus, the Haggadah, is read at ceremonial Seder meals on the first and second days of the festival, which begins on the 14th day of Nisan (Mar.-Apr.).

Shavuoth, Pentecost (Feast of Weeks): Observed 50 days after Passover, commemorating the anniversary of the revelation of the Law to Moses.

Purim: A joyous festival observed on the 14th day of Adar (Feb.-Mar.), commemorating the rescue of the Israelites from massacre by the Persians through the intervention of Esther. The festival is preceded by a day of fasting. A gift- and alms-giving custom became associated with it in medieval times.

Rosh Hashana (Feast of Trumpets, New Year): Observed on the first day of Tishri (Sept.-Oct.), the festival focuses attention on the ways of life and the ways of death. It is second in importance only to the most solemn observance of Yom Kippur.

Yom Kippur (Day of Atonement): The highest holy day, observed with strict fasting. It occurs 10 days after Rosh Hashana.

Yom HaShoah (Holocaust Memorial Day): Observed in the week after Passover; increasingly observed with joint Christian-Jewish services of remembrance.

CATHOLIC-JEWISH RELATIONS

The Second Vatican Council, in addition to the *Decree on Ecumenism* (concerning the movement for unity among Christians, stated the mind of the Church on a similar matter in *Nostra Aetate*, a" Declaration on the Relationship of the Church to Non-Christian Religions." This document, as the following excerpts indicate, backgrounds the reasons and directions of the Church's regard for the Jews. (Other portions of the document refer to Hindus, Buddhists and Muslims.)

Spiritual Bond

As this sacred Synod searches into the mystery of the Church, it recalls the spiritual bond linking the people of the New Covenant with Abraham's stock.

For the Church of Christ acknowledges that, according to the mystery of God's saving design, the beginnings of her faith and her election are already found among the patriarchs, Moses, and the prophets. She professes that all who believe in Christ, Abraham's sons according to faith (cf. Gal. 3:7), are included in the same patriarch's call, and likewise that the salvation of the Church was mystically foreshadowed by the Chosen People's exodus from the land of bondage.

The Church, therefore, cannot forget that she received the revelation of the Old Testament through the people with whom God in his inexpressible mercy deigned to establish the Ancient Covenant. Nor can she forget that she draws sustenance from the root of

that good olive tree onto which have been grafted the wild olive branches of the Gentiles (cf. Rom. 11:17-24). Indeed, the Church believes that by his cross Christ, our Peace, reconciled Jew and Gentile, making them both one in himself (cf. Eph. 2:14-16).

The Jews still remain most dear to God because of their fathers, for he does not repent of the gifts he makes nor of the calls he issues (cf. Rom. 11:28-29). In company with the prophets and the same Apostle (Paul), the Church awaits that day, known to God alone, on which all peoples will address the Lord in a single voice and "serve him with one accord" (Zeph. 3:9; cf. Is. 66:23; Ps. 65:4; Rom. 11:11-32).

Since the spiritual patrimony common to Christians and Jews is thus so great, this sacred Synod wishes to foster and recommend that mutual understanding and respect which is the fruit above all of biblical and theological studies, and of brotherly dialogues.

No Anti-Semitism

True, authorities of the Jews and those who followed their lead pressed for the death of Christ (cf. Jn. 19:6); still, what happened in his passion cannot be blamed upon all the Jews then living, without distinction, nor upon the Jews of today. Although the Church is the new People of God, the Jews should not be presented as repudiated or cursed by God, as if such views followed from the holy Scriptures. All should take pains, then, lest in catechetical instruction and in the preaching of God's Word they teach anything out of harmony with the truth of the Gospel and the spirit of Christ.

The Church repudiates all persecutions against any person. Moreover, mindful of her common patrimony with the Jews, and motivated by the Gospel's spiritual love and by no political considerations, she deplores the hatred, persecutions, and displays of anti-Semitism directed against the Jews at any time and from any source (No. 4).

The Church rejects, as foreign to the mind of Christ, any discrimination against men or harassment of them because of their race, color, condition of life, or religion (No. 5).

Bishops' Secretariat

The American hierarchy's first move toward implementation of the Vatican II "Declaration on the Relationship of the Church to Non-Christian Religions" (*Nostra Aetate*) was to establish, in 1965, a Subcommission for Catholic-Jewish Relations in the framework of its Commission for Ecumenical and Interreligious Affairs. Its moderator is Cardinal William H. Keeler of Baltimore. The Secretariat for Ecumenical and Interreligious Relations is located at 3211 Fourth St. N.E., Washington, DC 20017. Its Catholic-Jewish efforts are directed by Dr. Eugene J. Fisher.

According to the key norm of a set of guidelines issued by the secretariat Mar. 16, 1967, and updated Apr. 9, 1985: "The general aim of all Catholic-Jewish meetings (and relations) is to increase our understanding both of Judaism and the Catholic faith, to eliminate sources of tension and misunderstanding, to initiate dialogue or conversations on different levels, to multiply intergroup meetings between Catholics and Jews, and to promote cooperative social action."

Vatican Guidelines

In a document issued Jan. 3, 1975, the Vatican Commission for Religious Relations with the Jews offered a number of suggestions and guidelines for implementing the Christian-Jewish portion of the Second Vatican Council's Declaration on Relations with Non-Christian Religions.

Among "suggestions from experience" were those concerning dialogue, liturgical links between Christian and Jewish worship, the interpretation of biblical texts, teaching and education for the purpose of increasing mutual understanding, and joint social action.

Notes on Preaching and Catechesis

On June 24, 1985, the Vatican Commission for Religious Relations with the Jews promulgated its "Notes on the Correct Way to Present Jews and Judaism in Preaching and Catechesis in the Roman Catholic Church," with the intent of providing "a helpful frame of reference for those who are called upon in the course of their teaching assignments to speak about Jews and Judaism and who wish to do so in keeping with the current teaching of the Church in this area."

The document states emphatically that, since the relationship between the Church and the Jewish people is one "founded on the design of the God of the Covenant," Judaism does not occupy "an occasional and marginal place in catechesis," but an "essential" one that "should be organically integrated" throughout the curriculum on all levels of Catholic education.

The Notes discuss the relationship between the Hebrew Scriptures and the New Testament, focusing especially on typology, which is called "the sign of a problem unresolved." Underlined is the "eschatological dimension," that "the people of God of the Old and the New Testament are tending toward a like end in the future: the coming or return of the Messiah." Jewish witness to God's Kingdom, the Notes declare, challenges Christians to "accept our responsibility to prepare the world for the coming of the Messiah by working together for social justice and reconciliation."

The Notes emphasize the Jewishness of Jesus' teaching, correct misunderstandings concerning the portrayal of Jews in the New Testament and describe the Jewish origins of Christian liturgy. One section addresses the "spiritual fecundity" of Judaism to the present, its continuing "witness — often heroic — of its fidelity to the one God," and mandates the development of Holocaust curricula and a positive approach in Catholic education to the "religious attachment which finds its roots in biblical tradition" between the Jewish people and the Land of Israel, affirming the "existence of the State of Israel" on the basis of "the common principles of international law."

WE REMEMBER: A REFLECTION ON THE SHOAH

On Mar. 16, 1998, the Commission for Religious Relations with the Jews under Cardinal Edward Idris Cassidy, issued a long-awaited white paper on the Holocaust, entitled "We Remember: Reflections on the Shoah."

The document offered repentance for the failures of many Christians to oppose the policies of Nazi Germany and to resist the extermination of the Jews during the years of the Third Reich. It analyzed the history of anti-Semitism in the Church, while distinguishing between the historical anti-Judaism of Christian teaching over the centuries and the modern, racial ideology of Nazism that climaxed with the Holocaust.

"We Remember" defends Pope Pius XII and his efforts on behalf of the Jews during World War II, and at the same time acknowledges the need for a "call to

penitence" by the Church as a whole "for the failures of her sons and daughters in every age." Cardinal Cassidy, in an address given in May of 1998 to the American Jewish Committee responding to criticisms of the text, stated clearly that terms such as "sons and daughters" and "members of the Church" are not restricted to a single category, "but can include popes cardinals, bishops, priests and laity," and he acknowledged that Christian anti-Judaism paved the way for Nazi anti-Semitism, though distinct from it.

We Remember begins with a letter from Pope John Paul II expressing his hope that the document will indeed help to heal the wounds of past misunderstandings and injustices and enable memory to play its necessary part in the process of shaping a future in which the unspeakable iniquity of the Shoah will never again be possible."

The U.S. Conference of Catholic Bishops' Committee for Ecumenical and Interreligious Relations in 1998 published the text of "We Remember" along with the statements of European and American bishops' conferences similarly expressing repentance for Christian sins of omission and commission during the Shoah in a volume entitled, *Catholics Remember the Holocaust*. In 2001 the U.S. Bishops issued *Catholic Teaching on the Shoah: Implementing the Holy See's "We Remember"* urging and giving guidelines for Holocaust education in all Catholic schools, from elementary through college and university education.

Five-Part Document

"We Remember" begins with a letter from Pope John Paul II expressing his hope that the document "will indeed help to heal the wounds of past misunderstandings and injustices" and "enable memory to play its necessary part in the process of shaping a future in which the unspeakable iniquity of the Shoah will never again be possible."

Part I, "The Tragedy of the Shoah and the Duty of Remembrance," looks at the call by Pope John Paul II in *Tertio Millennio Adveniente*: "The Church should become more fully conscious of the sinfulness of her children," lamenting that the 20th century "has witnessed an unspeakable tragedy which can never be forgotten: the attempt by the Nazi regime to exterminate the Jewish people ... We ask all Christians to join us in meditating on the catastrophe which befell the Jewish people, and on the moral imperative to ensure that never again will selfishness and hatred grow to the point of sowing such suffering and death."

Part II, "What We Must Remember," declares that "such an event cannot be fully measured by the ordinary criteria of historical research alone," requiring a "reflection" on the conditions that made it possible. One important point is that the Shoah was perpetrated in Europe, raising the question of a relationship between Nazism and historical Christian anti-Semitism.

Part III, "Relations Between Jews and Christians," traces the "tormented" history of Christian-Jewish relations. The section explores the historical failure of Christians to follow Christ's teachings right up to the 19th century. It is noted that in that century, "there began to spread in varying degrees throughout most of Europe an anti-Judaism that was essentially more sociological and political than religious," in connection with ideas that "denied the unity of the human race." Of these, National Socialism was the most extreme expression, an ideology resisted, as the paper documents, by Church leaders in Germany and by Pope Pius XI.

Part IV, "Nazi Anti-Semitism and the Shoah," stresses that Nazism's anti-Semitism "had its roots outside of Christianity and, in pursuing its aims, it did not hesitate to oppose the Church and persecute her members also." Further, "the Nazi Party not only showed aversion to the ideas of divine Providence ... but gave proof of a definite hatred directed at God ... such an attitude led to a rejection of Christianity, and a desire to see the Church destroyed...."

Part V, "Looking Together to a Common Future," expresses Catholic hopes that by this act of repentance (teshuva), a new relationship will be possible. It calls upon all peoples to reflect upon the Shoah and resolve that "the spoiled seeds of anti-Judaism and anti-Semitism must never again be allowed to take root in any human heart."

PAPAL STATEMENTS

(*Courtesy of Dr. Eugene Fisher, associate director of the Bishops' Committee for Ecumenical and Interreligious Affairs.*)

Pope John Paul II, in a remarkable series of addresses beginning in 1979, has sought to promote and give shape to the development of dialogue between Catholics and Jews.

In a homily delivered June 7, 1979, at Auschwitz, which he called the "Golgotha of the Modern World," he prayed movingly for "the memory of the people whose sons and daughters were intended for total extermination."

In a key address delivered Nov. 17, 1980, to the Jewish community in Mainz, the Pope articulated his vision of the three "dimensions" of the dialogue: (1) "the meeting between the people of God of the Old Covenant and the people of the New Covenant"; (2) the encounter of "mutual esteem between today's Christian churches and today's people of the Covenant concluded with Moses"; (3) the "holy duty" of witnessing to the one God in the world and "jointly to work for peace and justice."

On Mar. 22, 1984, at an audience with members of the Anti-Defamation League of B'nai B'rith, the Pope commented on "the mysterious spiritual link which brings us close together, in Abraham and through Abraham, in God who chose Israel and brought forth the Church from Israel." He urged joint social action on "the great task of promoting justice and peace."

In receiving a delegation of the American Jewish Committee Feb. 14, 1985, the Holy Father confirmed that *Nostra Aetate* "remains always for us a teaching which is necessary to accept not merely as something fitting, but much more as an expression of the faith, as an inspiration of the Holy Spirit, as a word of the divine wisdom."

During his historic visit to the Great Synagogue in Rome Apr. 13, 1986, the Holy Father affirmed that God's covenant with the Jewish people is "irrevocable," and stated: "The Jewish religion is not 'extrinsic' to us, but in a certain way is 'intrinsic' to our own religion. With Judaism, therefore, we have a relationship which we do not have with any other religion."

Meeting with the Jewish community in Sydney, Australia, Nov. 26, 1986, the Holy Father termed the 20th century "the century of the Shoah" (Holocaust) and called "sinful" any "acts of discrimination or persecution against Jews."

On June 14, 1987, meeting with the Jewish community of Warsaw, the pope called the Jewish witness to the Shoah (Holocaust) a "saving warning before all of humanity" which reveals "your particular vocation, showing you (Jews) to be still the heirs of that election to which God is faithful."

A collection of Pope John Paul II's addresses, On Jews and Judaism 1979-1986, prepared by the NCCB Secretariat was sent to the pope Aug. 12, 1987. In a response of Aug. 17, the Pope reiterated his Warsaw statement and added: "Before the vivid memory of the extermination (Shoah), it is not permissible for anyone to pass by with indifference. The sufferings endured by the Jews are also for the Catholic Church a motive of sincere sorrow, especially when one thinks of the indifference and sometimes resentment which have divided Jews and Christians."

In 1995, an updated edition of the collection of papal texts entitled Spiritual Pilgrimage won the National Jewish Book Award and became the third best-selling "Jewish" book, according to the Jewish Book News.

Meeting with Jewish leaders Sept. 11, 1987, in Miami, the Pope praised the efforts in theological dialogue and educational reform implemented in the U.S. since the Second Vatican Council; affirmed the existence of the State of Israel "according to international law," and urged "common educational programs on the Holocaust so that never again will such a horror be possible. Never again!"

In an apostolic letter on the 50th anniversary of World War II (Aug. 27, 1989), the Pope stressed the uniqueness of the Jewish sufferings of the Shoah, "which will forever remain a shame for humanity."

On Aug. 14, 1991, during a visit to his home town of Wadowice, Poland, the Pope recalled with sadness the deaths of his Jewish classmates at the hands of the Nazis during World War II: "In the school of Wadowice there were Jewish believers who are no longer with us. There is no longer a synagogue near the school. It is true that your people (the Jews) were on the front lines. The Polish Pope has a special relationship to that period because, together with you, we lived through all that in our Fatherland."

On Apr. 7, 1994, the eve of Yom HaShoah, the Jewish day of prayer commemorating the victims of the Holocaust, Pope John Paul II hosted a memorial concert at the Vatican. It was, he noted, a moment of "common meditation and shared prayer," as the Kaddish, the prayer for the dead, and the Kol Nidre, the prayer for forgiveness and atonement, were recited.

Speaking Apr. 10, 1997, to Aharon Lopez, Israel's second ambassador to the Holy See, the Pope said: "The Catholic Church as a whole is committed to cooperating with the State of Israel in combating all forms of anti-Semitism, racism and religious intolerance, and in promoting mutual understanding and respect for human life and dignity. There can be no question that in these areas more can and must be done. It is precisely such renewed efforts that will give to the Great Jubilee of the Year 2000 a truly universal significance, not limited to Catholics or Christians but embracing every part of the world."

The Pope addressed members of the Pontifical Biblical Commission Apr. 11, 1997, saying: "Jesus' human identity is determined on the basis of his bond with the people of Israel, with the dynasty of David and his descent from Abraham. This does not mean only a physical belonging. By taking part in the synagogue celebrations where the Old Testament texts were read and commented on, Jesus nourished his mind and heart with the. . . . From her origins, the Church has well understood that the Incarnation is rooted in history and, consequently, she has fully accepted Christ's insertion into the history of the people of Israel. She has regarded the Hebrew Scriptures as the perennially valid word of God addressed to her as well as to the children of Israel. It is of primary importance to preserve and renew this ecclesial awareness."

To the Jewish people of Sarajevo on Apr. 13, 1997, the Pope declared: "The great spiritual patrimony which unites us in the divine word proclaimed in the Law and the Prophets is for all of us a constant and sure guide.... We (together are) the witnesses of the Ten Commandments.... Let us therefore go forward courageously as true brothers and heirs of the promises on the path of reconciliation and mutual forgiveness. This is the will of God."

MILLENNIUM EVENTS

During 2000 the London Philharmonic conducted by Maestro Gilbert Levine played a special series of concerts of Haydn's "Creation" for interreligious audiences in Baltimore, Paris, Jerusalem and, finally in Rome to celebrate the Holy Father's 80th birthday.

Pope John Paul II determined that the year marking the beginning of the 3rd millennium would be a year of repentance by the Church for the sins of its members during the 2nd millennium. On the first Sunday of Lent, during Mass in St. Peter's, he lead the Church in a liturgy of repentance in seven categories of Christian sins, one of which was the mistreatment of Jews and Judaism over the centuries including, especially the Shoah in the 20th Century.

A high point of the millennium year was the pope's pilgrimage to the Holy Land. In Israel, he visited not only Christian holy places, but places central to Jewish memory as well. At Yad VaShem in Jerusalem, Israel's memorial to the six million Jews murdered by Nazi Germany, he prayed for the deceased and embraced Jewish survivors, some of them from his own home town of Wadowice. The prime minister of Israel, Ehud Barak, spoke movingly for his people and his country in a warm response. At the Western Wall (the Kotel, the last remnant of the ancient Temple of Jerusalem), the Pope not only prayed but inserted into the Wall a written petition just as the humblest of Jews have done ever since the Temple's destruction in 70 C.E. Its wording summarizes one of the major themes of the millennium year and of the remarkable pontificate of Karol Wojtyla. Addressing the "God of our fathers," the pope prayed in the name of the whole Church: "We are deeply saddened by the behavior of those who in the course of history have caused these children of yours to suffer and, asking your forgiveness, we wish to commit ourselves to genuine brotherhood with the People of the Covenant." The note was reverently taken from the wall for permanent display at Yad VaShem.

In 2002 the Pontifical Biblical Commission issued "The Jewish People and Their Sacred Scriptures in the Christian Bible, " a 205 page volume fulfilling the pope's 1997 mandate to the Commission. The first section of the report stresses, contrary to Marcionism, that the Jewish Scriptures are a fundamental part of the Christian Bible. The second section shows how the New Testament attests "conformity" (continuity) to the Jewish Bible in "fulfilling the Scriptures" but also presents a "newness" ("discontinuity, progression") in the life and certain teachings of Christ (IIA). Still, major "fundamental themes" of revelation are shared by both testaments (II,B). Jewish readings of the Bible, from rabbinic times to the present, maintain their own integrity and validity based upon the integrity and validity of the Jewish Scriptures understood in their own terms.

The third section outlines the historical setting of the New Testament as a document of "post-exilic Judaism" (IIIA) and describes the portrait of Jews in each gospel (IIIB) and of Judaism in the Pauline Letters and other apostolic writings (IIIC). The document concludes with "pastoral orientations" urging Jews and Christians to continued dialogue over the "inexhaustible riches" of our shared sacred texts.

INTERNATIONAL LIAISON COMMITTEE

The International Catholic-Jewish Liaison Committee (ILC) was formed in 1971 and is the official link between the Commission for Religious Relations with the Jewish People and the International Jewish Committee for Interreligious Consultations. The committee meets every 18 months to examine matters of common interest.

Topics under discussion have included: mission and witness (Venice, 1977), religious education (Madrid, 1978), religious liberty and pluralism (Regensburg, 1979), religious commitment (London, 1981), the sanctity of human life in an age of violence (Milan, 1982), youth and faith (Amsterdam, 1984), the Vatican Notes on Preaching and Catechesis (Rome, 1985), the Holocaust (Prague, 1990), education and social action (Baltimore, 1992), family and ecology (Jerusalem, 1994), the Catholic Church and the Shoah (Rome, 1998), and theological understandings of one another (New York, 2001).

Pope John Paul, addressing in Rome a celebration of *Nostra Aetate* (the Second Vatican Council's "Declaration on the Relationship of the Church to Non-Christian Religions") by the Liaison Committee, stated: "What you are celebrating is nothing other than the divine mercy which is guiding Christians and Jews to mutual awareness, respect, cooperation and solidarity. The universal openness of *Nostra Aetate* is anchored in and takes its orientation from a high sense of the absolute singularity of God's choice of a particular people. The Church is fully aware that Sacred Scripture bears witness that the Jewish people, this community of faith and custodian of a tradition thousands of years old, is an intimate part of the mystery of revelation and of salvation."

Family Rights and Obligations

The Liaison Committee, at its May, 1994, meeting in Jerusalem, issued its first joint statement, on the family, in anticipation of the UN Cairo Conference subsequently held in September.

The statement affirmed that "the rights and obligations of the family do not come from the State but exist prior to the State and ultimately have their source in God the Creator. The family is far more than a legal, social or economic unit. For both Jews and Christians, it is a stable community of love and solidarity based on God's covenant."

Caring for God's Creation

During its March 23-26, 1998, meeting in the Vatican, the Liaison Committee issued its second joint statement, on the environment. Drawing deeply on the shared sacred text of Genesis, the Committee affirmed that "concern for the environment has led both Catholics and Jews to reflect on the concrete implications of their belief in God, creator of all things,"

especially "a recognition of the mutual dependence between the land and the human person." "Care for creation," the document concluded "is also a religious act."

In its April 2001, meeting, the Liaison Committee issued two statements, one affirming the need to preserve the sacred character of Christian and Jewish holy places, as well as the communities who give witness to them, and one urging review and revision where necessary of curriculum and course materials teaching about each other's traditions especially in institutions of theological education.

Protecting Religious Freedom and Holy Sites

At its May 2001, meeting in New York, the Liaison Committee issued a joint declaration on a subject of increasing concern, not only in the Middle East, but in Asia and Africa as well. With regard to the obligation of states, the document notes: "Government and political authorities bear special responsibility for protecting human and religious rights. Those responsible for law, order, and public security should feel themselves obligated to defend religious minorities and to use available legal remedies against those who commit crimes against religious liberty and the sanctity of holy places. Just as they are prohibited from engaging in anti-religious acts, governments must also be vigilant lest by inaction they effectively tolerate religious hatred or provide impunity for the perpetrators of anti-religious actions."

On Education in Catholic and Jewish Seminaries and Theological Schools

Also in New York, the Liaison Committee issued a statement calling on Catholic and Jewish seminaries to provide understanding of the other. In addition to expanding course work and examining existing courses for the treatment of the other, the statement concluded that "educational institutions in both our communities should make every effort to expose students to living Jewish and Christian communities through guest lecturers, field trips, involvement in local national and international dialogue groups and conferences."

Vatican-Israel Accord

On Dec. 30, 1993, a year of dramatic developments in the Middle East was capped by the signing in Jerusalem of a "Fundamental Agreement" between representatives of the Holy See and the State of Israel. The agreement acknowledged in its preamble that the signers were "aware of the unique nature of the relationship between the Catholic Church and the Jewish people, and of the historic process of reconciliation and growth in mutual understanding and friendship between Catholics and Jews." Archbishop (later Cardinal) William H. Keeler, president of the National Conference of Catholic Bishops, welcomed the accord together with the Israeli Ambassador to the United States at a ceremony at the NCCB headquar-

ters in Washington. (*See* also **News Events** .)In 1996, the Anti-Defamation League published a set of documents related to the accord, entitled "A Challenge Long Delayed," edited by Eugene Fisher and Rabbi Klenicki.

U.S. DIALOGUE

The National Workshop on Christian-Jewish Relations, begun in 1973 by the NCCB Secretariat, draws more than 1,000 participants from around the world. Recent workshops have been held in Baltimore (1986), Minneapolis (1987), Charleston, SC (1989), Chicago (1990), Pittsburgh (1992), Tulsa (1994), Stamford (1996), and Houston (1999).

In October, 1987, the Bishops' Committee for Ecumenical and Interreligious Affairs began a series of twice-yearly consultations with representatives of the Synagogue Council of America. Topics of discussion have included education, human rights, respect for life, the Middle East. The consultation has issued several joint statements: "On Moral Values in Public Education" (1990), "On Stemming the Proliferation of Pornography" (1993), "On Dealing with Holocaust Revisionism" (1994).

Ongoing relationships are maintained by the USCCB Secretariat with such Jewish agencies as the American Jewish Committee, the Anti-Defamation League, B'nai B'rith International, and the National Jewish Council for Public Affairs.

In June, 1988, the Bishops' Committee for Ecumenical and Interreligious Affairs published in Spanish and English Criteria for the Evaluation of Dramatizations of the Passion, providing for the first time Catholic guidelines for passion plays.

In January, 1989, the Bishops' Committee for the Liturgy issued guidelines for the homiletic presentation of Judaism under the title, "God's Mercy Endures Forever."

When the Synagogue Council of America dissolved in 1995, the Bishops' Committee for Ecumenical and Interreligious Affairs initiated separate consultations with the new National Council of Synagogues (Reform and Conservative), chaired by Cardinal William H. Keeler, and the Orthodox Union/Rabbinical Council, chaired by Cardinal John J. O'Connor, of blessed memory. The bishops have issued three joint statements

with the National Council of Synagogues: "Reflections on the Millennium" (1998), "To End the Death Penalty" (1999), and "Children and the Environment" (2001). Bishop William Murphy of the Diocese of Rockville Center has succeeded Cardinal O'Connor as co-chair of the dialogue with Orthodox Judaism.

Recent Developments

In December 1999, the Holy See's Commission and the International Jewish Committee for Interreligious Consultations announced the establishment of a committee of three Catholic and three Jewish scholars to look into the many complex historical and moral issues involving the Church and the Shoah beginning with an analysis of the thousands of archival documents for the period of World War II already made public by the Holy See in its 12 volume *Actes et Documents* (1965-80). The Committee met in New York in December 1999, in London in May of 2000, in Baltimore in July 2000, and finally in Rome in October 2000, where it issued its "Preliminary Report." The report affirmed the objectivity of the original team of four Jesuit scholars who selected the tens of thousands of texts from the Vatican archives for inclusion in the 11 volumes of the *Actes et Documents du Saint Siege Relatives a la Seconde Guerre Mondiale* (Libreria Editrice Vaticana, 1965-80), but also raised numerous questions for further study and documentation. The Joint Commission's Catholic Coordinator, Dr. Eugene Fisher praised the group's "achievement of so much consensus between Catholic and Jewish scholars on what are the questions that need to be faced today. Such solid consensus could by no means be presumed when the group started its work, so emotional and complex are the issues . . .The scholarly successors of this group will be forever in their debt" (*Catholic International*, May 2002, p. 68).

ISLAM

(*Courtesy of Dr. John Borelli, executive secretary for Interreligious Relations, USCCB.*)

Islam, meaning grateful surrender (to God), originated with Muhammad and the revelation he is believed to have received. Muslims acknowledge that this revelation, recorded in the *Qu'ran*, is from the one God and do not view Islam as a new religion. They profess that Muhammad was the last in a long series of prophets, most of whom are named in the Hebrew Bible and the New Testament, beginning with Adam and continuing through Noah, Abraham, Moses, Jesus and down to Muhammad.

Muslims believe in the one God, Allah in Arabic, and cognate with the Hebrew Elohim and the ancient Aramaic Elah. According to the *Qu'ran*, God is one and transcendent, Creator and Sustainer of the uni-

verse, all-merciful and all-compassionate Ruler and Judge. God possesses numerous other titles, known collectively as the 99 names of God. The profession of faith states: "There is no god but the God and Muhammad is the messenger of God."

The essential duties of Muslims are to: witness the faith by daily recitation of the profession of faith; worship five times a day facing in the direction of the holy city of Mecca; give alms; fast daily from dawn to dusk during the month of Ramadan; make a pilgrimage to Mecca once if possible.

Muslims believe in final judgment, heaven and hell. Morality and following divinely revealed moral norms are extremely important to Muslims. Some dietary regulations are in effect. On Fridays, the noon prayer is a congregational (juma) prayer which should be said in a mosque. The general themes of prayer are adoration and thanksgiving. Muslims do not have an ordained ministry.

The basis of Islamic belief is the *Qu'ran*, the created word of God revealed to Muhammad through the angel Gabriel over a period of 23 years. The contents of this sacred book are complemented by the Sunna, a collection of sacred traditions from the life of the prophet Muhammad, and reinforced by Ijma, the consensus of Islamic scholars of Islamic Law (Shariah) which guarantees them against errors in matters of belief and practice

Conciliar Statement

The attitude of the Church toward Islam was first stated in the Second Vatican Council's "Constitution on the Church": "But the plan of salvation also includes those who acknowledge the Creator, in the first place among whom are the Muslims: these profess to hold the faith of Abraham, and together with us they adore the one, merciful God, mankind's judge on the last day." (16) The Council's "Declaration on the Relation of the Church to Non-Christian Religions" (*Nostra Aetate*, No. 3) stated the position in further detail:

"The Church has a high regard for the Muslims. They worship God, who is one, living and subsistent, merciful and almighty, the Creator of heaven and earth, who has also spoken to men. They strive to submit themselves without reserve to the hidden decrees of God, just as Abraham submitted himself to God's plan, to whose faith Muslims eagerly link their own. Although not acknowledging him as God, they venerate Jesus as a prophet, his virgin Mother they also honor, and even at times devoutly invoke. Further, they await the day of judgment and the reward of God following the resurrection of the dead, For this reason, they highly esteem an upright life and worship God, especially by way of prayer, alms-deeds and fasting.

"Over the centuries many quarrels and dissensions have arisen between Christians and Muslims. The sacred Council now pleads with all to forget the past, and urges that a sincere effort be made to achieve mutual understanding; for the benefit of all men, let them together preserve and promote peace, liberty, social justice and moral values."

Dialogue

Pope John Paul II has met with Muslim leaders and delegations both in Rome and during his trips abroad. He has addressed large gatherings of Muslims in Morocco, Indonesia, Mali and elsewhere. In 1979 on a pastoral visit to Turkey, he suggested to the Catholic community: "My brothers, when I think of this spiritual heritage (Islam) and the value it has for man and for society, its capacity of offering, particularly in the young, guidance for life, filing the gap left by materialism, and giving a reliable foundation to social and juridical organization, I wonder if it is not urgent, precisely today when Christians and Muslims have entered a new period of history, to recognize and develop the spiritual bonds that unite us, in order to preserve and promote together for the benefit of all men, 'peace, liberty, social justice and moral values' as the Council calls upon us to do (*Nostra Aetate* 3). In *Tertio Millennio Adveniente*, he recommended

for the year 1999 that "the dialogue with Jews and the Muslims ought to have a pre-eminent place" and "meetings in places of significance for the great monotheistic religions." On Feb. 24, 2000, John Paul II traveled to Egypt as part of his Jubilee Year pilgrimages and was received by Grand Sheik Mohammed Sayyid Tantawi at al-Azhar University, the most influential Islamic university in the world. On pastoral visit to Syria in May 2001, John Paul II spoke of the significant relationship that exists between Muslims and Christians concluding with a citation to his first letter of the new millennium: "I am thinking too of the great cultural influence of Syrian Islam, which under the Umayyad caliphs reached the farthest shores of the Mediterranean. Today, in a world that is increasingly complex and interdependent, there is a need for a new spirit of dialogue and cooperation between Christians and Muslims. Together we acknowledge the one indivisible God, the Creator of all that exists. Together we must proclaim to the world that the name of the one God is 'a name of peace and a summons to peace' (*Novo Millennio Ineunte*, 55)!" On the same trip to Syria, on May 6, 2001, John Paul II made the first papal visit to a mosque when he was received at the Umayyad Mosque in Damascus by the Minister of the Waqf and the Grand Mufti of Syria. On Nov. 18, 2001, John Paul II asked Catholics to fast and pray for peace on Friday, December 14, the last Friday of the Ramadan fast that year. He also announced that he was intending to invite representatives of various world religions to Assisi for a day of prayer on January 24, 2002.

The Pontifical Council for Interreligious Dialogue holds formal dialogues with several Islamic organizations on a regular basis. In the U.S., the Bishops' Committee for Ecumenical and Interreligious Affairs holds regular consultations on relations with Muslims. Dialogue on a national level with the participation of Catholics and Muslims from several U.S. cities was initiated in October 1991 and was followed again in 1992. These and a series of conversations with Muslims on international and domestic issues were co-sponsored with the American Muslim Council. Then in the late 1990's, the Bishops' Committee initiated a series of regional dialogues with Muslims. In 1996, an annual regional dialogue in the Midwest with the co-sponsorship of the Islamic Society of North America in Indianapolis was initiated. In 1998, an annual dialogue in the Mid-Atlantic region with the co-sponsorship of the Islamic Circle of North America in Queens, New York held its first meeting. In 2000, the West Coast Dialogue of Muslims and Catholics began meeting in Orange, CA, with the co-sponsorship of several Islamic councils. All three regional dialogues continue to meet and are co-chaired by bishops and Islamic leaders. Also in 1995 a dialogue between representatives of the ministry of W.D. Mohammed and the United States Conference of Catholic Bishops began. Following a pilgrimage to Rome by Cardinal William Keeler and Imam Warith Deen Mohammed, the spiritual leader of African-American Muslims in the United States, the relationship between Imam Mohammad's American Society of Muslims and the Catholic Church has been served by the Focolare Movement. For the 1999 Interreligious Assembly hosted by the Pontifical Council for Interreligious Dialogue in Rome in preparation for the great jubilee year 2000, Imam Mohammed was selected as the Muslim spokesperson at the closing ceremony.

On September 14, 2001, following the events in New York, Washington, and Western Pennsylvania, Bishop Tod D. Brown, BCEIA chairman, issued a statement with five Muslims leaders, representing the various organizations who have been partners with the bishops' conference in dialogues, condemning terrorist acts, encouraging unity and cooperation, urging restraint, entreating Muslims and Catholics to join with others in services of prayer.

MESSAGE FOR THE END OF RAMADAN 'ID AL-FITR 1422 A.H./2002 A.D.

Christians and Muslims and the Ways to Peace

This message was issued by Archbishop Michael Fitzgerald, President of the Pontifical Council for Interreligious Dialogue, and was addressed to the Muslim community on the observance of the Muslim feast of 'Id al-Fitr at the end of Ramadan, the month of fasting.

Dear Muslims Friends,

1. It is a pleasure for me to address you on the occasion of '*Id al-Fitr*, which concludes the month of Ramadan, in order to offer you friendly greetings on behalf of the Pontifical Council for Interreligious Dialogue and indeed on behalf of the whole Catholic Church.

We are happy to receive an increasing number of replies to our Message and also greetings on the occasion of our own festivities, especially Christmas. We note too with pleasure that in many places, at the local level, contacts between Christians and Muslims are intensifying.

2. You are well aware, dear friends, how acute has become the question of peace in our world today. Situations where war prevails are like an open wound in the heart of humanity, above all those conflicts which have been going on for many years, whether in the Middle East, in Africa or in Asia. In several countries such conflicts result in numerous innocent victims, leading the population to despair of peace returning to their land in the near future.

3. The origin of the causes of conflict is often to be located in hearts which refuse to be open to God. Such hearts are characterised by egoism, by an immoderate desire for power, domination and wealth, at the expense of others and without any attention to the cry of distress of those who hunger and thirst for justice and peace. While the ultimate causes of wars are well known, we need above all to explore together the ways to peace.

4. As believers in the One God we see it as our duty to strive to bring about peace. Christians and Muslims, we believe that peace is above all a gift from God. This is why our two communities pray for peace; it is something they are always called to do. As you know, Pope John Paul II invited representatives of different religions to come to Assisi, the city of St Francis, on 24 January 2002, in order to pray and to commit themselves to peace in the world. Many Muslims, coming from different countries, contributed to the success of this day. All those present were exhorted not to allow the flame of hope, symbolised by the lamp held by each official representative, to be extinguished. Our Council, for its part, is examining the best way to fulfil this commitment.

5. In bringing about peace, and maintaining it, religions have an important role to play, one which in these days more than ever is being recognised by civil society and by Governments. In this respect, education is a domain in which religions can make a particular contribution. We are indeed convinced that the ways of peace include education, for through it one can learn to recognise one's own identity and that of the other. This identity will be clarified without coming into opposition with that of our brothers and sisters, as if humanity could be made up of antagonistic factions. Peace necessarily entails an approach to the human person in truth and justice. Education for peace also involves recognition and acceptance of diversity, just as it includes learning about crisis management, in order to prevent crises from degenerating into conflicts. We are happy to see that in several countries there is increased collaboration in this field among Muslims and Christians, especially as regards the equitable revision of text-books for schools.

6. It is at what is a very special time for you, the month of Ramadan in which fasting, prayer and solidarity bring you interior peace, that I am sharing with you these reflections on the ways to peace. I express to you, therefore, good wishes of peace, peace in your hearts, in your families and in your respective countries, and I invoke upon you the Blessing of the God of Peace.

Archbishop Michael L. Fitzgerald, President

HINDUISM AND BUDDHISM

(*Courtesy of Dr. John Borelli.*)

In its Declaration on the Relation of the Church to Non-Christian Religions, the Second Vatican Council stated: "In Hinduism men explore the divine mystery and express it both in the limitless riches of myth and the accurately defined insights of philosophy. They seek release from the trials of the present life by ascetical practices, profound meditation and recourse to God in confidence and love." (2)

Catholics, especially in India, have sought good relations with Hindus and have engaged in numerous dialogues and conferences. In papal visits to India, Paul VI in 1964 and John Paul II in 1986 and 1999, popes have addressed words of respect for Indian, particularly Hindu, religious leaders. Pope John Paul II said to Hindus in India in 1986: "Your overwhelming sense of the primacy of religion and of the greatness of the Supreme Being has been a powerful witness against a materialistic and atheistic view of life." In 1987, he said of Hinduism: "I hold in esteem your concern for inner peace and for the peace of the world, based not on purely mechanistic or materialistic political considerations, but on self-purification, unselfishness, love and sympathy for all."

In 1995, the Pontifical Council for Interreligious Dialogue began sending a general message to Hindus on the occasion of Diwali, a feast commemorating the victory of light over darkness. In 1999, John

Paul II was in India during the celebration and said these words to the religious leaders of India: "On the occasion of Diwali, the festival of lights, which symbolizes the victory of life over death, good over evil, I express the hope that this meeting will speak to the world of the things that unite us all: our common human origin and destiny, our shared responsibility for people's well-being and progress, our need of the light and strength that we seek in our religious convictions." In the United States, there are a few dialogues between Catholics and Hindus.

"Buddhism in its multiple forms acknowledges the radical insufficiency of this shifting world. It teaches a path by which men, in a devout and confident spirit, can either reach a state of absolute freedom or attain supreme enlightenment by their own efforts or by higher assistance." So stated the Second Vatican Council in its Declaration on the Relation of the Church to Non-Christian Religions.

Numerous delegations of Buddhists and leading monks have been received by the popes, and John Paul II has met with Buddhist leaders on many of his trips. Paul VI said to a group of Japanese Buddhists in 1973: "Buddhism is one of the riches of Asia: you teach men to seek truth and peace in the kingdom of the Eternal, beyond the horizon of visible things. You likewise strive to encourage the qualities of goodness, meekness and non-violence." In 1995, while in Sri Lanka, John Paul II said to Buddhists: "I express my highest regard for the followers of Buddhism, ... with its four great values of loving kindness, compassion, sympathy, and equanimity; with its ten transcendental virtues and the joys of the Sangha [the monastic community]. . . At the 1986 World Day of Prayer for Peace at Assisi, the Dalai Lama, principal teacher of the Gelugpa lineage, was placed immediately to the Holy Father's left. Numerous dialogues and good relations between Catholics and Buddhists exist in many countries.

In 1995, the Pontifical Council for Interreligious Dialogue organized a Buddhist-Christian colloquium hosted by the Fo Kuang Shan Buddhist order in Taiwan. A second colloquium was held in Bangalore, India, in 1998. A third was held in Tokyo in 2002. These grew out of the perceived need for greater ongoing contact between the Pontifical Council and Buddhist leaders and scholars. Each of these meetings has produced a report. Also in 1995, the council began sending a message to Buddhists on the feast of Vesakh, the celebration of Gautama Buddha's life.

A meeting of great significance between Buddhist and Catholic monastics took place at Our Lady of Gethsemani Abbey, Kentucky, in July 1996, which was organized and facilitated by Monastic Interreligious Dialogue, a network formed in 1981 of mostly monasteries of men and women following the rule of St. Benedict. "The Gethsemani Encounter," the result of several formal visits and hospitality between Catholic and Buddhist monks and nuns, focused on various aspects of monastic life. There were twenty-five participants on each side with numerous observers. The Buddhists represented the Theravada, Tibetan,

and Zen traditions. A second Gethsemani Encounter took place in April 2002.

In 1998, an ongoing dialogue between Buddhists and Catholics in Los Angeles hosted a retreat dialogue for 50 Catholic and Buddhist participants from different regions of the U.S. The retreat/dialogue was co-planned with the Faiths in the World Committee of the National Association of Diocesan Ecumenical Officers, a network of Catholic diocesan staff responsible for ecumenical and interreligious relations.

In 1996, Cardinal Arinze, in a letter to "Dear Buddhist Friends," wrote: "The pluralistic society in which we live demands more than mere tolerance. Tolerance is usually thought of as putting up with the other or, at best, as a code of public conduct. Yet, this resigned, lukewarm attitude does not create the right atmosphere for true harmonious coexistence. The spirit of our religions challenges us to go beyond this. We are commanded, in fact, to love our neighbors as ourselves." The cardinal wrote in the same vein to Muslims on the occasion of their 1996 celebration of Id al-Fitr.

Formal dialogues continue in the Archdiocese of Los Angeles and formal relations are developing in a few other dioceses. In 1989, the Bishops' Committee for Ecumenical and Interreligious Affairs convened its first national consultation on relations with Buddhists; a second consultation was held in 1990.

After a series of meetings in the San Francisco area, the Bishops' Committee inaugurated a Buddhist-Catholic dialogue in March 2003, following the model of its regional dialogues, with the Dharma Realm Buddhist Association and the San Francisco Zen Center as partners. The theme of the first dialogue was "Walking the Bodhisattva Path/Walking the Christ Path." The Northern California Chan/Zen-Catholic Dialogue will meet annual for three more years discussing topics of mutual interest.

Subcommittee on Interreligious Dialogue

With an increase in dialogues and other cooperative programs with Muslims, Buddhists, Hindus and others, the U. S. Bishops' Committee for Ecumenical and Interreligious Affairs decided that it would be helpful to its work if a Subcommittee were formed to oversee in greater detail interreligious relations. In December 2000, Bishop Tod D. Brown, BCEIA chairman, announced the formation of the Subcommittee on Interreligious Dialogue. Bishop Joseph J. Gerry, Diocese of Portland (Maine), who had served for more than 10 years as Bishop Moderator for Interreligious Relations, was the first chairman of the new Subcommittee. The first meeting was held in March 2001. In addition to discussing the various dialogues in progress and other items of mutual interest, the members decided to undertake a program of education in interreligious relations for the members of the bishops' conference. In March 2003, the first Institute for Bishops on Islam and Catholic-Muslim Relations was held under the sponsorship of the Subcommittee and with the financial assistance of the Catholic Near East Welfare Association.

MESSAGE FOR THE FEAST OF VESAKH 2003

Archbishop Michael Fitzgerald sent the following message on behalf of the Pontifical Council for Interreligious Dialogue to the Buddhists of the world on the occasion of 2003 celebration of the Feast of Vesakh.

Buddhists and Christians: Praying for Peace in the World

Dear Buddhist Friends,

1. As the new President of the Pontifical Council for Interreligious Dialogue, the office of His Holiness the Pope for relations with people of different religious traditions, I wish to greet you and send this congratulatory message on the occasion of the feast of *Vesakh*. This gesture of friendship, initiated in 1995 by my predecessor Cardinal Francis Arinze, has almost become a tradition. I wish to continue this good tradition and express my hearty congratulations to each and every one of you.

2. In this message, I would like to invite you, my dear Buddhist friends, to join in prayer for the cause of peace in the world. Observing the current international situation, we cannot but be aware of the acuteness of the question of peace in our world. Since the beginning of this new Millennium, marked by the dramatic events of 11 September 2001, we witness every day fresh scenes of bloodshed, violence, confrontation and crisis in almost all parts of the world. In the midst of this grave situation, we cannot lead our lives without committing ourselves to advancing the cause of peace in the world.

3. We Christians and Buddhists are convinced that the origin of all conflict is ultimately located in human hearts characterized by selfish desire, specifically by desire for power, domination and wealth often at the expense of others. It is also our common conviction that peace must inhabit people s hearts before it can become a social reality. For us, therefore, the most fundamental and efficient way to advance peace is to do our best to see that the deep-rooted selfishness of human hearts is overcome, so that people may be transformed into true artisans of peace.

4. Pope John Paul II has proclaimed the year from October 2002 to October 2003 the Year of the Rosary of the Virgin Mary. He has earnestly encouraged the frequent recitation of the Rosary in order to pray for peace in the world. His wish to revive the practice of the Rosary is closely connected with the present historical circumstances, which need more than ever constant supplication for the great gift of peace.

5. My Buddhists friends, is it not a wonderful coincidence that you also have a lengthy tradition of using the *Mala* for prayer? The Rosary for Catholics and the *Mala* for Buddhists are simple yet profound and meaningful prayer, despite essential differences in their form and content, based on our distinct doctrines and practices. For Catholics, the Rosary represents a most effective means of fostering contemplation of Jesus Christ. For Buddhists, the *Mala* is used to overcome the 108 sinful desires in order to reach the state of Nirvana. By virtue of their meditative character, these two prayers have in common a calming effect on those who pray them; they lead them to experience and to work for peace, and they produce fruits of love. For Catholics, the repetition and meditation of the holy names of the Persons of the Blessed Trinity and the Virgin Mary in the recitation of the Rosary makes us more willing to assimilate their love and compassion for others, especially for the poor and afflicted. In your Buddhist tradition, praying the Mala helps one to become a peacemaker.

6. Dear Buddhist friends, these are the thoughts I wish to share with you this year. I am convinced that by persevering in prayer we will contribute to advancing peace in the world both now and in the future. May this peace be with you and your families on the feast of *Vesakh* and at all times.

Archbishop Michael L. Fitzgerald, President

MESSAGE FOR THE FEAST OF DIWALI 2002

Cardinal Francis Arinze, then president of the Pontifical Council for Interreligious Dialogue sent this message to the Hindu faithful of the world on the occasion of the feast of Diwali.

Dear Hindu Friends,

1. Once again it is time for you to light tiny lamps, hang colourful lanterns on your homes, offer prayers to God, visit friends and neighbours and celebrate around the family table the joy which the festival of *Diwali* brings. I wish to extend my heartfelt greetings to all Hindus on this happy occasion. May the external joy which will be manifest throughout the Hindu world be an expression of a genuine religious sense, the fruit of genuine religious beliefs and convictions.

2. It has become customary for me to invite friends of different religious traditions, on the occasion of their respective feasts, to joint reflection on various aspects of our life, in society and in the world at large. This year, on the occasion of *Diwali* I should like to ask whether religious festivals, in the first place, are not also expressions of the desire of human beings to conquer over darkness by light, evil by good, untruth by truth and death by life? The mystery of life, from the moment of conception onwards through the stages after the birth of a child, is attended by prayers and ritual actions in the Hindu tradition. We Christians attribute particular value to human life because the Bible teaches us that the human person is created in the image and likeness of God. This gift of God is sealed by Christ's blood which he shed out of his love for every human being. Thus every individual is precious in the eyes of God.

3. Technology has made great progress in our days. Life has perhaps become safer, easier and longer. But what answers can we give to the following questions: Has technology helped better the quality of human life? Does technology help us to value human life? With the progress of technology life paradoxically seems to be more threatened than ever. Pope John Paul II observes that "In addition to the ancient scourges of poverty, hunger, endemic diseases, violence and war, new threats are emerging on an alarmingly vast scale" (*Evangelium Vitae*, "On the Value and Inviolability of Human Life," 3). The Pope continues: "with

new prospects opened up by scientific and technological progress there arise new forms of attacks on the dignity of the human being" (*Evangelium Vitae*, "On the Value and Inviolability of Human Life," 4). Modern genetic science has become a tool in the hands of man. He can use it or abuse it. Tempted at times to become a manipulator of life, or even an agent of death, man needs to rediscover his fundamental place in creation, namely, that he is created by God and that God is the sole Creator of all that exists.

4. Representatives of different religions gathered in Assisi last January to pray for world peace. The Hindu participant, in her testimony, described the meeting as a sign of the unity of the human family under the Fatherhood of God (*Vasudhaiva Kutumbakam*). Although the participants belonged to different religious traditions, they made a common commitment in favour of promoting each single life and the whole of life. We would do well to focus our attention on the second commitment, which declared: "We commit ourselves to educating peoples to mutual respect and esteem, in order to help bring about a peaceful and fraternal coexistence between individuals and among peoples…". Through our respective communities and institutions we could devise our own approach to educating people to promote respect for life. Here I would like to make special mention of young people, whose hearts are scandalized by and suffer from the tragic events they see with their own eyes. Education particularly of youth in respect for life should be one of our urgent priorities, so that strong ethical convictions and a culture of life may prevail among them. Only to the degree that ethical and religious considerations will prevail in the whole of society can we hope that the principle of respect for life will be enshrined in society's attitudes and laws.

5. Dear Hindu friends, I would like to conclude by sharing with you the strong impression which the image of lighted lamps made on me during the Day of Prayer for Peace in Assisi last January. The representatives of different religions held lighted lamps in their hands and after their common commitment they placed the lamps on a common stand, symbolizing the convergence of hopes and efforts for peace. The Pope blessed them, saying: "Go forward into the future holding high the lamp of peace. The world has need of light!" Happy *Diwali*.

Cardinal Francis Arinze, President

Index

ABOUT THE GENERAL EDITOR

Matthew Bunson, D.Min., was born in Germany and grew up in Hawaii. He is the author or co-author of more than 30 books, including *Our Sunday Visitor's Encyclopedia of Saints, Revised, Our Sunday Visitor's Encyclopedia of Catholic History, Encyclopedia of the Roman Empire, Papal Wisdom, Words of Hope and Inspiration from Pope John Paul II, The Encyclopedia of Saints, The Catholic Almanac's Guide to the Church*, and *The Angelic Doctor: The Life and World of St. Thomas Aquinas*. He is also general editor *Our Sunday Visitor's Catholic Almanac*. In addition to delivering lectures on a variety of topics, he has appeared on many radio and television programs. He has a B.A. in history, an M.A. in theology, and recently received his doctorate in ministry.

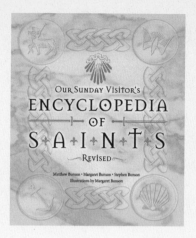

Our Sunday Visitor's Encyclopedia of Saints, Revised

by Matthew Bunson, Margaret Bunson, and Stephen Bunson

Virtually every person ever declared a saint by the Catholic Church is in this exhaustive reference — newly updated in 2003!

Hardcover, 1-931709-75-0 (ID# T41), 1,008 pages

To order: Call toll-free 1-800-348-2440, or e-mail us at osvbooks@osv.com. Order securely online on the web: www.osvbooks.com.

Availability of books is subject to change without notice.

The Catholic Almanac's Guide to the Church

YOUR CONCISE GUIDE TO ALL THINGS CATHOLIC
by Matthew Bunson

No matter what you want to know about the Catholic Church, you'll find the answer in this one-volume guide. From the composition of the Curia to contemporary saints, from major doctrines to the Third Secret of Fátima, if it's part of the Catholic world, it's here.

Topics include: Church councils; major documents and writings; American Catholic history; missionaries to the Americas; Catholics in the U.S. Government; the Pope and the Papacy; the Curia and Church government; Western and Eastern rites and their liturgies; canon law; major teachings; people and events of Scripture; Doctors of the Church; Mary, including her apparitions and the Third Secret of Fátima; Church calendar and Church year; liturgical life; sacraments, including an extensive section on marriage and divorce; saints; ecumenism and interreligious dialogue; glossary of terms; familiar prayers of the Church; and much more. If it's part of the Catholic world, you'll find it in **The Catholic Almanac's Guide to the Church**.

0-87973-914-2, (914) paper, 328 pp.

To order: Call toll-free 1-800-348-2440, or e-mail us at osvbooks@osv.com. Order securely online on the web: www.osvbooks.com.

Availability of books subject to change without notice.

Our Sunday Visitor . . .
Your Source for Discovering the Riches of the Catholic Faith

Our Sunday Visitor has an extensive line of materials for young children, teens, and adults. Our books, Bibles, booklets, CD-ROMs, audios, and videos are available in bookstores worldwide.

To receive a FREE full-line catalog or for more information, call **Our Sunday Visitor** at **1-800-348-2440**. Or write, **Our Sunday Visitor** / 200 Noll Plaza / Huntington, IN 46750.

- -

Please send me: __A catalog
Please send me materials on:
__Apologetics and catechetics   __Reference works
__Prayer books   __Heritage and the saints
__The family   __The parish
Name_____
Address_____Apt._____
City_____State_____Zip_____
Telephone (   ) _____

A39BBABP

- -

Please send a friend: __A catalog
Please send a friend materials on:
__Apologetics and catechetics   __Reference works
__Prayer books   __Heritage and the saints
__The family   __The parish
Name_____
Address_____Apt._____
City_____State_____Zip_____
Telephone (   ) _____

A39BBABP

- -

Our Sunday Visitor
200 Noll Plaza
Huntington, IN 46750
Toll free: **1-800-348-2440**
E-mail: osvbooks@osv.com
Website: www.osv.com